2018/2019
TWELFTH EDITION

Educators Resource Guide

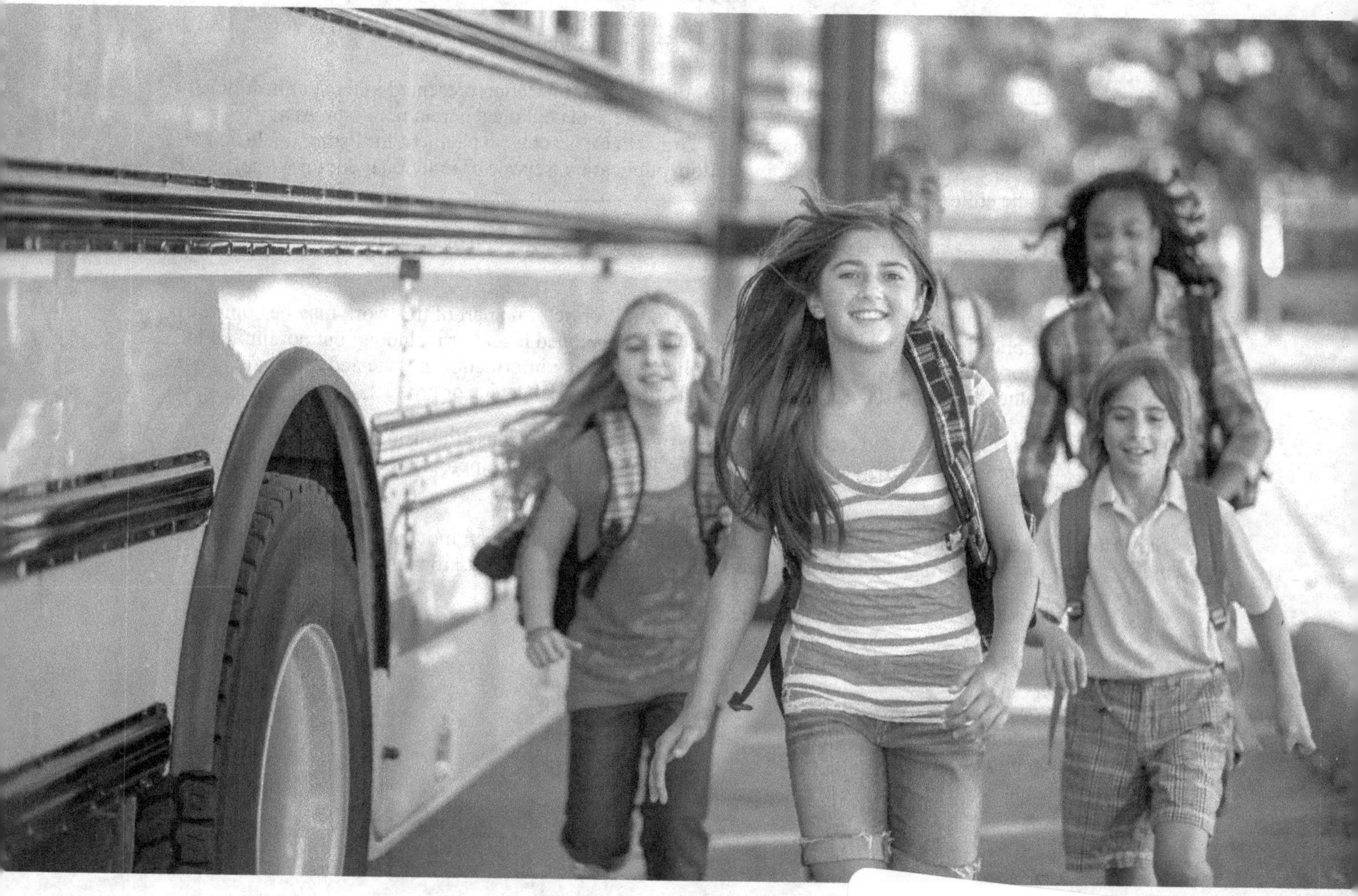

GREY HOUSE PUBLISHING

PUBLISHER: Leslie Mackenzie
EDITOR: Richard Gottlieb
EDITORIAL DIRECTOR: Laura Mars

PRODUCTION MANAGER & COMPOSITION: Kristen Hayes
STATISTICS: David Garoogian
MARKETING DIRECTOR: Jessica Moody

A Sedgwick Press Book
Grey House Publishing, Inc.
4919 Route 22
Amenia, NY 12501
518.789.8700
FAX 518.789.0545
www.greyhouse.com
e-mail: books@greyhouse.com

First edition published 1994
Twelfth edition published 2017
Printed in Canada

ISBN: 978-1-68217-350-3
ISSN: 1549-7224

Educators Resource Guide

Table of Contents

Introduction

This twelfth edition of *Educators Resource Guide*—formerly called *Educator's Resource Directory*—is a comprehensive resource designed to provide educators, administrators, and other education professionals access to a unique combination of educational resources and educational statistics and rankings.

Listings in *Educators Resource Guide* include associations, publications, trade shows, workshops and training programs designed not only to help educators advance professionally, but also to give them the resources they need to help their students, their schools, and their state meet educational standards. It provides tools for classroom and career management, and resources that truly make a difference in job, school, and student performance.

Listings in this comprehensive volume are thoughtfully organized in 13 chapters and 76 subchapters, making information significantly easier to access than the unfocused data available online or the scattered in dozens of different sources. Updated statistics and rankings are designed to help states, school districts, and individual educators better understand their educational environment, crucial to making informed decisions on careers, curriculum and funding.

Praise for previous edition:

> ". . . an important reference source overflowing with information educators may use for their own improvement or as an aid for winning a . . . Race to the Top grant. . . . The glossary is handy and the indexes are accurate. All school, public and academic libraries need an up to date education directory . . . and this is a worthy choice."
>
> ***American Reference Books Annual***

> ". . . This handy tool, appropriate for larger public and academic libraries as well as school districts, will be highly valuable to those writing education grants. . . "
>
> ***Library Journal***

SECTION ONE: RESOURCES

Educators Resource Guide includes approximately 6,500 listings in Section One. Hundreds of records have been updated and dozens of new records added. This section includes 8,082 key contact names, 4,308 fax numbers, 3,755 e-mail addresses, and 5,124 web sites, and is categorized as follows, for easy research:

Associations & Organizations disseminate information, host seminars, provide educational literature and promote study councils. This chapter organizes associations into 16 distinct categories from *Administration* to *Technology.*

The chapter on **Conferences & Trade Shows** lists everything from large conventions of classroom resources and equipment suppliers to small, specialized conferences that target rural education and specific teaching challenges. Events are listed regionally.

Consultants give information on educational consulting services, including curriculum-building guidance, school district organizations, and facility format.

Teaching Opportunities Abroad include not only U.S. government schools, but also American schools overseas. The chapter is organized geographically by region, and provides contact information, grade level and enrollment numbers.

Details on more than 600 grants, foundations and scholarships can be found in **Financial Resources**. Learn how to obtain funds for individual professional advancement, schools, programs, students, and education districts and communities.

The **Professional Development** listings include *Associations, Awards, Conferences* and *Training Materials.*

Publications list directories, magazines and journals, divided into 16 subjects. Find where to publish research findings, which testing materials best suit your needs, how to incorporate technology into your classroom, and where to find innovative classroom supplies.

Publishers include educational publishers of textbooks, testing resources and specific curriculums. Research results on general learning and training issues, and data on specific subjects, like *Gifted & Talented, Educational Media* and *Scientific Learning*, is easy to find from the **Research Centers** profiled in this edition.

The chapter on **School Supplies** focuses on the latest in *Classroom Technology, Scientific Equipment, Furniture* and *Sports & Playground Equipment.*

Software, Hardware & Internet Resources include 16 subchapters from *Administration* to *Technology in Education* that provide easy access to everything from educational computer programs to web sites with information on classroom resources for every level and subject.

Testing Resources include resources for written materials and web sites in six categories: *Elementary Education, Language Arts, Mathematics, Music & Art, Reading* and *Secondary Education.*

SECTION TWO: STATISTICS, RANKINGS & GLOSSARY

Section Two includes 347 tables and charts (111 more than last edition) across 25 categories. From educational attainment to post-secondary levels, these statistics and rankings include data not only on the American educational system, but also on Canadian and international education.

Main topics covered are: * Educational Attainment * Elementary & Secondary Education * Federal Funds for Eduation & Related Activities * Outcomes of Education * Post-secondary Education * Canadian Education Statistics. Specific topics include degrees, enrollment, completions, dropouts, faculty, revenues, expenditures, and student behavior. Many tables offer state-by-state rankings.

Using the most current data available, this section helps to complete the picture for educators making career development decisions, for school administrators interested in comparing fiscal health and educational scores, and for anyone doing educational research.

Following the statistics and rankings is a **Glossary** with over 100 education terms from Accountability to Vocational.

SECTION THREE: INDEXES

Entry & Publisher Name Index–alphabetical list of both entry names and the companies that publish the listed material. Publishers and parent organizations are boldfaced.

Geographic Index–state-by-state listing of all entries.

Subject Index–organized by core subjects plus Special Education and Technology.

Educators Resource Guide 2018/19 is also available for subscription via Grey House OnLine Database. Subscribers can do customized searches that instantly locate needed information. Visit http://gold.greyhouse.com or call 800-562-2139 to set up a free trial.

General

1 **A Better Chance**
253 W 35th Street
6th Floor
New York, NY 10001-2506
646-346-1310
800-562-7865
Fax: 646-346-1311
abetterchance.org
A Better Chance is an organization whose mission is to increase the number of well-educated young people of color through the creation of educational opportunities for students in grades 6-12.

Founded: 1963

Kurt Van Wagenen, Chair

2 **ASPIRA Association**
ASPIRA National Office
1444 I Street NW
Suite 800
Washington, DC 20005-6543
202-835-3600
Fax: 202-835-3613
info@aspira.org
www.aspira.org
The ASPIRA Association promotes the empowerment of the Puerto Rican and Latino community by developing and nurturing the leadership, intellectual, and cultural potential of its youth so that they may contribute to their communities. Some of ASPIRA's services include career and college counseling, financial aid, educational advocacy, leadership training and more.

Founded: 1961

Ronald Blackburn, President & CEO
John Villamil-Casanova, EVP & CIO

3 **Accelerated Christian Education Canada**
105 Anson Street
Southport, MB R0H-1N0
204-428-5332
800-976-7226
Fax: 204-428-5386
info@acecanada.net
www.acecanada.net
Offers individualized learning options for children, such as homeschooling, inspired by the basic values of Christianity.

Founded: 1974

Alfred MacLaren, Manager
Michele Yanchuk, Assistant Manager/Accountant

4 **Advance Program for Young Scholars**
ADVANCE program
175 Sam Sibley Drive
Suite 5671
Natchitoches, LA 71457
318-357-4500
Fax: 318-357-4547
palmerh@nsula.edu
advance.nsula.edu
ADVANCE is a residential program for talented youth in Louisiana, offering a specialized curriculum for students grades 8 through 12. The program also offers recreational and social activities.

Harriette Palmer, Associate Director

5 **American Academy of Pediatrics**
141 NW Point Boulevard
Elk Grove Village, IL 60007-1098
847-434-4000
800-433-9016
Fax: 847-434-8000
kidsdoc@aap.org
www.aap.org
Organization of pediatricians committed to serving children and adolescents to ensure their optimal physical, mental and social health. The organization offers its members professional resources, publications, conferences, advocacy and other resources to help them advance their practice.

Fernando Stein, MD, FAAP, President
Karen Remley, MD, MBA, FAAP, CEO & Executive VP

6 **American Association for Vocational Instructional Materials (AAVIM)**
220 Smithonia Road
Winterville, GA 30683-1418
706-742-5355
Fax: 706-742-7005
sales@aavim.com
www.aavim.com
Develops, produces and distributes instructional materials for career education instructors, students, and administrators.

Founded: 1949

Gary Farmer, Director

7 **American Council for Rural Special Education**
West Virginia University
509 Allen Hall
PO Box 6122
Morgantown, WV 26506-6122
304-293-3450
acres-sped@mail.wvu.edu
www.acres-sped.org
The organization is comprised of special educators, general educators, related service providers, administrators, teacher trainers, researchers and parents committed to the enhancement of services for students and individuals living in rural communities in America.

Founded: 1981

Matt Jameson, Chair
Melinda Jones Ault, Chair Elect

8 **American Council of Trustees and Alumni**
1730 M Street NW
Suite 600
Washington, DC 20036-4525
202-467-6787
Fax: 202-467-6784
info@goacta.org
www.goacta.org
An independent, non-profit organization working with alumni, trustees, and education leaders to support liberal arts education, uphold high academic standards and safeguard the free exchange of ideas on campus.

Founded: 1995

Michael B Poliakoff, Ph.D, President
Lauri Kempson, Senior Vice President

9 **American Council on Education**
1 Dupont Circle NW
Washington, DC 20036
202-939-9300
Fax: 202-833-4730
comments@ace.nche.edu
www.acenet.edu
Represents accredited degree-granting colleges and universities directly and through national and regional higher education associations. The council's mission is to advance education and serve as an advocate for adult education.

Judy C Miner, Chair
Barbara R Snyder, Vice Chair & Chair-Elect

10 **American Driver and Traffic Safety Education Association (ADTSEA)**
Highway Safety Services
1434 Trim Tree Road
Indiana, PA 15701
724-801-8246
877-485-7172
Fax: 724-349-5042
office@adtsea.org
www.adtsea.org
The purpose of the American Driver and Traffic Safety Education Association is to promote quality traffic safety education by publishing policies and guidelines. The association also offers conferences, workshops, seminars, consultative services and educational materials.

Wendy Bills, President
Allen Robinson, CEO

11 **American Federation of Teachers**
555 New Jersey Avenue NW
Washington, DC 20001
202-879-4400
Fax: 202-879-4556
online@aft.org
www.aft.org
The American Federation of Teachers is a union of professionals devoted to ensuring access to economic opportunity and quality public education, healthcare and public services for the students and families within their communities. The federation offers resources on topics such as immigration, retirement, public services and more.

Founded: 1916

Randi Weingarten, President
Mary Cathryn Ricke, Executive Vice President

12 **American Montessori Society**
116 East 16th Street
New York, NY 10003-2163
212-358-1250
Fax: 212-358-1256
ams@amshq.org
amshq.org
The Society advocates for quality Montessori education by offering services such as an information center for its members, the media, and the public; teacher resources; research and professional development events.

Founded: 1960

Mary Ellen Kordas, President
Timothy Purnell, EdD, Executive Director

13 **American School Health Association**
7918 Jones Branch Drive
Suite 300
McLean, VA 22102
703-506-7675
Fax: 703-506-3266
info@ashaweb.org
www.ashaweb.org
A non-profit organization founded to protect and improve the health and well-being of children and youth by supporting comprehensive, preschool-grade 12 school health programs.

Sharon Murray, MHSE, FASHA, President
Ty Oehrtman, MS,MCHES,FASHA, Vice President

14 **American Society for Engineering Education**
1818 N Street NW
Suite 600
Washington, DC 20036-2479
202-331-3500
Fax: 202-265-8504
aseeexec@asee.org
www.asee.org

A nonprofit organization of individuals and institutions committed to promoting the fields of engineering and engineering technology. The society develops policies and programs for engineering faculty members and offers publications, events, fellowships, job postings and more.

Founded: 1893

Louis A Martin-Vega, President
Norman Fortenberry, Executive Director

15 Association Montessori International

206 N Washington Street
Suite 330
Alexandria, VA 22314
703-746-9919
800-872-2643
montessori@amiusa.org
amiusa.org
The Association Montessori International USA applies the principles of Dr. Montessori to the education of children. The association oversees conferences and events, consultation programs, membership opportunities, training centers and other initiatives conneted to the education field.

Founded: 1929

Philip O'Brien, President

16 Association for Business Communication (ABC)

181 Turner Street NW
Blacksburg, VA 24061
540-231-8460
abcoffice@businesscommunication.org
www.businesscommunication.org
International, interdisciplinary organization engaged in fostering excellence in business communication scholarship, research, education and practice. The association offers resources, publications, conferences and membership benefits.

Founded: 1936

Jim Dubinsky, Ph.D, Executive Director
Marilyn Buerkens, Office Manager

17 Association for Childhood Education International

1200 18th Street NW
Suite 700
Washington, DC 20036
202-372-9986
800-423-3563
Fax: 202-372-9989
headquarters@acei.org
www.acei.org
The association promotes and supports the education, development, and well-being of children, from birth through adolescence. It also seeks to influence the professional growth of educators and the efforts of others who are committed to the needs of children in a changing society.

Founded: 1892

Pilar Fort, President
Diane Whitehead, Executive Director

18 Association for Environmental and Outdoor Education (AEOE)

560 Silver Strand Boulevard
Imperial Beach, CA 91932
714-838-8990
helen@aeoe.org
aeoe.org
The Association for Environmental and Outdoor Education supports and inspires educators in their quest for the knowledge, skills, and attitudes essential to help all learners understand, appreciate and care for their environment. The association also offers learning resources, job postings and events.

Founded: 1954

Reed Schneider, President & Chair
Helen M De La Maza, Membership Coordinator

19 Association for Interdisciplinary Studies

Oakland University
44575 Garfield Road
Building UC2, Suite 103
Clinton Township, MI 48038
248-370-2100
aisorg@oakland.edu
oakland.edu/ais
The Association for Interdisciplinary Studies is an interdisciplinary professional organization dedicated to promoting the interchange of ideas among scholars and administrators in the arts and science fields on intellectual and organizational issues.

Founded: 1979

James Welch, President
Tanya Augsburg, Ph.D, Vice-President, Relations

20 Association for Play Therapy

401 Clovis Avenue
Suite 107
Clovis, CA 93612
559-298-3400
Fax: 559-298-3410
info@a4pt.org
www.a4pt.org
The Association for Play Therapy promotes the value of play, play therapy and credentialed play therapists to advance the psychosocial development and mental health of all people. The association also sponsors and supports programs, services and related activities that promote public understanding of play therapy.

Founded: 1982

Jodi Crane, Chair
Kathryn Lebby, President & CEO

21 Association for Supervision & Curriculum Development (ASCD)

ASCD
1703 N Beauregard Street
Alexandria, VA 22311
703-578-9600
800-933-2723
Fax: 703-575-5400
press@ascd.org
www.ascd.org
A membership organization that develops programs, products, and services essential to the way educators learn, teach, and lead.

Founded: 1943

Ben Shuldiner, President
Deborah Delisle, CEO & Executive Director

22 Association of American Educators

25909 Pala Place
Suite 330
Mission Viejo, CA 92691
949-595-7979
800-704-7799
Fax: 949-595-7970
socialmedia@aaeteachers.org
www.aaeteachers.org
Provides professional benefits and services to educators, including liability insurance, scholarships and grants, and professional resources.

Founded: 1994

Gary Beckner, Chairman & President
Colin Sharkey, Executive Vice President

23 Association of Boarding Schools

1 N Pack Square
Suite 301
Asheville, NC 28801
828-258-5354
Fax: 828-258-6428
tabs@tabs.org
www.boardingschools.com
The association promotes awareness and understanding of boarding schools with the goal of expanding the pool of applicants for member institutions. The association also offers resources for educators seeking training, research, guidance and support on all issues pertaining to the residential school experience.

Founded: 1975

Susan Nelson, Chair
Peter Upham, Executive Director

24 Association of State Supervisors of Mathematics

E-mail: admin@statemathleaders.org
www.statemathleaders.org
The Association of State Supervisors of Mathematics is an organization whose members provide supervising and consulting services in the area of mathematics. Its membership is made up of current or previous state or provincial supervisors of mathematics.

Founded: 1960

Robin Hill, President
Dewey Gottlieb, President Elect

25 Association of Teacher Educators

11350 Random Hills Road
Suite 800, PMB 6
Fairfax, VA 22030
703-659-1708
Fax: 703-595-4792
info@ate1.org
www.ate1.org
The mission of the Association of Teacher Educators is to improve the effectiveness of teacher education through leadership in the development of training programs. The association analyzes issues and practices relating to professional development and provides opportunities for the personal and professional growth of Association members.

Founded: 1920

Karen Embry Jenlink, President
Patricia Tate, First Vice President

26 Attention Deficit Disorder Association

PO Box 103
Denver, PA 17517
800-939-1019
Fax: 800-939-1019
info@add.org
add.org
The Attention Deficit Disorder Association (ADDA) is an adult ADHD organization providing information, resources and networking opportunities to help adults with Attention Deficit/Hyperactivity Disorder (AD/HD) lead better lives.

Duane Gordon, President
David Teplin, Psy.D, Co-Chair

27 Awards and Personalization Association

8735 W Higgins Road
Suite 300
Chicago, IL 60631
847-375-4800
Fax: 847-375-6480
info@awardspersonalization.org
awardspersonalization.org
The purpose of the Awards and Personalization Association is to advance the capabilities and growth of businesses whose primary focus is the

manufacture, distribution or sales of awards and recognition goods and services.

Richard Korbyl, President
Louise Ristau, CAE, Executive Director

28 **CHADD: Children & Adults with Attention Deficit/Hyperactivity Disorder**
4601 Presidents Drive
Suite 300
Lanham, MD 20706
301-306-7070
Fax: 301-306-7090
customer_service@chadd.org
www.chadd.org
National nonprofit organization offering advocacy, education and support for patients and parents of children with attention deficit disorders. The organization maintains support groups, provides a forum for continuing education about ADHD, and offers a national resource center.

Founded: 1987

Michael MacKay, President
April Gower, Chief Operating Officer

29 **Canadian Association for Astrological Education**
226 Cromwell Avenue
Oshawa, ON L1J-4T8
905-725-9179
thecaae@gmail.com
www.thecaae.com
Offers a curriculum for the study of astrology and its applications covering the areas of relationships, vocation, horary astrology, consulting, mathematical techniques and chart rectification.

Founded: 1993

Joan Ann Evelyn, President
Lina Grosso, Secretary

30 **Canadian Association for Co-Operative Education (CAFCE)**
411 Richmond Street E
Suite 200
Toronto, ON M5A-3S5
416-483-3311
Fax: 416-929-5256
membership@cafce.ca
www.cafce.ca
Voice for post-secondary Co-operative Education in Canada. The association promotes national standards, offers a forum for practitioners to network and provides informational resources and professional development opportunities for those working in the co-op education field.

Anne Fannon, President
Jennie Benjamins, Membership Services

31 **Canadian Association for Prior Learning Assessment (CAPLA)**
E-mail: b.kennedy@quicklinks.on.ca
capla.ca
National advocate for recognizing prior learning in Canada. Members include adult learners, researchers, employers, academic and training institutions and more.

Founded: 1994

Patrick J Donahoe, Ph.D, Chair
Bonnie Kennedy, Executive Director

32 **Canadian Association for Teacher Education**
E-mail: info@cate-acfe.ca
cate-acfe.ca
Promotes the study of teacher education through publications, scholarly research, conferences and dialogues.

Jodi Nickel, President
Alexandre Mesquita, Communications Director

33 **Canadian Association for the Study of Indigenous Education**
E-mail: mkresswh@unb.ca
www.casieaceea.org
Promotes the study of Aboriginal/Indigenous education by offering platforms for dialogue, connecting professionals and students with a shared interest in the subject and encouraging scholary work.

Mark Aquash, Ph.D, President
Margaret Kress-White, Ph.D, Secretary-Treasurer

34 **Canadian Association for the Study of Adult Education**
260 Dalhousie Street
Suite 204
Ottawa, ON K1N-7E4
613-241-0018
Fax: 613-241-0019
casae.aceea@csse.ca
www.casae-aceea.ca
Organization supporting adult education scholarship through publications on practice as well as through conferences and other resources.

Founded: 1981

Melissa White, President
Erin Careless, Secretary

35 **Canadian Association of University Teachers**
2705 Queensview Drive
Ottawa, ON K2B-8K2
613-820-2270
Fax: 613-820-7244
acppu@caut.ca
www.caut.ca
National advocate for academic professionals, providing lobbying services for its members as well as research and publications touching upon academic freedom and other relevant issues.

Founded: 1951

James Compton, President
David Robinson, Executive Director

36 **Canadian Education Association**
60 St. Clair Avenue E
Suite 703
Toronto, ON M4T-1N5
416-591-6300
866-803-9549
Fax: 416-591-5345
info@edcan.ca
www.edcan.ca
National voice for K-12 education in Canada, bringing together education professionals to discuss and plan for the future of the institution. The association offers research and professional development opportunities for its members.

Max Cooke, Direct of Communications
Gilles Latour, Chief Operating Officer

37 **Center for Civic Education**
5115 Douglas Fir Road
Suite J
Calabasas, CA 91302-2590
818-591-9321
Fax: 818-591-9330
cce@civiced.org
www.civiced.org
Non-profit, nonpartisan educational corporation dedicated to fostering the development of informed, responsible participation in civic life by citizens. The center aims to help students understand how constitutional democracy works, as well as democratic procedures for making decisions.

Thomas A Craven, President
Charles N Quigley, Executive Director

38 **Center for Parent Information and Resources**
35 Halsey Street
4th Floor
Newark, NJ 07102
973-642-8100
malizo@spannj.org
www.parentcenterhub.org
The center provides information to Parent Centers serving children with disabilities and their families. Some of the services offered by the center include research material, workspaces for exchange of resources between centers and an e-newsletter.

Debra A Jennings, Director
Myriam Alizo, Project Assistant

39 **Center on Education Policy**
2100 Pennsylvania Avenue NW
Suite 310
Washington, DC 20052
202-994-9050
Fax: 202-994-8859
cep-dc@cep-dc.org
www.cep-dc.org
Provides research and information about public education so that Americans can see the role public education plays in a democracy, and understand the conflicting perceptions about the system. The long term goal of the center is to improve upon existing systems.

Founded: 1995

Maria Voles Ferguson, Executive Director
Diane Stark Rentner, Deputy Director

40 **Constitutional Rights Foundation**
601 S Kingsley Drive
Los Angeles, CA 90005-4128
213-487-5590
Fax: 213-386-0459
crf@crf-usa.org
www.crf-usa.org
The mission of the foundation is to help youth gain a deeper understanding of citizenship through values expressed in the Constitution and its Bill of Rights, and educate them to become active and responsible participants in society. The two main areas of focus are Law and Government and Civic Participation.

Marshall Croddy, President
Keri Doggett, Director of Programs

41 **Council for Advancement & Support of Education**
1307 New York Avenue NW
Suite 1000
Washington, DC 20005-4701
202-328-2273
Fax: 202-387-4973
membersupportcenter@case.org
www.case.org
An international membership association that provides educational institutions with knowledge, standards, advocacy and training designed to strengthen alumni relations, communications, fundraising, marketing and allied professionals. CASE helps members raise funds for campus projects, produce recruitment materials, market their institutions to prospective students, diversify the

profession and foster public support of education.

Founded: 1974

Sue Cunningham, President & CEO
Ron Mattocks, Chief Operating Officer

42 **Council for Christian Colleges and Universities**
321 Eighth Street NE
Washington, DC 20002
202-546-8713
council@cccu.org
www.cccu.org
Association dedicated to advancing the cause of Christ-centered higher education by ensuring scholarships, programs and services embody the Christian values and spirit.

Founded: 1976

Shirley V Hoogstra, JD, President
Kristen Erbelding, Director, Human Resources

43 **Council for Exceptional Children**
2900 Crystal Drive
Suite 100
Arlington, VA 22202-3557
703-620-3660
888-232-7733
Fax: 703-264-9494
service@cec.sped.org
www.cec.sped.org
The Council for Exceptional Children works to improve the educational success of individuals with disabilities and/or unique gifts and talents.

Founded: 1922

Mikki Garcia, President
Laurie VanderPloeg, President Elect

44 **Council for the Accreditation of Educator Preparation**
1140 19th Street NW
Suite 400
Washington, DC 20036
202-223-0077
caep@caepnet.org
www.caepnet.org
Professional accrediting organization for schools, colleges and departments of education as well as alternative educators. The focus is P-12 student education.

Founded: 1954

Christopher A Koch, President
Gina Burkhardt, Vice President

45 **Council of Graduate Schools**
1 Dupont Circle NW
Suite 230
Washington, DC 20036
202-223-3791
Fax: 202-331-7157
general_inquiries@cgs.nche.edu
cgsnet.org
The Council of Graduate Schools represents the graduate dean community. The council seeks to advance graduate education and research through advocacy in policy, innovative research and the development of best practices.

Nancy Marcus, Chair
Suzanne T Ortega, President

46 **Council of Independent Colleges**
1 Dupont Circle NW
Suite 320
Washington, DC 20036-1142
202-466-7230
Fax: 202-466-7238
cic@cic.nche.edu
www.cic.edu
The Council of Independent Colleges is an association of nonprofit independent colleges and universities. The mission of the council is to advance excellence in schools, support leadership in school communities, and educate the public on the benefits of private higher education. The council also offers its members conferences, seminars, and other programs that help institutions to improve and to increase their visibility.

Founded: 1956

Thomas L Hellie, Chair
Richard Ekman, President

47 **Disability Resource Center**
University Community Center
730 College Avenue
Norman, OK 73019
405-325-3852
Fax: 405-325-4491
drc@ou.edu
www.ou.edu/content/drc.html
The Disability Resource Center at The University of Oklahoma offers services and supports to students with disabilities. Services include accomodations, digital accessibility, campus accessibility maps and employee resources.

Chelle' Guttery, Ph.D, Director
Darcy Adams Maelzer, M.Ed, Associate Director

48 **EMPath: Economic Mobility Pathways**
1 Washington Mall
Boston, MA 02108
617-259-2900
Fax: 617-247-8826
info@empathways.org
www.empathways.org
EMPath supports governments and nonprofit organizations in serving low-income families by offering programs, research and advocacy. Their aim is to empower families so that people can increase their income, secure permanent housing, attain education, and break out of the cycle of poverty.

Elizabeth Gaydos De Montigny, Chair
Elisabeth Babcock, President & CEO

49 **Easterseals**
141 W Jackson Boulevard
Suite 1400A
Chicago, IL 60604
312-726-6200
800-221-6827
Fax: 312-726-1494
info@easterseals.com
www.easterseals.com
Easter Seals provides services, education, outreach, and advocacy to people living with autism and other disabilities so they can learn and live as a part of their communities.

Founded: 1934

Joe Kern, Chairman
Katherine Beh Neas, Executive Vice President

50 **Education Commission of the States**
700 Broadway
Suite 810
Denver, CO 80203
303-299-3600
Fax: 303-296-8332
ecs@ecs.org
www.ecs.org
The Commision's mission is to help states develop effective policy and practice for public education by providing data, research, analysis and leadership; and by facilitating collaboration, the exchange of ideas among the states and long-range strategic thinking.

Jeremy Anderson, President
Phil Bryant, Chair

51 **Education Development Center**
43 Foundry Avenue
Waltham, MA 02453-8313
617-969-7100
Fax: 617-969-5979
contact@edc.org
www.edc.org
The Education Development Center designs and evaluates programs addressing some of the world's challenges in education, health and economic opportunity. The center's mission is to improve education, health promotion and care, workforce preparation, communications technologies and civic engagement in communities.

Founded: 1958

Vivien Stewart, Chair
David Offensend, President & CEO

52 **Education Writers Association**
3516 Connecticut Avenue NW
Washington, DC 20008
202-452-9830
www.ewa.org
The Education Writers Association works to stregnthen the community of education writers by offering programs, training, information, support, and recognition.

Greg Toppo, President
Caroline W Hendrie, Executive Director

53 **Education, Training and Research Associates**
100 Enterprise Way
Suite G300
Scotts Valley, CA 95066
800-620-8884
Fax: 831-438-4284
customerservice@etr.org
www.etr.org
The Education, Training and Research Associates is a nonprofit dedicated to providing solutions in the areas of health and education for the benefit of people with behavioral health issues. Their mission is to advance the work of health, education and social service providers through research, publications, information resources and programs.

Vincent Lafronza, MS, EdD, Chair
Vignetta Charles, CEO

54 **Excelencia in Education**
1156 15th Street NW
Suite 1001
Washington, DC 20005
202-785-7350
contact@edexcelencia.org
www.edexcelencia.org
Nonprofit organization working to support the acedemic success of Latino students in higher education. Goals are met through the promotion of education policies and provision of data on the educational status of Latinos.

Sarita E Brown, President
Deborah Santiago, COO & VP for Policy

55 **FHI 360**
FHI 360 Headquarters
359 Blackwell Street
Suite 200
Durham, NC 27701
919-544-7040
Fax: 919-544-7261
eec@fhi360.org
www.fhi360.org
A nonprofit organization that develops programs and materials promoting bias-free learning in

school and after school. Some services offered include quality assurance, research, data analysis, monitoring and evaluation, training and technical assistance and more.

Patrick C Fine, MEd, CEO
Deborah Kennedy-Iraheta, MA, Chief Operating Officer

56 **Facing History & Ourselves**
16 Hurd Road
Brookline, MA 02445-6919
617-232-1595
800-856-9039
Fax: 617-232-0281
info@facing.org
www.facinghistory.org
Facing History is an international nonprofit that helps teachers and students link the past to moral choices they face today. Some of the subjects examined include racism, prejudice and antisemitism.

Founded: 1976

Julie Abrams Leff, Chair
Roger Brooks, President & CEO

57 **Family Centered Learning Alternatives (FCLA)**
Context Institute
PO Box 946
Langley, WA 98260
360-221-6044
Fax: 360-221-6045
www.context.org
Supports parents' right to choose the educational environment best suited to their children's needs and promotes homeschooling as a legal nationwide learning alternative.

Founded: 1979

Robert Gilman, Founder & Director

58 **Foundation for Student Communication**
Princeton University
48 University Place
Princeton, NJ 10028
609-258-1111
Fax: 609-258-1222
info@businesstoday.org
www.businesstoday.org
Run by Princeton University undergraduates, the Foundation for Student Communication works to create a platform for business leaders both current and future to make connections. Interactions are encouraged through magazines, conferences, Seminar Series events, and Online Journal blog posts.

Founded: 1968

Colleen Kang, President
Paul Kigawa, Director of Finance

59 **Friends Council on Education**
1507 Cherry Street
Philadelphia, PA 19102
215-241-7245
Fax: 215-241-7299
Info@friendscouncil.org
www.friendscouncil.org
A national organization of Quaker schools which assists teachers, students and families by providing publications and programs supporting Quaker values in the classroom and in the life of the school community. Programs include peer networks, workshops, seminars, pilgrimages and more.

Founded: 1931

Drew Smith, Executive Director
Betsy Torg, Director, Dev & Comm

60 **Girls Incorporated**
120 Wall Street
Suite 1804
New York, NY 10005-3902
212-509-2000
Fax: 212-509-8708
communications@girlsinc.org
www.girlsinc.org
A national nonprofit youth organization dedicated to inspiring all girls to develop into healthy, educated, and independent adults. Programs offered touch upon the areas of media and economic literacy, leadership, relationships and more.

Founded: 1864

Melanie Gray, Board Chair
Judy Vredenburgh, President & CEO

61 **Global Exploration for Educators Organization**
2945 Morris Road
Ardmore, PA 19003
877-600-0105
Fax: 610-667-8543
jesse@geeo.org
www.geeo.org
A nonprofit organization dedicated to encouraging and assisting teachers to travel abroad to broaden their knowledge and enrich the education of their own students upon returning to the classroom. The organization provides travel incentives, professional development credits, educational resources and more.

Founded: 2007

Jesse Weisz, Founder & Executive Director
Aaron Muderick, Treasurer

62 **Independent Schools Association of the Southwest (ISAS)**
Energy Square
505 N Big Spring Street
Suite 406
Midland, TX 79701
432-684-9550
Fax: 432-684-9401
webmaster@isasw.org
www.isasw.org
A voluntary membership association of private schools. The central purpose of the association is to encourage, support and develop the highest standard for independent schools of the region and to recognize by formal accreditation those schools in which these standards are maintained.

Founded: 1955

Mark Desjardins, President
Rhonda Durham, Executive Director

63 **Institute for Educational Leadership**
4301 Connecticut Avenue NW
Suite 100
Washington, DC 20008
202-822-8405
Fax: 202-872-4050
iel@iel.org
iel.org
The vision of the Institute for Educational Leadership is to encourage leadership in all levels of society, inspiring those such as policymakers, administrators, and practitioners to develop youth for higher education, careers and citizenship.

Founded: 1964

C. Kent McGuire, Chair
Johan Uvin, President

64 **InterAction - American Council for Voluntary International Action**
1400 16th Street NW
Suite 210
Washington, DC 20036
202-667-8227
ia@interaction.org
www.interaction.org
InterAction is an alliance of U.S. based international nongovernmental organizations using its collective voice to shape important policy decisions on disaster relief and long term development issues including foreign assistance, the environment, women, health, education and agriculture.

Lindsay Coates, President
Sam Worthington, CEO

65 **International Association of Educators for World Peace**
PO Box 3282
Huntsville, AL 35810-0282
256-534-5501
Fax: 256-536-1018
info@iaewp.org
iaewp.org
The mission of the association is to encourage people to practice peaceful co-existence through education and cooperation in order to achieve international understanding and world peace.

Charles Mercieca, Ph.D, Founder

66 **Jewish Educators Assembly**
Broadway & Locust Avenue
PO Box 413
Cedarhurst, NY 11516
516-569-2537
Fax: 516-295-9039
jewisheducators@aol.com
www.jewisheducators.org
Promotes excellence among educators committed to Conservative Jewish education by advancing professionalism, encouraging leadership, providing advocacy and certification, encouraing lifelong learning and building community.

Louis Nagel, Ph.D, CJE, President
Edward Edelstein, Executive Director

67 **Jewish Federation of Greater Seattle**
6th Avenue & Lenora Street
Seattle, WA 98121
206-443-5400
Fax: 206-770-6363
info@jewishinseattle.org
www.jewishinseattle.org
Works to sustain a vibrant Jewish cimmunity that is connected locally, in Israel and worldwide. The federation also serves the needs of the Jewish comunity in Puget Sound region by offering human services, education, and cultural opportunities.

Founded: 1928

Sarah Boden, Chair
Nancy B Greer, President & CEO

68 **John Dewey Society for the Study of Education & Culture**
www.johndeweysociety.org
The society fosters John Dewey's commitment to the use of critical and reflective intelligence to find solutions to problems in education and culture. The society also offers conferences, journals, books and resources.

Founded: 1935

A.G. Rud, President
Sarah Stitzlein, President-Elect

69 **Learning Disabilities Association of America (LDA)**
4156 Library Road
Pittsburgh, PA 15234-1349
412-341-1515
888-300-6710
Fax: 412-344-0224
info@ldaamerica.org
ldaamerica.org
The Learning Disabilities Association of America is a national network of service providers supporting individuals with learning disabilities, their families and the professionals who work with them. The association offers learning resources, advocacy services and conferences.

Founded: 1963

Patricia Lillie, President
Mary-Clare Reynolds, Executive Director

70 **Lutheran Education Association**
7400 Augusta Street
River Forest, IL 60305
708-209-3343
Fax: 708-209-3458
lea@lea.org
www.lea.org
Seeks to spark ideas, thoughts and practices among Lutherans. The Lutheran Education Association links, equips and affirms educators and workers in ministry for the purpose of maintaining the Lutheran understanding of Scriptures and the Christian faith.

Mike Oldenburg, Chair
Jonathan Laabs, Ed.D, Executive Director

71 **MATRIX: Parent Network and Resource Center**
94 Galli Drive
Suite C
Novato, CA 94949
415-884-3535
800-578-2592
Fax: 415-884-3555
info@matrixparents.org
www.matrixparents.org
Matrix provides training and information to parents of children with disabilities of all kinds (physical, cognitive, emotional or learning). The Matrix network consists of parent training and info centers, family empowerment centers and family resource centers.

Founded: 1983

Alexis Lynch, Board President
Nora Thompson, Executive Director

72 **McREL International**
4601 DTC Boulevard
Suite 500
Denver, CO 80237-2596
303-337-0990
800-858-6830
info@mcrel.org
www.mcrel.org
Provides educators with research-based, practical guidance on the issues and challenges facing education today. Some services offered include customized consulting, professional learning and instructional coaching, leadership development, personnel evaluation, data analysis and program evaluation and more.

Founded: 1966

Bryan Goodwin, CEO & President
Robin Jarvis, Chief Program Officer

73 **Music Teachers National Association**
MTNA National Headquarters
1 W 4th Street
Suite 1550
Cincinnati, OH 45202
513-421-1420
888-512-5278
Fax: 513-421-2503
mtnanet@mtna.org
www.mtna.org
Advances the value of music study and music making to society while supporting the careers and professionalism of teachers of music. The association also provides networking opportunities, continuing education, conferences, certification, publications, grants and more.

Scott McBride Smith, NCTM, President
Gary L Ingle, Executive Director & CEO

74 **National Academy of Education**
500 5th Street NW
Washington, DC 20001
202-334-1947
Fax: 202-334-2350
info@naeducation.org
naeducation.org
Advances quality education research and its use in policy formation and practice. The academy also offers professional development fellowship programs.

Founded: 1965

Michael Feuer, President
Gregory White, Executive Director

75 **National Alliance of Black School Educators (NABSE)**
National Alliance of Black School Educators
310 Pennsylvania Avenue SE
Washington, DC 20003
202-608-6310
800-221-2654
Fax: 202-608-6319
info@nabse.org
www.nabse.org
Nonprofit organization devoted to furthering the academic success of the nation's children, with an emphasis on children of African descent. NABSE is dedicated to improving both the educational experiences and accomplishments of African American youth through the development and use of instructional and motivational methods that lead to higher achievement.

Founded: 1970

Marietta English, President
Sheila Harrison-Williams, Ph.D, Treasurer

76 **National Association for Developmental Education (NADE)**
PO Box 963
Northport, AL 35476
205-331-5997
877-233-9455
Fax: 866-519-1331
office@thenade.org
thenade.org
Seeks to improve the theory and practice of developmental education and the professional skills of developmental educators as well as develop programs. The association offers advocacy, awards, publications and conference events to further this goal.

Robin Ozz, President
Mary Zimmerer, Ph.D, Vice President

77 **National Association for Gifted Children**
1331 H Street NW
Suite 1001
Washington, DC 20005
202-785-4268
Fax: 202-785-4248
nagc@nagc.org
www.nagc.org
Organization of parents, teachers, educators and other professionals committed to addressing the unique needs of children and youth with demonstrated gifts and talents. The organization's mission is to help children develop through education, advocacy, community building and research.

George Betts, President
M. Rene Islas, Executive Director

78 **National Association for Year-Round Education**
San Diego, CA 92171-1386
619-276-5296
Fax: 858-571-5754
spepper@pepper3.com
www.nayre.org
The National Association for Year-Round Education promotes year-round education by providing services on time and learning. The association provides publications, encourages research, and presents a clearinghouse of information on the benefits of year-round education.

David Hornak, Executive Director
Charles Ballinger, Ph.D, Executive Director Emeritus

79 **National Association for the Legal Support of Alternative Schools (NALSAS)**
18520 NW 67th Avenue
Suite 188
Miami, FL 33015
800-456-7784
educate@nalsas.org
www.nalsas.org
The National Association for the Legal Support of Alternative Schools was originally designed to help interested persons/organizations locate, evaluate, and create viable alternatives to traditional schooling approaches, such as home study. The association now offers a Certificate of Accreditation for homeschooling programs and other members.

Founded: 1973

Ed Nagel, CEO

80 **National Association of Career Colleges (NACC)**
44 Byward Market Square
Suite 270
Ottawa, ON K1N-7A2
613-800-0340
855-839-5151
Fax: 613-789-9669
aqueen@nacc.ca
nacc.ca
Organization bringing together professionals from career colleges to develop the programs that serve their students. Some services offered by the association include curriculums, professional development for instructors, conferences and resources for students and colleges.

Founded: 1896

Frank Gerencser, Chair
Serge Buy, CEO

81 **National Association of Catholic School Teachers**
1700 Sansom Street
Suite 903
Philadelphia, PA 19103
215-665-0993
Fax: 215-568-8270

nacst.nacst@verizon.net
www.nacst.com
The National Association of Catholic School Teachers unifies, advises and assists Catholic school teachers in matters of collective bargaining.

Founded: 1978

Rita C Schwartz, President

82 **National Association of Federally Impacted Schools**
Hall of the States
444 N Capitol Street NW
Suite 419
Washington, DC 20001
202-624-5455
Fax: 202-624-5468
bryan@nafisdc.org
www.nafisdc.org
Corporation of school districts throughout the country organized primarily to educate Congress on Impact Aid. The association works to ensure that the needs of federally connected children are met with adequate federal funds.

Jim Sarruda, President
Chad Blotsky, Vice President

83 **National Association of Special Education Teachers**
1250 Connecticut Avenue NW
Suite 200
Washington, DC 20036
800-754-4421
Fax: 800-754-4421
contactus@naset.org
www.naset.org
The National Association of Special Education Teachers (NASET) is the only national membership organization dedicated to meeting the needs of special education teachers and those preparing for the field of special education teaching. NASET offers publications, membership benefits and a career center.

Roger Pierangelo, Ph.D, Co-Executive Director
George Giuliani, Ph.D, Co-Executive Director

84 **National Association of State Boards of Education**
333 John Carlyle Street
Suite 530
Alexandria, VA 22314
703-684-4000
Fax: 703-836-2313
boards@nasbe.org
www.nasbe.org
The National Association of State Boards of Education works to strengthen state leadership in educational policymaking, promote excellence in education, advocate for equal opportunity, and assure continued support for public education.

Founded: 1958

Jay Barth, Chair
Kristen Amundson, President & CEO

85 **National Board for Professional Teaching Standards**
1525 Wilson Boulevard
Suite 700
Arlington, VA 22209
703-465-2700
800-228-3224
www.nbpts.org
The mission of the National Board for Professional Teaching Standards is to improve the quality of teaching and learning by developing professional standards for accomplished teaching, certifying teachers who meet those standards and integrating certified teachers into educational reform efforts.

Founded: 1987

Peggy Brookins, NBCT, President & CEO
Joe Doctor, Chief Operating Officer

86 **National Catholic Educational Association**
1005 N Glebe Road
Suite 525
Arlington, VA 22201
571-257-0010
800-711-6232
Fax: 703-243-0025
info@ncea.org
www.ncea.org
Rooted in the Gospel of Jesus Christ, the National Catholic Educational Association (NCEA) is a professional membership organization that provides leadership, direction and service to fulfill the teaching mission of Catholic schools.

Reverend George V. Murry, SJ, Chairman
Thomas W Burnford, D.Min, Ph.D, President & CEO

87 **National Center for Learning Disabilities**
32 Laight Street
2nd Floor
New York, NY 10013
212-545-7510
888-575-7373
Fax: 212-545-9665
info@ncld.org
www.ncld.org
The National Center for Learning Disabilities (NCLD) works to ensure that the nation's children, adolescents and adults with learning disabilities have every opportunity to succeed in school, work and life. NCLD provides advocacy services, programs and research to fulfil this purpose.

Founded: 1977

Frederic M Poses, Chairman
Mimi Corcoran, President & CEO

88 **National Center for School Engagement**
Pueblo, CO
719-248-8669
TerriMM@schoolengagement.net
schoolengagement.org
Provides training and technical assistance, research and evaluation to school districts, law enforcement agencies, courts, as well as state and federal agencies to encourage students to succeed in school. Special attention is given to at-risk students and the prevention of truancy, the dropout rate, and bullying.

Terri Martinez-McGraw, Co-Director
Joanna Zorn Heilbrunn, Co-Director

89 **National Coalition of Independent Scholars**
PO Box 120182
San Antonio, TX 78212
919-451-4801
info@ncis.org
www.ncis.org
Nonprofit corporation providing information for the creation of local organizations of independent scholars. The coalition seeks to improve access to research institutions and libraries, offer grants to members, provide information and advice about fellowships and publishing and more.

Founded: 1989

Amanda Haste, President
Tula Connell, Communications Officer

90 **National Commission for Cooperative Education**
WACE
600 Suffolk Street
Suite 503
Lowell, MA 01854
978-934-1867
Fax: 978-934-4084
marty_ford@uml.edu
www.waceinc.org
Organization linking higher institutions, employers and public authorities through research, programs, and services designed to advance learning where education and work experience intersect.

Founded: 1962

Paul J Stonely, Ph.D, CEO
Marty Ford, Director

91 **National Consortium for Academics and Sports**
University of Central Florida
4000 Central Florida Boulevard
Suite 113
Orlando, FL 32826
407-823-4770
Fax: 407-823-3542
keith.lee@ucf.edu
www.ncasports.org
The mission of the association is to use the power and appeal of sports as a tool with which to positively affect social change. Their services cover the areas of sports, diversity, education, social justice and ethical leadership.

Founded: 1985

Joseph Crowley, Ph.D, Chairman
Richard E Lapchick, Ph.D, Founder & President

92 **National Council for Black Studies**
University of Cincinnati, Africana Studies Dept
PO Box 210370
Cincinnati, OH 45221-0370
513-556-0785
info@ncbsonline.org
www.ncbsonline.org
Promotes academic excellence and social responsibility in the discipline of Africana/Black Studies through the production and dissemination of knowledge, professional development and training, and advocacy for social change and social justice.

Founded: 1975

Georgene Bess Montgomery, President
Amilcar Shabazz, Vice President

93 **National Council for Science and the Environment**
1101 17th Street NW
Suite 250
Washington, DC 20036
202-530-5810
ncse@ncseglobal.org
www.ncseglobal.org
Nonprofit organization seeking to improve the scientific basis of environmental decision making through fostering collaboration between leaders in the areas of interdisciplinary research, education, policy, and business.

Founded: 1990

James Buizer, Chair
Michelle Wyman, Executive Director

94 **National Council of Urban Education Associations (NCUEA)**
National Education Association (NEA)
1201 16th Street NW
Washington, DC 20036-3290

202-833-4000
Fax: 202-822-7974
ncuea@nea.org
www.nea.org
NCUEA is a caucus of local affiliates of the National Education Association (NEA), dedicated to strengthening and making NEA more responsive to member needs. NCUEA works to develop public education in urban schools by supporting local associations, leaders and members on issues around advocacy, diversity, communication, human rights and more.

Lily Eskelsen Garc¡a, President
Becky Pringle, Vice President

95 National Council on Measurement in Education

NCME
100 N 20th Street
Suite 400
Philadelphia, PA 19103
215-461-6263
Fax: 215-564-2175
ncme@fernley.com
www.ncme.org
The National Council on Measurement in Education is a professional organization for individuals involved in the work of educational measurement (such as assessment and testing). Council members include university faculty; test developers; state and federal testing and research directors, and testing specialists working in various fields. The council aims to develop educational measurement methods so that they can be more effective.

Randy Bennett, President
Rebecca Zwick, President Elect

96 National Council on Rehabilitation Education (NCRE)

1099 E Champlain Drive
Suite A, 137
Fresno, CA 93720
559-906-0787
Fax: 559-412-2550
info@ncre.org
ncre.org
A professional organization of educators dedicated to serving persons with disabilities through education and research. The council works to maintain excellence in the field of rehabilitation by addressing issues around training priorities, federal funding, and research activities.

Founded: 1955

Michael Accordino, D.Ed,CRC,LMHC, President
Denise Catalano, Ph.D., CRC, First Vice President

97 National Council on Student Development (NCSD)

NCSD National Office
301 Largo Road
Largo, MD 20774
866-972-0717
ncsd@ncsdonline.org
www.ncsd-aacc.com
The council's mission is to promote knowledge, expertise and professional development opportunities for student development professionals through advocacy and education.

Kevin J Wade, President
Linda Garcia, Treasurer

98 National Education Association (NEA)

National Education Association
1201 16th Street NW
Washington, DC 20036-3290
202-833-4000
Fax: 202-822-7974
nche@nea.org
www.nea.org
An organization made up of professional employees with the mission of advocating for public education, from pre-school to university programs, to ensure success of students. Some areas covered within their services include debt, educational funding, legislative action, human and civil rights, teaching strategies, grants and events and more.

Founded: 1857

Lily Eskelsen Garc¡a, President
Becky Pringle, Vice President

99 National Education Association-Retired

National Education Association
1201 16th Street NW
Washington, DC 20036-3290
202-833-4000
Fax: 202-822-7974
etcwjh@aol.com
www.nea.org/retired
NEA-Retired serves the needs of retired education employees. Some services offered by the program include the improvement of retirement pensions, intergenerational programs and activities and political action.

Tom Curran, President
John Jensen, Vice President

100 National Educational Association of Disabled Students

Carleton University
1125 Colonel by Drive
Room 514, Unicentre
Ottawa, ON K1S-5B6
613-380-8065
877-670-1256
Fax: 613-369-4391
info@neads.ca
www.neads.ca
Advocates for accessible education and employment for disabled graduates. The association provides support in the form of research, resources, projects, financial aid and more services offered to their members.

Founded: 1986

Frank Smith, National Coordinator
Mahadeo Sukhai, Director of Research

101 National Lekotek Center

2001 N Clybourn Avenue
1st Floor
Chicago, IL 60614
773-528-5766
Fax: 773-537-2992
lekotek@lekotek.org
www.lekotek.org
Nonprofit organization providing services for kids with special needs. The center offers a therapeutic toy lending library and play education for children ages 0-8 with disabilities, with the goal of helping them understand how to relate to their environment and their families.

Eric Gastevich, Chair
Rebecca Clark, Interim President & CEO

102 National Organization on Disability

77 Water Street
Suite 204
New York, NY 10005
646-505-1191
Fax: 646-505-1184
info@nod.org
www.nod.org
The National Organization on Disability is a nonprofit organization promoting the participation of people with disabilities in society. The organization works with employers and educational institutions to create strategies for disability inclusion.

Founded: 1982

Gov. Tom Ridge, Chair
Carol Glazer, President

103 National Rural Education Association

615 McCallie Avenue
Hunter Hall 212
Chattanooga, TN 37421
423-425-4539
allen-pratt@utc.edu
www.nrea.net
Organization made up of rural school administrators, teachers, board members, regional service agency personnel, researchers, business and industry representatives. The organization serves the educational needs of those living in rural communities.

Founded: 1907

Allison Nys, President
Allen Pratt, Ed.D, Executive Director

104 National School Boards Association

1680 Duke Street
2nd Floor
Alexandria, VA 22314-3493
703-838-6722
Fax: 703-683-7590
info@nsba.org
www.nsba.org
Nonprofit collective of state associations of school boards advocating for excellence in public education in the United States.

Kevin E Ciak, President
Thomas Gentzel, Executive Director & CEO

105 National School Public Relations Association

15948 Derwood Road
Rockville, MD 20855
301-519-0496
Fax: 301-519-0494
info@nspra.org
www.nspra.org
Provides communication training and services to school leaders with the aim of advancing education through responsible public relations. The association also offers resource and research files, contacts in the corporate communication industry, workshops and seminars.

Founded: 1935

Julie Thannum, APR, President
Rich Bagin, APR, Executive Director

106 National Society for Experiential Education

19 Mantua Road
Mount Royal, NJ 08061
856-423-3427
Fax: 856-423-3420
nsee@talley.com
www.nsee.org
The National Society for Experiential Education (NSEE) is a nonprofit membership association of educators, businesses and community leaders in-

terested in the development and improvement of experiential education programs nationwide.

Founded: 1971

Stephanie Thomason, President
Haley Brust, Executive Director

107 National Student Council (NatStuCo)

1904 Association Drive
Reston, VA 20191-1537
703-860-0200
NatStuCo@NatStuCo.org
www.nasc.us
Promotes student participation within school communities, encourages development of new student councils, assists state associations of student councils, provides leadership training for council members and advisors and encourages healthy living for young people.

Founded: 1931

Flora Sapsin, Region 1 Executive Director
Roberta Bittel, Region 2 Executive Director

108 National Student Exchange

National Student Exchange
2613 Northridge Parkway
Suite 106
Ames, IA 50010
515-450-5529
info@nse.org
www.nse.org
The National Student Exchange is a program offering undergraduate study opportunities across regional, provincial, and cultural borders. NSE students gain insight into the historical and cultural makeup of different regions, improve their communication skills with individuals from different backgrounds and prepare themselves to live and work in a culturally diverse society.

Founded: 1968

Debra Sanborn, Ph.D, President

109 National Women's Studies Association

11 E Mount Royal Avenue
Suite 100
Baltimore, MD 21202
410-528-0355
Fax: 410-528-0357
nwsaoffice@nwsa.org
www.nwsa.org
The National Women's Studies Association supports the production of educational materials on the subject of women and gender. Their mission is to demonstrate the value of women's studies and feminist scholarship in education.

Founded: 1977

Allison Kimmich, Executive Director
Patti Provance, Deputy Director

110 Nechi Training, Research and Health Promotions Institute

Nechi Institute
PO Box 2039, Station Main
St. Albert, AB T8N-2G3
800-459-1884
Fax: 780-458-1883
nechi@nechi.com
nechi.com
Offers accredited programs for Indigenous training, research and health. Nechi provides councellors, health care workers, social workers, educators, government agencies and other support agencies with knowledge and tools to help them address the issues faced by Indigenous people.

Betty Bastien, Ph.D, Chairperson
Colleen Courtoreille, CEO

111 New England School Development Council

28 Lord Road
Marlborough, MA 01752
508-481-9444
Fax: 508-481-5655
nesdec@nesdec.org
www.nesdec.org
Nonprofit educational organization helping schools to achieve and maintain high performance standards by providing planning and management, professional development, legal assistance, research and publications services.

Founded: 1946

Brendan F Minnihan, Ph.D, Chair
Arthur L Bettencourt, Ed.D, Executive Director

112 North American Association for Environmental Education (NAAEE)

2000 P Street NW
Suite 540
Washington, DC 20036
202-419-0412
Fax: 202-419-0415
naaeesocial@gmail.com
naaee.org
Teaches children and adults how to learn about and investigate their environment and to make intelligent, informed decisions about how they can take care of it. Environmental literacy and social engagement is fostered through education. NAAEE also offers consultation services, research, an affiliate network, policy initiatives, certification and more.

October

Charlotte Clark, Board Chair
Judy Braus, Executive Director

113 North American Association of Educational Negotiators

1523 Military Turnpike
Suite 100
Plattsburgh, NY 12901
518-603-3303
execdir@naen.org
www.naen.org
Improves the knowledge and performance of K-12 school district, community college, and university management negotiators by advancing their professional status, providing a forum for communication, and encouraging information exchanges with others in the same profession.

James B Fernow, President
Rachel M Rissetto, Executive Director

114 North American Students of Cooperation

NASCO Main Office
1100 W Cermak Road
Suite 514
Chicago, IL 60608
773-404-2667
Fax: 331-223-9727
info@nasco.coop
www.nasco.coop
Organizes and educates affordable group equity co-ops to promote a community oriented cooperative movement. The association provides education and technical assistance to its members, as well as public education about the co-op movement and spirit.

Founded: 1968

Alex Green, President
Syd Burke, Development Officer

115 Northwest Commission on Colleges and Universities

8060 165th Avenue NE
Suite 100
Redmond, WA 98052
425-558-4224
Fax: 425-376-0596
egossett@nwccu.org
www.nwccu.org
The mission of the Northwest Commission on Colleges and Universities is to assure educational quality and enhance institutional effectiveness of higher education schools in the Northwest region through the application of accreditation criteria and evaluation procedures.

Sandra E Elman, Ph.D, President
Pamela Goad, Ph.D, Senior Vice President

116 Oakland School

128 Oakland Farm Way
Troy, VA 22974
434-293-9059
Fax: 434-296-8930
information@oaklandschool.net
www.oaklandschool.net
Private boarding and day school specializing in helping students with learning difficulties. Oakland School provides an individualized academic program focused on reading, writing, math and study skills. It is a school for children ages 6 - 13 years old. A variety of recreational activities, including horseback riding, are also offered on a farm for Fall/Winter and Summer Programs.

Carol Williams, Head of School
Rebecca Tweel Jolin, Admissions & Marketing

117 Oklahoma State University - Education Outreach

Oklahoma State University
325R Willard Hall
Stillwater, OK 74078
405-744-6254
800-765-8933
Fax: 405-744-7713
education.outreach@okstate.edu
education.okstate.edu
Education Outreach provides courses and acedemic programs as well as support and services to educators. It also encourages collaboration between the college and other communities. Some programs offered by Education Outreach include faculty-led study abroad trips, distance learning, non-credit courses and professional development opportunities.

John S.C. Romans, Ph.D, Dean
Bert Jacobson, Ph.D, Associate Dean

118 PACER Center

8161 Normandale Boulevard
Bloomington, MN 55437
952-838-9000
888-248-0822
Fax: 952-838-0199
pacer@pacer.org
www.pacer.org
PACER Center serves children, youth, and young adults with disabilities, with the goal of improving their quality of life and creating opportunities. The center fosters a supportive environment where parents can help parents and recieve the education and programs they need to continue supporting their children in every stage of their lives.

Founded: 1977

Paula F Goldberg, Executive Director
Matthew Woods, President

119 **Parents, Let's Unite for Kids**
516 N 32nd Street
Billings, MT 59101-6003
406-255-0540
800-222-7585
Fax: 406-255-0523
info@pluk.org
www.pluk.org
Network of families and children with disabilities in Montana working to support one another, and share health and policy information for the benefit of their children.

Founded: 1984

J. Jill Charter, Vice President
Sheryl Shockley, Director of Operations

120 **Partnership for the Assessment of Readiness for College and Careers**
1747 Pennsylvania Avenue NW
Suite 600S
Washington, DC 20006-4604
202-748-8100
governingboard.info@dc.gov
parcc-assessment.org
The Partnership for Assessment of Readiness for College and Careers is a collection of states working to develop a set of assessments that measure whether students are on track to be successful in college and their careers. These high quality, computer-based K-12 assessments in mathematics and English language arts/literacy give teachers, schools, students and parents better information about student progress and needs.

Hanseul Kang, Chair
Bonnie O'Keefe, Committee Member

121 **Peace & Justice Studies Association**
100 Bishop Circle
375 Upham Hall
Oxford, OH 45056
202-681-2057
info@peacejusticestudies.org
www.peacejusticestudies.org
Brings together academics, K-12 teachers and grassroots activists to explore alternatives to violence and share strategies for social justice and social change. PJSA also serves as a professional association for scholars in the field of peace and conflict resolution studies, and is a member of the International Peace Research Association.

Founded: 2001

Laura Finley, Co-Chair
Michael Loadenthal, Executive Director

122 **Phoenix House**
New York, NY
888-671-9392
askph@phoenixhouse.org
www.phoenixhouse.org
Phoenix House offers treatment services to people with addiction issues through several treatment centers across the U.S. Centers offer services such as substance abuse evaluation, educational services, outpatient counseling, residential treatment, recovery plans, detoxification and more.

Benjamin R Nordstrom, MD, Ph.D, SVP & Chief Clinical Officer
Ann Bray, President & CEO

123 **Public Relations Student Society of America**
120 Wall Street
21st Floor
New York, NY 10005
212-460-1474
Fax: 212-995-0757
prssa@prsa.org
prssa.prsa.org
The Public Relations Student Society of America (PRSSA) is an organization dedicated to serving students interested in public relations and communications. PRSSA advocates for high academic standards, ethical principles and diversity in the field, while offering professional development and networking opportunities to students.

Founded: 1967

Andrew Cook, National President
Jeneen Garcia, Executive Director

124 **Reading Education Association**
Richmond Corporate Centre
1800 N 12th Street
Reading, PA 19604
610-374-7101
Fax: 610-374-3173
office@readingea.com
readingea.com
The Reading Education Association (REA) represents the educators and students of Reading, Pennsylvania . REA advocates for the equal education and educational opportunities for the school district of Reading.

Rebecca Titus, President
Priscilla Knight, Office Manager

125 **Religious Education Association (REA)**
765-225-8836
Fax: 203-432-5356
nc@religiouseducation.net
religiouseducation.net
Creates opportunities for exploring and advancing the interconnected practices of scholarship, research, teaching, and leadership in faith communities, academic institutions, and the wider world community.

Founded: 1903

Bert Roebben, President
Lucinda Huffaker, Executive Secretary

126 **STEM Education Coalition**
2000 M Street NW
Suite 520
Washington, DC 20036
202-400-2192
info@stemedcoalition.org
www.stemedcoalition.org
Works to raise awareness in congress, the Administration, and other organizations about the critical role that STEM education plays in ensuring the economic and technological expertise of the U.S. in the global marketplace.

Jodi Peterson, Chair
James Brown, Executive Director

127 **Sexuality Information & Education Council of the United States**
1012 14th Street NW
Suite 1108
Washington, DC 20005
202-265-2405
Fax: 202-462-2340
media@siecus.org
www.siecus.org
Promotes sexuality education for people of all ages, protects sexual rights, and expands access to sexual health services. The council trains educators, advocates for sound public policies related to sexuality, and provides information and resources on a host of sexuality topics.

Founded: 1964

Chitra Panjabi, President & CEO
Jennifer Driver, State Policy Director

128 **Smarter Balanced Assessment Consortium**
E-mail: sb@smarterbalanced.org
www.smarterbalanced.org
Smarter Balanced is a public agency offering an online assessment system informed by thousands of educators and aligned to the Common Core State Standards (CCSS). The agency also offers tools for educators to improve teaching and learning in the classroom.

Tony Alpert, Executive Director
Paisha Allmendinger, Director, Finance/Operations

129 **Society for the Advancement of Excellence in Education (SAEE)**
1889 Springfield Road
Suite 225
Kelowna, BC V1Y-5V5
250-717-1163
Fax: 250-717-1134
info@saee.ca
www.saee.ca
Provides non-partisan education research and information to policy-makers, education partners and the public in order to encourage higher performance throughout Canada's public education system.

Founded: 1996

Elizabeth Bredberg, Research Director

130 **Solution Tree**
555 N Morton Street
Bloomington, IN 47404
812-336-7700
800-733-6786
Fax: 812-336-7790
info@solutiontree.com
www.solutiontree.com
Strives to be the premier provider of books, videos, multimedia resources, and professional development opportunities designed to help educators throughout the world realize continuous school improvement and connect with youth at risk.

Founded: 1998

Ed Ackerman, President & COO
Erica Dooley-Dorocke, Marketing & Communications

131 **Summit Vision**
8111 Schott Road
Westerville, OH 43801
614-403-3891
trey@summit-vision.com
summit-vision.com
Summit Vision believes that through the use of adventure and experiential learning tools, people can develop valuable skills and traits such as problem-solving, conflict resolution, decision-making, leadership, perseverance and empathy. Services offered include play days, camp and fitness programs.

Founded: 1997

Trey McBane, President
Karen Burke, Office Manager

132 **Teach Plus**
27-43 Wormwood Street
Tower Point, Suite 410
Boston, MA 02210
617-533-9900
info@teachplus.org
teachplus.org
Offers programs to support teachers in making policy changes for the betterment of the education system for all.

Michelle Boyers, Board Chair
Roberto J Rodriguez, President & CEO

133 **The Gifted Child Society**
1 Myrtle Avenue
2nd Floor
Allendale, NJ 07401
201-444-6530
Fax: 201-444-9099
admin@gifted.org
www.gifted.org
Nonprofit organization providing educational enrichment and support services specifically designed for gifted children. Programs offered include workshops, day camps, IQ testing services, parent and guardian education and training for professionals and school educators.

Founded: 1957

Anastasia Ivanova, President
D'Arcy Natale, TGCS Managing Director

134 **The Jewish Federations of North America**
25 Broadway
17th Floor
New York, NY 10004
212-284-6500
info@JewishFederations.org
jewishfederations.org
The Jewish Federations of North America is made up of Federations and communities dedicated to serving the Jewish communities of North America by offering education, funding for services, advocacy, crisis relief and more.

Richard V Sandler, Chair
Jerry B Silverman, CEO

135 **US Israel Education Association**
E-mail: info@usieducation.org
usieducation.org
Provides resources to help build connections between the U.S. and Israeli leaders by offering educational tours and briefings about the systems of Israeli government.

Heather Johnston, Executive Director
Brant McDuffie, Managing Director

136 **United States Student Association**
1211 Connecticut Avenue NW
PO Box 33486
Washington, DC 20036
202-640-6570
ops@usstudents.org
usstudents.org
The United States Student Association provides leadership opportunities for students to make social change by developing grassroots campus bases and strategic campaigns, as well as providing training in order to challenge systems of oppression through education justice perspectives.

Breana Ross, President
Joseline Garcia, Vice President

137 **Wilderness Education Association**
PO Box 601
Dresden, OH 43821
740-607-9759
nationaloffice@weainfo.org
www.weainfo.org
The Wilderness Education Association is a nonprofit organization whose purpose is to educate the general public and outdoor leaders in the appropriate use of wildlands and protected areas by developing and implementing educational programs and by forming strategic alliances with federal land management agencies, conservation groups and all organizations that are affected by wildlands.

Founded: 1977

Kelli McMahan, President
Francois Guilleux, President Elect

138 **World Council for Curriculum and Instruction (WCCI)**
WCCI Secretariat
Alliant International University
10455 Pomerado Road
San Diego, CA 92131
858-635-4718
Fax: 858-635-4714
wcci@alliant.edu
wcci-international.org
A transnational educational organization with the goal of creating a just and peaceful world community through support of education and community development programs. The organization also has a special status with Economic and Social Council (ECOSOC) of the UN and UNESCO.

Jessica Kimmel, President
Estela C Matriano, Executive Director

139 **World Trade Centers Association**
120 Broadway
Suite 3350
New York, NY 10271
212-432-2626
800-937-8886
info@wtca.org
www.wtca.org
Fosters a global Trade Center Network that enhances the brand and promotes prosperity through trade and investment.

Founded: 1970

Scott Ferguson, CEO
Jennifer Guerrero, CPA, Chief Financial Officer

Administration

140 **American Association of Collegiate Registrars & Admissions Officers**
1 Dupont Circle NW
Suite 520
Washington, DC 20036
202-293-9161
Fax: 202-872-8857
reillym@aacrao.org
www.aacrao.org
Nonprofit professional organization bringing together those who work in higher education from around the world. The association provides professional development, guidelines, and professional standards to be used in the areas of records management, admissions, enrollment, information technology and student services.

Jim Bouse, President
Mike Reilly, Executive Director

141 **American Association of School Administrators**
1615 Duke Street
Alexandria, VA 22314
703-528-0700
Fax: 703-841-1543
info@aasa.org
www.aasa.org
The mission of the American Association of School Administrators is to support and develop effective school system leaders who are dedicated to ensuring the quality of public education.

Daniel A Domenech, Executive Director
Chuck Woodruff, Chief Operating Officer

142 **American Association of University Administrators**
10 Church Road
Wallingford, PA 19086
814-460-6498
Fax: 610-565-8089
dking@aaua.org
www.aaua.org
The mission of the American Association of University Administrators is to develop and advance superior standards for the profession of higher education administration.

Founded: 1970

Rosa Rivera-Hainaj, Chairperson
Dan L King, President & CEO

143 **American Finance Association (AFA)**
350 Main Street
Malden, MA 02148
781-388-8599
800-835-6770
cs-membership@wiley.com
www.afajof.org
Association working to promote awareness about financial economics. It aims to improve public understanding of financial problems, distribute knowledge through written and other media and to enourage finance as an educational study.

David Scharfstein, President
David Hirshleifer, Vice President

144 **Association for Supervision and Curriculum Development (ASCD)**
ASCD
1703 N Beauregard Street
Alexandria, VA 22311
703-578-9600
800-933-2723
Fax: 703-575-5400
press@ascd.org
www.ascd.org
A membership organization that develops programs, products, and services to support educators in excelling in their work. Some supports offered include publications, conferences, online courses and more.

Founded: 1943

Ben Shuldiner, President
Deb Delisle, Executive Director & CEO

145 **Association of Arts Administration Educators**
188 Hanford Street
Columbus, OH 43206
312-469-0795
info@artsadministration.org
www.artsadministration.org
The Association of Arts Administration Educators (AAAE) is an international organization representing college and university graduate and undergraduate programs in arts administration. Through their programs, the association offers students opportunities to develop knowledge and skills in arts leadership, management, entrepreneurship, cultural policy and more.

Founded: 1975

Sherburne Laughlin, President
Katy Coy, Executive Director

146 **Association of College Administration Professionals**
PO Box 1389
Staunton, VA 24402
540-885-1873
Fax: 540-885-6133
acap@cfw.com
acap.webstarts.com
The Association of College Administration Professionals provides career development services to college and university administrators. Among these services are monthly newsletters, articles and surveys, job postings and annual conferences.

Founded: 1995

Meg Murray, CEO

147 **Association of School Business Officials International**
11401 N Shore Drive
Reston, VA 20190-4232
866-682-2729
Fax: 703-478-0205
asboreq@asbointl.org
asbointl.org
Provides programs and services that promote high standards for school business management procedures and which support professional development. Among the services offered are certification options, scholarships, legislative resources, a global network and advocacy.

Founded: 1910

Anthony N Dragona, Ed.D., RSBA, President
John D Musso, CAE, RSBA, Executive Director

148 **Association of University Programs in Health Administration**
1730 M Street NW
Suite 407
Washington, DC 20036
202-763-7283
Fax: 703-894-0941
aupha@aupha.org
www.aupha.org
The Association of University Programs in Health Administration (AUPHA) is a global network of colleges, universities, faculty, individuals and organizations united by the goal of improving healthcare delivery through development in healthcare management and policy education. Some programs offered by AUPHA include baccalaureate, master's and doctoral degree programs in health administration education, workshops and international programs.

Keith Benson, Ph.D, Chair
Gerald Glandon, Ph.D, President & CEO

149 **Canadian Association of Principals**
E-mail: info@cdnprincipals.org
cdnprincipals.org
National organization advocating on behalf of school principals and vice principals with the goal of improving education for students. The association offers journals, reports and conferences for its members to get together and share ideas.

Maxine Gellar, President
Kyran Dwyer, President Elect

150 **Council for the Advancement of Standards in Higher Education**
PO Box 1369
Fort Collins, CO 80522-1369
202-862-1400
executive_director@cas.edu
www.cas.edu
The Council for the Advancement of Standards in Higher Education (CAS) promotes collaboration within campus and creates standards for conduct in student affairs, student services, and student development programs.

Founded: 1979

Deborah Garrett, President
Marybeth Drechsler Sharp, Executive Director

151 **Council of Chief State School Officers**
1 Massachusetts Avenue NW
Suite 700
Washington, DC 20001-1431
202-336-7000
Fax: 202-408-8072
communications@ccsso.org
www.ccsso.org
Nonprofit organization of education leaders providing leadership, advocacy, and technical assistance to resolve issues related to education. The council envisions a system of schooling in each state that ensures high standards of performance and prepares students to succeed as productive members of society.

Melody Schopp, President
Chris Minnich, Executive Director

152 **Council of Higher Education Management Associations**
NACUBO
1110 Vermont Avenue NW
Suite 800
Washington, DC 20005-3593
202-861-2584
Fax: 202-449-1246
rroberson@nacubo.org
www.chemanet.org
The Council of Higher Education Management Associations (CHEMA) is an informal assembly of management-oriented higher education associations in the U.S. and Canada. CHEMA members share information and experiences, and collaborate on projects in order to better serve the colleges and universities they represent.

Founded: 1971

Mary Lou Merkt, Chair
Lynne Schaefer, Vice Chair

153 **Independent Schools Association of the Central States**
ISACS Office
55 W Wacker Drive
Suite 701
Chicago, IL 60601
312-750-1190
Fax: 312-750-1193
info@isacs.org
www.isacs.org
The purpose of ISACS is to promote the development of strong learning communities characterized by high achievements, social responsibility, and independence of governance, programs and policies. ISACS provides professional development opportunities, consulting services, resources on the subject of independent school operations and networking events.

1165 pages

Claudia Daggett, President
Karen Zeitlin, Director of Programs

154 **NASPA - Student Affairs Administrators in Higher Education**
111 K Street NE
10th Floor
Washington, DC 20002
202-265-7500
Fax: 202-898-5737
office@naspa.org
www.naspa.org
Association dedicated to supporting the student affairs administration profession. Services, programs and knowledge are provided by the association for the purpose of cultivating student success in colleges and universities.

Founded: 1919

Deb Moriarty, Board Chair
Kevin Kruger, President

155 **National Adult Educational Professional Development Consortium**
444 N Capitol Street NW
Suite 422
Washington, DC 20001
202-624-5250
Fax: 202-624-1497
lmclendon@naepdc.org
naepdc.org
The mission of organization is to assist adult education staff in their professional development, attend to their public policy needs and establish and disseminate information on the field.

Founded: 1990

Reecie Stagnolia, Chair
Lennox McLendon, Ph.D, Executive Director

156 **National Association for Gifted Children**
1331 H Street NW
Suite 1001
Washington, DC 20005
202-785-4268
Fax: 202-785-4248
nagc@nagc.org
www.nagc.org
The National Association for Gifted Children offers education, advocacy, community building and research. Its mission is to provide families and K-12 education professionals with the necessary tools to help them develop gifted and talented children.

George Betts, President
M. Rene Islas, Executive Director

157 **National Association of Elementary School Principals**
1615 Duke Street
Alexandria, VA 22314
703-684-3345
800-386-2377
Fax: 703-549-5568
naesp@naesp.org
www.naesp.org
Professional organization serving elementary and middle school principals and other education leaders. The association offers advocacy, conferences, a learning center and other services to prepare leaders for success in their work with children, families and communities.

Founded: 1921

Brian K Partin, President
L Earl Franks, Ed.D., CAE, Executive Director

158 **National Association of Private Special Education Centers**
601 Pennsylvania Avenue NW
Suite 900 - South Building
Washington, DC 20004
202-434-8225
Fax: 202-434-8224
napsec@aol.com
www.napsec.org
Provides support for private services offered to students with disabilities. Members include those who provide intervention services, schools, residential therapeutic centers, postsecondary and adult living programs and more.

Founded: 1971

Sherry Kolbe, Executive Director & CEO

159 **National Association of Secondary School Principals**
1904 Association Drive
Reston, VA 20191-1537
703-860-0200
866-647-7253
Fax: 703-860-3422
nhs@nassp.org
www.nassp.org
Promotes excellence in school leadership and provides members with a wide variety of programs

and services to assist them in administration, supervision, curriculum planning, and effective staff development.

Founded: 1916

Daniel P Kelley, President
Christine Handy, President Elect

160 National Association of State Directors of Special Education

225 Reinekers Lane
Suite 420
Alexandria, VA 22314
703-519-3800
Fax: 703-519-3808
nasdse@nasdse.org
www.nasdse.org
A nonprofit corporation that promotes and supports education programs for students with disabilities in the United States and outlying areas. The association does this by building connections with providers of policies, educational and other programs serving individuals with disabilities.

Founded: 1938

Glenna Gallo, President
Bill East, Executive Director

161 National Association of Student Financial Aid Administrators

1801 Pennsylvania Avenue NW
Suite 850
Washington, DC 20006-3606
202-785-0453
Fax: 202-785-1487
info@nasfaa.org
www.nasfaa.org
Nonprofit corporation of postsecondary institutions, individuals, agencies and students interested in promoting the effective administration of student financial aid in the United States. The association provides advocacy, training, courses, technical supports, research, resources for councelors and more.

Billie Jo Hamilton, National Chair
Justin Draeger, President & CEO

162 National Center for the Improvement of Educational Assessment

31 Mount Vernon Street
Dover, NH 03820
603-516-7900
Fax: 603-516-7910
www.nciea.org
The Center strives to improve the assessment processes for education to enhance practices and ensure accountability in compliance with the Every Student Succeeds Act (ESSA). The center offers assessment systems, a library and conferences.

Mark Musick, Chair
Scott Marion, Executive Director

163 National Center on Educational Outcomes

University of Minnesota
150 Pillsbury Drive SE
207 Pattee Hall
Minneapolis, MN 55455
612-626-1530
Fax: 612-624-0879
nceo@umn.edu
nceo.info
The National Center on Educational Outcomes (NCEO) was established to provide national leadership in designing and building educational assessments and accountability systems that appropriately monitor educational results for all students, including students with disabilities and English Language Learners.

Founded: 1990

Martha Thurlow, Ph.D, Director
Sheryl Lazarus, Ph.D, Associate Director

164 National Council for Accreditation of Teacher Education

1140 19th Street
Suite 400
Washington, DC 20036
202-223-0077
Fax: 202-296-6620
caep@caepnet.org
www.ncate.org
The National Council for Accreditation of Teacher Education is an organization seeking to support the development of educators through evidence-based accreditation with the aim of improving P-12 student learning.

Founded: 1954

James G Cibulka, President
Mishaela Duran, Chief of Staff

165 National Orientation Directors Association

2829 University Avenue SE
Suite 415
Minneapolis, MN 55414
612-301-6632
866-521-6632
Fax: 612-624-2628
noda@umn.edu
www.nodaweb.org
The mission of the National Orientation Directors Association is to provide education, leadership and professional development in the fields of college student orientation, transition and retention.

Shawn Smee, President
Joyce Holl, Executive Director

166 National Policy Board for Educational Administration

NASSP
1904 Association Drive
Reston, VA 20191
703-518-6256
Huttonb@nassp.org
npbea.org
The National Policy Board for Educational Administration is a national consortium of major stakeholders in educational leadership and policy. The purpose of the Board is to provide a forum for collaborative actions by organizations interested in the advancement of school and school-system leadership.

JoAnn Bartoletti, Executive Director
Beverly J Hutton, Ph.D, Deputy Executive Director

167 National School Safety Center

30200 Agoura Road
Suite 260
Agoura Hills, CA 91301
805-373-9977
info@schoolsafety.us
www.schoolsafety.us
Advocates for safe, secure and peaceful schools worldwide as well as the prevention of school crime and violence. The center provides schools with information, resources, consultation and training services neccessary to ensure safe environments.

Founded: 1984

Ronald D Stephens, Executive Director

168 Pearson's Clinical Assessment Group

PO Box 599700
San Antonio, TX 78259
800-627-7271
Fax: 800-232-1223
clinicalcustomersupport@pearson.com
www.pearsonclinical.com
Offers tools to assist professionals in various fields, including schools, to promote effective education via assessments, research and innovative technologies.

Bob Whelan, President

169 The Heads Network

102 Wentworth Avenue
Nashville, TN 37215
615-533-6022
Fax: 615-523-1952
swade@headsnetwork.org
headsnetwork.org
Provides a forum for school leaders to learn from each other in the interest of the education and employment of girls and young women.

Founded: 1920

Sue Bosland, President
Margaret Wade, Ph.D, Executive Director

Early Childhood Education

170 Association for Early Learning Leaders

1250 S Capital of Texas Highway
Building 3, Suite 400
Austin, TX 78746
512-301-5557
800-537-1118
info@earlylearningleaders.org
www.earlylearningleaders.org
The Association for Early Learning Leaders is a nonprofit organization serving administrators and directors of early education programs by offering accreditation information, conferences, online training and more.

Founded: 1984

Mary Hornbeck, President
Colleen Tracy Haddad, Executive Director

171 Association to Benefit Children (ABC)

419 E 86th Street
New York, NY 10028
212-845-3821
Fax: 212-426-9488
abc@a-b-c.org
www.a-b-c.org
The Association to Benefit Children (ABC) is dedicated to helping create quality of life for disadvantaged children and their families through compassionate programs designed to break the cycles of abuse, neglect, sickness and homelessness. Some of their services include supportive housing, family programs, mental health supports and early childhood education.

Founded: 1986

Thomas Styron, Chairman
Gretchen Buchenholz, Executive Director

172 Building Blocks for Literacy

Stern Center for Language and Learning
183 Talcott Road
Suite 101
Williston, VT 05495-9209
802-878-2332
BBforLiteracy@Sterncenter.org
www.buildingblocksforliteracy.org
Promotes early literacy skills for children in child care and preschool by providing certifi-

cation, research, professional development and a video Family Forum online.

Founded: 1997

Will Billings, Chair
Blanche Podhajski, Ph.D, President

173 Child Care Aware of America

1515 N Courthouse Road
2nd Floor
Arlington, VA 22201
800-424-2246
news@usa.childcareaware.org
www.childcareaware.org

Child Care Aware is a hub of information for parents and child care providers covering topics such as types of childcare, financial assistance, military assistance, programs, training for professionals, videos and newsletters.

Lynette M Fraga, Ph.D, Executive Director
Steve Smith, MBA, Chief Operating Officer

174 Child Care Information Exchange

Exchange Press
17725 NE 65th Street
Suite B-275
Redmond, WA 98052
425-883-9394
800-221-2864
Fax: 425-861-9386
info@ChildCareExchange.com
www.childcareexchange.com

Promotes the exchange of ideas among leaders in early childhood programs worldwide through magazine, books, training products, training seminars and international conferences. Some topics covered include administration, environments, family, social and emotional development and teaching.

Jennifer Shiner, General Manager
Lindsey Kortum, Communications Specialist

175 Child Development Resources

150 Point O'Woods Road
Williamsburg, VA 23188
757-566-3300
Fax: 757-566-8977
development@cdr.org
www.cdr.org

A comprehensive resource for physicians, teachers, and parents covering questions about infants or toddlers. Areas served are Williamsburg, James City County, York County, and Poquoson, Virginia. Services include early intervention for children with disabilities and/or at-risk children.

Founded: 1965

Betsy C Anderson, Chair
Paul Scott, Executive Director

176 Children's Place Association, The

700 N Sacramento Boulevard
Suite 300
Chicago, IL 60612
312-733-9954
Fax: 312-243-7653
www.childrens-place.org

The Children's Place Association provides assistance to primarily low income families and children in Chicago, Illinois. The Association is focused on education, health, family, and financial stability and facilitates early childhood education, offering home based, and center based education initiatives at their Arthur E. Jones Early Childhood Care and Learning Center.

Founded: 1991

Cathy Krieger, LCSW, MA, MBA, President & CEO
John Sweeney, MBA, Deputy Executive Director

177 Division for Early Childhood

2900 Crystal Drive
Suite 100
Arlington, VA 22202-3557
310-428-7209
Fax: 855-678-1989
dec@dec-sped.org
www.dec-sped.org

An international education, the Division for Early Childhood (DEC) works to promote policy and implement evidence based practices that support the development of young children ages 0-8. The DEC is focused on helping children at risk for developmental delays and disabilities.

Peggy Kemp, Executive Director
Ben Rogers, Associate Director

178 Early Childhood Technical Assistance Center

ECTA Center
517 S Greensboro Street
Carrboro, NC 27510
919-962-2001
Fax: 919-966-7463
ectacenter@unc.edu
ectacenter.org

The Early Childhood Technical Assistance Center works to improve early childhood special education service systems by creating recommended practices and monitoring effectiveness of early intervention programs.

Joan Danaher, Associate Director
Betsy Ayankoya, Associate Director

179 Education Advisory Group

101 Market Street
San Francisco, CA 94105
415-974-2000
800-227-4133
publicweb.sf@sf.frb.org
www.frbsf.org

The Education Advisory Group is made up of 20 high school and community college educators from around the 12th District. The group works with the SF Fed's Education & Outreach Department to review ideas, teaching activities, FRBSF education resources, the use of technology and the subject of Federal Reserve and the U.S. economy.

Alexander R Mehran, Chair
John C Williams, President & CEO

180 HighScope Educational Research Foundation

600 North River Street
Ypsilanti, MI 48198-2898
800-587-5639
Fax: 734-485-0704
info@highscope.org
www.highscope.org

HighScope Educational Research Foundation is an independent nonprofit research, development, and outreach organization. The foundation supports early childhood education including the professional development of individuals in the field.

Founded: 1970

Cheryl Polk, PhD, President
Armen Hratchian, Chief Operating Officer

181 Military Child Education Coalition

909 Mountain Lion Circle
Harker Heights, TX 76548
254-953-1923
Fax: 254-953-1925
info@militarychild.org
www.militarychild.org

The Military Child Education Coalition (MCEC) is a nonprofit, international organization dedicated to equal and quality education for military children who are affected by mobility, family separation, and transition. The MCEC conducts research, develops resources, and maintains and fosters connections with school districts to facilitate communication.

Mary M. Keller, EdD, President & CEO
COL (Ret) John Ballantyne, Senior Vice President & COO

182 National AfterSchool Association

2961A Hunter Mill Road
Suite 626
Oakton, VA 22124
E-mail: info@naaweb.org
naaweb.org

The National AfterSchool Association (NAA) develops programs and provides after school education for children and youth in grades K-12. The NAA is a membership association comprised of individuals who work with children and provided extended learning opportunities.

Gina Warner, President & CEO
Heidi Ham, VP, Programs & Strategy

183 National Association for Family Child Care

1743 W Alexander Street
Suite 201
Salt Lake City, UT 84119
801-886-2322
nafcc@nafcc.org
www.nafcc.org

The National Association for Family Child Care is a nonprofit membership association representing early childhood care providers throughout the United States. The association offers public policy advocacy, conferences and accreditation opportunities for professionals.

Bill Hudson, CEO
Stacy Pagan, Director of Membership

184 National Association for the Education of Homeless Children and Youth

NAEHCY Business Office
P.O. Box 26274
Minneapolis, MN 55426
866-862-2562
Fax: 763-545-9499
info@naehcy.org
www.naehcy.org

Professional organization dedicated to meeting the educational needs of children and youth experiencing homelessness. The association provides professional development, resources, advocacy and training for those interested in supporting the academic success of children and youth challenged by homelessness.

Kerry Wrenick, Executive Committee Chair
Tim Stahlke, Vice President

185 National Association of Early Childhood Specialists in State Departments of Education

E-mail: information@naecs-sde.org
www.naecs-sde.org

The National Association of Early Childhood Specialists in State Departments of Education (NAECS-SDE) promotes quality early childhood education through the improvement of instruction, curriculum, and administration of programs.

Founded: 1972

John Pruette, President
Vincent J. Constanza, Vice President

186 National Child Care Association
PO Box 195
Morrisville, PA 19067
877-537-6222
admin@nccanet.org
www.nccanet.org
The National Child Care Association (NCCA) advocates for policies and regulations that positively impact children.

187 National Educational Systems
National Educational Systems, Inc.
6333 De Zavala
Suite 106
San Antonio, TX 78249
800-231-4380
Fax: 210-699-4674
info@shopnes.com
www.shopnes.com
The National Educational Systems (NES) offers quality instructional materials and support services to its clients. NES works to provides clients with the latest in instructional material, bilingual materials, dual language, special needs, and teacher resources.

Founded: 1991

188 National Head Start Association
1651 Prince Street
Alexandria, VA 22314
703-739-0875
866-677-8724
www.nhsa.org
The National Head Start Association (NHSA) is a nonprofit organization committed to supporting the needs of at risk children through policy change.

Founded: 1974

Yasmina Vinci, Executive Director
Gregg Porter, Director, Membership

189 National Institute for Early Education Research
73 Easton Avenue
New Brunswick, NJ 08901-1879
848-932-4350
info@nieer.org
www.nieer.org
The National Institute for Early Education Research (NIEER) provides independent research based information to support quality, effective early childhood education.

Founded: 2002

W. Steven Barnett, Sr. Co-Director & Founder
Ellen Frede, Sr. Co-Director

190 Professional Association for Childhood Education
1 Capitol Mall
Suite 800
Sacramento, CA 95814
800-924-2460
Fax: 916-444-7462
info@pacenet.org
www.pacenet.org
A nonprofit membership based association, the Professional Association for Childhood Education (PACE) advocates for early childhood education and represents its members on a state and national level. PACE hosts a variety of events including seminars, conferences, training, and roundtable discussions.

Founded: 1955

Kimberly Andosca, Executive Director
Lynette Ferguson Powe, Secretary

191 Southern Early Childhood Association
1123 S University Avenue
Suite 255
Little Rock, AR 72204
501-221-1648
800-305-7322
Fax: 501-221-5297
info@southernearlychildhood.org
www.southernearlychildhood.org
The Southern Early Childhood Association (SECA) provides a network for communication among childhood educators including preschool, kindergarten, primary teachers, administrators, and individuals interested in early childhood education. SECA members exchange ideas at local, state, and regional meetings, and provides access to publications including the Dimensions of Early Childhood journal.

Founded: 1948

Jo Carroll, President
Mark Polevoy, Executive Director

Elementary Education

192 Center for Play Therapy
425 S Welch Street
Complex 2
Denton, TX 76203
940-565-3864
Fax: 940-565-4461
cpt@unt.edu
cpt.unt.edu
Encourages the development and emotional growth of children through play therapy and a positive interpersonal relationship with a therapist trained in play therapy. The center also provides training, research, publications, counseling services and literature on the field.

Sue Bratton, Ph.D, Director
Garry L Landreth, Ed.D, Founder

193 National Association for the Education of Young Children
1313 L Street NW
Suite 500
Washington, DC 20005
202-232-8777
800-424-2460
Fax: 202-328-1846
webmaster@naeyc.org
www.naeyc.org
Supports those interested in serving and acting on behalf of the educational needs and rights of young children. The association engages in advancing practice, policy, and research in the field through accreditation programs and conferences.

Rhian Evans Allvin, CEO
Noordin Moloo, Deputy Chief Executive

194 Tribeca Learning Center-PS 150
334 Greenwich Street
New York, NY 10013
212-732-4392
Fax: 212-766-5895
Info@ps150.net
ps150.net
Tribeca Learning Center, PS 150 nurtures the development of students in all aspects of their lives through a curriculum that integrates arts, sciences, math, language and physical education.

Jenny Bonnet, Principal
Christine Walford, School Secretary

195 Voyager Sopris Learning
Cambium Learning Group
17855 Dallas Parkway
Suite 400
Dallas, TX 75287
800-547-6747
Fax: 888-819-7767
vslsocial@voyagersopris.com
www.voyagersopris.com
Voyager Sopris Learning is a provider of solutions and professional development services to preK-12 students and educators.

Founded: 1994

Jeff Elliott, President
Aaron Ingold, Senior VP of Sales

Employment

196 English Language Program
Center for Intercultural Education & Development
3300 Whitehaven Street
Suite 1000
Washington, DC 20007
800-308-7649
fellow@elprograms.org
www.elprograms.org
A program of the U.S Department of State, the English Language Programs sends United States English teachers abroad to U.S embassies to assist in delivering and maintaining quality English language programs.

Founded: 1969

Magdalena Potocka, Program Director
Toni Hull, Associate Director

197 Graphic Arts Education & Research Foundation
1899 Preston White Drive
Reston, VA 20191
703-264-7200
866-381-9839
Fax: 703-620-3165
gaerf@npes.org
www.gaerf.org
The Graphic Arts Education and Research Foundation (GAERF) is dedicated to advancing knowledge and education in graphic communications through programs that support workforce development.

Founded: 1983

Wayne Marshall, Chairman
Thayer Long, President

198 Health Occupations Students of America
HOSA - Future Health Professionals
548 Silicon Drive
Suite 101
Southlake, TX 76092
800-321-4672
hosa@hosa.org
www.hosa.org
An international student organization, HOSA works to enhance the quality of healthcare through the promotion of career opportunities in the healthcare industry.

Founded: 1976

Jim Koeninger, PhD, Executive Director
Karen Koeninger, Deputy Executive Director

199 Mountain Pacific Association of Colleges & Employers
700 R Street
Suite 200
Sacramento, CA 95811
925-934-3877
Fax: 925-906-0922
info@mpace.org
www.mpace.org
Comprised of career services professionals and employers, the Mountain Pacific Association of Colleges and Employers (MPACE) works with its members to help college students obtain jobs and internships.

Melissa Dixon, CAE, Executive Director
Michelle Foley, Director, Communications

200 National Association of Colleges and Employers
62 Highland Avenue
Bethlehem, PA 18017
610-868-1421
nace@naceweb.org
www.naceweb.org
The National Association of Colleges and Employment (NACE) connects college career services professionals with universities, colleges, and recruiting professionals. NACE provides information on employment, hiring trends, hiring practices, and student attitudes and outcomes.

Founded: 1956

Marilyn Mackes, Executive Director
Matthew Brink, Assistant Executive Director

201 National Association of Professional Employer Organizations
707 North Saint Asaph Street
Alexandria, VA 22314
703-836-0466
Fax: 703-836-0976
info@napeo.org
www.napeo.org
The National Association of Professional Employer Organizations (NAPEO) represents the PEO industry advocating for the interests of PEOs at all levels of government.

Founded: 1984

Pat Cleary, President & CEO
Melissa Viscovich, CAE, Senior Vice President & COO

202 National Business Education Association
1914 Association Drive
Reston, VA 20191-1596
703-860-8300
Fax: 703-620-4483
nbea@nbea.org
www.nbea.org
The National Business Education Association (NBEA) works to support individuals and groups who instruct, administer, research, and spread information regarding business. NBEA advances the professional interests of it members through programs that enhance professional growth and development.

Janet M. Trichel, Executive Director
Laura Sutherland, Director, Convention

203 National Student Employment Association
9600 Escarpment Boulevard
Suite 745 PMB 11
Austin, TX 78749
512-423-1417
Fax: 972-767-5131
nsea@nsea.info
www.nsea.info
The National Student Employment Association (NSEA) is a student employment association providing professional development and employment opportunities for college students. Membership is open to any individual with an interest in hiring students.

Linda Morgan, Office Manager
Shirley M. Govindasamy, President

Guidance & Counseling

204 American Association of Sex Educators, Counselors & Therapists
1444 I Street NW
Suite 700
Washington, DC 20005
202-449-1099
Fax: 202-216-9646
info@aasect.org
www.aasect.org
The American Association of Sexuality Educators, Counselors and Therapists (AASECT) promotes sexual health through the development and advancement of the sexual therapy, counseling, and education fields.

Founded: 1967

Michael Chan, Executive Director
Alphonsus Baggett, Deputy Executive Director

205 American College Counseling Association
1101 N Delaware Street
Indianapolis, IN 46202
855-220-8760
caseye@cmcglobal.com
www.collegecounseling.org
Primarily working in a higher education setting, the American College Counseling Association (ACCA) is comprised of mental health professionals and student members working to foster student development. The ACCA works to support and enhance college counselling, promote ethical practice, and facilitate communication among college counselors.

Founded: 1991

Janelle Johnson, President
Raime Thibodeaux, Secretary

206 American College Personnel Association
National Center for Higher Education
One Dupont Circle NW
Suite 300
Washington, DC 20036
202-835-2272
Fax: 202-827-0601
info@acpa.nche.edu
www.myacpa.org
The American College Personnel Association (ACPA) works to advance student affairs and engage students in activities. The ACPA represents 1,200 private and public institutions with 7,500 members across the United States and the globe.

Founded: 1924

Cindi Love, Ed.D., Executive Director
Tricia Fechter Gates, Deputy Executive Director

207 American Counseling Association
6101 Stevenson Avenue
Suite 600
Alexandria, VA 22304
800-347-6647
Fax: 800-473-2329
membership@counseling.org
www.counseling.org
A nonprofit professional and educational organization, the American Counselling Association (ACA) represents professional counselors working to grow and enhance the counseling profession.

Founded: 1952

Gerard Lawson, PhD, President

208 American School Counselor Association
1101 King Street
Suite 310
Alexandria, VA 22314
703-683-2722
800-306-4722
Fax: 703-997-7572
asca@schoolcounselor.org
www.schoolcounselor.org
The American School Counselor Association (ASCA) supports counselors at every level of education and works to promote professionalism and ethical practice. The ASCA offers its members professional development opportunities, provides current information related to professionalism, and supports research and evaluation in school counseling.

Richard Wong, Executive Director
Jill Cook, Assistant Director

209 Association for Financial Counseling & Planning Education
79 South State Street
Suite D3
Westerville, OH 43081
614-368-1055
Fax: 703-684-4485
rwiggins@afcpe.org
www.afcpe.org
A nonprofit organization, the Association for Financial Counseling & Planning Education (AFCPE) provides supports for professionals who offer counselling regarding financial planning to individuals and families. The AFCPE works with the government, military, and other organizations to establish policy that sets standards in the financial counseling, planning, and education fields.

Rebecca Wiggins, Executive Director
Katie Tornow, Director, Operations

210 Association for University and College Counseling Center Directors
1101 N Delaware Street
Suite 200
Indianapolis, IN 46202
317-635-4755
office@aucccd.org
www.aucccd.org
The Association for University and College Counseling Center Directors (AUCCCD) is a professional organization working to encourage the development and success of directors. The AUCCCD supports higher education by advocating for collegiate mental health.

Founded: 1950

Sharon Mitchell, PhD, President
Charles Davidshofer, PhD, Treasurer

211 Association of Educational Therapists
7044 S 13th Street
Oak Creek, WI 53154
414-908-4949
Fax: 414-768-8001
customercare@AETOnline.org
www.aetonline.org

The Association of Educational Therapists (AET) offers leadership, certification, and training for Educational Therapists. The AET promotes the ethical practice and sets standards in the Educational Therapy field.

Alice Pulliam, President

212 Canadian Education and Research Institute for Counselling
Foundation House
2 St Clair Avenue E
Suite 300
Toronto, ON M4T-2T5
416-929-2510
Fax: 416-923-2536
admin@ceric.ca
ceric.ca
A charitable organization dedicated to promoting the study of career counseling and career development. Some services offered by the organization include funds for projects, training programs for career professionals, publications and research.

Jennifer Browne, Chair
Riz Ibrahim, Executive Director

213 Council for Accreditation of Counseling & Related Educational Programs
1001 North Fairfax Street
Suite 510
Alexandria, VA 22314
703-535-5990
Fax: 703-739-6209
www.cacrep.org
An accrediting organization, the CACREP sets standards to promote excellence and enhance professional preparation among counseling and related educational programs. The CACREP works collaboratively with other organizations that are focused on accreditation.

Founded: 1981

Kelly Coker, Chair
Vilia Tarvydas, Vice Chair

214 Higher Education Consultants Association
800 Washington Avenue
Suite 131
St. Louis, MO 63101
800-662-6775
www.hecaonline.org
The Higher Education Consultants Association (HECA) is a professional organization focused on independent college admissions consulting.

Founded: 1997

Ping Wei, Executive Director
Joe Bernard, President

215 International Association of Counseling Services
101 S Whiting Street
Suite 211
Alexandria, VA 22304
703-823-9840
Fax: 703-823-9843
admin@iacsinc.org
www.iacsinc.org
Offering accreditation to universities, four-year colleges, and two-year community colleges counseling services, the International Association of Counseling Services (IACS) encourages counselling programs to provide and meet excellent professional standards.

Nancy E. Roncketti, Executive Director
Rattana Thanagosol, Executive Assistant

216 National Association of School Psychologists
4340 E West Highway
Suite 402
Bethesda, MD 20814
301-657-0270
866-331-6277
Fax: 301-657-0275
center@naspweb.org
www.nasponline.org
The National Association of School Psychologists (NASP) represents over 25,000 school psychologists, psychology students, and related professionals. The NASP works to promote effective school psychology practices that fosters students' learning, behavior, and mental health.

Susan Gorin, Executive Director
Laura Benson, Chief Operating Officer

International

217 Academic Travel Abroad
1155 Connecticut Avenue NW
Suite 300
Washington, DC 20036-4355
800-556-7896
info@academic-travel.com
www.academic-travel.com
Academic Travel Abroad is an educational travel provider for organizations, and university undergraduate programs across the United States.

Founded: 1950

Kate Simpson, President
Chase Poffenberger, Executive Vice President

218 Academy for International School Heads
494 Locust Place
Boulder, CO 80304
303-955-1655
Fax: 508-576-9490
office@academyish.org
www.academyish.org
The Academy for International School Heads (AISH) is a nonprofit organization providing a forum of communication and support for the Head or Deputy Head of international schools.

Founded: 1999

Deb Welch, Chief Executive Officer
Charles Barder, President

219 Alberta Association of Recreation Facility Personnel
312 3rd Street W
PO Box 100
Cochrane, AB T4C-1A4
403-851-7626
888-253-7544
Fax: 403-851-9181
office@aarfp.com
www.aarfp.com
The Alberta Association of Recreation Facility Personnel is a provincial nonprofit organization providing education, training, and consultation for people involved in recreation and recreation operations.

Founded: 1978

Stuart Ray, Executive Director
Monica Culic, Coordinator, Communications

220 Alberta Council on Admissions and Transfer
Commerce Place
10155-102 Street
8th Floor
Edmonton, AB T5J-4L5
780-422-9021
Fax: 780-422-3688
acat@gov.ab.ca
www.acat.gov.ab.ca
The Alberta Council on Admissions and Transfer works cooperatively with postsecondary institutions, develops policies, guidelines, and procedures to ensure the effective transition of transfer agreements between institutions.

Founded: 1974

221 American Councils For International Education
1828 L Street NW
Suite 1200
Washington, DC 20036
202-833-7522
Fax: 202-833-7523
general@americancouncils.org
www.americancouncils.org
American Councils for International Education is dedicated to creating educational opportunities, such as international academic exchange, for individuals and institutions to facilitate a better understanding of culture and global political, economic, and social challenges.

Founded: 1974

Lorne W. Craner, President
Dr. David Patton, Executive Vice President

222 Association for Asian Studies
Association For Asian Studies, Inc.
825 Victors Way
Suite 310
Ann Arbor, MI 48108
734-665-2490
Fax: 734-665-3801
mpaschal@asian-studies.org
www.asian-studies.org
A scholarly nonprofit professional organization, the Association for Asian Studies (AAS) is focused on the study of Asia, through the AAS' publications, resources, regional conferences, and annual conferences, the association provides members with professional development and networking opportunities. Membership is open to any individual interested in Asia.

Founded: 1941

Michael Paschal, Executive Director
Doreen Ilozor, Manager, Membership

223 Association for Canadian Education Resources
92 Lakeshore Road E
Suite 202
Mississauga, ON L4Y-3P5
905-891-6004
office@acer-acre.ca
www.acer-acre.ca
The Association for Canadian Educational Resources (ACER) develops and offers programs and resources to educate individuals in environmental sciences. Programs are specifically focused on climate change.

Alice Casselman, President
Nimesha Basnayaka, Program Manager

224 Association for Canadian Studies in the United States
University at Buffalo - SUNY
1004 Clemens Hall
Buffalo, NY 14260

716-645-8440
Fax: 716-645-5976
info@acsus.org
www.acsus.org
The Association for Canadian Studies in the United States (ACSUS) is a member based organization dedicated to fostering awareness and understanding of Canada and the relationship it has with the US.

James McHugh, President
Amy Sotherden, Secretary

225 Association for Learning Environments
11445 E Via Linda
Suite 2-440
Scottsdale, AZ 85259
480-391-0840
Fax: 480-391-0940
www.a4le.org
Formerly the CEFPI, the Association for Learning Environments is focused on improving the environments in which children learn.

Philip Idle, Chair
John K. Ramsey, CAE, Ex-Officio CEO

226 Association of Advancement of International Education
Mailman Hollywood Building
3301 College Avenue
Suite 314
Ft. Lauderdale, FL 33314
954-262-6937
yolanda@aaie.org
www.aaie.org
The Association for the Advancement of International Education (AAIE) is committed to developing and improving international education. Through the exchange of information and the establishment of professional networks, the AAIE works with educational institutions to promote the international exchange of ideas and research.

Founded: 1966

Yolanda Murphy Barrena, Executive Director & CEO
Derek Harwell, Coordinator, Program

227 Association of American Schools of Central America
E-mail: aascaonline.net@gmail.com
www.aascaonline.net
The Association of American Schools of Central America advocates for United States style education in Central America.

Founded: 1990

Ron Vair, President
Liliana Jenkins, Vice President & Treasurer

228 Association of American Schools of South America
1911 NW 150 Avenue
Suite 101
Pembroke Pines, FL 33028
954-436-4034
Fax: 954-436-4092
ppoore@aassa.com
www.aassa.com
A regional membership organization of American International schools in South America, the Association of American Schools in South America works to develop a better understanding of international education and to improve teaching techniques among Association schools.

Founded: 1977

Paul Poore, Executive Director
Paul Sicard, Deputy Director

229 Association of Christian Schools International
731 Chapel Hills Drive
PO Box 65130
Colorado Springs, CO 80920-5130
719-528-6906
800-367-5391
www.acsi.org
The Association of Christian Schools International, promotes Christian education and provides training and resources to Christian schools and educators.

Daniel Egeler, EdD, President
Stephen P. Dill, EdD, Senior Vice President

230 Association of International Education Administrators
Duke University
2204 Erwin Road
Room 030, Campus Box 90404
Durham, NC 27708
919-668-1928
Fax: 919-684-8749
aiea@duke.edu
www.aieaworld.org
The Association of International Education Administrators (AIEA) is a member based organization comprised of institutional leaders working to advance international components of higher education.

Founded: 1982

Darla K Deardorff, Ph.D, Executive Director

231 Atlantic Provinces Special Education Authority
5940 South Street
Halifax, NS
Canada B3H-1S6
902-424-8500
Fax: 902-423-8700
apsea@apsea.ca
www.apsea.ca
The Atlantic Provinces Special Education Authority (APSEA) is an interprovincial agency serving the educational needs of individuals with visual and hearing impairments, in New Brunswick, Newfoundland and Labrador, Nova Scotia, and Prince Edward Island.

Founded: 1975

Lisa Doucet, Superintendent

232 Canadian Association of Communicators in Education
1390 Prince of Wales Drive
Suite 310
Ottawa, ON K2C-3N6
E-mail: catherine.shedden@tldsb.on.ca
www.cace-acace.org
The Canadian Association of Communications in Education (CACE) is committed to encouraging communication in education. CACE provides resources for educational marketing and communication professionals to ensure effective communication.

Founded: 1984

Catherine Shedden, President
Maxeen Jolin, VP

233 Canadian Association of Independent Schools
264 Welland Avenue
2nd Floor, Suite P
St. Cathatines, ON L2R-2P8
905-684-5658
tnolan@cais.ca
www.cais.ca
A national network of member schools, the Canadian Association of Independent Schools (CAIS) supports collaborative efforts in leadership, education, management, and governance.

Founded: 1981

Patti MacDonald, Executive Director
Val Pighin, Coordinator, Accreditation

234 Canadian Bureau for International Education
220 Laurier W
Suite 1550
Ottawa, ON K1P-5Z9
613-237-4820
Fax: 613-237-1073
communication@cbie.ca
cbie.ca
National nonprofit membership organization engaged in providing services for international learners. Services include forums for educational exchanges, scholarships, awards and internships, technical assistance and more.

Founded: 1966

David Ross, Chair
Karen McBride, President & CEO

235 Canadian Council for the Advancement of Education
The Woolen Mill
4 Cataraqui Street
Suite 310
Kingston, ON K7K-1Z7
613-531-9213
Fax: 613-531-0626
admin@ccaecanada.org
www.ccaecanada.org
The Canadian Council for the Advancement of Education (CCAE) is an organization working to promote excellence in education advancement through professional learning opportunities. The CCAE provides programs covering new trends and techniques designed to meet the needs of the 4,400 members.

Mark Hazlett, Executive Director
Heather Dow, Operations Manager

236 Canadian Society for the Study of Education
260 Dalhousie Street
Suite 204
Ottawa, ON K1N-7E4
613-241-0018
Fax: 613-241-0019
csse-scee@csse.ca
www.csse-scee.ca
The Canadian Society for the Study of Education (CSSE) is an organization comprised of professors, students, researchers, and practitioners in education. The CSSE is represents individuals who create educational knowledge, prepare teachers and leaders, and apply research in schools.

Founded: 1972

Lynn Thomas, President
Kirk Anderson, Vice President

237 Commonwealth of Learning
4710 Kingsway
Suite 2500
Burnaby, BC V5H-4M2
604-775-8200
Fax: 604-775-8210
info@col.org
www.col.org
The Commonwealth of Learning (COL) is an intergovernmental organization dedicated to the development and sharing of open learning and distance education knowledge, resources, and technologies. The COL was established by the Commonwealth Heads of Government.

Founded: 1987

Asha S. Kanwar, President & CEO
Dr. K. Balasubramanian, Vice President

238 **Comparative and International Education Society**
Florida International University
11200 SW 8 Street
PC 244D
Miami, FL 33199
305-348-5464
oed@cies.us
www.cies.us
The Comparative and International Education Society (CIES) facilitates cross-cultural understanding, scholarship, academic achievement, and societal development through the study of the different facets of international education. The Society has over 2,500 members.

Founded: 1956

Hilary C. Landorf, Executive Director
Mariusz Galczynski, Managing Director

239 **Consortium for Educational Resources on Islamic Studies**
University of Pittsburgh
4100 Posvar Hall
Pittsburgh, PA 15260
412-648-2113
Fax: 412-624-4672
cerisnet@gmail.com
www.cerisnet.pitt.edu
The Consortium for Educational Resources on Islamic Studies (CERIS) is a collaborative effort of academic, nonprofit, and religious organizations in Ohio, Pennsylvania, and West Virginia working to develop and disseminate information on Islamic Studies.

Founded: 1990

Rachel Sternfeld, President
Elaine Linn, Executive Director

240 **Cordell Hull Foundation for International Education**
45 Rockefeller Plaza
20th Floor
New York, NY 10111
212-300-2138
Fax: 646-349-3455
cordellhull@aol.com
www.cordellhull.org
A nonprofit organization, The Cordell Hull for International Education, works to improve foreign relations through teacher exchange.

Founded: 1951

Marianne Mason, Director

241 **Council of Ministers of Education, Canada**
95 St Clair Avenue W
Suite 1106
Toronto, ON M4V-1N6
416-962-8100
Fax: 416-962-2800
information@cmec.ca
www.cmec.ca
The Council of Ministers of Education, Canada (CMEC) is an intergovernmental organization providing a forum of communication to discuss policy issues, consult with national and federal education organizations, and a tool to undertake activities and educational projects.

Founded: 1967

Chantal C. Beaulieu, Executive Director

242 **Council on International Educational Exchange**
300 Fore Street
Portland, ME 04101
207-553-4000
contact@ciee.org
www.ciee.org
The Council on International Educational Exchange (CIEE) offers study abroad, work exchange, and professional development programs to foster understanding, respect and the exchange of ideas and experiences between cultures.

Founded: 1947

James P. Pellow, President & CEO
Tim Propp, Chief Operating Officer

243 **Cultural Vistas**
440 Park Avenue S
2nd Floor
New York, NY 10016
212-497-3500
info@culturalvistas.org
www.culturalvistas.org
Cultural Vistas promotes cultural understanding and collaboration through international exchange.

Founded: 1963

Linda Boughton, Acting President & CEO
Dan Ewert, VP, Program Research

244 **Global Learning**
Global Learning NJ, Inc.
PO Box 1011
Chatham, NJ 07928
201-317-8796
global.learning.inc@gmail.com
www.globallearningnj.org
Global Learning offers professional development opportunities for educators.

Shay Coleman, Executive Director
Erik Yates, Director, Program

245 **Graphic Communications Education Association**
1899 Preston White Drive
Reston, VA 20191
E-mail: info@gceaonline.org
www.gceaonline.org
The Graphic Communications Education Association (GCEA) is a nonprofit organization focused on sharing theories, principles, techniques,and processes with educators and industry professionals.

Lexa Browning-Needham, President
Laura Roberts, Secretary

246 **IREX**
2121 K Street NW
Suite 600
Washington, DC 20005
202-628-8188
Fax: 202-628-8189
communications@irex.org
www.irex.org
IREX (International Research and Exchanges Board) is an independent, nonprofit organization committed to building a more inclusive world through equal access to quality education and information.

Founded: 1968

Kristin M. Lord, President & CEO
Taleb Salhab, VP, Global Programs

247 **Institute of Cultural Affairs**
4750 N Sheridan Road
Chicago, IL 60640
773-769-6363
Fax: 773-944-1582
Chicago@ica-usa.org
www.ica-usa.org/
The Institute of Cultural Affairs advocates for an equal and just society, working to strengthen communities and individuals through a variety of programs.

Founded: 1962

Ted Wysocki, Chief Executive Officer
Seva Gandhi, Director, Program

248 **Institute of International Education**
809 United Nations Plaza
New York, NY 10017-3580
212-883-8200
Fax: 212-984-5452
www.iie.org
The Institute of International Education (IIE) is committed to advancing international education and access to education across the globe. Through international exchange programs, the IIE promotes closer educational ties between the people of the United States and other countries.

Founded: 1919

Allan E. Goodman, President & CEO
Jaye Chen, Executive Vice President

249 **International Association Of Medical Science Educators**
IAMSE c/o JulNet Solutions LLC
1404 1/2 Adams Avenue
Huntington, WV 25704
304-522-1270
Fax: 304-523-9701
support@iamse.org
www.iamse.org
A professional development society, the International Association of Medical Science Educators advances medical education through faculty development.

Founded: 1988

Julie K. Hewett, CMP, Association Manager
Danielle Inscoe, Communications Manager

250 **International Association for Continuing Education & Training**
11130 Sunrise Valley Drive
Suite 350
Reston, VA 20191
703-234-4065
Fax: 703-435-4390
info@iacet.org
www.iacet.org
The International Association for Continuing Education and Training (IACET) is a nonprofit organization working to advance the global workforce through accreditation.

Joe McClary, CAE, Chief Executive Officer
Tracey Naughton, Program Manager

251 **International Association for the Exchange of Students for Technical Experience**
440 Park Avenue South
2nd Floor
New York, NY 10016
212-497-3530
iaeste@culturalvistas.org
www.iaesteunitedstates.org
A program of Cultural Vista, the International Association for the Exchange of Students for Technical Experiences (IAESTE) supports international exchange between students studying in the STEM fields.

Gina Del Tito, Associate Program Manager
Katerina Holubova, Senior Program Director

252 **International Baccalaureate**
7501 Wisconsin Avenue
Suite 200 W
Bethesda, MD 20814
301-202-3000
Fax: 301-202-3033
ibid@ibo.org
www.ibo.org
The International Baccalaureate (IB) is a nonprofit educational foundation working to develop the intellectual, personal, emotional, and social skills of youth ages 3-19, through 4

education programmes. There are over 600,000 IB students across 133 countries across the world at 2,400 schools.

Founded: 1968

Andrew Macdonald, Chief Schools Officer
Paula Wilcock, Chief Assessment Officer

253 International Education Council

1101 Vermont Avenue NW
Suite 400
Washington, DC 20005
202-289-3900
contact@internationaleducationcouncil.org
www.internationaleducationcouncil.org
The International Education Council (IEC) is a nonprofit association focused on issues and policies affecting international education.

Harrison Wadsworth, Executive Director
Jenny Roberts, President

254 International Education Exchange Council

San Francisco State University
1600 Holloway Avenue
Ceaser Chavez Student Center Room T-125
San Francisco, CA 94132
415-338-1293
IEEC@mail.sfsu.edu
www.sfsuieec.com
A program of San Francisco State University, the International Education Exchange Council, is a student run organization working to encourage international education through student exchange, study abroad programs, and the sharing of cultural experiences.

Akram Abdulrahman, President
Ayesha Midha, Co-President

255 International Schools Services

15 Roszel Road
PO Box 5910
Princeton, NJ 08543
609-452-0990
Fax: 609-452-2690
www.iss.edu
International Schools Services is a non-profit educational organization providing comprehensive and customized services to schools and educators. The organization recruits international teachers and helps to develop international schools.

Founded: 1955

Liz Duffy, President
Bruce McWilliams, Executive Vice President

256 International Society for Business Education

6302 Mineral Point Road
Unit 100
Madison, WI 53705-1596
608-273-8467
mrbsherry@comcast.net
www.siec-isbe.org
The International Society of Business Education is an international network of individuals, businesses, and organizations working to connect business and education.

Founded: 1901

Petra Bragadottir, International President
Lila Waldman, General Secretary

257 International Studies Association

362 Fairfield Way
Unit 4013
Storrs, CT 06269-4013
860-486-5850
isa@isanet.org
www.isanet.org
The International Studies Association (ISA) is a global organization promoting the study, education, and exchange of information centered on international studies. The ISA has over 6,500 members divided into 6 geographic subdivisions, 29 groups and 4 Caucuses.

Founded: 1959

Jennifer Fontanella, Director, Operations
Giulianna Franchetti, Program Coordinator

258 NAFSA: Association of International Educators

1307 New York Avenue NW
8th Floor
Washington, DC 20005-4701
202-737-3699
Fax: 202-737-3657
inbox@nafsa.org
www.nafsa.org
NAFSA: Association of International Educators is an organization of individuals committed to facilitating international education, exchange, and global workforce development. NAFSA supports international educators, institutions, and organizations through training, professional development and networking opportunities, and advocating for international education.

Founded: 1948

Esther Brimmer, Executive Director
Alan Williams, Deputy Executive Directory

259 National Registration Center for Study Abroad

PO Box 1393
Milwaukee, WI 53201
414-278-0631
Fax: 414-271-8884
study@nrcsa.com
www.nrcsa.com
Working to foster international understanding, the National Registration Center for Study Abroad (NRCSA) supports international educational exchanges for individuals of all ages.

Founded: 1968

Mike Wittig, General Manager

260 Odyssey of the Mind

Creative Competitions, Inc.
406 Ganttown Road
Sewell, NJ 08080
856-256-2797
Fax: 856-256-2798
info@odysseyofthemind.com
www.odysseyofthemind.com
An educational program that provides creative problem-solving activities for students from kindergarten through college. With creative and imaginative paths to problem solving, students learn skills that will provide them with the ability to solve problems for a lifetime.

Samuel Micklus, Ph.D, Founder

261 Ontario Cooperative Education Association

35 Reynar Drive
Quispamsis, NB E2G-1J9
Fax: 506-849-8375
OCEA@Rogers.com
www.ocea.on.ca
The Ontario Cooperative Education Association (OCEA) is nonprofit working to provide leadership and professional development opportunities for its members.

Carmine Romano, Chair
Susanna Scocchia, Secretary

262 Opportunities Industrialization Centers International

1875 Connecticut Avenue NW
10th Floor
Washington, DC 20009
202-846-6798
info@oici.org
www.oici.org
OIC International is dedicated to alleviating poverty through workforce development and education. OIC is primarily working in sub-Saharan Africa working to educate the growing workforce population in agriculture, customer service, health, and vocational training.

Crispian Kirk, President & CEO
Edmund D Cooke Jr, Chair of the Board

263 People to People International

2405 Grand Boulevard
Suite 500
Kansas City, MO 64108
816-531-4701
Fax: 816-561-7502
ptpi@ptpi.org
www.ptpi.org
People to People International is committed to fostering cultural understanding and friendship through education, cultural, and humanitarian activities and the exchange of ideas and experiences.

Founded: 1956

Mary Jean Eisenhower, President & CEO
Anna Bazan, Manager, Programs & Events

264 Phi Delta Kappa International

1525 Wilson Boulevard
Suite 705
PO Box 13090
Arlington, VA 22219
812-339-1156
800-766-1156
Fax: 812-339-0018
memberservices@pdkintl.org
www.pdkintl.org
PDK International is a professional association comprised of educational associations working to facilitate connection between educators, and leaders.

Albert Chen, Chief Operating Officer
Gislaine Ngounou, Chief Program Officer

265 TESOL International Association

1925 Ballenger Avenue
Suite 550
Alexandria, VA 22314-6820
703-836-0774
Fax: 703-836-7864
info@tesol.org
www.tesol.org
An international association, TESOL advocates for quality English teaching through professional development, research, and standard setting.

Luciana de Oliveira, President
Chirstopher Powers, Executive Director & CEO

266 Tri-Association - The Association of American Schools

2637 Ascot Drive
Florence, SC 29501
843-799-5754
skeller@tri-association.org
www.tri-association.org

The Tri-Association is a nonprofit organization dedicated to improving the quality of teaching and learning opportunities for schools in the region. The Association is supported by the United States State Department, Office of Overseas Schools, and covers schools located in Central America, Colombia-Caribbean, and Mexico.

Dr. Sonia Keller, Executive Director
Ron Vair, President

267 World Learning
1 Kipling Rd
PO Box 676
Brattleboro, VT 05302-0676
802-257-7751
800-257-7751
Fax: 802-258-3508
info@worldlearning.org
www.worldlearning.org
A nonprofit organization using education, development, and exchange programs, World Learning teaches educators ways in which to help students learn. With programs designed to improve education established in over 100 countries, World Learning helps to strengthen communities and institutions.

Carol Jenkins, President
Joel Colony, Director, Policy & Advocacy

268 iEARN
E-mail: ec@iearn.org
www.iearn.org
iEARN is an international education and resource network using online and communication technology to foster safe communication between schools, youth organizations, and students.

Founded: 1988

Language Arts

269 Academic Language Therapy Association
14070 Proton Road
Suite 100
Dallas, TX 75244
972-233-9107
Fax: 972-490-4219
office@altaread.org
www.altaread.org
The Academic Language Therapy Association (ALTA) is a national nonprofit working to establish, maintain, and promote the standards of Certified Academic Language Therapists.

Founded: 1986

Janna Curry-Dobbs, President
Christine Bedenbaugh, Secretary

270 Accrediting Council on Education in Journalism and Mass Communications
University of Kansas
Stauffer Flint Hall
1435 Jayhawk Boulevard
Lawrence, KS 66045
785-864-3973
Fax: 785-864-5225
sshaw@ku.edu
www.acejmc.org
The Accrediting Council on Education in Journalism and Mass Communication, promotes excellence in the professional education of journalism and mass communication, specifically education that is focused on incorporating technology into the professional field.

Susanne Shaw, Executive Director
Cheryl Klug, Office Staff

271 American Association of Teachers of French
302 N Granite Street
Marion, IL 62959-2346
815-310-0490
Fax: 815-310-5754
www.frenchteachers.org
The American Association of Teachers of French (AATF) is a national association of French teachers. The ATTF has almost 10,000 members.

Founded: 1927

Jayne Abrate, Executive Director
Catherine Danielou, President

272 American Comparative Literature Association
E-mail: info@acla.org
www.acla.org
The American Comparative Literature Association (ACLA) is comprised of scholars whose work promotes cross-cultural literacy.

Founded: 1960

Andy Anderson, Administrative Coordinator
Emily Apter, President

273 American Council on the Teaching of Foreign Languages
1001 N Fairfax Street
Suite 200
Alexandria, VA 22314
703-894-2900
Fax: 703-894-2905
membership@actfl.org
www.actfl.org
An individual membership organization of language educators and administrators, the American Council on the Teaching of Foreign Languages (ACTFL) works to improve and support the teaching and learning of all languages.

Founded: 1967

Marty Abbott, Executive Director
Candace Thompson, Office Manager

274 American Speech-Language-Hearing Association
2200 Research Boulevard
Rockville, MD 20852-3289
301-296-5700
800-638-8255
Fax: 301-296-8580
community@asha.org
www.asha.org
The American Speech-Language-Hearing Association (ASHA) is a national association committed to supporting audiologists, speech-language pathologists, and speech, language, and hearing scientists by advancing science, setting standards, and advocating for those who work to make effective communication accessible for all.

Founded: 1925

Elise Davis-McFarland, President
Arlene A. Pietranton, Chief Executive Officer

275 Association of Schools of Journalism and Mass Communication
234 Outlet Pointe Boulevard
Columbia, SC 29210-5667
803-798-0271
Fax: 803-772-3509
aejmchq@aol.com
www.asjmc.org
The Association of School of Journalism and Mass Communication (ASJMC) is a nonprofit association working to foster, encourage, and facilitate excellence in journalism and mass communication education.

Founded: 1917

Jennifer McGill, Executive Director
Sonya Duhe, President

276 Center for Applied Linguistics
4646 40th Street NW
Washington, DC 20016-1859
202-362-0700
Fax: 202-363-7204
info@cal.org
www.cal.org
The Center for Applied Linguistics (CAL), is a nonprofit organization dedicated to promoting language and cultural understanding as it relates to access and equality in education.

Joel Gomez, EdD, President & CEO
Ruben Rodriguez, COO & CFO

277 Children's Literature Assembly
E-mail:
info@childrensliteratureassembly.org
www.childrensliteratureassembly.org
Part of the National Council of Teachers of English, the Children's Literature Assembly (CLA) advocates for the presence of literature in the lives of youth. The CLA provides a forum for the exchange of information among teachers and works cooperatively with organizations to promote literature.

Jennifer Graff, President
Lauren Liang, Vice President

278 Children's Literature Association
1301 W 22nd Street
Suite 202
Oak Brook, IL 60523
630-571-4520
Fax: 708-876-5598
info@childlitassn.org
www.childlitassn.org
The Children's Literature Association (ChLA) is a nonprofit association dedicated to the academic study of children's literature. Members include scholars, critics, professors, students, teachers, and librarians.

Founded: 1973

Teya Rosenberg, President
Kate Capshaw, Vice President

279 International Dyslexia Association
40 York Road
4th Floor
Baltimore, MD 21204-2044
410-296-0232
800-222-3123
Fax: 410-321-5069
info@dyslexiaida.org
www.dyslexiaida.org
The International Dyslexia Association (IDA) is a nonprofit, educational organization dedicated to promoting literacy and education for individuals with dyslexia. The IDA advocates for better resources and educational tools, has 11,000 members with 47 branches across the United States and Canada.

Rick Smith, Chief Executive Officer
Newton Guerin, Chief Operating Officer

280 Journalism Education Association
828 Mid-Campus Drive S
105 Kedzie Hall
Manhattan, KS 66506-1505
785-532-5532
866-532-5532
Fax: 785-532-5563
staff@jea.org
jea.org

A nonprofit organization providing training and resources for educators teaching journalism. The Association offers national certification and publishes print and online resources for its members.

Founded: 1924

Sarah Nichols, President
Valerie Kibler, Vice President

281 Modern Language Association
85 Broad Street
Suite 500
New York, NY 10004-2434
646-576-5000
Fax: 646-458-0030
help@mla.org
www.mla.org
The Modern Language Association (MLA) provides a forum of communication for its members to discuss scholarly information and exchange teaching experiences in the field of humanities. The MLA hosts an annual convention, has a book publication program, and publishes 4 major periodicals.

Founded: 1883

Paula M. Krebs, Executive Director
Dennis Looney, Director, Programs

282 National Association for Bilingual Education
c/o Ana G. Mendez, University System
11006 Veirs Mill Rd
Suite L-1
Wheaton, MD 20902
240-450-3700
Fax: 240-450-3799
www.nabe.org
The National Association for Bilingual Education (NABE) is a nonprofit, membership organization dedicated to advocating for equal education for bilingual and multilingual students. NABE provides bilingual educators with resources, works to improve instruction, and helps to secure funding for programs serving children limited English proficiency.

Founded: 1975

Santiago V. Wood, Ed.D, National Executive Director
Nilda M. Aguirre, ED.S, Deputy Director

283 National Association for Poetry Therapy
E-mail: naptadmin@poetrytherapy.org
www.poetrytherapy.org
An international, nonprofit organization, the National Association for Poetry Therapy (NAPT) promotes growth and healing through language, including the written word, symbols, and stories.

Geri Chavis, President
Barbara Kreisberg, VP, Conference

284 National Council of Teachers of English
1111 W Kenyon Road
Urbana, IL 61801-1096
217-328-3870
877-369-6283
Fax: 217-328-9645
membership@ncte.org
www.ncte.org
The National Council of Teachers of English (NCTE) promotes literacy through the learning and teaching of English. The NCTE is a communication tool for english educators to connect with their peers and exchange information to improve literacy.

Founded: 1911

Emily Kirkpatrick, Executive Director
Lori Bianchini, Executive Assistant

285 National Federation of Modern Language Teachers Association
1809 Saint Andrews Place
Lincoln, NE 68512
www.nfmlta.org
The National Federation of Modern Language Teachers Association (NFMLTA) is dedicated to the improvement of the teaching of languages, literature, and culture across the United States. The NFMLTA improves teaching primarily through the publishing of The Modern Language Journal.

Founded: 1916

Dr. Lara Lomicka Anderson, President
Daryl Biallas, Treasurer

286 National Network for Early Language Learning
E-mail: info@nnell.org
www.nnell.org
Focused on K-8 education, the National Network for Early Language (NNELL) advocates for high quality education among elementary school students. The NNELL provides leadership and resources for educators, parents, and policymakers.

Founded: 1987

Kathleen Priceman, President
Dorie Perugini, Executive Secretary

287 National Research Center on English Learning & Achievement
School of Education
University of Albany
1400 Washington Avenue
Albany, NY 12222
518-442-4985
Fax: 518-442-4953
educationdean@uamail.albany.edu
www.albany.edu/cela
The Center on English Learning and Achievement (CELA) carries out research focused on improving English and literacy among students.

Founded: 1987

Arthur Applebee, Co-Director
Judith A. Langer, Co-Director

288 ReadWriteThink
c/o NCTE, Project Manager
1111 W Kenyon Road
Urbana, IL 61801
www.readwritethink.org
ReadWriteThink provides free language and reading instructional material to educators, parents, and afterschool professionals.

Lisa Storm Fink, Project Manager

289 Sigma Tau Delta, International English Honor Society
Northern Illinois University
Department of English
1425 Lincoln Highway
DeKalb, IL 60115
815-981-9974
sigmatd@niu.edu
www.english.org
Main purpose is to confer distinction upon students of the English language and literature in undergraduate, graduate and professional studies. Sigma Tau Dalta also recognizes the accomplishments of professional writers who have contributed to the fields of language and literature.

Founded: 1924

William C. Johnson PhD, Executive Director
Natasha McPartlin, Director, Operations

290 Teachers & Writers Collaborative
540 President Street
3rd Floor
New York, NY 11215
212-691-6590
Fax: 212-675-0171
info@twc.org
www.twc.org
The Teachers & Writers Collaborative (T&W) works to educate teachers and students through programs and publications focused on creative writing. Programs include writing workshops for students, professional development opportunities for educators, and poetry competitions.

Founded: 1967

Amy Swauger, Executive Director
Jade Triton, Director, Operations

Library Services

291 American Association of Law Libraries
105 W Adams Street
Suite 3300
Chicago, IL 60603-6225
312-939-4764
Fax: 312-431-1097
www.aallnet.org
The American Association of Law Libraries (AALL) is dedicated to supporting the professional development and recognition of law librarianship.

Founded: 1906

Gregory R. Lambert, President
Kate Hagan, Staff Liaison

292 American Council on Education Library & Information Service
1 Dupont Circle NW
Washington, DC 20036
202-939-9300
Fax: 202-833-4730
comments@ace.nche.edu
www.acenet.edu
The council seeks to provide leadership and a unifying voice on key higher education issues and to influence public policy through advocacy, research, and program initiatives.

Judy C Miner, Chair
Barbara R Snyder, Vice Chair & Chair-Elect

293 American Indian Library Association
E-mail: ailawebsite@gmail.com
ailanet.org
The American Indian Library Association (AILA) is dedicated to providing the library related needs of American Indians and Alaska Natives. The Association is membership based, comprised of individuals and institutions wishing to support the development and improvement of Indian library, cultural, and informational services in schools. The AILA is an affiliate of the American Library Association.

Founded: 1979

Heather Devine-Hardy, Executive Director
Aaron Lafromboise, Secretary

294 American Library Association
50 E Huron Street
Chicago, IL 60611-2795
312-944-6780
800-545-2433
Fax: 312-440-9374

ala@ala.org
www.ala.org
The American Library Association (ALA) promotes and develops the profession of librarianship and information services. The ALA is the oldest and largest library association in the world.

Founded: 1876

Mary Ghikas, Interim Executive Director
Cheryl Malden, Program Officer

295 American Theological Library Association
300 South Wacker Drive
Suite 2100
Chicago, IL 60606-6701
312-454-5100
888-665-2852
Fax: 312-454-5505
atla@atla.com
www.atla.com
The American Theological Library Association (ATLA) works to develop the study of theology and religion through fostering the improvement of theological and religious studies libraries and librarianship.

Founded: 1946

Brenda Bailey-Hainer, Executive Director
Gillian Harrison Cain, Director, Member Programs

296 Art Libraries Society of North America
7044 South 13th Street
Oak Creek, WI 53154
414-908-4954
800-817-0621
www.arlisna.org
The Art Libraries Society of North America (ARLIS/NA) provides an electronic forum for communication between art professionals, organizations, and art libraries.

Founded: 1972

Robert J. Kopchinski, Executive Director
Eumie Imm Stroukoff, President

297 Asian American Curriculum Project
529 E Third Avenue
San Mateo, CA 94401
650-375-8286
800-874-2242
Fax: 650-375-8797
aacpinc@asianamericanbooks.com
www.asianamericanbooks.com
The Asian American Curriculum Project (AACP), is a nonprofit educational organization working to educate the public about the Asian American experience through books. The AACP provides the most complete collection of Asian American books, with materials including, literature, folk tales, posters, magazines, tapes, reference books, and dictionaries.

Founded: 1969

Florence M. Hongo, President & General Manager
Shizue Yoshina, Vice President

298 Asian Pacific American Librarians Association
c/O Buenaventura Basco, Executive Director
PO Box 677593
Orlando, FL 32867-7593
www.apalaweb.org
A nonprofit organization, the Asian Pacific American Librarians Association (APALA) is a communication tool for Asian Pacific American librarians and libraries to discuss problems, exchange ideas, and recruit and mentor Asian Pacific American librarians.

Founded: 1980

Dora T. Ho, President
Buenaventura Basco, Executive Director

299 Association for Library & Information Science Education
2150 N 107 Street
Suite 205
Seattle, WA 98133
206-209-5267
Fax: 206-367-8777
office@alise.org
www.alise.org
The Association for Library and Information Science Education (ALISE) promotes the advancement of research, teaching, and service for educators and scholars in the Library and Information Science field. ALISE is comprised of 500 individual members and 60 institutions.

January

Andrewa Estep, Executive Director
Cecilia Salvatore, Director, Membership

300 Association of Research Libraries
21 Dupont Circle NW
Suite 800
Washington, DC 20036
202-296-2296
Fax: 202-872-0884
webmgr@arl.org
www.arl.org
The Association of Research Libraries (ARL) is a nonprofit organization working to influence scholarly communication and public policies that affect research libraries. The ARL is comprised of 123 research libraries.

Founded: 1932

Elliott Shore, Executive Director
Prudence S. Adler, Associate Executive Director

301 Black Caucus of the American Library Association
Winston-Salem State University
601 S Martin Luther King Dr.
Winston Salem, NC 27110
773-916-6970
bcalamarketing@gmail.com
www.bcala.org
The Black Caucus of the American Library Association (BCALA) supports the development, promotion, and improvement of library resources for the African American community.

Founded: 1969

Wanda Kay Brown, Director, Library Services
Richard Ashby, President

302 Center for Research Libraries
6050 S Kenwood Avenue
Chicago, IL 60637-2804
773-955-4545
800-621-6044
Fax: 773-955-4339
systems@crl.edu
www.crl.edu
An association of university, college, and independent research libraries, the Center for Research Libraries (CRL), provides primary resource material that supports research and quality teaching in all subjects.

Founded: 1949

Bernard Reilly, President
Gloria Johnson, Communications Coordinator

303 Institute of Museum and Library Services
955 L'Enfant Plaza North SW
Suite 4000
Washington, DC 20024-2135
202-653-4657
imlsinfo@imls.gov
www.imls.gov
The Institute of Museum and Library Services (IMLS) is committed to proving leadership through research, policy making, and the funding of libraries and museums.

Kathryn K. Matthew, PhD, MBA, Director
Michael D. Jerger, Chief Operating Officer

304 International Association of School Librarianship
PO Box 684
Jefferson City, MO 65102
Fax: 312-419-8950
www.iasl-online.org
The International Association of School Librarianship (IASL) provides a forum for individuals to promote effective school library programs as a tool in the educational process.

Katy Manck, President
Jennifer Branch-Mueller, Treasurer

305 Pro LiBRA Associates
436 Springfield Avenue
Summit, NJ 07901-2618
908-918-0077
800-262-0070
Fax: 908-918-0977
staffing@prolibra.com
www.prolibra.com
Pro LiBRA is a library service company involved in staffing libraries and information centers.

306 Southeastern Library Association
SELA Administrative Services
PO Box 950
Rex, GA 30273
678-466-4334
Fax: 678-466-4349
selaadminservices@selaonline.org
selaonline.org
Provides a forum for discussing library education and leadership for the expansion of public library services. The association also offers information in the areas of reference and public services, resources and technical services, school and children's librarians and more.

Linda Suttle Harris, President
Tim Dodge, President-Elect

307 Utah Library Association (ULA)
PO Box 708155
Sandy, UT 84070
801-200-3129
anna.neatrour@gmail.com
ula.org
The mission of the Utah Library Association is to serve the professional development and educational needs of its members and to provide leadership and direction in developing and improving library and information services in Utah.

Founded: 1912

Dan Compton, President
Barbara Hopkins, Executive Director

Mathematics

308 American Institute of Mathematics
600 E Brokaw Road
San Jose, CA 95112

408-350-2088
conrey@aimath.org
www.aimath.org
The American Institute of Mathematics (AIM) is dedicated to advancing mathematical knowledge and increased participation in the mathematical sciences at every level.

Founded: 1994

Brian Conrey, Executive Director
Estelle Basor, Deputy Director

309 American Mathematical Association of Two-Year Colleges
Southwest Tennessee Community College
5983 Macon Cove
Memphis, TN 38134
901-333-6243
Fax: 901-333-6251
amatyc@amatyc.org
www.amatyc.org
The American Mathematical Association of Two-Year College (AMATYC) provides a forum for the improvement of mathematical instruction in the first two years of college. The AMATYC offers professional development opportunities for educators through conferences, workshops, and publications.

Founded: 1974

Wanda L. Garner, Executive Director
Beverly Vance, Office Director

310 Association for Symbolic Logic
Vassar College
PO Box 742
124 Raymond Avenue
Poughkeepsie, NY 12604
845-437-7080
Fax: 845-437-7830
asl@vassar.edu
www.aslonline.org
An international organization, the Association for Symbolic Logic is dedicated to supporting research in logic. The Association provides a forum for the discussion of scholarly work.

Founded: 1936

Ulrich Kohlenbach, President
Julia Knight, Vice President

311 Association for Women in Mathematics
11240 Waples Mill Road
Suite 200
Fairfax, VA 22030
703-934-0163
Fax: 703-359-7562
awm@awm-math.org
sites.google.com/site/awmmath
The Association for Women in Mathematics (AWM) is a nonprofit organization supporting women and girls to study and have careers in mathematical sciences.

Founded: 1971

Ami Radunskay, President
Ellen Kirkman, Treasurer

312 Association of Mathematics Teacher Educators
AMTE, c/o Meredith College
3800 Hillsborough Street
Raleigh, NC 27607
919-760-8240
Fax: 919-760-8763
harpersr@miamioh.edu
amte.net
The Association of Mathematics Teacher Educators is a professional organization devoted to the improvement of education for K-12 teachers of mathematics. The association offers professional learning opportunities, conferences, publications, job listings and more.

Founded: 1991

Randy Philipp, President
Tim Hendrix, Executive Director

313 Institute for Operations Research and the Management Sciences
5521 Research Park Drive
Suite 200
Catonsville, MD 21228
443-757-3500
800-446-3676
Fax: 443-757-3515
informs@informs.org
www.informs.org
The Institute for Operations Research and the Management Sciences (INFORMS) is an international association comprised of professionals in operations research and analytics. INFORMS works to advance the profession of operations research through conferences, competitions, networking opportunities, and development services.

Melissa Moore, Executive Director
Jeff Cohen, Director, Marketing

314 Mathematical Association of America
1529 18th Street NW
Washington, DC 20036-1358
202-387-5200
800-741-9415
Fax: 202-265-2384
maahq@maa.org
www.maa.org
The Mathematical Association of America (MAA) is dedicated to advance mathematical sciences at the collegiate level.

Michael Pearson, Executive Director
Doug Ensley, Deputy Executive Director

315 National Academy of Sciences
2101 Constitution Avenue NW
Washington, DC 20418
202-334-2000
www.nasonline.org
The National Academy of Sciences (NAS) is a private nonprofit society of scholars that offers independent objective advice related to science and technology. Members of NAS are active contributors in the international scientific community.

Founded: 1863

Marcia McNutt, President
Diane Griffin, Vice President

316 National Council of Supervisors of Mathematics
NCSM
2851 S Parker Road
Suite 1210
Aurora, CO 80014
303-317-6595
Fax: 303-200-7099
office@mathedleadership.org
www.mathedleadership.org
The National Council of Supervisors of Mathematics (NCSM) is an organization providing professional development opportunities to education leaders, with the goal of preparing them to better support student academic success.

Connie S Schrock, President
Kimberly Morrow-Leong, First Vice President

317 National Council of Teachers of Mathematics
1906 Association Drive
Reston, VA 20191-1502
703-620-9840
800-235-7566
Fax: 703-476-2970
nctm@nctm.org
www.nctm.org
The National Council of Teachers of Mathematics (NCTM) supports and advocates for the increased quality in mathematic teaching. The NCTM has over 60,000 members and 230 affiliates across the United States and Canada.

Founded: 1920

Ken Krehbiel, Executive Director
David Shayka, COO & CFO

318 Society for Industrial and Applied Mathematics
3600 Market Street
6th Floor
Philadelphia, PA 19104-2688
215-382-9800
800-447-7426
Fax: 215-386-7999
membership@siam.org
www.siam.org
The Society for Industrials and Applied Mathematics (SIAM) facilitates connection and interaction between mathematics, scientific, and technological communities. SIAM provides members with activities, conferences, and publishes books and journals.

Founded: 1951

Nicholas Higham, President
Cynthia Phillips, Vice President, Programs

319 Society for Mathematical Biology
270-809-2491
membership@smb.org
www.smb.org
An international organization, the Society for Mathematical Biology (SMB) promotes interaction between the mathematical and biological sciences. Through the development and dissemination of research, the SMB works to further science and math by hosting an annual meeting and the publication of research.

Founded: 1973

Denise Kirschner, President
Ping Ye, Secretary

320 Society of Actuaries
475 North Martingale Road
Suite 600
Schaumburg, IL 60173
847-706-3500
Fax: 847-706-3599
customerservice@soa.org
www.soa.org
The Society of Actuaries (SOA) is an educational and research organization dedicated to advancing actuarial knowledge.

Founded: 1889

Greg Heidrich, Executive Director
Stacy Lin, Deputy Exec. Director & CFO

Music & Art

321 American Art Therapy Association
4875 Eisenhower Avenue
Suite 240
Alexandria, VA 22304
700-548-5860
888-290-0878
Fax: 703-783-8468
info@arttherapy.org
www.arttherapy.org

The American Art Therapy Association is a nonprofit organization is committed to the increased access and expansion of professional art therapists. The Association provides members with resources and networking opportunities to further the field of art therapy and encourages the highest quality of art therapy services.

Cynthia Woodruff, Executive Director
Christina Easterly, Coordinator, Operations

322 **American Dance Therapy Association**
10632 Little Patuxent Parkway
Suite 108
Columbia, MD 21044-3273
410-997-4040
Fax: 410-997-4048
info@adta.org
www.adta.org
The American Dance Therapy Association (ADTA) works to support the profession of dance/movement therapy . The ADTA provides communication among dance/movement therapists and related professions.

Founded: 1966

Gloria J. Farrow, Director, Operations
Renee Wolfe, Administrative Assistant

323 **American Guild of Music**
PO Box 599
Warren, MI 48090
248-686-1975
www.americanguild.org
An international organization, the American Guild of Music is dedicated to advancing the study of music and the promotion of artistic, educational, recreational, and commercial music. Membership to the Guild is open to music teachers, music store owners, teaching staff, music publishers, instrument manufacturers and music students.

Tracey King, President
Gina Selvaggi, 1st Vice President

324 **American Musicological Society**
American Musicological Society, Inc.
194 Mercer Street
Room 404
New York, NY 10012-1502
212-992-6340
877-679-7648
Fax: 212-995-4022
ams@ams-net.org
www.ams-net.org
The American Musicological Society is a nonprofit organization working to advance research in various fields of music through learning and scholarship. The Society publishes a journal, holds an annual meeting, and offers an array of awards.

Founded: 1934

Robert Judd, Executive Director
Katie VanDerMeer, Office Manager

325 **Americana Music Association**
PO Box 628
Franklin, TN 37065
615-386-6936
Fax: 615-386-6937
info@americanamusic.org
americanamusic.org
The Americana Music Association is a professional trade organization advocating for the authentic voice of American Roots Music around the world.

Founded: 1999

John Allen, Director
Jed Hilly, Executive Director

326 **Arts Education Partnership**
700 Broadway Street
#810
Denver, CO 80203
303-299-3631
www.aep-arts.org
Through research, policy and procedure, the Arts Education Partnership is a network of organizations dedicated to advancing and advocating for equal access to the arts in education.

Founded: 1995

Jane R. Best, PhD, Director
Cassandra Quillen, Communications

327 **Association for Public Art**
1528 Walnut Street
Suite 1000
Philadelphia, PA 19102-3627
215-546-7550
Fax: 215-546-2363
apa@associationforpublicart.org
associationforpublicart.org
The Association for Public Art (aPA) is a nonprofit civic organization dedicated to integrating public art and urban design in Philadelphia.

Founded: 1872

Penny Balkin Bach, Executive Director
Laura S. Griffith, Associate Director

328 **Civic Music Association**
900 Mulberry Street
Suite 203
Des Moines, IA 50309
515-280-4020
info@civicmusic.org
civicmusic.org
The Civic Music Association works to engage the central Iowa community with musical performances.

Founded: 1925

329 **College Art Association**
50 Broadway
21st Floor
New York, NY 10004
212-691-1051
Fax: 212-627-2381
nyoffice@collegeart.org
www.collegeart.org
The College Art Association (CAA) promotes the visual arts through practice and intellectual engagement.

Founded: 1911

Hunter O'Hanian, Executive Director
Tiffany Dugan, Director, Programs

330 **Country Music Association**
35 Music Square E
Suite 201
Nashville, TN 37203
615-244-2840
info@cmaworld.com
www.cmaworld.com
The Country Music Association (CMA) is a trade association dedicated to promoting country music. The CMA has over 7,500 members of industry professionals, representative of the business.

Founded: 1958

Sarah Trahern, Chief Executive Officer
Mechalle Myers, Executive Assistant

331 **Educational Theatre Association**
2343 Auburn Avenue
Cincinnati, OH 45219-2815
513-421-3900
Fax: 513-421-7077
info@schooltheatre.org
www.schooltheatre.org
The Education Theatre Association is a national nonprofit organization working to recognize, educate, influence the lives of individuals through theatre.

Founded: 1929

Julie Cohen Theobald, Executive Director
Doug Berlon, Deputy Executive Director

332 **Future Music Oregon**
School of Music
1225 University of Oregon
Eugene, OR 97403-1225
E-mail: stolet@uoregon.edu
pages.uoregon.edu/fmo/home
Future Music Oregon is dedicated to the exploration of sound and its creation.

Jeffrey Stolet, Director

333 **International Technology and Engineering Educators Association**
1914 Association Drive
Suite 201
Reston, VA 20191-1539
703-860-2100
Fax: 703-860-0353
iteea@iteea.org
www.iteea.org
The International Technology and Engineering Educators Association (ITEEA) promotes technological literacy through leadership, professional development, and publications. ITEEA supports the teaching of, and those who teach technology and engineering.

Steven A. Barbato, Executive Director
Dr. Jennifer Buelin, Dir, Digital Initiative

334 **National Art Education Association**
901 Price Street
Alexandria, VA 22314-1590
703-860-8000
800-299-8321
Fax: 703-860-2960
info@arteducators.org
www.arteducators.org
The National Art Education Association is a membership organization open to visual arts educators. The Association advocates for balanced learning of the visual arts by qualified art educators.

Founded: 1947

Deborah B. Reeve, EdD, Executive Director
Melanie R. Dixon, CAE, PHR, Chief Operating Officer

335 **National Association for Music Education**
1806 Robert Fulton Drive
Reston, VA 20191
800-336-3768
Fax: 703-860-1531
memberservices@nafme.org
www.nafme.org
The National Association for Music Education (NAfME) advocates at the local, state, and national level for all aspects of music education. NAfMe provides resources for teachers, parents, and administrators, and hosts professional development events.

Founded: 1907 72 pages
ISSN: 0027-4321

Mike Blakeslee, Executive Director & CEO
Christopher Woodside, Chief Operating Officer

336 **National Association of Schools of Music**
11250 Roger Bacon Drive
Suite 21
Reston, VA 20190-5248

703-437-0700
Fax: 703-437-6312
info@arts-accredit.org
nasm.arts-accredit.org/
An organization of schools, conservatories, colleges, and universities, the National Association of Schools of Music (NASM) establishes national standards for undergraduate and graduate degrees.

Founded: 1924

Karen P. Moynahan, Executive Director
Stacy McMahon, Office Manager

337 National Dance Education Organization
8609 Second Avenue
Suite 203-B
Silver Spring, MD 20910
301-585-2880
www.ndeo.org
The National Dance Education Organization (NDEO) is a nonprofit organization working to further dance education centered in the arts. The NDEO provides it members with a network of resources, support, and professional development opportunities.

Founded: 1998

Susan McGreevy-Nichols, Executive Director
Vilma Braja, Director, Finance

338 National Guild of Community Schools of the Arts
520 8th Avenue
Suite 302
New York, NY 10018
212-268-3337
Fax: 212-268-3995
guildinfo@nationalguild.org
www.nationalguild.org
The National Guild for Community Arts Education advocates for equal and accessible arts education for all. The Guild provides support for community art educators and members include community schools of the arts, art and cultural centers, preparatory programs, performing art companies, museums, and parks and recreation departments.

Founded: 1937

Jonathan Herman, Executive Director
Heather Ikemire, Chief Program Officer

339 National Institute of Art and Disabilities
551 23rd Street
Richmond, CA 94804
510-620-0290
www.niadart.org
The National Institute of Art and Disabilities is an art studio dedicated to the promotion of independent living for individuals with disabilities.

Deborah Dyer, Executive Director
Arden Fredman, Director, Client Services

Physical Education

340 American Canoe Association
ACA Canoe-Kayak-SUP-Raft Rescue
503 Sophia Street
Suite 100
Fredericksburg, VA 22401
540-907-4460
Fax: 888-229-3792
aca@americancanoe.org
www.americancanoe.org
The American Canoe Association (ACA) is a national nonprofit working to provide education and programs related to all aspects of paddling. The ACA promotes the stewardship and protection of paddling environments, and paddlesport competition.

Founded: 1880

Christopher Stec, Chief Operating Officer
Wade Blackwood, Executive Director

341 International Council for Health, Physical Education, Recreation, Sport, and Dance
1900 Association Drive
Reston, VA 20191-1598
703-476-3462
Fax: 703-476-9527
ichper@aahperd.org
www.ichpersd.org
The International Council for Health, Physical Education, Recreation, Sport, and Dance (ICHPERD-SD), is a membership organization of professors, teachers, researchers, coaches, educators, and administrators in the fields of health and physical activity.

Dr. Adel M. Elnashar, President
Dr. Shaikha Al Jeeb, Secretary General

342 National Alliance for Youth Sports
2050 Vista Parkway
West Palm Beach, FL 33411
561-684-1141
800-688-5437
Fax: 561-684-2546
nays@nays.org
www.nays.org
The National Alliance for Youth Sports (NAYS) provides programs, services, and resources to support and advocate for safe and positive sports for children.

Founded: 1981

John Engh, Executive Director
Kate Nematollahi, Director, Education Programs

343 National Association for Kinesiology in Higher Education
E-mail: clsmoore@mit.edu
www.nakhe.org
The National Association for Kinesiology in Higher Education works to fosters leadership in kinesiology administration and policy in relation to teaching and scholarship in higher education.

Carrie Sampson Moore, Executive Director
Betty Block, President

344 National Association of Collegiate Directors of Athletics
24651 Detroit Road
Westlake, OH 44145
919-513-1007
Fax: 919-513-0541
info@nfoura.org
www.nfoura.org
The National Association of Collegiate Directors of Athletics (NACDA) is a professional association of individuals in the field of athletics administration. The NACDA provides its members with professional educational and networking opportunities and is a forum for the exchange of information.

Founded: 1965

Bart Byrd, President
Jim Pignataro, President-Elect

345 National Athletic Trainers' Association
1620 Valwood Parkway
Suite 115
Carrollton, TX 75006
214-637-6282
Fax: 214-637-2206
toddc@nata.org
www.nata.org
The National Athletic Trainers' Association (NATA) is a membership association comprised of certified athletic trainers. NATA works to support and advocate for the recognition of athletic therapy as an essential practice that can advance healthcare.

Founded: 1950

Dave Sadd;Er, Executive Director
Rachael Oats, Associate Executive Director

346 National Collegiate Athletic Association
700 W. Washington Street
PO Box 6222
Indianapolis, IN 46206-6222
317-917-6222
Fax: 317-917-6888
www.ncaa.org
The National Collegiate Athletic Association is committed to support the long term success of college athletes.

Mark Emmert, President

347 President's Council on Fitness, Sports & Nutrition
1101 Wootton Parkway
Suite 560
Rockville, MD 20852
240-276-9567
Fax: 240-276-9860
fitness@hhs.gov
www.fitness.gov
The President's Council on Fitness, Sports & Nutrition (PCFSN) is dedicated to encouraging Americans in the adoption of a healthy lifestyle, including physical activity and good nutrition. The Council creates programs and campaigns focused on motivating people of all ages.

Founded: 1956

348 Shape America - Society of Health and Physical Educators
1900 Association Drive
Reston, VA 20191-1598
800-213-7193
Fax: 703-476-9527
www.shapeamerica.org
A nonprofit, member organization of health and physical educators, Shape America works to advance and promote physical education and activity. The organization provides programs and resources to support health and physical educators at every level, advocating for school health and physical education throughout the United States. Shape America has helped to implement the Presidential Youth Fitness Program, Active Schools and the Jump Rope For Heart/Hoops for Heart programs.

Founded: 1885

349 Women's Sports Foundation
E-mail: info@womenssportsfoundation.org
www.womenssportsfoundation.org
An educational organization, the Women's Sports Foundation is dedicated to advancing the lives of women and girls of all ages through sport and physical activity.

Founded: 1974

Reading

350 Center for Applied Linguistics
4646 40th Street NW
Washington, DC 20016-1859
202-362-0700
Fax: 202-363-7204
info@cal.org
www.cal.org
The Center for Applied Linguistics (CAL), is a nonprofit organization dedicated to promoting language and cultural understanding as it relates to access and equality in education.

Joel Gomez, EdD, President & CEO
Ruben Rodriguez, COO & CFO

351 College Reading & Learning Association
7044 S 13th Street
Oak Creek, WI 53154
414-908-4961
customercare@crla.net
www.crla.net
The College Reading & Learning Associations (CRLA) is dedicated to providing a forum for the exchange of ideas, methods, and information to improve student learning. The CRLA membership is comprised of, and open to professionals active in the fields of reading, learning assistance, developmental education, tutoring, and mentoring at the college/adult level.

Rosemarie Woodruff, President
Kathy Stein, Secretary

352 International Literacy Association
800 Barksdale Road
PO Box 8139
Newark, DE 19714-8139
302-731-1600
800-336-7323
Fax: 302-731-1057
customerservice@reading.org
www.literacyworldwide.org
An advocacy and membership organization, the International Literacy Association (ILA) fosters and encourages educators, students, and leaders to make literacy accessible for everyone. The ILA has a membership of 300,000 literacy educators in 84 countries.

Marci Craig Post, Executive Director
Stephen Sye, Associate Executive Director

353 National Summer Learning Association
575 South Charles Street
Suite 310
Baltimore, MD 21201
410-856-1370
Fax: 410-856-1146
info@summerlearning.org
www.summerlearning.org
The National Summer Learning Association (NSLA) is a national nonprofit organization focused on closing the education gap by providing summer learning opportunities for youth. The NSLA works with other national organizations to bring awareness and advocate for excellence in education for all.

Founded: 1992

Matthew Boulay, Founder & Interim CEO
Maleka Lawrence, Chief Operating Officer

354 Organization of Teacher Educators in Literacy
E-mail: kbates@emporia.edu
oter.coedu.usf.edu
A special interest group of the International Literacy Association, the Organization of Teacher Educators in Literacy (OTEL) provides a forum for members to communicate to debate and discuss issues and ways to improve reading instruction.

Rachael Waller, President
Karen Bates, Treasurer

355 ProLiteracy Worldwide
104 Marcellus Street
Syracuse, NY 13204
315-422-9121
888-528-2224
Fax: 315-422-6369
info@proliteracy.org
www.proliteracy.org
ProLiteracy is a membership organization advocating, and providing literacy and basic education to adults across both nationally and internationally. ProLiteracy supports 1,000 programs providing adult literacy instruction, advocates for the awareness, funding, and support for literacy, provides professional development, and produces of 400 instructional tools for students.

Kevin Morgan, President & CEO
Peter Waite, Executive Vice President

356 Reach Out and Read
89 South Street
Suite 201
Boston, MA 02111
617-455-0600
Fax: 617-455-0601
info@reachoutandread.org
www.reachoutandread.org
A nonprofit organization working to incorporate books into pediatric care. Reach Out and Read encourages families to read aloud together.

Founded: 1989

Brian Gallagher, Chief Executive Officer
Diane Malcolmson, MBA, MA, Director, Development

357 Reading Recovery Council of North America
500 W Wilson Bridge Road
Suite 250
Worthington, OH 43085
614-310-7323
Fax: 614-310-7345
membership@readingrecovery.org
www.readingrecovery.org
The Reading Recovery Council of North America is a nonprofit organization of Reading Recovery, offering opportunities for leadership and professional development.

Jady Johnson, Executive Director
Julie Reeves, Director, Membership

358 Reading to Kids
1600 Sawtelle Boulevard
Suite 210
Los Angeles, CA 90025
310-479-7455
Fax: 310-479-7435
info@readingtokids.org
readingtokids.org
Reading to Kids is dedicated to helping and inspiring underserved children through reading. The organization hosts monthly reading clubs, and offers parents training tools to encourage reading at home.

Founded: 1999

Charlie Orchard, Managing Director
Jessica Brown-Clark, Program Coordinator

359 Women's National Book Association
PO Box 237
FDR Station
New York, NY 10150
866-610-9622
info@wnba-books.org
www.wnba-books.org
The Women's National Book Association (WNBA) is an national organization dedicated to connecting, educating, and advocating for the literary community. The WNBA has 11 chapters across the United States, and is made up of women and men who work with and value books.

Founded: 1917

Jane Kinney Denning, President
Celine Keating, Secretary

Secondary Education

360 American Association for Adult and Continuing Education
Building 14
1827 Powers Ferry Road
Suite 100
Atlanta, GA 30339
678-271-4319
Fax: 404-393-9506
office@aaace.org
www.aaace.org
The American Association for Adult and Continuing Education (AAACE), is a nonprofit organization dedicated to providing leadership in the field of adult and continuing education. The AAACE works to expand opportunities for adult development , through research, information, and practice.

Founded: 1982

Sarah Berke, CAE, Managing Director
Donna Heavener, Association Manager

361 American Association of Colleges for Teacher Education
1307 New York Avenue NW
Suite 300
Washington, DC 20005
202-293-2450
Fax: 202-293-2450
aacte@aacte.org
www.aacte.org
The American Association of Colleges for Teacher Education (AACTE) advocates for high quality, evidence based educator preparation programs. AACTE represents over 800 postsecondary institutions, working to ensure that educators are prepared to teach at all levels.

Lynn M. Gangone, President & CEO
Gail Bozeman, Chief of Staff

362 American Driver & Traffic Safety Education Association
Highway Safety Services, LLC.
1434 Trim Tree Road
Indiana, PA 15701
724-801-8246
877-485-7172
Fax: 724-349-5042
office@adtsea.org
www.adtsea.org
A professional association, the American Driver and Traffic Safety Education Association (ADTSEA) represents traffic safety educators. The ADTSEA advocates for traffic safety education through the publication of policies and guidelines, hosts conferences, workshops and seminars, and provides consultation services.

Connie Sessoms, Jr., President
Stan Henderson, President-Elect

363 **Association for Institutional Research**
1983 Centre Pointe Boulevard
#101
Tallahassee, FL 32308
850-385-4155
Fax: 850-385-5180
air@airweb.org
www.airweb.org
The Association for Institutional Research (AIR) is an association of higher education professionals working in the institutional research, assessment, and planning education fields. AIR provides its members with professional development opportunities, and educational resources, working to support the process of collecting, analyzing, and converting data to aid in higher education decision information.
Christine M. Keller, Executive Director
Jason Lewis, Chief Financial Officer

364 **Association for Middle Level Education**
4151 Executive Parkway
Suite 300
Westerville, OH 43081
614-895-4730
800-528-6672
Fax: 614-895-4750
info@amle.org
www.amle.org
The Association for Middle Level Education is committed to meeting the educational and developmental needs of young adolescents by providing educators with the knowledge and resources to help them improve their services. The association offers workshops, publications and informational material.
Nancy Ruppert, President
William D. Waidelich, Ed.D, Executive Director

365 **Association for Supervision and Curriculum Development**
1703 N Beauregard Street
Alexandria, VA 22311-1714
703-578-9600
800-933-2723
Fax: 703-575-5400
press@ascd.org
www.ascd.org
The Association for Supervision and Curriculum Development (ASCD) works to develop and implement programs, products, and services to support all learners. ASCD is comprised of 115,000 members from over 128 countries.
Founded: 1943
Marge Scherer, Editor in Chief
Amy Azzam, Senior Associate Editor

366 **Close Up Foundation**
1330 Braddock Place
Suite 400
Alexandria, VA 22314
703-706-3300
800-336-5479
Fax: 703-706-0001
info@closeup.org
www.closeup.org
Close Up works to inform all citizens of their democratic rights and responsibilities. Close Up partners with schools, educators, and organizations to implement programs and develop skills to engage citizens in democracy.
Founded: 1971
Timothy S. Davis, Esq., President & CEO
Eric Adydan, Chief Operating Officer

367 **College Board**
The College Board National Office
250 Vesey Street
New York, NY 10281
212-713-8000
www.collegeboard.com
A nonprofit organization, the College Board is dedicated to expanding access to higher education by connecting students to college opportunities and programs, including an Advanced Placement Program, and SAT practice.
Founded: 1900
David Coleman, President & CEO
Jeremy Singer, Chief Operating Officer

368 **National Alliance for Secondary Education and Transition**
University of Minnesota, ATTN: Joe Timmons
6 Pattee Hall
150 Pillsbury Drive SE
Minneapolis, MN 55455
612-624-5659
Fax: 612-624-9344
ncset@umn.edu
www.nasetalliance.org
The National Alliance for Secondary Education and Transition (NASET) is a national coalition representing education and career organizations and advocacy groups focused on policy development and professional practice. NASET works in 5 areas, schooling, career preparatory experiences, youth development and leadership, family involvement and connecting activities.
Founded: 2003
Joe Timmons, NASET Contact

369 **National Business Education Association**
1914 Association Drive
Reston, VA 20191-1596
703-860-8300
Fax: 703-620-4483
nbea@nbea.org
www.nbea.org
The National Business Education Association (NBEA) works to support individuals and groups who instruct, administer, research, and spread information regarding business. NBEA advances the professional interests of it members through programs that enhance professional growth and development.
Janet M. Trichel, Executive Director
Laura Sutherland, Director, Convention

370 **National Parent Teacher Association**
1250 N Pitt Street
Alexandria, VA 22314
703-518-1200
800-307-4782
Fax: 703-836-0942
info@pta.org
www.pta.org
The National PTA is a nonprofit organization dedicated to the educational success of children, and parent involvement in schools.
Founded: 1897
Cynthia Gismegian, Executive Director
Fatima Collins, Manager, Governance

Science

371 **Academy of Applied Science**
24 Warren Street
Concord, NH 03301
603-228-4530
Fax: 603-228-4730
assistance@aas-world.org
www.aas-world.org
The Academy of Applied Science offers science, technology, engineering, and math programs for students. Programs are designed to promote the application of scientific knowledge and creativity.
Sheldon Apsell, CEO & Chairman

372 **American Association for the Advancement of Science**
1200 New York Avenue NW
Washington, DC 20005
202-789-4386
www.aaas.org
A nonprofit organization dedicated to the advancement of science. The American Association for the Advancement of Science (AAAS) is the largest multidisciplinary scientific society, with international membership. The AAAS is open to anyone interested in science for the benefit of people.
Founded: 1848
Barbara A. Schaal, Chair
Susan Hockfield, President

373 **American Association of Physics Teachers**
1 Physics Ellipse
College Park, MD 20740-3845
301-209-3311
Fax: 301-209-0845
eo@aapt.org
www.aapt.org
The American Association of Physics Teachers (AAPT) works to spread and improve physics knowledge and education through teaching.
Founded: 1930
Beth A. Cunningham, Executive Officer
Robert C. Hilborn, Associate Executive Officer

374 **American Dairy Science Association**
1800 S Oak Street
Suite 100
Champaign, IL 61820-6974
217-356-5146
Fax: 217-398-4119
ADSA@assochq.org
www.adsa.org
The American Dairy Science Association (ADSA) works to advance the dairy industry. The ADSA is an international organization comprised of diary educators, scientists, and industry representatives.
Founded: 1906
Peter Studney, MBA, CAE, Executive Director
Cara Tharp, Executive Assistant

375 **American Medical Student Association**
45610 Woodland Road
Suite 300
Sterling, VA 20166
703-620-6600
Fax: 703-620-6445
www.amsa.org
A student run national organization, the American Medical Student Association (AMSA), works to advocate for, and represent the concerns of physicians in training.
Founded: 1950
Joey Johnson, DO, President
Joshua Caulfield, IOM, Executive Director

376 **American Society for Clinical Laboratory Science, The**
1861 International Drive
Suite 200
McLean, VA 22102
571-748-3770
ascls@ascls.org
www.ascls.org
The American Society for Clinical Laboratory Science (ASCLS) is dedicated to impacting healthcare through the assurance of excellence in the practice of laboratory medicine.
Founded: 1936
Jim Flanigan, CAE, Executive Vice President
Karrie Hovis, MHS, MLS, CQIA, Project Manager

377 **American Society of Nephrology**
1510 H Street NW
Suite 800
Washington, DC 20005
202-640-4660
Fax: 202-637-9793
email@asn-online.org
www.asn-online.org
The American Society of Nephrology (ASN) is dedicated to preventing, treating and curing kidney disease. With nearly 15,000 physicians and scientists making up its membership, the ASN advocates policy makers on the importance of kidney health.
Tod Ibrahim, Executive Vice President
Bob Henkel, Director, Communications

378 **Association for Information Science and Technology**
8555 16th Street
Suite 850
Silver Spring, MD 20910
301-495-0900
Fax: 301-495-0810
asist@asist.org
www.asist.org
A professional organizations, the Association for Information Science and Technology (ASIS&T) works to bring together the practice of science and scientific research. Through the professional exchange of information, career development, research dissemination, and education, ASIS&T is committed to advancing information sciences.
Founded: 1937
Lydia Middleton, MBA, CAE, Executive Director
Maureen C. Markey, MBA, CAE, Director, Development

379 **Association for Science Teacher Education**
715-838-0893
Fax: 715-838-0893
theaste.org
The Association for Science Teacher Education (ASTE) works to promote leadership and support for those involved in the development of teachers of science.
Robert Hollon, Executive Director

380 **Association for the Advancement of Computing in Education**
PO Box 719
Waynesville, NC 28786
Fax: 828-246-9557
info@aace.org
www.aace.org
The Association for the Advancement of Computing in Education (AACE) is an international nonprofit association working to advance information technology and E-learning in education. The AACE offers conferences, publications, a digital library, and career center to provide professional growth opportunities for its members.
Founded: 1981

381 **Association of Science-Technology Centers**
818 Connecticut Avenue NW
7th Floor
Washington, DC 20006-2734
202-783-7200
Fax: 202-783-7207
info@astc.org
www.astc.org
An international organization, the Association of Science-Technology Centers (ASTC) represents, supports, and offers programming opportunities for science centers, museums, nature centers, aquariums, planetarium, zoos, and botanical gardens. The ASTC represents 600 members, from 50 countries worldwide, sponsoring an annual conference, and learning opportunities.
Founded: 1973
Gillian Thomas, Interim CEO
Cliff Reiss, Chief of Staff

382 **California Biomedical Research Association**
PO Box 19340
Sacramento, CA 95819-0340
916-558-1515
Fax: 916-558-1523
dsutton@ca-biomed.org
www.ca-biomed.org
The California Biomedical Research Association (CBRA) is a social welfare organization promoting and supporting biomedical research, and conducting public outreach on the role of research and medical care. The CBRA is comprised of academic institutions, voluntary health agencies, hospitals, nonprofit medical research institutions, and pharmaceutical companies based in California, Nevada, and the greater western region.

383 **Canadian Association for Medical Education**
2733 Chemin Lancaster Road
Suite 100
Ottawa, ON K1B-0A9
613-730-0687
Fax: 613-730-1196
came@afmc.ca
www.came-acem.ca
Organization of medical educators dedicated to promoting excellence in the field through advocacy, publications, professional development workshops and networking.
Allyn Walsh, Ph.D, President
Ming-Ka Chan, Ph.D, Membership Coordinator

384 **Energy Education Group**
The California Study, Inc.
664 Hilary Drive
Tiburon, CA 94920
415-435-4574
24hrcleanpower@gmail.com
www.energyforkeeps.org
A division of The California Study, Inc. the Energy Education Group is a nonprofit organization working to educate people on electricity and where it comes from.
Marilyn Nemzer, Executive Director

385 **Entomological Society of America**
3 Park Place
Suite 307
Annapolis, MD 21401-3722
301-731-4535
esa@entsoc.org
www.entsoc.org
The Entomological Society of America (ESA) is a nonprofit professional society working to advance the professional and scientific needs of entomologists. The ESA publishes 6 journals, a quarterly magazine, and organizes an annual meeting for entomologists and other scientists.
Founded: 1889
David Gammel, Executive Director
Nikki Olin, Executive Assistant

386 **Geothermal Education Office**
664 Hilary Drive
Tiburon, CA 94920
Fax: 415-435-7737
24hrcleanpower@gmail.com
www.geothermaleducation.org
The Geothermal Education Office (GEO) is a nonprofit organization dedicated to promoting and producing information about geothermal resources and its uses as a clean sustainable energy.
Marliyn Nemzer, Executive Director

387 **Green Communities Canada**
416 Chambers Street
2nd Floor
Peterborough, ON K9H-3V1
705-745-7479
Fax: 705-745-7294
info@greencommunitiescanada.org
greencommunitiescanada.org
National association of community organizations working to spread awareness about environmental health and reduce negative impacts on the environment through programs and initiatives.
Chris Birchall, Chair
Clifford Maynes, Executive Director

388 **History of Science Society**
University of Notre Dame
440 Geddes Hall
Notre Dame, IN 46556
574-631-1194
Fax: 574-631-1533
info@hssonline.org
www.hssonline.org
The History of Science Society is dedicated to understanding the relationship between history, science, technology, and medicine. The society has 3,000 members made up of individuals and institutions.
Founded: 1924
Robert J. Malone, Executive Director
Janet Browne, President

389 **Institute for Earth Education, The**
Cedar Cove
Greenville, WV
E-mail: info@ieetree.org
www.ieetree.org
The Institute for Earth Education (IEE) is an international nonprofit organization dedicated to earth education. The IEE creates and implement programs to promote interpretation, education and contemplation of earth education.
Founded: 1974
Dr. Andreas Hadjichamis, Director
Gabriella Deriv, Deputy Director

390 **National Association for Research in Science Teaching**
11130 Sunrise Valley Drive
Suite 350
Reston, VA 20191

703-234-4138
Fax: 703-435-4390
info@narst.org
www.narst.org
The National Association for Research in Science Teaching (NARST) is an international organization working to improve the teaching and learning of science through research. NARST promotes science literacy by encouraging and supporting research into the teaching and learning of science, disseminating research findings, and working with other educational and scientific societies to influence educational policies.

Founded: 1928

William C. Kyle, JR, Executive Director
Barbara Crawford, President

391 National Association of Biology Teachers
PO Box 3363
Warrenton, VA 20188
703-264-9696
888-501-6227
Fax: 202-962-3939
office@nabt.org
www.nabt.org
The National Association of Biology Teachers (NABT) supports educators to ensure students receive the highest quality of biology and life science education. The NABT represents teachers, students, and science organizations and is committed to the professional development of educators, through pedagogy, relevant and scientifically sound instructional content, and advocating for biology teachers.

Founded: 1938

Mark Little, President
Jaclyn Reeves-Pepin, Executive Director

392 National Association of Geoscience Teachers
NAGT c/O Science Education Resource Center
200 Division Street
Suite 210
Northfield, MN 55057
Fax: 507-222-5175
cmanduca@carleton.edu
www.nagt.org
The National Association of Geoscience Teachers (NAGT) is dedicated to improving geoscience education. NAGT membership is comprised of K-12 teachers, college and university faculty members, museums, and science centers.

Founded: 1938

Cathryn Manduca, Executive Director
Krista Herbstrith, Program Manager

393 National Center for Science Education
1904 Franklin Street
Suite 600
Oakland, CA 94612
510-601-7203
Fax: 510-601-7204
info@ncse.com
www.ncse.com
A nonprofit organization, the National Center for Science Education (NCSE) supports the accurate teaching of evolution and climate change. The NCSE works with teachers, scientists and communities to ensure scientific topics are taught without ideological interference.

ISSN: 1064-2358

Ann Reid, Executive Director
Glenn Branch, Deputy Director

394 National Earth Science Teachers Association
www.nestanet.org
The National Earth Science Teachers Association (NESTA) is a nonprofit, educational organization dedicated to advancing K-12, Earth and Space Science education in formal and informal settings.

Founded: 1983

Cheryl L. B. Manning, President
Dr. Carla McAuliffe, Executive Director

395 National Science Teachers Association
1840 Wilson Boulevard
Arlington, VA 22201
703-243-7100
Fax: 703-243-7177
pubinfo@nsta.org
www.nsta.org
The National Science Teachers Association (NSTA) is an international organization dedicated to improving and promoting excellence and innovation in science teaching.

Founded: 1944

Dr. David L. Evans, Executive Director
Dr. Christine Anne Royce, President

396 School Science and Mathematics Association
University of Alabama Birmingham
SSMA Central Office
1720 2nd Avenue S
Birmingham, AL 35924-1250
205-934-5067
office@ssma.org
www.ssma.org
The School Science and Mathematics Association (SSMA) is a professional community of educators and researchers promoting scholarship, research, and practices that improve social science, mathematics, and STEM. SSMA publishes a journal , newsletter, and hosts a national convention.

Founded: 1901

Melanie Shores, Co-Executive Director
Tommy Smith, Co-Executive Director

397 Society for Science & the Public
1719 N Street NW
Washington, DC 20036-2888
202-785-2255
member@societyforscience.org
www.societyforscience.org
A nonprofit, membership organization, the Society for Science & the Public, is focused on, and dedicated to expanding scientific literacy, effective STEM education, and research. The Society, formerly known as Science Service, advances science through information, education, and inspiration.

Founded: 1921

Maya Ajmera, President & CEO
Gayle Kansagor, CCO

398 Soil Science Society of America
5585 Guilford Road
Madison, WI 53711-5801
608-273-8080
Fax: 608-273-2021
certification@soils.org
www.soils.org
The Soil Science Society of America (SSSA) is an international scientific society dedicated to fostering the dissemination and implementation of sustainable soil practices. The SSSA provides information about soil as it relates to, crop production, environmental quality, ecosystems, waste management, recycling, and wise land use.

Founded: 1936

Sara Uttech, Senior Manager, Membership
Wes Meixelsperger, Chief Financial Officer

Social Studies

399 African-American Institute, The
420 Lexington Avenue
Suite 1706
New York, NY 10170-0002
212-949-5666
Fax: 212-682-6174
aainy@aaionline.org
www.aaionline.org
The Africa-America Institute (AAI) is an international education and policy organization working to foster engagement between Africa and America. The AAI seeks to advance higher education and the professional development of Africans, and raises funds to provide scholarships for under resourced students to attend African universities.

Founded: 1953

Kofi Appenteng, President & CEO
Steven Pfeiffer, Chair

400 American Association for History and Computing
Van Pelt-Dietrich Libary Center
3420 Walnut Street
Room 2016
Philadelphia, PA 19104-6206
www.historians.org
The American Association for History and Computing (AAHC) is dedicated to the promotion of the merging of history and computer technology. The AAHC meets once per year, publishes an electronic journal, and hosts summer workshops.

Founded: 1996

Aaron Marcavitch, President
Shawn Martin, Executive Director

401 American Association of Geographers
1710 16th Street NW
Washington, DC 20009-3198
202-234-1450
Fax: 202-234-2744
gaia@aag.org
www.aag.org
The American Association of Geographers (AAG) is a nonprofit, educational and scientific organization dedicated to the advancement of geography. The AAG provides a forum for its members and scholars to discuss theory, methods, and the practice of geography.

Founded: 1904

Douglas Richardson, Executive Director
Candida Mannozzie, Deputy Director, Operations

402 American Geographical Society
32 Court Street
Brooklyn, NY 11201
917-745-8354
Fax: 917-677-8328
ags@americangeo.org
americangeo.org
The American Geographical Society (AGS) advances and promotes geographic thinking in business, government, achedemic and social sectors. Their mission is to enhance the nation's geographic literacy and foster sound public policy, national security, and global wellbeing.

Founded: 1851

Christopher Tucker, Chairman
Marie Price, President

403 **American Political Science Association**
1527 New Hampshire Avenue NW
Washington, DC 20036-1206
202-483-2512
Fax: 202-483-2657
apsa@apsanet.org
www.apsanet.org
A professional organization, the American Political Science Association (APSA) promotes the study of political science. The APSA is comprised of 12,000 members from over 80 countries, working to bring together political scientists from a wide range of fields for scholarly research, the increase of academic and non-academic opportunities, and strengthening the professional environment of political science.

Founded: 1903

Steven Rathgeb Smith, Executive Director
Betsy Super, Deputy Director

404 **Canadian Association for Social Work Education**
383 Parkdale Avenue
Suite 410
Ottawa, ON K1Y-4R4
613-792-1953
888-342-6522
charmarkeh@caswe-acfts.ca
caswe-acfts.ca
A national nonprofit association comprised of faculties and school departments engaged in providing social work education. The association promotes excellence in the field by offering accreditation options, programs, research, a publication and an annual conference.

Susan Cadell, President
Alexandra Wright, Ph.D, Executive Director

405 **Canadian Association of Social Workers**
383 Parkdale Avenue
Suite 402
Ottawa, ON K1Y-4R4
613-729-6668
855-729-2279
casw@casw-acts.ca
casw-acts.ca
National organization engaged in overseeing general and financial policies that affect social work, as well as providing information and services for the development of social workers and their profession.

Founded: 1926

Jan Christianson-Wood, President
Fred Phelps, Executive Director

406 **Council for Economic Education**
212-730-7007
info@councilforeconed.org
www.councilforeconed.org
The Council for Economic Education (CEE) is focused on the economic and financial education of students from K-12. The Council works to educate teachers by providing curriculum tools, and pedagogical support in order to ensure youth are equipped to achieve financial and economic independence.

Nan J. Morrison, President & CEO
Sally Wood, COO & CFO

407 **Council of State Social Studies Specialists**
E-mail: fay.gore@dpi.nc.gov
cs4.socialstudies.org/home
The Council of State Social Studies Specialists is forum for the exchange of ideas between social studies specialists from different states and various state departments of education.

Founded: 1965

Fay Gore, President
Kris McDaniel, Chair

408 **Foundation for Teaching Economics**
260 Russell Boulevard
Suite B
Davis, CA 95616
530-757-4630
Fax: 530-757-4636
information@fte.org
www.fte.org
The Foundation for Teaching Economics is a nonprofit corporation working to introduce youth to economic, national, and international issues. The Foundation promotes the increased quality of economic education, provides workshops, and offers teachers tools to become more effective educators.

Thomas T. Tucker, Executive Director
Roger Ream, President

409 **National Council for Geographic Education**
1775 Eye Street NW
Suite 1150
Washington, DC 20006
202-587-5727
Fax: 202-618-6249
ncge@ncge.org
www.ncge.org
The National Council for Geographic Education (NCGE) is a nonprofit organization dedicated to promoting excellence among the geography teacher profession. The NCGE supports educators and students from kindergarten to university, with the council conducting and gathering research, producing journals, providing professional development opportunities, and organizing an annual conference.

Founded: 1915

Zachary R. Dulli, Chief Executive Officer
Melissa Lepak, Coordinator, Events

410 **National Council for the Social Studies**
8555 Sixteenth Street
Suite 500
Silver Spring, MD 20910
301-588-1800
800-683-0812
Fax: 301-588-2049
ncss@ncss.org
www.socialstudies.org
The National Council for the Social Studies (NCSS) advocates and supports social studies education. The Council is the largest professional association in the United States, and its membership is represented by K-12 teachers, college and university professors, and curriculum designers. Membership is open to any person or institution interested in social studies.

Founded: 1921

Lawrence M. Paska, Executive Director
Ana Post, Director, Communications

411 **National Council on Public History**
127 Cavanaugh Hall - IUPUI
425 University Boulevard
Indianapolis, IN 46202-5140
317-274-2716
Fax: 317-278-5230
ncph@iupui.edu
www.ncph.org
A membership association, the National Council on Public History (NCPH) works to establish professional standards, ethics, and practices, to encourage collaboration between historians and the public. The NCPH provides professional development and networking opportunities, and supports history education.

Founded: 1980

Stephanie Rowe, Executive Director
Meghan Hillman, Program Assistant

412 **New England History Teachers Association**
Dean College
99 Main Street
Franklin, MA 02038
E-mail: info@nehta.org
www.nehta.org
The New England History Teachers Association (NEHTA) provides teachers and students with academic opportunities to engage in history and social studies discussions through conferences, publications, and awards.

Founded: 1897

Stephen Armstrong, President
Kristen Borges, Treasurer

413 **Oral History Association**
25 Park Place
Suite 2020
Atlanta, GA 30303
404-413-5751
oha@gsu.edu
www.oralhistory.org
The Oral History Association (OHA) is dedicated to promoting the value of oral history. OHA advocates policy makers, educators, and historians to foster the collections, preservation, and dissemination of oral history.

Founded: 1966

Kristine Navarro-McElhaney, Executive Director
Gayle Knight, Program Associate

414 **Society for History Education**
1250 Bellblower Boulevard
Long Beach, CA 90840-1601
562-985-2573
info@thehistoryteacher.org
www.societyforhistoryeducation.org
The Society for History Education (SHE) is a nonprofit organization working to improve the learning experience in the classroom. SHE organizes and publishes the journal The History Teacher and is an affiliate of the American Historical Association.

Tim Keirn, President
David Shafer, Vice President

415 **Street Law**
Street Law, Inc.
1010 Wayne Avenue
Suite 870
Silver Spring, MD 20910
301-589-1130
Fax: 301-589-1131
learnmore@streetlaw.org
www.streetlaw.org
Street Law is a nonprofit organization that creates classroom and community programs focused on law, democracy, and human rights. Programs are created for teachers, lawyers, law students, non-governmental organizations, and law enforcement officers.

Founded: 1972

Lee Arbetman, Executive Director
Jos, A. Ar,valo, Chief Financial Officer

416 **Western History Association**
University of Nebraska at Omaha
Department of History
6001 Dodge Street
Omaha, NE 68182-6460

402-554-5999
westernhistoryassociation@gmail.com
www.westernhistory.org
The Western History Association (WHA) promotes the study of North American Western History. The WHA is comprised of historians, with 1,200 active members.

Founded: 1961

Donald Fixico, President
John W. Heaton, Executive Director

417 World History Association

Northeastern University
Meserve Hall
360 Huntington Avenue
Boston, MA 02115
617-373-6818
Fax: 617-373-2661
info@thewha.org
www.thewha.org
The World History Association (WHA) promotes the teaching, research, and publication of world history.

Michael Burns, Council Member
Diego Holstein, Council Member

Technology in Education

418 American Distance Education Consortium

Gainesville, FL
www.adec.edu
The American Distance Education Consortium (ADEC) is a nonprofit distance education consortium composed of state universities and land-grant colleges. ADEC works to promote high quality distance education programs and extend educational content to diverse populations.

Founded: 1989

Ian Tebbett, President
Oliver Grundmann, Executive Chair

419 American Technical Education Association

ATEA
Dunwoody College of Technology
818 Dunwoody Boulevard
Minneapolis, MN 55403
612-381-3315
Fax: 701-671-2260
info@ateaonline.org
www.ateaonline.org
International organization dedicated to the professional growth and development of postsecondary educators and industrial trainers. The American Technical Education Association provides leadership and networking opportunities with others working in the field.

Sandra Krebsbach, Ph.D, Executive Director
DeeAnn Bilben, Administrative Assistant

420 Association for Career & Technical Education

1410 King Street
Alexandria, VA 22314
800-826-9972
Fax: 703-683-7424
acte@acteonline.org
www.acteonline.org
The Association for Career and Technical Education is the largest national education association working to prepare youth and adults for their careers through the advancement of education.

Founded: 1926

LeAnn Wilson, Executive Director
Becky Cox, President

421 Association for Educational Communications & Technology

320 W 8th Street
Suite 101
Bloomington, IN 47404-3745
812-335-7675
877-677-2328
aect@aect.org
www.aect.org
The Association for Educational Communications and Technology (AECT) is a professional organization of educators dedicated to improving instruction through technology. AECT provides a forum for the exchange and dispersal of information between its members; with its members instrumental in the study, planning, application, and production of communications media for instruction.

Dr. Phillip Harris, Executive Director
Larry Vernon, Director Electronic Services

422 Association for the Advancement of Computing in Education

PO Box 719
Waynesville, NC 28786
Fax: 828-246-9557
info@aace.org
www.aace.org
The Association for the Advancement of Computing in Education (AACE) is an international nonprofit association working to advance information technology and E-learning in education. The AACE offers conferences, publications, a digital library, and career center to provide professional growth opportunities for its members.

Founded: 1981

423 CUE

CUE, Inc.
877 Ygnacio Valley Road
Suite 200
Walnut Creek, CA 94596
925-478-3460
Fax: 925-934-6799
cueinc@cue.org
www.cue.org
CUE is a nonprofit membership and educational corporation working to inspire learners and educators through community, personalized learning, technology, leadership development, and the advocating of educational opportunities. CUE is open to all education disciplines from preschool to college.

Founded: 1978

Mike Lawrence, Chief Executive Officer
Danielle Forst, Associate Executive Director

424 Canadian Network for Innovation in Education

CNIE/RCIE
204, 260 Dalhousie
Ottawa, ON K1N-7E4
613-241-0018
Fax: 613-241-0019
hello@cnie-rcie.ca
cnie-rcie.ca
National organization dedicated to supporting innovation in Canadian education of all levels. Services offered to members include conferences, publications and platforms for conversations about the use of technology in education.

Ruth Hickey, President
David Macdonald, Secretary & Treasurer

425 Center for Children & Technology

96 Morton Street
7th Floor
New York, NY 10014
212-807-4200
Fax: 212-633-8804
cct.edc.org
The Center for Children & Technology (CCT) researches how technology influences and enhances teaching. CCT uses a range of research tools, including classroom based research studies and international evaluations to understand the role of technology in education.

Founded: 1980

Shelley Pasnik, Director & Vice President
Bill Tally, Managing Project Director

426 Center for Educational Leadership & Technology

65 Boston Post Road W
Suite 200
Marlborough, MA 01752
508-624-4474
Fax: 508-624-6565
info@celtcorp.com
www.celtcorp.com
The Center for Educational Leadership and Technology (CELT) offers research, planning, and implementation services for educational institutions; including private and public schools, education agencies, education departments, universities and colleges, national education associations, and educational foundations. CELT is primarily focused on designing learner-centered data systems.

John Phillipo, Chairman & CEO
Richard Rozzelle, President & CIO

427 Center for Educational Technologies

Erma Ora Byrd Center for Educational Technologies
316 Washington Avenue
Wheeling, WV 26003-6243
304-243-2388
800-624-6992
Fax: 304-243-2497
webmaster@cet.edu
www.cet.edu
The Center for Education Technologies creates curriculum supplements to improve the teaching and learning of, science, technology, engineering, and math. The Center works with federal and state agencies, foundations, school districts, corporations, and educators by offering outreach, professional development, and onsite and distance learning opportunities.

Dr. Charles Wood, Executive Director
Dr. Laurie Ruberg, Associate Director

428 Consortium for School Networking

1325 G Street NW
Suite 420
Washington, DC 20005
202-861-2676
communications@cosn.org
www.cosn.org
Consortium for School Network (CoSN) is a professional association working to advocate for the use of technology to improve teaching and learning in K-12 classrooms.

Keith Krueger, Chief Executive Officer
Robert Duke, CAE, Chief Operating Officer

429 **Consortium of College and University Media Centers**
306 North Union Street
Indiana University
Bloomington, IN 47405-3888
812-855-6049
ccumc@ccumc.org
www.ccumc.org
The Consortium of College and University Media Centers (CCUMC) advocates for the accessibility of educational media, technology, and pedagogy. In addition, the CCUMC works to provide leadership and a forum for the exchange of information to the providers of media content, academic technology, and learning institutions.
Aileen Scales, Executive Director
Kirsten Phillips, Program Coordinator

430 **DANEnet**
517 N Segoe Rd
Suite 210
Madison, WI 53705
608-274-3107
www.danenet.org
Nonprofit organization offering on-site technical support, training, planning and consulting services to community agencies and science education groups in Dane County.
Founded: 1995
Dennis Lange, President
Alyssa Kenney, Executive Director

431 **EDUCAUSE**
1150 18th Street NW
Suite 900
Washington, DC 20036
303-449-4430
info@educause.edu
www.educause.edu
EDUCAUSE is a nonprofit association dedicated to improving and optimizing the impact of IT on higher education. EDUCAUSE is focused on building the IT profession, connecting and facilitating collaboration among IT professionals, research, and data analysis. Membership is comprised of 2,300 colleges, universities, and educational organizations, 300 corporations, and 68,000 individual members.
John O'Brien, President & CEO

432 **Instructional Technology Council**
PO Box 2406
Columbus, OH 43216
800-715-1451
itc@itcnetwork.org
www.itcnetwork.org
The Instructional Technology Council (ITC) is a nonprofit organization dedicated to advocating collaborating, researching, and the sharing of innovative educational technologies to its network of e-Learning providers with the purpose of advancing distance education.
Founded: 1977
Jennifer Starkey, Executive Director

433 **International Society for Technology in Education**
1530 Wilson Boulevard
Suite 730
Arlington, VA 22209
703-348-4784
800-336-5191
Fax: 703-348-6459
iste@iste.org
www.iste.org
Provides leadership and services to improve teaching and learning by advancing the effective use of technology in education.
Mila Thomas Fuller, Ed.D, President
Richard Culatta, CEO

434 **International Technology and Engineering Educators Association**
1914 Association Drive
Suite 201
Reston, VA 20191-1539
703-860-2100
Fax: 703-860-0353
iteea@iteea.org
www.iteea.org
The International Technology and Engineering Educators Association (ITEEA) promotes technological literacy through leadership, professional development, and publications. ITEEA supports the teaching of, and those who teach technology and engineering.
Steven A. Barbato, Executive Director
Dr. Jennifer Buelin, Dir, Digital Initiatives

435 **National Association of Media and Technology Centers**
NAMTC
PO Box 378
West Milton, PA 17886
570-701-4202
Fax: 570-710-4202
bettyge@namtc.org
www.namtc.org
The National Association of Media and Technology Centers (NAMTC) provides leadership opportunities, instructional technology, and professional development to foster the use of media and technology in education. Membership to NAMTC is open to regional, K-12, and higher education instructional technology media centers and commercial vendors.
Geoff Craven, Executive Director
Ron Cone, President

436 **National Center for Technology Innovation**
American Institutes for Research
1000 Thomas Jefferson Street NW
Washington, DC 20007
202-403-5000
Fax: 855-459-6213
ncti@air.org
www.nationaltechcenter.org
A program of the American Institutes for Research, the National Center for Technology Innovation (NCTI) works to advance learning opportunities for individuals with disabilities by promoting technological innovation. NCTI supports researchers, product developers, manufacturers, and publishers to create and commercialize technology products for students.
Tracy Gray, Managing Director

437 **National Center for Technology Planning**
PO Box 2393
Tupelo, MS 38803
662-844-9630
Fax: 662-844-9630
www.nctp.com
The National Center for Technology Planning (NCTP) provides a forum for the collection and exchange of information related to technology planning.
Dr. Larry S. Anderson, Founder & Director

438 **National Coalition for Technology in Education and Training**
Washington, DC
E-mail: Info@NCTET.org
www.nctet.org
The National Coalition for Technology in Education and Training (NCTET) is a nonprofit organization promoting the use of technology to improve education and training.
Founded: 1993
Jon Bernstein, Executive Director
Ally Bernstein, Project Manager

439 **Online Learning Consortium**
Online Learning Consortium, Inc.
PO Box 1238
Newburyport, MA 01950-8238
617-716-1414
info@onlinelearning-c.org
onlinelearningconsortium.org
Online Learning Consortium works to advance the quality of online learning through professional development, instruction, research, best-practice publications and connections to online learning organizations worldwide.
Founded: 1992
Kathleen Ives, Executive Director & CEO
Rpberta Vigliani, Chief Financial Officer

440 **State Educational Technology Directors Association**
PO Box 10
Glen Burnie, MD 21060
202-715-6636
www.setda.org
The State Educational Technology Directors Association (SETDA) is a nonprofit association dedicated to representing and supporting the use of technology in teaching and learning.
Dr. Tracy Weeks, Executive Director
Christine Fox, Deputy Executive Director

441 **Technology & Media Division**
The Council for Exceptional Children
2900 Crystal Drive
Suite 1000
Arlington, VA 22202-3557
E-mail: aevmenov@gmu.edu
www.tamcec.org
A division of the Council for Exceptional Children, the Technology and Media Division (TAM) promotes the use of technology and media for individuals with special learning needs.
Sean Smith, President
Marci Kinas Jerome, Treasurer

442 **Technology Student Association**
1914 Association Drive
Reston, VA 20191-1540
703-860-9000
888-860-9010
Fax: 703-758-4852
general@tsaweb.org
www.tsaweb.org
The Technology Student Association (TSA) works to promote personal development, leadership, and career opportunities in STEM. The TSA is open to students who are currently enrolled or were enrolled in technology education courses.

443 **United States Distance Learning Association**
76 Canal Street
Suite 301
Boston, MA 02114
617-399-1770
Fax: 617-399-1771
info@usdla.org
www.usdla.org
The United States Distance Learning Association (USDLA) supports distance learning

research and development across the United States.

Founded: 1987

Pat Cassella, President

444 **V-LINC**
2301 Argonne Drive
Baltimore, MD 21218
410-554-9134
info@linc.org
www.v-linc.org
V-LINC is a volunteer organization dedicated to the promotion of technology in schools, the workplace, and home to help individuals with disabilities lead productive and independent lives.

Founded: 2010

445 **WICHE Cooperative for Educational Technologies**
3035 Center Green Drive
Suite 200
Boulder, CO 80301-2204
303-541-0231
wcetinfo@wiche.edu
wcet.wiche.edu
WICHE Cooperative for Educational Technologies (WCET) is a national nonprofit working to bring together higher education institutions, organizations, and companies to improve the quality and reach of e-Learning programs. In addition, WCET promotes the adoption of effective practices and policies that advance technology in education.

Founded: 1989

Mike Abbiatti, Executive Director
Mollie McGill, Director, Programs

446 **eLearning Guild, The**
120 Stony Point Road
Suite 125
Santa Rosa, CA 95401
707-566-8990
Fax: 707-566-8963
service@elearningguild.com
www.elearningguild.com
The eLearning Guild is a member organization that produces conferences, online events, online training courses, eBooks, research reports, and a Learning Solutions Magazine. The Guild is source of information and a network for eLearning professionals.

Alabama

447 **Alabama Business Education Association**
National Business Education Association
1914 Association Drive
Reston, VA 20191-1596
703-860-8300
Fax: 703-620-4483
gkimble@hoover.k12.al.us
www.albusinessed.org
A professional association for business and marketing educators at the secondary and post-secondary levels. The association encourages professional growth among business teachers through events and networking.

Tiffany Stonecipher, President
Gerri M Kimble, Ed.S, President Elect

448 **Alabama Commission on Higher Education**
100 N Union Street
Montgomery, AL 36104-3758
334-242-1998
Fax: 334-242-0268
deborah.nettles@ache.alabama.gov
www.ache.alabama.gov
Coordinating board in the State of Alabama responsible for providing information on the state's education programs, colleges and universities, financial aid assistance programs, grants, scholarships, continuing education programs and career opportunities.

Jim Purcell, Ph.D, Executive Director
Deborah Nettles, Administrative Assistant

449 **Alabama Education Association**
422 Dexter Avenue
Montgomery, AL 36104
334-834-9790
800-392-5839
Fax: 334-262-8377
myaea@alaedu.org
www.myaea.org
Serves as an advocate for Alabama teachers and takes a lead role in the advancement of equitable and quality public education. The association provides legal assistance, member benefits and professional development resources.

Sheila Hocutt Remington, President
Sherry Tucker, Vice President

450 **Alabama Library Association**
6030 Monticello Drive
Montgomery, AL 36117
334-414-0113
www.ala.org
Nonprofit corporation formed to encourage and promote the welfare of libraries and professional interests of librarians in Alabama. The association provides leadership for the development, advocacy and improvement of library services.

Founded: 1904

Heather Cover, Chair

451 **Alabama Public Library Service**
6030 Monticello Drive
Montgomery, AL 36117
334-213-3900
800-723-8459
Fax: 334-213-3993
cburchett@apls.state.al.us
webmini.apls.state.al.us
The Alabama Public Library Service manages state funds provided by the State Legislature in making library services available to the citizens of Alabama, including those who are blind or disabled.

Ronald A Snider, District 1 Director
Carol Burchett, Finance

452 **Alabama State Council on the Arts**
201 Monroe Street
Montgomery, AL 36130-1800
334-242-4076
Fax: 334-240-3269
staff@arts.alabama.gov
www.arts.state.al.us
Promotes high-quality education in the arts. Areas covered include literary arts, performing arts, visual arts, community arts and more.

Albert B Head, Executive Director
Barbara Edwards, Deputy Director

453 **Alabama State Department of Education - Teaching and Learning Improvement Division**
50 N Ripley Street
PO Box 302101
Montgomery, AL 36104
334-242-9700
dtl@alsde.edu
www.alsde.edu/div/dtl/Pages/home.aspx
The Teaching and Learning Improvement Division is responsible for implementing Alabama's strategic PLAN 2020, to ensure that graduating students receive the kind of education that would make them college or career ready.

Barbara Cooper, Ph.D, Chief Academic Officer
Shanthia Washington, Assistant Superintendent

Alaska

454 **Alaska Association of School Librarians**
PO Box 101085
Anchorage, AK 99510-1085
907-269-6569
800-776-6566
association@akasl.org
akasl.org
Advances high standards for the school librarian profession and library information programs in the schools of Alaska. The association offers grants and awards, as well as development programs.

Karla Barkman, President
Jill Gann, President Elect

455 **Alaska Commission on Postsecondary Education**
ACPE
PO Box 110505
Juneau, AK 99811-0505
907-465-2962
800-441-2962
Fax: 907-465-5316
ACPE@alaska.gov
acpe.alaska.gov
Provides information on the state's education programs, colleges and universities, financial aid assistance programs, grants, scholarships, continuing education programs and career opportunities.

Randy Weaver, Chair
Stephanie Butler, Executive Director

456 **Alaska Education of Homeless Children and Youth Program**
801 W 10th Street
Suite 200
Juneau, AK 99811-0500
907-465-8704
877-854-5437
Fax: 907-465-4156
eed.webmaster@alaska.gov
education.alaska.gov/esea/titlex-c
Ensures that all homeless children and youth have equal access to the same free, appropriate public education.

Sheila Box, Youth Program Manager

457 **Alaska Library Association**
PO Box 81084
Fairbanks, AK 99708
907-543-4571
daniel.cornwall@alaska.gov
akla.org
Provides leadership and advocacy for the educational and political concerns of the library community in Alaska. The association encourages cooperation among libraries and related groups, safeguards intellectual freedom, and promotes access to information for all Alaskans.

Mollie Good, President
Stacey Glasser, Executive Officer

458 **Alaska State Council on the Arts**
161 Klevin Street
Suite 102
Anchorage, AK 99508-1506

907-269-6610
888-278-7424
Fax: 907-269-6601
aksca.info@alaska.gov
education.alaska.gov
Promotes high-quality education in the arts. The council offers art programs, publications, a photo gallery and grants.

Andrea Noble-Pelant, Executive Director
Keren Lowell, Office Manager

Arizona

459 **Arizona Commission for Postsecondary Education**
2020 N Central Avenue
Suite 650
Phoenix, AZ 85004
602-258-2435
Fax: 602-258-2483
acpe@azhighered.gov
www.azhighered.org
Provides information on the state's education programs, colleges and universities, financial aid assistance programs, continuing education programs and career opportunities.

April L Osborn, Ph.D, Executive Director
Cathy Guthrie, Business Manager

460 **Arizona Commission on the Arts**
417 W Roosevelt Street
Phoenix, AZ 85003-1326
602-771-6501
Fax: 602-256-0282
info@azarts.gov
azarts.gov
Promotes high-quality education in the arts by offering grants and development programs as well as publications to cultivate arts communities and make arts activities accessible.

Jaime Dempsey, Executive Director
Kim McCreary, Fiscal Office Manager

461 **Arizona Library Association**
950 E Baseline Road
Suite 104-1025
Tempe, AZ 85283
480-609-3999
admin@azla.org
www.azla.org
Promotes library service and librarianship in the state of Arizona. The accociation provides continuing education to school librarians, advocacy, job listings, awards and more.

Founded: 1926

Sandy Edwards, President
Gina Macaluso, President Elect

462 **Arizona School Boards Association**
2100 N Central Avenue
Suite 200
Phoenix, AZ 85004
602-254-1100
800-238-4701
Fax: 602-254-1177
asba-information@azsba.org
azsba.org
Nonprofit organization providing training, legislative advocacy, leadership and other services to public schools in Arizona.

Julie Bacon, President
Timothy L Ogle, Ph.D, Executive Director

463 **Arizona State Library, Archives and Public Records**
State Librarian & Library Services Director
1700 W Washington Street
7th Floor
Phoenix, AZ 85007
602-542-6200
800-228-4710
Fax: 602-256-7983
services@lib.az.us
www.azlibrary.gov
Offers archives and records management, books in accessible formats for those with visual disabilities, research materials, publications and a digital library and museum containing public records.

Michele Reagan, Secretary of State
Ted Hale, Ph.D, Director, Archives & Records

464 **Arizona State Office of Homeless Education**
1535 W Jefferson Street
Phoenix, AZ 85007
602-542-4963
800-352-4558
Fax: 602-542-5175
alexis.clermont@azed.gov
www.azed.gov/homeless
Ensures that all homeless children and youth have equal access to the same free, appropriate public education. The office offers programs and training for those interested in the cause.

Alexis Clermont, State Homeless Coordinator
JoAnne McCoy, Administrative Assistant

Arkansas

465 **Arkansas Arts Council**
1100 N Street
Little Rock, AR 72201
501-324-9150
Fax: 501-324-9207
info@arkansasarts.com
www.arkansasarts.com
Advances the arts in Arkansas by providing services and funding for arts programs (literary, performing or visual).

Founded: 1966

Patrick Ralston, Director
Jess Anthony, Grant Programs Manager

466 **Arkansas Business Education Association**
, AR
E-mail:
jennifer.curry@pottsvilleschools.org
www.abea.us
A professional association comprised of secondary and post secondary business and marketing educators, with the mission of developing quality education in the business field.

Founded: 1954

Tracie Opolka, President
Tonya Loe, Vice President

467 **Arkansas Department of Higher Education**
423 Main Street
Suite 400
Little Rock, AR 72201
501-320-3095
Fax: 501-371-8000
communications@adhe.edu
www.adhe.edu
Provides information on the state's education programs, colleges and universities, financial aid and grants.

Maria Markham, Ph.D, Director
Tara Smith, Deputy Director

468 **Arkansas Education Association**
1500 W 4th Street
Little Rock, AR 72201
501-375-4611
800-632-0624
Fax: 501-375-4620
www.aeaonline.org
Advocates for education professionals and unites members and the state to ensure that public education prepares students to succeed in a diverse world.

Cathy Koehler, President
Tracey-Ann Nelson, Executive Director

469 **Arkansas Library Association**
Benton, AR
501-860-7585
800-241-4590
info@arlib.org
arlib.org
Furthers the professional development of library staff members, fosters communication and cooperation among librarians and trustees, increases library visibility and serves as an advocate for librarians and libraries.

Founded: 1911

David Eckert, President
Lynn Valetutti, Secretary & Treasurer

470 **Arkansas State Education for Homeless Children and Youth**
4 Capitol Mall
Little Rock, AR 72201
501-683-3439
Fax: 501-682-5136
dana.davis@arkansas.gov
www.askansased.org
Provides programs to ensure that all homeless children and youth have equal access to free public education.

Dana Davis, Program Advisor
Bobby Lester, Federal Programs Coordinator

California

471 **California Arts Council**
1300 I Street
Suite 930
Sacramento, CA 95814
916-322-6555
800-201-6201
Fax: 916-322-6575
info@arts.ca.gov
www.cac.ca.gov
Promotes education in the arts through funding, programs, internships, research, policy development, workshops and more.

Donn Harris, Chair
Shelly Gilbride, Ph.D, Programs Officer

472 **California Association for Bilingual Education**
16033 E San Bernadino Road
Covina, CA 91722-3900
626-814-4441
Fax: 626-814-4640
info@bilingualeducation.org
www.gocabe.org
Nonprofit organization dedicated to supporting bilingual education for students in Cali-

fornia by offering services to teachers, administrators, parents and others.

Founded: 1976

Elodia Ortega-Lampkin, President
Jan Gustafson Corea, CEO

473 California Business Education Association
2607 Saklan Indian Drive
Walnut Creek, CA 94595
925-295-1104
cbeaquestions@cbeaonline.org
www.cbeaonline.org
The mission of the California Business Education Association is to recognize and promote excellence in business disciplines.

Bob Livingston, President
Frank Timpone, Treasurer

474 California Classical Association-Northern Section
San Francisco State University
Department of Classics, SFSU
1600 Holloway Avenue
San Francisco, CA 94132
415-205-6658
ccanorth@gmail.com
www.ccanorth.org
Funds support programs to enrich and promote Classical Studies.

Founded: 1969

Scott Roos, President
Dobbie Vasquez, Secretary

475 California Foundation for Agriculture in the Classroom
2300 River Plaza Drive
Sacramento, CA 95833-3293
916-561-5625
800-700-2482
Fax: 916-561-5697
info@learnaboutag.org
www.learnaboutag.org
The foundation's mission is to educate California's youth about the value of agriculture in their daily lives. The foundation offers programs, teaching resources, grants and professional training for educators.

Jamie Johansson, President
Judy Culbertson, Executive Director

476 California Library Association
1055 E Colorado Boulevard
5th Floor
Pasadena, CA 91106
626-204-4071
info@cla-net.org
www.cla-net.org
Provides supports and development services for libraries, librarianship and the library community. The association also offers resources for learning about new ideas and technology.

Helen McAlary, President
Trish Garone, Programs Manager

477 California Reading Association
638 Camino De Los Mares
Suite H130/476
San Clemente, CA 92673
949-547-6664
Fax: 949-481-8163
admin@californiareads.org
www.californiareads.org
An independent, self-governing organization dedicated to increasing literacy in California. Members include educators working in the fields of language arts education in all levels of the school system. The association offers advocacy, policy information, assessment standards and more.

Kathy Langham, President
Tawnya Shaw, Vice President

478 California School Library Association
6444 E Spring Street
Suite 237
Long Beach, CA 90815-1553
888-655-8480
Fax: 888-655-8480
info@csla.net
csla.net
Organization made up of librarians, teachers, paraprofessionals, coordinators of curriculum and others involved in the education system. The organization offers advocacy, publications, events and resources to support the education of all California students.

Terry Lai, President
Renee Ousley-Swank, President Elect

479 California State Homeless Education
1430 N Street
Sacramento, CA 95814-5901
916-319-0800
866-856-8214
homelessED@cde.ca.gov
www.cde.ca.gov
The program offers information and resources to ensure that all homeless children and youth have equal access to free, appropriate public education.

Leanne Wheeler, Consultant
Kathy Dobson, Executive Office

480 California Student Aid Commission
PO Box 419026
Rancho Cordova, CA 95741-9026
916-464-7222
888-224-7268
Fax: 916-464-8002
studentsupport@csac.ca.gov
www.csac.ca.gov
Provides information on the state's education programs, colleges and universities, financial aid assistance programs, continuing education and career opportunities.

Lupita Cortez Alcal , Executive Director
Keith Yamanaka, Chief Deputy Director

481 California Teachers Association
1705 Murchison Drive
Burlingame, CA 94010
650-697-1400
Fax: 650-552-5002
membership@cta.org
www.cta.org
Protects and promotes the well-being of California teachers by improving the conditions of teaching and learning and advancing the cause of universal education. The association offers professional development opportunities, resources for parents, publications, legal services and more.

Leslie Littman, Board of Director
Debby Baker, Executive Director

482 Northern California WestEd
730 Harrison Street
San Francisco, CA 94107
415-565-3000
877-493-7833
Fax: 415-565-3012
gtulley@wested.org
www.wested.org
WestEd's Assessment and Standards Development Services program has helped shape effective assessment and accountability systems nationwide. WestEd is a nonprofit research, development, and service agency working with education and other communities to promote excellence and equity in education for all students - regardless of their circumstances.

Founded: 1995

Susan H Fuhrman, President
Glen Harvey, CEO

Colorado

483 Colorado Association of Libraries
12011 Tejon Street
Suite 700
Westminster, CO 80234
303-463-6400
Fax: 303-458-0002
cal@cal-webs.org
www.cal-webs.org
The Colorado Association of Libraries (CAL) advocates for quality library services, supports access to information and fosters the professional development of its members.

Dana Abbey, President
Carol Smith, President Elect

484 Colorado Business Educators
, CO
E-mail: cswank@lps.k12.co.us
cbeducators.webs.com
Supports business educators in Colorado with curriculum material and career networking.

Caroline Swank, Membership Representative
Cassandra Bryning, Representative

485 Colorado Community College System
9101 E Lowry Boulevard
Denver, CO 80230-6011
303-620-4000
Fax: 303-620-4030
sarah.kane@cccs.edu
www.cccs.edu
The Colorado Community College System (CCCS) comprises the state's largest system of higher education. CCCS provides accessible, responsive learning environments that facilitate the achievement of educational, professional and personal goals.

Nancy McCallin, Ph.D, President
Russ Meyer, Ph.D, Board Chair

486 Colorado Creative Industries
1625 Broadway
Suite 2700
Denver, CO 80202
303-892-3840
Fax: 303-892-3848
oedit_creativeindustries@state.co.us
coloradocreativeindustries.org
Organization whose mission is to promote creative industries in Colorado to develop the economy, create jobs and enhance quality of life. Services offered by them include arts programs, arts spaces, education and grants.

Tim Schultz, Chair
Margaret Hunt, Executive Director

487 Colorado Department of Higher Education
1560 Broadway
Suite 1600
Denver, CO 80202
303-862-3001
Fax: 303-996-1329
departmentofhighereducation@dhe.state.co.us
highered.colorado.gov
Provides information on the state's education programs, colleges and universities, financial aid as-

sistance programs, grants, continuing education programs and career opportunities.

Kim Hunter Reed, Ph.D, Executive Director
Diane Duffy, Chief Operating Officer

488 **Colorado Education Association**
1500 Grant Street
Denver, CO 80203
303-837-1500
800-332-5939
Fax: 303-837-9006
www.coloradoea.org
The Colorado Education Association is a voluntary membership organization of K-12 teachers and education support professionals, retired educators and students interested in the field of teaching. The association provides advocacy, public education and networking.

Founded: 1875

Kerrie Dallman, President
Brad Bartels, Executive Director

489 **Colorado State Education for Homeless Children and Youth**
201 E Colfax Avenue
Denver, CO 80203
303-866-6600
Fax: 303-830-0793
homeless@serve.org
www.cde.state.co.us/dropoutprevention/homeless_index
Ensures that all homeless children and youth have equal access to free, appropriate public education.

Kerry Wrenick, State Coordinator
Tricia Walz, Program & Evaluation

Connecticut

490 **Connecticut Business & Industry Association (CBIA)**
350 Church Street
Hartford, CT 06103
860-244-1900
Fax: 860-278-8562
www.cbia.com
Serves as an advocate for the general business and industry community in Connecticut. The association promotes a business climate that is globally competitive and encourages communication and cooperation among businesses.

John Ciulla, Chair
Mary Kay Fenton, Vice Chair

491 **Connecticut Education Association (CEA)**
Capitol Place
21 Oak Street
Hartford, CT 06106
860-525-5641
800-842-4316
Fax: 860-725-6323
info@cea.org
www.cea.org
The Connecticut Education Association (CEA) advocates for teachers and public education by lobbying legislators for the resources public schools need and campaigning for high system standards.

Sheila Cohen, President
Donald E Williams, Jr, Executive Director

492 **Connecticut Office of Culture and Tourism**
1 Constitution Plaza
2nd Floor
Hartford, CT 06103
860-256-2800
Fax: 860-256-2811
leigh.johnson@ct.gov
www.cultureandtourism.org/cct/site/default.asp
Brings together arts, historic preservation and tourism. The office works to preserve and promote Connecticut's cultural and tourism assets to improve the economy and quality of life.

Founded: 2003

Kristina Newman-Scott, Director of Culture
Leigh Johnson, Executive Assistant

493 **Connecticut Office of Higher Education**
450 Columbus Boulevard
Suite 510
Hartford, CT 06103-1841
860-947-1800
Fax: 860-947-1310
HDao@ctohe.org
www.ctohe.org
Provides information on the state's education programs, colleges and universities, financial aid assistance programs, grants, continuing education programs and career opportunities. The office also offers advocacy for students, taxpayers and postsecondary schools.

Keith M Norton, Acting Executive Director
Latoya McPherson, Finance & Administration

494 **Connecticut State Education for Homeless Children and Youth**
450 Columbus Boulevard
Hartford, CT 06103-1841
860-807-2058
Fax: 860-807-2127
louis.tallarita@ct.gov
www.sde.ct.gov
Ensures that all homeless children and youth have equal access to free, appropriate public education.

Louis Tallarita, Contact

Delaware

495 **Delaware Division of Libraries**
121 Martin Luther King Jr. Blvd N
Dover, DE 19901
302-739-4748
800-282-8696
Fax: 302-739-6787
mary.e.bradley@state.de.us
libraries.delaware.gov
Provides leadership and support for the development of Delaware's libraries by ensuring accessibility to library resources for all.

Annie Norman, Ph.D, Director
Beth-Ann Ryan, Deputy Director

496 **Delaware Division of the Arts**
820 N French Street
4th Floor
Wilmington, DE 19801
302-577-8278
Fax: 302-577-6561
delarts@state.de.us
arts.delaware.gov
Works to cultivate and support the arts in Delaware by offering grants, programs, education and access to arts for all citizens.

Paul Weagraff, Director
Kristin Pleasanton, Deputy Director

497 **Delaware Higher Education Office**
The Townsend Building
401 Federal Street
Suite 2
Dover, DE 19901
302-735-4120
800-292-7935
Fax: 302-739-5894
dheo@doe.k12.de.us
www.doe.k12.de.us/domain/226
Provides information and financial assistance to students and their families to make postsecondary education more accessible.

Adrian Peoples, Education Associate
Alison May, Public Information Officer

498 **Delaware Library Association**
121 Martin Luther King Jr. Blvd. N
Dover, DE 19901
302-257-3014
dla@lib.de.us
dla.lib.de.us
Promotes the profession of librarianship and provides library information and media services to the people of Delaware through a unified library community.

Michelle Hughes, President
Cathay Keough, Executive Director

499 **Delaware State Education Association**
DSEA
136 E Water Street
Dover, DE 19901
866-734-5834
Fax: 302-674-8499
david.wright@dsea.org
www.dsea.org
The Delaware State Education Association is a union of public school employees that advocates for the rights and interests of its members and outstanding public education for all students.

Founded: 1919

Mike Matthews, President
Jeff Taschner, Executive Director

500 **Delaware State Local Homeless Education Liaisons**
The Townsend Building
401 Federal Street
Suite 2
Dover, DE 19901-3639
302-735-4000
dedoe@doe.k12.de.us
www.doe.k12.de.us
Ensures that all homeless children and youth have equal access to public education by monitoring school enrollment, attendance and the identification of homeless youth.

Rahel Torres, Liaison
Chavonne Stewart, Liaison

District of Columbia

501 **Associates for Renewal in Education (ARE)**
Brenda Strong Nixon Community Complex
45 P Street NW
Washington, DC 20001
202-483-9424
Fax: 202-667-5299

info@areinc.org
www.areinc.org
A multi project agency working to improve the quality of life and education of the young people of the District of Columbia, with an emphasis on at risk youth and under-served populations. The organization offers intervention, education and employment skills training towards this purpose.

Founded: 1971

Cubie A Bragg, Ph.D, Chairperson
Dayna Nokes-Minor, President & CEO

502 District of Columbia Commission on the Arts and Humanities
200 I Street SE
Washington, DC 20003
202-724-5613
Fax: 202-727-4135
cah@dc.gov
dcarts.dc.gov
Provides grants, professional opportunities, education and relevant programming to individuals involved in the arts so they may learn and contribute to the culture with their works.

Arthur Espinoza, Jr, Executive Director
Michael Bigley, Deputy Director

503 District of Columbia Library Association
50 Massachusetts Avenue SE
PO Box 1653
Washington, DC 20002
202-872-1112
dclamembers@gmail.com
dcla.org
Provides library services to the residents of D.C. and represents the region at the Council of the American Library Association. The District of Columbia Library Association offers networking events, advocacy, job support and library resources.

Candice Townsend, President
Kimberly Knight, Membership Director

504 District of Columbia Office of the State Superintendent of Education
810 1st Street NE
9th Floor
Washington, DC 20002
202-727-6436
osse@dc.gov
osse.dc.gov
The mission of the agency is to foster excellence in education for the residents of DC by offering programs and services to develop standards and increase accessibility.

Shana Young, Chief of Staff
Naomi Watson, Deputy Chief of Staff

Florida

505 Florida Association for Media in Education
PO Box 941169
Maitland, FL 32794-1169
863-585-6802
FAME@floridamediaed.org
www.floridamediaed.org
Association advocating for student access to library media programs as well as offering services to school librarians. Services include professional development programs, resources and the promotion of technology-integration initiatives.

Elizabeth Zdrodowski, President
Lorraine Stinson, Treasurer

506 Florida Business Technology Education Association
E-mail: sslarsen@bellsouth.net
www.fbtea.org
Fosters business education in the state of Florida by offering professional development services, leadership and education.

Melissa Anne Konkol, President
Susan Larsen, Treasurer

507 Florida Division of Cultural Affairs
329 N Meridian Street
Tallahassee, FL 32301
850-245-6470
Fax: 850-245-6454
info@florida-arts.org
dos.myflorida.com
The state agency of Florida committed to promoting the arts by offering programming, exhibitions, jobs and resources.

Founded: 1977

Sandy Shaughnessy, Division Director
Gaylen Phillips, Arts Administrator

508 Florida Education Association
213 S Adams Street
Tallahassee, FL 32301
850-201-2800
888-807-8007
Fax: 850-222-1840
Tammy.Manning@floridaea.org
feaweb.org
Advocates for the right to a free, quality public education for all. The association advances the professional growth, development and status of all who serve the students in Florida's public schools, by offering them advocacy, legal services and training opportunities.

Joanne McCall, President
Fedrick Ingram, Vice President

509 Florida Library Association (FLA)
541 E Tennessee Street
Suite 103
Tallahassee, FL 32308
850-270-9205
admin@flalib.org
www.flalib.org
The Florida Library Association (FLA) develops programs and undertakes activities to stregnthen libraries and the field of librarianship. FLA provides opportunities for librarians and support staff in Florida to advance their skills so that they can continue to be effective in the new information age.

Robin Shader, President
Sarah Hammill, Vice President

510 Florida State Office of Student Financial Assistance
1940 N Monroe Street
Suite 70
Tallahassee, FL 32303-4759
800-366-3475
Fax: 850-487-1809
OSFAStudentLoans@fldoe.org
www.floridastudentfinancialaid.org
Serves as a guarantor for the Federal Family Education Loan Program and the administrator of Florida's scholarship and grant programs. The office aims to make higher education more accessible and provides financial aid information to parents and students.

Pam Stewart, Commissioner

Georgia

511 Georgia Association of Educators
100 Crescent Center Parkway
Suite 500
Tucker, GA 30084
800-282-7142
Fax: 678-837-1100
chris.baumann@gae.org
pv.gae2.org
The Georgia Association of Educators is a professional organization serving public education professionals, through legal supports, programs and resources.

Chris Baumann, Executive Director
Karen Henderson, Executive Assistant

512 Georgia Business Education Association (GBEA)
PO Box 58
Covington, GA 30620
E-mail: gbea.online@gmail.com
www.gbea-online.org
Serves individuals and groups involved in instruction, administration, research and dissemination of information related to business. Teachers are given the opportunity to network with others working in the field and to develop their professional skills through conferences.

Laura Edwards, President
Shayna Moses, President Elect

513 Georgia Council for the Arts
Techonology Square
75 Fifth Street NW
Suite 1200
Atlanta, GA 30308
404-962-4078
Fax: 404-685-2788
EMurray@georgia.org
gaarts.org
Supports the arts in Georgia by providing grants, programs and education services to artists.

Karen L Paty, Executive Director
Emily Murray, Communications Specialist

514 Georgia Library Association
PO Box 793
Rex, GA 30273
678-466-4334
Fax: 678-466-4349
karamullen@clayton.edu
gla.georgialibraries.org
Provides support and encouragement for libraries to advance the educational, cultural and economic life of the state.

Elizabeth McKinney, President
Eli Arnold, Treasurer

515 Georgia Parent Teacher Association
114 Baker Street NE
Atlanta, GA 30308-3366
404-659-0214
800-782-8632
Fax: 404-525-0210
gapta@bellsouth.net
www.georgiapta.org
An organization representing the needs of children, families and communities by advocating for the education, engagement and empowerment of every child in the state of Georgia.

Debbie Snyder, Office Manager
Marty Berry, Event Coordinator

516 Georgia Public Library Service
1800 Century Place
Suite 150
Atlanta, GA 30345-4304
404-235-7200
Fax: 404-235-7201

jwalker@georgialibraries.org
www.georgialibraries.org
Provides support services to develop the libraries of Georgia, which includes offering leadership support, resources, technology services, publications, advocacy and more.

Julie Walker, State Librarian
Wendy Cornelisen, Assistant State Librarian

517 **Georgia State Education for Homeless Children and Youth**
Georgia Department of Education
205 Jesse Hill Jr Drive SE
Atlanta, GA 30334
404-651-7555
Fax: 404-344-4526
emcghee@doe.k12.ga.us
www.gadoe.org
Ensures that all homeless children and youth have equal access to appropriate public education. This mission is promoted through the McKinney-Vento Education for Homeless Children and Youth program, which identifies the challenges unique to the experience of homeless youth and recommends solutions.

Eric McGhee, Grants Program Manager
Debbie Caputo, Administrative Assistant

518 **Georgia Student Finance Commission**
2082 E Exchange Place
Tucker, GA 30084
770-724-9003
800-505-4732
Fax: 770-724-9089
waltr@gsfc.org
gsfc.georgia.gov
Provides information on the state's student financial aid assistance programs, grants and scholarships to students and their families to help in the process of school enrollment.

Founded: 1965

Shawn Ryan, President
Andy Parsons, Executive VP & CIO

Hawaii

519 **Hawaii Business Education Association**
, HI
E-mail: info@hbea.org
www.hbea.org
The Hawaii Business Education Association is devoted exclusively to serving individuals and groups teaching in the fields of business and information technology. The association provides conferences and other professional improvement opportunities to its members.

Cheryl Fujii, President
Warren Kawano, Vice President

520 **Hawaii Education Association (HEA)**
1953 S Beretania Street
Suite 5C
Honolulu, HI 96826
808-949-6657
866-653-9372
Fax: 808-944-2032
hea.office@hawaiieducationassociation.org
www.hawaiieducationassociation.org
Strengthens and supports quality education for all through the enrichment and development of future, current and retired educators. The association offers a variety of scholarships to educators and student teachers alongside other member benefits.

Founded: 1921

June Motokawa, President
Ron Toma, Vice President

521 **Hawaii Library Association**
PO Box 4441
Honolulu, HI 96812-4441
E-mail:
hawaii.library.association@gmail.com
hawaiilibraryassociation.weebly.com
Promotes library service and librarianship in Hawaii through programs, resources and education.

Kara Plamann Wagoner, President
Gwen Sinclair, Vice President

522 **Hawaii State Education for Homeless Children and Youth**
Hawai'i State Department of Education
1390 Miller Street
Honolulu, HI 96813
808-305-9869
doe_info@hawaiidoe.org
www.hawaiipublicschools.org
Ensures that children experiencing homelessness have access to public education.

Carole Kwock, Executive Assistant
Lisa Ann Silva, Private Secretary

523 **Hawaii State Foundation on Culture and the Arts**
250 S Hotel Street
2nd Floor
Honolulu, HI 96813
808-586-0300
Fax: 808-586-0308
hawaiisfca@hawaii.gov
sfca.hawaii.gov
Promotes the development of culture and the arts in Hawaii through grants, programs, education and more.

Jonathan Johnson, Executive Director
Margaret Lui, Secretary

524 **Hawaii State Teachers Association (HSTA)**
1200 Ala Kapuna Street
Honolulu, HI 96819
808-833-2711
Fax: 808-839-7106
kkerr@hsta.org
www.hsta.org
Supports the professional roles of teachers, advocates for teachers' interests, and assures quality education for Hawaii's youth.

Corey Rosenlee, President
Wilbert Holck, Executive Director

Idaho

525 **Idaho Commission for Libraries**
325 W State Street
Boise, ID 83702
208-334-2150
800-458-3271
Fax: 208-334-4016
jeannie.standal@libraries.idaho.gov
libraries.idaho.gov
The mission of the Idaho Commission for Libraries is to develop libraries in Idaho through funding, programs, policy guidance and events.

Ann Joslin, State Librarian
Dylan Baker, Library Consultant

526 **Idaho Commission on the Arts**
2410 Old Penitentiary Road
Boise, ID 83712
208-334-2119
800-278-3863
Fax: 208-334-2488
info@arts.idaho.gov
arts.idaho.gov
Promotes the arts in Idaho by providing arts education, guidelines for teachers of art, programs and advocacy.

Kay Hardy, Chair
Michael Faison, Executive Director

527 **Idaho Education Association**
620 N 6th Street
PO Box 2638
Boise, ID 83701
208-344-1341
800-727-9922
Fax: 208-336-6967
iea-mbc@idahoea.org
idahoea.org
Advocates for the professional and personal well-being of its members and the vision of excellence in public education. Members consist of education professionals and students.

Kari Overall, President
Sue Wigdorski, Executive Director

528 **Idaho Library Association**
PO Box 8533
Moscow, ID 83843-1033
208-334-2150
Fax: 208-334-4016
www.idaholibraries.org
Supports the library community in Idaho and encourages both students and professionals to engage with the services that libraries offer.

Amy Vecchione, President

529 **Idaho State Homeless Children and Youths Title IX-A**
650 W State Street
Boise, ID 83702
208-332-6904
800-432-4601
Fax: 208-334-2228
tmnaillon@sde.idaho.gov
www.sde.idaho.gov/federal-programs/homeless
Ensures that all homeless children and youth have access to public education, transportation and services.

Tina Naillon, Coordinator
Allison Westfall, Communications Director

Illinois

530 **Illinois Arts Council Agency**
James R. Thompson Center
100 W Randolph Street
Suite 10-500
Chicago, IL 60601
312-814-6750
800-237-6994
Fax: 312-814-1471
iac.info@illinois.gov
www.arts.illinois.gov
Responsible for developing the state's public arts policy, creating culturally diverse programs and approving grants to support the arts sector and arts education.

Founded: 1965

Encarnacion Teruel, Program Director
Susan Dickson, Program Director

531 Illinois Association of Private Special Education Centers
, IL
E-mail: ssover@coveschool.org
www.iapsec.org
A nonprofit organization consisting of private schools serving Illinois children with exceptional needs and working to maintain the quality of special education through the setting of high standards of care.
Sally Sover, President
Karoline Dean, Secretary

532 Illinois Association of School Administrators
2648 Beechler Court
Springfield, IL 62703-7305
217-753-2213
Fax: 217-753-2240
jgillespie@iasaedu.org
www.iasaedu.org
The state's advocacy organization for school administrators. The association supports excellence in education by offering its memembers professional development opportunities, leadership summits, member benefits, programs and more.
Founded: 1946
Thomas E Bertrand, Ph.D, President
Brent Clark, Ph.D, Executive Director

533 Illinois Association of School Business Officials
Northern Illinois University
108 Carroll Avenue
DeKalb, IL 60115
815-753-1276
Fax: 815-516-0184
jwarner@iasbo.org
www.iasbo.org
Provides its members a range of professional development activities and services in relation to the school business management profession.
Michael A Jacoby, Executive Director & CEO
Julie A Warner, Director, Human Resources

534 Illinois Business Education Association (IBEA)
3610 Hennepin Drive
Joliet, IL 60431
815-483-4056
ibea@ibea.org
www.ibea.org
Association supporting the profession of business education by offering conferences, information, scholarships and reports.
Diane Mahinda, President
Gary Hutchinson, Executive Director

535 Illinois Citizen Corps
2200 S Dirksen Parkway
Springfield, IL 62703
217-558-1334
Fax: 217-558-1335
citizen.corps@illinois.gov
www.illinois.gov
Works to strenthen citizens through education, training, and volunteer services with the aim of making communities safer and stronger. The Illinois Citizen Corps offers training for disaster relief response and other emergency situations that threaten the well-being of communities.
James K Joseph, Director
Joe Klinger, Assistant Director

536 Illinois Education Association
100 E Edwards Street
Springfield, IL 62704
217-544-0706
844-432-1800
Fax: 217-544-7383
ieaconnect@ieanea.org
ieanea.org
An association of teachers, higher education faculty and staff, educational support professionals, retired educators and students preparing to enter the teaching field. Services offered to members include professional development options, legal assistance, grants, advocacy and a host of member benefits.
Founded: 1853
Kathi Griffin, President
Al Llorens, Vice President

537 Illinois Homeless Education Program
100 N 1st Street
Springfield, IL 62777
217-782-4321
800-215-6379
Fax: 217-524-4928
www.isbe.net/Pages/Homeless.aspx
The purpose of the program is to ensures that all homeless children and youth have equal access to public education.
Emma Wilson, Principal Consultant

538 Illinois Library Association
33 W Grand Avenue
Suite 401
Chicago, IL 60654-6799
312-644-1896
Fax: 312-644-1899
ila@ila.org
www.ila.org
The association provides leadership for the development, promotion and improvement of library services in Illinois and for the library community in order to enhance learning and ensure access to information for all. Services offerred by the association include conferences, publications, legislative advocacy and a reading program.
Founded: 1896
Melissa Gardner, President
Robert P Doyle, Executive Director

539 Illinois School Library Media Association
PO Box 1326
Galesburg, IL 61402-1326
309-341-1099
Fax: 309-341-2070
execsecretary@islma.org
www.islma.org
Promotes student interaction and continuing education of school library media specialists, as well as collaboration among parents, community members, teachers and administrators as they prepare students for life-long learning.
Founded: 1988
Jacob Roskovensky, President
Mary Morgan Ryan, President Elect

540 Illinois Student Assistance Commission
1755 Lake Cook Road
Deerfield, IL 60015-5209
800-899-4722
Fax: 847-831-8549
isac.studentservices@isac.illinois.gov
www.isac.org
Provides information on the state's education programs, with an emphasis on student financial aid assistance.
Founded: 1957
Eric Zarnikow, Executive Director
Shoba Nandhan, Chief Financial Officer

Indiana

541 Indiana Arts Commission
100 N Senate Avenue
Room N505
Indianapolis, IN 46204
317-232-1268
Fax: 317-232-5595
breckert@iac.in.gov
www.in.gov/arts
Provides leadership, advocacy, programs and public stewardship of artistic resources for citizens of Indiana. The commission's long term goal is to shape the cultural, economic and educational climate of Indiana for the better.
Lewis C Ricci, Executive Director
Miah Michaelsen, Deputy Director

542 Indiana Association of School Business Officials
1 N Capitol Avenue
Suite 1215
Indianapolis, IN 46204-2095
317-639-3586
Fax: 765-374-0961
dcosterison@indiana-asbo.org
www.indiana-asbo.org
The Indiana Association of School Business Officials is a professional organization which promotes the advancement of those involved in school business affairs such as finance, accounting, purchasing, maintenance and operations, human resources, facilities and grounds, food service, technology and transportation.
Dennis L Costerison, Executive Director
Ella Adamson, Member Services Admin

543 Indiana Business Education Association
PO Box 3361
Carmel, IN 46082
765-484-4511
Fax: 765-489-4333
khirschy@sacs.k12.in.us
sites.google.com/site/indianaibea/about/home
Professional association of business educators, administrators and leaders with the mission of promoting business education. The association offers professional development opportunities, news and courses.
John Dawson, President
Karen Hirschy, Membership Director

544 Indiana Commission for Higher Education
101 W Ohio Street
Suite 300
Indianapolis, IN 46204-4206
317-464-4400
Fax: 317-464-4410
tlubbers@che.in.gov
www.in.gov/che/2376.htm
The commission's mission is to plan and coordinate Indiana's system of post-high school education, review budget appropriation requests, and handle other matters related to public institutions.
Founded: 1971
Teresa Lubbers, Commissioner
Dominick Chase, Associate Commissioner & CFO

545 Indiana Library Federation
941 E 86th Street
Suite 260
Indianapolis, IN 46240
317-257-2040
Fax: 317-257-1389
askus@ilfonline.org
ilfonline.site-ym.com
Works to advance library services of Indiana through member services such as technical assistance, mentoring programs, networking, advocacy and professional development opportunities for those working in the field.
David Peter, President
Lucinda Nord, Executive Director

546 Indiana State Teachers Association
150 W Market Street
Suite 900
Indianapolis, IN 46204
317-263-3400
844-275-4782
Fax: 317-655-3700
askista@ista-in.org
www.ista-in.org
Provides the resources necessary to enable people to effectively advocate for public schools and the education profession. Topics covered include compensation, working conditions, professional development and student well-being.
Teresa Meredith, President
Daniel Holub, Executive Director

Iowa

547 Iowa Arts Council
State Historical Building
600 E Locust Street
Des Moines, IA 50319
515-281-5111
Fax: 515-242-6498
iowaculture.gov
Responsible for encouraging creativity by giving artists opportunities for growth and development, including public spaces to share their talents.
Founded: 1967
Matthew Harris, Division Administrator
Liesl Voges, Community Development

548 Iowa Business Education Association
, IA
E-mail: webmaster@ibeaonline.org
www.ibeaonline.org
Works to discover and serve the needs of business educators in Iowa. The association offers research, awards, workshops, conferences and professional development programs.
Kyle Van Ausdall, President

549 Iowa College Student Aid Commission
430 E Grand Avenue
3rd Floor
Des Moines, IA 50309-1920
515-725-3400
877-272-4456
Fax: 515-725-3401
info@iowacollegeaid.org
www.iowacollegeaid.org
Provides information on the state's student financial aid assistance programs to increase the success of youth as they engage in higher education.
Founded: 1963
Janet Adams, Chair
Julie Leeper, Executive Officer 3

550 Iowa Library Association
6919 Vista Drive
West Des Moines, IA 50266
515-282-8192
800-452-5507
Fax: 515-282-9117
agalstad@coralville.org
www.iowalibraryassociation.org
The Iowa Library Association advocates for quality library services for all Iowans and provides leadership, education and support for members.
Founded: 1890
Alison Ames Galstad, Executive Board Member
Daniel Chibnall, Executive Board Member

551 Iowa State Education Association
777 Third Street
Des Moines, IA 50309
515-471-8000
800-445-9358
Fax: 515-471-8017
communications@isea.org
isea.org
Supports educators and other school staff by offering advocacy, professional development resources and member benefits. The association's mission is to improve public school education for all.
Tammy Wawro, President
Mary Jane Cobb, Executive Director

552 Iowa State Education for Homeless Children and Youth
400 E 14th Street
Des Moines, IA 50319-0146
515-281-6131
Fax: 515-242-5988
carolyn.paulaitis@iowa.gov
www.educateiowa.gov
Seeks to ensure that all homeless children and youth have access to public education regardless of their circumstances.
Carolyn Paulaitis, Consultant
Mary Bartlow, Administrative Assistant

Kansas

553 Kansas Association of School Librarians
, KS
E-mail: kasltechcommittee@gmail.com
www.ksschoollibrarians.org
An organization of school librarians in the state of Kansas that provides advocacy, education, workshops and networking for the development of library services and library media specialists.
Martha House, President
Barb Bahm, Executive Secretary

554 Kansas Board of Regents
1000 SW Jackson Street
Suite 520
Topeka, KS 66612-1368
785-430-4240
Fax: 785-296-0983
hmelby@ksbor.org
www.kansasregents.org
Functions as the govering board of the state's universities as well as coordinating board for public higher education institutions in Kansas. The board administers student financial aid, adult education and other education programs.
Blake Flanders, President & CEO
Hunter Melby, Administrative Specialist

555 Kansas Business Education Association
, KS
E-mail: michael.moseley@usd262.net
ksbea.org
Fosters business education in the state of Kansas by offering professional development programs and information to help business teachers increase their skills.
Kim Dhority, President
Michael Moseley, Secretary

556 Kansas Creative Arts Industries Commission
Kansas Department of Commerce
1000 SW Jackson Street
Suite 100
Topeka, KS 66612-1354
785-296-2178
Fax: 785-296-4989
peter.jasso@ks.gov
kansascommerce.gov/541/Creative-Arts-Commission
Supports the creative industries sector in Kansas by offering funding, grants, arts education and integration programs.
Peter Jasso, Director
Kevin Doel, Director of Communications

557 Kansas Library Association
Northwest Kansas Library System
2 Washington Sqare
Norton, KS 67654
785-877-5148
Fax: 785-580-4595
kansaslibraryassociation@yahoo.com
kslibassoc.org
Offers professional development opportunities for the library community of Kansas as well as information materials covering the issues that affect libraries, including policies and bylaws.
Gloria Creed-Dikeogu, President
George Seamon, First Vice President

558 Kansas National Education Association
715 SW 10th Avenue
Topeka, KS 66612-1686
785-232-8271
Fax: 785-232-6012
KNEAnews@knea.org
www.knea.org
Association of educators, school administrators and those studying to get into the teaching field. The association offers programs and services to promote public schools and the teaching profession, while developing its members professionally.
Founded: 1863
Mark Farr, President
Sherri Schwanz, Vice President

559 Kansas State Educating Homeless Children and Youth
900 SW Jackson Street
Topeka, KS 66612
785-296-6714
ttoedman@ksde.org
www.ksde.org
Offers assistance to districts so they could better serve their homeless youth and children by ensuring equal access to public education without barriers. Areas covered include law, policy, dispute resolution and data on homelessness.
Tate Toedman, Education Program Consultant

Kentucky

560 **Kentucky Arts Council**
1025 Capital Center Drive
3rd Floor
Frankfort, KY 40601
502-564-3757
888-833-2787
Fax: 502-564-2839
wendy.linale-cheatham@ky.gov
artscouncil.ky.gov
The Kentucky Arts Council is the state government agency responsible for developing and promoting the arts in Kentucky. The agency creates opportunities for people to find value in the arts, participate in the arts and benefit from the arts through programs, grants and services.
Lydia Bailey Brown, Executive Director
Wendy Linale-Cheatham, Administrative Associate

561 **Kentucky Department for Libraries and Archives**
300 Coffee Tree Road
Frankfort, KY 40601
502-564-8300
800-928-7000
Fax: 502-564-5773
renita.van@ky.gov
kdla.ky.gov
A collection of library resources, including government records, research materials, historical records and more. The department also offers information for libraries (programs, policies, funding and development).
Stacey Whitehouse, Executive Secretary
Renita Van, Administrative Specialist

562 **Kentucky Education for Homeless Children and Youth**
Kentucky Department of Education
300 Sower Boulevard
5th Floor
Frankfort, KY 40601
502-564-4770
Fax: 502-564-8149
sharma.aitken@education.ky.gov
education.ky.gov
Initiative to ensure that all homeless youth and children of Kentucky have access to public education.
Sharma Aitken, Contact
Tyson Harbin, Contact

563 **Kentucky Higher Education Assistance Authority**
PO Box 798
Frankfort, KY 40602-0798
502-696-7200
800-928-8926
Fax: 502-696-7496
verification@kheaa.com
www.kheaa.com
Public corporation and government agency responsible for administering financial aid programs and offering information on higher education programs in Kentucky.
Founded: 1966
Carl Rollins, Ph.D, Executive Director
Erin Klarer, VP, Government Relations

564 **Kentucky Library Association**
5932 Timber Ridge Drive
Suite 101
Prospect, KY 40059
502-223-5322
Fax: 502-223-4937
info@kylibasn.org
www.klaonline.org
Provides leadership, conferences and information to support libraries, information services and the profession of librarianship.
Dave Schroeder, President
John T Underwood, Executive Director

565 **Kentucky School Media Association**
School of Information Science
320 Little Fine Arts Library
Lexington, KY 40506-0039
859-218-0956
Fax: 859-257-4205
infosci@uky.edu
www.uky.edu/OtherOrgs/KSMA/ksma5.htm
Promotes the use of school library media by offering professional development activities to library media specialists.
Susan Melcher, President
Becky Stephens, Treasurer

566 **Mountain-Plains Business Education Association**
, NE
E-mail: tlandenb@gmail.com
www.mpbea.org
The Mountain-Plains Business Education Association is an affiliate of the National Business Education Association (NBEA), a professional organization serving individuals and groups engaged in instruction, administration, research, and dissemination of information related to business. Some services offered by them include professional publications, business conventions, networking opportunities and advocacy.
Carol Sessums, President
Toni Landenberger, Webmaster

Louisiana

567 **Louisiana Association of Business Educators**
Association for Career and Technical Education
1410 King Street
Alexandria, VA 22314
601-807-8478
jmercer@winnpsb.org
laabe.weebly.com
The mission of the association is to support business educators in the state of Louisiana by facilitating information sharing between professionals.
Marie Coleman, President
Jason Mercer, Vice President

568 **Louisiana Association of Educators**
8322 One Calais Avenue
Baton Rouge, LA 70809
225-343-9243
800-256-4523
Fax: 225-343-9272
advocacycenter@lae.org
www.lae.org
A membership organization dedicated to improving the education profession through advocacy, professional development opportunities and membership benefits.
Lynda Guidry, Executive Director
Laurie Guillot, Office Manager

569 **Louisiana Association of School Business Officials (LASBO)**
PO Box 1290
Prairieville, LA 70769
225-933-1309
Fax: 225-673-8867
tabs1@bellsouth.net
lasbo.org
Nonprofit professional association made up of school administrators working in the areas of business and operations. The association offers a certification program, networking opportunities and scholarships to promote excellence in the practice of public school business administration.
Founded: 1993
Mary Bonnette, CLSBA, President
Anya Randle, CLSBA, Vice President

570 **Louisiana Division of the Arts**
1051 N 3rd Street
Room 405
Baton Rouge, LA 70802
225-342-8180
Fax: 225-342-8173
arts@crt.la.gov
www.crt.state.la.us/cultural-development/arts
Responsible for offering arts programs, education, grants, services and supports towards the purpose of developing arts and culture in Louisiana.
Founded: 1977
Cheryl Castille, Executive Director
Paula White, Director, Grants & Programs

571 **Louisiana Education for Homeless Children and Youth**
Louisiana Department of Education
1201 N 3rd Street
Baton Rouge, LA 70802-5243
877-453-2721
louisianabelieves@la.gov
www.louisianabelieves.com
The Louisiana Education for Homeless Children and Youths Program is a grant provided to fund services and supports for students experiencing homelessness.
Martha Moore, Education Program Consultant
Laura Smith, Consultant

572 **Louisiana Library Association**
8550 United Plaza Boulevard
Suite 1001
Baton Rouge, LA 70809
225-922-4642
877-550-7890
Fax: 225-408-4422
office@llaonline.org
www.llaonline.org
The mission of the Louisiana Library Association is to promote library interests of Louisiana by offering news about the profession, resources, advocacy, scholarships and networking events to interested professionals.
Founded: 1925
Patricia Brown, President
Bland O'Connor, Executive Director

573 **Louisiana Office of Student Financial Assistance**
602 N 5th Street
Baton Rouge, LA 70802
800-259-5626
Fax: 225-208-1496
custserv@la.gov
www.osfa.la.gov
Offers information to students preparing to enroll in post-secondary education, with emphasis on matters of financial assistance.
Sujuan W Boutt,, Ed.D, Executive Director
Breanna Paul, Events Coordinator

Maine

574 **Maine Arts Commission**
193 State Street
Augusta, ME 04333-0025
207-287-2724
Fax: 207-287-2725
mainearts.info@maine.gov
mainearts.maine.gov
The Commission seeks to engage all sectors both public and private to support the arts, while offering services to artists such as grants, conferences, funding, internships, education and more.
Julie A Richard, Executive Director
Argy Nestor, Director, Arts Education

575 **Maine Association of School Libraries**
PO Box 634
Augusta, ME 04332-0634
E-mail: maslibraries@gmail.com
www.maslibraries.org
The association works to advance the library profession by supporting library programs and personnel through scholarships, advocacy, continuing education for librarians and more.
Tina Taggart, President
Janet Patterson, Treasurer

576 **Maine Education for Homeless Children and Youth**
Maine Department of Education
23 State House Station
Augusta, ME 04333-0023
207-624-6637
Fax: 207-624-6700
gayle.erdheim@maine.gov
www.maine.gov/doe/homeless
An initiative to help homeless students succeed in school with minimal disruptions due to living circumstances.
Gayle Erdheim, Contact

577 **Maine Library Association**
MLA Business Office
93 Saco Avenue
Old Orchard Beach, ME 04064
207-730-3028
mainelibrary@gmail.com
www.mainelibraries.org
The purpose of the Maine Library Association is to promote and enhance the value of libraries and librarianship, to foster cooperation among library professionals, and to ensure that information is accessible to all citizens.
Founded: 1891
Bryce Cundick, President
Jenna Blake Davis, Business Manager

Maryland

578 **Maryland Division of Library Development and Services**
Maryland State Department of Education
200 W Baltimore Street
Baltimore, MD 21201
410-767-0444
Fax: 410-333-2507
dnangle@msde.state.md.us
archives.marylandpublicschools.org
The state library agency responsible for administering funds and creating programs that advance the libraries of Maryland.
Founded: 1968
Irene M Padilla, Asst State Superintendent

579 **Maryland Higher Education Commission**
6 N Liberty Street
Baltimore, MD 21201
410-767-3300
800-974-0203
Fax: 410-332-0270
mdhighered@mhec.state.md.us
www.mhec.state.md.us
Responsible for administering financial aid programs for students and establishing policies and regulations for universities, colleges and career schools within the state.
James D Fielder, Jr., Ph.D, Higher Education Secretary
Michael Kiphart, Director, Academic Affairs

580 **Maryland Library Association**
1401 Hollins Street
Baltimore, MD 21223
410-947-5090
Fax: 410-947-5089
mla@mdlib.org
www.mdlib.org
Maryland Library Association provides leadership for those who are committed to libraries by offering them opportunities for professional development and communication and by advocating on behalf of the issues related to librarianship and library services.
Founded: 1923
Kathleen Teaze, President
Margaret Carty, Executive Director

581 **Maryland State Arts Council**
175 W Ostend Street
Suite E
Baltimore, MD 21230
410-767-6555
800-735-2258
Fax: 410-333-1062
john.harris@maryland.gov
www.msac.org
Provides supports such as grants and programs to artists and organizations with the goal of developing the arts in Maryland.
Shelley Morhaim, Chair
Pamela Dunne, Sr Program Director, Grants

582 **Maryland State Education Association**
140 Main Street
Annapolis, MD 21401
443-433-3676
dhelfman@mseanea.org
www.marylandeducators.org
Consists of teachers, education administrators, specialists and students. The mission of the association is to improve public education in Maryland by offering career development opportunities, legal supports, testing and resources.
Betty Weller, President
David Helfman, Executive Director

Massachusetts

583 **Massachusetts Board of Library Commissioners**
98 N Washington Street
Suite 401
Boston, MA 02114
617-725-1860
800-952-7403
Fax: 617-725-0140
answers@mblc.state.ma.us
mblc.state.ma.us
Government agency responsible for organizing, developing and coordinating library services throughout the Commonwealth. The agency administers programs and sets policies towards improving the overall function of Massachusetts libraries.
James Lonergan, Director
Celeste Bruno, Communications Director

584 **Massachusetts Business Educators Association**
, MA
E-mail: pmeggison@mbea-ma.org
mbea-ma.org
Supports business education professionals in the state of Massachusetts by offering conferences, programs and policy development.
Cynthia Durkee, President
Jo-Ann O'Brien, Vice President

585 **Massachusetts Cultural Council**
10 St. James Avenue
3rd Floor
Boston, MA 02116-3803
617-858-2700
800-232-0960
Fax: 617-727-0044
mcc@art.state.ma.us
www.massculturalcouncil.org
State agency promoting the arts and sciences through grant programs, partnerships and services offered to cultural organizations, schools, communities and artists.
Anita Walker, Executive Director
Jenifer Lawless, Operations Director

586 **Massachusetts Department of Higher Education**
1 Ashburton Place
Room 1401
Boston, MA 02108
617-994-6950
Fax: 617-727-0955
kabel@bhe.mass.edu
www.mass.edu
Provides information about student financial aid, colleges and universities to the citizens of Massachusetts. The Massachusetts Department of Higher Education is responsible for execution of policies set out by the Board of Higher Education for the purpose of coordinating the Commonwealth's higher education system.
Chris Gabrieli, Chairman
Katy Abel, External Affairs

587 **Massachusetts Library Association**
PO Box 21
Seekonk, MA 02771
781-698-7764
Fax: 781-998-0393
manager@masslib.org
www.masslib.org
Supports the Massachusetts library community by providing leadership, advocacy, professional development programs, conferences, networking opportunities and more.
Alexander Lent, President
William Adamczyk, Vice President

588 **Massachusetts Office for the Education of Homeless Children and Youth**
75 Pleasant Street
Malden, MA 02148-4906
781-338-6330
Fax: 781-338-3090
sslautterback@doe.mass.edu
www.doe.mass.edu
Responsible for ensuring that homeless children and youth have access to education and

are given the neccessary services to help them overcome barriers.

Peter D Cirioni, State Coordinator
Sarah Slautterback, Education Specialist

589 **Massachusetts Teachers Association**
2 Heritage Drive
8th Floor
Quincy, MA 02171-2119
617-878-8000
800-392-6175
Fax: 617-742-7046
contactus@massteacher.org
massteacher.org
The Massachusetts Teachers Association is a union dedicated to improving the workplace for all education employees and protecting their rights. The association is governed by democratic principles.

Barbara Madeloni, President
Erik Champy, Vice President

590 **New England Library Association**
55 N Main Street
Unit 49
Belchertown, MA 01007
413-813-5254
rscheier@nelib.org
nelib.org
Provides educational and leadership opportunities for library staff to support library services in New England.

Founded: 1963

Mary Danko, President
Robert Scheier, Administrator

Michigan

591 **Michigan Association for Media in Education**
1407 Rensen Street
Lansing, MI 48910
517-394-2808
Fax: 517-492-3878
mame@mimame.org
www.mimame.org
The Michigan Association for Media in Education is an independent, professional association of library media specialists dedicated to developing educational, literary and technological excellence in the library/media services of Michigan's schools.

Lisa Kelley, President
Bruce Popejoy, Treasurer

592 **Michigan Association of School Administrators**
1001 Centennial Way
Suite 300
Lansing, MI 48917-9279
517-327-5910
Fax: 517-327-0779
mitchsmith@gomasa.org
gomasa.org
Professional organization serving school leaders of Michigan by offering legal services, publications, professional development opportunities and resources so they can better serve students.

Chris Wigent, Executive Director
Margaret Helmer, Executive Assistant

593 **Michigan Council for Arts and Cultural Affairs**
300 N Washington Square
Lansing, MI 48913
517-241-4011
Fax: 517-241-3979
gillj@michigan.org
www.michigan.gov/arts
Supports the arts in Michigan by providing opportunities for visibility, supporting arts education and providing grants.

Andrew Buchholz, Chairman
John Bracey, Executive Director

594 **Michigan Education Association**
1216 Kendale Boulevard
East Lansing, MI 48823
517-332-6551
800-292-1934
Fax: 517-337-5587
webmaster@mea.org
www.mea.org
A self-governing education association representing teachers, faculty and education support staff throughout Michigan. The association offers its members advocacy, professional development events, financial services and information so they can better serve their communities.

Paula Herbart, President
Gretchen Dziadosz, Executive Director

595 **Michigan Education for Homeless Children and Youth**
608 W Allegan Street
PO Box 30008
Lansing, MI 48909
517-373-3324
www.michigan.gov/homeless
A branch in the Michigan Department of Education responsible for providing access to education for children and youth experiencing homelessness.

Brian Whiston, State Superintendent
Joetta Parker, Director, Human Resources

596 **Michigan Elementary & Middle School Principals Association**
1980 N College Road
Mason, MI 48854
517-694-8955
Fax: 517-694-8945
annette@memspa.org
memspa.org
Professional organization serving elementary and middle level principals as they deliver quality educational experiences to the students of Michigan. The association provides leadership, legislative advocacy, professional development and guidance to its members.

Jeremy Patterson, President
Paul Liabenow, Executive Director

597 **Michigan Library Association**
3410 Belle Chase Way
Suite 100
Lansing, MI 48911
517-394-2774
Fax: 517-394-2675
mla@milibraries.org
www.milibraries.org
The Michigan Library Association is a professional organization dedicated to the support of its members through advocacy and professional development events, the advancement of librarianship and the promotion of quality library service for all Michigan citizens.

Gail Madziar, Executive Director
Melissa Jo Scenga, Administrative Assistant

598 **Michigan Student Financial Services Bureau**
PO Box 30462
Lansing, MI 48909-7962
888-447-2687
mistudentaid@michigan.gov
www.michigan.gov/mistudentaid
Provides access to student financial resources and information available for students in Michigan to encourage the pursuit of higher education.

Nick A Khouri, Treasurer

Minnesota

599 **Education Minnesota**
41 Sherburne Avenue
St. Paul, MN 55103
651-227-9541
800-652-9073
Fax: 651-292-4802
webmaster@edmn.org
www.educationminnesota.org
Education Minnesota is an advocate for educators and public education in the state. Its main function is that of a union that helps teachers gain professional development, nagotiate job contracts and more.

Denise Specht, President
Paul Mueller, Vice President

600 **Minnesota Business Educators**
, MN
E-mail: mbeionline@gmail.com
www.mbite.org
A professional organization for business educators working in the areas of marketing, accounting, information technology and graphic design. The organization provides advocacy, professional development and networking opportunities to its members.

Callon Siebenhaler, President
Brenda Diekman, Communications Chair

601 **Minnesota Library Association**
400 S 4th Street
Suite 754E
Minneapolis, MN 55415
612-294-6549
office@mnlibraryassociation.org
www.mnlibraryassociation.org
Facilitates educational opportunities, upholds ethical standards and forms connections between the library community and other groups.

Founded: 1891

Amy Boese, President
Kate Anderson, Treasurer

602 **Minnesota PTA**
1667 Snelling Avenue
North Suite 111
Saint Paul, MN 55108
651-999-7320
800-672-0993
Fax: 651-999-7321
mnpta@mnpta.org
mnpta.org
Minnesota PTA aims to support and advocate for children and youth in school, educate parents and teachers on issues affecting children and youth and encourage parent participation in the school system.

Founded: 1922

Heather Starks, President
Michelle Utter, Office Manager

603 **Minnesota School Boards Association**
1900 W Jefferson Avenue
Saint Peter, MN 56082-3015

507-934-2450
800-324-4459
Fax: 507-931-1515
www.mnmsba.org
The purpose of the Association is to support, promote and enhance the work of public school boards.

Kirk Schneidawind, Executive Director
Tiffany Rodning, Deputy Executive Director

604 **Minnesota State Arts Board**
Park Square Court
400 Sibley Street
Suite 200
Saint Paul, MN 55101-1928
651-215-1600
800-866-2787
Fax: 651-215-1602
msab@arts.state.mn.us
www.arts.state.mn.us
State agency supporting the arts in Minnesota by providing grants and encouraging creativity.

Peggy Burnet, Chair
Sue Gens, Executive Director

605 **Office of Higher Education**
1450 Energy Park Drive
Suite 350
Saint Paul, MN 55108-5227
651-642-0567
800-657-3866
Fax: 651-642-0675
info.ohe@state.mn.us
www.ohe.state.mn.us
The Minnesota Office of Higher Education is a state agency responsible for providing financial aid programs to students as well as giving them the information they need when applying to higher education institutions.

Tim Geraghty, Chief Financial Officer
Sandy Connolly, Director of Communications

Mississippi

606 **Mississippi Arts Commission**
Woolfolk Building
501 NW Street
Suite 1101A
Jackson, MS 39201
601-359-6030
Fax: 601-359-6008
arts.ms.gov
Supports the arts in Mississippi by offering grant programs to nonprofit organizations and artists.

Steve Edds, Chair
Becky Beard, Commissioner

607 **Mississippi Association of Educators**
775 N State Street
Jackson, MS 39202
601-354-4463
800-530-7998
Fax: 601-352-7054
fholmes@nea.org
maetoday.org
The Mississippi Association of Educators supports teachers, higher education faculty and students by offering professional development programs, advocacy and membership benefits.

Joyce Helmick, President
Tyrone C Hendrix, Executive Director

608 **Mississippi Business Education Association**
, MS
E-mail: msmbea1950@gmail.com
msmbea1950.wordpress.com
Professional organization for business educators of Mississippi. The association supports the development of business and technology education.

Founded: 1950

Michelle Taylor, Ph.D, Contact

609 **Mississippi Education for Homeless Children and Youth**
Mississippi Department of Education
359 NW Street
Jackson, MS 39201
601-359-3499
Fax: 601-359-2587
pyoungblood@mdek12.org
www.mde.k12.ms.us/OFP/title-x
Serves youth and children who are experiencing homelessness by helping them access education.

Quentin Ransburg, Executive Director
Patricia Youngblood, Office Manager

610 **Mississippi Institutions of Higher Learning**
3825 Ridgewood Road
Jackson, MS 39211
601-432-6198
800-327-2980
Fax: 601-432-6972
hgriffin@ihl.state.ms.us
www.mississippi.edu
Responsible for regulating student affairs among various other sectors.

Hannah Griffin, Contact

611 **Mississippi Library Association**
PO Box 13687
Jackson, MS 39236-3687
601-981-4586
Fax: 601-981-4501
info@misslib.org
www.misslib.org
Provides professional leadership for the development, promotion, and improvement of library and information services in Mississippi. The association also provides advocacy and conferences to stregnthen the profession of librarianship.

Founded: 1909

Jenniffer Stephenson, President
Sarah Mangrum, Vice President

612 **Mississippi Library Commission**
3881 Eastwood Drive
Jackson, MS 39211
601-432-4111
800-647-7542
Fax: 601-432-4480
mslib@mlc.lib.ms.us
mlc.lib.ms.us
Provides information services for libraries on the subjects of technology and libary development so that all citizens of Mississippi would be able to access these resources.

Founded: 1926

Susan Cassagne, Executive Director
David Collins, Grant Program Director

Missouri

613 **Missouri Arts Council**
815 Olive Street
Suite 16
Saint Louis, MO 63101-1503
314-340-6845
866-407-4752
Fax: 314-340-7215
moarts@ded.mo.gov
www.missouriartscouncil.org
The Missouri Arts Council is the state agency dedicated to supporting the arts in the state through programming, arts education, grants, events and advocacy.

Founded: 1965

Michael Donovan, Executive Director
Virginia R Sanders, Executive Assistant

614 **Missouri Association of Elementary School Principals**
3550 Amazonas Drive
Jefferson City, MO 65109
573-638-2460
Fax: 573-556-6270
maesp@maesp.com
maesp.com
A statewide professional association made up of elementary and middle school principals and educators that aspire to become principals. Services offered by the association to its members include legal advice and professional development opportunities.

Jennifer Dittemore, President
Michael L Schooley, Ph.D, Executive Director

615 **Missouri Association of Secondary School Principals**
2409 W Ash Street
Columbia, MO 65203-0045
573-445-5071
Fax: 573-445-6416
gstevens@moassp.org
www.moassp.org
The mission of the Missouri Association of Secondary School Principals is to improve secondary education by offering professional development programs and workshops to the leaders of schools (principals and school administrator). The association provides information and leadership, promotes high educational standards and addresses state educational issues.

Chris Hoehne, President
Phil Lewis, Executive Director

616 **Missouri Business Education Association**
, MO
660-281-8538
andrew.reynolds@catnet.gen.mo.us
mbea.weebly.com
The mission of the association is to promote the professional growth of those working in the field of business education.

Becky Brownfield, President
Andrew Reynolds, Secretary

617 **Missouri Department of Higher Education**
205 Jefferson Street
PO Box 1469
Jefferson City, MO 65102-1469
573-751-2361
800-473-6757
Fax: 573-751-6635
info@dhe.mo.gov
dhe.mo.gov
The mission of the Missouri Department of Higher Education is to coordinate higher education policy and promote enrollment in Missouri 's public education institutions. The Department offers information to help students and families plan for college as well as development strategies for institutions.

Carolyn R Mahoney, Ph.D, Chair
Mike Thomson, Secretary

618 **Missouri Education for Homeless Children and Youth**
205 Jefferson Street
Jefferson City, MO 65101
573-522-8763
Fax: 573-526-6698
Donna.Cash@dese.mo.gov
dese.mo.gov
Responsible for ensuring homeless children and youth have access to education regardless of their circumstances.
Donna Cash, Homeless State Coordinator

619 **Missouri Library Association**
1190 Meramec Station Road
Suite 207
Ballwin, MO 63021-6902
573-449-4627
Fax: 573-449-4655
brekhusr@missouri.edu
molib.org
A nonprofit educational organization dedicated to promoting library service and the profession of librarianship.
Founded: 1900
Gerald Brooks, Chair
Rachel Brekhus, Web Manager

620 **Missouri National Education Association**
1810 E Elm Street
Jefferson City, MO 65101
573-634-3202
800-392-0236
Fax: 573-634-5646
deeann.aull@mnea.org
www.mnea.org
The Missouri National Education Association is an advocate for public schools and their students and employees. The association offers educational conferences and workshops for educators, legal services and advocacy.
Charles E Smith, President
DeeAnn Aull, Executive Director

621 **Missouri PTA**
2101 Burlington Street
Columbia, MO 65202
573-445-4161
Fax: 573-445-4163
office@mopta.org
mopta.org
Provides programs, activities and advocacy for children and youth of Missouri. The PTA works to ensure the health, welfare, safety and education of all.
Dorothy Gardner, President
Sonia Smith, Treasurer

622 **Missouri State Teachers Association**
407 S 6th Street
PO Box 458
Columbia, MO 65205
573-442-3127
800-392-0532
Fax: 573-443-5079
membercare@msta.org
www.msta.org
A grassroots organization of local community teachers associations. The mission of the association is to meet the needs of educators in Missouri by offering resources such as professional development, grants, learning standards and more.
Brett Hoch, President
Bruce Moe, Executive Director

Montana

623 **Montana Arts Council**
830 N Warren Street
PO Box 202201
Helena, MT 59620-2201
406-444-6430
800-282-3092
Fax: 406-444-6548
mac@mt.gov
art.mt.gov
State agency responsible for developing the arts in Montana. The agency offers funding, programs, advocacy and education towards realizing this mission.
Tatiana Gant, Executive Director
Jenifer Alger, Chief Financial Officer

624 **Montana Association of County School Superintendents**
School Administrators of Montana
900 N Montana Avenue
Suite A-4
Helena, MT 59601
406-442-2510
Fax: 406-442-2518
cmaloney@bsb.mt.gov
www.sammt.org/macss
Organization of school superintendents offering services and educational leadership in Montana.
Linda Marsh, President
Cathy Maloney, 1st Vice President

625 **Montana Business Education Association**
, MT
E-mail: blawrence@jordanpublicschools.org
www.mbea.info
Serves business educators by offering them opportunities for growth in their profession.
Chad Eichenlaub, President
Beth Lawrence, Secretary

626 **Montana Education for Homeless Children and Youth**
1227 11th Avenue
2nd Floor
Helena, MT 59601
406-444-2036
hdenny@mt.gov
opi.mt.gov
A program that seeks to make education accessible for children and youth experiencing homelessness.
Heather Denny, Education Coordinator

627 **Montana Library Association**
Lewis & Clark Public Library
120 S Last Chance Gulch
Helena, MT 59601-4133
406-447-1690
mbeckstr@mtlib.org
mtlib.org
Works to develop and promote library services and librarianship in Montana through advocacy, conferences and grants.
Debbi Kramer, Executive Director
Matt Beckstrom, MLA Postmaster

Nebraska

628 **Nebraska Arts Council**
1004 Farnam Street
Omaha, NE 68102
402-595-2122
800-341-4067
Fax: 402-742-1110
nac.info@nebraska.gov
www.artscouncil.nebraska.gov
Dedicated to promoting and cultivating the arts in Nebraska through grants, leadership, advocacy, education and exhibitions.
Founded: 1974
Candy Henning, Chair
Suzanne Wise, Executive Director

629 **Nebraska Education for Homeless Children and Youth**
301 Centennial Mall S
PO Box 94987
Lincoln, NE 68509-4987
402-471-1419
Fax: 402-471-0117
denise.fisher@nebraska.gov
www.education.ne.gov
Reponsible for implementing the guidelines of the McKinney-Vento Homeless Assistance Act and creating services so that homeless children and youth may access public education.
Cathy Mohnike, Consultant

630 **Nebraska Library Association**
c/o Executive Director
PO Box 21756
Lincoln, NE 68542-1756
402-826-2636
nebraskalibraries@gmail.com
www.nebraskalibraries.org
The Nebraska Library Association supports and promotes all libraries and library services in the state through advocacy and professional development programs.
Angela Kroeger, President
Joe Pittman, Executive Director

631 **Nebraska Library Commission**
The Atrium
1200 N Street
Suite 120
Lincoln, NE 68508-2023
402-471-2045
800-307-2665
Fax: 402-471-2083
maryjo.ryan@nebraska.gov
www.nlc.nebraska.gov
Part of the state's executive branch. The commission is responsible for the promotion and coordination of Nebraska libraries and library services through funding of programs, accreditation, training, accessible technology and more.
Founded: 1901
Rod Wagner, Library Commission Director
Mary Jo Ryan, Communications Coordinator

632 **Nebraska State Business Education Association**
, NE
E-mail: condonj@mpcc.edu
www.nsbea.org
Fosters education in business, marketing and information technology within the state of Nebraska by offering professional growth opportunities, networking and guidance.
Matt Maw, President
Jean Condon, State Membership Director

633 **Nebraska State Education Association**
605 S 14th Street
Suite 200
Lincoln, NE 68508
402-475-7611
800-742-0047
Fax: 402-475-2630
maddie.fennell@nsea.org
www.nsea.org

A member-directed union of professional educators and education support professionals dedicated to advocating for all education professionals in Nebraska.

Jenni Benson, President
Maddie Fennell, Executive Director

Nevada

634 Nevada Arts Council
716 N Carson Street
Suite A
Carson City, NV 89701
775-687-6680
Fax: 775-687-6688
infonvartscouncil@nevadaculture.org
nvculture.org
State agency supporting the arts in Nevada through grants, programs, education, arts promotion, publications and various other resources.

Julia Arger, Chair
Tony Manfredi, Executive Director

635 Nevada Education for Homeless Children and Youth
700 E 5th Street
Suite 113
Carson City, NV 89701
775-687-9235
Fax: 775-687-9250
mbwalker@doe.nv.gov
www.nde.doe.nv.gov
Offers assistance to homeless children and youth so that they may access public education.

Michael Walker, State Coordinator
Cyekeia Lee, Higher Education Specialist

636 Nevada Library Association
E-mail: cornm@lvccld.org
nevadalibraries.org
The purpose of the association is to promote library services of Nevada through advocacy, events and membership resources.

Amy Dodson, President
Mayra Corn, Executive Secretary

637 Nevada State Education Association
3511 E Harmon Avenue
Las Vegas, NV 89121
702-733-7330
800-248-6732
Fax: 702-733-6004
contact.nsea@nsea-nv.org
www.nsea-nv.org
Advocates for the professional rights and economic security of its members, while also serving as a voice for excellence in public education in Nevada.

Ruben Murillo, Jr., President
Brian Lee, Executive Director

New Hampshire

638 New Hampshire Business Education Association
200 Derry Road
Hudson, NH 03051
E-mail: info@nhbea.com
www.nhbea.com
Fosters business education in the state of New Hampshire by offering members opportunities to develop their skills and network with others working in the business education field.

Steve Foster, President
Michael Magoon, Vice President

639 New Hampshire Education Association
9 S Spring Street
Concord, NH 03301-2425
603-224-7751
866-556-3264
Fax: 603-224-2648
members@nhnea.org
neanh.org
The mission of the association is to strengthen and support public education by providing public school educators with the resources they need to develop their skills. The association also provides services for the children of New Hampshire so they can succeed in school.

Founded: 1857

Megan Tuttle, President
Rick Trombly, Executive Director

640 New Hampshire Education for Homeless Children and Youth
New Hampshire Department of Education
101 Pleasant Street
Concord, NH 03301-3494
603-271-6055
Fax: 603-271-2760
Kristine.Braman@doe.nh.gov
www.education.nh.gov
Provides resources and services to districts, schools and people in need of assistance so they can understand the regulations relating to the rights of homeless children and youth and thereby better serve these individuals.

Lynda Thistle-Elliott, Director
Kristine Braman, Program Assistant

641 New Hampshire Higher Education Commission
New Hampshire Department of Education
101 Pleasant Street
Concord, NH 03301-3494
603-271-0257
Patricia.Edes@doe.nh.gov
www.education.nh.gov/highered
The mission of the commission is to offer leadership and services in support of equal educational opportunities for the people of New Hampshire. Its divisions cover areas such as student assessment, educational technology, school health and safety, special education and more.

Todd J Leach, Ph.D, Chair
Patti Edes, Program Specialist IV

642 New Hampshire Library Association
c/o New Hampshire State Library
20 Park Street
Concord, NH 03301-6314
603-249-0645
kgabert@wadleighlibrary.org
nhlibrarians.org
The association is made up of library professionals working to advocate on behalf of the interests of its members, increase public awareness of library services, support the professional development of its members and encourage communication among professionals.

Marilyn Borgendale, President
Matthew Gunby, Secretary

643 New Hampshire State Council on the Arts
19 Pillsbury Street
1st Floor
Concord, NH 03301
603-271-2789
800-735-2964
Fax: 603-271-3584
julianne.gadoury@nh.gov
www.nh.gov/nharts
Supports the arts in New Hampshire through grants, arts education and other services.

Ginnie Lupi, Director
Julianne Gadoury, Grants Coordinator

New Jersey

644 New Jersey Education Association (NJEA)
180 W State Street
Trenton, NJ 08608
609-599-4561
Fax: 609-392-6321
www.njea.org
The mission of the New Jersey Education Association is to advance and protect the rights and interests of its members and promote excellence in public education. The association offers advocacy, training, grants and professional development in support of educators.

Marie Blistan, President
Matthew DiRado, Esq., HR Manager

645 New Jersey Education for Homeless Children and Youth
New Jersey Department of Education
PO Box 500
Trenton, NJ 08625-0500
609-984-4974
Fax: 609-292-1211
danielle.anderson-thomas@doe.state.nj.us
www.state.nj.us/education/students/homeless
Provides resources for parents, students and schools in order to make public education more accessible to young people experiencing homelessness.

Danielle Anderson Thomas, State Coordinator

646 New Jersey Higher Education Student Assistance Authority
HESAA
PO Box 545
Trenton, NJ 08625-0545
609-584-4480
800-792-8670
Fax: 609-588-7389
Jennifer_Azzarano@hesaa.org
www.hesaa.org
State agency with the mission of providing information on higher education matters (such as financial aid) to students and families in order to assist them in planning academic futures.

Christy Van Horn, Chairperson
Jennifer Azzarano, Communications Director

647 New Jersey Library Association
NJLA
PO Box 1534
Trenton, NJ 08607
609-394-8032
Fax: 609-394-8164
ptumulty@njla.org
njla.org
Advocates for the advancement of library services for the residents of New Jersey, provides continuing education and networking

opportunities for librarians and promotes access to library services for all.

Founded: 1890

Michael Maziekien, President
Patricia Tumulty, Executive Director

648 **New Jersey School-Age Care Coalition**
NJSACC
208 Lenox Avenue
Westfield, NJ 07090
908-789-0259
Fax: 908-789-4237
sac@njsacc.org
www.njsacc.org
Promotes out-of-school time programs and upholds the New Jersey Quality Afterschool Standards. The organization provides training, conferences and technical assistance for program development. It also works to improve State regulations and legislation to ensure that students have access to programs within their communities.

Diane Genco, Executive Director
Lee McDermott Schaefer, Policy Director

649 **New Jersey State Council on the Arts**
33 W State Street
4th Floor
Trenton, NJ 08608
609-292-6130
Fax: 609-989-1440
Feedback@sos.nj.gov
nj.gov/state/njsca/dos_njsca_about.html
Supports the arts in New Jersey by offering services, programs and grants to artists as well as by supporting arts education.

Founded: 1966

Robin Middleman, Senior Program Officer
Allison Tratner, Director of Communications

650 **New Jersey State Department of Education Learning Resource Centers**
NJ Department of Education
PO Box 500
Trenton, NJ 08625-0500
609-292-4469
877-900-6960
Fax: 609-777-2077
communications@doe.state.nj.us
www.nj.gov/education/lrc/services.htm
Provides in-service workshops, information, publications, training, conferences, consultations and technical assistance to educators and families of students with disabilities.

Arcelio Aponte, President
Andrew J Mulvihill, Vice President

New Mexico

651 **Mountain Plains Business Education Association (M-PBEA)**
E-mail: cjsessums@gmail.com
www.mpbea.org
The Mountain-Plains Business Education Association is a professional organization serving individuals and groups engaged in teaching and working in the field of business. The association provides its members opportunities to develop their professional skills, education, networking opportunities and other member benefits.

Carol Sessums, President
Sherrell Wheeler, President-Elect

652 **National Education Association of New Mexico**
2007 Botulph
Santa Fe, NM 87505
505-982-1916
Fax: 505-982-6719
neanmsf@gmail.com
www.nea-nm.org
Engaged in ensuring excellence in public education by advocating for the rights of students and education employees in New Mexico.

Betty Patterson, President
Charles Goodmacher, Director, Media Relations

653 **New Mexico Arts**
Bataan Memorial Building
407 Galisteo Street
Suite 270
Santa Fe, NM 87501
505-827-6490
800-879-4278
Fax: 505-827-6043
cynthiar.gonzales@state.nm.us
www.nmarts.org
A division of the Department of Cultural Affairs responsible for supporting the arts in New Mexico by funding arts services and programs.

Loie Fecteau, Executive Director
Phyllis Kennedy, Program Coordinator

654 **New Mexico Higher Education Department**
2044 Galisteo Street
Suite 4
Santa Fe, NM 87505-2100
505-476-8400
800-279-9777
Fax: 505-476-8453
Patrick.Lucero2@state.nm.us
www.hed.state.nm.us
Provides information on topics and issues related to higher education such as continuing education, grants, student financial aid options, credit transfers, information for school administrators and research data.

Barbara Damron, Cabinet Secretary
Robert McEntyre, Public Information Officer

655 **New Mexico Library Association (NMLA)**
PO Box 26074
Albuquerque, NM 87125
505-400-7309
Fax: 505-544-5740
contact@nmla.org
nmla.org
The New Mexico Library Association is a nonprofit organization dedicated to the support and promotion of libraries and library personnel through education, grants, conferences and legislative advocacy.

Lynette Schurdevin, President
Karla Hunt, Secretary

New York

656 **Business Teachers Association of New York State**
, NY
E-mail: treasurer@btanys.org
www.btanys.org
The Business Teachers Association of New York State provides networking, support and professional growth opportunities for business educators so they may effectively educate their students.

Tara Bellevue, President
Kristen Fry, Treasurer

657 **New York Education for Homeless Children and Youth**
NYS-TEACHS
151 W 30th Street
5th Floor
New York, NY 10001
800-388-2014
Fax: 212-807-6872
info@nysteachs.org
www.nysteachs.org
The New York State Technical and Education Assistance Center for Homeless Students provides support for young people experiencing homelessness by educating schools, social service providers, parents and others about the rights of these youth to access education.

Michelle Frank, Assistant Director
Daniel Kennedy, Education Specialist

658 **New York Library Association (NYLA)**
6021 State Farm Road
Guilderland, NY 12084
518-432-6952
Fax: 518-427-1697
marketing@nyla.org
www.nyla.org
Provides support in the form of advocacy and professional development events to libraries and library staff in New York. The association also acts as a voice on library matters to media and policymakers.

Founded: 1890

Jeremy Johannesen, Executive Director
Galina Tsvaygenbaum, Accounting Director

659 **New York State Council on the Arts**
300 Park Avenue S
10th Floor
New York, NY 10010
212-459-8800
800-510-0021
info@arts.ny.gov
www.nysca.org
Dedicated to preserving and supporting the arts in New York through grants, advisory support and public education on the value the arts brings to communities.

Mara Manus, Executive Director
Ronni Reich, Director, Public Information

660 **New York State Higher Education Services Corporation**
99 Washington Avenue
Albany, NY 12255
518-473-1574
888-697-4372
Fax: 518-474-2839
Teresa.Gehrer@hesc.ny.gov
www.hesc.ny.gov
The corporation is the agency of New York state responsible for administering and offering information on financial assistance available to students applying for higher education.

Guillermo Linares, Ph.D, Acting President
Elsa MaGee, Executive Vice President

661 **New York State United Teachers (NYSUT)**
800 Troy-Schenectady Road
Latham, NY 12110
518-213-6000
800-342-9810

mediarel@nysutmail.org
www.nysut.org
New York State United Teachers is a union of health care and education professionals dedicated to improving the professional and personal lives of its members and their families by advocating for excellence in education and healthcare for all New York citizens.

Andrew Pallotta, President
Jolene T DiBrango, Executive Vice President

North Carolina

662 North Carolina Arts Council
Department of Natural & Cultural Resources
4632 Mail Service Center
Raleigh, NC 27699-4600
919-807-6500
Fax: 919-807-6532
ncarts@ncdcr.gov
www.ncarts.org
Dedicated to developing the arts in North Carolina by providing education, grants, leadership and other resources useful for artists.

Stephen Hill, Chair
Wayne Martin, Executive Director

663 North Carolina Association for Career and Technical Education
NCACTE
7021 Goshen Road
Oxford, NC 27565
919-693-3962
Fax: 877-663-1146
tony.bello@gmail.com
www.ncacteonline.org
The association aims to act as a central agency, bringing together professionals working in various kinds of career and technical education in order to expand and promote the fields.

Carol Harper, President
Ruth Huff, Executive Director

664 North Carolina Association of Educators (NCAE)
700 S Salisbury Street
Raleigh, NC 27601
919-832-3000
800-662-7924
Fax: 919-829-1626
derevana.leach@ncae.org
www.ncae.org
The mission of the association is to advocate for members and students with the goal of enhancing public education and the education profession.

Mark Jewell, President
Rachelle Johnson, Executive Director

665 North Carolina Business Education Association (NCBEA)
E-mail: jtucker@centurylink.net
www.ncbea.org
NCBEA works to promote and improve the quality of business education through membership meetings and strives to create programs useful for the development of business educators in North Carolina.

Madeline Tucker, President
Janis Tucker, Secretary

666 North Carolina Department of Public Instruction (DPI)
Education Building
301 N Wilmington Street
Raleigh, NC 27601-2825
919-807-3300
Fax: 919-807-3445
information@dpi.nc.gov
www.ncpublicschools.org
The North Carolina Department of Public Instruction (DPI) is the agency responsible for implementing the State's public school laws and the State Board of Education's policies and procedures relating to pre-kindergarten through 12th grade public education. The agency provides leadership and services to local public school districts to assist in developing the areas of curriculum, assessments and instruction.

Mark Johnson, State Superintendent
Adam Levinson, Chief Financial Officer

667 North Carolina Homeless Education Program
The SERVE Center at UNCG
PO Box 5367
Greensboro, NC 27435
336-315-7400
800-659-3204
Fax: 336-315-7457
lphillip@serve.org
serve.uncg.edu/hepnc/about.php
Ensures that young people experiencing homelessness in North Carolina have the resources they need to access education.

Lisa Phillips, State Coordinator
Patricia Lentz, Program Specialist

668 North Carolina Library Association (NCLA)
1841 Capital Boulevard
Raleigh, NC 27604
919-839-6252
Fax: 888-977-3143
nclaonline@gmail.com
www.nclaonline.org
Statewide organization intent on promoting libraries, intellectual freedom, library services and library professions in North Carolina.

Rodney Lippard, President
Julie Humphrey, Secretary

669 North Carolina State Education Assistance Authority
10 TW Alexander Drive
Research Triangle Park, NC 27709
919-549-8614
Fax: 919-549-8481
www.ncseaa.edu
Provides services such as student financial assistance programs and information on financial assistance options for citizens of North Carolina.

James O Roberts, Chair
Elizabeth V McDuffie, Executive Director

North Dakota

670 North Dakota Council on the Arts
1600 E Century Avenue
Suite 6
Bismarck, ND 58503-0649
701-328-7590
Fax: 701-328-7595
comserv@nd.gov
www.nd.gov/arts
State agency with the mission of developing and promoting the arts in North Dakota through programs, education, grants and opportunities for professional development of artists.

Founded: 1967

Beth G Klingenstein, Ph.D, Executive Director
Robin Bosch, Administrative Officer

671 North Dakota Education for Homeless Children and Youth
North Dakota Department of Public Instruction
600 E Boulevard Avenue
Dept. 201
Bismarck, ND 58505-0440
701-328-3544
esteckler@nd.gov
www.nd.gov
Aims to ensure that youth and children experiencing homelessness have access to public education.

Beth Larson-Steckler, State Homeless Coordinator
Heidi Merkel, Contact

672 North Dakota Library Association
PO Box 1595
Bismarck, ND 58502-1595
E-mail: lwest@cityoffargo.com
ndla.info
The North Dakota Library Association is concerned with the right of all citizens of North Dakota to access library collections and services in their state.

Lesley Allan, President
Lori West, Professional Development

673 North Dakota United (NDU)
301 N 4th Street
Bismarck, ND 58501
701-223-0450
800-369-6332
Fax: 701-224-8535
comments@ndunited.org
ndunited.org
Works to provide public education and services to the citizens of North Dakota. Some services offered by the group include acting as a union to represent the rights of employees, support for improvement of institutions and professional development opportunities for members.

Nick Archuleta, President
Karen Christensen, Vice President of Education

Ohio

674 Ohio Arts Council
Rhodes State Office Tower
30 E Broad Street
33rd Floor
Columbus, OH 43215-3414
614-466-2613
Fax: 614-466-4494
communications@oac.ohio.gov
oac.ohio.gov
State agency supporting the arts in Ohio by offering grants, programs and other resources for artists and their supporters.

Geraldine Warner, Chair
Donna S Collins, Executive Director

675 Ohio Association of School Business Officials
8050 N High Street
Suite 170
Columbus, OH 43235
614-431-9116
844-838-5395

Fax: 614-431-9137
callie@oasbo-ohio.org
oasbo-ohio.org
The Ohio Association of School Business Officials is a nonprofit educational management organization dedicated to learning, utilizing and sharing the best methods and technology for school business administration.

Jim Rowan, Executive Director
Debbie Trzeciak, Chief Financial Officer

676 **Ohio Association of Secondary School Administrators**
8050 N High Street
Suite 180
Columbus, OH 43235-6484
614-430-8311
Fax: 614-430-8315
dcarlson@oassa.org
www.oassa.org
The Ohio Association of Secondary School Administrators is dedicated to advocating for the welfare of its members, while offering leadership, professional development and legislative influence.

Kenneth C Baker, Executive Director
Tim Freeman, Associate Executive Director

677 **Ohio Education for Homeless Children and Youth**
Ohio Department of Education
25 S Front Street
Mail Stop 404
Columbus, OH 43215
614-387-7725
Fax: 614-387-0963
Susannah.wayland@education.ohio.gov
education.ohio.gov
Represents initiatives and programs created to ensure that children and youth experiencing homelessness have access to education.

Susannah Wayland, Education Coordinator
Shannon D Teague, Assistant Director

678 **Ohio Library Council**
1105 Schrock Road
Suite 440
Columbus, OH 43229
614-410-8092
Fax: 614-410-8098
olc@olc.org
olc.org
The Ohio Library Council is the statewide professional association representing the interests of Ohio's public libraries and library staff. The council offers support for development of libraries through advocacy, education and collaboration.

Andrew Mangels, Chair
Douglas Evans, Executive Director

679 **Ohio Technology and Engineering Educators Association**
330-494-1100
tdouce@getsetsite.org
www.oteea.org
The mission of the Ohio Technology and Engineering Educators Association is to improve technological literacy for all Ohio students by providing professional development and networking opportunities to educators, as well as advocacy and public education on the value of technological literacy.

Richard F Miller, President
Victor Stefan, Executive Director

Oklahoma

680 **Oklahoma Arts Council**
Jim Thorpe Building
2101 N Lincoln Boulevard
Suite 640
Oklahoma City, OK 73105
405-521-2931
Fax: 405-521-6418
okarts@arts.ok.gov
www.arts.ok.gov
The Oklahoma Arts Council is responsible for helping to develop the arts in Oklahoma through grants, education, programs and initiatives.

Phyllis Stough, Chair
Amber Sharples, Executive Director

681 **Oklahoma Department of Libraries**
Allen Wright Memorial Library
200 NE 18th Street
Oklahoma City, OK 73105-3298
405-521-2502
Fax: 405-525-7804
info@libraries.ok.gov
libraries.ok.gov
Official state library of Oklahoma responsible for serving the state government's records management needs, assisting in developing libraries, coordinating projects and serving the public with programs and learning resources.

Susan McVey, Director
Vicki Sullivan, Deputy Director

682 **Oklahoma Education Association (OEA)**
323 E Madison Street
PO Box 18485
Oklahoma City, OK 73154
405-528-7785
800-522-8091
Fax: 405-524-0350
rkennedy@okea.org
okea.org
The Oklahoma Education Association (OEA) supports public education as the cornerstone of a democratic society. The association is comprised of public school teachers, counselors, administrators and others playing supporting roles in the education field. Some services offered by the association include legislative advocacy, professional development and other resources.

Alicia Priest, President
David DuVall, Executive Director

683 **Oklahoma Education for Homeless Children and Youth**
PO Box 36609
Oklahoma City, OK 73136
405-587-0106
Fax: 405-587-0642
webmaster@okcps.org
www.okcps.org
Initiative to offer supports for homeless children and youth, with the aim of making education more accessible to them.

Kathy Brown, Homeless Coordinator
Bryan Coleman, Assistant

684 **Oklahoma Library Association (OLA)**
PO Box 6550
Edmond, OK 73083
405-525-5100
Fax: 405-525-5103
exec_director@oklibs.org
www.oklibs.org
The Oklahoma Library Association supports libraries, library services and librarianship in Oklahoma. Members include library staff, library trustees, students, volunteers and others. The association offers advocacy, conferences and leadership resources.

Linda Pye, President
Natalie Currie, Secretary

Oregon

685 **AFT-Oregon (American Federation of Teachers-Oregon)**
7035 SW Hampton Street
Tigard, OR 97223-8313
503-595-3880
Fax: 503-595-3887
AFTOregon@aft-oregon.org
or.aft.org/
Charted in 1952, AFT-Oregon, a state affiliate of the American Federation of Teachers, AFL-CIO, is a non-profit organization representing some 11,000 Oregon workers in K-12, community college and higher education in faculty and classified positions; and child care workers, in both public and private sectors. AFT-Oregon, in coalition with other unions and community groups, advocates for quality education and health care for all Oregonians, and gives working people a voice in our state's capitol.

Mark Schwebke, President
Richard Schwarz, Executive VP

686 **Homeless Education Program**
255 Capitol St NE
Salem, OR 97310-0203
503-947-5781
Fax: 503-378-5156
www.ode.state.or.us/go/homelessed

687 **Oregon Arts Commission**
775 Summer St NE
Salem, OR 97301-1284
503-986-0082
Fax: 503-986-0082
www.oregonartcommission.org

688 **Oregon Association of Student Councils (OASC)**
707 13th Street SE
Suite 100
Salem, OR 97301-4035
503-480-7206
Fax: 503-581-9840
sara@oasc.org
www.oasc.org
The Oregon Association of Student Councils (OASC) is a non-profit member association, serving middle and high schools throughout the state. It provides leadership development to both students and advisors and is sponsored by the Confederation of Oregon School Administrators.

Sara S Nilles, Program Director

689 **Oregon Education Association (OEA)**
6900 SW Atlanta Street
Portland, OR 97223
503-684-3300
800-858-5505
Fax: 503-684-8063
larry.wolf@oregoned.org
www.oregoned.org
The mission of the Oregon Education Association (OEA) is to assure quality public education for every student in Oregon by providing a strong, positive voice for school employees. OEA's school funding priority, established in December 2002, seeks to restore stable and adequate funding for Oregon's schools and community colleges so that

all Oregon students have access to a quality public education.

Larry Wolf, President
Jerry Caruthers, Executive Director

690 **Oregon Educational Media Association**
PO Box 277
Terrebonne, OR 97760
503-625-7820
j23hayden@aol.com
www.oema.net
To provide progressive leadership to ensure that Oregon students and educators are effective users of ideas and information, and to pursue excellence in school library media programs by advocating information literacy for all student, supporting reading instruction and enjoyment of literature, supporting the highest levels of library media services in schools, strengthening member professionalism through communications and educational opportunities and promoting visibility in education, governme

Jim Hayden, Executive Director
Merrie Olson, President

691 **Oregon Library Association (OLA)**
P.O. Box 3067
La Grande, OR 97850-2042
503-370-7019
Fax: 503-587-8063
ola@olaweb.org
www.olaweb.org
The mission of the Oregon Library Association is to promote and advance library service through public and professional education and cooperation. Holds a conference in March and publishes two journals.

Mary Ginnane, President
Connie A Cohoon, Vice President

692 **Oregon Student Assistance Commission**
1500 Valley River Dr
Suite 100
Eugene, OR 97401
541-687-7400
800-452-8807
Fax: 541-687-7414
www.osac.state.or.us

Pennsylvania

693 **Office of Postsecondary Higher Education**
333 Market St
Harrisburg, PA 17126-0333
717-787-5041
Fax: 717-772-3622
www.pdehighered.state.pa.us/higher/site/default.asp

694 **Pennsylvania Council on the Arts**
215 Finance Building
Harrisburg, PA 17120
717-787-6883
Fax: 717-783-2538
www.pacouncilonthearts.org

695 **Pennsylvania Library Association (PaLA)**
220 Cumberland Parkway
Suite 10
Mechanicsburg, PA 17055
717-766-7663
800-622-3308
Fax: 717-766-5440
glenn@palibraries.org
www.palibraries.org
The Pennsylvania Library Association (PaLA) is a professional non-profit organization with strong volunteer leadership, dedicated to the support of its members, to the advancement of librarianship, and to the improvement and promotion of quality library service for citizens of the Commonwealth.

Glenn Miller, Executive Director
Mary O Garm, President

696 **Pennsylvania School Librarians Association**
9 Saint James Avenue
Somerville, MA 02144
617-628-4451
www.psla.org
Provides school librarians/media specialists with educational opportunities and current information through publications, workshops, seminars and conferences

Marg Foster, Secretary
Nancy S Latanision, President

697 **Pennsylvania State Education Association (PSEA)**
400 N 3rd Street
PO Box 1724
Harrisburg, PA 17105-1724
717-255-7000
800-944-7732
Fax: 717-255-7124
cdumaresq@psea.org
www.psea.org
PSEA's mission is to advocate for quality public education and our members through collective action. PSEA is a member-driven organization, headed by elected officers, an executive director and a board of directors.

James P Testerman, President
John F Springer, Executive Director

Rhode Island

698 **Higher Education Assistance Authority**
560 Jefferson Blvd
Suite 100
Warwick, RI 02886-1304
401-736-1100
800-922-9855
Fax: 401-732-3541
www.riheaa.org

699 **National Education Association Rhode Island (NEARI)**
99 Bald Hill Road
Cranston, RI 02920
401-463-9630
Fax: 401-463-5337
RWalsh@nea.org
www.neari.org/matriarch/default.asp
The NEA Rhode Island is both a union and a professional organization.

Robert A Walsh Jr, Executive Director
Vincent P Santaniello, Deputy Executive Director

700 **Rhode Island Association of School Business Officials**
600 Mount Pleasant Avenue
Building #16, RIC
Providence, RI 02908
401-272-9811
Fax: 401-272-9834
www.riasp.org
Is an umbrella association serving elementary, middle level, and high school leaders from all across Rhode Island. Affiliated with both the National Association of Elementary School Principals (NAESP) and the National Association of Secondary School Principals (NASSP)

Norma Cole, President
Arlene Miguel, Secretary

701 **Rhode Island Educational Media Association**
6946 Camp Avenue
Suite 402
North Kingstown, RI 02852
401-398-7500
Fax: 401-886-0855
www@ride.ri.net
www.ri.net
RINET provides complete Internet solutions for organizations that serve children, such as schools, libraries, municipalities, as well as high quality technology programs and services in support of K-12 teaching, learning and administration

Founded: 1999

Mike Mello, Membership Chairman
Sharon Hussey, Executive Director

702 **Rhode Island Library Association**
PO Box 6765
Providence, RI 02940
401-943-9080
Fax: 401-946-5079
book_n@yahoo.com
www.rilibraryassoc.org
The Rhode Island Library Association is a profesional association of Librarians, Library Staff, Trustees, and library supporters whose purpose is to promote the profession of librarianship and to improve the visibility, accessibility, responsiveness and effectiveness of library and information services throughout Rhode Island.

Christopher Laroux, President
Laura Marlane, Vice President

703 **State Council on the Arts**
One Capitol Hill
Providence, RI 02908
401-222-3880
Fax: 401-222-3018
www.arts.ri.gov

South Carolina

704 **Education for Homeless Children and Youth**
1429 Senate St
Suite 1114-E
Columbia, SC 29201
803-734-3215
Fax: 803-734-3043
www.ed.sc.gov/

705 **South Carolina Arts Commission**
1800 Gervais St
Columbia, SC 29201
803-734-8696
Fax: 803-734-8526
www.state.sc.us/arts

706 **South Carolina Commission on Higher Education**
1333 Main St
Suite 200
Columbia, SC 29201
803-737-2260
877-349-7183
Fax: 803-737-2297
www.che.sc.gov

707 **South Carolina Education Association (SCEA)**
421 Zimalcrest Drive
Columbia, SC 29210
803-772-6553
800-422-7232
Fax: 803-772-0922
help@thescea.org
www.thescea.org/
Professional association for educators in South Carolina.
Aaron Wallace, Executive Director
Carolyn Randolph, Assistant Executive Director

708 **South Carolina Library Association**
PO Box 1763
Columbia, SC 29202
803-252-1087
Fax: 803-252-0589
scla@capconsc.com
www.scla.org
Informs members of issues and to provide training and networking opportunities.
Libby Young, President
Rayburne Turner, Vice President

South Dakota

709 **Education for Homeless Children and Youth**
700 Governors Dr
Pierre, SD 57501
605-773-6400
Fax: 605-773-3782

710 **Mountain Plains Library Association (MPLA)**
14293 West Center Drive
Lakewood, CO 80228
303-985-7795
mpla_execsecretary@operamail.com
www.mpla.us
The Mountain Plains Library Association (MPLA) is a twelve state association of librarians, library paraprofessionals and friends of libraries in Arizona, Colorado, Kansas, Montana, Nebraska, Nevada, New Mexico, North Dakota, Oklahoma, South Dakota, Utah and Wyoming. Its purpose is to promote the development of librarians and libraries by providing significant educational and networking opportunities. Holds conferences in September, October and November. Also publishes a newsletter.
Judy Zelenski, Interim Executive Secretary
Dan Chaney, MPLA Webmaster

711 **South Dakota Arts Council**
711 E Wells Ave
Pierre, SD 57501-3369
605-773-3301
800-952-3625
Fax: 605-773-5657
www.artscouncil.sd.gov

712 **South Dakota Education Association (SDEA)**
441 E Capitol Avenue
Pierre, SD 57501
605-224-9263
800-529-0090
Fax: 605-224-5810
Bryce.Healy@sdea.org
www.sdea.org/
The South Dakota Education Association/SDEA advocates new directions for public education, providing professional services that benefit students, schools and the public.
Bryce Healy, Executive Director
Paul McCorkle, CFO/CIO

713 **South Dakota Library Association**
28363 472nd Ave
Worthing, SD 57707
605-343-3750
bkstand@rap.midco.net
www.sdlibraryassociation.org
The SD Library Association strives to promote library service of the highest quality for present and potential SD library users; to provide opportunities for professional involvement of all persons engaged in any phase of librarianship within the state; and to further the professional development of SD librarians, trustees, and library employees.
Jan Brue Enright, President
Laura Olson, Secretary/Treasurer

Tennessee

714 **Education for Homeless Children and Youth**
710 James Robertson Parkway
Nashville, TN 37243-0379
615-532-6309
Fax: 615-253-5706

715 **Tennessee Arts Commission**
401 Charlotte Ave
Nasville, TN 37243-0780
615-532-5934
Fax: 615-741-8559
www.arts.state.tn.us

716 **Tennessee Association of Secondary School Principals (TASSP)**
2671 Bebe Branch Lane
Knoxville, TN 37928
423-309-6187
866-737-2777
Fax: 865-687-2341
tassp@bellsouth.net
www.tnassp.org/
The mission of the Tennessee Association of Secondary School Principals is: to promote professional standards of practice for secondary school administrators; provide high quality professional development experiences for rural, urban, and suburban administrators, statewide, based on their common and unique professional development needs; and advocate on behalf of secondary administrators in their efforts to provide high quality education for all students.
Dana Finch, President
Tommy Everette, Executive Director

717 **Tennessee Higher Education Commission**
404 James Robertson Parkway
Suite 1900
Nashville, TN 37243-0830
615-741-3605
Fax: 615-741-6230
www.state.tn.us/thec

718 **Tennessee Library Association**
PO Box 241074
Memphis, TN 38124-1074
901-485-6952
Fax: 615-269-1807
arhuggins1@comcast.net
www.tnla.org
Promote the establishment, maintenance, and support of adequate library services for all people of the state.
Annelle R Huggins, Executive Director
Dinah Harris, President

719 **Tennessee School Boards Association**
525 Brick Church Park Drive
Nashville, TN 37207
615-815-3900
800-448-6465
Fax: 615-815-3911
webadmin@tsba.net
www.tsba.net
The mission of the Tennessee School Boards Association is to assist school boards in effectively governing school districts.
Founded: 1953
Tammy Grissom, Executive Director
David Pickler, President

Texas

720 **Texas Association of Secondary School Principals (TASSP)**
1833 S IH-35
Austin, TX 78741
512-443-2100
Fax: 512-442-3343
aarguello@tassp.org
www.tassp.org/
TASSP provides proactive leadership to systemically change schools into learning communities in which all students and other participants achieve their full potential as life long learners in a diverse and changing society.
Bob Alvey, President
Tom Leyden, Associate Executive Director

721 **Texas Commission on the Arts**
PO Box 13406
Austin, TX 78711-3406
512-463-5535
800-252-9415
Fax: 512-475-2699
www.arts.state.tx.us

722 **Texas Higher Education Coordinating Board**
PO Box 12788
Austin, TX 78711-2788
512-427-6101
800-242-3062
Fax: 512-427-6127
www.thecb.state.tx.us

723 **Texas Homeless Education Office**
2901 N IH35
Austin, TX 78722
512-475-8765
800-446-3142
Fax: 512-471-6193

724 **Texas Library Association (TLA)**
3355 Bee Cave Road
Suite 401
Austin, TX 78746-6763
512-328-1518
800-580-2852
Fax: 512-328-8852
tla@txla.org
www.txla.org
The Texas Library Association is a professional organization that promotes librarianship and library service in Texas. Through legislative advocacy, continuing education events, and networking channels, TLA offers members oppor-

tunities for service to the profession as well as for personal growth.

Patricia H Smith, Executive Director
Gloria Meraz, Communications Director

Utah

725 **Education for Homeless Children and Youth**
250 East 500 S
PO Box 144200
Salt Lake City, UT 84114-4200
801-538-7975
Fax: 801-538-7991
www.schools.utah.gov

726 **Utah Arts Council**
617 East South Temple
Salt Lake City, UT 84102
801-320-9794
Fax: 801-533-3210
www.arts.utah.gov

727 **Utah Education Association (UEA)**
875 E 5180 S
Murray, UT 84107-5299
801-266-4461
800-594-8996
Fax: 801-265-2249
mark.mickelsen@utea.org
www.utea.org
The mission of the Utah Education Association (UEA) is to advance the cause of public education in partnership with others: strengthen the teaching profession, promote quality schools for Utah's children, and advocate the well-being of members.

Kim Campbell, President
Mark Mickelsen, Executive Director

728 **Utah State Library Division**
250 North 1950 W
Suite A
Salt Lake City, UT 84116-7901
801-715-6777
800-433-1479
Fax: 801-715-6767
www.library.utah.gov

729 **Utah System of Higher Education**
60 South 400 W
Salt Lake City, UT 84101-1284
801-321-7103
Fax: 801-321-7156
www.utahsbr.edu

Vermont

730 **Education for Homeless Children and Youth**
120 State St
Montpelier, VT 05620-2501
802-828-5148
Fax: 802-828-0573
www.education.vermont.gov/new/html/pgm_homeless.html

731 **Vermont Arts Council**
136 State St
Montpelier, VT 05633-6001
802-828-3778
Fax: 802-828-3363
www.vermontartscouncil.org

732 **Vermont Department of Libraries**
109 State St
Montpelier, VT 05609-0601
802-828-3261
Fax: 802-828-2199
www.libraries.vermont.gov

733 **Vermont Library Association**
PO Box 803
Burlington, VT 05402
802-388-3845
Fax: 802-388-4367
vlaorg@sover.net
www.vermontlibraries.org
The Vermont Library Association is an educational Organization working to develop, promote, and improve library and information services and librarianship in the state of Vermont.

Judah S Hamer, President
David Clark, Chapter Councilor

734 **Vermont National Education Association (VTNEA)**
10 Wheelock Street
Montpelier, VT 05602-3737
802-223-6375
800-649-6375
Fax: 802-223-1253
vtnea@together.net
www.vtnea.org/
The Vermont National Education Association is a voluntary organization of 11,000 Vermont teachers and education support professionals, their purpose being to make sure that members have a satisfying work environment where they are acknowledged for the work they perform and where the work they perform helps students do their best.

Joel D Cook, Executive Director
Darren M Allen, Communications Director

735 **Vermont Student Assistance Corporation**
10 East Allen St
PO Box 2000
Winooski, VT 05404-2601
www.vsac.org

736 **Volunteers for Peace**
131 Main Street
Suite 201
Burlington, VT 05401
802-598-0052
vfp@vfp.org
vfp.org
Volunteers for Peace promotes intercultural education and volunteer opportunities abroad so that people from diverse backgrounds can learn to work together to develop communities.

Tom Sherman, President
Matt Messier, Executive Director

Virginia

737 **Division of Student Leadership Services**
701 East Franklin Street
Richmond, VA 23288-0001
804-285-2829
Fax: 804-285-1379
www.vaprincipals.org
Organization that sponsors the Virginia Student Councils Association; the Virginia Association of Honor Societies; and the Virginia Association of Student Activity Advisers.

Dr. Randy Barrack, President

738 **Eastern Business Education Association (EBEA)**
1914 Association Drive
Reston, VA 20191-1596
703-860-8300
Fax: 703-620-4483
nbea@nbea.org
www.nbea.org
NBEA is committed to the advancement of the professional interest and competence of its members and provides programs and services that enhance members' professional growth and development.

Sharon Fisher-Larson, President
Janet M Treichel, Executive Director

739 **Education for Homeless Children and Youth**
PO Box 8795
Williamsburg, VA 23187-8795
757-221-4002
877-455-3412
Fax: 757-221-5300
www.wm.edu/hope

740 **Organization of Virginia Homeschoolers**
PO Box 5131
Charlottesville, VA 22905
866-513-6173
Fax: 804-946-2263
info@vahomeschoolers.org
www.vahomeschoolers.org
The Organization of Virginia Homeschoolers' most effective action is screening legislation for potential impact on homeschoolers. We pay attention to a large list of topics: home instruction statute, tutor provision, religious exemption provision, driver training, truancy, curfews, tax credits, and more.

Parrish Mort, President
Kenneth L Payne, Executive Director

741 **Southern Association of Colleges & Schools**
Virginia Secondary & Middle School Committee
PO Box 7007
Radford, VA 24142-7007
540-831-5399
Fax: 540-831-6309
mdalderm@runet.edu
www.sacs.org
Public and private school accreditation organization. 12,000 member schools in 11 southern state regions. 430 middle and secondary SACS member schools in Virginia.

Dr. Emmett Sufflebarger, President
Lanny Holsinger, President-Elect

742 **State Council of Higher Education for Virginia**
101 North 14th St
Richmond, VA 23219
804-225-2600
Fax: 804-225-2604
www.schev.edu

743 **Virginia Alliance for Arts Education**
PO Box 70232
Richmond, VA 23255-0232
804-740-7865
Fax: 804-828-2335
www.socialarchive.iath.virginia.edu
To promote aesthetic and creative art education for the development of the individual at all levels in the commonwealth of Virginia. To assist teachers in improving the quality of art education. To organize and conduct panels, forums, lectures, and tours for art educators and the general public on art and art instruction. To keep the public informed of

the arts through whatever means are available.

Founded: 1974

Margaret Edwards, Division Director

744 **Virginia Association for Health, Physical Education, Recreation & Dance**
817 W Franklin Street
Box 842037
Richmond, VA 23284-2037
800-918-9899
Fax: 800-918-9899
www.vahperd.org
VAHPERD is a professional association of educators that advocate quality programs in health, physical education, recreation, dance and sport. The association seeks to facilitate the professional growth and educational practices and legislation that will impact the profession.

Judith Clark, President

745 **Virginia Association for Supervision and Curriculum Development**
33074 Clay Street
Hopewell, VA 23860
804-458-9554
vascd1@verizon.net
www.vaascd.org/
VASCD is an organization committed to excellence in education by providing programs and services that promote quality instruction for lifelong learning.

Linda Hyslop, Executive Director
Judy Lam, Administrative Coordinator

746 **Virginia Association for the Education ofthe Gifted**
PO Box 26212
Richmond, VA 23260-6212
804-355-5945
Fax: 804-355-5137
vagifted@comcast.net
www.vagifted.org
The Virginia Association for the Gifted supports research in gifted education and advocates specialized preparation for educators of the gifted. The association disseminates information, maintains a statewide network of communication, and cooperates with organizations and agencies to improve the quality of education in the Commonwealth of Virginia.

Liz Nelson, Executive Director

747 **Virginia Association of Elementary School Principals**
1805 Chantilly Street
Richmond, VA 23230
804-355-6791
Fax: 804-355-1196
info@vaesp.org
www.vaesp.org
Nonprofit professional association advocating for public education and equal educational opportunities. Promotes leadership of school administrators, principals as educational leaders, and provides professional development opportunities.

Thomas L Shortt, Executive Director
Jeanne Grady, Operations Director

748 **Virginia Association of Independent Specialized Education Facilities**
6802 Paragon Place
Suite 525
Richmond, VA 23230
804-282-3592
Fax: 804-282-3596
info@vais.org
www.vais.org
The Virginia Association of Independent Schools is a service organization that promotes educational, ethical and professional excellence. Through its school evaluation/accreditation program, attention to professional development and insistence on integrity, the Association safeguards the interests of its member schools.

Kimberly E Failon, Director Professional Develo
Sally K Boese, Executive Director

749 **Virginia Association of Independent Schools**
6802 Paragon Place
Suite 525
Richmond, VA 23230
804-282-3592
Fax: 804-282-3596
info@vais.org
www.vais.org
The Virginia Association of Independent Schools is a service organization that promotes educational, ethical and professional excellence. Through its school evaluation/accreditation program, attention to professional development and insistence on integrity, the Association safeguards the interests of its member schools.

Kimberly E Failon, Director Professional Develo
Sally K Boese, Executive Director

750 **Virginia Association of School Superintendents**
1805 Chantilly Street
PO Box 400265
Richmond, VA 2323-4265
804- 5-2
Fax: 434-982-2942
vass.edschool.virginia.edu/
The Virginia Association of School Superintendents (VASS) is a professional organization dedicated to the mission of providing leadership and advocacy for public school education throughout the Commonwealth of Virginia.

J Andrew Stamp, Associate Executive Director
Alfred R Butler IV, Executive Director

751 **Virginia Association of School Business Officials**
Williamsburg-James City County Public Schools
PO Box 8783
Williamsburg, VA 23187-8783
757-253-6748
Fax: 757-253-0173
www.vasbo.org/
The mission of the Virginia Association of School Business Officials is to promote the highest standards of school business practices for its membership through professional development, continuing education, networking, and legislative impact.

David C Papenfuse, Division Director

752 **Virginia Association of School Personnel Administrators**
800 E City Hall Avenue
Norfolk, VA 23510-2723
757-340-1217
Fax: 757-340-1889
president@vaspa.org
www.vaspa.org/
The Virginia Association of School Personnel Administrators helps personnel/human resources professionals improve their administrative skills and grow extensively in their profession.

Eddid P Antoine II, Division Director
Barbara Warren Jones, President

753 **Virginia Commission for the Arts**
223 Governor St
Richmond, VA 23219-2010
804-225-3132
Fax: 804-225-4327
www.arts.virigina.gov

754 **Virginia Congress of Parents & Teachers**
1027 Wilmer Avenue
Richmond, VA 23227-2419
804-264-1234
866-482-497
Fax: 804-264-4014
info@vapta.org
www.vapta.org
The Virginia Congress of Parents and Teachers, better known as the Virginia PTA is a volunteer child advocacy association working for ALL children and youth in the Commonwealth of Virginia.

Melissa S Nehrbass, President
Eugene A Goldberg, Executive Director

755 **Virginia Consortium of Administrators for Education of the Gifted**
RR 5 Box 680
Farmville, VA 23901-9011
804-225-2884
Fax: 814-692-3163
www.vagifted.org

Catherine Cottrell, Division Director

756 **Virginia Council for Private Education**
919 E Main Street
Suite 1150
Richmond, VA 23219
804-423-6435
Fax: 804-423-6436
office@vcpe.org
www.vcpe.org
The Virginia Council for Private Education (VCPE) oversees accreditation of nonpublic preschool, elementary and secondary schools in the Commonwealth.

Joanne L Webster, Executive Director

757 **Virginia Council of Administrators of Special Education**
Franklin County Public Schools
25 Bernard Road
Rocky Mount, VA 24151
703-493-0280
Fax: 540-483-5806
kkirst@k12albemarle.org
www.vcase.org
The Virginia Council of Administrators of Special Education is a professional organization that promotes professional leadership through the provision of collegial support and current information on recommended instructional practices as well as local, state and national trends in Special Education for professionals who serve students with disabilities in order to improve the quality and delivery of special education services in Virginia's public Schools

Dr. Sheila Bailey, President
Wyllys VanDerwerker, President-Elect

758 **Virginia Council of Teachers of Mathematics**
1033 Backwoods Road
Virginia Beach, VA 23455-6617
757-671-7316
gnelson@vctm.org.
www.vctm.org/

The purpose of the Virginia Council of Teachers of Mathematics is to stimulate an active interest in mathematics, to provide an interchange of ideas in the teaching of mathematics, to promote the improvement of mathematics education in Virginia, to provide leadership in the professional development of teachers, to provide resources for teachers and to facilitate cooperation among mathematics organizations at the local, state and national levels

Ellen Smith Hook, Division Director
Ian Shenk, President

759 Virginia Council on Economic Education

301 W Main Street
Box 844000
Richmond, VA 23284-4000
804-828-1627
Fax: 804-828-7215
shfinley@vcu.edu
www.vcee.org
Goal is for students to understand our economy and develop the life-long decision-making skills they need to be effective, informed citizens, consumers, savers, investors, producers and employees.

Yvonne Toms Allmond, Senior Vice President
Sallie Garrett, Contact

760 Virginia Education Association

116 S 3rd Street
Richmond, VA 23219
804-648-5801
800-552-9554
Fax: 804-775-8379
kboitnott@veanea.org
www.veanea.org/
VEA is a statewide community of more than 60,000 teachers and school support professionals working for the betterment of public education in the Commonwealth. First organized in 1863, VEA has consistently advocated for quality instruction and curriculum, adequate funding, and excellent working conditions for Virginia public employees.

Robert Whitehead, Executive Director
Kitty Boitnott, President

761 Virginia Educational Media Association

PO Box 2743
Fairfax, VA 22031-2743
703-764-0719
Fax: 703-272-3643
jremler@pen.k12.va.us
www.vema.gan.va.us
Aim is to promote literacy, information access and evaluation, love of literature, effective use of technology, collaboration in the teaching and learning process, intellectual freedom, professional growth, instructional leadership and lifelong learning.

Jean Remler, Executive Director
Terri Britt, President

762 Virginia Educational Research Association

3354 Taleen Court
Annandale, VA 22003-1161
703-698-1325
Fax: 703-698-0587
mpowell@ctb.com
www.va-edresearch.org
The mission of the Educational Research Service is to improve the education of children and youth by providing educators and the public with timely and reliable research and information.

Dr. Edith Carter, Assistant Professor
Michaeline M Powell, President

763 Virginia High School League

1642 State Farm Boulevard
Charlottesville, VA 22911-8609
434-977-8475
Fax: 434-977-5943
ktillry@vhsl.org
www.vhsl.org
The Virginia High School League is an alliance of Virginia's public high schools that promotes education, leadership, sportsmanship, character and citizenship for students by establishing and maintaining high standards for school activities and competitions.

Craig Barbrow, President
Susan Bechtol, Chairman

764 Virginia Library Association

PO Box 56312
Virginia Beach, VA 23503-0277
757-583-0041
Fax: 757-583-5041
lhahne@coastalnet.com
www.vla.org
The Virginia Library Association is a statewide organization whose purpose is to develop, promote, and improve library and information services and the profession of librarianship in order to advance literacy and learning and to ensure access to information in the Commonwealth of Virginia.

Linda Hahne, Executive Director

765 Virginia Middle School Association

11138 Marsh Road
Bealeton, VA 22712-9360
703-439-3207
Fax: 540-439-2051
www.vmsa.org/

Lisa Norris, President
Virginia Jones, President Elect

766 Virginia School Boards Association

200 Hansen Road
Charlottesville, VA 22911
434-295-8722
800-446-8722
Fax: 434-295-8785
www.vsba.org
The Virginia School Boards Association is a voluntary, nonpartisan association whose primary mission is the advancement of education through the unique American tradition of local citizen control of, and accountability for, the Commonwealth's public schools.

Gina Patterson, Assistant Executive Director
Frank E Barham, Executive Director

767 Virginia Student Councils Association

4909 Cutshaw Avenue
Richmond, VA 23230
804-355-2777
Fax: 804-285-1379
rbarrack@vassp.org
www.vassp.org/vsca.html
Assist school principals and assistant principals in providing leadership to their schools and communities for the purpose of improving the education of Virginia's youth.

Randy D Barrack, Executive Director
Lawrence W Lenz, President

768 Virginia Vocational Association

10259 Lakeridge Square Court
Suite G
Ashland, VA 23005-8159
804-365-4556

Jean Holbrook, President
Kathy Williams, Executive Director

769 Voices for Virginia's Children

701 E Franklin Street
Suite 807
Richmond, VA 23219
804-649-0184
Fax: 804-649-0161
info@vakids.org
www.vakids.org
Independent organization advocating for better lives and futures for the children and youth of Virginia. The organization makes recommendations for policy solutions, advises policymakers and develops leadership in support of policy initiatives.

Founded: 1994

Jamie Dyke Clancey, Board Chair
Margaret Nimmo Holland, Executive Director

Washington

770 Washington Education Association

32032 Weyerhaeuser Way S
PO Box 9100
Federal Way, WA 98001-9687
253-941-6700
800-622-3393
www.washingtonea.org
The mission of the Washington Education Association is to advance the professional interests of its members in order to make public education the best it can be for students, staff and communities

John Donaghy, Executive Director
Rod Regan, Director

771 Washington Library Association

PO Box 33808
Seattle, WA 98133
206-823-1138
info@wla.org
www.wla.org
The Washington Library Association provides the leadership needed to develop, improve and promote library services so that all Washington residents can benefit from these services to further their education and enhance their skills.

Kate Laughlin, Executive Director

772 Washington State Arts Commission

PO Box 42675
Olympia, WA 98504-2675
360-753-3860
Fax: 360-586-5351
www.arts.wa.gov

773 Washington State Higher Education Coordinating Board

917 Lakeridge Way
PO Box 43430
Olympia, WA 98504-3430
360-753-7800
Fax: 360-753-7808
www.hecb.wa.gov

West Virginia

774 Edvantia

1031 Quarrier Street
PO Box 1348
Charleston, WV 25325-1348
304-347-0400
800-624-9120

Fax: 304-347-0487
info@edvantia.org
www.edvantia.org
Edvantia is a nonprofit corporation committed to helping client-partners improve education and meet federal and state mandates. Schools, districts, and state education agencies-as well as publishers and service providers-rely on Edvantia's core capabilities in research, evaluation, professional development, and technical assistance to help them succeed.

Nancy Balow, Author
Patricia Hammer, Director of Communications
Carolyn Luzader, Communications Specialist

775 **West Virginia Division of Culture and History**
The Culture Center Capitol Complex
199 Kanawha Boulevard E
Charleston, WV 25305-0300
604-558-0240
Fax: 304-558-3560
www.wvculture.org
The West Virginia Division of Culture and History works to identify, preserve, protect, and promote the art, culture, and artifacts of West Virginia.

Randall Reid-Smith, Commissioner
Caryn Gresham, Deputy Commissioner

776 **West Virginia Education Association**
1558 Quarrier Street
Charleston, WV 25311
304-346-5315
800-642-8261
Fax: 304-346-4325
mail@wvea.org
www.wvea.org
The West Virginia Education Association (WVEA) is a voluntary membership organization dedicated to advocating for education employees and the public education system. The WVEA has 15,000 members, 100 local affiliates, and is associated with the National Education Association.

David Haney, Executive Director
Ladonna Campbell, Secretary

777 **West Virginia Higher Education Policy Commission**
1018 Kanawha Boulevard E
Suite 700
Charleston, WV 25301
304-558-0699
Fax: 304-558-1011
molly.george@wvhepc.edu
www.hepc.wvnet.edu
The West Virginia Higher Education Commission develops policy for West Virginia's four-year colleges and universities.

Paul L. Hill, Chancellor

778 **West Virginia Library Association**
, WV
wvla.org
The West Virginia Library Association (WVLA) promotes library services and librarianship in West Virginia.

Founded: 1914

Brenna Call, President
Kelly Funkhouser, Executive Director

779 **West Virginia Library Commission**
Culture Center, Building 9
1900 Kanawha Boulevard E
Charleston, WV 25305
304-558-2041
800-642-9021
www.librarycommission.lib.wv.us
The West Virginia Library Commission is focused on improving library and information services.

Karen Goff, Executive secretary
Jennifer Johnson, Admin Services Director

Wisconsin

780 **Division for Libraries and Technology**
Wisconsin Department of Public Instruction
125 S Webster St
Madison, WI 53707
608-266-3390
800-441-4563
www.dpi.wi.gov/dltcl
The Division for Libraries and Technology provides learning and information needs to Wisconsin citizens.

Tony Evers, State Superintendent

781 **Wisconsin Arts Board**
201 West Washington Avenue
PO Box 8690
Madison, WI 53708-8690
608-266-0190
Fax: 608-267-0380
artsboard.wisconsin.gov
A state agency, the Wisconsin Arts Board fosters arts, creativity, art education, community, and economic development and serves as a cultural resource for Wisconsin.

George Tzougros, Executive Director
Karen Goeschko, Assistant Director, Programs

782 **Wisconsin Education Association Council**
33 Nob Hill Drive
PO Box 8003
Madison, WI 53708-8003
608-276-7711
800-362-8034
Fax: 608-276-8203
www.weac.org
The Wisconsin Education Association Council (WEAC) is statewide educational organization representing public education employees including teachers, counselors, librarians, education support professionals, and university students studying to be teachers. WEAC supports a range of policies, reforms, and development opportunities designed to better public education.

Founded: 1853

Ron Martin, President
Peggy Wirtz-Olsen, Vice President

783 **Wisconsin Higher Educational Aids Board**
131 W Wilson Street, Suite 902
PO Box 7885
Madison, WI 53703-7885
608-267-2206; Fax: 607-267-2808
HEABmail@wi.gov
www.heab.state.wi.us
The Higher Educational Aids Board (HEAB) manages the states student financial aid system for residents in Wisconsin attending higher education institutions. HEAB provides financial aid programs, including grants, scholarships, and loan programs.

John Reinemann, Executive Secretary
Cassie Weisensel, Operations Program Associate

784 **Wisconsin Library Association**
4610 South Biltmore Lane
Suite 100
Madison, WI 53718-2153
608-245-3640; Fax: 608-245-3646
wla@wisconsinlibraries.org
wla.wisconsinlibraries.org
The Wisconsin Library Association advocates for and supports libraries, and library workers in the state of Wisconsin.

Plumer Lovelace, Executive Director
Vanessa Mauss, Membership Coordinator

Wyoming

785 **Wyoming Arts Council**
Barrett Building
2301 Central Avenue
2nd Floor
Cheyenne, WY 82002
307-777-7742
michael.lange@wyo.gov; wyoarts.state.wy.us
The Wyoming Arts Council (WAC) invests in resources that promote excellence in the arts; providing grants, and programs, and through partnerships the Council funds art projects across the state.

Michael Lange, Executive Director
Rachel Clifton, Assistant Director

786 **Wyoming Education Association**
115 E 22nd Street
Suite 1
Cheyenne, WY 82001-3795
307-634-7991
Fax: 800-778-8161
mkruse@nea.org; www.wyoea.org
The Wyoming Education Association (WEA) is dedicated to improving public education in the state of Wyoming. The WEA works at all levels of education, in schools, colleges, and universities and facilitates the improvement in teaching and learning. The Association has more than 6,300 members.

Founded: 1892

Ron Sniffin, Executive Director
Kathy Vetter, President

787 **Wyoming Library Association**
PO Box 1387
Cheyenne, WY 82003
307-632-7622
lauragrott@gmail.com; www.wyla.org
The Wyoming Library Association works to support, promote and educate the community on libraries, libranship, and services provided by libraries in Wyoming.

Laura Grott, Executive Secrerary

788 **Wyoming School Boards Association**
2323 Pioneer Avenue
Cheyenne, WY 82001
307-634-1112; Fax: 307-634-1114
wsba@wsba-wy.org
www.wsba-wy.org
The Wyoming School Boards Association (WSBA) represents local school boards advocating for improved educational opportunities in Wyoming public schools. Through resource sharing members of the WSBA provides educational services to students that would be otherwise economically unfeasible.

Brian Farmer, Executive Director
Richard Strahorn, Director, Member Services

International

789 **ACSI Professional Development Forum**
Assocation of Christian Schools International
731 Chapel Hills Drive
Colorado Springs, CO 80920
719-528-6906
Fax: 719-531-0631
press@acsi.org
www.acsi.org
Convention for administrators, school board members and educators. The convention encourages staff and volunteer development.
Dan Egeler, Ph.D, President

790 **AISA School Leaders' Retreat and Educators Conference**
Association of International Schools in Africa
Peponi Road
PO Box 14103, Nairobi
Kenya 00800
254-20-2697442
Fax: 254-20-4183272
info@aisa.or.ke
www.aisa.or.ke
Facilitates communications, cooperation, and professional growth among member schools. Promotes intercultural understanding and friendships as well as facilitating collaboration between its members, host country schools, and other regional and professional groups.
Annual/October
Peter Bateman, Executive Director

791 **Annual International Conference on ADHD**
PO Box 103
Denver, PA 17517
800-939-1019
Fax: 800-939-1019
info@add.org
add.org
A conference for adults with ADHD to learn about ADHD treatments and research, and to network with professionals and organizations serving those with ADHD.
November
Duane Gordon, President
David Teplin, Psy.D, Co-Chair

792 **Association for Experiential Education Annual Conference**
3775 Iris Avenue
Suite 4
Boulder, CO 80301-2043
303-440-8844
866-522-8337
Fax: 303-440-9581
membership@aee.org
www.aee.org
Annual international and regional conference dedicated to promoting, defining, developing, and applying the theories and practices of experiential education.
November
1,200 attendees
Mary Breunig, President
Leslie Stevens, Office Manager

793 **CIEE Annual Conference**
Council on International Educational Exchange
300 Fore Street
Portland, ME 04101
207-553-7600
800-407-8839
Fax: 207-553-7699
conference@ciee.org
www.ciee.org
Open to study-abroad advisors, administrators, faculty and other international education professionals. The conference is an opportunity to share ideas, keep up with developments in the field, and meet with colleagues from around the world.
November

794 **Center for Critical Thinking and Moral Critique Annual International**
Po Box196
Tomales, CA 94971
707-878-9100
800-833-3645
Fax: 707-878-9111
cct@criticalthinking.org
www.criticalthinking.org
Over 1,200 educators participate to discuss critical thinking and educational change.
March, July
Dr Linda Elder, President

795 **Council for Advancement and Support of Education**
1307 New York Avenue NW
Suite 1000
Washington, DC 20005-4701
202-328-2273
Fax: 202-387-4973
conferences@case.org
www.case.org
Offers numerous opportunities in the United States, Canada, Mexico, mainland Europe, and the United Kingdom to network with colleagues.
Fall/Winter
John Lippincott, President
Richard Salatiello, Sr Conference Program Coord.

796 **Council for Learning Disabilities International Conference**
1184 Antioch Road
Box 405
Overland Park, KS 66210
913-491-1011
Fax: 913-491-1012
cldinfo@cldinternational.org
www.cldinternational.org
Intensive interaction with and among professional educators and top LD researchers. Concise, informative and interesting forums on topics from effective instruction to self-reliance are presented by well-known professionals from across the country and around the world.
October
35 booths with 800 attendees
Diane Bryant, Conference Contact
Judy Voress, Conference Contact

797 **Council of British Independent Schools in the European Communities Annual Conference**
St. Mary's University Palace
Strawberry Hill
Twickenham, UK TW1-4SX
44(0) 208 240 4142
Fax: 44(0) 208 240 4255
excecutive.director@cobis.org.uk
www.cobis.org.uk
Conference for members of senior management educational teams.
May
75 attendees and 20 exhibits
Colin Bell, Executive Director
Suzanne Howarth, Membership

798 **European Council of International Schools**
146 Buckingham Palace Road
Fourth Floor
London, UK SW1W-9TR
+44 0 20 7824 7040
Fax: +44 0 20 7824 7041
ecis@ecis.org
www.ecis.org
Support professional development, curriculum and instruction, leadership and good governance in international schools located in Europe and around the world.
April, November
Michelle Clue, Conference Coordinator
Jean Vahey, Executive Director

799 **Hort School: Conference of the Association of American Schools**
International School of Panama
P.O. Box 0819-02588
Panama City
507-293-3000
Fax: 507-266-7808
isp@isp.edu.pa
www.isp.edu.pa
Educates and inspires our students to reach their full potential and contribute to the world by providing an exemplary English language education enriched by our multicultural community.
October
600 attendees and 35 exhibits
Rajiv Bhat, Director
Terry McCoy, President

800 **International Association of Teachers of English as a Foreign Language**
Darwin College
University of Kent
Canterbury, Kent, UK CT2-7NY
44-1227-824430
Fax: 44-1227-824431
generalenquires@iatefl.org
www.iatefl.org
Plenary sessions by eminent practitioners, a large number of workshops, talks and round tables given by other speakers, an ELT Resources Exhibition and Pre-Conference Events organized by Special Interest Groups.
April
80 booths with 1500 attendees
Alison Medland, Conference Organizer
Glenda Smart, Executive Director

801 **International Awards & Personalization Expo**
8735 W Higgins Road
Suite 300
Chicago, IL 60631
847-375-4800
Fax: 847-375-6480
info@awardspersonalization.org
awardspersonalization.org
The International Awards & Personalization Expo will offer opportunities for business leaders to learn about processes and products, experience hands-on training, and connect with industry colleagues on the subject of custom awards manufacturing.
February
Richard Korbyl, President
Louise Ristau, CAE, Executive Director

802 **International Awards Market**
Awards and Recognition Association
4700 W Lake Avenue
Glenview, IL 60025
847-375-4800
800-344-2148
Fax: 888-374-7257

info@ara.org
www.ara.org
Providing outstanding business and educational opportunities for both retailers and suppliers. Retailers can view the latest industry products, take advantage of special show offers and benefit from a full educational program.

Feb, March, Nov
200 booths with 6,000 attendees

Lori Warren, President

803 International Conference
World Association for Symphonic Bands & Ensembles
1037 Mill Street
San Luis Obispo, CA 93401
805-541-8000
Fax: 805-543-9498
admin@wasbe2005.com
www.wasbe.org
WASBE is a nonprofit, international association open to individuals, institutions, and industries interested in symphonic bands and wind ensembles. Dedicated to enhancing the quality of the wind band throughout the world and exposing its members to new worlds of repertoire, musical culture, people and places.

Every 2 years

Bert Aalders, President

804 International Congress for School Effectiveness & Improvement
International Congress Secretariat
86 Ellison Road
Springwood
Australia NSW-2777
61 2 4751 7974
Fax: 61 2 4751 7974
admin@icsei.net
www.icsei.net
The purpose of building and using an expanded base for advancing research, practice and policy in the area of school effectiveness and improvement. The Congress offers the opportunity to exchange information and networking for the educational community.

January
500 attendees

Dr. Lorna Earl, President
Dr. Alma Harris, President Elect

805 International Dyslexia Association Annual Conference
40 York Road
4th Floor
Baltimore, MD 21204-2044
410-296-0232
800-ABC-D123
Fax: 410-321-5069
info@interdys.org
www.interdys.org
Provide the most comprehensive range of information and services that address the full scope of dyslexia and related difficulties in learning to read and write.

November
3000 attendees

Darnella Parks, Conference Manager
Kristen Penczek, Conference Director

806 International Exhibit
National Institute for Staff & Organizational Dev.
University of Texas
1912 Speedway, Stop D5600
Austin, TX 78712-1607
512-471-7545
Fax: 512-471-9426
membership@nisod.oeg
www.nisod.org
The largest international conference to focus specifically on the celebration of teaching, learning, and leadership excellence.

May
1500 attendees

Sheryl Powell, Conference Director

807 International Listening Association Annual Convention
International Listening Association
Box 164
Belle Plaine, MN 56011
952-594-5697
Convention topics cover broad spectrum of listening practice and research. Papers, panels, courses, practice and workshops can be found at the convention in effort to network, spread research and new practices in effetcive listening training,

June

Dr. Nanette Johnson-Curiskis, Executive Director
Debra Worthington, Convention Planner

808 International Multicultural Institute (IMCI) Annual Conference
International Multicultural Institute
595 6th Street
Brooklyn, NY 11215
718-832-8625
www.imciglobal.org
Brings together practitioners from across the country and around the world to explore diversity and multiculturalism in both personal and professional contexts. Leaders from academia, business, and government present the latest thinking and action on diversity issues to conference participants.

June

Nancy J. Di Dia, Executive Director
Margaret Regan, President

809 International Reading Association Annual Convention
800 Barksdale Road
PO Box 8139
Newark, DE 19714-8139
302-731-1600
800-336-7323
Fax: 302-731-1057
customerservice@reading.org
www.reading.org
Contains exhibitors involved in various lectures and workshops dealing with illiteracy, literature and some library science courses.

May
800 booths with 13M attendees

Carrice C. Cummins, President
Marcie Craig Post, Executive Director

810 International Technology Education Association Conference
1914 Association Drive
Suite 201
Reston, VA 20191-1539
703-860-2100
Fax: 703-860-0353
iteea@iteea.org
www.iteea.org
Provides teachers with new and exciting ideas for educating students of all grade levels. The conference gives educators an opportunity for better understanding of the constant changes that take place in technology education.

varies
150 booths with 2,200+ attendees

Ken Starkman, Program Chair
Christine Maggio, Exhibit Opportunities

811 International Trombone Festival
International Trombone Association
PO Box 441
Coppell, TX 75019
888-684-2361
Fax: 888-684-2362
jon@trombonefestival.net
www.trombone.net
Annual festival giving trombonists the opportunity to meet and share with other trombonists for performances, lectures, exhibits, competitions and more.

June

John Drew, President
Jon Bohls, Festivals Director

812 Learning Disabilities Association of America International Conference
4156 Library Road
Pittsburgh, PA 15234-1349
412-341-1515
888-300-6710
Fax: 412-344-0224
info@ldaamerica.org
ldaamerica.org
The theme of the conference will be on discussing how people can create opportunities for those with learning disabilities through advocacy and collaboration.

February

Patricia Lillie, President
Mary-Clare Reynolds, Executive Director

National

813 2018 NADE Conference
PO Box 963
Northport, AL 35476
205-331-5997
877-233-9455
Fax: 866-519-1331
infonade2018@gmail.com
thenade.org
Conference for developmental education topics.

Johari Barnes, Conference Co-Chair
Karen Tompson-Wolfe, Conference Co-Chair

814 2018 NEA National Leadership Summit
National Education Association
1201 16th Street NW
Washington, DC 20036-3290
202-833-4000
Fax: 202-822-7974
leadershipsummits@nea.org
www.nea.org
Meant to empower NEA members and leaders, encouraging them to develop their leadership knowledge and skills. There will be interactive sessions and workshops exploring issues faced by the public education system.

March

Lily Eskelsen Garc¡a, President
Becky Pringle, Vice President

815 AAUW National Convention
American Association of University Women
1111 16th Street NW
Washington, DC 20036
202-785-7700
800-326-2289
Fax: 202-872-1425

convention@aauw.org
www.aauw.org
The nation's leading voice promoting education and equity for women and girls. Speakers, panels and workshops allow for networking with other AAUW members and explore opportunities to further empower women.
Katie Broendel, Media/PR Manager
Christy Jones, Membership Director

816 **ASCD Annual Conference & Exhibit Show**
1703 N Beauregard Street
Alexandria, VA 22311-1714
703-578-9600
800-933-2723
Fax: 703-575-5400
member@ascd.org
www.ascd.org
Explore the big ideas in education today, or examine new developments in your content area or grade level. Stretch your professional development learning into new areas, or pick an issue you care about most and examine it in depth.
March
12000 attendees
Barbara Gleason, Public Information Director
Christy Guilfoyle, Public Relations Specialist

817 **ASCD Educational Leadership Conference**
ASCD
1703 N Beauregard Street
Alexandria, VA 22311
703-578-9600
800-933-2723
Fax: 703-575-5400
press@ascd.org
www.ascd.org
The focus of the conference will be on instructional leadership, leveraging resources, and leading and supporting students and adults.
October
Ben Shuldiner, President
Deborah Delisle, CEO & Executive Director

818 **AZLA Conference**
Arizona Library Association
1030 E Baseline Road
Suite 105-1025
Tempe, AZ 85283
480-609-3999
Fax: 480-998-7838
admin@azla.org
www.azla.org
Advance the education advantages of the state through libraries, and to promote general interest in library extension (traveling libraries). Sometimes conference is a joint venture between two libraries(2014 held by AZLA and MPLA libraries).
November
90+ booths with 2,000 attendees
Rene Tanner, Conference Planning

819 **AdvancED**
National Study of School Evaluation
9115 Westside Parkway
Alpharetta, GA 30009-4958
678-392-2285
888-413-3669
Fax: 847-995-9088
contactus@advanc-ed.org
www.advanc-ed.org
Annual international summit held in Washington, DC. Share research on best educational practices, research based products. Research helps shape educational policy and strengthen learning practices worldwide.
November
Dr. Mark A Elgart, President/CEO

820 **American Association for Employment in Education Annual Conference**
American Association for Employment in Education
947 E. Johnstown Rd.
#170
Gahanna, OH 43230
614-485-1111
800-678-6010
Fax: 360-244-7802
aaee@osu.edu
www.aaee.org
Disseminate information on the educational marketplace, and job search process. Promote ethical standards and practices in the employment process. Promote dialogue and cooperation among institutions which prepare educators and institutions which provide employment opportunities.
November
20 booths with 150-200 attendees
Doug Peden, Executive Director
Diana Sanchez, Nat'l Conference Prog. Chair

821 **American Association of Colleges for Teacher Ed Annual Meeting and Exhibits**
1307 New York Avenue NW
Suite 300
Washington, DC 20005-4701
202-293-2450
Fax: 202-457-8095
aacte@aacte.org
www.aacte.org
Learning event for educator preparation professionals. Oppportunities for networking, advancing understanding of new concepts and theories, hear new research and discover innovative practices and programs.
Feb
75 booths with 2400 attendees
Sharon P Robinson, President/CEO
Gail M. Bozeman, VP Meetings and Events

822 **American Association of French Teachers Conference**
American Association of French Teachers
Mailcode 4510
Southern Illinois University
Carbondale, IL 62901-4510
618-453-5731
Fax: 618-453-5733
aatf@frenchteachers.org
www.frenchteachers.org/convention
Conventions regularly occur in French-speaking areas. Representing the French language in North America and to encourage the dissemination, both in the schools and in the general public, of knowledge concerning all aspects of the culture and civilization of France and the French-speaking world.
July
1100 attendees
Dr Jayne Abrate, Executive Director

823 **American Association of Physics Teachers National Meeting**
One Physics Ellipse
College Park, MD 20740-3311
301-209-3311
Fax: 301-209-0845
aapt-meet@aapt.org
www.aapt.org
Gives members the opportunity to network, discuss innovations in teaching methods and share the results of research about teaching and learning.
summer & winter
Tiffany Hayes, Director of Conferences
Cerena Cantrell, Associate Program Director

824 **American Association of School Librarians National Conference**
American Library Association
50 E Huron Street
Chicago, IL 60611
312-280-4382
800-545-2433
Fax: 312-280-5276
aasl@ala.org
www.ala.org/aasl
An open conference holding seminars, workshops and tours of local libraries and facilities.
October
3,000 attendees
Julie Walker, Executive Director
Melissa Jacobsen, Professional Development Mgr

825 **American Association of Sexuality Educators, Counselors & Therapists Conference**
1444 I Street NW
Suite 700
Washington, DC 20005-1960
202-449-1099
Fax: 202-216-9646
aasect@aasect.org
www.aasect.org
Facilitate productive discussions about identity and human sexuality; encourage interdisciplinary, intergenerational and cross-cultural collaboration and networking of current sexual health topics; provide opportunities for developing and refining skills in sexuality education, therapy, counseling and research
06/20-06/24
50 booths with 400-500 attendees
Dee Ann Walker, Executive Director
Carey Roth Bayer, Conference Co Chair

826 **American Camp Association National Conference**
American Camp Association
5000 State Road 67 N
Martinsville, IN 46151-7902
765-342-8456
800-428-2267
Fax: 765-342-2065
conference@ACAcamps.org
www.acacamps.org
Largest national camp conference hosted in the United States. Focuses on professional development, networking and commerce.
February
175 booths with 1500 attendees
Peg Smith, CEO
Kim Bruno, Marketing Manager

827 **American Council on Education Annual Meeting**
American Council on Education
1 Dupont Circle NW
Washington, DC 20036
202-939-9444
annualmeeting@ace.nche.edu
www.acenet.edu
Brings together higher education leaders from all sectors. The American Council on

Education annual meeting is seen as the go-to event to network with colleagues, hear about emerging trends from national thought leaders and learn about new approaches to campus challenges.

March
74 booths

Judy C Miner, Chair
Barbara R Snyder, Vice Chair & Chair-Elect

828 American Council on the Teaching of Foreign Languages Annual Conference
101 N Fairfax Street
Suite 200
Alexandria, VA 22314
703-894-2900
Fax: 703-894-2905
morehouse@actfl.org
www.actfl.org
More than 600 professional development opportunities, including pre and post convention workshops and sessions focused on all aspects of teachiing and learning languages and cultures.

November
250 booths with 6,000+ attendees

Julia Richardson, Convention Coordinator
Marty Abbott, Executive Director

829 American Counseling Association Annual Conference & Expo
American Counseling Association
5999 Stevenson Avenue
Alexandria, VA 22304-3302
703-823-9800
800-347-6647
Fax: 703-823-0252
rhayes@counseling.org
www.counseling.org
Education sessions, speakers, mental health training and time and space for networking with other professionals in the mental health field.

March
4000 attendees

Robin Hayes, Convention & Meeting Contact
Theresa Holmes, Convention & Meeting Contact

830 American Educational Research Association Annual Brown Lecture
American Educational Research Association
1430 K Street NW
Suite 1200
Washington, DC 20005
202-238-3200
Fax: 202-238-3250
flevine@aera.net
www.aera.net
Features lectures on the vital role research plays in improving equality and equity in education.

October

Deborah Loewenberg Ball, President
Felice J Levine, Executive Director

831 American Indian Science & Engineering Society Annual Conference
AISES
PO Box 9828
Albuquerque, NM 87119-9828
505-765-1052
Fax: 505-765-5608
info@aises.org
www.aises.org
Provides an opportunity for networking, educational workshops, a career fair, showcase academic research and study and how to bridge the waysbewtween tradition and STEM.

November
3000 attendees

Chris Echohawk, Vice Chair
Dr. Mary Jo Ondrechen, Chair

832 American Library Association (ALA) Annual Conference
American Library Association
50 E Huron
Chicago, IL 60611
312-944-6780
800-545-2433
Fax: 312-440-9374
ala@ala.org
www.ala.org
Programs, updates, conversations about key issues like digital content, e-books, technology in libraries, books, leadership, literacy advocacy, community engagement and library marketing. Also a great way to network with other librarians and libraries.

June/January
20000+ attendees

Alicia Babcock, Conference Services
Keith Fiels, Executive Director

833 American Mathematical Society
American Mathematical Society
201 Charles Street
Providence, RI 02904-2294
401-455-4000
800-321-4267
Fax: 401-331-3842
meet@ams.org
www.ams.org
Advance mathematical achievement, encouraging research and provide communication necessary to progress in the field. Preserve, supplement and utilize the results of the research of mathematicians throughout the world.

January

Dr. Donald McClure, Executive Director
Penny Pina, Director Meetings/Conference

834 American Montessori Society Conference
116 East 16th St
New York, NY 10003-2163
212-358-1250
Fax: 212-358-1256
ams@amshq.org
amshq.org
Promotes quality Montessori education for all children from birth to 18 years of age. Conference participants share knowledge and research and strengthen bonds while creating new networks. Conference workshops address curriculum, socio-emotional development, leadership, public policy, research and more.

March

Mary Ellen Kordas, President
Timothy Purnell, EdD, Executive Director

835 American Psychological Association Annual Conference
750 1st Street NE
Washington, DC 20002-4242
202-336-5500
800-374-2721
Fax: 202-336-6123
convention@apa.org
www.apa.org
A national conference attended by psychologists from around the world. The conference has workshops, lectures, discussions, roundtables and symposiums.

August
13,000 attendees

Donald N Bersoff, Ph.D, JD, President

836 American Public Health Association Annual Meeting
American Public Health Association
800 I Street NW
Washington, DC 20001-3710
202-777-2742
Fax: 202-777-2534
anna.keller@apha.org
www.apha.org
The premier platform to share successes and failures, discover exceptional best practices and learn from expert colleagues and the latest research in the field.

November
650 booths with 13000 attendees

Georges C. Benjamin, Executive Director
James E. Dale, CoA Chair

837 American School Health Association's National School Conference
Hilton St. Louis at the BallPark
1 S Broadway
St. Louis, MO 63102
703-506-7675
Fax: 703-506-3266
info@ashaweb.org
www.ashaweb.org
Attendees include school nurses, health educators, health counselors, physicians and students. During the conference, presentations are made by ASHA members, government officials and health education professionals covering a variety of issues centered around child and adolescent health.

October
40 booths with 500 attendees

Sharon Murray, MHSE, FASHA, President
Ty Oehrtman, MS,MCHES,FASHA, Vice President

838 American Speech-Language-Hearing Association Annual Convention
ASHA
2200 Research Blvd.
Rockville, MD 20850-3289
301-296-5700
800-638-8255
Fax: 301-296-8580
convention@asha.org
www.asha.org
A scientific and professional conference of speech-language pathology, audiology and other professionals. Opportunity to learn about latest evidence based research , enhance clinical skills, improve technique and gain new tools and resources to advance career.

Annual
November
400 booths with 12,000 attendees

Arlene A Pietranton, CEO
Patricia A. Prelock, President

839 American Technical Education Association Annual Conference
American Technical Education Association
Dunwoody College of Technology
818 Dunwoody Blvd.
Minneapolis, MN 55403
612-381-3315
info@ateaonline.org
www.ateaonline.org
Administrators/directors and faculty of various technical institutes, junior colleges, universities

and colleges. Topics cover all aspects of computer assisted instruction, distance education and technical education. Professional development opportunity for all involved in postsecondary technical education.

March
35 booths with 700 attendees and 75 exhibits

Dr. Sandra Krebsbach, Executive Director
DeeAnn Bilben, Administrative Assistant

840 Annual Effective Schools Conference
7227 North 16th Street
Suite 190
Phoenix, AZ 85020
866-626-7556
Fax: 888-756-7628
now@4aplus.com
www.effectiveschoolsconference2013.com
Latest research and methods for creating successful educational environments where all students can reach their academic potential. Gain valuable hands-on experience, learn proven implementation strategies and hear from some of the greatest minds in the field.

March

Amber Countiss
Annie Hanks

841 Annual International Conference on ADHD
4601 Presidents Drive
Suite 300
Lanham, MD 20706
301-306-7070
Fax: 301-306-7090
customer_service@chadd.org
www.chadd.org
The conference will feature research, practice, and public information on ADHD. It will bring together children and adults with ADHD, clinicians, educators, researchers, coaches, organizers, advocates, and others.

November
60 booths

Michael MacKay, President
April Gower, Chief Operating Officer

842 Annual NCEA Convention & Exposition
National Catholic Educational Association
1005 North Glebe Road
Suite 525
Arlington, VA 22201-3852
571-257-0010
800-711-6232
Fax: 703-243-0025
nceaadmin@ncea.org
www.ncea.org
Attendees represent all aspects of Catholic and faith based education from pre-school to universities, to local parishes and more. Provides development sessions, departmental meetings, special events in order to gain knowledge and network with fellow colleagues.

Annually
April

Regina M. Haney, Executive Director
Amy Durkin, Convention/Events

843 Association for Behavior Analysis Annual Convention
Association for Behavior Analysis
550 W. Centre Ave.
Portage, MI 49024-5364
269-492-9310
Fax: 269-492-9316
convention@abainternational.org
www.abainternational.org
Psychologists, psychology faculty and students, counselors and social workers are among the attendees of this conference offering over 25 exhibitors. The conference is research and education oriented.

43 booths

Maria E Malott, PhD, CEO

844 Association for Behavioral and Cognitive Therapies Annual Convention
305 7th Avenue
16th Floor
New York, NY 10001-6008
212-647-1890
Fax: 212-647-1865
mebrown@abct.org
www.abct.org
Provide participants with clinical knowledge of specific issues or new research in the field, networking possibilities, clinical roundtable, panel discussions on training and symposia of the presentation of data or research.

November
2,000 attendees

Mary Ellen Brown, Education/Mtg Services Dir.
Mary Jane Eimer, Executive Director

845 Association for Education Finance and Policy
6703 Madison Creek
Columbia, MO 65203
573-814-9878
Fax: 314-256-2831
info@aefpweb.org
www.aefpweb.org
The conference theme changes yearly; this year the focus is education renewal and reform and the fact that domestic policy and global economic competition challenge our education system. The conference will present, discuss and evaluate the latest research on education topics and current reforms and policy directions.

March
3000 attendees

Deborah Cunningham, President
Angela M. Hull, Executive Director

846 Association for Education in Journalism and Mass Communication Convention
AEJMC
234 Outlet Pointe Boulevard
Suite A
Columbia, SC 29210-5667
803-798-0271
Fax: 803-772-3509
www.aejmc.org
Featuring the latest in technology as well as special sessions on teaching, research and public service in the various components of journalism and mass communication — from advertising and public relations to radio and television journalism to media management and newspapers.

August
1,500 attendees

Fred Williams, Convention Manager
Jennifer McGill, Executive Director

847 Association for Interdisciplinary Studies Annual Conference
University of Maryland
1000 Hilltop Circle
Baltimore, MD 21250
410-455-2004
ais-2017@umbc.edu
ais2017.umbc.edu
The theme will be "applied and experiential learning through an interdisciplinary lens."

October

Eric Brown, Conference Coordinator

848 Association for Persons with Severe Handicaps Annual Conference
1001 Connecticut Ave NW
Suite 235
Washington, DC 20036
202-540-9020
Fax: 202-540-9019
info@tash.org
www.tash.org
Provides a forum for individuals with disabilities, families, researchers, educators, scholars, and others to create dialogue around creating action for social and systems reform.

December
2,500 attendees

Barbara Trader, Executive Director

849 Association for Play Therapy Conference
Marriott City Center
30 S 7th Street
Minneapolis, MN 55402
559-298-3400
Fax: 559-298-3410
info@a4pt.org
www.a4pt.org
Major interdisciplinary event for Play Therapists wishing to earn continuing education credits, network with popular authors, speakers and vendors and enjoy extra curricular activities with peers.

October

Jodi Crane, Chair
Kathryn Lebby, President & CEO

850 Association for Science Teacher Education Annual Meeting
The Association For Science Teacher Education
5040 Haley Center
Auburn, AL 36849
972-690-2496
executivedirector@theaste.org
www.theaste.com
Offers programs in science, mathematics and environmental education with a wide variety of teachers and professors attending.

January

Kathy Cabe Trundle, President
Bob Hollon, Executive Director

851 Association for the Advancement of International Education
Nova Southeastern University
11501 N. Military Trail
Palm Beach Gardens, FL 33418
561-805-2193
Fax: 561-805-2187
g.nicoll@nove.edu
www.aaie.org
Provides the organizational leadership to initiate and promote an understanding of the need for and the support of American/International education.

February
70 booths with 550 attendees

Elleana Austin, Administrative Assistant
Elsa Lamb, Executive Director

852 Association for the Education of Gifted Underachieving Students Conference
6 Wildwood Street
Burlington, MA 01803

651-962-5385
aegusquestions@gmail.com
www.aegus1.org
Attended by teachers, professors, administrators and social workers, this conference deals with cultural awareness and education of the disabled and gifted students.
April
Lois Baldwin, President
Terry Neu, Vice President

853 **Association for the Study of Higher Education Annual Meeting**
University Of Nevada
4505 S. Maryland Parkway
453068
Las Vegas, NV 89154-3068
702-895-2737
Fax: 702-895-4269
ashe@unlv.edu
www.ashe.ws
Promotes collaboration among its members and others engaged in the study of higher education; as a community of scholarly practice and as practicing scholars and educators.
November
Kim Nehls, Executive Director
Christal Allen, Conference Coordinator

854 **Association of American Colleges & Universities Annual Meeting**
Association of American Colleges & Universities
1818 R Street NW
Washington, DC 20009-1604
202-387-3760
Fax: 202-265-9532
www.aacu.org
Bringing together college educators from across institutional types, disciplines, and departments. Providing participants with innovative ideas and practices, and shaping the direction of their educational reform efforts.
January
1,200 attendees
Carol Geary, President

855 **Association of Community College Trustees Conference**
1233 20th Street NW
Suite 301
Washington, DC 20036-2907
202-775-4667
Fax: 202-223-1297
acctinfo@acct.org
www.acct.org
Exists to develop effective lay governing board leadership to strengthen the capacity of community colleges to achieve their missions on behalf of their communities.
1500+ attendees
J. Noah Brown, President/CEO
Lila Farmer, Conference Logistics Coord.

856 **Association of Mathematics Teacher Educators Annual Conference**
AMTE, c/o Meredith College
3800 Hillsborough Street
Raleigh, NC 27607
919-760-8240
Fax: 919-760-8763
harpersr@miamioh.edu
amte.net/conferences/conf2018
Annual conference for mathematics educators to come together and exchange the latest research and practice findings applicable to their fields of study.
February
Randy Philipp, President
Tim Hendrix, Executive Director

857 **Association of Science-Technology Centers Incorporated Conference**
Association of Science-Technology Centers Incorp.
1025 Vermont Avenue NW
Suite 500
Washington, DC 20005-3516
202-783-7200
Fax: 202-783-7207
conference@astc.org
www.astc.org
An organization of science centers and museums dedicated to furthering the public understanding of science. ASTC encourages excellence and innovation in informal science learning by serving and linking its members worldwide and advancing the common goals.
October
165 booths with 1600 attendees
David Corson, Mgr. Conference/Exhibit Hall
Nina Humes, Meetings/Conference Coord.

858 **Association of Teacher Educators Annual Meeting**
11350 Random Hills Road
Suite 800, PMB 6
Fairfax, VA 22030
703-659-1708
Fax: 703-595-4792
info@ate1.org
www.ate1.org
This conference will center on Academic proposals submitted online. The conference is a call for teacher educators to act as public intellectuals through social re-imagining, inquiry, and participation in educational policy-making.
February
Karen Embry Jenlink, President
Patricia Tate, First Vice President

859 **Center for Appalachian Studies Annual Conference**
Appalachian Studies Center
One John Marshall Drive
Huntington, WV 25755-0918
304-696-2904
mthomas@marshall.edu
www.appalachianstudies.org
Central theme each year about some facet of Appalachia- communities, landscapes, evoulution of their work together-history, etc.
March
Katherine Ledford, Conference Chair
Mary Thomas, Executive Director

860 **Center on Disabilities Conference**
Students with Disabilities Resources
1811 Nordhoff
Bayramian Hall 110
Northridge, CA 91330-8264
818-677-1200
conference@csun.edu
www.csun.edu/cod
Provides a setting for researchers, practitioners, exhibitors, end users, speakers and participants to share knowledge and best practices in the field of assistive technology.
March
130 booths with 4800 attendees
Wayne Fernades, Mktg/Events Manager
Sandy Plotin, Managing Director

861 **Choristers Guild's National Festival & Directors' Conference**
Choristers Guild
12404 Park Central Drive
Suite 100
Dallas, TX 75251-1802
469-398-3606
800-246-7478
Fax: 469-398-3611
conferences@mailcg.org
www.choristersguild.org
Enables leaders to nurture the spiritual and musical growth of children and youth.
June
Jim Rindelaub, Director
Eve Hehn, Conferences

862 **Closing the Gap**
526 Main Street
PO Box 68
Henderson, MN 56044-0068
507-248-3294
Fax: 507-248-3810
info@closingthegap.com
www.closingthegap.com
Conference themes change yearly. Always focus on technology and howit changes—primarily with assistive technology.
October
150+ booths with 2400 attendees
Jan Latzke, Conference Registration
Connie Kneip, VP/General Manager

863 **Conference for Advancement of Mathematics Teaching**
Texas Education Agency
PO Box 200669
Austin, TX 78720-0669
512-335-2268
Fax: 512-335-8517
camt@camtonline.org
www.camtonline.org
Exhibits educational materials useful to mathematics teachers; education of the use of technology on the classroom and effective use of manipulative materials in the classroom.
July
175 booths with 7.5M-8M attendees
Joyce Polanco, Program Chair

864 **Council for Exceptional Children Annual Convention**
The Council for Exceptional Children
2900 Crystal Drive
Suite 100
Arlington, VA 22202-3557
703-620-3660
888-232-7733
Fax: 703-264-9494
service@cec.sped.org
www.cec.sped.org
The convention & expo is a special education professional development event. The event features educational sessions, opportunities to network with others working with children and learn about new and pending legislation, as well as a chance to explore cutting edge products and services.
February
Mikki Garcia, President
Laurie VanderPloeg, President Elect

865 EDUCAUSE Anuual Convention
282 Century Place
Suite 5000
Louisville, KY 80027
303-449-4430
Fax: 303-440-0461
info@educause.edu
www.educause.edu
Provides opportunity for educators to network with colleagues and learn form each other by sharing experience, ideas and information through presentations and sessions.
October
4,000+ attendees and 180 exhibits
Diana Oblinger, President
Beverly Williams, Conference Director

866 Education Market Association
8380 Colesville Road
Silver Spring, MD 20910
301-495-0240
800-395-5550
Fax: 301-495-3330
awatts@nssea.org
www.edmarket.org
Lists 1,500 member dealers and manufacturers representatives for school supplies, equipment and instructional materials.
March
1200 booths with 5,000 attendees and 700 exhibits
Adrienne Dayton, VP of Marketing/Communicatio
Jim McGarry, President/ CEO

867 Education in the Digital Age
1615 Duke Street
Alexandria, VA 22314
703-528-0700
Fax: 703-841-1543
info@aasa.org
www.aasa.org
Conference for school administrators to hear education leaders, see exhibits and network. The theme of this year's meeting will be education in the digital age.
February
Daniel A Domenech, Executive Director
Chuck Woodruff, Chief Operating Officer

868 Educational Publishing Summit
Association of Educational Publishers
300 Martin Luther King Blvd.
Suite 200
Wilmington, DE 19801
302-295-8350
Fax: 302-656-2918
mail@aepweb.org
www.aepweb.org
Presents a range of informative and practical sessions that address all issues relating to the development and distribution of high-quality learning resources.
June
Charlene F Gaynor, CEO
JoAnn McDevitt, VP Sales/Mrktg/Business Dev.

869 Educational Theatre Association Conference
Educational Theatre Association
2343 Auburn Avenue
Cincinnati, OH 45219-2815
513-421-3900
Fax: 513-421-7077
mpeitz@edta.org
www.edta.org
Supports the association's mission by supporting educators through networking opportunities, educational workshops, speakers and resources that can enrich students' educational experience.
September
2,400 attendees
Julie Woffington, Executive Director
Gloria McIntyre, President

870 Foundation for Critical Thinking Regional Workshop & Conference
Foundation for Critical Thinking
PO Box 196
Tomales, CA 94971
707-878-9100
800-833-3645
Fax: 707-878-9111
cct@criticalthinking.org
www.criticalthinking.org
Investigates and reports on the value and use of analytical thinking programs and curriculum in the classroom.
July
Dr Linda Elder, President

871 INFOCOMM Tradeshow
InfoComm International
11242 Waples Mill Road
Suite 200
Fairfax, VA 22030
703-273-7200
800-659-7469
Fax: 703-273-5924
inief@chiefmfg.com
www.infocommshow.org
Designed for professionals in the audiovisual, information communications and system integration industries. Attendees can explore audiovisual products and services from the industry's leading manufacturers, and there are educational seminars, workshops and labs taught with a focus on technology, trends and the best practices in the country.
June
David Labuskes, Executive Director
Jason McGraw, Sr. VP Expositions

872 Independent Education Consultants Association Conference
3251 Old Lee Highway
Suite 510
Fairfax, VA 22030-1504
703-591-4850
800-888-4322
Fax: 703-591-4860
info@IECAonline.com
www.IECAonline.com
Attended by consultants, school, college and program admissions officers, administrators and staff and related service companies. Workshops and discussions led by leaders in their fields including specialists in educational trends, college admissions and boarding school issues, adolescent development, learning differences and emotional disorders and treatments.
Spring & Fall
400 booths with 800 attendees
Mark H Sklarow, Executive Director
Rachel King, Conference Manager

873 International Performance Improvement Conference
International Society for Performance
PO Box 13035
Silver Spring, MD 20910
301-587-8570
Fax: 301-587-8573
info@ispi.org
www.ispi.org
Provides educational opportunities with sessions in multiple formats across multiple tracks, keynote presentations, networking opportunities with other performance minded professionals across the spectrum of performance improvement disciplines.
April
60 booths with 1500 attendees
Ellen Kaplan, Conference Manager

874 Iteachk
Staff Development for Educators
10 Sharon Road
PO Box 577
Peterborough, NH 03458
603-924-9621
800-462-1478
Fax: 800-337-9929
www.sde.com
Explore new technology engaging teachers and students, new games and tools for students, meet and learn from nation's top kindergarten experts, use strategies right away and network with others.
Jim Grant, Executive Director/Founder
Terra Tarango, President

875 Journalism Education Association National Convention
828 Mid-Campus Drive S
105 Kedzie Hall
Manhattan, KS 66506-1505
785-532-5532
866-532-5532
Fax: 785-532-5563
staff@jea.org
jea.org
Semiannual gathering of high school journalists and advisers to discuss topics relevant to the profession of Journalism, to network and to participate in professional learning workshops.
November
Sarah Nichols, President
Valerie Kibler, Vice President

876 Lutheran Education Association National School Administrators Conference
Lutheran Education Association
7400 Augusta Street
River Forest, IL 60305
708-209-3343
Fax: 708-209-3458
lea@lea.org
www.lea.org
Conference will feature workshops, sectionals, plenary sessions, and a learning mall for administrators of schools.
Mike Oldenburg, Chair
Jonathan Laabs, Ed.D, Executive Director

877 MEMSPA Annual State Conference
Michigan Elementary & Middle School Principals
Association
1980 N. College Road
Mason, MI 48854
517-694-8955
800-227-0824
Fax: 517-694-8945
bob@memspa.org
www.memspa.org
Professional association for elementary & middle level principals.
Annual/December
Paul Liabenow, Executive Director
Rob Kauffman, President

878 MTNA National Conference
MTNA National Headquarters
1 W 4th Street
Suite 1550
Cincinnati, OH 45202
513-421-1420
888-512-5278
Fax: 513-421-2503
mtnanet@mtna.org
www.mtna.org
Brings together representatives of the Music Teachers National Association. The conference features performances by students, classes, technology and informational sessions, pedagogy sessions, an exhibit hall and more.
March
Scott McBride Smith, NCTM, President
Gary L Ingle, Executive Director & CEO

879 Modern Language Association Annual Conference
26 Broadway
3rd Floor
New York, NY 10004-1789
646-576-5000
Fax: 646-458-0030
convention@mla.org
www.mla.org
Opportunity for memberes to share scholarly findings and teaching experience and discuss trends in the academy.
January
2000+ attendees
Rosemary G. Feal, Executive Director

880 Music Teachers Association National Conference
Music Teachers National Association
441 Vine Street
Suite 3100
Cincinnati, OH 45202-3004
513-421-1420
888-512-5278
Fax: 513-421-2503
mtnanet@mtna.org
www.mtna.org
Supports and supplies music teachers with information on development and training.
March
160 booths with 2000 attendees
Brian Shepard, Deputy Executive Director
Gary L. Ingle, Executive Director/CEO

881 NAAEE Annual Conference
North American Assoc for Environmental Education
2000 P Street NW
Suite 540
Washington, DC 20036
202-419-0412
Fax: 212-419-0415
info@naaee.net
www.naaee.net
Promotes environmental education in the classroom and public, shares the latest research and information.
October
1000+ attendees
Judy Braus, Executive Director
Lori Mann, Conference Manager

882 NABSE Annual Conference
National Alliance of Black School Educators
310 Pennsylvania Avenue SE
Washington, DC 20003
202-608-6310
800-221-2654
Fax: 202-608-6319
info@nabse.org
www.nabse.org
Offers educational workshops, plenary sessions, informative presentations, public forums, networking and fellowship.
November
300 booths with 6,000 attendees
Marietta English, President
Sheila Harrison-Williams, Ph.D, Treasurer

883 NAESP Pre-K-8 Principals Conference
1615 Duke Street
Alexandria, VA 22314
703-684-3345
800-386-2377
Fax: 703-549-5568
naesp@naesp.org
www.naespconference.org
Conference for Pre-K-8 principals to connect with peers, learn the best practices within their profession and prepare for the challenges ahead. Some topics that will be covered include Leading Learning Communities, Technology and Social Media, Arts Education and High Leverage Leadership.
July
Brian K Partin, President
L Earl Franks, Ed.D., CAE, Executive Director

884 NAFSA: National Association of International Educators
1307 New York Ave. NW
8th Floor
Washington, DC 20005-4701
202-737-3699
800-836-4994
Fax: 202-737-3657
inbox@nafsa.org
www. nafsa.org
Annual meeting of professionals in the field of international education, for training workshops, educational sessions, networking opportunities and special events.
May
150 booths with 8,500 attendees
Marlene M. Johnson, Executive Director/CEO
Chris Seamens, Conference Program, Coord.

885 NASDSE National Conference
National Association of State Directors of Special
Education
225 Reinekers Lane, Suite 420
Alexandria, VA 22314
703-519-3800
Fax: 703-519-3808
nasdse@nasdse.org
www.nasdse.org
Multiple presentations, Annual business meeting for state directors and networking opportunities.
Colleen Riley, President
Bill East, Executive Director

886 NASPA Annual Conference
NASPA-Student Affairs Administrators in Higher
Education
111 K Street NE, 10th Floor
Washington, DC 20002
202-265-7500
Fax: 202-898-5737
office@naspa.org
www.naspa.org
Exchange ideas with peers, earn continuing education credits, build new partnerships with vendors, gain tools and ideas and remain current on issues.
Annual/March
5000 attendees
Kevin Kruger, President
Arlene Kidwell, Sr. Director of Meetings

887 NELA Annual Conference
New England Library Association
55 North Main Street
Unit 49
Belchertown, MA 01007
413-813-5254
Fax: 603-654-3526
rscheier@gmail.com
www.nelib.org
Bringing together librarians from New England in a forum to educate and network about moving libraries into the 21st century.
600 attendees
Robert Scheier, Association Administrator
Mary Ann Rupert, Conference Manager

888 NJLA Spring Conference
New Jersey Library Association
PO Box 1534
Trenton, NJ 08607
609-394-8032
Fax: 609-394-8164
ptumulty@njla.org
www.njla.org
1139 attendees
Patricia A Tumulty, Executive Director
Susan Rice, Office Manager

889 NSEE Annual Conference
National Society for Experiential Education
19 Mantua Road
Mount Royal, NJ 08061
856-423-3427
Fax: 856-423-3420
nsee@talley.com
www.nsee.org
The purpose of the conference is to foster the effective use of experience as an integral part of education, in order to empower learners and promote the common good.
September
Stephanie Thomason, President
Haley Brust, Executive Director

890 NSTA Annual Conference
National Science Teachers Association
1840 Wilson Boulevard
Arlington, VA 22201-3000
703-243-7100
888-400-6782
Fax: 703-243-7177
conferences@nsta.org
www.nsta.org
To promote excellence and innovation in science teaching and learning for all. Discover strategies for improving science teaching and learning, engage in professional discussions, receive the latest information of science education and network with colleagues from across the country and the globe.
April
Dr. Karen L. Ostlund, President
Dr. Gerald F. Wheeler, Interim Executive Director

891 National Academy Foundation NEXT
National Academy Foundation
218 West 40th Street
5th Floor
New York, NY 10018
212-635-2400
Fax: 212-635-2409
www.naf.org

Formerly the Institute for Staff Development, NEXT is a professional learning experience that will ignite innovation and spread effective practices across

July

JD Hoye, President
David Moore, Sr. VP Programs

892 National Art Education Association Annual Convention
National Art Education Association
1806 Robert Fulton Drive
Suite 300
Reston, VA 20191-1590
703-860-8000
Fax: 703-860-2960
info@arteducators.org
www.arteducators.org
Provides substantive professional development services that include the advancement of knowledge in all sessions, events and activities for the purpose of improving visual arts instruction in American schools.

March
171 booths with 5,000 attendees

Kathy Duse, Conference Manager
Deborah B. Reeve, Executive Director

893 National Association for Bilingual Education
8701 Georgia Avenue
Suite 700
Silver Spring, MD 20910-4018
240-450-3700
Fax: 240-450-3799
nabe@nabe.org
www.nabe.org
Contains publishers and Fortune 500 companies displaying educational materials and multi-media products. Educational materials, products and services for use in linguistically and culturally diverse learning environments.

March
350 booths with 2,000+ attendees

Dr. Santiago Wood, Executive Director
Nilda Aguirre, Conference Coordinator

894 National Association for College Admission Counseling Conference
Nat'l Association for College Admission Counseling
1050 N Highland Street
Suite 400
Arlington, VA 22201-2818
703-836-2222
800-822-6285
Fax: 703-243-9375
info@nacacnet.org
www.nacacnet.org
Membership association offering information to counselors and guidance professionals working in the college admissions office.

September
142 booths with 4,000 attendees

Joyce E. Smith, CEO
Bethany Blue Chirico, Director of Conference/Mtgs

895 National Association for Girls and Women in Sports Yearly Conference
1900 Association Drive
Reston, VA 20191-1598
703-476-3543
800-213-7193
Fax: 703-476-4566
nagws@aahperd.org
www.aahperd.org/nagws
An association providing information for girls and women in sports.

March/April
280 booths with 6,000 attendees

Lynda Ransdell, President
Sandra K. Sims, VP of Programs/Convention

896 National Association for Multicultural Education
NAME National Office
2100 M Street
Suite 170-245
Washington, DC 20037
202-628-6263
Fax: 202-628-6264
name@nameorg.org
www.nameorg.org
Opportunity to build networks, confront challenges and renews sense of possibility and hope in making schools and societies a better place through community advocacy and multicultural education.

Bette Tate Beaver, Executive Director

897 National Association of Biology Teachers Conference
1313 Dolley Madison Blvd.
Suite 402
McLean, VA 22101
703-264-9696
888-501-6228
Fax: 703-790-2672
office@nabt.org
www.nabt.org
Speakers, hands-on workshops, informative sessions teaching biology in the 21st century.

November
140 booths with 1,700 attendees

Jaclyn Reeves-Pepin, Executive Director
Matthew D. Wells, Conference Committee

898 National Association of Independent Schools Conference
National Association of Independent Schools
1129 20th Street NW
Suite 800
Washington, DC 20036-3425
202-973-9700
Fax: 888-316-3862
annualconference@nais.org
www.nais.org
New ways to cultivate leadership in independent schools- for administrators, faculty and students- with workshops and speakers.

February/March
166 booths with 4000 attendees

Patrick Bassett, President
Amy Ahart, Director Annual Conference

899 National Association of Private Schools for Exceptional Children Conference
1522 K Street NW
Suite 1032
Washington, DC 20005-1211
202-408-3338
Fax: 202-408-3340
napsec@aol.com
www.napsec.com
This in an annual conference that is held for administrators/directors/principals and private school educators.

January
300 attendees and 8 exhibits

Sherry L. Kolbe, Executive Director/CEO

900 National Association of School Psychologists Annual Convention
4340 EW Highway
Suite 402
Bethesda, MD 20814
301-657-0270
866-331-6277
Fax: 301-657-0275
convention@naspweb.org
www.nasponline.org
Gathering of school psychologists and related professionals, offering workshops, seminars, symposia, papers, presentations and exhibits on topics from solutions for individual children to answers to your most difficult professional challenges and find ways to be a more efficient and effective practitioner.

April
100 booths with 4000 attendees

Susan Gorin, Executive Director
Marcia Harvey, Manager, Conventions

901 National Association of State Directors of Teacher Education and Certification Conference
1629 K Street NW
Suite 300
Washington, DC 20006
202-204-2208
Fax: 202-204-2210
nasdtec@attbi.com
NASDTEC is the National Association of State Directors of Teacher Education and Certification. It is the organization that represents professional standards boards and commissions and state departments of education in all 50 states.

June

Phillip S. Rogers, Executive Director

902 National Association of Student Financial Aid Administrators Conference
1801 Pennsylvania Avenue NW
Suite 850
Washington, DC 20006-3606
202-785-0453
Fax: 202-785-1487
info@nasfaa.org
www.nasfaa.org
Provides opportunities to learn and teach best practices in student financial aid, discover new products and services, network with others in the field and more.

June
2,300 attendees

Billie Jo Hamilton, National Chair
Justin Draeger, President & CEO

903 National Black Child Development Institute Annual Conference
1313 L Street NW
Suite 110
Washington, DC 20005-4110
202-833-2220
800-556-2234
Fax: 202-833-8222
moreinfo@ndcdi.orh
www.nbcdi.org
Educators and professionals in early care and education; elementary and secondary education and administration; child welfare and youth development; research; and local, state and federal policy convene to gain knowledge and acquire skills needed to ensure a quality future for all children and youth.

October

Felicia DeHaney, Pd.D, President/CEO
Keami Harris, Director of Programs

904 **National Coalition for Aviation and Space Education**
Omni Rosen Hotel
Orlando, FL
334-953-5095
mail@ncase.info
www.ncase.info
Provides educators with the tools that make classroom learning fun.
April

905 **National Coalition of ESEA Title 1 Parents**
310 Pennsylvania Ave. SE
3rd Floor
Washington, DC 20003
205-923-7955
Fax: 205-925-5403
ethomas@nctic1p.org
www.nctic1p.org
Annual In-Service Professional Development conference on current education laws, legislation and educational issues with the assistance of the Department of Education.
October
Ernestine Thomas, President

906 **National Conference on Student Services**
Magna Publications
2718 Dryden Drive
Madison, WI 53704
608-246-3590
800-206-4805
Fax: 608-246-3597
carriej@magnapubs.com
www.magnapubs.com
Build strong foundation as a student leader, secure leadership skills and experience a possibly life-changing event.
April
35 booths with 500 attendees
Susan Liimata, Conference Manager
Catherine Stover, Managing Editor

907 **National Council on Alcoholism & Drug Abuse**
9355 Olive Boulevard
St. Louis, MO 63132
314-962-3456
Fax: 314-968-7394
info@ncada-stl.org
www.ncada-stl.org
A not-for-profit community health agency serving the metropolitan St. Louis area, provides educational materials on substance abuse and addiction, information and referral services, prevention and intervention.
Jim Murphy, President
Jenny Armbruster, Director, Community Services

908 **National Council on Rehabilitation Education Spring 2018 Conference**
1099 E Champlain Drive
Suite A, 137
Fresno, CA 93720
559-906-0787
Fax: 559-412-2550
info@ncre.org
ncre.org
The theme will be on the improvement of rehabilitation services for people with disabilities. Some topics to be addressed include Access to Treatment for disorders, Disability and Employment, Barriers to Service Among Marginalized Individuals, Public Policies and Legislation and more.
March
Michael Accordino, D.Ed,CRC,LMHC, President
Denise Catalano, Ph.D, CRC, First Vice President

909 **National Dropout Prevention Network Conference**
Clemson University
209 Martin Street
Clemson, SC 29631-1555
864-656-2599
864-656-2675
Fax: 864-656-0136
ndpc@clemson.edu
dropoutprevention.org
Networking opportunity for educators and counselors who work with at-risk students. Some subject areas that will be covered include absenteeism, workforce development, parent and family engagement, arts studies, alternative education and more.
October
Denise Gianforcaro, Registration
Debra Andrews, Coordination

910 **National Forum to Advance Rural Education**
National Rural Education Association
615 McCallie Avenue
Hunter Hall 212
Chattanooga, TN 37421
423-425-4539
allen-pratt@utc.edu
www.nrea.net
The National Forum to Advance Rural Education will address issues that affect rural educators.
October
35 booths
Allison Nys, President
Allen Pratt, Ed.D, Executive Director

911 **National Guild of Community Arts Education**
520 8th Avenue
Suite 302, 3rd Floor
New York, NY 10018
212-268-3337
Fax: 212-268-3995
info@natguild.org
www.nationalguild.org
The National Guild of Community Schools of the Arts fosters and promotes the creation and growth of high-quality arts education in communities across the country. The Guild provides community arts organizations with multiple levels of support, including training, advocacy, information resources, and high-profile leadership in arts education.
November
15 booths with 300 attendees and 15 exhibits
Jonathan Herman, Executive Director
Heather Ikemire, Director

912 **National Head Start Association Annual Conference**
1651 Prince Street
Alexandria, VA 22314
703-739-0875
866-677-8724
www.nhsa.org
Seeks to advance program development and policy as well as promote training of the Head Start program professionals.
September
Yasmina Vinci, Executive Director
Gregg Porter, Director, Membership

913 **National In-Service Conference**
National Association for Music Education (NAFME)
1806 Robert Fulton Drive
Reston, VA 20191-4348
703-860-4000
800-336-3768
Fax: 703-860-1531
www.musiced.nafme.org
Opportunities to network with peers from across the United States, professional development sessions giving tools and techniques for use in classrooms, receptions and keynote speakers.
April
Michael A. Butera, Executive Director/CEO

914 **National Parent-Teacher Association Annual Convention & Exhibition**
501 South College Street
Charlotte, NC 28202
703-518-1234
nptameetings@pta.org
www.pta.org
Addresses parent-teacher involvement in education. Includes lectures, workshops and seminars for parents and professionals.
June

915 **National Reading Styles Institute Conference**
PO Box 737
Syosset, NY 11791-3933
512-224-4555
800-331-3117
Fax: 516-921-5591
readingstyle@nrsi.com
www.nrsi.com
This conference addresses reading instruction and the problems of illiteracy.
July
Juliet Carbo, Conference Contact

916 **National Rehabilitation Education Conference**
1099 E Champlain Drive
Suite A, 137
Fresno, CA 93720
559-906-0787
Fax: 559-412-2550
info@ncre.org
ncre.org
A conference for professionals involved in training, recruiting, hiring and enhancing the development of rehabilitation counselors. Themes include evaluation processes, legislation and policy, employment, student development, inclusion and equity, career counseling and more.
October
Michael Accordino, D.Ed,CRC,LMHC, President
Denise Catalano, Ph.D., CRC, First Vice President

917 **National Rural Education Annual Convention**
National Rural Education Association
230 Education
Colorado State University
Fort Collins, CO 80523-0001
970-491-1101
Fax: 970-491-1317
www.nrea.net
Exchanges ideas, practices and better ways to enhance rural educational school systems.
October
30 booths with 400 attendees
Joseph T Newlin, PhD, Conference Contact

918 **National School Boards Annual Conference**
1680 Duke Street
Alexandria, VA 22314-3493
703-838-6722
Fax: 703-683-7590
info@nsba.org
www.nsba.org
The nation's largest policy and training conference for local education officials on national and federal issues affecting public schools in the U.S.
March
7,000 attendees and 300 exhibits
Sandra Folks, Conferences Manager
Karen Miller, Director, Exhibits

919 **National School Conference Institute**
11202 N 24th Street
Suite 103
Phoenix, AZ 85029
602-371-8655
888-399-8745
Fax: 602-371-8790
www.nscinet.com
Our purpose is to increase every student's opportunity for academic success.

920 **National Student Assistance Conference**
1270 Rakin Drive
Suite F
Troy, MI 48033-2843
800-453-7733
Fax: 800-499-5718
Learn to maintain and improve safe, drug free schools, student assistance programs. Develop skills to implement the Principles of Effectiveness. Choose from workshops and skill building sessions.

921 **National Women's History Project Annual Conference**
730 Second Street #469
PO Box 469
Santa Rosa, CA 95402
707-636-2888
Fax: 707-636-2909
nwhp1980@gmail.com
www.nwhp.org
Posters, reference books, curriculum materials and biographies of American women in all subjects for grades K-12.
July
72 attendees
Molly Murphy MacGregor, Executive Director/ Chair
Shona Rocco, Financial Manager

922 **Natural Learning Institute Seminar**
54385 Pine Crest Ave
Idyllwild, CA 92549
951-691-0139
Fax: 951-659-0242
www.naturallearninginstitute.org
Linda Hargan, President

923 **Neag Center for Gifted Education and Talent Development Conference**
University of Connecticut
2131 Hillside Road
Unit 3007
Storrs, CT 06269-3007
860-486-4826
Fax: 860-486-2900
www.gifted.uconn.edu
Provides educators with research based practical strategies for engagement and enrichment learning for all students, as well as meeting the needs of gifted and talented students.
Annual
JoAnn Easton, Confratute

924 **New Learning Technologies**
Society for Applied Learning Technology
50 Culpeper Street
Warrenton, VA 20186
540-347-0055
800-457-6812
Fax: 540-349-3169
info@lti.org
www.salt.org
To provide a comprehensive overview of the latest in research, design, and development in order to furnish attendees information on systems that are applicable to their organizations.

925 **New Learning Technologies Conference**
Society for Applied Learning Technology
50 Culpeper Street
Warrenton, VA 20186
540-347-0055
800-457-6812
Fax: 540-349-3169
info@lti.org
www.salt.org
For over 30 years the Society has sponsored conferences which are educational in nature and bring together senior professionals from government, industry, academia and the military to present the latest developments in the field of learning and training technologies.
August
20 booths with 400 attendees
Raymond G Fox, President

926 **North American Montessori Teachers' Association**
13693 Butternut Road
Burton, OH 44021
440-834-4011
Fax: 440-834-4016
staff@montessori-namta.org
www.montessori-namta.org/
Professional organization for Montessori teachers and administrators. Services include The NAMTA Journal and other publications, videos and slide shows. Conferences in January and March.
David J Kahn, Executive Director

927 **Parents as Teachers National Center Conference**
2228 Ball Drive
Saint Louis, MO 63146
314-432-4330
Fax: 314-432-8963
patnc@patnc.org
www.patnc.org
An international early childhood parent education and family support program designed to enhance child development and school achievement through parent education accessible to all families. Serves families throughout pregnancy and until their child enters kindergarten, usually age 5.
April-May
40 booths with 1400+ attendees
Susan S Stepleton, President/CEO
Cheryl Dyle-Palmer, Director Operations

928 **Reidy Interactive Lecture Series**
Center for Assessment
31 Mount Vernon Street
Dover, NH 03820
603-516-7900
Fax: 603-516-7910
www.nciea.org
The goal is to discuss the Next Generation Science Standards and how it applies to current issues.
September
Mark Musick, Chair
Scott Marion, Executive Director

929 **Retention in Education Today for All Indigenous Nations**
ConferencePROS
University of Oklahoma
1639 Cross Center Drive, Suite 101
Norman, OK 73072
405-325-3760
800-203-5494
Fax: 405-325-7075
lasmith@ou.edu
www.conferencepros.com
National conference designed to discuss and share retention strategies for indigenous students.
Laurie Smith, Manager/ Projects Director
Richard Feinberg, Media Specialist Manager

930 **SERVE Conference**
SERVE
5900 Summit Avenue, #201
Browns Summit, NC 27214
336-315-7400
800-755-3277
Fax: 336-315-7457
jsanders@serve.org
www.serve.org
The Regional Educational Laboratories are educational research and development organizations supported by contracts with the US Education Department, National Institute for Education Sciences. Specialty area: Expanded Learning Opportunities.
October-November
Elliott Wolf, Director of Operations
Greg LeePow, Technical Systems Director

931 **STEMtech Conference**
League for Innovation in the Community College
4505 East Chandler Boulevard
Suite 250
Phoenix, AZ 85048
480-705-8200
Fax: 480-705-8201
harris@league.org
www.league.org
Emphasizes student success in science, technology, engineering and mathematics (STEM) at all levels.
October
3,000 attendees
Robin Piccilliri, Meeting Planner

932 **School Equipment Show**
830 Colesville Road
Suite 250
Silver Spring, MD 20910-3297
301-495-0240
800-395-5550
Fax: 301-495-3330
customerservice@nnsea.org
www.nnsea.org
Annual show featuring exhibits from manufacturers of school equipment such as bleachers, classroom furniture, lockers, playground and athletic equipment, computer hardware, software, etc.
February
Elizabeth Bradley, Conference Contact

933 Sexual Assault and Harassment on Campus Conference
c/o Sexual Conference
PO Box 1338
Holmes Beach, FL 34218-1338
800-537-4903
www.ed.mtu.edu
Topics include gender based hate crime, sexual assault investigators, generational legacy of rape, innovations in the military, sexual harassment in K-12, updates on date-rape drugs and many more. Hosted by the Hyatt Orlando Hotel in Kissimmee, Florida.
Karen McLaughlin, Conference Co-Chair
Alan McEvoy, Conference Co-Chair

934 Society for Research in Child Development Conference
2950 S. State St.
Suite 401
Ann Arbor, MI 48104
734-926-0600
Fax: 734-926-0601
communications@srcd.org
www.srcd.org
Working to further research in the area of child development and education.
March/April
40 booths
Barbara Kahn, Conference Contact

935 Teacher Link: An Interactive National Teleconference
Center for the Study of Small/Rural Schools
555 E Constitution Street
Room 138
Norman, OK 73072-7820
405-325-1450
Fax: 405-325-7075
jcsimmons@ou.edu
cssrs.ou.edu
Prevention Series
Spring
5 booths with 100 attendees
Jan C Simmons, Program Director

936 Teachers of English to Speakers of Other Languages Convention and Exhibit
1925 Ballenger Avenue
Suite 550
Alexandria, VA 22314-6820
703-836-0774
888-547-3369
Fax: 703-836-6447
info@tesol.org
www.tesol.org
Leading worldwide professional development opportunity. Simulating program of presentations sponsored by nineteen interest sections, a half-dozen caucus groups and TESOL's advocacy division as well as sessions invited especially for their relevance to our work and our students.
March
245 booths with 8000 attendees
Rita Gainer, Executive Assistant
Rosa Aronson, Executive Director

937 Teaching for Intelligence Conference
SkyLight
2626 S Clearbrook Drive
Arlington Heights, IL 60005
847-290-6600
800-348-4474
Fax: 877-260-2530
info@irisskylight.com
www.iriskylight.com
Focuses on student achievement, brain-based learning and multiple intelligences.
April

938 Technology & Learning Schooltech Exposition & Conference
212-615-6030
www.SchoolTechExpo.com
Over 150 targeted sessions specifically designed for all education professionals: technology directors, teachers, principals, superintendents and district administrators.

939 Technology Student Conference
Technology Student Association
1914 Association Drive
Reston, VA 20191-1538
703-860-9000
Fax: 703-758-4852
www.tsawww.org
Devoted to the needs of technology education students and supported by educators, parents, and business leaders who believe in the need for a technologically literate society.
June
2,500 attendees
Rosanne White, Conference Manager

940 Technology in 21st Century Schools
National School Conference Institute
PO Box 37527
Phoenix, AZ 85069-7527
602-371-8655
Fax: 602-371-8790
www.nscinet.com
Conference will cover managing the Internet, literacy skills, Web Site designs, short and long term planning, creating curriculum, and staff development. Being held at the Boston Park Plaza Hotel in Boston, Massachusetts.
July
Alan November

941 Technology, Reading & Learning Difficulties Conference
International Reading Association
19 Calvert Court
Piedmont, CA 94611
510-594-1249
888-594-1249
Fax: 510-594-1838
www.trld.com
Focuses on ways to use technology for reading, learning difficulties, staff development, adult literacy, and more.
January

942 Training of Trainers Seminar
Active Parenting Publishers
1220 Kennestone Circle
Suite 130
Marietta, GA 30066-6022
770-429-0565
800-825-0060
Fax: 770-429-0334
cservice@activeparenting.com
www.activeparenting.com
Delivers quality education programs for parents, children and teachers to schools, hospitals, social services organizations, churches and the corporate market.
Michael H. Popkin, Ph.D., Founder/ President
Micole Mason, Training Coordinator

943 U.S. Conference on Adult Literacy (USCAL)
Proliteracy
104 Marcellus Street
Syracuse, NY 13204
315-422-9121
888-528-2224
Fax: 315-422-6369
infor@proliteracy.org
www.proliteracy.org
Bring together adult literacy advocates and educators to share new ideas, learn from leading thinkers and inspire one another.
November
50 booths with 1,000 attendees
Robyn Smith, Conference/Events Coord.
David Harvey, President

944 USC Summer Superintendents' Conference
University of Southern California, School of Ed.
Waite Philips Hall, Room 901
Los Angeles, CA 90089-0031
213-740-2182
Fax: 213-749-2707
lpicus@bcf.usc.edu
www.usc.edu
A select group of educational leaders nationwide engaged in reform practices offer discussions with nationally renowned speakers; tour innovative schools; and network with colleagues from the United States, Great Britain and Australia.
Lawrence O Picus, Conference Director
Carolyn Bryant, Conference Coordinator

Northeast

945 Clonlara School Annual Conference Home Educators
Clonlara Home Based Education Programs
1289 Jewett Street
Ann Arbor, MI 48104-6201
734-769-4511
Fax: 734-769-9629
info@clonlara.org
www.clonlara.org
Clonlara School is committed to illuminating educational rights and freedoms through our actions and deep dedication to human rights and dignity.
June
300 attendees
Terri Wheeler, Associate Director

946 Connecticut Library Association
234 Court St.
Middletown, CT 06457
860-346-2444
Fax: 860-344-9199
cla@ctlibrarians.org
ctlibraryassociation.org/index.php?bypassCookie=1
Holds a conference in April and publishes a journal.
April
1000 attendees and 100 exhibits
Dawn La Valle, President
Beth A Crowley, VP/ President Elect

947 Hoosier Science Teachers Association Annual Meeting
5007 W 14th Street
Indianapolis, IN 46224-6503
317-244-7238
Fax: 317-486-4838
Papers, workshops, demonstrations and presentations in each area of science.
February
78 booths
Edward Frazer, Conference Contact

948 **Illinois Library Association Annual Conference**
Illinois Library Association
33 W Grand Avenue
Suite 401
Chicago, IL 60654-6799
312-644-1896
Fax: 312-644-1899
ila@ila.org
www.ila.org
A conference exploring the topic of library services, featuring authors and special speakers interested in discussing how people can better their communities.
October
Melissa Gardner, President
Robert P Doyle, Executive Director

949 **Illinois Vocational Association Conference**
230 Broadway
Suite 150
Springfield, IL 62701-1138
217-585-9430
Fax: 217-544-0208
iva@eosinc.com
Equipment and supplies, publications, teaching aids, computers and food services.
February
75 booths with 600 attendees
Karen Riddle, Conference Contact

950 **New Jersey School Boards Association Annual Meeting**
413 W State Street
PO Box 909
Trenton, NJ 08605-0909
609-695-7600
888-886-5722
Fax: 609-695-0413
www.njsba.org
School/office supplies, furniture, equipment, counseling services and more.
October
630 booths with 9,000 attendees
Wendy L. Wilson, Conference Contact

951 **New York State Council of Student Superintendents Forum**
111 Washington Avenue
Suite 104
Albany, NY 12210-2210
518-449-1063
Fax: 518-426-2229
Offers educational products and related services.
February
12 booths
Dr. Claire Brown, Conference Contact

952 **Northeast Regional Christian Schools International Association**
P.O. Box 65130
Colorado Springs, CO 80962-5130
717-285-3022
800-367-0798
Fax: 719-531-0716
customerservices@acsi.org
www.acsi.org
40 booths.
November
Dr. Dan Egeler, President

953 **Ohio Library Council Convention and Expo**
Ohio Library Council
1105 Schrock Road
Suite 440
Columbus, OH 43229
614-410-8092
Fax: 614-410-8098
olc@olc.org
olc.org
The theme of the event will be "Libraries in Balance," exploring strategies to maintain a balance between traditional practices and the use of innovations such as digital materials.
October
Andrew Mangels, Chair
Douglas Evans, Executive Director

954 **Ohio School Boards Association Capital Conference & Trade Show**
Greater Columbus Convention Center
400 N. High St.
Columbus, OH 43215
614-891-6466
conference.ohioschoolboards.org
Provides school officials from Ohio an opportunity to gain information about products, equipment, materials and services.
November
425 booths
Richard Lewis, Conference Contact

955 **Satellites and Education Conference**
189 Schmucker Science Center
W Chester University
West Chester, PA 19383
610-436-1000
Fax: 610-436-2790
www.sated.org
The Satellite Educators Association was established in 1988 as a professional society to promote the innovative use of satellite technology in education and disseminate information nationally to all members.
March
15 booths with 200 attendees
Nancy McIntyre, Director

956 **UNI Overseas Recruiting Fair**
University of Northern Iowa Career Services
102 Gilchrist Hall
Cedar Falls, IA 50614-0390
319-273-2083
Fax: 319-273-6998
overseas.placement@uni.edu
www.uni.edu/placement/overseas
About 160 recruiters from 120 schools in 80 countries recruit at this fair for certified K-12 educators.
February
Tracy Roling, Coordinator

957 **Wisconsin Vocational Association Conference**
44 E Mifflin Street
Suite 104
Madison, WI 53703-2800
608-283-2595
Fax: 608-283-2589
Trade and industry vendor equipment and book publishers.
April
50 booths
Linda Stemper, Conference Contact

Northwest

958 **Montana High School Association Conference**
1 S Dakota Street
Helena, MT 59601-5111
406-442-6010
School athletic merchandise.
January
15 booths
Dan Freund, Conference Contact

959 **Nebraska School Boards Association Annual Conference**
140 S 16th Street
Lincoln, NE 68508-1805
402-475-4951
Fax: 402-475-4961
60 booths exhibiting products and services directed at the public school market.
November
60 booths
Burma Kroger, Conference Contact

960 **North Dakota Vocational Educational Planning Conference**
State Capitol
600 East Boulevard Avenue, Dept. 270
Bismarck, ND 58505-610
701-328-3180
Fax: 701-328-1255
cte@nd.gov
www.nd.gov/cte/
August
30 booths
Ernest Breznay, Conference Contact

961 **Pacific Northwest Library Association**
Boise Public Library
715 Capitol Boulevard
Boise, ID 83702
208-384-4026
Fax: 208-384-4156
sprice@pobox.ci.boise.id.us
www.pnla.org
Oldest regional library association in the United States and the only binational association in North America.
Honore Bray, President
Gwendolyn Haley, First VP/President-Elect

962 **WA-ACTE Career and Technical Exhibition for Career and Technical Education**
Washington Association for Career & Tech Education
PO Box 315
Olympia, WA 98507-0315
360-786-9286
Fax: 360-357-1491
wa-acte@wa-acte.org
www.wa-acte.org
August
40 booths with 1,000 attendees
Tim Knue, Executive Director
Tess Alviso, Executive Assistant

Southeast

963 **Association for Continuing Higher Education Conference**
Trident Technical College
PO Box 118067
Charleston, SC 29423-8067
843-722-5546
Fax: 843-574-6470
15 tabletops.
October
Dr. Wayne Whelan, Executive VP

964 Center for Play Therapy Summer Institute
425 S Welch Street
Complex 2
Denton, TX 76203
940-565-3864
Fax: 940-565-4461
cpt@unt.edu
cpt.unt.edu
Conference for practitioners and educators to gain play therapy training experience through didactic and experiential learning components.

Sue Bratton, Ph.D, Director
Garry L Landreth, Ed.D, Founder

965 Missouri Library Association Conference
Missouri Library Association
1190 Meramec Station Road
Suite 207
Ballwin, MO 63021-6902
573-449-4627
Fax: 573-449-4655
mlaconference2017@gmail.com
molib.org/conference/2017-conference
The conference will cover topics such as grant writing, graph making and development strategies. It will feature programming that supports libraries and the librarian profession.

October

Anna Strackeljahn, Conference Coordinator
Justin Megahan, Conference Coordinator

966 National Youth-At-Risk Conference
Georgia Southern University
1332 Southern Drive
Statesboro, GA 30458
912-478-4636
Fax: 912-681-0306
academics.georgiasouthern.edu
Stresses education and development for professionals working with at-risk students.

February

Sybil Fickle, Conference Contact

967 Technology and Learning Conference
National School Boards Association
1680 Duke Street
Alexandria, VA 22314
703-838-6722
Fax: 703-683-7590
info@nsba.org
www.nsba.org
This conference offers programs, equipment, services, and ideas. It will be held at the Dallas Convention Center.

Southwest

968 CBEA State Conference
Westin Hotel
400 West Broadway
San Diego, CA 92109
925-295-1104
cbeaquestions@cbeaonline.org
www.cbeaonline.org
Annual conference featuring computer workshops, information sessions, speakers, exhibitions, tours and more.

11/15-11/17 2013
200 attendees

Susan White, Office Manager

969 Children's Literature Festival
Department of Library Science
Sam Houston State University
PO Box 2236
Huntsville, TX 77341-2236
936-294-1614
Fax: 936-294-3780
This annual event is sponsored by the Department of Library Science at Sam Houston State University.

970 Colorado Library Association Conference
12011 Tejon Street
Suite 700
Westminister, CO 80234
303-463-6400
Fax: 303-458-0002
cal@cal-webs.org
www.cal-webs.org

October
60 booths with 450 attendees

Kari May, President
Dinah Kress, Secretary

971 Phoenix Learning Resources Conference
12 W 31st Street
New York, NY 10001-4415
212-629-3887
800-221-1274
Fax: 212-629-5648
Supplemental and remedial reading and language arts programs for early childhood, K-12, and adult literacy programs.

Alexander Burke, President
John Rothermich, Executive VP

972 Southwest Association College and University Housing Officers
624 W. University Drive
Suite 418
Denton, TX 76204
936-294-1812
Fax: 936-294-1920
swacuho@gmail.com
www.swacuho.org
Products and services for college and university housing.

Febuary/March
45 booths

Diane Brittingham, President

973 Texas Classroom Teachers Association Conference
PO Box 1489
Austin, TX 78767-1489
512-477-9415
Fax: 512-469-9527
www.tcta.org
Educational materials, fundraising and jewelry.

February
150 booths

Jan Lanfear, Conference Contact

974 Texas Library Association Conference
3355 Bee Cave Road
Suite 401
Austin, TX 78746-6763
512-328-1518
800-580-2852
Fax: 512-328-8852
pats@txla.org
www.txla.org
Established in 1902 to promote and improve library services in Texas.

March
750 booths with 6,000 attendees

Sharon Amastae, President
Patricia H. Smith, Executive Director

975 Texas Vocational Home Economics Teachers Association Conference
3737 Executive Center Drive
Suite 210
Austin, TX 78731-1633
512-794-8370

July/August

Terry Green, Conference Contact

976 Western History Association Annual Meeting
605 Gruening Bldg.
University of Alaska Fairbanks
Fairbanks, AK 99775
505-277-5234
Fax: 505-277-6023
westernhistoryassociation@gmail.com
www.westernhistoryassociation.wildapricot.org
Exhibits by book sellers.

October
45 booths

Paul Hutton, Conference Contact

General

977 **Accuracy Temporary Services Incorporated**
20674 Hall Road
Clinton Township, MI 48038
248-399-0220
800-297-2119
Fax: 586-465-9481
info@atsprojectsuccessworks.com
atsprojectsuccess.com
Educational consultant for public and private schools.
Howard Weaver, President

978 **Add Vantage Learning Incorporated**
6805 Route 202
New Hope, PA 18938
800-230-2213
Fax: 215-579-8391
www.vantagelearning.com/
Management and educational consultant for the general public.
Jim Pepitone, Chairman

979 **Advance Infant Development Program**
2232 D Street
Suite 203
LaVerne, CA 91750-5409
909-593-3935
Fax: 909-593-7969
Business and educational consultant for general trade.
Diane Hinds, President
Jeanine Coleman, Executive Director

980 **American International Schools**
2203 Franklin Road SW
Roanoak, VA 24014-1109
852-233-3812
Fax: 852-233-5276
asisadmin@ais.edu.hk
American International School is pledged to preparing students to contribute to an increasingly international and interdependent world. AIS strives to provide an atmosphere conducive to building interpersonal relationships and global awareness. AIS is committed to working closely with students and families to attain academic excellence and to inspire the growth of well-rounded individuals.
Andrew Hurst, President
Lewis C Smith Jr, Executive VP

981 **Area Cooperative Educational Services**
350 State Street
North Haven, CT 06473
203-498-6800
Fax: 203-498-6817
acesinfo@aces.org
www.aces.org
ACES is the regional educational service center for twenty-five school districts in south central Connecticut.
Erika Forte, Assistant Executive Director
Thomas M. Danehy Ed.D., Executive Director

982 **Aspira of Penna**
2726 N 6th Street
Philadelphia, PA 19133-2714
215-229-1226
Educational consultant for educational institutions.
Oscar Cardona, President

983 **Association for Refining Cross-Cultured International**
Japanese American Cultural Center
244 S San Pedro Street
Suite 505
Los Angeles, CA 90012
213-620-0696
Fax: 213-620-0930
support@eryugaku.org
www.arcint.com
Educational consultants for international studies.
Chiey Nomura, Director

984 **Association of Christian Schools International**
PO Box 69103
Colorado Springs, CO 80962-3509
719-528-6906
800-367-0798
Fax: 719-531-0631
customerservices@acsi.org
www.acsi.org
Educational consultant for Christian Schools.
Dr. Dan Egeler, President

985 **Basics Plus**
921 Aris Avenue
Suite C
Metairie, LA 70005-2200
504-832-5111
Fax: 504-832-5110
Educational consultants.
Scott Green, President

986 **Beacon Education Management**
112 Turnpike Road
Suite 107
Westborough, MA 01581
508-836-4461
800-789-1258
Fax: 508-836-2604
www.beaconedu.com
A K-12, education services company that offers contracted management services to public schools and charter school boards. Currently operating 27 charter schools in Massachusetts, Michigan, Missouri and North Carolina.

987 **Bluegrass Regional Recycling Corporation**
540 Recycle Drive
Richmond, KY 40475
859-626-9117
Fax: 859-233-7787
thebrrc@qx.net
www.thebrrc.com
Consultants for educational, training, and services for governments and school systems.
Douglas Castle, Chairman

988 **CPM Educational Program**
1233 Noonan Drive
Sacramento, CA 95822-2569
916-446-9936
Fax: 916-444-5263
lorraynegraham@cpm.org
www.cpm.org
Educational and training consultants for school districts.
Karen Wootton, Executive Director
Paul Chmelik, Director

989 **Caldwell Flores Winters**
2187 Newcastle Avenue
Suite 201
Cardiff, CA 92007-1848
760-634-4239
800-273-4239
Fax: 760-436-7357
cfw@cfwinc.com
www.cfwinc.com/index.html
Offers educational counsel to school districts.
Ernesto Flores, President
Scott Gaudineer, AIA, Program Executive

990 **Career Evaluation Systems**
1024 N Oakley Boulevard
Suite 4
Chicago, IL 60622-3586
773-772-9595
800-448-7552
Fax: 773-772-5010
Testing instruments for vocational evaluation.

991 **Carnegie Foundation for the Advancement of Teaching**
51 Vista Lane
Stanford, CA 94305
650-566-5100
Fax: 650-326-0278
publications@carnegiefoundation.org
www.carnegiefoundation.org/
Educational consultant for the educational field.
Tom Payzant, Chair
Anthony S Bryk, President

992 **Carney Sandoe & Associates**
44 Bromfield Street
Boston, MA 02108-4608
617-542-0260
800-225-7986
Fax: 617-542-9400
www.carneysandoe.com/
Educational consultant for private schools.
James H Carney, Chairman/President
Jonathan Ball, Managinf Associate

993 **Carter/Tardola Associates**
419 Pleasant Street
Suite 307
Beloit, WI 53511
608-365-3163
Fax: 608-365-5961
tardola@tucm.net
www.carter-tardola.com/
Evaluates program, administration, staff, resource and time organization, and utilization of resources. Proposal development, language skills development, diversity training.
Betty Tardola, Educational Consultant

994 **Center for Educational Innovation**
28 West 44th Street
Suite 300
New York, NY 10036-6600
212-302-8800
Fax: 212-302-0088
info@the-cei.org
www.the-cei.org
Educational consultant for private and commercial accounts.
Seymour Fliegel, President
John Falco, Vice President

995 **Center for Professional Development & Services**
1525 Wilson Blvd
Suite 705
Arlington, VA 22209-0789
812-339-1156
800-766-1156
Fax: 812-339-0018
membersevices@pdkintl.org
www.pdkintl.org
Examines school district curriculum management system. Determines how effectively a

school district designs and delivers its curriculum.

Patricia Williams, Chair
Douglas Christensen, Vice Chair

996 Center for Resource Management
1861 E. Beaumont Circle
Salt Lake City, UT 84121
801-509-5308
Fax: 603-427-6983
info@crm.org
www.crm.org
Employment, human resources, educational, development, training, computer software, organizational and management consultants for Human Service Agencies and Educational Institutions/ Schools.

Paul Parker, President
Colleen Parker, VP/ Office Manager

997 Child Like Consulting Limited
700 E Rambling Drive
Wellington, FL 33414-5010
561-798-5847
800-487-6725
Fax: 866-468-4555
Training in literacy, music, classroom and learning center management.

998 Children's Educational Opportunity Foundation
P.O Box 59
South Glastonbury, CT 06073
860-430-2756
855-326-4935
Fax: 479-273-9362
Educational consultant for institutions.

Mark R. Rousseau, President
Mary Jane Sullivan, Executive Director

999 Childs Consulting Associates
514 Lakeside Drive
P O Box 550
Mackinaw City, MI 49701
231-436-4099
Fax: 231-436-4101
info@childs.com
www.childs.com
Educational, schools and technology consultants for schools, banking and automotive industries.

John W Childs, President
Sheryl Childs, Executive Assistant

1000 Classroom
245 Fifth Avenue
Room 1901
New York, NY 10016-8728
212-545-8400
800-258-0640
Fax: 212-481-7178
www.classroominc.org
Technology based curriculum and teacher professional development for middle school and high school use.

Lewis W Bernard, Chairman
Lisa Holton, President

1001 Coalition of Essential Schools
482 Congress Street
Suite 500A
Portland, ME 04101
401-426-9638
Fax: 510-433-1455
info@essentialschools.org
essentialschools.org
The Coalition of Essential Schools (CES) is a leading comprehensive school reform organization, fundamentally changing the way people think about teaching and learning and transforming American education.

Hudi Podolsky, Executive Director

1002 College Bound
17316 Edwards Road
Suite 180
Cerritos, CA 90703
562-860-2127
Fax: 562-407-2131
info@collegeboundca.org
www.collegeboundca.org
Educational consultants.

Janice Criddle, Chair
Denise McLeod, Vice Chair

1003 College Entrance Examination Board
45 Columbus Avenue
New York, NY 10023-6917
212-713-8000
emonts@umich.edu
www.collegeboard.com
Educational, research, testing and financial consultant for learning institutions and students.

David Coleman, President
Jeremy Singer, Chief Operating Officer

1004 Community Connections
1865 W Broad Street
Suite C
Athens, GA 30606
706-353-1313
800-924-5085
Fax: 706-353-1375
info@communityconnection211.org
www.communityconnection211.org
Educational consultant for the general public.

Ashley Harp, President
Julia Weckbeck, Vice President

1005 Community Foundation for Jewish Education
30 S Wells-216
Chicago, IL 60606
312-673-3270
Fax: 312-913-1763
www.cfje.org
Educational consultant for the general public and schools.

Howard Swibel, President

1006 Connecting Link
387 Coopers Pond Drive
Suite 1
Lawrenceville, GA 30044-5231
770-979-5804
Fax: 770-931-6831
Business and educational consultants for teachers.

Dr. Bernard F Cleveland, President

1007 Conover Company
4 Brookwood Court
Appleton, WI 54914-8618
920-231-4667
800-933-1933
Fax: 800-933-1943
sales@conovercompany.com
www.conovercompany.com
Training and setting up workplace literacy programs; emotional intelligence assessment and skill enhancement; functional literacy software, career exploration and assessment software

Rebecca Schmitz, Member

1008 Consortium on Reading Excellence
1300 Clay Street
Suite 600
Oakland, CA 94612-1923
888-249-6165
Fax: 510-540-4242
orders@corelearn.com
www.corelearn.com
Educational consultant for public and private schools.

Bill Honig, President
Linda Diamond, CEO

1009 Continuous Learning Group Limited Liability Company
500 Cherrington Parkway
Suite 350
Pittsburgh, PA 15108
412-269-7240
Fax: 412-269-7247
info@clg.com
www.clg.com
Educational consultants.

Steve Jacobs, Non-Executive Chairman
Vikesh Mahendroo, President & CEO

1010 Corporate Design Foundation
20 Park Plaza
Suite 400
Boston, MA 02116-4303
617-566-7676
admin@cdf.org
www.cdf.org
Educational consultant for universities and colleges.

Peter G Lawrence, Chairman

1011 Corporate University Enterprise
909 North Washington Street
Suite 310
Alexandria, VA 22314
703-848-0070
866-848-1675
Fax: 703-848-0071
info@cuenterprise.com
www.cuenterprise.com
Corporate University Enterprise, Inc. is and educational consulting firm designed to bring a strategic approach to workforce education in both private and public organizations. The company was incorporated in 1998 and has since served clients throughout the United States, Europe, and Asia.

Teresa Sayasithsena, Vice President
Karen Barley, President

1012 Council for Aid to Education
215 Lexington Avenue
Floor 16
New York, NY 10016-1599
212-661-5800
Fax: 212-661-9766
www.cae.org
Non-profit educational consultant for government and commercial concerns.

Roger W Benjamin, President
James Hundley, Executive Vice President

1013 Council on Occupational Education
7840 Roswell Road
Suite 325
Atlanta, GA 30350-1903
770-396-3898
800-917-2081
Fax: 770-396-3790
bowmanh@council.org
www.council.org
Managerial and educational consultant for post secondary technical education institutions.

Al Salazar, Chair
James Spruel, Vice Chair

1014 Creative Learning Consultants
1990 Market Road
Marion, IL 62959-1906

800-729-5137
Fax: 800-844-0455
info@piecesoflearning.com
www.piecesoflearning.com
Educational consulting for school districts, teachers, book stores and parents.

Stanley Balsamo, Secretary/Treasurer
Kathy Balsamo, President

1015 Creative Learning Systems
2065 S Escondido Blvd
Suite 108
Escondido, CA 92025
800-458-2880
Fax: 858-592-7055
info@creativelearningsystems.com
www.creativelearningsystems.com
Educational consulting firm.

Matt Dickstein, Chief Executive Officer

1016 Dawson Education Cooperative
711 Clinton Street
Suite 201
Arkadelphia, AR 71923-5921
870-246-3077
Fax: 870-246-5892
rds@dawson.dsc.k12.ar.us
www.dawson.dsc.k12.ar.us
Educational consulting group.

Nathan Gills, President
Ron Wright, Director

1017 Dawson Education Service Cooperative
711 Clinton Street
Suite 201
Arkadelphia, AR 71923-5921
870-246-3077
Fax: 870-246-5892
www.dawson.dsc.k12.ar.us
Educational and organizational consultants for school districts

Ron Wright, Director
Beth Neel, Assisstant Director

1018 Designs for Learning
2233 University Ave W
Suite 450
St. Paul, MN 55114-1634
651-645-0200
Fax: 651-645-0240
dalley@designlearn.net
www.designlearn.net
Educational consultants for primary schools and the private sector.

David Alley, Chair
Pamela Meade, President

1019 Direct Instructional Support Systems
535 Lakeview Plaza Blvd.
Suite B
Worthington, OH 43085-4146
614-846-8946
Fax: 614-846-1794
Educational consultant for public and private agencies.

Gary Moore, President

1020 Dr. Anthony A Cacossa
4300 N Charles Street
Apartment 9B
Baltimore, MD 21218-1052
410-889-1806
Fax: 410-889-1806
Assists schools in marketing academic programs that offer internship opportunities.

1021 E.P.P.A Consulting
1116 Comanche Trail
Georgetown, KY 40324-1071
502-370-6341
eppa@juno.com
Provider of strategic and operational planning consulting services.

Theo R Leverenz, Ph.D, Contact, Owner

1022 EPIE Institute: Educational Products Information Exchange Institute
103 West Montauk Highway
PO Box 590
Hampton Bays, NY 11946-4006
631-728-9100
kkomoski@epie.org
www.epie.org
Curriculum development, training and evaluation of education products.

1023 East Bay Educational Collaborative
317 Market Street
Warren, RI 02885
401-245-4998
Fax: 401-245-9332
Karen.corr@ebecri.org
www.ebecri.org
Business and educational consultant for member school districts.

Kathryn Crowley, Chair
Gerald Kowalczyk, Executive Director

1024 East Central Educational Service Center
1601 Indiana Avenue
Connersville, IN 47331
765-825-1247
Fax: 765-825-2532
harrison@ecesc.k12.in.us
www.ecesc.k12.in.us
Educational services for school districts in East Central Indiana.

William J Harrison, Executive Director

1025 Edge Learning Institute
4807 Rockside Rd.
Ste. 720
Z, OH 44131-3320
216-674-1085
888-892-0300
Fax: 216-674-8204
info@legacycultures.com
legacycultures.com
Educational consultants for the general public, commercial concerns, government agencies and school districts.

Paul Meshanko, President & CEO
Todd Costello, VP Business Operations

1026 Edison Schools
485 Lexington Avenue
2nd Floor
New York, NY 10017
212-419-1600
Fax: 212-419-1746
information@edisonlearning.com
www.edisonschools.com
The country's largest private manager of public schools. Implemented its design in 79 public schools, including 36 charter schools, which it operates under management contracts with local school districts and charter school boards.

Jeff Wahl, President, CEO

1027 Education Concepts
9861 Strausser Street
Canal Fulton, OH 44614
330-497-1055
Fax: 330-966-8000
info@ed-concepts.com
www.ed-concepts.com
Professional development programs for early childhood educators.

1028 Education Data
1305 E Waterman
Witchata, KS 67211
800-248-4135
Expertise in organizational needs assessments.

1029 Education Development Center
43 Foundry Avenue
Waltham, MA 02453-8313
617-969-7100
Fax: 617-969-5979
contact@edc.org
www.edc.org
Offers consultation in design and development, evaluation, implementation, policy and research to improve the education system.

Vivien Stewart, Chair
David Offensend, President & CEO

1030 Education Management Consulting LLC
49 Coryell Street
Lambertville, NJ 08530
609-397-8989
800-291-0199
Fax: 609-397-1999
edragan@edmgt.com
www.edmgt.com
Consultation for schools on special education and administration consultation for lawyers working on education and school related issues.

Dr. Edward F Dragan, President

1031 Educational Consultants of Oxford
10431 Highway 51 S
Courtland, MS 38620
601-563-8954
All areas of educational information services, tutoring, scholarship information, and non-traditional and overseas training.

1032 Educational Credential Evaluators
101 W. Pleasant St. Suite 200
PO Box 514070
Milwaukee, WI 53212-3963
414-289-3400
Fax: 414-289-3411
eval@ece.org
www.ece.org
Evaluates foreign educational credentials.

James Frey, President
Margit Schatzman, VP

1033 Educational Data Service
236 Midland Avenue
Saddle Brook, NJ 07663-4604
973-340-8800
Fax: 973-340-0078
www.ed-data.com
Educational and school consulting for Boards of Education.

Gil Wohl, President
Alan Wohl, Chairman

1034 Educational Information & Resource Center
900 Hollydell Drive
Sewell, NJ 08080
856-582-7000
Fax: 856-582-4206
info@eirc.org
www.eirc.org
Programs and consulting services for schools, on many topics from teaching techniques to technical assistance.

Rena Alpert, Board of Director
Jack Hill, Board of Director

1035 **Educational Resources**
651-592-3688
info@eduresources.org
www.eduresources.org
Nonprofit educational organization seeking to promote understanding between different ethnic and religious groups through programs, lectures, curriculums and trips abroad.
Steven L Derfler, Director

1036 **Educational Services Company**
3535 East 96th Street
Suite 126
Indianapolis, IN 46240-1754
317-818-3535
888-351-3535
Fax: 317-818-3533
info@educationalservicesco.com
www.educationalservicesco.com
Educational and management consulting for primary and secondary schools.
Douglas Cassman, President
William McMaster, Secretary

1037 **Educational Specialties**
9923 S Wood Street
Chicago, IL 60643-1809
773-445-1000
Fax: 773-445-5574
www.educationalspecialties.com
Educational consultant for schools.
Elois W Steward, President

1038 **Educational Systems for the Future**
11415 Georgetown Circle
Tampa, FL 33625-1560
813-814-1192
Fax: 813-814-1193
info@esf-protainer.com
www.esf-protainer.com
Development of teaching skills, training needs analysis, and training management.
Dr. Mary Sullivan Esseff, President & Director
Dr. Peter J Esseff, Vice President

1039 **Educational Technology Design Consultants**
100 Allentown Parkway
Suite 110
Allen, TX 75002
972-727-1234
Fax: 972-727-1491
www.etdc.com/html/about_us.html
Developing system design for virtual campus control and support.

1040 **Educational Testing Service**
1800 K Street, NW,
Suite 900
Washington, DC 20006-0001
202-659-0616
Fax: 202-659-8075
etsinfo@ets.org
www.ets.org
Educational and professional consulting for schools.
Kurt M. Landgraf, President
Sharon Robison, COO, Senior VP

1041 **Edusystems Export**
820 Wisconsin Street
Walworth, WI 53184-9765
262-275-5761
Fax: 262-275-2009
sales@edusystems.com
Expertise in educational systems.

1042 **Effective Schools Products**
PO Box 1337
Okemos, MI 48805-5983
517-349-8841
800-827-8041
Fax: 517-349-8852
staff@effectiveschools.com
www.effectiveschools.com
Publishing consultants for schools, teachers, directors of planning and others in this field.
Ruth Lezotte, PhD, President
Dr. Carmen Granto, Superintendent

1043 **Effective Training Solutions**
93 Linden Street
Oakland, CA 94607-1447
510-834-1901
800-949-5035
Fax: 510-834-1905
boris@trainingsuccess.com
www.trainingsuccess.com
Design and implementation of training strategies. Proficiency training-performance improvement training.
Ingrid Gudenas, CEO

1044 **Efficacy Institute**
182 Felton Street
Waltham, MA 02453-4134
781-547-6060
Fax: 781-547-6077
info@efficacy.org
www.efficacy.org
Non-profit, educational consultants for educational and community service institutions.
Dr Jeff Howard, Chair
Barbara M. Logan, Vice President

1045 **Emerging Technology Consultants**
216 Heritage Lane
New Brighton, MN 55112
651-639-3973
Fax: 651-639-3973
Serves as a connection between technology producers and the education and training industries.
Richard Pollak, Chief Executive Officer
Rubyanna Pollak, President

1046 **Epistemological Engineering**
5269 Miles Avenue
Oakland, CA 94618-1044
510-653-3377
866-341-3377
Fax: 866-879-7797
publications@eeps.com
www.eeps.com
Educational consultants.
Tim Erickson, President

1047 **Examiner Corporation**
600 Marshall Avenue
Suite 100
St. Paul, MN 55102-1723
651-451-7360
800-395-6840
Fax: 651-451-6563
examine@xmn.com
www.xmn.com
Educational and certification evaluation instruments.
Gary C Brown, President
Michelle Smith, Sales and Marketing

1048 **Excell Education Centers**
3807 Wilshire Boulevard
Los Angeles, CA 90010-3101
213-386-1953
Educational and planning consultants.
Raymond Hahl, Owner

1049 **FPMI Communications**
707 Fiber Street NW
Huntsville, AL 35801-5833
256-539-1850
Fax: 256-539-0911
www.fmpi.com
Educational management consulting.

1050 **First District Resa**
201 West Lee Street
P.O. Box 780
Brooklet, GA 30415
912-842-5000
Fax: 912-842-5161
wmyers@fdresa.org
www.fdresa.org
Educational consultants for the general public and commercial concerns.
Dr. Whit Myers, Executive Director
Donna Mangrum, Chief Financial Officer

1051 **Foundation for Educational Innovation**
401 M Street SW
2nd Floor, Suite 1
Washington, DC 20024-2610
202-554-7400
Fax: 202-554-7401
Educational consultant for educational/school systems.
Archie Prioleau, President

1052 **George Dehne & Associates**
33 Main Street
Suite F
Old Saybrook, CT 06475
843-971-9088
860-388-3958
Fax: 843-971-7759
george@dehne.com
www.dehne.com
Educational and business consultants for commercial concerns and colleges.
George Dehne, President
Christopher Topher Small, Executive Vice President

1053 **Health Outreach Project**
825 Cascade Avenue
Atlanta, GA 30331-8362
404-755-6700
Educational consultants.
Sandra McDonald, President

1054 **Higher Education Consortium**
2233 University Avenue W
Suite 210
St. Paul, MN 55114
651-287-3300
Fax: 651-659-9421
hecua@hecua.org
www.hecua.org
Educational consultants.
Jenny Keyser, Executive Director
Patrick Mulvihill, Director of Operations

1055 **Highlands Program**
PO Box 76168
Atlanta, GA 30358-3915
404-497-0835
Educational consultants for educational institutions, corporations and consumers.
Don Hutcheson, President

1056 **Howard Greene Associates**
60 Post Road West
Westport, CT 06880-4208
203-226-4257
Fax: 203-226-5595
counseling@howardgreeneassociates.com
www.greenesguides.com

Educational consultants for school systems and individuals.

Howard R Greene, President & Founder
Ginger F.C. Miller, Director

1057 Huntley Pascoe
19125 N Creek Parkway
Bothel, WA 98011-8035
425-485-0900
Fax: 425-487-1825
Educational consultant for architects, utility companies, computer facilities, school districts and hospitals.

Roger Huntley, President

1058 Ingraham Dancu Associates
121 Bald Cypress Court
Pawleys Island, SC 29585
843-235-8709
Fax: 843-235-3422
dedancu@ingrahamdancu.com
www.ingrahamdancu.com
Development planning for educational and industrial clients.

Daniel E. Dancu, PhD, President

1059 Innovative Learning Group
514 East Fourth Street
Royal Oak, MI 48067
248-544-1568
Fax: 248-544-2159
www.innovativelg.com
Educational consultants for schools and the general public.

Lisa Toenniges, Owner/ CEO

1060 Innovative Programming Systems
9001poplar Bridge Road
Bloomington, MN 55437
612-835-1290
Development of instructional and training programs.

1061 Insight
12 S 6th Street
Suite 510
Minneapolis, MN 55402-1510
612-338-5777
Educational consultants for commercial concerns.

Mark Kovatch, President

1062 Institute for Academic Excellence
901 Deming Way
Suite 301
Madison, WI 53717-1964
608-664-0965
Fax: 608-664-382
Educational consultants for K-12 schools.

John Hickey, Chairman

1063 Institute for Development of Educational Activities
259 Regency Ridge
Dayton, OH 45459
937-434-6969
Fax: 937-434-5203
ideadayton@aol.com
www.idea.com
Assistance for administrators and teachers of elementary and secondary schools.

1064 Institute for Global Ethics
6824 University Avenue
Middleton, WI 53562
608-204-5902
888-607-0883
ethics@globalethics.org
www.globalethics.org
Mission-driven organization aimed at providing the practical tools to build ethical environments and cultures at home, school, the workplace and in society. The organization offers consulting, seminars, research and grants towards realizing this mission.

Anthony J Gray, President & CEO
Iakovos Balassi, Project Manager

1065 Interface Network
321 SW 4th Avenue
Suite 502
Portland, OR 97204-2323
503-222-2702
Fax: 503-222-7503
www.daggettt.com
info@leaderEd.com
Educational consultant for the United States Department of Education, businesses, school districts and other governmental agencies.

1066 International Center for Leadership in Education
1587 Route 146
Rexford, NY 12148
518-399-2776
Fax: 518-399-7607
info@leadered.com
www.leadered.com
Educational consultants for educational institutions, governments and commercial concerns.

Willard R Daggett, Chairman
Susan A. Gendron, President

1067 International Schools Association
1033 Diego Drive South
BOCA RATON, FL 33428
561-883-3854
39-011-645-967
Fax: 561-483-2004
Fax: 39-011-643-298
info@isaschools.org
www.isaschools.org
Provides advisory and consultative services to its international and internationally minded member schools, as well as to other organizations in the field of education, such as UNESCO. The Association promotes innovations in international education, conducts conferences and workshops and publishes various educational materials.

Luis Martinez-Zorzo, Chairman
Freida Pilus, Vice Chairman

1068 J&Kalb Associates
300 Pelham Road
Suite 5K
New Rochelle, NY 10805
914-636-6154
Consulting experience to school districts.

1069 JBS International
5515 Security Lane
Suite 800
North Bethesda, MD 20852-5007
301-495-1080
Fax: 650-348-0260
info@jbsinternational.com
www.jbsinternational.com
Educational, data, market analysis, statistical and research consultants for US Government Agencies.

Jerri Shaw, Co-CEO/ President
Gail Bassin, Co-CEO/ CFO

1070 JCB/Early Childhood Education Consultant Service
813 Woodchuck Place
Bear, DE 19701
302-836-8505
Program design and cross-cultural staff development through seminars.

1071 JJ Jones Consultants
1206 Harrison Avenue
Oxford, MS 38655-3904
662-234-6755
Educational consultant for high school and college students.

JJ Jones, Owner

1072 JP Associates Incorporated
131 Foster Avenue
Valley Stream, NY 11580-4726
516-561-7803
Fax: 516-561-4066
Educational consultant for schools.

Jane Dinapoli, President

1073 Janet Hart Heinicke
1302 W Boston Avenue
Indianola, IA 50125
515-961-8933
Fax: 515-961-8903
heinicke@simpson.edu
Development of new programs and maintenance strategies.

1074 Jewish Learning Venture
7607 Old York Road
Melrose Park, PA 19027-3010
215-320-036
Fax: 215-635-8946
info@jewishlearningventure.org
jewishlearningventure.org
Educational consultants.

Rabbi Philip Warmflash, Executive Director
Elana Rivel, Associate Director

1075 Jobs for California Graduates
2525 O Street
Merced, CA 95340-3634
209-385-8466
Educational consultants for high school students.

Obie Obrien, Director

1076 John McLaughlin Company
1524 S Summit Avenue
Sioux Falls, SD 57105
605-332-4900
Fax: 605-339-1662
www.mclaughlincompany.com
Advises companies regarding private-sector activities in K-12 and higher education.

John Laughlin, Owner

1077 Johnson & Johnson Associates
3970 Chain Bridge Road
Fairfax, VA 22030-3316
703-359-5969
800-899-6363
Fax: 703-359-5971
info@jjaconsultants.com
www.jjaconsultants.com
Educational consultants for governmental agencies and commercial concerns.

Dr. Johnson Edosomwan, President/CEO

1078 Joseph & Edna Josephson Institute
9841 Airport Blvd.
Suite 300
Los Angeles, CA 90045-6621
310-846-4800
800-711-2670
Fax: 310-846-4858
charactercounts.org
Educational consultant for organizations, government, businesses and the general public.

Scott Raecker, Chairman
Robert Holmes, Vice Chairman

1079 Kaludis Consulting Group
1050 Connecticut Avenue NW
10th Floor
Washington, DC 20036
202-772-3120
Fax: 202-331-1428
info@kaludisconsulting.com
www.kaludisconsulting.com
Educational consultants for colleges and universities.
George Kaludis, President/Chairman
Barry M Cohen, Senior Vice President

1080 Kentucky Association of School Administrators
152 Consumer Lane
Suite 154
Frankfort, KY 40601-8489
502-875-3411
800-928-kasa
Fax: 502-875-4634
webmaster@kasa.com
www.kasa.org
Educational consultant for school administrators.
Lu S. Young, President
Barry Lee, President-elect

1081 Kleiner & Associates
8636 SE 75th Place
Mercer Island, WA 98040-5235
206-236-0608
Educational consultants for public and private institutions.
Charles Kleiner, Owner

1082 Lawrence A Heller Associates
324 Freeport Road
Pittsburgh, PA 15238-3422
412-820-0670
Fax: 412-820-0669
Development and implementation of educational programs.

1083 Leona Group
7878 N. 16th St
Suite 150
Phoenix, AZ 85020
602-953-2933
Fax: 602-953-0831
www.leonagroup.com
Currently manages more than 40 school sites in Michigan, Arizona, Ohio and Indiana
Wieland Wettstein, Chairman
Dr. Bill Coats, CEO

1084 Linkage
200 Wheeler Road
3rd Floor South Tower
Burlington, MA 01803-7305
781-402-5555
Fax: 781-402-5556
info@linkageinc.com
www.linkageinc.com
Linkage, Inc. is a global organizational development company that specializes in leadership development.
Phil Harkins, Executive Chairman
Harley Ostis, President & CEO

1085 Logical Systems
605 East 1st Street
Suite 101
Rome, GA 30161-3109
706-234-9896
Fax: 706-290-0998
www.logsysinc.com
Educational consultants for school districts.
Francis Ranwez, President

1086 Los Angeles Educational Alliance for Restructuring Now
445 S Figueroa Street
Los Angeles, CA 90071
323-255-3276
Fax: 213-626-5830
asant@ccf-la.org
Educational consulting for school systems.
Mary Chambers, Vice President
Michael Roos, President

1087 Louisiana Children's Research Center for Development & Learning
1 Galleria Blvd.
Suite 903
Metairie, LA 70001-3036
504-840-9786
Fax: 504-840-9968
learn@cdl.org
www.cdl.org
Educational consultants for the general public.
Frank Williams, Chairman
Gregory N. Rattler, Vice Chairman

1088 MK & Company
132 Bronte Street
San Francisco, CA 94110
415-826-5923
Program development and project management for educational products, services and organizations.

1089 MPR Associates
3040 East Cornwallis Road
Post Office Box 12194
Research Triangle Park, NC 27709-2194
510-849-4942
Fax: 510-849-0794
info@mprinc.com
www.mprinc.com
Educational consultants for governmental, educational and commercial concerns including law firms.
Gary Hoachlander, President

1090 Magi Educational Services Incorporated
7-11 Broadway
Suite 402
White Plains, NY 10601-3546
914-682-1861
Fax: 914-682-1760
info@westchesterinst.com
www.westchesterinst.org
Educational consultant for educational institutions.
Dr. Ronald Szczypkowski, President

1091 Management Concepts
8230 Leesburg Pike
Suite 800
Tysons Corner, VA 22182-2639
703-790-9595
888-545-8571
Fax: 703-790-1371
info@managementconcepts.com
www.managementconcepts.com
Educational consultants for commercial and governmental concerns.
Stephen L. Maier, President
Thomas F. Dungan Ill, CEO

1092 Management Simulations
55 E Monroe
Chicago, IL 60093-1250
312-477-7200
877-477-8787
welcome@capsim.com
www.capsim.com
Educational consultants for commercial concerns and universities.
Daniel Smith, President
Shridhar Sampath, General Manager

1093 Marketing Education Resource Center
1375 King Avenue
PO Box 12279
Columbus, OH 43212-2220
614-486-6708
800-448-0398
Fax: 614-486-1819
www.mbaresearch.org
Educational, development and curriculum consulting for high schools and post secondary schools.
Trey Michael, Chair
James R Gleason Ph.D., President, CEO

1094 Maryland Educational Opportunity Center
2305 N. Charles St.
Suite 101
Baltimore, MD 21218
410-728-3400
888-245-2774
Fax: 410-523-6340
edhoward@meoconline.com
www.meoconline.com
Consultant services for educational institutions.
Ellen Howard, Executive Director
Lynn Drummond, Associate Director

1095 Maryland Elco Incorporated Educational Funding Company
4740 Chevy Chase Drive
Chevy Chase, MD 20815-6461
301-654-8677
Fax: 301-654-7750
info@efconline.com
www.efconline.com
Educational, accounting and billing consultants for service and vocational schools and businesses.
Nicholas Cokinos, Chairman
John Cokinos, President

1096 Mason Associates
142 N Mountain Avenue
Montclair, NJ 07042
201-744-9143
Educational services for independent secondary schools, colleges and universities.

1097 Matrix Media Distribution
28310 Roadside Drive
Suite 237
Agoura, CA 91301-4951
818-865-3470
Educational consultant for the educational market.
Paul Luttrell, President

1098 McKenzie Group
1100 17th Street NW
Suite 1100
Washington, DC 20036-4638
202-466-1111
Fax: 202-466-3363
Educational consultant for commercial concerns and government.
Floretta D McKenzie, President

1099 Measurement
423 Morris Street
Durham, NC 27701-2128
919-683-2413
Fax: 919-425-7726
www.measurementinc.com

Educational, research, testing and printing consultant for schools, state governments and private businesses.

Dr. Henry H Scherich, President
Dr. Michael B Bunch, Senior Vice President

1100 Measurement Learning Consultants
80920 Highway 10
Tolovana Park, OR 97145
503-436-1464
Business, educational, testing and development consultants for the general public and commercial concerns such as schools.

Albert G Bennyworth, Partner

1101 Merrimack Education Center
101 Mill Road
Chelmsford, MA 01824-4844
978-256-3985
Fax: 978-937-5585
www.mec.edu
Educational consultant for educational facilities.

John Barranco, Executive Director

1102 Michigan Education Council
40440 Palmer Road
Canton, MI 48188-2034
734-729-1000
Fax: 734-729-1004
Educational consultant for individuals.

Dawud Tauhidi, Director

1103 Midas Consulting Group
4600 S Syracuse Street
Suite 900
Denver, CO 80237
303-256-6500
Fax: 866-790-9500
info@midasconsultinggroup.com
www.midasconsultinggroup.com
Educational consultant for schools, universities, training centers and government agencies.

Michael Blimes, Executive Consultant

1104 Miller, Cook & Associates
1606 Bellview Avenue
Suite 1
Roanoke, VA 24014-4923
540-345-4393
800-591-1141
Fax: 239-394-2652
info@millercook.com
www.millercook.com
Educational consultants for colleges and universities.

William B Miller, President
Catherine R. Cook, Chief Executive Officer

1105 Model Classroom
4095 173rd Place SW
Bellvue, WA 98008-5929
425-746-0331
Educational consultant for school districts, commercial concerns and the Department of Education.

Cheryl Avena, Owner

1106 Modern Educational Systems
15 Limestone Terrace
Ridgefield, CT 06877-2621
203-431-4144
Educational consultant for schools.

Edward T McCormick, President

1107 Modern Red Schoolhouse Institute
1901 21st Avenue
South Nashville, TN 37212-1502
615-320-8804
888-275-6774
Fax: 615-320-5366
info@mrsh.com
www.mrsh.com
Educational consultant for school districts.

Sally B Kilgore, President

1108 Montana School Boards Association
863 Great Northern Blvd.
Suite 301
Helena, MT 59601-5156
406-442-2180
Fax: 406-442-2194
cwilson@mtsba.org
www.mtsba.org
Training, educational and school districts consultant for school boards.

Charles Wilson, President
Lance Melton, Executive Director

1109 Montgomery Intermediate Unit 23
1605 West Main Street
Suite B
Norristown, PA 19403-3268
610-539-8550
Fax: 610-539-5073
webmaster@mciu.org
www.mciu.org
Educational consultants for professional associations, groups and student organizations.

Marc Lieberson, President

1110 Moore Express
865 Pancheri Drive
Idaho Falls, ID 83402
208-523-6276
Educational consultant for public school districts, state and local governments and commercial concerns.

Lawry Wilde, President

1111 Mosaica Education
45 Broadway
17th Floor
New York, NY 10006
212-232-0305
Fax: 212-232-0309
partner@mosaicaeducation.com
www.mosaicaeducation.com
Manages public schools either under contract with local school districts or funded directly by states under charter school laws that permit private management.

Gene Eidelman, President
Michael J Connelly, Chief Executive Officer

1112 Multicorp
1912 Avenue K
Suite 210
Plano, TX 75074-5960
972-551-8899
Computer and educational consultant.

Fred Sammet, Chairman

1113 National Center on Education & the Economy
2121 K Street NW
Suite 700
Washington, DC 20037-4507
202-379-1800
Fax: 202-293-1560
info@ncee.org
www.ncee.org
Educational consultant for schools.

Marc S Tucker, President
Betsy Brown Ruzzi, Vice President

1114 National Evaluation Systems
30 Gatehouse Road
PO Box 226
Amherst, MA 01004
Fax: 413-256-8221
Educational testing, test development, and assessment for education agencies.

1115 National Heritage Academies
3850 Broadmoor Avenue SE
Suite 201
Grand Rapids, MI 49512
877-223-6402
Fax: 616-575-6801
info@heritageacademies.com
www.nhaschools.com
Manages 22 charter academies (K-8) in Michigan and North Carolina.

2007, Author
Harry Hurlburt, President, CEO
Todd McKee, Chief Academic Officer

1116 National Reading Styles Institute
PO Box 737
Syosset, NY 11791
516-921-5500
800-331-3117
Fax: 516-921-5591
readingstyle@nrsi.com
www.nrsi.com
Educational consultants for schools and educators.

Marie Carbo, Executive Director

1117 National School Safety and Security Services
PO Box 110123
Cleveland, OH 44111
216-251-3067
ken@schoolsecurity.org
www.schoolsecurity.org
National consulting firm specializing in school security and crisis preparedness training, security assessments, and related safety consulting for K-12 schools, law enforcement, and other youth safety providers.

Kenneth S Trump, President/CEO
Dr. Asia Jones, Director

1118 Noel/Levitz Centers
2350 Oakdale Blvd.
Coralville, IA 52241-9581
319-626-8380
800-876-1117
Fax: 319-626-8388
ContactUs@noellevitz.com
www.noellevitz.com
Educational consultant for colleges and universities.

Tom Williams, President/CEO

1119 Ome Resa
2230 Sunset Boulevard
Steubenville, OH 43952-1349
740-283-2050
Fax: 740-283-1500
angie.underwood@omeresa.net
www.omeresa.net
Educational consultants for school districts.

Dave Hire, Chair
John Wilson, Vice Chair

1120 Oosting & Associates
200 Seaboard Lane
Franklin, TN 37067-8237
615-771-7706
Fax: 615-771-7810
Educational consultants for colleges and universities.

Dr. Kenneth Oosting, President

1121 **Pamela Joy**
1049 Whipple Avenue
Suite A
Redwood City, CA 94062-1414
650-368-9968
Fax: 650-368-2794
Educational consultants for schools.
Pamela Joy, Owner

1122 **Parsifal Systems**
155 N Craig Street
Pittsburgh, PA 15213
412-682-8080
Fax: 412-682-6291
Educational consultants for commercial concerns and schools.
Marcia Morton, President

1123 **Paul H Rosendahl, PHD**
240 Mohouli Street
Hilo, HI 96720-2445
808-935-5233
Fax: 808-961-6998
Science, archaeology, historical, resources and management consultant for developers, government agencies, educational institutions, groups and individuals.
Paul H Rosendahl, Owner

1124 **Perfect PC Technologies**
15012 Red Hill Avenue
Tustin, CA 92780-6524
714-258-0800
Computer consultants for commercial concerns, schools and institutions.
Neil Lin, President

1125 **Performa**
124 N Broadway
De Pere, WI 54115
920-336-9929
Fax: 920-336-2899
jeffk@performaic.com
www.performainc.com
Planning and facility consultants for higher education, manufacturing and government agencies.
Doug Page, President
Jeff Kanzelberger, CEO

1126 **Poetry Alive!**
70 Woodfin Place
Suite WW4C
Asheville, NC 28801
828-255-7636
800-476-8172
Fax: 828-232-1045
poetry@poetryalive.com
www.poetryalive.com
Educational consultants for commercial concerns and school systems.
Bob Falls, President

1127 **Post Secondary Educational Assistance**
500 Century Park South
Suite 200
Birmingham, AL 35226-3920
205-930-4930
Fax: 205-930-4905
mystudentloanassistance
mystudentloanassistance.com
Educational consultant for commercial concerns.
Kenneth Horne, President

1128 **Prevention Service**
7614 Morningstar Avenue
Harrisburg, PA 17112-4226
717-651-9510
Educational consultant for corporations, private health clubs, school districts and other organizations.
Mark Everest, President

1129 **Princeton Review**
2315 Broadway
2nd Floor
New York, NY 10024-4332
212-874-8282
888-955-4600
Fax: 212-874-0775
www.princetonreview.com
Educational consultants for commercial concerns.
John Katzman, President

1130 **Priority Computer Services**
6561 Lonewolf Drive
Suite 110
South Bend, IN 46628
574-236-5979
866-661-9049
priority@pcserv-inc.com
www.prioritycomputer.biz
Computer consultant for commercial education.
Ben Hahaj, President

1131 **Prism Computer Corporation**
2 Park Plaza
Suite 1060
Irvine, CA 92614-8520
800-774-7622
Fax: 949-553-6559
Educational consultant for manufacturers, government agencies and colleges.
Micheal A Ellis, President

1132 **Professional Computer Systems**
849 SE Greenville Avenue
Winchester, IN 47394-8441
765-584-2288
Fax: 765-584-1283
www.pcswin.com
Computer consultants for businesses, schools and municipalities.
Steve Barnes, President

1133 **Professional Development Institute**
280 S County Road
Suite 427
Longwood, FL 32750-5468
407-834-5224
Educational consultants for US Department of Transportation and commercial concerns.
Elsom Eldridge, Jr, President

1134 **Profiles**
507 Highland Avenue
Iowa City, IA 52240-4516
319-354-7600
Fax: 319-354-6813
Educational consultants for school districts and commercial concerns.
Douglas Paul, President

1135 **Pyramid Educational Consultants**
13 Garfield Way
Newark, DE 19713
302-368-2515
888-732-7462
Fax: 302-368-2516
pyramid@pecs.com
www.pecsusa.com
Educational consultant for general trade, historical commissions and other public bodies.
Andrew Bondy, President
Lori A Frost, Vice President

1136 **Quality Education Development**
41 Central Park West
New York, NY 10023
212-724-3335
800-724-2215
Fax: 212-724-4913
info@qedconsulting.com
Structures courses that promote knowledge and understanding through interactive learning, and communication programs.

1137 **Quantum Performance Group**
5050 Rushmore Road
Palmyra, NY 14522-9414
315-986-9200
Educational consultant for commercial concerns, including schools.
Dr. Mark Blazey, President

1138 **Rebus**
4111 Jackson Road
Ann Arbor, MI 48103-1827
734-668-4870
Fax: 734-913-4750
Educational consultant for schools and school districts.
Linda Borgsdorf, President

1139 **Records Consultants**
10826 Gulfdale Street
San Antonio, TX 78216-3607
210-366-4127
Fax: 210-366-0776
Educational consultant for school districts and municipalities.
Lang Glotfelty, President

1140 **Regional Learning Service of Central New York**
770 James Street Office
Syracuse, NY 13203-1644
315-446-0500
Fax: 315-446-5869
Educational consultants for commercial concerns.
Rebecca Livengood, Executive Director

1141 **Reinventing Your School Board**
Aspen Group International,Inc
PO Box 260301
Highlands Ranch, CO 80163-0301
303-478-0125
Fax: 208-248-6084
Linda Dawson, Contact
Dr. Randy Quinn, Contact

1142 **Relearning by Design**
447 Forcina Hall
PO Box 7718
Ewing, NJ 08628-0718
609-771-2921
Fax: 609-637-5130
info@relearning.org
www.relearning.org
Grant Wiggins, Author/Editor
Jacquelyn Nance, Chair

1143 **Research Assessment Management**
816 Camarillo Springs Road
Camarillo, CA 93012-9441
805-987-5538
Fax: 805-987-2868
Educational consultants for governmental agencies and commercial concerns.
Adrienne McCollum, PhD, President

1144 **Robert E Nelson Associates**
120 Oak Brook Center
Suite 208
Oak Brook, IL 60523

630-954-5585
Fax: 630-954-5606
Consulting for private colleges, universities and secondary schools.

1145 Rookey Associates
1740 Little York Xing
Little York, NY 13087
607-749-2325
Educational consultant for school districts, public utility companies and the government.
Ernest J Rookey, President

1146 Root Learning
810 W S Boundary Street
Perrysburg, OH 43551-5200
419-874-0077
Fax: 419-874-4801
Business, educational, employment consultant for commercial concerns.
Randall Root, Chairman/CEO

1147 School Management Study Group
1649 Lone Peoh Drive
Salt Lake City, UT 84117
801-277-3725
Fax: 801-277-4547
Organization seeking to promote improvement of schools and to involve educators in critical school problems.
Donald Thomas, President
Dale Holden, Associate

1148 SchoolMatch by Public Priority Systems
2200 Lane Woods Drive
Columbus, OH 43221
973-831-1757
schoolmatch.com
An educational consultant for private and public schools.
William L. Bainbridge, Ph.D., FACFE, President/ CEO

1149 Sensa of New Jersey
110 Mohawk Trail
Wayne, NJ 07470-5030
973-831-1757
An educational consultant for private and public schools.
John Pinto, President

1150 Shirley Handy
4151 Wild Lilac Drive
Turlock, CA 95382-8308
209-668-4142
Fax: 209-668-1855
info@n-e-n.com
www.n-e-n.com
Educational consultants for school districts and teachers.
Shirley Handy, Owner

1151 Sidney Kreppel
704 E Benita Boulevard
Vestal, NY 13850-2629
607-754-6870
Educational consultants.
Sidney Kreppel, Owner

1152 Solutions Skills
545 E Tennessee Street
Tallahassee, FL 32308-4981
850-681-6543
Fax: 850-681-6543
www.solutionskills.com
Business and educational consultants for state and governments, educational, medical and legal publishing companies.
Randall Vickers, President

1153 Special Education Service Agency
3501 Denali Street
Suite 101
Anchorage, AK 99503-1068
907-563-8284
877-890-9269
Fax: 907-562-0545
sesa@sesa.org
www.sesa.org
Educational consultant for school districts.
Nancy Nagarkar, Executive Director
Laraine Adams, Secretary

1154 Sports Management Group
918 Parker Street
Suite A-13
Berkeley, CA 94710
510-849-3090
Fax: 510-849-3094
tsmq@sportsmqmt.com
www.sportsmgnt.com
Educational consulting for universities.
Lauren Livingston, President

1155 Stewart Howe Alumni Service of New York
3109 N Triphammer Road
Lansing, NY 14882
607-533-9200
Fax: 607-533-9218
programs@stewarthowe.com
www.stewarthowe.com
Educational consultants for college organizations.
Peter McChesney, Director
Mike Duesing, Managing Partner

1156 Strategies for Educational Change
11 Whitby Court
Mount Holly, NJ 08060
609-261-1702
barbd@prodigy.net
Development of programs for youths at risk.

1157 Success for All Foundation
300 E. Joppa Road
Suite 500
Baltimore, MD 21286
410-616-2300
800-548-4998
Fax: 410-324-4444
sfainfo@successforall.net
www.successforall.net
A not-for-profit organization dedicated to the development, evaluation and dissemination of proven reform models for preschool, elementary and middle schools.
Nancy Madden, Ph.D., CEO

1158 Teachers Curriculum Institute
P.O. Box 1327
Rancho Cordova, CA 95741
916-366-3686
800-497-6138
Fax: 800-343-6828
infor@teachtci.com
www.teachtci.com
Educational consultant for schools and teachers.
Bert Bower, President/ CEO
Amy Larson, Chief Operating Officer

1159 Teachers Service Association
1107 E Lincoln Avenue
Orange, CA 92865-1939
714-282-6342
Educational consultants for schools and teachers.
Richard Ghysels, Secretary Treasurer

1160 Tech Ed Services
One World Trade Center
8th Floor
Long Beach, CA 90831
562-869-1913
800-832-4411
Fax: 562-869-5673
info@techedservices.com
techedservices.com
Computer, planning and training consultant for k-12 educators and adult educators.
Patricia K Sanford, President/ CEO
Brenna Terrones, TES Senior Specialist

1161 Technical Education Research Centers
2067 Massachusetts Avenue
Cambridge, MA 02140-1340
617-873-9600
Fax: 617-873-9601
contactus@terc.edu
www.terc.edu
Educational consultant for the National Science Foundation and the Department of Education.
Arthur Nelson, Founder
George E. Hein, Chairman

1162 Tesseract Group
18 W 27th Street
11th Floor
New York, NY 10001
212-481-8304
Fax: 212-481-8306
info@tesseractllc.com
tesseractllc.com
An integrated education management company, serving private and public charter elementary, middle and high schools in six states.
Erica Payne, Founder

1163 Timothy Anderson Dovetail Consulting
936 Nantasket Avenue
Hull, MA 02045-1453
781-925-3078
Fax: 781-925-9830
Educational consultant for businesses.
Eric Anderson, Owner

1164 University Research
7200 Wisconsin Avenue
Suite 600
Bethesda, MD 20814-4811
301-654-8338
Fax: 301-941-8427
www.urc-chs.com
Educational consultants for the federal government along with other government and private sectors.
Barbara N. Turner, President

1165 University of Georgia-Instructional Technology
630 Aderhold Hall
Athens, GA 30602
706-542-4110
Fax: 706-542-4240
coeinfo@uga.edu
www.coe.uga.edu
Instructional design and development.
Aurthur M. Horne, Dean
Pedro R Portes, Professor

1166 Uplinc
48 Capital Drive
West Springfield, MA 01089
413-693-0700
sales@uplinc.com
www.uplinc.com

Computer consultants for commercial, general public and educational concerns.

Ron Marino, President

1167 William A Ewing & Company
505 S Main Street
Suite 700
Orange, CA 92868
714-245-1850
Fax: 714-456-1755
ewingo@aol.com
www.members.aol.com/ewingo
Expertise in compensation and classification.

1168 Wisconsin Technical College System Foundation
1 Foundation Circle
Waunakee, WI 53597-8914
608-849-2400
Fax: 608-849-2468
foundation@wtcsf.tec.wi.us
www.wtcsf.tec.wi.us
Educational consultant for educational institutions and businesses.

Loren Brumm, Executive Director

Africa

1169 **Alexandra House School**
King George V Avenue
Floreal
Mauritius
230-696-4108
Fax: 230-696-4108
admin@alexandrahouseschool.com
www.alexandrahouseschool.com
A private English Primary day school in Mauritius for boys and girls between 4 and 11 years of age. Cater for approximately 100 children and provide a British curriculum with a strong international flavour.
M Wrenn-Beejadhur, Principal

1170 **American International School-Dhaka**
United Nations Road Baridhara
Dhaka
Bangladesh
880-2-882-2414
Fax: 880-2-883-3175
info@ais-dhaka.net
www.ais-dhaka.net
Provides a program based on American educational principles to students from an international community, creates an academic and social environment that challenges students to achieve their potential, become life-long learners and contribute to changing global society.
Kyra Buchko, President
Diane Lindsey, Vice President

1171 **American International School-Johannesburg**
Private Bag X 4
Bryanston 2021
Republic of South Africa
011 464 1505
Fax: 27-11-464-1327
info@aisj-jhb.com
www.aisj-jhb.com
Serves a diverse community of students from around the world and provides a challenging education emphasizing academic excellence through a collaborative partnership with families and staff. Our program inspires and prepares the students to become responsible world citizens with a passion for life long learning.
Andy Page-Smith, Director
Ellinor Parkes, Admissions Coordinator

1172 **American International School-Zambia**
PO Box 31617
Lusaka
Zambia
260-211-260509 (10
Fax: 260-211-260-538
SpecialPerson@aislusaka.org
www.aislusaka.org
Committed to being a leading IB World School, offering a balanced, academically rigorous and internationally recognized college preparatory education and seeks to enable its students to become successful, lifelong learners, as well as humane, self-directed, confident and well-rounded individuals.
Chris Mulind, Director
Jim Anderson, Secondary Principal

1173 **American School of Kinshasa**
Unit 31550
APO AE
09828
243-884-6619
Fax: 243-884-1161
irene.epp@gmail.com
www.tasok.cd
rawing on the strengths of a committed and culturally diverse community, The American School of Kinshasa aims to provide a high quality American primary and secondary education for English speaking students living in the Democratic Republic of Congo
Irene Epp, Superintendent
Fiona M Merali, Business Manager

1174 **American School-Tangier**
Rue Christophe Colomb
Tangier 9000
Morocco
212-39 93 98 27/28
Fax: 212-39 94 75 35
ast@tangeroise.net.ma
www.theamericanschooloftangier.com/
An independent, coeducational day and boarding school which offers an educational program from prekindergarten through grade 12 for students of all nationalities.
Brian Horvath, Head of School

1175 **American School-Yaounde**
BP 7475
Yaounde
Cameroon
237-2223-0421
Fax: 237-2223-6011
school@asoy.org
asoy.org
Ensures that all students achieve high academic success, demonstrate critical thinking skills, and become responsible and compassionate, global citizens prepared for their next stage in life; as gained through an enriched, American curriculum and offered in a challenging, secure, and diverse environment.
Paul Sheppard, School Director

1176 **Arundel School**
28 Arundel School Road
PO Box MP 91 Mount Pleasant
Harere, Zimbabwe
263-4-302121
head@arundel.ac.zw
www.arundel.ac.zw
School providing an active educational program, which encompasses excellence in culture, sports and personal development.
P. Makoni, Head
K Shawatu, Deputy Head

1177 **Arusha International School**
PO Box 733
Moshi, Kilimanjaro
Tanzania
255-27-275-5004
Fax: 255-27-275-2877
director@ismoshi.net
www.ismoshi.org
Offers a fully accredited, academically rigorous international education for students of ages three to nineteen years old.
Barry Sutherland, CEO
Bob Woods, Director

1178 **Asmara International Community School**
117-19 Street, #6
PO Box 4941, Asmara
Eritrea
291-1-161-705
Fax: 291-1-161-705
johnston@gmail.com
www.aicsasmara.com
Grade levels pre K-12.
Paul Johnston, Director

1179 **Banda School**
PO Box 24722
Nairobi
Kenya 00502
254-20-8891220/260
Fax: 254-20-8890004
bandaschool@swiftkenya.com
www.bandaschool.com
Meet the educational needs of children living in and around Nairobi whose parents required a Preparatory School education for their children but who did not wish them to go to boarding school overseas.
Michael D Dickson, Headmaster
W Rutter, Deputy Head

1180 **Bishop Mackenzie International Schools**
PO Box 102
Lilongwe
Malawi
265-1-756-364
Fax: 265-1-751-374
info@bmismw.com
bmis.ecis.org
The mission of the school is to prepare students to become responsible, self-reliant, contributing and productive citizens of our ever-changing world.
Peter Todd, Director
Janette Johnson, Primary Head Teacher

1181 **Braeburn High School**
Kisongo Campus
Gitanga Road
PO Box 45112 GPO Nairobi
Kenya 00100
254-20-5018000
Fax: 254-20-3872310
andy.hill@braeburn.ac.ke
www.braeburn.com
This is a co-educational international boarding school following the British National Curriculum (University of Cambridge International General Certificate of Secondary Education Examinations IGCSE), with boarding options.
R E Diaper, Principal
Mr. Terry L. K. Childs, CEO

1182 **Braeburn School**
Gitanga Road
PO Box 45112 GPO Nairobi
Kenya 00100
254-722 68557
Fax: 254-2-572310
scott.webber@braeburn.ac.ke
www.braeburn.com
This school caters to close to 600 children from 61 different countries.
R E Diaper, Principal
Mr. Terry L. K. Childs, CEO

1183 **British International School Cairo**
km 38, Cairo-Alex Desert Road
Beverly Hills, 6th of October
Egypt, EG
202-3859-2000
Fax: 202-3859-1720
info@bisc.edu.eg
www.bisc.edu.eg
The School was established in 1976 to provide a balanced and challenging education based on British principles and curricula to meet the needs of the children of the expatriate British and Anglo-Egyptian communities; children from the Commonwealth and other countries with educational systems based upon British standards; children of the

English-speaking Egyptian community and other nationalities tied to British-type schooling.

Simon O'Grady, Assistant
Ahmed Ezz, Principal

1184 British School-Lom
BP 20050
Lome
Togo
228-222-606
Fax: 228-222-498
admin@bsl.tg
www.bsl.tg
We value not only academic success but encourage talent of all kinds, whether in academic studies, art, drama, music or games; and that we take the position that the pupil who is kind and helpful, who has a positive attitude to school life and fellow pupils, is considered every bit as worthwhile as the brilliant scholar, artist or athlete.

1185 British School-Lom,
228-226-46-06
Fax: 228-226-49-89
This school offers an English based curriculum for 120 day students and 95 boarding students (110 boys; 105 girls), ages 4-18. The school is an independent, co-educational day and boarding school. External exams from the University of London and Cambridge-UK plus International Baccalaureate (IB) is offered. Applications needed to teach include science, pre-school, French, math, social sciences, administration, Spanish, reading, German, English and physical education.

1186 British Yeoward School
Parque Taoro
Tenerife
Spain, ES 38400
00-34-922-384685
Fax: 00-34-922-37-35-65
office@yeowardschool.org
www.yeowardschool.org
The International British Yeoward School provides a high quality British education for children of all ages in an open, multi-cultural environment; allowing each child to achieve their full potential in a positive learning community

Karen Hernandez, Head of Primary Grades
Alan Halstead, Head of School

1187 Broadhurst Primary School
Private Bag BR 114 Broadhurst
Garborone
Botswana, BW
267-3971-221
Fax: 267-307987
broadhurst@info.bw
www.info.bw
To create, together with the family, a caring environment of learning and experience, in which children may develop their potential to the full, may acquire the knowledge and skills to equip them for living, may experience the best that the human spirit has achieved, may develop respect for themselves, for other people and the world around them and have the courage to make a difference to future

Rehana Khan, Head Teacher
Michael Eisen, Deputy Headteacher

1188 Brookhouse Preparatory School
PO Box 24987- 00502
Nairobi
Kenya
254-20-2430260
Fax: 254-20-891641
info@brookhouse.ac.ke
www.brookhouse.ac.ke
Provides education in general computer literacy.

Eric Mulind, School Coordinator

1189 Cairo American College
PO Box 39
Maadi 11431
Cairo, EG 11431
20-2-755-5505
Fax: 20-2-2519-6584
support@cacegypt.org
www.cacegypt.org
Cairo American College is a world class learning environment that affirms the voice, passions and talents of students and inspires them to use their hearts and minds as global citizens.

Nivine Captan-Amr, Board Chair
Elizabeth Bredin, Secretary

1190 Casablanca American School
Route de la Mecque,Lotissement Ougo
Casablanca, Morocco 20150
212-22-214-115
Fax: 212-22-212-488
cas@cas.ac.ma
www.cas.ac.ma
To offer the best possible U.S. and international university preparatory education program, curriculum and instruction for its students.

Simohamed Erroussafi, President
Karima Abisourour, Vice President

1191 Cavina School
PO Box 43090
Nairobi
Kenya
254-2-3866011
Fax: 254-2-3866676
cavina@iconnect.co.ke
www.cavina.ac.ke
Cavina aims to develop many qualities in the children who come through her gates - academic excellence, an inquiring mind, a sense of moral and social responsibility, and most of all a recognition of their relationship with their Creator who has revealed Himself through His son Jesus.

Massie Bloofield, Headmaster/Managing Director

1192 Dakar Academy
BP 3189 Route des Peres Maristes
Dakar, Senegal
West Africa
221-33-832-06-82
Fax: 221-33-832-17-21
office@dakar-academy.org
www.dakar-academy.org
Dakar Academy exists to partner in the advancement of the Kingdom of God through serving missionary families by providing education services for their children

Charlie Campbell, Chairman
Joseph Rosa, Director

1193 Greensteds School
Private Bag
Nakuru
Kenya
254 50 50770
Fax: 254 50 50775
office@greenstedsschool.com
www.greenstedsschool.com/
An international school for boys and girls.

MP Bentley, Headmaster

1194 Harare International School
66 Pendennis Road
Mount Pleasant
Harare, Zimbabwe
(263 4) 870514/5
Fax: 263-4-883-371
his@his.ac.zw
www.his-zim.com
Grade levels prekindergarten through twelfth, with enrollment of 376.

Marcel Gerrmann, Board Chair
Shannon Brauchli, Vice Chair

1195 Hillcrest Secondary School
PO Box 24819
Nairobi
Kenya 00502
254-20-882-222
Fax: 254-20-882-350
admin@hillcrest.ac.ke
www.hillcrest.ac.ke/secondary/
Mixed boarding school.

Christopher Drew, Head Teacher

1196 International Community School-Addis Ababa
PO Box 70282
Addis Adaba
Ethiopia
251-11-3-711-544
Fax: 251-11-371-0722
info@icsaddis.edu.et
www.icsaddis.edu.et/
An independent, coeducational day school which offers an educational program from prekindergarten through grade 12 for students of all nationalities.

Jim Laney, Director

1197 International School-Kenya
PO Box 14103
Nairobi
Kenya 00800
254-20-418-3622
Fax: 254-20-418-3272
info@isk.ac.ke
www.isk.ac.ke
Students from many backgrounds go to this school, which prepares them for successful transitions to other schools and universities around the world, offering both a North American Hogh School Diploma as well as the International Baccalaureate Diploma to its graduates.

John Roberts, Director
Jodi Lake, Curriculum Coordinator

1198 International School-Moshi
PO Box 733
Moshi, Kilimanjaro
Tanzania
255-27-275-5004
Fax: 255-27-275-2877
school@ismoshi.org
www.ismoshi.org
The school inspires individuals to be lifelong learners in a global community.

Bob Woods, Director of ISM
Keiron White, Head, Moshi Campus

1199 International School-Tanganyika
United Nations Road
PO Box 2651, Dar es Salaam
Tanzania
255-22-2151817/8
Fax: 255-22-2152077
ist@raha.com
www.istafrica.com
IST aspires to provide an outstanding international education. We value and respect cultural diversity and embrace the people and natural environment of Tanzania. Within this safe, secure

and caring community students reach their full potential as citizens of the world.

David Shawver, Director
Nazir Thawer, General Manager

1200 John F Kennedy International School
CH-3792 Saanen
Switzerland
41-033-744-1372
Fax: 41- 033-744-8982
lovell@jfk.ch
www.jfk.ch
Boarding day school for boys and girls aged 5-14 years.

William Lovell, Co-Director
Sandra Lovell, Co-Director

1201 Kabira International School
PO Box 34249
Kampala
Uganda
256-0414-530-472
Fax: 256-0414-543-444
office@kisu.com
www.kabiraschool.com
Grade levels Pre-K through 8, school year - September - July

Emma Whitney, Admissions
Elaine Whelen, Principal

1202 Kestrel Manor School
Ring Road Westlands
PO Box 14489, Nairobi
Kenya 00200
254-20-3740-311
info@kestrelmanorschool.com
www.kestrelmanorschool.com
Coeducational school for children Kindergarten through secondary schooling.

1203 Khartoum American School
PO Box 699
Khartoum
Sudan
249-15-577-0105
Fax: 249-183-512044
kas@krtams.org
www.krtams.org
An independent, coeducational day school which offers an educational program from prekindergarten through grade 12 for students of all nationalities.

Gregory Hughes, Superintendent
Brad Waugh, Principal

1204 Kigali International School
Caisse Sociale Estates, Gaculiro
BP 6558
Kigali, Rwanda
250-0783307282
Fax: 250-72128
office.kics@gmail.com
www.kicsrw.org
Non-profit, co-educational day school

Bryan Hixson, Chairman
Mark Thiessen, Vice Chairman

1205 Kingsgate English Medium Primary School
Box 169
Mafeteng, 900 Lesotho
Africa
Kingsgate is the only non-denominational primary school in the district. The curriculum is English-based offered to a total of 460 day students (240 boys; 220 girls), PreK-7. Overseas teachers are welcome with the length of stay being one year, with housing provided. Applications needed to teach include pre-school and reading.

M Makhothe, Principal

1206 Kisumu International School
PO Box 1276
Kisumu
Kenya
254-35-21678
admin@kis.co.ke
www.kisumu.braeburn.com
This school is located on the shores of Lake Victoria and offers a unique education to students of all nationalities and cultural backgrounds. The total enrollment of the school is 35 day students, in grades K-7. The school does participate in the teacher exchange programs, with the length of stay being two years with housing provided by the school. Applications needed to teach include science, preschool, math, social sciences, English and physical education.

Neena Sharma, Principal

1207 Lincoln Community School
American Embassy Accra
N126/21 Dedeibaa Street
Abelemkpe, Accra
Ghana, West Africa
233 30 277 4018
Fax: 233 302 78 09 85
headofschool@lincoln.edu.gh
www.lincoln.edu.gh
is committed to inspiring students to achieve the highest standards of intellectual and personal development through a stimulating and comprehensive program.

Dennis Larkin, Head of School
Sanjay Rughani Tanzanian, President

1208 Lincoln International School of Uganda
PO Box 4200
Kampala
Uganda
256-41-4200374/8/9
Fax: 256-41-200303
dtodd@isumail.ac.ug
www.lincoln.ac.ug
Grade levels Pre-K through 12, school year August - June

Daniel Todd, Dean of Studied/Admission
Jim Campbell, Chairman

1209 Maru A Pula School
Plot 4725
Maruapula Way
Botswana 00045
267-391-2953
Fax: 267-397-3338
principal.map@gmail.com
www.maruapula.org/
Maru-a-Pula is a dynamic, world-class school rooted in Botswana. We offer a rigorous curriculum that prepares students for entry to highly selective universities and to pursue challenging careers. Through programmes emphasizing self-discipline and community service, each student learns personal and social responsibility.

Andrew S Taylor, Principal

1210 Mombasa Academy
PO Box 86487
Mombasa
Kenya, KE
254-11-471629
Fax: 254-11-221484
msaacademy@swiftmombasa.com
www.msaacademy.com
Our aim is to help our pupils to reach their true potential. Within the academic and extra-curricular frameworks, staff offer pupils considerable personal support; warm and productive working relations are a distinguishing feature of our community and are instrumental in helping each girl and boy on the road towards maturity and self-fulfillment

Kishor Joshi, Headmaster
FJ Bentley, Founder

1211 Northside Primary School
PO Box 897
Gaborone
Botswana
267-395-2440
Fax: 267-395-3573
administration@northsideschool.net
www.northsideschool.net
In Gaborone, Botswana, Northside Primary School provides education in English and serves the needs of primary school children of all nationalities.

Mandy Watson, Headteacher

1212 Nsansa School
PO Box 70322
Ndola
Zambia
26-2-611753
Fax: 26-2-618465
This school offers an English curriculum to 185 day students (96 boys; 124 girls), in grades K-7. Length of stay for overseas teachers is one year with housing provided. Student/teacher ratio is 20:1.

Nel Mather, Principal

1213 Peterhouse
Private Bag 3741
Marondera
Zimbabwe
263 (0)279 - 22200
Fax: 263 (0)279 - 24200
peterhouse@peterhouse.co.zw
www.peterhouse.org
This Anglican school offers an English based curriculum for 19 day students and 790 boarding students (535 boys; 255 girls), in Form I-Form VI. The school is willing to participate in a teacher exchange program with the length of stay being one year, with housing provided. Applications needed to teach include science, math, and physical education.

JB Calderwood, Rector

1214 Rabat American School
1 Bis Rue Emir Ibn Abdelkade
Agdal, Rabat
Morocco 10000
212-537-671-476
Fax: 212-537-670
Fax: 212-537-670-963
info@ras.ma
www.ras.ma
We provide our students with a breadth of experiences which encourage them to realize their full potential and allow them to acquire the knowledge, skills, character, and confidence to contribute positively and responsibly to an ever-changing, interconnected world.

Paul W Johnson, Director

1215 Rift Valley Academy
PO Box 80
Kijabe, 00220
Kenya
254-20-3246-249
Fax: 254-20-3246-111
rva@rva.org
www.rva.org
RVA is a Christian boarding school located in central Kenya. The academy, a branch of Africa Inland Mission International, exists to provide a quality education in a nurturing en-

vironment for the children of missionaries serving in Africa.

Roy E Entwistle, Principal
Tim Cook, Superintendent

1216 Rosslyn Academy
PO Box 14146
Nairobi
Kenya 00800
254-20-263-5294
Fax: 254-20-263-5281
info@rosslynacademy.com
www.rosslynacademy.com
The purpose of Rosslyn Academy is to provide a K-12 North American and Christian-oriented educational program for children of missionaries. Rosslyn also welcomes children from privately sponsored families who are in sympathy with the philosophy of the school.

Phil Dow, Superintendent
Don McGavran, Director of Operations

1217 Sandford English Community School
PO Box 30056 MA
Addis Ababa
Ethiopia
251-11-123-38-92
Fax: 251-11-123-3728
admission@sandfordschool.org
www.sandfordschool.org
A co-educational, non-boarding, nursery to pre University institution. Its committed to providing a standard of education that is accepted within Ethiopia and by the international community.

Jon D P Lane, Head of Primary School
Tsegaye Kassa, Senior Manager

1218 Schutz American School
51 Schutz Street
PO Box 1000
Alexandria, Egypt 21111
(20) (3) 576-2205
Fax: (20) (3) 576-0229
jlujan@schutzschool.org.eg
www.schutzschool.org.eg
A single campus houses PreK-3 through grade twelve in two main classroom buildings and an auditorium/ classroom complex, as well as the administrative center, dining room, resident staff housing, clinic, art room, computer labs, libraries and snack bar. Sports facilities on the campus include basketball, volleyball, tennis and football courts, a half-size grass soccer pitch, and a swimming pool and weight training room.

Dr Joyce Lujan, Head of School
Nathan Walker, Upper School Principal

1219 Sifundzani School
PO Box A286, Swazi Plaza
Mbabane
Swaziland
268-404-2465
Fax: 268-404-0320
sifundzani@realnet.co.sz
A coeducational day school which offers an educational program from grades 1 through 10 for students of all nationalities.

Ella Magongo, Principal

1220 Sir Harry Johnston Primary School
Kalimbuka Road
Zomba PO Box 52
Malawi
265-1525280
Fax: 265 888202374
admin@shjzomba.com
www.shjzomba.com

Una Barras-Hargan, Headteacher

1221 St. Barnabas College
34 Langeberg Avenue Bostmont Johann
PO Box 88188 Newclare
South Africa 02112
011-27-474-2055
Fax: 011-27-474-2249
theronn@stbarnabas.co.za
www.stbarnabas.co.za
St Barnabas College is a co-educational secondary school in Johannesburg. It is well known as a centre of excellence. The school's mission is to provide quality secondary education to young people, the main criterion for admission being intellectual potential and the motivation to succeed.

Glynn Blignaut, Headmaster
Faizel Panker, Deputy Headmaster

1222 St. Mary's School
Rhapta Road, PO Box 40580- 00100
Nairobi
Kenya
254-020-4444569
Fax: 254-020-4446191
info@stmarys.ac.ke
www.stmarys.ac.ke
We are a Catholic Private School committed to our international character in the provision of a spiritual, intellectual and physical education. We aim at developing the gifts of the young in an atmosphere which encourages the ethos of self-expression and mutual respect with a view to their facing the future responsibly, with confidence and courage.

John Awiti, Head of School
Rosemary Abuodha Omogo, Deputy Principal

1223 St. Paul's College
St. Paul's United Theological College
Po Private Bag
Limuru
Kenya 00217
254 - 20 - 2020505
Fax: 254-66-73033
assistantregistrar@stpaulslimuru.ac.ke
www.stpaulslimuru.ac.ke/
The school prepares men and women for ministry in the Christian Church and present day society.

Samuel Kobia, Chancellor
Joseph Galgalo, Vice Chancellor

1224 Tigoni Girls Academy
Box 10
Limuru
Kenya
This Academy is a small, closely knit community of individuals from different cultures in which physical, emotional, creative and intellectual development is fortified in all aspects of daily life. Total enrollment is 40 boarding students, ages 11-16. Applications from overseas include science, math, social sciences, French, Spanish and English. Length of stay for overseas teachers is 2 years with housing provided. The Academy is affiliated with the Church of England.

Duncan Kelly, Principal

1225 Waterford-Kamhlaba United World College
PO Box 52
Mbabane
Swaziland
011-268-422-0866
Fax: 011-268-422-0088
admissions@waterford.sz
www.waterford.sz/index.php
This school offers a curriculum based in English for 181 day students and 295 boarding (251 boys; 226 girls), in grades 6-12. Overseas teachers length of stay is three years with housing provided. Applications needed to teach include math, English, and physical education.

Laurence Nodder, Principal
Bruce Wells, Deputy Principal

1226 Westwood International School
PO Box 2446
Gabarone
Botswana
011-267-390-6736
Fax: 011-267-390-6734
westwood-admissions@info.bw
www.westwoodis.com
Westwood International School shall provide students with a quality international education that shall effectively prepare them for access to tertiary study and the world of work, and enable them to confidently meet future challenges as life long learners

Phyllis Hildebrandt, Principal
Michael Francis, Director

1227 Windhoek International School
Private Bag
Windhoek
Namibia 16007
264-61-241-783
Fax: 264-61-243-127
k.jarman@wis.edu.na
www.wis.edu.na
The Windhoek International School prepares its students to be inquiring, knowledgeable and caring participants in the global arena through an international curriculum of the highest standard. WIS embraces the diversity of its students from the international community and Namibia, in an atmosphere of mutual respect, tolerance and educational enrichment for all

Catherine O'Connor-Smith, Secretary
Neville Field, Chairperson

Asia, Pacific Rim & Australia

1228 Aiyura International Primary School
PO Box 407
Ukarumpa Papua
New Guinea

Perry Bradford, Principal

1229 Ake Panya International School
158/1 Moo 3 Hangdong-Samoeng Road
Banpong, Hangdong, Chiang Mai 50230
Thailand
66-53-36-5303
Fax: 66-53-365-304
akepanya@cm.ksc.co.th
www.akepanya.co.th
Grade levels 1-12, school year August - June

Barry Sutherland, Headmaster
Holly Shaw, Director of Studies

1230 Alotau International Primary School
PO Box 154
Alotau, Milne Bay Province
Papua New Guinea
675-641-1078
Fax: 675-641-1627
alotauis@iea.ac.pg
www.iea.ac.pg

Lucy Kula, Principal

1231 **Amelia Earhart Intermediate School**
Unit 5166
APO AP 96368
Okinawa
011-81-611-734-132
Fax: 011-81-611-734-720
aeis_okinawa@pac.dodea.edu
www.earhart-is.pac.dodea.edu
Success in Education is a Partnership in Responsibility characterized by the opportunities and the guidance necessary to motivate learners, the desire and ability to be successful in human interactions, to access and process information, and to accept personal responsibility for all decisions made throughout one's lifetime.
Deborah Carlson, Principal

1232 **American International School-Dhaka**
P.O. Box: 6106
Gulshan, Dhaka 1212
Bangladesh
880-2-882-2452
Fax: 880-2-882-3175
info@ais-dhaka.net
www.ais-dhaka.net
Provides a program based on American educational principles to students from an international community, creates an academic and social environment that challenges students to achieve their potential, become life-long learners and contribute to changing global society.
Richard Boerner, Superintendent
Kyra Buchko, President

1233 **American International School-Guangzhou**
No 3 Yan Yu Street S
Ersha Island, Yuexiu District
Guangzhou PR China 51010
86-20-8735-3392
Fax: 86-20-8735-3339
admissions@aisgz.org
www.aisgz.org/
Prepares students for entrance into the very best universities in the world is enhanced by being in the cultural center of Guangzhou and Southern China.
Joseph Stucker, Director
Katherine Farrell, Chair

1234 **American School-Bombay**
SF 2 G Block
Bandra Kurla Complex
Mumbai 400 0
91 22 6772 7272
Fax: 91 22 6252 6666
admissions@asbindia.org
www.asbindia.org
ASB delivers a dynamic educational program that encourages each student to achieve her or his highest potential. While ASB is a U.S. style school, the Indian setting and multi-national community, representing over 51 countries, brings children who have varied experiences together to learn in a rich and unique environment
Paul M Fochtman, Superintendent

1235 **American School-Guangzhou (China)**
Number 3 Yan Yu Street S
Ersha Island, Yuexiu District
Guangzhou, China 51010
8620-8735-3393
Fax: 8620-8735-3339
admissions@aisgz.org
www.aisgz.org/
An independent, coeducational day school which offers an educational program from kindergarten through grade 12
Joseph Stucker, Director
Paul Wood, Principal

1236 **American School-Japan**
1-1 Nomizu 1
Chofu-shi, Tokyo
Japan 182-0
0422-34-5300
Fax: 0422-34-5303
info@asij.ac.jp
www.asij.ac.jp
The American School in Japan is a private, coeducational day school which offers an educational program from nursery through grade 12 for students of all nationalities, but it primarily serves the American community living in the Tokyo area. The school was founded in 1902. The school year comprises 2 semesters extending from September to January and January to June.
Ed Ladd, Headmaster

1237 **Aoba International School**
2-10-34 Aobadai
Meguro-Ku, Tokyo
Japan 153-0-42
03-3461-1442
Fax: 81-3-3463-9873
meguro@aobajapan.jp
www.aobaonline.jp
A co-educational school located on campuses in Meguro and Suginami. Over 550 students are enrolled in classes from pre-kindergarten to grade nine.
Neal Dilk, Head of School
Chiharu Uemura, VP

1238 **Ashgabat International School**
Berzengi, Ata Turk Street
Ashgabat
Turkmenistan
386-12-007870
Fax: 386-12-007871
ashgabat@qsi.org
tkm.qsi.org
Offers high quality education in the English language for elementary students from three years through thirteen years of age.
Brad Goth, Director

1239 **Bali International School**
PO Box 3259
Denpasar
Bali, Indonesia
62-361-288-770
Fax: 62-361-285-103
admin@baliis.net
www.baliinternationalschool.com
Provides educational excellence in a supportive, secure environment, preparing students to thrive and succeed as responsible citizens in a changing world. Offers the three IB Programs (PYP, MYP and DP) and is accredited by WASC.
Chris Akin, Director
Russell McGrath, PS-12 Assistant Principal

1240 **Bandung Alliance International School**
Jalan Bujanggamanik Kav 2
Kota Baru Parahyangan
Bandung, Indonesia 40553
62-22-8681-3949
Fax: 62-22-8681-3953
info@baisedu.org
www.baisedu.org
BAIS operates as a private non-profit school to serve the international community. BAIS provides quality education in the traditions of classic, conservative ethics and values.
Pete Simano, Director
Charity Lamertha, Elementary Principal

1241 **Bandung International School**
Jl Suria Sumantri No 61
Bandung
West Java, Indonesia 40164
62-22-201-4995
Fax: 62-22-201-2688
bisadmin@poboxes.com
www.bisdragons.com
At Bandung International Scholl, it is our vision to be a preeminent school providing world class secular education in the English language to the children of expatriates and others while maintaining strong links with the Indonesian community
Henri Behelmans, Head of School
Mark Holland, Chair

1242 **Bangalore International School**
Geddalahalli, Hennur Bagalur Road
Kothanur Post
Bangalore, India 560 0
91-802-846-5060
Fax: 91-802-846-5059
info@bisedu.co.in
www.bangaloreinternationalschool.com
Provides internationally recognized standards of education with an India ethos and enable students to fulfill their potential in a culturally rich atmosphere.
Anuradha Monga, Principal

1243 **Bangkok Patana School**
643 Lasalle road Sukhumvit 105 Bang
Bangkok, Thailand 10260
6602-398-0200
Fax: 6602-399-3179
reception@patana.ac.th
www.patana.ac.th
We are an academically directed school, focussed on our commitment to offer all of our students the best intellectual and physical preparation for higher education.
Tej Bunnag, Chairman
Kulvadee Siribhadra, Director

1244 **Beijing BISS International School**
No 17, Area 4 An Zhen Xi Li
Chaoyang District, Beijing
China 10002
86-10-6443-3151
Fax: 86-10-6443-3156
Admissions@biss.com.cn
www.biss.com.cn
To educate and empower our students to attain personal excellence and positively impact the world.
Chan Ching Oi, CEO
Ettie Zilber, Head of School

1245 **Bob Hope Primary School**
Unit 5166
APO AP 96368-5166
Okinawa, Japan 96368-5166
11-81-611-734-0093
Fax: 11-81-98-934-6806
bhps.okinawa@pac.dodea.edu
www.bob-hope-ps.pac.dodea.edu
The Bob Hope Primary School community is committed to teaching basic skills using developmentally appropriate strategies.
Jim Journey, Principal
Luldes Giraud, Vice Principal

1246 **Bogor Expatriate School**
PO Box 258
Jalan Papandayan 7, Bogor 16151
Indonesia

62-251-324360
Fax: 62-251-328512
Mission is to provide opportunities to foster positive attitudes towards learning.

Chris Rawlins, Head of School
Lance Kelly, Principal

1247 Bontang International School
15 Roszel Road
Po Box 5910
Princeton, NJ 08543
62-548551176
iss@iss.edu
An international school with an English/Japanese based curriculum for twenty day students (6 boys; 14 girls), grades PreK-8. Student/teacher ration 5:1.

Roger Hove, Executive Vice President

1248 Brent International School-Manila
Brentville Subdivision
Mamplasan, Bian, Laguna
Philippines 04024
63 (049) 511-4330
Fax: 632-633-8420
webmaster@brent.edu.ph
www.brent.edu.ph
Brent Schools, in a Christian ecumenical environment in the Philippines, are committed to develop individual students as responsible global citizens and leaders in their respective communities, with a multicultural and international perspective, and equipped for entry to colleges and universities throughout the world.

Dick B Robbins, Headmaster
Jeffrey W Hammett, Deputy Headmaster

1249 Brent School
Brent Road
PO Box 35, Baguio City
Philippines 02600
63 (074) 442-3628
Fax: 63 (074) 442-2260
webmaster@brent.edu.ph
www.brentschoolbaguio.com
Brent Schools, in a Christian ecumenical environment in the Philippines, are committed to develop individual students as responsible global citizens and leaders in their respective communities, with a multicultural and international perspective, and equipped for entry to colleges and universities throughout the world.

Dick B Robbins, Headmaster
Ursula Banga-an Daoey, Deputy Head

1250 British International School
Bintayo Jaya Sektor IX Jl
Raya Jomabang Ciledug Pondok Aren
Jakarta, ID 15227
62-21-745-1670
Fax: 62-21-745-1671
enquiries@bis.or.id
www.bis.or.id
The new premises and facilities enable the school to excel further in the range of opportunities and experiences that can be offered to its students.

Christian Barkei, Principal
Brian Dallamore, Chairman

1251 British School Manila
36th Street University Park Forth B
Fort Bonifacio Global City
Taguig, PH
63 2 860 4800
Fax: 63 2 860 4900
admissions@britishschoolmanila.org
www.britishschoolmanila.org
The British School Manila will deliver the highest standard of education in the Philippines for British children and for English speaking children of other nationalities The British School Manila provides outstanding education for English speaking children of all nationalities aged 3-18, based on an adapted form of the National Curriculum of England, and the I.B. Diploma

Chris Mantz, Head of School
Glenn Hardy, Head of Primary School

1252 British School-Muscat
PO Box 1907
Ruwi
Oman 00112
00968 24600842
Fax: 00968 24601062
admin@britishschoolmuscat.com
www.britishschoolmuscat.com
The Vision of the British School-Muscat is to offer the highest quality British education to children of wide ranging abilities and nationalities. It values cultural diversity and provides a caring, innovative and stimulating environment, realizing the full potential and celebrating the success of every student. The School's curriculum will also develop the child as a whole person, provide them with learning-to-learn skills and will prepare them to lead a successful life in an inter-cultural wor

Kai Vacher, Principal
Deirdre Selway, Registrar

1253 Calcutta International School Society
18 Lee Road
Calcutta 700 020
India
www.calcuttais.edu.in
This school offers an English-based curriculum to 480 day students (230 boys; 250 girls), grades Nursery-12. CIS follows GCE London Curriculum. The cultures represented by the student body include expatriates, NRIs, local children. The student body is mainly Indians. Highly qualified individuals offering excellent results. The school is willing to participate in a teacher exchange program with the length of stay being 1-2 years, with no housing provided.

N Chatterjee, Principal
L Chaturvedi, Faculty Head

1254 Caltex American School
CPI Rumbal
Pekanbaru, Sumatra Riau
Indonesia
62-765-995-501
Fax: 62-765-996-321
Grade level preK through 8.

Daniel Hovde, Superintendent

1255 Camberwell Grammar School
55 Mout Albert Road
Canterbury 3126, Victoria
Australia
61 3 9835 1777
Fax: 61 3 9836 0752
registrar@cgs.vic.edu.au
www.cgs.vic.edu.au
Independent boys school.

CF Black, Principal

1256 Canadian Academy
4-1 Koyo Cho Naka
Higashinada-Ku, Kobe
Japan 658-0-32
81-78-857-0100
Fax: 81-78-857-3250
hdmstr@canacad.ac.jp
www.canacad.ac.jp/canacad/welcome.html
Canadian Academy inspires students to inquire, reflect, and choose to compassionately impact the world throughout their lives.

Fred Wesson, Headmaster
Charles Kite, Assistant Headmaster

1257 Canadian School-India
14/1 Kodigehalli Main Road
Sahakar Nagar, Bangalore 560 092
India
91-80-343-8414
Fax: 91-80-343-6488
csib@vsnl.com
www.canschoolindia.org
Grade levels K-13, school year August - June

T Alf Mallin, Principal

1258 Canberra Grammar School
40 Monaro Crescent
Red Hill
Australia ACT 2
02-6260-9700
Fax: 02-6260-9701
headmaster@cgs.act.edu.au
www.cgs.act.edu.au
To develop a cultured man, ready for today's world and the future, balanced in intellectual, spiritual, emotional and physical aspects, with a love of learning and a willingness to serve fellow students and the wider community

Justin Garrick, Headmaster
Alan Ball, Head of Senior School

1259 Carmel School-Hong Kong
10 Borrett Road
Mid-Levels
Hong Kong
852-2964-1600
Fax: 852-2813-4121
admin@carmel.edu.hk
www.carmel.edu.hk
Carmel School is committed to providing children living in Hong Kong with the highest international standard of secular and Jewish education. Through small classes and individual attention, the school offers a supportive environment that develops students' confidence, imagination and skills, in both academic and social spheres.

Edwin Epstein, Head of School
Kaisha Chow, Operations Director

1260 Casa Montessori Internationale
17 Palm Avenue Forbes Park Makati
Etro Manila D-3117
Philippines
Pre-nursery, nursery and kindergarten classes.

Carina Lebron, Principal

1261 Cebu International School
Banilad Road
PO Box 735, Cebu City 6000
Philippines
(63 32) 401-1900
Fax: (63 32) 401-1904
deidref@cis.edu.ph
www.cis.edu.ph/main.aspx
The primary aim of Cebu International School is to develop well-balanced global citizens who are intelligent, dynamic, respectful of universal moral values within a multicultural environment, and able to cope responsibly in an ever-changing interdependent world.

Deidre Fischer, Superintendent
Jenny Basa, Dean of Student Services

1262 Central Java Inter-Mission School
Jl Nakula Sadewa Raya Number 55
Salatiga, Jateng
Indonesia 50722
62-298-311673
Fax: 62-298-321609

office@mountainviewics.org
www.mountainviewics.org
Primary intent of the school is that all students be thoroughly exposed to Scripture and that they find and sustain a vital relationship to Jesus Christ through Holy Spirit.

Willliam J Webb III, Superintendent
Kirk Thornton, Assistant Superintendent

1263 Central Primary School
Winston Churchill Avenue
Port Vila
Republic of Vanuatu
678-23122
Fax: 678-22526
central@vanuatu.com.vu
www.central.herts.sch.uk
Meet the needs of children from most countries and to provide an equivalent level of education for local children in an 'English as a First Language' context.

John Path, Chairman
John Lee Solomon, PEO

1264 Chiang Mai International School
PO Box 38
13 Chetupon Road
Thailand, TH 50000
665-324-2027
Fax: 665-324-2455
info@cmis.ac.th
www.cmis.ac.th
Encourage the development of students' abilities in critical, analytical, and independent thinking, demonstrated in fluent oral and written communication.

Lance Potter, Principal
Sinturong Pannavalee, Director

1265 Chinese International School
1 Hau Yuen Path
Braemar Hill, Hong Kong
China
852-2510-7288
Fax: 852-2510-7488
cis_info@cis.edu.hk
www.cis.edu.hk
Committed to the achievement of academic excellence and is characterized and enriched by its dual-language program in Chinese and English.

Theodore S Faunce, Headmaster
Li Bin, Deputy Head of School

1266 Chittagong Grammar School
Sarson Valley, 448/B Joynagar,
Chiottagong
Bangladesh
88-031-632900
cgslower@hotmail.com
www.chittagonggrammarschool.com
Dedicated to the total growth and development of each student. Provides the students a broad, challenging and sound education to enable children to achieve the highest standards of which they are capable.

Afran Sanchita, Teacher
Akther Sharmin, Teacher

1267 Colombo International School
28, Gregory's Road
Colombo 7
Sri Lanka
94-11-269-7587
Fax: 94-11-269-9592
management@cis.lk
www.cis.lk
English medium co-educational day school with separate Infant, Junior and Secondary sections.

M.J. Chappell, Principal
Armyne Wirasinha, Chairman

1268 Concordia International School-Shanghai
999 Mingyue Road, Jinqiao,Pudong
Shanghai
201206, China
86-21-5899-0380
Fax: 86-21-5899-1685
admissions@ciss.com.cn
www.ciss.com.cn
Concordia's vision to offer academic excellence in a faith-based, caring community finds its roots in the 150-year educational tradition of the Lutheran Church-Missouri Synod.

James Koerschen, Head of School
Carol Ann Tonn-Bourg, Director of Admissions

1269 Cummings Elementary School
Unit 5039
APO AP
Japan 96319-5039
81-3117-66-2226
Fax: 81-3117-62-5110
pcumming@pac.dodea.edu
www.cummings-es.pac.dodea.edu
We, the community of Cummings Elementary School, are committed to guiding our students to become successful learners and responsible citizens in an ever-changing world

Scott Sterry, Principal

1270 Dalat School
11200 Penang
Tanjung Bunga
Malaysia
60-4-899-2105
Fax: 60-4-890-2141
info@dalat.org
www.dalat.org
The mission of Dalat International School is to prepare young people to live fully for God in a rapidly changing world by enabling them to understand, evaluate, and reconcile that world with the foundation of God's unchanging values.

Karl Steinkamp, Director
Fred Colburn, High School Principal

1271 Dover Court Prep School
Dover Road
Singapore, 139644
Singapore
65-67757664
Fax: 65-67774165
admin@dover.edu.sg
www.dovercourt.org
To teach goals of the learning process, which is facilitated through encouraging pupils to pose and solve problems, take risks, demonstrate responsible attitudes and behaviour, adopt a critical and self-evaluative approach to their work.

Maureen Roach, Director
Catherine Alliott, Chief Executive Officer

1272 Ela Beach International School
PO Box 1137
Boroko
Papua New Guinea
675-325-2183
Fax: 675-325-7925
bmackinlay@temis.iea.ac.pg
This school consists of 262 boys and 222 girl day students in PreK-Grade 6. The length of stay for overseas teachers is three years with housing provided. School enrollment is made up of 260 PNG children, 224 non PNG children, overseas and PNG staff team teaching in mixed age group classrooms.

Bruce E Mackinlay, Principal

1273 Elsternwick Campus-Wesley College
577 Street Kilda Road
Melbourne
Australia 03004
61-3-8102-6100
Fax: 61 3 8102 6054
stkildaroad@wesleycollege.net
www.wesleycollege.net
Wesley College is a coeducational school of the Uniting Church which has enriched the lives of thousands of young people, since it opened on 18 January 1866 as a boy's boarding school. In its 140 year history, it has experienced the influence of 14 principals, each of whom has in turn, enriched the life of the College.

Jack Moshakis, Executive Director
Helen Drennen, Principal

1274 Faisalabad Grammar School
Kohinoor Nagar
Faisalabad 728593
Pakistan
www.fgschools.edu.pk
This Islamic school offers a curriculum taught in both English and Urdu to 2,000 day students (1,000 boys; 1,000 girls), in Junior Nursery up to eighteen years of age. The school runs 50% of classes in Matriculation Streams Local, and 50% in 'O' and 'A' level University of Cambridge UK examinations. Applications needed to teach include science, math, English and computers, with the length of stay for overseas teachers being one year.

RY Saigol Sarfraz, Principal
N Akhtar, VP

1275 Faith Academy
MCPO Box 2016
Makati City
Philippines 00706
11-632-248-5000
Fax: 63-2-658-0026
vanguard@faith.edu.ph
www.faith.edu.ph
Faith Academy envisions expanding children's educational delivery options to meet the needs of the missions enterprise throughout Asia.

Tom Hardeman, Superintendent
Mike Hause, Deputy Superindentent

1276 French International School
165 Blue Pool
Happy Valley, SAR, Hong Kong
China
852-257-76217
Fax: 852-257-79658
lfi@lfis.edu.hk
www.fis.edu.hk
To provide, together with families, a nurturing, culturally diverse community that inspires our young people to realize their true potential as confident, independent learners and responsible global citizens with moral values and integrity.

Francis Cauet, Headmaster
Samuel Hureau, Administrator

1277 Fukuoka International School
3-18-50 Momochi
Sawara-ku, Fukuoka
Japan 00814-6
81-92-841-7601
Fax: 81-92-841-7602
adminfis@fka.att.ne.jp
www.fis.ed.jp
To create a dynamic learning environment in which students can be educated in high international academic standards. We strive to be a model of unity in diversity in which the in-

dividual is respected in each student is challenged at his/her own level.

Linda Gush, Head of School
Daniel Habel, Dean of Students

1278 Garden International School
16 Jalan Kiara 3, Off Jalan Bukit K
Kuala Lumpur
Malaysia 50480
011-60-3-6209-6888
Fax: 011-60-3-6201-2468
admissions@gardenschool.edu.my
www.gardenschool.edu.my
Grade levels Pre-K through eleventh.

Simon Mann, Principal
Dato' Loy Teik Ngan, Chairman

1279 Geelong Grammar School-Glamorgan
14 Douglas Street
Toorak, Victoria
Australia 03142
011-61-3-9829-1444
Fax: 011-61-3-9826-2829
toorakcampus@ggs.vic.edu.au
www.ggs.vic.edu.au
Geelong Grammar School offers an exceptional Australian education. Our students are girls and boys who see the richness of the world through confident eyes.

Lisa Marchetti, Fundraising Coordinator
Stephen Meek, Principal

1280 German Swiss International School
11 Guildford Road, The Peak
Hong Kong
China
011-852-2849-6216
Fax: 011-852-2849-6347
gsis@gsis.edu.hk
www.gsis.edu.hk
Encourage and foster the talents of our students - as well-rounded individuals, responsible team members and open-minded citizens of the 21st century.

Hans Peter Naef, COO
Jens-Peter Green, Principal

1281 Glenunga International High School
99 L'Estrange Street
Glenuga
South Australia 05064
011-61-8-8379-5629
Fax: 011-61-8-8338-2518
glenunga@gihs.sa.edu.au
www.gihs.sa.edu.au
Grade levels 8-12.

Wendy Johnson, Principal
Jeremy Cogan, Deputy Principal

1282 Good Hope School-Kowloon
303 Clear Water Bay Road
Kowloon
Hong Kong
011-852- 2321-0250
Fax: 011-852- 2324-8242
goodhope@ghs.edu.hk
www.ghs.edu.hk
Provides equal opportunities to develop their moral, intellectual, physical, social, emotional and artistic aspects of life.

Pauline Yuen, Supervisor
Paul Chow, Principal

1283 Goroka International School
PO Box 845
Goroka EHP
Papua New Guinea
011-675-732-1452
Fax: 011-675-732-2146
gorokais@online.net.pg
www.iea.ac.pg
Provide education of a high academic standard from early childhood to grade 12

James M Masa, Principal

1284 Hebron School-Lushington Hall
Lushington Hall, Ootacamund
Tamil Nadu
India 64300
11-91-42-3244-2372
Fax: 11-91-42-3244-1295
admin@hebronooty.org
www.hebronooty.org
Independent, international Christian school.

Mark Noonan, Principal

1285 Hillcrest International School
PO Box 249
Sentani 99352
Papua, Indonesia
011-62-967-591460
Fax: 011-62-967-592673
director@hismk.org
www.hismk.org
HIS is a Christian international school. Teachers must raise their own support, normally with a mission. Enrollment consists of 97 day students and 24 boarding (53 boys; 68 girls), in grades K-12.

Margaret Hartzler, Director
Ryan Kennedy, Director

1286 Hiroshima International School
3-49-1 Kurakake
Asakita-Ku
Hiroshima, Japan 739-1
011-81-82-843-4111
Fax: 011-81-82-843-6399
info@hiroshima-is.ac.jp
www.hiroshima-is.ac.jp
The Hiroshima International School is an independent, coeducational day school which offers educational programs from preschool through grade 12. The school year comprises 2 semesters extending from early September to mid-June.

Peter MacKenzie, Principal

1287 Hokkaido International School
1-55, 5-Jo, 19-Chome
Hirahishi, Toyohira-Ku
Sapporo, Japan 062-0
011-81-11-816-5000
Fax: 011-81-11-816-2500
his@his.ac.jp
www.his.ac.jp
A private, coeducational day and boarding school which offers an America-style education from preschool through grade 12.

Michael Branson, Headmaster
Eri Kashiwabara, Business Manager

1288 Hong Kong International School
1 Red Hill Road
Tai Tam, Hong Kong
Republic of China
011-852-3149-7000
Fax: 011-852-2813-8740
Advancement@hkis.edu.hk
www.hkis.edu.hk
The Hong Kong International School is a private, Christian, coeducational day school which offers an educational program from pre-primary through grade 12 for students of all nationalities and religious backgrounds. The school year comprises 2 semesters extending approximately from August 19 to January 16 and from January 19 to June 12.

Doug Werth, Chair
David Condon, Head of School

1289 Ikego Elementary School
PSC 474 Box 300
FPO, AP
Japan 96351-300
011-81-46-806-8320
Fax: 011-81-46-806-8324
principal_ikegoes@pac.dodea.edu
www.ikego-es.pac.dodea.edu
Provides developmentally-appropriate learning experiences that teaches, problem solving, critical thinking, make responsible choices.

Scott Finlay, Principal

1290 International Christian School
1 On Muk Lane
Shek Mun
N.T. Hong Kong
011-852-3920 0010
Fax: 011-852-2336-6114
ics@ics.edu.hk
www.ics.edu.hk
International Christian School is an exceptional school for a number of reasons. Every ICS graduate has enrolled in a college or university somewhere in the world.

Jack Young, Board Chair
Noel Chu, Executive Assistant

1291 International Community School
1225 The Parkland Road
Khwaeng Bangna, Khet Bangna Bangkok
Thailand 10260
011-66-2-338-0777
Fax: 011-66-2-338-0778
info@icsbangkok.com
www.icsbangkok.com
Based on the Bible, in partnership with parents, we teach the whole student to know and apply wisdom for the good of our world and the glory of God.

Darren Gentry, Headmaster
Gary Opfer, High School Principal

1292 International School Manila
University Parkway
Fort Bonifacio Global City, Taguig
Philippines 01634
011-63-2-840-8400
Fax: 011-63-2-840-8405
superintendent@ismanila.com
www.ismanila.com
International School Manila is an independent international school whose structure, traditions and style emanate from the United States and whose curriculum and methodology reflect the best in worldwide educational research and practice. Our school is diverse and dynamic, and our students have the highest aspirations for their education and future lives.

William Brown, High School Principal
David Toze, Superintendent

1293 International School of the Sacred Heart
4-3-1 Hiroo, Shibuya-ku
Tokyo
Japan 150-0
011-81-3-3400-3951
Fax: 011-81-3-3400-3496
info@issh.ac.jp
www.issh.ac.jp
ISSH is a multicultural Catholic school that warmly welcomes students and families from many faiths. The Pre-Kindergarten and Kindergarten classes for 3, 4 and 5 year olds are for boys and girls, while grades 1-12 are for girls only.

Yvonne Hayes, Headmistress
Charmaine Young, High School Principal

1294 International School-Bangkok
39/7 Soi Nichada Thani,Samakee Road
Nonthaburi
Thailand 11120
011-66-2-963-5800
Fax: 011-66-2-583-5432
daladk@isb.ac.th
www.isb.ac.th
Our Vision states that our students will make extraordinary academic progress. They become smart about their own learning processes, understanding what does and does not work for them as learners.
Dr Bill Gerritz, Head of School
Dr Ugo Costessi, Deputy Head of School/CFO

1295 International School-Beijing
10 An Hua Street
Shunyi District,,Beijing
China 10131
86-10-8046-2345
Fax: 86-10-8046-2001
isb-info@isb.bj.edu.cn
www.isb.bj.edu.cn
Educate and inspire students to reach their unique potential and contribute positively to society by providing a world class education enriched by diversity and the Chinese culture.
Thomas Hawkins, Head of School
Rodney Fagg, High School Principal

1296 International School-Eastern Seaboard
PO Box 6
Banglamung, Chonburi
Thailand 20150
(6638) 372 591
Fax: (6638) 372 950
ise@ise.ac.th
www.ise.ac.th
Prepare an international student population for higher education and lifelong learning by emphasizing higher level thinking skills, effective communication, global responsibilities, and personal wellness within a cooperative and supportive school community.
Robert Brewitt, Superintendent
Heather Naro, Elementary Principal

1297 International School-Fiji
PO Box 10828
Laucala Beach Estate, Suva
Fiji Islands
11-679-3393-560
Fax: 11-679-3340-017
info@international.school.fj
www.international.school.fj
An independent co-educational day school offering pre-school, primary and secondary education and offers excellent education and a caring and nurturing environment for young people. The curriculum includes International Baccalaureate (Primary Years Programme, Middle Years Programme, Diploma Programme), University of Cambridge - International General Certificate of Secondary Education and the Australian Capital Territory Year 12 Certificate and University Admissions Index (UAI).
Dianne Korare, Principal
Sera Brown, Registrar

1298 International School-Ho Chi Minh City
16 Vo Truong Toan St
An Phu Ward, District 2, Ho Ci Minh City
Vietnam
84-8-898-9100
Fax: 84 (8) 3 519-4110
admissions@ishcmc.edu.vn
www.ishcmc.com
The school provides and teaches the students about intellectual, emotional, social, creative, linguistic, cultural, moral, aesthetic and physical needs of each students. The school seeks to involve parents in the education of their children through regular communication.
Sean O'Maonaigh, Headmaster
Chris Byrne, Admissions/Marketing

1299 International School-Kuala Lumpur
PO Box 12645
Kuala Lumpur
Malaysia 50784
603-4259-5600
Fax: 603-4257-9044
iskl@iskl.edu.my
www.iskl.edu.my
Offers its students a superior education to prepare them to be responsible world citizens who think creatively, reason critically, communicate effectively and learn enthusiastically throughout life.
Paul Chmelik, Headmaster
Amina O'Kane, Admissions Director

1300 International School-Lae
PO Box 2130
Lae, Morobe
Papua New Guinea 00411
011-675-479-1425
Fax: 011-675-472-3485
mail@tisol.iea.ac.pg
www.tisol.ac.pg
Offers high quality education, from ages 18 months to grade 8. The curriculum prepares students for national and international success.
Neal Mather, Principal

1301 International School-Manila
Univeristy Parkway
Fort Bonifacio, Taguig City
Philippines 01634
632-840-8488
Fax: 632-840-8489
superintendent@ismanila.com
www.ismanila.org
An independent international school whose structure, traditions and style emanate from the United States. It aims to build a community of reflective learners who are passionate, caring and responsible contributors to the world in which we live.
Ray Dempsey, President
David Toze, Superintendent

1302 International School-Penang-Uplands
Jalan Sungai Satu
Batu Feringgi, Penang
Malaysia 11100
011-604-8819-777
Fax: 011-604-8819-778
info@uplands.org
www.uplands.org
Uplands aims to provide excellent international education for students of all nationalities in a challenging multi-cultural environment. It favours methods of teaching which foster the joys of learning, discovery and enquiry, aiming to nurture students into thinking, learning, caring and striving to meet the needs of a better world.
John Horsfall, Acting Principal
M R Chandran, Chair

1303 International School-Phnom Penh, Cambodia
146 Norodom Boulevard
PO Box 138, Phnom Penh
Cambodia
855-23-213-103
Fax: 855-23-213-104
ispp@ispp.edu.kh
www.ispp.edu.kh
ISPP empowers students, in a caring international environment, to achieve their potential by pursuing personal and academic excellence, and to grow as responsible global citizens who celebrate diversity.
Barry Sutherland, Director
Laura Watson, Chairperson

1304 International School-Phnom Penh-Cambodia
146 Norodom Boulevard
PO Box 138, Phnom Penh
Cambodia
855-23-213-103
Fax: 855-23-361-002
ispp@ispp.edu.kh
www.ispp.edu.kh
ISPP empowers students, in a caring international environment, to achieve their potential by pursuing personal and academic excellence, and to grow as responsible global citizens who celebrate diversity.
Barry Sutherland, Director
Laura Watson, Chairperson

1305 International School-Pusan
798 Nae-ri, Gijang-eup
Gijang-gun, Busan 619-902
South Korea
82 51 742-3332
Fax: 82 51 742 3375
enquiries@bifskorea.org
www.isbusan.org
The school possess a caring, family-like ethos, giving the children a high level of self-confidence and esteem, and teaching them tolerance and respect for other cultures.
Stephen Palmer, Principal
Thomas Walker, Chairman

1306 International School-Singapore
25 Paterson Road
Singapore 23851
(65) 6235 5844
Fax: (65) 6732 5701
admissions@iss.edu.sg
www.iss.edu.sg
ISS mission is to provide a multicultural educational environment for our students in which they achieve academic success, personal growth and become socially responsible and active global citizens with an appreciation of learning as a life-long process.
Mak Lai Ying, Principal
Anthony Race, Headmaster

1307 International School-Ulaanbaatar
Four Seasons Garden, Khan-Uul Distr
1st Khoroo, PO Box 36/10
Ulaanbaatar, Mongolia 17032
976-70160010
Fax: 976-70160012
administration@isumongolia.edu.mn
www.isumongolia.edu.mn
The International School of Ulaanbaatar seeks to offer the best educational system possible, based on an international curriculum.
Gregory Rayl, Director
Tuul Arildii, Deputy Director

1308 Island School
20 Borrett Road
Mid Levels
Hong Kong
852-2524-7135
Fax: 852-2840-1673
school@mail.island.edu.hk
www.island.edu.hk
An international, co-educational, comprehensive school, providing secondary education for children of all nations who can benefit from an education through the medium of English.
Pinder Wong, Council Chairman
Chris Binge, Principal

1309 Ivanhoe Grammar School
PO Box 91
The Ridgeway, Ivanhoe, Victoria
Australia 03079
61 3 9490 1877
Fax: 61 3 9497 4060
info@ivanhoe.com.au
www.igs.vic.edu.au
Our mission is to be a community of learning that develops in students the skills and values that will prepare them for the challenges and responsibilities of adult citizenship.
Roderick D Fraser, Principal
Andrew Sloane, Head of School

1310 JN Darby Elementary School
PSC 485 Box 99
FPO, AP
Japan 96321
011-81-956-50-8800
Fax: 011-81-956-50-8804
Darby_ES@pac.dodea.edu
www.darby-es.pac.dodea.edu/
The Darby Community promotes academic and social excellence so all students can become positive contributors to society.
Joy Jaramillo, Principal

1311 Jakarta International School
PO Box 1078/JKS
Jakarta 12010
Indonesia
(62-21) 750-3644
Fax: 62-21-765-7852
parentnet@jisedu.org
www.jisedu.org
JIS is a place where people from almost 60 countries come together to share ideas, experiences and values.
Tim Carr, Head of School

1312 Japan International School
7-5-1 Hikarigaoka
Shibuya-Ku, Tokyo 168-0081
Japan
81-3-3335-6620
Fax: 81-3-3332-6930
hikarigaoka@aobajapan.jp
www.aobaonline.jp/
Student of all nationalities, and religions are welcome.
Charles S Barton, Headmaster

1313 John McGlashan College
2 Pilkington Street
Maori Hill, Dunedin
New Zealand
03-467-6620
Fax: 03-467-6622
www.mcglashan.school.nz
ohn McGlashan College is an integrated, Year 7-13, secondary school for boys. The roll comprises approximately 380 dayboys from Dunedin city and its surrounds and 110 boarders, most of whom come from rural Otago and Southland. In addition, up to 20 international students are enrolled each year
K Michael Corkery, Principal
Neil Garry, Deputy Principal

1314 Kansai Christian School
282-2 Oaza Misato, Heguri-cho, Ikom
Nara Ken 636-0904
Japan
0745-45-6422
Fax: 011-81-745-45-6422
office@kansaichristianschool.com
www.kansaichristianschool.com
Kansai Christian School was established in 1970 to provide a general education in a Christian environment for children of the evangelical missionary community
Albert Greeff, Principal

1315 Kaohsiung American School
35 Sheng Li Road
Tzuo-Ying District (813)
Taiwan
886-7-583-0112
Fax: 886-7-582-4536
dchang@kas.kh.edu.tw
www.kas.kh.edu.tw
Kaohsiung American School (KAS) is a private, non-profit Pre-K - 12 institution with 330 students offering college preparatory programs leading to a U.S. high school diploma. It is located in Kaohsiung, a city of 1.5 million in southwestern Taiwan.
Tom Farrell, Superintendent
Deborah Taylor, Assistant Director

1316 Kellett School
2 Wah Lok Path
Wah Fu, Pokfulam
Hong Kong
852-2551-8234
Fax: 852-2875-0262
admissions@kellettschool.com
www.kellettschool.com
Kellett School is an independent non-for-profit school catering to the English-speaking children living in Hong Kong. The school is operated by Kellett School Association Limited through a Board of Governors; seven of whom are parents, elected by the Association, and the remaining three are ex-officio members. All parents become members of the Association.
Ann McDonald, Principal

1317 Kilmore International School
40 White Street
Kilmore, Victoria
Australia 03764
61-357-822-211
Fax: 61-357-822-525
info@kilmore.vic.edu.au
www.kilmore.vic.edu.au
The Kilmore International School is an independent, non-denominational, co-educational boarding and day school for academically motivated students undertaking their secondary education (Years 7-12 inclusive).
John Settle, Principal

1318 Kinabalu International School
PO Box 12080
88822 Kota Kinabalu, Sabah
Malaysia
608-822-4526
Fax: 608-824-4203
kismy@streamyx.com
www.kis.edu.my
This school offers an English-based curriculum for 100 day students (50 boys; 50 girls), ages 3-13 years.
1973 pages
Stuart McLay, Principal
Elis Ho, Office Manager

1319 King George V School
2 Tin Kwong Road
Homantin, Kowloon
Hong Kong
852-2711-3029
Fax: 852-2760-7116
office@kgv.edu.hk
www.kgv.edu.hk
Non selective secondary school which provides a broad.
Ed Wickins, Principal
Richard Bradford, Vice Principal

1320 Kitakyushu International School
Yahata Higashi-ku, Takami 2,
Shinnittetsu, Shijo, Kitakyushu
Japan
81-93-652-0682
This school offers an English based curriculum for 8 day students (2 boys; 6 girls), in kindergarten through elementary. The school is always looking for dedicated and qualified teachers to teach children and adults in school and preschool (especially female teachers). Applications needed include preschool and English.
Ann Ratnayake, Principal

1321 Kodaikanal International School
Seven Roads Junction, PO Box 25
Kodaikanal, Tamil Nadu
India 624 1-0101
91-4542-247-500
Fax: 91-4542-241-109
contact@Kis.in
www.kis.in
Kodaikanal Internationa lSchool is an autonomous residential school with a broad college-oriented curriculum, serving young people from a wide diversity of cultures. The School's academic program is intentionally set within a community life based on the life and teaching of Jesus Christ and devoted to service in India and the whole human community.
Geoffrey Fisher, Principal
Gregg Faddegon, Vice Principal

1322 Kooralbyn International School
Shop 1, 29 Wellington Bundock Drive
Kooralbyn QLD 4285
Australia
61-7-5544-6111
Fax: 61-7-5544-6702
info@kooralbyn.com
www.tkis.qld.edu.au
Aims to provide students with a broad liberal education.
Geoff Mills, Principal

1323 Kowloon Junior School
20 Perth Street
Ho Man Tin, Kowloon
Hong Kong
852-2714-5279
Fax: 852 2760 4438
office@kjs.edu.hk
www.kjs.edu.hk
Primary students learn English, math, science, technology, history, geography, art, music and physical education.
Mark Cripps, Principal
Deborah Graham, ESF Representative

1324 Kyoto International School
Kitatawara-cho,Nakadachiuri-sagaru
Yoshiyamachi-Dori, Kamigyo-ku, Kyoto
Japan 00602-8247
81-75-451-1022
Fax: 81-75-451-1023
kis@kyotointernationalschool.org
www.kyoto-is.org
Independent day school, offering education from Preschool level through to Middle School

Annette Levy, Head of School
Amanda Gillis-Furutaku, Board Chair

1325 Lahore American School
American Consulate General Lahore
15 Upper Mall, Canal Bank
Lahore
Pakistan 54000
92-42-576-2406
Fax: 92-42-571-1901
las@las.edu.pk
www.las.edu.pk
An independent, coeducational day school which offers an educational program from nursery through grade 12 for students of all nationalities.

Kathryn Cochran, Superintendent
Imran Aslam, Board Chair

1326 Lanna International School Thailand
300 Grandview Moo 10
Chiang-Mai to Hang Dong, T Mae-hea, A. M
Thailand 50100
66-53-806-231
Fax: 66-53-271-159
head@lannaist.ac.th
www.lannaist.ac.th
t is the goal of Lanna International School to prepare its students to be responsible world citizens who demonstrate a commitment to life-long learning and the application of that learning to the improvement of self, and local and global communities.

Roy Lewis, Head of School
Ajarn Kannika, School Director

1327 Lincoln School
PO Box 2673
Rabi Bhawan, Kathmandu
Nepal
977-1-4270482
Fax: 977-142-7268
Fax: 977-1-4272685
info@lsnepal.com.np
www.lsnepal.com
is an independent, international school in Kathmandu, Nepal with an American Curriculum

Allan Bredy, Director
Craig Baker, Principal

1328 Malacca Expatriate School
2443-C Jalan Batang Tiga
Tanjung Kling, Melaka
Malaysia 76400
011-60-6-315-4970
Fax: 011-60-6-315-4970
sossb@pd.jaring.my
www.meschool.virtualave.net
Mission is provide a high standard of learning. The students benefit from a high level of individual attention because of their low student to teacher ratio.

Susheila Samuel, Principal

1329 Marist Brothers International School
1-2-1 Chimori-cho
Suma-ku, Kobe
Japan 654-0
011-81-787-326266
Fax: 011-81-787-326268
enquiries@marist.ac.jp
www.marist.ac.jp
The philosophy of MBIS is designed to awaken students to the realities of life and to prepare them for the future. school aims to give to each student a well-rounded education incorporating the academic, moral, social and physical aspects of life.

Ed Fitzgerald, Principal
Geraldo de Couto, Vice Principal

1330 Matthew C Perry Elementary School
PSC 561 Box 1874
FPO Iwakuni 96310 0019
Japan
011-81-827-79-3447
Fax: 011-81-827-79-6490
principal.perryes@pac.dodea.edu
www.perry-es.pac.dodea.edu/
Committed to promoting student achievement in a positive safe environment. It provides a quality education for every student based on the needs of each child.

Shelia Cary, Principal
Christopher Racek, Asst. Principal

1331 Matthew C Perry Middle & High School
PSC 561 Box 1874
FPO Iwakuni 96310 1874
Japan
011-81-827-79-5449
Fax: 011-81-827-79-4600
principal.perryhs@pac.dodea.edu
www.perry-es.pac.dodea.edu/

Morgan Nugent, Principal
Robert Funk, Assistant Principal

1332 Mentone Boys Grammar School
63 Venice Street
Mentone, Victoria
Australia 03194
011-61-3-9584-4211
Fax: 011-61-3-9581-3290
enquiry@mentonegrammar.net
www.mentonegrammar.net
We are a school for boys and girls providing a flexible and sensitive approach which considers what boys and girls need at various stages of their development.

Mal Cater, Principal
Simon Appel, Chairman

1333 Mercedes College
540 Fullarton Road
Springfield 5062
South Australia
011-61-8-8372-3200
Fax: 011-61-8-8379-9540
info@mercedes.adl.catholic.edu.au
www.mercedes.adl.catholic.edu.au/index.cfm
Mercedes College, in Adelaide, South Australia, is a Reception to Year 12 Catholic co-educational school in the Mercy tradition.

Peter Daw, Principal
Steve Bowley, Business Manager

1334 Methodist Ladies College
207 Barkers Road Kew
Victoria 3101
Australia
011-61-3-9274-6333
Fax: 011-61-3-9819-2345
college@mlc.vic.edu.au
www.mlc.vic.edu.au
This college prepares its students for the world of tomorrow by liberating their talents through challenge, enrichment, and opportunity in a supportive Christian environment. Committed to technology and to student initiated learning so each girl from year five onward works with her personal computer to understand the present and shape the future. Total enrollment: 2,135 day students; 105 boarding. Grade range K-12. The school is willing to participate in a teacher exchange program.

Rosa Swtorelli, Principal
Louise Adler, Chairperson

1335 Minsk International School
DOS/Administrative Officer
7010 Minsk Place
Washington, DC 20521-7010
375-172-343-035
Fax: 375-172-343-035
mis@open.by
www.minsk.qsischool.org
An independent, coeducational day school which offers an educational program from kindergarten through grade 8 for students of all nationalities. Enrollment 11.

Stanley Harrison Orr, Director

1336 Moreguina International Primary School
PO Box 438
Konedobu Papua
New Guinea

Wayne Coleman, Principal

1337 Morrison Christian Academy
136-1 Shui Nan Road
Taichung 40679
Taiwan, TW 40679
11-886-4-2297-3927
Fax: 11-886-4-2292-1174
mcgillt@mca.org.tw
www.mca.org.tw
Morrison Academy exists to meet the educational needs of the children of missionaries throughout Taiwan, helping fulfill Christ's commission to go into all the world. Morrison seeks to provide a Christ-centered school culture where all students, from missionary and non-missionary families, experience a Biblically-integrated quality education. Therefore, Morrison structures learning so that students may develop the knowledge, discernment, and ability to dynamically impact their world as Christian

Tim McGill, Superintendent
Matt Strange, Director of Curriculum

1338 Mount Hagen International School
PO Box 945
Mount Hagen
Papua New Guinea
675-542-1964
Fax: 675-542-1840
mhis@online.net.pg
www.iea.ac.pg
It is envisaged that students enrolled at the Mount Hagen International School will always remain encouraged by their schooling. They will earn an education of International standard, their learning will be contextualized within Papua New Guinea culture, and they will learn how to become productive members of their community

Bruce Imatana, Principal

1339 Mt Zaagham International School
PT Freeport
Tembagapura W Papua
Indonesia
62 901 407876
Fax: 62 901 403170
joecuthbertson@efmi.com
mzis.org

Grade levels Pre-K through 98, school year September - June. Two campuses Tembagapura and Kuala Kencana

Barney Latham, Superintendent
Richard Ledger, Principal

1340 Murray International School

PO Box 1137
Boroko
Papua New Guinea
675-325-2183
Fax: 675-325-7925
ssavage@temis.iea.ac.pg
www.elamurray.ac.pg
Non-profit, private, co-educational day school that provides quality international standard education for the expatriate and local community in Port Moresby.

Suzanne Savage, Principal
Marlene Filippi, Deputy Principal

1341 Murree Christian School

Jhika Gali, Murree Hills
Punjab
Pakistan 47180
0092-513-410321
Fax: 0092-513-411668
mcs@mcs.org.pk
www.mcs.org.pk
This school offers an English-based curriculum for 20 day students and 140 boarding students (75 boys; 85 girls), in grades K-12. Murree Christian School educates the children of missionaries from 14 different countries working in Pakistan and the region. Living allowances rather than salaries are awarded. Overseas teacher stay is two years with housing provided by the school.

Phil Billing, Director
Linda Fisher, HS Faculty Head

1342 Mussoorie International School

Srinagar Estate, Mussoorie 248179
Uttarakhand
India
91-135-2632007
Fax: 91-135-2631160
misadmission@gmail.com
www.misindia.net
One of the leading residential educational institutions for girls and is recognized for its progressive education with a definite account on India culture and traditions.

HK Rawal, Principal
A. Ghosh, Headmaster

1343 Nagoya International School

2686 Minamihara, Nakashidami
Moriyama-ku, Nagoya, 463-0002
Japan
81-52-736-2025
Fax: 81-52-736-3883
info@nis.ac.jp
www.nagoyais.jp
Envisions a school community devoted to developing the skills, attitudes, and values that allow students to realize their full potential, lead lives of purpose, and become responsible, global citizens.

Rob Risch, Headmaster

1344 Narrabundah College

Jerrabomberra Avenue
Narrabundah, ACT 2604
Australia
61-2-6205-6999
Fax: 61-2-6205-6969
laura.beacroft@cbit.net.au
www.narrabundahc.act.edu.au
This college is a government college for years 11 and 12 students - the final two years of secondary education. It offers a challenging curriculum in a caring environment and meets the needs of an international community.

Steve Kyburz, Head of School
Laura Beacroft, Board Chair

1345 New International School of Thailand

36 Sukhumvit Soi 15
Bangkok, TH 10110
66-2651-2065
Fax: 66-2253-3800
nist@nist.ac.th
www.nist.ac.th
Co-educational, day school, IBO World School

Simon Leslie, Headmaster
Adrian Watts, Deputy Head

1346 Nile C Kinnick High School

PSC 473 Box 95
FPO, AP
96349-95
011-81-46816-7392
Fax: 011-81-46-816-7278
Kinnick_Principal@pac.dodea.edu
www.kinnick-hs.pac.dodea.edu
The mission of Nile C. Kinnick High School is to challenge students to maximize potential in order to prepare them to be responsible and productive citizens in an ever-changing world.

Lorenzo Brown, Principal

1347 Nishimachi International School

2-14-7 Moto Azabu
Minato-ku Tokyo
Japan 106-0-46
81-3-3451-5520
Fax: 81-3-3456-0197
info@nishimachi.org
www.nishimachi.ac.jp
Offers a dual-language, multicultural program ro 430 student k-9.

Terence Christian, Headmaster

1348 Okinawa Christian School International

1835 Zakimi, Yomitan-son
Okinawa 904-0301
Japan
81-098-958-3000
800-446-6423
Fax: 81-098-958-6279
info@ocsi.org
www.ocsi.org
Provides a major educational support base for the international community living on Okinawa.

Rich Barnett, Contact
Randel J Hadley, Superintendent

1349 Osaka International School

4-4-16 Onohara Nishi
Mino-shi, Osaka, 562-0032
Japan
81-72-727-5050
Fax: 81-72-727-5055
addmissions@senri.ed.jp
www.senri.ed.jp
OIS is an English-language-based, preK-12 grade coeducational college-preparatory school.

John Searle, Head of School

1350 Osaka YMCA International High School

6-7-34 Benten Minato-ku
Osaka 552-0007
Japan
06-4395-1002
Fax: 06-4395-1004
general-inquiry@oyis.org
www.oyis.org
OYIS strives to be a leading provider of international education for the citizens and residents of Osaka and its environs.

John Murphy, Principal

1351 Osan American High School

Unit 2037
APO AP 96278-0005
Korea
011-82-31-661-9076
Fax: 011-82-31-661-9121
PRINCIPAL.OSANHS@pac.dodea.edu
www.osan-hs.pac.dodea.edu
Provides student with successful, productive and rewarding educational experiences.

Timothy Erickson, Principal
Truly Schramm, Assistant Principal

1352 Osan Elementary School

Unit 2037
APO, AP 96278-2037
Korea
011-82-31-661-6912
Fax: 011-82-31-661-5733
david.petree.pac.dodea.edu
www.osan-es.pac.dodea.edu
Provides quality and challenging educational opportunities for all students to become critical thinkers, life-long learners, and productive citizens in a global society.

Mia Plourde, Secretary
David Petree, Principal

1353 Overseas Children's School

PO Box 9, Pelawatte
Battaramulla
Sri Lanka
94 11 2784920-2
Fax: 94-11-2784999
admin@osc.lk
www.osc.lk
OSC develops the whole person as a responsible learner striving for personal excellence within a culturally diverse school

Areta Williams, Head of School
Jerry Huxtable, Chair

1354 Overseas Family School

25 F Paterson Road
Singapore 23851
65-6738-0211
Fax: 65-6733-8825
executive_director@ofs.edu.sg
www.ofs.edu.sg
To focus on the individual needs of every student and to provide a supportive atmosphere designed to help students achieve personal academic goals.

David Perry, Chairman
Irene Wong, Executive Director

1355 Overseas School of Colombo

Pelawatte
PO Box 9, Battaranmulla
Sri Lanka
94 11 2784920-2
Fax: 94 11 2784999
admin@osc.lk
www.osc.lk
OSC develops the whole person as a responsible learner striving for personal excellence within a culturally diverse school.

Areta Williams, Head of School
Jerry Huxtable, Chair

1356 Pacific Harbour International School

PO Box 50
Pacific Harbour, Deuba
Fiji Islands

679-450-0005
Fax: 679-450-566
www.isbi.com
Janet Tuni, Principal

1357 Pasir Ridge International
Unocal-po Box 3-tampines S
Balikpapan 9152
Singapore
62-542-543-474
Fax: 62-542-767-126
prschool@bpp.mega.net.id
pasirridgeinternationalschool.com
Grade levels preK through 8.
Kathryn Carter-Golden PhD, Principal

1358 Peak School
20 Plunketts Road
The Peak
Hong Kong
852-2849 7211
Fax: 852-2849 7151
office@peakschool.net
www.ps.edu.hk
Helping promote a better understanding of Americans on the part of the peoples served
Annette Ainsworth, Principal/Secretary
Bill Garnett, Vice Principal

1359 Phuket International Preparatory School
115/15 Moo 7 Thepkasattri Road
Thepkasattri, Thalang, Phuket 83110
Thailand
66 (0)76 336 000
Fax: 66 (0)76 336 081
info@phuketinternationalacademy.com
www.phuketinternationalacademy.com
Agnes Hebler, Principal

1360 Popondetta International School
PO Box 10
Popondetta, Papua
New Guinea
Michael Whitting, Principal

1361 Prahram Campus-Wesley College
577 St Kilda Road-Prahran
Melbourne
Australia
61 3 8102 6100
Fax: 61 3 8102 6054
stkildaroad@wesleycollege.net
www.wesleycollege.net
AB Conabere, Principal

1362 Pusan American School
Do DOS
Pusan 96259
South Korea
82-51-801-7528
Fax: 82-51-803-1729
pas@pac.odedodea.edu
Alexia Venglek, Principal

1363 Pusan Elementary & High School
Unit 15625
APO AP 96259-0005, Pusan
Korea
82-52-801-7528
Fax: 82-51-803-1729

1364 QSI International School-Phuket
Box 432 A Muang
Phuket 83000
Thailand
66-076-354-077
Fax: 66-76-354077
phuket@qsi.org
www.qsi.org
To keep this urge to learn alive in every child in QSI schools. Our schools are established to provide in the English language a quality education for students in the cities we serve.
Khun Janrita Hnobnorb, Administrative Coordinator
Alan Siporin, Director

1365 QSI International School-Zhuhai
No. 168 Anning Road
Xianzhou District
Zuhai, China 51900
86-756-815-6134
Fax: 86-756-8189021
zhuhai@qsi.org
www.qsi.org
To keep this urge to learn alive in every child in QSI schools. Our schools are established to provide in the English language a quality education for students in the cities we serve.
Matthew Farwell, Director

1366 Quarry Bay School
6 Hau Yuen Path Braemar Hill
North Point, Hong Kong
China
852 2566 4242
Fax: 852 2887 9849
debra.gardiner@qbs.edu.hk
www.qbs.edu.hk
Our aim is to encourage in our children the enjoyment of learning by providing activities both in and outside the classroom which help to develop confident, happy and successful individuals.
Mina Dunstan, Principal

1367 Rabaul International School
PO Box 855
Rabaul Enbp, Papua
New Guinea
675-982-8770
Fax: 675-982-8770
www.iea.ac.pg
Ian Smith, Principal

1368 Richard E Byrd Elementary School
PSC 472 Box 12
FPO
Japan, AP 96348-12
011-81-45-281-4815
Fax: 011-81-45-281-4870
www.byrd-es.pac.dodea.edu
Richard E. . Byrd envisions a school unbound by traditional school concepts of time, location and age requirements. Byrd Elementary School will provide all students with vast opportunities for learning and civic involvement
Gwen Baxter-Oakley, Principal

1369 Robert D Edgren High School
Unit 5040
APO
Japan, AP 96319-5040
011-81-176-77-4377
Fax: 011-81-176-77-4959
principal_*edgren_hs@pac.dodea.edu
www.edgren-hs.pac.dodea.edu
Committed to helping students develop academically, socially, physically and emotionally in a global community.
Gerogia Watters, Principal

1370 Ruamrudee International School
6 Ramkamhaeng 184 Road
Minburi, Bangkok
Thailand 10510
66-2-518-0320
Fax: 66-2-518-0334
info@rism.ac.th
www.rism.ac.th/risweb
Grade levels K-12, school year August - June
Fr. Leo Travis, Director
Dave Parsons HS Principal

1371 Saigon South International School
Tan Phong Ward
Ho Chi Minh City
Vietnam
(84-8) 5413-0901
Fax: (84-8) 5413-0902
info@ssis.edu.vn
www.ssischool.org
Saigon South International School is a college preparatory school committed to the intellectual and personal development of each student in preparation for a purposeful life as a global citizen.
Robert Crowther, Headmaster
Charles Barton, Head of School

1372 Saint Maur International School
83 Yamate-cho, Naka-ku
Yokohama
Japan, 231-8654
81-(0)45-641-5751
Fax: 81-(0)45-641-6688
office@stmaur.ac.jp
www.stmaur.ac.jp
International School in Japan providing Pre-school, Elementary and Secondary education for international students, bringing together people from different cultures and faiths.
Catherine Osias Endo, School Head
Richard Rucci, Director of Admissions

1373 Sancta Maria International School
41 Karasawa Minami-ku
Yokohama
Japan
Sr Mary Elizabeth Doll, Principal

1374 School at Tembagapura
PO Box 616 Cairns
Queensland 4870
Australia
Bruce Goforth, Principal

1375 Scots PGC College
60 Oxenham Street
Warwick, QLD
Australia 04370
61 7 4666 9811
Fax: 61 7 4666 9812
postbox@scotspgc.qld.edu.au
www.scotspgc.qld.edu.au
Our philosophy of schooling rests squarely on the belief that a true education encourages young people to question and explore, to develop a strong sense of personal identity, to strive to achieve one's best, and to value the act of serving without losing one's desire to lead.
Michael Harding, Principal
Nigel Grant, Director of Learning

1376 Seisen International School
12-15 Yoga 1-chome
Setagaya-Ku, Tokyo
Japan 158-0-97
03-3704-2661
Fax: 033701-1033
sisinfo@seisen.com
www.seisen.com
Seisen International School seeks to provide a happy, stable and secure environment in which students are prepared through teaching and example, to live in a world of tremendous challenge and rapid change.
Concesa Martin, Headmistress

1377 Semarang International School
Asad Ave-Mohammedpur
Semarang, Central Java
Indonesia 50254
62-24-8311-424
Fax: 62-24-8311-994
info@semarangis.or.id
www.semarangis.or.id '
Offer Semarang 's international community high quality and affordable education based on the International Baccalaureate Organization's Primary Years Programme, (PYP) philosophy. Provide an educational and motivational base from which each pupil may take his or her place with confidence in any school in any country in the medium of English.
Barry Burns, Principal

1378 Seoul Academy
988-5, Daechi-dong
Kangamku Seoul
Korea 135-2
82-02-554-1690
Fax: 82-2-562-0451
sais5541690@hanmail.net
www.seoulacademy.net/
Grade levels pre-K through eighth.
Thomas O'Connor, Director

1379 Seoul British School
55 Yonhi Dong Sudaemun Ku
Seoul
Korea
822-330-3100
www.seoulforeign.org
Richard Schlueter, Principal

1380 Seoul Elementary School
Unit 15549
APO, AP
Korea 96205-5549
011-82-2-7916-4613
Fax: 011-82-2-793-6925
principal.seoules@pac.dodea.edu
www.seoul-es.pac.dodea.edu
Provides standards based instruction in a safe learning environment which fosters independent thinking and respects cultural diversity through collaboration among staff, students, parents and community
Catherine Yurica, Principal

1381 Seoul Foreign School
55 Yonhi-Dong Sodaemun-Gu
Seoul
Korea 120-8-113
82-2-330-3100
Fax: 82-2-335-1857
sfsoffice@seoulforeign.org
www.sfs.or.kr
As has been true throughout our history, Seoul Foreign School is committed to academic excellence. Our rigorous college preparatory curriculum - which includes the International Baccalaureate diploma program - and our dynamic learning environment challenge students to achieve their full intellectual potential. Equally, we cherish Christian values which encourage our students to develop strong character, live and work with integrity, and accept responsibility for themselves and others.
John Engstrom, Head of School
Barry Benger, Director Human Resources

1382 Seoul High School
Unit 15549
APO, AP
South Korea 96205-5549
011+82-2-7918-5261
Fax: 011+82-2-7918-8822
www.seoul-hs.pac.dodea.edu
Seoul American High School is located on Yongsan Army Base in the center of Seoul, Korea. The school complex is comprised of eight buildings containing over 60 classrooms and special purpose rooms.
Richard Schlueter, Principal

1383 Shanghai American School
258 Jin Feng Lu
Huacao Town, Minhang Dist. Shanghai
China 20110
86-21-6221-1445
Fax: 86-21-6221-1269
admission@saschina.org
www.saschina.org
Shanghai American School, in partnership with parents, fosters the development of each student's personal potential through a balance of the academic, physical, social, emotional and ethical aspects of life. SAS provides a challenging American core curriculum with an international perspective that inspires a passion for learning and intellectual vitality.
Kerry Jacobson, Superintendent
Andrew Torris, Deputy Superintendent

1384 Shatin College
3 Lai Wo Lane
Sha Tin
Hong Kong
852 26991811
Fax: 852 26950592
info@shatincollege.edu.hk
www.shatincollege.edu.hk
Independent, coeducational, secondary school within the English Schools Foundation
David Cottam, Principal
Grahame Carder, Chairman

1385 Shatin Junior College
3A Lai Wo Lane
Fo Tan, New Terretories
Hong Kong
852 2692 2721
Fax: 852 2602 5572
info@sjs.esf.edu.hk
www.sjs.edu.hk/
At Sha Tin Junior School we aim to provide a secure and happy environment in which a child can develop their academic, social and physical potential to the full.
Perry Tunesi, Principal

1386 Shirley Lanham Elementary School
PSC 477 Box 38
FPO AP
Japan 96306-5
011-81-467-63-3664
Fax: 011-81-467-63-4476
Principal.lanhames@pac.dodea.edu
www.lanham-es.pac.dodea.edu
We are preparing all students to be responsible, positive contributors within a diverse, global community.
Dave Russell, Principal

1387 Singapore American School
40 Woodlands Street 41
Singapore 73854
65-6363-3403
Fax: 65-6363-3408
communications@sas.edu.sg
www.sas.edu.sg
The Singapore American School is committed to providing each student an exemplary American educational experience with an international perspective.
Brent Mutsch, Superintendent

1388 Sollars Elementary School
Unit 5041
APO, AP
Japan 96319-5041
011-81-176-77-3933
Fax: 011-81-176-77-3873
PRINCIPAL.SOLLARSES@pac.dodea.edu
www.sollars-es.pac.dodea.edu
Dana Chandler, Principal

1389 South Island School
50 Nam Fung Road
Aberdeen
Hong Kong
852-255- 931
Fax: 852-255- 881
sis@mail.sis.edu.hk
www.sis.edu.hk
School Aims to develop students' confidence, self-esteem and a range of positive values and personal qualities and to produce enthusiastic, active, independent and lifelong learners.
Graham Silverthorne, Principal
Roberta Kam, Admission

1390 St. Andrews International School-Bangkok
Pridi Banomyong 20/1
Sukhumvit Soi 71, Prakanong, Bangkok
Thailand 10110
(+66) 23 81 23 87-
Fax: (+66) 23 91 52 27
info@standrews.ac.th
www.standrews.ac.th/
Our mission is to provide an inclusive, international education in a happy, supportive and stimulating environment, where all the needs of the individual learner are met and students are inspired to achieve their full potential enabling them to become responsible global citizens
Paul Schofield, Head of School
Jamsai Anuvongchareon, Director

1391 St. Christopher's School
10 Nunn Road
Penang
Malaysia 10350
604-226-3589
Fax: 604-226-4340
principal@scips.org.my
www.scips.org.my
St. Christopher's International Primary School of Penang, caters for expatriates' and also Malaysian children. It is located in one of the most sought after residential areas on the island of Penang Malaysia.
John G Jones, Principal

1392 St. John's International School
Ladprao
Bangkok
Thailand 10900
662-513-8575
Fax: +66 2 513 5273
sjiadmin@stjohn.ac.th
www.international.stjohn.ac.th
A holistic British style school preparing students of all nationalities to become life long learners and effective communicators in the global community.
Chainarong Monthienvic, Principal

1393 St. Joseph International School
5-16-10 Shibamata, Katsushika-ku
Tokyo
Japan 125-0

035-694-4550
schray@stjoseph-k.org
www.stjoseph-k.org
Coeducational day/boarding school, preschool through grade 12.

James Mueller, Principal
Thomas Schray, Head Teacher

1394 St. Joseph's International Primary School
177 Currie Street
Nambour
New Guinea
54 -19 -22
www.stjosephsnambour.qld.edu.au

Barbara D'Arbon, Principal

1395 St. Mary's International School
1-6-19 Seta Setagaya-ku
Tokyo
Japan 158-8
813-370- 341
Fax: 813-370- 195
michelj@smis.ac.jp
www.smis.ac.jp
St. Mary's is committed to educating boys to be lifelong learners of good character who demonstrate academic, physical, artistic, and moral excellence, respect for religious and cultural beliefs, and responsibility as international citizens.

Michel Jutras, Headmaster
Br Lawrence G Lambert, Elementary School Principal

1396 St. Michael's International School
17-2 Nakayamate-dori 3-chome
Chuo-ku, Kobe-shi 650-0004
Japan
81-78-231-8885
Fax: 81-78-231-8899
head@smis.org
www.smis.org
Provides a distinctive Primary education within a positive culture of academic excellence and caring family community.

Aileen Pardon, Principal
Paul Grisewood, Head of School

1397 St. Stephen's International School
998 Viphavadi Rangsit Road
Lad Yao, Chatuchak, Bangkok
Thailand 10900
66-2-5130270
Fax: 66-2-9303307
info@sis.edu
www.sis.edu
To encourage all students in their studies, personal life and in all their interactions to strive for excellence on their journey to becoming effective and compassionate citizens and leaders. Our goal is to nurture a culture and a community of learners creating a unique East meets West environment .

Richard A Ralphs, School Director
Gary Rodbard, Principal

1398 St. Xavier's Greenherald School
Asad Ave-Mohammedpur
Dhaka 1207
Bangladesh

Mary Imelda, Principal

1399 Stearley Heights Elementary School
Unit 5166
APO Kadena 96368 5166
Okinawa 36368
001-81-611-694-452
Fax: 001-81- 98-934-681
Stearley-Heights.Principal@pac.dodea.edu
www.stearley-es.pac.dodea.edu

Thomas Godbold, Principal

1400 Sullivans Elementary School
PSC 473, Box 96
Yokosuka 96349 0096
Japan
011-81-468-16-7336
Fax: 011-81-468-16-7865
principal_*sullivan_es@pac.dodea.edu
www.sullivans-es.pac.dodea.edu

Walter Wilhoit, Principal

1401 Surabaya International School
CitraRaya International Village
Citra Raya, Lakarsantri
Tromol Pos 2/SBDK, Surabaya
Indonesia 60225
62-31-741-4300
Fax: 62-31-741-4334
sisadmin@sisedu.net
www.sisedu.net
The Surabaya International School Community is committed to developing the social, emotional, physical, creative, and intellectual abilities necessary for its students to become reasoning, responsible, contributing, successful members of our global community.

Larry Jones, Superintendent
Christopher Burke, Chairperson

1402 TEDA International School-Tianjin
Number 72 Third Avenue Teda
Tianjin, CN 30045
86 -2 6-2261
Fax: 86 -2 6-0018
Principal@tedainternationalschool.net
www.tedainternationalschool.net
provide outstanding education to the students of all nationalities.

Nick Bowley, Director
Joseph Azmeh, Headmaster

1403 Tabubil International School
PO Box 408 Tabubil
Tabubil
Papua New Guinea
675-548-9233
Fax: 675-542-9641
tabis@online.net.pg
www.tis.ac.pg
To provides a high quality international school education catering to the varied needs of Tabubil's multicultural mining community. The school employs a well motivated and productive staff, with good working conditions and a high degree of community involvement

SE Walker, Principal

1404 Taegu Elementary & High School
Unit 15623
APO Taegu 96218 0005
Korea
Leon Rivers, Principal

1405 Taipei American School
800 Chung Shan N Road Section 6
Taipei
Taiwan 11152
886-2-287-39900
Fax: 886-2-287-31641
admissions@tas.edu.tw
www.tas.edu.tw
Our mission is to inspire each student to be a confident, creative, caring and moral individual prepared to adapt and succeed anywhere in a rapidly changing world. We provide an American-based education with a global perspective that results in a love of learning, academic excellence, a balanced life, and service to others.

Sharon D Hennessy, Superintendent
Ira B Weislow, Business Manager

1406 Tanglin Trust Schools
95 Portsdown Road
Singapore 13929
65-67780711
Fax: 65-67775862
admissions@tts.edu.sg
www.tts.edu.sg
Our vision is to be the premier school, providing the highest quality learning experiences for 3 to 18 year olds, and cultivating strong relationships in an environment where the individual is important. Our students enjoy a rich and stimulating all-round education which prepares them thoroughly for life in a rapidly-changing and competitive world.

Ronald Stones, Head of School
Peter Derby-Crook, CEO

1407 Thai-Chinese International School
101/177 Moo 7 Soi Mooban Bangpleeni
Prasertsin Road Bangplee Yai
Samutprakarn, TH 10540
66-2-260-8202
tcis@schoolmail.com
www.tcis.ac.th
provide an education which allows each student to develop his/her full being in all areas of human development, academic, physical, emotional, spiritual and social, to interact as critical and compassionate thinkers, and to become a responsible member of our global society.

1408 Timbertop Campus
Timbertop PB-Mansfield
Victoria 3722
Australia
61 3 5733 6777
Fax: 61 3 5777 5772
timbertop@ggs.vic.edu.au
www.ggs.vic.edu.au/Contact.aspx

Stephen Meek, Principal

1409 Traill Preparatory School
34-36 S01
18 Ramkhamheng Road, Huamark Bangkok
Thailand
660-271- 877
Fax: 660-271- 854
www.traillschool.ac.th

AM Traill, Principal

1410 Ukarumpa High School
PO Box 406
Ukarumpa Via Lae, Papua
New Guinea
675-737-4498
Fax: 675-737-4618
www.ukarumpainternationalschool.org

Steve Walker, Principal

1411 United Nations International School-Hanoi
Phu Thuong Ward Lac Long Quan Road
Tay Ho District
Veitnam, VN
(84 4) 3758 1551
Fax: (84 4) 3758 1542
info@unishanoi.org
www.unishanoi.org
A private, nonprofit, English language, coeducational day school which offers an educational program from prekindergarten through grade 12 for the expatriate community of Hanoi.

Chip Barder, Head of School

1412 United World College-SE Asia
1207 Dover Road
PO Box 15, Singapore 9111
Singapore 13965
65 6775 5344
Fax: 65 6778 5846
info@uwcsea.edu.sg
www.uwcsea.edu.sg
The United World College Movement makes education a force to unite people, nations and cultures for peace and a sustainable future. We educate individuals to take responsibility for shaping a better world
Julian Whiteley, Head of College
Geraint Jones, Assistant Head of College

1413 University Vacancies in Australia
Australian Vice-Chancellors' Committee
GPO Box 1142
Canberra City
Australia
61-02-6285-8200
Fax: 60-02-6285-8211
contact@universitiesaustralia.edu.au
Universities Australia was established on 22 May 2007 as the industry peak body representing the university sector.
G Withers, Chief Executive Officer
P Rodely, Committee Executive Officer

1414 Vientiane International School
PO Box 3180
Phonesavanh Road, Saphanthong Tai Villag
Lao PDR
856 21 486001
Fax: 856 21 486009
contact@ourvis.com
www.vislao.com
Vientiane International School (VIS) is an independent, nonprofit day school offering an international-standard curriculum from Preschool through Grade 12. VIS is an IB World School.
Jane McGee, Director
Glenn Lawler, Primary Principal

1415 Wellesley College
PO Box 41037
Eastbourne, Lower Hutt 5047, Wellington
New Zealand
64 -56 -03
Fax: 64 -56 -28
office@wellesley.school.nz
www.wellesley.school.nz
Wellesley is a full independent primary day school for boys from Year 0 (aged five) to Year 8.
Warren Owen, Principal
Charlotte Gendall, Board member

1416 Wesley International School
Kotak Pos 275
Malang, East Java
Indonesia 65101
62-341-586410
Fax: 62-341-586413
wesley@wesleyinterschool.org
www.wesleyinterschool.org
Our mission at Wesley International School is to provide students with a Christ-centered education: one that inspires them to live a Godly life, that instills a biblical worldview, and produces academic excellence-an education that will prepare our students to impact and bless their world with knowledge, insight, action and love
Paul Richardson, HS Principal
Jonathan Heath, Director

1417 Western Academy of Beijing
PO Box 8547
10 Lai Guang Ying dong Lu, Beijing
10010
China
86-10-8456-4155
Fax: 86 10 6433-3974
wabinfo@wab.edu
www.wab.edu
The Western Academy of Beijing offers a challenging and caring, community based educational environment in which students are active participants in the learning process
Robert Landau, Director
Karen O'Connell, Deputy Chair

1418 Wewak International Primary School
PO Box 354
Wewak Esp, Papua
New Guinea
Darian Sullavan, Principal

1419 Woodstock School
Mussoorie
Uttarakhand
India 24817
91-135-632-610
Fax: 91-135-632-885
mail@woodstock.ac.in
www.woodstock.ac.in
Woodstock aims to develop responsible global citizens and leaders by providing a world-class international education, rooted in its Christian heritage and values, for a diverse group of students, especially from families in Christian or public service, in an Indian Himalayan environment
David Laurenson, Principal
Thomas Chandy, President

1420 Xiamen International School
262 Xingbei San Lu, Xinglin
Jimei, Xiamen, Fujian
China
86-592-625-6581
Fax: 86-592-625-6584
askxis@xischina.com
www.xischina.com
Develops confident, knowledgeable students who enjoy life-long learning, demonstrate global awareness and contribute compassionately to the world around them.
Paul Raschke, Headmaster
Yuan Yuan Deng, Vice Chairman

1421 Yew Chung Shanghai International School
18 W Rong Hua Road, Gubei New Area
Shanghai
China 20110
(8621) 6219 5910
Fax: (8621) 6219 0675
enquiry@ycef.com
www.ycis-sh.com
Provide an all-round education that nurtures the whole person - spiritual, academic, physical, social and emotional that includes relationships with others.
Andrew Mellor, Co-Principal
Julie Zheng, Co-Principal

1422 Yogyakarta International School
P.O. Box 1175
Yogyakarta 55011, Jalan Cendrawasih No.1
Indonesia
62-274-625965
Fax: 62-274-625966
board@ yis-edu.org
www.yis-edu.org/
Operates as a not for profit social foundation and is overseen by a School Board made up of both parents and non-parents.
Chris Scott, Principal

1423 Yokohama International School
258 Yamate-cho Naka-ku
Yokohama
Japan 231-0
81-45-622-0084
Fax: 81-45-621-0379
yis@yis.ac.jp
www.yis.ac.jp
Provides the highest-quality, balanced education to internationally minded students in an inquiring and supportive environment.
Simon Taylor, Headmaster
John Inge, Chairman

1424 Yokota High School
DoDDS P J YH Unit 5072
APO AP
Japan 96328-5072
011-81-3117-55-701
Fax: 011-81-3117-55-722
principal_*yokotahs@pac.dodea.edu
www.yokota-hs.pac.dodea.edu
Yokota High School, working in partnership with the family and local community, provides a safe, academically-inspiring environment in which all students will develop to their maximum potential as life-long learners and responsible participants in an ever-changing global society.
Darrell Mood, Principal

1425 Yokota West Elementary School
DoDDS P J YW Unit 5072
APO AP
Japan 96328-5072
011-81-3117-55-761
Fax: 011-81-3117-55-573
principal_*yokota_west_es@pac.dodea.edu
www.ywes.pac.dodea.edu
Sharon Carter, Principal

1426 Yonggwang Foreign School
Ceii Site Office
PO Box 9, Yonggwang-Kun 513-880
Korea
Eleanor Jones, Principal

1427 Zama Junior High & High School
USA Garrison, Camp Zama
APO, Honshu 96343 0005
Japan
Samuel Menniti, Principal

1428 Zukeran Elementary School
Unit 35017
FPO AP
Japan 96379-5017
011-81-611-7452576
Fax: 011-81-098-892-795
Zukeran.Principal@pac.dodea.edu
www.zukeran-es.pac.dodea.edu
Zukeran Elementary School shares the vision of creating a community of learners actively engaged in the pursuit of the knowledge, skills and experiences necessary to empower all children to meet the challenges of the 21st century.
Cindy Templeton, Principal
Roger Reade, Assistant Principal

Central & South America

1429 Academia Cotopaxi American International School
De las Higuerillas y Alondras
Quito
Ecuador
593-2-246-7411
Fax: 593-2-244-5195
info@cotopaxi.k12.ec
www.cotopaxi.k12.ec
Premier English-language school from early childhood through secondary school.

Kurt Kywi, President
Robert Moss, Vice President

1430 American Cooperative School
Lawton 20
Paramaribo
Suriname
597-49-9461
Fax: 597-498-853
acs_suriname@sil.org
www.acslp.org
A private, coeducational day school which offers an educational program from prekindergarten through grade 12 for students of all nationalities.

Frank Martens, Administrator

1431 American Elementary & High School
Caixa Postal 7432
01064-970, Sao Paulo
Brazil
55-11-3842-2499
Fax: 55-11-3842-9358
graded@eagle.aegsp.br
A private, coeducational day school which offers a full college-preparatory educational program from preschool through grade 12 for students of all nationalities.

Dr Gunther Brandt, Principal

1432 American International School-Bolivia
Casilla 5309
Cochabamba
Bolivia
591-4-428-8577
Fax: 591-4-428-8576
administracion@aisb.edu.bo
www.aisb.edu.bo
The American International School of Bolivia was founded in 1993 as an international, non-governmental, co-educational day school. The AIS/B educational system covers from Early Childhood education up to the IB program in grades 11 and 12 for students representing all nationalities and socio-economical levels.

Dr Silke Marina Scholer, Director General
Tatiana Jimenez BA, Chief Administrator

1433 American International School-Lincoln Buenos Aires
Andres Ferreyra 4073
B1637 AOS La Lucila, Buenos Aires
Argentina
(54)(11) 4851-1700
Fax: 54-11-479-02117
pacha_c@lincoln.edu.ar
www.lincoln.edu.ar
Provides education based on United States accredited curriculum in an environment of academic excellence that develops ethical, responsible and globally conscious world citizens.

Phil T Joslin, Superintendent

1434 American School
PO Box (01) 35
El Salvador
503-26-38-330
Fax: 503-26-38-385
recruiting@amschool.edu.sv
www.amschool.edu.sv
Founded in 1946 and is an independent, international, coeducational, college-preparatory institution

Yolanda de Lopez, Director of Admissions

1435 American School Foundation AC
Bondojito 215
Colonia Las Americas
Mexico City, Mexico 01120
52-55-5227-4900
Fax: 52-55-5273-4357
asf@asf.edu.mx
www.asf.edu.mx
is an academically rigorous, international, university preparatory school, which offers students from diverse backgrounds the best of American independent education

Julie Hellmund, Director

1436 American School Foundation-Guadalajara
Colomos 2100, Coronel Providencia
Guadalajara, Jalisco
Mexico 44640
52 (33) 3648-0299
Fax: 52-33-3817-3356
asfg@asfg.mx
www.asfg.mx
Educating students in a bilingual, bicultural and secular environment to be purposeful learners, critical and creative thinkers, effective communicators and community contributors, based on a foundation of honor, freedom and commitment

David McGrath, Principal
Jabet Heinze, Superintendent

1437 American School Foundation-Monterrey
Ave. Ignacio Morones Prieto No. 150
Col. San Isidro, Santa Catarina, N.L.
Nuevo Leon, Mexico 66190
(52)-81-5000-4400
Fax: (52)-81-5000-4428
jeff.keller@asfm.edu.mx
www.asfm.edu.mx
A private, nonprofit, coeducational day school which offers an educational program from nursery through grade 12 for students of all nationalities.

Dr. Jeffrey Keller, Superintendent

1438 American School-Belo Horizonte
Avenida Deputado Cristovan Chiaradia 120
Caixa Postal 1701
Bairro Buritis, Belo Horizonte 30575-440
Brazil
55-31-378-6700
Fax: 55-31-378-6878
eabh@eabh.com.br
www.eabh.com.
A coeducational, private day school which offers an educational program from prekindergarten through grade 12 for students of all nationalities.

Sid Stewart, Principal

1439 American School-Brasilia
SGAS 605
Bloco E, Lotes 34/37
Brasilia,DF,Brazil 70200-650
55 (61) 3442-9700
Fax: 55 (61) 3442-9729
kpuzic@eabdf.br
www.eabdf.br
A private, coeducational day school which offers an educational program from prekindergarten through grade 12 for students of all nationalities

Barry Dequanne, Headmaster
Beth Lopez, Lower School Principal

1440 American School-Campinas
Rua Cajamar, 35 - Jardim Alto da Ba
Campinas- SP
Brazil 13090
55 19 2102-1000
Fax: 55 19 2102-1016
www.escolaamericanadecampinas.com.br

Steve Herrara, Superintendent

1441 American School-Durango
Francisw Sarabia #416 Pte
Durango 34000
Mexico
(618) 813-36-36
Fax: (618) 811-28-39
colegio_americano@cadurango.edu.mx
www.cadurango.edu.mx

Dr Jorge O Nelson, Principal

1442 American School-Guatemala
11 Calle 1579 Zona 15 Vista Hermosa
Guatemala
Guatemala
502-690-
Fax: 502-698-
director@cag.edu.gt
www.cag.edu.gt
is to educate independent, critical-thinking, responsible, bilingual individuals prepared to meet the challenges of the future

Robert Gronniger, General Director
Edward Langlais, High School Principal

1443 American School-Guayaquil
PO Box 3304
Guayaquill
Ecuador
593-4-255-503
Fax: 593-4-250-453
dir_asg@gye.satnet.net
www.americanschool.edu.ec
Grade levels K-12, school year April - January

Francisco Andrade, Interim General Director
Patricia Ayala de Coronel, HS Principal

1444 American School-Laguna Verde
Veracruz, Mexico
Maurice H Blum, Principal

1445 American School-Lima
Apartado 18-0977
Lima 18
Peru
51-14-35-0890
Fax: 51 1 619-9301
fdr@amersol.edu.pe
www.amersol.edu.pe
is to empower our students to pursue their passion for learning, lead lives of integrity and create socially responsible solutions.

Caron Kluznik, Superintendent

1446 American School-Pachuca
Valle de Anahuac S/N Valle de San J
ZC: 42083 Pachuca de Soto Hidalgo
Mexico
01-771 713 9608
Fax: 52-771-85077
admisiones@americana.edu.mx
www.americana.edu.mx/
Grade levels prekindergarten through ninth.

Nic,foro Ramirez, General Director

1447 American School-Puebla
Apartado 665
Puebla
Mexico
www.cap.edu.mx/english/
Dr Arthur W Chaffee, Principal

1448 American School-Puerto Vallarta
PO Box 2-280
Puerto Vallarta, Jalisco 48300
Mexico
52 322-221-1525
Fax: (52) 322-226-7677
Info@aspv.edu.mx
www.aspv.edu.mx
Gerald Selitzer, Director

1449 American School-Recife
408 Se Souza Street
Boa Viagem
Brazil 51030-60
55 81 3341.4716
Fax: 55-81-341-0142
info@ear.com.br
www.ear.com.br
A private, coeducational day school which offers an instructional program from prekindergarten through grade 12 for students of all nationalities.
George Takacks, Superintendent

1450 American School-Tampico
Hidalgo # 100
Tancol, Tampico
Mexico
52-12-272-081
Fax: 52-12-280-080
racevedo@ats.edu.mx
www.ats.edu.mx
Grade levels N through tenth.
Emma deSalazar, Headmaster

1451 American School-Torreon
Paseo del Algodn y Boulevard Carlo
Fracc Los Viedos Torren, Coahuila
Mexico 27019
871 222 51 00 TO 0
Fax: 871 733 26 68
cat@cat.mx
www.cat.mx
A prestigious center of academic excellence dedicated to creating life-long learners and ethical leaders in a global and changing world.
Makhlouf Ouyed, Director General
Martha Martinez, Business Manager

1452 Anglo American School
PO Box 3188-1000
San Jose
Costa Rica
506-279-2626
Fax: 506-279-7894
angloam@racsa.co.cr
www.aas.ru
Grade levels Pre-K through 6, school year February - November
Virginia Hine Barrantes, Principal

1453 Anglo Colombian School
Apaptado Aereo 253393
Bogota
Colombia
www.anglocolombiano.edu.co
David Toze, Principal

1454 Anglo-American School
Calle 37
Avenida Central, 1000 San Jose
Costa Rica
495-231-447
angloam@sd.racsa.co.cr
www.aas.ru
Virginia Hine, Principal

1455 Antofagasta International School
Avda. Jaime Guzman Errazurz #04300
Antofagasta
Chile
56 - 55 - 694900
Fax: 56 - 55 - 694912
ais@ais.cl
www.ais.cl
A Pre-Kindergarten through 12th grade educational institution that is dedicated to offering a challenging, English-based curriculum to its students.
Carlos Ignacio Figueroa Ahumada, Principal
Carlos Arturo Calussen Calvo, Chairman

1456 Asociacion Colegio Granadino
AA 2138
Manizales, Caldas
Colombia
57-68-745-774
Fax: 57-68-746-066
granadino@emtelsa.multi.net.co
www.granadino.edu.co
Grade levels Pre-K through 12, school year August - June
Gonzalo Arango, General Director

1457 Asociacion Escuelas Lincoln
Andres Ferreyra 4073
B1636 AOS La Lucila, Buenos Aires
Argentina
(54)(11) 4851-1700
Fax: 54-11-4790-2117
joslin_p@lincoln.edu.ar
www.lincoln.edu.ar
Provide an education based on United States accredited curriculum
Phil Joslin, Superintendent
Claudia Pacha, Admissions

1458 Balboa Elementary School
Unit 9025
APO Balboa 34002
Panama
818-241-1801
www.gusd.net
Susan Beattie, Principal

1459 Balboa High School
Unit 9025
APO Balboa 34002
Panama
818-241-1801
www.gusd.net
Ernest Holland, Principal

1460 Barker College
91 Pacific Highway
Hornsby
NSW, Australia, 2077
61-2-9847-8399
Fax: 61-2-9847-8009
reception@barker.nsw.edu.au
www.barker.college
Barker College is an Anglican day and boarding school. In 2016, the School announced plans to become fully coeducational by 2022.
Phillip Heath, Head of Barker College
Peter Berkley, Chair

1461 Belgrano Day School
Juramento 3035
Ciudad de Buenos Aires
Argentina c1428
54 -1 -81
Fax: 54 -1 -786
rrpp@bdsnet.com.ar
www.bds.edu.ar
We cooperate with the family to offer bilingual education quality for the training of future leaders and citizens of the world committed to the common good, free, responsible, creative and respectful of diversity and dissent.
Maria Matilde V Green, President
Carol Halle, Faculty Head

1462 Bilingue School Isaac Newton
Chihuahua, Mexico
Lauya Gonzalez Valenzula, Principal

1463 British American School
AA 4368
Barranquilla
Colombia 28277
704-341-3236
britishschoolofcharlotte.org
Rafael Ortegon Rocha, Principal

1464 British School-Costa Rica
PO Box 8184-1000
San Jose
Costa Rica 02232-7833
50 - 2 -0 0
Fax: 50 - 2 -2 7
britsch@racsa.co.cr
www.thebritishschoolofcostarica.com/
David John Lloyd, Principal

1465 British School-Rio de Janeiro
R Real Grandeza 99
Botafogo, Rio de Janeiro
Brazil, BR 22281-30
55(21) 2539-2717
Fax: 55(21) 2244-5591
edu@britishschool.g12.br
www.britishschool.g12.br
The British School aims to develop responsible, well-informed, open-minded, confident and caring individuals by providing an educational community within which all pupils are motivated to realize their full potential through a challenging British-based education in a non-discriminatory and bi-cultural environment
Paul Wiseman, Director
Adam Reid, Chairman

1466 British School-Venezuela
Sector 8 and Sector 12
Panchkula
India 13410
91-172-5028556
tbs@thebritishschool.org
www.thebritishschool.org
aims to provide education with global standards. This will not only make students studying in the school eligible for higher education in the institutions across the world but also give NRI's settled abroad, an opportunity to send their children to such schools to have a better idea of the social system back home.
TBS Panchkula, Principal
U Sethi, Board Member

1467 Buenos Aires International Christian Academy
Red de Escuelas Mundiales Cristiana
Av Libertador General San Mart-n 2170
Buenos Aires, AR 01646
5411 4549 1300
Fax: 5411 4549 1300
info@baica.com
www.baica.com

Our school is unique in that we are home to both Argentineans and the expat community.

Andy Simon, Principal
Robert Newman, Director

1468 Caribbean International School
Box 1594
Cristobal Colon
Panama
507-445-0933
cis.edu.pa

Anderson, Principal

1469 Centro Cultural Brazil-Elementary School
Rua Jorge Tibirica 5
11100 Santos, Sao Paulo
Brazil

Newton Antonio Martin, Principal

1470 Cochabamba Cooperative School
Casilla 1395
Cochabamba
Bolivia 01395
591-42-987-61
Fax: 591-42-329-06
Cwieburg@ccs.edu.bo
www.ccs.edu.bo
President

Provide attendees

Carl Wieburg, Director
Jos Leonis, Manager

1471 Colegio Abraham Lincoln
Calle 170, # 51A-81
SedePrimaria Avenue Calle 170 #65-31
Columbia
571-676-7360
www.abrahamlincoln.edu.co
Promoting human development within a humanistic philosophy and pruricultural.

Amparo Rueda, Director

1472 Colegio Americano De Guayaquil
Juan Tanca Marengo Avenue PO Box 33
Guayaquil
Ecuador
593-4-255-03
Fax: 593-4-250-453
info@colegioamericano.edu.ec
www.colegioamericano.edu.ec
Provide an education with the highest standards of quality, thus contributing to the improvement of our society.

Stanley Whitman, Principal
Francisco Andrade, Association President

1473 Colegio Anglo Colombiano
Avenida 19 # 152A-48
Bogota
, DC
571-259-5700
admissions@anglocolombiano.edu.co
www.anglocolombiano.edu.co
Our purpose is to educate human beings with open minds, real social awareness and the power of critical thinking.

David Toze, Principal
Catherine Cushnan, Admission

1474 Colegio Bilingue Juan Enrigue
Pestalozzi AC
Veracruz
Mexico

Michael S Garber, Principal

1475 Colegio Bolivar
Calle 5 Number 122-21 V-a Pance
Cali
Colombia
(57-2) 684 8600
Fax: 57-2-555-2041
cbinfo@colegiobolivar.edu.co
www.colegiobolivar.edu.co
Colegio Bolivar is an educational community whose mission is to educate its students in a bilingual, democratic environment to be autonomous, and to demonstrate a spirit of inquiry and collaboration, a commitment to excellence, and the highest aspirations for the welfare of both the individual and society.

Joseph Nagy, Director
Richard Martin, Dean of Students

1476 Colegio Columbo Britanico
Apartado Aereo 5774
Cali
Colombia
www.colombobritanico.edu.co

Ian Watson, Principal

1477 Colegio Gran Breta¤a
Cra 51 #215-20
Bogot
Colombia
57-1-676-0391
Fax: 57-1-676-0426
admissions@cgb.edu.co
www.cgb.edu.co
School teaching primary and secondary grade levels.

Robert Tomalin, Director
Fiorella Rocha, Director, Marketing

1478 Colegio Granadino
AA 2138 Manizales
Colombia
57-6-874-57-74
Fax: 57-6-874-60-66
granadino@emtelsa.multi.net.com
www.granadino.edu.co
Early Childhood, Elementary, Middle School and High School

Gonzalo Arango, Principal
Robert Sims, Director

1479 Colegio Interamericano de la Montana
Boulevard La Montana
Finca El Socorro, Zona 16
Guatemala, GT 01016
502 2200.2990
Fax: 502-3-641-779
www.interamericano.edu.gt
The mission of Colegio Interamericano is to prepare its students for life and for studies anywhere in the world, by orienting them towards being responsible members of society.

Dr Michael Farr, General Director
Griselda de Amezquita, Head of Human Resources

1480 Colegio Jorge Washington
Zona Norte, Anillo Vial Km.12
Cartagena
Colombia, CO
57-5-673 5505
Fax: 57-5-665-6447
director@cojowa.edu.co
cojowa.edu.co
The mission of the George Washington School is to form bilingual and bicultural citizens who possess high ethical values and commitment to the search for academic excellence and success in life.

Pete Nonnenkamp, Director
Maritza Garcia, Assistant Director

1481 Colegio Karl C Parrish
Kilometer 2 Antigua Via a Puerto Co
Barranquilla
Colombia, CO 52962
57-5-359-8929
Fax: 57-5-359-8828
mail@kcparrish.edu.co
www.kcparrish.edu.co
strives to provide an environment that results in students displaying personal integrity and character in their relationships both within and outside the school.

Laura Horbal Rebolledo, Director
Hectalina Donado, Elementary School Principal

1482 Colegio Montelibano
AA 6823 Cerromatoso
Montelibano, Bogota
Colombia

Francisco Cajiao, Principal

1483 Colegio Nueva Granada
Carrera 2 Este Number 70-20
Bogota
Colombia, CO
57-1-2123511
Fax: 57-1-211-3720
sngrana@COL1.telecom.com.co
www.cng.edu
Prepare tomorrow's leaders by educating the mind, nurturing the spirit, and strengthening the body.

Barry McCombs PhD, Director
Michael Adams, Deputy Director

1484 Colegio Peterson SC
Apartado Postal 10-900
DF 11000
Mexico
52-5-81-30-11-4
Fax: 52-5-81-31-38-5
kapm@mail.internet.com.mx
www.peterson.edu

Marvin Peterson, Principal

1485 Colegio San Marcus
61 Ourense
Buenas Aires
Argentina 32004
988-247-4
Fax: 988- 39-5
csmarcos@csmarcos.com
www.csmarcos.com
Collegio San Marcos was established in 1988, when it began its first year of dentures, being recognized by the Galician regional government, as accredited Vocational Training Second Grade, under the Order of May 20 1.988 of the Department of Education and University (DOG num.110 June 1988).

Susana Raffo, Principal

1486 Colegio Ward
Hector Coucheiro 599
1706 DF Sarmiento, Ramos Mejia
Buenos Aires, Argentina
541- 46-8 03
info@ward.edu.ar
www.ward.edu.ar

Ruben Carlos Urcola, Principal
Daniel Campagna, Director

1487 Costa Rica Academy
Apartado Postal 4941
San Jose 1000
Costa Rica
506-239-03-76
Fax: 506-239-06-25
A private, coeducational school which offers an educational program from prekindergarten through grade 12 for students of all nationalities.

William D Rose, BS, Med, Principal

1488 Cotopaxi Academy
PO Box 17-11-6510
Quito
Ecuador
593-2-246-7411
Fax: 593-2-244-5195
info@cotopaxi.k12.ec
www.cotopaxi.k12.ec
Premier English-language early childhood through secondary school in Ecuador. The internationally recognized program is aggressively sought out by all National and International parents who truly want to join a partnership to provide the very best education possible for their children.
Eddie Wexler, Principal
Kurt Kywi, President

1489 Country Day School
Apartado 1139 - 1250
Escazu
Costa Rica
(506) 2289 - 0919
Fax: (506) 2228 - 2076
gloria_doll@cds.ed.cr
www.cds.ed.cr
CDS is an American School serving an international population. Accredited by the Middle States Association of Colleges and Schools in the United States, and by the Costa Rican Ministry of Education
Gloria Doll, Director
Maria Fernanda Cardona, Admissions Coordinator

1490 Crandon Institute
Casilla Correo 445
Montevideo
Uruguay
248- 33-5
www.crandon.edu.uy
This school offers a curriculum taught in Spanish for 2,000 day students (700 boys; 1,300 girls), in high school through junior college level (home economics, commercial). The school, affiliated with the Methodist church, employs 300 teachers.
Marcos Rocchietti, Principal

1491 Curundu Elementary School
Unit 0925
APO Curundu 34002 0005
Panama
Clifford Drexler, Principal

1492 Curundu Junior High School
Unit 0925
APO Curundu 34002 0005
Panama
Charles Renno, Principal

1493 Edron Academy-Calz Al Desierto
Desierto de los Leones 5578
Mexico City 01740
Mexico
5-585-30-49
Fax: 5-585-28-46
www.edron.edu.
Richard Gilby Travers, Principal

1494 El Abra School
Phelps Dodge Corporation
Calama
Chile
56-55-313-600
Fax: 56-55-315-182
elabraschool@hotmail.com
Grade levels K-11, school year August - June
Margaret Maclean, Head of School

1495 English School
AA 51284
Bogota
Colombia
Leonard Mabe, Principal

1496 Escola Americana do Rio de Janeiro
Estrada Da Gavea 132
Rio de Janeiro
Brazil 22451-263
(916) 458-5932
Fax: 55-21-259-4722
americanrio@ax.apc.org
www.earj.com.br
Escola Americana motivates engaged learners to become independent critical thinkers in a multicultural community.
Dr Dennis Klumpp, Principal
Caren Addis, Director of Admissions

1497 Escola Maria Imaculada
Rua Vig rio Joao de Pontes, 537, Ch
Sao Paulo
Brazil 04748
551- 2-01 7
Fax: 551- 55-1 77
www.chapelschool.com/
Gerald Gates, Principal

1498 Escuela Anaco
Avenue Jose Antonio Anzoategui, KM
Anaco
Venezuela
58 -82 -22 2
director@ESCUELAANACO.COM
princeton.iss.edu
Offers a United States High School Diploma with a full schooling program from Day Care through Grade 12. Also have on-line courses to enhance our program. Uses the best of the educational standards of the states of California, New York, and Virginia.
Francene Conte, Principal
Bill Kralovec, Director

1499 Escuela Bilingue Santa Barbara
Apartado 342-El Marchito
San Pedro Sila
Honduras
504-659-3053
Fax: 504-659-3059
mochitoschool@breakwater.hn
princeton.iss.edu
Grade levels preK through 8.
John P Leddy, Principal

1500 Escuela Bilingue Valle De Sula
Apartado 735
San Pedro Sula
Honduras
Carole A Black, Principal

1501 Escuela International Sampedrana
Col Gracias A Dios 500 mts W Hospit
San Pedro Sula
Honduras
504-566-2722
Fax: 504-566-1458
eperez@seishn.com
www.seishn.org
EIS seeks to be the premier school in the city of San Pedro Sula, the country of Honduras and region of Central America through the use of best teaching practices with the goal of reaching all of its students.
Gregorg E Werner, Principal
Ronald Vair, Superintendent

1502 Escuela Las Palmas
Apartdo 6-2637
Panama
797-530-
www.cmpuentealto.cl
Aleida Molina, Principal

1503 Foreign Students School
Avenue Station B
#6617-6615 Esquina 70
Miramar Havana City, Cuba
Gillian P Greenwood, Principal

1504 Fort Clayton Elementary School
2000 Park Place Avenue
APO, Fort Clayton 34004 0005
Panama, TX
817-814-5400
www.lilybclayton.org
Barbara Seni, Principal

1505 Fort Kobbe Elementary School
Unit 0714
APO, Fort Kobbe 34001 0005
Panama
Dr Vinita Swenty, Principal

1506 Fundacion Colegio Americano de Quito
Manuel Benigno Cueva N80 - 190 Urba
PO Box 17-01-157, Carcel,n, Quito
Ecuador, DC
(593) 2 3976 300
Fax: 593-2-472-972
dirgeneral@fcaq.k12.ec
www.fcaq.k12.ec
Grade levels Pre-K through 12, school year September - June.
Susan Barbara, Director General

1507 George Washington School
Apartado Aereo 2899
Cartagena
Colombia
57-5-665-3396
Fax: 57-5-665-6447
A private, coeducational day school which offers and educational program from prekindergarten through grade 12 for students of all nationalities.
Steven Fields, Principal

1508 Grange School
Casilla 218
Correo 12, Santiago
Chile
(56) 2- 5981500?
Fax: 56-2-227-1204
admissions@grange.cl
www.grange.cl
Places great importance on the idea of 'fair play', a concept with connotations of sportsmanship, rule obedience, and honesty
Mike Freeman, Headmaster
Carolina Varela, Deputy Headmaster

1509 Greengates School
Avenue Circumbalacion Pte 102
Baliones De San Mateo, Naucalpah
Edo de Mexico, Mexico 53200
52-55-5373-0088
Fax: 52-55-5373-0765
sarav@greengates.edu.mx
www.greengates.edu.mx
Grade levels prekindergarten through twelfth.
Susan E Mayer, Principal

1510 Howard Elementary School
805 Long Hollow Pike
Gallatin
Panama, TN 37066

615-452-3025
www.hes.sumnerschools.org
Jean Lamb, Principal

1511 Inst Tecnologico De Estudios
Apartado Postal 28B
Chihuahua
Mexico
528- 83-8 20
www.itesm.edu
Hector Chavrez Barron, Principal

1512 International Preparatory School
PO Box 20015-LC
Santiago
Chile
56-2-321-5800
Fax: 56-2-321-5821
info@tipschool.com
www.internationalpreparatoryschool.com
Grade levels Pre-K through 12, school year March - December
Lesley Easton-Allen, Headmistress
Pamela Thomson, Curriculum Coordinator

1513 International School Nido de Aguilas
Avenida El Rodeo 14200
Santiago
Chile
(562) 339-8105
Fax: 56-2-216-7603
abattistoni@nido.cl
www.nido.cl
The International School Nido de Aguilas is committed to offering each student excellence in the pursuit of academic achievement in preparation for attendance at a US, Chilean or other international university, all within the framework of a challenging US-based, English-language curriculum. We encourage open-mindedness, global diversity, environmental awareness, community service and the development of leadership skills, including integrity, responsibility and self-discipline.
Dr Don Bergman, Headmaster
Jared Harris, HS Principal

1514 International School-Curitiba
Av Dr Eug^nio Bertolli
3900 Santa Felicidade, Curitiba, Paran~
Brazil 18241
413-525-7400
Fax: 413-525-7499
isc@iscbrazil.com~
www.iscbrazil.com
It is a private, nonprofit, self-governed school that serves students and families from our local and international community; offers a U.S. based curriculum in English with American, Brazilian and International Baccalaureate diplomas; commits to academic and personal excellence and prepares students for universities around the world.
Elizabeth Mello, Principal 1-12
Bill Pearson, Superintendent

1515 International School-La Paz
CC1075870 Villa Dolores
La Paz, Cordoba
Argentina
LH Sullivan, Principal

1516 International School-Panama
PO Box 0819-02588
El Dorado
Panama
(507) 293-3000
Fax: 507-266-7808
isp@isp.edu.pa
www.isp.edu.pa
A private, coeducational day school which offers an educational program from prekindergarten through grade 12 for students of all nationalities.
Rajiv Bhatt, Director
Jania Jacob, Business Manager

1517 Karl C Parrish School
Km 2 Antigua via a Puerto
Barranquilla
Colombia
(57-5) 3598929
Fax: 57-5-3598828
mail@kcparrish.edu.co
www.kcparrish.edu.co
Karl C. Parrish is a private, non-sectarian, non-profit elementary and secondary school that is open to children of all nationalities.
Laura H Rebolledo, Director

1518 Liceo Pino Verde
Vereda Los Planes kilometro 5
V¡a Cerritos Entrada 16, El Tigre
Colombia
963-379368
info@liceopinoverde.edu.co
www.liceopinoverde.edu.co
This school teaches English as a second language; builds strong human values; develops logical thinking skills and prepares students for the world of technology and communication. Enrollment consists of 110 day students (57 boys; 53 girls, in grades PK-12. Overseas teachers are welcome to apply with the length of stay being two years, with housing provided. Applications needed to teach include science, math and English.
Luz Stella Rios Patino, Principal

1519 Limon School
P.O. Box 249
847 F Avenue
Limon, CO 80828
719-775-2350
Fax: 719-775-9052
limonbadgers.com
strive to provide a safe environment and develop responsible and productive citizens who have the knowledge and skills to seize their chosen opportunities
Chris Selle, Principal

1520 Lincoln International Academy
PO Box 52-7444
Miami, FL 33152
1 (305) 395-4825
lincoln@lincoln.edu.ni
www.lincoln.edu.ni
instilling in them solid Christian and human virtues as taught by the Catholic faith, challenging them to reach their full intellectual capacity and achieve a high integral academic excellence in order to face the challenges of today's world. providing them with English instruction while preserving our Hispanic-Nicaraguan culture.
Henningston Hammond, Operation Manager
Adolfo Gonzalez, General Director

1521 Mackay School
Vicuna Mackenna 700
Renaca
Chile
563-223- 660
Fax: 563-223- 667
www.mackay.cl
Nigel William Blackbur, Principal

1522 Marian Baker School
Apartado 4269
San Jose
Costa Rica 01000
560-273-3426
Fax: 506-273-4609
mbschool@sol.racsa.co.cr
www.mbs.ed.cr/
Marian Baker School (MBS) is an International English speaking school educating preschool through high school students.
Linda Niehaus, Director
Bonnie Heigold, Business Manager

1523 Marymount School
1026 Fifth Avenue
Barranquilla
Colombia, NY 10028
212-744-4486
Fax: 212-744-0163
www.marymountnyc.org
Dr. Kathleen Cunniffe, Principal

1524 Metropolitan School
7281 Sarah Avenue
Maplewood, MO 63143
314-644-0850
nsmith@metroschool.org
The School is dedicated to providing a highly individualized educational experience for middle and senior high school students whose potential has not been recognized and/or meaningfully challenged in traditional school settings.
Judi Thomas, Head of School

1525 Modern American School
Cerro del Hombre 18
Col. Romero de Terreros
Mexico
565-476-
www.modernamerican.edu.mx
To provide our students with the educational elements which will promote the optimum development of the intellect, instill social awareness and emotional sensitivity, encourage artistic creativity, and emphasize physical well-being, aiming for excellence toward future success
Northlands Day School

1526 Northlands Day School
Roma 1210
1636 Olivos, Buenos Aires
Argentina
541-147-1 84
Fax: 541- 47-1 84
www.northlands.org.ar/
This bilingual day school for girls offers modern facilities, sports, etc. on a spacious campus. Languages spoken include English and Spanish and total enrollment is 1,100 students, ranging in grade from K1-12. Overseas teachers are accepted, with the length of stay being 2-6 years with housing provided.
Susan Brooke Jackson, MA, Principal

1527 Our Lady of Mercy School
Rua Visconde de Caravelas
48, Botafogo, Rio de Janeiro
Brazil
336-722-7204
www.ourladyofmercyschool.org
Our Lady of Mercy School is an American Catholic English speaking school whose main purpose is to educate the whole student towards global understanding.
Charles Lyndaker, Superintendent

1528 Pan American Christian Academy
1730 Link Road
04829-310 Sao Paulo
Brazil

480.471.5339
Fax: 55-11-59289591
info@paca.com.br
www.paca.com.br
American international school located in the city of Sao Paulo, working with 350 students from different parts of the world with an American-style pre-school through high school education. Since 1960, we've served the local and international community of Sao Paulo.

Micheal Epp, Superintendent

1529 Pan American School-Bahia
Caixa Postal 231
Salvador
Brazil, SA 40901-970
55-71-3368-8400
Fax: 55-71-3368-8441
info@escolapanamericana.com
www.escolapanamericana.com
A private, coeducational day school which offers a program from preschool through grade 12 for students of all nationalities.

Mary Jo Heatherington, PhD, Superintendent

1530 Pan American School-Costa Rica
Apartado 474
Monterrey
Costa Rica, NL 64000
(81) 83-42-07-78
Fax: (81) 83-40-27-49
dadmission@pas.edu.mx
www.pas.edu.mx
Offer excellent educational programs in English that foster the integral development of students.

Robert Arpee, Director

1531 Pan American School-Monterrey
Hidalgo 656 Pte
Apartado Postal 474, Monterrey 64000
Mexico
(81) 83-42-07-78
www.pas.edu.mx
This school offers an English curriculum for 1,393 day students and 100 boarding students (709 boys; 684 girls), grades preschool through nine. The school is willing to participate in a teacher exchange program with the length of stay being one year. Applications needed to teach include science, preschool, math, reading, English, and physical education.

Tobert L Arpee, Principal
Lenor Arpee, Faculty Head

1532 Pan American School-Porto Alegre
Rua Joao Paetzel 440
91 330 Porto Alegre
Brazil
555- 33-4 58
www.panamerican.com.br

Jennifer Sughrue, Principal

1533 Panama Canal College
Unit 0925
APO Balboa 34002 0005
Panama
www.educationusapanama.wetpaint.com

1534 Prescott Anglo American School
PO Box 1036
Arequipa
Peru
www.prescott.edu.pe
This school offers a Spanish/English curriculum for 1,050 day students (450 boys; 600 girls) in grades K-12. Students are taught English three hours a day, so they can reach an intermediate level in grade 9, and high intermediate in grades 11-12.

Jorge Pachecot, Principal

1535 Redland School
272 Military Road
Cremorne
Chile, NS 02090
612-990- 313
Fax: 612-990- 322
www.redlands.nsw.edu.au
This school offers an English/Spanish curriculum to 820 day students (420 boys; 400 girls), in grades PreK-12. The student body is mostly Chilean and 90% of the teachers are Chilean. However, overseas teachers are welcome, with the applications being pre-school and English.

Richard Collingwood-Selby, Principal

1536 Reydon School for Girls
5178 Cruz Chica
Sierras de Cordoba, Cordoba
Argentina

NJ Milman, Principal

1537 Saint George's School
Carrera 92 No 156-88, Suba
Bogota
Colombia
057-168- 917
sanjorge@sgs.edu.co
www.sgs.edu.co

Mary De Acosta, Principal

1538 Santa Cruz Cooperative School
Barrio Las Palmas Calle Barcelona #
Casilla 753 Santa Cruz
Bolivia
(591) (3) 353-0808
Fax: (591) (3) 352-6993
william.j.mckelligott@gmail.com
www.sccs.edu.bo
College preparatory school equipping students with the necessary skills and values to be citizens and leaders for the 21st century. Preparing students to become productive citizens, leaders and life-long learners.

William J McKelligott, Director General
Hugo Paz, Board Director

1539 Santa Margarita School
22062 Antonio Parkway Rancho Santa
Surco, Lima
Peru, CA 92688
949-766-6000
www.smhs.org

Guillermo Descalzi, Principal

1540 St. Albans College
110 Clearwater Road
Lynnwood Glen Pretoria
South Africa
271-234- 122
Fax: 271-236- 191
robertr@stalbanscollege.com
www.stalbanscollege.com
St Alban's College is a learning community of boys, staff and parents. We are forward looking, committed to quality and service, and we pursue innovative strategies and encourage personal responsibility in the interest of all-round development of the boy as he journeys towards manhood.

Tom Hamilton, Headmaster
Carlos Palermo, Faculty Director

1541 St. Andrew's Scots School
Rosales 2809
Olivos
Argentina 01636
54-114-799-8318
Fax: 54-114-799-8318
admissions@sanandres.esc.edu.ar
www.sanandres.esc.edu.ar
St. Andrew's Scots School aims to graduate responsible citizens committed to serving Argentina and contributing to its equitable development through a well-balanced, bilingual education which meets high international standards and fosters a joy for learning.

Gabriel Rshaid, Headmaster
Ana Repila, Admissions Director

1542 St. Catherine's School
Carbajal 3250
1426 Capital Federal, Buenos Aires
Argentina
54-114-552-4353
Fax: 54-114-554-4113
stcath@ciudad.com.ar
www.redeseducacion.com.ar
Pre-K through 12, school year March-December

Mabel Manzitti, Principal

1543 St. George's College
Guido 800 CP
Quilmes, Buenos Aires
Argentina 01878
(5411) 4254-8237
Fax: 54-11-425-30030
info@stgeorge.com.ar
www.stgeorge.com.ar
Our mission is to provide students of varying abilities and backgrounds between the ages of 3 - 18 with a bilingual, fully integrated education of the highest calibre in order that they may develop their potential to the full in an appropriately resourced co-educational environment which nurtures individual development, independent thinking and the highest moral standards.

Derek Pringle, Headmaster
Peter Ashton, Deputy Headmaster

1544 St. Hilda's College
Cowley Place Oxford
OX4 1DY
England
44-1865-276884
Fax: 44-1865-276816
college.office@st-hildas.ox.ac.uk
www.st-hildas.ox.ac.uk
To promote the education of women within Oxford University and the tradition of excellence in women's education which it pioneered.

Sheila Forbes, Principal
Lucia Nixon, Senior Tutor

1545 St. John School
Casilla 284
Concepcion
Chile
www.sjs.org
St. John School is a bilingual school that caters to children from PK through grade twelve. The student body includes 1,170 day students (580 boys and 590 girls). The school does participate in teacher exchange programs with the length of stay for teachers being two years. The languages spoken include Spanish and English and the student/teacher ratio is 10:1.

Chris Pugh, Principal

1546 St. Margaret's British School-Girls
Calle Saint Margaret
150 Lomas de Montemar
Chile
451-00 -
admissions@stmargarets.cl
www.stmargarets.cl
St. Margarets objective is to protect in its pupil its motto: Recte Fac Nec Time (Do Right , Fear not) This implies assigning value to great ideals, act-

ing fairly and courteously, having sound judgement, enriched understanding, a discipline manner and making responsible use of their freedom.

Margery Byrne, Principal
Avril Cooper, Headmistress

1547 St. Paul's School
325 Pleasant Street
Concord, NH 03301-2591
603-229-4600
www.sps.edu
St. Paul's School is a fully residential academic community that pursues the highest ideals of scholarship. We strive to challenge our students intellectually and morally - to nurture a love for learning and a commitment to engage as servant leaders in a complex world.

Richardo Pons, Principal
William R Matthews, Jr, Rector

1548 St. Pauls School
1600 St Paul's Drive
Clearwater, FL 33764
727-536-2756
Fax: 727-531-2276
www.st.pauls.edu
To educate and inspire young minds in a challenging and nurturing community of learning.

AH Thurn, Principal
Angel W Kytle, Head of the School

1549 St. Peter's School
Pacheco 715
1640 Martinez, Buenos Aires
Argentina
www.st.peterspanchgani.org

Joy Headland, Principal

1550 Teaching Opportunities in Latin America for US Citizens
Organization of American States
17th & Constitution Avenue NW
Washington, DC 20036
202-458-3000
Fax: 202-458-3967
www.st.peterspanchgani.org
Supports teaching abroad opportunities.

1551 The American School Foundation of Monterrey
Ave. Ignacio Morones Prieto No. 150
Santa Catarina, N.L., C.P.
Mexico, MX 66190
(52)-81-5000-4400
Fax: (52)-81-5000-4428
jeff.keller@missouri.asfm.edu.mx
www.asfm.edu.mx
providing the type of learning environment which will prepare its students to successfully assume their role in the international community during the current millennium.

Jeff Keller, Superintendent
Jeff Farrington, Principal

1552 Uruguayan American School
Av Saldon de Rodriguez
Montevideo
Uruguay 11500-3360
598-2-600-7681
Fax: 598-2-606-1935
MSchramm@uas.edu.uy
www.uas.edu.uy
Uruguayan American School is to provide, together with the family, a balanced college preparatory education. UAS integrates a US style curriculum with Uruguayan studies to equip our national and international students to be successful in a diverse, ever changing world

Mike Schramm, Director
Cecilia Burgueo, UP Coordinator

1553 William T Sampson
Elementary & High School
PSC 1005 Box 49
FPO, Guantanamo Bay 09593 0005
Cuba

Eastern Europe

1554 American Academy Larnaca
Gregory Afxentious Avenue
PO Box 40112, Larnaca
Cyprus 06301
357-248-5400
Fax: 357-246-1046
info@academy.ac.cy
www.academy.ac.cy
Non-profit making school that is supported by an active multi-functional operation to achieve its core purpose: pre-school to University entrance education of the highest standard. It is a private, selective, co-educational, independent school, registered under the Private Schools' Law, 1971, of the Republic of Cyprus and uniquely, is run by its own graduates.

Doros Neocleous, Principal
Tom Widdows, Director

1555 American College of Sofia
PO Box 873
Sofia
Bulgaria, 1000
(359-2) 434 10 10
Fax: (359-2) 434 10 09
acs@acsbg.org
www.acs.bg
The American College of Sofia integrates the values and best practices of American pedagogy with the rich educational traditions of Bulgaria and Europe. The college aims to develop critical thinking, leadership and collaboration among multi-talented students of various social, cultural, economic and geographic backgrounds.

Richard T Ewing, Jr, Ph.D, President
Maria Angelova, Deputy Director

1556 American International School-Bucharest
Sos Pipera-Tunari 196
Voluntari Jud Ilfov 077190
Romania
40-21-2044300
Fax: 40-21-2044306
office@aisb.ro
www.aisb.ro
The American International School of Bucharest is a multicultural and international learning community, located in Romania. English is the principal language of instruction.

David Ottaviano Ed D, Director
Tamara Shreve, Elementary Principal

1557 American International School-Budapest
PO Box 53
Budapest
Hungary 01525
36 26 556 000
Fax: 36 26 556 003
admissions@nk.aisb.hu
www.aisb.hu
The American International School of Budapest (AISB) is a private and independent co-educational day school governed by a Board of Directors elected and appointed from the parent community. Established in 1973 by the United States Embassy to serve United States Government employees' dependents, AISB currently serves the needs of a rapidly expanding international population, including children of the local and expatriate business and diplomatic communities.

Ray Holliday Bersegeay, School Director
Larry Kinde, Chairman

1558 American International School-Cyprus
PO Box 23847, 11 Kassos Street
1086 Nisocia
Cyprus
357-22-316345
Fax: 357-22-316549
aisc@aisc.ac.cy
www.aisc.ac.cy
Founded in 1987, a private, coeducational, college preparatory day school providing a first class American and international university preparatory education within the Cyprus local community that incorporates a Greek as a First Language program for our Cypriot students.

Michelle Kleiss, Director
Terry Wolfson, Principal

1559 American International School-Krakow
Lusina ul. sw. Floriana 57
30-698 Krak¢w
Poland
48 12 270-1409
Fax: 48 12 270-1409
director@iskonline.org
www.aisk.kompit.com.pl
Affiliated with the American School of Warsaw, AISK is an independent, coeducational day school which offers an educational program from preschool through grade 8 for students of all nationalities.

Ellen Deitsch Stern, Director

1560 American International School-Vienna
Salmannsdorfer Strasse 47
A-1190 Vienna
Austria
43-1-40-132-0
Fax: 43-1-40-132-5
info@ais.at
www.ais.at
Provide a culture of educational excellence, a nurturing environment, and an atmosphere of open communication and aims to prepare a diverse student body for higher education; to inspire the youth to realize their potential; to foster life-long learning, tolerance, personal integrity, and democratic values; and to prepare students to become responsible adults, with respect for different cultures and beliefs.

Carol Kluznik, Director
Gail McMillan, HS Principal

1561 American School of Bucharest
Sos Pipera-Tunari 196
Voluntari Jud Ilfov
Romania 07719
40-21-2044300
Fax: 40-21-2044306
office@aisb.ro
www.aisb.ro
An independent, international, coeducational day school which offers an educational program from prekindergarten

through grade 12 for students of all nationalities.

David Ottaviano, Director
Jeri Guthrie Corn, Chair

1562 Asuncion Christian Academy
Avenida Santisimo Sacramento
1181 Casilla 1562
Asuncion, Paraguay-1209
011-595-21-607-378
Fax: 011-595-21-604-855
aca@aca.edu.py
www.acaknights.org/
Asuncion Christian Academy believes that the best education to prepare a student for adult life is an education based upon the truth of God's Word and having a growing and personal relationship with Jesus Christ.

Bethany Abreu, Director

1563 Falcon School
PO Box 23640
Nicosia
Cyprus 01685
357 22 424781
Fax: 357 22 313764
falconschool@cytanet.com.cy
www.falconschool.ac.cy/default.asp?id=261

Nikolas Michael Ieride, Principal

1564 Gimnazija Bezigrad
Periceva ulica 4
PO Box 2504
Ljubljana 01001-1001
Fax: 010-044-
info@gimb.org
www.gimb.org
Assistance to parents in raising gifted children to full and productive adulthood

Cyril Dominko, Principal
Janez Sustersic, Director

1565 International Elementary School-Estonia
Juhkentali 18
Tallinn
Estonia 10132
372-666-4380
Fax: 372-666-4383
office@ise.edu.ee
www.ise.edu.ee
Provide high-quality, international education; maximize personal potential; develop life-long learners who appreciate diversity; foster active, compassionate world citizens

Don Fitzmahan, Director
Terje Akke, PYP Coordinator

1566 International School-Belgrade
Temisvarska 19
Belgrade
Serbia 11040
381 11 206-9999
Fax: 381 11 206-9940
isb@isb.rs
www.isb.rs
An independent, coeducational day school which offers an educational program from kindergarten through grade 8 for students of all nationalities.

Dr. Eric Sands, Director
Sanja Ilic, Admissions Director

1567 International School-Budapest
P.O. Box 53
Budapest
Hungary 01525
36 26 556 000
Fax: 36 26 556 003
admissions@aisb.hu
www.aisb.hu
Grade levels N-8, school year August - June

Ray Holliday-Bersegeay, Director

1568 International School-Estonia
Juhkentali 18
Tallinn
Estonia 10132
372-666-4380
Fax: 372-666-4383
office@ise.edu.ee
www.ise.edu.ee
Provides high-quality, international education, maximize personal potential, develop life-long learners who appreciate diversity and foster active, compassionate world citizens.

Don Fitzmahan, Terje
Akke PYP Coordinator

1569 International School-Latvia
Viestura iela 6a
Jurmala
Latvia LV 20
(+371) 6775 5146
Fax: (+371) 6775 5009
merliha@isl.edu.lv
www.isl.edu.lv
Offers English-language, academically challenging programmes designed to develop life-long learners who are critical, creative and open-minded thinkers prepared and motivated to meet the diverse challenges of an ever-changing environment; act with integrity and responsibility locally and globally to transform their world in positive ways and appreciate and respect human diversity.

Larry Molacek, Director
Kevin Reimer, Deputy Director

1570 International School-Paphos
100 Aristotelous Savva Avenue
PO Box 62018, Paphos
Cyprus 08025
26 821700
Fax: 26 942541
info@isop-ed.org
www.isop-ed.org
The school caters for the needs of children from Kindergarten to Year 13. Its mission is to serve each and every one of the pupils as part of our school family and as an individual.

Litsa Olympiou, Headmistress

1571 International School-Prague
Nebusicka 700
164 00 Prague 6
Czech Republic
420 2 2038 4111
Fax: 420-2-2038-4555
ispmail@isp.cz
www.isp.cz
Educates students to be responsible, productive, ethical and healthy citizens with the ability to think creatively, reason critically, and communicate effectively through a variety of educational philosophies and methods, combining the best methodology and practices from a variety of national systems with an international perspective.

Rajiv Bhatt, Director
Barry Freckmann, Business Manager

1572 International Teachers Service
47 Papakyriazi Street
Larissa, Greece
41-253856
Fax: 41-251022
A recruitment service for teachers of English in Greece. Must have a BA/BS in education preferably English and/or EFL training or past experience in EFL and be a native speaker of English.

Fani Karatzou

1573 Kiev International School
3A Svyatoshinsky Provuluk
Kyiv
Ukraine 03115
380-44-452-2792
Fax: 380-44-452-2998
kiev@qsi.org
www.qsi.org
Kyiv International School, a private non-profit institution

Scott D'Alterio, Director
David Pera, Director Instruction

1574 Limassol Grammar-Junior School
10 Manoli Kalomiri & Theklas Lisiot
PO Box 51340
Limassol, Cyprus 03504
357-257-7933
Fax: 357-257-7818
junior@grammarschool.com.cy
www.grammarschool.com.cy/services.htm
The primary goal of the Grammar School is to provide its students with a solidly grounded liberal education. Thus, it seeks to encourage the intellectual, spiritual, and physical development of its students.

EWP Foley, Principal
Demetris Gregoriou, Director

1575 Logos School of English Education
33-35 Yialousa Street
PO Box 51075 Limassol
Cyprus 03501
357-25336061
Fax: 357-25335578
Principal@Logos.ac.cy
www.logos.ac.cy

Gary Love, Principal

1576 Magyar British International School
H-1519 Budapest
PO Box 219, Budapest
Hungary
361-466-9794
www.bisb.hu

Mary E Pazsit, Principal

1577 Melkonian Educational Institute
PO Box 1907
Nicosia
Cyprus
www.englishschool.ac.cy/?link=contact.php
An Armenian boarding school with high academic standards.

S Bedikan, Principal

1578 Private English Junior School
P.O Box 23575
Nicosia
Cyprus 01684
357-22 -9930
Fax: 357-22 -9930
info@englishschool.ac.cy
www.englishschool.ac.cy/?link=contact.php

Vassos Hajierou, BA, Principal

1579 QSI International School-Bratislava
Karloveska 64
Bratislava
Slovak Republic 842-2
421-2-6542-2844
Fax: 421-2-6541-1646

bratislava@qsi.org
www.qsi.org
To keep this urge to learn alive in every child in QSI schools. Our schools are established to provide in the English language a quality education for students in the cities we serve.

Britt Brantley, Director

1580 QSI International School-Ljubljana
Dolgi most 6A
1000 Ljubljana
Solvenia
386-1-2441750
Fax: 386-1-2441754
ljubljana@qsi.org
www.qsi.org
To keep this urge to learn alive in every child in QSI schools. Our schools are established to provide in the English language a quality education for students in the cities we serve.

Jay Loftin, Director

1581 QSI International School-Tbilisi
Village Zurgovani
Tbilisi
Republic of Georgia
995-32-53767
Fax: 995-32-322607
tbilisi@qsi.org
www.qsi.org
To keep this urge to learn alive in every child in QSI schools. Our schools are established to provide in the English language a quality education for students in the cities we serve.

James Rehberg, Director

1582 QSI International School-Yerevan
PO Box 82, Ashtarok Highway
Yerevan
Republic of Armenia 37501
374-10-349130
Fax: 374-10-397599
yerevan@qsi.org
www.qsi.org
To keep this urge to learn alive in every child in QSI schools. Our schools are established to provide in the English language a quality education for students in the cities we serve.

Douglas Shippert, Director

Middle East

1583 ACI & SEV Elementary School
Inonu Caddesi No 476
Goztepe, Izmir
Turkey 35290
90-232-285-3401
Fax: 90-232-246-1674
channa@aci.k12.tr
www.aci.k12.tr
Contribute to the growth of individuals who combine self-confidence with a firm sense of personal, social, and environmental responsibility. Enable students to be strong bilinguals in English and Turkish, well-educated adults, lifelong learners, and efficient communicators, who have developed skills, accountability, and attitudes for leading a fulfilling life and for serving their country and humanity.

Charles C Hanna, Director
Anet Gomel, Turkish First Vice Principal

1584 Abdul Hamid Sharaf School
PO Box 6008
Amman
Jordan 11118
962-615-2418
Fax: 962-651-2462
ahss@go.com.jo
www.ahss.edu.jo
A private, coeducational, K-12 day school serving the needs of a diverse group of students, international and local. Languages of instruction for the basic subjects are Arabic and English.

Sue Dahdah, Director

1585 Abquaiq Academy
PO Box 31677
Al-Khobar
Saudi Arabia 31952
966-3 5-6 04
Fax: 966-3 5-6 23
abqaiq@isgdh.org
The sole purpose of the school is for serving the educational needs of children from expatriate families.

Vineeta Dambal, Administrator/Principal

1586 Al Ain English Speaking School
PO Box 17939
Al Ain
United Arab Emirates
00971-3-7678636
Fax: 00971-3-767-1973
school@aaess.sch.ae
www.aaess.com
Al Ain English Speaking School is a member of the Association of British Schools in the Middle East and the Incorporated Association of Preparatory Schools (UK). The basic curriculum is that of the National Curriculum of England.

Peter Hodge, Principal

1587 Al Bayan Bilingual School
PO Box 24472
Safat 13105
Kuwait
965 2227 - 5000
Fax: 965 2227 - 5002
bbsjadm@bbs.edu.kw
www.bbs.edu.kw
A non-profit Arabic-English university preparatory educational institution, which fosters an environment for students to develop the intellectual qualities, ethical values, and positive attitudes required for effective participation and leadership in the overall development of Kuwait and the rapidly changing world.

Brian L McCauley, Director

1588 Al Khubairat Community School
PO Box 4001
Abu Dhabi
United Arab Emirates
971-244- 228
Fax: 971-244-6819
principal@britishschool.sch.ae
www.britishschool.sch.ae
British curriculum school for children aged 3 to 18.It is a non-profit school administered by a Board consisting of parent representatives and nominees of the British Ambassador.

Paul Coackley, Principal

1589 Al Rabeeh School
PO Box 41807
Abu Dhabi
United Arab Emirates
971 2 4482856
Fax: 971 2 4482854
www.alrabeeh.sch.ae/

HJ Kadri, Principal

1590 Al-Nouri English School
PO Box 46901
Fahaheel
Kuwait

PD Oldfield, Principal

1591 Al-Worood School
PO Box 46673
Abu Dhabi
United Arab Emirates
971-2-444-7655
Fax: 971-2-444-9732
alworood@emirates.net.ae
www.alworood.sch.ae/alworood/StaticContentDetails.asp
Grade levels N-12, school year September - June

Ahmed Osman, Academic Principal
Abdulla Al Nuwais, President

1592 American Collegiate Institute
Inonu Caddesi #476 Goztepe
Izmir
Turkey 35290
90-232-285-3401
Fax: 90-232-246-4128
channa@aci.k12.tr
www.aci.k12.tr
Offers a 1 + 4 year academic program. Students enter the school based upon a competitive national high-school entrance exam needing to improve their English language skills go into the intensive English one-year preparatory program before entering the school's rigorous four-year educational program.

Charles C Hanna, Director
Anet Gomel, First Vice Principal

1593 American Community School
Rue de Paris, Jel El Bahr
PO Box 11-8129, Riad El Solh
Beirut, Lebanon 01107-2260
961-1-374-370
Fax: 961-1-366-050
gdamon@acs.edu.lb
www.acs.edu.lb
Founded in 1905, an independent, non-profit, non-sectarian, pre-K-12 coeducational day school.

George Damon, Headmaster
David Warren, Deputy Headmaster

1594 American Community School-Abu Dhabi
PO Box 42114
Abu Dhabi
United Arab Emirates
971-2-681-5115
Fax: 971-2-681-6006
acs@acs.sch.ae
www.acs.sch.ae
The mission is to empower and inspire all students to define and shape their futures, pursue their dreams and contribute to society.

Dr George Robinson, Superintendent
Waheeda Al Tamimi, Administrative Assistant

1595 American Community School-Beirut
Rue de Paris, Jel El Bahr
PO Box 11-8129, Riad El Solh
Beirut, Lebanon 01107-2260
961-1-374-370
Fax: 961-1-366-050
gdamon@acs.edu.lb
www.acs.edu.lb
Founded in 1905, an independent, non-profit, non-sectarian, pre-K-12 coeducational day school. It draws students from both the Lebanese and international communities in Lebanon and embraces diversity in race, gender,

religion, national origin and economic background.

Dr George Robinson, Superintendent
David Warren, Deputy Headmaster

1596 **American International School**
PO Box 22090
Doha
Qatar
974-445-0150
Fax: 974-445-0157
info@asd.edu.qa
www.asd.edu.qa
The American School of Doha is an independent, U.S. accredited, college preparatory school, committed to provide the highest standard of educational excellence, through an enriched American curriculum.

Deborah Welch, Director
Michael Shahen, High School Principal

1597 **American International School-Abu Dhabi**
PO Box 5992
Abu Dhabi
United Arab Emirates
971-2-444-4333
Fax: 971-2-444-4005
admissions@aisa.sch.ae
www.aisa.sch.ae
Founded in 1995 to serve the needs of the local and expatriate residents of Abu Dhabi who want their children to pursue both American and International Baccalaureate curricula in an international setting.

Gareth Jones, Director
Abdulla Al-Hashly, Chairman

1598 **American International School-Israel**
PO Box 484, 65 Hashomron St
Even Yehuda
Israel 40500
972-9-890-1000
Fax: 972-9-890-1001
aisrael@wbais.org
www.wbais.org/~joomla/index.php?option=com_frontpage&
An independent, coeducational day school which offers an educational program from kindergarten through grade 12 for students of all nationalities.

Richard Detwiler, Principal

1599 **American International School-Kuwait**
PO Box 3267
Salmiya
Kuwait 22033
(965) 22255155
Fax: (965) 22255156
director@aiskuwait.org
www.aiskuwait.org
Grade levels kindergarten through twelfth.

Samera Al Rayes, Owner/Director
Noreen Hawley, Superintendent

1600 **American International School-Muscat**
PO Box 584
Azaiba Postal Code 130
Sultanate of Oman
968 24 595 180
Fax: 968 24 503 815
taism@omantel.net.com
www.taism.com
Pursues academic excellence for students in the international community through an American-based education that develops ethical, responsible, and globally conscious life-long learners.

Kevin Schafer, Director
Keith Boniface, High School Principal

1601 **American International School-Riyadh**
PO Box 990
Riyadh
Saudi Arabia 11421
966-1-491-4270
Fax: 966-1-491-7101
registration@ais-r.edu.sa
www.aisr.org
As a school committed to excellence, we will educate and inspire our students to be responsible, productive and ethical world citizens with the skills and passion to think creatively, reason critically, communicate effectively and learn continuously. We will accomplish this in an American educational environment characterized by high measurable standards and a clearly defined, appropriately interrelated college preparatory curriculum, implemented by a superior staff in partnership with parents a

Dr. Dennis Larkin, Superintendent

1602 **American School-Doha**
PO Box 22090
Doha
Qatar
974-4459-1500
Fax: 974-4459-1570
dwelch@asd.edu.ga
www.asd.edu.qa
is an independent, U.S. accredited, college preparatory school, committed to provide the highest standard of educational excellence, through an enriched American curriculum

Deborah Welch, Director
Colin Boudreau, High School Principal

1603 **American School-Kuwait**
PO Box 6735
Hawalli
Kuwait 32040
965-266-4341
Fax: 965-265-0438
ask@ask.edu.kw
www.ask.edu.kw
It is a privately owned, independent coeducational day school which offers a general academic curriculum for students of all nationalities

Bernard Mitchell, Superintendent
Fawsi Hasan, Arabic Studies Principal

1604 **American-British Academy**
PO Box 372
Medinat Al Sultan Qaboos
Sultanate of Oman PC 11
968-24603646
Fax: 968-24603544
admin@abaoman.edu.om
www.abaoman.edu.om
Provides an international education of the highest quality to enable students to be confident, responsible, caring life-long learners.

Mona Nashman-Smith, Superintendent
Rod Harding, Director of Operations

1605 **Amman Baccalaureate School**
PO Box 441
Sweileh Amman
Jordan 11910
962-6-541-1191/7
Fax: 962-6-541-2603
info@abs.edu.jo
www.abs.edu.jo
A coeducational and non-profit school which caters to students aged 3-18 years that offers an academically rigorous programme, enriched by extensive co-curricular activities, that culminates in the International Baccalaureate Diploma or Certificates.

Stuart Bryan, Principal
Robert Jones, Vice-Principal

1606 **Anglican International School-Jerusalem**
82 Rechov Haneviim
PO Box 191 Jerusalem
Israel 91001
972-2-567-7200
Fax: 972-2-538-474
hoskino@aisj.co.il
www.aisj.co.il
An internationally accredited, pre-Kindergarten to Grade 12 [ages 3-18] school. It creates student-focused academic and educational environment which aspires to achieve excellence.

Owen Hoskin, Director
Matthew Dufty, Deputy Principal

1607 **Ankara Elementary & High School**
PSC 89 Unit 7010
APO, Ankara 09822 7010
Turkey
011-90-312-287-253
Fax: 011-90-312-285-179
AnkaraEHS.Principal@eu.dodea.edu
www.anka-ehs.eu.dodea.edu/

Kathleen Reiss, Principal
Rosie Uluer, Assistant Principal

1608 **Arab Unity School**
PO Box 10563
Rashidiya, Dubai
United Arab Emirates
971-4-886-226
Fax: 971 4 2886321
auschool@amirates.net.ae
www.arabunityschool.com
Provide an equal opportunity, to all students, to develop their intellectual faculties and to awaken their latent, creative talents, irrespective of their ethnic background.

Zainab A Taher, Founder Director

1609 **Baghdad International School**
PO Box 571
Baghdad
Iraq

Amen A Rihani, Principal

1610 **Bahrain Bayan School**
PO Box 32411
Isa Town
Bahrain
973-682-227
Fax: 973-780-019
bayanschool@bayan.edu.bh
www.bayanschool.edu.bh
A bilingual, coeducational, college preparatory school with an international curriculum and faculty. It aims to preserve the tenets of Arabic /Islamic values, to assist students to a depth of cross-cultural knowledge and to promote the global perspective necessary for future world citizens.

Dr Nakhle Wehbe, Director General
Gilbert Daoura, Operations Manager

1611 **Bahrain Elementary & High School**
Psc 451 Box 690
FPO Bahrain
Bahrain 09834-5200
973 1772-7828
Fax: 973 1772-8583
www.bahr-ehs.eu.dodea.edu/

Grade levels K-12.
Gail Anderson, Principal

1612 Bahrain School
PO Box 934
Juffair
Bahrain
973 1772-7828
Fax: 973 1772-8583
BahrainEHS.Principal@eu.dodea.edu
www.bahr-ehs.eu.dodea.edu/
To provide a safe environment in which our students are challenged to their maximum potential as responsible members of a multi-cultural society.
Gail Anderson, Principal
Laura Bleck, Assistant Principal

1613 Bilkent University Preparatory School-Bilkent International School
East Campus
Bilkent Ankara
Turkey 06800
90 312 290 53 61
Fax: 90 312 266 49 63
school@bups.bilkent.edu.tr
www.bupsbis.bilkent.edu.tr
BUPS serves the educational needs of selected Turkish students while BIS serves the needs of selected international students in the Ankara area.
James Swetz, Director
Dan Keller, Associate Director

1614 Bishop's School
PO Box 2001
Amman
Jordan
962-6-653668
This Episcopal boy's school, founded in 1936, teaches both the Jordanian Curricula and the London University General Certification of Education Curriculum. Total enrollment is 855 day students in grades 1-12. Length of stay for teachers is one year with no housing provided. Languages spoken are English and Arabic.
Najib F Elfarr, Principal
Jamil Ismair, Faculty Head

1615 British Aircraft Corp School
PO Box 3843
Riyadh
Saudi Arabia
MR Pound, Principal

1616 British Embassy Study Group
Sehit Ersan Caddesi 46A, 06680
Cankaya Ankara
Turkey 06680
90 (312) 468 6563
Fax: 90 (312) 468 6239
admin@besg.org
www.besg.org
BESG is a co-educational primary school with 135 children aged between 3 and 11, representing nearly 26 countries. We are known as a friendly and caring British school, which values a holistic approach to education
Dawn Akyurek, Head Teacher
Katie Vincent, Deputy Head Teacher

1617 British International School-Istanbul
Dilhayat Sokak No:18 Etiler
Istanbul
Turkey, TR
90 (0) 212 257 51
Fax: 90-0-212-257 53 33
registrar2@bis.k12.tr
www.bis.k12.tr
The British International School Istanbul (BISI) provides a wide range of educational choices for international families. We are a private, coeducational school providing British-style international education for 520 students of 40 nationalities between the ages of 2r and 18.
Graham Pheby, Principal
Roger Short, Governor of the School

1618 Cairo American College
PO Box 39
Maadi 11431
Cairo, EG 11431
(20-2) 2755-5507
Fax: 20-2-519-6584
support@cacegypt.org
www.cacegypt.org
Cairo American College is a world class learning environment that affirms the voice, passions and talents of students and inspires them to use their hearts and minds as global citizens.
Nivine Captan-Amr, Board Chair
Elizabeth Bredin, Secretary

1619 Cambridge High School
PO Box 60835
Dubai
United Arab Emirates
971 - 4 282 4646
Fax: 971 - 4 282 4109
cambridge@cis-dxb.ae
www.gemscis-garhoud.com
David Mcaughlin, Principal
Nigel Cropley, Vice Principal

1620 Continental School (Sais British)
PO Box 6453
Jeddah 21442
Saudi Arabia
966-269-9001
Fax: 966-269-9194
conti@conti.sch.sa
www.continentalschool.com
Inspire in students a love of learning using a child centered, British style of education. Strive for excellence, recognizing, celebrating and encouraging a spirit of internationalism.
Bruce Gamwell, Director
Marina Alibhai, Registrar

1621 Dhahran Academy International School Group
PO Box 31677
Al Khobar 31952
Saudi Arabia 31952
966-3-330-0555
Fax: 966-3-330-2450
info@isgdh.org
www.isgdh.org
Grades preSchool-11, enrollment 994.
Norma Hudson, Superintendent

1622 Dhahran Central School
PO Box 31677
Dhahran 31311
Saudi Arabia 31952
966-3-330-0555
Fax: 966-3-330-2450
info@isgdh.org
www.isgdh.org
Norma Hudson, Principal

1623 Dhahran Hills School
PO Box 31677
Dhahran 31311
Saudi Arabia 31952
966-3-330-0555
Fax: 966-3-330-2450
info@isgdh.org
www.isgdh.org
Norma Hudson, Principal

1624 Doha College-English Speaking
PO Box 7660
Doha Qatar
Arabian Gulf
974-806-770
Fax: 974-806-311
dess@dess.org
www.dess.org
An independent, coeducational day school which offers an educational program from children of all nationalities from kindergarten through grade12.
E Goodwin, Principal
Emad Turkman, Chairman

1625 Doha English Speaking School
PO Box 7660
Doha
Qatar
(974) 44592750
Fax: (974) 44592761
dess@dess.org
www.dess.org
Create a happy, secure, stimulating and supportive learning environment
Emad Turkman, Chairman
Eddie Liptrot, Head Teacher

1626 Doha Independent School
PO Box 5404
Doha Qatar
Arabian Gulf
www.dohaacademy.net
SJ Williams, Principal

1627 Emirates International School
PO Box 6446
Dubai
United Arab Emirates
971-4-348-9804
Fax: 971-4-348-2813
mail@eischools.ae
www.eischools.ae
We offer a broad international education, in English, designed for local and expatriate students, that promotes excellence in all academic activities. It is our mission to enhance the educational, social and physical development of our students encouraging them to think analytically and creatively in preparation for the next stage of their education.
Daryle Russell, EdD, Headmaster
Jason Kirwin, HS Principal

1628 English School-Fahaheel
PO Box 7209
Fahaheel
Kuwait 64003
096-023-1010
Fax: 096-023-1054
esf@skee.com
www.skee.com
The English School Fahaheel recognizes the need for all students to be made aware of the demands placed upon them for Further Education and the world of work.
Ibrahim J Shuhaiber, Chairman
John J MacGregor, Principal

1629 English School-Kuwait
PO Box 379
Safat
Kuwait 13004
965-256-7205
Fax: 965-256-7147
www.tes.edu.kw
The English School was founded in 1953 under the auspices of the British Embassy and is

the longest established school in Kuwait catering for the expatriate community. The School operates as a not-for-profit independent co-educational establishment providing the highest standards in education for children of Pre-Preparatory and Preparatory School age.

William James Strath, Principal
Richard Davis, Chair

1630 English Speaking School

PO Box 2002
Dubai
United Arab Emirates
974-445- 275
Fax: 974-445- 276
dess@dessdubai.com
www.dessdxb.com
The school opened in 1963 in the upstairs room of a villa where expatriate workers were housed. There was one class which was taught by parents and a British Officer called Flight Lieutenant F. Loughman.

Bernadette McCarty, Principal
David Hammond, Headteacher

1631 Enka Okullari-Enka Schools

Sadi Gulcelik Spor Sitesi
Istinye, Istanbul
Turkey 34460
90-212-276-05-4547
Fax: 90-212-286-59-3035
mailbox@enkaschools.com
www.princeton.iss.edu
Enka Schools provide an international education for our students. We have a well qualified and passionate group of teachers from Turkey and overseas. Most of our students are Turkish while some of them have international backgrounds.

Darlene Fisher, Director
Ayten Yilmaz, Preschool Principal

1632 Gulf English School

PO Box 2440
Doha
Qatar
974-445-8 77
Fax: 974-448-1 25
info@gulfenglishschool.com
www.gulfenglishschool.com
Provide a positive and stimulating environment which facilitates individual learning, encourages experimentation, and develops critical thinking and problem solving skills. We must enable each student to achieve his or her best in the pursuit of academic excellence, and give them the confidence to be independent thinkers, able to assume responsibility and leadership and to take their place in the wider world

Paul Andrews, Principal
Tim Brosnan, Faculty Head

1633 Habara School

PO Box 26510
Bahrain
973-172- 173
www.ameinfo.com

PM Wrench, Principal

1634 IBN Khuldoon National School

Po Box 20511
Manama
Bahrain
973-16-687-073
Fax: 973-17-689-028
info@ikns.edu.bh
www.ikns.edu.bh
This IBN school is a private, fee paying, non-profit, coeducational, accredited middle states school. The curriculum offered to the 1,210 day students (630 boys and 580 girls) in grades K-12, is English/Arabic. The school is willing to participate in a teacher exchange program with the applications needed being science, math, social sciences, pre-school and English.

Kamal Abdel-Nour, President
Ghada R Bou Zeineddine, Principal

1635 Incirlik Elementary School

Unit 7180 Box 270
APO AE 09824
Turkey
011-90-322-316-310
Fax: 011-90-322-332-757
IncirlikEHS.Principal@eu.dodea.edu
www.inci-ehs.eu.dodea.edu/

Mary Davis, Principal

1636 Incirlik High School

Unit 7180 Box 270
APO AE 09824
Turkey
011-90-322-316-310
Fax: 011-90-322-332-757
IncirlikEHS.Principal@eu.dodea.edu
www.inci-ehs.eu.dodea.edu/

Dr. Donald Torrey, Principal

1637 Infant School-House #45

Khalil Kando Gardens Road, 5651
Manama
Bahrain

Maria Stiles, Principal

1638 International Community School

PO Box 2002
Amman
Jordan 11181
962-6 5-2 10
Fax: 962-6 5-2 71
office@ics-amman.edu.jo
www.ics-amman.edu.jo
Ours is a school where people matter. ~We want good results for each student, according to his or her own abilities in the classroom, in sport , music, drama or art.

John Light, Principal
Sue Hill, Primary Head

1639 International School of Choueifat

PO Box 7212
Abu Dhabi
United Arab Emirates
971-2-446-1444
Fax: 971-2-446-1048
iscad@sabis.net
www.iscad-sabis.net
Over the last 27 years hundreds of students have graduated from The International Schools of Choueifat in the region and then graduated from top universities in the world. In the UK, these universities include Oxford, Cambridge, LSE, Bristol, Edinburgh, Bath, Birmingham, Liverpool, The Imperial College of Science and Technology and all other Colleges of London University.

Marilyn Abu-Esber, Director

1640 Istanbul International Community School

Karaagac Mahallesi, G 72 Sokak No:1
Buyukcekmece , Istanbul
Turkey 34866
90-212-857-8264
Fax: 90-212-857-8270
jlewis@iics.k12.tr
www.iics.k12.tr
Through its challenging curriculum and strong staff-student relationships, IICS provides a caring environment that inspires each student to excel and to be inquisitive, creative, compassionate, balanced and internationally-minded.

Peter Welch, Headmaster
Sean Murphy, Primary Principal

1641 Izmir Elementary & High School

PSC 88
APO, Izmir 09821 0005
Turkey

Terry Emerson, Principal

1642 Jeddah Preparatory School

British Consulate, Box 6316
Jeddah 21442 Saudi Arabia
265-235-
Fax: 065-183-
registrar@jpgs.org
www.jpgs.org/

John GF Parsons, Principal

1643 Jubail British Academy

PO Box 10059 Madinat Al Jubail
Jubail 31961
Saudi Arabia
966.3.341.7550
Fax: 966.3.341.6990
mmcdougall@isgdh.org
www.isg-jubail.org/

Norman Edwards, Principal

1644 Jumeirah English Speaking School

PO Box 24942, Dubai
United Arab Emirates
971-4-394-5515
Fax: 971-4-394-3531
jess@jess.sch.ae
www.jess.sch.ae

CA Branson, Headmaster
RD Stokoe, Director

1645 King Faisal School

PO Box 94558, Riyadh 11614
Saudia Arabia
966-1-482-0802
Fax: 966-1-482-1521
kfs@kfs.sch.sa
www.kfs.sch.sa/English/adefault.aspx
Grade levels preK-12, enrollment 600.

Mohammed Al-Humood, Director General

1646 Koc School

PK 60-Tuzla
Istanbul
Turkey 34941
(90)216 585 6200
Fax: 90-216-304-1048
info@kocschool.k12.tr
www.kocschool.k12.tr
The goal of KoO School is to be respected nationally and internationally as a model K-12 school, offering an educational program of the highest academic and ethical standards.

Suna Kirac, Chairman

1647 Kuwait English School

PO Box 8640
Salmiya 22057
Kuwait
256-552-
Fax: 256-293-
keschool@kes.edu.kw
www.kes.edu.kw/?page_id=69

Craig Halsall, Principal

1648 Mohammed Ali Othman School

PO Box 5713
Taiz Yemen
Arab Republic

967-422-3671
Fax: 967-4 2-1495
maoschool.dx.am
Mohammed Ali Othman School is a well established school which has been running for over thirty years. At present it has around a thousand students from the Foundation Stage through to Year 12

Abdulla Ahmad, Principal
Fowzia Abdo Saeed, Deputy Head

1649 Nadeen Nursery & Infant School
PO Box 26367
Adliya
Bahrain
973-177- 888
Fax: 973-177- 888
info@nadeenschool.com
www.nadeenschool.info/
Nadeen School is dedicated to providing a caring, nurturing, and stimulating environment in which all children can learn and thrive. All of our students are treated with respect, care, and with the utmost sensitivity to their individual needs and requirements.

Pauline Puri, Principal

1650 New English School
PO Box 6156
Hawalli
Kuwait, KW 32036
[00965] 25318060
Fax: [00965] 25319924
admin@neskt.com
www.neskt.com
Private, co-educational day-school to offer a British style curriculum from Kindergarten to 'A' level.

Tareq S Rajab, Founder

1651 Pakistan International School-Peshawar
23 Sahibzada Abdual Qayyum Road
University Town
Peshawar
92-441-4428
Fax: 92-441-7272
www.isbi.com
An independent, coeducaional day school which offers an educational program from prekindergarten through grade 8 and supervised correspondence study for the high school grades for all expatriate nationalities.

Angela Coleridge, Principal

1652 Rahmaniah-Taif-Acad International School
American Consulate General, Dhahran
District Saudi Arabia
03 -30 -555
Fax: 03 -30 -450
www.isgdh.org

Dean May, Principal

1653 Ras Al Khaimah English Speaking School
PO Box 975
Ras Al Khaimah
United Arab Emirates
971-7-362-441
Fax: 971-7-362-445
www.rakess.net

Roy Burrows, Principal

1654 Ras Tanura School
PO Box 6140
Ras Tanura
Saudi Arabia 31311
067-367-
david.weston@aramco.com
www.saudiaramco.com

David Weston, Principal

1655 Sanaa International School
PO Box 2002
Sanaa
Yemen
967-1-370192
Fax: 967-1-370-193
qsi-sanaa@qsi.org
www.qsi.org
Sanaa International School, a non-profit institution that opened in September 1971 offers a high quality education in the English language for pre-school, elementary, and secondary students. The Campus is located on 34 acres on the outskirts of Sanaa constructed and entered in September 1978.

Mr. Philip Weirich, Director

1656 Saudi Arabian International British School
PO Box 85769
Riyadh
Saudi Arabia 11612
966- 12-8 23
Fax: 966- 12-8 23
principal@britishschoolriyadh.com
www.britishschoolriyadh.com
Improve standards of teaching, learning and citizenship within a safe and secure environment. Our Mission Statement and School Improvement Plan provide the direction for the future development of our pupils and the continuous improvement of our school.

Peter Wiles, Acting Principal
Terry Sayce, Chairman

1657 Saudi Arabian International School-Dhahran
SAIS-DD, Box 677
Dhahran International Airport
Dhahran 31932, Saudi Arabia
996-3-330-0555
Fax: 966-3-330-0555
brent_mutsch%sais@macexpress.org
www.isgdh.org/

Dr. Leo Ruberto, Principal

1658 Saudi Arabian International School-Riyadh
PO Box 990
Riyadh
Kingdom of Saudi Arabia 11421
966-1-491-4270
Fax: 966-1-491-7101
registration@ais-r.edu.sa
www.aisr.org
Educate and inspire our students to be responsible, productive and ethical world citizens with the skills and passion to think creatively, reason critically, communicate effectively and learn continuously. We will accomplish this in an American educational environment characterized by high measurable standards and a clearly defined, appropriately interrelated college preparatory curriculum, implemented by a superior staff in partnership with parents and community.

Daryle Russell, EdD, Principal
Brian Matthews, Superintendent

1659 Saudia-Saudi Arabian International School
PO Box 167, CC 100
Jeddah 21231
Saudi Arabia
www.saudigazette.com

John Hazelton, Principal

1660 Sharjah English School
PO Box 1600
Sharjah
United Arab Emirates
971-655- 930
Fax: 971- 55- 930
seschool@emirates.net.ae
www.seschool.ae
Not for profit school. It is self-supporting and financed by fees paid by parents for the education of their children.

David Throp, Principal
Jenefer Race, Primary Headteacher

1661 Sharjah Public School
PO Box 6125, Sharjah
United Arab Emirates
971-652- 124
www.sharjahpublicschool.ae

Nazim Khan, Principal

1662 St. Mary's Catholic High School
PO Box 52232
Dubai
United Arab Emirates
009-104-3370
Fax: 009-104-3368
maryscol@emirates.net.ae
www.stmarysdubai.com
St. Mary's Catholic High School is reputed for its high standards in academic work and also in the standards of discipline which we try to inspire in the children.

Sr Anne Marie Quigg, Principal
U D'Souza, Vice Principal

1663 Sultan's School
PO Box 665
Seeb
Sultanate of Oman 00121
968-24 -367
Fax: 968-24 -362
admissions@sultansschool.org
www.sultansschool.org
The Sultan's School is a co-educational school offering a bilingual Arabic-English education from early childhood to pre-university.

Anthony J Cashin, Principal

1664 Sunshine School
2 Dutcher Avenue
Pawling, NY 12564
845-855-9238
Fax: 845-855-0222
sunshineschool-pawling.org
Our goal is to provide a quality pre-school education for young children. We do this by addressing both the social and the intellectual development of the child.

David Brinded, Principal

1665 Tarsus American College and SEV Primary
Cengiz Topel Cd Caminur Mah 201 Sk
Tarsus/Mersin
Turkey 33440
90-324-613-5402
Fax: 90-324-624-6347
info@tac.k12.tr
www.tac.k12.tr
The mission of Tarsus American Schools is to contribute to the growth of individuals who combine self-confidence with a firm sense of personal and social responsibility.

Bernard Mitchell, PhD, Superintendent
Jale Sever, Primary School Principal

1666 Universal American School
PO Box 17035
Khalidiya
Kuwait 72451

965-562-0297/561
Fax: 965-562-5343
uas@qualitynet.net
www.uas.edu.kw
The Universal American School is a private, college-preparatory, N-12 school serving a multinational student body from the diverse populations residing in Kuwait
Nora Al-Ghanim, Administrative Director
Mike Church, Assistant Principal

1667 Uskudar American Academy
Vakif Sokak Number 1
Baglarbasi Istanbul
Turkey, TR
90-216-310-6823
Fax: 90-216-333-1818
wshepard@uaa.k12.tr
www.uaa.k12.tr
The mission of SEV/ABH Schools is to contribute to the growth of individuals who combine self-confidence with a firm sense of personal, social, and environmental responsibility. We aim to enable our students to be strong bilinguals in English and Turkish, well-educated adults, lifelong learners, and efficient communicators, who have developed skills, accountability, and attitudes for leading a fulfilling life and for serving their country and humanity
Whitman Shepard, Director
Dilek Yakar, Primary Principal

1668 Walworth Barbour American International School in Israel
65 Hashomron Street
PO Box 484
Israel 40500
972-9-961-8100
Fax: 972-9-961-8111
aisrael@wbais.org
www.american.hasharon.k12.il
Through a rigorous and dynamic American international curriculum, AIS, a private secular school in Israel, inspires each student to cultivate a respect for diversity, develop a passion for life-long learning, achieve academic potential, assume leadership, contribute actively to society, and resolve conflict through dialogue and understanding
Robert A Sills, Superintendent
John Chere, Chairman

Western Europe

1669 AC Montessori Kids
Route De Renipont 4
Lasne B-1380
Belgium
32-2-633-6652
Fax: 32-2-633-6652
info@acmontessorikids.com
www.acmontessorikids.com
A bilingual English/French Montessori School for children aged18 months - 12 years.
Laurence Randoux, Director
Mark Ciepers, Director

1670 AFCENT Elementary & High School
Unit 21606
APO AE 09703
Brunssum, Netherlands
www.afcent.org

1671 Abbotsholme School
Rocester (Uttoxeter, Staffordshire)
ST14 5BS
England
01889-590217
Fax: 01889-590001
admissions@abbotsholme.co.uk
www.abbotsholme.com
This interdenominational school offers an English-based curriculum for 78 day students and 166 boarding (152 boys; 92 girls), in grades 7-13.
Darrell J Farrant, MA, FRSA, Principal
Steve Fairclough, Head

1672 Academy-English Prep School
Apartado 1300 Palma D Mallorca
525 W 17th Street Bloomington
Spain, IN 47404
812-333-2882
Fax: 812-339-2253
www.theprepschool.info
CA Walker, Principal

1673 Ackworth School, Ackworth
Pontefract, West Yorkshire
England WF7 7
0977-611401
admissions@ackworthschool.com
www.ackworthschool.com
This school offers an English-based curriculum to 264 day students and 111 boarding students (180 boys; 195 girls), ages 11-18 years of age.
Peter J Simpson, Head
Jeffrey Swales, Deputy Head, Curriculum

1674 Alconbury Elementary School
Unit 5570 Box 60
APO AE 09470
Great Britain
011-44-1480-843620
Fax: 011-44-1480-843172
AlconburyES.Principal@eu.dodea.edu
www.alco-es.eu.dodea.edu
To provide a safe and productive learning environment in which all students reach their fullest potential by developing knowledge and skills.
Teddy Emerson, Principal

1675 Alconbury High School
Unit 5570 Box 60
APO AE 09470
Great Britain
441- 80-4 36
Fax: 441- 80-4 31
www.alco-hs.eu.dodea.edu
To develop healthy, adaptable, independently thinking, and socially responsible members of the global community.
Teddy Emerson, Principal
Lance Posey, Assistant Principal

1676 Alexander M Patch Elementary School
Unit 30401
APO AE 09107
Germany
071- 68- 520
Fax: 071- 68- 713
www.patch-es.eu.dodea.edu
Provide a standards-based curriculum that develops lifelong learners and promotes highest student achievement in partnership with our community.
Robert Allen, Principal
Ronald Lathrop, Assistant. Principal

1677 Alexander M Patch High School
Unit 30401
APO AE 09107-0401
Germany
071- 68- 520
Fax: 071- 68- 713
www.patch-es.eu.dodea.edu
Prepares all students to exceed challenging academic standards, know how to learn, communicate effectively, and make responsible decisions so that they can be continuous learners and productive citizens in a diverse society.
Robert Allen, Principal
Ronald Lathrop, Assistant. Principal

1678 Alfred T Mahan Elementary School
PSC 1003 Box 48
FPO Keflavik 09728
Iceland
Jan Long, Principal

1679 Alfred T Mahan High School
PSC 1003 Box 52
FPO Keflavik 09728 0352
Iceland
M Deatherage, Principal

1680 Amberg Elementary School
CMR 414
APO, Amberg 09173 0005
Germany
Letcher Connell, Principal

1681 Ambrit Rome International School
Via Filippo Tajani, 50
Rome, Italy 00149
39-06-559-5305
Fax: 39-06-559-5309
ambrit@ambrit-rome.com
www.ambrit-rome.com
Grade levels Pre-K through 8, school year September - June
Bernard C Mullane, Director
Loretta Nanini, Admissions Director

1682 American College-Greece
6 Gravias Street
Aghia Paraskevi
Athens, Greece GR-15
30-1-600-9800
Fax: 30-1-600-9811
info@acg.edu
www.acg.edu
Founded in 1875, combining the best of American education with the intellectual and cultural heritage of Greece, provide a unique foundation for international educational excellence.
David G Horner, President
Nicholas Jiavaras, Executive Vice President

1683 American Community School-Cobham
Heywood, Portsmouth Road
Cobham, Surrey
United Kingdom KT11
44-1932-869-744
Fax: 44-1932-869-789
hayoub@acs-england.co.uk
www.acs-england.co.uk
Promotes a high standard of scholarship, responsibility, and citizenship in a supportive, international community.
Tom Lehman, Head of School
Heidi Ayoub, Dean of Admissions

1684 American Community School-Egham
Woodlee London Road (A30)
Egham, Surrey
United Kingdom TW20
44-1784-430-611
Fax: 44-1784-430-626

jlove@acs-england.co.uk
www.acs-england.co.uk
Promotes high standards of scholarship, responsibility and citizenship in a supportive, international community

Julia Love, Dean of Admissions
Moyra Hadley, Head of School

1685 American Community School-Hillingdon
108 Vine Lane
Hillingdon, Middlesex
United Kingdom UB10
44-189-581-3734
Fax: 44-189-581-0634
HillingdonAdmissions@acs-england.co.uk
www.acs-england.co.uk
Foundes in 1978, has endeavoured to provide a quality education for a multi-national community in the London area.

Ginger Apple, Head of School
Rudianne Soltis, Dean of Admissions

1686 American Community Schools
108 Vine Court
Hillingdon, Uxbridge, Middlesex
UB100BE
England
44-189-581-3734
Fax: 44-189-581-0634
hmulkey@acs-england.co.uk
www.acs-england.co.uk
This school serves the needs of the international business families in Greater London. Programs are nonsectarian, coeducational day schools with lower, middle and high school divisions offering coordinate college preparatory curricula from pre-kindergarten through grade twelve.

Paul Berg, Headmaster

1687 American Community Schools-Athens
129 Aghias Paraskevis Avenue and Ka
Halandri, Athens
Greece 15343
301-639-3200
Fax: 301-639-0051
gialamas@acs.gr
www.acs.gr
Provides a student-centered environment where individuals excel academically and develop intellectually, socially and ethically to thrive as healthy, responsible members of global society.

Stefanos Gialamas, President
Steve Kakaris, Business Manager

1688 American Embassy School-Reykjavik
Lngul nu 8
210 Gardab'r
Iceland
354-590-3106
Fax: 354-590-3110
isi@internationalschool.is
www.internationalschool.is
The International School of Iceland (ISI) is a private elementary school housed in an Icelandic public school, Sj landssk›li. The school offers an international educational program to children in grades 1-7.

Berta Faber, Headmistress
Hanna Hilmarsdottir, Assistant Headmistress

1689 American International School-Carinthia
Friesacher Strasse 3 Audio ICC
A-9330 Althofen
Austria
www.cic-network.at
Ron Presswood, Principal

1690 American International School-Florence
Villa le Tavernule - via del Carota
Bagno a Ripoli, Florence
Italy, VA 50012
39-055-646-1007
Fax: 39-055-644-226
admin.tav@isfitaly.org
www.isfitaly.org
Business Manager
Provide attendees

Christopher Maggio, Head of School
Marie Jos , Manzini

1691 American International School-Genoa
Via Quarto 13-C
Genoa
Italy 16148
39-010-386-528
Fax: 39-010-398-700
info@aisge.it
www.aisge.it
Provides students of internationally- minded families with a high quality education in the English language, from Pre-School through to the 12th Grade.

Sheldon Friedman, Director
Raffaele Boccardo, President

1692 American International School-Lisbon
Rua Antonio Dos Reis, 95
Linho, 2710-301 Sintra
Portugal
351-21-923-98-00
Fax: 351-21-923-98-26
tesc0893@mail.telepac.pt
www.ecis.org
An independent, coeducational day school which offers an educational program from early childhood through grade 12 for student of all nationalities.

Blannie M Curtis, Director

1693 American International School-Rotterdam
Verhulstlaan 21
3055 WJ Rotterdam
Netherlands
31-10-422-5351
Fax: 31-10-422-4075
queries@aisr.nl
www.aisr.nl
Provides a comprehensive program of learning, with well-qualified and experienced faculty who prepare students Pre-School through Grade 12 for the ever-changing world in which we live.

Brian Atkins, Director
Anne-Marie Blitz, Elementary Principal

1694 American International School-Salzburg
Moosstrasse 106
Salzburg A-5020
Austria
43-662-824-617
Fax: 43-662-824-555
office@ais.salzburg.at
www.ais-salzburg.at
A boarding and day school committed to the college-preparatory education of conscientious young men and women. The academic and boarding programs nurture the students' intellectual growth and artistic potential, as well as their social, physical, and personal development.

Paul McLean, Headmaster
Felicia Gundringer, Admissions Coordinator

1695 American International School-Vienna
Salmannsdorfer Strasse 47
A-1190 Vienna
Austria
43-1-401-320
Fax: 43-1-401-325
info@ais.at
www.ais.at
Provide a culture of educational excellence, a nurturing environment, and an atmosphere of open communication and aims to prepare a diverse student body for higher education; to inspire the youth to realize their potential; to foster life-long learning, tolerance, personal integrity, and democratic values; and to prepare students to become responsible adults, with respect for different cultures and beliefs.

Ellen Stern, Director
Dr Greg Moncada, HS Principal

1696 American Overseas School-Rome
Via Cassia 811
Rome, IT 00189
39-06-3326-4841
Fax: 39-06-3326-2608
aosr@aosr.org
www.aosr.org
An independent, coeducational day school for students of all nationalities in prekindergarten through grade 13 and offers a boarding program for select students in grades 9-12.

Beth Kempler, Head of School

1697 American School of the Hague
Rijksstraatweg 200
2241 BX Wassenaar
The Netherlands
31-70-512-1060
Fax: 31-70-511-2400
info@ash.nl
www.ash.nl
educates students to excel in critical inquiry, creative thinking, clear communication, and commitment to others.

Paul De Minico, Superintendent
Douglas Buckley, Chair

1698 American School-Barcelona
Jaume Balmes 7
Esplugues de Llobregat
Spain 08950
34-93-371-4016
Fax: 34-93-473-4787
info@a-s-b.com
www.a-s-b.com
fully develop each student's unique potential by providing a high quality American/Spanish curriculum in an English-language based, respectful and diverse environment

Nancy Boyd, Elementary School Principal
Bill Volckok, Secondary School Principal

1699 American School-Bilbao
Soparda Bidea 10
Berang (Bizkaia)
Spain 48640
34-94-668-0860
Fax: 34-94-668-0452
asob@asob.es
www.asob.es/en
s a private, non-profit, International School, Offers students an American-style educational programme taught in English. The cur-

riculum has an international focus and leads to the American High School Diploma

Roger West, Director

1700 American School-Las Palmas
Carretera de los Hoyos, Km 1.7
Las Palmas de Gran Canaria
Las Palmas, Spain 35017
34-928-430-023
Fax: 34-928-430-017
info@dns.aslp.org
www.aslp.org
Supports students in becoming life long learners in the tradition of American education

Linnah Sanab, Director
Conchita Neyra, Assistant Director

1701 American School-London
One Waverly Place
London
United Kingdom NW8 0
44-207-449-1200
Fax: 44-207-449-1350
admissions@asl.org
www.asl.org
is to develop the intellect and character of each student by providing an outstanding American education with a global perspective.

Jodi Coats, Dean of Admissions

1702 American School-Madrid
Apartado 80
Madrid
Spain 28080
34-91-740-1900
Fax: 34-91-357-2678
info@asmadrid.org
www.amerschmad.org
Grade levels Pre-K through 12, school year September - June

Robert Thompson, Director
William O'Hale, Headmaster

1703 American School-Milan
Via K Marx 14
Noverasco di Opera, Milan
Italy 20090
39-02-530-001
Fax: 39-02-576-06274
director@asmilan.org
www.asmilan.org
s to provide a fulfilling educational environment where learners can discover and develop their capacities and achieve personal excellence.

Alen P Austen, Director
Samer Khoury, High School Principal

1704 American School-Paris
41, rue Pasteur
Saint Cloud
France 92210
33-1-411-28282
Fax: 33-1-460-22390
webteam@asparis.fr
www.asparis.org
We develop lifelong learners with an international focus who use their social, thinking and problem-solving skills to contribute constructively to a changing global society

Pilar Cabeza de Vaca, Headmistress
Jack Davis, Head of the School

1705 American School-Valencia
Avenida Sierra Calderona 29
Urb Los Monasterios, Puzol
Spain 46530
34-96-140-5412
Fax: 34-96-140-5039
asvalencia@asvalencia.org
www.asvalencia.org
An international, private, bilingual, university- preparatory school that provides a broad and balanced curriculum in a safe and positive learning environment that encourages students to seek challenges.

Saara Tatem, Director
Ildefonso Segura, Financial Director

1706 American School-the Hague
Rijkstraatweg 200
BX Wassenaar
Netherlands 02241
31-70-514-0113
Fax: 31-70-511-2400
info@ash.nl
www.ash.nl
Educates students to excel in critical inquiry, creative thinking, clear communication, and commitment to others.

Rick Spradling, Director

1707 Anatolia College
PO Box 21021
Pylea Thessaloniki
Greece 55510
30-31-398-201
Fax: 30-31-327-500
admissions@act.edu
www.anatolia.edu.gr
Offers undergraduate and graduate programs of study characterized by reasoned and open inquiry, acquisition of the breadth and depth of knowledge associated with traditional university curricula, and achievement of the highest possible standards in student-centered teaching and faculty scholarship, with emphasis on individual growth.

Richard L Jackson, President
Panayiotis Kanellis, Executive Vice President

1708 Anglo-American School-Moscow
American Embassy
Itainen Puistotie 14
Finland 00140
7-095-231-4488
Fax: 7-095-231-4477
director@aas.ru
www.aas.ru
An international learning community where students, teachers and parents demand excellence and engagement from one another.

Drew Alexander, Director
Nicolette Kirk, Admissions Officer

1709 Anglo-American School-St. Petersburg
c/o American Embassy
Itainen Puistotie 14, Box L, Helsinki
Finland
7-812-320-8925
Fax: 7-812-320-8926
nastia.smirnova@aas.ru
www.aas.ru/stpetersburg
An international learning community where students, teachers and parents demand excellence and engagement from one another.

Ronald Gleason, Principal
Ellen D Stren, Director

1710 Ansbach Elementary School
Unit 28614 APO AE 09177
Germany
011-49 -802
Fax: 011-46 -802
AnsbachES.Principal@eu.odedodea.edu
www.ansb-es.eu.dodea.edu
Provides many excellent opportunities to encouage and support all students intellectual, physical, social, emotional and creative developments and prepare them to meet the challengges of a dynamic and diverse world community.

Essie Grant, Principal

1711 Ansbach High School
Unit 28614
APO AE 09177
Germany
49-9802-223
Fax: 49-9802-1496
AnsbachHS.Principal@eu.dodea.edu
www.ansb-hs.eu.dodea.edu
A public school serving the children of American Army units.

Jennifer Rowland, Principal

1712 Antwerp International School
Veltwijcklaan 180
2180 Ekeren-Antwerpen
Belgium
32-3-543-9300
Fax: 32-3-541-8201
ais@ais-antwerp.be
www.ais-antwerp.be
Educates young people to be responsible, caring, and productive members of a democratic society in a global community, and to prepare them for continued education. It promotes integrity, self-realization, mutual respect and understanding in a multi-cultural environment of students and teachers.

Alun Cooper, Headmaster

1713 Argonner Elementary School
Unit 20193 Box 0015
APO, Hanau 09165 0015
Germany

Christine Holsten, Principal

1714 Athens College
420 Madison Avenue
New York, NY 10017
212-697-7071
Fax: 212-697-7093
trustees@athenscollege.org
www.athenscollege.org
The mission of Athens College is to provide, by international standards, the highest quality education to the most deserving candidates and to cultivate in its students those habits of mind, body, and spirit necessary for responsible citizenship in GReece and the world; moral courage, intellectual discipline, compassion, and an unswerving devotion to justice and truth. Our goal is to instill in our students, by teaching and by example, a strong sense of measure.

Walter McCanny Eggleston, Principal
Dr Nicholas G Bacopoulos, President

1715 Aviano Elementary School
Unit 6210 Box 180
APO, AE 09604-0180
Italy
011-39-0434-660921
avianoes.principal@eu.dodea.edu
www.avia-es.eu.dodea.edu

Lillian Hiyama, Principal
Phyllis Fuglaar, Assistant Principal

1716 Aviano High School
Unit 6210 Box 180
APO, AE 09604-0180
Italy
632-567-
Fax: 390- 34-6 09

avianohs.principal@eu.dodea.edu
www.avia-hs.eu.dodea.edu
Debra K Johnson, Principal

1717 BEPS 2 Limal International School
23 Avenue Franklin Roosevelt
Brussels
Belgium 01050
32-10-417-227
Fax: 32-2-687-2968
info@beps.com
www.beps.com
The schools share a common philosophy and approach to education. An average class size of 16 allows for a high level of individual attention in a caring and supportive environment.
Charles A Gellar, Head
Henny de Waal, Headmistress

1718 Babenhausen Elementary School
CMR 426 Unit 20219
APO, Babenhausen 09089 0005
Germany
Ida Rhodes, Principal

1719 Bad Kissingen Elementary School
CMR 464
APO, Bad Kissingen 09226 0005
Germany
Beatrice McWaters, Principal

1720 Bad Kreuznach Elementary School
CMR 441
APO, Bad Kreuznach 09525 0005
Germany
Peter Grenier, Principal

1721 Bad Kreuznach High School
Unit 24324
APO, Bad Krueznach 09252 0005
Germany
Jennifer Beckwith, Principal

1722 Bad Nauheim Elementary School
Unit 21103
APO, Bad Nauheim 09074 0005
Germany
Raymond Burkard, Principal

1723 Badminton School
Westbury-on-Trym, Bristol
BS9 3BA
England
0272-623141
admissions@badminton.bristol.sch.uk
www.badminton.bristol.sch.uk
The school combines excellent facilities and teaching standards with a friendly atmosphere and a strong emphasis on pastoral care. Badminton is also focused on ensuring that girls realise their potential so that they can be capable of achieving whatever they want to be when they leave school.
Jan Scarrow, Headmistress

1724 Bamberg Elementary School
USAG Bamberg, Unit 27539
APO AE 09139
Germany
469-761-
Fax: 095- 31-15
BambergES.Principal@eu.dodea.edu
www.bamb-es.eu.dodea.edu
John G Rhyne, Principal

1725 Bamberg High School
Unit 27539
APO AE 09139
Germany
469-088-
BambergHS.Principal@eu.dodea.edu
www.bamb-hs.eu.dodea.edu/
Preparing all students to achieve success and personal fulfillment in a dynamic global environment.
Dominick Calabria, Principal
Richard Jimenez, Assistant Principal

1726 Barrow Hills School
Roke Lane
Witley, Godalming
Surrey, England GU8 5
01428-683639
Fax: 01428-683639
sec@barrowhills.org.uk
www.barrowhills.org.uk
Michael Connolly, Headmaster

1727 Baumholder High School
Unit 23816 Box 30
APO, AE 09034-0034
Germany
011-49 -783
Fax: 011-49 -783
BaumholderHS.Principal@eu.dodea.edu
www.baum-hs.eu.dodea.edu
Danny Robinson, Principal
Patrick McDonald, Assistant Principal

1728 Bavarian International School
Haputstrasse 1
Schloss Haimbausen
Haimhausen, Germany 85778
49-8133-9170
Fax: 49-8133-917-135
k.lippacher@bis-school.com
www.bis-school.com
Inspiring young minds and challenging young individuals to achieve their intellectual and personal potential within a caring international environment
Bryan Nixon, Director

1729 Bedales School
Church Road Steep
Petersfield Hampshire
England, UK GU32
01730-300100
Fax: 01730-300500
admin@bedales.org.uk
www.bedales.org.uk
Keith Budge, Headmaster
Leo Winkley, Deputy Head

1730 Bedford School
De Parys Avenue Bedford
England, UK MK40
44-0-1234-362200
Fax: 44-0-1234-362283
info@bedfordschool.org.uk
www.bedfordschool.org.uk
We pride ourselves on the pursuit of excellence, on encouraging boys to develop their talent, discover new interests and prepare for the world beyond school.
John Moule, Head Master

1731 Bedgebury School
Goudhurst
Cranbrook
Kent TN17
0580-211954
bedgebury@bell-centres.com
www.bedgeburyschool.co.uk
Our goal at Bell Bedgebury is a simple one - to offer all our students the best possible preparation for their future educational careers.
Eric Squires, Headmaster
David Morse, Principal

1732 Belgium Antwerp International School
Veltwijcklaan 180
Ekeren-Antwerp
Belgium 02180
32-3-543-9300
Fax: 32-3-541-8201
ais@ais-antwerp.be
www.ais-antwerp.be
The school is concerned with the student's social, physical, emotional and intellectual development. It is committed to excellence and to providing the best possible opportunities for growth for each student.
Alun Cooper, Headmaster
Matthew Cox, Elementary School Principal

1733 Benjamin Franklin International School
Martorell i Pena 9
Barcelona
Spain 08017
34-93-434-2380
Fax: 34-93-417-3633
bfranklin@bfis.org
www.bfis.org
We view education as an opportunity for children to live fully and become global citizens able to build a more humane world.
David Penberg, Director
James Duval, Elementary Principal

1734 Berlin International School
Lentzeallee 8/14
Berlin
Germany 14195
49-30-790-00370
Fax: 49-30-3790-00370
office@berlin-international-school.de
www.berlin-international-school.de
Berlin International School is a private, non-profit, non-denominational day school offering student-centered learning to international and local students from pre-school through university entrance preparation.
Hubert Keulers, Acting Director
Michael Cunningham, Principal

1735 Berlin Potsdam International School
Am Hochwald 30, Haus 2
14 532 Kleinmachnow
Germany
49-332-086-760
Fax: 49-332-086-7612
office@bpis.de
www.bpis.de
Grade levels N-12, school year August - June
Stephen Middlebrook, Director

1736 Bitburg Elementary School
52 MSG/CCSE-B Unit 3820 Box 45
APO, AE
Germany 09126-45
119-661-
Fax: 119- 61-
BitburgES.Principal@eu.dodea.edu
www.bitb-es.eu.dodea.edu
Joseph Lovett, Principal

1737 Bitburg High School
52 MSG/CCSH-B Unit 3820 Box 50
APO, AE
Germany 09126-50
065-692-
Fax: 065- 90-0
webmaster@eu.dodea.edu
www.bitb-hs.eu.dodea.edu
David W Carlisle, Principal
Jennifer Remoy, Assistant Principal

1738 Bitburg Middle School
52 MSG/CCSM-B Unit 3820 Box 55
APO, AE
Germany 09126
561-946-3200
Fax: 065-611-2091
webmaster@eu.dodea.edu
www.bitb-ms.eu.dodea.edu
Douglas Carlson, Principal

1739 Bjorn's International School
Gartnerivej 5
Copenhagen
Denmark 02100
453-929-2937
Fax: 453-929-1938
kontoret.101152@skolekom.dk
www.b-i-s.dk
Lea Kroghly, Principal

1740 Black Forest Academy
Postfach 1109
Kandern
Germany 79396
49-7626-91610
Fax: 49-7626-8821
www.bfacademy.com
Black Forest Academy's vision is globally-minded Christians changing their world for Christ.
George Durance, Principal
Tim Shuman, Director

1741 Bloxham School
Bloxham
Banbury
Oxfordshire, UK OX15
01295-720206
Fax: 01295-721897
registar@bloxhamschool.com
www.bloxhamschool.com
As the largest group of Church of England Schools in the UK, Woodard was established in 1847 and today is known for providing academic excellence and an unrivalled supportive environment where individuals can flourish.
Mark Allbrook, Headmaster
B Hurst, Chairman

1742 Blue Coat School
Birmingham Street
Walsall
West Midlands, UK WS1 2
0121-456-3966
postbox@blue-coat-s.walsall.sch.uk
www.bluecoatschool.org
Brian Bissell, Principal
Ken Yeates, Headteacher

1743 Boeblingen Elementary School
Unit 30401
APO
AE 09107
070-1 1-2715
Fax: 070-1 2-1368
www.stut-esb.eu.dodea.edu
To inspire curiosity and ambition for life-long learning in every student.
Dale Moore, Principal
Toufy Haddad, Assistant Principal

1744 Bonn International School
Martin-Luther-King Strasse 14
Bonn
Germany 53175
49-228-308-540
Fax: 49-228-308-5420
admin@bis.bonn.org
www.bis.bonn.org
The mission of Bonn International School is to inspire and empower students, aged 3-19, to become balanced, responsible global citizens who are successful, independent thinkers with a passion for learning.
Peter Murphy, Director
Diane Lewthwaite, Secondary School Principal

1745 Bordeaux International School
252 rue Jadaique
Bordeaux
France 33000
33-557-870-211
Fax: 33-556-790-047
bis@bordeaux-school.com
www.bordeaux-school.com
Conveniently located in the centre of historic Bordeaux, the school is purpose-built around a secure, enclosed and partially covered courtyard, which provides a space for pupils across the school to socialise with each other.
Christine Cussac, Head Teacher

1746 Brillantmont International School
16, avenue Charles-Secretan
Lausanne
Switzerland, CH 01005
41-21-310-0400
Fax: 41-21-320-8417
info@brillantmont.ch
www.brillantmont.ch
Brillantmont International School houses some 100 boarding boys and girls and about 50 day students.
Philippe Pasche, Director
Geraldine Boland, Deputy Director

1747 British Council School-Madrid
Prado de Somosaguas
Pozuelo de Alarc›n
Madrid, UK 28223
34-91-337-3500
Fax: 34-91-337-3573
general.enquiries@britishcouncil.org
www.britishcouncil.org
The British Council School is one of the leading bilingual, bi-cultural schools in the world, offering the very best of British and Spanish education. The school is divided into three departments (Early Years, Primary and Secondary) and offers education from children aged three to eighteen years old.
Jack Cushman, Principal
Norman Roddom, Head of School

1748 British Kindergarten
Ctra Del La Coruna Km 17
Las Rozas, 28230 Madrid
Spain
www.britishnursery.com
Mary Jane Maybury, Principal

1749 British Primary School
Stationsstraat 3 Vossem
Tervuren, BE 03080
32-2-767-3098
Fax: 32-2-767-0351
info@stpaulsbps.com
www.isftervuren.org
Our aim at St Paul's is to provide 'The Best Possible Start in Life '. We offer a secure, nurturing and truly caring environment for children, whether settling into a new country or going to school for the first time.
Katie Tyrie, Headteacher
Bruce Guy, Financial Manager

1750 British Primary School-Stockholm
Vossem
182 68 Djursholm
Sweden
468-755-2375
www.britishinternationalprimaryschool.se
Gaye Elliot, Principal

1751 British School-Amsterdam
Anthonie van Dijckstraat 1
Amsterdam, ME 01077
31-20-347-1111
Fax: 31-20-347-1222
www.britishschoolofamsterdam.nl
Our school is commited to providing the best possible eduction for our students. This is achieved in a calm, friendly, purposeful learning environment. Our strong and experieced team of teaching professionals are supported with excellent resources and facilities.
John Light, Principal
K McCarthy, Chairman

1752 British School-Bern
Hintere Dorfgasse 20
Gumligen
Switzerland 03073
41-31-951-2358
Fax: 41-31-951-1710
britishschool@bluewin.ch
www.britishschool.ch
We aim to provide a high quality programme for children of all abilities that promotes the social, emotional, cognitive, moral, physical and aesthetic development of each child
Enid Potts, Head Teacher/Administrator
Joe Quinn, Support Staff

1753 British School-Brussels
Leuvensesteenweg 19
Tervuren
Belgium, BE 03080
322-767-4700
Fax: 322-767-8070
reception@britishschool.be
www.britishschool.be
The British School of Brussels, situated 30 minutes from the city centre on a beautiful campus, offers a British education to International families in the heart of Europe, with pupils from some 70 nationalities on roll.
Roland Chant, Principal
Brenda Despontin, Principal

1754 British School-Netherlands
Wheatfields
Tarwekamp 3
Netherlands 02592
071-616958
Fax: 071-617144
foundation@britishschool.nl
www.britishschool.nl
BSN provides the opportunity of becoming part of a student community defined by an ethos of mutual understanding and cultural harmony. We have high expectations of our students, so whilst appreciating the difference in the ability and achievement of individual children within the classroom, we expect the same high level of behaviour from all. Good behaviour, manners and a respect for teachers and other adults are everyday expectations of our students.
Martin Coles, Principal
Nigel Collins, Assistant Principal

1755 British School-Oslo
PO Box 7531, Skillebekk 0205
Oslo 2
Norway
Margaret Stark, Principal

1756 **British School-Paris**
21B Lavant Street
Petersfield
Hampshire GU32-3EL
01-34-80-45-94
Fax: 01-39-76-12-69
ecis@ecis.org
www.ecis.org
The European Council of International Schools (ECIS) is a collaborative network promoting the ideals and best practice of international education.

Pilar Cabeza de Vaca, Executive Director
Mary Langford de Donoso, Deputy Executive Director

1757 **Bromsgrove School**
Worcester Road
Bromsgrove
Worcestershire B61-7DU
44-0-1527-579679
Fax: 44-0-1527-576177
headmaster@bromsgrove-school.co.uk
www.bromsgrove-school.co.uk
This school offers an English curriculum to 840 day students and 350 boarding (700 boys; 490 girls), ages 3 to 18. The curriculum is English based but french, german and Spanish are also taught. Teachers from overseas are welcome with the length of stay being 1-2 years. Applications needed to teach include science, French, math, Spanish, reading, German, English and physical education.

Chris Edwards, Headmaster
John Rogers, Foundation Director

1758 **Brooke House College**
Market Harborough Leicestershire
Leicestershire
England LE16-7AU
44-0-1852-462452
Fax: 44-0-1858-462487
enquiries@brookehouse.com
www.brookehouse.com
Brooke House College is a co-educational, international boarding college, specialising in preparing students from all over the globe, and from Britain, for entrance to the most prestigious universities to which they can aspire in both the U.K. and U.S.A

K Anderton, Academic Tutor
A Burditt, Diploma Personal Assistant

1759 **Brussels American School**
Unit 8100 Box 13
APO AE 09714-9998
Belgium, BE
320-271-9552
Fax: 302-717-9577
BrusselsEHS.Principal@eu.dodea.edu
www.brus-ehs.eu.dodea.edu
Brussels American School (BAS) serves students in Kindergarten through Grade 12. The elementary section of the school consists of Kindergarten through Grade 5. It is housed in one of the four major buildings and has a playground and special learning facilities. Grades 6-8 serve as transitional grades between the elementary and secondary programs; students attend classes in both the elementary and high school buildings

Walter G Seely, Principal
Cheryl A Aeillo, Assistant Principal

1760 **Brussels English Primary School**
23 Avenue Franklin Roosevelt
Brussels
Belgium 01050
62-010-41-72-27
Fax: 62-010-40-10-43
info@beps.com
www.beps.com
Offering the Primary Years Programme, a prestigious programme supported by many international schools around the world (ages 3 to 11).

Henny de Waal, Head of School
Dominique Floridor, Secretary

1761 **Bryanston School**
Blandford
Dorset
UK DT11-0PX
0258-452411
development@bryanston.co.uk
www.bryanston.co.uk
Bryanston they are those which encourage independence, individuality, and thinking, as well as being able to learn from living in a loving community which fast becomes, and remains, a family

Paul Speakman, Treasurer
Robert Ware, Chair

1762 **Buckswood Grange International School**
Broomham Hall Rye Road Guestling
Nr Hastings E Suxxex
England TN35-4LT
44-182-574-7000
Fax: 44-182-576-5010
achieve@buckswood.co.uk
www.buckswood.co.uk
A multinational boarding school for British and foreign students which combines the British curriculum with specialist EFL tution and close attention to social skills in an international environment.

Michael Reiser, Principal
David Walker, Marketing Manager

1763 **Butzbach Elementary School**
CMR 452 Box 5500
APO, Butzbach 09045 0005
Germany

Carl Ford, Principal

1764 **Byron Elementary School**
202 New Dunbar Road
Byron, GA 31008
478-956-5020
Fax: 478-956-5910
dmartin@peachschools.org
bes.peachschools.org
Our teachers are dedicated, hard working educators who are life learners themselves. An enriched, standards-based instruction is provided through collegial partnerships and staff development. Teachers continue to refine their instructional skills through book study discussions, grade level meetings, and attending various workshops.

Martin Dannelly, Principal
Dennis Teresia, Assistant Principal

1765 **CIV International School-Sophia Antipolis**
BP 97, 190 rue Frederic Mistral
Sophia Antipolis 06902
France
33-4-929-65224
Fax: 33-4-936-52215
secretary@civissa.org
www.civissa.org
Grade levels 1-12, school year September-June

Andrew Derry, Head of Section

1766 **Calpe College International School**
Cta de Cadiz Km 171
29670 Malaga
Spain
95-278-1479
Fax: 95-278-9416
info@calpeactivanet.es
www.calpeschool.com

Luis Proetta, Principal

1767 **Campion School**
PO Box 67484
Pallini GR-15302
Greece
301-813-5901
Fax: 301-813-6492
dbaker@hol.gr
www.campionschool.in

Dennis MacKinnon, Principal

1768 **Canadian College Italy-The Renaissance School**
59 Macamo Courte
Maple, Ontario
Canada L6A-1G1
905-508-7108
800-422-0548
Fax: 905-508-5480
cciren@rogers.com
www.ccilanciano.com
A unique source of highest-quality English-language education, preparing students for university entrance in the U.S.A., U.K., Canada and Europe, become one of the pre-eminent high school boarding schools in Europe. Graduates from CCI's founding years earned acceptances, and a variety of scholarships

1769 **Cascais International School**
Rua Das Faias, Lt 7 Torre
2750 Cascais
Portugal
www.icsc.pt
An international nursery school, founded in 1996, that caters to children ages 1-6 years on a fulltime or part-time basis. The first language of the school is English and Portuguese is the second. Many other languages are spoken throughout the school. Offers an individual approach, flexible hours and transport. Total enrollment is 75 day students (45 boys; 30 girls).

Evan Lerven Sixma, Principal

1770 **Castelli Elementary School**
Via Dei Laghi, 8.60
Ligetta Di Marinus, Ag, 00047 Marina
Italy
39-06-9366-1311
Fax: 39-06-9366-1311
www.castelli-international.it

Diana Jaworska, Principal

1771 **Castelli International School**
Via Degli Scozzesi
13-Grottaferrata
Rome, Italy
39-06-943-15779
Fax: 39-06-943-15779
maryac@castelli-international.it
www.castelli-international.it/
To provide a stimulating educational environment for international families living south of Rome and in the Castelli Romani area. CIS believes that the children, being naturally curious, are eager to learn, and that they learn best through inquiry, experience, and trial and error

Marianne Palladino, BA, MA, PhD, Director of Studies

1772 **Casterton School**
Kirkby Lonsdale, Via Carnforth
Lancashire, United Kingdom LA6-2SG

052-42-71202
admissions@castertonschool.co.uk
www.castertonschool.co.uk
One of the most established academic girls boarding and day schools in the UK, with a national and international reputation.

P McLaughlin, Headmaster
G A Sykes, Deputy Head

1773 Caxton College
Ctra De Barcelona S/N 46530
Puzol Valencia
Spain
34-96-146-4500
Fax: 34-96142-0930
caxton@caxtoncollege.com
www.caxtoncollege.com
Aim to provide pupils with the skills necessary to form independent opinions enabling them to make personal decisions in response to situations which will arise in their lives.

Amparo Gil, Principal
Marta Gil, Vice Principal

1774 Center Academy
92 St John's Hill Battersea
London SW11 1SH
England
071-821-5760
www.centeracademy.com
To provide students with a learning environment that facilitates the development of self-confidence, motivation, and academic skills, and gives students the opportunity to achieve success in life.

Robert Detweiler, Principal
Mack R Hicks, Founder and Chairman

1775 Centre International De Valbonne
Civ-bp 097 06902 Sophia
Antipolis Cedex
France
33-4-929-652-24
Fax: 33-4-936-522-15
greta.antipolis languages @ ac-nice.fr
www.civfrance.com

Ian Hill, Principal

1776 Charters-Ancaster School
Penland Road, Bexhill on Sea
TN40 2JQ
England
0424-730499
Boarding girls ages eleven to eighteen; day school for boys three to eight and girls three-eighteen.

K Lewis, MA, Headmaster

1777 Children's House
Kornbergvegen 23-4050 Sola
Stavanger
Norway
www.hr.umich.edu

Christine Grov, Principal

1778 Cite Scolaire International De Lyon
2 Place De Montreal
69007 Lyon
France
33-04-78-69-60-06
Fax: 33-04-78-69-60-36
csi-lyon-gerland@ac-lyon.fr
www.csilyon.fr
Grade levels 1-12.

Donna Galiana, Director

1779 Cobham Hall
Cobham (Nr Gravesend, Kent)
DA12 3BL
England, UK
0474-82-3371
enquiries@cobhamhall.com
www.cobhamhall.com
Encouraged and supported to make the most of your talents, whether these are academic, musical, sporting ... or as yet undiscovered!

Paul Mitchel, Headmaster
C Sykes, Chairman

1780 Colegio Ecole
Santa Rosa 12
Lugo Llanera
Asturias 33690
985- 77-8
ecole1@colegioecole.com
www.colegioecole.com

Patrick Wilson, Principal

1781 Colegio International-Meres
Apartado 107
33080 Oviedo, Asturias
Spain
985-792-427
Fax: 985-794-582
www.colegiomeres.com

Belen Orejas Fernandez, Principal

1782 Colegio International-Vilamoura
Apt 856, 8125 Vilamoura
Loule Algarve
Portugal
www.civ.com

Lawrence James, Principal

1783 College Du Leman International School
74 Route De Sauverny
CH-1290 Versoix, Geneva
Switzerland
41-22-775-5555
Fax: 41-22-775-5559
admissions@cdl.ch
www.cdl.ch
Grade levels include N-13 with an enrollment of 1700.

Francis Clivaz, General Director
Cedric Chaffois, Director of Admission

1784 College International-Fontainebleau
48 Rue Guerin 77300
Fontainebleau
France
01-64-22-11-77
Fax: 01-64-23-43-17
glenyskennedy@compuserve.com
www.fontainebleau.fr

Mrs. G Kennedy, Principal

1785 College Lycee Cevenol International
43400 Le Chambon sur Lignon
France
04-71-59-72-52
Fax: 04-71-65-87-38
contact@lecevenol.org
www.lecevenol.org
he CollSge Lyc,e International C,venol (a private establishment under a contract of state sponsorship since 1971) today welcomes boarders and day students of local, regional, national and international origins.

Christiane Minssen, Principal
Robert Lassey, Headmaster

1786 Copenhagen International School
Hellerupvej 22-26
2900 Hellerup
Denmark
45-39-463-300
Fax: 45-39-612-230
cis@cisdk.dk
www.cis-edu.dk
Develop the potential of each student in a stimulating environment of cultural diversity, academic excellence and mutual respect.

Peter Wellby, Director
Simon Watson, Senior School Principal

1787 Croughton High School
Unit 5485 Box 15
APO Croughton, 09494 0005
Great Britain

Dr. Charles Recesso, Principal

1788 Danube International School
Josef Gall-Gassee 2
1020 Vienna
Austria
00-43-1-720-3110
Fax: 43-1-720-3110-40
info@ danubeschool.at
www.danubeschool.at
DIS started off life in 1992 in Schrutkagasse in the 13th District. The school had another name, then - 'Pawen International Community School' that now houses a Rudolf Steiner school

Peter Harding, Director
Sabine Biber-Brussmann, Registrar

1789 Darmstadt Elementary School
CMR 431
APO, Darmstadt 09175 0005
Germany

Sherry Templeton, Principal

1790 Darmstadt Junior High School
CMR 431
APO, Darmstadt 09175 0005
Germany

Daniel Basarich, Principal

1791 De Blijberg
Graaf Florisstraat 56
Rotterdam
Netherlands 3032C
010-448-2266
Fax: 010-448-2270
deblijberg_international@hotmail.com
international.blijberg.nl

Barbera Everaars, Director
Bart Loman, Director

1792 Dean Close School
Lansdown Road
Cheltenham
England GL51
0242-522640
squirrels@deanclose.org.uk
www.deanclose.co.uk
Aim to provide a rich variety of opportunities that will enable your son or daughter to develop in confidence and independance within our happy and caring community.

Sue Bennett, Headmistress
Anthony R Barchand, Faculty Head

1793 Dexheim Elementary School
Unit 24027
APO, Dexheim 09110 0005
Germany

Gary Waltner, Principal

1794 Downside School
Stratton-on-the-Fosse, Bath (Avon)
Radstock Bath
England, UK BA3
0761-232-206
admin@downside.co.uk
www.downside.co.uk
Downside is an independent Catholic co-educational boarding school for pupils aged 9 to 18.
Dom Leo Maidlow Davis, Head Master
AR Hobbs, Deputy Head Master

1795 Dresden International School
Annenstr 9
D-01067 Dresden
Germany
49-351-3400428
Fax: 49-351-3400430
dis@dredsen-is.de
www.dresden-is.de
Committed to the aim of continuous improvement, which has been such a feature of the school since it opened in 1996.
Chrissie Sorenson, Director
Steve Ellis, Secondary School Principal

1796 ECC International School
Jacob Jordaensstraat 85-87
2018 Antwerp
Belgium
Dr. X Nieberding, Principal

1797 Ecole Active Bilingue
70 rue du Theatre
Paris
France 75015
01-44-37-00-80
Fax: 01-45-79-06-66
info@eabjm.net
www.eabjm.org
An associated UNESCO school, EABJM is also contractually part of the French national education system. The high school prepares students for the French Baccalaureate, the French Baccalaureate with Option Internationale, or the International Baccalaureate. An official testing site for the SAT, EABJM is also accredited by the College Entrance Examination Board and the Cambridge University Local Examination Syndicate.
Danielle Monod, Principal

1798 Ecole Active Bilingue Jeannine Manuel
70 rue du Theatre
75015 Paris
France 75015
45-44-37-00-80
Fax: 01-45-79-06-66
info@eabjm.net
www.eabjm.com
Grade levels k-12.
Elizabeth Zeboulon, Directrice

1799 Ecole D'Humanite
CH-6085 Hasliberg-Goldern
Switzerland
41-33-972-9292
Fax: 41-33-972-9211
us.office@ecole.ch
www.ecole.ch
150 boys and girls, aged 6 to 20 and faculty live in small family-style groups. International, inter-racial student body. Main language is German, with special classes for beginners.
Kathleen Hennessy, Interim Director
Arsheles Curturils, Director

1800 Ecole Des Roches & Fleuris
3961 Bluche
Valais
Switzerland
Marcel Clivez, Principal

1801 Ecole Lemania
Chemin de Preville 3
CP500 1001 Lausanne
Switzerland
41-0-21-320-15-01
Fax: 41-0-21-312-67-00
info@lemania.com
www.lemania.com
This international college represents over 65 nationalities offering French and English intensive courses, summer programs, American academic studies at graduate and undergraduate levels, sports and cultural activities, and accommodation in boarding school. Total enrollment: 800 day students; 100 boarding (450 boys; 450 girls), in grades 1-10.
M JP du Pasquier, Principal

1802 Ecole Nouvelle Preparatoire
Route Du Lac 22, Ch-1094
Paudex
Switzerland
Marc Desmet, Principal

1803 Ecole Nouvelle de la Suisse Romande
Ch de Rovereaz 20, CP-161
CH-1000 Lausanne 12
Switzerland
41-21-654-65-00
Fax: 41-21-654-65-05
info@ensr.ch
www.ensr.ch
The mission of the school is to prepare its students
Isabel Matos, Director Administrative/Fina
Beth Krasna, President

1804 Edinburgh American School
29 Chester Street
Edinburgh EH37EN
Scotland
013-155- 460
Fax: 013-162- 499
www.edinburghacademy.org.uk
AW Morris, Principal

1805 Edradour School
Edradour House - Pitlochry
Perthshire PH165JW,
Scotland
JPA Romanes, Principal

1806 El Plantio International School Valencia
Urbanizacion El Plantio
Calle 233, N36, La Canada, Paterna
Spain
96-132-14-10
Fax: 96-132-18-41
plantiointernational@retemail.es
www.plantiointernational.com
To educate young people who can adapt to their environment and therefore our objective is based on providing our students with the necessary skills to enable a better knowledge of the modem world and maximising the ability to communicate in an ever-changing and broadening society.
Anthony C Nelson, Principal

1807 Ellerslie School
Abbey Road, Malvern
WR14 3HF
England
0684-575701
www.ellerslie.school.nz
Elizabeth M Baker, BA, Headmaster

1808 English Junior School
Lilla Danska Vagen 1
412 74 Gothenburg
Sweden
31-401819
Patricia Gabrielsson, Principal

1809 English Kindergarten
Valenjanpolku 2
05880 Hyvinkaa
Finland
www.theenglishkindergarten.co.in
Riva Rentto, Principal

1810 English Montessori School
C/ de la Salle S/N
Aravaca, Madrid
Spain 28023
91-357-26-67
Fax: 91-307-15-43
t.e.m.s@teleline.es
englishmontessorischool.com
Each year of school up to and including Year 10 at The English Montessori School is validated with the Spanish Educational System. The importance of this is that a students entering or leaving the school can transfer to the equivalent level in any other school.
Elaine Fitzpatrick, Headmistress
Milagros Alonso, Director

1811 English School-Helsinki
Mantytie 14
Helinski
Finland 00270
358-9-477-1123
Fax: 358-9-477-1980
english.school@edu.hel.fi
www.eschool.edu.hel.fi
The English School is a private, national language school based on Christian values. The Ministry of Education has placed a special responsibility on the school to familiarize the students with Finnish and English languages as well as the culture of Finnish and Anglo-Saxon language areas.
Erkki Lehto, Principal
Riitta Volanen, Secretary

1812 English School-Los Olivos
Avda Pino Panera 25, 46110 Godella
Valencia
Spain 46110
96-363-99-38
Fax: 96-364-48-63
www.school-losolivos.es
Jane Rodriguez, Principal

1813 European Business & Management School
Frederik de Merodestraat, 12-16
Antwerp
Belgium 02600
323-218-8182
Fax: 323-218-5868
info@ebms.edu
www.ebms.edu
Once a year, European Business and Management School organizes a cross-cultural business tour, providing our students with another opportunity to strengthen their competencies in global thinking in international business.
Luc Van Meli, Director

1814 European School-Brussels I
Avenue Du Vert Chasseur 46
Brussels
Belgium 01180
02-374-58-44
kari.kivinen@eursc.org
www.eeb1.org
The European Schools fulfil a task that national schools are unable to fulfil: to teach pupils from different countries in their respective mother tongues and to instil in them the cultural values of their home country room a European perspective.
J Marshall, Principal
Kari Kivinen, Director

1815 European School-Italy
Via Montello 118
21100 Varese
Italy
32 -297-5990
www.ec.europa.eu
Jorg Hoffman, Principal

1816 Evangelical Christian Academy
Calle La Manda 47
Camarma de Esteruelas, Madrid
Spain 28816
34-91-741-2900
Fax: 34-91-320-8606
secretary@ecaspain.com
www.ecaspain.com
The vision drives every facet of ECA's existence. ECA offers a challenging, college preparatory curriculum in an American-based system. Students at ECA study Bible each year, and a Christian worldview is integrated into every aspect of the curriculum.
Beth Hornish, Principal
Scot Musser, Business Manager

1817 Feltwell Elementary School
CCSE/F Unit 5185 Box 315
APO AE
Great Britain 09461-5315
011-44 -842
Fax: 018-2 8-7931
feltwell.attendance@eu.dodea.edu
www.felt-es.eu.dodea.edu
School where teachers, parents, and community share the responsibility for each child's learning.
Tom LaRue, Principal

1818 Frankfurt International School
An der Waldlust 15
Oberursel
Germany 61440
49-6171-2020
Fax: 49-6171-202384
admissions@fis.edu
www.fis.edu
To be the leading culturally diverse and family-oriented international school with English as the principal language of instruction. We inspire young individuals to develop their intellect, creativity and character to grow into adaptable, socially responsible global citizens by ensuring a dynamic, 21st-century, inquiry-driven education of the highest standard.
Jutta Kuehne, Director
Mark Ulfers, Head of School

1819 Frederiksborg Gymnasium
Carlsbergvej 15
3400 Hillerod
Denmark
800-055-7314
Fax: 482- 07-1
post@frborg-gymhf.dk
www.frborg-gymhf.dk
Peter Kuhlman, Principal

1820 Friends School
Saffron Walden, Essex
England CB11
0642-722141
admissions@friends.org.uk
www.friends.org.uk
Friends' School strives to be a unique community where the potential and talent of each individual is realised within a friendly and challenging environment based on Quaker principles.
Graham Wigley, Head

1821 Gaeta Elementary & Middle School
PSC Box 811
FPO Gaeta 09609 0005
Italy
Dr. Robert Kirkpatrick, Principal

1822 Garmisch Elementary School
Unit 24511
APO AE, Garmisch
Germany 09053
440-261-
Fax: 088-176-949
GarmischEMS.Webmaster@eu.dodea.edu
www.garm-es.eu.dodea.edu
To provide a challenging curriculum in an atmosphere respectful of individual needs and cultural diversity. All students will learn the academic and social skills necessary for their future success.
Debbie Strong, Principal

1823 Geilenkirchen Elementary School
Unit 8045
APO AE, Geilenkirchen 09104 0005
Germany 09104
024-1 9- 308
Fax: 024-1 9- 308
GeilenkirchenES.Webmaster@eu.dodea.edu
www.geil-es.eu.dodea.edu/
Educating our students to be responsible, productive and ethical citizens with the skills to think creatively, reason critically, communicate effectively and learn continuously.
James V Dierendonck, Principal

1824 Gelnhausen Elementary School
CMR 465
APO, Gelnhausen 09076 0005
Germany
Jim Harrison, Principal

1825 Geneva English School
36 Route de Malagny
1294 Genthod
Switzerland
41-22-755-18-55
Fax: 41-22-779-14-29
admin@genevaenglishschool.ch
www.geneva-english-school.ch
A private, nonprofit primary school that is owned and managed by an association which is composed of parents whose children attend the school. The main objective of the school is to offer education on British lines for children of primary school age living in or near Geneva, and to prepare them for secondary education in any English-speaking school.
Denis Unsworth, Principal
Gareth Davies, Headmaster

1826 Giessen Elementary School
414th BSB GSN, Unit 20911
APO, Giessen 09169 0005
Germany
496-414-6265
496-414-8333
www.aoshs.org
Mary Ann Burkard, Principal

1827 Giessen High School
414th BSB GSB, Unit 20911
APO, Giessen 09169 0005
Germany
496-414-6266
www.aoshs.org
Gordon Gartner, Principal

1828 Grafenwoehr Elementary School
Unit 28127
APO AE
Germany 09114-8127
964-183-7133
Fax: 964- 32-4
GrafenwoehrES.Principal@eu.dodea.edu
www.graf-es.eu.dodea.edu
To maintain a meaningful partnership with the community through which physical well being, cognitive growth, and emotional support are provided to all learners.
Crystal Bailey, Principal
David Eldredge, Assistant Principal

1829 Greenwood Garden School
Via Vito Sinisi 5
Rome
Italy
39-06-332-66703
Fax: 39-06-332-66703
greenwoodgarden@libero.it
www.greenwoodgardenschool.com
An international pre-school and kindergarten for children aging from 2-6 with teaching being done in English by mother-tongue educators experienced with young children
Donna Seibert, Directress

1830 Gstaad International School
Ahorn
Gstaad
Switzerland CH-37
41-33-744-2373
Fax: 41-33-744-3578
gis@gstaad.ch
www.gstaadschool.ch
The school's mission includes the building of endurance and stamina in both academics and sports, as well as stimulating personal achievement by teaching the values of respect, gratitude, humour and real caring for others. Students are continually presented with challenges and the opportunities to achieve where perhaps before they thought impossible.
Alain Souperbiet, Director

1831 Haagsche School Vereeniging
Nassaulaan 26
Den Haag-2514
003-170-363
info@hsvdenhaag.nl
www.hsvdenhaag.nl
HM Jongeling, Principal
Lorraine Dean, Director

1832 Hainerberg Elementary School
Unit 29647 Box 0086
APO AE, Wiesbaden
Germany 09096-86
337-516-
Fax: 011-49 -11 7
Wiesbadenes.principal@eu.dodea.edu
www.wies-esh.eu.dodea.edu

Provide exemplary educational programs that inspire and prepare all students for success in a global environment.

Maren James, Principal

1833 Halvorsen Tunner Elementary and Middle School
Unit 7565
APO, Rhein Main 09050 0005
Germany
Julie Gaski, Principal

1834 Hanau High School
Unit 20235
APO, Hanau 09165 0005
Germany
Allen Davenport, Principal

1835 Hanau Middle School
Unit 20193
APO, Hanau 09165 0016
Germany
Robert Sennett, Principal

1836 Harrow School
5 High Street
Harrow on the Hill
England HA1 3
01-423-2366
harrow@harrowschool.org.uk
www.harrowschool.org.uk
Barnaby Lenon, Headmaster

1837 Hatherop Castle School
Hatherop, Cirencester
England GL7 3
028-575-206
www.hatheropcastle.com
Paul Easterbrook, Headmaster

1838 Heidelberg High School
Unit 29237
APO AE
Germany 09102
370-800-
Fax: 062-213- 587
www.heid-hs.eu.dodea.edu
Kevin J Brewer, Principal

1839 Heidelberg Middle School
Unit 29237
APO AE
Germany 09102
221-338-9310
www.heid-ms.eu.dodea.edu
Donald Johnson, Principal

1840 Hellenic-American Education Foundation Athens College-Psychico College
15 Stefanou Delta
Psychico
Greece 154 5
30-1-671-2771
Fax: 30-1-674-8156
info@haef.gr
www.haef.gr
Grade levels 1-12, school year September - June
David William Rupp, President

1841 Helsingin Suomalainen
Isonnevantie 8
Helinski, Finland 00320
358- 47-1
www.syk.fi
Helsingin Suomalainen Yhteiskoulu (SYK) is an independent coeducational, which prepares its students either for the national matriculation exam or the International Baccalaureate, both of which give a student general university entry qualifications.
Anja-Liisa Alanko, Principal

1842 Het Nederlands Lyceum
Wijndaelerduin 1
Hague, Netherlands 02554
070-338-4567
Fax: 070-328-2049
primary@ishthehague.nl
www.ishthehague.nl
Offers young people of all nationalities between the ages of 4 and 18 top quality international education in a caring environment, which aim for academic success and encourage sporting and creative abilities in a community based on honesty, fairness, open-mindedness and tolerance.
Graeme Scott, Principal Primary School

1843 Het Rijnlands Lyceum
Appollolaan 1 2341 BA
Oegstgeest
Netherlands
31-3771-5155640
administratie@rijnlandslyceum-rlo.nl
www.rlo.nl
Lyceum is a state subsidized school with an international department offering IBMYP and IB. Offers an English/Dutch spoken curriculum to 1,190 day students and 60 boarding (650 boys; 600 girls), in grades 6 through 12. Student/teacher ratio is 15:1, and the school is willing to participate in a teacher exchange program, however, housing will not be provided by the school.
Drs LE Timmerman, Principal

1844 Hillhouse Montessori School
Avenida Alfonso Xiii 30 Y 34
Madrid 2
Spain
www.houseonthehill.com.sg
Judy Amick, Principal

1845 Hohenfels Elementary School
Unit 28214
APO AE
Germany 09173
466-400-
Fax: 094-2 8-32
www.hohe-es.eu.dodea.edu
Olaf Zwicker, Principal

1846 Hohenfels High School
CMR 414
APO, AE
Germany 09173
094-2 -9096
Fax: 094-2 8- 316
www.hohe-hs.eu.dodea.edu
Daniel J Mendoza, Principal

1847 Holmwood House
Chitts Hill, Lexden
Colchester, Essex
England CO3 9
44-0-1904-626183
Fax: 44-0-1904-670899
hst@holmwood.essex.sch.uk
www.holmwood.essex.sch.uk
Holmwood House is an independent coeducational day and boarding preparatory school. The total enrollment of the school is 310 day students and 50 boarding students (240 boys and 120 girls), ages 4 1/2 to 13 1/2.
Alexander Mitchell, Headmaster

1848 Hvitfeldtska Gymnasiet
Rektorsgatan 2, SE-411 33
Goteborg
Sweden
46-31-367-0623
Fax: 46-31-367-0602
agneta.santesson@educ.goteborg.se
www.hvitfeldt.educ.goteborg.se
State school, founded 1647, offers the International Baccalaureate curriculum to a total enrollment of 90 girls and 90 boys, in grades 10-12.
Christen Holmstrom, Principal
Agneta Santesson, Deputy Headmaster

1849 Illesheim Elementary and Middle School
CMR 416 Box J
APO, Hohenfels 09140 0005
Germany
49-9841-8408
Fax: 49-9841-8987
Donald J Ness, Principal

1850 Independent Bonn International School
Tulpenbaumweg 42
Bonn 53177
Germany
49-228-32-31-66
Fax: 49-228-32-39-58
ibis@ibis-school.com
www.ibis-school.com
IBIS is an international primary school.
Irene Bolik, Headteacher

1851 Independent Schools Information Service
Grosveror Gardens House 35-37
Frosvernor Gardens, London SW1W 0BS
England
020-77981575
Fax: 020-77981561
national@isis.org.uk
www.isis.org.uk
Provides information on 1400 elementary and secondary schools in the United Kingdom and Ireland.
David J Woodhead

1852 Innsbruck International High School
Schonger, Austria A-6141
0-5225-4201
Fax: 0-5225-4202
An accredited coeducational boarding and day school. The school offers an American college preparatory high school curriculum for grades 9-12.
Gunther Wenko, Director
John E Wenrick, Headmaster

1853 Institut Alpin Le Vieux Chalet
1837 Chateau D'oex
Switzerland
212-338-9743
Fax: 212-949-7534
www.christusrex.org
Jean Bach, Principal

1854 Institut Auf Dem Rosenberg
Hohenweg 60-9000 St Gallen
Switzerland
417- 27-0777
Fax: 417- 27- 982
info@instrosenberg.ch
www.instrosenberg.ch
Felicitas Scharli, Principal

1855 Institut Chateau Beau-Cedre
57 Av De Chillion
CH-1820 Territet Montreux
Switzerland
41-21-963-5341
Fax: 41-21-963-4783
info@monterosaschool.com
This Institut is an exclusive boarding and finishing international school for girls. American high school with a general culture section for 30 boarding students in grades 9 through twelve. Languages spoken include French and English and the student/teacher ratio is 1:6.

Pierre Gay, Principal

1856 Institut Le Champ Des Pesses
1618 Chatel-st-denis
Montreux
Switzerland

PL Racloz, Principal

1857 Institut Le Rosey
Chateau du Rosey
1180 Rolle
Switzerland
41-21-822-5500
Fax: 41-21-822-5555
rosey@rosey.ch
www.rosey.ch
Le Rosey's philosophy is inspired by what Harvard educationalist Howard Gardner has called multiple intelligences: its aim is to develop all Roseans' talents through academic, sporting and artistic programs.

Philippe Gudin, General Director
Michael Gray, Headmaster

1858 Institut Montana Bugerbug-American Schools
Zugerberg
CH 6300 Zug
Switzerland
41-41-711-1722
Fax: 41-41-711-5465
kob@montana.zug.ch
www.montana.zug.ch
Grade levels include 7-13 with a total enrollment of 111.

Daniel Fredez, Director

1859 Institut Monte Rosa
57, Ave de Chillon,
CH-1820 Territet/Montreux
Switzerland
021-963-5341
Fax: 021-963-4783
info@monterosa.ch
www.monterosa.ch

Bernhard Gademann, BS, MS, Principal

1860 Inter-Community School
Strubenacher 3 Postfach
Zumikon
Switzerland 08126
41-1-919-8300
Fax: 41-1-919-8320
www.icsz.ch
The Inter-Community School is committed to providing a supportive and enabling learning environment in which all members of the community are challenged to achieve their individual potential, encouraged to pursue their passions, and expected to fulfil their responsibilities

Michael Matthews, Head of School
Martin Hall, Secondary Principal

1861 International Academy
Via di Grottarossa 295
00189 Rome
Italy
39-340-731-4195
info@internationalacademy.in
www.internationalacademy.in

Joan Bafaloukas Bulgarini, Principal

1862 International College Spain
C/Vereda Norte 3
La Moraleja, Madrid
Spain 28109
34-91-650-2398
Fax: 34-91-650-1035
admissions@icsmadrid.org
www.icsmadrid.com
The philosophy of the school is to provide students with a high quality international education which places a strong emphasis on fostering respect for the world's nations and cultures.

Terry Hedger, Director
Hubert Keulers, Head of Primary School

1863 International Management Institute
Garden Square Building, Block-C Laa
Antwerp
Belgium 02610
32-3-21-85-431
Fax: 32-3-21-85-868
info@timi.edu
www.timi.edu
Our vision is to empower our students in terms of all the faculties required to pursue a career in the competitive globalized world. The focus of our curriculum is to enhance the learning perspective through customized modules and simulation exercises from globally renowned academicians and professionals.

Luc Van Mele, Director

1864 International Preparatory School
Rua Do Boror 12 Carcavelos
2775 Parede
Portugal
56-2-321-5800
Fax: 56-2-321-5821
info@tipschool.com
www.tipschool.com

1865 International School Beverweerd
Beverweerdseweg 60, 3985 RE
Werkhoven
Netherlands
03437-1341
Fax: 03437-2079
www.isbeverweerd.nl

Ray Kern, BA, MA, Principal

1866 International School-Aberdeen
296 N Deeside Road
Milltimber, Aberdeen
Scotland, UK AB13
44-1224-732267
Fax: 44-1224-735648
admin@isa.aberdeen.sch.uk
www.isa.aberdeen.sch.uk
The International School of Aberdeen (ISA) is an independent, non-profit school (K-12) that delivers excellence in education. We do this through a safe and caring learning environment where students are challenged to reach their maximum potential through academic success and personal growth, becoming socially responsible and active global citizens.

Daniel A Hovde PhD, Director
Don Newbury, Elementary Principal

1867 International School-Algarve
Apartado 80 Porches 8400
Lagoa Algarve
Portugal
www.algarveschool.com

Peter Maddison, Principal

1868 International School-Amsterdam
PO Box 920
AX Amstelveen
The Netherlands 01180
31-20-347-1111
Fax: 31-20-347-1222
info@isa.nl
www.isa.nl
The International School of Amsterdam (ISA) was founded in 1964 to serve the educational needs of the children of the international community living in and around Amsterdam. ISA is a nonsectarian, non-profit coeducational day school, enrolling students in Pre-School through Grade 12 (from 3 to 18 years of age).

Dr Edward Greene, Director
Sarah Grace, Head of Lower School

1869 International School-Basel
Fleischbachstrasse 2
4153 Reinach BL
Switzerland
41-61-426-96-26
Fax: 41-61-426-96-25
www.isbasel.ch
mission of the International School Basel is to provide an international education to the highest recognized academic standards

Geoff Tomlinson, Principal

1870 International School-Bergen
Vilhelm Bjerknesvei 15
Bergen
Norway 05081
47-55-30-63-30
Fax: 47-55-30-63-31
post@isob.no
www.isb.gs.hl.no
Provide an education for the children of expatriate oil company personnel in Bergen and to attract further corporate investment in the Bergen area.

June Murison, Director

1871 International School-Berne
170 Mattenstrasse
Gumligen
Switzerland 03073
41-31-951-2358
Fax: 41-31-951-1710
office@isberne.ch
www.isberne.ch
Creative learning community for students from all over the world, within the framework of the three International Baccalaureate Programmes, guided by ISBerne teachers and staff, students aged 3 - 18 have the opportunity to become open-minded, principled, knowledgeable, confident lifelong learners and multilingual citizens of the world, who respect themselves and others.

Kevin Page, Director
Cory Etchberger, Chair

1872 International School-Brussels
Kattenberg 19
Brussels 1170
Belguim
32-2-661-4211
Fax: 32-2-661-4200
admissions@isb.be
www.isb.be
Offers a challenging, inclusive international education designed to give every student opportunities for success within and beyond our school.

Kevin Bartlett, Director
Andrei Teixeira, Chairman

1873 International School-Cartagena
Manga Club Cp 30385 Cartagena
Los Belones Murcia
Spain
34-68-175000
isc@sendanet.es
www.cartagenainternationalschool.com

Robert Risch, Principal

1874 International School-Curacao
PO Box 3090
Koninginnelaan Emmastad, Curacao
Netherlands Antilles
599-9-737-3633
Fax: 599-90737-3142
iscmec@attglobal.net
www.isc.an
Offers a rigorous academic program in order to prepare students planning to pursue higher learning at colleges and universities around the world. The School's curriculum includes International Baccalaureate (IB) coursework that allows students the opportunity to receive the IB Diploma.

Margie Elhage, Director
Rene Romer, President

1875 International School-Dusseldorf
Niederrheinstrasse 336
Dusseldorf
Germany 40489
49-211-94066-799
Fax: 49-211-4080-744
nmcw@isdedu.de
www.isdedu.eu
Provide the students of the International School of D□sseldorf with the best possible program of academic and personal development in a challenging and supportive environment.

Neil A McWilliam, Director
Michael Coffey, Senior School Principal

1876 International School-Eerde
Kasteellaan 1
PJ Ommen
The Netherlands 07731
031-0529-451452
Fax: 031-0529-456377
info@eerde.nl
www.eerde.nl
Offers numerous programmes tailored to the individual needs of each student, including children with learning difficulties and dyslexia, as well as highly gifted children. Eerde carefully monitors the personal, academic, athletic and creative development of each individual student ages 4 to 19.

Herman Voogd, Principal

1877 International School-Friuli
Via Delle Grazie 1/A
Pordenone 33170
Italy
www.udineis.org

Susan Clarke, Principal

1878 International School-Geneva
62 route de Chene
Geneva
Switzerland CH-12
41-22-787-2400
Fax: 41-22-787-2410
administration@ecolint.ch
www.ecolint.ch
Aims to provide a distinctive high quality international education that prepares pupils for membership of a world community based on mutual understanding, tolerance and shared humanitarian values.

Nicholas Tate, Director General
John Douglas, Director

1879 International School-Hamburg
Holmbrook 20
Hamburg
Germany 22605
49-40-883-1101
Fax: 49-40-1881-1405
info@ishamburg.org
www.international-school-hamburg.de
A co-educational day school enrolling students from Primary 1 (age 3) to Grade 12. The school was founded in 1957 as the first international school in Germany.

Peter Gittin, Headmaster
Nick Ronai, Junior School Director

1880 International School-Hannover Region
Bruchmeisterstrasse 6
Hannover
Germany D-301
49-511-27041650
Fax: 49-511-557934
adminoffice@is-hr.de
www.is-hr.de
Provides a high quality, balanced educational program in the English language for children of internationally-minded families.Offer a dynamic environment where each student is challenged and supported to become a dedicated learner for life and a contributing member of the local and global community.

Patricia Baier, Director
Steffen Stegeman, Business Manager

1881 International School-Helsinki
Selkamerenkatu 11
Helsinki
Finland 00180
358-9-686-6160
Fax: 358-9-685-6699
mainoffice@ish.edu.hel.fi
www.ish.edu.hel.fi
Office Manager
Provide attendees

Bob Woods, Headmaster
Therese Thibault, Director

1882 International School-Iita
PMB 5320
Ibadan
Nigeria CR9 3
E-mail: iita@cgiar.org
www.iita.org
Provide a comprehensive, international curriculum in an environment which promotes confidence, caring and understanding, and prepares our students for successful learning here and in schools around the world.

Neil Jackson, Principal

1883 International School-Lausanne
Chemin de la Grangette 2
Le Mont-sur-Lausanne
Switzerland CH -
41-21-728-1733
Fax: 41-21-728-7868
info@isl.ch
www.isl.ch
The school is committed to excellence in education, it strives to fulfill the unique potential of each student in a supportive and challenging holistic learning environment that prepares the student for continuing education and an active and responsible role in a multicultural world.

Lyn Cheetham, Director
John Ivett, Assistant Director

1884 International School-Le Chaperon Rouge
3963 Crans Sur Sierre
Crans/Montana
Switzerland
41-27-4812-500
Fax: 41-27-4812-502
www.chaperonrouge.ch

Prosper Bagnoud, Principal

1885 International School-London
139 Gunnersbury Avenue
London
England W3 8L
44-20-8992-5823
Fax: 44-20-8993-7012
mail@ISLondon.com
www.islondon.com
Aims to maximize the achievement of its students throughout the curriculum and in personal and social fields. Drawing on the rich variety of cultures represented at the school, ISL aims to develop in each student a global outlook which seeks to understand and appreciate the attitudes and values of others.

Amin Makarem, Director
Sergio Pawel, Deputy Head, Curriculum

1886 International School-Lyon
80 chemin du Grand Roule
Ste-Foy-LSs-Lyon
France F-691
47 -86 -190
Fax: 47 -86 -198
info@islyon.org
www.islyon.org
The school's curriculum is based on the programmes and pedagogy of the International Baccalaureate Organization which aims to develop in the students the skills, values and knowledge that will help them to become responsible citizens in an increasingly interconnected world.

Donna Philip, Director
Michael Ford, Curriculum Coordinator

1887 International School-Naples
Viale della Liberazione, 1
Bagnoli, Napoli 80125
Italy
39-081-721-2037
Fax: 39-081-570-0248
info@isnaples.it
www.isnaples.it
Provide a nurturing environment where students can grow intellectually, socially, psychologically and physically. Through a dedicated partnership of parents and educators, we strive to prepare our students to become productive, global citizens of the twenty-first century.

Josephine Sessa, Principal
Patricia Montesano, Vice Principal

1888 International School-Nice
15 Avenue Claude Debussy
Nice
France 06200
33-493-210-400
Fax: 33-493-216-911
robert.silvetz@cote-azur.cci.fr
www.isn-nice.org
The school offers Pre-Kindergarten through grade 12 instruction and college preparatory education and provides an intellectually challenging programme of studies which aims to promote analytic understanding with an integrated view of the various academic disciplines and to encourage creativity and self-expression. Serves both the international community and local families who wish to offer their children an education in

English, which is both international and versatile.

Wylie Michael, Director

1889 International School-Paris
6 Rue Beethoven
Paris
France 75016
33-1-422-40954
Fax: 33-1-452-71593
info@isparis.edu
www.isparis.edu
ISP create a challenging and motivating English-speaking environment where students and staff from around the world use the programs of the International Baccalaureate Organisation and work in harmony to develop every student's full intellectual and human potential.

Audrey Peverelli, Headmaster
Catherine Hard, Head of Admissions

1890 International School-Sotogrande
Apartado 15
Sotogrande San Roque Cadiz
Spain 11310
34-956-79-59-02
Fax: 34-956-79-48-16
director@sis.ac
www.sis.ac
Our school is a learning organisation with a passion for learning. Learning is a complex process and it is vitally important that our teachers know how pupils learn best and that they create exciting opportunities for learning to take place.

Geroge O'Brien, Headmaster
Christopher TJ Charleson, Head of School

1891 International School-Stavanger
Treskeveien 3
Hafrsfjord
Norway 04043
47-51-559-100
Fax: 47-51-552-962
LDuevel@isstavanger.no
www.isstavanger.no
The International School of Stavanger is dedicated to providing its students with an English language education in a supportive, academically stimulating, and multi-cultural environment.

Linda Duevel, PhD, Director
Gareth Jones, High School Principal

1892 International School-Stockholm
Johannesgatan 18
Stockholm SE-111 38
Sweden
46-8-412-4000
Fax: 46-8-412-4001
admin@intsch.se
www.intsch.se
SIS vision is to enable students to learn, develop, grow, and fulfill their potential in an international environment, which is student-centered, safe, nurturing and rich with opportunities to learn.

Chris Mockrish, Principal
Richard Mast, Director

1893 International School-Stuttgart
Sigmaringer Street 257
Stuttgart
Germany 70597
49-7-11-76-9600-0
Fax: 49-7-11-76-9600-0
iss@issev.de
www.international-school-stuttgart.de
The International School of Stuttgart provides students of internationally-minded families with a high quality, English language education.

Timothy Kelley, Director
Sarah Kupke, Head of School

1894 International School-Trieste
Via Conconello 16 Opicina
Trieste Friuli - Venezia Giulia
Italy 34151
39-040-211-452
Fax: 39-040-213-122
istrieste@interbusiness.it
www.istrieste.org
It is our mission to provide students from the international and local community with a broad, balanced education using English both in curricular and extra-curricular life of the school.

Peter Metzger, Principal
Jim Pastore, Director

1895 International School-Turin
Vicolo Tiziano 10
Moncalieri
Italy 10024
391- 45-9
Fax: 39 -11 -43 2
info@acat-ist.it
www.acat-ist.it
The school's goal is to create self-motivated, independent learners who strive for excellence. The school community feels that this is best achieved in an environment which fosters trust and respect between the educational staff and the student body, demands accountability and team-work, while inspiring a general sense of well-being and self-confidence.

George Selby, BA, MA, Principal

1896 International School-Venice
Via Terraglio 30
Mestre, Venice
Italy 30174
04 -98 -711
Fax: 04 -98 -001
info@isvenice.com
www.isvenice.com
The fundamental aim of The International School of Venice is to give its pupils a bilingual education and an intellectual education based on tolerance, open-mindedness and an acceptance of diversity.

John Millerchip, Principal

1897 International School-Zug
Walterswil
Baar 6340
Switzerland
41-41-768-1188
Fax: 41-41-768-1189
office@isoz.ch
www.iszl.ch
Grade levels include preK-8 with a total enrollment of 354.

Martin Latter, Head of School

1898 International Schule-Berlin, Potsdam
Seestrasse 45
14467 Potsdam
Germany
49-332-086-760
Fax: 49-332-086-7612
office@isbp.p.bb.schule.de
www.shuttle.de/p/isbp
This school offers an English curriculum to 157 day students (87 boys and 64 girls) in grades PreK-12. Applications needed to teach include science, pre-school, math, social sciences, reading, English and physical education.

Matthias Truper, Principal

1899 International Secondary School-Eindhoven
Venetiestraat 43
RM Eindhoven
Netherlands 05632
040-413600
isse@issehv.nl
www.issehv.nl
By striving for excellence in education and by engaging with the international community, the ISSE seeks to be an asset to Eindhoven and the Noord-Brabant region.

JM Westerhout, Principal
M Watts, Acting Head of School

1900 Internationale Schule Frankfurt-Rhein-Main
Strasse zur Internationalen Schule
Frankfurt
Germany 65931
49-69-954-3190
Fax: 49-69-954-31920
isf@sabis.net
www.isf-net.de
ISF Internationale Schule-Rhein-Main, as a member of the SABISr School Network, is academically oriented without being highly selective.

Angus Slesser, School Director
Carl Bistany, Managing Director

1901 Interskolen
Engtoften 22
8260 Viby J
Denmark
45-8611-4560
Fax: 45-8614-9670
adm@interskolen.dk
www.interskolen.dk
Coeducational day program for ages five to seventeen.

Tommy Schou Christesen, Principal

1902 John F Kennedy International School
CH-3792 Saanen
Switzerland 03792
41-33-744-1372
Fax: 41-33-744-8982
lovell@jfk.ch
www.jfk.ch
Boarding day school for boys and girls aged 5-14 years.

William Lovell, Co-Director
Sandra Lovell, Co-Director

1903 John F Kennedy School-Berlin
Teltower Damm 87-93
Berlin
Germany 14167
49-30-6321-5711
Fax: 49-30-6321-6377
jfks-el-adm@t-online.de
www.jfks.de
The John F. Kennedy School is a bilingual, bicultural German-American tuition-free public school.

Herr Ulrich Schurmann, Managing Principal
HR Roth, German Principal

1904 Joppenhof/Jeanne D'arc Clg
PO Box 4050, 6202 Rb Maastricht
Netherlands
47 -77 -000
www.paguro.net
L Spronck, Principal

1905 Kaiserslautern Elementary School
Unit 3240 Box 425
APO
Germany, AE 09021
080- -520
063- 99-46
Fax: 063- 58-06
www.kais-es.eu.dodea.edu
Bariett Prince, Principal

1906 Kaiserslautern High School
Unit 3240 Box 425
APO
Germany, AE 09021
801- 1-20
063- 99-47
Fax: 063- 99-46
www.kais-hs.eu.dodea.edu
Bariett Prince, Principal
Richard Nicholson, Assistant Principal

1907 Kaiserslautern Middle School
Unit 3240 Box 425
APO
Germany, AE 09021
802- 1-20
063- 99-48
Fax: 063- 99-25
www.kais-ms.eu.dodea.edu
Bariett Prince, Principal
Marion Sutton, Assistant Principal

1908 Kendale Primary International School
Via Gradoli 86, Via Cassia Km 10300
00189 Rome
Italy
39-06-332-676-08
Fax: 39-06-332-676-08
kendale@diesis.com
www.diesis.com/kendale
Veronica Said Tani, Principal

1909 Kensington School
Carrer Dels Cavallers 31-33 Pedralb
Barcelona
Spain 08034
930-345-
Fax: 938-006-
info@kensingtonschoolbcn.com
www.kensingtonschoolbcn.com
EP Giles, Principal

1910 King Fahad Academy
Bromyard Avenue, Acton
London
United Kingdom W3-7HD9
020-7259-3350
academy@thekfa.org.uk
www.thekfa.org.uk
The idea for the establishment of an academy that caters for the educational needs of the Saudi Arabian, Arab and Muslim communities in the UK took its genesis in the creation of the King Fahad Academy in London in 1985 AD/1405 H
Dr. Ibtissam Al-Bassam, Dean
Mohammed Bin Na Al Saud, Chairman

1911 King's College
Paseo de los Andes, 35
Soto De Viuelas, Madrid
Spain
91-803-48-00
Fax: 91-803-65-57
info@kingscollege.es
www.kingscollege.es
to sustain and develop an educational environment in which all students are able to fulfil their maximum potential, both as individuals and as members of a community.
CA Clark, Principal
David Johnson, Headmaster

1912 Kitzingen Elementary School
Unit 26124
APO, Kitzingen 09031 0005
Germany
Fred Paesel, Principal

1913 Kleine Brogel Elementary School
701 MUNSS
Unit 8150, APO AE
Belgium 09719
001-179-2527
Fax: 001-179-0091
terry.emerson@eu.dodea.edu
www.kbro-es.eu.dodea.edu
Terry Emerson, Principal

1914 La Chataigneraie International School
Geneva La Chataigneraie, 1297
1208 Geneva
Switzerland
122-787-2400
www.ecolint.ch
Michael Lee, Principal

1915 La Maddalena Elementary School
PSC 816 Box 1755
FPO, La Maddalena, Sardinia 09612 0005
Italy
907-897- 820
www.aoshs.org
Janice Barber, Principal

1916 Lajes Elementary School
Unit 7725
APO AE
Portugal 09720
351-295-5741
Fax: 011-351-295
www.laje-ehs.eu.dodea.edu/index.htm
Mary Waller, Principal

1917 Lajes High School
Unit 7725
APO AE
Portugal 09720
351-295-5741
Fax: 351-295-5425
www.laje-hs.eu.dodea.edu/main1.htm
Virginia Briggs, Principal

1918 Lakenheath Elementary School
Unit 5185 Box 40
APO AE
Great Britain 09464-8540
016-805-3072
Fax: 016-8 5-3943
www.lake-es.eu.dodea.edu/index.htm
Lakenheath Elementary School serves the US Military overseas as part of the Department of Defense Dependent Schools
Charles Yahres, Principal
Rhonda Bennett, Assistant Principal

1919 Lakenheath High School
Unit 5185 Box 45
APO AE
Great Britain 09461-8545
044- 01- 852
Fax: 044- 01- 853
lakenheathhs.attendance@eu.dodea.edu
www.lake-hs.eu.dodea.edu
Lakenheath High School (LHS) serves three U.S. Air Force bases located in the East Anglia region of England; about 1.5 hours drive northeast of London. LHS is coeducational.
Kent Worford, Principal
Barbara Lee, Assistant Principal

1920 Lakenheath Middle School
Unit 5185 Box 55
APO AE
Great Britain 09461-8555
011-44 -638
Fax: 226-737-
LakenheathMS.Principal@eu.dodea.edu
www.lake-ms.eu.dodea.edu
Mary Zimmerman-Bayer, Principal
D J LaFon, Assistant Principal

1921 Lancing College
Lancing, West Sussex
BN15 ORW
England
0273-452213
Fax: 01273-464720
admissions@lancing.org.uk
www.lancingcollege.co.uk
One of Britain's leading independent schools for boys and girls aged 13 to 18
Jonathan W J Gillespie, Headmaster
Harry Brunjes, Chairman

1922 Landstuhl Elementary and Middle School
CMR 402
APO AE
Germany 09180-402
637-192-6508
Fax: 637-192-6514
LandstuhlEMS.Principal@eu.dodea.edu
www.lans-ems.eu.dodea.edu
Susan Ransom, Principal
Stephen Austin, Assistant Principal

1923 Leighton Park School
Shinfield Road
Reading RG2 7DH
England
4-118-987-9600
Fax: 44-118-987-9625
info@leightonpark.com
www.leightonpark.com
Life at Leighton Park reflects the school's Quaker foundation and is influenced by Quaker thinking and practice. We seek to create a community of tolerance and understanding within which a balance between discipline, especially self-discipline, freedom and exploration is maintained.
John Dunston, Headmaster
Elizabeth Thomas, Deputy Head

1924 Leipzig International School
Konneritzstrasse 47
Leipzig
Germany 04229
49-341-421-0574
Fax: 49-341-421-2154
admin@intschool-leipzig.com
www.intschool-leipzig.com
The Leipzig International School provides a quality education conducted primarily in English for children of all nationalities and cultures living in the Leipzig region. We seek to give all students the opportunity to discover and develop their intellectual, creative, social and physical potential to the full.
Michael Webster, Headmaster
Clemens Gerteiser, Commercial Editor

1925 Lennen Bilingual School
65 Quai d'Orsay
Paris
France 75007

01-47-05-66-55
Fax: 01-47-05-17-18
www.lennenbilingual.com
This school teaches a curriculum in English and French to 120 day students. The school is willing to participate in a teacher exchange program with the length of stay being one year, with no housing provided by the school. Bilingual education is offered in the preschool and grade school (until Grade 3).

Michelle Lennen, Principal

1926 Leys School
The Leys School
Cambridge CB2 7AD
England
44-1223-508-900
Fax: 44-1223-505-333
office@theleys.net
www.theleys.cambs.sch.uk
The Leys is one of England's premier independent schools.

Mark Slater, Headmaster

1927 Leysin American School
1854 Leysin
Switzerland
41-24-493-3777
Fax: 41-24-493-3790
admissions@las.ch
www.las.ch
At the core of Leysin American School is a guiding set of principles and beliefs that set the highest standards for our efforts every day.

Steven Oh, Executive Director
Vladimir Kuskovski, Headmaster

1928 Livorno Elementary School
Unit 31301 Box 65
APO, Livorno 09613 0005
Italy
www.livo-ems.eu.dodea.edu

Dr. Robert Kethcart, Principal

1929 Livorno High School
Unit 31301 Box 65
APO, Livorno 09613 0005
Italy, AE 09613-5
www.livo-ems.eu.dodea.edu

Dr. Frank Calvano, Principal

1930 London Central High School
PSC 821 Box 119
APO, High Wycombe 09421 0005
Great Britain, AE 09421-5
www.londoncentral.org

Dr. Charles Recesso, Principal

1931 Lorentz International School
Groningensingel 1245, 6835HZ
Arnhem
Netherlands
31-26-320-0110
Fax: 31-26-320-0113

Jan M Meens, Principal

1932 Lusitania International College Foundation
Apartado 328
8600 Lagos
Portugal

Krisine Byrne, Principal

1933 Lyce International-American Section
BP 230, rue du Fer A Cheval
St Germain-En-Laye, 78104 Cedex
France
033-051-7485
Fax: 139-100-914
american.lycee@wanadoo.fr
lycee-intl-american.org
pursues this mission through a rigorous and rewarding American curriculum which culminates in the French Baccalaureate with International Option, as well as through a broad and enriching co-curricular program including such activities as drama, community service, sports and student publications.

Sean Lynch, Director
Beth Heudebourg, President

1934 Lycee Francais De Belgique
9 Avenue Du Lycee Francais
1180 Brussels
Belgium
02-374-58-78
www.lyceefrancais-jmonnet.be

Jean-Claude Giudicelli, Principal

1935 Lyc,e International-American Section
33-1-345-17485
Fax: 33-1-308-70049
Grade levels Pre-K through 12, school year September - June

1936 Malvern College
College Road, Malvern
Worcestershire WR14 3DF
England
01684-581-500
generaloffice@malcol.org
www.malverncollege.org.uk
Boarding school.

Antony Clark, Headmaster

1937 Mannheim Elementary School
Unit 29938
APO AE
09086
380-4705
Fax: 0621-723-905
esmannattend@eu.dodea.edu
www.mann-es.eu.dodea.edu

Dr. Ardelle Hamilton PhD, Principal
Dr. Ellen Minette, Assistant Principal

1938 Mannheim High School
Unit 29939
APO AE
09267
380-409-
Fax: 062- 73-901
MannheimHS.Principal@eu.dodea.edu
www.mann-hs.eu.dodea.edu
is to equip all students to be conscientiously contributing citizens through a challenging curriculum and effective instruction

Sharon O'Donnell, Principal

1939 Margaret Danyers College
N Downs Road, Cheadle Hulme
Cheadle SK8 5HA
England
061-485-4372

Harry Tomlinson, BA, MA, MS, Headmaster

1940 Mark Twain Elementary School
Unit 29237
APO, Heidelberg 09102 0005
Germany 80909
www.mtwain.k12.ca.us

Joseph Newbury, Principal

1941 Marymount International School-Rome
Via di Villa Lauchli 180
00191 Rome
Italy
33-1-462-41051
Fax: 33-1-463-70750
marymount@marymountrome.org
www.marymountrome.org/
Marymount International School provides an education based on Christian values. Marymount is dedicated to fostering individual dignity in an atmosphere of love and respect in which students, faculty, staff and parents work and pray together.

Anne Marie Clancy, Headmistress

1942 Marymount International School-United Kingdom
George Road
Kingston upon Thames, Surrey, KT2 7PE
Surrey , United Kingdom KT2 7
44-20-8949-0571
Fax: 44-20-8336-2485
admissions@marymount.kingston.sch.uk
www.marymountlondon.com/home.php
Marymount London is a vibrant and dynamic learning community where all are respected and encouraged to contribute,committed to developing individuals.

Cathleen Fagan, Headmistress

1943 Mattlidens Gymnasium
Mattliden 1
02230 Esbo
Finland
09 -16 -30 5
Fax: 09 -16 -30 5
gun-maj.roiha@esbo.fi
www.mattliden.fi/gym/
Mattlidens Gymnasium is a coeducational Swedish-speaking upper secondary school

Tom Ginman, Headmaster

1944 Mayenne English School
Chateau les Courges 53420
Chailland
France

J Braillard, Principal

1945 Menwith Hill Estates & Middle School
PSC 45 Unit 8435
APO, High Wycombe 09468 0005
Great Britain
142-377-7778
Fax: 142-377-0236
www.mhil-ehs.eu.dodea.edu

Dr. Arnold Watland, Principal

1946 Millfield School
Butleigh Road Street
Somerset
England BA16-0YD
145-844-2291
office@millfieldschool.com
www.millfieldschool.com
With its outstanding facilities, a staff:pupil ratio of 1:7.5, an extraordinary range of academic courses and the unrivalled strength of its extra-curricular programme, Millfield strives to achieve all these aims. It also seeks to move with the times whilst maintaining the important traditions of good manners, discipline and respect for others

Craig Considine, Headmaster
Adrian E White, Chairman of the Governors

1947 Monkton Combe School
Church Lane
Monkton Combe, Bath
England BA2-7HG
01225-721102
Fax: 01225-721208

reception@monkton.org.uk
www.monktoncombeschool.com
Boarding and day school for girls and boys ages two to nineteen.

Chris Stafford, Headmaster
Richard Backhouse, Principal

1948 Monti Parioli English School
Via Monti Parioli 50
00197 Rome
Italy

Lynette Surtees, Principal

1949 Mougins School
615 Avenue Maurice Donat
CS 12180, 06252 Mougins Cedex
France
33-4-93-90-15-47
Fax: 33-4-93-75-31-40
information@mougins-school.com
www.mougins-school.com
The School has a capacity of 550 students, large enough to provide a stimulating environment and small enough to retain a caring family atmosphere. With over 40 nationalities, the School is culturally rich and aims to encourage pupils to develop morally, emotionally, culturally, intellectually and physically.

Brian G Hickmore, Headmaster
Johanna Povall, Deputy Head

1950 Mountainview School
Bosch 35-6331 Hunenberg
Switzerland

Brenda Moors, Principal

1951 Munich International School
Schloss Buchhof
Starnberg
Germany 82319
49-8151-366-100
Fax: 49-8151-366-109
admissions@mis-munich.de
www.mis-munich.de
MIS caters for the physical, social, emotional and educational development of its children by providing a student-centred, inquiry-based learning environment which fosters an appreciation in its students of their cultural heritage and the cultural richness of the global community.

Mary Sepalla, Head of School
Maha Kattoura, Chairman

1952 Naples Elementary School
PSC 808 Box 39
FPO, AE
Italy 09618
011-39 -8108
Fax: 011-39 -8108
NaplesES.Principal@eu.dodea.edu
www.napl-es.eu.dodea.edu

Dr. Jacqueline Hulbert, Principal

1953 Naples High School
PSC 808 Box 15
FPO, AE
Italy 09618
011-39 -8108
Fax: 011-39 -8108
NaplesHS.Principal@eu.dodea.edu
www.napl-hs.eu.dodea.edu
Students will be prepared to be critical thinkers, effective communicators, and accountable members in a global society.

Carl Albrecht, Principal

1954 Neubruecke Elementary School
Unit 23825
APO, Neubruecke 09034 0005
Germany

Margaret Hoffman-Otto, Principal

1955 Neuchatel Junior College
44 Victoria Street
Suite 1310
Toronto, ON M5C-1Y2
038-25-27-00
800-263-2923
Fax: 038-24-42-59
info@neuchatel.org
www.njc.ch
To provide students a rigorous university preparatory programme in a culturally rich and multi-lingual European setting where learning through educational travel, engagement with world affairs and service to others fosters personal growth and leadership.

Norman Southward, Principal
Dayle Leishman, Director

1956 New School Rome
Via Della Camilluccia 669
Roma
Italy 00135
39-329-4269
info@newschoolrome.com
www.newschoolrome.com
The School is a non-profit making organisation run by the Academic Council (all staff and seven student representatives) which also elects the headteacher, and by the Executive Council (three elected teachers and four elected parents).

Josette Fusco, Head Teacher
Richard Lydiker, Executive Chairman

1957 Newton College
Av Ricardo El as Aparicio 240
La Molina
Lima-Peru, PE
511-479-0460
Fax: 511-479-0430
college@newton.edu.pe
www.newton.edu.pe
Newton College is an Anglo-Peruvian, co-educational, bilingual, day school for students aged 2 to 18.

David Few, Principal

1958 Norra Reals Gymnasium
Roslagsgatan 1
Stockholm
Sweden 113 5
087-420-
Fax: 087-328-
infonorrareal@utbildning.stockholm.se
www.norrareal.stockholm.se
Offers two preparatory study programs: the science and social science.

Per Engback, Principal
Maria Sellberg, Assistant Principal

1959 Numont School
C/ Parma 16
Madrid
Spain 28043
349-130-0243
Fax: 349-759-
numont@telefonica.net
eoficina.e.telefonica.net
Provide a warm, happy and challenging atmosphere where children can derive pleasure from learning and achieving their personal goals. The emphasis is on the individual, so that all of the children, regardless of strengths and weaknesses, colour, creed or sex, feel valued and able to reach their full potential.

Margaret Ann Swanson, Principal

1960 Oak House School
Sant Pere Claver 12-18
Barcelona
Spain 08017
349-325- 402
Fax: 349-325- 402
sec@oakhouseschool.com
www.oakhouseschool.com
The training of students both personal and social is one of the main objectives of the educational work.

Teresa Armadans, Director of Finance
VicenØ Orobitg, Information Technology

1961 Oakham School
Chapel Close
Market Place
Oakham,Rutland, UK LE15
44-0-1572-758758
Fax: 44-0-1572-758595
registrar@oakham.rutland.sch.uk
www.oakham.rutland.sch.uk
A pioneer of full co-education, a boarding and day school for boys and girls aged 10 to 18 years that has become widely known for developing new ideas and making them work to the benefit of all Oakham's pupils.

Joseph AF Spence, Headmaster
Jon Wills, Registrar

1962 Oporto British School
Rua Da Cerca 326/338
PORTO
Portugal 4150-
226-666-
school@obs.edu.pt
www.obs.edu.pt
As the oldest British School in Continental Europe, the Oporto British School is committed to providing a high quality international education for its students.

Mark Rogers, Principal
David Butcher, Headmaster

1963 Oslo American School
Gml Ringeriksv 53, 1340 Bekkestua
Oslo
Norway 05507
www.oasalumni.org

James Mcneil, Principal

1964 Panterra American School
Via Ventre D'oca 41, Fontanella
Pescara 65131
Italy
www.panamterra.com

Virginia Simpson, Principal

1965 Paris American Academy
277 Rue Street Jacques
Paris
France 75005
001-449-
Fax: 01 -4 4- 99
www.parisamericanacademy.edu
To create and maintain a system of higher education that contributes to the transformation of students into

Peter Carman, President/Executive Director
Jean-Michel Ageron-Blanc, General Director

1966 Patrick Henry Elementary School
Unit 29237
APO, Heidelberg
Germany, AE 09102

388-905-
Fax: 062-1 7-5 49
PatrickHenryES.Principal@eu.dodea.edu
www.heid-esp.eu.dodea.edu
To educate all children by providing a nurturing environment and standards-based curriculum dedicated to meeting he diverse needs of every child.

Russ Claus, Principal
Marie Granger, Assistant Principal

1967 Perse School
Hills Road
Cambridge CB2 8QF
England
0223-248127
office@perse.co.uk
www.perse.co.uk

Edward Elliott, Head of Politics
Dan Cross, Deputy Head

1968 Pinewood Schools of Thessaloniki
PO Box 21001
555 10 Pilea
Greece
30-31-301-221
Fax: 30-31-323-196
pinewood@spark.net.gr
www.pinepeaceschool.k12.vi
Independent, coeducational schools which offer an educational program from prekindergarten through grade 12 and boarding facilities from grade 7 though grade 12 for students of all nationalities. The school year comprises 2 semesters extending from September to January and from January to June.

Peter B Baiter, Director

1969 Pordenone Elementary School
PSC 1
Aviano
Italy
39-0434-28462
Fax: 39-0434-28761

D Jean Waddell, Principal

1970 Priory School
West Bank, Dorking
Surrey RH4 3DG
England
130-688-7337
Fax: 130-688-8715
enquiries@staff.priorycofe.surrey.sch.uk
www.priorycofe.surrey.sch.uk
To provide an educational environment which encourages pupils to become confident, competent, self-reliant and happy members of society, fully prepared for adult life and the world of work

A C Sohatski, Headteacher
M Pinchin, Senior Deputy Headteacher

1971 Queen Elizabeth School
Queen's Road, Barnet
Hertfordshire
England, UK EN5 4
020-844-0464
Fax: 020-844-0750
enquiries@qebarnet.co.uk
www.qebarnet.co.uk
To produce boys who are confident, able and responsible.

John Marincowitz, Headmaster

1972 Queens College the English School
Juan De Saridakis 64
Palma de Malorca
Spain
809-393-2153
www.qc.cuny.edu
This Methodist affiliated school offers an English-based curriculum to a total of 1,200 female students, grades K1-12. The school does recruit from overseas, offering three year contracts with housing provided for one week at the beginning of the contract, while they find accommodations. Applications needed to teach include science, pre-school, French, math, Spanish, English and physical education.

Philip Cash, Principal

1973 Rainbow Elementary School
Unit 28614 Box 0040
APO, Ansbach 09177 0005
Germany
407-320-8450
www.rainbow.scps.k12.fl.us

Thomas Murdock, Principal

1974 Ramstein Elementary School
Unit 3240 Box 430
APO AE
Germany 09094
067-014-0 39
Fax: 067- 15- 835
www.rams-es.eu.dodea.edu
To provide a quality education for eligible minor dipendents of DoD military and civilian personnel stationed overseas.

Kathy Downs, Principal

1975 Ramstein High School
Unit 3240 Box 445
APO AE
Germany 09094-445
067-1 4-6095
Fax: 067-1 4-9 86
www.rams-hs.eu.dodea.edu
To provide a varied and challenging curriculum that will allow students to be life-long learners and responsible participants in a global community.

Greg Hatch, Principal

1976 Ramstein Intermediate School
Unit 3240 Box 600
APO AE
Germany 09094-600
067-1 4-6023
Fax: 067-1 5-238
www.rams-is.eu.dodea.edu
To provide an educational environment designed to maximize the potential of all Students.

Stanley B Caldwell, Principal

1977 Ramstein Junior High School
86 SPTG CCSI R, Unit 3240 Box 455
APO, Ramstein 09094 0005
Germany

Richard Snell, Principal

1978 Rathdown School
Upper Glenageary Road Glenageary
Co Dublin
Ireland
01-853133
admin@rathdownschool.ie
www.rathdownschool.ie/contact_us.php
Our aim is to offer a high-quality, modern, challenging and liberal education. In an inclusive and friendly environment, Rathdown School hopes to foster a love of learning which will enable each student to develop her own unique potential. Our purpose is to support and promote the student's academic, cultural, sporting, creative, musical and spiritual capabilities.

Barbara Ennis, Principal

1979 Rikkyo School in England
Guildford Road, Rudgwick, W Sussex
RH12 3BE
Great Britain
014-3 8-2107
Fax: 014-3 8-2535
eikoku@rikkyo.w-sussex.sch.uk
www.rikkyo.co.uk

M Usuki, Principal

1980 Riverside School
Walterswil
6340 Baar
Switzerland
41-41-724-5690
Fax: 41-41-724-5692
office.zug@iszl.ch
www.iszl.ch
The International School of Zug and Luzern (ISZL) provides a high quality Pre-School to Grade 12 international education to day students resident in the Cantons of central Switzerland.

Dominic Currer, Director
Elaine Tomlinson, Headmaster

1981 Robinson Barracks Elementary School
Unit 30401
APO
Germany, AE 09107
491-119-
Fax: 071- 85- 473
RobinsonBarracksES.Principal@eu.dodea.edu
www.rbar-es.eu.dodea.edu
The Robinson Barrack's school community provides a respectful environment where all members learn to recognize their strengths and gain confidence to become lifelong learners and leaders in an ever-changing world.

Shirley Sheck, Principal

1982 Rome International School
Via Panama 25
00198 Rome
Italy
039-06 -4482
Fax: 039-06 -4482
office@romeinternationalschool.it
www.romeinternationalschool.it
Provides a nurturing environment, in which children of all nationalities and faiths can explore and respect their own and each other's cultural and religious heritage.

Patricia Martin-Smith, Principal Primary School
Ivano Boragine, Managing Director

1983 Rosall School
Fleetwood
Lancashire
United Kingdom FY7 8
012- 37- 420
Fax: 012- 37- 205
enquiries@rossallcorporation.co.uk
www.rossall.co.uk
Providing a unique educational experience we offer a wide ranging choice of curriculums underpinned by a commitment to academic excellence.

RDW Rhodes, Principal
GSH Penelley, Faculty Head

1984 Rosemead
East Street, Littlehampton
BN17 6AL
England
0903-716065

J Bevis, BA, Headmaster

1985 Rota Elementary School
PSC 819 Box 19
FPO AE 09645 0019
Spain
345-624-
Fax: 011-34 -56 8

rotaes.principal@eu.dodea.edu
www.rota-es.eu.dodea.edu
Provides a standards-based educational program, which creates lifelong learners and responsible citizens.

Charles Callahan, Principal

1986 Rota High School
PSC 819 Box 63
FPO AE 09645 0005
Spain
345-624-
Fax: 011-34 -56 8
RotaHS.Principal@eu.dodea.edu
www.rota-hs.eu.dodea.edu

Lynne Michael, Principal

1987 Roudybush Foreign Service School
Place des Arcades, Sauveterre de Rouergue (Averyon)
France
This European school prepares men for the foreign service.

Franklin Roudybush, AB, MA, Headmaster

1988 Rugby School
Rugby, Warwickshire
United Kingdom CV22
44-178-854-3465
Fax: 44-178-856-9124
enquiries@rugbyschool.net
www.rugbyschool.net
Rugby School is an educational community whose philosophy embraces the challenges of academic excellence, spiritual awareness, responsibility and leadership, friendships and relationships and participation in a wide variety of activities

Patrick Derham, Headmaster
SK Fletcher, Deputy Head

1989 Runnymede College School
Calle Salvia 30
28109 La Moraleja, Madrid
Spain
34-91-650-8302
Fax: 34-91-650-8236
office@runnymede-college.com
www.runnymede-college.com
Provides an all-round, academic, liberal humanist education to all students regardless of their sex, race, religion or nationality. There is no religious instruction.

Frank M Powell, Headmaster
FJ Murphy, Deputy Head

1990 Rygaards International School
Bernstorffsvej 54, DK-2900
Hellerup
Denmark
45-39-62-10-53
Fax: 45-39-62-10-81
admin@rygaards.com
www.rygaards.com
Rygaards School is a private, Christian/Catholic, co-educational establishment. It is recognised by and subject to, Danish law and receives a subsidy from the Danish State.

Mathias Jepsen, Principal
Charles Dalton, Headmaster

1991 Salzburg International Preparatory School
Moosstrasse 106
A-5020 Salzburg
Austria
662-844485
Fax: 662-847711
www.ais-salzburg.a
A coeducational boarding school offering an American college preparatory high school curriculum for grades 7 to 12 as well as a post graduate course.

1992 Schiller Academy
51-55 Waterloo Road
London, SE1 8TX
United Kingdom
44-207-928-1372
Fax: 44-207-928-8089
office@schiller-academy.org.uk
www.schiller-academy.org.uk
Grade levels 9-12, school year August - June

George Selby, Headmaster
Renee Miller, Director Studies

1993 Schools of England, Wales, Scotland & Ireland
J. Burrow & Company
Imperial House, Lypiatt Road
Cheltenham 50201
England

1994 Schweinfurt American Elementary School
CMR 457
AP, AE
Germany 09033
09721-81893
Fax: 09721-803905
schweinfurtes.principal@eu.dodea.edu
www.schw-es.eu.dodea.edu
The mission of Schweinfurt Elementary School is to help all students become respectful, responsible citizens and life-long learners.

Wilma Holt, Principal
Beverly Erdmann, Assistant Principal

1995 Schweinfurt Middle School
CMR 457
AP, AE
Germany 09033-5
354-681-1800
Fax: 097-1 8-363
SchweinfurtMS.Principal@eu.dodea.edu
www.schw-ms.eu.dodea.edu
Schweinfurt Middle School will engage all students in meaningful experiences that develop 21st Century Skills, preparing them to be successful and responsible citizens in a technological, global society.

Dr George P Carpenter, Principal

1996 Sembach Elementary School
Unit 4240 Box 325
APO, AE
Germany 09136
063- 67-0
Fax: 063-271-
SembachES.Principal@eu.dodea.edu
www.semb-es.eu.dodea.edu

Monica Harvey, Principal

1997 Sembach Middle School
Unit 4240 Box 320
APO, AE
Germany 09136
063- 67-0
Fax: 063-271-
SembachMS.Principal@eu.dodea.edu
www.semb-ms.eu.dodea.edu

Bonnie B Hannan, Principal

1998 Sevenoaks School
Sevenoaks
Kent TN13 IHU
England
44 -017-245
Fax: 44 -017-245
enq@sevenoaksschool.org
www.sevenoaksschool.org
Sevenoaks School is an independent, co-educational boarding and day school, set in 100 acres in the heart of Southeast England. Half an hour from Central London, and half an hour from Gatwick International Airport, we are situated on the edge of Sevenoaks, overlooking the 15th century deer park of the Knole Estate.

Katy Ricks, Head of School
Tony Evans, Chairman

1999 Sevilla Elementary & Junior High School
496 ABS DODDS Unit 6585
APO Moron AB 09643 0005
Spain

Robert Ludwig, Principal

2000 Shape Elementary School
Unit 21420
APO, AE
Belgium 09705
011-32 -5044
Fax: 011-32 -31
ShapeES.Principal@eu.dodea.edu
www.shap-es.eu.dodea.edu
It is the mission of SHAPE Elementary School to educate all students in an integrated, multi-cultural environment to become productive thinkers, to achieve their maximum physical and mental potential, and to be literate, responsible members of a global society through excellence in teaching and learning.

Charlene Leister, Principal
Miles Shea, Assistant Principal

2001 Shape High School
Unit 21420
APO, AE
Belgium 09705
011-32 -5044
Fax: 011-32 -31
david.tran@eu.dodea.edu
www.shap-hs.eu.dodea.edu

David Tran, Principal
Arlena Ray, Assistant Principal

2002 Shape International School
Avenue de Reijkjavik 717
SHAPE
Belgium 07010
65-44-52-83
www.nato.int/shape/community/school.htm
Performs the operational duties previously undertaken by Allied Command Europe and Allied Command Atlantic

Jacques Laurent, Principal

2003 Sidcot School
Winscombe
N Somerset BS25 1PD
England
44-193-484-3102
Fax: 44-193-484-4181
addmissions@sidcot.org.uk
www.sidcot.org.uk
This friendly school with an international enrollment of 277 day students and 149 boarding students (255 boys; 171 girls), in grades K-12, is set in over one hundred acres of Somerset countryside. The school offers an English-based curriculum and the student/teacher ratio is 10:1.

John Walmsley, Headteacher
Ross Wallis, Head of Art

2004 Sierra Bernia School
La Caneta s/n
Alfaz del Pi Alicante
Spain 03580

96-687-51-49
Fax: 96-687-36-33
duncan@ctv.es
sierraberniaschool.com/news.php
Forefront of modern education. Combining both traditional and innovative methods of teaching made possible by the wealth and immense knowledge base of its fully qualified teaching body

Duncan Allan, Owner/Director
Iain Macinnes, Headteacher

2005 Sigonella Elementary & High School
PSC 824 Box 2630
FPO Signoella, Sicily 09627 2630
Italy
624-440-
www.sigo-es.eu.dodea.edu/

Dr. Peter Price, Principal

2006 Sigtunaskolan Humanistiska Laroverket
Manfred Bjorkquists Alle 6
Box 508, Sigtuna
Sweden 19328
46-8-592-57100
Fax: 46-8-592-57250
info@sshl.se
www.sshl.se
Grade levels include 7-12 with an enrollment of 543.

Kent Edberg, Principal
Rune Svaninger, Director

2007 Sir James Henderson School
Via Pisani Dossi 16
Milano
Italy 20134
39-02-264-13310
Fax: 39-02-264-13515
sirjames@bbs.infosquare.it
www.sjhschool.com
To ensure that its diverse student body grows to its full potential as independent learners in a caring British and international community, uniting the best of British educational tradition with the values, practices and beliefs of the International Baccalaureate

Stephen Anson, Principal
Jim Noble, Chairman

2008 Skagerak Gymnas
PO Box 1545-Veloy
3206 Sandefjord
Norway
473-345-6500
www.skagerak.org

Elisabeth Norr, Principal

2009 Smith Elementary School
Unit 23814 Box 30
APO, AE
Germany 09034-3814
067-783-5693
Fax: 067-783-8874
SmithES.Principal@eu.dodea.edu
www.baum-ess.eu.dodea.edu

Kent Bassett, Principal

2010 Southlands English School
Via Teleclide 40
Casalapalocco, Rome
Italy 00124
39 -605-5039
Fax: 06 -091-7192
www.southlands.it
Our aim is to give you a flavour of the quality educational experience available at Southlands and encourage you to visit the school so you can see for yourself the happy, successful community that Southlands nurtures.

Deryck M Wilson, Principal

2011 Spangdahlem Elementary School
52 MSG/CCSE S, Unit 3640 Box 50
APO, AE
Germany 09126-4050
065-056- 688
Fax: 065-056- 710
SpnagdahlemES.Principal@eu.dodea.edu
www.spang-es.eu.dodea.edu

Richard R Alix, Principal

2012 Spangdahlem Middle School
52 CSG CCSM, Unit 3640 Box 45
APO, AE
Germany 09126-4045
065-506- 725
Fax: 065-506-0279
SpangdahlemMS.Principal@eu.dodea.ed
u
www.spang-ms.eu.dodea.edu
Spangdhalem Middle School promotes high achievement and lifelong learning for all students through positive interactions and standards-based educational program.

Joseph Malloy, Principal

2013 Sportfield Elementary School
Unit 20193 Box 0014
APO, Hanau
Germany, AE 09165-14

John O'Reilly, Jr, Principal

2014 St. Andrew's College
19 Carillon Avenue
Newtown NSW
Australia 02042
02-9626-1999
principalassist@standrewscollege.edu.au
www.standrewscollege.edu.au
St Andrew's is proud of its reputation as a leading academic institution, fostering leaders within the community and moulding the leaders of tomorrow. The College places emphasis on academic and intellectual development and excellence as core to the development of the individual.

Wayne Erickson, Principal
Donna Wiemann, Development Manager

2015 St. Anne's School
Jarama 9
Madrid 2
Spain
www.stannes.edu.in

Margaret Raines, Principal

2016 St. Anthony's International College
Camino de Coin km 53.5
Mijas-Costa, Malaga
Spain 29649
00 -09 -247
Fax: 00 -09 -046
info@stanthonyscollege.com
www.stanthonyscollege.com
The school with its friendly, family atmosphere provides opportunities for our students to achieve their best. Trying not to cater just for high achievers we endeavour, through a broad and balanced education, to find courses for all abilities.

2017 St. Catherine's British School
PO Box 51019
Kifissia 145 10 Athens
Greece
301- 8-97
Fax: 301- 8-64
administrator@stcatherines.gr
www.stcatherines.gr
The school endeavors to foster a love of learning through a well taught, appropriately challenging, clearly defined and balanced curriculum. Our aim is to fully develop intellectual, social, physical and creative potential, giving students the foundatin to develop into sensitive, informed, and capable global citizens of the future.

Michael Toman, Principal
R Morton, Headmaster & CEO

2018 St. Christopher School
Barrington Road, Letchworth
Hertfordshire SG6 3JZ
England
0462-679301
Fax: 0462-481578
school.admin@stchris.co.uk
www.stchris.co.uk
St Christopher has a distinctive ethos, based on the development of each child's individuality whilst teaching a sense of responsibility towards others, towards the School and towards the local and global community.

Richard Palmer, Head of School
Emma-Kate Henry, Deputy Head of St Christophe

2019 St. Clare's Oxford
139 Banbury Road
Oxford OX2 7AL
England
44-186-555-2031
Fax: 44-186-551-3359
admissions@stclares.ac.uk
www.stclares.ac.uk
St. Clare's welcomes students and staff of all nationalities and cultures who will benefit from, and contribute to, our learning community. Living and studying together, we learn from one another. We are enriched and challenged by a diversity of views and ideas.

Paula Holloway, Principal
Tom Walsh, Vice Principal

2020 St. David's School
Justin Hall, Beckenham Road
West Wickham BR4 0QS
England
01784-252494
Fax: 01784-252494
office@stdavidsschool.com
www.sdsw.org
Boarding school for girls ages nine to eighteen; day school for girls ages four to eighteen.

Judith G Osborne, BA, Headmaster

2021 St. Dominic's International School
Outeiro de Polima-Arneiro
2785-816 Sao Domingos da Rana
Portugal
351-21-448-0550
351-214-5505
Fax: 351-21-444-3027
school@dominics-int.org
www.dominics-int.org
Our school mission is to offer an international education of the highest calibre enriched and enlivened by the Dominican tradition of study and education; promoting the development of each student's potential: physical, emotional, social, intellectual, moral and spiritual.

Maria do Ros ri Empis, Principal
Manuel Lucas, President of Supervision

2022 St. Dominic's Sixth Form College
Mount Park Avenue Harrow on the Hil
Middlesex HA1 3HX
England
020-84228084
208-422-3759

Fax: 020-8422-3759
stdoms@stdoms.ac.uk
www.stdoms.ac.uk
St. Dominic's is a Roman Catholic Sixth Form College committed to the pesonal and spiritual growth of all its members based on Christian values, academic excellence and high quality pastoral care.

Patrick Harty, Principal

2023 St. Georges English School
Via Cassia Km 16
La Storta Rome
Italy 00123
06-3790141
Fax: 06-3792490
Secretary@stgeorge.school.it
www.stgeorge.school.it
To develop the individual talents of young people and teach them to relate the experience of the classroom to the realities of the world outside.

Martyn Hales, Principal

2024 St. Georges School
Vila Goncalve, Quinta Loureiras
2750 Cascais
Portugal
112-602-4645
www.sgs.edu.in

MPB Hoare, Principal

2025 St. Georges School-Switzerland
Chemin de St Georges 19
Clarens Montreux
Switzerland 01815
21-964-34-11
Fax: 21-964-49-32
office@st-georges.ch
www.st-georges.ch
St. George's School encourages students to lift their eyes and recognise positive qualities within themselves and others and to nurture a caring and dynamic attitude in today's demanding world.

Dr Ilya V Eigenbrot, Principal
Francis Kahn, President of Directors

2026 St. Gerard's School
Thornhill Road, Bray Co Wicklow
Republic of Ireland
353-001-2821
Fax: 353-001-2821
info@stgerards.ie
www.stgerards.ie
To provide an opportunity for each student to realise his or her potential in all areas: academic, moral, personal, physical, social, spiritual and sporting.

Tom Geraghty, Headmaster
Victor Drummy, Deputy Principal

2027 St. Helen's School
Eastbury Road Northwood, Middlesex
England HA6-3AS
09274-28511
Fax: 0923-835824
enquiries@sthn.co.uk
www.sthn.co.uk
We aim to give every pupil an academic, innovative and stimulating education, developing her intellectual, creative and physical talents to the full. We provide a friendly, supportive and well-ordered environment in which every girl is treated as an individual and where integrity, personal responsibility and respect for others are highly valued.

YA Burne, Principal

2028 St. John's International School
Dreve Richelle 146
Waterloo
Belguim 01410
32-2-352-0610
Fax: 32-2-352-0630
contact@stjohns.be
www.stjohns.be
we exist to provide an English-speaking education that emphasizes Christian values, encourages academic excellence and stimulates social development within a culturally diverse environment. St. John's is also a caring environment where students are encouraged to reach their full potential, prepared to think globally, with a commitment to justice and challenged to act responsibly in a consistently changing society.

Joseph Doenges, Director
Judith Hoskins, Director Admissions

2029 St. Mary's School
Rhapta Road, PO Box 40580- 00100
Nairobi
Kenya
0990-23721
info@stmarys.ac.ke
www.stmarys.ac.ke
We are a Catholic Private School committed to our international character in the provision of a spiritual, intellectual and physical education. We aim at developing the gifts of the young in an atmosphere which encourages the ethos of self-expression and mutual respect with a view to their facing the future responsibly, with confidence and courage.

M Mark Orchard, IBVM, BA, Principal

2030 St. Michael's School
Otford Court
Otford TN14 5SA
England
095-92-2137
www.stmichaels-otford.co.uk

Keith Crombie, Headmaster

2031 St. Stephen's School
Via Aventina 3
Rome
Italy 00153
39-06-575-0605
Fax: 39-06-574-1941
ststephens@ststephens-rome.com
www.ststephens-rome.com

Philip Allen, Headmaster
Lesley Murphey, Head of the School

2032 Stavenger British School
Gauselbakken 107
4032 Gausel
Norway
475-195-0250
www.biss.no

Zelma Roisli, Principal

2033 Stover School
Newton Abbot
Devon
England TQ12
0626-54505
351-214-5505
mail@stover.co.uk
www.stover.co.uk

Susan Bradley, Principal

2034 Stowe School
Stowe
Buckingham
England MK18
44-1280-818000
351-214-5505
Fax: 44-1280-818181
enquiries@stowe.co.uk
www.stowe.co.uk
Our vision for Stowe, a co-educational independent boarding and day school in the heart of the English countryside, is of a school that delivers the highest academic and cultural achievement; and a school that continues to foster the development of Stoics who are as original and individual as their school.

Anthony Wallersteiner, Headmaster
GM Hornby, Faculty Head

2035 Summerfield School SRL
Via Tito Poggi 21 Divino Amore
00134 Rome
Italy
www.summerfields.co.in

Vivien Franceschini, Principal

2036 Summerhill School
Westward Ho
Leiston, Suffolk
England IP16
0728-830540
zoe@summerhillschool.co.uk
www.summerhillschool.co.uk
A S Neill's Summerhill School, a co-educational boarding school in Suffolk, England, is the original alternative 'free' school. Founded in 1921, it continues to be an influential model for progressive, democratic education around the world.

Zoe Readhead, Principal

2037 Sunny View School
C/ Teruel No 32, Cerro del Toril
Torremolinos Malaga
Spain 29620
345-283-
Fax: 345-272-
sunny@acade.es
www.sunnyviewschool.com
Sunny View is a privately owned day school, which accepts students of all nationalities from the age of 3 years to 18 years. It is a long-established International School.

Jane Barbadillo, Principal
David McConnell, HS Principal

2038 Sutton Park School
St Fintan's Road
Sutton, Dublin 13
Ireland
353-1-832-2940
Fax: 353-1-832-5929
info@sps.ie
www.suttonparkschool.com
Sutton Park School aims to provide its pupils with an educational environment that is intellectually, physically and culturally challenging, so that they can grow into balanced, mature and confident adults.

Laurence J Finnegan, Chief Executive
Michael Moretta, Head of School

2039 Sutton Valence School
Maidstone
Kent
England ME17
0622-842281
enquiries@svs.org.uk
www.svs.org.uk
Our aim today is to give our girls and boys an excellent all round education in an atmosphere of togetherness and trust, where day and boarding pupils benefit from the same supportive ethos.

Joe Davies, Headmaster
Kathy Webster, Admissions Officer

2040 Swans School
Capricho s/n
Marbella, Malaga
Spain 29600
95 -77 -248
Fax: 95 -77 -431
info@swansschool.net
www.swansschool.net
Swans' motto is Constancy and Truth.
TJ Swan, Principal
Nick Lee, Head Teacher

2041 TASIS Hellenic International School
PO Box 51051
Kifissia Gr-145 10
Greece
30-1-623-3888
Fax: 30-1-623-3160
info@tasis.edu.gr
www.tasis.com
Grade levels Pre-K through 12, school year September - June
Basile Daskalakis, President

2042 TASIS The American School in England
Coldharbour Lane
Thorpe, Surrey, TW20 8TE
England
44-1932-565-252
Fax: 44-1932-564-644
ukadmissions@tasis.com
www.tasis.com
Grade levels Pre-K through 12, school year August - June
Barry Breen, Headmaster

2043 Taunus International Montessori School
Altkonigstrasse 1 6370
Oberursel
Germany
496-171-9133
www.tims-frankfurt.com
Kathleen Hauer, Principal

2044 Teach in Great Britain
5 Netherhall Gardens
London, NW3, England
www.teachaway.com

2045 Thessaloniki International High School & Pinewood Elementary School
PO Box 21001
555 10 Pilea, Thessaloniki
Greece
30-31-301-221
Fax: 30-31-323-196
pinewood@spark.net.gr
www.users.otenet.gr/~pinewood
Grades preK-12, enrollment 256.
Peter B Baiter, Director

2046 Thomas Jefferson School
4100 South Lindbergh Boulevard
Saint Louis
Missouri, MO 63127
314-843-4151
www.tjs.org
The mission of Thomas Jefferson School is to give its students the strongest possible academic background, responsibility for their own learning, a concern for other people, and the resources to live happily as adults and become active contributors to society
William C Rowe, Head of School
Susan S Stepleton, Chair, Board of Trustees

2047 United Nations Nursery School
40 Rue Pierre Guerin
75016 Paris
France
33-1-452-72024
Fax: 33-1-428-87146
www.unns.net
Pre-K and kindergarten levels.
Brigitte Weill, Directrice

2048 United World College-Adriatic
Via Treste 29
Duino (TS)
Italy 34011
39 -40 -7391
Fax: 39 -40 -7392
www.uwcad.it
The United World Colleges offer students of all races and creeds the opportunity of developing international understanding through programmes which combine high quality academic study and activities which encourage
DB Sutcliffe, Principal
David Sutcliffe, Headmaster

2049 United World College-Atlantic
St Donats Castle Llantwit
Major S Glamorgan
United Kingdom
441- 46-9 90
www.atlanticcollege.org
a sense of adventure and social responsibility
Colin Jenkins, Principal

2050 Vajont Elementary School
PSC 1
Aviano
Italy
427-701553
Nick Suida, Principal

2051 Verdala International School
Fort Pembroke
Pembroke, STJ 14
Malta
356-332-361
Fax: 356-372-387
vis@maltanet.net
www.verdala.org
An independent, coeducational day and boarding school which offers an educational program from play school through grade 12 for students of all nationalities.
Adam Pleasance, Headmaster
Charles Zerafa, Business Manager

2052 Verona Elementary School
1011 Lee Highway
Verona, VA 24482
540-248-0141
Fax: 540-248-0562
www.augusta.k12.va.us
Marguerite McDonald, Principal

2053 Vicenza Elementary School
Unit 31401 Box 11
APO, Vicenza
Italy 09630-5
011-390-444
Fax: 011-39 -444
VicenzaES.Principal@eu.dodea.edu
www.vice-es.eu.dodea.edu/index.htm
Increase student achievement, we are committed to improving our children's ability to communicate in writing across all curricular areas, and to reason mathematically.
Martha Parsons, Principal

2054 Vicenza High School
Unit 31401 Box 11
APO, Vicenza
Italy 09630
011-390-444
Fax: 011-39 -444
VicenzaHS.Principal@eu.dodea.edu
www.vice-hs.eu.dodea.edu/
Lauri Kenney, Principal
Chris Beane, Assistant Principal

2055 Vicenza International School
Viale Trento 141
Vicenza 36100
Italy
39-0444-288-475
Fax: 39-0444-963-633
vix-ib@vip.it
Grade levels 11-13, school year September - June
Dionigio Tanello, PhD, Director

2056 Vienna Christian School
Wagramerstrasse 175
Panthgasse 6A
Wien, Austria A-122
43-1-25122-501
351-214-5505
office@vcs-austria.org
www.viennachristianschool.org/
VCS is an international school with a United States-based curriculum.
Ken Norman, Director
Nancy L Deibert, Athletic Director/PE

2057 Vienna International School
Strasse der Menschenrechte 1
Vienna, Austria 01220
43-1-203-5595
Fax: 43-1-203-0366
visinfo@vis.ac.at.
www.vis.ac.at
To serve the children of the United Nations and diplomatic community in Vienna. It is also open to children of the international business community and of Austrian families.
James S Walbran, Director
Neil Tomalin, Head Primary School

2058 Vilseck Elementary School
Unit 28040
APO, Vilseck
Germany 09112-14
011-490-662
Fax: 011-490-662
VilseckES.Principal@eu.dodea.edu
www.vils-es.eu.dodea.edu/
Vilseck Elementary School prepares students for lifelong learning within a safe, nurturing environment. Honoring the uniqueness of our military community, we foster respect for all people and for cultural diversity
Hammack, Principal, Assistant Principal

2059 Vilseck High School
Unit 20841
APO, Vilseck
Germany 09112-5
011-490-662
Fax: 011-490-662
Duane.Werner@eu.dodea.edu
www.vils-hs.eu.dodea.edu/
VHS is home to approximately 520 students, grades 9-12, who have the opportunity to participate in Engaged Learning projects in academic areas. They have a wide range of choices in elective areas to include art, band, chorus, German, Spanish, home economics and technical education.
Duane Werner, Principal

2060 Violen School, International Department
Violenstraat 3, 1214
CJ Hilversum
Netherlands
035-621-6053
www.ipsviolen.nl
This school offers an enrollment of 240 day students (125 boys and 115 girls), in grades K through 6. The primary education is in the English language for international mobile families, set up and supported by the Dutch government.
Atse R Spoor, Principal

2061 Vogelweh Elementary School
Unit 3240 Box 435
APO
Germany, AE 09021
011-49 -3109
Fax: 011-49 -3105
www.voge-es.eu.dodea.edu
Vogelweh Elementary School is committed to creating an environment that supports life-long learning in order for students to be successful in a global society.
Donna E Donaldson, Principal
Janie Page, Assistant Principal

2062 Volkel Elementary School
752 MUNSS Unit 6790
APO, Volkel 09717 5018
Netherlands
www.aoshs.org
Claudia Holtzclaw, Principal

2063 Westwing School
Kyneton House
Thornbury BS122JZ
England
0454-412311
westwing.dvusd.org
Marjorie Crane, MA, Headmaster

2064 Wetzel Elementary School
Unit 23815
APO, Baumholder 09034 0005
Germany
www.baum-esw.eu.dodea.edu
Robert Richards, Principal

2065 Wiesbaden Middle School
Unit 29647
APO, AE
Germany 09096
011-049- 110
Fax: 011-049- 110
wiesbadenMS.Webmaster@eu.dodea.edu
www.wies-ms.eu.dodea.edu
The entire WMS community strives to provide a positive school climate through which all students can mature socially, academically and physically, while developing a life-long love of learning.
Alexia Venglik, Principal

2066 Wolfert Van Borselen
Bredewater 24, Postbus 501
2700 AM Zoetermeer
Netherlands
E-mail: info@owinsp.nl
www.wolfert.nl/
Gilles Schuilenburg, Principal

2067 Worksop College
Worksop, Nottinghamshire
S80 3AP
England
0909-472391
enquiries@worksopcollege.notts.sch.uk
www.worksopcollege.notts.sch.uk/
Worksop College was founded as St Cuthbert's School in 1890 by Nathaniel Woodard. As a parish priest working in London in the 1840s Woodard was dismayed by the ignorance of the middle classes and believed that there was a need for something comparable to the National School's Christian schools for the poor in order to serve the needs of the trade classes.
Roy Collard, Headmaster

2068 Worms Elementary School
CMR 455
APO, Worms 09058 0005
Germany
011-490-662
www.wikimapia.org
Charles Raglan, Principal

2069 Wuerzburg Elementary School
CMR 475 Box 6
APO, Wuerzburg 09244 6627
Germany
011-490-662
www.wikimapia.org
Dee Ann Edwards, Principal

2070 Wuerzburg High School
CMR 475 Box 8
APO, Wuerzburg 09036 0005
Germany
011-490-662
www.wikimapia.org
Robert Kubarek, Principal

2071 Wuerzburg Middle School
CMR 475 Box 7
APO, Wuerzburg 09036 0005
Germany
011-490-662
www.wikimapia.org
Karen Kroon, Principal

2072 Zurich International School
Steinacherstrasse 140
8820 Wadenswill
Switzerland
41-43-833-2222
Fax: 41-43-833-2223
zis@zis.ch
www.zis.ch
Zurich International School is a co-educational international day school in the Zurich area for students aged 3 to 18 and is fully accredited by both the Council of International Schools and the New England Association of Schools and Colleges and is an IB World School.
Peter C Mott, Director
Jennifer Saxe, Director Development

West Indies & Carribean

2073 American School-Santo Domingo
Apartado 20212
Santo Domingo
Dominican Republic
809-565-7946
809-549-5841
info@assd.edu.do
www.assd.edu.do
The American School of Santo Domingo provides all students with quality educational opportunities to make life long learners while fostering moral values and physical development.
Lourdes Tomas, School Director

2074 Aquinas College
1607 Robinson Road SE
Grand Rapids, MI 49506-1799
616-632-8900
www.aquinas.edu
Emphasizes career preparation with a focus on leadership and service to others.
Vincent Ferguson, Principal

2075 Belair School
43 Decarteret Road
Mandeville
Jamaica
1-876-962-2168
Fax: 1-876-962-3396
admissions@belairschool.com
www.belairschool.com
The Belair School seeks to promote the academic, social and emotional development of students and a value system of integrity through an integrated curriculum, so that students will become self-assured and responsible citizens.
Sylvan Shields, Director

2076 Bermuda High School
19 Richmond Road
Pembroke
Bermuda HM 08
1-441-295-6153
Fax: 1-441-295-2754
info@bhs.bm
www.bhs.bm
This girls school offers an English-based curriculum for 620 total day students in grades 1-12.
Martina Harris, Primary Head
Jennifer Howarth, Primary Assistant

2077 Bermuda Institute-SDA
234 Middle Road
Southampton
Bermuda SN BX
441-238-1566
www.bermudainstitute.bm
The Bermuda Institute family exists to show children Jesus, nurture their love for Him and others, teach them to think, and empower them to serve.
Lois Tucker, Principal
Kathleen Allers, Elementary Vice Principal

2078 Bishop Anstey Junior School
Ariapita Road
Port of Spain
Trinidad and Tobago
868-624-1177
admin@bishopansteyjunior.edu.tt
www.bishopansteyjunior.edu.tt
To stimulate learning within the spiritual, academic, social , cultural and sporting disciplines aimed at developing rounded individuals, within an environment that allows the flexibility to cope with the challenges of the changing education landscape.
Grace Campbell, Principal

2079 Capitol Christian School
C-11 #3 Urb Real Santo Domingo
Dominican Republic
916-856-5630
Fax: 916-856-5609
www.ccscougars.org
Stacy Lee Blossom, Principal

2080 Ecole Flamboyant
PO Box 1744-A Schweitzer Hosp
Port-au-Prince
Haiti

509-381-141/2
Fax: 509-381-141
has-pap@acn.com
William Dunn, Principal

2081 International School-Aruba
Wayaca 238 A
Aruba
Dutch Caribbean
297-845-365
Fax: 297-847-341
info@isaruba.com
www.isaruba.com
A nonprofit, coeducational English-speaking day school serving students from prekindergarten to grade 12.
Paul D Sibley, Headmaster
Mary B Sibley, Academic Dean/Counselor

2082 International School-Curacao
PO Box 3090
Koninginnelaan Emmastad, Curacao
Netherlands Antilles
5-999-737-3633
Fax: 5-999-737-3142
iscmec@attglobal.net
www.isc.an
Offers a rigorous academic program in order to prepare students planning to pursue higher learning at colleges and universities around the world. The School's curriculum includes International Baccalaureate (IB) coursework that allows students the opportunity to receive the IB Diploma.
Margie Elhage PhD, Director
Rene Romer, President

2083 International School-West Indies
PO Box 278 Leeward
Providenciales
British West Indies
Alison Hodges, Principal

2084 Kingsway Academy
PO Box N-4378
Nassau
Bahamas
242-324-6887
Fax: 242-393-6917
www.kingswayacademy.com
Kingsway Academy endeavours to provide children with a sound education that is thoroughly Christian in its outlook and practices - Training Children in the King's Way .
Carol Harrison, Principal

2085 Mount Saint Agnes Academy
PO Box HM 1004
Hamilton HMDX
Bermuda
441-292-4134
Fax: 441-295-7265
msaoffice@msa.bm
www.msa.bm
The Mission of Mount Saint Agnes Academy is to provide quality education in a caring, Christian environment. Belief in Christ and fidelity to the Roman Catholic Church form the foundation upon which all academic learning and social interaction take place. To this end we make a strong commitment to recognize each child as an individual and to help him/her to develop according to his/her own potential in order to become a responsible member of the community
Sue Moench, Principal
Margaret DiGiacomo, Assistant Principal

2086 Queens College
PO Box N7127
Nassau
Bahamas
242-393-1666
Fax: 242-393-3248
info@qchenceforth.com
www.qchenceforth.com
Our interests lie not only in academic excellence but also in raising well-rounded, courteous, spiritually grounded global citizens.
Andrea Gibson, Principal

2087 Saltus Cavendish School
PO Box DV 209
Devonshire DV BX
Bermuda
441-236-3215
Fax: 441-292-0438
head.cavendish@saltus.bm
www.saltus.bm
Saltus Grammar School is a co-educational, independent day school of excellent reputation. It is the premier independent school in Bermuda and is well known in the international community.
Susan Furr, Headteacher
Stephanie Queary, Secretary

2088 St. Andrew's School
16 Valleton Avenue
Marraval Trinidad West Indies
Trinidad and Tobago
868-622-2630
Fax: 868-628-1857
principal@standrews.edu.tt
www.standrews.edu.tt
St. Andrew's is a progressive school that produces a caring, confident and responsible child. St. Andrew's also supports the development of social and moral values that allow the child to appreciate and respect diversity.
Sandra Farinha, Principal
Paula Moses, Vice Principal

2089 St. Anne's Parish School
PO Box SS6256
Nassau
Bahamas
868-622-2631
Fax: 868-628-1858
www.standrewsindia.com
Rev. Patrick Adderley, Principal

2090 St. John's College
PO Box N4858
Nassau
Bahamas
868-622-2632
Fax: 868-628-1859
www.standrewsindia.com
Arlene Ferguson, Principal

2091 St. Paul's Methodist College
PO Box F897
Freeport
Grand Bahamas
814-237-2163
stpaulsc.org
Annette Poitier, Principal

2092 Sunland Lutheran School
PO Box F2469
Freeport
Bahamas
www.sunlandbaptistacademy.org
J Pinder, Principal

2093 Tapion School
PO Box 511 La Toc
Castries, St Lucia
West Indies
758-452-2902
Fax: 758-453-0582
tapionsch@candw.lc
tapionschool.com
The Tapion School will endeavour to produce individuals who would be empowered to meet the demands of a changing society.
Laurena Primus, Principal
Margaret Francois, Administration Officer

U.S. Branches

2094 Aisha Mohammed International School
Washington, DC 20521-1
www.joh.cam.ac.uk
Daryl Barker, Principal

2095 Albania Tirana International School
DOS/Administrative Officer
9510 Tirana Place
Washington, DC 20521-9510
355-436-5239
qsialb@albaniaonline.net
www1.qsi.org/alb
Provides a quality education in the English language for expatriates living in Tirana and Albanian citizens who want their children to be educated in English.
Scott D'Alterio, Director
Sotiraq Trebicka, Administrative Coordinator

2096 Alexander Muss High School Israel
78 Randall Avenue
Rockville Centre, NY 11570
212-472-9300
800-327-5980
Fax: 212-472-9301
info@amiie.org
amiie.org
Provide a superior Israel education experience to learners of all ages in Israel and within communities throughout North America and abroad. The Institute promotes, builds and strengthens lifelong bonds between Jews and Israel through education, experiences and understanding.
Gideon Shavit, CEO
Chaim Fischgrund, Headmaster

2097 Almaty International School
DOS/Administrative Officer
7030 Almaty Place
Washington, DC 20521-7030
E-mail: director@ais.almaty.kz
www.state.gov/www/about_state/schools/oalmaty.html
Grades preK-12, enrollment 169.
Robert B Draper, Director

2098 American School
Col Lomas del Guijarro Avenue Repœb
Tegucigalpa
Honduras 02134
504-239-3333
Fax: 504-239-6162
eagurcia@amschool.org
www.amschool.org
Provides a student-centered, enriching, college-preparatory education that emphasizes social responsibility in a safe, bicultural, and disciplined learning environment.
Liliana F Jenkins, Superintendent
David Mendoza, Business Administrator

2099 American Cooperative School
Calle 10 y Pasaje Kantutas, Calacot
c/o American Embassy, La Paz, Bolivia
La Paz, Bolivia
519-2-792-302
Fax: 591-2-797-218
acs@acslp.org
www.acslp.org
Offers college prepatory North American education that enables our graduates to enter the best universities in the United States, Canada, Europe and Latin America.
Matthew Kirby, Superintendent
Robert Boni, Chair

2100 American Cooperative School of Tunis
6360 Tunis Place
Washington, DC 20521-6360
216-71-760-905
Fax: 216-71-761-412
acst@acst.intl.tn
www.acst.net
Dennis Sheehan, Superintendent

2101 American Embassy School
Department of State/AES
9000 New Delhi Place
Washington, DC 20521-9000
91-11-611-7140
Fax: 91-11-687-3320
aesindia@aes.ac.in
www.serve.com/aesndi
Grade levels Pre-K through 12, school year August - May
Rob Mochrish, PhD, Director

2102 American Embassy School of New Delhi
Chandragupta Marg
Chanakyapuri, New Delhi
India 11002
91-11-611-7140
Fax: 91-11-687-3320
aesindia@del2.vsnl.net.in
aes.ac.in
Serves students from the United States and other nations. It provides a quality American education that enables students to be inspired learners and responsible global citizens through the collaboration of a dedicated faculty and a supportive community.
Dr Robert Hetzel, Director
Linda McGinnis, Secretary, AES School Board

2103 American International School of Nouakchott
DOS/Administrative Officer
2430 Nouakchott Place
Washington, DC 20521-2430
222-2-52967
Fax: 222-2-52967
aisnsahara@yahoo.com
www.aisn.mr
At the American International School of Nouakchott, a partnership of educators and parents is committed to providing our culturally diverse students a safe, nurturing and respectful learning environment. We promote academic achievement through a curriculum founded on an American educational philosophy.
Sharon Orlins PhD, Director

2104 American International School-Abuja
DOS/Administrative Officer
8300 Abuja Place
Washington, DC 20521-8300
234-9-413-4464
Fax: 234-9-413-4464
info@aisabuja.com
www.aisabuja.com
Provide a quality education, utilizing an American curriculum for students of all nationalities from preschool through 12th grade.
Amy Uzoewulu, Director
Peter Williams, Primary Principal

2105 American International School-Bamako
DOS/Administrative Officer
2050 Bamako Place
Washington, DC 20189-2050
223-222-4738
Fax: 223-222-0853
aisb@aisbmali.org
www.aisbmali.org
An independent, coeducational day school which offers an educational program from prekindergarten through grade 10. Supervised study using the University of Nebraska High School correspondence courses for grades 12 may also be arranged.
David Henry, Director
Rob Van Doeselaar, Chairman

2106 American International School-Chennai
100 Feet Road
Taramani
Chennai 00600-113
91-44-499-0881
Fax: 91-44-466-0636
HeadofSchool@aisch.org
www.aisch.org
Embraces international diversity and strives to provide an academically challenging environment in order to foster intellectual curiosity and a sense of responsibility in our students. To fully educate the whole person, we are committed to cultivating lifelong learners and balanced, service-oriented citizens, who are thereby prepared to positively contribute in a globally competitive world.
Barry Clough, Head of School
Dr James R Fellabaum, High School Principal

2107 American International School-Costa Rica
Interlink 249
PO Box 02-5635
Miami, FL 33102
506-229-3256
Fax: 506-223-9062
ais@aiscr.com
www.aiscr.com
A private, non-profit school that was founded in 1970 under the name of Costa Rica Academy. AIS serves approximately 200 students from pre-school through 12th grade.
Austin Briggs Jr, Headmaster
Neli Santiago, Principal

2108 American International School-Freetown
Department of State/MGT
2160 Freetown Place
Washington, DC 20521-2160
232-22-232-480
Fax: 232-22-225-471
aisfinfo@yahoo.com
www.aisfreetown.websiteanimal.com
A private, non-profit, PreK-8th grade school providing an American curriculum to a multinational community in Freetown, Sierra Leone.
Ndye Njie, Director
Nielette Gordon, Administrative Assistant

2109 American International School-Kingston
1a Olivier Road
Kingston 8
Jamaica
876-977-3625
Fax: 876-977-3625
aiskoff@cwjamaica.com
www.aisk.com
A non-profit, non-sectarian, private day school funded by tuition income receiving small annual grants from the U.S. Government through it Office of Overseas Schools.
Sean Goudie, Director
Anna Wallace, Lower School Coordinator

2110 American International School-Lesotho
DOS/Administrative Officer
2340 Maseru Place
Washington, DC 20521-2340
266-322-987
Fax: 266-311-963
aisl@lesoff.co.za
www.aisl.lesoff.co.za
An independent, coeducational day school which offers an American education from preschool through grade 8. The school was founded in 1991 to serve the needs of the American community and other students seeking an English-language education.
Harvey Cohen, Principal

2111 American International School-Libreville
2270 Libreville Place
Washington, DC 20521-2270
241-76-20-03
Fax: 241-74-55-07
aisl@internetgabon.com
www.aisa.or.ke
Paul Sicard, Director

2112 American International School-Lome
DOS/Administrative Officer
2300 Lome Place
Washington, DC 20521-2300
E-mail: aisl@cafe.tg
www.aisa.or.ke
Established in 1967 as a private, coeducational day school offering an educational program to students of all nationalities in pre-kindergarten through grade 8.
Clover Afokpa, Director
Warace Tchamsi, Administrative Assistant

2113 American International School-Lusaka
PO Box 31617
Lusaka
Zambia
260-1-260-509
Fax: 260-1-260-538
SpecialPerson@aislusaka.org
www.aislusaka.org
Committed to being a leading IB World School, offering a balanced, academically rigorous and internationally recognized college preparatory education.
Chris Muller, Director
Shirley Mee, Business Manager

2114 American International School-Mozambique
DOS/Administrative Officer
2330 Maputo Place
Washington, DC 20521-2330
258-1-49-1994
Fax: 258-1-49-0596

aism@aism-moz.com
www.aisa.or.ke

Don Reeser, Director

2115 American International School-N'Djamena
DOS/Administrative Officer
2410 N'Djamena Place
Washington, DC 20521-2410
235-52-2103
Fax: 235-51-5654
aisn@intent.td
www.aisa.or.ke

Gay Mickle, Director

2116 American International School-Nouakchott
2430 Nouakchott Place
Washington, DC 20521-2430
222-2-52967
Fax: 222-2-52967
aisnsahara@yahoo.com
www.aisn.mr
Committed to provide culturally diverse students a safe, nurturing and respectful learning environment and promotes academic achievement through a curriculum founded on an American educational philosophy.

Sharon Orlins PhD, Director

2117 American Nicaraguan School
c/o American Embassy
Unit No 2710 Box 7, APO AA 34021
Washington, DC 20521-3240
505-278-0029
Fax: 505-267-3088
info@ans.edu.ni
www.ans.edu.ni
A private, nonsectarian coeducaitonal day school which offers an educaional program from prekindergarten through grade 12 for students of all nationalities.

Fredy Ramirez, Elementary School Principal
Joseph Azmeh, Secondary Principal

2118 American Samoa Department of Education
Pago Pago
American Samoa 96799
011-684-633-5237
Fax: 011-684-633-5733
www.doe.as
Is to ensure student success by providing high quality teaching and learning opportunities to all our children

Sili K Sataua

2119 American School Honduras
American Embassy Tegucigalpa
Department of State
Washington, DC 20521-3480
504-239-333
Fax: 504-239-6162
admin_assistant@asamadagascar.org
www.amschool.org
A private, coeducational day school which offers an educational program from nursery through grade 12 for students of all nationalities.

James Szoka, Principal

2120 American School of Bombay
SF2, G Block
Bandra-Kurla Complex Road
Bandra (E), Mumbai, 400098
91-22-6772-7272
personnel@asbindia.org
www.asbindia.org
International school in Mumbai with the mission of empowering and developing its students so they can gain the skills and inspiration they need to succeed in their goals. The school is a coeducational independent day school teaching children from Pre-K through Grade 12.

Craig Johnson, Superintendent
Alok Parashar, Chief Operating Officer

2121 American School-Algiers
American Embassy Algiers
Washington, DC 20520-1
202-265-2800
Fax: 202-667-2174

Richard Gillogly, Principal

2122 American School-Antananarivo
2040 Antananarivo Place
Dulles, VA 20189-2040
261-20-22-420-39
Fax: 261-20-22-345-39
miasaadm@gmail.com
www.asamadagascar.org
As the only English language institution in Madagascar offering a K-12 diploma program, we challenge our students to actively engage with the exceptional educational opportunities that are available to them in our school.

Jay Long, Director

2123 American School-Asuncion
Avenida Esapaa 1175
PO Box 10093
Asuncion, Paraguay
595-21-600-476
Fax: 595-21-603-518
asagator@asa.edu.py
www.asa.edu.py
A bilingual learning community of International and Paraguayan families, is to prepare responsible proactive world citizens in a student-centered, caring environment through a college preparatory program that adheres to the highest U.S. and Paraguayan standards of excellence

Dennis Klumpp, Director
David Warken, Elementary Principal

2124 American School-Dschang
Washington, DC 20521-1

Jane French, Principal

2125 American School-Guatemala
11 Calle 1579 Zona 1511 calle 15-79
Guatemala
Guatemala
502-236- 079
Fax: 502-236- 833
director@cag.edu.gt
www.cag.edu.gt
The school's goal is to educate independent, critical-thinking, responsible, bilingual individuals prepared to meet the challenges of the future.

Tracy Berry-Lazo, General Director
Fabio Corvaglia, High School Principal

2126 American School-Niamey
DOS/Administrative Officer
2420 Niamey Place
Dulles, VA 20189-2420
227-723-942
Fax: 227-723-457
asniger@intnet.ne
www.geocities.com/asniamey
A coeducational day school offering an educational program from prekindergarten through grade 9, and 10-12 correspondence.

Deborah M Robinson, Director

2127 American School-Port Gentil
1100 Louisiana Street
Suite 2500
Houston, TX 77002-5215

Keith Marriott, Principal

2128 American School-Tegucigalpa
Coronel Lomas del Guijarro
Avenue Repœblica Dominicana Calle Costa
Tegucigalpa, Honduras
504-239-3333
Fax: 504-239-6162
www.amschool.org
Provides a Student Centered, enriching, college-preparatory education that emphasizes social responsibility in a safe, bicultural, and disciplined learning enviroment

James Shepherd, Principal
Liliana Jerkins, Superintendent

2129 American School-Warsaw
Ul Warszawska 202
Konstancin-Jeziorna
Poland 05520
48-22-651-9611
Fax: 48-22-642-1506
admissions@asw.waw.pl
www.asw.waw.pl
Offers a rigorous, supportive and balanced PK-12 program in English for the international community of Warsaw that is driven by a strong commitment to prepare students for lives as responsible world citizens

Tony Gerlicz, Director
Rebecca Brown, Finance/Operations Director

2130 American School-Yaounde
BP 7475
Yaounde
Cameroon
234-223-0421
Fax: 237-223-6011
school@asoy.org
asoy.org
Ensures that all students achieve high academic success, demonstrate critical thinking skills, and become responsible and compassionate, global citizens prepared for their next stage in life; as gained through an enriched, American curriculum and offered in a challenging, secure, and diverse environment.

Nanci Shaw, School Director

2131 American-Nicaraguan School
Frente al Club Lomas de Monserrat
PO Box 2670, Managua
Nicaragua
505-2-782-565
Fax: 505-2-673-088
elementary@ans.edu.ni
www.ans.edu.ni
Provides its multicultural student community with a US-accredited college preparatory program, based on democratic and universal values, that develops critical thinkers and ethical individuals capable of realizing their leadership potential by making meaningful contributions to society.

Stan Key, Director General
Roberto Cardenal, Director of Finance

2132 Amoco Galeota School
PO Box 4381
Houston, TX 77210-4381

Barbara Punch, Principal

2133 Andersen Elementary & Middle School
Unit 14057
APO, Mariana Islands 96543 4057
Guam
www.extranet.guam.pac.dodea.edu

2134 Anzoategui International School
PO Box 020010, M-42
Jet Cargo International
Miami, FL 33102-10
58-82-22683
Fax: 58-82-22683
aishead@telcel.net.ve
www.anaco.net
Grade levels Pre-K through 12, school year August - June
Jorge Nelson EdD, Superintendent

2135 Armenia QSI International School-Yerevan
DOS/Administrative Officer
7020 Yerevan Place
Washington, DC 20521-7020
374-1-391-030
Fax: 374-1-151-438
qsiy@arminco.com
www.qsi.org
An independent, coeducational day school which offers an educational program from preschool (3-4 years) through grade 12 for students of all nationalities. Enrollment 45.
Arthur W Hudson, Director

2136 Atlanta International School
2890 N Fulton Drive NE
Atlanta, GA 30305-3155
404-841-3840
Fax: 404-841-3873
info@aischool.org
www.aischool.org
Continuing to develop and deserve a worldwide reputation as an exemplary center of teaching and learning, a school that achieves and sets, within the framework of the International Baccalaureate.Maintaining an optimal size composition of faculty and students so that opportunities for individual learning, mutual understanding, and community feeling are maximized.
Robert Brindley, Headmaster
Charlotte Smith, Executive Assistant

2137 Awty International School
7455 Awty School Lane
Houston, TX 77055-7222
713-686-4850
Fax: 713-686-4956
admissions@awty.org
www.awty.org
Grade level prekindergarten through twelfth, with total enrollment of 900 students.
David Watson, Headmaster
John Ransom, Chairman

2138 Azerbaijan Baku International School
Darnagul Qasabasi Street Ajami Nakc
Block 3097
Baku, Azerbaijan 01108
994-12-90-63-52
Fax: 994-12-90-63-51
baku@qsi.org
www.qsi.org
the primary purpose of the school is to meet the needs of the children in Baku who require this type of education with a view to continuing their education in their home countries with a minimum of adjustment problems.
Scott Root, Director
Arthur W Hudson, Director

2139 Baku International School
Darnagul Qasabasi Street Ajami Nakc
Block 3097
Baku, Azerbaijan, AZ 01108
994-12-656352
Fax: 991-12-4105951
baku@qsi.org
www.qsi.org
the primary purpose of the school is to meet the needs of the children in Baku who require this type of education with a view to continuing their education in their home countries with a minimum of adjustment problems.
Scott Root, Director
Arthur W Hudson, Director

2140 Ball Brothers Foundation
222 S Mulberry Street
Muncie, IN 47305
765-741-5500
Fax: 765-741-5518
info@ballfdn.org
www.ballfdn.org
The Foundation's primary focus is Muncie and East Central Indiana.The Foundation has been a philanthropic leader, serving as initiator, convener, and catalyst among donors and nonprofit organizations. Within Muncie, the Foundation seeks to forge active partnerships with effective nonprofit agencies by providing consultation and financial support to promote their success.
Jud Fisher, Executive Director/ COO
John W Fisher, Chairman & President

2141 Banjul American Embassy School
2070 Banjul Place
Dulles, VA 20189-2070
220-495-920
Fax: 220-497-181
baes@qanet.gm
www.baes.gm
The school demonstrates U.S. education abroad to a multi-ethnic, multi-cultural, diverse student body and otherwise increases mutual understanding through its emphasis on an American-based curriculum, use of American textbooks and supplemental materials, and its teaching staff, of whom four are American nationals trained in American universities.
Dianne Zemichael, Director
Leah Moore, Administrative Secretary

2142 Bingham Academy Ethiopia
SIM International
PO Box 4937
Addis Ababa, Ethiopia
East Africa
251-11 -791
Fax: 251-11 -791
director@binghamacademy.net
www.binghamacademy.net
The purpose of Bingham Academy is to provide high quality, culturally sensitive education, within a Christian environment, which challenges each student to impact the world for God's glory.
Murray Overton, Director

2143 Bishkek International School
14A Tynystanova Street
Bishkek
Kyrgyzstan 72005
996-312-66-35-03
Fax: 996-312-66-35-03
bishkek@qsi.org
www.qsi.org
The primary purpose of the school is to meet the needs of the children in Bishkek who require this type of education with a view to continuing their education in their home countries with a minimum of adjustment problems.
MaryKay Gudkova, Director

2144 Bosnia-Herzegovina QSI International School Sarajevo
Omladinska #12
Vogosca-Saravejo
Bosnia & Herzegovina 71320
387-33-434-756
Fax: 387-33-434-756
saravejo@qsi.org
www.qsi.org
The primary purpose of the school is to meet the needs of the expatriate children living in Sarajevo who require this type of education.
Jay Hamric, Director
Arthur W Hudson, Director

2145 Bratislava American International School
American Embassy Bratislava
Karloveska 64
Bratislava
Slovak Republic 842-2
421-7-722-844
Fax: 721-7-722-844
bratislava@qsi.org
www.qsi.sk
The primary purpose of the school is to meet the needs of the children in Bratislava who require this type of education with a view to continuing their education in their home countries with a minimum of adjustment problems.
Ronald Adams, Principal
Matthew Lake, Director

2146 Bulgaria Anglo-American School-Sofia
DOS/Administrative Officer
5740 Sophia Place
Washington, DC 20521-5740
359-2-974-4575
Fax: 359-2-974-4483
aasregist@infotel.bg
www.geocities.com/angloamericanschool
An independent, coeducational day school which offers an educational program from prekindergarten through grade 8 for students of all nationalities. The school year comprises 2 semesters extending from August to December and from January to June. Enrollment 140.
Brian M Garton, Director
Arthur W Hudson, Director

2147 Burma International School Yangon
DOS/Administrative Officer
4250 Rangoon Place
Washington, DC 20521-4250
95-1-512-793/795
Fax: 95-1-525-020
ISYDIRECTOR@mptmail.net.mm
www.internationalschoolyangon.org
Grades PK-12, enrollment 331.
Merry Wade, Director

2148 Burns Family Foundation
410 N Michigan Avenue
Room 1600
Chicago, IL 60611-4213
Offers support in secondary school education, higher education and youth services.

2149 Caribbean American School
5 Gates Court
Cranbury, NJ 08512-2926
509-257-7961
www.isbi.com
Ernestine Rochelle, Principal
Ernestine Roche Robinson, Director

2150 Caribbean-American School
PO Box 407139
Lynx Air
Ft Lauderdale, FL 33340-7139
509-257-7961
www.isbi.com
Grade levels Pre-K through 12, school year September - June

Ernestine Roche Robinson, Director
Ernestine Rochelle, Principal

2151 Chinese American International School
150 Oak Street
San Francisco, CA 94102
415-865-6000
Fax: 415-865-6089
caishead@aol.com
www.cais.org
Educates students for academic excellence, moral character and international perspective through immersion in American and Chinese culture and language.

Andrew W Corcoran, Executive Director

2152 Colegio Albania
PO Box 25573
Miami, FL 33102-5573

Eric Spindler, Principal

2153 Colegio Corazon de Maria
Ferrer y Ferrer-Santiago Igles
San Juan
Puerto Rico

M Cyril Stauss, Principal

2154 Colegio De Parvulos
263 Calle San Sebastian
San Juan 00901-1205
Puerto Rico

Maria Dolores Vice, Principal

2155 Colegio Del Buen Pastor
Camino Alejandrino Km 3.4
Rio Piedras 00927
Puerto Rico
www.colegiobuenpastor.com

Adria M Borges, Principal

2156 Colegio Del Sagrado Corazon
Obispado Final Urb La Alhambra
Ponce 00731
Puerto Rico
556- 14-2
www.sagradocorazon.edu.co

Joan G Dedapena, Principal

2157 Colegio Espiritu Santo
Box 191715 San Juan
Puerto Rico 00019-1715
787-754-0555
Fax: 754-715-
admision@colespiritusanto.com
www.colespiritusanto.com

Carmen Jovet, Principal

2158 Colegio Inmaculada
Carr Militar 2 Km 49.6
Manati 00674
Puerto Rico
www.colegioinmaculada.es

Sor Nichlasa Maderea, Principal

2159 Colegio Inmaculada Concepcion
2 Calle Isabela
Guayanilla 00656-1703
Puerto Rico
www.colegioinmaculada.es

Sor Alejandrina Torres, Principal

2160 Colegio Internacional-Carabobo
VLN 1010
PO Box 025685
Miami, FL 33102-5685
58-41-421-807
Fax: 58-41-426-510
admin@cic-valencia.org.ve
www.cic-valencia.org.ve
To develop young men and women of character through an international college-preparatory program, in English, based on high intellectual and moral standards

Frank Anderson, Superintendent
Joe Walker, Director

2161 Colegio Internacional-Caracas
PAKMAIL 6030
PO Box 025323
Miami, FL 33102-5304
58-2-945-0444
Fax: 58-2-945-0533
cic@cic-caracas.org
www.cic-caracas.org
Colegio Internacional de Caracas is an English-medium, Pre-Nursery to Grade 12 school dedicated to the intellectual and personal development of each student in a caring and supportive environment. CIC offers a challenging program to prepare an international student body to excel in a variety of the world's finest schools and universities.

Alan Benson, Superintendent
Carmen Sweeting, Director of Academics

2162 Colegio Internacional-Puerto La Cruz
11010 NW 30th Street
Suite 104
Miami, FL 33172-5032
58-281-277-6051
Fax: 58-281-274-1134
ciplc@telcel.net.ve
www.ciplc.net
Inspiring students to learn and serve by cultivating each student's full potential as an effective communicator, problem solver, and contributing global citizen.

Mike Martell, Superintendent
Frank Capuccio, Administrative Assistant

2163 Colegio La Inmaculada
1711 Ave Ponce De Leon
San Juan 00909-1905
Puerto Rico
787-754-0555
Fax: 754-715-
www.colegioinmaculada.es

Sor Teresa Del Rio, Principal

2164 Colegio La Milagrosa
107 Calle De Diego
San Juan 00925-3303
Puerto Rico
787-754-0555
Fax: 754-715-
www.colegioinmaculada.es

Maria Flores, Principal

2165 Colegio Lourdes
Box 190847
San Juan, PR 00919-847
787-767-6106
Fax: 787-767-5282
clourdes@coqui.net
www.colegiolourdes.net
Forming strong Christian faith and critical, able to make a commitment within the society and the church that is open to the realities and needs of his time, able to integrate into an attitude of service in a democratic society, as understand and explain the Preamble to the Constitution of Puerto Rico.

Paz Asiain, Director
Thalia Lopez, Principal

2166 Colegio Madre Cabrini
1564 Calle Encarnacion
San Juan 00920-4739
Puerto Rico
787-792-6180
www.madrecabrini.com.b

Anne Marie Gavin, Principal

2167 Colegio Maria Auxiliadora
PO Box 797
Carolina 00986-0797
Puerto Rico
787-792-6181
www.auxiliadora.ne

Leles Rodriguez, Principal

2168 Colegio Marista
Final Santa Ana Alt Torrimar
Guaynabo 00969
Puerto Rico
www.marista.org.br

Hilario Martinez, Principal

2169 Colegio Marista El Salvador
PO Box 462
Manati 00674-0462
Puerto Rico
www.marista.org.br

Hnio Efrain Romo, Principal

2170 Colegio Mater Salvatoris
RR 3 Box 3080
San Juan 00926-9601
Puerto Rico
821- 99- 963
Fax: 821- 99- 973
www.matersalvatoris.org

Maria Luisa Benito, Principal

2171 Colegio Notre Dame Nivel
PO Box 967
Caguas 00726-0967
Puerto Rico

Francisca Suarez, Principal

2172 Colegio Nuestra Senora de La Caridad
PO Box 1164
Caparra Heigh 00920
Puerto Rico
www.colegiosdepr.com

Madre Esperanza Sanchez, Principal

2173 Colegio Nuestra Senora de La Merced
PO Box 4048
San Juan 00936-4048
Puerto Rico
www.colegiolamercedpr.com

Ivette Lopez, Principal

2174 Colegio Nuestra Senora de Lourdes
1050 Demetrio Odaly-Country Club
Rio Piedras 00924
Puerto Rico

Rita Manzano, Principal

2175 Colegio Nuestra Senora de Valvanera
53 Calle Jose I Quinton # 53
Coamo 00769-3108
Puerto Rico

Cruz Victor Colon, Principal

2176 Colegio Nuestra Senora del Carmen
RR 2, Box 9KK, Carr Trujillo Alt
Rio Piedras 00721
Puerto Rico
Candida Arrieta, Principal

2177 Colegio Nuestra Senora del Pilar
PO Box 387
Canovanas 00729-0387
Puerto Rico
Sor Leonilda Mallo, Principal

2178 Colegio Nuestra Senora del Rosario
Aa7 Calle 5
Bayamon 00959-3719
Puerto Rico
341-425-9781
www.maristasrosario.com
Theresita Miranda, Principal

2179 Colegio Nuestra Sra del Rosario
PO Box 1334
Ciales 00638-0414
Puerto Rico
787-871-1318
Fax: 787-871-5797
www.maristasrosario.com
Parrochial School - Prekindergarten to 9th grade.
Angel Mendoza, Principal
Padre Gabriel M Jorres, Director

2180 Colegio Padre Berrios
PO Box 7717
San Juan 00916-7717
Puerto Rico
www.colegiopadreberrios.webs.com
Sor Enedina Santos, Principal

2181 Colegio Parroquial San Jose
PO Box 7718
San Juan 00916-7718
Puerto Rico 00644
www.colegiopadreberrios.webs.com
Sor Enedina Santos, Principal

2182 Colegio Ponceno
PO Box 7718
San Juan 00916-7718
Puerto Rico 00644
809-848-2525
www.colegiopadreberrios.webs.com
Sor Enedina Santos, Principal

2183 Colegio Reina de Los Angeles
M-19 Calle Frontera
San Juan, PR 00926
787-761-7455
Fax: 787-761-7440
info@reinaangeles.org
www.reinaangeles.org
Train Students education with a focus on physical, moral, intellectual, religious and social development within a framework of faith.
Victorina Ortega, Principal
Juana F Gomez, Director

2184 Colegio Rosa Bell
Calle Oviedo Number 42
Torrimar-Guaynabo, PR 00966
787-781-4240
Fax: 787-792-5415
exalumno@rosabell.com
rosabell.wordpress.com
The purpose of a good education is to maximize the capabilities of the individual: intellectually, socially, emotionally and physically.
Rose Rodriquez, Director
Miguel Arzola-Barris, Executive Director

2185 Colegio Sacred Heart
Palma Real Urb, Univ Gardens
San Juan 00927
Puerto Rico
Paul Marie, CSB, Principal

2186 Colegio Sagrada Familia
7 Hostos
Ponce
Puerto Rico 00731
www.safa.edu.uy
Sor Pilar Becerra, Principal

2187 Colegio Sagrados Corazones
A Esmeralda Urb, Ponce De Leon
Guaynabo 00969
Puerto Rico
home.coqui.net/sagrado
Ana Arce de Marrer, Principal

2188 Colegio San Agustin
PO Box 4263
Bayamon 00958-1263
Puerto Rico
csa.edu.ph
Georgina Ortiz, Principal

2189 Colegio San Antonio
PO Box 21350
San Juan 00928-1350
Puerto Rico
809-764-0090
www.colegio-san-antonio.org
Rev. Paul S Brodie, Principal

2190 Colegio San Antonio Abad
PO Box 729
Humacao 00792-0729
Puerto Rico
809-764-0090
www.colegio-san-antonio.org
Padre Eduardo Torrella, Principal

2191 Colegio San Benito
PO Box 728
Humacao 00792-0728
Puerto Rico
www.csb.cl
Hermana Carmen Davila, Principal

2192 Colegio San Conrado (K-12)
PO Box 7111
Ponce 00732-7111
Puerto Rico
Fax: 787-841-7303
sanconrado@pucpr.edu
Sister Nildred Rodriguez, Principal
Sister Wilma de Echevarria, Assistant Principal

2193 Colegio San Felipe
566 Ave San Luis # 673
Arecibo 00612-3600
Puerto Rico
809-878-3532
www.colegiosanfelipe.edu.mx
Veronica Oravec, Principal

2194 Colegio San Francisco De Asis
PO Box 789
Barranquitas
Puerto Rico 00794
787-857-2123
Fax: 787-857-2123
info@csfabarranquitas.com
www.csfabarranquitas.com
Founded in August 7, 1985
Hermana Maria Carbonell, Principal
Carlos Colon-Bernadi, Director

2195 Colegio San Gabriel
Gpo Box 347
San Juan 00936
Puerto Rico
www.sangabriel.cl
Sor Antonia Garatachea, Principal

2196 Colegio San Ignacio de Loyola
Urb Santa Mar a, 1940 Calle Saœco
San Juan
Puerto Rico 00927
787-765-3814
Fax: 787-758-4145
www.sanignacio.org
Dr Luis O Pino, Principal
Mario Alberto Torres, President

2197 Colegio San Jose
PO Box 21300
San Juan
Puerto Rico 00928-1300
787-751-8177
Fax: 787-767-7146
sanjose@csj-rpi.org
www.csj-rpi.org
Bro Francisco T Gonzalez, Principal
Sra Elaine Torrens, Vice Principal

2198 Colegio San Juan Bautista
PO Box E
Orocovis 00720
Puerto Rico
787-751-8177
Fax: 787-767-7146
www.colegiosanjuanbautista.com
Sor Maria Antonia Miya, Principal

2199 Colegio San Juan Bosco
PO Box 14367
San Juan 00916-4367
Puerto Rico
www.sanjuanboscosalamanca.eu
Rev. P Jose Luis Gomez, Principal

2200 Colegio San Luis Rey
43 Final SE, Urb Reparto Metro
San Juan 00921
Puerto Rico
Rosario Maria, Principal

2201 Colegio San Miguel
GPO Box 1714
San Juan 00936
Puerto Rico
www.sanluisrey.edu.co
Elvira Gonzalez, Principal

2202 Colegio San Rafael
PO Box 301
Quebradillas 00678-0301
Puerto Rico
www.maristas.com.a

2203 Colegio San Vicente Ferrer
PO Box 455
Catano 00963-0455
Puerto Rico
Maria Soledad Colon, Principal

2204 Colegio San Vicente de Paul
Calle Bolivar 709, Parada 24
San Juan
Puerto Rico 00909

787-727-4273
Fax: 787-728-2263
www.csvp-sj.org
Dra Isabel C Machado, Principal
P Evaristo Oliveras, Director

2205 Colegio Santa Clara
Via 14-2JL-456 Villa Fontana
Carolina 00983
Puerto Rico
www.colegiostaclara.com
Elsie Mujica, Principal

2206 Colegio Santa Cruz
PO Box 235
Trujillo Alto 00977-0235
Puerto Rico
113-024-5197
www.santacruz.g12.br
Maria Ramon Santiago, Principal

2207 Colegio Santa Gema
PO Box 1705
Carolina 00984-1705
Puerto Rico
491-711-5093
www.colegio-santagema.es
Lilia Luna De Anaya, Principal

2208 Colegio Santa Rita
Calle 9, Apartado 1557
Bayamon 00958
Puerto Rico
www.colegiosantarita.com.br
Elba N Villalba, Principal

2209 Colegio Santa Rosa
Calle Marti, 15 Esquina Maceo
Bayamon 00961
Puerto Rico
www.colegiosantarosa-pa.com.br
Ana Josefa Colon, Principal

2210 Colegio Santa Teresita
342 Victoria
Ponce 00731
Puerto Rico
015-278-1202
www.santateresita.edu.pe
Mary Terence, Principal

2211 Colegio Santiago Apostol
Calle 23 Bloque 23 #17, Urb Sierra
Bayamon
Puerto Rico 00961
787-786- 917
Fax: 787-269-3965
colegiosantiagoapostol@onlinkpr.net
www.colegiosantiagoapostol.net
Hilda Velazquez, Principal

2212 Colegio Santisimo Rosario
PO Box 26
Yauco 00698-0026
Puerto Rico
Judith Negron, Principal

2213 Colegio Santo Domingo
192 Calle Comerio
Bayamon 00959-5358
Puerto Rico
www.colegiosantodomingo.edu.do
Pura Huyke, Principal

2214 Colegio Santo Nino de Praga
PO Box 25
Penuelas 00624-0025
Puerto Rico
Aminta Santos, Principal

2215 Colegio Santos Angeles Custod
3 Sicilia Urb, San Jose
San Juan 00923
Puerto Rico
www.angelescustodios.com
Roberto Rivera, Principal

2216 Colegio de La Salle
PO Box 518
Bayamon 00960-0518
Puerto Rico
www.colsalle.edu.co
Wilfredo Perez De, Principal

2217 Commandant Gade Special Education School
St. Thomas, Virgin Islands 00801
Miss Jeanne Richards, Principal

2218 Community United Methodist School
PO Box 681
Frederiksted 00841-0681
Virgin Islands
Marva Oneal, Principal

2219 Country Day
RR 1 Box 6199
Kingshill, VI 00850
340-778-1974
Fax: 340-779-3331
bsinfield@stxcountryday.com
www.stxcountryday.com
An independent, multicultural, college preparatory educational community set on a 34-acre tropical campus.
William Sinfield, Headmaster
Mariska Nurse, Dean of Guidance

2220 Croatia American International School-Zagreb
Vocarska 106
10 000 Zagreb
Croatia-5080
385-1-4680-133
Fax: 385-1-4680-171
asz@asz.hr
www.aisz.hr
Grades K-8, enrollment 112.
Robin Heslip, Director

2221 Dallas International School
6039 Churchill Way
Dallas, TX 75230
972-991-6379
Fax: 972-991-6608
rwkdis@metronet.com
www.dallasinternationalschool.org
DIS students will have the skills to continue their studies at universities in the United States or abroad and launch a professional career which will take advantage of all the opportunities created by globalization
Mea Ahlberg, Director of Admissions
MylSne Dumont, Middle School Coordinator

2222 Dominican Child Development Center
PO Box 5668
Agana
Guam 96910
617-477-7228
Fax: 671-472-4782
Kindergarten and nursery school.
Lednor Flores, Principal

2223 Dorado Academy
Urb Dorado del Mar Calle Madre Perl
Dorado
Puerto Rico 00646
787-796-2180
Fax: 787-796-7398
mescabi@doradoacademy.org
www.doradoacademy.org
Its objective is to provide to all students an education that reflects the school's philosophy. The teachers strive to implement by instruction the school's philosophy and meet instructional goals and objectives.
Liutma Caballero, Principal
Nancy Escabi, Headmaster

2224 Dwight School
291 Central Park W
New York, NY 10024
212-724-7524
Fax: 212-724-2539
admissions@dwight.edu
www.dwight.edu
Dwight's rigorous IB program and world-class faculty prepare a future generation of well-educated and ethical global leaders who will seek to create an environment of equality and respect for all human beings.
Marina Bernstein, Director Admissions
Alyson Waldman, Associate Director

2225 Educare
4235 Reserve Road
Unit 202
Lexington, KY 40514
859-396-7087
Fax: 859-201-1064
mnaidu@educare.org
www.educare.org
To inspire children to achieve their very best; to educate children in character and leadership by drawing out their hidden character traits and leadership qualities.
Sara Connell, Principal

2226 Episcopal Cathedral School
PO Box 13305
Santurce
Puerto Rico 00908-3305
787-721-5478
Fax: 787-724-6668
esc@gocougars.com
www.gocougars.com
Founded in 1946.
Gary J DeHope, Director

2227 Escole Tout Petit
PO Box 1248
San Juan 00902
Puerto Rico
Vivian Aviles, Principal

2228 Escuela Beata Imelda
PO Box 804
Guanica 00653-0804
Puerto Rico
P Salvador Barber, Principal

2229 Escuela Bella Vista
Avenido Cecilio Acosta Calle 67 Ent
Maracaibo
Venezuela
58-61-966-696
Fax: 58-61-969-417
ebvnet@ebv.org.ve
www.ebv.org.ve
At EBV we offer an internationally enriched accredited U.S. program that prepares our students to participate actively, independently, cooperatively, and effectively in a multicultural, multilin-

gual world. It is our commitment to educate each student to his/her maximum potential.

Steve Sibley, Superintendent
Todd Zukewich, High School Principal

2230 Escuela Campo Alegre
8424 NW 56th Street
Suite CCS 00007
Miami, FL 33166
58-2-993-3230
Fax: 58-2-993-0219
info@eca.com.ve
www.eca.com.ve
ECA seeks to inspire its students toward the highest standards and expectations through a stimulating and comprehensive program of intellectual and personal development.

Bambi Betts, Director
Phil Redwine, Principal

2231 Escuela Campo Alegre-Venezuela
8424 NW 56th Street
Suite CCS00007
Miami, FL 33166
58-2-993-7135
Fax: 58-2-993-0219
info@eca.com.ve
www.eca.com.ve
A private, coeducational day school offering a program for students from prekindergarten through grade 12.

Phil Redwine, Principal

2232 Escuela Caribe Vista School
8424 NW 56th Street
Suite CCS00007
Miami, FL 33166
765-668-4009
info@eca.com.ve
www.eca.com.ve

Phil Redwine, Principal

2233 Escuela Las Morochas
Apartado Postal # 235
Ciudad Ojeda, Estado Zulia
Venezuela
58-265-6315-539
Fax: 58-265-6315-539
jtrudeau@escuelalasmorochas.com
www.escuela-lasmorochas.com
Escuela Las Morochas is an English medium international school that offers a challenging U.S. education that encourages students to be life-long learners and responsible global citizens.

Jeff Trudeau, Director
Zulay Marcano, Assistant Secretary

2234 Escuela Nuestra Senora Del Carmen
PO Box 116, Playa De Ponce
Ponce 00731
Puerto Rico 00731
266-282-
Fax: 266-253-
www.colegionuestrasradelcarmen.edu

Paquita Alvarado, Principal

2235 Escuela Superior Catolica
PO Box 4245
Bayamon 00958-1245
Puerto Rico

Eledis Diaz, Principal

2236 Evangelical School for the Deaf
HC-01 Buzon 7111
Luquillo
Puerto Rico 00773-9602
787-889-3488
866-928-2836
esdluquillo@gmail.com
www.esdluquillo.com
We believe that it is the obligation of the saved to witness by life and by words to the truths of Scripture, and to seek to proclaim the Gospel to all mankind.

Pamela Eadie, Principal
Hector Saroza, President

2237 Fajardo Academy
55 Calle Federico Garcia
PO Box 1146, Fajardo 00648
Puerto Rico
809-863-1001
fajardoacademy.org

Miguel A Rivera, BA, MA, MEd, Principal

2238 Freewill Baptist School
PO Box 6265
Christiansted 00823-6265
Virgin Islands
www.freewillschool.com

Joe Postlewaite, Principal

2239 French-American International School
150 Oak Street
San Francisco, CA 94102
415-558-2000
Fax: 415-558-2024
fais@fais-ihs.org
www.fais-ihs.org
Grade levels preK-12, with total student enrollment of 813.

Jane Camblin, Head of School

2240 George D Robinson School
5 Nairn Condado
Santurce 00907
Puerto Rico
845-344-2292
www.orangeahrc.org

Daniel W Sheehan, Principal

2241 Georgetown American School
3170 Georgetown Place
Washington, DC 20521-3170
592-225-1595
Fax: 592-226-1459
admin@amschoolguyana.net
www.geocities.com/Athens/Atlantis/6811

Thurston Riehl, Director

2242 Georgia QSI International School-Tbilisi
Village Zurgovani
Tbilisi
Republic of Georgia
995-32-982909
Fax: 995-32-322-607
tbilisi@qsi.org
www.qsi.org
A private non-profit organization, organizes and operates schools of excellence, identifies quality educators for these schools, and provides educational consulting services

Scott D'Alterio, Director
David Pera, Director Instruction

2243 Glynn Christian School
Club 6, Christian Hill
St Croix, Kingshill 00851
Virgin Islands
340-778-1932
www.virginislandsdailynews.com

Muriel Francis, Principal

2244 Good Hope School-St. Croix
Estate Good Hope Frederiksted
St Croix 00840
Virgin Islands
340-778-1932
www.virginislandsdailynews.com

Tanya L Nichols, Principal

2245 Good Shepherd School
PO Box 1069
St Croix, Kingshill 00851
Virgin Islands 00851
340-772-2280
Fax: 340-772-1021
www.virginislandsdailynews.com

Mary Ellen Mcencil, Director
Susan P Eversley, Assistant Director

2246 Grace Baptist Academy
7815 Shallowford Road
Chattanooga, TN 37421
423-892-8223
Fax: 423-892-1194
jmccurdy@gracechatt.org
www.gracechatt.org

Helen Yasper, Principal

2247 Guam Adventist Academy
1200 Aguilar Road
Yoa
Guam 96915
617-789-1515
Fax: 617-789-3547
Office@GAAsda.org
www.gaasda.org
Learn about God and His character through Bible study, aided by the study of nature and E.G. White's writings. Develop a personal friendship with Jesus Christ

John N Youngberg, Principal
Dori Talon, Accountant

2248 Guam Department of Education
PSC 455 Box 192
FPO, Mariana Islands 96540 1192
Guam 96915-1054
011-671-475-0457
Fax: 011-671-472-5003
www.gdoe.net
Develop a personal friendship with Jesus Christ

Rosie R Tainatongo, Director

2249 Guam High School
PSC 455 Box 192
FPO, Mariana Islands 96540 1192
Guam 96915-1054
671-475-0462
Fax: 671-472-5003
www.gdoe.net

Rosie R Tainatongo, Director

2250 Guam S Elementary & Middle School
PSC 455 Box 192
FPO, Mariana Islands 96540 1192
Guam 96915-1054
671-475-0462
Fax: 671-472-5003
www.gdoe.net

Rosie R Tainatongo, Director

2251 Guamani School
PO Box 3000
Guayama
Puerto Rico 00785
787-864-6880
Fax: 787-866-4947
edelgado@guamani.com
www.guamani.com
A private non-profit, co-educational, non-sectarian school committed in offering an English-based academic college preparatory program geared in preparing students to

become knowledgeable and responsible individuals for today's changing society.

Eduardo Delgado, Director
Pedro A Dominguez, Administrator

2252 Harvest Christian Academy
PO Box 23189
Barrigada
Guam 96921
671-477-6341
Fax: 671-477-7136
www.harvestministries.net
Harvest Christian Academy is a K-12th grade school. It is a ministry of Harvest Baptist Church.

John McGraw, Principal

2253 Hogar Colegio La Milagrosa
Ave Cotto 987 Barrio Cotto
Arecibo 00612
Puerto Rico 00612
787-878-0341
www.hogarcolegiolamilagrosa.com

Sor Trinidad Ibizarry, Principal

2254 India American Embassy School-New Delhi
Chandragupta Marg Chanakyapuri
New Delhi
India 11002
91-11-611-7140
Fax: 91-11-687-3320
aesindia@aes.ac.in
aes.ac.in
The American Embassy School serves students from the United States and other nations. It provides a quality American education that enables students to be inspired learners and responsible global citizens through the collaboration of a dedicated faculty and a supportive community.

Bob Hetzel, Director

2255 Inter-American Academy
Suite 8227
6964 NW 50th Street
Miami, FL 33166-5632
593-4-871-790
Fax: 593-4-873-358
bgoforth@acig.k12.ec
www.acig.k12.ec

Dr. Bruce Goforth, Executive Director

2256 International Community School-Abidjan
DOS/Administrative Officer
2010 Abidjan Place
Washington, DC 20521-2010
225-22-47-11-52
Fax: 225-22-47-19-96
rmockrish@icsa.ac.ci
www.icsa.ac.ci
American style curriculum from kindergarten through grade 12 for children of all nationalities.

Rob Mockrish, Director

2257 International High School-Yangon
4250 Rangoon Place
Department of State
Washington, DC 20521-4250
95-1-512-793
Fax: 95-1-525-020
isydirector@mptmail.net.mm
www.internationalschoolyangon.org

Merry Wade, Director

2258 International School of Port-of-Spain
#POS 1369 1601 NW 97th Avenue
PO Box 025307
Miami, FL 33102-5307
868-632-4591
Fax: 868-632-4595
elarson@isps.edu.tt
www.isps.edu.tt
ISPS will provide an outstanding educational programme for both international and resident families who want their children to pursue higher education.

Eric Larson, Director
John Horsfall, High School Principal

2259 International School-Conakry
2110 Conakry Place
Washington, DC 20521-2110
224-12-661-535
Fax: 224-41-15-22
isc@biasy.net
www.iscguinea.org
A private, coeducational school offering an educational program from pre-kindergarten through grade 12 for children from expatriate and host country families. Develop pupils' academic knowledge; learning, thinking, social, and communication skills; international attitudes; and appreciation for cultural diversity.

Greg Hughes, Director
Robert Merritt, Management Officer

2260 International School-Dakar
BP 5136
Dakar
Senegal
221-033- 250
Fax: 221-033- 250
admin_isd@orange.sn
www.isd.sn
An independent English-medium international school, which offers, in a nurturing environment, a rigorous, US-based, PK-12 curriculum enriched to reflect the needs and diversity of its international student body and faculty.

Wayne Rutherford, Director

2261 International School-Grenada
Washington, DC 20521-1
www.international-schoolfriends.com

Mary Delaney Dunn, Principal

2262 International School-Havana
Department of State
18 Street, 315 and 5th Avenue
Miramar, Havana City
Cuba 10600
053- 02- 281
Fax: 530-020-2740
office@ish.co.cu
www.ishav.org
The school offer high quality education to the children of the expatriate community in Cuba. Serves and can admit students who have a foreign (non-Cuban) citizenship, and are temporarily living in Cuba with their parent(s) or guardian(s), and as such form part of the diplomatic or expatriate non-diplomatic community in the country.

Ian Morris, Principal
Richard Fluit, Head, Secondary School

2263 International School-Islamabad
H-9/1, PO Box 1124
Islamabad
Pakistan 44000
92-51-434-950
Fax: 92-51-440-193
school@isoi.edu.pk
www.isoi.edu.pk
Offers an American- based curriculum to students of over 29 nationalities.

Rose C Puffer, Superintendent

2264 International School-Ouagadougou
s/c Ambassade des, Etats Unis
01 BP35, Ouagadougou
Burkina Faso
226-36-21-43
Fax: 226-36-22-28
iso@iso.bf
www.iso.bf
ISO strives to cultivate a student's intellect and character in an English-speaking environment, offering strong academic programs and promoting cultural understanding.

Larry Ethier, Director
Kim Overton, Curriculum Coordinator

2265 International School-Port of Spain
1601 NW 97th Avenue
PO Box 025307
Miami, FL 33102-5307
868-633-4777
Fax: 868-632-4595
elarson@isps.edu.tt
www.isps.edu.tt
Provides a college preparatory, holistic education for children in grades pre-kindergarten through grade 12, providing them with the skills, knowledge, and values necessary to be productive individuals in an interdependent world.

Eric Larson, Director
Jackie Fung-Kee-Fung, Admission Director/PR

2266 International School-Sfax
Brit Gas 1100 Louisiana
Houston, TX 77002

Sidney Norris, Principal

2267 International School-Yangon
20 Shwe Taungyar
Bahan Township, Yangon
Myanmar-1
512-93 -
Fax: 95 - 52-020
director@isy.net.mm
www.isy.net.mm
We inspire students with a challenging, international education, based on an American curriculum, in a nurturing learning environment that promotes respondibility and respect. We aim to develop socially engaged, self-motivated, creative, compassionate individuals who will be a force for positive change in their communities and the world.

DJ Condon, Middle/High School Principal
Dennis MacKinnon, Director

2268 Izmir American Institute
Friends-850 Third Avenue
18th Floor
New York, NY 10022
232-355-0555
www.aci.k12.tr

Richard Curtis, Principal

2269 John F Kennedy School-Queretaro
Sabinos #272, Jurica
Queretaro
Mexico 76100
442-218-0075
Fax: 442-218-1784
admissions@jfk.edu.mx
www.jfk.edu.mx
The American School of Queretaro, is to provide the whole individual an opportunity for high quality U.S. type, bilingual education that recognizes

individual talents and encourages lifelong learning

Dr. Francisco Galicia, Principal
Mirtha Stappung, General Director

2270 Jordan American Community School
PO Box 310, Dahiat Al-Amir Rashid
Amman 11831
Jordan
962-6-581-3944
Fax: 962-6-582-3357
school@acsamman.edu.jo
www.acsamman.edu.jo
ACS is fully accredited K-12 by the Middle States Association of Colleges and Schools and is a member in good standing of NESA, the Near East South Asia Association of Overseas Schools

Dr. Gray Duckett, Superintendent

2271 Karachi American Society School
American Consulate General Karachi
610 Karachi Place
Washington, DC 20521-6150
92-21-453-909619
Fax: 92-21-453-7305
www.kas.edu.pk

David Holmer, Principal

2272 Kongeus Grade School
44-46 Gade
St Thomas 00802
Virgin Islands 00802

Veronica Miller, Principal

2273 Lincoln International School-Kampala
Co of State
Washington, DC 20521-1

Margaret Bell, Principal

2274 Lincoln School
Lincoln School 565-20
PO Box 025331
Miami, FL 33102-5331
506-224- 660
Fax: 506-224- 670
director@ns.lincoln.ed.cr
www.lincoln.ed.cr
offer an integrated education, using English as the primary language of instruction, to motivate a continuing search for excellence and stimulate students to fully develop their potential to become responsible, enterprising, creative, open-minded citizens with solid ethical values, committed to democracy, and capable of being successful in a multicultural, global society.

Charles Prince, Principal

2275 Lincoln-Marti Schools
2700 SW 8 Street
Miami, FL 33135
305-643-4888
877-874-1999
Fax: 305-649-2767
info@lincoln-marti.com
www.lincolnmarti.com
Lincoln-Mart is an institution dedicated to educating the future of our community, both academically and socially.

Demitrio Perez, President

2276 Little People's Learning Center
9605 SE 7th Street
Vancouver, WA 98664
360-892-7570
info@lplc.net
www.lplc.net/home.html

Daphne Maynard, Principal
Becky Dolan, Director

2277 Little School House
47 Kongens Gade
St Thomas 00802
Virgin Islands
416-303-7282
www.littleschoolhouse.ca

Carol Struiell, Principal

2278 Luanda International School
Rua da Talatona Caixa 1566
Barrio da Talatona Luanda Sul Samba
Republica de Angola
244-2-44-3416
Fax: 244-2-44-3416
officesec@lisluanda.com
www.lisluanda.com
offers a balanced, academically challenging, English language education to the international community of Luanda, designed to develop individuals who are both independent learners and international citizens.

Anthony Baron, Director
Di Atkinson, Senior Administrator

2279 Lutheran Parish School
#1 Lille Taarne Gade
Charlotte Aml 00802
Puerto Rico 00802

Nancy Gotwalt, Principal

2280 Manor School
236 La Grande Princesse
Christiansted, VI 00820-4449
340-718-1448
Fax: 340-718-3651
jgadd@manorschoolstx.com
www.manorschoolstx.com
is dedicated to personal and academic growth in an extended-family environment. We promote academic confidence, creativity, community involvement and citizenship, a sense of respon-sibility, and positive decision-making. We strive to ensure that our graduates are person-ally and academically prepared to succeed in their future endeavors.

Judith C Gadd, Headmistress
Hanley Hamed, Office Manager

2281 Maranatha Christian Academy
9201 75th Avenue N
Brooklyn Park, MN 55428
612- 58- 285
Fax: 763-315-7294
info@mca.lwcc.org
www.maranathachristianacademy.org
is to offer a pre-kindergarten through 12th grade traditional classroom education providing a quality educational experience, which encourages and enables students to mature spiritually, intellectually, physically, emotionally, and socially in accordanc

Rev. Gary Sprunger, Principal
Brian Sullivan, Chief Administrator

2282 Martin De Porress Academy
621 Elmont Road
Elmont, NY 11003
516-502-2840
Fax: 516-502-2841
sfagin@mdp.org
www.mdp.org/
The Martin De Porress Academy program provides academic instruction based upon the NY State Learning Standards as well as hands on experiences in business enterprises, performing arts, home improvement skills, life skills, culinary arts, maintenance services and community services.

Raymond R Blixt, Executive Director
Philip E Chance, Assistant Executive Director

2283 Montessori House of Children
572 Dunholme Way
Suite 103
Sunnyvale, CA 94086
408-749-1602
www.sunnyvalemontessori.com
Our program is based on the premise that every child is an individual with his own needs and abilities. All children need affection and friendliness. They require affirmation, encouragement and understanding

William Myers, Principal
Priya Medelberg, Founder-Director

2284 Moravian School
4313 Green Pond Road
Bethlehem
Virgin Islands
610-868-4744
www.moravianacademy.org
This Moravian affiliated school offers a curriculum based in English for 200 day students (96 boys; 104 girls), in grades K-6. The school is willing to participate in a teacher exchange program, with the length of stay being one year, with housing provided. Applications include science, Spanish and computer skills.

Condon L Joseph, Principal

2285 Morrocoy International
MUN 4051
PO Box 025352
Miami, FL 33102-5352
58-286-9520016
Fax: 58-286-9521861
kempenich@telcel.net.ve
www.geocities.com/minaspov
Grade levels Pre-K through 10, school year August - June

Michael Kempenich, Headmaster

2286 Mount Carmel Elementary School
PO Box 7830
Agat 96928 0830
Guam-b830
256-852-7187
Fax: 256-852-0039
www.vrml.k12.la.us/mc
This Catholic school offers an English (primary) curriculum for 206 day students (100 boys; 106 girls), in Kinder 4 - 8th grade. Overseas teachers are accepted, with the length of stay being one year. Applications needed to teach include reading, English and counseling/counselor.

Bernadette Quintanilla, Sr, SSND, Principal
Augustin Gumataotao, Administrator

2287 Nazarene Christian School
385 Hazel Mill Road
Asheville, NC 28806
828-252-9713
ncsoffice@ashevillefirstnazarene.org
www.ashevillefirstnazarene.org
The Nazarene International Center provides support services to more than 1.2 million members worshiping in more than 11,800 churches in the United States, Canada, and 135 other world areas

Peggy Neighbors, Administrator

2288 Nepal Lincoln School
Kathmandu (LS)
Department of State
Washington, DC 20521-6190

977-1-270-482
Fax: 977-1-272-685
info@lsnepal.com.np
www.lsnepal.com
Lincoln School is an independent, international school in Kathmandu, Nepal with an American Curriculum. We are committed to nurture of the individual student, excellence in all spheres of achievement, pursuit of personal responsibility, appreciation of diversity, and love of learning
Allan Bredy, Director
Craig Baker, Principal

2289 Northern Mariana Islands Department of Education
PO Box 501370 CK
Siapan, MP 96950
011-670-664-3720
Fax: 011-670-664-3798
www.cnmipss.org
Rita Hocog Inos, Commissioner

2290 Notre Dame High School
480 S San Miguel Street
Talofofo
Guam 96930-4699
671-789-1676
www.ndhs.org
Notre Dame is a co-educational, year-round high school run by the School Sisters of Notre Dame. This Roman Catholic affiliated school offers a curriculum in English for 191 day students and 9 boarding (32 boys; 168 girls), in grades 9-12. Student/teacher ratio is 10:1, and the applications needed to teach include science, math, social sciences, and English.
Regina Paulino, SSND, Principal

2291 Nuestra Senora de La Altagracia
672 Calle Felipe Gutierrez #672
San Juan 00924-2225
Puerto Rico

2292 Nuestra Senora de La Providencia
PO Box 11610
San Juan 00922-1610
Puerto Rico

2293 Okinawa Christian School
1835 Zakimi
Yomitan, Okinawa
Japan 904-0
098-958-3000
Fax: 098-958-6279
info@ocsi.org
www.ocsi.org
A non-denominational mission whose purpose is to partner with families of the international community of Okinawa by offering an excellent Christian education in the English language.
Paul Gieschen, Principal

2294 Open Classroom
PO Box 4046
St Thomas 00803
Virgin Islands 00803
805-904-5931
805-289-1817
Fax: 852- 54- 133
www.openclassroom.stanford.edu
Janie Lang, Principal

2295 Osaka International School
4-16 Onohar Nishi 4-Chome
Mino, Osaki, 562-0032
Japan
072-727-5050
Fax: 072-727-5055
addmissions@senri.ed.jp
www.senri.ed.jp
OIS is an english-language-based, preK-12 grade coeducational college-preparatory school.
John Searle, Head of School

2296 Palache Bilingual School
PO Box 1832
Arecibo 00613-1832
Puerto Rico
Rev. David Valez, Principal

2297 Peace Corp
1111 20th Street NW
Washington, DC 20526
202-692-1470
800-424-8580
Fax: 202-692-1897
psa@peacecorps.gov
www.peacecorps.gov
Helping the people of interested countries in meeting their need for trained men and women. Helping promote a better understanding of Americans on the part of the peoples served

2298 Pine Peace School
PO Box 1657
St John, VI 00831
340-776-6595
pinepeace@viaccess.net
www.pinepeaceschool.k12.vi
An independent, non-profit, English language school that serves students without regard to sex, race, religion, or nationality.
Beth Knight, Headmistress

2299 Ponce Baptist Academy
72 Calle 1 Belgica
Ponce 00731
Puerto Rico
Vivian Medina, Principal

2300 Prophecy Elementary School
PO Box 10497
APO St Thomas 00801-3497
Virgin Islands 00801
340-775-7223
Fax: 340-714-5354
pai@prophecyacademy.org
www.prophecyacademy.net
Church of God of Prophecy Academy, Inc. offers a Christian atmosphere which develops the physical, spiritual, intellectual and the social skills of every student. Our primary purpose is to help train students while teaching them the Christian way of life.
Anne E Bramble-Johnson, Principal
VeronaCeleste Hutchinson, Secretary/Office Manager

2301 Puerto Rico Department of Education
PO Box 190759
San Juan
Puerto Rico 00919-759
787-759-2000
www.de.gobierno.pr
Cesar A Rey-Hernandez, Secretary

2302 QSI International School-Chisinau
18 Anton Crihan Street
Chisinau
Moldova 20521-7080
373-24-2366
chisinau@qsi.org
www.qsi.org
To keep this urge to learn alive in every child in QSI schools. Our schools are established to provide in the English language a quality education for students in the cities we serve.
Sandra Smith, Director

2303 QSI International School-Skopje
Inlindenska BB, Reon 55
1000 Skopie
Macedonia 20521-7120
389-91-367-678
Fax: 389-91-362-250
skopje@qsi.org
www.qsi.org
To keep this urge to learn alive in every child in QSI schools. Our schools are established to provide in the English language a quality education for students in the cities we serve.
Robert Tower, Director
Aleksandar Kostadinovski, Finance Manager

2304 QSI International School-Vladivostok
DOS/Administrative Officer
5880 Vladivostok Place
Washington, DC 20521-5880
7-4232-321-292
Fax: 7-4232-313-684
qsiisv@fastmail.vladivostok.ru
www.qsi.org
Grades preK-9, enrollment 18.
Harold M Strom Jr, Director

2305 Rainbow Development Center
PO Box 7618
Christiansted 00823-7618
Virgin Islands
408-215-1386
www.rainbowccc.com
Gloria Henry, Principal

2306 Rainbow Learning Institute
PO Box 75
Christiansted 00821-0075
Virgin Islands
408-215-1386
www.rainbowccc.com
Alda Lockhart, Principal

2307 Rainbow School
PO Box 422
Charlotte Aml 00801
Virgin Islands
408-215-1386
www.rainbowccc.com
Louise Thomas, Principal

2308 Robinson School
5 Nairn Street Condado
San Juan 00907
Puerto Rico 00907
1-787-728-6767
Fax: 1-787-727-7736
robinson_school@hotmail.com
www.robinsonschool.org
The Heart of Educational Excellence. Robinson offers its students a solid foundation for their future academic and career pursuits.
Giberto Quintana, Executive Director
Hugh Andrews, President

2309 Roosevelt Roads Elementary School
PO Box 420132
Roosevelt Roads 00742-0132
Puerto Rico
787-865-3073
Fax: 787-865-4891
www.netdial.caribe.net

2310 Roosevelt Roads Middle & High School
PO Box 420131
Roosevelt Roads 00742-0131
Puerto Rico

787-865-4000
Fax: 787-865-4893
wjames@caribe.net
www.antilles.odedodea.edu
Waynna James, Principal

2311 Saint Anthony School
529 Chalan San Antonio
Tamuning
Guam 96913
671-647-1140
Fax: 471-649-7130
stanthonyschoolguam.org/index.php
A Catholic co-educational elementary school in the Archdiocese of Agana, exists to educate the whole person by providing a rich integrated curriculum served by enabling adults.
Doris San Agustin, Principal
Elizabeth E San Nicolas, Vice-Principal

2312 Saint Eheresas Elementary School
2701 Indian Mound Trail
Coral Gables
American Samoa, F
305-446-1738
Fax: 305-446-2877
www.cotlf.org
Sister Katherine, Principal

2313 Saint Francis Elementary School
2701 Indian Mound Trail
Coral Gables
American Samoa, F
305-446-1738
Fax: 305-446-2877
www.cotlf.org
Sister Gaynor Ana, Principal

2314 Saint John's School
911 N Marine Corps Drive
Tumon Bay 96913
Guam
671-646-8080
Fax: 617-649-6791
info@stjohns.edu.gu
www.stjohns.edu.gu
St. John's students on average score in the top 20% on national scholastic achievement tests in all academic subjects in all grades K-12, a tangible result of an integrated academic program supported by a dedicated faculty, many with advanced degrees in their respective areas of instruction
Glenn Chapin, Headmaster
Imelda D Santos, Dean of Students

2315 Saint John's School, Puerto Rico
1454-66 Ashford Avenue
San Juan 00907
Puerto Rico
787-728-5343
Fax: 787-268-1454
www.sjspr.org
Saint John's School is a college preparatory, nonsectarian, coeducational day school founded in 1915. The school, located in a residential area of the Condado, has an enrollment of approximately 750 students from preschool to grade twelve. 84% come from Hispanic backgrounds, 8% percent from diverse backgrounds and 8% from the continental United States. With the exception of Spanish and French classes, instruction is in English.
Louis R Christiansen, Principal
Barry Farnham, Headmaster

2316 Saints Peter & Paul High School
900 High Street
Easton, MD
410-822-2275
Fax: 410-822-1767
jnemeth@ssppeaston.org
www.ssppeaston.org
Saints Peter and Paul High School is a parochial, Catholic, college preparatory,
James Nemeth, Principal
Carolyn Hayman, Administrative Assistant

2317 Samoa Baptist Academy
Tafuna
Pago Pago 96799
American Samoa
Janice Yerton, Principal

2318 San Carlos & Bishop McManus High School
PO Box Loo 9, Yumet
Aguadilla 00605
Puerto Rico
504-246-5121
questions@bishopmcmanus.ws
www.bishopmcmanus.ws
Nydia U Nieves, Principal

2319 San Vincente Elementary School
San Vincente School Drive
Soledad
Puerto Rico 96913
671-734-4242
www.soledad.monterey.k12.ca
This campus is on five acres of outside Barrigada Village. The average enrollment of 460 students consists of 234 boys and 226 girls in grades PreK-8. SVS holds a Certificate of Accreditation from the Western Association of Schools and Colleges until 1998. Length of stay for overseas teachers is two years, with housing provided. Applications needed to teach include English and physical education.
Adrian Cristobal, Principal
Tarcisia Sablan SSND, Faculty Head

2320 Santa Barbara School
274A W Santa Barbara Avenue
Dededo
Guam 96929
671-632-5578
Fax: 671-632-1414
www.santabarbaraschool.org
To ensure that each student is given the opportunity to realize his or her full potential according to God's design by recognizing and affirming the gifts of each child.
Sr Jeanette Mar Pangelinan, Principal
Sr Maria Rosari Gaite, Vice Principal

2321 Santiago Christian School
PO Box 5600
Santiago
Dominican Republic, FL 33310-5600
809-570-6140
www.santiagochristianschool.org
Lloyd Haglund, Principal

2322 School of the Good Shepherd
1069 Kinghill
St Croix 00851
Virgin Islands 00851
www.goodshepherdtvm.org
Linda Navarro, Principal

2323 Seventh Day Adventist
PO Box 7909
St Thomas 00801-0909
Virgin Islands
Josiah Maynard, Principal

2324 Shekou International School
Jing Shan Villas, Nan Hai Road Shek
Guangdong Province
China 51806
86-755-2669-3669
Fax: 86-755-2667-4099
sis@sis.org.cn
www.sis.org.cn
Shekou International School follows a rigorous college preparatory US style curriculum and is dedicated to meeting the outcomes of the Expected Student Learning Results.
Robert Dunseth, Director
Jennifer Lees, Curriculum Coordinator

2325 Slovak Republic QSI International School of Bratislava
Karloveska 64
Bratislava
Slovak Republic 84220
421-2-6541-1636
Fax: 421-2-6541-1646
bratislava@qsi.org
www.qsi.sk
THE PRIMARY PURPOSE of the school is to meet the needs of the children in Bratislava who require this type of education with a view to continuing their education in their home countries with a minimum of adjustment problems.
Ronald Adams, Principal
Matthew Lake, Director

2326 Slovenia QSI International School-Ljubljana
Dolgi Most 6A
Ljubljana
Slovenia 01000
386-1-439-6300
Fax: 386-1-439-6305
bratislava@qsi.org
www.qsi.org
THE PRIMARY PURPOSE of the school is to meet the needs of the children in Ljubljana who require this type of education with a view to continuing their education in their home countries with a minimum of adjustment problems.
Ronald Adams, Principal
Matthew Lake, Director

2327 South Pacific Academy
PO Box 520
Pago Pago 96799 0520
American Samoa
644-237-4072
www.spa.ac.nz
Tina Senrud, Principal

2328 Southern Peru Staff Schools-Peru
180 Maiden Lane
New York, NY 10038-4925
www.isbi.com
John Dansdill, Principal

2329 St. Croix Christian Academy
26-28 Golden Rock, Christiansted, S
PO Box 716
Virgin Islands, US 00821
340-718-4974
Fax: 340-718-6768
stccacademy@vipowernet.net
www.stcroixchristianacademy.com
The mission of the school is to foster knowledge of God and to give the children a solid academic foundation, along with effective Christian training.
Linus Gittens, Principal

2330 St. Croix Country Day School
Rt-01, Box 6199
Kingshill
Virgin Islands, US 00850
1-340-778-1974
Fax: 1-340-779-3331
bsinfield@stxcountryday.com
www.stxcountryday.com
It is dedicated to providing students with an enriched and challenging education, encouraging them to love learning, grow as individuals and be prepared for a productive and responsible future.
Bill Sinfield, Headmaster
Susan Gibbons, Business Manager

2331 St. Croix Moravian School
PO Box 117
St Thomas 00801
Virgin Islands
www.aavirginislands.org
Condon L Joseph, Principal

2332 St. Croix SDA School
PO Box 930
Kingshill 00851-0930
Virgin Islands
www.stcroixsdaschool.org
Peter Archer, Principal

2333 St. Joseph High School
PO Box 517
Frederiksted 00841-0517
Virgin Islands
Kevin Marin, Principal

2334 St. Patrick School
PO Box 988
Frderiksted 00841-0988
Virgin Islands
www.spsasansol.com
Juliette Clarke, Principal

2335 St. Peter & Paul Elementary School
PO Box 1706
St Thomas 00803
Virgin Islands
www.sppschool.org
Annamay Komment, Principal

2336 Sunbeam
36 Hospital Ground
St Thomas 00803
Virgin Islands
202-427-2383
Fax: 202-426-0308
www.sunbeaminfo.com
Ione Leonard, Principal

2337 Syria Damascus Community School
6110 Damascus Place
Dulles, VA 20189-6110
963-11-333-0331
Fax: 963-11-332-1457
dcs-dam@net.sy
www.dcssyria.org
An independent, coeducational day school which offers an American educational program from preschool through grade 12 for students of all nationalities.
John Gates, Director
Maura Connelly, Chairman

2338 Tashkent International School
7117 Tashkent Place
Dulles, VA 20189-7110
998-71-191-9671
Fax: 998-71-120-6621
office@tashschool.org
www.tashschool.org
To provide a high academic standard of education, educating students to become ethical, responsible, productive citizens of the world with the skills to think creatively, reason critically, and to communicate effectively
John Thomas, Director

2339 Teaching in Austria
Austrian Institute
11 E 52nd Street
New York, NY 10022-5301
212-579-5165

2340 Temple Christian School
PO Box 3009
Agana 96910
Guam 96910
Rev. Ray Fagan, Principal

2341 Tirana International School-Albania
Kutia Postare
Tirana
Albania, DC 01527-9510
355-4-365-239
Fax: 335-4-227-734
tirana@qsi.org
www.qsi.org
The school's educational philosophy, which includes a personalized approach to instruction, leads to teaching for mastery.
Ronald Adams, Principal
Matthew Lake, Director

2342 Trinity Christian School
1231 East Pleasant Run Road
Yiga 96929 0343
Cedar Hill, TX 75104
972-291-2505
Fax: 972-291-4739
www.trinitychristianschool.com
Being a Christian school means we assist parents in fulfilling their divine responsibility to thoroughly train each child to obey God in every area of life and make him or her a true disciple of Jesus Christ. Our program is designed to challenge and educate students of good moral character who are in the middle to upper range of academic ability
Kathleen L Watts, Superintendent
Rhonda Parker, Executive Assistant

2343 Turkmenistan Ashgabat International School
Box 2002
7070 Ashgabat Place
Washington, DC 20521-7070
967-1-234-437
Fax: 967-1-234-438
director@ais.cat.glasnet.ru
Grades K-11, enrollment 75.
Scott Root, Director

2344 Ukraine Kiev International School-An American Institution
EOS/Administrative Officer
5850 Kiev Place
Washington, DC 20521-5850
380-44-452-2792
Fax: 380-44-452-2998
kisukr@sovamua.com
www.kis.net.ua
An independent, coeducational day school which offers an educational program from prekindergarten through high school for students of all nationalities.
E Michael Tewalthomas, Director

2345 United Nations International School
24-50 FDR Drive
New York, NY 10010-4046
212-684-7400
Fax: 212-684-1382
admissions@unis.org
www.unis.org
The United Nations International School provides an international education that emphasizes academic excellence within a caring community for prekindergarten through twelfth grade students from the United Nations, as well as from other families seeking a similar education for their children.
Salvador Uy, Interim Executive Director
Susan Enzer, Executive Assistant

2346 University del Sagrado Corazon
PO Box 12383
San Juan
Puerto Rico 00914-383
787-728-1515
www.sagrado.edu

2347 Uruguayan American School
Av Saldœn de Rodriguez
Montevideo
Uruguay, DC 11500-3360
598-2-600-7681
Fax: 598-2-600-1935
info@uas.edu.uyuy
www.uas.edu.uy
Uruguayan American School is to provide, together with the family, a balanced college preparatory education. UAS integrates a US style curriculum with Uruguayan studies to equip our national and international students to be successful in a diverse, ever changing world
Thomas Oden, Director
Cecilia Burgueo, UP Coordinator

2348 Uruguayan American School-Montevideo
Av Saldœn de Rodriguez
Montevideo
Uruguay, DC 11500-3360
598-2-600-7681
Fax: 598-2-606-1935
info@uas.edu.uyuy
www.uas.edu.uy
Uruguayan American School is to provide, together with the family, a balanced college preparatory education. UAS integrates a US style curriculum with Uruguayan studies to equip our national and international students to be successful in a diverse, ever changing world
Thomas Oden, Director
Cecilia Burgueo, UP Coordinator

2349 Uzbekistan Tashkent International School
38 Sarikul Street
Tashkent, Uzbekistan 10000
998-71-191-9671
Fax: 998-71-120-6621
office@tashschool.org
www.tashschool.org
Tashkent International School (TIS), an IB World School, is a private, not for profit, independent, co-educational day school governed by a Board of Directors elected and appointed from the parent community. TIS offers an American based international curriculum from Kindergarten - grade 12. TIS is an IB World School offering: the full International Baccalaureate Diploma in grades 11 - 12, the Primary Years Program for Kindergarten - grade 5, and is a candidate school for the Middle Years Program
Kevin Glass, Director
John Zohrab, Treasurer

2350 Venezuela Colegio Internacional-Carabobo
PO Box 025685
Miami, FL 33102-5685
58-41-426-551
Fax: 58-41-426-510
admin@cic-valencia.org.ve
www.cic-valencia.org.ve
Colegio Internacional de Carabobo (CIC) is a school dedicated to the development of the whole child. Our teachers are innovative, skilled, and dedicated. Creativity and self-esteem are essential qualities for students to develop as they ascend the academic ladder.
Frank Anderson, Superintendent
Joe Walker, Director

2351 Venezuela Escuela Campo Alegre
8424 NW 56th Street
Suite CCS 00007
Miami, FL 33166
58-2-993-7135
Fax: 58-2-993-0219
info@eca.com.ve
www.eca.com.ve
Escuela Campo Alegre is a private non-profit English language school, designed primarily to serve the needs of the children from ages 3-18 of its shareholding members.
Jean K Vahey, Superintendent

2352 Venezuela International School-Caracas
Pakmail 6030
PO Box 025304
Miami, FL 33102-5304
58-2-945-0422
Fax: 58-2-945-0533
cic@cic-caracas.org
www.cic-caracus.org
Colegio Internacional de Caracas is an English-medium, Pre-Nursery to Grade 12 school dedicated to the intellectual and personal development of each student in a caring and supportive environment.
Alan Benson, Superintendent

2353 Virgin Island Montessori School
6936 Vessup Lane
Saint Thomas, VI 00802
340-775-6360
Fax: 340-775-3080
info@vimontessori.com
www.vimontessori.com/
Virgin Islands Montessori School and International Academy offers a unique environment and learning experience to over 200 students from two years of age through High School
Shournagh Mcweeney, Administrator
Michael Bornn, President

2354 Virgin Islands Department of Education
44-46 Kongens Gade
Saint Thomas, Virgin Islands 00802
340-774-2810
Fax: 340-774-7153
www.doe.vi/
The mission of the Department of Education is to provide the Territory's students with an education that makes them competitive with their peers in the rest of the Caribbean,the United States, and the World; take advantage of our uniqueness of being geographically Caribbean and politically American; integrate all discipline; and educate the whole child.
LaVerne Terry, Commissioner
Donna Frett-Gregory, Assistant Commissioner

2355 Washington International School
3100 Macomb Street NW
Washington, DC 20008-3324
202-243-1800
Fax: 202-243-1802
admissions@wis.edu
www.wis.edu
Washington International School (WIS) is a coeducational day school offering 890 students a challenging curriculum and rich language program from Pre-Kindergarten through Grade 12
Clayton W. Lewis, Head of School
Sandra Bourne, Middle School Principal

2356 We Care Child Development Center
PO Box 818
Christiansted 00821-0818
Virgin Islands
www.utexas.edu
Pauline Canton, Principal

2357 Wesleyan Academy
PO Box 1489
Guaynabo
Puerto Rico 00970-1489
787-008-
Fax: 787-790-0730
www.wesleyanacademy.org
We are a nonprofit, private, coeducational, English Christian school providing a Pre-Pre Kinder through Twelfth grade college preparatory education.
Jack Mann, Principal

2358 Yakistan International School-Karachi
DOS/Administrative Officer
6150 Karachi Place
Washington, DC 20521-6150
92-21-453-9096
Fax: 92-21-454-7305
ameschl@cyber.net.pk
www.isk.edu.pk
Grades N-12, enrollment 338.
Glen Shapin, Superintendent

2359 Zion Academy
7629 199th Street SW
Lynnwood, WA 98036
425-640-3311
info@zionacademy.com
www.zionacademy.com
Zion Academy is a fully accredited private school. Consists of students that wish to work at home and desire complete oversight and administrative services.
Evelyn Williams, Principal
Marigene Lindsey, Founder and Headmaster

International

2360 Center for Strategic and International Studies
1616 Rhode Island Avenue NW
Washington, DC 20036
202-887-0200
Fax: 202-775-3199
books@csis.org
www.csis.org
Provides strategic insights and policy solutions to decisionmakers in government, international institutions, the private sector and civil society.
John J Hamre, President & CEO
Thomas J Pritzker, Chairman

2361 Council for International Exchange of Scholars
3007 Tilden Street NW
Suite 5-L
Washington, DC 20008-3009
202-686-4000
Fax: 202-362-3442
apprequest@cies.iie.org
www.cies.org
Helped administer the Fulbright Scholar Program on behalf of the United States Department of State, Bureau of Educational and Cultural Affairs.
Michael A Brintnall, Executive Director
Judy Pehrson, Director External Relations

2362 Defense Language Institute-English Language Branch
US Civil Service Commission, San Antonio Area
2235 Andrews Avenue
Lackland, TX 78236-5514
210-671-3783
Fax: 210-671-5362
www.dlielc.org
The DLIELC is a Department of Defense (DOD) agency responsible for the management and operation of the Defense English Language Program (DELP) to train international military and civilian personnel to speak and teach English, manage the English as a second language program for the US military

2363 EF Educational Tours
2 Education Cir
Cambridge, MA 02141
800-637-8222
www.eftours.com
EF Educational Tours helps educators enrich classroom learing with international group travel. Students learn from experiencing the world's historic, cultural and natural sights.
Shane Steffens, President
Amar Dhotar, CPA, CA, Finance Manager

2364 Education Information Services which Employ Americans
Education Information Services
PO Box 620662
Newton, MA 02462-662
781-433-0125
Fax: 781-237-2842
www.alis.alberta.ca
Devoted to helping Americans who wish to teach in American overseas schools and International Schools in which English is the primary teaching language. Supports those wishing to teach English as a second language. Publish papers covering every country in the world, list of recruiting fairs, internships, volunteers, jobs, summer overseas jobs.
Frederic B Viaux, President

2365 Educational Information Services
PO Box 662
Newtown Lower Falls, MA 02162
617-964-4555
www.fulbright.jp
Offers information on employment opportunities including books, periodicals and more for the teaching professional who wishes to teach in American overseas schools, international schools, language (ESL) schools, and Department of Defense Dependencies Schools (DODDS).
Frederick B Viaux, President
Michelle V Curtin, Editor

2366 Educational Placement Sources-US
Education Information Services/Instant Alert
PO Box 620662
Newton, MA 02462-662
617-433-0125
Lists 100 organizations in the United States that find positions for teachers, educational administrators, counselors and other professionals. Listings are classified by type, listed alphabetically and offer all contact information.
4 pages Annual
FB Viaux, President

2367 Educational Staffing Program
International Schools Services
15 Roszel Road
PO Box 5910
Princeton, NJ 08543
609-452-0990
Fax: 609-452-2690
edustaffing@iss.edu
www.iss.edu/edustaff/edstaffingprog.htm l
The Educational Staffing Program has placed almost 15,000 K-12 teachers and administrators in overseas schools since 1955. Most candidates obtain their overseas teaching positions by attending our US-based International Recruitment Center where ISS candidates have the potential to interview with overseas school heads seeking new staff. You must be an active ISS candidate to attend an IRC. Applicants must have a bachelor's degree and two years of current relevant experience.

2368 European Council of International Schools
21B Lavant Street
Petersfield, Hampshire GU3 23EL
United Kingdom GU32
44-0-1730-268244
Fax: 44-0-1730-267914
ecis@ecis.org
www.ecis.org
The European Council of International Schools (ECIS) is a collaborative network promoting the ideals and best practice of international education.
T Michael Maybury, Executive Secretary
Pilar Cabeza de Vaca, CEO

2369 FRS National Teacher Agency
PO Box 298
Seymour, TN 37865-298
865-577-8143
www.ffiec.gov
Offers employment options to educators in the United States and abroad.

2370 Foreign Faculty and Administrative Openings
Education Information Services
PO Box 620662
Newton, MA 02462-662
617-433-0125
150 specific openings in administration, counseling, library and other professional positions for American teachers in American schools overseas and in international schools in which teaching language is English.
15 pages Every 6 Weeks
FB Viaux, Coordinating Education

2371 Fulbright Teacher Exchange
600 Maryland Avenue SouthWest
Suite 320
Washington, DC 20024-2520
202-314-3520
800-726-0479
Fax: 202-479-6806
fulbright@grad.usda.gov
www.fulbrightexchanges.org
An organization that offers opportunities for two-year college faculty and secondary school teachers who would like to exchange with teachers in Eastern or Western Europe, Latin America, Australia, Africa, and Canada. To qualify, teachers must be US citizens, have three years full-time teaching experience and be employed in a full-time academic position.

2372 International Educators Cooperative
212 Alcott Road
East Falmouth, MA 02536-6803
508-540-8173
Fax: 508-540-8173
www.icemenlo.com
In addition to year round recruitment, International Educators Cooperative hosts Recruitment Centers in the United States each year.
Dr. Lou Fuccillo, Director

2373 National Association of Teachers' Agencies
National Association of Teachers' Agencies
799 Kings Highway
Fairfield, CT 06432
203-333-0611
Fax: 203-334-7224
fairfieldteachers@snet.net
www.jobsforteachers.com
Provides placement services for those seeking professional positions at all levels of teaching/administration/support services worldwide.
Mark King, Secretary/Treasurer

2374 National Council of Independent Schools' Associations
1129 20th Street
PO Box 324
Australia
06-282-3488
Fax: 06-282-2926
www.nais.org
Services include career placement.
Fergus Thomson, President

2375 Overseas Employment Opportunities for Educators
Department of Defense, Office of Dependent Schools
2461 Eisenhower Avenue
Alexandria, VA 22331-3000
703-325-0867
This publication tells about teaching jobs in 250 schools operated for children of US military and civilian personnel stationed overseas. Applicants usually must qualify in two subject areas.

2376 Recruiting Fairs for Overseas Teaching
Education Information Services/Instant Alert
PO Box 620662
Newton, MA 02462-662
781-433-0125
Fax: 781-237-2842
Recruiting fairs and sponsors in the US and elsewhere for American educators who wish to teach outside of the United States.
FB Viaux, Coordinating Education

2377 UNI Overseas Recruiting Fair
University of Northern Iowa
102 Gilchrist Hall
Cedar Falls, IA 50614-390
319-273-2083
Fax: 319-273-6998
overseas.placement@uni.edu
www.uni.edu/placement/overseas
UNI is home to the oldest international recruitment event in the world. The event began in 1976 after the UNI Career Services staff and several school headmasters recognized the need for more efficient and cost-effective recruitment techniques. It became readily apparent that UNI was meeting a need for school recruiters and interested educators all over the globe. In addition to inventing the international recruitment fair, UNI developed fact sheets, credential files, vacancy listings, referral
February
Brian Atkins, Advisory Board
Susan Barba, Advisory Board

2378 WorldTeach
Center for International Development
79 John F Kennedy Street
Box 122
Cambridge, MA 02138
617-495-5527
800-483-2240
Fax: 617-495-1599
info@worldteach.org
www.worldteach.org
WorldTeach is a non-profit, non-governmental organization that provides opportunities for individuals to make a meaningful contribution to international education by living and working as volunteer teachers in developing countries
Laurie Roberts Belton, Executive Director
Eric Weiss, Program Manager

Alabama

2379 Auburn University at Montgomery Library
PO Box 244023
Montgomery, AL 36124-4023
334-244-3649
Fax: 334-244-3720
www.aumnicat.aum.edu
Member of The Foundation Center network, maintaining a collection of private foundation tax returns which provide information on the scope of grants dispensed by that particular foundation.
R Best, Dean Administration
T Bailey, ILL/ Reference

2380 Benjamin & Roberta Russell Educational and Charitable Foundation
PO Box 272
Alexander City, AL 35010-0272
256-329-4224
www.non-profit-organizations.findthebest.com
Offers giving in the areas of higher and public education, youth programs and a hospital.
James D Nabors, Executive Director

2381 Birmingham Public Library
Government Documents
2100 Park Place
Birmingham, AL 35203-2794
205-226-3600
Fax: 205-226-3729
www.bplonline.org
Member of The Foundation Center network, maintaining a collection of private foundation tax returns which provide information on the scope of grants dispensed by that particular foundation.

2382 Carolina Lawson Ivey Memorial Foundation
PO Box 340
Smiths, AL 36877-0340
334-826-5760
Scholarships are offered to college juniors and seniors who are pursuing careers of teaching social studies in middle or secondary grades. The grants are also offered to teachers in Alabama and west Georgia for curriculum planning and development, in-service training, the development of instructional materials for use in elementary and secondary schools, and other projects that focus on the cultural approach method of teaching.

2383 Huntsville Public Library
915 Monroe Street SW
Huntsville, AL 35801-5007
256-532-5940
www.hpl.lib.al.us/ .
Member of The Foundation Center network, maintaining a collection of private foundation tax returns which provide information on the scope of grants dispensed by that particular foundation.
Donna B Schremser, Library Director

2384 JL Bedsole Foundation
PO Box 1137
Mobile, AL 36633-1137
251-432-3369
Fax: 251-432-1134
www.jlbedsolefoundation.org
The foundation's primary interest is the support of educational institutions within the state of Alabama and civic and economic development which is limited to the geographical area of Southwest Alabama. The arts, social service and health programs receive limited grants. Organizations or projects outside of the State of Alabama are not considered for funding by the Foundation.
Mabel B Ward, Executive Director
Scott A Morton, Assistant Director

2385 Mildred Weedon Blount Educational and Charitable Foundation
PO Box 607
Tallassee, AL 36078-0007
334-283-4931
www.schoolsoup.com
Support for Catholic schools, public schools and a scholarship fund for secondary school students.
Arnold B Dopson, Executive Director

2386 Mitchell Foundation
PO Box 1126
Mobile, AL 36633
251-432-1711
Fax: 334-432-1712
www.cgmf.org
Places an emphasis on secondary and higher education, social services programs, youth agencies, and aid for the handicapped.
Augustine Meaher, Executive Director
Marilu Hastings, Director

2387 University of South Alabama
307 University Boulevard
Mobile, AL 36688-0002
251-460-7025
Fax: 251-460-7636
www.library.southalabama.edu
Richard Wood, Dean of Libraries

Alaska

2388 University of Alaska-Anchorage Library
3211 Providence Drive
Anchorage, AK 99508-8000
907-786-1848
Fax: 907-786-6050
www.lib.uaa.alaska.edu
Member of The Foundation Center network, maintaining a collection of private foundation tax returns which provide information on the scope of grants dispensed by that particular foundation.
Stephen J Rollins, Dean of Library

Arizona

2389 Arizona Department of Education
1535 W Jefferson Street
Phoenix, AZ 85007
602-542-5393
800-352-4558
Fax: 602-542-5440
www.ade.state.az.us
Implements procedures that ensure the proper allocation, distribution, and expenditure of all federal and state funds administerd by the department. The following links to our web pages contain information pertaining to educational grants funded from the state or federal programs.
Tom Horne, Superintendent

2390 Arizona Governor's Committee on Employment of People with Disabilities
Samaritan Rehabilitation Institute
1012 E Willetta Street
Phoenix, AZ 85006-3047
602-239-4762
Fax: 602-239-5256
Jim Bruzewski, Executive Director

2391 Education Services
Arizona Department of Education
1535 W Jefferson Street
Phoenix, AZ 85007-3280
602-364-1961
Fax: 602-542-5440
www.ade.state.az.us/edservices
Provides quality services and resources to schools, parent groups, government agencies, and community groups to enable them to achieve their goals.
Lillie Sly, Associate Superintendent

2392 Evo-Ora Foundation
2525 E Broadway Boulevard
Suite 111
Tucson, AZ 85716-5398
Giving is primarily aimed at education, especially Catholic high schools and universities.

2393 Flinn Foundation
1802 N Central Avenue
Suite 2300
Phoenix, AZ 85012-2513
602-744-6800
Fax: 602-744-6815
info@flinn.org
www.flinn.org
Supports nonprofit organizations in the state of Arizona for programs in health care, as well as an annual awards competition for Arizona's principal arts institutions and a college scholarship program for Arizona high school graduates. Scholarship provides expenses for four years, two summers of study-related travel abroad and other benefits.
John W Murphy, Executive Director

2394 Phoenix Public Library
Business & Sciences Department
12 E McDowell Road
Phoenix, AZ 85004-1627
602-262-4636
Fax: 602-261-8836
www.phxlib.org
Member of The Foundation Center network, maintaining a collection of private foundation tax returns which provide information on the scope of grants dispensed by that particular foundation.

2395 Special Programs
721 Broadway
12th Floor
New York, NY 10003
212-998-1800
tisch.special.info@nyu.edu
www.specialprograms.tisch.nyu.edu
Tom Horne, Superintendent

2396 Support Services
Arizona Department of Education
1535 W Jefferson Street
Phoenix, AZ 85007-3280
602-542-5393
Fax: 602-542-5440
Rachel Arroyo, School Finance

2397 Vocational Technological Education
Arizona Department of Education
1535 W Jefferson Street
Phoenix, AZ 85007-3280
602-542-5393
Fax: 602-542-5440
Tom Horne, Superintendent

Arkansas

2398 Charles A Frueauff Foundation
200 River Market Avenue
Suite 100
Little Rock, AR 72201-3848
501-324-2233
www.frueauff.org
Will review proposals from private four-year colleges and universities.
David Frueauff, President
Sue Frueauff, Chief Administrative Officer

2399 Northwest Arkansas Community College
Borham Library
One College Drive
Bentonville, AR 72904-7397
479-636-9222
800-995-6922
www.nwacc.edu
Member of The Foundation Center network, maintaining a collection of private foundation tax returns which provide information on the scope of grants dispensed by that particular foundation.
Daniel Shewmaker, Secretary
Ric Clifford, Chairman

2400 Roy and Christine Sturgis Charitable and Educational Trust
PO Box 92
Malvern, AR 72104-0092
501-337-5109
Giving is offered to Baptist and Methodist organizations, including schools, churches and higher and secondary education.
Katie Speer, Executive Director

2401 The Jones Center For Families
922 East Emma Avenue
Springdale, AR 72765
479-756-8090
www.thejonescenter.net
Focuses funds on education, medical resources and religious organizations in Arkansas.
HG Frost Jr, Executive Director
Grace Donoho, Director Of Education

2402 Walton Family Foundation
125 W Central Avenue
Room 217 Po Box 2030
Bentonville, AR 72712-5248
479-464-1570
Fax: 479-464-1580
www.wffhome.com
Offers giving for systemic reform of primary education (K-12) and early childhood development.
Stewart T Springfield, Executive Director

2403 William C & Theodosia Murphy Nolan Foundation
200 N Jefferson Avenue
Suite 308
El Dorado, AR 71730-5853
870-863-7118
Fax: 870-863-6528
Supports education and the arts (historic preservation, arts centers) as well as religious welfare and youth organizations in Northern Louisiana and Southern Arkansas.
William C Nolan, Executive Director

2404 Winthrop Rockefeller Foundation
225 East Markham Street
Suite 200
Little Rock, AR 72201-3999
501-376-6854
Fax: 501-374-4797
webfeedback@wrfoundation.org
www.wrfoundation.org
Dedicated to improving the quality of life and education in Arkansas. Grants go to schools that work to involve teachers and parents in making decisions; to universities and local schools to strengthen both levels of education; and for projects that promote stakeholder participation in the development of educational policy.
Sherece Y West, President
Jackie Cox-New, Sr Program Officer

California

2405 Ahmanson Foundation
9215 Wilshire Boulevard
Beverly Hills, CA 90210-5538
310-278-0770
info@theahmansonfoundation.org
www.theahmasonfoundation.org
Concentrates mainly on education, health and social services in Southern California.
Lee E Walcott, Executive Director
William H Ahmanson, President

2406 Alice Tweed Tuohy Foundation
205 E Carrillo Street
Suite 219
Santa Barbara, CA 93101-7186
805-962-6430
Priority consideration is given to applications from organizations serving: young people; education; selected areas of interest in health care and medicine; and community affairs.
Harris W Seed, President
Eleanor Van Cott, Executive VP

2407 Arrillaga Foundation
2560 Mission College Boulevard
Suite 101
Santa Clara, CA 95054-1217
408-980-0130
Fax: 408-988-4893
Giving is aimed at secondary schools and higher education in the state of California.
John Arrillaga, Executive Director

2408 Atkinson Foundation
1720 So.Amphlett Blvd
Suite 100
San Mateo, CA 94402-2710
650-357-1101
atkinfdn@aol.com
www.atkinsonfdn.org
Provides opportunities for people in San Mateo County, California to reach their highest potential and to improve the quality of their lives and to assist educational institutions and supporting organizations with the implementation of effective programs that reach and serve their target populations.
Elizabeth H Curtis, Administrator

2409 BankAmerica Foundation
Bank of America Center
PO Box 37000
San Francisco, CA 94137-0001
800-678-2632
Fax: 818-507-4023
banknote@bankamerica.com
www.bankamerica.com
Fields of interest include arts/cultural programs, higher education, community development and general federated giving programs.
Elizabeth Nachbaur, Program Director

2410 Bechtel Group Corporate Giving Program
Po Box 193965
San Francisco, CA 94119-3965
415-768-5974
Offers support for higher education and programs related to engineering and construction, math and science in grades K-12 and general charitable programs.
Kathryn M Bandarrae, Executive Director

2411 Bernard Osher Foundation
One Ferry Building
Suite 255
San Francisco, CA 94111
415-861-5587
Fax: 415-677-5868
nagle@osherfoundation.org
www.osherfoundation.org
Funds in the arts, post-secondary education and environmental education on San Francisco and Alameda Counties.
Patricia Nagle, Sr VP
Jeanie Hirokane, Corporate Secretary and Exec

2412 Boys-Viva Supermarkets Foundation
955 Carrillo Drive
Suite 103
Los Angeles, CA 90048-5400
Wide range of support for education of school-aged children, especially the at-risk population, tutoring, and social opportunities.
Fred Snowden, Executive Director

2413 California Community Foundation
221 S Figueroa Street
Suite 400
Los Angeles, CA 90012-1638
213-413-4130
Fax: 213-383-2046
www.calfund.org
Improving human condition through nonprofit agencies in Los Angeles County. Integral parts of eligible proposals are, hosting conferences, incurring debt, individuals, sectarian purposes or regranting.
Judy Spiegel, Sr VP of Programs
Antonia Hernandez, President/CEO

2414 Carrie Estelle Doheny Foundation
707 Wilshire Boulevard
Suite 4960
Los Angeles, CA 90017-2659
213-488-1122
Fax: 213-488-1544
www.dohenyfoundation.org
This foundation funds a myriad of organizations ranging from the education and medicine field to public health and science areas.
Robert A Smith III, Executive Director

2415 Dan Murphy Foundation
PO Box 711267
Los Angeles, CA 90071-9767
213-623-3120
Fax: 213-623-1421

Funds Roman Catholic institutions, with a primary interest in religious orders and schools.

Daniel J Donohue, Executive Director

2416 David & Lucile Packard Foundation
343 Second Street
Los Altos Hills, CA 94022-3643
650-948-7658
Fax: 650-941-3151
www.packard.org
Concentrates on four categories: education, the arts, conservation and child health. Also allocates funds to companies interested in public improvement and public policy.

Colburn S Wilbur, Executive Director

2417 Evelyn & Walter Haas Jr Fund
114 Sansome Street
Suite 600
San Francisco, CA 94104
415-856-1400
Fax: 415-856-1500
www.haasjr.org
Interested in strengthening neighborhoods, communities, and human services. Funds mainly in San Francisco Bay Area.

Ira Hirschfield, President
Clayton Juan, Grants Administrator

2418 Foundation Center-San Francisco
312 Sutter Street
Suite 606
San Francisco, CA 94108-4314
415-397-0902
Fax: 415-397-7670
www.fdncenter.org
One of five Foundation Centers nationwide, the Foundation Center - San Francisco is a library which collects information on private foundations, corporate philanthropy, nonprofit management, fundraising and other topics of interest to nonprofit organization representatives.

Melissa A Berman, President & CEO
John Colborn, Vice President

2419 Foundations Focus
Marin Community Foundation
5 Hamilton Landing
Suite 200
Novato, CA 94949
415-464-2500
Fax: 415-464-2555
www.marincf.org
Grants support projects that benefit residents of Marin County, CA.

Don Jen, Program Officer/Education
Thomas Peters, President/CEO

2420 Francis H Clougherty Charitable Trust
500 Newport Center Drive
Suite 910
Newport Beach, CA 92660-7009
Offers grants in the areas of elementary, secondary school and higher education in Southern California.

2421 Freitas Foundation
C/O Fiduciary Resources
874 Fourth St
Suite D
San Rafael, CA 94901-3246
Offers giving in the areas of elementary and secondary education, as well as theological education.

Margaret Boyden, Executive Director

2422 Fritz B Burns Foundation
4001 W Alameda Avenue
Suite 201
Burbank, CA 91505-4338
818-840-8802
Fax: 818-840-0468
Grants are primarily focused on education, hospitals and medical research organizations.

Joseph E Rawlinson, Executive Director

2423 George Frederick Jewett Foundation
235 Montgomery Street
Suite 612
San Francisco, CA 94104-2915
415-421-1351
Fax: 415-421-1351
Concerns itself mainly with voluntary, nonprofit organizations that promote human welfare.

2424 Grant & Resource Center of Northern California
2280 Benton Drive, Building C
Suite A
Redding, CA 96003
530-244-1219
Fax: 530-244-0905
library@grcnc.org
Member of The Foundation Center network, maintaining a collection of private foundation tax returns which provide information on the scope of grants dispensed by that particular foundation.

2425 Greenville Foundation
PO Box 4667
Scottsdale, AZ 85261-4667
707-938-9377
Fax: 707-939-9311
This foundation focuses its support on education, the environment and human rights. The main focus of the educational grants lie within the areas of elementary, secondary and higher education.

Virginia Hubbell, Executive Director
Virginia Hubbell, Administrator

2426 HN & Frances C Berger Foundation
PO Box 3064
Arcadia, CA 91006
626-447-3351
www.hnberger.org
Provides scholarships and endowments to colleges and universities.

Ronald M Auen, President/CEO
Christopher M McGuire, Vice President of Programs

2427 Henry J Kaiser Family Foundation
Quadrus
2400 Sand Hill Road
Menlo Park, CA 94025-6941
650-854-9400
Fax: 650-854-4800
www.kff.org
Concentrates on health care, minority groups and South Africa.

Drew Altman, President/CEO
Susan V Berresford, Former President

2428 Hon Foundation
25200 La Paz Road
Suite 210
Laguna Hills, CA 92653-5110
949-586-4400
Offers giving in the areas of elementary, secondary and higher education in the states of Hawaii and California.

2429 Hugh & Hazel Darling Foundation
520 S Grand Avenue
7th Floor
Los Angeles, CA 90071-2645
213-683-5200
Fax: 213-627-7795
Supports education in California with special emphasis on legal education; no grants to individuals; grants only to 501(c)(3) organizations.

Richard L Stack, Trustee

2430 Ingraham Memorial Fund
C/O Emrys J. Ross
301 E Colorado Boulevard
Suite 900
Pasadena, CA 91101-1916
626-796-9123
Offers giving in the areas of elementary, secondary and higher education, as well as theological education in Claremont and Pasadena, California.

2431 James G Boswell Foundation
101 W Walnut Street
Pasadena, CA 91103-3636
626-583-3000
Fax: 626-583-3090
Funds hospitals, pre-college private schools, public broadcasting and youth organizations.

James G Boswell II, Chairman
Sherman Railsback, EVP/COO

2432 James Irvine Foundation
575 Market Street
Suite 3400
San Francisco, CA 94105-1017
415-777-2244
Fax: 415-777-0869
www.irvine.org
Giving is primarily aimed at the areas of education, youth and health.

James E Canales, President/CEO
Kristin Nelson, Executive Assistant

2433 James S Copley Foundation
7776 Ivanhoe Avenue #1530
La Jolla, CA 92037-4520
858-454-0411
Fax: 858-729-7629
Support is offered for higher and secondary education, child development, cultural programs and community services.

Anita A Baumgardner, Executive Director

2434 John Jewett & H Chandler Garland Foundation
PO Box 550
Pasadena, CA 91102-0550
Support given primarily for secondary and higher education, social services and cultural and historical programs.

GE Morrow, Executive Director

2435 Joseph Drown Foundation
1999 Avenue of the Stars
Suite 2330
Los Angeles, CA 90067-4611
310-277-4488
Fax: 310-277-4573
www.jdrown.org
The Foundation's goal is to assist individuals in becoming successful, self-sustaining, contributing citizens. The foundation is interested in programs that break down any barrier that prevents a person from continuing to grow and learn.

Norman Obrow, Executive Director

2436 Jules & Doris Stein Foundation
PO Box 30
Beverly Hills, CA 90213-0030
213-276-2101
Supports charitable organizations.

2437 Julio R Gallo Foundation
PO Box 1130
Modesto, CA 95353-1130
209-579-3373
Offers grants and support to secondary schools and higher education universities.

Sam Gallo, Chairman

2438 Kenneth T & Eileen L Norris Foundation
11 Golden Shore Street
Suite 450
Long Beach, CA 90802-4214
562-435-8444
Fax: 562-436-0584
grants@ktn.org
www.norrisfoundation.org
Funding categories include medical, education/science, youth, cultural and community.

Ronald Barnes, Executive Director

2439 Koret Foundation
33 New Montgomery Street
Suite 1090
San Francisco, CA 94105-4526
415-882-7740
Fax: 415-882-7775
sandyedwards@koretfoundation.org
www.koretfoundation.org
Funding includes; public policy and selected programs in K-12 public education, higher education, youth programs, Jewish studies at colleges and universities, and Jewish education. The geographical area for grant-making is the San Francisco Bay area.

Tad Taube, President
Susan Koret, Board Chair

2440 Lane Family Charitable Trust
500 Almer Road
Apartment 301
Burlingame, CA 94010-3966
Offers giving in the areas of secondary schools and higher education facilities in California.

Ralph Lane, Trustee
Joan Lane, Trustee

2441 Levi Strauss Foundation
1155 Battery Street
Floor 7
San Francisco, CA 94111-1230
415-501-6000
Fax: 415-501-7112
www.levistrauss.com
Grants are made in four areas: AIDS prevention and care; economic empowerment; youth empowerment; and social justice. Grants are limited to communities where Levi Strauss and Company has plants or customer service centers.

Theresa Fay-Buslillos, Executive Director

2442 Louise M Davies Foundation
180 Montgomery St
Suite 1616
San Francisco, CA 94104-4235
Offers giving in the areas of elementary, secondary and higher education, as well as scholarship funding for California students.

Donald Crawford Jr, Executive Director

2443 Lowell Berry Foundation
3685 Mount Diablo Boulevard
Suite 269
Lafayette, CA 94549
925-284-4427
Fax: 925-284-4332
www.lowellberryfoundation.org
Assists Christian ministry at local church levels.

Debbie Coombe, Office Manager
Larry R Langdon, President

2444 Luke B Hancock Foundation
360 Bryant Street
Palo Alto, CA 94301-1409
650-321-5536
Fax: 650-321-0697
lhancock@lukebhancock.org
www.fdcenter.org/grantmaker/hancock
Provides funding for programs which promote the well being of children and youth. Priority is given to programs which address the needs of youth who are at risk of school failure. Additional funding is provided for early childhood development, music education and homeless families.

Ruth M Ramel, Executive Director

2445 Margaret E Oser Foundation
1911 Lyon Court
Santa Rosa, CA 95403-0974
949-553-4202
Offers grants in the areas of elementary and secondary and higher education, which will benefit women.

Carl Mitchell, Executive Director

2446 Marin Community Foundation
5 Hamilton Landing
Suite 200
Novato, CA 94949-1736
415-461-3333
Fax: 415-464-2555
www.marincf.org
Established as a nonprofit public benefit corporation to engage in educational and philanthropic activities in Marin County, California.

Thomas Peterson, President&CEO
Julie Absey, Vice President

2447 Mary A Crocker Trust
233 Post Street
Floor 2
San Francisco, CA 94108-5003
415-982-0138
Fax: 415-982-0141
staff@mactrust.org
www.mactrust.org
Giving is aimed at precollegiate education, as well as conservation and environmental programs.

Barbaree Jernigan, Executive Director

2448 Maurice Amado Foundation
3940 Laurel Canyon Boulevard
Suite 809
Studio City, CA 91604
818-980-9190
Fax: 818-980-9190
pkaizer@mauriceamadofdn.org
www.mauri
Concentrates on the Jewish heritage.

Pam Kaizer, Executive Director

2449 McConnell Foundation
PO Box 492050
800 Shasta View Drive
Redding, CA 96003
530-226-6200
Fax: 530-226-6210
www.mcconnellfoundation.org
Interested in cultural, community and health care related projects.

Ana Diaz, Program Assistant

2450 McKesson Foundation
1 Post Street
San Francisco, CA 94104-5203
415-983-8300
www.mckesson.com/foundation.html
Giving is primarily to programs for junior high school students and for emergency services such as food and shelter.

Marcia M Argyris, Executive Director

2451 Milken Family Foundation
C/O Foundations of the Milken Families
1250 4th Street
Floor 6
Santa Monica, CA 90401-1353
310-570-4800
Fax: 310-570-4801
www.mff.org
Offers support to the educational community to reward educational innovators, stimulate creativity among students, involve parents and other citizens in the school system, and help disadvantaged youth.

Dr. Julius Lesner, Executive Director
Lowell Milken, Chairman & Co Founder

2452 Miranda Lux Foundation
57 Post Street
Suite 510
San Francisco, CA 94104-5020
415-981-2966
admin@mirandalux.org
www.mirandalux.org
Offers support to promising proposals for pre-school through junior college programs in the fields of pre-vocational and vocational education and training.

Kenneth Blum, Executive Director

2453 Northern California Grantmakers
625 Market Street
3rd Floor
San Francisco, CA 94105
415-777-4111
Fax: 415-777-1714
ncg@ncg.org
www.ncg.org
Northern California Grantmakers is an association of foundations, corporate contributions programs and other private grantmakers. Its mission is to jpromote the well being of people and their communities in balance with a healthy environment by the thoughtful and creative use of private wealth and resources for the public benefit. To this end, NCG works to enhance the effectiveness of philanthropy, including nonprofit organizations, government, business, media, academia and the public at large.

Colin Lacon, President

2454 Pacific Telesis Group Corporate Giving Program
130 Kearny Street
San Francisco, CA 94108-4818
415-394-3000
Primary areas of interest include K-12 education reform, education of minorities, women and disabled individuals in the math, science, engineering, education and MBA fields; and specific K-12 issues such as dropouts, information technology and parent involvement.

Jere A Jacobs, Executive Director

2455 Peninsula Community Foundation
11742 Jefferson Avenue
Suite 350
Newport News, VA 23606-3049

757-327-0862
Fax: 757-327-0865
www.pcfvirginia.org
Serving a population from Daly City to Mountain View, the foundations focus is on children and youth, adult services, programs serving homeless families and children, prevention of homelessness and civic and public benefit grants.

Sterling K Speirn, Executive Director
Gregory F Lawson, President

2456 Peter Norton Family Foundation
225 Arizona Avenue
Floor 2
Santa Monica, CA 90401-1243
310-576-7700
Fax: 310-576-7701
Offers giving in the areas of early childhood education, elementary school education, higher education, childrens services and AIDS research.

Anne Etheridge, ED, Executive Director

2457 RCM Capital Management Charitable Fund
4 Embarcadero Center
Suite 2900
San Francisco, CA 94111-4189
415-954-5474
Fax: 415-954-8200
www.rcm.com
Giving is offered in many areas including youth development, early childhood education and elementary education.

Jami Weinman, Executive Director

2458 Ralph M Parsons Foundation
888 West Sixth Street
Suite 700
Los Angeles, CA 90017-5600
213-362-7600
Fax: 213-482-8878
www.rmpf.org
Giving is focused on higher and pre-collegiate education, with an emphasis on engineering, technology, and science; social impact programs serving families, children and the elderly; health programs targeting underserved populations; civic and cultural programs.

Wendy G Hoppe, Executive Director
Walter B Rose, Vice Chairman

2459 Riordan Foundation
PO Box 491190
Los Angeles, CA 90049-3110
310-472-2020
Fax: 310-472-1414
contact@riordanfoundation.org
www.riordanfoundation.org
Priorities of the foundation include early childhood literacy, youth programs, leadership programs, job training, direct medical services to young children, and cyclical, targeted mini-grants. When determining levels of support, priority is always given to programs which impact young children.

Jessica Flores, President
Jaime Kalenik, Program Coordinator

2460 Royal Barney Hogan Foundation
PMB 220,3000 S.Hulen
Ste 124
Forth Worth, TX
E-mail:
RoyalHoganFoundation@yahoo.com
www.royalhoganfoundation.org
Offers grants specifically for secondary education in the state of California.

Jacque Hogan, President/Treasurer
Robert L Towery, Secretary/Chief Executive Of

2461 SH Cowell Foundation
595 Market Street
Suite 950
San Francisco, CA 94105-4303
415-397-0285
Fax: 415-986-6786
www.shcowell.org
Offers support for educational programs, including pre-school and primary public educational programs.

JD Erickson, Executive Director
Anna Alpers, President

2462 Sacramento Regional Foundation
555 Capitol Mall
Suite 550
Sacramento, CA 95814-4502
916-492-6510
Fax: 916-492-6515
www.sacregfoundation.org
Primary interests of this foundation include the arts, humanities and education.

Stephen F Boutin, President
Janice Gow Pettey, CEO

2463 San Diego Foundation
2508 Historic Decatur Rd
Suite 200
San Diego, CA 92106-2434
619-235-2300
Fax: 619-239-1710
info@sdfoundation.org
www.sdfoundation.org
Offers grants in the areas of social services with emphasis on children and families, education and health for San Diego County.

Robert A Kelly, President/CEO
Rebecca Reichmann, VP Programs

2464 San Francisco Foundation
225 Bush Street
Suite 500
San Francisco, CA 94104-4224
415-733-8500
Fax: 415-477-2783
rec@sff.org
www.sff.org
Addresses community needs in the areas of community health, education, arts and culture, neighborhood revitalization, and environmental justice. Works to support families and communities to help children and youth succeed in school and provide opportunities for them to become confident, caring and contributing adults.

Sandra R Hernandez MD, CEO
Sara Ying Kelley, Director Public Affairs

2465 Santa Barbara Foundation
1111 Chapala Street
Suite 200
Santa Barbara, CA 93101-2780
805-963-1873
Fax: 805-966-2345
www.sbfoundation.org
Offers a student aid program with no interest-1/2 loan and 1/2 scholarship. Funding limited to long-term Santa Barbara County residents.

Claudia Armann, Program Officer
Peter MacDougall, Chairman

2466 Sega Youth Education & Health Foundation
255 Shoreline Drive
Suite 200
Redwood City, CA 94065-1428
Offers support only to organizations that address and promote youth education and health issues.

Trizia Carpenter, Executive Director

2467 Sidney Stern Memorial Trust
PO Box 893
Pacific Palisades, CA 90272-0893
310-459-2117
info@sidneysternmemorialtrust.org
www.sidneysternmemorialtrust.org
Funding offered includes education, community action groups, the arts and the disabled.

2468 Sol & Clara Kest Family Foundation
5150 Overland Avenue
Culver City, CA 90230-4914
213-204-2050
Offers support for Jewish organizations in the areas of education.

Sol Kest, Executive Director

2469 Szekely Family Foundation
3232 Dove Street
San Diego, CA 92103
619-295-2372
Offers giving in the areas of early childhood education, child development, elementary education, higher education, and adult and continuing education.

Deborah Szekely, Executive Director

2470 Thomas & Dorothy Leavey Foundation
10100 Santa Monica Boulevard
Suite 610
Los Angeles, CA 90067
310-551-9936
Focus is placed on college scholarships, medical research, youth groups and programs, and secondary and higher education purposes.

J Thomas McCarthy, Executive Director

2471 Times Mirror Foundation
202 West First Street
Los Angeles, CA 90012
213-237-3945
Fax: 213-237-2116
www.timesmirrorfoundation.org
Giving is largely for higher education purposes including liberal arts and business education.

Cassandra Malry, Executive Director

2472 Timken-Sturgis Foundation
7421 Eads Avenue
La Jolla, CA 92037-5037
619-454-2252
Offers support for education in Southern California and Nevada.

Joannie Barrancotto, Executive Director

2473 Toyota USA Foundation
19001 S Western Avenue
Torrance, CA 90501-1106
310-715-7486
800-331-4331
Fax: 310-468-7814
b_pauli@toyota
www.toyota.com/foundation
Supports K-12 education programs, with strong emphasis on math and science.

William Pauli, National Manager

2474 Turst Funds Incorporated
100 Broadway Street
Floor 3
San Francisco, CA 94111-1404
415-434-3323
Offers grants for Catholic Schools, including elementary and secondary education, in the San Francisco Bay Area.

James T Healy, President

2475 Ventura County Community Foundation
Funding & Information Resource Center
4001 Mission Oaks Blvd
Suite 150
Camarillo, CA 93012-8504
805-988-0196
Fax: 805-484-2700
vccf@vccf.org
www.vccf.org
Member of The Foundation Center network, maintaining a collection of private foundation tax returns which provide information on the scope of grants dispensed by that particular foundation.

Gary E Erickson, President/CEO
Virginia Weber, Program Officer

2476 WM Keck Foundation
550 S Hope Street
Suite 2500
Los Angeles, CA 90071
213-680-3833
Fax: 213-614-0934
info@wmkeck.org
www.wmkeck.org
The Foundation also gives some consideration, limited to Southern California, for the support of arts and culture, civic and community services, health care and precollegiate education. The foundation's grant-making is focused primarily on pioneering research efforts in the areas of science, engineering and medical research, and on higher education, including liberal arts.

Dorothy Fleisher, Program Director
Allison Keller, Executive Director and Chief

2477 Walter & Elise Haas Fund
1 Lombard Street
Suite 305
San Francisco, CA 94111-1130
415-398-4474
Fax: 415-986-4779
www.haassr.org
Supports education, arts, environment, human services, humanities and public affairs; is especially in projects which have a wide impact within their respective fields through enhancing public education and access to information, serving a central organizing role, addressing public policy, demonstrating creative approaches toward meeting human needs, or supporting the work of a major institution in the field.

Pamela H David, Executive Director
Peter E Hass Jr, President

2478 Walter S Johnson Foundation
1660 Bush Street
Suite 300
San Francisco, CA 94025-3447
415-561-6540
Fax: 415-561-6477
www.wsjf.org
Giving is centered on education in public schools and social service agencies concerned with the quality of public education in Northern California and Washoe County, Nevada.

Pancho Chang, Executive Director

2479 Wayne & Gladys Valley Foundation
1939 Harrison Street
Suite 510
Oakland, CA 94612-3535
510-466-6060
Fax: 510-466-6067
Supports four areas: education, medical research, community services and special projects.

Michael D Desler, Executive Director

2480 Weingart Foundation
1055 W 7th Street
Suite 3200
Los Angeles, CA 90017-2509
213-688-7799
Fax: 213-688-1515
www.weingartfnd.org
Offers support for community services including a student loan program.

William C Allen, Chairman & CEO
Fred J Ali, President/Chief Adm. Officer

2481 Wells Fargo Foundation
550 California Street
7th Floor MAC A0112-073
San Francisco, CA 94104
415-396-5830
Fax: 415-975-6260
www.wellsfargo.com
Offers support for elementary school education, secondary school education and community development.

Tim Hanlon, Executive Director

2482 Wilbur D May Foundation
C/O Brookhill Corporation
2716 Ocean Park Boulevard
Suite 2011
Santa Monica, CA 90405
Gives to youth organizations and hospitals.

2483 William & Flora Hewlett Foundation
2121 Sand Hill Road
Menlo Park, CA 94025-3448
650-234-4500
Fax: 650-234-4501
www.hewlett.org
The Hewlett Foundation concentrates its resources on the performing arts, education, population issues, environmental issues, conflict resolution and family and community development. Grants in the education program, specifically the elementary and secondary education part of it, are limited to K-12 areas in California programs, with primary emphasis on public schools in the San Francisco Bay area. The program favors schools, school districts and universities.

Larry Kramer, President
Walter B Hewlett, Chairman

2484 William C Bannerman Foundation
9255 Sunset Boulevard
Suite 400
West Hollywood, CA 90069
310-273-9933
Fax: 310-273-9931
Offers grants in the fields of elementary school, secondary schools, education, human services and youth programs K-12 in Los Angeles County, Adult Education and Vocational Training.

Elliot Ponchick, President

2485 Y&H Soda Foundation
1635 School Street
Moraga, CA 94556
925-631-1133
Fax: 925-631-0248
jNM@silcom.com
www.yhsodafoundation.org
Offers support in the areas of early childhood education, child development, elementary education and vocational and higher education.

Bob Uyeki, Executive Director

2486 Zellerbach Family Fund
575 Market Street
Suite 2950
San Francisco, CA 94105-4318
415-421-2629
Fax: 415-421-6713
www.zellerbachfamilyfoundation.org
Provides funds to nonprofit organizations in the San Francisco Bay Area.

Cindy Rambo, Executive Director
Linda Avidan, Program Director

Colorado

2487 Adolph Coors Foundation
4100 East Mississippi Avenue
Suite 1850
Denver, CO 80246
303-388-1636
Fax: 303-388-1684
www.adolphcoors.org
Giving is primarily offered for programs with an emphasis on education, human services, youth and health.

Sally W Rippey, Executive Director
Jeanne L Bistranin, Program Officers

2488 Boettcher Foundation
600 17th Street
Suite 2210
Denver, CO 80202-5422
303-534-1937
800-323-9640
www.boettcherfoundation.org
Offers grants to educational institutions, with an emphasis on scholarships and fellowships.

Timothy W Schultz, President/Executive Director

2489 Denver Foundation
55 Madison Street
8th Floor
Denver, CO 80206
303-300-1790
Fax: 303-300-6547
www.denverfoundation.org
The Foundation serves as the steward and the administrator of the endowment, charged with investing its earned income in programs that meet the community's growing and changing needs. The Foundation has a solid history of supporting a broad array of community efforts. Grants are awarded to nonprofit organizations that touch nearly every meaningful artistic, cultural, civic, educational, human service and health interest of metro Denver's citizens.

David Miller, President/CEO
Betsy Mangone, VP Philanthropic Services

2490 El Pomar Foundation
10 Lake Circle
Colorado Springs, CO 80906-4201
719-633-7733
800-554-7711
Fax: 719-577-5702
www.elpomar.org
Founded in 1937, the philosophy of this foundation is simply to help foster a climate for excel-

lence in Colorado's third sector, the nonprofit community, as well as the foundation's own responsibility to improve the quality of life for all residents of Colorado. The foundation gives grants to the arts and humanities, civic and community, education, health, human services, and youth in community service.

William J Hybl, Executive Director

2491 Gates Foundation
500 Fifth Avenue North
Seattle, WA 98109
206-709-3100
info@gatesfoundation.org
www.gatesfoundation.org
The purpose of this foundation is to aid, assist, encourage, initiate, or carry on activities that will promote the health, well-being, security and broad education of all people. Because of a deep concern for and confidence in the future of Colorado, the foundation will invest primarily in institutions and programs that will enhance the quality of life for those who live and work in the state.

Thomas C Stokes, Executive Director

2492 Ruth & Vernon Taylor Foundation
518 17th Street
Suite 1670
Denver, CO 80202
303-893-5284
Fax: 303-893-8263
Offers support for education, the arts, human services and conservation.

Friday A Green, Executive Director

2493 US West Foundation
915 Memorial Drive
Manitowoc, WI 54220
920-684-6110
Fax: 920-684-7381
info@westfoundation.us
www.westfoundation.us
Grants are given in the areas of health and human services, including programs for youth, early childhood, elementary, secondary, higher and other.

Janet Rash, Executive Director
Thomas Bare, President

Connecticut

2494 Aetna Foundation
151 Farmington Avenue
Hartford, CT 06156-0001
860-273-0123
Fax: 860-273-4764
www.aetna.com/foundation/
Aetna gives grants in various areas that improve the community and its citizens. Certain areas include; children's health, education for at-risk students, and community initiatives. Geographic emphasis is placed on organizations and initiatives in Aetna's Greater Hartford headquarters communities; organizations in select communities across the country where Aetna has a significant local presence; and national organizations that can influence state, local or federal policies and programs.

Marilda L Gandara, President
Dave Wilmont, Executive Assistant

2495 Community Foundation of Greater New Haven
70 Audubon Street
New Haven, CT 06510-1248
203-777-2386
Fax: 203-787-6584
contactus@cfgnh.org
www.cfgnh.org
Offers a wide variety of giving with an emphasis on social services, youth services, AIDS research and education.

William W Ginsberg, President/CEO
Ronda Maddox, Administrative Assistant

2496 Connecticut Mutual Financial Services
140 Garden Street
Hartford, CT 06154-0200
860-987-6500
Giving is aimed at education, primarily higher education, equal opportunity programs and social services.

Astrida R Olds, Executive Director

2497 Hartford Foundation for Public Giving
10 Columbus Boulevard
8th Floor
Hartford, CT 06106-2693
860-548-1888
Fax: 860-524-8346
hpfg@hpfg.org
www.hfpg.org
Offers grants for demonstration programs and capital purposes with emphasis on educational institutions, social services and cultural programs.

Michael R Bangser, Executive Director
Edward Forand Jr, Chairman

2498 Loctite Corporate Contributions Program
Hartford Square North
10 Columbus Boulevard
5th Floor
Hartford, CT 06106-1976
860-571-5100
Fax: 860-571-5430
Offers support in various fields of interest including funding for educational programs for inner city youths in grades K-12.

Kiren Cooley, Corporate Contributions

2499 Louis Calder Foundation
125 Elm Street
New Canaan, CT 06840
203-966-8925
Fax: 203-966-5785
www.louiscalderfdn.org
Offers support to organizations who promote education, health and welfare of children and youth in New York City.

Holly Nuechterlein, Program Manager

2500 Sherman Fairchild Foundation
71 Arch Street
Greenwich, CT 06830-6544
203-661-9360
Fax: 203-661-9360
Offers grants in higher education, fine arts and cultural institutions.

Patricia A Lydon, Executive Director

2501 Smart Family Foundation
74 Pin Oak Lane
Wilton, CT 06897-1329
203-834-0400
Fax: 203-834-0412
The foundation is interested in educational projects that focus on primary and secondary school children.

Raymond Smart, Executive Director

2502 Worthington Family Foundation
P.O Box 4311
Traverse City, MI 49685
203-255-9400
www.worthington-family-foundation.org
Offers grants in the areas of elementary school education and secondary school education in Connecticut.

Worthington Johnson, Executive Director
Ruth Worthington, President

Delaware

2503 Crystal Trust
Po Box 39
Montchanin, DE 19710-0039
302-651-0533
Grants are awarded for higher and secondary education and social and family services.

Stephen C Doberstein, Executive Director

2504 HW Buckner Charitable Residuary Trust
JP Morgan Services
PO Box 8714
Wilmington, DE 19899-8714
302-633-1900
Focuses giving on educational and cultural organizations in New York, Rhode Island and Massachusetts.

2505 Longwood Foundation
100 W 10th Street
Suite 1109
Wilmington, DE 19801-1694
302-654-2477
Fax: 302-654-2323
Limited grants are offered to educational institutions and cultural programs.

David D Wakefield, Executive Director

District of Columbia

2506 Abe Wouk Foundation
3255 N Street NW
Washington, DC 20007-2845
Offers grants in elementary, secondary education and federated giving programs.

Herman Wouk, Executive Director

2507 Eugene & Agnes E Meyer Foundation
1250 Connecticut Avenue
Suite 800
Washington, DC 20036-2215
202-483-8294
Fax: 202-328-6850
www.meyerfoundation.org
Offers grants in the areas of development and housing, education and community services, arts and humanities, law and justice, health and mental health.

Julie L Rogers, President
Barbara Krumsiek, Chairman

2508 Foundation Center-District of Columbia
1627 K Street NW
3rd Floor
Washington, DC 20006-1708
202-331-1400
Fax: 202-331-1739
www.fdncenter.org/washington/index.jhtml
Member of The Foundation Center network, maintaining a collection of private foundation tax returns which provide information on the scope of grants dispensed to nonprofit organizations by those particular foundations.

2509 Foundation for the National Capitol Region
1201 15th Street NW
Suite 420
Washington, DC 20005
202-955-5890
Fax: 202-955-8084
www.cfncr.org
Grants are focused on organization strengthening and regional collaboration. The Foundation wishes to foster collaborations that identify, address, and increase awareness of regional issues, as well as help strengthen the region's existing nonprofit organizations to improve their financial stability. The Foundation welcomes requests from organizations serving the Greater Washington area that are tax-exempt under Section 501(c)(3) of the Internal Revenue Code.
Terry Lee Freeman, President

2510 Gilbert & Jaylee Mead Family Foundation
2700 Virginia Avenue NW #701
Washington, DC 20037-1908
202-338-0208
Offers support for education (K-12), the performing arts and community service programs for Washington, DC, Montgomery County, Maryland, and Geneva, Switzerland.
Linda Smith, Executive Director

2511 Hitachi Foundation
1509 22nd Street NW
Washington, DC 20037-1073
202-457-0588
Fax: 202-296-1098
www.hitachi.org
The majority of projects supported by the foundation: promote collaboration across sectors and among institutions, organizations and individuals; reflect multi-or-interdisciplinary perspectives; respect and value diversity of thought, action, and ethnicity. Grants are given in the areas of community development, education, global citizenship and program related investments.
Barbara Dyer, President/CEO

2512 Morris & Gwendolyn Cafritz Foundation
1825 K Street NW
Suite 1400
Washington, DC 20006-1202
202-223-3100
Fax: 202-296-7567
www.cafritzfoundation.org
Gives grants to organizations in the metropolitan area, focusing on arts, humanities and scholarships.
Sara Cofrin, Program Assistant
Michael Bigley, Program Officer

2513 Public Welfare Foundation
1200 U Street NW
Washington, DC 20009-4443
202-965-1800
Fax: 202-265-8851
info@publicwelfare.org
www.publicwelfare.org
Offers grants to grass roots organizations in the US and abroad with emphasis on the environment and education.
Larry Kressley, Executive Director
Teresa Langston, Director Of Programs

2514 Washington Post Company Educational Foundation
1150 15th Street NW
Washington, DC 20071-0002
202-334-6000
Offers support for pre-college and higher education including student scholarships and awards for academic excellence.
Eric Grant, Director Contributions

Florida

2515 Applebaum Foundation
1111 Biscaynees Boulevard
Tower 3, Room 853
North Miami, FL 33181
Offers an emphasis on higher education.

2516 Benedict Foundation for Independent Schools
607 Lantana Lane
Vero Beach, FL 32963-2315
www.thebenedictfoundation.org
Support is offered primarily for independent secondary schools that have been members of the National Association of Independent Schools for ten consecutive years.
Nancy H Benedict, Executive Director
Davis M Benedict, Vice President & Director

2517 Chatlos Foundation
PO Box 915048
Longwood, FL 32791-5048
407-862-5077
Fax: 407-862-0708
www.chatlos.org
Bible colleges and seminaries, liberal arts colleges, vocation and domestic education, medical education; children, elderly, disabled and learning disabled. The Foundation is non-receptive to primary or secondary education, the arts, medical research, individual churches. No direct scholarship support to individuals.
William J Chatlos, Executive Director

2518 Citibank of Florida Corporate Giving Program
8750 Doral Boulevard
7th Floor
Miami, FL 33718
305-599-5775
Fax: 305-599-5520
Offers support for K-12 education for at-risk children. Funding is also available through the program for housing and community development in the state of Florida.
Susan Yarosz, Executive Director

2519 Dade Community Foundation
200 S Biscayne Boulevard
Suite 505
Miami, FL 33131-2343
305-371-2711
Fax: 305-371-5342
www.dadecommunityfoundation.org
Offers support for projects in the fields of education, arts and culture.
Ruth Shack, Executive Director

2520 Innovating Worthy Projects Foundation
Lakeview Corporate Center
4045 Sheridan Avenue
Miami, FL 33140-2904
305-861-5352
Fax: 305-868-4293
info@IWPF.org
www.iwpf.org
Offers grants and support for education in the areas of childhood education and elementary education.
Dr. Irving Packer, Executive Director

2521 Jacksonville Public Library
Business, Science & Documents
303 N Laura St
Jacksonville, FL 32202-3374
904-630-2665
Fax: 904-630-2431
www.jpl.coj.net
Member of The Foundation Center network, maintaining a collection of private foundation tax returns which provide information on the scope of grants dispensed by that particular foundation.
Gretchen Mitchell, Business/Science Department

2522 Jessie Ball duPont Fund
One Independent Drive
Suite 1400
Jacksonville, FL 32202-5011
904-353-0890
800-252-3452
Fax: 904-353-3870
smagill@dupontfund.org
www.dupontfund.org
Grants limited to those institutions to which the donor contributed personally during the five year period ending December 31, 1964. Among the 325 institutions eligible to recieve funds are higher and secondary education intitutions, cultural and historic preservation programs, social services organizations, hospitals, health agencies, churches and church-related organizations and youth agencies.
Dr. Sherry P Magill, President
JoAnn Bennett, Director Administration

2523 Joseph & Rae Gann Charitable Foundation
10185 Collins Avenue
Apartment 317
Bal Harbour, FL 33154-1606
Offers support in the areas of elementary, secondary and theological education.

2524 Orlando Public Library-Orange County Library System
Social Sciences Department
101 E Central Boulivard
Orlando, FL 32801-2471
407-835-7323
Fax: 407-835-7646
ajacobe@ocls.lib.fl.us
www.ocls.lib.fl.us
Member of The Foundation Center network, maintaining a collection on microfiche of Florida private foundation tax returns which provide information on the scope of grants dispensed by that particular foundation. Other available resources include directories of foundations, guide to funding, and materials on successful grant acquisition. FC Search Foundation Center CD Rom.
Angela C Jacobe, Head Social Science Dpt

2525 Peter D & Eleanore Kleist Foundation
12734 Kenwood Lane
Suite 89
Fort Myers, FL 33907-5638
Support is given to secondary school education and higher education.
Peter D Kleist, Executive Director

2526 Robert G Friedman Foundation
76 Isla Bahia Drive
Fort Lauderdale, FL 33316-2331

Giving is offered to elementary and high schools, with minor support to indigent individuals and charitable activities.

Robert G Friedman, Executive Director

2527 Southwest Florida Community Foundation
8771 College Parkway
Suite 201
Fort Myers, FL 33919
239-274-5900
Fax: 239-274-5930
swflcfo@earthlink.net
www.floridacommunity.com
Offers grants and support in the areas of education, higher education, children and youth services and general charitable giving to Lee, Charlotte, Hendry, Glades, and Collier Counties, Florida.

Paul B Flynn, Executive Director
Carol McLaughlin, Program Director

2528 Student Help and Assistance Program to Education
C/O Michael Bienes
141 Bay Colony Drive
Fort Lauderdale, FL 33308-2024
Offers grants and support in the areas of elementary and secondary education, music and dance.

2529 Thomas & Irene Kirbo Charitable Trust
550 Water St
Suite 1327
Jacksonville, FL 32202-5113
904-354-7212
Favors smaller colleges in Florida and Georgia.

Murray Jenks, Executive Director

2530 Thompson Publishing Group
PO Box 26185
Tampa, FL 33623
800-876-0226
grants.thompson.com
Assists education administrators and grant seekers in successful fundraising in the public and private sectors.

Joel M Drucker, Executive Director

Georgia

2531 Atlanta-Fulton Public Library
Foundation Collection/Ivan Allen Department
1 Margaret Mitchell Square NW
Atlanta, GA 30303-1089
404-730-1700
Fax: 404-730-1990
www.af.public.lib.ga.us.org
Member of The Foundation Center network, maintaining a collection of private foundation tax returns which provide information on the scope of grants dispensed by that particular foundation.

2532 BellSouth Foundation
C/O BellSouth Corporation
1155 Peachtree Street NE
Sutie 7H08
Atlanta, GA 30309-3600
404-249-2396
Fax: 404-249-5696
www.bellsouthfoundation.org
The foundation's purpose is to improve education in the South and to address the problem of the inadequate schooling in the region.

Mary D Boehm, President
Beverly Fleming, Administrative Assistant

2533 Bradley Foundation
1241 North Franklin Place
Milwaukee, WI 53202-2901
414-291-9915
Fax: 414-291-9991
www.bradleyfdn.org
Focuses on higher educational facilities, elementary and secondary education, human services and federated giving programs.

Terry Considine, Chairman

2534 Callaway Foundation
209 W Broome Street
#790
Lagrange, GA 30241-3101
706-884-7348
Fax: 706-884-0201
www.callawayfoundation.org
Offers giving in the areas of elementary, higher and secondary education, including libraries and community giving.

JT Gresham, Executive Director

2535 Coca-Cola Foundation
Po Box 1734
Atlanta, GA 30301
404-676-2568
Fax: 404-676-8804
www.thecoca-colacompany.com
Committed to serving communities through education. The foundation supports programs for early childhood education, elementary and secondary schools, public and private colleges and universities, teacher training, adult learning and global education programs, among others.

Donald R Greene, Executive Director

2536 J Bulow Campbell Foundation
3050 Peachtree Road
Suite 270
Atlanta, GA 30305
404-658-9066
Fax: 404-659-4802
www.jbcf.org
The purpose of this foundation is to offer grants and support to privately supported education, human welfare, youth services and the arts in the state of Georgia.

John W Stephenson, Executive Director

2537 JK Gholston Trust
C/O NationsBank of Georgia
PO Box 992
Athens, GA 30603-0992
706-357-6271
Support is offered to elementary school and higher education facilities in the Comer, Georgia area.

Janey M Cooley, Executive Director

2538 John & Mary Franklin Foundation
C/O Bank South N.A.
PO Box 4956
Atlanta, GA 30302
404-521-7397
Offers grants in secondary school/education, higher education and youth services.

Virlyn Moore Sr, Executive Director

2539 John H & Wilhelmina D Harland Charitable Foundation
2 Piedmont Center NE
Suite 710
Atlanta, GA 30305-1502
404-264-9912
Fax: 404-266-8834
info@harlandfoundation.org
www.harlandfoundation.org
Children and higher education.

Jane G Hardesty, Executive Director
Gail G Byers, Grants Manager

2540 Joseph B Whitehead Foundation
191 Peachtree Street NE
Suite 3540
Atlanta, GA 30303-2916
404-522-6755
Fax: 404-522-7026
fdns@woodruff.org
www.jbwhitehead.org
Offers grants in education, cultural programs, the arts and civic affairs.

Charles H McTier, Executive Director
James B William, Chairman

2541 Lettie Pate Evans Foundation
191 Peachtree Street NE
Suite 3540
Atlanta, GA 30303-2916
404-522-6755
Fax: 404-522-7026
fdns@woodruff.org
www.lpevans.org
Offers grants in the areas of higher education, and support for educational and cultural institutions.

Charles H McTier, Executive Director
James B William, Chairman

2542 McCamish Foundation
1 Buckhead Loop NE #3060
Atlanta, GA 30326-1528
www.mccamish.com
Offers grants for conservation and educational institutions.

2543 Metropolitan Atlanta Community Foundation
50 Hurt Plaza
Suite 449
Atlanta, GA 30303
404-688-5525
Fax: 404-688-3060
www.atlcf.org
This foundation was organized for the administration of funds placed in trust for the purposes of improving education, community development and civic health of the 19-county metropolitan area of Atlanta.

Winsome Hawkins Sr, Executive Director
Alicia Phillip, President

2544 Mill Creek Foundation
4400 Braselton Hwy
Hoschton, GA 30548-0190
478-237-0101
Fax: 478-237-6187
www.mccef.org
The foundation's primary interests are educational programs in all levels of study in Emanuel County, Georgia.

James H Morgan, Executive Director

2545 Mills Bee Lane Memorial Foundation
Nations Bank of Georgia
PO Box 9626
Savannah, GA 31412-9626
Offers support in various areas of education, including higher, secondary, and elementary.

2546 Peyton Anderson Foundation
577 Mulberry Street
Suite 830
Macon, GA 31201
478-743-5359
Fax: 912-742-5201
grants@pafdn.org
www.peytonanderson.org

Supports organizations and programs that center on elementary education, higher education, adult education, literacy and basic skills and youth services, in Bibb County, Georgia only.

Juanita T Jordan, Executive Director
Karen Lambert, President

2547 **Rich Foundation**
11 Piedmont Avenue NE
Atlanta, GA 30303
404-262-2266
Funds are allocated to social services, health, the arts and education.

Anne Berg, Executive Director

2548 **Robert & Polly Dunn Foundation**
PO Box 723194
Atlanta, GA 31139-0194
404-816-2883
Fax: 404-237-2150
Offers support in the areas of child development, education, higher education, and children and youth services.

Karen C Wilbanks, Executive Director

2549 **Sapelo Foundation**
4503 New Jesup Highway
Brunswick, GA 31520
912-265-0520
Fax: 912-265-1888
info@sapelofoundation.org
sapelofoundation.org
Promotes social change affecting rural communities, the environment and vulnerable people in Georgia. The foundation offers a scholarship program as well as grants to students of McIntosh County, Georgia.

Christine Reeves Strigaro, Executive Director
Seandra Pope, Trustee

2550 **Tull Charitable Foundation**
50 Hurt Plaza SE
Suite 1245
Atlanta, GA 30303-2916
404-659-7079
www.tullfoundation.org
Offers support to secondary schools, elementary schools and higher education facilities in the state of Georgia.

Barbara Cleveland, Executive Director

2551 **Warren P & Ava F Sewell Foundation**
PO Box 645
Bremen, GA 30110-0645
Offers support in elementary school, secondary school education and religion.

Jack Worley, Executive Director

Hawaii

2552 **Barbara Cox Anthony Foundation**
1132 Bishop Street #120
Honolulu, HI 96813-2807
Offers support to secondary schools, higher education, and human service organizations in Hawaii.

Barner Anthony, Executive Director

2553 **Cooke Foundation**
827 Fort Street Mall
Honolulu, HI 96813
808-537-6333
888-731-3863
Fax: 808-521-6286
foundations@hcf-hawaii.org
www.hawaiicommunityfoundation.org
The environment, the arts, education and social services are the priority areas for this foundation.

Lisa Schiff, Private Foundation Service
Samuel Cooke, President & Trustee

2554 **Harold KL Castle Foundation**
1197 Auloa Road
Kailua, HI 96734-2835
808-263-7073
Fax: 808-261-6918
www.castlefoundation.org
Grants are given in the area of education, community and cultural/community affairs.

Terrence R George, Executive Director
H Mitchell D'Olier, President

2555 **Hawaiian Electric Industries Charitable Foundation**
PO Box 730
Honolulu, HI 96808-0730
808-532-5862
www.hei.com
Offers support for education, including higher education, business education, educational associations and secondary schools.

Scott Shirai, Executive Director
Robert F Clark, President

2556 **James & Abigail Campbell Foundation**
1001 Kamokila Boulevard
Kapolei, HI 96707-2014
808-674-3167
Fax: 808-674-3349
keolal@jamescampbell.com
www.campbellfamilyfoundation.org
Offers support in education for schools and educational programs related to literacy or job training in Hawaii.

Theresia McMurdo, Public Relations
D. Keola Lloyd, Grants Manager

2557 **Oceanic Cablevision Foundation**
200 Akamainui Street
Mililani, HI 96789-3999
808-625-8359
Offers support in a variety of areas with an emphasis on education, especially early childhood and cultural programs.

Kit Beuret, Executive Director

2558 **Samuel N & Mary Castle Foundation**
733 Bishop Street
Suite 1275
Honolulu, HI 96813-2912
808-522-1101
Fax: 808-522-1103
acastle@aloha.net
www.fdncenter.org
Funding is offered in the areas of education, human services and the arts for the state of Hawaii.

Annually

Al Castle, Executive Director

2559 **University of Hawaii**
Hamilton Library
2550 The Mall
Honolulu, HI 96822-2233
808-956-7214
Fax: 808-956-5968
www.libweb.hawaii.edu/uhmlib
Member of The Foundation Center network, maintaining a collection of private foundation tax returns which provide information on the scope of grants dispensed by that particular foundation.

Idaho

2560 **Boise Public Library**
715 S Capitol Boulevard
Boise, ID 83702-7115
208-384-4076
www.boisepubliclibrary.org
Member of The Foundation Center network, maintaining a collection of private foundation tax returns which provide information on the scope of grants dispensed by that particular foundation.

2561 **The Whittenberger Foundation**
PO Box 1073
Caldwell, ID 83606-1073
E-mail: whittfnd@cableone.net
www.whittenberger.org
Provides funding for projects and initiatives that seek to improve quality of life for children and young people. Fields of interest to the foundation include education, arts and culture, health, social welfare, recreation and the environment.

Scott Gipson, Chair
Elaine Carpenter, Vice Chair

2562 **Walter & Leona Dufresne Foundation**
1150 W State Street
Boise, ID 83702-5327
Offers support in the areas of secondary school education and higher education.

Royce Chigbrow, Executive Director

Illinois

2563 **Ameritech Foundation**
30 S Wacker Drive
Floor 34
Chicago, IL 60606-7487
312-750-5223
Fax: 312-207-1098
www.ntlf.com
A foundation that offers grants to elementary school/education, secondary school/education and higher education.

Michael E Kuhlin, Executive Director

2564 **Carus Corporate Contributions Program**
315 5th Street
Peru, IL 61354-2859
815-223-1500
Offers support for higher, secondary, elementary and early childhood education.

Robert J Wilmot, Executive Director

2565 **Chauncey & Marion Deering McCormick Foundation**
410 N Michigan Avenue
Suite 590
Chicago, IL 60611-4220
312-644-6720
Preschool education, journalism and the improvement of socio-economic condition of Metropolitan Chicago are the main areas of giving for this foundation.

Charles E Schroeder, Executive Director

2566 **Chicago Community Trust**
225 North Michigan Avenue
Suite 2200
Chicago, IL 60601-1088
312-616-8000
Fax: 312-616-7955
sandy@cct.org
www.cct.org
A community foundation that offers support for general operating projects and specific programs

and projects in areas including child development, education and higher education.

Sandy Chears, Grants Manager
Terry Mazany, President

2567 Coleman Foundation
651 West Washington Boulevard
Suite 306
Chicago, IL 60661-2515
312-902-7120
Fax: 312-902-7124
info@colemanfoundation.org
www.colemanfoundation.org
A nonprofit, private foundation established in the state of Illinois in 1951. Major areas of support include health, educational, cultural, scientific and social programs. Grants generally focus on organizations within the Midwest and particularly within the state of Illinois and the Chicago Metropolitan area. No grants are made for programs outside of the United States. Ongoing support is not available, continuing programs must indicate how they will be sustained in the future.

Rosa Janus, Program Manager
Michael W Hennessy, President/CEO

2568 Dellora A & Lester J Norris Foundation
PO Box 4325
Saint Charles, IL 60174-9075
630-377-4111
Education, health and social services are the main concerns of this foundation, with Illinois, Colorado and Florida being their priority.

Eugene W Butler, Executive Director

2569 Dillon Foundation
PO Box 454
Boulder, MT 59632-0537
406-980-1588
info@dillonfoundation.org
www.dillonfoundation.org
Offers support for educational purposes, including higher education and community services.

Peter W Dillon, Executive Director

2570 Dr. Scholl Foundation
1033 Skokie Boulevard
Suite 230
Northbrook, IL 60062
847-559-7430
www.drschollfoundation.com
Applications for grants are considered in the following areas: private education at all levels including elementary, secondary schools, colleges and universities and medical and nursing institutions; general charitable organizations and programs, including grants to hospitals and programs for children, developmentally disabled and senior citizens; civic, cultural, social services, health care, economic and religious activities.

Pamela Scholl, Executive Director

2571 Evanston Public Library
1703 Orrington Avenue
Evanston, IL 60201-3886
847-866-0300
Fax: 847-866-0313
www.evanston.lib.il.us
Member of The Foundation Center network, maintaining a collection of private foundation tax returns which provide information on the scope of grants dispensed by that particular foundation.

Neal J Ney, Director

2572 Farny R Wurlitzer Foundation
PO Box 418
Sycamore, IL 60178-0418
Offers support in the areas of education, including programs for minorities, early childhood, elementary and secondary institutions, music education and organizations.

William A Rolfing, Executive Director

2573 Grover Hermann Foundation
1000 Hill Grove
Suite 200
Western Springs, IL 60558-6306
708-246-8331
Focus of giving is on higher education and private schooling activities.

Paul K Rhoads, Executive Director

2574 Joyce Foundation
70 W Madison Street
Suite 2750
Chicago, IL 60602
312-782-2464
Fax: 312-782-4160
info@joycefdn.org
www.joycefdn.org
Based in Chicago with assets of $1 billion, the Joyce foundation supports efforts to strengthen public policies in ways that improve the quality of life in the Great Lakes region. Last year the foundation made nearly $17 million in grants to groups working to inprove public education in Chicago, Cleveland, Detroit and Milwaukee.

Ellen Alberding, President

2575 Lloyd A Fry Foundation
120 S Lasalle Street
Suite 1950
Chicago, IL 60603-3419
312-580-0310
Fax: 312-580-0980
www.fryfoundation.org
The foundation primarily supports education, higher education, the performing arts, and social service organizations.

Unmi Song, Executive Director

2576 Northern Trust Company Charitable Trust
Community Affairs Division
50 S Lasalle Street
Chicago, IL 60603-1006
312-630-6000
www.ntrs.com
Offers grants in the areas of community development, education and early childhood education.

Marjorie W Lundy, Executive Director

2577 Palmer Foundation
734 15th Street NW
Suite 600
Washington, DC 20005
202-595-1020
Fax: 202-833-5540
admin@thepalmerfoundation.org
www.thepalmerfoundation.org
Offers grants in elementary and secondary education, as well as youth services and Protestant churches.

2578 Philip H Corboy Foundation
33 N Dearborn Street
Chicago, IL 60602-2502
312-346-3191
www.corboydemetrio.com
Offers grants in the areas of elementary, secondary, law school education and health care.

2579 Polk Brothers Foundation
20 W Kinzie Street
Suite 1100
Chicago, IL 60610-4600
312-527-4684
Fax: 312-527-4681
www.polkbrosfdn.org
Offers grants for new or ongoing programs to organizations whose work is based in the areas of education, social services and health care.

Nikki W Stein, Executive Director
Shiela A Robinson, Grants Administrator

2580 Prince Charitable Trust
303 West Madison Street
Suite 1900
Chicago, IL 60606-7407
312-419-8700
Fax: 312-419-8558
www.fdncenter.org/grantmaker/prince/chicago.html
Offers support for cultural programs, public school programming and social service organizations.

Benna B Wilde, Managing Director
Sharon L Robison, Grants Manager

2581 Regenstein Foundation
8600 W Bryn Mawr Avenue
Suite 705N
Chicago, IL 60631-3579
773-693-6464
Fax: 773-693-2480
Offers grants for educational and general charitable institutions within the metropolitan Chicago area and the state of Illinois.

Joseph Regenstein Jr, Executive Director

2582 Richard H Driehaus Foundation
333 N Michigan Avenue
Suite 510
Chicago, IL 60601-1604
312-641-5772
Fax: 312-641-5736
www.driehausfoundation.org
Offers support in elementary, secondary and higher education in the state of Illinois.

Susan Fischer, Executive Director
Peter Handler, Program Director

2583 Robert R McCormick Tribune Foundation
435 N Michigan Avenue
Suite 770
Chicago, IL 60611-4066
312-222-3512
Fax: 312-222-3523
www.rrmtf.org
Offers contributions for private higher education and rehabilitation services.

Nicholas Goodban, Senior VP/Philanthropy
Richard A Behrenhausen, President/CEO

2584 Sears-Roebuck Foundation
Sears Tower
Department 903-BSC 51-02
Chicago, IL 60684
312-875-8337
The foundation focuses its giving primarily on projects that address education and volunteerism.

Paula A Banke, Executive Director

2585 Spencer Foundation
875 N Michigan Avenue
Suite 3930
Chicago, IL 60611-1803
312-337-7000
Fax: 312-337-0282
www.spencer.org

Supports research aimed at the practice of understanding and expanding knowledge in the area of education.

Michael McPherson, President

2586 Sulzer Family Foundation
1940 W Irving Park Road
Chicago, IL 60613-2437
312-321-4700
Offers giving for education, including higher, secondary, elementary and adult education in the areas of Chicago, Illinois.

John J Hoellen, Executive Director

2587 United Airlines Foundation
1800 Massachusetts Avenue
Suite 400
Washington, DC 20036-0919
847-952-5714
www.unfoundation.org
Offers a wide variety of support programs with an emphasis on education and educational reform.

Eileen Younglove, Executive Director
Timothy E Wirth, President

2588 Valenti Charitable Foundation
Valenti Builders
PO Box 2534
Rancho Santa Fe, CA 92067-3311
858-759-9239
Fax: 858-759-1319
Irene@valentifoundation.org
www.valentifoundation.org
Offers support in elementary education, secondary school education, higher education and children and youth services.

Valenti Sr Trustee, Executive Director

Indiana

2589 Allen County Public Library
900 Library Plaza
Fort Wayne, IN 46802-3699
260-421-1200
Fax: 260-421-1386
www.acpl.lib.in.us
Member of The Foundation Center network, maintaining a collection of private foundation tax returns which provide information on the scope of grants dispensed by that particular foundation.

2590 Arvin Foundation
1 Noblitt Plaza #3000
Columbus, IN 47201-6079
812-379-3207
Fax: 812-379-3688
Giving is offered primarily to primary, secondary and higher education and technical training.

E Fred Meyer, Executive Director

2591 Clowes Fund
320 N Meridian Street Suite 316
The Chamber of Commerce Building
Indianapolis, IN 46204-1722
800-943-7209
Fax: 800-943-7286
www.clowesfund.org
Offers giving for higher and secondary education; the performing arts; marine biology and social service organizations.

Elizabeth Casselman, Executive Director
Alexander W Clowes, President

2592 Dekko Foundation
PO Box 548
Kendallville, IN 46755-0548
260-347-1278
Fax: 260-347-7103
Offers support for all levels of education and human service organizations.

Linda Speakman, Executive Director

2593 Eli Lilly & Company Corporate Contribution Program
Lilly Corporate Center D.C. 1627
Indianapolis, IN 46285
317-276-2000
Offers support in the areas of secondary school/education, higher education and health care programs.

Thomas King, President

2594 Foellinger Foundation
520 E Berry Street
Fort Wayne, IN 46802-2002
260-422-2900
Fax: 260-422-9436
info@foellinger.org
www.foellinger.org
Giving is aimed at higher education and other secondary and elementary projects, community programs and social service organizations.

Harry V Owen, Executive Director

2595 Indianapolis Foundation
615 N Alabama Street
Suite 119
Indianapolis, IN 46204-1498
317-634-2423
Fax: 317-684-0943
www.indyfund.org
Offers support in the areas of education and neighborhood services.

Kenneth Gladish, Executive Director

2596 John W Anderson Foundation
402 Wall Street
Valparaiso, IN 46383-2562
219-462-4611
Fax: 219-531-8954
Offers grants in the areas of higher education, youth programs, human services, and arts and humanities. Grants are limited primarily to Northwest Indian organizations.

William Vinovich, Vice Chairman/Trustee

2597 Lilly Endowment
2801 N Meridian Street
Indianapolis, IN 46208-0068
317-924-5471
Fax: 317-926-4431
www.lillyendowment.org
Supports the causes of religion, education and community development. Although the Endowment supports efforts of national significance, especially in the field of religion, it is primarily committed to its hometown, Indianapolis, and home state, Indiana.

Sue Ellen Walker, Communications Associate

2598 Moore Foundation
1661 Page Mill Road
Palo Alto, CA 94304-2158
317-848-2013
Fax: 317-571-0744
info@moore.org
www.moore.org
Offers support in elementary school and secondary school education, higher education, business school education and youth services in Indiana.

Eileen C Ryan, Executive Director
Gordon Moore, Chairman

2599 W Brooks Fortune Foundation
7933 Beaumont Green W Drive
Indianapolis, IN 46250-1652
317-842-1303
Support is limited to education-related programs in Indiana.

William Brooks Fortune, Executive Director

Iowa

2600 Cedar Rapids Public Library
Funding Information Center
500 1st Street SE
Cedar Rapids, IA 52401-2095
319-398-5123
Fax: 319-398-0476
www.crlibrary.org
Member of The Foundation Center network, maintaining a collection of private foundation tax returns which provide information on the scope of grants dispensed by that particular foundation.

Tamara Glise, Public Services Manager
Eileen C Ryan, Executive Director

2601 RJ McElroy Trust
425 Cedar Street
Suite 312
Waterloo, IA 50701
312
www.mcelroytrust.org
The trust funds grants to educational youth programs in the northeast quarter of Iowa. The trust guidelines do not include grants to individuals.

Linda L Klinger, Executive Director

Kansas

2602 Mary Jo Williams Charitable Trust
PO Box 660075
Dallas, TX 75266-0075
866-866-7509
Offers support in the areas of early childhood education, higher education, and children and youth services.

Michael E Collins, Executive Director

2603 Sprint Foundation
2330 Shawnee Mission Parkway
Westwood, KS 66205-2090
913-624-3343
www.sprint.com
Offers grants in a variety of areas with an emphasis on education, including business education, secondary education and higher education.

Don G Forsythe, Executive Director

2604 Wichita Public Library
223 S Main Street
Wichita, KS 67202-3795
316-261-8500
Fax: 316-262-4540
www.wichita.lib.ks.us
Member of The Foundation Center network, maintaining a collection of private foundation tax returns which provide information on the scope of grants dispensed by that particular foundation.

Kentucky

2605 Ashland Incorporated Foundation
50 E River Center Boulevard
Covington, KY 41012
859-815-3630
Fax: 859-815-4496
www.ashland.com

Offers support to educational organizations, colleges and universities, as well as giving an employee matching gift program to higher education and community funding.

James O'Brien, CEO

2606 Gheens Foundation
401 W Main Street
Suite 705
Louisville, KY 40202
502-584-4650
Fax: 502-584-4652
www.gheensfoundation.org
The foundation's support is aimed at higher and secondary education, ongoing teacher education, and social service agencies.

James N Davis, Executive Director
William G Duncan, Secretary

2607 James Graham Brown Foundation
4350 Brownsboro Road
Suite 200
Louisville, KY 40207
502-896-2440
Fax: 502-896-1774
info@jgbf.org
www.jgbf.org
Offers grants in the areas of higher education and social services.

Mason Rummel, Executive Director
Dodie L McKenzie, Program Officer

2608 Louisville Free Public Library
301 York Street
Louisville, KY 40203-2257
502-574-1611
Fax: 502-574-1657
www.lfpl.org
Member of The Foundation Center network, maintaining a collection of private foundation tax returns which provide information on the scope of grants dispensed by that particular foundation.

2609 Margaret Hall Foundation
6685 Walnutwood Circle
Baltimore, MD 21212-1727
443-708-3548
www.margarethallfoundation.org
Awards grants and scholarships to private, nonprofit secondary schools for innovative programming.

Helen R Burg, Executive Director

2610 VV Cooke Foundation Corporation
220 Mount Mercy Drive
Pewee Valley, KY 40056-9068
502-241-0303
Offers support in education and youth services with an emphasis on Baptist church and school support.

John B Gray, Executive Director

Louisiana

2611 Baton Rouge Area Foundation
402 N 4th Street
Baton Rouge, LA 70802
225-387-6126
877-387-6126
Fax: 225-387-6153
www.braf.org
Offers grants in the area of elementary and secondary education and health.

John G Davies, President

2612 Booth-Bricker Fund
826 Union Street
Suite 300
New Orleans, LA 70112-1421
504-581-2430
Fax: 504-566-4785
Does not have a formal grant procedure or grant application form; nor does it publish an annual report. The Booth-Bricker Fund makes contributions for the purposes of promoting, developing and fostering religious, charitable, scientific, literary or educational programs, primarily in the state of Louisiana. It does not make contributions to individuals.

Gray S Parker, Chairman

2613 East Baton Rouge Parish Library
Centroplex Branch Grants Collection
7711 Goodwood Boulevard
Baton Rouge, LA 70806
225-231-3750
www.ebrpl.com
Member of The Foundation Center network, maintaining a collection of private foundation tax returns which provide information on the scope of grants dispensed by that particular foundation.

2614 Fred B & Ruth B Zigler Foundation
Zigler Foundation
PO Box 986
Zigler Building
Jennings, LA 70546-0986
337-824-2413
Fax: 337-824-2414
frizler@bellsouth.net
www.ziglerfoundation.org
Offers support to higher, secondary and primary education.

Julie G Berry, President
Marie Romero, Secretary

2615 New Orleans Public Library
Business & Science Division
219 Loyola Avenue
New Orleans, LA 70112-2044
504-529-7323
Fax: 504-596-2609
www.nutrias.org
Member of The Foundation Center network, maintaining a collection of private foundation tax returns which provide information on the scope of grants dispensed by that particular foundation.

2616 Shreve Memorial Library
424 Texas Street
Shreveport, LA 71101-5452
318-226-5897
Fax: 318-226-4780
webmaster@shreve-lib.org
www.shreve-lib.org
Member of The Foundation Center network, maintaining a collection of private Louisiana foundation tax returns which provide information on the scope of grants dispensed by that particular foundation.

Carlos Colon, Reference Supervisor

Maine

2617 Clarence E Mulford Trust
PO Box 290
Fryeburg, ME 04037-0290
207-935-2061
Fax: 207-935-3939
Offers grants to charitable, educational and scientific organizations for the purpose of improving education.

David R Hastings II, Executive Director

2618 Harold Alfond Trust
C/O Dexter Shoe Company
Two Monument Square
Portland, ME 04101-0353
207-828-7999
info@haroldalfoundation.org
www.haroldalfondfoundation.org
Grants are offered to secondary and higher education in Maine and Maryland.

Keith Burden, Executive Director

Maryland

2619 Abell Foundation
111 S Calvert Street
Suite 2300
Baltimore, MD 21202-6182
410-547-1300
Fax: 410-539-6579
abell@abell.org
www.abell.org
The foundation supports education with an emphasis on public education, including early childhood and elementary, research, and minority education.

Robert C Embry Jr, Executive Director
Ellen Mullan, Controller

2620 Aegon USA
1111 N Charles Street
Baltimore, MD 21201-5505
410-576-4571
Fax: 410-347-8685
www.aegonins.com
Offers grants in elementary school, secondary school, higher education and medical school education.

Larry G Brown, Executive Director

2621 Clarence Manger & Audrey Cordero Plitt Trust
C/O First National Bank of Maryland
25 S Charles St
Baltimore, MD 21201-3330
410-566-0914
Offers grants to educational institutions for student loans and scholarships.

Mary M Kirgan, Executive Director

2622 Clark-Winchcole Foundation
Air Rights Building
3 Bethesda Metro Center
Suite 550
Bethesda, MD 20814
301-654-3607
Fax: 301-654-3140
Offers grants in the areas of higher education and social service agencies.

Laura E Philips, Executive Director

2623 Commonwealth Foundation
9737 Colesville Road
Suite 800
Silver Spring, MD 20910
301-495-4400
Offers grants in the areas of early childhood education, child development, elementary schools, secondary schools and youth services.

Barbara Bainum, Executive Director

2624 Dresher Foundation
4940 Campbell Boulevard
Suite 110
Baltimore, MD 21236
410-933-0384
web@jdgraphicdesign.com
www.jdgraphicdesign.com/dresher/dresherfoundation/

Offers giving in the areas of elementary school, early childhood education, meals on wheels, and food distribution.

2625 Edward E Ford Foundation
66 Pearl Street
Suite 322
Portland, ME 04101
207-774-2346
Fax: 207-774-2348
office@eeford.org
www.eeford.org
Offers giving to secondary schools and private education in the US and its protectorates.
Robert Hallett, Executive Director

2626 Enoch Pratt Free Library
Social Science & History Department
400 Cathedral Street
Baltimore, MD 21201-4484
301-396-5430
www.pratt.lib.md.us
Member of The Foundation Center network, maintaining a collection of private foundation tax returns which provide information on the scope of grants dispensed by that particular foundation.

2627 France-Merrick Foundation
The Exchange
2 Hamill Rd,Quadrangle East
Suite 302
Baltimore, MD 21210-2139
410-464-2004
Fax: 410-832-5704
rschaefer@france-merrickfdn-org
Offers grants in the areas of public education, private and higher education, health, social services and cultural activities.
Frederick W Lafferty, Executive Director

2628 Grayce B Kerr Fund
117 Bay Street
Easton, MD 21601-2769
410-822-6652
Fax: 410-822-4546
office@gbkf.org
www.gbkf.org
The major area of interest to the fund is education, including higher, elementary and early childhood education for the state of Maryland with focus on the Eastern Shore Counties.
Margaret van den Berg, Administrative Assistant
John R Valliant, President

2629 Henry & Ruth Blaustein Rosenberg Foundation
Blaustein Building
10 East Baltimore Street
Suite 1111
Baltimore, MD 21202
410-347-7201
Fax: 410-347-7210
info@blaufund.org
www.blaufund.org
Offers grants in the areas of secondary and higher education.
Betsy F Ringel, Executive Director
Henry A Rosenberg Jr, President

2630 James M Johnston Trust for Charitable and Educational Purposes
2 Wisconsin Circle
Suite 600
Chevy Chase, MD 20815-7003
301-907-0135
Grants are given to higher and secondary educational institutions located in Washington, DC and North Carolina.
Julie Sanders, Executive Director

2631 John W Kluge Foundation
15004 Sunflower CT
Rockville, MD 20853-0174
301-929-9340
Offers grants in higher education and secondary education.

2632 Marion I & Henry J Knott Foundation
3904 Hickory Avenue
Baltimore, MD 21211-1834
410-235-7068
Fax: 410-889-2577
info@knottfoundation.org
www.knottfoundation.org
Grantmaking limited to private nonsectarian schools and Catholic schools geographically located within the Archdiocese of Baltimore, Maryland.
Greg Cantori, Executive Director

2633 Robert G & Anne M Merrick Foundation
The Exchange
1122 Kenilworth Drive
Suite 118
Baltimore, MD 21204-2142
410-832-5700
Fax: 410-832-5704
Offers grants for public education, higher education and social services.
Frederick W Lafferty, Executive Director

Massachusetts

2634 Associated Grantmakers of Massachusetts
55 Court Street
Suite 520
Boston, MA 02108-4304
617-426-2606
Fax: 617-426-2849
www.agmconnect.org
Member of The Foundation Center network, maintaining a collection of private foundation tax returns which provide information on the scope of grants dispensed by that particular foundation.
Ron Ancrum, President
Martha Moore, Director Center Philanthropy

2635 Boston Foundation
75 Arlington Street
10th Floor
Boston, MA 02116-4407
617-338-1700
Fax: 617-338-1604
www.tbf.org
Supports local educational, social and housing programs and institutions.
Paul Grogan, President

2636 Boston Globe Foundation II
135 Morrissey Boulevard
Boston, MA 02107
617-929-2895
Fax: 617-929-7889
www.bostonglobe.com/community/foundation/partner.stm
The foundation's highest priority is community based agencies which understand, represent and are part of the following populations; children and youth with disabilities, children and youth with AIDS, refugees, low-birth weight babies, pregnant and nursing mothers and incarcerated youth.
Suzanne W Maas, Executive Director
Leah P Bailey

2637 Boston Public Library
Social Sciences Reference
700 Boylston Street
Boston, MA 02116-2813
617-536-5400
www.bpl.org
Member of The Foundation Center network, maintaining a collection of private foundation tax returns which provide information on the scope of grants dispensed by that particular foundation.
Bernard Margolis, President

2638 Dean Foundation for Little Children
C/O Boston Safe Deposit & Trust Company
PO Box 185
Pittsburgh, PA 15230-0185
Giving is centered on little children age twelve and under for the care and relief of destitute children. Provides support for preschools, day care, summer camps and other programs.
Nancy Criscitiello, Executive Director

2639 Hyams Foundation
50 Federal Street
Floor 9
Boston, MA 02110-2210
617-426-5600
Fax: 617-426-5696
www.hyamsfoundation.org
The foundation seeks to promote understanding and appreciation of diversity, including race, ethnicity, gender, sexual orientation, age, physical ability, class and religion. The foundation's primary objective is to meet the needs of low-income and other underserved populations, striving to address the causes of those needs, whenever possible. Foundation supports low-income communities in their efforts to identify their own problems, solve these problems and improve people's lives.
Elizabeth B Smith, Executive Director
Angela Brown, Director of Programs

2640 Irene E & George A Davis Foundation
C/O Ann T Keiser
1 Monarch Place
Suite 1450
Springfield, MA 01144-1300
413-734-8336
Fax: 413-734-7845
info@davisfdn.org
www.davisfdn.org
Education and social service organizations and programs in Western Massachusetts are the primary concern of this foundation.
Mary E Walachy, Executive Director

2641 James G Martin Memorial Trust
122 Pond Street
Jamaica Plain, MA 02130-2714
Giving is centered on elementary education and higher education in Massachusetts.
Ms Martin, Executive Director

2642 Jessie B Cox Charitable Trust
Grants Management Association
60 State Street
Boston, MA 02109-1899
617-227-7940
Fax: 617-227-0781
www.hemenwaybarnes.com/selectsrv/jbcox/cox.html
This trust makes grants for projects which will address important social issues in the trust's fields of interest and for which adequate funding from other sources cannot be obtained. The trust funds projects in New England in the areas of health, ed-

ucation and the environment. The trustees look to support special projects which will assist the applicants to achieve their long-range organizational goals.

Michaelle Larkins, Executive Director
Susan M Fish, Grants Administrator

2643 LG Balfour Foundation
Fleet Bank of Massachusetts
75 State Street
Boston, MA 02109-1775
617-346-4000
Offers support for scholarships and innovative projects designed to eliminate barriers and improve access to education for all potentially qualified students.

Kerry Herliney, Executive Director

2644 Little Family Foundation
33 Broad Street
Suite 10
Boston, MA 02109-4216
617-723-6771
Fax: 617-723-7107
Offers scholarships at various business schools and Junior Achievement programs in secondary schools.

Arthur D Little, Executive Director

2645 Rogers Family Foundation
10 Clay Street
Suite 200
Oakland, CA 94067-4501
510-899-7918
Fax: 978-685-1588
www.rogersfoundation.org
Offers support in the areas of secondary and higher education in the Lawrence, Massachusetts area.

Kathleen Rogers, President
Nicole Taylor, Secretary/Treasurer

2646 State Street Foundation
225 Franklin Street
12th Floor
Boston, MA 02110
617-664-1937
www.statestreet.com
Offers grants to organizations that help improve the quality of life in the greater Boston area. Interest includes human services, public and secondary education, vocational education, and arts and culture programs.

Madison Thompson, Executive Director

2647 Sudbury Foundation
326 Concord Road
Sudbury, MA 01776-1843
978-443-0849
Fax: 978-579-9536
www.sudburyfoundation.org
Offers college scholarships to local high school seniors who meet eligibility criteria.

Marilyn Martino, Executive Director
Tricia Brunner, Grants Administrator

2648 Trustees of the Ayer Home
PO Box 1865
Lowell, MA 01853-1865
978-452-5914
Fax: 978-452-5914
Funding (greater Lowell, MA only) educational programs (RLF, SMARTS). Primary interests are women and children.

D Donahue, Assistant Treasurer

2649 Weld Foundation
Peter Loring/Janice Palumbo
Loring, Wolcott & Coolidge
30 Congress Street
Boston, MA 02110-2409
617-523-6531
Fax: 617-523-6535
Grants are offered in the areas of elementary, secondary and higher education in Massachusetts.

2650 Western Massachusetts Funding Resource Center
65 Elliot Street
Springfield, MA 01105-1713
413-732-3175
Fax: 413-452-0618
www.diospringfield.org/wmfrc.html
Member of The Foundation Center network, maintaining a collection of private foundation tax returns which provide information on the scope of grants dispensed by that particular foundation.

Kathleen Dowd, Director
Jean Los, Administrative Assistant

2651 William E Schrafft & Bertha E Schrafft Charitable Trust
77 Summer Street
Boston, MA 02110
617-457-7327
www.schrafftcharitable.org
Giving is primarily allocated to educational programs in the Boston metropolitan area.

Arthur H Parker, Trustee
Lavinia B Chase, Trustee

2652 Woodstock Corporation
Woodstock Corporation
27 School Street
Suite 200
Boston, MA 02108-2301
617-227-0600
Fax: 617-523-0229
info@woodstockcorp.com
www.woodstockcorp.com
Offers support in the area of secondary school education in the state of Massachusetts.

2653 Worcester Public Library
Grants Resource Center
3 Salem Square
Worcester, MA 01608
508-799-1655
Fax: 508-799-1652
www.worcpublib.org
Member of The Foundation Center network, maintaining a collection of private foundation tax returns which provide information on the scope of grants dispensed by that particular foundation.

J Peck, Director Grants Resource

Michigan

2654 Alex & Marie Manoogian Foundation
21001 Van Born Road
Taylor, MI 48180-1340
313-274-7400
Fax: 313-792-6657
Supports higher and secondary education, cultural programs and human service organizations.

Alex Manoogian, Executive Director

2655 Charles Stewart Mott Foundation
Office of Proposal Entry
503 S Saginaw Street
Suite 1200
Flint, MI 48502-1851
810-238-5651
800-645-1766
Fax: 810-237-4857
infocenter@mott.org
www.mott.org
Grants are given to nonprofit organizations with an emphasis on programs of volunteerism, at-risk youth, environmental protection, economic development and education.

2656 Chrysler Corporate Giving Program
12000 Chrysler Drive
Detroit, MI 48288-0001
810-576-5741
Offers support for education, especially secondary education and leadership development.

Lynn A Feldhouse, Executive Director

2657 Community Foundation for Southeastern Michigan
333 W Fort Street
Suite 2010
Detroit, MI 48226-3134
313-961-6675
Fax: 313-961-2886
cfsem@cfsem.orq
www.cfsem.org
Supports projects in the areas of education, culture and social services.

Mariam C Noland, President

2658 Community Foundation of Greater Flint
500 South Saginaw Street
Flint, MI 48502-2013
810-767-8270
Fax: 810-767-0496
cfgf@cfgf.org
www.cfgf.org
A community foundation that makes grants to benefit residents of Genessee County, Michigan. Areas of interest include: arts, education, environment, community services and health and social services.

Kathi Horton, President
Evan M Albert, VP Program

2659 Cronin Foundation
203 E Michigan Avenue
Marshall, MI 49068-1545
616-781-9851
Fax: 616-781-2070
Offers support to expand educational, social and cultural needs of the community within the Marshall, Michigan school district.

Joseph E Schroeder, Executive Director

2660 Detroit Edison Foundation
2000 2nd Avenue
Room 1046
Detroit, MI 48226-1279
313-235-9271
Fax: 313-237-9271
www.my.dteenergy.com
Offers support for all levels of education, and local community social services and cultural organizations in Southeast Michigan.

Katharine W Hunt, Executive Director

2661 Ford Motor Company Fund
One American Road
PO Box 1899
Dearborn, MI 48126-2798
888-313-0102
Fax: 313-337-6680
www.ford.com
Ford Motor Company Fund continues the legacy of Henry Ford's commitment to innovative education at all levels. We remain dedicated to creating and enriching educational opportunities, especially in the areas of

science, engineering, math and business, while promoting diversity in education.

Sandra E Ulsh, President
Jim Graham, Manager Education Programs

2662 Frey Foundation
40 Pearl Street NW
Suite 1100
Grand Rapids, MI 49503-3023
616-451-0303
Fax: 616-451-8481
www.freyfdn.org
Awards grants and supports the needs of children in their early years, support for environmental education and protection of our natural resources.

Milton W Rohwer, President
Teresa J Crawford, Grants Manager

2663 General Motors Foundation
PO Box 33170
Detroit, MI 48232-5170
313-556-4260
www.gm.com/company/gmability/philanthropy
Offers support for higher education, cultural programs and civic affairs.

Ronald L Theis, Executive Director

2664 Grand Rapids Foundation
185 Oakes St SW
Grand Rapids, MI 49503
616-454-1751
Fax: 616-454-6455
grfound@grfoundation.org
www.grfoundation.org
A community foundation established in 1922. The foundation actively serves the people of Kent County by administering funds it receives and by making philanthropic grants to non-profit organizations in response to community needs. Various educational scholarships are offered on the basis of a competitive process which considers academic achievement, extracurricular activities, a statement of one's own personal aspirations and educational goals, and financial need. Kent County Residency required.

Ruth Bishop, Program Associate-Education
Diana Sieger, President

2665 Harry A & Margaret D Towsley Foundation
3055 Plymouth Road
Suite 200
Ann Arbor, MI 48105-3208
312-662-6777
Areas of support include pre-school education, social services, and continuing education.

Margaret Ann Riecker, Executive Director

2666 Henry Ford Centennial Library
Adult Services
16301 Michigan Avenue
Dearborn, MI 48126-2792
313-943-2330
Fax: 313-943-3063
www.dearborn.lib.mi.us/aboutus/adult.htm
Member of The Foundation Center network, maintaining a collection of private foundation tax returns which provide information on the scope of grants dispensed by that particular foundation.

2667 Herbert H & Grace A Dow Foundation
1018 W Main Street
Midland, MI 48640-4292
989-631-3699
Fax: 989-631-0675
www.hhdowfdn.org
Limited to organizations within Michigan. Has charter goals to improve the educational, religious, economic and cultural lives of Michigan's people.

Margaret Ann Riescker, President
Elysa M Rogers, Assistant VP

2668 Herrick Foundation
150 W Jefferson Avenue
Suite 2500
Detroit, MI 48226-4415
313-496-7585
Offers grants to colleges and universities, health agencies and social service organizations.

Dolores de Galleford, Executive Director

2669 Kresge Foundation
3215 W Big Beaver Road
Troy, MI 48084
248-643-9630
Fax: 313-643-0588
www.kresge.org
Giving is aimed at areas of interest including arts and humanities, social services and public policy.

John E Marshall III, Executive Director
Sandra McAlister Ambrozy, Senior Program Officer

2670 Malpass Foundation
PO Box 1206
East Jordan, MI 49727-1206
Offers giving in the areas of education and community development.

William J Lorne, Executive Director

2671 McGregor Fund
333 W Fort Street
Suite 2090
Detroit, MI 48226-3134
313-963-3495
Fax: 313-963-3512
info@mcgregorfund.org
www.mcgregorfund.org
Social services, health and education grants awarded to organizations located in Ohio, primarily the Detroit area.

C David Campbell, President
Kate Levin Markel, Program Officer

2672 Michigan State University Libraries
Social Sciences/Humanities
366 W Circle Drive
East Lansing, MI 48824
517-353-8700
Fax: 517-432-3532
www.lib.msu.edu
Member of The Foundation Center network, maintaining a collection of private foundation tax returns which provide information on the scope of grants dispensed by that particular foundation.

2673 Richard & Helen DeVos Foundation
190 Muncie NW
Suite 500
Grand Rapids, MI 49503
616-454-4114
Fax: 616-454-4654
Strong geographical preference to Western Michigan. Funding includes Christian education, cultural, community, education (not an individual basis) and government services. Donations are also made on a national level to organizations based in Washington, DC.

Stephanie Roy, Executive Director

2674 Rollin M Gerstacker Foundation
PO Box 1945
Midland, MI 48641-1945
989-631-6097
Fax: 517-832-8842
lanphear@concentric.net
www.tamu.edu/baum/gerstack.html
Primary purpose of this foundation is to carry on, indefinitely, financial aid to charities concentrated in the states of Michigan and Ohio. Grants are given in the areas of community support, schools, education, social services, music and the arts, youth activities, health care and research, churches and other areas.

Carl A Gerstacker, Executive Director

2675 Steelcase Foundation
PO Box 1967, CH-4E
Grand Rapids, MI 49501-1967
616-246-4695
Fax: 616-475-2200
sbroman@steelcse.com
www.steelcase.com
Offers support for human services and education, to improve the quality of life for children, the elderly and the disabled in the areas where there are manufacturing plants.

Susan Broman, Executive Director

2676 Wayne State University
Purdy-Kresge Library
5265 Cass Avenue
Detroit, MI 48202-3930
313-577-6424
www.lib.wayne.edu
Member of The Foundation Center network, maintaining a collection of private foundation tax returns which provide information on the scope of grants dispensed by that particular foundation.

2677 Whirlpool Foundation
2000 N M 63
MD 3106
Benton Harbor, MI 49022-2692
269-923-5584
Fax: 269-925-0154
www.whirlpoolcorp.com
Giving centers on learning, cultural diversity, adult education, and scholarships for children of corporation employees.

Ddaniel Hopp, President & Chairman
Pamela Silcox, Operations Manager

Minnesota

2678 Andersen Foundation
Andersen Corporation
100 4th Avenue N
Bayport, MN 55003-1058
651-264-5150
Fax: 651-264-5537
Grants are given in the areas of higher education, health, youth and the arts in Minnesota.

2679 Bush Foundation
E-900 First National Bank Building
332 Minnesota Street
Saint Paul, MN 55101-1314
651-227-0891
Fax: 651-297-6485
www.bushfoundation.org
The foundation is predominantly a regional grantmaking foundation, with broad interests in

education, human services, health, arts and humanities and in the development of leadership.

Anita M Pampusch, President
John Archabal, Senior Program Officer

2680 Cargill Foundation
PO Box 9300
Minneapolis, MN 55440-9300
952-742-4311
Fax: 612-742-7224
www.cargill.com
Offers grants in the areas of education, health, human service organizations, arts and cultural programs and social service agencies.

Audrey Tulberg, Executive Director

2681 Charles & Ellora Alliss Educational Foundation
800 Nicollet Mall
Minneapolis, MN 55402-1314
612-303-4411
Fax: 651-244-0860
allissfoundation@usbank.com
www.allissfoundation.org
The foundation is organized exclusively for support of the education of young people, up to and including the period of postgraduate study. As a matter of policy, the foundation generally has limited its program to universities and colleges located in Minnesota. Grants are made to such institutions in support of undergraduate scholarship programs administered by their student aid offices. The foundation makes no direct grants to individuals.

John Bultena, Executive Director
Anita M Pampusch, Board of Trustee

2682 Duluth Public Library
520 W Superior Street
Duluth, MN 55802-1578
218-723-3802
Fax: 218-723-3815
www.duluth.lib.mn.us
Member of The Foundation Center network, maintaining a collection of private foundation tax returns which provide information on the scope of grants dispensed by that particular foundation.

Elizabeth Kelly, Library Director

2683 FR Bigelow Foundation
Center 55th Street East
Suite 600
St. Paul, MN 55101-1797
651-224-5463
800-875-6167
Fax: 651-224-8123
info@frbiquelow.org
www.frbigelow.org
Offers support in early childhood education, elementary and secondary education, higher and adult education and human services.

Richard B Heydinger, Chair
Carleen K Rhodes, Secretary

2684 First Bank System Foundation
PO Box 522
Minneapolis, MN 55480-0522
612-973-2440
Offers support for public elementary and secondary education, arts and cultural programs.

Cheryl L Rantala, Executive Director

2685 Hiawatha Education Foundation
360 Vila Street
Winona, MN 55987-1500
507-453-5550
Giving is centered on Catholic high schools and colleges, as well as awarding scholarships to college-bound high school graduates.

Robert Kierlin, Executive Director

2686 IA O'Shaughnessy Foundation
2001 Killebrew Drive
Suite 120
Bloomington, MN 55425-0704
952-698-0959
Fax: 952-698-0959
www.iaoshaughessyfdn.org
Giving is centered on cultural programs, secondary and higher education, human services and medical programs.

John Bultena, Executive Director
John F O'Shaughnessy, President

2687 Marbrook Foundation
730 2nd Avenue
Suite 1300
Minneapolis, MN 55402
612-752-1783
Fax: 612-752-1780
jhara@marbrookfoundation.org
www.marbrookfoundation.org
Offers grants in the areas of the environment, the arts, social empowerment, spiritual endeavors, basic human needs and health.

Annual Report

Julie S Hara, Executive Director

2688 Medtronic Foundation
7000 Central Avenue NE
Minneapolis, MN 55432-3576
763-514-4000
800-328-2518
Fax: 763-514-8410
www.medtronic.com
Offers grants in the areas of education (especially at the pre-college level), community funding and social services.

Penny Hunt, Executive Director

2689 Minneapolis Foundation
800 Ids Center 80 S 8th Street
Minneapolis, MN 55402
612-672-3878
Fax: 612-672-3846
mplsfoundation.org
www.minneapolisfoundation.org
The foundation strives to strengthen the community for the benefit of all citizens. Grants are awarded for the purposes of achieving this goal in the areas of early childhood education, child development, and education.

Karen Kelley-Ariwoola, VP Community Philanthropy

2690 Minneapolis Public Library
Music, Art, Sociology & Humanities
250 S Marquette
Minneapolis, MN 55401-2188
612-630-6000
Fax: 612-630-6220
www.mplib.org
Member of The Foundation Center network, maintaining a collection of private foundation tax returns which provide information on the scope of grants dispensed by that particular foundation.

Katherine G Hadle, Director

2691 Otto Bremer Foundation
445 Minnesota Street
Suite 2250
Saint Paul, MN 55101-2135
651-227-8036
888-291-1123
Fax: 651-312-3665
www.ottobremer.org
Offers support for post-secondary education, human services and community affairs.

John Kostishack, Executive Director
Karen Starr, Senior Program Officer

2692 Saint Paul Foundation
55 Fifth Street East
Suite 600
St. Paul, MN 55101-1797
651-224-5463
800-875-6167
Fax: 651-224-8123
info@saintpaulfoundation.org
www.saintpaulfoundation.org
Offers support for educational, charitable and cultural purposes of a public nature.

Carleen K Rhodes, President
Mindy K Molumby, Grants Administrator

2693 TCF Foundation
Code EXO-02-C
200 Lake Street
East Wayzata, MN 55391-1693
952-745-2757
Fax: 612-661-8554
www.tcfexpress.com
Giving is primarily for education through grants and employee matching gifts, including secondary schools, higher education and organizations that increase public knowledge.

Neil I Whitehouse, Executive Director

Mississippi

2694 Foundation for the Mid South
134 East Amite Street
Jackson, MS 39201
601-355-8167
Fax: 601-355-6499
www.fndmidsouth.org
Makes grants in the area of education, as well as economic development and families and children.

George Penick, Executive Director
Kay Kelly Arnold, Vice Chairman

2695 Jackson-Hinds Library System
300 N State Street
Jackson, MS 39201-1705
601-968-5811
reference@jhlibrary.com
www.jhlibrary.com
Member of The Foundation Center network, maintaining a collection of private foundation tax returns which provide information on the scope of grants dispensed by that particular foundation.

Carolyn McCallum, Executive Director

2696 Mississippi Power Foundation
PO Box 4079
Gulfport, MS 39502-4079
228-864-1211
www.mississippipower.com
The foundation is dedicated to the improvement and enhancement of education in Mississippi from kindergarten to twelfth grade.

Huntley Biggs, Executive Director

2697 Phil Hardin Foundation
2750 North Park Drive
Meridian, MS 39305-5800
601-483-4282
Fax: 601-483-5665
info@philhardin.org
www.philhardin.org

Offers giving in Mississippi for schools and educational institutions and programs.

C Thompson Wacaster, Executive Director

Missouri

2698 Ameren Corporation Charitable Trust
Ameren Corporation
PO Box 66149
MC 100
Saint Louis, MO 63166-6149
314-554-2789
877-426-3736
Fax: 314-554-2888
sbell@ameren.com
www.ameren.com
Offers giving in the areas of education, environment, youth and seniors; giving restricted to nonprofits located in Ameren service area in Missouri and Illinois.

Annually

Susan M Bell, Sr Community Relations
Otis Cowan, Community Relations Manger

2699 Clearinghouse for Midcontinent Foundations
University of Missouri
5110 Cherry Street
Suite 310
Kansas City, MO 64110-2426
816-253-1176
Fax: 816-235-5727
Member of The Foundation Center network, maintaining a collection of private foundation tax returns which provide information on the scope of grants dispensed by that particular foundation.

2700 Danforth Foundation
205 E Butterfield Road
Suite 410
Elmhurst, IL 60126-2733
630-501-1235
Fax: 314-588-0035
meboozell@danforthfoundation.com
www.danforthfoundation.com
This foundation is aimed at enhancing human life through activities which emphasize the theme of improvement in teaching and learning. Serves the pre-collegiate education through grantmaking and program activities.

Dr. Bruce J Anderson, President

2701 Enid & Crosby Kemper Foundation
C/O UMB Bank, N.A.
PO Box 419692
Kansas City, MO 64141-6692
816-860-7711
Fax: 816-860-5690
Giving is primarily allocated to organizations and programs focusing on educational and cultural needs.

Stephen J Campbell, Executive Director

2702 Hall Family Foundation
Charitable & Crown Investment - 323
PO Box 419580
Kansas City, MO 64141-6580
816-274-8516
Fax: 816-274-8547
www.hallfamilyfoundation.org
Offers grants in the areas of all levels of education, performing and visual arts, community development, and children, youth and families.

William S Berkley, President & CEO
David A Warm, Executive Director

2703 James S McDonnell Foundation
1034 S Brentwood Boulevard
Suite 1850
Saint Louis, MO 63117-1284
314-721-1532
Fax: 314-721-7421
www.jsmf.org
Foundation Program, Cognitive Studies for Educational Practice, funding available through competition in broadly announced requests for proposals. Program grant guidelines are announced in 3 year cycles.

John T Bruer, President
Cheryl A Washington, Grants Manager

2704 Kansas City Public Library
14 West 10th Street
Kansas City, MO 64105
816-701-3400
Fax: 816-701-3401
www.kclibrary.org
Member of The Foundation Center network, maintaining a collection of private foundation tax returns which provide information on the scope of grants dispensed by that particular foundation.

Jonathan Kemper, President
David Mayta, Vice President

2705 Mary Ranken Jordan & Ettie A Jordan Charitable Foundation
Mercantile Bank
PO Box 387
Saint Louis, MO 63166-0387
314-231-7626
Giving is limited to charitable institutions with an emphasis on secondary education and cultural programs, as well as higher education and social services.

Fred Arnold, Executive Director

2706 McDonnell Douglas Foundation
PO Box 419692
M S 10203
Kansas City, MO 64141-6692
314-234-0360
Fax: 314-232-7654
Offers various grants with an emphasis on higher and other education and community funding.

AM Bailey, Executive Director

2707 Monsanto Fund
800 N Lindbergh Boulevard
Saint Louis, MO 63167-0001
314-694-1000
Fax: 314-694-7658
monsanto.fund@monsanto.com
monsanto.com
Giving is offered primarily in the area of education, specifically science and math.

Deborah J Patterson, President

Montana

2708 Eastern Montana College Library
Special Collections-Grants
1500 N 30th Street
Billings, MT 59101-0245
406-657-1662
800-565-6782
Fax: 406-657-2037
www.msubillings.edu/library
Member of The Foundation Center network, maintaining a collection of private foundation tax returns which provide information on the scope of grants dispensed by that particular foundation.

Joan Bares, Grants Manager

2709 Montana State Library
Library Services
1500 University Drive
Billings, MT 59101-4542
406-657-2011
800-565-6782
Fax: 406-444-5612
www.msl.state.mt.us/
Member of The Foundation Center network, maintaining a collection of private foundation tax returns which provide information on the scope of grants dispensed by that particular foundation.

Barbara Duke, Administrative Assistant

Nebraska

2710 Dr. CC & Mabel L Criss Memorial Foundation
US Bank
PO Box 64713
Saint Paul, MN 55614-0713
800-441-2117
Fax: 402-348-6666
Offers support for educational and scientific purposes, including higher education.

2711 Thomas D Buckley Trust
PO Box 647
Chappell, NE 69129-0647
308-874-2212
Fax: 308-874-3491
Offers giving in the areas of education, health care and youth and religion. Grants awarded in Chappell, NE, community and surrounding area.

Connie Loos, Secretary

2712 W Dale Clark Library
Social Sciences Department
215 S 15th Street
Omaha, NE 68102-1601
402-444-4826
Fax: 402-444-4504
www.omahapubliclibrary.org
Member of The Foundation Center network, maintaining a collection of private foundation tax returns which provide information on the scope of grants dispensed by that particular foundation.

Angela Green-Garland, President
Arun K Agarwal, Vice President

Nevada

2713 Conrad N Hilton Foundation
30440 Agoura Road
Agoura Hills, CA 91301-1988
818-851-3700
Fax: 775-323-4150
www.hiltonfoundation.org
Founded in 1944 as a Trust, this foundation is dedicated to fulfilling and expanding Conrad Hilton's philanthropic vision by carrying out grantmaking activities. The foundation's giving is focused primarily in two areas: the alleviation of human suffering, particularly among disadvantaged children; and the human services works of the Catholic Sisters through a separate entity as described under Major Projects (supportive housing, disabled, education and prevention of domestic violence).

Donald H Hubbs, Executive Director
Steven M Hilton, President

2714 Cord Foundation
E.L. Cord Foundation Center For Learning Literacy
1664 N Virginia Street
Reno, NV 89557-0208
775-784-4951
Fax: 775-784-4758
www.unr.edu/cll
Offers support for secondary and higher education, including youth organizations and cultural programs.
Donald Bear, Director/Professor

2715 Donald W Reynolds Foundation
1701 Village Center Circle
Las Vegas, NV 89134-6303
702-804-6000
Fax: 702-804-6099
generalquestions@dwrf.org
www.dwreynolds.org
Devotes funds to further the cause of free press and journalism education.
Fred Smith, Chairman
Wes Smith, Vice-Chairman

2716 EL Wiegand Foundation
Wiegand Center
165 W Liberty Street
Reno, NV 89501-1915
775-333-0310
Fax: 775-333-0314
Offers grants in of culture and the arts, organizations, health and medical institutions, with an emphasis on Roman Catholic organizations.
Kristen A Avansino, Executive Director

2717 Las Vegas-Clark County
Library District
7060 W Windmill Lane
Las Vegas, NV 89113-2030
702-382-5280
Fax: 702-382-5491
www.lvccld.org
Member of The Foundation Center network, maintaining a collection of private foundation tax returns which provide information on the scope of grants dispensed by that particular foundation.
Daniel L Walters, Executive Director
Kelly Benavidez, Chairman

2718 Washoe County Library
301 S Center Street
Reno, NV 89501-2102
775-327-8300
Fax: 775-327-8341
www.washoe.lib.nv.us/
Member of The Foundation Center network, maintaining a collection of private foundation tax returns which provide information on the scope of grants dispensed by that particular foundation.
Fred Lokken, Chairman

New Hampshire

2719 Lincolnshire
Liberty Lane
Hampton, NH 03842
Giving is primarily for secondary school education, business school education and recreation.
William Coffey, Executive Director

2720 New Hampshire Charitable Foundation
37 Pleasant Street
Concord, NH 03301-4005
603-225-6641
Fax: 603-225-1700
info@nhcf.org
www.nhcf.org
Offers grants for charitable and educational purposes including college scholarships, existing charitable organizations, child welfare, community services, health and social services and new programs that emphasize programs rather than capital needs.
Racheal Stuart, VP Program

2721 Plymouth State College
Herbert H. Lamson Library
17 High Street
Plymouth, NH 03264-1595
603-535-2258
Fax: 603-535-2445
www.plymouth.edu/psc/library
Member of The Foundation Center network, maintaining a collection of private foundation tax returns which provide information on the scope of grants dispensed by that particular foundation.

New Jersey

2722 Community Foundation of New Jersey
Knox Hill Road
PO Box 338
Morristown, NJ 07963-0338
973-267-5533
Fax: 973-267-2903
cfnj@bellatlantic.net
www.cfnj.org
Offers support for programs that offer a path of solution of community problems in the areas of education, leadership development and human services.
Hans Dekker, President

2723 Fund for New Jersey
Kilmer Square
One Palmer Square East
Suite 303
Princeton, NJ 08542-1242
609-356-0241
Fax: 732-220-8654
www.fundfornj.org
Offers grants on projects which provide the basis of action in education, AIDS research, minorities/immigrants, public policy and community development.
Mark M Murphy, Executive Director
Kiki Jamieson, President

2724 Hoechst Celanese Foundation
Route 202-206 N
PO Box 2500
Somerville, NJ 08876
908-522-7500
Fax: 908-598-4424
Provides support for education, particularly in the sciences.
Lewis F Alpaugh, Executive Director

2725 Honeywell Foundation
101 Columbia Road
Morristown, NJ 07962-4658
973-455-2000
877-841-2840
Fax: 973-455-4807
www.honeywell.com/about/foundation.html
Offers support for education, including fellowship and scholarship aid to colleges.

2726 Hyde & Watson Foundation
31-F Mountain Boulevard
Warren, NJ 07059-1454
908-753-3700
Fax: 908-753-0004
hydeandwatson@yahoo.com
www.fdncenter.org/grantmaker/hydeandwatson
Support of capital projects of lasting value which tend to increase quality, capacity, or efficiency of a grantee's programs or services, such as purchase or relocation of facilities, capital equipment, instructive materials development, and certain medical research areas. Broad fields include health, education, religion, social services, arts, and humanities. Geographic areas served include the New York City Metropolitan region and primarily Essex, Union, and Morris Counties in New Jersey.
Hunter W Corbin, President

2727 Mary Owen Borden Memorial Foundation
160 Hodge Road
Princeton, NJ 08540-3014
609-924-3637
Fax: 609-252-9472
tborden@ibm.net
www.fdncenter.org/grantmaker/borden/index.htm
Offers grants in the areas of childhood education, child development, education, conservation and health and human services.
Thomas Borden, Executive Director

2728 Merck Company Foundation
1 Merck Drive #100
Whitehouse Station, NJ 08889-0100
908-423-2042
www.merck.com
Offers support of education, primarily medical through community programs, grants and matching gift programs for colleges and secondary education.
John R Taylor, Executive Director
Kenneth C Fraizer, Chairman,President& CEO

2729 Prudential Foundation
Prudential Plaza
751 Broad Street
Floor 15
Newark, NJ 07102-3714
973-802-4791
www.prudential.com
Focus is on children and youth for services that can better their lives. Grants are made in the areas of education, health and human services, community and urban development, business and civic affairs, culture and the arts. Emphasis is placed on programs that serve the city of Newark and the surrounding New Jersey urban centers, programs in cities where The Prudential has a substantial presence and national programs that further the company's objectives.
Barbara L Halaburda, Executive Director

2730 Turrell Fund
21 Van Vleck Street
Montclair, NJ 07042-2358
973-783-9358
Fax: 973-783-9283
turrell@turrellfund.org
www.fdncenter.org/grantmaker/turrell
Offers grants to organizations and agencies that are dedicated to the care of children and youth under twelve years of age, with an emphasis on education, early childhood education, delinquency prevention and child and youth services.
E Belvin Williams, Executive Director

2731 **Victoria Foundation**
31 Mulberry Street
5th Floor
Newark, NJ 07102
973-792-9200
Fax: 793-792-1300
cmcfarvic@aol.com
www.victoriafoundation.org
Grants are limited to Newark, New Jersey in the following areas: elementary and secondary education, after school enrichment programs, teacher training and academic enrichment.
Catherine M McFarland, Executive Officer
Nancy K Zimmerman, Senior Program Officer

2732 **Warner-Lambert Charitable Foundation**
201 Tabor Road
Morris Plains, NJ 07950-2614
212-573-2323
Fax: 212-573-7851
Grants are given in the areas of education, health care, culture and the arts. Supports higher institutions of learning which concentrate on pharmacy, medicine, dentistry, the sciences and mathematics. Current support is aimed at the higher levels of education, but the foundation has begun to place more of its attention on the growing needs that impact elementary and secondary training.
Evelyn Self, Community Affairs
Richard Keelty, VP Investor Affair

2733 **Wilf Family Foundation**
820 Morris Tpke
Short Hills, NJ 07078-2619
973-467-5000
Awards grants in the areas of Jewish higher education and religion.
Joseph Wilf, Executive Director

New Mexico

2734 **Dale J Bellamah Foundation**
PO Box 36600
Albuquerque, NM 87176-6600
858-756-1154
Fax: 858-756-3856
Offers grants for higher education including military academies, hospitals and social service organizations.
AF Potenziani, Executive Director

2735 **New Mexico State Library**
Information Services
1209 Camino Carlos Rey
Santa Fe, NM 87507
505-476-9700
Fax: 505-476-9701
www.stlib.state.nm.us
Member of The Foundation Center network, maintaining a collection of private foundation tax returns which provide information on the scope of grants dispensed by that particular foundation.

2736 **RD & Joan Dale Hubbard Foundation**
PO Box 1679
Ruidoso Downs, NM 88346-1679
505-378-4142
Giving is offered in the areas of childhood education, elementary, secondary and higher education as well as other cultural programs.
Jim Stoddard, Executive Director

New York

2737 **Achelis Foundation**
767 3rd Avenue
4th Floor
New York, NY 10017-2023
212-644-0322
Fax: 212-759-6510
main@achelis-bodman-fnds.org
www.fdncenter.org/grantmaker/achelis-bodman
Grants include biomedical research at Rockefeller University, rebuilding the Hayden Planetarium at the American Museum of Natural History, support for the arts and culture, the charter school movement, youth organizations, and special efforts to curb father absence and strengthen family life with awards.
Russell P Pennoyer, President
Joseph S Dolan, Executive Director

2738 **Adrian & Jessie Archbold Charitable Trust**
401 East 60th Street
New York, NY 10022
212-371-1152
Eastern United States educational institutions and health care service organizations are the main recipients of the Trust.
Myra Mahon, Executive Director

2739 **Alfred P Sloan Foundation**
630 5th Avenue
Suite 2550
New York, NY 10111-0100
212-649-1649
Fax: 212-757-5117
www.sloan.org
A nonprofit foundation offering Sloan Research Fellowships which are awarded in chemistry, computer science, economics, mathematics, neuroscience and physics. These are competitive grants given to young faculty members with high research potential on the recommendation of department heads and other senior scientists.
Ralph E Gomory, President

2740 **Altman Foundation**
521 5th Avenue
35th Floor
New York, NY 10175
212-682-0970
info@altman.org
www.altmanfoundation.org
In education, the Altman Foundation supports programs that identify, sponsor and tutor talented disadvantaged youngsters and help them to obtain educations in non-public and independent schools. The Foundation awards grants only in New York State with an almost-exclusive focus on the five boroughs of New York City. The Foundation does not award grants or scholarships to individuals.
Karen L Rosa, VP/Executive Director

2741 **Ambrose Monell Foundation**
C/O Fulton, Duncombe & Rowe
1 Rockefeller Plaza
Room 301
New York, NY 10020-2002
212-586-0700
Fax: 212-245-1863
info@monellvetlesen.org
www.monellvetlesen.org
Broad range of allocation including education, social service, cultural organizations and the environment.
Ambrose K Monell, Executive Director
George Rowe, President,Treasurer and Dire

2742 **American Express Foundation**
American Express Company
World Financial Center
New York, NY 10285
212-640-5661
www.home3.americanexpress.com/corp/philanthropy/contacts.asp
The foundation's giving focuses on three areas including community service, education and employment.
Mary Beth Salerno, Executive Director
Angela Woods, Philanthropic Program

2743 **Andrew W Mellon Foundation**
140 E 62nd Street
New York, NY 10065-8187
212-838-8400
Fax: 212-888-4172
www.mellon.org
Offers grants in the areas of higher education, cultural affairs and public affairs.
W.Taylor Revely, President
Lewis W Bernard, Chairman

2744 **Arnold Bernhard Foundation**
220 E 42nd Street
Floor 6
New York, NY 10017-5806
212-907-1500
Offers funding in the areas of education with the emphasis placed on college and universities as well as college preparatory schools.
Jean B Buttner, Executive Director

2745 **Atran Foundation**
23-25 East 21st Street
3rd Floor
New York, NY 10010
212-505-9677
Offers grants and funding to nonprofit educational and religious organizations.

2746 **Beatrice P Delany Charitable Trust**
The Chase Manhattan Bank
1211 Avenue of the Americas
34th Floor
New York, NY 10036
212-935-9935
Giving is offered for education, especially higher education and religion.
John HF Enteman, Executive Director

2747 **Bodman Foundation**
767 3rd Avenue
4th Floor
New York, NY 10017-2023
212-644-0322
Fax: 212-759-6510
main@achelis-bodman-fnds.org
www.achelis-bodman-fnds.org
Grants include biomedical research at Rockefeller University, building the Congo Gorilla Forest Education Center at the Bronx Zoo through the Wildlife Conservation Society, rebuilding of the Hayden Planetarium for Science and Technology at the American Museum of Natural History, support for Symphony Space, the charter school movement, youth organizations, and the Rutgers University Foundation.
John N Irwin III, Chairman
John B Krieger, Executive Director

2748 **Bristol-Myers Squibb Foundation**
345 Park Avenue
Floor 43
New York, NY 10154-0004

212-546-4331
www.bms.com
Offers support for elementary and secondary school, math and science education reform, civic affairs and health care.

Cindy Johnson, Executive Director
Lamberto Andreotti, Chief Executive Officer

2749 Buffalo & Erie County Public Library
History Department
Lafayette Square
Buffalo, NY 14203
716-858-8900
Fax: 716-858-6211
www.buffalolib.org
Member of The Foundation Center network, maintaining a collection of private foundation tax returns which provide information on the scope of grants dispensed by that particular foundation.

Michael C Mahaney, Director

2750 Caleb C & Julia W Dula Educational & Charitable Foundation
C/O Chemical Bank
112 S Hanley RD
St Louis, MO 63105-3418
212-270-9066
Offers grants to charities with an emphasis on secondary and higher education.

G Price-Fitch, Executive Director

2751 Capital Cities-ABC Corporate Giving Program
77 W 66th St
New York, NY 10023-6201
212-456-7498
Fax: 212-456-7909
Offers support in adult education, literary and basic skills, reading, and AIDS research.

Bernadette Longford Williams, Executive Director

2752 Carl & Lily Pforzheimer Foundation
950 Third Ave
30th Floor
New York, NY 10022-2705
212-764-0655
Offers support primarily for higher and secondary education, cultural programs, public administration, and health care.

Carl H Pforzheimer III, Executive Director

2753 Carnegie Corporation of New York
437 Madison Avenue
New York, NY 10022-7001
212-374-3200
Fax: 212-754-4073
www.carnegie.org
The foundation has several program goals including education and healthy development of children and youth, including early childhood health and education, early adolescence educational achievement, science education and education reform.

Janet L Robinson, President
Kurt L Schmoke, Vice-Chairman

2754 Chase Manhattan Corporation Philanthropy Department
1 Chase Manhattan Plaza
Floor 9
New York, NY 10005-1401
212-552-7087
Offers support to various organizations to enhance the well-being of the communities Chase Manahattan serves. Grants are awarded in the areas of education, youth services, community and economic development, homeless, library science, health care and housing development.

Steven Gelston, Executive Director

2755 Christian A Johnson Endeavor Foundation
1060 Park Avenue
New York, NY 10128-1008
212-534-6620
www.csuohio.edu/uored/funding/johnson.htm
Offers support to private institutions of higher education at the baccalaureate level and on educational outreach programs.

Wilmot H Kidd, Executive Director

2756 Cleveland H Dodge Foundation
420 Lexington Avenue
Suite 2331
New York, NY 10170-3292
212-972-2800
Fax: 212-972-1049
www.chdodgefoundation.org
Bestows funding for nonprofit organizations aimed at improving higher education and youth organizations.

William D Rueckert, President
Bayard Dodge, Vice-President

2757 Cowles Charitable Trust
P.O Box 219
Rumson, NJ 07760
732-936-9826
www1.mville.edu/Grants/GrantDescriptionPages/Cowles.htm
Funding for higher education and cultural organizations.

Gardner Cowles, President

2758 Daisy Marquis Jones Foundation
1600 S Avenue
Suite 250
Rochester, NY 14620-3921
585-461-4950
Fax: 585-461-9752
mail@dmjf.org
www.dmjf.org
Offers grants for nonprofit organizations focusing on improving the lives of children, youth and the elderly, in Monroe and Yates counties in New York State.

Donald W Whitney, President
Marless A Honan, Administrative Assistant

2759 DeWitt Wallace-Reader's Digest Fund
5 Penn Plaza
7th Floor
New York, NY 10001-9301
212-251-9700
Fax: 212-679-6990
www.wallacefoundation.org
The mission of this foundation is to invest in programs and projects that enhance the quality of educational and career development opportunities for all school-age youth.

M Christine De Vita, President

2760 Edna McConnell Clark Foundation
415 Madison Avenue
10th Floor
New York, NY 10017
212-551-9100
Fax: 212-421-9325
www.emcf.org
Supports select youth, serving organizations working with children 9-24 during the non-school hours.

Michael Bailin, President

2761 Edward John Noble Foundation
32 E 57th Street
Floor 19
New York, NY 10022-2513
212-759-4212
Fax: 212-888-4531
Offers grants to major cultural organizations in New York City, especially for arts educational programs and management training internships.

June Noble Larkin, Chairman

2762 Edward W Hazen Foundation
333 Seventh Avenue
14 th Floor
New York, NY 10001
212-889-3034
Fax: 212-889-3039
hazen@hazenfoundation.org
www.hazenfoundation.org
The foundation focuses giving on public education and youth development in the area of public education.

Lori Bezahler, President
Sonia Jarvis, Chairman

2763 Edwin Gould Foundation for Children
126 East 31st Street
New York, NY 10016
212-251-0907
Fax: 212-982-6886
Supports projects that promote the welfare and education of children. Interests lies in early childhood education, higher education, children and youth services and family services.

Michael W Osheowitz, Executive Director

2764 Elaine E & Frank T Powers Jr Foundation
81 Skunks Misery Road
Locust Valley, NY 11560-1306
Offers support in the areas of secondary and higher education as well as youth services.

2765 Elmer & Mamdouha Bobst Foundation
Elmer Holmes Bobst Library, NYU
70 Washington Square S
New York, NY 10012-1019
212-998-2440
Fax: 212-995-4070
Offers grants and funding in the areas of youth, community development and the arts.

2766 Equitable Foundation
3rd Floor Champaca II Building
162 L.P Leviste Street, Salcedo Village
Makati City 10019-6018
E-mail: mail@equitablefoundation.com
www.equitablefoundation.com
Offers grants in the areas of secondary school education, arts, community services, art and cultural programs, and higher education.

Kathleen A Carlson, Executive Director
Darlene Ramos, Administrative Assistant

2767 Ford Foundation
320 E 43rd Street
New York, NY 10017-4890
212-573-5000
Fax: 212-351-3677
offsec@fordfound.rog
www.fordfound.org
Offers grants to advance public well-being and educational opportunities. Grants are given in the areas of education, secondary school/education, early childhood education,

development services, human services, citizenship, academics and more.

Barron M Tenny, Secretary
Luis Ubinas, President

2768 Frances & Benjamin Benenson Foundation
C/O Door County Community Foundation
P.O. Box 802
Sturgeon Bay, WI 54235-1006
920-746-1786
Fax: 212-755-0021
www.benensoncapital.com
Offers grants in elementary/secondary education, higher education and human services.

Cynthia Green Colin, Executive Director

2769 George F Baker Trust
C/O JPMorgan Chase Bank
N.A Philanthropic Services
270 Park Avenue
New York, NY 10017
212-473-1587
Fax: 212-464-2305
jonathan.q.horowitz@jpmchase.com
Offers giving in the areas of higher and secondary education, social services, civic affairs and international affairs.

Monica J Neal, Vice President

2770 George Link Jr Foundation
10 Rockefeller Plaza
16th Floor
New York, NY 10020
212-713-7654
Fax: 212-645-4055
Giving is primarily centered on higher education, secondary school/education and medical research.

Eve Weiss, Executive Director

2771 Gladys & Roland Harriman Foundation
51 Madison Avenue
30 th Floor
New York, NY 10010-1202
212-489-7700
Fax: 212-581-9541
hlf1@hluce.org
Giving is centered on education and support for youth and social service agencies.

Michael Gilligan, President
Margaret B Fitzgerald, Chairman

2772 Gladys Brooks Foundation
1055 Franklin Avenue
Garden City, NY 11530
212-943-3217
www.gladysbrooksfoundation.org
The purpose of this foundation is to provide for the intellectual, moral and physical welfare of the people of this country by establishing and supporting nonprofit libraries, educational institutions, hospitals and clinics. In the area of education, grant applications will be considered generally for (a) educational endowments to fund scholarships based solely on leadership and academic ability of the student; (b) endowments to support salaries of educators.

Harman Hawkins, Chairman
Robert E Hill, Executive Director

2773 Green Fund
14 E 60th Street
Suite 702
New York, NY 10022-1006
212-755-2445
Fax: 212-755-0021
Offers grants in the area of higher and secondary education.

Cynthia Green Colin, Executive Director

2774 Hagedorn Fund
C/O JPMorgan Private Bank
Private Foundation Services
270 Park Avenue, 16th floor
New York, NY 10017
212-473-1587
Fax: 212-464-2304
g.horowitz@jpmorgan.com
fdnweb.org
Offers support for higher and secondary education, youth agencies and social service agencies.

Jonathan Horowitz, Program Officer

2775 Hasbro Children's Foundation
10 Rockefeller Plaza
16th Floor
New York, NY 10020
212-713-7654
888-836-7025
Fax: 212-645-4055
www.hasbro.org
Offers support to improve the quality of life for children. Areas of interest include education, AIDS research, literacy, special education, and youth services.

Eve Weiss, Executive Director

2776 Henry Luce Foundation
51 Madison Avenue, 30th Floor
New York, NY 10010
212-489-7700
Fax: 212-581-9541
hlf1@hluce.org
www.hluce.org
Offers grants for specific programs and projects in the areas of higher education and scholarship, social sciences at private colleges and universities, American arts and public affairs.

Michael Gilligan, President
Ellen Holtzman, Program Director

2777 Herman Goldman Foundation
61 Broadway
Floor 18
New York, NY 10006-2701
212-797-9090
Fax: 212-797-9161
This foundation offers grants in the areas of social, legal and organizational approaches to aid for deprived or handicapped people; education for new or improved counseling for effective pre-school, vocational, and paraprofessional training; and the arts.

Richard K Baron, Executive Director

2778 Hess Foundation
1185 Avenue of the Americas
New York, NY 10036-2601
212-997-8500
Fax: 212-536-8390
webmaster@hess.com
www.hess.com
Offers grants that focus on higher education, performing arts, and welfare organizations.

Leon Hess, Executive Director

2779 Horace W Goldsmith Foundation
375 Park Avenue
Suite 1602
New York, NY 10152-1699
212-319-8700
800-319-2881
Fax: 212-319-2881
Offers giving and support for education, higher education, cultural programs and museums.

James C Slaughter, Executive Director

2780 IBM Corporate Support Program
Old Orchard Road
Armonk, NY 10504
914-765-1900
The mission of this fund is to improve the areas and the communities that IBM operates in. Grants are awarded in various areas including early childhood education, elementary education, secondary education, business school/education, and engineering school/education.

Stanley Litow, Executive Director

2781 JI Foundation
C/O Patterson, Belknap, Webb & Tyler
1133 Avenue of the Americas
New York, NY 10036
212-336-2000
Offers grants in the areas of elementary education, higher education, and general charitable giving.

2782 JP Morgan Charitable Trust
60 Wall Street
Floor 46
New York, NY 10005-2836
212-648-9673
Offers support in the area of education, housing, economic development, advocacy and international affairs.

Roberta Ruocco, Executive Director

2783 Joukowsky Family Foundation
410 Park Avenue
Suite 1610
New York, NY 10022-4407
212-355-3151
Fax: 212-355-3147
www.joukowsky.org
Giving is focused on higher and secondary education.

Nina J Koprulu, Director/President
Emily R Kessler, Executive Director

2784 Julia R & Estelle L Foundation
1 HSBC Center
Suite 3650
Buffalo, NY 14203-1217
716-856-9490
Fax: 716-856-9493
info@oisheifdt.com
www.oisheifdt.org
This fund offers grants in the areas of higher and secondary education, medical research, social services and support agencies.

Thomas E Baker, President
James M Wadsworth, Chairman

2785 Leon Lowenstein Foundation
575 Madison Avenue
New York, NY 10022-3613
212-605-0444
Fax: 212-688-0134
Support is given for New York City public education and medical research.

John F Van Gorder, Executive Director

2786 Levittown Public Library
1 Bluegrass Lane
Levittown, NY 11756-1292
516-579-8585
Fax: 516-735-3168
www.nassaulibrary.org/levtown/
Member of The Foundation Center network, maintaining a collection of private foundation tax returns which provide information on the scope of grants dispensed by that particular foundation.

Margaret Santer, President

2787 Louis & Anne Abrons Foundation
C/O First Manhattan Company
437 Madison Avenue
New York, NY 10022-7001
212-756-3376
Fax: 212-832-6698
Offers support in the areas of education, improvement programs, environmental and cultural projects.
Richard Abrons, Executive Director

2788 Margaret L Wendt Foundation
40 Fountain Plaza
Suite 277
Buffalo, NY 14202-2200
716-855-2146
Fax: 716-855-2149
Offers various grants with an emphasis on education, the arts and social services in Buffalo and Western New York.
Robert J Kresse, Executive Director

2789 New York Foundation
10 East 34th Street
10 th Floor
New York, NY 10016-2996
212-594-8009
Fax: 212-594-5918
webmaster@nyf.org
www.nyf.org
Provides support for the implementation of programs that offer support for the quality of life including educational services, health organizations, centers and services, civil rights, public policy, research and more.
Maria Mottola, Executive Director
Melissa Hall, Operations Manager

2790 Palisades Educational Foundation
C/O Gibney, Anthony & Flaherty
665 5th Avenue
Floor 2
New York, NY 10022-5305
Offers support for secondary and higher education in New York, New Jersey and Connecticut.
Ralph F Anthony, Executive Director

2791 Robert Sterling Clark Foundation
135 E 64th Street
New York, NY 10065-7307
212-288-8900
Fax: 212-288-1033
rscf@rsclark.org
www.rsclark.org
For more than 15 years, this foundation has provided support to New York City's cultural community. During this time, the Foundation has tried to structure a grants program so that it is flexible and meets the needs of the institutions and organizations. Grants are given in the areas of cultural institutions, arts advocacy, family planning services and supporting new initiatives in the area of arts and education.
Margaret C Ayers, President
James A Smith, Chairman

2792 Rochester Public Library
Business, Economics & Law
115 S Avenue
Rochester, NY 14604-1896
585-428-8045
Fax: 585-428-8353
www.rochester.lib.ny.us/central
Member of The Foundation Center network, maintaining a collection of private foundation tax returns which provide information on the scope of grants dispensed by that particular foundation.
Emeterio M Otero, President

2793 Ronald S Lauder Foundation
Rykestrasse 53
10405 Berlin
Berlin 10153-0023
212-572-6966
www.lauderfoundation.com
Offers giving in the areas of elementary/secondary education, human services and religion.
Marjorie S Federbush, Executive Director
Ronald S Lauder, Chairman & President

2794 SH & Helen R Scheuer Family Foundation
350 5th Avenue
Suite 3410
New York, NY 10118-0110
212-947-9009
Fax: 212-947-9770
Offers support in the areas of higher education, welfare funding and cultural programs.

2795 Samuel & May Rudin Foundation
345 Park Avenue
New York, NY 10154-0004
212-407-2544
Fax: 212-407-2540
Offers support for higher education, social services, religious welfare agencies, hospitals and cultural programs.
Susan H Rapaport, Executive Director

2796 Seth Sprague Educational and Charitable Foundation
C/O U.S. Trust Company of New York
114 W 47th Street
New York, NY 10036-1510
212-852-3683
Fax: 212-852-3377
Offers support in the areas of education, culture, the arts, human services, community development and government/public administration.
Maureen Augusciak, Executive Director

2797 Starr Foundation
399 Park Avenue
17th Floor
New York, NY 10022-0002
212-909-3600
Fax: 212-750-3536
www.fdncenter.org/grantmaker/starr
Support is given for educational projects with an emphasis on higher education, including scholarships under specific programs.
Ta Chun Hsu, Executive Director
Florence A Davis, President

2798 Tiger Foundation
101 Park Avenue
47th Floor
New York, NY 10178-0002
212-984-2565
Fax: 212-949-9778
info@tigerfoundation.org
www.tigerfoundation.org
Support is given primarily for early childhood education, youth programs and job training.
Phoebe Boyer, Executive Director

2799 Tisch Foundation
667 Madison Avenue
New York, NY 10021-8029
212-545-2000
Support is given in the area of education, especially higher education, and includes institutions in Israel and research-related programs.
Laurence A Tisch, Executive Director

2800 Travelers Group
388 Greenwich Street
New York, NY 10013-2375
212-816-8000
Fax: 212-816-5944
The main purpose of this foundation is to support public education, offering grants in the communities that the company serves.
Dee Topol, Executive Director

2801 White Plains Public Library
100 Martine Avenue
White Plains, NY 10601-2599
914-422-1400
Fax: 914-422-1462
www.whiteplainslibrary.org
Member of The Foundation Center network, maintaining a collection of private foundation tax returns which provide information on the scope of grants dispensed by that particular foundation.

2802 William Randolph Hearst Foundation
300 West 57th Street
26th Floor
New York, NY 10019-3741
212-649-3750
Fax: 212-586-1917
heart.ny@hearstfdn.org
www.hearstfdn.org
Offers support to programs that aid priority-level and minority groups, educational programs especially private secondary and higher education, health systems and cultural programs.
Paul ""Dino"" Dinovitz, Executive Director
Ligia Cravo, Senior Program Officer

2803 William T Grant Foundation
570 Lexington Avenue
Floor 18
New York, NY 10022-6837
212-752-0071
Fax: 212-752-1398
info@wtgrantfdn.org
www.wtgrantfoundation.org
The goal of the foundation is to help create a society that values people and helps them to reach their potenial. The Foundation is interested in environmentally friendly approaches
Edward Seidman, Senior VP Programs
Robert Granger, President

North Carolina

2804 AE Finley Foundation
P.O. Box 98266
Raleigh, NC 27624-8266
919-782-0565
Fax: 919-782-6978
lesa@aeffinc.org
www.aefinleyfoundationinc.org
Private foundation contributing and supporting to charitable, scientific, literary, religious and educational organizations. It endeavors to contribute to soundly managed and operated qualifying organizations which fundamentally give service with a broad scope and impact, aid all kinds of people and contribute materially to the general welfare.
Robert C Brown, Executive Director

2805 Cannon Foundation
PO Box 548
Concord, NC 28026-0548
704-786-8216
Fax: 704-785-2052
info@cannonfoundation.org
www.thecannonfoundationinc.org

Offers support for higher and secondary education, cultural programs, and grants to social service and youth agencies.

Frank Davis, Executive Director
William C Cannon Jr, President

2806 Dickson Foundation
301 S Tryon Street
Suite 1800
Charlotte, NC 28202
704-372-5404
Fax: 704-372-6409
Main focus is on areas of education & healthcare. Considers funding programs in the Southeast.

Susan Patterson, Secretary/Treasurer

2807 Duke Endowment
100 N Tryon Street
Suite 3500
Charlotte, NC 28202-4012
704-376-0291
Fax: 704-376-9336
www.dukeendowment.org
Support is given to higher education, children and youth services, churches and hospitals.

Eugene W Cochrané Jr, Executive Director
Minor M Shaw, Chairman

2808 First Union University
Two 1st Union Center
Charlotte, NC 28288
704-374-6868
Fax: 704-374-4147
Offers support for higher education and special programs for public elementary and secondary schools.

Ann D Thomas, Executive Director

2809 Foundation for the Carolinas
220 N Tryon Street
Charlotte, NC 28202
704-973-4500
800-973-7244
Fax: 704-376-1243
www.fftc.org
Offers support for education, the arts and health in North Carolina and South Carolina.

Ron Carter, President/CEO
Catherine P Bessant, Chairman

2810 Kathleen Price and Joseph M Bryan Family Foundation
3101 N Elm Street
Greensboro, NC 27408-3184
336-288-5455
Grants are primarily offered in the fields of higher, secondary, and early childhood education.

William Massey, Executive Director

2811 Mary Reynolds Babcock Foundation
2920 Reynolda Road
Winston Salem, NC 27106-4618
336-748-9222
Fax: 336-777-0095
www.mrbf.org
This foundation traditionally provides funds to programs in education, social services, the environment, the arts and citizen participation in the development of public policy. The foundation prefers to fund programs of two kinds: those particularly sensitive to the changing and emerging needs of society and those addressing society's oldest needs in new and imaginative ways.

Gayle W Dorman, Executive Director
Sandra H Mikush, Assitant Director

2812 Non-Profit Resource Center/Pack Memorial Library
Learning Resources Center
67 Haywood Street
Asheville, NC 28801-4897
828-254-4960
Fax: 828-251-2258
Cooperating collection of the Foundation Center. Other resources for non-profit organizations are also available.

Ed Sheary, Library Director

2813 State Library of North Carolina
Government & Business Services
109 E Jones Street
Raleigh, NC 27601-2806
919-807-7450
Fax: 919-733-5679
www.statelibrary.dcr.state.nc.us
Member of The Foundation Center network, maintaining a collection of private foundation tax returns which provide information on the scope of grants dispensed by that particular foundation.

2814 William R Kenan Jr Charitable Trust
Kenan Center
PO Box 3858
Chapel Hill, NC 27515-3858
919-962-0343
Fax: 919-962-3331
The focus of this foundation is on education, primarily at private institutions in the US. The emphasis now is on national literacy and the importance of early childhood education. Grants have just established an institute for the arts and an institute for engineering, technology and science. No grants are given to individuals for scholarships, for research or other special projects or for medical, public health or social welfare projects. This Trust does not accept unsolicited requests.

William C Friday, Executive Director

2815 Winston-Salem Foundation
860 W 5th Street
Winston Salem, NC 27101-2506
336-725-2382
Fax: 336-727-0581
www.wsfoundation.org
Educational grants and loans to residents of Forsyth County, North Carolina in most areas.

Scott Wierman, President
Donna Rader, VP Grants & Programs

2816 Z Smith Reynolds Foundation
102 West Third Street
Suite 1110
Winston Salem, NC 27101-3940
336-725-7541
800-443-8319
Fax: 336-725-6069
www.zsr.org
Grants are limited to the state of North Carolina. General purpose foundation provides for their current priorities including community economic development, women's issues, minority issues, environment and pre-collegiate education. No grants are given to individuals.

Thomas W Ross, Executive Director

North Dakota

2817 Myra Foundation
PO Box 13536
Grand Forks, ND 58208-3536
701-775-9420
jbotsford@myrafoundation.org
www.myrafoundation.org
Offers grants in the areas of secondary school, and higher education to residents of Grand Forks County, North Dakota.

Edward C Gillig, Executive Director

2818 Tom & Frances Leach Foundation
1720 Burnt Boat Drive
PO Box 1136
Bismarck, ND 58502-1136
701-255-0479
www.leachfoundation.org
Offers grants in the areas of higher and other education in North Dakota.

Clement C Weber, Executive Director

Ohio

2819 Akron Community Foundation
345 W Cedar Street
Akron, OH 44307-2407
330-376-8522
Fax: 330-376-0202
acf_fund@ix.netcom.com
www.akroncommunityfdn.org
The foundation receives donations to permanent endowment and makes grants to qualified nonprofit organizations within Summit County, Ohio.

Jody Bacon, President

2820 American Foundation Corporation
720 National City Bank Building
Cleveland, OH 44114
216-241-6664
Fax: 216-241-6693
Offers support in the areas of higher and secondary education, the arts and community funds.

Maria G Muth, Executive Director

2821 Burton D Morgan Foundation
22 Aurora Street
Hudson, OH 44236-1500
330-655-1660
Fax: 330-655-1673
admin@bdmorganfdn.org
www.bdmorganfdn.org
The foundation's present areas of interest include economics, education, mental health and organizations principally located in Northeast Ohio. No grants are made to individuals and few grants are made to social service organizations.

Deborah D Hoover, President
Denise M Griggs, Chief Financial Officer

2822 Dayton Foundation
500 Kettering Tower
Dayton, OH 45423-1395
937-222-0410
Fax: 937-222-0636
info@daytonfoundation.org
www.daytonfoundation.org
Educational and community service grants.

Michael M Parks, President
Ellen S Ireland, Vice-Chairman

2823 Eva L & Joseph M Bruening Foundation
1422 Euclid Avenue
Suite 966
Cleveland, OH 44115-1952

216-621-2632
Fax: 216-621-8198
www.fmscleveland.com/bruening
Support is offered in the fields of education, early childhood education, education fund-raising, higher education, youth services and health agencies.

Janet E Narten, Executive Director
Karen Noster, Chairman

2824 GAR Foundation
Andrew Jackson House
277 East Mill Street
Akron, OH 44308-1828
330-576-2926
800-686-2825
Fax: 330-437-2843
info@garfdn.org
www.garfdn.org
Established in 1967 as a charitable trust, the foundation offers grants to organizations located primarily in Akron, Ohio area or, secondarily, in Northeastern Ohio or elsewhere in the United States at the discretion of the Distribution Committee. Grants for research projects of educational or scientific institutions, capital improvement projects, or matching campaigns are the priorities of this foundation.

Richard A Chenoweth, Executive Director
Robert W Briggs, Co-Trustee

2825 George Gund Foundation
1845 Guildhall Building
45 Prospect Avenue
West Cleveland, OH 44115
216-241-3114
Fax: 216-241-6560
info@gundfdn.org
www.gundfdn.org
The primary interest of this foundation is in educational projects, with an emphasis on inventive movements in teaching and learning, and on increasing educational opportunities for the disadvantaged.

David Abbott, Executive Director
Marcia Egbert, Senior Program Officer

2826 Hoover Foundation
101 E Maple Street
North Canton, OH 44720-2517
330-499-9499
Fax: 330-497-5065
Offers grants for elementary education, secondary and higher education and youth agencies.

LR Hoover, Executive Director
Annette Bravard, Vice President of Marketing

2827 Kettering Fund
1480 Kettering Tower
Dayton, OH 45423-1001
937-228-1021
888-719-1185
www.cfketteringfamilies.com
Support is offered for social and educational studies and research as well as community development and cultural programs.

Judith M Thompson, Executive Director

2828 Kulas Foundation
Tower City Center
50 Public Square
Suite 600
Cleveland, OH 44113-2267
216-623-4770
Fax: 216-623-4773
www.fdncenter.org/grantmaker/kulas/
A major general interest foundation, but with an emphasis on music. Giving is limited to Cuyahoga County and its surrounding area. Provides support to musical educational programs at Baldwin Wallace College, Case Western Reserve University and Cleveland Institute of Music. Also provides tickets to cultural programs to students in 16 colleges and universities in the area. The Foundation does not provide grants or loans to individuals. Support is geared to local primary and secondary schools.

Nancy W McCann, President/Treasurer

2829 Louise H & David S Ingalls Foundation
20600 Chagrin Boulevard
Suite 301
Shaker Heights, OH 44122-5334
216-921-6000
Offers support to organizations whose primary interest in the improvement of the educational, physical and mental condition of humanity throughout the world. Grants are given in secondary, elementary, and educational research.

Jane W Watson, Executive Director

2830 Louise Taft Semple Foundation
425 Walnut Street
Suite 1800
Cincinnati, OH 45202-3948
513-381-2838
Fax: 513-381-0205
Support is offered in the areas of secondary school/education, higher education, human services and health care organizations.

Dudley S Taft, Executive Director

2831 Martha Holden Jennings Foundation
Advisory & Distribution Committee Office
1228 Euclid Avenue
Suite 710
Cleveland, OH 44115-1831
216-589-5700
Fax: 216-589-5730
www.mhjf.org
The purpose of this foundation is to foster the development of young people to the maximum possible extent through improving the quality of teaching in secular elementary and secondary schools.

William T Hiller, Executive Director
Kathy L Kooyman, Grants Manager

2832 Mead Corporation Foundation
Courthouse Plz NE
Dayton, OH 45463-0001
937-495-3883
Fax: 937-495-4103
Grants are given to elementary, secondary, higher and minority education.

Ronald F Budzik, Executive Director

2833 Nord Family Foundation
747 Milan Avenue
Amherst, OH 44001
440-984-3939
Fax: 440-984-3934
www.nordff.org
Offers support for a variety of programs, including giving for early childhood, secondary, and higher education, social services, cultural affairs and civic activities.

David R Ashenhurst, Executive Director

2834 Ohio Bell Telephone Contribution Program
45 Erieview Plaza
Room 870
Cleveland, OH 44114-1814
216-822-4445
800-257-0902
Offers support of elementary school/education, secondary school/education, higher education, literacy and basic skills.

William W Boag Jr, Executive Director

2835 Ohio State Library Foundation Center
Kent H. Smith Library
1480 West Lane Avenue
Columbus, OH 43221-2001
614-292-2141
Member of The Foundation Center network, maintaining a collection of private foundation tax returns which provide information on the scope of grants dispensed by that particular foundation.

John B Gerlach, Chairman & CEO
Martin Murrer, Vice-Chairman

2836 Owens-Corning Foundation
PO Box 1688
Toledo, OH 43603-1688
419-248-8000
Fax: 419-325-4273
Offers support for education, including religious schools and science and technology programs.

Emerson J Ross, Executive Director

2837 Procter & Gamble Fund
200 West Fourth Street
Cincinnati, OH 45202-2775
513-241-2880
Fax: 513-983-8250
info@gcfdn.org
www.gcfdn.org
Always considers the interests of the company's employees helping in the community, the arts, improving of schools and universities and to meet the needs of the less-fortunate neighbors. Some donations into the education program include grants to the United Negro College Fund, The National Hispanic Scholarship Fund, The Leadership Conference on Civil Rights Education Fund and more than 600 colleges and universities.

RL Wehling, President
G Talbot, VP

2838 Public Library of Cincinnati
Grants Resource Center
800 Vine Street #Library
Cincinnati, OH 45202-2009
513-369-6900
Fax: 513-665-3384
www.cincinnatilibrary.org
Member of The Foundation Center network, maintaining a collection of private foundation tax returns which provide information on the scope of grants dispensed by that particular foundation.

Kimber L Fender, Director

2839 Thomas J Emery Memorial
Frost & Jacobs
201 E 5th Street
Suite 2500
Cincinnati, OH 45202-4113
513-621-3124
Offers support in secondary school/education, higher education, health care, human services and arts/cultural programs.

Henry W Hobson Jr, Executive Director

2840 Timken Foundation of Canton
200 Market Avenue N
Suite 210
Canton, OH 44702-1622
330-452-1144
Fax: 330-455-1752
Offers support to promote the broad civic betterment including the areas of education,

conservation and recreation. Grants restricted to caption projects only.

Don D Dickes, Secretary
Nancy Kuvdsen

2841 Wolfe Associates
34 S 3rd Street
Columbus, OH 43215-4201
614-461-5220
Fax: 614-469-6126
The foundation supports those organizations whose programs educate the individual and cultivate the individual's ability to participate in and contribute to the community or which enhance the quality of life which the community can offer to its citizens. The foundation has six general program areas in which it focuses its support: health and medicine, religion, education, culture, community service and environment.

AK Pierce Jr, Executive Director

Oklahoma

2842 Grace & Franklin Bernsen Foundation
15 W 6th Street
Suite 1308
Tulsa, OK 74119-5407
918-584-4711
Fax: 918-584-4713
gfbersen@aol.com
www.bernsen.org
The foundation is limited by its policies to support of nonprofit organizations within the metropolitan area of Tulsa. The foundation discourages applications for general support or reduction of debt or for continuing or additional support for the same programs, although a single grant may cover several years. No grant is made to individuals or for the benefit of specific individuals and the applications must be received before the twelfth of each month.

John Strong Jr, Trustee

2843 Mervin Bovaird Foundation
100 W 5th Street
Suite 800
Tulsa, OK 74103-4291
918-583-1777
Fax: 918-592-5809
Awards scholarships to the University of Tulsa. Recipients are selected by Tulsa Area high schools and by Tulsa Junior College. No individual grants are made.

R Casey Cooper, President

2844 Oklahoma City University
Dulaney Brown Library
2501 N Blackwelder Avenue
Oklahoma City, OK 73106-1493
405-521-5000
Fax: 405-521-5291
www.okcu.edu
Member of The Foundation Center network, maintaining a collection of private foundation tax returns which provide information on the scope of grants dispensed by that particular foundation.

Victoria Swinney, Director

2845 Public Service Company of Oklahoma Corporate Giving Program
212 E 6th Street #201
Tulsa, OK 74119-1295
918-586-0420
www.psoklahoma
Offers support in the areas of elementary, secondary and higher education.

Mary Polfer, Executive Director

2846 Samuel Roberts Noble Foundation
2510 Sam Noble Parkway
Ardmore, OK 73401-2180
580-223-5810
Fax: 580-224-6380
www.noble.org
Offers support in the areas of higher education, agricultural research, human services and educational grants for health research pertaining to degenerative diseases, cancer and for health delivery systems.

Michael A Cawley, Executive Director
Emily Bynum, Administrative Assistant

Oregon

2847 Collins Foundation
1618 SW 1st Avenue
Suite 305
Portland, OR 97201-5708
503-227-7171
Fax: 503-295-3794
www.collinsfoundation.org
Offers general support with an emphasis on higher education, hospices and health agencies, youth programs and arts and culture.

Cynthia G Adams, Executive Vice President
Cindy Knowles, Director Of Programs

2848 Ford Family Foundation
1600 NW Stewart Parkway
Roseburg, OR 97471-1957
541-957-5574
Fax: 541-957-5720
info@tfff.org
www.tfff.org
Giving is centered on education, youth organizations and human service programs in Oregon and Siskiyou County in California.

Bart Howard, Director Scholarship Program
Sarah Reeve, Scholarship Program Officer

2849 Meyer Memorial Trust
425 NW 10th Avenue
Suite 400
Portland, OR 97209
503-228-5512
Fax: 503-228-5840
mmt@mmt.org
www.mmt.org
The Trust operates three different funding programs, all of which are restricted primarily to Oregon: 1) a broad-based General Purpose program that provides funds for education, arts, and humanities, health, social welfare, community development, and other activities; 2) a Small Grants program that provides up to $12,000 for small projects in the general purpose categories; and 3) the Support for Teacher Initiatives program, which provides grants of up to $7,000- to teachers.

Doug Stamm, Executive Director
Cathie Glennon, Executive Assistant

2850 Multnomah County Library
Government Documents
801 SW 10th Avenue
Portland, OR 97205-2597
503-988-5123
Fax: 503-988-8014
www.multcolib.org
Member of The Foundation Center network, maintaining a collection of private foundation tax returns which provide information on the scope of grants dispensed by that particular foundation.

2851 Oregon Community Foundation
1221 SW Yamhill
Suite 100
Portland, OR 97205
503-227-6846
Fax: 503-274-7771
www.ocfl.org
The purpose of this foundation is to improve the cultural, educational and social needs in all levels of society throughout the state of Oregon.

Gregory A Chaille, Executive Director

2852 Tektronix Foundation
PO Box 1000
Wilsonville, OR 97070-1000
503-627-7111
www.tek.com
Offers support for education, especially science, math and engineering, and some limited art grants.

Jill Kirk, Executive Director

Pennsylvania

2853 Alcoa Foundation
201 Isabella Street
Pittsburgh, PA 15212-5858
412-553-4545
Fax: 412-553-4498
www.alcoa.com
Grants are given for education, arts and cultural programs.

F Worth Hobbs, Executive Director

2854 Annenberg Foundation
St. David's Center
2000 Avenue of the Stars
Suite 1000 S
Los Angeles, CA 90067-5293
310-209-4560
Fax: 310-209-1631
info@annenbergfoundation.org
www.annenbergfoundation.org
Primary support is given to childhood and K-12 education.

Dr. Gail C Levin Sr, Executive Director
Wallis Annenberg, Chairman

2855 Arcadia Foundation
105 E Logan Street
Norristown, PA 19401-3058
215-275-8460
www.arcadiafoundation.org
Gives only in Eastern Pennsylvania, no personal scholarships, accepts proposals only between June 1-August 15. These will be considered for the following calendar year. Proposal has to be no more than 2 pages long and longer submissions will be discarded. Must have a copy of the IRS tax-identified letter with no other enclosures.

Marilyn Lee Steinbright, Executive Director

2856 Audrey Hillman Fisher Foundation
2000 Grant Building
Pittsburgh, PA 15219
412-338-3466
Fax: 412-338-3463
Offers support for secondary school/education, higher education, rehabilitation, science and engineering.

Ronald W Wertz, Executive Director

2857 Bayer Corporation
100 Bayer Court
Pittsburgh, PA 15205
412-777-2000
Fax: 412-777-3468
www.bayerus.com/about/community/
Support is given primarily in education, especially science programs, chemistry and the arts.

Rebecca Lucore, Executive Director

2858 Buhl Foundation
650 Smithfield Street
Pittsburgh, PA 15222-1207
412-566-2711
Fax: 412-566-2714
buhl@buhlfoundation.org
www.buhlfoundation.org
Grants are given to colleges and universities, secondary schools and educational associations, community educational and training programs, and other community programs offering health and education to the community. Grants are not made for building funds, overhead costs, accumulated deficits, ordinary operating budgets, general fund-raising campaigns, loans, scholarships and fellowships, other foundations, nationally funded organized groups or individuals.

Dr. Doreen Boyce, President

2859 Connelly Foundation
One Tower Bridge
Suite 1450
West Conshohocken, PA 19428-2873
610-834-3222
Fax: 610-834-0866
www.connellyfdn.org
Offers support for education, health, human service, culture and civic programs to nonprofit organizations located in the city of Philadelphia and the greater Delaware Valley region.

Victoria K Flaville, VP Administration
Josephine C Mandeville, President/CEO

2860 Eden Hall Foundation
Pittsburgh Office And Research Park
600 Grant Street
Suite 3232
Pittsburgh, PA 15219
412-642-6697
Fax: 412-642-6698
www.edenhallfdn.org
This foundation offers support for higher education, social welfare and the improvement of conditions of the poor and needy.

Sylvia V Fields, Program Director
George C Greer, Chairman/President

2861 Erie County Library System
160 E Front Street
Erie, PA 16507-1554
814-451-6927
Fax: 814-451-6969
www.ecls.lib.pa.us
Member of The Foundation Center network, maintaining a collection of private foundation tax returns which provide information on the scope of grants dispensed by that particular foundation.

2862 Foundation Center-Carnegie Library of Pittsburgh
Foundation Collection
4400 Forbes Avenue
Pittsburgh, PA 15213-4080
412-622-6277
Fax: 412-454-7001
foundati@carnegielibrary.org
www.clpgh.org/clp/Foundation
Member of the Foundation Center network, of cooperating collections; providing current, factual information about grants and grantmaking organizations, and other aspects of philanthropy to the local nonprofit community.

Jim Lutton, Manager
Herb Elish, Director

2863 HJ Heinz Company Foundation
PO Box 57
Pittsburgh, PA 15230-0057
412-456-5772
Fax: 412-456-7859
heinz.foundation@hjheinz.com
www.heinz.com/jsp/foundation.jsp
Offers support for higher education, employee matching gifts, social service agencies and cultural programs.

Loretta M Oken, Executive Director

2864 John McShain Charities
540 N 17th Street
Philadelphia, PA 19130-3988
215-564-2322
Offers support for higher and secondary education, Roman Catholic church support and social welfare.

Mary McShain, Executive Director

2865 Mary Hillman Jennings Foundation
625 Stanwix Street
Apt 2203
Pittsburgh, PA 15222-1408
412-434-5606
Fax: 412-434-5907
Offers grants to schools, youth agencies, and hospitals and health associations.

Paul Euwer Jr, Executive Director

2866 McCune Foundation
750 Six PPG Place
Pittsburgh, PA 15222
412-644-8779
Fax: 412-644-8059
www.mccune-db.mccune.org
The foundation provides support to independent higher education and human services.

Henry S Beukema, Executive Director

2867 Pew Charitable Trusts
One Commerce Square
2005 Market Street
Suite 1700
Philadelphia, PA 19103-7077
215-575-9050
Fax: 215-575-4939
info@pewtrusts.org
www.pewtrusts.com
Offers support for education (including theology), arts culture, as well as public policy and religion.

Rebecca W Rimel, Executive Director
Robert H Campbell, Board of Director

2868 Richard King Mellon Foundation
One Mellon Bank Center
500 Grant Street
Suite 4106
Pittsburgh, PA 15219-2502
412-392-2800
Fax: 412-392-2837
www.fdncenter.org/grantmaker/rkmellon/
Offers local grant programs with an emphasis on education, social services and the environment.

Seward Prosser Mellon, Trustee/President
Bruce King Mell Henderson, President

2869 Rockwell International Corporation Trust
625 Liberty Avenue
Pittsburgh, PA 15222-3110
414-212-5200
Fax: 414-212-5201
Offers support in the areas of K-12 math and science education, and higher education in the field of engineering and science.

William R Fitz, Executive Director

2870 Samuel S Fels Fund
1528 Walnut Street
Suite 1002
Philadelphia, PA 19102-5308
215-731-9455
Fax: 215-731-9457
www.samfels.org
Offers grants in continuing support that help prevent, lessen or resolve contemporary social problems including education, arts/cultural programs, and community development.

Helen Cunningham, Executive Director
Robin N Culmer, Office Administrator

2871 Sarah Scaife Foundation
Three Mellon Bank Center
301 Grant Street
Suite 3900
Pittsburgh, PA 15219-6401
412-392-2900
www.scaife.com
Offers grants in the areas of education and community development.

Joanne B Beyer, Executive Director
Michael W Gleba, Executive Vice President

2872 Shore Fund
C/O Melton Bank N.A.
PO Box 185
Pittsburgh, PA 15230-0185
412-234-4695
Fax: 412-234-3551
Although the foundation appreciates funding opportunities within the field of education, most grants given out have been to schools with which the foundation's trustees have been personally involved.

Helen M Collins, Executive Director

2873 Stackpole-Hall Foundation
44 S Saint Marys Street
Saint Marys, PA 15857-1667
814-834-1845
Fax: 814-834-1869
stackpolehall@windstream.net
www.stackpolehall.org
Offers support for higher education and secondary education, literacy and vocational projects, social services, arts and cultural programs, and community development.

William C Conrad, Executive Director

2874 United States Steel Foundation
600 Grant Street
Suite 639
Pittsburgh, PA 15219-2800
412-433-5237
Fax: 412-433-2792
www.psc.uss.com/usxfound
Grants are awarded for capital development, special projects or operating needs. Support is limited to organizations within the United States, with preference to those in the US Steel Corporation's operating areas. US Steel does not award grants for religious purposes. Additionally, grants are not awarded for conferences, seminars or symposia, travel, publication of papers, books or magazines, or

production of films, videotapes or other audiovisual materials.

Craig D Mallick, General Manager
Pamela E DiNardo, Program Administrator

2875 William Penn Foundation
2 Logan Square11th Floor
100 North 18th Street
Philadelphia, PA 19103-2757
215-988-1830
Fax: 215-988-1823
grants@williampennfoundation.org
www.williampennfoundation.org
The foundation supports culture, environment, human development, including programs for youth and elderly, education, including early childhood, secondary, elementary and higher.

Kathryn J Engebretson, President
Bergen Bruce, Director of Finance and Admi

Rhode Island

2876 Champlin Foundations
2000 Chapel View Boulevard
Suite 350
Cranston, RI 02920
401-944-9200
Fax: 401-944-9299
champlinfons@worldnet.att.net
www.fdncenter.org/grantmaker/champlin
Offers giving in the areas of higher, secondary and other education. Exclusively in Rhode Island.

David A King, Executive Director
Jonathan K Farnum, Distribution Committee Membe

2877 Providence Public Library
Reference Department
150 Empire Street
Providence, RI 02903-3219
401-455-8000
www.provlib.org
Member of The Foundation Center network, maintaining a collection of private foundation tax returns which provide information on the scope of grants dispensed by that particular foundation.

Dale Thompson, Director
Robert K Taylor, Chairman

2878 Rhode Island Foundation
One Union Station
Providence, RI 02903-4630
401-274-4564
Fax: 401-331-8085
www.rifoundation.org
Promotes charitable activities which tend to improve the living conditions and well-being of the residents of Rhode Island.

Ned Handy, President
David M Hirsch, Chairman

South Carolina

2879 Charleston County Library
68 Calhoun Street
Charleston, SC 29401
843-805-6930
Fax: 843-727-3741
www.ccpl.org
Member of The Foundation Center network, maintaining a collection of private foundation tax returns which provide information on the scope of grants dispensed by that particular foundation.

Janet Segal, Chairperson
Harlan Greene, Chairperson

2880 South Carolina State Library
1500 Senate Street
Columbia, SC 29201-3815
803-734-8666
Fax: 803-734-8676
www.state.sc.us/scsl/
Member of The Foundation Center network, maintaining a collection of private foundation tax returns which provide information on the scope of grants dispensed by that particular foundation.

James B Johnson Jr, Director

South Dakota

2881 South Dakota Community Foundation
1714 North Lincoln Ave
Box 296
Pierre, SD 57501-3159
605-224-1025
800-888-1842
Fax: 605-224-5364
www.sdcommunityfoundation.org
The mission of the foundation is to promote philanthropy, receive and administer charitable gifts and invest in a wide range of programs promoting the social and economic well being of the people of the South Dakota. Grants given in South Dakota only.

Bob Sutton, President
Stephanie Judson, Administrative Vice Presiden

2882 South Dakota State Library
Reference Department
800 Governors Drive
Pierre, SD 57501-2294
605-773-5070
Fax: 605-773-4950
www.sdstatelibrary.com
Member of The Foundation Center network, maintaining a collection of private foundation tax returns which provide information on the scope of grants dispensed by that particular foundation.

Tennesse

2883 Benwood Foundation
736 Market Street
Suite 1600
Chattanooga, TN 37402-4803
423-267-4311
Fax: 423-267-9049
www.benwood.org
The general purpose of this foundation is to support such religious, charitable, scientific, literary and educational activities as will promote the advancement of mankind in any part of the United States of America. It should be recognized by all prospective grantees that while the foundation is not limited to the Chattanooga, Tennessee area, the bulk of the grants are made to organizations in the immediate area.

Jean R McDaniel, Executive Director
Sarah Morgan, President

2884 Christy-Houston Foundation
1296 Dow Street
Murfreesboro, TN 37130-2413
615-898-1140
Fax: 615-895-9524
Offers grants for education, arts, culture and health care to residents and organizations of Rutherford County, Tennessee.

James R Arnhart, Executive Director

2885 Frist Foundation
3100 West End Avenue
Suite 1200
Nashville, TN 37203
615-292-3868
Fax: 615-292-5843
www.fristfoundation.org
Broad general-purposed charitable foundation whose grants are restricted primarily to Nashville.

Peter F Bird Jr, President/CEO
Thomas F Frist Jr, Chairman

2886 JR Hyde Foundation
17 West Pontotoc Ave
Suite 200
Memphis, TN 38103-0084
901-685-3400
Fax: 901-683-7478
info@hydefoundation.org
www.hydefoundation.org
Offers grants for higher education, including scholarships for the children of Malone and Hyde employees, community funds, secondary education and youth services.

JR Hyde III, Executive Director

2887 Lyndhurst Foundation
517 E 5th Street
Chattanooga, TN 37403-1826
423-756-0767
Fax: 423-756-0770
www.lyndhurstfoundation.org
Support local arts and culture and downtown revitalzation efforts in Chattanooga. Support the protection and enhancement of the natural environment of the Southern Appalachian Region. Support the elementary and secondary public schools in Chattanooga.

Jack E Murrah, President

2888 Nashville Public Library
Business Information Division
615 Church Street
Nashville, TN 37219
615-862-5800
www.library.nashville.org
Member of The Foundation Center network, maintaining a collection of private foundation tax returns which provide information on the scope of grants dispensed by that particular foundation.

Keith B Simmons, Board Chair

2889 Plough Foundation
6410 Poplar Avenue
Suite 710
Memphis, TN 38119-5736
901-761-9180
Fax: 901-761-6186
Offers grants for community projects, including a community fund, early childhood and elementary education, social service agencies and the arts.

Noris R Haynes Jr, Executive Director

2890 RJ Maclellan Charitable Trust
Provident Building
Suite 501
Chattanooga, TN 37402
423-755-1366
Supports higher and theological education, social services and youth programs.

Hugh O Maclellan Jr, Executive Director

Texas

2891 Albert & Ethel Herzstein Charitable Foundation
6131 Westview Drive
Houston, TX 77055-5421
713-681-7868
Fax: 713-681-3652
www.herzsteinfoundation.org
Concentrates support on temples and medical research with grants offered to medical schools.

L Michael Hajtman, President
Nathan H Topek, Chairman

2892 Burlington Northern Foundation
3800 Continental Plaza
777 Main Street
Fort Worth, TX 76102
817-352-6425
Fax: 817-352-7924
The major channel of philanthropy for Burlington Northern and its subsidiaries. The foundation administers a consistent contribution program in recognition of the company's opportunity to support and improve the general welfare and quality of life in communities it serves.

Beverly Edwards, President
Becky Blankenship, Grant Administrator

2893 Burnett Foundation
801 Cherry Street
Suite 1400
Fort Worth, TX 76102-6814
817-877-3344
Fax: 817-338-0448
Focus is on Fort Worth and Santa Fe, NM, seeking to be a positive force in the community, supporting the energy and creativity that exist in the nonprofit sector, and building capacity in organizations and people in the fields of education, health, community affairs, human services and arts and humanities.

Thomas F Beech, Executive Director

2894 Cooper Industries Foundation
PO Box 4446
Houston, TX 77210-4446
713-209-8400
Fax: 713-209-8982
evans@cooperindustries.com
www.cooperindustries.com
The policy of this foundation is to carry out the responsibilities of corporate citizenship, by supporting nonprofit organizations in areas where employees are located, which best serve the educational, health, welfare, civic, cultural and social needs of the foundation's communities. All gifts are consistent with the company's objectives to enhance the quality of life and to honor the principles and freedoms that have enabled the company to prosper and grow. Average Grant: $5,000.

Victoria Guennewig, President
Jennifer L Evans, Secretary

2895 Corpus Christi State University
Library-Reference Department
805 Comanche
Corpus Christi, TX 78401
361-880-7000
Fax: 361-880-7005
www.library.ci.corpus-christi.tx.us
Member of The Foundation Center network, maintaining a collection of private foundation tax returns which provide information on the scope of grants dispensed by that particular foundation.

Denise Landry

2896 Cullen Foundation
601 Jefferson Street
Floor 40
Houston, TX 77002-7900
713-651-8837
Fax: 713-651-2374
www.cullenfdn.org
Supports educational, medical purposes, community funds and conservation.

Alan M Stewart, Executive Director
Sue A Alexander, Grants Administrator

2897 Dallas Public Library
Urban Information
1515 Young Street
Dallas, TX 75201-5499
214-670-1400
Fax: 214-670-1451
www.dallaslibrary.org
Member of The Foundation Center network, maintaining a collection of private foundation tax returns which provide information on the scope of grants dispensed by that particular foundation.

2898 El Paso Community Foundation
333 North Oregon St
2nd Floor
El Paso, TX 79901
915-533-4020
Fax: 915-532-0716
www.epcf.org
Grants to 501(c)(3) organizations in the El Paso geographic area. Fields of interest are arts and humanities, education, environment, health and disabilities, human services and civic benefits. No grants to individuals are offered.

Janice Windle, President
Virginia Martinez, Executive VP

2899 Ellwood Foundation
PO Box 52482
Houston, TX 77052-2482
713-739-0763
Scholarships for social services and education.

H Wayne Hightower, Executive Director

2900 Eugene McDermott Foundation
1155 Union Circle
Suite 311580
Denton, TX 76203-5017
940-369-5200
Fax: 940-369-5248
www.tshaonline.org
Offers support primarily for higher and secondary education, health, cultural programs, and general community interests.

Eugene McDermott, Executive Director
Laurie E Jasinski, Research Editor

2901 Ewing Halsell Foundation
711 Navarro Street
Suite 535
San Antonio, TX 78205-1786
210-223-2649
Fax: 210-271-9089
www.ewinghalsell.org
Offers grants in the areas of art and cultural programs, education, medical research, human services and youth services.

Jackie Moczygemba

2902 Exxon Education Foundation
5959 Las Colinas Boulevard
Irving, TX 75039-2298
972-444-1106
Fax: 972-444-1405
www.exxon.mobile.com
Grants are given in the areas of environment, education, public information and policy research, united appeals and federated drives, health, civic and community service organizations, minority and women-oriented service organizations, arts, museums and historical associations. In the education area grants are awarded to mathematics education programs, elementary and secondary school improvement programs, undergraduate general education programs, research, training and support programs.

EF Ahnert, Executive Director

2903 Fondren Foundation
7 TCT 37
PO Box 2558
Houston, TX 77252
713-236-4403
Provides support in various areas of interest with an emphasis on higher and secondary education, social services and cultural organizations.

Melanie Scioneaus, Executive Director

2904 George Foundation
310 Morton Street
PMB Suite C
Richmond, TX 77469-3135
281-342-6109
Fax: 281-341-7635
www.thegeorgefoundation.org
Offers giving for religious, educational, charitable or scientific purposes.

Roland Adamson, Executive Director
Sandra Thompson, Chief Financial Officer

2905 Gordon & Mary Cain Foundation
8 E Greenway Plaza
Suite 702
Houston, TX 77046-0892
713-960-9283
Fax: 713-877-1824
The foundation is not limited to education but does contribute a large amount to that area. For a company to apply for a grant they must offer a statement of purpose or a summary of the project needing funding; budget with balance sheet, fund balance, distribution of funds, audited statement and number of employees; latest copy of IRS tax-exempt status letter 501(c)(3); current projects needing funding with amounts needed for entire project and the amount of the grant being requested.

James D Weaver, Executive Director

2906 Haggar Foundation
6113 Lemmon Avenue
Dallas, TX 75209-5715
214-352-8481
Fax: 214-956-4446
Offers support in various areas with an emphasis on higher and secondary education, including a program for children of company employees.

Mary Vaughan Rumble, Executive Director

2907 Hobby Foundation
2131 San Felipe Street
Houston, TX 77019-5620
713-521-4694
Fax: 713-521-3950
Offers grants to educational facilities in the state of Texas.

Oveta Culp Hobby, Executive Director

2908 Houston Endowment
600 Travis Street
Suite 6400
Houston, TX 77002-3000
713-238-8100
Fax: 713-238-8101

info@houstonendowment.org
www.houstonendowment.org
Offers support for charitable, religious or educational organizations.

H Joe Nelson III, Executive Director
Ann B Stern, President

2909 Houston Public Library
Bibliographic Information Center
500 McKinney Street
Houston, TX 77002-2534
832-238-9640
Fax: 832-393-1383
www.hpl.lib.tx.us/hpl/hplhome
Member of The Foundation Center network, maintaining a collection of private foundation tax returns which provide information on the scope of grants dispensed by that particular foundation.

2910 James R Dougherty Jr Foundation
PO Box 640
Beeville, TX 78104-0640
361-358-3560
Fax: 361-358-9693
Offers support for Roman Catholic church-related industries including education, higher, secondary and other education.

Hugh Grove Jr, Executive Director

2911 Leland Fikes Foundation
3050 Lincoln Plaza
500 N Akard
Dallas, TX 75201
214-754-0144
Fax: 214-855-1245
Giving is focused on education, youth services, family planning, public interest and cultural programs.

Nancy Solana, Executive Director

2912 MD Anderson Foundation
1515 Holcombe Blvd
Houston, TX 77030-2558
713-658-2316
www.mdanderson.org
The purpose of this foundation is to improve lives in the areas of health care, education, human service, youth and research.

John W Lowrie, Executive Director

2913 Meadows Foundation
3003 Swiss Avenue
Wilson Historic Block
Dallas, TX 75204-6049
214-826-9431
800-826-9431
Fax: 214-824-0642
besterline@mfi.org
www.mfi.org
Support is given in the area of arts and culture, civic and public affairs , education, health, including mental health, and human services.

Bruce Esterline, VP Grants
Carol Stabler, Director Communications

2914 Moody Foundation
2302 Post Office Street
Suite 704
Galveston, TX 77550-1994
409-797-1500
Fax: 409-763-5564
info@moodyf.org
www.moodyf.org
Provides major support for two foundation-initiated projects: the Transitional Learning Center, a residential rehabilitation and research facility for the treatment of traumatic brain injury, and Moody Gardens, a world-class education and recreation complex that includes a 1-acre enclosed rainforest, the area's largest aquarium, a space museum, IMAX theater, and the Moody Hospitality Institute.

Peter M Moore, Grants Director
Robert L Moody, Sr.Chairman

2915 Paul & Mary Haas Foundation
PO Box 2928
Corpus Christi, TX 78403-2928
361-887-6955
Offers scholastic grants to graduating high school seniors from Corpus Christi, Texas. The student must have above average grades and ability to prove financial need. The Foundation asks that the senior contact them in the Fall of his/her senior year in order to begin the in-house application process. The grant is a maximum of $1,500 per semester and is renewable for a total of eight semesters if the student maintains a 3.0 GPA. The student may attend college or university of his choice.

Karen Wesson, Executive Director

2916 Perot Foundation
12377 Merit Drive
Suite 1700
Dallas, TX 75251-2239
972-788-3000
Fax: 972-788-3091
Educational grants, medical research funding and grantmaking for the arts and cultural organizations.

Bette Perot, Executive Director

2917 RW Fair Foundation
PO Box 689
Tyler, TX 75710-0689
903-592-3811
Grants are given for secondary and higher education, church-related programs and legal education.

Wilton H Fair, Executive Director

2918 Sid W Richardson Foundation
309 Main Street
Fort Worth, TX 76102-4006
817-336-0494
Fax: 817-332-2176
www.sidrichardson.org
www.sidrichardson.org
This foundation was established for the purpose of supporting organizations that serve the people of Texas. Grants are given in the areas of education, health, the arts and human services.

Valleau Wilkie Jr, Executive Director

2919 Strake Foundation
712 Main Street
Suite 3300
Houston, TX 77002-3210
713-546-2400
Fax: 713-216-2401
Foundation gives primarily in Texas in the areas of operating budgets, continuing support, annual campaigns, special projects, research, matching funds and general purposes.

George W Strake Jr, Executive Director

2920 Trull Foundation
404 4th Street
Palacios, TX 77465-4812
361-972-5241
Fax: 361-972-1109
trullfdn@ncnet.net
www.trullfoundation.org
1. A concern for the needs of the Palacios, Matagorda county are, where the foundation has its roots. Local health care, the senior center, and other local projects were considered and supported. 2. A concern for children and families. Grants are given to direct and channel lives away from child abuse, neglect from hunger, and poverty. 3. A concern for those persons and families devastated by the effects of substance abuse.

Gail Purvis, Executive Director
Lucja White, Administrative Assistant

Utah

2921 Marriner S Eccles Foundation
79 S Main Street
Salt Lake City, UT 84111-1901
801-246-5155
General support for Utah's human services, education and the arts programs.

Erma E Hogan, Executive Director

2922 Ruth Eleanor Bamberger and John Ernest Bamberger Memorial Foundation
136 S Main Street
Salt Lake City, UT 84101-1690
801-364-2045
Fax: 801-322-5284
bambergermemfdn@qwestoffice.net
www.ruthandjohnbambergermemorialfdn.org
Offers support for secondary education, especially undergraduate scholarships for student nurses and for schools.

William H Olwell, Executive Director

2923 Salt Lake City Public Library
210 East 400 south
Salt Lake City, UT 84111-3280
801-524-8200
Fax: 801-524-8272
www.slcpl.lib.ut.us
Member of The Foundation Center network, maintaining a collection of private foundation tax returns which provide information on the scope of grants dispensed by that particular foundation.

Dana Tumtowsky, Comm Relations Coordinator
Nancy Tessman, Director

Vermont

2924 Vermont Community Foundation
PO Box 30
Three Court Street
Middlebury, VT 05753-0030
802-388-3355
Fax: 802-388-3398
www.vermontcf.org
Offers support for the arts and education, the environment, preservation of the community, public affairs and more for the betterment of Vermont.

David F Finney, President/CEO
John Killacky, Executive Director

2925 Vermont Department of Libraries
Reference Services
109 State Street
Montpelier, VT 05609-0001
802-828-3268
Fax: 802-828-2199
www.dol.state.vt.us
Member of The Foundation Center network, maintaining a collection of private foundation tax returns which provide information on the scope of grants dispensed by that particular foundation.

2926 William T & Marie J Henderson Foundation
PO Box 600
Stowe, VT 05672-0600
Offers grants in the areas of elementary and secondary education.
William T Henderson, Executive Director

Virginia

2927 Beazley Foundation
3720 Brighton Street
Portsmouth, VA 23707-3902
757-393-1605
Fax: 757-393-4708
info@beazleyfoundation.org
www.beazleyfoundation.org
The purpose of this foundation to further the causes of charity, education and religion. Offers support for higher, secondary and medical education, youth agencies, community agencies and development.
Judge Richard S Bray, President
Donna M Russell, Associate Director

2928 Flagler Foundation
PO Box 644
Richmond, VA 23205
804-648-5033
Offers support for secondary and higher education, cultural programs and restoration.
Lawrence Lewis Jr, Executive Director

2929 Hampton Public Library
22 Lincoln Street
Hampton, VA 23669-4200
757-727-6315
Fax: 757-728-3037
council@hampton.gov
www.hampton.va.us
Member of The Foundation Center network, maintaining a collection of private foundation tax returns which provide information on the scope of grants dispensed by that particular foundation.
Molly Joseph Ward, Mayor
George E Wallace, Vice Mayor

2930 Jeffress Memorial Trust
Bank Of America Private Bank
Po Box 8795
Williamsburg, VA 23187-8795
804-788-3698
Fax: 804-788-2700
www.wm.edu/grants/opps/jeffress.htm
Funds research in higher education.
Richard B Brandt, Advisor

2931 Kentland Foundation
267 Kentlands Boulevard
Gaithesrsburg, MD 20878-5442
301-926-6636
info@kentlands.org
www.kentlands.org
Focuses on civic affairs organizations and education.
Helene Walker, Executive Director

2932 Longview Foundation for Education in World Affairs/International Understanding
1069 West Broad Street
Suite 801
Falls Church, VA 22046
301-681-0899
Fax: 301-681-0925
globaled@longviewfdn.org
www.longviewfdn.org
Offers grants and scholarships with an emphasis on pre-collegiate education, primarily elementary education, and also supports teacher education.
Betsy Devlin-Foltz, Director
Stevenson McIlvaine, President

2933 Richmond Public Library
Business, Science & Technology Department
3100 Ellwood Avenue
Richmond, VA 23221-2193
804-646-1139
Fax: 804-646-4757
www.richmondpubliclibrary.org
Member of The Foundation Center network, maintaining a collection of private foundation tax returns which provide information on the scope of grants dispensed by that particular foundation.
Peter Blake, Chairman
Brenda Drew, Vice-Chairman

2934 Virginia Foundation for Educational Leadership
2204 Recreation Drive
Virginia Beach, VA 23456-6178
757-430-2412
Fax: 757-430-3247
George E McGovern, Division Director

Washington

2935 Comstock Foundation
3010 Gull Road
Kalamazoo, MI 49048
269-250-8900
Fax: 269-250-8901
www.comstockps.org
The Foundation contributes only to 501(c)(3) organizations, limited to Spokane County and its environs. In the field of general education, Comstock Foundation favors grants only to private institutions of higher learning, and no grants are made to individuals.
Horton Herman, Trustee
Charles M Leslie, Trustee

2936 Foster Foundation
13 Central Way
Kirland, WA 98033
206-726-1815
info@thefosterfoundation.org
www.thefosterfoundation.org
Offers support in art, culture, higher education, adult education, literacy and basic reading, health care and children and youth services.
Jill Goodsell, Executive Director

2937 MJ Murdock Charitable Trust
703 Broadway Street
Suite 701
Vancouver, WA 98660-3308
360-694-8415
Fax: 360-694-1819
www.murdock-trust.org
Offers support primarily for special projects of private organizations in the areas of education, higher education, human services and program development.
John Van Zytveld, Senior Program Director

2938 Seattle Foundation
1200 5th Avenue
Suite 1300
Seattle, WA 98101-3151
206-622-2294
Fax: 206-622-7673
www.seattlefoundation.org
A community foundation that facilitates charitable giving; administers charitable funds, trusts and bequests; and distributes grants to non-profit organizations that are making a positive difference in our community. Grants are awarded to organizations working in areas that include social service, children and youth, civic, culture, elderly, conservation, education and health/rehabilitation.
Phyllis J Campbell, President/CEO
Molly Stearns, Senior Vice President

2939 Seattle Public Library
Science, Social Science
1000 4th Avenue
Seattle, WA 98104-1109
206-386-4636
Fax: 206-386-4634
www.spl.org
Member of The Foundation Center network, maintaining a collection of private foundation tax returns which provide information on the scope of grants dispensed by that particular foundation.

2940 Spokane Public Library
Funding Information Center
906 West Main Street
Spokane, WA 99201-0903
509-444-5300
Fax: 509-444-5365
www.spokanelibrary.org
Member of The Foundation Center network, maintaining a collection of private foundation tax returns which provide information on the scope of grants dispensed by that particular foundation.
Pat Partovi, Director

West Virginia

2941 Clay Foundation
1426 Kanawha Boulevard E
Charleston, WV 25301-3084
304-344-8656
Fax: 304-344-3805
Private charitable foundation making grants for health, education and programs for the aging or disadvantaged children.
Charles M Avampao, Executive Director

2942 Kanawha County Public Library
123 Capitol Street
Charleston, WV 25301-2686
304-343-4646
Fax: 304-348-6530
www.kanawha.lib.wv.us
Member of The Foundation Center network, maintaining a collection of private foundation tax returns which provide information on the scope of grants dispensed by that particular foundation.
Michael Albert, President
Elizabeth O Lord, First Vice President

2943 Phyllis A Beneke Scholarship Fund
Security National Bank & Trust Company
PO Box 511
Wheeling, WV 26003-0064
Offers support and scholarships for secondary education.
GP Schramm Sr, Executive Director

Wisconsin

2944 **Faye McBeath Foundation**
101 W Pleasant Street
Suite 210
Milwaukee, WI 53212-3157
414-272-2626
Fax: 414-272-6235
info@fayemcbeath.org
www.fayemcbeath.org
The purpose of the foundation is to provide Wisconsin people the best in education, child welfare, homes and care for the elderly and research in civics and government.
Scott E Gelzer, Executive Director
Aileen Mayer, Executive Assistant

2945 **Lynde & Harry Bradley Foundation**
1241 N Franklin Place
Milwaukee, WI 53202-2901
414-291-9915
Fax: 414-291-9991
www.bradleyfdn.org
The Foundation encourages projects that focus on cultivating a renewed, healthier and more vigorous sense of citizenship among the American people, and among peoples of all nations, as well. Grants are awarded to organizations and institutions exempt from federal taxation under Section 501(c)(3) and publicly supported under section 509(a), favor projects which are not normally financed by public tax funds, consider requests from religious organizations and institutions as well.
Michael W Grebe, President/CEO
Terry Considine, Chairman

2946 **Marquette University Memorial Library**
1355 West Wisconsin Avenue
Milwaukee, WI 53233-2287
414-288-7556
Fax: 414-288-5324
www.marquette.edu/library/
Member of The Foundation Center network, maintaining a collection of private foundation tax returns which provide information on the scope of grants dispensed by that particular foundation.

2947 **Siebert Lutheran Foundation**
300 N Corporate Dr
Suite 200
Brookfield, WI 53045-1392
262-754-9160
Fax: 262-754-9162
contactus@siebertfoundation.org
www.siebertfoundation.org
Offers support in elementary and secondary, higher education and early childhood education.
Ronald D Jones, President
Deborah Engel, Administrative Assistant

2948 **University of Wisconsin-Madison**
Memorial Library
728 State Street
Madison, WI 53706-1418
608-262-3242
Fax: 608-262-8569
grantsinfo@library.wisc.edu
www.grants.library.wisc.edu
Member of The Foundation Center network, maintaining a collection of private foundation tax returns which provide information on the scope of grants dispensed by that particular foundation.

Wyoming

2949 **Natrona County Public Library**
307 E 2nd Street
Casper, WY 82601-2598
307-237-4935
Fax: 307-266-3734
www.library.natrona.net
Member of The Foundation Center network, maintaining a collection of private foundation tax returns which provide information on the scope of grants dispensed by that particular foundation.

Grants, Federal & Private

2950 **American Honda Foundation**
PO Box 2205
Torrance, CA 90509-2205
310-781-4090
Fax: 310-781-4270
www.hondacorporate.com/community
Offers support for national organizations whose areas of interest include youth and scientific education. Grants reach private elementary, secondary, higher, vocational and scientific education.
Kathryn A Carey, Manager

2951 **Awards for University Administrators and Librarians**
Association of Commonwealth Universities
John Foster House
36 Gordon Square
London WC1H OPF, England
171 3878572
Fax: 171 3872655
pubinfo@acu.ac.uk
Lists approximately 40 sources of financial assistance for administrative and library staff for universities worldwide. Includes name, address, phone, fax, tenure place and length, amount of aid, requirements for eligibility and application procedure, and frequency and number of grants available.
40 pages Biennial
ISSN: 0964-2714
Moira Hunter, Editor

2952 **Awards for University Teachers and Research Workers**
Association of Commonwealth Universities
36 Gordon Square
London
WC1H OPF, England
44-20-7380-6700
Fax: 44-20-7387-2655
info@devry.edu
www.devry.edu
Lists approximately 740 awards open to university teachers and research workers in one country for research, study visits or teaching at a university in another country. Offers fellowships, visiting professorships and lectureships and travel grants.
364 pages Biennial
ISSN: 0964-2706

2953 **Educational Foundation of America**
55 Walls Drive
Fairfield, CT 06824-3515
203-226-6498
Fax: 203-227-0424
www.efaw.org
Funds projects in arts, education and programs benefiting Native Americans.
Diane M Allison, Executive Director
Lynn P Babicka, President

2954 **Foundation Center**
79 5th Avenue
Floor 8
New York, NY 10003-3076
212-620-4230
Fax: 212-807-3677
www.fdncenter.org
A national service organization which disseminates information on private giving through public service programs, publications, and through a national network of library reference collections for free public use. Over 100 network members have sets of private foundation information returns, and the New York, Washington, DC, Cleveland and San Francisco reference collections operated by the Foundation offer a wide variety of services and collections of information on foundations and grants.
Cheryl Loe, Director Of Communications
Laura Cascio, Fulfillment Management

2955 **GTE Foundation**
PO Box 152257
Irving, TX 75015-2257
972-507-5434
Fax: 972-615-4310
www.gte.com
The emphasis of giving for the foundation is on higher education in math, science and technology. It also sponsors scholarships and supports community funds and social service agencies that emphasize literacy training.
Maureen Gorman, VP

2956 **George I Alden Trust**
370 Main Street
Worcester, MA 01608-1714
508-459-8005
Fax: 508-459-8305
trustees@aldentrust.org
www.aldentrust.org
Gives to higher education organizations and facilities with an emphasis on scholarship endowments.
Francis H Dewey III, Executive Director
Warner S Fletcher, Chairman

2957 **Gershowitz Grant and Evaluation Services**
505 Merle Hay Tower
Des Moines, IA 50310
515-270-1718
Fax: 515-270-8325
gershowitz@netins.net
To give schools an edge in funding their technology programs
Michael V Gershowitz, PhD
Steve Panyan, PhD

2958 **Grants and Contracts Service**
Department of Education/Regional Office Building
7th & D Streets
Suite 3124
Washington, DC 20202-0001
202-401-2000
Fax: 202-260-7225
To support improvements in teaching and learning and to help meet special needs of schools and students in elementary and secondary education
Gary J Rasmussen, Director

2959 **Grantsmanship Center**
PO Box 17220
Los Angeles, CA 90017-0220
213-482-9860
Fax: 213-482-9863

norton@tgci.com
www.tgci.com
The world's oldest and largest training organization for the nonprofit sector. Since it was founded in 1972, the has trained trains more than 75,000 staff members of public and private agencies; training provided includes grantsmanship, program management and fundraising. Center also produces publications on grantsmanship, fundraising, planning, management and personnel issues for nonprofit agencies.

Norton Kiritz, President

2960 John S & James L Knight Foundation

Wachovia Financial Center
Suite 3300
200south Biscayne Boulevard
Miami, FL 33131-2349
305-908-2600
Fax: 305-908-2698
web@knightfoundation.org
www.knightfdn.org
The foundation makes national grants in journalism, education and the field of arts and culture. It also supports organizations in communities where the Knight brothers were involved in publishing newspapers but is wholly separate from and independent of those newspapers.

James D Spaniolo, Executive Director

2961 National Academy of Education - Spencer Postdoctoral Fellowship

500 5th Street NW
Washington, DC 20001
202-334-1947
Fax: 202-334-2350
info@naeducation.org
naeducation.org
The Spencer Postdoctoral Fellowship is designed to promote scholarship in the United States and abroad on matters relevant to the improvement of education in all its forms.

Michael Feuer, President
Gregory White, Executive Director

2962 National Science Foundation

4201 Wilson Boulevard
Arlington, VA 22230
703-292-5111
Fax: 703-292-9184
www.nsf.gov
Offers grants, workshops and curricula for all grade levels.

Arden L Bement Jr, Director

2963 Trust to Reach Education Excellence

1904 Association Drive
Reston, VA 20191-1537
703-860-0200
800-253-7746
Fax: 703-476-5432
tree@principals.org
www.tree.principals.org
Founded to make grants to educators and students who would ordinarily not have access to outstanding NASSP programs, such as camps, programs and workshops on leadership, technology and school reform.

Dr. Anne Miller, Executive Director

2964 Union Carbide Foundation

39 Old Ridgebury Road
Danbury, CT 06817-0001
203-794-6945
Fax: 203-794-7031
www.unioncarbide.com
Offers grants in the areas of elementary and secondary education, with an emphasis on systemic reform; higher education with a focus on science and engineering; and environmental protection awareness.

Nancy W Deibler, Executive Director

2965 United States Institute of Peace

2301 Constitution Avenue
Washington, DC 20037
202-457-1700
Fax: 202-429-6063
www.usip.org
Includes grants, fellowships, a National Peace Essay Contest for high school students and teacher training institutes.

Richard H Solomon, President
Judy Ansley, Board of Director

2966 United States-Japan Foundation

145 E 32nd Street
Floor 12
New York, NY 10016-6055
212-481-8753
Fax: 212-481-8762
info@us-jf.org
www.us-jf.org
A nonprofit, philanthropic organization with the principal mission of promoting a greater mutual knowledge between United States and Japan and to contribute to a strengthened understanding of important public policy issues of interest to both countries. Currently the focus is on precollegiate education, policy studies, and communications and public opinion.

2967 Westinghouse Foundation

Westinghouse Electric Corporation
Po Box 355
ECE 575C
Pittsburgh, PA 15230-0355
412-374-6824
Fax: 412-642-4874
www.westinghousenuclear.com
Makes charitable contributions to community priorities primarily where Westinghouse has a presence. Areas of emphasis include: education, health and welfare, culture and the arts and civic and social grants. Support for education is central to Westinghouse's contributions program, particularly higher education in the areas of engineering, applied science and business. Also encourages educational programs that strengthen public schools through enhanced student learning opportunities.

G Reynolds Clark, Executive Director

2968 Xerox Foundation

800 Long Ridge Road #1600
Stamford, CT 06902-1227
203-968-3445
www.xerox.com
Offers giving in the areas of higher education to prepare qualified men and women for careers in business, government and education.

Joseph M Cahalan, Executive Director

Fundraising

2969 A&L Fund Raising

29 Carriage Drive
South Windsor, CT 06074-1140
860-242-2476
800-286-7247
www.alstudentservices.com
Offers many successful fundraising programs including Christmas gifts, designer gift wraps from Ashley Taylor and Geoffrey Boehm chocolates. A&L sells only the highest quality items at affordable prices with great service to schools and organizations.

Anita Brown

2970 A+ Enterprises

1426 Route 33
Hamilton Square, NJ 08690-1704
609-587-1765
800-321-1765
A promotional corporation offering a variety of fundraising programs for schools and educational institutions, ranging from Christmas campaigns to chocolates, as well as magnets and gift campaigns.

2971 Aid for Education

CD Publications
8204 Fenton Street
Sliver Spring, MD 20910
301-588-6380
800-666-6380
Fax: 301-588-0519
afe@cdpublications.com
www.cdpublications.com

18 pages Newsletter
ISSN: 1058-1324

Frank Kimko, Editor

2972 All Sports

21 Round Hill Road
Wethersfield, CT 06109
860-721-0273
800-829-0273
Fax: 860-257-9609
shirts2graduationshirts.com
www.graduationshirts.com
Fundraising and school promotion company offering crew sweatshirts, hoods, tees, jackets, caps, gymwear and specialty signature shirts for graduating classes.

Wally Schultz, Owner

2973 Art to Remember

5535 Macy Drive
Indianapolis, IN 46235
317-826-0870
800-895-8777
Fax: 317-823-2822
brackney@arttoremember.com
www.arttoremember.com
Raises funds for art departments and special school programs.

2974 Childrens Youth Funding Report

CD Publications
8204 Fenton Street
Sliver Spring, MD 20910
301-588-6380
800-666-6380
Fax: 301-588-6385
cye@cdpublications.com
www.cdpublications.com
Detailed coverage of federal and private grant opportunities and legislative initiatives effecting childrens programs in such areas as child welfare, education healthcare.

18 pages Monthly

Steve Albright, Editor

2975 Disability Rights Education & Defense Fund

3075 Adeline Street
Suite 210
Berkeley, CA 94703
510-644-2555
Fax: 510-841-8645
info@dredf.org
dredf.org
The Disability Rights Education and Defense Fund works to advance the civil and human rights of people with disabilities through le-

gal advocacy, training, education, public policy and legislative development.

Claudia Center, President & Chair
Susan Henderson, Executive Director

2976 Dutch Mill Bulbs
212 Piper Cir
Annville, PA 17003
800-533-8824
Fax: 800-556-0539
info@dutchmillbulbs.com
www.dutchmillbulbs.com
Raises funds for organizations, including high schools, by selling Spring and Fall flower bulbs.

Jeffrey E Ellenberger, President

2977 E-S Sports Screenprint Specialists
47 Jackson Street
Holyoke, MA 01040-5512
413-534-5634
800-833-3171
Fax: 413-538-8648
Scholastic Spirit Division offers screenprinted T-shirts, sweatshirts, shorts and apparel. This program offers schools and organizations an easy way to increase school spirit with no risk, no minimum orders and prompt delivery.

Aaron Porchelli, Division Director

2978 Fundraising USA
1395 State Route 23
Butler, NJ 07405-1736
973-283-1946
800-428-6178
Fundraiser offering a variety of programs for schools and organizations including Walk-A-Thons. This program is fast becoming the most popular way for schools to raise money. The walks are designed to take place at your own school, and children are not responsible for collecting any money. Fundraising USA collects all donations through the mail.

2979 Gold Medal Products
10700 Medallion Drive
Cincinnati, OH 45241-4807
513-769-7676
800-543-0862
Fax: 513-769-8500
info@gmpopcorn.com
www.gmpopcorn.com
Offers a full line of fundraising products popcorn poppers and supplies and programs including candy, clothing and sports programs for schools and colleges.

Chris Petroff
Dan Kroeger, President

2980 Human-i-Tees
400 Columbus Avenue
Valhalla, NY 10595-1335
800-275-2638
Fax: 914-745-1799
www.humanitees.com
Environmental T-shirt fundraisers that provide large profits while raising environmental awareness for thousands of school, youth and service organizations across the country.

2981 Hummel Sweets
PO Box 232
Forestville, MD 20747
800-998-8115
Offer fundraising programs with 45% to 50% profit.

2982 M&M Mars Fundraising
800 High Street
Hackettstown, NJ 07840-1552
908-852-1000
Fax: 908-850-2734
Offers America's favorite candies for fundraising programs throughout the year.

2983 QSP
Subsidiary of the Reader's Digest Association
PO Box 2003
Ridgefield, CT 06877-0903
203-756-3022
800-667-2536
Fax: 800-844-3568
customerservice@qsp.ca
www.qsp.ca
For twenty-seven years, this fundraiser has helped students raise more than $900,000,000 for extracurricular programs and projects that are essential to a meaningful, well-rounded education. With QSP programs, students earn money to fund worthwhile projects and learn about the business world at the same time. QSP offers various fundraising programs including: Family Reading Programs; The Music Package; Delightful Edibles; and The Parade of Gifts.

Robert L Metivier, Sales Manager

2984 Sally Foster Gift Wrap
PO Box 539
Duncan, SC 29334-0539
800-552-5875
Fax: 800-343-0809
www.sallyfoster.com
Fundraiser offers gift wrap packages to schools. Offers high quality merchandise, including the heaviest papers and foils available. This proven two-week program is quick, easy and profitable offering your school or organization the opportunity to raise thousands of dollars to buy computers, books, athletic equipment and more. Organizations and schools keep 50% of all the profits, and there are no up-front costs or risks.

Mark Metcalfe, Sr VP

2985 School Identifications
Chas. E. Petrie Comapny
PO Box 527
Woodburn, OR 97071-0012
503-982-0757
800-772-0798
Fax: 503-981-3038
info@schoolidents.com
www.schoolidents.com
An easy fundraising project for schools, offering school identification cards and tags for students.

2986 School Memories Collection
Fundcraft Publishing
PO Box 340
Collierville, TN 38027
901-853-7070
800-853-1363
Fax: 901-853-6196
info@fundcraft.com
www.schoolmemories.com
Memory books with games and activities.

Chris Bradley, Marketing Director

2987 Sports Shoes & Apparel
3 Moulton Drive
Londonderry, NH 03053-4061
603-437-7844
800-537-7844
Fax: 603-437-2300
Offers customized sweatshirts, T-shirts and beach towels at group discount, with several complete fund raising programs being available as well. Beach towels for fundraising.

Bill McMahon, Regional Manager

2988 Steve Wronker's Funny Business
39 Boswell Road
W Hartford, CT 06107-3708
860-233-6716
800-929-swfb
Fax: 860-561-8910
www.swfb.net/swfb.htm
Comedy and educational magic shows available for preschool and elementary school aged children. Award winning programs such as The Magic of Books and Magic from Around the World are available for any size audience. For middle schools and high schools, comedy hypnosis is a perfect venue for entertainment as a fundraising program, for high school after-prom parties, graduation parties, or just for an evening's entertainment.

Steve Wronker

2989 T-Shirt People/Wearhouse
10722 Hanna Street
Beltsville, MD 20705-2123
301-937-4843
800-638-7070
Fax: 301-937-2916
www.t-shirtpeople.com
Fundraiser offering customized T-shirts to boost school spirit, raise funds, instill school pride and save money.

2990 Troll Book Fairs
100 Corporate Drive
Mahwah, NJ 07430-2041
201-529-4000
Fax: 201-529-8282
A profit-making program designed to introduce children to the wonderful world of books.

2991 Union Pen Company
166 Wallins Corner Road
Amsterdam, NY 12010
800-203-9917
Fax: 800-688-4877
unionpen@aol.com
www.unionpen.com
This company offers advertising gifts including customized pens and key chains that will increase confidence, school spirit and community goodwill in education. Group discounts are available.

Matt Roberts, General Manager
Morton Tenny, President

2992 www.positivepins.com
802 E 6th Streetve
PO Box 52528
Tulsa, OK 74152
918-587-2405
800-282-0085
Fax: 918-382-0906
pinrus@aol.com
www.thepinman-pins.com
Fundraising organization used by educational organizations. Designer and manufacturer of lapel pins used for employee service, appreciation, volunteer recognition, donor incentives and recognition, public relations and spirit.

Bern L Gentry, President
Michelle Anderson, VP

Scholarships & Financial Aid

2993 **AFL-CIO Guide to Union Sponsored Scholarships, Awards & Student Aid**
AFL-CIO
1100 1st St NE
Suite 850
Washington, DC 20002-4104
202-637-5000
info@unionprivelege.org
www.unionplus.org
Lists international and national unions, local unions, state federations and labor councils offering scholarships, awards or financial aid to students.
100 pages Annual

2994 **American-Scandinavian Foundation**
58 Park Avenue at 38th Street
New York, NY 10016
212-779-3587
info@amscan.org
www.amscan.org
The Foundation provides information, scholarships and grants on the study programs in Scandinavia.
Edward P. Gallagher, President
Steven B. Peri, Deputy Chairman

2995 **Arts Scholarships**
Jewish Foundation for Education of Women
430 Park Ave
Suite 3A
Highland Park, IL 60035-1827
212-288-3931
Fax: 212-288-5798
fdnscholar@aol.com
www.scholarships.com
These scholarships are being offered at the Julliard School, Tisch School, of the Arts at New York University, and the Manhattan School of Music to qualified students enrolled in their programs. Faculty members will select recipients.
Marge Goldwater, Executive Director

2996 **CUNY Teacher Incentive Program**
Jewish Foundation for Education of Women
135 E 64th Street
New York, NY 10019-1827
212-288-3931
Fax: 212-288-5798
fdnscholar@aol.com
www.jfew.org
Provide stipends to CUNY graduates who are studying for a master's degree in education and interested in a teaching career in the New York City public school system. Contact the office of the Vice Chancellor for Academic Affairs at CUNY for further information.
Marge Goldwater, Executive Director

2997 **College Board**
45 Columbus Avenue
New York, NY 10023-6917
212-713-8000
Fax: 212-713-8282
www.collegeboard.org
The College Board is a national, nonprofit membership association that supports educational transitions through programs and services in assessment, guidance, admission, placement, financial aid, and educational reform.
David Coleman, President

2998 **Dissertation Fellowships in the Humanities**
Jewish Foundation for Education of Women
135 E 64th Street
New York, NY 10065-1827
212-288-3931
Fax: 212-288-5798
fdnscholar@aol.com
www.jfew.org
A small number of fellowships will be awarded through the CUNY Graduate Center to qualified applicants.
Marge Goldwater, Executive Director

2999 **George & Mary Kremer Foundation**
1100 5th Avenue S
Suite 411
Naples, FL 34102-7415
941-261-2367
Fax: 941-261-1494
www.kremerfoundation.com
Provides scholarship funding for needy children in elementary Catholic schools throughout the Continental United States.
Mary Anderson Goddard, Director
Sister MT Ballrach, Assistant Director

3000 **Intel Science Talent Search Scolarship**
1719 N Street NW
Washington, DC 20036-2888
202-785-2255
Fax: 202-785-1243
sciedu@sciserv.org
www.sciserv.org
Offers a variety of services to teachers and students, including Intel Science Talent Search Scholarship competition, science fairs and publications.

3001 **Jewish Foundation for Education of Women**
Jewish Foundation for Education of Women
135 E 64th Street
New York, NY 10019-1827
212-288-3931
Fax: 212-288-5798
fdnscholar@aol.com
www.jfew.org
The Jewish Foundation for Education of Women is a private, nonsectarian foundation providing scholarships to women for higher education in the New York City area. A variety of specific programs are available. Most programs are administered collaboratively with area schools and organizations; the Foundation's mission is to help women of all ages attain the education and training needed to make them productive, economically independent members of the community.
Marge Goldwater, Executive Director
Sharon L Weinberg, Chairman

3002 **Octameron Associates**
P.O Box 2748
Alexandria, VA 22301-0748
703-836-5480
Fax: 703-836-5650
info@octameron.com
www.octameron.com
Octameron is a publishing and consulting firm with over 25 years experience in financial aid and admissions.
Anna Leider, Publisher

3003 **Scholarship America**
One Scholarship Way
Saint Peter, MN 56082-1556
507-931-1682
800-537-4180
Fax: 507-931-9250
dsnatoff@aol.com
www.dollarsforscholars.org
Provides community volunteers with the tools and support to create, develop and sustain legally constituted community-based scholarship foundations. Over 15,000 volunteers are active on 760 Dollars for Scholars chapter boards and committees throughout the United States. In addition, 20,000 high school youth and community residents are active in fund-raising events and academic support programs. Since the late 1950's, over 155,000 students have received Dollars for Scholars scholarships.
David Bach, VP
Susan Ponwith, President&CEO

3004 **Scholarships in the Health Professions**
Jewish Foundation for Education of Women
135 E 64th Street
New York, NY 10021
212-288-3931
Fax: 212-288-5798
fdnscholar@aol.com
www.jfew.org
Provides scholarships to emigres from the former Soviet Union who are studying medicine, dentistry, nursing, pharmacy, OT, PT, dental hygiene, and physician assistanceship.
Marge Goldwater, Executive Director

Federal Listings

3005 Accounting & Financial Management Services
U.S. Department of Education
400 Maryland Avenue, SW
Washington, DC 20202-0001
800-872-5327
Fax: 202-401-0207
www2.ed.gov

Arne Duncan, Secretary of Education
Emma Vadehra, Chief of Staff

3006 Assistance to States Division
U.S. Department of Education
400 Maryland Avenue, SW
Washington, DC 20202
202-401-2000
800-872-5327
Fax: 202-260-7225
www2.ed.gov

Arne Duncan, Secretary of Education
Emma Vadehra, Chief of Staff

3007 Brody Professional Development
Brody Communications Ltd.
115 West Avenue
Suite 114
Jenkintown, PA 19046
215-886-1688
Fax: 215-886-1699
info@brodypro.com
www.brodypro.com
Brody offers tailored training programs, executive coaching and presentations in the areas of communication skills and professional development.

Miryam Roddy, Manager of Maximum Exposure

3008 Compensatory Education Program
US Department of Education
400 Maryland Avenue SW
Washington, DC 20202
202-401-2000
800-872-5327
Fax: 202-260-7764
www.ed.gov

Emma Vadehra, Chief of Staff
Richard Culatta, Director, Education Tech

3009 Elementary Secondary Bilingual & Research Branch
U.S. Department of Education
400 Maryland Avenue, SW
Suite 3653
Washington, DC 20202
202-401-0113
800-872-5327
Fax: 202-260-7225
www2.ed.gov

Arne Duncan, Secretary of Education
Emma Vadehra, Chief of Staff

3010 Elementary, Secondary & Vocational Analysis
U.S. Department of Education
400 Maryland Avenue SW
3043 Main Building
Washington, DC 20202-0001
202-401-0318
800-872-5327
Fax: 202-260-7225
www2.ed.gov

Arne Duncan, Secretary of Education
Emma Vadehra, Chief of Staff

3011 Management Services
U.S. Department of Education
400 Maryland Avenue SW
Washington, DC 20202-0001
202-401-0500
800-872-5327
Fax: 202-260-7225
www2.ed.gov

Arne Duncan, Secretary of Education
Emma Vadehra, Chief of Staff

3012 National Center for Education Statistics
1990 K Street NW
8th & 9th Floors
Washington, DC 20006
202-502-7300
Fax: 202-502-7466
www.nces.ed.gov

Sean P. Jack Buckley, Commissioner

3013 National Council on Disability
1331 F Street NW
Suite 850
Washington, DC 20004-1107
202-272-2004
Fax: 202-272-2022
ncd@ncd.gov
www.ncd.gov/
An independent federal agency comprised of 15 members appointed by the President and confirmed by the Senate.

Jonathan M. Young, Ph.D., Chairman
Aaron Bishop, Executive Director

3014 National Institute of Child Health and Human Development
Bldg.31, Room 2A32, MSC 2425
31 Center Drive
Bethesda, MD 20892-2425
800-370-2943
Fax: 866-760-5947
NICHDInformationResourceCenter@mail.nih.gov
www.nichd.nih.gov
Develops research to solve problems in the physical and mental evolution of development. Including some of the most emotionally draining disorders, learning disabilities, behavioral disabilities, birth defects and infant mortality. Acts as a clearinghouse of materials, information and referrals and more.

Ellie Brown Hochman, Administrative Officer
Brenda Hanning, Program Management Officer

3015 National Library of Education
U.S. Department of Education
400 Maryland Avenue, SW
Washington, DC 20202
202-401-2000
800-872-5327
Fax: 202-401-0547
library@ed.gov
www.ed.gov

Emma Vadehra, Chief of Staff
Richard Culatta, Director, Education Tech

3016 National Trust for Historic Preservation: Office of Education Initiatives
The Watergate Office Building
2600 Virginia Avenue, Suite 1000
Washington, DC 20037
202-588-6000
800-944-6847
Fax: 202-588-6038
info@savingplaces.org
www.nationaltrust.org
Teaching with Historic Places, a program offered by the National Park Service's National Register of Historic Places, and the National Trust for Historic Preservation Press.

Stephanie Meeks, President & CEO
Tabitha Almquist, Chief of Staff

3017 No Child Left Behind
U.S. Department of Education
400 Maryland Avenue, SW
Washington, DC 20202
202-401-2000
800-872-5327
Fax: 202-401-0689
www.ed.gov
Provides education standards and incentives for states in adopting academic standards that prepare students to succeed in college and the workplace.

Emma Vadehra, Chief of Staff
Richard Culatta, Director, Education Tech

3018 Office for Civil Rights
U.S. Department of Education
400 Maryland Avenue SW
Lyndon Baines Johnson Dept of Ed Bldg.
Washington, DC 20202-1100
202-401-2000
800-872-5327
Fax: 202-453-6012
ocr@ed.gov
www.ed.gov

Emma Vadehra, Chief of Staff
Richard Culatta, Director, Education Tech

3019 Office of Bilingual Education and Minority Languages Affairs
U.S. Department of Education
400 Maryland Avenue SW
Washington, DC 20202-6510
202-401-2000
800-872-5327
Fax: 202-260-7225
askncbe@ncbe.gwu.edu
www.ed.gov

Emma Vadehra, Chief of Staff
Richard Culatta, Director, Education Tech

3020 Office of Elementary & Secondary Education
U.S. Department of Education
400 Maryland Avenue SW
Washington, DC 20202
202-401-2000
800-872-5327
Fax: 202-205-0310
oese@ed.gov
www.ed.gov

Emma Vadehra, Chief of Staff
Richard Culatta, Director, Education Tech

3021 Office of Indian Education
U.S. Department of Education
400 Maryland Avenue SW
LBJ Building, 3E205
Washington, DC 20202-6335
202-401-2000
800-872-5327
Fax: 202-260-7779
indian.education@ed.gov
www.ed.gov

Emma Vadehra, Chief of Staff
Richard Culatta, Director, Education Tech

3022 Office of Legislation & Congressional Affairs
U.S. Department of Education
400 Maryland Avenue SW
Washington, DC 20202-3100
202-401-2000
800-872-5327
Fax: 202-401-1438

olca@ed.gov
www.ed.gov

Emma Vadehra, Chief of Staff
Richard Culatta, Director, Education Tech

3023 Office of Migrant Education
U.S. Department of Education
400 Maryland Avenue SW
Room 3E317 FOB-6
Washington, DC 20202-6135
202-401-2000
800-872-5327
Fax: 202-205-0089
www.ed.gov

Emma Vadehra, Chief of Staff
Richard Culatta, Director, Education Tech

3024 Office of Overseas Schools
US Department of State
Room H328, SA-1
Washington, DC 20522-0132
202-261-8200
Fax: 202-261-8224
OverseasSchools@state.gov
www.state.gov
Maintains detailed information on 190 overseas elementary and secondary schools which receive some assistance from the US Department of State. These schools provide an American-type education which prepares students for schools, colleges and universities in the United States.

Dr. Keith D Miller, Director

3025 Office of Planning, Evaluation and Policy Development
U.S. Department of Education
400 Maryland Avenue SW
Suite 4022
Washington, DC 20201-0001
202-401-2000
800-872-5327
Fax: 202-260-7225
judy.wurtzel.ed.gov
www.ed.gov

Emma Vadehra, Chief of Staff
Richard Culatta, Director, Education Tech

3026 Office of Special Education Programs
Department of Education/3086 Mary E. Switzer Bldg.
600 Independence Avenue SW
Washington, DC 20202-2570
202-205-5507
Fax: 202-260-7225
thomas_hehir@ed.gov
www.ed.gov

Thomas Hehir, Director

3027 Office of Student Financial Assistance Programs
U.S. Department of Education
400 Maryland Avenue SW
Washington, DC 20202-0001
202-401-2000
800-872-5327
www.ed.gov

Emma Vadehra, Chief of Staff
Richard Culatta, Director, Education Tech

3028 Planning & Evaluation Service
U.S. Department of Education
400 Maryland Avenue, SW
Washington, DC 20202
202-401-2000
800-872-5327
Fax: 202-260-7225
www.ed.gov

Emma Vadehra, Chief of Staff
Richard Culatta, Director, Education Tech

3029 Rehabilitation Services Administration
U.S. Department of Education
400 Maryland Avenue SW
Washington, DC 20202-2800
202-401-2000
800-872-5327
Fax: 202-260-7225
rsa.ed.gov
www.ed.gov

Emma Vadehra, Chief of Staff
Richard Culatta, Director, Education Tech

3030 Research to Practice Division
U.S. Department of Education
Ofc of Special Ed/Rehabilitative Sv
400 Maryland Avenue SW
Washington, DC 20202-7100
202-401-2000
800-872-5327
www.ed.gov

Emma Vadehra, Chief of Staff
Richard Culatta, Director, Education Tech

3031 School Assistance Division
U.S. Department of Education
400 Maryland Avenue, SW
Washington, DC 20202-2141
202-260-2270
800-872-5327
Fax: 202-260-7225
www2.ed.gov

Arne Duncan, Secretary of Education
Emma Vadehra, Chief of Staff

3032 School Improvement Grants
U.S. Department Of Education
400 Maryland Avenue SW
Washington, DC 20202
202-401-2000
800-872-5327
www.ed.gov

Emma Vadehra, Chief of Staff
Richard Culatta, Director, Education Tech

3033 School Improvement Programs-Equity and Educational Excellence Division
U.S. Department of Education
400 Maryland Avenue, SW
Washington, DC 20202-2141
202-260-3693
800-872-5327
Fax: 202-260-7225
www2.ed.gov

Arne Duncan, Secretary of Education
Emma Vadehra, Chief of Staff

3034 School Improvement Programs-Safe and Drug Free Schools
Office of Safe and Drug Free Schools
400 Maryland Avenue, SW
Washington, DC 20202
202-245-7896
800-872-5327
Fax: 202-485-0013
osdfs.safeschl@ed.gov
www.ed.gov
Works to promote safe schools that are free from drug abuse and violence.

Arne Duncan, Secretary of Education
Emma Vadehra, Chief of Staff

3035 US Department of Defense Dependents Schools
2461 Eisenhower Avenue
Alexandria, VA 22331-3000
571-325-0867

Marilyn Witcher

3036 US Department of Education
400 Maryland Avenue SW
Washington, DC 20202
800-872-5327
Fax: 202-401-0689
customerservice@inet.ed.gov
www.ed.gov
Ensures equal access to education and promotes educational excellence for all Americans.

Arne Duncan, Secretary of Education
Emma Vadehra, Chief of Staff

3037 Vocational & Adult Education
U.S. Department of Education
400 Maryland Avenue, SW
Washington, DC 20202
202-205-5451
800-872-5327
Fax: 202-260-7225
www2.ed.gov

Arne Duncan, Secretary of Education
Emma Vadehra, Chief of Staff

3038 Washington DC Department of Education
825 N Capitol Street NE
Suite 900
Washington, DC 20202-4210
202-442-5885
Fax: 202-442-5026

Paul L Varce, Superintendent

Alabama

3039 Alabama State Department of Education
50 N Ripley Street
PO Box 302101
Montgomery, AL 36104
334-242-9700
astarks@alsde.edu
www.alsde.edu
Mission is to provide a state system of education which is committed to academic excellence and which provides education of the highest quality to all Alabama students, preparing them for the 21st century. For certification information contact the Alabama certification office at 334-242-9977.

Dr. Joseph B Morton, State Superintendent of Ed.
Dr. Craig Pouncey, Deputy State Superintendent

3040 General Counsel
Alabama Department of Education
50 N Ripley Street
PO Box 302101
Montgomery, AL 36130-0624
334-242-9700
studor@alsde.edu
www.alsde.edu
Provides legal counsel to the State Superintendent of Education, State Board of Education and State Department of Education.

Larry Craven, General Counsel
Juliana Teixeira Dean, Associate General Counsel

3041 Instructional Services
Alabama Department of Education
50 N Ripley Street
P.O. Box 302101?
Montgomery, AL 36104

334-242-9700
Fax: 334-242-9708
www.alsde.edu

Charlie G Williams, Assistant Superintendent

3042 Professional Services
Alabama Department of Education
50 N Ripley Street
P.O. Box 302101?
Montgomery, AL 36104
334-242-9700
Fax: 334-242-9708
www.alsde.edu

Eddie R Johnson, Assistant Superintendent

3043 Rehabilitation Services
Alabama Department of Rehabilitation Services
602 S. Lawrence St.
Montgomery, AL 36104
334-293-7500
800-441-7607
Fax: 334-293-7383
www.rehab.alabama.gov
State agency that provides and services and assistance to Alabama's children and adults with disabilities and their families.

Steve Shrivers, Commissioner

3044 Special Education Services
Alabama Department of Education
50 N Ripley Street
P.O. Box 302101?
Montgomery, AL 36104
334-242-9700
Fax: 334-242-9192
www.alsde.edu

Bill East, Division Director

3045 Student Instructional Services
Alabama Department of Education
50 N Ripley Street
P.O. Box 302101?
Montgomery, AL 36104
334-242-9700
Fax: 334-242-9708
www.alsde.edu

Martha V Beckett, Assistant Superintendent

3046 Superintendent
Alabama Department of Education
50 N Ripley Street
P.O. Box 302101?
Montgomery, AL 36104
334-242-9700
Fax: 334-242-9708
www.alsde.edu

Ed Richardson, Superintendent

3047 Vocational Education
Alabama Department of Education
50 N Ripley Street
P.O. Box 302101?
Montgomery, AL 36104
334-242-9700
Fax: 334-353-8861
www.alsde.edu

Stephen B Franks, Division Director

Alaska

3048 Alaska Commission on Postsecondary Education
ACPE
PO Box 110505
Juneau, AK 99811-0505
907-465-2962
800-441-2962
Fax: 907-465-5316
ACPE@alaska.gov
acpe.alaska.gov
Provides information on the state's education programs, colleges and universities, financial aid assistance programs, grants, scholarships, continuing education programs and career opportunities.

Randy Weaver, Chair
Stephanie Butler, Executive Director

3049 Alaska Department of Education Administrative Services
801 W 10th Street
Suite 200
Juneau, AK 99801-1894
907-465-2802
Fax: 907-465-4156
For certification information visit www.eed.state.ak.us/TeacherCertification / or contact 907-465-2831.

Shirley J Halloway, Commissioner

3050 Alaska Department of Education & Early Development
801 W 10th Street, Suite 200
PO Box 110500
Juneau, AK 99811-500
907-465-2800
Fax: 907-465-4156
eed.webmaster@alaska.gov
www.educ.state.ak.us

Gerald Covey, Commissioner

3051 Libraries, Archives & Museums
PO Box 110571
333 Willoughby Avenue
Juneau, AK 99811-0571
907-465-2910
Fax: 907-465-2151
eed.webmaster@alaska.gov
www.lam.alaska.gov
Summer reading programs

Linda Thibodeau, Director
Bob Banghart, Chief Curator

3052 School Finance & Data Management
Alaska Department of Education & Early Development
801 W 10th Street, Suite 200
PO Box 110500
Juneau, AK 99811-0500
907-465-2800
Fax: 907-465-4156
eed.webmaster@alaska.gov
www.eed.state.ak.us
Public school funding programs

Cynthia Curran, Director
Paul Prussing, Deputy Director

3053 Teaching And Learning Support Program
Alaska Department of Education & Early Development
801 W 10th Street, Suite 200
PO Box 110500
Juneau, AK 99811-0500
907-465-2800
Fax: 907-465-4156
eed.webmaster@alaska.gov
www.eed.state.ak.us
To improve students performance as well as the administering of a variety of federal, state and private programs that provide support to school district staff across the state.

Cynthia Curran, Director
Paul Prussing, Deputy Director

3054 Vocational Rehabilitation
Alaska Department of Labor & Workforce Development
801 W 10th Street
Suite A
Juneau, AK 99801-1894
907-465-2814
800-478-2815
Fax: 907-465-2856
dawn.duval@alaska.gov
www.labor.state.ak.us
Helping individuals with disabilities to find employment

Cheryl Walsh, Director
John Cannon, Chairperson

Arkansas

3055 Arkansas Department of Education
4 Capitol Mall
Room 403-A
Little Rock, AR 72201-1071
501-682-4475
virginia.hill@arkansas.gov
www.arkansased.org
Mission is to provide the highest quality leadership, service, and support to school districts and schools in order that they may provide equitable, quality education for all to ensure that all public schools comply with the standards.

Samuel Ledbetter, Chair
Abby Cress, Administrative Analyst

3056 Arkansas Department of Education: Special Education
4 Capitol Mall
Room 403-A
Little Rock, AR 72201-1071
501-682-4475
virginia.hill@arkansas.gov
www.arkansased.org

Samuel Ledbetter, Chair
Abby Cress, Administrative Analyst

3057 Federal Programs
Arkansas Department of Education
4 Capitol Mall
Room 403-A
Little Rock, AR 72201-1011
501-682-4475
virginia.hill@arkansas.gov
www.arkansased.org

Samuel Ledbetter, Chair
Abby Cress, Administrative Analyst

California

3058 California Department of Education
1430 N Street
Sacramento, CA 95814-5901
916-319-0800
Fax: 916-657-4975
EHughes@cde.ca.gov.
www.cde.ca.gov
Works to encourage the highest achievement for students by defining the knowledge, concepts and skills that students should aquire in each grade level.

Tom Torlakson, St Superintendent Public Ins
Richard Zeiger, Chief Deputy Superintendent

3059 California Department of Education's Educational Resources Catalog
CDE Press Sales
1430 N Street
Suite 3207
Sacramento, CA 95814-5901

916-319-0800
800-995-4099
Fax: 916-323-0823
EHughes@cde.ca.gov.
www.cde.ca.gov
Offers new techniques and fresh perspectives in handbooks, guides, videos and more.

Tom Torlakson, St Superintendent Public Ins

3060 California Department of Special Education
1430 N Street
Sacramento, CA 95814-5901
913-319-0800
Fax: 916-327-3516
EHughes@cde.ca.gov
www.cde.ca.gov
Resources and information that serve the unique needs of persons with disabilities by helping them to meet or exceed high standards of achievement in both academic and nonacademic skills.

Tom Torlakson, St Superintendent Public Ins

3061 Curriculum & Instructional Leadership Branch
California Department of Education
1430 N Street
Sacramento, CA 95814-5901
916-319-0800
EHughes@cde.ca.gov.
www.cde.ca.gov
Works to improve students academic achievements

Tom Torlakson, St Superintendent Public Ins

3062 Region 9: Education Department
San Diego COE
6401 Linda Vista Road
Suite 321
North San Diego, CA 92111
858-569-5304
dbrashear@sdcoe.net
Part of a statewide system of school support established to meet state and federal requirements, the support system works within county offices offering intensive and sustained assistance to local schools and educational agencies receiving Title I funds, helping to increase the opportunity for all student's to meet the state academic content standards.

David Brashear, Director

3063 Specialized Programs Branch
California Department of Education
1430 N Street
Sacramento, CA 95814-5901
916-319-0800
EHughes@cde.ca.gov
www.cde.ca.gov
Works to ensure that all children have the opportunity to obtain high-quality education.

Tom Torlakson, St Superintendent Public Ins
Mary Payne, District/School Improvement

Colorado

3064 Colorado Department of Education
201 E Colfax Avenue
Denver, CO 80203-1799
303-866-6600
Fax: 303-866-6938
www.cde.state.co.us
For certification information visit www.cde.state.co.us/index_license.htm or contact 303-866-6628.

William T Moloney, Commissioner

3065 Educator Licensing Unit
Colorado Department of Education
201 E Colfax Avenue
Denver, CO 80203-1704
303-866-6628
Fax: 303-866-6866
Licensing applications for educators, career and technical education. Issues educators licenses, reviews content, induction/professional development and disciplinary actions

Ed Almon, Educator Licensing

3066 Office of Federal Program Administration
Colorado Department of Education
1560 Broadway
Suite 1450
Denver, CO 80202-5149
303-866-6600
Fax: 303-866-6637
Administers funds under the elementary and secondary education act as well as a variety of other state and federal competitive awards and grants with the main goal to help all students to reach proficiency in English language arts, mathematics and reading.

Patrick Chapman, Executive Director
Lynn Bamberry, Director

3067 State Library
Colorado Department of Education
201 E Colfax Avenue
Room 309
Denver, CO 80203-1704
303-866-6900
Fax: 303-866-6940
www.cde.state.co.us
Provides leadership and expertise in library related activities and policies and provides assistance to public and academic schools.

Eugene Hainer, Assistant Commissioner
Sharon Morris, Director

3068 Supplemental Educational Services
Colorado Department of Education
1560 Broadway
Suite 1450
Denver, CO 80202
303-866-6600
Fax: 303-866-6637
medler_l@cde.state.co.us
www.cde.state.co.us
SES offers tutoring outside the regular school day that is designed to increase the academic achievement in reading/mathematics and language arts to low-income students in low-income schools

Patrick Chapman, Executive Director
Lisa Medler, Title IIA Coordinator

Connecticut

3069 Connecticut Early Childhood Unit
Connecticut State Department of Education
165 Capital Avenue
Hartford, CT 06106
860-713-6740
Fax: 860-713-7018
www.sde.ct.gov
Offers programs for children, infants and toddlers with disabilities.

Steven Adamowski, Superintendent

3070 Connecticut Governor's Committee on Employment of the Handicapped
Labor Department Building
200 Constitution Ave. NW
Washington, DC 20210
860-263-6774
866-4 U-A DO
Fax: 860-263-6039
www.dol.gov

3071 Connecticut State Department of Education
165 Capitol Avenue
Hartford, CT 06106
860-713-6543
Fax: 860-722-8502
www.sde.ct.gov

Steven Adamowski, Superintendent

3072 Education Programs & Services
Connecticut Department of Education
25 Industrial Park Road
Middletown, CT 06457-1520
860-807-2005
Fax: 860-635-7125

Theodore S Sergi, Division Director

3073 Finance & Grants Department
Connecticut State Department of Education
Grants Management
165 Capitol Avenue
Hartford, CT 06106
860-713-0466
Fax: 860-713-7046
www.sde.ct.gov

Eugene Croce, Manager
Candace Madison, Secretary

3074 Office of State Coordinator of Vocational Education for Disabled Students
Vocational Prgs. for the Disabled & Disadvantaged
PO Box 2219
Hartford, CT 06145
860-807-2001
Fax: 860-807-2196

3075 Teaching & Learning Division
Connecticut State Department of Education
165 Capital Avenue
Hartford, CT 06106-1659
860-713-6740
Fax: 860-713-7018
ciquest@ct.gov
www.sde.ct.gov

George Coleman, Acting Commissioner

3076 Vocational-Technical School Systems
Connecticut Technical High School System
25 Industrial Park Road
Middletown, CT 06457-1520
800-822-6832
Fax: 860-807-2196
cthsinternet@ct.gov
www.cttech.org

Patricia Ciccone, Superintendent
Robert Lombardi, Assistant

Delaware

3077 Assessments & Accountability Branch Delaware Department of Education
The Townsend Building
401 Federal Street, Suite 2
Dover, DE 19901-3639

302-735-4000
Fax: 302-739-4654
www.doe.k12.de.us

Mark T. Murphy, Secretary of Education
Mary Kate McLaughlin, Chief of Staff

3078 Delaware Department of Education
The Townsend Building
401 Federal Street, Suite 2
Dover, DE 19901-3639
302-735-4000
Fax: 302-739-4654
dedoe@doe.k12.de.us
www.doe.k12.de.us
Our mission is to promote the highest quality education for every Delaware student by providing visionary leadership and superior service.
Mark T. Murphy, Secretary of Education
Mary Kate McLaughlin, Chief of Staff

3079 Delaware Department of Education: Administrative Services
The Townsend Building
401 Federal Street, Suite 2
Dover, DE 19901-3639
302-735-4000
Fax: 302-739-4654
dedoe@doe.k12.de.us
www.doe.k12.de.us
Mark T. Murphy, Secretary of Education
Mary Kate McLaughlin, Chief of Staff

3080 Improvement & Assistance Branch Delaware Department of Education
The Townsend Building
401 Federal Street, Suite 2
Dover, DE 19901-3639
302-735-4000
Fax: 302-739-4654
dedoe@doe.k12.de.us
www.doe.k12.de.us
Mark T. Murphy, Secretary of Education
Mary Kate McLaughlin, Chief of Staff

District of Columbia

3081 DC Office of Special Education
District of Columbia Public Schools
441 4th Street, NW, 700S
Washington, DC 20001
202-727-0252
Fax: 202-727-9385
ocp@dc.gov
www.ocp.dc.gov
Nancy Hapeman, Interim Director
Yinka Alao, Chief of Staff

3082 District of Columbia Department of Education
441 4th Street, NW, 700S
Washington, DC 20001
202-727-0252
Fax: 202-727-9385
ocp@dc.gov
www.ocp.dc.gov
Nancy Hapeman, Interim Director
Yinka Alao, Chief of Staff

Florida

3083 Florida Department of Education
Turlington Building Suite 1514
325 West Gaines Street
Tallahassee, FL 32399
850-245-0505
Fax: 850-245-9667
commissioner@fldoe.org
www.fldoe.org
Offers information on community colleges, vocational education, public schools, human resources, financial assistance, adult education and more.
Pam Stewart, Commissioner/Fl. Dept of Ed
Kathy Hebda, Chief of Staff

Georgia

3084 Georgia Department of Education
2054 Twin Towers East
205 Jesse Hill Jr. Drive SE
Atlanta, GA 30334
404-656-2800
800-311-3627
Fax: 404-651-6867
askdoe@doe.k12.ga.us
www.gadoe.org
Among many other features, this organization offers agriculture education, federal programs, Leadership Development Academy, school and community nutrition progams, Spanish language and cultural program, technology/career (vocational) education and more.
Richard Woods, Superintendent
Sue Goodman, Manager

Hawaii

3085 Career & Technical Education Center
University of Hawaii
Lunalilo Portable 1
Lower Campus Road
Honolulu, HI 96822-2489
808-956-7461
Fax: 808-956-9096
hicte@hawaii.edu
www.hawaii.edu/cte
Angela Meixell, Interim Director
Sherilyn Lau, Education Specialist

3086 Hawaii Department of Education
1390 Miller Street
PO Box 2360
Honolulu, HI 96813
808-586-3230
Fax: 808-586-3234
doe_info@notes.k12.hi.us
www.hawaiipublicschools.org
Kathryn Matayoshi, Superintendent
Ronn Nozoe, Deputy Superitendent

3087 Information & Telecommunications Services Branch
Hawaii Department of Education
1390 Miller St., Room 417
PO Box 2360
Honolulu, HI 96813
808-586-3230
Fax: 808-586-3234
doe_info@notes.k12.hi.us
www.hawaiipublicschools.org
Kathryn Matayoshi, Superintendent
Ronn Nozoe, Deputy Superitendent

3088 Office of Curriculum, Instruction and Student Support
Hawaii Department of Education
Queen Liliuokalani Bldg, Rm 316
1390 Miller St,
Honolulu, HI 96813
808-586-3446
Fax: 808-586-3429
doe_info@notes.k12.hi.us
www.ociss.k12.hi.us
Kathryn Matayoshi, Superintendent
Leila Hayashida, Acting Assis Superintendent

3089 Special Education Department
Hawaii Department of Education
1390 Miller Street
Ofc Curriculum/Instruction/Student Supp.
Honolulu, HI 96813
808-586-3230
Fax: 808-586-3234
doe_info@notes.k12.hi.us
www.hawaiipublicschools.org
Kathryn Matayoshi, Superintendent
Ronn Nozoe, Deputy Superitendent

3090 State Public Library System
Hawaii State Public Library System
478 South King Street
Honolulu, HI 96813-2901
808-586-3617
Fax: 808-586-3314
hawaii.sdp.sirsi.net
Richard P. Burns, State Librarian

Idaho

3091 Idaho State Department of Education
650 West State Street
PO Box 83720
Boise, ID 83720-0027
208-332-6800
800-432-4601
Fax: 208-334-2228
infosuperintendent@sde.idaho.gov
www.sde.idaho.gov
Tom Luna, Superintendent
Sherri Ybarra, Superitendent

3092 Special Education Division
Idaho State Department of Education
650 W. State Street
PO Box 83720
Boise, ID 83720-0027
208-332-6806
Fax: 208-334-2228
infosuperintendent@sde.idaho.gov
www.sde.idaho.gov
Committed to empower people with disabilities with appropriate resources to make informed choices about their futures.
Sherri Ybarra, Superitendent
Casandra Myers, Administrative Assistant

Illinois

3093 Educator & School Development
Illinois Department of Education
100 N. 1st Street
Springfield, IL 62777

217-782-4321
866-262-6663
www.isbe.state.il.us

Dr. Christopher Koch, State Superintendent
Gery J. Chico, Board Chair

3094 Educator Certification
Illinois Department of Education
100 N. 1st Street
Springfield, IL 62777
217-782-4321
866-262-6663
www.isbe.state.il.us

Dr. Christopher Koch, State Superintendent
Gery J. Chico, Board Chair

3095 Finance & Support Services
Illinois Department of Education
100 N. 1st Street
Springfield, IL 62777
217-782-4321
866-262-6663
finance@isbe.net
www.isbe.state.il.us

Dr. Christopher Koch, State Superintendent
Gery J. Chico, Board Chair

3096 Illinois Department of Education
100 N 1st Street
Springfield, IL 62777
217-782-4321
866-262-6663
www.isbe.state.il.us

Dr. Christopher Koch, State Superintendent
Gery J. Chico, Board Chair

3097 School Finance
Illinois State Department of Education
100 N. 1st Street
Springfield, IL 62777
217-782-4321
866-262-6663
finance@isbe.net
www.isbe.state.il.us

Dr. Christopher Koch, State Superintendent
Gery J. Chico, Board Chair

3098 School Improvement & Assessment Services
Illinois State Board of Education
100 N 1st Street
Springfield, IL 62777
217-782-4321
866-262-6663
www.isbe.state.il.us

Chris Koch, Superintendent
Gery J. Chico, Board Chair

3099 Special Education
Illinois State Board of Education
100 N 1st Street
Springfield, IL 62777
217-782-4321
866-262-6663
www.isbe.state.il.us

Dr. Christopher Koch, State Superintendent
Gery J. Chico, Board Chair

Indiana

3100 Center for School Assessment & Research
Indiana Department of Education
South Tower, Suite 600
115 W. Washington Street
Indianapolis, IN 46204-2203
317-232-6610
Fax: 317-232-8004
webmaster@doe.in.gov
www.doe.in.gov

Glenda Ritz, Superintendent

3101 Community Relations & Special Populations
Indiana Department of Education
South Tower, Suite 600
115 W. Washington Street
Indianapolis, IN 46204-2203
317-232-6610
Fax: 317-232-8004
webmaster@doe.in.gov
www.doe.in.gov

Glenda Ritz, Superintendent

3102 External Affairs
Indiana Department of Education
South Tower, Suite 600
115 W. Washington Street
Indianapolis, IN 46204-2203
317-232-6610
Fax: 317-232-8004
webmaster@doe.in.gov
www.doe.in.gov

Glenda Ritz, Superintendent

3103 Indiana Department of Education
South Tower, Suite 600
115 W. Washington Street
Indianapolis, IN 46204-2798
317-232-6610
Fax: 317-232-8004
webmaster@doe.in.gov
www.doe.in.gov
For certification information visit www.in.gov/psb or contact 866-542-3672.

Glenda Ritz, Superintendent

3104 Office of Legal Affairs
Indiana Department of Education
South Tower, Suite 600
115 W. Washington Street
Indianapolis, IN 46204-2203
317-232-6610
Fax: 317-232-8004
webmaster@doe.in.gov
www.doe.in.gov

Glenda Ritz, Superintendent

3105 Office of School Financial Management
Indiana Department of Education
South Tower, Suite 600
115 W. Washington Street
Indianapolis, IN 46204-2203
317-232-6610
Fax: 317-232-8004
webmaster@doe.in.gov
www.doe.in.gov

Glenda Ritz, Superintendent

3106 Office of the Deputy Superintendent
Indiana Department of Education
South Tower, Suite 600
115 W. Washington Street
Indianapolis, IN 46204-2203
317-232-6610
Fax: 317-232-8004
webmaster@doe.in.gov
www.doe.in.gov

Glenda Ritz, Superintendent

3107 School Improvement & Performance Center
Indiana Department of Education
South Tower, Suite 600
115 W. Washington Street
Indianapolis, IN 46204-2203
317-232-6610
Fax: 317-232-8004
webmaster@doe.in.gov
www.doe.in.gov

Glenda Ritz, Superintendent

Iowa

3108 Community Colleges Division
Iowa Department of Education
400 E. 14th Street
Des Moines, IA 50319-0146
515-281-5294
Fax: 515-281-5988
www.educateiowa.gov

Brad Buck, Director
Jeremy Varner, Administrator

3109 Division of Library Services
Iowa Department of Education
400 E. 14th Street
Des Moines, IA 50319-0146
515-281-5294
Fax: 515-281-5988
www.educateiowa.gov

Brad Buck, Director
Jeremy Varner, Administrator

3110 Educational Services for Children & Families
Iowa Department of Education
400 E. 14th Street
Des Moines, IA 50319-0146
515-281-5294
Fax: 515-281-5988
www.educateiowa.gov

Brad Buck, Director
Jeremy Varner, Administrator

3111 Elementary & Secondary Education
Iowa Department of Education
400 E. 14th Street
Des Moines, IA 50319-0146
515-281-5294
Fax: 515-281-5988
www.educateiowa.gov
Strives for higher levels of learning and achievement for students in public elementary and secondary schools

Brad Buck, Director
Jeremy Varner, Administrator

3112 Financial & Information Services
Iowa Department of Education
400 E. 14th Street
Des Moines, IA 50319-0146
515-281-5294
Fax: 515-242-5988
lee.tack@ed.state.ia.us
www.educateiowa.gov

Brad Buck, Director
Jeremy Varner, Administrator

3113 Iowa Department of Education
Iowa Department of Education
400 E. 14th Street
Des Moines, IA 50319-0146
515-281-5294
Fax: 515-281-5988
webmaster@ed.state.ia.us
www.educateiowa.gov
Serves the students of Iowa by providing leadership and resources for schools, area education agencies and community colleges. For certification information visit www.state.ia.us/boee or contact 515-281-3245.

Brad Buck, Director
Jeremy Varner, Administrator

3114 **Iowa Public Television**
Iowa Department of Education
400 E. 14th Street
Des Moines, IA 50319-0146
515-281-5294
Fax: 515-281-5988
www.educateiowa.gov
Brad Buck, Director
Jeremy Varner, Administrator

3115 **Vocational Rehabilitation Services**
Iowa Department of Education
400 E. 14th Street
Des Moines, IA 50319-0146
515-281-5294
Fax: 515-281-5988
www.educateiowa.gov
Brad Buck, Director
Jeremy Varner, Administrator

Kansas

3116 **Kansas Department of Education**
Kansas State Department of Education
900 SW Jackson Street
Topeka, KS 66612-1212
785-296-3201
Fax: 785-796-7933
contact@ksde.org
www.ksde.org
Dr. Diane DeBacker, Commissioner of Education
Brad Neuenswander, Interim Commissioner

3117 **Office of the Commissioner**
Kansas State Department of Education
900 SW Jackson Street
Topeka, KS 66612-1212
785-296-3201
Fax: 785-296-7933
contact@ksde.org
www.ksde.org
Dr. Diane DeBacker, Commissioner of Education
Brad Neuenswander, Interim Commissioner

3118 **Special Education Services Department**
Kansas State Department of Education
900 SW Jackson Street
Topeka, KS 66612-1212
785-296-3201
Fax: 785-296-7933
contact@ksde.org
www.ksde.org
Dr. Diane DeBacker, Commissioner of Education
Brad Neuenswander, Interim Commissioner

3119 **Teacher Education & Licensure**
Kansas State Department of Education
900 SW Jackson Street
Topeka, KS 66612-1212
785-296-3201
Fax: 785-296-7933
contact@ksde.org
www.ksde.org
Dr. Diane DeBacher, Commissioner of Education
Brad Neuenswander, Interim Commissioner

Kentucky

3120 **Communications Services**
Kentucky Department of Education
500 Mero Street
Frankfort, KY 40601-1957
502-564-4770
andrew.liaupsin@education.ky.gov
www.education.ky.gov
Terry Holliday, Ph.D, Commissioner of Education
Rebecca Blessing, General Counsel

3121 **Curriculum, Assessment & Accountability Council**
Kentucky Department of Education
??Capital Plaza Tower
500 Mero St.
Frankfort, KY 40601-1957
502-564-4770
Fax: 502-564-7749
rebecca.blessing@education.ky.gov
education.ky.gov/Pages/default.aspx
Terry Holliday, Ph.D, Commissioner of Education
Rebecca Blessing, General Counsel

3122 **Education Technology Office**
Kentucky Department of Education
500 Mero Street
16th Floor CPT
Frankfort, KY 40601-1957
502-564-4770
rebecca.blessing@education.ky.gov
education.ky.gov/Pages/default.aspx
Terry Holliday, Ph.D, Commissioner of Education
Rebecca Blessing, General Counsel

3123 **Kentucky Department of Education**
Kentucky Department of Education
500 Mero Street
Capital Plaza Tower
Frankfort, KY 40601-1957
502-564-4770
Fax: 502-564-5680
rebecca.blessing@education.ky.gov
education.ky.gov/Pages/default.aspx
For certification information visit www.kyepsb.net or contact 502-573-4606.
Terry Holliday PhD, Commissioner of Education
Rebecca Blessing, General Counsel

3124 **Regional Services Centers**
Kentucky Department of Education
500 Mero Street
18th Floor CPT
Frankfort, KY 40601-1957
502-564-4770
rebecca.blessing@education.ky.gov
education.ky.gov/Pages/default.aspx
Terry Holliday, Ph.D, Commissioner of Education
Rebecca Blessing, General Counsel

3125 **Special Education Services**
Kentucky Department of Education
500 Mero Street
8th Floor
Frankfort, KY 40601-1957
502-564-4770
Fax: 502-564-6721
rebecca.blessing@education.ky.gov
education.ky.gov/Pages/default.aspx
Terry Holliday, Ph.D, Commissioner of Education
Rebecca Blessing, General Counsel

3126 **Teacher Education & Certification**
Kentucky Department of Education
500 Mero Street
17th Floor
Frankfort, KY 40601-1957
502-564-4770
rebecca.blessing@education.ky.gov
education.ky.gov/Pages/default.aspx
Terry Holliday, Ph.D, Commissioner of Education
Rebecca Blessing, General Counsel

Louisiana

3127 **Academic Programs Office**
Louisiana Department of Education
1201 North Third Street
PO Box 94064
Baton Rouge, LA 70804-9064
877-453-2721
Fax: 225-342-0193
customerservice@la.gov
www.louisianabelieves.com
Paul Pastorek, State Superintendent of Educ
Rene Greer, Director, Public Affairs

3128 **Louisiana Department of Education**
1201 North Third Street
PO Box 94064
Baton Rouge, LA 70804-9064
504-342-3607
877-453-2721
Fax: 225-342-0193
www.louisianabelieves.com
Provides leadership and enacts policies that result in improved academic achievement and responsible citizenship for all students. For certification information visit www.louisianaschools.net or contact 225-342-3490.
Cecil J Picard, Superintendent

3129 **Management & Finance Office**
Louisana State Department of Education
1201 North Third Street
PO Box 94064
Baton Rouge, LA 70804-9064
225-342-3617
877-453-2721
Fax: 225-219-7538
mlangley@doe.state.la.us
www.louisianabelieves.com
Marlyn J Langley, Deputy Superintendent

3130 **Office of Educator Support**
Louisiana Department of Education
1201 North Third Street
PO Box 94064
Baton Rouge, LA 70804-9064
877-453-2721
Fax: 225-342-0193
customerservice@la.gov
www.louisianabelieves.com
Paul Pastorek, State Superintendent of Educ
Karen Burke, Acting Asst. Superintendent

3131 **Special Education Services**
Louisiana Department of Education
1201 North Third Street
PO Box 94064
Baton Rouge, LA 70804-9064
877-453-2721
Fax: 225-342-0193
customerservice@la.gov
www.louisianabelieves.com
Paul Pastorek, State Superintendent of Educ
Rene Greer, Director, Public Affairs

3132 **Standards, Assessments & Accountability**
Louisiana Department of Education
1201 North Third Street
PO Box 94064
Baton Rouge, LA 70804-9064
877-453-2721
Fax: 225-342-3600
customerservice@la.gov
www.louisianabelieves.com
Paul Pastorek, State Superintendent of Educ
Scott Norton, Assistant Superintendent

Maine

3133 **Administrator and Teacher Certification**
Maine Department of Education
Certification Office
23 State House Station
Augusta, ME 04333-0023
207-624-6600
Fax: 207-624-6700
commish.doe@maine.gov
www.maine.gov
Jim Rier, Commissioner
Charlene Tucker, Team Coordinator

3134 **Adult Education**
Maine Department of Education
23 State House Station
Augusta, ME 04333-0023
207-624-6600
Fax: 207-624-6700
commish.doe@maine.gov
www.maine.gov
Jim Rier, Commissioner
Charlene Tucker, Team Coordinator

3135 **Maine Department of Education**
23 State House Station
Augusta, ME 04333-0023
207-624-6600
Fax: 207-624-6700
commish.doe@maine.gov
www.maine.gov
Jim Rier, Commissioner
Charlene Tucker, Team Coordinator

Maryland

3136 **Career & Technology Education**
Maryland State Department of Education
200 W Baltimore Street
Baltimore, MD 21201-2595
410-767-0100
888-246-0016
Fax: 410-333-2099
pmikos@msde.state.md.us
www.marylandpublicschools.org
Pat Mikos, Program Manager
Kimberlee Schultz, Public Affair Officer

3137 **Certification & Accreditation**
Maryland State Department of Education
200 W. Baltimore Street
Baltimore, MD 21201-2595
410-767-0100
888-246-0016
www.marylandpublicschools.org
Nancy S. Grasmick, St Superintendent of Schools
Kimberlee Schultz, Public Affair Officer

3138 **Instruction Division**
Maryland State Department of Education
200 W Baltimore Street
Baltimore, MD 21201-2595
410-767-0100
888-246-0016
www.marylandpublicschools.org
Mary Cary, Assistant Superintendent
Kimberlee Schultz, Public Affair Officer

3139 **Library Development & Services**
Maryland State Department of Education
200 West Baltimore Street
Baltimore, MD 21201-2595
410-767-0100
888-246-0016
www.marylandpublicschools.org
www.marylandpublicschools.org
Irene Padilla, Asst St Superintendent Lib.
Kimberlee Schultz, Public Affair Officer

3140 **Maryland Department of Education**
Maryland State Department of Education
200 W Baltimore Street
Baltimore, MD 21201-2595
410-767-0100
888-246-0016
Fax: 410-333-6033
www.marylandpublicschools.org
Mission of MSDE is to provide leadership, support, and accountability for effective systems of public education, library services and rehabilitation services. For certification information visit www.certification.msde.state.md.us or contact 410-767-0412.
Nancy S Grasmick, Superintendent
Kimberlee Schultz, Public Affair Officer

3141 **Office of Special Education and Rehabilitative Services**
U.S. Department of Education
400 Maryland Avenue SW
Washington, DC 20202-7100
202-245-7459
www.ed.gov
Melody Musgrove, Director
Bill Wolf, Acting Deputy Director

3142 **Special Education/Early Intervention Services Division**
Maryland State Department of Education
200 W Baltimore Street
9th Floor
Baltimore, MD 21201-2595
410-767-0100
888-246-0016
Fax: 410-333-8165
www.marylandpublicschools.org
Nancy S. Grasmick, St Superintendent of Schools
Kimberlee Schultz, Public Affair Officer

Massachusetts

3143 **Massachusetts Department of Education**
75 Pleasant Street
Malden, MA 02148-4906
781-338-3000
Fax: 781-338-3770
boe@doe.mass.edu
www.doe.mass.edu
David P Driscoll, Commissioner

3144 **Massachusetts Department of Educational Improvement**
75 Pleasant Street
Malden, MA 02148-4906
781-388-3300
Fax: 781-338-3770
boe@doe.mass.edu
www.doe.mass.edu
Andrea Perrault, Division Director

3145 **Region 1: Education Department**
J.W. McCormick Post Office & Courthouse
540 McCormick Courthouse
Boston, MA 02109-4557
617-223-9317
Fax: 617-223-9324
Michael Sentance

Michigan

3146 **Administrative Services Office**
Michigan Department of Education
608 W Allegan Street
Lansing, MI 48933-1524
517-373-3324
877-932-6424
Fax: 517-335-4565
www.michigan.gov
Rick Snyder, Governor

3147 **Adult Extended Learning Office**
Michigan Department of Education
608 W Allegan Street
Lansing, MI 48933-1524
517-373-3324
877-932-6424
Fax: 517-335-4565
www.michigan.gov
Rick Snyder, Governor

3148 **Career & Technical Education**
Michigan Department of Education
608 W Allegan Street
Lansing, MI 48933-1524
517-373-3324
877-932-6424
Fax: 517-373-8776
www.michigan.gov
Rick Snyder, Governor

3149 **Higher Education Management Office**
Michigan Department of Education
608 W Allegan Street
Lansing, MI 48933-1524
517-373-3324
877-932-6424
Fax: 517-373-2759
www.michigan.gov
Rick Snyder, Governor

3150 **Instructional Programs**
Michigan Department of Education
608 W Allegan Street
Lansing, MI 48933-1524
517-373-3324
877-932-6424
Fax: 517-335-4565
www.michigan.gov
Rick Snyder, Governor

3151 **Michigan Department of Education**
Michigan Department of Education
608 W Allegan Street
PO Box 30008
Lansing, MI 48909
517-373-3324
877-932-6424
Fax: 517-335-4565
MDEweb@michigan.gov
www.michigan.gov/mde
Rick Snyder, Governor

3152 Office of School Management
Michigan Department of Education
608 W Allegan Street
Lansing, MI 48933-1524
517-373-3324
877-932-6424
Fax: 517-335-4565
www.michigan.gov
Rick Snyder, Governor

3153 Office of the Superintendent
Michigan Department of Education
608 W Allegan Street
Lansing, MI 48933-1524
517-373-3324
877-932-6424
Fax: 517-335-4565
www.michigan.gov
Rick Snyder, Governor

3154 Postsecondary Services
Michigan Department of Education
608 W Allegan Street
Lansing, MI 48909
517-373-3324
877-932-6424
Fax: 517-335-4565
www.michigan.gov
Rick Snyder, Governor

3155 School Program Quality
Michigan Department of Education
608 W Allegan Street
Lansing, MI 48933-1524
517-373-3324
877-932-6424
Fax: 517-373-4565
www.michigan.gov
Rick Snyder, Governor

3156 Special Education
Michigan Department of Education
608 W Allegan Street
Lansing, MI 48933-1524
517-373-3324
877-932-6424
Fax: 581-733-5456
www.michigan.gov
Rick Snyder, Governor

3157 Student Financial Assistance
Michigan Department of Education
608 W Allegan Street
Lansing, MI 48933-1524
517-373-3324
877-932-6424
Fax: 517-335-4565
www.michigan.gov
Rick Snyder, Governor

3158 Teacher & Administrative Preparation
Michigan Department of Education
608 W Allegan Street
Lansing, MI 48933-1524
514-373-3324
877-932-6424
Fax: 517-335-4565
www.michigan.gov
Rick Snyder, Governor

Minnesota

3159 Data & Technology
Minnesota Department of Education
1500 Highway 36 West
Roseville, MN 55113-2233
651-582-8200
mde.commissioner@state.mn.us
education.state.mn.us/mde
Brenda Cassellius, Commissioner
Charlene Briner, Chief of Staff

3160 Data Management
Minnesota Department of Education
1500 Highway 36 West
Roseville, MN 55113
651-582-8200
Fax: 651-582-8873
mde.commissioner@state.mn.us
education.state.mn.us/mde
Brenda Cassellius, Commissioner
Charlene Briner, Chief of Staff

3161 Education Funding
Minnesota Department of Education
1500 Highway 36 West
Roseville, MN 55113-2233
651-582-8200
mde.commissioner@state.mn.us
education.state.mn.us/mde
Brenda Cassellius, Commissioner
Charlene Briner, Chief of Staff

3162 Financial Conditions & Aids Payment
Minnesota Department of Education
1500 Highway 36 West
Roseville, MN 55113-2233
651-582-8200
mde.commissioner@state.mn.us
education.state.mn.us/mde
Brenda Cassellius, Commissioner
Charlene Briner, Chief of Staff

3163 Government Relations
Minnesota Department of Education
1500 Highway 36 West
Roseville, MN 55113-2233
651-582-8200
mde.commissioner@state.mn.us
education.state.mn.us/mde
Brenda Cassellius, Commissioner
Charlene Briner, Chief of Staff

3164 Human Resources Office
Minnesota Department of Education
1500 Highway 36 West
Roseville, MN 55113-2233
651-582-8200
mde.commissioner@state.mn.us
education.state.mn.us/mde
Brenda Cassellius, Commissioner
Charlene Briner, Chief of Staff

3165 Minnesota Department of Children, Families & Learning
Minnesota Department of Education
1500 Highway 36 W
Roseville, MN 55113-4266
651-582-8200
Fax: 651-582-8724
mde.commissioner@state.mn.us
education.state.mn.us/mde
Works to help communities to measurably improve the well-being of children through programs that focus on education, community services, prevention, and the preparation of young people for the world of work. All department efforts emphasize the achievement of positive results for children and their families.
Brenda Cassellius, Commissioner
Charlene Briner, Chief of Staff

3166 Minnesota Department of Education
Minnesota Department of Education
1500 Highway 36 W
Roseville, MN 55113-4266
651-582-8200
Fax: 651-582-8724
mde.commissioner@state.mn.us
www.education.state.mn.us
Brenda Cassellius, Commissioner
Charlene Briner, Chief of Staff

3167 Residential Schools
Minnesota Department of Education
1500 Highway 36 West
Roseville, MN 55113-2233
651-582-8200
mde.commissioner@state.mn.us
education.state.mn.us/mde
Brenda Cassellius, Commissioner
Charlene Briner, Chief of Staff

Mississippi

3168 Community Outreach Services
Mississippi Department of Education
PO Box 771
Jackson, MS 39205-0771
601-359-3513
Fax: 601-359-3033
www.mde.k12.ms.us
Sarah Beard, Division Director

3169 Educational Innovations
Mississippi Department of Education
PO Box 771
Jackson, MS 39205-0771
601-359-3513
Fax: 601-359-2587
www.mde.k12.ms.us
David Robinson, Division Director

3170 External Relations
Mississippi Department of Education
PO Box 771
372 Central High Building
Jackson, MS 39205-0771
601-359-3513
Fax: 601-359-3033
www.mde.k12.ms.us
Andrew P Mullins, Division Director

3171 Management Information Systems
Mississippi Department of Education
PO Box 771
Jackson, MS 39205-0771
601-359-3513
Fax: 601-359-3033
www.mde.k12.ms.us
Rusty Purvis, Division Director

3172 Mississippi Department of Education
Mississippi Department of Education
359 NW Street
PO Box 771
Jackson, MS 39205-0771
601-359-3513
Fax: 601-359-3242
www.mde.k12.ms.us
Dr.Henry Johnson, Superintendent

3173 Mississippi Employment Security Commission
Mississippi Department of Education
PO Box 771
Jackson, MS 39205-0771
601-359-3513
Fax: 601-961-7405
www.mde.k12.ms.us

3174 Office of Accountability
Mississippi Department of Education
PO Box 771
Jackson, MS 39205-0771
601-359-3513
Fax: 601-359-1748
www.mde.k12.ms.us
Judy Rhodes, Division Director

3175 Vocational Technical Education
Mississippi Department of Education
359 NW Street
PO Box 771
Jackson, MS 39205-0771
601-359-3513
Fax: 601-359-3989
www.mde.k12.ms.us
Samuel McGee, Division Director

Missouri

3176 Deputy Commissioner
Missouri Department of Education
205 Jefferson Street
PO Box 480 Floor 6
Jefferson City, MO 65101-0480
573-751-4212
Fax: 573-751-1179
dese.mo.gov
Margie Vandeven, Commissioner

3177 Division of Instruction
Missouri Department of Education
205 Jefferson Street
Floor 6
Jefferson City, MO 65101-0480
573-751-4212
Fax: 573-751-8613
dese.mo.gov
Margie Vandeven, Commissioner

3178 Missouri Department of Education
Missouri Department of Education
205 Jefferson Street, 6th Floor
PO Box 480
Jefferson City, MO 65101-0480
573-751-4212
Fax: 573-751-8613
pubinfo@mail.dese.state.mo.us
dese.mo.gov
A team of dedicated individuals working for the continuous improvement of education and services for all citizens. We believe that we can make a positive difference in the quality of life for all Missourians by providing exceptional service to students, educators, schools and citizens.
Margie Vandeven, Commissioner

3179 Region 7: Education Department
Missouri Department of Education
10220 NW Executive Hills Boulevard
Kansas City, MO 64153-2312
816-891-7972
Fax: 816-891-7972
dese.mo.gov
Margie Vandeven, Commissioner

3180 Special Education Division
Missouri Department of Education
205 Jefferson Street
PO Box 480 Floor 6
Jefferson City, MO 65101-0480
573-751-4212
Fax: 573-751-8613
communications@dese.mo.gov
dese.mo.gov
Margie Vandeven, Commissioner

3181 Urban & Teacher Education
Missouri Department of Education
205 Jefferson Street
Floor 6
Jefferson City, MO 65101-0480
573-751-4212
Fax: 573-751-8613
communications@dese.mo.gov
dese.mo.gov
Margie Vandeven, Commissioner

3182 Vocational & Adult Education
Missouri Department of Education
205 Jefferson Street, 5th Floor
PO Box 480
Jefferson City, MO 65101-0480
573-751-4212
Fax: 573-751-8613
communications@dese.mo.gov
dese.mo.gov
Margie Vandeven, Commissioner

3183 Vocational Rehabilitation
Missouri Department of Education
205 Jefferson Street
PO Box 480
Jefferson City, MO 65101-0480
573-751-4212
Fax: 573-751-8613
communications@dese.mo.gov
dese.mo.gov
Margie Vandeven, Commissioner

Montana

3184 Accreditation & Curriculum Services Department
Montana Department of Education
106 State Capitol
PO Box 200113
Helena, MT 59620-113
406-444-2511
Fax: 406-444-2701
mt.gov/education
Steve Bullock, Governor

3185 Division of Information-Technology Support
Montana Department of Education
106 State Capitol
PO Box 200113
Helena, MT 59620-113
406-444-2511
Fax: 406-444-2701
mt.gov/education
Steve Bullock, Governor

3186 Montana Department of Education
Montana Department of Education
1227 11th Avenue
PO Box 200113
Helena, MT 59620-113
406-444-2511
Fax: 406-444-2701
mt.gov/education
For certification information visit www.opi.state.mt.us or contact 406-444-3150.
Steve Bullock, Governor

3187 Operations Department
Montana Department of Education
106 State Capitol
PO Box 200113
Helena, MT 59620-113
406-444-2511
Fax: 406-444-2701
mt.gov/education
Steve Bullock, Governor

Nebraska

3188 Administrative Services Office
Nebraska Department of Education
301 Centennial Mall S
Lincoln, NE 68508-2529
402-471-2295
Fax: 402-471-6351
www.education.ne.gov
To provide quality services and support in the areas of finance human resource management continuous quality improvement, office/building services,and technical assistant.
Mike Stefkovich, Division Director

3189 Division of Education Services
Nebraska Department of Education
301 Centennial Mall S
Lincoln, NE 68508-2529
402-471-2783
Fax: 402-471-0117
www.education.ne.gov
Marge Harouff, Division Director

3190 Nebraska Department of Education
Nebraska Department of Education
301 Centennial Mall S
PO Box 94987
Lincoln, NE 68509-4987
402-471-5020
Fax: 402-471-4433
www.education.ne.gov
Douglas D Christensen, Commissioner

3191 Rehabilitation Services Division
Nebraska Department of Education
301 Centennial Mall S 6th Floor
PO Box 94987
Lincoln, NE 68509-2529
402-471-3649
877-637-3422
Fax: 402-471-0788
www.education.ne.gov
Frank C Lloyd, Director

Nevada

3192 Administrative & Financial Services
Nevada Department of Education
700 E. Fifth Street
Carson City, NV 89701-4204
775-687-9200
888-590-6726
Fax: 775-687-9101
www.doe.nv.gov
Dale A.R. Erquiaga, Superintendent
Steve Canavero, Ph.D., Deputy Superintendent

3193 Instructional Services Division
Nevada Department of Education
700 E. Fifth Street
Carson City, NV 89701-4204
775-687-9200
Fax: 775-687-9101
www.doe.nv.gov
Dale A.R. Erquiaga, Superintendent
Steve Canavero, Ph.D., Deputy Superintendent

3194 Nevada Department of Education
700 E 5th Street
Carson City, NV 89701-5096

775-687-9200
Fax: 775-687-9101
www.doe.nv.gov
Mission is to lead Nevada's citizens in accomplishing lifelong learning and educational excellence.
Dale A.R. Erquiaga, Superintendent
Steve Canavero, Ph.D., Deputy Superintendent

New Hampshire

3195 Information Services
New Hampshire Department of Education
101 Pleasent Street
Concord, NH 03301-3860
603-271-3494
Fax: 603-271-1953
www.education.nh.gov
New Hampshire schools enrollment, financial, assessment information.
Virginia M. Barry, Commissioner
Paul K. Leather, Deputy Commissioner

3196 New Hampshire Department of Education
New Hampshire Department of Education
101 Pleasant Street
State Office Park S
Concord, NH 03301-3860
603-271-3494
800-339-9900
Fax: 603-271-1953
llovering@ed.state.nh.us
www.education.nh.gov
Mission is to provide educational leadership and services which promote equal educational opportunities and quality practices and programs than enable New Hampshire residents to become fully productive members of society.
Virginia M. Barry, Commissioner
Paul K. Leather, Deputy Commissioner

3197 New Hampshire Division of Instructional Services
New Hampshire Department of Education
101 Pleasant Street
Concord, NH 03301-3860
603-271-3494
Fax: 603-271-1953
www.education.nh.gov
Virginia M. Barry, Commissioner
Paul K. Leather, Deputy Commissioner

3198 Standards & Certification Division
New Hampshire Department of Education
101 Pleasant St
Concord, NH 03301-3860
603-271-3494
Fax: 603-271-1953
www.education.nh.gov
Virginia M. Barry, Commissioner
Paul K. Leather, Deputy Commissioner

New Jersey

3199 New Jersey Department of Education
New Jersey Department of Education
100 Riverview Plaza
PO Box 500
Trenton, NJ 08625-0500
609-292-4450
877-900-6960
Fax: 609-777-4099
www.state.nj.us/education
Develops and implements policies that address the major education issues in New Jersey. The State Board will engage in an effort to ensure that all children receive a quality public education that prepares them to succeed as responsible, productive citizens in a global society.
David C. Hespe, Commissioner
Bari Anhalt Erlichson, Chief Performance Officer

3200 New Jersey Department of Education: Finance
New Jersey Department of Education
100 Riverview Plaza
PO Box 500
Trenton, NJ 08625-0500
609-292-4421
877-900-6960
Fax: 609-292-6794
www.state.nj.us/education
David C. Hespe, Commissioner
Bari Anhalt Erlichson, Chief Performance Officer

3201 New Jersey Division of Special Education
New Jersey Department of Education
100 Riverview Plaza
PO Box 500
Trenton, NJ 08625-0500
609-292-0147
877-900-6960
Fax: 609-984-8422
www.state.nj.us/education
David C. Hespe, Commissioner
Bari Anhalt Erlichson, Chief Performance Officer

3202 New Jersey State Library
New Jersey Department of Education
PO Box 520
Trenton, NJ 08625-0500
609-292-6200
877-900-6960
Fax: 609-292-2746
nblake@njstatelib.org
www.state.nj.us/education
David C. Hespe, Commissioner
Bari Anhalt Erlichson, Chief Performance Officer

3203 Professional Development & Licensing
New Jersey Department of Education
PO Box 500
Trenton, NJ 08625-0500
609-292-2070
877-900-6960
Fax: 609-292-3768
www.state.nj.us/education
David C. Hespe, Commissioner
Bari Anhalt Erlichson, Chief Performance Officer

3204 Urban & Field Services
New Jersey Department of Education
100 Riverview Plaza
PO Box 520
Trenton, NJ 08625-0500
609-292-4442
877-900-6960
Fax: 609-292-3830
www.state.nj.us/education
David C. Hespe, Commissioner
Bari Anhalt Erlichson, Chief Performance Officer

New Mexico

3205 Agency Support
New Mexico Department of Education
300 Don Gaspar
Education Building
Santa Fe, NM 87501-2786
505-827-5800
ped.state.nm.us/ped
Tres Giron, Division Director

3206 Learning Services
New Mexico Department of Education
300 Don Gaspar
Education Building
Santa Fe, NM 87501
505-827-5800
Fax: 505-827-6689
ped.state.nm.us/ped
Albert Zamora, Division Director

3207 New Mexico Department of Education
New Mexico Department of Education
300 Don Gaspar
Education Building
Santa Fe, NM 87501-2786
505-827-5800
Fax: 505-827-6520
ped.state.nm.us/ped
Michael J Davis, Superintendent

3208 New Mexico Department of School-Transportation & Support Services
New Mexico Department of Education
300 Don Gaspar
Education Building
Santa Fe, NM 87501
505-827-5800
ped.state.nm.us/ped
Susan Brown, Division Director

3209 School Management Accountability
New Mexico Department of Education
300 Don Gaspar
Education Building
Santa Fe, NM 87501
505-827-5800
Fax: 505-827-6689
ped.state.nm.us/ped
Michael J Davis, Division Director

3210 Vocational Education
New Mexico Department of Education
300 Don Gaspar
Education Building
Santa Fe, NM 87501
505-827-5800
ped.state.nm.us/ped
Tom Trujillo, Division Director

New York

3211 Cultural Education
New York Department of Education
89 Washington Avenue
Albany, NY 12234
518-474-3852
Fax: 518-474-2718
SiteSupport@mail.nysed.gov
www.nysed.gov
Carole F Huxley, Division Director

3212 **Elementary, Middle & Secondary Education**
New York Department of Education
89 Washington Avenue
Albany, NY 12234-0001
518-474-3852
Fax: 518-474-2718
SiteSupport@mail.nysed.gov
www.nysed.gov
James Kadamus, Deputy

3213 **Higher & Professional Education**
New York Department of Education
89 Washington Avenue
Albany, NY 12234-0001
518-474-3852
Fax: 518-474-2718
SiteSupport@mail.nysed.gov
www.nysed.gov
Johanna Duncan-Poitier, Deputy Commissioner

3214 **New York Department of Education**
New York Department of Education
89 Washington Avenue
Albany, NY 12234
518-474-3852
Fax: 518-473-4909
SiteSupport@mail.nysed.gov
www.nysed.gov
Richard P Mills, President

3215 **Professional Responsibility Office**
New York Department of Education
89 Washington Avenue
Albany, NY 12234-2643
518-474-3852
Fax: 518-485-9361
SiteSupport@mail.nysed.gov
www.nysed.gov

3216 **Region 2: Education Department**
New York Department of Education
89 Washington Avenue
Albany, NY 12234
518-474-3852
Fax: 212-264-4427
SiteSupport@mail.nysed.gov
www.nysed.gov

3217 **Vocational & Educational Services for Disabled**
New York Department of Education
89 Washington Avenue
Albany, NY 12234
518-474-3852
800-272-5448
Fax: 518-457-4562
SiteSupport@mail.nysed.gov
www.nysed.gov
David Segalla, Regional Coordinator

North Carolina

3218 **Auxiliary Services**
North Carolina Department of Education
301 N Wilmington Street
Raleigh, NC 27601-2825
919-807-3300
Fax: 919-733-5279
www.ncpublicschools.org
Charles Weaver, Division Director

3219 **Financial & Personnel Services**
North Carolina Department of Education
301 N Wilmington Street
Raleigh, NC 27601-2825
919-807-3300
www.ncpublicschools.org
James O Barber, Division Director

3220 **North Carolina Department of Education**
North Carolina Department of Education
301 N Wilmington Street
Raleigh, NC 27601-2825
919-807-3300
Fax: 919-807-3279
www.ncpublicschools.org
Bob R Etheridge, Division Director

3221 **North Carolina Department of Instructional Services**
North Carolina Department of Education
301 N Wilmington Street
Raleigh, NC 27601-2825
919-807-3300
Fax: 919-807-3279
www.ncpublicschools.org
Henry Johnson, Division Director

3222 **Staff Development & Technical Assistance**
North Carolina Department of Education
301 N Wilmington Street
Raleigh, NC 27601-2825
919-807-3300
www.ncpublicschools.org
Nancy Davis, Division Director

North Dakota

3223 **North Dakota Department of Education**
North Dakota Department of Education
600 E Boulevard Avenue
Dept. 201
Bismarck, ND 58505-0440
701-328-2260
Fax: 701-328-2461
dpi@nd.gov
www.dpi.state.nd.us
Wayne G Sanstead, Superintendent
Kirsten Baesler, State Superintendent

3224 **North Dakota Department of Public Instruction Division**
North Dakota Department of Education
600 E Boulevard Avenue
Dept. 201
Bismarck, ND 58505-0440
701-328-2260
Fax: 701-328-2461
dpi@nd.gov
www.dpi.state.nd.us
Kirsten Baesler, State Superintendent

3225 **North Dakota State Board for Vocational & Technical Education**
North Dakota Department of Education
600 E Boulevard Avenue
Dept. 201
Bismarck, ND 58505-0440
701-328-2260
Fax: 701-328-2461
dpi@nd.gov
www.dpi.state.nd.us
Kirsten Baesler, State Superintendent
Reuben Guenthner, Division Director

3226 **Study & State Film Library**
North Dakota Department of Education
600 E Boulevard Avenue
Dept. 201
Bismarck, ND 58505-0440
701-328-2260
dpi@nd.gov
www.dpi.state.nd.us
Kirsten Baesler, State Superintendent
Robert Stone, Division Director

Ohio

3227 **Blind School**
Ohio Department of Education
25 S Front Street
Columbus, OH 43215-4131
614-466-3641
877-644-6338
Fax: 614-752-1713
contact.center@education.ohio.gov
education.ohio.gov
Richard A. Ross, Superitendent
Tom Gunlock, President

3228 **Curriculum, Instruction & Professional Development**
Ohio Department of Education
25 S Front Street
Columbus, OH 43215-4131
614-466-2761
877-644-6338
Fax: 704-992-5168
contact.center@education.ohio.gov
education.ohio.gov
Richard A. Ross, Superitendent
Tom Gunlock, President

3229 **Early Childhood Education**
Ohio Department of Education
25 S Front Street
Columbus, OH 43215-4131
614-466-0224
877-644-6338
Fax: 614-728-2338
contact.center@education.ohio.gov
education.ohio.gov
Richard A. Ross, Superitendent
Tom Gunlock, President

3230 **Federal Assistance**
Ohio Department of Education
25 S Front Street
Columbus, OH 43215-4131
614-466-4161
877-644-6338
Fax: 704-992-5168
contact.center@education.ohio.gov
education.ohio.gov
Richard A. Ross, Superitendent
Tom Gunlock, President

3231 **Ohio Department of Education**
Ohio Department of Education
25 S Front Street
7th Floor
Columbus, OH 43215-4183
614-466-7578
877-644-6338
Fax: 614-728-4781
contact.center@education.ohio.gov
education.ohio.gov
Works in partnership with school districts to assure high achievements for all learners, promote a safe and orderly learning environment, provide leadership, support, and build capacity, and provide support to school districts particularly those who need it most.
Richard A. Ross, Superitendent
Tom Gunlock, President

3232 Personnel Services
Ohio Department of Education
25 S Front Street
Columbus, OH 43215-4131
614-466-3763
877-644-6338
Fax: 704-992-5168
contact.center@education.ohio.gov
education.ohio.gov

Richard A. Ross, Superintendent
Tom Gunlock, President

3233 School Finance
Ohio Department of Education
25 S Front Street
Columbus, OH 43215-4183
614-466-6266
877-644-6338
Fax: 704-992-5168
contact.center@education.ohio.gov
education.ohio.gov

Richard A. Ross, Superintendent
Tom Gunlock, President

3234 School Food Service
Ohio Department of Education
25 S Front Street
Columbus, OH 43215-4131
614-466-2945
877-644-6338
Fax: 704-992-5168
contact.center@education.ohio.gov
education.ohio.gov

Richard A. Ross, Superintendent
Tom Gunlock, President

3235 School for the Deaf
Ohio Department of Education
25 S Front Street
Columbus, OH 43215-4131
614-466-3641
877-644-6338
Fax: 704-992-5168
contact.center@education.ohio.gov
education.ohio.gov

Richard A. Ross, Superintendent
Tom Gunlock, President

3236 Special Education
Ohio Department of Education
25 S Front Street
Worthington, OH 43085
614-466-2650
877-644-6338
Fax: 704-992-5168
contact.center@education.ohio.gov
education.ohio.gov

Richard A. Ross, Superintendent
Tom Gunlock, President

3237 Student Development
Ohio Department of Education
25 S Front Street
Columbus, OH 43215-4131
614-466-3641
877-644-6338
Fax: 704-992-5168
contact.center@education.ohio.gov
education.ohio.gov

Richard A. Ross, Superintendent
Tom Gunlock, President

3238 Teacher Education & Certification
Ohio Department of Education
25 S Front Street
Columbus, OH 43215-4131
614-466-3430
877-644-6338
Fax: 704-992-5168
contact.center@education.ohio.gov
education.ohio.gov

Richard A. Ross, Superintendent
Tom Gunlock, President

3239 Vocational & Career Education
Ohio Department of Education
25 S Front Street
Columbus, OH 43215-4131
614-466-3430
877-644-6338
Fax: 704-992-5168
contact.center@education.ohio.gov
education.ohio.gov

Richard A. Ross, Superintendent
Tom Gunlock, President

Oklahoma

3240 Accreditation & Standards Division
Oklahoma State Department of Education
2500 N Lincoln Boulevard
Oklahoma City, OK 73105-4599
405-521-3301
Fax: 405-521-6205
sdeservicedesk@sde.ok.gov
www.ok.gov/sde

Joy Hofmeister, Superintendent
Liz Young, Executive Assistant

3241 Federal/Special/Collaboration Services
Oklahoma State Department of Education
2500 N Lincoln Boulevard
Oklahoma City, OK 73105-4599
405-521-3301
Fax: 405-521-6205
sdeservicedesk@sde.ok.gov
www.ok.gov/sde

Joy Hofmeister, Superintendent
Liz Young, Executive Assistant

3242 Oklahoma Department of Career and Technology Education
Oklahoma Department of Career and Technology Educa
1500 W 7th Avenue
Stillwater, OK 74074-4398
405-377-2000
Fax: 405-743-5541
Paula.Bowles@careertech.ok.gov
www.okcareertech.org

Roy Peters Jr, Division Director
Paula Bowles, Chief Comm Officer/CMO

3243 Oklahoma Department of Education
Oklahoma State Department of Education
2500 N Lincoln Boulevard
Hodge Education Building
Oklahoma City, OK 73105-4599
405-521-3301
Fax: 405-521-6205
sdeservicedesk@sde.ok.gov
www.ok.gov/sde

Joy Hofmeister, Superintendent
Liz Young, Executive Assistant

3244 Oklahoma Department of Education; Financial Services
Oklahoma State Department of Education
2500 N Lincoln Boulevard
Oklahoma City, OK 73105-4599
405-521-3301
Fax: 405-521-6205
sdeservicedesk@sde.ok.gov
www.ok.gov/sde

Joy Hofmeister, Superintendent
Liz Young, Executive Assistant

3245 Professional Services
Oklahoma State Department of Education
2500 N Lincoln Boulevard
Oklahoma City, OK 73105-4599
405-521-3301
Fax: 405-521-6205
sdeservicedesk@sde.ok.gov
www.ok.gov/sde

Joy Hofmeister, Superintendent
Liz Young, Executive Assistant

3246 School Improvement
Oklahoma State Department of Education
2500 N Lincoln Boulevard
Oklahoma City, OK 73105-4599
405-521-3301
Fax: 405-521-6205
sdeservicedesk@sde.ok.gov
www.ok.gov/sde

Joy Hofmeister, Superintendent
Liz Young, Executive Assistant

Oregon

3247 Assessment & Evaluation
Oregon Department of Education
255 Capitol Street NE
Salem, OR 97310-0203
503-378-3600
Fax: 503-378-5156
ode.frontdesk@ode.state.or.us
www.ode.state.or.us

Rob Saxton, Deputy Superintendent

3248 Community College Services
Oregon Department of Education
225 Capitol Street NE
Salem, OR 97310-1341
503-378-3600
Fax: 503-378-5156
ode.frontdesk@ode.state.or.us
www.ode.state.or.us

Rob Saxton, Deputy Superintendent

3249 Compensatory Education Office
Oregon Department of Education
225 Capitol Street NE
Salem, OR 97310-1341
503-378-3569
Fax: 503-378-5156
ode.frontdesk@ode.state.or.us
www.ode.state.or.us

Rob Saxton, Deputy Superintendent

3250 Deputy Superintendent Office
Oregon Department of Education
225 Capitol Street NE
Salem, OR 97310-1341
503-378-3573
Fax: 503-378-5156
ode.frontdesk@ode.state.or.us
www.ode.state.or.us

Rob Saxton, Deputy Superintendent

3251 Early Childhood Council
Oregon Department of Education
225 Capitol Street NE
Salem, OR 97310-1341
503-378-5585
Fax: 503-378-5156
ode.frontdesk@ode.state.or.us
www.ode.state.or.us

Rob Saxton, Deputy Superintendent

3252 **Government Relations**
Oregon Department of Education
225 Capitol Street NE
Salem, OR 97310-1341
503-378-8549
Fax: 503-378-5156
ode.frontdesk@ode.state.or.us
www.ode.state.or.us
Rob Saxton, Deputy Superitendent

3253 **Management Services**
Oregon Department of Education
225 Capitol Street NE
Salem, OR 97310-1341
503-378-8549
Fax: 503-378-5156
ode.frontdesk@ode.state.or.us
www.ode.state.or.us
Rob Saxton, Deputy Superitendent

3254 **Office of Field, Curriculum & Instruction Services**
Oregon Department of Education
225 Capitol Street NE
Salem, OR 97310-1341
503-378-8004
Fax: 503-378-5156
ode.frontdesk@ode.state.or.us
www.ode.state.or.us
Rob Saxton, Deputy Superitendent

3255 **Oregon Department of Education**
Oregon Department of Education
225 Capitol Street NE
Salem, OR 97310-0203
503-378-3569
Fax: 503-378-5156
ode.frontdesk@ode.state.or.us
www.ode.state.or.us
Rob Saxton, Deputy Superitendent

3256 **Professional Technical Education**
Oregon Department of Education
225 Capitol Street NE
Salem, OR 97310-1341
503-378-3584
Fax: 503-378-5156
ode.frontdesk@ode.state.or.us
www.ode.state.or.us
Rob Saxton, Deputy Superitendent

3257 **Special Education**
Oregon Department of Education
225 Capitol Street NE
Salem, OR 97310-1341
503-378-3600
Fax: 503-378-5156
ode.frontdesk@ode.state.or.us
www.ode.state.or.us
Rob Saxton, Deputy Superitendent

3258 **Student Services Office**
Oregon Department of Education
225 Capitol Street NE
Salem, OR 97310-1341
503-378-5585
Fax: 503-378-5156
ode.frontdesk@ode.state.or.us
www.ode.state.or.us
Rob Saxton, Deputy Superitendent

3259 **Twenty First Century Schools Council**
Oregon Department of Education
225 Capitol Street NE
Salem, OR 97310-1341
503-378-3600
Fax: 503-378-5156
ode.frontdesk@ode.state.or.us
www.ode.state.or.us
Rob Saxton, Deputy Superitendent

Pennsylvania

3260 **Chief Counsel**
Pennsylvania Department of Education
333 Market Street
Harrisburg, PA 17126-2210
717-783-6788
Fax: 717-783-0347
www.education.state.pa.us
Carolyn Dumaresq, Acting Secretary

3261 **Chief of Staff Office**
Pennsylvania Department of Education
333 Market Street
Harrisburg, PA 17126-2210
717-783-6788
Fax: 717-787-7222
www.education.state.pa.us
Carolyn Dumaresq, Acting Secretary

3262 **Higher Education/Postsecondary Office**
Pennsylvania Department of Education
333 Market Street
Harrisburg, PA 17126-2210
717-783-6788
Fax: 717-783-0583
www.education.state.pa.us
Carolyn Dumaresq, Acting Secretary

3263 **Office of Elementary and Secondary Education**
Pennsylvania Department of Education
333 Market Street
5th Floor
Harrisburg, PA 17126
717-783-6788
Fax: 717-783-6802
dhaines@state.pa.us
www.education.state.pa.us
Carolyn Dumaresq, Acting Secretary

3264 **Office of the Comptroller**
Pennsylvania Department of Education
333 Market Street
Harrisburg, PA 17126-2210
717-783-6788
Fax: 717-787-3593
www.education.state.pa.us
Carolyn Dumaresq, Acting Secretary

3265 **Pennsylvania Department of Education**
Pennsylvania Department of Education
333 Market Street
Harrisburg, PA 17126
717-783-6788
Fax: 717-787-7222
www.education.state.pa.us
Carolyn Dumaresq, Acting Secretary

3266 **Region 3: Education Department**
Pennsylvania Department of Education
333 Market Street
Harrisburg, PA 17126-3309
717-783-6788
www.education.state.pa.us
Carolyn Dumaresq, Acting Secretary

Rhode Island

3267 **Career & Technical Education**
Rhode Island Department of Education
255 Westminster Street
Providence, RI 02903-3414
401-222-4600
Fax: 401-222-2537
www.ride.ri.gov
Deborah Gist, Commissioner
Andy Andrade, Commissioner Support

3268 **Equity & Access Office**
Rhode Island Department of Education
255 Westminster Street
Providence, RI 02903-3414
401-222-4600
Fax: 401-222-2537
www.ride.ri.gov
Deborah Gist, Commissioner
Andy Andrade, Commissioner Support

3269 **Human Resource Development**
Rhode Island Department of Education
255 Westminster Street
Providence, RI 02903-3414
401-222-4600
Fax: 401-222-2537
www.ride.ri.gov
Deborah Gist, Commissioner
Andy Andrade, Commissioner Support

3270 **Instruction Office**
Rhode Island Department of Education
255 Westminster Street
Providence, RI 02903-3414
401-222-4600
Fax: 401-222-2537
www.ride.ri.gov
Deborah Gist, Commissioner
Andy Andrade, Commissioner Support

3271 **Office of Finance**
Rhode Island Department of Education
255 Westminster Street
Providence, RI 02903-3414
401-222-4600
Fax: 401-222-2537
www.ride.ri.gov
Deborah Gist, Commissioner
Andy Andrade, Commissioner Support

3272 **Outcomes & Assessment Office**
Rhode Island Department of Education
255 Westminster Street
Providence, RI 02903-3414
401-222-4600
Fax: 401-222-2537
www.ride.ri.gov
Deborah Gist, Commissioner
Andy Andrade, Commissioner Support

3273 **Resource Development**
Rhode Island Department of Education
255 Westminster Street
Providence, RI 02903-3414
401-222-4600
Fax: 401-222-6033
www.ride.ri.gov
Deborah Gist, Commissioner
Andy Andrade, Commissioner Support

3274 **Rhode Island Department of Education**
Rhode Island Department of Education
255 Westminster Street
Providence, RI 02903
401-222-4600
Fax: 401-222-6178

ride0001@ride.ri.net
www.ride.ri.gov
Goal of all our work is to improve student performance and help all students meet or exceed a high level of performance. Standards, instruction, and assessment intertwine to provide a system that ensures a strong education for our students.
Deborah Gist, Commissioner
Andy Andrade, Commissioner Support

3275 School Food Services Administration
Rhode Island Department of Education
255 Westminster Street
Providence, RI 02903-3414
401-222-4600
Fax: 401-222-3080
www.ride.ri.gov
Deborah Gist, Commissioner
Andy Andrade, Commissioner Support

3276 Special Needs Office
Rhode Island Department of Education
255 Westminster Street
Providence, RI 02903-3414
401-456-9331
Fax: 401-456-8699
www.ride.ri.gov
Deborah Gist, Commissioner
Andy Andrade, Commissioner Support

3277 Teacher Education & Certification Office
Rhode Island Department of Education
255 Westminster Street
Providence, RI 02903-3414
401-222-4600
Fax: 401-222-2048
www.ride.ri.gov
Deborah Gist, Commissioner
Andy Andrade, Commissioner Support

South Carolina

3278 Budgets & Planning
South Carolina Department of Education
1429 Senate Street
Suite 950
Columbia, SC 29201-3730
803-734-8500
Fax: 803-734-0645
SCSuptED@ed.sc.gov
ed.sc.gov
Molly Spearman, Superitendent

3279 Communications Services
South Carolina Department of Education
1429 Senate Street
Columbia, SC 29201-3730
803-734-8500
Fax: 803-734-3389
SCSuptED@ed.sc.gov
ed.sc.gov
Molly Spearman, Superitendent

3280 General Counsel
South Carolina Department of Education
1429 Senate Street
Columbia, SC 29201-3730
803-734-8500
Fax: 803-734-4384
SCSuptED@ed.sc.gov
ed.sc.gov
Molly Spearman, Superitendent

3281 Internal Administration
South Carolina Department of Education
1429 Senate Street
Columbia, SC 29201-3730
803-734-8500
Fax: 803-734-6225
SCSuptED@ed.sc.gov
ed.sc.gov
Molly Spearman, Superitendent

3282 Policy & Planning
South Carolina Department of Education
1429 Senate Street
Columbia, SC 29201-3730
803-734-8500
Fax: 803-734-8624
SCSuptED@ed.sc.gov
ed.sc.gov
Molly Spearman, Superitendent

3283 South Carolina Department of Education
South Carolina Department of Education
1429 Senate Street
Columbia, SC 29201
803-734-8500
Fax: 803-734-3389
SCSuptED@ed.sc.gov
ed.sc.gov
Provides leadership and services to ensure a system of public education in which all students become educated, responsible, and contributing citizens. For certification information visit www.myscschools.com or contact 803-734-5280.
Molly Spearman, Superitendent

3284 Support Services
South Carolina Department of Education
1429 Senate Street
Columbia, SC 29201-3730
803-734-8500
Fax: 803-734-8254
SCSuptED@ed.sc.gov
ed.sc.gov
Molly Spearman, Superitendent

South Dakota

3285 Finance & Management
South Dakota Department of Education
800 Governors Drive
Pierre, SD 57501-2291
605-773-3248
Fax: 605-773-6139
doe.sd.gov
Stacy Krusemark, Division Director

3286 Services for Education
South Dakota Department of Education
800 Governors Drive
Pierre, SD 57501-2291
605-773-4699
Fax: 605-773-3782
doe.sd.gov
Donlynn Rice, Division Director

3287 South Dakota Department of Education & Cultural Affairs
South Dakota Department of Education
800 Governors Drive
Pierre, SD 57501-2291
605-773-2291
Fax: 605-773-6139
ray.christensen@state.sd.us
doe.sd.gov
Advocates for education, facilitate the delivery of statewide educational and cultural services, and promote efficient, appropriate, and quality educational opportunities for all persons residing in South Dakota.
Ray Christensen, Secretary
Patrick Keating, Division Director

3288 South Dakota State Historical Society
South Dakota Dept of Education & Cultural Affairs
800 Governors Drive
Pierre, SD 57501-2291
605-773-3458
Fax: 605-773-6041
jay.vogt@state.sd.us
doe.sd.gov
Program areas: Archaeology, archives, historic preservation, museum, research, and publishing
Jay D Vogt, History Manager

3289 Special Education Office
South Dakota Department of Education
800 Governors Drive
Pierre, SD 57501-2291
605-773-3678
Fax: 605-773-3782
doe.sd.gov
Michelle Powers, Division Director

Tennessee

3290 Special Education
Tennessee Department of Education
710 James Robertson Parkway
6th Floor
Nashville, TN 37243-5158
615-741-2851
Fax: 615-532-9412
www.tn.gov
Kevin S. Huffman, Commissioner
Kathleen Airhart, Deputy Commissioner

3291 Teaching and Learning
Tennessee Department of Education
710 James Robertson Parkway
5th Floor
Nashville, TN 37243-5158
615-532-6195
Fax: 615-741-1837
wprotoe@mail.state.tn.us
www.tn.gov
Kevin S. Huffman, Commissioner
Kathleen Airhart, Deputy Commissioner

3292 Tennessee Department of Education
Tennessee Department of Education
710 James Robertson Parkway
6th Floor
Nashville, TN 37243-5158
615-741-2731
Fax: 615-741-6236
jwalters@mail.state.tn.us
www.tn.gov
Kevin S. Huffman, Commissioner
Kathleen Airhart, Deputy Commissioner

3293 Vocational Education
Tennessee Department of Education
710 James Robertson Parkway
4th Floor
Nashville, TN 37243-5158
615-532-2800
Fax: 615-532-8226
www.tn.gov
Kevin S. Huffman, Commissioner
Kathleen Airhart, Deputy Commissioner

Texas

3294 Accountability Reporting and Research
Texas Education Agency
1701 N. Congress Avenue
WBT Building Room 3-111
Austin, TX 78701-1494
512-463-9734
Fax: 512-463-9838
ccloudt@tmail.tea.state.tx.us
tea.texas.gov
Rick Perry, Commissioner

3295 Chief Counsel
Texas Department of Education
1701 N. Congress Avenue
Austin, TX 78701-1402
512-463-9734
Fax: 512-463-9838
tea.texas.gov
Rick Perry, Commissioner

3296 Continuing Education
Texas Education Agency
1701 N. Congress Avenue
Austin, TX 78701-1402
512-463-9734
Fax: 512-463-9838
wtillian@tea.state.tx.us
tea.texas.gov
Rick Perry, Commissioner

3297 Curriculum Development & Textbooks
Texas Department of Education
1701 N. Congress Avenue
Austin, TX 78701-1402
512-463-9734
Fax: 512-463-9838
tea.texas.gov
Rick Perry, Commissioner

3298 Curriculum, Assessment & Professional Development
Texas Department of Education
1701 N. Congress Avenue
Austin, TX 78701-1402
512-463-9734
Fax: 512-463-9838
tea.texas.gov
Rick Perry, Commissioner

3299 Curriculum, Assessment and Technology
Texas Department of Education
1701 N. Congress Avenue
Austin, TX 78701-1402
512-463-9734
Fax: 512-463-9838
asmisko@tea.tetn.net
tea.texas.gov
Rick Perry, Commissioner

3300 Education of Special Populations & Adults
Texas Department of Education
1701 N. Congress Avenue
Austin, TX 78701-1402
512-463-9734
Fax: 512-463-9838
tea.texas.gov
Rick Perry, Commissioner

3301 Field Services
Texas Department of Education
1701 N. Congress Avenue
Austin, TX 78701-1402
512-463-9734
Fax: 512-463-9838
tea.texas.gov
Rick Perry, Commissioner

3302 Internal Operations
Texas Department of Education
1701 N. Congress Avenue
Austin, TX 78701-1402
512-463-9734
Fax: 512-463-9838
tea.texas.gov
Rick Perry, Commissioner

3303 Operations & School Support
Texas Department of Education
1701 N. Congress Avenue
Austin, TX 78701-1494
512-463-9734
Fax: 512-463-9838
tea.texas.gov
Rick Perry, Commissioner

3304 Permanent School Fund
Texas Department of Education
1701 N. Congress Avenue
Room 5-120
Austin, TX 78701-1402
512-463-9734
Fax: 512-463-9838
tea.texas.gov
Rick Perry, Commissioner

3305 Region 6: Education Department
Texas Department of Education
1200 Main Tower
Dallas, TX 75202-4325
512-463-9734
Fax: 512-463-9838
tea.texas.gov
Rick Perry, Commissioner

3306 Texas Department of Education
Texas Department of Education
1701 N Congress Avenue
William B Travis Building
Austin, TX 78701-1494
512-463-9734
Fax: 512-463-9838
tea.texas.gov
Rick Perry, Commissioner

Utah

3307 Applied Technology Education Services
Utah Department of Education
250 E 500 S
PO Box 144200
Salt Lake City, UT 84111-3204
801-538-7840
Fax: 801-538-7868
rbrems@usoe.kiz.ut.us
www.schools.utah.gov
State agency for career and technical education.
Rod Brems, Associate Superintendent
Mark Peterson, Director

3308 Instructional Services Division
Utah Department of Education
250 E 500 S
PO Box 144200
Salt Lake City, UT 84111-3204
801-538-7515
Fax: 801-538-7768
www.schools.utah.gov
Jerry P Peterson, Division Director
Mark Peterson, Director

3309 Schools for the Deaf & Blind
Utah Department of Education
250 E 500 S
PO Box 144200
Salt Lake City, UT 84111-3204
801-629-4700
Fax: 801-629-4896
www.schools.utah.gov
Wayne Glaus, Division Director
Mark Peterson, Director

3310 Utah Office of Education
Utah Department of Education
250 E 500 South
PO Box 144200
Salt Lake City, UT 84111-3204
801-538-7510
Fax: 801-538-7768
www.schools.utah.gov
Steven O Laing, Superintendent
Mark Peterson, Director

3311 Utah Office of Education; Agency Services Division
Utah Department of Education
250 E 500 S
PO Box 144200
Salt Lake City, UT 84114-4200
801-538-7500
Fax: 801-538-7768
www.schools.utah.gov
Patrick Ogden, Associate Superintendent
Mark Peterson, Director

Vermont

3312 Career & Lifelong Learning
Vermont Department of Education
120 State Street
Montpelier, VT 05620-0001
802-479-1030
Fax: 802-828-3146
AOE.EdInfo@state.vt.us
education.vermont.gov
Rebecca Holcombe, Secretary
John Fischer, Deputy Secretary

3313 Core Services
Vermont Department of Education
120 State Street
Montpelier, VT 05620-0001
802-479-1030
Fax: 802-828-3140
AOE.EdInfo@state.vt.us
education.vermont.gov
Rebecca Holcombe, Secretary
John Fischer, Deputy Secretary

3314 Family & School Support
Vermont Department of Education
120 State Street
Montpelier, VT 05620-0001
802-479-1030
Fax: 802-828-3140
AOE.EdInfo@state.vt.us
education.vermont.gov
Rebecca Holcombe, Secretary
John Fischer, Deputy Secretary

3315 Financial Management Team
Vermont Department of Education
120 State Street
Montpelier, VT 05620-0001

802-479-1030
Fax: 802-828-3140
AOE.EdInfo@state.vt.us
education.vermont.gov

Rebecca Holcombe, Secretary
John Fischer, Deputy Secretary

3316 School Development & Information
Vermont Department of Education
120 State Street
Montpelier, VT 05620-0001
802-479-1030
Fax: 802-828-3140
AOE.EdInfo@state.vt.us
education.vermont.gov

Rebecca Holcombe, Secretary
John Fischer, Deputy Secretary

3317 Teaching & Learning
Vermont Department of Education
120 State Street
Montpelier, VT 05620-0001
802-479-1030
Fax: 802-828-3140
AOE.EdInfo@state.vt.us
education.vermont.gov

Rebecca Holcombe, Secretary
John Fischer, Deputy Secretary

3318 Vermont Department of Education
Vermont Department of Education
120 State Street
Montpelier, VT 05620-0001
802-479-1030
Fax: 802-828-3140
AOE.EdInfo@state.vt.us
education.vermont.gov
For certification information visit www.pen.k12.va.us or contact 804-225-2022.

Rebecca Holcombe, Secretary
John Fischer, Deputy Secretary

3319 Vermont Special Education
Vermont Department of Education
120 State Street
Montpelier, VT 05620-0001
802-479-1030
AOE.EdInfo@state.vt.us
education.vermont.gov

Rebecca Holcombe, Secretary
John Fischer, Deputy Secretary

Virginia

3320 Administrative Services
Virginia Department of Education
14th & Franklin Streets
PO Box 2120
Richmond, VA 23218
804-225-3252
Fax: 804-786-5828
www.doe.virginia.gov

Steven R. Staples, Superitendent

3321 Policy, Assessment, Research & Information Systems
Virginia Department of Education
101 N 4th Street
PO Box 2120
Richmond, VA 23218-2120
804-225-2102
800-292-3820
Fax: 804-371-8978
charris@pen.k12.va.us
www.doe.virginia.gov

Steven R. Staples, Superitendent

3322 Student Services
Virginia Department of Education
14th & Franklin Streets
PO Box 2120
Richmond, VA 23218
804-225-2757
Fax: 804-786-5828
www.doe.virginia.gov

Steven R. Staples, Superitendent

3323 Virginia Centers for Community Education
Virginia Department of Education
101 N 4th Street
PO Box 2120
Richmond, VA 23218-2120
804-225-2293
Fax: 804-786-5828
www.doe.virginia.gov

Steven R. Staples, Superitendent

3324 Virginia Department of Education
Virginia Department of Education
James Monroe Building
101 N 14th Street
Richmond, VA 23219
804-225-2023
800-292-3820
Fax: 804-371-2099
rlayman@pen.k12.va.us
www.doe.virginia.gov

Steven R. Staples, Superitendent

Washington

3325 Region 10: Education Department
US Department of Education
915 2nd Avenue
Room 3362
Seattle, WA 98174-1001
206-220-7800
Fax: 202-220-7806
www.ed.gov

3326 Washington Department of Education
Washington State Board of Education
600 Washington Street SE
P.O. Box 47206
Olympia, WA 98504-7200
360-725-6025
Fax: 360-753-6712
sbe@k12.wa.us
www.sbe.wa.gov

Theresa Bergeson, Superintendent
Isabel Munoz-Colon, Chair

3327 Washington Department of Education; Instruction Program
Washington State Board of Education
600 Washington Street SE
P.O. Box 47206
Olympia, WA 98504-7200
360-725-6025
Fax: 360-586-0247
sbe@k12.wa.us
www.sbe.wa.gov

John Pearson, Division Director
Isabel Munoz-Colon, Chair

3328 Washington Department of Education; Commission on Student Learning Administration
Washington State Board of Education
600 Washington Street SE
P.O. Box 47206
Olympia, WA 98504-7200
360-725-6025
Fax: 360-664-3028
sbe@k12.wa.us
www.sbe.wa.gov

Terry Bergeson, Division Director
Isabel Munoz-Colon, Chair

3329 Washington Department of Education; Executive Services
Washington State Board of Education
600 Washington Street SE
P.O. Box 47206
Olympia, WA 98504-7200
360-725-6025
Fax: 360-753-6754
sbe@k12.wa.us
www.sbe.wa.gov

Ken Kanikeberg, Division Director
Isabel Munoz-Colon, Chair

3330 Washington Department of Education; School Business & Administrative Services
Washington State Board of Education
600 Washington Street SE
P.O. Box 47206
Olympia, WA 98504-7200
360-725-6025
sbe@k12.wa.us
www.sbe.wa.gov

David Moberly, Division Director
Isabel Munoz-Colon, Chair

West Virginia

3331 Division of Administrative Services
West Virginia Department of Education
1900 Kanawha Boulevard E
Building 6
Charleston, WV 25305-0009
304-558-2441
Fax: 304-558-8867
www.wvde.state.wv.us

Carolyn Arrington, Division Director

3332 Research, Accountability & Professional
West Virginia Department of Education
1900 Kanawha Boulevard E
Building 6
Charleston, WV 25305-0009
304-558-3762
Fax: 304-558-8867
www.wvde.state.wv.us

William J Luff Jr, Division Director

3333 Student Services & Instructional Services
West Virginia Department of Education
1900 Kanawha Boulevard E
Building 6
Charleston, WV 25305-0009
304-558-2691
Fax: 304-558-8867
wvde.state.wv.us

Keith Smith, Division Director

3334 Technical & Adult Education Services
West Virginia Department of Education
1900 Kanawha Boulevard E
Building 6
Charleston, WV 25305-0009
304-558-2346
Fax: 304-558-8867
www.wvde.state.wv.us

Adam Sponaugle, Division Director

3335 **West Virginia Department of Education**
West Virginia Department of Education
1900 Kanawha Boulevard E
Building 6, Room B-358
Charleston, WV 25305-0330
304-558-2681
Fax: 304-558-0048
www.wvde.state.wv.us
The constitutional mission is to provide supervision of the K-12 education system.

David Stewart, Superintendent
Audrey Horne, President

Wisconsin

3336 **Division for Learning Support: Equity & Advocacy**
Wisconsin Department of Education
125 S Webster Street
PO Box 7841
Madison, WI 53707-7841
608-266-3390
800-441-4563
Fax: 608-267-3746
dpi.wi.gov

Tony Evers, Superintendent
Carolyn Stanford-Taylor, Division Director

3337 **Instructional Services Division**
Wisconsin Department of Education
125 S Webster Street
PO Box 7841
Madison, WI 53707-7841
608-266-3390
800-441-4563
Fax: 608-267-3746
dpi.wi.gov

Tony Evers, Superintendent
Pauline Nikolay, Division Director

3338 **Library Services Division**
Wisconsin Department of Education
2109 S. Stoughton Road
PO Box 7841
Madison, WI 53707-7841
608-266-3390
800-441-4563
Fax: 608-267-3746
dpi.wi.gov

Tony Evers, Superintendent
William Wilson, Division Director

3339 **School Financial Resources & Management**
Wisconsin Department of Education
125 S Webster Street
PO Box 7841
Madison, WI 53707-7841
608-266-3390
800-441-4563
Fax: 608-267-3746
dpi.wi.gov

Tony Evers, Superintendent
Bambi Statz, Division Director

3340 **Wisconsin College System Technical**
Wisconsin Department of Education
125 S Webster Street
PO Box 7841
Madison, WI 53707-7841
608-266-3390
800-441-4563
Fax: 608-266-1285
wtcsb@board.tec.wi.us
dpi.wi.gov

Tony Evers, Superintendent
Richard Carpenter, President

3341 **Wisconsin Department of Public Instruction**
Wisconsin Department of Education
125 S Webster Street
PO Box 7841
Madison, WI 53707-7841
608-266-3390
800-441-4563
Fax: 608-266-5188
statesuperintendent@dpi.wi.gov
www.dpi.wi.gov

Tony Evers, Superintendent
Mike Thompson, Deputy State Superintendent

Wyoming

3342 **Accounting, Personnel & School Finance Unit**
Wyoming Department of Education
2300 Capitol Avenue
Hathaway Building, 2nd Floor
Cheyenne, WY 82002-2060
307-777-7675
Fax: 307-777-6234
edu.wyoming.gov

Ron Micheli, Chairman
Barry Nimmo, Division Director

3343 **Applied Data & Technology Unit**
Wyoming Department of Education
2300 Capitol Avenue
Hathaway Building, 2nd Floor
Cheyenne, WY 82002-2060
307-777-7675
Fax: 307-777-6234
edu.wyoming.gov

Ron Micheli, Chairman
Steven King, Division Director

3344 **Services for Individuals with Hearing Loss**
Wyoming Department of Education
2300 Capitol Avenue
Hathaway Building, 2nd Floor
Cheyenne, WY 82002-2060
307-777-7675
Fax: 307-777-6234
edu.wyoming.gov

Ron Micheli, Chairman
Tim Sanger, Division Director

3345 **Support Programs & Quality Results Division**
Wyoming Department of Education
2300 Capitol Avenue
Hathaway Building, 2nd Floor
Cheyenne, WY 82002-2060
307-777-7675
Fax: 307-777-6234
edu.wyoming.gov

Ron Micheli, Chairman
Dr. Alan Sheinker, Division Director

3346 **Wyoming Department of Education**
Wyoming Department of Education
2300 Capitol Avenue
Hathaway Building, 2nd Floor
Cheyenne, WY 82002-2060
307-777-7675
Fax: 307-777-6234
edu.wyoming.gov

Dr.Trent Blankenship, Superintendent
Ron Micheli, Chairman

Associations

3347 Agency for Instructional Technology
Agency for Instructional Technology
8111 N. Lee Paul Road
Box A
Bloomington, IN 47404-7916
812-339-2203
800-457-4509
Fax: 812-333-4218
info@ait.net
www.ait.net
AIT's mission is to be the premier provider of services and products to enhance student learning. A nonprofit organization and is one of the largest providers of instructional TV programs in North America.

Robert E. Yocum, President and CEO
Cynthia M. Mosca, Director

3348 American Association for Higher Education & Accreditation
2020 Pennsylvania Avenue NW
#975
Washington, DC 20006
202-293-6440
Fax: 877-510-4240
admin@aahea.org
www.aahea.org
The individual membership organization that promotes the changes higher education must make to ensure its effectiveness in a complex, interconnected world. The association equips individuals and institutions committed to such changes with the knowledge they need to bring those changes about.

Jose Luis Gomez, President
Ken Rabac, International Director

3349 American Association of Colleges for Teacher Education
1307 New York Avenue NW
Suite 300
Washington, DC 20005
202-293-2450
Fax: 202-457-8095
aacte@aacte.org
www.aacte.org
A national alliance of educator preparation programs dedicated to the highest quality professional development of teachers and school leaders in order to enhance PK-12 student learning.

Sharon P Robinson, President/CEO
Jerry Wirth, Chief Operating Officer

3350 American Educational Research Association
1430 K Street NW
Suite 1200
Washington, DC 20005
202-238-3200
Fax: 202-238-3250
flevine@aera.net
www.aera.net
Supports the improvement of the educational process through the encouragement of scholarly inquiry related to education, and the practical application of research results. The association also holds an annual conference and publishes books, videos and magazines.

Deborah Loewenberg Ball, President
Felice J Levine, Executive Director

3351 American Educational Studies Association
Department of Education
235 Morton Hall
Huntsville, AL 35899
330-972-7111
www.educationalstudies.org
An international learned society for students, teachers, research scholars, and administrators who are interested in the foundations of education. A society primarily comprised of college and university professors who teach and research in the field of education utilizing one or more of the liberal arts disciplines of philosophy, history, politics, sociology, anthropology, or economics as well as comparative/international and cultural studies.

Audrey Thompson, President
Susan Laird, Vice President

3352 American Foundation for Negro Affairs
117 S 17th Street
Suite 1200
Philadelphia, PA 19103-5011
215-854-1470
Fax: 215-854-1487
Offers a model for educational programs preparing minority students for professional careers.

Samuel L Evans, President

3353 American Society for Training and Development Information Center
1640 King Street
Box 1443
Alexandria, VA 22313-1443
703-683-8100
800-628-2783
Fax: 703-683-8103
customercare@astd.org
www.td.org
Dedicated to workplace learning and performance professionals. Members come from more than 100 countries and connect locally in more than 130 U.S. chapters and with more than 30 international partners.

Charles Fred, Chair
Tony Bingham, President and CEO

3354 Association of Teacher Educators
11350 Random Hills Road
Suite 800, PMB 6
Fairfax, VA 22030
703-659-1708
Fax: 703-595-4792
info@ate1.org
www.ate1.org
The mission of the Association of Teacher Educators is to improve the effectiveness of teacher education through leadership in the development of training programs.

Karen Embry Jenlink, President
Patricia Tate, First Vice President

3355 Canadian Association for University Continuing Education (CAUCE)
University of Saskatchewan
Williams Building
221 Cumberland Avenue N
Saskatoon, SK S7N-1M3
306-966-5604
Fax: 306-966-5590
cauce.secretariat@usask.ca
cauce-aepuc.ca
Association of professionals working in the field of university continuing education in Canada. The association offers services and resources for the development of its members and their careers.

Gary Hepburn, President
Gordon Michael, Secretary Treasurer

3356 Center for Rural Studies
University of Vermont
206 Morrill Hall
146 University Place
Burlington, VT 05405
802-656-3021
Fax: 802-656-1423
crs@uvm.edu
www.uvm.edu/crs
A nonprofit, fee-for-service research and resource center that works with people and communities to address social, economic, and resource-based challenges. CRS supports the research and teaching missions of the university through its work in applied research, community outreach, program evaluation, and consulting services.

Fred Schmidt, Founder/Director Emeritus
Jane Kolodinsky, Director

3357 Committee on Continuing Education for School Personnel
Kean College of New Jersey
Academic Services
Union, NJ 07083
908-737-5326
Fax: 908-737-5845
Develops activities for professional and personal growth among teachers and educators.

George Sisko, Director

3358 Council for Learning Disabilities
11184 Antioch Road
PO Box 405
Overland Park, KS 66210
913-491-1011
Fax: 913-491-1012
CLDInfo@ie-events.com
www.cldinternational.org
An international organization that promotes evidence-based teaching, collaboration, research, leadership, and advocacy. Comprised of professionals who represent diverse disciplines and are committed to enhancing the education and quality of life for individuals with learning disabilities and others who experience challenges in learning.

Silvana Watson, President
Mary Beth Calhoon, Vice President

3359 Council of Administrators of Special Education
Osigian Office Centre
101 Katelyn Circle, Suite E
Warner Robins, GA 31088
478-333-6892
Fax: 478-333-2453
lpurcell@casecec.org
www.casecec.org
An international professional educational organization which is affiliated with the Council for Exceptional Children (CEC) whose members are dedicated to the enhancement of the worth, dignity, potential, and uniqueness of each individual in society.

Dr. Mary Lynn Boscardin, President
Julie Bost, Secretary

3360 Distance Education & Training Council
1601 18th Street NW
Suite 2
Washington, DC 20009
202-234-5100
Fax: 202-332-1386
info@deac.org
www.deac.org
A voluntary, non-governmental, educational organization that was founded to promote sound ed-

ucational standards and ethical business practices within the correspondence field.

Leah K. Matthews, Executive Director
Sally R. Welch, Associate Director

3361 ERIC Clearinghouse on Teaching and Teacher Education
American Association of Colleges for Teacher Ed.
1307 New York Avenue NW
Suite 300
Washington, DC 20005-4701
202-293-2450
Fax: 202-457-8095
aacte@aacte.org
www.aacte.org
To promote the learning of all PK-12 students through high-quality, evidence-based preparation and continuing education for all school personnel.

Mary Dilworth, Director
Deborah Newby, Associate Director

3362 Educational Leadership Institute
4301 Connecticut Ave NW
Suite 100
Washington, DC 20008
202-822-8405
Fax: 202-822-8405
iel@iel.org
www.iel.org
A non-profit, nonpartisan organization that envisions a society that uses its resources effectively to achieve better futures for all children and youth. IEL's mission continues to be to build the capacity of individuals and organizations in education and related fields to work together, across policies, programs and sectors.

S. Decker Anstrom, Chair
June Atkinson, Superintendent

3363 International Council on Education for Teaching
National-Louis University
1000 Capitol Drive
Wheeling, IL 60090
847-947-5881
Fax: 847-947-5881
contact@icet4u.org
icet4u.org
An international association of policy and decision-makers in education, government and business dedicated to global development through education. ICET provides programs and services that give its members access to a worldwide resource base of organizations, programs, specialized consultative services and research and training opportunities at the university level.

Maria Assuncao Flores, Chairman
James O'Meara, President

3364 National Association of State Directors of Teacher Education & Certification
1629 K Street, NW
Suite 300
Washington, DC 20006
202-204-2208
Fax: 202-204-2210
rje@nasdtec.com
www.nasdtec.org
The organization that represents professional standards boards and commissions and state departments of education in all 50 states, the District of Columbia, the Department of Defense Education Activity, the U.S. Territories, Alberta, British Columbia, and Ontario that are responsible for the preparation, licensure, and discipline of educational personnel.

D. T. Magee, President
Elisabeth Keller, Vice President

3365 National Center for Community Education
1017 Avon Street
Flint, MI 48503-2797
810-238-0463
800-811-1105
Fax: 810-238-9211
info@nccenet.org
www.nccenet.org
It is the mission of the National Center for Community Education to promote community and educational change emphasizing community schools by providing state-of-the-art leadership development, training and technical assistance.

Maxine Murray, Operations Director
Marion Baldwin, Chief Administrator

3366 National Middle School Association
4151 Executive Parkway
Suite 300
Westerville, OH 43081
614-895-4730
800-528-6672
Fax: 614-895-4750
info@amle.org
www.amle.org
NMSA has been a voice for those committed to the educational and developmental needs of young adolescents. NMSA is the only national education association dedicated exclusively to those in the middle level grades.

Ashley Smith, President
William D. Waidelich, EdD, Executive Director

3367 National Staff Development Council
504 S Locust Street
Oxford, OH 45056
513-523-6029
800-727-7288
Fax: 513-523-0638
office@learningforward.org
learningforward.org
The largest non-profit professional association committed to ensuring success for all students through staff development and school improvement. The purpose of the NSDC is that every educator engages in effective professional learning every day so every student achieves.

Deborah Renee Jackson, President
Scott Laurence, Superintendent

3368 National Women's Studies Association
11 E Mount Royal Avenue
Suite 100
Baltimore, MD 21202
410-528-0355
Fax: 410-528-0357
nwsaoffice@nwsa.org
www.nwsa.org
A professional organization dedicated to leading the field of women's studies and gender studies through its teaching, learning, research and services in various settings.

Allison Kimmich, Executive Director
Patti Provance, Deputy Director

3369 Recruiting New Teachers
385 Concord Avenue
Suite 103
Belmont, MA 02478-3037
617-489-6000
800-45 -EACH
Fax: 617-489-6005
rnt@rnt.org
www.rnt.org/channels/clearinghouse
Conducts public service advertising campaign encouraging people to consider teaching careers.

Mildred Hudson, CEO

3370 Search Associates
PO Box 636
Dallas, PA 18612-636
570-696-4600
Fax: 570-696-9500
SearchCentralHQ@cs.com
www.search-associates.com
Each year Search Associates places over 1,500 teachers, administrators and interns in international schools throughout the world, making us the largest of the International School placement organizations. However, it is our personalized approach to the schools and candidates we serve which we would most like to emphasize.

John Magagna, Founding Director
Robert Barlas, Senior Associate

Awards & Honors

3371 Apple Education Grants
Apple Computer
1 Infinite Loop
Cupertino, CA 95014
408-996-1010
800-800-2775
Fax: 512-919-2992
www.apple.com
Awarded each year to teams of K-12 educators working on educational technology plans. Potential awardees find innovative uses of technology in the classroom and come from schools that would otherwise have limited access to technology.

3372 Bayer/NSF Award for Community Innovation
105 Terry Drive
Suite 120
Newtown, PA 18940
215-579-8590
800-291-6020
Fax: 215-579-8589
success@edumedia.com
A community-based science and technology competition to give all sixth, seventh and eighth-graders a hands-on experience with real-world problems using the scientific method.

Stephanie Hallman, Program Manager
Stacey Gall, Competition Coordinator

3373 Excellence in Teaching Cabinet Grant
Curriculm Associates
PO Box 2001
North Billerica, MA 01862
800-225-0248
Fax: 800-366-1158
Awarded to educators who wish to implement unique educational projects. Potential awardees propose projects using a variety of teaching tools, including technology and print.

3374 Magna Awards
American School Board Journal
1680 Duke Street
Alexandria, VA 22314
703-838-6722
www.asbj.com
A national recognition program co-sponsored by American School Board Journal, the National School Boards Association, and

Sodexo School Services that honors school board best practices and innovative programs that advance student learning.

Thomas J Gentzel, Publisher
Kathleen Vail, Managing Editor

3375 NSTA Fellow Award
National Science Teachers Association
1840 Wilson Boulevard
Arlington, VA 22201
703-243-7100
Fax: 703-243-7177
www.nsta.org
This award recognizes NSTA members who have made extraordinary contributions to science education through personal commitment to education, specifically science teaching or science; educational endeavors and original work that position recipients as exemplary leaders in their field; significant contributions to the profession that reflect dedication to NSTA as well the entire educational community.

Dr. Juliana Texley, President
David L. Evans, Executive Director

3376 NSTA Legacy Award
National Science Teachers Association
1840 Wilson Boulevard
Arlington, VA 22201
703-243-7100
Fax: 703-243-7177
www.nsta.org
This NSTA award posthumously recognizes long-standing members of NSTA for significant lifelong service to NSTA and contributions to science education.

Dr. Juliana Texley, President
David L. Evans, Executive Director

3377 National Teachers Hall of Fame
National Teachers Hall of Fame
1200 Commercial
Box 4017
Emporia, KS 66801
620-341-5660
800-968-3224
Fax: 620-341-5912
hallfame@emporia.edu
www.nthf.org
The mission of The National Teachers Hall of Fame is to recognize and honor exceptional career teachers, encourage excellence in teaching, and preserve the rich heritage of the teaching profession in the United States.

Roberts T Jones, President
Dr Anne L Bryant, Executive Director

3378 Presidential Awards for Excellence in Mathematics and Science Teaching
National Science Foundation
4201 Wilson Boulevard
Arlington, VA 22230
703-292-8620
Fax: 703-292-9044
msaul@nsf.gov
www.ehr.nsf.gov
This award is the nation's highest commendation for K-12 math and science teachers. Approximately 108 teachers are recognized annually with this prestigious award.

Mark Saul, Director

3379 Senior Researcher Award
Music Education Research Council
Deptartment of Music
138 Fine Arts Center
Columbia, MO 65211
573-884-1604
Fax: 573-884-7444
For recognition of a significant scholarly achievement maintained over a period of years.

3380 Toyota Tapestry Grants for Teachers
National Science Teachers Association
1840 Wilson Boulevard
Arlington, VA 22201
703-243-7100
Fax: 703-243-7177
www.nsta.org
Awards 50 grants of up to $10,000 each to K-12 teachers of science in the fields of environmental science education.

Dr. Juliana Texley, President
David L. Evans, Executive Director

Conferences

3381 AACRAO Annual Meeting
American Assoc of Collegiate Registrars/Admissions
1 Dupont Circle NW
Suite 520
Washington, DC 20036
202-293-9161
Fax: 202-872-8857
meetings@aacrao.org
www.aacrao.org
The American Association of Collegiate Registrars & Admissions Officers will hold its annual meeting in March, 2018. The meeting will feature workshops, sessions, roundtables and networking opportunities for those interested in learning more about education administration.

March

Jim Bouse, President
Mike Reilly, Executive Director

3382 AASA National Conference on Education
American Association of School Administrators
1615 Duke Street
Suite 700
Alexandria, VA 22314-1730
703-528-0700
Fax: 703-841-1543
info@aasa.org
www.aasa.org
Where America's school leaders go for a vision of the future in public education; to explore new thinking, new products, new services and new technologies.

February

Daniel A Domenech, Executive Director
Christopher Daw, Meetings Director

3383 ACE Fellows Program
American Council on Education
One Dupont Circle NW
Washington, DC 20036-1193
202-939-9300
fellows@ace.nche.edu
www.acenet.edu
The nation's premier higher education leadership development program in preparing senior leaders to serve American colleges and universities. Enables participants to immerse themselves in the culture, policies, and decision-making processes of another institution.

Jim Sirianni, Director
Deborah Ingram Allen, Program Coordinator

3384 AFT Convention
American Federation of Teachers AFL-CIO
555 New Jersey Avenue NW
Washington, DC 20001
202-879-4400
online@aft.org
www.aft.org
The AFT represents one million teachers, school support staff, higher education faculty and staff, health care professionals, and state and municipal employees. AFT is an affiliated international union of the AFL-CIO.

Randi Weingarten, President
Mary Cathryn Ricker, Executive Vice President

3385 Alaska Department of Education Bilingual& Bicultural Education Conference
University of Alaska, Conference & Special Events
117 Eielson Building
Fairbanks, AK 99775-7680
907-474-7436
Fax: 907-474-6586
www.uaf.edu/anla/contact-us/
Stresses the importance of literacy and multicultural education for Alaskan educators.

February

Gary Holton, Director

3386 American Society for Training & Development International Conference & Exposition
American Society for Training & Development
1640 King Street
Box 1443
Alexandria, VA 22314-1443
703-683-8100
800-628-2783
Fax: 703-683-8103
customercare@td.org
www.td.org
This premier event for workplace learning and performance professionals welcomes attendees from more than 70 countries. The conference features 200+ educational sessions from industry leading experts, and a world-class EXPO filled with the latest products and services available from top suppliers.

Annual/May

Charles Fred, Chair
Tony Bingham, President/CEO

3387 Annual Building Championship Schools Conference
Center for Peak Performing Schools
2021 Clubhouse Drive
Greeley, CO 80634
970-339-9277
Interested in curriculum development and instructional assessment. Members include administrators at all levels of education.

February

3388 Annual New England Kindergarten Conference
Lesley University
29 Everett Street
Cambridge, MA 02138
617-349-8544
800-999-1959
Fax: 617-349-8125
hr@lesley.edu
www.lesley.edu
Committed to active learning, scholarly research, critical inquiry, and diverse forms of artistic prac-

tice through close mentoring relationships among students, faculty, and practitioners in the field

November
1000 attendees

Mary Mindess, Conference Coordinator
Kari Nygaard, Conference Manager

3389 Annual State Convention of Association of Texas Professional Educators

Association of Texas Professional Educators
305 E Huntland Drive
Suite 300
Austin, TX 78752
800-777-2873
Fax: 512-467-2203
info@atpe.org
www.atpe.org
A member-owned, member-governed professional association with more than 112,000 members leading educators' association in the state and the largest independent association for public school educators in the nation.

March
100 booths with 1,300 attendees

Richard Wiggins, President
Cory Colby, Vice President

3390 Association for Educational Communications & Technology Annual Convention

Assoc for Educational Communications & Technology
320 W. 8th St.
Suite 101
Bloomington, IN 47404-3745
812-335-7675
Fax: 812-335-7678
aect@aect.org
www.aect.org
Provide leadership in educational communications and technology by linking a wide range of professionals holding a common interest in the use of educational technology and its application learning process.

November

Stephen Harmon, President
Ellen Hoffman, Executive Secretary

3391 Association for Library & Information Science Education Annual Conference

ALISE
2150 N 107th St
Suite 205
Seattle, WA 98133-7246
206-209-5267
Fax: 206-367-8777
office@alise.org
www.alise.org
Promotes excellence in education for library and information sciences as a means of increasing library services.

January

Clara Chu, President
Samantha K. Hastings, Vice President

3392 CASE Annual Convention

Colorado Association of School Executives
4101 S Bannock Street
Englewood, CO 80110-4606
303-762-8762
Fax: 303-762-8697
case@co-case.org
www.co-case.org

July

Bruce Caughey, Executive Director
Melissa Gibson, Director

3393 CCAE/COABE National Conference

California Council for Adult Education
19332 Peachtree Lane
PO Box 978
Los Alamitos, CA 90720
626-825-9363
888-542-2231
Fax: 866-941-5129
membership@ccaestate.org
www.ccaestate.org

April
1200 attendees

Lariann Torrez, President
Adriana Sanchez-Aldana, Executive Director

3394 CSBA Education Conference & Trade Show

California School Boards Association
3100 Beacon Boulevard
West Sacramento, CA 95691
800-266-3382
Fax: 916-371-3407
dfernandes@csba.org
www.csba.org
Premier continuing education program - delivering practical solutions to help governance teams from districts and county offices of education improve student learning and achievement.

Annual/December
200 booths

Jesus Holguin, President
Sherri Reusche, Vice President

3395 California Kindergarten Conference and PreConference Institute

California Kindergarten Association
1014 Chippendale Way
Roseville, CA 95661
916-780-5331
Fax: 916-780-5330
cka@ckanet.org
www.ckanet.org
The original conference for teachers by teachers.

January
120 booths with 2,000 attendees and 100 exhibits

Ada Hand, President
Debra Weller, President

3396 Central States Conference on the Teaching of Foreign Languages

7141A Ida Red Road
Egg Harbor, WI 54209
414-405-4645
Fax: 920-868-1682
csctfl@aol.com
www.csctfl.org
Foreign language organization serving a number of states through annual spring conferences featuring approximately 140 workshops and sessions on the subject of second-language learning and teaching.

Annual/March

Mary Goodwin, Chair
Patrick T Raven, Executive Director

3397 Chicago Principals Association Education Conference

221 N Lasalle Street
Suite 3316
Chicago, IL 60601-1505
312-263-7767
Fax: 312-263-2012
Educational or fund raising products including copy machines, computers, book companies, etc.

February

Beverly Tunney, Conference Coordinator

3398 Classroom Connect

6277 Sea Harbor Drive
Orlando, FL 32887
800-638-1639
888-801-8299
Fax: 650-351-5300
help@classroom.com
www.classroom.com
A leading provider of professional development programs and online instructional content for K-12 education.

October

Jim Bowler, President
Melinda Cook, Vice President Sales

3399 Florida Elementary School Principals Association Conference

206 S Monroe Street
Suite B
Tallahassee, FL 32301-1801
800-593-3626
Fax: 850-224-3892
Exhibitors from fundraisers to computer companies.

November
50 booths

Lisa Begue, Conference Coordinator

3400 Florida School Administrators Association Summer Conference

Florida Association of School Administrators
206B S. Monroe St.
Tallahassee, FL 32301
850-224-3626
800-593-3626
Fax: 850-224-3892
www.fasa.net
Exhibits include computer software, textbooks and school supplies, fundraising companies, schoolyear book and ring companies, video and audio companies, furniture suppliers and other school related products.

Annual/July

Bob Jones, President
Mark Shanoff, President

3401 Florida Vocational Association Conference

1420 N Paul Russell Road
Tallahassee, FL 32301-4835
850-878-6860
Fax: 850-878-5476
Curriculum materials, industrial equipment and supplies, computer hardware and software, medical equipment and other materials utilized by vocational educators.

July
150 booths

Donna Harper, Conference Coordinator

3402 Foundation for Critical Thinking Annual Conference

PO Box 196
Tomales, CA 94971
707-878-9100
800-833-3645
Fax: 707-878-9111
cct@criticalthinking.org
www.criticalthinking.org
Provides a unique opportunity to improve understanding of critical thinking, as well as one's ability to foster it in the classroom and other aspects in work/life.

July-August
1200 attendees

Dr. Richard Paul, Fellow
Dr. Linda Elder, Fellow

3403 IASB Convention
Iowa Association of School Boards
6000 Grand Avenue
Des Moines, IA 50312-1417
515-288-1991
800-795-4272
Fax: 515-243-4992
www.ia-sb.org
IASB is an organization of elected school board members dedicated to assisting school boards in achieving their goal of excellence and equity in public education.
Annual/November
LouAnn Gvist, Convention Director
Veronica Stalker, Interim Executive Director

3404 IASB Joint Annual Conference
Illinois Association of School Boards
2921 Baker Drive
Springfield, IL 62703-5929
217-528-9688
www.iasb.com
Recognized as one of the nation's largest state education conferences, the event was open to local school board members, superintendents and secretaries, school administrators, state and regional educators and officials, school attorneys, university professors, exhibitors, and guests.
November
235 booths with 9500+ attendees
Roger L. Eddy, Executive Director
Ben Schwarm, Deputy Executive Director

3405 IASSIST Annual Conference
Int'l Assoc for Social Science Info Service & Tech
405 Hilgard Avenue
Attn: Wendy Treadwell
Los Angeles, CA 90095-9000
612-624-4389
Fax: 612-626-9353
melanie@essex.ac.uk
www.iassistdata.org
IASSIST is an international organization of professionals working with information technology and data services to support research and teaching in the social sciences. Its 300 members work in a variety of settings, including data archives, statistical agencies, research centers, libraries, academic departments, government departments, and non-profit organizations.
May-June
Bill Block, President
Tuomas J. Alatera, Vice President

3406 ISBA/IAPSS Annual Conference
Indiana School Board Association
1 N Capitol Avenue
Suite 1215
Indianapolis, IN 46204-2225
317-639-0330
Fax: 317-639-3591
mwagers@isba-ind.org
www.isba-ind.org
Jointy sponsored by the Indiana School Boards Association and Indiana Association of Public School Superintendents. A comprehensive program, designed by the ISBA and IAPPS, that brings the latest information and some of the most informed experts on current topics in education.
Fall
Sally Krouse, President
Bill Wilson, Vice President

3407 Illinois Assistant Principals Conference
Illinois Principals Association
2940 Baker Drive
Springfield, IL 62703
217-525-1383
Fax: 217-525-7264
support@ilprincipals.org
www.ilprincipals.org
Where assistant principals and deans attend annually to hear outstanding educational leaders; participate in educational sessions and to network with colleagues across the state
Annual/February
120 booths with 200 attendees
Jason Leahy, Executive Director
Jean Smith, Professional Development Dir

3408 Illinois Resource Center Conference of Teachers of Linguistically Diverse Students
Illinois Resource Center
2626 Clearbrook Drive
Arlington Heights, IL 60005-4626
224-366-8555
Fax: 847-649-0551
www.thecenterweb.org/irc/
A conference that caters to those educators involved with teaching multi-licensed pupils.
March

3409 Iowa Council Teachers of Math Conference
Iowa Council of Teachers of Mathematics
1712 55th Street
Des Moines, IA 50310-1548
515-242-7846
www.iowamath.org
Math teachers conference.
Annual/February
48 booths
Megan Balong, President
Maureen Busta, Executive Secretary

3410 Iowa Reading Association Conference
Iowa Reading Association
512 Lynn Avenue
Ames, IA 50014-7320
712-754-3636
jneal@jefferson0scranton.k12.ia.us
www.iowareading.org
Nationally prominent speakers, published authors, and experienced instructors will anchor the conference, sharing current research and creative reading strategies.
Annual/April
Deb Mortensen, President
Nancy White, Conference Chair

3411 KSBA Annual Conference
Kentucky School Boards Association
260 Democrat Drive
Frankfort, KY 40601
800-372-2962
Fax: 502-695-5451
www.ksba.org
February
Allen Kennedy, President
Mike Armstrong, Executive Director

3412 Kansas School Boards Association Conference
1420 SW Arrowhead Road
Topeka, KS 66604-4024
785-273-3600
800-432-2471
Fax: 785-273-7580
ahartzell@kasb.org
www.kasb.org
Wide variety of school district vendors and contacts for products and services.
December
70 booths
Dennis Depew, President
Frank Henderson, President-Elect

3413 Kentucky School Superintendents Association Meeting
152 Consumer Lane
Frankfort, KY 40601
502-875-3411
800-928-5272
Fax: 502-875-4634
webmaster@kasa.org
www.kasa.org
KASA is dedicated to serving school administrators throughout Kentucky through advocacy, professional development, research and leadership.
June
36 booths
Dr. Roland Haun, Conference Contact
Wayne Young, Executive Director

3414 LSBA Convention
Louisiana School Boards Association
7912 Summa Avenue
Baton Rouge, LA 70809
225-769-3191
877-664-5722
Fax: 225-769-6108
www.lsba.com
Annual/March
John Smith, President
Russ Wise, Vice President

3415 Lilly Conference on College Teaching
Miami University
317 Laws Hall
551 East High St.
Oxford, OH 45056
513-529-9266
Fax: 513-529-9984
lillycon@miamioh.edu
www.units.muohio.edu/lillycon
One of the nation's most renowned conferences presenting the scholarship of teaching and learning. Teacher-scholars from across the U.S. and internationally gather to share innovative pedagogies and discuss questions, challenges, and insights about teaching and learning.
Annual/November
660 attendees
Melody Barton, Administrative Associate
Milton Cox, Conference Director

3416 MASB Annual Fall Conference
Michigan Association of School Boards
1001 Centennial Way
Suite 400
Lansing, MI 48917-8249
517-327-5900
Fax: 517-327-0775
info@masb.org
www.masb.org
The premier leadership event that features nationally acclaimed speakers addressing current education topics.
October
110 booths with 500 attendees and 110 exhibits
Kathy Hayes, Executive Director
Nanette Pearson, Chief Financial Officer

3417 MESPA Spring Conference
Massachusetts Elementary School Principals Assoc
28 Lord Road
Suite 125
Marlborough, MA 01752
508-624-0500
Fax: 508-485-9965
mespa@mespa.org
www.mespa.org
Features nationally-known speakers, numerous workshops on relevant topics, awards presentation, and an outstanding exhibition of school-related vendors.
Annual/May
100 booths
Jennifer Chapin, President
Kirk Downing, Vice President

3418 MNEA Fall Conference
Missouri National Education Association
1810 E Elm Street
Jefferson City, MO 65101
573-634-3202
800-392-0236
Fax: 573-634-5646
chris.guinther@mnea.org
www.mnea.org
Free and open to the public. Includes workshops, exhibits and features a keynote address presented by Diane Ravitch
Annual/November
95 booths with 1,500 attendees
Charles Smith, President
Brent Fullington, Vice President

3419 MSBA Annual Conference
Missouri School Boards Association
2100 I-70 Drive SW
Columbia, MO 65203
800-221-6722
Fax: 573-445-9981
info@msbanet.org
www.msbanet.org
September/October
125 booths
Dr Carter Ward, Executive Director
Jaime Fessler, Conference/Events Manager

3420 Maine Principals Association Conference
50 Industrial Drive
PO Box 2468
Augusta, ME 04330-2468
207-622-0217
Fax: 207-622-1513
mpa@mpa.cc
www.mpa.cc
To assure a quality education for all students, promote the principalship
April
Barbara Proko, Conference Contact
Mary Martin, President

3421 Massachusetts School Boards Association Meeting
One Mckinley Square
Boston, MA 02109-1650
617-523-8454
800-392-6023
www.masc.org
May
100 booths
Capt. Edward Bryant, NCCC, Conference Contact
Glen Koocher, Executive Director

3422 Michigan Association of Elementary and Middle School Principals Conference
1980 N College Road
Mason, MI 48854
517-694-8955
Fax: 517-694-8945
www.memspa.org
Exhibits offer books, fundraisers, camps, insurance groups and non-profit organizations.
October
100 booths
William Hays, Jr, Conference Contact

3423 Michigan Science Teachers Association Annual Conference
Michigan Science Teachers Association
1390 Eisenhower Place
Ann Arbor, MI 48108
734-973-0433
Fax: 734-677-3287
cchopp@kamsc.k12.mi.us
www.msta-mich.org
A conference that aims to supply science teachers with information and research.
February
Charles Bucienski, President
Robby Cramer, Executive Director

3424 Mid-South Educational Research Association Annual Meeting
Louisiana State University, School of Dentistry
1100 Florida Avenue
#223
New Orleans, LA 70119-2714
504-619-8700
Fax: 504-619-8740
www.dtm10.cep.msstate.edu/
Focuses on assessment and involvement in education by releasing research and statistics.
November
Diana Gardiner PhD, Conference Contact

3425 Middle States Council for the Social Studies Annual Regional Conference
P.O Box 1196
Savona, NY 14879
717-865-2117
www.mscssonline.org
Seeks to develop and implement new curriculum into the social studies area.
April
Dan Sidelnick, Conference Contact
Rebecca Herndon, President

3426 Minnesota Leadership Annual Conference
Minnesota School Boards Association
1900 W Jefferson Avenue
Saint Peter, MN 56082-3015
507-934-2450
800-324-4459
Fax: 507-931-1515
gabbott@mnmsba.org
www.mnmsba.org
The purpose of the Association is to support, promote and enhance the work of public school boards
January
200+ booths with 2,000+ attendees
Kevin Donovan, President
Kirk Schneidawind, Executive Director

3427 Minnesota School Administrators Association
1884 Como Avenue
Saint Paul, MN 55108-2715
651-645-6272
866-444-5251
Fax: 651-645-7518
members@mnasa.org
www.mnasa.org
MASA's Educational Leaderswill establish the statewide agenda for children, serve as the preeminent voice for public education and empower members through quality services and support.
October
70 booths
Gary Amoroso, Executive Director
Mia Urick, Director of Communications

3428 Minnesota School Boards Association Leadership Conference
1900 W Jefferson Avenue
Saint Peter, MN 56082-3015
507-934-2450
800-324-4459
Fax: 507-931-1515
www.mnmsba.org
The theme of the conference will be "Student Achievement: Passion, Perseverance and Possibility". The program will include workshops and guest speakers.
January
Kirk Schneidawind, Executive Director
Tiffany Rodning, Deputy Executive Director

3429 Missouri State Teachers Association Convention
407 S 6th Street
PO Box 458
Columbia, MO 65205
573-442-3127
800-392-0532
Fax: 573-443-5079
membercare@msta.org
www.msta.org
The convention will feature an assembly of delegates, committee progress reports and an open discussion on issues facing the education profession.
November
Brett Hoch, President
Bruce Moe, Executive Director

3430 Montana Association of Elementary School Principals Conference
1134 Butte Avenue
Helena, MT 59601-5178
406-442-2510
Fax: 406-442-2518
January/Febuary
20 booths
Loran Frazier, Conference Contact

3431 NAAEE Annual Conference
North American Assoc for Environmental Education
2000 P Street NW
Suite 540
Washington, DC 20036
202-419-0412
Fax: 202-419-0415
communicator@naaee.org
www.naaee.org
October
Jose Marcos-Iga, President
Judy Braus, Executive Director

3432 NCASA Annual Conference
North Carolina Association of School Administrator
333 Fayetteville Street
Suite 1410
Raleigh, NC 27601

919-828-1426
Fax: 919-828-6099
info@ncasa.net
www.ncasa.net
Delivers a powerful agenda packed with essential training and sessions led by key education leaders and political insiders in the state and nation.
March-April
40 booths
Rodney Shotwell, President
Katherine Joyce, Executive Director

3433 NCTM Annual Meeting & Exposition
National Council of Teachers of Mathematics
1906 Association Drive
Reston, VA 20191-1502
703-620-9840
800-235-7566
Fax: 703-476-2970
nctm@nctm.org
www.nctm.org
Covers topics like differentiated instruction, common core standards, intervention, technology and more
April
650 booths with 18M attendees
Diane J. Briars, President
Bob Doucette, Executive Director

3434 NELMS Annual Conference
New England League of Middle Schools
120 Water Street
Suite 403
North Andover, MA 01983
978-557-9311
Fax: 978-557-9312
nelms@nelms.org
www.nelms.org
April
160+ booths with 3800+ attendees
Esther Asbell, Chair
Brenda Needham, Executive Director

3435 NMSA Annual Education Conference & Exhibit
National Middle School Association
4151 Executive Parkway
Suite 300
Westerville, OH 43016
614-895-4730
800-528-6672
Fax: 614-895-4750
info@amle.org
www.amle.org
Provides information, tools, and encouragement necessary to provide a high-quality education for every young adolescent.
November
Ashley Smith, President
William D. Waidelich, EdD, Executive Director

3436 NSBA Annual Confernce & Exposition
National School Boards Association
1680 Duke Street
Alexandria, VA 22314
703-838-6722
Fax: 703-683-7590
info@nsba.org
www.nsba.org
The largest national gathering of elected officials and offers an impressive collection of professional development opportunities for school board members and other education leaders. Offers a great opportunity to improve leadership skills and learn what is happening in public education.
April
550 booths
Anne M. Byrne, President
Miranda A. Beard, Secretary-Treasurer

3437 NSTA National Conference
National Science Teachers Association
1840 Wilson Boulevard
Arlington, VA 22201
703-243-7100
Fax: 703-243-7177
conferences@nsta.org
www.nsta.org
March
Dr. Juliana Texley, President
David L. Evans, Executive Director

3438 NYSSBA Annual Convention & Expo
New York School Board Association
24 Century Hill Drive
Suite 200
Latham, NY 12210-2125
518-783-0200
Fax: 518-783-0211
info@nyssba.org
www.nyssba.org
Join your fellow school board colleagues from all corners of the state for an unsurpassed opportunity to learn, network with peers, and hear about the latest products and services impacting education at this all-important event.
October
Lynne L. Lenhardt, President
Timothy G. Kremer, Executive Director

3439 National Association of State Boards of Education Conference
333 John Carlyle Street
Suite 530
Alexandria, VA 22314
703-684-4000
Fax: 703-836-2313
boards@nasbe.org
www.nasbe.org
Speakers will cover topics such as ESSA implementation, education equity and excellence, leadership development, school funding, personalized learning and more.
November
Jay Barth, Chair
Kristen Amundson, President & CEO

3440 National Career Development Association Conference
National Career Development Association
305 N Beech Circle
Broken Arrow, OK 74012
918-663-7060
866-367-6232
Fax: 918-663-7058
webeditor@ncda.org
www.ncda.org
Mark Danaher, President
Deneen Pennington, Executive Director

3441 National Conference on Education
American Association of School Administrators
1615 Duke Street
Suite 700
Alexandria, VA 22314-1730
703-528-0700
info@aasa.org
www.aasa.org
Rich with content about the issues and challenges in public education. Take this opportunity to hear recognized speakers discuss solutions, beest practices, challenges and more.
Annual/February
Molly O'Neill, Meetings Manager

3442 National Conference on Standards and Assessment
National School Conference Institute
Riviera Hotel
Las Vegas, NV 89101
602-371-8655
Fax: 602-371-8790
www.nscinet.com
Two pre-conference workshops: The five most important things that educators need to know when using information for continuous program improvement, and The key to sustained leadership effectiveness. Conference will also hold over 60 breakout sessions.
April
Bill Daggett
Bob Marzano

3443 National Council for Geographic Education Annual Meeting
National Council for Geographic Education
1101 14 Street, NW
Suite 350
Washington, DC 20005-5647
202-216-0942
Fax: 202-618-6249
www.ncge.org
Where geography educators from across the country and around the world meet to exchange ideas, research, resources, and best practices in geogrpahy education.
October
45 booths with 800 attendees
Eric J. Fournier, Chair
Susan E. Hume, President

3444 National Council for History Education Conference
National Council for History Education
13940 Cedar Road
Suite 393
University Heights, OH 44118
240-696-6600
Fax: 240-523-0245
nche@nche.net
www.nche.net
bring school and university people together to tackle all the issues that concern them—from curricular design, K to Ph.D., through state, local, and university standards and requirements, teacher education, certification, and professional development, to the implications of the assessment movement, of new technologies, and of school re-structuring.
March-April
750 attendees and 75 exhibits
Dale Steiner, Chairman
Justin Jakovac, Executive Director

3445 National Council for Social Studies Annual Conference
National Council for the Social Studies
8555 Sixteenth Street
Suite 500
Silver Spring, MD 20910
301-588-1800
800-683-0812
Fax: 301-588-2049
sgriffin@ncss.org
www.socialstudies.org
Provides new ideas, resources, techniques, and skills that will pay off in the classroom, school, district, and invigorate your career. Features more than 400 sessions, workshops, poster presenta-

tions, clinics, tours, speakers and panels, and social events.

December

Michelle Herczog, President
Peggy Jackson, Vice President

3446 National Council of Teachers of English 2018 Annual Convention
National Council of Teachers of English
1111 W Kenyon Road
Urbana, IL 61801
217-328-3870
877-369-6283
Fax: 217-328-9645
public_info@ncte.org
www.ncte.org
Brings together educators, experts, authors, administrators, publishers and others to discuss the profession of teaching.

Annual/November

Franki Sibberson, Program Chair
Emily Kirkpatrick, Executive Director

3447 National Education Association Annual Meeting
National Education Association (NEA)
1201 16th Street NW
Washington, DC 20036-3290
202-833-4000
Fax: 202-822-7974
ncuea@nea.org
www.nea.org
A general conference that addresses all facets and concerns of the educator.

July

Gloria Durgin, Conference Contact
Dennis Van Roekel, President

3448 National Educational Computing Conference
Washington State Convention & Trade Center
Walter E Washington Convention Cent
Washington, DC 20001
800-336-5191
Fax: 206-694-5399
neccinfo@iste.org
www.center.uoregon.edu/ISTE
NECC has been the premier forum in which to learn, exchange, and survey the field of educational technology.

June
417 booths with 12,500 attendees

Dr Heidi Rogers, First Executive Director
Trina Davis, President

3449 National Occupational Information Coordinating Committee Conference
2100 M Street NW
Suite 156
Washington, DC 20037-1207
202-653-7680
Focuses on policy, social issues and social services addressing career development and occupational information.

August

Mary Susan Vickers, Conference Contact

3450 National Principals Conference
1904 Association Drive
Reston, VA 20191-1537
703-860-0200
800-253-7746
Fax: 703-476-5432
conference@nassp.org
www.principalsconference.org
Offers programming addressing the needs and challenges of K-12 school leaders.

July
290 booths

Daniel P Kelley, President
Christine Handy, President Elect

3451 New Mexico School Boards Association Conference
New Mexico School Boards Association
300 Galisteo Street
Suite 204
Santa Fe, NM 87501
505-983-5041
Fax: 505-983-2450
nmsba@nmsba.org
www.nmsba.org
The New Mexico School Boards Association aspires to be recognized as the premier source of development and support for local boards of education in New Mexico.

February
20 booths

Joe Guillen, Executive Director
Elizabeth Egelhoff, Programs Director

3452 New York School Superintendents Association Annual Meeting
111 Washington Avenue
Suite 404
Albany, NY 12210-2210
518-449-1063
Fax: 518-426-2229
Provides leadership and membership services through a professional organization of school superintendents.

October
50 booths

Dr. Claire Brown, Conference Contact

3453 New York Science Teachers Association Annual Meeting
2449 Union Boulevard
Apartment 20B
Islip, NY 11751-3117
516-783-5432
Fax: 516-783-5432
Education related publications, equipment, supplies and services.

November
110 booths

Harold Miller, Conference Contact

3454 New York State United Teachers Conference
159 Wolf Road
Albany, NY 12205-1106
518-213-6000
Fax: 518-213-6415
www.nysut.org

February
40 booths

Anthony Bifaro, Conference Contact

3455 New York Teachers Math Association Conference
92 Governor Drive
Scotia, NY 12302-4802
518-399-0149

October-November
50 booths

Phil Reynolds, Conference Contact

3456 North Central Association Annual Meeting
North Central Association Commission on Accred.
9115 Westside Parkway
Alpharetta, GA 30009-1008
866-837-2229
800-525-9517
Fax: 480-773-6901
denz@ncacasi.org
www.ncacasi.org
Founded in 1895, NCA CASI accredits over 8,500 public and private schools in 19 states, the Navajo Nation, and the Department of Defense Schools. NCA CASI is an accreditation division of AdvancED.

April
30 booths with 1,800 attendees

William Fisher, CEO
Jay Cummings, Dean, College of Education,

3457 North Central Conference on Summer Sessions Conference
North Central Conference on Summer Sessions
University of Wisconsin
410 S 3rd Street
River Falls, WI 54022
715-425-3851
Fax: 715-425-3785
www.nccss.org
This conference attracts a wide variety range of attendees, from faculty, admissions personnel, registrars, business office and marketing representatives, and a wide variety of academic and student affairs administrators with responsibility for overseeing or directing some aspect of their institution's summer session activities.

Annual/March

Molly Berger, President
Diane Dingfelder, President-Elect

3458 Northeast Conference on the Teaching of Foreign Languages
Northeast Conference at Dickinson College
PO Box 1773
Carlisle, PA 17013-2896
717-243-5121
800-644-1773
Fax: 717-245-1976
nectfl@dickinson.edu
www.nectfl.org
NECTFL aspires to serve the diverse community of language professionals through responsive leadership in its outreach activities and its annual conference.

April
160 booths with 2500 attendees

Rebecca Kline, Executive Director
Susan M Shaffer, Associate Executive Director

3459 Northeast Teachers Foreign Language Conference
Northeast Conference at Dickinson College
PO Box 1773
Carlisle, PA 17013-2896
717-243-5121
800-644-1773
Fax: 802-654-2595
nectfl@dickinson.edu
www.nectfl.org
Foreign language textbooks, supplementary materials, audio equipment, computer software, travel abroad program materials and other related teaching aids and publications.

April
130 booths

Rebecca Kline, Executive Director

3460 Northwest Association of Schools & Colleges Annual Meeting
1910 University Drive
Boise, ID 83725-1060

208-426-1000
Fax: 208-334-3228
www.boisestate.edu
The university offers more than 190 fields of interest. Undergraduate, graduate and technical programs are available in seven colleges: Arts and Sciences, Business and Economics, Education, Engineering, Graduate Studies, Health Sciences, and Social Sciences and Public Affairs. Students can also study abroad and participate in one of the largest internship programs in the Northwest.

December
120 attendees

Bob Kustra, President
Martin Schimpf, Vice President for Academic

3461 Northwest Regional Educational Laboratory Conference
101 SW Main Street
Suite 500
Portland, OR 97204-3213
503-275-9500
800-547-6339
Fax: 503-275-0660
info@nwrel.org
www.nwrel.org
The mission of the Northwest Regional Educational Laboratory (NWREL) is to improve learning by building capacity in schools, families, and communities through applied research and development

October/November

Jeffrey Weldon, Chairperson
Steve Bradshaw, Vice Chairperson

3462 Ohio Business Teachers Association
Wright State University, Lake Campus
2350 Westbelt Drive
Columbus, OH 43228-2921
419-586-0337
Fax: 419-586-0368
MCWhite@itt-tech.edu
www.obta-ohio.org
Promote among educators the desire to find better techniques and methods in an effort to improve instruction in the field of business so that the students are well prepared to take their place in the business world.

October
40 booths

Daniel McCarthy, President
Stella Hull, Treasurer

3463 Ohio Public School Employees Association Convention
6805 Oak Creek Drive
Columbus, OH 43229
614-890-4770
800-786-2773
Fax: 614-890-3540
www.oapse.org
Committed in developing the most effective programs in the labor movement today.

May
15 booths

Joseph P Rugola, Executive Director
JoAnn Johntony, State President

3464 Ohio Secondary School Administrators Association Conference
Ohio Association of Secondary School Administrator
8050 N High Street
Suite 180
Columbus, OH 43235-6484
614-430-8311
Fax: 614-430-8315
www.oassa.org
Offers school secretaries the opportunity to network with colleagues while gaining valuable information that will add to their performance. Current administrators, representatives from the business community, OASSA legal counsel, and fellow secretaries combine to update these valuable employees.

April
42 booths

Kenneth C. Baker, Executive Director
John Richard, Associate Executive Director

3465 Oklahoma School Boards Association & School Administrators Conference
2801 N Lincoln Boulevard
Suite 125
Oklahoma City, OK 73105-4223
405-528-3571
888-528-3571
Fax: 405-528-5695
www.ossba.org
The mission of the Oklahoma State School Boards Association shall be to offer services to safeguard,represent and improve public education.The Association shall represent the interests of public school boards before the legislature; provide training programs for school board members; provide school system services; and provide to the individual school board members a variety of other services and information that will improve the quality of educational leadership for each school district in Okla

August
195 booths

Joann Yandell, Conference Contact
Beth Schieber, President

3466 Oregon School Boards Association Annual Convention
Oregon School Boards Association
1201 Court Street NE
Suite 400
Salem, OR 97301
503-588-2800
800-578-6722
Fax: 503-588-2813
info@osba.org
www.osba.org
To improve student achievement through advocacy, leadership and services to Oregon public school boards.

November

Betsy Miller-Jones, Executive Director
Jim Green, Deputy Executive Director

3467 PDK International Conference
Int'l Honor and Professional Assoc in Education
PO Box 7888
Bloomington, IN 47407-7888
812-339-1156
800-766-1156
Fax: 812-339-0018
plt@pdkintl.org
www.pilambda.org
Conference on Innovations in Teaching and Learning was selected because of its relevance to educators everywhere as new and effective educational practices continue to emerge. Includes interactive sessions, research presentations, and networking events.

Annual/February
400 attendees

Dan Brown, Executive Director
Bill Bushaw, Chief Executive Officer

3468 PSBA School Board Secretaries and Affiliates Conference
Pennsylvania School Boards Association
400 Bent Creek Blvd.
PO Box 2042
Mechanicsburg, PA 17050-1873
717-506-2450
800-932-0588
Fax: 717-506-2451
trustinfo@psba.org
www.psba.org
To promote excellence in school board governance through leadership, service and advocacy for public education.

October
140 booths

William S. LaCoff, President
Mark B. Miller, Vice President

3469 Pacific Northwest Council on Languages Annual Conference
5290 University of Oregon
Eugene, OR 97403
541-346-5699
Fax: 541-346-6303
pncfl@uoregon.edu
www.pncfl.org
The Pacific Northwest Council for Languages unites, serves, and supports all world language educators in Alaska, Idaho, Montana, Oregon, Washington, and Wyoming.

April

Brenda Gaver, President
Laura Kiolet, Executive Director

3470 Pennsylvania Council for the Social Studies Conference
Pennsylvania Council for the Social Studies
1212 Smallman Street
Senator John Heinz Regional Histiry Cnt
Pittsburgh, PA 15222-4200
717-238-8768
JKEARNEY@CBSD.ORG
www.pcssonline.org
The PCSS promotes quality Social Studies education from kindergarten to higher learning by advocating the Social Studies at all levels of education in Pennsylvania.

October
50 booths with 500 attendees

David Trevaskis, President elect
Don Imler, Executive Secretary

3471 Pennsylvania Science Teachers Association
Center for Science & Technology Education
PO Box 330
Shippenville, PA 16254-330
814-782-6301
www.pascience.org
Work towards the advancement, improvement, and coordination of science education in all areas of science at all educational levels.

December
70 booths

Don Kine, President
Kathleen Jones, Vice President

3472 Principals' Center Spring Institute Conference
Harvard Graduate School of Education
6 Appian Way
#336
Cambridge, MA 02138-3704
617-495-1825
Fax: 617-495-5900
www.gse.harvard.edu
Administrative professionals get together to discuss issues, policy and procedures.
April
Nindy Leroy, Conference Contact

3473 Restructuring Curriculum Conference
National School Conference Institute
PO Box 35099
Phoenix, AZ 85069-5099
602-674-8990
Presents research, studies, and new information relevant to curriculum development.
January

3474 SAI Annual Conference
School Administrators of Iowa
12199 Stratford Drive
Clive, IA 50325
515-267-1115
Fax: 515-267-1066
dsmith@sai-iowa.org
www.sai-iowa.org
August
Deron Durflinger, President
Paul Wenger, Vice President

3475 SchoolTech Forum
Miller Freeman
600 Harrison Street
San Francisco, CA 94109
415-947-6657
Fax: 415-947-6015
National forum for educational technology professional development and exhibits, devoted to intensive instruction by today's leading practitioners, eye-opening special events, unparalleled networking opportunities, and exposure to products and services.

3476 South Carolina Library Association Conference
South Carolina Library Association
PO Box 1763
Columbia, SC 29202
803-252-1087
Fax: 803-252-0589
scla@capconsc.com
www.scla.org
Annual/October
125 booths with 350 attendees
Crystal Johnson, President
John Kennerly, 1st Vice President

3477 Southern Association Colleges & Schools
1866 Southern Lane
Decatur, GA 30033-4097
404-679-4500
Fax: 404-679-4556
www.sacs.org
Exhibits publications, data and word processing equipment, school photography, charter bus services and more.
December
50 booths with 3700 attendees
Dr. James Rogers, Chief Academic Officer

3478 Southern Early Childhood Annual Convention
Southern Early Childhood Association
1123 S University Avenue
Suite 255
Little Rock, AR 72204
501-221-1648
800-305-7322
Fax: 501-221-5297
info@southernearlychildhood.org
www.southernearlychildhood.org
Southern Early Childhood Association unites preschool, kindergarten, and primary educators and administrators, as well as other staff members working with and for families. The next conference will be called 'Every Child Needs a Champion', dedicated to promoting care and education for young children.
March
Jo Carroll, President
Mark Polevoy, Executive Director

3479 Superintendents Work Conference
Teachers College, Columbia University
525 W 120th Street
PO Box 179
New York, NY 10027-6696
212-678-7449
Fax: 212-678-3682
swc@tc.columbia.edu
www.superintendentsworkconference.com
Offers practicing school superintendents a unique opportunity for professional growth in stimulating surroundings.
July
60 attendees
Thomas Sobol, Conference Chair
Gibran Matdalany, Associate Chair

3480 TASA/TASB Convention
Texas Association of School Boards
PO Box 400
Austin, TX 78767-0400
512-467-0222
800-580-8272
Fax: 512-467-3554
tasb@tasb.org
www.tasb.org
Offers school board members and school administrators the opportunity to earn almost 17 hours of continuing education credit, hear outstnading keynote speakers, explore a tradeshow with hundreds of exhibitors, and network with more than 6,000 public school officials.
September-October
James B Crow, Executive Director
Grover Campbell, Associate Executive Director

3481 Teachers Association in Instruction Conference
150 W Market Street
Indianapolis, IN 46204-2806
317-634-1515
Exhibits a wide variety of teaching materials and information from Grades K-12.
October
150 booths
Barbara Stainbrook, Conference Contact

3482 Tennessee School Boards Association Conference
525 Brick Church Park Drive
Nashville, TN 37207-2884
615-815-3900
800-448-6465
Fax: 615-815-3911
webadmin@tsba.net
www.tsba.net
The mission of the Tennessee School Boards Associationis to assisst school boards in effectively governing school districts.
November
60 booths with 1,000 attendees
Tammy Grissom, Executive Director
David Pickler, President

3483 Texas Middle School Association Conference
Texas Middle School Association
PO Box 152499
Austin, TX 78715-2499
512-468-1168
888-529-8672
Fax: 512-462-0991
tmsa2@austin.rr.com
www.tmsanet.org
To promote the implementation of student-centered programs and highly effective practices by providing vision, knowledge, and resources which meet the unique individual needs of adolescents in an ever-changing society.
February
Thad Spears, President
Cecil Floyd, Executive Director

3484 Texas State Teachers Association
316 W 12th Street
Austin, TX 78701-1815
877-275-8782
Fax: 512-476-9555
www.tsta.org
The Texas State Teachers Association will unite, organize and empower public education advocates to shape public education in Texas thus providing a quality public school for every child
April
120 booths
Carla Bond, Conference Contact
Rita Haecker, President

3485 Training & Presentations
Chief Manufacturing, Inc.
6436 City West Parkway
Eden Prairie, MN 55344-4839
612-894-6280
800-582-6480
Fax: 877-894-6918
chief@chiefmfg.com
www.chiefmfg.com
Providing top quality mounting solutions for projectors, monitors, and flat panel TVs. Committed to responding to industry needs in Commercial, Residential and Workstation/IT markets, Chief is dedicated to producing solutions that packed with form, function, and flexibility
Chicago, Illinois
February
Kris Murray, Director Customer Service/Pr
Yvette Danz, Manager Customer Service

3486 UPCEA Annual Conference
University Professional/Continuing Education Assoc
One Dupont Circle
Suite 615
Washington, DC 20036
202-659-3130
Fax: 202-785-0374
nkats@upcea.edu
www.upcea.edu
The largest single gathering of higher education professionals who develop, implement, and promote professional and continuing ed-

ucation and online learning in North America.

April
70 booths with 1,000 attendees

Robert Hansen, CEO/Executive Director
Lori Derkay, Chief Operating Officer

3487 USA Kansas Annual Convention
United School Administrators of Kansas
515 S Kansas Avenue
Suite 201
Topeka, KS 66603
785-232-6566
Fax: 785-232-9776
usaoffice@usa-ks.org
www.usakansas.org
Offers quality professional development opportunities for education administrators and leaders. During the convention, administrators are able to participate in professional workshops or learning clusters.

180 booths

Cheryl Semmel, Executive Director

3488 VAIS Conference
Virginia Association of Independent Schools
6802 Paragon Place
Suite 525
Richmond, VA 23230
804-282-3592
Fax: 804-282-3596
info@vais.org
www.vais.org
The Virginia Association of Independent Schools is a service organization that promotes educational, ethical and professional excellence. Through its school evaluation/accreditation program, attention to professional development and insistence on integrity, the Association safeguards the interests of its member schools.

November
1,500 attendees

Henry D. Berg, President
Betsy Hunroe, Executive Director

3489 Virginia ASCD Conference
Virginia ASCD
2516 Old Lynchburg Rd
North Garden, VA 22959
434-293-3290
vascded@gmail.com
vaascd.org
Dedicated to advancing excellence in Teaching, Learning and Leadership.

December
30 booths with 600 attendees

Daniel Smith, President
Laurie McCullough, Executive Director

3490 Virginia Association of Elementary School Principals Conference
Virginia Assoc of Elementary School Principals
1805 Chantilly Street
Richmond, VA 23230
804-355-6791
Fax: 804-355-1196
info@vaesp.org
www.vaesp.org
Nonprofit professional association advocating for public education and equal educational opportunities. Promotes leadership of school administrators, principal as educational leaders, and provides professional development opportunities.

50 booths with 300 attendees

Shane Wolfe, President
Jim Baldwin, Executive Director

3491 Virginia School Boards Association Conference
Virginia School Boards Association
200 Hansen Road
Charlottesville, VA 22911
434-295-8722
800-446-8722
Fax: 434-295-8785
www.vsba.org
A voluntary, self-supporting and nonpartisan organization that promotes quality education through its services for local school boards. Provides member boards with services, training, and advocacy so that they may exercise effective leadership in public school governance on behalf of public education for all the children of the Commonwealth.

Annual/November

Juandiego R. Wade, President
Gina G Patterson, Executive Director

3492 Wisconsin Association of School Boards Annual Conference
Wisconsin Association of School Boards
122 W Washington Avenue
Suite 400
Madison, WI 53703-2761
608-257-2622
Fax: 608-257-8386
info@wasb.org
www.wasb.org
The WASB provides background and support for elected school leaders as they do the difficult work of democracy: weighing and balancing the unique values of their communities.

January
370 booths with 3,000 attendees

John Ashley, Executive Director
Patti Welch, Administrative Assistant

3493 Wisconsin Association of School District Administrators Conference
Wisconsin Assoc of School District Administrators
4797 Hayes Road
Suite 201
Madison, WI 53704
608-242-1090
Fax: 608-242-1290
mturner@wasda.org
www.wasda.org
The premiere collaborative leadership association, serves superintendents by providing professional support and expanding their capacity to be effective, innovative leaders.

Annual/May
70 booths

Kristine Gilmore, President
Jon Bales, Executive Director

3494 Wisconsin School Administrators Association Conference
Association of Wisconsin School Administrators
4797 Hayes Road
Suite 103
Madison, WI 53704
608-241-0300
Fax: 608-249-4973
patricia@awsa.org
www.awsa.org
The Association of Wisconsin School Administrators exists to coordinate the collective interests and needs of school administrators and to enhance their professional growth and competency for the purpose of improving the quality of educational opportunities for the youth of Wisconsin

October
60 booths

Jim Lynch, Executive Director
Kelly Meyers, Associate Executive Director

Directories & Handbooks

3495 American Association of Colleges for Teacher Education-Directory
American Association of Colleges for Teacher Ed.
1307 New York Avenue NW
Suite 300
Washington, DC 20005
202-293-2450
Fax: 202-457-8095
aacte@aacte.org
www.aacte.org
Promote the learning of all PK-12 students through high-quality, evidence-based preparation and continuing education for all school personnel.

144 pages Annual
ISSN: 0516-9313

Sharon P Robinson, President/CEO
Jeannette Knight-Mills, Associate Director Executive

3496 American Society for Training/Development-Training Video
American Society for Training & Development
1640 King Street
Box 1443
Alexandria, VA 22313-1443
703-683-8100
800-628-2783
Fax: 703-683-8103
customercare@astd.org
www.astd.org
Serves as the educational society for persons engaged in training and development of business, industry, education and government personnel.

Tony Bingham, President/CEO
Cindy Huggett, Chair

3497 Appropriate Inclusion and Paraprofessionals
National Education Association (NEA)
1201 16th Street NW
Washington, DC 20036-3290
202-833-4000
Fax: 202-822-7974
ncuea@nea.org
www.nea.org
A book offering information on mainstreaming disabled students and the work of paraprofessionals in the education process.

10 pages

Dennis Van Roekel, President
Lily Eskelsen, Vice President

3498 Assessing Student Performance: Exploring the Purpose and Limits of Testing
Jossey-Bass/Pfeiffer
989 Market Street
San Francisco, CA 94103-1741
415-433-1740
Fax: 415-433-0499
info@wiley.com
www.josseybass.com
Clarifies the limits of testing in an assessment system. Analyzes problematic practices in test design and formats that prevent students from explaining their answers by showing that assessment is more

than testing and intellectual performance is more than right answers.

336 pages Softcover
ISBN: 0-7879-5047-5

3499 Association for Continuing Higher Education Directory
1700 Asp Avenue
Norman, OK 73072-6400
405-329-0249
800-807-2243
Fax: 405-325-7196
admin@acheinc.org
www.acheinc.org
Dedicated to promoting lifelong learning and excellence in continuing higher education. Encourage professional development, research and exchange of information for its members and continuing higher education as a means of enhancing and improving society.

102 pages Annual/March
10 booths with 250 attendees

James P Pappas, Executive VP
Rick E Osborn, President

3500 BBX Teacher Clearinghouse
175 Norwood Road
Silver Spring, MD 20905
301-628-9776
Fax: 301-989-9606
CEO@BBXOnline.com
www.teachersclearinghouse.com
BBX's Teacher Clearinghouse is a comprehensive resume databank where elementary and secondary school teachers, administrators, and education majors can post their resumes at no charge for review by subscribing school districts. Subscribers are public and private schools with an interest in receiving applications from, and importantly, a commitment to hiring, members of the African American/Black communities.

J R Moore, Administrator

3501 Before the School Bell Rings
Phi Delta Kappa Educational Foundation
320 W Eight Street
Suite 216
Bloomington, IN 47404
812-339-1156
800-766-1156
Fax: 812-339-0018
memberservices@pdkintl.org
www.pdkintl.org
Early childhood teachers and administrators, childcare providers and parents will enjoy and learn from this practical, insightful book.

84 pages Paperback
ISBN: 0-87367-476-6

Carol B Hillman, Author
George Kersey, Executive Director
Donovan R Walling, Editor, Special Publications

3502 Beyond Tracking: Finding Success in Inclusive Schools
Phi Delta Kappa Educational Foundation
PO Box 7888
Bloomington, IN 47407-7888
812-339-1156
800-766-1156
Fax: 812-339-0018
memberservices@pdkintl.org
www.pdkintl.org
Research data, practical ideas and reports from educators involved in untracking schools make this an authoritative and useful collection of important articles.

293 pages Hardcover
ISBN: 0-87367-470-7

Harbison Pool and Jane A Page, Author
George Kersey, Executive Director
Donovan R Walling, Dir Publications/Research

3503 Book of Metaphors, Volume II
AEE and Kendall/Hunt Publishing Company
4050 Westmark Drive
P.O Box 1840
Dubuque, IA 52004-1840
563-589-1000
800-228-0810
Fax: 800-772-9165
orders@kendallhunt.com
www.kendallhunt.com
A compilation of presentations designed to enhance learning for those participating in adventure-based programs. Practitioners share how they prepare experiences for presentations.

256 pages Paperback
ISBN: 0-7872-0306-8

AEE, Author
Karen Berger, Customer Service Assistant

3504 Brief Legal Guide for the Independent Teacher
441 Vine Street
Suite 505
Cincinnati, OH 45202-2811
Offering insights into the most common legal issues faced by independent music teachers.

28 pages

3505 Building Life Options: School-Community Collaborations
Academy for Educational Development
1255 23rd Street NW
Washington, DC 20037-1125
202-884-8800
Fax: 202-884-8400
A handbook for family life educators on how to prevent pregnancy in the middle grades.

3506 Center on Education and Work
Center on Education and Work
1025 W Johnson Street
Room 964
Madison, WI 53706-1796
608-265-6700
800-862-1071
Fax: 608-262-3063
cewmail@cew.wisc.edu
cew.wisc.edu
A training center offering programs in vocational-technical education and career development, with a focus on teaching careers.

Jane Kwiecinski, Operations
Jun Zheng, Lead Programmer Director

3507 Closing the Achievement Gap
Master Teacher
Leadership Lane
PO Box 1207
Manhattan, KS 66505-1207
785-539-0555
800-669-9633
Fax: 800-669-1132
www.masterteacher.com
A complete step-by-step approach to building a system that narrows the gap between student potenial and student performance—between success and failure.

162 pages
ISBN: 0-914607-73-1

Kristy Meeks, Author

3508 Coming Up Short? Practices of Teacher Educators Committed to Character
Character Education Partnership
1025 Connecticut Avenue NW
Suite 1011
Washington, DC 20036
202-296-7743
800-988-8081
Fax: 202-296-7779
rsipos@character.org
www.character.org
Nonprofit, nonpartisan, nonsectarian coalition of organizations and individuals committed to fostering effective character education in our nation's K-12 schools.

Henry Huffman, Author
Rebecca Sipos, Director Communications
Anne Bryant, Executive Director

3509 Competency-Based Framework for Professional Development of Certified Health Specialists
Nat'l Health Education Credentialing
1541 Alta Drive
Suite 303
Whitehall, PA 18052-5642
484-223-0770
888-624-3248
Fax: 800-813-0727
www.nchec.org
Aims to help the health education profession provide the leadership necessary for improving health in a rapidly changing, culturally pluralistic and technologically complex society. Provides universities, professional organizations, and accreditation a common basis of skills for the development, assessment, and improvement of professional preparation for health educators.

Linda Lysoby, Executive Director
Melissa Rehrig, Communication Director

3510 Contracting Out: Strategies for Fighting Back
National Education Association (NEA)
1201 16th Street NW
Washington, DC 20036-3290
202-833-4000
Fax: 202-822-7974
ncuea@nea.org
www.nea.org
The voice of education professionals. Advocate for education professionals

John I Wilson, Executive Director
Dennis Van Roekel, President

3511 Directory of Curriculum Materials Centers
PO Box 399
Addison, IL 60101-0399
630-833-5300
877-850-2300
Fax: 630-833-5303
info@telusys.net
www.telusys.com
Listing of over 275 centers that have collections of curriculum materials to aid in elementary and secondary teaching preparation.

200 pages

Jackie Bedell, Supervisor
Ruth Miller, Supervisor

3512 Distance Learning Directory
Virginia A Ostendorf
PO Box 2896
Littleton, CO 80161-2896
303-797-3131
Fax: 303-797-3524
ostendorf@vaostendorf.com
Comprehensive list of distance learning practitioners and vendors. Each listing includes

names, addresses, e-mail, fax and phones, credits awarded, program content, peripherals and technologies used, class configurations and more. Includes a lists of vendors offering descriptions of distance learning products, services and programming.

308 pages Annual

Virginia A Ostendorf, President
Ronald Ostendorf, VP

3513 Education Index
H.W. Wilson Company
950 University Avenue
Bronx, NY 10452-4224
718-588-8400
800-367-6770
Fax: 718-590-1617
rsky@hwwilson.com
www.hwwilson.com
Contains more than 456,000 citations to articles, interviews, editorials and letters, reviews of books, educational films, and software for approximately 427 English-language periodicals, monographs and yearbooks in the field of education. Available electronically on the Web with index, abstracts and full text versions.

Monthly

Roseward Sky, Assistant Manager/Marketing
Harold Regan, President

3514 Educational Administration Resource Centre Database
3-300 Edmonton Clinic Health Academy
11405-87 Ave
Edmonton, AB G1C9
780-492-0560
Fax: 780-492-0364
school.publichealth@ualberta.ca
www.publichealth.ualberta.ca
Over 3,650 bibliographic descriptions of the Centre's collection of educational administration print and audiovisual materials.

Laing Lory, Interim Dean

3515 Ethical Issues in Experiential Education
AEE and Kendall/Hunt Publishing Company
4050 Westmark Drive
Dubuque, IA 52002-2624
319-589-1000
800-228-0810
Fax: 800-772-9165
www.kendallhunt.com
An examination of ethical issues in the field of adventure programming and experiential education. Topics include ethical theory, informed consent, sexual issues, student rights, environmental concerns and programming practices.

144 pages
ISBN: 0-7872-93083

Karen Berger, Customer Service Assistant

3516 Finishing Strong: Your Personal Mentoring & Planning Guide for the Last 60 Days of Teaching
Master Teacher
Leadership Lane
PO Box 1207
Manhattan, KS 66505-1207
785-539-0555
800-669-9633
Fax: 800-669-1132
www.masterteacher.com
In this book we've selected from the 32 years of The Master Teacher, the writings we know you would most like your teachers to have to support that last 60 days of the school year.

132 pages
ISBN: 1-58992-095-3

Robert L De Bruyn, Author

3517 How to Raise Test Scores
Skylight Professional Development
1900 E Lake Avenue
Glenview, IL 60025
847-657-7450
800-348-4474
Fax: 847-486-3183
info@skylightedu.com
www.skylightedu.com
Addresses the teaching and learning process at its most basic and important level-the classroom.

30 pages Softcover
ISBN: 1575171635

Robin Fogarty, Author

3518 Inclusion: The Next Step DVD
Master Teacher
Leadership Lane
PO Box 1207
Manhattan, KS 66505-1207
785-539-0555
800-669-9633
Fax: 800-669-1132
www.masterteacher.com
Offers practical help for regular classroom teachers and special education teachers in meeting the challenges of inclusion.

225 pages
ISBN: 0-914607-69-3

Wendy Dover, Author

3519 Law of Teacher Evaluation: A Self-Assessment Handbook
Phi Delta Kappa Educational Foundation
PO Box 7888
Bloomington, IN 47407-7888
812-339-1156
800-766-1156
Fax: 812-339-0018
www.pdkintl.org
This handy guidebook provides a concise, authoritative overview of US state statutes, regulations and guidelines regarding the performance evaluation of educators.

51 pages Paperback
ISBN: 0-87367-488-X

Perry A. Zirkel, Author
DR Walling, Director Publications/Resear

3520 Learning for Life
1329 W Walnut Hill Lane
PO Box 152225
Irving, TX 75015-2225
972-580-2433
855-806-9992
Fax: 972-580-2137
exploring@lflmail.org
www.learning-for-life.org
Learning for Life is designed to support schools and other youth-serving organizations in their efforts toward preparing youth to successfully handle the complexities of today's society and to enhance their self-confidence, motivation, and self-worth.

Diane E Thornton, National Director
William Taylor, Director of Criminal Justice

3521 Lesson Plans for the Substitue Teacher: Elementary Edition
Master Teacher
Po Box 1207
Manhattan, KS 66505-1207
785-539-0555
800-669-9633
Fax: 800-669-1132
www.masterteacher.com
Gives you more than 100 lessons developed and tested by teachers across the curriculum and at all grade levels.

145 pages
ISBN: 1-58992-107-0

Robert L DeBruyn, Author

3522 Libraries Unlimited
PO Box 1911
Santa Barbara, CA 93116-1911
800-368-6868
800-225-5800
Fax: 805-968-1911
CustomerService@abc-clio.com
www.lu.com
Publisher of resource books written by educators for educators. The books offer innovative ideas, practical lessons, and classroom-tested activities in the areas of math, science, social studies, whole language literature and library connections.

Debby LaBoon, Manager of Authors/Workshops

3523 Life Skills Training
711 Westchester Avenue
White Plains, NY 10604
914-421-2525
800-293-4969
Fax: 914-421-2007
lstinfo@nhpamail.com
www.LifeSkillsTraining.com
Botvin LifeSkills Training (LST) is a research-validated substance abuse prevention program proven to reduce the risks of alcohol, tobacco, drug abuse, and violence by targeting the major social and psychological factors that promote the initiation of substance use and other risky behaviors.

Gilbert J Botvin, Developer

3524 List of Regional, Professional & Specialized Accrediting Association
Educational Information Services
PO Box 662
Newton Lower Falls, MA 02162
617-964-4555
A list of those associations involved in accreditation for the education fields.

3525 MacMillan Guide to Correspondence Study
MacMillan Publishing Company
175 Fifth Avenue
New York, NY 10010
888-330-8477
Fax: 609-409-0298
press.inquiries@macmillan.com
us.macmillan.com
Contaings a list of accredited and non-accredited institutions offering independent study programs.

782 pages

Modoc Press, Author
Michael Messineo, Senior Purchasing Manager
Alison Lazarus, President, Sales Division

3526 Middle Grades Education in an Era of Reform
Academy for Educational Development
1255 23rd Street NW
Washington, DC 20037-1125
202-884-8800
Fax: 202-884-8400
Reviews middle-grades educational reform policies and practices.

3527 Middle School Teachers Guide to FREE Curriculum Materials
Educators Progress Service
214 Center Street
Randolph, WI 53956-1408
920-326-3126
888-951-4469
Fax: 920-326-3127
epsinc@centurytel.net
www.freeteachingaids.com
Lists and describes free supplementary teaching aids for the middle school and junior high level.
290 pages Annual
ISBN: 87708-401-7
Kathy Nehmer, President

3528 NASDTEC Knowledge Base
1629 K Street NW
Suite 300
Washington, DC 20006
202-204-2208
Fax: 202-204-2210
rje@nasdtec.com
www.nasdtec.org
It is the organization that represents professional standards boards and commissions and state departments of education in all 50 states, the District of Columbia, the Department of Defense Education Activity, the U.S. Territories, Alberta, British Columbia, and Ontario that are responsible for the preparation, licensure, and discipline of educational personnel.
Annually
ISBN: 0-9708628-3-0
Phillip Rogers, Executive Director

3529 Orators & Philosophers: A History of the Idea of Liberal Education
College Board Publications
45 Columbus Avenue
New York, NY 10023-6992
212-713-8165
800-323-7155
Fax: 212-713-8143
aces@info.collegeboard.org
www.collegeboard.org
A cogent study of the historical evolution of the idea of liberal education. Clearly and forcefully argued, the book portrays this evolution as a struggle between two contending points of view, one oratorical and the other philosophical.
308 pages
Bruce A Kimball, Author
David Coleman, President

3530 Parent Training Resources
PACER Center
8161 Normandale Boulevard
Bloomington, MN 55437
952-838-0190
800-537-2237
Fax: 952-838-0199
pacer@pacer.org
www.pacer.org
A Minnesota nonprofit, tax-exempt organization that provides information, training, and assistance to parents of children and young adults with all disabilities; physical, learning, cognitive, emotional, and health
130 pages
Paula F Goldberg, Executive Director
Mary Schrock, Chief Operating and Developm

3531 Personal Planner and Training Guide for the Paraprofessional
Master Teacher
Po Box 1207
Manhattan, KS 66505-1207
785-539-0555
800-669-9633
Fax: 800-669-1132
www.masterteacher.com
Includes numerous forms which allow each para to keep track of vital information he or she will need in working with specific teachers and their special students.
128 pages
ISBN: 0-914607-39-1
Wendy Dover, Author

3532 Practical Handbook for Assessing Learning Outcomes in Continuing Education
International Association for Continuing Education
1760 Old Meadow Road
Suite 500
McLean, VA 22102
703-506-3275
Fax: 703-506-3266
www.iacet.org
Innovative guide offers readers a series of steps to help select an assessment plan which will work for any organization.
Michael Todd Shinholster, President
Kristopher Newbauer, President-Elect

3533 Principles of Good Practice in Continuing Education
International Association for Continuing Education
1760 Old Meadow Road
Suite 500
McLean, VA 22102
703-506-3275
Fax: 703-506-3266
www.iacet.org
Principles from many sources for the field of continuing education, placing a pervasive emphasis on learning outcomes for the individual learner.
Michael Todd Shinholster, President
Kristopher Newbauer, President-Elect

3534 Professional Learning Communities at Work
National Educational Service
65 West Shore Drive
Enfield, CT 06082
860-763-2609
800-733-6786
Fax: 812-336-7790
nes@nesonline.com
www.nesonline.com
This publication provides specific, practical, how-to information on the best practices in use in schools through the US and Canada for curriculum development, teacher preparation, school leadership, professional development programs, school-parent partnerships, assessment practices and much more.

3535 Programs for Preparing Individuals for Careers in Special Education
The Council for Exceptional Children
1920 Association Drive
Reston, VA 20191-1545
703-620-3660
800-232-7323
Fax: 703-264-1637
This directory offers over 600 colleges and universities with programs in special education. Information includes institution name, address, contact person, telephone, fax, Internet, accreditation status, size of faculty, level of program, and areas of specialty.
256 pages

3536 Quality School Teacher
National Professional Resources
25 South Regent Street
Port Chester, NY 10573-8295
914-937-8897
800-453-7461
Fax: 914-937-8879
service@nprinc.com
www.nprinc.com
Provides the specifics that classroom teachers are asking for as they begin the move to quality schools. It is written for educators who are trying to give up the old system of boss-managing, and to create classrooms that produce quality work.
144 pages
ISBN: 0060-952857
William Glasser, Author
Robert Hanson, President
Helene Hanson, VP

3537 Requirements for Certification of Teachers & Counselors
University of Chicago Press
5801 S Ellis Avenue
Floor 4
Chicago, IL 60637-5418
312-702-7700
800-621-2736
Fax: 800-621-8476
A list of state and local departments of education for requirements including teachers, counselors, librarians, and administrators for elementary and secondary schools.
256 pages Annual
ISBN: 0-226-42850-8
Elizabeth Kaye, Author
John Tryneski, Coordinating Education

3538 Research for Better Schools Publications
123 South Broad Street
Philadelphia, PA 19109-2471
215-568-6150
Fax: 215-568-7260
info@rbs.org
www.rbs.org
RBS is a private, nonprofit educational organization funded primarily through grants and contracts from the U.S. Department of Education, the National Science Foundation, Mid-Atlantic state departments of education, institutions of higher education, foundations, and school districts.
Dr. Keith M Kershner, Executive Director
Rev. John F Bloh, President

3539 Resources for Teaching Middle School Science
National Academy Press
901 D Street SW
Suite 704B
Washington, DC 20024-403
202-633-2966
Fax: 202-287-7309
shulers@si.edu
www.nsrconline.org
The NSRC is an intermediary organization that bridges research on how children learn with best practices for the classroom.
496 pages
National Science Resources Center, Author
Sally Goetz Shuler, Executive Director
Tanya Miller, Executive Assistant

3540 Restructuring in the Classroom: Teaching, Learning, and School Organization
Jossey-Bass/Pfeiffer
989 Market Street
San Francisco, CA 94103-1741
415-433-1740
Fax: 415-433-0499
www.josseybass.com
Teaching, learning and school organization.
288 pages Hardcover
ISBN: 0-7879-0239-X
Riched Elmore, Penelope Peterson & Sara McCarthey, Author

3541 Revolution Revisited: Effective Schools and Systemic Reform
Phi Delta Kappa Educational Foundation
320 W Eight Street
Suite 216
Bloomington, IN 47404-3800
812-339-1156
800-766-1156
Fax: 812-339-0018
memberservices@pdkintl.org
www.pdkintl.org
The authors examine the Effective Schools movement of the past quarter century as a school reform philosophy and renewal process for today and for the coming years.
132 pages Paperback
ISBN: 0-873674-83-9
BO Taylor and P Bullard, Author
Donovan R Walling, Director Publications/Resear
Kathleen Andreson, President

3542 Seminar Information Service
250 El Camino Real
Suite 112
Tustin, CA 92780-4469
714-508-0340
877-736-4636
Fax: 714-734-8027
info@seminarinformation.com
www.seminarinformation.com
In 1981, Catherine Bellizzi and Mona Piontkowski founded Seminar Information Service, Inc. (SIS). Their idea was to fill a void - thousands of seminars were taking place, but there wasn't any one central source to tell someone where and when they were being held.
1,000 pages Annual
Mona Pointkowski, Co-Founder
Catherine Bellizzi, Co-Founder

3543 Service-Learning and Character Education: One Plus One is More Than Two
Character Education Partnership
1025 Connecticut Avenue NW
Suite 1011
Washington, DC 20036
202-296-7743
800-988-8081
Fax: 202-296-7779
jmazzola@character.org
www.character.org
Leading the nation in helping schools develop people of good character for a just and compassionate society.
Rebecca Sipos, Director Communications
Joe Mazzola, Executive Director

3544 Teacher Created Resources
Teacher Created Resources
6421 Industry Way
Westminster, CA 92683-3652
888-343-4335
800-662-4321
Fax: 800-525-1524
custserv@teachercreated.com
www.teachercreated.com
We publish quality resource books at the early childhood, elementary, and middle school levels. Our books cover all aspects of the curriculum—language arts, social studies, math, science, technology, and the arts.
Ina Levin, Managing Editor
Karen Goldfluss, Managing Editor

3545 Teachers as Educators of Character: Are the Nations Schools of Education Coming Up Short?
Character Education Partnership
1025 Connecticut Avenue NW
Suite 1011
Washington, DC 20036
202-296-7743
800-988-8081
Fax: 202-296-7779
rsipos@character.org
www.character.org
Leading the nation in helping schools develop people of good character for a just and compassionate society.
Henry Huffman, Author
Rebecca Sipos, Director Communications
Joseph W Mazzola, Executive Director

3546 Teachers as Leaders
Phi Delta Kappa Educational Foundation
PO Box 7888
Bloomington, IN 47407-7888
812-339-1156
800-766-1156
Fax: 812-339-0018
www.pdkintl.org
Examines teacher recruitment, retention, professional development and leadership. The central theme of these twenty essays is excellence in education and how to achieve it.
320 pages Hardcover
ISBN: 0-873674-68-5
Donovan R Walling, Author
Donovan R Walling, Director Publications/Resear

3547 Teachers in Publishing
Pike Publishing Company
221 Town Center W
Suite 112
Santa Maria, CA 93458-5083
Editorial, research, sales, consulting, in office positions or travel to learn teachers' needs and instruct new texts.

3548 Teaching About Islam & Muslims in the Public School Classroom
9300 Gardenia Avenue
#B3
Fountain Valley, CA 92708-2253
714-839-2929
Fax: 714-839-2714
117 pages
ISBN: 1-930109-008
Susan Douglas, Author
Shabbir Mansuri, Founding Director

3549 Teaching as the Learning Profession: Handbookof Policy and Practice
Jossey-Bass/Pfeiffer
989 Market Street
San Francisco, CA 94103-1741
415-433-1740
Fax: 415-433-0499
Provides the best essays about the status of teaching, and the contributing writers are among the best thinkers in education today.
426 pages Hardcover
Linda Darling-Hammond, Editor
Gary Sykes, Editor

3550 Teaching for Results
Master Teacher
Leadership Lane
PO Box 1207
Manhattan, KS 66505-1207
800-669-9633
Fax: 800-669-1132
www.masterteacher.com
An easy-to-implement powerful method for helping to ensure sucess in the classroom.
45 pages
ISBN: 1-58992-120-8

3551 Their Best Selves: Building Character Education and Service Learning Together
Character Education Partnership
1025 Connecticut Avenue NW
Suite 1011
Washington, DC 20036
202-296-7743
800-988-8081
Fax: 202-296-7779
rsipos@character.org
www.character.org
Character Education Partnership (CEP) is one of the world's premier character education organizations. It is recognized as a leader in the field and a foremost advocate for developing young people of good character and civic virtue
Joseph Mazzola, Executive Director
David W Fisher, Chairman

3552 Theory of Experiential Education
AEE and Kendall/Hunt Publishing Company
4050 Westmark Drive
PO Box 1840
Dubuque, IA 52004-2624
319-589-1000
800-228-0810
Fax: 563-589-1253
www.kendallhunt.com
This groundbreaking resource looks at the theoretical foundations of experiential education from philosophical, historical, psychological, social and ethical perspectives.
496 pages
ISBN: 0-7872-0262-2
AEE, Author
Karen Berger, Customer Service Assistant

3553 Time to Teach, Time to Learn: Changing the Pace of School
1615 Duke Street
Alexandria, VA 22314
703-528-0700
800-360-6332
Fax: 413-774-1129
info@aasa.org
Giving students the chance to learn and their teachers the chance to teach.
322 pages Softcover
Chip Wood, Author

3554 Top Quality School Process (TQSP)
National School Services
390 Holbrook Drive
Wheeling, IL 60090-5812
847-541-2768
800-262-4511
Fax: 847-541-2553
A customized School Improvement Program that incorporates input from all stakeholders in the educational process to establish baseline data, im-

plement a continuous process of school improvement, and select quality programs for professional development.

3555 US Department of Education: Office of Educational Research & Improvement

National Library of Education
555 New Jersey Avenue NW
Washington, DC 20208-5573
202-219-2230
Fax: 202-219-2030
www2.ed.gov/pubs/TeachersGuide/oeri.htm l

Offers a variety of publications for professional development. The list of sources includes statistical reports, topical reports and effective programs, schools and practices.

John Blake, Reference/Information
Nancy Cavanaugh, Collection Development

3556 Understanding and Relating To Parents Professionally

Master Teacher
Leadership Lane
PO Box 1207
Manhattan, KS 66505-1207
800-669-9633
Fax: 800-669-1132
www.masterteacher.com

From one man with a mission to over sixty employees and growing, The MASTER Teacher has developed and matured. We will continue to provide educators with cutting-edge professional development solutions as we advance into the future.

70 pages
ISBN: 0-914607-65-0

Robert L DeBruyn, Author

3557 Welcome to Teaching and our Schools

Master Teacher
Leadership Lane
PO Box 1207
Manhattan, KS 66505-1207
800-669-9633
800-669-9633
Fax: 800-669-1132
www.masterteacher.com

Sets the stage for teachers so that they can have an enthusiastic and successful year in the classroom.

50 pages
ISBN: 0-914607-49-9

Robert L DeBryon, Author

3558 World Exchange Program Directory

Center for U.N. Studies, GPO Box 2786
Ramna
Dacca 1000, Bangladesh

Offers listings, by geographical location, of exchange programs available to United States and abroad students. Listings include all contact information, schedules, fields and levels of study and bilingual information.

Biennial

3559 You Can Handle Them All

Master Teacher
Leadership Lane
PO Box 1207
Manhattan, KS 66505-1207
800-669-9633
Fax: 800-669-1132
www.masterteacher.com

Encyclopedia of student misbehaviors offering answers that work. one hundred seventeen student misbehaviors are covered.

320 pages
ISBN: 0-914607-04-9

Robert L DeBruyn, Author

3560 Your Personal Mentoring & Planning Guide forthe First 60 Days of Teaching

Master Teacher
Leadership Lane
PO Box 1207
Manhattan, KS 66505-1207
800-669-9633
Fax: 800-669-1132
www.masterteacher.com

In this book we've selected from 32 years of The Master Teacher, the writings we know you would most like your teachers to have to support the first 60 days of the school year.

116 pages
ISBN: 1-58992-056-2

Periodicals

3561 ATEA Journal

ATEA
Dunwoody College of Technology
818 Dunwoody Boulevard
Minneapolis, MN 55403
612-381-3315
Fax: 701-671-2260
info@ateaonline.org
www.ateaonline.org

Official journal of the American Technical Education Association, dedicated to topics related to postsecondary technical education.

Sandra Krebsbach, Ph.D, Executive Director
DeeAnn Bilben, Administrative Assistant

Periodicals

3562 AACTE Briefs

American Association of Colleges for Teacher Ed.
1307 New York Avenue NW
Suite 300
Washington, DC 20005-4701
202-293-2450
Fax: 202-457-8095
aacte@aacte.org
www.aacte.org

To promote the learning of all PK-12 students through high-quality, evidence-based preparation.

4-12 pages Monthly
ISSN: 0731-602x

Kristin McCabe, Publications Specialist/Edit
Aimee J Hall, Meetings Coordinator

3563 Action in Teacher Education

University of Georgia, College of Education
820 Van Vleet Oval
Rome 100
Norman, OK 73019
405-325-1081
Fax: 706-542-4277
educationinformation@ou.edu
www.ou.edu/action

The official publication of the Association of Teacher Educators, serving as a forum for the exchange of information and ideas related to the improvement of teacher education at all levels.

Quarterly

John J Chiodo, Editor
Laura Bolf-Beliveau, Editor

3564 American Educational Research Journal

Columbia University Teachers College
PO Box 51
New York, NY 10027
212-678-3498
Fax: 212-678-4048
www.aer.sagepub.com

Publishes research articles that explore the processes and outcomes of teaching, learning, and human development at all educational levels and in both formal and informal settings.

Quarterly

Lois Weis, Editor
Philip Altbach, Associate Editor

3565 American Educator

American Federation of Teachers
555 New Jersey Avenue NW
Washington, DC 20001-2029
202-879-4420
ae@aft.org
www.aft.org/ae

The professional journal of the American Federation of Teachers is a quarterly magazine covering research and subjects related to K-12 education.

Quarterly

Amy M Hightower, Editor
Jennifer Dubin, Managing Editor

3566 Arts Management in Community Institutions: Summer Training

National Guild of Community Schools of the Arts
520 8th Avenue
Suite 302
New York, NY 10018
212-268-3337
Fax: 212-268-3995
info@natguild.org
www.nationalguild.org

Advances high-quality, community arts education so all people may participate in the arts according to their interests and abilities. Support the creation and development of community arts education organizations by providing research and information resources, professional development and networking opportunities, advocacy, and high-profile leadership.

June

Jonathan Herman, Executive Director
Kenneth T Cole, Associate Director

3567 Balance Sheet

ITP South-Western Publishing
5101 Madison Road
Cincinnati, OH 45227-1427
513-271-8811
800-824-5179
Fax: 800-487-8488

Informational publication for high school accounting educators. Articles contain information about innovations in teaching accounting, producing an extensive line of educational texts and software for K-postsecondary markets.

2x Year

Larry Qualls, Editor
Carol Bross-McMahon, Coordinating Editor

3568 Better Teaching
The Parent Institute
PO Box 7474
Fairfax Station, VA 22039-7474
703-323-9170
800-756-5525
Fax: 703-323-9173
www.parent-institute.com
Newsletter for teachers (grades 1-12) that offers tips and techniques to improve student learning.
Monthly
ISSN: 1061-1495
John Wherry, President

3569 C/S Newsletter
Center for Instructional Services
Purdue University
W. Lafayette, IN 47907
317-494-9454
Contains descriptions of CIS services and articles about instructional techniques.
4 pages 7x Year
Vickie Lojek

3570 Curriculum Brief
International Technology Education Association
1914 Association Drive
Reston, VA 20191-1538
703-860-2100
Fax: 703-860-0353
Seeks to advance technological literacy through professional development activities and publications.
4x Year
Kendall Starkweather, Executive Director

3571 Education & Treatment of Children
Pressley Ridge School
PO Box 6295
Morgantown, WV 26506-3016
304-293-8400
Fax: 304-293-6585
fdowney@wvu.edu
www.educationandtreatmentofchildren.net
A journal devoted to the dissemination of information concerning the development and improvement of services for children and youth. Its primary criterion for publication is that the material be of direct value to educators and other child care professionals in improving their teaching/training effectiveness. Various types of material are appropriate for publication including originial experimental research, experimental replications, adaptations of previously reported research and reviews.
Quarterly
Bernie Fabry, Managing Editor
Daniel E Hursh, Senior Editor

3572 Educational Placement Sources-US
Education Information Services/Instant Alert
PO Box 620662
Newton, MA 2462-662
617-433-0125
Lists 100 organizations in the United States that find positions for teachers, educational administrators, counselors and other professionals. Listings are classified by type, listed alphabetically and offers all contact information.
4 pages Annual
FB Viaux, President

3573 Exceptional Child Education Resources
The Council for Exceptional Children
2900 Crystal Drive
Suite 1000
Arlington, VA 22202-3557
703-620-3660
888-232-7733
Fax: 703-264-1637
askeric@ericir.syr.edu
www.cec.sped.org
A quarterly abstract journal that helps teachers stay abreast of the book, nonprint media, and journal literature in special and gifted education.
Quarterly
ISSN: 0160-4309
Robin D. Brewer, President
Alexander T. Graham, Executive Director

3574 Extensions - Newsletter of the High/Scope Curriculum
High/Scope Educational Research Foundation
600 N River Street
Ypsilanti, MI 48198-2898
734-485-2000
800-587-5639
Fax: 734-485-0704
info@highscope.org
www.highscope.org
Teacher guide for users of the High/Scope curriculum. Articles on classroom strategies, training techniques, problem-solving ideas, and news from the field. Also includes updated training data.
8 pages BiMonthly
ISSN: 0892-5135
Cheryl Polk, President
Steven Schwartz, Chief Financial Officer

3575 Guild Notes Bi-Monthly Newswletter
National Guild of Community Schools of the Arts
520 8th Avenue
Suite 302, 3rd Floor
New York, NY 10018
212-268-3337
Fax: 212-268-3995
info@natguild.org
www.nationalguild.org
Bi-Monthly
Terry Hueneke, Chairman
Jonathan Herman, Executive Director

3576 Infocus: A Newsletter of the University Continuing Education Association
University Continuing Education Association
1 Dupont Circle NW
Suite 615
Washington, DC 20036-1134
202-659-3130
Fax: 202-785-0374
kjkohl@ucea.edu
www.upcea.edu
Reports on higher education activities, federal legislation and government agencies, innovative programming at institutions across the country; member institutions; trends in continuing and part-time education; resources; professional development opportunities within the field; and changes in member personnel.
12-20 pages Monthly
Roger Whitaker, President
Robert Hansen, Chief Executive Officer

3577 Innovator
Alumni Association of the University of Michigan
200 Fletcher St.
Ann Arbor, MI 48109-1007
734-764-0394
800-874-4764
Fax: 734-615-3151
m.alumni@umich.edu
alumni.umich.edu
For professional educators and alumni of University of Michigan's School of Education.
20 pages Quarterly
Eric Warden, Contact

3578 International Journal of Instructional Media
Westwood Press
149 Goose Lane
Tolland, CT 6084-3822
860-875-5484
PLSleeman@aol.com
www.adprima.com
A professional journal directly responsive to the need for precise information on the application of media to your instructional and training needs.
Quarterly
Dr Phillip J Sleeman, Executive Editor
Dr Bruce R Ledford, Associate Editor

3579 Intervention in School and Clinic
Pro-Ed., Inc.
8700 Shoal Creek Boulevard
Austin, TX 78757-6897
512-451-3246
800-897-3202
Fax: 800-397-7633
general@proedinc.com
www.proedinc.com
The hands-on how-to resource for teachers and clinicians working with students (especially LD and BD) for whom minor curiculum and environmental medications are ineffective.
64 pages 5x Year Magazine
ISSN: 1053-4512
Judith K Voress, Periodicals Director
Brenda Smith Myles, Editor

3580 Journal of Classroom Interaction
University of Houston-University Park
4800 Calhoun Rd
University of Houston
Houston, TX 77204-5026
713-743-2255
Fax: 713-743-8664
jci@bayou.uh.edu
www.uh.edu
The Journal is a semi-annual publication devoted to empirical investigations and theoretical papers dealing with observation techniques, research on student and teacher behavior, and other issues relevant to the domain of classroom interaction.
Bi-Annually
Renu Khator, Chancellor
Paula Myrick Short, Vice Chancellor

3581 Journal of Economic Education
Heldref Publications
1319 18th Street NW
Washington, DC 20036-1802
202-296-6267
800-365-9753
Fax: 202-296-5149
www.indiana.edu/~econed/index.html
The Journal of Economic Education offers original articles on innovations in and evaluations of teaching techniques, materials, and programs in economics
Quarterly
William E Becker, Executive Editor

3582 **Journal of Experiential Education**
Association for Experiential Education
1435 Yarmouth Ave
Suite 104
Boulder, CO 80304-2043
303-440-8844
866-522-8337
Fax: 303-440-9581
webmaster@aee.org
www.aee.org
Association for Experiential Education develops and promotes experiential education. The association is committed to supporting professional development, theoretical advancement and the evaluation of experiential education worldwide.
64 pages 3x Year
ISSN: 1053-8259
Maurie Lung, President
Marin Burton, Secretary

3583 **Journal on Excellence in College Teaching**
Miami University
Miami University
Oxford, OH 45056
513-529-9265
Fax: 531-529-9264
wentzegw@muohio.edu
celt.muohio.edu/ject
A peer-reviewed journal published by and for faculty at colleges and universities to increase student learning through effective teaching, interest in and enthusiasm for the profession of teaching, and communication among faculty about their classroom experiences. The Journal provides a scholarly forum for faculty to share proven, innovative pedagogies and thoughtful, inspirational insights about teaching.
Journal 3x/Yr
ISSN: 1052-4800
Gregg Wentzell, Author
Gregg Wentzell, Managing Editor
Milton D. Cox, Editor-in-Chief

3584 **Journalism Education Today Magazine**
Journalism Education Association
828 Mid-Campus Drive S
105 Kedzie Hall
Manhattan, KS 66506-1505
785-532-5532
866-532-5532
Fax: 785-532-5563
bradleywilson08@gmail.com
jea.org
A publication providing educational perspectives on the subjects of teaching, scholastic media strategy, pedagogical updates, journalism research and more to the members of the Journalism Education Association.
Bradley Wilson, Ph.D, Publications Editor
Pam Boller, Advertising Coordinator

3585 **NCRTL Special Report**
National Center for Research on Teacher Education
Michigan State University
East Lansing, MI 48824
517-355-9302
floden@msu.edu
ncrtl.msu.edu
Membership news and updates.
Robert E. Floden, Contact

3586 **NCSIE Inservice**
National Council of States on Inservice Education
Syracuse University
402 Huntington Hall
Syracuse, NY 13244
315-443-1870
Fax: 315-443-9082
Professional development, staff development and inservice education.
20 pages Quarterly
James Collins

3587 **On The Go! for the Educational Office Professional**
Master Teacher
One Leadership Lane
PO Box 1207
Manhattan, KS 66502-1207
800-669-9633
Fax: 800-669-1132
www.masterteacher.com
Positive, practical, and successful insights and techniques to help you manage and work with your support staff.
1 pages Monthly Newsletter
Tracey H DeBruyn, Executive Editor

3588 **On-The-Go For Educational Office Professionals**
Master Teacher
One Leadership Lane
PO Box 1207
Manhattan, KS 66502-1207
785-539-0555
800-669-9633
Fax: 800-669-1132
www.masterteacher.com
The publication that provides you with great articles to complete your in-house newsletters and newsletters to parents, without fear of copyright violations.
1 pages Monthly Newsletter
Erica Parkinson, Executive Editor

3589 **Paraeducator's Guide to Instructional & Curricular Modifications**
Master Teacher
One Leadership Lane
PO Box 1207
Manhattan, KS 66502-1207
800-669-9633
Fax: 800-669-1132
www.masterteacher.com
An indispensible tool your paras can use to understand, plan for and carry out appropriate modification for students with all types of special needs.
100 pages
ISBN: 0-914607-88-X
Wendy Dover, Author

3590 **Pennsylvania Education**
Pennsylvania Department of Education
333 Market Street
Harrisburg, PA 17126-2210
717-783-6788
Fax: 717-783-8230
ra-edwebmaster@pa.gov
www.pde.state.pa.us
The mission of the Pennsylvania Department of Education is to assist the General Assembly, the Governor, the Secretary of Education and Pennsylvania educators in providing for the maintenance and support of a thorough and efficient system of education.
8-10 pages 8x Year
Gary Tuma, Press Secretary
Beth Boyer, Information Specialist

3591 **Performance Improvement Journal**
International Society for Performance
PO Box 13035
Suite 260
Silver Spring, MD 20910-2753
301-587-8570
Fax: 301-587-8573
info@ispi.org
www.ispi.org
To develop and recognize the proficiency of its members and advocate the use of Human Performance Technology.
48 pages Monthly
ISSN: 1090-8811
Mary Ellen Kassotakis, President
Rhonda Buckley, Interim Executive Director

3592 **Preventing School Failure**
Heldref Publications
325 Chestnut Street
Suite 800
Philadelphia, PA 19106-1802
215-625-8900
800-354-1420
Fax: 202-296-5149
customer.service@taylorandfrancis.com
www.heldref.org
The journal for educators and parents seeking strategies to promote the success of students who have learning and behavior problems. It includes practical examples of programs and practices that help children and youth in schools, clinics, correctional institutions, and other settings. Articles are written by educators and concern teaching children with various kinds of special needs.
48 pages Quarterly
ISSN: 1045-988X
Mary O'Donnell, Managing Editor

3593 **Prevention Researcher**
Integrated Research
333 South Hope Street
Floor 48
Los Angeles, CA 90071
541-683-9278
800-929-2955
Fax: 541-683-2621
orders@TPRonline.org
globalsportsdevelopment.org
A quarterly journal that uses a straightforward and easy-to-read approach to present the most current research and developments in adolescent behavioral research. In addition to cutting-edge, evidence-based research it also examines exemplary prevention programs and strategies that can help youth workers see which of today's best practices are most successful.
24 pages Magazine/Quarterly
ISSN: 1086-4385
Melanie Raffle, Vice President of Operations
Brooke Lusk, Director of Communication

3594 **Progressive Teacher**
Progressive Publishing Company
2678 Henry Street
Augusta, GA 30904-4656
770-868-1691
Offers new information and updates for the improvement and development of higher education.
Quarterly
ISSN: 0033-0825
MS Adcock

3595 **Retaining Great Teachers**
Master Teacher
One Leadership Lane
PO Box 1207
Manhattan, KS 66502-1207
800-669-9633
Fax: 800-669-1132
www.masterteacher.com

The Retaining Great Teachers Book is a systemic approach for attracting, mentoring, supporting, and retaining new and veteran teacher.

85 pages
ISBN: 1-58992-097-X

Michael J Lovett PhD, Author

3596 Rural Educator-Journal for Rural and Small Schools

National Rural Education Association
Colorado State University
Fort Collins, CO 80523-1588
970-491-6444
Fax: 970-491-1317
presofc@lamar.colostate.edu
www.colostate.edu

Official journal of the NREA. A nationally recognized publication that features timely and informative articles written by leading rural educators from all levels of education. All NREA members are encouraged to submit research articles and items of general information for publication.

40 pages Quarterly Magazine
ISSN: 0273-446X

Anthony A Frank, President
Joseph T Newlin, Editor

3597 TED Newsletter

The Council for Exceptional Children
1920 Association Drive
Reston, VA 20191-1545
703-620-3660
888-232-7733
Fax: 703-264-9494
www.tedcec.org

Newsletter of the Teacher Education Division offering information about TED activities, upcoming events, current trends and practices, state and national legislation, recently published materials and practical information of interest to persons involved in the preparation and continuing professional development of effective professionals in special education and related service fields.

3x Year

Mary Anne Prater, President
Marcia Rock, Vice President

3598 TESOL Journal: A Journal of Teaching and Classroom Research

Teachers of English to Speakers of Other Languages
1925 Ballenger Avenue
Suite 550
Alexandria, VA 22314-6820
703-836-0774
Fax: 703-836-7864
info@tesol.org
www.tesol.org

TESOL's mission is to develop the expertise of its members and others involved in teaching English to speakers of other languages to help them foster communication in diverse settings. The association advances standards for professional preparation and employment, continuing education, and student programs, produces programs, services, and products, and promotes advocacy to further the profession. TESOL has 91 affiliates worldwide.

50 pages Quarterly

Yilin Sun, President
Rosa Aronson, Executive Director

3599 Teacher Education Reports

Feistritzer Publishing
4401-A Connecticut Avenue NW
#212
Washington, DC 20008-2302
202-822-8280
Fax: 202-822-8284
www.ncei.com

Covers the field of teacher education for elementary and secondary schools, including pre-service preparation, in-service training and professional development, related federal programs, legislation and funding.

8 pages BiWeekly

David T Chester, Editor

3600 Teacher Education and Special Education

The Council for Exceptional Children
1920 Association Drive
Reston, VA 20191-1545
703-620-3660
Fax: 352-392-7159
eric.ed.gov

Contains information on current research, exemplary practices, timely issues, legislation, book reviews, and new programs and materials relative to the preparation and continuing professional development of effective professionals in special education and related service fields.

Quarterly

Vivian Correa, Editor

3601 Teacher Magazine

6935 Arlington Road
Suite 100
Bethesda, MD 20814-5233
301-280-3100
800-346-1834
Fax: 301-280-3250
webeditors@epe.org
www.edweek.org

Our primary mission is to help raise the level of awareness and understanding among professionals and the public of important issues in American education.

Kevin Bushweller, Executive Editor
Gregory Chronister, Executive Editor

3602 Teacher's Guide to Classroom Management

Economics Press
12 Daniel Road
Fairfield, NJ 7004-2507
973-227-1224
www.marketingconsultants.cc

Bulletins showing teachers how to solve problems and avoid problematic situations.

BiWeekly

Alan Yohalem, President

3603 Teachers in Touch

ISM Independent School Management
1316 N Union Street
Wilmington, DE 19806-2594
302-656-4944
800-955-4944
Fax: 302-656-0647
smedina@isminc.com
isminc.com

Faculty professional development publication with strategies for career satisfaction, good teaching practices and stress-reducing techniques. The forum for professional sharing for private-independent school educators.

4 pages 5x Year

Rozanne S Elliott, Publisher
Kelly Rawlings, Editor

3604 Teaching Education

University of South Carolina, College of Education
Wardlaw College
Room 231
Columbia, SC 29208-1
803-777-6301
Fax: 803-777-3068
www.ashe.ws

Focuses on the actual profession of teaching and new methodology by which to learn.

2x Year

Laura Perna, President
James T. Sears, PhD, Editor

3605 Techniques-Connecting Education and Careers

Association for Career and Technical Education
1410 King Street
Alexandria, VA 22314-2749
703-683-3111
800-826-9972
Fax: 703-683-7424
sackley@acteonline.org
www.acteonline.org

To provide leadership in developing an educated, prepared, adaptable and competitive workforce.

Newsletter/Magazine

Peter Magnuson, Director of Programs/Communi
Jan Bray, Executive Director

3606 Technology Integration for Teachers

Master Teacher
One Leadership Lane
Po Box 1207
Manhattan, KS 66502-1207
785-539-0555
800-669-9633
Fax: 800-669-1132
www.masterteacher.com

The publication that provides teachers with innovative strategies for integratinjg technology into the classroom.

Monthly Newsletter

Brad Roberts, Executive Editor

3607 The Board

Master Teacher
One Leadership Lane
Po Box 1207
Manhattan, KS 66502-1207
785-539-0555
800-669-9633
Fax: 800-669-1132
www.masterteacher.com

A complete program of in-service training for school board members.

Robert DeBruyn, Executive Editor

3608 The Professor In The Classroom

Master Teacher
One Leadership Lane
PO Box 1207
Manhattan, KS 66502-1207
785-539-0555
800-669-9633
Fax: 800-669-1132
www.masterteacher.com

From one man with a mission to over sixty employees and growing, The MASTER Teacher has developed and matured. We will continue to provide educators with cutting-edge professional development solutions as we advance into the future.

1 pages Semi-Monthly

Robert DeBruyn, Author

3609 Today's Catholic Teacher
2621 Dryden Road
Suite 300
Dayton, OH 45439
937-293-1415
800-523-4625
Fax: 937-293-1310
service@peterli.com
www.catholicteacher.com
Today's Catholic Teacher magazine is written for you, a teacher in a Catholic school. Each issue is filled with information that will help you succeed in the classroom
72 pages Bimonthly
ISSN: 0040-8441
Cullen Schippe, President/ Publisher
Chris Orsborne, VP/ COO

3610 Training Research Journal: The Science and Practice of Training
Educational Technology Publications
700 Paliside Avenue
Englewood Cliffs, NJ 7632
Fax: 201-871-4009
contact @mcweadon.com
mcweadon.com
Peer-reviewed publication, published once yearly by Educational Technology Publications, is now in its fourth volume. Provides a high-quality, peer-reviewed forum for theoretical and empirical work relevant to training.
Annually
Badrul H. Khan, Founder
Kelee Plagis, Advisor

Software, Hardware & Internet Resources

3611 Analog & Digital Peripherals
PO Box 499
Troy, OH 45373-3585
937-339-2241
800-758-1041
Fax: 937-339-0070
info@adpi.com
www.adpi.com
Established in 1978 to provide OEM manufacturers and end users with practical solutions in data logging, storage, and retrieval as well as program loading and back-up.
Lyle Ellicott

3612 E-Z Grader Software
E-Z Grader Company
PO Box 23608
Chagrin Falls, OH 44023
800-432-4018
Fax: 800-689-2772
ezgrader@voyager.net
www.ezgrader.com
Electronic guidebook designed by teachers for teachers.

3613 K12jobs.Com
PO Box 210811
West Palm Beach, FL 33421
E-mail: beth@k12jobs.com
k12jobs.com
To provide schools with an efficient and cost-effective recruiting tool, providing service and opportunities to institutions and job seekers alike.
Also: K-12jobs.Com
Beth Jones, CSR & General Information

3614 KidsCare Childcare Management Software
770 Cochituate Road
Framingham, MA 1701-4672
508-875-3451
Sells software programs to education professionals involved in childcare to aid their development and understanding.

3615 Mental Edge
Learning ShortCuts
PO Box 382367
Germantown, TN 38183-2367
901-218-8163
Fax: 309-406-5358
feedback@learningshortcuts.com
www.learningshortcuts.com
The Mental Edge is specifically designed to facilitate review and reinforcement. It is the quickest, easiest, and most thorough way to bring the things that have been learned back to mind in preparation for any testing scenario.

3616 The Center For The Future of Teaching and Learning
Center for the Future of Teaching & Learning
730 Harrison Street
Suite 220
San Francisco, CA 94170
415-565-3000
877-493-7833
Fax: 415-565-3012
info@cftl.org
www.cftl.org
A not-for-profit organization dedicated to strengthening teacher development policy and practice.
Margaret Gaston, President/Executive Director
Tacy C. Ashby, Vice President

3617 www.aasa.org
American Association of School Administrators
1615 Duke Street
Suite 700
Alexandria, VA 22314-1730
703-528-0700
Fax: 703-841-1543
info@aasa.org
www.aasa.org
Supports and develops effective school system leaders who are dedicated to the highest quality public education for all children.
Randall H Collins, President
Mark T Bielang, President-Elect

3618 www.classbuilder.Com
Class Builder
www.classbuilder.com
Free teachers toolbox! Grade book, Create tests, Reports, Lessons, Distance Learning Courseware, and more.
Internet Only Access
Edhelper.Com, Author

3619 www.ed.gov/free
Federal Resources for Educational Excellence
202-401-1444
tech@ed.gov
tech.ed.gov
Teaching and learning resources from Federal Agencies
Richard Culatta, Director
Bernadette Adams, Senior Policy Advisor

3620 www.eduverse.com
eduverse.com
Leading Internet e-Knowledge software developer building core technologies for powering international distance education.

3621 www.freeteachingaids.com
Free Teaching Aids.com
214 Center Street
Beaver Dam, WI 53956
920-210-3684
888-951-4469
info@monumentalhosting.com
www.monumentalhosting.com
Guides for finding free resources for teachers.

3622 www.gsn.org
Global SchoolNet Foundation
270 N. El Camino Real
Suitte 395
Encinitas, CA 92024
760-635-0001
Fax: 760-635-0003
helper2009@globalschoolnet.org
www.globalschoolnet.org
Collaborative projects, communication tools and professional development.
Yvonne Marie Andres, President
John St. Clair, Vice President

3623 www.imagescape.com/helpweb/www/oneweb.html
An Overview of the World Wide Web
E-mail: webmaster@imagescape.com
www.imagescape.com/helpweb/www/oneweb.html

3624 www.learningpage.com
1840 E River Road
Suite 320
Tucson, AZ 85718
E-mail: learningpage@learningpage.com.
www.learningpage.com
LearningPage provides a huge collection of professionally produced instructional materials you can download and print.

3625 www.mmhschool.com
McGraw Hill School Division
220 E Danieldale Road
Desoto, TX 75115
800-442-9685
Fax: 972-228-1982
www.mhschool.com
Dedicated to educating children and to helping educational professionals by providing the highest quality materials and services.
John Predmore, Privacy Official

3626 www.nprinc.com
National Professional Resources
25 S Regent Street
Port Chester, NY 10573
914-937-8879
800-453-7461
Fax: 914-937-9327
service@nprinc.com
www.nprinc.com
Produces videos/DVDs and publishes books on the most significant and current topical areas in the educational arena. New to this product line are laminated reference guides that provide a succinct summary of the topic being addressed.
Robert M. Hanson, Founder/ President
Helene Hanson, Vice President

3627 www.onlinelearning.net
OnlineLearning.net
12975 Coral Tree Place
Los Angeles, CA 90066

800-669-9011
customerservice@laureate-inc.com
www.canter.net
Source for teacher education online.

Susan Ko, Vice President

3628 www.pagestarworld.com
Pagestar
E-mail: orders@pagestarworld.com
www.scrase.com
Software products that are specifically designed for teachers. Over 600 electronic forms that are commonly used by teachers for planning, administering, delivering and assessing student learning.

3629 www.pbs.org
PBS TeacherSource
2100 Crystal Drive
Arlington, VA 22202
www.pbs.org
Offers all Americans the opportunity to explore new ideas and new worlds through television and online content.

Jonathan Barzilay, Chief Operating Officer

3630 www.pbs.org/uti/quicktips.html
QuickTips
2100 Crystal Drive
Arlington, VA 22202
www.pbs.org
On understanding and using the Internet, you'll find tips on navigating the Web.

Jonathan Barzilay, Chief Operating Officer

3631 www.rhlschool.com
RHL School
E-mail: webmaster@rhlschool.net
www.rhlschool.com
Free ready to use quality worksheets for teaching, reinforcement,and review.

3632 www.sanjuan.edu/select/structures.html
San Juan Select - Structures
E-mail: info@sanjuan.edu
www.sanjuan.edu
A Web site that examines various ways to structure and facilitate student projects using Internet capabilities. Each suggestion is accompanied by a specific example of how that structure can be or is being used on the Internet.

San Juan, Contact

3633 www.schoolrenaissance.com
School Renaissance Model
2911 Peach Street
PO Box 8036
Wisconsin Rapids, WI 54495-8036
715-424-3636
800-338-4204
Fax: 715-424-4242
answers@renlearn.com
www.renaissance.com
Advance technology for essential practice. Makes the practice component of reading, math, and writing curriculum more personalized and effective.

John J. Luynch, CEO
Mary T. Minch, VP/ CFO

3634 www.teachingjobs.com
The Teachers Employment Network
510-653-1521
info@teachingjobs.com
www.teachingjobs.com
Leading resource for education employment.

3635 www.usajobs.opm.gov/b1c.htm
Overseas Employment Info- Teachers
US Office of Personnel Management
1900 E Street, NW
Washington, DC 20415-1000
202-606-1800
www.opm.gov
Covers eligibility, position categories and special requirements, application procedures, program information and entitlement, housing, living/working conditions, shipment of household goods, and complete application forms and guidance.

Katherine Archuleta, Director
Earl L. Gay, Senior Advisor

3636 www.webworkshops.com
Web Work Shops
www.webworkshops.com
A series of on-line courses, designed to prepare teachers to integrate both the Internet and classroom computer applications into daily lessons.

Training Materials

3637 At-Risk Students: Identification and Assistance Strategies
Center for the Study of Small/Rural Schools
555 E Constitution Street
Room 138
Norman, OK 73072-7820
405-325-1450
Fax: 405-325-7075
jcsimmons@ou.edu
cssrs.ou.edu
The Center for the Study of Small/Rural Schools is a cooperative effort between the University of Oklahoma's Colleges of Education and Continuing Education. Endorsed by the National Rural Education Association as one of its five recognized rural education research

Video

Jan C Simmons, Program Director

3638 Character Education: Making a Difference
Character Education Partnership
1634 I Street NW
Suite 550
Washington, DC 20036
202-296-7743
800-988-8081
Fax: 202-296-7779
information@character.org
www.character.org
Leading the nation in helping schools develop people of good character for a just and compassionate society.

Becky Sipos, President/ CEO
Sheril Morgan, Director

3639 Character Education: Restoring Respect & Responsibility in our Schools
Master Teacher
One Leadership Lane
Po Box 1207
Manhattan, KS 66502-1207
785-539-0555
800-669-9633
Fax: 800-669-1132
www.masterteacher.com
Provides a comprehensive model for character education in our nations schools. Specific classroom stategies as well as school wide approaches are outlines in a clear and compelling fashion.

Thomas Lickona PhD, Author

3640 Cisco Educational Archives
University of North Carolina at Chapel Hill
170 W Tasman Drive
Po Box 1207
San Jose, CA 95134-3455
408-526-4000
800-553-6387
www.cisco.com
Focus on business operations, product innovation and design, and customer solutions. We develop products with minimal environmental impact and extend our technology to reduce environmental footprints globally.

John T Chambers, Chairman / CEO
Frank Calderoni, Executive VP/CFO

3641 Classroom Teacher's Guide for Working with Paraeducators Video Set
Master Teacher
One Leadership Lane
PO Box 1207
Manhattan, KS 66502-1207
785-539-0555
800-669-9633
Fax: 800-669-1132
www.masterteacher.com
Covers a range of nuts-and-bolts topics including why the job duties of paras have changed so much over the years, what a classroom teacher needs to know to get started working effectively with a para. Useful tips for managing another adult, and how para factor into the planning process.

Wendy Dover, Author

3642 Clinical Play Therapy Videos: Child-Centered Developmental & Relationship Play Therapy
University of North Texas
425 S. Welch St.
Complex 2
Denton, TX 76203-829
940-565-3864
Fax: 940-565-4461
cpt@unt.edu
cpt.unt.edu
Encourage the unique development and emotional growth of children through the process of play therapy, a dynamic interpersonal relationship between a child and a therapist trained in play therapy procedures.

Garry Landreth PhD, Founder
Sue Bratton PhD, Director

3643 Conferencing with Students & Parents Video Series
Master Teacher
One Leadership Lane
PO Box 1207
Manhattan, KS 66502-1207
800-669-9633
800-669-9633
Fax: 800-669-1132
www.masterteacher.com
Will help teachers turn both formal and informal conferences with students and parents into opportunities for student success.

Robert L DeBruyn, Author/Publisher

3644 Conflict Resolution Strategies in Schools
Center for the Study of Small/Rural Schools
555 E Constitution Street
Room 138
Norman, OK 73072-7820
405-325-1450
Fax: 405-325-7075
jcsimmons@ou.edu
cssrs.ou.edu

Series IV
Video
Jan C Simmons, Program Director

3645 Conover Company
4 Brookwood Court
Appleton, WI 54914-8618
800-933-1933
Fax: 800-933-1943
sales@conovercompany.com
www.conovercompany.com
Developing training programs for industry. Provide off-the-shelf as well as custom sales and marketing, training, presentation, and application programs that connect learning to the workplace
Rebecca Schmitz, Member

3646 Cooperative Learning Strategies
Center for the Study of Small/Rural Schools
555 E Constitution Street
Room 138
Norman, OK 73072-7820
405-325-1450
Fax: 405-325-7075
jcsimmons@ou.edu
cssrs.ou.edu
Series I
Video
Jan C Simmons, Program Director

3647 Creating Schools of Character Video Series
Master Teacher
One Leadership Lane
PO Box 1207
Manhattan, KS 66502-1207
785-539-0555
800-669-9633
Fax: 800-669-1132
www.masterteacher.com
Visit a Blue Ribbon School of excellence and hear staff and others discuss how to create or improve a whole school charecter education program.

ISBN: 0-914607-90-1

3648 Crisis Management in Schools
Center for the Study of Small/Rural Schools
555 E Constitution Street
Room 138
Norman, OK 73072-7820
405-325-1450
Fax: 405-325-7075
jcsimmons@ou.edu
cssrs.ou.edu
Series IV
Video
Jan C Simmons, Program Director

3649 Critical Thinking Video Set
Master Teacher
One Leadership Lane
PO Box 1207
Manhattan, KS 66502-1207
785-539-0555
800-669-9633
Fax: 800-669-1132
www.masterteacher.com
Will help teachers challange students to think in a new way. Research shows that when we engage students in critical and creative though, retention increases tremendously.

ISBN: 1-58992-079-1

3650 Curriculum Alignment: Improving Student Learning
Center for the Study of Small/Rural Schools
555 E Constitution Street
Room 138
Norman, OK 73072-7820
405-325-1450
Fax: 405-325-7075
jcsimmons@ou.edu
cssrs.ou.edu
Series I
Video
Jan C Simmons, Program Director

3651 Datacad
20 Tower Lane
P.O. Box 815
Simsbury, CT 6070
860-217-0490
800-394-2231
Fax: 860-217-1866
info@datacad.com
www.datacad.com
DATACAD's product development, sales, and marketing activities are managed at the corporate headquarters in Avon, Connecticut
Mark F Madura, President/CEO
David A Giessleman, Senior Vice President and CT

3652 Discipline Techniques you can Master in a Minute Video Series
Master Teacher
One Leadership Lane
PO Box 1207
Manhattan, KS 66502-1207
800-669-9633
Fax: 800-669-1132
www.masterteacher.com
he MASTER Teacher provides essential solutions to meet the professional development needs of educators at all levels-from the paraeductor to the superintendent. For over 30 years, we have provided practical strategies to inspire, enrich, and motivate educators.

ISBN: 1-58992-040-6
Robert L DeBruyn, Founder

3653 Educational Productions Inc
7101 Wisconsin Avenue
Suite 700
Bethesda, MD 20814
800-950-4949
800-637-3652
Fax: 301-634-0826
custserv@edpro.com
teachingstrategies.com
To increase the skills and understanding of the adults who work with, teach and care for young children.
Linda Freedman, President
Rae Latham, Vice-President

3654 Eleven Principals of Effective Character Education
Master Teacher
One Leadership Lane
PO Box 1207
Manhattan, KS 66502-1207
800-669-9633
Fax: 800-669-1132
www.masterteacher.com
Takes you to schools in Maryland, New York, and Missouri, where quality character education programs are being implemented by skilled and resourceful staff.

ISBN: 1-887943-13-7
Thomas Lickona PhD, Author

3655 Eleven Principles of Effective Character Education
Character Education Partnership
1634 I Street NW
Suite 550
Washington, DC 20036
202-296-7743
800-988-8081
Fax: 202-296-7779
information@character.org
www.character.org
Leading the nation in helping schools develop people of good character for a just and compassionate society.
Becky Sipos, President/ CEO
Sheril Morgan, Director

3656 Eye on Education
7625 Empire Drive
Florence, KY 41042-2919
888-299-5350
800-634-7064
Fax: 914-833-0761
orders@taylorandfrancis.com
www.routledge.com
Books on performance-based learning and assessment.

3657 Great Classroom Management Series DVD
Master Teacher
One Leadership Lane
PO Box 1207
Manhattan, KS 66502-1207
800-669-9633
Fax: 800-669-1132
www.masterteacher.com
Effestive classroom management is getting more difficult everday. teachers face increasing demands and expectations in ebery aspect of their jobs.

ISBN: 0-914607-90-1

3658 Great Classroom Management Video Series VHS
Master Teacher
One Leadership Lane
PO Box 1207
Manhattan, KS 66502-1207
800-669-9633
Fax: 800-669-1132
www.masterteacher.com
Effective classroom management is getting more difficult everyday. teachers face increasing demands and expectations in everyday. Teachers face increasing demands and expectations in every aspect of their jobs.

ISBN: 1-58992-121-6

3659 Handling Chronically Disruptive Students at Risk Video Series
Master Teacher
One Leadership Lane
PO Box 1207
Manhattan, KS 66502-1207
800-669-9633
Fax: 800-669-1132
www.masterteacher.com
Implement and utlize a CARE couscil, develop and individual Action plan, strategies for enhancing individual action plan.

ISBN: 1-58992-031-7

3660 Hearlihy & Company
Po Box 1708
Pittsburg, KS 66762-1747
866-622-1003
Fax: 800-443-2260

orders@hearlihy.com
www.hearlihy.com
Training and installation for schools purchasing modular labratories.

Kevin Bolte, Contact

3661 Improving Parent/Educator Relationships
Center for the Study of Small/Rural Schools
555 E Constitution Street
Room 138
Norman, OK 73072-7820
405-325-1450
Fax: 405-325-7075
jcsimmons@ou.edu
cssrs.ou.edu
Series I

Video

Jan C Simmons, Program Director

3662 Improving Student Thinking in the Content Area
Center for the Study of Small/Rural Schools
555 E Constitution Street
Room 138
Norman, OK 73072-7820
405-325-1450
Fax: 405-325-7075
jcsimmons@ou.edu
cssrs.ou.edu
Series II

Video

Jan C Simmons, Program Director

3663 Inclusion: The Next Step the Video Series
Master Teacher
One Leadership Lane
PO Box 1207
Manhattan, KS 66502-1207
800-669-9633
Fax: 800-669-1132
www.masterteacher.com
Will help you propel your inclusion efforts to a new level of success giving you the necessary insights and stategies for building consensus; weighing your program, curriculum, and instructional options.

ISBN: 1-58992-012-0

Wendy Dover, Author

3664 Integrating Technology into the Curriculum Video Series
Master Teacher
One Leadership Lane
PO Box 1207
Manhattan, KS 66502-1207
800-669-9633
Fax: 800-669-1132
www.masterteacher.com
Gives teachers the tools and strategies they need to make information technology work for then and for students while empowering then to teach the skills necessary for students to be productive in a technology driven world.

ISBN: 1-58992-007-Y

3665 International Clearinghouse for the Advancement of Science Teaching
University of Maryland
Benjamin Building
Room 226
College Park, MD 20742-1100
301-405-1000
Fax: 301-314-9055
www.umd.edu
Provides curriculum information about science and mathematics teaching.

Wallace D. Loh, President
Mary Ann Rankin, Vice President

3666 Lesson Plans and Modifications for Inclusionand Collaborative Classrooms
Master Teacher
One Leadership Lane
PO Box 1207
Manhattan, KS 66502-1207
800-669-9633
Fax: 800-669-1132
www.masterteacher.com
Discover specific strategies lesson plans and activity modifications to enhance learning for all students in the inclusive classroom.

ISBN: 1-58992-022-8

3667 Managing Students Without Coercion
Center for the Study of Small/Rural Schools
555 E Constitution Street
Room 138
Norman, OK 73072-7820
405-325-1450
Fax: 405-325-7075
jcsimmons@ou.edu
cssrs.ou.edu
Series II

Video

Jan C Simmons, Program Director

3668 Mentoring Teachers to Mastery Video Series
Master Teacher
One Leadership Lane
PO Box 1207
Manhattan, KS 66502-1207
800-669-9633
Fax: 800-669-1132
www.masterteacher.com
The MASTER Teacher's e-learning solutions provide cost-effective, subscription-based systems that help meet educators' time demands and continuous learning needs.

ISBN: 1-58992-001-5

3669 Motivating Students in the Classroom Video Series
Master Teacher
One Leadership Lane
PO Box 1207
Manhattan, KS 66502-1207
800-669-9633
Fax: 800-669-1132
www.masterteacher.com
The MASTER Teacher has developed and matured.We will continue to provide educators with cutting-edge professional development solutions as we advance into the future

ISBN: 1-58992-074-0

3670 Multicultural Education: Teaching to Diversity
Center for the Study of Small/Rural Schools
555 E Constitution Street
Room 138
Norman, OK 73072-7820
405-325-1450
Fax: 405-325-7075
jcsimmons@ou.edu
cssrs.ou.edu
Series II

Video

Jan C Simmons, Program Director

3671 Outcome-Based Education: Making it Work
Center for the Study of Small/Rural Schools
555 E Constitution Street
Room 138
Norman, OK 73072-7820
405-325-1450
Fax: 405-325-7075
jcsimmons@ou.edu
cssrs.ou.edu
Series III

Video

Jan C Simmons, Program Director

3672 Overview of Prevention: A Social Change Model
Center for the Study of Small/Rural Schools
555 E Constitution Street
Room 138
Norman, OK 73072-7820
405-325-1450
Fax: 405-325-7075
jcsimmons@ou.edu
cssrs.ou.edu
Prevention Series

Video

Jan C Simmons, Program Director

3673 Quality School
Center for the Study of Small/Rural Schools
555 E Constitution Street
Room 138
Norman, OK 73072-7820
405-325-1450
Fax: 405-325-7075
jcsimmons@ou.edu
cssrs.ou.edu
Series II

Video

Jan C Simmons, Program Director

3674 SAP Today
Performance Resource Press
1270 Rankin Drive
Suite F
Troy, MI 48083-2843
800-453-7733
Fax: 800-499-5718
Overview offers the basics of student assistance.

3675 School-Wide Strategies for Retaining Great Teachers Video Series
Master Teacher
One Leadership Lane
PO Box 1207
Manhattan, KS 66502-1207
800-669-9633
Fax: 800-669-1132
www.masterteacher.com
You will hear proven strategies for supporting new teachers through all those typical expirences that cansabatage their efforts and cause them to leave your district or even abandon teaching all together.

ISBN: 1-58992-098-8

3676 Site-Based Management
Center for the Study of Small/Rural Schools
555 E Constitution Street
Room 138
Norman, OK 73072-7820

405-325-1450
Fax: 405-325-7075
jcsimmons@ou.edu
cssrs.ou.edu
Series III

Video

Jan C Simmons, Program Director

3677 Strategic Planning for Outcome-Based Education
Center for the Study of Small/Rural Schools
555 E Constitution Street
Room 138
Norman, OK 73072-7820
405-325-1450
Fax: 405-325-7075
jcsimmons@ou.edu
cssrs.ou.edu
Series II

Video

Jan C Simmons, Program Director

3678 Strengthening the Family: An Overview of a Holistic Family Wellness Model
Center for the Study of Small/Rural Schools
555 E Constitution Street
Room 138
Norman, OK 73072-7820
405-325-1450
Fax: 405-325-7075
jcsimmons@ou.edu
cssrs.ou.edu
Prevention Series

Video

Jan C Simmons, Program Director

3679 Students-at-Risk Video Series
Master Teacher
One Leadership Lane
PO Box 1207
Manhattan, KS 66502-1207
800-669-9633
Fax: 800-669-1132
www.masterteacher.com
Gives you specific stategies for reaching those students who are giving up.

ISBN: 1-58992-060-0

Mildred Odom Bradley, Author

3680 Superintendent/School Board Relationships
Center for the Study of Small/Rural Schools
555 E Constitution Street
Room 138
Norman, OK 73072-7820
405-325-1450
Fax: 405-325-7075
jcsimmons@ou.edu
cssrs.ou.edu
Series I

Video

Jan C Simmons, Program Director

3681 TQM: Implementing Quality Management in Your School
Center for the Study of Small/Rural Schools
555 E Constitution Street
Room 138
Norman, OK 73072-7820
405-325-1450
Fax: 405-325-7075
jcsimmons@ou.edu
cssrs.ou.edu
Series III

Video

Jan C Simmons, Program Director

3682 Teachers as Heros
Center for the Study of Small/Rural Schools
555 E Constitution Street
Room 138
Norman, OK 73072-7820
405-325-1450
Fax: 405-325-7075
jcsimmons@ou.edu
cssrs.ou.edu
Series IV

Video

Jan C Simmons, Program Director

3683 Teaching for Intelligent Behavior
Center for the Study of Small/Rural Schools
555 E Constitution Street
Room 138
Norman, OK 73072-7820
405-325-1450
Fax: 405-325-7075
jcsimmons@ou.edu
cssrs.ou.edu
Series IV

Video

Jan C Simmons, Program Director

3684 The Master Teacher
Master Teacher
One Leadership Lane
PO Box 1207
Manhattan, KS 66502-1207
800-669-9633
Fax: 800-669-1132
www.masterteacher.com
From one man with a mission to over sixty employees and growing, The MASTER Teacher has developed and matured. We will continue to provide educators with cutting-edge professional development solutions as we advance into the future.

2 pages Weekly

3685 Training Video Series for the Substitute Teacher
Master Teacher
One Leadership Lane
PO Box 1207
Manhattan, KS 66502-1207
800-669-9633
Fax: 800-669-1132
www.masterteacher.com
From one man with a mission to over sixty employees and growing, The MASTER Teacher has developed and matured. We will continue to provide educators with cutting-edge professional development solutions as we advance into the future.

ISBN: 0-914607-95-2

3686 Voices in the Hall: High School Principals at Work
Phi Delta Kappa Educational Foundation
320 W. Eighth Street
Suite 216
Bloomington, IN 47404-3800
812-339-1156
800-766-1156
Fax: 812-339-0018
memberservices@pdkintl.org
www.pdkintl.org
The mission of Phi Delta Kappa International is to promote high-quality education, in particular publicly supported education, as essential to the development and maintenance of a democratic way of life. This mission is accomplished through leadership, research, and service in education
William E Webster, Author
Dan Brown, Executive Director
Bill Bushaw, Chief Executive Officer

3687 Wavelength
4753 N Broadway
Suite 818
Chicago, IL 60640
773-784-1012
877-528-47 2
Fax: 773-784-1079
info@wavelengthinc.com
www.wavelengthinc.com
Wavelength offers a fresh perspective on the key challenges in education today. Our programs are founded on the tenet that humor heals and enlightens. Of course, we also realized that by focusing our humor on education, we'd never run out of material

3688 You Can Handle Them All Discipline Video Series
Master Teacher
One Leadership Lane
PO Box 1207
Manhattan, KS 66502-1207
800-669-9633
Fax: 800-669-1132
www.masterteacher.com
Based upon the best selling books You Can Handle Them All and BEfore you can Discipline by Robert L Debruyn. It contains the vital professional foundations that must underpin and solid philosophy of discipline.

ISBN: 1-58992-035-X

Robert L DeBruyn, Author

Workshops & Programs

3689 ACE Fellows Program
American Council on Education
1 Dupont Circle NW
Washington, DC 20036-1193
202-939-9300
Fax: 202-785-8056
comments@ace.nche.edu
www.acenet.edu
Provides comprehensive leadership development for senior faculty and administrators of universities and colleges. Offers mentor-intern relationships programs. Special institutional grants available for candidates from community colleges, tribal colleges and private historical black universities and colleges.
James H. Mullen, Chairman
Renu Khator, Vice Chair

3690 ART New England Summer Workshops
Massachusetts College of Art and De
621 Huntington Avenue
Boston, MA 2115-5801
617-879-7175
Nancy.Mccarthy@massart.edu
ane.massart.edu
Offers painting, drawing, photography, jewelry making, sculpting, computer imaging and ceramics.
Nancy McCarthy, Administrator

3691 Annual Conductor's Institute of South Carolina
University of South Carolina
School of Music
Columbia, SC 29208
803-777-7500
Fax: 803-777-9774
charl@mailbox.sc.edu
www.conductorsinstitute.com
Since its inception, more than 600 conductors have traveled to Columbia to study with guest

conductors and composers. Academic credit is available.

Donald Portnoy, Director

3692 Annual Summer Institute for Secondary Teachers

Rock and Roll Hall of Fame
E-mail: soehler@rockhall.org
www.rockhall.com/programs/institute.asp
The institute provides teachers with the knowledge and tools needed to bring popular music into the curriculum. The program includes a rock and roll history survey; guest speakers; discussions and workshops.

June

Susan Oehler, Education Programs Manager

3693 Ball State University

2000 W University Avenue
Muncie, IN 47306
765-289-1241
800-382-8540
askus@bsu.edu
cms.bsu.edu
At Ball State, we're more than just educators-we're educational entrepreneurs. Combining top-flight talent with the˜top-notch resources Ball State has to offer, our students and faculty inject endless energy and creativity into what they teach and how they learn. The result-a university The Princeton Review calls one of the best in the Midwest.

Rick Hall, Chairman
Frank Hancock, Vice Chair

3694 Bryant and Stratton College

1259 Central Avenue
Albany, NY 12205-142
518-437-1802
Fax: 716-821-9343
rpferrell@bryantstratton.edu
www.bryantstratton.edu
For 150 years, Bryant & Stratton College has been helping students develop meaningful career skills in a concise, contemporary and effective manner - providing graduates with the marketable job skills they need to succeed in an increasingly competitive marketplace

Bryant H Prentice, Chairman of the Board
David J Ament, Managing Partner

3695 Center for Educational Leadership Trinity University

Trinity University
One Trinity Place
San Antonio, TX 78212-7200
210-999-7207
Fax: 210-999-8164
admissions@trinity.edu
new.trinity.edu
Offers three Masters degree programs for Arts, Teaching, Psychology and School Administration. The school also offers summer institutes and training programs for educators and administrators. Also see information regarding the Master of Education: School Administration at carme.cs.trinity.edu/education/graduate/medschoolleadership.htm

Paul Kelleher, Chairman
Sonia L Mireles, Senior Secretary

3696 Center for Global Education

Augsbury College
2211 Riverside Avenue
Minneapolis, MN 55454-1350
612-330-1000
800-299-8889
Fax: 612-330-1695
globaled@augsburg.edu
www.augsburg.edu/global
To provide cross-cultural educational opportunities in order to foster critical analysis of local and global conditions so that personal and systemic change takes place leading to a more just and sustainable world.

Orval Gingerich, Associate Dean
Regina McGoff, Associate Director

3697 Center for Image Processing in Education

1155 15TH STREET NW
SUITE 700
Washington, DC 20005-3750
202-721-9200
800-322-9884
Fax: 202-721-9250
kRISR@evisual.org
www.cipe.com
CIPE promotes computer-aided visualization as a tool for inquiry-based learning. In support of that mission, it develops instructional materials and conducts workshops that use digital image analysis and geographic information systems technologies as platforms for teaching about science, mathematics, and technology.

Greg Lebedev, Chair
Karen Karrigan, Vice Chair

3698 Center for Learning Connections

Edmonds Community College
20000 68th Ave West
Lynnwood, WA 98036-9800
425-640-1463
Fax: 425-640-1826
peter.schmidt@edcc.edu
www.learningconnections.org
The mission of the Center for Learning Connections is to prepare learners to manage change and create successful futures.

Peter Schmidt, Executive Director
Cal Crow, Program Director

3699 Center for Occupational Research & Development

4901 Bosque Blvd.
2nd Floor
Waco, TX 76710
254-772-8756
800-231-3015
Fax: 254-776-2306
twarner@cord.org
www.cord.org
The Center for Occupational Research and Development (CORD) is a national nonprofit organization dedicated to leading change in education

Richard Hinckley, President/ CEO
Ann-Claire Anderson, Assistant Vice President

3700 Center for Play Therapy Fall Conference

425 S Welch Street
Complex 2
Denton, TX 76203
940-565-3864
Fax: 940-565-4461
cpt@unt.edu
cpt.unt.edu
Features a one day workshop led by a recognized authority in the field of play therapy. This workshop enables professionals in the field of mental health to broaden their knowledge and clinical skills in play therapy.

September

Sue Bratton, Ph.D, Director
Garry L Landreth, Ed.D, Founder

3701 Classroom Connect

6277 Sea Harbor Drive
Orlando, FL 32887
800-638-1639
888-801-8299
Fax: 650-351-5300
support@classroom.tv
www.classroom.tv
A leading provider of professional development programs and online instructional content for K-12 education.

October

Eduardo Abeliuk, Founder
Nicolas Velasco, Operations

3702 College of the Ozarks

1 Industrial Place
PO Box 17
Point Lookout, MO 65726
417-334-6411
800-222-0525
Fax: 417-335-2618
webmaster@cofo.edu
www.cofo.edu
The College of the Ozarks began as a dream. In 1905, young Presbyterian missionary James Forsythe was assigned to serve the region that encompassed Sparta, Mansfield, and Forsyth, Missouri

Jerry C Davis, President

3703 Connect

Synergy Learning
116 Birge Street
PO Box 60
Brattleboro, VT 5302-60
802-257-2629
800-769-6199
Fax: 802-254-5233
info@synergylearning.org
www.synergylearning.org
To engage in publishing and professional development for educators, pre-K through middle school

28 pages
ISSN: 1041-682X

Casey Murrow, Executive Director
Susan Hathaway, Circulation Manager

3704 Critical Issues in Urban Special Education: The Implications of Whole-School Change

Harvard Graduate School of Education
Appian Way
Fifth Floor
Cambridge, MA 2138
617-495-3572
800-545-1849
Fax: 617-496-8051
webeditor@gse.harvard.edu
www.gse.harvard.edu/~ppe
A one-week summer seminar that examines the implications of whole-school change on students with disabilities, policy, procedure, and practice. The program will clarify competing agendas, illuminate various models, and identify unified approaches to ensuring measurable benefits to all children.

Genet Jeanjean, Program Coordinator
Al Written, Interim Director

3705 Critical and Creative Thinking in the Classroom
National Center for Teaching Thinking
1703 N. Beauregard St.
Suite 8
Alexandria, VA 22311
703-578-9600
800-933-2723
Fax: 703-575-5400
www.ascd.org
A unique summer program of courses for K-12 teachers, curriculum developers, staff-development specialists, school/district administrators, teacher educators and college faculty.
Nancy Gibson, President
Marie Adair, Executive Director

3706 Curriculum Center - Office of Educational Services
Southern Illinois University Carbondale
1263 Lincoln Drive
Suite 114
Carbondale, IL 62901-6899
618-453-2121
Fax: 217-786-3020
oesiscc@siu.edu
coas.siu.edu
Programs in vocational areas, career awareness, career development, integration, technology, tech preparation.
Mickey A. Latour, Dean

3707 Darryl L Sink & Associates
1 Cielo Vista Place
Suite 101
Monterey, CA 93940
831-649-8384
800-650-7465
Fax: 831-649-3914
jane@dsink.com
www.dsink.com
DSA encourages customers to evaluate such adult learning strategies as cognitive apprenticeship, problem-based learning, goal-based scenarios, and real world authentic learning activities as the cornerstones of efficient, effective, and appealing learning experiences.

3708 DeVry University
One Tower Lane
Oakbrook Terrace, IL 60181
602-216-7700
866-338-7937
Fax: 602-943-4108
www.devry.edu
Subjects include communications, computer technology, electronics, graphic communications, and training and development.
Peter Anderson, Chief Strategist
Richard L Ehrlickman, Executive Vice President

3709 Delmar Thomson Learning
10650 Toebben Drive
Independence, KY 41051
518-464-3500
800-354-9706
Fax: 518-464-7000
info@delmar.com
solutions.cengage.com/brands/Delmar/
Subjects include welding, HVAC-R, electrical, electronics, automotive, CADD and drafting, construction, blueprint reading, and fire science.
Josef Blumenfeld, Senior Vice President
Lindsay Stanley, Senior Director

3710 Depco
689 S. Hwy. 69
PO Box 178
Pittsburg, KS 66762
620-231-0019
800-767-1062
Fax: 620-231-0024
tcoon@depcollc.com
www.depcollc.com
DEPCO (Dependable Education Products Company) was introduced as a manufacturers' representative organization, which represented manufacturers of vocational education products

3711 Eastern Illinois University School of Technology
1014 Klehm Hall
600 Lincoln Avenue
Charleston, IL 61920-3099
217-581-3226
Fax: 217-581-6607
www.eiu.edu/tech/
Subjects include manufacturing, construction, electronics, graphic communications, training and development.
Austin Cheney, Chair
Rendong Bai, Associate Professor

3712 Edison Welding Institute
EWI
1250 Arthur E Adams Drive
Columbus, OH 43221-3585
614-688-5000
Fax: 614-688-5001
info@ewi.org
www.ewi.org
The NJC's mission is to enhance the life-cycle affordability and mission capability of critical Navy weapon systems through the implementation of materials joining technology
Richard Rogovin, Chair
Henry Cialone, President/ CEO

3713 Educational Summit
The Principals' Center
20 Nassau Street
Suite 211
Princeton, NJ 8542-4509
609-497-1907
Fax: 609-497-1927
An educational summit held in August for school principals to explore, debate and design new models for schooling in America with implications for choice, charters and the community.

3714 Effective Strategies for School Reform
Harvard Graduate School of Education
Appian Way
5th Floor
Cambridge, MA 2138
617-495-3572
800-545-1849
Fax: 617-496-8051
webeditor@gse.harvard.edu
www.gse.harvard.edu/~ppe
To enrich the professional practice of individuals and institutions worldwide that share our commitment to improving education.
Rosanne Boyle, Program Coordinator
Jennifer Stine, Managing Director/Profession

3715 Electronics Industries Alliance/CEA
2500 Wilson Boulevard
Arlington, VA 22201-3834
703-907-7670
Fax: 703-907-7968
www.CEMAweb.org
Electronics workshops.

3716 Elementary Education Professional Development School
Pennsylvania State University
228 Chambers Building
Pennsylvania State University
University Park, PA 16802
814-865-0488
n78@psu.edu
www.ed.psu.edu
The first goal is to enhance the educational experiences of all children. The second goal focuses on ensuring high quality field experiences for new teachers.
David H. Monk, Dean
Greg J. Kelly, Associate Dean

3717 Emco Maier Corporation
46850 Magellan Drive
Unit 160
Novi, MI 48377-2448
248-313-2700
Fax: 248-313-2701
info@emcomaier-usa.com
www.emco-world.us
The EMCO success story began in 1947 with the production of conventional lathes. In the years to follow, EMCO repeatedly impressed the market with extraordinary, innovative solutions.
Josh Dack, Sales Manager
Karen Fahy, Sales/Marketing Coordinator

3718 Energy Concepts
1001 Cottonwood Drive NE
PO Box 628
Willmar, MN 56201
320-235-9079
800-621-1247
Fax: 847-837-8171
info@energyconceptsinc.com
www.energyconceptsinc.com
Subjects include material science technology, principles of technology year I&II.

3719 Fastech
1750 Westfield Drive
Findlay, OH 45840
419-425-2233
Fax: 419-425-9431
info@fastechinc.net
www.fastechinc.net
Subjects include mastercam training, and FMMT CD's.
Roger J. Darr, President

3720 Festo Corporation
395 Moreland Road
PO Box 18023
Hauppauge, NY 11788
631-435-0800
Fax: 631-435-8026
customer.service@us.festo.com
www.festo-usa.com
Subjects include fluid power, PLC, industrial automation.
Fred Zieram, Sales Manager
Petra Milks, Product Coordinator

3721 Foundation for Critical Thinking
PO Box 196
Tomales, CA 94971
707-878-9100
800-833-3645
Fax: 707-878-9111
cct@criticalthinking.org
www.criticalthinking.org
The work of the Foundation is to integrate the Center's research and theoretical developments, and to create events and resources designed to help educators improve their instruction. Materials developed through the Foundation for Critical Thinking include

books, thinker's guides, videos, and other teaching and learning resources.

Dr Richard Paul, Fellow
Dr Linda Elder, Fellow

3722 Four State Regional Technology Conference
Pittsburg State University
College of Technology
1701 S Broadway
Pittsburg, KS 66762
620-235-7000
800-854-7488
Fax: 620-235-4343
tbaldwin@pittstate.edu
www.pittstate.edu
Subjects include educational technology and technology management.

November
30 booths with 250 attendees

Tom Baldwin, Dean, College of Technology
Steve Scott, President

3723 Graduate Programs for Professional Educators
North Central Association of Colleges & Schools
Walden University
155 5th Avenue S
Minneaoplis, MN 55401
800-444-6795
Fax: 941-498-4266
request@waldenu.edu
www.northcentralassociation.org
Both the MS and PhD in Education allow study from home or work. The Master of Science in Education serves classroom teachers and the PhD in education serves the advanced learning needs of educators from a wide range that serves practice fields and levels.

Benny Gooden, President
David Ho, Vice President

3724 Grand Canyon University College of Education
3300 W Camelback Road
Phoenix, AZ 85017-3030
602-639-7500
800-800-9776
Fax: 312-263-7462
cmosby@gcu.edu
www.gcu.edu
Prepares learners to become global citizens, critical thinkers, effective communicators, and responsible leaders by providing an academically challenging, values-based curriculum from the context of our Christian heritage.

Brain Mueler, President/ CEO
Stan Meyer, Chief Operating Officer

3725 Harvard Institute for School Leadership
Harvard Graduate School of Education
Appian Way
Fifth Floor
Cambridge, MA 2138
617-495-3572
800-545-1849
Fax: 617-496-8051
webeditor@gse.harvard.edu
www.gse.harvard.edu/ppe
An intensive residential program for leadership teams from school districts. Participants will gain new perspectives on the processes and goals of school reform and practical skills for leading change in their districts.

July

3726 Harvard Seminar for Superintendents
Harvard Graduate School of Education
Appian Way
Fifth Floor
Cambridge, MA 2138
617-495-3572
800-545-1849
Fax: 617-496-8051
webeditor@gse.harvard.edu
www.gse.harvard.edu/ppe
Veteran superintendents from around the country participate in a week of intellectually stimulating conversations with Harvard faculty and networking with colleagues. Topics discussed include the arts, science, social science, and current events.

July

Julia Bean, Program Assistant

3727 Hobart Institute of Welding Technology
400 Trade Square East
Troy, OH 45373
800-332-9448
Fax: 937-332-9550
info@welding.org
www.welding.org
Preparation course for CWI/CWE exams. Instructor course devoted to welding theory and hand-son practice.

Elmer Swank, Contact

3728 Indiana University-Purdue University of Indianapolis, IUPUI
Department of Construction Technology
420 University Blvd.
ET 209
Indianapolis, IN 46202-5160
317-274-5555
Fax: 317-274-4567
askiu@iu.edu
www.iupui.edu
Subjects include architectural technology, civil engineering technology, construction technology, interior design.

Charles R. Bantz, Chancellor
Nasser H. Paydar, Executive Vice Chancellor

3729 Industrial Training Institute
3385 Wheeling Road
Lancaster, OH 43130
740-687-5262
800-638-4180
Fax: 740-687-5262
drbillstevens1@msn.com
www.dvdcoach.com
Subjects include basic electricity, motors, controls, PLC's, NEC and process control; custom designed training and consulting.

3730 Institute of Higher Education
General Board of Higher Education & Ministry/UMC
1001 19th Avenue S
P. O. Box 340007
Nashville, TN 37203-7
615-340-7400
Fax: 615-340-7379
scu@gbhem.org
www.gbhem.org
An annual seminar for administrators and faculty of United Methodist-related educational institutions addressing current themes related to the college's mission.

June
125 attendees

James E. Dorff, President
Lanther Marie Mills, Vice President

3731 International Curriculum Management Audit Center
Phi Delta Kappa International
320 W Eight Street
Suite 216
Bloomington, IN 47404
812-339-1156
800-766-1156
Fax: 812-339-0018
memberservices@pdkintl.org
www.pdkintl.org
The mission of Phi Delta Kappa International is to promote high-quality education, in particular publicly supported education, as essential to the development and maintenance of a democratic way of life. This mission is accomplished through leadership, research, and service in education.

William Bushaw, Executive Director
Diana Daugherty, Administrative Assistant

3732 International Graduate School
Berne University
35 Center Street
Suite 18
Wolfeboro Falls, NH 03896-1080
603-569-8648
866-755-5557
Fax: 603-569-4052
berne@berne.edu
www.berne.edu
Doctoral Degrees in one to two years, Specialist Diplomas in six to twelve months in: business, education (all specialties), government, health services, international relations, psychology, religion, social work and human services.

3733 International Workshops
187 Aqua View Road
Cedarburg, WI 53012
262-377-7062
Fax: 262-377-7096
thintz@internationalworkshops.org
www.internationalworkshops.org
International Workshops creates an international community of artists and teachers in a site that combines touristic and cultural interest.

400 attendees

Tori Hintz, Manager
Gerald F Fischbach, Director

3734 Island Drafting & Technical Institute
128 Broadway
Amityville, NY 11701-2704
631-691-8733
Fax: 631-691-8738
info@idti.edu
www.idti.edu
Our aim is to graduate students well-trained and technically qualified so that they may enter their chosen field or continue their education at the baccalaureate or higher level.

John G Diliberto, VP

3735 Janice Borla Vocal Jazz Camp
N Central College, Music Department
30 N Brainard Street
Naperville, IL 60540
630-416-3911
Fax: 630-416-6249
jborla@aol.com
www.janiceborlavocaljazzcamp.org
The camp's mission is to enable jazz vocalists to develop and enhance their individual performing skills and musical creativity, regardless of prior experience level, by studying with and attending performances of professional artists actively engaged in the field of jazz performance.

Janice Borla, Director
Jay Clayton, Faculty

3736 Jefferson State Community College
2601 Carson Road
Birmingham, AL 35215
205-853-1200
800-239-5900
Fax: 205-856-8572
workforcedev@jeffstateonline.com
www.jeffstateonline.com
Certificate and degree programs in automated manufacturing, electromechanical systems, industrial maintenance, and CAD.

3737 July in Rensselaer
St Joseph's College, Graduate Dept
PO Box 984
Rensselaer, IN 47978
219-866-6352
Fax: 219-866-6102
jamesc@saintjoe.edu
Solo, ensemble, liturgy, accompanying, history, improvisation, private lessons, technique, repertoire, sight reading, workshops, theory and sacred choral music.
Rev. James Challancin, Director

3738 K'nex Education Division
2990 Bergey Road
PO Box 700
Hatfield, PA 19440
888-ABC-KNEX
Fax: 215-996-4222
abcknex@knex.com
www.knexeducation.com
Introductory, set specific, regional and design your own professional development programs offered for any/all K-12 technology, math and science sets.

3739 Kaleidoscope
Consulting Psychologists Press
3803 E Bayshore Road
Palo Alto, CA 94303-4300
800-624-1765
Fax: 650-969-8608
An institute for educators that develops insights into teaching styles and learning styles; administers and interprets the Myers-Briggs Type Indicator (personality inventory); learn new techniques to help children understand and value their unique qualities; create and deliver lessons that enlighten all students and more.
July

3740 Kent State University
375 Terrace Drive
Van Deusen Hall
Kent, OH 44242
330-672-2892
Fax: 330-672-2894
lepps@kent.edu
www.tech.kent.edu
Subjects include aeronautics, electronics, manufacturing engineering, computer technology, and automotive engineering technology.
Verna Fitzsimmons, Interim Dean
Isaac Richmond Nettey, Associate Dean

3741 Kentucky State University
400 East Main Street
Frankfort, KY 40601
502-597-6000
Fax: 502-227-6236
webadmin@kysu.edu
www.kysu.edu
Associates in applied science in drafting and design technology and applied science in electronics technology.
Mary Evans Sias, President
Stephen Mason, Executive Assistant to the P

3742 Kodaly Teaching Certification Program
DePaul University, School of Music
804 West Belden Avenue
Chicago, IL 60614
773-325-4355
Fax: 773-325-7263
Music education, pedagogy and workshops.
Robert Krueger, Director Operations

3743 Lab Volt Systems
1710 State Highway 34
Farmingdale, NJ 07727
732-938-2000
800-522-2658
Fax: 732-774-8573
us@labvolt.com
www.labvolt.com
Global leader in the design and manufacture of hands-on training laboratories for public education, industry, and the military.
Eric Maynard, Contact

3744 Leadership and the New Technologies
Harvard Graduate School of Education
44 Brattle Street
Fifth Floor
Cambridge, MA 02138
800-545-1849
800-545-1849
Fax: 617-496-8051
ppe@gse.harvard.edu
www.gse.harvard.edu/~ppe
Programs designed to help teams of school leaders anticipate the far-reaching impacts that new technologies can have on students, teachers, curriculum, and communication. Participants make long-term plans for the use of technology in their schools and districts and learn how to take advantage of federal and state technology initiatives.
July
Ann Doyle, Program Coordinator

3745 Learning & The Enneagram
National Enneagram Institute at Milton Academy
230 Atherton Street
Milton, MA 02186-2424
617-898-1798
Fax: 617-898-1712
An educational enterprise dedicated to guiding individuals and organizations in the most responsible and effective format for their needs. Programs include exploration of what every educator needs to know; why we learn in the way we do; and how we teach.
July
Regina Pyle, Coordinator

3746 Learning Materials Workshop
58 Henry Street
Burlington, VT 05401
800-693-7164
Fax: 802-862-8399
info@learningmaterialswork.com
www.learningmaterialswork.com
Learning Materials Workshop Blocks are learning tools in the hands of young children. They are open-ended, yet carefully designed in a variety of colors, sizes, shapes, and textures that stimulate and develop perpetual, motor, and language skills. Learning Materials Workships are designed for early childhood/primary grade teachers, paraprofessionals, curriculum coordinators, special education teachers, ESL teachers, and teachers of the gifted and talented to help develop the learning process.
Karen Hewitt, President

3747 Light Machines
444 E Industrial Park Avenue
Manchester, NH 03109-5317
800-221-2763
Fax: 603-625-2137
industrialsales@intelitek_usa.com
www.lightmachines.com
Subjects include demonstrations and comprehensive training on CNC routers, turning machines and milling machines, and CAD/CAM software.

3748 MPulse Maintenance Software
PO Box 22906
Eugene, OR 97402
541-302-6677
800-944-1796
Fax: 541-302-6680
info@mpulsesoftware.com
www.mpulsesoftware.com
Deliver simply better EAM / CMMS software that is easier to use and faster to implement. Keep it affordable by controlling the cost of sales and marketing. Design it to keep up with their needs today, their challenges of tomorrow, while maintaining the history of what they did yesterday. And do it better than anyone else
Steve Brous, President & CEO

3749 Marcraft International Corporation
1350 Spaulding Ave
Suite 302
Kennwick, WA 99352
509-374-1951
800-441-6006
Fax: 509-374-9250
sales@marcraft.com
www.marcraft.com
s to develop exceptional products for effectively teaching and training people the technical IT, computer, and electronics training skills in demand today and in the future.
Robert Krug, National Sales Manager

3750 Maryland Center for Career and Technology Education
1415 Key Highway
Baltimore, MD 21230
410-685-1648
Fax: 410-685-0032
Subjects include technology education and occupational education certification.

3751 Media and American Democracy
Harvard Graduate School of Education
Programs in Professional Education
Appian Way
Cambridge, MA 02138
617-495-3572
800-545-1849
Fax: 617-496-8051
ppe@harvard.edu
www.gse.harvard.edu/~ppe
Participants learn about the interaction between the media and American democratic process, develop curriculum units, and examine ways to help students become thoughtful consumers of media messages about politics. Designed for secondary school teachers of history, social studies, English, journalism, and humanities.
August
Tracy Ryder, Program Assistant

3752 Millersville University
PO Box 1002
1 South George Street
Millersvile, PA 17551
717-872-3011
800-426-4553
Fax: 877-327-8132
www.millersville.edu

With a student population of 7,259 undergraduate and 1,047 graduate students, Millersville University offers all the advantages you would expect from a university: competitive programs, great facilities, a diverse student community and a variety of campus programming all offered in an accessible, intimate and close-knit atmosphere more frequently found at a smaller college

Michael G Warfel, Chairman
Paul G Wedel, Vice Chairman

3753 Morehead State University

150 University Boulevard
Morehead, KY 40351
606-783-2221
Fax: 606-783-5000
admissions@moreheadstate.edu
www.morehead-st.edu

Morehead State University was founded upon and continues to embrace the ideal that all persons should have opportunity to participate in higher education. With immense pride in its past and great promise for its future, the University intends to emerge in the first decade of the 21st century as an even stronger institution recognized for superb teaching and learning with exemplary programs in teacher education, space-related science and technology, entrepreneurship, visual and performing arts, r

Beth Patrick, Vice President
Dayna Seelig, Special Assistant to the Pre

3754 Musikgarten

507 Arlington Street
Greensboro, NC 27406
336-272-5303
800-216-6864
Fax: 336-272-0581
musgarten@aol.com
www.musikgarten.org

Early childhood music education workshops teaching music and understanding children.

Lorna Heyge, President

3755 NASA Educational Workshop

NSTA
1840 Wilson Boulevard
Arlington, VA 22201-3000
703-243-7100
888-400-6782
Fax: 703-243-7177
businessoffice@nsta.org
www.nsta.org

Two week workshop at a NASA Center, professional development opportunity for K-12 teachers in mathematics, science, and technology, teachers and curriculum specialists at the K-12 levels; media specialists, resource teachers, elementary curriculum developers, counselors, and others with special interest in mathematics, science, technology, and geography.

Karen Ostlund, President
Bill Badders, President-Elect

3756 NCSS Summer Workshops

National Council for the Social Studies
8555 Sixteenth Street
Suite 500
Silver Spring, MD 20910
301-588-1800
800-683-0812
Fax: 301-588-2049
sgriffin@ncss.org
www.socialstudies.org

Social studies educators teach students the content knowledge, intellectual skills, and civic values necessary for fulfilling the duties of citizenship in a participatory democracy.

July

Susan Griffin, Executive Director
Sojan Alex, Finance Assistant

3757 National Center for Construction Education & Research

13614 Progress Boulevard
Alachua, FL 32615
386-518-6500
888-622-3720
Fax: 386-518-6303
info@nccer.org
www.nccer.org

Our mission is to build a safe, productive, and sustainable workforce of craft professionals.

Don Whyte, President
Cathy Tyler, Executive Assistant

3758 National Computer Systems

4401 L Street NW
Suite 550
Edina, MN 55435
612-995-8997
800-328-6172
Fax: 952-830-8564
www.ncsus.net

Programs offer skills to teach technology in the classroom.

3759 National Education Association Student Program

National Education Association
1201 16th Street NW
Washington, DC 20036-3290
202-833-4000
Fax: 202-822-7974
amuscarella@nea.org
www.nea.org/home/1600.htm

Strives to promote community partnerships; foster leadership through pre-professional opportunities and peer mentoring; promote membership among diverse populations; supplement teacher-education training; promote national accreditation of teacher-education training and more.

Ashley Muscarella, Student Program Chair
Marti Garza, Associate Director

3760 National Head Start Association

1651 Prince Street
Alexandria, VA 22314
703-739-0875
866-677-8724
www.nhsa.org

Nonprofit organization offering professional development training to those working with at risk children.

Yasmina Vinci, Executive Director
Gregg Porter, Director, Membership

3761 Northern Arizona University

South San Francisco Street
Flagstaff, AZ 86011
928-523-9011
Fax: 520-523-6395
tlc2@dana.ucc.nau.edu
www.nau.edu

Provide an outstanding undergraduate residential education strengthened by research, graduate and professional programs, and sophisticated methods of distance delivery.

John D Haeger, President
Tracy Cooper, Lab Assistant

3762 Orff-Schulwerk Teacher Certification Program

DePaul University, School of Music
804 West Belden Avenue
Chicago, IL 60614
773-325-7260
Fax: 773-325-7264
ahutchen@wppost.depaul.edu.

Music education, pedagogy and workshops.

Judy Bundra, Associate Dean

3763 Owens Community College

PO Box 10000
Toledo, OH 43699-1947
567-661-7000
800-466-9367
Fax: 419-661-7664
www.owens.edu

We believe in serving our students and our communities. Your success is our misssion.

Diana H Talmage, Chairman
R J Molter, Vice Chair

3764 Paideia Group

608 Garden Leaf Court
St. Louis, MO 63011
636-220-9300
Fax: 919-932-3905
bethsymes@psideiagroup.com
www.paideiagroup.com

To help people understand what it means to be customer-focused. Participants focus on the skills, attitudes, and automatic behaviors that must be developed to reach a common goal of becoming a customer-focused organization.

Beth Symes, Principal and Founder

3765 Pamela Sims & Associates

54 Mozart Crescent
Brampton, Ontario
Canada L6Y-2W7
905-455-7331
888-610-7467
Fax: 905-455-0207
loveofkids@aol.com
www.pamelasims.com

Seminars and workshops for educators and parents.

Pamela Sims, President
Kelly Smith, Marketing Director

3766 Pennsylvania State University-Workforce Education & Development Program

411D Keller Building
University Park, PA 16802
814-863-3858
Fax: 814-863-7532
eif1@psu.edu
www.ed.psu.edu

To promote excellence, opportunity, and leadership among professionals in the workforce education and development field including, but not limited to, those employed in secondary or postsecondary education institutions, social services industries, and employee groups and private businesses.

Edgar I Farmer, Department Head
Judith A Kolb, Professor-in-Charge

3767 Performance Learning Systems

72 Lone Oak Drive
Cadiz, KY 42211
270-522-2000
866-757-2527
Fax: 270-522-2010
info@plsweb.com
www.plsweb.com

The mission of Performance Learning Systems, Inc. is to enhance education through the development of educational services.

Jackie Futrell, Resource Manager
Stephen G Barkley, Master teacher-of-teachers

3768 Piano Workshop
Goshen College
1700 S Main Street
Goshen, IN 46526
574-535-7000
Fax: 574-535-7949
beverlykl@goshen.edu
www.goshen.edu/music/Piano%20Workshop/Main
The Goshen College Piano Workshop and Academy comprises lectures, master classes and recital performances presented by distinguished clinicians, composers and performers. Teachers participating in the Workshop hear inspiring lectures relevant to piano pedagogy, performance and literature.

Beverly K Lapp, Associate Professor of Music

3769 Pittsburg State University
College of Technology
1701 S Broadway
Pittsburg, KS 66762
620-231-7000
800-854-7488
Fax: 620-235-4343
psuinfo@pittstate.edu
www.pittstate.edu
A comprehensive regional university, provides undergraduate and graduate programs and services to the people of southeast Kansas, but also to others who seek the benefits offered.

Bruce Dallman, Dean, College of Technology
Steve Scott, President

3770 Polaroid Education Program
565 Technology Square
#3B
Cambridge, MA 02139-3539
781-386-2000
Fax: 781-386-3925
This program offers workshops for professional educators, preK-12; the Visual Learning Workshop and an Instant Image Portfolio Workshop.

3771 Professional Development Institutes
Center for Professional Development & Services
2730 University Boulevard
Suite 301
Kensington, MD 20895
301-949-1771
800-766-1156
Fax: 301-949-5441
info@pditraining.net
www.pditraining.net
Offers a wide variety of courses for Real Estate professionals around the US to meet their pre-licensing, post-licensing, and continuing education needs. Also offers non-credit courses on Technology, Business, Accounting, and Project Management, among others to further any career.

3772 Professional Development Workshops
Rebus
4111 Jackson Road
Ann Arbor, MI 48103
734-668-4870
800-435-3085
Fax: 734-668-4728
www.rebusinc.com
Workshops that promote success by assessing children in the context of active learning.

June/July

Sam Meisels, CEO
Linda Borgsdorf, President

3773 Project Zero Classroom
Harvard Graduate School of Education
Programs in Professional Education
Appian Way
Cambridge, MA 02138
617-495-3572
800-545-1849
Fax: 617-496-8051
ppe@harvard.edu
www.gse.harvard.edu/~ppe
Renowned educators Howard Gardner and David Perkins and their Project Zero colleagues work with K-12 educators to help them reshape their classroom practices to promote student understanding. The week focuses on five concepts: teaching for understanding, multiple intelligences, the thinking classroom, authentic assessment, and learning with and through the arts.

July

Tracy Ryder, Program Assistant

3774 Robert McNeel & Associates
3670 Woodland Park Avenue N
Seattle, WA 98103
206-545-7000
Fax: 206-545-7321
bob@mcneelcom
www.en.na.mcneel.com
3D modeling workshop for design, drafting, graphics, and technology educators.

3775 Rockford Systems
4620 Hydraulic Road
Rockford, IL 61109-2695
815-874-7891
800-922-7533
Fax: 815-874-6144
sales@rockfordsystems.com
www.rockfordsystems.com
Machine safegaurding seminar for technology educators.

3776 SUNY College at Oswego
7060 Route 104
Oswego, NY 13126-3599
315-312-2500
Fax: 315-312-2863
stanley@oswego.edu
www.oswego.edu
The chief goal of the Oswego College Foundation, Inc. is to raise and manage private support to advance SUNY Oswego's mission.

October
26 booths with 350-400 attendees

Deborah F Stanley, President
Howard Gordon, Executive Assistant to Presi

3777 School of Music
Georgia State University
PO Box 4097
Atlanta, GA 30302-4097
404-413-5900
Fax: 404-413-5910
music@gsu.edu
www.music.gsu.edu
The mission of the School of Music is to provide a comprehensive, rigorous, and innovative academic program that is consistent with the urban context and mission of Georgia State University, and that serves the pursuit of artistic, professional, and scholarly excellence through experiences of lasting value to all stakeholders.

W Dwight Coleman, Director
Robert J Ambrose, Associate Director

3778 Southern Polytechnic State University
1100 S Marietta Parkway
Marietta, GA 30060-2896
678-915-7778
800-635-3204
Fax: 678-915-7490
coned@spsu.edu
www.oce.spsu.edu
Specialize in the delivery of comprehensive real-world training on a grand scale. Whether it be High-Tech, Business Professional or Engineering

3779 Southwestern Oklahoma State University
Industrial and Engineering Technology Department
100 Campus Drive
Weatherford, OK 73096
580-774-3063
Fax: 580-774-3795
admissions@swosu.edu
www.swosu.edu
The mission of Southwestern Oklahoma State University is to provide educational opportunities in higher education that meet the needs of the state and region; contribute to the educational, economic, and cultural environment; and support scholarly activity.

Gary Bell, Chair
Jeff Short, Program Coordinator

3780 Specialized Solutions
24703 US Highway 19-N
Suite 200
Clearwater, FL 33763
240-252-5070
888-840-2378
Fax: 877-200-5959
cameron@specializedsolutions.com
www.specializedsolutions.com
Technology based training and certification self study programs.

Sheri Nash, Contact

3781 Staff Development Workshops & Training Sessions
National School Conference Institute
PO Box 37527
Phoenix, AZ 85069-7527
602-371-8655
Fax: 602-371-8790
Offers twenty relevant and leading edge programs including curriculum instruction assessment, restructuring your school, improving student performance and gifted at-risk students. Ten monthly sessions of each program are available, with monthly feedback to follow-up. Accelerates restructuring efforts and also offers graduate credit.

3782 Standards and Accountability: Their Impact on Teaching and Assessment
Harvard Graduate School of Education
Programs in Professional Education
339 Gutman Library
Cambridge, MA 02138
617-495-3572
800-545-1849
Fax: 617-496-8051
ppe@harvard.edu
www.gse.harvard.edu/~ppe
Examines educational and policy issues by new approaches to standards, assessment, and accountability. Focuses on issues of excellence and equity, aligning assessments with standards, strengthening professional

development, impacts of challenges on school communities, and political and legal issues surrounding standards and forms of accountability. Designed for public school leaders whose responsibilities include evaluation and testing.

July

Tracy Ryder, Program Assistant

3783 Storytelling for Educational Enrichment The Magic of Storytelling
2709 Oak Haven Drive
San Marcos, TX 78666-5065
512-392-0669
800-322-3199
Fax: 512-392-9660
krieger@corridor.net
Teacher in-service and training in storytelling and puppetry for teachers of Pre-K through third grades. The Magic of Storytelling is for all ages and levels, specializing in original stories of enlightenment and environmental education. Over ten years experiences with many national and regional conferences and training.

Cherie Krieger, President

3784 Summer Institute in Siena
University of Siena-S/American Universities
595 Prospect Road
Waterbury, CT 06706
203-754-5741
Fax: 203-753-8105
siena@sienamusic.org
www.sienamusic.org
Programs offered in cooperation with the University of Siena-S and American Universities and Colleges. The program in Siena Italy is open to qualified graduates, undergraduates, professionals, teachers, 19 years of age or above. Special diploma; credit or non-credit; in-service credit; auditions; trips to Rome, Florence, Assisi, Venice, Pisa, three days in Switzerland; a Puccini Opera.

Joseph Del Principe, Music Director

3785 Summer Programs for School Teams
National Association of Elementary School Principa
1615 Duke Street
Alexandria, VA 22314-3345
703-684-3345
800-386-2377
Fax: 703-518-6281
www.naesp.org
Events focused on the key to exceptional instruction. Effective teaching and learning for school teams, must include the principal.

Ann R Walker, Assistant Executive Director
Herrie Hahn, Director Programs

3786 Supplemental Instruction, Supervisor Workshops
University of Missouri-Kansas City
5100 Rockhill Road
SASS 210
Kansas City, MO 64110-2499
816-235-1174
Fax: 816-235-5156
cad@umkc.edu
www.umkc.edu/cad/si
Supplemental Instruction (SI) is an academic assistance program that utilizes peer-assisted study sessions.

Kim Wilcox, Coordinator of Training
Glen Jacobs, Executive Director

3787 Syracuse University Disability Studies
805 S Crouse Avenue
105 Hoople Building
Syracuse, NY 13244-2280
315-443-4486
Fax: 315-443-0193
sudcc@syr.edu
disabilitystudies.syr.edu
Promotes its mission of inclusion by developing and sponsoring academic programs and courses, conferences and publications, research and training programs, and public education and advocacy efforts on behalf of, and with, people with disabilities.

Diane R Wiener, Ph.D, LMSW, Director

3788 THE Institute & Knowvation
1105 Media 9201 Oakdale Avenue
Suite 101
Chatsworth, CA 91311
818-734-1520
800-840-0003
Fax: 818-734-1522
kodell@1105media.com
www.thejournal.com/institute
T.H.E. Institute believes that in order for students to be successful in the 21st century, technology must be an integral part of every aspect of education.

Geoffrey H Fletcher, Executive Director

3789 TUV Product Service
Westendstra e 199
Munich, MA D-806
49 -9 5-91 0
800-TUV-0123
Fax: 978-762-7637
info@tuev-sued.de
www.tuvglobal.com
As process partners with comprehensive industry knowledge our teams of specialists provide early consultation and continuous guidance, thus achieving the optimisation of technology, systems and expertise

Axel Stepken, Chief Executive Officer
Manfred Bayerlein, Chief Operations Officer

3790 Teacher Education Institute
1079 W Morse Boulevard
Suite A
Winter Park, FL 32789-3751
800-331-2208
Fax: 800-370-2600
tei@teachereducation.com
www.teachereducation.com
TEI was founded in 1981 to meet the needs of classroom teachers for quality education and training in practical, proven skills and methods that make a tangible and positive difference in their relationships and interactions with students and colleagues.

Vince Welsh, President

3791 Teachers College: Columbia University
Center for Technology & School Change
525 W 120th Street
New York, NY 10027
212-678-3000
Fax: 212-678-4048
webcomments@tc.columbia.edu
www.tc.columbia.edu
bring educational opportunities to all members of society, and whose faculty and students, time and again during more than a century of leadership, have demonstrated the power of ideas to change the world.

Howard Budin, Director Center for Technolo
Susan H Fuhrman, President

3792 Technology Training for Educators
Astronauts Memorial Foundation
Kennedy Space Center
, FL 32899
321-452-2887
800-792-3494
Fax: 321-452-6244
amfreg@amfcse.org
www.amfcse.org
Microsoft NT Administration; Technology Specialist; Management of Technology; Advanced Technology Specialist.

3793 Tooling University
3615 Superior Avenue
Building 44,6th Floor
Cleveland, OH 44114-3898
216-706-6600
866-706-8665
Fax: 216-706-6601
info@toolingu.com
www.toolingu.com
Toolingu.com is the leading online training provider focused on the unique needs of manufacturers. Our roots are in manufacturing, and our business started by recognizing the industry's specific needs

Gene Jones, Director Marketing

3794 Total Quality Schools Workshop
Pennsylvania State University
302F Rackley Building
University Park, PA 16802
814-843-3765
hli@psu.edu
www.ed.psu.edu
Designed for public school educators at the state, national, and international level, this training program provides information in the philosophy, tools, and techniques of total quality management in education. The three day-six week program focuses on leadership, reform models, and education decision making.

William Hartman, Director

3795 University of Arkansas at Little Rock
2801 S University Avenue
Little Rock, AR 72204-1099
501-683-7302
Fax: 501-683-7304
admissions@ualr.edu
www.ualr.edu
With more than 100 programs of study, UALR has an academic program to suit your interests. We offer everything from computer science to fine arts, and we're sure you will find your niche on our campus

Sandra Bates, President
Tammy Starks, Vice President

3796 University of Central Florida
3100 Technology Parkway
Suite 264
Orlando, FL 32826-3281
407-823-4910
Fax: 407-207-4911
distrib@ucf.edu
www.distrib.ucf.edu
The University of Central Florida is one of the most dynamic universities in the country. Offering 223 degree programs, it has become an academic and research leader in numerous fields, such as optics, modeling and simulation, engineering and computer science, business administration, education, science, hospitality management and digital media.

John C Hitt, President/Corporate Secretar
John Schell, Vice President

3797 University of Michigan-Dearborn Center for Corporate & Professional Development
4901 Evergreen Road
CCPD-2000
Dearborn, MI 48128-2406
313-593-5000
Fax: 313-593-5111
info@umich.edu
www.umd.umich.edu
We offer undergraduate, graduate, and professional education to a diverse, highly motivated, and talented student body. Our programs are responsive to the changing needs of society; relevant to the goals of our students and community partners; rich in opportunities for independent and collaborative study, research, and practical application; and reflective of the traditions of excellence, innovation, and leadership that distinguish the University of Michigan

Daniel Little, Chancellor
Ray Metz, Chief of Staff

3798 Wavelength
4753 N Broadway
Suite 808
Chicago, IL 60640
773-784-1012
877-528-47 2
Fax: 773-784-1079
info@wavelengthinc.com
www.wavelengthinc.com
Wavelength offers a fresh perspective on the key challenges in education today. Our programs are founded on the tenet that humor heals and enlightens.

3799 Wids Learning Design System
1 Foundation Circle
Waunakee, WI 53597
800-677-9437
800-821-6313
Fax: 608-849-2468
info@wids.org
www.wids.org
WIDS strives to enhance the quality of learning through the development, implementation, support, and continuous improvement of the WIDS Learning Design System, a comprehensive methodology, supported by application and professional development tools, for designing and planning performance-based assessment learning and teaching.

Lisa Laabs, Office Manager
Judy Neill, Director

3800 Workforce Education and Development
Southern Illinois University Carbondale
475 Clocktower Drive
Mailcode 4605
Carbondale, IL 62901-4605
618-453-3321
Fax: 618-453-1909
wed@siu.edu
www.wed.siu.edu/Public/
The Department of Workforce Education and Development is one of the largest education, training, and development departments in the United States. A recent external evaluation team recognized the Department as among the top ten in the nation.

Keith Waugh, Associate Professor/Chairman

Directories & Handbooks / General

3801 106 Ways Parents Can Help Students Achieve
American Association of School Administrators
1615 Duke Street
Suite 700
Alexandria, VA 22314-1730
703-528-0700
Fax: 703-841-1543
info@aasa.org
www.aasa.org
Provides parents with useful information about the importance of parental involvement, concrete ways to work with children and schools to promote success, and a list of resources for further reading.
Set of 10
ISBN: 0-8108-4220-3

3802 A Personal Planner & Training Guide for the Substitute Teacher
Master Teacher
One Leadership Lane
PO Box 1207
Manhattan, KS 66502-1207
800-669-9633
Fax: 800-669-1132
www.masterteacher.com
Helps substitute teachers set the tone for a positive experience.
90 pages
ISBN: 0-914607-89-8
John Eller, Author

3803 Academic Year & Summer Programs Abroad
American Institute for Foreign Study
1 High Ridge Park
Stamford, CT 06905-5504
203-399-5000
866-906-2437
Fax: 203-399-5590
info@aifs.com
www.aifs.com
Offers school names, addresses, courses offered, tuition and fee information.
224 pages Annual
Cyril Taylor, Founder/ Chairman
William L. Gertz, President/ CEO

3804 Accredited Institutions of Postsecondary Education
MacMillan Publishing Company
1633 Broadway
New York, NY 10019
212-654-8500
888-247-8269
Fax: 800-835-3202
ope.ed.gov/accreditation/
Lists over 5,000 accredited institutions and programs for postsecondary education in the United States.
600 pages Annual

3805 Activities and Strategies for Connecting Kids with Kids: Elementary Edition
Master Teacher
One Leadership Lane
PO Box 1207
Manhattan, KS 66502-1207
800-669-9633
Fax: 800-669-1132
www.masterteacher.com
Activities, lesson plans, and strategies that celebrate each student's individual differences while developing cooperation, tolerance, understanding, sharing and caring.
159 pages
ISBN: 0-914607-74-X

3806 Activities and Strategies for Connecting Kids with Kids: Secondary Edition
Master Teacher
One Leadership Lane
PO Box 1207
Manhattan, KS 66502-1207
800-669-9633
Fax: 800-669-1132
www.masterteacher.com
Activities, lesson plans, and strategies that celebrate each student's individual differences while developing cooperation, tolerance, understanding, sharing and caring.
136 pages
ISBN: 0-914607-75-8

3807 American School Directory
PO Box 20002
Murfreesboro, TN 37129
866-273-2797
Fax: 800-929-3408
support@asddataservices.com
www.asd.com
More than 104,000 school sites are loaded with pictures, art, calendars, menus, local links and notes from students, parents and alumni. Choose the school by name, state list, or by ASD number.

3808 Amusing and Unorthodox Definitions
Careers/Consultants Consultants in Education
3050 Palm Aire Drive N
#310
Pompano Beach, FL 33069
954-974-5477
Fax: 954-974-5477
carconed@aol.com
Collection of amusing and unorthodox definitions. The meanings, purposes and implications assigned to the words appearing here will delight audiences, enliven conversations and keep you chuckling.
ISBN: 0-7392-0089-5
ISSN: 99-94623
Dr. Robert M Bookbinder, President/Author

3809 Associated Schools Project in Education for International Co-operation
UNESCO Associated Schools Project Network
7 Place de Fontenoy
75352 Paris 07 SP
France
33 -0 1-45 6
1-45681000
www.unesco.org
Lists 1,970 secondary and primary schools, teacher training institutions and nursery schools in 95 countries that participate in the UNESCO Associated School Project.
200 pages Annual

3810 Awakening Brilliance: How to Inspire Children to Become Successful Learners
Pamela Sims & Associates
54 Mozart Crescent
Canada L6Y 2W7
905-455-7331
888-610-7467
Fax: 905-455-0207
loveofkids@aol.com
www.pamelasims.com
Seminars and workshops for educators and parents. Upcoming workshops include themes of awakening students' potential and team leadership skills.
248 pages Paperback
ISBN: 0-9651126-0-8
Pamela Sims, Author/Editor
Kelly Smith, Marketing Director

3811 Beyond the Bake Sale
Master Teacher
One Leadership Lane
PO Box 1207
Manhattan, KS 66502-1207
800-669-9633
Fax: 800-669-1132
www.masterteacher.com
A notebook containing 101 detailed plans that not only provide you with fundraising ideas, but get you started, keep you on track, and lead your team through the finishing touches.
101 pages
ISBN: 1-58992-119-4

3812 Biographical Membership Directory
American Educational Research Association
1430 K Street, NW
Suite 1200
Washington, DC 20005-3078
202-238-3200
Fax: 202-238-3250
www.aera.net
Membership directory of more than 23,000 persons involved in education research and development, including the names, addresses, phone numbers, highest degree held and year received, occupational specialization areas, e-mail addresses and more.
420 pages Bi-Annual
Felice J. Levine, Executive Director
Gerald E. Sroufe, Senior Advisor

3813 CASE Directory of Advancement Professionals in Education
Council for Advancement & Support of Education
1307 New York Avenue NW
Suite 1000
Washington, DC 20005-4701
202-328-2273
Fax: 202-387-4973
info@case.org
www.case.org
Membership directory of 16,000 professionals in alumni relations, communications and fund raising at educational institutions worldwide.
Publication Date: 1995 200 pages Annual
ISBN: 0-899643-10-8
John Lippincott, President
Donald Falkenstein, Vice President

3814 Cabells Directory of Publishing Opportunities in Educational Curriculum & Methods
Cabell Publishing Company
Box 5428
Tobe Hahn Station
Beaumont, TX 77726
409-898-0575
Fax: 409-866-9554
info@cabells.com
www.cabells.com
Provides information on editor's contact information, manuscript guidelines, acceptance rate, re-

view information and circulation data for over 350 academic journals.

799 pages Annual
ISBN: 0-911753-27-3

David WE Cabell, Editor
Deborah L English, Editor

3815 Cadet Gray: Your Guide to Military Schools-Military Colleges & Cadet Programs
Reference Desk Books
PO Box 22925
Santa Barbara, CA 93121
805-772-8806
This is a comprehensive reference book which describes 55 American military schools, grade schools, high schools, junior colleges, senior colleges, and the federal service academies. Descriptions include school histories, academic requirements, military environment, extracurricular activities and costs.

Publication Date: 1990 212 pages
ISBN: 0-962574-90-2

3816 Carnegie Communications, LLC
Porter Sargent Publishers
2 LAN Drive
Suite 100
Westford, MA 01886-3028
978-692-5092
800-342-7470
Fax: 978-692-4174
info@carnegiecomm.com
www.carnegiecomm.com
Lists and authoritatively describes 800 elementary and secondary schools in 130 countries. Written for the educator, personnel advisor, student and parent as well as diplomatic and corporate officials, this unique guide is an indispensable reference for American students seeking preparatory schooling overseas. Hardcover.

Publication Date: 1991 544 pages BiAnnual

Joe Moore, President/ CEO
Meghan Dalesandro, EVP, Operation

3817 Character Education Evaluation Tool Kit
Character Education Partnership
1634 I Street NW
Suite 550
Washington, DC 20036
202-296-7743
800-988-8081
Fax: 202-296-7779
information@character.org
www.character.org

Julea Posey, Matthew Davison, Meg Korpi, Author
Becky Sipos, President and CEO
Sheril Morgan, Director

3818 Character Education Kit: 36 Weeks of Success: Elementary Edition
Master Teacher
One Leadership Lane
PO Box 1207
Manhattan, KS 66502-1207
800-669-9633
Fax: 800-669-1132
www.masterteacher.com
Takes the guesswork out of delivering your character education message by providing you with all the pieces of a well-rounded program including important components for 36 character traits.

428 pages
ISBN: 1-58992-096-1

3819 Choosing Your Independent School in the United Kingdom & Ireland
Independent Schools Information Service
56 Buckingham Gate
London SW1E 6AG
England
71-63087934
1,400 independent schools in the United Kingdom and Ireland with contact information, entry requirements, fees, scholarships available, subjects and exam boards.

293 pages Annual/September

3820 Classroom Teacher's Guide for Working with Paraeducators
Master Teacher
One Leadership Lane
PO Box 1207
Manhattan, KS 66502-1207
800-669-9633
Fax: 800-669-1132
www.masterteacher.com
This workbook includes numerous forms that allow teachers to communicate more effectively to paras the vital information they will need in working with special students.

60 pages
ISBN: 1-58992-127-5

Wendy Dover, Author

3821 Commonwealth Universities Yearbook
Association of Commonwealth Universities
20-24 Tavistock Square
London WC1H 0PF
England
207-380-6700
44-20-7380-6700
Fax: 207-387-2655
Fax: 44-20-738-2655
info@acu.ac.uk
www.acu.ac.uk
Offers information on over 700 university institutions of recognized academic standing in 36 Commonwealth countries or regions, including Africa, Asia, Australia, Britain, Canada and the Pacific.

2,600 pages Annual
ISBN: 0-85143-188-7
ISSN: 0069-7745

Olive Mugenda, Chairman
Jan Thomas, Vice Chairman

3822 Complete Learning Disabilities Directory
Grey House Publishing
5979 North Elm Avenue
Suite 113
Millerton, NY 12546
518-789-8700
800-562-2139
Fax: 518-789-0556
books@greyhouse.com
www.greyhouse.com
A one-stop sourcebook for people of all ages with learning disabilities and those who work with them. This comprehensive database in print includes information about associations and organizations, schools, government agencies, testing materials, camps, books, newsletters and more.

800 pages Annual/Softcover
ISBN: 1-59237-049-7

Leslie Mackenzie, Publisher
Richard Gottlieb, Editor

3823 Computer and Web Resources for People with Disabilities
Alliance for Technology Access/Hunter House
1119 Old Humboldt Road
Suite 240
Jackson, TN 38305
731-554-5282
800-914-3017
Fax: 731-554-5283
atainfo@ataccess.org
www.ataccess.org
This directory shows how America's forty-five million people with disabilities can potentially benefit from using computer technology to achieve goals and change their lives. Written by experts in the field, this important work provides a comprehensive, step-by-step guide to approaching computer innovations. It explains how to identify the appropriate technology, how to seek funding, how to set it up and what to consider.

Publication Date: 1996 400 pages Paperback/CD ROM
ISBN: 0-89793-433-4

James Allison, President
Bob Van der Linde, Vice President

3824 Conservation Education and Outreach Techniques
North American Assoc for Environmental Education
2000 P Street NW
Suite 540
Washington, DC 20036
202-419-0412
Fax: 212-419-0415
info@naaee.org
www.naaee.org
Presents the theory and practice for creating effective education and outreach programmes for conservation. An exciting array of techniques for enhancing school resources, marketing environmental messages, using mass media, developing partnerships for conservation, and designing on-site programmes for natural areas and community centres.

ISBN: 0-19-856772-3

Jose Marcos-Iga, President
Judy Braus, Executive Director

3825 Contemporary World Issues: Public Schooling in America
ABC-CLIO
130 Cremona Drive
#1911
Santa Barbara, CA 93117-5599
805-963-4221
800-368-6868
Fax: 805-685-9685
www.abc-clio.com
Offers information on organizations and agencies involved with public education systems.

3826 Cornocopia of Concise Quotations
Careers/Consultants Consultants in Education
3050 Palm Aire Drive N
#310
Pompano Beach, FL 33069
954-974-5477
Fax: 954-974-5477
carconed@aol.com
Wealth of practical reminders of the enduring ideas. The book furthers humane understand-

ings by gathering and preserving the wisdom of the wise and experienced.

ISBN: 0-7392-0275-8
ISSN: 99-95201

Dr. Robert M Bookbinder, President

3827 Council for Educational Development and Research Directory
National Education Association (NEA)
1201 16th Street NW
Washington, DC 20036-3290
202-833-4000
Fax: 202-822-7974
ncuea@nea.org
www.nea.org
Offers 15 member educational research and development institutions.

50 pages Annual

Lily Eskelsen Garc¡a, President
Becky Pringle, Vice President

3828 Digest of Supreme Court Decisions
Phi Delta Kappa Educational Foundation
320 W. Eighth Street
Suite 216
Bloomington, IN 47404-0789
812-339-1156
800-786-1156
Fax: 812-339-0018
memberservices@pdkintl.org
www.pdkintl.org
Designed as a ready reference, this edition of a popular digest provides a concise set of individual summaries of cases decided by the Supreme Court. Fully indexed.

256 pages Paperback
ISBN: 0-87367-835-4

Perry A Zirkel, Author
Dan Brown, Executive Director
Bill Bushaw, Chief Executive Officer

3829 Directory for Exceptional Children
Porter Sargent Publishers, Inc.
2 LAN Drive
Suite 100
Westford, MA 01886-3028
978-692-5092
800-342-7470
Fax: 617-523-1021
info@portersargent.com
www.portersargent.com
A comprehensive survey of 2,500 schools, facilities and organizations across the country serving children and young adults with developmental, physical and medical disabilities. With 15 distinct chapters covering a range of disabilities, this work is an invaluable aid to parents and professionals seeking the optimal environment for special-needs children. Hardcover.

Publication Date: 1994 1152 pages BiAnnual
ISSN: 0070-5012

Dan McKeever, Senior Editor

3830 Directory of Catholic Special Educational Programs & Facilities
National Catholic Educational Association
1005 North Glebe Road
Suite 525
Arlington, VA 22201-3829
202-337-6232
800-711-6232
Fax: 703-243-0025
www.ncea.org
Lists approximately 950 Catholic schools and day and residential school programs for children and adolescents with special education needs.

Publication Date: 1989 100 pages

Blas, Cupich, Chairman
Robert Bimonte, President

3831 Directory of Central Agencies for Jewish Education
Jewish Education Service of North America
247 West 37th Street
5th Floor
New York, NY 10018
212-284-6882
Fax: 212-284-6951
info@jesna.org
www.jesna.org
Offers educational resources for professionals in Jewish education, including general education information, materials and services.

Cass Gottlieb, Chair
Sandra Gold, Vice Chair

3832 Directory of College Cooperative Education Programs
National Commission for Cooperative Education
600 Suffolk Street
Suite 25
Lowell, MA 01854-5096
617-373-3770
Fax: 617-373-3463
ncce@neu.edu
www.waceinc.org
A publication providing detailed information on cooperative education programs at 460 colleges throughout the United States.

Publication Date: 1962 219 pages
ISBN: 0-89774-998-4

Mauritis van Rooijen, Chair
Sampan Silapanad, Chair

3833 Directory of ERIC Information Service Providers
Educational Resources Information Ctr./Access ERIC
1600 Research Boulevard
Rockville, MD 20850-3172
301-656-9723
eric.ed.gov
Offers information on more than 1,000 government agencies, nonprofit and profit organizations, individuals and foreign organizations that provide access to ERIC microfiche collections, search services and abstract journal collections.

100 pages Biennial

3834 Directory of Graduate Programs
Graduate Record Examinations Program/ ETS
PO Box 6000
Princeton, NJ 08541-6000
609-771-7670
866-473-4373
Fax: 610-290-8975
www.ets.org/gre
Accredited institutions that offer graduate degrees.

1,400 pages 4 Volumes

3835 Directory of Indigenous Education
Floyd Beller - Wested
730 Harrison Street
San Francisco, CA 94107
415-565-3000
877-493-7833
Fax: 415-565-3012
fbeller@WestEd.org
www.wested.org
This revised and expanded edition incorporates a wider scope of information, including a list of Head Start, Child Care and Title IX programs and JOM contractors, which enhances our principal goal of improving educational services to native students and communities.

Publication Date: 1998 94 pages

Tacy C. Ashby, Vice President
Jorge Ayala, Superitendent

3836 Directory of International Internships: A World of Opportunities
International Studies & Programs
Michigan State University
427 N. Shaw Lane, Room 207
East Lansing, MI 48824-1035
517-353-2350
Fax: 517-353-7254
gliozzo@msu.edu
www.isp.msu.edu
A directory containing information about a wide range of overseas internship oppotunities. Over 500 entries of international internships sponsored by educational institutions, government agencies, and private organizations. There are indexes of topics in geographical areas listed by countries and geographical areas listed by topic.

Adedayo Adekson, Assistant Dean
Deandra Beck, Associate Dean

3837 Directory of Member Institutions and Institutional Representatives
Council of Graduate Schools
1 Dupont Circle NW
Suite 230
Washington, DC 20036-1136
202-223-3791
Fax: 202-331-7157
general_inquiries@cgs.nche.edu
www.cgsnet.org
Offers listings of over 400 member graduate schools in the US and Canada.

85 pages Annually

Barbara A. Knuth, Chair
Suzanne T. Ortega, President

3838 Directory of Overseas Educational Advising Centers
College Board Publications
45 Columbus Avenue
New York, NY 10023-6917
212-713-8000
800-323-7155
Fax: 800-525-5562
www.collegeboard.org
This directory has been developed as a means through which institutions of higher education can communicate directly with overseas education advisers and through which advisers can communicate more directly with each other.

Publication Date: 1995 165 pages

David Coleman, President/ CEO
Jeremy Singer, Chief Operating Officer

3839 Directory of Postsecondary Institutions
National Center for Education Statistics
K Street NW
Washington, DC 20006
202-502-7300
877-4ED-PUBS
Fax: 301-470-1244
edpubs@inet.ed.gov
www.edpubs.gov
Postsecondary institutions in the US, Puerto Rico, Virgin Islands and territories in the Pacific United States. Two volumes: Volume I Degree-Granting Institutions, Volume II Non-Degree-Granting Institutions.

Publication Date: 1990 500 pages Biennial

3840 Directory of Youth Exchange Programs
UN Educational, Scientific & Cultural Association
Youth Division, 1 Rue Miollis
Paris F-75015
France
1-4563842
Offers about 370 nonprofit organizations and governmental agencies in 95 countries that organize youth and student exchanges, study tours and correspondence exchanges.
Publication Date: 1992 225 pages

3841 Diversity, Accessibility and Quality
College Board Publications
45 Columbus Avenue
New York, NY 10023-6917
212-713-8000
800-323-7155
Fax: 800-525-5562
www.collegeboard.org
Primarily for non-Americans, this overview is designed to examine aspects of US education that have particular importance in programs of student exchange.
Publication Date: 1995 47 pages
ISBN: 0-874474-24-8
Clifford F Sjogren, Author
David Coleman, President/ CEO
Jeremy Singer, Chief Operating Officer

3842 ERIC - Education Resources Information Center
655 15th Street NW
Suite 500
Washington, DC 20005
800-538-3742
ericrequest@ed.gov
eric.ed.gov
The mission of the center is to provide a comprehensive, easy-to-use, searchable, Internet-based bibliographic and full-text database of education research and information that meets the requirements of the Education Sciences Reform Act of 2002.
Publication Date: 1965

3843 Education Sourcebook: Basic Information about National Education Expectations and Goals
Omnigraphics
155 West Congress
Suite 200
Detroit, MI 48226
313-961-1340
800-234-1340
Fax: 313-961-1383
contact@omnigraphics.com
www.omnigraphics.com
A collection of education-related documents and articles for parents and students.
1123 pages
ISBN: 0-7808-0179-2
Jeanne Gough, Author
Paul Rogers, Publicity Associate

3844 Educational Placement Sources-Abroad
Education Information Services/Instant Alert
PO Box 620662
Newton, MA 02462-0662
617-433-0125
Lists 150 organizations, arranged by type, in the United States and abroad that place English-speaking teachers and education administrators in positions abroad.
19 pages Annual
FB Viaux, President

3845 Educational Rankings Annual
Gale Group
27500 Drake Road
Farmington Hills, MI 48331-3535
248-699-GALE
800-877-4253
Fax: 877-363-4253
galeord@galegroup.com
www.cengage.com
Top 10 lists from popular and scholarly periodicals, government publications, and others. The lists cover all facets of education.
890 pages Annual Hardcover
ISBN: 0-7876-7419-2
Lynn C Hattendorf Westney, Author
Josef Blumenfeld, Senior Vice President
Lindsay Stanley, Senior Director

3846 Educational Resources Catalog
CDE Press
1430 N Street
PO Box 271
Sacramento, CA 95814-0271
916-445-1260
800-995-4099
Fax: 916-323-0823
www.cde.ca.gov
Resource catalog from the California Department of Education.

3847 Educator's Desk Reference: A Sourcebook of Educational Information & Research
MacMillan Publishing Company
1633 Broadway
New York, NY 10019
212-654-8500
Fax: 800-835-3202
Directory includes national and regional education organizations.
Publication Date: 1989

3848 Educator's Scrapbook
Careers/Consultants Consultants in Education
3050 Palm Aire Drive N
#310
Pompano Beach, FL 33069
954-974-5477
Fax: 954-974-5477
carconed@aol.com
Collection of education morsels offered to those who who would seek to redefine and clarify the aims and purposes of today's education. The book attepts to help its readers refocus upon the real purposes of education and their relationships to current education practices.

ISBN: 0-9703623-0-7
ISSN: 00-93185
Dr. Robert M Bookbinder, President

3849 Educators Guide to FREE Computer Materials and Internet Resources
Educators Progress Service
214 Center Street
Beaver Dam, WI 53956-1408
920-210-3684
888-951-4469
Fax: 920-326-3127
info@monumentalhosting.com
www.monumentalhosting.com
Lists and describes almost 2000 web sites of educational value. Available in two grade specific editions.
317 pages Annual
ISBN: 87708-362-2
Kathy Nehmer, President

3850 Educators Guide to FREE Films, Filmstrips and Slides
Educators Progress Service
214 Center Street
Beaver Dam, WI 53956-1408
920-210-3684
888-951-4469
Fax: 920-326-3127
info@monumentalhosting.com
www.monumentalhosting.com
Lists and describes free and free-loan films, filmstrips, slides, and audiotapes for all age levels.
135 pages Annual
ISBN: 87708-400-9
Kathy Nehmer, President

3851 Educators Guide to FREE Multicultural Material
Educators Progress Service
214 Center Street
Beaver Dam, WI 53956-1408
920-210-3684
888-951-4469
Fax: 920-326-3127
info@monumentalhosting.com
www.monumentalhosting.com
Lists and describes FREE films, videotapes, filmstrips, slides, web sites, and hundreds of free printed materials in the field of multicultural and diversity education for all age levels.
198 pages Annual
ISBN: 87708-412-2
Kathy Nehmer, President

3852 El-Hi Textbooks and Serials in Print
RR Bowker Reed Reference
2104 21st Avenue South
Birmingham, NJ 35223-1541
205-870-4693
Fax: 908-665-6688
frankflemingart.com
Listing of about 995 publishers of elementary and secondary level textbooks and related teaching materials.
Annual

3853 Environmental Education Materials: Guidelines for Excellence
North American Assoc for Environmental Education
2000 P Street NW
Suite 540
Washington, DC 20036
202-419-0412
Fax: 212-419-0415
info@naaee.org
www.naaee.org
A set of recommendations for developing and selecting environmental education materials. These guidelines aim to help developers of activity guides, lesson plans, and other instructional materials produce high wuality products, and to provide educators with a tool to evaluate the wide array of available environmental education materials.
23 pages
ISBN: 1-884008-41-0
Jose Marcos-Iga, President
Judy Braus, Executive Director

3854 Evaluating Your Environmental Education Programs: A Workbook for Practitioners
North American Assoc for Environmental Education
2000 P Street NW
Suite 540
Washington, DC 20036

202-419-0412
Fax: 212-419-0415
info@naaee.org
www.naaee.org
Walks you through how to design and conduct an evaluation. Throughout the workbook, 23 exercises as you to check your understanding (the answers are included). In addition, 47 application exercises point you to tasks that will help you develop your own evaluation.

Jose Marcos-Iga, President
Judy Braus, Executive Director

3855 Excellence in Environmental Education: Guidelines for Learning (PreK-12)

North American Assoc for Environmental Education
2000 P Street NW
Suite 540
Washington, DC 20036
202-419-0412
Fax: 212-419-0415
info@naaee.org
www.naaee.org
The guidelines support state and local environmental education efforts by: setting expectations for performance and achievement in fourth, eighth, and twelfth grades; suggesting a framework for effective and comprehensive environmental education programs and curricula; demonstrating how environmental edcuation can be used to meet standards set by the traditional disciplines and to give students opportunities to synthesize knowledge and experience across disciplines.

121 pages
ISBN: 1-884008-75-5

Jose Marcos-Iga, President
Judy Braus, Executive Director

3856 Exceptional Children Education Resources

The Council for Exceptional Children
2900 Crystal Drive
Suite 1000
Arlington, VA 22202-3557
703-620-3660
888-232-7733
Fax: 703-264-9494
cec@cec.sped.org
www.cec.sped.org
A proprietary database that includes bibliographic data and abstract information on journal articles, and audiovisual materials in special education, and gifted education.

ISSN: 0160-4309

Robin D. Brewer, President
Sharon Raimondi, Treasurer

3857 Family Services Report

CD Publictions
8204 Fenton Street
Sliver Spring, MD 20910
301-588-6380
855-237-1396
Fax: 301-588-0519
info@cdpublications.com
cdpublications.com
Private grants for family service programs

18 pages
ISSN: 1524-9484

Ray Sweeney, Editor
Mary Crompton, Publisher

3858 Fifty State Educational Directories

Career Guidance Foundation
1327 E. Kemper Rd
Suite 3000
Cincinnati, OH 45246-1906
513-834-8780
Fax: 513-834-8779
collegesource.com
A collection on microfiche consisting of reproductions of the state educational directories published by each individual state department of education.

3859 Funny School Excuses

Careers/Consultants Consultants in Education
3050 Palm Aire Drive N
#310
Pompano Beach, FL 33069
954-974-5477
Fax: 954-974-5477
carconed@aol.com
Collection of illustrations, cartoons and excuses gathered from authentic notes written by parents and sometimes their children. The book is wonderfully entertaining and recommended for its unusual humor, variety, and revelations of human nature.

ISBN: 0-7392-0309-6
ISSN: 99-95349

Dr. Robert M Bookbinder, President

3860 Ganley's Catholic Schools in America

Fisher Publishing Company
PO Box 15070
Sun City West, AZ 85376-5070
623-328-8326
800-759-7615
Fax: 480-657-9422
publisher@ganleyscatholicschools.com
www.ganleyscatholicschool.com
Comprehensive listings on all Catholic Schools in America. Listings include phone numbers, addresses, names of administrators, number of students, complete diocesan, state, regional and national statistics. Includes an extensive analysis of demographic trends within Catholic elementary and secondary education, prepared by the National Catholic Education Association.

450+ pages Annual/June
ISBN: 1-558331-59-0

Millard T Fischer, Publisher

3861 Graduate & Undergraduate Programs & Courses in Middle East Studies in the US, Canada

Middle East Studies Association of North America
University of Arizona
633 Third Ave
New York, NY 10017-6795
520-697-1505
Fax: 520-626-9095
mesana@u.arizona.edu
www.acls.org

Pauline Yu, President
Steven C. Wheatley, Vice President

3862 Guide to International Exchange, Community Service & Travel for Persons with Disabilities

Mobility International USA
132 E. Broadway
Suite 343
Eugene, OR 97401
541-343-1284
Fax: 541-343-6812
info@miusa.org
www.miusa.org
This directory lists an impressive array of information regarding international study, living, travel, funding and contact organizations for people with disabilities.

Publication Date: 1981
ISBN: 1-880034-24-7

Susan Sygall, Chief Executive Officer
Cerise Roth-Vinson, Chief Operating Officer

3863 Guide to Summer Camps & Schools

Porter Sargent Publishers
2 LAN Drive
Suite 100
Westford, MA 01886-3028
978-692-5092
800-342-7470
Fax: 617-523-1021
info@portersargent.com
www.portersargent.com
Covers the broad spectrum of recreational and educational summer opportunities. Current facts from 1,500 camps and schools, as well as programs for those with special needs or learning disabilities, makes the guide a comprehensive and convenient resource.

816 pages Biannual
ISBN: 0-875581-33-1

HJ Lane Coordinating Editor, Author
J Yonce, General Manager
Daniel McKeever, Sr Editor

3864 Guidelines for Effective Character Education Through Sports

Character Education Partnership
1634 I Street NW
Suite 550
Washington, DC 20036
202-296-7743
800-988-8081
Fax: 202-296-7779
information@character.org
www.character.org
Guidelines for turning sports and physical education programs into the powerful, positive forces they should be.

Becky Sipos, President/ CEO
Sheril Morgan, Director

3865 Guidelines for the Preparation and Professional Development of Environmental Educato

North American Assoc for Environmental Education
2000 P Street NW
Suite 540
Washington, DC 20036
202-419-0412
Fax: 212-419-0415
info@naaee.org
www.naaee.org
Recommendations about the basic knowledge and abilities educators need to provide high quality environmental education. The guidelines are designed to apply: within the context of pre-service teacher education programs and environmental education courses offered to students with varied backgrounds such as environmental studies, geography, liberal studies, or natural resources.

43 pages
ISBN: 1-884008-78-X

Jose Marcos-Iga, President
Judy Braus, Executive Director

3866 HEATH Resource Center at the National Youth Transitions Center

HEATH Resource Center
2134 G Street NW
Suite 308
Washington, DC 20052-0001

202-973-0904
800-544-3284
Fax: 202-973-0908
askheath@gwu.edu
www.heath.gwu.edu
A national clearinghouse on postsecondary education for people with disabilities, managed by the George Washington University Graduate School and the HSC Foundation. HEATH develops training modules and publishes resource papers, fact sheets, directories, and website information. The center also fosters a network of professionals in disability issues.

Publication Date: 2000

Joan Kester, Ph.D, Principal Investigator
Christopher Nace, Research Assistant

3867 Handbook of Private Schools
Porter Sargent Publishers
2 LAN Drive
Suite 100
Westford, MA 01886-3028
978-692-5092
800-342-7470
Fax: 617-523-1021
info@portersargent.com
www.portersargent.com
Continuing a tradition that began in 1915, this handbook provides optimal guidance in the choice of educational environments and opportunities for students. Totally revised and updated, this 83rd edition presents current facts on 1,700 elementary and secondary boarding and day schools across the United States. Complete statistical data on enrollments, tuition, graduates, administrators and faculty have been compiled and objectively reported. Hardcover.

1472 pages Annual
ISBN: 0-875581-44-7

J Yonce, General Manager
Daniel McKeever, Sr Editor

3868 Handbook of United Methodist-Related Schools, Colleges, Universities & Theological Schools
General Board of Higher Education & Ministry/UMC
1001 19th Avenue
PO Box 340007
Nashville, TN 37203-0007
615-340-7400
Fax: 615-340-7379
scu@gbhem.org
www.gbhem.org
Includes two pages of information about each of United Methodist's 123 institutions, a chart indicating major areas of study, information about United Methodist loan and scholarship programs, as well as information about how to select a college. Published every four years.

344 pages Paperback

James E. Dorff, President
Lanther Marie Mills, Vice President

3869 Hidden America
Place in the Woods
3900 Glenwood Avenue
Golden Valley, MN 55422-5302
763-374-2120
Fax: 952-593-5593
placewoods@aol.com
Set of five reference-essay books on American minorities (African America; Hispanic America, the People (Native Americans); American women; My Own Book! classroom reference for elementary through secondary).

36+ pages Paperback Book

Roger Hammer, Publisher

3870 Higher Education Directory
Higher Education Publications
1801 Robert Fulton Drive
Suite 555
Reston, VA 20191-5499
571-313-0478
888-349-7715
Fax: 571-313-0526
info@hepinc.com
www.hepinc.com
Lists over 4,364 degree granting colleges and universities accredited by approved agencies, recognized by the US Secretary of Education successor to the Department of Education's: Education Directory, Colleges and Universities and Council for Higher Education Accreditation (CHEA).

Publication Date: 1994 1,040 pages Annual/Paperback
ISBN: 0-914927-44-2
ISSN: 0736-0197

Jeanne Burke, Editor
Fred Hafner JR, Vice President Operations

3871 Higher Education Opportunities for Women & Minorities: Annotated Selections
U.S. Office of Postsecondary Education
400 Maryland Avenue SW
Room 3915
Washington, DC 20202-0001
202-708-9180
Programs of public and private organizations and state and federal government agencies that offer loans, scholarships and fellowship opportunities for women and minorities.

143 pages Biennial

3872 Home from Home (Educational Exchange Programs)
Central Bureau for Educational Visits & Exchanges
10 Spring Gardens
London, SW1A 2BN, England
171-389-4004
Fax: 171-389-4426
150 organizations and agencies worldwide that arrange stays with families for paying guests or on an exchange basis. Organizations are geographically listed including a description of program, costs, insurance information, overseas representation and language instruction.

216 pages

3873 Homeschooler's Guide to FREE Teaching Aids
Educators Progress Service
214 Center Street
Beaver Dam, WI 53956-1408
920-210-3684
888-951-4469
Fax: 920-326-3127
info@monumentalhosting.com
www.monumentalhosting.com
Lists and describes free print materials specifically available to homeschoolers with students of all age levels.

277 pages
ISBN: 87708-375-4

Kathy Nehmer, President

3874 Homeschooler's Guide to FREE Videotapes
Educators Progress Service
214 Center Street
Beaver Dam, WI 53956-1408
920-210-3684
888-951-4469
Fax: 920-326-3127
info@monumentalhosting.com
www.monumentalhosting.com
Lists and describes free and free-loan videotapes specifically available to homeschoolers with students of all age levels.

248 pages Annual
ISBN: 87708-411-4

Kathy Nehmer, President

3875 IIEPassport: Academic Year Abroad 2007
Institute of International Education
809 United Nations Plaza
New York, NY 10017-3580
412-741-0930
Fax: 212-984-5496
iiebooks@abdintl.com
www.iiebooks.org
Over 3,100 undergraduate and graduate study-abroad programs conducted worldwide during the academic year by United States and foreign colleges, universities, and private organizations.

Publication Date: 2007 Annual
ISBN: 87206-279-1

Marie O'Sullivan, Author
Daniel Obst, Sr Editor

3876 ISS Directory of Overseas Schools
International Schools Services
15 Roszel Road
PO Box 5910
Princeton, NJ 08540-6729
609-452-0990
Fax: 609-452-2690
jlarsson@iss.edu
www.iss.edu
The only comprehensive guide to American and international schools around the world. The Directory is carefully researched and compiled to include current and complete information on over 600 international schools.

590 pages Paperback
ISBN: 0-913663-13-1

Jane Larsson, Director Of Education

3877 Inclusion Guide for Handling Chronically Disruptive Behavior
Master Teacher
One Leadership Lane
PO Box 1207
Manhattan, KS 66502-1207
800-669-9633
Fax: 800-669-1132
www.masterteacher.com
A comprehensive process for ensuring that no disruptive behavior is tolerated, no student is turned away, and all students are served.

150 pages
ISBN: 0-914607-40-5

Teresa VanDover, Author

3878 Incorporating Multiple Intelligences into the Curriculum and into the Classroom: Elementary
Master Teacher
One Leadership Lane
PO Box 1207
Manhattan, KS 66502-1207
800-669-9633
Fax: 800-669-1132
www.masterteacher.com
Contains lesson plans and teaching methods that address the needs of students and help them identify their strengths according to the domains of multiple intelligences.

181 pages
ISBN: 0-914607-63-4

3879 Incorporating Multiple Intelligences into the Curriculum and into the Classroom: Secondary
Master Teacher
One Leadership Lane
PO Box 1207
Manhattan, KS 66502-1207
800-669-9633
Fax: 800-669-1132
www.masterteacher.com
Contains lesson plans and teaching methods that address the needs of students and help them identify their strengths according to the domains of multiple intelligences.
147 pages
ISBN: 0-914607-64-2

3880 Independent Schools Association of the Southwest-Membership List
Energy Square
505 N Big Spring Street
Suite 406
Midland, TX 79701
432-684-9550
Fax: 432-684-9401
webmaster@isasw.org
www.isasw.org
A geographical index of independent schools accredited by the Independent Schools Association.
Mark Desjardins, President
Rhonda Durham, Executive Director

3881 Independent Study Catalog
Peterson's Guides
PO Box 2123
Princeton, NJ 08543-2123
800-338-3282
Fax: 609-896-4531
A comprehensive listing of over 10,000 correspondence course offerings at 100 accredited colleges and universities nationwide, for those seeking the flexibility and convenience of at-home study.
293 pages
ISBN: 1-560794-60-7

3882 International Federation of Organizations for School Correspondence/Exchange
FIOCES
29, rue d'ulm, F-75230 Paris
F-75230 Paris
France
Governmental agencies and other organizations concerned with scholastic correspondence and student exchange programs.
Publication Date: 1991 3 pages

3883 International Schools Directory
European Council of International Schools
Fourth Floor, 146 Buckingham Palace
London, SW1W 9TR
United Kingdom
44 -0 2- 782
1730-268244
Fax: 1730-267914
ecis@ecis.org
www.ecis.org
Over 420 ECIS schools in more than 90 countries; 300 affiliated colleges and universities worldwide; educational publishers and equipment suppliers.
Publication Date: 1965 550 pages Annual
Kevin J. Ruth, Ph.D., Executive Director
Darlene Fisher, People & Programmes Lead

3884 International Study Telecom Directory
WorldWide Classroom
PO Box 1166
Milwaukee, WI 53201-1166
414-224-3476
Fax: 414-224-3466
info@worldwide.edu
www.worldwide.edu
Comprehensive directory for locating educational resources both internationally and throughout the US Provides contact information on educational institutions including address, phone, fax, e-mail and URL. New icon system offers additional information on the type of programs offered. Resource guide at beginning includes useful web sites, airline and car rental contact numbers, currency converters, international organizations and international publications.
Mike Witley, President
Stacy Hargarten, Classroom Publications

3885 International Voluntary Service Directory
Volunteers for Peace
1034 Tiffany Road
Belmont, VT 05730
802-259-2759
Fax: 802-259-2922
vfp@vfp.org
www.vfp.org
Comprehensive listing of over 3,400 workcamps in 100 countries around the world. Organized by country.
289 pages Annual
ISBN: 0-945617-20-B
Peter Coldwell, Director

3886 International Who's Who in Education
International Biographical Centre/Melrose Press
3 Regal Lane, Soham, Ely
Cambridgeshire CB7 5BA
United Kingdom
353-721091
Lists about 5,000 persons at all levels of teaching and educational administration.
1,000 pages

3887 International Yearbook of Education: Education in the World
UN Educational, Scientific & Cultural Assn.
7, place de Fontenoy
F-75700 Paris
France
1-45681000
Describes and offers information on educational systems worldwide.
Publication Date: 1989 200 pages

3888 Job Search Handbook for Educators
American Association for Employment in Education
947 E. Johnstown Road
#170
Gahanna, OH 43230
614-485-1111
Fax: 360-244-7802
execdir@aaee.org
www.aaee.org
Resume writing, interviewing tips, as well as articles on how to select the kind of school system you want, job fair networking and other related articles.
212 pages Bi-Annually
Doug Peden, Executive Director
Todd Fukai, Board President

3889 Legal Basics: A Handbook for Educators
Phi Delta Kappa International
320 W. Eighth Street
Suite 216
Bloomington, IL 47404-0789
812-339-1156
800-766-1156
Fax: 812-339-0018
memberservices@pdkintl.org
www.pdkintl.org
Superintendents, principals, counselors, teachers, and paraprofessionals need to pay close attention to their actions in schools and classrooms because, from a legal standpoint, those settings may contain hazardous conditions. Legal Basics points out the pitfalls and how to avoid them.
Publication Date: 1906 120 pages Paperback
ISBN: 0-8736-806-0
Evelyn B Kelly, Author
Patricia Williams, Chair
Douglas Christensen, Vice Chair

3890 Lesson Plans and Modifications for Inclusion and Collaborative Classrooms
Master Teacher
One Leadership Lane
PO Box 1207
Manhattan, KS 66502-1207
800-669-9633
Fax: 800-669-1132
www.masterteacher.com
Each modification is a complete lesson plan that gives the teacher a description of the activity and objetive the materials need and a step-by-step guide of how to carry out the learning process.
Publication Date: 1969 242 pages
ISBN: 0-914607-37-5

3891 Lesson Plans for Character Education: Elementary Edition
Master Teacher
One Leadership Lane
PO Box 1207
Manhattan, KS 66502-1207
800-669-9633
Fax: 800-669-1132
www.masterteacher.com
Gives you more than 140 practical lessons developed and tested by teachers across the curriculum and in all grade levels.
Publication Date: 1969 207 pages
ISBN: 0-914607-53-7

3892 List of Over 70 Higher Education Association
Educational Information Services
PO Box 662
Newton Lower Falls, MA 02162
617-964-4555
Provides descriptions and contact information on associations for individuals in higher education.

3893 List of State Boards of Higher Education
Educational Information Services
PO Box 662
Newton Lower Falls, MA 02162
617-964-4555
A compilation of the boards of education for all the states in the union.

3894 List of State Community & Junior College Board Offices
Educational Information Services
PO Box 662
Newton Lower Falls, MA 02162
617-964-4555

A list of the board officers and state officers within community, junior and university institutions.

3895 MDR School Directory
Market Data Retrieval
6 Armstrong Road
Suite 301
Shelton, CT 06484-6216
203-926-4800
800-333-8802
Fax: 203-929-5253
mdrinfo@dnb.com
mdreducation.com
MDR's school directories provide comprehensive data on every public school district and school throughout the United States and the District of Columbia. Each state directory contains current names and job titles of key decision makers, school and district addresses, phone numbers, current enrollments and much more. The content is also available on CD-ROM and diskette.
Publication Date: 1969 51 Volume Set
Aaron Stibel, GM, CEO MDR Education
Kristina James, Director of Marketing

3896 Minority Student Guide to American Colleges
Paoli Publishing
P.O. Box 190
Suite 287
Paoli, IN 47454-1553
812-723-2572
Fax: 812-723-2592
paolinewsrepublican.com
Covers colleges, military schools, and financial aid information for minority students.
89 pages

3897 Monograph 1-Using a Logic Model to Review and Analyze an Environmental Education Program
North American Association for Environmental Educa
2000 P Street NW
Suite 540
Washington, DC 20036
202-419-0412
Fax: 212-419-0415
info@naaee.org
www.naaee.org
Reviews and analyzes a long-standing and well-documented program in environmental education, Hungerford et al.'s issue-and-action instruction program (1973-). Logic models provide conceptual guidance and visual support for this review and analysis. These models were adapted from work in Aquatic Resource Education by Peyton, and the literature on logic modeling in program evaluation.
72 pages
ISBN: 1-884008-86-0
Jose Marcos-Iga, President
Susan McGuire, Secretary

3898 Monograph 2-Preparing Effective Environmental Educators
North American Association for Environmental Educa
2000 P Street NW
Suite 540
Washington, DC 20036
202-419-0412
Fax: 212-419-0415
info@naaee.org
www.naaee.org
Focuses on the methods used to prepare those who teach environmental education. Research and evaluation related to three main audiences for environmental education preparedness training - pre-service teachers, in-service teachers, and nonformal education - are examined. The five papers presented represent an interesting and instructive array of research and evaluation that can be used to spur our thinking about the preparation of environmental educators.
89 pages
ISBN: 1-884008-88-7
Jose Marcos-Iga, President
Susan McGuire, Secretary

3899 NAFSA's Guide to Education Abroad for Advisers & Administrators
NAFSA: Association of International Educators
1307 New York Avenue NW
8th Floor
Washington, DC 20005-4701
202-737-3699
800-836-4994
Fax: 202-737-3657
inbox@nafsa.org
www.nafsa.org
Publication Date: 1948
Marlene M Johnson, Executive Director & CEO
Vic Johnson, Senior Advisor

3900 NEA Almanac of Higher Education
National Education Association (NEA)
1201 16th Street NW
Washington, DC 20036-3290
202-833-4000
Fax: 202-822-7974
nche@nea.org
www.nea.org
Publication Date: 1857 Annually
ISSN: 0743-670X
Con Lehane, Author
Lily Eskelsen Garcia, President
Becky Pringle, VP

3901 NSEE Perspectives
NSEE Headquarters
19 Mantua Road
Mount Royal, NJ 08061
856-423-3427
Fax: 856-423-3420
nsee@talley.com
www.nsee.org
Book exploring the theory and practice of experiential education and conflicting opinions on the meaning of "the common good" within service learning and civic engagement.
John S. Duley, Author

3902 National Directory of Children, Youth & Families Services
Contexo Media
9737 Washingtonian Blvd
Suite 200
Gaithersburg, MD 20878
800-334-5724
Fax: 301-287-2535
customersupport@contexomedia.com
www.contexomedia.com
Organized by state and county, this directory lists over 30,000 organizations and 46,000 contacts that focus on helping anyone who is committed to providing the best possible service to our nation's at-risk children, youth and families.
Publication Date: 0 1456 pages Annually
Treavor Peterson, President
Kim Luna, Product Manager

3903 National Guide to Educational Credit for Training Programs
American Council on Education
1 Dupont Circle NW
Suite 535
Washington, DC 20036-1110
202-939-9430
Fax: 202-833-4762
www.acenet.edu
More than 4,500 courses offered by over 280 government agencies, business firms and nonprofit groups.
1,018 pages Annual
James H. Mullen Jr., Chair
Renu Khator, Vice Chair/ Chair-elect

3904 National Reference Directory of Year-Round Education Programs
National Association for Year-Round Education
PO Box 711386
San Diego, CA 92171-1386
619-276-5296
Fax: 858-571-5754
info@nayre.org
www.nayre.org
Six hundred fifty school districts in the US with year-round programs are covered in this directory, listed by geographical location, including all contact information and descriptions.
178 pages Annual Paperback
Charles Ballinger, Executive Director Emeritus
Samuel Pepper, Executive Director

3905 National Schools of Character: Best Practices and New Perspectives
Character Education Partnership
1634 I Street NW
Suite 550
Washington, DC 20006
202-296-7743
800-988-8081
Fax: 202-296-7779
www.character.org
Becky Sipos, President and CEO
Sheril Morgan, Director

3906 National Schools of Character: Practices to Adopt & Adapt
Character Education Partnership
1634 I Street NW
Suite 550
Washington, DC 20006
202-296-7743
800-988-8081
Fax: 202-296-7779
www.character.org
Becky Sipos, President and CEO
Sheril Morgan, Director

3907 New England Association of Schools and Colleges
New England Association of Schools and Colleges
3 Burlington Woods Drive
Suite 100
Burlington, MA 01803-1433
781-425-7700
855-886-3272
Fax: 781-425-1001
www.neasc.org
Listing of over 1,575 institutions of higher education, public and independent schools and vocational-technical schools in New England.
Publication Date: 1885 65 pages Annual
Mary Lyons, Chair
William L. Burke III, Secretary-Treasurer

3908 Nonformal Environmental Education Programs: Guidelines for Excellence
North American Assoc for Environmental Education
2000 P Street NW
Suite 540
Washington, DC 20036
202-419-0412
Fax: 212-419-0415
info@naaee.org
www.naaee.org
A set of recommendations for developing and administering high quality nonformal environmental education programs. These recommendations provide a tool that can be used to ensure a firm foundation for new programs or to trigger improvements in existing ones. The overall goal of these guidelines is to facilitate a superior educational process leading to the environmental quality that people desire.

ISBN: 1-884008-89-5
Jose Marcos-Iga, President
Susan McGuire, Secretary

3909 Overseas American-Sponsored Elementary and Secondary Schools
US Department of State, Office Overseas Schools
2201 C Street NW
Washington, DC 20520
202-647-4000
Fax: 202-261-8224
www.state.gov/m/a/os
Lists nearly 180 independent schools overseas and 10 regional associations of schools.
30 pages Annual
Antony Blinken, Deputy Secretary

3910 Paradigm Lost: Leading America Beyond It's Fear of Educational Change
American Association of School Administrators
1615 Duke Street
Suite 700
Alexandria, VA 22314-1730
703-528-0700
Fax: 703-841-1543
info@aasa.org
www.aasa.org
Explores the beliefs and assumptions upon which schools operate, provides powerful and practical insights and improvement strategies.
Publication Date: 1998 158 pages Softcover
ISBN: 0-87652-232-0
Daniel A. Domenech, Executive Director
Sharon Adams-Taylor, Associate Executive Director

3911 Patterson's American Education
Educational Directories Inc
Po Box 68097
Schaumburg, IL 60168-97
847-891-1250
800-357-6183
Fax: 847-891-0945
info@ediusa.com
www.ediusa.com
Lists more than 11,000 public school districts; 300 parochial superintendents; 400 territorial schools; 400 state department of education personnel; and 400 educational associations in one easy to use consistent format. Arranged alphabetically by state then by city. City listings include the city name, telephone area code, city population, county name, public school district name, enrollment, grade range, superintendent's name, address and phone number. Index of secondary schools included.
Publication Date: 1904 974 pages Annual
ISBN: 0-9771602-3-8
ISSN: 0079-0230
Linda Moody, Office Manager

3912 Patterson's Schools Classified
Educational Directories Inc.
1025 W Wise Road
PO Box 68097
Schaumburg, IL 60168-97
847-891-1250
800-357-6183
Fax: 847-891-0945
info@ediusa.org
www.ediusa.org
Contains 7,000 accredited postsecondary schools, the broadest assortment available in a single directory. Universities, colleges, community colleges, junior colleges, career schools and teaching hospitals are co-mingled under 50 academic disciplines but retain their school type identification. School professional accreditation is shown in 32 classifications. The basic entry includes school name, mailing address and contact person, with additional descriptive material supplied by the school.
Publication Date: 1904 302 pages Annual
ISBN: 0-9771602-2-X
Wayne Moody, Coordinating Education

3913 Peterson's Competitive Colleges
Peterson's, A Nelnet Company
Princeton Pike Corporate Center
461 From Road
Paramus, NJ 07652
609-896-1800
800-338-3282
Fax: 402-458-3042
support@petersons.com
www.petersons.com
The most trusted source of advice for excellent students searching for high-quality schools. Provides objective criteria to compare more than 440 leading colleges and universities.
Publication Date: 1975 524 pages
ISBN: 1-560795-98-0

3914 Peterson's Guide to Four-Year Colleges
Peterson's, A Nelnet Company
Princeton Pike Corporate Center
461 From Road
Paramus, NJ 07652
609-896-1800
800-338-3282
Fax: 402-458-3042
support@petersons.com
www.petersons.com
Includes descriptions of over 2,000 colleges, providing guidance on selecting the right school, getting in and financial aid.
Publication Date: 1975 2,922 pages

3915 Peterson's Guide to Two-Year Colleges
Peterson's, A Nelnet Company
Princeton Pike Corporate Center
461 From Road
Paramus, NJ 07652
609-896-1800
800-338-3282
Fax: 402-458-3042
support@petersons.com
www.petersons.com
The only two-year college guide available, this new and expanded directory is the most complete source of information on institutions that grant an associate as their highest degree.
Publication Date: 1975 712 pages
ISBN: 1-560796-05-7

3916 Peterson's Regional College Guide Set
Peterson's, A Nelnet Company
Princeton Pike Corporate Center
461 From Road
Paramus, NJ 07652
609-896-1800
800-338-3282
Fax: 402-458-3042
support@petersons.com
www.petersons.com
Six individual regional guides that help students compare colleges in a specific geographic area.
Publication Date: 1975

3917 Power of Public Engagement Book Set
Master Teacher
One Leadership Lane
PO Box 1207
Manhattan, KS 66502-1207
800-669-9633
Fax: 800-669-1132
www.masterteacher.com
Learn how to engage your community to make the changes needed to ensure the best education for its children.
Publication Date: 1969
ISBN: 1-58992-128-3
William G O'Callaghan Jr, Author

3918 PreK-12 Excellence In Environmental Educatio Education
North American Assoc for Environmental Education
2000 P Street NW
Suite 540
Washington, DC 20036
202-419-0412
Fax: 212-419-0415
info@naaee.org
www.naaee.org
Offers a vision of environmental education and promotes progress toward sustaining a healthy environment and quality of life. The Guidelines support state and local environmental efforts by: setting expectations for performance and achievement in fourth, eighth, and twelfth grades; suggesting a framework for effective and comprehensive environmental education programs.

ISBN: 1-884008-77-1
Jose Marcos-Iga, President
Susan McGuire, Secretary

3919 Private Independent Schools
Bunting & Lyon
238 N Main Street
Wallingford, CT 06492-3728
203-269-3333
Fax: 203-269-5697
BuntingandLyon@aol.com
www.macraesbluebook.com
Provides information on more than 1,100 elementary and secondary private schools and summer programs in the United States and abroad. This annual guide, now in its 56th edition, is the most concise, current resource available on private school programs.
Publication Date: 1996 644 pages Annual Hardcover
ISBN: 0-913094-56-0
ISSN: 0079-5399
Peter G Bunting, Publisher

3920 Private School Law in America
Progressive Business Publications
370 Technology Drive
Malvern, PA 19355
610-695-8600
800-220-5000
Fax: 610-647-8089
customer_service@pbp.com
www.pbp.com
An up-to-date compilation of summarized federal and state appellate court decisions which affect private education. The full legal citation is supplied for each case. A brief introductory note on the American judicial system is provided along with updated appendices of recent US Supreme Court cases and recently published law review articles. Also included are portions of the US Constitution which are most frequently cited in private education cases.
Publication Date: 1959 500 pages Annually
ISBN: 0-939675-80-3
Ed Satell, Founder

3921 Public Schools USA: A Comparative Guide to School Districts
Peterson's, A Nelnet Company
Princeton Pike Corporate Center
461 From Road
Paramus, NJ 07652
609-896-1800
800-338-3282
Fax: 402-458-3042
support@petersons.com
www.petersons.com
Lists over 400 school districts in 52 metropolitan areas throughout the United States.
Publication Date: 1975 490 pages Annual
Charles Hampton Harrison, Author

3922 School Foodservice Who's Who
Information Central
PO Box 3900
Prescott, AZ 86302-3900
520-778-1513
Listing of over 2,500 food service programs in public and Catholic school systems.
110 pages Triennial

3923 School Guide
School Guide Publications
210 N Avenue
New Rochelle, NY 10801-6402
914-632-7771
800-433-7771
Fax: 914-632-3412
mridder@schoolguides.com
schoolguides.com
Listing of over 3,000 colleges, vocational schools and nursing schools in the US.
Publication Date: 1886 280 pages Annual/Paperback
ISBN: 1-893275-30-2
Janette Aiello, Editor

3924 Schools-Business & Vocational Directory
American Business Directories
5711 S 86th Circle
Omaha, NE 68127-4146
402-593-4600
888-999-1307
Fax: 402-331-5481
www.americanbusinessandservicedirectory.com
A complete listing of business and vocational schools nationwide. Includes phone numbers, contact names, employee sizes and more.
Annual
Jerry Venner, Coordinating Education

3925 Treasury of Noteworthy Proverbs
Morris Publishing
P.O. Box 2110
Kearney, NE 68848
954-974-5477
800-650-7888
Fax: 308-237-0263
carconed@aol.com
www.morrispublishing.com
Tapestry of maxims, aphorisims, and pithy sayings. A revealing picture of the wisdom, philosophy, and humor of the people of this and many other nations throughout the world.
Publication Date: 1933
ISBN: 0-7392-0208-1
ISSN: 99-943-75
Dr. Robert M Bookbinder, President

3926 US Supreme Court Education Cases
Progressive Business Publications
370 Technology Drive
Malvern, PA 19355
610-695-8600
800-220-5000
Fax: 610-647-8089
customer_service@pbp.com
www.pbp.com
A compilation of summarized US Supreme Court decisions since 1954 which affect education. The full legal citation is supplied for each case. Also included are portions of the US Constitution which are most frequently cited in education cases.
Publication Date: 1959 Annually
Liz Webb, Senior Corporate Recruiter
Ed Satell, Founder

3927 VincentCurtis Educational Register
VincentCurtis
PO Box 724
Falmouth, MA 02541-0724
508-457-6473
Fax: 508-457-6499
register@vincentcurtis.com
www.theeducationalregister.com
An online guide to a variety of private boarding and day schools as well as resident summer programs in the United States, Canada and Europe. The guide includes articles, information and advice on the subject of independent education.
Publication Date: 1941
Stan Vincent, Editor

3928 Western Association of Schools and Colleges
Western Association of Schools and Colleges
533 Airport Boulevard
Suite 200
Burlingame, CA 94010-2009
650-696-1060
Fax: 650-696-1867
mail@acswasc.org
www.acswasc.org
Listing of schools and colleges in California, Hawaii, Guam, American Samoa and East Asia.
130 pages Annual
Fred Van Leuven, Executive Director
Marilyn S. George, Associate Executive Director

3929 What's Fair Got to Do With It
North American Assoc for Environmental Education
2000 P Street NW
Suite 540
Washington, DC 20036
202-419-0412
Fax: 212-419-0415
info@naaee.org
www.naaee.org
Educators will find these cases a powerful tool for professional development. Each case is a candid, dramatic, and highly readable first-person account that makes concrete the challenges of fairness, expectations, respect, and communication when people who share goals, perhaps, but not cultures, interact.
119 pages
ISBN: 0-914409-20-4
Jose Marcos-Iga, President
Susan McGuire, Secretary

3930 Whole Nonprofit Catalog
Grantmanship Center
PO Box 17720
Los Angeles, CA 90017
213-482-9860
800-421-9512
Fax: 213-482-9863
Info@tgci.com
www.tgci.com
Offers information on training programs offered by the Center, publications and other services available to the nonprofit sector.
Publication Date: 1972
Cathleen Kiritz, President
Barbara Floersch, Executive Director

3931 Working Together: A Guide to Community-Based Educational Resources
Research, Advocacy & Legislation/Council of LaRaza
1126 16th Street, NW
Suite 600
Washington, DC 20036-4845
202-289-1380
comments@nclr.org
www.nclr.org
Listing of about 30 community-based organizations nationwide providing educational services to Hispanic Americans.
35 pages
Jorge A. Plasencia, Chair
Renata Soto, Vice Chair

3932 World of Learning
Gale Group
27500 Drake Road
Farmington Hills, MI 48331
248-699-4253
800-877-4253
Fax: 877-363-4253
galeord@galegroup.com
www.cengage.com
Contains information for over 26,000 universities, colleges, schools of art and music, libraries, archives, learned societies, research institutes, museums and art galleries in more than 180 countries.

ISBN: 0-7876-5004-8
Michael E. Hansen, CEO
Fernando Bleichmar, Chief Strategy Officer

Directories & Handbooks / Administration

3933 American School & University - Who's Who Directory & Buyer's Guide
Prism Business Media
9800 Metcalf Avenue
Overland Park, KS 66212-2286
913-967-1960
Fax: 913-967-1905

jagron@asumag.com
www.asumag.com
Comprehensive directory of suppliers and products for facility needs; listings of architects by region; listing of associations affiliated with the education industry; article index for quick and easy reference; in-depth calendar of events.

Publication Date: 1928 Annual

Joe Agron, Editor-In-Chief
Gregg Herring, VP, Market Leader

3934 Bricker's International Directory
Peterson's, A Nelnet Company
Princeton Pike Corporate Center
461 From Road
Paramus, NJ 07652
609-896-1800
800-338-3282
Fax: 402-458-3042
support@petersons.com
www.petersons.com
Offers over 400 residential management development programs at academic institutions in the United States and abroad.

Publication Date: 1975 Annual

3935 Cabells Directory of Publishing Opportunities in Educational Psychology and Administration
Cabell Publishing Company
Box 5428
Tobe Hahn Station
Beaumont, TX 77726
409-898-0575
Fax: 409-866-9554
info@cabells.com
www.cabells.com
Provides information on editor contact information, manuscript guidelines, acceptance rate, review information and circulation data for over 225 academic journals.

Publication Date: 1978 799 pages Annual
ISBN: 0-911753-28-1

David WE Cabell, Editor
Deborah L English, Associate Editor

3936 Character Education Questions & Answers
Character Education Partnership
1634 I Street NW
Suite 550
Washington, DC 20006
202-296-7743
800-988-8081
Fax: 202-296-7779
information@character.org
www.character.org

Becky Sipos, President/ CEO
Sheril Morgan, Director

3937 Character Education Resource Guide
Character Education Partnership
1634 I Street NW
Suite 550
Washington, DC 20006
202-296-7743
800-988-8081
Fax: 202-296-7779
information@character.org
www.character.org

Becky Sipos, President/ CEO
Sheril Morgan, Director

3938 Character Education: The Foundation for Teacher Education
Character Education Partnership
1634 I Street NW
Suite 550
Washington, DC 20006
202-296-7743
800-988-8081
Fax: 202-296-7779
information@character.org
www.character.org

Becky Sipos, President/ CEO
Sheril Morgan, Director

3939 Continuing Education Guide
International Association for Continuing Education
7918 Jones Branch Drive
Suite 300
McLean, VA 22102-0001
703-506-3275
Fax: 703-506-3266
www.iacet.org
Explores how to interpret and use the Continuing Education Unit or other criteria used for continuing education programs. This guide, written by continuing education and training consultant, Louis Phillips, is a reference source complete with sample forms, charts, checklists and everything you need to plan, develop and evaluate your school's continuing education program.

Sandra Williams, President
Lori Schaeffer, President-Elect

3940 Creating Quality Reform: Programs, Communities and Governance
Pearson Education Communications
1 Lake Street
Upper Saddle River, NJ 07458
201-236-7000
Fax: 877-260-2530
communications@pearsoned.com
www.pearsoned.com

Publication Date: 2002

J Thomas Owens, Editor
Jan C Simmons, Editor

3941 Designing & Implementing a Leadership Academy in Character Education
Character Education Partnership
1634 I Street NW
Suite 550
Washington, DC 20006
202-296-7743
800-988-8081
Fax: 202-296-7779
information@character.org
www.character.org

Becky Sipos, President/ CEO
Sheril Morgan, Director

3942 Deskbook Encyclopedia of American School Law
Progressive Business Publications
370 Technology Drive
Malvern, PA 19355
610-695-8600
800-220-5000
Fax: 610-647-8089
customer_service@pbp.com
www.pbp.com
An up-to-date compilation of summarized federal and state appellate court decisions which affect education. The full legal citation is supplied for each case with a brief introductory note on the American judicial system is provided along with updated appendices of recent US Supreme Court cases and recently published law review articles.

Publication Date: 1959 Annually

Liz Webb, Senior Corporate Recruiter
Ed Satell, Founder

3943 Developing a Character Education Program
Character Education Partnership
1634 I Street NW
Suite 550
Washington, DC 20006
202-296-7743
800-988-8081
Fax: 202-296-7779
information@character.org
www.character.org

Henry Huffman, Author
Becky Sipos, President/ CEO
Sheril Morgan, Director

3944 Development Education: A Directory of Non-Governmental Practitioners
U.N. Non-Governmental Liaison Service
Palais des Nations, CH 1211
Geneva 10
Switzerland
E-mail: ngls@unctad.org
www.un-ngls.org
Lists about 800 national non-governmental organizations in industrialized countries and international non-governmental networks concerned with developmental education.

Publication Date: 1975 400 pages

Beth Peoch, Officer in Charge
David Vergari, Administration

3945 Directory of Chief Executive Officers of United Methodist Schools, Colleges & Universities
General Board of Higher Education & Ministry/UMC
1001 19th Avenue South
PO Box 340007
Nashville, TN 37203-0007
615-340-7406
Fax: 615-340-7379
scu@gbhem.org
www.gbhem.org
123 United Methodist educational institutions including theology schools, professional schools, two year colleges and colleges and universities with all contact information arranged by institution type. Paperback.

32 pages Annual

James E. Dorff, Presiden
Ianther Marie Mills, Vice President

3946 Directory of Organizations in Educational Management
ERIC Clearinghouse on Educational Management
1501 Kincaid Street
Eugene, OR 97403-1299
541-346-3053
800-438-8841
Fax: 541-346-3485
sales@oregon.uoregon.edu
scholarsbank.uoregon.edu
Offers listings of 163 organizations in the field of educational management at the elementary and secondary school levels.

Dr. Philip Piele, Director
Stuart C Smith, Associate Director

3947 Directory of State Education Agencies
Council of Chief State School Officers
1 Massachusette Avenue NW
Suite 700
Washington, DC 20001-1431

202-336-7000
Fax: 202-408-8072
communications@ccsso.org
www.ccsso.org
A reference to state and national education agency contracts. Arranged state-by-state, it includes state education agency personnel titles, addresses, phone numbers, and fax numbers when applicable. National information includes key contacts and information for 33 national education associations and 5 pages of names, titles, addresses, and numbers for the US Department of Education.

103 pages
ISBN: 1-884037-66-6

June Atkinson, President
Lillian Lowery, President-elect

3948 Educating for Character
Master Teacher
One Leadership Lane
PO Box 1207
Manhattan, KS 66502-1207
800-669-9633
Fax: 800-669-1132
www.masterteacher.com
Dr. Licona has developed a 12 point program that offers practical strategies designed to create a working coalition of parents, teachers and communities.

428 pages
ISBN: 0-553-37052-9

Thomas Lickona PhD, Author

3949 Educating for Character: How Our Schools Can Teach Respect and Responsibility
Character Education Partnership
1634 I Street NW
Suite 550
Washington, DC 20006
202-296-7743
800-988-8081
Fax: 202-296-7779
information@character.org
www.character.org

Tom Likona, Author
Becky Sipos, President/ CEO
Sheril Morgan, Director

3950 Education Budget Alert
Committee for Education Funding
1640 Rhode Island Ave., NW
Suite 600
Washington, DC 20036-2109
202-383-0083
Fax: 202-463-4803
jchang@cef.org
www.cef.org
Federal programs currently help over 63 million Americans to engage in formal learning. This guidebook explains what these programs do, what types of activities are supported, the reasons the federal government initiated these programs, and their level at funding.

Publication Date: 2012 150 pages Annually

Noelle Ellerson, President
Makese Motley, Vice-President

3951 Educational Consultants Directory
American Business and Service Directory
5711 S 86th Circle
PO Box 27347
Omaha, NE 68127
402-593-4600
800-555-6124
Fax: 402-331-5481
info@usabsd.com
www.americanbusinessandservicedirectory.com
A list of more than 5,000 entries, including name, address, phone, size of advertisement, name of owner or manager and number of employees.

3952 Educational Dealer-Buyers' Guide Issue
Fahy-Williams Publishing
171 Reed St.
PO Box 1080
Geneva, NY 14456-2137
315-789-0458
800-344-0559
Fax: 315-789-4263
www.fwpi.com
List of approximately 2,000 suppliers of educational materials and equipment.

Annual

J. Kevin Fahy, Publisher
Tina Manzer, Editorial Director

3953 Executive Summary Set
Master Teacher
One Leadership Lane
PO Box 1207
Manhattan, KS 66502
800-669-9633
Fax: 800-669-1132
www.masterteacher.com
An easy, effective and practical way to orient new board members before they attend their first meeting. Executive Summary Sets cover the vital information board members must have in eight areas: tenets of education; powers and responsibilities; decision making; communication for maximum results; resource management; assessment of programs; assessment of personnel and conflict resolution.

Robert DeBruyn, Editor

3954 Grants and Contracts Handbook
Association of School Business Officials Int'l
11401 N Shore Drive
Reston, VA 20190-4232
703-478-0405
866-682-2729
Fax: 703-478-0205
asbointl.org
This is a basic reference for grant applicants, executors, project managers, administrators and staff. The ideas are school-tested and based on information gathered from institutions and agencies over the past two decades.

Publication Date: 1910 32 pages
ISBN: 0-910170-52-5

Mark C. Pepera, President
Brenda R. Burkett, Vice President

3955 Hispanic Yearbook-Anuario Hispano
TIYM Publishing
8370 Greensboro Dr.
#1009
McLean, VA 22102
703-734-1632
Fax: 703-356-0787
TIYM@aol.com
www.tiym.com
This guide lists Hispanic organizations, publications, radio and TV stations, through not specifically for grant-giving purposes.

Publication Date: 1985 Annually

John O Zavala, COO
Ramon Palencia, Director PR

3956 Leading to Change: The Challenge of the New Superintendency
Jossey-Bass/Pfeiffer
One Montgomery Street
Suite 1200
San Francisco, CA 94104-1741
415-433-1740
Fax: 415-433-0499
www.josseybass.com
The challenge of the new superintendency.

Publication Date: 1814 352 pages
ISBN: 0-7879-0214-4

Susan Moore Johnson, Author
Stephen M. Smith, President and CEO
John Kritzmacher, EVP, CFO

3957 Legal Basics: A Handbook for Educators
Phi Delta Kappa International
320 W. Eighth Street
Suite 216
Bloomington, IL 47404-0789
812-339-1156
800-766-1156
Fax: 812-339-0018
memberservices@pdkintl.org
www.pdkintl.org
Superintendents, principals, counselors, teachers, and paraprofessionals need to pay close attentioh to their actions in schools and classrooms because, from a legal standpoint, those settings may contain hazardous conditions. Legal Basics points out the pitfalls and how to avoid them.

Publication Date: 1906 120 pages Paperback
ISBN: 8-87367-806-0

Evelyn B Kelly, Author
Dan Brown, Executive Director
Douglas Christensen, Vice Chair

3958 Legal Issues and Education Technology
National School Board Association
1680 Duke Street
Alexandria, VA 22314
703-838-6722
800-706-6722
Fax: 703-683-7590
info@nsba.org
www.nsba.org
Helps administrators craft an acceptable-use policy.

Publication Date: 1999
ISSN: 0314510

Thomas Gentzel, Executive Director
Heather Francis, Executive Assistant

3959 Lifeworld of Leadership: Creating Culture, Community, and Personal Meaning in Our Schools
Jossey-Bass Publishers
One Montgomery Street
Suite 1200
San Francisco, CA 94104-1741
415-433-1740
Fax: 415-433-0499
www.josseybass.com
Explores the crucial link between school improvement and school character.

Publication Date: 1814 240 pages Paperback
ISBN: 0-7879-7277-6

Stephen M. Smith, President and CEO
John Kritzmacher, EVP, CFO

3960 Looking at Schools: Instruments & Processes for School Analysis
Research for Better Schools
123 South Broad Street
Suite 1860
Philadelphia, PA 19109
215-568-6150
Fax: 215-568-7260
www.rbs.org
Thirty-five institutions that offer instruments and processes to assess the performance of students, teachers and administrators, school

climate effectiveness and school-community relations.

Publication Date: 1966 140 pages

Carol Crociante, Executive Assistant
Keith M Kershner, Executive Director

3961 Market Data Retrieval-National School Market Index

Market Data Retrieval
6 Armstrong Road
Suite 301
Shelton, CT 06484-0947
203-926-4800
800-333-8802
Fax: 203-929-5253
msubrizi@dnb.com
schooldata.com

An annual report on school spending patterns for instructional materials in the United States. The Index now in its twenty-fifth year of publication, lists the expenditures for instructional materials for all 15,000 US senior districts.

Publication Date: 1996
ISBN: 0-897708-25-3

Mike Subrizi, Marketing Director

3962 National Association of Principals of Schools for Girls Directory

National Association of Principals/Girls Schools
23490 Caraway Lakes Dr.
Bonita Springs, FL 34135-8317
239-947-4323
Fax: 828-693-1490
bruce@headsnetwork.org
www.headsnetwork.org

List of 575 principals and deans of private and secondary schools for girls and coeducational schools, colleges and admissions officers.

Publication Date: 1920 Annual

Bruce W. Galbraith, Executive Director

3963 National School Public Relations Association Directory

15948 Derwood Road
Rockville, MD 20855
301-519-0496
Fax: 301-519-0494
info@nspra.org
www.nspra.org

Lists over 1,500 members of the association, creating networking possibilities with school communication professionals for those who want to exchange knowledge.

Julie Thannum, APR, President
Rich Bagin, APR, Executive Director

3964 National School Supply & Equipment Association Membership/Buyers' Guide Directory

Education Market Association
8380 Colesville Rd
Suite 250
Silver Spring, MD 20910
301-495-0240
800-395-5550
Fax: 301-495-3330
awatts@nssea.org
www.edmarket.org

Lists 1,500 member dealers, manufacturers and manufacturers' representatives for school supplies, equipment and instructional materials.

200 pages Annual

Adrienne Watts, Author
Jim McGarry, President/ CEO
Adrienne Dayton, VP, Marketing & Comm.

3965 National Schools of Character

Character Education Partnership
1634 I Street NW
Suite 550
Washington, DC 20006
202-296-7743
800-988-8081
Fax: 202-296-7779
information@character.org
www.character.org

Becky Sipos, President/ CEO
Sheril Morgan, Director

3966 Proactive Leadership in the 21st Century

Master Teacher
One Leadership Lane
PO Box 1207
Manhattan, KS 66502-1207
800-669-9633
Fax: 800-669-1132
www.masterteacher.com

Contain the laws and principals of leadership and people management as they had never been defined and described before giving school administrators a set of guidelines that if followed would guarantee success.

ISBN: 0-914607-44-8

Robert L DeBruyn, Author

3967 QED's State School Guides

Quality Education Data
601 E. Marshall St
Suite 250
Sweet Springs, MO 65351
303-860-1832
800-776-6373
Fax: 660-335-4157
info@qeddata.com
www.qeddata.com

Complete directories of every US school district and public, Catholic and private school. Directories are available for individual states, geographic regions and the entire United States. Each directory includes names of district administrators, school principals and school librarians, as well as addresses, phone numbers and enrollment information. QED's State school guide also includes key demographic and instructional technology data for each district and school.

Publication Date: 1993 Yearly
ISBN: 0-887476-49-0

John F. Hood, President
Peter Long, CEO

3968 School Promotion, Publicity & Public Relations: Nothing but Benefits

Master Teacher
One Leadership Lane
PO Box 1207
Manhattan, KS 66502-1207
785-539-0555
800-669-9633
Fax: 785-539-7739
www.masterteacher.com

Contains the vital foundations an administrator must have to understand and implement a program of publicity, promotion and public relations, in a school or school district.

327 pages
ISBN: 0-914607-25-1

Tracey H DeBruyn, Author

3969 Schoolwide Discipline Strategies that Make a Difference in Teaching & Learning

Master Teacher
One Leadership Lane
PO Box 1207
Manhattan, KS 66502-1207
800-669-9633
Fax: 800-669-1132
www.masterteacher.com

This approach to discipline will help your school or district eliminate the dependecy on one individual, provide guidance for present and new teachers, allow disipline to become a K-12 program, an bring about consistancy in the handling of all student misbehaviors.

150 pages
ISBN: 1-58992-000-7

Larry Dixon, Author

3970 The Teaching Professor

Magna Publications
2718 Dryden Drive
Madison, WI 53704
608-246-3590
Fax: 608-246-3597
support@magnapubs.com
www.magnapubs.com

This newsletter has been a leading source of information and inspiration for educators committed to creating a better learning environment.

Publication Date: 1972 530 pages Paperback
November
1000 attendees and 10+ exhibits

William Haight, President
Jody Glynn Patrick, Vice President

Directories & Handbooks / Early Childhood Education

3971 Early Childhood Environmental Education Programs: Guidelines for Excellence

North American Association for Environmental Educa
2000 P Street NW
Suite 540
Washington, DC 20036
202-419-0412
Fax: 212-419-0415
info@naaee.org
www.naaee.org

A set of recommendations for developing and administering high-quality environmental education programs for young children from birth to age eight, with a focus on ages three to six. These guidelines provide a tool that can be used to ensure a firm foundation for new programs or to trigger improvements in existing ones.

Jose Marcos-Iga, President
Susan McGuire, Secretary

Directories & Handbooks / Elementary Education

3972 Educational Impressions

P.O. Box 377
Franklin, NJ 07414-0377
973-423-4666
800-451-7450
Fax: 201-644-0907

awpeller@worldnet.att.net
www.edimpressions.com
Educational workbooks, activity books, literature guides, and audiovisuals. Grades K-8, with emphasis on intermediate and middle grades.

Paperback/Video/Audi

Neil Peller, Marketing Director
Lori Brown, Sales/Marketing

3973 Educators Guide to FREE Videotapes-Elementary/ Middle School Edition
Educators Progress Service
214 Center Street
Randolph, WI 53956-1408
920-326-3126
888-951-4469
Fax: 920-326-3127
epsinc@centurytel.net
www.freeteachingaids.com
Lists and describes free and free-loan videotapes for the elementary and middle school level.

Annual
ISBN: 0-877082-67-7

Kathy Nehmer, President

3974 Educators Guide to FREE Videotapes-Secondary Edition
Educators Progress Service
214 Center Street
Randolph, WI 53956-1408
920-326-3126
888-951-4469
Fax: 920-326-3127
epsinc@centurytel.net
www.freeteachingaids.com
Lists and describes free and free-loan videotapes for the elementary and middle school level.

Annual
ISBN: 0-877082-67-7

Kathy Nehmer, President

3975 Elementary Teachers Guide to FREE Curriculum Materials
Educators Progress Service
214 Center Street
Randolph, WI 53956-1408
920-326-3126
888-951-4469
Fax: 920-326-3127
epsinc@centurytel.net
www.freeteachingaids.com
Lists and describes free supplementary teaching aids for the elementary level.

Annual
ISBN: 0-877082-64-2

Kathy Nehmer, President

3976 KIDSNET Media Guide and News
KIDSNET
6856 Eastern Avenue NW
Suite 208
Washington, DC 20012
202-291-1400
Fax: 202-882-7315
kidsnet@kidsnet.org
www.kidsnet.org
Contains children's television, radio and video listings. Also lists related teaching materials and copyright guidelines.

150 pages Monthly

3977 Lesson Plans, Integrating Technology into the Classroom: Elementary Edition
Master Teacher
One Leadership Lane
PO Box 1207
Manhattan, KS 66502-1207
800-669-9633
Fax: 800-669-1132
www.masterteacher.com
Gives teachers practical lessons developed and tested by teachers across the curriculum, with students of all levels of ability in using technology.

Publication Date: 1969 130 pages
ISBN: 0-914607-59-6

3978 Nursery Schools & Kindergartens Directory
American Business Directories
5711 S 86th Circle
Omaha, NE 68127-4146
402-593-4600
888-999-1307
Fax: 402-331-5481
www.americanbusinessandservicedirectory.com
A geographical listing of 34,900 nursery schools and kindergartens including all contact information, first year in Yellow Pages and descriptions. Also available are regional editions and electronic formats.

Annual

Jerry Venner, Coordinating Education

3979 Parent Involvement Facilitator: Elementary Edition
Master Teacher
One Leadership Lane
PO Box 1207
Manhattan, KS 66502-1207
800-669-9633
Fax: 800-669-1132
www.masterteacher.com
Packed with ideas for you and your teachers to implement along with the exact steps for you to follow.

169 pages
ISBN: 0-914607-45-6

3980 Patterson's Elementary Education
Educational Directories Inc.
1025 W Wise Road
PO Box 68097
Schaumberg, IL 60168-97
847-891-1250
800-357-6183
Fax: 847-891-0945
info@ediusa.org
www.ediusa.com
A directory to more than 13,000 public school districts; 71,000 public, private and Catholic elementary and middle schools; 1,600 territorial schools; and 400 state department of education personnel in one easy to use consistent format. Arranged alphabetically by state then city. City listings include city name, telephone area code, city population, county name, public school district name, enrollment, grade range, superintendent's name, address and phone number.

Publication Date: 1994 870 pages Annual
ISBN: 0-910536-59-7

Douglas Moody, Coordinating Education

3981 Teaching Our Youngest-A Guide for Preschool Teachers and Child Care and Family Providers
ED Pubs
P.O. Box 22207
Alexandria, VA 22304-1398
877-4ED-PUBS
Fax: 703-605-6794
edpubs@inet.ed.gov
www.edpubs.org
This booklet draws from scientifically based research about what can be done to help children develop their language abilities, increase their knowledge, become familiar with books and other printed materials,learn letters and sounds, recognize numbers and learn to count.

Directories & Handbooks / Employment

3982 AAEE Job Search Handbook for Educators
American Association for Employment in Education
947 E. Johnstown Road
#170
Gahanna, OH 43230
614-485-1111
Fax: 614-485-9609
aaee@osu.edu
www.aaee.org
Information for those pursuing work as educators.

72 pages Annually

Doug Peden, Executive Director
Deborah Snyder, President

3983 Cabell's Directory of Publishing Opportunities in Education
Cabell Publishing
Box 5428
Tobe Hahn Station
Beaumont, TX 77726-5428
409-898-0575
Fax: 409-866-9554
info@cabells.com
www.cabells.com
Includes list of more than 430 education journals that consider manuscripts for publication. Includes contact names and addresses for submitting manuscripts, topics considered, publication guidelines, fees, and circulation information.

Publication Date: 1978 1,200 pages

David WE Cabell, Editor
Deborah L English, Associate Editor

3984 Cabell's Directory of Publishing Opportunities in Accounting
Cabell Publishing Company
Box 5428
Tobe Hahn Station
Beaumont, TX 77726
409-898-0575
Fax: 409-866-9554
info@cabells.com
www.cabells.com
Contains information on 130 journal. Entries include manuscript guidelines for authors: editor's address, phone, fax and e-mail. Review process and the time required, acceptance rates, readership circulation and subscription prices. The Index classifies journals by 15 topics areas and provides information on type of review, acceptance rate and review time.

Publication Date: 1978 425 pages Annual
ISBN: 0-911753-13-3

David WE Cabell, Editor
Deborah L English, Editor

3985 Cabell's Directory of Publishing Opportunities in Economics & Finance

Cabell Publishing Company
Box 5428
Tobe Hahn Station
Beaumont, TX 77726-5428
409-898-0575
Fax: 409-866-9554
info@cabells.com
www.cabells.com

Contains information on 350 journals. Each journal entry includes manuscript guidelines for authors: editor's address, phone, fax and e-mail, review process and time required, acceptance rates, readership, circulation and subscription prices. The Index classifies journals by 15 topic areas and provides information on type of review, acceptance rate and review time.

Publication Date: 1978 1100 pages Annual
ISBN: 0-911753-14-1

David WE Cabell, Editor
Deborah L English, Associate Editor

3986 Cabells Directory of Publishing Opportunities in Management

Cabell Publishing Company
Box 5428
Tobe Hahn Station
Beaumont, TX 77726
409-898-0575
Fax: 409-866-9554
info@cabells.com
www.cabells.com

Provides editor contact information, acceptance rates, review information, manuscript guidelines and circulation data for over 540 academic journals.

Publication Date: 1978 648 pages
ISBN: 0-911753-15-X

David WE Cabell, Editor
Deborah L English, Associate Editor

3987 Career Book

VGM Career Books
4255 W Touhy Avenue
Lincolnwood, IL 60712
732-329-6991
Fax: 732-329-6994

Offers information on educational employment opportunities in America and abroad.

BiAnnual Hard/Paper

Joyce Lain Kennedy & Darryl Laramore, Author

3988 Career Information Center; 13 Volumes

MacMillan Publishers
175 Fifth Avenue
New York, NY 10010
646-307-5151
888-330-8477
Fax: 800-835-3202
customerservice@mpsvirginia.com
us.macmillan.com

13 volumes covering 3,000 careers, 633 job summaries with 800 photos. Up-to-date information on salaries and occupational outlooks for nearly 3,000 careers.

2.6M pages Triennial
ISBN: 0-028974-52-2

3989 Careers Information Officers in Local Authorities

Careers Research & Advisory Centre/Hobsons Pub.
Sheraton House, Castle Park
Cambridge CB3 0AX
England
44 -0 1-23 4
223-354551
enquiries@crac.org.uk
www.crac.org.uk

1,100 United Kingdom institutions offering collections of career information and audio-visual materials covering career opportunities and current job markets. Arranged alphabetically listing address, phone, contact name and titles, type of materials held and a description of the facilities.

Publication Date: 1964 165 pages 12.95 pounds

Ellen Pearce, Chief Executive
Alison Mitchell, Director of Development

3990 Certification and Accreditation Programs Directory

Gale Research
27500 Drake Road
Farmington Hills, MI 48331-3535
248-699-4253
800-877-4253
Fax: 877-363-4253
galeord@gale.com
www.cengage.com

Directory of private organizations that offer more than 1,700 voluntary certification programs and approximately 300 accreditation programs. Also on CD-ROM.

Publication Date: 1995 620 pages
ISSN: 1084-2128

Michael E. Hansen, CEO
Fernando Bleichmar, Chief Strategy Officer

3991 Council of British Independent Schools in the European Communities-Members Directory

Council of British International Schools
St Mary's University, Strawberry Hi
Twickenham, TW1 4SX
United Kingdom
44-1303-260857
Fax: 44-1303-260857
ceo@cobis.org.uk
www.cobis.org.uk

Annual

Colin Bell, CEO
Sarah Wooldridge, Finance Officer

3992 Directory of English Language Schools in Japan Hiring English Teachers

Information Career Opportunities Research Center
Box 1100, Station F
Toronto M4Y 2T7
Canada
416-925-8878

English-language schools in Japan.

15 pages Annual

3993 Directory of International Internships Michigan State University

MSU: Dean's Office of Int'l Studies and Programs
427 N. Shaw Lane
Room 207
East Lansing, MI 48824-1035
517-355-2350
Fax: 517-353-7254
infonew@isp.msu.edu
www.isp.msu.edu

International internships sponsored by academic institutions, private corporations and the federal government.

Publication Date: 1994 168 pages Paperback

Rachel Warner, Director of Communications
Julie Norton, Secretary

3994 Directory of Schools, Colleges, and Universities Overseas

Overseas Employment Services
EBSCO Industries
PO Box 1943
Birmingham, AL 35201
205-991-1330
Fax: 205-995-1582

Directory of 300 educational institutions worldwide that hire teachers to teach different subjects in English.

21 pages Annual

Leonard Simcoe, Editor

3995 Directory of Work and Study in Developing Countries

Vacation-Work Publishers
9 Park End Street
Oxford OX1 1HJ
England
865-241978

Offers information on about 420 organizations worldwide offering employment and study opportunities in over 100 developing countries.

215 pages

3996 Earn & Learn: Cooperative Education Opportunities

Octameron Associates
1900 Mount Vernon Avenue
PO Box 2748
Alexandria, VA 22301-0748
703-836-5480
Fax: 703-836-5650
info@octameron.com
www.octameron.com

Explains how students may participate in cooperative work-study education programs with federal government agencies.

Publication Date: 1997 48 pages BiAnnual
ISBN: 1-57509-023-6

3997 English in Asia: Teaching Tactics for New English Teachers

Global Press
350 Rhode Island Street
Suite 240
San Francisco, CA 94103-1135
415-570-9114
info@globalpressinstitute.org
globalpressinstitute.org

Directory covering 1,000 private English-language schools in Asia, to which applications can be sent to teach.

Publication Date: 1992 180 pages

Danforth Austin, Chairman
Cristi Hegranes, Secretary

3998 European Council of International Schools Directory

European Council of International Schools
Fourth Floor, 146 Buckingham Palace
London, SW1W 9TR, London
United Kingdom
004- 0-20 7
44-1730-26-8244
Fax: 44-1730-267914
ecis@ecis.org
www.ecis.org

More than 420 member elementary and secondary international schools in Europe and worldwide.

Publication Date: 1965 480 pages Annual

Kevin J Ruth, PhD, President
Darlene Fisher, People & Programmes Lead

3999 Faculty Exchange Center Directory and House Exchange Supplement
Faculty Exchange Center
University of Dayton
300 College Park
Dayton, OH 45469-3116
937-229-1000
info@udayton.edu
https://www.udayton.edu
Offers information for college and faculty members wishing to exchange positions and/or homes temporarily with faculty members at other institutions.

35 pages Annual

Steven D. Cobb, Chair
Rev. Martin A. Solma, Vice Chair

4000 Foreign Faculty and Administrative Openings
Education Information Services
PO Box 620662
Newton, MA 02462-0662
617-433-0125
150 specific openings in administration, counseling, library and other professional positions for American teachers in American schools overseas and in international schools in which teaching language is English.

15 pages Every 6 Weeks

FB Viaux, Coordinating Education

4001 Guide to Educational Opportunities in Japan
Embassy of Japan
2520 Massachusetts Avenue NW
Washington, DC 20008
202-238-6700
Fax: 202-328-2187
www.embjapan.org
This guide describes opportunities for study in Japan and outlines different forms of financial assistance.

4002 How to Create a Picture of Your Ideal Job or Next Career
Ten Speed Press
6001 Shellmound Street
Emeryville, CA 94608-0123
510-285-3000
800-841-BOOK
Fax: 510-285-2979
www.randomhouse.com
Offers handy tips on how to choose the right career, and then go out and get it.

Publication Date: 1989

Richard Nelson Bolles, Author

4003 Leading Educational Placement Sources in the US
Educational Information Services
PO Box 662
Newton Lower Falls, MA 02162
617-964-4555
An index of the host placement agencies in America for education professionals.

4004 List of Over 200 Executive Search Consulting Firms in the US
Educational Information Services
PO Box 662
Newton Lower Falls, MA 02162
617-964-4555
www.nypl.org
Covers companies with active search committees in America.

4005 List of Over 600 Personnel & Employment Agencies
Educational Information Services
PO Box 662
Newton Lower Falls, MA 02162
617-964-4555
www.nypl.org
Contains information on personnel and employment agencies.

4006 Living in China: A Guide to Studying, Teaching & Working in the PRC & Taiwan
China Books & Periodicals
360 Swift Avenue
Suite 48
South San Francisco, CA 94080
650-872-7076
800-818-2017
Fax: 650-872-7808
info@chinabooks.com
www.chinabooks.com
America's #1 source of publications about China since 1960.

284 pages Paperback
ISBN: 0835125823
November

Chellis Ying, Marketing Director
Chris Robyn, Senior Managing Editor

4007 National Directory of Internships
National Society for Experiential Education
19 Mantua Road
Suite 207
Mt. Royal, NJ 08061-7235
856-423-3427
Fax: 856-423-3420
nsee@talley.com
www.nsee.org
Directory contains internship descriptions for hundreds of organizations in 85 fields in nonprofit organizations, government and corporations. Lists work and service experiences for high school, college and graduate students, people entering the job market, mid-career professionals and retired persons. Includes indexes by field of interest, location and host organization.

Publication Date: 1995 703 pages
ISBN: 0-536-01123-0

Jim Colbert, President
Stephanie Thomason, President Elect

4008 Opening List in US Colleges, Public & Private Schools
Education Information Services/Instant Alert
PO Box 620662
Newton, MA 02462-0662
617-433-0125
Offers about 150 current professional openings in US colleges and public and private schools.

10 pages Every 6 weeks

FB Viaux, Coordinating Education

4009 Opening List of Professional Openings in American Overseas Schools
Education Information Services/Instant Alert
PO Box 620662
Newton, MA 02462-0662
617-433-0125
About 150 current professional openings for teachers, administrators, counselors, librarians and educational specialists in American overseas schools and international schools at which the teaching language is primarily English.

FB Viaux, Coordinating Education

4010 Overseas Employment Opportunities for Educators
Department of Defense, Office of Dependent Schools
4800 Mark Center Drive
Alexandria, VA 22350-1400
571-372-0590
www.dodea.edu
This publication tells about teaching jobs in 250 schools operated for children of US military and civilian personnel stationed overseas. Applicants usually must qualify in two subject areas.

4011 Private School, Community & Junior College Four Year Colleges & Universities
Educational Information Services
PO Box 662
Newton Lower Falls, MA 02162
617-964-4555
Names, addresses and phones for any state or region in the United States offering employment opportunities.

4012 Research, Study, Travel, & Work Abroad
US Government Publishing Office
710 North Capitol Street N.W.
Washington, DC 20401-1
202-512-1800
866-512-1800
Fax: 202-512-2104
ContactCenter@gpo.gov
www.gpo.gov

Publication Date: 1861

Davita Vance-Cooks, Director
Jim Bradley, Deputy Director

4013 Teaching Overseas
KSJ Publishing Company
PO Box 2311
Sebastopol, CA 95473-2311
A directory of information on how to find jobs teaching overseas.

Publication Date: 1992 89 pages 2nd Edition
ISBN: 0-962044-55-5

4014 Thirty-Four Activities to Promote Careers in Special Education
The Council for Exceptional Children
2900 Crystal Drive
Suite 1000
Arlington, VA 22202-3557
703-620-3660
888-232-7733
Fax: 703-264-1637
www.cec.sped.org
This guide introduces individuals to the opportunities, rewards and delights of working with children with exceptionalities. It provides directions on how to plan, develop, and implement activities in the school and community that will increase people's awareness of careers in special education and related services.

Publication Date: 1996 120 pages
ISBN: 0-865862-77-0

Robin D. Brewer, President
James P. Heiden, President Elect

4015 VGM's Careers Encyclopedia
VGM Career Books/National Textbook Company
4255 W Touhy Avenue
Lincolnwood, IL 60646-1933
708-679-5500

A list of over 200 professional associations that provide career guidance information.

4016 Work Abroad: The Complete Guide to Finding a Job Overseas
Transitions Abroad
P.O. Box 1369
Amherst, MA 01004
413-992-6486
Fax: 802-442-4827
editor@transitionsabroad.com
www.transitionsabroad.com
Resource for finding both short- and long-term jobs abroad. Organized by region and country, includes websites and phone numbers.
Publication Date: 1977
Dr. Joanna Hubbs, President
Gregory Hubbs, Editor-in-Chief

4017 Workforce Preparation: An International Perspective
The Johns Hopkins University Press
2715 North Charles Street
Baltimore, MD 21218-4319
410-516-6989
800-530-9673
Fax: 410-516-8805
muse@press.jhu.edu
muse.jhu.edu
Excellent collection of material by 20 prominent educators describes efforts in developed and developing countries worldwide to prepare youth and adults for work.
Dean Smith, Director
Wendy Queen, Deputy Director

4018 World of Learning
Europa Publications
18 Bedford Square
London WC1B 3JN
England
00 -00 - 7 8
171-580-8236
Fax: 171-636-1664
europa.eu
Details over 26,000 educational, cultural and scientific institutions throughout the world, together with an exhaustive directory of over 150,000 people active within them.
2,072 pages Annual
ISBN: 0-946653-92-5

Directories & Handbooks / Financial Aid

4019 Catalog of Federal Domestic Assistance
Office of Management & Budget
Washington, DC 20402
https://www.cfda.gov/
Offers information from all federal agencies that have assistance programs (loans, scholarships and technical assistance as well as grants) and compiles these into the CFDA. The individual entries are grouped by Department of Agency and includes an excellent set of instructions and several indices. Indices allow the user to search for grants by subject matter, agency, deadline date or eligibility criteria.

4020 Chronicle Financial Aid Guide
Chronicle Guidance Publications
66 Aurora Street
Moravia, NY 13118-3569
315-497-0330
800-622-7284
Fax: 315-497-3359
customerservice@chronicleguidance.com
www.chronicleguidance.com
Financial aid programs offered primarily by noncollegiate organizations, independent and AFL-CIO affiliated labor unions and federal and state governments for high school seniors and undergraduate and graduate students.
Publication Date: 1938 460 pages Annual
ISBN: 1-5563-310-1
Janet Seemann, Author
Cheryl Fickeisen, President and CEO
Gary Fickeisen, Vice President

4021 College Costs and Financial Aid Handbook
College Board Publications
45 Columbus Avenue
New York, NY 10023-6917
212-713-8000
800-323-7155
Fax: 888-321-7183
www.collegeboard.org
A step-by-step guide providing the most up-to-date facts on costs plus financial aid and scholarship availability at 3,200 two- and four-year institutions.
Publication Date: 1900
ISBN: 0-874476-83-6
David Coleman, President and CEO
Jeremy Singer, Chief Operating Officer

4022 College Financial Aid Annual
Arco/Macmillan
1633 Broadway
Floor 7
New York, NY 10019-6708
212-654-8933
Lists of private businesses, academic institutions and other organizations that provide awards and scholarships for financial aid; guide to federal and state financial aid.

4023 Directory of Educational Contests for Students K-12
ABC-CLIO
130 Cremona Drive
#1911
Santa Barbara, CA 93117-5599
805-895-5623
800-368-6868
Fax: 805-685-9685
internationalsales@abc-clio.com
www.abc-clio.com
Offers about 200 competitive scholarship programs and other educational contests for elementary and secondary school students.
Publication Date: 1991 253 pages

4024 Directory of Financial Aid for Women
Reference Service Press
2310 Homestead Rd
Suite C1 #219
Los Altos, CA 94024
650-861-3170
Fax: 650-861-3171
rspinfo@aol.com
www.rspfunding.com
Offers information on more than 1,500 scholarships, fellowships, loan sources, grants, awards and internships.
490 pages
Gail Schlachter, President
R. David Weber, Editor-in-Chief

4025 Directory of Institutional Projects Funded by Office of Educational Research
U.S. Office of Educational Research & Improvement
555 New Jersey Avenue NW
Washington, DC 20208-5573
202-219-2079
Fax: 202-219-2135
https://www2.ed.gov/pubs/TeachersGuide/oeri.html
Publication Date: 1990 60 pages

4026 Directory of International Grants & Fellowships in the Health Sciences
National Institutes of Health
9000 Rockville Pike
Building 31, Room B2C29
Bethesda, MD 20892-2220
301-496-4000
Fax: 301-594-1211
NIHinfo@od.nih.gov
www.nih.gov
Fellowships and grants listed separately in this guide. Each listing includes a complete program description with contact information.
Publication Date: 1887
Francis S. Collins, M.D., Ph.D., Director

4027 Don't Miss Out: The Ambitous Students Guide to Financial Aid
Octameron Associates
1900 Mt Vernon Avenue
P.O. Box 2748
Alexandria, VA 22301-0748
703-836-5480
Fax: 703-836-5650
info2octameon.com
www.octameron.com
Publication Date: 0 192 pages Anually

4028 Fellowships in International Affairs-A Guide to Opportunities in the US & Abroad
Lynne Rienner Publishing
1800 30th Street
Suite 314
Boulder, CO 80301
303-444-6684
Fax: 303-444-0824
questions@rienner.com
www.rienner.com
This guide lists fellowships meant to encourage women to pursue careers in international security.
Publication Date: 1984

4029 Fellowships, Scholarships and Related Opportunities
Center for International Ed./University of TN
1620 Melrose Avenue
University of Tennessee
Knoxville, TN 37996-3531
865-974-3177
Fax: 865-974-2985
international@utk.edu
international.utk.edu
140 grants, scholarships and fellowships available to citizens of the United States for study or research abroad.
50 pages Biennial

4030 Financial Aid for Research & Creative Activities Abroad
Reference Service Press
2310 Homestead Rd
Suite C1 #219
Los Altos, CA 94024
650-861-3170
Fax: 650-861-3171
webagent@rspfunding.com
www.rspfunding.com

This book lists opportunities fir high school students and undergraduates, graduates, postdoctoral students, professionals and others.

432 pages
ISBN: 1588410625

Gail Schlachter, President
R.David Weber, Editor-in-Chief

4031 Financial Aid for Study Abroad: a Manual for Advisers & Administrators

NAFSA: Association of International Educators
1307 New York Avenue NW
8th Floor
Washington, DC 20005-4701
202-737-3699
800-836-4994
Fax: 202-737-3657
inbox@nafsa.org
www.nafsa.org

Publication Date: 1948 105 pages

Marlene M Johnson, Director/CEO
Vic Johnson, Senior Adviser

4032 Financial Resources for International Study

Institute of International Education
P.O. Box 1020
Sewickley, PA 15143-1020
412-741-0930
Fax: 212-984-5452
iiebooks@abdintl.com
www.iiebooks.org
Directory of more than 600 awards that can be used for international study.

Publication Date: 1996 320 pages
ISBN: 087206-220-1

4033 Foundation Grants to Individuals

Foundation Center
79 Fifth Avenue/16th Street
New York, NY 10003-3076
212-260-4230
Fax: 212-807-3677
foundationcenter.org
Features current information for grant seekers.

Publication Date: 1956

Melissa Berman, President and CEO
Patrick Collins, CFO

4034 Free Money for College: Fifth Edition

Facts On File
132 West 31st Street
17th Floor
New York, NY 10001
800-322-8755
custserv@factsonfile.com
www.factsonfile.com
1,000 grants and scholarships.

Publication Date: 1999 240 pages Annual Hardcover
ISBN: 081603947X

Laurie Blum, Author
Laurie Likoff, Editorial Director

4035 Free Money for Foreign Study: A Guide to 1,000 Grants for Study Abroad

Facts On File
132 West 31st Street
17th Floor
New York, NY 10001
800-322-8755
custserv@factsonfile.com
www.factsonfile.com
Lists organizations and institutions worldwide offering scholarships and grants for study outside the United States.

262 pages

Laurie Likoff, Editorial Director

4036 Fulbright and Other Grants for USIA Graduate Study Abroad

U.S. Student Programs Division
809 United Nations Plaza
New York, NY 10017-3580
212-984-5330
Fax: 212-984-5325
www.iie.org
Mutual educational exchange grants for pre-doctoral students offered by foreign governments.

Publication Date: 1919 90 pages Annual

Allan E. Goodman, President and CEO
Reter Thompson, Executive Vice President

4037 Fund Your Way Through College: Uncovering 1,100 Opportunities in Aid

Visible Ink Press/Gale Research
43311 Joy Road
#414
Canton, MI 48187-2075
734-667-3211
Fax: 734-667-4311
www.visibleinkpress.com
1,100 scholarships, grants, loans, awards and prizes for undergraduate students.

470 pages

4038 German-American Scholarship Guide-Exchange Opportunities for Historians and Social Scientist

German Historical Institute
1607 New Hampshire Avenue NW
Washington, DC 20009-2562
202-387-3355
Fax: 202-387-6437
www.ghi-dc.org
This guide is divided into two sections: scholarships for study and research in the US and scholarships for study and research in Germany.

Hartmut Berghoff, Director
Uwe Spiekmann, Deputy Director

4039 Getting Funded: The Complete Guide to Writing Grant Proposals

Continuing Education Press
400 W First St
Chico, CA 95929-0250
530-898-6105
866-647-7377
Fax: 530-898-6105
rce@csuchico.edu
rce.csuchico.edu
A step-by-step guide to writing successful grants and proposals. An indispensible reference for experienced and first-time grant writers alike.

180 pages Paperback
ISBN: 0-87678-071-0

Mary Hall, Author
Debra Barger, Administration
Joe Picard, Director

4040 Graduate Scholarship Book

Pearson Education
1 Lake Street
Upper Saddle River, NJ 07458
201-909-6200
Fax: 201-767-5029
www.pearsoned.com
A complete guide to scholarships, grants and loans for graduate and professional study.

441 pages Biennial

4041 Grant Opportunities for US Scholars & Host Opportunities for US Universities

International Research & Exchange Board
1275 K Street NW
Suite 600
Washington, DC 20005
202-628-8188
Fax: 202-628-8189
irex@irex.org
www.irex.org
This pamphlet lists programs in advanced research, language and development, short-term travel, special projects and institutional opportunities.

Publication Date: 1968

Kristin M. Lord, President and CEO
Joyce Warner, SVP, Chied of Staff

4042 Grant Writing Beyond The Basics: Proven Strategies Professionals Use To Make Proposals

Continuing Education Press
400 W First St
Chico, CA 95929-0250
530-898-6105
866-647-7377
Fax: 530-898-6105
rce@csuchico.edu
rce.csuchico.edu
Designed to inspire those with grant writing experience who want to take their development strategies to the next level.

128 pages Paperback
ISBN: 0-87678-117-2

Michael K Wells, Author
Debra Barger, Administration
Joe Picard, Director

4043 Grants & Awards Available to American Writers

PEN American Center
588 Broadway
Suite 303
New York, NY 10012
212-334-1660
Fax: 212-334-2181
ftw@pen.org
www.pen.org
Includes a full program description and is then broken down by type of writing. Awards for work in a particular country are listed alphabetically by country.

340 pages Paperback
ISBN: 0-934638-20-9

Peter Godwin , President
John Troubh, Executive Vice-President

4044 Grants Register

St. Martin's Press
175 5th Avenue
New York, NY 10010
212-674-5151
888-330-8477
Fax: 212-674-6132
firstname.lastname@stmartins.com
us.macmillan.com/smp
This directory offers a comprehensive list of programs organized alphabetically with special attention to eligibility requirements. Index by subject.

4045 Grants, Fellowships, & Prizes of Interest to Historians

American Historical Association
400 A Street SE
Washington, DC 20003-3889

202-544-2422
Fax: 202-544-8307
aha@theaha.org
www.historians.org
This guide offers information on awards for historians from undergraduate to postgraduate grants, fellowships, prizes, internships and awards.
Publication Date: 1884
Jim Grossman, Executive Director
Shatha Almutawa, Associate Editor

4046 Guide to Department of Education Programs
US Department of Education
400 Maryland Avenue SW
Washington, DC 20202-0001
202-401-2000
800-872-5327
www.ed.gov
Programs of financial aid offered by the Department of Education.
Publication Date: 1980 35 pages Annual
Emma Vadehra, Chief of Staff
James Cole, Jr., General Counsel

4047 Harvard College Guide to Grants
Office of Career Services
Harvard University
54 Dunster Street
Cambridge, MA 02138
617-495-2595
Fax: 617-495-3584
www.ocs.fas.harvard.edu
This guide describes national and regional grants and fellowships for study in the US, study abroad and work and practical experience.
234 pages Paperback

4048 How to Find Out About Financial Aid & Funding
Reference Service Press
2310 Homestead Rd.
Suite C1 #219
Los Altos, CA 94024
650-861-3170
Fax: 650-861-3171
rspinfo@aol.com
www.rspfunding.com
Over 700 financial aid directories and Internet sites described and evaluated.
432 pages Hardcover
ISBN: 1588410935
Gail A Schlachter, Author
Gail Schlachter, President
R. David Weber, Editor-in-Chief

4049 International Foundation Directory
Europa Publications
11 New Fetter Lane
London
England EC4P 4EE
00 -00 - 7 8
44-0-20-7842-2110
Fax: 44-0-20-7842-2249
europa.eu
A world directory of international foundations, trusts and similar non-profit institutions. Provides detailed information on over 1,200 institutions in some 70 countries throughout the world.
Publication Date: 1994 736 pages
ISBN: 1-857430-01-8
Paul Kelly, Editorial Director

4050 International Scholarship Book: The Complete Guide to Financial Aid
Pearson Education
1 Lake Street
Upper Saddle River, NJ 07458
201-909-6200
Fax: 201-767-5029
www.pearsoned.com
Offers information on private organizations providing financial aid for university students interested in studying in foreign countries.
335 pages Cloth

4051 Journal of Student Financial Aid
University of Notre Dame
Office of Financial Aid
Notre Dame, IN 46556
574-631-5000
www.nd.edu
Offers a listing of private and federal sources of financial aid for college bound students.
3x Year
Rev. John I. Jenkins, President
Thomas G. Burish, Provost

4052 Loans and Grants from Uncle Sam
Octameron Associates
1900 Mount Vernon Avenue
PO Box 2748
Alexandria, VA 22301-0748
703-836-5480
Fax: 703-836-5650
info@octameron.com
www.octameron.com
Offers information on federal student loan and grant programs and state loan guarantee agencies.
72 pages Annual
ISBN: 1-57509-097-X
Anna Leider, Author

4053 Money for Film & Video Artists
American for the Art
1000 Vermont Avenue NW
6th Floor
Washington, DC 20005
202-371-2830
Fax: 202-371-0424
www.artsusa.org
The listings are organized by sponsoring organization and entries include basic application and program information.
Abel Lopez, Chair
Ramona Baker, Vice Chair

4054 Money for International Exchange in the Arts
American for the Art
1000 Vermont Avenue NW
6th Floor
Washington, DC 20005
202-371-2830
Fax: 202-371-0424
www.artsusa.org
A guide to the various resources available to support artists and arts organizations in international work.
Abel Lopez, Chair
Ramona Baker, Vice Chair

4055 Money for Visual Artists
America for the Art
1000 Vermont Avenue NW
6th Floor
Washington, DC 20005
202-371-2830
Fax: 202-371-0424
www.artsusa.org
Programs are listed alphabetically by sponsor with detailed program description.
Abel Lopez, Chair
Ramona Baker, Vice Chair

4056 National Association of State Scholarship and Grant Program Survey Report
National Association of State Scholarship Programs
8 W. 38TH ST
Suite 503
New York, NY 10018-1324
917-551-6770
contact@nas.org
www.nas.org
Listing of over 50 member state agencies administering scholarship and grant programs for student financial aid.
Publication Date: 1987 150 pages
Peter Wyatt Wood, President
Ashley Thorne, Executive Director

4057 National Association of Student Financial Aid Administrators Directory
1801 Pennsylvania Avenue NW
Suite 850
Washington, DC 20006-3606
202-785-0453
Fax: 202-785-1487
info@nasfaa.org
www.nasfaa.org/Directory_of_Associations
Offers information on institutions of postsecondary education and their financial aid administrators.
Billie Jo Hamilton, National Chair
Justin Draeger, President & CEO

4058 Need A Lift?
The American Legion
700 N Pennsylvania Street
P.O. Box 36460
Indianapolis, IN 46236-1050
317-630-1200
888-453-4466
Fax: 317-630-1381
emblem@legion.org
www.EMBLEM.legion.org
Sources of career, scholarship and loan information or assistance.
144 pages Annual/Paperback
Robert Caudell, Author

4059 Peterson's Grants for Graduate and Postdoctoral Study
Peterson's, A Nelnet Company
Princeton Pike Corporate Center
461 From Road
Paramus, NJ 07652
609-698-1800
800-338-3282
Fax: 402-458-3042
support@petersons.com
www.petersons.com
Only comprehensive source of current information on grants and fellowships exclusively for graduate and postdoctoral students.
Publication Date: 1998 5th Edition
ISBN: 1-560794-01-1

4060 Peterson's Sports Scholarships and College Athletic Programs
Peterson's, A Nelnet Company
Princeton Pike Corporate Center
461 From Road
Paramus, NJ 08648
609-896-1800
800-338-3282
Fax: 402-458-3042
support@petersons.com
www.petersons.com

A college-by-college look at scholarships designated exclusively for student athletes in 32 men's and women's sports.

Publication Date: 2004 624 pages 5th Edition
ISBN: 0768915244

4061 Scholarship Handbook
The College Board
45 Columbus Avenue
New York, NY 10023
212-713-8000
800-323-7155
www.collegeboard.org
Useful text for college-bound students, their families and guidance counselors. Offers more than 2,000 descriptions of national and state level award programs, public and private education loan programs, intership opportunities and more.

David Coleman, President and CEO
Jeremy Singer, COO

4062 Scholarships for Emigres Training for Careers in Jewish Education
Jewish Foundation for Education of Women
135 E 64th Street
New York, NY 10065
212-288-3931
Fax: 212-288-5798
fdnscholar@aol.com
www.jfew.org
Open to emigres from the former Soviet Union who are pursuing careers in Jewish education. Candidates in Jewish education, rabbinical and cantorial studies, and Jewish studies are invited to write the Foundation.

Elizabeth Leiman Kraiem, Executive Director
Jill Weber Smith, Chair

4063 Scholarships, Fellowships and Loans
Gale Research
27500 Drake Road
Farmington Hills, MI 48231-5477
800-877-4253
Fax: 877-363-4253
www.cengage.com
Written especially for professionals, students, counselors, parents and others interested in education. This resource provides more than 3,700 sources of education-related financial aid and awards at all levels of study.

Publication Date: 1995 1,290 pages Annual
ISBN: 0-810391-14-7

Michael E. Hansen, CEO
Fernando Bleichmar, Chief Strategy Officer

4064 Student Guide
Federal Student Aid Information Center
PO Box 84
Washington, DC 20044-0084
800-433-3243
800-433-3243
https://studentaid.ed.gov
Describes the federal student aid programs, and general information about the eligibility criteria, application procedures and award levels, and lists important deadlines and phone numbers.

54 pages

John J McCarthy, Director

4065 Study Abroad
U.N. Educational, Scientific & Cultural Assn.
7, place de Fontenoy
F-75700 Paris
France
1-45681123
Listing of over 200,000 scholarships, fellowships and educational exchange opportunities offered for study in 124 countries.

1,300 pages Biennial

4066 Write Now: A Complete Self-Teaching Programfor Better Handwriting
Continuing Education Press
400 W First St
Chico, CA 95929-0250
530-898-6105
866-647-7377
Fax: 530-898-4020
rce@csuchico.edu
rce.csuchico.edu
A step-by-step guide to improving one's handwriting. Develop clean and legible italic handwriting with regular practice.

128 pages Paperback
ISBN: 0-87678-089-3

Barbara Getty & Inga Dubay, Author
Debra Barger, Administration
Joe Picard, Director

Directories & Handbooks / Guidance & Counseling

4067 Accredited Institutions of Postsecondary Education
MacMillan Publishers
175 Fifth Avenue
New York, NY 10010
646-307-5151
888-330-8477
Fax: 800-835-3202
customerservice@mpsvirginia.com
us.macmillan.com
Lists over 5,000 accredited institutions and programs for postsecondary education in the United States.

600 pages Annual

4068 Adolescent Pregnancy Prevention Clearinghouse
Children's Defense Fund Education & Youth Develop.
25 E Street NW
#400
Washington, DC 20001-2109
202-628-8787
800-233-1200
Fax: 202-662-3560
cdfinfo@childrensdefense.org
www.childrensdefense.org
Provides information and clarification on the connection between pregnancy and broader life questions for youth.

Marian Wright Edelman, President
Richard Gollub, Chief Financial Officer

4069 COLLEGESOURCE
Career Guidance Foundation
8090 Engineer Road
San Diego, CA 92111-1906
858-560-8051
800-854-2670
Fax: 858-278-8960
www.collegesource.org
CD-ROM and Web College Catalog Collection. Contains colleges and universitie's catalogs from throughout the US, over 2,600. Also a college search program that can be searched by major, tuition costs, and more. Foreign catalogs available.

Annette Crone, Account Coordinator
David Hunt, Account Coordinator

4070 Cabells Directory of Publishing Opportunities in Educational Psychology and Administration
Cabell Publishing Company
Box 5428
Tobe Hahn Station
Beaumont, TX 77726
409-898-0575
Fax: 409-866-9554
info@cabells.com
www.cabells.com
Provides information on editor contact information, manuscript guidelines, acceptance rate, review information and circulation data for over 225 academic journals.

Publication Date: 1978 799 pages Annual
ISBN: 0-911753-19-2

David WE Cabell, Editor
Deborah L English, Associate Editor

4071 Career & Vocational Counseling Directory
American Business Directories
5711 S 86th Circle
Omaha, NE 68127-4146
402-593-4600
888-999-1307
Fax: 402-331-5481
www.americanbusinessandservicedirectory.com
Nationwide listing of 3,300 companies/consultants available in print, computer magnetic tape and diskette, mailing labels, and index cards listing the name, address, phone, size of advertisement, contact person and number of employees.

Annual

Jerry Venner, Coordinating Education

4072 College Handbook
College Board Publications
45 Columbus Avenue
New York, NY 10023-6992
212-713-8000
Fax: 800-525-5562
puborderinfo@collegeboard.org
www.collegeboard.org
Descriptions of 3,200 colleges and universities.

Publication Date: 1994 1728 pages Annually

David Coleman, President and CEO
Jeremy Singer, COO

4073 College Handbook Foreign Student Supplement
College Board Publications
45 Columbus Avenue
New York, NY 10023-6917
212-713-8000
Fax: 800-525-5562
aces@info.collegeboard.org
www.collegeboard.org
Lists about 2,800 colleges and universities that are open to foreign students.

Publication Date: 1994 288 pages Annual
ISBN: 0-877474-83-3

David Coleman, President and CEO
Jeremy Singer, COO

4074 College Transfer Guide
School Guide Publications
210 N Avenue
New Rochelle, NY 10801-6402
914-632-7771
800-433-7771
Fax: 914-632-3412
mridder@schoolguides.com
www.schoolguides.com
Five hundred four-year colleges in the Northeast and Midwest that accept transfer students listing transfer requirements,

deadlines, fees, enrollment, costs and contact information. Circulation, 60,000.

125 pages Annual/January

4075 Community College Exemplary Instructional Programs
Massachusetts Bay Community College Press
50 Oakland Street
Wellesley Hills, MA 02181
781-239-3000
Fax: 781-237-1061
www.massbay.edu
Community college programs identified as outstanding by the National Council of Instructional Administrators.

Publication Date: 1961

John O'Donnell, President

4076 Comparative Guide to American Colleges for Students, Parents & Counselors
HarperCollins
195 Broadway
New York, NY 10007-5244
212-207-7000
Fax: 212-207-7145
www.harpercollins.com
Accredited four-year colleges in the United States.

800 pages Cloth

4077 Directory of Play Therapy Training
University of North Texas
PO Box 310829
425 S. Welch St., Complex 2
Denton, TX 76203
940-565-3864
Fax: 940-565-4461
cpt@unt.edu
www.centerforplaytherapy.com
Provides training, research publications and serves as a clearinghouse for literature in the field.

Paperback

Rinda Thomas, Office Manager
Sue C Bratton, Center Director

4078 Educators Guide to FREE Guidance Materials
Educators Progress Service
214 Center Street
Randolph, WI 53956-1408
920-326-3126
888-951-4469
Fax: 920-326-3127
epsinc@centurytel.net
www.freeteachingaids.com
Lists and describes free films, videotapes, filmstrips, slides, web sites, and hundreds of free printed materials in the field of career education and guidance for all age levels.

190 pages Annual
ISBN: 87708-406-8

Kathy Nehmer, President

4079 Index of Majors and Graduate Degrees
College Board Publications
45 Columbus Avenue
New York, NY 10023-6992
212-713-8000
Fax: 800-525-5562
www.collegeboard.org
Includes descriptions of over 600 majors and identifies the 3,200 colleges, universities, and graduate schools that offer them.

Annual
ISBN: 0-87447-592-9

David Coleman, President and CEO
Jeremy Singer, COO

4080 Tests: a Comprehensive Reference for Psychology, Education & Business
PRO-ED
8700 Shoal Creek Boulevard
Austin, TX 78757-6897
512-451-3246
800-897-3202
Fax: 800-397-7633
general@proedinc.com
www.proedinc.com
This fifth edition groups updated information on approximately 2,000 assessment instruments into three primary classifications-psychology, education, and business-and 89 subcategories, enabling users to readily identify the tests that meet their assessment needs. Each entry contains a statement of the instrument's purpose, a concise description of the instrument, scoring procedures, cost, and publisher information.

Publication Date: 1991 809 pages Paperback/Hardcover
ISBN: 0-89079-709-9

Taddy Maddox, General Editor

4081 Vocational Biographies
Vocational Biographies
PO Box 31
Sauk Centre, MN 56378-0031
320-352-6516
800-255-0752
Fax: 320-352-5546
careers@vocbio.com
www.vocbio.com
Real life career success stories of persons in every walk of life that allow students to see a career through the eyes of a real person. New for 2005: Internet Access to 1001 Career Success Stories.

Toby Behnen, President
Roxann Behnen, Customer Service/Sales

4082 What Works and Doesn't With at Risk Students
BKS Publishing
3109 150th Place SE
Mill Creek, WA 98012-4864
425-745-3029
Fax: 425-337-4837
DocBlokk@aol.com
www.literacyfirst.com

Publication Date: 1919 162 pages Paperback
ISBN: 0-9656713-0-5

Jan Glaes, Author
Bill Blokker, Owner

4083 World of Play Therapy Literature
Center for Play Therapy
PO Box 311337
5308 Valley Ridge Plaza
Middleton, WI 53562
608-203-8646
Fax: 608-203-5872
cpt@coefs.coe.unt.edu
www.playtherapymadison.com
Author and topical listings of over 6,000 books, dissertations, documents, and journal articles on play therapy, updated every two years.

Publication Date: 1995 306 pages

Landreth, Homeyer, Bratton, Kale, Hipl, Schumann, Author

Directories & Handbooks / Language Arts

4084 Classroom Strategies for the English Language Learner
Master Teacher
One Leadership Lane
PO Box 1207
Manhattan, KS 66502-1207
800-669-9633
Fax: 800-669-1132
www.masterteacher.com
A practical model for accelerating both oral language and literacy development, based on the latest research for effective instruction of both Native English speakers and English language learners.

266 pages
ISBN: 1-58992-068-6

Socrro Herrera EdD, Author

4085 Italic Handwriting Series-Book A
Continuing Education Press
400 W First St
Chico, CA 95929-0250
530-898-6105
866-647-7377
Fax: 530-898-4020
rce@csuchico.edu
rce.csuchico.edu
Book A is the first workbook of a seven-part series. Designed for the beginning reader and writer, it introduces the alphabet one letter at a time. Illustrated.

64 pages Paperback
ISBN: 0-87678-092-3

Barbara Getty & Inga Dubay, Author
Debra Barger, Administration
Joe Picard, Director

4086 Italic Handwriting Series-Book B
Continuing Education Press
400 W First St
Chico, CA 95929-0250
530-898-6105
866-647-7377
Fax: 530-898-4020
rce@csuchico.edu
rce.csuchico.edu
Book B is the second workbook of a seven-part series. Designed for the beginning reader and writer. Introduces words and sentences, lowercase and capitol print script, one letter per page. Illustrated.

59 pages Paperback
ISBN: 0-87678-093-1

Barbara Getty & Inga Dubay, Author
Debra Barger, Administration
Joe Picard, Director

4087 Italic Handwriting Series-Book C
Continuing Education Press
400 W First St
Chico, CA 95929-0250
530-898-6105
866-647-7377
Fax: 530-898-4020
rce@csuchico.edu
rce.csuchico.edu
Book C is the third workbook of a seven-part series. Covers basic italic and introduces the cursive. Words and sentences include days of week,

months of year, modes of transportation, and tongue twisters. Illustrated.

60 pages Paperback
ISBN: 0-87678-094-X

Barbara Getty & Inga Dubay, Author
Debra Barger, Administration
Joe Picard, Director

4088 Italic Handwriting Series-Book D
Continuing Education Press
400 W First St
Chico, CA 95929-0250
530-898-6105
866-647-7377
Fax: 530-898-4020
rce@csuchico.edu
rce.csuchico.edu
Book D is the fourth workbook of a seven-part series. Reviews basic italic and covers the total cursive program. Includes prefixes, suffixes, capitalization, and playful poems. Explores history of the alphabet. Illustrated.

80 pages Paperback
ISBN: 0-87678-095-8

Barbara Getty & Inga Dubay, Author
Debra Barger, Administration
Joe Picard, Director

4089 Italic Handwriting Series-Book E
Continuing Education Press
400 W First St
Chico, CA 95929-0250
530-898-6105
866-647-7377
Fax: 530-898-4020
rce@csuchico.edu
rce.csuchico.edu
Book E is the fifth workbook of a seven-part series. Reviews basic italic and covers the total cursive program. Writing practice covers natural history— plants, volcanoes, cities. Explores history of the alphabet. Illustrated.

56 pages Paperback
ISBN: 0-87678-096-6

Barbara Getty & Inga Dubay, Author
Debra Barger, Administration
Joe Picard, Director

4090 Italic Handwriting Series-Book F
Continuing Education Press
400 W First St
Chico, CA 95929-0250
530-898-6105
866-647-7377
Fax: 530-898-4020
rce@csuchico.edu
rce.csuchico.edu
Book F is the sixth workbook of a seven-part series. Reviews basic italic and covers the total cursive program. Writing practice emphasizes figures of speech (e.g. homophones, puns, metaphors, acronyms). Explores history of the alphabet. Illustrated.

56 pages Paperback
ISBN: 0-87678-097-4

Barbara Getty & Inga Dubay, Author
Debra Barger, Administration
Joe Picard, Director

4091 Italic Handwriting Series-Book G
Continuing Education Press
400 W First St
Chico, CA 95929-0250
530-898-6105
866-647-7377
Fax: 530-898-4020
rce@csuchico.edu
rce.csuchico.edu
Book G is the seventh workbook of a seven-part series. A comprehensive self-instruction program in basic and cursive italic. Writing content follows a central theme-the history of our alphabet. Suitable for older students. Illustrated.

56 pages Paperback
ISBN: 0-87678-098-2

Barbara Getty & Inga Dubay, Author
Debra Barger, Administration
Joe Picard, Director

4092 Language Schools Directory
American Business Directories
5711 S 86th Circle
Omaha, NE 68127-4146
402-593-4600
888-999-1307
Fax: 402-331-5481
www.americanbusinessandservicedirectory.com
A listing of language schools, arranged by geographic location, offering contact information which is updated on a continual basis, and printed on request. Directory is also available in electronic formats.

Jerry Venner, Coordinating Education

4093 Picture Book Learning Volume-1
Picture Book Learning Inc.
PO Box 270075
Louisville, CO 80027
303-548-2809
todd@picturebooklearning.com
www.picturebooklearning.com
Teachers can use this fun method of teaching elementary children basic language arts skills through the use of picture books.

60 pages
ISBN: 0-9760725-0-5

Todd Osborne, Co-President
Corinne Osborne, Editor

4094 Process of Elimination - a Method of Teaching Basic Grammar - Teacher Ed
Scott & McCleary Publishing Company
2482 11th Street SW
PO Box 3830
Akron, OH 44314-0830
702-566-8756
800-765-3564
Fax: 702-568-1378
jscott7576@aol.com
www.scottmccleary.com
Series of 7 steps designed to teach basic grammar skills to students in middle grades through college. Available in a teacher edition and a student workbook.

50 pages
ISBN: 0-9636225-2-8
ISSN: 0-9636225-

Milton Metheny, Author
Janet Scott, Publisher
Sheila McCleary, Publisher

4095 Process of Elimination: A Method of Teaching Basic Grammar - Student Ed
Scott & McCleary Publishing Company
2482 11th Street SW
PO Box 3830
Akron, OH 44314-0830
702-566-8756
800-765-3564
Fax: 702-568-1378
jscott7576@aol.com
www.scottmccleary.com
Series of 7 steps designed to teach basic grammar skills to students in middle grades through college. Available in a teacher edition and a student workbook.

Milton Metheny, Author
Janet Scott, Publisher
Sheila McCleary, Publisher

4096 Put Reading First: The Research Building Blocks For Teaching Children To Read
ED Pubs
P.O. Box 22207
Alexandria, VA 22304-1398
877-4ED-PUBS
Fax: 703-605-6794
edpubs@inet.ed.gov
www.edpubs.org
Provides analysis and discussion in five areas of reading instruction: phonemic awareness, phonics, fluency, vocabulary and text comprehension.

4097 Write Now: A Complete Self Teaching Program for Better Handwriting
Continuing Education Press
400 W First St
Chico, CA 95929-0250
530-898-6105
866-647-7377
Fax: 530-898-4020
rce@csuchico.edu
rce.csuchico.edu
Finally, a handwriting improvement book for adults. Teach yourself to write legibly and retain it over time using this step-by-step guide to modern italic handwriting with complete instructions as well as practice exercises and tips. The secret to legible handwriting is the absence of loops in letterform, making it easier to write and easier to read.

96 pages Paperback
ISBN: 0-87678-089-3

Barbara Getty & Inga Dubay, Author
Debra Barger, Administration
Joe Picard, Director

Directories & Handbooks / Library Services

4098 Directory of Manufacturers & Suppliers
Special Libraries Association
331 S Patrick Street
Alexandria, VA 22314-3501
703-647-4900
Fax: 703-647-4901
sla@sla.org
www.sla.org
The SLA network consists of nearly 15,000 librarians and information professionals who specialize in the arts, communication, business, social science, biomedical sciences, geosciences and environmental studies, and industry, business, research, educational and technical institutions, government, special departments of public and university libraries, newspapers, museums, and public or private organizations that provide or require specialized information.

Doug Newcomb, Deputy CEO
Linda Broussard, Chief Financial Officer

4099 Directory of Members of the Association for Library and Information Science Education
Association for Library and Information Science Ed
2150 N 107th St
Suite 205
Seattle, WA 98133
206-209-5267
Fax: 206-367-8777
office@alise.org
www.alise.org
The Directory is designed to serve as a handbook for the association, including a list of officers, committees, and interest groups and strategic planning information for the association. Also listed are graduate schools of library and information science and their faculty.
Annual Paperback
Clara Chu, President
Samantha K. Hastings, Vice President

4100 Libraries Unlimited Academic Catalog
Libraries Unlimited
88 Post Road W
Westport, CT 06881
203-226-3571
Fax: 203-222-1502
lu-books@lu.com
www.abc-clio.com/LibrariesUnlimited.aspx
Catalog includes reference, collection development, library management, cataloging, and technology.
Kathryn Su rez, Publisher

4101 Managing Info Tech in School Library Media Center
Libraries Unlimited
88 Post Road West
Westport, CT 06881
203-226-3571
800-225-5800
Fax: 203-222-1502
lu-books@lu.com
www.abc-clio.com/LibrariesUnlimited.aspx
Publication Date: 2000 290 pages Hardcover
ISBN: 1-56308-724-3
Kathryn Su rez, Publisher

4102 Managing Media Services Theory and Practice
Libraries Unlimited
88 Post Road West
Westport, CT 06881
203-226-3571
800-225-5800
Fax: 203-222-1502
lu-books@lu.com
www.abc-clio.com/LibrariesUnlimited.aspx
Publication Date: 2002 418 pages Cloth
ISBN: 1-56308-530-5
Kathryn Su rez, Publisher

Directories & Handbooks / Music & Art

4103 College Guide for Visual Arts Majors
Peterson's, A Nelnet Company
Princeton Pike Corporate Center
461 From Road
Paramus, NJ 07652
609-896-1800
800-338-3282
Fax: 402-458-3042
support@petersons.com
www.petersons.com
Offers descriptions of over 700 accredited US colleges and universities, music conservatories, and art/design schools that grant undergraduate degrees in the areas of studio art.
Publication Date: 2006 404 pages
ISBN: 1-560795-36-0

4104 Community Outreach and Education for the Arts Handbook
Music Teachers National Association
PO Box 261452
Littleton, CO 80163-1452
303-565-5351
888-512-5278
Fax: 555-555-1212
mtnanet@mtaa.org
www.mtaa.org
Resource booklet for independent music teachers.
Paperback
March
150 booths with 2500 attendees
Chad Schwatbach, Pr/Marketing Associate

4105 Italic Letters
Continuing Education Press
400 W First St
Chico, CA 95929-0250
530-898-6105
866-647-7377
Fax: 530-898-4020
rce@csuchico.edu
rce.csuchico.edu
Italic Letters is for professional and amateur calligraphers, art teachers, and enthusiasts of the book arts. Numerous tips on letter shapes, spacing, slant, pen edge angle, and other secrets to handsome writing.
128 pages Paperback
ISBN: 0-87678-091-5
Barbara Getty & Inga Dubay, Author
Debra Barger, Administration
Joe Picard, Director

4106 Money for Film & Video Artists
American for the Art
1000 Vermont Avenue NW
6th Floor
Washington, DC 20005
202-371-2830
Fax: 202-371-0424
www.artsusa.org
The listings are organized by sponsoring organization and entries include basic application and program information.
Abel Lopez, Chair
Ramona Baker, Vice Chair

4107 Money for Visual Artists
America for the Art
1000 Vermont Avenue NW
12th Floor
Washington, DC 20005
202-371-2830
Fax: 202-371-0424
www.artsusa.org
Programs are listed alphabetically by sponsor with detailed program description.
Abel Lopez, Chair
Ramona Baker, Vice Chair

4108 Music Teachers Guide to Music Instructional Software
Music Teachers National Association
1 W. 4th St.
Ste. 1550
Cincinnati, OH 45202-2811
513-421-1420
888-512-5278
Fax: 513-421-2503
mtnanet@mtna.org
www.mtna.org
Evaluations of music software for the macintosh and PC, including CD-ROMs, music skills and keyboard technique drill software, sequencers and soundequipment controllers.
Publication Date: 1876
Kenneth J. Christensen, President
Rebecca Grooms Johnson, President-elect

4109 Resource Booklet for Independent Music Teachers
Music Teachers National Association
1 W. 4th St.
Ste. 1550
Cincinnati, OH 45202-2811
513-421-1420
888-512-5278
Fax: 513-421-2503
mtnanet@mtna.org
www.mtna.org
A booklet for organizing information about community resources.
Publication Date: 1876
Kenneth J. Christensen, President
Rebecca Grooms Johnson, President-elect

4110 School Arts
Davis Publications, Inc.
50 Portland Street
Worcester, MA 01608
800-533-2847
Fax: 508-753-3834
www.schoolartsdigital.com
Companies offering products, materials, and art education resources or programs that focus on the history of art, multicultural resources such as Fine Art, reproductions, CD-Roms, museum education, programs, slides, books, videos, exhibits, architecture, timelines, and resource kits.

Directories & Handbooks / Physical Education

4111 Educators Guide to FREE HPER Materials
Educators Progress Service
214 Center Street
Randolph, WI 53956-1408
920-326-3126
888-951-4469
Fax: 920-326-3127
epsinc@centurytel.net
www.freeteachingaids.com
Lists and describes free films, videotapes, filmstrips, slides, web sites, and hundreds of free printed materials in the field of health, physical education, and recreation for all age levels.
184 pages Annual
ISBN: 87708-407-6
Kathy Nehmer, President

4112 Schools & Colleges Directory
Association for Experiential Education
3775 Iris Avenue
Suite 4
Boulder, CO 80301-2043
303-440-8844
Fax: 303-440-9581

publications@aee.org
www.aee.org
Provides information about many schools, colleges and universities that have programs or offer degrees related to the field of outdoor/experiential education. Listings include programs in high schools and independent organizations as well as institutions of higher learning. Paperback.

Publication Date: 1995 Paperback

Maurie Lung, President
Bobbi Beale, President-Elect

Directories & Handbooks / Reading

4113 Diagnostic Reading Inventory for Bilingual Students in Grades 1-8

Scott & McCleary Publishing Company
2482 11th Street SW
PO Box 3830
Akron, OH 44314-0830
702-566-8756
800-765-3564
Fax: 702-568-1378
jscott7576@aol.com
www.scottmccleary.com
Series of 13 tests designed to access reading performance. IRI, spelling, phonics, visual and auditory discrimination and listening comprehension are just some of the tests included.

155 pages
ISBN: 0-9636225-1-X

Janet M Scott, Co-Author
Sheila C McCleary, Co-Author

4114 Diagnostic Reading Inventory for Primary and Intermediate Grades K-8

Scott & McCleary Publishing Company
2482 11th Street SW
PO Box 3830
Akron, OH 44314-0830
702-566-8756
800-765-3564
Fax: 702-568-1378
jscott7576@aol.com
www.scottmccleary.com
Designed to assess reading performance in grades K-8. Tests include: word recognition, oral reading inventory, comprehension, listening comprehension, auditory and visual discrimination, auditory and visual memory, learning modalities inventory, phonics mastery tests, structural analysis, word association and a diagnostic spelling test.

260 pages
ISBN: 0-9636225-4-4

Janet M Scott, Co-Author
Sheila C McCleary, Co-Author

4115 Educational Leadership

Assn. for Supervision & Curriculum Dev. (ASCD)
1703 N Beauregard Street
Alexandria, VA 22311-1714
703-578-9600
800-933-2723
Fax: 703-575-5400
el@ascd.org
www.ascd.org
For educators by educators. With a circulation of 175,000, Educational Leadership is acknowledged throughout the world as an authoritative source of information about teaching and learning, new ideas and practices relevant to practicing educators, and the latest trends and issues affecting prekindergarten through higher education.

Publication Date: 1943

Marge Scherer, Executive Editor

4116 Laubach Literacy Action Directory

Laubach Literacy Action
222 Waverly Avenue
Syracuse, NY 13244-2010
315-422-9121
888-528-2224
Fax: 315-422-6369
info@laubach.org
library.syr.edu
Listing of over 1,100 local literacy councils and associates who teach the Laubach Method.

Publication Date: 1955 90 pages Annual

4117 Ready to Read, Ready to Learn

ED Pubs
P.O. Box 22207
Alexandria, VA 22304-1398
703-605-6794
Fax: 703-605-6794
edpubs@inet.ed.gov
www.edpubs.org

4118 Tips for Reading Tutors

ED Pubs
P.O. Box 22207
Alexandria, VA 22304-1398
877-4ED-PUBS
Fax: 703-605-6794
edpubs@inet.ed.gov
www.edpubs.org
Basic tips for reading tutors

Directories & Handbooks / Secondary Education

4119 College Board Guide to High Schools

College Board Publications
45 Columbus Avenue
New York, NY 10023-6917
212-713-8000
800-323-7155
Fax: 800-525-5562
www.collegeboard.org
Offers listings and information on over 25,000 public and private high schools nationwide.

Publication Date: 1994 2,024 pages
ISBN: 0-874474-66-3

David Coleman, President and CEO
Jeremy Singer, COO

4120 Compendium of Tertiary & Sixth Forum Colleges

SCOTVIC: S McDonald, Principal
Ridge College
Manchester
England
61-4277733
Offers listings of over 200 Sixth Form and Tertiary Colleges in the United Kingdom offering courses preparing secondary students for university study.

Publication Date: 1990 200 pages Biennial

4121 Directory of Public Elementary and Secondary Education Agencies

US National Center for Education Statistics
1990 K Street, NW
8th & 9th Floors
Washington, DC 20006-5651
202-502-7300
800-424-1616
Fax: 202-502-7466
nces.ed.gov
Directory of approximately 17,000 local education agencies that operate their own schools or pay tuition to other local education agencies.

400 pages Annual

Peggy G. Carr, Acting Commissioner
Lena McDowell, Contact

4122 Educators Guide to FREE Family and Consumer Education Materials

Educators Progress Service
214 Center Street
Randolph, WI 53956-1408
920-326-3126
888-951-4469
Fax: 920-326-3127
epsinc@centurytel.net
www.freeteachingaids.com
Lists and describes free films, videotapes, filmstrips, slides, web sites, and hundreds of free printed materials in the field of home econominics and consumer education for all age levels.

161 pages Annual
ISBN: 87708-408-4

Kathy Nehmer, President

4123 Focus on School

ABC-CLIO
130 Cremona Drive
#1911
Santa Barbara, CA 93117-5599
805-968-1911
800-368-6868
Fax: 805-685-9685
www.abc-clio.com
Hotlines, print and nonprint resources on education for young adults.

Publication Date: 1990

4124 Great Source Catalog

Great Source Education Group
PO Box 7050
Wilmington, MA 01887
800-289-4490
Fax: 800-289-3994
www.hmhco.com
Alternative, affordable, student-friendly K-12 materials to make teaching and learning fun for educators and students.

4125 Helping Your Child Succeed In School: Elementary and Secondary Editions

Master Teacher
One Leadership Lane
Manhattan, KS 66502-1207
785-539-0555
800-669-9633
Fax: 800-669-1132
www.masterteacher.com
Provides a way for school administrators to help parents help their children succeed in school. Published in English and Spanish.

Erica Paronson, Executive Editor

4126 Lesson Plans for Integrating Technology into the Classroom: Secondary Edition

Master Teacher
One Leadership Lane
PO Box 1207
Manhattan, KS 66502-1207
800-669-9633
Fax: 800-669-1132
www.masterteacher.com
Gives teachers practical lessons developed and tested by teachers across the curriculum,

with students of all levels of ability in using technology.

104 pages
ISBN: 1-58992-152-6

4127 Lesson Plans for Problem-Based Learning: Secondary Edition
Master Teacher
One Leadership Lane
PO Box 1207
Manhattan, KS 66502-1207
800-669-9633
Fax: 800-669-1132
www.masterteacher.com
An instructional technique which organizes the curriculum around a major problem that students work to solve over the weeks or months.

117 pages
ISBN: 0-914607-87-1

4128 Lesson Plans for the Substitute Teacher: Secondary Edition
Master Teacher
One Leadership Lane
PO Box 1207
Manhattan, KS 66502-1207
800-669-9633
Fax: 800-669-1132
www.masterteacher.com
Gives you more than 100 lessons developed and tested by teachers across the curriculum and at all grade levels.

177 pages
ISBN: 1-58992-108-9

4129 Peterson's Private Secondary Schools
Peterson's, A Nelnet Company
Princeton Pike Corporate Center
461 From Road
Paramus, NJ 07652-2123
609-896-1800
800-338-3282
Fax: 402-458-3042
support@petersons.com
www.petersons.com
Listing of over 1,400 accredited and state-approved private secondary schools in the US and abroad.

1,300 pages Annual

4130 Secondary Teachers Guide to FREE Curriculum Materials
Educators Progress Service
214 Center Street
Randolph, WI 53956-1408
920-326-3126
888-951-4469
Fax: 920-326-3127
epsinc@centurytel.net
www.freeteachingaids.com
Lists and describes free supplementary teaching aids for the high school and college level.

296 pages Annual
ISBN: 87708-399-1

Kathy Nehmer, President

Directories & Handbooks / Science

4131 Earth Education: A New Beginning
Institute for Earth Education
Cedar Cove
PO Box 115
Greenville, WV 24945
304-832-6404
Fax: 304-832-6077
info@ieetree.org
www.eartheducation.org
This book proposes another direction-an alternative that many environmental leaders and teachers around the world have already taken. It is called The Earth Education Path, and anyone can follow it in developing a genuine program made up of magical learning adventures.

334 pages Paperback
ISBN: 0917011023

Steve Van Matre, Chairman

4132 Earthkeepers
Institute for Earth Education
Cedar Cove
PO Box 115
Greenville, WV 24945
304-832-6404
Fax: 304-832-6077
iee1@aol.com
www.eartheducation.org
This book will give you the best picture of what a complete earth education program involves. Even if you can't set up the complete Earthkeepers program, there are many activities you can use to build an earth education program in your own settting and situation.

108 pages Paperback
ISBN: 0917011015

Bruce Johnson, Chairman

4133 Educators Guide to FREE Science Materials
Educators Progress Service
214 Center Street
Randolph, WI 53956-1408
920-326-3126
888-951-4469
Fax: 920-326-3127
epsinc@centurytel.net
www.freeteachingaids.com
Lists and describes free films, videotapes, filmstrips, slides, web sites, and hundreds of free printed materials in the field of science for all age levels.

Annual

Kathy Nehmer, President

4134 K-6 Science and Math Catalog
Carolina Biological Supply Co.
2700 York Road
PO Box 6010
Burlington, NC 27216-6010
336-584-0381
800-334-5551
Fax: 336-538-6330
quotations@carolina.com
www.carolina.com
Service teaching materials for grades Pre K through 8, including charts, computers, software, books, living animals and plants, microscopes, microscope slides, models, teaching kits and more.

Publication Date: 1927

4135 Science for All Children; A Guide to Improving Science Education
National Academy Press
Smithsonian Information
P.O. Box 23293
Washington, DC 20026-3293
202-633-1000
Fax: 202-287-2070
info@si.edu
www.si.edu/nsrc
Provides concise and practical guidelines for implementing science education reform at local level, including the elements of an effective, inquiry-based, hands-on science program. Produced by the National Science Resources Center. Published by National Academy Press.

240 pages
ISBN: 0-309-05297-1

National Science Resources Center, Author
John McCarter Jr., Chair
Shirley Ann Jackson, Vice Chair

4136 Sunship Earth
Institute for Earth Education
Cedar Cove
PO Box 115
Greenville, WV 24945
304-832-6404
Fax: 304-832-6077
iee1@aol.com
www.eartheducation.org
Contains clear descriptions of key ecological concepts and concise reviews of important learning principals, plus over 200 additional pages of ideas, activities and guidelines for setting up a complete Sunship Earth Study Station.

265 pages Paperback
ISBN: 0876030460

Bruce Johnson, Chairman

4137 Sunship III
Institute for Earth Education
Cedar Cove
PO Box 115
Greenville, WV 24945
304-832-6404
Fax: 304-832-6077
iee1@aol.com
www.eartheducation.org
Examines perception and choice in our daily habits and routines. It is about exploration and discovery in the larger context of where and how we live, and examining alteratives and making sacrifices on behalf of a healthier home planet.

133 pages Paperback
ISBN: 0917011031

Bruce Johnson, Chairman

4138 UNESCO Sourcebook for Out-of-School Science & Technology Education
U.N. Educational, Scientific & Cultural Assn.
7, place de Fontenoy
F-75700 Paris
France
Offers information on science clubs, societies and congresses, science fairs and museums.

145 pages

Directories & Handbooks / Social Studies

4139 Directory of Central America Classroom Resources
Central American Resource Center
2845 West 7th Street
Los Angeles, CA 90005-2012
213-385-7800
Fax: 213-385-1094
info@carecen-la.org
www.carecen-la.org
Offers information on suppliers of education resource materials about Central America, including curricula, materials, directories and organizations providing related services.

Publication Date: 1990 200 pages

Angela Sanbrano, President
Gloria Annicchiarico, Vice President

4140 **Educators Guide to FREE Social Studies Materials**
Educators Progress Service
214 Center Street
Randolph, WI 53956-1408
920-326-3126
888-951-4469
Fax: 920-326-3127
epsinc@centurytel.net
www.freeteachingaids.com
Lists and describes free films, videotapes, filmstrips, slides, web sites, and hundreds of free printed materials in the field of social studies for all age levels.
287 pages Annual
ISBN: 87708-405-X
Kathy Nehmer, President

4141 **Geography: A Resource Guide for Secondary Schools**
ABC-CLIO
130 Cremona Drive
#1911
Santa Barbara, CA 93117-5599
805-968-1911
800-368-6868
Fax: 805-685-9685
www.abc-clio.com
List of organizations and associations to use as resources for secondary education geography studies.

Directories & Handbooks / Technology in Education

4142 **American Trade Schools Directory**
Croner Publications
10951 Sorrento Valley Road
Suite 1D
San Diego, CA 92121
858-546-1954
800-441-4033
Fax: 858-546-1955
paul@croner.com
ww.croner.com
Loose leaf binder directory listing trade and technical schools throughout the United States, in alphabetical order, by state, then city, then school name.
411 pages
ISBN: 0-875140-02-5
Rosa Padilla, Office Manager

4143 **Association for Educational Communications & Technology: Membership Directory**
Association for Educational Communications & Tech.
320 W. 8th St.
Ste 101
Bloomington, IN 47404-3745
812-335-7675
877-677-AECT
aect@aect.org
www.aect.org
Five thousand audiovisual and instructional materials specialists and school media specialists, with audio-visual and TV production personnel. Also listed are committees, task force divisions, auxiliary affiliates, state organizations and directory of corporate members.
200 pages Annual/Spring
Stephen Harmon, President
Ellen Hoffman, Executive Secretary

4144 **Chronicle Vocational School Manual**
Chronicle Guidance Publications
66 Aurora Street
Moravia, NY 13118-3569
315-497-0339
800-899-0454
Fax: 315-497-3359
customerservice@chronicleguidance.com
www.chronicleguidance.com
A geographical index of more than 3,500 vocational schools including all contact information, programs, admissions requirements, costs, financial aid programs and student services.
Publication Date: 1938 300 pages Annual
ISBN: 1-556312-50-4
Cheryl Fickeisen, President/ CEO
Gary Fickeisen, Vice President

4145 **Directory of Public Vocational-Technical Schools & Institutes in the US**
Media Marketing Group
Voorhees Town Center
220 Laurel Road
Voorhees, NJ 08043-0611
856-782-6000
Fax: 856-385-7155
www.2mg.com
Offers information on over 1,400 post secondary vocational and technical education programs in public education; private trade and technical schools are not included.
Publication Date: 1994 400 pages Biennial
ISBN: 0-933474-51-2
Frank Palmieri, President

4146 **Directory of Vocational-Technical Schools**
Media Marketing Group
Voorhees Town Center
220 Laurel Road
Voorhees, NJ 08043-0611
856-782-6000
Fax: 856-385-7155
www.2mg.com
Offers information on public, postsecondary schools offering degree and non-degree occupational education.
Publication Date: 1996 450 pages Biennial
ISBN: 0-933474-52-0
Frank Palmieri, President

4147 **Educational Film & Video Locator**
RR Bowker Reed Reference
121 Chanlon Road
New Providence, NJ 07974-1541
908-665-2834
Fax: 908-464-3553
www.sabre.org
Producers and distributors of educational films.
Publication Date: 1990

4148 **Guide to Vocational and Technical Schools East & West**
Peterson's, A Nelnet Company
Princeton Pike Corporare Center
461 From Road
Paramus, NJ 07652
609-896-1800
800-338-3282
Fax: 402-458-3042
support@petersons.com
www.petersons.com
These two directories cover the full range of training programs in over 240 career fields divided into the categories of Business, Technology, Trade, Personal Services, and Health Care. East edition covers East of Mississippi; West edition covers West of the Mississippi.
Publication Date: 2006 579 pages Per Volume

4149 **Industrial Teacher Education Directory**
National Assn. of Industrial Teacher Educators
University of Northern Iowa
Cedar Falls, IA 50614-0178
319-273-2561
Fax: 319-273-5818
www.uni.edu/indtech
Listing of about 2,800 industrial education faculty members at 250 universities and four-year colleges in the United States, Canada, Australia, Japan and Taiwan.
108 pages Annual
M Fahmy, Professor/Head of Department
Charles Johnson, Coordinator of Tech Ed. Prog

4150 **Information Literacy: Essential Skills for the Information Age**
Syracuse University
900 South Crouse Ave
Syracuse, NY 13244-0001
315-443-1870
800-464-9107
Fax: 315-443-5448
eric@ericir.sye.edu
www.syr.edu
Traces history, development, and economic necessity of information literacy. Reports on related subject matter standards. Includes reports on the National Educational Goals (1991), the Secretary's Commission on Achieving Necessary Skills Report (1991), and the latest updates from ALA's Information Power (1998).
377 pages
ISBN: 0-937597-44-9
Richard L. Thompson, Chairman
Kenneth E. Goodman, Vice Chair

4151 **Internet Resource Directory for Classroom Teachers**
Regulus Communications
140 N 8th Street
Suite 201
Lincoln, NE 68508-1358
402-432-2680
regulus.com/
Directory offering information on all resources available on-line for classroom teachers, including e-mail addresses, Home Page URL's, phone and fax numbers, surface-mail addresses, classroom contacts and teaching resources. Available in paper and electronic formats.
Publication Date: 1996 272 pages Paper Format
Jane A Austin, Coordinating Education

4152 **K-12 District Technology Coordinators**
Quality Education Data
601 E. Marshall St
Suite 250
Sweet Springs, MO 65351-4715
303-860-1832
800-776-6373
Fax: 660-335-4157
info@qeddata.com
www.qeddata.com
The first in QED's National Educator Directories, this comprehensive directory of technology coordinators combines QED's exclusive database of technology and demographic data with names of technology coordinators in the 7,000 largest US school

districts. The directory includes district phone number, number of students in the district, number of computers, student/computer ratio and predominant computer brand.

Publication Date: 1994 400 pages

Peter Long, CEO
John F. Hood, President

4153 NetLingo Internet Dictionary
805-794-8687
info@netlingo.com
www.netlingo.com
A smart looking easy-to-understand dictionary of 3000 internet terms, 1200 chat acronyms, and much more. Modem reference book for international students, educators, industry professionals and online businesses and organizations.

Publication Date: 0

Erin Jansen, Author

4154 Quick-Source
AM Educational Publishing
P.O. Box 247
Suite D
Harrisonburg, VA 22801-3048
866-293-5313
800-296-5750
Fax: 540-433-5640
info@quicksourcelearning.com
https://www.quicksourcelearning.com/
Educational technology directory with over 1,100 names, addresses, phones/faxes, and brief descriptions of the products/services of companies/organizations; supports major works/word processors (MS-DOS/MAC); conferences and other educational technology listings.

Annual/September

4155 Schools Industrial, Technical & Trade Directory
American Business Directories
5711 S 86th Circle
Omaha, NE 68127-4146
402-593-4600
888-999-1307
Fax: 402-331-5481
www.americanbusinessandservicedirectory.com
A geographical listing of over 3,750 schools with all contact information, size of advertisement and first year in Yellow Pages. Also available in electronic formats.

Annual

Jerry Venner, Coordinating Education

4156 TESS: The Educational Software Selector
EPIE Institute
103 W Montauk Highway
PO Box 590
Hampton Bays, NY 11946-4003
631-728-9100
Fax: 631-728-9228
kkomoski@epie.org
www.epie.org
A list of over 1,200 suppliers of educational software and over 18,000 educational software products (on CD-ROM) for pre-school through college information. Includes description of program, grade level data, price, platform and review citations.

Publication Date: 1967

Nancy Boland, Coordinating Education

4157 Tech Directions-Directory of Federal & Federal and State Officials Issue
Prakken Publications
416 Longshore Drive
PO Box 8623
Ann Arbor, MI 48107-8623
734-975-2800
Fax: 313-577-1672
https://www.techdirections.com
Listing of federal and state officials concerned with vocational, technical, industrial trade and technology education in the United States and Canada.

Annual

Susanne Peckham, Managing Editor
Pam Moore, Assistant Editor

4158 Technology in Public Schools
Quality Education Data
601 E. Marshall St
Suite 250
Sweet Springs, MO 65351-4715
303-860-1832
800-776-6373
Fax: 660-335-4157
info@qeddata.com
www.qeddata.com
Annual survey of instructional technology represents more than 67% of all US K-12 students. Includes computer brand and processor type market share, CD-ROM, networks, LAN, modem, cable and in-depth internet access installed base information.

Publication Date: 1994 160 pages Yearly
ISBN: 0-88947-925-1

Peter Long, CEO
John F. Hood, President

Periodicals / General

4159 AACS Newsletter
American Association of Christian Schools
602 Belvoir Avenue
East Ridge, TN 37412-2221
423-629-4280
Fax: 423-622-7461
www.aacs.org
Association news offering the most up-to-date information relating to Christian education.

Publication Date: 1972 4 pages Monthly

Dr. Carl Herbster, Contact

4160 AAHE Bulletin
American Association for Higher Education
4505 S. Maryland Parkway
Box 453068
Las Vegas, NV 89154-3068
702-895-2737
Fax: 702-895-4269
ASHE@unlv.edu
www.ashe.ws
Electronic newsletter

16 pages Monthly

Kim Nehls, Ph.D, Executive Director
Holly Schneider, Conference Coordinator

4161 ACJS Today
Academy of Criminal Justice Services
7339 Hanover Parkway
Suite A
Greenbelta, MD 20770
301-446-6300
800-757-2257
Fax: 301-446-2819
www.acjs.org
Provides upcoming events, news releases, ACJS activities, ads, book reviews and miscellaneous information.

24-32 pages Quarterly

Brian Payne, President
Brandon Applegate, 1st Vice President

4162 ASCD Update
Assn. for Supervision & Curriculum Development
1703 N Beauregard Street
Alexandria, VA 22311-1714
703-578-9600
Fax: 703-575-5400
www.ascd.org
News on contemporary education issues and information on ASCD programs.

Publication Date: 1943

Ronald Brandt, Publisher
John O'Neil, Editor

4163 ASSC Newsletter
Arkansas School Study Council
500 Woodlane Street
Suite 256
Little Rock, AR 72201
501-682-1010
Fax: 479-442-2038
www.sos.arkansas.gov
Monthly up-date on education, finance, new legislation, mandates for Arkansas public schools.

3-10 pages

Judith Crouch, Human Resources
Laura Labay, Public Affairs

4164 AV Guide Newsletter
Educational Screen
380 E NW Highway
Des Plaines, IL 60016-2201
847-298-6622
Fax: 847-390-0408
Provides concise and practical information on audiovisually oriented products with an emphasis on new ideas and methods of using learning media, including educational computer software.

Monthly
ISSN: 0091-360X

HS Gillette, Publisher
Natalie Ferguson, Editor

4165 Academe
American Association of University Professors
1133 Nineteenth Street, NW
Suite 200
Washington, DC 20036-3406
202-737-5900
Fax: 202-737-5526
aaup@aaup.org
www.aaup.org
A thoughtful and provocative review of developments affecting higher education faculty. With timely features and informative departments, Academe delivers the latest on the state of the profession, legal and legislative trends, and issues in academia.

BiMonthly

Lawrence Hanley, Editor, Author
Julie Schmid, Executive Director
Elona M. Jouben, Executive Assistant

4166 Aero Gramme
Alternative Education Resource Organizations
417 Roslyn Road
Roslyn Heights, NY 11577-2620
516-621-2195
800-769-4171
Fax: 516-625-3257
info@educationrevolution.org
www.educationrevolution.org

Networks all forms of educational alternatives, from public and private alternative schools to homeschooling.

Quarterly

Jerry Mintz, Director
Chri Mercogliano, Course Instructor

4167 Agenda: Jewish Education
Jewish Education Service of North America
247 West 37th Street
5th Floor
New York, NY 10018
212-284-6950
Fax: 212-284-6951
info@jesna.org
www.jesna.org
Seeks to create a community of discourse on issues of Jewish public policy dealing with Jewish education and the indications of policy options for the practice of Jewish education.

Quarterly
ISSN: 1072-1150

Cass Gottlieb, Chair
Sandra Gold, Vice Chair

4168 American Journal of Education
University of Chicago
5801 South Ellis Avenue
Chicago, IL 60637
773-702-1234
Fax: 773-702-6207
aje@uchicago.edu
www.uchicago.edu

Quarterly

Robert Dreeben and Zalman Usiskin, Author
Robert J. Zimmer, President
Eric D. Isaacs, Provost

4169 American Scholar
1785 Massachusetts Avenue NW
4th Floor
Washington, DC 20036-2117
202-265-3808
A general interest magazine that includes articles on science, literature, and book reviews.

Quarterly

Anne Fadiman, Editor

4170 American Students & Teachers Abroad
US Government Printing Office
732 N Capitol Street NW
Washington, DC 20401
202-512-1800
Fax: 202-512-2104
admin@access.gpo.gov
www.access.gpo.gov

4171 Annual Report
Jessie Ball duPont Fund
One Dependent Drive
Suite 1400
Jacksonville, FL 32202-5011
904-353-0890
800-252-3452
Fax: 904-353-3870
contactus@dupontfund.org
www.dupontfund.org
Focused on a variety of good work aimed at growing the capacity of the nonprofit sector.

Publication Date: 0 Annually

4172 Association of Orthodox Jewish Teachers of the New York Public Schools
Association of Orthodox Jewish Teachers of the NY
1577 Coney Island Avenue
Brooklyn, NY 11230-4715
718-258-3585
Fax: 718-258-3586
aojt@juno.com
www.aojt.org
Newsletter representing observant Jewish teachers in the New York City Public Schools.

Publication Date: 1963 8-12 pages Quarterly Newsletter

Nechemia Aaron Oberstein, President
Rachel B. Lieff, Vice President

4173 Between Classes-Elderhostel Catalog
Road Scholar
11 Avenue de Lafayette
Boston, MA 02111-1913
617-426-7788
Fax: 617-426-8351
www.roadscholar.org
Seasonal listings of elderhostel educational programs offered by educational cultural institutions in the US and 60 countries overseas.

120 pages Quarterly

Heather Baynes, Contact

4174 Blumenfeld Education Newsletter
PO Box 45161
Boise, ID 83711-5161
www.howtotutor.com/bel.htm
Providing knowledge to parents and educators who want to save children of America from destructive forces that endanger them. Children in public schools are at grave risk in 4 ways: academically, spiritually, morally, physically, and only a well-informed public will be able to reduce these risks.

8 pages

Peter F Watt, Publisher
Samuel L Blumenfeld, Editor

4175 Brighton Times
Brighton Academy/Foundation of Human Understanding
1121 NE 7th Street
PO Box 1000
Grants Pass, OR 97528-1421
541-474-6865
800-877-3227
Fax: 541-956-6705
https://www.fhu.com/aboutroy.html
Home schooling information.

Monthly

Cynthia Coumoyer, Contact

4176 Brochure of American-Sponsored Overseas Schools
Office of Overseas Schools, Department of State
Room H328
SA-1
Washington, DC 20522-132
202-261-8200
Fax: 202-261-8224
OverseasSchools@state.gov
www.state.gov

Dr. Keith D. Miller, Director
Antony Blinken, Deputy Secretary

4177 Business-Education Insider
Heritage Foundation
214 Massachusetts Avenue NE
Washington, DC 20002-4999
202-546-4400
Fax: 202-546-8328
www.heritage.org
Deals with issues relating to the corporate/business world, and the effects it has on education.

Monthly

George Adams, Senior Production Specialist
David S. Addington, Group VP, Research

4178 CBE Report
Association for Community Based Education
1806 Vernon Street NW
PO BOX 70587
Washington, DC 20024-0587
202-462-6333
www.faqs.org
Educational institutions covering news, workshops and resources.

Monthly

4179 CEDS Communique
The Council for Exceptional Children
2900 Crystal Drive
Suite 1000
Arlington, VA 22202-1545
703-620-3660
888-232-7733
Fax: 703-264-9494
www.cec.sped.org
Reports on the activities of the Council for Educational Diagnostic Services and information about special programs, upcoming events, current trends and practices, and other topical matters.

Quarterly

Alison Heron, Director
Diane Shinn, Marketing & Communications

4180 Center Focus
Center of Concern
1225 Otis Street NE
Washington, DC 20017-2516
202-635-2757
Fax: 202-832-9494
coc@coc.org
www.coc.org
Newsletters addressing the everchanging needs and concerns in the education field.

6 pages BiMonthly

Raymond W. Baker, President
Claire M. Cifaloglio, M.D., Pediatrician

4181 Center for Continuing Education of Women Newsletter
University of Michigan
Ann Arbor, MI 48109
734-763-1400
Fax: 734-936-1641
Association news focusing on the concerns of women in education.

4 pages

4182 Center for Parent Education Newsletter
81 Wyman Street
Wapham, MA 02160
617-964-2442
Offers information and tips to address parent involvement in the education of their children.

BiMonthly

4183 Change
Taylor & Francis
325 Chestnut Street
Suite 800
Philadelphia, PA 19106-1802

215-625-8900
800-365-9753
Fax: 202-296-5149
customer.service@taylorandfrancis.com
www.heldref.org
Perspectives on the critical issues shaping the world of higher education. It is not only issue-oriented and reflective, but challenges the status quo in higher education.

BiMonthly

Margaret A Miller, President
Theodore J Marchese, VP/Editor

4184 Clearing House: A Journal of Educational Research

Taylor & Francis
325 Chestnut Street
Suite 800
Philadelphia, PA 19106-1826
215-625-8900
800-365-9753
Fax: 202-296-5149
customer.service@taylorandfrancis.com
www.heldref.org
Each issue offers a variety of articles for teachers and administrators of middle schools and junior and senior high schools. It includes experiments, trends and accomplishments in courses, teaching methods, administrative procedures and school programs.

4 pages BiMonthly
ISSN: 0009-8655

Deborah N Cohen, Promotions Manager
Judy Cusick, Managing Editor

4185 Commuter Perspectives

National Clearinghouse for Commuter Programs
Western Illinois University
3300 River Drive
Moline, IL 61265-9634
309-762-8843
Fax: 301-314-9874
nccp@accmail.umd.edu
www.wiu.edu
A quarterly newsletter published by the National Clearinghouse for Commuter Programs for professionals who work for, with, and on behalf of commuter students.

8 pages Quarterly

Dr. Kristi Mindrup, Co-Director
Dr. Melissa Mahan, Co-Director

4186 Congressional Digest

301-528-7777
Fax: 301-634-3189
support@congressionaldigest.com
congressionaldigest.com
An independent, scholarly publication featuring debates within the U.S. Supreme Court, presented in a neutral manner.

Publication Date: 1921

Sarah Orrick, Editor

4187 ConneXions

Association of International Schools in Africa
Peponi Road
PO Box 14103, Nairobi
Kenya 00800
254- 20- 269
254-20-2697442
Fax: 254- 20- 418
Fax: 254-20-4183272
info@aisa.or.ke
www.aisa.or.ke
Published twice per year, ConneXions is AISA's print and online newsletter

Peter Bateman, Executive Director
Thomas Shearer, Chairperson

4188 Contemporary Education

Indiana State University, School of Education
200 North Seventh Street
Terre Haute, IN 47809-9989
877-856-8005
Fax: 812-856-8088
coe.indstate.edu
A readable and currently informative journal of topics in the mainstream of educational thought.

Quarterly
ISSN: 0010-7476

Todd Whitaker, Editor
Beth Whitaker, Editor

4189 Contemporary Issues in Technology and Teacher Education (CITE)

AMTE, c/o Meredith College
3800 Hillsborough Street
Raleigh, NC 27607
919-760-8240
Fax: 919-760-8763
harpersr@miamioh.edu
amte.net/publications/cite-journal
An online, peer-reviewed journal including articles on the cross-section of teacher education and technology integration.

Quarterly

Randy Philipp, President
Tim Hendrix, Executive Director

4190 Creative Child & Adult Quarterly

National Association for Gifted Children
1331 H Street, NW
Suite 1001
Washington, DC 20005-1352
202-785-4268
Fax: 202-785-4248
www.nagc.org

Quarterly

Tracy L. Cross, President
George Betts, President-Elect

4191 Creativity Research Journal

Lawrence Erlbaum Associates
10 Industrial Avenue
Mahwah, NJ 07430-2262
201-258-2200
800-926-6579
Fax: 201-236-0072
journals@erlbaum.com
www.erlbaum.com
A peer-reviewed journal covering a full range of approaches including behavioral, cognitive, clinical developmental, educational, social and organizational. Online access is available by visiting LEAonline.com

Quarterly
ISSN: 1040-0419

Mark A Runco, PhD., Editor

4192 Currents

Council for Advancement & Support of Education
1307 New York Avenue NW
Suite 1000
Washington, DC 20005-4726
703-379-4611
Fax: 202-387-4973
memberservicecenter@case.org
www.case.org
Published nine times a year and distributed to 19,000 professional members, Currents delivers essential information, insight and ideas that empower those who support education to master challenges and act decisively to create a better future for their institutions and the world.

John Lippincott, President
Donald Falkenstein, VP

4193 DCDT Network

The Council for Exceptional Children
2900 Crystal Drive
Suite 1000
Arlington, VA 22202-1545
703-620-3660
888-232-7733
Fax: 703-264-9494
www.cec.sped.org
Newsletter of the Division on Career Development and Transition. Provides the latest information on legislation, projects, resource materials and implementation strategies in the field of career development and transition for persons with disabilities and/or who are gifted. Carries information about Division activities, upcoming events, announcements and reports of particular interest to DCDT members.

3x Year

Alison Heron, Director
Diane Shinn, Marketing & Communications

4194 DECA Dimensions

1908 Association Drive
Reston, VA 20191-1503
703-860-5000
Fax: 703-860-4013
info@deca.org
www.deca.org
An educational nonprofit association news management for marketing education students across the country, Canada, Guam and Puerto Rico. Offers information on DECA activities, leadership, business and career skills, which help develop future leaders in business, marketing and management.

36 pages Quarterly
ISSN: 1060-6106

Carol Lund, Author
Chuck Beatty, Project Manager
Cindy Allen, Director

4195 DLD Times

The Council for Exceptional Children
2900 Crystal Drive
Suite 1000
Arlington, VA 22202-1589
703-620-3660
800-CEC-SPED
Fax: 703-264-1637
www.cec.sped.org
Information concerning education and welfare of children and youth with learning disabilities.

8 pages TriQuarterly

Alison Heron, Director
Diane Shinn, Marketing & Communications

4196 Decision Line

Decision Sciences Institute
334 Melcher Hal
Suite 325
Houston, TX 77204-6021
713-743-4815
Fax: 713-743-8984
info@decisionsciences.org
www.decisionsciences.org
Contains articles on education, business and decision sciences as well as available positions and textbook advertising.

32 pages 5x Year

E. Powell Robinson, Jr., Interim Executive Director
Dana L. Evans, Program Director

4197 Desktop Presentations & Publishing
Doron & Associates
291 Farmington Avenue
Farmington, CT 6032-5421
860-677-8666
866-764-5378
Fax: 860-677-5839
dental_associates@sbcglobal.net
www.dasmile.com/doc_doron.htm
Computer generated presentations and visual aids for education and business.
16 pages BiMonthly
Tom Doron, Contact

4198 Development and Alumni Relations Report
LRP Publications
360 Hiatt Drive
Suite 700
Palm Beach Gardens, FL 33418
561-622-6520
800-341-7874
Fax: 561-622-1375
custserve@lrp.com
www.lrp.com
Provides colleges and universities with innovative ideas for improving: alumni relations; the involvement of alumni in clubs and chapters; annual giving; endowment and capital campaigns; and planned giving. Plus, you can recieve free e-mail updates on crucial news affecting your job with your paid subscription.
Monthly Newsletter
Kenneth F. Kahn, President

4199 Different Books
Place in the Woods
111 Third Avenue South
Suite 290
Minneapolis, MN 55401-5302
612-627-1970
Fax: 612-627-1980
ump@umn.edu
www.upress.umn.edu
Special imprint of books by, for and about persons on a different path. Features main characters with disabilities as heroes and heroines in storyline. For hi-lo reading in early elementary grades (3-7).
Publication Date: 1925 Paperback
Roger Hammer, Publisher

4200 Directions
AFS Intercultural Programs USA
71 West 23rd Street
6th Floor
New York, NY 10010-4102
212-807-8686
Fax: 212-807-1001
www.afs.org
News of AFS US volunteers.
6 pages Monthly
Dr. Vincenzo Morlini, President/ CEO
Dr. Urs-Rainer von Arx, VP, CFO & Operation Officer

4201 Disability Compliance for Higher Education
LRP Publications
360 Hiatt Drive
Suite 700
Palm Beach Gardens, FL 33418
561-622-6520
800-341-7874
Fax: 561-622-1375
custserve@lrp.com
www.lrp.com
Newsletter helps colleges determine if they're complying with the Americans with Disabilities Act (ADA) and Section 504 of the Rehabilitation Act- so they can avoid costly litigation. Gives tips on how to provide reasonable accommodations in test-taking, grading, admissions, and accessibility to programs and facilities.
Monthly
ISSN: 1086-1335
Edward Filo, Author
Kenneth F. Kahn, President

4202 Diversity 2000
Holocaust Resource Center
Kean College
1000 Morris Avenue
Union, NJ 07083
Offers ideas and issues on multicultural school education programs.
BiMonthly
Janice Kroposky, Director
Helen Walzer, Assistant Director

4203 ERIC/CRESS Bulletin
AEL, Inc.
102 E. Keefe Ave
Milwaukee, WI 53212-1348
414-265-7630
866-656-1486
Fax: 414-265-7628
sales@aelseating.com
https://www.aelseating.com
Announces new developments in the ERIC system nationally, and publications and events relevant to American Indians, Alaska Natives, Mexican Americans, migrants, outdoor education and rural, small schools.
3x Year Newsletter
Patricia Hammer Cahape, Associate Director

4204 Eagle Forum
Eagle Education Fund
P.O. BOX 17113
Fountain Hills, AZ 85269-8110
www.fhgeef.org
News on the Eagle Education Fund.
Quarterly
Ralph Norman, President
Pam McNeil, 1st Vice President

4205 EdPress News
PreK-12 Learning Group
325 Chestnut St.
Ste. 1110
Philadelphia, PA 19106
267-351-4310
Fax: 267-351-4317
prek12learning@publishers.org
www.aepweb.org
The Association supports the growth of educational publishing and it's positive effects on learning and teaching. EdPress provides information and analysis of markets and trends, education and legislative policy, learning and teaching research, and intellectual property. The Association also provides training and staff development programs, promotes supplemental learning resources as essential curriculum materials, and advocates on issues relevant to its constituents.
Jay Diskey, Executive Director
Stacey Pusey, Editorial Director

4206 Education
Project Innovation
1362 Santa Cruz Court
Chula Vista, CA 91910-7114
760-630-9938
rcassel5@aol.com
www.rcassel.com
Original investigations and theoretical articles dealing with education. Preference given to innovations, real or magical, which promise to improve learning.
160 pages Quarterly
ISSN: 0013-1172
Dr. Russell Cassel, Editor
Lan Mieu Cassel, Managing Editor

4207 Education Digest
Prakken Publications
PO Box 8623
3970 Varsity Drive
Ann Arbor, MI 48107-8623
734-975-2800
800-530-9673
Fax: 734-975-2787
publisher@techdirectories.com
www.eddigest.com
Offers outstanding articles condensed for quick review from over 200 magazines, monthlies, books, newsletters and journals, timely and important for professional educators and others interested in the field.
80 pages Monthly
ISSN: 0013-127X
George F Kennedy, Publisher
Kenneth Schroeder, Managing Editor

4208 Education Hotline
Editorial Projects in Education
6935 Arlington Road
Suite 100
Bethesda, MD 20814
301-280-3100
800-445-8250
Fax: 301-280-3250
ads@epe.org
www.edweek.org
Education newsletter.

4209 Education Newsletter Library Counterpoint
LRP Publications
360 Hiatt Drive
Suite 700
Palm Beach Gardens, FL 33418
561-622-6520
800-341-7874
Fax: 561-622-1375
custserve@lrp.com
www.lrp.com
Offers its readers concise, informative and timely articles covering innovative practices in special education. Covers: special education news from the states; updates on curriculum; developments in special education technology; classified ads; descriptions of new products and publications; and more.
On-Line
Kenneth F. Kahn, President

4210 Education Newsline
National Association of Christian Educators
PO Box 3200
Costa Mesa, CA 92628-3200
949-251-9333
naceoffice.com
Articles pertinent to public education for teachers and parents, current trends and solutions and the work of Citizens for Excellence in Education.
Publication Date: 1972 8 pages BiMonthly
Robert Simonds, Publisher
Kathi Hudson, Editor

4211 Education Now and in the Future
Northwest Regional Educational Laboratory
101 SW Main Street
Suite 500
Portland, OR 97204-3213

503-275-9500
800-597-6339
Fax: 503-275-0458
info@nwrel.org
www.nwrel.org
Contains articles about products, events, research and publications produced or sponsored by the NW Regional Educational Laboratory, a private nonprofit educational institution whose mission is to help schools improve outcomes for all students.

Steve Fleischman, CEO
Barbara Adams, Chairperson

4212 Education Quarterly
New Jersey State Department of Education
100 Riverview Plaza
PO Box 500
Trenton, NJ 08625-500
877-900-6960
www.state.nj.us/education
New Jersey education information and updates.

6 pages Quarterly

Richard Vespucci, Contact

4213 Education USA
LRP Publications
360 Hiatt Drive
Suite 1106
Palm Beach Gardens, FL 33418
561-622-6520
800-341-7874
Fax: 561-622-1375
custserve@lrp.com
www.lrp.com
Offers information on court decisions, federal funding, the national debate over standards, education research, school finance, and more. Subscribers receive biweekly reports on Education Department policies on Title I, special education, bilingual education, drug-free schools and other issues affecting schools nationwide.

8-10 pages BiWeekly

Kenneth F. Kahn, President

4214 Education Update
Heritage Foundation
214 Massachusetts Avenue NE
Washington, DC 20002-4999
202-546-4400
Fax: 202-544-7330
www.heritage.org
Contains analyses of policy issues and trends in US education.

4215 Education Week
Editorial Projects in Education, Inc.
6935 Arlington Road
Suite 100
Bethesda, MD 20814-5233
301-280-3100
800-346-1834
Fax: 301-280-3250
ads@epe.org
www.edweek.org
For principals, superintendents, director, managers and other administrators.

4216 Education in Focus
Books for All Times
PO Box 2
Alexandria, VA 22313-0002
703-548-0457
jdavid@bfat.com
Examines failures and successes of public and private education by looking beneath the surface for answers and explanations.

6 pages BiAnnually
ISSN: 1049-7250

Joe David, Editor

4217 Educational Forum
University of Colorado-Denver, School of Education
PO Box 173364
Campus Box 106
Denver, CO 80217-3364
303-556-3402
Fax: 303-556-4479
education@cudenver.edu
www.ucdenver.edu
The university is recognized as one of the leading public universities in the nation and offers a broad range of academic opportunities to students.

Quarterly

Hank Brown, President
Michel Dahlin, Interim Vice President

4218 Educational Freedom Spotlight On Homeschooling
Clonlara Home Based Education Programs
1289 Jewett Street
Ann Arbor, MI 48104-6201
734-769-4511
Fax: 734-769-9629
clonlara@wash.k12.mi.us
www.clonlara.org
Clonlara School is committed to illuminating educational rights and freedoms through our actions and deep dedication to human rights and dignity.

12 pages Monthly

Susan Andrews, Editor
Carmen Amabile, Coordinator

4219 Educational Horizons
P. Lambda Theta, Int'l Honor & Professional Assn.
P.O. Box 7888
Bloomington, IN 47407-7888
812-339-1156
Fax: 812-339-0018
root@pilambda.org
www.pilambda.org
Founded in the spirit of academic excellence in order to provide leadership in addressing educational, social and cultural issues of national and international significance and to enhance the status of educators by providing a recognized forum for sharing new perspectives, research findings and scholarly essays.

48 pages Quarterly
ISSN: 0013-175X

Dan Brown, Executive Director
Bill Bushaw, Chief Executive Officer

4220 Educational Research Forum
American Educational Research Association
1430 K Street, NW
Suite 1200
Washington, DC 20005-3078
202-238-3200
Fax: 202-238-3250
aera@gmu.edu
www.aera.net
Contains news and information on educational research, teaching, counseling and school administration.

Felice J. Levine, Executive Director
Joyce E. King, President

4221 Educational Researcher
American Educational Research Association
1430 K Street, NW
Suite 1200
Washington, DC 20005-3078
202-238-3200
Fax: 202-238-3250
aera@gmu.edu
www.aera.net
Publishes research news and commentary on events in the field of educational research and articles of a wide interest to anyone involved in education.

9x Year

Felice J. Levine, Executive Director
Joyce E. King, President

4222 Educational Theory
University of Illinois at Urbana
901 West Illinois Street
Urbana, IL 61801-6925
217-333-0302
Fax: 217-244-3711
edtheory@uiuc.edu
illinois.edu
The purpose of this journal is to foster the continuing development of educational theory and encourage wide and effective discussion of theoretical problems with the educational profession. Publishes articles and studies in the foundations of education and in related disciplines outside the field of education which contribute to the advancement of education theory.

570 pages Quarterly
ISSN: 0013-2004

Nicholas C Burbules, Editor
Diane E Beckett, Business Manager

4223 Exceptional Children
The Council for Exceptional Children
2900 Crystal Drive
Suite 100
Arlington, VA 22202-3557
703-620-3660
888-232-7733
Fax: 703-264-3494
service@cec.sped.org
www.cec.sped.org
Original research on the education and development of infants, toddlers, children and youth with exceptionalities and articles on professional issues of concern to special educators. Published quarterly, free to members or $86.00 per year to individuals.

Quarterly
ISSN: 0014-4029

Anitra Davis, Senior Customer Service Rep
Alison Heron, Director

4224 Focus on Autism
Pro-Ed., Inc.
8700 Shoal Creek Boulevard
Austin, TX 78757-6897
512-451-3246
800-897-3202
Fax: 512-451-8542
www.proedinc.com
Hands-on tips, techniques, methods and ideas from top authorities for improving the quality of assessment, instruction and management.

Brenda Smith Myles, PhD, Editor

4225 Focus on Research
The Council for Exceptional Children
2900 Crystal Drive
Suite 100
Arlington, VA 22202-1545
703-620-3660
888-232-7733
Fax: 703-264-9494
www.cec.sped.org

Contains member opinion articles, debates on research issues, descriptions and dates of specific projects, notices of funded program priorities in special education, the availability of research dollars, and the discussion of emerging issues that may affect research in special education.

3x Year

Anitra Davis, Senior Customer Service Rep
Alison Heron, Director

4226 Foreign Student Service Council
2263 12th Place NW
Washington, DC 20009-4405
202-232-4979
Non-profit organization dedicated to promoting understanding between international students and Americans.

Quarterly

4227 Fortune Education Program
2890 Gateway Oaks Drive
Suite 100
Sacramento, CA 95833-1872
916-924-8633
800-448-3399
Fax: 916-924-8664
www.fortuneschool.us
Professional program that offers 75% off the cover price of Fortune magazine, a free educator's desk reference, a free 2-page teaching guide, fast delivery, choice of billing options. Plus quality customer service.

Paulette Brown Hinds, Managing Partner
Carolyn Lawson, Chief Information Officer

4228 Forum
Educators for Social Responsibility
23 Garden Street
Cambridge, MA 02138-3623
617-492-1764
Fax: 617-864-5164
educators@esrnational.org
www.esrnational.org
Edited for educators concerned with teaching in the nuclear age.

12 pages Quarterly

Barry Berman, Chief Financial Officer
Deborah Childs-Bowen, Executive Director

4229 Foundation for Exceptional Children: Focus
The Council for Exceptional Children
2900 Crystal Drive
Suite 100
Arlington, VA 22202-1545
703-620-3660
888-232-7733
Fax: 703-264-9494
www.cec.sped.org
Membership and association news.

6 pages TriQuarterly

Anitra Davis, Senior Customer Service Rep
Alison Heron, Director

4230 Fulbright News
American Friends Service Committee
1501 Cherry St.
Room 450
Philadelphia, PA 19102-2269
215-241-7000
Fax: 212-941-6291
https://afsc.org
A four page newsletter distributed 5 times a year to visiting Fulbright scholars in the New York area. Contains a scholar profile, information about activities, tips for living in the United States, events in the New York area, and relevant announcements.

4 pages

Kristen Pendleton, Publisher

4231 GED Items
Adult Learning Center
1340 Braddock Place
7th Floor
Alexandria, VA 22314-1110
703-619-8027
www.acps.k12.va.us/adulted
Newsletter of the GED Testing Service with articles focusing on adult education programs, teaching tips, GED graduate success stories and administration of GED testing.

12 pages BiMonthly

4232 Harvard Education Letter
Harvard Education Publishing Group
8 Story Street
1st Floor
Cambridge, MA 02138
617-495-3432
800-513-0763
Fax: 617-496-3584
editor@edletter.org
www.edletter.org
Published by the Harvard Graduate School of Education and reports on current research and innovative practice in PreK-12.

Publication Date: 1985 8 pages Bi-Monthly
ISSN: 8755-3716

Douglas Clayton, Publisher
Nancy Walser, Editor

4233 Health in Action
American School Health Association
7918 Jones Branch Drive
Suite 300
McLean, VA 22102-0013
703-506-7675
800-445-2742
Fax: 703-506-3266
info@ashaweb.org
www.ashaweb.org

24 pages Quarterly
ISSN: 1540-2479

Linda Morse, President
Ty Oehrtman, Vice President

4234 Help! I'm in Middle School... How Will I Survive?
Northern Research Station
11 Campus Blvd.
Suite 200
Newtown Square, PA 19073
610-557-4017
info@englishthrough.com
www.nrs.fs.fed.us/pubs
The goal of NRS Publications is the success of every child. We provide a varity of books, educational games, posters, educational dice, overhead tiles, science kits, the SHAPES parts of speech learning system and creative play toys to help meet that goal.

Merry L Gumm, President
Tanya L Hein, Vice President

4235 Higher Education & National Affairs
American Council on Education
1 Dupont Circle NW
Suite 800
Washington, DC 20036-1132
202-939-9300
www.acenet.edu
National newsletter with Capitol Hill and Administration updates on issues that affect colleges and universities. Includes stories on the federal budget, student financial aid, tax laws, Education Department regulations and research, legal issues and minorities in higher education.

James H. Mullen Jr., Chair
Renu Khator, Vice Chair

4236 History of Education Quarterly
Indian University
School of Education
107 S. Indiana Ave.
Bloomington, IN 47405-7000
812-855-4848
Fax: 812-855-3631
www.iu.edu
Discusses current and historical movements in education.

Quarterly

Charles R. Bantz, Executive VP
MaryFrances McCourt, Senior VP, CFO

4237 Homeschooling Marketplace Newsletter
13106 Patrici Circle
Omaha, NE 68164
Offers information, strategies and tips for homeschooling.

Clarice Routh, Contact

4238 IDRA Newsletter
Intercultural Development Research Association
5835 Callaghan Road
Suite 101
San Antonio, TX 78228-1125
210-444-1710
Fax: 210-444-1714
feedback@idra.org
www.idra.org
Mini-journal covering topics in the education of minority, poor and language-minority students in public institutions. It provides research-based solutions and editorial materials for education.

Monthly

Maria Robledo Montecel, President & CEO
Abelardo Villarreal, Chief of Operations

4239 IEA Reporter
Idaho Education Association
620 N 6th Street
P.O. Box 2638
Boise, ID 83701-5542
208-344-1341
800-727-9922
Fax: 208-336-6967
www.idahoea.org

Quarterly

Diana Mikesell, VP
Kathy Phelan, President

4240 Inclusive Education Programs
LRP Publications
360 Hiatt Drive
Suite 700
Palm Beach Gardens, FL 33418
561-622-6520
800-341-7874
Fax: 561-622-1375
custserve@lrp.com
www.lrp.com
Newsletter covers the legal and practical issues of educating children with disabilities in regular education environments. It provides practical, how-to-advice, real life examples, and concise case summaries of the most recent judicial case laws.

Monthly
ISSN: 1076-8548

Kenneth F. Kahn, President

4241 Independent Scholar
National Coalition of Independent Scholars
PO Box 120182
San Antonio, TX 78212-0743
510-704-0990
www.ncis.org

A newsletter for independent scholars and their organizations.

Quarterly

Mona Berman, President
Janet Wasserman, Secretary

4242 Innovative Higher Education
Kluwer Academic/Human Sciences Press
233 Spring Street
New York, NY 10013
212-620-8000
800-221-9369
Fax: 212-463-0742
www.wkpa.nl
Provides educators and scholars with the latest creative strategies, programs and innovations designed to meet contemporary challenges in higher education. Professionals throughout the world contribute high-quality papers on the changing rules of vocational and liberal arts education, the needs of adults reentering the education process, and the reconciliation of faculty desires to economic realities, among other topics.

Quarterly
ISSN: 0742-5627

Carol Bischoff, Publisher
Ronald Simpson, Editor

4243 Insight
Independent Education Consultants Association
3251 Old Lee Highway
Suite 510
Fairfax, VA 22030-1504
703-591-4850
800-888-4322
Fax: 703-591-4860
requests@IECAonline.com
www.IECAonline.com
Publication of national professional association of educational counselors working in private practice. Association provides counseling in college, secondary schools, learning disabilities and wilderness therapy programs.

Rebecca Peek, Author
Gail Meyer, President
Pamela Jobin, Vice President

4244 International Debates
Congressional Digest Corp.
4416 East West Highway
Suite 400
Bethesda, MD 20814-4568
301-634-3113
800-637-9915
Fax: 301-634-3189
griff.thomas@pro-and-con.org
www.pro-and-con.org
An independent publication featuring global controversies in the United Nations and other international forums, pro and cons.

ISSN: 1542-0345

Delores Baisden, Assistant

4245 International Education
University of Tennessee
College of Education
Health & Human Services
Knoxville, TN 37996-3400
865-974-1000
Fax: 865-974-8718
scarey@utk.edu
www.utk.edu
Publishes articles related to various international topics.

Publication Date: 1997 BiAnnual/Paperback
ISSN: 0160-5429

Sue Carey, Managing Editor

4246 International Journal of Qualitive Studies in Education
Taylor & Francis Group, LLC Books
6000 Broken Sound Parkway, NW
Suite 300
Boca Raton, FL 33487
561-994-0555
Fax: 561-241-7856
orders@taylorandfrancis.com
www.tandF.co.uk/journals
Aims to enhance the theory of qualitative research in education.

6 Issues Per Year

Jim Scheurich, Editor
Angela Valenzuela, Editor

4247 International Volunteer
Volunteers for Peace
7 Kilburn Street
Suite 316
Burlington, VT 05401-9988
802-540-3060
Fax: 802-259-2922
info@vfp.org
www.vfp.org
Newsletter of Volunteers for Peace, which provides intercultural education and community services.

8 pages Annual

Peter Coldwell, Author
Megan Brook, Executive Director
Maddie Craig, Coordinator

4248 Issues in Integrative Studies
Association for Integrative Studies
Miami University
Oxford, OH 45056
513-529-2659
Fax: 513-529-5849
aisorg@muohio.edu
www.units.muohio.edu/aisorg
An annual, refereed professional journal for members.

ISBN: 1081-4760

Rick Szostak, Editor

4249 It Starts in the Classroom
National School Public Relations Association
15948 Derwood Road
Suite 201
Rockville, MD 20855-1109
301-519-0496
Fax: 301-519-0494
www.nspra.org
Devoted to classroom and teacher public relations techniques and ideas.

8 pages Monthly

Jim Cummings, President
Susan Hardy Brooks, President-elect

4250 Journal of Behavioral Education
Kluwer Academic/Human Sciences Press
233 Spring Street
New York, NY 10013
212-620-8000
800-221-9369
Fax: 212-463-0742
www.wkpa.nl
Provides the first single-source forum for the publication of research on the application of behavioral principles and technology to education. Publishes original empirical research and brief reports covering behavioral education in regular, special and adult education settings. Subject populations include handicapped, at-risk, and non-handicapped students of all ages.

Quarterly
ISSN: 1053-0819

Carol Bischoff, Publisher
Christopher Skinner, Co-Editor

4251 Journal of Creative Behavior
Creative Kids Education Foundation
11726 San Vicente Blvd.
Suite 370
Los Angeles, CA 90049
310-234-8604
800-447-2774
Fax: 413-559-6615
creativekidsfoundation@gmail.com
creativekidseducationfoundation.org
Devoted to the serious general reader with vocational/avocational interests in the fields of creativity and problem solving. Its articles are authored not only by established writers in the field, but by up-and coming contributors as well. The criteria for selecting articles include reference, clarity, interest and overall quality.

Quarterly

Jama Laurent, President
Byron Adams, Professor of Music

4252 Journal of Curriculum Theorizing
Colgate University
Department of Education
13 Oak Drive
Hamilton, NY 13346
315-228-7000
Fax: 315-228-7998
www.colgate.edu
Analyzes and provides insights to curriculum movements and evolution.

Quarterly

JoAnne Pagano, Editor

4253 Journal of Disability Policy Studies
Pro-Ed., Inc.
8700 Shoal Creek Boulevard
Austin, TX 78757-6897
512-451-3246
800-897-3202
Fax: 512-302-8542
proed1@aol.com
www.proedinc.com
Devoted exclusively to disability policy topics and issues.

Quarterly Magazine
ISSN: 1044-2073

Craig R Fiedler, JD, PhD, Editor
Billie Jo Rylance, PhD, Editor

4254 Journal of Educational Research
Taylor & Francis
325 Chestnut Street
Suite 800
Philadelphia, PA 19106-1826
215-625-8900
800-354-1420
Fax: 202-296-5149
customer.service@taylorandfrancis.com
www.heldref.org
Since 1920, this journal has contributed to the advancement of educational practice in elementary and secondary schools. Authors experiment with new procedures, evaluate traditional practices, replicate previous research for validation and perform other work central to understanding and improving the education of today's students and teachers. This Journal is a valuable resource for

teachers, counselors, supervisors, administrators, planners and educational researchers.

64 pages BiMonthly
ISSN: 0022-0671

Deborah Cohen, Promotions Editor

4255 Journal of Experimental Education
Taylor & Francis
325 Chestnut Street
Suite 800
Philadelphia, PA 19106-1826
215-625-8900
800-354-1420
Fax: 202-296-5149
customer.service@taylorandfrancis.com
www.heldref.org
Aims to improve educational practice by publishing basic and applied research studies using the range of quantitative and qualitative methodologies found in the behavioral, cognitive and social sciences. Published studies address all levels of schooling, from preschool through graduate and professional education, and various educational context, including public and private education in the United States and abroad.

96 pages Quarterly

Paige Jackson, Managing Editor

4256 Journal of Law and Education
University of South Carolina Law School
701 Main Street
Columbia, SC 29208
803-777-4155
Fax: 803-777-9405
lawweb@law.sc.edu
www.law.sc.edu
A periodical offering information on the newest laws and legislation affecting education.

Quarterly

Ronbert M. Wilcox, Dean
Jaclyn A. Cherry, Associate Dean

4257 Journal of Learning Disabilities
Pro-Ed., Inc.
8700 Shoal Creek Boulevard
Austin, TX 78757-6897
512-451-3246
800-897-3202
Fax: 512-451-8542
proed1@aol.com
www.proedinc.com
Special series, feature articles and research articles.

Bi-Monthly Magazine
ISSN: 0022-2194

Wayne P Hresko, PhD, Editor-in-Chief

4258 Journal of Negro Education
Howard University
2400 Sixth Street, NW
Washington, DC 20059-0001
202-806-6100
Fax: 202-806-8434
jne@howard.edu
www.howard.edu
A Howard University quarterly review of issues incident to the education of Black people; tracing educational developments and presenting research on issues confronting Black students in the US and around the world.

120+ pages Quarterly
ISSN: 0022-2984

D. Kamili Anderson, Associate Editor
Dr. Sylvia T. Johnson, Editor-in-Chief

4259 Journal of Positive Behavior Interventions
Pro-Ed., Inc.
8700 Shoal Creek Boulevard
Austin, TX 78757-6897
512-451-3246
800-897-3202
Fax: 512-302-9129
www.proedinc.com
Sound, research-based principles of positive behavior support for use in home, school and community settings for people with challenges in behavioral adaptation.

Glen Dunlap, PhD, Editor
Robert L Koegel, PhD, Editor

4260 Journal of Research and Development in Education
University of Georgia, College of Education
G3 Aderhold Hall
110 Carlton Street,
Athens, GA 30602
404-542-1154
www.coe.uga.edu
A magazine offering insight and experimental and theoretical studies in education.

Quarterly

Craig H. Kennedy, Dean
Laura Lee Bierema, Associate Dean

4261 Journal of Research in Character Education
Character Education Partnership
1634 I Street NW
Suite 550
Washington, DC 20006
202-296-7743
800-988-8081
Fax: 202-296-7779
information@character.org
www.character.org

Becky Sipos, President & CEO
Sheril Morgan, Director

4262 Journal of Research in Rural Education
University of Maine, College of Education
5766 Shibles Hall
Orono, ME 04469-5766
207-581-2493
Fax: 207-581-2423
www.umaine.edu
Publishes the results of educational research relevant to rural settings.

3x Year Journal

Theodore Coladarci, Editor
Sara Sheppard, Managing Editor

4263 Journal of School Health
American School Health Association
7918 Jones Branch Drive
Suite 300
McLean, VA 22102-0013
703-506-7675
800-445-2742
Fax: 703-506-3266
info@ashaweb.org
www.ashaweb.org
Contains material related to health promotion in school settings. A non-profit organization founded in 1927, ASHA's mission is to protect and improve the health and well-being of children and youth by supporting comprehensive, preschool-12 school health programs. ASHA and its 4,000 members (school nurses, health educators, and physicians) work to improve school health services and school health environments.

40 pages Monthly
ISSN: 0022-4391

Linda Morse, President
Ty Oehrtman, Vice President

4264 Journal of Special Education
Pro-Ed., Inc.
8700 Shoal Creek Boulevard
Austin, TX 78757-6897
512-451-3246
800-897-3202
Fax: 512-302-9129
www.proedinc.com
Timely, sound special education research.

Lynn S Fuchs, PhD, Editor
Douglas Fuchs, PhD, Editor

4265 Journal of Urban & Cultural Studies
University of Massachusetts at Boston
Department of English
100 Morrissey Blvd.
Boston, MA 02125-3393
617-287-5000
Fax: 617-287-4000
www.umb.edu/
Explores various issues in education that deal with urban and cultural affairs.

Donaldo Macedo, Editor

4266 Journal of the Alliance of Black School Educators
National Alliance of Black School Educators
310 Pennsylvania Avenue SE
Washington, DC 20003
501-247-4731
800-221-2654
Fax: 202-608-6319
jabse@nabse.org
www.nabse.org
Journal published by the National Alliance of Black School Educators (NABSE), containing conceptual and empirical articles that cover the subject of education development, with a focus on students of African descent.

Lloyd Sain, Ph.D, JABSE Editor

4267 Kaleidoscope
Evansville-Vanderburgh School Corporation
951 Walnut St
Evansville, IN 47713-1821
812-435-8599
district.evscschools.com
A staff publication for and about employees of the Evansville-Vanderburgh School Corporation.

8 pages Monthly

Patti S Coleman, Contact

4268 LD Forum
Council for Learning Disabilities
Box 405
11184 Antioch Road
Overland Park, KS 68210
913-491-1011
Fax: 913-491-1011
www.council-for-learning-disabilities.org/
Provides updated information and research on the activities of the Council for Learning Disabilities.

60 pages Quarterly
ISSN: 0731-9487

Steve Chamberlain, President
Mary Beth Calhoon, Vice President

4269 Learning Disability Quarterly
Council for Learning Disabilities
Box 405
11184 Antioch Road
Overland Park, KS 68210-4303
913-491-1011
Fax: 913-491-1011
www.council-for-learning-disabilities.org/
Aimed at learning disabled students, their parents and educators. Accepts advertising.
Quarterly
Steve Chamberlain, President
Mary Beth Calhoon, Vice President

4270 Learning Point Magazine Laboratory
North Central Regional Educational Laboratory
1000 Thomas Jefferson Street NW
Suite 300
Washington, DC 20007-1447
202-403-5000
Fax: 202-403-5001
info@ncrel.org
www.ncrel.org
Applies research and technology to learning.
16 pages Quarterly
Jeri Nowakowski, Director

4271 Learning Unlimited Network of Oregon
31960 SE Chin Street
Boring, OR 97009-9708
503-663-5153
Cuts through all barriers to communication and learning; institutional, personal, physical, psychological, spiritual. It focuses on basic communication/language skills but sets no limits on means or tools, subjects or participants in seeking maximum balance and productivity for all.
10 pages 9x Year
Gene Lehman, Contact

4272 Let It Grow. Let It Grow. Let It Grow. Hands-on Activities to Explore the Planet Kingdom
NSR Publications
1482 51st Road
Douglass, KS 67039
620-986-5472
info@englishthrough.com
www.nsrpublications.com
The goal of NSR Publication is the success of every child. We provide a variety of books, educational games, posters, educational dice, overhead tiles, science kits, the SHAPES parts of speech learning system and creative play toys to help meet that goal.
58 pages
Merry L Gumm, President
Tanya L Hein, Vice President

4273 Liaison Bulletin
National Assn. of State Directors of Special Ed.
225 Reinekers Lane
Suite 420
Alexandria, VA 22314-2840
703-519-3800
Fax: 703-519-3808
www.nasdse.org
Membership news for persons affiliated with the National Association of State Directors of Special Education.
BiWeekly
Dr. William Schipper, Editor
Frank Podobnik, Director

4274 Liberal Education
Association of American Colleges & Universities
1818 R Street NW
Washington, DC 20009-1604
202-387-3760
Fax: 202-265-9532
www.aacu-edu.org
Concentrates on issues currently affecting American higher education. Promotes and strengthens undergraduate curriculum, classroom teaching and learning, collaborative leadership, faculty leadership, diversity. Other publications on higher education include books, monographs, peer review, and on campus with women.
64 pages Quarterly
ISSN: 0024-1822
Kenneth P. Ruscio, Chair
Edward J. Ray, Vice Chair

4275 Link
AEL, Inc.
102 E. Keefe Ave
Milwaukee, WI 53212-1348
414-265-7630
866-656-1486
Fax: 414-265-7628
sales@aelseating.com
www.aelseating.com
A newsletter for educators providing research summaries, education news, and news of AEL products, services and events.
12 pages Quarterly Newsletter
Patricia Hammer Cahape, Associate Director

4276 Lisle-Interaction
433 W Sterns Street
Temperance, MI 48182-9568
734-847-7126
800-477-1538
Fax: 512-259-0392
www.lisleinternational.org
Reports on domestic and international programs, annual meetings and board meetings of the Lisle Fellowship which seeks to broaden global awareness and appreciation of different cultures. Occasional special articles on topics such as racism, book reviews. News of members are also included.
16 pages Quarterly
Mark Kinney, Executive Director
Dianne Brause, VP

4277 MEA Today
Montana Education Association
1232 E 6th Avenue
Helena, MT 59601-3927
406-442-4250
800-398-0826
Fax: 406-443-5081
www.mea-mft.org
National and state association news, legislative policies, and classroom features.
8 pages Monthly
Eric Feaver, President
Melanie Charlson , VP

4278 MTNA E-Journal
MTNA National Headquarters
1 W 4th Street
Suite 1550
Cincinnatti, OH 45202
513-421-1420
888-512-5278
Fax: 513-421-2503
mtnaejournal@mtna.org
www.mtna.org
Peer-reviewed online journal presenting scholarly research-oriented articles on music and the music teaching profession.
Linda Essick Cockey, NCTM, Chair
Michelle Conda, Editorial Commitee Member

4279 Massachusetts Home Learning Association Newsletter
23 Mountain Street
Sharon, MA 02067-2234
781-784-8006
www.mhla.org
A source for information gleaned from all the major national magazines and many state newsletters. Calendar of events for Massachusetts homeschooling and several feature articles on legal, educational or familial issues.
24 pages Quarterly
Sharon Terry, Editor
Patrick Terry, Editor

4280 Mel Gabler's Newsletter
Educational Research Analysts
PO Box 7518
Longview, TX 75607-7518
972-753-5993
www.textbookreviews.org/
Educational information pertaining to curricula used in schools.
8 pages SemiAnnually
Mel Gabler, Publisher
Chad Rosenberger, Editor

4281 Minnesota Education Update
Office of Library Development & Services
200 West Baltimore Street
550 Cedar Street
Baltimore, MD 21201-2595
410-767-0444
Fax: 410-333-2507
www.marylandpublicschools.org
Policies and activities in elementary and secondary education in the state of Minnesota.
8 pages Monthly
Amber Massaquoi, Executive Assistant
Dennis Nangle, Branch Chief

4282 Missouri Schools
Missouri Department of Education
PO Box 480
Jefferson City, MO 65102-0480
573-751-4212
Fax: 573-751-8613
dese.mo.gov
State education policy.
28 pages BiMonthly
Margie Vandeven, Commissioner
Jay Nixon, Governor

4283 Momentum
National Catholic Educational Association
1005 North Glebe Road
Suite 525
Arlington, VA 22201
202-337-6232
800-711-6232
Fax: 703-243-0025
www.ncea.org
The association offers a quarterly publication, conducts research, works with voluntary groups and government agencies on educational prob-

lems, conducts seminars and workshops for all levels of educators.

Quarterly

Reverend Blase Cupich, Chairman
Brother Robert Bimonte, FSC, President

4284 Montana Schools

Montana Office of Public Instruction
State Capitol
Helena, MT 59620
406-444-3095
Fax: 406-444-2893
opi.mt.gov
Information about people and programs in the Montana education system.

12 pages 5x Year

Ellen Meloy

4285 Montessori Observer

International Montessori Society
9525 Georgia Avenue
Suite 200
Silver Spring, MD 20910
301-589-1127
800-301-3131
Fax: 301-920-0764
havis@imsmontessori.org
imsmontessori.org
Provides news and information about Montessori education and the work of the International Montessori Society.

Publication Date: 1979
ISSN: 0889-5643

Lee Havis, Editor

4286 NADE Digest

PO Box 963
Northport, AL 35476
205-331-5997
877-233-9455
Fax: 866-519-1331
office@thenade.org
thenade.org
A publication by the National Association for Developmental Education, containing articles on the practical issues in post-secondary developmental education.

Naomi Ludman, NADE Digest Editor

4287 NAEIR Advantage

Nat'l Assn. for Exchange of Industrial Resources
560 McClure Street
Galesburg, IL 61401-4286
309-343-0704
800-562-0955
Fax: 309-343-3519
member.naeir@misslink.net
www.naeir.org
News of the National Association for the Exchange of Industrial Resources, which collects donations of new excess inventory from corporations and redistributes them to American schools and nonprofits.

Publication Date: 1977 8 pages BiMonthly

Gary C Smith, President/CEO
Robert B. Gilstrap, Vice President/CFO

4288 NAEN Bulletin

Nort American Association of Education Negotiators
PO Box 1068
Salem, OR 97308
519-503-0098
Fax: 503-588-2813
execdir@naen.org
www.naen.org
Association news and notes.

Members Only

Tim Alexander, President
Michael R. Weinert, Executive Director

4289 NAFSA Newsletter

NAFSA: Association of International Educators
1307 New York Avenue NW
8th Floor
Washington, DC 20005-4701
202-737-3699
800-836-4994
Fax: 202-737-3657
inbox@nafsa.org
www.nafsa.org
Publishes news and information related to international education and exchange.

Publication Date: 1948 40 pages Weekly & Quarterly

Fanta Aw, PhD, Chair/ President
Marlene Johnson, Executive Director/ CEO

4290 NAPSEC News

Assn. of Private Schools for Exceptional Children
1522 K Street NW
Suite 1032
Washington, DC 20005-1202
202-408-3338
Fax: 202-408-3340
www.napsec.org
Association news and events.

8-12 pages Quarterly

Sherry L Kolbe, Executive Director/CEO
Barb DeGroot, Manager

4291 NEA Higher Education Advocate

National Education Association (NEA)
1201 16th Street NW
Washington, DC 20036-3290
202-833-4000
Fax: 202-822-7974
ncuea@nea.org
www.nea.org
Reports on NEA and general higher education news.

Publication Date: 1857 4 pages Monthly

Lily Eskelsen Garcia, President
Becky Pringle, Vice President

4292 NEA Today

National Education Association (NEA)
1201 16th Street NW
Washington, DC 20036-3290
202-833-4000
Fax: 202-822-7974
ncuea@nea.org
www.nea.org
Contains news and features of interest to classroom teachers and other employees of schools.

Publication Date: 1857 8x Year

Lily Eskelsen Garcia, President
Becky Pringle, Vice President

4293 NEWSLINKS

International Schools Services
15 Roszel Road
P.O. Box 5910
Princeton, NJ 08543
609-452-0990
Fax: 609-452-2690
newslinks@iss.edu
www.iss.edu
Regularly published newspaper of International Schools Services that is distributed free of charge to overseas teachers, school administrators and libraries, US universities, educational organizations, multinational corporations, school supply companies and educational publishers.

Publication Date: 1955 32-40 pages Quarterly

Roger Hove, President
Kristin Evins, Chief Financial Officer

4294 NJEA Review

New Jersey Education Association
180 W State Street
Trenton, NJ 08607-1211
609-599-4561
Fax: 609-392-6321
webmaster@njea.org
www.njea.org
Monthly educational journal of the New Jersey Education Association which focuses on educational news and issues related to New Jersey public schools. Its readers are active and retired teaching staff members and support staff, administrators, board members, teacher education students, and others in New Jersey public schools and colleges.

Publication Date: 1853 80 pages Monthly
ISSN: 0027-6758

Wendell F. Steinhauer, Chair/ President
Marie Blistan, Vice President

4295 NREA News

National Rural Education Association
Colorado State University
Fort Collins, CO 80523
Fax: 970-491-1317
jnewlin@lamar.colostate.edu
www.colostate.edu
Keeps all members up-to-date on Association activities, events, rural education conferences and meetings, and research projects in progress.

Publication Date: 1870 8 pages Quarterly Newsletter
ISSN: 0273-4460

Joseph T Newlin, Editor

4296 National Accrediting Commission of Cosmetology, Arts and Sciences

National Accrediting Commission of Cosmetology
4401 Ford Avenue
Suite 1300
Arlington, VA 22302-1432
703-600-7600
Fax: 703-379-2200
naccas@naccas.org
www.naccas.org
Information on accreditation, cosmetology schools and ahy federal regulations affecting accreditation and postsecondary education.

Publication Date: 1969 20 pages 6x Year

Tony Mirando, MS, DC, Executive Director
Eddie Broomfield, Asst. to Executive Director

4297 National Homeschool Association Newsletter

National Homeschool Association
PO Box 290
Hartland, MI 48353-0290
425-432-1544
Information on what's happening in the homeschooling community.

28 pages Quarterly

4298 National Monitor of Education

CA Monitor of Education
1331 Fairmount Avenue
Suite 61
El Cerrito, CA 94530
510-527-4430
Fax: 510-528-9833
jsod@aol.com
www.e-files.org

Supports traditional moral and academic values in education. Reports on litigation and reviews various education publications. Issues reported on include parents' rights and movement to restore basic academics.

8 pages Bi-Monthly/Paperback

Susan O'Donnell, Publisher
Susan Sweet, Newsletter Design

4299 New Hampshire Educator

National Education Association, New Hampshire
103 N State Street
Concord, NH 03301-2425
603-224-7751
Fax: 603-224-2648
neanh.org
Reports on the advancements in education in the state and nation and promotes the welfare of educators.

Publication Date: 1854 10 pages Monthly

Scott McGilvray, President
Megan Tuttle, Vice President

4300 New Images

METCO
55 Dimock Street
Boston, MA 02119-1029
617-427-1545
Mailed to METCO parents and educational institutions local and national.

4 pages Quarterly

JM Mitchell

4301 New York Teacher

New York State United Teachers
800 Troy-Schenectady Road
Latham, NY 12110-2455
518-213-6000
800-342-9810
Fax: 518-213-6415
mediarel@nysutmail.org
www.nysut.org
Edited primarily for teaching personnel in elementary, intermediate and high schools and colleges. News and features cover organizations' development, progress of legislation affecting education at local state and national levels and news of the labor movement.

BiWeekly

Karen E. Magee, President
Andrew Pallotta, Executive Vice President

4302 News N' Notes

NTID at Rochester Institute of Technology
52 Lomb Memorial Drive
Rochester, NY 14623
585-475-6400
gbuckley@ntid.rit.edu
www.ntid.rit.edu
Convention news, membership information, education legislation advocacy and personal contributions to the scholarly society.

Publication Date: 1829 12 pages Quarterly

Dr. Gerard J. Buckley, President
Bernard Hurwitz, J.D., Executive Assistant

4303 Non-Credit Learning News

Learning for All Seasons
6 Saddle Club Road
#579X
Lexington, MA 02420-2115
781-861-0379
Marketing information for directors and marketers of non-credit programs.

8 pages 10x Year

Susan Capon

4304 Notes from the Field

Jessie Ball duPont Fund
One Dependent Drive
Suite 1400
Jacksonville, FL 32202-5011
904-353-0890
800-252-3452
Fax: 904-353-3870
contactus@dupontfund.org
www.dupontfund.org
Provides information on the various organizations and institutes the Jessie Ball duPont Fund reaches out to every year.

Publication Date: 1977 3x

Sherry P. Magill, President
Mark D. Constantine, Senior Vice President

4305 Occupational Programs in California Community Colleges

Leo A Myer Associates/LAMA Books
2381 Sleepy Hollow Avenue
Hayward, CA 94545-3429
510-785-1091
888-452-6244
Fax: 510-785-1099
lama@lmabooks.com
www.lamabooks.com
Writers and publishers of HVAC books.

186 pages Bi-Annually
ISBN: 0-88069

Steve Meyer, President

4306 Our Children: The National PTA Magazine

1250 N. Pitt Street
Alexandria, VA 22314
703-518-1200
800-307-4782
Fax: 703-836-0942
info@pta.org
www.pta.org
Written by, for and about the National PTA. A nonprofit organization of parents, educators, students, and other citizens active in their schools and communities.

5x Year

Otha Thornton, President
Shannon Sevier, Vice President Advocacy

4307 PTA National Bulletin

National Association of Hebrew Day School PTA'S
160 Broadway
New York, NY 10038-4201
212-227-1000
Fax: 212-406-6934
Educational events in day school relating to PTA movement. News of national and regional groups.

Quarterly

4308 PTA in Pennsylvania

Pennsylvania PTA
4804 Derry Street
Harrisburg, PA 17111-3440
717-564-8985
Fax: 717-564-9046
info@papta.org
www.papta.org
Topical articles about issues affecting education and children, such as safety and health, AIDS, parents involvement and guidance, environmental concerns and special education.

24 pages Quarterly
ISSN: 1072-3242
250 attendees and 40-50 exhibits

Deborah Dunstone, President
Christine Harty, Secretary

4309 Parents as Teachers National Center

2228 Ball Drive
Saint Louis, MO 63146
314-432-4330
Fax: 314-432-8963
patnc@patnc.org
www.parentsasteachers.org
Provides information, training and technical assistance for those interested in adopting the home-school-community partnership program. Offers parents the information and support needed to give their children the best possible start in life.

Quarterly

Julie Robbens, Editor, Author
Scott Hippert, President/CEO
Cheryl Dyle-Palmer, M.A., EVP/ COO

4310 Passing Marks

San Bernadino City Unified School District
777 N F Street
San Bernardino, CA 92410
909-381-1250
Fax: 909-388-1451
www.sbcusd.k12.ca.us
Educational resume of school activities, covering instruction, personnel, administration, board of education, etc.

12 pages Monthly

Michael J. Gallo, President
Bobbie Perong, Vice President

4311 Pennsylvania Home Schoolers Newsletter

RR 2 Box 117
Kittanning, PA 16201-9311
724-783-6512
Fax: 724-783-6512
A support newsletter directed to home schooling families in Pennsylvania. Articles, reviews of curriculum, advice, calendar, support group listing, children's writing section.

32 pages Quarterly

Howard Richman, Publisher
Susan Richman, Editor

4312 Pennsylvania State Education Association

400 N 3rd Street
PO Box 1724
Harrisburg, PA 17105-1724
717-255-7000
800-944-7732
Fax: 717-255-7124
www.psea.org

Publication Date: 1852 16 pages 9x Year
ISSN: 0896-6605

Michael J. Crossey, President
W. Gerard Oleksiak, Vice President

4313 Phi Delta Kappa Educational Foundation

P.O. Box 7888
Bloomington, IN 47407-7888
812-339-1156
800-766-1156
Fax: 812-339-0018
memberservices@pdkintl.org
www.pdkintl.org

Articles concerned with educational research, service, and leadership; issues, trends and policy are emphazied.

Publication Date: 1906 350 pages 10x Year
ISBN: 0-87367-835-4
November
600 attendees and 30 exhibits

Perry A. Zirkel, Author
Patricia Williams, Chair
Douglas Christensen, Vice Chair

4314 Phi Delta Kappan

Phi Delta Kappa International
320 W. Eighth Street
Suite 216
Bloomington, IN 47404
812-339-1156
800-766-1156
Fax: 812-339-0018
memberservices@pdkintl.org
www.pdkintl.org

Published 8 times a year and is Phi Delta Kappa International's professional education magazine distributed to more than 35,000 individuals. Addresses policy/practice for teachers, administrators, education faculty. Advocates research-based school reform and covers professinal development, research, federal policy, and standards. Includes annual PDK/Gallup poll on public education and features full text of current issues available to online subscribers.

Publication Date: 1906
ISBN: 0031-7217

Patricia Williams, Chair
Douglas Christensen, Vice Chair

4315 Planning for Higher Education

Society for College and University Planning (SCUP)
1330 Eisenhower Place
Ann Arbor, MI 48108
734-669-3270
Fax: 734-661-0157
info@scup.org
www.scup.org/phe

A quarterly, peer-reviewed journal devoted to the advancement and application of the best planning practices for colleges and universities.

70+ pages Quarterly Journal
ISSN: 0736-0983
July
150 booths with 1,200 attendees and 150 exhibits

Ellen Stanton Milstone, Chair
Philip G. Stack, Vice Chair

4316 Policy & Practice

American Public Human Services Association
1133 19th Street, NW
Suite 400
Washington, DC 20036
202-682-0100
Fax: 202-289-6555
www.aphsa.org

This quarterly magazine presents a comprehensive look at issues important to public human services administrators. It also features a wide spectrum of views by the best thinkers in social policy.

Publication Date: 1930 52 pages Quarterly
ISSN: 1520-801X

Reggie Bicha, President
Tracy Wareing, Executive Director

4317 Population Educator

Population Connection
1400 16th Street NW
Suite 320
Washington, DC 20036-2215
202-332-2200
800-767-1956
Fax: 202-332-2302
poped@populationconnection.org
www.populationeducation.org

Offers population education news, classroom activities and workshop schedules for grades K-12.

4 pages Quarterly

Pamela Wasseman

4318 Public Education Alert

Public Education Association
39 W 32nd Street
New York, NY 10001-3803
212-868-1640
Fax: 212-302-0088
info@peaonline
www.pea-online.org

Provides information and consumer-oriented analysis of law policy issues and current developments in New York City public education. PEA Alert back issues; e-guide to New York City's public high school offering comparative data.

Ray Domanico, Publisher
Jessica Wolfe, Editor

4319 QEG

Friends Council on Education
1507 Cherry Street
Philadelphia, PA 19102
215-241-7245
info@friendscouncil.org
friendscouncil.org

Informal news sheet for Quaker schools.

4 pages BiMonthly

Irene McHenry

4320 QUIN: Quarterly University International News

University of Minnesota, Office in Education
231 Pillsbury Drive S.E
Minneapolis, MN 55455-213
612-625-1915
800-752-1000
Fax: 612-624-1693
admissions.tc.umn.edu

International campus update for students, faculty, staff and the community.

TriQuarterly

Rachelle Hernandez, Associate Vice Provost

4321 Reclaiming Children and Youth

Pro-Ed., Inc.
8700 Shoal Creek Boulevard
Austin, TX 78757-6897
512-451-3246
800-897-3202
Fax: 512-451-8542
general@proedinc.com
www.proedinc.com

Provides positive, creative solutions to professionals serving youth in conflict.

Quarterly Magazine

Nicholas J Long, PhD, Editor
Larry K Brendtro, PhD, Editor

4322 Recognition Review

Awards and Recognition Association
8735 W. Higgins Road
Suite 300
Chicago, IL 60631
847-375-4800
800-344-2148
Fax: 847-375-6480
info@ara.org
www.ara.org

Published monthly by the Awards and Recognition Association. Recognition Review is the leading voice of the awards, engraving and recognition industry.

Publication Date: 1964 Monthly

Jeanette Brewer Richardson, CRS, President
Louise Ristau, CAE, Executive Director

4323 Regional Spotlight

Southern Regional Education Board
592 10th Street NW
Atlanta, GA 30318-5776
404-875-9211
Fax: 404-872-1477
www.sreb.org

News of educational interest directed to 15 SREB-member states.

9 pages

Steve Beshear, Chair
Dave Spence, President

4324 Rehabilitation Research, Policy, and Education

National Council on Rehabilitation Education
1099 E Champlain Drive
Suite A, 137
Fresno, CA 93720
559-906-0787
Fax: 559-412-2550
info@ncre.org
ncre.org

A quarterly journal exploring the subject of rehabilitation education. Topics covered include issues related to licensing, certification, accreditation, innovative methodology, employment trends, educational media and more.

quarterly

David Strauser, Ph.D, CRC, Journal Editor

4325 Remedial and Special Education

Pro-Ed., Inc.
8700 Shoal Creek Boulevard
Austin, TX 78757-6897
512-451-3246
800-897-3202
Fax: 512-451-8542
general@proedinc.com
www.proedinc.com

Highest-quality interdisciplinary scholarship that bridges the gap between theory and practice involving the education of individuals for whom typical instruction is not effective.

Bi-Monthly Magazine
ISSN: 0741-9325

Edward A Polloway, EdD, Editor-in-Chief

4326 Renaissance Educator

Renaissance Educational Associates
4817 N County Road 29
Loveland, CO 80538-9515
970-679-4300

Quarterly publication highlighting educators around the world who are revealing the effectiveness of integrity in education.

8 pages Quarterly

Kristy Clark

4327 Research in Higher Education

Kluwer Academic/Human Sciences Press
233 Spring Street
New York, NY 10013
212-620-8000
800-221-9369
Fax: 212-463-0742
www.wkpa.nl

Essential source of new information for all concerned with the functioning of postsecondary educational institutions. Publishes original, quantitative research articles which contribute to an increased understanding of an institution, aid faculty in making more informed decisions about current or future operations, and improve the efficiency of an institution.

Bimonthly
ISSN: 0361-0365

Carol Bischoff, Publisher
John C Smart, Editor

4328 Research in the Schools
Mid-South Educational Research Association
University of Alabama
Tuscaloosa, AL 35487-0001
Fax: 205-348-6873
ktcampbell@selu.edu
msera.org
A nationally refereed journal sponsored by the Mid-South Educational Research Association and the University of Alabama. RITS publishes original contributions in the following areas: 1) Research in practice; 2) Topical Articles; 3) Methods and Techniques; 4) Assessment and 5) Other topics of interest dealing with school-based research. Contributions should follow the guidelines in the latest edition of the Publications Manual of the American Psychological Association.

Publication Date: 1972

Kathy Campbell, President
Cliff Hofwolt, Executive Director

4329 Roeper Review: A Journal on Gifted Education
Roeper Institute
PO Box 329
Bloomfield Hills, MI 48303-0329
248-203-7321
Fax: 248-203-7310
tcross@bsu.edu
www.roeperreview.org
A journal that focuses on gifted and talented education, the Roeper Review applies the highest standards of peer review journalism to cover a broad range of issues. For professionals who work with teachers and for professionals who work directly with gifted and talented children and their families, the journal provides readable coverage of policy issues. Each issue covers one or more subjects. Regular departments include research reports and book reviews.

60-80 pages Quarterly
ISSN: 0278-3193

Tracy L Cross PhD, Editor
Vicki Rossbach, Subsciption

4330 Rural Educator: Journal for Rural and Small Schools
National Rural Education Association
Colorado State University
Fort Collins, CO 80523
970-491-7022
Fax: 970-491-1317
jnewlin@lamar.colostate.edu
www.colostate.edu
Official journal of the NREA. A nationally recognized publication that features timely and informative articles written by leading rural educators from all levels of education. All NREA members are encouraged to submit research articles and items of general information for publication.

Publication Date: 1870 40 pages TriAnnual

Joseph T Newlin, Editor

4331 SEDL Letter
Southwestern Educational Development Laboratory
4700 Mueller Boulevard
Austin, TX 78723
512-476-6861
800-476-6861
Fax: 512-476-2286
information@sedl.org
www.sedl.org
A biannual letter that complements and draws on work and performed by SEDL under a variety of funding sources, including the US Department of Education and the US government.

Publication Date: 1960
ISBN: 520-7315

Linda Villarreal, Chair
Gwenneth Price-Picard, Vice Chair

4332 SKOLE: A Journal of Alternative Education
Down-To-Earth Books
72 Philip Street
Albany, NY 12202-1729
518-432-1578
Publishes articles, poems, and research by people engaged in alternative education.

200 pages SemiAnnually

Mary Leue

4333 SNEA Impact: The Student Voice of the Teaching Profession
National Education Association (NEA)
1201 16th Street NW
Washington, DC 20036-3290
202-833-4000
Fax: 202-822-7974
www.nea.org
Offers articles and views on current events and the educational system through students' eyes for education professionals.

Publication Date: 1857 7x Year

Lily Eskelsen, President
Becky Pringle, Vice President

4334 Safety Forum
Safety Society
1900 Association Drive
Reston, VA 20191-1502
703-476-3440
Offers articles and up-to-date information on school safety.

4 pages TriQuarterly

Linda Moore

4335 School Bus Fleet
Bobit Business Media
3520 Challenger Street
Torrance, CA 90503
310-533-2400
Fax: 310-533-2512
info@schoolbusfleet.com
www.schoolbusfleet.com
Provides coverage of federal vehicle and education regulations that affect pupil transportation, policy and management issues as well as how to improve the safety of children riding yellow buses. Special sections cover transportation for students with disabilities.

Publication Date: 1956

James Blue, General Manager
Thomas McMahon, Executive Editor

4336 School Foodservice & Nutrition
School Nutrition Association
1600 Duke Street
Floor 7
Alexandria, VA 22314-3421
703-739-3900
800-877-8822
Fax: 703-739-3915
schoolnutrition.org
For foodservice professionals presenting current articles on industry issues, management events, legislative issues, public relations programs and professional development news.

11x Year

Adrienne Gall Tufts, Editor

4337 School Law Bulletin
Quinlan Publishing
23 Drydock Avenue
Boston, MA 02210-2336
617-542-0048
Covers cases and laws pertaining to schools.

8 pages Monthly

4338 School Safety
National School Safety Center
141 Duesenberg Drive
Suite 7B
Westlake Village, CA 91362
805-373-9977
800-453-7461
Fax: 805-373-9277
info@schoolsafety.us
www.schoolsafety.us
For educators, law enforcers, judges and legislators on the prevention of drugs, gangs, weapons, bullying, discipline problems and vandalism; also on-site security and character development as they relate to students and schools.

Monthly

Dr. Ronald D Stephens, Executive Director
June Lane Arnette, Editor

4339 School Transportation News
STN Media Company Inc.
P.O. Box 789
Redondo Beach, CA 90277
310-792-2226
Fax: 310-792-2231
bpaul@stnonline.com
www.stnonline.com
Covers school district and contractor fleets, special needs and prekindergarten transportation, Head Start, and more on a monthly basis. Reports developments affecting public school transportation supervisors and directors, state directors of school transportation, school bus contractors, special needs transportation, Head Start transportation, private school transportation, school business officials responsible for transportation and industry suppliers.

Publication Date: 1991 Magazine/Monthly
100 booths

Bill Paul, Author
Ryan Gray, Editor-in-Chief
Tony Corpin, Publisher

4340 School Zone
West Aurora Public Schools, District 129
80 S River Street
#14
Aurora, IL 60506-5178
630-844-4400
www.sd129.org
Informs the community of what is happening in their schools, with their students, and with their tax dollars.

4 pages 5x Year

Laurel Chivari

4341 Shaping the Future
Lutheran Education Association
7400 Augusta Street
River Forest, IL 60305
708-209-3343
Fax: 708-209-3458

lea@lea.org
www.lea.org
Newsletter for LEA members to focus on the unique spiritual and professional needs of church workers and to celebrate life in the ministry. Resource information for the organization, upcoming events, encouragement for pre-planning.

Daniel Czaplewski, Chair
Candyce Seider, Vice Chair

4342 Sharing Space
Creative Urethanes, Children's Creative Response
PO Box 271
Nyack, NY 10960-0271
845-358-4601
Trains all those working with children to communicate positivity and cooperation.

12 pages TriAnnually

4343 Special Education Leadership
LifeWay Church Resources
One LifeWay Plaza
Nashville, TN 37234
615-251-2000
800-588-7222
Fax: 615-251-5933
www.lifeway.com
Covers special education issues relating to religious education.

Publication Date: 1891 52 pages Quarterly

Thom S. Rainer, President/ CEO
Brad Waggoner, Executive Vice President

4344 Special Educator
LRP Publications
360 Hiatt Drive
Palm Beach Gardens, FL 33418
703-516-7002
800-341-7874
Fax: 561-622-2423
custserve@lrp.com
www.lrp.com
Covers important issues in the field of special education, including such topics as law and administrative policy.

Publication Date: 1977 22 pages 22 Issues Per Year
ISSN: 1047-1618

Kenneth F. Kahn, President

4345 Star News
Jefferson Center for Character Education
PO Box 1283
Monrovia, CA 91017-1283
949-770-7602
Fax: 949-450-1100
Mission is to produce and promote programs to teach children the concepts, skills and behavior of good character, common core values, personal and civic responsibility, workforce readiness and citizenship.

Quarterly

Robert Jamieson, CEO
Sharon McClenahan, Administrative Assistant

4346 Statewise: Statistical & Research Newsletter
State Board of Education, Planning & Research
PO Box 1402
Dover, DE 19903-1402
302-736-4601
Fax: 302-739-4654
Statistical data relating to Delaware public schools.

2 pages

4347 Street Scenes
(APO Street College of Education
610 W 112th Street
New York, NY 10025-1898
212-222-6700
Fax: 212-222-6700
New ideas in education.

8 pages SemiAnnually

Renee Creange

4348 Teacher$ Talk
Teachers Insurance and Annuity Association
730 3rd Avenue
New York, NY 10017-3206
212-490-9000
Fax: 800-914-8922
www.tiaa-cref.org
Offers timely information and helpful hints about savings, investments, finance and insurance for teachers and educators.

Publication Date: 1918 Quarterly

Roger Ferguson, President/ CEO
Ron Pressman, EVP/ COO

4349 Teaching Exceptional Children
Council for Exceptional Children
2900 Crystal Drive
Suite 1000
Arlington, VA 22202-3557
703-620-3660
888-232-7733
Fax: 703-264-9494
robin.brewer@unco.edu
www.cec.sped.org
Features practical articles that present methods and materials for classroom use as well as current issues in special education teaching and learning. Published four times per year, free with membership or $86.00 for individual subscription.

Publication Date: 1922

Robin D. Brewer, President
Alexander T. Graham, Executive Director/Secretary

4350 Telluride Newsletter
217 West Ave.
Ithaca, NY 14850
607-273-5011
Fax: 607-272-2667
telluride@tellurideassociation.org
www.tellurideassociation.org
News of interest to alumni of Telluride Association sponsored programs.

Publication Date: 1891 8 pages TriQuarterly

Eric Lemer

4351 Tennessee Education
University of Tennessee
College of Education
Knoxville, TN 37996-0001
865-974-5252
Fax: 865-974-8718
admissions@utk.edu
www.utk.edu
Publishes articles on topics related to K through higher education.

BiAnnually
ISSN: 0739-0408

Mary Lucal, Assistant Vice Chancellor

4352 Tennessee School Board Bulletin
Tennessee School Boards Association
525 Brick Church Park Drive
Nashville, TN 37207
615-815-3900
800-448-6465
Fax: 615-815-3911
www.tsba.net
Articles of interest to boards of education.

Publication Date: 1939 6 pages

Susan Lodal, President
Wayne Blair, Vice President

4353 The Sounds and Spelling Patterns of English: P Honics for Teachers and Parents
Oxton House Publishers, LLC
Po Box 209
Farmington, ME 04938
207-779-1923
800-539-7323
Fax: 207-779-0623
info@oxtonhouse.com
www.oxtonhouse.com
A clear, concise, practical, jargon-free overview of the sounds that make up the English language and the symbols that we use to represent them in writing. It includes a broad range of strategies for helping beginning readers develop fluent decoding skills.

62 pages

Jill Fulkerson, Representative, Colorado
Phillip Neill, Representative, Texas

4354 Theory Into Practice
Ohio State University, College of Education
122 Ramseyer Hall
29 W Woodruff Avenue
Columbus, OH 43210
614-292-3407
Fax: 614-292-7900
tip@osu.edu
www.coe.ohio-state.edu
Nationally recognized for excellence in educational journalism; thematic format, providing comprehensive discussion of single topic with many diverse points of view.

Quarterly
ISSN: 0040-5841

Anita Woolfolk Hey, Author
Anita Woolfolk Hey, Editor

4355 This Active Life
National Education Association (NEA)
1201 16th Street NW
Washington, DC 20036-3290
202-833-4000
Fax: 202-822-7974
www.nea.org/retired
Serves as a resource in the maintenance of quality public education.

Publication Date: 1857 20 pages Bi-Monthly
ISSN: 1526-9342

Lily Eskelsen, President
Becky Pringle, Vice President

4356 Three R'S for Teachers: Research, Reports & Reviews
Master Teacher
Po Box 1207
Manhattan, KS 66502
785-539-0555
800-669-9633
Fax: 800-669-1132
www.masterteacher.com
The publication that synthesizes the most recent educational research, data and trends on specific topics for teachers.

Publication Date: 1969 Quarterly

Dr. Joanna Hubbs, President
Gregory Hubbs, Editor-in-Chief

4357 Tidbits
Assn. for Legal Support of Alternative Schools
PO Box 2823
Santa Fe, NM 87504-2823
505-471-6928

Information and legal advice to those involved in non-public educational facilities.

12 pages Quarterly

Ed Nagel

4358 Transitions Abroad: The Guide to Learning, Living, & Working Abroad

Transitions Abroad
P.O. Box 1369
Amherst, MA 1004
413-992-6486
Fax: 802-442-4827
webeditor@TransitionsAbroad.com
www.transitionsabroad.com

This magazine contains articles and bibliographies on travel, study, teaching, internships and work abroad.

Publication Date: 1977 Bi-Monthly

4359 Unschoolers Network

Unschoolers Network
2 Smith Street
Farmingdale, NJ 07727
732-938-2473
UnNet@unschooling.org
www.unschooling.org/UnNet

Information and support for families teaching their children at home.

Publication Date: 1977 14 pages Monthly

Nancy Plent

4360 VSBA Newsletter

Vermont School Boards Association
2 Prospect Street
Montpelier, VT 05602
802-223-3580
800-244-8722
sdale@vtvsba.org
www.vtvsba.org

General information.

Publication Date: 1936 16 pages Monthly

Stephen Dale, Executive Director
Kerri Lamb, Operations Manager

4361 WCER Highlights

Wisconsin Center for Education Research
1025 W Johnson Street
Suite 785
Madison, WI 53706
608-263-4200
Fax: 608-263-6448
uw-wcer@education.wisc.edu
www.wcer.wisc.edu

News about research conducted at the Wisconsin Center for Education Research.

Publication Date: 1964 8 pages Quarterly
ISSN: 1073-1882

Robert Mathieu, Director
Paul Baker, Specialist

4362 WestEd: Systems Framework

The Center on School Turnaround
730 Harrison Street
San Francisco, CA 94107
415-565-3000
877-493-7833
Fax: 415-565-3012
gtulley@wested.org
www.wested.org

The 'Four Domains for Rapid School Improvement: A Systems Framework' is a publication designed to help states, districts, and schools manage school improvement in the areas of leadership, talent development, instructional transformation and culture.

48 pages

Susan H Fuhrman, President
Glen Harvey, CEO

4363 Western Journal of Black Studies

Washington State University
Heritage House
Pullman, WA 99164-0001
509-335-3564
888-468-6978
Fax: 509-335-8338
admissions@wsu.edu
www.wsu.edu

A journal which canvasses topical issues affecting Black studies and education.

Publication Date: 1890 Quarterly

Elson S. Floyd, Ph.D., President
Daniel J. Bernardo, Provost & EVP

4364 World Gifted

World Council for Gifted & Talented Children
Western Kentucky University
Gary A. Ransdell Hall, Room 2007, 1906 C
Bowling Green, KY 42101-1030
270-745-4123
Fax: 270-745-4124
headquarters@world-gifted.org
www.world-gifted.org

Offers information and articles on gifted education for the professional.

4365 Young Audiences Newsletter

Young Audiences New York
One East 53rd Street
New York, NY 10128-1688
212-319-9269
Fax: 212-319-9272
info@yany.org
www.yany.org

Organization news of performing arts education programs in schools and communities.

Publication Date: 1952 Annual

Kim Greenberg, Chair
Robert Riesenberg, President

Periodicals / Administration

4366 AACRAO Data Dispenser

American Association of Collegiate Registrars
1 Dupont Circle NW
Suite 520
Washington, DC 20036
202-293-9161
Fax: 202-872-8857
myers.7@osu.edu
www.aacrao.org

Association newsletter for US and foreign postsecondary education institution professionals involved in admissions, records and registration.

12 pages 10x Year

Brad Myers, President
Nicole Rovig, VP, Information Technology

4367 AASA Bulletin

American Association of School Administrators
1615 Duke Street
Alexandria, VA 22314
703-528-0700
Fax: 703-841-1543
info@aasa.org
www.aasa.org

The AASA Bulletin is a supplement to The School Administrator. It contains the Job Bulletin and information for school leaders about the many products, services and events available to them from AASA.

Publication Date: 1865

Ginger O'Neil, Editor
Kari Arfstrom, Project Director

4368 ACCT Advisor

Association of Community College Trustees
1101 17th Street NW
Suite 300
Washington, DC 20036
202-775-4667
Fax: 202-223-1297
acctinfo@acct.org
www.acct.org

Provides news of association events, federal regulations, activities, state activities, legal issues and other news of interest to community college governing board members.

Robin M. Smith, Chair
Bakari Lee, Vice Chair

4369 AVA Update

Association for Volunteer Administration
PO Box 4584
Boulder, CO 80306-4584
303-447-0558

Information of value to administrators of volunteer services.

4 pages BiMonthly

Martha Martin

4370 Accreditation Fact Sheet

NAPNSC Accrediting Commission for Higher Education
182 Thompson Road
Grand Junction, CO 81503-2246
970-243-5441
Fax: 970-242-4392
director@napnsc.org
www.napnsc.org

Newsletter reporting on the origin, history, developments, procedures and changes of educational institution accreditation.

Annually

H. Earl Heusser, Author
H Earl Heusser, Executive Director

4371 Administrative Information Report

Nat'l Association of Secondary School Principles
1904 Association Drive
Reston, VA 20191-1537
703-860-0200
800-253-7746
Fax: 703-620-6534
www.principals.org

Offers school statistics and administrative updates for secondary school principals and management officers.

Publication Date: 1916 4 pages Monthly

G.A. Buie, President
JoAnn D. Bartoletti, Executive Director

4372 American School & University Magazine

Intertec Publishing
PO Box 12960
Overland Park, KS 66282-2960
913-967-1960
Fax: 913-967-1905

Directed at business and facilities administrators in the nation's public and private schools.

Monthly

Joe Agron, Editor

4373 American School Board Journal
National School Boards Association
1680 Duke Street
Alexandria, VA 22314
703-838-6722
Fax: 703-683-7590
info@nsba.org
www.nsba.org
Published primarily for school board members and school system superintendents serving public elementary and secondary schools in the United States and Canada.
Monthly
Anne M. Byrne, President
Heather Francis, Executive Asst.

4374 Board
Master Teacher
PO Box 1207
Manhattan, KS 66502
785-539-0555
800-669-9633
Fax: 800-669-1132
www.masterteacher.com
Designed to be a continuous form of communication to help board members know and understand the duties, responsibilities, and commitments of the office; view the superintendent of schools as the educational leader; improve administrator-board working relationships; better understand the purpose of education; and work at their responsibilities in a prudent, calm, and rational manner.
Publication Date: 1969 Monthly
Dr. Joanna Hubbs, President
Gregory Hubbs, Editor-in-Chief

4375 Building Leadership Bulletin
2990 Baker Drive
Springfield, IL 62703-2800
217-525-1383
Fax: 217-525-7264
www.ipa.vsta.net
Topical, timely issues.
8 pages 11x Year
Julie Weichert, Associate Director

4376 Business Education Forum
National Business Education Association
1914 Association Drive
Reston, VA 20191-1596
703-860-8300
Fax: 703-620-4483
www.nbea.org
A journal of distinctive articles dealing with current issues and trends, future directions and exemplary programs in business education at all instructional levels. Articles focus on international business, life-long learning, cultural diversity, critical thinking, economics, state-of-the-art technology and the latest research in the field.
Publication Date: 1939 200 pages Quarterly
Maurice S. Henderson, President
Janet M Treichel, Executive Director

4377 CASE Currents
1307 New York Avenue NW
Suite 1000
Washington, DC 20036-1226
202-328-2273
Fax: 202-387-4973
MemberSupportCenter@case.org
www.case.org
Covers the world of fund raising, alumni administration, public relations, periodicals, publications and student recruitment in higher education.
Publication Date: 1974 10x Year
John Lippincott, President
Christina Antoniewicz, Educational Programs Manager

4378 CASE Newsletter
The Council for Exceptional Children
2900 Crystal Drive
Suite 1000
Arlington, VA 22202-3557
703-620-3660
888-232-7733
Fax: 703-264-9494
www.cec.sped.org
News about CASE activities, upcoming events, current trends and practices, state and national legislation, and other practical information relevant to the administration of special education programs.
Publication Date: 1922 5x Year
Robin D. Brewer, President
Alexander T. Graham, Executive Director/Secretary

4379 CASE in Point
The Council for Exceptional Children
2900 Crystal Drive
Suite 1000
Arlington, VA 22202-3557
703-620-3660
888-232-7733
Fax: 703-264-9494
www.cec.sped.org
A journal reporting on emerging promising practices, current research, contact points for expanded information, and field-based commentary relevant to the administration of special education programs.
Publication Date: 1922 BiAnnual
Robin D. Brewer, President
Alexander T. Graham, Executive Director/Secretary

4380 California Schools Magazine
California School Boards Association
3251 Beacon Boulevard
West Sacramento, CA 95691
916-371-4691
800-266-3382
Fax: 916-372-3369
www.csba.org
For school board members, superintendents and school business managers, responsible for the operation of California's public schools. Articles of interest to parents, teachers, community members and anyone else concerned with public education.
20 pages Quarterly
ISSN: 1081-8936
Jesus Holguin, President
Sherri Reusche, Vice President

4381 Clearing House: A Journal of Educational Research
Heldref Publications
325 Chestnut Street
Suite 800
Philadelphia, PA 19106
215-625-8900
800-365-9753
Fax: 202-296-5149
customer.service@taylorandfrancis.com
www.heldref.org
Each issue offers a variety of articles for teachers and administrators of middle schools and junior and senior high schools. It includes experiments, trends and accomplishments in courses, teaching methods, administrative procedures and school programs.
4 pages BiMonthly
ISSN: 0009-8655
Deborah N Cohen, Promotions Manager
Judy Cusick, Managing Editor

4382 Connection
National Association of State Boards of Education
1680 Duke Street
Alexandria, VA 22314
703-838-6722
Fax: 703-683-7590
info@nsba.org
www.nsba.org
Quarterly magazine for state board of education members.
10 pages
Anne M. Byrne, President
Heather Francis, Executive Asst.

4383 Developer
National Staff Development Council
504 South Locust St.
Oxford, OH 45056-0240
513-523-6029
Fax: 513-523-0638
learningforward.org
Devoted to staff development for educational personnel.
Publication Date: 1969 8 pages 10x Year
Deborah Jackson, President
Stephanie Hirsh, Executive Director

4384 ERS Spectrum
Educational Research Service
1001 N. Fairfax Street
Suite 500
Arlington, VA 22314-1587
703-243-2100
800-791-9308
Fax: 703-243-1985
ers@ers.org
www.ers.org
A quarterly journal of school research and information. Publishes practical research and information for school decisions. Authors include practicing administrators and other educators in local school districts.
Publication Date: 1958 48 pages Quarterly
ISSN: 0740-7874
Lester Strong, Chair
Christopher Curran, Vice Chair

4385 Education Daily
LRP Publications
360 Hiatt Drive
Palm Beach Gardens, FL 33418
703-516-7002
800-341-7874
Fax: 561-622-2423
custserve@lrp.com
www.lrp.com
News on national education policy. Offers daily reports of Education Department policies, initiatives and priorities— how they are developed and how they affect school programs.
Publication Date: 1977 6-8 pages Daily
Kenneth F. Kahn, President

4386 Educational Administration Quarterly
University of Wisconsin, Milwaukee
PO Box 413
Milwaukee, WI 53201-0413
414-229-1122
Fax: 414-229-5300
www4.uwm.edu

Deals with administrative issues and policy.

Quarterly

Mark Mone, Chancellor
Johannes Britz, Provost/ Vice Chancellor

4387 Electronic Learning

Scholastic
555 Broadway
New York, NY 10012-3919
212-343-6100
800-724-6527
Fax: 212-343-4801

Published for the administrative level, education professionals who are directly responsible for the implementing of electronic technology at the district, state and university levels.

8x Year

Lynn Diamond, Advertising Director
Therese Mageau, Editor

4388 Enrollment Management Report

LRP Publications
360 Hiatt Drive
Palm Beach Gardens, FL 33418
703-516-7002
800-341-7874
Fax: 561-622-2423
custserve@lrp.com
www.lrp.com

Provides colleges and universities with solutions and strategies for recruitment, admissions, retention and financial aid. Reviews the latest trends, research studies and their findings and gives a profile on how other institutions are handling their enrollment management issues.

Publication Date: 1977 Monthly
ISSN: 1094-3757

Kenneth F. Kahn, President

4389 Galileo For Superintendents And District Level Administrators

Master Teacher
Po Box 1207
Manhattan, KS 66505
785-539-0555
800-669-9633
Fax: 800-669-1132
www.masterteacher.com

The monthly web and print service provides direction & strategies for superintendents and district level administrators.

Publication Date: 1969 Monthly Newsletter

Dr. Joanna Hubbs, President
Gregory Hubbs, Editor-in-Chief

4390 HR on Campus

LRP Publications
360 Hiatt Drive
Palm Beach Gardens, FL 33418
703-516-7002
800-341-7874
Fax: 561-622-2423
custserve@lrp.com
www.lrp.com

This monthly newsletter provides coverage of the latest and most inovative programs higher education institutions use to handle their human resource challenges. Plus, you can recieve free e-mail updates on crucial news affecting your job with your paid subscription.

Publication Date: 1977 Monthly
ISSN: 1098-9293

Kenneth F. Kahn, President

4391 IPA Newsletter

2990 Baker Drive
Springfield, IL 62703-2800
217-525-1383
Fax: 217-525-7264
www.ipa.vsta.net

Provides current information on Illinois principals and the profession.

8 pages 11x Year

David Turner, Author
Julie Weichert, Associate Director

4392 Integrated Pathways

Association of Integrative Studies
Miami University
Oxford, OH 45056
513-529-2659
Fax: 513-529-5849
rszostak@ualberta.ca
www.units.muohio.edu/aisorg

AIS news, including updates on AIS conferences, decisions of the AIS Board of Directors, and membership announcements. Published quarterly.

Publication Date: 1979
ISSN: 1081-647X

Rick Szostak, President
James Welch, Vice President, Development

4393 Journal of Curriculum & Supervision

Association for Supervision & Curriculum Develop.
1703 N Beauregard Street
Alexandria, VA 22311-1714
512-471-4611
800-933-ASCD
Fax: 512-471-8460
oldavisjr@mail.uteyas.edu
www.ascd.org

Offers professional updates and news as well as membership/association information.

Publication Date: 1943 Quarterly Paperback

Nancy Gibson, President
Judy Seltz, Executive Director

4394 Journal of Education for Business

Heldref Publications
325 Chestnut Street
Suite 800
Philadelphia, PA 19106
215-625-8900
800-365-9753
Fax: 202-296-5149
customer.service@taylorandfrancis.com
www.heldref.org

Offers information to instructors, supervisors, and administrators at the secondary, postsecondary and collegiate levels. The journal features basic and applied research-based articles in accounting, communications, economics, finance, information systems, management, marketing and other business disciplines.

BiMonthly

4395 Keystone Schoolmaster Newsletter

Pennsylvania Assn. of Secondary School Principals
PO Box 39
122 Valley Road
Summerdale, PA 17093
717-732-4999
Fax: 717-732-4890
www.paessp.org

Reports achievements, honors, problems and innovations by officers and established authorities.

Publication Date: 1960 4 pages Monthly

Jacqueline Clarke Havrilla, President
Paul M. Healey, PhD, Executive Director

4396 LSBA Quarter Notes

Louisiana School Boards Association
7912 Summa Avenue
Baton Rouge, LA 70809
225-769-3191
877-664-5722
Fax: 225-769-6108
www.lsba.com

News articles relative to the association, feature stories on research.

Publication Date: 1938 6 pages BiMonthly

John Smith, President
Russ Wise, Vice President

4397 Legal Notes for Education

Progressive Business Publications
370 Technology Drive
Malvern, PA 19355
610-695-8600
800-220-5000
Fax: 610-647-8089
customer_service@pbp.com
www.pbp.com

Reports the latest school law cases and late-breaking legislation along with the most recent law review articles affecting education. Federal and state appellate court decisions are summarized and the full legal citation is supplied for each case.

Publication Date: 1959 Monthly

Ed Satell, Founder
Liz Webb, Human Resources

4398 Maintaining Safe Schools

LRP Publications
360 Hiatt Drive
Palm Beach Gardens, FL 33418
703-516-7002
800-341-7874
Fax: 561-622-2423
custserve@lrp.com
www.lrp.com

Focuses on the legal and practical issues involved in preventing and responding to violent acts by students in schools, and highlights successful violence prevention programs in school districts across the country. Offers strategies for mediation, discipline and crisis managment.

Publication Date: 1977 Monthly
ISSN: 1082-4774

Kenneth F. Kahn, President

4399 Managing School Business

LRP Publications
360 Hiatt Drive
Palm Beach Gardens, FL 33418
703-516-7002
800-341-7874
Fax: 561-622-2423
custserve@lrp.com
www.lrp.com

Newsletter provides school business managers with tips on how to solve the problems they face in managing finance, operations, personnel, and their own career.

Publication Date: 1977 Biweekly
ISSN: 1092-2229

Angela Childers, Author
Kenneth F. Kahn, President

4400 Memo to the President

American Assn. of State Colleges & Universities
1307 New York Avenue NW
5th Floor
Washington, DC 20005
202-293-7070
Fax: 202-296-5819
www.aascu.org

Monitors public policies at national, state and campus level on higher education issues. Reports on activities of the Association and member institutions.

20 pages Monthly
November

J. Keith Motley, Chair
Muriel A. Howard, President

4401 NASPA Forum

National Assn. of Student Personnel Administrators
111 K Street NE
10th Floor
Washington, DC 20002
202-265-7500
Fax: 202-797-1157
office@naspa.org
www.naspa.org
Offers information for personnel administrators and strategies, updates and tips on the education system.

Publication Date: 1918 Monthly

Patricia Whitely, Chair
Kevin Kruger, President

4402 National Faculty Forum

National Faculty of Humanities, Arts & Sciences
1676 Clifton Road NE
Atlanta, GA 30329-4050
404-727-5788
Offers administrative news and updates for persons in higher education.

TriQuarterly

4403 Network

National School Public Relations Association
15948 Derwood Road
Rockville, MD 20855
301-519-0496
Fax: 301-519-0494
nspra@nspra.org
www.nspra.org
Monthly newsletter for and about our members. Some articles about school public relations, issues that affect school public relations people.

Jim Cummings, APR, President
Stephen Nichols, VP for Diversity Engagement

4404 OASCD Journal

Oklahoma Curriculum Development
3705 S. 98th East Avenue
Tulsa, OK 74146
918-627-4403
Fax: 918-627-4433
A refereed journal which prints contributions on curriculum theory and practices, leadership in education, staff development and supervision. The Editorial Board welcomes photographs, letters to the editor, program descriptions, interviews, research reports, theoretical pieces, reviews of books and non-print media, poetry, humor, cartoons, satire and children's art and writing, as well as expository articles.

Annual

Blaine Smith, Executive Secretary

4405 On Board

New York State School Boards Association
24 Century Hill Drive
Suite 200
Latham, NY 12110-2125
518-783-0200
800-342-3360
Fax: 518-783-0211
info@nyssba.org
www.nyssba.org
Contains general educational news, state and federal legislative activity, legal and employee relations issues, commentary, issues in education, and successful education programs around the state.

Publication Date: 1896 21x Year

Lynne L. Lenhardt, President
Susan Bergtraum, 1st VP & Area 11 Director

4406 Perspectives for Policymakers

New Jersey School Boards Association
413 W State Street
#909
Trenton, NJ 08618-5617
609-695-7600
888-88N-SBA
info@njsba.org
www.njsba.org
Each issue focuses on a specific topic in education providing background, activities and resources.

8 pages SemiAnnually

Donald Webster, Jr., President
Daniel T. Sinclair, VP, County Activities

4407 Planning & Changing

Illinois State University
College of Education
Campus Box 5300
Normal, IL 61790-5300
309-438-2399
Fax: 309-438-8683
coe.ilstu.edu/eafdept/pandc.htm
An educational leadership and policy journal. This journal attempts to disseminate timely and useful reports of practice and theory with particular emphasis on change, and planning in K-12 educational settings and higher education settings. Paperback.

Publication Date: 1857 64 pages Quarterly
ISSN: 0032-0684

Perry Schoon, Chair, College Faculty
Alan Bates, College Faculty

4408 Principal

Nat'l Association of Elementary School Principals
1615 Duke Street
Alexandria, VA 22314-3406
703-684-3345
Fax: 800-396-2377
A professional magazine edited for elementary and middle school principals and others interested in education.

5x Year

Leon E Greene, Editor
Louanne M Wheeler, Production Manager

4409 Principal Communicator

National School Public Relations Association
15948 Derwood Road
Rockville, MD 20855
301-519-0496
Fax: 301-519-0494
nspra@nspra.org
www.napra.org
Tips for building public relations people.

6 pages Monthly

Andy Grunig, Manager of Communications

4410 Private Education Law Report

Progressive Business Publications
370 Technology Drive
Malvern, PA 19355
610-695-8600
800-220-5000
Fax: 610-647-8089
customer_service@pbp.com
www.pbp.com
Reports the latest school law cases and late-breaking legislation along with the most recent law review articles affecting private education. Federal and state appellate court decisions are summarized and the full legal citation is supplied for each case.

Publication Date: 1959 Monthly

Ed Satell, Founder
Liz Webb, Human Resources

4411 Public Personnel Management

International Personnel Management Association
1617 Duke Street
Alexandria, VA 22314-3406
703-549-7100
Fax: 703-684-0948
Caters to those professionals in human resource management.

Quarterly

Sarah AI Shiffert, Editor

4412 Rural Educator-Journal for Rural and Small Schools

National Rural Education Association
Colorado State University
Fort Collins, CO 80523
970-491-7022
Fax: 970-491-1317
jnewlin@lamar.colostate.edu
www.colostate.edu
Official journal of the NREA. A nationally recognized publication that features timely and informative articles written by leading rural educators from all levels of education. All NREA members are encouraged to submit research articles and items of general information for publication.

Publication Date: 1870 40 pages Quarterly
Magazine
ISSN: 0273-446X

Joseph T Newlin, Editor

4413 School Administrator

American Association of School Administrators
801 N Quincy Street
Suite 700
Arlington, VA 22203-1730
703-528-0700
Fax: 703-841-1543
info@aasa.org
www.aasa.org
Ensures the highest quality education systems for all learners through the support and development of leadership on the building, district and state levels.

52 pages Monthly

Paul D Houston, Executive Director

4414 School Business Affairs

Association of School Business Officials Int'l
11401 N Shore Drive
Reston, VA 20190-4232
703-478-0405
Fax: 703-478-0205
For school business administrators responsible for the administration and purchase of products and services for the schools.

Monthly

Peg D Kirkpatrick, Editor/Publisher
Robert Gluck, Managing Editor

4415 School Law Briefings

LRP Publications
360 Hiatt Drive
Palm Beach Gardens, FL 33418
703-516-7002
800-341-7874
Fax: 561-622-2423

custserve@lrp.com
www.lrp.com
Gives you summaries of general education, special education, and early childhood court cases, as well as administrative hearings.

Publication Date: 1977 Monthly
ISSN: 1094-3749

Kenneth F. Kahn, President

4416 School Law News
LRP Publications
360 Hiatt Drive
Palm Beach Gardens, FL 33418
703-516-7002
800-341-7874
Fax: 561-622-2423
custserve@lrp.com
www.lrp.com
Advises administrators to avoid legal pitfalls by monitoring education-related court action across the nation. With School Law News, administrators receive the latest information on issues like sexual harassment liability, special education, religion in the schools, affirmative action, youth violence, student-faculty rights, school finance, desegregation and much more.

Publication Date: 1977 8-10 pages Monthly

Kenneth F. Kahn, President

4417 School Planning & Management
Peter Li Education Group
2621 Dryden Road
Suite 300
Dayton, OH 45439
937-293-1415
800-523-4625
Fax: 800-370-4450
www.peterli.com
For the business needs of school administrators featuring issues, ideas and technology at work in public, private and independent schools.

Monthly
ISSN: 1086-4628

Peter J Li, Publisher
Deborah Moore, Editor

4418 Section 504 Compliance Advisor
LRP Publications
360 Hiatt Drive
Palm Beach Gardens, FL 33418
703-516-7002
800-341-7874
Fax: 561-622-2423
custserve@lrp.com
www.lrp.com
Newsletter examines the requirements of Section 504 of the Rehabilitation Act and analyzes their impact on disciplining students. Provides educators and administrators with detailed tips and advice to help them solve the discipline problems they face everyday and keep their policies and programs in compliance.

Publication Date: 1977 Monthly
ISSN: 1094-3730

Kenneth F. Kahn, President

4419 Special Education Law Monthly
LRP Publications
360 Hiatt Drive
Palm Beach Gardens, FL 33418
703-516-7002
800-341-7874
Fax: 561-622-2423
custserve@lrp.com
www.lrp.com
Covers court decisions and administrative rulings affecting the education of students with disabilities.

Publication Date: 1977 Monthly
ISSN: 1094-3773

Kenneth F. Kahn, President

4420 Special Education Law Report
Progressive Business Publications
370 Technology Drive
Malvern, PA 19355
610-695-8600
800-220-5000
Fax: 610-647-8089
customer_service@pbp.com
www.pbp.com
Reports the latest school law cases and late-breaking legislation along with the most recent law review articles affecting special education. Federal and state appellate court decisions are summarized and the full legal citation is supplied for each case.

Publication Date: 1959 Monthly

Ed Satell, Founder
Liz Webb, Human Resources

4421 Special Education Report
LRP Publications
360 Hiatt Drive
Palm Beach Gardens, FL 33418
703-516-7002
800-341-7874
Fax: 561-622-2423
custserve@lrp.com
www.lrp.com
The special education administrator's direct pipeline to federal legislation, regulation and funding of programs for children and youths with disabilities.

Publication Date: 1977 6-8 pages Monthly

Kenneth F. Kahn, President

4422 Student Affairs Today
LRP Publications
360 Hiatt Drive
Palm Beach Gardens, FL 33418
703-516-7002
800-341-7874
Fax: 561-622-2423
custserve@lrp.com
www.lrp.com
Newsletter provides strategies and tips for handling higher education institutions' student affairs challenges and problems involving: sexual harassment, binge drinking, fraternity and sorority activities, student housing and more. Gives profiles of other colleges programs.

Publication Date: 1977 Monthly
ISSN: 1098-5166

Kenneth F. Kahn, President

4423 Superintendents Only Notebook
Master Teacher
Leadership Lane
PO Box 1207
Manhattan, KS 66502
800-669-9633
Fax: 800-669-1132
www.masterteacher.com
Offers superintendents hundreds of solid ideas to help their jobs run more smoothly. Written by practicing superintendents and business executives, this publication saves hundreds of hours of anguish over the course of the year.

Publication Date: 1969 Monthly

Dr. Joanna Hubbs, President
Gregory Hubbs, Editor-in-Chief

4424 THE Journal Technology Horizons in Education
T.H.E Journal
1105 Media
9201 Oakdale Ave., Suite 101
Chatsworth, CA 91311
818-734-1520
Fax: 818-734-1522
editorial@thejournal.com
www.thejournal.com
A forum for administrators and managers in school districts to share their experiences in the use of technology-based educational aids.

Publication Date: 1972

Rajeev Kapur, Chief Executive Officer
Henry Allain, Chief Operating Officer

4425 Thrust for Educational Leadership
Association of California School Administrators
1029 J Street
Suite 500
Sacramento, CA 95814
916-444-3216
800-608-2272
Fax: 916-444-3739
rdelling@lausd.net
www.acsa.org
Designed for school administrators who must stay abreast of educational developments, management and personnel practices, social attitudes and issues that impact schools.

Publication Date: 1971 7x Year

Randall V. Delling, President
Ralph Gomez Porras, Vice President

4426 Title I Handbook
Thompson Publishing Group, Inc.
P.O. Box 41868
Austin, TX 78704
800-677-3789
Fax: 800-999-5661
service@thompson.com
www.titleionline.com
Two-volume looseleaf provides complete, up-to-date coverage of Title I, the largest federal program of aid for elementary and secondary education. The book contains all the laws, regulations and guidance needed to sucessfully operate the grant program, and insightful articles on key Title I topics, ongoing budget coverage, and special reports on issues like Title I testing, schoolwide programs, and audits. Also included is a compilation of official Title I policy letters, found nowhere else.

Publication Date: 1972 1,500 pages Quarterly

Cheryl L. Sattler, Author
Jeannette Burke, Director, Product Marketing
Mark Reishus, Energy Regulation

4427 Title I Monitor
Thompson Publishing Group, Inc.
P.O. Box 41868
Austin, TX 78704
202-872-4000
800-677-3789
Fax: 800-999-5661
service@thompson.com
www.titleionline.com
This newsletter provides continuing coverage of Title I, the largest federal program of aid for elementary and secondary education. Title I is at the heart of the debate over education reform, and the Monitor ensures that educators have the most up-to-date information about developments in this ever-changing program. Breaking news about the Title I budget, new legislation and regulations, court cases and other issues.

Publication Date: 1972 Monthly
ISSN: 1086-2455

Cheryl L Sattler, Author
Jeannette Burke, Director, Product Marketing
Mark Reishus, Energy Regulation

4428 Training Magazine
Lakewood Publications
P.O. Box 247
27020 Noble Road
Excelsior, MN 55331
847-559-7596
800-328-4329
Fax: 847-559-7596
ntrn@omeda.com
www.trainingmag.com
Focuses on corporate training and employee development, as well as management and human performance issues.

Monthly

Mike Murrell, President/ Publisher
Bryan Powell, VP - Finance/Operations

4429 Updating School Board Policies
National School Boards Association
1680 Duke Street
Alexandria, VA 22314
703-838-6722
Fax: 703-683-7590
info@nsba.org
www.nsba.org
Offers information and statistics for school boards and administrative offices across the country.

16 pages BiMonthly
ISSN: 1081-8286

Anne M. Byrne, President
Heather Francis, Executive Assistant

Periodicals / Early Childhood Education

4430 Child Development
Arizona State University
University Drive and Mill Avenue
Tempe, AZ 85287
480-965-9011
Fax: 480-965-8544
www.asu.edu
Offers professionals working with children news on childhood education, books, reviews, questions and answers and professional articles of interest.

BiMonthly

Michael M. Crow, President
Morgan R. Olsen, VP, Business & Finance

4431 Child Study Journal
Buffalo State College
1300 Elmwood Avenue
Buffalo, NY 14222
716-878-4000
suny.buffalostate.edu
Articles of interest related to childhood education.

Publication Date: 1871 Quarterly

Katherine S. Conway-Turner, President

4432 Children Today
ACF Office of Public Affairs
370 L'Enfant Promenade, S.W.
4th Floor
Washington, DC 20447
202-401-9215
888-747-1861
Fax: 202-205-9688
www.acf.hhs.gov/office-of-public-affairs
An interdisciplinary magazine published by the Administration for Children and Families (ACF). The content is a mix of theory and practice, research and features, news and opinions for its audience.

Quarterly

Jeff Hild, Chief of Staff
Mark Greenberg, Assistant Secretary

4433 Children and Families
National Head Start Association
1651 Prince Street
Alexandria, VA 22314
703-739-0875
866-677-8724
Fax: 703-739-0878
www.nhsa.org
Designed to support the Head Start programs, directors, staff, parents and volunteers.

Publication Date: 1973 Quarterly
ISSN: 1091-7578

Vanessa Rich, Vice Chairman
Alvin Jones, Vice Chairman

4434 Division for Children with Communication Disorders Newsletter
The Council for Exceptional Children
2900 Crystal Drive
Suite 1000
Arlington, VA 22202-3557
703-620-3660
888-232-7733
Fax: 703-264-1637
www.cec.sped.org
Information concerning education and welfare of children with communication disorders.

Publication Date: 1922 12 pages SemiAnnually

Robin D. Brewer, President
Alexander T. Graham, Executive Dir./ Secretary

4435 Early Childhood Education Journal
Kluwer Academic/Human Sciences Press
233 Spring Street
New York, NY 10013
212-620-8000
Fax: 212-463-0742
www.wkpa.nl
Provides professional guidance on instructional methods and materials, child development trends, funding and administrative issues and the politics of day care.

Quarterly
ISSN: 1082-3301

Carol Bischoff, Publisher
Mary Renck Jalongo, Editor

4436 Early Childhood Report
LRP Publications
360 Hiatt Drive
Palm Beach Gardens, FL 33418
703-516-7002
800-341-7874
Fax: 561-622-2423
custserve@lrp.com
www.lrp.com
Educational newsletter for parents and professionals involved at the local state and federal levels responsible for the design and implementation of early childhood programs.

Publication Date: 1977 Monthly
ISSN: 1058-6482

Kenneth F. Kahn, President

4437 Early Childhood Research Quarterly
Department of Individuals & Family Syudies
111 Alison Annex
University of Delaware
Newark, DE 19716
302-831-6500
Fax: 302-831-8776
hdfs-dept@udel.edu
www.hdfs.udel.edu
Addresses various topics in the development and education of young children.

Quarterly

Dr. Marion Hyson, Editor

4438 Early Childhood Today
Scholastic
555 Broadway
New York, NY 10012
212-343-6100
800-724-6527
Fax: 212-343-4801
ect@scholastic.com
www.scholastic.com
The magazine for all early childhood professionals working with infants to six-year-olds. Each issue provides child development information resources, staff development information and parent communication information.

Publication Date: 1920 8x Year
ISSN: 1070-1214

Richard Robinson, Chair/ President/ CEO
Maureen O'Connell, EVP/ CFO/ CAO

4439 Highlights for Children
Highlights for Children
PO Box 269
1800 Watermark Drive
Columbus, OH 43216-0269
888-372-6433
www.highlights.com/working-for-highlights
Magazine featuring Fun with a Purpose, to all children preschool to preteen. Features stories, hidden pictures, reading and thinking exercises, crafts, puzzles, and more.

Publication Date: 1946

Kent S. Johnson, CEO
Christine French Cully, Editor in Chief

4440 Journal of Early Intervention
The Council for Exceptional Children
2900 Crystal Drive
Suite 1000
Arlington, VA 22202-3557
703-620-3660
888-232-7733
Fax: 703-264-1637
www.cec.sped.org

Publication Date: 1922 Quarterly
ISSN: 0885-3460

Robin D. Brewer, President
Alexander T. Graham, Executive Dir./ Secretary

4441 Journal of Research in Childhood Education
Association for Childhood Education International
1101 16th St. N.W.
Suite 300
Washington, DC 20036
202-372-9986
800-423-3563
Fax: 202-372-9989
acei.org
Current research in education and related fields. It is intended to advance knowledge and theory of the education of children, from infancy through early adolescence. The journal seeks to stimulate the exchange of research ideas through publication of: reports of empirical research; theroretical articles; ethnographic and case studies; cross-cultural studies and studies addressing international

concerns; participant observation studies and, studies, deriving data collected.

142 pages BiAnnual
ISSN: 0256-8543

Carrie Whaley, President
Diane Whitehead, Executive Director

4442 NHSA Journal
National Head Start Association
1651 Prince Street
Alexandria, VA 22314
703-739-0875
866-677-8724
Fax: 703-739-0878
www.nhsa.org
Edited for Head Start communities serving children 3 to 5 years of age throughout the country. The journal is an invaluable resource containing current research, innovative programming ideas, details on the Head Start conferences and training events.

Publication Date: 1973 Quarterly

Vanessa Rich, Chairman
Alvin Jones, Vice Chairman

4443 National Guild of Community Schools of the Arts
National Guild of Community Schools of the Arts
520 8th Avenue
Suite 302
New York, NY 10018
212-268-3337
Fax: 212-268-3995
info@natguild.org
www.nationalguild.org
National association of community based arts education institutions employment opportunities, guildnotes newsletter, and publications catalog. See www.nationalguild.org.

Monthly

Terry Hueneke, Chairman
Carol Ross, Vice Chairman

4444 Parents Make the Difference!: School Readiness Edition
The Parent Institute
PO Box 7474
Fairfax Station, VA 22039-7474
703-323-9170
800-756-5525
Fax: 703-323-9173
support@parent-institute.com
www.parent-institute.com
Newsletter focusing on parent involvement in education. Focuses on parents of children ages infant to five.

Publication Date: 1989 Monthly
ISSN: 1089-3075

John H. Wherry, Ed.D., President

4445 Pre-K Today
Scholastic
555 Broadway
New York, NY 10012
212-343-6100
800-724-6527
Fax: 212-343-4801
www.scholastic.com
Edited to serve the needs of early childhood professionals, owners, directors, teachers and administrators in preschools and kindergarten.

Publication Date: 1920 8x Year

Richard Robinson, Chair/ President/ CEO
Maureen O'Connell, EVP/ CFO/ CAO

4446 Report on Preschool Programs
Business Publishers
2222 Sedwick Drive
Durham, NC 27713
301-587-6300
800-223-8720
Fax: 800-508-2592
custserv@bpinews.com
www.bpinews.com
Reports on information about Head Start regulations, federal funding policies, state trends in Pre-K and research news. Also covers information on grant and contract opportunities.

Publication Date: 1963 8 pages BiWeekly

Eric Easton, Publisher
Chuck Devarics, Editor

4447 Topics in Early Childhood Special Education
Pro-Ed
8700 Shoal Creek Boulevard
Austin, TX 78757-6897
512-451-3246
800-897-3202
Fax: 512-451-8542
general@proedinc.com
www.proedinc.com
Provides program developers, advocates, researchers, higher education faculty and other leaders with the most current, relevant research on all aspects of early childhood education for children with special needs.

Judith J Carta, PhD, Editor

4448 Totline Newsletter
Frank Schaffer Publications
23740 Hawthorne Boulevard
Torrance, CA 90505
310-378-1137
800-421-5533
Fax: 800-837-7260
fspcustsrv@aol.com
www.frankschaffer.com
Creative activities for working with toddlers and preschool children.

32 pages BiMonthly

4449 Vision
SERVE
5900 Summit Avenue, #201
Browns Summit, NC 27214
336-315-7400
800-755-3277
Fax: 336-315-7457
cahearn@serve.org
www.serve.org
Publication of the Regional Educational Laboratories, an educational research and development organization supported by contracts with the US Education Department, National Institute for Education Sciences. Specialty area: Extended Learning Opportunity including Before and After School programs and Early Childhood.

Quarterly

Charles Ahearn, Author
Wendy McColskey, Program Director
Elliot Wolf, Operations Director

Periodicals / Elementary Education

4450 Children's Literature in Education
Kluwer Academic/Human Sciences Press
233 Spring Street
New York, NY 10013
212-620-8000
Fax: 212-463-0742
www.wkpa.nl
Source for stimulating articles and interviews on noted children's authors, incisive critiques of classic and contemporary writing for young readers, and original articles describing successful classroom reading projects. Offers timely reviews on a variety of reading-related topics for teachers and teachers-in-training, librarians, writers and interested parents.

Quarterly
ISSN: 0045-6713

Margaret Mackey & Geoff Fox, Editors, Author
Carol Bischoff, Publisher

4451 Creative Classroom
Creative Classroom Publishing
149 5th Avenue
12th Floor
New York, NY 10010
212-353-3639
Fax: 212-353-8030
www.creativeclassroom.com
A magazine for teachers of K-8, containing innovative ideas, activities, classroom management tips and information on contemporary social problems facing teachers and students.

BiMonthly

Susan Eveno, Editorial Director
Laura Axler, Associate Editor

4452 Dragonfly
National Science Teachers Association
1840 Wilson Boulevard
Arlington, VA 22201
703-243-7100
800-782-6782
Fax: 703-243-7177
boardofdirectors@nsta.org
www.nsta.org
A fun-filled interdisciplinary magazine for children grades 3-6. A teacher's companion is also available. The teacher's companion is designed to help you integrate Dragonfly into your curriculum.

Publication Date: 1944

Juliana Texley, President
Dr. David L. Evans, Executive Director

4453 Educate@Eight
US Department of Education, Region VIII
1244 Speer Boulevard
Suite 310
Denver, CO 80204-3582
303-844-3544
Fax: 303-844-2524
www.ed.gov

8 pages

Helen Littlejohn, Author

4454 Elementary School Journal
University of Missouri
1507 E Broadway
Hillcrest Hall
Columbia, MO 65211
573-882-2121
missouri.edu
Academic journal publishing primarily original studies but also reviews of research and conceptual analyses for researchers and practitioners interested in elementary schooling. Emphasizes papers dealing with educational theory and research and their implications.

Publication Date: 1839 5x Year

R. Bowen lLoftin, Chancellor
Kenneth D. Dean, Interim Provost

4455 Elementary Teacher's Ideas and Materials Workshop
Princeton Educational Publishers
117 Cuttermill Road
NY, NY 11021-3101
516-466-9300
Articles on teaching for elementary schools.
16 pages 10x Year
Barry Pavelec

4456 Helping Your Child Succeed in Elementary School
Rowman & Littlfield Education
4501 Forbes Boulevard
Suite 200
NY, MD 20706
301-459-3366
Fax: 301-429-5748
customercare@rowman.com
www.rowmaneducation.com
Provides parents with useful information about the importance of parental involvement, concrete ways to work with children and schools to promote success, and a list of resources for further reading.
Tom Koerner, PhD, VP & Publisher
Dean Roxanis, Sr. Marketing Manager

4457 Highlights for Children
Highlights for Children
PO Box 269
1800 Watermark Drive
Columbus, OH 43216-0269
888-372-6433
Fax: 614-876-8564
www.highlights.com/working-for-highlights
Magazine featuring Fun with a Purpose, to all children preschool to preteen. Features stories, hidden pictures, reading and thinking exercises, crafts, puzzles, and more.
Publication Date: 1946
Kent S. Johnson, CEO
Christine French Cully, Editor in Chief

4458 Independent School
National Association of Independent Schools
1129 20th Street, NW
Suite 800
Washington, DC 20036-3425
202-973-9700
Fax: 888-316-3862
www.nais.org
Contains information and opinion about secondary and elementary education in general and independent education in particular.
TriAnnually
Thomas W Leonhardt, Editor
Kurt R Murphy, Advertising/Editor

4459 Instructor
Scholastic
555 Broadway
New York, NY 10012
212-343-6100
800-724-6527
Fax: 212-343-4801
www.scholastic.com
Edited for teachers, curriculum coordinators, principals and supervisors of primary grades through junior high school.
Publication Date: 1920 Monthly
Richard Robinson, Chair/ President/ CEO
Maureen O'Connell, EVP/ CFO/ CAO

4460 Journal of Research in Childhood Education
Association for Childhood Education International
1101 16th St., N.W.
Suite 300
Washington, DC 20036
202-372-9986
800-423-3563
Fax: 202-372-9989
cwhaley@uu.edu
acei.org
Current research in education and related fields. It is intended to advance knowledge and theory of the education of children, from infancy through early adolescence. The journal seeks to stimulate the exchange of research ideas through publication of: reports of empirical research; theroretical articles; ethnographic and case studies; cross-cultural studies and studies addressing international concerns; participant observation studies and, studies, deriving data collected.
Publication Date: 1892 142 pages BiAnnual
ISSN: 0256-8543
Carrie Whaley, President
Diane Whitehead, Executive Director

4461 Montessori LIFE
American Montessori Society
281 Park Avenue S
6th Floor
New York, NY 10010
212-358-1250
Fax: 212-358-1256
kate@amshq.org
www.amshq.org
Magazine for parents and educators.
Publication Date: 1960 Quarterly
ISSN: 1054-0040
Joy Turner, Author
Joyce S. Pickering, President
Dane L. Peters, Vice President

4462 Parents Make the Difference!
The Parent Institute
PO Box 7474
Fairfax Station, VA 22039-7474
703-323-9170
800-756-5525
Fax: 703-323-9173
support@parent-institute.com
www.parent-institute.com
Newsletter focusing on parent involvement in children's education. Focuses on parents of preschool-aged children.
Publication Date: 1989 9x Year
John H. Wherry, Ed.D., President

4463 Teaching K-8 Magazine
Early Years
40 Richards Avenue
Norwalk, CT 06854-2319
203-855-2650
800-249-9363
Fax: 203-855-2656
patricia@teachingk-8.com
www.teachingk-8.com
Written for teachers in the elementary grades, kindergarten through eighth, offering classroom tested ideas and methods.
Monthly Magazine
ISSN: 0891-4508
November-December
Allen A Raymond, Publisher
Patricia Broderick, Editorial Director

Periodicals / Employment

4464 AACE Careers Update
American Association for Career Education
2900 Amby Place
Hermosa Beach, CA 90254
310-376-7378
Fax: 310-376-2926
Connects careers, education and work through career education for all ages. Career awareness, exploration, decision making, and preparation. Employability, transitions, continuing education, paid and nonpaid work, occupations, career tips, resources, partnerships, conferences and workshops. Awards and recognition, trends and futures. A newsletter is published.
8+ pages Quarterly/Newsletter
ISBN: 1074-9551
Dr.Pat Nellor Wickwire, Author
Dr. Pat Nellor Wickwire, Editor

4465 Career Development for Exceptional Individuals
The Council for Exceptional Children
2900 Crystal Drive
Suite 1000
Arlington, VA 22202-3557
703-620-3660
888-232-7733
Fax: 703-264-9494
www.cec.sped.org
Contains articles dealing with the latest research activities, model programs, and issues in career development and transition planning for individuals with disabilities and/or who are gifted.
Publication Date: 1922 2x Year
Robin D. Brewer, President
Alexander T. Graham, Executive Dir./ Secretary

4466 Career Education News
Diversified Learning
72300 Vallat Road
Rancho Mirage, CA 92270-3906
619-346-3336
Reports on programs, materials and training for career educators.
4 pages BiWeekly
Webster Wilson Jr, Publisher
Webster Wilson, Editor

4467 Careers Bridge Newsletter
St. Louis Public Schools
801 N. 11th Street
Saint Louis, MO 63101
314-231-3720
www.slps.org
Available to educators and business/community persons on collaborative activities and promotion of career and self-awareness education in preschool to grade 12.
BiMonthly
Dr. Kelvin Adams, Superintendent
Roger CayCe, Interim Chief of Staff

4468 Chronicle of Higher Education
Subscription Department
163 E. Center Street
Marion, OH 43302
740-387-0400
800-347-6969
www.marionstar.com
Newspaper published weekly advertising many teaching opportunities overseas.
Weekly
Adam Trabitz, Sales Director
Kelly Gearhart, Sales Manager

4469 Current Openings in Education in the USA
Education Information Services
100 Walnut Street
Newton, MA 02460
617-559-6000
www.newton.k12.ma.us
This publication is a booklet listing about 140 institutions or school systems, each with one to a dozen or more openings for teachers, librarians, counselors and other personnel.
15 pages Every 6 Weeks
F Viaux, Coordinating Education

4470 Education Jobs
National Education Service Center
PO Box 1279
Riverton, WY 82501-1279
307-856-0170
Offers information on employment in the education field.
Weekly
Lucretia Ficht, Contact

4471 Employment Opportunities
National Guild of Community Schools of the Arts
520 8th Avenue
Suite 302
New York, NY 10018
212-268-3337
Fax: 212-268-3995
info@natguild.org
www.nationalguild.org
Monthly
Terry Hueneke, Chairman
Carol Ross, Vice Chairman

4472 Faculty, Staff & Administrative Openings in US Schools & Colleges
Educational Information Services
PO Box 662
Newton Lower Falls, MA 02162
617-964-4555
A listing of available positions in the educational system in the United States.
Monthly

4473 International Educator
The International Educator
PO Box 513
Cummaquid, MA 02637
508-790-1990
877-375-6668
Fax: 508-790-1922
tie@tieonline.com
www.tieonline.com/contact_us.cfm
A newspaper listing over 100 teaching positions overseas.
Publication Date: 1986 Quarterly
Daniel Lincoln, Editor
Nikki Gundry, Ad Sales Rep.

4474 Jobs Clearinghouse
Association for Experiential Education
1435 Yarmouth Ave
#104
Boulder, CO 80304
303-440-8844
Fax: 303-440-9581
jch@aee.org
www.aee.org
A newsletter that is one of the most comprehensive and widely-used monthly listings of full-time, part-time, and seasonal employment and internship opportunities in the experiential/adventure education field for both employers and job seekers.
Monthly
Maurie Lung, President
Robert Smariga, CEO

4475 Journal of Cooperative Education
University of Waterloo
200 University Avenue West
Waterloo, ON N2L 3
519-888-4567
519-885-1211
uwaterloo.ca
Dedicated to the publication of thoughtful and timely articles concerning work-integrated education. It invites manuscripts which are essays that analyze issues, reports of research, descriptions of innovative practices.
Publication Date: 1957 3x Year
Feridun Hamdullahpur, President/ Vice-Chancellor
Ian Orchard, VP Academic & Provost

4476 Journal of Vocational Education Research
Colorado State University
202 Education
Fort Collins, CO 80523
970-491-6835
Fax: 970-491-1317
questions@online.colostate.edu
www.colostate.edu
Publishes refereed articles dealing with research and research-related topics in vocational education. Manuscripts based on original investigations, comprehensive reviews of literature, research methodology and theoretical constructs in vocational education are encouraged.
Quarterly
Brian Cobb, Editor

4477 New Jersey Education Law Report
Whitaker Newsletters
313 S Avenue
#340
Fanwood, NJ 07023-1364
908-889-6336
800-359-6049
Fax: 908-889-6339
Court decisions and rulings on employment in New Jersey schools.
8 pages
ISSN: 0279-8557
Joel Whitaker, Publisher
Fred Rossu, Editor

4478 SkillsUSA Champions
SkillsUSA Inc.
14001 SkillsUSA Way
Leesburg, VA 20176-5494
703-777-8810
Fax: 703-777-8999
anyinfo@skillsusa.org
www.skillsusa.org
To individuals interested in cultivating leaderships skills, SkillsUSA is a dynamic resource that inspires and connencts all members creating a virtual community through its revalent and useful content.
28 pages Quarterly
ISSN: 1040-4538
Ahmad Shawwal, President
Dalton Lee Crump, Vice President

4479 VEWAA Newsletter
Vocational Evaluation & Work Adjustment Assn.
1234 Haley Circle
Auburn University
Auburn, AL 36849
334-844-3800
Info@vewaa.com
www.vewaa.com
News and information about the practice of vocational evaluation and work adjustment.
8 pages Quarterly
Ronald Fru, Publisher
Clarence D Brown, Editor

4480 Views & Visions
Wisconsin Vocational Association
44 E Mifflin Street
Suite 104
Madison, WI 53703-2800
608-283-2595
Fax: 608-283-2589
For teachers of vocational and adult education.
8 pages BiMonthly
Linda Stemper

4481 Vocational Training News
Aston Publications
701 King Street
Suite 444
Alexandria, VA 22314-2944
703-683-4100
800-453-9397
Fax: 703-739-6517
Contains timely, useful reports on the federal Job Training Partnership Act and the Carl D Perkins Vocational Education Act. Other areas include literacy, private industry councils and training initiatives.
10 pages Weekly
Cynthia Carter, Publisher
Matthew Dembicki, Editor

Periodicals / Financial Aid

4482 American-Scandinavian Foundation Magazine
American-Scandinavian Foundation
58 Park Avenue
New York, NY 10016-5025
212-779-3587
info@amscan.org
www.amscan.org
Covers politics, culture and lifestyles of Denmark, Finland, Iceland, Norway and Sweden.
100 pages Quarterly Magazine
Edward P Gallagher, President
Christian Sonne, Deputy Chairman

4483 Education Grants Alert
LPR Publications
360 Hiatt Drive
Palm Beach Gardens, FL 33418-2944
703-516-7002
800-341-7874
Fax: 561-622-2423
custserve@lrp.com
www.lrp.com
Dedicated to helping schools increase funding for K-12 programs. This newsletter will uncover new and recurring grant competitions from federal agencies that fund school projects, plus scores of corporate and foundation sources.
Publication Date: 1977 Weekly
Kenneth F. Kahn, President

4484 **Federal Research Report**
Business Publishers
2222 Sedwick Drive
Durham, NC 27713
301-587-6300
800-223-8720
Fax: 800-508-2592
custserv@bpinews.com
www.bpinews.com
Identifies critical funding sources supplying administrator's with contact names, addresses, telephone numbers, RFP numbers and other vital details.
Publication Date: 1963 8 pages Weekly
Eric Easton, Publisher
Leonard Eiserer, Editor

4485 **Foundation & Corporate Grants Alert**
LRP Publishing
360 Hiatt Drive
Palm Beach Gardens, FL 33418
703-516-7002
800-341-7874
Fax: 561-622-2423
custserv@lrp.com
www.lrp.com
Offers information on funding trends, new foundations and hard-to-find regional funders. You'll also get to foundation and corporate funders from the inside, with foundation profiles and interviews with program officers.
Publication Date: 1977 Monthly
Kenneth F. Kahn, President

4486 **Grants for School Districts Monthly**
Quinlan Publishing
23 Drydock Avenue
Boston, MA 02210-2336
617-542-0048
Listing of grants available for schools across the country.
Monthly

4487 **Informativo**
LASPAU (Latin America Scholarship Program)
25 Mount Auburn Street
Suite 300
Cambridge, MA 02138-6095
617-495-5255
angelica_natera@harvard.edu
www.laspau.harvard.edu
Administers scholarships for staff members nominated by Latin American and Caribbean education and development organizations and other public and private sector entities.
Publication Date: 1964 8 pages SemiAnnually
Jeff Coburn, Chair
Fernando Reimers, Vice Chair

4488 **NASFAA Newsletter**
National Assn. of Student Financial Aid Admin.
1101 Connecticut Avenue NW
Suite 1100
Washington, DC 20036-4303
202-785-0453
Fax: 202-785-1487
www.nasfaa.org
News covering student financial aid legislation and regulations.
24 pages SemiMonthly
Eileen O'Leary, National Chair
Justin Draeger, President/ CEO

4489 **United Student Aid Funds Newsletter**
PO Box 6180
Indianapolis, IN 46206-6180
317-578-6094
USA Funds Education Loan products and services information.
8 pages BiMonthly
Nelson Scharadin, Publisher
Dena Weisbard, Editor

Periodicals / Guidance & Counseling

4490 **ASCA Counselor**
American Counseling Association
6101 Stevenson Ave.
Alexandria, VA 22304
703-823-9800
800-347-6647
Fax: 703-823-0252
membership@counseling.org
www.counseling.org
Aimed at the guidance counselor.
16 pages BiMonthly
Robert L. Smith, Ph.D., NCC, FPPR, President
Richard Yep, CEO

4491 **Adolescence**
Libra Publishers
3089C Clairemont Drive
San Diego, CA 92117-6802
858-571-1414
Fax: 858-571-1414
librapublishers@juno.com
Articles contributed by professionals spanning issues relating to teenage education, counseling and guidance. Paperback.
256 pages Quarterly
ISSN: 0001-8449
Jon Kroll, Editor
William Kroll, Author

4492 **Attention**
CHADD
4601 Presidents Drive
Suite 300
Lanham, MD 20706
301-306-7070
800-233-4050
Fax: 301-306-7090
help@chadd.org
www.chadd.org
Magazine for children and adults with Attention Deficit/Hyperactivity Disorder, and their families.
Publication Date: 1987 48 pages Bi-Monthly
ISSN: 1551-0980
70+ booths with 1,400 attendees and 70+ exhibits
Michael F. MacKay, JD, CPA, MSIA, President
Susan Buningh, MRE, Executive Editor

4493 **Before You Can Discipline**
Master Teacher
Leadership Lane
PO Box 1207
Manhattan, KS 66505-1207
800-669-9633
Fax: 800-669-1132
www.masterteacher.com
Understand exactly how student's primary and secondary needs can and do influence acceptable and unacceptable behavior. Develop professional attitudes toward discipline problems and learn the laws and principals of managing people.
Publication Date: 1969 170 pages
ISBN: 0-914607-03-0
Robert L DeBruyn, Author
Dr. Joanna Hubbs, President
Gregory Hubbs, Editor-in-Chief

4494 **Child Psychiatry & Human Development**
Kluwer Academic/Human Sciences Press
233 Spring Street
New York, NY 10013
212-620-8000
800-221-9369
Fax: 212-463-0742
www.wkpa.nl
Interdisciplinary international journal serving the groups represented by child psychiatry, clinical child/pediatric/family psychology, pediatrics, social science, and human development. Publishes research on diagnosis, assessment, treatment, epidemiology, development, advocacy, training, cultural factors, ethics, policy, and professional issues as related to clinical disorders in children, adolescents and families.
Quarterly
ISSN: 0009-398X
Carol Bischoff, Publisher
Kenneth J Tarnowski, Editor

4495 **Child Welfare**
Child Welfare League of America
440 1st Street NW
Suite 310
Washington, DC 20001-2085
202-688-4200
Fax: 202-833-1689
cwla@cwla.org
www.cwla.org
Publication Date: 1920 BiMonthly
Joesph M. Costa, Chair
Julie Sweeney-Springwater, Vice Chair

4496 **Child and Adolescent Social Work Journal**
Kluwer Academic/Human Sciences Press
233 Spring Street
New York, NY 10013
212-620-8000
800-221-9369
Fax: 212-463-0742
www.wkpa.nl
Features original articles that focus on clinical social work practice with children, adolescents and their families. The journal addresses current issues in the field of social work drawn from theory, direct practice, research, and social policy, as well as focuses on problems affecting specific populations in special settings.
Bimonthly
ISSN: 0738-0151
Carol Bischoff, Publisher
Thomas Kenemore, Editor

4497 **College Board News**
College Board Publications
45 Columbus Avenue
New York, NY 10023
212-713-8000
800-323-7155
Fax: 800-525-5562
www.collegeboard.org
Sent free to schools and colleges several times a year, the News reports on the activities of the College Board. Its articles inform readers about the Board's services in such areas as high school, guidance, college admis-

sion, curriculum and placement, testing, financial aid, adult education and research.

Publication Date: 1900

David Coleman, President/ CEO
Jeremy Singer, COO

4498 College Board Review
College Board Publications
45 Columbus Avenue
New York, NY 10023
212-713-8000
800-323-7155
Fax: 800-525-5562
www.collegeboard.org
Each issue of the Review probes key problems and trends facing education professionals concerned with student transition from high school to college.

Publication Date: 1900

David Coleman, President/ CEO
Jeremy Singer, COO

4499 College Times
College Board Publications
45 Columbus Avenue
New York, NY 10023
212-713-8000
800-323-7155
Fax: 800-525-5562
www.collegeboard.org
This annual magazine is a one-stop source to college admission. It provides valuable advice to help students through the complex college selection, application and admission process.

Publication Date: 1900 32 pages Package of 50

David Coleman, President/ CEO
Jeremy Singer, COO

4500 Communique
National Association of School Psychologists
4340 EW Highway
Suite 402
Bethesda, MD 20814
301-657-0270
866-331-NASP
Fax: 301-657-0275
sgorin@naspweb.org
www.nasponline.org

50 pages 8x Year
ISSN: 0164-775X

Stephen E. Brock, President
Susan Gorin, Executive Director

4501 Counseling & Values
American Counseling Association
6101 Stevenson Ave.
Alexandria, VA 22304
703-823-9800
800-347-6647
Fax: 703-823-0252
membership@counseling.org
www.counseling.org
Editorial content focuses on the roles of values and religion in counseling and psychology.

3x Year

Robert L. Smith, Ph.D., NCC, FPPR, President
Richard Yep, CEO

4502 Counseling Today
American Counseling Association
6101 Stevenson Ave.
Alexandria, VA 22304
703-823-9800
800-347-6647
Fax: 703-823-0252
membership@counseling.org
www.counseling.org
Covers national and international counseling issues and reports legislative and governmental activities affecting counselors.

Monthly

Robert L. Smith, Ph.D., NCC, FPPR, President
Richard Yep, CEO

4503 Counselor Education & Supervision
American Counseling Association
6101 Stevenson Ave.
Alexandria, VA 22304
703-823-9800
800-347-6647
Fax: 703-823-0252
membership@counseling.org
www.counseling.org
Covers counseling theories, techniques and skills, teaching and training.

Quarterly

Robert L. Smith, Ph.D., NCC, FPPR, President
Richard Yep, CEO

4504 ERIC Clearinghouse on Counseling & Student Services
ERIC Clearinghouse on Counseling and Student Servi
201 Ferguson Building UNCG
Greensboro, NC 27412
910-334-4114
800-414-9769
Fax: 910-334-4116
ericcas2@hamlet.uncg.edu
cecp.air.org/teams/stratpart/ericccss.asp
Covers news about ERIC and the counseling clearinghouse and developments in the fields of education and counseling.

4 pages Quarterly

David Osher, Director
Mary Quinn, Deputy Director

4505 Educational & Psychological Measurement
Sage Publications
2455 Teller Road
Thousand Oaks, CA 91320
805-499-9774
800-818-7243
Fax: 800-583-2665
journals@sagepub.com
www.sagepub.com

Quarterly

Sara Miller Mccune, Founder/ Chairman
Blaise R. Simqu, President & CEO

4506 Elementary School Guidance & Counseling
American Counseling Association
6101 Stevenson Ave.
Alexandria, VA 22304-3300
703-823-9800
800-347-6647
Fax: 703-823-0252
membership@counseling.org
www.counseling.org
Journal concerned with enhancing the role of the elementary, middle school and junior high school counselor.

Quarterly
ISSN: 0013-5976

Robert L. Smith, Ph.D., NCC, FPPR, President
Richard Yep, CEO

4507 Family Relations
Miami University
501 E. High St.
Oxford, OH 45056
513-529-4909
Fax: 513-529-7270
miamioh.edu

Publication Date: 1809 Quarterly

Dr. David C. Hodge, President
Robin Parker, General Counsel

4508 Family Therapy: The Journal of the California Graduate School of Family Psychology
Libra Publishers
3089C Clairemont Drive
San Diego, CA 92117-6802
858-571-1414
Fax: 858-571-1414
Articles contributed by professionals spanning issues relating to teenage education, counseling and guidance. Paperback.

96 pages Quarterly
ISSN: 0091-6544

William Kroll, Editor

4509 Health & Social Work
National Association of Social Workers
750 First Street NE
Suite 800
Washington, DC 20002
202-408-8600
800-638-8799
Fax: 202-336-8311
membership@naswdc.org
www.socialworkers.org
Covers practice, innovation, research, legislation, policy , planning, and all the professional issues relevant to social work services in all levels of education.

Publication Date: 1955

Darrell P. Wheeler, PhD, MPH, ACSW, President
Angelo McClain, PhD, LICSW, CEO

4510 ICA Quarterly
Western Illinois University
1 University Circle
Macomb, IL 61455
309-298-1414
Fax: 309-298-3253
info@wiu.edu
www.wiu.edu
Official publication of the Illinois Counseling Association. Focus is on material of interest and value to professional counselors.

Publication Date: 1899 Quarterly

Dr. Jack Thomas, President
Dr. Kenneth Hawkinson, Provost & Academic VP

4511 International Journal of Play Therapy
401 Clovis Avenue
Suite 107
Clovis, CA 93612
559-298-3400
Fax: 559-298-3410
info@a4pt.org
www.a4pt.org
Qarterly peer-reviewed journal presenting scholarly articles on the subject of play therapy and related research, case studies, theoretical applications and current practices.

Quarterly

Edward Hudspeth, Clinical Editor

4512 Journal for Specialists in Group Work
American Counseling Association
6101 Stevenson Ave.
Alexandria, VA 22304-3302

703-823-9800
800-347-6647
Fax: 703-823-0252
membership@counseling.org
www.counseling.org
Contains theory, legal issues and current literature reviews.

Quarterly

Robert L. Smith, Ph.D., NCC, FPPR, President
Richard Yep, CEO

4513 Journal of Child and Adolescent Group Therapy
Kluwer Academic/Human Sciences Press
233 Spring Street
New York, NY 10013
212-620-8000
800-221-9369
Fax: 212-463-0742
www.wkpa.nl
Addresses the whole spectrum of professional issues relating to juvenile and parent group treatment. Promotes the exchange of new ideas from a wide variety of disciplines concerned with enhancing treatments for this special population. The multidisciplinary contributions include clinical reports, illustrations of new technical methods, and studies that contribute to the advancement of therapeutic results, as well as articles on theoretical issues, applications, and the group process.

Quarterly
ISSN: 1053-0800

Carol Bischoff, Publisher
Edward S Soo, Editor

4514 Journal of College Admission
Nat'l Association for College Admission Counseling
1050 N Highland Street
Suite 400
Alexandria, VA 22201
703-836-2222
800-822-6285
Fax: 703-243-9375
info@nacacnet.org
www.nacac.com
Membership association offering information to counselors and guidance professionals working in the college admissions office.

Publication Date: 1937 32 pages Quarterly
ISSN: 0734-6670

Elaina Loveland, Author
Jeff Fuller, President
Joyce E. Smith, CEO

4515 Journal of Counseling & Development
American Counseling Association
6101 Stevenson Ave.
Alexandria, VA 22304
703-823-9800
800-347-6647
Fax: 703-823-0252
membership@counseling.org
www.counseling.org
A quarterly journal that publishe articles that have broad interest for a readership composed mostly of couselors and other mental health professionals who work in private practice, schools, colleges, community agencies, hospitals and government.

ISBN: 0748-9633

Robert L. Smith, Ph.D., NCC, FPPR, President
Richard Yep, CEO

4516 Journal of Counseling and Development
American Counseling Association
6101 Stevenson Ave.
Alexandria, VA 22304-3302
703-823-9800
800-347-6647
Fax: 703-823-0252
membership@counseling.org
www.counseling.org
Edited for counseling and human development specialists in schools, colleges and universities.

Monthly

Robert L. Smith, Ph.D., NCC, FPPR, President
Richard Yep, CEO

4517 Journal of Drug Education
California State University
18111 Nordhoff Street
Northridge, CA 91330
818-677-1200
Fax: 818-677-2045
www.csun.edu
Offers information to counselors and guidance professionals dealing with areas of drug and substance abuse education in the school system.

Publication Date: 1958 Quarterly

Dianne F. Harrison, President
Colin Doanhue, VP & CFO

4518 Journal of Emotional and Behavioral Disorders
Pro-Ed
8700 Shoal Creek Boulevard
Austin, TX 78757-6897
512-451-3246
800-897-3202
Fax: 512-451-8542
general@proedinc.com
www.proedinc.com
Presents high-quality interdisciplinary scholarship in the area of emotional and behavioral disabilities. Explores issues including youth violence, emotional problems among minority children, long-term foster care placement, mental health services, social development and educational strategies.

Michael H Epstein, EdD, Editor
Douglas Cullinan, EdD, Editor

4519 Journal of Employment Counseling
American Counseling Association
6101 Stevenson Ave.
Alexandria, VA 22304-3302
703-823-9800
800-347-6647
Fax: 703-823-0252
membership@counseling.org
www.counseling.org
Editorial content includes developing trends in case studies and newest personnel practices.

Quarterly

Robert L. Smith, Ph.D., NCC, FPPR, President
Richard Yep, CEO

4520 Journal of Humanistic Education and Development
Ohio University
1 Ohio University
345 Baker University Center
Athens, OH 45701
740-593-1000
Fax: 740-593-0569
deanofstudents@ohio.edu
www.ohio.edu
Focuses on the humanities and promotes their place in the educational system.

Publication Date: 1786 Quarterly

David Brightbill, Chair
David A. Wolfort, Vice Chair

4521 Journal of Multicultural Counseling & Development
American Counseling Association
6101 Stevenson Ave.
Alexandria, VA 22304-3302
703-823-9800
800-347-6647
Fax: 703-823-0252
membership@counseling.org
www.counseling.org
Contains articles with focus on research, theory and program application related to multicultural counseling.

Quarterly

Robert L. Smith, Ph.D., NCC, FPPR, President
Richard Yep, CEO

4522 Journal of Sex Education & Therapy
American Association of Sexuality Educators Counse
1444 I Street, NW
Suite 700
Washington, DC 20005
202-449-1099
Fax: 202-216-9646
info@aasect.org
www.aasect.org
Provides education and training in all areas of sexual health.

Publication Date: 1967 110 pages Quarterly
ISSN: 0161-4576

Michael Plant, Author
Pat Schiller, MA, JD, Founder

4523 Measurement & Evaluation in Counseling and Development
American Counseling Association
6101 Stevenson Ave.
Alexandria, VA 22304-3302
703-823-9800
800-347-6647
Fax: 703-823-0252
membership@counseling.org
www.counseling.org
Editorial focuses on research and applications in counseling and guidance.

Quarterly

Robert L. Smith, Ph.D., NCC, FPPR, President
Richard Yep, CEO

4524 NACAC Bulletin
Nat'l Association for College Admission Counseling
1050 N Highland Street
Suite 400
Alexandria, VA 22201
703-836-2222
800-822-6285
Fax: 703-243-9375
info@nacacnet.org
www.nacac.com
Membership association offering information to counselors and guidance professionals working in the college admissions office.

Publication Date: 1937 Monthly

Jeff Fuller, President
Joyce E. Smith, CEO

4525 NASW News
National Association of Social Workers
750 First Street NE
Suite 800
Washington, DC 20002
202-408-8600
800-638-8799
Fax: 301-206-7989
membership@naswdc.org
www.naswdc.org
Features in-depth coverage of developments in social work practice, news of national social policy developments, political and legislative news in social services, noteworthy achievements of social workers and association news.

Publication Date: 1955 Monthly

Darrell P. Wheeler, PhD, MPH, ACSW, President
Angelo McClain, PhD, LICSW, CEO

4526 National Coalition for Sex Equity in Education
PO Box 534
Annandale, NJ 08801
908-735-5045
Fax: 908-735-9674
info@ncsee.org
www.ncsee.org
The only national organization for gender equity specialists and educators. Individuals and organizations committed to reducing sex role stereotyping for females and males. Services include an annual national training conference, a quarterly newsletter and a membership directory. Members may join task forces dealing with equity related topics such as computer/technology issues, early childhood, male issues, sexual harassment prevention, sexual orientation and vocational issues.

Quarterly Newsletter

Theodora Martin, Business Manager

4527 New Horizons
National Registration Center for Study Abroad
PO Box 1393
Milwaukee, WI 53201
414-278-0631
Fax: 414-271-8884
study@nrcsa.com
www.nrcsa.com
Provides information about member institution's programs and establishes standards for treatment of visitors from abroad including the appointment of bilingual housing officers and counselors to deal with culture shock.

Publication Date: 1968 16 pages Quarterly
ISBN: 1-977864-43-3

Anne Wittig, Author
Mike Wittig, General Manager

4528 Rehabilitation Counseling Bulletin
Pro-Ed
8700 Shoal Creek Boulevard
Austin, TX 78757-6897
512-451-3246
800-897-3202
Fax: 512-451-8542
general@proedinc.com
www.proedinc.com
International journal providing original empirical research, essays of a theoretical nature, methodological treatises and comprehensive reviews of the literature, intensive case studies and research critiques.

Quarterly Magazine
ISSN: 0034-3552

Douglas Strohmer, PhD, Editor

4529 School Counselor
American Counseling Association
6101 Stevenson Ave.
Alexandria, VA 22304-3302
703-823-9800
800-347-6647
Fax: 703-823-0252
membership@counseling.org
www.counseling.org
Includes current issues and information affecting teens and how counselors can deal with them.

5x Year

Robert L. Smith, Ph.D., NCC, FPPR, President
Richard Yep, CEO

4530 School Psychology Review
National Association of School Psychologists
4340 EW Highway
Suite 402
Bethesda, MD 20814
301-657-0270
866-331-NASP
Fax: 301-657-0275
sgorin@naspweb.org
www.nasponline.org

170 pages Quarterly
ISSN: 0279-6015

Susan Gorin, Executive Director
Laura Benson, COO

4531 Social Work Research Journal
National Association of Social Workers
750 First Street NE
Suite 800
Washington, DC 20002
202-408-8600
800-638-8799
Fax: 202-336-8311
membership@naswdc.org
www.socialworkers.org
Contains orginal research papers that contribute to knowledge about social work issues and problems. Topics include new technology, strategies and methods, and research results.

Publication Date: 1955 Quarterly
ISSN: 1070-5309

Darrell P. Wheeler, PhD, MPH, ACSW, President
Angelo McClain, PhD, LICSW, CEO

4532 Social Work in Education
National Association of Social Workers
750 First Street NE
Suite 800
Washington, DC 20002
202-408-8600
Fax: 202-336-8310
membership@naswdc.org
www.socialworkers.org
Covers practice, innovation, research, legislation, policy, planning, and all the professional issues relevant to social work services in all levels of education.

Publication Date: 1955

Darrell P. Wheeler, PhD, MPH, ACSW, President
Angelo McClain, PhD, LICSW, CEO

4533 SocialWork
National Association of Social Workers
750 First Street NE
Suite 800
Washington, DC 20002
202-408-8600
800-638-8799
Fax: 202-336-8311
membership@naswdc.org
www.socialworkers.org
Covers important research findings, critical analyses, practice issues, and information on current social issues such as AIDS, homelessness, and federal regulation of social programs. Case management, third-party reimbursement, credentialing, and other professional issues are addressed.

Publication Date: 1955

Darrell P. Wheeler, PhD, MPH, ACSW, President
Angelo McClain, PhD, LICSW, CEO

4534 Today's School Psychologist
LRP Publications
360 Hiatt Drive
Palm Beach Gardens, FL 33418
703-516-7002
800-341-7874
Fax: 561-622-2423
custserve@lrp.com
www.lrp.com/ed
An in-depth guide to a school psychologist's job, offering practical strategies and tips for handling day-to-day responsibilites, encouraging change, and improving professional standing and performance.

Publication Date: 1977 Monthly
ISSN: 1098-9277

Kenneth F. Kahn, President

4535 Washington Counseletter
Chronicle Guidance Publications
66 Aurora Street
Moravia, NY 13118-3569
315-497-0330
800-622-7284
Fax: 315-497-3359
customerservice@chronicleguidance.com
www.chronicleguidance.com
Monthly report highlighting federal, state, and local developments affecting the counseling and education professions. Items list events, programs, activities and publications of interest to counselors and educators.

Publication Date: 1938 8 pages 8x Year

Cheryl Fickeisen, President/ CEO
Gary Fickeisen, Vice President

Periodicals / Language Arts

4536 AATF National Bulletin
American Association of Teachers of French
P.O. Box 2617
Carbondale, IL 62902-2617
815-310-0490
Fax: 815-310-5754
abrate@siu.edu
www.frenchteachers.org
Announcements and short articles relating to the association on French language and cultural activities.

Publication Date: 1995 30-50 pages 5x Year

Mary Helen Kashuba, SSJ, President
Jayne Abrate, Executive Director

4537 ACTFL Newsletters
American Council on the Teaching of Foreign Lang.
1001 N. Fairfax Street
Suite 200
Alexandria, VA 22314
703-894-2900
Fax: 914-963-1275
www.actfl.org/
A quarterly newsletter containing topical and timely information on matters of interest to foreign language educators. Regular columns in-

clude Languages in the News and Washington Watch.

20 pages Quarterly

Jacque Bott Van Houten, President
Marty Abbott, Executive Director

4538 ADE Bulletin
Association of Departments of English
26 Broadway
Third Floor
New York, NY 10004-1789
646-576-5133
Fax: 646-835-4056
dlaurence@mla.org
www.ade.org
This bulletin concentrates on developments in scholarship, curriculum and teachers in English.

64 pages
ISSN: 0001-0888

David Laurence, Director
Doug Steward, Associate Director

4539 Beyond Words
1534 Wells Drive NE
Albuquerque, NM 87112-6383
505-275-2558
Offers information on literature, language arts and English for the teaching professional.

10x Year

4540 Bilingual Research Journal
National Association for Bilingual Education
8701 Georgia Ave.
Suite 700
Siver Spring, MD 20910
240-450-3700
Fax: 240-450-3799
nabe@nabe.org
www.nabe.org
Journal published by National Association for Bilingual Education.

Publication Date: 1972 Quarterly
8,000 attendees

Julio Cruz, Ed.D., President
Jose A. Ruiz-Escalante, Ed.D., Vice President

4541 Bilingual Review Press
Arizona State University
PO Box 877705
Tempe, AZ 85287-7705
480-965-8972
Fax: 480-965-0865
www.asu.edu
Offers information and reviews on books, materials and the latest technology available to bilingual educators.

3x Year

Gary D Keller, President

4542 CEA Forum
E-mail: jmcdaniel30@radford.edu
journals.tdl.org
Online peer-reviewed journal publishing articles on professional issues and pedagogy related to the teaching of college English.

Jamie McDaniel, Editor
Morgan Ebbs, Assistant Editor

4543 Classroom Notes Plus
National Council of Teachers of English
1111 W Kenyon Road
Urbana, IL 61801-1096
217-328-3870
877-369-6283
Fax: 217-328-9645
executivecommittee@ncte.org
www.ncte.org
Secondary periodical for English/Language Arts featuring usable teaching ideas for teachers by teachers.

Publication Date: 1911 16 pages Quarterly

Kathy G. Short, President
Susan Houser, Vice President

4544 Communication Disorders Quarterly
Pro-Ed., Inc.
8700 Shoal Creek Boulevard
Austin, TX 78757-6897
512-451-3246
800-897-3202
Fax: 512-451-8542
general@proedinc.com
www.proedinc.com
Research, intervention and practice in speech, language and hearing.

Quarterly Magazine
ISSN: 1525-7401

Alejandro Brice, Editor

4545 Communication: Journalism Education Today
Truman High School
3301 S Noland Road
Independence, MO 64055
816-521-2710
Fax: 816-521-2913
sites.isdschools.org/truman
Provides educational perspectives to JEA members— mostly high schools journalism editors— on a wide variety of topics such as teaching/advising issues, scholastic media strategy, pedagogical updates, current journalism research and other professional and technological concerns.

Publication Date: 1964 Quarterly
ISBN: 1536
ISSN: 9129

Pam Boatright, President
Bradley Wilson, Editor

4546 Composition Studies Freshman English News
De Paul University
1 E. Jackson Blvd.
Chicago, IL 60604
312-362-8000
800-4DE-PAUL
Fax: 773-325-7328
dpcl@depaul.edu
www.depaul.edu/
Theoretical and practical articles on rhetorical theory.

Publication Date: 1898 44 pages SemiAnnually

Rev. Dennis H. Holtschneider, CM, EdD, President
Robert L. Kozoman, EVP

4547 Council-Grams
National Council of Teachers of English
1111 W Kenyon Road
Urbana, IL 61801-1096
217-328-3870
800-369-6283
Fax: 217-328-9645
executivecommittee@ncte.org
www.ncte.org
Offers information and updates in the areas of English, language arts and reading.

Publication Date: 1911 16 pages 5x Year

Kathy G. Short, President
Susan Houser, Vice President

4548 Counterforce
Society for the Advancement of Good English
4501 Riverside Avenue
#30
Anderson, CA 96007-2759
530-365-8026
Offers updates and information for English teachers and professors.

Quarterly

4549 English Education
NYU Steinhardt
239 Greene Street
6th Floor
New York, NY 10003
212-998-5460
Fax: 212-998-4049
ce33@nyu.edu
steinhardt.nyu.edu/teachlearn/english
Offers information about educational programs for English teachers and professors to develop their skills for the classroom.

Maryrose Cordero, Operations Administrator
Cherrelle Hall, Department Administrator

4550 English Journal
National Council of Teachers of English
1111 W Kenyon Road
Urbana, IL 61801-1096
217-328-3870
800-369-6283
Fax: 217-328-9645
executivecommittee@ncte.org
www.ncte.org
An ideal magazine for middle school, junior and senior high school English teachers.

Publication Date: 1911 Biannual
ISSN: 0013-8274

Kathy G. Short, President
Susan Houser, Vice President

4551 English Leadership Quarterly
National Council of Teachers of English
1111 W Kenyon Road
Urbana, IL 61801-1096
217-328-3870
800-369-6283
Fax: 217-328-9645
executivecommittee@ncte.org
www.ncte.org
Teaching of English for secondary school English Department chairpersons.

Publication Date: 1911 12 pages Quarterly

Kathy G. Short, President
Susan Houser, Vice President

4552 English for Specific Purposes
University of Michigan
500 South State Street
Ann Arbor, MI 48109
734-764-1817
Fax: 619-594-6530
sgrafton@umich.edu
www.umich.edu
Concerned with English education and its importance to the developing student.

Publication Date: 1817 3x Year

Janey Lack, Chair
Steve Grafton, President/ CEO

4553 Foreign Language Annals
American Council on the Teaching of Foreign Lang.
1001 N. Fairfax Street
Suite 200
Alexandria, VA 22314
703-894-2900
Fax: 914-963-1275
www.actfl.org

Dedicated to advancing all areas of the profession of foreign language teaching. It seeks primarily to serve the interests of teachers, administrators and researchers, regardless of educational level of the language with which they are concerned. Preference is given in this scholarly journal to articles that describe innovative and successful teaching methods, that report educational research or experimentation, or that are relevant to the concerns and problems of the profession.

128 pages Quarterly

Jacque Bott Van Houten, President
Marty Abbott, Executive Director

4554 Journal of Basic Writing
City University of NY, Instructional Resource Ctr.
535 E 80th Street
New York, NY 10021-0767
212-794-5445
Fax: 212-794-5706
Publishes articles of theory, research and teaching practices related to basic writing. Articles are referred by members of the Editorial Board and the editors.

Spring & Fall

Karen Greenberg, Editor
Trudy Smoke, Editor

4555 Journal of Children's Communication Development
The Council for Exceptional Children
2900 Crystal Drive
Suite 1000
Arlington, VA 22202-3557
703-620-3660
888-232-7733
Fax: 703-264-9494
robin.brewer@unco.edu
www.cec.sped.org
Provides in-depth research and practical application articles in communication assessment and intervention. The journal frequently contains a practitioner's section that addresses professional questions, reviews tests and therapy materials, and describes innovative programs and service delivery models.

Publication Date: 1922 2x Year
ISSN: 0735-3170

Robin D. Brewer, President
Alexander T. Graham, Executive Dir./Secretary

4556 Journal of Teaching Writing
Indiana Teachers of Writing
425 University Boulevard CA 345
Indianapolis, IN 46202
317-274-4777
Fax: 317-278-1287
jtw@iupui.edu
www.iupui.edu/~jtw
A refereed journal for classroom teachers and researchers at all academic levels whose interest or emphasis is the teaching of writing. Appearing semiannually, JTW publishes articles on the theory, practice, and teaching of writing throughout the curriculum. Each issue covers a range of topics, from composition theory and discourse analysis to curriculum development and innovative teaching techniques. Contributors are reminded to tailor their writing for a diverse readership.

12-20 pages Semiannually

Dr. Kim Brian Lovejoy, Editor
Kay Halasek, Reviews Editor

4557 Journalism Quarterly
George Washington University
2121 Eye Street, NW
Washington, DC 20052
202-994-1000
Fax: 202-994-5806
www.gwu.edu
Information on all facets of writing and journalism for the student and educator.

Publication Date: 1821 Quarterly

Nelson A. Carbonell, Jr., Chair
Steven Knapp, President

4558 Language & Speech
Kingston Press Services, Ltd.
43 Derwent Road, Whitton
Twickenham, Middlesex TW2 7HQ
United Kingdom
0-20-8893-3015
Fax: 208-893-3015
sales@kingstonepress.com
www.kingstonepress.com
Includes psychological research articles, speech perception, speech production, psycholinguistics and reading.

Quarterly

4559 Language Arts
National Council of Teachers of English
1111 W Kenyon Road
Urbana, IL 61801-1096
217-328-3870
800-369-6283
Fax: 217-328-9645
executivecommittee@ncte.org
www.ncte.org
Edited for instructors in language arts at the elementary level.

Publication Date: 1911 Monthly

Kathy G. Short, President
Susan Houser, Vice President

4560 Language, Speech & Hearing Services in School
Ohio State University
281 W. Lane Ave.
Columbus, OH 43210
614-292-OHIO
Fax: 614-292-7504
www.osu.edu
Interested in innovative technology and growth in language development in schools.

Jeffery Wadsworth, Chair
Ronald A. Ratner, Vice Chair

4561 Merlyn's Pen: Fiction, Essays and Poems by America's Teens
11 South Angell St.
Suite 301
Providence, RI 02906
401-751-3766
800-247-2027
Fax: 401-751-3766
merlyn@merlynspen.org
www.merlynspen.com
Merlyns' Pen magazine is a selective publisher of model writing by America's students in grades 6-12. Products include Merlyn's Pen magazine (a reproducible annual magazine) and the American Teen Writer Series, collections of anthologized short fiction and nonfiction by brilliant teen writers. Used for models, inspiration, and instruction in literature and writing.

Publication Date: 1985 100 pages Annually
ISSN: 0882-2050

R. James Stahl, Editor

4562 Modern Language Journal
Case Western Reserve University
10900 Euclid Ave.
Cleveland, OH 44106
216-368-2000
Fax: 216-368-2216
www.case.edu

Publication Date: 1826 Quarterly

Barbara R. Snyder, President
William A. Baeslack III, Provost & EVP

4563 NABE News
National Association for Bilingual Education
8701 Georgia Ave.
Suite 700
Siver Spring, MD 20910-4018
240-450-3700
Fax: 240-450-3799
nabe@nabe.org
www.nabe.org
Magazine published by the National Association for Bilingual Education.

Publication Date: 1972 Bi-Monthly

Julio Cruz, Ed.D., President
Jose A. Ruiz-Escalante, Ed.D., Vice President

4564 NASILP Journal
Temple University
1801 N. Broad Street
Philadelphia, PA 19122
215-204-7000
www.temple.edu
Articles, news and book reviews on language instructional methodology.

Publication Date: 1884 12 pages SemiAnnually

Neil D. Theobald, President

4565 National Clearinghouse for Bilingual Education Newsletter
George Washington University
2121 Eye Street, NW
Washington, DC 20052
202-994-1000
800-321-6223
askncbe@ncbe.gwu.edu
www.gwu.edu
Provides information to practitioners on the education of language minority students.

Publication Date: 1821 Weekly

Nelson A. Carbonell, Jr., Chair
Steven Knapp, President

4566 PCTE Bulletin
Williamsport Area Community College
One College Avenue
Williamsport, PA 17701
570-326-3761
800-367-9222
www.pct.edu
Focuses on Pennsylvania literacy issues.

Publication Date: 1970 SemiAnnually

Sen. Gene Yaw, Chair
Dave Jane Gilmour, Ph.D., President

4567 Quarterly Journal of Speech
National Communication Association
1765 N Street NW
Washington, DC 20036
202-464-4622
Fax: 202-464-4600
inbox@natcom.org
www.natcom.org
Main academic journal in the speech/communication field of education.

Publication Date: 1914 Quarterly

Carole Blair, President
Christina S. Beck, 1st VP

4568 Quarterly Review of Doublespeak
National Council of Teachers of English
1111 W Kenyon Road
Urbana, IL 61801-1096
217-328-3870
800-369-6283
Fax: 217-328-9645
executivecommittee@ncte.org
www.ncte.org
Provides information on the misuses and abuse of language.
Publication Date: 1911 8 pages Quarterly
Kathy G. Short, President
Susan Houser, Vice President

4569 Quarterly of the NWP
National Writing Project
2105 Bancroft Way
Suite 1042
Berkeley, CA 94720-1042
510-642-0963
Fax: 510-642-4545
nwp@nwp.org
www.writingproject.org
Journal on the research in and practice of teaching writing at all grade levels.
40 pages Quarterly Magazine
ISSN: 0896-3592
Art Peterson, Amy Bauman; Editors, Author
Judith Warren Little, Chair
Elyse Eidman-Aadahl, Executive Director

4570 Quill and Scroll
University of Iowa School of Journalism
100 Adler Journalism Builing
Iowa City, IA 52242
319-335-3457
Fax: 319-335-3989
quill-scroll@uiowa.edu
www.uiowa.edu
Founded and distributed for the purpose of encouraging and rewarding individual achievements in journalism and allied fields. This magazine is published bimonthly during the school year and has a variety of pamphlets and lists of publications available as resources.
BiMonthly
Richard P Johns, Executive Director

4571 Research in the Teaching of English
Harvard Graduate School of Education
Larsen Hall
Appian Way
Cambridge, MA 02138
617-495-3521
Fax: 617-495-0540
www.gse.harvard.edu
A research journal devoted to original research on the relationships between teaching and learning for language development in reading, writing and speaking at all age levels.
Publication Date: 1920 Quarterly
Sandra Stotsky, Editor

4572 Rhetoric Review
University of Arizona
Department of English
Tucson, AZ 85721
520-621-2211
Fax: 520-621-7397
www.arizona.edu
A journal of rhetoric and composition publishing scholarly and historical studies, theoretical and practical articles, views of the profession, review essays of professional books, personal essays about writing and poems.
Publication Date: 1885 200+ pages Quarterly
ISSN: 0735-0198
Ann Weaver Hart, President
Andrew DuMont, Executive Communication Mngr

4573 Slate Newsletter
National Council of Teachers of English
1111 W Kenyon Road
Urbana, IL 61801-1096
217-328-3870
800-369-6283
Fax: 217-328-9645
executivecommittee@ncte.org
www.ncte.org
Short articles on topics such as censorship, trends and issues and testing.
Publication Date: 1911
Kathy G. Short, President
Susan Houser, Vice President

4574 Studies in Second Language Acquisition
Cambridge University Press
1105 Atwater
Bloomington, IN 47401-5020
812-855-6874
Fax: 812-855-2386
ssla@indiana.edu
www.indiana.edu/~ssla
Referred journal devoted to problems and issues in second and foreign language acquisition of any language.
140 pages Quarterly Paperback
ISSN: 0272-2631
Albert Valdman, Editor

4575 TESOL Journal: A Journal of Teaching and Classroom Research
Teachers of English to Speakers of Other Languages
1925 Ballenger Avenue
Suite 550
Alexandria, VA 22314-6820
703-836-0774
888-547-3369
Fax: 703-836-7864
info@tesol.org
www.tesol.org
TESOL's mission is to develop the expertise of its members and others involved in teaching English to speakers of other languages to help them foster communication in diverse settings. The association advances standards for professional preparation and employment, continuing education, and student programs, produces programs, services, and products, and promotes advocacy to further the profession. TESOL has 91 affiliates worldwide.
Publication Date: 1963 50 pages Quarterly
Yilin Sun, President
Rosa Aronson, Executive Dir./ Secretary

4576 TESOL Quarterly
Teachers of English to Speakers of Other Languages
1925 Ballenger Avenue
Suite 550
Alexandria, VA 22314-6820
703-836-0774
888-547-3369
Fax: 703-836-7864
info@tesol.org
www.tesol.org
TESOL Quarterly is our scholarly journal containing articles on academic research, theory, reports, reviews. Articles about linguistics, ethnographies, and more describe the theoretic basis for ESL/EFL teaching practices. Readership is approximately 23,400.
Publication Date: 1963 830 pages Quarterly
Yilin Sun, President
Rosa Aronson, Executive Dir./ Secretary

4577 Writing Lab Newsletter
Purdue University, Department of English
500 Oval Drive
W. Lafayette, IN 47907
765-494-3740
Fax: 765-494-3780
wln@purdue.edudue.edu
www.cla.purdue.edu/english
Monthly newsletter for readers involved in writing centers and/or one-to-one instruction in writing skills.
Publication Date: 1955 16 pages Monthly/Newsletter
ISSN: 1040-3779
Nancy Peterson, Department Head
Ryan Schneider, Dir. Of Graduate Studies

Periodicals / Library Services

4578 ALA Editions Catalog
American Library Association
50 East Huron Street
Chicago, IL 60611-2795
312-944-6780
800-545-2433
Fax: 312-836-9958
ala@ala.org
www.ala.org
Contains over 1,000 job listings, news and reports on the latest technologies in 11 issues annually. Also scholarships, grants and awards are possibilities.
Publication Date: 1853 Annually
Courtney Young, President
Keith Michael Fiels, Executive Director

4579 American Libraries
American Library Association
50 East Huron Street
Chicago, IL 60611-2795
312-944-6780
800-545-2433
Fax: 312-836-9958
ala@ala.org
www.ala.org
The magazine of the American Library Association that is published six times a year and distributed to more than 65,000 individuals.
Publication Date: 1853
ISBN: 0002-9769
Courtney Young, President
Keith Michael Fiels, Executive Director

4580 Booklist
American Library Association
50 East Huron Street
Chicago, IL 60611-2795
312-944-6780
800-545-2433
Fax: 312-836-9958
ala@ala.org
www.ala.org
A guide to current print and audiovisual materials worthy of consideration for purchase by small and medium-sized public libraries and school library media centers.
Publication Date: 1853 Semimonthly
Courtney Young, President
Keith Michael Fiels, Executive Director

4581 Catholic Library World
Catholic Library Association
8550 United Plaza Blvd.
Baton Rouge, LA 19041-1412
225-408-4417
sbaron@regent.edu
www.cathla.org
A periodical geared toward the professional librarian in order to keep them abreast of new publications, library development, association news and technology.
Publication Date: 1921 Quarterly
Sara R. Baron, President
Mary Kelleher, VP/ Treasurer

4582 Choice
Current Reviews for Academic Libraries
100 Riverview Center
Middletown, CT 06457-3445
860-347-6933
Fax: 860-346-8586
adsales@ala-choice.org
www.ala.org/acrl/choice
A magazine distributed to librarians and other organizations that analyzes various materials, offers book reviews and information on the latest technology available for the library acquisitions departments.
11x Year
Steven Conforti, Subscriptions Manager
Stuart Foster, Advertising Manager

4583 ILA Reporter
The Illinois Library Association
33 W Grand Avenue
Suite 401
Chicago, IL 60654-6799
312-644-1896
Fax: 312-644-1899
ila@ila.org
www.ila.org
30 pages
ISSN: 0018-9979
Jeannie Dilger, President
Betsy Adamowski, VP/ President Elect

4584 Information Technology & Libraries
University of the Pacific
3601 Pacific Avenue
Stockton, CA 95211
209-946-2285
Fax: 209-946-2805
President@Pacific.edu
www.pacific.edu
Offers information on the latest technology, systems and electronics offered to the library market.
Quarterly
Pamela Eibeck, President
Ken Mullen, VP, Business & Finance

4585 Journal of Education for Library and Information Sciences
Kent State University
800 E. Summit St.
Kent, OH 44240
330-672-3000
Fax: 330-672-7965
info@kent.edu
www.kent.edu
The latest information on books, publications, electronics and technology for the librarian.
Publication Date: 1910 Quarterly
Beverly Warren, President
Edward G. Mahon, Vice President

4586 Libraries & Culture
University of Texas at Austin/Univ. of Texas Press
PO Box 7819
Austin, TX 78713-7819
512-471-3434
Fax: 512-232-7178
dgdavis@gslis.utexas.edu
www.utexas.edu
An interdisciplinary journal that explores the significance of collections of recorded knowledge. Scholarly articles and book reviews cover international topics dealing with libraries, books, reviews, archives, personnel, and their history; for scholars, librarians, historians, readers interested in the history of books and libraries.
Publication Date: 1883 100 pages Quarterly
ISSN: 0894-8631
William Powers, Jr., President
Gregory L. Fenves, EVP & Provost

4587 Library Collections, Acquisitions & Technical Services
Pergamon Press, Elsevier Science
The Boulevard, Lanngford Lane
Kidlington, Oxford
United Kingdom
614-292-4738
Fax: 614-292-7859
deidrichs.1@osu.edu
www.elsvier.com
Offers information on policy, practice, and research on the collection management and technical service areas of libraries.
500 pages Quarterly
ISSN: 1464-9055
Carol Pitts Diedrichs, Editor

4588 Library Issues: Briefings for Faculty and Administrators
Mountainside Publishing Company
PO Box 8330
Ann Arbor, MI 48107
734-662-3925
Fax: 734-662-4450
sales@libraryissues.com
www.libraryissues.com
Offers overviews of the trends and problems affecting campus libraries. Explained in layman's terms as they relate to faculty, administrators and the parent institution.
Publication Date: 1980 4-6 pages
Bi-Monthly
ISSN: 0734-3035
Richard M. Dougherty, Editor
Ann P. Dougherty, Managing Editor

4589 Library Quarterly
Indiana University, School of Library Science
1320 E. 10th Street
LI 011
Bloomington, IN 47405-3907
812-855-2018
888-335-7547
Fax: 812-855-6166
ilsmain@indiana.edu
www.ils.indiana.edu
Updates, information, statistics, book reviews and publications for librarians.
Quarterly
David Cole, Manager, IT Hardware
Jane M. Lewis, ILS Business Dir.

4590 Library Resources & Technical Services
Columbia University, School of Library Sciences
116th Street and Broadway
New York, NY 10027
212-854-1754
Fax: 212-854-8951
askcuit@columbia.edu
www.columbia.edu
Publication Date: 1754 Quarterly
Lee C. Bollinger, President
John H. Coatsworth, Provost

4591 Library Trends
Grad. School Library & Info. Science
501 E Daniel Street
MC-493
Champaign, IL 61820-6211
217-333-3280
Fax: 217-244-3302
dstroud@illinois.edu
www.lis.illinois.edu
A scholarly quarterly devoted to invited papers in library and information science. Each issue is devoted to a single theme.
208 pages Quarterly
Allen Renear, Chair
Carol Tilley, Chair, Admissions

4592 Media & Methods Magazine
American Society of Educators
1429 Walnut Street
Philadelphia, PA 19102-3218
215-563-6005
Fax: 215-587-9706
info@media-methods.com
www.media-methods.com
Leading pragmatic magazine for K-12 educators and administrators. The focus is on how to integrate today's technologies and presentation tools into the curriculum. Very up-to-date and well respected national source publication. Loyal readers are media specialists, school librarians, technology coordinators, administrators and classroom teachers.
5x Year
Michele Sokoloff, Publisher
Christine Weiser, Editor

4593 NEWSletter
New Jersey Library Association
PO Box 1534
Trenton, NJ 08607
609-394-8032
Fax: 609-394-8164
ptumulty@njla.org
njla.org
A quarterly newsletter and distributed to more than 1,800 members, serves as a vehicle for communication of library issues and activities among members of NJLA.
Terrie McColl, President
James Keehbler, Vice President

4594 Read, America!
Place in the Woods
3900 Glenwood Avenue
Golden Valley, MN 55422-5302
763-374-2120
Fax: 952-593-5593
readamerica10732@aol.com
News, book reviews, ideas for librarians and reading program leaders; short stories and poetry pages for adults and children; and an annual Read America! collection with selections of new books solicited from 350 publishers.
12 pages Quarterly Newsletter
ISSN: 0891-4214
Roger Hammer, Editor/Publisher

4595 School Library Journal
School Library Journal
123 William St., Suite 802
New York, NY 10038
646-380-0700
Fax: 646-380-0756

slj@mediasourceinc.com
www.schoollibraryjournal.com
For children, young adults and school librarians.

Kathy Ishizuka, Executive Editor
Rebecca T. Miller, Editor-in-Chief

4596 School Library Media Activities Monthly
LMS Associates
2205 West Division
Suite A-9
Arlington, TX 76012
301-685-8621
800-725-7377
lms@lmsassociates.com
lmsassociates.com

Monthly

Steve Langston, President
Michael Fiedler, GM/ Sales Rep.

4597 School Library Media Quarterly
American Library Association
50 East Huron Street
Chicago, IL 60611-2795
312-944-6780
800-545-2433
Fax: 312-836-9958
ala@ala.org
www.ala.org
For elementary and secondary building level library media specialists, district supervisors and others concerned with the selection and purchase of print and nonprint media.

Publication Date: 1853 Quarterly

Courtney Young, President
Keith Michael Fiels, Executive Director

4598 Southeastern Librarian (SELn)
Southeastern Library Association
PO Box 950
Rex, GA 30273
678-466-4334
Fax: 678-466-4349
gordonbaker@clayton.edu
selaonline.org
This quarterly publication seeks to publish articles, announcements and news of professional interest to the library community in the southeast. The publication also represents a significant means for addressing the Association's research objective. Two newsletter-style issues serve as a vehicle for conducting Association business, and two issues include juried articles.

Publication Date: 1920

Camille McCutcheon, President
Sue Alexander, Secretary

4599 Special Libraries
Special Libraries Association
331 South Patrick Street
Alexandria, VA 22314-3501
703-647-4900
Fax: 703-647-4901
www.sla.org
Includes information and manuscripts on the administration, organization and operation of special libraries.

Publication Date: 1909 Quarterly

Jill Strand, President
Linda Broussard, CFO

4600 Specialist
Special Libraries Association
1700 18th Street NW
Washington, DC 20009-2514
703-647-4900
Fax: 703-647-4901
www.sla.org
Contains news and information about the special library/information field.

Publication Date: 1909 Monthly

Jill Strand, President
Linda Broussard, CFO

4601 TLACast
Texas Library Association
3355 Bee Cave Road
Suite 401
Austin, TX 78746-6763
512-328-1518
800-580-2852
Fax: 512-328-8852
tla@txla.org
www.txla.org
The association's online newsletter that is published several times a year to keep members informed on TLA issues and events.

Publication Date: 1902

Sharon Amastae, President
Patricia H. Smith, Executive Director

4602 Teacher Librarian
301-805-2191
dlevitov@teacherlibrarian.com
teacherlibrarian.com
Professional journal targeted to the specific needs and concerns of librarians and teachers working with K-12 students. The focus is on the role of the school librarian, as an educator.

Deborah D Levitov, Ph.D, Editor
Christie Kaaland, Associate Editor

4603 Texas Library Journal
Texas Library Association
3355 Bee Cave Road
Suite 401
Austin, TX 78746-6763
512-328-1518
800-580-2852
Fax: 512-328-8852
tla@txla.org
www.txla.org

Publication Date: 1902
ISBN: 0040-4446

Sharon Amastae, President
Patricia H. Smith, Executive Director

Periodicals / Mathematics

4604 Focus on Learning Problems in Math
Center for Teaching/Learning Math
754 Old Connecticut Path
Framingham, MA 01701-7747
508-877-7895
Fax: 508-788-3600
mahesh@mathematicsforall.org
www.mathematicsforall.org
An interdisciplinary journal. Edited jointly by the Research Council for Diagnostic and Prescription Mathematics and the Center for Teaching/Learning of Mathematics. The objective of focus is to make available the current research, methods of identification, diagnosis, and remediation of learning problems in mathematics. Contribution from the fields of education psychology and mathematics having the potential to import on classroom or clinical practice are valued.

64-96 pages Quarterly

Mahesh Sharma, Editor/ Founder

4605 Journal for Research in Mathematics Education
National Council of Teachers of Mathematics
1906 Association Drive
Reston, VA 20191-1502
703-620-9840
Fax: 703-476-2970
nctm@nctm.org
www.nctm.org
A forum for disciplined inquiry into the teaching and learning of math at all levels—from preschool through adult. Available in print or online version.

5x Year
ISSN: 0021-8251

Diane J. Briars, President
Bob Doucette, Executive Director

4606 Journal of Computers in Math & Science
PO Box 2966
Charlottesville, VA 22902-2966
804-973-3087
Fax: 703-997-8760

Quarterly

4607 Journal of Recreational Mathematics
4761 Bigger Road
Kettering, OH 45440-1829
631-691-1470
Fax: 631-691-1770
Promotes the creative practice of mathematics for educational learning.

Quarterly

Joseph S Madachy, Editor

4608 Math Notebook
Center for Teacher/Learning Math
754 Old Connecticut Path
Framingham, MA 01701-7747
508-877-7895
Fax: 508-788-3600
mahesh@mathematicsforall.org
www.mathematicsforall.org
A publication for teachers and parents to improve mathematics instruction.

4x/5x Year

Mahesh Sharma, Editor/ Founder

4609 Mathematics & Computer Education
MAYTC Journal
PO Box 158
Old Bethpage, NY 11804-0158
516-822-5475
Contains a variety of articles pertaining to the field of mathematics.

TriAnnually

George Miller, Editor

4610 Mathematics Teacher
National Council of Teachers of Mathematics
1906 Association Drive
Reston, VA 20191-1502
703-620-9840
Fax: 703-476-2970
nctm@nctm.org
www.nctm.org
Devoted to the improvement of mathematics instruction in grades 9 and higher.

Monthly
ISSN: 0025-5769

Diane J. Briars, President
Bob Doucette, Executive Director

4611 Mathematics Teaching in the Middle School
National Council of Teachers of Mathematics
1906 Association Drive
Reston, VA 20191-1593
703-620-9840
Fax: 703-476-2970
nctm@nctm.org
www.nctm.org
Addresses the learning needs of students in grades 5-9.
Monthly
ISSN: 1072-0839
Diane J. Briars, President
Bob Doucette, Executive Director

4612 NCTM News Bulletin
National Council of Teachers of Mathematics
1906 Association Drive
Reston, VA 20191-9988
703-620-9840
Fax: 703-476-2970
nctm@nctm.org
www.nctm.org
Publication that reaches all of NCTM's individual and institutional members of more than 107,000 math teachers and school personnel.
Diane J. Briars, President
Bob Doucette, Executive Director

4613 Notices of the American Mathematical Society
American Mathematical Society
201 Charles Street
Providence, RI 2904-2294
401-455-4000
800-321-4267
Fax: 401-331-3842
www.ams.org
Announces programs, meetings, conferences and symposia of the AMS and other mathematical groups.
Publication Date: 1888 10x Year
David A. Vogan, Jr., President
Dr. Donald McClure, Executive Director

4614 SSMart Newsletter
School Science & Mathematics Association
University of Alabama Birmingham
School of Education EB 246B
Birmingham, AL 35924-1250
205-934-5067
Fax: 570-389-3894
office@ssma.org
www.ssma.org
Membership news offering information, updates, reviews, articles and association news for professionals in the science and mathematics fields of education.
8 pages Quarterly
Gilbert Naizer, President
Carla Johnson, Editor

4615 Teaching Children Mathematics
National Council of Teachers of Mathematics
1906 Association Drive
Reston, VA 20191-1502
703-620-9840
Fax: 703-476-2970
nctm@nctm.org
www.nctm.org
Concerned primarily with the teaching of mathematics from Pre-K through grade 6.
Monthly
ISSN: 1073-5836
Diane J. Briars, President
Bob Doucette, Executive Director

Periodicals / Music & Art

4616 American Academy of Arts & Sciences Bulletin
American Academy of Arts & Sciences
136 Irving Street
Cambridge, MA 02138
617-576-5000
Fax: 617-576-5050
www.amacad.org
Covers current news of the Academy as well as developments in the arts and sciences.
Publication Date: 1780
Don M. Randel, Chair
Jonathan F. Fanton, President

4617 Art Education
National Art Education Association
1806 Robert Fulton Drive
Suite 300
Reston, VA 20191
703-860-8000
Fax: 703-860-2960
info@arteducators.org
www.arteducators.org
A professional journal in the field of art education devoted to articles on all education levels.
Publication Date: 1947 6x Year
Dennis Inhulsen, President
Dr. Deborah B. Reeve, Executive Director

4618 Arts & Activities
Arts & Activities Magazine
12345 World Trade Drive
San Diego, CA 92128
858-605-0242
subs@artsandactivities.com
www.artsandactivities.com
For classroom teachers, art teachers and other school personnel teaching visual art from kindergarten through college levels.
Monthly
ISSN: 0004-3931

4619 Arts Education Policy Review
Heldref Publications
325 Chestnut Street
Suite 800
Philadelphia, PA 19106
215-625-8900
800-365-9753
Fax: 202-296-5149
customer.service@taylorandfrancis.com
www.heldref.org
Discusses major policy issues concerning K-12 education in the various arts. The journal presents a variety of views rather than taking sides and emphasizes analytical exploration. Its goal is to produce the most insightful, comprehensive and rigorous exchange of ideas ever available on arts education. The candid discussions are a valuable resource for all those involved in the arts and concerned about their role in education.
40 pages BiWeekly
ISSN: 1063-2913
Leila Saad, Managing Editor

4620 CCAS Newsletter
Council of Colleges of Arts & Sciences
c/o The College of William & Mary
PO Box 8795
Williamsburg, VA 23187-8795
757-221-1784
Fax: 757-221-1776
ccas@wm.edu
www.ccas.net
Membership newsletter to inform deans about arts and sciences issues in education.
Publication Date: 1965 4-10 pages BiMonthly
Timothy D. Johnston, President
Kate Conley, Treasurer

4621 Choral Journal
American Choral Directors Association
PO Box 6310
Lawton, OK 73506-0310
903-935-7963
Fax: 903-934-8114
jmoore@etbu.edu
acda.org/page.asp%3Fpage%3Dwomenschoirhistory
Publishes scholarly, practical articles and regular columns of importance to professionals in the fields of choral music and music education. Articles explore conducting teachnique, rehearsal strategies, historical performance practice, choral music history and teaching materials.
Publication Date: 1980 Monthly
Amy Blosser, Chair
Karen Fulmer, President

4622 Clavier
The Instrumentalist
200 Northfield Road
Northfield, IL 60093
847-446-5000
Fax: 847-446-6263
members@schooltheatre.org
www.schooltheatre.org
Published 10 times each year for piano and organ teachers, with issues in all months except June and August.
Monthly

4623 Dramatics
Educational Theatre Association
2343 Auburn Avenue
Cincinnati, OH 45219-2815
513-421-3900
Fax: 513-421-7077
members@schooltheatre.org
www.schooltheatre.org
Magazine published by Educational Theatre Association, a professional association for theatre educators/artists.
Monthly
Jay Seller, Ph.D., President
Frank Pruet, Vice President

4624 Flute Talk
The Instrumentalist
200 Northfield Road
Northfield, IL 60093
847-446-5000
888-446-6888
Fax: 847-446-6263
advertising@theinstrumentalist.com
theinstrumentalist.com
Published 10 times each year for flute teachers and intermediate or advanced students, with issues every month except June and August.
Monthly

4625 Instrumentalist
The Instrumentalist
200 Northfield Road
Northfield, IL 60093

847-446-5000
888-446-6888
Fax: 847-446-6263
advertising@theinstrumentalist.com
theinstrumentalist.com
Published 12 times each year for band and orchestra directors and teachers of instruments in these groups.
Monthly

4626 Journal of Experiential Education
Association of Experiential Education
1435 Yarmouth Ave
#104
Boulder, CO 80304
303-440-8844
Fax: 303-440-9581
aewert@indiana.edu
www.aee.org
A professional journal that publishes articles in outdoor adventure programming, service learning, environmental education, therapeutic applications, research and theory, the creative arts, and much more. An invaluable reference tool for anyone in the field of experiential education.
3x Year
ISSN: 1053-8259
Maurie Lung, President
Robert Smariga, CEO

4627 Journal of the American Musicological Society
American Musicological Society
6010 College Station
Brunswick, ME 04011
207-798-4243
877-679-7648
Fax: 207-798-4254
ams@ams-net.org
www.ams-net.org
One of the premier journals in the field, the Journal of the American Musicological Society(JAMS) publlishes scholarship from all fields of musicalinquiry:from historical musicology, critical theory, music analysis, iconographyand organology, to performance practice, aesthetics and hermeneutics, ethnomusicology, gender and sexuality, popular music and cultural studies.
ISBN: 0003
ISSN: 0139
Annegret Fauser, Editor-in-Chief
Louise Goldberg, Assistant Editor

4628 Music Educators Journal
National Association for Music Education
1806 Robert Fulton Drive
Reston, VA 20191
703-860-4000
Fax: 703-860-1531
memberservices@nafme2.org
www.nafme.org
Offers informative, timely and accurate articles, editorials, and features to a national audience of music educators.
Publication Date: 1907 BiMonthly
ISSN: 0027-4321
Frances Ponick, Editor, Author
Glenn E. Nierman, President/ Chair
Michael A. Butera, Executive Director/ CEO

4629 Music Educators Journal and Teaching Music
National Association for Music Education
1806 Robert Fulton Drive
Reston, VA 20191
703-860-4000
Fax: 703-860-4826
memberservices@nafme2.org
www.nafme.org
Informative, timely and accurate articles, editorials, and features to a national audience of music educators.
Publication Date: 1907 BiMonthly
ISSN: 1069-7446
Glenn E. Nierman, President/ Chair
Michael A. Butera, Executive Director/ CEO

4630 NAEA News
National Art Education Association
1806 Robert Fulton Drive
Suite 300
Reston, VA 20191
703-860-8000
Fax: 703-860-2960
info@arteducators.org
www.naea-reston.org
National, state and local news affecting visual arts education.
24 pages BiMonthly
Dr. Thomas Hatfield, Executive Director

4631 National Guild of Community Schools of the Arts
National Guild of Community Schools of the Arts
520 8th Avenue
Suite 302
New York, NY 10018
212-268-3337
Fax: 212-268-3995
info@natguild.org
www.nationalguild.org
National association of community based arts education institutions employment opportunities, guildnotes newsletter, and publications catalog.
Monthly
Terry Hueneke, Chairman
Carol Ross, Vice Chairman

4632 Oranatics Journal
Educational Theatre Association
2343 Auburn Avenue
Cincinnati, OH 45219-2815
513-451-3900
Fax: 513-421-7077
members@schooltheatre.org
www.schooltheatre.org
Promotes and strengthens theatre in education - primarily middle school and high school. Sponsors an honor society, various events, numerous publications, and arts education advocacy activities.
9x Year
Jay Seller, Ph.D., President
Frank Pruet, Vice President

4633 SchoolArts
Davis Publications
50 Portland Street
Worcester, MA 01608
508-754-7201
800-533-2847
Fax: 508-791-3834
VSullivan@DavisArt.com
www.davisart.com
Davis has promoted and advocated for art education at both the local and national levels, providing good ideas for teachers and celebrating cultural diversity and the contributions of world cultures through a wide range of art forms.
Publication Date: 1901
Wyatt Wade, President
Valerie Sullivan, Publications

4634 SchoolArts Magazine
Davis Publications
50 Portland Street
Worcester, MA 01608
508-754-7201
800-533-2847
Fax: 508-791-3834
VSullivan@DavisArt.com
www.davisart.com
Aimed at art educators in public and private schools, elementary through high school. Articles offer ideas and information involving art media for the teaching profession and for use in classroom activities.
Publication Date: 1901 Monthly
ISSN: 0036-3463
Wyatt Wade, President
Valerie Sullivan, Publications

4635 Studies in Art Education
Louisiana State University, Dept. of Curriculum
Baton Rouge, LA 70803-0001
225-578-3202
Fax: 225-578-9135
webmaster@lsu.edu
www.lsu.edu
Reports on developments in art education.
Quarterly
Karen A Hamblen, Editor

4636 Teaching Journal
Educational Theatre Association
2343 Auburn Avenue
Cincinnati, OH 45219-2815
513-421-3900
Fax: 513-421-7077
members@schooltheatre.org
www.schooltheatre.org
Journal published by Educational Theatre Association, a professional association for theatre educators/artists.
Quarterly
Jay Seller, Ph.D., President
Frank Pruet, Vice President

4637 Teaching Music
National Association for Music Education
1806 Robert Fulton Drive
Reston, VA 20191-4348
703-860-4000
Fax: 703-860-4826
memberservices@nafme2.org
www.nafme.org
Offers informative, timely and accurate articles, editorials, and features to a national audience of music educators.
Publication Date: 1907 BiMonthly
ISSN: 1069-7446
Glenn E. Nierman, President/ Chair
Michael A. Butera, Executive Director/ CEO

4638 Ultimate Early Childhood Music Resource
Miss Jackie Music Company
10001 El Monte Street
Shawnee Mission, KS 66207-3631
913-381-3672
jsilberg@interserv.com
www.jackiesilberg.com
Designed to assist parents and teachers engaged in early childhood.
16 pages Quarterly
Jackie Weissman, Publisher
Emily Smith, Editor

Periodicals / Physical Education

4639 Athletic Director
National Association for Sport & Physical Ed.
1900 Association Drive
Reston, VA 20191
703-476-3410
800-213-7193
Fax: 703-476-9527
board@shapeamerica.org
www.shapeamerica.org
Of interest to athletic directors and coaches.
Publication Date: 1885 4 pages SemiAnnually
Dolly D. Lambdin, Ed.D., President
E. Paul Roetert, CEO

4640 Athletic Management
College Athletic Administrator
2488 N Triphammer Road
Ithaca, NY 14850
607-274-3209
Fax: 607-273-0701
athletics.ithaca.edu/staff.aspx
Offers information on how athletic managers can improve their operations, focusing on high school and college athletic departments.
BiMonthly
Andrea McClatchie, Operations and Events
Kathy Farley, Administrative Assistant

4641 Athletic Training
National Athletic Trainers' Association
1620 Valwood Parkway
Suite 115
Carrollton, TX 75006
214-637-6282
860-437-5700
Fax: 214-637-2206
jthornton@clarion.edu
www.nata.org
Edited for athletic trainers.
Publication Date: 1950 100 pages Quarterly Magazine
Jim Thornton, MS, ATC, CES, President
MaryBeth Horodyski, Vice President

4642 Athletics Administration
NACDA
PO Box 16428
Cleveland, OH 44116
440-892-4000
Fax: 440-892-4007
burkeg@nsula.edu
www.nacda.com
The official publication of the National Association of Collegiate Directors of Athletics (NACDA), Athletics Administration focuses on athletics facilities, new ideas in marketing, promotions, development, legal ramifications and other current issues in collegiate athletics administrations.
Publication Date: 1965 44-48 pages BiMonthly
ISSN: 0044-9873
Jim Phillips, President
Bob Vecchione, Executive Dir.

4643 Journal of Environmental Education
Heldref Publications
325 Chestnut Street
Suite 800
Philadelphia, PA 19106
215-625-8900
800-365-9753
Fax: 202-296-5149
customer.service@taylorandfrancis.com
www.heldref.org
An excellent resource for department chairpersons and directors of programs in environmental, resources, and outdoor education.
48 pages Quarterly
ISSN: 0095-8964
B Alison Panko, Managing Editor

4644 Journal of Experiential Education
Association for Experiential Education
1435 Yarmouth Ave
#104
Boulder, CO 80304
303-440-8844
800-787-7979
Fax: 303-440-9581
simps_sv@mail.uwlax.edu
www.aee.org
A professional journal that publishes articles in outdoor adventure programming, service learning, environmental education, therapeutic applications, research and theory, the creative arts, and much more. An invaluable reference tool for anyone in the field of experiential education.
3x Year
Maurie Lung, President
Robert Smariga, CEO

4645 Journal of Physical Education, Recreation and Dance
American Alliance for Health, Phys. Ed. & Dance
1900 Association Drive
Reston, VA 20191-1502
703-476-3495
800-213-7193
Fax: 703-476-9527
board@shapeamerica.org
www.shapeamerica.org
Presents new books, teaching aids, facilities, equipment, supplies, news of the profession and related groups.
Publication Date: 1885 9x Year
Dolly D. Lambdin, Ed.D., President
E. Paul Roetert, CEO

4646 Journal of Teaching in Physical Education
Human Kinetics Incorporation
PO Box 5076
Champaign, IL 61825-5076
217-351-5076
800-747-4457
Fax: 217-351-1549
info@hkusa.com
www.humankinetics.com/jtpe
Journal for in-service and pre-service teachers, teacher educators, and administrators, that presents research articles based on classroom and laboratory studies, descriptive and survey studies, summary and review articles, as well as discussions of current topics.
132 pages Quarterly
ISSN: 0273-5024
Brian Moore, Managing Editor
Skip Maier, Journals Division Dir.

4647 Marketing Recreation Classes
Learning Resources Network
P.O. Box 9
River Falls, WI 54022
715-426-9777
800-678-5376
Fax: 888-234-8633
info@lern.org
www.lern.org
Successful new class ideas and promotion techniques for recreation instructors.
8 pages Monthly
William A. Draves, President
Greg Marsello, VP, Development

4648 National Association for Sport & Physical Education News
National Association for Sport & Physical Ed.
1900 Association Drive
Reston, VA 20191-1502
703-476-3410
800-213-7193
Fax: 703-476-9527
board@shapeamerica.org
www.shapeamerica.org
News of conventions, new publications, workshops, and more, all tailored for people in the field of sports, physical education, coaching, etc. Legislative issues are covered as well as news about the over 20 structures in NASPE.
Publication Date: 1885 12 pages Monthly
Dolly D. Lambdin, Ed.D., President
E. Paul Roetert, CEO

4649 National Standards for Dance Education News
National Dance Association
1900 Association Drive
Reston, VA 20191-1502
703-476-3400
800-213-7193
Fax: 703-476-9527
board@shapeamerica.org
www.shapeamerica.org
News of the National Dance Association activities, national events in dance education and topics of interest to recreation and athletic directors.
Publication Date: 1885 12 pages Quarterly
Dolly D. Lambdin, Ed.D., President
E. Paul Roetert, CEO

4650 Physical Education Digest
Physical Education Update
11 Cerilli Crescent
Sudbury
Ontario, Ca P3E5R
705-805-9245
800-455-8782
Fax: 705-805-9245
coach@pedigest.com
www.physicaleducationupdate.com
Edited for physical educators and scholastic coaches. Condenses practical ideas from periodicals and books.
36 pages Quarterly
ISSN: 0843-2635
Dick Moss, Editor/ Publisher

4651 Physical Educator
Arizona State University
University Drive and Mill Avenue
Tempe, AZ 85287
480-965-9011
Fax: 480-965-2569
www.asu.edu
Offers articles for the physical educator.
Quarterly
Michael M. Crow, President
Morgan R. Olsen, VP, Business & Finance

4652 Quest
Louisiana State University/Dept. of Kinesiology
Huey Room 112
Baton Rouge, LA 70803-0001
225-388-2036
Fax: 225-388-3680
www.southeastern.edu

Publishes articles concerning issues critical to physical education in higher education. Its purpose is to stimulate professional development within the field.

Publication Date: 1925 Quarterly

Dr. John Crain, President
Dr. Tammy Bourg, Provost/ VP

4653 Teaching Elementary Physical Education
Human Kinetics Publishers
1607 N Market Street
P.O. Box 5076
Champaign, IL 61820
217-351-5076
800-747-4457
Fax: 217-351-1459
info@hkusa.com
www.humankinetics.com
A resource for elementary physical educators, by physical educators. Each 32-page issue includes informative articles on current trends, teaching hints, activity ideas, current resources and events, and more.

32 pages BiMonthly Magazine
ISSN: 1045-4853

Brian Holding, CEO
Margery Robinson, Managing Editor

Periodicals / Reading

4654 Beyond Words
20827 NW Cornell Rd.
Suite 500
Hillsboro, OR 97124
503-531-8700
Fax: 503-531-8773
www.beyondword.com
Offers information on literature, language arts and English for the teaching professional.

Publication Date: 1983 10x Year

Richard Cohn, President/ Publisher
Tim Schroeder, Chief Operating Officer

4655 Christian Literacy Outreach
Christian Literacy Association
541 Perry Highway
Pittsburgh, PA 15229
412-364-3777
www.pghpresbytery.org
Association news offering membership information, convention news, books and articles for the Christian education professional.

Publication Date: 1975 4 pages Quarterly

Joseph Mosca

4656 Exercise Exchange
Appalachian State University
222 Duncan Hall
Boone, NC 28608
828-262-2000
Fax: 828-262-2128
admissions@appstate.edu
www.appstate.edu
Bi-annual journal which features classroom-tested approaches to the teaching of English language arts from middle school through college; articles are written by classroom practitioners.

Publication Date: 1899 BiAnnual
ISSN: 0531-531X

Dr. Randy Edwards, Chief of Staff
Melody C. Miller, Executive Assistant

4657 Forum for Reading
Fitchburg State College, Education Department
160 Pearl Street
Fitchburg, MA 01420-2697
978-665-3000
800-705-9692
admissions@fitchburgstate.edu
www.fitchburgstate.edu/academics/academic-departments/educat
Offers articles, reviews, question and answer columns and more for educators and students.

Publication Date: 1894 2x Year

Dr. Ronald P. Colbert, Chair
Beth Lawrence, Secretary

4658 Journal of Adolescent & Adult Literacy
International Reading Association
800 Barksdale Road
Newark, DE 19711-3204
302-731-1600
800-336-7323
Fax: 302-731-1057
customerservice@reading.org
www.reading.org
Carries articles and departments for those who teach reading in adolescent and adult programs. Applied research, instructional techniques, program descriptions, training of teachers and professional issues.

Publication Date: 1956 80-96 pages 8x Year
ISSN: 1081-3004

Jill Lewis-Spector, President
Diane Barone, Vice President

4659 Journal of Reading Recovery
Reading Recovery Council of North America
500 W. Wilson Bridge Road
Suite 250
Worthington, OH 43085
614-310-7323
877-883-7323
Fax: 614-310-7345
jjohnson@readingrecovery.org
www.readingrecovery.org
The Journal of Reading Recovery is published twice per year, and is primarily a practitioners journal offering current information on Reading Recovery teaching theory, implementation and research for K-6 classroom literacy.

Janet Behrend, President
Lindy Harmon, Vice President

4660 Laubach LitScape
Laubach Literacy Action
1320 Jamesville Avenue
Syracuse, NY 13210
315-422-9121
888-528-2224
Fax: 315-422-6369
info@laubach.org
www.laubach.org
Includes articles about national literacy activities as well as support and information on tutoring, resources, training, new readers, program management, and recruitment and retention of students and volunteers.

12 pages Quarterly

Linda Church, Managing Editor

4661 Literacy Advocate
Laubach Literacy Action
1320 Jamesville Avenue
Syracuse, NY 13210
315-422-9121
888-528-2224
Fax: 315-422-6369
info@laubach.org
www.laubach.org
Covers United States and international programs and membership activities.

8 pages Quarterly

Beth Kogut, Editor

4662 News for You
Laubach Literacy Action
1320 Jamesville Avenue
Syracuse, NY 13210
315-422-9121
888-528-2224
Fax: 315-422-6369
info@laubach.org
www.laubach.org
A newspaper for older teens and adults with special reading needs. Includes US and world news written at a 4th to 6th grade reading level.

4 pages Weekly
ISSN: 0884-3910

Heidi Stephens, Editor

4663 Phonics Institute
The Phonics Instuite
PO Box 98682
Steilacoom, WA 98388
253-588-3436
read@readingstore.com
www.readingstore.com
Restoration of intensive phonics to beginning reading instruction.

8 pages 5x Year

4664 RIF Newsletter
Smithsonian Institution
PO Box 37012
SI Building, Room 153, MRC 010
Washington, DC 20013-7012
202-357-2888
Fax: 202-786-2564
info@si.edu
www.si.edu
Describes RIF's nationwide reading motivation program.

Publication Date: 1846 TriQuarterly

John W. McCarter, Jr., Chair
Shirley Ann Jackson, Vice Chair

4665 Read, America!
Place in the Woods
3900 Glenwood Avenue
Golden Valley, MN 55422-5302
763-374-2120
Fax: 952-593-5593
readamerica10732@aol.com
News, book reviews, ideas for librarians and reading program leaders; short stories and poetry pages for adults and children; and an annual Read America! collection with selections of new books solicited from 350 publishers.

12 pages Quarterly Newsletter
ISSN: 0891-4214

Roger Hammer, Editor/Publisher

4666 Reading Improvement
Project Innovation of Mobile
PO Box 8508
Mobile, AL 36608
251-610-8333
philfeldman@projectinnovation.com
www.projectinnovation.com
A journal dedicated to improving reading and literacy in America.

Quarterly

Phil Feldman, Ph.D, Editor

4667 **Reading Psychology**
Texas A&M University, College of Education
Department of Education
College Station, TX 77843-0001
979-845-7093
Fax: 979-845-9663
www.tamu.edu/about/departments.html
Publication Date: 1862 Quarterly
Dr. Mark A. Hussey, President
Dr. Karan L. Watson, Provost/ EVP

4668 **Reading Research Quarterly**
Ohio State University
281 W. Lane Ave.
Columbus, OH 43210
614-292-OHIO
Fax: 614-292-1816
www.osu.edu
Delves into reading ratings and special concerns in the field of literacy.
Quarterly
Jeffery Wadsworth, Chair
Ronald A. Rtaner, Vice Chair

4669 **Reading Research and Instruction**
Appalachian State University, College of Education
Dept. of Curriculum & Instruction
Boone, NC 28608
828-262-2000
admissions@appstate.edu
www.appstate.edu
Publication Date: 1899 Quarterly
John C. Fennebresque, Chair
W. Louis Bissette, Jr., Vice Chair

4670 **Reading Teacher**
International Reading Association
800 Barksdale Road
Newark, DE 19711-3204
302-731-1600
800-336-7323
Fax: 301-731-1057
customerservice@reading.org
www.reading.org
Carries articles and departments for those who teach reading in preschool and elementary schools. Applied research, instructional techniques, program descriptions, the training of teachers, professional issues and special feature reviews of children's books and ideas for classroom practice.
Publication Date: 1956 8x Year
Jill Lewis-Spector, President
Marcie Craig Post, Executive Director

4671 **Reading Today**
International Reading Association
800 Barksdale Road
Newark, DE 19711-3204
302-731-1600
800-336-7323
Fax: 302-731-1057
customerservice@reading.org
www.reading.org
Edited for IRA individual and institutional members offering information for teachers, news of the education profession and information for and relating to parents, councils and international issues.
Publication Date: 1956 36-44 pages Bi-Monthly
Jill Lewis-Spector, President
Marcie Craig Post, Executive Director

4672 **Recording for the Blind & Dyslexic**
Learning Ally
20 Roszel Road
Princeton, NJ 08540
609-750-1830
800-221-4792
Fax: 609-750-9653
bvidialogue@LearningAlly.org
www.learningally.org
Textbooks on tape for students who cannot read standard print.
Publication Date: 1948
Andrew Friedman, President/ CEO
Jim Halliday, Executive Vice President

4673 **Report on Literacy Programs**
Business Publishers
2222 Sedwick Drive
Durham, NC 27713
301-587-6300
800-223-8720
Fax: 800-508-2592
custserv@bpinews.com
www.bpinews.com
Reports on the efforts of business and government to provide literacy training to adults— focusing on the effects of literacy on the workforce.
8-10 pages BiWeekly
Eric Easton, Publisher
Dave Speights, Editor

4674 **Visual Literacy Review & Newsletter**
International Visual Literacy Association
Virginia Tech
Old Security Building
Blacksburg, VA 24061
540-231-8992
jhethorn@udel.edu
www.ivla.org
Forum for sharing research and practice within an educational context in the area of visual communication.
8 pages BiMonthly
Janet Hethorn, President
Cindy Kovalik, Vice President

4675 **What's Working in Parent Involvement**
The Parent Institute
PO Box 7474
Fairfax Station, VA 22039-7474
703-323-9170
800-756-5525
Fax: 703-323-9173
custsvc@parent-institute.com
www.parent-institute.com
Focuses on parent involvement in children's reading education.
10x Year
John H. Wherry, Ed.D., President

Periodicals / Secondary Education

4676 **ACTIVITY**
American College Testing
2201 Dodge
Iowa City, IA 52243-0001
319-337-1410
Fax: 319-337-1014
Distributed free of charge to more than 100,000 persons concerned with secondary and postsecondary education. ACT, an independent nonprofit organization provides a broad range of educational programs and services throughout this country and abroad.
Quarterly
Dan Lechay, Editor

4677 **Adolescence**
Libra Publishers
3089C Clairemont Drive
PNB 383
San Diego, CA 92117-6802
858-571-1414
Fax: 858-571-1414
Articles contributed by professionals spanning issues relating to teenage education, counseling and guidance. Paperback.
256 pages Quarterly
ISSN: 0001-8449
William Kroll, Editor

4678 **American Secondary Education**
Bowling Green State University
Education Room 531
Bowling Green, OH 43403-0001
419-372-2531
Fax: 419-372-8265
joelo@bgsu.edu
www.bgsu.edu
Serves those involved in secondary education—administrators, teachers, university personnel and others. Examines and reports on current issues in secondary education and provides readers with information on a wide range of topics that impact secondary education professionals. Professionals are provided with the most up-to-date theories and practices in their field.
Quarterly
Joel O'Dorisio, Chair
Allen Rogel, Vice Chair

4679 **Child and Youth Care Forum**
Kluwer Academic/Human Sciences Press
233 Spring Street
New York, NY 10013
212-620-8000
800-221-9369
Fax: 212-463-0742
www.wkpa.nl
Independent, professional publication committed to the improvement of child and youth care practice in a variety of day and residential settings and to the advancement of this field. Designed to serve child and youth care practitioners, their supervisors, and other personnel in child and youth care settings, the journal provides a channel of communication and debate including material on practice, selection and training, theory and research, and professional issues.
Bimonthly
ISSN: 1053-1890
Carol Bischoff, Publisher
Doug Magnuson, Co-Editor

4680 **Family Therapy: The Journal of the California Graduate School of Family Psychology**
Libra Publishers
3089C Clairemont Drive
PNB 383
San Diego, CA 92117-6802
858-571-1414
Fax: 858-571-1414
Articles contributed by professionals spanning issues relating to teenage education, counseling and guidance. Paperback.
96 pages Quarterly
ISSN: 0091-6544
William Kroll, Editor

4681 **High School Journal**
University of North Carolina
CB 3500 Peabody Hall
Chapel Hill, NC 27599-3500
919-966-1346
Fax: 919-962-1533
soe.unc.edu/hsj

The Journal publishes articles dealing with adolescent growth, development, interests, beliefs, values, learning, etc., as they effect school practice. In addition, it reports on research dealing with teacher, administrator and student interaction within the school setting. The audience is primarily secondary school teachers and administrators, as well as college level educators.

Publication Date: 1918 60 pages Quarterly
ISSN: 0018-1498

Zan Crowder, Editor
Hillary Parkhouse, Associate Editor

4682 Independent School
National Association of Independent Schools
1129 20th Street, NW
Suite 800
Washington, DC 20036-3425
202-973-9700
Fax: 888-316-3862
www.nais.org
Contains information and opinion about secondary and elementary education in general and independent education in particular.

TriAnnually

John E. Chubb, President
Kurt R Murphy, Advertising/Editor

4683 Journal of At-Risk Issues
Clemson University
209 Martin Street
Clemson, SC 29631-1555
864-656-2599
Fax: 864-656-0136
ndpc@clemson.edu
dropoutprevention.org
A journal published by the National Dropout Prevention Center/Network presenting research articles on the subject of dropout prevention and at-risk youth.

Publication Date: 0

Greg Hickman, Ph.D, Editor
Gary J Burkholder, Ph.D, Assistant Editor

4684 NASSP Bulletin
National Assn. of Secondary School Principals
1904 Association Drive
P.O. Box 417939
Reston, VA 20191-1537
703-860-0200
800-253-7746
Fax: 703-620-6534
nassp@nassp.org
www.principals.org
For administrators at the secondary school level dealing with subjects that range from the philosophical to the practical.

TriAnnual

G.A. Buie, President
Michael Allison, President Elect

4685 Parents Still Make the Difference!
The Parent Institute
PO Box 7474
Fairfax Station, VA 22039-7474
703-323-9170
800-756-5525
Fax: 703-323-9173
custsvc@parent-institute.com
www.parent-institute.com
Newsletter focusing on parent involvement in children's education. Focuses on parents of children in grades 7-12.

Monthly
ISSN: 1523-2395

Betsie Millar, Author
John H. Wherry, Ed.D., President

4686 Parents Still Make the Difference!: Middle School Edition
The Parent Institute
PO Box 7474
Fairfax Station, VA 22039-7474
703-323-9170
800-756-5525
Fax: 703-323-9173
custsvc@parent-institute.com
www.parent-institute.com
Newsletter focusing on parent involvement in children's education. Focuses on parents of children in grades 7-12.

Monthly
ISSN: 1071-5118

John H. Wherry, Ed.D., President

Periodicals / Science

4687 American Biology Teacher
National Association of Biology Teachers
12100 Sunset Hills Road
Suite 130
Reston, VA 20190
703-264-9696
888-501-NABT
Fax: 703-435-4390
office@nabt.org
www.nabt.org
Edited for elementary, secondary school, junior college, four-year college and university teachers of biology.

80 pages 9 times a year

Stacey Kiser, President
Jane Ellis, President Elect

4688 AnthroNotes
Smithsonian Information
PO Box 37012
SI Building, Room 153, MRC 010
Washington, DC 20013-7012
202-633-1000
Fax: 202-357-2208
info@si.edu
www.mnh.si.edu
Offers archeological, anthropological research in an engaging style.

20 pages

Ann Krupp, Editor

4689 Appraisal: Science Books for Young People
Children's Science Book Review Committee
Boston University
School of Education
Boston, MA 02215
617-353-4150
This is a journal dedicated to the review of science books for children and young adults. Now in its 27th year of publication, Appraisal reviews nearly all of the science books published yearly for pre-school through high-school age young people. Each book is examined by a children's librarian and by a specialist in its particular discipline.

Quarterly

Diane Holzheimer, Editor

4690 Association of Science-Technology Centers Dimensions
818 Connecticut Avenue, NW
7th Floor
Washington, DC 20006-2734
202-783-7200
Fax: 202-783-7207
info@astc.org
www.astc.org

Publication Date: 1973 20 pages
ISSN: 1528-820X

Carolyn Sutterfield, Author
Chevy Humphrey, Chair
Linda Conlon, Chair-Elect

4691 CCAS Newsletter
Council of Colleges of Arts & Sciences
PO Box 8795
Williamsburg, VA 23187-8795
757-221-1784
Fax: 757-221-1776
ccas@wm.edu
www.ccas.net
Membership newsletter to inform deans about arts and sciences issues in education.

Publication Date: 1965 4-10 pages BiMonthly

Dr. Anne-Marie McCartan, Executive Director
Nichelle Wright, Office Specialist

4692 Cream of the Crop
California Foundation for Agriculture
2300 River Plaza Drive
Sacramento, CA 95833-3293
916-561-5625
800-700-2482
Fax: 916-561-5697
info@learnaboutag.org
www.LearnAboutAg.org
E-newsletter released monthly with articles about agriculture related resources, ideas, information and CFAITC event overviews.

Judy Culbertson, Executive Director
Mindy DeRohan, Communications Coordinator

4693 Journal of College Science Teaching
National Science Teachers Association
1840 Wilson Boulevard
Arlington, VA 22201-3000
703-243-7100
800-782-6782
Fax: 703-243-7177
www.nsta.org
Professional journal for college and university teachers of introductory and advanced science with special emphasis on interdisciplinary teaching of nonscience majors. Contains feature articles and departments including a science column, editorials, lab demonstrations, problem solving techniques and book reviews.

6x Year

Juliana Texley, President
Carolyn Hayes, President Elect

4694 Journal of Environmental Education
Taylor & Francis
325 Chestnut Street
Suite 800
Philadelphia, PA 19106
215-625-8900
800-354-1420
Fax: 202-296-5149
customer.service@taylorandfrancis.com
www.heldref.org
A vital research journal for everyone teaching about the environment. Each issue features case studies of relevant projects, evaluation of new research, and discussion of public policy and philosophy in the area of environmental education. The Journal is an excellent resource for department chairpersons and directors of programs in outdoor education.

Quarterly

Kerri P Kilbane, Editor

4695 Journal of Research in Science Teaching

Wiley InterScience
Wiley Corporate Headquarters
111 River Street
Hoboken, NJ 07030-5774
866-465-3817
Fax: 201-748-5715
onlinelibrarysales@wiley.com
www.interscience.wiley.com

10x Year

4696 NSTA Reports!

National Science Teachers Association
1840 Wilson Boulevard
Arlington, VA 22201-3000
703-243-7100
800-782-6782
Fax: 703-243-7177
www.nsta.org

The association's timely source of news on issues of interest to science teachers of all levels. Includes national news, information on teaching materials, announcements of programs for teachers and students, and advance notice about all NSTA programs, conventions and publications.

52 pages BiMonthly

Juliana Texley, President
Carolyn Hayes, President Elect

4697 Odyssey

Cobblestone Publishing
30 Grove Street
Suite C
Peterborough, NH 03458-1453
603-924-7209
800-821-0115
Fax: 603-924-7380
custsvc@cobblestonepub.org
www.odysseymagazine.com

Secrets of science are probed with each theme issue's articles, interviews, activities and math puzzles. Astronomical concepts are experienced with Jack Horkheimer's Star Gazer cartoon and Night-Sky Navigation.

48 pages Monthly
ISSN: 0163-0946

Elizabeth E Lindstrom, Editor

4698 Physics Teacher

American Association of Physics Teachers
One Physics Ellipse
College Park, MD 20740-3845
301-209-3311
Fax: 301-209-0845
webmaster@aapt.org
www.aapt.org

Published by the American Association of Physics Teachers and dedicated to the improvement of the teaching of introductory physics at all levels.

9x Year

Mary Elizabeth Mogge, President
Janelle M. Bailey, President Elect

4699 Quantum

National Science Teachers Association
1840 Wilson Boulevard
Arlington, VA 22201-3000
703-243-7100
800-782-6782
Fax: 703-243-7177
www.nsta.org

Illustrated magazine containing material translated from Russian magazine Kvant as well as original material specifically targeted to American students. In addition to feature articles and department pieces, Quantum offers olympiad-style problems and brainteasers. Each issue also contains an answer section.

BiMonthly

Juliana Texley, President
Carolyn Hayes, President Elect

4700 Reports of the National Center for Science Education

National Center for Science Education
420 40th Street
Suite 2
Oakland, CA 94609-2688
510-601-7203
800-290-6006
Fax: 510-601-7204
info@ncse.com
www.ncseweb.org

An examination of issues and current events in science education with a focus on evolutionary science, and the evolution/creation controversy.

36-44 pages BiMonthly Newsletter
ISSN: 1064-2358

Brian Alters , President
Lorne Trottier, Vice President/ Treasurer

4701 Science Activities

Heldref Publications
325 Chestnut Street
Suite 800
Philadelphia, PA 19106
215-625-8900
800-365-9753
Fax: 202-296-5149
customer.service@taylorandfrancis.com
www.heldref.org

A storehouse of up-to-date creative science projects and curriculum ideas for the K-12 classroom teacher. A one-step source of experiments, projects and curriculum innovations in the biological, physical and behavioral sciences, the journal's ideas have been teacher tested, providing the best of actual classroom experiences. Regular departments feature news notes, computer news, book reviews and new products and resources for the classroom.

48 pages Quarterly
ISSN: 0036-8121

Betty Bernard, Managing Editor

4702 Science News Magazine

Society for Science & The Public
1719 N Street NW
Washington, DC 20036-2888
202-785-2255
800-552-4412
Fax: 202-659-0365
member@societyforscience.org
www.societyforscience.org

Information and programs in all areas of science.

Publication Date: 1921 Weekly

Maya Ajmera, CEO/ President/ Publisher
Tom Bakry, Chief Technology Officer

4703 Science Scope

National Science Teachers Association
1840 Wilson Boulevard
Arlington, VA 22201-3000
703-243-7100
800-782-6782
Fax: 703-243-7177
www.nsta.org

Specifically for middle-school and junior-high science teachers. Science Scope addresses the needs of both new and veteran teachers. The publication includes classroom activities, posters and teaching tips, along with educational theory on the way adolescents learn.

8x Year

Juliana Texley, President
Carolyn Hayes, President Elect

4704 Science Teacher

National Science Teachers Association
1840 Wilson Boulevard
Arlington, VA 22201-3000
703-243-7100
800-782-6782
Fax: 703-243-7177
www.nsta.org

Professional journal for junior and senior high school science teachers. Offers articles on a wide range of scientific topics, innovative teaching ideas and experiments, and current research news. Also offers reviews, posters, information on free or inexpensive materials, and more.

9x Year

Juliana Texley, President
Carolyn Hayes, President Elect

4705 Science and Children

National Association of Science Teachers
1840 Wilson Boulevard
Arlington, VA 22201-3000
703-243-7100
800-782-6782
Fax: 703-243-7177
www.nsta.org

Dedicated to preschool through middle school science teaching provides lively how-to articles, helpful hints, software and book reviews, colorful posters and inserts, think pieces and on-the-scene reports from classroom teachers.

8x Year

Juliana Texley, President
Carolyn Hayes, President Elect

4706 Sea Frontiers

International Oceanographic Foundation
4600 Rickenbacker Causeway
Key Biscayne, FL 33149-1031
305-361-4888

A general interest magazine about science education including underwater studies.

BiMonthly

Bonnie Gordon, Editor

4707 Teacher Resource Guide

California Foundation for Agriculture
2300 River Plaza Drive
Sacramento, CA 95833
916-561-5625
800-722-2482
Fax: 916-561-5697
infolearnaboutag.org
www.LearnAboutAg.org

This is a must have tool for professional and volunteers encouraging the agriculturalliteracy of California's youth. Resources that assist in teaching about agriculture are plentiful. This guide provides an all-encompassing look at the array of materials that readily support such an endeavor.

Judy Culbertson, Executive Director
Mindy DeRohan, Communications Coordinator

4708 Universe in the Classroom

Astronomical Society of the Pacific
390 Ashton Avenue
San Francisco, CA 94112-1722
415-337-1100
Fax: 415-337-5205
astroed@astrosociety.org
www.astrosociety.org/uitc

On teaching astronomy in grades 3-12, including astronomical news, plain-English explanations, teaching resources and classroom activities.

8 pages Quarterly

Gordon Myers, President
Connie Walker, Vice President

Periodicals / Social Studies

4709 **Alumni Newsletter**
The Jewish Federations of North America
25 Broadway
17th Floor
New York, NY 10004
212-477-0707
Fax: 212-477-1918
info@jewishlabor.org
jewishfederations.org
Newsletter of American public secondary school teachers who teach about the Holocaust and Jewish Resistance.

8 pages SemiAnnually

Richard V Sandler, Chair
Cynthia D Shapira, Vice Chair

4710 **American Sociological Review**
Pennsylvania State University
211 Oswald Tower, Department of Soc
University Park, PA 16802
814-865-2527
Fax: 814-863-7216
sociology@la.psu.edu
www.psu.edu/
Addresses most aspects of sociology in a general range of categories for academic and professional sociologists.

Bimonthly

David Baker, Professor of Education
Duane Alwin, Director

4711 **AnthroNotes**
Smithsonian Information
PO Box 37012
SI Building, Room 153, MRC 010
Washington, DC 20013-7012
202-633-1000
Fax: 202-357-2208
info@si.edu
www.mnh.si.edu
Offers archeological, anthropological research in an engaging style.

4712 **AppleSeeds**
Cobblestone Publishing
30 Grove Street
Suite C
Peterborough, NH 03458-1453
603-924-7209
800-821-0115
Fax: 603-924-7380
custsvc@cobblestonepub.com
www.cobblestonepub.com
A delightful way to develop love of non-fiction reading in grades 2-4. Full color articles, photographs, maps, activities that grab student and teacher interest. Children's doings and thinking around the world in Mail Bag.

Publication Date: 1973 32 pages Monthly
ISSN: 1099-7725

Susan Buckey, Barb Burt, Editors, Author
Lou Waryncia, Managing Editor

4713 **Boletin**
Center for the Teaching of the Americas
Immaculata College
Immaculata, PA 19345
610-647-4400
School teaching of the Americas.

Quarterly

Sr. Mary Consuela

4714 **California Weekly Explorer**
California Weekly Reporter
285 E Main Street
Suite 3
Tustin, CA 92780-4429
714-730-5991
Fax: 714-730-3548
Resources, events, awards and reviews relating to California history.

16 pages Weekly

Don Oliver

4715 **Calliope**
Cobblestone Publishing
30 Grove Street
Suite C
Peterborough, NH 03458-1453
603-924-7209
800-821-0115
Fax: 603-924-7380
custsvc@cobblestonepub.com
www.cobblestonepub.com
Invests in world history with reality not only through articles, stories and maps but also current events and resource lists. Calliope's themes are geared to topics studied in world history classrooms.

48 pages Monthly
ISSN: 1058-7086

Lou Waryncia, Managing Editor
Charles F Baker, Editors

4716 **Capitalism for Kids**
National Schools Commitee for Economic Education
250 East 73rd Street
Suite 12G
New York, NY 10021-8641
212-535-9534
Fax: 212-535-4167
info@nscee.org
www.nscee.org
Teaches young people about capitalism and the free enterprise system in a clear and entertaining styl. Disscusses the practical aspects of starting a small business.

247 pages

Edward H. Crane, Jr., Chairman
John G. Murphy, Ph.D, President

4717 **Cobblestone**
Cobblestone Publishing
30 Grove Street
Suite C
Peterborough, NH 03458-1453
603-924-7209
800-821-0115
Fax: 603-924-7380
custsvc@cobblestonepub.com
www.cobblestonepub.com
Blends sound information with excellent writing, a combination that parents and teachers appreciate. Cobblestone offers imaginative approaches to introduce young readers to the world of American history.

48 pages Monthly
ISSN: 0199-5197

Lou Waryncia, Managing Editor
Meg Chorlian, Editor

4718 **Colloquoy on Teaching World Affairs**
World Affairs Council of North California
312 Sutter Street
Suite 200
San Francisco, CA 94108-4311
415-293-4600
Fax: 415-982-5028
www.worldaffairs.org
Offers information, articles and updates for the history teacher.

3x Year

Peter J. Robertson, Chairman
Jane M. Wales, President/ CEO

4719 **Faces**
Cobblestone Publishing
30 Grove Street
Suite C
Peterborough, NH 03458-1453
603-924-7209
800-821-0115
Fax: 603-924-7380
custsvc@cobblestonepub.com
www.cobblestonepub.com
The world is brought to the classroom through the faces of its people. World culture encourages young readers' perspectives through history, folk tales, news and activities.

48 pages Monthly
ISSN: 0749-1387

Lou Waryncia, Managing Editor
Elizabeth Crooker Carpentiere, Editor

4720 **Focus**
Freedoms Foundation at Valley Forge
PO Box 706
Valley Forge, PA 19482-0706
215-933-8825
800-896-5488
Fax: 610-935-0522
tsueta@ffvf.org
www.ffvf.org
Strives to teach America and promote responsible citizenship through educational programs and awards designed to recognize outstanding Americans.

6 pages Quarterly

Thomas M Sueat, Editor

4721 **Footsteps**
Cobblestone Publishing
30 Grove Street
Suite C
Peterborough, NH 03458-1453
603-924-7209
800-821-0115
Fax: 603-924-7380
custsvc@cobblestonepub.com
www.cobblestonepub.com
Celebrates heritage of African Americans and explores their contributions to culture from colonial times to present. Courage, perserverance mark struggle for freedom and equality in articles, maps, photos, etc.

48 pages 9x Year
ISSN: 1521-5865

Lou Waryncia, Managing Editor
Charles Baker, Editor

4722 **History Matters Newsletter**
National Council for History Education
13940 Cedar Rd. #393
University Heights, OH 44118
240-696-6600
Fax: 240-523-0245
NCHE@nche.net
www.nche.net
Serves as a resource to help members improve the quality and quantity of history learning.

8 pages Monthly
ISSN: 1090-1450

Justin Jakovac, Executive Director
John Csepegi, Director of Membership

4723 Inquiry in Social Studies: Curriculum, Research & Instruction
University of North Carolina-Charlotte
Dept of Curriculum & Instruction
Charlotte, NC 28223
704-547-4500
Fax: 704-547-4705
An annual journal of North Carolina Council for the Social Studies with a readership of 1,400.
Annual
John A Gretes, Editor
Jeff Passe, Editor

4724 Journal of American History
Organization of American Historians
112 N. Bryan Avenue
Bloomington, IN 47408-4141
812-855-7311
800-446-8923
Fax: 812-855-0696
www.oah.org/meetings-events/2015/
Contains articles and essays concerning the study and investigation of American history.
Quarterly
Patricia Limerick, President
Jon Butler, President-Elect

4725 Journal of Economic Education
Heldref Publications
325 Chestnut Street
Suite 800
Philadelphia, PA 19106
215-625-8900
800-365-9753
Fax: 202-296-5149
customer.service@taylorandfrancis.com
www.heldref.org
Offers original articles on innovations in and evaluations of teaching techniques, materials and programs in economics.
Quarterly
ISSN: 0022-4085

4726 Journal of Geography
National Council for Geographic Education
1101 14 Street, NW
Suite 350
Washington, DC 20005-5647
202-216-0942
Fax: 202-618-6249
ncge@jsu.edu
www.ncge.org
Stresses the essential value of geographic education and knowledge in schools.
Quarterly
ISSN: 0022-1341
Susan Hume, President
Eric J. Fournier, Board Chair

4727 Magazine of History
Organizations of American History
112 N. Bryan Avenue
Bloomington, IN 47408-4141
812-855-7311
800-446-8923
Fax: 812-855-0696
oah@oah.org
www.oah.org
Includes informative articles, lesson plans, current historiography and reproducible classroom materials on a particular theme. In addition to topical articles, such columns as Dialogue, Studentspeak and History Headlines allow for the exchange of ideas from all levels of the profession.
70-90 pages Quarterly Magazine
ISSN: 0882-228X
Patricia Limerick, President
Jon Butler, President-Elect

4728 New England Journal of History
Bentley College
Dept of History
175 Forest Street
Waltham, MA 02452
781-891-2000
Fax: 781-891-2896
www.bentley.edu
Covers all aspects of American history for the professional and student.
3x Year
Gloria Cordes Larson, Esq., President
Victor Schlitzer, Director, Marketing & Adv.

4729 News & Views
Pennsylvania Council for the Social Studies
11533 Clematis Boulevard
Pittsburgh, PA 15235-3105
717-238-8768
lguru1@aol.com
www.pcss.org
Offers news, notes, and reviews of interest to social studies educators.
20 pages 5x Year
ISSN: 0894-8712
Jack Suskind, Executive Secretary
Leo R West, Editor

4730 Perspective
Association of Teachers of Latin American Studies
PO Box 620754
Flushing, NY 11362-0754
718-428-1237
Fax: 718-428-1237
Promotes the teaching of Latin America in US schools and colleges.
10 pages BiMonthly
Daniel Mugan

4731 Social Education
National Council for the Social Studies
8555 Sixteenth Street
Suite 500
Silver Spring, MD 20910
301-588-1800
800-683-0812
Fax: 301-588-2049
sgriffin@ncss.org
www.socialstudies.org
Journal for the social studies profession serves middle school, high school and college and university teachers. Social Education features research on significant topics relating to social studies, lesson plans that can be applied to various disciplines, techniques for using teaching materials in the classroom and information on the latest instructional technology.
7x Year
ISSN: 0337-7724
Michelle Herczog, President
Kim O'Neil, President Elect

4732 Social Studies
Heldref Publications
325 Chestnut Street
Suite 800
Philadelphia, PA 19106
215-625-8900
800-365-9753
Fax: 202-296-5149
customer.service@taylorandfrancis.com
www.heldref.org
Offers K-12 classroom teachers, teacher educators and curriculum administrators an independent forum for publishing their ideas about the teaching of social studies at all levels. The journal presents teachers' methods and classroom-tested suggestions for teaching social studies, history, geography and the social sciences.
48 pages BiMonthly
Helen Kress, Managing Editor

4733 Social Studies Journal
Pennsylvania Council for the Social Studies
11533 Clematis Boulevard
Pittsburgh, PA 15235-3105
717-238-8768
lguru1@aol.com
www.pcss.org
Delves into matters of social studies, history, research and statistics for the education professional and science community.
80 pages Annual
Leo R West, Editor
Dr. Saundra McKee, Editor

4734 Social Studies Professional
National Council for the Social Studies
8555 Sixteenth Street
Suite 500
Silver Spring, MD 20910
301-588-1800
800-683-0812
Fax: 301-588-2049
sgriffin@ncss.org
www.socialstudies.org
Newsletter focusing on strategies, tips and techniques for the social studies educator. New product announcements, professional development opportunities, association news, state and regional meetings.
6 Times
Michelle Herczog, President
Kim O'Neil, President Elect

4735 Social Studies and the Young Learner
National Council for the Social Studies
8555 Sixteenth Street
Suite 500
Silver Spring, MD 20910
301-588-1800
800-683-0812
Fax: 301-588-2049
sgriffin@ncss.org
www.socialstudies.org
This publication furthers creative teaching in grades K-6, meeting teachers' needs for new information and effective teaching activities.
Quarterly
Steven S. Lapham, Editor

4736 Society For History Education/History Teacher
California State University - Long Beach
CSULB, 1250 Bellflower Blvd.
Long Beach, CA 90840-1601
562-985-2573
Fax: 562-985-5431
historytacherjournal@gmail.com
www.thehistoryteacher.org
The most widely recognized journal in the United States suppoting all areas of history education, pre-collegiate through university level, with practical and insightful professional analyses of both traditional and innovative teaching techniques.
150 pages Quarterly
ISSN: 0018-2745
Jane Dabel, Editor
Elisa Herrera, Executive Director

4737 Teaching Georgia Government Newsletter
Carl Vinson Institute of Government
201 N Milledge Avenue
Athens, GA 30602-5482
706-542-2736
Fax: 706-542-9301
www.cviog.uga.edu
Substantive and supplementary material for social studies teachers in Georgia. Topics of government, history, archaeology, geography, citizenship, etc. are covered. Publications available and upcoming social studies meetings in the state are also announced.
8 pages TriAnnually
Stacy Jones, Associate Director
Laura Meadows, Director

4738 Theory and Research in Social Education
National Council for the Social Studies
8555 Sixteenth Street
Suite 500
Silver Spring, MD 20910
301-588-1800
800-683-0812
Fax: 301-588-2049
sgriffin@ncss.org
www.socialstudies.org
Features articles covering a variety of topics: teacher training, learning theory, and child development research; instructional strategies; the relationship of the social sciences, philosophy, history and the arts to social education; models and theories used in developing social studies curriculum; and schemes for student participation and social action.
Quarterly
Michelle Herczog, President
Kim O'Neil, President Elect

4739 Wall Street Journal - Classroom Edition
PO Box 7019
Chicopee, MA 01021
800-544-0522
Fax: 413-598-2332
classroom.edition@wsj.com
www.wsjclassroom.com
Monthly student newspaper, with stories drawn from the daily journal that show international, business, economic, and social issues affect students' lives and futures. The newspaper is supported by posters, monthly teacher guides, and videos. Regular features on careers, enterprise, marketing, personal finance and technology. Helps teachers prepare students for the world of work by combining timely articles with colorful graphics, etc.
Monthly
Krishnan Anantharamanz, Editor

4740 Women's History Project News
National Women's History Project
730 Second Street #469
PO Box 469
Santa Rosa, CA 95402
707-636-2888
Fax: 707-636-2909
nwhp1980@gmail.com
www.nwhp.org
Monthly E-mail newsletter about US women's history, for educators, researchers, program planners, and general women's history enthusiasts.
Monthly
Molly Murphy MacGregor, Chair/ Co-Founder
Shona Rocco, Financial Manager

Periodicals / Technology in Education

4741 Connections/EdTech News
Commonwealth of Learning
4710 Kingsway, Suite 2500
Burnaby, BC V5H -4M2
604-775-8200
Fax: 604-775-8210
info@col.org
www.col.org/connections
Published three times per year to, these newsletters provide a continually updated mailing list of over 9,000 government officials, education leaders and international agencies with information on COL's work with its partners as well as other developments worldwide.
Asha S. Kanwar, President/ CEO
Vis Naidoo, Vice President

4742 E-School News
7920 Norfolk Avenue
Suite 900
Bethesda, MD 20814
301-913-0115
800-394-0115
Fax: 301-913-0119
ndavid@eschoolnews.com
www.eschoolnews.com
Monthly newspaper dedicated to providing news and information to help educators use technology to improve education.
Monthly
Gregs Downey, Publisher
Nancy David, Customer Relations Director

4743 EDUCAUSE Quarterly
EDUCAUSE
282 Century Place
Suite 5000
Louisville, CO 80027
303-449-4430
Fax: 303-440-0461
info@educause.edu
www.educause.edu
Strategic policy advocacy; teaching and learning initiatives; applied research; special interest collaboration communities; awards for leadership and exemplary practices; and extensive online information services.
Quarterly Magazine
ISSN: 1528-5324
Nancy Hays, Author
Diana G. Oblinger, President/ CEO
Kay Rhodes, Asso. Vice Chancellor & CIO

4744 EDUCAUSE Review
EDUCAUSE
282 Century Place
Suite 5000
Louisville, CO 80027-2408
303-449-4430
Fax: 303-440-0461
info@educause.edu
www.educause.edu
Strategic policy advocacy; teaching and learning initiatives applied research; special interest collaboration communities; awards for leadership and exemplary practices; and extensive online information services.
Monthly
ISSN: 1527-6619
Nancy Hays, Author
Diana G. Oblinger, President/ CEO
Kay Rhodes, Asso. Vice Chancellor & CIO

4745 Education Technology News
Business Publishers
2222 Sedwick Drive
Durham, NC 27713
301-587-6300
800-223-8720
Fax: 800-508-2592
custserv@bpinews.com
www.bpinews.com
Offers information on computer hardware, multimedia products, software applications, public and private funding and integration of technology into K-12 classrooms.
8 pages BiWeekly
Eric Easton, Publisher
Brian Love, Editorial Coordinato

4746 Educational Technology
700 E Palisade Avenue
Englewood Cliffs, NJ 07632-3040
201-871-4007
800-952-BOOK
Fax: 201-871-4009
Published since 1961, periodical covering the entire field of educational technology. Issues feature essays by leading authorities plus a Research Section. With many special issues covering aspects of the field in depth. Readers are found in some 120 countries.
9x Year
Lawrence Lipsitz, Editor

4747 Electronic Learning
Scholastic
555 Broadway
New York, NY 10012-3919
212-343-6100
800-724-6527
Fax: 212-343-4801
Published for the administrative level, education professionals who are directly responsible for the implementing of electronic technology at the district, state and university levels.
8x Year
Lynn Diamond, Advertising Director
Therese Mageau, Editor

4748 Electronic School
1680 Duke Street
Alexandria, VA 22314
703-838-6722
Fax: 703-683-7590
cwilliams@nsba.org
www.electronic-school.com
The school technology authority.
Cheryl S Williams, Director
Ann Lee Flynn, Director Education

4749 Information Searcher
Datasearch Group
14 Hadden Road
Scarsdale, NY 10583-3328
914-723-1995
Fax: 914-723-1995
www.infosearcher.com
Quarterly newsletter for the Internet and curriculum-technology integration in school.
32 pages
Pam Berger, President
Bill Berger, Treasurer

4750 Journal of Computing in Childhood Education
AACE
PO Box 2966
Charlottesville, VA 22902-2966
757-623-7588
Fax: 703-997-8760
www.aace.org

Discusses the realm of software and technology now merging with primary education.

Quarterly

4751 Journal of Educational Technology Systems
58 New Mill Road
Smithtown, NY 11787-3342
516-632-8767
A compendium of articles submitted by professionals regarding the newest technology in the educational field.

Quarterly

Dr. Thomas Liao, Editor

4752 Journal of Information Systems Education
Bryant University
1150 Douglas Pike
Smithfield, RI 02917-1284
401-232-6000
800-622-7001
Fax: 401-232-6319
admission@bryant.edu
www.bryant.edu
Publishes original articles on current topics of special interest to Information Systems Educators and Trainers. Focus is applications-oriented articles describing curriculum, professional development or facilities issues. Topics include course projects/cases, lecture materials, curriculum design and/or implementation, workshops, faculty/student intern/extern programs, hardware/software selection and industry relations.

Quarterly

Richard Glass, Contact

4753 Journal of Research on Computing in Education
International Society for Technology in Education
1530 Wilson Boulevard
Suite 730
Arlington, VA 22209
703-348-4784
800-336-5191
Fax: 703-348-6459
iste@iste.org
www.iste.org
A quarterly journal of original research and detailed system and project evaluations. It also defines the state of the art and future horizons of educational computing.

Quarterly

Diane McGrath, Editor
Brian Lewis, M.A., C.A.E., CEO

4754 Journal of Special Education Technology
The Council for Exceptional Children
1920 Association Drive
Reston, VA 20191-1589
703-620-3660
888-232-7733
Fax: 703-264-9494
cec@cec.sped.org
cecp.air.org/teams/stratpart/cec.asp
Provides professionals in the field with information on new technologies, current research, exemplary practices, relevant issues, legislative events and more concerning the availability and effective use of technology and media for individuals with disabilities and/or who are gifted.

Quarterly

Herbert Rieth, Editor

4755 Matrix Newsletter
Department of CCTE, Teachers College/Communication
PO Box 8
New York, NY 10027-0008
212-678-3344
Fax: 212-678-8227
Newsletter describing activities and interests of Department of Communication, Computing and Technology.

14 pages SemiAnnually

Marie Sayer

4756 MultiMedia Schools
Information Today
143 Old Marlton Pike
Medford, NJ 08055-8750
609-654-6266
800-300-9868
Fax: 609-654-4309
custserv@infotoday.com
www.infotoday.com
A practical journal of multimedia, CD-Rom, online and Internet in K-12.

Thomas H Hogan, Publisher
Ferdi Serim, Editor

4757 National Forum of Instructional Technology Journal
McNeese State University
4205 Ryan Stree
Lake Charles, LA 70601-5915
337-475-5000
800-622-3352
Fax: 318-475-5467
www.mcneese.edu

Publication Date: 1939

Dr. J Mark Hunter, Editor

4758 Society for Applied Learning Technology
50 Culpeper Street
Warrenton, VA 20186
540-347-0055
800-457-6812
Fax: 540-349-3169
info@lti.org
www.salt.org

Publication Date: 1972 Quarterly

4759 TAM Connector
The Council for Exceptional Children
1920 Association Drive
Reston, VA 20191-1589
703-620-3660
888-232-7733
Fax: 703-264-9494
cec@cec.sped.org
cecp.air.org/teams/stratpart/cec.asp
Contains information about upcoming events, current trends and practices, state and national legislation, recently published materials and practical information relative to the availability and effective use of technology and media for individuals who are gifted or are disabled.

Quarterly

Cynthia Warger, Editor

4760 TECHNOS Quarterly for Education & Technolgy
Agency for Instructional Technology
8111 N. Lee Paul Road
Bloomington, IN 47404-7916
812-339-2203
800-457-4509
Fax: 812-333-4218
info@ait.net
www.ait.net
TECHNOS Quarterly is a forum for the discussion of ideas about the use of technology in education, with a focus on reform.

36 pages Quarterly
ISSN: 1060-5649

Michael F Sullivan, Executive Director
Carole Novak, Manager TECHNOS Press

4761 Tech Directions
Prakken Publications
275 Meity Drive
P.O. Box 8623
Ann Arbor, MI 48107-8623
734-975-2800
Fax: 734-975-2787
publisher@techdirections.com
www.eddigest.com
Issues programs, projects for educators in career-technical and technology education and monthly features on technology, computers, tech careers.

Monthly
ISSN: 1062-9351

Tom Bowden, Managing Editor

4762 Technology & Learning
NewBay Media
28 East 28th Street
12th Floor
New York, NY 10016
212-378-0400
800-607-4410
Fax: 212-378-0470
www.techlearning.com
Product reviews; hard-hitting, straightforward editorial features; ideas on challenging classroom activities; and more. Tailor made to the special needs of a professional and an educator.

Publication Date: 2006 60-80 pages Monthly Magazine
ISSN: 1053-6728
March & October

Susan McLester, Author
Judy Salpeter, Editor-in-Chief
Jo-Ann McDevitt, Publisher

4763 Technology Integration for Teachers
Master Teacher
One Leadership Lane
PO Box 1207
Manhattan, KS 66502-1207
800-669-9633
Fax: 800-669-1132
www.masterteacher.com

4 pages Monthly

4764 Technology Teacher
International Technology Education Association
1914 Association Drive
Suite 201
Reston, VA 20191-1538
703-860-2100
Fax: 703-860-0353
itea@iris.org
www.iteawww.org
Seeks to advance technological literacy through professional development activities and publications.

40 pages 8x Year

Kendall Starkweather, Executive Director
Kathleen de la Paz, Editor

4765 Technology in Education Newsletter
111 E 14th Street
#140
New York, NY 10003-4103
800-443-7432
This newsletter for K-12 educators and administrators, covers national trends of technology in education.

4766 Web Feet Guides
Thomson Gale
Thomson Gale World Headquarters
27500 Drake Road
Farmington Hills, MI 48331-3535
248-699-4253
800-877-4253
Fax: 877-363-4253
www.webfeetguides.com
The premier subject guides to the Internet, rigorously reviewed by librarians and educators, fully annotated, expanded and updated monthly. Appropriate for middle school through adult. Available in print, online, or MARC records. For more information, free trials and free samples.
Monthly

General

4767 **ABC Feelings Adage Publications**
Po Box 7280
Ketchum, ID 83340
208-788-5399
Fax: 208-788-4195
info@abcfeelings.com
www.abcfeelings.com
Interactive line of children's products that relate feelings to each letter of the alphabet. Encourages dialogue, understanding, communication, enhances self-esteem. Books, audiotape, poster, placemats, charts, activity cards, t-shirts and multicultural activity guides, floor puzzles,feelings dictionary, carpets.
Ages 3-10
Dr. Alexandra Delis-Abrams, President

4768 **ABDO Publishing Company**
P.O Box 398166
Minneapolis, MN 55439-5300
452-831-2120
800-800-1312
Fax: 800-862-3480
info@abdopublishing.com
www.abdopub.com
K-8 nonfiction books, including Abdo and Daughters imprint, high/low books for reluctant readers and Checkerboard Library with K-3 science, geography, and biographics for beginning readers. Sand Castle for pre-K to second grade, graduated reading program.
Jill Abdo Hansen, President
James Abdo, Publisher

4769 **ADL-A World of Difference Institute**
212-885-7700
education@adl.org
www.adl.org
Provider of anti-bias education materials and training for schools, universities, law enforcement agencies and community organizations.
Marvin D Nathan, National Chair
Jonathan Greenblatt, CEO & National Director

4770 **AGS**
4201 Woodland Road
Circle Pines, MN 55014-1796
763-786-4343
800-328-2560
Fax: 800-471-8457
Major test publisher and distributor of tests for literature, reading, English, mathematics, sciences, aptitude, and various other areas of education. Includes information on timing, scoring, teacher's guides and student's worksheets.

4771 **AIMS Education Foundation**
1595 S Chestnut Avenue
Fresno, CA 93702-4706
559-255-4094
888-733-2467
Fax: 559-255-6396
aimsed@fresno.edu
www.aimsedu.org
A nonprofit educational foundation that focuses on preparing materials for science and mathematics areas of education.

4772 **Ablex Publishing Corporation**
PO Box 811
Stamford, CT 06904-0811
201-767-8450
Fax: 201-767-8450
Publishes academic books and journals dealing with many different subject areas. Some of these include: education, linguistics, psychology, library science, computer and cognitive science, writing research and sociology.
Kristin K Butter, President

4773 **Acorn Naturalists**
155 El Camino Real
Tustin, CA 92780
714-838-4888
800-422-8886
Fax: 714-838-5309
www.acornnaturalists.com
Publishes and distributes science and environmental education materials for teachers, naturalists and outdoor educators. A complete catalog is available.
World Wildlife Fund, Author
Jennifer Rigby, Director
Mika Stonehawk, Operations Manager

4774 **Active Child**
PO Box 2346
Salem, OR 97308-2346
503-371-0865
Publishes creative curriculum for young children.

4775 **Active Learning**
10744 Hole Avenue
Riverside, CA 92505-2867
909-689-7022
Fax: 909-689-7142
Interactive learning center publishing materials for childhood education.

4776 **Active Parenting Publishers**
1220 Kennestone Circle
Suite 130
Marietta, GA 30066-6022
770-429-0565
800-825-0060
Fax: 770-429-0334
cservice@activeparenting.com
www.activeparenting.com
Produces and sells books and innovative video-based programs for use in parent education, self-esteem education and loss education groups/classes.

4777 **Addison-Wesley Publishing Company**
2725 Sand Hill Road
Menlo Park, CA 94025-7019
650-854-0300
Publisher and distributor of a wide range of fiction, nonfiction and textbooks for grades K-12 in the areas of mathematics, reading, language arts, science, social studies and counseling.

4778 **Advance Family Support & Education Program**
301 S Frio Street
Suite 103
San Antonio, TX 78207-4422
210-270-4630
Fax: 210-270-4612
Offers books and publications on counseling and support for the family, student and educator.

4779 **Alarion Press**
PO Box 1882
Boulder, CO 80306-1882
303-443-9039
800-523-9177
Fax: 303-443-9098
info@alarion.com
www.alarion.com
Video programs, posters, activities, manuals and workbooks dealing with History Through Art and Architecture for grades K-12.

4780 **Albert Whitman & Company**
250 South Northwest Highway
Suite 320
Park Ridge, IL 60068-2723
847-232-2800
800-255-7675
Fax: 847-581-0039
mail@awhitmanco.com
www.albertwhitman.com
Children's books.

4781 **Allyn & Bacon**
160 Gould Street
Needham Heights, MA 02194
781-455-1250
Fax: 781-455-1220
Publisher of college textbooks and professional reference books.

4782 **Alpha Publishing Company**
1910 Hidden Point Road
Annapolis, MD 21401-6002
410-757-5404
Educational materials for K-12 curricula.

4783 **American Association for State & Local History**
1717 Church Street
Nashville, TN 37203-2921
615-320-3203
Fax: 615-327-9013
www.aaslh.org
How-to books for anyone teaching history or social studies.

4784 **American Association of School Administrators**
1615 Duke Street
Alexandria, VA 22314
703-528-0700
Fax: 703-841-1543
info@aasa.org
www.aasa.org
Publishes a variety of educational materials and resources on education administration. Topics covered include scholarship and practice, children's program publications, policy, news and media, district-level change and more.
Daniel A Domenech, Executive Director
Chuck Woodruff, Chief Operating Officer

4785 **American Guidance Service**
4201 Woodland Road
Circle Pines, MN 55014-1796
612-786-4343
800-328-2560
Fax: 763-783-4658
Largest distributor of educational materials focusing on guidance counselors and educators in the field of counseling. Materials include books, pamphlets, workshops and information on substance abuse, childhood education, alcoholism, inner-city subjects and more.
Matt Keller, Marketing Director

4786 **American Institute of Physics**
2 Huntington Quadrangle
Suite 1NO1
Melville, NY 11747
516-576-2200
Fax: 516-349-9704
www.aip.org
Physics books.
Marc Brodsky, Executive Director

4787 **American Nuclear Society**
Outreach Department
555 N Kensington Avenue
La Grange Park, IL 60526-5592

708-352-6611
800-323-3044
Fax: 708-352-0499
outreach@ans.org
www.aboutnuclear.com
Nuclear science and technology, supplemental educational materials for grades K-12. ReActions newsletters.

4788 American Physiological Society
9650 Rockville Pike
Bethesda, MD 20814-3991
301-530-7132
Fax: 301-634-7098
www.the-aps.org
Videotapes, tracking materials and free teacher resource packets.

4789 American Technical Publishers
10100 Orland Parkway
Suite 200
Orland Parkway, IL 60467-5756
708-957-1100
800-323-3471
Fax: 708-957-1101
service@americantech.net
www.go2atp.com
Offers instructional materials for a variety of vocational and technical training areas.

4790 American Water Works Association
6666 W Quincy Avenue
Denver, CO 80235-3098
303-794-7711
800-926-7337
Fax: 303-347-0804
www.awwa.org
Activity books, teacher guides and more on science education.

Gary McCoy, Director-at-large

4791 Ampersand Press
750 Lake Street
Port Townsend, WA 98368
360-379-5187
800-624-4263
Fax: 360-379-0324
info@ampersandpress.com
www.ampersandpress.com
Nature and science educational games.

Lou Haller, Owner

4792 Amsco School Publications
315 Hudson Street
New York, NY 10013-1085
212-886-6500
800-969-8398
Fax: 212-675-7010
www.amscopub.com
Basal textbooks, workbooks and supplementary materials for grades 7-12.

4793 Anderson's Bookshops
123 West Jefferson
Naperville, IL 60540-3832
630-355-2665
Fax: 630-355-3470
www.andersonsbookshop.com
The very latest and best trade books to use in the classroom.

4794 Annenberg/CPB Project
1301 Pennsylvania Avenue NW
Suite 302
Washington, DC 20004-2037
202-783-0500
Fax: 202-783-0333
order@learner.org
www.learner.org
Offers teaching resources in chemistry, geology, physics and environmental science.

Pete Neal, General Manager
Larisa M Kirgan, Operations Officer

4795 Art Image Publications
PO Box 160
Derby Line, VT 05830-0568
800-361-2598
Fax: 800-559-2598
www.artimagepublications.com
Offers various products including art appreciation kits, art image mini-kits and visual arts programs for grades K-12.

Rachel Ross, President
Rachel Ross, Art Educational Consultant

4796 Art Visuals
PO Box 925
Orem, UT 84059-0925
801-226-6115
Fax: 801-226-6115
artvisuals@sisna.com
www.artvisuals.tripod.com
Social studies and art history products including an Art History Timeline, 20 feet long that represents over 50 different styles, ranging from prehistoric to contemporary art; Modern Art Styles, set of 30 posters depicting 20th century styles; Multicultural Posters, Africa, India, China, Japan and the World of Islam, with 18 posters in each culture. Sets on women artists and African American Artists. Each set is printed on hard cardstock, laminated and ultraviolet protected.

Diane Asay, Owner

4797 Asian American Curriculum Project
529 East Third Avenue
San Mateo, CA 94401
650-375-8286
800-874-2242
Fax: 650-375-8797
aacpinc@best.com
www.asianamericanbooks.com
Develops, promotes and disseminates Asian-American books to schools, libraries and Asian-Americans. Over 1,500 titles.

Florence M Hongo, General Manager

4798 Association for Science Teacher Education
University of Florida
11000 University Parkway
Pensacola, FL 32514-5732
850-474-2000
Fax: 850-474-3205
www.theaste.org
Yearbooks, journals, newsletters and information on AETS.

John Tilloston, President

4799 Association for Supervision & Curriculum Development
ASCD
1703 N Beauregard Street
Alexandria, VA 22311
703-578-9600
800-933-2723
Fax: 703-575-5400
press@ascd.org
www.ascd.org
Publishers of educational leadership books, audios and videos focusing on teaching and learning in all subjects and grade levels.

Ben Shuldiner, President
Deborah Delisle, CEO & Executive Director

4800 Association of American Publishers
71 5th Avenue
Floor 12
New York, NY 10003
212-255-0200
Fax: 212-255-7007
www.publishers.org
Association for the book publishing industry.

4801 Atheneum Books for Children
MacMillan Publishing Company
1633 Broadway
New York, NY 10019
212-512-2000
Fax: 800-835-3202
Hardcover trade books for children and young adults.

4802 Australian Press-Down Under Books
15235 Brand Boulevard
Suite A107
Mission Hills, CA 91345-1423
818-837-3755
Big Books, models for writing, small books and teacher's ideas books from Australia.

4803 Avon Books
1350 Avenue of the Americas
New York, NY 10019-4702
212-481-5600
Fax: 212-532-2172
Focuses on middle grade paperbacks for the classroom and features authors such as Cleary, Avi, Borks, Hous, Reeder, Hobbs, Hahn, Taylor and Prish.

4804 Ballantine/Del Rey/Fawcett/Ivy
201 E 50th Street
New York, NY 10022-7703
212-782-9000
800-638-6460
Fax: 212-782-8438
Offer paperback books for middle school and junior and senior high.

4805 Barron's Educational Series
250 Wireless Boulevard
Hauppauge, NY 11788-3924
631-434-3311
800-645-3476
Fax: 631-434-3217
barrons@barronseduc.com
www.barronseduc.com
Educational books, including a full line of juvenile fiction and non-fiction, and titles for test prep and guidance, ESL, foreign language, art history and techniques, business, and reference.

Frederick Glasser, Director School/Library Sale

4806 Baylor College of Medicine
One Baylor Plaza
Houston, TX 77030
713-798-4951
Fax: 713-798-6521
www.bcm.edu
Offers materials and programs in the scientific area from Texas Scope, Sequence and Coordination projects.

Peter G Traber, President
Robert H Allen, Chairman

4807 Beech Tree Books
1350 Avenue of the Americas
New York, NY 10019-4702
212-261-6500
Fax: 212-261-6518
Curriculum offering reading materials, fiction and nonfiction titles.

4808 Black Butterfly Children's Books
625 Broadway
Floor 10
New York, NY 10012-2611
212-982-3158
A wide variety of books focusing on children, hardcover and paperback.

4809 Blake Books
2222 Beebee Street
San Luis Obispo, CA 93401-5505

805-543-7314
800-727-8550
Fax: 805-543-1150
Photo books on nature, endangered species, habitats, etc. for ages 10 and up.
Paige Torres, President

4810 Bluestocking Press Catalog
Bluestocking Press
PO Box 1014
Placerville, CA 95997-1014
530-622-8586
800-959-8586
Fax: 530-642-9222
Jane@bluestockingpress.com
www.bluestockingpress.com
Approximately 800 items with a concentration in American History, economics and law. That includes fiction, nonfiction, primary source material, historical documents, facsimile newspapers, historical music, hands-on-kits, audio history, coloring books and more.
Jane A Williams, Coordinating Editor

4811 Boyds Mill Press
815 Church Street
Honesdale, PA 18431-1889
570-253-1164
Fax: 570-253-0179
Publishes books for children from preschool to young adult.

4812 BridgeWater Books
100 Corporate Drive
Mahwah, NJ 07430-2041
Distinctive children's hardcover books featuring award-winning authors and illustrators, including Laurence Yep, Babette Cole, Joseph Bruchac and others. An imprint of Troll Associates.

4813 Bright Ideas Charter School
2507 Central Freeway East
Wichita Falls, TX 76302-5802
940-767-1561
Fax: 940-767-1904
lydiaplmr@aol.com
K-12 curriculum framework for educators struggling to move toward a global tomorrow.
Lynda Plummer, President

4814 Brown & Benchmark Publishers
25 Kessel Court
Madison, WI 63711
608-273-0040
College textbooks in language arts and reading.

4815 Bureau for At-Risk Youth Guidance Channel
Guidance Channel
135 Dupont Street
PO Box 760
Plainview, NY 11803-0760
516-349-5520
800-999-6884
Fax: 800-262-1886
info@at-risk.com
www.at-risk.com
Publisher and distributor of educational curriculums, videos, publications and products for at-risk youth and the counselors and others who work with them. Bureau products focus on areas such as violence and drug prevention, character education, parenting skills and more.
Sally Germain, Editor-in-Chief

4816 Business Publishers
PO Box 17592
Baltimore, MD 21297
301-587-6300
800-274-6737
Fax: 301-585-9075
bpinews@bpinews.com
www.bpinews.com
Publishes education related materials.

4817 CLEARVUE/eav
6465 N Avondale Avenue
Chicago, IL 60631
773-775-9433
800-253-2788
Fax: 773-775-9855
slucas@clearvue.com
www.clearvue.com
CLEARVUE/eav offers educators the largest line of curriculum-oriented media in the industry. CLEARVUE/eav programs have, and will continue to enhance students' interest, learning, motivation and skills.
Sarah M Lucas, Communications Coordinator
Kelli Campbell, VP

4818 Calculators
7409 Fremont Avenue S
Minneapolis, MN 55423-3971
800-533-9921
Fax: 612-866-9030
Calculators and calculator books for K thru college level instruction. Calculator products by Texas Instruments, Casio, Sharp and Hewlett-Packard.
Richard Nelson, President

4819 Cambridge University Press
Edinburgh Building
Shaftesbury Road
Cambridge, England CB22RU
www.cup.cam.ac.uk
Curriculum materials and textbooks for science education for grades K-12.

4820 Candlewick Press
2067 Massachusetts Avenue
Cambridge, MA 02140-1340
617-661-3330
Fax: 617-661-0565
High quality trade hardcover and paperback books for children and young adults.

4821 Capstone Press
151 Good Counsel Drive
Mankato, MN 56001-3143
952-224-0529
888-262-6135
Fax: 888-262-0705
timadsen@capstone-press.com
www.capstonepress.com
PreK-12 Nonfiction publisher
Tim Mandsen, Director Marketing

4822 Careers/Consultants in Education Press
3050 Palm Aire Drive N
#310
Pompano Beach, FL 33069
954-974-3511
Fax: 954-974-5477
carconed@aol.com
Current education job lists for teacher and administrator positions in schools and colleges. Plus nine differently titled desk/reference paperback books.
Dr. Robert M Bookbinder, President

4823 Carolrhoda Books
A Division of Lerner Publishing Group
241 1st Avenue N
Minneapolis, MN 55401-1607
612-332-3344
800-328-4929
Fax: 612-332-7615
www.lernerbooks.com
Fiction and nonfiction for readers K through grade 6. List includes picture books, biographies, nature and science titles, multicultural and introductory geography books, and fiction for beginning readers.
Rebecca Poole, Submissions Editor

4824 Carson-Dellosa Publishing Company
PO Box 35665
Greensboro, NC 27425-5665
336-632-0084
800-321-0943
Fax: 336-632-087
Textbooks, manuals, workbooks and materials aimed at increasing students reading skills.

4825 Center for Play Therapy
425 S Welch Street
Complex 2
Denton, TX 76203
940-565-3864
Fax: 940-565-4461
cpt@unt.edu
cpt.unt.edu
Offers literature covering topics in the field of play therapy.
Sue Bratton, Ph.D, Director
Garry L Landreth, Ed.D, Founder

4826 Central Regional Educational Laboratory
2550 S Parker Road
Suite 500
Aurora, CO 80014
303-337-0990
Fax: 303-337-3005
twaters@mcrel.org
The Regional Educational Laboratories are educational research and development organizations supported by contracts with the US Education Department, Office of Educational Research and Improvement. Specialty area: curriculum, learning and instruction.
Dr. J Timothy Waters, Executive Director

4827 Charles Scribner & Sons
MacMillan Publishing Company
1633 Broadway
New York, NY 10019
212-632-4944
Fax: 800-835-3202
Hardcover trade books for children and young adults.

4828 Chicago Board of Trade
141 W Jackson Boulevard
Chicago, IL 60604-2992
312-435-3500
Educational materials including a new economics program entitled Commodity Challenge.

4829 Children's Book Council
12 West 37th Street
2nd Floor
New York, NY 10018-7480
212-966-1990
800-999-2160
Fax: 212-966-2073
staff@cbcbooks.org
www.cbcbooks.org
The Children's Book Council, Inc is the nonprofit trade association of publishers and packagers of trade books and related materials for children and young adults.
JoAnn Sabatino-Falkenstein, VP Marketing

4830 Children's Press
Grolier Publishing
90 Sherman Turnpike
Danbury, CT 06816

800-621-1115
Fax: 800-374-4329
publishing.grolier.com
Leading supplier of reference and children's nonfiction and fiction books.

4831 Children's Press/Franklin Watts
PO Box 1330
Danbury, CT 06813-1330
203-797-3500
Fax: 203-797-3197
K-12 curriculum materials.

4832 Children's Television Workshop
1 Lincoln Plaza
New York, NY 10023-7129
212-875-6809
Fax: 212-875-7388
Hands-on books for elementary school use in the area of science education.

Brenda Pilson, Review Coordinator
Elaine Israel, Editor-in-Chief

4833 Chime Time
2440-C Pleasantdale Road
Atlanta, GA 30340-1562
770-662-5664
Early childhood products and publications.

4834 Choices Education Project
Watson Institute for International Studies
Brown University
PO Box 1948
Providence, RI 02912-1948
401-863-3155
Fax: 401-863-1247
choices@brown.edu
www.choices.edu
Develops interactive, supplementary curriculum resources on current and historical international issues. Makes complex current and historic international issues accessible for secondary school students. Materials are low-cost, reproducible, updated annually.

Annually

4835 Close Up Publishing
44 Canal Center Plaza
Alexandria, VA 22314-1592
800-765-3131
Fax: 703-706-3564
Offers textbooks, workbooks and other publications focusing on self-esteem, learning and counseling.

4836 Cognitive Concepts
PO Box 1363
Evanston, IL 60204-1363
888-328-8199
Fax: 847-328-5881
www.cogcon.com
Leading provider of language and literacy software, books, internet services and staff development. Specialize in integrating technology with scientific principles and proven instructional methods to offer effective and affordable learning solutions for educators, specialists and families.

4837 College Board
45 Columbus Avenue
New York, NY 10023-6992
212-713-8000
Fax: 212-713-8282
www.collegeboard.org
Publishers of books of interest to educational researchers, policymakers, students, counselors, teachers; products to prepare students for college and test prep materials.

4838 Coloring Concepts
1732 Jefferson Street
Suite 7
Napa, CA 94559-1737
707-257-1516
800-257-1516
Fax: 707-253-2019
chris@coloringconcepts.com
www.coloringconcepts.com
Colorable active learning books for middle school through college that combine scientifically correct text with colorable illustrations to provide an enjoyable and educational experience that helps the user retain more information than during normal reading. Subjects include Anatomy, Marine Biology, Zoology, Botany, Human Evolution, Human Brain, Microbiology and biology.

Christopher Elson, Operations

4839 Comprehensive Health Education Foundation
22419 Pacific Hwy S
Seattle, WA 98198-5106
206-824-2907
800-833-6388
info@chef.org
www.chef.org
Primarily Health gives K-3 kids a dynamic, hands-on health program while teaching academic skills.

Larry Clark, President
Marvin Hamanishi, Vice President

4840 Computer Learning Foundation
PO Box 60007
Palo Alto, CA 94306-0007
408-720-8898
Fax: 408-730-1191
clf@computerlearning.org
www.computerlearning.org
Publishes books and videos on using technology.

4841 Computer Literacy Press
Computer Literacy Press
PO Box 562
Earlysville, VA 22936
513-600-3455
513-530-0110
Fax: 800-833-5413
info@complitpress.com
www.complitpress.com
Instructional materials using hands-on, step-by-step format, appropriate for courses in adult and continuing education, business education, computer literacy and applications, curriculum integration, Internet instruction, and training and staff development. Products are available for ranging from middle school through high school as well as post secondary, teacher training and adult/senior courses.

Robert First, President

4842 Concepts to Go
PO Box 10043
Berkeley, CA 94709-5043
510-848-3233
Fax: 510-486-1248
Develops and distributes manipulative activities for language arts and visual communications for ages 3-8.

4843 Congressional Quarterly
1414 22nd Street NW
Washington, DC 20037-1003
202-887-8500
Fax: 202-293-1487
Comprehensive publications and reference and paperback books pertaining to Congress, US Government and politics, the presidency, the Supreme Court, national affairs and current issues.

4844 Continental Press
520 E Bainbridge Street
Elizabethtown, PA 17022-2299
717-367-1836
800-233-0759
Fax: 717-367-5660
cpeducation@continentalpress.com
www.continentalpress.com
Publisher of print for PreK-12 (plus adult education). Programs relate to skill areas in reading, math, comprehension, phonics, etc. Producers of Testlynx Software.

4845 Cottonwood Press
107 Cameron Drive
Suite 398
Fort Collins, CO 80525
970-204-0715
800-864-4297
Fax: 970-204-0761
cottonwood@cottonwwodpress.com
www.cottonwoodpress.com
Publishes books focusing on teaching language arts and writing, grades 5-12.

Cheryl Thurston

4846 Council for Exceptional Children
The Council for Exceptional Children
2900 Crystal Drive
Suite 100
Arlington, VA 22202-3557
703-620-3660
888-232-7733
Fax: 703-264-9494
service@cec.sped.org
www.cec.sped.org
The Council for Exceptional Children is a major publisher of special education literature and produces a catalog semiannually.

Mikki Garcia, President
Laurie VanderPloeg, President Elect

4847 Creative Teaching Press
Po Box 2723
Huntington Beach, CA 92647-0723
800-287-8879
Fax: 800-229-9929
customerservice@creativeteaching.com
www.creativeteaching.com
Offers language and literature-based books including Teaching Basic Skills through Literature, Literature-Based Homework Activities, I Can Read! I Can Write!, Multicultural Art Activities, Responding to Literature, and Linking Math and Literature.

Jim Connelly, President
Luella Connelly, Co-Founder

4848 Cricket Magazine Group
315 5th Street
Peru, IL 61354-2859
815-223-1500
Magazines of high quality children's literature.

4849 Curriculum Associates
PO Box 2001
North Billerica, MA 01862-0901
978-667-8000
800-225-0248
Fax: 800-366-1158
cainfo@curriculumassociates.com
www.curriculumassociates.com
Supplementary educational materials; cross-curriculum, language arts, reading, study skills, test preparation, diagnostic assessments, emergent readers, videos, and software.

4850 DC Heath & Company
125 Spring Street
Lexington, MA 02421-7801
781-862-6650

Publishes resources for all academic levels ranging from textbooks, fiction and nonfiction titles to business and college guides.

4851 DLM Teaching Resources
PO Box 4000
Allen, TX 75013-1302
972-248-6300
800-527-4747
Offers a variety of teacher's resources and guides for testing in all areas of education.

4852 Dawn Publications
14618 Tyler Foote Road
Nevada City, CA 95959-9316
530-478-7540
800-545-7475
Fax: 530-478-0112
Specializes in nature, children and health and healing books, tapes and videos and dedicated to helping people experience unity and harmony.
Bob Rinzler, Publisher
Glenn Hoveman, Editor

4853 Delta Education
80 Northwest Blvd.
Nashua, NH 03061-3000
800-258-1302
Fax: 800-282-9560
Science programs, materials and curriculum kits.

4854 Dial Books for Young Readers
345 Hudson Street
New York, NY 10014-3658
212-366-2800
Fax: 212-366-2938
www.penguinputnam.com
General hardcover, children's books, from toddler through young adult, fiction and nonfiction.

4855 Didax Educational Resources
PO Box 507
Rowley, MA 01969-0907
978-948-2340
800-458-0024
Fax: 978-948-2813
info@didaxinc.com
www.didaxinc.com
High quality educational materials featuring Unifix and hundreds of math and reading supplements.
Brian Scarlett, President
Martin Kennedy, VP

4856 Dinah-Might Activities
PO Box 39657
San Antonio, TX 78218-6657
210-698-0123
Fax: 210-698-0095
Learn how to integrate language arts, math, map and globe skills and more into a science curriculum. Books include The Big Book of Books and Activities, Organizing the Integrated Classroom, Write Your Own Thematic Units and Reading and Writing All Day Long.

4857 Dinocardz Company
146 5th Avenue
San Francisco, CA 94118-1310
415-751-5809
Dinosaur curriculums for grades 1-3 and 4-6.

4858 Disney Press
Disney Juvenile Publishing
114 5th Avenue
New York, NY 10011-5604
212-633-4400
Fax: 212-633-5929
Hardcover trade and library editions and paperback books for children, grades K-12.
Liisa-Ann Fink, President

4859 Dominic Press
1949 Kellogg Avenue
Carlsbad, CA 92008-6582
619-481-3838
Offers a range of materials for the Reading Recovery Program and Chapter 1 programs.

4860 Dorling Kindorley Company
95 Madison Avenue
New York, NY 10016
212-213-4800
Fax: 212-689-5254
Science books for all grade levels.

4861 Dover Publications
31 E 2nd Street
Mineola, NY 11501
516-294-7000
Fax: 516-742-6953
Fun and educational storybooks, coloring, activity, cut-and-assemble toy books, science for children.
Clarence Strowbridge, President

4862 Dutton Children's Books
375 Hudson Street
New York, NY 10014-3658
212-366-2000
Fax: 212-366-2948
General hardcover children's books from toddler through young adult, fiction and nonfiction.

4863 DynEd International
1350 Bayshore Highway
Suite 850
Burlingame, CA 94010
800-765-4375
Fax: 650-375-7017
www.dyned.com
Pre-K-adult listening and speaking skill development English language acquisition software.
Steven Kearney, Sales
Sue Young, Operations

4864 EBSCO Publishing
EBSCO Publishing
10 Estes Street
Ipswich, MA 01938
800-653-2726
Fax: 978-356-6565
information@ebscohost.com
www.ebscohost.com
Database and eBook provider for libraries and other institutions — more than 375 full-text and secondary research databases and more than 300,000 eBooks available via the EBSCOhost platform. EBSCO's content services K-12 students to public library patrons, from academic, corporate and medical researchers to clinicians and governments around the world.
Tim Collins, President
Sam Brooks, EVP Sales/Marketing

4865 ERICAE Clearinghouse on Assessment & Evaluation
University of Maryland
1129 Shriver Laboratory
Building 075
College Park, MD 20742-5701
301-405-7449
800-464-3742
Fax: 301-405-8134
feedback3@ericae.net
ericae.net
Provides information on topics pertaining to tests and other measurement devices, research design and methodology.

4866 ETA - Math Catalog
620 Lakeview Parkway
Vernon Hills, IL 60061-1828
847-816-5050
800-445-5985
Fax: 847-816-5066
info@etauniverse.com
www.etauniverse.com
Offers a full line of mathematics products, materials, books, textbooks and workbooks for grades K-12.
Mary Cooney, Product Development Manager
Monica Butler, Director Marketing

4867 ETR Associates
4 Carbonero Way
Scotts Valley, CA 95066
831-438-4060
800-321-4407
Fax: 800-435-8433
www.etr.org
ETR Associate's mission is to enhance the well-being of individuals, families and communities by providing leadership, educational resources, training and research in health promotion with an emphasis on sexuality and health education.
Robert Keet, President
Arnold W. Kriegel, Vice President

4868 EVAN-Motor Corporation
18 Lower Ragsdale Drive
Monterey, CA 93940-5728
831-649-5901
Fax: 800-777-4332
Resource materials for K-6 science educational programs.

4869 Early Start-Fun Learning
PO Box 350187
Jacksonville, FL 32235-0187
904-641-6138
Preschool materials for the educator.

4870 Earth Foundation
5151 Mitchelldale
B11
Houston, TX 77092-7200
713-686-9453
Fax: 713-686-6561
Join the largest active network of educators working to save endangered ecosystems and their species! Multi-disciplinary, hands-on curriculum and videos for the classroom.
Cynthia Everage, President

4871 Editorial Projects in Education
6935 Arlington Road
Suite 100
Bethesda, MD 20814-5233
301-280-3100
800-346-1834
Fax: 301-280-3250
customercare@epe.org
www2.edweek.org
Publishes various newsletters and publications in the fields of history and education.
Christopher B Swanson, Director
Carole Vinograd Bausell, Assistant Director

4872 Edmark
Riverdeep Inc.
100 Pine Street
Suite 1900
San Francisco, CA 94111
415-659-2000
888-242-6747
Fax: 415-659-2020

info@riverdeep.net
www.edmark.com
Develops innovative and effective educational materials for children.

Barry O'Callaghan, Chairman
Tony Mulderry, Executive Vice President

4873 Education Center
3515 W Market Street
Greensboro, NC 27403-1309
336-273-9409
Publishers of the Mailbox, teacher's helper magazines, learning centers clubs, classroom beautiful bulletin board clubs, the storybook club and more.

4874 Educational Marketer
SIMBA Information
11 Riverbend Drive
PO Box 4234
Stamford, CT 06907-0234
800-307-2529
Fax: 203-358-5824
Contains a range of print and electronic tools, including software and multimedia materials for educational institutions.

4875 Educational Press Association of America
Glassboro State College
Glassboro, NJ 08028
609-445-7349
Offers various publications and bibliographic data focusing on all aspects of education.

4876 Educational Productions
9000 SW Gemini Drive
Beaverton, OR 97008
503-644-7000
800-950-4949
Fax: 503-350-7000
custserv@edpro.com
www.edpro.com
Video training programs that help increase parenting skills and help every teacher meet performance standards. Offers training on preventing discipline problems, increasing parenting skills, supporting literacy efforts and more.

4877 Educational Teaching Aids
620 Lakeview Pkwy
Vernon Hills, IL 60061-1838
847-816-5050
800-445-5985
Fax: 847-816-5066
info@etauniverse.com
www.etauniverse.com
Manipulatives to enhance understanding of basic concepts and to help bridge the gap between the concrete and the abstract.

4878 Educators Progress Service
214 Center Street
Randolph, WI 53956
920-326-3127
888-951-4469
Fax: 920-326-3126
www.freeteachingaids.com
A complete spectrum of curriculum and mixed media resources for allgrade levels.

4879 Educators Publishing Service
31 Smith Place
Cambridge, MA 02138-1089
617-547-6706
800-225-5750
Fax: 617-547-0412
www.epsbooks.com
Supplementary workbooks and teaching materials in reading, spelling, vocabulary, comprehension, and elementary math, as well as materials for assessment and learning differences.

4880 Edumate-Educational Materials
2231 Morena Boulevard
San Diego, CA 92110-4134
619-275-7117
Multicultural and multilingual materials in the form of toys, puzzles, books, videos, music, visuals, games, dolls and teacher resources. Special emphasis on Spanish and other languages. Literature offered from North and South America.

Gustavo Blankenburg, President

4881 Ellis
406 W 10600 S
Suite 610
Salt Lake City, UT 84003
801-374-3424
888-756-1570
Fax: 801-374-3495
www.ellis.com
Publish software that teaches English.

4882 Encyclopaedia Britannica
333 N La Salle Street
Chicago, IL 60610
312-347-7159
800-323-1229
Fax: 312-294-2104
www.britannica.com
Books and related educational materials.

4883 Energy Learning Center
USCEA
1776 I Street NW
Suite 400
Washington, DC 20006-3700
703-741-5000
Fax: 703-741-6000
Energy learning materials.

4884 Essential Learning Products
PO Box 2590
Columbus, OH 43216-2590
800-357-3570
Fax: 614-487-2272
Publishers of phonics workbooks.

4885 Ethnic Arts & Facts
PO Box 20550
Oakland, CA 94620-0550
510-465-0451
888-278-5652
Fax: 510-465-7488
eaf@ethnicartsnfacts.com
www.ethnicartsnfacts.com
Kit titles include: Traditional Africa, Urban Africa, China, Guatemala, Peru, Huichol Indians of Mexico, Chinese Shadow Puppet Kit. African-American Music History Mini-Kit. Artifact kits/resource booklets designed to enhance appreciation of cultural diversity, improve geographic literacy and sharpen critical thinking and writing skills.

Susan Drexler, Curriculum Specialist

4886 Evan-Moor Corporation
18 Lower Ragsdale Drive
Monterey, CA 93940-5728
How to Make Books with Children and other fine teacher resources and reproducible materials for all curriculum areas grades PreK-6.

4887 Everyday Learning Corporation
PO Box 812960
Chicago, IL 60681-2960
800-382-7670
Fax: 312-233-7860
University of Chicago school mathematics project. Everyday Mathematics enriched curriculum for grades K-6.

4888 Exploratorium
3601 Lyon Street
San Francisco, CA 94123-1099
415-563-7337
Fax: 415-561-0307
www.exploratorium.edu
Exploratorium is dedicated to the formal and informal teaching of science using innovative interactive methods of inquiry. It publishes materials for educators and provides professional development opportunities both in print and online.

Quarterly/Monthly

4889 Extra Editions K-6 Math Supplements
PO Box 38
Urbana, IL 61803-0038
Fax: 614-794-0107
Special needs math supplements offering 70 single-topic units from K-6 that reach students your basic math program misses. Extra Editions newspaper-like format uses animation with a hands-on approach to show real life necessity for computational skills, time, money, problem solving, critical thinking, etc. Ideal for Chapter One, Peer-Tutoring, Parental Involvement, Home Use, and more.

Craig Rucker, General Manager
Earl Ockenga, Author/Owner

4890 F(G) Scholar
Future Graph
538 Street Road
Suite 200
Southhampton, PA 18966-3780
215-396-0721
Fax: 215-396-0724
A revolutionary program for teaching, learning and using math. This single program allows students and teachers easy answers to Algebra, Trigonometry, Pre-Calculus, Calculus, Statistics, Probability and more. It combines all of the power of a graphing calculator, spreadsheet, drawing tools, mathematics and programming/scripting language and much more, and makes it simple and fun to use.

4891 Facts on File
11 Penn Plaza
New York, NY 10001
212-967-8800
800-322-8755
Fax: 212-967-9196
llikoff@factsonfile.com
www.factsonfile.com
Reference books for teacher education, software, hardware and educational computer systems.

9 Hardcover Books

Laurie Likoff, Editorial Director

4892 Farrar, Straus & Giroux
19 Union Square W
New York, NY 10003-3304
212-741-6900
Fax: 212-633-9385
Children's, young adult and adult trade books in hardcover and paperback, including Sunburst Books, Aerial Miraso/libros juveniles and Hill and Wang.

4893 First Years
1 Kiddie Drive
Avon, MA 02322-1171
508-588-1220
Early childhood books, hardcover and paperback.

4894 Forbes Custom Publishing
60 5th Avenue
New York, NY 10011-8802
513-229-1000
800-355-9983
Fax: 800-451-3661

fcpinfo@forbes.com
www.forbescp.com
Offers educators and teachers the opportunity to select unique teaching material to create a book designed specifically for their courses.

4895 Formac Distributing
5502 Atlantic Street
Halifax, NS E3HIG-4
902-421-7022
800-565-1905
Fax: 902-425-0166
Contemporary and historical fiction for ages 6-15. Multicultural themes featuring Degrassi Y/A series; first novel chapter books.

4896 Frank Schaffer Publications
3195 Wilson Drive NW
Grand Rapids, MI 49534
800-417-3261
Fax: 888-203-9361
cpg_custserve@schoolspecialty.com
www.frankschaffer.com
Best-selling supplemental materials including charts, literature notes, resource materials and more.

4897 Franklin Watts
Grolier Publishing
Sherman Turnpike
Danbury, CT 06816
800-621-1115
800-843-3749
Fax: 800-374-4329
Publisher of library bound books, paperback and Big Books for literature based, multicultural classrooms and school libraries.

4898 Free Spirit Publishing
217 Fifth Avenue North
Suite 200
Minneapolis, MN 55401-1299
612-338-2068
800-736-7323
Fax: 612-337-5050
Free Spirit is the leading publisher of learning tools that support young people's social and emotional health.

4899 Frog Publications
PO Box 280996
Tampa, FL 33682
813-935-5845
Fax: 813-935-3764
www.frog.com
An organized system of cooperative games for K-5 reading, language arts, thinking skills, math, social studies, Spanish and multicultural studies. Parental Involvement Program, Learning Centers, Test Preperation, Afterschool Program Materials. Drops in the Bucket daily practice books.

4900 Gareth Stevens
330 W Olive Street
Suite 100
Milwaukee, WI 53212
414-332-3520
800-542-2595
Fax: 414-336-0156
info@gsinc.com
garethstevens.com
Complete display of supplemental children's reading material for grades K-6, including our New World Almanac Library imprint grades 6-12.
Bi-Annually
ISSN: 0-8368
Mark Sachner, Author
Juanita Jones, Marketing Manager
Jonathan Strickland, National Sales Manager

4901 Goethe House New York
1014 5th Avenue
New York, NY 10028-0104
Teaching materials on Germany for the social studies classroom in elementary, middle and high schools.

4902 Goodheart-Willcox Publisher
18604 W Creek Drive
Tinley Park, IL 60477-6243
800-323-0440
Fax: 888-409-3900
custerv@goodheartwillcox.com
www.goodheartwillcox.com
Comprehensive text designed to help young students learn about themselves, others, and the environment. Readers will develop skills in clothing, food, decision making, and life management. Case studies throughout allow students to apply learning to real-life situations.

4903 Greenhaven Press
PO Box 9187
Farmington Hills, MI 48333-9187
800-231-5163
800-231-5163
Fax: 248-699-8035
info@greenhaven.com
Publishers of the Opposing Viewpoints Series, presenting viewpoints in an objective, pro/con format on some of today's controversial subjects.

4904 Greenwillow Books
1350 Avenue of the Americas
New York, NY 10019-4702
212-261-6500
Fax: 212-261-6518
Offers publications for all reading levels.

4905 Grey House Publishing
4419 Route 22
Amenia, NY 12501
518-789-8700
800-562-2139
Fax: 518-789-0545
books@greyhouse.com
www.greyhouse.com
Publisher of educational reference directories, and encyclopedias.
Richard Gottlieb, President
Leslie Mackenzie, Publisher

4906 Grolier Publishing
90 Sherman Turnpike
Danbury, CT 06816
203-797-3500
800-621-1115
Fax: 203-797-3197
www.publishing.grolier.com
Publisher of library bound and paperback books in the areas of social studies, science, reference, history, and biographies for schools and libraries for grades K-12.

4907 Gryphon House
Gryphon House
PO Box 275
Mount Rainier, MD 20712-0275
301-779-6200
Fax: 301-595-0051
info@ghbooks.com
www.ghbooks.com
Resource and activity books for early childhood teachers and directors.
Cathy Callootte, Marketing Director

4908 H. W. Wilson
Grey House Publishing
2 University Plaza
Suite 310
Hackensack, NJ 07601
201-968-0500
800-221-1592
Fax: 201-968-0511
info@hwwilsoninprint.com
www.hwwilsoninprint.com
H. W. Wislon publishes database and reference resources to serve libraries, schools and corporations.

4909 Hands-On Prints
PO Box 5899-268
Berkeley, CA 94705
510-601-6279
Fax: 510-601-6278
Specializes in cultural and language materials for children with an emphasis on internationalism and multiculturalism.
Christina Cheung, President

4910 Hardcourt Religion Publishers
6277 Sea Harbor Drive
Orlando, FL 32887
563-557-3700
800-922-7696
Fax: 563-557-3719
hardcourtreligion.com
Publishers of religion education materials for schools and parishes.

4911 Hazelden Educational Materials
PO Box 176
Center City, MN 55012-0176
651-257-4010
Fax: 651-213-4590
Educational publisher of materials supporting both students and faculty in areas of substance abuse and related topics.

4912 Heinemann
361 Hanover Street
Portsmouth, NH 03801-3959
603-431-7894
Fax: 203-750-9790
Holistic/student-centered publications, videotapes and workshops for parents, teachers and administrators.

4913 Henry Holt & Company
175 Fifth Avenue
New York, NY 10010
646-307-5095
800-628-9658
Fax: 212-633-0748
Books and materials for classroom teachers, grades 6-adult, including programs on science literacy.

4914 Henry Holt Books for Young Readers
115 W 18th Street
New York, NY 10011-4113
800-628-9658
Fax: 212-647-0490
Hardcover and paperback trade books for preschool through young adult, fiction and nonfiction. Also, big books and promotional materials are available.

4915 High Touch Learning
PO Box 754
Houston, MN 55943-0754
507-896-3500
800-255-0645
Fax: 507-896-3243

Classroom interactive learning maps promoting the hands-on approach to the teaching of social studies.

4916 HighScope Educational Research Foundation
600 N River Street
Ypsilanti, MI 48198-2898
800-587-5639
Fax: 734-485-0704
publications@highscope.org
highscope.org
Provides early childhood educational materials, with over 300 titles of books, videos, cassettes and CDs to choose from. Research and training materials as well as curriculum and development materials are based on the HighScope active learning approach.
Sue Bredekamp, Ph.D, Chair
Cheryl Polk, Ph.D, President

4917 Holiday House
425 Madison Avenue
New York, NY 10017-1110
212-688-0085
Fax: 212-688-0395
Hardcover and paperback children's books. General fiction and nonfiction, preschool through high school.

4918 Hoover's
5800 Airport
Dallas, TX 78752-3812
512-374-4500
Fax: 512-374-4501
Everything educational, for the early childhood and K-12 market. As a partner for over 100 years, the company is eager to extend their commitment to produce quality, timely shipping and customer service to the public. Offer over 10,000 products for infants, toddlers, pre-school and school age educational needs.

4919 Horn Book Guide
Horn Book
56 Roland Street
Suite 200
Boston, MA 02129
617-628-0225
800-325-1170
Fax: 617-628-0882
info@hbook.com
www.hbook.com
The most comprehensive review source of children's and young adult books available. Published each spring and fall, the Guide contains concise, critical reviews of almost every hardcover trade children's and young adult book published in the United States - nearly 2,000 books each issue.
BiAnnually
ISSN: 1044-405X
Anne Quirk, Marketing Manager
Roger Sutton, Editor

4920 Houghton Mifflin Books for Children
222 Berkeley Street
Boston, MA 02116-3748
617-351-5000
800-225-3362
Fax: 617-351-1111
www.hmco.com
Wide variety of children's and young adult books, fiction and nonfiction.

4921 Houghton Mifflin Company: School Division
222 Berkeley Street
Boston, MA 02116-3748
617-351-5000
Fax: 617-651-1106
Children's literature; K-12 reading and language arts print and software programs; and testing and evaluation for K-12.

4922 Hyperion Books for Children
114 5th Avenue
New York, NY 10011-5604
212-633-4400
Fax: 212-633-5929
Children's books in paperback and hardcover editions.

4923 ITP South-Western Publishing Company
5101 Madison Road
Cincinnati, OH 45227-1427
800-824-5179
Fax: 800-487-8488
Innovative instructional materials for teaching integrated science.

4924 Idea Factory
10710 Dixon Drive
Riverview, FL 33569-7406
813-677-6727
Teacher resource books, science project ideas, materials and more for elementary and middle school teachers.

4925 Illinois Early Intervention Clearinghouse
University of Illinois at Urbana-Champaign
51 Gerty Drive
Champaign, IL 61820-7469
217-333-1386
877-275-3227
ecap@illinois.edu
eiclearinghouse.org
The Illinois Early Intervention Clearinghouse provides publications and information to the early childhood and parenting communities on topics relating to the development of children with special needs and their families.
Meghan Burke, Co-Principal Investigator
Amy Santos, Ph.D, Co-Principal Investigator

4926 Institute for Chemical Education
University of Wisconsin
1101 University Avenue
Madison, WI 53706-1322
608-262-3033
800-991-5534
Fax: 608-265-8094
ice@chem.wisc.edu
ice.chem.wisc.edu
Hands-on activities, publications, kits and videos.

4927 Institute for Educational Leadership - Publications
4301 Connecticut Avenue NW
Suite 100
Washington, DC 20008
202-822-8405
Fax: 202-872-4050
iel@iel.org
iel.org
The Institute's list of publications on educational trends and policies is available to the public.
C. Kent McGuire, Chair
Johan Uvin, President

4928 IntelliTools
1720 Corporate Circle
Petaluma, CA 94954
707-773-2000
800-899-6687
Fax: 707-773-2001
www.intellitools.com
Provider of hardware and software giving students with special needs comprehensive access to learning.

4929 Intellimation
130 Cremona Drive
Santa Barbara, CA 93117-5599
805-968-2291
800-346-8355
Fax: 805-968-8899
Educational materials in all areas of curriculum for early learning through college level. Over 400 titles are available in video, and software and multimedia exclusively for the Macintosh. Free catalogs avaiable.
Karin Fisher, Marketing Associate
Marlene Carlyle, Marketing Supervisor

4930 Intercultural Press
100 City Hall Plaza
Suite 501
Boston, MA 02108
617-523-3801
888-273-2539
Fax: 617-523-3708
books@interculturalpress.com
www.interculturalpress.com
Publishes over 100 titles.
Judy Carl-Hendrick, Managing Editor

4931 J Weston Walch, Publisher
PO Box 658
Portland, ME 04104-0658
207-772-2846
800-558-2846
Fax: 207-772-3105
www.walch.com
Walch Publishing is an independent, family-owned publisher of educational supplemental materials for grades 3 through 12 and adult makets.

4932 Jacaranda Designs
3000 Jefferson Street
Boulder, CO 80304-2638
707-374-2543
Fax: 707-374-2543
Authentic African children's books from Kenya, including modern concept stories for K-3 in bilingual editions, folktales, and traditional cultural stories for older readers. All books are written and illustrated by African Kenyans.
Carrie Jenkins Williams, President

4933 Jarrett Publishing Company
PO Box 1460
Ronkonkoma, NY 11779
631-981-4248
Fax: 631-588-4722
Offers a wide range of books for today's educational needs.

4934 JayJo Books
Guidance Channel
135 Dupont Street
PO Box 760
Plainview, NY 11803
516-349-5520
800-999-6884
Fax: 516-349-5521
jayjobooks@guidancechannel.com
www.jayjo.com
Publisher of books to help teachers, parents and children cope with chronic illnesses, special needs and health education in classroom, family and social settings.
Sally Germain, Editor-in-Chief

4935 John Wiley & Sons
111 River Street
Hoboken, NJ 07030-5774

201-748-6000
Fax: 201-748-6088
Publish science and nature books for children and adults.

4936 Jossey-Bass: An Imprint of Wiley
Jossey-Bass/Pfeiffer
989 Market Street
San Francisco, CA 94103-1741
415-433-1740
Fax: 415-433-0499
www.josseybass.com
Creating educational incentives that work.
Adrianne Biggs, Publicity/Manager
Jennifer A O'Day, Editor

4937 Junior Achievement
1 Education Way
Colorado Springs, CO 80906-4477
719-540-8000
Fax: 719-540-6127
Provides business and economics-related materials and programs to students in grades K-12. All programs feature volunteers from the local business community. Materials are free, but available only from local Junior Achievement offices.

4938 Kaeden Corporation
PO Box 16190
19915 Lake Road
Rocky River, OH 44116
440-356-0030
800-890-7323
Fax: 440-356-5081
lcowan@kaedeen.com
www.kaeden.com
Books for emergent readers at the K, 1 and 2 levels, ideal for Title 1 and Reading Recovery and other at-risk reading programs.
Laura Cowan, Sales Manager
Joan Hoyer, Office Manager

4939 Kane/Miller Book Publishers
PO Boxn 8515
La Jolla, CA 92038-0529
858-456-0540
Fax: 858-456-9641
info@kanemiller.com
www.kanemiller.com
English translation of foreign children's picture books. Distributors of Spanish language children's books.
Byron Parnell, Sales Manager
Kira Lynn, President

4940 Keep America Beautiful
1010 Washington Boulevard
Stamford, CT 06901
203-323-8987
Fax: 203-325-9199
info@kab.org
www.kab.org
K-12 curriculum specializing in litter prevention and environmental education. Education posters with lesson plans printed right on the back of each poster and school recycling guides.

4941 Kendall-Hunt Publishing Company
4050 Westmark Drive
Dubuque, IA 52002-2624
319-589-1000
800-228-0810
Fax: 800-772-9165
webmaster@kendallhunt.com
www.kendallhunt.com
A leading custom publisher in the United States with over 6,000 titles in print. Kendall/Hunt publishes educational materials for kindergarten through college to continuing education creditation and distance learning courses.
Karen Berger, Customer Service Assistant

4942 Knowledge Adventure
2377 Crenshaw Blvd
Suite 302
Torrance, CA 90501
310-533-3400
Fax: 310-533-3700
editorial@education.com
www.knowledgeadventure.com
Develops, publishes, and distributes best-selling multimedia educational software for use in both homes and schools.

4943 Knowledge Unlimited
PO Box 52
Madison, WI 53701-0052
800-356-2303
Fax: 608-831-1570
www.newscurrents.com
NewsCurrents, the most effective current events programs for grades 3-12. Now available on DVD or Online.

4944 Kraus International Publications
358 Saw Mill River Road
Millwood, NY 10546-1035
914-762-2200
800-223-8323
Fax: 914-762-1195
Offers teacher resource notebooks with complete resource information for teachers and administrators at all levels. Great for program planning, quick reference, inservice training. Also offers books on early childhood education, English/language arts, mathematics, science, health education and visual arts.
Barry Katzen, President

4945 Lake Education
AGS/Lake Publishing Company
500 Harbor Boulevard
Belmont, CA 94002-4075
650-592-1606
800-328-2560
Fax: 800-471-8457
Alternative learning materials for underachieving students grades 6-12, RSL and adult basic education. High interest, low readability fiction, adapted classic literature, lifeskills and curriculum materials to supplement and support many basal programs.
Phil Schlenter
Carol Hegarty, VP Editorial

4946 Langenseheidt Publishing
515 Valley Street
Maplewood, NJ 07040-1337
800-526-4953
Fax: 908-206-1104
edusales@hammond.com
www.hammondmap.com
World maps, atlases, general reference guides and CD-Roms.

4947 Lawrence Hall of Science
University of California
Berkeley, CA 94720
510-642-5132
Fax: 510-642-1055
lhsinfo@uclink.berkeley.edu
www.lawrencehallofscience.org
Offers programs and materials in the field of science and math education for teachers, families and interested citizens. Exhibits include Equals, Family Math, CePUP and FOSS.
Linda Schneider, Marketing Manager
Mike Salter, Marketing/PR Associate

4948 Leap Frog Learning Materials
6401
Suite 100
Emeryville, CA 94608-1071
510-596-3333
800-701-5327
Learning materials, books, posters, games and toys for children.

4949 Learning Connection
19 Devane Street
Frostproof, FL 33843-2017
863-635-5610
800-338-2282
Fax: 863-635-4676
Thematic, literature-based units with award-winning books, media and hands-on for PK-12 including parent involvement, early childhood, bilingual, literacy, math, writing, science and multicultural.

4950 Learning Disabilities Association of America
4156 Library Road
Pittsburgh, PA 15234-1349
412-341-1515
888-300-6710
Fax: 412-344-0224
info@ldaamerica.org
ldaamerica.org
The national office has a resource center with over 500 publications for sale. Publications explore the subject of disability, with empasis on learning disabilities.
Patricia Lillie, President
Mary-Clare Reynolds, Executive Director

4951 Learning Links
2300 Marcus Avenue
New Hyde Park, NY 11042-1083
516-437-9075
800-724-2616
Fax: 516-437-5392
learningLx@aol.com
www.learinglinks.com
All you need for literature based instruction; Noveltie, study guides, thematic units books and more.

4952 Lee & Low Books
95 Madison Avenue
Suite 606
New York, NY 10016-3303
212-779-4400
Fax: 212-683-1894
info@leeandlow.com
www.leeandlow.com
A multicultural children's book publisher. Our primary focus is on picture books, especially stories set in contemporary America. Spanish language titles are available.
Craig Low, VP Publisher
Louise May, Executive Editor

4953 Leo A Myer Associates/LAMA Books
20956 Corsair Boulevard
Hayward, CA 94545-1002
510-785-1091
Fax: 510-785-1099
lama@lmabooks.com
Writers and publishers of HVAC books.
Barbara Ragura, Marketing Assistant

4954 Lerner Publishing Group
A Division Lerner Publications Group
241 1st Avenue N
Minneapolis, MN 55401-1607
612-332-3344
800-328-4929

Fax: 612-332-7615
www.lernerbooks.com
Primarily nonfiction for readers of all grade levels. List includes titles encompassing nature, geography, natural and physical science, current events, ancient and modern history, world art, special interests, sports, world cultures, and numerous biography series. Some young adult and middle grade fiction.

Jennifer Martin, Submissions Editor

4955 Linden Tree Children's Records & Books
170 State Street
Los Altos Hills, CA 94022-2863
650-949-3390
Fax: 650-949-0346
Offers a wide variety of books, audio cassettes and records for children.

4956 Listening Library
One Park Avenue
Old Greenwich, CT 06870-1727
203-637-3616
800-243-4504
Fax: 800-454-0606
moreinfo@listeninglib.com
www.listeninglib.com
A producer of quality unabridged audiobooks for listeners of all ages. Specializing in children's literature and adult classics.

BiAnnually

Annette Imperati, Director Sales/Marketing

4957 Little, Brown & Company
3 Center Plaza
Boston, MA 02108-2084
617-227-0730
Fax: 617-263-2854
Trade books for children and young adults, hardcover and paper, including Sierra Club Books for Children.

4958 Lodestar Books
375 Hudson Street
New York, NY 10014-3658
212-366-2000
General hardcover children's books from toddler through young adult, fiction and nonfiction.

4959 Lothrop, Lee & Shepard Books
1350 Avenue of the Americas
New York, NY 10019-4702
212-261-6500
Fax: 212-261-6518
Children's books.

4960 Lynne Rienner Publishing
1800 30th Street
Suite 314
Boulder, CO 80301
303-333-3003
800-803-8488
Fax: 303-333-4037
karen-hemmes@mindspring.com
www.fireflybooks.com
Publishes academic-level books with a focus on international and domestic social sciences.

Karen Hemmes, Publicist
Mary Kay Opicka, Publicist

4961 MHS
PO Box 950
North Tonawanda, NY 14120-0950
416-492-2627
800-456-3003
Fax: 416-492-3343
customer_service@mhs.com
www.mhs.com
Publishers and distributors of professional assessment materials.

Steven J Stein, PhD, President

4962 MacMillan Learning
16365 James Madison Highway
Gordonsville, VA 22942
888-330-8477
Fax: 800-672-2054
orders@mpsvirginia.com
www.macmillanlearning.com
Offers educational content incorporating interactive teaching tools. A wide variety of subjects are covered such as Astronomy, Biochemistry, Communication, Economics, Nutrition and Health, English, Political Science, Psychology and more.

Ken Michaels, CEO
Susan Winslow, Managing Director

4963 Macmillan Education
266 Elmwood Avenue
Suite 134
Buffalo, NY 14222
866-518-4170
Fax: 416-850-0834
info@englishcentral.net
www.macmillaneducation.com
Publishes educational materials, such as English language teaching content and higher education content covering various subjects. They also offer a Spanish curriculum.

Jane Carlin, Chief Financial Officer
Nidhi Upadhyay, HR Consultant

4964 Macro Press
18242 Peters Court
Fountain Valley, CA 92708-5873
310-823-9556
Fax: 310-306-2296
Includes resources to conduct thematic hands-on science lessons and integrated curriculum; and, student materials offering a Scientist's Notebook and reading materials to integrate hands-on (grade specific) scientific thinking, problem solving and documenting skills to benefit all students. Nine award-winning K-6 teachers (200+ years combined experience) joined together to address the real needs of today's high student load.

Leigh Hoven Swenson, President

4965 Magna Publications
2718 Dryden Drive
Madison, WI 53704
608-227-8109
800-206-4805
Fax: 608-246-3597
carriej@magnapubs.com
www.magnapubs.com
Produces eight subscriptions newsletters in the field of higher education.

Carrie Jenson, Conference Manager
David Burns, Associate Publisher

4966 Major Educational Resources Corporation
10153 York Road
Suite 107
Hunt Valley, MD 21030-3340
800-989-5353
Multimedia curriculum tools for educators.

4967 Margaret K McElderry Books
1633 Broadway
New York, NY 10019
212-512-2000
Fax: 800-835-3202
Hardcover trade books for children and young adults.

4968 Mari
3215 Pico Boulevard
Santa Monica, CA 90405-4603
310-829-2212
800-955-9494
Fax: 310-829-2317
www.mariinc.com
The best literature learning materials for K-12. Offers Mini-Units for writing and critical thinking skills, Literature Extenders that extend literature across the curriculum and Basic Skills Through Literature that combine literature and skill work.

4969 MasterTeacher
Leadership Lane
PO Box 1207
Manhattan, KS 66505-1207
800-669-9633
Fax: 800-669-1132
www.masterteacher.com
A publisher of videotapes for the professional. Offers programs on inclusion, tests and testing, student motivation, discipline and more.

4970 MathSoft
101 Main Street
Cambridge, MA 02142
617-577-1017
800-628-4223
Fax: 617-577-8829
www.mathsoft.com
Provider of math, science and engineering software for business, academia, research and government.

4971 McCracken Educational Services
PO Box 3588
Blaine, WA 98231
360-332-1881
800-447-1462
Fax: 360-332-7332
mes@mccrackened.com
www.mccrackened.com
Materials for beginning reading, writing and spelling. Big Books, manipulative materials, teacher resource books, spelling through phonics, posters and both audio and video tapes.

Robert & Marlene McCracken, Author

4972 McGraw Hill Children's Publishing
PO Box 1650
Grand Rapids, MI 49501-1650
616-363-1290
Fax: 800-543-2690
New self-esteem literature based reading and multicultural literature based reading.

4973 Mel Bay Publications
4 Industrial Drive
PO Box 66
Pacific, MO 63069-0066
637-257-3970
800-863-5229
Fax: 636-257-5062
email@melbay.com
www.melbay.com
Music supply distributors.

Sheri Stephens, Customer Service Supervisor

4974 Merriam-Webster
47 Federal Street
#281
Springfield, MA 01105-3805
413-734-3134
Fax: 413-734-0257
A wide variety of titles for students and teachers of all grade levels.

4975 Millbrook Press
1251 Washington Avenue N
Minneapolis, MN 55401
203-740-2220
800-328-4929
Fax: 800-332-1132
www.millbrookpress.com
Exceptional nonfiction juvenile and young adult books for schools and public libraries.

4976 Milton Roy Company
820 Linden Avenue
Rochester, NY 14625-2710
716-248-4000
Teacher support materials, scientific kits and manuals.

4977 Mimosa Publications
90 New Montgomery Street
San Francisco, CA 94105-4501
415-982-5350
A language based K-3 math program featuring big books, language and activity based math topics and multicultural math activities.

4978 Model Technologies
2420 Van Layden Way
Modesto, CA 95356-2454
209-575-3445
Curriculum guides and scientific instruction kits.

4979 Mondo Publishing
980 Avenue Of The Americas
New York, NY 10018
Fax: 888-532-4492
mondopub@aol.com
www.mondopub.com
Offers multicultural big books and music cassettes: Folk Tales from Around the World series; Exploring Habitats series; and, Let's Write and Sing a Song, whole language activities through music.

4980 Morning Glory Press
6595 San Haroldo Way
Buena Park, CA 90620-3748
714-828-1998
888-612-8254
Fax: 714-828-2049
info@morningglorypress.com
www.morningglorypress.com
Publishes books and materials for teenage parents.

Quarterly

Jeanne Lindsay, President
Carole Blum, Promotion Director

4981 Music for Little People
PO Box 1460
Redway, CA 95560-1460
707-923-3991
Fax: 707-923-3241
Science and environmental education materials set to music for younger students.

4982 N&N Publishing Company
18 Montgomery Street
Middletown, NY 10940-5116
Low-cost texts and workbooks.

4983 NASP Publications
National Association of School Psychologists
4340 EW Highway
Suite 402
Bethesda, MD 20814
301-657-0270
Fax: 301-657-0275
center@naspweb.org
www.naspionline.org
Over 100 hard-to-find books and videos centering on counseling, psychology and guidance for students.

Betty Somerville, President

4984 NCTM Educational Materials
National Council of Teachers of Mathematics
1906 Association Drive
Reston, VA 20191-1502
703-620-9840
Fax: 703-476-2970
nctm@nctm.org
www.nctm.org
Publications, videotapes, software, posters and information to improve the teaching and learning of mathematics.

Harry B Tunis, Publications Director
Cynthia C Rosso, Director Marketing Services

4985 NYSTROM
3333 N Elston Avenue
Chicago, IL 60618-5898
773-463-1144
800-621-8086
Fax: 773-463-0515
Maps, globes, hands-on geography and history materials.

4986 National Aeronautics & Space Administration
NASA Headquarters
300 E Street SW
Washington, DC 20546
202-358-0000
Fax: 202-358-3251
Over 10 different divisions offering a wide variety of classroom and educational materials in the areas of science, physics, aeronautics and more.

4987 National Center for Science Teaching & Learning/Eisenhower Clearinghouse
1929 Kenny Road
Columbus, OH 43210-1015
Collects and creates the most up-to-date listing of science and mathematics curriculum materials in the nation.

4988 National Council for the Social Studies
8555 Sixteenth Street
Suite 500
Silver Spring, MD 20910
301-588-1800
800-683-0812
Fax: 301-588-2049
sgriffin@ncss.org
www.ncss.org
Publishes books, videotapes and journals in the area of social education and social studies.

4989 National Council on Economic Education
1140 Avenue of the Americas
New York, NY 10036-5803
212-730-7007
Offers various programs including their latest, US History: Eyes on the Economy, a council program for secondary education teachers.

4990 National Geographic School Publishing
1145 17th Street NW
Washington, DC 20036
800-368-2728
Fax: 515-362-3366
Books, magazines, videos, and software in the areas of science, geography and social studies.

4991 National Geographic Society
PO Box 10041
Des Moines, IA 50340-0597
800-548-9797
Fax: 301-921-1575
www.nationalgeographic.com
Science materials, videos, CD-ROM's and telecommunications program.

4992 National Head Start Association
1651 Prince Street
Alexandria, VA 22314
703-739-0875
866-677-8724
www.nhsa.org
Nonprofit organization serving America's low-income children and families. The association publishes books, periodicals and resource guides on aspects of early education and practice.

Yasmina Vinci, Executive Director
Gregg Porter, Director, Membership

4993 National Textbook Company
4255 W Touhy Avenue
Lincolnwood, IL 60646-1975
847-679-5500
800-323-4900
Fax: 847-679-2494
Offers various textbooks for students grades K-college level.

4994 National Women's History Project
3343 Industrial Drive
Suite #4
Santa Rosa, CA 95403
707-636-2888
Fax: 707-636-2909
nwhp@aol.com
www.nwhp.org
Non-profit organization, the clearinghouse for information about multicultural US women's history. Initiated March as National Women's History Month; issues a catalog of women's history materials. Provides teacher-training nationwide; coordinates the Women's History Network; produces videos, posters, curriculum units and other curriculum materials.

Molly Murphy MacGregor, Exec. Dir./Co-Founder

4995 National Writing Project
University of California, Berkeley
2105 Bancroft Way
#1042
Berkeley, CA 94720-1042
510-642-6096
Fax: 510-642-4545
www.writingproject.org
Technical reports and occasional paper series: a series of research reports and essays on the research in and practice of teaching writing at all grade levels.

4996 New Canaan Publishing Company
PO Box 752
New Canaan, CT 06840
203-966-3408
800-705-5698
Fax: 203-966-3408
www.newcanaanpublishing.com
Children's publications.

4997 New Press
38 Greene Street
4th Floor
New York, NY 10013
212-629-8802
Fax: 212-629-8617
Multicultural teaching materials, focusing on the social studies.

4998 NewsBank
5020 Tamiami Trail N
Suite 110
Naples, FL 34103-2837
941-263-6004
Electronic information services that support the science curriculum.

4999 North South Books
11 E 26th Street
17 Floor
New York, NY 10010-2007
212-706-4545
Fax: 212-706-4544
Publisher of quality children's books by authors and illustrators from around the world.

5000 Nystrom, Herff Jones
3333 N Elston Avenue
Chicago, IL 60618-5811
913-432-8100
Fax: 913-432-3958
Charts for earth, life and physical science for upper elementary and high school grades.

5001 Options Publishing
PO Box 1749
Merrimack, NH 03054
603-429-2698
800-782-7300
Fax: 603-424-4056
serviceoptionspublishing.com m
www.optionspublishing.com
Publishers of supplemental materials in reading, math and language arts.
Marty Furlong, VP

5002 Organization of American Historians
112 N Bryan Avenue
Bloomington, IN 47408-4136
812-855-7311
800-446-8923
Fax: 812-855-0696
oah@oah.org
www.oah.org
Offers various products and literature dealing with American history, as well as job registries, Magazine of History, Journal of American History, OAH Newsletter, and more.
Damon Freeman, Marketing Manager
Michael Regoli, Publications Director

5003 Oxton House Publishers, LLC
Po Box 209
Farmington, ME 04938
207-779-1923
800-539-7323
Fax: 207-779-0623
info@oxtonhouse.com
www.oxtonhouse.com
Publishes high quality, innovative, affordable materials for teaching, reading and mathematics and for dealing with learning disabilities.
William Berlinghoff, Managing Editor
Bobby Brown, Marketing Director

5004 PF Collier
1315 W 22nd Street
Suite 250
Oak Brook, IL 60523-2061
A leading educational publisher for more than 110 years, creating the home learning center. Products include: Collier's Encyclopedia, Quickstart and Early Learning Fun.

5005 PRO-ED
8700 Shoal Creek Boulevard
Austin, TX 78757-6897
512-451-3246
800-897-3202
Fax: 800-397-7633
info@proedinc.com
www.proedinc.com
A leading publisher of assessments, therapy materials and resource/reference books in the areas of speech, language, and hearing; psychology; special education; and occupational therapy.

5006 Parenting Press
PO Box 75267
11065 5th Avenue NE
Seattle, WA 98125-0267
206-364-2900
800-992-6657
Fax: 206-364-0702
office@ParentingPress.com
www.ParentingPress.com
Publishes books for parents, children, and professionals who work with them. Nonfiction books include topics on parenting, problem solving, dealing with feelings, safety, and special issues.
Carolyn J Threadgill, Publisher

5007 Penguin USA
375 Hudson Street
New York, NY 10014-3658
212-366-2000
Fax: 212-366-2934
www.penguinputnam.com
Children's and adult hardcover and paperback general trade books, including classics and multiethnic literature.

5008 Perfection Learning Corporation
Perfection Learning
10520 New York Avenue
Des Moines, IA 50322
303-333-3003
800-803-8488
Fax: 303-333-4037
karen-hemmes@mindspring.com
www.fireflybooks.com
Perfection Learning publishes high interest-low reading level fiction and non-fiction books for young adults.
Karen Hemmes, Publicist
Mary Kay Opicka, Publicist

5009 Perma Bound Books
E Vandalia Road
Jacksonville, IL 62650
217-243-5451
800-637-6581
Fax: 800-551-1169
Thematically arranged for K-12 classroom use with 480,000 titles available in durable Perma-Bound bindings; related library services also available.
Ben Mangum, President

5010 Personalizing the Past
1534 Addison Street
Berkeley, CA 94703-1454
415-388-9351
Museum quality artifact history kits complete with integrated lesson plan teachers guide. Copy-ready student worksheets, literature section, videos and audio tapes. United States and ancient world history.

5011 Perspectives on History Series
Discovery Enterprises, Ltd.
31 Laurelwood Drive
Carlisle, MA 01741
978-287-5401
800-729-1720
Fax: 978-287-5402
ushistorydocs@aol.com
www.ushistorydocs.com
Primary and secondary source materials for middle school to college levels; bibliographies; plays for grades 5-9 on American history topics. Educators curriculum guides for using primary source documents. 75-volumes of primary source documents on American history may be purchased individually or in sets. New Researching American History Series presents documents with summaries and vocabulary on each page (20 volumes) sold individually or in sets.
JoAnne Deitch, President

5012 Peytral Publications Inc
PO Box 1162
Minnetonka, MN 55345
952-949-8707
877-739-8725
Fax: 952-906-9777
inquiry@peytral.com
www.peytral.com
Books and videos for educators.
Peggy Hammeken, Owner

5013 Phelps Publishing
PO Box 22401
Cleveland, OH 44122
216-752-4938
Fax: 216-752-4941
earl@phelpspublishing.com
www.phelpspublishing.com
Publisher of art instruction books for ages 8 to 108.
Earl Phelps, President

5014 Phoenix Learning Resources
12 W 31st Street
New York, NY 10001-4415
212-629-3887
800-221-1274
Fax: 212-629-5648
Phoenix Learning Resources provides all students with the skills to be successful, lifelong learners.
Alexander Burke, President
John Rothermich, Executive VP

5015 Pleasant Company Publications
8400 Fairway Pl
Middleton Branch, WI 53562-2554
608-836-4848
800-233-0264
Fax: 800-257-3865
The American Girls Collection historical fiction series.

5016 Pocket Books/Paramount Publishing
1230 Avenue of the Americas
New York, NY 10020-1513
212-698-7000
Books for children and young adults in hardcover and paperback originals and reprints of bestselling titles.

5017 Population Connection
1400 16th Street NW
Suite 320
Washington, DC 20036-2290
800-767-1956
Fax: 202-332-2302
poped@populationconnection.org
www.populationconnection.org
Curriculum materials for grades K-12 to teach students about population dynamics and their social, political and environmental effects in the United States and the world.
Pamela Wasserman, Director Education

5018 Prentice Hall School Division
340 Rancheros Drive
Suite 160
San Marcos, CA 92069
760-510-0222
Fax: 760-510-0230

Superb language arts textbooks and ancillaries for students grades 6-12.

5019 Prentice Hall School Division - Science
1 Lake Street
Upper Saddle River, NJ 07458
201-236-7000
Fax: 201-236-3381
Science textbooks and ancillaries for grades 6-12 and advanced placement students.

5020 Prentice Hall/Center for Applied Researchin Education
1 Lake Street
Upper Saddle River, NJ 07458
201-236-7000
Fax: 201-236-3381
Publisher of practical, time and work saving teaching/learning resources for PreK-12 teachers and specialists in all content areas.

5021 Project Learning Tree
American Forest Foundation
1111 19th Street NW
Suite 780
Washington, DC 20036-3603
202-463-2462
Fax: 202-463-2461
Pre-K through grade 12 curriculum materials containing hundreds of hands-on science activities. PLT uses the forest as a window into the natural world to increase students' understanding of our complex environment. Stimulates critical and creative thinking; develops the ability to make informed decisions on environmental issues; and instills the confidence and commitment to take action on them.
Kathy McGlauflin, President

5022 Prufrock Press
PO Box 8813
Waco, TX 76714
800-998-2208
Fax: 800-240-0333
www.prufrock.com
Exciting classroom products for gifted and talented education.

5023 Puffin Books
375 Hudson Street
New York, NY 10014-3658
212-366-2819
Fax: 212-366-2040
Offers the Puffin Teacher Club set.
Lisa Crosby, President

5024 RR Bowker
ProQuest Affiliate
121 Chanlon Road
New Providence, NJ 07974-1541
908-464-6800
Fax: 908-665-6688
A leading information provider to schools and libraries for over one hundred years, RR Bowker provides quality resources to help teachers and librarians make informed reading selections for children and young adults.

5025 Raintree/Steck-Vaughn
Harcourt Achieve
6277 Sea Harbor Drive
Orlando, FL 32887
800-531-5015
Fax: 800-699-9459
www.steck-vaughn.com
Reference materials for K-8 students and texts for underachieving students K-12.
Tim McEwen, President
Martijn Tel, Chief Financial Officer

5026 Rand McNally
8255 Central Park Avenue
Skokie, IL 60076-2970
847-674-2151
Cross-curricular products featuring reading/language arts in the social studies.

5027 Random House
201 E 50th Street
New York, NY 10022-7703
212-751-2600
Fax: 212-572-8700
Offers a line of science trade books for grades K-8.

5028 Random House/Bullseye/Alfred A Knopf/Crown Books for Young Readers
201 E 50th Street
New York, NY 10022-7703
212-751-2600
Fax: 212-572-8700
Publisher of hardcover books, paperbacks, books and cassettes and videos for children.

5029 Recorded Books
270 Skipjack Road
Prince Frederick, MD 20678-3410
800-638-1304
Professionally narrated, unabridged books on standard-play audio cassettes, classroom ideas and combinations of print book, cassettes and teacher's guides.
Linda Hirshman, President

5030 Redleaf Press
10 Yorkton Court
Saint Paul, MN 55117-1065
800-428-8309
Fax: 800-641-0115
jward@redleafpress.org
www.redleafpress.org
Publisher of curriculum, activity, and childrens books for early childhood professionals.
Sid Farrer, Editor In Chief
JoAnne Voltz, Marketing Manager

5031 Reference Desk Books
430 Quintana Road
Suite 146
Morro Bay, CA 93442-1948
805-772-8806
Offers a variety of books for the education professional.

5032 Rhythms Productions
PO Box 34485
Los Angeles, CA 90034-0485
310-836-4678
800-544-7244
Fax: 310-837-1534
Producer and publisher of songs and games for learning through music. Cassettes, CDs, books for birth through elementary featuring rhythms, puppet play, art activities, and more. Titles include Lullabies, Singing Games, Watch Me Grow series, Mr. Windbag concept stories, phonics, First Reader's Kit, Hear-See-Say-Do Musical Math series, Themes, and more. Also publishes a line of folk dances from elementary through adult.
Audio
Ruth White, President

5033 Richard C Owen Publishers
PO Box 585
Katonah, NY 10536
914-232-3903
800-336-5588
Fax: 914-232-3977
mfrund@rcowen.com
www.rcowen.com
Focus child-centered learning, Books for Young Learners, professional books, the Learning Network and Meet the Author series.
Mary Frundt, Marketing

5034 Riverside Publishing Company
425 Spring Lake Drive
Ithaca, IL 60143
630-467-7000
800-323-9540
Fax: 630-467-7192
www.riverpub.com
Offers a full line of reading materials, including fiction and nonfiction titles for all grade levels.

5035 Roots & Wings Educational Catalog-Australiafor Kids
PO Box 19678
Boulder, CO 80308-2678
303-776-4796
800-833-1787
Fax: 303-776-6090
roos@boulder.net
www.rootsandwingscatalog.com/
www.australiaforkids.com
Catalog company providing materials for the education of the young child, specializing in the following topics: Australia, multiculturalism, parenting and families, teaching, special needs, environment and peace.
Susan Ely, President/Sales
Anne Wilson, VP/Marketing

5036 Rosen Publishing Group
29 E 21st Street
New York, NY 10010-6209
212-777-3017
800-237-9932
Fax: 888-436-4643
Nonfiction books on self-help and guidance for young adults. Books also available for reluctant readers on self-esteem, values and drug abuse prevention.

5037 Routledge/Europa Library Reference
Taylor & Francis Books
29 W 35 Street
New York, NY 10001-2299
212-216-7800
800-634-7064
Fax: 212-564-7854
reference@routledge-ny.com
www.reference.routlege-ny.com
Publisher of a wide range of print and online library reference titles, including the renowned Europa World Yearbook and the award-winning Routledge Encyclopedia of Philosophy (both available in online and print formats), Garland Encyclopedia of World Music, Routledge Religion and Society Encyclopedias, Chronological History of US Foreign Relations, and many other acclaimed resources.
Koren Thomas, Sr Marketing/Library Ref
Elizabeth Sheehan, Marketing/Library Reference

5038 Runestone Press
A Divisions of Lerner Publishing Group
241 1st Avenue N
Minneapolis, MN 55401-1607
612-332-3344
800-328-4929
Fax: 612-332-7615
www.lernerbooks.com

Nonfiction for readers in Grades 5 and up. Newly revised editions of previously out-of-print books. List includes Buried Worlds archaeology series and titles of Jewish and Native American interest. Complete catalog is available.

Harry J Lerner, President
Mary M Rodgers, Editorial Director

5039 Saddleback Educational

Three Watson
Irvine, CA 92618-2767
949-860-2500
800-637-8715
Fax: 888-734-4010
Supplementary curriculum materials for K-12 and adult students.

5040 SafeSpace Concepts

1424 N Post Oak Road
Houston, TX 77055-5401
713-956-0820
800-622-4289
Fax: 713-956-6416
safespacec@aol.com
www.safespaceconcepts.com
Manufactures young children's play equipment and furnishings.

Barbara Carlson, PhD, President
Jerry Johnson, Marketing Director

5041 Sage Publications

Sage Publications
2455 Teller Road
Thousand Oaks, CA 91320
303-333-3003
800-803-8488
Fax: 303-333-4037
karen-hemmes@mindspring.com
www.fireflybooks.com
Sage Publications publishes handbooks and guides with a focus on research and science.

Karen Hemmes, Publicist
Mary Kay Opicka, Publicist

5042 Salem Press

Grey House Publishing
2 University Plaza
Suite 310
Hackensack, NJ 07601
201-968-0500
Fax: 201-968-0511
sales@salempress.com
www.salempress.com
Salem Press delivers award-winning literary, historical, medical and science reference content to the public library, academic and high school markets.

Richard Gottlieb, President
Pam Brunke, Sales Manager

5043 Santillana Publishing

901 W Walnut Street
Compton, CA 90220-5109
310-763-0455
800-245-8584
Fax: 305-591-9145
Publishers of K-12 and adult titles in Spanish.Imprints include: Altea, Alfagunea, Taurus and Aguilar.

Marla Norman, Publisher/Trade Book
Antonio de Marco, President

5044 Scholastic

555 Broadway
New York, NY 10012
212-343-6100
800-724-6527
Fax: 212-343-4801
www.scholastic.com
Publisher and distributor of children's books. Provides professional and classroom resources for K-12.

5045 School Book Fairs

PO Box 835105
Richardson, TX 75083
972-231-9838
A children's book publisher that provides distribution of leisure reading materials to elementary and middle schools through book fair fund-raising events via a North American network with 97 locations.

5046 Science Inquiry Enterprises

14358 Village View Lane
Chino Hills, CA 91709-1706
530-295-3338
Fax: 530-295-3334
Selected science teaching materials.

5047 Scott & McCleary Publishing Company

2482 11th Street SW
Akron, OH 44314-1712
702-566-8756
800-765-3564
Fax: 702-568-1378
jscott7576@aol.com
www.scottmccleary.com
Diagnostic reading and testing material.

Janet M Scott, Publisher
Sheila C McCleary, Publisher

5048 Scott Foresman Company

1900 E Lake Avenue
Glenview, IL 60025-2086
800-554-4411
Fax: 800-841-8939
Science tests and reading/language arts materials for teachers and students. Celebrate Reading! is the K-8 literature-based reading/integrated language arts program designed to meet the needs of all children. Book Festival is a literature learning center that offers teachers a collection of trade books for independent reading.

Bert Crossland, Reading Product Manager
Jim Fitzmaurice, VP Editor Group

5049 Sharpe Reference

M.E. Sharpe, Inc.
80 Business Park Drive
Armonk, NY 10504
914-273-1800
800-541-6563
Fax: 914-273-2106
custserv@mesharpe.com
www.mesharpe.com
Historical, political, geographical and art reference books.

Diana McDermott, Director Marketing

5050 Signet Classics

375 Hudson Street
New York, NY 10014-3658
212-366-2000
Fax: 212-366-2888
Publishes books on literature, poetry and reading.

5051 Silver Moon Press

160 5th Avenue
Suite 622
New York, NY 10010-7003
212-242-6499
800-874-3320
Fax: 212-242-6799
Informational and entertaining books for young readers. Subjects include history, multiculturalism and science.

5052 Simon & Schuster Children's Publishing

1230 Avenue of the Americas
New York, NY 10020
212-698-7000
Fax: 212-698-7007
www.simonsayskids.com
Fiction and nonfiction, in hardcover and paperback editions, for preschool through young adult.

5053 Social Issues Resources Series

1100 Holland Drive
Boca Raton, FL 33487-2701
561-994-0079
Fax: 561-994-2014
Provides information systems in print format and CD-ROM format.

5054 Social Science Education Consortium

Box 21270
Boulder, CO 80308-4270
303-492-8154
Fax: 303-449-3925
singletl@stripe.colorado.edu
www.ssecinc.org
Produces curriculum guides, instructional units and collections of lesson plans on US history, law-related education, global studies, public issues and geography. Develops projects for social studies teachers and evaluates social studies programs.

James Cooks, Executive Director
Laurel Singleton, Associate Director

5055 Social Studies School Service

10200 Jefferson Boulevard
Culver City, CA 90232-3598
310-839-2436
800-421-4246
Fax: 310-839-2249
access@socialstudies.com
www.socialstudies.com
Supplemental materials in all areas of social studies, language arts.

5056 Special Education & Rehabilitation Services

330 C Street
Washington, DC 20202
202-205-5465
Fax: 202-260-7225

Judith E Heuman, Assistant Secretary

5057 Speech Bin

1965 25th Avenue
Vero Beach, FL 32960-3000
561-770-0007
800-477-3324
Fax: 561-770-0006
Publisher and distributor of books and materials for professionals in rehabilitation, speech-language pathology, occupational and physical therapy, special education, and related fields. Major product lines include professional and children's books, computer software, diagnostic tests.

Jan J Binney, VP

5058 Stack the Deck Writing Program

PO Box 5352
Chicago, IL 60680-0429
312-675-1000
Fax: 312-765-0453
stockthedeck@sbcglobal.net
www.stackthedeck.com
Composition textbooks, grades 1-12, plus computer software.

5059 **Stenhouse Publishers**
477 Congress Street
Suite 4B
Portland, ME 04101-3417
888-363-0566
Fax: 800-833-9164
www.stenhouse.com
Professional materials for teachers by teachers.

5060 **Story Teller**
PO Box 921
Salem, UT 84653-0921
801-423-2560
Fax: 801-423-2568
patti@thestoryteller.com
www.thestoryteller.com
Felt board stories books and educational sets.
Patti Gardner, VP Sales

5061 **Summit Learning**
7755 Rockwell Avenue
PO Box 755
Fort Atkinson, WI 53538-0755
800-777-8817
800-777-8817
Fax: 800-317-2194
info@summitlearning.com
www.summitlearning.com
Summit learning is a distributor of manipulative-based math and science materials, provides you with a carefully selected group of the most popular high-quality products at low prices.
Gary Otto, Marketing Manager

5062 **Sunburst Technology**
1550 Executive Drive
Elgin, IL 60123
914-747-3310
800-338-3457
Fax: 914-747-4109
www.sunburst.com
K-12 educational software, guidance and health materials, and online teacher resources.

5063 **Sundance Publishing**
234 Taylor Street
PO Box 1326
Littleton, MA 01460
978-486-9201
800-343-8204
Fax: 978-486-8759
kjasmine@sundancepub.com
www.sindancepub.com
A supplementary educational publisher of instructional materials for shared, guided, and independent reading, phonics, and comprehension skills for grades K-9. Some of its programs include AlphKids, SunLit Fluency, Popcorns and Little Readers. Its Second Chance Reading Program for below-level readers features high-interest titles, written for upper elementary/middle school students. It also distributes paperback editions of some of the most widely taught literature titles for grades K-1
Katherine Jasmine, VP Marketing

5064 **Synergistic Systems**
2297 Hunters Run Drive
Reston, VA 20191-2834
703-758-9213
Science education curriculum materials.

5065 **TASA**
PO Box 382
Brewster, NY 10509-0382
845-277-8100
800-800-2598
Fax: 845-277-3548
Degrees of Literacy Power Program; English Language Profiles, primary, standard and advanced DRP tests, Degrees of World Meaning Tests.

5066 **TL Clark Incorporated**
5111 SW Avenue
St. Louis, MO 63110
314-865-2525
800-859-3815
Fax: 314-865-2240
general@tlclarkinc.com
www.tlclarkinc.com
Educational products for grades Pre-K-3. Rest time products including cots and mats, sand and water play tubs, active play items including tunnels, tricycles and foam play items.
Jim Fleminla, President

5067 **TMC/Soundprints**
353 Main Avenue
Norwalk, CT 06851-1508
203-846-2274
800-228-7839
Fax: 203-846-1776
sndprnts@ixinctcom.com
www.soundprints.com
Children's story books for children ages 4 through 8 under the license of the Smithsonian Institute and the National Wildlife Federation. Each 32 page four color book highlights a unique aspect of the animal featured in the book so as to provide education while still being entertaining. Each book can be bought with an audiocassette read-a-long and plush toy. Over 80 books in print.
Ashley Anderson, Associate Publisher
Chelsea Shriver

5068 **Tambourine Books**
1350 Avenue of the Americas
New York, NY 10019-4702
212-261-6500
Fax: 212-261-6518
A wide variety of books to increase creativity and reading skills in students.

5069 **Taylor & Francis Publishers**
7625 Empire Drive
Florence, KY 41042
800-624-7064
Fax: 800-248-4724
Publisher of professional texts and references in several fields including the behavioral sciences; arts, humanities, social sciences, science technology and medicine.
Chris Smith, Customer Service Manager

5070 **Teacher's Friend Publications**
3240 Trade Center Drive
Riverside, CA 92507
909-682-4748
800-343-9680
Fax: 909-682-4680
Complete line of the original monthly and seasonal Creative Idea Books. Plus, two new cooperative-learning language series and much more.
Karen Sevaly, Author
Richard Sevaly, President/CEO
Kim Marsh, National Sales Manager

5071 **Teaching Comprehension: Strategies for Stories**
Oxton House Publishers, LLC
Po Box 209
Farmington, ME 04938
207-779-1923
800-539-7323
Fax: 207-779-0623
info@oxtonhouse.com
www.oxtonhouse.com
A detailed roadmap for providing students with effective strategies for comprehending and remembering stories. It includes story-line masters for helping students to organize their thinking and to accurately depict character and sequence events.
62 pages
William Berlinghoff, Managing Editor
Bobby Brown, Marketing Director

5072 **The Narrative Press**
4392 US Highway 26/85
Torrington, WY 82240
307-532-3495
Fax: 307-532-3495
mike.bond@narrativepress.com
www.narrativepress.com
Publisher of first person narratives of adventure and exploration, useful for teaching about the U.S. Western history covering mountain men and trappers, Asian history and African History. Also published by The Narrative Press are books on sea travel, autobiographies and California history.
Vickie Zimmer, Editor

5073 **Theme Connections**
Perfection Learning
PO Box 500
Logan, IA 51546-0500
800-831-4190
Fax: 712-644-2392
Features 135 best-selling literature titles and related theme libraries for students to develop lifelong learning strategies.

5074 **Ther-A-Play Products**
PO Box 2030
Lodi, CA 95241-2030
209-368-6787
800-308-6749
Fax: 209-365-2157
madgic@attbi.com
Children's books, play therapy books, sandplay and sandtray manipulatives, puppets, games, doll houses and furniture. Playmobile and educational toys, specializing in counselors' tools. Books on abuses, illness, death, behavior and parenting.
Madge Geiszler, Owner

5075 **Thomson Learning**
115 5th Avenue
New York, NY 10003-1004
212-979-2210
800-880-4253
Fax: 248-699-8061
Book publisher of library and classroom-oriented educational resources for children and young adults. Over 200 books are available in 30 different subjects.

5076 **Time-Life Books**
2000 Duke Street
Alexandria, VA 22314-3414
703-838-7000
Fax: 703-838-7166
A wide-ranging selection of quality reference and supplemental books for students from elementary to high school.

5077 **Tiny Thought Press**
1427 S Jackson Street
Louisville, KY 40208-2720
502-637-6916
Fax: 502-634-1693
Children's books that build character and self-esteem.

5078 **Tom Snyder Productions**
80 Coolidge Hill Road
Watertown, MA 02472

800-342-0236
Fax: 800-304-1254
ask@tomsynder.com
www.tomsynder.com
Developer and publisher of educational software.

John McAndrews, Contact

5079 Tor Books/Forge/SMP
175 5th Avenue
New York, NY 10010-7703
212-388-0100
Fax: 212-388-0191
Science-fiction and fantasy children's books, mysteries, Westerns, general fiction and classics publications.

5080 Tricycle Press
PO Box 7123
Berkeley, CA 94707-0123
510-559-1600
800-841-2665
Fax: 510-559-1637
Publisher of books and posters for children ages 2-12 and their grown-ups. Catalog available.

Christine Longmuir, Publicity/Marketing

5081 Troll Associates
100 Corporate Drive
Mahwah, NJ 07430-2322
201-529-4000
Fax: 201-529-8282
Publisher of children's books and products, including paperbacks and hardcovers, special theme units, read-alongs, videos, software and big books.

5082 Trumpet Club
1540 Broadway
New York, NY 10036-4039
212-492-9595
School book club featuring hardcover and paperback books, in class text sets and author video visits.

5083 Turn-the-Page Press
203 Baldwin Avenue
Roseville, CA 95678-5104
916-786-8756
800-959-5549
Fax: 916-786-9261
mleeman@ibm.net
www.turnthepage.com
Books, cassettes and videos focusing on early childhood education.

Michael Leeman, President

5084 USA Today
1000 Wilson Boulevard
Arlington, VA 22209-3901
703-276-3400
Fax: 703-854-2103
Educational programs focusing on social studies.

5085 Upstart Books
PO Box 800
Fort Atkinson, WI 53538-0800
920-563-9571
800-558-2110
Fax: 920-563-7395
www.hpress.highsmith.com
Publishes teacher activity resources, reading activities, library and information seeking skills, Internet.

Matt Mulder, Director
Virginia Harrison, Editor

5086 Useful Learning
711 Meadow Lane Court
Apartment 12
Mount Vernon, IA 52314-1549
319-895-6155
800-962-3855
The Useful Spelling Textbook series for Grades 2-8, represents a curriculum based upon the scientific knowledge of research studies conducted during the past 80 years at The University of Iowa, Iowa City, IA. Incorporates the New Iowa Spelling Scale and is composed of qualitative curriculum, qualitative learning practices and qualitative instructional procedures.

Larry D. Zenor, PhD, President
Bradley M Loomer, PhD, Board Chairman

5087 VIDYA Books
PO Box 7788
Berkeley, CA 94707-0788
510-527-9932
Fax: 510-527-2936
Supplemental materials about India and the surrounding region for K-12 lesson plans.

5088 Viking Children's Books
375 Hudson Street
New York, NY 10014-3658
212-941-8780
General hardcover children's books, from toddler through young adult, fiction and nonfiction.

5089 Vision 23
Twenty-Third Publications
185 Willow Street
Mystic, CT 06355-2636
860-536-2611
Fax: 800-572-0788
A wide variety of children's products including books, games, clothing and toys.

5090 WH Freeman & Company
41 Madison Avenue
New York, NY 10010-2202
212-576-9400
Fax: 212-481-1891
Books relating to the world of mathematics.

5091 Wadsworth Publishing School Group
10 Davis Drive
Belmont, CA 94002-3002
650-595-2350
Fax: 800-522-4923
College and advanced placement/honors high school materials in biology, chemistry and environmental science.

5092 Walker & Company
104 Fifth Avenue
New York, NY 10011
212-727-8300
800-289-2553
Fax: 212-727-0984
www.walkerbooks.com
Hardcover and paperback trade titles for Pre-K-12th grade, including picture books, photo essays, fiction and nonfiction titles appropriate for every curriculum need.

5093 Warren Publishing House
11625-G Airport Road
Everett, WA 98204-3790
425-353-3100
New Totline Teaching Tales with related activities plus quality whole language teacher activity books including Alphabet Theme-A-Saurus and Piggyback Songs.

5094 Waterfront Books
85 Crescent Road
Burlington, VT 05401-4126
802-658-7477
800-639-6063
Fax: 802-860-1368
helpkids@waterfrontbooks.com
www.waterfrontbooks.com
Publishes and distributes books on special issues for children: barriers to learning, coping skills, mental health, prevention strategies, family/parenting, etc. for grades K-12. Titles include: The Divorce Workbook; Josh, a Boy with Dyslexia; What's a Virus, Anyway? The Kids' Book About AIDS and more.

Sherrill N Musty, Publisher
Michelle Russell, Order Fulfillment

5095 Web Feet Guides
Rock Hill Communications
14 Rock Hill Road
Bala Cynwyd, PA 19004
610-667-2040
888-762-5445
Fax: 610-667-2291
info@rockhillcommunications.com
www.webfeetguides.com
The premier subject guides to the Internet, rigorously reviewed by librarians and educators, fully annotated, expanded and updated monthly. Appropriate for middle school through adult. Available in print, online, or marc records. For more information, free trials and Web casts, and free interactive Web Quests for your K-8 students, visit our Web site.

Linda Smith, Marketing Coordinator

5096 West Educational Publishing
620 Opperman Drive
#645779
Saint Paul, MN 55123-1340
A leader in quality social studies textbooks and ancillaries for grades K-12.

5097 Western Psychological Services
12031 Wilshire Boulevard
Los Angeles, CA 90025-1251
310-478-2061
800-648-8857
Fax: 310-478-7838
www.wpspublish.com
Assessment tools for professionals in education, psychology and allied fields. Offer a variety of tests, books, software and therapeutic games.

5098 Wildlife Conservation Society
Bronx Zoo
Education Department
2300 Southern Boulevard
Bronx, NY 10460
718-220-5131
800-937-5131
Fax: 718-733-4460
sscheio@wes.org
www.wcs.com
Environmental science and conservation biology curriculum materials and information regarding teacher training programming for Grades K-12, on site or off site, nationally and locally. Science programming for grades pre-K-12 available on site.

Sydell Schein, Manager/Program Services
Ann Robinson, Director National Programs

5099 William Morrow & Company
1350 Avenue of the Americas
New York, NY 10019-4702
212-261-6500
Fax: 212-261-6518
High quality hardcover and paperback books for children.

5100 Winston Derek Publishers
101 French Landing Drive
Nashville, TN 37228-1511
615-321-0535
A cross section of African American books and educational materials, including preschool and primary grade books.

5101 **Wisconsin State Reading Association**
WSRA
909 Rock Ridge Road
Burlington, WI 53105
262-514-1450
Fax: 262-514-1450
wsra@wsra.org
www.wsra.org
The Wisconsin State Reading Association is a professional organization providing leadership, advocacy and expertise for those working in the field of literacy education.
Gale Gerharz, President
Cindy Cate, Vice President

5102 **Wolfram Research, Inc.**
100 Trade Center Drive
Champaign, IL 61820-7237
217-398-0700
800-965-3726
Fax: 217-398-0747
info@wolfram.com
www.wolfram.com
Offers mathematics publications, statistics and information to educators of grades K-12.
Stephen Wolfram, Founder/CEO
Jean Buck, Dir., Corp Communications

5103 **Workman Publishing**
708 Broadway
New York, NY 10003-9508
212-254-5900
Fax: 212-254-8098
Children's curriculum, books, textbooks, workbooks, fiction and nonfiction titles.

5104 **World & I**
News World Communications
2800 New York Avenue NE
Washington, DC 20002-1945
202-636-3365
800-822-2822
Fax: 202-832-5780
ckim@worldandimag.com
www.worldandi.com
With over 40 articles each month, The World & I presents an enlightening look at our changing world through the eyes of noted scholars and experts covering current issues, the arts, science, book reviews, lifestyles, cultural perspectives, philosophical trends, and the millennium. For educators, students and libraries. Free teacher's guides year round. Also, online archives available at www.worldandi.com.
Charles Kim, Business Director

5105 **World Association of Publishers, Manufacturers& Distributors**
Worlddidac
Bollwerk 21, PO Box 8866 CH-3001
Berne
Switzerland
41-31-3121744
Fax: 41-31-3121744
info@worlddidac.org
A worldwide listing of over 330 publishers, manufacturers and distributors of educational materials. Listings include all contact information, products and school levels/grades.
160 pages Annual
Beat Jost, Coordinating Education

5106 **World Bank**
1818 H Street NW
Room T-8061
Washington, DC 20433-0002
202-477-1234
Fax: 202-477-6391
Maps, poster kits, case studies and videocassettes that teach about life in developing countries.

5107 **World Book Educational Products**
525 W Monroe Street
20th Floor
Chicago, IL 60661
312-729-5800
Fax: 312-729-5600
Reference books and the World Book Encyclopedia on CD-Rom.

5108 **World Eagle**
111 King Street
Littleton, MA 01460-1527
978-486-9180
800-854-8273
Fax: 978-486-9652
info@ibaradio.org
www.worldeagle.com
Publishes an online, social studies educational resource magazine: comparative data, graphs, maps and charts on world issues. Publishes world regional atlases, and supplies maps and curriculum materials.
Valentina Bardawil Powers, Author
Martine Crandall-Hollick, President

5109 **World Resources Institute**
10 G Street, NE
Suite 800
Washington, DC 20002
202-729-7600
Fax: 202-729-7610
The world Resources Institute is an environmental think tank that goes beyond research to create practical ways to protect the Earth and improve people's lives. our mission is to move human society to live in ways that protect Earth's environment for surrent and future generations.
Jonathan Lash, President

5110 **World Scientific Publishing Company**
27 Warren Street
Suite 401-402
Hackensack, NJ 07601
201-487-9655
Fax: 201-487-9695
wspc@wspc.com
www.wspc.com
This is one of the world's leading academic publishers. It now publishes more than 400 books and 100 journals a year in diverse fields of science technology, medicine, business and management.
Ruth Zhou, Marketing Executive

5111 **Worth Publishers**
33 Irving Plaza
New York, NY 10003-2332
212-475-6000
Fax: 212-689-2383
A balanced and comprehensive account of the U.S. past is accompanied by an extensive set of supplements.

5112 **Wright Group**
19201 120th Avenue NE
Bothell, WA 98011-9507
800-523-2371
Fax: 425-486-7704
www.wrightgroup.com
Supplementary program materials for reading education.

5113 **Write Source Educational Publishing House**
PO Box 460
Burlington, WI 53105-0460
262-763-8258
Fax: 262-763-2651
Publishes Writers Express, a writing, thinking and learning handbook series for grades 4 and 5. Also offer the latest editions of Write Source 2000 and Writers INC for grades 6-8 and 9-12.

5114 **You Call This Living?**
William Kingsley Publishing
3036 Big Oaks Drive
Garland, TX 75044
972-220-9959
seabed999@yahoo.com
www.billkingsley.com
The book explored the human condition and the need for a drastic overhaul of the educational system.
274 pages
ISBN: 978-578-12522
Bill Kingsley, Author
Bill Kingsley

5115 **Zaner-Bloser K-8 Catalog**
2200 W 5th Avenue
Columbus, OH 43215
614-486-0221
800-421-3018
Fax: 614-487-2699
www.zaner-bloser.com
Publisher of handwriting materials and reading, writing, spelling and study skills programs.
Robert Page, President

5116 **Zephyr Press**
814 North Franklin Street
Chicago, IL 60610-3109
312-337-5985
800-232-2187
Fax: 312-337-5985
neways2learn@zephyrpress.com
www.zephyrpress.com
Zephyr Press publishes effective, state-of-the-art-teaching materials for classroom use.
Joey Tanner MEd, President

5117 **ZooBooks**
ZooBooks/Wildlife Education. Ltd.
12233 Thatcher Court
Poway, CA 92064-6880
619-513-7600
800-477-5034
Fax: 858-513-7660
animals@zoobooks.com
www.zoobooks.com
Reference books offering fascinating insights into the world of wildlife. Created in collaboration with leading scientists and educators, these multi-volume Zoobooks make important facts and concepts about nature, habitat and wildlife understandable to children. From alligators to zebras, aquatic to exotic, each Zoobook is colorful, scientifically accurate and easy to read.

General

5118 AVKO Educational Research Foundation
3084 Willard Road
Birch Run, MI 48415-9404
810-686-9283
Fax: 810-686-1101
avkoemail@aol.com
www.avko.org
Comprised of teachers and individuals interested in helping others learn to read and spell, while researching the causes of learning disabilities. The foundation develops reading training materials for individuals with dyslexia or other learning disabilities using a method involving audio, visual, kinesthetic and oral diagnosis and remediation.
Don McCabe, President/Research Director
Linda Heck, Vice President

5119 Assistive Technology Clinics
Children's Hospital
1056 E 19th Avenue
#030
Denver, CO 80218-1007
303-861-6250
Fax: 303-764-8214
A diagnostic clinic providing evaluation, information and support to families with children with disabilities in the areas of seating and mobility. Offers augmentative communication and assistive technology access.
Tracey Kovach, Coordinator

5120 Center for Equity and Excellence in Education
George Washington University
1555 Wilson Boulevard
Suite 515
Arlington, VA 22209-2004
703-528-3588
800-925-3223
Fax: 703-528-5973
ceeeinfo@ceee.gwu.edu
www.ceee.gwu.edu
Mission is to advance education reform so that all students achieve high standards. Operates under the umbrella of the Institute for Education Policy Studies within the Graduate School of Education and Human Development. Designs and conducts program evaluation for states, districts and schools and conducts program evalutaion, policy and applied research effecting equitable educational opportunities for all students.
Charlene Rivera, Executive Director
Kristina Anstrom, Assistant Director

5121 Center for Learning
The Center for Learning
PO Box 910
2105 Evergreen Road
Villa Maria, PA 16155
724-964-8083
800-767-9090
Fax: 724-964-8992
customerservice@centerforlearning.org
www.centerforlearning.org
To improve education by writing and publishing values-based curriculum materials that enable teachers to foster student responsibility for learning

5122 Center for Organization of Schools
Johns Hopkins University
2701 N Charles Street
Suite 300
Baltimore, MD 21218-2404
410-516-8800
Fax: 410-516-8890
mmaushard@csos.jhu.edu
www.csos.jhu.edu
Conduct research, development, evaluation, and dissemination of replicable strategies designed to transform low-performing schools so that al lstudents graduate ready for college, career and life. Products include curricula that help all students achieve at a high level. Programs in early learning; school, family and community partnerships; a financial literacy program called Stocks ain the Future, and the Baltimore Education Research Consortium, plus Talent development Secondary reform
James McPartland, Co-Director
Mary Maushard, Communication Director

5123 Center for Research on the Context of Teaching
Stanford University
CERAS Building
4th Floor 520 Galvez Mall
Stanford, CA 94305-3084
650-725-1845
Fax: 650-736-2296
www.stanford.edu/group/CRC/
Conducts research on ways in which secondary school teaching and learning are affected by their contexts.
Milbrey W McLaughlin, Co-Director
Joan E Talbert, Co-Director

5124 Center for Social Organization of Schools
Johns Hopkins University
3003 N Charles Street
Suite 200
Baltimore, MD 21218-3888
410-516-8800
Fax: 410-516-8890
jmcpartland@csos.jhu.edu
www.csos.jhu.edu
Conduct programmatic research to improve the education system, as well as full-time support staff engaged in developing curricula and providing technical assistance to help schools use the Center's research.
Jim McPartland, Director
Mary Maushard, Communication Director

5125 Center for Technology in Education
Bank Street College of Education
6740 Alexander Bell Drive
Suite 302
Columbia, MD 21046-1898
410-516-9800
Fax: 410-516-9818
cte@jhu.edu
cte.jhu.edu
Improve the quality of life of children and youth, particularly those with special needs, through teaching, research, and leadership in the use of technology.
Jacqueline A Nunn, Director
K Lynne Harper Mainzer, Deputy Director

5126 Center for the Study of Reading
University of Illinois
158 Children's Research Center
51 Gerty Drive
Champaign, IL 61820
217-333-2552
Fax: 217-244-4501
csrrca@uiuc.edu
csr.ed.uiuc.edu
Conduct reading research and development must be to discover and put into practice the means for reaching children who are failing to read.
Richard C Anderson, Director
Kim Nguyen-Jahiel, Associate Director

5127 Center for the Study of Small/Rural Schools
University of Oklahoma
555 E Constitution Street
Suite 138
Norman, OK 73072-7820
405-325-1450
Fax: 405-325-7075
jcsimmons@ou.edu
cssrs.ou.edu
Assists small and rural schools in building and maintaining necessary knowledge bases, founded on state-of-the-art research in the areas of school improvement and reform, restructuring, staff development, administration, and teaching.
Jan C Simmons, Director

5128 Center on Families, Schools, Communities & Children's Learning
Northeastern University
50 Nightingale Hall
Boston, MA 02215
617-373-2595
Fax: 617-373-8924
Examines how families, communities and schools can work in partnership to promote children's motivation, learning and development, including disseminating information.
Nancy Ames, Vice President

5129 Center on Organization & Restructuring of Schools
1025 W Johnson Street
Madison, WI 53706-1706
608-263-7575
Fax: 608-263-6448
Focuses on restructuring K-12 schools in various areas of student development and progress.
Fred M Newman, Director

5130 Council for Educational Development and Research
National Education Association (NEA)
1201 16th Street NW
Washington, DC 20036-3290
202-833-4000
Fax: 202-822-7974
www.nea.org
The voice of education professionals. Advocate for education professionals
John I Wilson, Executive Director
Dennis Van Roekel, President

5131 Curriculum Research and Development Group
University of Hawaii
1776 University Avenue
Honolulu, HI 96822-2463
808-956-4969
800-799-8111
Fax: 808-956-6730
crdg@hawaii.edu
www.hawaii.edu/crdg
Conducts research and creates, evaluates, disseminates, and supports educational programs that serve students, teachers, parents, and other educators in grades preK-12.
Helen Au, Assistant Director
Dr. Kathleen F. Berg, Director

5132 Division for Research
The Council for Exceptional Children
2000 Broadway
Oakland, CA 94612
510-891-3400
www.dor.kaiser.org
The Division of Research aims to conduct, publish, and disseminate high-quality epidemiologic and health services research to improve the health and medical care of Kaiser

Permanente members and the society at large.

Joe Selby, Director
Morris Collen, Founder

5133 Early Childhood Technical Assistance Center Resources
ECTA Center
517 S Greensboro Street
Carrboro, NC 27510
919-962-2001
Fax: 919-966-7463
ectacenter@unc.edu
ectacenter.org
Provides access to primary sources, research and reference materials for the benefit of those working in the special education system: administrators, researchers, policy makers, practitioners, families and advocates.

Joan Danaher, Associate Director
Betsy Ayankoya, Associate Director

5134 Educational Information & Resource Center
Research Department
606 Delsea Drive
Sewell, NJ 08080-9399
856-582-7000
Fax: 856-582-4206
info@eirc.org
www.eirc.org
EIRC is committed to continuously improving the education, safety, physical and emotional health of children. EIRC meets this commitment by developing and delivering a comprehensive array of support services to those who teach, raise, care for and mentor children.

Charles Ivory, Executive Director
John Henry, Program Director

5135 Educational Research Service
1001 N Fairfax Street
Suite 500
Alexandria, VA 22314-1587
703-243-2100
800-791-9308
Fax: 703-243-1985
ers@ers.org
www.ers.org
For over 30 years Educational Research Service has been the nonprofit organization serving the research and information needs of the nation's K-12 education leaders and the public.

John C Draper EdD, CEO
Katherine A Behrens, Chief Operating Officer

5136 Educational Testing Service
Rosedale Road
Princeton, NJ 08541
609-921-9000
Fax: 609-734-5410
www.ets.org
To advance quality and equity in education by providing fair and valid assessments, research and related services. Our products and services measure knowledge and skills, promote learning and educational performance, and support education and professional development for all people worldwide.

Susan Keipper, Program Director
Kurt Landgraf, President and CEO

5137 Florida Atlantic University-Multifunctional Resource Center
1515 W Commercial Boulevard
Suite 303
Boco Raton, FL 33309-3095
561-297-3000
800-328-6721
Fax: 561-297-2141
Provides training and technical assistance to Title VII-funded classroom instructional projects and other programs serving limited-English proficient students.

Dr Ann C Willig, Director
Elaine Sherr, Research Assistant

5138 Higher Education Center
National Education Association (NEA)
1201 16th Street NW
Washington, DC 20036-3290
202-833-4000
Fax: 202-822-7974
ncuea@nea.org
www.nea.org
The center provides data and other research products to NEA higher education affiliates. The Research Advisory Group, composed of higher education leaders and staff, meets twice a year to review products from the NEA Research Center for Higher Education and make recommendations about additional research needs. The center currently provides salary reports, Higher Education Contract Analysis System, and budget analysis.

Dennis Van Roekel, President
John I Wilson, Executive Director

5139 Information Center on Education
Eba Room 385
Albany, NY 12234-1
518-474-8716
Fax: 518-473-7737
Coordinates data collection procedures within the New York State Education Department.

Leonard Powell, Director

5140 Information Exchange
Maine State Library
64 State House Station
Augusta, ME 04333-64
207-287-5620
800-322-8899
Fax: 207-287-5624
Provides access to the latest education research and information for teachers.

Edna M Comstock, Director

5141 Institute for Research in Learning Disabilities
The University of Kansas
3060 Robert
Lawrence, KS 66045-1
785-864-4780
Fax: 785-864-5728
Although the focus of the Institute's research is children, they have a sizeable publication list with some of their research having relevance for adults.

5142 Instructional Materials Laboratory
University of Missouri-Columbia
8 London Hall
Columbia, MO 65211-2230
800-669-2465
800-669-2465
Fax: 573-882-1992
iml@missouri.edu
www.iml.missouri.edu/
Prepares and disseminates instructional materials for the vocational education community.

Dana Tannehill, Director
Richard Branton, Assistant Director

5143 Learning Research and Development Center
University of Pittsburgh
3939 O'Hara Street
Pittsburgh, PA 15260
412-624-7487
Fax: 412-624-3051
lrangel@pitt.edu
www.lrdc.pitt.edu
LRDC fosters an environment in which research initiatives relating to the science, practice, organization and technology of learning, teaching and training are born and thrive.

Charles Perfetti, Director
Alan Lesgold, Senior Scientist/Research Sc

5144 Life Lab Science Program
1156 High Street
Santa Cruz, CA 95064
831-459-2001
Fax: 831-459-3483
lifelab@lifelab.org
www.lifelab.org
Life Lab Science Program is nationally acknowledged as an expert leader in the development and dissemination of garden-centered educational programs.

Gail Harlamoff, Executive Director
Whitney Cohen, Education Director

5145 Merrimack Education Center
101 Mill Road
Chelmsford, MA 01824-4899
978-256-3985
Fax: 978-256-6890
cjeffers@meccorp.mec.edu
www.mec.edu/
Merrimack Education Center (MEC) is a diversified educational and technological resource for schools, cities and towns and other non-profit organizations. MEC offers a broad range of special education, professional development, facilities management and technology programs and solutions.

John Barranco, Director

5146 Mid-Atlantic Regional Educational Laboratory
1301 Cecil B Moore Avenue
Philadelphia, PA 19122-6091
215-204-3000
Fax: 215-204-5130
robert.sullivan@temple.edu
www.temple.edu
The Regional Educational Laboratories are educational research and development organizations supported by contracts with the US Education Department. Specialty area: Education Leadership.

William Evans, Director

5147 Mid-Continent Regional Educational Laboratory
2550 S Parker Road
Suite 500
Aurora, CO 80014-1678
303-337-0990
Fax: 303-337-3005
Focuses on improvement of education practices in Colorado, Kansas, Missouri, Nebraska, Wyoming, North Dakota and South Dakota.

C. Lawrence Hutchins, Director

5148 Midwestern Regional Educational Laboratory
1900 Spring Road
Suite 300
Oak Brook, IL 60521
630-649-6500
Fax: 630-649-6700
nowakows@ncrel.org
The Regional Educational Laboratories are educational research and development organizations supported by contracts with the US Education Department, Office of Educational Research and Improvement. Specialty area: Technology.
Dr. Jeri Nowakowski, Executive Director

5149 Missouri LINC
401 E Stewart Road
Columbia, MO 65211
573-882-2733
800-392-0533
Fax: 573-882-5071
Serves students with special needs through a resource and technical assistance center.
Linda Bradley, Director

5150 NEA Foundatrion for the Improvement of Education
1201 16th Street NW
Washington, DC 20036
202-822-7840
Fax: 202-822-7779
info@neafoundation@list.nea.org
www.neafoundation.org
The NEA Foundation, through the unique strength of its partnership with educators, advances student achievement by investing in public education that will prepare each of America's children to learn and thrive in a rapidly changing world.
Aaron J Pope, Communications Associate
John I Wilson, Executive Director

5151 National Black Child Development Institute
1313 L Street, NW
Suite 110
Washington, DC 20005-4110
202-833-2220
800-556-2234
Fax: 202-833-8222
moreinfo@nbcdi.org
www.nbcdi.org
NBCDI's mission is to improve and protect the quality of life of Black children and families.
Carol Brunson Day, President
Gillian Shurland, Contact

5152 National Center for Improving Science Education
2000 L Street NW
Suite 616
Washington, DC 20036-4917
202-467-0652
Fax: 202-467-0659
Promotes change in state and local policies and practices in science curricula, teaching, and assessment.
Senta A Raizen, Director

5153 National Center for Research in Mathematical Sciences Education
University of Wisconsin-Madison
1025 W Johnson Street
#557
Madison, WI 53706-1706
608-263-4285
Fax: 608-263-3406
Provides a research base for the reform of school mathematics.
Thomas A Romberg, Director

5154 National Center for Research in Vocational Education
University of California, Berkeley
2030 Addison Street
Suite 500
Berkeley, CA 94720-1674
510-642-4004
800-762-4093
Fax: 510-642-2124
NCRVE@berkeley.edu
vocserve.berkeley.edu
The mission of the National Center for Research in Vocational Education (NCRVE) is to strengthen education to prepare all individuals for lasting and rewarding employment and lifelong learning.
David Stern, Director
Phyllis Hudecki, Associate Director

5155 National Center for Research on Teacher Learning
Michigan State University, College of Education
116 Erickson Hall
East Lansing, MI 48824-1034
517-355-9302
Fax: 517-432-2795
floden_@_msu.edu
ncrtl.msu.edu
The NCRTL extended its findings about learning from students-as-learners to teachers-as-learners in order to understand how teachers learn to teach.
Robert E Floden, Director
G Williamson McDiarmid, Director

5156 National Center for Science Teaching & Learning
Ohio State University
1314 Kinnear Road
Columbus, OH 43212-1156
614-292-3339
Fax: 614-292-0263
Seeks to understand how non-curricular factors affect how science is taught in grades K-12.
Arthur L White, Director

5157 National Center for the Study of Privatizationin Education
525 W 120th Street
Box 181, 230 Thompson Hall
New York, NY 10027-6696
212-678-3259
Fax: 212-678-3474
ncspe@columbia.edu
www.ncspe.org
The goal of the National Center for the Study of Privatization in Education is to provide an independent, non-partisan source of analysis and information on privatization in education.
Henry M Levin, Director
Clive Belfield, Associate Director

5158 National Center on Education & the Economy
555 13th Street, NW
Suite 500 W
Washington, DC 20004
202-783-3668
888-361-6233
Fax: 202-783-3672
info@ncee.org
www.ncee.org
NCEE is committed not just to research, analysis and advocacy, but also to following through on its recommendations by creating the training, professional development, technical assistance and materials that professionals in the system need to implement the proposals we make.
Marc Tucker, President/Founder
Rich Moglia Cannon, Chief Financial Officer

5159 National Center on Education in the Inner Cities
Temple University
13th Street & Cecil B Moore Avenue
Philadelphia, PA 19122
215-893-8400
Fax: 215-735-9718
Conducts systematic studies of innovative initiatives for improving the quality and outcomes of schooling and broad-based efforts to strengthen and improve education.
Margaret C Wang, Director

5160 National Child Labor Committee
1501 Broadway
Suite 1908
New York, NY 10036-5592
212-840-1801
Fax: 212-768-0963
info@nationalchildlabor.org
www.nationalchildlabor.org
The National Child Labor Committee (NCLC) is a private, non-profit organization founded in 1904 and incorporated by an Act of Congress in 1907 with the mission of promoting the rights, awareness, dignity, well-being and education of children and youth as they relate to work and working.
Jeffrey F Newman, President/Executive Director
Erik Butler, President

5161 National Clearinghouse for Alcohol & Drug Information
PO Box 2345
Rockville, MD 20847-2345
240-221-4019
800-729-6686
Fax: 240-221-4292
ncadi.samhsa.gov
SAMHSA's National Clearinghouse for Alcohol and Drug Information (NCADI) is the Nation's one-stop resource for information about substance abuse prevention and addiction treatment.
John Noble, Director

5162 National Clearinghouse for Bilingual Education
George Washington University
2011 Eye Street NW
Suite 300
Washington, DC 20006
202-467-0867
800-321-6223
Fax: 202-467-4283
askncela@ncela.gwu.edu
www.ncela.gwu.edu
OELA's National Clearinghouse collects, coordinates and conveys a broad range of research and resources in support of an inclusive approach to high quality education for ELLs.
Nancy Zelasko, Director
Minerva Gorena, Director

5163 National Clearinghouse for Information on Business Involvement in Education
National Association for Industry-Education Co-op
235 Hendricks Boulevard
Buffalo, NY 14226-3304

716-834-7047
Fax: 718-834-7047
www2.pecom/naiec
www2.pecom.net/naiec
Seeks to foster industry-education cooperation in the US and Canada in the areas of school improvement, career education and human resource/economic development.

Dr. Donald Clark, Director

5164 National Dropout Prevention Center
Clemson University
209 Martin Street
Clemson, SC 29631-1555
864-656-2599
Fax: 864-656-0136
ndpc@clemson.edu
dropoutprevention.org
Provides knowledge and promotes networking for researchers, practitioners, policymakers and families to increase opportunities for at-risk youth to help them succeed in high school.

Sandy Addis, Ph.D, Director
Jennie Cole, Research Associate

5165 National Information Center for Educational Media
PO Box 8640
Albuquerque, NM 87198-8640
505-998-0800
800-926-8328
Fax: 505-256-1080
mhlava@accessinn.com
www.nicem.com
The world's most comprehensive audiovisual database for over 35 years and a crucial reference tool for librarians, media specialists, training directors, faculty, teachers and researchers.

Marjorie Hlava, President
Jay Van Eman, Chief Executive Officer

5166 National Research Center on the Gifted & Talented
University of Connecticut
2131 Hillside Road
Unit 3007
Storrs, CT 06269-3007
860-486-4826
Fax: 860-486-2900
www.gifted.uconn.edu
Studies focusing on meeting the needs of gifted and talented youth have received national and international attention for over 40 years.

Joseph S Renzulli, Director
Phillip E Austin, President

5167 National Resource Center on Self-Care & School-Age Child Care
American Home Economics Association
1555 King Street
Alexandria, VA 22314-2738
703-706-4620
800-252-SAFE
Fax: 703-706-4663
Provides materials to parents, educators, child care professionals and others concerned about the number of latchkey children and about quality school-age child care.

Dr. Margaret Plantz, Director

5168 National School Boards Association Library
1680 Duke Street
2nd Floor
Alexandria, VA 22314-3493
703-838-6722
Fax: 703-683-7590
info@nsba.org
www.nsba.org
Maintains an up-to-date collection of resources concerning education issues, with an emphasis on school board policy issues. Publications include amicus briefs, reports, school law resources, conference presentations, surveys and newsletters.

Kevin E Ciak, President
Thomas Gentzel, Executive Director & CEO

5169 National School Safety Center
30200 Agoura Road
Suite 260
Agoura Hills, CA 91301
805-373-9977
info@schoolsafety.us
www.schoolsafety.us
Serves as an advocate for safe schools and the prevention of school crime and violence. The center also offers research materials, statistics and books on the subject.

Ronald D Stephens, Executive Director

5170 National Science Resources Center
901 D Street SW
Suite 704B
Washington, DC 20024
202-633-2966
Fax: 202-287-2070
nsrcinfo@si.edu
www.nsrconline.org
Intermediary organization that bridges research on how children learn with best practices for the classroom.

Sally Shuler, Executive Director
Jennifer Childress, Director

5171 North Central Regional Educational Laboratory
1120 East Diehl Road
Suite 200
Naperville, IL 60563-1486
630-649-6500
Fax: 630-649-6700
info@ncrel.org
www.ncrel.org
Being an educator is a great responsibility. At Learning Point Associates, we accept responsibility in order to deserve the trust that has been placed in us and our work

Gina Burkhard, Chief Executive Officer
Robert Davis, Chief Financial Officer

5172 Northeast Regional Center for Drug-Free Schools & Communities
12 Overton Avenue
Sayville, NY 11782-2437
718-340-7000
Fax: 516-589-7894
Works to support the prevention of alcohol and other drug use in the northeast region of the United States.

Dr. Gerald Edwards, Director

5173 Northeast and Islands Regional Educational Laboratory
222 Richmond Street
Suite 300
Providence, RI 02903
401-274-9548
800-521-9550
Fax: 401-421-7650
info@lab.brown.edu
Promotes educational change to provide all students equitable opportunities to succeed. We advocate for populations whose access to excellent education has been limited or denied.

Oaxaca Schroder, Administrative Assistant
Sunitha Appikatla, Senior Programmer/Analyst

5174 Northwest Regional Educational Laboratory
101 SW Main Street
Suite 500
Portland, OR 97204-3213
503-275-9500
800-547-6339
Fax: 503-275-0660
info@nwrel.org
www.nwrel.org
The mission of the Northwest Regional Educational Laboratory (NWREL) is to improve learning by building capacity in schools, families, and communities through applied research and development

Jerry Colonna, Chairperson
Rob Larson, Vice Chairperson

5175 Pacific Regional Educational Laboratory
1099 Alakea Street
Suite 2500
Honolulu, HI 96813
808-969-3482
Fax: 808-969-3483
kofelj@prel.hawaii.edu
The Regional Educational Laboratories are educational research and development organizations supported by contracts with the U.S. Education Department, Office of Educational Research and Improvement. Specialty area: Language and Cultural Diversity.

Dr. John Kofel, Executive Director

5176 Parent Educational Advocacy Training Center
100 N Washington Street
Suite 234
Falls Church, VA 22046-4523
703-923-0010
800-869-6782
Fax: 800-693-3514
partners@peatc.org
www.peatc.org
Mission is to build positive futures for children in Virginia by working collaboratively with families, schools and communities in order to improve opportunities for excellence in education and success in school and community life.

Michael Jefferson, President
Betsy McGuire, Vice President

5177 Parents as Teachers National Center
2228 Ball Drive
Saint Louis, MO 63146
314-432-4330
866-728-4968
Fax: 314-432-8963
info@parentsasteachers.org
www.patnc.org
To provide the information, support and encouragement parents need to help their children develop optimally during the crucial early years of life.

Sue Stepleton, President/CEO
Cheryl Dyle-Palmer, COO

5178 Public Education Fund Network
601 13th Street NW
Suite 710 S
Washington, DC 20005-3808
202-628-7460
Fax: 202-628-1893
PEN@PublicEducation.org
www.publiceducation.org
To build public demand and mobilize resources for quality public education for all children

through a national constituency of local education funds and individuals.

Wendy D Puriefoy, Director
Richard J. Vierk, Chairman

5179 Quality Education Data
1050 Seventeenth Street
Suite 1100
Denver, CO 80265
303-209-9400
800-525-5811
Fax: 303-209-9444
info@qeddata.com
www.qeddata.com
Gathers information about K-12 schools, colleges and other educational institutions, offers an on-line database on education, directories of public and nonpublic schools and research reports.

Jeanne Hayes, President
Katie Bukovsky, Sales Executive

5180 Regional Laboratory for Educational Improvement of the Northeast
555 New Jersey Ave NW
Washington, DC 20208
800-347-4200
Fax: 781-481-1120
Seeks to improve education in Connecticut, Maine, Massachusetts, New Hampshire, New York, Rhode Island, Vermont, Puerto Rico and the Virgin Islands.

David P Crandall, Director

5181 Research for Better Schools
112 N Broad Street
Philadelphia, PA 19102-2471
215-568-6150
Fax: 215-568-7260
info@rbs.org
www.rbs.org
RBS is a private, nonprofit educational organization funded primarily through grants and contracts from the U.S. Department of Education, the National Science Foundation, Mid-Atlantic state departments of education, institutions of higher education, foundations, and school districts.

Dr. Keith M Kershner, Executive Director
Rev. John F Bloh, President

5182 SERVE
PO Box 5367
Greensboro, NC 27435
336-315-7400
800-755-3277
Fax: 336-315-7457
info@serve.org
www.serve.org
Its mission is to support and promote teaching and learning excellence in the Pre-kindergarten to Grade 12 education community.

Ludwig Van Broekhuizen, Executive Director
Francena Cummings, Director, Technical Assistan

5183 SIGI PLUS
Educational Testing Service
105 Terry Drive
Suite 120
Newtown, PA 18940-1872
800-257-7444
Fax: 215-579-8589
A computerized career guidance program developed by Educational Testing Service. Covers all the major aspects of career decision making and planning through a carefully constructed system of nine separate but interrelated sections, including a Tech Prep module and Internet Hydrolink Connectivity.

Annie Schofer, Sales Manager

5184 Satellite Educational Resources Consortium
939 S Stadium Road
Columbia, SC 29201-4724
803-252-2782
Fax: 803-252-5320
www.adec.edu
Seeks to expand educational opportunities by employing the latest telecommunication technologies to make quality education in math, science, and foreign languages available equally and cost-effectively to students regardless of their geographic location.

Wilbur H Hinton, Executive Director

5185 Scientific Learning
300 Frank H Ogawa Plaza
Suite 600
Oakland, CA 94612-2040
888-665-9707
888-665-9707
Fax: 510-444-3580
customerservice@scilearn.com
www.scientificlearning.com
Scientific Learning bases their products and services on neuroscience research and scientifically validated efficacy and deliver them using the most efficient technologies. We also provide beneficial products and services to our customers that are easy to use and access.

Robert C Bowen, Chairman/CEO
Andy Myers, President/COO

5186 Smithsonian Institution/Office of Elementary& Secondary Education
PO Box 37012
SI Building, Room 153, MRC 010
Washington, DC 20013-7012
202-633- 100
Fax: 202-357-2116
info@si.edu
si.edu
Helps K-12 teachers incorporate museums and other community resources into their curricula.

Ann Bay, Director
G Wayne Clough, Secretary

5187 Society for Research in Child Development
University of Chicago Press
2950 S State Street
Suite 401
Ann Arbor, MI 48104
734-926-0600
Fax: 734-926-0601
info@srcd.org
www.srcd.org
The Society is a multidisciplinary, not-for-profit, professional association with a membership

Barbara Kahn, Business Manager
Lonnie Sherrod, Executive Director

5188 Southeast Regional Center for Drug-Free Schools & Communities
Spencerian Office Plaza
Louisville, KY 40292-1
502-588-0052
800-621-7372
Fax: 502-588-1782
Works to support the prevention of alcohol and drug use among youth in the Southeast region.

Nancy J Cunningham, Director

5189 Southern Regional Education Board
592 10th Street NW
Atlanta, GA 30318-5776
404-875-9211
Fax: 404-872-1477
evalutech@sreb.org
www.sreb.org
Nonprofit, nonpartisan organization that helps government and education leaders in its 16 member states work together to advance education and improve the social and economic life of the region.

Mark D Musick, Director
David S Spence, President

5190 Southwest Comprehensive Regional Assistance Center-Region IX
New Mexico Highlands University
121 Tijeras Avenue NE
Suite 2100
Albuquerque, NM 87102-3461
800-247-4269
Fax: 505-243-4456
National network of 15 technical assistance centers, funded through the US Department of Education, designed to support federally funded educational programs. Specifically, these centers will provide comprehensive training and technical assistance under the Improving America's Schools Act (IASA) to States, Tribes, community based organizations, local education agencies, schools and other recipients of funds under the Act.

Paul E Martinez EdD, Director

5191 Southwestern Educational Development Laboratory
4700 Mueller Boulevard
Austin, TX 78723
512-476-6861
800-476-6861
Fax: 512-476-2286
information@sedl.org
www.sedl.org
SEDL is a private, nonprofit corporation dedicated to fulfilling its mission with clients and other education stakeholders on a national, regional, state, and local basis through diverse and interrelated funding, partnerships, and projects.

Dr. Wesley A Hoover, President/ CEO
Vicki Dimock, Chief Program Officer

5192 Special Interest Group for Computer Science Education
Computer Science Department
University of Texas at Austin
Austin, TX 78712
512-471-9539
Fax: 512-471-8885
www.sigcse.org
Provides a forum for solving problems common in developing, implementing and evaluating computer science education programs and courses.

Nell B Dale, Director

5193 TACS/WRRC
1268 University of Oregon
Eugene, OR 97403
541-346-5641
Fax: 541-346-0322
wrrc@oregon.uoregon.edu
wrrc.uoregon.edu/tacs
Supports state education agencies in their task of ensuring quality programs and services for children with disabilities and their families.

Richard Zeller, Co-Director
Caroline Moore, Project Director

5194 TERC
2067 Massachusetts Avenue
Cambridge, MA 2140-1340
617-873-9600
Fax: 617-873-9601

contactus@terc.edu
www.terc.edu
We imagine a future in which learners from diverse communities engage in creative, rigorous, and reflective inquiry as an integral part of their lives.

24 pages
ISSN: 0743-0221

Laurie Brennan, President
Nira Voss, Chief Financial Officer

5195 UCLA Statistical Consulting
University of California, Los Angeles
8130 MSB, UCLA
PO Box 951554
Los Angeles, CA 90095-1554
310-825-8299
Fax: 310-206-5658
www.ats.ucla.edu
Provides statistical consulting services to UCLA and off-campus students. The staff is faculty members, graduate students and the Department of Statistics. Specializes in the quantitative analysis of research problems in a wide variety of fields.

Debbie Barrera, Administrator
Richard Berk, Director

Audio Visual Materials

5196 AGC/United Learning
Discovery Education
1560 Sherman Avenue
Suite 100
Evanston, IL 60201
847-328-6700
800-323-9084
Fax: 847-328-6706
www.discoveryed.com
A publisher/producer of educational videos and digital content K-College curriculum based.
Coni Rechner, Director Marketing
Ronald Reed, Sr. Vice President

5197 Active Parenting Publishing
1220 Kennestone Circle
Suite 130
Marietta, GA 30066-6022
770-429-0565
800-825-0060
Fax: 770-429-0334
cservice@activeparenting.com
www.activeparenting.com
Videos and books on parenting, character education, substance abuse prevention, divorce and step-parenting, ADHD and more.
Dr. Michael H. Popkin, Founder

5198 Agency for Instructional Technology/AIT
8111 N. Lee Paul Road
Bloomington, IN 47404-7916
800-457-4509
info@ait.net
www.ait.net
Videodiscs, videocassettes, films and electronics.

5199 Allied Video Corporation
PO Box 702618
Tulsa, OK 74170-2618
918-587-6477
800-926-5892
Fax: 918-587-1550
allied@farpointer.net
www.allied-video.com/default.aspx
Produces the educational video series, The Assistant Professor. Animations and three-dimensional graphics clearly illustrate concepts in mathematics, science and music. Companion supplementary materials are also available.
Video
Charles Brown, President

5200 Altschul Group Corporation
1560 Sherman Avenue
Suite 100
Evanston, IL 60201-4817
800-323-9084
Video and film educational programs.

5201 Ambrose Video Publishing Inc
145 West 45th Street
New York, NY 10036
212-768-7373
800-526-4663
Fax: 212-768-9282
customerservice@ambrosevideo.com
www.ambrosevideo.com
A leading distributor of broadcast quality documentation/educational videos to individuals (in the home) and schools, libraries and other institutions. The company also sells through catalog, sales staff and television advertising.

5202 Anchor Audio
5931 Darwin Court
Carlsbad, CA 92008
310-784-2300
800-262-4671
Fax: 760-827-7105
sales@anchoraudio.com
www.anchoraudio.com
Various audio visual products for the school and library.
Alex Jacobs, VP, Sales
Nick Craig, Sales

5203 Association for Educational Communications & Technology
1025 Vermont Avenue NW
Suite 820
Washington, DC 20005-3516
202-347-7834
Offers a full line of videotapes and films for the various educational fields including language arts, science and social studies.

5204 BUILD Sucess Through the Values of Excellence
Center for the Study of Small/Rural Schools
555 E Constitution Street
Room 138
Norman, OK 73072-7820
405-325-1450
Fax: 405-325-7075
jcsimmons@ou.edu
cssrs.ou.edu
Series IV
Video
Jan C Simmons, Ph.D., Program Director

5205 Bergwall Productions
540 Baltimore Pike
Chadds Ford, PA 19317-9304
800-645-3565
Educational videotapes and films.

5206 Cedrus
1420 Buena Vista Avenue
McLean, VA 22101-3510
703-883-0986
Videodiscs, videocassettes and filmstrips for educational purposes.

5207 Cengage Learning
2493 Du Bridge Avenue
Irvine, CA 92606-5022
949-660-0727
800-233-7078
Fax: 949-660-0206
info@conceptmedia.com
www.cengage.co.in/
Videos for students and professionals focused on child development, early childhood education, and the challenges facing many young children. Effective educational media for development specialists, regular and special education staff in elementary school, preschool teachers, childcare providers, health care workers and parents.
Dennis Timmerman, Sr Account Executive

5208 Character Education
Center for the Study of Small/Rural Schools
555 E Constitution Street
Room 138
Norman, OK 73072-7820
405-325-1450
Fax: 405-325-7075
jcsimmons@ou.edu
cssrs.ou.edu
Series IV
Video
Jan C Simmons, Ph.D., Program Director

5209 Chip Taylor Communications
2 East View Drive
Derry, NH 03038-5728
603-434-9262
800-876-2447
Fax: 603-432-2723
chip@chiptaylor.com
www.chiptaylor.com
Offers worldwide Digital and DVD program distribution for Broadcast, Digital, Theatrical, Education, Library, Museum, Institution, Organization, In-flight, At Sea, Medical, Business, Home and Retail markets.
Video
Chip Taylor, President

5210 Churchill Media
6677 N NW Highway
Chicago, IL 60631-1304
310-207-6600
800-334-7830
Fax: 800-624-1678
Videos, videodiscs and curriculum packages for schools and libraries.

5211 College Board Publications
College Board Publications
45 Columbus Avenue
New York, NY 10023-6992
212-713-8000
800-323-7155
Fax: 800-525-5562
aces@info.collegeboard.org
www.collegeboard.org
Offers a variety of educational videotapes and publications focusing on college issues.
David Coleman, President/ CEO
Jack Buckley, SVP, Research

5212 Computer Prompting & Captioning Company
1010 Rockville Pike
Suite 306
Rockville, MD 20852-3035
301-738-8487
800-977-6678
Fax: 301-738-8488
info@cpcweb.com
www.cpcweb.com
Closed captioning systems and service.
Sid Hoffman, Project Manager

5213 Crystal Productions
5320 Carpinteria Ave
Suite K
Carpinteria, CA 93013-2107
847-657-8144
800-255-8629
Fax: 800-657-8149
custserv@crystalproductions.com
www.crystalproductions.com
Producer and distributor of educational resource material in art and sciences. Resources include videotapes, posters, books, videodiscs, CD-Rom, reproductions, games.
132 pages
Amy Woodworth, President

5214 Dukane Corporation
Audio Visual Products Division
2900 Dukane Drive
St Charles, IL 60174-3395
630-584-2300
Fax: 630-584-5156
www.dukane.com
Full line of audio visual products, LCD display panels, computer data projectors, overhead projectors, microfilm readers and silent and sound filmstrip projectors.
Michael W. Ritschdorff, President/ CEO
Terry Goldman, VP, Administration

5215 Early Advantage
270 Monroe Turnpike
P.O. Box 743
Fairfield, CT 6824-9853
888-248-0480
Fax: 800-409-9928
customerservice@early-advantage.com
www.earlyadvantage.com
Features the Muzzy video collection for teaching children beginning second language skills.

5216 Educational Video Group
291 S Wind Way
Greenwood, IN 46142-9190
317-888-6581
Fax: 317-888-5857
evg@insightbb.com
www.evgonline.com
Award-winning video programs and textbooks in education, presenting new offerings in speech, government and historic documentaries.
Roger Cook, President

5217 English as a Second Language Video Series
Master Teacher
One Leadership Lane
PO Box 1207
Manhattan, KS 66502-1207
800-669-9633
Fax: 800-669-1132
www.masterteacher.com
Assessing the needs of culturally diverse learners, you will learn what must be done to evaluate the learning needs and progress of ESL students.

ISBN: 1-58992-045-7

5218 Fase Productions
4801 Wilshire Boulevard
Suite 215
Los Angeles, CA 90010-3813
213-965-8794
Educational videotapes and films.

5219 Films for Humanities & Sciences
PO Box 2053
Princeton, NJ 08543-2053
609-419-8000
800-257-5126
Fax: 609-419-8071
www.wiley.com
A leading publisher/distributor of over four thousand educational programs, including NOVA and TV Ontario, for school and college markets. Also a leader in the production and distribution of videotapes and videodiscs to the educational, institutional and government markets.

5220 First Steps/Concepts in Motivation
18105 Town Center Drive
Olney, MD 20832-1479
301-774-9429
800-947-8377
Educational videotapes and accessories promoting physical fitness for preschoolers and young children. Using choreographed dance movement, familiar and fun children's music, colorful mats, bean bags and rhythm sticks, First Steps teaches balance, gross and fine motor skills, rhythm, coordination, and primary learning skills.
Dale Rimmey, Marketing Director
Larry Rose, President/Owner

5221 Future of Rural Education
Center for the Study of Small/Rural Schools
555 E Constitution Street
Room 138
Norman, OK 73072-7820
405-325-1450
Fax: 405-325-7075
jcsimmons@ou.edu
cssrs.ou.edu
Series I
Video
Jan C Simmons, Ph.D., Program Director

5222 GPN Year 2005 Literacy Catalog
Destination Education
4910 S 75th St
Lincoln, NE 68516
402-472-2007
800-228-4630
Fax: 402-435-0110
slenzen@shopdei.com
www.gpn.unl.edu
DVD, VHS, CD-ROM and slides for K-12 libraries and higher education. Free previews and satisfaction guaranteed. The sole source of Reading Rainbow and many other quality programs seen on PBS.
Annually/Video
Steve Lenzen, President and co-founder
John Vondracek, Director Marketing

5223 Gangs in Our Schools: Identification, Response, and Prevention Strategies
Center for the Study of Small/Rural Schools
555 E Constitution Street
Room 138
Norman, OK 73072-7820
405-325-1450
Fax: 405-325-7075
jcsimmons@ou.edu
cssrs.ou.edu
Series III
Video
Jan C Simmons, Ph.D., Program Director

5224 Guidance Associates
31 Pine View Road
PO Box 1000
Mount Kisco, NY 10549-7000
800-431-1242
Fax: 914-666-5319
willg1961@gmail.com
www.guidanceassociates.com
Curriculum based videos in health/guidance, social studies, math, science, English, the humanities and career education.
Will Goodman, President

5225 Health Connection
55 West Oak Ridge Drive
Hagerstown, MD 21740
800-548-8700
Fax: 888-294-8405
sales@healthconnection.org
www.healthconnection.org
Tools for freedom from tobacco and other drugs.

5226 Human Relations Media
175 Tompkins Avenue
Pleasantville, NY 10570-3144
800-431-2050
Fax: 914-244-0485
Offers a wide variety of videotapes and videodiscs in the areas of guidance, social services, human relations, self-esteem and student services.

5227 IIEPassport: Short Term Study Abroad
Institute of International Education
809 United Nations Plaza
New York, NY 10017-3580
412-741-0930
Fax: 212-984-5496
iiebooks@abdintl.com
www.iiebooks.org
Over 2,900 short-term study abroad programs offered by universities, schools, associations and other organizations.
Annual
ISBN: 087206-296-1
Daniel Obst, Sr Editor

5228 INSIGHTS Visual Productions
374-A N Highway 101
Encinitas, CA 92024-2527
760-942-0528
Fax: 760-944-7793
Science video for K-12 and teacher training.

5229 INTELECOM Intelligent Telecommunications
150 E Colorado Boulevard
Suite 300
Pasadena, CA 91105-1937
626-796-7300
800-576-2988
Fax: 626-577-4282
wharden@intelecom.org
www.intelecomonline.net
Videos and educational films.
Bob Miller, VP Marketing/Sale

5230 In Search of Character
Performance Resource Press
1270 Rankin Drive
Suite F
Troy, MI 48083-2843
800-453-7733
Fax: 800-499-5718
www.pronline.net
Character education videos.

5231 Instructional Resources Corporation
1819 Bay Ridge Avenue
Annapolis, MD 21403-2835
800-922-1711
Fax: 410-268-8320
bwhite@historypictures.com
www.historypictures.info
American History Videodisc.

5232 Intermedia
5600 Rainier Ave S
Suite 203
Seattle, WA 98118
206-284-2995
800-553-8336
Fax: 206-283-0778
info@intermedia-inc.com
www.intermedia-inc.com
Distributes a wide range of high-quality, social interest videos on topics such as teen pregnancy prevention, substance abuse prevention, domestic violence, sexual harassment, dating violence, date rape, gang education, cultural diversity, AIDS prevention and teen patenting. Offer free 30 day previews of the programs which are developed to address the needs of educators who must deal with the pressing social problems of today.
Paperback/Video
Susan Hoffman, President
Ted Fitch, General Manager

5233 International Historic Films
3533 S Archer Avenue
Chicago, IL 60609-1135
773-927-2900
Fax: 773-927-9211
intrvdeo@ix.netcom.com
www.ihffilm.com

Military, political and social history of the 20th century.

Video/Audio

5234 January Productions
PO Box 66
Hawthorne, NJ 07507-0066
973-423-4666
800-451-7450
Fax: 973-423-5569
anpeller@worldnet.att.net
Educational videotapes, read-a-long books, and CD-Rom.

Paperback/Video/Audi

Lori Brown, Sales/Marketing

5235 Karol Media
375 Stewart Road
Hanover, PA 18706
570-822-8899
Fax: 570-822-8226
www.karolmedia.com
Science videos.

Carol Kincheloe, Founder
Mick Kincheloe, Founder

5236 Kimbo Educational
PO Box 477
Long Branch, NJ 07740-0477
732-229-4949
800-631-2187
service@kimboed.com
www.kimboeddownloads.com
Manufacturer of children's audio-musical learning fun. Also offers videos and music by other famous children's artists such as Raffi, Sharon, Lois and Bram.

Jim Kimble, President

5237 Leadership: Rethinking the Future
Center for the Study of Small/Rural Schools
555 E Constitution Street
Room 138
Norman, OK 73072-7820
405-325-1450
Fax: 405-325-7075
jcsimmons@ou.edu
cssrs.ou.edu
Series IV

Video

Jan C Simmons, Ph.D., Program Director

5238 MPC Multimedia Products Corp
1010 Sherman Avenue
Hamden, CT 06514
203-407-4623
800-243-2108
Fax: 203-407-4636
sales@800-pickmpc.com
www.800-pickmpc.com
Over 5,000 most frequently requested high quality audio, visual and video products and materials offered at deep discount prices. Manufacturer of high quality tape records,CD's record players, PA systems, headphones

148 pages BiAnnual

T. Guercia, Author
T Guercia, VP
A Melillo, Sales Manager

5239 Main Street Foundations: Building Community Teams
Center for the Study of Small/Rural Schools
555 E Constitution Street
Room 138
Norman, OK 73072-7820
405-325-1450
Fax: 405-325-7075
jcsimmons@ou.edu
cssrs.ou.edu
Prevention Series

Video

Jan C Simmons, Ph.D., Program Director

5240 Marshmedia
Marsh Media
P.O. Box 8082
Shawnee Mission, KS 66208-82
816-523-1059
800-821-3303
Fax: 816-333-7421
info@marshmedia.com
www.marshmedia.com
Children's educational videotapes, books and teaching guides.

32 pages Bi-Annual
ISBN: 1-55942-xxx

Joan K Marsh, President

5241 Media Projects
5215 Homer Street
Dallas, TX 75206-6623
214-826-3863
Fax: 214-826-3919
mail@mediaprojects.org
www.mediaprojects.org
Educational videotapes in all areas of interest, including drug education, violence prevention, women's studies, history, youth issues and special education.

Allen Mondell, Director, Writer, Producer

5242 Middle School: Why and How
Center for the Study of Small/Rural Schools
555 E Constitution Street
Room 138
Norman, OK 73072-7820
405-325-1450
Fax: 405-325-7075
jcsimmons@ou.edu
cssrs.ou.edu
Series III

Video

Jan C Simmons, Ph.D., Program Director

5243 Multicultural Educations: Valuing Diversity
Center for the Study of Small/Rural Schools
555 E Constitution Street
Room 138
Norman, OK 73072-7820
405-325-1450
Fax: 405-325-7075
jcsimmons@ou.edu
cssrs.ou.edu
Series I

Video

Jan C Simmons, Ph.D., Program Director

5244 NUVO, Ltd.
PO Box 1729
Chula Vista, CA 91912
619-426-8440
Fax: 619-691-1525
nuvoltd@aol.com
Produces and distributes how-to videotapes for teens and adults on beginning reading and decorative napkin folding useful in classroom instruction and individual practice. Also distributes two bilingual (Spanish/English) books by psychologist Dr. Jorge Espinoza.

5245 National Film Board
1251 Avenue of the Americas
New York, NY 10020-1104
800-542-2164
Fax: 845-774-2945
Educational films and videos ranging from documentaries on nature and science to social issues such as teen pregnancy.

5246 National Geographic School Publishing
PO Box 10579
Washington, DC 20090-8019
800-368-2728
Fax: 515-362-3366
Offers a wide variety of videodiscs, videotapes and educational materials in the area of social studies, geography, science and social sciences.

5247 PBS Video
1320 Braddock Pl
Alexandria, VA 22314-1649
703-739-5380
800-424-7963
Fax: 703-739-5269
Award-winning programs from PBS, public television's largest video distributors. Video and multimedia programming including interactive videodiscs for schools, colleges and libraries. The PBS Video Resource Catalog is organized into detailed subject categories.

5248 PICS Authentic Foreign Video
University of Iowa
270 International Center
Iowa City, IA 52242-1802
319-335-3500
800-373-PICS
Fax: 319-335-0280
webmaster@uiowa.edu
housing.uiowa.edu
Provides educators with authentic foreign language videos in French, German and Spanish on videotapes and videodisc. Also offers software to accompany the videodiscs as well as written materials in the form of transcripts and videoguides with pedagogical hints and tips.

Sally Mason, President
Anny Ewing, French Coll Editor

5249 Penton Overseas
2470 Impala Drive
Carlsbad, CA 92008-7226
800-748-5804
Fax: 760-431-8110
Educational videotapes and videodiscs in a wide variety of interests for classroom use.

5250 Phoenix Films/BFA Educ Media/Coronet/MII
Phoenix Learning Group
141 Millwell Dr.
Suite A
St. Louis, MO 63043
314-569-0211
800-221-1274
Fax: 314-569-2834
phoenixdealer@aol.com
www.phoenixlearninggroup.com
Educational multi-media - VHS, CD-Rom, DVD, streaming & broadcast.

Video

Kathy Longsworth, Vice President, Market Dev

5251 Presidential Classroom
2201 Old Ivy Road
P.O. Box 400406
Charlottesville, VA 22904
434-924-7236
800-441-6533
Fax: 434-982-2739
eriedel@presidentialclassroom.org
www.presidentialclassroom.org
Video of civic education programs in Washington, DC for high school juniors and seniors. Each one week program provides students with an inside view of the federal

government in action and their role as responsible citizens and future leaders.
Annual
400 attendees
Jack Buechner, President/CEO
William Antholis, Director and CEO

5252 Rainbow Educational Media Charles Clark Company
4540 Preslyn Drive
Raleigh, NC 27616
919-954-7550
800-331-4047
Fax: 919-954-7554
karencf@rainbowedumedia.com
www.rainbowedumedia.com
Educational videocassettes and CD-Roms.
Karen C Francis, Business Analyst

5253 Rainbow Educational Video
170 Keyland Court
Bohemia, NY 11716-2638
800-331-4047
Producer and distributor of educational videos.
Wesley Clark, Marketing Director

5254 Reading & O'Reilly: The Wilton Programs
PO Box 302
Wilton, CT 06897-0302
800-458-4274
Producers and distributors of award-winning audiovisual educational programs in art appreciation, history, multicultural education, social studies and music. Titles include: African-American Art and the Take-a-Bow, musical production series. Free catalog is available of full product line.
Lee Reading, President
Gretchen O'Reilly, VP

5255 SAP Today
Performance Resource Press
1270 Rankin Drive
Suite F
Troy, MI 48083-2843
800-453-7733
Fax: 800-499-5718
store.amplifiedlifenetwork.com
Overview offers the basics of student assistance.

5256 SVE: Society for Visual Education
55 E Monroe Street
Suite 3400
Chicago, IL 60603-5710
312-849-9100
800-829-1900
Fax: 800-624-1678
Producer and distributor of curriculum based instructional materials including videodisc, microcomputer software, video cassettes and filmstrips for grade levels PreK-12.

5257 Slow Learning Child Video Series
Master Teacher
One Leadership Lane
PO Box 1207
Manhattan, KS 66502-1207
800-669-9633
Fax: 800-669-1132
www.masterteacher.com
Provides a full understandging of the slow learning child and allows all educators to share in the excitment of teaching this invidual in ways that develop his or her emerging potenial to the fullest.

ISBN: 1-58992-157-0
Mildred Odom Bradley, Author

5258 Spoken Arts
PO Box 100
New Rochelle, NY 10802-0100
727-578-7600
Literature-based audio and visual products for library and K-12 classrooms.

5259 Teacher's Video Company
8150 S Krene Road
Tempe, AZ 85284
800-262-8837
Fax: 800-434-5638
www.teachersvideo.com
Video for teachers.

5260 Teen Court: An Alternative Approach to Juvenile Justice
Center for the Study of Small/Rural Schools
555 E Constitution Street
Room 138
Norman, OK 73072-7820
405-325-1450
Fax: 405-325-7075
jcsimmons@ou.edu
cssrs.ou.edu
Prevention Series
Video
Jan C Simmons, Ph.D., Program Director

5261 Tools to Help Youth
529 S 7 Street
Suite 570
Minneapolis, MN 55415
800-328-0417
Fax: 612-342-2388
www.communityintervention.com
Books and videos on counseling, character education, anger management, life skills, and achohol, tobacco and other drug uses.

5262 Training Video Series for the Professional School Bus Driver
Master Teacher
One Leadership Lane
PO Box 1207
Manhattan, KS 66502-1207
800-669-9633
Fax: 800-669-1132
www.masterteacher.com
Will help you provide bus drivers with consistent direction and training for the many situations thay will encounter beyond driving safety.

ISBN: 1-58992-082-1

5263 True Colors
Center for the Study of Small/Rural Schools
555 E Constitution Street
Room 138
Norman, OK 73072-7820
405-325-1450
Fax: 405-325-7075
jcsimmons@ou.edu
cssrs.ou.edu
Series III
Video
Jan C Simmons, Ph.D., Program Director

5264 United Transparencies
435 Main Street
#104
Johnson City, NY 13790-1935
607-729-6512
800-477-6512
Fax: 607-729-4820
A full line of overhead transparencies for Junior-Senior high school and colleges and technical programs.
D Hetherington

5265 Video Project
P.O. Box 411376
San Francisco, CA 94141-1376
800-475-2638
Fax: 888-562-9012
support@videoproject.com
www.videoproject.org
Distributor of environmental videos with a collection of over 500 programs for all grade levels, including Oscar and Emmy award winners. Many videotapes come with teacher's guides. Free catalogs available.
Steve Michelson, President
Craig Malina, Director of Business Affairs

5266 Weston Woods Studios
265 Post Road West
Westport, CT 06880
203-845-0197
800-243-5020
Fax: 203-845-0498
wstnwoods@aol.com
Audiovisual adaptations of classic children's literature.
Video
Cindy Cardozo, Marketing Coordinator

Classroom Materials

5267 ABC School Supply
3312 N Berkeley Lake Road NW
Duluth, GA 30096-3024
Instructional materials and supplies.

5268 ADP Lemco
5970 W Dannon Way
West Jordan, UT 84081
801-280-4000
800-575-3626
Fax: 801-280-4040
customerservice@adplemco.com
www.adplemco.com
Announcement boards, schedule boards, chalkboards, tackboard, marker boards, trophy cases, athletic equipment, gym divider curtains and basketball backstops.
David L Hall, Sr VP

5269 APCO
388 Grant Street SE
Atlanta, GA 30312-2227
404-688-9000
877-988-APCO
Fax: 404-577-3847
www.apcosigns.com
Classroom supplies including announcement and chalkboards.
Anne M Gallup

5270 AbleNet
2625 Patton Road
Roseville, MN 55113-1308
651-294-2200
800-322-0956
Fax: 651-294-2259
customerservice@ablenetinc.com
www.ablenetinc.com

Adaptive devices for students with disabilities from Pre-K through adult, as well as activities and games for students of all abilities.

Bill Sproull, Board Chairman
Jennifer Thalhuber, President/CEO

5271 **Accounter Systems USA**
1107 S Mannheim Road
Suite 305
Westchester, IL 60154-2560
800-229-8765
Sports timers and clocks and classroom supplies.

5272 **Accu-Cut Systems**
1035 E Dodge Street
Fremont, NE 68025
402-721-4134
800-288-1670
Fax: 402-721-5778
info@accucut.com
www.accucut.com
Manufacturer of die cutting machines dies.

5273 **Airomat Corporation**
2916 Engle Road
Fort Wayne, IN 46809-1198
260-747-7408
800-348-4905
Fax: 260-747-7409
airomat@airomat.com
www.airomat.com
Mats and matting.

Jody Feasel, VP
Janie Feasel, President/CEO

5274 **Airspace USA**
89 Patton Avenue
Asheville, NC 28801
828-258-1319
800-872-1319
Fax: 828-258-1390
sales@airspace-usa.com
www.airspacesolutions.com
Airspace Soft Center Play and Learn Systems provide a comprehensive range of play, learning and physical development opportunities using commercial grade and foam filled play equipment. Play manual provided.

Daniel Brenman, VP Sales/Marketing
Tracy Syxes, Administrator

5275 **All Art Supplies**
Art Supplies Wholesale
4 Enon Street
North Beverly, MA 01915
800-462-2420
Fax: 978-922-1495
info@allartsupplies.com
www.allartsupplies.com
Art supplies at wholesale prices.

5276 **American Foam**
HC 37 Box 317 H
Lewisburg, WV 24901
304-497-3000
800-344-8997
Fax: 304-497-3001
www.bfoam.com
Carving blocks of foam.

5277 **American Plastics Council**
700 Second St., NE
Washington, DC 20002
202-249-7000
800-243-5790
Fax: 202-249-6100
www.plastics.org
Offers classroom materials on recycling and environmental education.

5278 **Anatomical Chart Company**
8221 Kimball Avenue
Skokie, IL 60076-2956
847-679-4700
www.anatomical.com
Maps and charts for educational purposes.

5279 **Angels School Supply**
600 E Colorado Boulevard
Pasadena, CA 91101-2006
626-584-0855
Fax: 626-584-0888
www.angelschoolsupply.com
School and classroom supplies.

Jennifer , Sales Representitive

5280 **Aol@School**
22070 Broderick Drive
Dulles, VA 20166
888-468-3768
aol at school@aol.com
www.school.aol.com
Age-appropriate, high-quality educational content tailored for K-12 students and educators. Aol@School focuses and filters the Web for us, providing appropriate, developmental access to the vast educational resources on the internet.

5281 **Armada Art Materials**
Armada Art Inc.
142 Berkeley Street
Boston, MA 02116
617-859-3800
800-435-0601
Fax: 617-859-3808
info@armadaart.com
www.armadaart.com

5282 **Art Materials Catalog**
United Art and Education
PO Box 9219
Fort Wayne, IN 46899-9219
260-478-1121
800-322-3247
Fax: 800-858-3247
www.unitednow.com
Art materials.

5283 **Art Supplies Wholesale**
4 Enon Street
North Beverly, MA 01915
800-462-2420
Fax: 978-922-1495
info@allartsupplies.com
www.allartsupplies.com
Wholesale art supplies.

5284 **Art to Remember**
5535 Macy Drive
Indianapolis, IN 46235
317-826-0870
800-895-8777
Fax: 317-823-2822
info@arttoremember.com
www.arttoremember.com
A unique program that encourages your students' artistic creativity while providing an opportunity to raise funds for schools.

Patty Arbuckle, Program Coordinator
Kathy Robinson, Program Coordinator

5285 **Artix**
PO Box 25008
Kelowna, BC V1W3Y
250-861-5345
800-665-5345
www.artix.bc.ca
Papermaking kits.

5286 **Assessories by Velma**
PO Box 2580
Shasta, CA 96087-2580
Multicultural education-related products.

5287 **At-Risk Resources**
135 Dupont Street
PO Box 760
Plainview, NY 11803-0706
800-999-6884
Fax: 800-262-1886
Dealing with drug violence prevention, character education, self-esteem, teen sexuality, dropout prevention, safe schoolks, career development, parenting crisis and trauma, and professional development.

5288 **Atlas Track & Tennis**
19495 SW Teton Avenue
Tualatin, OR 97062-8846
800-423-5875
Fax: 503-692-0491
Specialty sport surfaces; synthetic running tracks, tennis courts, and athletic flooring for schools.

5289 **Audio Forum**
69 Broad Street
Guildford, CT 06437
203-453-9794
Fax: 203-453-9774
info@audioforum.com
www.audioforum.com
Cassettes, CD's and books for language study.

5290 **Badge-A-Minit**
345 N. Lewis Ave.
Oglesby, IL 61348
815-883-8822
800-223-4103
Fax: 815-883-9696
questions@badgeaminit.com
www.badgeaminit.com
Awards, trophies, emblems and badges for educational purposes.

5291 **Bag Lady School Supplies**
9212 Marina Pacifica Drive N
Long Beach, CA 90803-3886
Classroom supplies.

5292 **Bale Company**
PO Box 6400
Providence, RI 02940-6400
800-822-5350
Fax: 401-831-5500
www.bale.com
Awards, medals, pins, plaques and trophies.

5293 **Bangor Cork Company**
William & D Streets
Pen Argyl, PA 18072
610-863-9041
Fax: 610-863-6275
www.bangorcork.com
Announcement boards.

Janice Cory, Customer Services Rep

5294 **Baumgarten's**
144 Ottley Drive NE
Atlanta, GA 30324-4016
404-874-7675
800-247-5547
Fax: 800-255-5547
mlynch@baumgartens.com
www.baumgartens.com
Products available include pencil sharpeners, pencil grips, pocket binders, disposable aprons, American flags, practical colorful clips, fastening devices in a variety of shapes and sizes, identification security items, lamination, magnifiers and key chains.

David Baumgarten, Vice President
Michael Lynch, National Sales Manager

5295 **Best Manufacturing Sign Systems**
1202 N. Park Avenue
PO Box 577
Montrose, CO 81401-3171
970-249-2378
800-235-2378
Fax: 970-249-0223
sales@bestsigns.com
www.bestsigns.com
Architectural and ADA signs, announcement boards.

Mary Phillips, Sales Manager

5296 **Binney & Smith**
1100 Church Lane
Easton, PA 18044-431
610-253-6271
800-CRA-YOLA
Fax: 610-250-5768
www.crayola.com
Crayons.

Mike Perry, President, CEO
Smith Holland, CFO, EVP

5297 **Black History Month**
Guidance Channel
135 Dupont Street
PO Box 760
Plainview, NY 44803-0706
800-999-6884
Fax: 800-262-1886
Products to celebrate Black history, multicultutral resources.

5298 **Blackboard Resurfacing Company**
50 N 7th Street
Bangor, PA 18013-1731
610-588-0965
Fax: 610-863-1997
Chalk and announcement boards.

Karin Karpinski, Administrative Assistant

5299 **Bob's Big Pencils**
1848 E 27th Street
Hays, KS 67601-2108
Large novelty pencils, plaques, bookends and many pencil related items.

5300 **Book It!/Pizza Hut**
9111 E Douglas Avenue
Wichita, KS 67207-1205
316-687-8401
National reading incentive program with materials, books and incentive display items to get students interested in reading.

5301 **Borden**
Home & Professional Products Group
180 E Broad Street
Columbus, OH 43215-3799
614-225-7479
Fax: 614-225-7167
Arts and crafts supplies, maintenance and repair supplies.

5302 **Bulman Products**
1650 Mc Reynolds Ave NW
Grand Rapids, MI 49504
616-363-4416
Fax: 616-363-0380
bulman@macatawa.com
bulmanproducts.com
Art craft paper.

5303 **Bydee Art**
8603 Yellow Oak Street
Austin, TX 78729-3739
512-474-4343
Fax: 512-474-5749
Prints, books, T-shirts with the Bydee People focusing on education.

5304 **C-Thru Ruler Company**
6 Britton Drive
Bloomfield, CT 06002-3632
860-243-0303
Fax: 860-243-1856
www.CThruRuler.com
Arts, crafts and classroom supplies.

Ross Zachs, Manager

5305 **CHEM/Lawrence Hall of Science**
University of California
1 Centennial Drive #5200
Berkeley, CA 94720-5200
510-642-6000
Fax: 510-642-1055
lhsinfo@uclink.berkley.edu
www.lawrencehallofscience.org
Activities for grades 5-6 and helps students understand the use of chemicals in our daily lives.

Elizabeth K. Stage, Director
Rena Dorph, Research

5306 **CORD Communications**
324 Kelly Street
Waco, TX 76710-5709
254-776-1822
Fax: 254-776-3906
Instructional materials for secondary and postsecondary applications in science education.

5307 **Califone International**
1145 Arroyo Avenue, # A
San Fernando, CA 91340
818-407-2400
800-722-0500
Fax: 877-402-2248
www.califone.com
Multisensory, supplemental curricula on magnetic cards for use with all Card Reader/Language master equipment.

Nelly Spievak, Sales Coordinator

5308 **Cardinal Industries**
PO Box 1430
Grundy, VA 24614-1430
276-935-4545
800-336-0551
Fax: 276-935-4970
Awards, emblems, trophies and badges.

5309 **Carousel Productions**
1100 Wilcrest Drive
Suite 100
Houston, TX 77042-1642
281-568-9300
Fax: 281-568-9498
Moments in History T-shirts, as well as other various educational gifts and products.

5310 **Cascade School Supplies**
1 Brown Street
PO Box 780
North Adams, MA 01247
800-628-5078
Fax: 866-298-6578
president@cascadeschoolsupplies.com
cascadeschoolsupplies.com
Offers a variety of school supplies and more.

Peter L. Cote, President

5311 **Celebrate Diversity**
Guidance Channel
135 Dupont Street
PO Box 760
Plainview, NY 44803-0706
800-999-6884
Fax: 800-262-1886
Educational resources that celebrate diversity.

5312 **Celebrate Earth Day**
Guidance Channel
135 Dupont Street
PO Box 760
Plainview, NY 44803-0706
800-999-6884
Fax: 800-262-1886
Educational resources for celebrating earth day.

5313 **Center Enterprises**
PO Box 33161
West Hartford, CT 06110
860-953-4423
Fax: 800-373-2923
Clifford individual curriculum and storybook stamp sets, individual, grading, curriculum based and Sweet Arts rubber stamp line, stamp pads, embossing inks and powders.

5314 **Center for Learning**
10200 Jefferson Blvd.
Box 802
Culver City, CA 90232
440-331-1404
800-421-4246
Fax: 800-944-5432
customerservice@centerforlearning.org
www.centerforlearning.org
Supplementary curriculum units for all grade levels in biography, language arts, novel/drama and social studies.

5315 **Center for Teaching International Relations**
University of Denver
2199 S. University Blvd.
Denver, CO 80208
303-871-3106
www.du.edu
Reproducible teaching activities and software promoting multicultural understanding and international relations in the classroom for grades K-adult.

Rebecca Chopp, Chancellor
Gregg Kvistad, Executive Vice Chancellor

5316 **Childcraft Education Corporation**
20 Kilmer Avenue
Edison, NJ 08817
732-572-6100
Distributes children's toys, products, materials and publications to schools.

5317 **Childswork/Childsplay**
The Guidence Channel
135 Dupont Street
PO Box 760
Plainview, NY 11803-0760
800-962-1141
Fax: 800-262-1886
www.childswork.com
Contains over 450 resources to address the social and emotional needs of children and adolescents.

Lawrence C Shapiro, PhD, President
Constance H Logan, Development Coordinator

5318 **Chroma**
205 Bucky Drive
Lititz, PA 17543
717-626-8866
800-257-8278
Fax: 717-626-9292
infousa@chromaonline.com
www.chromaonline.com
Tempera and acrylic paints.

5319 **Chroma-Vision Sign & Art System**
PO Box 434
Greensboro, NC 27402-0434
336-275-0602
Refillable and renewable felt tip markers used with non-toxic, water soluable, fast drying colors

for making signs, posters, and general art work with no messy cleanup.

S Gray, President

5320 Citizenship Through Sports and Fine Arts Curriculum
National Federation of State High School Assoc.
PO Box 690
Indianapolis, IN 46206
317-972-6900
800-776-3462
Fax: 317-822-5700
www.nfhs.org
High school activities curriculum package that includes an introductory video, Rekindling the Spirit, along with the Overview booklet, plus two insightful books covering eight targets of the curriculum.

Tom Mezzanotte, President
Tom Welter, Presideny- Elect

5321 Claridge Products & Equipment
Claridge Products & Equipment
601 Highway 62-65 S
PO Box 910
Harrison, AR 72602-0910
870-743-2200
Fax: 870-743-1908
claridge@claridgeproducts.com
www.claridgeproducts.com
Claridge manufactures chalkboards, markerboards, bulletin boards, display and trophy cases, bulletin and directory board cabinets, easels, lecterns, speakers' stands, wood lecture units with matching credenzas and much more.

Terry McCutchen, Sales Manager

5322 Collins & Aikman Floorcoverings
311 Smith Industrial Boulevard
Dalton, GA 30722
800-248-2878
Fax: 706-259-2666
tellis@powerbond.com
www.powerbond.com
An alternative to conventional carpet to improve indoor air quality and reduce maintenance cost. Powerboard floor covering.

T Ellis, General Manager/Edu Markets

5323 Columbia Cascade Company
1300 S.W. Sixth Avenue
Suite 310
Portland, OR 97201-3464
503-223-1157
800-547-1940
Fax: 503-223-4530
hq@timberform.com
www.timberform.com
Playground equipment and site furniture.

Dale Gordon, Sales Manager

5324 Creative Artworks Factory
19031 McGuire Road
Perris, CA 92570-8305
909-780-5950
Screenprinted T-shirts, posters and gifts for educational purposes.

5325 Creative Educational Surplus
9801 James Avenue S
#C
Bloomington, MN 55431-2919
Art and classroom materials.

5326 Crown Mats & Matting
2100 Commerce Drive
Fremont, OH 43420-1048
419-332-5531
800-628-5463
Fax: 800-544-2806
sales@crown-mats.com
www.crown-mats.com
Mats, matting and flooring for schools.

Vincent J. DePhillips , President

5327 Dahle USA
49 Vose Farm Road
Peterborough, NH 03458
603-924-0003
800-995-1379
Fax: 603-924-1616
info@dahleusa.com
www.dahleusa.com
Arts and crafts supplies, school and office products, office shreddars and more.

5328 Designer Artwear I
8475 C-1 Highway 6 N
Houston, TX 77095
281-446-6641
Specialty clothing, accessories, etc. all educationally designed.

5329 Dexter Educational Toys
Dexter Educational Toys, Inc.
PO Box 630861
Aventura, FL 33163-0861
305-931-7425
800-291-4515
Fax: 305-931-0552
dexterplay@bellsouth.net
www.dexterplay.com
Manufacturer and distributor of education material. Dress-ups for children 2-7 years. Multicultural hand puppets, finger puppets, head masks puppet theaters, rag dolls, dress-ups for teddy bears and dolls, cloth books, export manufacturing under special designs and orders.

Genny Silverstein, VP Secretary

5330 Dick Blick Art Materials
PO Box 1267
Galesburg, IL 61402-1267
309-343-6181
800-723-2787
Fax: 800-621-8293
info@dickblick.com
www.dickblick.com
Classroom art supplies.

5331 Dinorock Productions
407 Granville Drive
Silver Spring, MD 20901-3238
301-588-9300
www.dinorock.com
Musical, Broadway puppet shows for early childhood fun and education.

5332 Discovery Toys
12443 Pine Creek Road
Cerritos, CA 90703-2044
562-809-0331
800-341-8697
Fax: 562-809-0331
contact@discoverytoys.net
www.discoverytoyslink.com/elizabeth
Emphasizes child physical, social and educational development through creative play. Educational toys, games and books are available for all ages. Services include home demonstrations, fund raisers, phone and catalog orders. New Book of Knowledge Encyclopedia and patenting video tapes are also available.

Jerry Salerno, CEO
Jim Myers, COO

5333 Disney Educational Productions
500 S Buena Vista Street
Burbank, CA 91521-0001
800-777-8100
Creates and manufactures classroom aids for the educational field.

5334 Dixie Art Supplies
5440 Mounes St.
Suite 108
New Orleans, LA 70123-3290
504-733-6509
800-783-2612
Fax: 504-733-0668
artdixie@aol.com
www.dixieart.com
Fine art supplier.

5335 Dr. Playwell's Game Catalog
Guidance Channel
135 Dupont Street
PO Box 760
Plainview, NY 44803-0706
800-999-6884
Fax: 800-262-1886
Games that develop character and life skills.

5336 Draper
411 South Pearl Street
Spiceland, IN 47385
765-987-7999
800-238-7999
Fax: 765-987-7142
draper@draper.com
www.draperinc.com
Projection screens, video projector mounts and lifts, plasma display mounts, presentation easels, window shades and gymnasium equipment.

Chris Broome, Contract Market Manager
Bob Mathes, AV/Video Market Manager

5337 Draw Books
Peel Productions
PO Box 546
Columbus, NC 28722-0546
828-859-3879
800-345-6665
Fax: 801-365-9898
www.drawbooks.com
How-to-draw books for elementary and middle school.

Paperback
ISBN: 0-939217

5338 Dupont Company
Corlan Products
CRP-702
Wilmington, DE 19880
302-774-1000
800-436-7426
Fax: 800-417-1266
www.dupont.com/
Arts and crafts supplies.

5339 Durable Corporation
75 N Pleasant Street
Norwalk, OH 44857-1218
419-668-8138
800-419-8622
Fax: 800-537-6287
www.durablecorp.com
Furniture, classroom supplies, arts and crafts and educational products.

5340 EZ Grader
PO Box 23698
Chagrin Falls, OH 44023
800-732-4018
Fax: 800-689-2772
ezgrader@voyager.net
www.ezgrader.com
Electronic gradebook designed by teachers for teachers. It is an incredible time saver and computes percentage scores accurately, quickly and easily.

5341 **Early Ed**
3110 Sunrise Drive
Crown Point, IN 46307-8905
Teacher sweatshirts, cardigans, T-shirts, tote bags and jewelry.

5342 **Education Department**
Wildlife Conservation Society
2300 Southern Boulevard
Bronx, NY 10460
718-220-5100
800-937-5131
Fax: 718-733-4460
membership@wcs.org
www.wcs.org
Year round programs for school and general audience. Teacher training, grades K-12.
Sydell Schein, Manager/Program Services
Ann Robinson, Director/National Programs

5343 **Educational Equipment Corporation of Ohio**
845 Overholt Road
Kent, OH 44240-7529
330-673-4881
Fax: 330-673-4915
mkaufman@mkco.com
www.mkco.com
Chalkboards, tackboards, trophy cases, announcement boards.
Michael Kaufman, General Manager
Eric Baughman, Sales Manager

5344 **Electronic Book Catalog**
Franklin Learning Resources
1 Franklin Plaza
Burlington, NJ 08016-4908
800-BOO-MAN
Fax: 609-387-1787
Electronic translation machines, calculators and supplies.

5345 **Ellison Educational Equipment**
25862 Commercentre Drive
Lake Forest, CA 92630-8804
800-253-2238
Fax: 800-253-2240
europecustomerservices@ellison.com
www.ellison.com
Serves the educational and craft community with time-saving equipment, supplies and ideas.

5346 **Endura Rubber Flooring**
2 University Office Park
Waltham, MA 02453-3421
781-647-5375
Fax: 781-647-4543
Floorcoverings, mats and matting for schools.

5347 **Fairgate Rule Company**
3718 New York 9G
Sawkill Industrial Park
Rhinebeck, NY 12572
845-876-3063
Fax: 845-265-4128
sales@fairgate.com
www.fairgate.com
Arts and crafts supplies.

5348 **Family Reading Night Kit**
Renaissance Learning
2911 Peach Street
PO Box 8036
Wisconsin Rapids, WI 54495-8036
715-424-3636
800-338-4204
Fax: 715-424-4242
answers@renaissance.com
www.renlearn.com
Kit to start a family reading night where parents and children spent quality time together sharing enthusiasm over books.
Mary T. Minch, EVP, Finance, CFO
Samir Joglekar, EVP, Sales

5349 **Fascinating Folds**
PO Box 10070
Glendale, AZ 85318
602-375-9979
Fax: 602-375-9978
www.fascinating-folds.com
World's large supplier of origami and paper arts products.

5350 **Fiskars Corporation**
2537 Daniels St.
Madison, WI 53718
608-233-1649
866-348-5661
Fax: 608-294-4790
www.fiskars.com
School scissors.

5351 **Flipside Products**
7624 Reinhold Drive
Cincinnati, OH 45237
513-527-4521
800-926-0704
Fax: 513-527-4526
info@flipsideproducts.com
www.flipsideproducts.com
Suppliers of certificates, awards, graduation supplies, dry erase boards, chalk boards, project sheets and more school-related and office products.
Bryan Sharpe, VP, Operations
Meghan O'Brien, Sales Coordinator

5352 **Fox Laminating Company**
84 Custer Street
W Hartford, CT 06110-1955
860-953-4884
800-433-2468
Fax: 860-953-1277
sales@foxlaminating.com
www.foxlam.com
Easy, simple, and inexpensive do-it-yourself laminators. A piece of paper can be laminated for just pennies. Badges, ID's and luggage tags can also be made. Also laminated plaques for awards, diplomas, and mission statements.
Joe Fox, President
John Mills, Marketing Manager

5353 **George F Cram Company**
PO Box 426
Indianapolis, IN 46206-0426
317-635-5564
Fax: 317-687-2845
Classroom geography maps, state maps, social studies skills and globes.

5354 **Gift-in-Kind Clearinghouse**
PO Box 850
Davidson, NC 28036-0850
704-892-7228
Fax: 704-892-3825
Educational and classroom supplies, computers and gifts for teachers.

5355 **Gold's Artworks**
2100 N Pine St.
Lumberton, NC 28358
910-739-9605
800-356-2306
Fax: 910-739-9605
www.goldsartworks.20m.com
Papermaking supplies.

5356 **Golden Artist Colors**
188 Bell Road
New Berlin, NY 13411-9527
607-847-6154
800-959-6543
Fax: 607-847-6767
goldenart@goldenpaints.com
www.goldenpaints.com
Acrylic paints.
Barbara Schindler, President/ COO
Mark Golden, CEO

5357 **Graphix**
5800 Pennsylvania Ave.
Maple Heights, OH 44137
216-581-9050
800-447-2349
Fax: 216-581-9041
info@grafixarts.com
www.grafixarts.com
Art and crafts supplies and a source for creative plastic films.
Tanya Lutz, National Sales Manager

5358 **Grolier Multimedial Encyclopedia**
Grolier Publishing
PO Box 1716
Danbury, CT 06816
203-797-3703
800-371-3908
Fax: 203-797-3899
Encyclopedia software.

5359 **Hands-On Equations**
Borenson & Associates
PO Box 3328
Allentown, PA 18106
610-398-6908
800-993-6284
Fax: 610-398-7863
info@borenson.com
www.borenson.com
System to teach algebraic concepts to elementary and middle school students.

5360 **Harrisville Designs**
Center Village
PO Box 806
Harrisville, NH 03450
603-827-3333
800-338-9415
Fax: 603-827-3335
www.harrisville.com
Award-winning weaving products for children.

5361 **Henry S Wolkins Company**
605 Myles Standish Boulevard
Taunton, MA 02780
800-233-1844
Fax: 877-965-5467
www.wolkins.com
Art and craft materials, teaching aids, early learning products, furniture, general school equipment.

5362 **Hooked on Phonics Classroom Edition**
665 3rd Street
Suite 225
San Francisco, CA 94107
714-437-3450
800-222-3334
customerservice@hop.com
www.hop.com
Program that teaches students to learn letters and sounds to decoding words, and then reading books.

5363 **Hydrus Galleries**
PO Box 4944
San Diego, CA 92164-4944
800-493-7299
Fax: 619-283-7466
info@hydra9.com
www.hydra9.com

Curriculum-based classroom activities including papyrus outlines for students to paint.

5364 Insect Lore
PO Box 1535
Shafter, CA 93263
800-548-3284
Fax: 661-746-0334
livebug@insectlore.com
www.insectlore.com
Science materials for elementary and preschoolstudents.

5365 J&A Handy-Crafts
165 S Pennsylvania Avenue
Lindenhurst, NY 11757-5058
631-226-2400
888-252-1130
Fax: 631-226-2564
info@jacrafts.com
www.jacrafts.com
Arts, crafts and educational supplies.
Paul Siegelman, Marketing

5366 Jiffy Printers Products
35070 Maria Road
Cathedral City, CA 92234
760-321-7335
Fax: 760-770-1955
jiffyprod@aol.com
Adhesive wax sticks.
Ivan Zwelling, Owner

5367 Key-Bak
Division of West Coast Chain Manufacturing Co.
4245 Pacific Privado
Ontario, CA 91761
909-923-7800
800-685-2403
Fax: 909-923-0024
sales@keybak.com
www.keybak.com
Badges, awards and emblems for educational purposes.

5368 Keyboard Instructor
Advanced Keyboard Technology, Inc.
PO Box 2418
Paso Robles, CA 93447-2418
805-237-2055
Fax: 805-239-8973
www.keyboardinstructor.com
Mobile keyboarding lab with individualized instruction.

5369 Kids Percussion Buyer's Guide
Percussion Marketing Council
PO Box 33252
Cleveland, OH 44133
440-582-7006
Fax: 440-230-1346
DLevine360@aol.com
www.playdrums.com
This guide is divided into two sections- recreational instruments and those for beginning traditional drummers.

5370 Kids at Heart & School Art Materials
PO Box 94082
Seattle, WA 98124-9482
Classroom and art materials.

5371 Kidstamps
PO Box 18699
Cleveland Heights, OH 44118-0699
216-291-6884
Fax: 216-291-6887
kidstamps@apk.net
www.kidstamps.com
Rubber stamps, T-shirts, bookplates and mugs designed by leading children's illustrators.

5372 Knex Education Catalog
Knex Education
2990 Bergey Road
PO Box 700
Hatfield, PA 19440-0700
800-KID-KNEX
email@knex.com
www.knexeducation.com
Hands-on, award-winning curriculum supported K-12 math, science and technology sets.
Joel Glickman, Chairman
Bob Glickman, Vice Chairman

5373 Lauri
PO Box 0263
Smethport, PA 16749
800-451-0520
Fax: 207-639-3555
Lacing puppets craft kits, crepe rubber picture puzzles, phonics kits and math manipulatives for pre- K and up. Catalog offers 200 manipulatives for early childhood.

5374 Learning Materials Workshop
58 Henry Street
Burlington, VT 05401-3621
802-802-8399
800-693-7164
Fax: 802-862-0794
info@learningmaterialswork.com
www.learningmaterialswork.com
Designs and produces open-ended blocks and construction sets for early childhood classrooms. An education guide and video, as well as training workshops are offered.
Karen Hewitt, President/ Founder

5375 Learning Needs Catalog
Riverdeep Interactive Learning
PO Box 97021
Redmond, WA 98073-9721
800-362-2890
www.learningneeds.com
Hardware, software and print products designed for specialized student needs for Pre-K to grade 12.

5376 Learning Power and the Learning Power Workbook
Great Source Education Group
181 Ballardvale
Wilmington, MA 01887
800-289-4490
Student materials for 8th and 9th grade critical thinking, study skills, life management, and other student success course.
218 pages
ISBN: 0-963813-33-1

5377 Learning Well
111 Kane Street
Baltimore, MD 21224-1728
800-645-6564
Fax: 800-413-7442
learningwell@wclm.com
Drawing compass/ruler.

5378 Linray Enterprises
167 Corporation Road
Hyannis, MA 02601-2204
800-537-9752
Mats and matting for gym classes.

5379 Loew-Coenell
300 Gap Way
Erlanger, KY 41018-3160
866-227-9206
Fax: 201-836-7070
sales@loew-cornell.com
www.loew-cornell.com
Leader in art and craft brushes, painting accessories and artists'tools.

5380 Longstreth
28 Wells Road
Spring City, PA 19475-0475
610-495-7022
800-545-1329
Fax: 610-495-7023
www.longstreth.com
Awards, emblems, badges and trophies, sports timers and clocks.

5381 Love to Teach
693 Glacier Pass
Westerville, OH 43081-1295
614-899-2115
800-326-8361
Fax: 614-899-2070
www.lovetoteach.com
Gifts for teachers.
Linda Vollmer, Contact

5382 Lyra
78 Browne Street
Suite 3
Brookline, MA 02146
888-PEN-LYRA
mshoham@aol.com
Drawing supplies.

5383 MPI School & Instructional Supplies
PO Box 24155
Lansing, MI 48909-4155
517-393-0440
Fax: 517-393-8884
School and classroom supplies, arts and crafts.

5384 Magnetic Aids
201 Ann Street
P.O. Box 2502
Newburgh, NY 12550
845-863-1400
800-426-9624
Fax: 845-863-1490
info@magneticaids.com
www.magneticaids.com
Announcement and chalkboards, office supplies and equipment. Magnetic book supports.
Paul Pecka, VP Sales

5385 Mailer's Software
970 Calle Negocio
San Clemente, CA 92673-6201
949-492-7000
Fax: 949-589-5211
Charts, maps, globes and software for the classroom.

5386 Marsh Industries
Div. of Marsh Lumber Company
2301 E. High Avenue
PO Box 1000
New Philadelphia, OH 44663-5100
330-308-8667
800-426-4244
Fax: 330-308-5325
vpsales@marsh-ind.com
www.marsh-ind.com
Marker boards chalkboards, and tacknoards for new rennovative construction projects. Glass enclosed bulletin and directory boards. Map rail and accessories.
William Singhaus, Sales Manager

5387 Master Woodcraft
1312 College Street
Oxford, NC 27565

919-693-8811
800-333-2675
Fax: 919-693-1707
Announcement and classroom chalkboards, arts and craft supplies. Cork bulletin boards, dry erase melamine boards, easels, floor and table top.

J Moss, VP

5388 Material Science Technology
Energy Concepts
595 Bond Street
Lincolnshire, IL 60069
800-621-1247
www.energy-concepts-inc.com
Provides practical knowledge of the use and development of materials in todays world. Each unit combines theory with hands-on experience.

5389 Math Through the Ages: A Gentle History for Teachers and Others
Oxton Publishers, LLC
124 Main St., Suite 203
PO Box 209
Farmington, ME 04938
207-779-1923
800-539-7323
Fax: 207-779-0623
info@oxtonhouse.com
www.oxtonhouse.com
An easy-to-use tool for teachers who want some history for their math classes, this book contains 25 independent 4-to-6 page historical summaries of particular topics from elementary and secondary math, a 56-page overview and an extensive bibliography.

224 pages

William Berlinghoff, Managing Editor
Bobby Brown, Marketing Director

5390 Midwest Publishers Supply
4640 N Olcott Avenue
Harwood Heights, IL 60706
800-621-1507
Fax: 800-832-3189
info@mps-co.com
www.mps-co.com
Arts and crafts supplies.

Bonnie Cready, Sales Manager

5391 Miller Multiplex
1555 Larkin Williams Road
Fenton, MO 63026-3008
636-343-5700
800-325-3350
Fax: 636-326-1716
info@millermultiplex.com
Announcement boards, classroom displays, charts and photography, books towers, posters, frames, kiosk displays, presentation displays.

12 pages Annually

Kathy Webster, Director Marketing

5392 Monsanto Company
800 N Lindbergh Boulevard
Saint Louis, MO 63167-0001
314-694-1000
Fax: 314-694-7625
monsanto.com
Arts and crafts supplies.

Hugh Grant, Chairman/ CEO
Brett D. Begemann, President/ COO

5393 MooreCo
2885 Lorraine Avenue
Temple, TX 76501-7402
254-778-4727
800-749-2258
Fax: 254-773-0500
support@moorecoinc.com
www.moorecoinc.com
Producer of visual display products including a complete line of chalk, marker, tack, bulletin, fabric and projection boards. Also offered in their catalogue are display and trophy cases, beginner boards, reversible boards, mobile easels, desk-top and floor carrels and early childhood products.

Greg Moore, President & CEO
Jonathan Vogelsang, Director, Educational Sales

5394 Morrison School Supplies
400 Industrial Road
San Carlos, CA 94070-6285
650-592-3000
800-950-4567
Fax: 650-592-1679
www.morrisonschoolsupplies.com
School supplies, classroom equipment, furniture and toys.

5395 Names Unlimited
2300 Spikes Lane
Lansing, MI 48906-3996
Chalkboard and markerboard slates and tablets.

5396 Nasco Arts & Crafts Catalog
Nasco
901 Janesville Avenue
PO Box 901
Fort Atkinson, WI 53538-0901
920-563-2446
800-558-9595
Fax: 920-563-8296
custserv@enasco.com
www.eNASCO.com
Complete line of arts and craft materials for the art educator and individual artist.

Norman Eckley, Founder
Kris Bakke, Arts & Crafts Director

5397 Nasco Early Learning & Afterschool Essential Catalogs
Nasco
901 Janesville Avenue
PO Box 901
Fort Atkinson, WI 53538-0901
920-563-2446
800-558-9595
Fax: 920-563-8296
custserv@enasco.com
www.eNasco.com
Features low prices on classroom supplies, materials, furniture and equipment for early childhood and afterschool programs.

Norman Eckley, Founder
Scott J Beyer, Director, Sales & Marketing

5398 Nasco Math Catalog
Nasco
901 Janesville Avenue
PO Box 901
Fort Atkinson, WI 53538-0901
920-563-2446
800-558-9595
Fax: 920-563-8296
custserv@enasco.com
www.eNasco.com
Features hands-on manipulatives and real-life problem-solving projects.

Norman Eckley, Founder

5399 National Teaching Aids
401 Hickory Street
PO Box 2121
Fort Collins, CO 80522
970-484-7445
800-289-9299
Fax: 970-484-1198
custserv@amep.com
www.hubbardscientific.com
Learning math, alphabet, and geography skills is easy with our Clever Catch Balls. These colorful 24-inch inflatable vinyl balls provide an excellent way for children to practice math, alphabet and geography skills. Excellent learning tool in organized classroom activities, on the playground, or at home.

Michael Warring, President
Candace Coffman, National Sales Manger

5400 New Hermes
2200 Northmont Parkway
Duluth, GA 30096
770-623-0331
800-843-7637
Fax: 770-814-7203
sales@us.gravotech.com
www.newhermes.com
Announcement boards, trophies, badges, emblems.

Gerard Guyard, Chairman

5401 Newbridge Discovery Station
33 Boston Post Road West
Suite 440
Marlborough, MA 1752
800-867-0307
Fax: 800-456-2419
www.newbridgeonline.com
Monthly quick tips and activities for teachers.

5402 Newbridge Jumbo Seasonal Patterns
PO Box 5267
Clifton, NJ 07015
Art projects, games, bulletin boards, flannel boards, story starters, learning center displays, costumes, masks and more for grades Pre K-3.

5403 NewsCurrents
Knowledge Unlimited
2320 Pleasant View Road
PO Box 52
Madison, WI 53701
608-836-6660
800-356-2303
Fax: 800-618-1570
csis@newscurrents.com
www.newscurrents.com
Current issues discussion programs for grades 3 and up.

5404 Partners in Learning Programs
1065 Bay Boulevard
Suite H
Chula Vista, CA 91911-1626
619-407-4744
Fax: 619-407-4755
Manufacturers and produces books, manuals, materials, supplies and gifts, such as banners for classroom purposes.

5405 Pearson Education Technologies
827 W Grove Avenue
Mesa, AZ 85210
520-615-7600
800-222-4543
Fax: 520-615-7601
www.pearsonedtech.com
SuccessMaker is a multimedia K-Adult learning system which includes math, reading, language arts and science courseware.

5406 Pentel of America
2715 Columbia Street
Torrance, CA 90503
310-320-3831
800-421-1419
Fax: 310-533-0697
www.pentel.com
Office supplies and equipment.

5407 **Pin Man**
Together Inc.
802 E 6th Street
PO Box 52528
Tulsa, OK 74105-3264
918-587-2405
800-282-0085
Fax: 918-382-0906
www.thepinmanok.com
Manufacturer of custom designed lapel pins, totes for Chapter 1, reading, scholastic achievement, honor roll, parent involvement, staff awards and incentives with over 25,000 items available for imprint.
Bern Gentry, CEO

5408 **PlayConcepts**
2275 Huntington Drive
#305
San Marino, CA 91108-2640
800-261-2584
Fax: 626-795-1177
Creative, 3-D scenery that stimulates dramatic play. The scenes complement integrated curriculum. They are age and developmentally appropriate, non-biased, and effective for groups or individuals.

5409 **Polyform Products Company**
1901 Estes Avenue
Elk Grove Village, IL 60007
847-427-0020
Fax: 847-427-0020
polyform@sculpey.com
www.sculpey.com
Manufacturer of sculpey modeling clay.

5410 **Presidential Classroom**
2201 Old Ivy Road
P.O. Box 400406
Charlottesville, VA 22904
434-924-7236
800-441-6533
Fax: 434-982-2739
eriedel@presidentialclassroom.org
www.presidentialclassroom.org
Civic education programs in Washington, DC for high school juniors and seniors. Each one week program provides students with an inside view of the federal government in action and their role as responsible citizens and future leaders.
Jan-March, June+July
400 attendees
Jack Buechner, President/CEO
William Antholis, Director/ CEO

5411 **Professor Weissman's Software**
Professor Weissman's Software
246 Crafton Avenue
Staten Island, NY 10314-4227
347-528-7837
Fax: 718-698-5219
mathprof@math911.com
www.math911.com
Algebra comic books, learn by example algebra flash cards, step-by-step software tutorials for algebra, trigonometry, precalculus, statistics, network versions for all software.
Martin Weissman, Owner
Keith Morse, VP

5412 **Pumpkin Masters**
PO Box 61456
Denver, CO 80206-8456
303-860-8006
Fax: 303-860-9826
Classroom pumpkin carving kits featuring whole language curriculum with safer and easier carving tools and patterns.

5413 **Puppets on the Pier**
Pier 39
Box H4
San Francisco, CA 94133
415-379-9544
800-443-4463
Fax: 415-379-9544
puppetshop@gmail.com
www.puppetdream.com
Puppets, arts, crafts and other creative educational products for children.
Arthur Partner

5414 **Qwik-File Storage Systems**
1000 Allview Drive
Crozet, VA 22932-3144
804-823-4351
Schedule boards and classroom supplies.

5415 **RC Musson Rubber Company**
1320 East Archwood Avenue
P.O. Box 7038
Akron, OH 44306-2825
330-773-7651
800-321-3281
Fax: 330-773-3254
info@mussonrubber.com
www.mussonrubber.com
Rubber floorcoverings, mats and athletic matting.
Mark Reese, Customer Service Manager
Robert Segers, VP

5416 **RCA Rubber Company**
1833 East Market St.
P.O. Box 9240
Akron, OH 44305-0240
330-784-1291
800-321-2340
Fax: 330-794-6446
commercialsales@rcarubber.com
www.rcarubber.com
Floorcoverings, athletic mats and more for the physical education class.

5417 **Reading is Fundamental**
600 Maryland Avenue SW
Suite 600
Washington, DC 20024-2520
202-673-1641
Fax: 202-673-1633
Distributor of posters, bookmarks, and parent guide brochures.

5418 **Reconnecting Youth**
National Educational Service
304 W Kirkwood Avenue
Suite 2
Bloomington, IN 47404-5132
812-336-7700
800-733-6786
Fax: 812-336-7790
nes@nesonline.com
www.nesonline.com
Curriculum to help discouraged learners achieve in school, manage their anger, and decrease drug use, depression, and suicide risk. The program was piloted for five years with over 600 urban Northwestern public high school students with funding from the National Institute on Drug Abuse and the National Institute of Mental Health, and has since been successful in many educational settings.
3 Ring Binder Circul
ISBN: 1-879639-42-4
Jane St. John, Sales Marketing Director

5419 **Red Ribbon Resources**
135 Dupont Street
PO Box 760
Plainview, NY 11803
800-646-7999
Fax: 800-262-1886
www.redribbonresources.com
Over 250 low cost giveaways to promote your safe and drug-free school and community.

5420 **Renaissance Graphic Arts**
69 Steamwhistle Drive
Ivyland, PA 18974
215-357-5705
888-833-3398
Fax: 215-357-5258
pat@printmaking-materials.com
www.printmaking-materials.com
Tools, papers, plates, inks and assorted products necessary for printmaking.

5421 **Rock Paint Distributing Corporation**
365 Sunnyside Drive
PO Box 482
Milton, WI 53563
608-868-6873
800-236-6873
Fax: 800-715-7625
handyart@handyart.com
www.handyart.com
Tempera paint, India ink, acrylic paint, block inc, washable paint, fabric paint.
Chuck Jackson, President

5422 **S&S Worldwide**
S&S Arts & Crafts
75 Mill Street
PO Box 513
Colchester, CT 06415-1263
860-537-3451
800-243-9232
Fax: 800-566-6678
cservice@ssww.com
www.ssww.com
Arts and crafts, classroom games and group paks.

5423 **Safe & Drug Free Catalog**
Performance Resource Press
1270 Rankin Drive
Suite F
Troy, MI 48083-2843
800-453-7733
Fax: 800-499-5718
www.pronline.net
Books, videos, CD-Roms, phamlets and posters toassist students with social skills, counseling, drug and violence prevention.

5424 **Sakura of America**
30780 San Clemente Street
Hayward, CA 94544-7131
510-475-8880
800-776-6257
Fax: 510-475-0973
express@sakuraofamerica.com
www.gellyroll.com
Producer of writing and drawing materials such as Gelly Roll Pens, Cray pas Oil pastels, Fantasia Watercolors, Pigma Micron Pens, Pentouch, Koi Watercolors, Pigma Pro Brush, Zentangle, Identipen, Microperm, Pigma Calligrapher and Mechanical Pencils.
Robert Kahre, National Accounts Manager
Julia Reed, Marketing Manager

5425 **Sanford Corporation**
A Lifetime of Color
2711 Washington Boulevard
Bellwood, IL 60104-1970
708-547-6650
800-323-0749
Fax: 708-547-6719
consumer.service@sanfordcorp.com
www.sanfordcorp.com
Writing instruments, art supplies.
Angela Nigl, Author
Sharon Meyers, PR Manager

5426 Sax Visual Art Resources
Sax Arts and Crafts
2725 S Moorland Road
bept. SA
New Berlin, WI 53151
800-558-6696
Fax: 800-328-4729
catalog@saxfcs.com
www.saxfcs.com
Variety of resources for slides, books, videos, fine art posters and CD-Roms.

5427 School Mate
PO Box 2225
Jackson, TN 38302
731-935-2000
Fax: 800-668-7610
school@schoolmateinc.com
Pre-school and elementary art products.

5428 SchoolMatters
Current
The Current Building
Colorado Springs, CO 80941-0001
800-525-7170
Fax: 800-993-3232
Offers a variety of creative classroom ideas including stickers, mugs, posters, signs and more for everyday and holidays and everyday of the year.

5429 Scott Sign Systems
7525 Pennsylvania Avenue
Suite 101
Sarasota, FL 34243
941-355-5171
800-237-9447
Fax: 941-351-1787
info@scottsigns.com
www.scottsigns.com
Educational supplies including announcement, letters, signs, graphics and chalkboards.
Kathy Hannon, Regional Sales Manager
Lisa Pyrcz, Account Mgr, Southeast/West

5430 Scratch-Art Company
PO Box 303
Avon, MA 02322
508-583-8085
800-377-9003
Fax: 508-583-8091
info@scratchart.com
www.scratchart.com
Offers materials for drawing, sketching and rubbings.

5431 Sea Bay Game Company
77 Cliffwood Avenue, Suite 1-D
Cliffwood, NJ 07721
732-583-7902
800-568-0188
Fax: 732-583-7284
www.seabaygame.com
Manufacturer and distributor of products, games and creative play to nursery schools and preschools.

5432 Seton Identification Products
20 Thompson Road
PO Box 819
Branford, CT 06405-819
855-544-7992
800-243-6624
Fax: 800-345-7819
help@seton.com
www.seton.com
Manufacturer of all types of identification products including signs, tags, labels, traffic control, OSHA, ADA and much more.

5433 Shapes, Etc.
532 North Plymouth Avenue
Rochester, NY 14608
585-335-6619
800-888-6580
Fax: 585-335-6070
info@shapesetc.com
www.shapesetc.com
Notepads and craft materials for creative writing projects. Coordinates with literature themes. Perfect for storystarters, bulletin boards, awards and motivators.

5434 Sign Product Catalog
Scott Sign Systems, Inc.
7525 Pennsylvania Avenue
Suite 101
Sarasota, FL 34243
941-355-5171
800-237-9447
Fax: 941-351-1787
info@scottsigns.com
www.scottsigns.com
Educational supplies including announcement, letters, signs, graphics and chalkboards.
Kathy Hannon, Regional Sales Manager
Lisa Pyrcz, Account Mgr, Southeast/West

5435 Small Fry Originals
2700 S Westmoreland Road
Dallas, TX 75233-1312
214-330-8671
800-248-9443
Children's original artwork preserved in plastic plates and mugs.

5436 Southwest Plastic Binding Corporation
109 Millwell Court
Maryland Heights, MO 63043-2509
314-739-4400
800-325-3628
Fax: 800-942-2010
www.swbindinglaminating.com
Overhead transparencies, maps, charts and classroom supplies.

5437 Spectrum Corporation
10048 Easthaven Boulevard
Houston, TX 77075-3298
713-944-6200
800-392-5050
Fax: 713-944-1290
sherrig@specorp.com
www.spectrumstuff.com
Announcement boards, scoreboards and sports equipment, sports timers and clocks.

5438 Speedball Art Products Company
2301 Speedball Road
PO Box 5157
Statesville, NC 28677
704-838-1475
800-898-7224
Fax: 704-838-1472
tonyahill@speedballart.com
www.speedballart.com
Art products for stamping, calligraphy, printmaking, drawing and painting.
Walt Glazer, CEO
Tonya Hill, Director of Sales

5439 Sponge Stamp Magic
525 S Anaheim Hills Road
Apartment C314
Anaheim, CA 92807-4726
Rubber stamps and games for classroom use.

5440 Staedtler
5725 McLaughlin Road
Mississauga, On L5R 3
905-501-9008
800-776-5544
Fax: 905-501-9117
info@staedtler.ca
www.staedtler-usa.com
Arts and crafts supplies, office supplies and equipment.
Dick Hoye, National Sales Manager

5441 Sylvan Learning Systems
1000 Lancaster Street
Baltimore, MD 21202
410-843-6828
888-779-5826
Fax: 410-783-3832
www.sylvanlearning.com
Provides public school academic programs that are traditional sylvan programs modified to fit the needs of individual school districts and performance guarantees.
Jody Madron, Contact

5442 Tandy Leather Company
PO Box 791
Fort Worth, TX 76101-0791
817-451-1480
Fax: 817-451-5254
Arts and crafts supplies, computer peripherals and systems.

5443 Teacher Appreciation
Guidance Channel
135 Dupont Street
PO Box 760
Plainview, NY 44803-0706
800-999-6884
Fax: 800-262-1886
Products for celebrating teacher appreciation week.

5444 Teachers Store
PO Box 24155
Lansing, MI 48909-4155
517-393-0440
Fax: 517-393-8884
School and classroom supplies, arts and crafts.

5445 Texas Instruments
12500 TI Boulevard
P.O. Box 660199
Dallas, TX 75243-4136
972-995-2011
800-336-5236
Fax: 972-995-4360
www.ti.com
Manufacturer of calculators.
Rich Templeton, Chairman/ President
Brian Crutcher, EVP, Business Operations

5446 Triarco Arts & Crafts
9900 13th Ave. N.
Suite 1015
Plymouth, MN 55441-5035
763-559-5590
800-328-3360
Fax: 736-559-2215
info@triarcoarts.com
www.etriarco.com
Art supplies.

5447 Vanguard Crafts
1081 E 48th Street
Brooklyn, NY 11234
718-377-5188
800-662-7238
Fax: 888-692-0056
Arts and crafts supplier.

5448 Wagner Zip-Change
3100 W Hirsch Avenue
Melrose Park, IL 60160-1741
708-681-4100
800-323-0744
Fax: 800-243-4924
sales@wagnerzip.com
www.wagnerzip.com

Non-lighted changeable letter message activity signs, changeable letters in all sizes and colors.

CJ Krasula, Marketing VP
Jim Leone, Sales Manager

5449 Walker Display
6520 Grand Avenue
P.O. Box 16955
Duluth, MN 55807-2242
218-624-8990
800-234-7614
Fax: 888-695-4647
www.walkerdisplay.com
Arts, crafts, classroom supplies and displays.

5450 Wellness Reproductions
Guidance Channel
135 Dupont Street
PO Box 760
Plainview, NY 44803-0706
800-999-6884
Fax: 800-262-1886
Mental and life skills educational materials.

5451 What So Proudly We Hail
1730 M Street NW
Suite 905
Washington, DC 20036
202-499-5267
cheryl@whatsoproudlywehail.org
www.whatsoproudlywehail.org
What So Proudly We Hail is an e-curriculum of literary resources to aid in the classroom education of American History, civics, social studies, and language arts. Resources are American based, with speeches, stories, songs, and anthology.

5452 Wikki Stix One-of-a-Kind Creatables
Omnicor
11034 N. 23rd Drive
#103
Phoenix, AZ 85029-4735
602-870-9937
800-869-4554
Fax: 602-870-9877
info@wikkistix.com
www.wikkistix.com
Unique, one-of-a-kind twistable, stickable, creatable, hands-on teaching tools. Ideal for Pre-K through 8 for science, language arts, math, arts and crafts, positive behavior rewards, rainy day recess, classroom display, diagrams and 3-D work. Self-stick; no glue needed.

Kem Clark, President
Gloria Porter, General Manager

5453 Wilson Language Training
47 Old Webster Road
Oxford, MA 1540
508-368-2399
800-899-8454
Fax: 508-368-2300
www.wilsonlanguage.com
Multisensory language program.

5454 Wilton Art Appreciation Programs
Reading & O'Reilley
PO Box 646
Botsford, CT 06404
203-270-6336
800-458-4274
Fax: 203-270-5569
ror@wiltonart.com
www.wiltonart.com
Materials for art appreciation including CD-ROMS, videos, fine art prints, slides, workbooks, teacher' guides, lessons, puzzles and games.

Diana O'Neill, President

5455 Young Explorers
P.O. Box 3338
Chelmsford, MO 1824-938
800-239-7577
Fax: 888-876-8847
www.youngexplorers.com
Educational material for children.

Electronic Equipment

5456 AIMS Multimedia
9710 De Soto Avenue
Chatsworth, CA 91311-4409
818-773-4300
800-367-2467
Fax: 818-341-6700
info@aimsmultimedia.com
www.aimsmultimedia.com
Film, video, laserdisc producer and distributor, offering a free catalog available materials. Also provides internet video streaming.

David Sherman, President
Biff Sherman, President

5457 Advance Products Company
1101 E Central Avenue
Wichita, KS 67214-3922
316-263-4231
Fax: 316-263-4245
Manufacturer of steel mobile projection and television tables, video cabinets, easels, computer furniture, wall and ceiling TV mounts, and study tables and carrels.

Paul Keck

5458 All American Scoreboards
Everbrite
401 South Main Street
Pardeeville, WI 53954
608-429-2121
800-356-8146
Fax: 877-505-9405
scoreboardsales@everbrite.com
www.allamericanscoreboards.com
Scoreboards.

Doug Winkelmann, Product Manager

5459 American Time & Signal Company
140 3rd Avenue S
Dassel, MN 55325
800-328-8996
Fax: 800-789-1882
theclockexperts@atsclock.com
www.atsclock.com
Sports timers and clocks.

Jeff Baumgartner, CEO/ Owner

5460 Arts & Entertainment Network
235 E 45th Street
Floor 9
New York, NY 10017-3354
212-210-1400
Fax: 212-210-9755
www.aenetworks.com
Cable network offering free educational programming to schools.

5461 Barr Media/Films
12801 Schabarum Avenue
Irwindale, CA 91706-6808
626-338-7878
K-12 film, video and interactive Level I and III laserdisc programs.

5462 C-SPAN Classroom
4000 N Capitol Street NW
Washington, DC 20001
202-737-3220
800-523-7586
Fax: 202-737-6226
www.c-span.org
C-SPAN School Bus travels through more than 80 communities during each school year. This bus is a mobile television production studio and learning center designed to give hands-on experience with C-SPAN's programming.

John Evans, CEO/ Chairman
Thomas O. Might, President/ CEO

5463 CASIO
570 Mount Pleasant Avenue
Dover, NJ 07801-1631
973-361-5400
Fax: 570-868-6898
www.casio.com
Cameras, overhead projectors and electronics.

5464 CASPR
100 Park Center Plaza
Suite 550
San Jose, CA 95113-2204
800-852-2777
www.caspr.com
Leader in the field of library automation for schools. Integrated library automation-cross platforms: Macintosh, Windows, Apple IIe/IIGS. Multimedia source.

Norman Kline, President

5465 Canon USA
1 Canon Plaza
Melville, NY 11747
631-330-5000
Fax: 516-328-5069
pr@cusa.canon.com
www.usa.canon.com/cusa/home
School equipment and supplies including a full line of electronics, cameras, calculators and other technology.

5466 Caulastics
5955 Mission Street
Daly City, CA 94014-1397
415-585-9600
Overhead projectors, transparencies and electronics.

5467 Cheshire Corporation
Cheshire Corporation
PO Box 61109
Denver, CO 80206-8109
303-333-3003
Fax: 303-333-4037
karen-hemmes@mindspring.com
Cheshire corporation is a publicist for book, video, CD-ROM and internet publishers in the school and library market.

Karen Hemmes, Publicist
Mary Kay Opicka, Publicist

5468 Chief Manufacturing
6436 City West Parkway
Eden Prairie, MN 55344
952-894-6280
800-582-6480
Fax: 877-894-6918
orders@chiefmfg.com
www.chiefmfg.com
Manufacturer of Communications Support Systems for audio visual and video equipment. Chief's product includes a full-line of mounts, electric lifts, carts, and accessories for LCD/DLP projectors, plasma displays and TV/monitors.

Liz Sorensen, Marketing Assistant
Sharon McCubbin, Marketing Manager

5469 Chisholm
7019 Realm Drive
San Jose, CA 95119-1321
408-329-4305
800-888-4210

info@chisholm.com
www.chisholm.com
Computer peripherals, overhead projectors and overhead transparencies.

5470 Daktronics
201 Daktronics Dr.
Brookings, SD 57006-5128
605-697-4300
800-325-8766
Fax: 605-697-4300
sales@daktronics.com
www.daktronics.com
Scoreboards, electronic message displays statistics software.

Gary Gramm, HSPR Market Manager

5471 Depco- Millennium 3000
3305 Airport Drive
PO Box 178
Pittsburg, KS 66762
316-231-0019
800-767-1062
Fax: 316-231-0024
sales@depcoinc.com
www.depcoinc.com
Program tracks and schedules for you, the test taker delivers tests electronically, as well as, automatic final exams. There are workstation security features to help keep students focused on their activities.

5472 Discovery Networks
7700 Wisconsin Avenue
Bethesda, MD 20814-3578
301-986-0444
www.discovery.com
Manages and operates The Discovery Channel, offering the finest in nonfiction documentary programming, as well as The Learning Channel, representing a world of ideas to learners of all ages.

5473 Echolab
175 Bedford Street
Burlington, MA 01803-2794
781-273-1512
Fax: 978-250-3335
Cameras, equipment, projectors and electronics.

5474 Eiki International
Audio Visual/Video Products
26794 Vista Terrace Drive
Lake Forest, CA 92630
949-457-0200
Fax: 949-457-7878
Video projectors, overhead projectors and transparencies.

5475 Elmo Manufacturing Corporation
1478 Old Country Road
Plainview, NY 11803-5034
516-501-1400
800-947-3566
Fax: 516-501-0429
www.elmousa.com
Overhead projectors and transparencies.

5476 Fair-Play Scoreboards
1700 Delaware Avenue
Des Moines, IA 50317-2999
800-247-0265
Fax: 515-265-3364
sales@fair-play.com
www.fair-play.com
Scoreboards and sports equipment.

5477 Festo Corporation
395 Moreland Road
PO Box 18023
Hauppauge, NY 11788
631-435-0800
800-993-3786
Fax: 631-435-3847
product.support@us.festo.com
www.festo-usa.com

5478 General Audio-Visual
333 West Merrick Road
Valley Stream, NY 11580-5219
516-825-8500
Fax: 516-568-2057
www.gavi.com
Offers a full line of audio-visual equipment and supplies, cameras, projectors and various other electronics for the classroom.

5479 Hamilton Electronics
2003 W Fulton Street
Chicago, IL 60612-2365
312-421-5442
Fax: 312-421-0818
www.hamiltonbuhl.com
Electronics, equipment and supplies.

5480 JR Holcomb Company
3205 Harvard Avenue
Cleveland, OH 44101
216-341-3000
800-362-9907
Fax: 216-341-5151
A full line of electronics including calculators, overhead projectors and overhead transparencies.

5481 JVC Professional Products Company
41 Slater Drive
Elmwood Park, NJ 07407-1311
201-794-3900
Electronics line including cameras, projectors, transparencies and other technology for the classroom.

5482 Labelon Corporation
10 Chapin Street
Canandaigua, NY 14424-1589
585-394-6220
800-428-5566
Fax: 585-394-3154
www.labelon.com
Electronics, supplies and equipment for schools.

5483 Learning Channel
7700 Wisconsin Avenue
Bethesda, MD 20814
800-346-0032
Offers educational programming for schools.

5484 Learning Station/Hug-a-Chug Records
3950 Bristol Court
Melbourne, FL 32904-8712
321-728-8773
800-789-9990
Fax: 321-722-9121
thelearningstation@cfl.rr.com
www.learningstationmusic.com
Early childhood products including OMH, cassettes, CD's and videos. Also, the Learning Station performs children and family concerts and are internationally acclaimed for their concert/keynote presentations for early childhood conferences and other educational organizations.

Don Monopoli, President
Laurie Monopoli, VP

5485 Learning Well
2200 Marcus Avenue
#3759
New Hyde Park, NY 11042-1042
800-645-6564
Fax: 800-638-6499
Instructional material including computer and board games, videos, cassettes, audio tapes, theme units, manipulatives for grades PreK-8.

Mona Russo, President

5486 Leightronix
1125 N Cedar Rd
Mason, MI 48854
517-694-5589
800-243-5589
Fax: 517-694-1600
sales@leightronix.com
www.leightronix.com
Educational cable programming for schools and institutions.

5487 MCM Electronics
650 Congress Park Drive
Centerville, OH 45459
888-235-4692
800-543-4330
Fax: 800-765-6960
www.mcmelectronics.com
Offers a full line of electronics products and components for use in the classroom or at home. Over 40,000 parts.

5488 Magna Plan Corporation
71 Meadowbank Drive
Ottawa, On K2G0P
613-563-8727
800-361-1192
Fax: 518-298-2368
info@visualplanning.com
www.visualplanning.com
Overhead projectors.

Joseph P Josephson, Managing Director
Joel Boloten, Manager Consultation Service

5489 Mitsubishi Professional Electronics
200 Cottontail Lane
Somerset, NJ 08873-1231
732-560-4500
Fax: 732-560-4535
www.mitsubishielectric.com
Video projectors and electronics.

5490 Multi-Video
PO Box 35444
Charlotte, NC 28235-5444
704-563-4279
800-289-0111
Fax: 704-568-0219
Cameras, projectors and equipment.

5491 Naden Scoreboards
505 Fair Avenue
PO Box 636
Webster City, IA 50595-0636
515-832-4290
800-467-4290
Fax: 515-832-4293
naden@ncn.net
www.naden.com
Electronic scoreboards for sports.

Russ Naden, President

5492 Navitar
200 Commerce Drive
Rochester, NY 14623
585-359-4000
800-828-6778
Fax: 585-359-4999
info@navitar.com
www.navitar.com
Overhead projectors and transparencies.

Julian Goldstein, Co-President
Jeremy Goldstein, Co-President

5493 Neumade Products Corporation
30 Pecks Lane
Newtown, CT 06470-2361
203-270-1100
Fax: 203-270-7778

neumadeGJ@aol.com
www.neumade.com
Overhead projectors, overhead transparencies, video projectors and electronics.

Gregory Jones, VP Sales

5494 Nevco Scoreboard Company
301 East Harris Avenue
Greenville, IL 62246-2151
618-664-0360
800-851-4040
Fax: 618-664-0398
sales@nevco.com
www.nevco.com
Nevco is a premier manufacturer and distributor of scoreboards, message centers and video displays.

G.D. Moore, President
Phil Robertson, Sales Manager

5495 Panasonic Communications & System Company
1 Panasonic Way
Secaucus, NJ 07094-2917
201-392-4818
800-524-1064
Fax: 201-392-4044
Cameras, projectors, equipment, players, CD-ROM equipment and school supplies.

5496 Quickset International
3650 Woodhead Drive
Northbrook, IL 60062-1895
800-247-6563
Fax: 847-498-1258
www.moogs3.com
Telecommunication equipment, cameras, projectors and electronics.

5497 RMF Products
1275 Paramount Pkwy.
PO Box 520
Batavia, IL 60510-0520
630-879-0020
Fax: 630-879-6749
info@rmfproducts.com
www.rmfproducts.com
Complete line of slide-related products including two and three-projector dissolve controls, programmers, multi-track tape recorders, audio-visual cables, remote controls and slide mounts.

Richard Frieders, President

5498 RTI-Research Technology International
4700 Chase
Lincolnwood, IL 60712-1689
847-677-3000
800-323-7520
Fax: 800-784-6733
sales@rtico.com
www.rti-us.com
TapeChek Videotape Cleaner/Inspector/Rewinders make videotapes last longer and perform better. Find damage before tape is circulated. Also available is videotape/laser disc storage, shipping and care products.

Ray Short, President/ CEO
Tom Boyle, Senior VP, RTI Sales

5499 Recreation Equipment Unlimited
PO Box 4700
Pittsburgh, PA 15206-0700
412-731-3000
Fax: 412-731-3052
Scoreboards and sports/recreation equipment.

5500 Reliance Plastics & Packaging
25 Prospect Street
Newark, NJ 07105-3300
973-473-7200
Fax: 973-589-6440
Vinyl albums for audio or video cassettes, video discs, slides, floppy disks, CDs Protect, store and circulate valuable media property.

5501 Resolution Technology
26000 Avenida Aeropuerto Spc 22
San Juan Capistrano, CA 92675-4736
949-661-6162
Fax: 949-661-0114
Video systems and videomicroscopy equipment.

5502 RobotiKits Direct
17141 Kingsview Avenue
Suite B
Carson, CA 90746-1207
310-515-6800
877-515-6652
Fax: 310-515-0927
info@owirobot.com
www.owirobot.com
New science and robotic kits for the millenium.

Craig Morioka, President
Armer Amante, General Manger

5503 S'Portable Scoreboards
3058 Alta Vista Drive
Fallbrook, CA 92028-8738
800-323-7745
Fax: 270-759-0066
Portable scoreboards, manual and electronic, sports timers and clocks.

5504 SONY Broadcast Systems Product Division
1 Sony Drive
Park Ridge, NJ 07656
800-472-SONY
Interactive videodisc players for multimedia applications, VTRs, monitors, projection systems, video cameras, editing systems, printers and scanners, video presentation stands, audio cassette duplicators and video library systems.

5505 Scott Resources/ Hubbard Scientific
National Training Aids
401 Hickory Street
PO Box 2121
Fort Collins, CO 80522-2121
970-484-7445
800-289-9299
Fax: 970-484-1198
custserv@amep.com
www.hubbardscientific.com
Microslide system is a comprehensive, classroom-ready to help students learn. The microslide system combines superb photo-materials with detaled curriculum material and reproducible student activity sheets at an affrdable price.

Michael Warring, President
Candace Coffman, National Sales Manager

5506 Shure Brothers
222 Hartrey Avenue
Evanston, IL 60202-3696
847-866-2200
Fax: 847-866-2551
Electronics, hardware and classroom supplies.

5507 Swift Instruments
1190 N 4th Street
San Jose, CA 95112
408-293-2380
800-523-4544
Fax: 408-292-7967
www.swiftmicroscope.com
Capture live or still microscopic images through your compound or stereo microscope and background sound images through your VCR or computer.

5508 Tech World
Lab-Volt
PO Box 686
Farmingdale, NJ 07727
732-938-2000
800-522-8658
Fax: 732-774-8573
us@labvolt.com
www.labvolt.com
Tech World provides superior hands-on instruction using state-of-the-art technology and equipment. Lab-Volt also offers a full line of attractive, durable, and flexible modular classroom furniture.

5509 Technical Education Systems
56 East End Drive
Gilberts, IL 60136
847-428-3085
800-451-2169
Fax: 847-428-3286
www.tii-tech.com
Hands-on application-oriented training systems integrating today's real world technologies in a flexible and easy-to-understand curriculum format.

5510 Telex Communications
12000 Portland Avenue S
Burnsville, MN 55337
952-884-4051
800-828-6107
Fax: 952-884-0043
www.telex.com
Telex manufactures a variety of products for the educational market, including multimedia headphones, headsets and microphones; LCD computer and multimedia projection panels, group listening centers, video projectors, slide projectors, portable sound systems, wired and wireless intercoms, and wired and wireless microphones.

Dawn Wiome, Marketing Coordinator

5511 The Transcription Studio
The Transcription Studio, LLC
2267 Honolulu Ave
Suite 2
Montrose, CA 91020
818-248-3400
Fax: 818-846-8933
Operations@TranscriptionStudio.com
www.transcriptionstudio.com
We transcribe and provide closed-captioning services to the education and academic fields.

Jeff Zedlar, CEO
Deborah Hargreaves, Director of Operations

5512 Three M Visual Systems
3M Austin Center
6801 River Place Boulevard
Austin, TX 78726-4530
512-984-1800
800-328-1371
Fax: 512-984-6529
www.solutions.3m.com
Overhead projectors, audiovisual carts and tables, and overhead transparencies.

5513 Tom Snyder Productions
100 Talcott Avenue
Watertown, MA 02472-5703
617-926-6000
800-342-0236
Fax: 800-304-1254
dealer@tomsnyder.com
www.tomsnyder.com

Educational videotapes, videodiscs and computer programs.
Bridget Dalton, Ed.D., Author
Peggy Healy Stearns, Ph.D., Author

5514 Varitronics Systems
PO Box 234
Minneapolis, MN 55440
800-637-5461
Fax: 800-543-8966
Computer electronics, hardware, software and systems.

5515 Wholesale Educational Supplies
PO Box 120123
East Haven, CT 06512-0123
800-243-2518
Fax: 800-452-5956
wes4@snet.net
www.discountav.com
Over 5,000 audio visual and video equipment and supplies offered at deep discount prices. Free 148 page catalog.
J Fields, President

Furniture & Equipment

5516 ASRS of America
304 Park Avenue South
11th Floor
New York, NY 10010
212-760-1607
Fax: 212-760-1614
info@elecompack.com
www.elecompack.com
Offers Elecompack, high density compact shelving which offers double storage capacity, automatic passive safety systems and custom front panels.
Walter M Kaufman

5517 Adden Furniture
710 Chelmsford Street
Lowell, MA 01851
978-454-7848
800-625-3876
Fax: 978-453-1449
fsafran@addenfurniture.com
www.addenfurniture.com
Manufacturer of dormitory furniture, bookcases and shelving products.
Linda Kane, President
Patrick Furnari, CEO

5518 Air Technologies Corporation
25641 White Sands Street
Dana Point, CA 92629
949-661-5060
800-759-5060
Fax: 949-661-2454
ken@airtech.net
www.airtech.net
Develop and manufacture professional ergonomic computer products.

5519 Alma Industries
1300 Prospect Street
High Point, NC 27260-8329
336-578-5700
Fax: 336-578-0105
Bookcases and shelving for educational purposes.

5520 Angeles Group
9 Capper Drive
Dailey Industrial Park
Pacific, MO 63069
636-257-0533
800-346-6313
Fax: 636-257-5473
www.angeles-group.com
Housekeeping furniture and children play kitchen's made of durable and sturdy molded polyethylene. Baseline Furniture: tables, chairs, lockers, cubbies, bookcases, bookracks, silver rider trikes, spaceline cots, basic trikes, and bye bye buggies.
Tim Lynch, Director of Sales
David Curry, General Manager

5521 Anthro Corporation Technology Furniture
10450 SW Manhasset Dr.
Tualatin, OR 97062
503-691-2556
800-325-3841
Fax: 800-325-0045
www.anthro.com
Durable computer workstations and accessories; educational discounts; and dozens of shapes and sizes.
Shoaib Tureen, Co-Founder, President
Cathy Filgas, Co-Founder, VP-Sales

5522 Architectural Precast
10210 Winstead Lane
Cincinnati, OH 45246
513-772-4670
800-542-1738
Fax: 513-772-4672
est@archprecast.com
www.archprecast.com
Furniture, tables, playground equipment, desks.

5523 Blanton & Moore Company
PO Box 70
Barium Springs, NC 28010-0070
704-528-4506
Fax: 704-528-6519
www.blantonandmoore.com
Standard and custom library furniture crafted from fine hardwoods.
Billy Galliher, Manager Sales Administration

5524 Borroughs Corporation
3002 N Burdick Street
Kalamazoo, MI 49004-3483
616-342-0161
800-748-0227
Fax: 269-342-4161
www.borroughs.com
Bookcases and shelving products for educational purposes.
Zac Sweetland, VP, Sales
Tom Gambon, VP Finance & Administration

5525 Brady Office Machine Security
11056 S Bell Avenue
Chicago, IL 60643-3935
773-779-8349
800-326-8349
Fax: 773-779-9712
b.brady1060@aol.com
The Brady Office Machine Security physically protects all office machines, computer components, faxes, printers, VCRs, have wall and ceiling mounts for TVs.
Bernadette Brady, President
Don Brady, VP

5526 Bretford Manufacturing
9715 Soreng Avenue
Schiller Park, IL 60176-2186
540-678-2545
www.bretford.com
Manufacturer of a full line of AV and computer projection screens, television mounts, wood office furniture and a full line of combination wood shelving and steel library shelving.

5527 Brixey
13030 Inglewood Avenue
Suite 200
Hawthorne, CA 90250
310-263-7025
877-694-0752
Fax: 310-263-7250
brixey@brixey.com
www.brixey.com
Furniture for the classroom.

5528 Brodart Company, Automation Division
500 Arch Street
Williamsport, PA 17701
570-326-2461
800-233-8467
Fax: 570-326-1479
support@brodart.com
www.brodart.com
Brodart's Automation Division has been providing library systems, software, and services for over 25 years. Products include: library management systems, media management systems, Internet solutions, cataloged web sites, cataloging resource tools, union catalog solutions, public access catalogs, and bibliographic services.
Kasey Dibble, Marketing Coordinator
Sally Wilmoth, Director Marketing/Sales

5529 Buckstaff Company
Buckstaff Company
PO Box 2851
Oshkosh, WI 54903
920-235-5890
800-755-5890
Fax: 920-235-2018
sales@buckstaff.com
www.buckstaff.com
The premier manufacturer of library furniture in the United States. Quality and durability has been the Buckstaff trademark for 150 years.
Tom Mugerauer, Sales Manager, National

5530 Carpets for Kids Etc...
115 SE 9th Avenue
Portland, OR 97214-1301
503-232-1203
Fax: 503-232-1394
customerservice@carpetsforkids.com
www.carpetsforkids.com
Carpets, flooring and floorcoverings for educational purposes.

5531 Children's Factory
505 N Kirkwood Road
Saint Louis, MO 63122-3913
314-821-1441
Fax: 877-726-1714
Manufactures children's indoor play furniture.

5532 Children's Furniture Company
Gressco Ltd.
328 Moravian Valley Road
Waunakee, WI 53597-339
608-849-6300
800-345-3480
Fax: 608-849-6304
info@gressoltd.com
www.gressco.com
Commercial quality furniture for children of all ages.
Robert Childers, President
Caroline Ashmore, Marketing/Sales

5533 Community Playthings
PO Box 901
Rifton, NY 12471-0901
800-777-4244
Fax: 800-336-5948
sales@bruderhof.com
Unstructured maple toys and furniture including innovative products, especially for infants and toddlers.

5534 Continental Film
1466 Riverside Drive, Suite E
PO Box 5126
Chattanooga, TN 37406
423-622-1193
888-909-3456
Fax: 423-629-0853
info@continentalfilm.com
www.continentalfilm.com
LCD projectors, distance learning systems, interactive white boards, document cameras.

Jim Webster, President
Courtney Sisk, VP

5535 Counterpoint
17237 Van Wagoner Road
Spring Lake, MI 49456-9702
800-628-1945
Fax: 616-847-3109
Audiovisual carts and tables.

5536 CyberStretch By Jazzercise
2460 Impala Drive
Carlsbad, CA 92010
760-476-1750
Fax: 760-602-7180
customercare@jazzercise.com
www.jazzercise.com
To foster and promote wellness through the production of free interactive software programs for business, government, educational and personal use.

Kathy Missett, Contact

5537 Da-Lite Screen Company
3100 North Detroit Street
Warsaw, IN 46582
574-267-8101
800-622-3737
Fax: 877-325-4832
info@da-lite.com
www.da-lite.com
Projection screens, monitor mounts, audiovisual carts and tables, overhead projectors and transparencies.

5538 DeFoe Furniture 4 Kids
910 S Grove Avenue
Ontario, CA 91761-8011
909-947-4459
Fax: 909-947-3377
Furniture, floorcoverings, toys, constructive playthings and more for children grades PreK-5.

5539 Decar Corporation
7615 University Avenue
Middleton Branch, WI 53562-3142
606-836-1911
Library shelving, storage facilities and furniture.

5540 DecoGard Products
Construction Specialties
Route 405
PO Box 400
Muncy, PA 17756
570-546-5941
Fax: 570-546-5169
Physical fitness and athletic floor coverings and mats.

5541 Engineering Steel Equipment Company
560 Central Drive
Suite 104
Virginia Beach, VA 23454
757-627-0762
Fax: 757-625-5754
al@engineeringsteel.com
www.engineeringsteel.com
Audiovisual carts and tables, bookcases and library shelving.

5542 Environments
PO Box 1348
Beaufort, SC 29901-1348
843-846-8155
800-348-4453
Fax: 843-846-2999
Publishes a catalog featuring equipment and materials for child care and early education. Offers durable and easy-to-maintain products with values that promote successful preschool, kindergarden, special needs and multi-age programs.

5543 Flagship Carpets
PO Box 1189
Chatsworth, GA 30705-1189
www.flagshipcarpets.com
Carpets, flooring and floorcoverings.

5544 Fleetwood Group
PO Box 1259
Holland, MI 49422-1259
616-396-1142
800-257-6390
Fax: 616-820-8300
www.fleetwoodfurniture.com
Offers library and school furniture including shelving, check out desks and multimedia units.

5545 Fordham Equipment Company
3308 Edson Avenue
New York, NY 10469
718-379-7300
800-249-5922
Fax: 718-379-7312
alrobbi@attglobal.net
www.fordhamequip.com
Distributor and manufacturer of complete line of library supplies. Specialize in professional library shelving and furniture (wood and metal), mobile shelving and displayers. Catalog on request.

Al Robbins, President

5546 Good Sports
6031 Broad Street Mall
Pittsburgh, PA 15206-3009
412-661-9500
Mats, matting, floorcoverings and athletic training mats.

5547 Grafco
ERD
PO Box 71
Catasauqua, PA 18032-0071
800-367-6169
Fax: 610-782-0813
info@grafco.com
www.grafco.com
GRAFCO manufacturers sturdy and durable computer furniture and tables designed for the educational environment.

Art Grafenberg, President

5548 Grammer
6989 N 55th Street
Suite A
Oakdale, MN 55128
651-770-6515
800-367-7328
www.grammerusa.com
Leading manufacturer and designer of ergonomically sound seating. Offers a chair designed especially for children.

5549 Greeting Tree
2709 Oak Haven Drive
San Marcos, TX 78666
512-392-0669
800-322-3199
Fax: 512-392-9660
krieger@corridor.net
www.greetingtree.com
Solid wood furniture for Reading Recovery, Reading Library, Primary and Early Childhood. Specializes in quality and customized furniture for today's classroom. Kitchen learning centers, storage units of all sizes and sorts, easels with over fourteen different display front possibilities.

BiAnnually

Cherie Krieger, Owner

5550 Gressco Ltd.
Gressco
328 Moravian Valley Road
PO Box 339
Waunakee, WI 53597-339
608-849-6300
800-345-3480
Fax: 608-849-6304
info@gresscoltd.com
www.gressco.com
Gressco is a supplier of a complete line of commercial children's HABA furniture and library displays for all types of medias. Kwik-case for the security protection of CDs, videos, and audiocassettes. Catalog available.

Caroline Ashmore, Marketing/Sales

5551 H Wilson Company
2245 Delany Road
Waukegan, IL 60087
708-339-5111
800-245-7224
Fax: 800-245-8224
info@hwilson.com
www.hwilson.com
Manufacturer of furniture for audio, video, and computers. Complete line of TV wall and ceiling mounts. Makers of the famous Tuffy color carts.

Matthew Glowiak, Director Sales/Marketing

5552 HON Company
200 Oak Street
Muscatine, IA 52761-4341
563-272-7100
800-466-8694
Fax: 563-264-7505
HONGSATeam@honcompany.com
www.hon.com
Bookcases and shelving units.

5553 Haworth
One Haworth Center
Holland, MI 49423-9576
616-393-3000
800-344-2600
Fax: 616-393-1570
www.haworth.com
Steel and wood desks, systems furniture, seating, files, bookcases, shelving units, and tables.

5554 Joy Carpets
104 West Forrest Road
Fort Oglethorpe, GA 30742-3675
706-866-3335
800-645-2787
Fax: 706-866-7928
joycarpets@joycarpets.com
www.joycarpets.com
Manufacturer of recreational and educational carpet for the classroom, home, or business. With a 10 year wear warranty, Class #1 Flammability rating, anti-stain and anti-bacterial treatment.

Joy Dobosh, Director Marketing

5555 KI
PO Box 8100
Green Bay, WI 54308-8100

920-468-8100
Fax: 920-468-2232
Library shelving, furniture, bookcases and more.

5556 Kensington Technology Group
2855 Campus Drive
San Mateo, CA 94403
650-572-2700
Fax: 650-572-9675
www.kensington.com
Offers several ergonomic mice.

5557 Kimball Office Furniture Company
1600 Royal Street
Jasper, IN 47549-1001
800-482-1818
800-482-1616
Fax: 812-482-8300
www.kimball.com
Bookcases, office equipment and shelving units for educational institutions.

5558 Lee Metal Products
PO Box 6
Littlestown, PA 17340-0006
717-359-4111
Fax: 717-359-4414
www.leemetal.com
Carts, tables, bookcases and storage cabinets.
Richard Kemper, President

5559 Library Bureau
172 Industrial Road
Fitchburg, MA 01420
978-345-7942
800-221-6638
Fax: 978-345-0188
melvil@librarybureau.com
www.librarybureau.com
Library shelving, bookcases, cabinets, circulation desks, carrels, computer workstations, upholstered seating.
Dennis Ruddy, Sr Project Manager

5560 Library Store
Library Store
112 E S Street
PO Box 0964
Tremont, IL 61568-964
309-925-5571
800-548-7204
Fax: 800-320-7706
customerservice@thelibrarystore.com
www.thelibrarystore.com
The Library Store offers through its full-line catalog, supplies and furniture items for librarians, schools, and churches. Free catalog available containing special product discounts.
Janice Smith, Marketing Director

5561 Little Tikes Company
2180 Barlow Road
Hudson, OH 44236-4199
330-656-3906
800-321-0183
Fax: 330-650-3221
www.littletikes.com
Offers a wide variety of furniture, educational games and toys and safety products for young children.

5562 Lucasey Manufacturing Company
2744 E 11th Street
Oakland, CA 94601-1429
510-534-1435
800-582-2739
Fax: 510-534-6828
janrence@lucasey.com
www.lucasey.com
Audiovisual carts , tables, and TV mounts
Jan RenceTurnbull, National Accountant

5563 Lundia
600 Capitol Way
Jacksonville, IL 62650-1096
800-726-9663
Fax: 800-869-9663
www.lundiausa.com
Bookcases and shelving products, as well as furniture for educational institutions.

5564 Lyon Metal Products
PO Box 671
Aurora, IL 60507-0671
630-892-8941
800-433-8488
Fax: 630-892-8966
lyon@lyonworkspace.com
www.lyonworkspace.com
Bookcases and library shelving.

5565 Mateflex-Mele Corporation
2007 Beechgrove Place
Utica, NY 13501
315-733-1412
844-244-8464
Fax: 315-735-4372
www.mateflex.com
Manufacturers of Mateflex gymnasium flooring for basketball/gym courts. Mateflex II tennis court surfaces and Mateflex/Versaflex gridded safety floor tiles.
Gabe Martini, Sales Manager

5566 Microsoft Corporation
One Microsoft Way
Redmond, WA 98502-6399
425-882-8080
Fax: 206-703-2641
www.microsoft.com
Strives to produce innovative products and services that meet our costomers' evolving needs.

5567 Miller Multiplex
1610 Design Way
Dupo, IL 62239-1820
636-343-5700
800-325-3350
Fax: 618-286-6202
info@Miller-Group.com
www.multiplexdisplays.com
Announcement boards, classroom displays, charts and pghtography, books towers, posters, frames, kiosk displays, presentation displays.
12 pages
Kathy Webster, Director Marketing

5568 ModuForm
ModuForm, Inc.
172 Industry Road
Fitchburg,, MA 01420
978-345-7942
800-221-6638
Fax: 978-345-0188
guestlog@moduform.com
www.moduform.com
Residence hall furniture, loung seating, tables, stacking chairs, fully upholstered seating.
Robert Kushnir, Nationals Sales Manager
Darlene Bailey, VP Sales/Marketing

5569 Morgan Buildings, Pools, Spas, RV's
12700 Hillcrest Rd Suite 278
PO Box 660280
Dallas, TX 75230
972-864-7300
800-935-0321
Fax: 972-864-7382
rmoran@morganusa.com
www.morganusa.com
Classrooms, campus and other buildings custom designed to meet your projects needs. Permanent and relocatable modular classrooms or complete custom facilities. Rent, lease or purchase options available.

5570 Norco Products
Division of USA McDonald Corporation
4985 Blue Mountain Road
PO Box 4227
Missoula, MT 59806
406-251-3800
800-662-2300
Fax: 406-251-3824
jim@norcoproducts.com
www.norcoproducts.com
Mobile cabinets, YRE funiture, tables, science labs, home economics displays, bookcases and shelving units, laboratory equipment, casework, cabinets, computer labs, podiums, award display cabinets, flags and flag poles.
Jim McDonald, President
Patti McDonald, Vice President

5571 Nova
421 W Industrial Avenue
PO Box 725
Effingham, IL 62401
800-730-6682
Fax: 800-940-6682
novadesk@effingham.net
www.novadesk.com
Patented furniture solution for computer mounting incorporates the downward gaze, our visual system's natural way of viewing close objects. Scientific evidence indicates that viewing a computer monitor at a downward gaze angle is a better solution than with traditional monitor placement.

5572 Oscoda Plastics
5585 North Huron Avenue
PO Box 189
Oscoda, MI 48750
989-739-6900
800-544-9538
Fax: 800-548-7678
sales@oscodaplastics.com
protect-allflooring.com
Oscoda Plastics manufactures Protect-All Specialty Flooring from 100% recycled post-industrial vinyls. Protect-All is perfect for use in locker rooms, kitchen/walk-in cooler floors, fitness areas, weight rooms, gym floors, or as a temporary gym floor cover.
Joe Brinn, National Sales Manager
Rick Maybury, Sales Coordinator

5573 Palmer Snyder
201 High Street
Conneautville, PA 16406
814-587-6313
800-762-0415
Fax: 814-587-2375
Tables are built with the highest quality materials for long life and low maintenance. A complete range of rugged options.

5574 Paragon Furniture
2224 East Randol Mill Road
Arlington, TX 76011
817-633-3242
800-451-8546
Fax: 817-633-2733
customerservice@paragoninc.com
www.paragoninc.com
Offers a line of furniture for classroom, labs, science, and libraries.
Carl Brockway, VP Sales
Mark Hubbard, President

5575 Pawling Corporation
Borden Lane
Wassaic, NY 12592
845-373-9300
800-431-3456
Fax: 800-451-2200
sales@pawling.com
Pawling is an approved manufacturer by E&I cooperative buying for athletic flooring, traffic safety products, wall and corner protection and entrance mat systems.

Richard Meyer, Sales Manager

5576 Peerless Sales Company
1980 N Hawthorne Avenue
Melrose Park, IL 60160-1167
708-865-8870
Fax: 708-865-2941
Auidovisual carts and tables.

5577 RISO
300 Rosewood Drive
Suite 210
Danvers, MA 01923-4527
978-777-7377
800-876-7476
Fax: 978-777-2517
The Risograph digital printer offers high speed copy/duplicating at up to 130 pages per minute. A 50-sheet document feeder lets people print multi-page documents quickly and inexpensively. Specifically designed to handle medium run length jobs that are too strenuous for copiers. Offers various other products and office equipment available to the education community.

5578 Research Technology International
4700 Chase Avenue
Lincolnwood, IL 60646-1689
847-677-3000
800-323-7520
Fax: 847-677-1311
sales@rtico.com
www.ritco.com
Tape check, Video tape cleaner, disk chack optical, disc rejestor.

5579 Russ Bassett Company
8189 Byron Road
Whittier, CA 90606-2615
562-945-2445
800-350-2445
Fax: 562-698-8972
info@russbassett.com
www.russbassett.com
Shelving units, furniture and bookcases for educational institutions.

5580 SNAP-DRAPE
2045 Westgate Drive
Suite 100
Carrollton, TX 75006-5116
972-466-1030
800-527-5147
Fax: 800-230-1330
info@snapdrape.com
www.snapdrape.com
Table and stage skirting

Melissa Acton, Marketing/Sales Assistant

5581 Screen Works
2201 W Fulton Street
Chicago, IL 60612
312-243-8265
800-294-8111
Fax: 312-243-8290
screens@thescreenworks.com
www.thescreenworks.com
Manufacturers the E-Z Fold brand of portable projection screens and offers a full line of portable presentation accessories and services, including: an extensive screen rental inventory; audio-visula roll carts; lecterns and PaperStand flip charts. Custom screen sizes, screen surface cleaning and frame repair service also available.

David Hull, National Sales Manager

5582 Spacemaster Systems
155 W Central Avenue
Zeeland, MI 49464-1601
616-772-2406
Fax: 616-772-2100
Standard and Custom Shelving Systems and USEFUL AISLE Storage Systems.

5583 Spacesaver Corporation
1450 Janesville Avenue
Fort Atkinson, WI 53538-2798
920-563-6362
800-255-8170
Fax: 920-563-2702
info@spacesaver.com
www.spacesaver.com
Flexible Spacesaver custom designs high-density mobile storage systems. Will double your storage and filing capacity while increasing usable floor space. Store files, supplies, manuals, books, drawings, multi-media, etc.

5584 Synsor Corporation
1920 Merrill Creek Pkwy
Everett, WA 98203-5859
425-551-1300
800-426-0193
Fax: 425-551-1313
info@synsor.com
www.synsor.com
Offers a full line of educational furniture.

5585 Tab Products Company
1400 Page Mill Road
Palo Alto, CA 94304-1124
800-672-3109
Fax: 920-387-1802
Bookcases and shelving products for library/media centers.

5586 Tepromark International
206 Mosher Avenue
Woodmere, NY 11598-1662
516-569-4533
800-645-2622
Fax: 516-295-5991
Trolley Rail wall guards, corner guards, wall guards with hand rails, door plates, chair rolls, kick plates, vinyl floor mats and carpet mats. All mats promote safety from slipping in wet areas.

Robert Rymers

5587 Tesco Industries
1038 E Hacienda Street
Bellville, TX 77418-2828
979-865-3176
800-699-5824
Fax: 979-865-9026
tesco@tesco-ind.com
www.tesco-ind.com
Bookcases and shelving units.

5588 Texwood Furniture
1353 N 2nd Street
Taylor, TX 76574
512-352-3000
888-878-0000
Fax: 512-352-3084
ajohnson@texwood.com
www.texwood.com
Wood library furniture, shelving, computer tables and circulation desks and early childhood furniture.

Andrea Johnson, Director Marketing
Dave Gaskers, VP Sales/Marketing

5589 Tot-Mate by Stevens Industries
704 West Main Street
Teutopolis, IL 62467-1212
217-857-7100
800-397-8687
Fax: 217-857-7101
timw@stevens.com
www.stevensind.com
Early learning furniture manufactured by Stevens Industries. Features include 16 color choices, plastic laminate surfacing, rounded corners, beveled edges, safe and strong designs. Items offered include change tables, storage shelving, book displays, teacher cabinets, housekeeping sets and locker cubbies.

Randy Ruholl, Sales Representative
Paul Jones, Customer Service

5590 University Products
University Products
517 Main Street
PO Box 101
Holyoke, MA 1040
413-532-3372
800-628-1912
Fax: 413-532-9281
info@universityproducts.com
www.universityproducts.com
University Products specializes in top-quality archival materials for conservation and preservation as well as library and media centers supplies, equipment, and furnishings.

Scott E. Magoon, President/ COO

5591 W. C. Heller & Company
Heller
201 W Wabash Avenue
Montpelier, OH 43543
419-485-3176
Fax: 419-485-8694
wcheller@hotmail.com
Complete line of wood library furniture in oak and birch, custom cabinetry and special modifications. Over 110 years in business.

Robert L Heller II, VP Sales

5592 Wheelit
PO Box 352800
Toledo, OH 43635-2800
419-531-4900
800-523-7508
Fax: 419-531-6415
Carts and storage containers.

5593 White Office Systems
50 Boright Avenue
Kenilworth, NJ 07033
908-272-6700
800-275-1442
Fax: 908-931-0840
whitesystems.com
Shelving, bookcases, furniture and products for libraries, media centers, schools and offices.

5594 Whitney Brothers Company
PO Box 644
Keene, NH 03431-0644
603-352-2610
Fax: 603-357-1559
www.whitneybros.com
Manufactures children's furniture products for preschools and day care centers.

5595 Winsted Corporation
10901 Hampshire Avenue S
Minneapolis, MN 55438
952-944-9050
800-447-2257
Fax: 800-421-3839
info@winsted.com
www.winsted.com

Video furniture, accessories, tape storage systems and lan rack systems.

Rich McPherson, Western Regional Manager
Kim Richter, Western Regional Manager

5596 **Wood Designs**
PO Box 1308
Monroe, NC 28111-1308
704-283-7508
800-247-8465
Fax: 704-289-1899
p.schneider@tip-me-not.com
www.wooddesigns.org
Manufactures wooden educational equipment and teaching toys for early learning environments. Sold through school supply dealers and stores.

Dennis Gosney, President
Paul Schneider, VP Sales/Marketing

5597 **Worden Company**
199 E 17th Street
Holland, MI 49423
800-748-0561
Fax: 616-392-2542
info@wordencompany.com
www.wordencompany.com
Furniture for office, business, school or library.

Maintenance

5598 **American Locker Security Systems**
2701 Regent Blvd
Suite 200
DFW Airport, TX 75261
817-329-1600
800-828-9118
Fax: 817-421-8618
info@americanlocker.com
www.americanlocker.com
Lockers featuring coin operated lockers.

David L Henderson, VP/General Manager

5599 **Atlantic Fitness Products**
PO Box 300
Linthicum Hts, MD 21090-0300
410-859-3907
800-445-1855
www.atlanticfitnessproducts.com
School lockers and fitness/physical education products and equipment.

5600 **Barco Products**
24 N. Washington Ave.
Batavia, IL 60510
800-338-2697
sales@barcoproducts.com
www.barcoproducts.com
Maintenance and safety products made from recycled materials.

Cyril Matter, CEO
Judy Leonard, Marketing Manager

5601 **Blaine Window Hardware**
17319 Blaine Drive
Hagerstown, MD 21740
800-678-1919
Fax: 888-250-3960
parts@Blainewindow.com
www.blainewindow.com
Producers of window and door parts including window repair hardware, custom screens locker hardware, chair glides, panic exit hardware, balance systems, door closers and motorized operators.

David Crouse, President
Robert Slick, Purchasing Agent

5602 **Bleacherman, M.A.R.S.**
105 Mill Street
Corinth, NY 12822
518-654-9084
800-628-1332
Fax: 518-654-2232
info@bleacherman.com
www.mars-bleachers.com
School lockers.

5603 **Burkel Equipment Company**
14670 Hanks Drive
Red Bluff, CA 96080-9475
800-332-3993
School lockers, hardware and security equipment, maintenance and repair supplies.

5604 **Chemtrol**
Santa Barbara Control Systems
5375 Overpass Road
Santa Barbara, CA 93111-5879
800-621-2279
Fax: 805-683-1893
chemtrol@slocontrol.com
www.ccdc.ucsb.edu
Maintenance supplies for educational institutions.

Karl Johan Astrom, Mechanical Engineering
Bassam Bamieh, Mechanical Engineering

5605 **Contact East**
Stanley Supply & Services, Inc.
335 Willow Street
North Andover, MA 01845-5995
978-682-9844
800-225-5370
Fax: 800-743-8141
sales@contacteast.com
www.contacteast.com
Maintenance supplies and equipment.

5606 **DeBourgh Manufacturing Company**
27505 Otero Avenue
PO Box 981
La Junta, CO 81050
719-384-8161
800-328-8829
Fax: 719-384-7713
sales@debourgh.com
www.debourgh.com
Security equipment, hardware, storage and school lockers.

Ralph Malers, Employee

5607 **Dow Corning Corporation**
2200 W. Salzburg Rd.
PO Box 0994
Midland, MI 48686-0994
989-496-4000
Fax: 989-496-4572
www.dowcorning.com/content/publishedlit/Global_Fast_Facts.pd
Maintenance supplies and equipment.

Robert D. Hansen, President/ CEO
Cathy Yang, Global Media Relations,China

5608 **Dri-Dek Corporation**
Kendall Products
P.O. Box 8656
Naples, FL 34101
239-643-0448
800-348-2398
Fax: 800-828-4248
info@dri-dek.com
www.dri-dek.com
Oxy-BI vinyl compound in the Dri-Dek flooring systems helps halt the spread of infectious fungus and bacteria in areas with barefooted traffic. This compound makes Dri-Dek's anti-skid, self-draining surface ideal for use in the wettest conditions.

5609 **Esmet**
1406 5th Street SW
Canton, OH 44702
330-452-9132
800-321-0870
Fax: 330-452-2557
info@esmet.com
www.esmet.com
Lockers for the educational institution.

5610 **Ex-Cell Metal Products**
11240 Melrose Avenue
Franklin, IL 60131
847-451-0451
Fax: 847-451-0458
Maintenance supplies and repair equipment.

5611 **Facilities Network**
PO Box 868
Mahopac, NY 10541-0868
845-621-1664
School lockers and security system units.

5612 **Fibersin Industries**
37031 E Wisconsin Avenue
PO Box 88
Oconomowoc, WI 53066-88
262-567-4427
Fax: 262-567-4814
info@fiberesin.com
www.fiberesin.com
School lockers and maintenance supplies. Desks, cradenzas, bookcases for school adm. Tables for cafeteria and adm.

5613 **Flagpole Components**
4150A Kellway Circle
Addison, TX 75001
972-250-0893
800-634-4926
Fax: 972-380-5143
www.concordindustries.com
Maintenance and repair supplies and equipment.

5614 **Flexi-Wall Systems**
PO Box 89
208 Carolina Dr.
Liberty, SC 29657-0089
864-843-3104
800-843-5394
Fax: 864-843-9318
flexiwall@bellsouth.net
www.flexiwall.com/pages/home_page.htm
Maintenance and repair supplies for educational institutions.

5615 **Flo-Pac Corporation**
700 Washington Avenue N
Suite 400
Minneapolis, MN 55401-1130
612-332-6240
Fax: 612-344-1663
Maintenance and repair supplies.

5616 **Four Rivers Software Systems**
400 Penn Center Blvd
Suite 450
Pittsburgh, PA 15235
412-256-9020
Fax: 412-273-6420
www.frsoft.com
Maintenance and repair supplies, business and administrative software and supplies.

Pierre Harrison, Regional VP,Healthcare
M. Lynn O'Donnell, Dir. Of Marketing

5617 **Friendly Systems**
3878 Oak Lawn Avenue
#1008-300
Dallas, TX 75219-4460
972-857-0399
Maintenance and repair supplies.

5618 GE Capitol Modular Space
40 Liberty Boulevard
Malvern, PA 19355
610-225-2836
800-523-7918
Fax: 610-225-2762
www.modspace.com
School lockers, shelving and storage facilities.

5619 Glen Products
13765 Alton Parkway
Suite A
Irvine, CA 92618-1627
800-486-4455
Storage facilities, lockers and security systems.

5620 Global Occupational Safety
22 Harbor Park Drive
Port Washington, NY 11050-4650
516-625-4466
Safety storage facilities, shelving, lockers and hardware.

5621 Graffiti Gobbler Products
6428 Blarney Stone Court
Springfield, VA 22152-2106
800-486-2512
Educational maintenance and repair supplies and equipment.

5622 H&H Enterprises
PO Box 585
Grand Haven, MI 49417-9430
616-846-8972
800-878-7777
Fax: 616-846-1004
hhenterprises@novagate.com
handhent.com
Maintenance and repair supplies.

5623 HAZ-STOR
75 Camrose Cres.
Underwood., Ql 4119
073-341-6200
800-727-2067
Fax: 073-341-6211
sales@haz-stor.net
haz-stor.net
Manufacturer of pre-fabricated steel structures including hazardous material storage buildings and outdoor flammables lockers as well as waste compactors and drum crushers, secondary containment products and process shelters.
Roger Quinlan, National Sales Manager
Antoinette Balthazor, Marketing Coordinator

5624 HOST/Racine Industries
1405 16th Street
Racine, WI 53403-2249
800-558-9439
Fax: 262-637-1624
Maintenance and repair supplies.

5625 Hako Minuteman
14N845 U.S. Route 20
Pingree Grove, IL 60140
847-264-5400
Fax: 847-683-5207
www.minutemanintl.com
Maintenance and repair supplies for educational institutions.

5626 Haws Corporation
1455 Kleppe Ln
Sparks, NV 89431
775-359-4712
888-640-4297
Fax: 775-359-7424
haws@hawsco.com
www.hawsco.com
Manufacturer of drinking fountains, electric water coolers, emergency drench showers and eyewashes.
Tom White, President
Aaron Cross, Jr., VP of Operations

5627 Honeywell
Home & Building Control
PO Box 524
Minneapolis, MN 55440-0524
973-455-2001
Fax: 973-455-4807
Maintenance and cleaning products for educational purposes.

5628 Insta-Foam Products
2050 N Broadway Street
Joliet, IL 60435-2571
800-800-FOAM
Fax: 800-326-1054
Maintenance supplies, cleaning products and repair hardware.

5629 Interstate Coatings
1005 Highway 301 S
Wilson, NC 27895
800-533-7663
Hardware, repair, maintenance and cleaning supplies.

5630 J.A. Sexauer
PO Box 1000
White Plains, NY 10602
800-431-1872
Fax: 888-499-0441
customercare@sexauer.com
www.casinovendors.com/vendor/j-a-sexaue
r
Cleaning and maintenance supplies for educational institutions.

5631 Karnak Corporation
330 Central Avenue
Clark, NJ 07066
732-388-0300
800-526-4236
Fax: 732-388-9422
www.karnakcorp.com/Contact.aspx
Maintenance and cleaning supplies.
Sarah J. Jelin, Chairwoman, President
John McDermott, Vice-Chairman

5632 Kool Seal
Unifex Professional Maintenance Products
1499 Enterprise Pkwy
Twinsburg, OH 44087-2241
800-321-0572
Fax: 330-425-9778
Maintenance, repair and cleaning supplies.

5633 LDSystems
407 Garden Oaks
Houston, TX 77018
713-695-9400
Fax: 713-695-8015
info@ldsystems.com
www.ldsystems.com
Environmentally-safe bottom pump air powered spray containers to dispense cleaning supplies such as window sprays, for cooling during workouts and general storage containers.
Dick Stark

5634 List Industries
401 Jim Moran Blvd.
PO Box 9601
Deerfield Beach, FL 33442
954-429-9155
800-776-1342
Fax: 954-428-3843
www.listindustries.com
School lockers and storage facilities.
JR List, President
Max H. List, Founder

5635 Maintenance
1051 W Liberty Street
Wooster, OH 44691-3307
330-264-6262
800-892-6701
Fax: 800-264-2578
Provides pavement maintenance products for parking lots, driveways, tennis courts, etc.
Robert E Huebner

5636 Master Bond
154 Hobart Street
Hackensack, NJ 07601
201-343-8983
Fax: 201-343-2132
main@masterbond.com
www.masterbond.com
Repair hardware, maintenance and cleaning products for schools.
Dr. Walter Brenne, Technical Director

5637 Master Builders
Admixture Division
23700 Chagrin Boulevard
Cleveland, OH 44122-5554
216-831-5500
Fax: 216-839-8815
School hardware, maintenance and repair supplies and equipment.

5638 Medart
Division of Carriage Industries
PO Box 435
Garrettsville, OH 44231-0435
662-453-2506
School lockers.

5639 Modular Hardware
8190 N Brookshire Court
Tucson, AZ 85741-4037
520-744-4424
800-533-0042
Fax: 800-533-7942
School hardware, for repair and maintenance purposes.

5640 Penco Products
1820 Stonehenge Drive
Greenville, NC 27858
610-666-0500
800-562-1000
Fax: 610-666-7561
general@pencoproducts.com
www.pencoproducts.com
School lockers.
L. Lewis Sagendorph, Founder
Sarah Crandell, Accounts Payable

5641 Permagile Industries
910 Manor Lane
Bay Shore, NY 11706-7512
516-349-1100
Maintenance and cleaning products and supplies.

5642 Powr-Flite Commercial Floor Care Equipment
3301 Wichita Court
Fort Worth, TX 76140
817-551-0700
800-880-2913
Fax: 817-551-0719
info@powr-flite.com
www.powrflite.com
School maintenance supplies focusing on floor care equipment products, accessories and parts.
Curtis Walton, Contact

5643 **ProCoat Products**
260 Centre Street
Suite D
Holbrook, MA 02343
781-767-2270
Fax: 781-767-2271
info@procoat.com
www.procoat.com
Designed to restore aged and discolored acoustical ceiling tiles. Acoustical and fire retarding qualities are maintained. Ceiling restoration is cost effective, time efficient and avoids solid waste disposal. Products available also for preventative maintenance programs.
Kenneth Woolf, Borad Chairman, Founder
Lisa Ploss, President

5644 **Rack III High Security Bicycle Rack Company**
675 Hartz Avenue
Suite 306
Danville, CA 94526-3859
800-733-1971
Lockers, bicycle racks, storage facilities and hardware.

5645 **Republic Storage Systems Company**
1038 Belden Avenue NE
Canton, OH 44705-1454
330-438-5800
800-477-1255
Fax: 330-454-7772
republicstorage.com
Storage facilities, containers, maintenance products, shelving and lockers.
John Berger, Co-Founder
Wilson Berger, Co-Founder

5646 **Safety Storage**
855 N. 5th Street
Charleston, IL 61920
800-344-6539
Fax: 831-637-7405
www.safetystorage.com
Equipment, supplies and storage containers for maintenance and educational purposes.
Lynn Dufek, CEO

5647 **Salsbury Industries**
1010 E 62nd Street
Los Angeles, CA 90001-1598
323-846-6700
800-624-5269
Fax: 323-846-6800
salsbury@mailboxes.com
www.mailboxes.com
School lockers, maintenance products and storage facilities.

5648 **Servicemaster**
Education Management Services
860 Ridge Lake Boulevard
Downers Grove, IL 60515
800-926-9700
ems.educationmgt.com
A provider of facility management support services to education.
Mark A. Smith, Ed.D, President
Joshua T. Fischer, PhD, VP of Operations

5649 **Sheffield Plastics**
Bayer MaterialScience LLC
119 Salisbury Road
Sheffield, MA 01257
413-229-8711
800-628-5084
Fax: 413-229-8717
sfdinfo@bayer.com
www.sheffieldplastics.com
Maintenance and cleaning products for schools.

5650 **Southern Sport Surfaces**
PO Box 1817
Cumming, GA 30028-1817
770-887-3508
800-346-1632
Maintenance and cleaning products for schools.

5651 **System Works**
3301 Windy Ridge Parkway
Marietta, GA 30067
770-952-8444
800-868-0497
Fax: 770-955-2977
Addresses the capacity, quality and safety requirements of maintenance operations. Comprehensive and interactive it maximizes maintenance resources, people, tools and replacement parts, for increased productivity and equipment reliability, reduced inventories and accurate cost accounting.
Karen Kharlead

5652 **TENTEL Corporation**
330 Industrial Drive # 4
Placerville, CA 95667
530-344-0183
800-538-6894
Fax: 530-344-0186
info@tentel.com
www.tentel.com
Cleaning, repair and maintenance products for educational institutions.

5653 **Tiffin Systems**
450 Wall Street
Tiffin, OH 44883-1366
419-447-8414
800-537-0983
Fax: 419-447-8512
mdysard@tiffinmetal.com
www.tiffinmetal.com
Lockers, storage containers and shelving.
Matt Dysard, President/ COO
Will Heddles, CEO

5654 **Topog-E Gasket Company**
1224 N Utica
Tulsa, OK 74110
918-587-6649
Fax: 918-587-6961
info@topog-e.com
www.topog-e.com
Maintenance supplies and products.

5655 **Tru-Flex Recreational Coatings**
Touraine Paints
1760 Revere Beach Pkwy
Everett, MA 02149-5906
800-325-0017
Maintenance, floor care, coatings and repair supplies for upkeep of schools and institutions.

5656 **Wagner Spray Tech Corporation**
1770 Fernbrook Lane N
Minneapolis, MN 55447
763-553-0759
Fax: 763-553-7288
www.wagnerspraytech.com
Maintenance supplies, floor care, cleaning and repair products and equipment.

5657 **Wilmar**
303 Harper Drive
Moorestown, NJ 08057
800-345-3335
800-345-3000
Fax: 800-220-3291
customercare@wilmar.com
www.wilmar.com
Maintenance and repair products, hardware and supplies.

5658 **Witt Company**
4454 Steel Place
Cincinnati, OH 45209-1184
513-979-3127
800-543-7417
Fax: 513-979-3134
Lockers, maintenance supplies and storage containers for educational purposes.

5659 **Zep Manufacturing**
1310 Seaboard Industrial Dr.
Atlanta, GA 30318
404-352-1680
877-428-9937
www.zep.com
Maintenance and cleaning supplies.

Scientific Equipment

5660 **Adventures Company**
435 Main Street
Johnson City, NY 13790-1935
607-729-6512
800-477-6512
Fax: 607-729-4820
A full line of supplies and equipment for science and technology education.
D Hetherington

5661 **Alfa Aesar**
26 Parkridge Rd
Ward Hill, MA 01835
978-521-6300
800-343-0660
Fax: 978-521-6350
www.alfa.com
Laboratory equipment and supplies.

5662 **American Chemical Society**
1155 16th Street NW
Washington, DC 20036
202-872-4600
800-333-9511
Fax: 202-833-7732
service@acs.org
www.@acs.org
Exhibits hands-on activities and programs for K-12 and college science curriculum.
Pat N. Confalone, Chair
Diane Grob Schmidt, President

5663 **Arbor Scientific**
PO Box 2750
Ann Arbor, MI 48106-2750
734-477-9370
800-367-6695
Fax: 734-477-9373
mail@arborsci.com
www.arborsci.com
Innovative products for Science Education.
56 pages Bi-Annual Catalog
Dave Barnes, Marketing Director

5664 **Astronomy to Go**
1115 Melrose Avenue
Melrose Park, PA 19027-3017
215-831-0485
Fax: 215-831-0486
astro2go@aol.com
www.astronomytogo.com
Programs include Starlab Planetarium presentations, hands-on demonstrations, slides and lecture shows and energy observing sessions with our many telescopes. We are funded through our traveling museum shop which carries a large assortment of t-shirts, jewelry, gifts, books, and

teaching supplies as well as an extensive selection of meterorites.

Bob Summerfield, Director/ Founder

5665 CEM Corporation
3100 Smith Farm Road
Matthews, NC 28104
704-821-7015
Fax: 704-821-7894
www.cem.com
Laboratory and scientific supplies, furniture, casework and equipment.

5666 Carolina Biological Supply Company
2700 York Road
Burlington, NC 27215-3398
336-584-0381
800-334-5551
Fax: 800-222-7112
carolina@carolina.com
www.carolina.com
Educational products for teachers and students of biology, molecular biology, biotechnology, chemistry, earth science, space science, physics, and mathematics. Carolina serves elementary schools through universities with living and preserved animals and plants, prepared microscope slides, microscopes, audiovisuals, books, charts, models, computer software, games, apparatus, and much more.

5667 Challenger Center for Space Science Education
422 1st St. SE
3rd Floor
Washington, DC 20003
202-827-1580
800-969-5747
Fax: 703-683-7546
mail@challenger.org
www.challenger.org
Is a global not-for-profit education organization created in 1986 by familes of the astronauts tragically lost during the last flight of the Challenger Space Shuttle. Dedicated to the educaltional spirit of that mission, Challenger center develops Learning Centers and othe educational programs worldwide to continue the mission to engage students in science and math education

Dr. Lance Bush, President/ CEO
Steven Goldberg, CFO

5668 ChronTrol Corporation
7525-D Mission Gorge Rd.
San Diego, CA 92120
619-282-8686
800-854-1999
Fax: 619-563-6563
info@chrontrol.com
www.chrontrol.com
Scientific equipment, laboratory supplies and furniture.

5669 Classic Modular Systems
1911 Columbus Street
Two Rivers, WI 54241
414-793-2269
800-558-7625
Fax: 414-793-2896
info@classicmodular.com
www.classicmodular.com
Laboratory equipment, shelving, cabinets and markerboards.

Cathy Albers, Advertising Manager

5670 Columbia University's Biosphere 2 Center
Highway 77 & Biosphere Road
Oracle, AZ 85623
520-838-6155
Fax: 520-838-6136
info@email.arizona.edu
b2science.org
Educational programs and products.

Pierre Meystre, Director
Joaquin Ruiz, Director

5671 Connecticut Valley Biological Supply Company
82 Valley Road
PO Box 326
Southampton, MA 01073
413-527-4030
800-628-7748
Fax: 800-355-6813
connval@ctvalleybio.com
www.connecticutvalleybiological.com
Cultures and specimens, instruments, equipment, hands-on kits, books, software, audiovisuals, models and charts for teaching botany, zoology, life science, anatomy, physiology, genetics, astronomy, entomology, microscopy, AP Biology, microbiology, horticulture, biotechnology, earth science, natural history and environmental science.

Marschall P. Lohr, Founder

5672 Crow Canyon Archaeological Center
23390 Road K
Cortez, CO 81321
970-565-8975
800-422-8975
Fax: 970-565-4859
webmanager@crowcanyon.org
www.crowcanyon.org
Experiential education programs in archaeology and Native American history. Programs offered for school groups, teachers and other adults.

ISBN: 0-7872-6748-1

M Elaine Davis and Marjorie R Connelly, Author
W. Bruce Milne, Chair
Barbara L. Schwietert, Vice-Chairman

5673 Cuisenaire Company of America
10 Bank Street
#5026
White Plains, NY 10606-1933
914-997-2600
Fax: 914-684-6137
Science materials and equipment.

5674 DISCOVER Science Program
105 Terry Drive
Suite 120
Newtown, PA 18940-1872
800-448-3399
Fax: 215-579-8589
Features the newest developments in a wide range of science topics and provides an easy way for teachers to stay current and up-to-date in the world of science. The DISCOVER Program offers the DISCOVER magazine at the lowest possible price.

5675 Delta Biologicals
PO Box 26666
Tucson, AZ 85726-6666
520-790-7737
800-821-2502
Fax: 520-745-7888
customerservice@deltabio.com
www.deltabio.com
Products and supplies for science and biology educators for over 30 years. Preserves specimens, laboratory furniture, microscopes, anatomy models, balances and scales, dissection supplies, lab safety supplies, multimedia, plant presses.

Lynn Hugins, Marketing
Darlene Harris, Customer Service Manager

5676 Delta Biologicals Catalog
PO Box 26666
Tucson, AZ 85726-6666
520-790-7737
800-821-2502
Fax: 520-745-7888
customerservice@deltabio.com
www.deltabio.com
96 pages

Lynn Hugins, Marketing
Darlene Harris, Customer Service Manager

5677 Detecto Scale Corporation
203 E Daugherty Street
Webb City, MO 64870
417-673-4631
800-641-2008
Fax: 417-673-5001
detecto@cardet.com
www.detectoscale.com
Scientific equipment and supplies for educational laboratories.

Johnathan Sabo, VP Marketing

5678 Dickson Company
930 S Westwood Avenue
Addison, IL 60101-4997
630-543-3747
800-757-3747
Fax: 800-676-0498
dicksoncsr@dicksondata.com
www.dicksondata.com
Laboratory instruments, electronics, furniture and equipment.

Mike Unger, President
Mark Kohlmeier, CFO

5679 Donald K. Olson & Associates
PO Box 858
Bonsall, CA 92003-0858
Fax: 19-4 -
Mineral and fossil samples for educational purposes.

5680 Dranetz Technologies
1000 New Durham Road
Edison, NJ 08818-4019
732-287-3680
800-372-6832
Fax: 732-287-9014
www.dranetz.com
Laboratory instruments, equipment and supplies.

5681 Edmund Scientific - Scientifics Catalog
E726 Edscorp Building
Department 16A1
Barrington, NJ 08007
856-547-3488
Fax: 856-573-6295
Over 5,000 products including a wide selection of microscopes, telescopes, astronomy aids, fiber optic kits, demonstration optics, magnets and science discover products used in science fair projects.

Nancy McGonigle, President

5682 Educational Products
1342 N I35 E
Carrollton, TX 75006
972-245-9512
Fax: 972-245-5468
Science display boards, workshop materials and science fair accessories.

5683 Edwin H. Benz Company
73 Maplehurst Avenue
Providence, RI 02908
401-331-5650
Fax: 401-331-5685

engineering@benztesters.com
www.benztesters.com
Laboratory equipment.

Ted Benz, President

5684 Electro-Steam Generator Corporation
50 Indel Ave.
PO Box 438
Rancocas, NJ 08073-0438
609-288-9071
866-617-0764
Fax: 609-288-9078
jharlineclectrostream.com
www.electrosteam.com
Laboratory equipment and supplies. Manufacture steam generators for sterilizers, autoclaves, clean rooms, pure steam humidification, laboratories, steam rooms, and cleaning of all kinds.

Jack Harlin, Sales/Marketing Associate

5685 Estes-Cox Corporation
PO Box 227
Penrose, CO 81240-0227
719-372-6565
800-820-0202
Fax: 719-372-3217
webcs@centurims.com
www.esteseducator.com
Supplier of model rockets, engines and supporting videos, curriculums and educational publications for K-12.

Ann Grimm, Director Education

5686 FOTODYNE
950 Walnut Ridge Drive
Hartland, WI 53029
262-369-7000
800-362-3642
Fax: 262-369-7017
info@fotodyne.com
www.fotodyne.com
Biotechnology curriculum equipment.

Brian Walsh, President & Owner
Dennis Devitt, Board Member

5687 First Step Systems
PO Box 2304
Jackson, TN 38302-2304
800-831-0877
Fax: 216-361-0829
Developed an effective, safe and less expensive approach to blood exposure safety for schools and classrooms that both help comply with OSHA requirements and is easy to purchase and resupply.

Susan Staples, Account Manager
Renee Carr, Bid Support

5688 Fisher Scientific Company
1410 Wayne Avenue
Indiana, PA 15701-3940
724-357-1000
Fax: 724-357-1019
A full line of laboratory and scientific supplies and equipment for educational institutions.

5689 Fisher Scientific/EMD
3970 John Creek Court
Suite 500
Suwanee, GA 30024
770-871-4500
800-766-7000
Fax: 800-926-1166
Supplier of chemistry, biology and physics laboratory supplies and equipment.

5690 Fisons Instruments
8 Forge Parkway
Franklin, MA 02038-3157
978-524-1000
Laboratory equipment and instruments for the scientific classroom.

5691 Flinn Scientific
PO Box 219
Batavia, IL 60510
630-879-6900
800-452-1261
Fax: 866-452-1436
flinn@flinnsci.com
www.flinnsci.com
Laboratory safety supplies.

5692 Forestry Supplies
PO Box 8397
205 West Rankin St.
Jackson, MS 39284-8397
601-354-3565
800-647-5368
Fax: 800-543-4203
fsi@forestry-suppliers.com
www.forestry-suppliers.com
Field and lab equipment for earth, life and environmental sciences.

Ken Peacock, VP Marketing
Debbie Raddin, Education Specialist

5693 Frank Schaffer Publications
23740 Hawthorne Boulevard
Torrance, CA 90505-5927
310-378-1133
800-421-5565
Fax: 800-837-7260
Charts, animal posters, floor puzzles, resource books and more.

5694 Frey Scientific
PO Box 300
Nashua, NH 03061-3000
800-225-3739
Fax: 800-226-3739
customercare.frey@schoolspeciality
www.freyscientific.com
Name brand scientific products including Energy Physics, Earth Science, Chemistry and Applied Science. Over 12,000 products and kits for grades 5-14 are available.

5695 Great Adventure Tours
1717 Old Topanga Canyon Road
Topanga, CA 90290-3934
800-642-3933
Educational science field trips and adventures.

5696 Guided Discoveries
PO Box 1360
Claremont, CA 91711
800-45 -423
Fax: 909-625-7305
info@guideddiscoveries.org
guideddiscoveries.org
Outdoor educational science programs.

Ross Turner, President/ CEO/ Co-Founder
Kristi Turner, CFO/ Co-Founder

5697 HACH Company
PO Box 389
Loveland, CO 80539
970-669-3050
800-227-4224
Fax: 970-669-2932
www.hach.com
Water and soil test kits for field and laboratory work.

5698 Heathkit Educational Systems
455 Riverview Drive
Benton Harbor, MI 49022-5015
616-925-6000
800-253-0570
Fax: 616-925-3895
Electronics educational products from basic electricity to high-tech lasers and microscopes and beyond. Comprehensive line of different media to fit varied applications. Including Computer-Aided Instruction and Computer-Aided Troubleshooting services and Heathkit's PC Servicing, Troubleshooting and Networking courses.

Carolyn Feltner, Sales Coordinator
Patrick Beckett, Marketing Manager

5699 Holometrix
25 Wiggins Avenue
Bedford, MA 01730-2314
781-275-3300
Fax: 781-275-3705
Laboratory instruments.

5700 Howell Playground Equipment
3728 Salem Rd.
Enterprise, AL 36330
217-442-0482
800-239-1370
Fax: 334-347-9563
howellequipment@aol.com
www.primestripe.com
Playground equipment and bicycle racks.

Nina Payne, President

5701 Hubbard Scientific
PO Box 2121
401 Hickory St.
Fort Collins, CO 80522
970-484-7445
800-289-9299
Fax: 970-484-1198
custserv@amep.com
www.amep.com
Earth science and life science models, kits, globes and curriculum materials.

5702 Innova Corporation
115 George Lamb Road
Bernardston, MA 01337-9742
Science kits and globes.

5703 Insect Lore
PO Box 1535
Shafter, CA 93263
661-746-6047
800-548-3284
Fax: 661-746-0334
orders@insectlore.com
www.insectlore.com
Science and nature materials for preschool through grade 6. Raises butterflies, frogs, ladybugs and more. Features books, curriculum units, videos, puppet, posters, and other nature oriented products.

5704 Insights Visual Productions
PO Box 230644
Encinitas, CA 92023-0644
800-942-0528
Laboratory instruments, manuals, and supplies.

5705 Instron Corporation
100 Royall Street
Canton, MA 02021-1089
781-828-2500
Fax: 781-575-5776
www.instron.com
Laboratory and scientific equipment, supplies and furniture.

5706 Johnsonite
16910 Munn Road
Chagrin Falls, OH 44023
440-543-8916
800-899-8916
Fax: 440-543-8920
info@johnsonite.com
www.johnsonite.com/ContactUs.aspx
Physical education mats, matting and floors.

5707 Justrite Manufacturing Company
2454 E Dempster Street
Suite 300
Des Plaines, IL 60016
847-298-9250
800-798-9250
Fax: 847-298-9261
justrite@justritemfg.com
www.justritemfg.com
Supplies and equipment aimed at the scientific classroom or laboratory.

5708 KLM Bioscientific
8888 Clairemont Mesa Boulevard
Suite D
San Diego, CA 92123-1137
858-571-5562
Fax: 858-571-5587
labsuppliesUSA.com
A mail order company that provides high quality, reasonably priced, on time living and preserved biological specimens. The Biology Store also carries a wide range of instructional materials including books, charts, models and videos. Also available is a wide range of general labware.
Loli Victorio, President

5709 Ken-a-Vision Manufacturing Company
5615 Raytown Road
Kansas City, MO 64133-3388
816-353-4787
Fax: 816-358-5072
info@ken-a-vision.com
www.ken-a-vision.com
Video Flex, Vison Viewer, Pupil CAM, Microscopes and Microrojectors
Steve Dunn, Domestic/International Op.
Ben Hoke, Sales Manger

5710 Kepro Circuit Systems
3640 Scarlet Oak Boulevard
Kirkwood, MO 63122-6606
800-325-3878
Fax: 636-861-9109
Laboratory equipment.

5711 Kewaunee Scientific Corporation
2700 W Front Street
Statesville, NC 28677
704-873-7202
800-824-6626
Fax: 704-873-5160
humanresources@kewaunee.com
www.kewaunee.com
Developer of science and laboratory supplies such as casework, fume hoods, adaptable modular systems, moveable workstations and various other technical furniture.
David M Rausch, President & CEO
Thomas D Hull III, Vice President & CFO

5712 Knex Education Catalog
Knex Education
2990 Bergey Road
PO Box 700
Hatfield, PA 19440-0700
888-KID-KNEX
email@knex.com
www.knexeducation.com
Hands-on, award-winning curriculum supported K-12 math, science and technology sets.
Michael Araten, President

5713 Koffler Sales Company
785 Oakwood Road
Suite C-100
Lake Zurich, IL 60047-1524
847-438-1152
800-355-MATS
Fax: 847-438-1514
info@kofflersales.com
www.kofflersales.com
Floor mats, Matting and stair treads.
Ron Starr, President
Pat Starr, CEO

5714 Komodo Dragon
PO Box 822
The Dalles, OR 97058-0822
541-773-5808
Museum-quality fossils and minerals.

5715 Kreonite
715 E 10th Street N
Wichita, KS 67214-2918
316-263-1111
Fax: 316-263-6829
Laboratory equipment, furniture and hardware.

5716 Kruger & Eckels
1406 E Wilshire Avenue
Santa Ana, CA 92705
714-547-5165
Fax: 714-547-2009
www.krugerandeckels.com
Laboratory and scientific instruments for institutional or educational use.

5717 LEGO Data
PO Box 1600
Enfield, CT 06083-1600
860-749-2291
Fax: 860-763-7477
Curriculum programs and materials for science education.

5718 LINX System
Science Source
PO Box 727
Waldoboro, ME 04572-0727
207-832-6344
800-299-5469
Fax: 207-832-7281
info@thesciencesource.com
www.thesciencesource.com
A building system that integrates science, mathematics and technology at the K-9 level.

5719 Lab Safety Supply
PO Box 1368
401 S Wright Rd.
Janesville, WI 53547-1368
608-754-2345
800-356-0783
Fax: 608-754-1806
custserv@labsafety.com
www.labsafety.com
Extensive variety of school products, including lab and safety apparel and floorcoverings.

5720 Lab Volt Systems
PO Box 686
Farmingdale, NJ 07727-0686
Educational materials and equipment for the science educator.

5721 Lab-Aids
17 Colt Court
Ronkonkoma, NY 11779
631-737-1133
800-381-8003
Fax: 631-737-1286
mkt@lab-aids.com
www.lab-aids.com
Science kits, published curriculum materials.
John Weatherby, Sales/Marketing Director
David M Frank, President

5722 Labconco Corporation
8811 Prospect Avenue
Kansas City, MO 64132-2696
816-333-8811
800-821-5525
Fax: 816-363-0130
labconco@labconco.com
www.labconco.com
Laboratory equipment and supplies.
Mark Schmitz, VP, Research & Engineering

5723 Lakeside Manufacturing
1977 S Allis Street
Milwaukee, WI 53207-1295
414-481-3900
Fax: 414-481-9313
Laboratory and scientific instruments, equipment, furniture and supplies.

5724 Lane Science Equipment Company
225 W 34th Street
Suite 1412
New York, NY 10122-1496
212-563-0663
Fax: 212-465-9440
Scientific equipment, technology and supplies.

5725 Lasy USA
1309 Webster Avenue
Fort Collins, CO 80524-2756
800-444-2126
Fax: 970-221-4352
Building sets that encourage children to encounter technology through problem solving activities, planning, co-operation and perseverance. Allows students to build and learn programming skills in areas of communication, construction, manufacturing and transportation.
Dave Nayak

5726 Learning Technologies
40 Cameron Avenue
Somerville, MA 02144-2404
617-628-1459
800-537-8703
Fax: 617-628-8606
starlab@starlab.com
www.starlab.com
STARLAB portable planetarium systems and the Project STAR hands-on science materials.
Jane Sadler, President

5727 Leica Microsystems EAD
PO Box 123
Buffalo, NY 14240-0123
716-686-3000
Fax: 716-686-3085
Educational microscopes for elementary through university applications.

5728 Life Technologies
7335 Executive Way
Frederick, MD 21704
240-379-4328
800-952-9166
Fax: 716-774-6727
learnlifetechnologies.com
Supplier of biology and cell culture products.

5729 Lyon Electric Company
1690 Brandywine Avenue
Chula Vista, CA 91911
619-216-3400
Fax: 619-216-3434
lyonelec@acts.com
www.lyonelectric.com
Electrical tabletop incubators for science classrooms and tabletop animal intensive care units, hatchers and brooders.
Caroline Vazquez, Sales Manager
Jose Madrigal, Marketing Manager

5730 Magnet Source
747 S Gilbert Street
Castle Rock, CO 80104
303-688-3966
888-525-3536
Fax: 303-688-5303
magnet@magnetsource.com
www.magnetsource.com
Educational magnetic products and magnetic toys designed to stimulate creativity and encourage exploration of science with fun magnets. Kits include experiments, fun games, activities and powerful magnets. Moo Magnets, rare earth magnets, horseshoes, and bulk magnets.
Jim Madsen, Sales Manager

5731 Meiji Techno America
Meiji Techno America
5895 Rue Ferrari
San Jose, CA 95138
408-226-3454
800-832-0060
Fax: 408-226-0900
info@meijitechno.com
www.meijitechno.com
A full line of elementary, secondary, grade school and college-level microscopes and accessories.
James J Dutkiewicz, General Manager

5732 Metrologic Instruments
Coles Road at Route 42
Blackwood, NJ 08012
800-436-3876
Fax: 856-228-0653
Manufactures low-power lasers and laser accessories for the classroom, a range of helium-neon lasers, a modulated VLD laser, optics lab, sandbox holography kit, speed of light lab, optics bench system and digital laser power meter, as well as a selection of pin carriers, mounting pins, lenses and mirrors. Sponsors the Physics Bowl, a yearly national physics competition for high school students by the American Association of Physics Teachers.
Betty Williams

5733 Modern School Supplies
PO Box 958
Hartford, CT 06143
860-243-2329
Fax: 800-934-7206
sales@modernss.com
www.modernss.com
Products for hands-on science education.

5734 Mohon International
1600 Porter Court
Paris, TN 38242
731-642-4251
Fax: 731-642-4262
Classroom equipment and supplies, directed at the scientific classroom and laboratory.

5735 Museum Products Company
84 Route 27
Mystic, CT 06355-1226
860-536-6433
800-395-5400
Fax: 860-572-9589
museumprod@aol.com
www.museumproducts.net
Field guides, rock collections, environmental puzzles, posters, charts, books, magnets, magnifiers, microscopes and other lab equipment. Also weather simulators, physics demonstration, games, toys in space, animal track replicas and fossils. Free catalog.
John Bannister, President

5736 Nalge Company
PO Box 20365
Rochester, NY 14602-0365
585-586-8800
800-625-4327
Fax: 585-586-8987
Plastic labware and safety products for the scientific classroom.

5737 National Instruments
6504 Bridge Point Parkway
Austin, TX 78730-5039
512-794-0100
Fax: 512-683-5794
Laboratory/scientific instruments.

5738 National Optical & Scientific Instruments
6508 Tri-County Pkwy.
Schertz, TX 78154
210-590-7010
800-275-3716
Fax: 210-590-1104
natlopt@sbcglobal.net
www.nationaloptical.com
Wholesale distributor of national comppound, stero and digital miocroscopes for K-12 and college.
Michael Hart, Sales Manager
Cynthia Syverson-Mercer, Director

5739 Ohaus Corporation
19-A Chapin Road
Pine Brook, NJ 07058
973-377-9000
800-672-7722
Fax: 973-593-0359
www.distribuidoramuller.com.ar/equipos/ohaus/traveler.pdf
Scientific supplies and equipment for the classroom or laboratory.

5740 PASCO Scientific
10101 Foothills Boulevard
Roseville, CA 95747-7100
916-786-3800
800-772-8700
Fax: 916-786-7565
jbrown@pasco.com
ww.pasco.com
US manufacturers of physics apparatus and probe warer that enable teachers to improve science literacy and meet the standards
Justine Brown, Copy Writer

5741 Quest Aerospace Education
350 E 18th Street
Yuma, AZ 85364
602-595-9506
Fax: 520-783-9534
A complete line of model rockets and related teaching materials.

5742 Resources for Teaching Elementary School Science
National Academy Press
Arts & Industries Bldg Room 1201
900 Jefferson Drive SW
Washington, DC 20560-0403
202-287-2063
Fax: 202-287-2070
outreach@nas.edu
www.si.edu
Resource guides for elementary, middle school, and high school science teachers. Annotated guides to hands-on, inquiry-centered curriculum materials and sources of help in teaching science from kindergarten through sixth grades. Produced by the National Science Resources Center.
National Science Resources Center, Author
Douglas Lapp, Executive Director

5743 Rheometrics
1 Possumtown Road
Piscataway, NJ 08854-2100
732-560-8550
Laboratory/science supplies and equipment.

5744 SARUT
107 Horatio Street
New York, NY 10014-1569
212-691-9453
fair.mingluji.com/SARUT_INC
Science and nature-related educational tools.

5745 Safe-T-Rack Systems
4325 Dominguez Road
Suite A
Rocklin, CA 95677
916-632-1121
Fax: 916-632-1173
www.safe-t-racksystems.com
Laboratory furniture, safety storage containers and equipment.

5746 Sargent-Welch Scientific Company
PO Box 92912
Rochester, NY 14692-9012
847-459-6625
800-727-4368
Fax: 800-676-2540
www.sargentwelch.com
Models, books and instruments for the scientific classroom.

5747 Science Instruments Company
6122 Reisterstown Road
Baltimore, MD 21215-3423
410-358-7810
Develops, manufactures and markets unique hands-on programs in biotechnology, biomedical instrumentation, telecommunications, electronics and industrial controls.

5748 Science Source
86475 Gene Lasserre Blvd.
Yulee, FL 32097
904-225-5558
800-875-3214
Fax: 904-225-2228
info@sciencefirst.com
www.thesciencesource.com
Design technology books, teacher resource and student books on design and technology, design technology materials, equipment and supplies used in the construction of design challenges.
Michelle Winter, Sales/Marketing Support
Rudolf Graf, President

5749 Science for Today & Tomorrow
1840 E 12th Street
Mishawaka, IN 46544
574-258-5397
Fax: 574-258-5594
Hands-on science activities packaged for K-3 students.

5750 Scientific Laser Connection, Incorporated
5021 N 55th Avenue
Suite 10
Glendale, AZ 85301-7535
623-939-6711
877-668-7844
Fax: 623-939-3369
sales@slclaser.com
www.slclasers.com
Laser education modules.
Don Morris, President
Travis Gatrin, Service

5751 **Shain/Shop-Bilt**
509 Hemlock Street
Philipsburg, PA 16866-2937
814-342-2820
Fax: 814-342-6180
Laboratory casework and cabinets.

5752 **Sheldon Lab Systems**
PO Box 836
Crystal Springs, MS 39059-0836
601-892-2731
Fax: 601-892-4364
Laboratory casework and technical equipment for K-12, college and university level.

5753 **Skilcraft**
CRAFT House Corporation
328 N Westwood Avenue
Toledo, OH 43607-3317
419-537-9090
Fax: 419-537-9160
Microchemistry sets.

5754 **Skullduggery Kits**
624 S B Street
Tustin, CA 92780-4318
800-336-7745
Fax: 714-832-1215
Social studies kits offers hands-on learning, art projects, complete lesson plans, authentic replicas, and challenging products designed for small groups of students with increasing levels of difficulty.

5755 **Skulls Unlimited International**
10313 S Sunnylane
Oklahoma City, OK 73160
405-794-9300
800-659-SKUL
Fax: 405-794-6985
sales@skullsunlimited.com
www.skullsunlimited.com
Leading supplier of specimen supplies to the educational community.

Jay Villemarette, President

5756 **Society of Automotive Engineers**
400 Commonwealth Drive
Warrendale, PA 15086-7511
724-776-4841
877-606-7323
Fax: 724-776-5760
info@sae.org
www.sae.org
Award-winning science unit for grades 4-6.

Jamie Ferguson, Development Officer
Lori Gatmaitan, Director

5757 **Southern Precision Instruments Company**
3419 E Commerce Street
San Antonio, TX 78220-1322
210-212-5055
800-417-5055
Fax: 210-212-5062
spico@flash.net
www.flash.net/spico
Microscopes and microprojectors for grades K-1-K-12 and college levels. Stereo and compound microscopes, along with CCTV color systems.

Victor Spiroff, VP/General Manager

5758 **Southland Instruments**
17741 Metzler Lane
Unit A
Huntington Beach, CA 92647-6246
714-847-5007
Fax: 714-893-3613
Microscopes.

5759 **Spectronics Corporation**
956 Brush Hollow Road
Westbury, NY 11590
516-333-4840
800-274-8888
Fax: 800-491-6868
info@spectroline.com
www.spectroline.com
Laboratory and scientific classroom equipment, hardware and shelving.

Gloria Blusk, Manager Customer Service
Vincent McKenna, Publicist

5760 **Spitz**
700 Brandywine Drive
Chadds Ford, PA 19317
610-459-5200
Fax: 610-459-3830
spitz@spitzinc.com
www.spitzinc.com
Offers scientific and laboratory instruments and accessories.

Jon Shaw, President/ CEO
Paul Dailey, CFO

5761 **Swift Instruments**
1190 N 4th Street
San Jose, CA 95112-4946
408-293-2380
Educational microscopes and other laboratory instruments.

5762 **TEDCO**
498 S Washington Street
Hagerstown, IN 47346-1596
765-489-4527
800-654-6357
Fax: 765-489-5752
sales@tedcotoys.com
www.tedcotoys.com
Bill Nye Extreme Gyro, Prisms, Educational Toys Solar Science Kit.

Raplh Teetor, Founder
Marjorie Teetor, Owner

5763 **Telaire Systems**
6489 Calle Real
Goleta, CA 93117-1538
805-964-1699
Fax: 805-964-2129
Laboratory instruments and hardware.

5764 **Tooltron Industries**
103 Parkway
Boerne, TX 78006
830-249-8277
800-293-8134
Fax: 830-755-8134
easykut@gvtc.com
www.tooltron.com
Scientific hardware and laboratory equipment, including instruments and accessories. School scissors and craft supplies.

Thomas Love, Owner/VP Marketing

5765 **Triops**
PO Box 11369
Pensacola, FL 32524
850-479-4415
800-200-3466
Fax: 850-479-3315
triopsinc@aol.com
www.triops.com
Classroom activities and kits in environmental, ecological and biological sciences.

Dr. Eugene Hull, President
Peter Bender, Office Manager

5766 **Trippense Planetarium Company**
Science First
86475 Gene Lasserre Blvd.
Yulee, FL 32097
904-225-5558
800-875-3214
Fax: 904-225-2228
info@sciencefirst.com
www.sciencefirst.com
Astronomy and earth science models and materials, including the Trippense planetarium, Elementary planetarium, Copernican and Ptolemic solar systems, Milky Way model, Explore Celestial Globes and the patented top quality educational astronomy models since 1905.

Kris Spors, Customer Service Manager
Nancy Bell, President

5767 **Unilab**
967 Mabury Road
San Jose, CA 95133
800-288-9850
Fax: 408-975-1035
unilab@richnet.net
www.unilabinc.com
Designs and manufactures products for teaching science and technology.

Gerald A Beer, VP

5768 **Vibrac Corporation**
16 Columbia Drive
PO Box 840
Amherst, NH 03031
603-882-6777
Fax: 603-886-3857
vibrac@concentric.net
www.vibrac.com
Scientific instruments and hardware.

5769 **Wild Goose Company**
5181 S 300 W
Murray, UT 84107-4709
801-466-1172
Hands-on science kits for elementary-aged students 3 and up and resource books for all levels of general science.

5770 **Wildlife Supply Company**
86475 Gene Lasserre Blvd.
Yulee, FL 32097
904-225-9889
800-799-8115
Fax: 904-225-2228
goto@wildco.com
www.wildco.com
Aquatic sampling equipment including Fieldmaster Field Kits, Water Bottle Kits, Secchi Disks, line and messengers and a NEW Mini Ponar bottom grab. Also, a variety of professional Wildco bottom grabs, water bottles, plankton nets, hand corers and other materials.

Aaron Bell, Product Manager
Bruce Izard, Customer Service Manager

5771 **WoodKrafter Kits**
PO Box 808
Yarmouth, ME 04096-0808
207-846-3722
Fax: 207-846-1019
Science kits, hands-on curriculum-based science kits for ages 4 and up, classroom packs, supplies and science materials also available.

Sports & Playground Equipment

5772 **American Playground Corporation**
6406 Production Drive
Anderson, IN 46013-9408
765-642-0288
800-541-1602
Fax: 765-649-7162

sales@american-playgroud.com
www.american-playground.com
Playground equipment and supplies.

Julie Morson, Inside Sales Manager
Marty Bloyd, General Manager

5773 American Swing Products
9120 Double Diamond Parkway
Suite 1062
Reno, NV 89521
800-433-2573
800-433-2573
Fax: 775-883-2384
play@americanswing.com
www.americanswing.com
Producer of playground equipment and products such as swing seats, swing hangers, tire swivels, slides and more. Materials used include stainless steel and carbon steel.

Susan Simon, President
Karen Gonzalez, Office Manager

5774 BCI Burke Company
660 Van Dyne Road
PO Box 549
Fond Du Lac, WI 54936-0549
920-921-9220
800-266-1250
Fax: 920-921-9566
pr@bciburke.com
www.bciburke.com
Playground equipment.

5775 Backyard Dreams
Backyard Dreams Denver
5370 N Broadway
Denver, CO 80216
303-868-9916
info@backyard-dreams.com
www.backyard-dreams.com
Produces playground equipment such as AlleyOop Trampolines and Redwood Playsets.

Joey Delmore, Owner

5776 Belson Manufacturing
111 N River Road
North Aurora, IL 60542-1396
800-323-5664
Playground equipment.

5777 Colorado Time Systems
1551 E 11th Street
Loveland, CO 80537
970-667-1000
800-279-0111
Fax: 970-667-5876
sales@coloorадotimes.com
www.coloradotime.com
Been the system of choice for sports timing and scoring. Has a timing system for almost every sport including swimming, basketball, football, baseball, track, soccer and most others. Has a wide variety of displays ranging from fixed digit scoreboards to animation LED boards to fullcolor video displays and ribbon boards.

Randy Flint, Sr Sales Representative
Rick Connell, CDS Sales Manager

5778 Constructive Playthings
Action For Children
1227 E 119th Street
Grandview, MO 64030-1178
312-823-1100
www.actforchildren.org/
Playground, recreational and indoor fun equipment for children grades PreK-3.

5779 Creative Outdoor Designs
142 Pond Drive
Lexington, SC 29073-8009
803-957-9259
Fax: 803-957-7152
Playground equipment.

5780 Curtis Marketing Corporation
2550 Rigel Road
Venice, FL 34293-3200
941-493-8085
Playground equipment.

5781 GameTime
150 PlayCore Dr. SE
Fort Payne, AL 35967
256-845-5610
800-235-2440
Fax: 256-845-9361
info@gametime.com
www.gametime.com
Playground equipment.

Doris Dellinger, Marketing Service Manager

5782 Gared Sports
9200 E 146th Street
Building A
Noblesville, IN 46060
317-774-9840
800-325-2682
Fax: 314-421-6014
koughton@garedholdings.com
www.garedsports.com
Gared offers a full line of basketball, volleyball, soccer and lacrosse equipment, as well as bleachers and seating for various types of indoor and outdoor facilities.

Laura St. George, VP, Sales & Marketing
Mark Cicotte, Team Dealer Sales Manager

5783 Gerstung/Gym-Thing
6308 Blair Hill Lane
Baltimore, MD 21209-2102
800-922-3575
Physical education mats, matting and floorcoverings.

5784 Grounds for Play
1050 Columbia Dr.
Carrollton, GA 30117
817-477-5482
800-552-7529
Fax: 817-477-1140
jimdempsey@groundsforplay.com
www.groundsforplay.com
Playground equipment, flooring, floorcoverings, play eviroment design, lanscape architecure, insatllation, and safety insepection.

Jim Dempsey, Senior VP
Emily Smith, Office Manager

5785 Iron Mountain Forge
One Iron Mountain Drive
Farmington, MO 63640
800-325-8828
Fax: 573-760-7441
Playground equipment.

5786 JCH International
978 E Hermitage Road NE
Rome, GA 30161-9641
800-328-9203
Coverings, mats and physical education matting.

5787 Jaypro
Jaypro Sports
976 Hartford Tpke
Waterford, CT 06385
860-447-3001
800-243-0533
Fax: 860-444-1779
info@jaypro.com
www.jaypro.com
Sports equipment.

Linda Andels, Marketing Manager
Bill Wild, VP Sales/Marketing

5788 Kidstuff Playsystems
5400 Miller Avenue
Gary, IN 46403-2844
800-255-0153
Fax: 219-938-3340
rhagelberg@kidstuffplaysystems.com
www.fun-zone.com
Preschool and grade school playground equipment, Health Trek Fitness Course, park site furnishings.

Dick Hagelberg, CEO

5789 Kompan
7717 New Market Street
Olympia, WA 98501
360-943-6374
800-426-9788
Fax: 360-943-5575
www.kompan.com
Unique playgrond equipment.

Tom Grover, Marketing Director

5790 LA Steelcraft Products
1975 Lincoln Avenue
Pasadena, CA 91103
626-798-7401
800-371-2438
Fax: 626-798-1482
info@lasteelcraft.com
www.lasteelcraft.com
Manufacturer of quality athletic, park and playground equipment for schools, parks and industry. Features indoor/outdoor fiberglass furniture, court and field equipment, site furnishings, bike racks, flagpoles, baseball and basketball backstops.

James D Holt, President
John C Gaudesi, COO

5791 Landscape Structures
PO Box 198
601 7th St.
Delano, MN 55328-0198
763-972-3391
888-4FU-LSI
Fax: 763-972-3185
www.playlsi.com
Playground equipment.

Bill Jannott, Board Member
Rick Jannott, Board Member

5792 MMI-Federal Marketing Service
PO Box 241367
Montgomery, AL 36124-1367
334-286-0700
Fax: 334-286-0711
Playground equipment, sports timers, clocks and school supplies.

5793 Matworks
Division of Janitex Rug Service Corporation
11900 Old Baltimore Pike
Beltsville, MD 20705-1265
800-523-5179
Fax: 301-595-0740
info@thematworks.com
www.thematworks.com
Mats, matting and floorcoverings for entrances, gymnasiums, and all other facilities where the potential for slip and fall exists.

Robert Burman, Chairman
Robert B. Collins, CEO and President

5794 Miracle Recreation Equipment Company
878 E Highway 60
PO Box 420
Monett, MO 65708-0420
417-235-6917
888-458-2752
Fax: 417-235-6816
www.miracle-recreation.com
Playground and recreation equipment.

5795 National Teaching Aids
401 Hickory Street
PO Box 2121
Fort Collins, CO 80522
970-484-7445
800-289-9299
Fax: 970-484-1198
bevans@amep.com
www.amep.com
Learning math, alphabet, and geography skills is easy with our Clever Catch Balls. These colorful 24-inch inflatable vinyl balls provide an excellent way for children to practice math, alphabet and geography skills. Excellent learning tool in organized classroom activities, on the playground, or at home.

Michael Warring, President
Candace Coffman, National Sales Manger

5796 New Braunfels General Store International
3150 Interstate H 35 S
New Braunfels, TX 78130-7927
830-620-4000
Fax: 830-620-0598
Playground equipment, supplies and classroom supplies.

5797 Outback Play Centers
1280 W Main Street
Sun Prairie, WI 53590-0010
608-825-2140
800-338-0522
Fax: 608-825-2114
www.outbackplaycenters.com
Playground equipment.

Jack Garczynskl, President

5798 Playground Environments
22 Old Country Road
PO Box 578
Quogue, NY 11959
516-653-5465
800-662-0922
Fax: 516-653-2933
peplay@mindspring.com
www.ncsu.edu
Designs and manufactures integrated play and recreational areas for children, providing them with new experiences in a safe, accessible, educationally supportive and fun environment.

Suzanne Crocitto, Contact
Claire Dudley, Ass. Landscape Architect

5799 Playworld Systems
1000 Buffalo Road
Lewisburg, PA 17837-9795
570-522-9800
800-233-8404
Fax: 570-522-3030
info@PlayworldSystems.com
www.playworldsystems.com
Playground and recreational equipment.

Mathew M. Miller, Chief Executive Officer

5800 Porter Athletic Equipment Company
Porter Athletic Equipment Company
601 Mercury Drive
Champaign, IL 61822-9648
217-367-8438
800-637-3090
Fax: 217-367-8440
porter@porter-ath.com
www.porterathletic.com
Athletic equipment, floorcoverings, mats and supplies.

Dan Morgan, VP Sales/Marketing

5801 Quality Industries
130 Jones Boulevard
PO Box 765
La Vergne, TN 37086-0765
800-745-8613
Fax: 615-793-2347
sales@qualityind.com
www.qualityind.com
Recycled plastic park and playground equipment.

5802 Real ACT Prep Guide
Peterson's, A Nelnet Company
Princeton Pike Corporate Center
2000 Lenox Drive PO Box 67005
Lawrenceville, NJ 08648
609-896-1800
800-338-3282
Fax: 609-896-4531
Familiarizes students with the test's format, reviews skills, and provides the all-important practice that helps build confidence.

621 pages
ISBN: 0-768919-75-4

Elaine Bender, Mark Weinfeld, et al., Author

5803 Recreation Creations
PO Box 955
Hillsdale, MI 49242-0955
517-439-0300
800-888-0977
Fax: 517-439-0303
rec-creations.com
Heavy duty park and playground equipment for school and public use. Equipment is both colorful and safe.

DC Shaneour

5804 Roppe Corporation
1602 N Union Street
Fostoria, OH 44830-1158
419-435-8546
800-537-9527
Fax: 419-435-1056
sales@roppe.com
www.roppe.com
Floorcoverings, mats and matting.

5805 Safety Play
10460 Roosevelt Boulevard
#295
St Petersburgh, FL 33716-3818
727-522-0061
888-878-0244
Fax: 727-522-0061
safetyplay@mindspring.com
www.safetyplay.net
Playground and recreational accident consultants. Experienced in insepctions, design, expert witness. Creators of Playground Safety Signs as required to be on the playground.

Scott Burmon, Contact

5806 Sport Court
5445 W Harold Gatty Dr.
Salt Lake City, UT 84116-1504
801-972-0260
800-421-8112
Fax: 801-401-3504
info@sportcourt.com
www.sportcourt.com
Sport flooring, portable flooring, outdoor-indoor educational institutions.

Finnika Lundmark, Director Marketing

5807 Sport Floors
6651 Reese Road
PO Box 1478
Memphis, TN 38133-1478
901-452-9492
800-881-6440
Fax: 901-452-9250
www.sportsfloorsinc.com
Sport floors, flooring, floorcoverings, mats and matting.

5808 Sportmaster
6031 Broad Street Mall
Pittsburgh, PA 15206-3009
412-243-5100
Fax: 412-731-3052
Playground equipment, sports timers and clocks.

5809 Stackhouse Athletic Equipment Company
1450 McDonald St NE
Salem, OR 97301-6949
503-363-1840
800-285-3640
Fax: 503-363-0511
bob@stackhouseathletic.com
www.stackhouseathletic.com
Volleyball, soccer, football and baseball hardgoods.

Greg Henshaw, VP Marketing

5810 Swedes Systems - HAGS Play USA
2180 Stratingham Drive
Dublin, OH 43016-8907
Fax: 614-889-9026
Playground safety consultants.

5811 Ultra Play Systems
Parek Stuff
1675 Locust Street
Red Bud, IL 62278-1000
800-458-5872
www.ultraplay.com
Playground and recreational equipment.

5812 Wausau Tile
PO Box 1520
Wausau, WI 54402-1520
715-359-3121
800-388-8728
Fax: 715-355-4627
wtile@wausautile.com
www.wausautile.com
Playground and recreation equipment.

Rob Geurink, Furnishings Division Manager

5813 Wear Proof Mat Company
2156 W Fulton Street
Chicago, IL 60612-2392
312-733-4570
Fax: 800-322-7105
www.notracks.com
Mats, matting and floorcoverings for the physical education class.

5814 Wolverine Sports
745 State Circle
Ann Arbor, MI 48108-1647
734-761-5690
800-521-2832
Fax: 800-654-4321
www.wolverinesports.com
Playground, sports and physical fitness furniture and equipment.

General

5815 A-V Online
National Information Center for Educational Media
4725 Indian School Road NE
Suite 100
Albuquerque, NM 87198-8640
505-265-3591
800-926-8328
Fax: 505-256-1080
info-request@nicem.com
www.nicem.com
A CD-ROM that contains over 400,000 citations with abstracts, to non-print educational materials for all educational levels. It is available on an annual subscription basis and comes with semiannual updates.
Lisa Savard, Marketing and Sales

5816 AASA Daily News
American Association of School Administrators
1615 Duke Street
Suite 700
Alexandria, VA 22314-1730
703-528-0700
Fax: 703-841-1543
info@aasa.org
www.aasa.org
Daniel A. Domenech, Executive Director
Sharon Adams-Taylor, Associate Executive Director

5817 ACT
2201 N Dodge Street
PO Box 168
Iowa City, IA 52243-0168
319-337-1000
Fax: 319-339-3021
www.act.org
Help individuals and organizations make informed decisions about education and work.
Jon L. Erickson, President
Jon Whitmore, Chief Executive Officer

5818 AMX Corporation
3000 Research Drive
Richardson, TX 75243-5481
469-624-7400
800-222-0193
Fax: 972-624-7153
www.amx.com
Multiple products, equipment and supplies.
Rashid Skaf, President

5819 ASC Electronics
2 Kees Pl
Merrick, NY 11566-3625
516-623-3206
Fax: 516-378-2672
High tech multimedia system. Completely software driven, featuring interactive video, audio and data student drills. Novell network. System includes CD-ROM, laserdisc and digital voice card technology.

5820 Accelerated Math
Renaissance Learning
2911 Peach Street
PO Box 8036
Wisconsin Rapids, WI 54495-8036
715-424-3636
800-338-4204
Fax: 715-424-4242
answers@renaissance.com
www.renaissance.com
Math management software that helps teachers increase student math achievement in grades 1 through calculus.
John J. Lynch, Chief Executive Officer
Mary T. Minch, EVP, Finance & CFO

5821 Accelerated Reader
Renaissance Learning
2911 Peach Street
PO Box 8036
Wisconsin Rapids, WI 54495-8036
715-424-3636
800-338-4204
Fax: 715-424-4242
answers@renaissance.com
www.renaissance.com
Software program that helps teachers manage literature-based reading.
John J. Lynch, Chief Executive Officer
Mary T. Minch, EVP, Finance & CFO

5822 Actrix Systems
6315 San Ignacio Avenue
San Jose, CA 95119-1202
800-422-8749
Fax: 509-744-2851
Computer networks.

5823 Allen Communications
5 Triac Center
5th Floor
Salt Lake Cty, UT 84180
801-537-7800
Fax: 801-537-7805
Software.

5824 Alltech Electronics Company
602 Garrison Street
Oceanside, CA 92054-4865
760-721-0093
Fax: 760-732-1460
Computer hardware.

5825 Anchor Pad Products
Anchor Pad Products
11105 Dana Circle
Cypress, CA 90630-5133
714-799-4071
800-626-2467
Fax: 714-799-4094
kris@anchor.com
www.anchorpad.com
Cost effective physical security systems for computers, computer peripherals and office equipment.
Kris Jones, Marketing Associate
Melanie Rustle, Marketing Associate

5826 Apple Computer
1 Infinite Loop
Cupertino, CA 95014-2084
408-996-1010
800-692-7753
Fax: 408-974-2786
www.apple.com
Offers a wide selection of software systems and programs for the student, educator, professional and classroom use. Program areas include reading, science, social studies, history, language arts, mathematics and more.
Tim Cook, CEO
Angela Ahrendts, Senior Vice President

5827 Ascom Timeplex
400 Chestnut Ridge Road
Woodcliff Lake, NJ 07675-7604
201-646-1571
Fax: 201-646-0485
Computer networks.

5828 BGS Systems
128 Technology Drive
Waltham, MA 02453-8909
617-891-0000
Facility planning and evaluation software.

5829 BLS Tutorsystems
5153 W Woodmill Drive
Wilmington, DE 19808-4067
800-545-7766
Computer software.

5830 Broderbund Software
500 Redwood Boulevard
Novato, CA 94947-6921
319-395-9626
800-223-8941
Fax: 319-395-7449
Educational software.

5831 Bulletin Boards for Busy Teachers
www.geocities.com/VisionTeacherwv/
Bulletin board tips and education links.

5832 CASL Software
6818 86th Street E
Puyallup, WA 98371-6450
206-845-7738
Educational software for schools and institutions in all areas of interest.

5833 CCU Software
PO Box 6724
Charleston, WV 25362-0724
800-843-5576
Fax: 800-321-4297
Educational software.

5834 CCV Software
5602 36th Street S
Fargo, ND 58104-6768
800-541-6078
Fax: 800-457-6953
All varieties of software and hardware for the educational fields of interest including language arts, math, social studies, science, history and more.

5835 Cambridge Development Laboratory
86 West Street
Waltham, MA 02451-1110
781-890-4640
800-637-0047
Fax: 781-890-2894
customerservice@edumatch.com
www.edumatch.com
Meets all educational software needs in language arts, mathematics, science, social studies early learning and special education.

5836 Chariot Software Group
2645 Financial Court
Suite 1
San Diego, CA 92117-3002
858-270-0202
800-242-7468
Fax: 858-270-2027
info@chariot.com
www.chariot.com
Academic software.

5837 Child's Play Software
5785 Emporium Square
Columbus, OH 43231-2802
614-833-1836
Fax: 614-833-1837
Markets learning games and creative software to schools.

5838 Claris Corporation
5201 Patrick Henry Drive
Santa Clara, CA 95054-1171
800-747-7483
Educational software.

5839 Classroom Direct
20200 E 9 Mile Road
Saint Clair Shores, MI 48080-1791
800-777-3642
Fax: 800-628-6250
Full line of hardware and software for Mac, IBM and Apple II at discount prices.

5840 College Board/SAT
45 Columbus Avenue
New York, NY 10023-6992
217-713-8000
877-999-7723
Fax: 646-607-2881
SpringBoard@collegeboard.org
www.collegeboard.org
David Coleman, President and CEO
Jeremy Singer, Chief Operating Officer

5841 Computer City Direct
2000 Two Tandy Center
Fort Worth, TX 76102
800-538-0586
Hardware.

5842 Computer Friends
10200 SW Eastridge Street
Portland, OR 97225
800-547-3303
Fax: 503-643-5379
cfi@cfriends.com
www.cfriends.com
Computer hardware, software and networks, printer support products.
Jimmy Moglia, Marketing Director

5843 Data Command
PO Box 548
Kankakee, IL 60901-0548
800-528-7390
Educational software.

5844 Davidson & Associates
19840 Pioneer Avenue
Torrance, CA 90503-1690
800-545-7677
Educational software and systems.

5845 Dell Computer Corporation
9595 Arboretum Boulevard
Austin, TX 78759-6337
512-338-4400
800-388-1450
Hardware.

5846 Digital Divide Network
19 Duncan Street
Suite 505
Toronto, ON
416-977-9363
Fax: 416-352-1898
www.digitaldivide.net
Knowledge to help everyone succeed in the digital age.
Adam Clare, Lead Editor
Kristen Jordan, Project Coordinator

5847 Digital Equipment Corporation
Educational Computer Systems Group
2 Iron Way
Marlboro, MA 01752
Computer hardware and networks.

5848 Don Johnston Developmental Equipment
26799 West Commerce Drive
Suite 115
Volo, IL 60073-1190
847-740-0749
800-999-4660
Fax: 847-740-7326
info@donjohnston.com
donjohnston.com
Develops educational software for special needs. Products include the Ukandu Series for emergent literacy, LD, ESL, students Co-Writer and Write: OutLoud.

5849 Edmark Corporation
6727 185th Avenue NE
PO Box 97021
Redmond, WA 98052-5037
425-556-8400
800-691-2986
Fax: 425-556-8430
Markets educational software.

5850 EduQuest, An IBM Company
PO Box 2150
Atlanta, GA 30301-2150
Offers exciting educational software in various fields of interest including history, social studies, reading, math and language arts, as well as computers.

5851 Educational Activities
1937 Grand Avenue
P.O. Box 87
Baldwin, NY 11510-2889
516-223-4666
800-797-3223
Fax: 516-623-9282
www.edact.com
Supplemental materials.
Carol Stern, VP
Roni Hofbauer, Office Manager

5852 Educational Resources
1550 Executive Drive
Elgin, IL 60123-9330
630-213-8681
Fax: 630-213-8681
The largest distributor of educational software and technology in the education market. Features Mac, APL, ligs and IBM school versions, lab packs, site licenses, networking and academic versions. Hardware, accessories and multimedia is also available.

5853 Electronic Specialists Inc.
75 Middlesex Ave
PO Box 389
Natick, MA 01760-0004
508-655-1532
810-225-4876
Fax: 508-653-0268
clipprx@ix.netcom.com
www.electspec.com
Computer and electronics, including networks and computer systems plus transformers and power converters.
Frank Stifter, President

5854 Environmental Systems Research Institute
380 New York Street
Redlands, CA 92373-8100
909-793-2853
888-377-4575
www.esri.com
Demonstrates a full range of geographic information system software products.
Jack Dangermond, Founder

5855 Eversan Inc.
34 Main Street
Whitesboro, NY 13492
315-736-3967
800-383-6060
Fax: 315-736-4058
sales&eversan.com
www.eversan.com
Announcement boards, scoreboards and classroom supplies, sports timers and clocks.
Michelle Moran, Sales Representative
Elsa Kucherna, Sales Representative

5856 GAMCO Educational Materials
PO Box 1911
Big Spring, TX 79721-1911
800-351-1404
Publishes software in math, language arts, reading, social studies, early childhood education and teacher tools for Macintosh, Apple, IBM and MS-DOS compatible.

5857 Games2Learn
1936 East Deere Avenue
Suite 120
Santa Ana, CA 92705
714-751-4263
888-713-4263
Fax: 714-442-0869
CustomerService@Games2Learn.com
www.games2learn.com
Develops, markets and provides children and adults with quality, fun, interactive educational products designed to increase their skills in language, math and general knowledge. Creator of The Phonics Game.

5858 Gateway Learning Corporation
665 3rd Street
Suite 225
San Francisco, CA 94107
800-544-7323
www.hop.com
Develop and sell innovative educational products for home learning.
Lionel Guerin, Chairman
Frederic Gagey, Chief Financial Officer

5859 Greene & Associates
1100 NW Loop 410
Suite 700
San Antonio, TX 78213-5857
210-366-8768
Fax: 210-366-0198
greeneandassociates.com
Educational software.
Barbara A. F. Greene, Chief Executive Officer

5860 Grolier
PO Box 1716
Danbury, CT 06816
800-371-3908
Fax: 800-456-4402
Multimedia software for education.

5861 Hubbell
Kellems Division
40 Waterview Drive
Shelton, CT 06378-2604
475-882-4800
800-288-6000
Fax: 203-882-4852
www.hubbell-wiring.com
Computer hardware, software, systems, and networks.

5862 Indiana Cash Drawer
1315 S Miller Street
Shelbyville, IN 46176-2424
317-398-6643
Fax: 317-392-0958
Computer peripherals.

5863 Ingenuity Works
325 Howe St
Suite 407
Vancouver, BC 98230-9702
604-484-8053
800-665-0667
Fax: 604-431-7996
information@ingenuityworks.com
www.ingenuityworks.com
Publishes K-12 educational software for classroom use. Key curriculum areas include

geography, keyboarding, and math (K-9). Network and district licenses are available.

Brigetta , Director Marketing

5864 Instructional Design
WIDS-Worldwide Instructional Design System
1 Foundation Circle
Waunakee, WI 53597-8914
608-849-2411
800-677-9437
Fax: 608-849-2468
info@wids.org
www.wids.org
Performance-based curriculum design software and professional devlopment tools. Use software to write curriculum, implement standards, create assessments, and build in learning styles. Excellent upfront online design tool.

Leah Osborn, Director
Terri Johnson, Associate Director

5865 Instructor
Scholastic
555 Broadway
New York, NY 10012-3919
212-343-6100
800-724-6527
Fax: 212-343-4801
www.scholastic.com/instructor
Edited for teachers, curriculum coordinators, principals and supervisors of primary grades through junior high school.

Monthly

Dick Robinson, President and CEO
Lynn Diamond, Advertising Director

5866 Jostens Learning Corporation
4920 Pacific Heights Boulevard
Suite 500
San Diego, CA 92121
858-587-0087
800-521-8538
Fax: 858-587-1629
Educational software and CD-ROM's.

5867 Journey Education
5212 Tennyson Pkwy.
Suite 130
Plano, TX 75024
800-876-3507
Fax: 972-245-3585
sales@journeyed.com
www.journeyed.com
Software for students.

5868 Ken Cook Education Systems
9929 W Silver Spring Drive
PO Box 25267
Milwaukee, WI 53225-1024
414-466-6060
800-362-2665
Fax: 414-466-0840
BoatingManuals@kencook.com
www.boatpubs.com
Classroom curricular software.

5869 Kensington Microwave
2855 Campus Drive
San Mateo, CA 94403-2510
650-572-2700
800-535-4242
Fax: 650-572-9675
www.kensington.com
Computer systems and peripherals.

5870 Lapis Technologies
1100 Marina Village Parkway
Alameda, CA 94501-1043
510-748-1600
Computer peripherals.

5871 Laser Learning Technologies
120 Lakeside Avenue
#3240
Seattle, WA 98122-6533
800-722-3505
Educational CD-ROM's and interactive videos.

5872 Lawrence Productions
6146 West Main St
Suite A
Kalamazoo, MI 49009-9687
269-903-2395
800-421-4157
Fax: 616-665-7060
sales@lpi.com
www.lpi.com
More than 60 proven software titles for PreK to adult, covering problem solving, early learning and leadership skills.

5873 Learning Company
500 Redwood Boulevard
Novato, CA 94947
415-881-8000
800-825-4420
Fax: 877-864-2275
www.sphinxaur.com/learning-company/novato-ca/
School educational software.

5874 Library Corporation, Sales & Marketing
1501 Regency Way
Woodstock, GA 30189-5487
770-591-0089
Computer networks.

Gary Kirk, Branch Manager

5875 LinkNet
Introlink
1400 E Touhy Avenue
Suite 260
Des Plaines, IL 60018-3339
847-390-8700
Fax: 847-390-9435
Computer networks.

5876 MECC
6160 Summit Drive N
Minneapolis, MN 55430-2100
800-685-MECC
www.mecc.co
Educational software, hardware and overhead projectors.

5877 Mamopalire of Vermont
PO Box 24
Warren, VT 05674
802-496-4095
888-496-4094
Fax: 802-496-4096
bethumpd@wcvt.com
www.bethumpd.com
Provides quality educational books and board games for the whole family.

Rebecca Cahilly, President
Glenn Cahilly, CEO

5878 McGraw-Hill Education
PO Box 182605
Columbus, OH 43218
800-338-3987
Fax: 800-953-8691
hep_customer-service@mheducation.com
www.mheducation.com
Provides educational software for PreK-12 and higher education teaching as well as reference and trade publications for the medical, business and engineering professions.

David Levin, President & CEO
Angelo T DeGenaro, Chief Information Officer

5879 Microsoft Corporation
1 Microsoft Way
Redmond, WA 98052-8300
425-882-8080
Fax: 425-936-7329
www.microsoft.com
One of the largest publishers and distributors of educational software, hardware, equipment and supplies.

Bill Gates, Founder
Paul Allen, Founder

5880 Misty City Software
11866 Slater Avenue NE
Kirkland, WA 98034-4103
206-820-2219
800-795-0049
Fax: 425-820-4298
Publisher of Grade Machine, gradebook software for Macintosh, MS-DOS, and Apple II. Grade Machine used by thousands of teachers in hundreds of schools worldwide. Grade Machine has full-screen editing, flexible reports, large class capacity, excellent documentation and reasonable cost.

Roberta Spiro, Business Manager
Russell Cruickshanks, Sales Manager

5881 NCR Corporation
1700 S Patterson Boulevard
Dayton, OH 45479-0002
937-445-5000
Computer networks, systems (large, mini, micro, medium and personal).

5882 NetLingo The Internet Dictionary
PO Box 627
Ojai, CA 93024
805-794-8687
Fax: 805-640-3654
info@netlingo.com
www.NetLingo.com
A smart-looking and easy to understand dictionary of 3000 internet terms, 1200 chat acronyms, and much more. NetLingo is a modern reference book fo international students, educators, industry professionals, and online businesses and organizations.

528 pages Paperback
ISBN: 0-9706396-7-8

Erin Jansen, Author
Erin Jansen, Author/Publisher

5883 NetZero
2555 Townsgate Road
Westlake Village, CA 91361-2650
805-418-2020
Fax: 805-418-2075
www.netzero.com
Free Internet access.

5884 New Century Education Corporation
220 Old New Brunswick Road
P.O. Box 43052
Upper Montclair, NJ 07043
732-981-0820
800-833-6232
Fax: 732-981-0552
jharrison@ncecorp.com
www.newcenturyeducation.org
ILS systems.

Janice Harrison, Marketing Representative

5885 OnLine Educator
faldo.atmos.uiuc.edu/CLA
A comprehensive archive of educational sites with useful search capabilities and descriptions of the sites.

5886 Online Computer Systems
1 Progress Drive
Horsham, PA 19044-3502

CD-ROM networking, CD-ROM titles and CD-ROM tower units.

5887 PBS TeacherSource
2100 Crystal Drive
Arlington, VA 22202
www.pbslearningmedia.org
Includes an on-line inventory of more than 1,000 free lesson plans, teacher guides and other activities designed to complement PBS television programs.

5888 Parent Link
Parlant Technology
290 N University Avenue
PO Box 50240
Provo, UT 84605
801-373-9669
800-735-2930
Fax: 801-373-9697
info@parlant.com
www.parlant.com
School to home communication systems allow scholls to create messages — emails, telephone calls, web content, printed letters, about student information, grades, attendance, homework, and activities. Also provides inbound access via internet and telephone.
George Joeckel, Marketing

5889 Peopleware
1621 114th Avenue SE
Suite 120
Bellevue, WA 98004-6905
425-454-6444
Fax: 425-454-7634
peopleware.com
Classroom curricular software.

5890 Phillips Broadband Networks
100 Fairgrounds Drive
Manlius, NY 13104-2437
315-682-9105
Fax: 315-682-1022
Computer networks.

5891 Pioneer New Media Technologies
2265 E 220th Street
Long Beach, CA 90810-1639
800-LAS-R ON
www.pioneerelectronics.com
DRM-604X CD-ROM mini-changer, world's fastest CD-ROM drive for multimedia. Also offers special packages including The Mystery Reading Bundle, CLD-V2400RB which includes the CLD-V2400 LaserDisc player, educator's remote control, UC-V109BC barcode reader and membership in the Pioneers in Learning Club and The Case of the Missing Mystery Writer videodisc from Houghton Mifflin.

5892 Polaroid Corporation
575 Tech Square
Cambridge, MA 02139
781-386-2000
Fax: 781-386-3925
Computer repair, hardware and peripherals, equipment and various size systems.

5893 Power Industries
37 Walnut Street
Wellsley Hills, MA 02181
800-395-5009
Educational software.

5894 Quetzal Computers
1708 E 4th Street
Brooklyn, NY 11223-1925
718-375-1186
Computer systems and networks, peripherals and hardware.

5895 RLS Groupware
Realtime Learning Systems
2700 Connecticut Avenue NW
Washington, DC 20008-5330
202-483-1510
Classroom curricular software.

5896 Radio Shack
100 Throckmorton Street
Suite 1800
Ft. Worth, TX 76102
817-415-3700
Fax: 817-415-2335
Computer networks and peripherals.
Laura Moore, Sr VP Public Relations

5897 Rose Electronics
10850 Wilcrest Drive
Suite 900
Houston, TX 77099-3599
281-933-7673
Fax: 281-933-0044
Computer peripherals and hardware.

5898 STAR Reading & STAR Math
Renaissance Learning
2911 Peach Street
PO Box 8036
Wisconsin Rapids, WI 54495-8036
715-424-3636
800-338-4204
Fax: 715-424-4242
answers@renaissance.com
www.renaissance.com
Computer-adaptive tests provide instructional levels, grade equivalents and percentile ranks.
John J. Lynch, Chief Executive Officer
Mary T. Minch, EVP, Finance & CFO

5899 SVE & Churchill Media
6677 N NW Highway
Chicago, IL 60631
773-775-9550
800-829-1900
Fax: 773-775-5091
slucas@svemedia.com
www.svemedia.com
Has brought innovative media technology into america's pre-K through high school classrooms. By producing programs to satisfy state curriculum standards, SVE consistantly provides educators with high-quality and award-winning videos, CD-ROMs, eLMods, and DVDs in science, social studies, English and health/guidance.
Sarah M Lucas, Communications Coordinator
Kelli Campbell, VP Marketing/Development

5900 School Cruiser
Time Cruiser Computing Corporation
9 Law Drive
3rd Floor, Ottawa, Ontario
Canada K1N 7G1
613-562-9847
877-450-9482
Fax: 613-562-4768
www.epals.com
School Cruiser provides online tools and resources to promote academic and community interaction. It lets you access and share school calenders, lesson plans, homework assignments, announcements and other school related information.

5901 School Specialty
PO Box 1579
Appleton, WI 54912-1579
1-419-589-1600
888-388-3224
Fax: 888-388-6344
orders@schoolspecialty.com
www.schoolspecialty.com
A classroom superstore that features the leading suppliers of educational products and services such as Crayola, 3M, Elmer's and more. The company also provides their own brands among educational resources such as instructional materials, playground equipment, art supplies, office supplies, furniture and more.
Joseph Yorio, President & CEO
Laura Vartanian, SVP, Human Resources

5902 SchoolHouse
www.encarta.msn.com/schoolhouse/maincontent.asp
The Encarta Lesson Collection and other educational resources.

5903 Seaman Nuclear Corporation
7315 S 1st Street
Oak Creek, WI 53154-2095
414-762-5100
Fax: 414-762-5106
Facility planning and evaluation software.
Scott C. Seamen, President
Todd Seaman, Vice President

5904 Skills Bank Corporation
7104 Ambassador Road
Suite 1
Baltimore, MD 21244-2732
800-451-5726
Educational manufacturing company offering computer and electronic resources, software, programs and systems focusing on home education and tutoring.

5905 Sleek Software Corporation
2404 Rutland Drive,Suite 600
P.O. Box 170100
Austin, TX 78717
512-833-0352
800-337-5335
Fax: 512-833-9718
info@sleek.com
www.sleek.com
Specializes in Algorithm-Based tutorial and test-generating software.

5906 Smartstuff Software
PO Box 82284
Portland, OR 97282-0284
415-763-4799
800-671-3999
Fax: 877-278-7456
info@smartstuff.com
www.smartstuff.com
Foolproof Security is a dual platform desktop security product that prevents unwanted changes to the desktop and a product line for the internet that protects browser settings, filters content, and allows guided activities.

5907 Society for Visual Education
1345 W Diversey Parkway
Chicago, IL 60614-1249
773-775-9550
Fax: 800-624-1678
Educational software dealing specifically with special education.

5908 SofterWare
132 Welsh Road
Suite 140
Horsham, PA 19044-2217
215-628-0400
800-220-4111
Fax: 215-628-0585
info@softerware.com
www.softerware.com
Offers software, support and administrative solutions to four markets: childcare centers,

public and private schools, nonprofit organizations and institutions, and camps.

Nathan Relles, President and Co-Founder
Douglas Schoenberg, CEO/ Co-Founder

5909 SpecialNet
GTE Educational Network Services
5525 N Macarthur Boulevard
Suite 320
Irving, TX 75038-2600
214-518-8500
800-927-3000
Fax: 757-852-8277
Contains news and information on trends and developments in educational services and programs. Databases, bulletin boards, school packages, student/teacher packages, online magazines, distance learning, vocational education, school health, educational laws, and more.

5910 Student Software Guide
800-874-9001
journey.com
Discounts on a variety of software materials.

5911 Sun Microsystems
2550 Garcia Avenue
#6-13
Mountain View, CA 94043-1100
714-643-2688
800-555-9786
Fax: 650-934-9776
Computer networks and peripherals.

5912 Sunburst/Wings for Learning
101 Castleton Street
Pleasantville, NY 10570-3405
914-747-3310
800-338-3457
Fax: 914-747-4109
Educational materials, including software, print materials, videotapes, videodisc and interdisciplinary packages.

5913 Support Systems International Corporation
136 S 2nd Street
Richmond, CA 94804-2110
510-234-9090
800-777-6269
Fax: 510-233-8888
Sales@FiberMailbox.com
www.fiberopticcableshop.com
Fiber optic patch cables, converters, and switches.

Ben Parsons, General Manager

5914 Surfside Software
PO Box 1112
East Orleans, MA 02643-1112
800-942-9008
Educational software.

5915 Target Vision
1160 Pittsford Victor Road
Suite K
Pittsford, NY 14534-3825
800-724-4044
Fax: 585-248-2354
TVI DeskTop expands your show directly to desktop PC utilizing existing LANS. View information by topics or as a screen saver. Features: graphic importing, VCR interface, advanced scheduling and more.

5916 Teacher Universe
5900 Hollis Street
Suite A
Emeryville, CA 94608
877-248-3224
Fax: 415-763-4917
info@teacheruniverse.com
www.teacheruniverse.com
Creates technology-rich solutions for improving the quality of life and work for teachers worldwide.

5917 Technolink Corporation
2609 Reach Rd
Williamsport, PA 17701-4004
570-323-9057
Fax: 814-693-5901
sales@technolinkcorp.com
www.technolinkcorp.com
Computer systems and electronics.

5918 Tom Snyder Productions
100 Talcott Avenue
Watertown, MA 02472-5703
800-342-0236
Fax: 800-304-1254
dealer@tomsnyder.com
www.tomsnyder.com
Educational CD-ROM products and Internet services for schools.

Tom Synder, Founder

5919 Tripp Lite
1111 West 35th Street
Chicago, IL 60610-4117
773-869-1111
international@tripplite.com
www.tripplite.com
Peripherals, hardware and computer systems.

Moti Shulak, Sales Representative

5920 True Basic
12 Commerce Avenue
West Lebanon, NH 03784-1669
800-436-2111
Fax: 603-298-7015
john@truebasic.com
www.truebasic.com
Educational software.

5921 U.S. Public School Universe Database
U.S. National Center for Education Statistics
555 New Jersey Avenue NW
Washington, DC 20001-2029
202-219-1335
85,000 public schools of elementary and secondary levels, public special education, vocational/technical education and alternative education schools.

5922 USA CityLink Project
USA CityLink Project
Floppies for Kiddies
4060 Highway 59
Mandevelle, LA 70471
985-898-2158
Fax: 985-892-8535
www.usacitylink.com
Collects used and promotional disketts from the masses for redistribution to school groups and nonprofits throughout the county.

Carol Blake, Contact

5923 Unisys
PO Box 500
Blue Bell, PA 19424-0001
215-986-3501
Fax: 215-986-3279
www.unisys.com
A full line of computers (sizes ranging from mini/micro to medium/large and personal).

Peter Altabef, President and CEO
Quincy Allen, Chief Marketing Officer

5924 Ventura Educational Systems
910 Ramona Avenue
P.O. Box 1622
Arroyo Grande, CA 93421-1622
805-473-7383
800-336-1022
Fax: 805-556-4469
sales@venturaes.com
www.venturaes.com
Publishers of curriculum based educational software for all grade levels, specializing in interactive math and science software. Programs include teacher's guide with student worksheets.

Fred Ventura, Software Developer
Marne Ventura, Teacher

5925 Viziflex Seels
406 N Midland Ave
Saddle Brook, NJ 07663-6895
201-487-8080
800-627-7752
Fax: 201-487-3266
info@viziflex.com
www.viziflex.com
Peripherals, hardware and electronics, floorcoverings, mats and matting.

5926 Waterford Institute
1590 E 9400 S
Sandy, UT 84093-3009
801-349-2200
800-767-9976
Fax: 801-572-1667
www.waterford.org
Produces children's educational software for math and reading.

Dustin Heuston, Chairman
Benjamin Heuston, President and COO

5927 Web Connection
Education Week
6935 Arlington Road
Bethesda, MD 20814
301-280-3100
800-346-1834
ads@epe.org
www.edweek.org
Information about education suppliers.

Larry Berger, Chairman
Gina Burkhardt, Secretary

5928 Wiremold Company
60 Woodlawn Street
W Hartford, CT 06110-2383
800-243-8421
Computer networks and peripherals.

5929 Wisconsin Technical College System Foundation
4622 University Avenue
PO Box 7874
Madison, WI 53707-7874
608-266-1207
800-821-6313
Fax: 608-266-1690
foundation@wtcsf.tec.wi.us
www.wtcsystem.edu
Interactive videodiscs, self-paced instruction or with barcodes. Students learn faster, become more motivated and retain more information. Math, algebra and electronics courseware are also available.

Drew Petersen, President
John Schwantes, Vice President

5930 Word Associates
3226 Robincrest Drive
Northbrook, IL 60062-5125
847-291-1101
Fax: 847-291-0931
microlrn@aol.com
www.wordassociates.com

Software tutorials featuring lessons in question format, with tutorial and test mode. 15 titles include Math SAT, 2 English SAT; US Constitution Tutor; Phraze Maze; Geometry: Planely Simple, Concepts and Proofs, Right Triangles; Life Skills Math; Algebra; Reading: Myths and More Myths, Magic and Monsters; Economics; American History. Windows, Macintosh, CD's or disks.

Software

Myrna Helfand, President
Sherry Azaria, Marketing

5931 Ztek Company
PO Box 967
Lexington, KY 40588-1768
859-281-1611
800-247-1603
Fax: 859-281-1521
cs@ztek.com
www.ztek.com
Offers physics multimedia lessons on CD-ROM, DVD, videodisc and videotape. Also, carries Pioneer New Media DVD and videodisc players as well as Bretford Manufacturing's line of audio-visual furniture.

5932 ePALS.com
Classroom Exchange
World's largest online classroom community, connecting over 3 million students and teachers through 41,044 profiles.

5933 ericir.syr.edu
AskERIC
Ask a question about education and receive a personalized e-mail response in two business days.

5934 gsn.bilkent.edu.tr
Ballad of an EMail Terrorist
Global SchoolNet Foundation
One pitfall of the internet is danger of vulgarity and/or obscenity to a child via e-mail.

5935 suzyred.home.texas.net
The Little Red School House
Offers sections on music, writing, quotes, web quests, jokes, poetry, games, activities and more.

5936 www.FundRaising.Com
FundRaising.Com
800-443-5353
Internet fundraising company.

5937 www.abcteach.com
P.O. Box 1217
Union Lake, MI 48387-1217
Fax: 248-493-6565
support@abcteach.com
Offers ideas and activities for kids, parents, students and teachers. Features section on many topics in education, including writing, poetry, word searches, crosswords, games, maps, mazes and more.

5938 www.abctooncenter.com
ABC Toon Center
This family orientated site offers games, cartoons, storybook, theater, information stations and more. This site is open to children of differnt languages. Can be translated into Italian, French, Spanish, German and Russian.

5939 www.americatakingaction.com
America Taking Action
Provides every school with a free, 20 page website with resources for teachers, parents, students and the community. Created entirely by involved parents, teachers and community leaders as a public service.

5940 www.awesomelibrary.org
Awesome Library
Organizes the Web with 15,000 carefully reviewed resources, including the top 5 percent in education. Offers sections of mathematics, science, social studies, english, health, physical education, technology, languages, special education, the arts and more. Features a section involved with today's current issues facing our world, like pollution, gun control, tobacco, and other changing 'hot' topics. Site can be browsed in English, German, Spanish, French or Portuguese.

5941 www.bigchalk.com
Big Chalk-The Education Network
800-521-0600
Fax: 734-997-4268
Educational web site tailored to fit teachers' and students' needs.

5942 www.brunchbunch.org
Brunch Bunch
The foundation names all of the grants it makes after teachers who have demonstrated excellence. The foundation regularly makes significant grants to aid teachers' efforts.

5943 www.busycooks.com
BusyCooks.com
A hit with home economics teachers, enjoying free recipes and online cooking shows. Tapping into the experience of thousands to nuture your culinary creativity.

5944 www.chandra.harvard.edu
Chandra X-ray Observatory Center
60 Garden Street
Cambridge, MA 2138
617-496-7941
Fax: 617-495-7356
cxcpub@cfa.harvard.edu
Find teacher-developed, classroom-ready materials based on results from the Chandra mission. Classroom-ready activities, interactive games, activities, quizzes, and printable activities which will keep students absorbed with interest.

5945 www.cherrydale.com
Cherrydale Farms
707 N. Valley Forge Rd.
Lansdale, PA 19446
800-333-4525
CDFinfo@Cherrydale.com
Website offers company information, fund raising products and information, online mega mall, card shop, career opportunities and much more. Produces fine chocolates and confections. Many opportunities for schools to raise funds with various Cherrydale programs.

5946 www.cleverapple.com
Education Station
E-mail: info@cleverapple.com
Offers links to many sites involved with education.

5947 www.edhelper.com
edhelper.com
Keeps you up to date with the latest educational news.

5948 www.education-world.com
Education World
75 Mill St.
Colchester, CT 6415
800-227-0831
webmaster@educationworld.com
Features and education-specific search engine with links to over 115,000 sites. Offers monthly reviews of other educational web sites, and other original content on a weekly basis.

5949 www.eduverse.com
Software developer building core technologies for powering international distance education. Features an online distance education engine, product information, news releases and more.

5950 www.efundraising.com
efundraising.com
C/O FedEx Trade Networks
156 Lawrence Paquette Ind'l Drive, PMW#
Champlain, NY 12919
866-825-2921
Fax: 877-275-8664
online@fundraising.com
Provides non-profit groups with quality products, low prices and superior service. Helping thousands of schools, youth sports teams and community groups reach their fundraising goals each year.

5951 www.embracingthechild.com
Embracing the Child
E-mail: pk@embracingthechild.org
Educational resource for teachers and parents that provides a structural resource for home and classroom use, lesson planning, as well as a child-safe site, for children's research, classroom use and homework fulfillment.

5952 www.enc.org
ENC Learning Inc.
1585 Central Ave.
Ste C-5 #293
Summerville, SC 29483
614-378-4567
Fax: 843-832-2063
info@goENC.com
For math and science teachers-anywhere in the K-12 spectrum. This organization contains a wealth of information, activities, resources, and demonstrations for the sciences and math.

5953 www.englishhlp.com
English Help
E-mail: englishhlpr@hotmail.com
This page is a walk through of Microsoft Power Point. The goal is to show in a few simple steps how to make your own website. Created by Rebecca Holland.

5954 www.expage.com/Just4teachers
Just 4 Teachers
The ultimate website for educators! Teaching tips, resources, themeunits, search engines, classroom management and sites for kids.

5955 www.fraboom.com
Fraboom
FR Productions, LLC
1427 NW Raleigh St
Portland, OR 97209
503-208-2315
support@fraboom.com
This site's tools let you specify areas within your state's standards and search for a list of 'Flying Rhinoceros' lessons that meet your criteria. Offers other information sources for teachers and students.

5956 www.globalschoolnet.org
Global SchoolNet Foundation
270 N. El Camino Real
Ste. 395
Encinitas, CA 92024
760-635-0001
helper2014@globalschoolnet.org
Connects teachers, administrators, and parents with options and possibilities the Internet has to offer the schools of the world.

Dr. Yvonne Marie Andres, President
John St. Clair, Vice President

5957 www.gradebook.org/
The Classroom
Dedicated to the students and teachers of the world.

5958 www.homeworkspot.com
HomeworkSpot
A free online homework resource center developed by educators, students, parents and journalists for K-12 students. It simplifies the search for homework help, features a top-notch reference cetner, current events, virtual field trips and expeditions, extracurricular activities and study breaks, parent and teacher resources and much more.

5959 www.iearn.org
iEARN USA
Utilizes projects for students ages 6 through 19. Projects are concerned with the environment as well as arts, politics, and the health and welfare of all the Earth's citizens.

5960 www.jasonproject.org
Jason Project
Founded in 1989 as a tool for live, interactive programs for students in the fourth through eighth grades. Annual projects are funded through a variety of public corporations and governmental organizations.

Dr. Eleanor Smalley, EVP/ COO
Sean Smith, SVP/ CTO

5961 www.k12planet.com
Chancery Software
Chancery Software is announcing a new school to home extension that will provide student information systems to give parents, students, and educators access to accurate information about students in one, easy-to-use website.

5962 www.kiddsmart.com
Institute for Child Development
E-mail: dcornell@kiddsmart.com
The ICD develops educational materials and resources designed to facilitate children's social and emotional development. Offers the previous materials as well as research summaries, lesson plans, training, workshops, games, multi-cultural materials and other resources to teachers, educational centers, parents, counselors, corporations, non-profits and others involved in the child-care professions.

5963 www.lessonplansearch.com
Lesson Plan Search
220 lesson plans from cooking to writing.

5964 www.lessonplanspage.com
HotChalk
1999 S. Bascom Avenue
Suite 1020
Campbell, CA 95008
888-468-2336
Fax: 408-608-1679
support@hotchalk.com
A collection of over 1,000 free lesson plans for teachers to use in their classrooms. Lesson plans are organized by subject and grade level.

5965 www.library.thinkquest.org
Think Quest Library of Entries
The Arti FAQS 2100 Project is designed to predict how art will influence our lives in the next hundred years. Students can use available data to make reasonable predictions for the future.

5966 www.ncspearson.com
NCS Pearson
E-mail: info@ncs.com
NCS Pearson is at the forefront of the education space with curriculum, contant, tools, assessment, and interface to enterprise systems

5967 www.negaresa.org
Northeast Georgia RESA
E-mail: keith.everson@negaresa.org
For teachers, electronic web-based grade book aplication eGRader 2000. Many educational resource links as well has discussion groups, a news and events section, and even links to online shopping.

Dr. Keith Everson, Executive Director
Debra Wallace, Business/ Finance Director

5968 www.netrover.com/~kingskid/108.html
Room 108
An educational activity center for kids. Offers lots of fun for children with educational focus; like songs, art, math, kids games, children's stories and much more. Sections with pen pal information, puzzles, crosswords, teachers store, spelling, kids sites, email, music, games and more.

5969 www.pcg.cyberbee.com
IwayNet Communications
614-294-9292
support@iwaynet.net
Offered to classes all over the world via the internet. Your class commits to exchanging picture postcards with all other participants. Appropriate for all ages, for public and private schools, for youth groups and for home- schools.

5970 www.pitt.edu
EdIndex
724-244-4939
poole@pitt.edu
A web resource for teachers and students, offers course information, MS Office tutorials, personal and professional pages, and more.

5971 www.riverdeep.net
Riverdeep Interactive Learning
617-351-5316
800-426-657
Sales_Support@hmhco.com
Riverdeep's interactive science, language and math arts programs deliver high quality educational experiences.

5972 www.safedayeducation.com
Safe Day Education
E-mail: info@safedayeducation.com
The leader in bully prevention and street proofing education for kids; safe dating preparation programs for teens; and re-empowerment and assault prevention training for women.

5973 www.safekids.com/child_safety.htm
SafeKids.Com
E-mail: larry@safekids.com
Cyberspace is a fabulous tool for learning, but some of it can be exploitative and even criminal.

Larry Magid, Founder/ Editor

5974 www.sdcoe.k12.ca.us
Researches a coral reef and creates a diorama for The Cay by Theodore Taylor.

5975 www.shop2gether.com
Collective Publishing Service
We are committed to helping all schools buy better by shopping together. Building upon a scalable, dynamic procurement platform and group buying technology, we also provide a unique ecommerce system, delivering next generation procurement services over the Internet.

5976 www.spaceday.com
Space Day
Program engineered to build problem-solving and teamwork skills.

5977 www.specialednews.com
Special Education News
E-mail: info@specialednews.com
Consists of breaking news stories from Washington and around the country. These stories are complied together in the Special Education News letter is sent via e-mail once a week.

5978 www.straightscoop.org
Straight Scoop News Bureau
SSNB increases the frequency of anti-drug themes and messages in junior high and high school student media.

5979 www.tcta.org
Texas Classroom Teachers Association
PO Box 1489
Austin, TX 78767-1489
512-477-9415
888-879-8282
Fax: 512-469-9527
Compromised of Texas educators, provides interest for teachers everywhere. Education laws and codes are presented here.

Terrill Q. Littlejohn, President
Teresa Koehler, President-Elect

5980 www.teacherszone.com
TeachersZone.Com
Lesson plans, free stuff for teachers, contests, sites for kids, conferences and workshops, schools and organizations, job listings, products for school.

5981 www.teacherweb.com
TeacherWeb
PO BOX 06290
Chicago, IL 60606
TeacherWeb, your free personal website that's as easy to use as the bulletin board in your classroom. This site offers a secure, password-protected service.

5982 www.teachingheart.com
Teaching is A Work of Heart
Chock-full of ideas, projects, motivational thoughts, behavior ideas.

5983 www.thelearningworkshop.com
Learning Workshop.com
Services for teachers, students, and parents. For teachers online gradebooks and grade tracking, students can check their grades online, parents enjoy articles written expressly for them and a tutor search by zip code.

5984 www.tutorlist.com
TutorList.com
Offers information on tips on how to find and choose a tutor, what a tutor does, educational news and more.

5985 www.worksafeusa.org
WorkSafeUSA
Addresses the alarming injury and death rates experienced by America's adolescent workers. This non-profit site publishes and distributes A Teen Guide to Workplace Safety, available in English and Spanish.

5986 **www1.hp.com**
Hewlett-Packard Development Company
3000 Hanover Street
Palo Alto, CA 94304-1185
650-857-1501
Compaq is one of the leading corporations in educational technology, working on developing solutions that will connect students, teachers and the community.

Administration

5987 **ASQC**
611 E Wisconsin Avenue
Milwaukee, WI 53202-4695
800-248-1946
Fax: 414-272-1734
Business and administrative software.

5988 **Anchor Pad**
Anchor Pad Products
11105 Dana Cir
Cypress, CA 90630-5133
714-799-4071
800-626-2467
Fax: 714-799-4094
anchor@anchor.com
Computer and office security
Caroline Jones, COO
Melanie Ruste, Sales/Marketing Associate

5989 **Applied Business Technologies**
55 S.E. 2nd Avenue
Delray Beach, FL 33444
561-272-1232
800-683-6590
Fax: 610-359-9420
info@appliedcorp.com
Computer networks and administrative software.

5990 **AskSam Systems**
PO Box 1831
Perry, FL 32348
850-584-6590
800-800-1997
Fax: 850-584-7481
info@asksam.com
Business and administrative free form database software.
Dottie Sheffield, Sales Manager

5991 **Autodesk Retail Products**
1725 220th Street
Suite C101
Bothell, WA 98021-8809
425-487-2233
Fax: 425-486-1636
Administrative and business software.

5992 **Avcom Systems**
250 Cox Lane
PO Box 977
Cutchogue, NY 11935-1303
631-734-5080
800-645-1134
Fax: 631-734-7204
Supplies for making and mounting transparencies. Products includes economy and self-adhesive mounts; transparent rolls and sheets; markers, pens and cleaners; thermo, computer graphics and plain-paper copier transparency films and laminating supplies.
Joseph K Lukas

5993 **Bobbing Software**
67 Country Oaks Drive
Buda, TX 78610-9338
800-688-6812
Administrative software and systems.

5994 **Bull HN Information Systems**
285 Billerica Road
Chelmsford, MA 01824
978-294-6000
Fax: 978-244-0085
Computer networks, computers (large, medium, micro and mini), and supplies.

5995 **Bureau of Electronic Publishing**
745 Alexander Road
#728
Princeton, NJ 08540-6343
973-808-2700
Administrative software, hardware and systems.

5996 **CRS**
17440 Dallas Parkway
Suite 120
Dallas, TX 75287-7307
800-433-9239
Administrative software and systems.

5997 **Campus America**
900 E Hill Avenue
Suite 205
Knoxville, TN 37915-2580
865-523-4477
877-536-0222
Fax: 617-492-9081
Computer supplies, equipment, systems and networks.

5998 **Century Consultants**
150 Airport Road
Suite 1500
Lakewood, NJ 08701-3309
732-363-9300
Fax: 732-363-9374
marketing@centuryltd.com
Develops, markets, and services Oracle based web-enabled Management software, STAR_BASE, for school districts K-12.

5999 **Computer Resources**
1037 Calef Highway
Barrington, NH 03825-0060
603-664-5811
888-641-9922
Fax: 603-664-5864
The Modular Management System for Schools is a school administrative software system designed to handle all student record keeping and course scheduling needs. A totally integrated modular system built around a central Student Master File. Additional modules handle student scheduling, grades, attendance and discipline reporting.
Raymond J Perreault, VP Marketing
Robert W Cook, National Sales Manager

6000 **Computer Supply People, The**
N93 W14636 Whittaker Way
Menomonee Falls, WI 53051-1629
262-251-5511
800-242-2090
Fax: 262-251-4737
medmgt@computersupplypeople.com
www.computersupplypeople.com
Computer supplies, equipment and systems, Koss headphones.
John Schimberg, Education Sales

6001 **Cyborg Systems**
2 N Riverside Plaza
Chicago, IL 60606-2600
312-454-1865
Administrative and business software programs.

6002 **Diskovery Educational Systems**
1860 Old Okeechobee Road
Suite 105
West Palm Beach, FL 33409-5281
561-683-8410
800-331-5489
Fax: 561-683-8416
info@diskovery.com
www.diskovery.com
Computer supplies, equipment, and various size systems.

6003 **Doron Precision Systems**
Doron Precision Systems
150 Corporate Drive
PO Box 400
Binghamton, NY 13902-0400
607-772-1610
Fax: 607-772-6760
sales@doronprecision.com
www.doronprecision.com
Business and classroom curriculum software. Driving Simulation Systems and Entertainment Simulation Systems.

6004 **Educational Data Center**
180 De La Salle Drive
Romeoville, IL 60446-1895
800-451-7673
Fax: 815-838-9412
Administration software.

6005 **EnrollForecast: K-12 Enrollment Forecasting Program**
Association of School Business Officials Int'l
11401 N Shore Drive
Reston, VA 20190-4232
703-478-0405
Fax: 703-478-0205
A powerful planning tool that helps project student enrollment.
Peg D Kirkpatrick, Editor/Publisher
Robert Gluck, Managing Editor

6006 **Epson America**
3840 Kilroy Airport Way
Long Beach, CA 90806
800-289-7766
Webmaster@ea.epson.com
www.epson.com
Computer repair and peripherals.
John Lang, President/ CEO
Keith Kratzberg, SVP, Sales & Marketing

6007 **FMJ/PAD.LOCK Computer Security Systems**
520 W. Central Ave.
Brea, CA 92821
714-990-3218
800-872-9562
Fax: 714-990-5409
dealerinquiry@fmjpadlock.com
www.fmjpadlock.com
Computer peripherals, supplies and equipment.
Tom Separa

6008 **Geist**
Geist Manufacturing
1821 Yolande Avenue
Lincoln, NE 68521-1835
402-474-3400
800-432-3219
Fax: 402-474-4369
products@geistmfg.com
www.geistmfg.com
Power distribution for racks, cabinets and data centers.
Terri Rockeman, Customer Service Supervisor

6009 **Global Computer Supplies**
11 Harbor Park Drive
Port Washington, NY 11050-4622
516-625-6200
800-446-9662

Fax: 516-484-8533
www.globalcomputer.com
Computer supplies, equipment, hardware, software and systems.

6010 Harrington Software
658 Ridgewood Road
Maplewood, NJ 07040-2536
201-761-5914
Administrative and business software.

6011 Information Design
7009 S Potomac Street
Suite 110
Englewood, CO 80112
303-792-2990
800-776-2469
Fax: 303-792-2378
sales@idesgninc.com
www.idesigninc.com
Administrative and business software including systems focusing on payroll, personnel, financial accounting, purchasing, budgeting, fixed asset accounting and salary administration.

6012 International Rotex
7171 Telegraph Road
Los Angeles, CA 90040-3227
800-648-1871
Computer supplies.

6013 Jay Klein Productions Grade Busters
118 N. Tejon St.
Suite 304
Colorado Springs, CO 80903
719-599-8786
Fax: 719-380-9997
support@gradebusters.com
www.gradebusters.com
A line of teacher productivity tools, the most highly recognized integrated gradebooks, attendance records, seating charts and scantron packages in K-12 education today (Mac, DOS, Windows, Apple II).

Jay A Klein, President
Angela C Wormley, Office Manager

6014 Jostens Learning Corporation
5521 Norman Center Drive
Minneapolis, MN 55437-1040
800-635-1429
The leading provider of comprehensive multimedia instruction, including hardware, software and service.

6015 MISCO Computer Supplies
1 Misco Plaza
Holmdel, NJ 07733-1033
800-876-4726
Computer supplies, networks, equipment and accessories.

6016 Mathematica
Wolfram Research, Inc.
100 Trade Centre Drive
Champaign, IL 61820-7237
217-398-0700
800-965-3726
Fax: 217-398-0747
info@wolfram.com
www.wolfram.com
Classroom curricular software and business/administrative software.

Stephen Wolfram, Founder/CEO
Jean Buck, Dir., Corp Communications

6017 MicroAnalytics
Student Transportation Systems
2300 Clarendon Boulevard
Suite 404
Arlington, VA 22201-3331
703-841-0414
Fax: 703-527-1693
Automates bus routing and scheduling for school districts with fleets of 5 to 500 buses. BUSTOPS is flexible, affordable and easy to use. Offers color maps and graphics, efficient routing, report writing, planning and more to improve your pupil transportation system.

Mary Buchanan, Sales Manager

6018 MicroLearn Tutorial Series
Word Associates
3226 Robincrest Drive
Northbrook, IL 60062-5125
847-291-1101
Fax: 847-291-0931
microlrn@aol.com
www.wordassociates.com
Software tutorials featuring lessons in question format, with tutorial and test mode. 15 titles include Math SAT, 2 English SAT; US Constitution Tutor; Phraze Maze; Geometry: Planely Simple, Concepts and Proofs, Right Triangles; Life Skills Math; Algebra; Reading: Myths and More Myths, Magic and Monsters; Economics; American History. Windows, Macintosh, CD's or disks.

Software

Myrna Helfand, President

6019 NCS Marketing
11000 Prairie Lakes Drive
Eden Prairie, MN 55344-3885
800-447-3269
Fax: 612-830-7788
www.ncspearson.com
OpScan optical mark reading scanners from NCS process data at speeds of up to 10,000 sheets per hour for improved accuracy and faster turnaround. Also provides software and scanning applications and services that manage student, financial, human resources, instructional and assessment information.

Sheryl Kyweriga

6020 National Computer Systems
11000 Prairie Lakes Drive
Minneapolis, MN 55440
800-447-3269
Fax: 952-830-8564
Administrative software and systems.

6021 Parlant Technologies
PO Box 50240
Provo, UT 84605
801-373-9669
800-735-2930
Fax: 801-373-9697
info@parlant.com
www.parlant.com
Administrative software and systems.

6022 Quill Corporation
P.O. Box 37600
Philadelphia, PA 19101-0600
847-634-4800
800-982-3400
Fax: 800-789-8955
www.quill.com
Computer and office supplies and equipment.

6023 Rauland Borg
1802 West Central Road
Mount Prospect, IL 60056
847-679-0900
Fax: 800-217-0977
www.rauland.com
Administrative software and systems.

Kidder's Rauland-Borg, President/ CEO
Peipert , SVP, Finance

6024 Rediker Administration Software
2 Wileraham Road
Hampden, MA 01036-9685
413-566-3463
800-213-9860
Fax: 413-566-2274
APSupport@rediker.com
www.rediker.com
School administrative software for the teaching professional.

Rich Rediker, CEO
Andrew Anderlonis, President

6025 Scantron Corporation
1313 Lone Oak Road
Eagan, MN 55121
949-639-7500
800-722-687
www.scantron.com
Computer peripherals, administrative software and services.

6026 SourceView Software International
PO Box 578
Concord, CA 94522-0578
925-825-1248
Classroom curricular, business and administrative software.

6027 Systems & Computer Technology Services
4 Country View Road
Malvern, PA 19355-1408
610-647-5930
Fax: 610-578-7778
Administrative and business software programs and services.

6028 Trapeze Software
8360 East Via de Ventura
Suite L-200
Scottsdale, AZ 85258
480-627-8400
Fax: 480-627-8411
info@trapezegroup.com
www.trapezegroup.com
Computerized bus routing, boundary planning and redistricting software and services, and AVL (automatic vehicle locator software).

Clint Rooley, Director of Sales

6029 University Research Company
7200 Wisconsin Avenue
Suite 600
Bethesda, MD 20814
301-654-8338
800-526-4972
Fax: 301-941-8427
www.urc-chs.com
Supplies Quiz-A-Matic electronics for quiz competitions.

Barbara N. Turner, President

6030 Velan
4153 24th Street
Suite 1
San Francisco, CA 94114-3667
415-949-9150
Administrative software and systems.

6031 WESTLAW
West Group
610 Opperman Drive
Eagan, MN 55123-1340
612-687-7000
800-937-8529
Fax: 651-687-5827
www.westlaw.com

Online service concerning the complete text of U.S. federal court decisions, state court decisions from all 50 states, regulations, specialized files, and texts dealing with education.

6032 teacherfiles.homestead.com/index~ns4
Homestead
800-986-0958
www.homestead.com
Offers sections on clip art, quotes, slogans, lesson plans, organizations, web quests, political involvement, grants, publications, special education, professional development, humor and more.

6033 www.abcteach.com
Abcteach
P.O. Box 1217
Union Lake, MI 48387-1217
Fax: 248-493-6565
support@abcteach.com
www.abcteach.com
Free printable materials for kids, parents, student teachers and teachers. Theme units, spelling word searches, research help, writing skills and much more.

6034 www.apple.com
PowerSchool
PowerSchool's web-based architecture makes it easy to learn and easy to use.

6035 www.atozteacherstuff.com
A to Z Teacher Stuff
E-mail: webmaster@atozteacherstuff.com
atozteacherstuff.com
Features quick indexes to online lesson plans and teacher resources, educational sites for teachers, articles, teacher store and more.

6036 www.awesomelibrary.org
Awesome Library
www.awesomelibrary.org
Organizes the Web with 15,000 carefully reviewed resources, including the top 5 percent in education. Offers sections of mathematics, science, social studies, english, health, physical education, technology, languages, special education, the arts and more. Features a section involved with today's current issues facing our world, like pollution, gun control, tobacco, and other changing 'hot' topics. Site can be browsed in English, German, Spanish, French or Portuguese.

6037 www.easylobby.com
HID Global
611 Center Ridge Drive
Austin, TX 78753
www.hidglobal.com
The complete electronic visitor management system.

Denis H,bert, President/ CEO
Michele DeWitt, SVP, Human Resources

6038 www.fraboom.com
FR Productions, LLC
1427 NW Raleigh St
Portland, OR 97209
503-208-2315
support@fraboom.com
fraboom.com
This site's tools let's you specify areas within your state's standards and search for a list of 'Flying Rhinoceros' lessons that meet your criteria. Offers other information sources for teachers and students.

6039 www.fundraising.com
PO BOX 305142
Nashville, TN 37230-5142
800-443-5353
filter.efr@gafundraising.com
www.fundraising.com
Internet fundraising company.

6040 www.hoagiesgifted.org
Hoagies Gifted Education Page
256 Eagleview Boulevard PMB 123
Exton, PA 19341
E-mail: webmaster@hoagiesgifted.org
www.hoagiesgifted.org
Features the latest research on parenting and educating gifted children. Offers ideas, solutions and other things to try for parents of gifted children. Sections with world issues facing children and other important social topics.

Carolyn K. Founder/ Director

6041 www.kiddsmart.com
Institute for Child Development
E-mail: dcornell@kiddsmart.com
The ICD develops educational materials and resources designed to facilitate children's social and emotional development. Offers the previous materials as well as research summaries, lesson plans, training, workshops, games, multi-cultural materials and other resources to teachers, educational centers, parents, counselors, corporations, non-profits and others involved in the child-care professions.

6042 www.nycteachers.com
NYCTeachers.com
www.nycteachers.com
Designed for NYC teachers that work within public school systems. Speaks out on controversial issues facing the broadening, funding, development, staffing and other concerns about public schools. Welcomes your suggestions and comments about the site and the issues involved.

6043 www.songs4teachers.com
O'Flynn Consulting
c/o Mary Flynn
494 St. Vincent Street
Barrie, ON L4M 7
705-728-6528
Fax: 705-728-6528
mary@songs4teachers.com
www.songs4teachers.com
Offers many resources for teachers including songs made especially for your classroom. Sections with songs and activities for holidays, seasons and more. Features books and audios with 101 theme songs for use in the classroom or anywhere children gather to sing.

6044 www.thecanadianteacher.com
The Canadian Teacher Marketplace
www.thecanadianteacher.com
Site where educators can find the latest links to free resources, materials, lesson plans, software, samples and computers. Some links are for Canadians only.

6045 www.welligent.Com
Welligent
5205 Colley Avenue
Norfolk, VA 23508
888-317-5960
info@welligent.com
www.welligent.com
A web-based software program that improves student health management and your school's finances at the same time.

Early Childhood Education

6046 Jump Start Math for Kindergartners
Knowledge Adventure
Torrance, CA
800-545-7677
www.knowledgeadventure.com
The program covers important and essential kindergarten math skills such as, writing numbers, sorting, and problem solving/following directions.

David Lord, President/ CEO
Jim Czulewicz, Chief Revenue Officer

6047 Mindplay
4400 E. Broadway Blvd.
Suite 400
Tucson, AZ 85711
520-888-1800
800-221-7911
Fax: 520-888-7904
mail@mindplay.com
www.mindplay.com
Educational software focusing on early childhood education and adult literacy.

Stacie Johnson, Communication Coordinator
Judith Bliss, Founder/ Chairwoman

6048 Nordic Software
PO Box 5403
Lincoln, NE 68505
402-489-1557
800-306-6502
Fax: 402-489-1560
info@nordicsoftware.com
www.nordicsoftware.com
Specializes in developing and publishing educational software titles. Well-known for its software titles that make it easy for children to learn while playing on the computer. Develops and publishes elementary software products for the Macintosh and Windows platforms. Products include Turbo Math Facts, Clock Shop, Coin Critters, Language Explorer and Preschool Parade, and more.

Tammy Hurlbut, Finance/Operations

6049 Personalized Software
PO Box 359
Phoenix, OR 97535
541-535-8085
800-553-2312
Fax: 541-535-8889
info@childcaremanager.com
www.childcaremanager.com
Offers a full line of childcare management and development software programs.

6050 Science for Kids
9950 Concord Church Road
Lewisville, NC 27023-9720
336-945-9000
800-572-4362
Fax: 336-945-2500
sci4kids@aol.com
www.scienceforkids.com
Developers and publishers of CD-ROM science and early learning programs for children ages 5-14; for Macintosh and Windows computers; school and home programs available.

Charles Moyer, Executive VP

Elementary Education

6051 Educational Institutions Partnership Program
Defense Information Systems Agency
Automation Resources Information
701 S Courthouse Road
Arlington, VA 22204-2199
703-607-6900
Fax: 703-607-4371
Makes available used computer equipment for donation of transfer to eligible schools, including K-12 schools recognized by the US Department of Education, Universities, colleges, Minority Institutions and nonporfit groups.

6052 Houghton Mifflin Company
222 Berkeley Street
Boston, MA 02116-3748
617-351-5000
Fax: 617-351-1106
www.hmhco.com
Offers literature-based technology products for grades K-8 including CD's Story Time, a Macintosh based CD-ROM programs for grades 1 and 2 and Channel R.E.A.D., a videodisc series for grades 3-8.
Linda K. Zecher, President/ CEO/ Director
Eric Shuman, Chief Financial Officer

6053 Kid Keys 2.0
Knowledge Adventure
800-545-7677
schoolsales@jumpstart.com
www.knowledgeadventure.com
Keyboarding for grades K-2.

6054 Kinder Magic
1680 Meadowglen Lane
Encinitas, CA 92024-5652
760-632-6693
Fax: 760-632-9995
www.kindermagic.com
Educational software for ages 4-11.
Dr. Ilse Ortabasi, President

6055 Micrograms Publishing
9934 N Alpine Road
Suite 108
Machesney Park, IL 61115-8240
800-338-4726
Fax: 815-877-1482
www.micrograms.com
Micrograms develops educational software for schools and homes.

6056 Tudor Publishing Company
17218 Preston Road
Suite 400
Dallas, TX 75252-4018
Grade level evaluation (GLE) is a computer-adaptive assessment program for elementary and secondary students.

6057 Wordware Publishing
2320 Los Rios Boulevard
#200
Plano, TX 75074-8157
214-423-0090
Fax: 972-881-9147
Publisher of computer reference tutorials, regional Texas and Christian books. Educational division produces a diagnostic and remediation software for grade levels 3-8. Content covers over 3,000 objectives in reading, writing and math. Contact publisher for dealer information.
Eileen Schnett, Product Manager

6058 World Classroom
Global Learning Corporation
PO Box 201361
Arlington, TX 76006-1361
214-641-3356
800-866-4452
An educational telecommunications network that prepares students, K-12 to use real-life data to make real-life decisions about themselves and their environment. Participating countries have included Argentina, Australia, Belgium, Canada, Denmark, France, Germany, Hungary, Iceland, Indonesia, Kenya, Russia, Lithuania, Mexico, Singapore, Taiwan, the Netherlands, the United States and Zimbabwe.

6059 k-6educators....education/k-6educators
About Education Elementary Educators

6060 www.etacuisenaire.com/index.htm
ETA hand2mind
500 Greenview Court
Vernon Hills, IL 60061
847-816-5050
800-288-9920
Fax: 800-875-9643
www.hand2mind.com
Over 5,000 manipulative-based education and supplemental materials for grades K-12.
Bill Chiasson, President
Dr. Barbara diSioudi, VP, Product Development

6061 www.wnet.org/wnetschool
wNet School
212-560-2713
www.wnet.org/education
Helps K-12 teachers by providing free standards based lesson plans, classroom activities, multimedia primers, online mentors, links to model technology schools, and more. Online workshops are also included in the WNET TV site.
Carole Wacey, Vice President
Christopher Brande, National Segment Producer

6062 www.cherrydale.com/
Cherrydale Farms
707 N. Valley Forge Rd.
Lansdale, PA 19446
800-333-4525
CDFinfo@Cherrydale.com
www.cherrydale.com
Website offers company information, fund raising products and information, online mega mall, card shop, career opportunities and much more. Produces fine chocolates and confections. Many opportunities for schools to raise funds with various Cherrydale programs.

6063 www.efundraising.com
Fundraising
C/O FedEx Trade Networks
156 Lawrence Paquette Ind'l Drive, PMW#
Champlain, NY 12919
866-825-2921
Fax: 877-275-8664
online@fundraising.com
www.efundraising.com
Provides non-profit groups with quality products, low prices and superior service. Helping thousands of schools, youth sports teams and community groups reach their fundraising goals each year.

6064 www.hoagiesgifted.org
Hoagies' Gifted Education Page
256 Eagleview Boulevard PMB 123
Exton, PA 19341
E-mail: webmaster@hoagiesgifted.org
www.hoagiesgifted.org
Features the latest research on parenting and educating gifted children. Offers ideas, solutions and other things to try for parents of gifted children. Sections with world issues facing children and other important social topics.
Carolyn K. Founder/ Director

6065 www.netrover.com/~kingskid/108.html
Room 108
www.netrover.com
An educational activity center for kids. Offers lots of fun for children with educational focus; like songs, art, math, kids games, children's stories and much more. Sections with pen pal information, puzzles, crosswords, teachers store, spelling, kids sites, email, music, games and more.

6066 www.netrox.net
Dr. Labush's Links to Learning
www.mylinkstolearning.com
General links for teachers with internet help, coloring pages, and enrichment programs.

6067 www.primarygames.com
PrimaryGames.com
E-mail: webmaster@primarygames.com
www.primarygames.com
Contains educational games for elementary students.

6068 www.usajobs.opm.gov/b1c.htm
Overseas Employment Info-Teachers

Employment

6069 Educational Placement Service
90 S Cascade
Suite 1110
Colorado Springs, CO 80903
www.teacherjobs.com
Largest teacher placement service in the U.S.

6070 Job Bulletin
American Association of School Administrators
1615 Duke Street
Alexandria, VA 22314
703-528-0700
Fax: 703-841-1543
info@aasa.org
www.aasa.org
The Job Bulletin was made to help employers and job candidates save time finding one another.
Jay Goldman, Editor
Kelly Beckwith, Project Director

6071 Teachers@Work
PO Box 430
Vail, CO 81658
970-476-5008
Fax: 970-476-1496
support@teachersatwork.com
teachersatwork.com
Electronic employment service designed to match the professional staffing needs of schools with teacher applicants.

6072 www.SchoolJobs.com
SchoolJobs.com
Provides principals, superintendents and other administrators the ability to market their job openings to a national pool of candidates, also gives educational professionals the chance to search for opportunities matching their skills.

6073 **www.aasa.org**
American Association of School Administrators
1615 Duke Street
Suite 700
Alexandria, VA 22314-1730
703-528-0700
Fax: 703-841-1543
info@aasa.org
www.aasa.org
Leadership news online.
Jay Goldman, Editor
Kelly Beckwith, Project Director

Guidance & Counseling

6074 **Alcohol & Drug Prevention for Teachers, Law Enforcement & Parent Groups**
PO Box 4656
Reading, PA 19606
610-582-2090
Fax: 610-404-0406
nodrugs@earthlink.net
www.nodrugs.com
Local organizations and international groups against drugs.

6075 **Live Wire Media**
P.O. Box 848
Mill Valley, CA 94942
415-564-9500
800-359-5437
Fax: 415-552-4087
sales@livewiremedia.com
www.livewiremedia.com/
Videos for youth guidance and character development, and teacher training.
Christine Hollander, Director Marketing

6076 **Phillip Roy Multimedia Materials**
PO Box 130
Indian Rocks Beach, FL 34635
727-593-2700
800-255-9085
Fax: 727-595-2685
ruth@philliproy.com
www.philliproy.com
Multimedia materials for use with alternative education, Chapter 1, dropout prevention, Even Start, Head Start, JTPA/PIC, special education students, at-risk students, transition to work programs. Focuses on basic skills, conflict resolution, remediation, vocational education, critical thinking skills, communication skills, reasoning and decision making skills. Materials can be duplicated networked at no cost.
Phil Padol, Consultant
Regina Jacques, Customer Support

6077 **www.goodcharacter.com**
Character Education
P.O. BOX 848
Mill Valley, CA 94942
415-564-9500
800-359-KIDS
Fax: 415-552-4087
www.goodcharacter.com
Teaching guides for k-12 character education, packed with discussion questions, assignments, and activities that you can use as your own lesson plans.

International

6078 **FHI 360**
FHI 360
359 Blackwell Street
Suite 200
Durham, NC 27701
919-544-7040
Fax: 919-544-7261
www.fhi360.org
The site provides information on international exchange, fellowshipand training.
Patrick C. Fine, Med, Chief Executive Officer
Manisha Bharti, MPH, MBA, Chief Stategy Officer

6079 **www.asce.org**
American Society of Civil Engineers
1801 Alexander Bell Drive
Reston, VA 20191
703-295-6300
800-548-2723
www.asce.org
This site lists scholarships and fellowships available only to ASCE members.
Robert D. Stevens, President
Dennis D. Truax, Treasurer

6080 **www.cie.uci.edu**
International Opportunities Program
1100 Student Services II
Irvine, CA 92697-2475
949-824-6343
Fax: 949-824-9133
studyabroad@uci.edu
www.cie.uci.edu
Valuable links for exploring opportunities for study and research abroad.
Marcella Khelif, Associate Director
Sharon Parks, Assistant Director

6081 **www.ciee.org**
Council on International Educational Exchange
300 Fore St.
Portland, ME 4101
207-553-4000
Fax: 207-553-4299
contact@ciee.org
www.ciee.org
Study abroad programs by region, work abroad opportunities, international volunteer projects and Council-administered financial aid and grant information .
Dr. James P. Pellow, President/ CEO
Jorge Barroso, Chief Information Officer

6082 **www.cies.org**
Council for International Exchange of Scholars
1400 K Street, NW
Suite 700
Washington, DC 20005
202-686-4000
Fax: 202-686-4029
Scholars@iie.org
www.cies.org
Information on the Fulbright Senior Scholar Program which is made available to Fulbright alumni,grantees, prospective applicants and public at large.
Jeff Hopper, Director
Peter VanDerwater, Director of Outreach

6083 **www.daad.org**
German Academic Exchange Service (DADD)
871 United Nations Plaza
New York, NY 10017
212-758-3223
Fax: 212-755-5780
daadny@daad.org
www.daad.org
Promotes international academic relations and contains links to research grants, summer language grants,annual grants, grants in German studies andspecial programs.
Dr. Nina Lemmens, Director
Peter Kerrigan, Deputy & Marketing Director

6084 **www.ed.gov**
US Department of Education
400 Maryland Avenue, SW
Washington, DC 20202
800-872-5327
answers.ed.gov
www2.ed.gov
This site describes programs and fellowships offered by the International Education and Graduate Programs office of the US Department of Education.
Arne Duncan, Secretary of Education
Emma Vadehra, Chief of Staff

6085 **www.finaid.org**
FinAid
A free, comprehensive, independent and ojective guide to student financial aid.
Mark Kantrowitz, Founder

6086 **www.iie.org**
Institute of International Education
P.O. Box 1020
Sewickley, PA 15143-1020
412-741-0930
Fax: 212-984-5452
iiebooks@abdintl.com
www.iiebooks.org
The largest not-for-profit international educational organization in the United States. This site provides information regarding IIE's programs, services and resources, including the Filbright Fellowship.

6087 **www.iiepassport.org**
Institute of International Education
IIE Passport: Study Abroad
1350 Edgmont Avenue Suite 1100
Chester, PA 19013
877-404-0338
Fax: 610-499-9205
iiesupport@naylor.com
www.iiepassport.org
A student guide on the web to 5,000 learning oppurtunities worldwide.

6088 **www.irex.org**
International Research and Exchange Board
E-mail: questions@finaid.org
www.finaid.org
Academic exchanges between the United States and Russia. Lists a variety of programs as well as grant and fellowship oppurtunities.

6089 **www.isp.msu.edu/ncsa**
Michigan State University
National Consortium for Study in Af in Africa
E-mail: ncsa@msu.edu
www.istc.umn.edu
Provides a comprehensive lists of sponsors for African exchange.

6090 **www.istc.umn.edu/**
University of Minnesota
International Study and Travel Center
Comprehensive and searchable links to study, work and travel abroad opportunities.

6091 **www.languagetravel.com**
Language Travel Magazine
Resource for finding study abroad language immersion courses.

6092 **www.nsf.gov/**
National Science Foundation
4201 Wilson Blvd
Arlington, VA 22230
703-292-5111
info@nsf.gov
www.nsf.gov
Encourages exchange in science and engineering. The site has inter-national component, providing links with valuable information on fellowships grants and awards, summer institutes, workshops,research and education projects and international programs.
Dr. France A. Cørdova, Director
Dr. Richard O. Buckius, Chief Operating Officer

6093 **www.si.edu/**
Smithsonian Institution
600 Maryland Ave.
Suite 1005
Washington, DC 20024
202-633-5330
Fax: 202-633-5489
learning@si.edu
www.smithsonianeducation.org
Fellowships link to Smithsonian Oppurtunities for research and study.
Patricia Bartlett, Chief of Staff
Claudine Brown, Assistant Secretary

6094 **www.studiesinaustralia.com/study**
Studies in Australia
E-mail:
enquiries@studiesinaustralia.com
www.studiesinaustralia.com
Listing of study abroad oppurtunities in Australia, providing details of academic and training institutions and the programs they offer to prospective international students and education professionals.
Denis Whelan, Vice President of Sales
Elysia Singam, Advertising Copy Controller

6095 **www.studyabroad.com/**
StudyAbroad.com
3803 West Chester Pk.
Suite 125
Newtown Sq, PA 19073
484-766-2920
Fax: 610-499-9205
webmaster@studyabroad.com
www.studyabroad.com
Study abroad information resource listing study abroad programs worldwide.

6096 **www.studyabroad.com/.**
StudyAbroad.com
3803 West Chester Pk.
Suite 125
Newtown Sq, PA 19073
484-766-2920
Fax: 610-499-9205
webmaster@studyabroad.com
www.studyabroad.com
A commercial site with thousands of study abroad programs in over 100 countries with links to study abroad program home pages.

6097 **www.ucis.pitt.edu/crees**
University of Pittsburgh
Center for Russian/European Studies
4400 Wesley W. Posvar Hall, 230 South Bo
Pittsburgh, PA 15260
412-648-7407
Fax: 412-648-7002
crees@pitt.edu
www.ucis.pitt.edu/crees
Index of electronic resources for the student interested in Russian and European language and culture study.
Andrew Konitzer, Acting Director
Dawn Seckler, Acting Associate Director

6098 **www.upenn.edu/oip/scholarships.html**
University of Pennsylvania
Scholarships/Graduate Study Abroad
Provides links for graduate study abroad and scholarship opportunities.

6099 **www.usc.edu**
University of Southern California
Resources for Colleges and Universities in International Exchange
Links for browsing all aspects of international exchange, including study, research, work and teaching abroad, financial aid, grants and scholarships.

6100 **www.usinfo.state/gov**
US Department of State International Information Programs
Comprehensive desriptions of all IIP programs, sections on policy issues, global and regional issues and IIP publications.

6101 **www.wes.org**
World Education Services
Bowling Green Station
P.O. Box 5087
New York, NY 10274-5087
212-966-6311
Fax: 212-739-6100
www.wes.org
Features information on WES' foreign credentials evaluation services, world education workshops, and the journals World Education and News Reviews.

6102 **www.world-arts-resources.com/**
World Wide Arts Resources
P.O. Box 150
Granville, OH 43023
646-455-1425
wwar.com
Focuses solely on the arts, this site provides links for funding sources, university programs and arts organizations all over the world.

6103 **www.yfu.org/**
Youth for Understanding (YFU)
641 S Street, NW.
Suite 200
Washington, DC 20001
202-774-5200
yfuusa.org
Oppurtunities for young people around the world to spend a summer, semester or year with a host family in another country.

6104 **wwww.sas.upenn.edu**
African Studies Center, University of Pennsylvania
647 Williams Hall
255 S 36th Street
Philadelphia, PA 19104-6305
215-898-6971
Fax: 215-573-7379
www.africa.upenn.edu
Links to Africa-related internet sources, African Studies Association and UPenn African Studies Center.
Carol Muller, Ph.D, Director
Ali B. Ali-Dinar, Ph.D, Associate Director

Language Arts

6105 **Advantage Learning Systems**
Renaissance Learning
2911 Peach Street
Wisconsin Rapids, WI 54494
715-424-3636
800-338-4204
Fax: 715-424-4242
answers@renlearn.com
www.renlearn.com
Accelerated Reader software and manuals that motivate K-12 students to read more and better books. The program boosts reading scores and library circulation. Lets educators quickly and accurately assess student reading while motivating students to read more and better books.
John J. Lynch Jr., Chief Executive Officer
Mary T. Minch, EVP, Finance & CFO

6106 **Bytes of Learning Incorporated**
266 Elmwood Avenue #256
Buffalo, NY 14222
905-947-4646
800-465-6428
Fax: 905-475-8650
www.bytesoflearning.com
Single and site licensed software for Macintosh, Apple II, DOS and Windows-network compatible too. Keyboarding, language arts, career exploration and more on diskette and CD-ROM.

6107 **Humanities Software**
408 Columbia Street
#950
Hood River, OR 97031-2044
503-386-6737
800-245-6737
Fax: 541-386-1410
Over 150 whole language, literature-based language arts software titles for grades K-12.
Karen Withrow, Marketing Assistant
Charlotte Arnold, Marketing Director

6108 **Teacher Support Software**
3542 NW 97th Boulevard
Gainesville, FL 32606-7322
352-332-6404
800-228-2871
Fax: 352-332-6779
tss@tssoftware.com
www.tssoftware.com
Language arts, Title 1, special ed, at-risk and ESL, curriculum-based networkable software for grades K-12. Vocabulary software that develops sight word recognition, provides basal correlated databases, tests reading comprehension, tracks student's progress and provides powerful teacher tools.

6109 **Weaver Instructional Systems**
6161 28th Street SE
Grand Rapids, MI 49546-6931
616-942-2891
800-634-8916
Fax: 616-942-1796
wisesoft@aol.com
www.wisesoft.com
Reading and language arts computer software programs for K-college.

6110 **www.caslt.org**
Canadian Association of Second Language Teachers
2490 Don Reid Drive
Ottawa, ON K1H 1
613-727-0994
877-727-0994
info@caslt.org
www.caslt.org

Promotes the advancement of second language education throughout Canada.

Guy Leclair, Executive Director
Diane Paquette, Finance Manager

6111 www.riverdeep.net
Riverdeep Interactive Learning
617-351-5316
800-426-6577
Sales_Support@hmhco.com
forms.hmhco.com
Riverdeep's interactive science, language and math arts programs deliver high quality educational experiences.

6112 www.signit2.com
Aylmer Press
Box 2302
Madison, WI 53701
608-441-5277
steve@signit2.com
www.signit2.com
Website hosted by Aylmer Press which produces video's to teach kids sign language as well as music.

6113 www.usajobs.opm.gov/b1c.html
Overseas Employment Info- Teachers
US Office of Personnel Management

Library Services

6114 American Econo-Clad Services
2101 N Topeka
Topeka, KS 66601
800-255-3502
Fax: 785-233-3129
A full service supplier of educational materials for the library, curriculum and software resource needs including MatchMaker, CD-ROM and ABLE (Analytically Budgeted Library Expenditures) computer systems.

6115 Anchor Audio Portable Sound Systems
5931 Darwin Court
Carlsbad, CA 92008
310-784-2300
800-262-4671
Fax: 760-827-7105
sales@anchoraudio.com
www.anchoraudio.com
Various audio visual products for the school and library.

Alex Jacobs, VP, Sales

6116 Baker & Taylor
2550 West Tyvola Road
Suite 300
Charlotte, NC 28217
704-998-3100
800-775-1800
www.baker-taylor.com
Nation's leading wholesale supplier of audio, computer software, books, videocassettes and other accessories to schools and libraries.

George F. Coe, President/ CEO
Jeff Leonard, Chief Financial Officer

6117 Brodart Company, Automation Division
500 Arch Street
Williamsport, PA 17701
570-326-2461
800-233-8467
Fax: 570-326-1479
support@brodart.com
www.brodart.com
Brodart's Automation Division has been providing library systems, software, and services for over 25 years. Products include: library management systems, media management systems, Internet solutions, cataloged web sites, cataloging resource tools, union catalog solutions, public access catalogs, and bibliographic services.

Kasey Dibble, Marketing Coordinator
Sally Wilmoth, Director Marketing/Sales

6118 Catalog Card Company
12219 Nicollet Avenue
Burnsville, MN 55337-1650
612-882-8558
800-442-7332
Fax: 785-290-1223
MARC records compatible with all software for retrospective conversions and new book orders. Catalog Card's conversion services include barcode labels to complement circulation software. MARC records generated from Dewey/Sears and Library of Congress databases are in standard USMARC or MicroLIF format.

6119 Data Trek
5838 Edison Place
Carlsbad, CA 92008-6519
800-876-5484
Turn-key library automation systems and computer networks.

6120 Demco
PO Box 7488
Madison, WI 53707-7488
800-356-1200
Fax: 800-245-1329
custserv@demco.com
www.demco.com
A leader in educational and library supplies for more than 80 years, Demco offers library audio and visual supplies and equipment plus display furniture.

6121 Dewey Decimal Classification
OCLC Forest Press
6565 Frantz Road
Dublin, OH 43017-3395
614-764-6000
800-848-5878
Fax: 614-764-6096
oclc@oclc.org
www.oclc.org
OCLC Forest Press publishes the Dewey Decimal Classification (DDC) system and many related print and CD-ROM products that teach librarians and library users about the DDC.

Skip Prichard, Chief Executive Officer
Rick Schwieterman, Chief Financial Officer

6122 Ebsco Subscription Services
International Headquarters
10 Estes Street
Ipswich, MA 01938
205-991-1480
800-653-2726
Fax: 978-356-6565
information@ebsco.com
www.ebsco.com
Periodical subscription and ordering and customer service equipment, computer and CD-ROM supplies, products and hardware for libraries.

Tim Collins, President
Sam Brooks, EVP

6123 Electronic Bookshelf
5276 S Country Road, 700 W
Frankfort, IN 46041
765-324-2182
Fax: 765-324-2183
Reading motivation, testing management system and various computer systems and networks for educational purposes.

Rosalie Carter

6124 Filette Keez Corporation/Colorworks Diskette Organizing System
3204 Channing Lane
Bedford, TX 76021-6506
817-283-5428
Produces ten filing inventions for classroom library, lab and district technology resources management. SelecTsideS folders store multimedia in Press-an-Inch Technology Slings and keep instruction, printouts, pamphlets and blackliners altogether. The diskette/CD portfolio color coordinates with the student/magazine Spbinder, plastic LaceLox fastener and all systems paper supplies: CD envelopes, storage box dividers, sheeted cards, perforated tractor labels and keys, available in 7 tech colors.

Roxanne Kay Harbert, Founder/President
Ray L Harbert, VP

6125 Follett School Solutions
1391 Corporate Drive
McHenry, IL 60050-7041
815-344-8700
800-323-3397
Fax: 800-807-3623
sales@winnebago.com
www.follettsoftware.com
Comprehensive, user-friendly circulation and catalog software for Windows, Mac OS, and MS-DOS systems-plus Internet technology, online periodical databases, outstanding customer support, and retrospective conversion services-all developed within the quality guidelines of Winnebago's ISO 9001 certification with TickIT accreditation.

6126 Follett Software Company
1391 Corporate Drive
McHenry, IL 60050-7041
815-344-8700
800-323-3397
Fax: 815-344-8774
marketing@fsc.follett.com
www.fsc.follett.com
Helping K-12 schools and districts create a vital library-to-classroom link to improve student achievement. FSC combines award-winning library automation with practical applications of the Internet. From OPAC data enhancement and easy-to-implement Internet technology to innovative information literacy solutions, FSC helps simplify resource management, increase access to resources inside and outside your collection and provide tools to integrate technology into the curriculum.

Patricia Yonushonis, Marketing Manager
Ann Reist, Conference Manager

6127 Foundation for Library Research
1200 Bigley Avenue
Charleston, WV 25302-3752
304-343-6480
Fax: 304-343-6489
The Automated Library Systems integrated library automation software.

Robert Evans

6128 Gaylord Brothers
PO Box 4901
Syracuse, NY 13221-4901
800-448-6160
Fax: 800-272-3412
www.gaylord.com

Library, AV supplies and equipment; security systems; and library furniture.

Tim Krein

6129 Highsmith Company
W5527 Highway 106
Fort Atkinson, WI 53538
414-563-9571
Catalog of microcomputer and multimedia curriculum products and software.

Barbara R Endl

6130 Information Access Company
362 Lakeside Drive
Foster City, CA 94404-1171
800-227-8431
Offers automation products and electronics for library/media centers.

6131 LePAC NET
Brodart Automation
500 Arch Street
Williamsport, PA 17701
570-326-2461
800-233-8467
Fax: 570-326-1479
support@brodart.com
www.brodart.com
Software for searching thousands of library databases with a single search. Schools can use to take multiple individual library databases and consolidate them, while deleting duplicate listings, into a union database.

Shawn Knight, Assistant Marketing Manager
Denise Macafee, Marketing Manager

6132 Library Corporation
Library Corporation
Research Park
Inwood, WV 25428-9733
304-229-0100
800-325-7759
Fax: 304-229-0295
info@TLCdelivers.com
www.tlcdelivers.com
Web-based library management systems allows patrons to have easy and immediate access to books and other library resources.

Annette Harwood Murphy, President/CEO/Chair
Calvin Whittington, Director, Finance & Admin

6133 Lingo Fun
International Software
PO Box 486
Westerville, OH 43086-0486
800-745-8258
Providers of microcomputer software including CD-ROM's for Macintosh and MPC, on-line dictionaries, translation assistants; teaching programs for elementary presentation, review and reinforcement, test preparation, and literary exploration.

6134 MARCIVE
PO Box 47508
San Antonio, TX 78265-7508
210-646-6161
800-531-7678
Fax: 210-646-0167
info@marcive.com
www.marcive.com
Economical, fast 100% conversion. Full MARC records with SEARS or LC headings. Free authorities processing smart barcode labels, reclassification, MARC Record enrichment

Robert Fleming, President
Scott Fleming, Chief Operating Officer

6135 Medianet/Dymaxion Research Limited
5515 Cogswell Street
Halifax, No B3J 1
902-422-1973
Fax: 902-421-1267
info@medianet.ns.ca
www.medianet.ns.ca
Medianet is the scheduling system for equipment and media that has consistently been rated as best in its class. Features include book library system integration, time-of-day booking, catalog production, WWW and touch tone phone booking by patrons.

Peter Mason, President

6136 Mitinet/Marc Software
PO Box 505
Bethany, MO 64424-0505
608-845-2300
800-824-6272
Fax: 660-425-3998
www.mitinet.com
Import/export USMARC, MICROLIF to USMARC conversions.

Bart Fitzgerald, Owner/ President
Cindy Beerkircher, Office Manager

6137 Orange Cherry Software
69 Westchester Avenue
PO Box 390
Pound Ridge, NY 10576-1702
914-764-4104
800-672-6002
Fax: 914-764-0104
www.orangecherry.com
Educational software products for libraries and media centers.

Biannual

Nicholas Vazzana, President

6138 Pearson Education
3001 Wayburne Drive
Burnbay
Canada V5G 4W3
604-294-1233
877-873-1550
Fax: 604-294-2225
proded@pearson.com
www.pearsonschoolsystems.com
Online catalog searches and checking materials in and out.

6139 Right on Programs
27 Bowdon Road
Suite B
Greenlawn, NY 11740
631-424-7777
Fax: 631-424-7207
riteonsoft@aol.com
www.rightonlibrarysoftware.com
Computer software for Windows and networks for library management including circulation, cataloging, periodicals, catalog cardmaking, inventory and thirty more. Used in more than 24,000 schools and libraries of all sizes.

D Farren, VP

6140 SOLINET, Southeastern Library Network
1438 W Peachtree Street NW
Suite 200
Atlanta, GA 30309-2955
404-892-0943
800-999-8558
Fax: 404-892-7879
information@solinet.net
www.solinet.net
SOLINET provides access, training and support for OCLC products and services; offers discounted library products and services, including licensed databases; provides electronic information solutions; workflow consulting, training and customized workshops; and supports a regional preservation of materials program.

Cathie Gharing, Marketing Coordinator
Liz Hornsby, Editor

6141 SirsiDynix
3300 North Ashton Blvd
Suite 500
Lehi, UT 84043
801-223-5200
800-288-8020
Fax: 801-331-7770
marketing@sirsidynix.com
www.sirsi.com
Unicorn Collection Management Systems are fully integrated UNIX-based library systems, automating all of a library's operation. Modules include: cataloging, authority control, public access, materials booking, circulation, academic reserves, acquisitions, serials control, reference database manager and electronic mail. Modules can be configured for all types and sizes of libraries.

Bill Davison, Chief Executive Officer
Scott Wheelhouse, SVP, Operations

6142 Social Issues Resources Series
PO Box 2348
Boca Raton, FL 33427
561-994-0079
800-521-0600
Fax: 561-994-4704
ars.sirs.com
Publisher of CD-ROM reference systems for PC and Macintosh computers. Databases of full-text articles carefully selected from 1,000 domestic and international sources. Also provides PC-compatible and stand-alone and network packages.

Paula Jackson, Marketing Director
Suzanne Panek, Customer Service

6143 TekData Systems Company
1111 W Park Avenue
Libertyville, IL 60048-2952
847-367-8800
Fax: 847-367-0235
tekdata@tekdata.com
www.tekdata.com
Scheduling and booking systems for intranets and internets.

Randy Kick, Sales Manager

6144 Three M Library Systems
Three M Center
Building 225-4N-14
St. Paul, MN 55144
800-328-0067
Fax: 800-223-5563
Materials Flow Management system is the first comprehensive system for optimizing the handling, processing and security of your library materials - from processing to checkout to check-in. The SelfCheck System and Staff Workstation automate the processing of virtually all of your library materials, while the Tattle-Tape Security Strips and Detection Systems help ensure the security of those materials.

6145 UMI
300 N Zeeb Road
Ann Arbor, MI 48103-1553
800-521-0600
Fax: 800-864-0019
Information products in microform, CD-ROM, online and magnetic tape.

6146 **University Products**
517 Main Street
#101
Holyoke, MA 01040-5514
413-532-3372
800-628-1912
Fax: 413-452-0618
info@universityproducts.com
www.universityproducts.com
Complete selection of library and media center supplies and equipment.
Juhn Dunpay

6147 **WLN**
PO Box 3888
Lacey, WA 98509-3888
360-923-4000
800-342-5956
Fax: 360-923-4009
School and media librarians experience 95% hit rates with WLN's LaserCat, CD-ROM database, a cataloging product and MARC record service.

6148 **www.awesomelibrary.org**
Awesome Library
www.awesomelibrary.org
Organizes the Web with 15,000 carefully reviewed resources, including the top 5 percent in education. Offers sections of mathematics, science, social studies, english, health, physical education, technology, languages, special education, the arts and more. Features a section involved with today's current issues facing our world, like pollution, gun control, tobacco, and other changing 'hot' topics. Site can be browsed in English, German, Spanish, French or Portuguese.

6149 **www.techlearning.com**
Technology & Learning
28 East 28th Street
12th floor
New York, NY 10016
212-378-0400
Fax: 212-378-0470
www.techlearning.com
Open 24 hours, every day of the week, with an extensive and up-to-date catalog of over 53,000 software and hardware products. Powerful search engine will help you find the right education-specific products.

Mathematics

6150 **Accelerated Math**
Renaissance Learning
2911 Peach Street
Wisconsin Rapids, WI 54494
715-424-3636
800-338-4204
Fax: 715-424-4242
answers@renlearn.com
www.renlearn.com
Accelerated Math provides 17 different reports, providing individualized, constructive feedback to students, parents, and teachers.
John J. Lynch Jr., Chief Executive Officer
Mary T. Minch, EVP, Finance & CFO

6151 **Applied Mathematics Program**
Prime Technology Corporation
PO Box 2407
Minneola, FL 34755-2407
352-394-7558
Fax: 352-394-3778
www.primetechnology.net
Provides students with comprehensive instruction in 11 math areas. In working with this program, students develop employment and life skills. The program will also lead the student to greater success on the mathematics sections of any standardized test.
Paul Scime, President

6152 **CAE Software**
3608 Shepherd Street
Chevy Chase, MD 20815-4132
301-907-9845
800-354-3462
Provides educational software for mathematics, grades 3-12. Simulations, tutorials, games, and problem solving. Titles include Mathematics Life Skills Services, Reading and Making Graphs Series, MathLab Series, Meaning of Fractions, Using Fractions and Using Decimals, ALG Football, GEO Pool and GEO Billiards, Paper Route, Mathematics Achievement Project, and others.
Alan R Chap, President

6153 **EME Corporation**
PO Box 1949
Stuart, FL 34995-1949
772-285-2131
800-848-2050
Fax: 561-219-2209
emecorp@aol.com
www.emescience.com
Publishers of award-winning science and math software, elementary through high school levels.

6154 **Logal Software**
125 Cambridgepark Drive
Cambridge, MA 02140-2329
617-491-4440
Fax: 617-491-5855
Math and science products for high school through college.
Martha Cheng, President

6155 **MathType**
Design Science
140 Pine Avenue
4th Floor
Long Beach, CA 90803-1502
562-432-2920
800-827-0685
Fax: 562-432-2857
info@dessci.com
www.dessci.com
Designed to make the creation of complex equations on a computer simple and fast. It works in conjunction with the software applications you already own, such as word processing programs, graphics programs, presentation programs, and web-authoring applications. Create research papers, tests, slides, books or web pages quickly and easily. MathType is the powerful, professional version of the Equation Editor in Microscoft Word, and Wordperfect.
Bruce Virga, EVP Sales/BD, COO
Paul R. Topping, President/ CEO

6156 **Mathematica**
Wolfram Research, Inc.
100 Trade Center Drive
Champaign, IL 61820-7237
217-398-0700
800-965-3726
Fax: 217-398-0747
info@wolfram.com
www.wolfram.com
Mathematica is an indispensable tool for finding and communicating solutions quickly and easily.
Stephen Wolfram, Founder/CEO
Jean Buck, Dir., Corp Communications

6157 **MindTwister Math**
Edmark Corporation
PO Box 97021
Redmond, WA 98073-9721
425-556-8400
800-691-2986
Fax: 425-556-8430
edmarkteam@edmark.com
www.edmark.com
Software to help students in grade 3 and 4 build math fact fluency, practice mental math and improve estimating skills as they compete in a series of math challenges.

6158 **Multimedia - The Human Body**
Sunburst Digital, Inc.
3150 W Higgins Rd
Ste 140
Hoffman Estates, IL 60169
914-747-3310
800-321-7511
Fax: 914-747-4109
service@sunburst.com
www.sunburst.com
Multimedia production of the intricate workings of the human body.

6159 **Texas Instruments**
Consumer Relations
12500 TI Boulevard
Dallas, TX 75243
972-995-2011
800-842-2737
Fax: 972-917-0874
www.ti.com
Instructional calculators offer features matched to math concepts taught at each of conceptional development. Classroom accessories and teacher support programs that support the Texas Instruments products enhance instruction and learning. TI also offers a complete range of powerful notebook computers and laser printers for every need.
Rich Templeton, Chairman/ President/ CEO
Steve Anderson Analog, SVP

6160 **William K. Bradford Publishing Company**
35 Forest Ridge Road
Concord, MA 01742-5414
800-421-2009
Fax: 978-318-9500
www.wkbradford.com
Educational software for grades K-12. Especially math and grade book.
Hal Wexler, VP

6161 **www.mathgoodies.com**
Mrs. Glosser's Math Goodies
75 Mill Street
Colchester, CT 6415
914-736-0286
Fax: 866-776-9170
www.mathgoodies.com
Free educational site featuring interactive math lessons. Use a problem-solving approach and actively engage students in the learning process.

6162 **www.mathstories.com**
MathStories.com
1426 Pine Grove Way
San Jose, CA 95129
E-mail: Customerservice@Mathstories.com
www.mathstories.com
The goal of this site is to help grade school children improve their math problem-solving and critical thinking skills. Offers over 4000 math word problems for children.

6163 **www.riverdeep.net**
Riverdeep Interactive Learning
617-351-5316
800-426-6577

Sales_Support@hmhco.com
forms.hmhco.com
Riverdeep's interactive science, language and math arts programs deliver high quality educational experiences.

6164 www.themathemagician.8m.com
The Mathemagician
310-452-0655
themathemagician_us@yahoo.com
www.themathemagician.8m.com
Offers the help of a real live person to help students correct and understand math and other home work problems.

Music & Art

6165 Harmonic Vision
1433 Rapids Trl
Nekoosa, WI 54457
715-325-3252
800-474-0903
Fax: 866-422-6686
www.harmonicvision.com
Leading musical education software to teach effectiveness of music in the home, school and studio.

6166 Midnight Play
Simon & Schuster Interactive
1230 Avenue of the Americas
New York, NY 10020
212-698-7000
800-793-9972
www.simonandschuster.com
Electronic picture book with an unusual look at creativity.

Carolyn Reidy, President/ CEO
Jon Anderson, EVP & Publisher

6167 Music Teacher Find
33 W 17th Street
10th Floor
New York, NY 10011
212-242-2464
www.MusicTeacherFind.com
Comprehensive Music Teacher Database designed to help music students find quality teachers in their neighborhood.

6168 Music and Guitar
www.nl-guitar.com
Original music programs for schools, courses and encounterswith music.

6169 Pure Gold Teaching Tools
PO Box 16622
Tuscon, AZ 85732
520-747-5600
866-692-6500
Fax: 520-571-9077
info@puregoldteachingtools.com
www.puregoldteachingtools.com
Exciting teaching methods and fabulous gifts for teachers, parents, students, pre-schoolers, homeschoolers and music therapists.

Heidi Goldman, President

6170 library.thinkquest.org
Think Quest
gitso-outage.oracle.com/thinkquest
The Arti FAQS 2100 Project is designed to predict how art will influence our lives in the next hundred years. Students can use available data to make reasonable predictions for the future.

6171 members.truepath.com/headofthec lass
Head of The Class
Offers three galleries with clip art for teachers and children, several lesson plans, teaching tips, songs for teachers, lounge laughs, teacher tales and more.

6172 www.billharley.com
Round River Productions
301 Jacob Street
Seekonk, MA 2771
508-336-9703
800-682-9522
Fax: 508-336-2254
debbie@billharley.com
www.billharley.com
Humerous, yet meaningful songs which chronicle the lives of children at school and at home. His recordings of songs and stories can be used most effectively in the classroom as inspirational tools for the motivation of learning.

6173 www.sanford-artedventures.com
Sanford- A Lifetime of Color
800-323-0749
Teaches students about art and color theory while they play a game. Lessons plans, newsletter and product information.

6174 www.songs4teachers.com
O'Flynn Consulting
E-mail: oflynn4@home.com
Offers many resources for teachers including songs made especially for your classroom. Sections with songs and activities for holidays, seasons and more. Features books and audios with 101 theme songs for use in the classroom or anywhere children gather to sing.

6175 www.ushistory.com
History Happens
www.songsabouthistory.com
Teaches integrating art, music, literature, science, math, library skills, and American history. The Primary source is stories from American history presented in musci video style.

Physical Education

6176 InfoUse
2560 9th Street
Suite 216
Berkeley, CA 94710-2557
510-549-6520
Fax: 510-549-6512
An award-winning, multimedia development and products firm, features CD-ROM, websites on health, education and disability. For training, education or presentations, our services include: research, instructional design, interface design, graphics, animation, content acquisition, videoing, analog and digital editing and evaluation. Products include SafeNet, (HIV prevention for fifth and sixth grade children), Place Math and Math Pad (math tools and lessons for students with disabilities).

Lewis E Kraus, VP
Susan Stoddard, President

6177 www.sports-media.org
Sports Media
www.sports-media.org
A tool for p.e. teachers, coaches, students and everyone who is interested in p.e./fitness and sports. Interactive p.e. lesson plans, sports pen-apls for the kids, European p.e. mailing list, and developing teaching skills in physical education.

Dr. Zan Gao, Editor-in-Chief
Guy Van Damme, Co-Chief editor

Reading

6178 Accelerated Reader
Renaissance Learning
2911 Peach Street
Wisconsin Rapids, WI 54494
715-424-3636
800-338-4204
Fax: 715-424-4242
answers@renlearn.com
www.renlearn.com
Helps teachers increase literature-based reading practice for all k-12 students

John J. Lynch Jr., Chief Executive Officer
Mary T. Minch, EVP, Finance & CFO

Secondary Education

6179 New York Times
New York, NY
646-698-8000
Fax: 646-698-8344
www.nytimes.com/learning
A resource for educators, parents and students in grades six through 12. Provides a daily lesson plan and comprehensive interactive resources based on newspaper content.

Katherine Schulte, Editor
Michael Gonchar, Deputy Editor

6180 Wm. C. Brown Communications
2460 Kerper Boulevard
Dubuque, IA 52001-2224
College textbooks, software, CD-ROM and more for grades 10-12.

6181 adulted.about.com/education/adulted
Adult/Continuing Education

6182 englishhlp.www5.50megs.com
English Help
E-mail: englishhlpr@hotmail.com
This page is a walk through of Microsoft Power Point. The goal is to show in a few simple steps how to make your own website. Created by Rebecca Holland.

6183 www.number2.com
Number2.com
Currently offer SAT and GRE prep along with a vocabulary builder. Practice questions and word drill are adapted to the ability level of the user.

Science

6184 Academic Software Development Group
University of Maryland
University of Maryland
Computer Science Center
College Park, MD 20742-0001
301-405-5100
Fax: 301-405-0726
Offers BioQuest Library which is a set of peer-reviewed resources for science education.

6185 Accu-Weather
385 Science Park Road
State College, PA 16803-2215
814-237-0309
Fax: 814-238-1339
www.accuweather.com

Offers a telecommunications weather and oceanography database.

Dr. Joel N. Myers, Founder/ Chairman/ President
Barry Lee Myers, CEO

6186 AccuLab Products Group
614 Senic Drive
Suite 104
Modesto, CA 95350
209-522-8874
Fax: 209-522-8875
Science laboratory software.

6187 Learning Team
10 Long Pond Road
Armonk, NY 10504-2625
914-273-2226
800-793-TEAM
Fax: 914-273-2227
Offers CD-ROM, including MathFinder, Science Helper and Small Blue Planet and Redshift, the Learning Team edition.

Thomas Laster

6188 Problem Solving Concepts
611 N Capitol Avenue
Indianapolis, IN 46204-1205
317-267-9827
800-755-2150
Fax: 317-262-5044
Pro Solv provides students with a new approach to learning introductory physics problem solving techniques. Multi-experiential exercises with supporting text introduce students to relevant variables and their interrelations, principles, graphing and the development of problem solving skills through the quiz/tutorial mode.

Thomas D Feigenbaum, President
Gean R Shelor, Administrative Assistant

6189 Quantum Technology
PO Box 8252
Searcy, AR 72145-8252
A microcomputer database collection system that allows users to perform experiments in chemistry, biology and applied physics.

6190 SCI Technologies
SCI Technologies
2002 W. Huron St.
Chicago, IL 60612
312-243-1977
800-421-9881
Fax: 312-243-1972
create@scitechnologies.com
www.scitechnologies.com
A computer-based interface with an integrated hardware and software package that allows the focus of a science lab to shift from data collection to data analysis and experiment design.

Colleen Greenblatt, Sales Manager
Michelle Trexler, Event Coordinator

6191 Videodiscovery
1700 Westlake Avenue N
Suite 600
Seattle, WA 98109-3040
206-285-5400
800-548-3472
Fax: 206-285-9245
Publishers of award winning science videodiscs and multimedia software for kindergarten through post-secondary classes.

6192 www.kidsastronomy.com
KidsAstronomy.com
www.kidsastronomy.com
Offers information on astronomy, deep space, the solar system, space exploration, a teachers corner and more.

6193 www.riverdeep.net
Riverdeep Interactive Learning
617-351-5316
800-426-6577
Sales_Support@hmhco.com
Riverdeep's interactive science, language and math arts programs deliver high quality educational experiences.

Social Studies

6194 AccuNet/AP Multimedia Archive
AccuWeather, Inc.
385 Science Park Road
State College, PA 16803
814-235-8600
800-249-5389
Fax: 814-235-8669
apsupport@accuweather.com
ap.accuweather.com
The Photo Archive is an on-line database containing almost a half-million of Associated Press's current and historic images for the last 150 years.

Michael Warfield, Southeastern Sales Manager
Richard Towne, Northeastern Sales Manager

6195 Cengage Learning
10650 Toebben Drive
Independence, KY 41051
800-354-9706
Fax: 800-487-8488
order.samples@cengage.com
www.cengage.com
Offers CD-Rom information that offer students contextual understanding of the most commonly-studies persons, events and social movements in U.S. history; concepts, theories, discoveries and people involved in the study of science; current geopolitical data with cultural information on 200 nations of the world as well as all U.S. states and dependencies; poetry and literary information; and more in various databases for education.

Michael E. Hansen, Chief Executive Officer
Sandi Kirshner, Chief Marketing Officer

6196 World Geography Web Site
ABC-CLIO Schools
130 Cremona Drive
#1911
Santa Barbara, CA 93117-5599
805-968-1911
800-368-6868
Fax: 805-685-9685
www.abc-clio.com
Provides convenient internet access to curriculum-based reference and research materials for media specialist, educators and students.

CD-ROM

Judy Fay, Managing Editor
Valerie Mercado, Customer Service

6197 WorldView Software
11 Barby Lane
Plainview, NY 11803
516-681-1773
history@worldviewsoftware.com
www.worldviewsoftware.com
WorldView Software's interactive social studies programs for middle school and high school are comprehensive, curriculum-based tools that may be used along with or in place of textbooks. Each program contains Socratic learning sessions, writing activities, thousands of test or study questions (with explanations), and a plethora of resource material: biographies, chronologies, glossaries, original source documents and more.

Jerrold Kleinstein, President

6198 faculty.acu.edu
M.I. Smart Program
Abilene Christian University
Abilene, TX 79699
325-674-2000
800-460-6228
www.acu.edu
Site designed for teacher and students. Offers electronic resources for historical and cultural geography. Features games, quizzes, trivia and virtual tours for students and thier teachers.

Dr. Phil Schubert, President
Steven Holley, Chief Financial Officer

Technology in Education

6199 BLINKS.Net
PO Box 79321
Atlanta, GA 30357
404-243-5202
Fax: 404-241-4992
info@blinks.net
www.blinks.net
Fastest growing free Internet service provider and community portal for information and resources for the African American, Caribbean, Latino, and African markets.

6200 Boyce Enterprises
360 Sharry Lane
Santa Maria, CA 93455
805-937-4353
Fax: 805-934-1765
Development of computer-based vocational curriculums.

6201 Center for Educational Outreach and Innovation
Teachers College-Columbia University
525 W 120th Street
Box 132
New York, NY 10027
212-678-3000
800-209-1245
Fax: 212-678-8417
ceoi-mail@tc.columbia.edu
www.tc.columbia.edu
Lifelong learning programs, including distance learning courses, certificates and workshoops in education related topics.

Dr. Susan H. Fuhrman, President
Dr. Thomas James, Provost/ Dean

6202 Depco
3305 Airport Drive
PO Box 178
Pittsburg, KS 66762
316-231-0019
800-767-1062
Fax: 316-231-0024
sales@depcoinc.com
www.depcoinc.com
Program tracks and schedules for you, the test taker delivers tests electronically, as well as, automatic final exams. There are workstation security features to help keep students focused on their activities.

6203 Dialog Information Services
Worldwide Headquaters
3460 Hillview Avenue
#10010
Palo Alto, CA 94304-1338
415-858-3785
800-334-2564
Fax: 650-858-7069

The world's most comprehensive online information source offering over 450 databases containing over 330 million articles, abstracts and citations - covering an unequaled variety of topics, with particular emphasis on news, business, science and technology. Dialog has offices throughout the United States and around the world.

6204 Distance Education Database
International Centre for Distance Learning
Open University, Walton Hall
Milton Keynes
England
441-085-3537
Fax: 441-086-4173
Contains information on distance education, including more than 22,000 distance-taught programs and courses in the Commonwealth of Learning, an organization created by the Commonwealth Heads of Government. On-line and CD-Rom versions of the database contain detailed information on over 30,000 distance-taught courses, 900 distance teaching instructions, and nearly 9,000 books, journals, reports and papers.
Keith Harry, Director

6205 EDUCAUSE
1150 18th Street, NW
Suite 900
Washington, DC 20036-4822
202-872-4200
Fax: 202-872-4318
info@educause.edu
www.educause.edu
Aims to link practitioners in primary and secondary education through computer-mediated communications networks.
Malcolm Brown, Director
Dr. Diana G. Oblinger, President/ CEO

6206 Educational Structures
NCS Pearson
827 W Grove Avenue
Mesa, AZ 85210
800-736-4357
www.ncspearson.com
Features complete lesson plans and resources in social studies, mathematics, science, and language arts.

6207 Gibson Tech Ed
31500 Grape St. Bldg 3-364
Lake Elsinore, CA 92532
800-422-1100
Fax: 951-471-4981
gary@gibsonteched.com
www.gibsonteched.com
Educational materials to teach electronics, from middle, junior, high school and college.
Gary Gibson, Founder
Tim Gibson, President

6208 Grolier Interactive
Grolier Publishing
90 Sherman Turnpike
Danbury, CT 06816
800-371-3908
Fax: 800-456-4402
publishing.grolier.com
Instructional software including reference, science, mathematics, music, social studies, early learning, art and art history, language arts/literature.

6209 Heifner Communications
4451 Interstate 70 Drive NW
Columbia, MO 65202-3271
573-445-6163
800-445-6164
Fax: 512-527-2395
Offers educational-merit, cable-programming available via satellite. HCI Distance Learning systems are designed for dependable services and ease of operation and competitive prices.
Vicky Roberts

6210 In Focus
27700 B SW Parkway Avenue
Wilsonville, OR 97070-9215
503-685-8887
800-294-6400
Fax: 503-685-8887
LCD panels, video projectors and systems.

6211 JonesKnowledge.com
Jones Knowledge Group
9697 E Mineral Avenue
Centennial, CO 80112
800-350-6914
www.jonesknowledge.com
For administrators, that means and integrated solution-with no minimum commitment, or upfront investment. For instructors, it means getting your course online your way, without being a web expert, and for students it means, an accessible and convenient online experience.

6212 Mastercam
CNC Software
5717 Wollochet Drive NW
Suite 2A
Gig Harbor, WA 98335
800-275-6226
Fax: 253-858-6737
mcinfo@mastercam.com
www.mastercamedu.com

6213 Merit Audio Visual
Merit Software
121 West 27th Street
Suite 1200
New York, NY 10001
212-675-8567
800-753-6488
Fax: 646-351-0423
sales@meritsoftware.com
www.meritsoftware.com
Easy to use, interactive basic skills software for Windows 9x/ME/NT/2000/XP computers. Lessons for reading, writing, grammar and math with appropriate graphics for teens and adults.
Ben Weintraub, Marketing Manager

6214 National Information Center for Educational Media
4725 Indian School Road NE
Suite 100
Albuquerque, NM 87198-8640
505-265-3591
800-926-8328
Fax: 505-256-1080
info-request@nicem.com
www.nicem.com
NICEM maintains a comprehensive database describing educational media materials for all ages and subjects. It is available on CD-ROM and online.
Lisa Savard, Sales/Marketing Director

6215 NoRad Corporation
4455 Torrance Boulevard
#2806513
Torrance, CA 90503-4398
310-605-0808
Fax: 323-934-2101
Mini, personal, medium and large computer systems for educational institutions.

6216 Proxima Corporation
9440 Carroll Park Drive
San Diego, CA 92121
858-457-5500
800-294-6400
Fax: 503-685-7239
www.proxima.com
Proxima Corporation is a global leader in the multimedia projection market, providing world class presentation solutions to corporate enterprises, workgroups, mobile professionals, trainers, and professional public speakers.
Kim Gallagher, Public Relations Manager
Kathy Bankerd, Director Marketing Programs

6217 RB5X: Education's Personal Computer Robot
General Robotics Corporation
760 S Youngfield Court
Suite 8
Lakewood, CO 80228-2813
303-988-5636
800-422-4265
Fax: 303-988-5303
cbrown@generalrobotics.com
www.edurobot.com
RB5X: Education's Personal Computer Robot. All grade levels. Self learn, self teach, hands on modular system. Problem solving, basic learning skills, increases self-esteem. Expanable open-ended, motivation at its best.
Constant Brown, President

6218 SEAL
550 Spring Street
Naugatuck, CT 06770-1906
203-729-5201
Complete line of systems and electronics for schools.

6219 Sharp Electronics Corporation
LCD Products Group
Sharp Plaza
Mall Stop One
Mahwah, NJ 07430
201-529-8200
800-237-4277
Fax: 201-529-9636
aquosadvantage@sharpusa.com
www.sharpusa.com
Offers a full line of LCD-based video and computer multimedia projectors and projection panels for use in a wide range of educational applications. Sharp's product line also includes industrial VHS format VCRs, color TV monitors.
J Ganguzza, Director/Marketing

6220 The NCTA Foundation
25 Massachusetts Avenue NW
Suite 100
Washington, DC 20001
202-222-2300
webmaster@ncta.com
www.ncta.com
The foundation assists its member organizations by helping them develop programs to promote responsible and effective use of cable's broadband technology, services and content in learning and teaching. Some topics covered by them include the future of Wi-Fi, open Internet, protecting consumer privacy, preventing robocalls and more.
Michael Powell, President & CEO
Dave Pierce, Executive Director

6221 Valiant
80 Little Falls Road
Fairfield, NJ 07004
800-825-4268
Fax: 800-453-6338
sales@valiantnational.com
www.valiantnational.com
Distributors of LCD projection panels, P/A systems, overhead/slide and filmstrip projectors,

cassette recorders, classroom record players, laser pointers, laminating equipment, lecturns, listening centers and headphones.

Sheldon Goldstein

6222 Vernier Software
13979 SW Millikan Way
Beaverton, OR 97005
503-277-2299
888-VER-ER
Fax: 503-277-2440
info@vernier.com
www.vernier.com
Laboratory interacting software for the Macintosh, IBM and Apple II.

6223 Websense
10240 Sorrento Valley Road
San Diego, CA 92121
858-320-8000
800-723-1166
Fax: 858-458-2950
www.websense.com
Internet filtering.

John R. McCormack, Chief Executive Officer
John Borgerding, President/ COO

6224 di...elearn/cs/eductechnology/index.htm
About Education Distance Learning

6225 futurekids.com
FUTUREKIDS School Technology Solutions
330 East 85th Street
New York, NY 10028
212-717-0110
Fax: 212-717-0259
info1@futurekidsnyc.com
www.futurekidsnyc.com
Helping schools use technology to transform education.

6226 online.uophx.edu
University of Phoenix Online
www.university-of-phoenix-online.net
Offers you the convenience and flexibility of attending classes from your personal computer. Students are discussing issues, sharing ideas, testing theories, essentially enjoying all of the advantages of an on-campus degree programs. Interaction is included like e-mail, so you practice at your convenience.

6227 www.crossteccorp.com
NetOp
500 NE Spanish River Blvd.
Suite 201
Boca Raton, FL 33431
561-391-6560
800-675-0729
Fax: 561-391-5820
sales@crosstecsoftware.com
www.crossteccorp.com
A powerful combination of seven essential tools for networked classrooms. Based on the award winning technology of NetOp Remote Control and is easy-to-use software only solution.

6228 www.growsmartbrains.com
GrowSmartBrains.com
Website for parents and educators who want research based information and practical stradegies for raising children in a media age.

6229 www.zdnet.com
ZDNet
www.zdnet.com
Full-service destination for people looking to buy, use and learn more about technology.

Larry Dignan, Editor-in-Chief
David Grober, Senior Editor

6230 www.21ct.org
Twenty First Century Teachers Network
A nationwide, non-profit initiative of the McGuffey Project, dedicated to assisting k-12 teachers learn, use and effectively integrate technology in the curriculum for improved student learning.

6231 www.aboutonehandtyping.com/
One Hand Typing and Keyboarding Resources
740 Purdue Dr.
Claremont, CA 91711
909-398-1228
Fax: 408-228-8752
www.aboutonehandtyping.com
This site dishes up a blend of messages and stories, resources for one-hand typists, links to alternative keyboards, teaching links, and more.

6232 www.digitaldividenetwork.org
Digital Divide Network
c/o TakingITGlobal
19 Duncan Street, Suite 505
Toronto, ON M5H 3
416-977-9363
Fax: 416-352-1898
ddn@takingitglobal.org
www.digitaldivide.net
The goal of bridging the divide is to use communications technology to help improve the quality of life of all communities and their citizens; provide them with the tools, skills and information they need to help them realize their socioeconomic, educational and cultural potential.

Adam Clare, Volunteer Lead Editor
Kirsten Jordan, DDN Project Coordinator

6233 www.getquizzed.com
GetQuizzed
Designed as a free service that provides a database that allows users to create, store and edit Multiple Choice or Question and Answer quizzes, under password protected conditions.

6234 www.guidetogeekdom.com
Guide to Geekdom
E-mail: info@guidetogeekdom.com
www.guidetogeekdom.com
Designed especially for Homeschoolers, step-by-step lessons teach students how to use the computer and troubleshoot computer problems. Offers workbooks, sample lesson and more.

6235 www.happyteachers.com
HappyTeachers.com
Information about technical and vocational education programs, products and curriculum.

6236 www.integratingit.com
Integrating Information Technology for the Classroom, School, & District
Dedicated to providing the education community a place to find real world strategies, solutions, and resources for integrating technology. Organized by the perspective of the classroom teacher, the school administrator, and the district.

6237 www.livetext.com
LiveText Curriculum Manager
1 W. Harris Avenue
2nd Floor
La Grange, IL 60525
866-548-3839
Fax: 708-588-1793
edu-solutions@livetext.com
www.livetext.com
Provides tools for engaged learning classroom projects and provides online professional development for teachers.

6238 www.ncrel.org
North Central Regional Educational Laboratory
1120 East Diehl Road
Suite 200
Naperville, IL 60563-1486
Fax: 630-649-6730
info@ncrel.org
www.ncrel.org
Offers research results regarding the effective use of technology.

Gina Burkhardt, CEO
Sabrina Laine, Chief Officer, R&D

6239 www.ncrtec.org
N Central Regional Technology in Education Consortiums
www.ncrtec.org
Provides a variety of tools and information to improve technology-related professional development programs.

Elementary Education

6240 **Curriculum Associates**
153 Rangeway Road
No. Billerica, MA 01862
978-667-8000
800-225-0248
Fax: 800-366-1158
www.curriculumassociates.com
Test preparation material with a guarantee of success; skill instruction and assessment.
Frank E. Ferguson, Chairman
Robert Waldron, Chief Executive Officer

6241 **Diagnostic Reading Inventory for Primaryand Intermediate Grades K-8**
Scott and McCleary Publishing Co.
PO Box 3830
Akron, OH 44314-0830
702-566-8756
800-765-3564
Fax: 702-568-1378
jscott7576@aol.com
www.scottmccleary.com
A series of 13 tests at each grade level, 10 can be given in a group setting. 3 Forms of the IRI teacher friendly. Easy to administer.
Spiral Paperback
ISBN: 0-9636225-4-4
Janet M. Scott and Sheila C. McCeary, Author
Janet Scott, Co-Author
Sheila McCleary, Co-Author

6242 **Lexia Learning Systems**
200 Baker Ave Ext.
Concord, MA 01742
978-405-6200
800-435-3942
Fax: 978-287-0062
info@lexialearning.com
www.lexialearning.com
Reading software and assessment programs for children and adults, professional development programs for teachers, principals and administrators.
Elizabeth C. Crawford Brooke, VP, Education & Research
Collin Earnst, VP, Marketing

6243 **National Study of School Evaluation**
1699 E Woodfield Road
Suite 406
Schaumburg, IL 60173-4958
847-995-9080
800-843-6773
Fax: 847-995-9088
schoolimprovement@nsse.org
www.nsse.org
Provides educational leaders with state-of-the-art assessment and evaluation materials to enhance and promote student growth and school improvement.
Dr. Kathleen A. Fitzpatrick, Executive Director

6244 **Pro-Ed, Inc.**
8700 Shoal Creek Blvd
Austin, TX 78757-6897
800-897-3202
Fax: 800-397-7633
info@proedinc.com
www.linguisystems.com
Offers tests and print materials for speech language pathologists, teachers of the learning disabled, middle school language arts and reading teachers.

6245 **Testing Miss Malarky**
Bloomsbury Publishing Inc.
1385 Broadway
5th Floor
New York, NY 10018
212-419-5300
888-330-8477
Fax: 212-727-0984
ebookhelp@bloomsbury.com
www.bloomsbury.com
Author and artist exploit the mania that accompanies the classes first standardized test.
32 pages
ISBN: 0-8027-8737-1
Judy Finchler, Contact

Language Arts

6246 **DRC/CTB**
20 Ryan Ranch Road
Monterey, CA 93940
800-538-9547
Fax: 763-268-3000
customer_service_ind@ctb.com
www.ctb.com
A division of the Data Recognition Corporation and publisher of educational assessments such as K-12 achievement tests, early literacy assessment, language proficiency evaluation, adult basic skills tests and test management/instructional planning software.
Laurie Bauer, Test Development Specialist
Rob Mann, Director, DRC Info Systems

6247 **SLEP Program Office**
PO Box 6155
Princeton, NJ 08541-6155
Offers information on the Secondary Level English Proficiency Test.

Mathematics

6248 **Psychological Assessment Resources**
16204 North Florida Avenue
Lutz, FL 33549
813-961-2196
800-331-TEST
Fax: 800-727-9329
www.parinc.com
Catalog of professional testing resources.

6249 **Summing It Up: College Board Mathematics Assessment Programs**
College Board Publications
45 Columbus Avenue
New York, NY 10023-6992
212-713-8000
800-323-7155
Fax: 800-525-5562
www.collegeboard.org
An overview of SAT I: Reasoning Tests and PSAT/NMSQT, SAT II: Subject Tests, Descriptive Tests of Mathematical Skills (DTMS), CPTs in Mathematics, CLEP Mathematics Examinations, AP Exams in Mathematics, AP Exams in Computer Sciences, and Pacesetter Mathematics.
30 pages
David Coleman, President/ CEO
Jeremy Singer, Chief Operating Officer

Music & Art

6250 **A&F Video's Art Catalog**
PO Box 264
Geneseo, NY 14454
www.aandfvideo.com
New listing of titles for Art Teachers and Art Lovers.

6251 **All Art Supplies**
Art Supplies Wholesale
4 Enon Street
North Beverly, MA 01915
800-462-2420
Fax: 978-922-1495
info@allartsupplies.com
www.allartsupplies.com
Art supplies at wholesale prices.

6252 **American Art Clay Company**
6060 Guion Road
Indianapolis, IN 46254
317-244-6871
800-374-1600
Fax: 317-248-9300
salessupport@amaco.com
www.amaco.com
Provides ceramic materials and equipment.

6253 **Arnold Grummer**
PO Box 13245
Milwaukee, WI 53213
800-453-1485
Fax: 414-453-1495
webmaster@arnoldgrummer.com
www.arnoldgrummer.com
Products and information to meet most any papermaking need.

6254 **Arrowmont School of Arts & Crafts**
556 Parkway
Gainsburg, TN 37738
865-438-5860
Fax: 865-438-4101
info@arrowmont.org
www.arrowmont.org
The art school of tomorrow.
Marty Begalla, President
Susie Glenn, Vice President

6255 **Art & Creative Materials Institute**
99 Derby St.
Suite 200
Hingham, MA 02043
781-556-1044
Fax: 781-207-5550
debbiem@acminet.org
www.acminet.org
A non-profit trade association whose memebers are manufacturers of art and creative materials. Sponsors a certification program to ensure that art materials are non-toxic or affixed with health warning labels where appropriate. Publishes a booklet on the safe use of art materials and a listing of products that are approved under its certification program. Both of these publications are free of charge.
Debbie Gustafson, Deputy Director
David H Baker, Executive Director

6256 **Art Instruction Schools**
3309 Broadway Street NW
Minneapolis, MN 55413
www.artists-ais.com

6257 **Art to Remember**
5535 Macy Drive
Indianapolis, IN 46235
317-826-0870
800-895-8777
Fax: 317-823-2822
info@arttoremember.com
www.arttoremember.com

A unique program that encourages your students' artisic creativity while providing an oppurtunity to raise funds for schools.

6258 ArtSketchbook.com
487 Hulsetown Road
Campbell Hall, NY 10916
845-496-4709
www.artsketchbook.com
Provides instructions and work examples by an elementary student, secondary student and a professional artist.

6259 Arts Institutes International
Education Management Corporation
210 Sixth Avenue
33rd Floor
Pittsburgh, PA 15222
888-624-0300
csprogramadmin@edmc.edu
www.artinstitutes.edu
Post-secondary career education. Offers associate's, bachelor's and non-degree programs in design, media arts, technology, culinary arts and fashion.

6260 Museum Stamps
PO Box 356
New Canaan, CT 06840
800-659-2787
Fax: 203-966-2729
www.museumstamps.com
Rubber stamps of famous works of art, stamp accessories, classroom projects.

6261 Music Ace 2
Harmonic Vision
1433 Rapids Trl
Nekoosa, WI 54457
715-325-3252
800-474-0903
Fax: 866-422-6686
www.harmonicvision.com
Introduces concepts such as standard notation, rhythm, melody, time signatures, harmony, intervals and more.

6262 www.ilford.com
Ilford
www.ilford.com
Partners in imaging.

6263 www.schoolrenaissance.com
Renaissance Learning
2911 Peach Street
Wisconsin Rapids, WI 54494
715-424-3636
800-338-4204
Fax: 715-424-4242
answers@renaissance.com
www.renaissance.com
The School Renaissance Model combines the #1 software in education with professional development and consulting services to help you dramatically improve student performance.

John J. Lynch Jr., Chief Executive Officer
Mary T. Minch, EVP, Finance & CFO

6264 www.speedballart.com
2301 Speedball Road
Statesville, NC 28677
800-898-7224
www.speedballart.com
Speedball lesson plans and teaching aids for calligraphy, stamping, printmaking, drawing, painting and more.

Walt Glazer, Chief Executive

Reading

6265 Advantage Learning Systems
2911 Peach Street
PO Box 8036
Wisconsin Rapids, WI 54495-8036
800-338-4204
Fax: 715-424-4242
mail@advlearn.com
www.advlearn.com
New computer-adaptive tests that assess student reading and math levels in just 15 minutes or less.

6266 Educational Testing Service/Library
Test Collection
Rosedale Road
Princeton, NJ 08541
609-734-5686
Fax: 609-734-5410
Provides information on tests and related materials to those in research and advisory services and educational activities.

Janet Williams, President

6267 National Foundation for Dyslexia
4801 Hermitage Road
Richmond, VA 23227-3332
804-262-0586
800-SOS-READ
Provides screenings for schools or individuals and assists individuals with IEP's. Provides information about support groups and organizations and teacher training workshops.

Jo Powell, Executive Director

6268 Psychological Assessment Resources
16204 North Florida Avenue
Lutz, FL 33549
813-961-2196
800-331-TEST
Fax: 800-727-9329
www.parinc.com
Catalog of professional testing resources.

6269 www.schoolrenaissance.com
Renaissance Learning
2911 Peach Street
Wisconsin Rapids, WI 54494
715-424-3636
800-338-4204
Fax: 715-424-4242
answers@renaissance.com
www.renaissance.com
The School Renaissance Model combines the #1 software in education with professional development and consulting services to help you dramatically improve student performance.

John J. Lynch Jr., Chief Executive Officer
Mary T. Minch, EVP, Finance & CFO

6270 www.voyagerlearning.com
Cambium Learning Group
17855 Dallas Parkway
Suite 400
Dallas, TX 75287
www.voyagersopris.com
Improves students performance in reading for those at different grade levels.

Secondary Education

6271 ACT
PO Box 4060
Iowa City, IA 52243-0001
319-337-1000
800-498-6065
Offers a full-service catalog of tests for intermediate and secondary schools organized by assessment, career and educational planning, study skills, surveys and research services.

Catalog

6272 Admission Officer's Handbook for the New SAT Program
College Board Publications
45 Columbus Avenue
New York, NY 10023-6992
212-713-8000
800-323-7155
Fax: 800-525-5562
www.collegeboard.org
Designed to help college admission staff quickly find information on the new SAT program, the Handbook has detailed descriptions of score reports and special services for colleges.

56 pages

David Coleman, President/ CEO
Jeremy Singer, Chief Operating Officer

6273 American College Testing
ACT
2201 Dodge
#168
Iowa City, IA 52243-0001
319-337-1028
Fax: 319-337-1014
gullettk@act.org
www.act.org
Provides educational assessment services to students and their parents, high schools, colleges and professional associations. Also workforce development services, including a network of ACT Centers and the Workkeys program.

Jon Whitmore, Chief Executive Officer
Janet E. Godwin, Chief Operating Officer

6274 College-Bound Seniors
College Board Publications
45 Columbus Avenue
New York, NY 10023-6992
212-713-8000
800-323-7155
Fax: 800-525-5562
www.collegeboard.org
Profile of SAT and achievement test takers, national report.

13 pages

David Coleman, President/ CEO
Jeremy Singer, Chief Operating Officer

6275 CollegeChoice, StudentChoice
College Board Publications
45 Columbus Avenue
New York, NY 10023-6992
212-713-8000
800-323-7155
Fax: 800-525-5562
www.collegeboard.org
This video provides a reassuring perspective on the SAT's importance and how the college admission process really works. It shows how SAT scores are only one of many elements in the admission picture and emphasizes academic preparation for college and discusses the SAT within the context of the entire admission process.

15 Minutes

David Coleman, President/ CEO
Jeremy Singer, Chief Operating Officer

6276 Counselor's Handbook for the SAT Program
College Board Publications
45 Columbus Avenue
New York, NY 10023-6992

212-713-8000
800-323-7155
Fax: 800-525-5562
www.collegeboard.org
Easy-to-use reference provides details on the new SAT program tests and services.

64 pages

David Coleman, President/ CEO
Jeremy Singer, Chief Operating Officer

6277 Destination College: Planning with the PSAT/NMSQT
College Board Publications
45 Columbus Avenue
New York, NY 10023-6992
212-713-8000
800-323-7155
Fax: 800-525-5562
www.collegeboard.org
This new video offers schools an ideal format for explaining the features and benefits of the PSAT/NMSQT Score Report to groups of students.

18 Minutes

David Coleman, President/ CEO
Jeremy Singer, Chief Operating Officer

6278 Educational Testing Service
660 Rosedale Road
Princeton, NJ 08541
609-921-9000
Fax: 609-734-5410
www.ets.org
Private educational measurement institution and a leader in educational research.

Susan Keipper, Program Director

6279 Focus on the SAT: What's on it, How to Prepare & What Colleges Look For
College Board Publications
45 Columbus Avenue
New York, NY 10023-6992
212-713-8000
800-323-7155
Fax: 800-525-5562
www.collegeboard.org
The authoritative video for students on how to prepare for the SAT and PSAT/NMSQT. It provides test-taking tips, sample test questions, and an explanation of how SAT is developed.

20 Minutes

David Coleman, President/ CEO
Jeremy Singer, Chief Operating Officer

6280 GED Testing Service
American Council on Education
1 Dupont Cir NW
Washington, DC 20036-1110
202-939-9490
877-392-6433
Fax: 202-775-8578
help@GEDtestingservice.com
www.gedtestingservice.com
The largest testing service in the United States. Maintains a full line of tests and testing resources for all areas of education and all grade levels K-college level testing.

Randy Trask, President/ CEO

6281 Guide to the College Board Validity Study Service
College Board Publications
45 Columbus Avenue
New York, NY 10023-6992
212-713-8000
800-323-7155
Fax: 800-525-5562
www.collegeboard.org
The purpose of this manual is to assist Validity Study Service users in designing and interpreting validity studies. It provides design suggestions, sample admission and placement studies, advice on interpreting studies, and a discussion of basic statistical concepts.

60 pages

David Coleman, President/ CEO
Jeremy Singer, Chief Operating Officer

6282 Look Inside the SAT I: Test Prep from the Test Makers Video
College Board Publications
45 Columbus Avenue
New York, NY 10023-6992
212-713-8000
800-323-7155
Fax: 800-525-5562
www.collegeboard.org
Brings the College Board's test-taking tips to life through interviews with people from different backgrounds who recount their SAT experiences.

30 Minutes
ISBN: 0-874475-29-5

David Coleman, President/ CEO
Jeremy Singer, Chief Operating Officer

6283 Master The GMAT
Peterson's, A Nelnet Company
461 From Road
Paramus, NJ 07652
609-896-1800
800-338-3282
Fax: 402-458-3042
custsvc@petersons.com
www.petersons.com
Helps test takers get ready, develop test-preparation strategies and manage test anxiety constructively, whether they have seven weeks to prepare or just one day.

672 pages Book & Disk

Martinson, Author

6284 Master The SAT
Peterson's, A Nelnet Company
461 From Road
Paramus, NJ 07652
609-896-1800
800-338-3282
Fax: 402-458-3042
custsvc@petersons.com
www.petersons.com
Features easily accessible Red Alert sections offering essential tips for test-taking success. Provides students with the critical skills they need to tackle the SAT.

821 pages Book & Disk
ISBN: 1-560796-06-5

John Davenport Carris with Michael R. Crystal, Author

6285 National Center for Fair & Open Testing
P.O. Box 300204
Jamaica Plain, MA 02130
617-477-9792
Fax: 617-497-2224
www.fairtest.org
Dedicated to ensuring that America's students and workers are assessed using fair, accurate, relevant and open tests.

Cinthia Schuman, President

6286 National Study of School Evaluation
1699 E Woodfield Road
Suite 406
Schaumburg, IL 60173-4958
847-995-9080
800-843-6773
Fax: 847-995-9088
schoolimprovement@nsse.org
www.nsse.org
Provides educational leaders with state-of-the-art assessment and evaluation materials to enhance and promote student growth and school improvement.

Dr. Kathleen A. Fitzpatrick, Executive Director

6287 Official Guide to the SAT II: Subject Tests
College Board Publications
45 Columbus Avenue
New York, NY 10023-6992
212-713-8000
800-323-7155
Fax: 800-525-5562
www.collegeboard.org
The authoritative preparation guide for students taking the SAT II: Subject Tests. The guide includes full-length practice Subject Tests, along with answer sheets, answer keys, and scoring instructions for Writing, Literature, American History, World History, Math I, Math IIC, Biology, Chemistry and Physics. It also includes minitests in French (reading only), German (reading only), Italian, Latin, Modern Hebrew, and Spanish.

380 pages
ISBN: 0-874474-88-4

David Coleman, President/ CEO
Jeremy Singer, Chief Operating Officer

6288 One-On-One with the SAT
College Board Publications
45 Columbus Avenue
New York, NY 10023-6992
212-713-8000
800-323-7155
Fax: 800-525-5562
www.collegeboard.org
Gives students easy access to proven advice and test-taking strategies directly from the test makers, as well as a unique chance to take a real SAT on computer. This program also includes password protection for each student record and toll-free technical support.

Home License

David Coleman, President/ CEO
Jeremy Singer, Chief Operating Officer

6289 Panic Plan for the SAT
Peterson's, A Nelnet Company
461 From Road
Paramus, NJ 07652
609-896-1800
800-338-3282
Fax: 402-458-3042
custsvc@petersons.com
www.petersons.com
An excellent, two-week review, featuring actual questions from the SAT. Helps students make the most out of the limited time they have left to study.

368 pages
ISBN: 1-560794-32-1

Michael R Crystal, Author

6290 Pearson's Clinical Assessment Group
PO Box 599700
San Antonio, TX 78259
800-627-7271
Fax: 800-232-1223
clinicalcustomersupport@pearson.com
www.pearsonclinical.com
Provides assessment materials for teachers in all areas of curricula.

Bob Whelan, President

6291 Preventing School Failure
Taylor & Francis
325 Chestnut Street
Suite 800
Philadelphia, PA 19106
215-625-8900
800-354-1420
Fax: 202-296-5149
customer.service@taylorandfrancis.com
www.heldref.org
The articles cover a broad array of specific topics, from important technical aspects and adaptions of functional behavioral assessment to descriptions of projects in which functional behavioral assessment is being used to provide technical assistance to preschools, schools, and families who must deal eith children and adolescents who present serious challenging behaviors.

Quarterly
ISSN: 1045-988X

Sheldon Braaten, Executive Editor

6292 Psychometric Affiliates
PO Box 807
Murfreeboro, TN 37133
615-890-6296
Testing instruments for use by educational institutions.

Jeannette Heritage

6293 Real SAT's
College Board Publications
45 Columbus Avenue
New York, NY 10023-6992
212-713-8000
800-323-7155
Fax: 800-525-5562
www.collegeboard.org
The only preparation guide that contains actual scorable tests. It has been developed to help the millions of students taking the tests each year to do their best on the PSAT/NMSQT and SAT and to improve their scores.

396 pages
ISBN: 0-874475-11-2

David Coleman, President/ CEO
Jeremy Singer, Chief Operating Officer

6294 Registration Bulletin
College Board Publications
45 Columbus Avenue
New York, NY 10023-6992
212-713-8000
800-323-7155
Fax: 800-525-5562
www.collegeboard.org
Available in five regional and a New York State edition, the Bulletin provides information on how to register for the SAT I and SAT II, and on how to use the related services.

24 pages

David Coleman, President/ CEO
Jeremy Singer, Chief Operating Officer

6295 SAT Services for Students with Disabilities
College Board Publications
45 Columbus Avenue
New York, NY 10023-6992
212-713-8000
800-323-7155
Fax: 800-525-5562
www.collegeboard.org
Describes arrangements for students with physical, hearing, visual and learning disabilities who wish to take the SAT I and/or SAT II.

6 pages

David Coleman, President/ CEO
Jeremy Singer, Chief Operating Officer

6296 Scholastic Testing Service
480 Meyer Road
Bensenville, IL 60106-1617
630-766-7150
800-642-6787
Fax: 630-766-8054
sts@ststesting.com
www.ststesting.com
Publisher of assessment materials from birth into adulthood, ability and achievement tests for kindergarten through grade twelve. Tests are also constructed on contract for educational agencies and school districts. Publish the Torrance Tests of Creative Thinking, Thinking Creatively in Action and Movement, the STS High School Placement Test and Educational Development Series.

OF Anderhalter, President
John D Kauffman, VP Marketing

6297 TOEFL Test and Score Manual
College Board Publications
45 Columbus Avenue
New York, NY 10023-6992
212-713-8000
800-323-7155
Fax: 800-525-5562
www.collegeboard.org
Focuses on information that college admissions officers, foreign student advisers and other users of TOEFL score reports need to know about the operation of the TOEFL program, the test itself, and the interpretation of scores.

48 pages

David Coleman, President/ CEO
Jeremy Singer, Chief Operating Officer

6298 Taking the SAT I: Reasoning Test
College Board Publications
45 Columbus Avenue
New York, NY 10023-6992
212-713-8000
800-323-7155
Fax: 800-525-5562
www.collegeboard.org
A complete guide for students who plan to take the SAT I: Reasoning Test.

80 pages

David Coleman, President/ CEO
Jeremy Singer, Chief Operating Officer

6299 Taking the SAT II: The Official Guide to the SAT II: Subject Tests
College Board Publications
45 Columbus Avenue
New York, NY 10023-6992
212-713-8000
800-323-7155
Fax: 800-525-5562
www.collegeboard.org
Provides information about the content and format of each of the SAT II: Subject Tests, as well as test-taking advice and sample questions.

95 pages

David Coleman, President/ CEO
Jeremy Singer, Chief Operating Officer

6300 TestSkills
College Board Publications
45 Columbus Avenue
New York, NY 10023-6992
212-713-8000
800-323-7155
Fax: 800-525-5562
www.collegeboard.org
A preparation program for the PSAT/NMSQT that helps students, particularly those from minority and disadvantaged groups, sharpen skills and increase confidence needed to succeed on the tests.

Spiral-Bound

David Coleman, President/ CEO
Jeremy Singer, Chief Operating Officer

6301 Think Before You Punch: Using Calculators on the New SAT I and PSAT/NMSQT
College Board Publications
45 Columbus Avenue
New York, NY 10023-6992
212-713-8000
800-323-7155
Fax: 800-525-5562
www.collegeboard.org
This video looks at the pros and cons of calculators usage on a test. In it, students talk about using them, and College Board and ETS staff explain the new calculator policy. It works through math questions that may or may not best be answered with the help of a calculator.

12 Minutes

David Coleman, President/ CEO
Jeremy Singer, Chief Operating Officer

Secondary Education

6302 American Council on Education: GED Testing Service
1919 M Street NW
Suite 600
Washington, DC 20036
877-392-6433
communications@gedtestingservice.com
www.gedtestingservice.com
A test delivered via computer to adult learners, to help them gain the skills and knowledge they need to be employable.

Randy Trask, President & CEO
Vicki Greene, VP, Operations

EDUCATION STATISTICS

Table 104.10. Rates of high school completion and bachelor's degree attainment among persons age 25 and over, by race/ethnicity and sex: Selected years, 1910 through 2015

[Standard errors appear in parentheses]

Sex, high school or bachelor's degree attainment, and year	Total, percent of all persons age 25 and over	White[1]	Black[1]	Hispanic	Asian/Pacific Islander			American Indian/ Alaska Native	Two or more races
					Total	Asian	Pacific Islander		
1	2	3	4	5	6	7	8	9	10
Total									
High school completion or higher[2]									
1910[3]	13.5 (—)	— (†)	— (†)	— (†)	— (†)	— (†)	— (†)	— (†)	— (†)
1920[3]	16.4 (—)	— (†)	— (†)	— (†)	— (†)	— (†)	— (†)	— (†)	— (†)
1930[3]	19.1 (—)	— (†)	— (†)	— (†)	— (†)	— (†)	— (†)	— (†)	— (†)
1940	24.5 (—)	26.1 (—)	7.7 (—)	— (†)	— (†)	— (†)	— (†)	— (†)	— (†)
1950	34.3 (—)	36.4 (—)	13.7 (—)	— (†)	— (†)	— (†)	— (†)	— (†)	— (†)
1960	41.1 (—)	43.2 (—)	21.7 (—)	— (†)	— (†)	— (†)	— (†)	— (†)	— (†)
1970	55.2 (—)	57.4 (—)	36.1 (—)	— (†)	— (†)	— (†)	— (†)	— (†)	— (†)
1975	62.5 (—)	65.8 (—)	42.6 (—)	38.5 (—)	— (†)	— (†)	— (†)	— (†)	— (†)
1980	68.6 (0.20)	71.9 (0.21)	51.4 (0.81)	44.5 (1.18)	— (†)	— (†)	— (†)	— (†)	— (†)
1985	73.9 (0.18)	77.5 (0.19)	59.9 (0.74)	47.9 (0.99)	— (†)	— (†)	— (†)	— (†)	— (†)
1986	74.7 (0.18)	78.2 (0.19)	62.5 (0.72)	48.5 (0.96)	— (†)	— (†)	— (†)	— (†)	— (†)
1987	75.6 (0.17)	79.0 (0.18)	63.6 (0.71)	50.9 (0.94)	— (†)	— (†)	— (†)	— (†)	— (†)
1988	76.2 (0.17)	79.8 (0.18)	63.5 (0.70)	51.0 (0.92)	— (†)	— (†)	— (†)	— (†)	— (†)
1989	76.9 (0.17)	80.7 (0.18)	64.7 (0.69)	50.9 (0.89)	82.3 (1.17)	— (†)	— (†)	— (†)	— (†)
1990	77.6 (0.17)	81.4 (0.17)	66.2 (0.67)	50.8 (0.88)	84.2 (1.09)	— (†)	— (†)	— (†)	— (†)
1991	78.4 (0.16)	82.4 (0.17)	66.8 (0.66)	51.3 (0.86)	84.2 (1.05)	— (†)	— (†)	— (†)	— (†)
1992	79.4 (0.16)	83.4 (0.16)	67.7 (0.65)	52.6 (0.85)	83.7 (1.02)	— (†)	— (†)	— (†)	— (†)
1993	80.2 (0.16)	84.1 (0.16)	70.5 (0.63)	53.1 (0.83)	84.2 (1.00)	— (†)	— (†)	— (†)	— (†)
1994	80.9 (0.15)	84.9 (0.16)	73.0 (0.61)	53.3 (0.78)	84.8 (0.98)	— (†)	— (†)	— (†)	— (†)
1995	81.7 (0.15)	85.9 (0.16)	73.8 (0.61)	53.4 (0.78)	83.8 (1.06)	— (†)	— (†)	— (†)	— (†)
1996	81.7 (0.16)	86.0 (0.16)	74.6 (0.53)	53.1 (0.68)	83.5 (0.82)	— (†)	— (†)	— (†)	— (†)
1997	82.1 (0.14)	86.3 (0.15)	75.3 (0.52)	54.7 (0.54)	85.2 (0.75)	— (†)	— (†)	— (†)	— (†)
1998	82.8 (0.14)	87.1 (0.14)	76.4 (0.50)	55.5 (0.53)	84.9 (0.74)	— (†)	— (†)	— (†)	— (†)
1999	83.4 (0.14)	87.7 (0.14)	77.4 (0.49)	56.1 (0.52)	84.7 (0.73)	— (†)	— (†)	— (†)	— (†)
2000	84.1 (0.13)	88.4 (0.14)	78.9 (0.48)	57.0 (0.51)	85.7 (0.71)	— (†)	— (†)	— (†)	— (†)
2001	84.3 (0.13)	88.7 (0.13)	79.5 (0.47)	56.5 (0.50)	87.8 (0.60)	— (†)	— (†)	— (†)	— (†)
2002	84.1 (0.09)	88.7 (0.10)	79.2 (0.34)	57.0 (0.34)	87.7 (0.44)	— (†)	— (†)	— (†)	— (†)
2003	84.6 (0.09)	89.4 (0.09)	80.3 (0.33)	57.0 (0.33)	87.8 (0.43)	87.8 (0.44)	88.2 (1.87)	77.2 (1.64)	86.1 (0.97)
2004	85.2 (0.09)	90.0 (0.09)	81.1 (0.32)	58.4 (0.32)	86.9 (0.43)	86.9 (0.44)	88.5 (1.91)	77.8 (1.61)	87.2 (0.91)
2005	85.2 (0.14)	90.1 (0.16)	81.4 (0.44)	58.5 (0.53)	87.8 (0.62)	87.7 (0.62)	90.1 (2.69)	75.6 (2.02)	88.6 (0.83)
2006	85.5 (0.15)	90.5 (0.15)	81.2 (0.43)	59.3 (0.58)	87.5 (0.71)	87.5 (0.71)	85.7 (2.51)	78.5 (2.11)	88.1 (0.90)
2007	85.7 (0.15)	90.6 (0.15)	82.8 (0.39)	60.3 (0.56)	88.0 (0.79)	87.9 (0.81)	88.6 (2.30)	80.3 (2.27)	89.3 (0.87)
2008	86.6 (0.15)	91.5 (0.15)	83.3 (0.40)	62.3 (0.58)	89.0 (0.62)	88.8 (0.64)	94.4 (1.00)	78.4 (2.74)	89.5 (1.12)
2009	86.7 (0.15)	91.6 (0.15)	84.2 (0.44)	61.9 (0.56)	88.4 (0.61)	88.3 (0.63)	90.8 (1.76)	81.5 (1.83)	87.4 (0.96)
2010	87.1 (0.13)	92.1 (0.14)	84.6 (0.41)	62.9 (0.53)	89.1 (0.67)	89.1 (0.68)	90.2 (1.95)	80.8 (1.76)	88.9 (0.90)
2011	87.6 (0.13)	92.4 (0.14)	84.8 (0.41)	64.3 (0.54)	88.8 (0.55)	88.7 (0.57)	90.4 (1.61)	82.3 (1.77)	89.4 (1.00)
2012	87.6 (0.15)	92.5 (0.14)	85.7 (0.40)	65.0 (0.59)	89.2 (0.59)	89.0 (0.61)	91.6 (1.33)	81.8 (1.69)	91.0 (0.89)
2013	88.2 (0.14)	92.9 (0.13)	85.9 (0.42)	66.2 (0.52)	90.2 (0.51)	90.2 (0.53)	89.5 (1.72)	82.2 (1.68)	92.6 (0.75)
2014	88.3 (0.15)	93.1 (0.17)	86.7 (0.45)	66.5 (0.57)	89.5 (0.62)	89.5 (0.64)	88.8 (2.15)	81.0 (2.01)	93.3 (0.88)
2015	88.4 (0.12)	93.3 (0.13)	87.7 (0.37)	66.7 (0.48)	88.9 (0.49)	89.1 (0.51)	85.1 (2.04)	83.8 (1.64)	91.6 (0.87)
Bachelor's or higher degree[4]									
1910[3]	2.7 (—)	— (†)	— (†)	— (†)	— (†)	— (†)	— (†)	— (†)	— (†)
1920[3]	3.3 (—)	— (†)	— (†)	— (†)	— (†)	— (†)	— (†)	— (†)	— (†)
1930[3]	3.9 (—)	— (†)	— (†)	— (†)	— (†)	— (†)	— (†)	— (†)	— (†)
1940	4.6 (—)	4.9 (—)	1.3 (—)	— (†)	— (†)	— (†)	— (†)	— (†)	— (†)
1950	6.2 (—)	6.6 (—)	2.2 (—)	— (†)	— (†)	— (†)	— (†)	— (†)	— (†)
1960	7.7 (—)	8.1 (—)	3.5 (—)	— (†)	— (†)	— (†)	— (†)	— (†)	— (†)
1970	11.0 (—)	11.6 (—)	6.1 (—)	— (†)	— (†)	— (†)	— (†)	— (†)	— (†)
1975	13.9 (—)	14.9 (—)	6.4 (—)	6.6 (—)	— (†)	— (†)	— (†)	— (†)	— (†)
1980	17.0 (0.16)	18.4 (0.18)	7.9 (0.44)	7.6 (0.63)	— (†)	— (†)	— (†)	— (†)	— (†)
1985	19.4 (0.16)	20.8 (0.19)	11.1 (0.47)	8.5 (0.55)	— (†)	— (†)	— (†)	— (†)	— (†)
1986	19.4 (0.16)	20.9 (0.19)	10.9 (0.47)	8.4 (0.53)	— (†)	— (†)	— (†)	— (†)	— (†)
1987	19.9 (0.16)	21.4 (0.19)	10.8 (0.46)	8.6 (0.53)	— (†)	— (†)	— (†)	— (†)	— (†)
1988	20.3 (0.16)	21.8 (0.19)	11.2 (0.46)	10.0 (0.55)	— (†)	— (†)	— (†)	— (†)	— (†)
1989	21.1 (0.16)	22.8 (0.19)	11.7 (0.46)	9.9 (0.53)	41.5 (1.51)	— (†)	— (†)	— (†)	— (†)
1990	21.3 (0.16)	23.1 (0.19)	11.3 (0.45)	9.2 (0.51)	41.7 (1.47)	— (†)	— (†)	— (†)	— (†)
1991	21.4 (0.16)	23.3 (0.19)	11.5 (0.45)	9.7 (0.51)	40.3 (1.42)	— (†)	— (†)	— (†)	— (†)
1992	21.4 (0.16)	23.2 (0.19)	11.9 (0.45)	9.3 (0.49)	39.3 (1.35)	— (†)	— (†)	— (†)	— (†)
1993	21.9 (0.16)	23.8 (0.19)	12.2 (0.45)	9.0 (0.48)	42.1 (1.35)	— (†)	— (†)	— (†)	— (†)
1994	22.2 (0.16)	24.3 (0.19)	12.9 (0.46)	9.1 (0.45)	41.3 (1.34)	— (†)	— (†)	— (†)	— (†)
1995	23.0 (0.16)	25.4 (0.19)	13.3 (0.47)	9.3 (0.45)	38.5 (1.40)	— (†)	— (†)	— (†)	— (†)
1996	23.6 (0.17)	25.9 (0.20)	13.8 (0.42)	9.3 (0.40)	42.3 (1.09)	— (†)	— (†)	— (†)	— (†)
1997	23.9 (0.16)	26.2 (0.19)	13.3 (0.41)	10.3 (0.33)	42.6 (1.04)	— (†)	— (†)	— (†)	— (†)
1998	24.4 (0.16)	26.6 (0.19)	14.8 (0.42)	11.0 (0.33)	42.3 (1.02)	— (†)	— (†)	— (†)	— (†)
1999	25.2 (0.16)	27.7 (0.19)	15.5 (0.43)	10.9 (0.33)	42.4 (1.01)	— (†)	— (†)	— (†)	— (†)
2000	25.6 (0.16)	28.1 (0.19)	16.6 (0.44)	10.6 (0.32)	44.4 (1.00)	— (†)	— (†)	— (†)	— (†)
2001	26.1 (0.16)	28.6 (0.19)	16.1 (0.43)	11.2 (0.32)	48.0 (0.92)	— (†)	— (†)	— (†)	— (†)
2002	26.7 (0.11)	29.4 (0.14)	17.2 (0.31)	11.1 (0.21)	47.7 (0.66)	— (†)	— (†)	— (†)	— (†)
2003	27.2 (0.11)	30.0 (0.14)	17.4 (0.31)	11.4 (0.21)	48.8 (0.65)	50.0 (0.67)	27.0 (2.56)	12.6 (1.30)	22.0 (1.17)
2004	27.7 (0.11)	30.6 (0.14)	17.7 (0.31)	12.1 (0.21)	48.9 (0.64)	49.7 (0.66)	32.4 (2.81)	14.3 (1.36)	21.8 (1.13)
2005	27.7 (0.23)	30.6 (0.29)	17.6 (0.45)	12.0 (0.31)	49.3 (0.91)	50.4 (0.93)	24.6 (3.67)	14.5 (1.51)	23.2 (1.19)

See notes at end of table.

Table 104.10. Rates of high school completion and bachelor's degree attainment among persons age 25 and over, by race/ethnicity and sex: Selected years, 1910 through 2015—Continued

[Standard errors appear in parentheses]

Sex, high school or bachelor's degree attainment, and year	Total, percent of all persons age 25 and over		White[1]		Black[1]		Hispanic		Asian/Pacific Islander: Total		Asian/Pacific Islander: Asian		Asian/Pacific Islander: Pacific Islander		American Indian/ Alaska Native		Two or more races	
1	2		3		4		5		6		7		8		9		10	
2006	28.0	(0.20)	31.0	(0.25)	18.6	(0.47)	12.4	(0.32)	49.1	(1.04)	50.0	(1.06)	26.9	(3.42)	12.9	(1.60)	23.1	(1.28)
2007	28.7	(0.21)	31.8	(0.27)	18.7	(0.51)	12.7	(0.31)	51.2	(1.02)	52.5	(1.03)	23.8	(3.30)	13.1	(1.24)	23.7	(1.30)
2008	29.4	(0.21)	32.6	(0.26)	19.7	(0.51)	13.3	(0.29)	51.9	(0.95)	52.9	(0.97)	28.4	(2.86)	14.9	(1.52)	24.4	(1.36)
2009	29.5	(0.21)	32.9	(0.26)	19.4	(0.45)	13.2	(0.34)	51.6	(0.91)	52.8	(0.95)	28.3	(2.68)	17.5	(2.08)	25.5	(1.34)
2010	29.9	(0.19)	33.2	(0.24)	20.0	(0.51)	13.9	(0.31)	51.6	(1.04)	52.8	(1.09)	25.6	(2.89)	16.0	(1.77)	25.3	(1.30)
2011	30.4	(0.19)	34.0	(0.24)	20.2	(0.50)	14.1	(0.34)	49.5	(0.92)	50.8	(0.96)	22.1	(2.73)	16.1	(1.73)	27.4	(1.27)
2012	30.9	(0.21)	34.5	(0.27)	21.4	(0.53)	14.5	(0.35)	50.7	(0.92)	51.9	(0.94)	24.5	(2.75)	16.7	(1.82)	27.1	(1.34)
2013	31.7	(0.21)	35.2	(0.26)	22.0	(0.49)	15.1	(0.34)	52.5	(0.92)	53.9	(0.93)	25.6	(2.66)	15.4	(1.72)	30.6	(1.35)
2014	32.0	(0.27)	35.6	(0.35)	22.8	(0.66)	15.2	(0.39)	51.3	(1.00)	52.7	(1.02)	22.3	(3.27)	13.8	(1.43)	31.2	(1.81)
2015	32.5	(0.22)	36.2	(0.28)	22.9	(0.52)	15.5	(0.31)	52.9	(0.84)	54.4	(0.87)	22.8	(2.39)	19.8	(1.32)	30.6	(1.52)
Males																		
High school completion or higher[2]																		
1940	22.7	(—)	24.2	(—)	6.9	(—)	—	(†)	—	(†)	—	(†)	—	(†)	—	(†)	—	(†)
1950	32.6	(—)	34.6	(—)	12.6	(—)	—	(†)	—	(†)	—	(†)	—	(†)	—	(†)	—	(†)
1960	39.5	(—)	41.6	(—)	20.0	(—)	—	(†)	—	(†)	—	(†)	—	(†)	—	(†)	—	(†)
1970	55.0	(—)	57.2	(—)	35.4	(—)	—	(†)	—	(†)	—	(†)	—	(†)	—	(†)	—	(†)
1980	69.2	(0.29)	72.4	(0.31)	51.2	(1.21)	44.9	(1.71)	—	(†)	—	(†)	—	(†)	—	(†)	—	(†)
1990	77.7	(0.24)	81.6	(0.25)	65.8	(1.01)	50.3	(1.25)	86.0	(1.49)	—	(†)	—	(†)	—	(†)	—	(†)
1995	81.7	(0.22)	86.0	(0.22)	73.5	(0.91)	52.9	(1.11)	85.8	(1.46)	—	(†)	—	(†)	—	(†)	—	(†)
1996	81.9	(0.23)	86.1	(0.23)	74.6	(0.80)	53.0	(0.97)	86.2	(1.10)	—	(†)	—	(†)	—	(†)	—	(†)
1997	82.0	(0.21)	86.3	(0.21)	73.8	(0.79)	54.9	(0.76)	87.5	(1.00)	—	(†)	—	(†)	—	(†)	—	(†)
1998	82.8	(0.20)	87.1	(0.21)	75.4	(0.77)	55.7	(0.74)	87.9	(0.98)	—	(†)	—	(†)	—	(†)	—	(†)
1999	83.4	(0.20)	87.7	(0.20)	77.2	(0.74)	56.0	(0.75)	86.9	(1.00)	—	(†)	—	(†)	—	(†)	—	(†)
2000	84.2	(0.19)	88.5	(0.20)	79.1	(0.72)	56.6	(0.73)	88.4	(0.94)	—	(†)	—	(†)	—	(†)	—	(†)
2001	84.4	(0.19)	88.6	(0.19)	80.6	(0.69)	55.6	(0.72)	90.6	(0.78)	—	(†)	—	(†)	—	(†)	—	(†)
2002	83.8	(0.14)	88.5	(0.14)	79.0	(0.51)	56.1	(0.48)	89.8	(0.58)	—	(†)	—	(†)	—	(†)	—	(†)
2003	84.1	(0.13)	89.0	(0.14)	79.9	(0.50)	56.3	(0.46)	89.8	(0.58)	89.8	(0.59)	89.8	(2.61)	76.5	(2.33)	87.2	(1.36)
2004	84.8	(0.13)	89.9	(0.13)	80.8	(0.49)	57.3	(0.45)	88.8	(0.59)	88.8	(0.60)	88.9	(2.65)	77.1	(2.31)	87.8	(1.29)
2005	84.9	(0.19)	89.9	(0.20)	81.4	(0.60)	57.9	(0.69)	90.4	(0.65)	90.5	(0.66)	88.5	(3.62)	75.6	(2.57)	89.0	(1.19)
2006	85.0	(0.20)	90.2	(0.21)	80.7	(0.63)	58.5	(0.77)	89.5	(0.84)	89.7	(0.86)	85.8	(3.10)	78.1	(2.77)	88.0	(1.36)
2007	85.0	(0.21)	90.2	(0.22)	82.5	(0.55)	58.2	(0.80)	90.0	(0.81)	90.1	(0.82)	88.1	(2.75)	78.3	(3.58)	89.4	(1.28)
2008	85.9	(0.19)	91.1	(0.20)	82.1	(0.61)	60.9	(0.72)	91.0	(0.66)	90.8	(0.69)	95.8	(1.40)	77.3	(3.37)	89.6	(1.21)
2009	86.2	(0.19)	91.4	(0.20)	84.2	(0.60)	60.6	(0.72)	90.8	(0.66)	90.7	(0.68)	92.1	(2.18)	80.0	(2.33)	87.3	(1.26)
2010	86.6	(0.17)	91.8	(0.19)	84.2	(0.57)	61.4	(0.68)	91.4	(0.78)	91.5	(0.79)	89.3	(2.84)	78.9	(2.46)	88.1	(1.36)
2011	87.1	(0.18)	92.0	(0.17)	84.2	(0.55)	63.6	(0.71)	90.6	(0.68)	90.6	(0.69)	91.5	(2.22)	80.6	(2.35)	88.1	(1.40)
2012	87.3	(0.19)	92.2	(0.18)	85.1	(0.56)	64.0	(0.73)	90.6	(0.68)	90.5	(0.70)	93.3	(1.84)	81.8	(2.39)	90.2	(1.45)
2013	87.6	(0.17)	92.7	(0.17)	84.9	(0.62)	64.6	(0.66)	91.6	(0.57)	91.7	(0.57)	89.3	(2.48)	81.0	(2.11)	93.3	(1.03)
2014	87.7	(0.19)	92.5	(0.22)	86.3	(0.58)	65.1	(0.74)	91.8	(0.70)	91.9	(0.72)	90.0	(2.68)	80.2	(2.30)	93.8	(1.08)
2015	88.0	(0.16)	93.0	(0.16)	87.2	(0.48)	65.5	(0.63)	90.9	(0.56)	91.3	(0.58)	84.9	(2.83)	81.9	(2.12)	92.5	(1.23)
Bachelor's or higher degree[4]																		
1940	5.5	(—)	5.9	(—)	1.4	(—)	—	(†)	—	(†)	—	(†)	—	(†)	—	(†)	—	(†)
1950	7.3	(—)	7.9	(—)	2.1	(—)	—	(†)	—	(†)	—	(†)	—	(†)	—	(†)	—	(†)
1960	9.7	(—)	10.3	(—)	3.5	(—)	—	(†)	—	(†)	—	(†)	—	(†)	—	(†)	—	(†)
1970	14.1	(—)	15.0	(—)	6.8	(—)	—	(†)	—	(†)	—	(†)	—	(†)	—	(†)	—	(†)
1980	20.9	(0.26)	22.7	(0.29)	7.7	(0.65)	9.2	(0.99)	—	(†)	—	(†)	—	(†)	—	(†)	—	(†)
1990	24.4	(0.25)	26.7	(0.28)	11.9	(0.69)	9.8	(0.74)	45.9	(2.14)	—	(†)	—	(†)	—	(†)	—	(†)
1995	26.0	(0.25)	28.9	(0.29)	13.7	(0.71)	10.1	(0.67)	42.3	(2.06)	—	(†)	—	(†)	—	(†)	—	(†)
1996	26.0	(0.26)	28.8	(0.30)	12.5	(0.61)	10.3	(0.59)	46.9	(1.59)	—	(†)	—	(†)	—	(†)	—	(†)
1997	26.2	(0.24)	29.0	(0.28)	12.5	(0.60)	10.6	(0.47)	48.0	(1.51)	—	(†)	—	(†)	—	(†)	—	(†)
1998	26.5	(0.24)	29.3	(0.28)	14.0	(0.62)	11.1	(0.47)	46.0	(1.50)	—	(†)	—	(†)	—	(†)	—	(†)
1999	27.5	(0.24)	30.6	(0.28)	14.3	(0.62)	10.7	(0.46)	46.3	(1.48)	—	(†)	—	(†)	—	(†)	—	(†)
2000	27.8	(0.24)	30.8	(0.28)	16.4	(0.65)	10.7	(0.45)	48.1	(1.47)	—	(†)	—	(†)	—	(†)	—	(†)
2001	28.0	(0.24)	30.9	(0.28)	15.9	(0.64)	11.1	(0.45)	52.9	(1.33)	—	(†)	—	(†)	—	(†)	—	(†)
2002	28.5	(0.17)	31.7	(0.20)	16.5	(0.47)	11.0	(0.30)	51.5	(0.96)	—	(†)	—	(†)	—	(†)	—	(†)
2003	28.9	(0.17)	32.3	(0.20)	16.8	(0.47)	11.2	(0.29)	52.8	(0.96)	54.2	(0.98)	25.7	(3.76)	13.1	(1.85)	21.9	(1.69)
2004	29.4	(0.17)	32.9	(0.20)	16.6	(0.46)	11.8	(0.30)	52.9	(0.93)	54.0	(0.95)	31.9	(3.94)	15.6	(1.99)	20.7	(1.60)
2005	28.9	(0.29)	32.4	(0.37)	16.0	(0.64)	11.8	(0.43)	53.0	(1.10)	54.3	(1.13)	25.1	(4.70)	17.0	(2.30)	23.1	(1.67)
2006	29.2	(0.24)	32.8	(0.31)	17.5	(0.63)	11.9	(0.40)	51.9	(1.33)	53.1	(1.35)	26.6	(4.67)	13.7	(2.07)	22.6	(1.75)
2007	29.5	(0.25)	33.2	(0.33)	18.1	(0.62)	11.8	(0.37)	54.2	(1.31)	55.8	(1.32)	19.2	(4.14)	12.7	(1.89)	21.5	(1.81)
2008	30.1	(0.25)	33.8	(0.33)	18.7	(0.67)	12.6	(0.39)	54.9	(1.24)	56.1	(1.24)	27.5	(3.64)	14.6	(2.15)	22.7	(1.62)
2009	30.1	(0.28)	33.9	(0.36)	17.9	(0.57)	12.5	(0.41)	54.8	(1.14)	56.5	(1.17)	23.0	(3.35)	16.1	(2.96)	24.4	(1.92)
2010	30.3	(0.23)	34.2	(0.30)	17.9	(0.59)	12.9	(0.37)	54.6	(1.26)	56.2	(1.30)	18.0	(3.74)	13.5	(2.61)	24.8	(1.86)
2011	30.8	(0.23)	35.0	(0.29)	18.4	(0.64)	13.1	(0.44)	52.4	(1.15)	54.0	(1.21)	19.1	(3.55)	14.1	(1.98)	25.7	(1.91)
2012	31.4	(0.27)	35.5	(0.33)	19.5	(0.62)	13.3	(0.45)	53.1	(1.26)	54.4	(1.29)	24.1	(3.34)	16.1	(2.27)	25.2	(1.85)
2013	32.0	(0.25)	36.0	(0.31)	20.2	(0.64)	13.9	(0.43)	55.1	(1.17)	56.9	(1.20)	23.1	(3.32)	14.0	(2.13)	29.0	(1.78)
2014	31.9	(0.32)	35.9	(0.41)	21.0	(0.88)	14.2	(0.51)	53.7	(1.33)	55.5	(1.34)	16.7	(3.42)	14.8	(2.46)	29.2	(2.56)
2015	32.3	(0.27)	36.3	(0.35)	21.1	(0.63)	14.3	(0.38)	55.6	(1.11)	57.3	(1.16)	24.4	(2.87)	18.1	(2.14)	27.2	(2.14)

See notes at end of table.

Table 104.10. Rates of high school completion and bachelor's degree attainment among persons age 25 and over, by race/ethnicity and sex: Selected years, 1910 through 2015—Continued

[Standard errors appear in parentheses]

Sex, high school or bachelor's degree attainment, and year	Total, percent of all persons age 25 and over		White[1]		Black[1]		Hispanic		Asian/Pacific Islander: Total		Asian/Pacific Islander: Asian		Asian/Pacific Islander: Pacific Islander		American Indian/ Alaska Native		Two or more races	
1	2		3		4		5		6		7		8		9		10	
Females																		
High school completion or higher[2]																		
1940	26.3	(—)	28.1	(—)	8.4	(—)	—	(†)	—	(†)	—	(†)	—	(†)	—	(†)	—	(†)
1950	36.0	(—)	38.2	(—)	14.7	(—)	—	(†)	—	(†)	—	(†)	—	(†)	—	(†)	—	(†)
1960	42.5	(—)	44.7	(—)	23.1	(—)	—	(†)	—	(†)	—	(†)	—	(†)	—	(†)	—	(†)
1970	55.4	(—)	57.7	(—)	36.6	(—)	—	(†)	—	(†)	—	(†)	—	(†)	—	(†)	—	(†)
1980	68.1	(0.28)	71.5	(0.30)	51.5	(1.08)	44.2	(1.63)	—	(†)	—	(†)	—	(†)	—	(†)	—	(†)
1990	77.5	(0.23)	81.3	(0.24)	66.5	(0.90)	51.3	(1.23)	82.5	(1.57)	—	(†)	—	(†)	—	(†)	—	(†)
1995	81.6	(0.21)	85.8	(0.22)	74.1	(0.81)	53.8	(1.09)	81.9	(1.54)	—	(†)	—	(†)	—	(†)	—	(†)
1996	81.6	(0.22)	85.9	(0.22)	74.6	(0.71)	53.3	(0.97)	81.0	(1.21)	—	(†)	—	(†)	—	(†)	—	(†)
1997	82.2	(0.20)	86.3	(0.20)	76.5	(0.68)	54.6	(0.76)	82.9	(1.11)	—	(†)	—	(†)	—	(†)	—	(†)
1998	82.9	(0.19)	87.1	(0.20)	77.1	(0.67)	55.3	(0.75)	82.3	(1.09)	—	(†)	—	(†)	—	(†)	—	(†)
1999	83.3	(0.19)	87.6	(0.19)	77.5	(0.66)	56.3	(0.73)	82.8	(1.06)	—	(†)	—	(†)	—	(†)	—	(†)
2000	84.0	(0.19)	88.4	(0.19)	78.7	(0.64)	57.5	(0.71)	83.4	(1.03)	—	(†)	—	(†)	—	(†)	—	(†)
2001	84.2	(0.18)	88.8	(0.19)	78.6	(0.64)	57.4	(0.70)	85.2	(0.91)	—	(†)	—	(†)	—	(†)	—	(†)
2002	84.4	(0.13)	88.9	(0.13)	79.4	(0.45)	57.9	(0.48)	85.7	(0.64)	—	(†)	—	(†)	—	(†)	—	(†)
2003	85.0	(0.13)	89.7	(0.13)	80.7	(0.44)	57.8	(0.46)	86.1	(0.62)	86.1	(0.64)	86.9	(2.63)	77.9	(2.30)	85.1	(1.38)
2004	85.4	(0.12)	90.1	(0.12)	81.2	(0.43)	59.5	(0.46)	85.3	(0.63)	85.1	(0.64)	88.1	(2.76)	78.6	(2.24)	86.5	(1.29)
2005	85.5	(0.15)	90.3	(0.18)	81.5	(0.53)	59.1	(0.63)	85.4	(0.76)	85.2	(0.78)	91.7	(2.46)	75.6	(2.29)	88.1	(1.12)
2006	85.9	(0.16)	90.8	(0.17)	81.5	(0.51)	60.1	(0.59)	85.6	(0.82)	85.6	(0.81)	85.7	(3.08)	78.9	(2.18)	88.2	(1.11)
2007	86.4	(0.15)	91.0	(0.16)	83.0	(0.49)	62.5	(0.56)	86.1	(0.93)	86.0	(0.97)	89.1	(2.40)	81.9	(1.91)	89.2	(1.22)
2008	87.2	(0.17)	91.8	(0.18)	84.2	(0.49)	63.7	(0.61)	87.2	(0.75)	87.0	(0.78)	93.0	(1.57)	79.2	(2.95)	89.5	(1.53)
2009	87.1	(0.16)	91.9	(0.17)	84.2	(0.48)	63.3	(0.59)	86.4	(0.73)	86.3	(0.75)	89.7	(2.33)	82.7	(1.96)	87.6	(1.16)
2010	87.6	(0.15)	92.3	(0.17)	85.0	(0.46)	64.4	(0.59)	87.2	(0.72)	87.1	(0.75)	90.9	(2.41)	82.5	(1.95)	89.7	(1.13)
2011	88.0	(0.15)	92.8	(0.16)	85.3	(0.50)	65.1	(0.57)	87.1	(0.64)	87.0	(0.66)	89.5	(2.25)	83.8	(2.00)	90.7	(1.22)
2012	88.0	(0.17)	92.7	(0.18)	86.1	(0.46)	66.0	(0.65)	87.9	(0.64)	87.8	(0.66)	90.1	(2.11)	81.8	(1.84)	91.6	(1.13)
2013	88.6	(0.16)	93.2	(0.16)	86.6	(0.46)	67.9	(0.55)	89.0	(0.61)	88.9	(0.63)	89.6	(2.01)	83.1	(2.16)	92.0	(0.95)
2014	88.9	(0.17)	93.7	(0.20)	87.0	(0.55)	67.9	(0.61)	87.4	(0.76)	87.4	(0.77)	87.8	(2.98)	81.6	(2.78)	92.8	(1.28)
2015	88.8	(0.14)	93.5	(0.15)	88.2	(0.43)	67.8	(0.53)	87.1	(0.60)	87.2	(0.62)	85.3	(2.46)	85.6	(2.10)	90.9	(1.14)
Bachelor's or higher degree[4]																		
1940	3.8	(—)	4.0	(—)	1.2	(—)	—	(†)	—	(†)	—	(†)	—	(†)	—	(†)	—	(†)
1950	5.2	(—)	5.4	(—)	2.4	(—)	—	(†)	—	(†)	—	(†)	—	(†)	—	(†)	—	(†)
1960	5.8	(—)	6.0	(—)	3.6	(—)	—	(†)	—	(†)	—	(†)	—	(†)	—	(†)	—	(†)
1970	8.2	(—)	8.6	(—)	5.6	(—)	—	(†)	—	(†)	—	(†)	—	(†)	—	(†)	—	(†)
1980	13.6	(0.20)	14.4	(0.23)	8.1	(0.59)	6.2	(0.79)	—	(†)	—	(†)	—	(†)	—	(†)	—	(†)
1990	18.4	(0.21)	19.8	(0.25)	10.8	(0.59)	8.7	(0.69)	37.8	(2.01)	—	(†)	—	(†)	—	(†)	—	(†)
1995	20.2	(0.22)	22.1	(0.26)	13.0	(0.62)	8.4	(0.61)	35.0	(1.90)	—	(†)	—	(†)	—	(†)	—	(†)
1996	21.4	(0.23)	23.2	(0.27)	14.8	(0.58)	8.3	(0.53)	38.0	(1.50)	—	(†)	—	(†)	—	(†)	—	(†)
1997	21.7	(0.21)	23.7	(0.25)	14.0	(0.56)	10.1	(0.46)	37.4	(1.43)	—	(†)	—	(†)	—	(†)	—	(†)
1998	22.4	(0.21)	24.1	(0.25)	15.4	(0.58)	10.9	(0.47)	38.9	(1.39)	—	(†)	—	(†)	—	(†)	—	(†)
1999	23.1	(0.22)	25.0	(0.26)	16.5	(0.59)	11.0	(0.46)	39.0	(1.37)	—	(†)	—	(†)	—	(†)	—	(†)
2000	23.6	(0.22)	25.5	(0.26)	16.8	(0.59)	10.6	(0.44)	41.0	(1.37)	—	(†)	—	(†)	—	(†)	—	(†)
2001	24.3	(0.22)	26.5	(0.26)	16.3	(0.58)	11.3	(0.45)	43.4	(1.26)	—	(†)	—	(†)	—	(†)	—	(†)
2002	25.1	(0.15)	27.3	(0.19)	17.7	(0.42)	11.2	(0.31)	44.2	(0.91)	—	(†)	—	(†)	—	(†)	—	(†)
2003	25.7	(0.15)	27.9	(0.19)	18.0	(0.43)	11.6	(0.30)	45.3	(0.89)	46.3	(0.92)	28.0	(3.50)	12.2	(1.81)	22.2	(1.61)
2004	26.1	(0.15)	28.4	(0.19)	18.5	(0.43)	12.3	(0.31)	45.2	(0.88)	45.7	(0.90)	32.9	(4.01)	13.1	(1.84)	22.7	(1.59)
2005	26.5	(0.23)	28.9	(0.30)	18.9	(0.51)	12.1	(0.42)	46.0	(1.08)	46.8	(1.10)	24.1	(4.08)	12.2	(2.00)	23.3	(1.43)
2006	26.9	(0.22)	29.3	(0.28)	19.5	(0.55)	12.9	(0.39)	46.6	(1.11)	47.3	(1.15)	27.2	(4.03)	12.3	(1.81)	23.6	(1.70)
2007	28.0	(0.23)	30.6	(0.29)	19.2	(0.59)	13.7	(0.44)	48.6	(1.07)	49.5	(1.10)	27.9	(4.16)	13.4	(1.53)	25.8	(1.58)
2008	28.8	(0.24)	31.5	(0.29)	20.5	(0.58)	14.1	(0.37)	49.3	(0.99)	50.1	(1.02)	29.3	(3.82)	15.1	(1.75)	26.1	(1.92)
2009	29.1	(0.21)	31.9	(0.26)	20.6	(0.56)	14.0	(0.41)	48.8	(0.98)	49.7	(1.02)	32.9	(3.74)	18.8	(1.91)	26.6	(1.67)
2010	29.6	(0.21)	32.4	(0.26)	21.6	(0.63)	14.9	(0.42)	49.1	(1.12)	49.9	(1.19)	32.2	(4.11)	18.2	(1.83)	25.7	(1.59)
2011	30.1	(0.22)	33.1	(0.28)	21.7	(0.60)	15.2	(0.43)	47.0	(1.04)	48.0	(1.07)	24.7	(3.52)	17.9	(2.17)	28.9	(1.70)
2012	30.6	(0.23)	33.5	(0.30)	22.9	(0.61)	15.8	(0.45)	48.6	(0.93)	49.7	(0.94)	24.9	(3.70)	17.2	(2.13)	28.8	(1.88)
2013	31.4	(0.24)	34.4	(0.31)	23.4	(0.61)	16.2	(0.42)	50.2	(0.94)	51.3	(0.96)	28.0	(3.44)	16.6	(2.05)	32.0	(1.89)
2014	32.0	(0.32)	35.3	(0.42)	24.2	(0.75)	16.1	(0.50)	49.3	(1.12)	50.4	(1.15)	27.1	(4.38)	13.1	(1.92)	33.1	(2.08)
2015	32.7	(0.25)	36.1	(0.32)	24.3	(0.60)	16.6	(0.42)	50.4	(0.82)	51.8	(0.85)	21.3	(3.13)	21.3	(1.71)	33.4	(1.96)

—Not available.
†Not applicable.
[1]Includes persons of Hispanic ethnicity for years prior to 1980.
[2]Data for years prior to 1993 are for persons with 4 or more years of high school. Data for later years are for high school completers—i.e., those persons who graduated from high school with a diploma as well as those who completed high school through equivalency programs, such as a GED program.
[3]Estimates based on Census Bureau reverse projection of 1940 census data on education by age.
[4]Data for years prior to 1993 are for persons with 4 or more years of college.

NOTE: Beginning in 2005, standard errors were computed using replicate weights, which produced more precise values than the generalized variance function methodology used in prior years. For 1960 and prior years, data were collected in April. For later years, data were collected in March. Race categories exclude persons of Hispanic ethnicity except where otherwise noted.
SOURCE: U.S. Department of Commerce, Census Bureau, *U.S. Census of Population: 1960*, Vol. I, Part 1; J.K. Folger and C.B. Nam, *Education of the American Population* (1960 Census Monograph); Current Population Reports, Series P-20, various years; and Current Population Survey (CPS), Annual Social and Economic Supplement, 1970 through 2015. (This table was prepared November 2015.)

Table 104.20. Percentage of persons 25 to 29 years old with selected levels of educational attainment, by race/ethnicity and sex: Selected years, 1920 through 2015

[Standard errors appear in parentheses]

Sex, selected level of educational attainment, and year	Total	White[1]	Black[1]	Hispanic	Asian/Pacific Islander: Total	Asian/Pacific Islander: Asian	Asian/Pacific Islander: Pacific Islander	American Indian/ Alaska Native	Two or more races
1	2	3	4	5	6	7	8	9	10
Total									
High school completion or higher[2]									
1920[3]	— (†)	22.0 (—)	6.3 (—)	— (†)	— (†)	— (†)	— (†)	— (†)	— (†)
1940	38.1 (—)	41.2 (—)	12.3 (—)	— (†)	— (†)	— (†)	— (†)	— (†)	— (†)
1950	52.8 (—)	56.3 (—)	23.6 (—)	— (†)	— (†)	— (†)	— (†)	— (†)	— (†)
1960	60.7 (—)	63.7 (—)	38.6 (—)	— (†)	— (†)	— (†)	— (†)	— (†)	— (†)
1970	75.4 (—)	77.8 (—)	58.4 (—)	— (†)	— (†)	— (†)	— (†)	— (†)	— (†)
1980	85.4 (0.40)	89.2 (0.40)	76.7 (1.64)	58.0 (2.59)	— (†)	— (†)	— (†)	— (†)	— (†)
1990	85.7 (0.38)	90.1 (0.37)	81.7 (1.37)	58.2 (1.94)	91.5 (2.09)	— (†)	— (†)	— (†)	— (†)
1995	86.8 (0.39)	92.5 (0.36)	86.7 (1.23)	57.1 (1.80)	90.8 (2.26)	— (†)	— (†)	— (†)	— (†)
2000	88.1 (0.37)	94.0 (0.33)	86.8 (1.13)	62.8 (1.22)	93.7 (1.27)	— (†)	— (†)	— (†)	— (†)
2005	86.2 (0.42)	92.8 (0.39)	87.0 (1.03)	63.3 (1.32)	95.6 (0.88)	95.5 (0.92)	‡ (†)	80.2 (4.77)	91.4 (3.91)
2006	86.4 (0.36)	93.4 (0.35)	86.3 (1.09)	63.2 (1.17)	96.4 (0.88)	96.6 (0.86)	‡ (†)	79.8 (5.19)	89.3 (3.96)
2007	87.0 (0.36)	93.5 (0.33)	87.7 (1.16)	65.0 (1.06)	96.8 (0.91)	97.5 (0.73)	‡ (†)	84.5 (4.41)	90.5 (4.30)
2008	87.8 (0.36)	93.7 (0.38)	87.5 (1.29)	68.3 (1.16)	95.9 (0.86)	95.8 (0.91)	‡ (†)	86.7 (3.36)	94.2 (3.82)
2009	88.6 (0.36)	94.6 (0.33)	88.9 (0.98)	68.9 (1.16)	95.4 (0.91)	95.8 (0.95)	91.6 (3.46)	81.1 (4.26)	88.5 (3.61)
2010	88.8 (0.32)	94.5 (0.31)	89.6 (0.93)	69.4 (1.22)	93.7 (1.18)	94.0 (1.24)	89.7 (5.05)	89.9 (2.98)	88.5 (3.86)
2011	89.0 (0.34)	94.4 (0.34)	88.1 (0.98)	71.5 (1.12)	95.4 (0.87)	95.3 (0.91)	‡ (†)	84.9 (3.95)	90.7 (3.79)
2012	89.7 (0.38)	94.6 (0.37)	88.5 (0.96)	75.0 (1.16)	96.2 (0.73)	96.1 (0.77)	98.6 (0.83)	84.5 (3.94)	92.8 (2.22)
2013	89.9 (0.35)	94.1 (0.35)	90.3 (0.92)	75.8 (1.10)	95.4 (0.77)	95.4 (0.81)	95.5 (2.72)	84.7 (3.47)	97.4 (1.11)
2014	90.8 (0.39)	95.6 (0.41)	91.9 (0.93)	74.7 (1.31)	96.6 (0.76)	96.6 (0.79)	‡ (†)	83.9 (4.67)	96.0 (2.01)
2015	91.2 (0.31)	95.4 (0.32)	92.5 (0.78)	77.1 (1.02)	95.3 (0.92)	95.8 (0.87)	87.2 (6.60)	86.7 (2.65)	94.9 (1.54)
Bachelor's or higher degree[4]									
1920[3]	— (†)	4.5 (—)	1.2 (—)	— (†)	— (†)	— (†)	— (†)	— (†)	— (†)
1940	5.9 (—)	6.4 (—)	1.6 (—)	— (†)	— (†)	— (†)	— (†)	— (†)	— (†)
1950	7.7 (—)	8.2 (—)	2.8 (—)	— (†)	— (†)	— (†)	— (†)	— (†)	— (†)
1960	11.0 (—)	11.8 (—)	5.4 (—)	— (†)	— (†)	— (†)	— (†)	— (†)	— (†)
1970	16.4 (—)	17.3 (—)	10.0 (—)	— (†)	— (†)	— (†)	— (†)	— (†)	— (†)
1980	22.5 (0.47)	25.0 (0.55)	11.6 (1.24)	7.7 (1.39)	— (†)	— (†)	— (†)	— (†)	— (†)
1990	23.2 (0.46)	26.4 (0.55)	13.4 (1.20)	8.1 (1.07)	43.0 (3.71)	— (†)	— (†)	— (†)	— (†)
1995	24.7 (0.49)	28.8 (0.62)	15.4 (1.31)	8.9 (1.04)	43.1 (3.87)	— (†)	— (†)	— (†)	— (†)
2000	29.1 (0.52)	34.0 (0.67)	17.8 (1.28)	9.7 (0.75)	54.3 (2.60)	— (†)	— (†)	— (†)	— (†)
2005	28.8 (0.55)	34.5 (0.78)	17.6 (1.21)	11.2 (0.81)	60.0 (2.20)	62.1 (2.25)	‡ (†)	16.4 (3.56)	28.0 (3.79)
2006	28.4 (0.52)	34.3 (0.78)	18.7 (1.33)	9.5 (0.66)	59.6 (2.39)	61.9 (2.44)	‡ (†)	9.5 ! (4.26)	23.3 (3.14)
2007	29.6 (0.54)	35.5 (0.75)	19.5 (1.21)	11.6 (0.61)	59.4 (2.24)	61.5 (2.26)	‡ (†)	6.4 ! (2.99)	26.3 (3.44)
2008	30.8 (0.51)	37.1 (0.70)	20.4 (1.35)	12.4 (0.69)	57.9 (2.26)	60.2 (2.32)	‡ (†)	14.3 (3.17)	26.6 (3.75)
2009	30.6 (0.57)	37.2 (0.85)	18.9 (1.36)	12.2 (0.80)	56.4 (2.25)	60.3 (2.28)	12.5 ! (4.44)	15.9 (3.73)	29.7 (3.84)
2010	31.7 (0.51)	38.6 (0.72)	19.4 (1.20)	13.5 (0.80)	52.5 (2.32)	55.8 (2.47)	10.0 ! (4.40)	18.6 (4.80)	29.8 (3.22)
2011	32.2 (0.62)	39.2 (0.88)	20.1 (1.25)	12.8 (0.73)	56.0 (2.50)	57.2 (2.52)	‡ (†)	17.3 (4.45)	32.4 (3.85)
2012	33.5 (0.58)	39.8 (0.78)	23.2 (1.38)	14.8 (0.90)	59.6 (2.17)	61.7 (2.24)	25.5 (6.12)	10.4 (2.87)	32.9 (3.72)
2013	33.6 (0.55)	40.4 (0.77)	20.5 (1.38)	15.7 (0.82)	58.0 (2.16)	60.1 (2.18)	24.7 ! (7.54)	16.6 (4.89)	29.6 (3.45)
2014	34.0 (0.75)	40.8 (1.05)	22.4 (1.82)	15.1 (0.97)	60.8 (2.44)	63.2 (2.50)	‡ (†)	5.6 ! (2.24)	32.4 (4.12)
2015	35.6 (0.55)	43.0 (0.83)	21.3 (1.33)	16.4 (0.78)	62.8 (2.25)	66.0 (2.27)	11.4 ! (4.64)	15.3 (3.21)	29.6 (3.62)
Master's or higher degree									
1995	4.5 (0.24)	5.3 (0.31)	1.8 (0.48)	1.6 (0.46)	10.9 (1.85)	— (†)	— (†)	— (†)	— (†)
2000	5.4 (0.26)	5.8 (0.33)	3.7 (0.63)	2.1 (0.36)	15.5 (1.70)	— (†)	‡ (†)	— (†)	— (†)
2005	6.3 (0.31)	7.5 (0.45)	2.6 (0.44)	2.1 (0.38)	16.9 (1.93)	17.5 (2.01)	‡ (†)	‡ (†)	7.0 ! (2.49)
2006	6.4 (0.29)	7.5 (0.42)	3.2 (0.58)	1.5 (0.25)	20.1 (2.00)	21.1 (2.10)	‡ (†)	‡ (†)	7.1 (1.83)
2007	6.3 (0.30)	7.6 (0.42)	3.5 (0.59)	1.5 (0.25)	17.5 (1.84)	18.5 (1.93)	‡ (†)	‡ (†)	6.2 ! (2.38)
2008	7.0 (0.28)	8.2 (0.40)	4.4 (0.64)	2.0 (0.28)	19.9 (1.84)	21.0 (1.96)	‡ (†)	‡ (†)	6.9 ! (2.57)
2009	7.4 (0.30)	8.9 (0.45)	4.2 (0.54)	1.9 (0.26)	21.1 (1.98)	22.9 (2.16)	‡ (†)	‡ (†)	6.5 ! (2.02)
2010	6.8 (0.26)	7.7 (0.38)	4.7 (0.60)	2.5 (0.37)	17.9 (1.87)	19.2 (1.99)	‡ (†)	‡ (†)	5.3 ! (1.63)
2011	6.9 (0.32)	8.1 (0.45)	4.0 (0.52)	2.7 (0.37)	16.7 (1.78)	17.5 (1.85)	‡ (†)	‡ (†)	6.1 (1.59)
2012	7.2 (0.35)	8.2 (0.51)	5.1 (0.66)	2.7 (0.36)	17.8 (1.85)	18.9 (1.92)	‡ (†)	2.6 ! (1.28)	4.1 ! (1.49)
2013	7.4 (0.31)	8.6 (0.50)	3.3 (0.50)	3.0 (0.37)	20.6 (1.73)	21.8 (1.79)	# (†)	‡ (†)	4.8 ! (1.54)
2014	7.6 (0.41)	9.0 (0.58)	3.9 (0.77)	2.9 (0.43)	17.9 (1.84)	18.8 (1.92)	‡ (†)	# (†)	7.1 ! (2.32)
2015	8.7 (0.33)	10.1 (0.51)	5.0 (0.60)	3.2 (0.41)	21.6 (1.85)	22.8 (1.97)	‡ (†)	‡ (†)	7.8 (1.79)
Males									
High school completion or higher[2]									
1980	85.4 (0.49)	89.1 (0.48)	74.7 (1.97)	57.0 (3.45)	— (†)	— (†)	— (†)	— (†)	— (†)
1990	84.4 (0.56)	88.6 (0.57)	81.4 (2.03)	56.6 (2.69)	95.3 (1.78)	— (†)	— (†)	— (†)	— (†)
1995	86.3 (0.56)	92.0 (0.53)	88.4 (1.72)	55.7 (2.51)	90.5 (2.37)	— (†)	— (†)	— (†)	— (†)
2000	86.7 (0.55)	92.9 (0.51)	87.6 (1.67)	59.2 (1.76)	92.1 (1.83)	— (†)	— (†)	— (†)	— (†)
2005	85.0 (0.58)	91.8 (0.53)	86.6 (1.76)	63.2 (1.72)	96.8 (1.09)	96.7 (1.15)	‡ (†)	‡ (†)	89.1 (3.07)
2006	84.4 (0.54)	92.3 (0.52)	84.2 (2.02)	60.5 (1.64)	97.2 (1.01)	97.2 (1.06)	‡ (†)	‡ (†)	89.2 (3.81)
2007	84.9 (0.50)	92.7 (0.48)	87.4 (1.65)	60.5 (1.59)	95.9 (1.13)	96.3 (1.10)	‡ (†)	‡ (†)	92.9 (2.64)
2008	85.8 (0.54)	92.6 (0.58)	85.7 (1.99)	65.6 (1.55)	95.6 (1.23)	95.4 (1.31)	‡ (†)	‡ (†)	92.7 (2.68)
2009	87.5 (0.51)	94.4 (0.46)	88.8 (1.56)	66.2 (1.54)	96.4 (1.17)	96.2 (1.25)	‡ (†)	‡ (†)	92.0 (3.01)
2010	87.4 (0.44)	94.6 (0.42)	87.9 (1.52)	65.7 (1.52)	93.8 (1.83)	93.5 (1.95)	‡ (†)	93.2 (3.47)	87.9 (4.32)
2011	87.5 (0.49)	93.4 (0.48)	88.0 (1.43)	69.2 (1.62)	94.2 (1.30)	93.9 (1.36)	‡ (†)	84.5 (5.28)	86.2 (4.41)
2012	88.4 (0.51)	93.8 (0.50)	86.2 (1.58)	73.3 (1.57)	96.1 (1.04)	96.0 (1.09)	‡ (†)	‡ (†)	91.0 (3.58)
2013	88.3 (0.52)	93.3 (0.53)	87.8 (1.60)	73.1 (1.64)	94.4 (1.13)	94.3 (1.21)	‡ (†)	‡ (†)	96.8 (1.77)
2014	90.1 (0.53)	95.4 (0.60)	93.5 (1.18)	72.4 (1.76)	96.1 (1.10)	96.1 (1.14)	‡ (†)	‡ (†)	96.9 (2.02)
2015	90.5 (0.45)	95.1 (0.45)	91.8 (1.22)	75.7 (1.41)	95.9 (1.23)	97.1 (0.96)	75.8 (12.49)	83.2 (4.73)	98.0 (1.27)
Bachelor's or higher degree[4]									
1980	24.0 (0.59)	26.8 (0.69)	10.5 (1.39)	8.4 (1.94)	— (†)	— (†)	— (†)	— (†)	— (†)
1990	23.7 (0.65)	26.6 (0.79)	15.1 (1.87)	7.3 (1.41)	47.6 (4.19)	— (†)	— (†)	— (†)	— (†)
1995	24.5 (0.70)	28.4 (0.88)	17.4 (2.04)	7.8 (1.35)	42.0 (3.98)	— (†)	— (†)	— (†)	— (†)
2000	27.9 (0.73)	32.3 (0.93)	18.4 (1.96)	8.3 (0.98)	55.5 (3.37)	— (†)	— (†)	— (†)	— (†)
2005	25.5 (0.68)	30.7 (0.98)	14.2 (1.57)	10.2 (0.99)	58.5 (3.11)	61.0 (3.17)	‡ (†)	‡ (†)	24.5 (4.13)

See notes at end of table.

Table 104.20. Percentage of persons 25 to 29 years old with selected levels of educational attainment, by race/ethnicity and sex: Selected years, 1920 through 2015—Continued

[Standard errors appear in parentheses]

Sex, selected level of educational attainment, and year	Total	White[1]	Black[1]	Hispanic	Asian/Pacific Islander			American Indian/ Alaska Native	Two or more races
					Total	Asian	Pacific Islander		
1	2	3	4	5	6	7	8	9	10
2006	25.3 (0.67)	31.4 (0.98)	15.2 (1.66)	6.9 (0.70)	58.7 (3.46)	60.9 (3.52)	‡ (†)	‡ (†)	20.8 (4.65)
2007	26.3 (0.72)	31.9 (0.98)	18.9 (1.86)	8.6 (0.71)	58.5 (3.45)	60.4 (3.54)	‡ (†)	‡ (†)	23.3 (4.88)
2008	26.8 (0.64)	32.6 (0.89)	19.0 (1.94)	10.0 (0.86)	54.1 (3.41)	55.8 (3.53)	‡ (†)	‡ (†)	25.7 (4.45)
2009	26.6 (0.66)	32.6 (1.04)	14.8 (1.82)	11.0 (1.04)	55.2 (3.07)	59.2 (3.24)	‡ (†)	‡ (†)	24.6 (5.77)
2010	27.8 (0.68)	34.8 (0.96)	15.0 (1.72)	10.8 (1.06)	49.0 (3.12)	52.3 (3.31)	‡ (†)	18.9 ! (7.12)	24.9 (4.91)
2011	28.4 (0.82)	35.5 (1.16)	17.0 (1.83)	9.6 (0.90)	50.8 (3.42)	52.1 (3.55)	‡ (†)	15.4 ! (4.80)	34.1 (6.62)
2012	29.8 (0.82)	36.0 (1.06)	19.1 (1.74)	12.5 (1.20)	55.0 (3.15)	56.9 (3.16)	‡ (†)	‡ (†)	30.4 (5.44)
2013	30.2 (0.68)	37.1 (1.00)	17.4 (1.63)	13.1 (1.06)	53.0 (3.03)	55.1 (3.13)	‡ (†)	‡ (†)	29.3 (4.61)
2014	30.9 (0.93)	37.7 (1.36)	20.8 (2.40)	12.4 (1.22)	56.9 (3.55)	59.0 (3.59)	‡ (†)	‡ (†)	26.4 (6.13)
2015	32.4 (0.74)	39.5 (1.12)	17.6 (1.83)	14.5 (1.04)	60.9 (3.13)	63.8 (3.12)	‡ (†)	‡ (†)	26.7 (5.07)
Master's or higher degree									
1995	4.9 (0.35)	5.6 (0.45)	2.2 ! (0.80)	2.0 ! (0.70)	12.6 (2.68)	— (†)	— (†)	— (†)	— (†)
2000	4.7 (0.34)	4.9 (0.43)	2.1 ! (0.72)	1.5 (0.43)	17.2 (2.56)	— (†)	— (†)	— (†)	— (†)
2005	5.2 (0.38)	6.2 (0.55)	1.1 ! (0.43)	1.7 (0.46)	19.7 (3.13)	20.5 (3.30)	‡ (†)	‡ (†)	‡ (†)
2006	5.1 (0.37)	5.8 (0.51)	1.7 ! (0.52)	1.1 (0.32)	20.5 (2.68)	21.8 (2.83)	‡ (†)	‡ (†)	5.9 ! (2.66)
2007	5.0 (0.39)	5.7 (0.50)	3.3 (0.99)	0.6 ! (0.19)	18.4 (2.89)	19.3 (3.00)	‡ (†)	‡ (†)	9.8 ! (4.28)
2008	5.3 (0.34)	5.9 (0.49)	3.4 (0.90)	1.2 (0.32)	20.9 (2.94)	22.1 (3.07)	‡ (†)	‡ (†)	7.8 ! (2.85)
2009	6.1 (0.37)	7.4 (0.60)	3.2 (0.73)	1.2 (0.28)	20.4 (2.48)	22.0 (2.69)	‡ (†)	‡ (†)	5.0 ! (2.38)
2010	5.2 (0.32)	6.3 (0.50)	2.9 (0.69)	1.5 (0.39)	15.0 (2.19)	16.2 (2.36)	‡ (†)	‡ (†)	# (†)
2011	5.1 (0.38)	5.9 (0.49)	1.9 (0.54)	1.8 (0.41)	18.0 (2.58)	19.1 (2.71)	‡ (†)	‡ (†)	‡ (†)
2012	5.6 (0.42)	6.3 (0.59)	2.7 (0.72)	2.4 (0.50)	16.2 (2.46)	17.2 (2.60)	‡ (†)	‡ (†)	‡ (†)
2013	5.7 (0.38)	6.3 (0.53)	1.5 ! (0.56)	2.1 (0.43)	20.8 (2.49)	22.1 (2.60)	‡ (†)	‡ (†)	5.9 ! (2.47)
2014	5.9 (0.51)	7.0 (0.72)	2.6 ! (0.82)	2.2 (0.52)	15.9 (2.56)	16.6 (2.65)	‡ (†)	‡ (†)	‡ (†)
2015	7.0 (0.40)	8.2 (0.62)	2.5 (0.75)	2.3 (0.56)	21.1 (2.65)	22.4 (2.78)	‡ (†)	‡ (†)	5.6 ! (2.37)
Females									
High school completion or higher[2]									
1980	85.5 (0.48)	89.2 (0.48)	78.3 (1.71)	58.9 (3.38)	— (†)	— (†)	— (†)	— (†)	— (†)
1990	87.0 (0.51)	91.7 (0.49)	82.0 (1.85)	59.9 (2.79)	85.1 (2.82)	— (†)	— (†)	— (†)	— (†)
1995	87.4 (0.54)	93.0 (0.50)	85.3 (1.75)	58.7 (2.60)	91.2 (2.50)	— (†)	— (†)	— (†)	— (†)
2000	89.4 (0.49)	95.2 (0.43)	86.2 (1.53)	66.4 (1.69)	95.2 (1.39)	— (†)	— (†)	— (†)	— (†)
2005	87.4 (0.44)	93.8 (0.47)	87.3 (1.22)	63.4 (1.54)	94.6 (1.36)	94.4 (1.41)	‡ (†)	‡ (†)	94.2 (2.26)
2006	88.5 (0.44)	94.6 (0.41)	88.0 (1.14)	66.6 (1.41)	95.6 (1.44)	96.0 (1.31)	‡ (†)	‡ (†)	89.4 (3.81)
2007	89.1 (0.45)	94.2 (0.44)	87.9 (1.46)	70.7 (1.30)	97.7 (1.05)	98.5 (0.68)	‡ (†)	90.2 (4.49)	87.9 (3.82)
2008	89.9 (0.39)	94.7 (0.44)	89.2 (1.43)	71.9 (1.34)	96.1 (1.12)	96.2 (1.18)	‡ (†)	84.2 (4.68)	95.9 (2.44)
2009	89.8 (0.41)	94.8 (0.44)	89.0 (1.12)	72.5 (1.34)	94.5 (1.20)	95.3 (1.18)	‡ (†)	83.4 (4.81)	84.8 (3.57)
2010	90.2 (0.39)	94.4 (0.42)	91.1 (0.96)	74.1 (1.53)	93.6 (1.25)	94.5 (1.27)	‡ (†)	86.8 (4.80)	89.1 (3.55)
2011	90.7 (0.36)	95.5 (0.42)	88.2 (1.24)	74.3 (1.26)	96.6 (0.89)	96.6 (0.92)	‡ (†)	85.3 (6.02)	94.0 (2.52)
2012	91.1 (0.44)	95.3 (0.46)	90.6 (1.11)	76.9 (1.39)	96.3 (0.98)	96.1 (1.04)	‡ (†)	85.8 (4.53)	94.7 (2.35)
2013	91.5 (0.38)	94.9 (0.43)	92.5 (0.95)	78.8 (1.17)	96.2 (0.96)	96.3 (1.01)	‡ (†)	82.0 (5.40)	98.2 (1.15)
2014	91.5 (0.50)	95.9 (0.54)	90.5 (1.62)	77.4 (1.56)	97.1 (0.96)	97.1 (0.99)	‡ (†)	84.1 (6.05)	95.2 (3.44)
2015	91.8 (0.39)	95.8 (0.41)	93.2 (0.90)	78.6 (1.34)	94.8 (1.18)	94.6 (1.25)	96.7 (1.86)	89.3 (3.52)	91.5 (2.99)
Bachelor's or higher degree[4]									
1980	21.0 (0.56)	23.2 (0.65)	12.4 (1.36)	6.9 (1.74)	— (†)	— (†)	— (†)	— (†)	— (†)
1990	22.8 (0.64)	26.2 (0.78)	11.9 (1.56)	9.1 (1.64)	37.4 (3.83)	— (†)	— (†)	— (†)	— (†)
1995	24.9 (0.70)	29.2 (0.89)	13.7 (1.70)	10.1 (1.59)	44.5 (4.38)	— (†)	— (†)	— (†)	— (†)
2000	30.1 (0.73)	35.8 (0.96)	17.4 (1.69)	11.0 (1.12)	53.1 (3.26)	— (†)	— (†)	— (†)	— (†)
2005	32.2 (0.75)	38.2 (1.00)	20.5 (1.68)	12.4 (1.07)	61.4 (3.06)	63.1 (3.11)	‡ (†)	‡ (†)	32.1 (5.70)
2006	31.6 (0.70)	37.2 (0.99)	21.7 (1.77)	12.8 (1.05)	60.4 (2.76)	62.8 (2.82)	‡ (†)	‡ (†)	25.7 (4.72)
2007	33.0 (0.72)	39.2 (1.03)	20.0 (1.38)	15.4 (1.10)	60.3 (2.83)	62.5 (2.88)	‡ (†)	‡ (†)	29.6 (5.17)
2008	34.9 (0.71)	41.7 (0.98)	21.6 (1.57)	15.5 (1.11)	61.6 (2.67)	64.4 (2.71)	‡ (†)	12.2 ! (3.69)	27.7 (5.57)
2009	34.8 (0.78)	42.0 (1.12)	22.6 (1.75)	13.8 (1.09)	57.6 (3.00)	61.3 (3.03)	‡ (†)	16.3 (4.42)	35.0 (5.07)
2010	35.7 (0.68)	42.4 (0.96)	23.3 (1.72)	16.8 (1.20)	55.8 (2.93)	58.9 (3.00)	‡ (†)	18.4 ! (6.68)	34.0 (4.96)
2011	36.1 (0.71)	43.0 (1.03)	22.9 (1.62)	16.8 (1.10)	61.0 (2.74)	62.0 (2.75)	‡ (†)	19.7 ! (6.64)	31.2 (4.36)
2012	37.2 (0.69)	43.6 (0.97)	26.7 (1.78)	17.4 (1.10)	64.0 (2.38)	66.2 (2.46)	‡ (†)	14.0 ! (4.55)	35.5 (5.50)
2013	37.0 (0.71)	43.8 (0.95)	23.2 (2.03)	18.6 (1.10)	62.4 (2.51)	64.3 (2.54)	‡ (†)	16.4 ! (6.57)	30.0 (5.26)
2014	37.2 (1.00)	43.9 (1.36)	23.8 (2.61)	18.3 (1.40)	64.3 (3.23)	66.9 (3.29)	‡ (†)	‡ (†)	38.4 (5.96)
2015	38.9 (0.74)	46.6 (1.06)	24.6 (1.72)	18.5 (1.21)	64.5 (2.74)	68.1 (2.73)	‡ (†)	21.8 (4.51)	32.9 (5.20)
Master's or higher degree									
1995	4.1 (0.32)	5.0 (0.42)	1.4 ! (0.59)	1.2 ! (0.58)	8.9 (2.50)	— (†)	— (†)	— (†)	— (†)
2000	6.2 (0.38)	6.7 (0.50)	4.9 (0.96)	2.7 (0.58)	13.9 (2.26)	— (†)	— (†)	— (†)	— (†)
2005	7.3 (0.44)	8.8 (0.64)	4.0 (0.70)	2.6 (0.51)	14.4 (2.08)	15.0 (2.15)	‡ (†)	‡ (†)	10.0 ! (4.26)
2006	7.8 (0.42)	9.2 (0.63)	4.5 (0.93)	2.0 (0.41)	19.7 (2.33)	20.4 (2.44)	‡ (†)	‡ (†)	8.3 ! (2.89)
2007	7.6 (0.43)	9.4 (0.63)	3.7 (0.66)	2.6 (0.53)	16.5 (2.39)	17.7 (2.54)	‡ (†)	‡ (†)	‡ (†)
2008	8.7 (0.44)	10.4 (0.64)	5.2 (0.87)	2.9 (0.46)	18.9 (2.30)	19.9 (2.44)	‡ (†)	‡ (†)	‡ (†)
2009	8.8 (0.45)	10.4 (0.66)	5.1 (0.80)	2.7 (0.43)	21.7 (2.45)	23.7 (2.70)	‡ (†)	‡ (†)	7.9 ! (2.84)
2010	8.5 (0.39)	9.2 (0.56)	6.2 (0.94)	3.8 (0.56)	20.6 (2.60)	21.8 (2.75)	‡ (†)	‡ (†)	10.0 ! (3.06)
2011	8.8 (0.48)	10.4 (0.72)	5.8 (0.85)	3.8 (0.63)	15.4 (1.98)	15.9 (2.03)	‡ (†)	‡ (†)	9.9 (2.61)
2012	8.8 (0.45)	10.0 (0.67)	7.1 (1.00)	3.0 (0.45)	19.3 (2.23)	20.4 (2.31)	‡ (†)	‡ (†)	6.3 ! (2.49)
2013	9.2 (0.44)	10.8 (0.71)	4.8 (0.74)	4.0 (0.59)	20.4 (1.91)	21.6 (2.00)	‡ (†)	‡ (†)	3.3 ! (1.56)
2014	9.3 (0.56)	11.1 (0.84)	5.0 (1.17)	3.6 (0.63)	19.7 (2.33)	20.8 (2.47)	‡ (†)	# (†)	7.5 ! (3.00)
2015	10.4 (0.51)	12.0 (0.73)	7.2 (0.98)	4.1 (0.60)	22.0 (2.51)	23.2 (2.67)	‡ (†)	‡ (†)	10.2 ! (3.20)

—Not available.
†Not applicable.
#Rounds to zero.
!Interpret data with caution. The coefficient of variation (CV) for this estimate is between 30 and 50 percent.
‡Reporting standards not met. Either there are too few cases for a reliable estimate or the coefficient of variation (CV) is 50 percent or greater.
[1]Includes persons of Hispanic ethnicity for years prior to 1980.
[2]Data for years prior to 1993 are for persons with 4 or more years of high school. Data for later years are for high school completers—i.e., those persons who graduated from high school with a diploma as well as those who completed high school through equivalency programs, such as a GED program.
[3]Estimates based on Census Bureau reverse projection of 1940 census data on education by age.
[4]Data for years prior to 1993 are for persons with 4 or more years of college.
NOTE: Beginning in 2005, standard errors were computed using replicate weights, which produced more precise values than the generalized variance function methodology used in prior years. For 1960 and prior years, data were collected in April. For later years, data were collected in March. Race categories exclude persons of Hispanic ethnicity except where otherwise noted.
SOURCE: U.S. Department of Commerce, Census Bureau, *U.S. Census of Population: 1960*, Vol. I, Part 1; J.K. Folger and C.B. Nam, *Education of the American Population* (1960 Census Monograph); Current Population Reports, Series P-20, various years; and Current Population Survey (CPS), Annual Social and Economic Supplement, 1970 through 2015. (This table was prepared October 2015.)

Table 104.30. Number of persons age 18 and over, by highest level of educational attainment, sex, race/ethnicity, and age: 2015

[Numbers in thousands. Standard errors appear in parentheses]

Sex, race/ethnicity, and age	Total		Elementary school (kindergarten–8th grade)		High school: 1 to 3 years		High school: 4 years, no completion		High school: Completion[1]		Postsecondary education: Some college, no degree		Postsecondary education: Associate's degree		Postsecondary education: Bachelor's degree		Postsecondary education: Master's degree		Postsecondary education: First-professional or doctor's degree	
1	2		3		4		5		6		7		8		9		10		11	
Total, 18 and over	**242,248**	**(96.9)**	**10,353**	**(186.4)**	**15,177**	**(209.1)**	**4,130**	**(101.9)**	**71,654**	**(411.7)**	**46,212**	**(331.8)**	**22,537**	**(242.5)**	**46,515**	**(361.2)**	**18,683**	**(225.6)**	**6,988**	**(153.5)**
18 and 19 years old	7,900	(82.2)	88	(14.2)	2,379	(61.6)	690	(34.6)	2,340	(68.3)	2,298	(65.1)	78	(13.7)	‡	(†)	‡	(†)	‡	(†)
20 to 24 years old	22,215	(21.7)	369	(33.8)	1,142	(56.8)	410	(33.5)	6,739	(113.8)	8,751	(137.2)	1,592	(69.2)	2,994	(103.0)	207	(23.5)	‡	(†)
25 years old and over	212,132	(45.8)	9,896	(179.2)	11,656	(185.2)	3,030	(82.3)	62,575	(382.7)	35,164	(285.3)	20,867	(213.8)	43,500	(327.7)	18,471	(223.5)	6,974	(153.9)
25 to 29 years old	21,867	(38.9)	496	(36.9)	1,048	(47.8)	384	(33.1)	5,690	(102.7)	4,259	(99.9)	2,197	(71.2)	5,889	(108.4)	1,492	(66.2)	412	(35.0)
30 to 34 years old	21,139	(35.6)	659	(36.1)	1,201	(51.0)	305	(24.3)	5,275	(96.8)	3,683	(86.2)	2,280	(63.4)	4,970	(94.9)	2,068	(75.6)	698	(48.5)
35 to 39 years old	19,916	(33.8)	923	(47.7)	1,134	(46.1)	270	(22.4)	5,134	(92.8)	3,228	(81.4)	2,049	(69.5)	4,457	(91.5)	2,002	(64.7)	719	(42.2)
40 to 49 years old	40,567	(41.6)	1,779	(63.2)	2,019	(68.2)	558	(34.2)	11,148	(148.0)	6,365	(110.9)	4,258	(84.4)	9,022	(136.2)	3,977	(105.2)	1,441	(58.6)
50 to 59 years old	43,652	(70.4)	1,818	(65.3)	2,249	(74.4)	631	(38.9)	13,581	(173.5)	7,113	(129.7)	4,724	(92.1)	8,542	(135.4)	3,624	(87.6)	1,369	(57.1)
60 to 64 years old	18,998	(113.0)	791	(40.2)	855	(48.6)	256	(26.4)	5,832	(123.3)	3,308	(87.7)	1,960	(70.3)	3,537	(89.8)	1,770	(68.8)	690	(41.1)
65 years old and over	45,994	(88.1)	3,431	(88.7)	3,150	(92.3)	626	(40.4)	15,915	(196.1)	7,207	(126.9)	3,398	(86.9)	7,082	(125.9)	3,539	(108.2)	1,645	(69.5)
Males, 18 and over	**117,051**	**(76.2)**	**5,158**	**(118.1)**	**7,580**	**(144.5)**	**2,133**	**(72.6)**	**36,008**	**(251.5)**	**22,129**	**(208.1)**	**9,718**	**(152.4)**	**22,027**	**(222.7)**	**8,221**	**(146.3)**	**4,077**	**(106.8)**
18 and 19 years old	3,962	(59.1)	46	(9.2)	1,246	(47.4)	381	(24.7)	1,228	(48.8)	1,019	(43.1)	‡	(†)	‡	(†)	‡	(†)	‡	(†)
20 to 24 years old	11,201	(21.1)	201	(24.2)	599	(39.6)	209	(21.3)	3,783	(79.4)	4,337	(92.9)	679	(42.9)	1,327	(67.2)	61	(11.7)	‡	(†)
25 years old and over	101,887	(44.2)	4,911	(113.9)	5,735	(129.4)	1,543	(61.6)	30,997	(234.9)	16,772	(177.0)	9,006	(139.4)	20,696	(203.7)	8,157	(145.2)	4,070	(107.3)
25 to 29 years old	10,984	(38.0)	269	(27.8)	550	(32.9)	223	(27.6)	3,286	(77.2)	2,122	(70.6)	980	(52.6)	2,783	(74.8)	599	(40.5)	172	(20.2)
30 to 34 years old	10,444	(35.3)	385	(25.8)	635	(37.4)	177	(18.4)	2,911	(64.5)	1,797	(62.4)	1,021	(44.8)	2,298	(59.3)	852	(47.2)	367	(30.3)
35 to 39 years old	9,830	(32.2)	500	(31.4)	641	(34.4)	146	(17.2)	2,799	(63.9)	1,597	(57.4)	903	(41.2)	2,071	(60.2)	839	(40.0)	334	(26.7)
40 to 49 years old	19,889	(40.1)	919	(45.7)	1,063	(48.7)	297	(26.1)	6,053	(108.3)	3,076	(73.0)	1,765	(56.7)	4,160	(84.3)	1,787	(68.8)	769	(40.0)
50 to 59 years old	21,174	(52.4)	914	(40.7)	1,237	(52.8)	336	(28.5)	6,884	(109.5)	3,323	(76.0)	2,039	(56.5)	4,000	(87.3)	1,604	(57.5)	836	(42.8)
60 to 64 years old	9,128	(105.2)	389	(25.7)	418	(31.1)	125	(16.9)	2,762	(80.9)	1,621	(62.1)	869	(44.4)	1,788	(60.9)	734	(43.3)	422	(33.4)
65 years old and over	20,439	(88.1)	1,535	(56.4)	1,191	(52.3)	240	(26.3)	6,301	(112.4)	3,236	(77.3)	1,428	(57.6)	3,596	(89.9)	1,742	(70.1)	1,170	(54.3)
Females, 18 and over	**125,197**	**(65.1)**	**5,195**	**(101.4)**	**7,597**	**(129.3)**	**1,996**	**(62.4)**	**35,646**	**(268.7)**	**24,084**	**(230.8)**	**12,819**	**(164.8)**	**24,488**	**(238.3)**	**10,462**	**(147.6)**	**2,911**	**(83.1)**
18 and 19 years old	3,938	(61.3)	‡	(†)	1,133	(45.4)	309	(23.9)	1,112	(44.8)	1,278	(46.7)	‡	(†)	‡	(†)	‡	(†)	‡	(†)
20 to 24 years old	11,014	(3.9)	168	(20.2)	543	(34.4)	200	(24.3)	2,956	(72.3)	4,414	(88.1)	913	(50.1)	1,668	(75.0)	146	(21.7)	‡	(†)
25 years old and over	110,245	(14.2)	4,985	(97.8)	5,921	(114.1)	1,487	(51.2)	31,578	(246.7)	18,391	(201.8)	11,861	(150.7)	22,804	(217.1)	10,314	(143.7)	2,903	(82.8)
25 to 29 years old	10,884	(6.2)	228	(21.9)	499	(31.6)	161	(18.7)	2,403	(65.8)	2,137	(60.5)	1,217	(44.1)	3,106	(73.5)	893	(50.1)	240	(24.3)
30 to 34 years old	10,695	(6.0)	273	(21.3)	566	(34.7)	128	(16.8)	2,364	(64.4)	1,886	(56.6)	1,260	(46.5)	2,672	(67.0)	1,216	(51.3)	330	(28.2)
35 to 39 years old	10,086	(7.6)	422	(27.9)	493	(28.4)	124	(15.8)	2,335	(62.0)	1,631	(51.0)	1,146	(46.9)	2,386	(58.5)	1,163	(47.2)	386	(27.0)
40 to 49 years old	20,678	(6.6)	860	(38.1)	956	(45.0)	261	(20.4)	5,095	(91.5)	3,289	(72.4)	2,493	(65.3)	4,862	(91.2)	2,190	(65.0)	672	(34.8)
50 to 59 years old	22,478	(45.3)	903	(43.1)	1,012	(43.6)	295	(24.1)	6,697	(117.2)	3,790	(93.2)	2,685	(70.2)	4,542	(91.3)	2,020	(67.6)	533	(36.8)
60 to 64 years old	9,870	(44.9)	402	(27.6)	437	(31.8)	131	(17.8)	3,070	(79.4)	1,687	(58.0)	1,091	(49.8)	1,750	(61.4)	1,035	(48.0)	267	(23.5)
65 years old and over	25,555	(0.6)	1,896	(55.9)	1,959	(67.5)	386	(29.3)	9,613	(129.3)	3,971	(99.9)	1,970	(65.5)	3,486	(89.4)	1,798	(68.2)	475	(32.9)
White, 18 and over	**157,151**	**(114.9)**	**2,713**	**(107.6)**	**7,273**	**(145.1)**	**1,809**	**(72.8)**	**46,241**	**(371.5)**	**29,928**	**(284.8)**	**15,957**	**(211.1)**	**34,072**	**(306.4)**	**13,904**	**(199.9)**	**5,254**	**(137.3)**
18 and 19 years old	4,293	(61.3)	‡	(†)	1,306	(46.1)	321	(25.5)	1,244	(49.3)	1,328	(52.5)	‡	(†)	‡	(†)	‡	(†)	‡	(†)
20 to 24 years old	12,219	(33.8)	143	(21.2)	409	(33.8)	126	(20.7)	3,471	(90.8)	4,857	(109.8)	955	(53.5)	2,129	(89.1)	124	(20.6)	‡	(†)
25 years old and over	140,638	(106.2)	2,536	(104.5)	5,558	(129.7)	1,362	(65.6)	41,526	(339.1)	23,743	(239.6)	14,964	(190.6)	31,927	(278.2)	13,776	(197.7)	5,247	(137.2)
25 to 29 years old	12,396	(36.2)	71	(13.0)	362	(32.2)	136	(18.9)	2,891	(78.5)	2,244	(74.5)	1,358	(58.3)	4,080	(92.0)	973	(55.5)	280	(29.6)
30 to 34 years old	12,185	(43.1)	107	(19.4)	421	(32.2)	109	(16.3)	2,682	(70.4)	2,100	(62.8)	1,530	(55.9)	3,351	(79.0)	1,401	(60.8)	484	(41.6)
35 to 39 years old	11,390	(41.2)	112	(16.7)	394	(28.6)	80	(12.1)	2,831	(77.6)	1,837	(62.6)	1,322	(53.7)	2,992	(76.1)	1,364	(52.7)	458	(34.1)
40 to 49 years old	24,868	(55.5)	255	(30.8)	748	(45.6)	204	(20.6)	6,614	(127.0)	4,060	(89.0)	2,860	(65.8)	6,362	(115.1)	2,766	(88.3)	997	(48.3)
50 to 59 years old	30,284	(52.0)	375	(31.0)	1,154	(59.5)	316	(32.8)	9,442	(152.7)	5,114	(111.7)	3,567	(85.1)	6,508	(117.5)	2,745	(78.7)	1,063	(50.3)
60 to 64 years old	13,788	(89.8)	184	(24.2)	402	(32.9)	136	(21.0)	4,201	(108.8)	2,518	(82.1)	1,543	(61.9)	2,744	(80.9)	1,486	(64.7)	574	(40.1)
65 years old and over	35,727	(91.2)	1,431	(65.7)	2,076	(73.3)	380	(35.2)	12,865	(180.6)	5,870	(118.4)	2,783	(84.6)	5,890	(121.8)	3,040	(103.3)	1,391	(63.4)
Black, 18 and over	**28,369**	**(81.3)**	**703**	**(41.2)**	**2,341**	**(73.9)**	**712**	**(42.0)**	**9,741**	**(146.4)**	**6,490**	**(117.8)**	**2,628**	**(79.2)**	**3,742**	**(89.5)**	**1,611**	**(65.0)**	**401**	**(35.0)**
18 and 19 years old	1,094	(35.6)	‡	(†)	379	(27.0)	106	(14.0)	328	(29.9)	252	(22.6)	‡	(†)	‡	(†)	‡	(†)	‡	(†)
20 to 24 years old	3,249	(23.7)	‡	(†)	205	(21.4)	93	(15.5)	1,153	(47.9)	1,346	(46.7)	187	(22.0)	238	(25.7)	‡	(†)	‡	(†)
25 years old and over	24,026	(64.2)	679	(40.8)	1,758	(64.4)	513	(36.6)	8,259	(130.4)	4,892	(99.6)	2,429	(75.4)	3,501	(85.6)	1,594	(64.2)	401	(35.0)
25 to 29 years old	2,858	(25.1)	‡	(†)	127	(16.1)	‡	(†)	997	(43.0)	760	(40.0)	280	(24.0)	466	(35.1)	119	(16.2)	‡	(†)
30 to 34 years old	2,585	(23.3)	‡	(†)	139	(18.5)	‡	(†)	876	(40.9)	597	(36.7)	290	(25.1)	434	(30.4)	172	(17.9)	‡	(†)
35 to 39 years old	2,482	(19.0)	‡	(†)	121	(14.8)	‡	(†)	765	(35.5)	550	(31.4)	291	(25.2)	446	(28.6)	209	(22.1)	‡	(†)
40 to 49 years old	4,937	(28.4)	62	(12.6)	261	(22.3)	95	(14.6)	1,698	(55.9)	971	(40.2)	527	(30.3)	777	(40.5)	422	(31.9)	124	(17.2)
50 to 59 years old	5,085	(54.5)	109	(15.9)	388	(22.8)	128	(15.7)	1,812	(53.1)	973	(39.7)	561	(31.7)	699	(35.5)	318	(27.8)	97	(13.4)
60 to 64 years old	2,066	(52.0)	67	(10.4)	209	(21.3)	44	(8.1)	710	(34.8)	401	(25.6)	193	(18.4)	271	(23.4)	132	(16.3)	‡	(†)
65 years old and over	4,013	(24.2)	374	(28.1)	513	(31.1)	101	(14.3)	1,400	(46.4)	641	(31.5)	286	(23.2)	407	(28.4)	221	(19.4)	69	(13.0)

See notes at end of table.

Table 104.30. Number of persons age 18 and over, by highest level of educational attainment, sex, race/ethnicity, and age: 2015—Continued

[Numbers in thousands. Standard errors appear in parentheses]

Sex, race/ethnicity, and age	Total		Elementary school (kindergarten–8th grade)		High school						Postsecondary education									
					1 to 3 years		4 years, no completion		Completion[1]		Some college, no degree		Associate's degree		Bachelor's degree		Master's degree		First-professional or doctor's degree	
1	2		3		4		5		6		7		8		9		10		11	
Hispanic, 18 and over	**37,509**	**(44.1)**	**6,040**	**(133.4)**	**4,546**	**(111.7)**	**1,295**	**(58.6)**	**11,529**	**(140.5)**	**6,440**	**(113.9)**	**2,565**	**(77.5)**	**3,611**	**(85.2)**	**1,099**	**(46.2)**	**384**	**(27.6)**
18 and 19 years old	1,771	(39.3)	‡	(†)	473	(25.9)	213	(20.2)	587	(32.5)	440	(23.3)	‡	(†)	‡	(†)	‡	(†)	‡	(†)
20 to 24 years old	4,717	(7.4)	198	(25.2)	466	(32.2)	155	(17.2)	1,685	(49.2)	1,603	(46.8)	322	(28.4)	270	(22.4)	‡	(†)	‡	(†)
25 years old and over	31,020	(13.0)	5,806	(124.9)	3,607	(95.9)	927	(49.3)	9,257	(121.3)	4,397	(99.5)	2,225	(65.5)	3,338	(80.9)	1,085	(46.4)	378	(27.8)
25 to 29 years old	4,487	(30.7)	366	(30.6)	496	(33.0)	166	(18.7)	1,399	(49.0)	907	(43.6)	416	(31.9)	595	(33.2)	120	(17.3)	‡	(†)
30 to 34 years old	4,307	(28.8)	518	(33.5)	563	(34.2)	140	(15.3)	1,366	(44.9)	697	(34.4)	307	(21.6)	513	(29.3)	154	(18.9)	50	(9.4)
35 to 39 years old	4,172	(30.6)	755	(40.4)	568	(36.8)	125	(15.5)	1,222	(40.3)	582	(35.2)	292	(23.5)	440	(28.8)	132	(14.7)	56	(9.9)
40 to 49 years old	7,246	(38.9)	1,361	(52.3)	880	(43.3)	217	(20.2)	2,125	(54.3)	936	(41.2)	535	(33.2)	814	(39.8)	292	(22.5)	87	(12.2)
50 to 59 years old	5,302	(46.8)	1,166	(51.8)	544	(30.2)	135	(15.6)	1,593	(54.0)	658	(34.7)	365	(26.2)	553	(29.0)	212	(21.2)	76	(11.6)
60 to 64 years old	1,870	(39.3)	437	(27.2)	178	(19.4)	59	(10.9)	576	(29.8)	225	(17.8)	127	(14.8)	184	(17.7)	56	(8.8)	‡	(†)
65 years old and over	3,636	(5.5)	1,204	(41.6)	378	(25.6)	85	(12.0)	976	(35.7)	392	(22.7)	183	(18.3)	239	(20.1)	120	(15.1)	60	(10.2)
Asian, 18 and over	**13,723**	**(106.4)**	**754**	**(43.7)**	**512**	**(33.4)**	**208**	**(24.0)**	**2,516**	**(84.4)**	**1,974**	**(65.0)**	**850**	**(40.3)**	**4,247**	**(89.9)**	**1,806**	**(67.9)**	**857**	**(47.9)**
18 and 19 years old	379	(21.2)	‡	(†)	77	(10.9)	‡	(†)	80	(10.9)	188	(16.0)	‡	(†)	‡	(†)	‡	(†)	‡	(†)
20 to 24 years old	1,268	(29.6)	‡	(†)	‡	(†)	‡	(†)	162	(20.2)	643	(33.9)	69	(13.0)	295	(26.2)	‡	(†)	‡	(†)
25 years old and over	12,077	(96.6)	740	(43.1)	418	(32.6)	159	(20.9)	2,274	(81.9)	1,143	(53.0)	776	(36.9)	3,952	(85.6)	1,760	(65.9)	855	(47.9)
25 to 29 years old	1,451	(30.9)	‡	(†)	‡	(†)	‡	(†)	202	(24.3)	147	(15.7)	83	(12.6)	627	(32.2)	256	(27.2)	75	(13.8)
30 to 34 years old	1,501	(34.9)	‡	(†)	‡	(†)	‡	(†)	189	(19.1)	165	(19.4)	96	(13.6)	543	(27.7)	306	(27.6)	135	(17.5)
35 to 39 years old	1,372	(39.0)	‡	(†)	‡	(†)	‡	(†)	181	(19.7)	124	(14.7)	99	(12.5)	484	(30.8)	260	(23.1)	164	(21.4)
40 to 49 years old	2,622	(51.0)	88	(13.6)	77	(13.8)	‡	(†)	478	(33.2)	181	(20.2)	210	(19.9)	899	(43.4)	448	(34.0)	214	(20.1)
50 to 59 years old	2,206	(53.8)	143	(18.3)	87	(14.6)	‡	(†)	473	(30.9)	235	(21.0)	136	(16.8)	666	(37.7)	301	(22.2)	120	(15.3)
60 to 64 years old	932	(36.5)	92	(14.6)	53	(11.1)	‡	(†)	239	(23.4)	99	(13.3)	65	(10.2)	262	(22.6)	72	(12.3)	43	(10.0)
65 years old and over	1,994	(37.8)	357	(31.3)	115	(16.8)	‡	(†)	511	(31.9)	191	(19.8)	86	(11.8)	470	(31.2)	117	(14.7)	105	(17.1)

†Not applicable.
‡Reporting standards not met. Either there are too few cases for a reliable estimate or the coefficient of variation (CV) is 50 percent or greater.
[1]Includes completion of high school through equivalency programs, such as a GED program.

NOTE: Total includes other racial/ethnic groups not shown separately. Race categories exclude persons of Hispanic ethnicity. Detail may not sum to totals because of rounding. Standard errors were computed using replicate weights.
SOURCE: U.S. Department of Commerce, Census Bureau, Current Population Survey (CPS), Annual Social and Economic Supplement, 2015. (This table was prepared November 2015.)

Table 104.40. Percentage of persons 18 to 24 years old and age 25 and over, by educational attainment, race/ethnicity, and selected racial/ethnic subgroups: 2009 and 2014

[Standard errors appear in parentheses]

Year and race/ethnicity	18 to 24 years old							Age 25 and over					
	Less than high school completion	High school completion[1] or higher						Less than high school completion	High school completion[1] or higher				
		Total, high school or higher	High school only	At least some college					Total, high school or higher	High school only	Some college, no degree	Associate's degree	Bachelor's or higher degree
				Total, at least some college	Some college, no degree	Associate's degree	Bachelor's or higher degree						
1	2	3	4	5	6	7	8	9	10	11	12	13	14
2009													
Total[2]	**16.4 (0.11)**	**83.6 (0.11)**	**30.2 (0.11)**	**53.4 (0.15)**	**39.7 (0.14)**	**4.7 (0.05)**	**9.0 (0.08)**	**14.7 (0.04)**	**85.3 (0.04)**	**28.5 (0.04)**	**21.4 (0.04)**	**7.5 (0.02)**	**27.9 (0.06)**
White	11.7 (0.10)	88.3 (0.10)	29.2 (0.14)	59.1 (0.16)	42.6 (0.18)	5.4 (0.07)	11.2 (0.11)	9.6 (0.04)	90.4 (0.04)	29.3 (0.05)	22.0 (0.04)	8.0 (0.02)	31.1 (0.06)
Black	21.7 (0.27)	78.3 (0.27)	33.0 (0.36)	45.3 (0.39)	37.6 (0.36)	3.1 (0.12)	4.6 (0.12)	18.4 (0.11)	81.6 (0.11)	31.6 (0.14)	25.0 (0.12)	7.3 (0.06)	17.7 (0.12)
Hispanic	28.9 (0.32)	71.1 (0.32)	32.8 (0.25)	38.3 (0.32)	30.7 (0.29)	3.7 (0.10)	3.8 (0.11)	39.1 (0.16)	60.9 (0.16)	26.0 (0.11)	16.9 (0.10)	5.3 (0.06)	12.7 (0.11)
Cuban	13.4 (1.31)	86.6 (1.31)	31.4 (1.57)	55.2 (1.53)	37.0 (1.68)	8.8 (0.79)	9.3 (0.84)	24.4 (0.55)	75.6 (0.55)	27.4 (0.58)	15.8 (0.41)	8.6 (0.34)	23.8 (0.54)
Dominican	22.1 (1.55)	77.9 (1.55)	28.4 (1.52)	49.5 (1.65)	38.0 (1.58)	5.0 (0.72)	6.5 (0.83)	36.4 (0.74)	63.6 (0.74)	25.4 (0.73)	17.4 (0.55)	6.0 (0.35)	14.8 (0.67)
Mexican	30.8 (0.37)	69.2 (0.37)	34.2 (0.30)	35.0 (0.35)	28.9 (0.34)	3.2 (0.12)	2.9 (0.15)	44.8 (0.18)	55.2 (0.18)	25.8 (0.15)	15.9 (0.12)	4.4 (0.07)	9.0 (0.12)
Puerto Rican	24.6 (0.79)	75.4 (0.79)	34.6 (0.77)	40.8 (0.84)	31.8 (0.79)	4.2 (0.37)	4.8 (0.41)	27.2 (0.34)	72.8 (0.34)	28.9 (0.39)	20.8 (0.30)	7.4 (0.21)	15.6 (0.30)
Spaniard	14.6 (2.04)	85.4 (2.04)	26.7 (2.54)	58.7 (3.06)	46.4 (2.98)	3.4 (0.76)	8.9 (1.39)	11.7 (0.60)	88.3 (0.60)	22.8 (0.77)	25.7 (0.83)	8.1 (0.54)	31.7 (0.93)
Central American[3]	38.7 (0.88)	61.3 (0.88)	26.5 (0.86)	34.8 (0.92)	27.5 (0.84)	3.5 (0.31)	3.8 (0.35)	47.0 (0.49)	53.0 (0.49)	23.9 (0.40)	14.0 (0.32)	4.0 (0.16)	11.0 (0.28)
Costa Rican	21.2 (5.23)	78.8 (5.23)	24.5 (5.60)	54.4 (5.62)	36.7 (5.02)	8.4 ! (3.09)	9.2 ! (3.20)	17.9 (2.02)	82.1 (2.02)	27.1 (2.14)	23.0 (1.90)	7.0 (1.10)	25.0 (1.88)
Guatemalan	51.2 (1.59)	48.8 (1.59)	24.2 (1.48)	24.5 (1.54)	19.2 (1.38)	2.7 (0.52)	2.6 (0.58)	55.2 (1.01)	44.8 (1.01)	21.2 (0.87)	12.0 (0.55)	3.2 (0.30)	8.4 (0.50)
Honduran	44.3 (2.90)	55.7 (2.90)	26.0 (2.73)	29.7 (2.21)	23.1 (2.25)	2.6 (0.73)	4.1 (0.96)	49.3 (1.30)	50.7 (1.30)	24.1 (0.96)	12.4 (0.91)	4.3 (0.50)	9.9 (0.78)
Nicaraguan	17.5 (2.26)	82.5 (2.26)	29.1 (2.64)	53.4 (2.92)	39.6 (2.45)	7.2 (1.68)	6.6 (1.50)	24.5 (1.31)	75.5 (1.31)	29.8 (1.60)	18.0 (1.13)	7.3 (0.80)	20.4 (1.12)
Panamanian	10.5 ! (3.21)	89.5 (3.21)	28.4 (4.31)	61.1 (5.01)	47.2 (5.88)	6.2 ! (1.95)	7.8 ! (2.61)	9.5 (1.15)	90.5 (1.15)	25.5 (1.86)	25.9 (2.01)	7.7 (0.75)	31.4 (1.94)
Salvadoran	36.1 (1.36)	63.9 (1.36)	27.5 (1.40)	36.5 (1.41)	30.1 (1.31)	3.2 (0.51)	3.1 (0.44)	53.3 (0.67)	46.7 (0.67)	23.6 (0.58)	12.7 (0.47)	3.1 (0.22)	7.3 (0.34)
South American	14.3 (0.89)	85.7 (0.89)	28.3 (1.00)	57.5 (1.16)	42.7 (1.18)	6.5 (0.53)	8.2 (0.73)	17.4 (0.41)	82.6 (0.41)	26.3 (0.47)	19.8 (0.45)	7.5 (0.27)	29.0 (0.40)
Chilean	9.6 (2.74)	90.4 (2.74)	21.5 (4.23)	68.9 (5.05)	56.3 (5.07)	7.4 ! (3.49)	5.3 ! (2.11)	10.6 (1.26)	89.4 (1.26)	23.9 (1.92)	22.0 (1.93)	9.2 (1.11)	34.3 (2.14)
Colombian	13.8 (1.26)	86.2 (1.26)	29.7 (1.88)	56.6 (1.82)	41.0 (2.03)	7.6 (0.99)	7.9 (1.11)	15.7 (0.69)	84.3 (0.69)	27.0 (0.82)	20.3 (0.66)	7.7 (0.49)	29.3 (0.67)
Ecuadorian	21.4 (2.69)	78.6 (2.69)	26.0 (2.56)	52.6 (3.09)	39.4 (2.87)	7.2 (1.42)	6.1 (1.19)	31.2 (1.24)	68.8 (1.24)	26.6 (1.02)	18.4 (0.97)	6.1 (0.54)	17.6 (0.83)
Peruvian	9.7 (1.39)	90.3 (1.39)	27.8 (2.73)	62.5 (2.98)	50.2 (2.90)	3.9 (1.05)	8.3 (1.27)	12.0 (0.68)	88.0 (0.68)	30.4 (0.99)	20.7 (0.97)	7.5 (0.59)	29.4 (1.04)
Venezuelan	9.8 (2.53)	90.2 (2.53)	25.5 (4.53)	64.7 (4.93)	41.2 (4.56)	9.9 (2.90)	13.6 (3.42)	8.3 (1.12)	91.7 (1.12)	15.8 (1.18)	17.6 (1.28)	10.8 (0.87)	47.5 (1.91)
Other South American	13.9 (2.32)	86.1 (2.32)	33.2 (2.59)	52.9 (3.34)	37.5 (3.29)	4.6 (1.10)	10.8 (1.66)	15.0 (0.97)	85.0 (0.97)	24.7 (1.13)	19.7 (1.01)	7.0 (0.58)	33.6 (1.19)
Other Hispanic	23.4 (1.30)	76.6 (1.30)	30.6 (1.35)	46.0 (1.53)	38.0 (1.49)	4.0 (0.57)	4.1 (0.60)	23.5 (0.59)	76.5 (0.59)	29.0 (0.59)	24.4 (0.62)	6.8 (0.34)	16.4 (0.44)
Asian	8.8 (0.29)	91.2 (0.29)	20.7 (0.37)	70.5 (0.43)	46.6 (0.57)	5.0 (0.26)	19.0 (0.44)	14.6 (0.14)	85.4 (0.14)	16.0 (0.20)	13.0 (0.13)	6.6 (0.10)	49.9 (0.23)
Chinese[4]	6.5 (0.55)	93.5 (0.55)	18.2 (0.72)	75.3 (0.83)	49.2 (1.19)	2.9 (0.38)	23.2 (0.86)	18.7 (0.37)	81.3 (0.37)	14.7 (0.36)	8.8 (0.24)	5.9 (0.22)	51.9 (0.46)
Filipino	7.9 (0.70)	92.1 (0.70)	23.3 (1.14)	68.8 (1.27)	48.0 (1.48)	8.0 (0.67)	12.8 (0.90)	7.8 (0.22)	92.2 (0.22)	14.8 (0.32)	20.1 (0.32)	9.2 (0.29)	48.0 (0.48)
Japanese	7.1 (1.29)	92.9 (1.29)	22.2 (2.38)	70.8 (2.51)	46.0 (2.83)	8.3 (1.88)	16.4 (1.89)	5.6 (0.27)	94.4 (0.27)	20.9 (0.57)	16.3 (0.52)	9.6 (0.37)	47.5 (0.66)
Korean	8.7 (1.03)	91.3 (1.03)	18.4 (1.19)	72.8 (1.42)	53.4 (1.33)	3.7 (0.64)	15.8 (1.21)	8.4 (0.39)	91.6 (0.39)	19.6 (0.61)	13.8 (0.47)	5.9 (0.27)	52.3 (0.72)
South Asian[5]	7.8 (0.65)	92.2 (0.65)	16.1 (0.84)	76.2 (0.96)	41.3 (1.33)	4.7 (0.51)	30.1 (1.25)	9.3 (0.27)	90.7 (0.27)	10.8 (0.37)	7.4 (0.23)	4.1 (0.18)	68.4 (0.56)
Asian Indian	6.6 (0.62)	93.4 (0.62)	15.8 (0.92)	77.6 (1.09)	40.0 (1.40)	4.2 (0.54)	33.3 (1.40)	8.4 (0.30)	91.6 (0.30)	10.1 (0.37)	6.8 (0.26)	3.8 (0.18)	70.8 (0.56)
Bangladeshi	17.3 ! (6.46)	82.7 (6.46)	20.4 (4.11)	62.3 (6.84)	40.4 (6.65)	9.1 ! (2.78)	12.8 ! (4.66)	19.4 (2.21)	80.6 (2.21)	14.4 (1.69)	10.6 (2.27)	4.5 (0.86)	51.1 (2.76)
Bhutanese	— (†)	— (†)	— (†)	— (†)	— (†)	— (†)	— (†)	— (†)	— (†)	— (†)	— (†)	— (†)	— (†)
Nepalese	— (†)	— (†)	— (†)	— (†)	— (†)	— (†)	— (†)	— (†)	— (†)	— (†)	— (†)	— (†)	— (†)
Pakistani	12.1 (2.28)	87.9 (2.28)	18.5 (2.49)	69.4 (3.01)	45.9 (3.05)	7.1 (2.01)	16.4 (2.32)	14.2 (0.97)	85.8 (0.97)	15.8 (1.29)	11.2 (0.88)	5.7 (0.71)	53.0 (1.71)
Southeast Asian	13.1 (0.88)	86.9 (0.88)	28.1 (1.34)	58.8 (1.44)	43.6 (1.36)	4.9 (0.60)	10.2 (0.67)	30.3 (0.51)	69.7 (0.51)	21.8 (0.55)	16.0 (0.40)	7.5 (0.29)	24.5 (0.44)
Burmese	— (†)	— (†)	— (†)	— (†)	— (†)	— (†)	— (†)	— (†)	— (†)	— (†)	— (†)	— (†)	— (†)
Cambodian	19.9 (2.85)	80.1 (2.85)	39.0 (3.59)	41.0 (3.55)	32.2 (2.89)	4.5 ! (1.53)	4.4 (1.28)	39.0 (1.80)	61.0 (1.80)	24.8 (1.62)	16.9 (1.18)	6.3 (0.67)	13.0 (1.15)
Hmong	17.1 (2.54)	82.9 (2.54)	36.5 (3.15)	46.4 (3.28)	36.0 (2.89)	4.8 (1.17)	5.6 (1.64)	37.3 (2.30)	62.7 (2.30)	23.4 (1.94)	18.0 (1.54)	7.9 (1.17)	13.5 (1.80)
Laotian	16.3 (2.71)	83.7 (2.71)	35.0 (3.73)	48.7 (4.18)	42.9 (4.16)	‡ (†)	4.9 ! (1.87)	38.5 (2.54)	61.5 (2.54)	27.5 (1.79)	16.5 (1.21)	6.2 (0.96)	11.4 (1.16)
Thai	7.8 ! (3.19)	92.2 (3.19)	19.8 (4.41)	72.3 (5.05)	49.7 (5.01)	6.0 ! (2.05)	16.6 (3.42)	18.7 (1.36)	81.3 (1.36)	16.8 (1.25)	12.9 (1.26)	6.6 (0.95)	44.9 (1.84)
Vietnamese	10.7 (1.16)	89.3 (1.16)	22.6 (1.59)	66.7 (1.93)	47.7 (2.02)	5.8 (0.93)	13.3 (1.01)	30.0 (0.59)	70.0 (0.59)	21.5 (0.66)	16.1 (0.48)	7.9 (0.37)	24.5 (0.52)
Other Southeast Asian[6]	‡ (†)	99.1 (0.91)	19.0 (4.51)	80.2 (4.60)	59.6 (6.60)	‡ (†)	16.3 (4.38)	8.8 (2.64)	91.2 (2.64)	15.2 (1.80)	14.1 (1.68)	8.0 (1.45)	53.8 (2.77)
Other Asian	12.9 (1.41)	87.1 (1.41)	19.4 (1.97)	67.7 (2.29)	46.9 (2.74)	7.4 (1.42)	13.4 (1.68)	18.5 (1.05)	81.5 (1.05)	16.4 (0.98)	14.3 (0.73)	6.5 (0.59)	44.4 (1.27)
Pacific Islander	17.9 (2.21)	82.1 (2.21)	39.8 (2.64)	42.4 (3.33)	34.3 (2.68)	3.1 ! (1.09)	4.9 ! (1.54)	14.4 (0.81)	85.6 (0.81)	37.4 (0.95)	26.1 (1.14)	7.7 (0.59)	14.4 (0.83)
American Indian/Alaska Native	27.0 (1.06)	73.0 (1.06)	36.6 (1.04)	36.4 (1.19)	29.4 (1.11)	3.6 (0.50)	3.4 (0.49)	19.6 (0.45)	80.4 (0.45)	31.7 (0.55)	27.1 (0.50)	7.8 (0.32)	13.7 (0.33)
Two or more races	15.1 (0.69)	84.9 (0.69)	32.0 (0.76)	52.9 (0.93)	41.0 (0.78)	4.5 (0.36)	7.5 (0.46)	11.5 (0.29)	88.5 (0.29)	25.1 (0.35)	28.1 (0.39)	9.1 (0.23)	26.1 (0.36)
White and Black	17.6 (1.30)	82.4 (1.30)	34.4 (1.67)	48.0 (1.71)	38.7 (1.79)	3.4 (0.60)	6.0 (0.68)	10.5 (0.87)	89.5 (0.87)	24.1 (1.09)	27.8 (0.97)	9.7 (0.64)	27.9 (1.14)
White and Asian	8.0 (0.85)	92.0 (0.85)	25.4 (1.44)	66.6 (1.53)	45.4 (1.64)	6.5 (0.97)	14.6 (1.14)	4.7 (0.40)	95.3 (0.40)	16.4 (0.75)	24.7 (0.81)	9.1 (0.55)	45.0 (0.88)
White and American Indian/Alaska Native	18.5 (1.28)	81.5 (1.28)	34.4 (1.53)	47.1 (1.87)	39.5 (1.70)	3.9 (0.58)	3.7 (0.69)	14.9 (0.48)	85.1 (0.48)	29.2 (0.57)	28.6 (0.55)	8.8 (0.37)	18.5 (0.47)
Other Two or more races	14.8 (1.25)	85.2 (1.25)	32.7 (1.59)	52.5 (1.66)	41.3 (1.45)	4.4 (0.76)	6.8 (0.99)	11.2 (0.47)	88.8 (0.47)	25.0 (0.59)	29.7 (0.74)	9.4 (0.37)	24.8 (0.64)

See notes at end of table.

Table 104.40. Percentage of persons 18 to 24 years old and age 25 and over, by educational attainment, race/ethnicity, and selected racial/ethnic subgroups: 2009 and 2014—Continued

[Standard errors appear in parentheses]

Year and race/ethnicity	18 to 24 years old: Less than high school completion	18 to 24 years old: High school completion[1] or higher: Total, high school or higher	18 to 24 years old: High school completion[1] or higher: High school only	18 to 24 years old: High school completion[1] or higher: At least some college: Total, at least some college	18 to 24 years old: High school completion[1] or higher: At least some college: Some college, no degree	18 to 24 years old: High school completion[1] or higher: At least some college: Associate's degree	18 to 24 years old: High school completion[1] or higher: At least some college: Bachelor's or higher degree	Age 25 and over: Less than high school completion	Age 25 and over: High school completion[1] or higher: Total, high school or higher	Age 25 and over: High school completion[1] or higher: High school only	Age 25 and over: High school completion[1] or higher: Some college, no degree	Age 25 and over: High school completion[1] or higher: Associate's degree	Age 25 and over: High school completion[1] or higher: Bachelor's or higher degree
1	2	3	4	5	6	7	8	9	10	11	12	13	14
2014													
Total[2]	**13.8 (0.08)**	**86.2 (0.08)**	**30.2 (0.11)**	**56.0 (0.11)**	**40.8 (0.14)**	**5.1 (0.06)**	**10.1 (0.08)**	**13.1 (0.04)**	**86.9 (0.04)**	**27.7 (0.05)**	**21.0 (0.04)**	**8.2 (0.03)**	**30.1 (0.06)**
White	10.6 (0.09)	89.4 (0.09)	29.0 (0.14)	60.3 (0.16)	42.1 (0.20)	5.8 (0.07)	12.4 (0.11)	8.0 (0.03)	92.0 (0.03)	28.2 (0.05)	21.5 (0.05)	8.7 (0.03)	33.6 (0.06)
Black	17.6 (0.26)	82.4 (0.26)	33.3 (0.35)	49.1 (0.39)	40.0 (0.37)	3.6 (0.12)	5.5 (0.16)	15.5 (0.09)	84.5 (0.09)	31.7 (0.15)	25.0 (0.12)	8.1 (0.08)	19.8 (0.12)
Hispanic	20.8 (0.20)	79.2 (0.20)	33.1 (0.26)	46.1 (0.28)	36.8 (0.26)	4.4 (0.11)	4.9 (0.12)	34.6 (0.16)	65.4 (0.16)	27.1 (0.11)	17.9 (0.10)	6.0 (0.06)	14.4 (0.10)
Cuban	15.0 (1.19)	85.0 (1.19)	30.3 (1.61)	54.7 (1.46)	37.6 (1.41)	7.9 (0.85)	9.2 (0.85)	19.7 (0.45)	80.3 (0.45)	29.9 (0.62)	17.0 (0.41)	8.1 (0.31)	25.5 (0.53)
Dominican	18.8 (1.03)	81.2 (1.03)	28.7 (1.27)	52.5 (1.29)	39.8 (1.38)	6.4 (0.84)	6.4 (0.62)	30.5 (0.77)	69.5 (0.77)	26.0 (0.69)	18.0 (0.53)	7.5 (0.43)	18.1 (0.59)
Mexican	21.1 (0.24)	78.9 (0.24)	34.8 (0.30)	44.1 (0.33)	36.4 (0.31)	3.8 (0.10)	3.9 (0.14)	40.1 (0.21)	59.9 (0.21)	27.3 (0.17)	17.1 (0.12)	5.1 (0.08)	10.4 (0.11)
Puerto Rican	19.5 (0.78)	80.5 (0.78)	34.2 (0.88)	46.4 (0.90)	35.5 (0.78)	5.2 (0.44)	5.7 (0.38)	22.5 (0.43)	77.5 (0.43)	29.3 (0.42)	21.7 (0.33)	8.6 (0.23)	18.0 (0.36)
Spaniard	12.0 (1.69)	88.0 (1.69)	26.7 (2.20)	61.3 (2.91)	47.0 (3.00)	5.1 (0.88)	9.2 (1.53)	10.2 (0.56)	89.8 (0.56)	20.5 (0.80)	25.1 (0.89)	9.9 (0.61)	34.3 (0.91)
Central American[3]	29.6 (1.01)	70.4 (1.01)	30.1 (0.89)	40.2 (0.82)	31.8 (0.81)	3.9 (0.30)	4.5 (0.39)	44.1 (0.54)	55.9 (0.54)	25.0 (0.42)	14.3 (0.29)	4.8 (0.17)	11.8 (0.27)
Costa Rican	12.2 ! (4.00)	87.8 (4.00)	29.5 (5.43)	58.3 (6.07)	45.5 (5.71)	‡ (†)	9.4 ! (3.07)	15.2 (1.77)	84.8 (1.77)	28.4 (2.14)	22.7 (1.67)	6.1 (0.97)	27.5 (2.08)
Guatemalan	40.2 (1.80)	59.8 (1.80)	27.9 (1.74)	31.9 (1.43)	25.3 (1.37)	2.4 (0.47)	4.2 (0.62)	53.6 (0.93)	46.4 (0.93)	21.8 (0.73)	12.2 (0.55)	4.1 (0.39)	8.3 (0.46)
Honduran	32.5 (2.41)	67.5 (2.41)	28.9 (2.19)	38.6 (2.46)	32.4 (2.40)	2.6 (0.78)	3.6 (0.88)	46.9 (1.08)	53.1 (1.08)	26.5 (1.09)	13.4 (0.68)	3.7 (0.36)	9.4 (0.68)
Nicaraguan	15.1 (1.99)	84.9 (1.99)	23.5 (2.75)	61.4 (3.12)	44.7 (3.11)	10.6 (2.25)	6.1 (1.16)	23.4 (1.39)	76.6 (1.39)	27.7 (1.19)	19.3 (1.06)	8.0 (0.66)	21.5 (1.16)
Panamanian	3.6 ! (1.18)	96.4 (1.18)	34.9 (3.88)	61.5 (3.92)	44.5 (4.30)	5.8 ! (1.82)	11.3 (2.73)	9.2 (1.03)	90.8 (1.03)	20.8 (1.87)	26.5 (1.68)	11.7 (1.29)	31.9 (1.73)
Salvadoran	28.2 (1.53)	71.8 (1.53)	32.2 (1.33)	39.5 (1.54)	31.7 (1.36)	3.9 (0.49)	4.0 (0.57)	48.1 (0.87)	51.9 (0.87)	25.7 (0.62)	12.9 (0.44)	4.0 (0.24)	9.2 (0.41)
South American	10.8 (0.79)	89.2 (0.79)	24.1 (0.85)	65.1 (1.06)	46.4 (1.11)	7.5 (0.65)	11.1 (0.84)	14.6 (0.36)	85.4 (0.36)	24.8 (0.47)	20.0 (0.35)	8.2 (0.27)	32.4 (0.45)
Chilean	6.4 ! (2.96)	93.6 (2.96)	28.9 (5.22)	64.7 (5.11)	40.5 (5.48)	8.6 ! (3.67)	15.6 (3.80)	9.9 (1.31)	90.1 (1.31)	23.0 (1.95)	24.4 (1.89)	7.1 (0.82)	35.6 (2.66)
Colombian	9.3 (1.28)	90.7 (1.28)	22.8 (1.64)	67.9 (1.73)	48.0 (1.93)	8.8 (1.23)	11.1 (1.17)	14.1 (0.57)	85.9 (0.57)	25.6 (0.75)	18.8 (0.70)	9.0 (0.40)	32.5 (0.67)
Ecuadorian	15.4 (2.39)	84.6 (2.39)	26.8 (2.24)	57.8 (3.20)	42.5 (2.69)	6.1 (1.38)	9.2 (1.46)	27.1 (1.35)	72.9 (1.35)	27.8 (1.07)	17.0 (0.92)	7.2 (0.65)	20.8 (0.79)
Peruvian	11.8 (1.68)	88.2 (1.68)	23.6 (2.41)	64.7 (2.99)	45.1 (3.14)	8.6 (1.70)	11.0 (1.84)	9.4 (0.64)	90.6 (0.64)	26.7 (0.91)	24.6 (0.92)	8.9 (0.66)	30.4 (0.96)
Venezuelan	7.6 (1.97)	92.4 (1.97)	24.2 (2.99)	68.3 (2.89)	44.7 (3.18)	9.0 (1.97)	14.6 (2.61)	5.4 (0.62)	94.6 (0.62)	14.4 (1.19)	17.9 (1.19)	9.0 (0.90)	53.2 (1.53)
Other South American	10.7 (1.90)	89.3 (1.90)	22.7 (2.54)	66.6 (2.83)	52.7 (2.47)	3.6 (1.02)	10.4 (1.75)	13.1 (0.89)	86.9 (0.89)	23.2 (1.15)	20.7 (0.96)	6.7 (0.56)	36.4 (1.27)
Other Hispanic	19.8 (1.15)	80.2 (1.15)	28.9 (1.42)	51.3 (1.62)	39.8 (1.81)	5.4 (0.63)	6.0 (0.73)	21.1 (0.61)	78.9 (0.61)	29.1 (0.66)	23.6 (0.62)	8.0 (0.33)	18.2 (0.57)
Asian	7.7 (0.27)	92.3 (0.27)	20.0 (0.39)	72.3 (0.44)	45.3 (0.49)	4.8 (0.17)	22.2 (0.43)	13.6 (0.12)	86.4 (0.12)	15.3 (0.15)	12.6 (0.14)	6.8 (0.09)	51.7 (0.22)
Chinese[4]	4.8 (0.36)	95.2 (0.36)	18.0 (0.63)	77.2 (0.60)	43.9 (1.12)	3.3 (0.37)	29.9 (1.01)	17.4 (0.31)	82.6 (0.31)	14.2 (0.30)	8.6 (0.23)	5.8 (0.15)	54.0 (0.42)
Filipino	7.8 (0.77)	92.2 (0.77)	22.6 (0.97)	69.6 (1.27)	46.9 (1.36)	8.0 (0.65)	14.7 (1.03)	7.0 (0.25)	93.0 (0.25)	14.8 (0.37)	20.0 (0.40)	9.9 (0.29)	48.2 (0.51)
Japanese	4.1 (1.16)	95.9 (1.16)	22.4 (2.82)	73.5 (2.88)	55.7 (2.84)	3.4 ! (1.09)	14.4 (1.96)	4.5 (0.31)	95.5 (0.31)	19.2 (0.65)	15.6 (0.53)	10.1 (0.48)	50.6 (0.69)
Korean	6.4 (0.76)	93.6 (0.76)	16.8 (1.19)	76.9 (1.31)	53.6 (1.74)	5.4 (0.65)	17.9 (1.39)	7.2 (0.32)	92.8 (0.32)	18.5 (0.57)	14.4 (0.48)	6.2 (0.27)	53.8 (0.66)
South Asian[5]	8.7 (0.70)	91.3 (0.70)	17.2 (0.78)	74.1 (0.93)	41.1 (1.00)	4.5 (0.42)	28.5 (1.13)	10.2 (0.26)	89.8 (0.26)	10.0 (0.31)	7.2 (0.22)	4.1 (0.16)	68.4 (0.41)
Asian Indian	6.2 (0.62)	93.8 (0.62)	15.3 (0.94)	78.5 (1.12)	40.9 (1.22)	4.1 (0.47)	33.4 (1.34)	8.4 (0.25)	91.6 (0.25)	8.9 (0.29)	6.6 (0.22)	3.5 (0.16)	72.6 (0.41)
Bangladeshi	11.3 (3.10)	88.7 (3.10)	17.1 (2.77)	71.6 (3.74)	48.8 (4.71)	8.2 ! (2.86)	14.6 (3.25)	15.8 (1.63)	84.2 (1.63)	17.7 (2.00)	11.2 (1.28)	8.6 (1.51)	46.8 (2.07)
Bhutanese	‡ (†)	‡ (†)	‡ (†)	‡ (†)	‡ (†)	‡ (†)	‡ (†)	59.0 (6.93)	41.0 (6.93)	22.1 (4.85)	9.7 ! (3.13)	5.1 ! (1.72)	4.1 ! (1.86)
Nepalese	40.2 (6.90)	59.8 (6.90)	17.9 (3.83)	41.9 (6.63)	27.5 (5.26)	4.2 ! (1.93)	10.2 (3.05)	31.9 (2.79)	68.1 (2.79)	14.0 (2.28)	7.6 (1.38)	6.8 (1.17)	39.7 (3.37)
Pakistani	8.9 (1.74)	91.1 (1.74)	24.4 (2.35)	66.7 (2.53)	44.5 (2.80)	6.0 (1.61)	16.2 (1.97)	14.3 (1.07)	85.7 (1.07)	14.3 (1.02)	10.9 (0.87)	7.1 (0.74)	53.4 (1.56)
Southeast Asian	12.1 (0.83)	87.9 (0.83)	24.8 (0.99)	63.1 (1.19)	45.6 (1.06)	4.4 (0.46)	13.1 (0.79)	26.6 (0.41)	73.4 (0.41)	22.2 (0.48)	16.2 (0.35)	7.9 (0.25)	27.3 (0.49)
Burmese	45.6 (6.19)	54.4 (6.19)	25.6 (5.53)	28.8 (5.20)	25.5 (4.96)	‡ (†)	2.5 ! (1.00)	50.3 (3.09)	49.7 (3.09)	14.8 (2.05)	7.1 (1.00)	1.5 (0.41)	26.4 (2.31)
Cambodian	15.9 (2.76)	84.1 (2.76)	29.4 (3.74)	54.7 (3.72)	44.7 (3.62)	5.7 (1.32)	4.3 (1.18)	29.8 (1.45)	70.2 (1.45)	25.2 (1.57)	19.3 (1.32)	8.1 (0.92)	17.6 (1.20)
Hmong	13.1 (1.83)	86.9 (1.83)	34.4 (3.60)	52.5 (3.60)	40.9 (3.55)	5.1 (1.31)	6.5 (1.74)	27.8 (2.03)	72.2 (2.03)	23.7 (2.14)	21.2 (1.86)	10.2 (1.06)	17.0 (1.34)
Laotian	19.8 (3.80)	80.2 (3.80)	30.5 (4.37)	49.7 (4.66)	41.0 (4.13)	‡ (†)	6.6 ! (2.01)	26.8 (1.72)	73.2 (1.72)	29.0 (1.88)	19.0 (1.40)	9.3 (1.17)	15.9 (1.33)
Thai	13.5 (3.29)	86.5 (3.29)	32.8 (4.75)	53.6 (5.62)	34.5 (4.85)	‡ (†)	17.0 (4.36)	19.1 (1.13)	80.9 (1.13)	20.7 (1.63)	11.8 (1.16)	7.5 (1.04)	40.8 (1.87)
Vietnamese	7.8 (0.98)	92.2 (0.98)	20.8 (1.33)	71.4 (1.62)	50.1 (1.58)	4.9 (0.67)	16.4 (1.18)	26.3 (0.56)	73.7 (0.56)	21.6 (0.57)	16.1 (0.43)	7.6 (0.33)	28.3 (0.62)
Other Southeast Asian[6]	‡ (†)	98.0 (1.21)	19.7 (4.40)	78.3 (4.49)	47.6 (6.77)	3.1 ! (1.38)	27.6 (5.81)	5.4 (1.30)	94.6 (1.30)	16.0 (1.90)	12.9 (1.86)	11.2 (1.72)	54.4 (2.68)
Other Asian	6.2 (1.20)	93.8 (1.20)	24.9 (1.99)	68.9 (2.23)	43.7 (2.72)	6.1 (1.41)	19.2 (1.96)	14.2 (0.86)	85.8 (0.86)	14.4 (0.86)	16.0 (0.81)	7.6 (0.62)	47.8 (1.27)
Pacific Islander	16.1 (1.72)	83.9 (1.72)	37.7 (2.66)	46.2 (3.20)	35.9 (3.09)	5.2 (1.30)	5.1 (1.18)	12.3 (0.82)	87.7 (0.82)	39.1 (1.26)	24.2 (0.97)	8.9 (0.55)	15.4 (0.84)
American Indian/Alaska Native	22.4 (1.06)	77.6 (1.06)	38.4 (1.28)	39.1 (1.50)	32.5 (1.42)	3.6 (0.54)	3.0 (0.50)	18.1 (0.39)	81.9 (0.39)	33.3 (0.46)	25.8 (0.48)	8.4 (0.27)	14.3 (0.38)
Two or more races	13.0 (0.47)	87.0 (0.47)	29.7 (0.63)	57.3 (0.73)	43.3 (0.72)	4.9 (0.32)	9.1 (0.44)	9.7 (0.24)	90.3 (0.24)	22.8 (0.32)	26.4 (0.32)	9.1 (0.23)	32.0 (0.35)
White and Black	15.3 (0.96)	84.7 (0.96)	32.6 (1.23)	52.1 (1.37)	42.0 (1.34)	3.6 (0.50)	6.4 (0.72)	9.2 (0.58)	90.8 (0.58)	23.8 (0.87)	30.4 (0.87)	8.6 (0.61)	28.0 (0.81)
White and Asian	9.1 (0.92)	90.9 (0.92)	24.7 (1.05)	66.2 (1.42)	44.5 (1.33)	5.6 (0.64)	16.1 (0.99)	6.2 (0.52)	93.8 (0.52)	15.7 (0.62)	21.6 (0.64)	8.1 (0.39)	48.4 (0.86)
White and American Indian/Alaska Native	16.8 (0.96)	83.2 (0.96)	32.0 (1.44)	51.2 (1.65)	40.5 (1.71)	4.3 (0.69)	6.3 (0.80)	11.9 (0.39)	88.1 (0.39)	27.2 (0.57)	28.2 (0.54)	9.7 (0.40)	23.0 (0.50)
Other Two or more races	10.8 (0.85)	89.2 (0.85)	28.9 (1.47)	60.2 (1.47)	45.9 (1.52)	6.4 (0.73)	7.9 (0.64)	10.2 (0.39)	89.8 (0.39)	23.1 (0.51)	26.2 (0.60)	9.3 (0.40)	31.2 (0.67)

—Not available.

†Not applicable.

!Interpret data with caution. The coefficient of variation (CV) for this estimate is between 30 and 50 percent.

‡Reporting standards not met. Either there were too few cases for a reliable estimate or the coefficient of variation (CV) is 50 percent or greater.

[1]High school completers include diploma recipients and those completing high school through alternative credentials, such as a GED.

[2]Total includes other racial/ethnic groups not shown separately.

[3]Includes other Central American subgroups not shown separately.

[4]Includes Taiwanese.

[5]In addition to the subgroups shown, also includes Sri Lankan.

[6]Consists of Indonesian and Malaysian.

NOTE: Race categories exclude persons of Hispanic ethnicity. Detail may not sum to totals because of rounding.

SOURCE: U.S. Department of Commerce, Census Bureau, American Community Survey (ACS), 2009 and 2014. (This table was prepared January 2016.)

Table 104.50. Persons age 25 and over who hold a bachelor's or higher degree, by sex, race/ethnicity, age group, and field of bachelor's degree: 2014

[Standard errors appear in parentheses]

Field of bachelor's degree	Total	Sex: Males	Sex: Females	Race/ethnicity: White	Race/ethnicity: Black	Race/ethnicity: Hispanic	Race/ethnicity: Asian/Pacific Islander	Race/ethnicity: American Indian/ Alaska Native	Age: 25 to 29 years old	Age: 30 to 49 years old	Age: 50 years old and over
1	2	3	4	5	6	7	8	9	10	11	12
Total population, 25 and over (in thousands)	**213,806 (50.0)**	**103,072 (31.3)**	**110,734 (31.9)**	**142,046 (14.8)**	**24,637 (23.9)**	**30,698 (21.0)**	**11,821 (21.2)**	**1,290 (12.0)**	**21,843 (23.1)**	**83,187 (30.3)**	**108,776 (37.8)**
Percent of population with bachelor's degree	**30.1 (0.01)**	**29.9 (0.06)**	**30.2 (0.07)**	**33.6 (0.06)**	**19.8 (0.12)**	**14.4 (0.10)**	**50.8 (0.22)**	**14.3 (0.38)**	**32.4 (0.15)**	**33.2 (0.09)**	**27.2 (0.05)**
Bachelor's degree holders	Number (in thousands)										
Total	**64,303 (137.5)**	**30,831 (71.4)**	**33,472 (81.9)**	**47,757 (92.0)**	**4,867 (30.8)**	**4,432 (33.3)**	**6,001 (28.6)**	**185 (5.4)**	**7,078 (33.6)**	**27,645 (78.4)**	**29,581 (63.2)**
Agriculture/forestry	671 (9.6)	461 (7.0)	210 (5.7)	565 (8.2)	23 (1.8)	27 (2.1)	43 (2.8)	3 (0.6)	66 (3.5)	248 (6.5)	358 (5.5)
Art/architecture	3,058 (22.6)	1,328 (14.2)	1,729 (15.8)	2,368 (18.1)	145 (4.9)	228 (6.0)	247 (6.3)	7 (1.1)	465 (9.7)	1,362 (16.4)	1,231 (13.4)
Business/management	13,117 (40.1)	7,331 (30.2)	5,786 (23.7)	9,525 (32.6)	1,156 (15.0)	1,045 (13.4)	1,162 (11.6)	36 (2.4)	1,356 (16.4)	6,041 (30.2)	5,719 (24.5)
Communications	2,396 (18.8)	991 (12.2)	1,404 (14.6)	1,851 (14.8)	223 (7.4)	156 (4.9)	117 (4.3)	3 (0.7)	391 (8.1)	1,277 (13.9)	728 (10.0)
Computer and information sciences	1,902 (19.9)	1,366 (16.1)	536 (9.3)	1,103 (13.5)	176 (5.9)	125 (5.0)	451 (8.6)	5 (0.8)	245 (7.4)	1,149 (13.9)	508 (9.2)
Education	8,635 (39.5)	2,115 (17.9)	6,519 (34.0)	7,082 (32.2)	626 (9.7)	508 (10.0)	298 (6.8)	32 (1.8)	550 (7.9)	2,656 (22.0)	5,430 (27.8)
Engineering	5,016 (29.7)	4,293 (27.9)	723 (9.8)	3,327 (22.3)	207 (7.4)	381 (7.9)	1,010 (12.0)	9 (1.0)	499 (9.5)	2,123 (20.8)	2,393 (18.0)
English/literature	2,077 (17.3)	690 (9.4)	1,388 (14.2)	1,689 (15.4)	112 (4.7)	90 (3.6)	146 (4.8)	4 (0.7)	219 (5.6)	848 (11.9)	1,010 (10.3)
Foreign languages	692 (9.9)	196 (5.2)	496 (7.9)	512 (7.9)	24 (1.7)	69 (3.5)	71 (3.5)	‡ (†)	75 (3.1)	275 (6.3)	342 (6.5)
Health sciences	4,633 (28.3)	827 (11.4)	3,806 (24.0)	3,311 (22.9)	425 (8.6)	283 (7.3)	525 (8.3)	14 (1.4)	491 (8.5)	1,955 (19.6)	2,188 (17.2)
Liberal arts/humanities	942 (12.6)	377 (7.4)	566 (9.8)	694 (10.7)	72 (3.4)	78 (4.0)	76 (3.4)	3 (0.6)	79 (4.7)	410 (8.6)	453 (8.6)
Mathematics/statistics	972 (12.3)	576 (9.5)	396 (7.9)	738 (9.8)	52 (2.5)	40 (2.9)	126 (4.3)	‡ (†)	75 (3.3)	347 (7.6)	549 (8.5)
Natural sciences (biological and physical)	5,032 (27.0)	2,852 (19.6)	2,180 (16.3)	3,605 (21.3)	301 (6.9)	284 (8.3)	736 (10.9)	11 (1.3)	624 (9.5)	2,151 (18.9)	2,257 (15.8)
Philosophy/religion/theology	904 (11.8)	635 (10.0)	268 (6.9)	712 (10.3)	73 (3.3)	47 (3.0)	56 (2.9)	2 (0.5)	90 (4.0)	331 (7.4)	483 (8.7)
Pre-professional	1,081 (11.9)	651 (9.3)	430 (7.1)	727 (8.9)	169 (5.9)	129 (4.9)	28 (1.9)	7 (1.1)	171 (5.2)	610 (10.9)	301 (5.5)
Psychology	3,013 (20.1)	947 (11.4)	2,066 (18.9)	2,248 (15.5)	281 (6.6)	245 (6.9)	169 (4.8)	8 (1.1)	409 (7.9)	1,425 (15.2)	1,180 (11.9)
Social sciences/history	6,156 (33.1)	3,465 (24.0)	2,691 (18.1)	4,730 (27.6)	434 (8.8)	409 (8.3)	455 (7.1)	15 (1.4)	705 (12.2)	2,590 (19.4)	2,860 (20.6)
Other fields	4,008 (28.2)	1,730 (16.0)	2,278 (20.0)	2,972 (22.1)	370 (8.1)	287 (7.3)	286 (6.8)	21 (1.5)	568 (9.7)	1,848 (19.3)	1,591 (16.4)
	Percentage distribution, by field										
Total	**100.0 (†)**	**100.0 (†)**	**100.0 (†)**	**100.0 (†)**	**100.0 (†)**	**100.0 (†)**	**100.0 (†)**	**100.0 (†)**	**100.0 (†)**	**100.0 (†)**	**100.0 (†)**
Agriculture/forestry	1.0 (0.01)	1.5 (0.02)	0.6 (0.02)	1.2 (0.02)	0.5 (0.04)	0.6 (0.05)	0.7 (0.05)	1.8 (0.35)	0.9 (0.05)	0.9 (0.02)	1.2 (0.02)
Art/architecture	4.8 (0.03)	4.3 (0.04)	5.2 (0.04)	5.0 (0.04)	3.0 (0.10)	5.1 (0.12)	4.1 (0.10)	4.0 (0.59)	6.6 (0.14)	4.9 (0.06)	4.2 (0.04)
Business/management	20.4 (0.06)	23.8 (0.09)	17.3 (0.06)	19.9 (0.07)	23.8 (0.26)	23.6 (0.25)	19.4 (0.18)	19.3 (1.07)	19.2 (0.22)	21.9 (0.10)	19.3 (0.08)
Communications	3.7 (0.03)	3.2 (0.04)	4.2 (0.04)	3.9 (0.03)	4.6 (0.15)	3.5 (0.11)	1.9 (0.07)	1.9 (0.35)	5.5 (0.11)	4.6 (0.05)	2.5 (0.03)
Computer and information sciences	3.0 (0.03)	4.4 (0.05)	1.6 (0.03)	2.3 (0.03)	3.6 (0.12)	2.8 (0.12)	7.5 (0.14)	2.7 (0.43)	3.5 (0.10)	4.2 (0.05)	1.7 (0.03)
Education	13.4 (0.05)	6.9 (0.05)	19.5 (0.09)	14.8 (0.06)	12.9 (0.19)	11.5 (0.21)	5.0 (0.11)	17.6 (0.95)	7.8 (0.10)	9.6 (0.07)	18.4 (0.09)
Engineering	7.8 (0.04)	13.9 (0.08)	2.2 (0.03)	7.0 (0.04)	4.2 (0.16)	8.6 (0.17)	16.8 (0.16)	4.6 (0.51)	7.1 (0.13)	7.7 (0.07)	8.1 (0.06)
English/literature	3.2 (0.03)	2.2 (0.03)	4.1 (0.04)	3.5 (0.03)	2.3 (0.09)	2.0 (0.08)	2.4 (0.08)	2.1 (0.39)	3.1 (0.08)	3.1 (0.04)	3.4 (0.03)
Foreign languages	1.1 (0.01)	0.6 (0.02)	1.5 (0.02)	1.1 (0.02)	0.5 (0.03)	1.6 (0.08)	1.2 (0.06)	0.5 ! (0.20)	1.1 (0.04)	1.0 (0.02)	1.2 (0.02)
Health sciences	7.2 (0.04)	2.7 (0.04)	11.4 (0.07)	6.9 (0.05)	8.7 (0.17)	6.4 (0.16)	8.7 (0.14)	7.7 (0.73)	6.9 (0.12)	7.1 (0.07)	7.4 (0.06)
Liberal arts/humanities	1.5 (0.02)	1.2 (0.02)	1.7 (0.03)	1.5 (0.02)	1.5 (0.07)	1.8 (0.09)	1.3 (0.06)	1.6 (0.33)	1.1 (0.07)	1.5 (0.03)	1.5 (0.03)
Mathematics/statistics	1.5 (0.02)	1.9 (0.03)	1.2 (0.02)	1.5 (0.02)	1.1 (0.05)	0.9 (0.06)	2.1 (0.07)	0.9 (0.21)	1.1 (0.05)	1.3 (0.03)	1.9 (0.03)
Natural sciences (biological and physical)	7.8 (0.04)	9.2 (0.06)	6.5 (0.05)	7.5 (0.04)	6.2 (0.13)	6.4 (0.17)	12.3 (0.17)	6.1 (0.68)	8.8 (0.13)	7.8 (0.06)	7.6 (0.05)
Philosophy/religion/theology	1.4 (0.02)	2.1 (0.03)	0.8 (0.02)	1.5 (0.02)	1.5 (0.07)	1.1 (0.07)	0.9 (0.05)	1.3 (0.28)	1.3 (0.06)	1.2 (0.03)	1.6 (0.03)
Pre-professional	1.7 (0.02)	2.1 (0.03)	1.3 (0.02)	1.5 (0.02)	3.5 (0.12)	2.9 (0.11)	0.5 (0.03)	3.8 (0.58)	2.4 (0.07)	2.2 (0.04)	1.0 (0.02)
Psychology	4.7 (0.03)	3.1 (0.04)	6.2 (0.05)	4.7 (0.03)	5.8 (0.14)	5.5 (0.15)	2.8 (0.08)	4.4 (0.60)	5.8 (0.11)	5.2 (0.05)	4.0 (0.04)
Social sciences/history	9.6 (0.05)	11.2 (0.07)	8.0 (0.05)	9.9 (0.05)	8.9 (0.17)	9.2 (0.18)	7.6 (0.12)	8.4 (0.69)	10.0 (0.16)	9.4 (0.07)	9.7 (0.06)
Other fields	6.2 (0.04)	5.6 (0.05)	6.8 (0.06)	6.2 (0.05)	7.6 (0.15)	6.5 (0.16)	4.8 (0.11)	11.5 (0.78)	8.0 (0.13)	6.7 (0.07)	5.4 (0.06)

†Not applicable.
!Interpret data with caution. The coefficient of variation (CV) for this estimate is between 30 and 50 percent.
‡Reporting standards not met (too few cases for a reliable estimate).

NOTE: Totals include other racial/ethnic groups not separately shown. Race categories exclude persons of Hispanic ethnicity. Detail may not sum to totals because of rounding.
SOURCE: U.S. Department of Commerce, Census Bureau, American Community Survey (ACS), 2014. (This table was prepared December 2015.)

Table 104.60. Number of persons 25 to 34 years old and percentage with a bachelor's or higher degree, by undergraduate field of study, sex, race/ethnicity, and U.S. nativity and citizenship status: 2014

[Standard errors appear in parentheses]

			Percentage distribution of bachelor's degree holders													
				Bachelor's degree in a science, technology, engineering, or mathematics (STEM) field									Bachelor's degree in a non-STEM field			
Sex, race/ethnicity, and U.S. nativity and citizenship status	Total population ages 25 to 34 (in thousands)	Percent of population with bachelor's or higher degree	Total, all fields	STEM total	Agriculture/ natural resources	Architecture	Computer and information sciences	Engineering/ engineering technologies	Biology/ biomedical sciences	Mathematics/ statistics	Physical/ social sciences	Health studies	Non-STEM total	Business	Education	All other fields of study
1	2	3	4	5	6	7	8	9	10	11	12	13	14	15	16	17
Total	**43,279 (33.9)**	**33.4 (0.12)**	**100.0 (†)**	**40.6 (0.16)**	**1.5 (0.05)**	**0.8 (0.03)**	**4.1 (0.08)**	**7.9 (0.10)**	**5.7 (0.07)**	**1.1 (0.03)**	**12.9 (0.12)**	**6.6 (0.08)**	**59.4 (0.16)**	**19.8 (0.13)**	**8.3 (0.09)**	**31.3 (0.17)**
Sex																
Male	21,780 (23.5)	29.4 (0.13)	100.0 (†)	43.8 (0.28)	1.8 (0.07)	1.1 (0.05)	6.9 (0.15)	13.8 (0.18)	5.1 (0.10)	1.5 (0.06)	11.1 (0.18)	2.6 (0.07)	56.2 (0.28)	22.7 (0.20)	4.0 (0.10)	29.5 (0.23)
Female	21,500 (23.2)	37.5 (0.16)	100.0 (†)	38.0 (0.19)	1.3 (0.05)	0.6 (0.03)	1.8 (0.06)	3.2 (0.08)	6.2 (0.11)	0.8 (0.04)	14.3 (0.16)	9.9 (0.12)	62.0 (0.19)	17.6 (0.16)	11.6 (0.14)	32.8 (0.21)
Race/ethnicity																
White	24,638 (12.9)	39.7 (0.15)	100.0 (†)	37.6 (0.18)	1.9 (0.06)	0.8 (0.03)	3.0 (0.07)	6.4 (0.11)	5.4 (0.08)	1.1 (0.04)	12.5 (0.13)	6.5 (0.08)	62.4 (0.18)	19.4 (0.16)	9.8 (0.11)	33.2 (0.20)
Black	5,665 (20.1)	20.6 (0.24)	100.0 (†)	37.2 (0.62)	0.7 (0.10)	0.3 (0.07)	3.7 (0.25)	4.3 (0.31)	5.2 (0.25)	0.6 (0.09)	14.6 (0.51)	7.7 (0.37)	62.8 (0.62)	22.6 (0.58)	6.7 (0.30)	33.6 (0.60)
Hispanic	8,779 (19.8)	15.1 (0.19)	100.0 (†)	37.8 (0.58)	0.6 (0.10)	1.1 (0.10)	2.9 (0.21)	7.4 (0.33)	4.3 (0.23)	0.7 (0.10)	14.6 (0.45)	6.0 (0.28)	62.2 (0.58)	21.9 (0.50)	7.1 (0.30)	33.2 (0.60)
Asian	2,796 (16.5)	63.4 (0.40)	100.0 (†)	60.9 (0.51)	0.7 (0.07)	0.8 (0.09)	11.0 (0.32)	18.7 (0.41)	8.5 (0.21)	1.7 (0.12)	12.2 (0.37)	7.5 (0.24)	39.1 (0.51)	19.2 (0.38)	2.4 (0.16)	17.5 (0.38)
Pacific Islander	88 (3.5)	12.7 (1.42)	100.0 (†)	48.7 (5.44)	‡ (†)	‡ (†)	4.3 ! (2.01)	9.1 ! (3.22)	10.2 ! (3.80)	‡ (†)	16.7 (4.28)	8.0 ! (3.29)	51.3 (5.44)	18.1 (5.16)	‡ (†)	30.7 (5.18)
American Indian/ Alaska Native[1]	285 (6.1)	13.0 (0.77)	100.0 (†)	37.2 (3.33)	5.1 ! (1.55)	‡ (†)	2.8 ! (0.88)	6.6 (1.70)	4.8 (1.34)	‡ (†)	10.5 (1.77)	6.4 (1.79)	62.8 (3.33)	20.3 (2.65)	10.6 (1.72)	31.9 (3.06)
American Indian	246 (5.5)	13.2 (0.85)	100.0 (†)	36.5 (3.51)	5.8 (1.72)	‡ (†)	1.9 ! (0.70)	6.5 (1.80)	4.4 ! (1.33)	‡ (†)	10.0 (1.86)	7.1 (2.07)	63.5 (3.51)	19.6 (2.89)	11.4 (1.87)	32.5 (3.42)
Alaska Native	14 (1.0)	6.0 ! (2.39)	100.0 (†)	‡ (†)	‡ (†)	‡ (†)	‡ (†)	‡ (†)	‡ (†)	‡ (†)	‡ (†)	‡ (†)	‡ (†)	‡ (†)	‡ (†)	‡ (†)
Some other race[2]	99 (5.4)	39.0 (2.01)	100.0 (†)	44.3 (4.19)	‡ (†)	‡ (†)	5.9 ! (2.21)	8.4 (2.14)	5.5 (1.44)	‡ (†)	11.6 (2.18)	6.9 (1.86)	55.7 (4.19)	22.5 (3.02)	3.9 ! (1.78)	29.3 (3.35)
Two or more races	928 (15.8)	35.5 (0.69)	100.0 (†)	43.9 (1.31)	1.5 (0.26)	0.9 (0.19)	3.7 (0.44)	8.6 (0.55)	8.1 (0.61)	1.2 (0.23)	14.5 (0.95)	5.4 (0.55)	56.1 (1.31)	17.1 (0.83)	4.4 (0.43)	34.6 (1.11)
Race/ethnicity by sex																
Male																
White	12,466 (9.0)	35.2 (0.17)	100.0 (†)	40.3 (0.30)	2.3 (0.09)	1.1 (0.06)	5.5 (0.13)	11.7 (0.21)	4.9 (0.11)	1.5 (0.07)	10.9 (0.19)	2.4 (0.08)	59.7 (0.30)	23.3 (0.25)	4.6 (0.12)	31.8 (0.27)
Black	2,706 (14.3)	16.5 (0.33)	100.0 (†)	36.5 (1.04)	1.0 (0.17)	0.6 (0.16)	6.5 (0.57)	8.2 (0.59)	4.8 (0.44)	0.8 (0.13)	11.5 (0.68)	3.1 (0.39)	63.5 (1.04)	24.1 (0.93)	4.9 (0.45)	34.4 (1.10)
Hispanic	4,590 (14.0)	12.4 (0.19)	100.0 (†)	40.6 (0.97)	0.7 (0.15)	1.5 (0.17)	5.6 (0.48)	13.3 (0.64)	4.1 (0.31)	1.0 (0.17)	11.9 (0.62)	2.5 (0.28)	59.4 (0.97)	24.0 (0.85)	4.1 (0.37)	31.3 (0.95)
Asian	1,326 (10.0)	61.8 (0.64)	100.0 (†)	68.4 (0.75)	0.7 (0.12)	0.7 (0.13)	15.2 (0.54)	28.0 (0.71)	6.8 (0.30)	2.1 (0.21)	11.4 (0.49)	3.5 (0.24)	31.6 (0.75)	18.0 (0.56)	0.7 (0.13)	12.9 (0.52)
Pacific Islander	43 (2.4)	10.7 (1.90)	100.0 (†)	48.5 (8.85)	‡ (†)	‡ (†)	9.5 ! (4.57)	11.3 ! (4.96)	‡ (†)	‡ (†)	11.6 ! (5.29)	‡ (†)	51.5 (8.85)	27.5 ! (8.51)	‡ (†)	23.1 ! (6.99)
American Indian/ Alaska Native[1]	141 (4.2)	10.6 (1.12)	100.0 (†)	34.6 (5.20)	‡ (†)	‡ (†)	4.6 ! (1.82)	11.2 ! (3.43)	4.3 ! (1.45)	‡ (†)	8.9 (2.56)	‡ (†)	65.4 (5.20)	26.5 (5.32)	6.0 ! (2.19)	32.8 (5.32)
American Indian	120 (4.0)	11.0 (1.20)	100.0 (†)	33.1 (5.41)	‡ (†)	‡ (†)	3.1 ! (1.42)	10.0 ! (3.47)	4.5 ! (1.54)	‡ (†)	9.3 (2.79)	‡ (†)	66.9 (5.41)	25.3 (5.73)	6.8 ! (2.48)	34.8 (5.88)
Alaska Native	7 (0.7)	‡ (†)	100.0 (†)	‡ (†)	‡ (†)	‡ (†)	‡ (†)	‡ (†)	‡ (†)	‡ (†)	‡ (†)	‡ (†)	‡ (†)	‡ (†)	‡ (†)	‡ (†)
Some other race[2]	52 (3.3)	33.3 (2.73)	100.0 (†)	49.7 (5.97)	‡ (†)	‡ (†)	11.5 ! (4.23)	16.0 (3.90)	4.1 ! (1.78)	‡ (†)	7.0 ! (2.14)	‡ (†)	50.3 (5.97)	20.0 (4.74)	‡ (†)	28.2 (4.63)
Two or more races	456 (11.2)	32.6 (0.89)	100.0 (†)	46.3 (1.88)	1.7 (0.44)	1.1 (0.30)	6.6 (0.89)	14.4 (1.11)	6.5 (0.87)	1.4 (0.40)	11.9 (1.11)	2.6 (0.53)	53.7 (1.88)	19.6 (1.28)	2.3 (0.63)	31.8 (1.51)
Female																
White	12,172 (7.0)	44.3 (0.20)	100.0 (†)	35.3 (0.23)	1.6 (0.07)	0.5 (0.04)	1.0 (0.06)	2.0 (0.08)	5.7 (0.12)	0.8 (0.05)	13.8 (0.18)	9.9 (0.14)	64.7 (0.23)	16.2 (0.20)	14.1 (0.19)	34.4 (0.27)
Black	2,960 (12.0)	24.4 (0.34)	100.0 (†)	37.6 (0.77)	0.5 (0.13)	0.2 ! (0.07)	1.9 (0.20)	1.9 (0.27)	5.4 (0.32)	0.6 (0.11)	16.6 (0.68)	10.5 (0.55)	62.4 (0.77)	21.6 (0.73)	7.8 (0.42)	33.0 (0.67)
Hispanic	4,189 (13.9)	18.1 (0.30)	100.0 (†)	35.6 (0.66)	0.6 (0.12)	0.9 (0.13)	1.0 (0.13)	3.0 (0.27)	4.4 (0.35)	0.5 (0.10)	16.7 (0.60)	8.6 (0.45)	64.4 (0.66)	20.3 (0.61)	9.4 (0.47)	34.7 (0.76)
Asian	1,470 (9.9)	64.9 (0.52)	100.0 (†)	54.5 (0.59)	0.7 (0.09)	0.8 (0.11)	7.4 (0.34)	10.7 (0.35)	9.9 (0.28)	1.3 (0.14)	12.8 (0.48)	10.9 (0.39)	45.5 (0.59)	20.2 (0.46)	3.8 (0.26)	21.5 (0.47)
Pacific Islander	45 (2.5)	14.6 (1.99)	100.0 (†)	48.8 (6.78)	‡ (†)	‡ (†)	‡ (†)	‡ (†)	‡ (†)	‡ (†)	20.4 ! (6.23)	10.6 ! (4.72)	51.2 (6.78)	11.5 ! (4.52)	‡ (†)	36.1 (7.14)
American Indian/ Alaska Native[1]	144 (3.6)	15.3 (1.12)	100.0 (†)	38.9 (4.22)	5.6 ! (2.16)	‡ (†)	‡ (†)	3.5 ! (1.46)	5.2 ! (2.05)	‡ (†)	11.6 (2.37)	10.1 (2.71)	61.1 (4.22)	16.1 (2.48)	13.7 (2.42)	31.3 (3.78)
American Indian	126 (3.2)	15.3 (1.26)	100.0 (†)	38.9 (4.43)	6.5 ! (2.41)	‡ (†)	‡ (†)	4.0 ! (1.68)	4.4 ! (2.07)	‡ (†)	10.4 (2.48)	11.1 (3.21)	61.1 (4.43)	15.7 (2.62)	14.6 (2.55)	30.8 (4.12)
Alaska Native	7 (0.6)	8.7 ! (3.65)	100.0 (†)	‡ (†)	‡ (†)	‡ (†)	‡ (†)	‡ (†)	‡ (†)	‡ (†)	‡ (†)	‡ (†)	‡ (†)	‡ (†)	‡ (†)	‡ (†)
Some other race[2]	48 (3.1)	45.2 (2.79)	100.0 (†)	40.0 (4.88)	‡ (†)	‡ (†)	‡ (†)	‡ (†)	6.6 ! (2.13)	‡ (†)	15.3 (3.53)	8.7 (2.51)	60.0 (4.88)	24.5 (4.36)	5.3 ! (2.36)	30.2 (4.15)
Two or more races	473 (10.4)	38.3 (0.92)	100.0 (†)	42.0 (1.54)	1.3 (0.26)	0.8 ! (0.25)	1.4 (0.35)	3.9 (0.55)	9.4 (0.82)	1.0 (0.27)	16.6 (1.31)	7.6 (0.79)	58.0 (1.54)	15.1 (1.01)	6.0 (0.60)	36.9 (1.43)
Nativity																
Hispanic																
U.S.-born[3]	4,836 (28.5)	19.7 (0.27)	100.0 (†)	36.2 (0.61)	0.5 (0.09)	1.0 (0.12)	2.8 (0.21)	5.4 (0.32)	4.2 (0.27)	0.7 (0.11)	15.4 (0.51)	6.1 (0.34)	63.8 (0.61)	20.1 (0.56)	7.3 (0.32)	36.4 (0.61)
Foreign-born	3,943 (24.2)	9.5 (0.21)	100.0 (†)	41.8 (1.17)	1.0 (0.22)	1.5 (0.25)	3.3 (0.43)	12.5 (0.79)	4.4 (0.48)	0.7 (0.19)	12.7 (0.86)	5.8 (0.52)	58.2 (1.17)	26.5 (1.00)	6.6 (0.58)	25.1 (1.13)
Asian																
U.S.-born[3]	866 (11.7)	61.5 (0.68)	100.0 (†)	51.8 (0.83)	0.7 (0.14)	0.9 (0.18)	4.6 (0.35)	8.8 (0.49)	11.5 (0.51)	1.2 (0.21)	16.1 (0.72)	8.0 (0.53)	48.2 (0.83)	21.2 (0.77)	2.4 (0.29)	24.6 (0.81)
Foreign-born	1,930 (17.1)	64.3 (0.48)	100.0 (†)	64.9 (0.55)	0.6 (0.08)	0.8 (0.10)	13.7 (0.44)	22.9 (0.52)	7.2 (0.25)	1.9 (0.14)	10.5 (0.37)	7.3 (0.29)	35.1 (0.55)	18.3 (0.44)	2.4 (0.19)	14.5 (0.39)
Citizenship status																
U.S.-born citizen	35,600 (46.5)	33.8 (0.13)	100.0 (†)	37.4 (0.17)	1.7 (0.05)	0.8 (0.03)	2.9 (0.06)	5.9 (0.09)	5.5 (0.08)	1.0 (0.04)	13.1 (0.13)	6.6 (0.08)	62.6 (0.17)	19.6 (0.15)	9.2 (0.10)	33.8 (0.19)
Naturalized citizen	2,266 (22.1)	39.5 (0.43)	100.0 (†)	49.2 (0.76)	0.7 (0.10)	1.0 (0.16)	5.9 (0.34)	9.5 (0.46)	8.1 (0.30)	1.3 (0.15)	13.6 (0.47)	9.2 (0.49)	50.8 (0.76)	24.9 (0.62)	3.6 (0.30)	22.3 (0.57)
Noncitizen	5,413 (32.2)	28.2 (0.28)	100.0 (†)	60.4 (0.51)	0.9 (0.10)	1.0 (0.11)	11.9 (0.41)	22.2 (0.40)	6.1 (0.24)	1.9 (0.15)	10.9 (0.37)	5.5 (0.24)	39.6 (0.51)	18.4 (0.32)	3.6 (0.20)	17.6 (0.43)

†Not applicable.

!Interpret data with caution. The coefficient of variation (CV) for this estimate is between 30 and 50 percent.

‡Reporting standards not met. Either there are too few cases for a reliable estimate or the coefficient of variation (CV) is 50 percent or greater.

[1]Includes persons reporting American Indian alone, persons reporting Alaska Native alone, and persons from American Indian and/or Alaska Native tribes specified or not specified.

[2]Respondents who wrote in some other race that was not included as an option on the questionnaire.

[3]Includes those born in the 50 states, the District of Columbia, Puerto Rico, American Samoa, Guam, the U.S. Virgin Islands, and the Northern Marianas, as well as those born abroad to U.S.-citizen parents.

NOTE: Estimates are for the entire population in the indicated age range, including persons living in households and persons living in group quarters (such as college residence halls, residential treatment centers, military barracks, and correctional facilities). The first bachelor's degree major reported by respondents was used to classify their field of study, even though they were able to report a second bachelor's degree major and may possess advanced degrees in other fields. STEM fields, as defined here, consist of the fields specified in columns 6 through 13. Data were assembled based on major field aggregations, except that management of STEM activities was counted as a STEM field instead of a business field. Detail may not sum to totals because of rounding. Race categories exclude persons of Hispanic ethnicity.

SOURCE: U.S. Department of Commerce, Census Bureau, American Community Survey (ACS), 2014. (This table was prepared December 2015.)

Table 104.70. Number and percentage distribution of 5- to 17-year-olds, by parent's highest level of educational attainment, household type, and child's race/ethnicity: 2009 and 2014

[Standard errors appear in parentheses]

Year, household type, and race/ethnicity	Total, all 5- to 17-year-olds: Number (in thousands)	Total, all 5- to 17-year-olds: Percentage distribution	Highest level of education attained by any parent residing with child[1]: Total, all levels	Less than high school completion	High school completion[2]	Some college, no degree	Associate's degree	Bachelor's or higher degree: Total	Bachelor's degree	Master's degree	Doctor's degree
1	2	3	4	5	6	7	8	9	10	11	12
2009											
Total, both household types	**50,507 (34.0)**	**100.0 (†)**	**100.0 (†)**	**11.2 (0.09)**	**20.3 (0.10)**	**23.3 (0.10)**	**10.0 (0.07)**	**35.2 (0.14)**	**20.5 (0.11)**	**9.9 (0.07)**	**4.8 (0.05)**
White	28,882 (16.9)	57.2 (0.04)	100.0 (†)	3.8 (0.08)	17.6 (0.12)	22.8 (0.12)	11.3 (0.09)	44.5 (0.16)	25.6 (0.12)	12.8 (0.10)	6.1 (0.07)
Black	6,745 (22.9)	13.4 (0.04)	100.0 (†)	12.5 (0.24)	26.6 (0.36)	31.2 (0.32)	9.9 (0.18)	19.8 (0.26)	12.9 (0.20)	5.3 (0.16)	1.7 (0.09)
Hispanic	10,624 (15.0)	21.0 (0.02)	100.0 (†)	31.7 (0.27)	25.6 (0.23)	21.0 (0.22)	6.8 (0.14)	15.0 (0.19)	9.8 (0.16)	3.5 (0.08)	1.7 (0.06)
Asian	2,087 (11.6)	4.1 (0.02)	100.0 (†)	9.5 (0.32)	12.0 (0.34)	11.8 (0.38)	6.3 (0.24)	60.4 (0.58)	30.1 (0.49)	18.2 (0.42)	12.1 (0.33)
Pacific Islander	69 (3.0)	0.1 (0.01)	100.0 (†)	5.9 (1.29)	31.2 (3.05)	33.7 (3.56)	7.7 (1.31)	21.4 (2.37)	14.9 (2.12)	5.6 (1.48)	0.9 ! (0.28)
American Indian/Alaska Native	348 (6.7)	0.7 (0.01)	100.0 (†)	10.7 (0.81)	25.9 (1.06)	33.2 (1.16)	10.4 (0.83)	19.8 (1.09)	13.5 (0.96)	4.8 (0.53)	1.5 (0.31)
Some other race	155 (6.4)	0.3 (0.01)	100.0 (†)	13.4 (1.51)	17.7 (1.54)	17.8 (1.58)	8.9 (1.16)	42.1 (2.26)	20.8 (1.87)	12.8 (1.26)	8.6 (1.23)
Two or more races	1,597 (16.0)	3.2 (0.03)	100.0 (†)	5.2 (0.27)	17.8 (0.50)	28.2 (0.61)	11.6 (0.38)	37.2 (0.58)	20.8 (0.41)	10.5 (0.35)	5.9 (0.31)
Two-parent household	33,893 (61.5)	100.0 (†)	100.0 (†)	7.3 (0.07)	16.0 (0.12)	21.1 (0.12)	10.7 (0.09)	44.9 (0.13)	25.4 (0.12)	13.0 (0.09)	6.5 (0.06)
White	21,930 (40.9)	64.7 (0.09)	100.0 (†)	1.8 (0.06)	14.0 (0.12)	20.9 (0.13)	11.6 (0.11)	51.7 (0.15)	29.1 (0.13)	15.2 (0.12)	7.4 (0.08)
Black	2,315 (25.4)	6.8 (0.07)	100.0 (†)	3.3 (0.21)	17.3 (0.49)	29.6 (0.49)	12.8 (0.43)	37.0 (0.54)	22.7 (0.45)	10.4 (0.32)	3.9 (0.23)
Hispanic	6,619 (26.1)	19.5 (0.06)	100.0 (†)	27.9 (0.30)	24.1 (0.31)	21.0 (0.31)	7.7 (0.19)	19.3 (0.28)	12.4 (0.24)	4.6 (0.12)	2.4 (0.09)
Asian	1,753 (12.0)	5.2 (0.04)	100.0 (†)	7.6 (0.37)	10.5 (0.35)	10.6 (0.41)	6.3 (0.27)	65.0 (0.65)	31.4 (0.56)	20.1 (0.45)	13.5 (0.38)
Pacific Islander	45 (2.7)	0.1 (0.01)	100.0 (†)	2.4 ! (0.91)	29.0 (3.71)	32.0 (4.37)	7.8 (1.51)	28.8 (3.60)	19.5 (3.11)	7.8 (2.18)	1.4 ! (0.45)
American Indian/Alaska Native	173 (5.9)	0.5 (0.02)	100.0 (†)	4.1 (0.64)	20.5 (1.50)	32.9 (1.70)	13.4 (1.27)	29.1 (1.65)	18.5 (1.46)	8.5 (0.98)	2.0 (0.42)
Some other race	101 (5.1)	0.3 (0.01)	100.0 (†)	7.8 (1.87)	13.8 (1.60)	16.2 (1.76)	8.5 (1.44)	53.7 (2.79)	25.3 (2.23)	16.1 (1.80)	12.4 (1.75)
Two or more races	957 (12.4)	2.8 (0.04)	100.0 (†)	1.6 (0.17)	11.6 (0.51)	23.8 (0.63)	12.1 (0.48)	51.0 (0.84)	27.6 (0.64)	14.6 (0.51)	8.7 (0.45)
Single-parent household	16,614 (71.1)	100.0 (†)	100.0 (†)	19.1 (0.18)	29.2 (0.18)	27.8 (0.17)	8.6 (0.12)	15.4 (0.16)	10.6 (0.13)	3.5 (0.08)	1.3 (0.05)
White	6,952 (38.1)	41.8 (0.14)	100.0 (†)	10.2 (0.23)	29.0 (0.29)	28.8 (0.29)	10.4 (0.22)	21.6 (0.27)	14.7 (0.23)	4.9 (0.14)	2.0 (0.08)
Black	4,430 (29.5)	26.7 (0.14)	100.0 (†)	17.3 (0.33)	31.4 (0.42)	32.1 (0.43)	8.3 (0.21)	10.9 (0.25)	7.7 (0.19)	2.6 (0.14)	0.5 (0.05)
Hispanic	4,005 (28.2)	24.1 (0.13)	100.0 (†)	38.0 (0.41)	28.0 (0.38)	21.0 (0.35)	5.4 (0.21)	7.7 (0.22)	5.5 (0.19)	1.6 (0.09)	0.6 (0.06)
Asian	334 (8.6)	2.0 (0.05)	100.0 (†)	19.8 (1.05)	19.8 (1.23)	17.9 (1.20)	6.4 (0.57)	36.1 (1.30)	23.2 (1.09)	8.2 (0.69)	4.8 (0.55)
Pacific Islander	24 (2.4)	0.1 (0.01)	100.0 (†)	12.5 (3.25)	35.2 (4.63)	36.8 (5.27)	7.6 ! (2.42)	7.9 ! (2.54)	6.3 ! (2.31)	‡ (†)	‡ (†)
American Indian/Alaska Native	175 (5.3)	1.1 (0.03)	100.0 (†)	17.2 (1.50)	31.2 (1.74)	33.5 (1.81)	7.4 (0.87)	10.6 (1.07)	8.6 (1.04)	1.2 (0.34)	0.9 ! (0.39)
Some other race	54 (3.9)	0.3 (0.02)	100.0 (†)	23.9 (3.26)	25.0 (3.34)	20.7 (2.90)	9.8 (2.16)	20.5 (2.95)	12.4 (2.54)	‡ (†)	‡ (†)
Two or more races	640 (10.5)	3.9 (0.06)	100.0 (†)	10.7 (0.59)	27.1 (0.85)	34.9 (0.98)	10.8 (0.63)	16.5 (0.60)	10.7 (0.46)	4.2 (0.38)	1.6 (0.23)
2014											
Total, both household types	**50,852 (31.7)**	**100.0 (†)**	**100.0 (†)**	**10.8 (0.08)**	**19.0 (0.12)**	**21.6 (0.10)**	**10.4 (0.08)**	**38.1 (0.15)**	**21.2 (0.10)**	**11.8 (0.08)**	**5.2 (0.05)**
White	26,906 (20.5)	52.9 (0.04)	100.0 (†)	3.6 (0.06)	15.3 (0.14)	20.4 (0.13)	11.9 (0.11)	48.8 (0.18)	26.8 (0.14)	15.3 (0.11)	6.8 (0.08)
Black	6,728 (22.5)	13.2 (0.04)	100.0 (†)	10.3 (0.25)	25.6 (0.36)	29.6 (0.37)	10.8 (0.23)	23.7 (0.31)	14.0 (0.25)	7.6 (0.20)	2.2 (0.10)
Hispanic	12,136 (17.0)	23.9 (0.03)	100.0 (†)	28.7 (0.26)	25.4 (0.21)	21.0 (0.19)	7.5 (0.15)	17.4 (0.19)	11.1 (0.14)	4.5 (0.11)	1.8 (0.07)
Asian	2,377 (14.4)	4.7 (0.03)	100.0 (†)	7.8 (0.28)	11.0 (0.36)	10.8 (0.33)	6.6 (0.24)	63.7 (0.48)	30.2 (0.48)	21.2 (0.42)	12.4 (0.31)
Pacific Islander	84 (3.2)	0.2 (0.01)	100.0 (†)	7.7 (1.62)	30.0 (2.47)	26.4 (2.40)	16.8 (2.23)	19.1 (2.14)	12.4 (1.87)	4.0 (1.08)	2.7 ! (0.91)
American Indian/Alaska Native	363 (7.2)	0.7 (0.01)	100.0 (†)	9.9 (0.73)	26.5 (0.98)	31.5 (1.07)	10.5 (0.71)	21.6 (0.98)	13.3 (0.91)	6.2 (0.53)	2.2 (0.34)
Some other race	152 (5.4)	0.3 (0.01)	100.0 (†)	13.7 (1.51)	18.0 (1.55)	18.9 (1.84)	6.4 (0.93)	43.0 (1.88)	23.1 (1.55)	13.1 (1.22)	6.8 (1.21)
Two or more races	2,107 (20.7)	4.1 (0.04)	100.0 (†)	5.4 (0.31)	15.7 (0.44)	25.7 (0.57)	11.9 (0.40)	41.3 (0.53)	21.9 (0.46)	12.5 (0.27)	6.9 (0.24)
Two-parent household	33,073 (60.6)	100.0 (†)	100.0 (†)	7.0 (0.09)	14.0 (0.12)	18.8 (0.12)	10.9 (0.10)	49.2 (0.17)	26.2 (0.14)	15.7 (0.11)	7.2 (0.07)
White	20,034 (54.6)	60.6 (0.13)	100.0 (†)	1.8 (0.06)	11.1 (0.13)	18.1 (0.16)	12.0 (0.13)	57.0 (0.20)	30.4 (0.18)	18.3 (0.14)	8.3 (0.10)
Black	2,340 (27.4)	7.1 (0.08)	100.0 (†)	2.6 (0.24)	15.1 (0.46)	25.9 (0.55)	13.0 (0.48)	43.5 (0.64)	23.5 (0.53)	15.1 (0.46)	4.8 (0.27)
Hispanic	7,185 (35.4)	21.7 (0.10)	100.0 (†)	24.5 (0.31)	23.8 (0.33)	20.5 (0.27)	8.1 (0.19)	23.1 (0.27)	14.2 (0.20)	6.2 (0.16)	2.6 (0.10)
Asian	1,974 (13.5)	6.0 (0.04)	100.0 (†)	6.1 (0.25)	9.2 (0.37)	9.9 (0.33)	6.1 (0.27)	68.7 (0.54)	31.2 (0.53)	23.5 (0.50)	14.0 (0.35)
Pacific Islander	55 (3.0)	0.2 (0.01)	100.0 (†)	3.7 ! (1.11)	27.1 (3.27)	28.7 (2.98)	14.6 (2.30)	26.0 (2.95)	17.3 (2.70)	4.7 (1.37)	4.0 ! (1.35)
American Indian/Alaska Native	172 (5.3)	0.5 (0.02)	100.0 (†)	2.6 (0.50)	20.9 (1.34)	31.5 (1.56)	11.8 (1.08)	33.2 (1.40)	18.9 (1.35)	10.2 (1.04)	4.2 (0.66)
Some other race	96 (5.2)	0.3 (0.02)	100.0 (†)	12.4 (1.79)	13.5 (1.67)	14.4 (1.79)	7.0 (1.27)	52.8 (2.46)	26.1 (1.94)	18.2 (1.74)	8.5 (1.42)
Two or more races	1,216 (16.7)	3.7 (0.05)	100.0 (†)	1.2 (0.25)	9.1 (0.49)	20.1 (0.60)	12.5 (0.53)	57.1 (0.72)	27.9 (0.64)	18.4 (0.45)	10.8 (0.40)
Single-parent household	17,779 (69.4)	100.0 (†)	100.0 (†)	17.8 (0.17)	28.2 (0.20)	26.8 (0.17)	9.6 (0.11)	17.6 (0.17)	11.8 (0.14)	4.4 (0.08)	1.4 (0.04)
White	6,872 (49.3)	38.7 (0.21)	100.0 (†)	8.9 (0.16)	27.5 (0.32)	27.0 (0.29)	11.6 (0.23)	25.0 (0.30)	16.5 (0.23)	6.3 (0.14)	2.3 (0.07)
Black	4,388 (31.2)	24.7 (0.15)	100.0 (†)	14.4 (0.35)	31.2 (0.47)	31.5 (0.44)	9.7 (0.27)	13.2 (0.33)	8.9 (0.28)	3.6 (0.16)	0.7 (0.07)
Hispanic	4,951 (35.6)	27.8 (0.18)	100.0 (†)	34.8 (0.43)	27.7 (0.34)	21.8 (0.31)	6.5 (0.21)	9.2 (0.23)	6.5 (0.19)	2.1 (0.11)	0.6 (0.05)
Asian	403 (9.5)	2.3 (0.05)	100.0 (†)	16.3 (0.97)	19.9 (1.07)	15.6 (0.97)	8.9 (0.70)	39.3 (1.25)	25.2 (1.19)	9.7 (0.75)	4.5 (0.46)
Pacific Islander	29 (2.7)	0.2 (0.02)	100.0 (†)	15.3 (3.77)	35.6 (4.80)	22.2 (3.84)	21.1 (5.19)	5.9 ! (2.05)	3.0 ! (1.38)	‡ (†)	‡ (†)
American Indian/Alaska Native	191 (5.4)	1.1 (0.03)	100.0 (†)	16.5 (1.28)	31.5 (1.40)	31.6 (1.52)	9.3 (0.89)	11.1 (1.22)	8.2 (1.11)	‡ (†)	‡ (†)
Some other race	56 (3.8)	0.3 (0.02)	100.0 (†)	16.1 (2.60)	25.7 (3.39)	26.7 (3.84)	5.3 (1.43)	26.1 (2.97)	18.0 (2.66)	4.3 (1.10)	3.8 ! (1.85)
Two or more races	890 (16.7)	5.0 (0.10)	100.0 (†)	11.0 (0.61)	24.8 (0.78)	33.3 (1.00)	11.1 (0.59)	19.8 (0.71)	13.6 (0.57)	4.5 (0.28)	1.6 (0.20)

†Not applicable.
!Interpret data with caution. The coefficient of variation (CV) for this estimate is between 30 and 50 percent.
‡Reporting standards not met. Either there are too few cases for a reliable estimate or the coefficient of variation (CV) is 50 percent or greater.
[1]Includes adoptive and stepparents, but excludes parents not residing in the same household as their children.
[2]Includes parents who completed high school through equivalency programs, such as a GED program.

NOTE: Table includes only 5- to 17-year-olds who resided with at least one of their parents (including an adoptive or stepparent). The 5- to 17-year-olds in single-parent households resided with only one parent, while those in two-parent households resided with two parents. Race categories exclude persons of Hispanic ethnicity. Detail may not sum to totals because of rounding.
SOURCE: U.S. Department of Commerce, Census Bureau, American Community Survey (ACS), 2009 and 2014. (This table was prepared January 2016.)

Table 104.80. Percentage of persons 18 to 24 years old and age 25 and over, by educational attainment and state: 2000 and 2014

[Standard errors appear in parentheses]

State	Percent of 18- to 24-year-olds who were high school completers[1]		Percent of population 25 years old and over, by educational attainment										
			2000					2014					
			Less than high school completion	High school completion[1] or higher	Bachelor's or higher degree			Less than high school completion	High school completion[1] or higher		Bachelor's or higher degree		
	2000	2014			Total	Bachelor's degree	Graduate degree		Total	High school only	Total	Bachelor's degree	Graduate degree
1	2	3	4	5	6	7	8	9	10	11	12	13	14
United States	**74.7 (0.02)**	**86.2 (0.08)**	**19.6 (0.01)**	**80.4 (0.01)**	**24.4 (0.01)**	**15.5 (0.01)**	**8.9 (#)**	**13.1 (0.04)**	**86.9 (0.04)**	**27.7 (0.05)**	**30.1 (0.06)**	**18.6 (0.04)**	**11.4 (0.04)**
Alabama	72.2 (0.15)	84.6 (0.74)	24.7 (0.06)	75.3 (0.06)	19.0 (0.05)	12.1 (0.04)	6.9 (0.03)	15.4 (0.29)	84.6 (0.29)	31.7 (0.38)	23.0 (0.30)	14.5 (0.25)	8.5 (0.20)
Alaska	76.9 (0.40)	86.6 (1.65)	11.7 (0.12)	88.3 (0.12)	24.7 (0.16)	16.1 (0.13)	8.6 (0.10)	8.1 (0.65)	91.9 (0.65)	25.8 (0.99)	29.1 (1.15)	18.7 (0.96)	10.4 (0.73)
Arizona	69.2 (0.19)	82.9 (0.61)	19.0 (0.06)	81.0 (0.06)	23.5 (0.07)	15.1 (0.06)	8.4 (0.04)	13.8 (0.22)	86.2 (0.22)	24.4 (0.29)	27.4 (0.24)	17.3 (0.23)	10.1 (0.17)
Arkansas	75.4 (0.19)	86.0 (0.83)	24.7 (0.07)	75.3 (0.07)	16.7 (0.06)	11.0 (0.05)	5.7 (0.04)	14.4 (0.34)	85.6 (0.34)	35.1 (0.46)	21.4 (0.47)	14.1 (0.35)	7.3 (0.27)
California	70.7 (0.07)	87.0 (0.20)	23.2 (0.03)	76.8 (0.03)	26.6 (0.03)	17.1 (0.02)	9.5 (0.02)	17.9 (0.09)	82.1 (0.09)	20.9 (0.10)	31.7 (0.13)	19.9 (0.10)	11.8 (0.08)
Colorado	75.1 (0.15)	86.7 (0.76)	13.1 (0.05)	86.9 (0.05)	32.7 (0.06)	21.6 (0.06)	11.1 (0.04)	9.5 (0.20)	90.5 (0.20)	21.9 (0.32)	38.0 (0.30)	24.1 (0.27)	13.9 (0.19)
Connecticut	78.2 (0.21)	88.9 (0.67)	16.0 (0.06)	84.0 (0.06)	31.4 (0.08)	18.1 (0.07)	13.3 (0.06)	9.9 (0.28)	90.1 (0.28)	27.5 (0.40)	37.9 (0.37)	21.3 (0.36)	16.7 (0.28)
Delaware	77.6 (0.41)	84.4 (1.47)	17.4 (0.14)	82.6 (0.14)	25.0 (0.16)	15.6 (0.14)	9.4 (0.11)	10.9 (0.56)	89.1 (0.56)	31.6 (0.76)	30.3 (0.69)	17.9 (0.56)	12.4 (0.57)
District of Columbia	79.4 (0.40)	88.8 (1.61)	22.2 (0.18)	77.8 (0.18)	39.1 (0.21)	18.1 (0.17)	21.0 (0.18)	9.9 (0.52)	90.1 (0.52)	17.8 (0.71)	54.8 (0.73)	24.5 (0.69)	30.2 (0.81)
Florida	71.7 (0.11)	83.5 (0.32)	20.1 (0.04)	79.9 (0.04)	22.3 (0.04)	14.2 (0.03)	8.1 (0.02)	12.8 (0.10)	87.2 (0.10)	29.5 (0.17)	27.4 (0.14)	17.5 (0.12)	9.9 (0.10)
Georgia	70.0 (0.15)	83.7 (0.55)	21.4 (0.05)	78.6 (0.05)	24.3 (0.05)	16.0 (0.05)	8.3 (0.04)	14.4 (0.17)	85.6 (0.17)	28.3 (0.25)	29.0 (0.22)	18.1 (0.19)	10.9 (0.15)
Hawaii	85.8 (0.25)	90.7 (1.15)	15.4 (0.10)	84.6 (0.10)	26.2 (0.12)	17.8 (0.10)	8.4 (0.08)	8.6 (0.36)	91.4 (0.36)	28.3 (0.63)	31.6 (0.70)	20.9 (0.63)	10.7 (0.37)
Idaho	77.3 (0.25)	86.4 (1.26)	15.3 (0.09)	84.7 (0.09)	21.7 (0.10)	14.9 (0.09)	6.8 (0.06)	9.9 (0.38)	90.1 (0.38)	28.3 (0.70)	25.2 (0.63)	17.1 (0.56)	8.2 (0.34)
Illinois	76.0 (0.09)	87.5 (0.36)	18.6 (0.03)	81.4 (0.03)	26.1 (0.03)	16.6 (0.03)	9.5 (0.02)	11.6 (0.13)	88.4 (0.13)	26.6 (0.23)	33.0 (0.19)	20.2 (0.18)	12.8 (0.15)
Indiana	76.5 (0.15)	83.2 (0.70)	17.9 (0.05)	82.1 (0.05)	19.4 (0.05)	12.2 (0.04)	7.2 (0.04)	11.3 (0.21)	88.7 (0.21)	34.4 (0.26)	24.8 (0.30)	15.8 (0.22)	9.0 (0.18)
Iowa	81.4 (0.16)	89.7 (0.86)	13.9 (0.06)	86.1 (0.06)	21.2 (0.07)	14.7 (0.06)	6.5 (0.04)	7.8 (0.26)	92.2 (0.26)	31.5 (0.44)	27.9 (0.41)	18.4 (0.35)	9.4 (0.29)
Kansas	78.3 (0.18)	86.5 (0.89)	14.0 (0.06)	86.0 (0.06)	25.8 (0.08)	17.1 (0.06)	8.7 (0.05)	9.8 (0.35)	90.2 (0.35)	26.7 (0.45)	31.5 (0.37)	20.1 (0.37)	11.5 (0.29)
Kentucky	74.9 (0.15)	86.3 (0.70)	25.9 (0.06)	74.1 (0.06)	17.1 (0.05)	10.2 (0.04)	6.9 (0.03)	15.5 (0.31)	84.5 (0.31)	33.3 (0.33)	22.7 (0.31)	13.3 (0.24)	9.4 (0.22)
Louisiana	72.3 (0.15)	80.3 (0.82)	25.2 (0.06)	74.8 (0.06)	18.7 (0.05)	12.2 (0.04)	6.5 (0.03)	16.4 (0.28)	83.6 (0.28)	33.9 (0.39)	22.9 (0.30)	15.0 (0.25)	7.8 (0.20)
Maine	78.9 (0.28)	88.4 (1.20)	14.6 (0.08)	85.4 (0.08)	22.9 (0.10)	15.0 (0.09)	7.9 (0.06)	7.8 (0.35)	92.2 (0.35)	32.1 (0.76)	29.7 (0.72)	19.5 (0.57)	10.2 (0.42)
Maryland	79.6 (0.16)	87.5 (0.59)	16.2 (0.05)	83.8 (0.05)	31.4 (0.07)	18.0 (0.06)	13.4 (0.05)	10.3 (0.23)	89.7 (0.23)	25.5 (0.26)	38.2 (0.31)	20.9 (0.25)	17.3 (0.25)
Massachusetts	82.2 (0.13)	89.9 (0.50)	15.2 (0.05)	84.8 (0.05)	33.2 (0.06)	19.5 (0.05)	13.7 (0.04)	10.4 (0.19)	89.6 (0.19)	24.6 (0.27)	41.4 (0.29)	23.3 (0.24)	18.0 (0.21)
Michigan	76.5 (0.10)	86.7 (0.41)	16.6 (0.03)	83.4 (0.03)	21.8 (0.04)	13.7 (0.03)	8.1 (0.02)	10.1 (0.18)	89.9 (0.18)	29.4 (0.22)	27.4 (0.21)	16.4 (0.17)	11.0 (0.14)
Minnesota	79.3 (0.13)	89.0 (0.67)	12.1 (0.04)	87.9 (0.04)	27.4 (0.06)	19.1 (0.05)	8.3 (0.03)	7.4 (0.19)	92.6 (0.19)	26.0 (0.33)	34.0 (0.36)	22.3 (0.31)	11.6 (0.26)
Mississippi	71.3 (0.18)	82.6 (0.88)	27.1 (0.08)	72.9 (0.08)	16.9 (0.06)	11.1 (0.05)	5.8 (0.04)	17.3 (0.37)	82.7 (0.37)	30.0 (0.44)	20.9 (0.44)	12.9 (0.35)	8.0 (0.28)
Missouri	76.5 (0.13)	86.9 (0.53)	18.7 (0.05)	81.3 (0.05)	21.6 (0.05)	14.0 (0.04)	7.6 (0.03)	11.2 (0.22)	88.8 (0.22)	31.2 (0.31)	27.5 (0.31)	17.1 (0.25)	10.5 (0.21)
Montana	78.6 (0.31)	87.2 (1.60)	12.8 (0.10)	87.2 (0.10)	24.4 (0.13)	17.2 (0.11)	7.2 (0.08)	7.8 (0.50)	92.2 (0.50)	30.8 (0.71)	28.1 (0.74)	18.5 (0.59)	9.6 (0.44)
Nebraska	80.0 (0.21)	88.7 (1.08)	13.4 (0.07)	86.6 (0.07)	23.7 (0.09)	16.4 (0.08)	7.3 (0.06)	9.5 (0.28)	90.5 (0.28)	27.9 (0.58)	30.2 (0.56)	20.8 (0.49)	9.5 (0.34)
Nevada	66.7 (0.32)	81.7 (1.00)	19.3 (0.10)	80.7 (0.10)	18.2 (0.10)	12.1 (0.08)	6.1 (0.06)	14.6 (0.34)	85.4 (0.34)	28.3 (0.47)	22.9 (0.36)	15.1 (0.31)	7.8 (0.21)
New Hampshire	77.8 (0.29)	89.4 (1.33)	12.6 (0.08)	87.4 (0.08)	28.7 (0.11)	18.7 (0.10)	10.0 (0.07)	7.4 (0.42)	92.6 (0.42)	28.7 (0.62)	35.3 (0.60)	22.0 (0.53)	13.2 (0.35)
New Jersey	76.3 (0.14)	87.5 (0.45)	17.9 (0.04)	82.1 (0.04)	29.8 (0.05)	18.8 (0.04)	11.0 (0.04)	11.0 (0.16)	89.0 (0.16)	28.5 (0.21)	37.2 (0.25)	23.0 (0.24)	14.2 (0.20)
New Mexico	70.5 (0.24)	81.9 (1.30)	21.1 (0.09)	78.9 (0.09)	23.5 (0.09)	13.7 (0.07)	9.8 (0.06)	15.5 (0.43)	84.5 (0.43)	26.2 (0.52)	26.6 (0.50)	15.4 (0.44)	11.2 (0.34)
New York	76.1 (0.09)	87.5 (0.32)	20.9 (0.03)	79.1 (0.03)	27.4 (0.04)	15.6 (0.03)	11.8 (0.03)	14.2 (0.13)	85.8 (0.13)	26.5 (0.17)	34.7 (0.16)	19.7 (0.16)	15.0 (0.14)
North Carolina	74.2 (0.11)	86.7 (0.46)	21.9 (0.04)	78.1 (0.04)	22.5 (0.04)	15.3 (0.04)	7.2 (0.03)	13.6 (0.19)	86.4 (0.19)	26.6 (0.20)	28.7 (0.23)	18.6 (0.18)	10.1 (0.13)
North Dakota	84.4 (0.24)	88.7 (1.52)	16.1 (0.10)	83.9 (0.10)	22.0 (0.12)	16.5 (0.10)	5.5 (0.06)	7.1 (0.44)	92.9 (0.44)	27.4 (0.95)	25.7 (0.96)	19.1 (0.87)	6.7 (0.50)
Ohio	76.8 (0.09)	86.1 (0.48)	17.0 (0.03)	83.0 (0.03)	21.1 (0.03)	13.7 (0.03)	7.4 (0.02)	10.7 (0.14)	89.3 (0.14)	34.0 (0.25)	26.5 (0.20)	16.6 (0.17)	9.9 (0.14)
Oklahoma	74.8 (0.16)	83.7 (0.77)	19.4 (0.06)	80.6 (0.06)	20.3 (0.06)	13.5 (0.05)	6.8 (0.04)	12.5 (0.23)	87.5 (0.23)	31.8 (0.44)	24.1 (0.42)	15.7 (0.35)	8.5 (0.21)
Oregon	74.2 (0.17)	86.8 (0.76)	14.9 (0.05)	85.1 (0.05)	25.1 (0.06)	16.4 (0.06)	8.7 (0.04)	10.3 (0.28)	89.7 (0.28)	24.0 (0.36)	30.6 (0.33)	19.0 (0.27)	11.5 (0.23)
Pennsylvania	79.8 (0.09)	87.8 (0.44)	18.1 (0.03)	81.9 (0.03)	22.4 (0.03)	14.0 (0.03)	8.4 (0.02)	10.5 (0.15)	89.5 (0.15)	36.3 (0.19)	28.8 (0.21)	17.5 (0.17)	11.3 (0.13)
Rhode Island	81.3 (0.32)	88.4 (1.10)	22.0 (0.13)	78.0 (0.13)	25.6 (0.14)	15.9 (0.12)	9.7 (0.10)	14.5 (0.55)	85.5 (0.55)	28.3 (0.67)	30.2 (0.73)	18.0 (0.54)	12.2 (0.49)
South Carolina	74.3 (0.18)	85.1 (0.59)	23.7 (0.07)	76.3 (0.07)	20.4 (0.07)	13.5 (0.06)	6.9 (0.04)	14.0 (0.29)	86.0 (0.29)	30.3 (0.31)	26.2 (0.30)	16.5 (0.23)	9.7 (0.20)
South Dakota	78.2 (0.33)	81.5 (2.15)	15.4 (0.12)	84.6 (0.12)	21.5 (0.13)	15.5 (0.12)	6.0 (0.08)	8.5 (0.45)	91.5 (0.45)	31.1 (0.84)	26.5 (0.86)	19.9 (0.87)	6.7 (0.42)
Tennessee	75.1 (0.16)	88.0 (0.45)	24.1 (0.06)	75.9 (0.06)	19.6 (0.06)	12.8 (0.05)	6.8 (0.03)	14.2 (0.21)	85.8 (0.21)	33.1 (0.27)	25.4 (0.28)	16.4 (0.23)	9.1 (0.15)
Texas	68.6 (0.08)	83.9 (0.29)	24.3 (0.03)	75.7 (0.03)	23.2 (0.03)	15.6 (0.03)	7.6 (0.02)	17.7 (0.12)	82.3 (0.12)	25.1 (0.16)	27.9 (0.14)	18.2 (0.13)	9.7 (0.08)
Utah	80.3 (0.16)	85.7 (0.87)	12.3 (0.07)	87.7 (0.07)	26.1 (0.09)	17.8 (0.08)	8.3 (0.06)	8.5 (0.32)	91.5 (0.32)	23.1 (0.48)	31.2 (0.44)	20.8 (0.35)	10.4 (0.27)
Vermont	83.0 (0.28)	92.1 (1.49)	13.6 (0.10)	86.4 (0.10)	29.4 (0.13)	18.3 (0.11)	11.1 (0.09)	8.0 (0.58)	92.0 (0.58)	29.9 (0.95)	36.2 (1.07)	21.9 (0.89)	14.2 (0.82)
Virginia	79.4 (0.13)	89.1 (0.53)	18.5 (0.05)	81.5 (0.05)	29.5 (0.06)	17.9 (0.05)	11.6 (0.04)	11.4 (0.19)	88.6 (0.19)	24.6 (0.25)	36.6 (0.26)	20.5 (0.20)	16.1 (0.20)
Washington	75.3 (0.16)	84.6 (0.61)	12.9 (0.05)	87.1 (0.05)	27.7 (0.06)	18.4 (0.05)	9.3 (0.04)	9.6 (0.19)	90.4 (0.19)	22.8 (0.22)	33.2 (0.29)	21.3 (0.23)	12.0 (0.18)
West Virginia	78.2 (0.22)	86.0 (1.07)	24.8 (0.09)	75.2 (0.09)	14.8 (0.07)	8.9 (0.06)	5.9 (0.05)	14.4 (0.42)	85.6 (0.42)	41.3 (0.48)	19.3 (0.41)	11.7 (0.36)	7.6 (0.27)
Wisconsin	78.9 (0.13)	89.1 (0.60)	14.9 (0.04)	85.1 (0.04)	22.4 (0.05)	15.2 (0.04)	7.2 (0.03)	8.5 (0.18)	91.5 (0.18)	32.1 (0.34)	28.5 (0.34)	18.8 (0.28)	9.7 (0.22)
Wyoming	79.0 (0.41)	88.1 (1.77)	12.1 (0.13)	87.9 (0.13)	21.9 (0.16)	14.9 (0.14)	7.0 (0.10)	7.8 (0.62)	92.2 (0.62)	27.5 (0.78)	25.9 (0.80)	16.9 (0.80)	9.0 (0.54)

#Rounds to zero.

[1]High school completers include those graduating from high school with a diploma as well as those completing high school through equivalency programs, such as a GED program.

NOTE: Detail may not sum to totals because of rounding.

SOURCE: U.S. Department of Commerce, Census Bureau, Census 2000 Summary File 3, retrieved October 11, 2006, from http://factfinder2.census.gov/faces/tableservices/jsf/pages/productview.xhtml?pid=DEC_00_SF3_QTP20&prodType=table; Census Briefs, *Educational Attainment: 2000*; and 2014 American Community Survey (ACS) 1-Year Public Use Microdata Sample (PUMS) data. (This table was prepared December 2015.)

Table 104.85. Rates of high school completion and bachelor's degree attainment among persons age 25 and over, by race/ethnicity and state: 2014

[Standard errors appear in parentheses]

State	Percent with high school completion[1] or higher						Percent with bachelor's degree or higher					
	Total[2]	White	Black	Hispanic	Asian	Two or more races	Total[2]	White	Black	Hispanic	Asian	Two or more races
1	2	3	4	5	6	7	8	9	10	11	12	13
United States	**86.9 (4)**	**92.0 (3)**	**84.5 (9)**	**65.4 (0.16)**	**86.4 (0.12)**	**90.3 (0.24)**	**30.1 (6)**	**33.6 (6)**	**19.8 (0.12)**	**14.4 (0.10)**	**51.7 (0.22)**	**32.0 (0.35)**
Alabama	84.6 (0.29)	87.4 (0.29)	79.8 (0.57)	59.4 (2.68)	86.5 (2.44)	89.2 (2.32)	23.0 (0.30)	25.6 (0.34)	15.1 (0.69)	17.4 (1.80)	52.1 (3.69)	24.5 (3.23)
Alaska	91.9 (0.65)	95.0 (0.65)	84.6 (7.68)	85.2 (4.46)	83.3 (4.17)	91.4 (3.54)	29.1 (1.15)	34.8 (1.47)	‡ (†)	23.1 (5.02)	37.8 (4.88)	15.4 (3.84)
Arizona	86.2 (0.22)	94.2 (0.16)	89.9 (0.94)	65.4 (0.62)	86.3 (1.27)	92.7 (1.30)	27.4 (0.24)	33.5 (0.32)	25.2 (1.39)	11.4 (0.41)	49.1 (1.64)	29.3 (2.16)
Arkansas	85.6 (0.34)	88.1 (0.33)	83.7 (0.91)	50.7 (2.53)	89.9 (2.56)	90.1 (2.41)	21.4 (0.47)	22.8 (0.55)	15.1 (0.87)	9.1 (1.03)	54.3 (4.22)	24.2 (3.61)
California	82.1 (9)	94.5 (9)	89.8 (0.32)	60.9 (0.24)	87.3 (0.20)	91.5 (0.54)	31.7 (0.13)	41.6 (0.20)	22.8 (0.47)	11.2 (0.15)	50.2 (0.36)	37.6 (0.84)
Colorado	90.5 (0.20)	95.6 (0.16)	89.9 (1.15)	69.7 (0.97)	83.5 (1.86)	93.1 (1.54)	38.0 (0.30)	43.9 (0.36)	24.1 (1.78)	13.9 (0.65)	51.6 (2.14)	36.0 (2.40)
Connecticut	90.1 (0.28)	93.5 (0.25)	86.8 (0.80)	72.3 (1.19)	91.1 (1.33)	88.2 (2.90)	37.9 (0.37)	41.7 (0.45)	22.9 (1.36)	17.8 (1.09)	66.3 (1.86)	33.2 (3.53)
Delaware	89.1 (0.56)	92.0 (0.62)	86.5 (1.41)	67.7 (3.70)	90.5 (3.09)	86.1 (5.59)	30.3 (0.69)	31.4 (0.82)	23.8 (1.60)	15.4 (2.50)	69.0 (4.37)	28.2 ! (9.40)
District of Columbia	90.1 (0.52)	98.9 (0.34)	86.9 (0.77)	67.2 (3.39)	91.7 (2.64)	98.9 (0.85)	54.8 (0.73)	89.6 (0.74)	24.7 (1.21)	41.3 (3.42)	75.4 (3.71)	85.0 (4.62)
Florida	87.2 (0.10)	92.0 (0.11)	81.3 (0.39)	78.0 (0.35)	85.0 (0.76)	89.1 (1.07)	27.4 (0.14)	30.9 (0.20)	17.3 (0.35)	21.7 (0.32)	44.6 (1.09)	28.5 (1.67)
Georgia	85.6 (0.17)	89.5 (0.20)	84.1 (0.36)	58.9 (1.12)	85.9 (0.90)	90.3 (1.54)	29.0 (0.22)	33.3 (0.27)	20.7 (0.47)	15.2 (0.78)	51.5 (1.41)	36.5 (2.68)
Hawaii	91.4 (0.36)	96.7 (0.52)	97.9 (0.90)	91.4 (1.32)	87.3 (0.61)	94.1 (0.80)	31.6 (0.70)	45.8 (1.39)	28.4 (4.82)	20.7 (1.86)	31.2 (0.97)	25.5 (1.52)
Idaho	90.1 (0.38)	93.5 (0.34)	76.2 (10.48)	58.1 (2.45)	85.4 (6.54)	92.1 (2.01)	25.2 (0.63)	26.8 (0.70)	26.7 ! (9.49)	8.1 (1.29)	45.7 (8.39)	22.0 (4.97)
Illinois	88.4 (0.13)	93.5 (0.12)	84.5 (0.47)	64.9 (0.64)	91.2 (0.60)	93.5 (0.95)	33.0 (0.19)	36.7 (0.25)	21.0 (0.53)	14.0 (0.51)	63.3 (1.03)	37.8 (2.50)
Indiana	88.7 (0.21)	90.3 (0.22)	86.3 (0.75)	65.1 (1.56)	87.5 (1.81)	88.8 (1.87)	24.8 (0.30)	25.5 (0.33)	16.5 (0.94)	13.6 (1.13)	58.3 (2.76)	26.2 (3.00)
Iowa	92.2 (0.26)	93.7 (0.25)	84.4 (2.30)	63.1 (2.49)	87.1 (2.20)	90.9 (3.23)	27.9 (0.41)	28.0 (0.46)	20.9 (3.13)	14.6 (1.72)	56.6 (4.49)	31.1 (6.12)
Kansas	90.2 (0.35)	93.6 (0.29)	85.9 (1.86)	60.2 (2.20)	86.2 (2.59)	92.3 (1.92)	31.5 (0.37)	33.9 (0.42)	17.7 (1.87)	12.4 (1.10)	53.0 (3.25)	28.0 (2.96)
Kentucky	84.5 (0.31)	84.9 (0.32)	86.3 (1.25)	64.5 (2.55)	83.5 (2.78)	85.2 (2.89)	22.7 (0.31)	23.1 (0.35)	15.2 (0.99)	17.1 (1.95)	54.4 (3.21)	23.9 (3.07)
Louisiana	83.6 (0.28)	87.3 (0.34)	78.0 (0.63)	73.2 (1.97)	75.5 (2.51)	81.6 (3.87)	22.9 (0.30)	26.8 (0.38)	14.0 (0.44)	19.9 (1.79)	40.7 (2.89)	20.4 (2.83)
Maine	92.2 (0.35)	92.4 (0.34)	76.8 (8.33)	95.9 (1.71)	84.4 (5.84)	88.9 (3.54)	29.7 (0.72)	29.7 (0.73)	20.3 ! (6.85)	35.9 (6.94)	45.9 (8.79)	19.2 (4.60)
Maryland	89.7 (0.23)	93.0 (0.25)	89.8 (0.44)	63.6 (1.93)	91.1 (0.77)	91.1 (1.42)	38.2 (0.31)	43.2 (0.33)	27.8 (0.60)	21.4 (1.00)	61.7 (1.19)	40.3 (2.83)
Massachusetts	89.6 (0.19)	93.1 (0.16)	83.8 (0.88)	67.3 (1.20)	83.3 (0.98)	89.1 (1.87)	41.4 (0.29)	44.4 (0.36)	23.5 (1.08)	17.9 (0.85)	56.2 (1.48)	37.3 (2.66)
Michigan	89.9 (0.18)	91.8 (0.16)	84.0 (0.53)	72.2 (1.29)	87.5 (1.28)	87.1 (1.84)	27.4 (0.21)	28.4 (0.25)	17.1 (0.47)	16.7 (1.09)	63.8 (1.49)	26.0 (1.77)
Minnesota	92.6 (0.19)	95.0 (0.15)	83.0 (1.65)	68.3 (2.50)	78.8 (1.83)	91.1 (2.33)	34.0 (0.36)	35.4 (0.36)	19.0 (1.93)	19.7 (1.89)	39.5 (2.41)	33.8 (3.57)
Mississippi	82.7 (0.37)	86.9 (0.37)	76.8 (0.64)	62.9 (3.25)	80.9 (3.77)	87.4 (4.34)	20.9 (0.44)	24.4 (0.50)	14.9 (0.72)	11.6 (1.80)	37.6 (4.40)	24.2 (6.62)
Missouri	88.8 (0.22)	9 (0.22)	85.3 (0.64)	70.4 (2.59)	87.5 (1.92)	82.6 (1.90)	27.5 (0.31)	28.5 (0.33)	17.2 (0.81)	20.6 (1.80)	61.3 (2.39)	25.1 (2.24)
Montana	92.2 (0.50)	93.0 (0.49)	‡ (†)	78.8 (5.96)	95.6 (2.73)	89.7 (4.02)	28.1 (0.74)	29.4 (0.78)	‡ (†)	19.1 (4.33)	34.5 ! (11.34)	20.6 (5.80)
Nebraska	90.5 (0.28)	94.3 (0.23)	85.4 (2.29)	52.8 (2.68)	77.4 (4.28)	93.2 (2.38)	30.2 (0.56)	32.0 (0.65)	25.5 (3.28)	9.5 (1.47)	47.3 (5.51)	32.2 (6.49)
Nevada	85.4 (0.34)	92.7 (0.35)	85.8 (1.35)	63.6 (1.01)	90.3 (1.00)	94.3 (1.23)	22.9 (0.36)	27.6 (0.47)	13.6 (1.31)	9.0 (0.61)	37.6 (1.62)	28.0 (2.66)
New Hampshire	92.6 (0.42)	92.9 (0.43)	95.1 (2.69)	82.2 (3.83)	91.6 (2.81)	92.4 (3.19)	35.3 (0.60)	35.2 (0.64)	3 (5.89)	17.6 (3.09)	64.4 (4.78)	29.1 (4.97)
New Jersey	89.0 (0.16)	93.3 (0.15)	88.0 (0.51)	72.6 (0.71)	92.7 (0.43)	94.2 (1.17)	37.2 (0.25)	41.0 (0.33)	23.6 (0.60)	17.1 (0.48)	67.2 (0.91)	38.6 (2.72)
New Mexico	84.5 (0.43)	95.4 (0.29)	88.8 (2.25)	73.9 (0.94)	83.9 (4.19)	92.6 (2.46)	26.6 (0.50)	39.0 (0.81)	26.6 (4.01)	14.6 (0.62)	57.7 (4.18)	40.2 (6.35)
New York	85.8 (0.13)	92.5 (0.11)	83.4 (0.34)	67.6 (0.49)	78.5 (0.62)	86.5 (1.16)	34.7 (0.16)	40.7 (0.18)	23.4 (0.46)	17.7 (0.39)	44.8 (0.71)	36.1 (1.78)
North Carolina	86.4 (0.19)	90.3 (0.19)	84.0 (0.38)	55.2 (1.17)	85.6 (1.40)	88.8 (1.46)	28.7 (0.23)	32.4 (0.29)	19.3 (0.43)	11.9 (0.68)	53.6 (2.11)	32.9 (2.52)
North Dakota	92.9 (0.44)	94.0 (0.41)	‡ (†)	70.3 (9.12)	88.1 (6.94)	‡ (†)	25.7 (0.96)	26.6 (0.99)	‡ (†)	‡ (†)	59.1 (7.47)	‡ (†)
Ohio	89.3 (0.14)	90.5 (0.16)	83.8 (0.55)	73.8 (1.27)	88.8 (1.10)	87.1 (1.35)	26.5 (0.20)	27.4 (0.21)	16.2 (0.60)	19.7 (1.10)	63.0 (1.69)	22.4 (1.67)
Oklahoma	87.5 (0.23)	90.5 (0.23)	88.8 (0.88)	58.8 (1.76)	84.0 (2.75)	89.5 (1.02)	24.1 (0.42)	26.4 (0.50)	18.6 (1.40)	8.7 (0.93)	40.2 (3.69)	22.9 (1.55)
Oregon	89.7 (0.28)	92.9 (0.23)	87.5 (1.89)	62.0 (1.76)	88.9 (1.37)	88.2 (2.18)	30.6 (0.33)	32.3 (0.39)	24.2 (3.32)	12.0 (0.90)	47.9 (2.24)	25.6 (2.14)
Pennsylvania	89.5 (0.15)	91.7 (0.15)	85.3 (0.56)	67.7 (1.17)	81.2 (1.03)	89.2 (1.81)	28.8 (0.21)	30.3 (0.23)	16.5 (0.65)	13.6 (0.73)	54.3 (1.45)	31.7 (2.09)
Rhode Island	85.5 (0.55)	88.9 (0.53)	86.4 (2.63)	63.7 (2.30)	73.4 (4.65)	87.3 (3.78)	30.2 (0.73)	33.1 (0.84)	21.7 (2.89)	13.1 (1.76)	34.4 (4.96)	29.8 (5.95)
South Carolina	86.0 (0.29)	9 (0.29)	79.8 (0.55)	59.5 (2.17)	87.0 (1.95)	86.7 (2.48)	26.2 (0.30)	30.9 (0.38)	14.7 (0.51)	13.6 (1.29)	5 (3.50)	27.4 (3.61)
South Dakota	91.5 (0.45)	93.0 (0.45)	74.3 (16)	77.1 (5.50)	69.5 (8.01)	89.6 (3.67)	26.5 (0.86)	28.0 (0.93)	12.8 ! (6.30)	28.5 (7.94)	31.9 ! (9.92)	20.4 (4.84)
Tennessee	85.8 (0.21)	87.2 (0.23)	85.2 (0.59)	58.6 (1.70)	84.5 (1.87)	82.6 (2.05)	25.4 (0.28)	26.9 (0.32)	18.5 (0.61)	13.4 (1.18)	50.2 (2.36)	22.9 (2.36)
Texas	82.3 (0.12)	93.4 (0.11)	88.2 (0.25)	62.7 (0.26)	86.9 (0.53)	91.8 (0.95)	27.9 (0.14)	36.4 (0.21)	21.9 (0.40)	13.0 (0.18)	58.1 (0.80)	34.9 (1.41)
Utah	91.5 (0.32)	95.5 (0.26)	89.1 (3.36)	65.5 (1.83)	87.3 (2.40)	91.8 (2.62)	31.2 (0.44)	34.0 (0.50)	27.8 (5.49)	12.2 (1.03)	39.8 (3.97)	38.0 (5.06)
Vermont	92.0 (0.58)	92.6 (0.53)	‡ (†)	96.3 (3.46)	60.4 (13.45)	97.6 (1.96)	36.2 (1.07)	36.2 (1.05)	‡ (†)	40.3 (9.32)	32.4 ! (9.77)	28.4 ! (9.06)
Virginia	88.6 (0.19)	91.7 (0.17)	84.4 (0.45)	69.3 (1.29)	89.1 (0.72)	92.9 (1.08)	36.6 (0.26)	40.1 (0.32)	21.2 (0.54)	22.5 (1.12)	59.9 (1.10)	44.3 (2.38)
Washington	90.4 (0.19)	94.2 (0.18)	87.9 (1.10)	63.1 (1.13)	86.9 (0.90)	93.0 (0.88)	33.2 (0.29)	34.8 (0.34)	22.1 (1.51)	14.5 (0.75)	47.8 (0.97)	33.0 (1.64)
West Virginia	85.6 (0.42)	85.5 (0.43)	87.9 (1.81)	85.2 (4.19)	92.0 (2.94)	89.0 (3.30)	19.3 (0.41)	19.1 (0.43)	15.3 (2.43)	26.8 (7.30)	58.9 (5.45)	23.2 (4.39)
Wisconsin	91.5 (0.18)	93.6 (0.20)	84.1 (1.27)	63.0 (1.64)	84.7 (1.80)	91.6 (2.25)	28.5 (0.34)	29.9 (0.38)	12.8 (1.21)	14.6 (1.45)	44.5 (2.81)	30.6 (3.23)
Wyoming	92.2 (0.62)	94.6 (0.49)	‡ (†)	66.7 (4.14)	92.3 (3.32)	85.8 (6.51)	25.9 (0.80)	27.7 (0.83)	‡ (†)	9.3 (2.45)	50.8 (10.92)	22.4 ! (7.01)

†Not applicable.

!Interpret data with caution. The coefficient of variation (CV) for this estimate is between 30 and 50 percent.

‡Reporting standards not met. Either there are too few cases for a reliable estimate or the coefficient of variation (CV) is 50 percent or greater.

[1]Includes completion of high school through equivalency programs, such as a GED program.

[2]Total includes racial/ethnic groups not shown separately.

NOTE: Race categories exclude persons of Hispanic ethnicity.

SOURCE: U.S. Department of Commerce, Census Bureau, 2014 American Community Survey (ACS) 1-Year Public Use Microdata Sample (PUMS) data. (This table was prepared December 2015.)

Table 104.88. Rates of high school completion and bachelor's degree attainment among persons age 25 and over, by sex and state: 2014

[Standard errors appear in parentheses]

State	Number of persons age 25 and over (in thousands)						Percent with high school completion[1] or higher						Percent with bachelor's or higher degree					
	Total		Male		Female		Total		Male		Female		Total		Male		Female	
1	2		3		4		5		6		7		8		9		10	
United States	**213,806**	**(50.5)**	**103,072**	**(31.5)**	**110,734**	**(32.0)**	**86.9**	**(0.04)**	**86.3**	**(0.05)**	**87.5**	**(0.05)**	**30.1**	**(0.06)**	**29.9**	**(0.06)**	**30.2**	**(0.07)**
Alabama	3,259	(3.6)	1,536	(3.0)	1,723	(2.7)	84.6	(0.29)	83.7	(0.41)	85.5	(0.31)	23.0	(0.30)	22.7	(0.40)	23.3	(0.43)
Alaska	468	(2.5)	243	(2.3)	225	(2.2)	91.9	(0.65)	92.6	(0.69)	91.3	(1.05)	29.1	(1.15)	25.3	(1.30)	33.1	(1.56)
Arizona	4,438	(3.8)	2,167	(2.8)	2,271	(3.4)	86.2	(0.22)	85.6	(0.33)	86.7	(0.23)	27.4	(0.24)	27.8	(0.33)	27.0	(0.37)
Arkansas	1,970	(3.4)	946	(2.6)	1,024	(2.4)	85.6	(0.34)	85.0	(0.46)	86.1	(0.43)	21.4	(0.47)	20.7	(0.52)	22.0	(0.56)
California	25,656	(8.4)	12,515	(6.7)	13,141	(5.3)	82.1	(0.09)	81.8	(0.12)	82.3	(0.10)	31.7	(0.13)	32.0	(0.14)	31.4	(0.15)
Colorado	3,587	(3.3)	1,776	(3.2)	1,811	(2.9)	90.5	(0.20)	89.7	(0.29)	91.3	(0.24)	38.0	(0.30)	37.4	(0.43)	38.6	(0.38)
Connecticut	2,478	(2.8)	1,183	(2.7)	1,295	(2.1)	90.1	(0.28)	89.8	(0.38)	90.4	(0.31)	37.9	(0.37)	37.7	(0.47)	38.2	(0.50)
Delaware	639	(1.7)	302	(1.3)	337	(1.1)	89.1	(0.56)	88.0	(0.83)	90.1	(0.64)	30.3	(0.69)	29.3	(0.91)	31.2	(0.96)
District of Columbia	465	(1.0)	217	(0.9)	247	(0.7)	90.1	(0.52)	89.3	(0.76)	90.8	(0.60)	54.8	(0.73)	54.0	(1.03)	55.5	(0.88)
Florida	14,042	(6.4)	6,722	(5.8)	7,320	(4.4)	87.2	(0.10)	86.5	(0.18)	87.9	(0.12)	27.4	(0.14)	28.1	(0.23)	26.7	(0.18)
Georgia	6,576	(6.0)	3,114	(4.7)	3,462	(4.1)	85.6	(0.17)	84.2	(0.25)	86.9	(0.20)	29.0	(0.22)	28.8	(0.29)	29.3	(0.29)
Hawaii	974	(2.2)	481	(1.8)	493	(1.6)	91.4	(0.36)	92.4	(0.45)	90.4	(0.47)	31.6	(0.70)	30.5	(0.90)	32.6	(0.83)
Idaho	1,045	(2.1)	513	(2.2)	532	(1.9)	90.1	(0.38)	89.2	(0.55)	91.0	(0.40)	25.2	(0.63)	26.5	(0.80)	24.0	(0.84)
Illinois	8,640	(5.6)	4,153	(4.6)	4,487	(4.1)	88.4	(0.13)	87.9	(0.17)	88.8	(0.17)	33.0	(0.19)	32.7	(0.26)	33.3	(0.23)
Indiana	4,344	(4.2)	2,093	(3.2)	2,251	(3.3)	88.7	(0.21)	88.3	(0.29)	89.0	(0.23)	24.8	(0.30)	24.2	(0.33)	25.2	(0.38)
Iowa	2,063	(3.1)	1,007	(2.8)	1,056	(2.4)	92.2	(0.26)	91.0	(0.36)	93.2	(0.30)	27.9	(0.41)	26.8	(0.53)	28.8	(0.54)
Kansas	1,881	(4.0)	917	(3.2)	964	(2.8)	90.2	(0.35)	89.6	(0.42)	90.7	(0.40)	31.5	(0.37)	31.4	(0.52)	31.6	(0.44)
Kentucky	2,969	(4.1)	1,433	(3.0)	1,535	(2.6)	84.5	(0.31)	83.2	(0.34)	85.6	(0.36)	22.7	(0.31)	21.9	(0.39)	23.5	(0.40)
Louisiana	3,063	(4.3)	1,461	(3.4)	1,602	(2.8)	83.6	(0.28)	81.9	(0.37)	85.1	(0.36)	22.9	(0.30)	21.6	(0.33)	24.0	(0.40)
Maine	957	(1.6)	457	(1.7)	500	(1.6)	92.2	(0.35)	91.0	(0.51)	93.2	(0.47)	29.7	(0.72)	28.7	(0.94)	30.6	(0.77)
Maryland	4,066	(4.2)	1,924	(3.5)	2,142	(2.9)	89.7	(0.23)	88.8	(0.32)	90.5	(0.24)	38.2	(0.31)	38.2	(0.37)	38.3	(0.37)
Massachusetts	4,653	(3.3)	2,208	(3.3)	2,445	(2.4)	89.6	(0.19)	89.3	(0.27)	89.8	(0.24)	41.4	(0.29)	41.2	(0.36)	41.5	(0.38)
Michigan	6,689	(5.2)	3,219	(4.2)	3,471	(4.1)	89.9	(0.18)	89.1	(0.24)	90.7	(0.21)	27.4	(0.21)	27.1	(0.25)	27.7	(0.27)
Minnesota	3,683	(5.1)	1,807	(4.2)	1,876	(3.8)	92.6	(0.19)	92.6	(0.22)	92.6	(0.28)	34.0	(0.36)	32.9	(0.48)	35.0	(0.42)
Mississippi	1,948	(2.7)	920	(2.0)	1,029	(2.0)	82.7	(0.37)	81.0	(0.55)	84.3	(0.40)	20.9	(0.44)	18.9	(0.57)	22.7	(0.48)
Missouri	4,077	(4.6)	1,959	(3.5)	2,118	(3.2)	88.8	(0.22)	88.4	(0.29)	89.2	(0.27)	27.5	(0.31)	26.7	(0.37)	28.3	(0.42)
Montana	694	(2.0)	343	(1.5)	351	(1.7)	92.2	(0.50)	91.9	(0.71)	92.4	(0.58)	28.1	(0.74)	27.8	(0.92)	28.5	(1.00)
Nebraska	1,225	(2.7)	600	(2.4)	625	(2.2)	90.5	(0.28)	89.7	(0.46)	91.2	(0.36)	30.2	(0.56)	29.7	(0.71)	30.7	(0.69)
Nevada	1,919	(2.3)	953	(2.1)	967	(1.7)	85.4	(0.34)	85.2	(0.49)	85.6	(0.42)	22.9	(0.36)	23.3	(0.48)	22.6	(0.47)
New Hampshire	930	(1.5)	452	(1.4)	478	(1.3)	92.6	(0.42)	91.1	(0.68)	94.0	(0.43)	35.3	(0.60)	34.5	(0.76)	36.0	(0.81)
New Jersey	6,129	(3.5)	2,927	(3.1)	3,201	(3.1)	89.0	(0.16)	88.7	(0.23)	89.4	(0.21)	37.2	(0.25)	37.7	(0.33)	36.8	(0.31)
New Mexico	1,371	(3.3)	663	(2.8)	708	(2.2)	84.5	(0.43)	83.8	(0.50)	85.3	(0.56)	26.6	(0.50)	25.6	(0.62)	27.5	(0.62)
New York	13,546	(6.1)	6,423	(5.0)	7,123	(4.6)	85.8	(0.13)	85.7	(0.15)	85.9	(0.17)	34.7	(0.16)	34.2	(0.20)	35.1	(0.20)
North Carolina	6,666	(6.9)	3,155	(5.5)	3,511	(3.7)	86.4	(0.18)	84.7	(0.27)	87.9	(0.23)	28.7	(0.23)	27.8	(0.33)	29.4	(0.25)
North Dakota	477	(1.5)	239	(1.4)	238	(1.5)	92.9	(0.44)	92.4	(0.57)	93.3	(0.55)	25.7	(0.96)	23.3	(1.23)	28.2	(1.16)
Ohio	7,858	(4.9)	3,765	(4.4)	4,093	(3.5)	89.3	(0.14)	88.6	(0.20)	89.9	(0.20)	26.5	(0.20)	26.8	(0.26)	26.3	(0.24)
Oklahoma	2,536	(3.8)	1,230	(3.0)	1,306	(2.9)	87.5	(0.23)	86.8	(0.31)	88.1	(0.30)	24.1	(0.42)	23.3	(0.52)	25.0	(0.55)
Oregon	2,748	(3.7)	1,336	(3.0)	1,412	(2.7)	89.7	(0.28)	89.2	(0.36)	90.1	(0.35)	30.6	(0.33)	30.4	(0.37)	30.8	(0.48)
Pennsylvania	8,875	(6.1)	4,262	(5.3)	4,613	(4.4)	89.5	(0.15)	88.9	(0.20)	90.1	(0.19)	28.8	(0.21)	28.6	(0.30)	29.0	(0.24)
Rhode Island	726	(1.3)	344	(1.1)	382	(1.2)	85.5	(0.55)	84.3	(0.74)	86.5	(0.67)	30.2	(0.73)	31.1	(1.00)	29.3	(0.85)
South Carolina	3,261	(4.0)	1,546	(3.7)	1,715	(2.5)	86.0	(0.29)	84.5	(0.39)	87.4	(0.32)	26.2	(0.30)	26.0	(0.42)	26.4	(0.38)
South Dakota	556	(2.1)	276	(1.9)	280	(1.8)	91.5	(0.45)	90.1	(0.72)	92.8	(0.56)	26.5	(0.86)	24.3	(1.11)	28.7	(1.12)
Tennessee	4,422	(3.9)	2,105	(3.7)	2,317	(3.1)	85.8	(0.21)	84.8	(0.28)	86.7	(0.30)	25.4	(0.28)	25.4	(0.39)	25.5	(0.34)
Texas	17,099	(8.4)	8,325	(6.6)	8,774	(5.6)	82.3	(0.12)	81.6	(0.15)	82.8	(0.14)	27.9	(0.14)	27.8	(0.19)	28.0	(0.17)
Utah	1,708	(2.8)	849	(2.4)	860	(2.3)	91.5	(0.32)	91.1	(0.45)	91.8	(0.34)	31.2	(0.44)	34.1	(0.54)	28.3	(0.58)
Vermont	439	(1.2)	211	(1.0)	228	(1.1)	92.0	(0.58)	91.3	(0.77)	92.8	(0.74)	36.2	(1.07)	35.3	(1.50)	37.0	(1.18)
Virginia	5,622	(5.5)	2,707	(4.6)	2,915	(3.6)	88.6	(0.19)	87.6	(0.26)	89.5	(0.21)	36.6	(0.26)	36.8	(0.31)	36.5	(0.31)
Washington	4,787	(5.3)	2,357	(4.0)	2,431	(3.9)	90.4	(0.19)	90.2	(0.25)	90.7	(0.24)	33.2	(0.29)	34.0	(0.36)	32.5	(0.36)
West Virginia	1,296	(2.1)	630	(1.6)	666	(1.8)	85.6	(0.42)	85.1	(0.56)	86.0	(0.55)	19.3	(0.41)	18.2	(0.54)	20.4	(0.57)
Wisconsin	3,896	(4.6)	1,906	(4.0)	1,990	(3.3)	91.5	(0.18)	90.6	(0.29)	92.3	(0.24)	28.5	(0.34)	27.7	(0.43)	29.3	(0.46)
Wyoming	390	(1.9)	196	(1.5)	193	(1.3)	92.2	(0.62)	91.5	(0.84)	92.8	(0.80)	25.9	(0.80)	25.0	(1.20)	26.8	(1.03)

[1]Includes completion of high school through equivalency programs, such as a GED program.
NOTE: Detail may not sum to totals because of rounding.

SOURCE: U.S. Department of Commerce, Census Bureau, 2014 American Community Survey (ACS) 1-Year Public Use Microdata Sample (PUMS) data. (This table was prepared December 2015.)

Table 104.90. Percentage distribution of spring 2002 high school sophomores, by highest level of education completed through 2012 and selected student characteristics: 2012

[Standard errors appear in parentheses]

Selected student characteristic	Total		Less than high school completion		High school completion		Some postsecondary (no credential)		Postsecondary certificate		Associate's degree		Bachelor's degree		Master's or higher degree	
1	2		3		4		5		6		7		8		9	
Total, all students	**100.0**	**(†)**	**3.1**	**(0.23)**	**12.6**	**(0.44)**	**32.3**	**(0.47)**	**10.1**	**(0.32)**	**8.7**	**(0.35)**	**26.6**	**(0.65)**	**6.7**	**(0.26)**
Sex																
Male	100.0	(†)	3.7	(0.31)	16.0	(0.67)	33.9	(0.72)	8.4	(0.43)	8.0	(0.46)	25.1	(0.87)	4.9	(0.31)
Female	100.0	(†)	2.5	(0.26)	9.3	(0.51)	30.7	(0.68)	11.8	(0.46)	9.4	(0.50)	28.1	(0.80)	8.3	(0.42)
Race/ethnicity																
White	100.0	(†)	1.8	(0.22)	11.7	(0.51)	28.9	(0.60)	8.7	(0.40)	9.1	(0.47)	31.6	(0.80)	8.2	(0.36)
Black	100.0	(†)	4.7	(0.70)	13.2	(1.10)	40.2	(1.31)	14.6	(0.93)	7.5	(0.80)	16.1	(1.07)	3.7	(0.56)
Hispanic	100.0	(†)	6.6	(0.75)	14.6	(1.10)	38.7	(1.27)	12.3	(0.84)	9.1	(0.87)	15.8	(1.26)	2.8	(0.49)
Asian	100.0	(†)	1.6	(0.46)	5.9	(0.96)	27.6	(1.60)	8.5	(0.93)	5.6	(0.87)	39.8	(2.08)	11.1	(0.97)
Pacific Islander	100.0	(†)	#	(†)	22.7 !	(8.56)	35.0	(8.93)	‡	(†)	‡	(†)	29.5 !	(10.00)	‡	(†)
American Indian/Alaska Native	100.0	(†)	8.1 !	(3.31)	22.7	(5.00)	33.7	(4.82)	11.3 !	(3.57)	7.1 !	(2.59)	13.7 !	(4.28)	‡	(†)
Two or more races	100.0	(†)	3.4	(0.89)	18.5	(2.00)	32.6	(2.69)	9.0	(1.51)	8.6	(1.60)	22.2	(2.12)	5.7	(1.20)
Parents' educational attainment in 2002																
High school completion or less	100.0	(†)	6.4	(0.53)	21.1	(0.80)	33.5	(0.81)	12.5	(0.72)	9.3	(0.63)	14.7	(0.80)	2.5	(0.32)
Some college	100.0	(†)	2.2	(0.27)	13.4	(0.65)	36.8	(0.83)	12.1	(0.57)	9.5	(0.53)	21.7	(0.82)	4.3	(0.38)
Bachelor's degree	100.0	(†)	1.6	(0.30)	6.6	(0.58)	30.2	(1.13)	7.5	(0.58)	8.5	(0.74)	36.4	(1.21)	9.2	(0.76)
Master's or higher degree	100.0	(†)	1.3	(0.30)	4.4	(0.62)	23.5	(1.24)	5.5	(0.64)	6.1	(0.65)	44.0	(1.41)	15.1	(0.85)
Parents' socioeconomic status in 2012[1]																
Low quartile	100.0	(†)	7.0	(0.58)	21.3	(0.92)	36.2	(1.03)	12.8	(0.72)	8.2	(0.63)	12.3	(0.86)	2.2	(0.30)
Middle two quartiles	100.0	(†)	2.4	(0.26)	12.9	(0.54)	34.7	(0.68)	11.1	(0.48)	9.9	(0.52)	24.2	(0.78)	4.9	(0.32)
High quartile	100.0	(†)	0.5	(0.15)	3.1	(0.41)	23.6	(1.07)	5.4	(0.51)	6.7	(0.58)	45.9	(1.13)	14.7	(0.70)
Student's educational expectation in 10th grade																
High school completion or less	100.0	(†)	12.3	(1.44)	36.0	(1.88)	31.5	(1.94)	11.3	(1.38)	5.3	(0.92)	3.3	(0.70)	‡	(†)
Some college	100.0	(†)	5.7	(0.88)	22.8	(1.45)	37.5	(1.70)	14.5	(1.31)	10.7	(1.16)	7.9	(0.91)	1.0 !	(0.36)
Bachelor's degree	100.0	(†)	1.7	(0.27)	10.3	(0.66)	33.3	(0.88)	10.6	(0.57)	10.0	(0.64)	29.0	(0.92)	5.0	(0.37)
Master's or higher degree	100.0	(†)	1.0	(0.19)	4.1	(0.40)	29.3	(0.79)	8.0	(0.53)	7.7	(0.47)	37.9	(0.88)	12.1	(0.57)
Don't know	100.0	(†)	5.0	(0.88)	21.2	(1.58)	36.7	(1.92)	11.5	(1.06)	7.7	(0.98)	14.7	(1.38)	3.2	(0.66)
2002 high school type																
Public	100.0	(†)	3.3	(0.25)	13.4	(0.47)	33.0	(0.49)	10.4	(0.35)	8.8	(0.37)	25.0	(0.69)	6.1	(0.28)
Catholic	100.0	(†)	‡	(†)	1.6	(0.45)	23.7	(1.26)	6.4	(0.66)	6.2	(0.68)	47.3	(1.76)	14.6	(1.15)
Other private	100.0	(†)	‡	(†)	3.9	(0.98)	23.9	(2.00)	6.4	(1.01)	8.5	(1.26)	44.3	(2.44)	12.8	(1.38)
Cumulative high school grade point average																
0.00–1.99	100.0	(†)	11.3	(0.90)	25.7	(1.22)	41.8	(1.29)	12.5	(0.79)	5.4	(0.58)	3.1	(0.46)	‡	(†)
2.00–2.49	100.0	(†)	2.4	(0.47)	18.3	(1.00)	44.5	(1.11)	12.5	(0.77)	9.9	(0.79)	11.4	(0.83)	1.0	(0.24)
2.50–2.99	100.0	(†)	0.6	(0.17)	11.1	(0.91)	35.8	(1.21)	12.4	(0.86)	12.5	(0.90)	24.1	(1.13)	3.5	(0.50)
3.00–3.49	100.0	(†)	‡	(†)	5.0	(0.54)	25.9	(1.06)	9.0	(0.66)	9.8	(0.83)	41.9	(1.22)	8.2	(0.69)
3.50+	100.0	(†)	‡	(†)	1.6	(0.32)	13.1	(0.85)	2.9	(0.42)	5.7	(0.61)	55.0	(1.34)	21.7	(0.99)
Students with subsequent postsecondary enrollment																
Timing of first postsecondary enrollment																
Within 3 months of high school completion	100.0	(†)	†	(†)	†	(†)	28.8	(0.65)	8.5	(0.40)	10.2	(0.48)	41.9	(0.80)	10.7	(0.42)
Between 4 and 12 months of high school completion	100.0	(†)	†	(†)	†	(†)	45.2	(1.65)	17.8	(1.52)	10.7	(1.05)	21.2	(1.41)	5.1	(0.80)
13 or more months after high school completion	100.0	(†)	†	(†)	†	(†)	65.7	(1.27)	18.4	(1.05)	9.9	(0.85)	5.5	(0.74)	0.5 !	(0.17)
Type of postsecondary institution first attended																
Public	100.0	(†)	†	(†)	†	(†)	40.1	(0.67)	10.6	(0.43)	10.9	(0.50)	31.5	(0.75)	6.9	(0.33)
Private nonprofit	100.0	(†)	†	(†)	†	(†)	24.2	(1.31)	5.1	(0.65)	4.7	(0.65)	49.1	(1.42)	17.0	(0.98)
Private for-profit	100.0	(†)	†	(†)	†	(†)	46.8	(2.13)	30.4	(2.13)	15.5	(1.59)	6.6	(1.01)	0.7 !	(0.35)
Selectivity and level of postsecondary institution first attended																
Highly selective 4-year	100.0	(†)	†	(†)	†	(†)	14.8	(1.02)	2.5	(0.45)	1.7	(0.37)	60.7	(1.39)	20.3	(0.98)
Moderately selective 4-year	100.0	(†)	†	(†)	†	(†)	26.1	(1.17)	5.0	(0.42)	5.7	(0.62)	49.4	(1.19)	13.7	(0.91)
Inclusive 4-year	100.0	(†)	†	(†)	†	(†)	40.9	(2.01)	7.3	(1.04)	10.9	(1.51)	33.0	(2.06)	7.8	(1.08)
2-year	100.0	(†)	†	(†)	†	(†)	51.7	(0.92)	15.8	(0.71)	16.1	(0.79)	15.2	(0.78)	1.3	(0.20)
Less-than-2-year	100.0	(†)	†	(†)	†	(†)	41.8	(3.14)	51.9	(3.19)	4.9	(1.07)	1.3 !	(0.64)	‡	(†)

†Not applicable.
#Rounds to zero.
!Interpret data with caution. The coefficient of variation (CV) for this estimate is between 30 and 50 percent.
‡Reporting standards not met. Either there are too few cases for a reliable estimate or the coefficient of variation (CV) is 50 percent or greater.
[1]Socioeconomic status (SES) was measured by a composite score on parental education and occupations, and family income.
NOTE: Race categories exclude persons of Hispanic ethnicity. Detail may not sum to totals because of rounding.
SOURCE: U.S. Department of Education, National Center for Education Statistics, Education Longitudinal Study of 2002 (ELS:2002), Third Follow-up. (This table was prepared May 2014.)

Table 104.91. Number and percentage distribution of spring 2002 high school sophomores, by highest level of education completed, and socioeconomic status and selected student characteristics while in high school: 2013

[Standard errors appear in parentheses]

Socioeconomic status (SES) and selected student characteristic	Total: Number (in thousands)		Total: Percentage distribution		Highest level of education completed through 2013[1]: All levels		Less than high school completion		High school completion		Some postsecondary education (no credential)		Postsecondary certificate		Associate's degree		Bachelor's or higher degree	
1	2		3		4		5		6		7		8		9		10	
Total, all SES[2] groups	**3,242**	**(49.0)**	**100.0**	**(†)**	**100.0**	**(†)**	**3.2**	**(0.23)**	**13.4**	**(0.47)**	**31.1**	**(0.53)**	**8.2**	**(0.31)**	**8.4**	**(0.31)**	**35.8**	**(0.79)**
Low SES[2]	**810**	**(24.4)**	**100.0**	**(†)**	**100.0**	**(†)**	**7.8**	**(0.61)**	**22.6**	**(0.92)**	**35.5**	**(1.07)**	**10.8**	**(0.68)**	**8.1**	**(0.59)**	**15.2**	**(0.90)**
Sex																				
Male	370	(12.9)	45.7	(0.94)	100.0	(†)	10.4	(1.08)	27.7	(1.49)	34.8	(1.57)	7.4	(0.83)	7.3	(0.91)	12.4	(1.11)
Female	440	(15.8)	54.3	(0.94)	100.0	(†)	5.5	(0.64)	18.3	(1.11)	36.2	(1.45)	13.6	(0.95)	8.9	(0.77)	17.6	(1.21)
Race/ethnicity																				
White	311	(15.1)	38.4	(1.53)	100.0	(†)	5.5	(0.77)	27.4	(1.51)	31.4	(1.68)	11.0	(1.24)	9.1	(0.96)	15.7	(1.34)
Black	162	(10.6)	20.1	(1.26)	100.0	(†)	9.3	(1.54)	19.1	(2.07)	40.2	(2.66)	12.0	(1.62)	5.7	(1.08)	13.8	(1.75)
Hispanic	251	(16.9)	30.9	(1.71)	100.0	(†)	10.1	(1.20)	19.1	(2.04)	39.4	(2.21)	9.7	(1.12)	9.0	(1.34)	12.6	(1.64)
Asian	38	(3.5)	4.7	(0.45)	100.0	(†)	4.6	(1.32)	12.8	(2.71)	29.2	(3.08)	9.2	(1.76)	7.6	(1.76)	36.6	(3.39)
Pacific Islander	‡	(†)	0.2 !	(0.07)	100.0	(†)	‡	(†)	‡	(†)	‡	(†)	‡	(†)	‡	(†)	‡	(†)
American Indian/Alaska Native	11 !	(3.4)	1.4 !	(0.43)	100.0	(†)	‡	(†)	‡	(†)	36.7	(8.47)	‡	(†)	‡	(†)	‡	(†)
Two or more races	35	(3.8)	4.3	(0.45)	100.0	(†)	7.1 !	(2.69)	34.4	(5.23)	29.8	(5.46)	8.7 !	(3.22)	7.0 !	(3.10)	13.0	(3.66)
Reading achievement quartile[3]																				
First (lowest)	324	(14.0)	40.6	(1.16)	100.0	(†)	12.0	(1.17)	28.3	(1.62)	34.9	(1.69)	10.0	(1.08)	7.8	(0.85)	7.1	(1.04)
Second	246	(10.8)	30.8	(1.05)	100.0	(†)	6.4	(0.97)	21.6	(1.80)	37.6	(1.85)	13.8	(1.36)	6.9	(0.97)	13.7	(1.33)
Third	140	(8.6)	17.6	(0.89)	100.0	(†)	3.6	(0.95)	16.5	(1.84)	39.1	(2.51)	9.3	(1.54)	10.1	(1.64)	21.3	(2.24)
Fourth (highest)	88	(5.8)	11.0	(0.70)	100.0	(†)	‡	(†)	12.1	(2.27)	29.9	(3.23)	6.3	(1.63)	9.6	(2.12)	40.6	(3.27)
Math achievement quartile[3]																				
First (lowest)	320	(14.1)	40.2	(1.17)	100.0	(†)	11.9	(1.16)	29.4	(1.59)	35.3	(1.81)	11.6	(1.05)	6.3	(0.79)	5.5	(0.87)
Second	239	(12.0)	30.0	(1.09)	100.0	(†)	6.8	(1.00)	19.1	(1.51)	39.2	(2.19)	11.6	(1.33)	9.8	(1.19)	13.4	(1.35)
Third	160	(8.7)	20.1	(1.01)	100.0	(†)	3.6	(1.03)	17.7	(1.98)	37.5	(2.30)	8.3	(1.62)	8.1	(1.47)	24.8	(2.30)
Fourth (highest)	78	(5.4)	9.8	(0.68)	100.0	(†)	‡	(†)	12.8	(2.10)	25.0	(3.00)	8.5	(2.13)	10.7	(2.62)	42.0	(3.41)
Middle SES[2]	**1,631**	**(31.5)**	**100.0**	**(†)**	**100.0**	**(†)**	**2.6**	**(0.28)**	**13.9**	**(0.58)**	**33.8**	**(0.72)**	**9.2**	**(0.44)**	**9.3**	**(0.47)**	**31.2**	**(0.85)**
Sex																				
Male	810	(20.1)	49.6	(0.83)	100.0	(†)	2.7	(0.37)	18.5	(0.90)	36.8	(1.18)	7.9	(0.61)	7.9	(0.62)	26.2	(1.16)
Female	822	(21.3)	50.4	(0.83)	100.0	(†)	2.5	(0.40)	9.4	(0.70)	31.0	(0.89)	10.4	(0.61)	10.7	(0.72)	36.1	(1.08)
Race/ethnicity																				
White	1,027	(26.7)	62.9	(1.14)	100.0	(†)	1.8	(0.32)	13.7	(0.71)	31.2	(0.89)	8.3	(0.55)	9.4	(0.60)	35.6	(1.08)
Black	241	(14.2)	14.7	(0.82)	100.0	(†)	3.9	(0.82)	13.4	(1.51)	41.2	(1.99)	13.1	(1.42)	9.0	(1.07)	19.4	(1.61)
Hispanic	215	(12.3)	13.2	(0.70)	100.0	(†)	4.9	(1.01)	14.1	(1.47)	39.3	(1.92)	10.4	(1.33)	10.8	(1.52)	20.5	(1.79)
Asian	53	(4.2)	3.2	(0.26)	100.0	(†)	‡	(†)	6.1	(1.49)	27.7	(2.20)	6.0	(1.52)	6.5	(1.33)	53.0	(2.86)
Pacific Islander	‡	(†)	0.2	(0.06)	100.0	(†)	‡	(†)	‡	(†)	‡	(†)	‡	(†)	‡	(†)	‡	(†)
American Indian/Alaska Native	16	(3.3)	1.0	(0.20)	100.0	(†)	‡	(†)	32.6	(7.74)	29.0	(7.20)	‡	(†)	‡	(†)	15.5 !	(6.41)
Two or more races	77	(5.9)	4.7	(0.36)	100.0	(†)	2.7 !	(1.02)	18.5	(3.17)	36.4	(3.23)	7.9	(1.91)	8.2	(2.07)	26.3	(3.34)
Reading achievement quartile[3]																				
First (lowest)	358	(14.4)	22.0	(0.82)	100.0	(†)	6.2	(0.86)	23.5	(1.52)	39.7	(1.80)	12.6	(1.00)	8.7	(0.96)	9.3	(0.93)
Second	427	(15.5)	26.3	(0.72)	100.0	(†)	2.7	(0.56)	15.7	(1.05)	37.1	(1.48)	10.9	(1.01)	10.6	(0.92)	23.0	(1.28)
Third	462	(15.0)	28.4	(0.73)	100.0	(†)	1.1 !	(0.32)	10.7	(1.06)	32.3	(1.36)	8.8	(0.74)	10.1	(0.89)	37.1	(1.62)
Fourth (highest)	379	(13.5)	23.3	(0.76)	100.0	(†)	0.8 !	(0.29)	6.1	(0.67)	26.8	(1.45)	4.4	(0.71)	7.7	(0.90)	54.2	(1.72)
Math achievement quartile[3]																				
First (lowest)	353	(14.8)	21.7	(0.83)	100.0	(†)	6.6	(0.89)	24.1	(1.35)	39.1	(1.67)	13.1	(1.04)	8.8	(0.95)	8.4	(0.98)
Second	448	(15.5)	27.5	(0.71)	100.0	(†)	2.7	(0.55)	15.7	(1.11)	37.5	(1.35)	11.9	(0.93)	11.6	(0.95)	20.6	(1.22)
Third	443	(13.5)	27.2	(0.69)	100.0	(†)	1.1	(0.31)	10.6	(0.94)	32.5	(1.41)	7.9	(0.85)	9.6	(0.90)	38.3	(1.56)
Fourth (highest)	382	(13.9)	23.5	(0.76)	100.0	(†)	‡	(†)	5.6	(0.79)	26.6	(1.50)	3.9	(0.66)	7.0	(0.84)	56.6	(1.76)
High SES[2]	**801**	**(27.1)**	**100.0**	**(†)**	**100.0**	**(†)**	**0.6**	**(0.17)**	**3.5**	**(0.43)**	**21.2**	**(1.11)**	**3.6**	**(0.43)**	**6.5**	**(0.54)**	**64.5**	**(1.19)**
Sex																				
Male	411	(17.3)	51.3	(1.19)	100.0	(†)	0.8 !	(0.29)	4.7	(0.66)	25.8	(1.61)	2.8	(0.50)	6.8	(0.73)	59.1	(1.61)
Female	390	(15.7)	48.7	(1.19)	100.0	(†)	‡	(†)	2.3	(0.48)	16.3	(1.14)	4.6	(0.67)	6.2	(0.78)	70.3	(1.45)
Race/ethnicity																				
White	616	(23.3)	76.9	(1.08)	100.0	(†)	0.4 !	(0.16)	3.1	(0.43)	19.6	(1.12)	3.0	(0.47)	6.4	(0.63)	67.5	(1.26)
Black	61	(5.9)	7.7	(0.70)	100.0	(†)	‡	(†)	6.3 !	(2.19)	36.7	(4.72)	6.9	(2.04)	5.7 !	(1.88)	44.2	(4.45)
Hispanic	53	(5.3)	6.6	(0.63)	100.0	(†)	‡	(†)	6.5 !	(2.03)	28.5	(4.09)	6.8	(1.95)	7.1	(1.94)	48.8	(4.08)
Asian	39	(3.7)	4.9	(0.46)	100.0	(†)	‡	(†)	‡	(†)	12.6	(1.99)	3.3 !	(1.19)	4.1 !	(1.36)	78.2	(2.61)
Pacific Islander	‡	(†)	‡	(†)	100.0	(†)	‡	(†)	‡	(†)	‡	(†)	‡	(†)	‡	(†)	‡	(†)
American Indian/Alaska Native	‡	(†)	‡	(†)	100.0	(†)	‡	(†)	‡	(†)	‡	(†)	‡	(†)	‡	(†)	‡	(†)
Two or more races	27	(3.0)	3.4	(0.38)	100.0	(†)	‡	(†)	‡	(†)	19.8	(4.26)	5.4 !	(2.68)	11.4 !	(3.82)	58.6	(5.54)
Reading achievement quartile[3]																				
First (lowest)	70	(5.8)	8.7	(0.70)	100.0	(†)	5.3 !	(1.75)	15.4	(2.82)	34.5	(3.62)	14.9	(2.72)	7.0	(1.82)	22.8	(2.90)
Second	120	(7.9)	15.0	(0.86)	100.0	(†)	‡	(†)	4.7	(1.24)	30.2	(2.58)	6.5	(1.35)	9.6	(1.84)	49.0	(2.90)
Third	239	(11.9)	29.9	(0.99)	100.0	(†)	‡	(†)	3.0	(0.72)	22.6	(1.94)	2.6	(0.77)	7.4	(1.12)	64.3	(2.12)
Fourth (highest)	370	(15.3)	46.4	(1.18)	100.0	(†)	‡	(†)	1.1 !	(0.36)	14.9	(1.22)	1.3	(0.33)	4.8	(0.70)	77.9	(1.42)
Math achievement quartile[3]																				
First (lowest)	68	(6.6)	8.5	(0.79)	100.0	(†)	4.4 !	(1.67)	15.4	(3.14)	35.7	(3.82)	13.5	(2.49)	5.4	(1.27)	25.5	(3.38)
Second	125	(7.3)	15.6	(0.81)	100.0	(†)	‡	(†)	4.2	(1.21)	30.3	(2.81)	8.0	(1.44)	13.5	(1.95)	43.3	(2.82)
Third	222	(10.0)	27.9	(0.90)	100.0	(†)	‡	(†)	3.3	(0.81)	22.5	(1.59)	2.3	(0.66)	7.5	(1.10)	64.3	(1.85)
Fourth (highest)	383	(17.0)	48.0	(1.18)	100.0	(†)	‡	(†)	1.2	(0.35)	14.9	(1.27)	1.3	(0.33)	3.8	(0.61)	78.7	(1.46)

†Not applicable.

!Interpret data with caution. The coefficient of variation (CV) for this estimate is between 30 and 50 percent.

‡Reporting standards not met. Either there are too few cases for a reliable estimate or the coefficient of variation (CV) is 50 percent or greater.

[1]Postsecondary transcripts from 2013 were used to update self-reported attainment of highest degree for all respondents with complete transcripts as well as for respondents whose partial transcripts indicated higher attainment than was self-reported in 2012.

[2]Socioeconomic status (SES) was measured by a composite score on parental education and occupations, and family income in 2002. The "low" SES group is the lowest quartile; the "middle" SES group is the middle two quartiles; and the "high" SES group is the upper quartile.

[3]Reading and math achievement quartiles reflect students' scores on assessments conducted in 2002.

NOTE: Race categories exclude persons of Hispanic ethnicity. Detail may not sum to totals because of rounding and survey item nonresponse. Some data have been revised from previously published figures.

SOURCE: U.S. Department of Education, National Center for Education Statistics, Education Longitudinal Study of 2002 (ELS:2002), Base Year through Postsecondary Transcript Study. (This table was prepared June 2016.)

Table 104.92. Number and percentage distribution of spring 2002 high school sophomores, by highest level of education completed, socioeconomic status and educational expectations while in high school, and college enrollment status 2 years after high school: 2013

[Standard errors appear in parentheses]

Socioeconomic status (SES), educational expectations, and college enrollment status	Total: Number (in thousands)		Total: Percentage distribution		Highest level of education completed through 2013[1]: All levels		Less than high school completion		High school completion		Some postsecondary education (no credential)		Postsecondary certificate		Associate's degree		Bachelor's or higher degree	
1	2		3		4		5		6		7		8		9		10	
Low SES[2]	**810**	**(24.4)**	**100.0**	**(†)**	**100.0**	**(†)**	**7.8**	**(0.61)**	**22.6**	**(0.92)**	**35.5**	**(1.07)**	**10.8**	**(0.68)**	**8.1**	**(0.59)**	**15.2**	**(0.90)**
Educational expectations in 2002																		
Don't know	94	(6.5)	12.6	(0.75)	100.0	(†)	8.9	(2.14)	29.1	(2.82)	35.5	(3.02)	9.7	(1.87)	6.4	(1.82)	10.4	(2.01)
Less than high school	13	(2.1)	1.7	(0.26)	100.0	(†)	21.3 !	(7.71)	42.0	(8.08)	34.6	(7.92)	‡	(†)	‡	(†)	‡	(†)
High school diploma or GED	92	(6.5)	12.4	(0.71)	100.0	(†)	16.2	(2.36)	43.4	(3.40)	26.1	(2.87)	8.6	(2.00)	4.4	(1.24)	1.3 !	(0.55)
Attend or complete 2-year college	66	(5.2)	8.8	(0.60)	100.0	(†)	9.7	(2.38)	28.8	(3.41)	33.9	(3.76)	15.2	(2.80)	6.6	(1.53)	5.8	(1.57)
Attend college, 4-year degree incomplete.	43	(4.0)	5.7	(0.48)	100.0	(†)	11.3	(2.90)	26.1	(4.66)	35.8	(5.08)	8.2 !	(2.56)	10.5	(3.03)	8.2	(2.42)
Bachelor's degree	247	(10.9)	33.1	(0.94)	100.0	(†)	4.8	(0.98)	18.5	(1.59)	38.4	(1.88)	13.4	(1.33)	9.3	(1.05)	15.6	(1.51)
Advanced degree	191	(9.7)	25.6	(1.06)	100.0	(†)	3.9	(0.88)	10.4	(1.34)	38.3	(2.20)	8.3	(1.33)	9.9	(1.25)	29.2	(2.00)
Educational expectations in 2004																		
Don't know	114	(7.5)	14.3	(0.82)	100.0	(†)	14.3	(2.25)	34.6	(3.23)	33.1	(2.69)	9.6	(2.08)	5.4	(1.49)	3.1 !	(1.02)
Less than high school	‡	(†)	0.7	(0.21)	100.0	(†)	‡	(†)	‡	(†)	‡	(†)	‡	(†)	‡	(†)	‡	(†)
High school diploma or GED	88	(6.6)	11.0	(0.77)	100.0	(†)	17.1	(2.54)	47.2	(3.51)	22.2	(2.77)	7.3	(1.75)	4.2 !	(1.50)	2.0 !	(0.88)
Attend or complete 2-year college	176	(10.6)	22.0	(1.08)	100.0	(†)	6.3	(1.37)	26.7	(2.09)	40.1	(2.51)	15.7	(1.74)	8.5	(1.36)	2.8	(0.74)
Attend college, 4-year degree incomplete.	40	(4.1)	5.0	(0.51)	100.0	(†)	‡	(†)	23.6	(4.56)	44.4	(4.99)	10.7 !	(3.39)	9.5 !	(3.33)	7.8 !	(2.97)
Bachelor's degree	202	(10.0)	25.2	(1.02)	100.0	(†)	2.8	(0.78)	9.8	(1.40)	39.9	(2.18)	9.7	(1.42)	12.2	(1.47)	25.6	(2.08)
Advanced degree	173	(8.8)	21.6	(0.93)	100.0	(†)	2.9 !	(1.02)	8.2	(1.25)	37.2	(2.82)	9.5	(1.74)	8.6	(1.29)	33.7	(2.50)
College enrollment status in 2006																		
Enrolled in a 4-year college	152	(7.7)	21.0	(1.00)	100.0	(†)	‡	(†)	‡	(†)	31.9	(2.39)	7.0	(1.24)	8.1	(1.60)	53.0	(2.62)
Enrolled in a 2-year college	207	(12.4)	28.6	(1.36)	100.0	(†)	‡	(†)	‡	(†)	50.6	(2.15)	16.2	(1.61)	16.9	(1.65)	15.9	(1.50)
Enrolled in a less-than-2-year college.	25	(3.2)	3.5	(0.43)	100.0	(†)	‡	(†)	12.9 !	(4.56)	35.3	(7.00)	42.3	(6.72)	5.4 !	(2.28)	‡	(†)
Not enrolled	340	(14.3)	46.9	(1.39)	100.0	(†)	15.5	(1.31)	45.4	(1.60)	28.3	(1.51)	7.1	(0.93)	2.9	(0.54)	0.8 !	(0.26)
Middle SES[2]	**1,631**	**(31.5)**	**100.0**	**(†)**	**100.0**	**(†)**	**2.6**	**(0.28)**	**13.9**	**(0.58)**	**33.8**	**(0.72)**	**9.2**	**(0.44)**	**9.3**	**(0.47)**	**31.2**	**(0.85)**
Educational expectations in 2002																		
Don't know	149	(7.5)	9.8	(0.44)	100.0	(†)	5.3	(1.16)	21.7	(2.22)	36.7	(2.68)	11.8	(1.58)	6.3	(1.29)	18.2	(2.15)
Less than high school	14	(2.6)	0.9	(0.16)	100.0	(†)	20.9 !	(7.98)	34.2	(8.99)	31.4	(8.37)	‡	(†)	‡	(†)	‡	(†)
High school diploma or GED	105	(6.7)	6.9	(0.41)	100.0	(†)	9.7	(1.83)	34.5	(2.84)	34.6	(3.03)	11.7	(1.92)	5.5	(1.25)	4.1	(1.13)
Attend or complete 2-year college	110	(7.0)	7.2	(0.39)	100.0	(†)	3.2 !	(1.19)	24.8	(2.90)	38.0	(2.93)	13.0	(1.98)	12.9	(2.07)	8.0	(1.63)
Attend college, 4-year degree incomplete.	59	(4.8)	3.9	(0.28)	100.0	(†)	‡	(†)	19.1	(3.05)	42.8	(4.20)	13.9	(2.59)	7.9	(2.11)	11.8	(2.37)
Bachelor's degree	562	(15.3)	36.9	(0.74)	100.0	(†)	1.2	(0.30)	11.5	(0.97)	34.1	(1.13)	8.4	(0.68)	11.4	(0.84)	33.5	(1.29)
Advanced degree	523	(15.8)	34.4	(0.74)	100.0	(†)	0.9 !	(0.27)	5.5	(0.66)	31.4	(1.40)	7.4	(0.72)	8.3	(0.71)	46.5	(1.33)
Educational expectations in 2004																		
Don't know	150	(8.8)	9.2	(0.50)	100.0	(†)	9.2	(1.55)	26.3	(2.33)	32.8	(2.48)	11.2	(1.82)	8.0	(1.51)	12.5	(1.98)
Less than high school	‡	(†)	‡	(†)	100.0	(†)	‡	(†)	‡	(†)	‡	(†)	‡	(†)	‡	(†)	‡	(†)
High school diploma or GED	97	(7.2)	5.9	(0.42)	100.0	(†)	7.9	(1.98)	46.9	(3.44)	27.3	(3.03)	8.1	(1.63)	4.6	(1.30)	5.2 !	(1.63)
Attend or complete 2-year college	281	(11.7)	17.2	(0.62)	100.0	(†)	3.1	(0.70)	23.9	(1.79)	39.2	(1.89)	17.2	(1.63)	11.6	(1.27)	4.9	(0.83)
Attend college, 4-year degree incomplete.	68	(6.0)	4.2	(0.35)	100.0	(†)	‡	(†)	15.0	(2.87)	48.9	(3.85)	8.2	(2.32)	12.7	(2.93)	13.7	(2.91)
Bachelor's degree	547	(15.7)	33.5	(0.73)	100.0	(†)	0.8	(0.22)	7.1	(0.77)	34.7	(1.40)	6.7	(0.67)	11.2	(0.95)	39.5	(1.52)
Advanced degree	489	(14.8)	29.9	(0.78)	100.0	(†)	‡	(†)	3.6	(0.60)	28.8	(1.35)	5.9	(0.69)	7.5	(0.76)	53.7	(1.51)
College enrollment status in 2006																		
Enrolled in a 4-year college	574	(16.7)	39.4	(1.00)	100.0	(†)	‡	(†)	‡	(†)	24.4	(1.03)	3.9	(0.51)	7.3	(0.69)	64.3	(1.21)
Enrolled in a 2-year college	451	(16.7)	30.9	(0.94)	100.0	(†)	‡	(†)	‡	(†)	46.0	(1.52)	12.9	(1.01)	17.8	(1.11)	23.0	(1.23)
Enrolled in a less-than-2-year college.	32	(3.8)	2.2	(0.26)	100.0	(†)	‡	(†)	14.6	(4.05)	31.5	(5.28)	39.6	(5.40)	7.7 !	(2.87)	‡	(†)
Not enrolled	402	(15.5)	27.5	(0.87)	100.0	(†)	8.6	(0.92)	43.6	(1.50)	31.4	(1.32)	9.7	(0.79)	4.4	(0.66)	2.3	(0.49)
High SES[2]	**801**	**(27.1)**	**100.0**	**(†)**	**100.0**	**(†)**	**0.6**	**(0.17)**	**3.5**	**(0.43)**	**21.2**	**(1.11)**	**3.6**	**(0.43)**	**6.5**	**(0.54)**	**64.5**	**(1.19)**
Educational expectations in 2002																		
Don't know	42	(4.0)	5.6	(0.48)	100.0	(†)	‡	(†)	6.3 !	(2.27)	34.3	(4.34)	4.2 !	(1.87)	9.2	(2.52)	45.6	(4.84)
Less than high school	‡	(†)	0.3 !	(0.10)	100.0	(†)	‡	(†)	‡	(†)	‡	(†)	‡	(†)	‡	(†)	‡	(†)
High school diploma or GED	14	(2.4)	1.9	(0.29)	100.0	(†)	‡	(†)	25.3	(7.29)	29.4	(8.30)	13.8 !	(6.19)	‡	(†)	16.3 !	(7.56)
Attend or complete 2-year college	19	(2.8)	2.5	(0.35)	100.0	(†)	‡	(†)	20.7 !	(7.21)	41.5	(7.90)	‡	(†)	20.6	(5.39)	12.0 !	(3.87)
Attend college, 4-year degree incomplete.	13	(2.2)	1.7	(0.28)	100.0	(†)	‡	(†)	17.5 !	(7.75)	39.0	(8.02)	‡	(†)	‡	(†)	27.7	(7.47)
Bachelor's degree	262	(12.2)	35.0	(1.01)	100.0	(†)	‡	(†)	3.2	(0.64)	23.5	(1.70)	4.2	(0.75)	7.2	(0.97)	61.5	(2.02)
Advanced degree	396	(14.8)	52.9	(1.06)	100.0	(†)	‡	(†)	1.2 !	(0.37)	16.3	(1.21)	2.8	(0.53)	4.7	(0.58)	74.8	(1.42)
Educational expectations in 2004																		
Don't know	37	(4.2)	4.6	(0.51)	100.0	(†)	4.2 !	(1.98)	13.8	(3.78)	31.0	(4.77)	8.7	(2.58)	13.4	(3.94)	28.9	(4.40)
Less than high school	‡	(†)	‡	(†)	100.0	(†)	‡	(†)	†	(†)	‡	(†)	‡	(†)	‡	(†)	‡	(†)
High school diploma or GED	13	(2.4)	1.7	(0.30)	100.0	(†)	‡	(†)	23.2 !	(9.42)	37.6	(11.14)	‡	(†)	‡	(†)	‡	(†)
Attend or complete 2-year college	43	(4.3)	5.3	(0.50)	100.0	(†)	‡	(†)	11.1 !	(3.57)	52.1	(5.15)	14.6	(3.61)	12.7	(3.31)	8.8	(2.25)
Attend college, 4-year degree incomplete.	22	(3.3)	2.7	(0.40)	100.0	(†)	‡	(†)	18.3 !	(7.40)	37.1	(7.61)	‡	(†)	15.4 !	(5.72)	22.1	(6.52)
Bachelor's degree	268	(12.1)	33.2	(1.06)	100.0	(†)	‡	(†)	1.7	(0.39)	24.0	(1.71)	4.0	(0.80)	6.5	(0.90)	63.6	(1.87)
Advanced degree	423	(17.6)	52.4	(1.15)	100.0	(†)	‡	(†)	0.9 !	(0.30)	13.6	(1.15)	1.4	(0.34)	4.8	(0.67)	79.2	(1.32)
College enrollment status in 2006																		
Enrolled in a 4-year college	527	(21.4)	70.5	(1.27)	100.0	(†)	‡	(†)	‡	(†)	13.5	(1.00)	1.4	(0.32)	3.4	(0.46)	81.6	(1.05)
Enrolled in a 2-year college	150	(9.1)	20.1	(1.06)	100.0	(†)	‡	(†)	‡	(†)	38.0	(2.64)	7.9	(1.46)	16.6	(1.77)	37.4	(2.48)
Enrolled in a less-than-2-year college.	6	(1.6)	0.8	(0.21)	100.0	(†)	‡	(†)	‡	(†)	36.6 !	(12.87)	30.3 !	(10.70)	‡	(†)	‡	(†)
Not enrolled	64	(5.4)	8.6	(0.70)	100.0	(†)	6.2 !	(1.98)	36.2	(4.18)	35.5	(4.21)	5.4	(1.55)	4.4 !	(1.77)	12.4	(2.42)

†Not applicable.

!Interpret data with caution. The coefficient of variation (CV) for this estimate is between 30 and 50 percent.

‡Reporting standards not met. Either there are too few cases for a reliable estimate or the coefficient of variation (CV) is 50 percent or greater.

[1]Postsecondary transcripts from 2013 were used to update self-reported attainment of highest degree for all respondents with complete transcripts as well as for respondents whose partial transcripts indicated higher attainment than was self-reported in 2012.

[2]Socioeconomic status (SES) was measured by a composite score on parental education and occupations, and family income in 2002. The "low" SES group is the lowest quartile; the "middle" SES group is the middle two quartiles; and the "high" SES group is the upper quartile.

NOTE: Detail may not sum to totals because of rounding and survey item nonresponse. Some data have been revised from previously published figures.

SOURCE: U.S. Department of Education, National Center for Education Statistics, Education Longitudinal Study of 2002 (ELS:2002), Base Year through Postsecondary Transcript Study. (This table was prepared June 2016.)

Table 104.93. Sources of college information for spring 2002 high school sophomores who expected to attend a postsecondary institution, by highest level of education completed and socioeconomic status while in high school: 2013

[Standard errors appear in parentheses]

Socioeconomic status (SES) and sources of college information	Percent of students obtaining college information from each source													
	All students who expected to attend a postsecondary institution		Highest level of education completed through 2013[1]											
			Less than high school completion		High school completion		Some postsecondary education (no credential)		Postsecondary certificate		Associate's degree		Bachelor's or higher degree	
1	2		3		4		5		6		7		8	
Low SES[2]														
Information sources as of 2002														
School counselor	40.8	(1.43)	25.9	(5.37)	35.5	(3.17)	40.5	(2.23)	39.4	(3.88)	41.9	(4.68)	50.8	(2.59)
Teacher	35.5	(1.29)	31.0	(5.50)	29.7	(2.65)	37.5	(2.18)	34.7	(3.96)	37.2	(4.50)	37.7	(3.10)
Coach	7.5	(0.68)	‡	(†)	6.4	(1.53)	10.4	(1.29)	3.1 !	(1.28)	6.4 !	(2.02)	6.5	(1.36)
Parent	42.0	(1.28)	29.8	(5.37)	36.9	(2.93)	42.7	(2.26)	41.7	(3.70)	48.8	(4.46)	45.6	(2.89)
Friend	39.5	(1.18)	30.0	(5.28)	35.9	(2.93)	40.8	(2.08)	41.3	(4.03)	31.2	(3.42)	46.0	(3.04)
Sibling	23.4	(1.13)	8.2 !	(2.86)	21.4	(2.70)	22.8	(1.91)	24.1	(3.81)	27.6	(3.86)	28.1	(2.64)
Other relative	27.2	(1.22)	26.3	(5.15)	21.9	(2.52)	29.2	(2.03)	29.2	(3.55)	28.8	(4.21)	26.6	(2.44)
College publication or website	29.9	(1.20)	12.8 !	(4.11)	21.8	(2.72)	30.3	(2.10)	22.0	(3.35)	36.4	(3.87)	43.1	(2.93)
College representative	15.2	(1.07)	‡	(†)	13.4	(1.83)	15.8	(1.71)	13.5	(2.86)	21.0	(3.88)	16.3	(2.55)
College search guide	28.7	(1.23)	18.8	(4.94)	21.6	(2.65)	28.6	(2.09)	21.5	(3.14)	26.3	(3.60)	43.9	(3.05)
Information sources as of 2004														
School counselor	77.7	(1.41)	‡	(†)	67.9	(3.96)	74.6	(2.44)	78.4	(3.54)	78.2	(4.23)	91.2	(1.81)
Teacher	46.1	(1.66)	‡	(†)	39.8	(3.79)	43.1	(2.65)	49.0	(4.52)	39.3	(5.45)	56.3	(3.59)
Coach	9.0	(0.89)	‡	(†)	‡	(†)	12.6	(1.68)	8.1 !	(3.43)	6.2 !	(2.36)	9.5	(1.76)
Parent	42.8	(1.41)	‡	(†)	36.7	(3.86)	41.7	(2.16)	47.7	(4.17)	40.2	(5.07)	47.4	(3.38)
Friend	25.9	(1.47)	‡	(†)	17.7	(2.72)	24.1	(2.18)	32.4	(4.40)	25.2	(4.69)	30.9	(2.89)
Sibling	32.6	(1.44)	‡	(†)	22.4	(3.42)	30.7	(2.01)	36.3	(4.05)	32.9	(4.91)	42.1	(3.10)
Other relative	53.1	(1.53)	‡	(†)	44.4	(4.32)	51.1	(2.56)	50.7	(4.21)	48.1	(5.39)	65.9	(3.06)
College publication or website	53.9	(1.50)	‡	(†)	36.8	(4.11)	52.9	(2.58)	56.1	(4.17)	53.5	(5.44)	67.8	(2.83)
College representative	50.7	(1.58)	‡	(†)	31.1	(3.78)	49.6	(2.43)	40.2	(4.36)	48.9	(5.31)	73.0	(3.10)
College search guide	43.0	(1.73)	‡	(†)	28.6	(3.51)	45.3	(2.59)	27.9	(4.02)	42.3	(4.65)	57.6	(3.03)
Middle SES[2]														
Information sources as of 2002														
School counselor	44.3	(1.06)	26.0	(6.59)	40.5	(2.83)	43.1	(1.41)	42.9	(2.72)	39.3	(2.77)	49.0	(1.64)
Teacher	31.6	(0.91)	41.4	(7.34)	32.0	(2.64)	32.0	(1.42)	31.0	(2.76)	24.1	(2.22)	32.9	(1.50)
Coach	9.3	(0.55)	‡	(†)	12.0	(1.86)	8.7	(0.81)	8.9	(1.66)	8.0	(1.56)	9.5	(0.96)
Parent	55.2	(0.90)	49.1	(8.17)	48.1	(2.89)	55.0	(1.39)	52.6	(3.23)	54.5	(2.60)	58.6	(1.51)
Friend	39.2	(0.86)	36.1	(9.25)	39.3	(2.89)	36.5	(1.50)	41.4	(2.81)	38.3	(2.71)	41.7	(1.40)
Sibling	23.6	(0.71)	20.8 !	(6.99)	17.4	(2.19)	20.7	(1.13)	24.0	(2.46)	23.9	(2.50)	28.3	(1.24)
Other relative	26.5	(0.84)	24.6	(6.88)	29.1	(2.46)	26.8	(1.47)	28.3	(2.72)	20.9	(2.11)	26.5	(1.34)
College publication or website	33.5	(0.86)	22.1	(5.71)	23.8	(2.58)	30.5	(1.32)	29.6	(2.81)	28.7	(2.62)	42.1	(1.44)
College representative	14.3	(0.67)	16.0 !	(6.32)	14.5	(1.87)	14.3	(1.05)	14.9	(1.94)	14.4	(2.24)	14.0	(1.04)
College search guide	31.0	(0.80)	30.5	(7.15)	20.8	(2.33)	28.4	(1.22)	28.8	(2.39)	28.3	(2.65)	37.8	(1.30)
Information sources as of 2004														
School counselor	79.6	(0.97)	‡	(†)	67.4	(3.23)	78.6	(1.44)	74.5	(3.09)	77.4	(2.86)	84.6	(1.23)
Teacher	43.6	(1.03)	‡	(†)	38.0	(3.39)	42.8	(1.97)	45.9	(3.48)	38.1	(3.05)	46.6	(1.71)
Coach	12.1	(0.77)	‡	(†)	8.2	(2.03)	11.8	(1.21)	6.9	(1.70)	11.5	(1.90)	14.2	(1.39)
Parent	58.5	(1.04)	‡	(†)	44.4	(3.47)	56.7	(1.89)	64.1	(3.33)	57.7	(2.98)	62.2	(1.48)
Friend	25.2	(0.81)	‡	(†)	22.9	(2.73)	20.9	(1.36)	21.9	(2.68)	23.7	(2.38)	30.1	(1.31)
Sibling	28.6	(1.00)	‡	(†)	28.3	(3.15)	27.8	(1.67)	34.6	(3.58)	26.2	(2.69)	28.8	(1.53)
Other relative	52.0	(0.97)	‡	(†)	45.8	(3.69)	49.7	(1.89)	50.6	(3.23)	47.8	(2.74)	56.7	(1.52)
College publication or website	59.3	(1.16)	‡	(†)	37.7	(3.47)	56.9	(2.01)	48.5	(3.49)	54.6	(2.91)	69.3	(1.72)
College representative	65.1	(1.01)	‡	(†)	38.6	(3.30)	58.4	(1.75)	49.6	(3.54)	64.9	(2.75)	79.6	(1.45)
College search guide	48.2	(1.11)	‡	(†)	31.8	(3.32)	41.1	(1.89)	42.7	(3.55)	45.7	(2.88)	59.3	(1.43)
High SES[2]														
Information sources as of 2002														
School counselor	46.3	(1.24)	‡	(†)	45.9	(7.73)	44.9	(2.32)	51.8	(6.69)	41.0	(5.26)	47.0	(1.41)
Teacher	30.7	(1.10)	‡	(†)	37.8	(8.19)	31.1	(2.36)	27.7	(6.30)	24.5	(3.78)	31.0	(1.32)
Coach	10.8	(0.70)	‡	(†)	14.9 !	(6.09)	10.2	(1.43)	12.5 !	(4.59)	5.4 !	(1.84)	11.2	(0.89)
Parent	68.4	(1.10)	‡	(†)	61.2	(8.52)	61.4	(2.54)	57.8	(6.34)	67.0	(4.61)	71.6	(1.22)
Friend	42.1	(1.09)	‡	(†)	45.4	(7.68)	37.4	(2.54)	36.8	(6.26)	43.5	(4.77)	43.5	(1.46)
Sibling	29.2	(0.94)	‡	(†)	23.7	(6.84)	26.1	(2.12)	20.5	(5.23)	29.8	(4.23)	30.7	(1.17)
Other relative	26.3	(0.97)	‡	(†)	37.1	(8.57)	26.8	(2.20)	23.2	(5.38)	23.6	(4.21)	26.0	(1.20)
College publication or website	44.4	(1.18)	‡	(†)	28.6	(7.35)	35.6	(2.52)	38.4	(6.87)	42.1	(4.83)	48.4	(1.49)
College representative	15.3	(0.78)	‡	(†)	10.9 !	(4.79)	17.9	(1.69)	23.7	(6.40)	14.2	(3.24)	14.4	(0.93)
College search guide	39.7	(1.13)	‡	(†)	21.1 !	(6.65)	34.2	(2.33)	29.4	(6.33)	33.5	(4.47)	43.3	(1.53)
Information sources as of 2004														
School counselor	80.9	(1.12)	‡	(†)	74.9	(8.21)	79.3	(2.48)	75.4	(6.62)	78.5	(4.24)	81.9	(1.23)
Teacher	42.7	(1.23)	‡	(†)	43.0	(8.66)	40.3	(2.97)	39.5	(7.32)	36.1	(5.21)	44.0	(1.45)
Coach	14.9	(0.88)	‡	(†)	‡	(†)	12.0	(1.82)	7.3 !	(3.50)	11.7	(3.23)	16.4	(1.13)
Parent	72.7	(1.29)	‡	(†)	69.5	(9.34)	65.9	(2.88)	61.4	(7.59)	67.0	(5.16)	75.5	(1.33)
Friend	30.0	(1.09)	‡	(†)	21.0 !	(7.21)	27.1	(2.34)	31.5	(6.84)	24.4	(4.56)	31.4	(1.20)
Sibling	28.0	(1.09)	‡	(†)	32.4	(8.55)	27.6	(2.89)	21.2	(5.48)	27.7	(4.46)	28.2	(1.35)
Other relative	53.2	(1.28)	‡	(†)	46.9	(8.79)	51.0	(2.78)	47.6	(7.90)	43.5	(4.84)	55.0	(1.48)
College publication or website	64.0	(1.23)	‡	(†)	40.2	(8.41)	55.5	(3.03)	49.4	(7.54)	44.7	(5.27)	69.0	(1.44)
College representative	79.5	(1.03)	‡	(†)	44.7	(9.51)	71.7	(2.75)	52.7	(8.05)	71.4	(4.38)	84.5	(1.10)
College search guide	59.6	(1.38)	‡	(†)	31.1	(8.61)	53.2	(3.12)	37.6	(7.23)	55.5	(4.71)	63.5	(1.52)

†Not applicable.

!Interpret data with caution. The coefficient of variation (CV) for this estimate is between 30 and 50 percent.

‡Reporting standards not met. Either there are too few cases for a reliable estimate or the coefficient of variation (CV) is 50 percent or greater.

[1]Postsecondary transcripts from 2013 were used to update self-reported attainment of highest degree for all respondents with complete transcripts as well as for respondents whose partial transcripts indicated higher attainment than was self-reported in 2012.

[2]Socioeconomic status (SES) was measured by a composite score on parental education and occupations, and family income in 2002. The "low" SES group is the lowest quartile; the "middle" SES group is the middle two quartiles; and the "high" SES group is the upper quartile.

NOTE: Students who reported that they planned to attend postsecondary education were asked, "Where have you gone for information about the entrance requirements of various colleges?" Because each student could indicate multiple sources, percentages do not sum to 100. Some data have been revised from previously published figures.

SOURCE: U.S. Department of Education, National Center for Education Statistics, Education Longitudinal Study of 2002 (ELS:2002), Base Year through Postsecondary Transcript Study. (This table was prepared June 2016.)

Table 104.95. Number of persons age 25 and over in metropolitan areas with populations greater than 1 million and rates of high school completion and bachelor's degree attainment among persons in this age group, by sex: 2014

[Standard errors appear in parentheses]

Metropolitan area	Number of persons 25 years old and over (in thousands)			Percent with high school completion or higher			Percent with bachelor's or higher degree		
	Total	Males	Females	Total	Male	Female	Total	Male	Female
1	2	3	4	5	6	7	8	9	10
Atlanta-Sandy Springs-Marietta, GA CBSA	3,591 (259.9)	1,719 (126.0)	1,873 (143.8)	90.9 (1.42)	88.9 (2.10)	92.8 (1.30)	38.7 (2.82)	39.9 (3.18)	37.6 (3.20)
Austin-Round Rock, TX CBSA	1,370 (133.2)	729 (76.4)	641 (65.8)	90.1 (2.68)	89.8 (3.21)	90.3 (2.50)	50.0 (4.08)	48.3 (5.10)	51.8 (4.06)
Birmingham-Hoover, AL CBSA	887 (93.5)	429 (52.4)	458 (46.0)	87.5 (2.32)	83.2 (4.42)	91.5 (2.49)	30.1 (4.53)	27.9 (5.18)	32.1 (5.16)
Boston-Worcester-Manchester, MA-NH-CT-ME CSA[1]	3,820 (132.2)	1,795 (77.1)	2,025 (69.7)	91.6 (1.32)	91.5 (1.74)	91.7 (1.31)	44.8 (2.31)	45.7 (2.54)	44.0 (2.67)
Buffalo-Niagara Falls, NY CBSA	759 (84.3)	354 (42.8)	405 (47.2)	92.3 (1.81)	89.1 (3.00)	95.0 (2.02)	24.4 (3.49)	23.9 (6.69)	24.9 (4.15)
Charlotte-Gastonia-Concord, NC-SC CBSA	1,291 (133.7)	602 (68.6)	689 (71.7)	82.5 (2.71)	81.7 (3.32)	83.2 (3.47)	30.9 (3.67)	32.3 (4.64)	29.6 (4.50)
Chicago-Naperville-Michigan City, IL-IN-WI CSA	6,218 (318.7)	2,993 (163.7)	3,224 (165.9)	89.0 (0.99)	87.7 (1.36)	90.3 (0.94)	38.2 (1.79)	37.2 (2.11)	39.1 (1.91)
Cincinnati-Middletown, OH-KY-IN CBSA[1]	1,344 (123.8)	668 (63.6)	676 (69.0)	89.0 (2.37)	92.0 (2.69)	86.1 (3.08)	29.3 (3.08)	31.8 (4.23)	26.9 (3.16)
Cleveland-Akron-Elyria, OH CSA	1,908 (145.4)	926 (81.0)	982 (77.2)	89.9 (1.63)	87.8 (2.43)	91.8 (1.60)	30.5 (3.09)	33.5 (3.98)	27.7 (2.91)
Columbus, OH CSA	1,174 (134.8)	565 (72.3)	608 (69.9)	90.9 (2.28)	89.9 (3.02)	91.8 (2.63)	32.3 (4.57)	34.3 (5.55)	30.5 (4.98)
Dallas-Fort Worth-Arlington, TX CBSA	4,565 (177.5)	2,248 (103.2)	2,317 (92.3)	85.6 (1.63)	84.2 (1.89)	86.9 (1.63)	33.7 (2.04)	35.4 (2.70)	32.1 (2.16)
Denver-Aurora-Boulder, CO CSA	2,086 (90.9)	1,042 (52.9)	1,044 (44.5)	93.1 (0.96)	92.7 (1.27)	93.6 (1.04)	48.7 (3.31)	47.2 (3.71)	50.2 (3.45)
Detroit-Warren-Flint, MI CSA	3,849 (249.4)	1,876 (132.9)	1,973 (123.8)	89.3 (1.35)	89.6 (1.65)	89.1 (1.56)	30.4 (2.06)	28.3 (2.63)	32.5 (2.38)
Fresno-Madera, CA CSA	688 (155.1)	345 (84.1)	342 (71.8)	84.5 (2.56)	86.0 (3.45)	83.0 (3.22)	18.4 (4.20)	17.0 (4.52)	19.8 (4.83)
Grand Rapids-Muskegon-Holland, MI CSA	895 (180.2)	418 (72.9)	477 (109.6)	96.7 (0.91)	96.7 (1.78)	96.7 (1.43)	33.2 (4.45)	30.3 (5.68)	35.7 (4.79)
Greensboro-Winston-Salem-High Point, NC CSA	1,040 (111.1)	488 (60.2)	551 (61.3)	86.8 (2.52)	84.7 (4.20)	88.7 (2.95)	21.4 (3.55)	22.3 (5.34)	20.7 (3.19)
Hartford-West Hartford, CT CBSA	789 (60.4)	384 (32.3)	406 (31.1)	89.7 (1.57)	87.7 (2.24)	91.6 (1.47)	38.5 (3.10)	37.3 (3.76)	39.7 (3.32)
Houston-Baytown-Sugarland, TX CBSA	4,044 (217.8)	1,944 (106.9)	2,100 (127.9)	83.0 (1.47)	81.1 (1.89)	84.8 (1.53)	31.8 (2.31)	30.5 (2.56)	32.9 (2.80)
Indianapolis-Anderson-Columbus, IN CSA	1,299 (108.4)	588 (54.0)	711 (61.4)	92.2 (2.00)	90.4 (2.69)	93.7 (1.81)	32.4 (4.20)	29.8 (5.06)	34.5 (4.22)
Jacksonville, FL CBSA	995 (99.7)	454 (49.3)	541 (55.4)	93.1 (1.87)	96.3 (1.89)	90.3 (2.19)	36.2 (4.26)	38.6 (5.45)	34.2 (4.69)
Kansas City, MO-KS CSBA	1,369 (92.3)	637 (49.1)	732 (49.7)	95.5 (0.96)	93.4 (1.44)	97.4 (0.92)	37.7 (3.03)	38.7 (3.92)	36.8 (3.39)
Las Vegas-Paradise, NV CBSA	1,259 (55.4)	630 (34.2)	630 (25.9)	89.9 (1.43)	90.6 (1.44)	89.1 (1.92)	23.4 (1.81)	22.5 (2.32)	24.4 (2.19)
Los Angeles-Long Beach-Riverside, CA CSA	11,824 (184.4)	5,696 (117.5)	6,128 (95.1)	80.7 (1.01)	80.7 (1.28)	80.6 (0.99)	32.4 (1.09)	33.0 (1.38)	31.8 (1.25)
Louisville, KY-IN CBSA	883 (112.4)	437 (74.5)	446 (44.4)	93.0 (1.37)	92.8 (2.01)	93.2 (2.21)	29.9 (2.87)	32.7 (5.19)	27.1 (4.31)
Memphis, TN-MS-AR CBSA[1]	896 (87.3)	396 (44.4)	500 (51.7)	84.8 (3.34)	87.7 (4.58)	82.6 (5.17)	31.6 (4.59)	26.8 (6.88)	35.4 (4.69)
Miami-Fort Lauderdale-Miami Beach, FL CBSA	3,893 (183.7)	1,822 (97.6)	2,071 (99.6)	88.9 (1.10)	89.7 (1.59)	88.2 (1.21)	31.7 (1.86)	32.7 (2.41)	30.8 (1.95)
Milwaukee-Racine-Waukesha, WI CSA	1,174 (243.7)	569 (119.6)	606 (126.4)	91.3 (1.68)	90.2 (2.54)	92.4 (1.44)	30.8 (3.49)	25.9 (4.42)	35.5 (3.41)
Minneapolis-St. Paul-St. Cloud, MN-WI CSA[1]	2,254 (97.4)	1,081 (54.3)	1,173 (50.9)	93.4 (0.90)	93.4 (1.10)	93.4 (1.07)	39.2 (1.97)	37.1 (2.17)	41.2 (2.34)
Nashville-Davidson-Murfreesboro, TN CBSA	1,159 (191.4)	552 (94.2)	607 (101.7)	87.5 (2.85)	89.6 (3.25)	85.6 (3.59)	37.2 (4.15)	39.5 (4.59)	35.1 (4.50)
New Orleans-Metairie-Kenner, LA CBSA	789 (88.1)	372 (46.0)	417 (47.9)	86.9 (2.95)	85.2 (4.23)	88.5 (3.02)	32.3 (4.08)	37.2 (5.40)	27.8 (5.40)
New York-Newark, NY-NJ-PA CSA	14,815 (254.8)	6,872 (160.0)	7,943 (128.1)	87.9 (0.72)	88.2 (0.92)	87.7 (0.74)	40.3 (1.12)	38.8 (1.44)	41.7 (1.19)
Oklahoma City, OK CBSA	937 (66.4)	412 (35.8)	524 (36.4)	89.5 (2.39)	88.0 (2.93)	90.7 (2.57)	29.4 (3.35)	32.1 (4.61)	27.4 (3.39)
Orlando, FL CBSA	1,496 (134.5)	750 (75.9)	746 (67.4)	92.7 (1.81)	91.0 (2.56)	94.5 (1.73)	29.4 (3.36)	28.4 (4.36)	30.4 (3.57)
Philadelphia-Camden-Vineland, PA-NJ-DE-MD CSA	4,274 (161.6)	2,029 (91.3)	2,244 (87.0)	93.1 (0.85)	92.6 (1.05)	93.6 (1.05)	36.6 (2.25)	37.4 (2.77)	35.9 (2.28)
Phoenix-Mesa-Scottsdale, AZ CBSA	2,805 ! (1,357.4)	1,425 ! (681.2)	1,380 ! (676.3)	85.0 (0.32)	83.1 (0.48)	86.9 (0.22)	31.3 (0.34)	33.3 (0.55)	29.2 (0.36)
Pittsburgh-New Castle, PA CBSA	1,742 (130.9)	818 (72.1)	923 (71.5)	93.2 (1.33)	90.1 (2.12)	96.0 (1.50)	37.7 (3.53)	37.6 (4.37)	37.7 (3.97)
Portland-Vancouver-Beaverton, OR-WA CBSA	1,552 (231.7)	773 (116.2)	779 (117.7)	92.7 (1.13)	95.4 (1.12)	90.1 (1.95)	36.2 (2.73)	34.6 (3.08)	37.7 (3.21)
Providence-Fall River-Warwick, RI-MA CBSA	876 (50.5)	419 (27.5)	457 (25.3)	84.8 (1.59)	86.0 (1.62)	83.8 (2.02)	35.8 (2.53)	38.5 (3.29)	33.4 (2.81)
Raleigh-Durham-Cary, NC CSA	1,382 (125.4)	648 (70.0)	734 (63.9)	86.3 (3.12)	83.6 (4.04)	88.7 (2.87)	44.7 (4.76)	45.6 (5.38)	44.0 (5.27)
Richmond, VA CBSA	976 (102.6)	466 (50.1)	510 (58.7)	90.4 (2.32)	89.3 (2.98)	91.4 (2.74)	34.5 (4.67)	30.4 (4.92)	38.3 (5.77)
Rochester, NY CBSA	806 (81.1)	398 (46.3)	408 (43.1)	93.6 (2.38)	92.3 (2.84)	94.9 (2.58)	34.7 (5.11)	34.1 (6.06)	35.2 (5.04)
Sacramento-Arden-Arcade-Roseville, CA CBSA	1,462 (86.0)	704 (49.0)	758 (51.2)	88.1 (2.25)	88.1 (3.27)	88.1 (2.28)	30.9 (2.92)	35.0 (3.58)	27.1 (2.93)
Salt Lake City-Ogden-Clearfield, UT CSA	1,053 (64.3)	521 (37.5)	532 (32.0)	91.5 (1.75)	90.5 (2.38)	92.5 (1.65)	32.5 (3.11)	35.4 (4.20)	29.7 (2.84)
San Antonio, TX CBSA	1,433 (121.2)	748 (66.4)	685 (65.5)	78.9 (2.50)	75.5 (3.18)	82.5 (2.45)	24.1 (3.01)	24.5 (3.68)	23.7 (3.46)
San Diego-Carlsbad-San Marcos, CA CBSA	2,087 (111.4)	1,018 (60.0)	1,069 (61.6)	90.7 (1.59)	92.7 (1.83)	88.8 (1.93)	41.3 (2.82)	43.4 (3.69)	39.2 (3.14)
San Jose-San Francisco-Oakland, CA CSA	5,604 (233.3)	2,838 (124.4)	2,766 (123.1)	89.0 (1.09)	89.6 (1.33)	88.4 (1.10)	45.7 (1.99)	47.1 (2.19)	44.3 (2.34)
Seattle-Tacoma-Olympia, WA CSA	2,808 (128.8)	1,331 (68.7)	1,477 (67.8)	92.6 (1.19)	92.2 (1.42)	92.9 (1.29)	41.5 (2.46)	39.7 (2.85)	43.2 (2.70)
St. Louis, MO-IL CBSA	1,951 (124.6)	954 (69.0)	997 (65.3)	91.8 (1.57)	90.8 (1.68)	92.6 (1.95)	32.2 (2.63)	30.4 (3.12)	34.0 (3.03)
Tampa-St. Petersburg-Clearwater, FL CBSA	2,321 (220.5)	1,120 (114.2)	1,202 (114.4)	90.1 (1.47)	92.3 (1.88)	88.2 (1.99)	30.4 (3.15)	32.3 (3.61)	28.6 (3.69)
Virginia Beach-Norfolk-Newport News, VA-NC CBSA[1]	1,114 (85.2)	515 (42.1)	598 (50.6)	91.7 (1.82)	88.9 (2.79)	94.2 (1.55)	27.4 (3.15)	25.6 (3.96)	29.0 (3.40)
Washington-Baltimore-Northern Virginia, DC-MD-VA-WV CSA[1]	5,989 (143.3)	2,890 (78.8)	3,099 (81.6)	92.0 (0.82)	91.5 (0.99)	92.5 (0.96)	49.1 (1.42)	49.9 (1.53)	48.3 (1.75)

!Interpret data with caution. The coefficient of variation (CV) for this estimate is between 30 and 50 percent.

[1]Information on metropolitan status was suppressed for a small portion of sample observations. As a result, population estimates for these areas may be slightly underestimated.

NOTE: A Core Based Statistical Area (CBSA) consists of one or more counties associated with at least one population core of at least 10,000 people, plus adjacent counties having a high degree of social and economic integration with the core as measured through commuting ties. A Combined Statistical Area (CSA) consists of two or more adjacent CBSAs that have social and economic ties as measured by commuting, but at lower levels than are found within each component CBSA. Detail may not sum to totals because of rounding. Standard errors were computed using replicate weights.

SOURCE: U.S. Department of Commerce, Census Bureau, Current Population Survey (CPS), March 2014. (This table was prepared March 2015.)

Table 221.10. Average National Assessment of Educational Progress (NAEP) reading scale score, by sex, race/ethnicity, and grade: Selected years, 1992 through 2015

[Standard errors appear in parentheses]

Grade and year	All students	Sex: Average reading scale score: Male	Sex: Average reading scale score: Female	Sex: Gap between female and male score	Race/ethnicity: Average reading scale score: White	Black	Hispanic	Asian/Pacific Islander: Total	Asian/Pacific Islander: Asian[1]	Asian/Pacific Islander: Pacific Islander[1]	American Indian/Alaska Native	Two or more races[1]	Gap between White and Black score	Gap between White and Hispanic score
1	2	3	4	5	6	7	8	9	10	11	12	13	14	15
Grade 4														
1992[2]	217 (0.9)	213 (1.2)	221 (1.0)	8 (1.6)	224 (1.2)	192 (1.7)	197 (2.6)	216 (2.9)	— (†)	— (†)	‡ (†)	— (†)	32 (2.1)	27 (2.9)
1994[2]	214 (1.0)	209 (1.3)	220 (1.1)	10 (1.7)	224 (1.3)	185 (1.8)	188 (3.4)	220 (3.8)	— (†)	— (†)	211 (6.6)	— (†)	38 (2.2)	35 (3.6)
1998	215 (1.1)	212 (1.3)	217 (1.3)	5 (1.8)	225 (1.0)	193 (1.9)	193 (3.2)	215 (5.6)	— (†)	— (†)	‡ (†)	— (†)	32 (2.2)	32 (3.3)
2000	213 (1.3)	208 (1.3)	219 (1.4)	11 (1.9)	224 (1.1)	190 (1.8)	190 (2.9)	225 (5.2)	— (†)	— (†)	214 (6.0)	— (†)	34 (2.1)	35 (3.1)
2002	219 (0.4)	215 (0.4)	222 (0.5)	6 (0.7)	229 (0.3)	199 (0.5)	201 (1.3)	224 (1.6)	— (†)	— (†)	207 (2.0)	— (†)	30 (0.6)	28 (1.4)
2003	218 (0.3)	215 (0.3)	222 (0.3)	7 (0.5)	229 (0.2)	198 (0.4)	200 (0.6)	226 (1.2)	— (†)	— (†)	202 (1.4)	— (†)	31 (0.5)	28 (0.6)
2005	219 (0.2)	216 (0.2)	222 (0.3)	6 (0.4)	229 (0.2)	200 (0.3)	203 (0.5)	229 (0.7)	— (†)	— (†)	204 (1.3)	— (†)	29 (0.4)	26 (0.5)
2007	221 (0.3)	218 (0.3)	224 (0.3)	7 (0.4)	231 (0.2)	203 (0.4)	205 (0.5)	232 (1.0)	— (†)	— (†)	203 (1.2)	— (†)	27 (0.5)	26 (0.6)
2009	221 (0.3)	218 (0.3)	224 (0.3)	7 (0.4)	230 (0.3)	205 (0.5)	205 (0.5)	235 (1.0)	— (†)	— (†)	204 (1.3)	— (†)	26 (0.6)	25 (0.6)
2011	221 (0.3)	218 (0.3)	225 (0.3)	7 (0.5)	231 (0.2)	205 (0.5)	206 (0.5)	235 (1.2)	236 (1.3)	216 (1.9)	202 (1.3)	227 (1.2)	25 (0.5)	24 (0.6)
2013	222 (0.3)	219 (0.3)	225 (0.3)	7 (0.5)	232 (0.3)	206 (0.5)	207 (0.5)	235 (1.1)	237 (1.1)	212 (2.5)	205 (1.3)	227 (1.0)	26 (0.6)	25 (0.6)
2015	223 (0.4)	219 (0.4)	226 (0.4)	7 (0.6)	232 (0.3)	206 (0.5)	208 (0.8)	239 (1.4)	241 (1.6)	215 (2.9)	205 (1.5)	227 (1.2)	26 (0.6)	24 (0.9)
Grade 8														
1992[2]	260 (0.9)	254 (1.1)	267 (1.0)	13 (1.5)	267 (1.1)	237 (1.7)	241 (1.6)	268 (3.9)	— (†)	— (†)	‡ (†)	— (†)	30 (2.0)	26 (2.0)
1994[2]	260 (0.8)	252 (1.0)	267 (1.0)	15 (1.4)	267 (1.0)	236 (1.8)	243 (1.2)	265 (3.0)	— (†)	— (†)	248 (4.7)	— (†)	30 (2.1)	24 (1.5)
1998	263 (0.8)	256 (1.0)	270 (0.8)	14 (1.3)	270 (0.9)	244 (1.2)	243 (1.7)	264 (7.1)	— (†)	— (†)	‡ (†)	— (†)	26 (1.5)	27 (1.9)
2000	— (†)	— (†)	— (†)	— (†)	— (†)	— (†)	— (†)	— (†)	— (†)	— (†)	— (†)	— (†)	— (†)	— (†)
2002	264 (0.4)	260 (0.5)	269 (0.5)	9 (0.7)	272 (0.4)	245 (0.7)	247 (0.8)	267 (1.7)	— (†)	— (†)	250 (3.5)	— (†)	27 (0.9)	26 (0.9)
2003	263 (0.3)	258 (0.3)	269 (0.3)	11 (0.4)	272 (0.2)	244 (0.5)	245 (0.7)	270 (1.1)	— (†)	— (†)	246 (3.0)	— (†)	28 (0.5)	27 (0.7)
2005	262 (0.2)	257 (0.2)	267 (0.2)	10 (0.3)	271 (0.2)	243 (0.4)	246 (0.4)	271 (0.8)	— (†)	— (†)	249 (1.4)	— (†)	28 (0.5)	25 (0.5)
2007	263 (0.2)	258 (0.3)	268 (0.3)	10 (0.4)	272 (0.2)	245 (0.4)	247 (0.4)	271 (1.1)	— (†)	— (†)	247 (1.2)	— (†)	27 (0.4)	25 (0.5)
2009	264 (0.3)	259 (0.3)	269 (0.3)	9 (0.5)	273 (0.2)	246 (0.4)	249 (0.6)	274 (1.1)	— (†)	— (†)	251 (1.2)	— (†)	26 (0.5)	24 (0.7)
2011	265 (0.2)	261 (0.3)	270 (0.2)	9 (0.4)	274 (0.2)	249 (0.5)	252 (0.5)	275 (1.0)	277 (1.0)	254 (2.2)	252 (1.2)	269 (1.2)	25 (0.5)	22 (0.5)
2013	268 (0.3)	263 (0.3)	273 (0.3)	10 (0.4)	276 (0.3)	250 (0.4)	256 (0.5)	280 (0.9)	282 (0.9)	259 (2.6)	251 (1.0)	271 (0.9)	26 (0.5)	21 (0.5)
2015	265 (0.2)	261 (0.2)	270 (0.3)	10 (0.4)	274 (0.2)	248 (0.5)	253 (0.4)	280 (1.3)	281 (1.3)	255 (2.4)	252 (1.7)	269 (1.1)	26 (0.5)	21 (0.5)
Grade 12														
1992[2]	292 (0.6)	287 (0.7)	297 (0.7)	10 (1.0)	297 (0.6)	273 (1.4)	279 (2.7)	290 (3.2)	— (†)	— (†)	‡ (†)	— (†)	24 (1.5)	19 (2.7)
1994[2]	287 (0.7)	280 (0.8)	294 (0.8)	14 (1.2)	293 (0.7)	265 (1.6)	270 (1.7)	278 (2.4)	— (†)	— (†)	274 (5.8)	— (†)	29 (1.8)	23 (1.9)
1998	290 (0.6)	282 (0.8)	298 (0.8)	16 (1.1)	297 (0.7)	269 (1.4)	275 (1.5)	287 (2.7)	— (†)	— (†)	‡ (†)	— (†)	27 (1.6)	22 (1.6)
2000	— (†)	— (†)	— (†)	— (†)	— (†)	— (†)	— (†)	— (†)	— (†)	— (†)	— (†)	— (†)	— (†)	— (†)
2002	287 (0.7)	279 (0.9)	295 (0.7)	16 (1.1)	292 (0.7)	267 (1.3)	273 (1.5)	286 (2.0)	— (†)	— (†)	‡ (†)	— (†)	25 (1.5)	20 (1.6)
2003	— (†)	— (†)	— (†)	— (†)	— (†)	— (†)	— (†)	— (†)	— (†)	— (†)	— (†)	— (†)	— (†)	— (†)
2005	286 (0.6)	279 (0.8)	292 (0.7)	13 (1.1)	293 (0.7)	267 (1.2)	272 (1.2)	287 (1.9)	— (†)	— (†)	279 (6.3)	— (†)	26 (1.4)	21 (1.4)
2007	— (†)	— (†)	— (†)	— (†)	— (†)	— (†)	— (†)	— (†)	— (†)	— (†)	— (†)	— (†)	— (†)	— (†)
2009	288 (0.7)	282 (0.7)	294 (0.8)	12 (1.1)	296 (0.6)	269 (1.1)	274 (1.0)	298 (2.4)	— (†)	— (†)	283 (3.7)	— (†)	27 (1.3)	22 (1.2)
2011	— (†)	— (†)	— (†)	— (†)	— (†)	— (†)	— (†)	— (†)	— (†)	— (†)	— (†)	— (†)	— (†)	— (†)
2013	288 (0.6)	284 (0.6)	293 (0.7)	10 (0.9)	297 (0.6)	268 (0.9)	276 (0.9)	296 (1.9)	296 (2.0)	289 (6.0)	277 (3.5)	291 (2.5)	30 (1.0)	22 (1.0)
2015	287 (0.5)	282 (0.6)	292 (0.7)	10 (1.0)	295 (0.7)	266 (1.1)	276 (0.9)	297 (2.1)	297 (2.1)	‡ (†)	279 (6.2)	295 (2.9)	30 (1.3)	20 (1.1)

—Not available.
†Not applicable.
‡Reporting standards not met (too few cases for a reliable estimate).
[1]Prior to 2011, separate data for Asian students, Pacific Islander students, and students of Two or more races were not collected.
[2]Accommodations were not permitted for this assessment.
NOTE: Scale ranges from 0 to 500. Includes public and private schools. For 1998 and later years, includes students tested with accommodations (1 to 13 percent of all students, depending on grade level and year); excludes only those students with disabilities and English language learners who were unable to be tested even with accommodations (2 to 6 percent of all students). Data on race/ethnicity are based on school reports. Race categories exclude persons of Hispanic ethnicity.
SOURCE: U.S. Department of Education, National Center for Education Statistics, National Assessment of Educational Progress (NAEP), 1992, 1994, 1998, 2000, 2002, 2003, 2005, 2007, 2009, 2011, 2013, and 2015 Reading Assessments, retrieved June 10, 2016, from the Main NAEP Data Explorer (http://nces.ed.gov/nationsreportcard/naepdata/). (This table was prepared June 2016.)

Table 221.12. Average National Assessment of Educational Progress (NAEP) reading scale score and percentage of students attaining selected NAEP reading achievement levels, by selected school and student characteristics and grade: Selected years, 1992 through 2015

[Standard errors appear in parentheses]

Grade and year	Percent of students in school eligible for free or reduced-price lunch: Average reading scale score[2]: 0–25 percent eligible (low poverty)	26–50 percent eligible	51–75 percent eligible	76–100 percent eligible (high poverty)	Gap between low-poverty and high-poverty score	English language learner (ELL) status: Average reading scale score[2]: ELL	Non-ELL	Gap between non-ELL and ELL score	Disability status[1]: Average reading scale score[2]: Identified as student with disability (SD)	Not identified as SD	Gap between non-SD and SD score	Percent of all students attaining reading achievement levels: Below *Basic*[3]	At or above *Basic*[3]	At or above *Proficient*[4]
1	2	3	4	5	6	7	8	9	10	11	12	13	14	15
Grade 4														
1992[5]	— (†)	— (†)	— (†)	— (†)	— (†)	‡ (†)	‡ (†)	‡ (†)	‡ (†)	‡ (†)	‡ (†)	38 (1.1)	62 (1.1)	29 (1.2)
1994[5]	— (†)	— (†)	— (†)	— (†)	— (†)	‡ (†)	‡ (†)	‡ (†)	‡ (†)	‡ (†)	‡ (†)	40 (1.0)	60 (1.0)	30 (1.1)
1998	231 (1.4)	218 (1.6)	205 (1.8)	187 (3.1)	44 (3.4)	174 (5.2)	217 (1.0)	43 (5.3)	176 (4.6)	217 (1.1)	41 (4.7)	40 (1.2)	60 (1.2)	29 (0.9)
2000	231 (1.5)	218 (1.3)	205 (2.1)	184 (2.8)	48 (3.2)	167 (5.2)	216 (1.1)	49 (5.3)	167 (4.8)	217 (1.2)	50 (4.9)	41 (1.4)	59 (1.4)	29 (1.1)
2002	233 (0.4)	221 (0.5)	210 (0.7)	196 (0.7)	37 (0.9)	183 (2.1)	221 (0.3)	38 (2.1)	187 (0.8)	221 (0.5)	34 (0.9)	36 (0.5)	64 (0.5)	31 (0.4)
2003	233 (0.4)	221 (0.5)	211 (0.5)	194 (0.5)	39 (0.7)	186 (0.8)	221 (0.3)	35 (0.8)	185 (0.6)	221 (0.3)	36 (0.6)	37 (0.3)	63 (0.3)	31 (0.3)
2005	234 (0.3)	221 (0.3)	211 (0.4)	197 (0.4)	37 (0.5)	187 (0.5)	222 (0.2)	35 (0.6)	190 (0.5)	222 (0.2)	32 (0.6)	36 (0.3)	64 (0.3)	31 (0.2)
2007	235 (0.4)	223 (0.4)	212 (0.4)	200 (0.5)	35 (0.7)	188 (0.6)	224 (0.3)	36 (0.6)	191 (0.6)	224 (0.3)	33 (0.7)	33 (0.3)	67 (0.3)	33 (0.3)
2009	237 (0.4)	223 (0.5)	215 (0.5)	202 (0.5)	35 (0.6)	188 (0.8)	224 (0.3)	36 (0.8)	190 (0.7)	224 (0.3)	35 (0.7)	33 (0.3)	67 (0.3)	33 (0.4)
2011	238 (0.5)	226 (0.5)	217 (0.4)	203 (0.5)	35 (0.7)	188 (0.8)	225 (0.3)	36 (0.9)	186 (0.5)	225 (0.3)	39 (0.6)	33 (0.3)	67 (0.3)	34 (0.4)
2013	240 (0.4)	227 (0.5)	218 (0.6)	203 (0.4)	37 (0.6)	187 (0.7)	226 (0.3)	38 (0.7)	184 (0.6)	227 (0.3)	42 (0.7)	32 (0.3)	68 (0.3)	35 (0.3)
2015	241 (0.5)	228 (0.5)	219 (0.6)	205 (0.6)	36 (0.8)	189 (1.1)	226 (0.3)	37 (1.1)	187 (0.7)	228 (0.3)	41 (0.8)	31 (0.4)	69 (0.4)	36 (0.4)
Grade 8														
1992[5]	— (†)	— (†)	— (†)	— (†)	— (†)	‡ (†)	‡ (†)	‡ (†)	‡ (†)	‡ (†)	‡ (†)	31 (1.0)	69 (1.0)	29 (1.1)
1994[5]	— (†)	— (†)	— (†)	— (†)	— (†)	‡ (†)	‡ (†)	‡ (†)	‡ (†)	‡ (†)	‡ (†)	30 (0.9)	70 (0.9)	30 (0.9)
1998	273 (1.1)	262 (1.3)	252 (2.1)	240 (1.8)	33 (2.1)	218 (2.5)	264 (0.7)	46 (2.6)	224 (3.7)	266 (0.7)	42 (3.7)	27 (0.8)	73 (0.8)	32 (1.1)
2000	— (†)	— (†)	— (†)	— (†)	— (†)	— (†)	— (†)	— (†)	— (†)	— (†)	— (†)	— (†)	— (†)	— (†)
2002	276 (0.6)	264 (0.6)	254 (0.8)	240 (1.1)	36 (1.3)	224 (1.4)	266 (0.4)	42 (1.4)	228 (1.0)	268 (0.4)	39 (1.0)	25 (0.5)	75 (0.5)	33 (0.5)
2003	275 (0.4)	263 (0.4)	253 (0.6)	239 (1.0)	36 (1.1)	222 (1.5)	265 (0.3)	43 (1.5)	225 (0.6)	267 (0.3)	42 (0.6)	26 (0.3)	74 (0.3)	32 (0.3)
2005	274 (0.3)	262 (0.3)	252 (0.4)	240 (0.6)	34 (0.7)	224 (0.9)	264 (0.2)	40 (0.9)	227 (0.5)	266 (0.2)	39 (0.5)	27 (0.2)	73 (0.2)	31 (0.2)
2007	275 (0.4)	263 (0.4)	253 (0.5)	241 (0.7)	34 (0.8)	223 (1.1)	265 (0.2)	42 (1.1)	227 (0.6)	266 (0.2)	39 (0.6)	26 (0.2)	74 (0.2)	31 (0.2)
2009	277 (0.5)	265 (0.4)	256 (0.6)	243 (0.7)	34 (0.8)	219 (1.0)	266 (0.2)	47 (1.0)	230 (0.6)	267 (0.3)	37 (0.7)	25 (0.3)	75 (0.3)	32 (0.4)
2011	279 (0.4)	268 (0.4)	258 (0.5)	247 (0.5)	32 (0.7)	224 (1.0)	267 (0.2)	44 (1.0)	231 (0.5)	269 (0.2)	38 (0.6)	24 (0.3)	76 (0.3)	34 (0.3)
2013	282 (0.5)	270 (0.5)	261 (0.4)	249 (0.5)	33 (0.7)	225 (0.9)	270 (0.2)	45 (1.0)	232 (0.6)	272 (0.2)	39 (0.7)	22 (0.3)	78 (0.3)	36 (0.3)
2015	281 (0.5)	269 (0.5)	261 (0.6)	248 (0.6)	33 (0.8)	223 (0.9)	268 (0.2)	45 (0.9)	230 (0.6)	270 (0.2)	40 (0.6)	24 (0.3)	76 (0.3)	34 (0.3)
Grade 12														
1992[5]	— (†)	— (†)	— (†)	— (†)	— (†)	‡ (†)	‡ (†)	‡ (†)	‡ (†)	‡ (†)	‡ (†)	20 (0.6)	80 (0.6)	40 (0.8)
1994[5]	— (†)	— (†)	— (†)	— (†)	— (†)	‡ (†)	‡ (†)	‡ (†)	‡ (†)	‡ (†)	‡ (†)	25 (0.7)	75 (0.7)	36 (1.0)
1998	296 (0.9)	284 (1.7)	275 (2.0)	272 (3.3)	23 (3.4)	244 (2.6)	291 (0.6)	46 (2.7)	244 (3.2)	292 (0.6)	48 (3.2)	24 (0.7)	76 (0.7)	40 (0.7)
2000	— (†)	— (†)	— (†)	— (†)	— (†)	— (†)	— (†)	— (†)	— (†)	— (†)	— (†)	— (†)	— (†)	— (†)
2002	293 (0.9)	282 (1.6)	275 (2.6)	268 (2.4)	25 (2.6)	245 (2.4)	288 (0.7)	43 (2.5)	247 (2.0)	289 (0.7)	42 (2.1)	26 (0.8)	74 (0.8)	36 (0.8)
2003	— (†)	— (†)	— (†)	— (†)	— (†)	— (†)	— (†)	— (†)	— (†)	— (†)	— (†)	— (†)	— (†)	— (†)
2005	292 (1.1)	282 (1.1)	273 (1.8)	266 (2.0)	26 (2.3)	247 (2.4)	288 (0.6)	40 (2.4)	244 (1.8)	289 (0.6)	45 (1.9)	27 (0.8)	73 (0.8)	35 (0.7)
2007	— (†)	— (†)	— (†)	— (†)	— (†)	— (†)	— (†)	— (†)	— (†)	— (†)	— (†)	— (†)	— (†)	— (†)
2009	299 (1.1)	286 (0.8)	276 (1.1)	266 (1.0)	33 (1.5)	240 (2.1)	290 (0.7)	50 (2.2)	253 (1.4)	291 (0.7)	38 (1.6)	26 (0.6)	74 (0.6)	38 (0.8)
2011	— (†)	— (†)	— (†)	— (†)	— (†)	— (†)	— (†)	— (†)	— (†)	— (†)	— (†)	— (†)	— (†)	— (†)
2013	302 (1.1)	289 (0.9)	280 (0.9)	268 (1.5)	35 (1.9)	237 (1.9)	290 (0.5)	53 (2.0)	252 (1.4)	292 (0.6)	40 (1.5)	25 (0.6)	75 (0.6)	38 (0.7)
2015	— (†)	— (†)	— (†)	— (†)	— (†)	— (†)	— (†)	— (†)	— (†)	— (†)	— (†)	— (†)	— (†)	— (†)

—Not available.
†Not applicable.
‡Reporting standards not met (too few cases for a reliable estimate).
[1]The student with disability (SD) variable used in this table includes students who have a 504 plan, even if they do not have an Individualized Education Plan (IEP).
[2]Scale ranges from 0 to 500.
[3]*Basic* denotes partial mastery of the knowledge and skills that are fundamental for proficient work at a given grade.
[4]*Proficient* represents solid academic performance. Students reaching this level have demonstrated competency over challenging subject matter.
[5]Accommodations were not permitted for this assessment.
NOTE: Includes public and private schools. For 1998 and later years, includes students tested with accommodations (1 to 13 percent of all students, depending on grade level and year); excludes only those students with disabilities and English language learners who were unable to be tested even with accommodations (2 to 6 percent of all students).
SOURCE: U.S. Department of Education, National Center for Education Statistics, National Assessment of Educational Progress (NAEP), 1992, 1994, 1998, 2000, 2002, 2003, 2005, 2007, 2009, 2011, 2013, and 2015 Reading Assessments, retrieved October 28, 2015, from the Main NAEP Data Explorer (http://nces.ed.gov/nationsreportcard/naepdata/). (This table was prepared October 2015.)

Table 221.20. Percentage of students at or above selected National Assessment of Educational Progress (NAEP) reading achievement levels, by grade and selected student characteristics: Selected years, 1998 through 2015

[Standard errors appear in parentheses]

Grade and selected student characteristic	1998 At or above *Basic*[1]	1998 At or above *Proficient*[2]	2003 At or above *Basic*[1]	2003 At or above *Proficient*[2]	2005 At or above *Basic*[1]	2005 At or above *Proficient*[2]	2007 At or above *Basic*[1]	2007 At or above *Proficient*[2]	2009 At or above *Basic*[1]	2009 At or above *Proficient*[2]	2011 At or above *Basic*[1]	2011 At or above *Proficient*[2]	2013 At or above *Basic*[1]	2013 At or above *Proficient*[2]	2015 At or above *Basic*[1]	2015 At or above *Proficient*[2]
1	2	3	4	5	6	7	8	9	10	11	12	13	14	15	16	17
4th grade, all students	**60 (1.2)**	**29 (0.9)**	**63 (0.3)**	**31 (0.3)**	**64 (0.3)**	**31 (0.2)**	**67 (0.3)**	**33 (0.3)**	**67 (0.3)**	**33 (0.4)**	**67 (0.3)**	**34 (0.4)**	**68 (0.3)**	**35 (0.3)**	**69 (0.4)**	**36 (0.4)**
Sex																
Male	57 (1.3)	27 (1.1)	60 (0.4)	28 (0.3)	61 (0.4)	29 (0.3)	64 (0.4)	30 (0.3)	64 (0.3)	30 (0.4)	64 (0.4)	31 (0.4)	65 (0.3)	32 (0.4)	66 (0.5)	33 (0.5)
Female	62 (1.5)	32 (1.2)	67 (0.4)	35 (0.4)	67 (0.3)	34 (0.3)	70 (0.3)	36 (0.4)	70 (0.4)	36 (0.4)	71 (0.4)	37 (0.5)	72 (0.4)	38 (0.4)	72 (0.4)	39 (0.5)
Race/ethnicity																
White	70 (1.3)	37 (1.2)	75 (0.3)	41 (0.4)	76 (0.3)	41 (0.3)	78 (0.3)	43 (0.4)	78 (0.3)	42 (0.4)	78 (0.3)	44 (0.4)	79 (0.3)	46 (0.4)	79 (0.3)	46 (0.5)
Black	36 (1.8)	10 (1.1)	40 (0.5)	13 (0.4)	42 (0.5)	13 (0.3)	46 (0.6)	14 (0.4)	48 (0.8)	16 (0.5)	49 (0.6)	17 (0.5)	50 (0.6)	18 (0.5)	52 (0.6)	18 (0.5)
Hispanic	37 (3.2)	13 (1.7)	44 (0.7)	15 (0.5)	46 (0.7)	16 (0.5)	50 (0.6)	17 (0.6)	49 (0.7)	17 (0.5)	51 (0.8)	18 (0.5)	53 (0.6)	20 (0.6)	55 (1.0)	21 (0.7)
Asian/Pacific Islander	58 (6.1)	30 (4.5)	70 (1.5)	38 (1.4)	73 (0.9)	42 (0.9)	77 (1.0)	46 (1.4)	80 (1.0)	49 (1.3)	80 (1.2)	49 (1.7)	80 (1.0)	51 (1.2)	82 (1.3)	55 (1.8)
Asian	— (†)	— (†)	— (†)	— (†)	— (†)	— (†)	— (†)	— (†)	— (†)	— (†)	81 (1.2)	50 (1.7)	82 (1.0)	53 (1.2)	84 (1.4)	57 (2.0)
Pacific Islander	— (†)	— (†)	— (†)	— (†)	— (†)	— (†)	— (†)	— (†)	— (†)	— (†)	61 (2.4)	28 (3.2)	57 (3.2)	27 (3.0)	60 (3.7)	28 (3.7)
American Indian/Alaska Native	‡ (†)	‡ (†)	47 (2.0)	16 (1.5)	48 (1.5)	18 (1.0)	49 (1.4)	18 (1.1)	50 (1.7)	20 (1.4)	47 (1.7)	18 (1.4)	51 (1.6)	21 (1.4)	52 (2.1)	21 (1.9)
Two or more races	— (†)	— (†)	— (†)	— (†)	— (†)	— (†)	— (†)	— (†)	— (†)	— (†)	50 (1.7)	20 (1.4)	73 (1.2)	40 (1.4)	73 (1.4)	40 (1.6)
Eligibility for free or reduced-price lunch																
Eligible	39 (1.8)	13 (1.0)	45 (0.4)	15 (0.3)	46 (0.4)	16 (0.3)	50 (0.4)	17 (0.3)	51 (0.4)	17 (0.3)	52 (0.4)	18 (0.3)	53 (0.4)	20 (0.3)	56 (0.5)	21 (0.4)
Not eligible	73 (0.9)	40 (1.2)	76 (0.3)	42 (0.5)	77 (0.2)	42 (0.3)	79 (0.3)	44 (0.4)	80 (0.3)	45 (0.4)	82 (0.3)	48 (0.5)	83 (0.3)	51 (0.5)	83 (0.3)	52 (0.6)
Unknown	69 (3.0)	37 (3.8)	76 (0.9)	43 (1.1)	77 (1.1)	45 (1.4)	80 (1.3)	46 (1.8)	81 (1.9)	50 (1.9)	82 (1.0)	48 (1.3)	83 (1.6)	51 (2.1)	81 (1.3)	52 (1.8)
8th grade, all students	**73 (0.8)**	**32 (1.1)**	**74 (0.3)**	**32 (0.3)**	**73 (0.2)**	**31 (0.2)**	**74 (0.2)**	**31 (0.2)**	**75 (0.3)**	**32 (0.4)**	**76 (0.3)**	**34 (0.3)**	**78 (0.3)**	**36 (0.3)**	**76 (0.3)**	**34 (0.3)**
Sex																
Male	67 (1.2)	26 (1.2)	69 (0.3)	27 (0.3)	68 (0.3)	26 (0.3)	69 (0.4)	26 (0.3)	71 (0.4)	28 (0.4)	72 (0.4)	29 (0.3)	74 (0.4)	31 (0.4)	72 (0.3)	29 (0.4)
Female	80 (0.9)	39 (1.3)	79 (0.3)	38 (0.3)	78 (0.2)	36 (0.3)	79 (0.3)	36 (0.3)	79 (0.4)	37 (0.5)	80 (0.3)	38 (0.4)	82 (0.3)	42 (0.4)	80 (0.3)	39 (0.5)
Race/ethnicity																
White	81 (0.9)	39 (1.3)	83 (0.2)	41 (0.3)	82 (0.2)	39 (0.3)	84 (0.3)	40 (0.3)	84 (0.2)	41 (0.4)	85 (0.2)	43 (0.4)	86 (0.2)	46 (0.4)	85 (0.2)	44 (0.4)
Black	53 (1.8)	13 (1.5)	54 (0.6)	13 (0.4)	52 (0.6)	12 (0.4)	55 (0.6)	13 (0.4)	57 (0.6)	14 (0.5)	59 (0.7)	15 (0.5)	61 (0.6)	17 (0.5)	58 (0.7)	16 (0.5)
Hispanic	53 (2.4)	14 (1.0)	56 (0.9)	15 (0.6)	56 (0.6)	15 (0.4)	58 (0.5)	15 (0.4)	61 (0.8)	17 (0.6)	64 (0.8)	19 (0.5)	68 (0.7)	22 (0.6)	66 (0.6)	21 (0.5)
Asian/Pacific Islander	75 (8.8)	33 (5.6)	79 (1.2)	40 (1.6)	80 (0.8)	40 (1.2)	80 (1.1)	41 (1.1)	83 (1.1)	45 (1.7)	83 (1.0)	47 (1.4)	86 (0.7)	52 (1.3)	86 (1.0)	52 (1.8)
Asian	— (†)	— (†)	— (†)	— (†)	— (†)	— (†)	— (†)	— (†)	— (†)	— (†)	84 (1.0)	49 (1.5)	87 (0.7)	54 (1.3)	87 (1.0)	54 (1.9)
Pacific Islander	— (†)	— (†)	— (†)	— (†)	— (†)	— (†)	— (†)	— (†)	— (†)	— (†)	63 (2.7)	24 (3.2)	70 (3.5)	27 (3.7)	66 (3.3)	24 (3.0)
American Indian/Alaska Native	‡ (†)	‡ (†)	57 (3.3)	17 (1.7)	59 (2.1)	17 (1.7)	56 (1.9)	18 (1.3)	62 (2.0)	21 (1.2)	63 (1.4)	22 (1.7)	62 (1.8)	19 (1.6)	63 (2.2)	22 (1.8)
Two or more races	— (†)	— (†)	— (†)	— (†)	— (†)	— (†)	— (†)	— (†)	— (†)	— (†)	79 (1.7)	39 (1.5)	81 (1.1)	40 (1.4)	79 (1.2)	38 (1.6)
Eligibility for free or reduced-price lunch																
Eligible	56 (1.3)	14 (1.0)	57 (0.5)	16 (0.3)	57 (0.4)	15 (0.3)	58 (0.4)	15 (0.2)	60 (0.5)	16 (0.3)	63 (0.5)	18 (0.3)	66 (0.4)	20 (0.2)	64 (0.4)	20 (0.4)
Not eligible	80 (1.0)	38 (1.5)	82 (0.3)	40 (0.4)	81 (0.3)	39 (0.2)	83 (0.3)	40 (0.4)	85 (0.3)	42 (0.5)	86 (0.3)	45 (0.4)	87 (0.3)	48 (0.4)	87 (0.3)	47 (0.5)
Unknown	80 (1.9)	43 (2.5)	81 (0.9)	42 (1.2)	84 (1.0)	45 (1.3)	86 (1.0)	48 (1.6)	89 (1.3)	51 (1.8)	90 (0.8)	54 (1.4)	92 (0.9)	59 (2.4)	89 (0.9)	53 (1.5)
12th grade, all students	**76 (0.7)**	**40 (0.7)**	**— (†)**	**— (†)**	**73 (0.8)**	**35 (0.7)**	**— (†)**	**— (†)**	**74 (0.6)**	**38 (0.8)**	**— (†)**	**— (†)**	**75 (0.6)**	**38 (0.7)**	**— (†)**	**— (†)**
Sex																
Male	70 (0.9)	32 (0.9)	— (†)	— (†)	67 (0.9)	29 (0.9)	— (†)	— (†)	69 (0.8)	32 (0.9)	— (†)	— (†)	70 (0.7)	33 (0.7)	— (†)	— (†)
Female	83 (0.8)	48 (1.1)	— (†)	— (†)	78 (0.9)	41 (0.9)	— (†)	— (†)	80 (0.6)	43 (1.0)	— (†)	— (†)	79 (0.7)	42 (0.9)	— (†)	— (†)
Race/ethnicity																
White	82 (0.7)	47 (0.9)	— (†)	— (†)	79 (0.8)	43 (0.9)	— (†)	— (†)	81 (0.5)	46 (0.8)	— (†)	— (†)	83 (0.6)	47 (0.8)	— (†)	— (†)
Black	57 (1.9)	17 (1.4)	— (†)	— (†)	54 (1.5)	16 (1.2)	— (†)	— (†)	57 (1.3)	17 (1.2)	— (†)	— (†)	56 (1.2)	16 (0.9)	— (†)	— (†)
Hispanic	62 (2.5)	24 (1.5)	— (†)	— (†)	60 (1.9)	20 (1.3)	— (†)	— (†)	61 (1.1)	22 (1.3)	— (†)	— (†)	64 (1.2)	23 (1.0)	— (†)	— (†)
Asian/Pacific Islander	74 (3.1)	38 (2.9)	— (†)	— (†)	74 (2.3)	36 (2.3)	— (†)	— (†)	81 (1.5)	49 (2.9)	— (†)	— (†)	80 (1.8)	47 (2.5)	— (†)	— (†)
Asian	— (†)	— (†)	— (†)	— (†)	— (†)	— (†)	— (†)	— (†)	— (†)	— (†)	— (†)	— (†)	80 (1.9)	48 (2.6)	— (†)	— (†)
Pacific Islander	— (†)	— (†)	— (†)	— (†)	— (†)	— (†)	— (†)	— (†)	— (†)	— (†)	— (†)	— (†)	75 (8.2)	39 (8.4)	— (†)	— (†)
American Indian/Alaska Native	‡ (†)	‡ (†)	— (†)	— (†)	67 (10.1)	26 (8.6)	— (†)	— (†)	70 (6.4)	29 (5.5)	— (†)	— (†)	65 (5.0)	26 (4.8)	— (†)	— (†)
Two or more races	— (†)	— (†)	— (†)	— (†)	— (†)	— (†)	— (†)	— (†)	— (†)	— (†)	— (†)	— (†)	77 (2.9)	38 (3.4)	— (†)	— (†)

—Not available.
†Not applicable.
‡Reporting standards not met (too few cases for a reliable estimate).
[1]*Basic* denotes partial mastery of the knowledge and skills that are fundamental for proficient work at a given grade.
[2]*Proficient* represents solid academic performance. Students reaching this level have demonstrated competency over challenging subject matter.

NOTE: Includes public and private schools. Includes students tested with accommodations (1 to 12 percent of all students, depending on grade level and year); excludes only those students with disabilities and English language learners who were unable to be tested even with accommodations (2 to 6 percent of all students). Race categories exclude persons of Hispanic ethnicity. Prior to 2011, separate data for Asian students, Pacific Islander students, and students of Two or more races were not collected.
SOURCE: U.S. Department of Education, National Center for Education Statistics, National Assessment of Educational Progress (NAEP), 1998, 2003, 2005, 2007, 2009, 2011, 2013, and 2015 Reading Assessments, retrieved November 3, 2015, from the Main NAEP Data Explorer (http://nces.ed.gov/nationsreportcard/naepdata/). (This table was prepared November 2015.)

Table 221.30. Average National Assessment of Educational Progress (NAEP) reading scale score and percentage distribution of students, by age, amount of reading for school and for fun, and time spent on homework and watching TV/video: Selected years, 1984 through 2012

[Standard errors appear in parentheses]

Amount of reading for school and for fun, time spent on homework and watching TV/video	9-year-olds					13-year-olds					17-year-olds				
	1984	1994	1999	2008	2012	1984	1994	1999	2008	2012	1984	1994	1999	2008	2012
1	2	3	4	5	6	7	8	9	10	11	12	13	14	15	16
	Average scale score[1]														
Pages read daily in school and for homework															
5 or fewer	208 (0.9)	203 (2.3)	202 (1.8)	210 (1.1)	207 (1.1)	250 (0.8)	249 (1.7)	249 (2.0)	250 (1.2)	251 (1.8)	273 (0.8)	271 (1.9)	273 (2.7)	271 (1.3)	274 (1.1)
6–10	215 (1.0)	214 (1.7)	212 (1.7)	219 (1.3)	219 (1.5)	261 (0.6)	261 (1.4)	262 (1.7)	258 (1.2)	261 (1.5)	287 (0.9)	284 (2.1)	285 (1.7)	284 (1.4)	283 (1.2)
11–15	220 (1.4)	217 (2.3)	221 (2.4)	224 (1.4)	225 (1.3)	264 (1.0)	266 (1.8)	263 (2.1)	263 (1.1)	266 (1.8)	294 (0.9)	288 (1.9)	292 (2.1)	290 (1.6)	289 (1.5)
16–20	215 (1.4)	209 (2.9)	214 (2.0)	225 (1.5)	226 (1.2)	263 (1.1)	263 (2.3)	264 (2.6)	267 (1.6)	268 (1.8)	296 (1.1)	298 (2.8)	292 (2.9)	296 (1.5)	297 (1.5)
More than 20	215 (1.6)	217 (2.4)	217 (2.1)	226 (1.2)	227 (1.0)	261 (1.5)	261 (2.0)	265 (2.0)	267 (1.4)	271 (1.3)	300 (1.2)	304 (2.2)	302 (1.9)	303 (1.3)	301 (1.5)
Frequency of reading for fun															
Almost every day	214 (1.1)	215 (2.3)	215 (2.4)	225 (1.2)	226 (0.9)	264 (1.4)	272 (3.2)	272 (3.2)	274 (1.4)	276 (1.4)	297 (1.5)	302 (4.2)	301 (4.9)	302 (1.3)	302 (1.3)
Once or twice a week	212 (1.7)	214 (3.1)	215 (2.6)	225 (1.3)	226 (0.9)	255 (1.4)	255 (3.1)	263 (3.2)	264 (1.1)	267 (1.4)	290 (1.7)	286 (4.1)	289 (2.9)	291 (1.7)	294 (1.4)
Once or twice a month	204 (3.3)	213 (5.8)	211 (4.2)	221 (1.7)	219 (2.0)	255 (2.1)	255 (5.7)	260 (3.7)	261 (1.3)	264 (1.7)	290 (1.8)	286 (4.5)	286 (4.8)	288 (1.3)	288 (1.5)
A few times a year	197 (4.2)	‡ (†)	‡ (†)	212 (2.0)	211 (1.9)	252 (3.6)	252 (5.4)	253 (4.4)	254 (1.3)	258 (1.6)	279 (2.7)	281 (8.2)	283 (4.4)	287 (1.5)	288 (1.3)
Never or hardly ever	198 (2.7)	193 (3.9)	195 (3.3)	211 (1.2)	208 (1.9)	239 (2.5)	237 (5.1)	242 (5.3)	247 (0.9)	249 (1.3)	269 (2.4)	258 (5.2)	262 (5.0)	269 (1.1)	272 (1.4)
TV/video watched on school day															
None	212 (3.4)	212 (4.8)	221 (4.6)	223 (3.0)	222 (3.1)	264 (2.7)	270 (5.1)	265 (6.0)	267 (3.0)	276 (3.5)	300 (1.6)	308 (3.4)	300 (2.8)	292 (2.4)	292 (2.5)
1 hour or less	217 (1.5)	216 (1.8)	218 (2.1)	225 (1.2)	229 (1.2)	269 (1.1)	270 (1.5)	270 (1.6)	266 (1.2)	269 (1.2)	300 (1.2)	299 (2.0)	298 (2.0)	293 (1.2)	292 (1.3)
2 hours	222 (1.1)	219 (2.1)	221 (1.7)	229 (1.1)	227 (1.1)	268 (0.8)	268 (1.4)	268 (1.6)	266 (1.1)	266 (1.5)	295 (0.9)	292 (1.8)	292 (2.1)	290 (1.1)	290 (1.3)
3 hours	220 (1.2)	218 (2.2)	218 (2.3)	227 (1.3)	226 (1.4)	264 (0.7)	262 (1.4)	263 (1.5)	262 (1.3)	261 (1.5)	288 (1.0)	284 (2.0)	282 (2.3)	284 (1.3)	284 (1.2)
4 hours	219 (1.0)	212 (1.8)	214 (2.4)	223 (1.4)	224 (1.4)	262 (0.9)	254 (2.2)	254 (2.4)	255 (1.5)	259 (1.5)	284 (1.0)	276 (4.1)	273 (2.2)	276 (2.3)	277 (2.1)
5 hours	214 (1.4)	209 (2.7)	208 (3.0)	219 (2.2)	213 (2.1)	257 (1.0)	250 (3.0)	253 (3.2)	255 (2.6)	255 (2.1)	277 (1.5)	269 (4.0)	275 (3.8)	273 (2.4)	275 (3.9)
6 hours or more	199 (0.8)	192 (2.7)	191 (1.7)	205 (1.2)	205 (1.2)	245 (1.0)	234 (3.1)	238 (1.8)	238 (1.4)	241 (1.4)	269 (1.5)	256 (3.7)	256 (5.2)	256 (2.3)	261 (2.6)
	Percentage distribution														
Pages read daily in school and for homework															
5 or fewer	36 (0.8)	28 (1.4)	28 (1.4)	25 (0.9)	22 (0.7)	27 (0.7)	26 (0.9)	23 (1.0)	26 (0.8)	23 (0.8)	21 (0.8)	21 (1.2)	23 (1.4)	30 (0.9)	29 (0.7)
6–10	25 (0.4)	26 (0.6)	24 (0.9)	20 (0.5)	17 (0.6)	34 (0.5)	31 (0.9)	31 (1.1)	24 (0.6)	22 (0.8)	26 (0.6)	25 (0.9)	24 (0.8)	23 (0.5)	22 (0.6)
11–15	14 (0.4)	14 (0.5)	15 (0.7)	14 (0.5)	12 (0.4)	18 (0.4)	17 (0.6)	18 (0.8)	17 (0.5)	17 (0.5)	18 (0.3)	18 (0.6)	17 (0.6)	16 (0.5)	15 (0.4)
16–20	13 (0.4)	14 (0.9)	14 (0.7)	14 (0.6)	15 (0.6)	11 (0.2)	13 (0.5)	13 (0.7)	13 (0.4)	14 (0.5)	14 (0.5)	13 (0.6)	14 (0.8)	12 (0.4)	12 (0.5)
More than 20	13 (0.5)	17 (1.0)	19 (1.0)	28 (0.8)	34 (1.1)	11 (0.5)	14 (0.8)	16 (1.0)	22 (0.9)	24 (1.1)	21 (0.9)	23 (1.5)	22 (1.2)	19 (0.7)	22 (0.7)
Frequency of reading for fun															
Almost every day	53 (1.0)	58 (1.6)	54 (1.7)	48 (0.7)	53 (0.8)	35 (1.0)	32 (1.8)	28 (1.7)	26 (0.7)	27 (0.7)	31 (0.8)	30 (2.6)	25 (1.7)	20 (0.6)	19 (0.6)
Once or twice a week	28 (0.8)	25 (1.5)	25 (1.5)	23 (0.6)	23 (0.6)	35 (1.2)	32 (2.1)	36 (1.6)	25 (0.6)	26 (0.6)	33 (1.1)	31 (1.9)	28 (2.7)	22 (0.5)	21 (0.6)
Once or twice a month	7 (0.6)	5 (0.6)	6 (0.6)	8 (0.3)	7 (0.4)	14 (0.8)	14 (1.7)	17 (1.6)	13 (0.4)	14 (0.4)	17 (0.5)	15 (1.5)	19 (1.7)	17 (0.5)	16 (0.4)
A few times a year	3 (0.3)	3 (0.6)	4 (0.7)	8 (0.4)	7 (0.3)	7 (0.5)	10 (1.2)	10 (1.1)	12 (0.4)	11 (0.4)	10 (0.5)	12 (1.5)	12 (1.4)	16 (0.5)	18 (0.6)
Never or hardly ever	9 (0.5)	9 (0.8)	10 (0.8)	14 (0.6)	11 (0.4)	8 (0.6)	12 (1.7)	9 (1.4)	24 (0.7)	22 (0.7)	9 (0.6)	12 (1.4)	16 (2.4)	24 (0.6)	27 (0.6)
Time spent on homework yesterday															
No homework assigned	35 (1.3)	32 (2.1)	26 (1.6)	18 (1.3)	22 (1.6)	22 (0.7)	23 (1.4)	24 (1.2)	23 (1.2)	21 (1.2)	22 (0.9)	23 (1.4)	26 (1.0)	28 (0.8)	27 (0.9)
Didn't do assignment	4 (0.3)	4 (0.4)	4 (0.3)	5 (0.3)	4 (0.4)	4 (0.2)	6 (0.6)	5 (0.4)	7 (0.3)	5 (0.3)	11 (0.3)	11 (0.6)	13 (0.7)	12 (0.4)	11 (0.4)
Less than 1 hour	41 (1.0)	48 (1.7)	53 (1.4)	60 (1.2)	57 (1.3)	36 (0.6)	34 (1.0)	37 (1.4)	43 (1.2)	44 (0.8)	26 (0.4)	27 (0.9)	26 (1.0)	27 (0.5)	26 (0.8)
1 to 2 hours	13 (0.4)	11 (0.7)	12 (0.7)	12 (0.5)	12 (0.6)	29 (0.5)	28 (1.0)	26 (1.0)	21 (0.7)	23 (0.9)	27 (0.5)	26 (1.2)	23 (0.8)	22 (0.5)	23 (0.6)
More than 2 hours	6 (0.2)	4 (0.4)	5 (0.5)	5 (0.3)	5 (0.3)	9 (0.3)	9 (0.7)	8 (0.8)	6 (0.4)	7 (0.5)	13 (0.5)	13 (0.9)	12 (0.9)	10 (0.5)	13 (0.7)
TV/video watched on school day															
None	3 (0.2)	2 (0.2)	4 (0.8)	4 (0.3)	6 (0.3)	2 (0.2)	3 (0.3)	4 (0.6)	5 (0.3)	6 (0.3)	5 (0.3)	6 (0.8)	6 (0.3)	6 (0.3)	10 (0.3)
1 hour or less	14 (0.3)	23 (1.0)	24 (0.9)	24 (0.6)	27 (0.7)	12 (0.4)	20 (1.0)	22 (0.8)	25 (0.7)	29 (0.6)	25 (0.5)	31 (0.9)	34 (0.9)	33 (0.6)	34 (0.6)
2 hours	16 (0.4)	23 (0.7)	21 (0.9)	18 (0.5)	18 (0.5)	23 (0.5)	27 (0.7)	29 (0.8)	25 (0.5)	27 (0.7)	26 (0.3)	26 (0.8)	26 (0.9)	27 (0.6)	25 (0.5)
3 hours	15 (0.3)	16 (0.5)	14 (0.6)	13 (0.4)	12 (0.5)	23 (0.4)	22 (0.8)	20 (0.9)	18 (0.5)	15 (0.5)	20 (0.3)	18 (0.8)	17 (0.7)	16 (0.5)	16 (0.6)
4 hours	12 (0.2)	11 (0.5)	9 (0.4)	9 (0.4)	8 (0.4)	17 (0.4)	12 (0.7)	11 (0.6)	10 (0.4)	8 (0.3)	12 (0.3)	9 (0.6)	8 (0.5)	8 (0.4)	8 (0.3)
5 hours	9 (0.3)	6 (0.4)	6 (0.4)	6 (0.3)	6 (0.3)	10 (0.3)	7 (0.4)	5 (0.3)	5 (0.3)	4 (0.2)	6 (0.2)	5 (0.5)	4 (0.4)	4 (0.2)	3 (0.2)
6 hours or more	30 (0.7)	20 (0.8)	22 (1.2)	26 (0.8)	23 (0.8)	13 (0.4)	10 (0.9)	9 (0.6)	13 (0.4)	10 (0.5)	6 (0.2)	5 (0.4)	5 (0.6)	6 (0.4)	5 (0.3)

†Not applicable.
‡Reporting standards not met (too few cases for a reliable estimate).
[1]Scale ranges from 0 to 500. Students scoring 150 (or higher) are able to follow brief written directions and carry out simple, discrete reading tasks. Students scoring 200 are able to understand, combine ideas, and make inferences based on short uncomplicated passages about specific or sequentially related information. Students scoring 250 are able to search for specific information, interrelate ideas, and make generalizations about literature, science, and social studies materials. Students scoring 300 are able to find, understand, summarize, and explain relatively complicated literary and informational material.
NOTE: Includes public and private schools. For 1984, 1994, and 1999, accommodations were not permitted. For 2008 and later years, includes students tested with accommodations; excludes only those students with disabilities and English language learners who were unable to be tested even with accommodations (2 to 4 percent of all students, depending on age and assessment year). Detail may not sum to totals because of rounding.
SOURCE: U.S. Department of Education, National Center for Education Statistics, National Assessment of Educational Progress (NAEP), *NAEP Trends in Academic Progress*, 1996 and 1999; and 2008 and 2012 NAEP Long-Term Trend Reading Assessments, retrieved June 24, 2009, and July 02, 2013, from the Long-Term Trend NAEP Data Explorer (http://nces.ed.gov/nationsreportcard/naepdata/). (This table was prepared July 2013.)

Table 221.40. Average National Assessment of Educational Progress (NAEP) reading scale score of 4th-grade public school students and percentage attaining reading achievement levels, by state: Selected years, 1992 through 2015

[Standard errors appear in parentheses]

State	Average scale score[1]											Percent attaining reading achievement levels, 2015		
	1992[2]	1994[2]	1998	2002	2003	2005	2007	2009	2011	2013	2015	At or above *Basic*[3]	At or above *Proficient*[4]	At *Advanced*[5]
1	2	3	4	5	6	7	8	9	10	11	12	13	14	15
United States	**215 (1.0)**	**212 (1.1)**	**213 (1.2)**	**217 (0.5)**	**216 (0.3)**	**217 (0.2)**	**220 (0.3)**	**220 (0.3)**	**220 (0.3)**	**221 (0.3)**	**221 (0.4)**	**68 (0.4)**	**35 (0.4)**	**8 (0.2)**
Alabama	207 (1.7)	208 (1.5)	211 (1.9)	207 (1.4)	207 (1.7)	208 (1.2)	216 (1.3)	216 (1.2)	220 (1.3)	219 (1.2)	217 (1.4)	65 (1.8)	29 (1.7)	5 (0.7)
Alaska	— (†)	— (†)	— (†)	— (†)	212 (1.6)	211 (1.4)	214 (1.0)	211 (1.2)	208 (1.1)	209 (1.0)	213 (1.3)	61 (1.4)	30 (1.4)	6 (0.8)
Arizona	209 (1.2)	206 (1.9)	206 (1.4)	205 (1.5)	209 (1.2)	207 (1.6)	210 (1.6)	210 (1.2)	212 (1.2)	213 (1.4)	215 (1.3)	62 (1.6)	30 (1.5)	7 (0.8)
Arkansas	211 (1.2)	209 (1.7)	209 (1.6)	213 (1.4)	214 (1.4)	217 (1.1)	217 (1.2)	216 (1.1)	217 (1.0)	219 (0.9)	218 (1.1)	65 (1.3)	32 (1.5)	6 (0.8)
California[6,7]	202 (2.0)	197 (1.8)	202 (2.5)	206 (2.5)	206 (1.2)	207 (0.7)	209 (1.0)	210 (1.5)	211 (1.8)	213 (1.2)	213 (1.7)	59 (2.1)	28 (1.7)	6 (0.9)
Colorado	217 (1.1)	213 (1.3)	220 (1.4)	— (†)	224 (1.2)	224 (1.1)	224 (1.1)	226 (1.2)	223 (1.3)	227 (1.0)	224 (1.6)	71 (1.7)	39 (1.8)	10 (1.0)
Connecticut	222 (1.3)	222 (1.6)	230 (1.6)	229 (1.1)	228 (1.1)	226 (1.0)	227 (1.3)	229 (1.1)	227 (1.3)	230 (0.9)	229 (1.1)	74 (1.2)	43 (1.5)	13 (1.0)
Delaware[8]	213 (0.6)	206 (1.1)	207 (1.7)	224 (0.6)	224 (0.7)	226 (0.8)	225 (0.7)	226 (0.5)	225 (0.7)	226 (0.8)	224 (0.8)	70 (1.2)	37 (1.2)	9 (0.7)
District of Columbia	188 (0.8)	179 (0.9)	179 (1.2)	191 (0.9)	188 (0.9)	191 (1.0)	197 (0.9)	202 (1.0)	201 (0.8)	206 (0.9)	212 (0.9)	56 (1.2)	27 (0.9)	8 (0.7)
Florida	208 (1.2)	205 (1.7)	206 (1.4)	214 (1.4)	218 (1.1)	219 (0.9)	224 (0.8)	226 (1.0)	225 (1.1)	227 (1.1)	227 (1.0)	75 (1.2)	39 (1.5)	8 (0.9)
Georgia	212 (1.5)	207 (2.4)	209 (1.4)	215 (1.0)	214 (1.3)	214 (1.2)	219 (0.9)	218 (1.1)	221 (1.1)	222 (1.1)	222 (1.2)	68 (1.5)	34 (1.6)	7 (0.9)
Hawaii	203 (1.7)	201 (1.7)	200 (1.5)	208 (0.9)	208 (1.4)	210 (1.0)	213 (1.1)	211 (1.0)	214 (1.0)	215 (1.0)	215 (1.0)	61 (1.2)	29 (1.2)	6 (0.6)
Idaho	219 (0.9)	‡ (†)	— (†)	220 (1.1)	218 (1.0)	222 (0.9)	223 (0.8)	221 (0.9)	221 (0.8)	219 (0.9)	222 (1.0)	69 (1.3)	36 (1.4)	8 (0.7)
Illinois	— (†)	— (†)	‡ (†)	‡ (†)	216 (1.6)	216 (1.2)	219 (1.2)	219 (1.4)	219 (1.1)	219 (1.4)	222 (1.2)	68 (1.3)	35 (1.5)	9 (0.9)
Indiana	221 (1.3)	220 (1.3)	— (†)	222 (1.4)	220 (1.0)	218 (1.1)	222 (0.9)	223 (1.1)	221 (0.9)	225 (1.0)	227 (1.1)	75 (1.3)	40 (1.6)	9 (0.8)
Iowa[6,7]	225 (1.1)	223 (1.3)	220 (1.6)	223 (1.1)	223 (1.1)	221 (0.9)	225 (1.1)	221 (1.2)	221 (0.8)	224 (1.1)	224 (1.1)	71 (1.4)	38 (1.6)	9 (0.8)
Kansas[6,7]	— (†)	— (†)	221 (1.4)	222 (1.4)	220 (1.2)	220 (1.3)	225 (1.1)	224 (1.3)	224 (1.0)	223 (1.3)	221 (1.5)	68 (1.6)	35 (1.8)	9 (1.0)
Kentucky	213 (1.3)	212 (1.6)	218 (1.5)	219 (1.1)	219 (1.3)	220 (1.1)	222 (1.1)	226 (1.1)	225 (1.0)	224 (1.2)	228 (1.2)	75 (1.3)	40 (1.6)	10 (1.1)
Louisiana	204 (1.2)	197 (1.3)	200 (1.6)	207 (1.7)	205 (1.4)	209 (1.3)	207 (1.6)	207 (1.1)	210 (1.4)	210 (1.3)	216 (1.5)	63 (1.9)	29 (1.6)	6 (1.0)
Maine[8]	227 (1.1)	228 (1.3)	225 (1.4)	225 (1.1)	224 (0.9)	225 (0.9)	226 (0.9)	224 (0.9)	222 (0.7)	225 (0.9)	224 (0.9)	71 (1.2)	36 (1.3)	8 (0.7)
Maryland	211 (1.6)	210 (1.5)	212 (1.6)	217 (1.5)	219 (1.4)	220 (1.3)	225 (1.1)	226 (1.4)	231 (0.9)	232 (1.3)	223 (1.3)	68 (1.5)	37 (1.7)	10 (0.9)
Massachusetts[6]	226 (0.9)	223 (1.3)	223 (1.4)	234 (1.1)	228 (1.2)	231 (0.9)	236 (1.1)	234 (1.1)	237 (1.0)	232 (1.1)	235 (1.0)	82 (1.2)	50 (1.5)	14 (1.0)
Michigan	216 (1.5)	‡ (†)	216 (1.5)	219 (1.1)	219 (1.2)	218 (1.5)	220 (1.4)	218 (1.0)	219 (1.2)	217 (1.4)	216 (1.3)	63 (1.8)	29 (1.6)	5 (0.8)
Minnesota[6,7]	221 (1.2)	218 (1.4)	219 (1.7)	225 (1.1)	223 (1.1)	225 (1.3)	225 (1.1)	223 (1.3)	222 (1.2)	227 (1.2)	223 (1.3)	71 (1.4)	39 (1.5)	9 (1.0)
Mississippi	199 (1.3)	202 (1.6)	203 (1.3)	203 (1.3)	205 (1.3)	204 (1.3)	208 (1.0)	211 (1.1)	209 (1.2)	209 (0.9)	214 (1.0)	60 (1.4)	26 (1.3)	5 (0.6)
Missouri	220 (1.2)	217 (1.5)	216 (1.3)	220 (1.3)	222 (1.2)	221 (0.9)	221 (1.1)	224 (1.1)	220 (0.9)	222 (1.0)	223 (1.1)	70 (1.2)	36 (1.5)	9 (0.8)
Montana[6,7,9]	— (†)	222 (1.4)	225 (1.5)	224 (1.8)	223 (1.2)	225 (1.1)	227 (1.0)	225 (0.8)	225 (0.6)	223 (0.8)	225 (0.8)	72 (1.2)	37 (1.2)	8 (0.6)
Nebraska[8,9]	221 (1.1)	220 (1.5)	— (†)	222 (1.5)	221 (1.0)	221 (1.2)	223 (1.3)	223 (1.0)	223 (1.0)	223 (1.0)	227 (1.1)	74 (1.3)	40 (1.5)	9 (1.0)
Nevada	— (†)	— (†)	206 (1.8)	209 (1.2)	207 (1.2)	207 (1.2)	211 (1.2)	211 (1.1)	213 (1.0)	214 (1.1)	214 (1.2)	61 (1.4)	29 (1.3)	6 (0.7)
New Hampshire[6,8,9]	228 (1.2)	223 (1.5)	226 (1.7)	— (†)	228 (1.0)	227 (0.9)	229 (0.9)	229 (1.0)	230 (0.8)	232 (0.9)	232 (1.0)	79 (1.2)	46 (1.5)	12 (0.8)
New Jersey[8]	223 (1.4)	219 (1.2)	— (†)	— (†)	225 (1.2)	223 (1.3)	231 (1.2)	229 (0.9)	231 (1.2)	229 (1.3)	229 (1.4)	75 (1.5)	43 (1.8)	12 (1.2)
New Mexico	211 (1.5)	205 (1.7)	205 (1.4)	208 (1.6)	203 (1.5)	207 (1.3)	212 (1.3)	208 (1.4)	208 (1.0)	206 (1.1)	207 (1.0)	54 (1.4)	23 (1.2)	4 (0.5)
New York[6,7,8]	215 (1.4)	212 (1.4)	215 (1.6)	222 (1.5)	222 (1.1)	223 (1.0)	224 (1.0)	224 (1.0)	222 (1.1)	224 (1.2)	223 (1.1)	68 (1.2)	36 (1.5)	9 (0.9)
North Carolina	212 (1.1)	214 (1.5)	213 (1.6)	222 (1.0)	221 (1.0)	217 (1.0)	218 (0.9)	219 (1.1)	221 (1.2)	222 (1.1)	226 (1.1)	73 (1.4)	38 (1.5)	9 (1.0)
North Dakota[7]	226 (1.1)	225 (1.2)	— (†)	224 (1.0)	222 (0.9)	225 (0.7)	226 (0.9)	226 (0.8)	226 (0.5)	224 (0.5)	225 (0.7)	73 (1.0)	37 (0.9)	7 (0.7)
Ohio	217 (1.3)	— (†)	— (†)	222 (1.3)	222 (1.2)	223 (1.4)	226 (1.1)	225 (1.1)	224 (1.0)	224 (1.2)	225 (1.2)	72 (1.3)	38 (1.7)	8 (1.0)
Oklahoma	220 (0.9)	— (†)	219 (1.2)	213 (1.2)	214 (1.2)	214 (1.1)	217 (1.1)	217 (1.1)	215 (1.1)	217 (1.1)	222 (1.1)	71 (1.4)	33 (1.5)	6 (0.7)
Oregon	— (†)	— (†)	212 (1.8)	220 (1.4)	218 (1.3)	217 (1.4)	215 (1.4)	218 (1.2)	216 (1.1)	219 (1.3)	220 (1.4)	67 (1.6)	34 (1.6)	8 (0.9)
Pennsylvania[9]	221 (1.3)	215 (1.6)	— (†)	221 (1.2)	219 (1.3)	223 (1.3)	226 (1.0)	224 (1.4)	227 (1.2)	226 (1.3)	227 (1.8)	74 (1.9)	41 (2.0)	11 (1.0)
Rhode Island[9]	217 (1.8)	220 (1.3)	218 (1.4)	220 (1.2)	216 (1.3)	216 (1.2)	219 (1.0)	223 (1.1)	222 (0.8)	223 (0.9)	225 (0.9)	72 (1.1)	40 (1.3)	10 (0.8)
South Carolina	210 (1.3)	203 (1.4)	209 (1.4)	214 (1.3)	215 (1.3)	213 (1.3)	214 (1.2)	216 (1.1)	215 (1.2)	214 (1.2)	218 (1.4)	65 (1.4)	33 (1.6)	8 (0.9)
South Dakota	— (†)	— (†)	— (†)	— (†)	222 (1.2)	222 (0.5)	223 (1.0)	222 (0.6)	220 (0.9)	218 (1.0)	220 (0.9)	68 (1.2)	35 (1.1)	8 (0.7)
Tennessee[7,9]	212 (1.4)	213 (1.7)	212 (1.4)	214 (1.2)	212 (1.6)	214 (1.4)	216 (1.2)	217 (1.2)	215 (1.1)	220 (1.4)	219 (1.4)	66 (1.7)	33 (1.7)	8 (1.0)
Texas	213 (1.6)	212 (1.9)	214 (1.9)	217 (1.7)	215 (1.0)	219 (0.8)	220 (0.9)	219 (1.2)	218 (1.5)	217 (1.1)	218 (1.7)	64 (1.9)	31 (1.9)	7 (0.9)
Utah	220 (1.1)	217 (1.3)	216 (1.2)	222 (1.0)	219 (1.0)	221 (1.0)	221 (1.2)	219 (1.0)	220 (1.0)	223 (1.1)	226 (1.1)	74 (1.1)	40 (1.5)	10 (1.1)
Vermont	— (†)	— (†)	— (†)	227 (1.1)	226 (0.9)	227 (0.9)	228 (0.8)	229 (0.8)	227 (0.6)	228 (0.6)	230 (0.8)	76 (1.0)	45 (1.4)	12 (0.9)
Virginia	221 (1.4)	213 (1.5)	217 (1.2)	225 (1.3)	223 (1.5)	226 (0.8)	227 (1.1)	227 (1.2)	226 (1.1)	229 (1.3)	229 (1.7)	74 (1.8)	43 (2.1)	14 (1.4)
Washington[7]	— (†)	213 1.5	218 (1.4)	224 (1.2)	221 (1.1)	223 (1.1)	224 (1.4)	221 (1.2)	221 (1.1)	225 (1.4)	226 (1.5)	71 (1.5)	40 (1.8)	12 (1.2)
West Virginia	216 (1.3)	213 (1.1)	216 (1.7)	219 (1.2)	219 (1.0)	215 (0.8)	215 (1.1)	215 (1.0)	214 (0.8)	215 (0.8)	216 (1.2)	64 (1.3)	30 (1.5)	6 (0.7)
Wisconsin[6,9]	224 (1.0)	224 (1.1)	222 (1.1)	‡ (†)	221 (0.8)	221 (1.0)	223 (1.2)	220 (1.1)	221 (0.8)	221 (1.6)	223 (1.1)	71 (1.4)	37 (1.5)	8 (0.7)
Wyoming	223 (1.1)	221 (1.2)	218 (1.5)	221 (1.0)	222 (0.8)	223 (0.7)	225 (0.5)	223 (0.7)	224 (0.8)	226 (0.6)	228 (0.7)	75 (1.0)	41 (1.2)	10 (0.7)
Department of Defense dependents schools[10]	— (†)	— (†)	220 (0.7)	224 (0.4)	224 (0.5)	226 (0.6)	229 (0.5)	228 (0.5)	229 (0.5)	232 (0.6)	234 (0.7)	83 (1.1)	47 (1.3)	9 (0.9)

—Not available.
†Not applicable.
‡Reporting standards not met. Participation rates fell below the required standards for reporting.
[1]Scale ranges from 0 to 500.
[2]Accommodations were not permitted for this assessment.
[3]*Basic* denotes partial mastery of the knowledge and skills that are fundamental for proficient work at the 4th-grade level.
[4]*Proficient* represents solid academic performance for 4th-graders. Students reaching this level have demonstrated competency over challenging subject matter.
[5]*Advanced* signifies superior performance.
[6]Did not meet one or more of the guidelines for school participation in 1998. Data are subject to appreciable nonresponse bias.
[7]Did not meet one or more of the guidelines for school participation in 2002. Data are subject to appreciable nonresponse bias.
[8]Did not meet one or more of the guidelines for school participation in 1992. Data are subject to appreciable nonresponse bias.
[9]Did not meet one or more of the guidelines for school participation in 1994. Data are subject to appreciable nonresponse bias.
[10]Prior to 2005, NAEP divided the Department of Defense (DoD) schools into two jurisdictions, domestic and overseas. In 2005, NAEP began combining the DoD domestic and overseas schools into a single jurisdiction. Data shown in this table for years prior to 2005 were recalculated for comparability.

NOTE: For 1998 and later years, includes public school students who were tested with accommodations; excludes only those students with disabilities (SD) and English language learners (ELL) who were unable to be tested even with accommodations. SD and ELL populations, accommodation rates, and exclusion rates vary from state to state. Some data have been revised from previously published estimates.

SOURCE: U.S. Department of Education, National Center for Education Statistics, National Assessment of Educational Progress (NAEP), 1992, 1994, 1998, 2002, 2003, 2005, 2007, 2009, 2011, 2013, and 2015 Reading Assessments, retrieved November 11, 2015, from the Main NAEP Data Explorer (http://nces.ed.gov/nationsreportcard/naepdata/). (This table was prepared November 2015.)

Table 221.50. Average National Assessment of Educational Progress (NAEP) reading scale score of 4th-grade public school students, by race/ethnicity, school's level of free or reduced-price lunch eligibility, and state: 2015

[Standard errors appear in parentheses]

State	Race/ethnicity							Percent of students in school eligible for free or reduced-price lunch			
	White	Black	Hispanic	Asian	Pacific Islander	American Indian/Alaska Native	Two or more races	0–25 percent eligible (low poverty)	26–50 percent eligible	51–75 percent eligible	76–100 percent eligible (high poverty)
1	2	3	4	5	6	7	8	9	10	11	12
United States	**232 (0.3)**	**206 (0.5)**	**208 (0.8)**	**240 (1.7)**	**212 (2.2)**	**206 (1.5)**	**226 (1.0)**	**241 (0.5)**	**228 (0.5)**	**219 (0.7)**	**205 (0.7)**
Alabama	226 (1.6)	204 (2.0)	199 (3.1)	‡ (†)	‡ (†)	‡ (†)	‡ (†)	232 (3.5)	226 (3.0)	218 (2.0)	205 (2.2)
Alaska	228 (1.6)	209 (5.4)	215 (3.0)	210 (3.8)	211 (5.0)	184 (3.4)	217 (3.1)	232 (2.4)	219 (2.0)	213 (3.3)	190 (4.7)
Arizona	229 (1.7)	217 (3.7)	204 (1.7)	‡ (†)	‡ (†)	191 (4.1)	‡ (†)	241 (3.2)	232 (2.7)	212 (3.0)	200 (1.7)
Arkansas	224 (1.2)	202 (2.2)	210 (2.9)	‡ (†)	‡ (†)	‡ (†)	‡ (†)	‡ (†)	227 (2.7)	219 (1.3)	209 (2.0)
California	231 (1.8)	198 (4.0)	201 (2.1)	237 (4.3)	‡ (†)	‡ (†)	228 (7.5)	243 (2.6)	220 (2.5)	212 (2.9)	197 (2.5)
Colorado	236 (1.4)	214 (5.0)	206 (1.9)	‡ (†)	‡ (†)	‡ (†)	232 (4.7)	243 (2.1)	225 (2.5)	222 (3.3)	201 (2.5)
Connecticut	240 (1.5)	205 (2.3)	210 (1.8)	235 (3.5)	‡ (†)	‡ (†)	‡ (†)	241 (1.8)	225 (2.2)	216 (2.9)	204 (2.5)
Delaware	236 (1.1)	210 (1.7)	210 (2.2)	240 (4.4)	‡ (†)	‡ (†)	229 (5.1)	246 (2.1)	229 (1.7)	223 (1.6)	210 (1.6)
District of Columbia	260 (2.3)	204 (1.0)	207 (2.8)	‡ (†)	‡ (†)	‡ (†)	‡ (†)	243 (2.1)	235 (4.0)	211 (3.6)	201 (1.2)
Florida	235 (1.5)	213 (1.9)	224 (1.4)	250 (3.2)	‡ (†)	‡ (†)	226 (3.1)	243 (2.2)	234 (2.5)	232 (1.5)	216 (1.7)
Georgia	232 (1.4)	212 (1.8)	211 (2.3)	241 (4.5)	‡ (†)	‡ (†)	222 (4.5)	243 (5.2)	232 (1.8)	224 (1.6)	211 (1.9)
Hawaii	233 (2.2)	‡ (†)	212 (4.2)	220 (1.4)	201 (1.5)	‡ (†)	225 (2.9)	241 (2.5)	221 (2.0)	211 (1.8)	195 (2.6)
Idaho	227 (1.0)	‡ (†)	200 (2.4)	‡ (†)	‡ (†)	‡ (†)	‡ (†)	232 (3.2)	230 (1.4)	218 (1.6)	207 (3.2)
Illinois	233 (1.5)	202 (2.2)	211 (1.5)	248 (4.5)	‡ (†)	‡ (†)	224 (4.4)	240 (3.2)	229 (2.5)	222 (2.4)	204 (2.4)
Indiana	231 (1.1)	212 (2.3)	216 (3.0)	‡ (†)	‡ (†)	‡ (†)	228 (4.3)	241 (1.8)	229 (1.5)	227 (1.6)	214 (2.8)
Iowa	228 (1.2)	195 (3.8)	209 (2.3)	233 (5.7)	‡ (†)	‡ (†)	227 (4.5)	239 (1.8)	226 (1.5)	216 (1.4)	205 (4.5)
Kansas	227 (1.4)	198 (5.4)	208 (1.9)	237 (5.4)	‡ (†)	‡ (†)	218 (4.3)	245 (2.9)	228 (1.9)	219 (1.6)	200 (2.3)
Kentucky	231 (1.3)	212 (2.4)	216 (2.8)	‡ (†)	‡ (†)	‡ (†)	225 (4.7)	‡ (†)	238 (2.0)	226 (1.4)	218 (1.3)
Louisiana	226 (1.6)	204 (1.8)	217 (4.3)	‡ (†)	‡ (†)	‡ (†)	‡ (†)	‡ (†)	229 (3.0)	223 (1.8)	210 (2.1)
Maine	225 (0.9)	196 (8.4)	‡ (†)	‡ (†)	‡ (†)	‡ (†)	‡ (†)	238 (2.1)	227 (1.4)	219 (1.5)	207 (4.8)
Maryland	235 (1.7)	208 (1.4)	210 (3.2)	238 (3.9)	‡ (†)	‡ (†)	236 (4.0)	242 (2.5)	228 (2.9)	213 (2.5)	202 (1.9)
Massachusetts	242 (1.1)	217 (2.9)	215 (1.8)	249 (3.9)	‡ (†)	‡ (†)	233 (4.3)	248 (1.6)	236 (2.0)	221 (5.2)	212 (2.5)
Michigan	221 (1.5)	192 (2.3)	206 (3.3)	236 (4.2)	‡ (†)	‡ (†)	223 (5.2)	233 (2.1)	222 (2.3)	212 (1.8)	198 (2.6)
Minnesota	232 (1.2)	195 (4.0)	199 (4.5)	222 (6.0)	‡ (†)	198 (6.8)	218 (4.0)	237 (2.3)	225 (1.8)	221 (2.5)	197 (4.8)
Mississippi	227 (1.2)	202 (1.4)	210 (3.9)	‡ (†)	‡ (†)	‡ (†)	‡ (†)	‡ (†)	230 (2.3)	218 (1.6)	206 (1.7)
Missouri	229 (1.1)	202 (3.0)	209 (4.6)	‡ (†)	‡ (†)	‡ (†)	215 (5.8)	239 (1.9)	228 (1.9)	221 (2.0)	207 (2.3)
Montana	229 (0.8)	‡ (†)	219 (3.9)	‡ (†)	‡ (†)	199 (3.1)	222 (3.3)	235 (1.7)	229 (1.3)	224 (1.9)	204 (2.5)
Nebraska	234 (1.0)	208 (3.1)	208 (2.1)	‡ (†)	‡ (†)	‡ (†)	219 (4.7)	240 (1.8)	228 (1.6)	226 (1.9)	210 (2.5)
Nevada	228 (1.9)	200 (2.9)	204 (1.5)	234 (3.6)	‡ (†)	‡ (†)	223 (3.6)	236 (2.7)	222 (2.2)	215 (3.0)	201 (2.2)
New Hampshire	233 (1.0)	‡ (†)	217 (3.1)	241 (3.5)	‡ (†)	‡ (†)	‡ (†)	238 (1.1)	229 (1.7)	218 (3.1)	‡ (†)
New Jersey	239 (1.7)	213 (2.3)	216 (2.7)	250 (3.7)	‡ (†)	‡ (†)	‡ (†)	243 (2.6)	229 (1.9)	218 (2.9)	210 (4.1)
New Mexico	225 (1.6)	‡ (†)	202 (1.2)	‡ (†)	‡ (†)	184 (4.9)	‡ (†)	‡ (†)	216 (2.7)	213 (1.9)	196 (2.1)
New York	234 (1.4)	208 (2.5)	209 (1.5)	236 (3.6)	‡ (†)	‡ (†)	‡ (†)	238 (2.6)	229 (2.9)	222 (2.7)	208 (2.4)
North Carolina	236 (1.3)	214 (1.6)	212 (2.0)	242 (5.2)	‡ (†)	198 (7.4)	228 (4.6)	245 (2.2)	233 (2.4)	221 (2.0)	213 (1.6)
North Dakota	229 (0.7)	208 (3.8)	205 (4.0)	‡ (†)	‡ (†)	204 (2.9)	‡ (†)	230 (1.1)	225 (1.1)	221 (2.5)	202 (3.9)
Ohio	230 (1.3)	205 (1.8)	210 (4.5)	‡ (†)	‡ (†)	‡ (†)	221 (3.8)	241 (2.3)	228 (1.4)	221 (2.0)	209 (2.8)
Oklahoma	226 (1.3)	205 (3.1)	213 (2.3)	‡ (†)	‡ (†)	223 (2.1)	225 (2.9)	242 (4.5)	227 (1.6)	223 (2.2)	212 (1.8)
Oregon	227 (1.4)	‡ (†)	202 (2.4)	232 (4.2)	‡ (†)	192 (7.5)	223 (3.4)	239 (2.4)	232 (3.0)	217 (2.1)	208 (2.2)
Pennsylvania	234 (1.4)	205 (2.8)	201 (2.9)	233 (5.9)	‡ (†)	‡ (†)	222 (4.7)	244 (1.8)	229 (1.7)	222 (2.4)	197 (3.0)
Rhode Island	234 (1.0)	215 (2.9)	207 (1.7)	223 (4.1)	‡ (†)	‡ (†)	221 (3.8)	240 (1.1)	231 (1.5)	224 (2.4)	205 (2.2)
South Carolina	230 (1.6)	200 (1.8)	203 (4.6)	‡ (†)	‡ (†)	‡ (†)	219 (4.9)	241 (3.3)	230 (2.9)	218 (2.0)	204 (2.0)
South Dakota	227 (1.0)	202 (5.4)	202 (4.0)	‡ (†)	‡ (†)	192 (3.2)	220 (3.8)	233 (1.5)	225 (1.3)	213 (2.7)	194 (2.9)
Tennessee	225 (1.6)	199 (2.2)	214 (3.5)	‡ (†)	‡ (†)	‡ (†)	225 (5.2)	236 (6.1)	235 (3.2)	216 (2.4)	204 (2.1)
Texas	235 (2.3)	205 (2.9)	210 (1.8)	248 (6.1)	‡ (†)	‡ (†)	225 (5.5)	241 (2.7)	229 (2.1)	218 (2.8)	206 (1.6)
Utah	231 (1.2)	‡ (†)	204 (2.3)	‡ (†)	‡ (†)	‡ (†)	‡ (†)	234 (1.5)	226 (2.5)	219 (3.0)	203 (3.5)
Vermont	231 (0.8)	‡ (†)	‡ (†)	‡ (†)	‡ (†)	‡ (†)	‡ (†)	239 (1.9)	233 (1.3)	225 (1.5)	211 (4.0)
Virginia	238 (1.5)	208 (2.6)	217 (3.1)	248 (3.8)	‡ (†)	‡ (†)	237 (3.7)	246 (2.3)	230 (3.0)	219 (2.0)	205 (3.6)
Washington	234 (1.6)	215 (4.2)	203 (2.0)	248 (3.7)	‡ (†)	198 (8.9)	225 (3.5)	243 (2.7)	231 (2.8)	217 (2.1)	207 (3.5)
West Virginia	217 (1.3)	210 (4.6)	‡ (†)	‡ (†)	‡ (†)	‡ (†)	211 (4.4)	‡ (†)	227 (2.1)	215 (1.8)	208 (2.1)
Wisconsin	231 (1.0)	193 (3.0)	209 (2.7)	222 (5.0)	‡ (†)	207 (7.1)	‡ (†)	238 (2.0)	228 (2.0)	214 (2.5)	198 (2.3)
Wyoming	232 (0.8)	‡ (†)	216 (1.9)	‡ (†)	‡ (†)	204 (4.5)	‡ (†)	233 (1.7)	231 (0.9)	221 (1.7)	214 (4.1)
Department of Defense dependents schools	237 (1.1)	228 (2.1)	228 (1.6)	236 (2.9)	‡ (†)	‡ (†)	237 (2.0)	237 (1.4)	234 (1.2)	228 (2.3)	‡ (†)

†Not applicable.
‡Reporting standards not met (too few cases for a reliable estimate).
NOTE: Scale ranges from 0 to 500. Includes public school students who were tested with accommodations; excludes only those students with disabilities (SD) and English language learners (ELL) who were unable to be tested even with accommodations. SD and ELL populations, accommodation rates, and exclusion rates vary from state to state. Race/ethnicity based on school records. Race categories exclude persons of Hispanic ethnicity.
SOURCE: U.S. Department of Education, National Center for Education Statistics, National Assessment of Educational Progress (NAEP), 2015 Reading Assessment, retrieved November 4, 2015, from the Main NAEP Data Explorer (http://nces.ed.gov/nationsreportcard/naepdata/). (This table was prepared November 2015.)

Table 221.60. Average National Assessment of Educational Progress (NAEP) reading scale score of 8th-grade public school students and percentage attaining reading achievement levels, by state: Selected years, 1998 through 2015

[Standard errors appear in parentheses]

State	Average scale score[1]									Percent attaining reading achievement levels, 2015		
	1998	2002	2003	2005	2007	2009	2011	2013	2015	At or above *Basic*[2]	At or above *Proficient*[3]	At *Advanced*[4]
1	2	3	4	5	6	7	8	9	10	11	12	13
United States	**261 (0.8)**	**263 (0.5)**	**261 (0.2)**	**260 (0.2)**	**261 (0.2)**	**262 (0.3)**	**264 (0.2)**	**266 (0.2)**	**264 (0.2)**	**75 (0.3)**	**33 (0.3)**	**3 (0.1)**
Alabama	255 (1.4)	253 (1.3)	253 (1.5)	252 (1.4)	252 (1.0)	255 (1.1)	258 (1.5)	257 (1.2)	259 (1.1)	71 (1.6)	26 (1.4)	2 (0.4)
Alaska	— (†)	— (†)	256 (1.1)	259 (0.9)	259 (1.0)	259 (0.9)	261 (0.9)	261 (0.8)	260 (1.1)	71 (1.4)	31 (1.5)	3 (0.4)
Arizona	260 (1.1)	257 (1.3)	255 (1.4)	255 (1.0)	255 (1.2)	258 (1.2)	260 (1.2)	260 (1.1)	263 (1.2)	74 (1.3)	31 (1.7)	2 (0.5)
Arkansas	256 (1.3)	260 (1.1)	258 (1.3)	258 (1.1)	258 (1.0)	258 (1.2)	259 (0.9)	262 (1.1)	259 (1.2)	70 (1.5)	27 (1.6)	2 (0.5)
California[5,6]	252 (1.6)	250 (1.8)	251 (1.3)	250 (0.6)	251 (0.8)	253 (1.2)	255 (1.0)	262 (1.2)	259 (1.2)	70 (1.4)	28 (1.5)	3 (0.4)
Colorado	264 (1.0)	— (†)	268 (1.2)	265 (1.1)	266 (1.0)	266 (0.8)	271 (1.4)	271 (1.1)	268 (1.4)	78 (1.3)	38 (2.0)	3 (0.6)
Connecticut	270 (1.0)	267 (1.2)	267 (1.1)	264 (1.3)	267 (1.6)	272 (0.9)	275 (0.9)	274 (1.0)	273 (1.1)	82 (1.0)	43 (1.7)	6 (0.9)
Delaware	254 (1.3)	267 (0.5)	265 (0.7)	266 (0.6)	265 (0.6)	265 (0.7)	266 (0.6)	266 (0.7)	263 (0.8)	73 (1.1)	31 (1.0)	3 (0.5)
District of Columbia	236 (2.1)	240 (0.9)	239 (0.8)	238 (0.9)	241 (0.7)	242 (0.9)	242 (0.9)	248 (0.9)	248 (1.0)	56 (1.4)	19 (1.0)	3 (0.5)
Florida	255 (1.4)	261 (1.6)	257 (1.3)	256 (1.2)	260 (1.2)	264 (1.2)	262 (1.0)	266 (1.1)	263 (1.0)	75 (1.1)	30 (1.4)	2 (0.4)
Georgia	257 (1.4)	258 (1.0)	258 (1.1)	257 (1.3)	259 (1.0)	260 (1.0)	262 (1.1)	265 (1.2)	262 (1.3)	73 (1.5)	30 (1.8)	3 (0.7)
Hawaii	249 (1.0)	252 (0.9)	251 (0.9)	249 (0.9)	251 (0.8)	255 (0.6)	257 (0.7)	260 (0.8)	257 (0.9)	68 (1.2)	26 (1.1)	2 (0.4)
Idaho	— (†)	266 (1.1)	264 (0.9)	264 (1.1)	265 (0.9)	265 (0.9)	268 (0.7)	270 (0.8)	269 (0.9)	81 (1.0)	37 (1.4)	3 (0.5)
Illinois	‡ (†)	‡ (†)	266 (1.0)	264 (1.0)	263 (1.0)	265 (1.2)	266 (0.8)	267 (1.0)	267 (1.0)	77 (1.1)	35 (1.5)	4 (0.7)
Indiana	— (†)	265 (1.3)	265 (1.0)	261 (1.1)	264 (1.1)	266 (1.0)	265 (1.0)	267 (1.2)	268 (1.1)	80 (1.1)	37 (1.6)	4 (0.6)
Iowa	— (†)	— (†)	268 (0.8)	267 (0.9)	267 (0.9)	265 (0.9)	265 (1.0)	269 (0.8)	268 (1.0)	81 (1.2)	36 (1.6)	3 (0.6)
Kansas[5,6]	268 (1.4)	269 (1.3)	266 (1.5)	267 (1.0)	267 (0.8)	267 (1.1)	267 (1.0)	267 (1.0)	267 (1.2)	79 (1.3)	35 (1.8)	3 (0.5)
Kentucky	262 (1.4)	265 (1.0)	266 (1.3)	264 (1.1)	262 (1.0)	267 (0.9)	269 (0.8)	270 (0.8)	268 (1.0)	78 (1.2)	36 (1.5)	4 (0.6)
Louisiana	252 (1.4)	256 (1.5)	253 (1.6)	253 (1.6)	253 (1.1)	253 (1.6)	255 (1.5)	257 (1.0)	255 (1.2)	66 (1.8)	23 (1.4)	2 (0.3)
Maine	271 (1.2)	270 (0.9)	268 (1.0)	270 (1.0)	270 (0.8)	268 (0.7)	270 (0.8)	269 (0.8)	268 (0.9)	81 (1.0)	36 (1.5)	2 (0.5)
Maryland[5]	261 (1.8)	263 (1.7)	262 (1.4)	261 (1.2)	265 (1.2)	267 (1.1)	271 (1.2)	274 (1.1)	268 (1.1)	76 (1.1)	37 (1.6)	5 (0.6)
Massachusetts	269 (1.4)	271 (1.3)	273 (1.0)	274 (1.0)	273 (1.0)	274 (1.2)	275 (1.0)	277 (1.0)	274 (1.1)	83 (1.2)	46 (1.5)	6 (0.8)
Michigan	— (†)	265 (1.6)	264 (1.8)	261 (1.2)	260 (1.2)	262 (1.4)	265 (0.9)	266 (1.0)	264 (1.2)	76 (1.3)	32 (1.6)	3 (0.5)
Minnesota[5]	265 (1.4)	‡ (†)	268 (1.1)	268 (1.2)	268 (0.9)	270 (1.0)	270 (1.0)	271 (1.0)	270 (1.1)	81 (1.1)	40 (1.5)	4 (0.8)
Mississippi	251 (1.2)	255 (0.9)	255 (1.4)	251 (1.3)	250 (1.1)	251 (1.0)	254 (1.2)	253 (1.0)	252 (1.0)	63 (1.5)	20 (1.1)	1 (0.3)
Missouri	262 (1.3)	268 (1.0)	267 (1.0)	265 (1.0)	263 (1.0)	267 (1.0)	267 (1.1)	267 (1.1)	267 (1.1)	77 (1.3)	36 (1.5)	3 (0.5)
Montana[5,6]	271 (1.3)	270 (1.0)	270 (1.0)	269 (0.7)	271 (0.8)	270 (0.6)	273 (0.6)	272 (0.8)	270 (0.8)	82 (1.0)	37 (1.4)	3 (0.5)
Nebraska	— (†)	270 (0.9)	266 (0.9)	267 (0.9)	267 (0.9)	267 (0.9)	268 (0.7)	269 (0.8)	269 (0.9)	81 (1.1)	38 (1.5)	3 (0.5)
Nevada	258 (1.0)	251 (0.8)	252 (0.8)	253 (0.9)	252 (0.8)	254 (0.9)	258 (0.9)	262 (0.7)	259 (0.9)	71 (1.2)	27 (1.4)	2 (0.4)
New Hampshire	— (†)	— (†)	271 (0.9)	270 (1.2)	270 (0.9)	271 (1.0)	272 (0.7)	274 (0.8)	275 (0.9)	85 (0.9)	45 (1.3)	5 (0.7)
New Jersey	— (†)	— (†)	268 (1.2)	269 (1.2)	270 (1.1)	273 (1.3)	275 (1.2)	276 (1.1)	271 (1.0)	80 (1.3)	41 (1.4)	6 (0.8)
New Mexico	258 (1.2)	254 (1.0)	252 (0.9)	251 (1.0)	251 (0.8)	254 (1.2)	256 (0.9)	256 (0.8)	253 (0.9)	65 (1.3)	20 (1.3)	1 (0.3)
New York[5,6]	265 (1.5)	264 (1.5)	265 (1.3)	265 (1.0)	264 (1.1)	264 (1.2)	266 (1.1)	266 (1.1)	263 (1.4)	73 (1.4)	33 (1.7)	4 (0.7)
North Carolina	262 (1.1)	265 (1.1)	262 (1.0)	258 (0.9)	259 (1.1)	260 (1.2)	263 (0.9)	265 (1.1)	261 (1.3)	72 (1.4)	30 (1.6)	3 (0.6)
North Dakota[6]	— (†)	268 (0.8)	270 (0.8)	270 (0.6)	268 (0.7)	269 (0.6)	269 (0.7)	268 (0.6)	267 (0.6)	80 (0.9)	34 (1.1)	2 (0.4)
Ohio	— (†)	268 (1.6)	267 (1.3)	267 (1.3)	268 (1.2)	269 (1.3)	268 (1.1)	269 (1.0)	266 (1.5)	76 (1.7)	36 (1.7)	4 (0.5)
Oklahoma	265 (1.2)	262 (0.8)	262 (0.9)	260 (1.1)	260 (0.8)	259 (0.9)	260 (1.1)	262 (0.9)	263 (1.3)	76 (1.5)	29 (1.6)	2 (0.4)
Oregon[6]	266 (1.5)	268 (1.3)	264 (1.2)	263 (1.1)	266 (0.9)	265 (1.0)	264 (0.9)	268 (0.9)	268 (1.3)	79 (1.2)	36 (1.8)	4 (0.7)
Pennsylvania	— (†)	265 (1.0)	264 (1.2)	267 (1.3)	268 (1.2)	271 (0.8)	268 (1.3)	272 (1.0)	269 (1.5)	78 (1.6)	39 (2.0)	5 (0.7)
Rhode Island	264 (0.9)	262 (0.8)	261 (0.7)	261 (0.7)	258 (0.9)	260 (0.6)	265 (0.7)	267 (0.6)	265 (0.7)	76 (0.9)	35 (1.2)	4 (0.6)
South Carolina	255 (1.1)	258 (1.1)	258 (1.3)	257 (1.1)	257 (0.9)	257 (1.2)	260 (0.9)	261 (1.0)	260 (1.2)	71 (1.5)	28 (1.5)	2 (0.4)
South Dakota	— (†)	— (†)	270 (0.8)	269 (0.6)	270 (0.7)	270 (0.5)	269 (0.8)	268 (0.8)	267 (1.0)	80 (1.4)	34 (1.3)	2 (0.4)
Tennessee[6]	258 (1.2)	260 (1.4)	258 (1.2)	259 (0.9)	259 (1.0)	261 (1.1)	259 (1.0)	265 (1.1)	265 (1.4)	76 (1.5)	33 (1.8)	3 (0.7)
Texas	261 (1.4)	262 (1.4)	259 (1.1)	258 (0.6)	261 (0.9)	260 (1.1)	261 (1.0)	264 (1.1)	261 (1.0)	72 (1.1)	28 (1.6)	2 (0.4)
Utah	263 (1.0)	263 (1.1)	264 (0.8)	262 (0.8)	262 (1.0)	266 (0.8)	267 (0.8)	270 (0.9)	269 (1.0)	81 (1.2)	38 (1.4)	4 (0.6)
Vermont	— (†)	272 (0.9)	271 (0.8)	269 (0.7)	273 (0.8)	272 (0.6)	274 (0.9)	274 (0.7)	274 (0.8)	83 (1.0)	44 (1.4)	6 (0.7)
Virginia	266 (1.1)	269 (1.0)	268 (1.1)	268 (1.0)	267 (1.1)	266 (1.1)	267 (1.2)	268 (1.3)	267 (1.2)	77 (1.2)	36 (1.8)	3 (0.6)
Washington[6]	264 (1.2)	268 (1.2)	264 (0.9)	265 (1.3)	265 (0.9)	267 (1.1)	268 (1.0)	272 (1.0)	267 (1.2)	77 (1.2)	37 (1.6)	4 (0.6)
West Virginia	262 (1.0)	264 (1.0)	260 (1.0)	255 (1.2)	255 (1.0)	255 (0.9)	256 (0.9)	257 (0.9)	260 (0.9)	72 (1.3)	27 (1.3)	2 (0.5)
Wisconsin[5]	265 (1.8)	‡ (†)	266 (1.3)	266 (1.1)	264 (1.0)	266 (1.0)	267 (0.9)	268 (0.9)	270 (1.1)	79 (1.1)	39 (1.7)	4 (0.7)
Wyoming	263 (1.3)	265 (0.7)	267 (0.5)	268 (0.7)	266 (0.7)	268 (1.0)	270 (1.0)	271 (0.6)	269 (0.7)	81 (1.0)	36 (1.2)	3 (0.5)
Department of Defense dependents schools[7]	269 (1.3)	273 (0.5)	272 (0.6)	271 (0.7)	273 (1.0)	272 (0.7)	272 (0.7)	277 (0.7)	277 (0.7)	90 (0.9)	47 (1.6)	3 (0.7)

—Not available.
†Not applicable.
‡Reporting standards not met. Either there are too few cases for a reliable estimate or item response rates fell below the required standards for reporting.
[1]Scale ranges from 0 to 500.
[2]*Basic* denotes partial mastery of the knowledge and skills that are fundamental for proficient work at the 8th-grade level.
[3]*Proficient* represents solid academic performance for 8th-graders. Students reaching this level have demonstrated competency over challenging subject matter.
[4]*Advanced* signifies superior performance.
[5]Did not meet one or more of the guidelines for school participation in 1998. Data are subject to appreciable nonresponse bias.
[6]Did not meet one or more of the guidelines for school participation in 2002. Data are subject to appreciable nonresponse bias.
[7]Prior to 2005, NAEP divided the Department of Defense (DoD) schools into two jurisdictions, domestic and overseas. In 2005, NAEP began combining the DoD domestic and overseas schools into a single jurisdiction. Data shown in this table for years prior to 2005 were recalculated for comparability.
NOTE: Includes public school students who were tested with accommodations; excludes only those students with disabilities (SD) and English language learners (ELL) who were unable to be tested even with accommodations. SD and ELL populations, accommodation rates, and exclusion rates vary from state to state. Some data have been revised from previously published figures.
SOURCE: U.S. Department of Education, National Center for Education Statistics, National Assessment of Educational Progress (NAEP), 1998, 2002, 2003, 2005, 2007, 2009, 2011, 2013, and 2015 Reading Assessments, retrieved November 11, 2015, from the Main NAEP Data Explorer (http://nces.ed.gov/nationsreportcard/naepdata/). (This table was prepared November 2015.)

Table 221.65. Average National Assessment of Educational Progress (NAEP) reading scale score of 8th-grade public school students, by race/ethnicity, parent's highest level of education, and state: 2015

[Standard errors appear in parentheses]

State	Race/ethnicity							Highest level of education attained by either parent[1]			
	White	Black	Hispanic	Asian	Pacific Islander	American Indian/ Alaska Native	Two or more races	Did not finish high school	Graduated high school	Some education after high school	Graduated college
1	2	3	4	5	6	7	8	9	10	11	12
United States	**273 (0.2)**	**247 (0.5)**	**253 (0.4)**	**280 (1.4)**	**254 (2.4)**	**253 (1.7)**	**267 (1.0)**	**249 (0.6)**	**253 (0.4)**	**267 (0.5)**	**274 (0.3)**
Alabama	267 (1.0)	243 (2.0)	252 (3.9)	‡ (†)	‡ (†)	‡ (†)	‡ (†)	250 (2.9)	246 (2.0)	265 (2.2)	268 (1.4)
Alaska	276 (1.3)	248 (4.1)	263 (3.0)	260 (3.0)	242 (4.0)	231 (2.3)	270 (3.1)	‡ (†)	‡ (†)	‡ (†)	‡ (†)
Arizona	276 (1.4)	249 (4.0)	254 (1.3)	‡ (†)	‡ (†)	244 (4.4)	‡ (†)	254 (2.4)	254 (1.9)	267 (1.8)	274 (1.5)
Arkansas	266 (1.6)	238 (1.9)	255 (2.7)	‡ (†)	‡ (†)	‡ (†)	‡ (†)	252 (2.4)	249 (2.0)	262 (2.0)	268 (1.9)
California	274 (1.6)	248 (2.6)	249 (1.2)	279 (3.5)	‡ (†)	‡ (†)	263 (6.4)	246 (2.3)	249 (1.8)	266 (2.4)	273 (1.5)
Colorado	277 (1.7)	255 (3.8)	253 (1.7)	290 (4.0)	‡ (†)	‡ (†)	272 (5.1)	244 (2.7)	254 (2.4)	269 (2.4)	280 (1.5)
Connecticut	282 (1.3)	251 (2.5)	256 (2.6)	282 (3.9)	‡ (†)	‡ (†)	‡ (†)	249 (4.1)	260 (2.4)	271 (2.5)	282 (1.1)
Delaware	273 (1.1)	249 (1.4)	253 (2.3)	284 (5.3)	‡ (†)	‡ (†)	‡ (†)	249 (2.6)	248 (2.2)	272 (2.0)	271 (1.3)
District of Columbia	299 (3.2)	242 (1.1)	249 (2.9)	‡ (†)	‡ (†)	‡ (†)	‡ (†)	238 (3.4)	236 (1.9)	253 (2.6)	259 (1.6)
Florida	272 (1.1)	251 (1.8)	260 (1.3)	283 (4.9)	‡ (†)	‡ (†)	261 (5.3)	255 (2.4)	257 (1.7)	265 (1.5)	271 (1.2)
Georgia	273 (1.7)	248 (1.7)	257 (2.1)	281 (5.4)	‡ (†)	‡ (†)	279 (6.0)	249 (3.0)	255 (1.6)	269 (2.0)	269 (2.0)
Hawaii	270 (2.3)	258 (4.2)	258 (3.1)	263 (1.2)	245 (1.3)	‡ (†)	264 (3.1)	249 (4.8)	244 (1.6)	260 (1.6)	266 (1.3)
Idaho	273 (1.0)	‡ (†)	253 (2.3)	‡ (†)	‡ (†)	‡ (†)	‡ (†)	253 (3.3)	254 (1.9)	274 (2.0)	277 (1.1)
Illinois	276 (1.3)	247 (1.5)	257 (1.8)	290 (3.4)	‡ (†)	‡ (†)	‡ (†)	253 (3.2)	256 (1.8)	269 (1.8)	276 (1.3)
Indiana	272 (1.3)	252 (2.5)	257 (3.0)	‡ (†)	‡ (†)	‡ (†)	260 (4.7)	255 (3.1)	258 (1.9)	272 (1.9)	277 (1.5)
Iowa	271 (1.1)	245 (3.1)	256 (2.7)	‡ (†)	‡ (†)	‡ (†)	‡ (†)	250 (3.6)	254 (1.8)	270 (2.4)	275 (1.3)
Kansas	272 (1.2)	246 (3.8)	254 (2.6)	‡ (†)	‡ (†)	‡ (†)	258 (4.0)	255 (3.1)	255 (2.9)	267 (1.9)	276 (1.2)
Kentucky	271 (1.2)	247 (2.0)	266 (3.0)	275 (7.7)	‡ (†)	‡ (†)	261 (5.6)	251 (2.4)	260 (1.7)	270 (1.8)	277 (1.4)
Louisiana	266 (1.5)	243 (1.6)	258 (3.6)	‡ (†)	‡ (†)	‡ (†)	‡ (†)	245 (3.0)	248 (2.1)	263 (1.8)	261 (1.4)
Maine	269 (0.9)	246 (4.7)	‡ (†)	‡ (†)	‡ (†)	‡ (†)	‡ (†)	‡ (†)	257 (2.0)	271 (1.8)	275 (0.9)
Maryland	279 (1.4)	251 (1.5)	258 (2.3)	292 (4.3)	‡ (†)	‡ (†)	275 (4.2)	251 (3.6)	255 (2.1)	264 (2.0)	277 (1.3)
Massachusetts	281 (0.9)	252 (2.6)	249 (2.3)	290 (3.3)	‡ (†)	‡ (†)	279 (5.0)	248 (2.9)	260 (2.4)	272 (1.9)	284 (1.2)
Michigan	270 (1.1)	243 (1.8)	263 (3.7)	282 (3.6)	‡ (†)	‡ (†)	‡ (†)	249 (4.5)	252 (1.7)	263 (1.7)	272 (1.3)
Minnesota	276 (1.2)	247 (3.0)	260 (3.3)	264 (3.8)	‡ (†)	250 (5.9)	260 (5.1)	242 (4.2)	253 (2.7)	271 (2.0)	279 (1.2)
Mississippi	266 (1.0)	240 (1.4)	‡ (†)	‡ (†)	‡ (†)	‡ (†)	‡ (†)	243 (3.1)	244 (1.8)	258 (2.0)	258 (1.6)
Missouri	271 (1.1)	246 (2.0)	258 (4.8)	‡ (†)	‡ (†)	‡ (†)	‡ (†)	254 (3.5)	258 (2.1)	272 (2.2)	274 (1.3)
Montana	273 (0.9)	‡ (†)	257 (3.9)	‡ (†)	‡ (†)	249 (2.2)	‡ (†)	256 (3.1)	260 (1.7)	269 (1.9)	278 (1.0)
Nebraska	275 (1.0)	245 (3.5)	257 (1.9)	‡ (†)	‡ (†)	‡ (†)	‡ (†)	257 (2.9)	253 (2.5)	269 (2.4)	278 (1.2)
Nevada	270 (1.6)	249 (2.4)	250 (1.1)	276 (3.1)	‡ (†)	‡ (†)	265 (4.0)	247 (2.2)	254 (1.9)	269 (1.9)	270 (1.4)
New Hampshire	275 (0.8)	‡ (†)	262 (4.6)	290 (6.5)	‡ (†)	‡ (†)	‡ (†)	252 (4.2)	264 (2.3)	276 (2.1)	281 (1.1)
New Jersey	278 (1.3)	253 (2.3)	254 (2.0)	294 (2.5)	‡ (†)	‡ (†)	‡ (†)	253 (4.7)	256 (2.5)	272 (2.1)	279 (1.3)
New Mexico	268 (1.5)	‡ (†)	249 (1.0)	‡ (†)	‡ (†)	243 (3.1)	‡ (†)	241 (2.4)	245 (1.8)	259 (1.9)	263 (1.3)
New York	273 (1.6)	248 (2.1)	254 (2.0)	272 (3.0)	‡ (†)	‡ (†)	‡ (†)	247 (3.2)	251 (2.1)	264 (2.2)	274 (1.6)
North Carolina	271 (1.6)	243 (2.0)	252 (1.9)	279 (4.8)	‡ (†)	250 (6.4)	269 (4.5)	245 (2.6)	249 (2.1)	263 (2.4)	272 (1.6)
North Dakota	270 (0.6)	255 (2.9)	261 (3.4)	‡ (†)	‡ (†)	245 (3.0)	‡ (†)	249 (3.8)	257 (1.9)	266 (2.2)	273 (0.8)
Ohio	271 (1.2)	245 (3.2)	255 (6.0)	272 (19.6)	‡ (†)	‡ (†)	260 (4.9)	244 (5.2)	253 (2.0)	265 (2.1)	277 (1.4)
Oklahoma	268 (1.3)	244 (3.2)	257 (1.9)	‡ (†)	‡ (†)	261 (2.4)	263 (4.0)	248 (3.3)	255 (1.9)	268 (1.6)	270 (1.5)
Oregon	274 (1.4)	‡ (†)	252 (1.9)	274 (4.8)	‡ (†)	‡ (†)	272 (3.7)	252 (2.5)	259 (2.5)	272 (2.2)	278 (1.5)
Pennsylvania	276 (1.3)	245 (2.7)	250 (4.2)	291 (5.3)	‡ (†)	‡ (†)	260 (4.5)	250 (3.8)	257 (1.9)	267 (2.4)	279 (1.5)
Rhode Island	275 (1.0)	248 (3.0)	245 (1.5)	279 (5.9)	‡ (†)	‡ (†)	266 (4.8)	247 (3.0)	253 (2.0)	268 (1.9)	277 (1.0)
South Carolina	271 (1.6)	244 (1.6)	249 (3.6)	‡ (†)	‡ (†)	‡ (†)	267 (4.8)	248 (3.0)	252 (2.0)	263 (2.1)	268 (1.5)
South Dakota	271 (0.9)	259 (3.7)	260 (3.1)	‡ (†)	‡ (†)	247 (2.2)	‡ (†)	254 (3.2)	257 (2.2)	269 (2.4)	273 (1.1)
Tennessee	270 (1.5)	247 (2.3)	257 (3.2)	‡ (†)	‡ (†)	‡ (†)	‡ (†)	247 (2.9)	254 (1.7)	267 (1.6)	275 (1.7)
Texas	274 (1.7)	251 (2.2)	252 (1.2)	284 (3.9)	‡ (†)	‡ (†)	274 (5.2)	251 (2.0)	252 (1.9)	265 (1.7)	271 (1.3)
Utah	274 (1.1)	‡ (†)	252 (2.4)	‡ (†)	‡ (†)	247 (7.1)	270 (4.9)	‡ (†)	‡ (†)	‡ (†)	‡ (†)
Vermont	275 (0.8)	‡ (†)	‡ (†)	‡ (†)	‡ (†)	‡ (†)	‡ (†)	‡ (†)	255 (2.3)	277 (2.2)	284 (1.0)
Virginia	274 (1.6)	249 (2.1)	257 (2.7)	287 (3.1)	‡ (†)	‡ (†)	267 (3.1)	249 (3.0)	252 (1.9)	265 (2.2)	278 (1.5)
Washington	275 (1.2)	250 (4.6)	250 (2.1)	282 (2.8)	‡ (†)	251 (4.5)	262 (3.2)	252 (2.6)	257 (2.5)	271 (1.7)	279 (1.4)
West Virginia	261 (1.0)	250 (3.1)	‡ (†)	‡ (†)	‡ (†)	‡ (†)	‡ (†)	248 (3.4)	248 (1.6)	264 (1.9)	269 (1.2)
Wisconsin	275 (1.2)	241 (2.6)	255 (2.4)	271 (6.0)	‡ (†)	253 (6.8)	‡ (†)	243 (4.4)	253 (2.2)	269 (2.1)	278 (1.4)
Wyoming	272 (0.7)	‡ (†)	258 (2.2)	‡ (†)	‡ (†)	‡ (†)	‡ (†)	252 (2.6)	257 (1.9)	269 (1.9)	278 (1.1)
Department of Defense dependents schools	281 (1.4)	273 (1.9)	273 (1.8)	274 (3.7)	‡ (†)	‡ (†)	279 (2.6)	‡ (†)	268 (2.4)	279 (2.1)	281 (1.0)

†Not applicable.

‡Reporting standards not met. Either there are too few cases for a reliable estimate or item response rates fell below the required standards for reporting.

[1]Excludes students who responded "I don't know" to the question about educational level of parents.

NOTE: Scale ranges from 0 to 500. Includes public school students who were tested with accommodations; excludes only those students with disabilities (SD) and English language learners (ELL) who were unable to be tested even with accommodations. SD and ELL populations, accommodation rates, and exclusion rates vary from state to state. Race/ethnicity based on school records. Race categories exclude persons of Hispanic ethnicity.

SOURCE: U.S. Department of Education, National Center for Education Statistics, National Assessment of Educational Progress (NAEP), 2015 Reading Assessment, retrieved November 13, 2015, from the Main NAEP Data Explorer (http://nces.ed.gov/nationsreportcard/naepdata/). (This table was prepared November 2015.)

Table 221.70. Average National Assessment of Educational Progress (NAEP) reading scale scores of 4th- and 8th-graders in public schools and percentage scoring at or above selected reading achievement levels, by English language learner (ELL) status and state: 2015

[Standard errors appear in parentheses]

State	4th-graders							8th-graders						
	English language learners				Not English language learners			English language learners				Not English language learners		
	Percent of all students assessed	Average scale score[1]	Percent At or above *Basic*[2]	Percent At or above *Proficient*[3]	Average scale score[1]	Percent At or above *Basic*[2]	Percent At or above *Proficient*[3]	Percent of all students assessed	Average scale score[1]	Percent At or above *Basic*[2]	Percent At or above *Proficient*[3]	Average scale score[1]	Percent At or above *Basic*[2]	Percent At or above *Proficient*[3]
1	2	3	4	5	6	7	8	9	10	11	12	13	14	15
United States	**11 (0.3)**	**189 (1.1)**	**32 (1.2)**	**8 (0.6)**	**225 (0.3)**	**72 (0.3)**	**38 (0.4)**	**6 (0.2)**	**223 (0.9)**	**28 (1.2)**	**3 (0.4)**	**267 (0.2)**	**78 (0.3)**	**35 (0.4)**
Alabama	2 (0.3)	‡ (†)	‡ (†)	‡ (†)	218 (1.3)	65 (1.8)	29 (1.7)	1 (0.2)	‡ (†)	‡ (†)	‡ (†)	259 (1.1)	72 (1.6)	26 (1.4)
Alaska	15 (1.0)	165 (4.3)	19 (2.9)	4 (1.2)	221 (1.1)	69 (1.4)	34 (1.6)	11 (1.0)	211 (2.8)	18 (3.7)	1 (0.6)	266 (1.2)	77 (1.4)	35 (1.8)
Arizona	10 (0.8)	165 (3.8)	12 (2.7)	1 (#)	221 (1.3)	67 (1.6)	33 (1.6)	4 (0.6)	206 (4.1)	8 (3.1)	# (†)	265 (1.2)	76 (1.4)	32 (1.8)
Arkansas	8 (1.1)	204 (3.1)	50 (4.3)	16 (3.4)	219 (1.1)	66 (1.4)	33 (1.5)	7 (0.7)	245 (2.6)	56 (4.4)	11 (2.8)	260 (1.3)	71 (1.4)	28 (1.7)
California	28 (1.7)	183 (2.7)	27 (2.9)	6 (1.1)	224 (1.4)	71 (1.7)	36 (2.0)	14 (0.9)	215 (2.4)	21 (2.7)	2 (0.9)	266 (1.2)	78 (1.4)	33 (1.7)
Colorado	14 (1.2)	185 (2.3)	29 (3.1)	5 (1.5)	230 (1.4)	77 (1.5)	44 (1.9)	11 (0.8)	229 (2.7)	33 (4.1)	3 (1.4)	273 (1.4)	84 (1.3)	43 (2.1)
Connecticut	7 (0.6)	190 (3.2)	33 (4.8)	7 (2.4)	232 (1.1)	77 (1.2)	46 (1.6)	3 (0.4)	217 (6.1)	24 (6.6)	2 (#)	275 (1.0)	84 (1.0)	45 (1.7)
Delaware	5 (0.4)	177 (4.1)	23 (5.1)	4 (2.2)	226 (0.8)	72 (1.2)	39 (1.3)	2 (0.2)	‡ (†)	‡ (†)	‡ (†)	263 (0.8)	74 (1.2)	32 (1.0)
District of Columbia	6 (0.3)	177 (4.5)	20 (4.7)	3 (#)	214 (0.9)	58 (1.2)	29 (1.0)	5 (0.4)	218 (4.1)	26 (6.3)	3 (#)	249 (1.0)	57 (1.4)	19 (1.0)
Florida	9 (0.7)	201 (1.8)	41 (3.5)	9 (1.6)	230 (1.1)	78 (1.3)	42 (1.6)	5 (0.4)	226 (2.9)	30 (4.9)	2 (1.1)	265 (0.9)	77 (1.1)	32 (1.4)
Georgia	5 (1.0)	188 (4.2)	23 (6.6)	5 (#)	224 (1.2)	70 (1.5)	35 (1.6)	3 (0.4)	233 (4.8)	42 (6.5)	6 (3.9)	263 (1.3)	74 (1.5)	31 (1.8)
Hawaii	7 (0.5)	164 (4.3)	12 (4.1)	2 (1.1)	219 (1.0)	65 (1.2)	31 (1.2)	6 (0.4)	214 (3.0)	17 (4.0)	1 (#)	260 (0.9)	71 (1.2)	27 (1.2)
Idaho	4 (0.4)	160 (4.8)	8 (3.9)	# (†)	225 (1.0)	72 (1.4)	38 (1.4)	2 (0.3)	‡ (†)	‡ (†)	‡ (†)	270 (0.9)	83 (0.9)	38 (1.4)
Illinois	10 (1.1)	184 (2.7)	25 (3.1)	4 (1.7)	226 (1.3)	73 (1.5)	39 (1.6)	5 (0.5)	219 (3.1)	26 (5.5)	3 (#)	269 (1.0)	80 (1.2)	37 (1.5)
Indiana	7 (1.0)	199 (3.6)	42 (4.4)	14 (4.2)	230 (1.1)	77 (1.4)	42 (1.7)	5 (0.6)	249 (3.8)	61 (7.2)	13 (4.1)	269 (1.1)	80 (1.0)	38 (1.7)
Iowa	7 (1.0)	197 (3.0)	42 (4.1)	11 (3.0)	226 (1.2)	74 (1.5)	40 (1.7)	4 (0.5)	235 (3.6)	44 (6.1)	6 (2.4)	270 (1.1)	82 (1.3)	37 (1.6)
Kansas	13 (1.2)	201 (3.0)	45 (4.2)	15 (2.8)	224 (1.5)	71 (1.6)	38 (1.9)	11 (0.8)	250 (4.1)	61 (4.9)	18 (4.7)	269 (1.1)	81 (1.1)	37 (1.8)
Kentucky	3 (0.3)	201 (5.4)	40 (8.1)	13 (6.1)	229 (1.3)	75 (1.3)	41 (1.6)	1 (0.2)	236 (6.2)	42 (8.9)	5 (3.3)	268 (1.0)	78 (1.1)	37 (1.5)
Louisiana	2 (0.4)	‡ (†)	‡ (†)	‡ (†)	217 (1.5)	64 (1.8)	29 (1.6)	1 (0.2)	‡ (†)	‡ (†)	‡ (†)	256 (1.2)	66 (1.8)	23 (1.4)
Maine	3 (0.3)	186 (8.3)	33 (7.9)	6 (3.7)	225 (0.9)	72 (1.2)	37 (1.3)	3 (0.3)	239 (5.1)	45 (7.1)	11 (5.0)	269 (0.9)	82 (1.0)	36 (1.5)
Maryland	8 (1.4)	193 (4.1)	35 (5.5)	7 (2.2)	225 (1.3)	70 (1.5)	39 (1.8)	2 (0.3)	232 (4.8)	36 (9.0)	7 (4.3)	269 (1.1)	77 (1.1)	38 (1.6)
Massachusetts	9 (0.8)	200 (2.7)	44 (3.8)	12 (2.5)	239 (1.0)	85 (1.1)	53 (1.5)	5 (0.6)	225 (3.8)	35 (5.5)	6 (2.8)	277 (1.0)	86 (1.1)	48 (1.5)
Michigan	4 (0.8)	202 (4.9)	48 (6.5)	16 (4.8)	217 (1.4)	64 (1.8)	29 (1.6)	3 (0.6)	237 (4.0)	43 (7.1)	6 (4.4)	265 (1.2)	77 (1.4)	33 (1.6)
Minnesota	10 (0.9)	179 (4.8)	28 (4.5)	6 (2.3)	228 (1.1)	75 (1.3)	42 (1.5)	6 (0.7)	234 (3.5)	43 (5.2)	6 (2.6)	273 (1.0)	84 (1.1)	42 (1.5)
Mississippi	2 (0.4)	‡ (†)	‡ (†)	‡ (†)	214 (1.0)	61 (1.4)	26 (1.3)	1 (0.2)	‡ (†)	‡ (†)	‡ (†)	253 (1.0)	63 (1.5)	20 (1.1)
Missouri	3 (0.4)	203 (4.4)	50 (7.7)	14 (5.6)	223 (1.2)	70 (1.3)	37 (1.5)	2 (0.4)	‡ (†)	‡ (†)	‡ (†)	268 (1.1)	78 (1.3)	37 (1.5)
Montana	3 (0.3)	175 (5.8)	17 (6.1)	1 (#)	226 (0.8)	74 (1.2)	38 (1.2)	2 (0.2)	‡ (†)	‡ (†)	‡ (†)	271 (0.8)	83 (1.0)	37 (1.4)
Nebraska	7 (0.7)	193 (3.1)	32 (4.6)	7 (2.7)	229 (1.0)	77 (1.3)	42 (1.5)	2 (0.3)	‡ (†)	‡ (†)	‡ (†)	270 (0.9)	83 (1.1)	39 (1.5)
Nevada	24 (1.1)	190 (1.8)	33 (2.1)	8 (1.5)	222 (1.2)	70 (1.5)	36 (1.5)	15 (0.6)	226 (1.8)	30 (2.7)	3 (1.2)	265 (1.1)	78 (1.3)	32 (1.6)
New Hampshire	3 (0.3)	206 (4.4)	51 (6.2)	19 (6.4)	233 (0.9)	80 (1.1)	47 (1.5)	1 (0.2)	‡ (†)	‡ (†)	‡ (†)	275 (0.9)	85 (1.0)	45 (1.3)
New Jersey	3 (0.6)	‡ (†)	‡ (†)	‡ (†)	231 (1.5)	77 (1.5)	44 (1.8)	2 (0.3)	‡ (†)	‡ (†)	‡ (†)	272 (1.0)	81 (1.2)	41 (1.4)
New Mexico	16 (0.7)	171 (2.9)	18 (2.3)	4 (1.2)	214 (0.9)	61 (1.4)	27 (1.3)	13 (0.7)	219 (1.9)	22 (3.1)	2 (1.0)	258 (0.9)	72 (1.4)	23 (1.4)
New York	7 (0.8)	184 (3.1)	26 (3.5)	5 (2.0)	226 (1.0)	72 (1.3)	38 (1.5)	6 (0.6)	215 (3.2)	22 (4.3)	3 (1.4)	266 (1.3)	76 (1.3)	35 (1.7)
North Carolina	6 (0.5)	187 (3.0)	29 (4.7)	5 (2.1)	229 (1.1)	76 (1.4)	41 (1.6)	4 (0.5)	217 (4.0)	25 (5.0)	1 (#)	263 (1.3)	74 (1.4)	32 (1.7)
North Dakota	2 (0.2)	‡ (†)	‡ (†)	‡ (†)	226 (0.7)	74 (1.0)	37 (1.0)	2 (0.2)	‡ (†)	‡ (†)	‡ (†)	268 (0.6)	81 (1.0)	34 (1.1)
Ohio	4 (0.7)	202 (4.8)	49 (7.0)	12 (5.2)	226 (1.2)	73 (1.3)	39 (1.7)	3 (1.5)	227 (11.8)	31 (14.2)	7 (#)	267 (1.3)	77 (1.6)	36 (1.6)
Oklahoma	6 (0.5)	197 (4.4)	42 (7.0)	9 (3.4)	224 (1.1)	73 (1.3)	34 (1.5)	5 (0.7)	239 (3.3)	47 (5.6)	7 (3.5)	264 (1.3)	77 (1.6)	31 (1.8)
Oregon	13 (1.0)	180 (3.1)	26 (3.5)	3 (1.2)	226 (1.2)	74 (1.4)	39 (1.6)	3 (0.3)	207 (5.6)	11 (5.2)	1 (#)	269 (1.2)	81 (1.2)	37 (1.9)
Pennsylvania	3 (0.5)	170 (5.5)	16 (4.4)	3 (#)	229 (1.6)	76 (1.8)	43 (1.9)	2 (0.4)	218 (6.7)	20 (7.2)	6 (3.5)	270 (1.4)	79 (1.5)	40 (2.0)
Rhode Island	7 (0.5)	182 (3.3)	25 (3.6)	5 (2.1)	229 (0.9)	76 (1.1)	43 (1.4)	5 (0.3)	209 (3.8)	17 (5.1)	1 (#)	268 (0.7)	78 (0.9)	36 (1.3)
South Carolina	8 (1.0)	201 (4.7)	47 (5.1)	21 (3.9)	219 (1.3)	66 (1.4)	35 (1.6)	4 (0.5)	242 (4.3)	48 (7.6)	11 (3.8)	261 (1.2)	72 (1.4)	29 (1.6)
South Dakota	3 (0.2)	170 (7.5)	20 (6.0)	5 (2.8)	222 (0.9)	69 (1.2)	35 (1.2)	2 (0.3)	‡ (†)	‡ (†)	‡ (†)	268 (1.0)	81 (1.3)	35 (1.3)
Tennessee	4 (0.6)	200 (5.1)	47 (7.1)	16 (5.2)	219 (1.4)	66 (1.8)	34 (1.7)	2 (0.4)	‡ (†)	‡ (†)	‡ (†)	266 (1.3)	77 (1.4)	33 (1.8)
Texas	22 (1.9)	198 (2.1)	41 (3.3)	12 (2.2)	224 (1.8)	70 (1.9)	36 (2.2)	11 (0.6)	224 (2.2)	29 (3.3)	2 (1.2)	265 (1.2)	78 (1.3)	31 (1.8)
Utah	4 (0.5)	174 (6.3)	19 (5.5)	8 (3.5)	228 (1.0)	77 (1.0)	41 (1.5)	3 (0.4)	213 (4.6)	16 (6.1)	1 (#)	271 (0.9)	83 (1.1)	39 (1.4)
Vermont	3 (0.3)	‡ (†)	‡ (†)	‡ (†)	231 (0.8)	76 (1.0)	45 (1.4)	1 (0.2)	‡ (†)	‡ (†)	‡ (†)	275 (0.8)	84 (1.0)	44 (1.4)
Virginia	6 (0.9)	189 (3.0)	30 (4.0)	7 (2.5)	232 (1.8)	77 (1.8)	45 (2.2)	5 (0.6)	231 (2.7)	31 (5.8)	3 (1.8)	269 (1.3)	80 (1.3)	38 (1.9)
Washington	13 (1.2)	189 (2.1)	28 (2.8)	5 (1.6)	231 (1.5)	77 (1.5)	46 (2.0)	6 (0.7)	223 (3.5)	26 (4.9)	3 (1.6)	270 (1.1)	80 (1.1)	40 (1.6)
West Virginia	1 (0.2)	‡ (†)	‡ (†)	‡ (†)	216 (1.2)	64 (1.3)	30 (1.5)	1 (0.2)	‡ (†)	‡ (†)	‡ (†)	260 (0.9)	72 (1.3)	27 (1.3)
Wisconsin	7 (0.8)	198 (2.9)	40 (4.5)	9 (2.1)	225 (1.1)	73 (1.4)	39 (1.5)	4 (0.5)	234 (3.2)	38 (5.4)	6 (3.1)	271 (1.2)	81 (1.2)	40 (1.7)
Wyoming	3 (0.2)	‡ (†)	‡ (†)	‡ (†)	229 (0.7)	77 (1.0)	42 (1.3)	2 (0.2)	‡ (†)	‡ (†)	‡ (†)	270 (0.8)	82 (1.0)	37 (1.2)
Department of Defense dependents schools	8 (0.4)	213 (2.5)	62 (4.2)	18 (3.5)	236 (0.7)	85 (1.1)	50 (1.4)	5 (0.5)	249 (4.1)	61 (7.5)	12 (5.5)	279 (0.8)	92 (0.9)	49 (1.8)

†Not applicable.
#Rounds to zero.
‡Reporting standards not met (too few cases for a reliable estimate).
[1]Scale ranges from 0 to 500.
[2]*Basic* denotes partial mastery of the knowledge and skills that are fundamental for proficient work at a given grade.
[3]*Proficient* represents solid academic performance. Students reaching this level have demonstrated competency over challenging subject matter.

NOTE: The results for English language learners are based on students who were assessed and cannot be generalized to the total population of such students. Although testing accommodations were permitted, some English language learners did not have a sufficient level of English proficiency to participate in the 2015 Reading Assessment.
SOURCE: U.S. Department of Education, National Center for Education Statistics, National Assessment of Educational Progress (NAEP), 2015 Reading Assessment, retrieved November 9, 2015, from the Main NAEP Data Explorer (http://nces.ed.gov/nationsreportcard/naepdata/). (This table was prepared November 2015.)

Table 221.75. Average National Assessment of Educational Progress (NAEP) reading scale score and standard deviation, by selected student characteristics, percentile, and grade: Selected years, 1992 through 2015

[Standard errors appear in parentheses]

Selected student characteristic, percentile, and grade	1992[1]	1994[1]	1998	2000	2002	2003	2005	2007	2009	2011	2013	2015 Total	2015 Male	2015 Female
1	2	3	4	5	6	7	8	9	10	11	12	13	14	15
							Average reading scale score[2]							
All students														
4th grade	217 (0.9)	214 (1.0)	215 (1.1)	213 (1.3)	219 (0.4)	218 (0.3)	219 (0.2)	221 (0.3)	221 (0.3)	221 (0.3)	222 (0.3)	223 (0.4)	219 (0.4)	226 (0.4)
8th grade	260 (0.9)	260 (0.8)	263 (0.8)	— (†)	264 (0.4)	263 (0.3)	262 (0.2)	263 (0.2)	264 (0.3)	265 (0.2)	268 (0.3)	265 (0.2)	261 (0.2)	270 (0.3)
12th grade	292 (0.6)	287 (0.7)	290 (0.6)	— (†)	287 (0.7)	— (†)	286 (0.6)	— (†)	288 (0.7)	— (†)	288 (0.6)	— (†)	— (†)	— (†)
Eligibility for free or reduced-price lunch														
4th grade														
Eligible	— (†)	— (†)	196 (1.7)	193 (1.7)	203 (0.7)	201 (0.3)	203 (0.3)	205 (0.3)	206 (0.3)	207 (0.3)	207 (0.3)	209 (0.4)	206 (0.5)	213 (0.4)
Not eligible	— (†)	— (†)	227 (0.9)	226 (1.2)	230 (0.4)	229 (0.3)	230 (0.2)	232 (0.3)	232 (0.3)	235 (0.3)	236 (0.3)	237 (0.3)	234 (0.4)	240 (0.4)
Unknown	— (†)	— (†)	223 (2.7)	225 (2.3)	226 (1.6)	230 (0.9)	232 (0.9)	233 (1.3)	236 (1.3)	235 (0.8)	237 (1.4)	236 (1.3)	234 (1.9)	239 (1.6)
8th grade														
Eligible	— (†)	— (†)	245 (1.0)	— (†)	249 (0.5)	247 (0.4)	247 (0.3)	247 (0.3)	249 (0.3)	252 (0.3)	254 (0.2)	253 (0.3)	248 (0.4)	258 (0.3)
Not eligible	— (†)	— (†)	269 (1.0)	— (†)	272 (0.4)	271 (0.3)	270 (0.2)	271 (0.3)	273 (0.3)	275 (0.3)	278 (0.3)	277 (0.3)	272 (0.4)	282 (0.4)
Unknown	— (†)	— (†)	272 (2.0)	— (†)	271 (1.4)	272 (1.0)	275 (1.1)	277 (1.3)	280 (1.3)	283 (0.9)	286 (1.8)	282 (0.9)	278 (1.3)	285 (1.1)
12th grade														
Eligible	— (†)	— (†)	270 (1.1)	— (†)	273 (1.4)	— (†)	271 (1.0)	— (†)	273 (0.7)	— (†)	274 (0.7)	— (†)	— (†)	— (†)
Not eligible	— (†)	— (†)	293 (0.6)	— (†)	289 (0.9)	— (†)	290 (0.7)	— (†)	294 (0.8)	— (†)	296 (0.6)	— (†)	— (†)	— (†)
Unknown	— (†)	— (†)	295 (1.6)	— (†)	294 (1.5)	— (†)	295 (1.9)	— (†)	296 (2.4)	— (†)	302 (2.6)	— (†)	— (†)	— (†)
Read for fun on own time														
4th grade														
Almost every day	223 (1.2)	223 (1.2)	219 (1.5)	218 (1.7)	225 (0.5)	225 (0.3)	225 (0.3)	227 (0.3)	228 (0.4)	228 (0.4)	229 (0.4)	229 (0.5)	227 (0.6)	232 (0.5)
1–2 times a week	218 (1.2)	213 (1.1)	217 (1.2)	216 (1.2)	220 (0.5)	219 (0.3)	220 (0.3)	223 (0.3)	221 (0.4)	221 (0.4)	223 (0.4)	224 (0.5)	222 (0.6)	226 (0.6)
1–2 times a month	210 (1.6)	208 (2.1)	211 (1.9)	212 (1.6)	210 (0.8)	211 (0.5)	213 (0.4)	216 (0.4)	214 (0.4)	214 (0.4)	216 (0.4)	219 (0.5)	217 (0.7)	221 (0.6)
Never or hardly ever	199 (1.8)	197 (1.9)	202 (1.9)	201 (1.8)	208 (0.5)	207 (0.4)	208 (0.3)	211 (0.4)	210 (0.3)	210 (0.5)	211 (0.4)	212 (0.5)	210 (0.5)	214 (0.7)
8th grade														
Almost every day	277 (1.1)	277 (1.4)	277 (1.0)	— (†)	279 (0.6)	279 (0.4)	279 (0.3)	281 (0.4)	282 (0.4)	284 (0.4)	286 (0.4)	284 (0.4)	278 (0.7)	286 (0.5)
1–2 times a week	263 (1.0)	264 (1.1)	267 (1.1)	— (†)	266 (0.5)	265 (0.4)	265 (0.3)	265 (0.3)	267 (0.4)	268 (0.3)	271 (0.4)	269 (0.4)	266 (0.6)	272 (0.5)
1–2 times a month	258 (1.2)	257 (0.8)	263 (0.9)	— (†)	264 (0.6)	262 (0.3)	261 (0.3)	261 (0.4)	261 (0.4)	263 (0.3)	266 (0.3)	263 (0.4)	260 (0.4)	266 (0.6)
Never or hardly ever	246 (1.4)	246 (1.1)	251 (1.1)	— (†)	255 (0.4)	253 (0.3)	252 (0.3)	253 (0.3)	253 (0.4)	255 (0.3)	257 (0.3)	255 (0.3)	253 (0.4)	258 (0.6)
12th grade														
Almost every day	304 (0.9)	302 (1.1)	304 (1.0)	— (†)	304 (1.1)	— (†)	302 (1.2)	— (†)	305 (0.9)	— (†)	306 (0.8)	— (†)	— (†)	— (†)
1–2 times a week	296 (0.7)	294 (1.0)	298 (0.9)	— (†)	292 (1.1)	— (†)	292 (1.0)	— (†)	295 (1.0)	— (†)	297 (0.8)	— (†)	— (†)	— (†)
1–2 times a month	290 (0.9)	285 (1.0)	289 (0.7)	— (†)	288 (0.9)	— (†)	285 (0.8)	— (†)	288 (0.8)	— (†)	289 (0.6)	— (†)	— (†)	— (†)
Never or hardly ever	279 (1.0)	273 (1.1)	275 (1.0)	— (†)	275 (1.0)	— (†)	274 (0.8)	— (†)	275 (0.6)	— (†)	276 (0.7)	— (†)	— (†)	— (†)
Percentile[3]														
4th grade														
10th	170 (1.9)	159 (1.5)	163 (2.1)	159 (2.3)	170 (0.9)	169 (0.5)	171 (0.4)	174 (0.4)	175 (0.5)	174 (0.4)	174 (0.6)	174 (0.7)	169 (1.0)	179 (0.6)
25th	194 (1.1)	189 (1.1)	191 (1.7)	189 (1.4)	196 (0.5)	195 (0.4)	196 (0.3)	199 (0.3)	199 (0.4)	200 (0.4)	200 (0.3)	201 (0.5)	197 (0.6)	205 (0.5)
50th	219 (1.3)	219 (1.3)	217 (1.3)	218 (1.7)	221 (0.5)	221 (0.3)	221 (0.2)	224 (0.3)	223 (0.3)	224 (0.3)	225 (0.3)	226 (0.4)	223 (0.5)	229 (0.4)
75th	242 (1.1)	243 (1.3)	242 (0.9)	243 (0.8)	244 (0.5)	244 (0.3)	244 (0.3)	246 (0.3)	245 (0.3)	246 (0.3)	247 (0.3)	248 (0.4)	246 (0.5)	250 (0.4)
90th	261 (1.4)	263 (1.7)	262 (0.9)	262 (1.4)	263 (0.4)	264 (0.3)	263 (0.3)	264 (0.4)	264 (0.3)	264 (0.4)	265 (0.4)	266 (0.4)	264 (0.4)	268 (0.6)
8th grade														
10th	213 (1.2)	211 (1.9)	216 (1.7)	— (†)	220 (0.5)	217 (0.6)	216 (0.3)	217 (0.4)	219 (0.5)	221 (0.3)	223 (0.4)	220 (0.5)	214 (0.6)	226 (0.5)
25th	237 (1.1)	236 (1.1)	241 (0.7)	— (†)	244 (0.5)	242 (0.3)	240 (0.2)	242 (0.3)	243 (0.4)	244 (0.3)	246 (0.2)	244 (0.3)	239 (0.5)	249 (0.3)
50th	262 (1.1)	262 (0.7)	266 (0.7)	— (†)	267 (0.5)	266 (0.3)	265 (0.2)	265 (0.2)	267 (0.3)	267 (0.2)	269 (0.3)	268 (0.2)	263 (0.3)	272 (0.4)
75th	285 (0.8)	286 (1.1)	288 (1.0)	— (†)	288 (0.4)	288 (0.3)	286 (0.2)	287 (0.2)	288 (0.4)	289 (0.3)	291 (0.3)	290 (0.3)	285 (0.4)	294 (0.4)
90th	305 (1.3)	305 (1.2)	306 (0.8)	— (†)	305 (0.5)	306 (0.2)	305 (0.2)	305 (0.2)	305 (0.4)	307 (0.2)	310 (0.4)	308 (0.3)	303 (0.4)	312 (0.4)
12th grade														
10th	249 (0.8)	239 (0.9)	240 (0.6)	— (†)	237 (1.5)	— (†)	235 (1.1)	— (†)	238 (0.8)	— (†)	239 (1.0)	— (†)	— (†)	— (†)
25th	271 (0.8)	264 (0.9)	267 (0.8)	— (†)	263 (1.3)	— (†)	262 (0.8)	— (†)	264 (0.8)	— (†)	264 (0.8)	— (†)	— (†)	— (†)
50th	294 (0.8)	290 (0.6)	293 (0.6)	— (†)	289 (0.7)	— (†)	288 (0.8)	— (†)	291 (0.7)	— (†)	290 (0.7)	— (†)	— (†)	— (†)
75th	315 (0.5)	313 (0.8)	317 (0.7)	— (†)	312 (0.6)	— (†)	313 (1.1)	— (†)	315 (0.9)	— (†)	315 (0.7)	— (†)	— (†)	— (†)
90th	333 (0.7)	332 (1.2)	336 (0.8)	— (†)	332 (0.9)	— (†)	333 (1.1)	— (†)	335 (0.9)	— (†)	335 (0.6)	— (†)	— (†)	— (†)
							Standard deviation of the reading scale score[4]							
All students														
4th grade	36 (0.6)	41 (0.6)	39 (0.7)	42 (0.9)	36 (0.3)	37 (0.2)	36 (0.1)	36 (0.2)	35 (0.2)	36 (0.1)	37 (0.2)	37 (0.3)	38 (0.3)	36 (0.3)
8th grade	36 (0.3)	37 (0.4)	35 (0.5)	— (†)	34 (0.3)	35 (0.2)	35 (0.1)	35 (0.2)	34 (0.2)	34 (0.1)	34 (0.1)	35 (0.2)	35 (0.2)	34 (0.2)
12th grade	33 (0.4)	37 (0.5)	38 (0.4)	— (†)	37 (0.4)	— (†)	38 (0.4)	— (†)	38 (0.3)	— (†)	38 (0.3)	— (†)	— (†)	— (†)

—Not available.
†Not applicable.
[1]Accommodations were not permitted for this assessment.
[2]Scale ranges from 0 to 500.
[3]The percentile represents a specific point on the percentage distribution of all students ranked by their reading score from low to high. For example, 10 percent of students scored at or below the 10th percentile score, while 90 percent of students scored above it.
[4]The standard deviation provides an indication of how much the test scores varied. The lower the standard deviation, the closer the scores were clustered around the average score. About two-thirds of the student scores can be expected to fall within the range of one standard deviation above and one standard deviation below the average score. For example, the average score for all 4th-graders in 2015 was 223, and the standard deviation was 37. This means that we would expect about two-thirds of the students to have scores between 260 (one standard deviation above the average) and 186 (one standard deviation below). Standard errors also must be taken into account when making comparisons of these ranges.

NOTE: Includes public and private schools. For 1998 and later years, includes students tested with accommodations (1 to 13 percent of all students, depending on grade level and year); excludes only those students with disabilities and English language learners who were unable to be tested even with accommodations (2 to 6 percent of all students). On the student questionnaire, the format of the question about reading for fun on your own time changed slightly beginning with the 2002 assessment year. In 1992 through 2000, reading for fun was one of several activities included in the same question ("How often do you do each of the following?"), and the response options were listed in order from most frequent to least frequent (that is, "Almost every day" was listed first, and "Never or hardly ever" was listed last); starting in 2002, reading for fun was the only activity in the question, and the order of the response options was reversed.

SOURCE: U.S. Department of Education, National Center for Education Statistics, National Assessment of Educational Progress (NAEP), 1992, 1994, 1998, 2000, 2002, 2003, 2005, 2007, 2009, 2011, 2013, and 2015 Reading Assessments, retrieved November 10, 2015, from the Main NAEP Data Explorer (http://nces.ed.gov/nationsreportcard/naepdata/). (This table was prepared November 2015.)

Table 221.80. Average National Assessment of Educational Progress (NAEP) reading scale scores of 4th- and 8th-grade public school students and percentage attaining selected reading achievement levels, by race/ethnicity and jurisdiction or specific urban district: 2009, 2011, 2013, and 2015

[Standard errors appear in parentheses]

Grade level and jurisdiction or specific urban district	Average reading scale score[1]												Percent of students	
	2009	2011	2013					2015					2015	
	All students	All students	All students	White	Black	Hispanic	Asian	All students	White	Black	Hispanic	Asian	At or above *Basic*[2]	At or above *Proficient*[3]
1	2	3	4	5	6	7	8	9	10	11	12	13	14	15
4th grade														
United States	220 (0.3)	220 (0.3)	221 (0.3)	231 (0.3)	205 (0.5)	207 (0.5)	237 (1.1)	221 (0.4)	232 (0.3)	206 (0.5)	208 (0.8)	240 (1.7)	68 (0.4)	35 (0.4)
All large cities[4]	210 (0.7)	211 (0.7)	212 (0.7)	235 (1.0)	202 (0.8)	204 (0.8)	229 (2.5)	214 (0.8)	235 (1.2)	204 (0.9)	206 (0.8)	233 (4.1)	59 (0.9)	27 (1.0)
Selected urban districts														
Albuquerque (NM)	— (†)	209 (1.6)	207 (1.5)	232 (2.4)	‡ (†)	199 (1.7)	‡ (†)	207 (1.6)	227 (2.6)	‡ (†)	202 (1.8)	‡ (†)	54 (1.9)	24 (1.7)
Atlanta (GA)	209 (1.5)	212 (1.4)	214 (1.3)	252 (1.9)	204 (1.4)	208 (3.5)	‡ (†)	212 (1.6)	251 (2.2)	202 (1.9)	205 (4.7)	‡ (†)	54 (2.0)	26 (1.6)
Austin (TX)	220 (1.8)	224 (2.3)	221 (1.6)	250 (2.2)	206 (5.4)	208 (2.1)	‡ (†)	220 (1.8)	248 (2.3)	‡ (†)	207 (2.2)	‡ (†)	65 (2.1)	35 (2.1)
Baltimore City (MD)	202 (1.7)	200 (1.7)	204 (1.6)	233 (5.2)	201 (1.7)	‡ (†)	‡ (†)	199 (1.7)	217 (3.8)	196 (1.9)	200 (4.4)	‡ (†)	40 (2.1)	11 (1.3)
Boston (MA)	215 (1.2)	217 (0.8)	214 (1.1)	237 (2.2)	205 (1.9)	210 (1.7)	234 (3.3)	219 (1.4)	241 (2.5)	214 (2.1)	214 (1.8)	230 (3.7)	65 (1.8)	29 (2.0)
Charlotte (NC)	225 (1.6)	224 (1.2)	226 (1.6)	245 (1.8)	215 (2.0)	212 (2.9)	238 (4.9)	226 (1.6)	245 (2.1)	216 (2.3)	212 (2.6)	246 (5.4)	72 (1.9)	39 (1.8)
Chicago (IL)	202 (1.5)	203 (1.3)	206 (1.6)	239 (4.1)	198 (2.5)	203 (1.6)	235 (4.7)	213 (1.4)	250 (2.3)	205 (2.4)	205 (1.6)	248 (5.0)	58 (1.6)	27 (1.5)
Cleveland (OH)	194 (2.0)	193 (0.9)	190 (1.9)	206 (3.7)	185 (2.2)	191 (4.1)	‡ (†)	197 (2.0)	210 (3.1)	193 (2.7)	199 (4.3)	‡ (†)	39 (2.3)	11 (1.3)
Dallas (TX)	— (†)	204 (1.6)	205 (1.4)	231 (4.9)	201 (2.1)	204 (1.8)	‡ (†)	204 (1.9)	240 (4.6)	202 (3.4)	200 (2.1)	‡ (†)	47 (2.4)	17 (1.8)
Detroit (MI)	187 (1.9)	191 (2.0)	190 (2.2)	‡ (†)	188 (2.6)	199 (3.4)	‡ (†)	186 (2.0)	‡ (†)	184 (2.2)	195 (4.0)	‡ (†)	27 (2.5)	6 (1.2)
District of Columbia (DC)	203 (1.2)	201 (1.0)	206 (1.2)	260 (2.6)	192 (1.4)	211 (2.6)	‡ (†)	214 (1.0)	262 (2.5)	202 (1.3)	206 (3.2)	‡ (†)	56 (1.4)	30 (1.3)
Duval County (FL)	— (†)	— (†)	— (†)	— (†)	— (†)	— (†)	— (†)	225 (1.5)	236 (2.0)	212 (2.1)	225 (2.7)	‡ (†)	73 (1.9)	35 (2.4)
Fresno (CA)	197 (1.7)	194 (2.4)	196 (1.7)	218 (2.9)	187 (3.0)	192 (1.9)	199 (3.0)	199 (1.6)	220 (4.7)	186 (3.8)	196 (2.0)	207 (3.8)	42 (2.1)	13 (1.6)
Hillsborough County (FL)	— (†)	231 (1.7)	228 (1.3)	237 (1.8)	214 (3.1)	223 (1.6)	247 (4.0)	230 (1.9)	242 (2.0)	216 (3.2)	221 (2.0)	‡ (†)	76 (2.4)	41 (2.7)
Houston (TX)	211 (1.7)	213 (1.6)	208 (1.3)	238 (3.3)	202 (2.7)	204 (1.3)	245 (4.7)	210 (1.9)	246 (4.3)	207 (3.3)	204 (1.9)	‡ (†)	54 (2.1)	23 (2.1)
Jefferson County (KY)	219 (1.8)	223 (1.3)	221 (1.2)	233 (1.7)	203 (1.9)	221 (3.5)	‡ (†)	222 (2.0)	232 (2.4)	208 (2.3)	217 (3.6)	‡ (†)	67 (2.2)	36 (2.6)
Los Angeles (CA)	197 (1.1)	201 (1.2)	205 (1.6)	237 (3.4)	204 (2.9)	199 (1.3)	222 (4.3)	204 (1.8)	233 (4.2)	202 (4.9)	197 (1.7)	237 (5.0)	50 (1.8)	21 (1.6)
Miami-Dade (FL)	221 (1.2)	221 (1.5)	223 (1.5)	239 (2.8)	209 (2.2)	225 (1.7)	‡ (†)	226 (1.3)	239 (4.5)	210 (3.3)	229 (1.6)	‡ (†)	74 (1.6)	39 (2.0)
Milwaukee (WI)	196 (2.0)	195 (1.7)	199 (1.9)	223 (3.8)	190 (2.3)	200 (2.6)	201 (8.2)	— (†)	— (†)	— (†)	— (†)	— (†)	— (†)	— (†)
New York City (NY)	217 (1.4)	216 (1.2)	216 (1.4)	231 (3.1)	210 (1.8)	208 (1.6)	233 (3.2)	214 (1.5)	233 (4.7)	206 (1.7)	205 (2.0)	236 (2.6)	59 (1.8)	26 (1.7)
Philadelphia (PA)	195 (1.8)	199 (1.8)	200 (1.7)	214 (3.2)	196 (2.0)	193 (3.0)	215 (4.9)	201 (2.2)	216 (4.3)	198 (1.8)	188 (4.4)	221 (4.6)	44 (2.7)	14 (1.8)
San Diego (CA)	213 (2.1)	215 (1.7)	218 (1.6)	240 (2.2)	205 (4.0)	204 (2.4)	229 (3.9)	216 (2.0)	240 (3.1)	201 (6.2)	204 (2.7)	223 (4.5)	61 (2.3)	30 (2.0)
8th grade														
United States	262 (0.3)	264 (0.2)	266 (0.2)	275 (0.2)	250 (0.4)	255 (0.4)	280 (1.0)	264 (0.2)	273 (0.2)	247 (0.5)	253 (0.4)	280 (1.4)	75 (0.3)	33 (0.3)
All large cities[4]	252 (0.5)	255 (0.5)	258 (0.8)	276 (1.0)	246 (0.9)	253 (0.7)	273 (2.8)	257 (0.9)	277 (1.3)	246 (0.8)	251 (1.0)	272 (2.4)	67 (0.9)	25 (1.0)
Selected urban districts														
Albuquerque (NM)	— (†)	254 (1.2)	256 (1.0)	275 (2.6)	‡ (†)	250 (1.1)	‡ (†)	251 (1.2)	267 (2.2)	‡ (†)	246 (1.3)	‡ (†)	62 (1.6)	19 (1.6)
Atlanta (GA)	250 (1.5)	253 (1.0)	255 (1.0)	294 (2.8)	249 (1.2)	254 (4.5)	‡ (†)	252 (1.4)	290 (2.9)	246 (1.5)	258 (3.7)	‡ (†)	61 (2.0)	20 (1.6)
Austin (TX)	261 (2.0)	261 (1.5)	261 (1.4)	286 (2.9)	245 (3.5)	251 (1.6)	‡ (†)	261 (1.5)	290 (3.1)	241 (5.0)	249 (1.6)	‡ (†)	70 (1.6)	33 (2.3)
Baltimore City (MD)	245 (1.7)	246 (1.6)	252 (1.5)	275 (5.6)	249 (1.5)	‡ (†)	‡ (†)	243 (1.7)	268 (5.9)	240 (2.0)	246 (5.1)	‡ (†)	51 (2.7)	13 (1.7)
Boston (MA)	257 (1.5)	255 (1.2)	257 (1.0)	281 (2.8)	247 (1.8)	250 (1.5)	278 (3.5)	258 (1.2)	282 (3.1)	250 (2.1)	249 (2.3)	281 (3.9)	67 (1.7)	28 (1.4)
Charlotte (NC)	259 (1.0)	265 (0.9)	266 (1.2)	286 (2.0)	253 (1.8)	259 (3.1)	‡ (†)	263 (1.6)	284 (2.1)	251 (2.4)	254 (3.7)	‡ (†)	73 (1.8)	33 (2.0)
Chicago (IL)	249 (1.6)	253 (1.1)	253 (1.0)	279 (2.6)	244 (1.6)	255 (1.6)	278 (4.3)	257 (1.8)	289 (5.0)	247 (1.6)	257 (1.6)	‡ (†)	67 (1.6)	24 (2.2)
Cleveland (OH)	242 (1.6)	240 (1.7)	239 (1.6)	250 (3.2)	235 (1.8)	241 (3.6)	‡ (†)	240 (1.6)	251 (3.4)	238 (2.1)	238 (3.3)	‡ (†)	48 (2.5)	11 (1.4)
Dallas (TX)	— (†)	248 (1.0)	251 (1.3)	‡ (†)	244 (2.4)	253 (1.6)	‡ (†)	250 (1.3)	‡ (†)	241 (2.5)	251 (1.5)	‡ (†)	60 (2.2)	17 (1.7)
Detroit (MI)	232 (2.4)	237 (1.0)	239 (1.6)	‡ (†)	239 (1.6)	242 (4.7)	‡ (†)	237 (1.2)	‡ (†)	235 (1.5)	245 (3.1)	‡ (†)	44 (2.4)	7 (1.2)
District of Columbia (DC)	240 (1.5)	237 (1.2)	245 (1.3)	301 (4.0)	237 (1.4)	247 (3.6)	‡ (†)	245 (1.4)	299 (3.8)	236 (1.8)	244 (3.7)	‡ (†)	52 (1.9)	19 (1.4)
Duval County (FL)	— (†)	— (†)	— (†)	— (†)	— (†)	— (†)	— (†)	264 (1.4)	272 (2.2)	254 (1.5)	262 (3.6)	‡ (†)	75 (2.0)	31 (2.0)
Fresno (CA)	240 (2.4)	238 (1.8)	245 (1.4)	265 (3.4)	236 (3.3)	241 (1.6)	247 (3.1)	242 (1.9)	256 (4.5)	238 (3.9)	238 (2.2)	249 (3.9)	51 (2.5)	13 (1.7)
Hillsborough County (FL)	— (†)	264 (1.5)	267 (1.2)	277 (1.6)	252 (2.3)	263 (1.8)	‡ (†)	261 (1.7)	274 (2.1)	246 (3.4)	254 (2.3)	‡ (†)	71 (2.5)	29 (2.3)
Houston (TX)	252 (1.2)	252 (0.9)	252 (1.2)	284 (3.2)	245 (2.2)	250 (1.4)	284 (5.6)	252 (1.8)	280 (4.1)	246 (2.6)	247 (1.5)	‡ (†)	61 (1.6)	20 (2.2)
Jefferson County (KY)	259 (1.0)	260 (1.1)	261 (1.0)	271 (1.6)	243 (1.4)	258 (4.5)	‡ (†)	261 (1.8)	271 (2.7)	247 (1.9)	260 (4.6)	‡ (†)	70 (2.2)	31 (2.2)
Los Angeles (CA)	244 (1.1)	246 (1.1)	250 (1.4)	276 (3.2)	240 (3.8)	245 (1.1)	272 (3.1)	251 (1.4)	273 (3.2)	248 (5.3)	246 (1.3)	274 (4.8)	62 (2.0)	20 (1.6)
Miami-Dade (FL)	261 (1.4)	260 (1.4)	259 (1.0)	278 (2.8)	245 (2.0)	261 (1.1)	‡ (†)	265 (1.8)	279 (4.5)	254 (3.1)	266 (1.9)	‡ (†)	77 (2.0)	32 (2.4)
Milwaukee (WI)	241 (2.0)	238 (1.6)	242 (1.4)	262 (3.3)	232 (1.7)	253 (2.5)	‡ (†)	— (†)	— (†)	— (†)	— (†)	— (†)	— (†)	— (†)
New York City (NY)	252 (1.4)	254 (1.8)	256 (1.2)	274 (4.0)	253 (2.0)	249 (2.0)	271 (3.1)	258 (1.7)	276 (3.7)	247 (2.0)	254 (2.2)	270 (3.5)	67 (1.8)	27 (2.2)
Philadelphia (PA)	247 (2.5)	247 (1.5)	249 (1.8)	261 (3.1)	244 (2.4)	243 (3.3)	265 (5.4)	248 (2.0)	263 (4.8)	240 (2.2)	244 (3.6)	276 (5.3)	58 (2.1)	16 (2.4)
San Diego (CA)	254 (2.8)	256 (2.1)	260 (1.5)	281 (2.4)	244 (3.7)	247 (2.1)	266 (3.6)	262 (2.0)	283 (2.9)	252 (4.4)	248 (2.9)	266 (4.1)	73 (2.3)	32 (2.2)

—Not available.
†Not applicable.
‡Reporting standards not met (too few cases for a reliable estimate).
[1]Scale ranges from 0 to 500.
[2]*Basic* denotes partial mastery of prerequisite knowledge and skills that are fundamental for proficient work at a given grade.
[3]*Proficient* represents solid academic performance. Students reaching this level have demonstrated competency over challenging subject matter.
[4]Includes public school students from all cities in the nation with populations of 250,000 or more, including the participating districts.

NOTE: Race categories exclude persons of Hispanic ethnicity. Totals include racial/ethnic groups not shown separately.

SOURCE: U.S. Department of Education, National Center for Education Statistics, National Assessment of Educational Progress (NAEP), 2009, 2011, 2013, and 2015 Reading Assessments, retrieved November 3, 2015, from the Main NAEP Data Explorer (http://nces.ed.gov/nationsreportcard/naepdata/). (This table was prepared November 2015.)

Table 221.85. Average National Assessment of Educational Progress (NAEP) reading scale score, by age and selected student characteristics: Selected years, 1971 through 2012

[Standard errors appear in parentheses]

Selected student characteristic	1971	1975	1980	1984	1988	1990	1992	1994	1996	1999	2004[1] Previous format	2004[1] Revised format	2008	2012
1	2	3	4	5	6	7	8	9	10	11	12	13	14	15
9-year-olds														
All students	**208 (1.0)**	**210 (0.7)**	**215 (1.0)**	**211 (0.8)**	**212 (1.1)**	**209 (1.2)**	**211 (0.9)**	**211 (1.2)**	**212 (1.0)**	**212 (1.3)**	**219 (1.1)**	**216 (1.0)**	**220 (0.9)**	**221 (0.8)**
Sex														
Male	201 (1.1)	204 (0.8)	210 (1.1)	207 (1.0)	207 (1.4)	204 (1.7)	206 (1.3)	207 (1.3)	207 (1.4)	209 (1.6)	216 (1.4)	212 (1.1)	216 (1.1)	218 (0.9)
Female	214 (1.0)	216 (0.8)	220 (1.1)	214 (0.9)	216 (1.3)	215 (1.2)	215 (0.9)	215 (1.4)	218 (1.1)	215 (1.5)	221 (1.0)	219 (1.1)	224 (0.9)	223 (0.9)
Gap between female and male score	13 (1.5)	12 (1.1)	10 (1.6)	7 (1.3)	9 (1.9)	11 (2.0)	10 (1.6)	7 (1.9)	11 (1.8)	6 (2.2)	5 (1.8)	8 (1.5)	7 (1.4)	5 (1.3)
Race/ethnicity														
White	214 [2] (0.9)	217 (0.7)	221 (0.8)	218 (0.9)	218 (1.4)	217 (1.3)	218 (1.0)	218 (1.3)	220 (1.2)	221 (1.6)	226 (1.1)	224 (0.9)	228 (1.0)	229 (0.8)
Black	170 [2] (1.7)	181 (1.2)	189 (1.8)	186 (1.3)	189 (2.4)	182 (2.9)	185 (2.2)	185 (2.3)	191 (2.6)	186 (2.3)	200 (2.2)	197 (1.8)	204 (1.7)	206 (1.9)
Hispanic	[3] (†)	183 (2.2)	190 (2.3)	187 (3.0)	194 (3.5)	189 (2.3)	192 (3.1)	186 (3.9)	195 (3.4)	193 (2.7)	205 (1.7)	199 (1.5)	207 (1.5)	208 (1.5)
Gap between White and Black score	44 (1.9)	35 (1.4)	32 (1.9)	32 (1.6)	29 (2.8)	35 (3.2)	33 (2.4)	33 (2.6)	29 (2.8)	35 (2.8)	26 (2.5)	27 (2.1)	24 (2.0)	23 (2.1)
Gap between White and Hispanic score	† (†)	34 (2.4)	31 (2.4)	31 (3.1)	24 (3.8)	28 (2.6)	26 (3.2)	32 (4.1)	25 (3.6)	28 (3.2)	21 (2.1)	25 (1.8)	21 (1.8)	21 (1.7)
13-year-olds														
All students	**255 (0.9)**	**256 (0.8)**	**258 (0.9)**	**257 (0.6)**	**257 (1.0)**	**257 (0.8)**	**260 (1.2)**	**258 (0.9)**	**258 (1.0)**	**259 (1.0)**	**259 (1.0)**	**257 (1.0)**	**260 (0.8)**	**263 (1.0)**
Sex														
Male	250 (1.0)	250 (0.8)	254 (1.1)	253 (0.7)	252 (1.3)	251 (1.1)	254 (1.7)	251 (1.2)	251 (1.2)	254 (1.3)	254 (1.2)	252 (1.1)	256 (1.0)	259 (1.3)
Female	261 (0.9)	262 (0.9)	263 (0.9)	262 (0.7)	263 (1.0)	263 (1.1)	265 (1.2)	266 (1.2)	264 (1.2)	265 (1.2)	264 (1.3)	262 (1.2)	264 (0.9)	267 (0.9)
Gap between female and male score	11 (1.3)	13 (1.2)	8 (1.4)	9 (1.0)	11 (1.7)	13 (1.6)	11 (2.1)	15 (1.7)	13 (1.7)	12 (1.8)	10 (1.8)	10 (1.6)	8 (1.3)	8 (1.6)
Race/ethnicity														
White	261 [2] (0.7)	262 (0.7)	264 (0.7)	263 (0.6)	261 (1.1)	262 (0.9)	266 (1.2)	265 (1.1)	266 (1.0)	267 (1.2)	266 (1.0)	265 (1.0)	268 (1.0)	270 (1.3)
Black	222 [2] (1.2)	226 (1.2)	233 (1.5)	236 (1.2)	243 (2.4)	241 (2.2)	238 (2.3)	234 (2.4)	234 (2.6)	238 (2.4)	244 (2.0)	239 (1.9)	247 (1.6)	247 (1.6)
Hispanic	[3] (†)	232 (3.0)	237 (2.0)	240 (2.0)	240 (3.5)	238 (2.3)	239 (3.5)	235 (1.9)	238 (2.9)	244 (2.9)	242 (1.6)	241 (2.1)	242 (1.5)	249 (1.3)
Gap between White and Black score	39 (1.4)	36 (1.4)	32 (1.6)	26 (1.3)	18 (2.6)	21 (2.4)	29 (2.7)	31 (2.7)	32 (2.8)	29 (2.7)	22 (2.3)	25 (2.1)	21 (1.9)	23 (2.1)
Gap between White and Hispanic score	† (†)	30 (3.1)	27 (2.1)	23 (2.1)	21 (3.6)	24 (2.5)	27 (3.7)	30 (2.2)	28 (3.1)	23 (3.1)	24 (1.9)	24 (2.4)	26 (1.8)	21 (1.8)
Parents' highest level of education														
Did not finish high school	— (†)	— (†)	239 (1.1)	240 (1.2)	246 (2.1)	241 (1.8)	239 (2.6)	237 (2.4)	239 (2.8)	238 (3.4)	240 (2.7)	238 (2.3)	239 (1.9)	248 (2.0)
Graduated high school	— (†)	— (†)	253 (0.9)	253 (0.8)	253 (1.2)	251 (0.9)	252 (1.7)	251 (1.4)	251 (1.5)	251 (1.8)	251 (1.6)	249 (1.1)	251 (1.1)	248 (1.7)
Some education after high school	— (†)	— (†)	268 (1.0)	266 (1.1)	265 (1.7)	267 (1.7)	265 (2.7)	266 (1.9)	268 (2.3)	269 (2.4)	264 (2.0)	261 (1.4)	265 (1.1)	264 (1.5)
Graduated college	— (†)	— (†)	273 (0.9)	268 (0.9)	265 (1.6)	267 (1.1)	271 (1.5)	269 (1.2)	269 (1.4)	270 (1.2)	270 (1.0)	266 (1.2)	270 (1.2)	273 (1.3)
17-year-olds														
All students	**285 (1.2)**	**286 (0.8)**	**285 (1.2)**	**289 (0.8)**	**290 (1.0)**	**290 (1.1)**	**290 (1.1)**	**288 (1.3)**	**288 (1.1)**	**288 (1.3)**	**285 (1.2)**	**283 (1.1)**	**286 (0.9)**	**287 (0.9)**
Sex														
Male	279 (1.2)	280 (1.0)	282 (1.3)	284 (0.8)	286 (1.5)	284 (1.6)	284 (1.6)	282 (2.2)	281 (1.3)	281 (1.6)	278 (1.5)	276 (1.4)	280 (1.1)	283 (1.1)
Female	291 (1.3)	291 (1.0)	289 (1.2)	294 (0.9)	294 (1.5)	296 (1.2)	296 (1.1)	295 (1.5)	295 (1.2)	295 (1.4)	292 (1.3)	289 (1.2)	291 (1.0)	291 (1.0)
Gap between female and male score	12 (1.8)	12 (1.4)	7 (1.8)	10 (1.2)	8 (2.1)	12 (2.0)	11 (1.9)	13 (2.7)	15 (1.8)	13 (2.1)	14 (2.0)	14 (1.8)	11 (1.5)	8 (1.5)
Race/ethnicity														
White	291 [2] (1.0)	293 (0.6)	293 (0.9)	295 (0.9)	295 (1.2)	297 (1.2)	297 (1.4)	296 (1.5)	295 (1.2)	295 (1.4)	293 (1.1)	289 (1.2)	295 (1.0)	295 (1.0)
Black	239 [2] (1.7)	241 (2.0)	243 (1.8)	264 (1.2)	274 (2.4)	267 (2.3)	261 (2.1)	266 (3.9)	266 (2.7)	264 (1.7)	264 (2.7)	262 (1.9)	266 (2.4)	269 (1.6)
Hispanic	[3] (†)	252 (3.6)	261 (2.7)	268 (2.9)	271 (4.3)	275 (3.6)	271 (3.7)	263 (4.9)	265 (4.1)	271 (3.9)	264 (2.9)	267 (2.5)	269 (1.3)	274 (1.5)
Gap between White and Black score	53 (2.0)	52 (2.1)	50 (2.0)	32 (1.5)	20 (2.7)	29 (2.6)	37 (2.5)	30 (4.2)	29 (3.0)	31 (2.3)	29 (2.9)	27 (2.3)	29 (2.6)	26 (1.9)
Gap between White and Hispanic score	† (†)	41 (3.6)	31 (2.9)	27 (3.0)	24 (4.4)	22 (3.8)	26 (3.9)	33 (5.2)	30 (4.2)	24 (4.2)	29 (3.1)	22 (2.8)	26 (1.6)	21 (1.9)
Parents' highest level of education														
Did not finish high school	— (†)	— (†)	262 (1.5)	269 (1.4)	267 (2.0)	270 (2.8)	271 (3.9)	268 (2.7)	267 (3.2)	265 (3.6)	259 (3.4)	259 (2.7)	266 (2.1)	266 (2.1)
Graduated high school	— (†)	— (†)	277 (1.0)	281 (0.8)	282 (1.3)	283 (1.4)	280 (1.6)	276 (1.9)	273 (1.7)	274 (2.1)	274 (1.6)	271 (1.4)	274 (1.4)	270 (1.6)
Some education after high school	— (†)	— (†)	295 (1.2)	298 (0.9)	299 (2.2)	295 (1.9)	293 (1.9)	294 (1.6)	295 (2.2)	295 (1.8)	286 (1.9)	285 (1.5)	288 (1.1)	287 (1.1)
Graduated college	— (†)	— (†)	301 (1.0)	302 (0.9)	300 (1.4)	302 (1.5)	301 (1.7)	300 (1.7)	299 (1.5)	298 (1.3)	298 (1.3)	295 (1.2)	298 (1.1)	300 (1.0)

—Not available.
†Not applicable.
[1]In 2004, two assessments were conducted—one using the same format that was used in previous assessments, and one using a revised assessment format that provides accommodations for students with disabilities and for English language learners. The 2004 data in column 12 are for the format that was used in previous assessment years, while the 2004 data in column 13 are for the revised format. In subsequent years, only the revised format was used.
[2]Data for 1971 include persons of Hispanic ethnicity.
[3]Test scores of Hispanics were not tabulated separately.
NOTE: Scale ranges from 0 to 500. Students scoring 150 (or higher) are able to follow brief written directions and carry out simple, discrete reading tasks. Students scoring 200 are able to understand, combine ideas, and make inferences based on short uncomplicated passages about specific or sequentially related information. Students scoring 250 are able to search for specific information, interrelate ideas, and make generalizations about literature, science, and social studies materials. Students scoring 300 are able to find, understand, summarize, and explain relatively complicated literary and informational material. Includes public and private schools. For assessment years prior to 2004, accommodations were not permitted. For 2004 (revised format) and later years, includes students tested with accommodations; excludes only those students with disabilities and English language learners who were unable to be tested even with accommodations (2 to 5 percent of all students, depending on age and assessment year). Race categories exclude persons of Hispanic ethnicity, except where noted. Totals include other racial/ethnic groups not shown separately.
SOURCE: U.S. Department of Education, National Center for Education Statistics, National Assessment of Educational Progress (NAEP), *NAEP 2012 Trends in Academic Progress*; and 2012 NAEP Long-Term Trend Reading Assessment, retrieved June 27, 2013, from Long-Term Trend NAEP Data Explorer (http://nces.ed.gov/nationsreportcard/naepdata/). (This table was prepared June 2013.)

Table 221.90. Percentage of students at or above selected National Assessment of Educational Progress (NAEP) reading score levels, by age, sex, and race/ethnicity: Selected years, 1971 through 2012

[Standard errors appear in parentheses]

Age, sex, race/ethnicity, and score level	1971	1975	1980	1984	1988	1990	1992	1994	1996	1999	2004	2008	2012
1	2	3	4	5	6	7	8	9	10	11	12	13	14
9-year-olds													
Total													
Level 150[1]	91 (0.5)	93 (0.4)	95 (0.4)	92 (0.4)	93 (0.7)	90 (0.9)	92 (0.4)	92 (0.7)	93 (0.6)	93 (0.7)	94 (0.5)	96 (0.4)	96 (0.4)
Level 200[2]	59 (1.0)	62 (0.8)	68 (1.0)	62 (0.8)	63 (1.3)	59 (1.3)	62 (1.1)	63 (1.4)	64 (1.3)	64 (1.4)	69 (1.0)	73 (0.9)	74 (0.9)
Level 250[3]	16 (0.6)	15 (0.6)	18 (0.8)	17 (0.7)	17 (1.1)	18 (1.0)	16 (0.8)	17 (1.2)	17 (0.8)	16 (1.0)	19 (0.7)	21 (0.8)	22 (0.7)
Male													
Level 150[1]	88 (0.7)	91 (0.5)	93 (0.5)	90 (0.5)	90 (0.9)	88 (1.4)	90 (0.8)	90 (1.0)	92 (0.8)	91 (1.1)	92 (0.6)	94 (0.6)	94 (0.6)
Level 200[2]	53 (1.2)	56 (1.0)	63 (1.1)	58 (1.0)	58 (1.8)	54 (1.9)	57 (1.6)	59 (1.5)	58 (2.0)	61 (1.8)	64 (1.3)	70 (1.2)	71 (1.0)
Level 250[3]	12 (0.6)	12 (0.6)	15 (0.9)	16 (0.8)	16 (1.4)	16 (1.2)	14 (1.0)	15 (1.2)	14 (1.3)	15 (1.3)	17 (0.8)	19 (1.0)	21 (0.8)
Female													
Level 150[1]	93 (0.5)	95 (0.3)	96 (0.4)	94 (0.5)	95 (1.0)	92 (1.1)	94 (0.6)	94 (0.8)	95 (0.6)	95 (0.8)	96 (0.5)	97 (0.4)	97 (0.4)
Level 200[2]	65 (1.1)	68 (0.8)	73 (1.0)	65 (1.0)	67 (1.4)	64 (1.2)	67 (1.2)	67 (1.9)	70 (1.6)	67 (1.6)	73 (1.2)	77 (1.1)	77 (1.1)
Level 250[3]	19 (0.8)	18 (0.8)	21 (1.0)	18 (0.8)	19 (1.2)	21 (1.2)	18 (1.1)	18 (1.5)	19 (1.3)	17 (1.3)	20 (1.0)	22 (1.0)	23 (0.9)
White													
Level 150[1]	94 [5] (0.4)	96 (0.3)	97 (0.2)	95 (0.3)	95 (0.7)	94 (0.9)	96 (0.5)	96 (0.5)	96 (0.6)	97 (0.4)	97 (0.4)	98 (0.4)	98 (0.4)
Level 200[2]	65 [5] (1.0)	69 (0.8)	74 (0.7)	69 (0.9)	68 (1.6)	66 (1.4)	69 (1.2)	70 (1.5)	71 (1.5)	73 (1.6)	77 (1.0)	81 (1.0)	82 (0.8)
Level 250[3]	18 [5] (0.7)	17 (0.7)	21 (0.9)	21 (0.8)	20 (1.5)	23 (1.2)	20 (1.0)	20 (1.5)	20 (1.1)	20 (1.4)	24 (0.8)	27 (1.1)	28 (0.8)
Black													
Level 150[1]	70 [5] (1.7)	81 (1.1)	85 (1.4)	81 (1.2)	83 (2.4)	77 (2.7)	80 (2.2)	79 (2.4)	84 (1.9)	82 (2.5)	88 (1.7)	91 (1.1)	94 (1.0)
Level 200[2]	22 [5] (1.5)	32 (1.5)	41 (1.9)	37 (1.5)	39 (2.9)	34 (3.4)	37 (2.2)	38 (2.8)	42 (3.2)	36 (3.0)	50 (2.3)	58 (2.3)	61 (2.1)
Level 250[3]	2 [5] (0.5)	2 (0.3)	4 (0.6)	5 (0.6)	6 (1.2)	5 (1.5)	5 (0.8)	4 (1.5)	6 (1.1)	4 (1.1)	7 (0.8)	9 (0.9)	10 (1.1)
Hispanic													
Level 150[1]	[6] (†)	81 (2.5)	84 (1.8)	82 (3.0)	86 (3.5)	84 (1.8)	83 (2.6)	80 (4.6)	86 (2.4)	87 (3.3)	89 (1.3)	93 (0.8)	92 (1.1)
Level 200[2]	[6] (†)	35 (3.0)	42 (2.6)	40 (2.7)	46 (3.3)	41 (2.7)	43 (3.5)	37 (4.6)	48 (3.8)	44 (3.4)	53 (1.7)	62 (1.7)	63 (1.8)
Level 250[3]	[6] (†)	3 (0.5)	5 (1.4)	4 (0.7)	9 (2.3)	6 (2.0)	7 (2.3)	6 (1.6)	7 (3.2)	6 (1.7)	7 (0.8)	10 (1.2)	11 (1.0)
13-year-olds													
Total													
Level 200[2]	93 (0.5)	93 (0.4)	95 (0.4)	94 (0.3)	95 (0.6)	94 (0.6)	93 (0.7)	92 (0.6)	92 (0.7)	93 (0.7)	92 (0.6)	94 (0.4)	94 (0.4)
Level 250[3]	58 (1.1)	59 (1.0)	61 (1.1)	59 (0.8)	59 (1.3)	59 (1.0)	62 (1.4)	60 (1.2)	60 (1.3)	61 (1.5)	59 (1.1)	63 (0.8)	66 (1.3)
Level 300[4]	10 (0.5)	10 (0.5)	11 (0.5)	11 (0.4)	11 (0.8)	11 (0.6)	15 (0.9)	14 (0.8)	14 (1.0)	15 (1.1)	12 (0.8)	13 (0.5)	15 (1.0)
Male													
Level 200[2]	91 (0.7)	91 (0.5)	93 (0.6)	92 (0.4)	93 (1.0)	91 (0.9)	90 (1.1)	89 (1.1)	89 (1.2)	91 (0.9)	89 (0.8)	92 (0.6)	93 (0.7)
Level 250[3]	52 (1.2)	52 (1.1)	56 (1.2)	54 (0.9)	52 (1.9)	52 (1.5)	55 (2.0)	53 (1.9)	53 (1.6)	55 (1.9)	55 (1.3)	59 (1.2)	62 (1.6)
Level 300[4]	7 (0.5)	7 (0.4)	9 (0.7)	9 (0.5)	9 (0.9)	8 (0.8)	13 (1.1)	10 (0.7)	10 (1.0)	11 (1.1)	11 (0.9)	11 (0.7)	13 (1.1)
Female													
Level 200[2]	95 (0.4)	95 (0.4)	96 (0.4)	96 (0.3)	97 (0.6)	96 (0.6)	95 (0.7)	95 (0.6)	95 (0.6)	96 (0.7)	95 (0.6)	96 (0.5)	96 (0.4)
Level 250[3]	64 (1.1)	65 (1.2)	65 (1.1)	64 (0.8)	65 (1.4)	65 (1.5)	68 (1.4)	68 (1.7)	66 (1.6)	66 (1.9)	65 (1.3)	66 (1.0)	69 (1.4)
Level 300[4]	12 (0.6)	13 (0.7)	13 (0.6)	13 (0.6)	13 (0.9)	14 (0.9)	18 (1.1)	18 (1.1)	17 (1.3)	18 (1.7)	14 (1.0)	16 (0.9)	17 (1.1)
White													
Level 200[2]	96 [5] (0.3)	96 (0.2)	97 (0.2)	96 (0.2)	96 (0.6)	96 (0.6)	96 (0.6)	95 (0.7)	95 (0.5)	96 (0.6)	95 (0.5)	96 (0.4)	96 (0.6)
Level 250[3]	64 [5] (0.9)	65 (0.9)	68 (0.8)	65 (0.8)	64 (1.5)	65 (1.2)	68 (1.4)	68 (1.3)	69 (1.4)	69 (1.7)	68 (1.1)	72 (1.2)	74 (1.8)
Level 300[4]	11 [5] (0.5)	12 (0.5)	14 (0.6)	13 (0.6)	12 (0.9)	13 (0.9)	18 (1.1)	17 (1.0)	17 (1.3)	18 (1.4)	16 (0.9)	18 (0.8)	19 (1.0)
Black													
Level 200[2]	74 [5] (1.7)	77 (1.3)	84 (1.7)	85 (1.2)	91 (2.2)	88 (2.3)	82 (2.7)	81 (2.3)	82 (3.2)	85 (2.3)	86 (1.5)	91 (1.1)	90 (1.3)
Level 250[3]	21 [5] (1.2)	25 (1.6)	30 (2.0)	35 (1.3)	40 (2.3)	42 (3.5)	38 (2.7)	36 (3.5)	34 (3.9)	38 (2.7)	40 (2.3)	48 (2.3)	48 (2.5)
Level 300[4]	1 [5] (0.2)	2 (0.3)	2 (0.5)	3 (0.6)	5 (1.2)	5 (0.8)	6 (1.4)	4 (1.2)	3 (0.9)	5 (1.4)	4 (0.7)	6 (0.8)	6 (0.9)
Hispanic													
Level 200[2]	[6] (†)	81 (2.3)	87 (2.4)	86 (1.7)	87 (2.6)	86 (2.4)	83 (3.5)	82 (2.7)	85 (3.2)	89 (2.8)	85 (1.9)	87 (1.3)	91 (1.2)
Level 250[3]	[6] (†)	32 (3.6)	35 (2.6)	39 (2.3)	38 (4.4)	37 (2.9)	41 (5.1)	34 (3.9)	38 (3.7)	43 (3.8)	44 (2.3)	44 (1.8)	51 (1.7)
Level 300[4]	[6] (†)	2 (1.0)	2 (0.6)	4 (1.0)	4 (1.9)	4 (1.2)	6 (1.9)	4 (1.8)	5 (1.7)	6 (1.8)	5 (1.2)	5 (0.6)	6 (0.5)
17-year-olds													
Total													
Level 250[3]	79 (0.9)	80 (0.7)	81 (0.9)	83 (0.6)	86 (0.8)	84 (1.0)	83 (0.8)	81 (1.0)	82 (0.8)	82 (1.0)	79 (0.9)	80 (0.6)	82 (0.6)
Level 300[4]	39 (1.0)	39 (0.8)	38 (1.1)	40 (1.0)	41 (1.5)	41 (1.0)	43 (1.1)	41 (1.2)	39 (1.4)	40 (1.4)	36 (1.2)	39 (0.8)	39 (0.9)
Male													
Level 250[3]	74 (1.0)	76 (0.8)	78 (1.0)	80 (0.7)	83 (1.4)	80 (1.4)	78 (1.2)	76 (1.5)	77 (1.2)	77 (1.5)	73 (1.2)	76 (0.8)	79 (0.8)
Level 300[4]	34 (1.1)	34 (1.0)	35 (1.3)	36 (1.0)	37 (2.3)	36 (1.5)	38 (1.6)	36 (1.9)	34 (1.9)	34 (1.7)	32 (1.2)	35 (0.9)	36 (1.2)
Female													
Level 250[3]	83 (1.0)	84 (0.9)	84 (1.0)	87 (0.6)	88 (1.1)	89 (1.0)	87 (1.1)	86 (1.2)	87 (1.0)	87 (1.0)	84 (0.9)	84 (0.8)	85 (0.7)
Level 300[4]	44 (1.2)	44 (0.9)	41 (1.2)	45 (1.1)	44 (2.0)	47 (1.3)	48 (1.5)	46 (1.5)	45 (1.7)	45 (1.8)	41 (1.6)	43 (1.0)	42 (1.1)
White													
Level 250[3]	84 [5] (0.7)	86 (0.6)	87 (0.6)	88 (0.5)	89 (0.9)	88 (1.1)	88 (0.9)	86 (1.1)	87 (0.8)	87 (1.3)	83 (0.9)	87 (0.6)	87 (0.6)
Level 300[4]	43 [5] (0.9)	44 (0.8)	43 (1.1)	47 (1.1)	45 (1.6)	48 (1.2)	50 (1.4)	48 (1.4)	46 (1.5)	46 (1.5)	42 (1.3)	47 (1.0)	47 (1.3)
Black													
Level 250[3]	40 [5] (1.6)	43 (1.6)	44 (2.0)	65 (1.5)	76 (2.4)	69 (2.8)	61 (2.3)	66 (4.1)	68 (4.0)	66 (2.5)	64 (2.2)	67 (2.4)	70 (1.4)
Level 300[4]	8 [5] (0.9)	8 (0.7)	7 (0.8)	16 (1.0)	25 (3.1)	20 (1.8)	17 (2.5)	22 (3.7)	18 (2.2)	17 (1.7)	16 (1.8)	21 (1.5)	22 (1.5)
Hispanic													
Level 250[3]	[6] (†)	53 (4.1)	62 (3.1)	68 (2.4)	71 (4.8)	75 (4.7)	69 (4.0)	63 (4.4)	65 (4.2)	68 (4.3)	67 (2.4)	70 (1.5)	74 (1.3)
Level 300[4]	[6] (†)	13 (2.7)	17 (2.1)	21 (3.0)	23 (3.7)	27 (3.3)	27 (3.2)	20 (3.0)	20 (4.8)	24 (3.8)	23 (2.1)	22 (1.0)	26 (1.3)

†Not applicable.
[1]Students scoring 150 (or higher) are able to follow brief written directions and carry out simple, discrete reading tasks.
[2]Students scoring 200 (or higher) are able to understand, combine ideas, and make inferences based on short uncomplicated passages about specific or sequentially related information.
[3]Students scoring 250 (or higher) are able to search for specific information, interrelate ideas, and make generalizations about literature, science, and social studies materials.
[4]Students scoring 300 (or higher) are able to find, understand, summarize, and explain relatively complicated literary and informational material.
[5]Data for 1971 include persons of Hispanic ethnicity.
[6]Test scores of Hispanics were not tabulated separately.

NOTE: The NAEP reading scores have been evaluated at certain performance levels, as outlined in footnotes 1 through 4. Scale ranges from 0 to 500. Includes public and private schools. For assessment years prior to 2004, accommodations were not permitted. For 2004 and later years, includes students tested with accommodations; excludes only those students with disabilities and English language learners who were unable to be tested even with accommodations (2 to 5 percent of all students, depending on age and assessment year). Race categories exclude persons of Hispanic ethnicity, except where noted. Totals include other racial/ethnic groups not shown separately.

SOURCE: U.S. Department of Education, National Center for Education Statistics, National Assessment of Educational Progress (NAEP), *NAEP 1999 Trends in Academic Progress*; and 2004, 2008, and 2012 Long-Term Trend Reading Assessments, retrieved May 12, 2009, and July 15, 2013, from the Long-Term Trend NAEP Data Explorer (http://nces.ed.gov/nationsreportcard/naepdata/). (This table was prepared July 2013.)

Table 222.10. Average National Assessment of Educational Progress (NAEP) mathematics scale score, by sex, race/ethnicity, and grade: Selected years, 1990 through 2015

[Standard errors appear in parentheses]

Grade and year	All students	Sex			Race/ethnicity									
		Average mathematics scale score		Gap between female and male score	Average mathematics scale score								Gap between White and Black score	Gap between White and Hispanic score
								Asian/Pacific Islander						
		Male	Female		White	Black	Hispanic	Total	Asian[1]	Pacific Islander[1]	American Indian/Alaska Native	Two or more races[1]		
1	2	3	4	5	6	7	8	9	10	11	12	13	14	15
Grade 4														
1990[2]	213 (0.9)	214 (1.2)	213 (1.1)	-1 (1.7)	220 (1.0)	188 (1.8)	200 (2.2)	225 (4.1)	— (†)	— (†)	‡ (†)	— (†)	32 (2.0)	20 (2.4)
1992[2]	220 (0.7)	221 (0.8)	219 (1.0)	-2 (1.2)	227 (0.8)	193 (1.4)	202 (1.5)	231 (2.1)	— (†)	— (†)	‡ (†)	— (†)	35 (1.6)	25 (1.7)
1996	224 (1.0)	224 (1.1)	223 (1.1)	# (†)	232 (1.0)	198 (1.6)	207 (1.9)	229 (4.2)	— (†)	— (†)	217 (5.6)	— (†)	34 (1.8)	25 (2.1)
2000	226 (0.9)	227 (1.0)	224 (0.9)	-3 (1.4)	234 (0.8)	203 (1.2)	208 (1.5)	‡ (†)	— (†)	— (†)	208 (3.5)	— (†)	31 (1.5)	27 (1.7)
2003	235 (0.2)	236 (0.3)	233 (0.2)	-3 (0.3)	243 (0.2)	216 (0.4)	222 (0.4)	246 (1.1)	— (†)	— (†)	223 (1.0)	— (†)	27 (0.4)	22 (0.5)
2005	238 (0.1)	239 (0.2)	237 (0.2)	-3 (0.2)	246 (0.1)	220 (0.3)	226 (0.3)	251 (0.7)	— (†)	— (†)	226 (0.9)	— (†)	26 (0.3)	20 (0.3)
2007	240 (0.2)	241 (0.2)	239 (0.2)	-2 (0.3)	248 (0.2)	222 (0.3)	227 (0.3)	253 (0.8)	— (†)	— (†)	228 (0.7)	— (†)	26 (0.4)	21 (0.4)
2009	240 (0.2)	241 (0.3)	239 (0.3)	-2 (0.4)	248 (0.2)	222 (0.3)	227 (0.4)	255 (1.0)	— (†)	— (†)	225 (0.9)	— (†)	26 (0.4)	21 (0.5)
2011	241 (0.2)	241 (0.2)	240 (0.2)	-1 (0.3)	249 (0.2)	224 (0.4)	229 (0.3)	256 (1.0)	257 (1.0)	236 (2.1)	225 (0.9)	245 (0.6)	25 (0.4)	20 (0.4)
2013	242 (0.2)	242 (0.3)	241 (0.2)	-1 (0.4)	250 (0.2)	224 (0.3)	231 (0.4)	258 (0.8)	259 (0.8)	236 (2.0)	227 (1.1)	245 (0.7)	26 (0.4)	19 (0.5)
2015	240 (0.3)	241 (0.3)	239 (0.3)	-2 (0.4)	248 (0.3)	224 (0.4)	230 (0.5)	257 (1.2)	259 (1.2)	231 (2.3)	227 (1.0)	245 (0.8)	24 (0.5)	18 (0.5)
Grade 8														
1990[2]	263 (1.3)	263 (1.6)	262 (1.3)	-1 (2.1)	270 (1.3)	237 (2.7)	246 (4.3)	275 (5.0)	— (†)	— (†)	‡ (†)	— (†)	33 (3.0)	24 (4.5)
1992[2]	268 (0.9)	268 (1.1)	269 (1.0)	1 (1.5)	277 (1.0)	237 (1.3)	249 (1.2)	290 (5.9)	— (†)	— (†)	‡ (†)	— (†)	40 (1.7)	28 (1.5)
1996	270 (0.9)	271 (1.1)	269 (1.1)	-2 (1.5)	281 (1.1)	240 (1.9)	251 (1.7)	‡ (†)	— (†)	— (†)	‡ (†)	— (†)	41 (2.2)	30 (2.0)
2000	273 (0.8)	274 (0.9)	272 (0.9)	-2 (1.3)	284 (0.8)	244 (1.2)	253 (1.3)	288 (3.5)	— (†)	— (†)	259 (7.5)	— (†)	40 (1.5)	31 (1.6)
2003	278 (0.3)	278 (0.3)	277 (0.3)	-2 (0.4)	288 (0.3)	252 (0.5)	259 (0.6)	291 (1.3)	— (†)	— (†)	263 (1.8)	— (†)	35 (0.6)	29 (0.7)
2005	279 (0.2)	280 (0.2)	278 (0.2)	-2 (0.3)	289 (0.2)	255 (0.4)	262 (0.4)	295 (0.9)	— (†)	— (†)	264 (0.9)	— (†)	34 (0.4)	27 (0.5)
2007	281 (0.3)	282 (0.3)	280 (0.3)	-2 (0.4)	291 (0.3)	260 (0.4)	265 (0.4)	297 (0.9)	— (†)	— (†)	264 (1.2)	— (†)	32 (0.5)	26 (0.5)
2009	283 (0.3)	284 (0.3)	282 (0.4)	-2 (0.5)	293 (0.3)	261 (0.5)	266 (0.6)	301 (1.2)	— (†)	— (†)	266 (1.1)	— (†)	32 (0.5)	26 (0.6)
2011	284 (0.2)	284 (0.3)	283 (0.2)	-1 (0.4)	293 (0.2)	262 (0.5)	270 (0.5)	303 (1.0)	305 (1.1)	269 (2.4)	265 (0.9)	288 (1.3)	31 (0.5)	23 (0.5)
2013	285 (0.3)	285 (0.3)	284 (0.3)	-1 (0.4)	294 (0.3)	263 (0.4)	272 (0.5)	306 (1.1)	309 (1.1)	275 (2.3)	269 (1.2)	288 (1.2)	31 (0.5)	22 (0.5)
2015	282 (0.3)	282 (0.3)	282 (0.4)	# (†)	292 (0.3)	260 (0.5)	270 (0.5)	306 (1.5)	307 (1.5)	276 (2.9)	267 (1.3)	285 (1.1)	32 (0.6)	22 (0.6)
Grade 12														
1990[2]	[3] (†)	[3] (†)	[3] (†)	[3] (†)	[3] (†)	[3] (†)	[3] (†)	[3] (†)	[3] (†)	[3] (†)	[3] (†)	[3] (†)	[3] (†)	[3] (†)
1992[2]	[3] (†)	[3] (†)	[3] (†)	[3] (†)	[3] (†)	[3] (†)	[3] (†)	[3] (†)	[3] (†)	[3] (†)	[3] (†)	[3] (†)	[3] (†)	[3] (†)
1996	[3] (†)	[3] (†)	[3] (†)	[3] (†)	[3] (†)	[3] (†)	[3] (†)	[3] (†)	[3] (†)	[3] (†)	[3] (†)	[3] (†)	[3] (†)	[3] (†)
2000	[3] (†)	[3] (†)	[3] (†)	[3] (†)	[3] (†)	[3] (†)	[3] (†)	[3] (†)	[3] (†)	[3] (†)	[3] (†)	[3] (†)	[3] (†)	[3] (†)
2003	— (†)	— (†)	— (†)	— (†)	— (†)	— (†)	— (†)	— (†)	— (†)	— (†)	— (†)	— (†)	— (†)	— (†)
2005	150 (0.6)	151 (0.7)	149 (0.7)	-3 (1.0)	157 (0.6)	127 (1.1)	133 (1.3)	163 (2.0)	— (†)	— (†)	134 (4.1)	— (†)	31 (1.2)	24 (1.4)
2007	— (†)	— (†)	— (†)	— (†)	— (†)	— (†)	— (†)	— (†)	— (†)	— (†)	— (†)	— (†)	— (†)	— (†)
2009	153 (0.7)	155 (0.9)	152 (0.7)	-3 (1.1)	161 (0.6)	131 (0.8)	138 (0.8)	175 (2.7)	— (†)	— (†)	144 (2.8)	— (†)	30 (1.0)	23 (1.0)
2011	— (†)	— (†)	— (†)	— (†)	— (†)	— (†)	— (†)	— (†)	— (†)	— (†)	— (†)	— (†)	— (†)	— (†)
2013	153 (0.5)	155 (0.6)	152 (0.6)	-3 (0.9)	162 (0.6)	132 (0.8)	141 (0.8)	172 (1.3)	174 (1.3)	151 (2.8)	142 (3.2)	155 (1.7)	30 (1.0)	21 (1.0)
2015	152 (0.5)	153 (0.7)	150 (0.6)	-3 (0.9)	160 (0.6)	130 (1.0)	139 (0.8)	170 (2.0)	171 (1.9)	‡ (†)	138 (2.8)	157 (2.2)	30 (1.2)	22 (1.0)

—Not available.
†Not applicable.
#Rounds to zero.
‡Reporting standards not met (too few cases for a reliable estimate).
[1]Prior to 2011, separate data for Asian students, Pacific Islander students, and students of Two or more races were not collected.
[2]Accommodations were not permitted for this assessment.
[3]Because of major changes to the framework and content of the grade 12 assessment, scores from 2005 and later assessment years cannot be compared with scores from earlier assessment years. Therefore, this table does not include scores from the earlier grade 12 assessment years (1990, 1992, 1996, and 2000). For data pertaining to scale score comparisons between earlier years, see the *Digest of Education Statistics 2009*, table 138 (http://nces.ed.gov/programs/digest/d09/tables/dt09_138.asp).

NOTE: For the grade 4 and grade 8 assessments, the scale ranges from 0 to 500. For the grade 12 assessment, the scale ranges from 0 to 300. Includes public and private schools. For 1996 and later years, includes students tested with accommodations (1 to 14 percent of all students, depending on grade level and year); excludes only those students with disabilities and English language learners who were unable to be tested even with accommodations (1 to 4 percent of all students). Race categories exclude persons of Hispanic ethnicity.
SOURCE: U.S. Department of Education, National Center for Education Statistics, National Assessment of Educational Progress (NAEP), 1990, 1992, 1996, 2000, 2003, 2005, 2007, 2009, 2011, 2013, and 2015 Mathematics Assessments, retrieved June 10, 2016, from the Main NAEP Data Explorer (http://nces.ed.gov/nationsreportcard/naepdata/). (This table was prepared June 2016.)

Table 222.12. Average National Assessment of Educational Progress (NAEP) mathematics scale score and percentage of students attaining selected NAEP mathematics achievement levels, by selected school and student characteristics and grade: Selected years, 1990 through 2015

[Standard errors appear in parentheses]

Grade and year	Percent of students in school eligible for free or reduced-price lunch					English language learner (ELL) status			Disability status[1]			Percent of all students attaining mathematics achievement levels		
	Average mathematics scale score[2]				Gap between low-poverty and high-poverty score	Average mathematics scale score[2]		Gap between non-ELL and ELL score	Average mathematics scale score[2]		Gap between non-SD and SD score			
	0–25 percent eligible (low poverty)	26–50 percent eligible	51–75 percent eligible	76–100 percent eligible (high poverty)		ELL	Non-ELL		Identified as student with disability (SD)	Not identified as SD		Below *Basic*[3]	At or above *Basic*[3]	At or above *Proficient*[4]
1	2	3	4	5	6	7	8	9	10	11	12	13	14	15
Grade 4														
1990[5]	— (†)	— (†)	— (†)	— (†)	— (†)	‡ (†)	‡ (†)	‡ (†)	‡ (†)	‡ (†)	‡ (†)	50 (1.4)	50 (1.4)	13 (1.2)
1992[5]	— (†)	— (†)	— (†)	— (†)	— (†)	‡ (†)	‡ (†)	‡ (†)	‡ (†)	‡ (†)	‡ (†)	41 (1.0)	59 (1.0)	18 (1.0)
1996	— (†)	— (†)	— (†)	— (†)	— (†)	201 (3.6)	225 (0.9)	24 (3.7)	204 (2.9)	225 (1.1)	22 (3.1)	37 (1.3)	63 (1.3)	21 (1.1)
2000	239 (1.2)	227 (1.2)	216 (1.5)	205 (1.2)	34 (1.7)	199 (2.0)	227 (0.8)	28 (2.1)	198 (2.2)	228 (0.9)	30 (2.4)	35 (1.3)	65 (1.3)	24 (1.0)
2003	247 (0.3)	237 (0.3)	229 (0.4)	216 (0.5)	31 (0.6)	214 (0.6)	237 (0.2)	23 (0.6)	214 (0.4)	237 (0.2)	23 (0.4)	23 (0.3)	77 (0.3)	32 (0.3)
2005	250 (0.3)	240 (0.3)	232 (0.3)	220 (0.3)	30 (0.4)	216 (0.5)	240 (0.1)	24 (0.5)	219 (0.4)	240 (0.2)	22 (0.4)	20 (0.2)	80 (0.2)	36 (0.2)
2007	252 (0.3)	242 (0.3)	234 (0.3)	222 (0.4)	30 (0.5)	217 (0.5)	242 (0.2)	25 (0.5)	220 (0.4)	242 (0.2)	22 (0.4)	18 (0.2)	82 (0.2)	39 (0.3)
2009	254 (0.4)	242 (0.4)	234 (0.4)	223 (0.4)	31 (0.6)	218 (0.6)	242 (0.2)	24 (0.7)	221 (0.5)	242 (0.2)	21 (0.5)	18 (0.3)	82 (0.3)	39 (0.3)
2011	255 (0.4)	245 (0.4)	237 (0.3)	226 (0.3)	29 (0.6)	219 (0.5)	243 (0.2)	24 (0.5)	218 (0.4)	244 (0.2)	26 (0.5)	18 (0.2)	82 (0.2)	40 (0.3)
2013	257 (0.4)	246 (0.4)	238 (0.5)	226 (0.5)	31 (0.6)	219 (0.6)	244 (0.2)	25 (0.6)	218 (0.5)	245 (0.2)	26 (0.5)	17 (0.2)	83 (0.2)	42 (0.3)
2015	257 (0.7)	245 (0.5)	237 (0.5)	226 (0.5)	30 (0.8)	218 (0.7)	243 (0.3)	25 (0.8)	218 (0.5)	244 (0.3)	26 (0.5)	18 (0.3)	82 (0.3)	40 (0.4)
Grade 8														
1990[5]	— (†)	— (†)	— (†)	— (†)	— (†)	‡ (†)	‡ (†)	‡ (†)	‡ (†)	‡ (†)	‡ (†)	48 (1.4)	52 (1.4)	15 (1.1)
1992[5]	— (†)	— (†)	— (†)	— (†)	— (†)	‡ (†)	‡ (†)	‡ (†)	‡ (†)	‡ (†)	‡ (†)	42 (1.1)	58 (1.1)	21 (1.0)
1996	— (†)	— (†)	— (†)	— (†)	— (†)	226 (3.2)	272 (1.0)	46 (3.4)	231 (2.7)	273 (0.9)	42 (2.9)	39 (1.0)	61 (1.0)	23 (1.0)
2000	287 (1.1)	270 (1.4)	260 (1.8)	246 (2.2)	41 (2.4)	234 (2.7)	274 (0.8)	40 (2.8)	230 (2.1)	276 (0.8)	47 (2.3)	37 (0.9)	63 (0.9)	26 (0.8)
2003	291 (0.4)	278 (0.4)	266 (0.7)	251 (0.7)	40 (0.8)	242 (1.0)	279 (0.3)	38 (1.0)	242 (0.6)	282 (0.3)	39 (0.6)	32 (0.3)	68 (0.3)	29 (0.3)
2005	293 (0.4)	280 (0.3)	268 (0.4)	254 (0.6)	38 (0.7)	244 (0.8)	281 (0.2)	37 (0.8)	245 (0.5)	283 (0.2)	38 (0.5)	31 (0.2)	69 (0.2)	30 (0.2)
2007	296 (0.4)	282 (0.4)	271 (0.6)	259 (0.7)	37 (0.8)	246 (0.8)	283 (0.3)	38 (0.8)	246 (0.6)	285 (0.3)	38 (0.7)	29 (0.3)	71 (0.3)	32 (0.3)
2009	298 (0.5)	284 (0.5)	274 (0.7)	260 (0.7)	38 (0.8)	243 (0.9)	285 (0.3)	42 (0.9)	249 (0.5)	287 (0.3)	38 (0.6)	27 (0.3)	73 (0.3)	34 (0.3)
2011	300 (0.5)	287 (0.5)	276 (0.7)	264 (0.7)	36 (0.9)	244 (1.0)	286 (0.2)	42 (1.0)	250 (0.6)	288 (0.2)	38 (0.7)	27 (0.2)	73 (0.2)	35 (0.2)
2013	301 (0.5)	289 (0.5)	277 (0.4)	265 (0.6)	36 (0.8)	246 (0.8)	287 (0.3)	41 (0.8)	249 (0.5)	289 (0.3)	40 (0.6)	26 (0.3)	74 (0.3)	35 (0.3)
2015	301 (0.6)	287 (0.5)	276 (0.7)	264 (0.7)	38 (1.0)	246 (0.8)	284 (0.3)	38 (0.8)	247 (0.5)	287 (0.3)	40 (0.6)	29 (0.3)	71 (0.3)	33 (0.3)
Grade 12														
1990[5]	[6] (†)	[6] (†)	[6] (†)	[6] (†)	[6] (†)	[6] (†)	[6] (†)	[6] (†)	[6] (†)	[6] (†)	[6] (†)	[6] (†)	[6] (†)	[6] (†)
1992[5]	[6] (†)	[6] (†)	[6] (†)	[6] (†)	[6] (†)	[6] (†)	[6] (†)	[6] (†)	[6] (†)	[6] (†)	[6] (†)	[6] (†)	[6] (†)	[6] (†)
1996	[6] (†)	[6] (†)	[6] (†)	[6] (†)	[6] (†)	[6] (†)	[6] (†)	[6] (†)	[6] (†)	[6] (†)	[6] (†)	[6] (†)	[6] (†)	[6] (†)
2000	[6] (†)	[6] (†)	[6] (†)	[6] (†)	[6] (†)	[6] (†)	[6] (†)	[6] (†)	[6] (†)	[6] (†)	[6] (†)	[6] (†)	[6] (†)	[6] (†)
2003	— (†)	— (†)	— (†)	— (†)	— (†)	— (†)	— (†)	— (†)	— (†)	— (†)	— (†)	— (†)	— (†)	— (†)
2005	158 (1.0)	147 (1.0)	136 (1.3)	122 (2.7)	36 (2.8)	120 (2.5)	151 (0.6)	31 (2.5)	114 (1.8)	153 (0.6)	39 (1.9)	39 (0.8)	61 (0.8)	23 (0.7)
2007	— (†)	— (†)	— (†)	— (†)	— (†)	— (†)	— (†)	— (†)	— (†)	— (†)	— (†)	— (†)	— (†)	— (†)
2009	166 (1.3)	150 (0.7)	140 (1.2)	130 (1.7)	36 (2.1)	117 (1.7)	154 (0.7)	38 (1.9)	120 (1.2)	156 (0.7)	36 (1.4)	36 (0.8)	64 (0.8)	26 (0.8)
2011	— (†)	— (†)	— (†)	— (†)	— (†)	— (†)	— (†)	— (†)	— (†)	— (†)	— (†)	— (†)	— (†)	— (†)
2013	169 (1.0)	155 (0.6)	143 (1.0)	134 (1.2)	35 (1.6)	109 (1.7)	155 (0.5)	46 (1.8)	119 (1.0)	157 (0.5)	38 (1.2)	35 (0.7)	65 (0.7)	26 (0.6)
2015	— (†)	— (†)	— (†)	— (†)	— (†)	— (†)	— (†)	— (†)	— (†)	— (†)	— (†)	— (†)	— (†)	— (†)

—Not available.
†Not applicable.
‡Reporting standards not met (too few cases for a reliable estimate).
[1]The student with disability (SD) variable used in this table includes students who have a 504 plan, even if they do not have an Individualized Education Plan (IEP).
[2]For the grade 4 and grade 8 assessments, the scale ranges from 0 to 500. For the grade 12 assessment, the scale ranges from 0 to 300.
[3]*Basic* denotes partial mastery of the knowledge and skills that are fundamental for proficient work at a given grade.
[4]*Proficient* represents solid academic performance. Students reaching this level have demonstrated competency over challenging subject matter.
[5]Accommodations were not permitted for this assessment.
[6]Because of major changes to the framework and content of the grade 12 assessment, results from 2005 and later assessment years cannot be compared with results from earlier assessment years. Therefore, this table does not include results from the earlier grade 12 assessment years (1990, 1992, 1996, and 2000). For data pertaining to comparisons between earlier years, see the *Digest of Education Statistics 2009*, table 138 (http://nces.ed.gov/programs/digest/d09/tables/dt09_138.asp).
NOTE: Includes public and private schools. For 1996 and later years, includes students tested with accommodations (1 to 14 percent of all students, depending on grade level and year); excludes only those students with disabilities and English language learners who were unable to be tested even with accommodations (1 to 4 percent of all students).
SOURCE: U.S. Department of Education, National Center for Education Statistics, National Assessment of Educational Progress (NAEP), 1990, 1992, 1996, 2000, 2003, 2005, 2007, 2009, 2011, 2013, and 2015 Mathematics Assessments, retrieved October 29, 2015, from the Main NAEP Data Explorer (http://nces.ed.gov/nationsreportcard/naepdata/). (This table was prepared October 2015.)

Table 222.20. Percentage of students at or above selected National Assessment of Educational Progress (NAEP) mathematics achievement levels, by grade and selected student characteristics: Selected years, 1996 through 2015

[Standard errors appear in parentheses]

Grade and selected student characteristic	1996		2003		2005		2007		2009		2011		2013		2015	
	At or above *Basic*[1]	At or above *Proficient*[2]	At or above *Basic*[1]	At or above *Proficient*[2]	At or above *Basic*[1]	At or above *Proficient*[2]	At or above *Basic*[1]	At or above *Proficient*[2]	At or above *Basic*[1]	At or above *Proficient*[2]	At or above *Basic*[1]	At or above *Proficient*[2]	At or above *Basic*[1]	At or above *Proficient*[2]	At or above *Basic*[1]	At or above *Proficient*[2]
1	2	3	4	5	6	7	8	9	10	11	12	13	14	15	16	17
4th grade, all students	**63 (1.3)**	**21 (1.1)**	**77 (0.3)**	**32 (0.3)**	**80 (0.2)**	**36 (0.2)**	**82 (0.2)**	**39 (0.3)**	**82 (0.3)**	**39 (0.3)**	**82 (0.2)**	**40 (0.3)**	**83 (0.2)**	**42 (0.3)**	**82 (0.3)**	**40 (0.4)**
Sex																
Male	63 (1.5)	22 (1.2)	78 (0.4)	35 (0.4)	81 (0.2)	38 (0.2)	82 (0.2)	41 (0.3)	82 (0.3)	41 (0.4)	83 (0.3)	42 (0.4)	82 (0.3)	43 (0.4)	82 (0.4)	42 (0.5)
Female	63 (1.4)	20 (1.4)	76 (0.3)	30 (0.3)	80 (0.2)	34 (0.3)	82 (0.2)	37 (0.4)	82 (0.3)	37 (0.4)	82 (0.3)	39 (0.4)	83 (0.2)	41 (0.4)	82 (0.3)	38 (0.5)
Race/ethnicity																
White	76 (1.2)	27 (1.3)	87 (0.2)	43 (0.3)	90 (0.2)	47 (0.2)	91 (0.2)	51 (0.4)	91 (0.2)	51 (0.4)	91 (0.2)	52 (0.4)	91 (0.2)	54 (0.4)	90 (0.3)	51 (0.5)
Black	27 (2.0)	3 (0.6)	54 (0.6)	10 (0.3)	60 (0.5)	13 (0.3)	64 (0.6)	15 (0.4)	64 (0.6)	16 (0.5)	66 (0.6)	17 (0.5)	66 (0.6)	18 (0.5)	65 (0.7)	19 (0.6)
Hispanic	40 (2.7)	7 (1.4)	62 (0.7)	16 (0.5)	68 (0.5)	19 (0.3)	70 (0.5)	22 (0.4)	71 (0.7)	22 (0.4)	72 (0.5)	24 (0.5)	73 (0.7)	26 (0.6)	73 (0.6)	26 (0.7)
Asian/Pacific Islander	67 (5.7)	27 (5.0)	87 (0.8)	48 (1.9)	90 (0.5)	55 (1.1)	91 (0.7)	58 (1.3)	92 (0.6)	60 (1.5)	91 (0.6)	62 (1.6)	91 (0.6)	64 (1.2)	91 (0.8)	62 (1.7)
Asian	— (†)	— (†)	— (†)	— (†)	— (†)	— (†)	— (†)	— (†)	— (†)	— (†)	93 (0.5)	64 (1.6)	92 (0.6)	66 (1.2)	93 (0.7)	65 (1.7)
Pacific Islander	— (†)	— (†)	— (†)	— (†)	— (†)	— (†)	— (†)	— (†)	— (†)	— (†)	77 (2.7)	34 (3.2)	77 (3.1)	33 (3.2)	68 (4.0)	30 (2.8)
American Indian/Alaska Native	57 (7.5)	‡ (†)	64 (1.7)	17 (1.2)	68 (1.5)	21 (1.2)	70 (1.2)	25 (1.1)	66 (1.6)	21 (1.2)	66 (1.2)	22 (1.2)	68 (1.7)	23 (1.4)	69 (1.8)	23 (1.7)
Two or more races	— (†)	— (†)	— (†)	— (†)	— (†)	— (†)	— (†)	— (†)	— (†)	— (†)	87 (0.7)	45 (1.2)	85 (1.0)	46 (1.4)	86 (0.9)	45 (1.3)
Eligibility for free or reduced-price lunch																
Eligible	40 (1.8)	8 (0.9)	62 (0.5)	15 (0.3)	67 (0.3)	19 (0.2)	70 (0.4)	22 (0.3)	70 (0.4)	22 (0.3)	72 (0.3)	24 (0.3)	73 (0.4)	25 (0.4)	72 (0.4)	24 (0.4)
Not eligible	76 (1.2)	27 (1.2)	88 (0.3)	45 (0.4)	90 (0.2)	49 (0.3)	91 (0.2)	53 (0.4)	91 (0.3)	54 (0.4)	92 (0.2)	57 (0.4)	93 (0.2)	59 (0.4)	92 (0.3)	58 (0.6)
Unknown	72 (3.0)	28 (4.1)	84 (0.9)	41 (1.2)	87 (0.7)	45 (1.2)	90 (0.9)	48 (1.5)	88 (1.3)	47 (1.7)	90 (0.8)	52 (1.4)	90 (1.0)	52 (2.2)	89 (1.2)	50 (1.7)
8th grade, all students	**61 (1.0)**	**23 (1.0)**	**68 (0.3)**	**29 (0.3)**	**69 (0.2)**	**30 (0.2)**	**71 (0.3)**	**32 (0.3)**	**73 (0.3)**	**34 (0.3)**	**73 (0.2)**	**35 (0.2)**	**74 (0.3)**	**35 (0.3)**	**71 (0.3)**	**33 (0.3)**
Sex																
Male	62 (1.2)	25 (1.2)	69 (0.4)	30 (0.4)	70 (0.3)	31 (0.3)	72 (0.3)	34 (0.4)	73 (0.3)	36 (0.4)	73 (0.4)	36 (0.3)	74 (0.3)	36 (0.4)	71 (0.4)	34 (0.4)
Female	60 (1.2)	22 (1.2)	67 (0.4)	27 (0.3)	69 (0.3)	28 (0.3)	71 (0.3)	30 (0.3)	72 (0.4)	32 (0.4)	73 (0.2)	34 (0.3)	74 (0.4)	35 (0.4)	72 (0.4)	33 (0.4)
Race/ethnicity																
White	73 (1.3)	30 (1.3)	80 (0.3)	37 (0.4)	80 (0.2)	39 (0.3)	82 (0.3)	42 (0.3)	83 (0.3)	44 (0.4)	84 (0.3)	44 (0.3)	84 (0.2)	45 (0.4)	82 (0.3)	43 (0.4)
Black	25 (1.8)	4 (0.8)	39 (0.8)	7 (0.3)	42 (0.5)	9 (0.3)	47 (0.7)	11 (0.3)	50 (0.6)	12 (0.5)	51 (0.6)	13 (0.4)	52 (0.7)	14 (0.5)	48 (0.9)	13 (0.5)
Hispanic	39 (2.0)	8 (1.1)	48 (0.8)	12 (0.5)	52 (0.6)	13 (0.4)	55 (0.7)	15 (0.4)	57 (0.8)	17 (0.6)	61 (0.7)	20 (0.6)	62 (0.6)	21 (0.5)	60 (0.7)	19 (0.6)
Asian/Pacific Islander	‡ (†)	‡ (†)	78 (1.1)	43 (1.3)	81 (0.8)	47 (1.2)	83 (0.8)	50 (1.1)	85 (1.0)	54 (1.8)	86 (1.0)	55 (1.2)	87 (0.8)	60 (1.3)	87 (0.9)	59 (1.7)
Asian	— (†)	— (†)	— (†)	— (†)	— (†)	— (†)	— (†)	— (†)	— (†)	— (†)	88 (0.9)	58 (1.3)	89 (0.8)	63 (1.3)	88 (0.9)	61 (1.7)
Pacific Islander	— (†)	— (†)	— (†)	— (†)	— (†)	— (†)	— (†)	— (†)	— (†)	— (†)	59 (4.7)	22 (1.9)	67 (3.5)	24 (2.9)	63 (4.2)	29 (3.9)
American Indian/Alaska Native	‡ (†)	‡ (†)	52 (2.7)	15 (1.7)	53 (1.3)	14 (1.2)	53 (1.8)	16 (1.2)	56 (1.5)	18 (1.3)	55 (1.5)	17 (1.2)	59 (1.7)	21 (1.5)	57 (1.8)	20 (1.7)
Two or more races	— (†)	— (†)	— (†)	— (†)	— (†)	— (†)	— (†)	— (†)	— (†)	— (†)	78 (1.1)	39 (1.7)	76 (1.2)	38 (1.4)	74 (1.5)	36 (1.3)
Eligibility for free or reduced-price lunch																
Eligible	38 (2.1)	8 (1.2)	48 (0.5)	12 (0.4)	51 (0.4)	13 (0.2)	55 (0.5)	15 (0.3)	57 (0.5)	17 (0.3)	59 (0.4)	19 (0.3)	60 (0.4)	20 (0.3)	58 (0.4)	18 (0.3)
Not eligible	69 (1.5)	28 (1.3)	79 (0.3)	37 (0.4)	79 (0.2)	39 (0.3)	81 (0.3)	42 (0.4)	83 (0.3)	45 (0.4)	84 (0.2)	47 (0.4)	86 (0.3)	49 (0.4)	84 (0.3)	48 (0.5)
Unknown	70 (2.6)	30 (2.6)	75 (1.1)	36 (1.2)	79 (1.1)	40 (1.4)	81 (1.7)	43 (1.7)	83 (1.3)	48 (1.9)	85 (0.9)	48 (1.5)	84 (1.3)	50 (2.6)	81 (1.5)	46 (1.9)
12th grade, all students	**[3] (†)**	**[3] (†)**	**— (†)**	**— (†)**	**61 (0.8)**	**23 (0.7)**	**— (†)**	**— (†)**	**64 (0.8)**	**26 (0.8)**	**— (†)**	**— (†)**	**65 (0.7)**	**26 (0.6)**	**— (†)**	**— (†)**
Sex																
Male	[3] (†)	[3] (†)	— (†)	— (†)	62 (0.9)	25 (1.0)	— (†)	— (†)	65 (0.9)	28 (1.0)	— (†)	— (†)	66 (0.8)	28 (0.8)	— (†)	— (†)
Female	[3] (†)	[3] (†)	— (†)	— (†)	60 (1.0)	21 (0.8)	— (†)	— (†)	63 (0.8)	24 (0.8)	— (†)	— (†)	64 (0.9)	24 (0.7)	— (†)	— (†)
Race/ethnicity																
White	[3] (†)	[3] (†)	— (†)	— (†)	70 (0.8)	29 (0.8)	— (†)	— (†)	75 (0.7)	33 (0.8)	— (†)	— (†)	75 (0.8)	33 (0.8)	— (†)	— (†)
Black	[3] (†)	[3] (†)	— (†)	— (†)	30 (1.7)	6 (0.8)	— (†)	— (†)	37 (1.2)	6 (0.6)	— (†)	— (†)	38 (1.5)	7 (0.6)	— (†)	— (†)
Hispanic	[3] (†)	[3] (†)	— (†)	— (†)	40 (2.1)	8 (1.0)	— (†)	— (†)	45 (1.1)	11 (0.8)	— (†)	— (†)	50 (1.3)	12 (0.7)	— (†)	— (†)
Asian/Pacific Islander	[3] (†)	[3] (†)	— (†)	— (†)	73 (2.6)	36 (3.0)	— (†)	— (†)	84 (1.9)	52 (3.4)	— (†)	— (†)	81 (1.4)	47 (2.0)	— (†)	— (†)
Asian	[3] (†)	[3] (†)	— (†)	— (†)	— (†)	— (†)	— (†)	— (†)	— (†)	— (†)	— (†)	— (†)	83 (1.5)	49 (2.0)	— (†)	— (†)
Pacific Islander	[3] (†)	[3] (†)	— (†)	— (†)	— (†)	— (†)	— (†)	— (†)	— (†)	— (†)	— (†)	— (†)	65 (7.3)	16 (6.0)	— (†)	— (†)
American Indian/Alaska Native	[3] (†)	[3] (†)	— (†)	— (†)	42 (8.6)	6 (2.9)	— (†)	— (†)	56 (5.4)	12 (3.3)	— (†)	— (†)	54 (5.8)	12 (4.0)	— (†)	— (†)
Two or more races	[3] (†)	[3] (†)	— (†)	— (†)	— (†)	— (†)	— (†)	— (†)	— (†)	— (†)	— (†)	— (†)	67 (3.0)	26 (2.7)	— (†)	— (†)

—Not available.
†Not applicable.
‡Reporting standards not met (too few cases for a reliable estimate).
[1]*Basic* denotes partial mastery of the knowledge and skills that are fundamental for proficient work.
[2]*Proficient* represents solid academic performance. Students reaching this level have demonstrated competency over challenging subject matter.
[3]Because of major changes to the framework and content of the grade 12 assessment, results from 2005 and later assessment years cannot be compared with results from earlier assessment years. Therefore, this table excludes grade 12 results from 1996.

NOTE: Includes public and private schools. Includes students tested with accommodations (1 to 14 percent of all students, depending on grade level and year); excludes only those students with disabilities and English language learners who were unable to be tested even with accommodations (1 to 4 percent of all students). Race categories exclude persons of Hispanic ethnicity. Prior to 2011, separate data for Asian students, Pacific Islander students, and students of Two or more races were not collected.
SOURCE: U.S. Department of Education, National Center for Education Statistics, National Assessment of Educational Progress (NAEP), 1996, 2003, 2005, 2007, 2009, 2011, 2013, and 2015 Mathematics Assessments, retrieved October 29, 2015, from the Main NAEP Data Explorer (http://nces.ed.gov/nationsreportcard/naepdata/). (This table was prepared October 2015.)

Table 222.30. Average National Assessment of Educational Progress (NAEP) mathematics scale score of 8th-graders with various attitudes toward mathematics and percentage reporting these attitudes, by selected student characteristics: 2015

[Standard errors appear in parentheses]

Student characteristic	Math work is engaging and interesting: Never or hardly ever	Sometimes	Often	Always/ almost always	Math work is challenging: Never or hardly ever	Sometimes	Often	Always/ almost always	Math work is too easy: Never or hardly ever	Sometimes	Often	Always/ almost always
1	2	3	4	5	6	7	8	9	10	11	12	13
						Average scale score[1]						
All students	**276 (0.4)**	**282 (0.4)**	**288 (0.4)**	**286 (0.6)**	**295 (0.6)**	**284 (0.4)**	**281 (0.4)**	**272 (0.6)**	**282 (0.5)**	**281 (0.3)**	**286 (0.5)**	**289 (0.8)**
Sex												
Male	277 (0.5)	282 (0.5)	287 (0.5)	285 (0.7)	297 (0.9)	284 (0.4)	281 (0.5)	270 (0.8)	281 (0.6)	281 (0.4)	286 (0.6)	291 (0.9)
Female	275 (0.5)	282 (0.4)	288 (0.6)	286 (0.8)	293 (0.8)	284 (0.5)	281 (0.6)	273 (0.7)	283 (0.7)	281 (0.4)	285 (0.6)	287 (1.1)
Race/ethnicity												
White	282 (0.5)	292 (0.4)	298 (0.4)	298 (0.6)	301 (0.6)	293 (0.4)	291 (0.5)	281 (0.7)	289 (0.6)	291 (0.3)	296 (0.5)	298 (0.9)
Black	258 (1.0)	260 (0.8)	264 (0.7)	263 (0.9)	272 (1.6)	263 (0.6)	260 (0.8)	252 (1.2)	261 (1.1)	260 (0.6)	265 (0.8)	265 (1.5)
Hispanic	264 (1.0)	269 (0.7)	274 (0.8)	273 (1.0)	281 (1.6)	272 (0.7)	269 (0.8)	264 (1.3)	271 (1.0)	269 (0.5)	273 (0.9)	277 (1.9)
Asian	300 (2.0)	306 (2.0)	312 (2.2)	310 (2.8)	325 (2.7)	308 (1.9)	305 (1.7)	293 (3.3)	305 (2.9)	305 (2.0)	311 (1.8)	318 (2.9)
Pacific Islander	271 (5.3)	273 (5.1)	291 (4.2)	266 (6.2)	296 (6.1)	277 (3.9)	277 (6.3)	260 (4.2)	286 (7.7)	275 (4.7)	274 (5.9)	287 (7.4)
American Indian/ Alaska Native	262 (3.0)	269 (2.2)	272 (2.3)	270 (3.9)	284 (6.1)	272 (1.9)	265 (2.2)	259 (2.9)	268 (2.8)	266 (1.7)	273 (3.3)	279 (5.9)
Two or more races	274 (1.8)	287 (1.8)	289 (2.0)	291 (2.5)	294 (2.9)	285 (1.4)	286 (2.2)	275 (2.9)	283 (2.3)	286 (1.5)	284 (2.1)	292 (3.7)
Eligibility for free or reduced-price lunch												
Eligible	264 (0.5)	267 (0.5)	273 (0.5)	271 (0.6)	280 (0.8)	271 (0.4)	267 (0.5)	258 (0.6)	266 (0.5)	267 (0.4)	272 (0.5)	275 (1.2)
Not eligible	286 (0.5)	295 (0.4)	302 (0.6)	303 (0.8)	306 (0.7)	297 (0.4)	295 (0.5)	287 (0.8)	294 (0.6)	295 (0.4)	299 (0.6)	304 (1.0)
Unknown	282 (2.4)	298 (1.7)	298 (1.7)	299 (2.6)	308 (3.9)	294 (1.6)	294 (1.8)	283 (2.7)	292 (2.3)	294 (1.7)	300 (2.6)	303 (3.3)
Highest education level of either parent[2]												
Did not finish high school	260 (1.2)	265 (0.9)	269 (1.3)	268 (1.7)	275 (2.2)	269 (1.0)	263 (1.1)	256 (1.6)	261 (1.4)	264 (0.8)	270 (1.3)	276 (2.2)
Graduated high school	265 (0.8)	267 (0.8)	272 (0.7)	269 (1.2)	279 (1.5)	270 (0.6)	267 (0.7)	257 (1.1)	267 (1.1)	267 (0.6)	2712 (0.9)	270 (1.6)
Some education after high school	278 (0.9)	282 (0.7)	285 (0.8)	286 (1.1)	293 (1.3)	284 (0.6)	281 (0.7)	272 (1.1)	278 (0.9)	282 (0.6)	287 (0.9)	292 (1.7)
Graduated college	285 (0.5)	294 (0.5)	299 (0.6)	298 (0.7)	305 (0.8)	295 (0.5)	293 (0.5)	285 (0.7)	293 (0.6)	293 (0.4)	296 (0.6)	300 (0.8)
						Percent of students						
All students	**20 (0.2)**	**35 (0.3)**	**29 (0.3)**	**15 (0.2)**	**11 (0.2)**	**44 (0.3)**	**34 (0.3)**	**12 (0.1)**	**18 (0.2)**	**55 (0.2)**	**20 (0.2)**	**7 (0.1)**
Sex												
Male	20 (0.3)	33 (0.3)	30 (0.3)	16 (0.2)	11 (0.2)	43 (0.3)	35 (0.3)	11 (0.2)	16 (0.2)	55 (0.3)	22 (0.3)	7 (0.2)
Female	20 (0.3)	37 (0.3)	29 (0.3)	15 (0.2)	11 (0.3)	44 (0.4)	33 (0.4)	12 (0.2)	20 (0.4)	55 (0.3)	19 (0.3)	6 (0.2)
Race/ethnicity												
White	23 (0.3)	35 (0.3)	28 (0.3)	14 (0.3)	12 (0.2)	43 (0.4)	34 (0.3)	11 (0.2)	21 (0.3)	54 (0.3)	18 (0.2)	6 (0.2)
Black	18 (0.5)	34 (0.6)	28 (0.5)	20 (0.5)	9 (0.3)	43 (0.6)	33 (0.6)	15 (0.3)	16 (0.4)	55 (0.6)	22 (0.5)	7 (0.3)
Hispanic	17 (0.4)	36 (0.5)	31 (0.6)	16 (0.5)	9 (0.4)	44 (0.6)	35 (0.6)	11 (0.3)	13 (0.4)	58 (0.6)	22 (0.5)	7 (0.3)
Asian	14 (1.0)	33 (1.4)	34 (0.9)	19 (1.3)	14 (0.9)	48 (1.3)	29 (1.1)	9 (0.7)	10 (0.9)	54 (1.2)	27 (1.2)	10 (0.7)
Pacific Islander	17 (4.1)	29 (3.4)	36 (4.1)	18 (2.6)	11 (2.6)	43 (3.7)	35 (2.9)	11 (1.8)	13 (2.5)	56 (3.7)	21 (3.2)	10 (2.6)
American Indian/Alaska Native	19 (1.5)	35 (1.9)	32 (2.1)	14 (1.0)	9 (1.3)	41 (2.2)	38 (2.3)	12 (1.0)	18 (1.4)	55 (2.1)	20 (1.8)	7 (1.0)
Two or more races	22 (1.0)	34 (1.3)	30 (1.3)	14 (0.9)	12 (0.8)	42 (1.6)	36 (1.8)	11 (0.7)	19 (1.1)	55 (1.3)	20 (1.1)	6 (0.6)
Eligibility for free or reduced-price lunch												
Eligible	19 (0.3)	35 (0.3)	30 (0.3)	17 (0.3)	10 (0.2)	44 (0.4)	34 (0.4)	12 (0.2)	15 (0.3)	56 (0.3)	22 (0.3)	7 (0.2)
Not eligible	22 (0.3)	35 (0.4)	29 (0.3)	14 (0.3)	12 (0.2)	43 (0.4)	34 (0.4)	11 (0.2)	20 (0.3)	55 (0.4)	19 (0.3)	6 (0.2)
Unknown	21 (1.2)	34 (1.1)	29 (1.3)	17 (0.9)	11 (0.9)	41 (1.1)	37 (1.2)	11 (0.7)	23 (1.3)	55 (1.2)	16 (1.0)	5 (0.5)
Highest education level of either parent[2]												
Did not finish high school	20 (0.6)	36 (0.7)	29 (0.7)	15 (0.7)	9 (0.5)	43 (1.0)	35 (1.0)	13 (0.6)	15 (0.6)	56 (0.9)	22 (0.6)	7 (0.5)
Graduated high school	21 (0.5)	36 (0.6)	28 (0.5)	15 (0.4)	9 (0.3)	44 (0.5)	35 (0.6)	12 (0.3)	16 (0.4)	58 (0.6)	20 (0.5)	6 (0.3)
Some education after high school	21 (0.4)	36 (0.5)	29 (0.5)	14 (0.4)	11 (0.5)	45 (0.7)	33 (0.7)	11 (0.4)	19 (0.4)	55 (0.5)	20 (0.5)	6 (0.3)
Graduated college	20 (0.3)	34 (0.4)	30 (0.3)	16 (0.3)	12 (0.2)	43 (0.3)	34 (0.4)	11 (0.2)	19 (0.3)	54 (0.3)	20 (0.3)	7 (0.2)

[1]Scale ranges from 0 to 500.
[2]Based on student reports. The category of students whose parents have an unknown level of education is not shown, although data for these students is included in table totals.
NOTE: Includes public and private schools. Includes students tested with accommodations (12 percent of all 8th-grade students); excludes only those students with disabilities and English language learners who were unable to be tested even with accommodations (2 percent of all 8th-grade students). Race categories exclude persons of Hispanic ethnicity. Detail may not sum to totals because of rounding.
SOURCE: U.S. Department of Education, National Center for Education Statistics, National Assessment of Educational Progress (NAEP), 2015 Mathematics Assessment, retrieved October 29, 2015, from the Main NAEP Data Explorer (http://nces.ed.gov/nationsreportcard/naepdata/). (This table was prepared October 2015.)

Table 222.35. Average National Assessment of Educational Progress (NAEP) mathematics scale score of 12th-graders with various attitudes toward mathematics and percentage reporting these attitudes, by selected student characteristics: 2013

[Standard errors appear in parentheses]

Student characteristic	Math work is engaging and interesting				Math work is challenging				Math work is too easy			
	Never or hardly ever	Sometimes	Often	Always/ almost always	Never or hardly ever	Sometimes	Often	Always/ almost always	Never or hardly ever	Sometimes	Often	Always/ almost always
1	2	3	4	5	6	7	8	9	10	11	12	13
	Average scale score[1]											
All students	**145 (0.6)**	**155 (0.6)**	**165 (0.8)**	**166 (1.0)**	**158 (1.4)**	**157 (0.7)**	**158 (0.6)**	**154 (1.0)**	**156 (0.7)**	**156 (0.6)**	**158 (1.0)**	**162 (1.1)**
Sex												
Male	146 (0.9)	158 (0.8)	167 (1.1)	169 (1.3)	161 (1.8)	160 (0.9)	158 (0.8)	155 (1.2)	157 (1.1)	157 (0.8)	163 (1.2)	165 (1.5)
Female	145 (0.8)	153 (0.8)	163 (1.0)	164 (1.4)	154 (1.8)	153 (0.9)	157 (0.9)	154 (1.3)	156 (0.8)	154 (0.8)	152 (1.2)	157 (1.8)
Race/ethnicity												
White	152 (0.8)	164 (0.7)	175 (1.1)	179 (1.4)	165 (1.5)	165 (0.8)	166 (0.8)	163 (1.2)	163 (0.9)	165 (0.8)	168 (1.1)	169 (1.4)
Black	127 (1.3)	133 (1.3)	139 (1.4)	135 (2.4)	136 (2.4)	134 (1.3)	134 (1.3)	129 (1.6)	133 (1.7)	132 (1.1)	134 (1.9)	136 (2.6)
Hispanic	135 (1.3)	142 (1.0)	147 (1.3)	154 (1.7)	141 (3.5)	144 (0.9)	144 (1.1)	141 (1.5)	144 (1.4)	142 (0.9)	144 (1.6)	150 (2.7)
Asian	167 (2.9)	173 (2.3)	182 (2.3)	187 (3.1)	188 (4.0)	179 (2.0)	174 (2.2)	176 (3.3)	181 (2.2)	174 (2.3)	176 (2.7)	185 (3.6)
Pacific Islander	‡ (†)	‡ (†)	‡ (†)	‡ (†)	‡ (†)	‡ (†)	‡ (†)	‡ (†)	‡ (†)	‡ (†)	‡ (†)	‡ (†)
American Indian/Alaska Native	137 (7.7)	149 (4.3)	140 (5.8)	‡ (†)	‡ (†)	140 (7.3)	145 (5.2)	‡ (†)	145 (3.8)	141 (4.8)	‡ (†)	‡ (†)
Two or more races	145 (3.9)	156 (2.4)	168 (5.3)	‡ (†)	‡ (†)	159 (3.8)	158 (3.3)	153 (3.7)	158 (3.7)	153 (3.1)	160 (6.2)	‡ (†)
Eligibility for free or reduced-price lunch												
Eligible	133 (0.9)	139 (0.8)	146 (1.2)	148 (1.9)	143 (1.8)	142 (0.9)	141 (1.0)	137 (1.3)	139 (1.2)	139 (1.0)	143 (1.4)	149 (1.8)
Not eligible	151 (0.8)	164 (0.7)	175 (0.9)	177 (1.2)	166 (1.6)	165 (0.7)	166 (0.7)	163 (1.2)	163 (0.8)	165 (0.7)	167 (1.1)	169 (1.5)
Unknown	155 (2.8)	165 (2.3)	175 (3.6)	183 (3.9)	174 (4.8)	169 (3.1)	166 (2.8)	165 (2.9)	166 (2.6)	167 (2.9)	169 (4.3)	‡ (†)
Highest education level of either parent[2]												
Did not finish high school	131 (2.0)	136 (1.4)	144 (1.8)	148 (3.2)	137 (4.3)	139 (1.6)	140 (1.7)	136 (1.5)	136 (1.6)	138 (1.5)	141 (2.0)	148 (3.9)
Graduated high school	134 (1.2)	141 (1.1)	147 (1.4)	152 (2.4)	147 (2.9)	142 (1.1)	142 (1.2)	137 (1.8)	140 (1.5)	141 (0.9)	142 (2.1)	150 (2.9)
Some education after high school	141 (1.1)	153 (1.0)	161 (1.4)	162 (1.9)	156 (2.5)	152 (1.2)	153 (1.0)	152 (1.3)	151 (1.0)	152 (0.9)	155 (1.5)	159 (2.0)
Graduated college	155 (0.9)	167 (0.8)	177 (1.0)	178 (1.4)	169 (1.7)	168 (0.8)	169 (0.8)	166 (1.2)	167 (0.9)	167 (0.8)	171 (1.2)	171 (1.5)
	Percent of students											
All students	**26 (0.5)**	**36 (0.5)**	**27 (0.5)**	**11 (0.4)**	**7 (0.2)**	**35 (0.5)**	**37 (0.5)**	**21 (0.4)**	**32 (0.5)**	**47 (0.5)**	**15 (0.3)**	**6 (0.3)**
Sex												
Male	25 (0.6)	35 (0.6)	28 (0.7)	12 (0.5)	8 (0.4)	36 (0.7)	37 (0.7)	18 (0.5)	27 (0.6)	48 (0.7)	18 (0.4)	7 (0.4)
Female	27 (0.7)	37 (0.7)	25 (0.5)	11 (0.4)	6 (0.3)	34 (0.7)	36 (0.6)	23 (0.6)	36 (0.8)	47 (0.7)	13 (0.4)	4 (0.3)
Race/ethnicity												
White	28 (0.6)	35 (0.6)	27 (0.6)	10 (0.4)	8 (0.4)	35 (0.6)	37 (0.7)	21 (0.5)	34 (0.7)	45 (0.7)	14 (0.4)	6 (0.3)
Black	27 (1.0)	37 (1.0)	24 (1.0)	13 (0.9)	8 (0.5)	37 (1.3)	34 (1.0)	22 (1.2)	32 (1.0)	48 (1.2)	14 (0.8)	6 (0.5)
Hispanic	24 (0.9)	35 (1.0)	28 (0.8)	13 (0.7)	6 (0.3)	35 (1.0)	39 (1.0)	20 (0.8)	25 (0.8)	52 (1.0)	18 (0.8)	6 (0.5)
Asian	13 (1.1)	37 (1.5)	32 (1.6)	17 (1.4)	6 (1.1)	36 (1.8)	36 (1.7)	21 (1.6)	24 (1.7)	49 (2.1)	20 (1.7)	8 (1.1)
Pacific Islander	20 (5.5)	42 (7.2)	18 (4.6)	20 (6.7)	7 (3.9)	32 (7.0)	31 (7.1)	31 (5.8)	36 (7.7)	41 (6.5)	19 (6.1)	4 (2.5)
American Indian/Alaska Native	27 (4.9)	40 (5.1)	22 (4.8)	11 (3.0)	10 (3.1)	30 (6.9)	38 (5.8)	22 (4.0)	30 (6.0)	50 (6.0)	11 (4.2)	10 (3.6)
Two or more races	28 (2.6)	40 (3.3)	22 (2.7)	10 (1.7)	6 (1.3)	36 (3.3)	37 (3.2)	21 (2.7)	35 (3.3)	46 (3.0)	13 (2.2)	6 (1.6)
Eligibility for free or reduced-price lunch												
Eligible	25 (0.6)	35 (0.7)	27 (0.8)	12 (0.6)	7 (0.4)	36 (0.8)	35 (0.8)	21 (0.6)	27 (0.6)	50 (0.9)	17 (0.5)	6 (0.5)
Not eligible	27 (0.7)	36 (0.6)	26 (0.6)	11 (0.4)	7 (0.3)	35 (0.7)	37 (0.8)	21 (0.6)	34 (0.7)	46 (0.6)	15 (0.4)	6 (0.3)
Unknown	25 (2.0)	37 (1.5)	28 (1.8)	10 (1.3)	6 (0.9)	33 (1.9)	40 (1.6)	21 (1.6)	38 (2.1)	44 (1.9)	14 (1.6)	4 (0.8)
Highest education level of either parent[2]												
Did not finish high school	25 (1.3)	35 (1.0)	26 (1.1)	14 (0.9)	7 (0.7)	38 (1.5)	35 (1.4)	20 (1.2)	24 (1.3)	49 (1.4)	20 (1.0)	7 (0.8)
Graduated high school	29 (1.1)	36 (1.0)	26 (0.9)	10 (0.6)	8 (0.5)	36 (1.1)	37 (1.1)	19 (0.7)	29 (1.0)	49 (1.1)	15 (0.8)	6 (0.5)
Some education after high school	27 (0.9)	38 (1.0)	25 (0.9)	9 (0.6)	8 (0.5)	35 (0.9)	36 (0.9)	21 (0.8)	32 (0.8)	47 (0.8)	15 (0.6)	5 (0.4)
Graduated college	25 (0.7)	35 (0.6)	28 (0.6)	12 (0.5)	7 (0.3)	35 (0.7)	37 (0.8)	21 (0.6)	34 (0.7)	46 (0.7)	14 (0.4)	6 (0.3)

†Not applicable.
‡Reporting standards not met (too few cases for a reliable estimate).
[1]Scale ranges from 0 to 300.
[2]Based on student reports. The category of students whose parents have an unknown level of education is not shown, although data for these students is included in table totals.
NOTE: Includes public and private schools. Includes students tested with accommodations (9 percent of all 12th-grade students); excludes only those students with disabilities and English language learners who were unable to be tested even with accommodations (2 percent of all 12th-grade students). Race categories exclude persons of Hispanic ethnicity. Detail may not sum to totals because of rounding.
SOURCE: U.S. Department of Education, National Center for Education Statistics, National Assessment of Educational Progress (NAEP), 2013 Mathematics Assessment, retrieved October 20, 2014, from the Main NAEP Data Explorer (http://nces.ed.gov/nationsreportcard/naepdata/). (This table was prepared October 2014.)

Table 222.40. Average National Assessment of Educational Progress (NAEP) mathematics scale score of high school graduates at grade 12, by highest mathematics course taken in high school and selected student and school characteristics: 2009

[Standard errors appear in parentheses]

Selected student or school characteristic	Algebra I or below[1]		Geometry		Algebra II/ trigonometry		Analysis/ precalculus		Statistics/ probability		Advanced mathematics, other[2]		Calculus	
1	2		3		4		5		6		7		8	
Total[3]	**114**	**(1.1)**	**127**	**(1.0)**	**143**	**(0.6)**	**166**	**(0.9)**	**164**	**(1.8)**	**154**	**(1.3)**	**193**	**(1.2)**
Sex														
Male	117	(1.7)	128	(1.2)	145	(0.8)	169	(1.0)	165	(2.2)	156	(1.5)	197	(1.4)
Female	111	(1.6)	126	(1.1)	142	(0.8)	163	(1.0)	162	(2.0)	153	(1.4)	190	(1.2)
Race/ethnicity														
White	117	(1.6)	133	(1.3)	150	(0.8)	172	(0.9)	169	(1.5)	160	(1.3)	194	(1.1)
Black	104	(2.8)	114	(1.8)	129	(0.9)	147	(1.6)	139	(4.0)	138	(2.1)	170	(2.7)
Hispanic	109	(2.2)	122	(1.0)	136	(0.8)	155	(1.6)	154	(3.2)	142	(2.3)	179	(2.5)
Asian/Pacific Islander	‡	(†)	129	(3.9)	149	(4.1)	170	(2.3)	176	(4.1)	164	(2.9)	203	(1.8)
American Indian/Alaska Native	‡	(†)	‡	(†)	143	(3.8)	‡	(†)	‡	(†)	‡	(†)	‡	(†)
Student with disabilities (SD) status														
SD[4]	103	(1.7)	114	(2.5)	126	(2.1)	166	(5.0)	136	(6.3)	134	(3.5)	197	(3.7)
Non-SD	122	(1.2)	129	(0.9)	144	(0.6)	166	(0.9)	164	(1.7)	156	(1.3)	193	(1.2)
English language learner (ELL) status														
ELL	104	(4.5)	113	(2.8)	121	(2.1)	144	(6.1)	‡	(†)	129	(4.8)	‡	(†)
Non-ELL	114	(1.2)	128	(1.0)	144	(0.6)	166	(0.9)	164	(1.8)	155	(1.3)	193	(1.2)
School type														
Traditional public	114	(1.2)	127	(1.0)	143	(0.7)	166	(0.9)	164	(1.8)	155	(1.4)	193	(1.3)
Public charter	‡	(†)	‡	(†)	137	(10.3)	141	(6.8)	132	(1.6)	‡	(†)	‡	(†)
Private	‡	(†)	123	(3.3)	146	(3.3)	169	(2.7)	168	(3.9)	146	(4.0)	193	(3.3)
Percentage of students eligible for free or reduced-price lunch														
0–25 percent	116	(3.0)	134	(2.0)	151	(1.3)	173	(1.5)	173	(1.5)	162	(1.9)	199	(1.6)
26–50 percent	115	(1.5)	127	(1.4)	144	(1.0)	165	(1.1)	162	(2.9)	154	(1.7)	189	(1.0)
51–75 percent	111	(3.0)	123	(1.8)	136	(1.1)	156	(1.3)	149	(3.6)	146	(3.7)	179	(2.8)
76–100 percent	107	(5.4)	115	(3.1)	126	(2.0)	144	(3.7)	137	(4.1)	131	(2.6)	163	(3.9)
School locale														
City	110	(2.6)	125	(1.7)	140	(1.8)	163	(2.1)	163	(3.3)	151	(3.0)	195	(2.3)
Suburban	112	(2.3)	127	(1.9)	144	(1.0)	169	(1.4)	167	(2.4)	157	(2.0)	195	(2.0)
Town	114	(2.5)	129	(1.9)	144	(1.6)	166	(1.6)	164	(3.1)	152	(3.8)	191	(2.1)
Rural	117	(2.0)	129	(1.4)	145	(1.3)	165	(1.9)	157	(4.9)	155	(2.1)	187	(2.0)

†Not applicable.
‡Reporting standards not met (too few cases for a reliable estimate).
[1]Includes basic math, general math, applied math, prealgebra, and algebra I.
[2]Includes courses such as actuarial sciences, pure mathematics, discrete math, and advanced functions and modeling.
[3]Includes other racial/ethnic groups not shown separately, as well as students for whom information on race/ethnicity or sex was missing.
[4]SD estimates include both students with an Individualized Education Plan (IEP) and students with a plan under Section 504 of the Rehabilitation Act (a "504 plan"). IEPs are only for students who require specialized instruction, whereas 504 plans apply to students who require accommodations but may not require specialized instruction.

NOTE: Scale ranges from 0 to 300. Includes students tested with accommodations (6 percent of all 12th-graders); excludes only those students with disabilities and English language learners who were unable to be tested even with accommodations (3 percent of all 12th-graders). For a transcript to be included in the analyses, it had to meet three requirements: (1) the graduate received either a standard or honors diploma, (2) the graduate's transcript contained 16 or more Carnegie credits, and (3) the graduate's transcript contained more than 0 Carnegie credits in English courses. Race categories exclude persons of Hispanic ethnicity.
SOURCE: U.S. Department of Education, National Center for Education Statistics, National Assessment of Educational Progress (NAEP), 2009 Mathematics Assessment; and 2009 High School Transcript Study (HSTS). (This table was prepared September 2012.)

Table 222.50. Average National Assessment of Educational Progress (NAEP) mathematics scale score of 4th-grade public school students and percentage attaining mathematics achievement levels, by state: Selected years, 1992 through 2015

[Standard errors appear in parentheses]

State	Average scale score[1]										Percent attaining mathematics achievement levels, 2015		
	1992[2]	1996[3]	2000	2003	2005	2007	2009	2011	2013	2015	At or above *Basic*[4]	At or above *Proficient*[5]	At *Advanced*[6]
1	2	3	4	5	6	7	8	9	10	11	12	13	14
United States	**219 (0.8)**	**222 (1.0)**	**224 (1.0)**	**234 (0.2)**	**237 (0.2)**	**239 (0.2)**	**239 (0.2)**	**240 (0.2)**	**241 (0.2)**	**240 (0.3)**	**81 (0.3)**	**39 (0.4)**	**7 (0.2)**
Alabama	208 (1.6)	212 (1.2)	217 (1.2)	223 (1.2)	225 (0.9)	229 (1.3)	228 (1.1)	231 (1.0)	233 (1.0)	231 (0.9)	75 (1.4)	26 (1.5)	2 (0.5)
Alaska[7]	— (†)	224 (1.3)	— (†)	233 (0.8)	236 (1.0)	237 (1.0)	237 (0.9)	236 (0.9)	236 (0.8)	236 (1.1)	78 (1.3)	35 (1.5)	6 (0.8)
Arizona	215 (1.1)	218 (1.7)	219 (1.3)	229 (1.1)	230 (1.1)	232 (1.0)	230 (1.1)	235 (1.1)	240 (1.2)	238 (1.0)	79 (1.2)	38 (1.5)	6 (0.9)
Arkansas[7]	210 (0.9)	216 (1.5)	216 (1.1)	229 (0.9)	236 (0.9)	238 (1.1)	238 (0.9)	238 (0.8)	240 (0.9)	235 (0.8)	79 (1.2)	32 (1.5)	3 (0.5)
California[8]	208 (1.6)	209 (1.8)	213 (1.6)	227 (0.9)	230 (0.6)	230 (0.7)	232 (1.2)	234 (1.4)	234 (1.2)	232 (1.4)	72 (1.5)	29 (2.1)	5 (1.0)
Colorado	221 (1.0)	226 (1.0)	— (†)	235 (1.0)	239 (1.1)	240 (1.0)	243 (1.0)	244 (0.9)	247 (0.8)	242 (1.0)	82 (1.1)	43 (1.5)	8 (0.8)
Connecticut	227 (1.1)	232 (1.1)	234 (1.1)	241 (0.8)	242 (0.8)	243 (1.1)	245 (1.0)	242 (1.3)	243 (0.9)	240 (0.9)	81 (1.2)	41 (1.4)	7 (0.7)
Delaware	218 (0.8)	215 (0.6)	— (†)	236 (0.5)	240 (0.5)	242 (0.4)	239 (0.5)	240 (0.6)	243 (0.7)	239 (0.6)	82 (0.9)	37 (1.1)	5 (0.5)
District of Columbia	193 (0.5)	187 (1.1)	192 (1.1)	205 (0.7)	211 (0.8)	214 (0.8)	219 (0.7)	222 (0.7)	229 (0.7)	231 (0.6)	69 (1.1)	31 (1.0)	7 (0.6)
Florida	214 (1.5)	216 (1.2)	— (†)	234 (1.1)	239 (0.7)	242 (0.8)	242 (1.0)	240 (0.8)	242 (0.8)	243 (1.0)	85 (1.0)	42 (1.8)	7 (0.7)
Georgia	216 (1.2)	215 (1.5)	219 (1.1)	230 (1.0)	234 (1.0)	235 (0.8)	236 (0.9)	238 (0.7)	240 (1.0)	236 (1.2)	78 (1.4)	35 (1.8)	5 (0.8)
Hawaii	214 (1.3)	215 (1.5)	216 (1.0)	227 (1.0)	230 (0.8)	234 (0.8)	236 (1.1)	239 (0.7)	243 (0.8)	238 (0.9)	79 (1.1)	38 (1.3)	7 (0.8)
Idaho[8]	222 (1.0)	— (†)	224 (1.4)	235 (0.7)	242 (0.7)	241 (0.7)	241 (0.8)	240 (0.6)	241 (0.9)	239 (0.9)	80 (1.1)	38 (1.5)	6 (0.7)
Illinois[8]	— (†)	— (†)	223 (1.9)	233 (1.1)	233 (1.0)	237 (1.1)	238 (1.0)	239 (1.1)	239 (1.2)	237 (1.2)	77 (1.4)	37 (1.5)	8 (0.9)
Indiana[8]	221 (1.0)	229 (1.0)	233 (1.1)	238 (0.9)	240 (0.8)	245 (0.8)	243 (0.9)	244 (1.0)	249 (0.9)	248 (1.1)	89 (1.1)	50 (1.8)	9 (1.2)
Iowa[7,8]	230 (1.0)	229 (1.1)	231 (1.2)	238 (0.7)	240 (0.7)	243 (0.8)	243 (0.8)	243 (0.8)	246 (0.9)	243 (0.9)	84 (1.0)	44 (1.5)	9 (0.9)
Kansas[8]	— (†)	— (†)	232 (1.6)	242 (1.0)	246 (1.0)	248 (0.9)	245 (1.0)	246 (0.9)	246 (0.8)	241 (1.0)	83 (1.1)	41 (1.7)	7 (0.8)
Kentucky	215 (1.0)	220 (1.1)	219 (1.4)	229 (1.1)	231 (0.9)	235 (0.9)	239 (1.1)	241 (0.8)	241 (0.9)	242 (1.1)	84 (1.2)	40 (1.8)	7 (1.1)
Louisiana	204 (1.5)	209 (1.1)	218 (1.4)	226 (1.0)	230 (0.9)	230 (1.0)	229 (1.0)	231 (1.0)	231 (1.2)	234 (1.1)	78 (1.3)	30 (1.9)	4 (0.6)
Maine[8]	232 (1.0)	232 (1.0)	230 (1.0)	238 (0.7)	241 (0.8)	242 (0.8)	244 (0.8)	244 (0.7)	246 (0.7)	242 (0.8)	85 (1.0)	41 (1.4)	7 (0.8)
Maryland	217 (1.3)	221 (1.6)	222 (1.2)	233 (1.3)	238 (1.0)	240 (0.9)	244 (0.9)	247 (0.9)	245 (1.3)	239 (1.0)	79 (1.2)	40 (1.5)	8 (0.9)
Massachusetts	227 (1.2)	229 (1.3)	233 (1.2)	242 (0.8)	247 (0.8)	252 (0.8)	252 (0.9)	253 (0.8)	253 (1.0)	251 (1.2)	90 (1.1)	54 (1.9)	13 (1.2)
Michigan[7,8]	220 (1.7)	226 (1.3)	229 (1.6)	236 (0.9)	238 (1.2)	238 (1.3)	236 (1.0)	236 (1.1)	237 (1.1)	236 (1.2)	77 (1.5)	34 (1.6)	5 (0.9)
Minnesota[8]	228 (0.9)	232 (1.1)	234 (1.3)	242 (0.9)	246 (1.0)	247 (1.0)	249 (1.1)	249 (0.9)	253 (1.1)	250 (1.2)	87 (1.1)	53 (1.8)	14 (1.2)
Mississippi	202 (1.1)	208 (1.2)	211 (1.1)	223 (1.0)	227 (0.9)	228 (1.0)	227 (1.0)	230 (0.9)	231 (0.7)	234 (0.9)	78 (1.3)	30 (1.5)	3 (0.5)
Missouri	222 (1.2)	225 (1.1)	228 (1.2)	235 (0.9)	235 (0.9)	239 (0.9)	241 (1.2)	240 (0.9)	240 (0.8)	239 (0.9)	82 (1.1)	38 (1.5)	5 (0.7)
Montana[7,8]	— (†)	228 (1.2)	228 (1.7)	236 (0.8)	241 (0.8)	244 (0.8)	244 (0.7)	244 (0.6)	244 (0.6)	241 (0.7)	84 (0.9)	41 (1.4)	6 (0.6)
Nebraska	225 (1.2)	228 (1.2)	225 (1.8)	236 (0.8)	238 (0.9)	238 (1.1)	239 (1.0)	240 (1.0)	243 (1.0)	244 (0.9)	86 (1.0)	46 (1.5)	7 (0.8)
Nevada[7]	— (†)	218 (1.3)	220 (1.0)	228 (0.8)	230 (0.8)	232 (0.9)	235 (0.9)	237 (0.8)	236 (0.8)	234 (1.1)	76 (1.5)	32 (1.7)	4 (0.6)
New Hampshire	230 (1.2)	— (†)	— (†)	243 (0.9)	246 (0.8)	249 (0.8)	251 (0.8)	252 (0.6)	253 (0.8)	249 (0.8)	91 (0.7)	51 (1.5)	10 (0.7)
New Jersey[7]	227 (1.5)	227 (1.5)	— (†)	239 (1.1)	244 (1.1)	249 (1.1)	247 (1.0)	248 (0.9)	247 (1.1)	245 (1.2)	86 (1.3)	47 (2.0)	9 (1.2)
New Mexico	213 (1.4)	214 (1.8)	213 (1.5)	223 (1.1)	224 (0.8)	228 (0.9)	230 (1.0)	233 (0.8)	233 (0.7)	231 (0.8)	73 (1.3)	27 (1.2)	3 (0.4)
New York[7,8]	218 (1.2)	223 (1.2)	225 (1.4)	236 (0.9)	238 (0.9)	243 (0.8)	241 (0.7)	238 (0.8)	240 (1.0)	237 (0.9)	79 (1.2)	35 (1.4)	5 (0.7)
North Carolina	213 (1.1)	224 (1.2)	230 (1.1)	242 (0.8)	241 (0.9)	242 (0.8)	244 (0.8)	245 (0.7)	245 (0.9)	244 (1.0)	85 (1.0)	44 (1.5)	8 (1.0)
North Dakota	229 (0.8)	231 (1.2)	230 (1.2)	238 (0.7)	243 (0.5)	245 (0.5)	245 (0.6)	245 (0.4)	246 (0.5)	245 (0.5)	88 (0.7)	45 (1.1)	8 (0.6)
Ohio[8]	219 (1.2)	— (†)	230 (1.5)	238 (1.0)	242 (1.0)	245 (1.0)	244 (1.1)	244 (0.8)	246 (1.1)	244 (1.2)	85 (1.2)	45 (1.9)	8 (0.9)
Oklahoma	220 (1.0)	— (†)	224 (1.0)	229 (1.0)	234 (1.0)	237 (0.8)	237 (0.9)	237 (0.8)	239 (0.7)	240 (1.0)	84 (1.2)	37 (1.8)	5 (0.8)
Oregon[8]	— (†)	223 (1.4)	224 (1.8)	236 (0.9)	238 (0.8)	236 (1.0)	238 (0.9)	237 (0.9)	240 (1.3)	238 (1.1)	79 (1.2)	37 (1.7)	6 (0.8)
Pennsylvania[7]	224 (1.3)	226 (1.2)	— (†)	236 (1.1)	241 (1.2)	244 (0.8)	244 (1.1)	246 (1.1)	244 (1.0)	243 (1.4)	83 (1.4)	45 (2.0)	10 (1.1)
Rhode Island	215 (1.5)	220 (1.4)	224 (1.1)	230 (1.0)	233 (0.9)	236 (0.9)	239 (0.8)	242 (0.7)	241 (0.8)	238 (0.7)	80 (1.0)	37 (1.2)	6 (0.6)
South Carolina[7]	212 (1.1)	213 (1.3)	220 (1.4)	236 (0.9)	238 (0.9)	237 (0.8)	236 (0.9)	237 (1.0)	237 (1.0)	237 (1.1)	79 (1.2)	36 (1.9)	6 (0.8)
South Dakota	— (†)	— (†)	— (†)	237 (0.7)	242 (0.5)	241 (0.7)	242 (0.5)	241 (0.6)	241 (0.5)	240 (0.7)	83 (1.0)	40 (1.4)	4 (0.6)
Tennessee	211 (1.4)	219 (1.4)	220 (1.4)	228 (1.0)	232 (1.2)	233 (0.9)	232 (1.1)	233 (0.9)	240 (0.9)	241 (1.1)	82 (1.2)	40 (1.9)	7 (0.9)
Texas	218 (1.2)	229 (1.4)	231 (1.1)	237 (0.9)	242 (0.6)	242 (0.7)	240 (0.7)	241 (1.1)	242 (0.9)	244 (1.3)	86 (1.2)	44 (2.1)	8 (1.1)
Utah	224 (1.0)	227 (1.2)	227 (1.3)	235 (0.8)	239 (0.8)	239 (0.9)	240 (1.0)	243 (0.8)	243 (0.9)	243 (1.0)	84 (1.1)	44 (1.6)	7 (0.8)
Vermont[7,8]	— (†)	225 (1.2)	232 (1.6)	242 (0.8)	244 (0.5)	246 (0.5)	248 (0.4)	247 (0.5)	248 (0.6)	243 (0.7)	85 (1.0)	43 (1.3)	9 (0.8)
Virginia	221 (1.3)	223 (1.4)	230 (1.0)	239 (1.1)	240 (0.9)	244 (0.9)	243 (1.0)	245 (0.8)	246 (1.1)	247 (1.3)	87 (1.2)	47 (1.9)	10 (1.2)
Washington	— (†)	225 (1.2)	— (†)	238 (1.0)	242 (0.9)	243 (1.0)	242 (0.8)	243 (0.9)	246 (1.1)	245 (1.3)	83 (1.2)	47 (1.7)	12 (1.3)
West Virginia	215 (1.1)	223 (1.0)	223 (1.3)	231 (0.8)	231 (0.7)	236 (0.9)	233 (0.8)	235 (0.7)	237 (0.8)	235 (0.8)	78 (1.2)	33 (1.4)	5 (0.6)
Wisconsin	229 (1.1)	231 (1.0)	‡ (†)	237 (0.9)	241 (0.9)	244 (0.9)	244 (0.9)	245 (0.8)	245 (1.0)	243 (1.1)	83 (1.1)	45 (1.8)	9 (1.0)
Wyoming	225 (0.9)	223 (1.4)	229 (1.1)	241 (0.6)	243 (0.6)	244 (0.5)	242 (0.6)	244 (0.4)	247 (0.4)	247 (0.6)	88 (0.8)	48 (1.2)	9 (0.7)
Department of Defense dependents schools[9]	— (†)	224 (0.6)	227 (0.6)	237 (0.4)	239 (0.5)	240 (0.4)	240 (0.5)	241 (0.4)	245 (0.4)	248 (0.5)	90 (0.8)	49 (1.1)	8 (0.8)

—Not available.
†Not applicable.
‡Reporting standards not met. Participation rates fell below the required standards for reporting.
[1]Scale ranges from 0 to 500.
[2]Accommodations were not permitted for this assessment.
[3]The 1996 data in this table do not include students who were tested with accommodations. Data for students tested with accommodations are not available at the state level for 1996.
[4]*Basic* denotes partial mastery of the knowledge and skills that are fundamental for proficient work at the 4th-grade level.
[5]*Proficient* represents solid academic performance for 4th-graders. Students reaching this level have demonstrated competency over challenging subject matter.
[6]*Advanced* signifies superior performance.
[7]Did not meet one or more of the guidelines for school participation in 1996. Data are subject to appreciable nonresponse bias.
[8]Did not meet one or more of the guidelines for school participation in 2000. Data are subject to appreciable nonresponse bias.
[9]Prior to 2005, NAEP divided the Department of Defense (DoD) schools into two jurisdictions, domestic and overseas. In 2005, NAEP began combining the DoD domestic and overseas schools into a single jurisdiction. Data shown in this table for years prior to 2005 were recalculated for comparability.
NOTE: For 2000 and later years, includes public school students who were tested with accommodations; excludes only those students with disabilities (SD) and English language learners (ELL) who were unable to be tested even with accommodations. SD and ELL populations, accommodation rates, and exclusion rates vary from state to state. Some data have been revised from previously published figures.
SOURCE: U.S. Department of Education, National Center for Education Statistics, National Assessment of Educational Progress (NAEP), 1992, 1996, 2000, 2003, 2005, 2007, 2009, 2011, 2013, and 2015 Mathematics Assessments, retrieved November 4, 2015, from the Main NAEP Data Explorer (http://nces.ed.gov/nationsreportcard/naepdata/). (This table was prepared November 2015.)

Table 222.55. Average National Assessment of Educational Progress (NAEP) mathematics scale score of 4th-grade public school students, by race/ethnicity, school's level of free or reduced-price lunch eligibility, and state: 2015

[Standard errors appear in parentheses]

State	Race/ethnicity							Percent of students in school eligible for free or reduced-price lunch			
	White	Black	Hispanic	Asian	Pacific Islander	American Indian/ Alaska Native	Two or more races	0–25 percent eligible (low poverty)	26–50 percent eligible	51–75 percent eligible	76–100 percent eligible (high poverty)
1	2	3	4	5	6	7	8	9	10	11	12
United States	**248 (0.3)**	**224 (0.4)**	**230 (0.5)**	**259 (1.2)**	**226 (2.2)**	**228 (1.1)**	**244 (0.8)**	**257 (0.7)**	**245 (0.5)**	**237 (0.5)**	**226 (0.5)**
Alabama	239 (1.3)	217 (1.4)	221 (2.3)	‡ (†)	‡ (†)	‡ (†)	‡ (†)	250 (3.1)	238 (2.5)	232 (1.7)	219 (1.5)
Alaska	246 (1.3)	221 (2.9)	235 (2.8)	239 (3.0)	216 (4.2)	219 (2.2)	243 (2.2)	254 (2.4)	240 (1.5)	232 (2.0)	219 (2.5)
Arizona	251 (1.6)	231 (3.1)	229 (1.1)	‡ (†)	‡ (†)	220 (3.1)	‡ (†)	257 (3.3)	248 (2.7)	233 (2.1)	227 (1.4)
Arkansas	240 (0.9)	221 (1.6)	231 (2.2)	‡ (†)	‡ (†)	‡ (†)	‡ (†)	‡ (†)	243 (2.1)	236 (1.1)	228 (1.7)
California	246 (1.9)	222 (2.5)	222 (1.2)	254 (3.2)	‡ (†)	‡ (†)	257 (7.0)	260 (3.0)	237 (2.5)	230 (2.3)	219 (1.7)
Colorado	253 (1.0)	221 (4.3)	227 (1.2)	‡ (†)	‡ (†)	‡ (†)	252 (3.1)	258 (1.4)	244 (2.1)	235 (2.3)	224 (2.0)
Connecticut	249 (1.0)	218 (2.0)	224 (1.5)	259 (2.8)	‡ (†)	‡ (†)	‡ (†)	251 (1.5)	240 (1.9)	229 (2.0)	218 (2.4)
Delaware	247 (0.8)	227 (0.9)	232 (1.4)	258 (2.7)	‡ (†)	‡ (†)	241 (2.8)	255 (1.6)	243 (1.2)	237 (1.4)	230 (1.1)
District of Columbia	274 (1.7)	223 (0.8)	231 (1.8)	‡ (†)	‡ (†)	‡ (†)	‡ (†)	257 (1.7)	244 (3.1)	232 (2.5)	222 (0.9)
Florida	251 (1.3)	228 (1.8)	240 (1.1)	262 (3.5)	‡ (†)	‡ (†)	244 (3.7)	259 (1.8)	251 (2.2)	245 (1.2)	232 (1.4)
Georgia	245 (1.5)	224 (1.6)	234 (1.8)	262 (5.5)	‡ (†)	‡ (†)	238 (3.4)	257 (5.3)	246 (2.2)	241 (1.4)	226 (1.8)
Hawaii	248 (1.8)	‡ (†)	236 (2.4)	244 (1.4)	226 (1.5)	‡ (†)	241 (3.1)	257 (1.6)	244 (1.7)	234 (1.5)	220 (2.9)
Idaho	243 (1.0)	‡ (†)	221 (1.5)	‡ (†)	‡ (†)	‡ (†)	‡ (†)	254 (2.0)	243 (1.6)	236 (1.3)	224 (2.0)
Illinois	248 (1.4)	215 (1.9)	228 (1.7)	262 (3.7)	‡ (†)	‡ (†)	244 (4.0)	253 (4.2)	243 (2.5)	236 (2.3)	221 (1.8)
Indiana	252 (1.0)	229 (1.9)	240 (2.2)	‡ (†)	‡ (†)	‡ (†)	244 (3.3)	260 (2.5)	252 (1.7)	246 (1.7)	236 (3.5)
Iowa	248 (0.9)	222 (3.1)	226 (2.2)	251 (5.1)	‡ (†)	‡ (†)	235 (3.5)	255 (1.7)	247 (1.3)	237 (1.9)	226 (3.4)
Kansas	247 (1.0)	218 (2.3)	228 (1.7)	255 (3.8)	‡ (†)	‡ (†)	240 (2.8)	258 (2.0)	243 (1.6)	241 (1.3)	225 (2.1)
Kentucky	244 (1.2)	226 (1.3)	234 (2.4)	258 (9.3)	‡ (†)	‡ (†)	243 (3.1)	‡ (†)	251 (2.6)	241 (1.6)	233 (1.4)
Louisiana	242 (1.2)	224 (1.3)	238 (2.4)	‡ (†)	‡ (†)	‡ (†)	‡ (†)	‡ (†)	244 (2.6)	238 (1.8)	230 (1.6)
Maine	243 (0.8)	223 (4.1)	‡ (†)	‡ (†)	‡ (†)	‡ (†)	‡ (†)	258 (2.7)	243 (1.1)	239 (1.3)	229 (3.4)
Maryland	252 (1.4)	224 (1.1)	229 (1.5)	262 (3.1)	‡ (†)	‡ (†)	245 (3.2)	255 (2.0)	245 (1.7)	231 (1.6)	221 (1.8)
Massachusetts	256 (1.3)	230 (2.2)	232 (1.9)	273 (3.5)	‡ (†)	‡ (†)	253 (4.3)	263 (2.1)	249 (1.6)	237 (3.9)	231 (2.3)
Michigan	241 (1.0)	212 (2.6)	223 (3.7)	254 (7.4)	‡ (†)	‡ (†)	‡ (†)	252 (2.4)	240 (1.7)	232 (1.3)	216 (2.8)
Minnesota	257 (1.1)	227 (3.1)	232 (3.1)	244 (6.1)	‡ (†)	223 (3.8)	248 (3.2)	263 (2.6)	251 (1.5)	245 (2.4)	226 (3.0)
Mississippi	245 (1.1)	224 (1.1)	229 (3.6)	‡ (†)	‡ (†)	‡ (†)	‡ (†)	‡ (†)	247 (2.4)	238 (1.3)	226 (1.4)
Missouri	244 (0.9)	220 (2.4)	233 (3.5)	‡ (†)	‡ (†)	‡ (†)	243 (4.7)	253 (3.0)	246 (1.6)	236 (1.7)	226 (1.6)
Montana	245 (0.8)	‡ (†)	231 (2.9)	‡ (†)	‡ (†)	216 (2.1)	239 (3.1)	249 (1.9)	245 (1.0)	240 (1.5)	224 (2.0)
Nebraska	251 (1.0)	217 (1.8)	230 (1.4)	‡ (†)	‡ (†)	‡ (†)	234 (3.0)	257 (1.6)	247 (1.3)	240 (1.8)	227 (1.6)
Nevada	246 (1.3)	218 (2.5)	227 (1.1)	251 (3.5)	‡ (†)	‡ (†)	237 (2.7)	253 (2.1)	242 (2.6)	231 (2.2)	223 (1.7)
New Hampshire	250 (0.8)	‡ (†)	237 (3.5)	262 (3.3)	‡ (†)	‡ (†)	‡ (†)	255 (0.9)	246 (1.2)	237 (2.7)	‡ (†)
New Jersey	254 (1.4)	228 (1.9)	232 (1.4)	270 (2.7)	‡ (†)	‡ (†)	‡ (†)	258 (2.5)	244 (1.8)	236 (2.7)	228 (2.3)
New Mexico	241 (1.5)	‡ (†)	229 (1.0)	‡ (†)	‡ (†)	218 (3.2)	‡ (†)	‡ (†)	236 (2.3)	236 (1.6)	224 (1.3)
New York	245 (1.1)	221 (1.8)	228 (1.2)	253 (3.6)	‡ (†)	‡ (†)	‡ (†)	248 (3.3)	244 (2.6)	234 (1.8)	226 (2.3)
North Carolina	253 (1.3)	229 (1.5)	235 (1.4)	260 (5.9)	‡ (†)	229 (4.4)	249 (3.8)	258 (2.3)	251 (2.2)	242 (1.4)	229 (1.5)
North Dakota	249 (0.6)	231 (3.2)	224 (3.4)	‡ (†)	‡ (†)	225 (1.9)	‡ (†)	251 (0.9)	243 (0.7)	238 (1.7)	228 (2.5)
Ohio	249 (1.2)	220 (1.6)	236 (2.5)	‡ (†)	‡ (†)	‡ (†)	237 (2.8)	258 (1.8)	248 (1.5)	240 (2.8)	227 (2.9)
Oklahoma	245 (1.2)	223 (2.9)	232 (1.4)	‡ (†)	‡ (†)	235 (1.7)	242 (2.5)	262 (4.4)	244 (2.3)	243 (1.8)	230 (1.4)
Oregon	243 (1.1)	217 (4.6)	224 (1.5)	253 (4.4)	‡ (†)	‡ (†)	240 (2.8)	256 (2.2)	246 (1.7)	233 (1.4)	229 (1.5)
Pennsylvania	250 (1.3)	219 (2.1)	226 (2.8)	260 (3.1)	‡ (†)	‡ (†)	243 (4.4)	258 (3.1)	246 (1.9)	239 (3.3)	216 (2.5)
Rhode Island	246 (0.9)	222 (2.7)	223 (1.2)	239 (4.7)	‡ (†)	‡ (†)	231 (3.5)	253 (1.3)	241 (1.7)	234 (2.0)	223 (1.5)
South Carolina	247 (1.2)	221 (1.1)	233 (3.9)	‡ (†)	‡ (†)	‡ (†)	240 (3.7)	254 (2.8)	249 (2.1)	238 (1.8)	225 (1.5)
South Dakota	246 (0.8)	218 (4.2)	227 (2.6)	‡ (†)	‡ (†)	216 (1.7)	236 (2.8)	251 (1.4)	242 (1.0)	236 (1.9)	219 (2.0)
Tennessee	246 (1.3)	226 (2.0)	235 (2.5)	‡ (†)	‡ (†)	‡ (†)	‡ (†)	258 (5.0)	247 (2.6)	240 (1.5)	231 (1.7)
Texas	255 (1.9)	233 (2.1)	239 (1.4)	271 (3.8)	‡ (†)	‡ (†)	252 (5.3)	272 (3.2)	248 (2.3)	242 (1.8)	234 (1.5)
Utah	247 (0.9)	‡ (†)	226 (2.4)	‡ (†)	‡ (†)	‡ (†)	‡ (†)	249 (1.5)	243 (1.9)	238 (1.7)	221 (3.2)
Vermont	244 (0.7)	‡ (†)	‡ (†)	‡ (†)	‡ (†)	‡ (†)	‡ (†)	255 (1.7)	244 (1.1)	236 (1.3)	233 (2.7)
Virginia	253 (1.2)	231 (1.9)	235 (1.9)	270 (2.3)	‡ (†)	‡ (†)	249 (3.3)	258 (2.1)	251 (2.4)	240 (1.6)	230 (3.2)
Washington	251 (1.2)	229 (4.4)	228 (2.1)	268 (3.8)	‡ (†)	216 (4.2)	244 (3.3)	263 (2.8)	250 (2.2)	236 (2.1)	230 (3.1)
West Virginia	236 (0.8)	218 (3.0)	‡ (†)	‡ (†)	‡ (†)	‡ (†)	228 (5.2)	‡ (†)	244 (2.4)	233 (1.3)	228 (1.5)
Wisconsin	250 (1.1)	212 (2.9)	229 (2.8)	251 (4.6)	‡ (†)	231 (4.5)	246 (4.0)	259 (1.9)	247 (1.4)	235 (2.2)	218 (2.7)
Wyoming	250 (0.6)	‡ (†)	234 (1.6)	‡ (†)	‡ (†)	220 (4.0)	‡ (†)	252 (1.3)	249 (0.7)	241 (1.4)	244 (2.9)
Department of Defense dependents schools	251 (0.8)	236 (1.5)	244 (1.3)	257 (2.6)	‡ (†)	‡ (†)	249 (1.8)	250 (1.2)	246 (1.0)	241 (2.2)	‡ (†)

†Not applicable.
‡Reporting standards not met (too few cases for a reliable estimate).
NOTE: Scale ranges from 0 to 500. Includes public school students who were tested with accommodations; excludes only those students with disabilities (SD) and English language learners (ELL) who were unable to be tested even with accommodations. SD and ELL populations, accommodation rates, and exclusion rates vary from state to state. Race/ethnicity based on school records. Race categories exclude persons of Hispanic ethnicity.
SOURCE: U.S. Department of Education, National Center for Education Statistics, National Assessment of Educational Progress (NAEP), 2015 Mathematics Assessment, retrieved November 16, 2015, from the Main NAEP Data Explorer (http://nces.ed.gov/nationsreportcard/naepdata/). (This table was prepared November 2015.)

Table 222.60. Average National Assessment of Educational Progress (NAEP) mathematics scale score of 8th-grade public school students and percentage attaining mathematics achievement levels, by state: Selected years, 1990 through 2015

[Standard errors appear in parentheses]

State	Average scale score[1]											Percent attaining mathematics achievement levels, 2015		
	1990[2]	1992[2]	1996[3]	2000	2003	2005	2007	2009	2011	2013	2015	At or above *Basic*[4]	At or above *Proficient*[5]	At *Advanced*[6]
1	2	3	4	5	6	7	8	9	10	11	12	13	14	15
United States	**262 (1.4)**	**267 (1.0)**	**271 (1.2)**	**272 (0.9)**	**276 (0.3)**	**278 (0.2)**	**280 (0.3)**	**282 (0.3)**	**283 (0.2)**	**284 (0.2)**	**281 (0.3)**	**70 (0.3)**	**32 (0.3)**	**8 (0.2)**
Alabama	253 (1.1)	252 (1.7)	257 (2.1)	264 (1.8)	262 (1.5)	262 (1.5)	266 (1.5)	269 (1.2)	269 (1.4)	269 (1.3)	267 (1.2)	56 (1.6)	17 (1.2)	3 (0.4)
Alaska[7]	— (†)	— (†)	278 (1.8)	— (†)	279 (0.9)	279 (0.8)	283 (1.1)	283 (1.0)	283 (0.8)	282 (0.9)	280 (1.0)	71 (1.2)	32 (1.2)	7 (0.7)
Arizona[8]	260 (1.3)	265 (1.3)	268 (1.6)	269 (1.8)	271 (1.2)	274 (1.1)	276 (1.2)	277 (1.4)	279 (1.2)	280 (1.2)	283 (1.4)	72 (1.4)	35 (1.8)	8 (1.0)
Arkansas[7]	256 (0.9)	256 (1.2)	262 (1.5)	257 (1.5)	266 (1.2)	272 (1.2)	274 (1.1)	276 (1.1)	279 (1.0)	278 (1.1)	275 (1.4)	66 (2.0)	25 (1.5)	4 (0.7)
California[8]	256 (1.3)	261 (1.7)	263 (1.9)	260 (2.1)	267 (1.2)	269 (0.6)	270 (0.8)	270 (1.3)	273 (1.2)	276 (1.2)	275 (1.3)	64 (1.5)	27 (1.3)	6 (1.0)
Colorado	267 (0.9)	272 (1.0)	276 (1.1)	— (†)	283 (1.1)	281 (1.2)	286 (0.9)	287 (1.4)	292 (1.1)	290 (1.2)	286 (1.5)	73 (1.6)	37 (1.7)	10 (1.0)
Connecticut	270 (1.0)	274 (1.1)	280 (1.1)	281 (1.3)	284 (1.2)	281 (1.4)	282 (1.5)	289 (1.0)	287 (1.1)	285 (1.1)	284 (1.2)	72 (1.4)	36 (1.4)	10 (0.8)
Delaware	261 (0.9)	263 (1.0)	267 (0.9)	— (†)	277 (0.7)	281 (0.6)	283 (0.6)	284 (0.5)	283 (0.7)	282 (0.7)	280 (0.7)	69 (1.4)	30 (0.9)	7 (0.6)
District of Columbia	231 (0.9)	235 (0.9)	233 (1.3)	235 (1.1)	243 (0.8)	245 (0.9)	248 (0.9)	254 (0.9)	260 (0.7)	265 (0.9)	263 (0.9)	51 (1.3)	19 (0.9)	4 (0.5)
Florida	255 (1.2)	260 (1.5)	264 (1.8)	— (†)	271 (1.5)	274 (1.1)	277 (1.3)	279 (1.1)	278 (0.8)	281 (0.8)	275 (1.4)	64 (1.7)	26 (1.2)	5 (0.5)
Georgia	259 (1.3)	259 (1.2)	262 (1.6)	265 (1.2)	270 (1.2)	272 (1.1)	275 (1.0)	278 (0.9)	278 (1.0)	279 (1.2)	279 (1.2)	67 (1.4)	28 (1.4)	7 (0.8)
Hawaii	251 (0.8)	257 (0.9)	262 (1.0)	262 (1.4)	266 (0.8)	266 (0.7)	269 (0.8)	274 (0.7)	278 (0.7)	281 (0.8)	279 (0.8)	70 (1.2)	30 (1.1)	6 (0.7)
Idaho[8]	271 (0.8)	275 (0.7)	— (†)	277 (1.0)	280 (0.9)	281 (0.9)	284 (0.9)	287 (0.8)	287 (0.8)	286 (0.7)	284 (0.9)	75 (1.1)	34 (1.4)	6 (0.6)
Illinois[8]	261 (1.7)	— (†)	— (†)	275 (1.7)	277 (1.2)	278 (1.1)	280 (1.1)	282 (1.2)	283 (1.1)	285 (1.0)	282 (1.3)	72 (1.4)	32 (1.6)	7 (1.0)
Indiana[8]	267 (1.2)	270 (1.1)	276 (1.4)	281 (1.4)	281 (1.1)	282 (1.0)	285 (1.1)	287 (0.9)	285 (1.0)	288 (1.1)	287 (1.2)	77 (1.3)	39 (1.5)	9 (0.9)
Iowa[7]	278 (1.1)	283 (1.0)	284 (1.3)	— (†)	284 (0.8)	284 (0.9)	285 (0.9)	284 (1.0)	285 (0.9)	285 (0.9)	286 (1.2)	76 (1.2)	37 (1.6)	9 (0.8)
Kansas[8]	— (†)	— (†)	— (†)	283 (1.7)	284 (1.3)	284 (1.0)	290 (1.1)	289 (1.0)	290 (0.9)	290 (1.0)	284 (1.3)	76 (1.5)	33 (1.6)	6 (0.7)
Kentucky	257 (1.2)	262 (1.1)	267 (1.1)	270 (1.3)	274 (1.2)	274 (1.2)	279 (1.1)	279 (1.1)	282 (0.9)	281 (0.9)	278 (0.9)	68 (1.3)	28 (1.3)	5 (0.6)
Louisiana	246 (1.2)	250 (1.7)	252 (1.6)	259 (1.5)	266 (1.5)	268 (1.4)	272 (1.1)	272 (1.6)	273 (1.2)	273 (0.9)	268 (1.4)	57 (1.8)	18 (1.5)	3 (0.5)
Maine[8]	— (†)	279 (1.0)	284 (1.3)	281 (1.1)	282 (0.9)	281 (0.8)	286 (0.8)	286 (0.7)	289 (0.8)	289 (0.7)	285 (0.7)	76 (0.8)	35 (1.1)	8 (0.7)
Maryland[7]	261 (1.4)	265 (1.3)	270 (2.1)	272 (1.7)	278 (1.0)	278 (1.1)	286 (1.2)	288 (1.1)	288 (1.2)	287 (1.1)	283 (1.2)	71 (1.5)	35 (1.7)	10 (0.8)
Massachusetts	— (†)	273 (1.0)	278 (1.7)	279 (1.5)	287 (0.9)	292 (0.9)	298 (1.3)	299 (1.3)	299 (0.8)	301 (0.9)	297 (1.4)	81 (1.5)	51 (1.6)	18 (1.1)
Michigan[7,8]	264 (1.2)	267 (1.4)	277 (1.8)	277 (1.9)	276 (2.0)	277 (1.5)	277 (1.4)	278 (1.6)	280 (1.4)	280 (1.3)	278 (1.3)	68 (1.6)	29 (1.5)	7 (0.7)
Minnesota[8]	275 (0.9)	282 (1.0)	284 (1.3)	287 (1.4)	291 (1.1)	290 (1.2)	292 (1.0)	294 (1.0)	295 (1.0)	295 (1.0)	294 (1.0)	82 (1.0)	48 (1.4)	13 (1.0)
Mississippi	— (†)	246 (1.2)	250 (1.2)	254 (1.1)	261 (1.1)	262 (1.2)	265 (0.8)	265 (1.2)	269 (1.4)	271 (0.9)	271 (1.1)	60 (1.5)	22 (1.1)	3 (0.4)
Missouri	— (†)	271 (1.2)	273 (1.4)	271 (1.5)	279 (1.1)	276 (1.3)	281 (1.0)	286 (1.0)	282 (1.1)	283 (1.0)	281 (1.2)	71 (1.6)	31 (1.5)	7 (0.8)
Montana[7,8]	280 (0.9)	— (†)	283 (1.3)	285 (1.4)	286 (0.8)	286 (0.7)	287 (0.7)	292 (0.9)	293 (0.6)	289 (0.9)	287 (0.8)	79 (1.0)	39 (1.1)	8 (0.8)
Nebraska	276 (1.0)	278 (1.1)	283 (1.0)	280 (1.2)	282 (0.9)	284 (1.0)	284 (1.0)	284 (1.1)	283 (0.8)	285 (0.9)	286 (0.8)	77 (1.0)	38 (1.2)	8 (0.8)
Nevada	— (†)	— (†)	‡ (†)	265 (0.8)	268 (0.8)	270 (0.8)	271 (0.8)	274 (0.7)	278 (0.8)	278 (0.7)	275 (0.7)	65 (1.1)	26 (0.9)	5 (0.5)
New Hampshire	273 (0.9)	278 (1.0)	‡ (†)	— (†)	286 (0.8)	285 (0.8)	288 (0.7)	292 (0.9)	292 (0.7)	296 (0.8)	294 (0.9)	84 (0.9)	46 (1.3)	12 (1.0)
New Jersey	270 (1.1)	272 (1.6)	‡ (†)	— (†)	281 (1.1)	284 (1.4)	289 (1.2)	293 (1.4)	294 (1.2)	296 (1.1)	293 (1.2)	79 (1.1)	46 (1.4)	16 (1.5)
New Mexico	256 (0.7)	260 (0.9)	262 (1.2)	259 (1.3)	263 (1.0)	263 (0.9)	268 (0.9)	270 (1.1)	274 (0.8)	273 (0.7)	271 (1.0)	61 (1.3)	21 (1.2)	3 (0.4)
New York[7,8]	261 (1.4)	266 (2.1)	270 (1.7)	271 (2.2)	280 (1.1)	280 (0.9)	280 (1.2)	283 (1.2)	280 (0.9)	282 (0.9)	280 (1.4)	69 (1.4)	31 (1.7)	7 (0.8)
North Carolina	250 (1.1)	258 (1.2)	268 (1.4)	276 (1.3)	281 (1.0)	282 (0.9)	284 (1.1)	284 (1.3)	286 (1.0)	286 (1.1)	281 (1.6)	69 (1.5)	33 (1.8)	9 (1.1)
North Dakota	281 (1.2)	283 (1.1)	284 (0.9)	282 (1.1)	287 (0.8)	287 (0.6)	292 (0.7)	293 (0.7)	292 (0.6)	291 (0.5)	288 (0.7)	80 (1.0)	39 (1.0)	7 (0.6)
Ohio	264 (1.0)	268 (1.5)	— (†)	281 (1.6)	282 (1.3)	283 (1.1)	285 (1.2)	286 (1.0)	289 (1.0)	290 (1.1)	285 (1.6)	75 (1.6)	35 (1.6)	9 (0.8)
Oklahoma	263 (1.3)	268 (1.1)	— (†)	270 (1.3)	272 (1.1)	271 (1.0)	275 (0.9)	276 (1.0)	279 (1.0)	276 (1.0)	275 (1.3)	67 (1.8)	23 (1.6)	3 (0.4)
Oregon[8]	271 (1.0)	— (†)	276 (1.5)	280 (1.5)	281 (1.3)	282 (1.0)	284 (1.1)	285 (1.0)	283 (1.0)	284 (1.1)	283 (1.2)	73 (1.2)	34 (1.5)	7 (0.8)
Pennsylvania	266 (1.6)	271 (1.5)	— (†)	— (†)	279 (1.1)	281 (1.5)	286 (1.1)	288 (1.3)	286 (1.2)	290 (1.0)	284 (1.5)	72 (1.7)	36 (1.7)	10 (1.0)
Rhode Island	260 (0.6)	266 (0.7)	269 (0.9)	269 (1.3)	272 (0.7)	272 (0.8)	275 (0.7)	278 (0.8)	283 (0.5)	284 (0.6)	281 (0.7)	72 (0.8)	32 (1.2)	6 (0.6)
South Carolina[7]	— (†)	261 (1.0)	261 (1.5)	265 (1.5)	277 (1.3)	281 (0.9)	282 (1.0)	280 (1.3)	281 (1.1)	280 (1.1)	276 (1.3)	65 (1.5)	26 (1.5)	5 (0.6)
South Dakota	— (†)	— (†)	— (†)	— (†)	285 (0.8)	287 (0.6)	288 (0.8)	291 (0.5)	291 (0.5)	287 (0.7)	285 (0.9)	77 (1.2)	34 (1.2)	6 (0.6)
Tennessee	— (†)	259 (1.4)	263 (1.4)	262 (1.5)	268 (1.8)	271 (1.1)	274 (1.1)	275 (1.4)	274 (1.2)	278 (1.3)	278 (1.8)	68 (1.8)	29 (2.0)	6 (1.0)
Texas	258 (1.4)	265 (1.3)	270 (1.4)	273 (1.6)	277 (1.1)	281 (0.6)	286 (1.0)	287 (1.3)	290 (0.9)	288 (1.0)	284 (1.2)	75 (1.4)	32 (1.6)	7 (0.9)
Utah	— (†)	274 (0.7)	277 (1.0)	274 (1.2)	281 (1.0)	279 (0.7)	281 (0.9)	284 (0.9)	283 (0.8)	284 (0.9)	286 (1.1)	76 (1.3)	38 (1.4)	8 (0.8)
Vermont[7,8]	— (†)	— (†)	279 (1.0)	281 (1.5)	286 (0.8)	287 (0.7)	291 (0.7)	293 (0.6)	294 (0.7)	295 (0.7)	290 (0.7)	79 (0.9)	42 (1.2)	11 (0.9)
Virginia	264 (1.5)	268 (1.2)	270 (1.6)	275 (1.3)	282 (1.3)	284 (1.1)	288 (1.1)	286 (1.1)	289 (1.1)	288 (1.2)	288 (1.2)	76 (1.2)	38 (1.6)	10 (1.1)
Washington	— (†)	— (†)	276 (1.3)	— (†)	281 (0.9)	285 (1.0)	285 (1.0)	289 (1.0)	288 (1.0)	290 (1.0)	287 (1.3)	74 (1.2)	39 (1.5)	11 (0.9)
West Virginia	256 (1.0)	259 (1.0)	265 (1.0)	266 (1.2)	271 (1.2)	269 (1.0)	270 (1.0)	270 (1.0)	273 (0.7)	274 (0.9)	271 (0.9)	62 (1.5)	21 (1.1)	3 (0.5)
Wisconsin[7]	274 (1.3)	278 (1.5)	283 (1.5)	‡ (†)	284 (1.3)	285 (1.1)	286 (1.1)	288 (0.9)	289 (1.0)	289 (0.9)	289 (1.3)	78 (1.5)	41 (1.5)	11 (1.0)
Wyoming	272 (0.7)	275 (0.9)	275 (0.9)	276 (1.0)	284 (0.7)	282 (0.7)	287 (0.7)	286 (0.6)	288 (0.6)	288 (0.5)	287 (0.7)	78 (0.9)	35 (1.2)	7 (0.7)
Department of Defense dependents schools[9]	— (†)	— (†)	274 (0.9)	277 (1.1)	285 (0.7)	284 (0.7)	285 (0.8)	287 (0.9)	288 (0.8)	290 (0.8)	291 (0.7)	83 (1.2)	40 (1.1)	9 (1.0)

—Not available.
†Not applicable.
‡Reporting standards not met. Participation rates fell below the required standards for reporting.
[1]Scale ranges from 0 to 500.
[2]Accommodations were not permitted for this assessment.
[3]The 1996 data in this table do not include students who were tested with accommodations. Data for students tested with accommodations are not available at the state level for 1996.
[4]*Basic* denotes partial mastery of the knowledge and skills that are fundamental for proficient work at the 8th-grade level.
[5]*Proficient* represents solid academic performance for 8th-graders. Students reaching this level have demonstrated competency over challenging subject matter.
[6]*Advanced* signifies superior performance.
[7]Did not meet one or more of the guidelines for school participation in 1996. Data are subject to appreciable nonresponse bias.
[8]Did not meet one or more of the guidelines for school participation in 2000. Data are subject to appreciable nonresponse bias.
[9]Prior to 2005, NAEP divided the Department of Defense (DoD) schools into two jurisdictions, domestic and overseas. In 2005, NAEP began combining the DoD domestic and overseas schools into a single jurisdiction. Data shown in this table for years prior to 2005 were recalculated for comparability.
NOTE: For 2000 and later years, includes public school students who were tested with accommodations; excludes only those students with disabilities (SD) and English language learners (ELL) who were unable to be tested even with accommodations. SD and ELL populations, accommodation rates, and exclusion rates vary from state to state. Some data have been revised from previously published figures.
SOURCE: U.S. Department of Education, National Center for Education Statistics, National Assessment of Educational Progress (NAEP), 1990, 1992, 1996, 2000, 2003, 2005, 2007, 2009, 2011, 2013, and 2015 Mathematics Assessments, retrieved October 29, 2015, from the Main NAEP Data Explorer (http://nces.ed.gov/nationsreportcard/naepdata/). (This table was prepared November 2015.)

Table 222.70. Average National Assessment of Educational Progress (NAEP) mathematics scale score of 8th-grade public school students, by race/ethnicity, parents' highest level of education, and state: 2015

[Standard errors appear in parentheses]

State	Race/ethnicity: White	Black	Hispanic	Asian	Pacific Islander	American Indian/ Alaska Native	Two or more races	Highest level of education attained by either parent[1]: Did not finish high school	Graduated high school	Some education after high school	Graduated college
1	2	3	4	5	6	7	8	9	10	11	12
United States	**291 (0.3)**	**260 (0.5)**	**269 (0.6)**	**307 (1.5)**	**277 (2.5)**	**267 (1.3)**	**283 (1.1)**	**265 (0.6)**	**268 (0.5)**	**282 (0.4)**	**293 (0.4)**
Alabama	276 (1.4)	248 (1.8)	260 (3.2)	‡ (†)	‡ (†)	‡ (†)	‡ (†)	254 (2.5)	252 (2.3)	271 (1.9)	276 (1.4)
Alaska	295 (1.2)	269 (4.5)	279 (2.9)	282 (2.5)	‡ (†)	257 (2.6)	285 (2.6)	‡ (†)	‡ (†)	‡ (†)	‡ (†)
Arizona	297 (1.9)	269 (4.1)	273 (1.2)	‡ (†)	‡ (†)	260 (4.4)	‡ (†)	269 (2.3)	271 (2.7)	285 (1.9)	297 (2.0)
Arkansas	283 (1.5)	255 (2.2)	269 (2.8)	‡ (†)	‡ (†)	‡ (†)	‡ (†)	266 (2.4)	262 (2.4)	280 (1.9)	283 (1.6)
California	291 (1.8)	260 (3.3)	263 (1.5)	304 (3.6)	‡ (†)	‡ (†)	289 (9.7)	261 (2.0)	263 (2.3)	278 (2.2)	293 (1.7)
Colorado	297 (1.7)	260 (4.9)	269 (1.6)	308 (5.3)	‡ (†)	‡ (†)	290 (4.8)	266 (2.6)	270 (2.3)	284 (2.3)	299 (1.6)
Connecticut	295 (1.2)	256 (2.9)	261 (2.3)	310 (5.6)	‡ (†)	‡ (†)	‡ (†)	254 (4.2)	265 (2.1)	275 (2.4)	297 (1.4)
Delaware	291 (1.1)	263 (1.3)	270 (2.2)	317 (4.0)	‡ (†)	‡ (†)	‡ (†)	264 (2.8)	267 (2.0)	280 (1.8)	290 (1.1)
District of Columbia	316 (2.7)	257 (1.0)	265 (2.6)	‡ (†)	‡ (†)	‡ (†)	‡ (†)	258 (3.6)	250 (2.0)	269 (2.3)	276 (1.6)
Florida	285 (1.6)	258 (2.2)	272 (1.4)	297 (3.6)	‡ (†)	‡ (†)	282 (3.5)	264 (2.5)	266 (2.1)	280 (2.0)	285 (1.6)
Georgia	291 (1.7)	264 (1.5)	270 (2.1)	317 (6.2)	‡ (†)	‡ (†)	277 (5.3)	269 (2.4)	264 (1.9)	281 (2.0)	289 (1.5)
Hawaii	286 (2.2)	‡ (†)	271 (2.9)	289 (1.4)	268 (1.4)	‡ (†)	285 (2.6)	270 (4.4)	264 (1.7)	284 (1.6)	289 (1.2)
Idaho	288 (0.9)	‡ (†)	264 (2.2)	‡ (†)	‡ (†)	‡ (†)	‡ (†)	262 (2.6)	267 (2.5)	286 (1.9)	294 (1.2)
Illinois	290 (1.5)	261 (2.4)	273 (1.4)	309 (4.6)	‡ (†)	‡ (†)	‡ (†)	270 (3.1)	268 (2.0)	282 (1.7)	293 (1.8)
Indiana	294 (1.2)	257 (3.2)	271 (3.1)	‡ (†)	‡ (†)	‡ (†)	281 (4.6)	268 (3.1)	274 (1.7)	288 (2.0)	297 (1.4)
Iowa	291 (1.2)	254 (3.0)	269 (3.1)	292 (5.1)	‡ (†)	‡ (†)	283 (5.6)	261 (3.5)	272 (2.4)	283 (2.0)	296 (1.3)
Kansas	289 (1.2)	263 (3.8)	274 (2.8)	302 (5.5)	‡ (†)	‡ (†)	278 (3.1)	268 (4.1)	272 (2.4)	282 (1.8)	293 (1.3)
Kentucky	281 (1.0)	257 (2.3)	274 (2.9)	‡ (†)	‡ (†)	‡ (†)	266 (5.9)	260 (2.6)	268 (1.6)	281 (1.6)	288 (1.1)
Louisiana	280 (1.7)	255 (1.4)	271 (3.7)	‡ (†)	‡ (†)	‡ (†)	‡ (†)	258 (2.5)	259 (2.2)	270 (1.9)	277 (1.6)
Maine	286 (0.7)	‡ (†)	‡ (†)	‡ (†)	‡ (†)	‡ (†)	‡ (†)	267 (4.4)	272 (1.9)	283 (1.8)	295 (1.0)
Maryland	297 (1.5)	263 (1.3)	273 (2.4)	314 (3.6)	‡ (†)	‡ (†)	290 (3.9)	265 (3.4)	263 (1.9)	282 (2.0)	295 (1.6)
Massachusetts	304 (1.3)	268 (3.6)	271 (3.1)	324 (4.3)	‡ (†)	‡ †	‡ (†)	267 (4.6)	277 (2.7)	293 (2.2)	308 (1.4)
Michigan	285 (1.3)	251 (2.2)	269 (4.0)	313 (4.7)	‡ (†)	‡ †	‡ (†)	261 (3.7)	263 (2.1)	275 (2.2)	288 (1.5)
Minnesota	302 (1.2)	262 (2.7)	272 (3.2)	293 (4.1)	‡ (†)	261 (5.8)	284 (5.0)	275 (3.3)	278 (2.9)	290 (1.8)	304 (1.2)
Mississippi	284 (1.2)	257 (1.7)	269 (4.9)	‡ (†)	‡ (†)	‡ (†)	‡ (†)	258 (3.0)	259 (2.0)	279 (2.5)	277 (1.5)
Missouri	285 (1.3)	258 (2.7)	270 (3.5)	‡ (†)	‡ (†)	‡ (†)	‡ (†)	257 (2.9)	268 (2.0)	285 (2.0)	291 (1.4)
Montana	292 (0.8)	‡ (†)	275 (4.9)	‡ (†)	‡ (†)	256 (2.9)	287 (4.1)	272 (3.7)	270 (2.3)	286 (1.8)	296 (1.0)
Nebraska	295 (0.9)	254 (3.6)	266 (2.1)	‡ (†)	‡ (†)	‡ (†)	285 (5.3)	262 (2.7)	267 (2.1)	288 (2.3)	298 (1.0)
Nevada	288 (1.3)	256 (2.5)	266 (1.1)	300 (3.8)	‡ (†)	‡ (†)	281 (3.3)	263 (2.0)	266 (1.5)	283 (1.7)	288 (1.3)
New Hampshire	295 (0.9)	‡ (†)	270 (4.3)	313 (6.9)	‡ (†)	‡ (†)	‡ (†)	269 (4.4)	278 (1.9)	290 (1.7)	304 (1.0)
New Jersey	301 (1.3)	269 (3.0)	272 (2.0)	332 (3.6)	‡ (†)	‡ (†)	‡ (†)	267 (4.5)	273 (2.2)	291 (2.1)	303 (1.6)
New Mexico	285 (2.1)	‡ (†)	266 (1.1)	‡ (†)	‡ (†)	259 (2.8)	‡ (†)	261 (2.2)	260 (1.6)	277 (1.9)	283 (1.4)
New York	290 (1.5)	264 (2.9)	268 (1.7)	298 (3.7)	‡ (†)	‡ (†)	‡ (†)	267 (3.0)	269 (2.5)	283 (1.9)	290 (1.6)
North Carolina	292 (1.7)	263 (2.0)	273 (2.5)	311 (6.3)	‡ (†)	261 (4.7)	274 (4.4)	264 (2.4)	267 (2.1)	281 (1.8)	294 (2.0)
North Dakota	293 (0.7)	263 (4.7)	276 (3.3)	‡ (†)	‡ (†)	260 (3.1)	‡ (†)	266 (3.4)	274 (2.3)	286 (1.6)	296 (0.9)
Ohio	291 (1.3)	259 (3.1)	266 (8.8)	304 (25.4)	‡ (†)	‡ (†)	280 (3.6)	259 (4.6)	272 (2.1)	284 (2.0)	296 (1.4)
Oklahoma	281 (1.4)	260 (2.7)	266 (2.9)	‡ (†)	‡ (†)	269 (1.8)	273 (3.8)	263 (3.0)	265 (1.8)	277 (2.1)	284 (1.7)
Oregon	289 (1.4)	‡ (†)	266 (1.7)	308 (5.9)	‡ (†)	‡ (†)	281 (4.2)	268 (2.4)	271 (1.9)	283 (2.1)	295 (1.6)
Pennsylvania	292 (1.3)	253 (2.3)	261 (3.7)	317 (6.1)	‡ (†)	‡ (†)	274 (4.9)	261 (3.4)	265 (3.3)	284 (2.3)	297 (1.6)
Rhode Island	290 (0.8)	258 (3.1)	265 (1.1)	300 (4.0)	‡ (†)	‡ (†)	274 (4.3)	268 (2.5)	269 (1.8)	285 (2.0)	293 (1.0)
South Carolina	288 (1.3)	256 (1.9)	272 (4.3)	‡ (†)	‡ (†)	‡ (†)	‡ (†)	271 (3.6)	263 (2.3)	278 (2.2)	284 (1.3)
South Dakota	290 (0.7)	‡ (†)	272 (4.5)	‡ (†)	‡ (†)	260 (2.9)	‡ (†)	265 (4.1)	269 (1.9)	287 (1.9)	292 (1.1)
Tennessee	285 (1.7)	253 (3.0)	273 (4.0)	‡ (†)	‡ (†)	‡ (†)	‡ (†)	265 (3.1)	266 (2.0)	281 (2.0)	291 (2.2)
Texas	298 (1.5)	267 (2.9)	277 (1.4)	312 (3.2)	‡ (†)	‡ (†)	293 (6.1)	272 (1.9)	275 (1.8)	284 (2.0)	296 (1.6)
Utah	292 (1.0)	‡ (†)	262 (2.6)	‡ (†)	‡ (†)	240 (9.0)	‡ (†)	‡ (†)	‡ (†)	‡ (†)	‡ (†)
Vermont	291 (0.8)	‡ (†)	‡ (†)	‡ (†)	‡ (†)	‡ (†)	‡ (†)	266 (3.6)	277 (2.0)	288 (2.5)	301 (1.1)
Virginia	295 (1.4)	265 (1.8)	279 (2.4)	317 (4.1)	‡ (†)	‡ (†)	293 (3.3)	268 (3.2)	272 (2.0)	281 (1.9)	298 (1.6)
Washington	294 (1.4)	257 (3.4)	269 (2.5)	312 (3.7)	‡ (†)	264 (7.0)	285 (3.7)	266 (3.0)	272 (2.6)	288 (1.8)	300 (1.4)
West Virginia	272 (0.9)	256 (3.1)	‡ (†)	‡ (†)	‡ (†)	‡ (†)	‡ (†)	255 (2.9)	261 (1.6)	275 (1.8)	280 (1.4)
Wisconsin	296 (1.1)	249 (4.2)	271 (2.6)	296 (4.8)	‡ (†)	274 (7.0)	‡ (†)	263 (3.8)	271 (2.4)	289 (2.1)	299 (1.2)
Wyoming	290 (0.8)	‡ (†)	273 (1.9)	‡ (†)	‡ (†)	251 (4.0)	‡ (†)	272 (2.8)	272 (1.7)	285 (1.8)	297 (1.0)
Department of Defense dependents schools	298 (1.2)	271 (2.1)	287 (2.1)	298 (3.3)	‡ (†)	‡ (†)	290 (2.6)	‡ (†)	276 (2.5)	291 (1.9)	295 (1.0)

†Not applicable.
‡Reporting standards not met. Either there are too few cases for a reliable estimate or item response rates fell below the required standards for reporting.
[1]Excludes students who responded "I don't know" to the question about educational level of parents.
NOTE: Scale ranges from 0 to 500. Includes public school students who were tested with accommodations; excludes only those students with disabilities (SD) and English language learners (ELL) who were unable to be tested even with accommodations. SD and ELL populations, accommodation rates, and exclusion rates vary from state to state. Race/ethnicity based on school records. Race categories exclude persons of Hispanic ethnicity.
SOURCE: U.S. Department of Education, National Center for Education Statistics, National Assessment of Educational Progress (NAEP), 2015 Mathematics Assessment, retrieved October 29, 2015, from the Main NAEP Data Explorer (http://nces.ed.gov/nationsreportcard/naepdata/). (This table was prepared October 2015.)

Table 222.80. Average National Assessment of Educational Progress (NAEP) mathematics scale scores of 4th- and 8th-grade public school students and percentage attaining selected mathematics achievement levels, by race/ethnicity and jurisdiction or specific urban district: 2009, 2011, 2013, and 2015

[Standard errors appear in parentheses]

Grade level and jurisdiction or specific urban district	Average mathematics scale score[1]												Percent of students	
	2009	2011	2013					2015					2015	
	All students	All students	All students	White	Black	Hispanic	Asian	All students	White	Black	Hispanic	Asian	At or above *Basic*[2]	At or above *Proficient*[3]
1	2	3	4	5	6	7	8	9	10	11	12	13	14	15
4th grade														
United States	239 (0.2)	240 (0.2)	241 (0.2)	250 (0.2)	224 (0.3)	230 (0.4)	260 (0.8)	240 (0.3)	248 (0.3)	224 (0.4)	230 (0.5)	259 (1.2)	81 (0.3)	39 (0.4)
All large cities[4]	231 (0.5)	233 (0.6)	235 (0.7)	254 (0.9)	223 (0.6)	229 (0.8)	258 (2.1)	234 (0.6)	251 (1.0)	222 (0.6)	230 (0.7)	253 (2.0)	75 (0.6)	32 (0.9)
Selected urban districts														
Albuquerque (NM)	— (†)	235 (1.3)	235 (1.0)	253 (2.0)	‡ (†)	229 (1.2)	‡ (†)	231 (1.1)	249 (2.2)	‡ (†)	226 (1.3)	‡ (†)	72 (1.7)	28 (1.6)
Atlanta (GA)	225 (0.8)	228 (0.7)	233 (0.7)	269 (1.4)	222 (0.9)	233 (2.7)	‡ (†)	228 (1.2)	267 (1.9)	218 (1.4)	225 (3.6)	‡ (†)	65 (2.1)	26 (1.4)
Austin (TX)	240 (1.0)	245 (1.1)	245 (0.9)	264 (1.7)	228 (3.4)	237 (1.2)	‡ (†)	246 (1.4)	268 (2.0)	226 (3.1)	237 (1.6)	‡ (†)	85 (1.5)	47 (1.9)
Baltimore City (MD)	222 (1.0)	226 (1.1)	223 (1.2)	250 (4.0)	220 (1.2)	227 (3.9)	‡ (†)	215 (1.5)	232 (3.6)	212 (1.6)	223 (3.3)	‡ (†)	51 (2.2)	12 (1.6)
Boston (MA)	236 (0.7)	237 (0.6)	237 (0.8)	255 (1.6)	228 (1.4)	233 (1.1)	259 (2.2)	236 (1.3)	253 (2.5)	228 (1.8)	230 (2.0)	259 (3.3)	78 (1.9)	33 (1.8)
Charlotte (NC)	245 (1.3)	247 (1.1)	247 (1.6)	264 (2.0)	235 (2.2)	242 (2.0)	255 (4.1)	248 (1.3)	264 (2.0)	236 (1.7)	243 (2.2)	268 (4.2)	87 (1.2)	51 (2.3)
Chicago (IL)	222 (1.2)	224 (0.9)	231 (1.3)	261 (2.8)	221 (2.1)	230 (1.2)	256 (5.8)	232 (1.2)	262 (2.7)	221 (1.8)	230 (1.6)	265 (4.3)	71 (1.5)	30 (1.7)
Cleveland (OH)	213 (1.0)	216 (0.7)	216 (0.9)	233 (2.2)	210 (1.1)	221 (2.6)	‡ (†)	219 (1.3)	233 (2.4)	215 (1.6)	221 (3.4)	‡ (†)	58 (2.1)	13 (1.5)
Dallas (TX)	— (†)	233 (1.3)	234 (1.0)	‡ (†)	226 (1.7)	235 (1.1)	‡ (†)	238 (1.3)	259 (7.8)	228 (2.8)	238 (1.2)	‡ (†)	82 (1.9)	34 (1.9)
Detroit (MI)	200 (1.7)	203 (1.4)	204 (1.6)	‡ (†)	201 (1.6)	214 (2.9)	‡ (†)	205 (1.6)	‡ (†)	202 (1.8)	215 (3.1)	‡ (†)	36 (2.9)	5 (1.1)
District of Columbia (DC)	220 (0.8)	222 (1.0)	229 (0.8)	277 (2.2)	218 (1.0)	226 (2.3)	‡ (†)	232 (0.9)	275 (1.9)	220 (1.1)	233 (2.3)	‡ (†)	68 (1.5)	33 (1.2)
Duval County (FL)	— (†)	— (†)	— (†)	— (†)	— (†)	— (†)	— (†)	243 (1.3)	254 (1.8)	230 (1.7)	240 (2.4)	‡ (†)	86 (1.5)	41 (2.3)
Fresno (CA)	219 (1.4)	218 (0.9)	220 (1.2)	241 (2.2)	211 (2.5)	217 (1.5)	221 (2.7)	218 (1.3)	235 (3.6)	213 (3.8)	214 (1.5)	226 (3.1)	55 (2.2)	14 (1.5)
Hillsborough County (FL)	— (†)	243 (1.1)	243 (0.9)	254 (1.4)	227 (1.9)	238 (1.3)	263 (3.2)	244 (1.4)	253 (1.9)	230 (1.6)	237 (1.9)	‡ (†)	86 (1.5)	43 (2.7)
Houston (TX)	236 (1.2)	237 (0.8)	236 (1.1)	261 (1.9)	227 (2.3)	235 (1.0)	‡ (†)	239 (1.4)	266 (2.8)	231 (2.4)	235 (1.1)	‡ (†)	80 (1.5)	36 (2.4)
Jefferson County (KY)	233 (1.6)	235 (0.9)	234 (1.0)	245 (1.2)	220 (1.4)	224 (3.0)	‡ (†)	236 (1.5)	245 (1.7)	225 (1.6)	226 (3.1)	‡ (†)	77 (1.8)	34 (2.3)
Los Angeles (CA)	222 (1.2)	223 (0.8)	228 (1.3)	254 (3.4)	223 (2.3)	224 (0.9)	252 (2.4)	224 (1.4)	247 (2.6)	216 (3.6)	218 (1.1)	255 (3.2)	64 (1.8)	22 (1.8)
Miami-Dade (FL)	236 (1.3)	236 (1.0)	237 (1.1)	251 (2.2)	227 (1.9)	238 (1.2)	‡ (†)	242 (1.1)	257 (2.6)	230 (2.2)	243 (1.1)	‡ (†)	86 (1.3)	41 (2.0)
Milwaukee (WI)	220 (1.5)	220 (1.0)	221 (1.6)	246 (2.8)	209 (1.8)	227 (2.2)	234 (7.5)	— (†)	— (†)	— (†)	— (†)	— (†)	— (†)	— (†)
New York City (NY)	237 (1.0)	234 (1.2)	236 (1.1)	251 (2.7)	225 (1.5)	228 (1.5)	257 (2.6)	231 (1.0)	242 (2.5)	220 (1.5)	226 (1.4)	254 (1.9)	73 (1.2)	26 (1.4)
Philadelphia (PA)	222 (1.4)	225 (1.2)	223 (1.5)	237 (3.3)	218 (1.3)	217 (2.2)	246 (3.9)	217 (1.9)	235 (4.1)	211 (1.7)	211 (2.3)	246 (4.0)	54 (2.5)	15 (2.0)
San Diego (CA)	236 (1.6)	239 (1.3)	241 (1.2)	260 (1.9)	228 (3.1)	228 (1.6)	253 (2.8)	233 (1.5)	254 (2.5)	217 (3.6)	222 (2.0)	243 (3.3)	73 (2.0)	31 (2.0)
8th grade														
United States	282 (0.3)	283 (0.2)	284 (0.2)	293 (0.3)	263 (0.4)	271 (0.4)	308 (1.1)	281 (0.3)	291 (0.3)	260 (0.5)	269 (0.6)	307 (1.5)	70 (0.3)	32 (0.3)
All large cities[4]	271 (0.7)	274 (0.7)	276 (0.8)	295 (1.2)	261 (0.8)	269 (0.8)	301 (2.2)	274 (1.0)	296 (1.4)	258 (0.9)	268 (1.2)	301 (2.0)	62 (1.1)	26 (0.9)
Selected urban districts														
Albuquerque (NM)	— (†)	275 (1.0)	274 (1.2)	295 (2.6)	‡ (†)	267 (1.5)	‡ (†)	271 (1.4)	289 (2.9)	‡ (†)	264 (1.5)	‡ (†)	61 (1.7)	21 (1.4)
Atlanta (GA)	259 (1.6)	266 (1.3)	267 (1.2)	311 (3.0)	261 (1.3)	262 (3.7)	‡ (†)	266 (1.2)	318 (2.4)	258 (1.2)	271 (4.4)	‡ (†)	51 (1.7)	20 (1.0)
Austin (TX)	287 (0.9)	287 (1.2)	285 (1.0)	312 (1.9)	267 (2.5)	273 (1.3)	‡ (†)	284 (1.3)	313 (2.4)	260 (3.4)	271 (1.4)	‡ (†)	70 (1.5)	35 (1.7)
Baltimore City (MD)	257 (1.9)	261 (1.3)	260 (2.0)	286 (6.0)	257 (2.0)	‡ (†)	‡ (†)	255 (1.8)	281 (6.4)	251 (1.9)	261 (5.2)	‡ (†)	41 (2.5)	12 (1.6)
Boston (MA)	279 (1.3)	282 (0.9)	283 (1.2)	309 (2.4)	271 (1.8)	275 (1.8)	318 (3.7)	281 (1.2)	311 (3.3)	269 (2.1)	271 (2.1)	318 (5.0)	67 (1.6)	34 (1.4)
Charlotte (NC)	283 (0.9)	285 (0.8)	289 (1.2)	313 (1.9)	271 (1.8)	279 (3.4)	314 (6.1)	286 (1.5)	312 (2.1)	268 (1.9)	275 (3.8)	314 (5.1)	71 (1.7)	39 (2.0)
Chicago (IL)	264 (1.4)	270 (1.0)	269 (1.0)	294 (2.4)	259 (1.5)	270 (1.4)	306 (5.4)	275 (2.4)	317 (5.6)	262 (1.5)	275 (1.8)	‡ (†)	62 (2.1)	25 (2.4)
Cleveland (OH)	256 (1.0)	256 (2.1)	253 (1.3)	265 (2.9)	249 (1.5)	252 (3.4)	‡ (†)	254 (1.5)	273 (3.1)	249 (2.1)	257 (3.5)	‡ (†)	40 (1.9)	9 (1.0)
Dallas (TX)	— (†)	274 (0.9)	275 (1.0)	304 (4.7)	263 (2.0)	277 (1.1)	‡ (†)	271 (1.3)	‡ (†)	261 (2.1)	272 (1.5)	‡ (†)	60 (1.9)	20 (1.5)
Detroit (MI)	238 (2.7)	246 (1.2)	240 (1.7)	‡ (†)	239 (1.7)	243 (4.0)	‡ (†)	244 (1.7)	‡ (†)	242 (1.9)	253 (3.3)	‡ (†)	27 (1.8)	4 (0.7)
District of Columbia (DC)	251 (1.3)	255 (0.9)	260 (1.3)	315 (4.1)	253 (1.4)	262 (3.6)	‡ (†)	258 (1.3)	314 (3.3)	248 (1.5)	263 (3.3)	‡ (†)	46 (1.8)	17 (1.3)
Duval County (FL)	— (†)	— (†)	— (†)	— (†)	— (†)	— (†)	— (†)	275 (1.0)	285 (1.6)	264 (1.4)	266 (3.3)	298 (4.9)	64 (1.7)	22 (1.3)
Fresno (CA)	258 (1.2)	256 (0.9)	260 (1.4)	279 (3.0)	247 (4.0)	256 (1.6)	270 (2.8)	257 (1.5)	281 (3.7)	242 (5.0)	252 (1.9)	270 (3.8)	44 (1.8)	12 (1.1)
Hillsborough County (FL)	— (†)	282 (1.5)	284 (1.1)	296 (1.8)	264 (2.5)	278 (1.9)	‡ (†)	276 (1.7)	290 (2.1)	260 (2.6)	266 (2.2)	‡ (†)	64 (2.3)	27 (1.6)
Houston (TX)	277 (1.2)	279 (1.0)	280 (1.1)	312 (3.3)	271 (1.7)	279 (1.2)	314 (7.2)	276 (1.4)	313 (3.7)	265 (2.6)	273 (1.2)	319 (6.6)	65 (1.7)	27 (1.5)
Jefferson County (KY)	271 (0.9)	274 (1.0)	273 (1.0)	285 (1.5)	257 (1.7)	265 (3.7)	‡ (†)	272 (1.7)	285 (2.2)	252 (2.2)	266 (4.5)	‡ (†)	58 (1.8)	26 (1.8)
Los Angeles (CA)	258 (1.0)	261 (1.3)	264 (1.5)	293 (3.2)	256 (3.4)	258 (1.3)	298 (3.3)	263 (1.6)	285 (4.4)	255 (4.1)	259 (1.4)	296 (5.9)	52 (2.0)	15 (1.4)
Miami-Dade (FL)	273 (1.1)	272 (1.1)	274 (1.5)	295 (3.4)	259 (2.9)	275 (1.3)	‡ (†)	274 (1.8)	299 (2.8)	255 (3.3)	277 (2.0)	‡ (†)	64 (2.1)	26 (1.7)
Milwaukee (WI)	251 (1.5)	254 (1.7)	257 (1.4)	282 (3.5)	247 (1.8)	266 (2.2)	‡ (†)	— (†)	— (†)	— (†)	— (†)	— (†)	— (†)	— (†)
New York City (NY)	273 (1.5)	272 (1.6)	274 (1.1)	301 (3.8)	263 (1.9)	263 (1.7)	304 (3.1)	275 (2.1)	294 (4.6)	261 (3.2)	267 (1.8)	303 (3.1)	62 (2.1)	27 (2.3)
Philadelphia (PA)	265 (2.0)	265 (2.0)	266 (1.7)	287 (2.8)	258 (2.2)	261 (4.1)	297 (4.9)	267 (1.9)	282 (4.0)	257 (2.1)	259 (3.2)	303 (6.0)	53 (2.3)	20 (1.9)
San Diego (CA)	280 (2.0)	278 (1.7)	277 (1.4)	300 (2.3)	260 (4.5)	260 (2.2)	294 (2.9)	280 (1.6)	302 (2.3)	261 (4.0)	266 (2.2)	293 (3.3)	70 (1.9)	32 (1.8)

—Not available.
†Not applicable.
‡Reporting standards not met (too few cases for a reliable estimate).
[1]Scale ranges from 0 to 500.
[2]*Basic* denotes partial mastery of the knowledge and skills that are fundamental for proficient work at a given grade.
[3]*Proficient* represents solid academic performance. Students reaching this level have demonstrated competency over challenging subject matter.
[4]Includes public school students from all cities in the nation with populations of 250,000 or more, including the participating districts.
NOTE: Race categories exclude persons of Hispanic ethnicity. Totals include racial/ethnic groups not shown separately.
SOURCE: U.S. Department of Education, National Center for Education Statistics, National Assessment of Educational Progress (NAEP), 2009, 2011, 2013, and 2015 Mathematics Assessments, retrieved October 29, 2015, from the Main NAEP Data Explorer (http://nces.ed.gov/nationsreportcard/naepdata/). (This table was prepared October 2015.)

Table 222.85. Average National Assessment of Educational Progress (NAEP) mathematics scale score, by age and selected student characteristics: Selected years, 1973 through 2012

[Standard errors appear in parentheses]

Selected student characteristic	1973	1978	1982	1986	1990	1992	1994	1996	1999	2004[1] Previous format	2004[1] Revised format	2008	2012
1	2	3	4	5	6	7	8	9	10	11	12	13	14
9-year-olds													
All students	**219 (0.8)**	**219 (0.8)**	**219 (1.1)**	**222 (1.0)**	**230 (0.8)**	**230 (0.8)**	**231 (0.8)**	**231 (0.8)**	**232 (0.8)**	**241 (0.9)**	**239 (0.9)**	**243 (0.8)**	**244 (1.0)**
Sex													
Male	218 (0.7)	217 (0.7)	217 (1.2)	222 (1.1)	229 (0.9)	231 (1.0)	232 (1.0)	233 (1.2)	233 (1.0)	243 (1.1)	239 (1.0)	242 (0.9)	244 (1.2)
Female	220 (1.1)	220 (1.0)	221 (1.2)	222 (1.2)	230 (1.1)	228 (1.0)	230 (0.9)	229 (0.7)	231 (0.9)	240 (1.1)	240 (1.0)	243 (1.0)	244 (1.0)
Gap between female and male score	2 (1.3)	3 (1.3)	4 (1.7)	# (†)	1 (1.4)	-2 (1.4)	-2 (1.4)	-4 (1.4)	-2 (1.3)	-3 (1.5)	1 (1.4)	1 (1.3)	# (†)
Race/ethnicity													
White	225 (1.0)	224 (0.9)	224 (1.1)	227 (1.1)	235 (0.8)	235 (0.8)	237 (1.0)	237 (1.0)	239 (0.9)	247 (0.9)	245 (0.8)	250 (0.8)	252 (1.1)
Black	190 (1.8)	192 (1.1)	195 (1.6)	202 (1.6)	208 (2.2)	208 (2.0)	212 (1.6)	212 (1.4)	211 (1.6)	224 (2.1)	221 (2.1)	224 (1.9)	226 (1.8)
Hispanic	202 (2.4)	203 (2.2)	204 (1.3)	205 (2.1)	214 (2.1)	212 (2.3)	210 (2.3)	215 (1.7)	213 (1.9)	230 (2.0)	229 (2.0)	234 (1.2)	234 (0.9)
Gap between White and Black score	35 (2.1)	32 (1.5)	29 (2.0)	25 (2.0)	27 (2.4)	27 (2.2)	25 (1.8)	25 (1.8)	28 (1.8)	23 (2.2)	24 (2.2)	26 (2.1)	25 (2.1)
Gap between White and Hispanic score	23 (2.6)	21 (2.4)	20 (1.7)	21 (2.3)	21 (2.3)	23 (2.5)	27 (2.5)	22 (2.0)	26 (2.1)	18 (2.2)	16 (2.1)	16 (1.4)	17 (1.5)
13-year-olds													
All students	**266 (1.1)**	**264 (1.1)**	**269 (1.1)**	**269 (1.2)**	**270 (0.9)**	**273 (0.9)**	**274 (1.0)**	**274 (0.8)**	**276 (0.8)**	**281 (1.0)**	**279 (1.0)**	**281 (0.9)**	**285 (1.1)**
Sex													
Male	265 (1.3)	264 (1.3)	269 (1.4)	270 (1.1)	271 (1.2)	274 (1.1)	276 (1.3)	276 (0.9)	277 (0.9)	283 (1.2)	279 (1.0)	284 (1.0)	286 (1.3)
Female	267 (1.1)	265 (1.1)	268 (1.1)	268 (1.5)	270 (0.9)	272 (1.0)	273 (1.0)	272 (1.0)	274 (1.1)	279 (1.0)	278 (1.2)	279 (1.0)	284 (1.1)
Gap between female and male score	2 (1.7)	1 (1.7)	-1 (1.7)	-2 (1.9)	-2 (1.5)	-2 (1.5)	-3 (1.6)	-4 (1.4)	-3 (1.4)	-3 (1.6)	-1 (1.6)	-4 (1.4)	-2 (1.7)
Race/ethnicity													
White	274 (0.9)	272 (0.8)	274 (1.0)	274 (1.3)	276 (1.1)	279 (0.9)	281 (0.9)	281 (0.9)	283 (0.8)	288 (0.9)	287 (0.9)	290 (1.2)	293 (1.1)
Black	228 (1.9)	230 (1.9)	240 (1.6)	249 (2.3)	249 (2.3)	250 (1.9)	252 (3.5)	252 (1.3)	251 (2.6)	262 (1.6)	257 (1.8)	262 (1.2)	264 (1.9)
Hispanic	239 (2.2)	238 (2.0)	252 (1.7)	254 (2.9)	255 (1.8)	259 (1.8)	256 (1.9)	256 (1.6)	259 (1.7)	265 (2.0)	264 (1.5)	268 (1.2)	271 (1.4)
Gap between White and Black score	46 (2.1)	42 (2.1)	34 (1.9)	24 (2.6)	27 (2.6)	29 (2.1)	29 (3.7)	29 (1.6)	32 (2.7)	27 (1.8)	30 (2.1)	28 (1.7)	28 (2.2)
Gap between White and Hispanic score	35 (2.4)	34 (2.1)	22 (1.9)	19 (3.2)	22 (2.1)	20 (2.0)	25 (2.1)	25 (1.9)	24 (1.9)	23 (2.2)	23 (1.8)	23 (1.7)	21 (1.8)
Parents' highest level of education													
Did not finish high school	— (†)	245 (1.2)	251 (1.4)	252 (2.3)	253 (1.8)	256 (1.0)	255 (2.1)	254 (2.4)	256 (2.8)	262 (2.2)	263 (1.9)	268 (1.3)	266 (2.5)
Graduated high school	— (†)	263 (1.0)	263 (0.8)	263 (1.2)	263 (1.2)	263 (1.2)	266 (1.1)	267 (1.1)	264 (1.1)	271 (1.7)	270 (1.3)	272 (1.1)	270 (1.1)
Some education after high school	— (†)	273 (1.2)	275 (0.9)	274 (0.8)	277 (1.0)	278 (1.0)	277 (1.6)	277 (1.4)	279 (0.9)	283 (1.0)	282 (1.4)	285 (1.1)	286 (1.4)
Graduated college	— (†)	284 (1.2)	282 (1.5)	280 (1.4)	280 (1.0)	283 (1.0)	285 (1.2)	283 (1.2)	286 (1.0)	292 (0.9)	289 (1.1)	291 (1.0)	296 (1.3)
17-year-olds													
All students	**304 (1.1)**	**300 (1.0)**	**298 (0.9)**	**302 (0.9)**	**305 (0.9)**	**307 (0.9)**	**306 (1.0)**	**307 (1.2)**	**308 (1.0)**	**307 (0.8)**	**305 (0.7)**	**306 (0.6)**	**306 (0.8)**
Sex													
Male	309 (1.2)	304 (1.0)	301 (1.0)	305 (1.2)	306 (1.1)	309 (1.1)	309 (1.4)	310 (1.3)	310 (1.4)	308 (1.0)	307 (0.9)	309 (0.7)	308 (1.0)
Female	301 (1.1)	297 (1.0)	296 (1.0)	299 (1.0)	303 (1.1)	305 (1.1)	304 (1.1)	305 (1.4)	307 (1.0)	305 (0.9)	304 (0.8)	303 (0.8)	304 (0.8)
Gap between female and male score	-8 (1.6)	-7 (1.4)	-6 (1.4)	-5 (1.5)	-3 (1.5)	-4 (1.5)	-4 (1.8)	-5 (1.9)	-3 (1.7)	-3 (1.4)	-3 (1.2)	-5 (1.1)	-4 (1.3)
Race/ethnicity													
White	310 (1.1)	306 (0.9)	304 (0.9)	308 (1.0)	309 (1.0)	312 (0.8)	312 (1.1)	313 (1.4)	315 (1.1)	313 (0.7)	311 (0.7)	314 (0.7)	314 (1.0)
Black	270 (1.3)	268 (1.3)	272 (1.2)	279 (2.1)	289 (2.8)	286 (2.2)	286 (1.8)	286 (1.7)	283 (1.5)	285 (1.6)	284 (1.4)	287 (1.2)	288 (1.3)
Hispanic	277 (2.2)	276 (2.3)	277 (1.8)	283 (2.9)	284 (2.9)	292 (2.6)	291 (3.7)	292 (2.1)	293 (2.5)	289 (1.8)	292 (1.2)	293 (1.1)	294 (1.1)
Gap between White and Black score	40 (1.7)	38 (1.6)	32 (1.5)	29 (2.3)	21 (3.0)	26 (2.4)	27 (2.1)	27 (2.2)	31 (1.9)	28 (1.8)	27 (1.6)	26 (1.4)	26 (1.6)
Gap between White and Hispanic score	33 (2.5)	30 (2.4)	27 (2.0)	24 (3.0)	26 (3.1)	20 (2.8)	22 (3.9)	21 (2.5)	22 (2.7)	24 (1.9)	19 (1.4)	21 (1.3)	19 (1.5)
Parents' highest level of education													
Did not finish high school	— (†)	280 (1.2)	279 (1.0)	279 (2.3)	285 (2.2)	285 (2.3)	284 (2.4)	281 (2.4)	289 (1.8)	287 (2.4)	287 (1.2)	292 (1.3)	290 (1.4)
Graduated high school	— (†)	294 (0.8)	293 (0.8)	293 (1.0)	294 (0.9)	298 (1.7)	295 (1.1)	297 (2.4)	299 (1.6)	295 (1.1)	294 (0.9)	296 (1.2)	291 (1.1)
Some education after high school	— (†)	305 (0.9)	304 (0.9)	305 (1.2)	308 (1.0)	308 (1.1)	305 (1.3)	307 (1.5)	308 (1.6)	306 (1.1)	305 (0.9)	306 (0.8)	306 (0.9)
Graduated college	— (†)	317 (1.0)	312 (1.0)	314 (1.4)	316 (1.3)	316 (1.0)	318 (1.4)	317 (1.3)	317 (1.2)	317 (0.9)	315 (0.9)	316 (0.7)	317 (0.8)

—Not available.
†Not applicable.
#Rounds to zero.
[1]In 2004, two assessments were conducted—one using the same format that was used in previous assessments, and one using a revised assessment format that provides accommodations for students with disabilities and for English language learners. The 2004 data in column 11 are for the format that was used in previous assessment years, while the 2004 data in column 12 are for the revised format. In subsequent years, only the revised format was used.
NOTE: Scale ranges from 0 to 500. Students scoring 150 (or higher) know some basic addition and subtraction facts. Students scoring 200 have a considerable understanding of two-digit numbers and know some basic multiplication and division facts. Students scoring 250 have an initial understanding of the four basic operations and are developing an ability to analyze simple logical relations. Students scoring 300 can perform reasoning and problem solving involving fractions, decimals, percents, elementary geometry, and simple algebra. Students scoring 350 can perform reasoning and problem solving involving geometry, algebra, and beginning statistics and probability. Includes public and private schools. For assessment years prior to 2004, accommodations were not permitted. For 2004 (revised format) and later years, includes students tested with accommodations; excludes only those students with disabilities and English language learners who were unable to be tested even with accommodations (1 to 4 percent of all students, depending on age and assessment year). Race categories exclude persons of Hispanic ethnicity. Totals include other racial/ethnic groups not shown separately.
SOURCE: U.S. Department of Education, National Center for Education Statistics, National Assessment of Educational Progress (NAEP), *NAEP 2012 Trends in Academic Progress*; and 2012 NAEP Long-Term Trend Mathematics Assessment, retrieved August 29, 2013, from Long-Term Trend NAEP Data Explorer (http://nces.ed.gov/nationsreportcard/naepdata/). (This table was prepared August 2013.)

Table 222.90. Percentage of students at or above selected National Assessment of Educational Progress (NAEP) mathematics score levels, by age, sex, and race/ethnicity: Selected years, 1978 through 2012

[Standard errors appear in parentheses]

Sex, race/ethnicity, and year	9-year-olds: Level 150[1]	9-year-olds: Level 200[2]	9-year-olds: Level 250[3]	13-year-olds: Level 200[2]	13-year-olds: Level 250[3]	13-year-olds: Level 300[4]	17-year-olds: Level 250[3]	17-year-olds: Level 300[4]	17-year-olds: Level 350[5]
1	2	3	4	5	6	7	8	9	10
Total									
1978	96.7 (0.25)	70.4 (0.92)	19.6 (0.73)	94.6 (0.46)	64.9 (1.18)	18.0 (0.73)	92.0 (0.50)	51.5 (1.14)	7.3 (0.44)
1982	97.1 (0.35)	71.4 (1.18)	18.8 (0.96)	97.7 (0.37)	71.4 (1.18)	17.4 (0.95)	93.0 (0.50)	48.5 (1.28)	5.5 (0.43)
1986	97.9 (0.29)	74.1 (1.24)	20.7 (0.88)	98.6 (0.25)	73.3 (1.59)	15.8 (1.01)	95.6 (0.48)	51.7 (1.43)	6.5 (0.52)
1990	99.1 (0.21)	81.5 (0.96)	27.7 (0.86)	98.5 (0.21)	74.7 (1.03)	17.3 (0.99)	96.0 (0.52)	56.1 (1.43)	7.2 (0.63)
1996	99.1 (0.18)	81.5 (0.76)	29.7 (1.02)	98.8 (0.20)	78.6 (0.87)	20.6 (1.24)	96.8 (0.42)	60.1 (1.72)	7.4 (0.77)
1999	98.9 (0.17)	82.5 (0.84)	30.9 (1.07)	98.7 (0.25)	78.8 (1.02)	23.2 (0.95)	96.8 (0.45)	60.7 (1.63)	8.4 (0.83)
2004	98.7 (0.19)	87.0 (0.77)	40.9 (0.89)	98.1 (0.19)	81.1 (0.98)	27.8 (1.09)	95.8 (0.40)	58.3 (1.12)	6.1 (0.47)
2008	99.0 (0.18)	89.1 (0.69)	44.5 (1.01)	98.2 (0.19)	83.4 (0.63)	30.0 (1.08)	96.0 (0.37)	59.4 (0.87)	6.2 (0.40)
2012	98.7 (0.21)	88.7 (0.69)	46.7 (1.28)	98.5 (0.21)	84.7 (0.71)	34.0 (1.38)	95.7 (0.31)	59.7 (1.22)	7.0 (0.51)
Male									
1978	96.2 (0.48)	68.9 (0.98)	19.2 (0.64)	93.9 (0.49)	63.9 (1.32)	18.4 (0.85)	93.0 (0.52)	55.1 (1.21)	9.5 (0.57)
1982	96.5 (0.55)	68.8 (1.29)	18.1 (1.06)	97.5 (0.55)	71.3 (1.44)	18.9 (1.18)	93.9 (0.58)	51.9 (1.51)	6.9 (0.70)
1986	98.0 (0.51)	74.0 (1.45)	20.9 (1.10)	98.5 (0.32)	73.8 (1.76)	17.6 (1.12)	96.1 (0.63)	54.6 (1.78)	8.4 (0.91)
1990	99.0 (0.26)	80.6 (1.05)	27.5 (0.96)	98.2 (0.34)	75.1 (1.75)	19.0 (1.24)	95.8 (0.77)	57.6 (1.42)	8.8 (0.76)
1996	99.1 (0.20)	82.5 (1.10)	32.7 (1.74)	98.7 (0.25)	79.8 (1.43)	23.0 (1.64)	97.0 (0.66)	62.7 (1.77)	9.5 (1.32)
1999	98.8 (0.28)	82.6 (0.92)	32.4 (1.25)	98.5 (0.27)	79.3 (1.12)	25.4 (1.19)	96.5 (0.81)	63.1 (2.12)	9.8 (1.09)
2004	98.3 (0.27)	86.1 (0.89)	40.7 (1.03)	97.7 (0.29)	80.5 (1.08)	29.9 (1.27)	95.6 (0.45)	60.8 (1.31)	7.3 (0.68)
2008	99.0 (0.27)	88.4 (0.87)	44.4 (1.18)	98.2 (0.28)	84.3 (0.75)	33.4 (1.29)	96.2 (0.47)	62.9 (0.96)	7.6 (0.61)
2012	98.6 (0.24)	88.0 (0.79)	47.0 (1.47)	98.2 (0.27)	84.7 (0.84)	35.7 (1.55)	95.5 (0.43)	61.5 (1.33)	9.0 (0.75)
Female									
1978	97.2 (0.27)	72.0 (1.05)	19.9 (1.00)	95.2 (0.49)	65.9 (1.17)	17.5 (0.75)	91.0 (0.57)	48.2 (1.29)	5.2 (0.66)
1982	97.6 (0.33)	74.0 (1.30)	19.6 (1.11)	98.0 (0.27)	71.4 (1.29)	15.9 (1.00)	92.1 (0.56)	45.3 (1.37)	4.1 (0.42)
1986	97.8 (0.38)	74.3 (1.32)	20.6 (1.28)	98.6 (0.31)	72.7 (1.95)	14.1 (1.31)	95.1 (0.65)	48.9 (1.73)	4.7 (0.59)
1990	99.1 (0.26)	82.3 (1.26)	27.9 (1.31)	98.9 (0.18)	74.4 (1.32)	15.7 (1.00)	96.2 (0.84)	54.7 (1.84)	5.6 (0.79)
1996	99.1 (0.36)	80.7 (0.93)	26.7 (1.07)	98.8 (0.27)	77.4 (1.09)	18.4 (1.48)	96.7 (0.57)	57.6 (2.21)	5.3 (0.80)
1999	99.0 (0.19)	82.5 (1.15)	29.4 (1.36)	99.0 (0.40)	78.4 (1.22)	21.0 (1.38)	97.2 (0.40)	58.5 (1.89)	7.1 (1.06)
2004	99.0 (0.22)	87.8 (0.96)	41.1 (1.13)	98.4 (0.25)	81.7 (1.10)	25.7 (1.24)	95.9 (0.58)	55.9 (1.18)	4.9 (0.48)
2008	99.0 (0.21)	89.9 (0.78)	44.6 (1.18)	98.2 (0.25)	82.5 (0.86)	26.7 (1.13)	95.7 (0.43)	55.8 (1.25)	4.6 (0.34)
2012	98.8 (0.29)	89.4 (0.80)	46.5 (1.34)	98.8 (0.23)	84.7 (0.91)	32.2 (1.42)	96.0 (0.37)	57.9 (1.45)	5.1 (0.60)
White									
1978	98.3 (0.19)	76.3 (1.00)	22.9 (0.87)	97.6 (0.27)	72.9 (0.85)	21.4 (0.73)	95.6 (0.30)	57.6 (1.14)	8.5 (0.48)
1982	98.5 (0.25)	76.8 (1.22)	21.8 (1.13)	99.1 (0.14)	78.3 (0.94)	20.5 (1.00)	96.2 (0.33)	54.7 (1.41)	6.4 (0.54)
1986	98.8 (0.24)	79.6 (1.33)	24.6 (1.03)	99.3 (0.27)	78.9 (1.69)	18.6 (1.17)	98.0 (0.36)	59.1 (1.69)	7.9 (0.68)
1990	99.6 (0.16)	86.9 (0.86)	32.7 (1.04)	99.4 (0.14)	82.0 (1.01)	21.0 (1.23)	97.6 (0.28)	63.2 (1.59)	8.3 (0.73)
1996	99.6 (0.15)	86.6 (0.80)	35.7 (1.38)	99.6 (0.16)	86.4 (1.02)	25.4 (1.50)	98.7 (0.37)	68.7 (2.18)	9.2 (1.02)
1999	99.6 (0.12)	88.6 (0.78)	37.1 (1.35)	99.4 (0.29)	86.7 (0.92)	29.0 (1.26)	98.7 (0.40)	69.9 (1.96)	10.4 (1.07)
2004	99.2 (0.18)	91.9 (0.61)	47.2 (0.97)	99.1 (0.16)	89.3 (0.82)	35.1 (1.21)	97.5 (0.28)	66.8 (1.08)	7.6 (0.63)
2008	99.6 (0.12)	94.0 (0.52)	52.9 (1.29)	98.9 (0.17)	90.4 (0.83)	39.2 (1.60)	98.2 (0.26)	70.5 (1.09)	8.1 (0.55)
2012	99.4 (0.18)	93.2 (0.58)	55.9 (1.54)	99.2 (0.15)	91.6 (0.57)	41.4 (1.65)	97.9 (0.33)	70.3 (1.56)	9.1 (0.71)
Black									
1978	88.4 (1.01)	42.0 (1.44)	4.1 (0.64)	79.7 (1.48)	28.7 (2.06)	2.3 (0.48)	70.7 (1.73)	16.8 (1.57)	0.5 (—)
1982	90.2 (0.97)	46.1 (2.35)	4.4 (0.81)	90.2 (1.60)	37.9 (2.51)	2.9 (0.96)	76.4 (1.47)	17.1 (1.51)	0.5 (—)
1986	93.9 (1.37)	53.4 (2.47)	5.6 (0.92)	95.4 (0.95)	49.0 (3.70)	4.0 (1.42)	85.6 (2.53)	20.8 (2.83)	0.2 (—)
1990	96.9 (0.88)	60.0 (2.76)	9.4 (1.72)	95.4 (1.10)	48.7 (3.56)	3.9 (1.61)	92.4 (2.20)	32.8 (4.49)	2.0 (1.04)
1996	97.3 (0.84)	65.3 (2.38)	10.0 (1.24)	96.2 (1.27)	53.7 (2.56)	4.8 (1.08)	90.6 (1.33)	31.2 (2.51)	0.9 (—)
1999	96.4 (0.64)	63.3 (2.11)	12.3 (1.48)	96.5 (1.06)	50.8 (4.01)	4.4 (1.37)	88.6 (1.95)	26.6 (2.70)	1.0 (—)
2004	97.1 (0.65)	74.3 (2.61)	22.0 (1.72)	95.3 (0.78)	61.5 (2.47)	9.7 (1.35)	89.1 (1.63)	29.4 (2.07)	0.4 (—)
2008	96.9 (0.86)	75.6 (2.31)	24.6 (1.67)	96.6 (0.68)	67.6 (1.69)	10.2 (1.17)	90.6 (1.42)	31.8 (1.60)	0.8 (0.23)
2012	97.5 (0.66)	77.2 (1.56)	26.3 (2.01)	96.7 (0.66)	67.3 (2.10)	14.2 (1.61)	89.8 (1.03)	33.8 (2.04)	1.1 (0.32)
Hispanic									
1978	93.0 (1.20)	54.2 (2.80)	9.2 (2.49)	86.4 (0.94)	36.0 (2.92)	4.0 (0.95)	78.3 (2.29)	23.4 (2.67)	1.4 (0.58)
1982	94.3 (1.19)	55.7 (2.26)	7.8 (1.74)	95.9 (0.95)	52.2 (2.48)	6.3 (0.97)	81.4 (1.86)	21.6 (2.16)	0.7 (0.36)
1986	96.4 (1.29)	57.6 (2.95)	7.3 (2.81)	96.9 (1.43)	56.0 (5.01)	5.5 (1.15)	89.3 (2.52)	26.5 (4.48)	1.1 (—)
1990	98.0 (0.76)	68.4 (3.03)	11.3 (3.49)	96.8 (1.06)	56.7 (3.32)	6.4 (1.70)	85.8 (4.18)	30.1 (3.09)	1.9 (0.78)
1996	98.1 (0.73)	67.1 (2.14)	13.8 (2.26)	96.2 (0.78)	58.3 (2.28)	6.7 (1.17)	92.2 (2.24)	40.1 (3.47)	1.8 (—)
1999	98.1 (0.71)	67.5 (2.47)	10.5 (1.63)	97.2 (0.60)	62.9 (2.50)	8.2 (1.37)	93.6 (2.21)	37.7 (4.15)	3.1 (1.12)
2004	98.0 (0.46)	80.5 (2.03)	30.2 (2.17)	96.4 (0.66)	68.5 (1.86)	13.7 (1.44)	92.3 (1.05)	38.1 (2.12)	1.9 (0.60)
2008	98.9 (0.28)	85.1 (1.25)	33.5 (1.46)	97.0 (0.44)	73.3 (1.71)	14.4 (1.09)	92.2 (1.10)	41.1 (1.69)	1.5 (0.41)
2012	98.3 (0.40)	84.7 (1.00)	34.6 (1.22)	97.3 (0.54)	76.4 (1.94)	18.5 (1.45)	92.9 (0.59)	43.3 (1.91)	2.4 (0.44)

—Not available.

[1]Students scoring 150 (or higher) know some basic addition and subtraction facts.

[2]Students scoring 200 (or higher) have a considerable understanding of two-digit numbers and know some basic multiplication and division facts.

[3]Students scoring 250 (or higher) have an initial understanding of the four basic operations and are developing an ability to analyze simple logical relations.

[4]Students scoring 300 (or higher) can perform reasoning and problem solving involving fractions, decimals, percents, elementary geometry, and simple algebra.

[5]Students scoring 350 (or above) can perform reasoning and problem solving involving geometry, algebra, and beginning statistics and probability.

NOTE: The NAEP mathematics scores have been evaluated at certain performance levels, as outlined in footnotes 1 through 5. Scale ranges from 0 to 500. Includes public and private schools. For assessment years prior to 2004, accommodations were not permitted. For 2004 and later years, includes students tested with accommodations; excludes only those students with disabilities and English language learners who were unable to be tested even with accommodations (1 to 4 percent of all students, depending on age and assessment year). Race categories exclude persons of Hispanic ethnicity. Totals include other racial/ethnic groups not shown separately.

SOURCE: U.S. Department of Education, National Center for Education Statistics, National Assessment of Educational Progress (NAEP), *NAEP Trends in Academic Progress*, 1996 and 1999; and 2004, 2008, and 2012 Long-Term Trend Mathematics Assessments, retrieved May 4, 2009, and July 20, 2013, from the Long-Term Trend NAEP Data Explorer (http://nces.ed.gov/nationsreportcard/naepdata/). (This table was prepared July 2013.)

Table 222.95. National Assessment of Educational Progress (NAEP) mathematics performance of 17-year-olds, by highest mathematics course taken, sex, and race/ethnicity: Selected years, 1978 through 2012

[Standard errors appear in parentheses]

Year, sex, and race/ethnicity	Percent of students	Average scale score by highest mathematics course taken: All students	Prealgebra or general mathematics	Algebra I	Geometry	Algebra II	Precalculus or calculus	Percent of students at or above score levels: 200	250	300	350
1	2	3	4	5	6	7	8	9	10	11	12
1978											
All students	**100 (†)**	**300 (1.0)**	**267 (0.8)**	**286 (0.7)**	**307 (0.7)**	**321 (0.7)**	**334 (1.4)**	**100 (†)**	**92 (0.5)**	**52 (1.1)**	**7 (0.4)**
Sex											
Male	49 (0.5)	304 (1.0)	269 (1.0)	289 (0.9)	310 (1.0)	325 (0.8)	337 (2.0)	100 (†)	93 (0.5)	55 (1.2)	10 (0.6)
Female	51 (0.5)	297 (1.0)	264 (0.9)	284 (1.0)	304 (0.8)	318 (0.9)	329 (1.8)	100 (†)	91 (0.6)	48 (1.3)	5 (0.7)
Race/ethnicity											
White	83 (1.3)	306 (0.9)	272 (0.6)	291 (0.6)	310 (0.6)	325 (0.6)	338 (1.1)	100 (†)	96 (0.3)	58 (1.1)	8 (0.5)
Black	12 (1.1)	268 (1.3)	247 (1.6)	264 (1.5)	281 (1.9)	292 (1.4)	297 (6.5)	99 (0.3)	71 (1.7)	17 (1.6)	# (†)
Hispanic	4 (0.5)	276 (2.3)	256 (2.3)	273 (2.8)	294 (4.4)	303 (2.9)	‡ (†)	99 (0.4)	78 (2.3)	23 (2.7)	1 (0.6)
Other[1]	1 (0.1)	313 (3.3)	‡ (†)	‡ (†)	‡ (†)	323 (2.9)	‡ (†)	100 (†)	94 (2.6)	65 (4.9)	15 (3.2)
1990											
All students	**100 (†)**	**305 (0.9)**	**273 (1.1)**	**288 (1.2)**	**299 (1.5)**	**319 (1.0)**	**344 (2.7)**	**100 (†)**	**96 (0.5)**	**56 (1.4)**	**7 (0.6)**
Sex											
Male	49 (0.9)	306 (1.1)	274 (1.7)	291 (1.6)	302 (1.6)	323 (1.2)	347 (2.4)	100 (†)	96 (0.8)	58 (1.4)	9 (0.8)
Female	51 (0.9)	303 (1.1)	271 (1.8)	285 (1.8)	296 (1.8)	316 (1.1)	340 (4.0)	100 (†)	96 (0.8)	55 (1.8)	6 (0.8)
Race/ethnicity											
White	73 (0.5)	309 (1.0)	277 (1.1)	292 (1.6)	304 (1.3)	323 (0.9)	347 (2.8)	100 (†)	98 (0.3)	63 (1.6)	8 (0.7)
Black	16 (0.3)	289 (2.8)	264 (2.2)	278 (4.0)	285 (3.5)	302 (3.2)	‡ (†)	100 (†)	92 (2.2)	33 (4.5)	2 (1.0)
Hispanic	7 (0.4)	284 (2.9)	‡ (†)	‡ (†)	‡ (†)	306 (3.3)	‡ (†)	100 (†)	86 (4.2)	30 (3.1)	2 (0.8)
Other[1]	4 (0.5)	312 (5.2)	‡ (†)	‡ (†)	‡ (†)	321 (3.8)	‡ (†)	100 (†)	98 (‡)	62 (7.0)	16 (4.3)
1996											
All students	**100 (†)**	**307 (1.2)**	**269 (1.9)**	**283 (1.3)**	**298 (1.3)**	**316 (1.3)**	**339 (1.7)**	**100 (†)**	**97 (0.4)**	**60 (1.7)**	**7 (0.8)**
Sex											
Male	50 (1.2)	310 (1.3)	272 (2.5)	286 (1.5)	302 (1.7)	320 (1.7)	342 (2.3)	100 (†)	97 (0.7)	63 (1.8)	9 (1.3)
Female	50 (1.2)	305 (1.4)	265 (2.2)	278 (2.2)	294 (1.5)	313 (1.4)	335 (2.2)	100 (†)	97 (0.6)	58 (2.2)	5 (0.8)
Race/ethnicity											
White	71 (0.6)	313 (1.4)	273 (2.3)	287 (2.0)	304 (1.6)	320 (1.4)	342 (1.9)	100 (†)	99 (0.4)	69 (2.2)	9 (1.0)
Black	15 (0.3)	286 (1.7)	‡ (†)	272 (2.4)	280 (3.0)	299 (2.2)	‡ (†)	100 (†)	91 (1.3)	31 (2.5)	1 (—)
Hispanic	9 (0.7)	292 (2.1)	‡ (†)	‡ (†)	‡ (†)	306 (2.8)	‡ (†)	100 (†)	92 (2.2)	40 (3.5)	2 (—)
Other[1]	4 (0.7)	312 (5.7)	‡ (†)	‡ (†)	‡ (†)	‡ (†)	‡ (†)	100 (†)	97 (1.2)	64 (7.2)	14 (5.0)
1999											
All students	**100 (†)**	**308 (1.0)**	**278 (2.8)**	**285 (1.7)**	**298 (1.2)**	**315 (0.8)**	**341 (1.4)**	**100 (†)**	**97 (0.5)**	**61 (1.6)**	**8 (0.8)**
Sex											
Male	48 (1.0)	310 (1.4)	281 (3.2)	288 (2.6)	301 (1.8)	317 (1.3)	343 (1.9)	100 (†)	96 (0.8)	63 (2.1)	10 (1.1)
Female	52 (1.0)	307 (1.0)	274 (3.2)	282 (2.5)	295 (1.3)	314 (1.1)	340 (2.0)	100 (†)	97 (0.4)	58 (1.9)	7 (1.1)
Race/ethnicity											
White	72 (0.5)	315 (1.1)	282 (3.4)	290 (2.2)	303 (1.5)	320 (0.9)	343 (1.5)	100 (†)	99 (0.4)	70 (2.0)	10 (1.1)
Black	15 (0.4)	283 (1.5)	‡ (†)	267 (2.9)	281 (2.5)	293 (1.4)	‡ (†)	100 (†)	89 (2.0)	27 (2.7)	1 (—)
Hispanic	10 (0.5)	293 (2.5)	‡ (†)	‡ (†)	‡ (†)	308 (3.0)	‡ (†)	100 (†)	94 (2.2)	38 (4.1)	3 (1.1)
Other[1]	4 (0.2)	320 (4.0)	‡ (†)	‡ (†)	‡ (†)	320 (4.4)	‡ (†)	100 (†)	100 (†)	76 (6.3)	14 (4.1)
2008											
All students	**100 (†)**	**306 (0.6)**	**270 (1.9)**	**280 (1.1)**	**295 (0.8)**	**307 (0.7)**	**333 (0.8)**	**— (†)**	**96 (0.4)**	**59 (0.9)**	**6 (0.4)**
Sex								— (†)			
Male	50 (0.5)	309 (0.7)	273 (2.9)	283 (1.5)	300 (0.8)	310 (0.8)	336 (1.1)	— (†)	96 (0.5)	63 (1.0)	8 (0.6)
Female	50 (0.5)	303 (0.8)	267 (2.8)	276 (1.6)	289 (1.0)	303 (0.8)	331 (0.9)	— (†)	96 (0.4)	56 (1.3)	5 (0.3)
Race/ethnicity								— (†)			
White	59 (1.5)	314 (0.7)	275 (2.3)	287 (1.3)	301 (0.9)	314 (0.8)	337 (0.8)	— (†)	98 (0.3)	71 (1.1)	8 (0.5)
Black	14 (1.4)	287 (1.2)	‡ (†)	266 (2.6)	282 (1.6)	291 (1.5)	312 (2.6)	— (†)	91 (1.4)	32 (1.6)	1 (0.2)
Hispanic	19 (1.2)	293 (1.1)	261 (3.2)	274 (2.3)	289 (1.3)	296 (1.2)	320 (1.9)	— (†)	92 (1.1)	41 (1.7)	1 (0.4)
Other[1]	7 (0.5)	316 (1.8)	‡ (†)	‡ (†)	297 (2.8)	311 (1.9)	340 (2.2)	— (†)	98 (0.7)	71 (2.2)	13 (1.8)
2012											
All students	**100 (†)**	**306 (0.8)**	**263 (3.6)**	**272 (1.5)**	**290 (1.3)**	**305 (1.0)**	**334 (0.8)**	**— (†)**	**96 (0.3)**	**60 (1.2)**	**7 (0.5)**
Sex											
Male	49 (0.5)	308 (1.0)	266 (4.4)	276 (1.7)	293 (1.6)	308 (1.1)	337 (1.2)	— (†)	95 (0.4)	62 (1.3)	9 (0.8)
Female	51 (0.5)	304 (0.8)	‡ (†)	267 (2.0)	287 (1.3)	302 (1.1)	331 (1.0)	— (†)	96 (0.4)	58 (1.4)	5 (0.6)
Race/ethnicity											
White	56 (1.6)	314 (1.0)	268 (5.2)	278 (2.1)	298 (1.8)	311 (1.2)	337 (0.8)	— (†)	98 (0.3)	70 (1.6)	9 (0.7)
Black	13 (1.2)	288 (1.3)	‡ (†)	260 (2.7)	280 (1.6)	290 (1.0)	317 (2.5)	— (†)	90 (1.0)	34 (2.0)	1 (0.3)
Hispanic	22 (1.5)	294 (1.1)	‡ (†)	269 (2.5)	284 (1.4)	296 (1.0)	324 (2.0)	— (†)	93 (0.6)	43 (1.9)	2 (0.4)
Other[1]	8 (0.8)	318 (2.4)	‡ (†)	‡ (†)	293 (3.7)	308 (2.4)	338 (2.1)	— (†)	98 (0.8)	73 (3.0)	14 (2.3)

—Not available.
†Not applicable.
#Rounds to zero.
‡Reporting standards not met (too few cases for a reliable estimate).
[1]Includes Asians/Pacific Islanders and American Indians/Alaska Natives.

NOTE: Scale ranges from 0 to 500. Students scoring 200 (or higher) have a considerable understanding of two-digit numbers and know some basic multiplication and division facts. Students scoring 250 have an initial understanding of the four basic operations and are developing an ability to analyze simple logical relations. Students scoring 300 can perform reasoning and problem solving involving fractions, decimals, percents, elementary geometry, and simple algebra. Students scoring 350 can perform reasoning and problem solving involving geometry, algebra, and beginning statistics and probability. Includes public and private schools. For assessment years prior to 2004, accommodations were not permitted. For 2004 and later years, includes students tested with accommodations; excludes only those students with disabilities and English language learners who were unable to be tested even with accommodations (1 to 4 percent of all students, depending on age and assessment year). Race categories exclude persons of Hispanic ethnicity. Detail may not sum to totals because of rounding.

SOURCE: U.S. Department of Education, National Center for Education Statistics, National Assessment of Educational Progress (NAEP), *NAEP Trends in Academic Progress*, 1996 and 1999; and 2004, 2008, and 2012 Long-Term Trend Mathematics Assessments, retrieved June 4, 2009, and August 12, 2013, from the Long-Term Trend NAEP Data Explorer (http://nces.ed.gov/nationsreportcard/naepdata/). (This table was prepared August 2013.)

Table 223.10. Average National Assessment of Educational Progress (NAEP) science scale score, standard deviation, and percentage of students attaining science achievement levels, by grade level, selected student and school characteristics, and percentile: 2009 and 2011

[Standard errors appear in parentheses]

Selected characteristic, percentile, and achievement level	Grade 4			Grade 8						Grade 12		
	2009			2009			2011			2009		
	Total, all students	Male	Female	Total, all students	Male	Female	Total, all students	Male	Female	Total, all students	Male	Female
1	2	3	4	5	6	7	8	9	10	11	12	13
	Average science scale score[1]											
All students	**150 (0.3)**	**151 (0.3)**	**149 (0.3)**	**150 (0.3)**	**152 (0.4)**	**148 (0.3)**	**152 (0.3)**	**154 (0.3)**	**149 (0.3)**	**150 (0.8)**	**153 (0.9)**	**147 (0.9)**
Race/ethnicity												
White	163 (0.2)	164 (0.3)	162 (0.3)	162 (0.2)	164 (0.3)	160 (0.3)	163 (0.2)	166 (0.3)	161 (0.3)	159 (0.7)	162 (0.9)	156 (0.8)
Black	127 (0.4)	126 (0.6)	128 (0.5)	126 (0.4)	125 (0.6)	126 (0.5)	129 (0.5)	130 (0.7)	128 (0.6)	125 (1.2)	127 (1.6)	123 (1.5)
Hispanic	131 (0.5)	132 (0.7)	130 (0.6)	132 (0.6)	134 (0.8)	130 (0.7)	137 (0.5)	140 (0.8)	134 (0.8)	134 (1.3)	138 (2.3)	130 (1.5)
Asian/Pacific Islander	160 (1.2)	159 (1.4)	160 (1.4)	160 (1.0)	162 (1.3)	158 (1.3)	159 (1.3)	161 (1.6)	157 (1.7)	164 (3.0)	161 (2.9)	166 (3.8)
American Indian/Alaska Native	135 (1.3)	135 (1.5)	135 (1.8)	137 (1.4)	141 (1.8)	133 (2.0)	141 (1.4)	143 (2.1)	139 (1.5)	144 (3.7)	‡ (†)	‡ (†)
Highest education level of either parent												
Did not finish high school	— (†)	— (†)	— (†)	131 (0.6)	135 (1.0)	128 (0.7)	132 (0.7)	136 (1.2)	130 (1.0)	131 (1.4)	136 (1.9)	128 (1.8)
Graduated high school	— (†)	— (†)	— (†)	139 (0.4)	141 (0.6)	137 (0.5)	140 (0.4)	143 (0.7)	138 (0.6)	138 (1.2)	140 (1.5)	136 (1.4)
Some education after high school	— (†)	— (†)	— (†)	152 (0.4)	154 (0.5)	150 (0.4)	153 (0.4)	156 (0.7)	151 (0.6)	147 (0.9)	150 (1.3)	144 (1.1)
Graduated college	— (†)	— (†)	— (†)	161 (0.4)	162 (0.5)	159 (0.3)	162 (0.3)	164 (0.4)	160 (0.4)	161 (0.7)	163 (0.9)	159 (1.0)
Eligibility for free or reduced-price lunch												
Eligible	134 (0.3)	134 (0.4)	133 (0.3)	133 (0.4)	135 (0.5)	131 (0.4)	137 (0.3)	139 (0.4)	135 (0.4)	132 (1.0)	135 (1.1)	130 (1.1)
Not eligible	163 (0.3)	164 (0.3)	163 (0.3)	161 (0.3)	163 (0.4)	159 (0.4)	164 (0.3)	166 (0.4)	161 (0.4)	157 (0.9)	159 (1.1)	154 (1.0)
Unknown	162 (1.3)	163 (1.7)	161 (1.3)	164 (1.2)	167 (1.4)	161 (1.2)	164 (1.6)	168 (2.2)	159 (2.2)	156 (2.7)	156 (3.6)	156 (3.0)
School type												
Public	149 (0.3)	149 (0.3)	148 (0.3)	149 (0.3)	151 (0.4)	147 (0.3)	151 (0.2)	153 (0.3)	148 (0.3)	— (†)	— (†)	— (†)
Private	163 (0.9)	165 (1.2)	162 (1.0)	164 (0.9)	167 (1.2)	161 (1.0)	163 (1.4)	168 (1.9)	158 (1.9)	— (†)	— (†)	— (†)
School locale												
City	142 (0.6)	142 (0.6)	142 (0.7)	142 (0.6)	144 (0.7)	141 (0.7)	144 (0.6)	146 (0.8)	142 (0.7)	146 (1.8)	148 (1.6)	144 (2.2)
Suburban	154 (0.4)	154 (0.6)	153 (0.4)	154 (0.5)	155 (0.6)	152 (0.5)	155 (0.5)	158 (0.5)	153 (0.6)	154 (1.4)	157 (1.8)	150 (1.5)
Town	150 (0.6)	151 (0.8)	149 (0.6)	149 (1.0)	152 (1.1)	147 (0.9)	153 (0.7)	155 (0.9)	150 (0.8)	150 (1.2)	153 (1.5)	146 (1.6)
Rural	155 (0.5)	156 (0.7)	154 (0.5)	154 (0.4)	156 (0.5)	152 (0.5)	156 (0.5)	159 (0.6)	153 (0.6)	150 (1.2)	153 (1.5)	146 (1.4)
Percentile[2]												
10th	104 (0.6)	103 (0.6)	104 (0.5)	103 (0.6)	103 (0.7)	103 (0.6)	106 (0.5)	107 (0.9)	105 (0.7)	104 (1.2)	106 (1.8)	103 (1.1)
25th	128 (0.4)	128 (0.5)	128 (0.4)	128 (0.4)	130 (0.5)	127 (0.5)	131 (0.4)	133 (0.5)	129 (0.6)	126 (0.8)	128 (1.0)	125 (1.5)
50th	153 (0.3)	154 (0.4)	152 (0.4)	153 (0.3)	156 (0.4)	151 (0.3)	155 (0.3)	158 (0.5)	152 (0.4)	151 (1.1)	154 (1.4)	148 (1.1)
75th	175 (0.3)	176 (0.3)	174 (0.4)	175 (0.2)	178 (0.4)	172 (0.2)	176 (0.4)	179 (0.3)	173 (0.4)	174 (1.0)	178 (1.2)	171 (1.1)
90th	192 (0.3)	194 (0.4)	191 (0.5)	192 (0.3)	195 (0.2)	188 (0.4)	193 (0.4)	196 (0.4)	189 (0.5)	194 (1.0)	198 (0.9)	190 (1.4)
	Standard deviation of the science scale score[3]											
All students	35 (0.2)	36 (0.2)	34 (0.2)	35 (0.2)	36 (0.2)	34 (0.2)	34 (0.2)	35 (0.2)	33 (0.3)	35 (0.4)	36 (0.5)	34 (0.5)
	Percent of students attaining science achievement levels											
Achievement level												
Below *Basic*	28 (0.3)	27 (0.4)	28 (0.3)	37 (0.4)	35 (0.5)	38 (0.4)	35 (0.3)	32 (0.4)	37 (0.5)	40 (1.0)	37 (1.1)	42 (1.3)
At or above *Basic*[4]	72 (0.3)	73 (0.4)	72 (0.3)	63 (0.4)	65 (0.5)	62 (0.4)	65 (0.3)	68 (0.4)	63 (0.5)	60 (1.0)	63 (1.1)	58 (1.3)
At or above *Proficient*[5]	34 (0.3)	35 (0.3)	32 (0.3)	30 (0.3)	34 (0.4)	27 (0.3)	32 (0.4)	35 (0.5)	28 (0.5)	21 (0.8)	24 (1.0)	18 (0.8)
At *Advanced*[6]	1 (0.1)	1 (0.1)	1 (0.1)	2 (0.1)	2 (0.1)	1 (0.1)	2 (0.1)	2 (0.1)	1 (0.1)	1 (0.2)	2 (0.3)	1 (0.2)

—Not available.
†Not applicable.
‡Reporting standards not met (too few cases for a reliable estimate).
[1]Scale ranges from 0 to 300 for all three grades, but scores cannot be compared across grades. For example, the average score of 163 for White 4th-graders does not denote higher performance than the score of 159 for White 12th-graders.
[2]The percentile represents a specific point on the percentage distribution of all students ranked by their science score from low to high. For example, 10 percent of students scored at or below the 10th percentile score, while 90 percent of students scored above it.
[3]The standard deviation provides an indication of how much the test scores varied. The lower the standard deviation, the closer the scores were clustered around the average score. About two-thirds of the student scores can be expected to fall within the range of one standard deviation above and one standard deviation below the average score. For example, the average score for all 4th-graders was 150, and the standard deviation was 35. This means that we would expect about two-thirds of the students to have scores between 185 (one standard deviation above the average) and 115 (one standard deviation below). Standard errors also must be taken into account when making comparisons of these ranges. For a discussion of standard errors, see Appendix A: Guide to Sources.
[4]*Basic* denotes partial mastery of the knowledge and skills that are fundamental for proficient work.
[5]*Proficient* represents solid academic performance. Students reaching this level have demonstrated competency over challenging subject matter.
[6]*Advanced* signifies superior performance.
NOTE: In 2011, only 8th-grade students were assessed in science. Includes students tested with accommodations (7 to 11 percent of all students, depending on grade level and year); excludes only those students with disabilities and English language learners who were unable to be tested even with accommodations (2 to 3 percent of all students). Race categories exclude persons of Hispanic ethnicity.
SOURCE: U.S. Department of Education, National Center for Education Statistics, National Assessment of Educational Progress (NAEP), 2011 Science Assessment, retrieved August 1, 2012, from the Main NAEP Data Explorer (http://nces.ed.gov/nations reportcard/naepdata/). (This table was prepared August 2012.)

Table 223.20. Average National Assessment of Educational Progress (NAEP) science scale scores of 8th-grade public school students, by race/ethnicity and state: 2009 and 2011

[Standard errors appear in parentheses]

State	2009					2011				
		Race/ethnicity					Race/ethnicity			
	Total, all students	White	Black	Hispanic	Asian/Pacific Islander	Total, all students	White	Black	Hispanic	Asian/Pacific Islander
1	2	3	4	5	6	7	8	9	10	11
United States	**149 (0.3)**	**161 (0.2)**	**125 (0.4)**	**131 (0.6)**	**159 (1.0)**	**151 (0.2)**	**163 (0.2)**	**128 (0.5)**	**136 (0.5)**	**159 (1.2)**
Alabama	139 (1.1)	152 (1.1)	115 (1.8)	129 (3.5)	‡ (†)	140 (1.4)	152 (1.3)	118 (1.4)	136 (3.6)	‡ (†)
Alaska	— (†)	— (†)	— (†)	— (†)	— (†)	153 (0.7)	166 (0.9)	133 (3.2)	147 (2.7)	145 (2.2)
Arizona	141 (1.3)	157 (1.3)	126 (3.2)	127 (1.5)	159 (5.5)	144 (1.3)	158 (1.3)	128 (2.9)	132 (1.6)	‡ (†)
Arkansas	144 (1.3)	154 (0.9)	111 (2.1)	134 (3.0)	‡ (†)	148 (1.1)	158 (1.0)	119 (2.1)	138 (2.1)	‡ (†)
California	137 (1.4)	157 (2.0)	122 (2.8)	122 (1.3)	154 (2.2)	140 (1.3)	159 (1.6)	124 (3.4)	128 (1.4)	157 (2.8)
Colorado	156 (1.0)	166 (1.0)	135 (3.7)	137 (1.6)	161 (3.7)	161 (1.3)	171 (1.4)	149 (3.7)	141 (1.8)	162 (4.5)
Connecticut	155 (0.9)	164 (0.8)	126 (2.3)	128 (1.8)	169 (3.5)	155 (1.1)	165 (1.0)	128 (2.3)	129 (2.5)	170 (4.2)
Delaware	148 (0.6)	159 (0.9)	133 (1.0)	141 (2.2)	160 (4.3)	150 (0.6)	161 (0.8)	134 (1.3)	139 (2.0)	168 (3.3)
District of Columbia	— (†)	— (†)	— (†)	— (†)	— (†)	112 (1.0)	174 (3.3)	107 (1.1)	116 (2.6)	‡ (†)
Florida	146 (1.0)	158 (1.4)	126 (1.4)	139 (1.2)	163 (4.1)	148 (1.1)	161 (1.1)	127 (2.0)	144 (1.5)	161 (4.5)
Georgia	147 (1.0)	161 (1.2)	129 (1.3)	137 (2.2)	172 (2.7)	151 (1.4)	166 (1.6)	133 (1.8)	143 (3.1)	168 (3.9)
Hawaii	139 (0.7)	153 (1.5)	133 (5.0)	148 (4.3)	136 (1.0)	142 (0.7)	157 (1.8)	‡ (†)	144 (3.3)	139 (0.9)
Idaho	158 (0.9)	162 (0.9)	‡ (†)	137 (1.4)	‡ (†)	159 (0.7)	163 (0.7)	‡ (†)	139 (1.8)	‡ (†)
Illinois	148 (1.4)	162 (1.2)	118 (1.5)	131 (1.5)	167 (3.2)	147 (1.0)	161 (1.1)	120 (1.9)	135 (1.2)	163 (4.4)
Indiana	152 (1.2)	159 (1.0)	126 (3.9)	135 (3.5)	‡ (†)	153 (0.9)	160 (1.0)	125 (2.7)	136 (3.7)	‡ (†)
Iowa	156 (0.9)	160 (0.8)	127 (3.5)	133 (3.2)	‡ (†)	157 (0.8)	161 (0.8)	128 (3.7)	143 (3.1)	‡ (†)
Kansas	— (†)	— (†)	— (†)	— (†)	— (†)	156 (0.8)	163 (0.8)	129 (3.2)	134 (2.1)	156 (5.2)
Kentucky	156 (0.8)	159 (0.9)	137 (1.8)	145 (3.5)	‡ (†)	157 (0.8)	160 (0.9)	135 (1.7)	149 (3.0)	‡ (†)
Louisiana	139 (1.7)	155 (1.5)	120 (1.9)	‡ (†)	‡ (†)	143 (1.7)	156 (1.6)	125 (2.1)	142 (5.2)	‡ (†)
Maine	158 (0.8)	159 (0.8)	126 (4.5)	‡ (†)	‡ (†)	160 (0.5)	160 (0.6)	‡ (†)	‡ (†)	‡ (†)
Maryland	148 (1.1)	164 (1.2)	127 (1.5)	136 (2.8)	169 (2.5)	152 (1.2)	167 (1.2)	131 (1.8)	142 (2.2)	164 (4.3)
Massachusetts	160 (1.1)	167 (1.1)	132 (2.6)	131 (2.7)	168 (4.1)	161 (1.1)	169 (1.1)	133 (4.3)	130 (2.6)	170 (4.1)
Michigan	153 (1.4)	162 (1.0)	121 (2.1)	139 (3.4)	‡ (†)	157 (1.0)	165 (0.8)	124 (2.8)	146 (3.3)	166 (6.9)
Minnesota	159 (1.0)	166 (0.9)	128 (2.8)	132 (3.7)	141 (3.0)	161 (1.0)	168 (1.0)	129 (2.5)	137 (4.0)	149 (3.9)
Mississippi	132 (1.2)	150 (1.2)	114 (1.1)	‡ (†)	‡ (†)	137 (1.3)	156 (1.1)	119 (1.4)	‡ (†)	‡ (†)
Missouri	156 (1.1)	161 (0.9)	129 (2.5)	150 (3.8)	167 (4.7)	156 (1.1)	162 (0.8)	130 (3.5)	‡ (†)	‡ (†)
Montana	162 (0.7)	166 (0.7)	‡ (†)	155 (3.3)	‡ (†)	163 (0.7)	167 (0.7)	‡ (†)	‡ (†)	‡ (†)
Nebraska	— (†)	— (†)	— (†)	— (†)	— (†)	157 (0.7)	164 (0.7)	126 (3.5)	135 (1.9)	‡ (†)
Nevada	141 (0.7)	153 (0.9)	127 (2.4)	129 (1.0)	148 (2.4)	144 (0.8)	157 (1.3)	123 (3.3)	133 (1.1)	154 (2.6)
New Hampshire	160 (0.8)	161 (0.8)	‡ (†)	131 (4.2)	‡ (†)	162 (0.7)	164 (0.6)	‡ (†)	137 (4.3)	‡ (†)
New Jersey	155 (1.5)	165 (1.0)	127 (3.3)	138 (2.7)	174 (2.6)	155 (1.2)	166 (1.2)	131 (2.5)	134 (1.9)	173 (2.8)
New Mexico	143 (1.4)	163 (1.4)	‡ (†)	135 (1.4)	‡ (†)	145 (0.8)	161 (1.4)	‡ (†)	139 (0.8)	‡ (†)
New York	149 (1.2)	164 (1.0)	123 (1.8)	125 (1.7)	161 (2.3)	149 (1.0)	163 (1.3)	130 (2.2)	129 (1.7)	154 (2.6)
North Carolina	144 (1.3)	158 (1.3)	121 (1.6)	132 (2.3)	165 (7.1)	148 (1.1)	160 (1.1)	125 (1.8)	138 (2.4)	160 (6.5)
North Dakota	162 (0.5)	166 (0.6)	‡ (†)	‡ (†)	‡ (†)	164 (0.7)	168 (0.8)	‡ (†)	‡ (†)	‡ (†)
Ohio	158 (1.0)	164 (0.9)	126 (2.1)	140 (4.6)	‡ (†)	158 (1.0)	165 (1.0)	132 (2.6)	151 (5.3)	‡ (†)
Oklahoma	146 (0.9)	155 (1.0)	124 (2.6)	127 (2.6)	‡ (†)	148 (1.1)	156 (1.0)	126 (3.6)	135 (2.8)	‡ (†)
Oregon	154 (1.0)	160 (1.1)	135 (4.1)	130 (1.8)	160 (3.5)	155 (0.9)	162 (1.0)	‡ (†)	135 (1.4)	159 (4.3)
Pennsylvania	154 (1.1)	162 (0.9)	123 (2.0)	121 (4.4)	159 (4.1)	151 (1.3)	163 (0.9)	120 (2.3)	118 (4.8)	163 (4.9)
Rhode Island	146 (0.6)	155 (0.8)	125 (2.6)	119 (1.9)	146 (5.3)	149 (0.7)	161 (0.7)	122 (3.4)	120 (1.9)	151 (4.6)
South Carolina	143 (1.6)	158 (1.1)	124 (1.7)	129 (4.2)	‡ (†)	149 (1.0)	163 (1.0)	128 (1.6)	139 (3.0)	‡ (†)
South Dakota	161 (0.6)	165 (0.6)	141 (5.5)	135 (4.1)	‡ (†)	162 (0.5)	166 (0.6)	‡ (†)	151 (4.1)	‡ (†)
Tennessee	148 (1.2)	157 (0.9)	122 (2.0)	139 (3.8)	‡ (†)	150 (1.0)	160 (0.9)	121 (1.6)	137 (3.1)	‡ (†)
Texas	150 (1.2)	167 (1.4)	133 (2.5)	141 (1.5)	170 (3.6)	153 (1.0)	167 (1.2)	137 (2.3)	146 (1.3)	172 (4.3)
Utah	158 (1.0)	164 (1.1)	‡ (†)	129 (1.7)	147 (3.9)	161 (0.8)	167 (0.8)	‡ (†)	137 (2.0)	153 (4.7)
Vermont	— (†)	— (†)	— (†)	— (†)	— (†)	163 (0.8)	164 (0.9)	‡ (†)	‡ (†)	‡ (†)
Virginia	156 (1.1)	166 (1.1)	135 (2.0)	144 (2.2)	168 (3.1)	160 (1.0)	169 (1.3)	138 (1.7)	145 (2.8)	172 (2.4)
Washington	155 (1.0)	161 (1.1)	135 (3.7)	132 (2.3)	157 (3.0)	156 (0.9)	163 (1.0)	133 (3.1)	141 (2.5)	156 (2.8)
West Virginia	145 (0.8)	146 (0.8)	127 (2.8)	‡ (†)	‡ (†)	149 (1.0)	150 (1.0)	136 (2.7)	‡ (†)	‡ (†)
Wisconsin	157 (0.9)	165 (0.8)	120 (1.5)	134 (3.9)	152 (3.5)	159 (1.0)	166 (0.9)	121 (3.1)	140 (4.8)	149 (4.7)
Wyoming	158 (0.7)	162 (0.7)	‡ (†)	137 (1.8)	‡ (†)	160 (0.5)	164 (0.6)	‡ (†)	143 (2.0)	‡ (†)
Department of Defense dependents schools	162 (0.7)	170 (1.0)	144 (1.4)	155 (2.0)	160 (2.3)	161 (0.8)	169 (1.1)	143 (2.2)	158 (2.5)	155 (3.2)

—Not available.
†Not applicable.
‡Reporting standards not met (too few cases for a reliable estimate).
NOTE: Scale ranges from 0 to 300. Includes students tested with accommodations (10 percent of all students in 2009 and 9 percent of all students in 2011); excludes only those students with disabilities and English language learners who were unable to be tested even with accommodations (2 percent of all students in both years). Race categories exclude persons of Hispanic ethnicity. Totals include other racial/ethnic groups not shown separately.
SOURCE: U.S. Department of Education, National Center for Education Statistics, National Assessment of Educational Progress (NAEP), 2009 and 2011 Science Assessment, retrieved August 12, 2012, from the Main NAEP Data Explorer (http://nces.ed.gov/nationsreportcard/naepdata/). (This table was prepared August 2012.)

Table 223.25. Average National Assessment of Educational Progress (NAEP) science scale scores of 8th-graders with various attitudes toward science and percentage reporting these attitudes, by selected student characteristics: 2011

[Standard errors appear in parentheses]

Student characteristic	Take science only because it will help in future: Strongly disagree	Take science only because it will help in future: Disagree	Take science only because it will help in future: Agree	Take science only because it will help in future: Strongly agree	Like science: Strongly disagree	Like science: Disagree	Like science: Agree	Like science: Strongly agree	Take science only because required: Strongly disagree	Take science only because required: Disagree	Take science only because required: Agree	Take science only because required: Strongly agree
1	2	3	4	5	6	7	8	9	10	11	12	13
	Average scale score[1]											
All students	**154 (0.5)**	**161 (0.4)**	**150 (0.3)**	**143 (0.5)**	**136 (0.6)**	**144 (0.5)**	**155 (0.3)**	**166 (0.5)**	**164 (0.5)**	**160 (0.4)**	**146 (0.3)**	**138 (0.5)**
Sex												
Male	156 (0.7)	163 (0.4)	153 (0.4)	145 (0.7)	136 (0.9)	146 (0.7)	157 (0.4)	168 (0.7)	166 (0.6)	162 (0.5)	148 (0.5)	140 (0.7)
Female	152 (0.9)	158 (0.5)	148 (0.5)	141 (0.6)	136 (0.8)	144 (0.6)	153 (0.5)	162 (0.7)	161 (0.7)	158 (0.6)	144 (0.5)	137 (0.6)
Race/ethnicity												
White	164 (0.6)	169 (0.4)	161 (0.3)	158 (0.6)	148 (0.6)	156 (0.5)	165 (0.3)	175 (0.5)	174 (0.5)	170 (0.4)	157 (0.4)	150 (0.6)
Black	132 (1.3)	137 (1.3)	130 (0.8)	123 (0.9)	120 (1.1)	124 (0.8)	131 (0.6)	141 (1.2)	139 (1.6)	137 (0.7)	126 (0.7)	121 (0.8)
Hispanic	140 (1.6)	145 (1.0)	135 (0.7)	132 (1.0)	124 (1.3)	129 (1.1)	140 (0.6)	151 (1.3)	149 (1.1)	144 (0.9)	132 (0.9)	129 (0.9)
Asian	165 (2.8)	170 (1.9)	159 (2.1)	156 (2.0)	140 (3.3)	151 (2.2)	162 (1.7)	177 (2.1)	176 (2.4)	167 (2.1)	155 (2.0)	144 (2.3)
Pacific Islander	143 (6.5)	146 (3.9)	139 (2.2)	137 (5.1)	117 (5.3)	130 (3.4)	147 (3.1)	153 (3.6)	150 (4.8)	150 (3.4)	134 (3.8)	126 (3.4)
American Indian/Alaska Native	140 (4.4)	151 (2.2)	141 (1.9)	134 (2.2)	126 (3.2)	138 (2.3)	146 (2.2)	150 (3.1)	149 (3.3)	150 (2.0)	140 (2.7)	132 (3.2)
Two or more races	158 (5.0)	161 (1.8)	153 (1.6)	155 (4.2)	139 (4.6)	147 (2.3)	159 (1.2)	170 (3.6)	167 (3.9)	163 (1.7)	152 (2.2)	139 (2.6)
Eligibility for free or reduced-price lunch												
Eligible	140 (0.7)	146 (0.5)	136 (0.4)	130 (0.6)	125 (0.7)	131 (0.7)	140 (0.4)	149 (0.6)	147 (0.5)	145 (0.5)	133 (0.5)	128 (0.6)
Not eligible	165 (0.7)	170 (0.4)	162 (0.4)	158 (0.6)	147 (0.6)	156 (0.6)	166 (0.4)	176 (0.5)	175 (0.6)	170 (0.5)	158 (0.5)	150 (0.5)
Unknown	168 (3.9)	170 (2.3)	161 (2.4)	154 (3.7)	147 (5.4)	156 (2.6)	166 (1.9)	177 (3.4)	174 (3.1)	170 (2.5)	157 (2.4)	147 (5.1)
Parents' highest level of education												
Did not finish high school	134 (1.9)	142 (1.3)	130 (1.4)	128 (1.5)	125 (1.8)	126 (1.6)	136 (0.9)	144 (1.8)	140 (1.6)	140 (1.3)	128 (1.2)	129 (1.5)
Graduated high school	143 (1.4)	148 (0.9)	139 (0.6)	132 (1.1)	129 (1.0)	135 (0.8)	143 (0.6)	153 (1.0)	151 (1.2)	148 (0.7)	136 (0.7)	132 (0.7)
Some education after high school	156 (1.3)	160 (0.8)	152 (0.6)	145 (0.9)	140 (1.3)	146 (0.9)	156 (0.5)	165 (1.0)	164 (0.9)	160 (0.8)	149 (0.7)	141 (0.9)
Graduated college	165 (0.8)	170 (0.4)	161 (0.4)	153 (0.7)	145 (0.9)	155 (0.6)	164 (0.4)	174 (0.5)	173 (0.6)	169 (0.4)	156 (0.5)	146 (0.8)
	Percent of students											
All students	**12 (0.2)**	**32 (0.3)**	**39 (0.2)**	**18 (0.2)**	**12 (0.2)**	**19 (0.3)**	**50 (0.3)**	**19 (0.3)**	**18 (0.2)**	**34 (0.3)**	**30 (0.2)**	**17 (0.2)**
Sex												
Male	14 (0.3)	33 (0.4)	36 (0.4)	16 (0.3)	11 (0.2)	16 (0.3)	51 (0.4)	22 (0.4)	21 (0.3)	35 (0.4)	27 (0.3)	17 (0.2)
Female	10 (0.2)	30 (0.4)	41 (0.4)	19 (0.3)	12 (0.3)	23 (0.4)	49 (0.4)	16 (0.3)	15 (0.2)	34 (0.4)	33 (0.4)	18 (0.3)
Race/ethnicity												
White	13 (0.2)	36 (0.4)	37 (0.4)	13 (0.2)	10 (0.2)	19 (0.3)	50 (0.4)	20 (0.3)	20 (0.2)	37 (0.4)	28 (0.3)	16 (0.2)
Black	12 (0.5)	22 (0.7)	37 (0.7)	29 (0.6)	16 (0.5)	20 (0.6)	46 (0.6)	19 (0.6)	17 (0.7)	28 (0.6)	30 (0.7)	25 (0.5)
Hispanic	11 (0.4)	27 (0.6)	42 (0.6)	20 (0.6)	13 (0.5)	21 (0.7)	50 (0.6)	16 (0.5)	15 (0.5)	33 (0.6)	35 (0.6)	18 (0.5)
Asian	9 (0.8)	26 (1.4)	42 (1.7)	22 (1.1)	8 (0.8)	16 (0.8)	57 (1.4)	19 (1.1)	19 (0.9)	37 (1.4)	30 (1.4)	14 (0.8)
Pacific Islander	11 (2.5)	26 (3.3)	39 (3.7)	23 (3.3)	15 (2.9)	21 (3.1)	50 (4.3)	15 (2.6)	14 (2.9)	37 (3.9)	30 (2.8)	18 (2.9)
American Indian/Alaska Native	10 (1.2)	27 (1.8)	44 (2.0)	18 (1.1)	14 (1.3)	19 (1.2)	52 (1.6)	15 (1.3)	14 (1.3)	29 (1.5)	37 (1.7)	19 (1.5)
Two or more races	13 (1.4)	33 (2.0)	36 (1.9)	18 (1.7)	14 (1.8)	18 (1.0)	47 (2.0)	21 (1.8)	20 (2.4)	34 (1.9)	28 (1.7)	19 (1.5)
Eligibility for free or reduced-price lunch												
Eligible	12 (0.2)	27 (0.3)	40 (0.3)	21 (0.3)	14 (0.3)	20 (0.3)	49 (0.3)	17 (0.3)	16 (0.3)	31 (0.4)	32 (0.3)	21 (0.3)
Not eligible	12 (0.2)	35 (0.3)	38 (0.3)	15 (0.3)	10 (0.2)	18 (0.3)	51 (0.4)	20 (0.3)	20 (0.3)	37 (0.4)	28 (0.3)	15 (0.2)
Unknown	12 (1.9)	38 (2.9)	35 (2.7)	15 (1.6)	10 (1.2)	20 (2.1)	48 (2.5)	22 (2.1)	22 (2.1)	36 (2.5)	30 (2.4)	12 (1.4)
Parents' highest level of education												
Did not finish high school	12 (0.6)	27 (1.1)	40 (1.0)	20 (0.9)	16 (0.7)	23 (0.9)	45 (1.1)	15 (0.7)	14 (0.6)	29 (0.9)	34 (1.0)	23 (0.9)
Graduated high school	12 (0.4)	31 (0.6)	39 (0.6)	18 (0.5)	13 (0.4)	21 (0.4)	50 (0.6)	16 (0.6)	15 (0.5)	32 (0.6)	32 (0.6)	20 (0.4)
Some education after high school	12 (0.3)	31 (0.5)	39 (0.5)	17 (0.4)	12 (0.4)	20 (0.5)	50 (0.6)	18 (0.5)	18 (0.4)	35 (0.6)	29 (0.5)	18 (0.5)
Graduated college	12 (0.3)	33 (0.4)	38 (0.4)	17 (0.3)	10 (0.3)	18 (0.4)	51 (0.5)	22 (0.3)	21 (0.3)	37 (0.5)	28 (0.4)	15 (0.3)

[1]Scale ranges from 0 to 300.

NOTE: Includes public and private schools. Includes students tested with accommodations (11 percent of all 8th-graders); excludes only those students with disabilities and English language learners who were unable to be tested even with accommodations (2 percent of all 8th-graders). Detail may not sum to totals because of rounding. Race categories exclude persons of Hispanic ethnicity.

SOURCE: U.S. Department of Education, National Center for Education Statistics, National Assessment of Educational Progress (NAEP), 2011 Science Assessment, retrieved November 22, 2013, from the Main NAEP Data Explorer (http://nces.ed.gov/nationsreportcard/naepdata/). (This table was prepared November 2013.)

Table 223.30. Average National Assessment of Educational Progress (NAEP) science scale scores of 12th-graders with various educational goals and attitudes toward science, and percentage reporting these goals and attitudes, by selected student characteristics: 2009

[Standard errors appear in parentheses]

Student characteristic	Educational goals[1]				Like science				Take science only because required			
	Graduate high school	Some education after high school	Graduate college	Go to graduate school	Strongly disagree	Disagree	Agree	Strongly agree	Strongly disagree	Disagree	Agree	Strongly agree
1	2	3	4	5	6	7	8	9	10	11	12	13
	Average scale score[2]											
All students	**114 (1.9)**	**131 (1.3)**	**148 (0.6)**	**171 (1.0)**	**132 (1.3)**	**141 (0.9)**	**153 (0.9)**	**172 (1.1)**	**169 (1.1)**	**159 (0.9)**	**142 (0.9)**	**134 (1.0)**
Sex												
Male	121 (2.6)	134 (1.8)	152 (0.8)	177 (1.3)	130 (1.7)	141 (1.4)	155 (1.2)	175 (1.3)	172 (1.4)	162 (1.2)	143 (1.2)	134 (1.3)
Female	103 (2.6)	127 (1.9)	143 (0.8)	166 (1.2)	133 (1.8)	141 (1.1)	150 (0.9)	169 (1.8)	165 (1.8)	156 (0.9)	140 (1.2)	134 (1.4)
Race/ethnicity												
White	127 (2.1)	140 (1.6)	156 (0.7)	178 (1.0)	140 (1.6)	150 (1.1)	161 (0.9)	180 (1.0)	176 (1.1)	167 (0.8)	151 (1.0)	143 (1.4)
Black	89 (3.6)	107 (3.2)	124 (1.1)	144 (1.8)	113 (2.0)	120 (2.0)	128 (1.5)	142 (2.4)	140 (2.6)	135 (2.3)	121 (1.6)	115 (1.7)
Hispanic	106 (3.7)	122 (2.7)	136 (1.2)	154 (2.3)	123 (2.6)	127 (1.5)	135 (1.8)	157 (2.4)	152 (2.9)	143 (1.7)	128 (1.6)	125 (2.3)
Asian/Pacific Islander	‡ (†)	‡ (†)	154 (2.9)	181 (3.4)	141 (5.2)	149 (3.8)	166 (2.9)	188 (4.5)	181 (4.2)	171 (3.3)	154 (3.2)	141 (4.5)
American Indian/Alaska Native	‡ (†)	‡ (†)	‡ (†)	‡ (†)	‡ (†)	‡ (†)	‡ (†)	‡ (†)	‡ (†)	‡ (†)	‡ (†)	‡ (†)
Eligibility for free or reduced-price lunch												
Eligible	105 (2.9)	120 (2.0)	134 (0.8)	151 (2.0)	120 (1.8)	125 (1.4)	135 (1.1)	152 (2.0)	147 (2.7)	142 (1.4)	127 (1.1)	121 (1.6)
Not eligible	122 (2.0)	138 (1.8)	153 (0.8)	176 (1.0)	137 (1.5)	148 (1.1)	159 (1.1)	179 (1.3)	175 (1.2)	165 (1.0)	148 (1.1)	140 (1.4)
Unknown	‡ (†)	‡ (†)	151 (2.4)	169 (3.5)	139 (3.1)	146 (3.6)	158 (2.9)	177 (3.8)	175 (3.6)	164 (3.3)	149 (2.6)	138 (3.3)
Parents' highest level of education												
Did not finish high school	112 (3.7)	124 (2.8)	134 (1.5)	145 (3.1)	119 (2.7)	125 (2.5)	134 (2.0)	153 (3.5)	147 (3.1)	138 (2.5)	127 (2.3)	121 (2.2)
Graduated high school	109 (2.8)	129 (2.7)	141 (1.3)	158 (2.1)	124 (2.2)	132 (1.5)	141 (1.3)	158 (2.7)	149 (2.7)	149 (1.6)	133 (1.8)	126 (1.9)
Some education after high school	126 (4.0)	135 (2.2)	146 (0.9)	162 (2.1)	133 (1.5)	138 (1.2)	149 (1.2)	168 (1.7)	164 (2.3)	156 (1.3)	140 (1.1)	133 (1.7)
Graduated college	120 (3.9)	140 (2.4)	155 (0.8)	177 (0.9)	141 (1.7)	151 (1.3)	163 (1.0)	181 (1.3)	180 (1.3)	168 (1.0)	152 (1.0)	143 (1.2)
	Percent of students											
All students	**5 (0.3)**	**7 (0.3)**	**59 (0.7)**	**26 (0.8)**	**14 (0.4)**	**21 (0.4)**	**48 (0.5)**	**16 (0.3)**	**15 (0.4)**	**34 (0.5)**	**31 (0.4)**	**19 (0.4)**
Sex												
Male	6 (0.4)	9 (0.4)	59 (0.8)	22 (0.8)	12 (0.5)	18 (0.5)	52 (0.7)	18 (0.5)	17 (0.5)	37 (0.6)	29 (0.7)	17 (0.5)
Female	4 (0.3)	6 (0.4)	58 (0.9)	31 (1.0)	16 (0.5)	25 (0.6)	45 (0.7)	14 (0.5)	14 (0.6)	31 (0.7)	33 (0.6)	21 (0.6)
Race/ethnicity												
White	4 (0.3)	7 (0.3)	60 (0.7)	26 (0.8)	13 (0.5)	21 (0.5)	49 (0.7)	17 (0.5)	17 (0.5)	36 (0.6)	29 (0.6)	18 (0.5)
Black	6 (0.8)	6 (0.6)	60 (1.3)	25 (1.4)	20 (1.0)	23 (0.9)	43 (1.3)	14 (0.9)	11 (0.8)	28 (1.2)	33 (1.0)	28 (1.1)
Hispanic	7 (0.7)	12 (0.8)	59 (1.4)	18 (1.1)	13 (0.7)	24 (0.9)	49 (1.1)	14 (0.9)	12 (0.8)	31 (1.1)	38 (1.0)	19 (0.9)
Asian/Pacific Islander	3 (0.8)	2 (0.5)	42 (2.6)	50 (2.8)	9 (1.0)	18 (1.7)	55 (1.5)	18 (1.5)	19 (1.6)	40 (1.3)	28 (1.9)	13 (1.1)
American Indian/Alaska Native	‡ (†)	‡ (†)	‡ (†)	‡ (†)	‡ (†)	‡ (†)	‡ (†)	‡ (†)	‡ (†)	‡ (†)	‡ (†)	‡ (†)
Eligibility for free or reduced-price lunch												
Eligible	8 (0.5)	10 (0.6)	60 (1.2)	18 (1.1)	16 (0.7)	23 (0.9)	47 (1.0)	14 (0.6)	13 (0.7)	30 (0.8)	34 (0.7)	22 (0.8)
Not eligible	4 (0.3)	7 (0.4)	59 (0.8)	29 (0.9)	13 (0.4)	21 (0.5)	49 (0.6)	17 (0.4)	16 (0.5)	35 (0.6)	30 (0.6)	18 (0.5)
Unknown	2 (0.7)	4 (1.0)	56 (2.4)	35 (2.7)	13 (1.2)	21 (1.3)	48 (1.9)	18 (1.6)	16 (1.6)	36 (2.3)	29 (1.8)	19 (1.6)
Parents' highest level of education												
Did not finish high school	11 (1.1)	13 (1.0)	53 (2.2)	16 (1.8)	19 (1.4)	22 (1.4)	47 (1.7)	13 (1.2)	13 (1.2)	30 (1.6)	35 (1.7)	23 (1.3)
Graduated high school	10 (0.6)	12 (0.8)	62 (1.4)	13 (1.0)	16 (0.8)	25 (1.0)	46 (1.2)	12 (0.7)	12 (0.7)	31 (1.3)	35 (1.1)	22 (1.1)
Some education after high school	4 (0.4)	9 (0.5)	65 (1.0)	20 (1.1)	15 (0.8)	22 (1.0)	48 (1.2)	15 (0.8)	14 (0.9)	33 (1.0)	32 (0.9)	21 (0.8)
Graduated college	2 (0.2)	4 (0.3)	56 (0.8)	37 (0.9)	12 (0.6)	19 (0.6)	50 (0.7)	19 (0.5)	18 (0.4)	37 (0.7)	28 (0.6)	17 (0.6)

†Not applicable.
‡Reporting standards not met (too few cases for a reliable estimate).
[1]The educational goals columns exclude the 1 percent of students who reported that they would not finish high school and the 2 percent who reported that they did not know how much education they would complete.
[2]Scale ranges from 0 to 300.

NOTE: Includes students tested with accommodations (7 percent of all 12th-graders); excludes only those students with disabilities and English language learners who were unable to be tested even with accommodations (3 percent of all 12th-graders). Race categories exclude persons of Hispanic ethnicity.
SOURCE: U.S. Department of Education, National Center for Education Statistics, National Assessment of Educational Progress (NAEP), 2009 Science Assessment, retrieved May 26, 2011, from the Main NAEP Data Explorer (http://nces.ed.gov/nationsreportcard/naepdata/). (This table was prepared May 2011.)

Table 224.10. Average National Assessment of Educational Progress (NAEP) arts scale score of 8th-graders, percentage distribution by frequency of instruction, and percentage participating in selected activities, by subject and selected characteristics: 2008

[Standard errors appear in parentheses]

Selected characteristic	Average score			Percentage distribution of students by school-reported frequency of instruction								Percent of students reporting participation in musical activities in school		
	Music,[1] responding scale score (0 to 300)	Visual arts[2]		Music				Visual arts						
		Responding scale score (0 to 300)	Creating task score (0 to 100)	Subject not offered	Less than once a week	Once or twice a week	At least 3 or 4 times a week	Subject not offered	Less than once a week	Once or twice a week	At least 3 or 4 times a week	Play in band	Play in orchestra	Sing in chorus or choir
1	2	3	4	5	6	7	8	9	10	11	12	13	14	15
All students	**150 (1.2)**	**150 (1.2)**	**52 (0.6)**	**8 (2.0)**	**8 (2.0)**	**27 (3.1)**	**57 (3.2)**	**14 (2.4)**	**10 (2.5)**	**30 (3.5)**	**47 (3.9)**	**16 (0.9)**	**5 (0.5)**	**17 (1.2)**
Sex														
Male	145 (1.3)	145 (1.4)	49 (0.7)	9 (2.1)	8 (2.1)	27 (3.1)	56 (3.2)	14 (2.6)	10 (2.5)	30 (3.6)	46 (4.1)	18 (1.0)	3 (0.5)	9 (1.2)
Female	155 (1.4)	155 (1.2)	54 (0.7)	8 (2.0)	7 (1.9)	28 (3.2)	57 (3.2)	13 (2.3)	10 (2.5)	29 (3.3)	48 (3.8)	14 (1.0)	6 (0.6)	26 (1.8)
Race/ethnicity														
White	161 (1.3)	160 (1.2)	55 (0.5)	6 (2.5)	8 (2.5)	29 (4.0)	57 (3.6)	11 (2.6)	11 (3.4)	34 (4.4)	44 (4.6)	19 (1.2)	5 (0.6)	19 (1.6)
Black	130 (2.0)	129 (2.4)	43 (1.5)	10 (2.9)	8 (4.5)	26 (5.5)	56 (7.0)	18 (4.9)	10 (4.9)	24 (4.5)	49 (5.7)	13 (1.2)	4 (1.0)	21 (1.9)
Hispanic	129 (1.9)	134 (1.9)	46 (1.1)	14 (4.3)	6 (2.3)	21 (4.1)	59 (4.5)	17 (4.5)	5 (2.0)	23 (4.7)	56 (6.0)	8 (1.2)	3 (0.6)	10 (1.6)
Asian/Pacific Islander	159 (4.7)	156 (4.2)	54 (2.0)	7 (4.1)	8 (3.4)	25 (6.6)	60 (8.7)	5 (2.5)	11 (4.6)	29 (6.0)	54 (8.4)	21 (3.5)	6 (2.1)	16 (2.9)
Free or reduced-price lunch eligibility														
Eligible	132 (1.3)	132 (1.4)	46 (1.0)	10 (2.1)	6 (2.1)	26 (3.4)	58 (3.9)	18 (3.4)	9 (3.2)	26 (3.7)	47 (4.7)	12 (1.2)	3 (0.6)	15 (1.4)
Not eligible	161 (1.4)	161 (1.2)	55 (0.6)	8 (2.6)	8 (2.6)	26 (4.0)	59 (4.0)	10 (2.4)	10 (3.2)	30 (4.1)	50 (4.6)	19 (1.0)	5 (0.6)	19 (1.6)
Unknown	156 (5.6)	156 (5.9)	57 (2.6)	4 †	19 (8.7)	54 (11.5)	23 (10.5)	16 (10.3)	13 (8.4)	47 (13.6)	24 (10.6)	14 (6.3)	5 (2.3)	13 (2.0)
Control of school														
Public	149 (1.3)	149 (1.2)	51 (0.7)	8 (2.1)	7 (2.1)	24 (3.2)	61 (3.5)	13 (2.4)	10 (2.7)	26 (3.5)	51 (4.2)	17 (0.9)	5 (0.5)	18 (1.3)
Private	163 (2.8)	159 (5.2)	60 (1.3)	10 (6.0)	15 (6.9)	71 (8.8)	3 (†)	17 (8.2)	10 (6.1)	70 (10.2)	3 (0.9)	9 (1.9)	1 (0.4)	13 (2.1)
School location														
City	142 (2.0)	144 (2.1)	49 (1.2)	13 (4.0)	10 (3.8)	24 (5.7)	52 (5.6)	12 (2.6)	9 (3.5)	24 (4.9)	55 (5.4)	14 (1.0)	4 (0.6)	13 (1.3)
Suburban	155 (1.9)	155 (1.8)	54 (0.7)	3 (2.2)	7 (3.5)	32 (5.6)	57 (6.3)	10 (3.1)	10 (4.6)	33 (6.4)	46 (6.1)	14 (1.5)	6 (1.0)	16 (1.6)
Town	156 (3.5)	149 (2.8)	50 (1.2)	4 (1.0)	# (†)	18 (9.0)	78 (9.0)	16 (8.4)	# (†)	23 (9.2)	60 (10.5)	23 (3.0)	4 (1.3)	23 (3.4)
Rural	150 (2.6)	151 (3.0)	52 (1.5)	13 (5.0)	8 (4.8)	29 (5.7)	50 (7.7)	20 (7.3)	17 (6.8)	35 (7.8)	28 (6.7)	18 (2.5)	3 (1.0)	21 (3.4)
Region														
Northeast	154 (3.1)	160 (2.3)	52 (0.9)	10 (5.3)	13 (5.8)	40 (9.0)	37 (8.6)	5 (3.3)	5 (†)	50 (6.2)	39 (9.3)	16 (2.7)	6 (0.9)	17 (2.6)
Midwest	158 (2.9)	155 (2.3)	53 (1.3)	12 (6.6)	# (†)	25 (7.2)	63 (5.8)	9 (2.0)	15 (7.7)	26 (6.7)	50 (7.3)	22 (2.1)	6 (1.3)	24 (3.1)
South	147 (1.9)	147 (2.2)	51 (1.0)	6 (1.8)	10 (4.0)	25 (3.9)	59 (5.7)	19 (5.3)	9 (3.8)	26 (5.0)	46 (6.4)	16 (1.2)	4 (0.6)	16 (2.0)
West	144 (2.0)	143 (2.1)	51 (1.1)	8 (3.7)	8 (3.5)	24 (6.9)	60 (5.4)	15 (4.9)	9 (4.0)	25 (9.0)	51 (8.2)	9 (1.2)	3 (0.6)	12 (1.7)
Frequency of instruction														
Subject not offered	139 (6.3)	138 (4.2)	— (†)	† (†)	† (†)	† (†)	† (†)	† (†)	† (†)	† (†)	† (†)	17 (4.0)	4 (1.5)	11 (2.1)
Less than once a week	149 (6.4)	154 (5.3)	— (†)	† (†)	† (†)	† (†)	† (†)	† (†)	† (†)	† (†)	† (†)	11 (2.4)	4 (1.5)	10 (2.0)
Once or twice a week	152 (2.8)	154 (2.6)	— (†)	† (†)	† (†)	† (†)	† (†)	† (†)	† (†)	† (†)	† (†)	12 (1.7)	3 (0.8)	17 (2.2)
At least 3 or 4 times a week	149 (1.8)	149 (1.8)	— (†)	† (†)	† (†)	† (†)	† (†)	† (†)	† (†)	† (†)	† (†)	17 (1.4)	5 (0.7)	20 (1.6)

—Not available.
†Not applicable.
#Rounds to zero.
[1]Students were asked to analyze and describe aspects of music they heard, critique instrumental and vocal performances, and demonstrate their knowledge of standard musical notation and music's role in society.
[2]The visual arts assessment measured students' ability to respond to and create visual arts. Responding questions asked students to analyze and describe works of art and design, while creating questions required students to create works of art and design of their own.

NOTE: Excludes students unable to be tested due to limited proficiency in English or due to a disability (if the accommodations provided were not sufficient to enable the test to properly reflect the students' music or visual arts proficiency). Detail may not sum to totals because of rounding. Race categories exclude persons of Hispanic ethnicity. Totals include other racial/ethnic groups not shown separately.
SOURCE: U.S. Department of Education, National Center for Education Statistics, National Assessment of Educational Progress (NAEP), 2008 Arts Assessment, retrieved June 30, 2009, from the Main NAEP Data Explorer (http://nces.ed.gov/nationsreportcard/naepdata/). (This table was prepared June 2009.)

Table 224.20. Average National Assessment of Educational Progress (NAEP) civics scale score and percentage of students attaining civics achievement levels, by grade level, selected student characteristics, and percentile: 1998, 2006, 2010, and 2014

[Standard errors appear in parentheses]

Selected student characteristic	4th-graders			8th-graders				12th-graders		
	1998	2006	2010	1998	2006	2010	2014	1998	2006	2010
1	2	3	4	5	6	7	8	9	10	11
	Average civics scale score[1]									
All students	**150 (0.7)**	**154 (1.0)**	**157 (0.8)**	**150 (0.7)**	**150 (0.8)**	**151 (0.8)**	**154 (1.1)**	**150 (0.8)**	**151 (0.9)**	**148 (0.8)**
Sex										
Male	149 (1.0)	153 (1.1)	153 (1.0)	148 (0.9)	149 (1.0)	150 (0.9)	154 (1.2)	148 (1.1)	150 (1.1)	148 (0.9)
Female	151 (0.9)	155 (1.1)	160 (0.8)	152 (0.8)	151 (0.8)	152 (0.8)	154 (1.1)	152 (0.8)	152 (1.0)	148 (0.9)
Race/ethnicity										
White	158 (0.9)	164 (0.9)	167 (0.8)	158 (0.9)	161 (0.8)	160 (0.8)	164 (1.0)	157 (1.0)	158 (1.0)	156 (0.9)
Black	130 (1.1)	140 (1.5)	143 (1.2)	131 (1.2)	133 (1.5)	135 (1.6)	137 (2.1)	130 (1.6)	131 (1.4)	127 (1.6)
Hispanic	123 (2.2)	138 (1.3)	140 (1.6)	127 (1.3)	131 (1.1)	137 (1.1)	141 (1.4)	132 (1.1)	134 (1.1)	137 (1.4)
Asian/Pacific Islander	147 (4.0)	154 (3.8)	164 (2.0)	151 (8.9)	154 (3.2)	158 (2.5)	165 (3.1)	149 (5.2)	155 (3.1)	153 (2.6)
Asian[2]	— (†)	— (†)	— (†)	— (†)	— (†)	— (†)	166 (3.1)	— (†)	— (†)	— (†)
Pacific Islander[2]	— (†)	— (†)	— (†)	— (†)	— (†)	— (†)	‡ (†)	— (†)	— (†)	— (†)
American Indian/Alaska Native	‡ (†)	124 (7.6)	143 (7.0)	‡ (†)	127 (7.3)	136 (12.6)	‡ (†)	‡ (†)	131 (3.5)	134 (14.6)
Two or more races[2]	— (†)	— (†)	— (†)	— (†)	— (†)	— (†)	160 (2.8)	— (†)	— (†)	— (†)
Parents' highest level of education[3]										
Did not finish high school	— (†)	— (†)	— (†)	123 (3.2)	129 (1.6)	134 (1.3)	134 (1.5)	124 (2.1)	126 (1.8)	128 (1.4)
Graduated high school	— (†)	— (†)	— (†)	144 (1.2)	140 (1.3)	139 (1.1)	140 (1.7)	140 (1.2)	138 (1.0)	137 (1.2)
Some education after high school	— (†)	— (†)	— (†)	143 (1.0)	153 (1.0)	155 (1.1)	155 (1.1)	145 (1.1)	150 (0.9)	147 (1.1)
Graduated college	— (†)	— (†)	— (†)	160 (0.8)	162 (0.9)	162 (0.8)	164 (1.0)	160 (0.9)	162 (1.1)	158 (0.9)
Eligibility for free or reduced-price lunch										
Eligible	132 (0.9)	139 (1.1)	143 (0.9)	131 (1.1)	132 (1.0)	136 (0.9)	139 (1.2)	130 (1.4)	133 (1.0)	132 (1.0)
Not eligible	160 (1.1)	166 (0.8)	169 (0.8)	157 (1.0)	160 (0.8)	163 (0.7)	166 (1.1)	153 (1.0)	156 (1.0)	155 (0.9)
Unknown	154 (2.2)	167 (2.1)	171 (2.7)	156 (2.2)	171 (2.4)	166 (2.3)	166 (2.1)	153 (1.3)	160 (2.4)	159 (3.3)
Percentile[4]										
10th	102 (1.6)	111 (1.9)	115 (1.6)	103 (1.6)	102 (1.6)	106 (1.9)	110 (1.8)	103 (1.2)	104 (1.2)	101 (1.8)
25th	128 (0.9)	134 (1.2)	138 (1.0)	128 (1.1)	128 (1.5)	131 (1.1)	133 (1.7)	128 (1.4)	128 (1.2)	126 (1.4)
50th	153 (1.3)	156 (1.1)	159 (1.2)	153 (0.7)	154 (1.1)	155 (0.9)	157 (1.2)	153 (0.8)	154 (1.1)	152 (1.0)
75th	175 (0.8)	176 (0.9)	179 (1.2)	175 (1.0)	175 (1.0)	175 (0.8)	177 (1.4)	175 (0.8)	176 (1.0)	173 (0.8)
90th	192 (0.7)	192 (1.1)	194 (1.0)	192 (0.7)	191 (0.6)	191 (0.5)	193 (1.0)	192 (0.7)	194 (0.9)	190 (1.3)
	Standard deviation of the civics scale score[5]									
All students	**35 (0.5)**	**31 (0.5)**	**31 (0.5)**	**35 (0.4)**	**35 (0.5)**	**34 (0.4)**	**33 (0.5)**	**35 (0.4)**	**35 (0.4)**	**35 (0.4)**
	Percent of students achieving civics achievement levels									
Achievement level										
Below *Basic*	31 (1.0)	27 (1.2)	23 (1.0)	30 (0.9)	30 (1.1)	28 (1.0)	26 (1.3)	35 (0.9)	34 (1.1)	36 (1.0)
At or above *Basic*[6]	69 (1.0)	73 (1.2)	77 (1.0)	70 (0.9)	70 (1.1)	72 (1.0)	74 (1.3)	65 (0.9)	66 (1.1)	64 (1.0)
At or above *Basic* by sex										
Male	68 (1.2)	72 (1.3)	73 (1.3)	67 (1.1)	68 (1.3)	70 (1.1)	74 (1.4)	62 (1.2)	64 (1.5)	63 (1.0)
Female	70 (1.0)	75 (1.4)	81 (1.0)	73 (1.2)	72 (1.2)	74 (1.1)	75 (1.4)	68 (1.2)	67 (1.2)	64 (1.3)
At or above *Basic* by sex by race/ethnicity										
White	78 (1.3)	85 (1.0)	87 (0.9)	78 (1.1)	82 (0.9)	82 (1.0)	86 (1.0)	73 (1.1)	74 (1.2)	73 (1.0)
Black	45 (1.7)	57 (2.3)	62 (2.2)	49 (1.7)	50 (2.0)	53 (2.3)	55 (3.4)	41 (2.0)	42 (1.9)	38 (1.9)
Hispanic	40 (2.8)	55 (2.0)	58 (2.3)	44 (2.3)	50 (2.2)	56 (1.4)	61 (1.7)	45 (1.9)	46 (1.7)	50 (1.8)
Asian/Pacific Islander	66 (5.5)	75 (4.5)	82 (2.3)	69 (9.5)	73 (4.0)	78 (2.5)	83 (2.8)	63 (4.8)	68 (3.7)	70 (3.1)
Asian[2]	— (†)	— (†)	— (†)	— (†)	— (†)	— (†)	84 (2.8)	— (†)	— (†)	— (†)
Pacific Islander[2]	— (†)	— (†)	— (†)	— (†)	— (†)	— (†)	‡ (†)	— (†)	— (†)	— (†)
American Indian/Alaska Native	‡ (†)	38 (11.3)	63 (10.9)	‡ (†)	46 (9.5)	56 (18.0)	‡ (†)	‡ (†)	42 (8.0)	47 (17.3)
Two or more races[2]	— (†)	— (†)	— (†)	— (†)	— (†)	— (†)	80 (3.4)	— (†)	— (†)	— (†)
At or above *Proficient*[7]	23 (0.9)	24 (1.0)	27 (0.9)	22 (0.8)	22 (0.8)	22 (0.8)	23 (1.1)	26 (0.9)	27 (1.0)	24 (0.9)
At *Advanced*[8]	2 (0.3)	1 (0.2)	2 (0.2)	2 (0.2)	2 (0.2)	1 (0.1)	2 (0.3)	4 (0.4)	5 (0.4)	4 (0.3)

—Not available.
†Not applicable.
‡Reporting standards not met (too few cases for a reliable estimate).
[1]Scale ranges from 0 to 300 for all three grades, but scores cannot be compared across grades. For example, the average score of 167 for White 4th-graders in 2010 does not denote higher performance than the score of 160 for White 8th-graders in 2010.
[2]In civics assessments prior to 2014, separate data for Asians, Pacific Islanders, and students of Two or more races were not collected.
[3]These data are based on students' responses to questions about their parents' education level. Because the wording of the questions was different in 1998 than in the later assessment years, data from 1998 are not directly comparable to data from 2006, 2010, and 2014. For all assessment years, data for students whose parents have an unknown level of education are included in table totals, but not shown separately.
[4]The percentile represents a specific point on the percentage distribution of all students ranked by their civics score from low to high. For example, 10 percent of students scored at or below the 10th percentile score, while 90 percent of students scored above it.
[5]The standard deviation provides an indication of how much the test scores varied. The lower the standard deviation, the closer the scores were clustered around the average score. About two-thirds of the student scores can be expected to fall within the range of one standard deviation above and one standard deviation below the average score. For example, the average score for all 8th-graders in 2014 was 154, and the standard deviation was 33. This means that about two-thirds of the students would be expected to have scores between 187 (one standard deviation above the average) and 121 (one standard deviation below). Standard errors also must be taken into account when making comparisons of these ranges.
[6]*Basic* denotes partial mastery of the knowledge and skills that are fundamental for proficient work.
[7]*Proficient* represents solid academic performance. Students reaching this level have demonstrated competency over challenging subject matter.
[8]*Advanced* signifies superior performance.
NOTE: In 2014, only 8th-grade students were assessed in civics. Includes public and private schools. Includes students tested with accommodations (1 to 13 percent of all students, depending on grade level and year); excludes only those students with disabilities and English language learners who were unable to be tested even with accommodations (1 to 5 percent of all students). Race categories exclude persons of Hispanic ethnicity. Detail may not sum to totals because of rounding.
SOURCE: U.S. Department of Education, National Center for Education Statistics, National Assessment of Educational Progress (NAEP), 1998, 2006, 2010, and 2014 Civics Assessments, retrieved April 30, 2015, from the Main NAEP Data Explorer (http://nces.ed.gov/nationsreportcard/naepdata/). (This table was prepared April 2015.)

Table 224.30. Average National Assessment of Educational Progress (NAEP) economics scale score of 12th-graders, percentage attaining economics achievement levels, and percentage with different levels of economics coursework, by selected characteristics: 2006 and 2012

[Standard errors appear in parentheses]

Selected characteristic	Average scale score[1]	Percent of students attaining achievement levels: At or above *Basic*[2]	At or above *Proficient*[3]	At *Advanced*[4]	Percentage distribution of students by highest level of economics coursework taken: No economics courses	Combined course	Consumer economics/ business	General economics	Advanced economics[5]
1	2	3	4	5	6	7	8	9	10
2006									
All students	**150 (0.9)**	**79 (0.8)**	**42 (1.1)**	**3 (0.3)**	**13 (0.9)**	**12 (0.7)**	**11 (0.7)**	**49 (1.4)**	**16 (0.7)**
Sex									
Male	152 (1.0)	79 (0.8)	45 (1.3)	4 (0.5)	13 (1.0)	10 (0.6)	10 (0.7)	50 (1.4)	16 (0.8)
Female	148 (0.9)	79 (0.9)	38 (1.3)	2 (0.3)	12 (0.9)	13 (0.9)	11 (0.8)	48 (1.6)	15 (0.8)
Race/ethnicity									
White	158 (0.8)	87 (0.7)	51 (1.2)	4 (0.4)	15 (1.1)	12 (0.8)	11 (0.8)	49 (1.6)	13 (0.9)
Black	127 (1.2)	57 (1.9)	16 (1.3)	# (†)	8 (0.8)	11 (0.9)	11 (1.2)	49 (1.7)	21 (1.1)
Hispanic	133 (1.2)	64 (1.6)	21 (1.2)	# (†)	8 (1.7)	13 (1.1)	7 (0.9)	55 (2.6)	18 (1.2)
Asian/Pacific Islander	153 (3.5)	80 (4.0)	44 (4.5)	4 (1.4)	13 (1.8)	10 (1.8)	10 (1.4)	45 (4.1)	22 (1.9)
American Indian/Alaska Native	137 (4.1)	72 (5.6)	26 (4.8)	2 (†)	11 (3.9)	18 (2.7)	17 (3.2)	41 (4.9)	13 (3.1)
Parents' highest level of education									
Not high school graduate	129 (1.4)	59 (2.1)	17 (1.7)	# (†)	10 (1.7)	13 (1.4)	10 (1.4)	53 (3.2)	14 (1.3)
Graduated high school	138 (1.2)	69 (1.5)	27 (1.4)	1 (0.3)	11 (1.2)	12 (1.0)	12 (1.0)	52 (1.7)	13 (0.9)
Some college	150 (0.8)	82 (1.1)	39 (1.4)	1 (0.4)	11 (1.0)	13 (0.9)	12 (1.0)	51 (1.9)	14 (1.0)
Graduated college	160 (0.9)	87 (0.8)	54 (1.3)	5 (0.6)	14 (1.0)	11 (0.8)	10 (0.7)	47 (1.5)	17 (1.0)
Free or reduced-price lunch eligibility									
Eligible	132 (0.9)	62 (1.1)	20 (1.1)	1 (0.2)	9 (0.7)	13 (1.1)	10 (0.9)	50 (1.6)	18 (0.8)
Not eligible	155 (0.9)	84 (0.8)	48 (1.2)	4 (0.4)	13 (1.1)	12 (0.8)	12 (0.9)	48 (1.6)	16 (0.9)
Unknown	157 (1.9)	86 (1.7)	50 (2.8)	4 (1.1)	16 (3.0)	12 (1.6)	7 (1.1)	54 (3.1)	11 (1.4)
Region									
Northeast	153 (2.0)	81 (1.7)	46 (2.6)	4 (0.9)	26 (2.6)	7 (1.1)	11 (1.3)	43 (3.2)	13 (1.4)
Midwest	153 (1.5)	83 (1.4)	45 (2.0)	3 (0.6)	12 (2.2)	12 (1.6)	15 (1.5)	51 (2.6)	10 (1.0)
South	147 (1.4)	77 (1.4)	37 (1.7)	2 (0.5)	6 (1.1)	14 (1.2)	9 (1.3)	49 (2.0)	22 (1.5)
West	‡ (†)	‡ (†)	‡ (†)	‡ (†)	‡ (†)	‡ (†)	‡ (†)	‡ (†)	‡ (†)
2012									
All students	**152 (0.8)**	**82 (0.8)**	**42 (1.1)**	**3 (0.3)**	**9 (1.0)**	**9 (0.8)**	**10 (1.2)**	**54 (2.0)**	**18 (0.9)**
Sex									
Male	155 (0.9)	83 (1.0)	47 (1.3)	4 (0.4)	8 (0.9)	9 (0.8)	10 (1.2)	54 (2.0)	18 (1.0)
Female	149 (0.9)	80 (1.0)	37 (1.3)	2 (0.2)	10 (1.2)	9 (0.9)	10 (1.3)	53 (2.2)	18 (1.1)
Race/ethnicity									
White	160 (1.0)	89 (0.9)	53 (1.6)	4 (0.4)	10 (1.4)	9 (1.0)	11 (1.6)	54 (2.4)	15 (1.1)
Black	131 (1.4)	61 (2.1)	16 (1.3)	1 (0.2)	6 (1.2)	8 (1.1)	9 (1.2)	54 (2.9)	23 (1.4)
Hispanic	138 (1.4)	71 (2.0)	25 (1.4)	1 (0.3)	5 (1.1)	9 (1.0)	7 (1.2)	57 (2.9)	21 (2.0)
Asian	160 (1.9)	86 (1.9)	53 (2.4)	6 (1.3)	10 (1.5)	9 (1.2)	7 (1.2)	45 (2.7)	29 (2.6)
Pacific Islander	‡ (†)	‡ (†)	‡ (†)	‡ (†)	‡ (†)	‡ (†)	‡ (†)	‡ (†)	‡ (†)
American Indian/Alaska Native	136 (4.7)	72 (7.8)	20 (5.6)	2 (†)	4 (2.7)	7 (2.9)	19 (9.9)	54 (8.0)	16 (4.6)
Two or more races	154 (3.4)	87 (3.0)	42 (5.2)	3 (1.8)	10 (2.9)	6 (1.4)	7 (1.8)	57 (4.5)	20 (2.8)
Parents' highest level of education									
Not high school graduate	134 (1.5)	66 (2.1)	21 (1.9)	# (†)	4 (0.7)	10 (1.3)	10 (1.4)	59 (2.4)	17 (1.5)
Graduated high school	139 (1.1)	71 (1.7)	27 (1.6)	1 (0.2)	7 (1.2)	9 (1.1)	11 (1.2)	56 (2.3)	16 (1.0)
Some college	150 (0.8)	84 (1.0)	38 (1.2)	1 (0.3)	8 (1.2)	9 (0.9)	10 (1.5)	56 (2.3)	16 (1.6)
Graduated college	161 (0.9)	89 (1.0)	55 (1.4)	5 (0.5)	10 (1.4)	9 (1.0)	10 (1.3)	51 (2.3)	20 (1.2)
Free or reduced-price lunch eligibility									
Eligible	138 (0.9)	70 (1.3)	25 (1.1)	# (†)	7 (0.9)	9 (0.7)	10 (1.2)	57 (2.1)	18 (1.3)
Not eligible	159 (0.9)	88 (0.8)	52 (1.4)	4 (0.4)	10 (1.3)	9 (1.1)	11 (1.4)	51 (2.3)	19 (1.1)
Unknown	164 (3.3)	90 (2.3)	59 (4.2)	5 (1.4)	13 (4.7)	8 (1.8)	6 (1.6)	58 (5.0)	15 (1.9)
School location									
City	147 (1.8)	77 (1.9)	37 (2.3)	3 (0.5)	8 (1.5)	9 (1.3)	8 (1.4)	54 (3.3)	22 (1.8)
Suburb	156 (0.9)	85 (1.0)	48 (1.1)	4 (0.4)	12 (1.8)	10 (1.1)	11 (1.6)	50 (2.1)	17 (1.5)
Town	149 (2.7)	81 (2.4)	39 (3.8)	2 (0.6)	9 (2.8)	8 (1.2)	10 (2.4)	57 (3.5)	16 (3.8)
Rural	152 (1.5)	83 (1.5)	42 (2.5)	2 (0.6)	5 (1.2)	9 (1.4)	12 (2.8)	57 (4.0)	17 (2.1)
Region									
Northeast	154 (1.7)	84 (1.8)	46 (2.0)	3 (0.7)	27 (4.0)	9 (1.9)	11 (1.4)	39 (5.5)	14 (2.2)
Midwest	157 (1.6)	86 (1.1)	50 (2.2)	4 (0.7)	5 (1.2)	9 (2.3)	18 (3.4)	57 (4.3)	11 (1.0)
South	149 (1.8)	79 (1.7)	38 (2.7)	2 (0.5)	3 (1.5)	8 (1.2)	5 (0.9)	55 (3.6)	29 (2.0)
West	148 (1.1)	79 (1.4)	40 (1.5)	2 (0.3)	7 (1.2)	11 (1.1)	9 (3.1)	60 (3.0)	13 (1.0)

†Not applicable.
#Rounds to zero.
‡Reporting standards not met. Either there are too few cases for a reliable estimate or item response rates fell below the required standards for reporting.
[1]Scale ranges from 0 to 300.
[2]*Basic* denotes partial mastery of the knowledge and skills that are fundamental for proficient work at a given grade.
[3]*Proficient* represents solid academic performance. Students reaching this level have demonstrated competency over challenging subject matter.
[4]*Advanced* signifies superior performance for a given grade.
[5]Advanced economics includes Advanced Placement, International Baccalaureate, and honors courses.

NOTE: Includes public and private schools. Includes students tested with accommodations; excludes only those students with disabilities and English language learners who were unable to be tested even with accommodations (3 percent of all students in both assessment years). Detail may not sum to totals because of rounding. Race categories exclude persons of Hispanic ethnicity. Totals include other racial/ethnic groups not shown separately.

SOURCE: U.S. Department of Education, National Center for Education Statistics, National Assessment of Educational Progress (NAEP), 2006 and 2012 Economics Assessment, retrieved May 08, 2013, from the NAEP Data Explorer (http://nces.ed.gov/nationsreportcard/naepdata/). (This table was prepared May 2013.)

Table 224.40. Average National Assessment of Educational Progress (NAEP) geography scale score, standard deviation, and percentage of students attaining geography achievement levels, by grade level, selected student characteristics, and percentile: Selected years, 1994 through 2014

[Standard errors appear in parentheses]

Selected student characteristic	4th-graders			8th-graders				12th-graders		
	1994[1]	2001	2010	1994[1]	2001	2010	2014	1994[1]	2001	2010
1	2	3	4	5	6	7	8	9	10	11
	Average geography scale score[2]									
All students	**206 (1.2)**	**208 (0.9)**	**213 (0.8)**	**260 (0.7)**	**260 (1.0)**	**261 (0.7)**	**261 (1.0)**	**285 (0.7)**	**284 (0.8)**	**282 (0.6)**
Sex										
Male	208 (1.4)	210 (1.0)	215 (0.9)	262 (0.9)	262 (1.2)	263 (0.8)	263 (1.1)	288 (0.8)	287 (1.0)	285 (0.6)
Female	203 (1.4)	206 (1.3)	211 (0.9)	258 (0.8)	258 (1.0)	259 (0.8)	260 (1.0)	281 (0.9)	281 (0.8)	280 (0.8)
Race/ethnicity										
White	218 (1.5)	219 (1.1)	224 (0.9)	269 (0.8)	269 (1.4)	272 (0.6)	273 (1.0)	290 (0.8)	291 (0.8)	290 (0.5)
Black	166 (2.4)	180 (1.8)	192 (1.3)	229 (1.7)	233 (1.6)	241 (1.1)	240 (1.1)	258 (1.4)	258 (1.5)	261 (1.2)
Hispanic	177 (3.3)	185 (2.5)	197 (1.2)	238 (2.0)	237 (2.0)	244 (1.0)	248 (1.1)	269 (1.7)	268 (1.6)	270 (1.2)
Asian/Pacific Islander	211 (4.0)	214 (3.5)	224 (3.3)	262 (5.3)	264 (2.7)	268 (2.7)	275 (2.5)	283 (3.1)	284 (5.0)	285 (1.7)
Asian[3]	— (†)	— (†)	— (†)	— (†)	— (†)	— (†)	275 (2.6)	— (†)	— (†)	— (†)
Pacific Islander[3]	— (†)	— (†)	— (†)	— (†)	— (†)	— (†)	‡ (†)	— (†)	— (†)	— (†)
American Indian/Alaska Native	‡ (†)	‡ (†)	201 (3.5)	251 (5.5)	261 (5.3)	250 (3.9)	‡ (†)	‡ (†)	‡ (†)	277 (2.5)
Two or more races[3]	— (†)	— (†)	— (†)	— (†)	— (†)	— (†)	264 (2.5)	— (†)	— (†)	— (†)
Parents' highest level of education[4]										
Did not finish high school	— (†)	— (†)	— (†)	238 (1.7)	236 (1.8)	243 (1.3)	243 (1.2)	263 (1.2)	266 (1.7)	263 (1.2)
Graduated high school	— (†)	— (†)	— (†)	250 (1.2)	251 (1.2)	251 (1.1)	250 (1.3)	274 (1.1)	275 (0.9)	274 (0.8)
Some education after high school	— (†)	— (†)	— (†)	265 (1.0)	264 (1.1)	262 (1.0)	261 (0.9)	286 (1.0)	284 (0.9)	280 (0.7)
Graduated college	— (†)	— (†)	— (†)	272 (1.0)	273 (1.0)	272 (0.7)	272 (1.2)	294 (0.9)	293 (1.0)	291 (0.7)
Eligibility for free or reduced-price lunch										
Eligible	— (†)	185 (1.4)	197 (0.7)	— (†)	239 (1.3)	246 (0.9)	248 (1.0)	— (†)	268 (1.7)	269 (0.8)
Not eligible	— (†)	221 (1.1)	227 (0.8)	— (†)	269 (1.2)	272 (0.7)	274 (1.2)	— (†)	287 (1.0)	288 (0.5)
Unknown	— (†)	219 (2.8)	227 (3.7)	— (†)	265 (2.3)	276 (2.6)	277 (3.0)	— (†)	288 (1.6)	289 (2.2)
Percentile[5]										
10th	146 (1.9)	159 (2.6)	169 (1.8)	213 (1.3)	213 (1.2)	220 (1.2)	220 (1.2)	244 (0.9)	246 (1.1)	247 (0.8)
25th	179 (1.5)	184 (1.4)	192 (1.2)	237 (1.0)	238 (1.3)	241 (0.7)	242 (1.3)	265 (1.1)	266 (1.2)	265 (0.8)
50th	211 (1.1)	211 (1.0)	216 (1.1)	263 (1.1)	264 (1.2)	263 (0.9)	263 (1.0)	287 (0.9)	286 (0.9)	284 (0.7)
75th	237 (1.3)	235 (1.4)	236 (0.7)	285 (0.9)	285 (1.1)	284 (0.9)	283 (0.9)	306 (1.0)	304 (0.9)	301 (0.7)
90th	257 (2.0)	254 (1.3)	253 (0.9)	302 (1.9)	302 (1.1)	300 (0.7)	300 (1.3)	321 (1.0)	319 (1.3)	315 (0.7)
	Standard deviation of the geography scale score[6]									
All students	**44 (0.8)**	**37 (0.8)**	**33 (0.4)**	**35 (0.4)**	**35 (0.5)**	**31 (0.3)**	**31 (0.5)**	**30 (0.4)**	**28 (0.4)**	**26 (0.3)**
	Percent of students achieving geography achievement levels									
Achievement level										
Below *Basic*[7]	30 (1.1)	27 (1.0)	21 (0.9)	29 (1.0)	28 (1.2)	26 (0.9)	25 (1.1)	30 (0.9)	29 (1.0)	30 (0.9)
At or above *Basic*[7]	70 (1.1)	73 (1.0)	79 (0.9)	71 (1.0)	72 (1.2)	74 (0.9)	75 (1.1)	70 (0.9)	71 (1.0)	70 (0.9)
At or above *Basic* by sex										
Male	71 (1.3)	74 (0.9)	80 (1.0)	72 (1.3)	73 (1.5)	75 (1.0)	76 (1.1)	73 (1.1)	74 (1.3)	73 (1.0)
Female	68 (1.4)	71 (1.5)	78 (1.1)	69 (1.1)	71 (1.1)	73 (1.1)	74 (1.2)	67 (1.2)	68 (1.2)	66 (1.2)
At or above *Basic* by race/ethnicity										
White	81 (1.3)	84 (1.1)	89 (1.0)	81 (0.9)	82 (1.5)	86 (0.7)	88 (0.9)	78 (0.9)	81 (0.9)	81 (0.8)
Black	33 (2.4)	43 (2.5)	57 (2.1)	34 (3.0)	39 (2.4)	49 (1.7)	48 (2.1)	33 (2.3)	33 (2.0)	36 (1.8)
Hispanic	44 (3.1)	50 (3.1)	64 (1.7)	49 (3.8)	45 (2.5)	55 (1.5)	61 (1.7)	48 (3.0)	48 (2.9)	52 (2.0)
Asian/Pacific Islander	72 (4.4)	77 (4.2)	87 (3.2)	72 (6.7)	77 (3.6)	80 (3.3)	87 (2.0)	67 (3.8)	70 (6.2)	73 (2.7)
Asian[3]	— (†)	— (†)	— (†)	— (†)	— (†)	— (†)	87 (2.0)	— (†)	— (†)	— (†)
Pacific Islander[3]	— (†)	— (†)	— (†)	— (†)	— (†)	— (†)	‡ (†)	— (†)	— (†)	— (†)
American Indian/Alaska Native	‡ (†)	‡ (†)	68 (6.4)	62 (7.7)	74 (4.8)	62 (7.2)	‡ (†)	‡ (†)	‡ (†)	62 (5.1)
Two or more races[3]	— (†)	— (†)	— (†)	— (†)	— (†)	— (†)	79 (3.5)	— (†)	— (†)	— (†)
At or above *Proficient*[8]	22 (1.2)	20 (0.9)	21 (0.8)	28 (1.0)	29 (1.3)	27 (0.8)	27 (1.2)	27 (1.2)	24 (1.2)	20 (0.8)
At *Advanced*[9]	3 (0.4)	2 (0.3)	2 (0.2)	4 (0.4)	4 (0.5)	3 (0.2)	3 (0.4)	2 (0.5)	1 (0.3)	1 (0.1)

—Not available.

†Not applicable.

‡Reporting standards not met (too few cases for a reliable estimate).

[1]Accommodations were not permitted for this assessment.

[2]Scale ranges from 0 to 500.

[3]In geography assessments prior to 2014, separate data for Asians, Pacific Islanders, and students of Two or more races were not collected.

[4]Based on student reports. Data for students whose parents have an unknown level of education are included in table totals, but not shown separately.

[5]The percentile represents a specific point on the percentage distribution of all students ranked by their geography score from low to high. For example, 10 percent of students scored at or below the 10th percentile score, while 90 percent of students scored above it.

[6]The standard deviation provides an indication of how much the test scores varied. The lower the standard deviation, the closer the scores were clustered around the average score. About two-thirds of the student scores can be expected to fall within the range of one standard deviation above and one standard deviation below the average score. For example, the average score for all 8th-graders in 2014 was 261, and the standard deviation was 31. This means that about two-thirds of the students would be expected to have scores between 292 (one standard deviation above the average) and 230 (one standard deviation below). Standard errors also must be taken into account when making comparisons of these ranges.

[7]*Basic* denotes partial mastery of the knowledge and skills that are fundamental for proficient work.

[8]*Proficient* represents solid academic performance. Students reaching this level have demonstrated competency over challenging subject matter.

[9]*Advanced* signifies superior performance.

NOTE: In 2014, only 8th-grade students were assessed in geography. Includes public and private schools. For 2001 and later years, includes students tested with accommodations (3 to 13 percent of all students, depending on grade level and year); excludes only those students with disabilities and English language learners who were unable to be tested even with accommodations (1 to 4 percent of all students). Race categories exclude persons of Hispanic ethnicity. Detail may not sum to totals because of rounding.

SOURCE: U.S. Department of Education, National Center for Education Statistics, National Assessment of Educational Progress (NAEP), 1994, 2001, 2010, and 2014 Geography Assessments, retrieved April 30, 2015, from the Main NAEP Data Explorer (http://nces.ed.gov/nationsreportcard/naepdata/). (This table was prepared April 2015.)

Table 224.50. Average National Assessment of Educational Progress (NAEP) U.S. history scale score, standard deviation, and percentage of students attaining achievement levels, by grade level, selected student characteristics, and percentile: Selected years, 1994 through 2014

[Standard errors appear in parentheses]

Selected student characteristic	4th-graders				8th-graders					12th-graders			
	1994[1]	2001	2006	2010	1994[1]	2001	2006	2010	2014	1994[1]	2001	2006	2010
1	2	3	4	5	6	7	8	9	10	11	12	13	14
	Average U.S. history scale score[2]												
All students	**205 (1.0)**	**208 (0.9)**	**211 (1.1)**	**214 (0.8)**	**259 (0.6)**	**260 (0.8)**	**263 (0.8)**	**266 (0.8)**	**267 (1.0)**	**286 (0.8)**	**287 (0.9)**	**290 (0.7)**	**288 (0.8)**
Sex													
Male	203 (1.5)	207 (1.1)	211 (1.2)	215 (1.0)	259 (0.8)	261 (0.9)	264 (0.9)	268 (0.8)	270 (1.1)	288 (0.8)	288 (1.1)	292 (0.9)	290 (0.8)
Female	206 (1.1)	209 (1.2)	211 (1.1)	213 (0.9)	259 (0.7)	260 (0.9)	261 (0.8)	263 (0.8)	265 (0.9)	285 (0.9)	286 (0.9)	288 (0.8)	286 (1.0)
Race/ethnicity													
White	214 (1.3)	217 (1.3)	223 (1.1)	224 (1.1)	266 (0.8)	268 (0.9)	273 (0.6)	274 (0.7)	277 (0.9)	292 (0.8)	292 (1.0)	297 (0.8)	296 (0.7)
Black	176 (1.6)	186 (2.0)	191 (1.9)	198 (1.9)	238 (1.6)	240 (1.9)	244 (1.2)	250 (1.1)	251 (1.3)	265 (1.5)	267 (1.4)	270 (1.3)	268 (1.5)
Hispanic	175 (2.6)	184 (2.6)	194 (1.9)	198 (1.2)	243 (1.4)	240 (2.0)	248 (1.2)	252 (1.0)	257 (0.9)	267 (1.7)	271 (1.9)	275 (1.0)	275 (1.3)
Asian/Pacific Islander	204 (3.6)	216 (3.7)	214 (5.1)	221 (2.4)	261 (5.0)	264 (2.8)	270 (3.0)	275 (1.8)	279 (2.5)	283 (3.5)	294 (6.0)	296 (2.6)	293 (2.5)
Asian[3]	— (†)	— (†)	— (†)	— (†)	— (†)	— (†)	— (†)	— (†)	280 (2.5)	— (†)	— (†)	— (†)	— (†)
Pacific Islander[3]	— (†)	— (†)	— (†)	— (†)	— (†)	— (†)	— (†)	— (†)	‡ (†)	— (†)	— (†)	— (†)	— (†)
American Indian/Alaska Native	‡ (†)	‡ (†)	190 (5.9)	193 (6.2)	245 (3.4)	255 (4.4)	244 (6.3)	259 (5.0)	‡ (†)	272 (3.0)	283 (4.2)	278 (4.1)	278 (4.2)
Two or more races[3]	— (†)	— (†)	— (†)	— (†)	— (†)	— (†)	— (†)	— (†)	276 (1.9)	— (†)	— (†)	— (†)	— (†)
Parents' highest level of education[4]													
Did not finish high school	— (†)	— (†)	— (†)	— (†)	241 (1.3)	241 (2.8)	244 (1.2)	249 (0.9)	250 (1.3)	263 (1.4)	266 (1.6)	268 (1.3)	268 (1.7)
Graduated high school	— (†)	— (†)	— (†)	— (†)	251 (0.8)	251 (1.0)	252 (1.3)	255 (0.9)	255 (1.1)	276 (1.1)	274 (1.1)	278 (1.0)	277 (1.0)
Some education after high school	— (†)	— (†)	— (†)	— (†)	264 (0.8)	264 (1.0)	265 (0.9)	267 (0.9)	269 (0.8)	287 (1.2)	286 (0.8)	290 (0.8)	286 (0.8)
Graduated college	— (†)	— (†)	— (†)	— (†)	270 (0.8)	273 (0.9)	274 (0.8)	276 (0.8)	277 (1.1)	296 (0.9)	298 (1.2)	300 (0.8)	298 (0.8)
Eligibility for free or reduced-price lunch													
Eligible	— (†)	188 (1.4)	195 (1.1)	199 (0.9)	— (†)	242 (1.3)	247 (1.1)	253 (0.7)	254 (0.9)	— (†)	269 (1.4)	273 (1.0)	273 (1.0)
Not eligible	— (†)	219 (1.4)	224 (1.0)	227 (0.8)	— (†)	267 (1.1)	273 (0.7)	275 (0.8)	279 (1.0)	— (†)	289 (1.2)	295 (0.8)	294 (0.7)
Unknown	— (†)	217 (2.8)	227 (3.9)	225 (6.1)	— (†)	266 (2.0)	281 (2.7)	278 (2.0)	281 (2.5)	— (†)	294 (2.1)	300 (2.4)	300 (2.5)
Percentile[5]													
10th	147 (2.1)	157 (1.4)	165 (2.3)	169 (1.4)	217 (1.1)	216 (1.3)	221 (1.4)	227 (1.2)	229 (1.1)	243 (1.2)	244 (1.2)	249 (1.3)	246 (1.3)
25th	180 (1.5)	184 (1.4)	189 (1.3)	192 (1.6)	239 (0.9)	239 (0.9)	243 (0.9)	246 (0.9)	248 (1.0)	265 (1.2)	266 (1.1)	270 (1.0)	267 (1.3)
50th	210 (0.9)	211 (1.1)	213 (1.0)	216 (0.6)	261 (1.1)	262 (1.1)	265 (0.7)	267 (0.9)	269 (1.0)	288 (0.8)	288 (1.1)	291 (0.9)	290 (0.7)
75th	234 (1.2)	234 (1.0)	235 (1.1)	238 (0.9)	282 (0.7)	284 (1.0)	285 (0.7)	286 (0.7)	288 (1.0)	309 (0.9)	309 (1.0)	312 (0.7)	311 (0.6)
90th	253 (1.4)	254 (1.4)	254 (1.0)	256 (1.4)	299 (0.6)	302 (0.7)	302 (1.0)	302 (1.1)	303 (1.0)	326 (1.0)	326 (1.5)	329 (0.9)	328 (1.0)
	Standard deviation of the U.S. history scale score[6]												
All students	**41 (0.7)**	**38 (0.7)**	**34 (0.5)**	**34 (0.7)**	**32 (0.3)**	**33 (0.4)**	**32 (0.4)**	**29 (0.3)**	**29 (0.4)**	**32 (0.4)**	**32 (0.6)**	**31 (0.3)**	**32 (0.4)**
	Percent of students achieving U.S. history achievement levels												
Achievement level													
Below *Basic*[7]	36 (1.1)	34 (1.2)	30 (1.3)	27 (0.8)	39 (0.9)	38 (1.0)	35 (1.0)	31 (1.0)	29 (1.3)	57 (1.1)	57 (1.2)	53 (1.1)	55 (1.0)
At or above *Basic*[7]	64 (1.1)	66 (1.2)	70 (1.3)	73 (0.8)	61 (0.9)	62 (1.0)	65 (1.0)	69 (1.0)	71 (1.3)	43 (1.1)	43 (1.2)	47 (1.1)	45 (1.0)
At or above *Basic* by sex													
Male	62 (1.6)	65 (1.3)	69 (1.5)	73 (1.0)	61 (1.0)	62 (1.1)	67 (1.3)	71 (1.1)	74 (1.5)	45 (1.2)	45 (1.6)	50 (1.2)	49 (1.1)
Female	65 (1.4)	67 (1.4)	70 (1.2)	73 (1.0)	61 (1.3)	61 (1.2)	64 (1.0)	67 (1.2)	69 (1.4)	40 (1.4)	40 (1.2)	44 (1.2)	41 (1.4)
At or above *Basic* by race/ethnicity													
White	73 (1.3)	76 (1.5)	84 (1.2)	83 (1.0)	70 (1.1)	71 (1.1)	79 (0.8)	80 (0.9)	84 (1.2)	50 (1.2)	49 (1.3)	56 (1.3)	55 (1.2)
Black	35 (1.5)	41 (2.3)	46 (2.5)	54 (2.6)	32 (2.4)	35 (2.1)	40 (1.7)	48 (2.1)	47 (2.5)	17 (1.5)	19 (1.5)	20 (1.6)	20 (1.2)
Hispanic	36 (3.2)	40 (2.8)	49 (2.7)	56 (1.6)	41 (2.2)	36 (2.6)	46 (2.2)	52 (1.7)	59 (1.5)	22 (2.4)	24 (2.3)	27 (1.4)	28 (1.4)
Asian/Pacific Islander	62 (4.3)	74 (4.5)	71 (4.8)	82 (3.1)	60 (6.9)	65 (3.0)	75 (4.4)	78 (2.1)	82 (2.6)	40 (4.7)	51 (6.7)	54 (3.5)	50 (3.2)
Asian[3]	— (†)	— (†)	— (†)	— (†)	— (†)	— (†)	— (†)	— (†)	84 (2.6)	— (†)	— (†)	— (†)	— (†)
Pacific Islander[3]	— (†)	— (†)	— (†)	— (†)	— (†)	— (†)	— (†)	— (†)	‡ (†)	— (†)	— (†)	— (†)	— (†)
American Indian/Alaska Native	‡ (†)	‡ (†)	41 (7.7)	49 (5.4)	42 (6.2)	57 (6.5)	43 (6.1)	61 (6.3)	‡ (†)	21 (6.3)	37 (7.8)	32 (7.3)	29 (5.9)
Two or more races[3]	— (†)	— (†)	— (†)	— (†)	— (†)	— (†)	— (†)	— (†)	81 (2.5)	— (†)	— (†)	— (†)	— (†)
At or above *Proficient*[8]	17 (1.0)	18 (0.9)	18 (1.0)	20 (0.7)	14 (0.6)	16 (0.7)	17 (0.8)	17 (0.8)	18 (0.9)	11 (0.7)	11 (0.9)	13 (0.7)	12 (0.5)
At *Advanced*[9]	2 (0.3)	2 (0.3)	2 (0.3)	2 (0.3)	1 (0.1)	1 (0.2)	1 (0.1)	1 (0.1)	1 (0.2)	1 (0.2)	1 (0.3)	1 (0.2)	1 (0.1)

—Not available.

†Not applicable.

‡Reporting standards not met (too few cases for a reliable estimate).

[1]Accommodations were not permitted for this assessment.

[2]Scale ranges from 0 to 500.

[3]In U.S. history assessments prior to 2014, separate data for Asians, Pacific Islanders, and students of Two or more races were not collected.

[4]Based on student reports. Data for students whose parents have an unknown level of education are included in table totals, but not shown separately.

[5]The percentile represents a specific point on the percentage distribution of all students ranked by their U.S. history score from low to high. For example, 10 percent of students scored at or below the 10th percentile score, while 90 percent of students scored above it.

[6]The standard deviation provides an indication of how much the test scores varied. The lower the standard deviation, the closer the scores were clustered around the average score. About two-thirds of the student scores can be expected to fall within the range of one standard deviation above and one standard deviation below the average score. For example, the average score for all 8th-graders in 2014 was 267, and the standard deviation was 29. This means that about two-thirds of the students would be expected to have scores between 296 (one standard deviation above the average) and 238 (one standard deviation below). Standard errors also must be taken into account when making comparisons of these ranges.

[7]*Basic* denotes partial mastery of the knowledge and skills that are fundamental for proficient work.

[8]*Proficient* represents solid academic performance. Students reaching this level have demonstrated competency over challenging subject matter.

[9]*Advanced* signifies superior performance.

NOTE: In 2014, only 8th-grade students were assessed in U.S. history. Includes public and private schools. For 2001 and later years, includes students tested with accommodations (3 to 13 percent of all students, depending on grade level and year); excludes only those students with disabilities and English language learners who were unable to be tested even with accommodations (1 to 3 percent of all students). Race categories exclude persons of Hispanic ethnicity. Detail may not sum to totals because of rounding.

SOURCE: U.S. Department of Education, National Center for Education Statistics, National Assessment of Educational Progress (NAEP), 1994, 2001, 2006, 2010, and 2014 U.S. History Assessments, retrieved April 30, 2015, from the Main NAEP Data Explorer (http://nces.ed.gov/nationsreportcard/naepdata/). (This table was prepared April 2015.)

Table 224.60. Average National Assessment of Educational Progress (NAEP) writing scale score of 8th- and 12th-graders, standard deviation, and percentage of students attaining writing achievement levels, by selected student and school characteristics and percentile: 2011

[Standard errors appear in parentheses]

Selected student or school characteristic	8th-graders: Total, all students	8th-graders: Eligibility for free or reduced-price lunch: Eligible	8th-graders: Not eligible	8th-graders: Unknown	12th-graders: Total, all students	12th-graders: Eligibility for free or reduced-price lunch: Eligible	12th-graders: Not eligible	12th-graders: Unknown
1	2	3	4	5	6	7	8	9
	Average writing scale score[1]							
All students	**150 (0.7)**	**134 (0.6)**	**161 (0.8)**	**163 (2.2)**	**150 (0.5)**	**133 (0.7)**	**157 (0.6)**	**167 (1.7)**
Sex								
Male	140 (0.7)	125 (0.7)	151 (0.9)	154 (2.6)	143 (0.6)	126 (0.8)	150 (0.6)	162 (1.9)
Female	160 (0.7)	144 (0.6)	171 (0.8)	171 (2.5)	157 (0.6)	140 (0.7)	165 (0.6)	173 (1.9)
Race/ethnicity								
White	158 (0.8)	142 (0.8)	163 (0.9)	166 (2.3)	159 (0.7)	144 (1.0)	161 (0.7)	172 (1.6)
Black	132 (1.1)	127 (1.1)	145 (1.4)	140 (4.6)	130 (1.0)	124 (1.1)	140 (1.2)	148 (3.6)
Hispanic	136 (0.7)	130 (0.8)	150 (1.0)	150 (5.4)	134 (0.7)	128 (0.8)	142 (1.0)	149 (3.6)
Asian/Pacific Islander	163 (2.4)	146 (2.8)	171 (2.4)	175 (4.0)	158 (1.6)	146 (2.3)	163 (2.0)	162 (4.9)
Asian	165 (2.0)	148 (2.7)	172 (2.2)	175 (4.0)	158 (1.5)	146 (2.5)	164 (1.7)	162 (5.0)
Native Hawaiian/Pacific Islander	141 (6.3)	‡ (†)	‡ (†)	‡ (†)	144 (6.0)	‡ (†)	‡ (†)	‡ (†)
American Indian/Alaska Native	145 (4.0)	139 (4.3)	‡ (†)	‡ (†)	145 (3.5)	135 (4.4)	153 (4.4)	‡ (†)
Two or more races	155 (1.9)	141 (2.3)	165 (2.5)	‡ (†)	158 (2.3)	137 (4.2)	163 (2.8)	‡ (†)
Parents' highest level of education								
Did not finish high school	133 (1.0)	131 (1.0)	142 (2.0)	‡ (†)	129 (0.9)	127 (1.0)	135 (1.6)	‡ (†)
Graduated high school	138 (0.8)	131 (0.8)	149 (1.3)	146 (4.4)	138 (0.7)	131 (1.0)	145 (0.9)	153 (3.5)
Some education after high school	150 (0.9)	143 (0.9)	158 (1.2)	155 (3.8)	149 (0.5)	140 (0.9)	155 (0.6)	158 (2.2)
Graduated college	160 (0.8)	141 (0.8)	166 (0.9)	167 (2.3)	160 (0.7)	139 (1.1)	164 (0.7)	173 (1.5)
Student's attitude and experience								
Agreed or strongly agreed that "Writing is one of my favorite activities"	157 (0.8)	141 (0.8)	170 (0.9)	172 (2.5)	157 (0.6)	139 (0.8)	165 (0.6)	175 (2.0)
Uses a computer for writing school assignments once or twice a week	157 (0.9)	140 (0.7)	168 (1.2)	169 (2.9)	154 (0.6)	136 (0.8)	161 (0.7)	167 (1.4)
School locale								
City	144 (1.2)	130 (1.0)	160 (1.4)	164 (4.3)	146 (1.0)	131 (0.8)	156 (1.2)	168 (2.5)
Suburban	155 (1.3)	137 (1.0)	165 (1.3)	164 (4.4)	154 (0.9)	135 (1.1)	160 (0.9)	167 (2.1)
Town	148 (1.1)	137 (1.3)	156 (1.3)	157 (3.8)	149 (2.0)	134 (3.1)	156 (1.8)	‡ (†)
Rural	150 (1.4)	137 (1.5)	158 (1.3)	158 (5.3)	149 (1.1)	135 (1.5)	154 (1.0)	164 (5.4)
Percentile[2]								
10th	104 (1.0)	92 (1.1)	119 (1.1)	121 (3.8)	104 (0.9)	90 (0.9)	114 (1.1)	126 (4.6)
25th	127 (0.8)	113 (0.6)	140 (1.0)	142 (2.6)	127 (0.8)	111 (0.9)	136 (0.8)	149 (2.3)
50th	151 (0.8)	135 (0.6)	163 (0.9)	163 (2.6)	152 (0.7)	135 (1.1)	159 (0.8)	170 (2.2)
75th	175 (0.7)	157 (0.8)	184 (1.1)	185 (2.6)	175 (0.6)	156 (0.6)	180 (0.5)	189 (1.7)
90th	194 (0.9)	176 (0.9)	201 (1.4)	203 (3.5)	194 (0.7)	176 (0.8)	198 (0.8)	205 (3.2)
	Standard deviation of the writing scale score[3]							
All students	35 (0.3)	33 (0.3)	32 (0.3)	32 (1.1)	35 (0.3)	33 (0.3)	33 (0.3)	31 (0.9)
	Percent of students attaining writing achievement levels							
Achievement level								
Below *Basic*[4]	20 (0.6)	32 (0.8)	10 (0.6)	10 (1.6)	21 (0.6)	36 (0.9)	14 (0.5)	9 (1.3)
At or above *Basic*	80 (0.6)	68 (0.8)	90 (0.6)	90 (1.6)	79 (0.6)	64 (0.9)	86 (0.5)	91 (1.3)
At or above *Basic* by race/ethnicity								
White	87 (0.6)	76 (1.1)	91 (0.6)	94 (1.6)	87 (0.6)	76 (1.2)	88 (0.6)	95 (1.1)
Black	65 (1.7)	59 (1.7)	79 (2.1)	74 (6.4)	61 (1.5)	54 (1.7)	71 (1.9)	82 (3.9)
Hispanic	69 (0.9)	63 (1.1)	82 (1.2)	80 (5.4)	65 (0.9)	59 (1.1)	74 (1.4)	79 (4.7)
Asian/Pacific Islander	88 (2.3)	76 (3.4)	93 (1.8)	96 (2.1)	85 (1.4)	78 (2.7)	89 (1.4)	83 (4.4)
Asian	89 (1.9)	79 (3.0)	94 (1.7)	95 (2.2)	85 (1.4)	78 (2.9)	89 (1.3)	83 (4.4)
Native Hawaiian/Pacific Islander	70 (7.3)	‡ (†)	‡ (†)	‡ (†)	78 (5.0)	‡ (†)	‡ (†)	‡ (†)
American Indian/Alaska Native	78 (4.7)	74 (6.6)	‡ (†)	‡ (†)	76 (4.3)	66 (7.2)	84 (5.0)	‡ (†)
Two or more races	87 (1.7)	79 (3.9)	92 (1.9)	‡ (†)	86 (2.7)	70 (7.1)	90 (3.1)	‡ (†)
At or above *Proficient*[5]	27 (0.7)	12 (0.4)	37 (1.0)	39 (2.9)	27 (0.6)	12 (0.5)	33 (0.7)	46 (2.3)
At *Advanced*[6]	3 (0.2)	1 (0.1)	5 (0.4)	5 (1.2)	3 (0.2)	1 (0.1)	4 (0.3)	7 (1.2)

†Not applicable.

‡Reporting standards not met (too few cases for a reliable estimate).

[1]Scale ranges from 0 to 300.

[2]The percentile represents a specific point on the percentage distribution of all students ranked by their writing score from low to high. For example, 10 percent of students scored at or below the 10th percentile score, while 90 percent of students scored above it.

[3]The standard deviation provides an indication of how much the test scores varied. The lower the standard deviation, the closer the scores were clustered around the average score. About two-thirds of the student scores can be expected to fall within the range of one standard deviation above and one standard deviation below the average score. For example, the average score for all 12th-graders was 150 and the standard deviation was 35. This means that we would expect about two-thirds of the students to have scores between 185 (one standard deviation above the average) and 115 (one standard deviation below). Standard errors also must be taken into account when making comparisons of these ranges.

[4]*Basic* denotes partial mastery of the knowledge and skills that are fundamental for proficient work.

[5]*Proficient* represents solid academic performance. Students reaching this level have demonstrated competency over challenging subject matter.

[6]*Advanced* signifies superior performance.

NOTE: Writing scores from 2011 cannot be compared with writing scores from earlier assessment years. The 2011 writing assessment was developed under a new framework and is NAEP's first computer-based writing assessment. Includes public and private schools. Includes students tested with accommodations (8 percent of all 8th-graders and 7 percent of all 12th-graders); excludes only those students with disabilities and English language learners who were unable to be tested even with accommodations (2 percent of all students at both grades). Race categories exclude persons of Hispanic ethnicity. Detail may not sum to totals because of rounding.

SOURCE: U.S. Department of Education, National Center for Education Statistics, National Assessment of Educational Progress (NAEP), 2011 Writing Assessment, retrieved October 1, 2012, from the Main NAEP Data Explorer (http://nces.ed.gov/nationsreportcard/naepdata/). (This table was prepared October 2012.)

Table 203.10. Enrollment in public elementary and secondary schools, by level and grade: Selected years, fall 1980 through fall 2025
[In thousands]

Year	All grades	Elementary												Secondary					
		Total	Pre-kinder-garten	Kinder-garten	1st grade	2nd grade	3rd grade	4th grade	5th grade	6th grade	7th grade	8th grade	Un-graded	Total	9th grade	10th grade	11th grade	12th grade	Un-graded
1	2	3	4	5	6	7	8	9	10	11	12	13	14	15	16	17	18	19	20
1980	40,877	27,647	96	2,593	2,894	2,800	2,893	3,107	3,130	3,038	3,085	3,086	924	13,231	3,377	3,368	3,195	2,925	366
1985	39,422	27,034	151	3,041	3,239	2,941	2,895	2,771	2,776	2,789	2,938	2,982	511	12,388	3,439	3,230	2,866	2,550	303
1990	41,217	29,876	303	3,306	3,499	3,327	3,297	3,248	3,197	3,110	3,067	2,979	541	11,341	3,169	2,896	2,612	2,381	284
1991	42,047	30,503	375	3,311	3,556	3,360	3,334	3,315	3,268	3,239	3,181	3,020	542	11,544	3,313	2,915	2,645	2,392	278
1992	42,823	31,086	505	3,313	3,542	3,431	3,361	3,342	3,325	3,303	3,299	3,129	536	11,737	3,352	3,027	2,656	2,431	272
1993	43,465	31,502	545	3,377	3,529	3,429	3,437	3,361	3,350	3,356	3,355	3,249	513	11,963	3,487	3,050	2,751	2,424	250
1994	44,111	31,896	603	3,444	3,593	3,440	3,439	3,426	3,372	3,381	3,404	3,302	492	12,215	3,604	3,131	2,748	2,488	244
1995	44,840	32,338	637	3,536	3,671	3,507	3,445	3,431	3,438	3,395	3,422	3,356	500	12,502	3,704	3,237	2,826	2,487	247
1996	45,611	32,762	670	3,532	3,770	3,600	3,524	3,454	3,453	3,494	3,464	3,403	399	12,849	3,801	3,323	2,930	2,586	208
1997	46,127	33,071	695	3,503	3,755	3,689	3,597	3,507	3,458	3,492	3,520	3,415	440	13,056	3,819	3,376	2,972	2,673	216
1998	46,539	33,344	729	3,443	3,727	3,681	3,696	3,592	3,520	3,497	3,530	3,480	449	13,195	3,856	3,382	3,021	2,722	214
1999	46,857	33,486	751	3,397	3,684	3,656	3,691	3,686	3,604	3,564	3,541	3,497	415	13,371	3,935	3,415	3,034	2,782	205
2000	47,204	33,686	776	3,382	3,636	3,634	3,676	3,711	3,707	3,663	3,629	3,538	334	13,517	3,963	3,491	3,083	2,803	177
2001	47,672	33,936	865	3,379	3,614	3,593	3,653	3,695	3,727	3,769	3,720	3,616	304	13,736	4,012	3,528	3,174	2,863	159
2002	48,183	34,114	915	3,434	3,594	3,565	3,623	3,669	3,711	3,788	3,821	3,709	285	14,069	4,105	3,584	3,229	2,990	161
2003	48,540	34,201	950	3,503	3,613	3,544	3,611	3,619	3,685	3,772	3,841	3,809	255	14,339	4,190	3,675	3,277	3,046	150
2004	48,795	34,178	990	3,544	3,663	3,560	3,580	3,612	3,635	3,735	3,818	3,825	215	14,618	4,281	3,750	3,369	3,094	122
2005	49,113	34,204	1,036	3,619	3,691	3,606	3,586	3,578	3,633	3,670	3,777	3,802	205	14,909	4,287	3,866	3,454	3,180	121
2006	49,316	34,235	1,084	3,631	3,751	3,641	3,627	3,586	3,602	3,660	3,716	3,766	170	15,081	4,260	3,882	3,551	3,277	110
2007	49,291	34,204	1,081	3,609	3,750	3,704	3,659	3,624	3,600	3,628	3,700	3,709	139	15,086	4,200	3,863	3,557	3,375	92
2008	49,266	34,286	1,180	3,640	3,708	3,699	3,708	3,647	3,629	3,614	3,653	3,692	117	14,980	4,123	3,822	3,548	3,400	87
2009	49,361	34,409	1,223	3,678	3,729	3,665	3,707	3,701	3,652	3,644	3,641	3,651	119	14,952	4,080	3,809	3,541	3,432	90
2010	49,484	34,625	1,279	3,682	3,754	3,701	3,686	3,711	3,718	3,682	3,676	3,659	77	14,860	4,008	3,800	3,538	3,472	42
2011	49,522	34,773	1,291	3,746	3,773	3,713	3,703	3,672	3,699	3,724	3,696	3,679	77	14,749	3,957	3,751	3,546	3,452	43
2012	49,771	35,018	1,307	3,831	3,824	3,729	3,719	3,690	3,673	3,723	3,746	3,699	76	14,753	3,975	3,730	3,528	3,477	43
2013	50,045	35,251	1,328	3,834	3,885	3,791	3,738	3,708	3,697	3,684	3,748	3,753	85	14,794	3,980	3,761	3,526	3,476	52
	Projected																		
2014	50,132	35,249	1,290	3,723	3,877	3,851	3,799	3,735	3,714	3,714	3,708	3,753	85	14,883	4,038	3,765	3,555	3,474	52
2015	50,268	35,298	1,294	3,733	3,765	3,843	3,859	3,796	3,741	3,731	3,737	3,713	85	14,970	4,038	3,820	3,558	3,502	52
2016	50,385	35,402	1,298	3,746	3,775	3,733	3,851	3,856	3,802	3,759	3,755	3,743	85	14,983	3,995	3,820	3,611	3,506	52
2017	50,477	35,451	1,293	3,730	3,788	3,742	3,740	3,848	3,862	3,820	3,782	3,761	85	15,026	4,027	3,779	3,611	3,557	52
2018	50,528	35,491	1,293	3,732	3,772	3,755	3,750	3,737	3,854	3,881	3,844	3,788	85	15,037	4,046	3,810	3,572	3,557	52
2019	50,618	35,543	1,303	3,761	3,774	3,739	3,763	3,747	3,744	3,872	3,905	3,850	85	15,075	4,075	3,827	3,601	3,519	52
2020	50,774	35,559	1,313	3,788	3,803	3,741	3,747	3,760	3,753	3,761	3,897	3,911	85	15,215	4,142	3,855	3,618	3,548	52
2021	50,928	35,541	1,322	3,816	3,831	3,770	3,749	3,744	3,766	3,771	3,785	3,903	85	15,387	4,208	3,918	3,644	3,564	52
2022	51,084	35,558	1,331	3,842	3,859	3,798	3,778	3,746	3,750	3,784	3,795	3,791	85	15,526	4,199	3,980	3,704	3,590	52
2023	51,225	35,712	1,340	3,867	3,886	3,825	3,806	3,775	3,752	3,768	3,807	3,800	85	15,514	4,078	3,972	3,762	3,649	52
2024	51,338	35,878	1,348	3,890	3,911	3,852	3,833	3,803	3,781	3,770	3,792	3,813	85	15,460	4,089	3,858	3,754	3,707	52
2025	51,420	36,052	1,355	3,911	3,934	3,877	3,860	3,830	3,809	3,799	3,794	3,798	86	15,368	4,103	3,868	3,647	3,699	52

NOTE: Due to changes in reporting and imputation practices, prekindergarten enrollment for years prior to 1992 represent an undercount compared to later years. The total ungraded counts of students were prorated to the elementary and secondary levels based on prior reports. Detail may not sum to totals because of rounding.

SOURCE: U.S. Department of Education, National Center for Education Statistics, *Statistics of Public Elementary and Secondary School Systems, 1980–81*; Common Core of Data (CCD), "State Nonfiscal Survey of Public Elementary/Secondary Education," 1985–86 through 2013–14; and National Elementary and Secondary Enrollment Projection Model, 1972 through 2025. (This table was prepared January 2016.)

Table 203.20. Enrollment in public elementary and secondary schools, by region, state, and jurisdiction: Selected years, fall 1990 through fall 2025

Region, state, and jurisdiction	Actual total enrollment													Percent change in total enrollment, 2008 to 2013	Projected total enrollment						Percent change in total enrollment, 2013 to 2025
	Fall 1990	Fall 2000	Fall 2003	Fall 2004	Fall 2005	Fall 2006	Fall 2007	Fall 2008	Fall 2009	Fall 2010	Fall 2011	Fall 2012	Fall 2013		Fall 2014	Fall 2015	Fall 2016	Fall 2017	Fall 2020	Fall 2025	
1	2	3	4	5	6	7	8	9	10	11	12	13	14	15	16	17	18	19	20	21	22
United States	**41,216,683**	**47,203,539**	**48,540,215**	**48,795,465**	**49,113,298**	**49,315,842**	**49,290,559**	**49,265,572**	**49,360,982**	**49,484,181**	**49,521,669**	**49,771,118**	**50,044,522**	**1.6**	**50,131,600**	**50,268,100**	**50,385,200**	**50,477,400**	**50,774,000**	**51,419,700**	**2.7**
Region																					
Northeast	7,281,763	8,222,127	8,292,315	8,271,259	8,240,160	8,257,889	8,122,022	8,052,985	8,092,029	8,071,335	7,953,981	7,959,128	7,961,243	-1.1	7,918,000	7,888,600	7,866,000	7,841,700	7,761,000	7,578,400	-4.8
Midwest	9,943,761	10,729,987	10,808,977	10,775,409	10,818,815	10,819,248	10,770,210	10,742,973	10,672,171	10,609,604	10,573,792	10,559,230	10,572,920	-1.6	10,549,100	10,534,500	10,517,100	10,493,400	10,409,900	10,283,600	-2.7
South	14,807,016	17,007,261	17,672,745	17,891,987	18,103,166	18,293,633	18,422,773	18,490,770	18,651,889	18,805,000	18,955,932	19,128,376	19,298,714	4.4	19,432,000	19,576,400	19,699,500	19,804,500	20,134,800	20,810,400	7.8
West	9,184,143	11,244,164	11,766,178	11,856,810	11,951,157	11,945,072	11,975,554	11,978,844	11,944,893	11,998,242	12,037,964	12,124,384	12,211,645	1.9	12,232,500	12,268,600	12,302,700	12,337,800	12,468,300	12,747,200	4.4
State																					
Alabama	721,806	739,992	731,220	730,140	741,761	743,632	742,919	745,668	748,889	755,552	744,621	744,637	746,204	0.1	743,900	741,100	739,500	737,500	734,100	734,700	-1.5
Alaska	113,903	133,356	133,933	132,970	133,288	132,608	131,029	130,662	131,661	132,104	131,167	131,489	130,944	0.2	130,900	131,400	132,100	132,700	135,700	140,100	7.0
Arizona	639,853	877,696	1,012,068	1,043,298	1,094,454	1,068,249	1,087,447	1,087,817	1,077,831	1,071,751	1,080,319	1,089,384	1,102,445	1.3	1,108,100	1,116,000	1,123,900	1,134,900	1,174,100	1,250,700	13.4
Arkansas	436,286	449,959	454,523	463,115	474,206	476,409	479,016	478,965	480,559	482,114	483,114	486,157	489,979	2.3	490,500	490,800	491,300	491,700	493,800	500,400	2.1
California	4,950,474	6,140,814	6,413,867	6,441,557	6,437,202	6,406,750	6,343,471	6,322,528	6,263,438	6,289,578	6,287,834	6,299,451	6,312,623	-0.2	6,288,100	6,271,300	6,256,300	6,244,400	6,219,700	6,221,200	-1.4
Colorado	574,213	724,508	757,693	765,976	779,826	794,026	801,867	818,443	832,368	843,316	854,265	863,561	876,999	7.2	885,900	895,100	902,500	908,800	925,500	957,900	9.2
Connecticut	469,123	562,179	577,203	577,390	575,059	575,100	570,626	567,198	563,968	560,546	554,437	550,954	546,200	-3.7	538,200	531,700	525,100	518,000	498,500	468,600	-14.2
Delaware	99,658	114,676	117,668	119,091	120,937	122,254	122,574	125,430	126,801	129,403	128,946	129,026	131,687	5.0	132,400	133,300	134,500	135,500	138,100	139,900	6.2
District of Columbia	80,694	68,925	78,057	76,714	76,876	72,850	78,422	68,681	69,433	71,284	73,911	76,140	78,153	13.8	80,100	82,500	85,200	87,900	96,400	108,900	39.4
Florida	1,861,592	2,434,821	2,587,628	2,639,336	2,675,024	2,671,513	2,666,811	2,631,020	2,634,522	2,643,347	2,668,156	2,692,162	2,720,744	3.4	2,746,700	2,770,600	2,792,800	2,811,400	2,882,100	3,034,200	11.5
Georgia	1,151,687	1,444,937	1,522,611	1,553,437	1,598,461	1,629,157	1,649,589	1,655,792	1,667,685	1,677,067	1,685,016	1,703,332	1,723,909	4.1	1,737,800	1,750,500	1,760,400	1,768,500	1,797,200	1,873,600	8.7
Hawaii	171,708	184,360	183,609	183,185	182,818	180,728	179,897	179,478	180,196	179,601	182,706	184,760	186,825	4.1	187,700	188,900	190,400	191,800	194,900	195,800	4.8
Idaho	220,840	245,117	252,120	256,084	261,982	267,380	272,119	275,051	276,299	275,859	279,873	284,834	296,476	7.8	302,200	308,400	313,400	317,200	329,500	346,700	17.0
Illinois	1,821,407	2,048,792	2,100,961	2,097,503	2,111,706	2,118,276	2,112,805	2,119,707	2,104,175	2,091,654	2,083,097	2,072,880	2,066,990	-2.5	2,061,600	2,055,400	2,051,100	2,044,600	2,015,500	1,961,200	-5.1
Indiana	954,525	989,267	1,011,130	1,021,348	1,035,074	1,045,940	1,046,764	1,046,147	1,046,661	1,047,232	1,040,765	1,041,369	1,047,385	0.1	1,042,400	1,038,600	1,034,500	1,029,500	1,014,200	1,008,700	-3.7
Iowa	483,652	495,080	481,226	478,319	483,482	483,122	485,115	487,559	491,842	495,775	495,870	499,825	502,964	3.2	504,500	506,800	508,700	509,800	513,100	514,200	2.2
Kansas	437,034	470,610	470,490	469,136	467,525	469,506	468,295	471,060	474,489	483,701	486,108	489,043	496,440	5.4	498,600	502,100	504,800	507,300	512,800	517,600	4.3
Kentucky	636,401	665,850	663,369	674,796	679,878	683,152	666,225	670,030	680,089	673,128	681,987	685,167	677,389	1.1	673,300	671,000	669,200	667,600	663,300	661,800	-2.3
Louisiana	784,757	743,089	727,709	724,281	654,526	675,851	681,038	684,873	690,915	696,558	703,390	710,903	711,491	3.9	712,400	714,500	715,700	716,500	718,500	724,900	1.9
Maine	215,149	207,037	202,084	198,820	195,498	193,986	196,245	192,935	189,225	189,077	188,969	185,739	183,995	-4.6	182,000	180,100	178,000	176,100	170,800	161,900	-12.0
Maryland	715,176	852,920	869,113	865,561	860,020	851,640	845,700	843,861	848,412	852,211	854,086	859,638	866,169	2.6	871,800	879,200	886,800	894,400	912,200	922,200	6.5
Massachusetts	834,314	975,150	980,459	975,574	971,909	968,661	962,958	958,910	957,053	955,563	953,369	954,773	955,739	-0.3	951,500	947,900	943,700	939,700	927,500	910,700	-4.7
Michigan	1,584,431	1,720,626	1,757,604	1,751,290	1,742,282	1,722,656	1,692,739	1,659,921	1,649,082	1,587,067	1,573,537	1,555,370	1,548,841	-6.7	1,532,800	1,518,300	1,503,100	1,488,900	1,449,800	1,407,500	-9.1
Minnesota	756,374	854,340	842,854	838,503	839,243	840,565	837,578	836,048	837,053	838,037	839,738	845,404	850,973	1.8	858,900	864,900	871,700	877,300	890,100	893,200	5.0
Mississippi	502,417	497,871	493,540	495,376	494,954	495,026	494,122	491,962	492,481	490,526	490,619	493,650	492,586	0.1	490,900	489,900	488,400	486,200	479,800	471,200	-4.3
Missouri	816,558	912,744	905,941	905,449	917,705	920,353	917,188	917,871	917,982	918,710	916,584	917,900	918,288	#	916,200	915,300	913,800	912,500	911,000	911,200	-0.8
Montana	152,974	154,875	148,356	146,705	145,416	144,418	142,823	141,899	141,807	141,693	142,349	142,908	144,129	1.6	144,800	145,700	146,600	147,400	150,900	157,300	9.1
Nebraska	274,081	286,199	285,542	285,761	286,646	287,580	291,244	292,590	295,368	298,500	301,296	303,505	307,677	5.2	308,900	310,800	312,400	313,600	315,400	318,100	3.4
Nevada	201,316	340,706	385,401	400,083	412,395	424,766	429,362	433,371	428,947	437,149	439,634	445,707	451,831	4.3	455,700	461,500	466,800	471,700	487,500	516,200	14.2
New Hampshire	172,785	208,461	207,417	206,852	205,767	203,572	200,772	197,934	197,140	194,711	191,900	188,974	186,310	-5.9	183,300	180,500	177,700	175,200	168,200	159,100	-14.6
New Jersey	1,089,646	1,313,405	1,380,753	1,393,347	1,395,602	1,388,850	1,382,348	1,381,420	1,396,029	1,402,548	1,356,431	1,372,203	1,370,295	-0.8	1,365,700	1,362,000	1,358,700	1,355,200	1,341,400	1,309,600	-4.4
New Mexico	301,881	320,306	323,066	326,102	326,758	328,220	329,040	330,245	334,419	338,122	337,225	338,220	339,244	2.7	339,400	339,300	339,900	339,700	339,800	342,500	1.0
New York	2,598,337	2,882,188	2,864,775	2,836,337	2,815,581	2,809,649	2,765,435	2,740,592	2,766,052	2,734,955	2,704,718	2,710,703	2,732,770	-0.3	2,726,300	2,725,200	2,727,900	2,730,200	2,730,500	2,693,100	-1.5
North Carolina	1,086,871	1,293,638	1,360,209	1,385,754	1,416,436	1,444,481	1,489,492	1,488,645	1,483,397	1,490,605	1,507,864	1,518,465	1,530,857	2.8	1,536,900	1,544,000	1,549,300	1,553,700	1,566,500	1,610,100	5.2
North Dakota	117,825	109,201	102,233	100,513	98,283	96,670	95,059	94,728	95,073	96,323	97,646	101,111	103,947	9.7	106,900	110,000	112,900	115,900	125,000	135,000	29.9
Ohio	1,771,089	1,835,049	1,845,428	1,840,032	1,839,683	1,836,722	1,827,184	1,817,163	1,764,297	1,754,191	1,740,030	1,729,916	1,724,111	-5.1	1,714,400	1,707,600	1,698,700	1,689,500	1,660,900	1,621,000	-6.0
Oklahoma	579,087	623,110	626,160	629,476	634,739	639,391	642,065	645,108	654,802	659,911	666,120	673,483	681,848	5.7	686,400	693,100	698,800	703,500	717,200	736,300	8.0
Oregon	472,394	546,231	551,273	552,505	552,194	562,574	565,586	575,393	582,839	570,720	568,208	587,564	593,000	3.1	594,600	597,800	600,300	602,800	612,500	627,500	5.8
Pennsylvania	1,667,834	1,814,311	1,821,146	1,828,089	1,830,684	1,871,060	1,801,971	1,775,029	1,785,993	1,793,284	1,771,395	1,763,677	1,755,236	-1.1	1,742,300	1,734,200	1,729,200	1,722,700	1,703,400	1,662,000	-5.3
Rhode Island	138,813	157,347	159,375	156,498	153,422	151,612	147,629	145,342	145,118	143,793	142,854	142,481	142,008	-2.3	141,000	140,200	139,500	139,600	137,600	133,900	-5.7
South Carolina	622,112	677,411	699,198	703,736	701,544	708,021	712,317	718,113	723,143	725,838	727,186	735,998	745,657	3.8	754,600	763,200	769,900	775,100	791,200	815,900	9.4
South Dakota	129,164	128,603	125,537	122,798	122,012	121,158	121,606	126,429	123,713	126,128	128,016	130,471	130,890	3.5	131,600	132,900	134,400	135,800	139,800	142,600	9.0
Tennessee	824,595	909,161	936,682	941,091	953,928	978,368	964,259	971,950	972,549	987,422	999,693	993,496	993,556	2.2	995,800	999,100	1,002,700	1,005,300	1,018,600	1,051,300	5.8
Texas	3,382,887	4,059,619	4,331,751	4,405,215	4,525,394	4,599,509	4,674,832	4,752,148	4,850,210	4,935,715	5,000,470	5,077,659	5,153,702	8.4	5,221,000	5,291,000	5,348,300	5,399,800	5,545,700	5,825,000	13.0
Utah	446,652	481,485	495,981	503,607	508,430	523,386	576,244	559,778	571,586	585,552	598,832	613,279	625,461	11.7	635,600	646,100	655,300	663,200	688,800	739,300	18.2

See notes at end of table.

Table 203.20. Enrollment in public elementary and secondary schools, by region, state, and jurisdiction: Selected years, fall 1990 through fall 2025—Continued

Region, state, and jurisdiction	Actual total enrollment													Percent change in total enrollment, 2008 to 2013	Projected total enrollment						Percent change in total enrollment, 2013 to 2025
	Fall 1990	Fall 2000	Fall 2003	Fall 2004	Fall 2005	Fall 2006	Fall 2007	Fall 2008	Fall 2009	Fall 2010	Fall 2011	Fall 2012	Fall 2013		Fall 2014	Fall 2015	Fall 2016	Fall 2017	Fall 2020	Fall 2025	
1	2	3	4	5	6	7	8	9	10	11	12	13	14	15	16	17	18	19	20	21	22
Vermont	95,762	102,049	99,103	98,352	96,638	95,399	94,038	93,625	91,451	96,858	89,908	89,624	88,690	-5.3	87,800	86,900	86,100	85,100	83,100	79,600	-10.3
Virginia	998,601	1,144,915	1,192,092	1,204,739	1,213,616	1,220,440	1,230,857	1,235,795	1,245,340	1,251,440	1,257,883	1,265,419	1,273,825	3.1	1,279,200	1,286,000	1,292,000	1,297,000	1,310,700	1,331,100	4.5
Washington	839,709	1,004,770	1,021,349	1,020,005	1,031,985	1,026,774	1,030,247	1,037,018	1,035,347	1,043,788	1,045,453	1,051,694	1,058,936	2.1	1,065,400	1,072,200	1,079,200	1,086,200	1,109,600	1,149,300	8.5
West Virginia	322,389	286,367	281,215	280,129	280,866	281,939	282,535	282,729	282,662	282,879	282,870	283,044	280,958	-0.6	278,400	276,600	274,800	273,100	269,700	268,800	-4.3
Wisconsin	797,621	879,476	880,031	864,757	875,174	876,700	874,633	873,750	872,436	872,286	871,105	872,436	874,414	0.1	872,200	871,900	870,900	868,600	862,500	853,400	-2.4
Wyoming	98,226	89,940	87,462	84,733	84,409	85,193	86,422	87,161	88,155	89,009	90,099	91,533	92,732	6.4	93,900	95,000	96,000	96,900	99,800	102,700	10.8
Jurisdiction																					
Bureau of Indian Education	—	46,938	45,828	45,828	50,938	—	—	40,927	41,351	41,962	—	—	—	—	—	—	—	—	—	—	—
DoD, overseas	—	73,581	71,053	68,327	62,543	60,891	57,247	56,768	—	—	—	—	—	—	—	—	—	—	—	—	—
DoD, domestic	—	34,174	30,603	29,151	28,329	26,631	27,548	28,013	—	—	—	—	—	—	—	—	—	—	—	—	—
Other jurisdictions																					
American Samoa	12,463	15,702	15,893	16,126	16,438	16,400	—	—	—	—	—	—	—	—	—	—	—	—	—	—	—
Guam	26,391	32,473	31,572	30,605	30,986	—	—	—	—	31,618	31,243	31,186	33,414	—	—	—	—	—	—	—	—
Northern Marianas	6,449	10,004	11,244	11,601	11,718	11,695	11,299	10,913	10,961	11,105	11,011	10,646	10,638	-2.5	—	—	—	—	—	—	—
Puerto Rico	644,734	612,725	584,916	575,648	563,490	544,138	526,565	503,635	493,393	473,735	452,740	434,609	423,934	-15.8	—	—	—	—	—	—	—
U.S. Virgin Islands	21,750	19,459	17,716	16,429	16,750	16,284	15,903	15,768	15,493	15,495	15,711	15,192	14,953	-5.2	—	—	—	—	—	—	—

—Not available.
#Rounds to zero.
NOTE: DoD = Department of Defense. Detail may not sum to totals because of rounding. Some data have been revised from previously published figures.

SOURCE: U.S. Department of Education, National Center for Education Statistics, Common Core of Data (CCD), "State Nonfiscal Survey of Public Elementary/Secondary Education," 1990–91 through 2013–14; and State Public Elementary and Secondary Enrollment Projection Model, 1980 through 2025. (This table was prepared January 2016.)

Table 203.25. Public school enrollment in prekindergarten through grade 8, by region, state, and jurisdiction: Selected years, fall 1990 through fall 2025

Region, state, and jurisdiction	Actual enrollment													Percent change in enrollment, 2008 to 2013	Projected enrollment						Percent change in enrollment, 2013 to 2025
	Fall 1990	Fall 2000	Fall 2003	Fall 2004	Fall 2005	Fall 2006	Fall 2007	Fall 2008	Fall 2009	Fall 2010	Fall 2011	Fall 2012	Fall 2013		Fall 2014	Fall 2015	Fall 2016	Fall 2017	Fall 2020	Fall 2025	
1	2	3	4	5	6	7	8	9	10	11	12	13	14	15	16	17	18	19	20	21	22
United States	**29,875,914**	**33,686,421**	**34,200,741**	**34,177,565**	**34,203,962**	**34,234,751**	**34,204,081**	**34,285,564**	**34,409,260**	**34,624,530**	**34,772,751**	**35,017,893**	**35,250,792**	**2.8**	**35,249,000**	**35,297,700**	**35,401,900**	**35,451,100**	**35,559,400**	**36,051,800**	**2.3**
Region																					
Northeast	5,188,795	5,839,970	5,751,561	5,689,094	5,622,955	5,573,729	5,504,400	5,476,224	5,494,080	5,540,276	5,479,174	5,493,308	5,502,015	0.5	5,471,100	5,451,600	5,444,000	5,424,500	5,351,800	5,203,300	-5.4
Midwest	7,129,501	7,523,246	7,501,579	7,438,674	7,425,308	7,404,578	7,359,028	7,373,391	7,361,959	7,349,334	7,358,792	7,368,484	7,394,141	0.3	7,358,200	7,331,200	7,318,800	7,293,900	7,199,300	7,132,900	-3.5
South	10,858,800	12,314,176	12,675,179	12,780,160	12,881,836	12,989,696	13,085,045	13,166,980	13,300,643	13,434,553	13,578,211	13,711,284	13,830,129	5.0	13,883,100	13,953,300	14,047,000	14,129,500	14,378,800	14,808,200	7.1
West	6,698,818	8,009,029	8,272,422	8,269,637	8,273,863	8,266,748	8,255,608	8,268,969	8,252,578	8,300,367	8,356,574	8,444,817	8,524,507	3.1	8,536,600	8,561,600	8,592,100	8,603,200	8,629,500	8,907,400	4.5
State																					
Alabama	527,097	538,634	525,313	521,757	529,347	528,664	525,978	528,078	529,394	533,612	527,006	527,434	527,499	-0.1	524,300	522,800	523,200	523,800	525,300	522,800	-0.9
Alaska	85,297	94,442	93,695	91,981	91,225	90,167	88,980	89,263	90,824	91,990	92,057	93,069	92,714	3.9	93,000	93,600	94,600	95,700	97,700	100,000	7.9
Arizona	479,046	640,564	704,322	722,203	739,535	759,656	771,056	771,749	760,420	751,992	759,494	767,734	775,280	0.5	783,800	793,200	802,500	809,800	830,900	891,100	14.9
Arkansas	313,505	318,023	321,508	328,187	335,746	336,552	339,920	341,603	344,209	345,808	346,022	347,631	349,709	2.4	349,500	349,600	350,400	351,300	355,100	357,100	2.1
California	3,613,734	4,407,035	4,539,777	4,507,355	4,465,615	4,410,105	4,328,968	4,306,258	4,264,022	4,293,968	4,308,447	4,331,807	4,357,989	1.2	4,337,200	4,325,200	4,316,200	4,295,600	4,232,300	4,319,400	-0.9
Colorado	419,910	516,566	536,325	540,695	549,875	559,041	565,726	580,304	591,378	601,077	610,854	617,510	627,619	8.2	631,600	635,200	638,100	639,300	645,400	673,200	7.3
Connecticut	347,396	406,445	407,794	404,169	399,705	398,063	394,034	392,218	389,964	387,475	383,377	380,709	377,162	-3.8	371,400	366,100	361,700	355,900	341,300	323,100	-14.3
Delaware	72,606	80,801	82,898	83,599	84,639	84,996	85,019	86,811	87,710	90,279	90,624	91,004	93,204	7.4	93,700	94,500	95,200	95,500	95,800	97,600	4.7
District of Columbia	61,282	53,692	59,489	57,118	55,646	52,391	55,836	50,779	51,656	53,548	56,195	58,273	60,379	18.9	62,100	64,500	67,400	70,200	77,600	85,100	40.9
Florida	1,369,934	1,759,902	1,832,376	1,857,798	1,873,395	1,866,562	1,855,859	1,849,295	1,850,901	1,858,498	1,876,102	1,892,560	1,913,710	3.5	1,928,900	1,945,000	1,965,000	1,984,700	2,040,100	2,134,000	11.5
Georgia	849,082	1,059,983	1,103,181	1,118,379	1,145,446	1,166,508	1,178,577	1,185,684	1,194,751	1,202,479	1,211,250	1,222,289	1,233,877	4.1	1,237,600	1,241,600	1,248,100	1,255,300	1,278,900	1,336,500	8.3
Hawaii	122,840	132,293	130,054	128,788	127,472	126,008	125,556	125,910	127,477	127,525	131,005	133,590	135,925	8.0	136,700	138,100	139,100	139,700	140,700	139,900	2.9
Idaho	160,091	170,421	175,424	178,221	182,829	187,005	191,171	193,554	194,728	194,144	198,064	202,203	209,333	8.2	213,000	216,400	219,900	223,000	229,000	237,300	13.4
Illinois	1,309,516	1,473,933	1,492,725	1,483,644	1,480,320	1,477,679	1,472,909	1,479,195	1,463,713	1,454,793	1,453,156	1,448,201	1,445,459	-2.3	1,435,400	1,425,700	1,418,400	1,406,200	1,365,800	1,351,200	-6.5
Indiana	675,804	703,261	716,819	720,006	724,467	730,108	729,550	730,021	730,599	729,414	724,605	725,040	731,035	0.1	725,800	719,200	716,000	714,400	708,500	705,900	-3.4
Iowa	344,804	333,750	326,831	324,169	326,160	326,218	329,504	335,566	341,333	348,112	350,152	355,041	357,953	6.7	358,500	360,300	361,800	362,300	362,200	359,800	0.5
Kansas	319,648	323,157	322,491	321,176	320,513	326,201	326,771	331,079	332,997	342,927	347,129	349,695	355,929	7.5	356,600	358,000	360,000	361,000	362,800	364,400	2.4
Kentucky	459,200	471,429	478,254	485,794	487,429	487,165	469,373	472,204	484,466	480,334	488,456	491,065	485,001	2.7	481,400	478,700	478,300	476,700	474,700	476,400	-1.8
Louisiana	586,202	546,579	536,390	533,751	482,082	492,116	499,549	504,213	509,883	512,266	518,802	524,792	523,310	3.8	521,800	522,300	523,000	524,100	528,700	530,300	1.3
Maine	155,203	145,701	139,420	136,275	133,491	132,338	130,742	129,324	128,646	128,929	130,046	127,924	127,071	-1.7	125,600	124,300	123,300	122,000	117,500	111,500	-12.3
Maryland	526,744	609,043	605,862	597,417	588,571	579,065	576,479	576,473	581,785	588,156	594,216	602,802	612,580	6.3	618,700	626,400	631,900	635,900	642,200	638,200	4.2
Massachusetts	604,234	702,575	692,130	682,175	675,398	670,628	666,926	666,538	666,551	666,402	666,314	667,267	668,261	0.3	663,400	659,500	656,800	653,000	643,800	635,000	-5.0
Michigan	1,144,878	1,222,482	1,229,121	1,211,698	1,191,397	1,170,558	1,136,823	1,118,569	1,114,611	1,075,584	1,070,873	1,061,930	1,060,065	-5.2	1,044,900	1,032,700	1,024,400	1,015,200	990,100	970,900	-8.4
Minnesota	545,556	577,766	564,049	558,447	557,757	558,445	558,180	560,184	564,661	569,963	575,544	583,363	589,564	5.2	594,800	598,600	603,000	605,100	604,000	601,900	2.1
Mississippi	371,641	363,873	360,881	361,057	358,030	356,382	353,512	351,807	351,652	350,885	352,999	356,364	356,432	1.3	354,200	353,400	352,800	352,900	350,100	338,600	-5.0
Missouri	588,070	644,766	632,227	628,667	635,142	634,275	631,746	635,411	638,082	642,991	645,376	647,530	649,061	2.1	646,900	646,300	647,000	647,000	645,600	644,000	-0.8
Montana	111,169	105,226	100,160	98,673	97,770	97,021	96,354	96,869	97,868	98,491	99,725	100,819	101,991	5.3	103,000	103,800	104,600	105,300	107,300	111,900	9.7
Nebraska	198,080	195,486	195,417	194,816	195,055	195,769	200,095	202,912	206,860	210,292	213,504	215,432	219,122	8.0	218,900	219,200	219,100	218,600	216,600	222,100	1.4
Nevada	149,881	250,720	280,734	288,753	295,989	302,953	307,573	308,328	305,512	307,297	309,360	313,730	319,240	3.5	322,500	326,500	330,500	334,400	345,800	362,400	13.5
New Hampshire	126,301	147,121	142,031	140,241	138,584	136,188	134,359	132,995	132,768	131,576	129,632	128,169	126,933	-4.6	124,900	123,000	121,100	119,300	114,200	109,500	-13.8
New Jersey	783,422	967,533	978,440	975,856	970,592	963,418	954,418	956,765	968,332	981,255	947,576	956,070	956,379	#	951,900	949,100	947,600	944,100	930,400	903,800	-5.5
New Mexico	208,087	224,879	226,032	227,900	229,552	230,091	229,718	231,415	235,343	239,345	239,481	240,978	241,528	4.4	241,100	240,500	240,400	240,400	239,800	242,700	0.5
New York	1,827,418	2,028,906	1,978,181	1,942,575	1,909,028	1,887,284	1,856,315	1,843,080	1,847,003	1,869,150	1,857,574	1,868,561	1,884,845	2.3	1,879,000	1,880,600	1,886,900	1,888,400	1,884,200	1,838,400	-2.5
North Carolina	783,132	945,470	974,019	985,740	1,003,118	1,027,067	1,072,324	1,058,926	1,053,801	1,058,409	1,074,063	1,080,090	1,089,594	2.9	1,090,300	1,091,300	1,094,800	1,097,800	1,116,700	1,142,400	4.8
North Dakota	84,943	72,421	67,870	67,122	65,638	64,395	63,492	63,955	64,576	66,035	67,888	70,995	73,527	15.0	76,400	79,000	81,600	83,900	88,900	92,300	25.5
Ohio	1,257,580	1,293,646	1,278,202	1,267,088	1,261,331	1,253,193	1,241,322	1,239,494	1,225,346	1,222,808	1,217,226	1,211,299	1,208,500	-2.5	1,199,000	1,191,300	1,185,900	1,179,500	1,159,300	1,131,200	-6.4
Oklahoma	424,899	445,402	450,310	452,942	456,954	459,944	462,629	467,960	476,962	483,464	490,196	496,144	501,504	7.2	502,800	506,600	511,000	513,900	522,700	533,000	6.3
Oregon	340,243	379,264	378,052	376,933	379,680	380,576	383,598	395,421	404,451	392,601	391,310	409,325	414,405	4.8	416,100	418,900	422,100	424,600	431,200	437,700	5.6
Pennsylvania	1,172,164	1,257,824	1,235,624	1,234,828	1,227,625	1,220,074	1,205,351	1,194,327	1,200,446	1,209,766	1,204,850	1,204,732	1,201,169	0.6	1,195,500	1,190,800	1,189,500	1,185,700	1,168,400	1,134,600	-5.5
Rhode Island	101,797	113,545	111,209	107,040	103,870	101,996	99,159	97,983	98,184	97,734	97,659	97,809	98,738	0.8	98,500	97,800	97,200	96,500	94,500	92,100	-6.7
South Carolina	452,033	493,226	500,743	504,264	498,030	501,273	504,566	507,602	512,124	515,581	519,389	527,350	533,822	5.2	537,900	542,400	548,000	553,100	565,000	573,500	7.4
South Dakota	95,165	87,838	86,015	83,891	83,530	83,137	83,424	87,477	85,745	87,936	90,529	93,204	94,251	7.7	94,800	96,300	97,600	98,700	100,300	100,600	6.7
Tennessee	598,111	668,123	675,277	670,880	676,576	691,971	681,751	684,549	686,668	701,707	712,749	711,525	709,668	3.7	710,300	712,200	715,900	719,400	729,900	754,900	6.4
Texas	2,510,955	2,943,047	3,132,584	3,184,235	3,268,339	3,319,782	3,374,684	3,446,511	3,520,348	3,586,609	3,636,852	3,690,146	3,742,266	8.6	3,773,100	3,804,000	3,840,500	3,870,200	3,965,600	4,165,600	11.3
Utah	324,982	333,104	348,840	355,445	357,644	371,272	410,258	404,469	413,343	424,979	434,536	444,202	451,332	11.6	456,100	461,400	466,300	470,200	484,900	526,200	16.6

See notes at end of table.

Table 203.25. Public school enrollment in prekindergarten through grade 8, by region, state, and jurisdiction: Selected years, fall 1990 through fall 2025—Continued

Region, state, and jurisdiction	Actual enrollment													Percent change in enrollment, 2008 to 2013	Projected enrollment						Percent change in enrollment, 2013 to 2025
	Fall 1990	Fall 2000	Fall 2003	Fall 2004	Fall 2005	Fall 2006	Fall 2007	Fall 2008	Fall 2009	Fall 2010	Fall 2011	Fall 2012	Fall 2013		Fall 2014	Fall 2015	Fall 2016	Fall 2017	Fall 2020	Fall 2025	
1	2	3	4	5	6	7	8	9	10	11	12	13	14	15	16	17	18	19	20	21	22
Vermont	70,860	70,320	66,732	65,935	64,662	63,740	63,096	62,994	62,186	67,989	62,146	62,067	61,457	-2.4	60,900	60,400	59,900	59,400	57,600	55,200	-10.1
Virginia	728,280	815,748	837,258	839,687	841,299	841,685	850,444	855,008	864,020	871,446	881,225	889,444	896,573	4.9	897,900	900,700	905,000	908,900	915,800	927,300	3.4
Washington	612,597	694,367	699,248	695,405	699,482	694,858	697,407	704,794	705,387	714,172	718,184	724,560	730,868	3.7	735,200	740,700	748,700	755,600	774,200	793,600	8.6
West Virginia	224,097	201,201	198,836	197,555	197,189	197,573	198,545	199,477	200,313	201,472	202,065	202,371	201,001	0.8	198,500	197,300	196,500	195,900	194,800	195,100	-3.0
Wisconsin	565,457	594,740	589,812	577,950	583,998	584,600	585,212	589,528	593,436	598,479	602,810	606,754	609,675	3.4	606,100	604,700	604,000	601,900	595,200	588,500	-3.5
Wyoming	70,941	60,148	59,759	57,285	57,195	57,995	59,243	60,635	61,825	62,786	64,057	65,290	66,283	9.3	67,300	68,200	69,100	69,500	70,600	72,100	8.7
Jurisdiction																					
Bureau of Indian Education	—	35,746	33,671	33,671	36,133	—	—	30,612	31,381	31,985	—	—	—	—	—	—	—	—	—	—	—
DoD, overseas	—	59,299	56,226	53,720	48,691	47,589	44,418	43,931	—	—	—	—	—	—	—	—	—	—	—	—	—
DoD, domestic	—	30,697	27,500	26,195	25,558	24,052	24,807	25,255	—	—	—	—	—	—	—	—	—	—	—	—	—
Other jurisdictions																					
American Samoa	9,390	11,895	11,772	11,873	11,766	11,763	—	—	—	—	—	—	—	—	—	—	—	—	—	—	—
Guam	19,276	23,698	22,551	21,686	21,946	—	—	—	—	21,561	21,223	21,166	23,301	—	—	—	—	—	—	—	—
Northern Marianas	4,918	7,809	8,192	8,416	8,427	8,504	8,140	7,816	7,743	7,688	7,703	7,396	7,340	-6.1	—	—	—	—	—	—	—
Puerto Rico	480,356	445,524	418,649	408,671	399,447	382,647	372,514	355,115	347,638	334,613	318,924	305,048	294,976	-16.9	—	—	—	—	—	—	—
U.S. Virgin Islands	16,249	13,910	12,738	11,650	11,728	11,237	10,770	10,567	10,409	10,518	10,576	10,302	10,283	-2.7	—	—	—	—	—	—	—

—Not available.
#Rounds to zero.
NOTE: DoD = Department of Defense. Detail may not sum to totals because of rounding. Some data have been revised from previously published figures.

SOURCE: U.S. Department of Education, National Center for Education Statistics, Common Core of Data (CCD), "State Nonfiscal Survey of Public Elementary/Secondary Education," 1990–91 through 2013–14; and State Public Elementary and Secondary Enrollment Projection Model, 1980 through 2025. (This table was prepared January 2016.)

Table 203.30. Public school enrollment in grades 9 through 12, by region, state, and jurisdiction: Selected years, fall 1990 through fall 2025

Region, state, and jurisdiction	Actual enrollment													Percent change in enrollment, 2008 to 2013	Projected enrollment						Percent change in enrollment, 2013 to 2025
	Fall 1990	Fall 2000	Fall 2003	Fall 2004	Fall 2005	Fall 2006	Fall 2007	Fall 2008	Fall 2009	Fall 2010	Fall 2011	Fall 2012	Fall 2013		Fall 2014	Fall 2015	Fall 2016	Fall 2017	Fall 2020	Fall 2025	
1	2	3	4	5	6	7	8	9	10	11	12	13	14	15	16	17	18	19	20	21	22
United States	**11,340,769**	**13,517,118**	**14,339,474**	**14,617,900**	**14,909,336**	**15,081,091**	**15,086,478**	**14,980,008**	**14,951,722**	**14,859,651**	**14,748,918**	**14,753,225**	**14,793,730**	**-1.2**	**14,882,600**	**14,970,400**	**14,983,400**	**15,026,300**	**15,214,600**	**15,367,900**	**3.9**
Region																					
Northeast	2,092,968	2,382,157	2,540,754	2,582,165	2,617,205	2,684,160	2,617,622	2,576,761	2,597,949	2,531,059	2,474,807	2,465,820	2,459,228	-4.6	2,446,900	2,437,000	2,422,000	2,417,300	2,409,200	2,375,100	-3.4
Midwest	2,814,260	3,206,741	3,307,398	3,336,735	3,393,507	3,414,670	3,411,182	3,369,582	3,310,212	3,260,270	3,215,000	3,190,746	3,178,779	-5.7	3,190,900	3,203,300	3,198,300	3,199,500	3,210,600	3,150,700	-0.9
South	3,948,216	4,693,085	4,997,566	5,111,827	5,221,330	5,303,937	5,337,728	5,323,790	5,351,246	5,370,447	5,377,721	5,417,092	5,468,585	2.7	5,548,900	5,623,100	5,652,500	5,674,900	5,756,000	6,002,200	9.8
West	2,485,325	3,235,135	3,493,756	3,587,173	3,677,294	3,678,324	3,719,946	3,709,875	3,692,315	3,697,875	3,681,390	3,679,567	3,687,138	-0.6	3,695,900	3,707,000	3,710,600	3,734,600	3,838,800	3,839,800	4.1
State																					
Alabama	194,709	201,358	205,907	208,383	212,414	214,968	216,941	217,590	219,495	221,940	217,615	217,203	218,705	0.5	219,600	218,300	216,300	213,700	208,800	211,900	-3.1
Alaska	28,606	38,914	40,238	40,989	42,063	42,441	42,049	41,399	40,837	40,114	39,110	38,420	38,230	-7.7	37,900	37,800	37,500	37,000	38,000	40,100	4.8
Arizona	160,807	237,132	307,746	321,095	354,919	308,593	316,391	316,068	317,411	319,759	320,825	321,650	327,165	3.5	324,300	322,800	321,400	325,100	343,200	359,600	9.9
Arkansas	122,781	131,936	133,015	134,928	138,460	139,857	139,096	137,362	136,350	136,306	137,092	138,526	140,270	2.1	141,000	141,200	141,000	140,500	138,600	143,300	2.2
California	1,336,740	1,733,779	1,874,090	1,934,202	1,971,587	1,996,645	2,014,503	2,016,270	1,999,416	1,995,610	1,979,387	1,967,644	1,954,634	-3.1	1,951,000	1,946,100	1,940,100	1,948,800	1,987,500	1,901,800	-2.7
Colorado	154,303	207,942	221,368	225,281	229,951	234,985	236,141	238,139	240,990	242,239	243,411	246,051	249,380	4.7	254,400	259,900	264,400	269,500	280,100	284,700	14.1
Connecticut	121,727	155,734	169,409	173,221	175,354	177,037	176,592	174,980	174,004	173,071	171,060	170,245	169,038	-3.4	166,800	165,600	163,400	162,100	157,200	145,500	-13.9
Delaware	27,052	33,875	34,770	35,492	36,298	37,258	37,555	38,619	39,091	39,124	38,322	38,022	38,483	-0.4	38,600	38,900	39,300	40,000	42,300	42,300	10.0
District of Columbia	19,412	15,233	18,568	19,596	21,230	20,459	22,586	17,902	17,777	17,736	17,716	17,867	17,774	-0.7	18,000	18,000	17,800	17,700	18,800	23,900	34.2
Florida	491,658	674,919	755,252	781,538	801,629	804,951	810,952	781,725	783,621	784,849	792,054	799,602	807,034	3.2	817,800	825,600	827,800	826,700	842,000	900,300	11.6
Georgia	302,605	384,954	419,430	435,058	453,015	462,649	471,012	470,108	472,934	474,588	473,766	481,043	490,032	4.2	500,100	508,900	512,300	513,200	518,300	537,100	9.6
Hawaii	48,868	52,067	53,555	54,397	55,346	54,720	54,341	53,568	52,719	52,076	51,701	51,170	50,900	-5.0	51,100	50,700	51,200	52,100	54,200	55,900	9.8
Idaho	60,749	74,696	76,696	77,863	79,153	80,375	80,948	81,497	81,571	81,715	81,809	82,631	87,143	6.9	89,200	92,000	93,500	94,200	100,500	109,400	25.5
Illinois	511,891	574,859	608,236	613,859	631,386	640,597	639,896	640,512	640,462	636,861	629,941	624,679	621,531	-3.0	626,100	629,700	632,700	638,400	649,700	610,000	-1.9
Indiana	278,721	286,006	294,311	301,342	310,607	315,832	317,214	316,126	316,062	317,818	316,160	316,329	316,350	0.1	316,600	319,400	318,500	315,100	305,700	302,800	-4.3
Iowa	138,848	161,330	154,395	154,150	157,322	156,904	155,611	151,993	150,509	147,663	145,718	144,784	145,011	-4.6	146,000	146,500	146,900	147,600	150,900	154,400	6.5
Kansas	117,386	147,453	147,999	147,960	147,012	143,305	141,524	139,981	141,492	140,774	138,979	139,348	140,511	0.4	142,100	144,100	144,800	146,300	149,900	153,200	9.0
Kentucky	177,201	194,421	185,115	189,002	192,449	195,987	196,852	197,826	195,623	192,794	193,531	194,102	192,388	-2.7	191,900	192,300	190,800	190,900	188,600	185,300	-3.7
Louisiana	198,555	196,510	191,319	190,530	172,444	183,735	181,489	180,660	181,032	184,292	184,588	186,111	188,181	4.2	190,600	192,300	192,600	192,500	189,800	194,700	3.5
Maine	59,946	61,336	62,664	62,545	62,007	61,648	65,503	63,611	60,579	60,148	58,923	57,815	56,924	-10.5	56,400	55,700	54,700	54,000	53,300	50,400	-11.5
Maryland	188,432	243,877	263,251	268,144	271,449	272,575	269,221	267,388	266,627	264,055	259,870	256,836	253,589	-5.2	253,200	252,800	254,900	258,400	270,000	284,100	12.0
Massachusetts	230,080	272,575	288,329	293,399	296,511	298,033	296,032	292,372	290,502	289,161	287,055	287,506	287,478	-1.7	288,100	288,400	286,900	286,700	283,800	275,700	-4.1
Michigan	439,553	498,144	528,483	539,592	550,885	552,098	555,916	541,352	534,471	511,483	502,664	493,440	488,776	-9.7	487,800	485,600	478,800	473,700	459,700	436,600	-10.7
Minnesota	210,818	276,574	278,805	280,056	281,486	282,120	279,398	275,864	272,392	268,074	264,194	262,041	261,409	-5.2	264,100	266,300	268,700	272,100	286,000	291,200	11.4
Mississippi	130,776	133,998	132,659	134,319	136,924	138,644	140,610	140,155	140,829	139,641	137,620	137,286	136,154	-2.9	136,700	136,400	135,500	133,300	129,700	132,600	-2.6
Missouri	228,488	267,978	273,714	276,782	282,563	286,078	285,442	282,460	279,900	275,719	271,208	270,370	269,227	-4.7	269,400	269,000	266,800	265,400	265,300	267,200	-0.8
Montana	41,805	49,649	48,196	48,032	47,646	47,397	46,469	45,030	43,939	43,202	42,624	42,089	42,138	-6.4	41,900	41,900	42,000	42,100	43,600	45,400	7.7
Nebraska	76,001	90,713	90,125	90,945	91,591	91,811	91,149	89,678	88,508	88,208	87,792	88,073	88,555	-1.3	90,100	91,600	93,300	95,000	98,800	95,900	8.3
Nevada	51,435	89,986	104,667	111,330	116,406	121,813	121,789	125,043	123,435	129,852	130,274	131,977	132,591	6.0	133,100	135,100	136,400	137,400	141,800	153,800	16.0
New Hampshire	46,484	61,340	65,386	66,611	67,183	67,384	66,413	64,939	64,372	63,135	62,268	60,805	59,377	-8.6	58,500	57,500	56,600	55,900	54,000	49,600	-16.4
New Jersey	306,224	345,872	402,313	417,491	425,010	425,432	427,930	424,655	427,697	421,293	408,855	416,133	413,916	-2.5	413,700	412,900	411,100	411,100	410,900	405,800	-2.0
New Mexico	93,794	95,427	97,034	98,202	97,206	98,129	99,322	98,830	99,076	98,777	97,744	97,242	97,716	-1.1	98,300	98,800	99,500	99,300	100,000	99,800	2.1
New York	770,919	853,282	886,594	893,762	906,553	922,365	909,120	897,512	919,049	865,805	847,144	842,142	847,925	-5.5	847,300	844,600	841,000	841,700	846,200	854,700	0.8
North Carolina	303,739	348,168	386,190	400,014	413,318	417,414	417,168	429,719	429,596	432,196	433,801	438,375	441,263	2.7	446,600	452,700	454,400	455,800	449,900	467,600	6.0
North Dakota	32,882	36,780	34,363	33,391	32,645	32,275	31,567	30,773	30,497	30,288	29,758	30,116	30,420	-1.1	30,500	31,000	31,300	31,900	36,200	42,700	40.5
Ohio	513,509	541,403	567,226	572,944	578,352	583,529	585,862	577,669	538,951	531,383	522,804	518,617	515,611	-10.7	515,400	516,300	512,800	510,000	501,600	489,700	-5.0
Oklahoma	154,188	177,708	175,850	176,534	177,785	179,447	179,436	177,148	177,840	176,447	175,924	177,339	180,344	1.8	183,600	186,400	187,900	189,600	194,500	203,300	12.7
Oregon	132,151	166,967	173,221	175,572	172,514	181,998	181,988	179,972	178,388	178,119	176,898	178,239	178,595	-0.8	178,500	178,900	178,200	178,300	181,400	189,800	6.3
Pennsylvania	495,670	556,487	585,522	593,261	603,059	650,986	596,620	580,702	585,547	583,518	566,545	558,945	554,067	-4.6	546,800	543,400	539,700	536,900	535,100	527,300	-4.8
Rhode Island	37,016	43,802	48,166	49,458	49,552	49,616	48,470	47,359	46,934	46,059	45,195	44,672	43,270	-8.6	42,500	42,400	42,400	43,100	43,100	41,800	-3.5
South Carolina	170,079	184,185	198,455	199,472	203,514	206,748	207,751	210,511	211,019	210,257	207,797	208,648	211,835	0.6	216,700	220,800	222,000	222,000	226,200	242,300	14.4
South Dakota	33,999	40,765	39,522	38,907	38,482	38,021	38,182	38,952	37,968	38,192	37,487	37,267	36,639	-5.9	36,800	36,700	36,800	37,100	39,500	42,000	14.7
Tennessee	226,484	241,038	261,405	270,211	277,352	286,397	282,508	287,401	285,881	285,715	286,944	281,971	283,888	-1.2	285,500	286,900	286,800	285,800	288,700	296,400	4.4
Texas	871,932	1,116,572	1,199,167	1,220,980	1,257,055	1,279,727	1,300,148	1,305,637	1,329,862	1,349,106	1,363,618	1,387,513	1,411,436	8.1	1,447,900	1,487,000	1,507,800	1,529,600	1,580,100	1,659,500	17.6
Utah	121,670	148,381	147,141	148,162	150,786	152,114	165,986	155,309	158,243	160,573	164,296	169,077	174,129	12.1	179,600	184,600	189,000	193,100	203,900	213,200	22.4

See notes at end of table.

Table 203.30. Public school enrollment in grades 9 through 12, by region, state, and jurisdiction: Selected years, fall 1990 through fall 2025—Continued

Region, state, and jurisdiction	Actual enrollment													Percent change in enrollment, 2008 to 2013	Projected enrollment						Percent change in enrollment, 2013 to 2025
	Fall 1990	Fall 2000	Fall 2003	Fall 2004	Fall 2005	Fall 2006	Fall 2007	Fall 2008	Fall 2009	Fall 2010	Fall 2011	Fall 2012	Fall 2013		Fall 2014	Fall 2015	Fall 2016	Fall 2017	Fall 2020	Fall 2025	
1	2	3	4	5	6	7	8	9	10	11	12	13	14	15	16	17	18	19	20	21	22
Vermont	24,902	31,729	32,371	32,417	31,976	31,659	30,942	30,631	29,265	28,869	27,762	27,557	27,233	-11.1	26,900	26,500	26,200	25,700	25,600	24,400	-10.5
Virginia	270,321	329,167	354,834	365,052	372,317	378,755	380,413	380,787	381,320	379,994	376,658	375,975	377,252	-0.9	381,300	385,300	387,000	388,100	394,800	403,900	7.1
Washington	227,112	310,403	322,101	324,600	332,503	331,916	332,840	332,224	329,960	329,616	327,269	327,134	328,068	-1.3	330,200	331,500	330,500	330,600	335,400	355,700	8.4
West Virginia	98,292	85,166	82,379	82,574	83,677	84,366	83,990	83,252	82,349	81,407	80,805	80,673	79,957	-4.0	79,900	79,300	78,300	77,100	74,900	73,800	-7.7
Wisconsin	232,164	284,736	290,219	286,807	291,176	292,100	289,421	284,222	279,000	273,807	268,295	265,682	264,739	-6.9	266,000	267,200	266,800	266,600	267,300	265,000	0.1
Wyoming	27,285	29,792	27,703	27,448	27,214	27,198	27,179	26,526	26,330	26,223	26,042	26,243	26,449	-0.3	26,600	26,800	26,900	27,300	29,200	30,700	16.0
Jurisdiction																					
Bureau of Indian Education	—	11,192	12,157	12,157	14,805	—	—	10,315	9,970	9,977	—	—	—	—	—	—	—	—	—	—	—
DoD, overseas	—	14,282	14,827	14,607	13,852	13,302	12,829	12,837	—	—	—	—	—	—	—	—	—	—	—	—	—
DoD, domestic	—	3,477	3,103	2,956	2,771	2,579	2,741	2,758	—	—	—	—	—	—	—	—	—	—	—	—	—
Other jurisdictions																					
American Samoa	3,073	3,807	4,121	4,253	4,672	4,637	—	—	—	—	—	—	—	—	—	—	—	—	—	—	—
Guam	7,115	8,775	9,021	8,919	9,040	—	—	—	—	10,057	10,020	10,020	10,113	—	—	—	—	—	—	—	—
Northern Marianas	1,531	2,195	3,052	3,185	3,291	3,191	3,159	3,097	3,218	3,417	3,308	3,250	3,298	6.5	—	—	—	—	—	—	—
Puerto Rico	164,378	167,201	166,267	166,977	164,043	161,491	154,051	148,520	145,755	139,122	133,816	129,561	128,958	-13.2	—	—	—	—	—	—	—
U.S. Virgin Islands	5,501	5,549	4,978	4,779	5,022	5,047	5,133	5,201	5,084	4,977	5,135	4,890	4,670	-10.2	—	—	—	—	—	—	—

—Not available.
NOTE: DoD = Department of Defense. Detail may not sum to totals because of rounding. Some data have been revised from previously published figures.

SOURCE: U.S. Department of Education, National Center for Education Statistics, Common Core of Data (CCD), "State Nonfiscal Survey of Public Elementary/Secondary Education," 1990–91 through 2013–14; and State Public Elementary and Secondary Enrollment Projection Model, 1980 through 2025. (This table was prepared January 2016.)

Table 203.40. Enrollment in public elementary and secondary schools, by level, grade, and state or jurisdiction: Fall 2013

State or jurisdiction	Total, all grades	Elementary												Secondary					
		Total	Prekindergarten	Kindergarten	Grade 1	Grade 2	Grade 3	Grade 4	Grade 5	Grade 6	Grade 7	Grade 8	Elementary ungraded	Total	Grade 9	Grade 10	Grade 11	Grade 12	Secondary ungraded
1	2	3	4	5	6	7	8	9	10	11	12	13	14	15	16	17	18	19	20
United States	**50,044,522**	**35,250,792**	**1,328,434**	**3,833,526**	**3,884,820**	**3,791,122**	**3,737,690**	**3,707,733**	**3,696,718**	**3,684,476**	**3,747,574**	**3,753,357**	**85,342**	**14,793,730**	**3,979,521**	**3,760,559**	**3,525,617**	**3,476,132**	**51,901**
Alabama	746,204	527,499	9,415	59,757	60,315	56,909	56,003	55,719	55,699	56,428	58,455	58,799	0	218,705	62,069	56,144	51,527	48,965	0
Alaska	130,944	92,714	3,247	10,632	10,529	10,208	9,902	9,722	9,543	9,518	9,736	9,677	0	38,230	9,904	9,284	9,542	9,500	0
Arizona	1,102,445	775,280	8,791	86,258	88,553	85,814	85,149	84,282	84,535	83,495	84,315	83,849	239	327,165	83,995	81,410	77,448	84,291	21
Arkansas	489,979	349,709	14,984	39,900	39,720	36,244	36,090	36,321	36,146	36,564	36,876	36,660	204	140,270	37,934	36,447	34,158	31,646	85
California	6,312,623	4,357,989	75,951	506,831	470,812	485,674	474,323	470,515	469,645	462,125	465,592	472,381	4,140	1,954,634	491,493	484,993	477,425	498,403	2,320
Colorado	876,999	627,619	31,741	67,225	68,509	67,460	66,429	66,140	66,326	65,161	64,808	63,820	0	249,380	64,753	62,510	59,281	62,836	0
Connecticut	546,200	377,162	16,922	38,274	40,005	39,024	39,629	39,810	40,857	40,058	41,123	41,460	0	169,038	45,055	42,211	40,997	40,775	0
Delaware	131,687	93,204	1,413	10,488	10,370	10,487	10,220	10,069	10,209	9,965	9,990	9,993	0	38,483	11,418	9,718	8,811	8,536	0
District of Columbia	78,153	60,379	11,867	7,174	6,787	6,005	5,479	4,826	4,648	4,452	4,617	4,425	99	17,774	6,116	4,448	3,827	3,326	57
Florida	2,720,744	1,913,710	56,470	209,318	216,003	208,256	212,806	198,411	197,996	200,499	207,253	206,698	0	807,034	219,016	206,599	197,997	183,422	0
Georgia	1,723,909	1,233,877	45,427	136,658	137,101	133,003	131,114	129,329	128,527	129,456	131,967	131,295	0	490,032	148,721	128,105	110,112	103,094	0
Hawaii	186,825	135,925	1,577	17,561	16,271	15,419	15,269	14,810	14,631	13,952	13,090	13,228	117	50,900	14,595	13,132	12,154	10,925	94
Idaho	296,476	209,333	4,081	23,396	23,954	23,213	23,118	22,803	22,268	22,093	22,416	21,991	0	87,143	23,011	22,078	20,991	21,063	0
Illinois	2,066,990	1,445,459	80,953	145,117	152,879	149,990	151,750	152,779	151,364	152,129	153,920	154,578	0	621,531	165,333	159,174	152,458	144,566	0
Indiana	1,047,385	731,035	14,586	80,611	81,471	78,613	78,508	77,584	76,451	78,726	82,656	80,754	1,075	316,350	82,622	80,353	77,504	75,871	0
Iowa	502,964	357,953	28,075	41,240	37,397	36,717	36,026	35,617	35,606	35,371	35,666	36,238	0	145,011	36,944	36,349	35,460	36,258	0
Kansas	496,440	355,929	18,746	38,534	38,403	37,280	36,669	36,435	36,536	35,907	36,412	36,457	4,550	140,511	36,955	35,699	33,204	32,989	1,664
Kentucky	677,389	485,001	27,142	52,267	54,401	51,484	49,972	49,770	49,779	49,134	50,519	50,203	330	192,388	52,710	49,972	45,842	43,732	132
Louisiana	711,491	523,310	29,319	57,377	59,386	55,212	53,429	56,770	50,511	53,268	53,196	54,842	0	188,181	56,215	48,460	42,388	41,118	0
Maine	183,995	127,071	5,004	13,451	13,562	13,354	13,493	13,550	13,371	13,469	13,842	13,975	0	56,924	14,365	14,540	14,055	13,964	0
Maryland	866,169	612,580	29,811	67,548	68,373	66,320	64,855	64,629	63,817	63,243	61,662	62,322	0	253,589	69,952	64,688	59,835	59,114	0
Massachusetts	955,739	668,261	28,189	69,853	71,911	70,323	69,700	70,862	71,179	70,948	72,050	72,116	1,130	287,478	76,415	73,464	70,170	67,429	0
Michigan	1,548,841	1,060,065	40,660	106,166	113,323	111,901	110,437	113,420	112,175	113,458	117,440	118,440	2,645	488,776	126,842	127,799	116,270	116,607	1,258
Minnesota	850,973	589,564	14,556	65,618	65,960	64,575	63,654	63,979	62,900	61,871	63,552	62,899	0	261,409	64,424	63,815	64,080	69,090	0
Mississippi	492,586	356,432	4,329	41,948	42,925	39,096	37,301	36,959	36,118	37,018	37,516	37,896	5,326	136,154	37,991	34,605	30,560	29,412	3,586
Missouri	918,288	649,061	30,339	70,845	71,555	69,250	68,316	67,908	67,344	67,026	68,077	68,401	0	269,227	71,149	69,057	65,303	63,718	0
Montana	144,129	101,991	1,440	12,038	11,611	11,570	11,047	11,028	10,848	10,898	10,876	10,635	0	42,138	11,228	10,726	10,272	9,912	0
Nebraska	307,677	219,122	14,457	24,025	21,980	23,249	22,911	23,097	22,644	22,441	22,229	22,089	0	88,555	22,051	21,925	21,611	22,968	0
Nevada	451,831	319,240	4,707	35,073	37,162	35,414	34,491	33,827	33,863	34,478	34,886	34,541	798	132,591	34,497	33,935	32,682	31,450	27
New Hampshire	186,310	126,933	3,464	11,615	13,524	13,519	13,563	13,953	13,962	14,265	14,378	14,690	0	59,377	15,766	15,131	14,340	14,140	0
New Jersey	1,370,295	956,379	36,024	92,017	100,557	98,842	97,686	98,832	98,388	97,952	99,801	99,950	36,330	413,916	104,627	101,728	97,390	95,646	14,525
New Mexico	339,244	241,528	7,865	27,368	27,504	26,251	25,779	25,597	25,275	25,284	25,543	25,062	0	97,716	29,729	25,491	22,363	20,133	0
New York	2,732,770	1,884,845	48,968	201,930	209,128	203,908	198,174	196,988	198,824	197,036	199,676	203,267	26,946	847,925	223,440	213,861	192,944	190,081	27,599
North Carolina	1,530,857	1,089,594	30,978	122,209	123,140	119,088	115,962	108,034	116,515	116,654	119,049	117,965	0	441,263	126,737	114,718	103,355	96,453	0
North Dakota	103,947	73,527	2,054	8,822	8,608	8,405	7,857	7,824	7,536	7,471	7,598	7,352	0	30,420	7,813	7,749	7,469	7,389	0
Ohio	1,724,111	1,208,500	28,477	131,003	132,883	129,681	128,124	128,668	129,598	130,755	134,269	135,042	0	515,611	147,490	134,963	118,551	114,607	0
Oklahoma	681,848	501,504	42,770	54,923	56,067	51,556	49,975	49,603	49,276	48,587	48,751	48,583	1,413	180,344	50,284	47,179	42,850	39,498	533
Oregon	593,000	414,405	25,902	42,728	44,741	43,602	42,649	42,858	42,752	42,449	43,202	43,522	0	178,595	44,396	44,491	42,633	47,075	0
Pennsylvania	1,755,236	1,201,169	8,499	129,360	133,419	131,275	129,889	132,216	131,917	131,345	135,962	137,287	0	554,067	144,721	140,209	133,554	135,583	0
Rhode Island	142,008	98,738	2,242	10,490	10,823	10,697	10,676	11,037	10,751	10,865	10,864	10,293	0	43,270	10,912	11,304	10,651	10,403	0

See notes at end of table.

Table 203.40. Enrollment in public elementary and secondary schools, by level, grade, and state or jurisdiction: Fall 2013—Continued

State or jurisdiction	Total, all grades	Elementary												Secondary					
		Total	Prekindergarten	Kindergarten	Grade 1	Grade 2	Grade 3	Grade 4	Grade 5	Grade 6	Grade 7	Grade 8	Elementary ungraded	Total	Grade 9	Grade 10	Grade 11	Grade 12	Secondary ungraded
1	2	3	4	5	6	7	8	9	10	11	12	13	14	15	16	17	18	19	20
South Carolina	745,657	533,822	24,295	58,226	60,401	57,286	55,331	54,672	54,512	55,267	57,070	56,762	0	211,835	63,304	55,463	48,444	44,624	0
South Dakota	130,890	94,251	2,865	11,898	10,855	10,446	10,310	9,842	9,621	9,499	9,384	9,531	0	36,639	10,062	9,385	8,707	8,485	0
Tennessee	993,556	709,668	25,756	78,601	80,082	77,373	75,382	74,401	74,124	73,970	75,070	74,909	0	283,888	77,917	72,827	67,290	65,854	0
Texas	5,153,702	3,742,266	248,150	391,731	409,446	394,449	390,023	383,586	382,945	376,623	385,527	379,786	0	1,411,436	408,892	362,937	330,538	309,069	0
Utah	625,461	451,332	12,373	50,386	51,413	50,197	49,048	49,041	48,483	47,161	46,821	46,409	0	174,129	45,902	44,431	42,469	41,327	0
Vermont	88,690	61,457	5,667	6,215	6,246	6,017	6,254	6,159	6,108	6,163	6,296	6,332	0	27,233	7,137	6,828	6,723	6,545	0
Virginia	1,273,825	896,573	33,166	96,058	99,806	97,162	95,384	95,625	93,994	94,524	95,076	95,778	0	377,252	102,293	96,496	89,754	88,709	0
Washington	1,058,936	730,868	11,957	81,559	83,314	80,412	79,203	78,929	78,538	77,603	79,400	79,953	0	328,068	82,991	81,205	79,162	84,710	0
West Virginia	280,958	201,001	15,472	21,541	21,319	20,284	20,224	20,418	20,164	20,543	20,402	20,634	0	79,957	22,257	20,688	18,713	18,299	0
Wisconsin	874,414	609,675	56,777	61,522	62,479	60,999	60,697	61,393	60,768	60,505	61,814	62,721	0	264,739	67,985	64,958	65,450	66,346	0
Wyoming	92,732	66,283	514	8,141	7,837	7,609	7,410	7,086	7,131	6,804	6,884	6,867	0	26,449	7,093	6,877	6,303	6,176	0
Bureau of Indian Education	—	—	—	—	—	—	—	—	—	—	—	—	—	—	—	—	—	—	—
DoD, overseas	—	—	—	—	—	—	—	—	—	—	—	—	—	—	—	—	—	—	—
DoD, domestic	—	—	—	—	—	—	—	—	—	—	—	—	—	—	—	—	—	—	—
Other jurisdictions																			
American Samoa	—	—	—	—	—	—	—	—	—	—	—	—	—	—	—	—	—	—	—
Guam	33,414	23,301	828	3,113	2,818	2,788	2,243	2,337	2,244	2,251	2,315	2,364	0	10,113	3,284	3,063	2,000	1,766	0
Northern Marianas	10,638	7,340	462	544	770	730	720	750	773	782	926	814	69	3,298	1,084	862	696	656	0
Puerto Rico	423,934	294,976	1,410	27,752	32,864	30,684	31,193	31,076	30,264	31,073	34,510	34,365	9,785	128,958	33,525	32,990	29,971	27,374	5,098
U.S. Virgin Islands	14,953	10,283	—	1,167	1,112	1,141	1,117	1,150	1,137	1,175	1,213	1,071	0	4,670	1,573	1,093	992	1,012	0

—Not available.
NOTE: DoD = Department of Defense. The total ungraded counts of students were prorated to the elementary and secondary levels based on prior reports.
SOURCE: U.S. Department of Education, National Center for Education Statistics, Common Core of Data (CCD), "State Nonfiscal Survey of Public Elementary/Secondary Education," 2013–14. (This table was prepared August 2015.)

Table 203.45. Enrollment in public elementary and secondary schools, by level, grade, and state or jurisdiction: Fall 2012

State or jurisdiction	Total, all grades	Elementary												Secondary					
		Total	Prekindergarten	Kindergarten	Grade 1	Grade 2	Grade 3	Grade 4	Grade 5	Grade 6	Grade 7	Grade 8	Elementary ungraded	Total	Grade 9	Grade 10	Grade 11	Grade 12	Secondary ungraded
1	2	3	4	5	6	7	8	9	10	11	12	13	14	15	16	17	18	19	20
United States	**49,771,118**	**35,017,893**	**1,306,991**	**3,830,982**	**3,823,604**	**3,729,465**	**3,719,135**	**3,690,224**	**3,672,977**	**3,723,354**	**3,746,485**	**3,698,977**	**75,699**	**14,753,225**	**3,975,264**	**3,729,960**	**3,528,256**	**3,477,025**	**42,720**
Alabama	744,637	527,434	9,032	59,428	58,287	56,361	55,868	55,859	56,523	58,240	59,685	58,151	0	217,203	61,642	56,229	50,387	48,945	0
Alaska	131,489	93,069	3,131	10,569	10,393	10,109	9,950	9,756	9,677	9,844	9,834	9,806	0	38,420	9,724	9,415	9,585	9,696	0
Arizona	1,089,384	767,734	9,304	86,265	86,474	84,763	83,883	83,892	83,093	83,540	83,568	82,769	183	321,650	82,291	80,074	77,518	81,751	16
Arkansas	486,157	347,631	14,290	40,463	37,093	36,450	36,362	36,140	36,569	36,727	36,693	36,607	237	138,526	37,978	36,343	33,373	30,734	98
California	6,299,451	4,331,807	74,360	489,274	489,420	474,656	470,243	468,007	462,439	463,024	470,054	465,967	4,363	1,967,644	497,945	487,566	482,903	496,754	2,476
Colorado	863,561	617,510	30,375	66,951	67,369	66,134	65,667	65,921	64,727	64,448	63,658	62,260	0	246,051	63,859	60,842	58,847	62,503	0
Connecticut	550,954	380,709	16,393	39,410	39,558	39,858	39,867	40,895	40,196	40,979	41,533	42,020	0	170,245	45,166	42,144	42,192	40,743	0
Delaware	129,026	91,004	1,291	10,128	10,393	10,123	9,963	10,089	9,619	9,699	9,983	9,716	0	38,022	11,056	9,670	8,931	8,365	0
District of Columbia	76,140	58,273	11,428	6,980	6,163	5,629	4,991	4,631	4,575	4,627	4,559	4,202	488	17,867	6,275	4,245	3,740	3,317	290
Florida	2,692,162	1,892,560	55,124	210,489	208,344	202,517	209,027	195,358	197,412	204,704	205,469	204,116	0	799,602	215,693	206,662	194,054	183,193	0
Georgia	1,703,332	1,222,289	45,252	136,837	133,482	130,176	129,257	128,538	129,054	130,803	130,458	128,432	0	481,043	146,953	124,928	108,084	101,078	0
Hawaii	184,760	133,590	1,509	17,497	15,555	15,264	14,810	14,572	14,383	13,315	13,772	12,791	122	51,170	14,786	13,307	12,255	10,721	101
Idaho	284,834	202,203	2,683	22,409	22,535	22,508	22,247	21,884	22,000	22,304	21,963	21,670	0	82,631	21,987	20,812	20,702	19,130	0
Illinois	2,072,880	1,448,201	81,475	147,315	150,312	150,336	154,232	151,409	151,508	154,031	155,078	152,505	0	624,679	165,536	160,924	151,946	146,273	0
Indiana	1,041,369	725,040	9,114	80,681	80,151	77,465	80,476	75,678	78,450	82,158	80,959	79,908	0	316,329	82,545	80,253	78,645	74,886	0
Iowa	499,825	355,041	27,729	41,381	36,730	35,891	35,455	35,492	35,142	35,469	36,058	35,694	0	144,784	36,752	36,240	35,538	36,254	0
Kansas	489,043	349,695	18,475	38,379	37,304	36,399	36,009	36,167	35,546	35,962	35,963	35,447	4,044	139,348	37,060	34,486	33,499	32,810	1,493
Kentucky	685,167	491,065	26,753	53,875	54,028	51,296	51,215	50,583	49,999	51,550	51,154	50,259	353	194,102	53,562	49,561	46,806	44,032	141
Louisiana	710,903	524,792	29,426	58,691	58,085	54,765	53,691	57,434	51,799	53,866	54,528	52,507	0	186,111	55,745	46,920	43,267	40,179	0
Maine	185,739	127,924	4,890	13,727	13,449	13,575	13,628	13,345	13,427	13,778	13,978	14,127	0	57,815	14,684	14,421	14,248	14,462	0
Maryland	859,638	602,802	29,671	66,896	66,274	64,595	64,272	63,703	63,204	61,120	62,159	60,908	0	256,836	71,360	64,841	60,657	59,978	0
Massachusetts	954,773	667,267	28,245	69,669	70,629	69,549	70,673	70,952	70,826	71,588	72,012	72,048	1,076	287,506	77,458	72,264	69,928	67,856	0
Michigan	1,555,370	1,061,930	36,769	107,986	113,035	110,939	113,332	112,068	112,720	116,465	118,538	117,640	2,438	493,440	128,111	128,144	117,453	118,564	1,168
Minnesota	845,404	583,363	14,695	65,745	64,520	63,357	63,659	62,523	61,355	62,547	62,627	62,335	0	262,041	63,743	64,278	63,510	70,510	0
Mississippi	493,650	356,364	4,026	43,208	40,851	38,001	37,735	36,663	37,336	37,646	39,034	36,745	5,119	137,286	37,825	34,874	31,434	29,676	3,477
Missouri	917,900	647,530	29,684	71,778	70,072	68,570	68,043	67,493	67,269	67,959	68,605	68,057	0	270,370	72,240	68,242	65,737	64,151	0
Montana	142,908	100,819	1,321	11,709	11,678	11,031	11,036	10,861	10,822	10,842	10,624	10,895	0	42,089	11,256	10,676	10,373	9,784	0
Nebraska	303,505	215,432	13,831	22,095	23,331	22,836	23,057	22,583	22,370	21,998	21,893	21,438	0	88,073	21,796	21,725	21,400	23,152	0
Nevada	445,707	313,730	4,599	35,008	35,429	34,266	33,557	33,462	33,787	34,364	34,373	34,192	693	131,977	34,025	33,462	32,527	31,939	24
New Hampshire	188,974	128,169	3,260	11,892	13,692	13,531	13,861	13,907	14,253	14,284	14,705	14,784	0	60,805	16,321	15,243	14,641	14,600	0
New Jersey	1,372,203	956,070	35,128	94,830	98,464	97,499	98,305	98,152	97,328	98,744	99,624	100,052	37,944	416,133	105,857	101,466	96,504	97,048	15,258
New Mexico	338,220	240,978	7,509	27,662	26,932	26,208	25,818	25,474	25,573	25,490	25,135	25,177	0	97,242	29,217	25,711	21,755	20,559	0
New York	2,710,703	1,868,561	48,712	202,670	205,963	199,600	199,088	198,361	196,709	198,595	202,583	200,642	15,638	842,142	225,291	215,312	193,257	192,112	16,170
North Carolina	1,518,465	1,080,090	30,329	121,389	120,038	116,691	107,832	116,264	116,351	118,514	117,535	115,147	0	438,375	126,694	113,605	103,428	94,648	0
North Dakota	101,111	70,995	1,848	8,578	8,367	7,710	7,725	7,380	7,292	7,339	7,256	7,500	0	30,116	7,801	7,536	7,432	7,347	0
Ohio	1,729,916	1,211,299	27,558	131,874	131,637	128,867	129,079	129,295	130,392	133,468	135,174	133,955	0	518,617	148,752	133,301	118,941	117,623	0
Oklahoma	673,483	496,144	42,154	55,115	54,039	50,660	49,840	49,274	48,675	48,486	48,640	47,856	1,405	177,339	49,577	45,628	42,200	39,407	527
Oregon	587,564	409,325	23,850	42,642	43,438	42,436	42,532	42,401	42,235	42,916	43,297	43,578	0	178,239	44,662	43,751	43,103	46,723	0
Pennsylvania	1,763,677	1,204,732	10,109	129,624	131,691	129,861	131,638	131,315	130,592	134,359	137,172	136,775	1,596	558,945	144,396	140,180	136,531	136,357	1,481
Rhode Island	142,481	97,809	2,068	10,786	10,429	10,737	10,968	10,831	10,820	10,900	10,299	9,971	0	44,672	12,014	11,330	10,819	10,509	0

See notes at end of table.

Table 203.45. Enrollment in public elementary and secondary schools, by level, grade, and state or jurisdiction: Fall 2012—Continued

State or jurisdiction	Total, all grades	Elementary												Secondary					
		Total	Prekindergarten	Kindergarten	Grade 1	Grade 2	Grade 3	Grade 4	Grade 5	Grade 6	Grade 7	Grade 8	Elementary ungraded	Total	Grade 9	Grade 10	Grade 11	Grade 12	Secondary ungraded
1	2	3	4	5	6	7	8	9	10	11	12	13	14	15	16	17	18	19	20
South Carolina	735,998	527,350	23,786	58,641	58,030	55,275	54,354	54,058	54,541	56,493	56,807	55,365	0	208,648	61,897	54,033	47,963	44,755	0
South Dakota	130,471	93,204	3,117	11,901	10,546	10,316	9,874	9,657	9,458	9,377	9,550	9,408	0	37,267	10,018	9,548	8,885	8,816	0
Tennessee	993,496	711,525	27,096	81,186	79,010	75,716	74,934	74,425	74,311	75,116	75,272	74,459	0	281,971	76,794	71,810	67,068	66,299	0
Texas	5,077,659	3,690,146	250,911	390,636	396,903	389,225	382,990	378,750	376,426	380,202	377,246	366,857	0	1,387,513	403,136	350,949	328,003	305,425	0
Utah	613,279	444,202	12,329	50,378	50,171	48,872	48,926	48,362	46,991	46,540	46,246	45,387	0	169,077	44,379	42,760	41,164	40,774	0
Vermont	89,624	62,067	5,705	6,273	6,096	6,269	6,196	6,133	6,190	6,291	6,373	6,541	0	27,557	7,004	6,980	6,817	6,756	0
Virginia	1,265,419	889,444	32,852	96,935	97,267	95,231	95,405	94,005	93,941	94,874	95,147	93,787	0	375,975	101,867	94,931	90,206	88,971	0
Washington	1,051,694	724,560	12,466	80,789	80,494	78,904	78,723	78,244	77,331	78,966	79,371	79,272	0	327,134	82,972	80,696	78,485	84,981	0
West Virginia	283,044	202,371	15,781	21,785	20,788	20,459	20,483	20,181	20,698	20,623	21,052	20,521	0	80,673	22,741	20,397	18,832	18,703	0
Wisconsin	872,436	606,754	55,008	62,422	61,037	60,585	61,243	60,670	60,253	61,369	62,310	61,857	0	265,682	67,699	64,507	66,346	67,130	0
Wyoming	91,533	65,290	540	8,131	7,628	7,394	7,116	7,127	6,790	6,811	6,879	6,874	0	26,243	7,122	6,738	6,337	6,046	0
Bureau of Indian Education	—	—	—	—	—	—	—	—	—	—	—	—	—	—	—	—	—	—	—
DoD, overseas	—	—	—	—	—	—	—	—	—	—	—	—	—	—	—	—	—	—	—
DoD, domestic	—	—	—	—	—	—	—	—	—	—	—	—	—	—	—	—	—	—	—
Other jurisdictions																			
American Samoa	—	—	—	—	—	—	—	—	—	—	—	—	—	—	—	—	—	—	—
Guam	31,186	21,166	13	2,207	2,329	2,317	2,408	2,325	2,348	2,364	2,383	2,472	0	10,020	3,101	3,269	2,089	1,561	0
Northern Marianas	10,646	7,396	462	582	745	686	740	776	799	825	934	792	55	3,250	1,078	794	748	630	0
Puerto Rico	434,609	305,048	1,050	27,887	33,453	32,372	31,647	31,345	32,116	33,811	36,096	35,547	9,724	129,561	34,414	32,839	30,216	27,169	4,923
U.S. Virgin Islands	15,192	10,302	—	1,052	1,146	1,118	1,108	1,144	1,243	1,129	1,278	1,084	0	4,890	1,651	1,193	1,051	995	0

—Not available.
NOTE: DoD = Department of Defense. The total ungraded counts of students were prorated to the elementary and secondary levels based on prior reports.
SOURCE: U.S. Department of Education, National Center for Education Statistics, Common Core of Data (CCD), "State Nonfiscal Survey of Public Elementary/Secondary Education," 2012–13. (This table was prepared October 2014.)

Table 203.50. Enrollment and percentage distribution of enrollment in public elementary and secondary schools, by race/ethnicity and region: Selected years, fall 1995 through fall 2025

Region and year	Enrollment (in thousands)							Percentage distribution						
	Total	White	Black	Hispanic	Asian/ Pacific Islander	American Indian/ Alaska Native	Two or more races	Total	White	Black	Hispanic	Asian/ Pacific Islander	American Indian/ Alaska Native	Two or more races
1	2	3	4	5	6	7	8	9	10	11	12	13	14	15
United States														
1995	44,840	29,044	7,551	6,072	1,668	505	—	100.0	64.8	16.8	13.5	3.7	1.1	†
2000	47,204	28,878	8,100	7,726	1,950	550	—	100.0	61.2	17.2	16.4	4.1	1.2	†
2001	47,672	28,735	8,177	8,169	2,028	564	—	100.0	60.3	17.2	17.1	4.3	1.2	†
2002	48,183	28,618	8,299	8,594	2,088	583	—	100.0	59.4	17.2	17.8	4.3	1.2	†
2003	48,540	28,442	8,349	9,011	2,145	593	—	100.0	58.6	17.2	18.6	4.4	1.2	†
2004	48,795	28,318	8,386	9,317	2,183	591	—	100.0	58.0	17.2	19.1	4.5	1.2	†
2005	49,113	28,005	8,445	9,787	2,279	598	—	100.0	57.0	17.2	19.9	4.6	1.2	†
2006	49,316	27,801	8,422	10,166	2,332	595	—	100.0	56.4	17.1	20.6	4.7	1.2	†
2007	49,291	27,454	8,392	10,454	2,396	594	—	100.0	55.7	17.0	21.2	4.9	1.2	†
2008	49,266	27,057	8,358	10,563	2,451	589	247[1]	100.0	54.9	17.0	21.4	5.0	1.2	0.5[1]
2009	49,361	26,702	8,245	10,991	2,484	601	338[1]	100.0	54.1	16.7	22.3	5.0	1.2	0.7[1]
2010	49,484	25,933	7,917	11,439	2,466	566	1,164	100.0	52.4	16.0	23.1	5.0	1.1	2.4
2011	49,522	25,602	7,827	11,759	2,513	547	1,272	100.0	51.7	15.8	23.7	5.1	1.1	2.6
2012	49,771	25,386	7,803	12,104	2,552	534	1,393	100.0	51.0	15.7	24.3	5.1	1.1	2.8
2013	50,045	25,160	7,805	12,452	2,593	523	1,511	100.0	50.3	15.6	24.9	5.2	1.0	3.0
2014[2]	50,132	25,007	7,828	12,740	2,637	516	1,404	100.0	49.9	15.6	25.4	5.3	1.0	2.8
2015[2]	50,268	24,789	7,817	13,030	2,678	508	1,445	100.0	49.3	15.6	25.9	5.3	1.0	2.9
2016[2]	50,385	24,566	7,806	13,306	2,723	499	1,484	100.0	48.8	15.5	26.4	5.4	1.0	2.9
2017[2]	50,477	24,340	7,796	13,563	2,769	490	1,519	100.0	48.2	15.4	26.9	5.5	1.0	3.0
2018[2]	50,528	24,128	7,776	13,791	2,799	483	1,552	100.0	47.8	15.4	27.3	5.5	1.0	3.1
2019[2]	50,618	23,993	7,754	13,964	2,846	472	1,590	100.0	47.4	15.3	27.6	5.6	0.9	3.1
2020[2]	50,774	23,882	7,756	14,142	2,892	463	1,638	100.0	47.0	15.3	27.9	5.7	0.9	3.2
2021[2]	50,928	23,777	7,774	14,300	2,934	457	1,685	100.0	46.7	15.3	28.1	5.8	0.9	3.3
2022[2]	51,084	23,686	7,799	14,437	2,979	451	1,731	100.0	46.4	15.3	28.3	5.8	0.9	3.4
2023[2]	51,225	23,614	7,819	14,541	3,029	447	1,777	100.0	46.1	15.3	28.4	5.9	0.9	3.5
2024[2]	51,338	23,544	7,832	14,615	3,083	443	1,821	100.0	45.9	15.3	28.5	6.0	0.9	3.5
2025[2]	51,420	23,465	7,836	14,677	3,139	439	1,863	100.0	45.6	15.2	28.5	6.1	0.9	3.6
Northeast														
1995	7,894	5,497	1,202	878	295	21	—	100.0	69.6	15.2	11.1	3.7	0.3	†
2000	8,222	5,545	1,270	1,023	361	24	—	100.0	67.4	15.4	12.4	4.4	0.3	†
2003	8,292	5,455	1,284	1,124	403	27	—	100.0	65.8	15.5	13.6	4.9	0.3	†
2005	8,240	5,317	1,282	1,189	425	27	—	100.0	64.5	15.6	14.4	5.2	0.3	†
2008	8,053	5,041	1,226	1,267	467	27	25[1]	100.0	62.6	15.2	15.7	5.8	0.3	0.3[1]
2009	8,092	5,010	1,230	1,308	487	27	30[1]	100.0	61.9	15.2	16.2	6.0	0.3	0.4[1]
2010	8,071	4,876	1,208	1,364	500	27	96	100.0	60.4	15.0	16.9	6.2	0.3	1.2
2011	7,954	4,745	1,166	1,394	510	27	113	100.0	59.7	14.7	17.5	6.4	0.3	1.4
2012	7,959	4,665	1,161	1,444	523	27	138	100.0	58.6	14.6	18.1	6.6	0.3	1.7
2013	7,961	4,593	1,158	1,492	533	28	158	100.0	57.7	14.5	18.7	6.7	0.3	2.0
Midwest														
1995	10,512	8,335	1,450	438	197	92	—	100.0	79.3	13.8	4.2	1.9	0.9	†
2000	10,730	8,208	1,581	610	239	92	—	100.0	76.5	14.7	5.7	2.2	0.9	†
2003	10,809	8,055	1,644	751	262	97	—	100.0	74.5	15.2	7.0	2.4	0.9	†
2005	10,819	7,950	1,654	836	283	96	—	100.0	73.5	15.3	7.7	2.6	0.9	†
2008	10,743	7,734	1,632	963	314	99	—	100.0	72.0	15.2	9.0	2.9	0.9	†
2009	10,672	7,622	1,606	1,000	318	98	29[1]	100.0	71.4	15.0	9.4	3.0	0.9	0.3[1]
2010	10,610	7,327	1,505	1,077	312	94	294	100.0	69.1	14.2	10.2	2.9	0.9	2.8
2011	10,574	7,240	1,485	1,127	321	90	311	100.0	68.5	14.0	10.7	3.0	0.9	2.9
2012	10,559	7,175	1,464	1,167	330	89	334	100.0	68.0	13.9	11.1	3.1	0.8	3.2
2013	10,573	7,111	1,464	1,212	341	87	358	100.0	67.3	13.8	11.5	3.2	0.8	3.4
South														
1995	16,118	9,565	4,236	1,890	280	148	—	100.0	59.3	26.3	11.7	1.7	0.9	†
2000	17,007	9,501	4,516	2,468	352	170	—	100.0	55.9	26.6	14.5	2.1	1.0	†
2003	17,673	9,437	4,656	2,980	410	189	—	100.0	53.4	26.3	16.9	2.3	1.1	†
2005	18,103	9,381	4,738	3,334	456	194	—	100.0	51.8	26.2	18.4	2.5	1.1	†
2008	18,491	9,190	4,771	3,790	537	203	—	100.0	49.7	25.8	20.5	2.9	1.1	†
2009	18,652	9,074	4,710	4,039	555	219	55[1]	100.0	48.6	25.3	21.7	3.0	1.2	0.3[1]
2010	18,805	8,869	4,545	4,206	555	207	424	100.0	47.2	24.2	22.4	3.0	1.1	2.3
2011	18,956	8,830	4,535	4,353	577	198	463	100.0	46.6	23.9	23.0	3.0	1.0	2.4
2012	19,128	8,780	4,545	4,513	595	191	504	100.0	45.9	23.8	23.6	3.1	1.0	2.6
2013	19,299	8,722	4,561	4,671	614	185	546	100.0	45.2	23.6	24.2	3.2	1.0	2.8
West														
1995	10,316	5,648	662	2,866	896	244	—	100.0	54.7	6.4	27.8	8.7	2.4	†
2000	11,244	5,624	733	3,625	998	264	—	100.0	50.0	6.5	32.2	8.9	2.4	†
2003	11,766	5,496	765	4,156	1,070	280	—	100.0	46.7	6.5	35.3	9.1	2.4	†
2005	11,951	5,356	771	4,428	1,115	281	—	100.0	44.8	6.5	37.1	9.3	2.4	†
2008	11,979	5,092	728	4,543	1,133	261	222[1]	100.0	42.5	6.1	37.9	9.5	2.2	1.9[1]
2009	11,945	4,997	699	4,645	1,124	256	223[1]	100.0	41.8	5.9	38.9	9.4	2.1	1.9[1]
2010	11,998	4,861	659	4,792	1,100	237	349	100.0	40.5	5.5	39.9	9.2	2.0	2.9
2011	12,038	4,787	642	4,886	1,105	233	385	100.0	39.8	5.3	40.6	9.2	1.9	3.2
2012	12,124	4,766	632	4,978	1,104	227	417	100.0	39.3	5.2	41.1	9.1	1.9	3.4
2013	12,212	4,733	623	5,077	1,105	224	449	100.0	38.8	5.1	41.6	9.1	1.8	3.7

—Not available.
†Not applicable.
[1]For this year, data on students of Two or more races were reported by only a small number of states. Therefore, the data are not comparable to figures for 2010 and later years.
[2]Projected.
NOTE: Race categories exclude persons of Hispanic ethnicity. Enrollment data for students not reported by race/ethnicity were prorated by state and grade to match state totals. Prior to 2008, data on students of Two or more races were not collected. Some data have been revised from previously published figures. Detail may not sum to totals because of rounding.
SOURCE: U.S. Department of Education, National Center for Education Statistics, Common Core of Data (CCD), "State Nonfiscal Survey of Public Elementary and Secondary Education," 1995–96 through 2013–14; and National Elementary and Secondary Enrollment by Race/Ethnicity Projection Model, 1972 through 2025. (This table was prepared January 2016.)

Table 203.60. Enrollment and percentage distribution of enrollment in public elementary and secondary schools, by race/ethnicity and level of education: Fall 1999 through fall 2025

Level of education and year	Enrollment (in thousands) Total	White	Black	Hispanic	Asian/Pacific Islander Total	Asian	Pacific Islander	American Indian/ Alaska Native	Two or more races	Percentage distribution Total	White	Black	Hispanic	Asian/Pacific Islander Total	Asian	Pacific Islander	American Indian/ Alaska Native	Two or more races
1	2	3	4	5	6	7	8	9	10	11	12	13	14	15	16	17	18	19
Total																		
1999	46,857	29,035	8,066	7,327	1,887	—	—	542	—	100.0	62.0	17.2	15.6	4.0	†	†	1.2	†
2000	47,204	28,878	8,100	7,726	1,950	—	—	550	—	100.0	61.2	17.2	16.4	4.1	†	†	1.2	†
2001	47,672	28,735	8,177	8,169	2,028	—	—	564	—	100.0	60.3	17.2	17.1	4.3	†	†	1.2	†
2002	48,183	28,618	8,299	8,594	2,088	—	—	583	—	100.0	59.4	17.2	17.8	4.3	†	†	1.2	†
2003	48,540	28,442	8,349	9,011	2,145	—	—	593	—	100.0	58.6	17.2	18.6	4.4	†	†	1.2	†
2004	48,795	28,318	8,386	9,317	2,183	—	—	591	—	100.0	58.0	17.2	19.1	4.5	†	†	1.2	†
2005	49,113	28,005	8,445	9,787	2,279	—	—	598	—	100.0	57.0	17.2	19.9	4.6	†	†	1.2	†
2006	49,316	27,801	8,422	10,166	2,332	—	—	595	—	100.0	56.4	17.1	20.6	4.7	†	†	1.2	†
2007	49,291	27,454	8,392	10,454	2,396	—	—	594	—	100.0	55.7	17.0	21.2	4.9	†	†	1.2	†
2008	49,266	27,057	8,358	10,563	2,451	2,405	46	589	247 [1]	100.0	54.9	17.0	21.4	5.0	4.9	0.1	1.2	0.5 [1]
2009	49,361	26,702	8,245	10,991	2,484	2,435	49	601	338 [1]	100.0	54.1	16.7	22.3	5.0	4.9	0.1	1.2	0.7 [1]
2010	49,484	25,933	7,917	11,439	2,466	2,296	171	566	1,164	100.0	52.4	16.0	23.1	5.0	4.6	0.3	1.1	2.4
2011	49,522	25,602	7,827	11,759	2,513	2,334	179	547	1,272	100.0	51.7	15.8	23.7	5.1	4.7	0.4	1.1	2.6
2012	49,771	25,386	7,803	12,104	2,552	2,372	180	534	1,393	100.0	51.0	15.7	24.3	5.1	4.8	0.4	1.1	2.8
2013	50,045	25,160	7,805	12,452	2,593	2,417	176	523	1,511	100.0	50.3	15.6	24.9	5.2	4.8	0.4	1.0	3.0
2014[2]	50,132	25,007	7,828	12,740	2,637	2,463	174	516	1,404	100.0	49.9	15.6	25.4	5.3	4.9	0.3	1.0	2.8
2015[2]	50,268	24,789	7,817	13,030	2,678	2,506	172	508	1,445	100.0	49.3	15.6	25.9	5.3	5.0	0.3	1.0	2.9
2016[2]	50,385	24,566	7,806	13,306	2,723	2,553	170	499	1,484	100.0	48.8	15.5	26.4	5.4	5.1	0.3	1.0	2.9
2017[2]	50,477	24,340	7,796	13,563	2,769	2,600	168	490	1,519	100.0	48.2	15.4	26.9	5.5	5.2	0.3	1.0	3.0
2018[2]	50,528	24,128	7,776	13,791	2,799	2,633	167	483	1,552	100.0	47.8	15.4	27.3	5.5	5.2	0.3	1.0	3.1
2019[2]	50,618	23,993	7,754	13,964	2,846	2,682	164	472	1,590	100.0	47.4	15.3	27.6	5.6	5.3	0.3	0.9	3.1
2020[2]	50,774	23,882	7,756	14,142	2,892	2,730	162	463	1,638	100.0	47.0	15.3	27.9	5.7	5.4	0.3	0.9	3.2
2021[2]	50,928	23,777	7,774	14,300	2,934	2,775	160	457	1,685	100.0	46.7	15.3	28.1	5.8	5.4	0.3	0.9	3.3
2022[2]	51,084	23,686	7,799	14,437	2,979	2,821	158	451	1,731	100.0	46.4	15.3	28.3	5.8	5.5	0.3	0.9	3.4
2023[2]	51,225	23,614	7,819	14,541	3,029	2,872	157	447	1,777	100.0	46.1	15.3	28.4	5.9	5.6	0.3	0.9	3.5
2024[2]	51,338	23,544	7,832	14,615	3,083	2,926	157	443	1,821	100.0	45.9	15.3	28.5	6.0	5.7	0.3	0.9	3.5
2025[2]	51,420	23,465	7,836	14,677	3,139	2,981	158	439	1,863	100.0	45.6	15.2	28.5	6.1	5.8	0.3	0.9	3.6
Prekindergarten through grade 8																		
1999	33,486	20,327	5,952	5,512	1,303	—	—	391	—	100.0	60.7	17.8	16.5	3.9	†	†	1.2	†
2000	33,686	20,130	5,981	5,830	1,349	—	—	397	—	100.0	59.8	17.8	17.3	4.0	†	†	1.2	†
2001	33,936	19,960	6,004	6,159	1,409	—	—	405	—	100.0	58.8	17.7	18.1	4.2	†	†	1.2	†
2002	34,114	19,764	6,042	6,446	1,447	—	—	415	—	100.0	57.9	17.7	18.9	4.2	†	†	1.2	†
2003	34,201	19,558	6,015	6,729	1,483	—	—	415	—	100.0	57.2	17.6	19.7	4.3	†	†	1.2	†
2004	34,178	19,368	5,983	6,909	1,504	—	—	413	—	100.0	56.7	17.5	20.2	4.4	†	†	1.2	†
2005	34,204	19,051	5,954	7,216	1,569	—	—	412	—	100.0	55.7	17.4	21.1	4.6	†	†	1.2	†
2006	34,235	18,863	5,882	7,465	1,611	—	—	414	—	100.0	55.1	17.2	21.8	4.7	†	†	1.2	†
2007	34,204	18,679	5,821	7,632	1,660	—	—	412	—	100.0	54.6	17.0	22.3	4.9	†	†	1.2	†
2008	34,286	18,501	5,793	7,689	1,705	1,674	31	410	187 [1]	100.0	54.0	16.9	22.4	5.0	4.9	0.1	1.2	0.5 [1]
2009	34,409	18,316	5,713	7,977	1,730	1,697	33	419	254 [1]	100.0	53.2	16.6	23.2	5.0	4.9	0.1	1.2	0.7 [1]
2010	34,625	17,823	5,495	8,314	1,711	1,589	122	394	887	100.0	51.5	15.9	24.0	4.9	4.6	0.4	1.1	2.6
2011	34,773	17,654	5,470	8,558	1,744	1,616	128	384	963	100.0	50.8	15.7	24.6	5.0	4.6	0.4	1.1	2.8
2012	35,018	17,535	5,473	8,804	1,773	1,644	129	375	1,057	100.0	50.1	15.6	25.1	5.1	4.7	0.4	1.1	3.0
2013	35,251	17,390	5,483	9,054	1,809	1,683	126	367	1,148	100.0	49.3	15.6	25.7	5.1	4.8	0.4	1.0	3.3
2014[2]	35,249	17,258	5,486	9,246	1,834	1,710	124	361	1,064	100.0	49.0	15.6	26.2	5.2	4.9	0.4	1.0	3.0
2015[2]	35,298	17,079	5,473	9,438	1,860	1,737	122	355	1,093	100.0	48.4	15.5	26.7	5.3	4.9	0.3	1.0	3.1
2016[2]	35,402	16,940	5,480	9,623	1,886	1,765	121	349	1,123	100.0	47.9	15.5	27.2	5.3	5.0	0.3	1.0	3.2
2017[2]	35,451	16,791	5,495	9,764	1,905	1,786	120	344	1,152	100.0	47.4	15.5	27.5	5.4	5.0	0.3	1.0	3.2
2018[2]	35,491	16,662	5,510	9,881	1,920	1,802	118	341	1,177	100.0	46.9	15.5	27.8	5.4	5.1	0.3	1.0	3.3
2019[2]	35,543	16,618	5,507	9,930	1,952	1,836	116	333	1,204	100.0	46.8	15.5	27.9	5.5	5.2	0.3	0.9	3.4
2020[2]	35,559	16,560	5,500	9,948	1,985	1,871	115	327	1,238	100.0	46.6	15.5	28.0	5.6	5.3	0.3	0.9	3.5
2021[2]	35,541	16,496	5,482	9,949	2,021	1,907	114	323	1,271	100.0	46.4	15.4	28.0	5.7	5.4	0.3	0.9	3.6
2022[2]	35,558	16,449	5,468	9,966	2,054	1,940	114	319	1,301	100.0	46.3	15.4	28.0	5.8	5.5	0.3	0.9	3.7
2023[2]	35,712	16,456	5,480	10,029	2,099	1,985	114	316	1,331	100.0	46.1	15.3	28.1	5.9	5.6	0.3	0.9	3.7
2024[2]	35,878	16,469	5,501	10,087	2,142	2,027	114	314	1,365	100.0	45.9	15.3	28.1	6.0	5.6	0.3	0.9	3.8
2025[2]	36,052	16,483	5,523	10,150	2,184	2,070	115	313	1,399	100.0	45.7	15.3	28.2	6.1	5.7	0.3	0.9	3.9
Grades 9 through 12																		
1999	13,371	8,708	2,114	1,815	584	—	—	151	—	100.0	65.1	15.8	13.6	4.4	†	†	1.1	†
2000	13,517	8,747	2,119	1,896	601	—	—	153	—	100.0	64.7	15.7	14.0	4.4	†	†	1.1	†
2001	13,736	8,774	2,173	2,011	619	—	—	159	—	100.0	63.9	15.8	14.6	4.5	†	†	1.2	†
2002	14,069	8,854	2,257	2,148	642	—	—	168	—	100.0	62.9	16.0	15.3	4.6	†	†	1.2	†
2003	14,339	8,884	2,334	2,282	663	—	—	177	—	100.0	62.0	16.3	15.9	4.6	†	†	1.2	†
2004	14,618	8,950	2,403	2,408	679	—	—	178	—	100.0	61.2	16.4	16.5	4.6	†	†	1.2	†
2005	14,909	8,954	2,490	2,570	709	—	—	186	—	100.0	60.1	16.7	17.2	4.8	†	†	1.2	†
2006	15,081	8,938	2,540	2,701	720	—	—	181	—	100.0	59.3	16.8	17.9	4.8	†	†	1.2	†
2007	15,086	8,775	2,571	2,821	736	—	—	183	—	100.0	58.2	17.0	18.7	4.9	†	†	1.2	†
2008	14,980	8,556	2,565	2,874	746	731	15	179	59 [1]	100.0	57.1	17.1	19.2	5.0	4.9	0.1	1.2	0.4 [1]
2009	14,952	8,385	2,532	3,014	754	738	16	182	84 [1]	100.0	56.1	16.9	20.2	5.0	4.9	0.1	1.2	0.6 [1]
2010	14,860	8,109	2,422	3,125	755	707	49	171	277	100.0	54.6	16.3	21.0	5.1	4.8	0.3	1.2	1.9
2011	14,749	7,948	2,357	3,202	769	719	50	163	309	100.0	53.9	16.0	21.7	5.2	4.9	0.3	1.1	2.1
2012	14,753	7,851	2,330	3,300	779	727	51	158	335	100.0	53.2	15.8	22.4	5.3	4.9	0.3	1.1	2.3
2013	14,794	7,770	2,322	3,398	784	733	51	156	363	100.0	52.5	15.7	23.0	5.3	5.0	0.3	1.1	2.5

See notes at end of table.

Table 203.60. Enrollment and percentage distribution of enrollment in public elementary and secondary schools, by race/ethnicity and level of education: Fall 1999 through fall 2025—Continued

Level of education and year	Enrollment (in thousands) Total	White	Black	Hispanic	Asian/Pacific Islander Total	Asian	Pacific Islander	American Indian/ Alaska Native	Two or more races	Percentage distribution Total	White	Black	Hispanic	Asian/Pacific Islander Total	Asian	Pacific Islander	American Indian/ Alaska Native	Two or more races
1	2	3	4	5	6	7	8	9	10	11	12	13	14	15	16	17	18	19
2014[2]	14,883	7,749	2,342	3,494	804	753	50	155	340	100.0	52.1	15.7	23.5	5.4	5.1	0.3	1.0	2.3
2015[2]	14,970	7,710	2,345	3,592	819	769	50	153	352	100.0	51.5	15.7	24.0	5.5	5.1	0.3	1.0	2.3
2016[2]	14,983	7,626	2,326	3,683	837	788	49	150	361	100.0	50.9	15.5	24.6	5.6	5.3	0.3	1.0	2.4
2017[2]	15,026	7,550	2,300	3,800	863	815	48	146	367	100.0	50.2	15.3	25.3	5.7	5.4	0.3	1.0	2.4
2018[2]	15,037	7,466	2,266	3,909	879	831	48	142	375	100.0	49.6	15.1	26.0	5.8	5.5	0.3	0.9	2.5
2019[2]	15,075	7,375	2,247	4,034	894	846	48	139	386	100.0	48.9	14.9	26.8	5.9	5.6	0.3	0.9	2.6
2020[2]	15,215	7,322	2,256	4,194	907	860	47	136	400	100.0	48.1	14.8	27.6	6.0	5.7	0.3	0.9	2.6
2021[2]	15,387	7,281	2,292	4,351	913	868	46	134	415	100.0	47.3	14.9	28.3	5.9	5.6	0.3	0.9	2.7
2022[2]	15,526	7,237	2,331	4,470	924	880	44	133	430	100.0	46.6	15.0	28.8	6.0	5.7	0.3	0.9	2.8
2023[2]	15,514	7,158	2,339	4,512	929	886	43	131	445	100.0	46.1	15.1	29.1	6.0	5.7	0.3	0.8	2.9
2024[2]	15,460	7,075	2,331	4,528	942	899	43	129	455	100.0	45.8	15.1	29.3	6.1	5.8	0.3	0.8	2.9
2025[2]	15,368	6,982	2,313	4,527	955	912	43	127	464	100.0	45.4	15.1	29.5	6.2	5.9	0.3	0.8	3.0

—Not available.
†Not applicable.
[1]For this year, data on students of Two or more races were reported by only a small number of states. Therefore, the data are not comparable to figures for 2010 and later years.
[2]Projected.
NOTE: Race categories exclude persons of Hispanic ethnicity. Enrollment data for students not reported by race/ethnicity were prorated by state and grade to match state totals. Prior to 2008, data on students of Two or more races were not collected separately. Total counts of ungraded students were prorated to prekindergarten through grade 8 and grades 9 through 12 based on prior reports. Some data have been revised from previously published figures. Detail may not sum to totals because of rounding.
SOURCE: U.S. Department of Education, National Center for Education Statistics, Common Core of Data (CCD), "State Nonfiscal Survey of Public Elementary and Secondary Education," 1998–99 through 2013–14; and National Elementary and Secondary Enrollment by Race/Ethnicity Projection Model, 1972 through 2025. (This table was prepared January 2016.)

Table 203.70. Percentage distribution of enrollment in public elementary and secondary schools, by race/ethnicity and state or jurisdiction: Fall 2003 and fall 2013

State or jurisdiction	Percentage distribution, fall 2003						Percentage distribution, fall 2013							
	Total	White	Black	Hispanic	Asian/ Pacific Islander	American Indian/ Alaska Native	Total	White	Black	Hispanic	Asian	Pacific Islander	American Indian/ Alaska Native	Two or more races
1	2	3	4	5	6	7	8	9	10	11	12	13	14	15
United States	**100.0**	**58.7**	**17.2**	**18.5**	**4.4**	**1.2**	**100.0**	**50.3**	**15.6**	**24.8**	**4.8**	**0.4**	**1.0**	**3.0**
Alabama	100.0	59.9	36.4	2.1	0.9	0.8	100.0	57.0	33.6	5.5	1.4	0.1	0.8	1.6
Alaska	100.0	58.9	4.7	3.9	6.5	26.0	100.0	49.2	3.4	6.6	6.2	2.4	23.9	8.3
Arizona	100.0	49.2	4.8	37.2	2.2	6.6	100.0	40.7	5.2	44.1	2.8	0.3	4.8	2.2
Arkansas	100.0	69.9	23.1	5.3	1.1	0.6	100.0	63.1	21.0	11.2	1.5	0.6	0.6	2.0
California	100.0	32.9	8.2	46.7	11.3	0.8	100.0	25.0	6.2	53.3	11.1	0.5	0.6	3.3
Colorado	100.0	64.5	5.8	25.3	3.1	1.2	100.0	55.0	4.7	32.8	3.1	0.2	0.7	3.5
Connecticut	100.0	68.3	13.6	14.6	3.2	0.3	100.0	58.5	12.9	21.2	4.7	0.1	0.3	2.4
Delaware	100.0	57.3	31.9	7.9	2.6	0.3	100.0	47.7	31.2	14.5	3.5	0.1	0.4	2.5
District of Columbia	100.0	4.3	84.7	9.5	1.5	0.1	100.0	8.8	73.6	14.4	1.4	0.1	0.1	1.6
Florida	100.0	51.3	24.3	22.1	2.0	0.3	100.0	40.9	22.9	30.0	2.6	0.1	0.3	3.2
Georgia	100.0	52.1	38.3	6.9	2.5	0.2	100.0	42.7	37.0	13.3	3.5	0.1	0.2	3.1
Hawaii	100.0	20.2	2.4	4.5	72.4	0.5	100.0	13.6	2.1	10.0	32.0	32.0	0.4	9.9
Idaho	100.0	84.1	0.9	12.0	1.5	1.6	100.0	76.8	1.1	17.2	1.3	0.3	1.3	2.0
Illinois	100.0	57.4	21.1	17.7	3.6	0.2	100.0	49.9	17.6	24.6	4.5	0.1	0.3	3.1
Indiana	100.0	81.5	12.4	4.8	1.1	0.2	100.0	70.9	12.3	10.2	1.9	0.1	0.2	4.5
Iowa	100.0	88.2	4.5	4.9	1.8	0.6	100.0	79.0	5.3	9.7	2.2	0.2	0.4	3.2
Kansas	100.0	76.4	8.9	11.0	2.3	1.4	100.0	65.9	7.2	18.4	2.7	0.2	1.0	4.7
Kentucky	100.0	87.0	10.4	1.5	0.8	0.2	100.0	79.3	10.8	5.3	1.5	0.1	0.1	3.0
Louisiana	100.0	48.5	47.7	1.8	1.3	0.7	100.0	46.8	44.5	4.8	1.5	0.1	0.7	1.6
Maine	100.0	95.8	1.7	0.8	1.2	0.5	100.0	90.9	3.2	1.8	1.5	0.1	0.8	1.6
Maryland	100.0	50.4	37.9	6.4	4.9	0.4	100.0	40.9	34.9	13.6	6.1	0.1	0.3	4.1
Massachusetts	100.0	74.6	8.8	11.5	4.7	0.3	100.0	64.9	8.7	17.0	6.1	0.1	0.2	2.9
Michigan	100.0	72.7	20.1	4.1	2.2	1.0	100.0	68.3	18.3	6.8	2.9	0.1	0.7	2.8
Minnesota	100.0	80.2	7.8	4.6	5.4	2.1	100.0	70.7	9.7	8.2	6.4	0.1	1.7	3.3
Mississippi	100.0	47.3	50.7	1.1	0.7	0.2	100.0	45.4	49.3	2.9	1.0	#	0.2	1.1
Missouri	100.0	77.7	18.0	2.6	1.4	0.4	100.0	73.2	16.5	5.4	1.9	0.2	0.4	2.4
Montana	100.0	85.1	0.7	2.1	1.0	11.0	100.0	80.0	0.9	4.1	0.8	0.2	11.3	2.6
Nebraska	100.0	79.5	7.1	10.1	1.7	1.6	100.0	68.9	6.7	17.3	2.3	0.1	1.4	3.3
Nevada	100.0	50.8	10.7	30.2	6.7	1.7	100.0	36.0	9.9	40.6	5.6	1.3	1.1	5.6
New Hampshire	100.0	94.2	1.4	2.4	1.7	0.3	100.0	88.0	1.9	4.4	3.0	0.1	0.3	2.3
New Jersey	100.0	57.9	17.7	17.2	7.0	0.2	100.0	48.9	16.1	24.2	9.3	0.2	0.1	1.2
New Mexico	100.0	32.8	2.4	52.5	1.2	11.2	100.0	24.6	1.9	60.7	1.2	0.1	10.1	1.4
New York	100.0	53.9	19.7	19.4	6.6	0.5	100.0	46.5	18.2	24.5	8.8	0.0	0.6	1.5
North Carolina	100.0	58.3	31.6	6.7	2.0	1.5	100.0	51.4	26.0	14.5	2.8	0.1	1.4	3.8
North Dakota	100.0	88.0	1.2	1.4	0.8	8.5	100.0	81.4	3.1	3.7	1.4	0.2	8.7	1.5
Ohio	100.0	79.4	17.0	2.1	1.3	0.1	100.0	72.6	16.3	4.5	1.9	0.1	0.1	4.5
Oklahoma	100.0	61.5	10.9	7.6	1.5	18.5	100.0	51.7	9.2	15.0	1.8	0.3	15.0	7.1
Oregon	100.0	76.6	3.1	13.6	4.4	2.3	100.0	63.8	2.5	22.4	3.9	0.7	1.6	5.1
Pennsylvania	100.0	76.3	15.8	5.5	2.3	0.1	100.0	69.1	15.1	9.5	3.4	0.1	0.1	2.7
Rhode Island	100.0	71.2	8.5	16.4	3.2	0.6	100.0	61.5	8.1	23.4	2.9	0.2	0.7	3.2
South Carolina	100.0	54.2	41.3	3.2	1.1	0.3	100.0	52.5	35.1	7.5	1.4	0.1	0.3	3.1
South Dakota	100.0	84.9	1.5	1.8	1.0	10.7	100.0	76.9	2.7	4.5	1.7	0.1	11.5	2.6
Tennessee	100.0	70.7	25.0	2.8	1.3	0.2	100.0	65.6	22.9	7.8	1.8	0.1	0.2	1.6
Texas	100.0	38.7	14.3	43.8	2.9	0.3	100.0	29.5	12.7	51.8	3.7	0.1	0.4	1.9
Utah	100.0	83.4	1.1	11.0	2.9	1.5	100.0	76.3	1.3	16.0	1.7	1.5	1.1	2.0
Vermont	100.0	95.9	1.2	0.8	1.5	0.6	100.0	91.6	1.9	1.6	1.9	0.1	0.3	2.6
Virginia	100.0	61.1	27.1	6.6	4.7	0.5	100.0	52.2	23.3	13.1	6.3	0.1	0.3	4.7
Washington	100.0	71.5	5.7	12.3	7.9	2.7	100.0	58.2	4.5	21.1	7.2	1.0	1.4	6.7
West Virginia	100.0	94.1	4.6	0.5	0.6	0.1	100.0	91.1	4.7	1.4	0.7	#	0.1	2.0
Wisconsin	100.0	78.8	10.5	5.8	3.4	1.4	100.0	72.4	9.7	10.5	3.6	0.1	1.2	2.4
Wyoming	100.0	86.0	1.4	8.2	1.0	3.5	100.0	79.4	1.2	13.1	0.9	0.1	3.4	1.9
Bureau of Indian Education	100.0	0.0	0.0	0.0	0.0	100.0	—	—	—	—	—	—	—	—
DoD, overseas	100.0	55.2	20.0	13.5	10.5	0.9	—	—	—	—	—	—	—	—
DoD, domestic	100.0	48.6	23.6	22.7	4.2	1.0	—	—	—	—	—	—	—	—
Other jurisdictions														
American Samoa	100.0	0.0	0.0	0.0	100.0	0.0	—	—	—	—	—	—	—	—
Guam	100.0	1.3	0.3	0.2	98.1	0.1	100.0	0.6	0.2	0.2	25.1	71.6	#	2.2
Northern Marianas	100.0	0.4	#	0.0	99.6	0.0	100.0	0.6	#	0.1	40.0	56.8	0.0	2.4
Puerto Rico	100.0	0.0	0.0	100.0	0.0	0.0	100.0	0.1	#	99.9	#	#	#	0.0
U.S. Virgin Islands	100.0	0.8	84.3	14.5	0.2	0.2	100.0	1.5	78.5	18.6	0.5	0.1	0.1	0.7

—Not available.
#Rounds to zero.
NOTE: Percentage distribution based on students for whom race/ethnicity was reported, which may be less than the total number of students in the state. Race categories exclude persons of Hispanic ethnicity. DoD = Department of Defense. Detail may not sum to totals because of rounding.

SOURCE: U.S. Department of Education, National Center for Education Statistics, Common Core of Data (CCD), "State Nonfiscal Survey of Public Elementary/Secondary Education," 2003–04 and 2013–14. (This table was prepared August 2015.)

Table 203.75. Enrollment and percentage distribution of enrollment in public schools, by family poverty rate of 5- to 17-year-olds living in the school district, student race/ethnicity, region, and school locale: 2013–14

Student race/ethnicity, region, and school locale	Enrollment in public schools					Percentage distribution of enrollment				
		Family poverty rate[1] of 5- to 17-year-olds[2] living in the school district					Family poverty rate[1] of 5- to 17-year-olds[2] living in the school district			
	Total	0 to 12.0 percent	12.1 to 20.0 percent	20.1 to 28.0 percent	More than 28.0 percent	Total	0 to 12.0 percent	12.1 to 20.0 percent	20.1 to 28.0 percent	More than 28.0 percent
1	2	3	4	5	6	7	8	9	10	11
Total	**49,481,720**	**12,301,079**	**12,922,300**	**12,094,711**	**12,163,630**	**100.0**	**24.9**	**26.1**	**24.4**	**24.6**
White	24,845,481	8,692,937	7,476,122	5,691,098	2,985,324	100.0	35.0	30.1	22.9	12.0
Black	7,719,312	771,004	1,488,381	1,905,234	3,554,693	100.0	10.0	19.3	24.7	46.0
Hispanic	12,339,568	1,431,637	2,658,932	3,529,446	4,719,553	100.0	11.6	21.5	28.6	38.2
Asian	2,398,012	889,457	655,025	404,814	448,716	100.0	37.1	27.3	16.9	18.7
Pacific Islander	174,671	25,723	93,798	35,346	19,804	100.0	14.7	53.7	20.2	11.3
American Indian/Alaska Native	514,311	72,506	117,958	139,649	184,198	100.0	14.1	22.9	27.2	35.8
Two or more races	1,490,365	417,815	432,084	389,124	251,342	100.0	28.0	29.0	26.1	16.9
Region										
Northeast	**7,868,890**	**3,384,038**	**1,474,912**	**756,386**	**2,253,554**	**100.0**	**43.0**	**18.7**	**9.6**	**28.6**
White	4,530,450	2,644,675	1,025,428	435,433	424,914	100.0	58.4	22.6	9.6	9.4
Black	1,141,778	166,961	146,847	106,649	721,321	100.0	14.6	12.9	9.3	63.2
Hispanic	1,483,514	261,431	212,600	170,445	839,038	100.0	17.6	14.3	11.5	56.6
Asian	524,451	237,102	51,055	23,392	212,902	100.0	45.2	9.7	4.5	40.6
Pacific Islander	6,405	3,190	1,470	555	1,190	100.0	49.8	23.0	8.7	18.6
American Indian/Alaska Native	26,723	6,379	4,654	2,860	12,830	100.0	23.9	17.4	10.7	48.0
Two or more races	155,569	64,300	32,858	17,052	41,359	100.0	41.3	21.1	11.0	26.6
Midwest	**10,404,086**	**3,628,774**	**3,008,289**	**1,883,607**	**1,883,416**	**100.0**	**34.9**	**28.9**	**18.1**	**18.1**
White	6,999,851	2,946,827	2,286,115	1,174,966	591,943	100.0	42.1	32.7	16.8	8.5
Black	1,433,910	166,580	209,790	272,151	785,389	100.0	11.6	14.6	19.0	54.8
Hispanic	1,197,286	232,755	304,204	282,979	377,348	100.0	19.4	25.4	23.6	31.5
Asian	326,685	156,921	78,301	53,191	38,272	100.0	48.0	24.0	16.3	11.7
Pacific Islander	10,657	3,324	3,147	2,684	1,502	100.0	31.2	29.5	25.2	14.1
American Indian/Alaska Native	84,113	15,354	27,889	20,904	19,966	100.0	18.3	33.2	24.9	23.7
Two or more races	351,584	107,013	98,843	76,732	68,996	100.0	30.4	28.1	21.8	19.6
South	**19,199,289**	**2,655,102**	**4,900,385**	**6,295,205**	**5,348,597**	**100.0**	**13.8**	**25.5**	**32.8**	**27.9**
White	8,671,331	1,491,574	2,548,037	3,073,684	1,558,036	100.0	17.2	29.4	35.4	18.0
Black	4,531,913	370,816	974,166	1,324,676	1,862,255	100.0	8.2	21.5	29.2	41.1
Hispanic	4,657,701	443,158	1,004,917	1,520,883	1,688,743	100.0	9.5	21.6	32.7	36.3
Asian	586,656	208,822	174,145	127,583	76,106	100.0	35.6	29.7	21.7	13.0
Pacific Islander	25,989	3,897	6,479	8,281	7,332	100.0	15.0	24.9	31.9	28.2
American Indian/Alaska Native	182,604	21,618	42,807	56,866	61,313	100.0	11.8	23.4	31.1	33.6
Two or more races	543,095	115,217	149,834	183,232	94,812	100.0	21.2	27.6	33.7	17.5
West	**12,009,455**	**2,633,165**	**3,538,714**	**3,159,513**	**2,678,063**	**100.0**	**21.9**	**29.5**	**26.3**	**22.3**
White	4,643,849	1,609,861	1,616,542	1,007,015	410,431	100.0	34.7	34.8	21.7	8.8
Black	611,711	66,647	157,578	201,758	185,728	100.0	10.9	25.8	33.0	30.4
Hispanic	5,001,067	494,293	1,137,211	1,555,139	1,814,424	100.0	9.9	22.7	31.1	36.3
Asian	960,220	286,612	351,524	200,648	121,436	100.0	29.8	36.6	20.9	12.6
Pacific Islander	131,620	15,312	82,702	23,826	9,780	100.0	11.6	62.8	18.1	7.4
American Indian/Alaska Native	220,871	29,155	42,608	59,019	90,089	100.0	13.2	19.3	26.7	40.8
Two or more races	440,117	131,285	150,549	112,108	46,175	100.0	29.8	34.2	25.5	10.5
School locale										
City	**15,033,168**	**1,534,603**	**2,801,732**	**3,828,456**	**6,868,377**	**100.0**	**10.2**	**18.6**	**25.5**	**45.7**
White	4,469,681	832,736	1,259,612	1,333,178	1,044,155	100.0	18.6	28.2	29.8	23.4
Black	3,605,174	124,911	359,545	793,345	2,327,373	100.0	3.5	10.0	22.0	64.6
Hispanic	5,296,601	259,359	780,337	1,314,327	2,942,578	100.0	4.9	14.7	24.8	55.6
Asian	1,014,109	216,841	241,298	189,312	366,658	100.0	21.4	23.8	18.7	36.2
Pacific Islander	58,505	6,841	23,252	16,015	12,397	100.0	11.7	39.7	27.4	21.2
American Indian/Alaska Native	108,738	14,031	21,442	35,715	37,550	100.0	12.9	19.7	32.8	34.5
Two or more races	480,360	79,884	116,246	146,564	137,666	100.0	16.6	24.2	30.5	28.7
Suburban	**19,681,922**	**7,934,194**	**5,641,891**	**4,085,643**	**2,020,194**	**100.0**	**40.3**	**28.7**	**20.8**	**10.3**
White	10,125,473	5,497,938	2,777,160	1,456,154	394,221	100.0	54.3	27.4	14.4	3.9
Black	2,688,333	553,707	892,296	738,779	503,551	100.0	20.6	33.2	27.5	18.7
Hispanic	4,889,909	962,617	1,354,169	1,561,821	1,011,302	100.0	19.7	27.7	31.9	20.7
Asian	1,183,661	605,471	349,149	172,738	56,303	100.0	51.2	29.5	14.6	4.8
Pacific Islander	73,890	15,103	41,847	13,326	3,614	100.0	20.4	56.6	18.0	4.9
American Indian/Alaska Native	90,382	30,705	31,517	19,458	8,702	100.0	34.0	34.9	21.5	9.6
Two or more races	630,274	268,653	195,753	123,367	42,501	100.0	42.6	31.1	19.6	6.7
Town	**5,656,097**	**757,138**	**1,660,327**	**1,699,017**	**1,539,615**	**100.0**	**13.4**	**29.4**	**30.0**	**27.2**
White	3,659,321	634,632	1,239,716	1,143,382	641,591	100.0	17.3	33.9	31.2	17.5
Black	573,219	15,760	54,892	144,836	357,731	100.0	2.7	9.6	25.3	62.4
Hispanic	1,042,256	65,144	241,442	302,533	433,137	100.0	6.3	23.2	29.0	41.6
Asian	73,683	12,231	29,025	18,934	13,493	100.0	16.6	39.4	25.7	18.3
Pacific Islander	24,396	1,266	18,165	3,180	1,785	100.0	5.2	74.5	13.0	7.3
American Indian/Alaska Native	124,190	10,245	27,541	31,038	55,366	100.0	8.2	22.2	25.0	44.6
Two or more races	159,032	17,860	49,546	55,114	36,512	100.0	11.2	31.2	34.7	23.0

See notes at end of table.

Table 203.75. Enrollment and percentage distribution of enrollment in public schools, by family poverty rate of 5- to 17-year-olds living in the school district, student race/ethnicity, region, and school locale: 2013–14—Continued

Student race/ethnicity, region, and school locale	Enrollment in public schools: Total	Family poverty rate[1] of 5- to 17-year-olds[2] living in the school district: 0 to 12.0 percent	12.1 to 20.0 percent	20.1 to 28.0 percent	More than 28.0 percent	Percentage distribution of enrollment: Total	Family poverty rate[1] of 5- to 17-year-olds[2] living in the school district: 0 to 12.0 percent	12.1 to 20.0 percent	20.1 to 28.0 percent	More than 28.0 percent
1	2	3	4	5	6	7	8	9	10	11
Rural	**9,110,533**	**2,075,144**	**2,818,350**	**2,481,595**	**1,735,444**	**100.0**	**22.8**	**30.9**	**27.2**	**19.0**
White	6,591,006	1,727,631	2,199,634	1,758,384	905,357	100.0	26.2	33.4	26.7	13.7
Black	852,586	76,626	181,648	228,274	366,038	100.0	9.0	21.3	26.8	42.9
Hispanic	1,110,802	144,517	282,984	350,765	332,536	100.0	13.0	25.5	31.6	29.9
Asian	126,559	54,914	35,553	23,830	12,262	100.0	43.4	28.1	18.8	9.7
Pacific Islander	17,880	2,513	10,534	2,825	2,008	100.0	14.1	58.9	15.8	11.2
American Indian/Alaska Native	191,001	17,525	37,458	53,438	82,580	100.0	9.2	19.6	28.0	43.2
Two or more races	220,699	51,418	70,539	64,079	34,663	100.0	23.3	32.0	29.0	15.7

[1]A family is in poverty if its income falls below the Census Bureau's poverty threshold, which is a dollar amount that varies depending on a family's size and composition and is updated annually to account for inflation. In 2013, for example, the poverty threshold for a family of four with two children was $23,624. The family poverty rate of 5- to 17-year-olds is the percentage of children in this age group whose families are in poverty. Includes only children classified as "related" and "relevant" (see footnote 2).
[2]Includes only those children who live in households and meet both of the following conditions: (1) The children are related to the householder by birth, marriage, or adoption (except a child who is the spouse of the householder). The householder is the person (or one of the people) who owns or rents (maintains) the housing unit. (2) The children are relevant to the school district. Children are relevant if they reside within the geographical boundaries of the district and are at a grade level served by the district, even if they do not attend a school in the district.
NOTE: School enrollment data were obtained from the Common Core of Data and poverty rate data were obtained from the Census Bureau. To create the school district categories, public school districts were ranked and divided into quarters based on the family poverty rate of their 5- to 17-year-old population; the cut points between the four quarters were chosen so that, at the national level, each quarter contains approximately the same number of students. For the approximately 3 percent of public school students who attended charter or other special districts, no data were available on their school district's family poverty rate. The rate for their district was imputed to be the same as the rate for the regular public school district within which their charter or other special district was geographically located. Race categories exclude persons of Hispanic ethnicity. Detail may not sum to totals because of rounding.
SOURCE: U.S. Department of Education, National Center for Education Statistics, Common Core of Data (CCD), "Public Elementary/Secondary School Universe Survey," 2013–14. U.S. Department of Commerce, Census Bureau, Small Area Income and Poverty Estimates (SAIPE) Program, 2013 Poverty Estimates for School Districts. (This table was prepared March 2016.)

Table 203.80. Average daily attendance (ADA) in public elementary and secondary schools, by state or jurisdiction: Selected years, 1969–70 through 2012–13

State or jurisdiction	1969–70	1979–80	1989–90	1999–2000	2004–05	2005–06	2006–07	2007–08	2008–09	2009–10	2010–11	2011–12	2012–13
1	2	3	4	5	6	7	8	9	10	11	12	13	14
United States	**41,934,376**	**38,288,911**	**37,799,296**	**43,806,726**	**45,625,458**	**45,931,617**	**46,132,663**	**46,155,880**	**46,173,477**	**45,919,206**	**46,118,737**	**46,400,465**	**46,567,834**
Alabama	777,123	711,432	683,833	725,212	706,588	714,197	714,302	731,161	712,179	698,208	709,225	715,402	688,614
Alaska	72,489	79,945	98,213	122,412	121,699	122,010	120,988	119,882	119,330	120,118	119,949	119,799	119,873
Arizona	391,526	481,905	557,252	782,851	911,640	933,663	972,404	973,689	999,386	968,764	964,683	969,825	973,369
Arkansas	414,158	423,610	403,025	422,958	430,290	435,278	436,804	439,347	439,432	435,676	443,118	443,125	470,644
California[1]	4,418,423	4,044,736	4,893,341	5,957,216	6,373,959	6,349,270	6,351,774	6,365,266	6,365,278	6,017,381 [2]	6,029,786 [2]	6,034,192 [2]	6,021,550 [2]
Colorado	500,388	513,475	519,419	656,700	700,485	712,476	722,168	735,549	747,845	762,190	763,147	779,747	784,242
Connecticut	618,881	507,362	439,524	533,779	559,478	558,423	555,428	553,445	549,776	548,787	537,104	534,846	534,350
Delaware	120,819	94,058	89,838	106,444	110,393	113,986	113,992	116,472	119,092	119,879	121,959	122,864	124,676
District of Columbia	138,600	91,576	71,468	65,371	70,817	59,137	61,799	61,636	68,447	68,217	69,575	71,910	76,486
Florida	1,312,693	1,464,461	1,646,583	2,175,453	2,463,323	2,494,778	2,527,431	2,494,397	2,468,060	2,493,694	2,541,022	2,575,910	2,600,989
Georgia	1,019,427	989,433	1,054,097	1,326,713	1,460,767	1,499,317	1,542,305	1,561,935	1,569,767	1,596,180	1,621,397	1,646,051	1,646,352
Hawaii	168,140	151,563	157,360	171,180	169,825	168,009	165,415	166,179	166,118	165,766	169,926	171,763	173,092
Idaho	170,920	189,199	203,987	230,828	241,590	247,009	251,278	255,523	258,712	262,238	263,001	263,377	264,786
Illinois	2,084,844	1,770,435	1,587,733	1,789,089	1,862,046	1,871,619	1,879,288	1,881,810	1,881,276	1,887,561	1,863,017	1,858,409	1,867,289
Indiana	1,111,043	983,444	884,568	929,281	944,944	966,967	976,373	969,976	973,342	976,503	976,225	976,337	977,509
Iowa	624,403	510,081	450,224	471,384	456,559	477,491	481,528	492,922	451,403	455,579	459,613	462,585	471,263
Kansas	470,296	382,019	388,986	426,853	411,455	407,812	422,142	418,751	418,495	435,745	443,131	454,740	453,778
Kentucky	647,970	619,868	569,795	565,693	574,380	580,937	583,102	585,775	585,556	587,102	593,323	594,440	618,774
Louisiana	776,555	727,601	727,125	701,957	670,238	648,243	625,916	631,163	637,764	643,374	654,093	664,640	673,721
Maine	225,146	211,400	195,089	194,554	184,374	180,223	178,870	175,161	173,357	168,213	165,067	166,483	164,339
Maryland	785,989	686,336	620,617	791,133	804,696	800,553	795,473	793,881	793,333	795,577	798,953	803,656	806,686
Massachusetts	1,056,207	935,960	763,231	913,502	930,338	930,151	933,697	917,181	913,976	912,792	910,568	906,736	907,954
Michigan	1,991,235	1,758,427	1,446,996	1,574,894	1,583,496	1,574,023	1,556,297	1,528,815	1,498,107	1,477,312	1,452,125	1,438,279	1,422,806
Minnesota	864,595	748,606	699,001	818,819	788,354	787,521	791,417	790,206	791,427	785,455	786,838	792,437	795,827
Mississippi	524,623	454,401	476,048	468,746	463,816	461,112	462,251	461,459	460,797	460,327	460,894	460,703	461,356
Missouri	906,132	777,269	729,693	836,105	851,114	859,441	858,821	852,106	853,580	852,460	839,997	840,917	843,762
Montana	162,664	144,608	135,406	142,313	130,998	129,948	128,872	132,104	131,982	130,704	130,949	133,266	132,579
Nebraska	314,516	270,524	254,754	261,767	260,725	262,805	263,800	264,810	266,536	269,590	271,468	285,837	288,023
Nevada	113,421	134,995	173,149	305,067	378,186	383,403	395,536	395,355	406,792	405,097	406,965	411,919	419,638
New Hampshire	140,203	154,187	154,915	200,283	201,242	199,952	198,004	195,383	192,890	191,969	188,913	185,947	183,571
New Jersey	1,322,124	1,140,111	997,561	1,222,438	1,341,156	1,358,562	1,348,279	1,340,220	1,342,419	1,343,405	1,339,012	1,340,367	1,336,336
New Mexico	259,997	253,453	290,245	323,963	322,046	323,964	327,244	326,034	327,562	331,152	334,272	335,165	335,773
New York	3,099,192	2,530,289	2,244,110	2,595,070	2,581,772	2,556,705	2,542,259	2,520,932	2,510,519	2,516,922	2,513,770	2,512,327	2,500,382
North Carolina	1,104,295	1,072,150	1,012,274	1,185,737	1,289,444	1,319,335	1,343,357	1,364,608	1,374,267	1,366,164	1,377,899	1,393,621	1,400,981
North Dakota	141,961	118,986	109,659	105,123	94,823	92,843	91,078	91,972	91,816	91,114	92,440	94,310	97,135
Ohio	2,246,282	1,849,283	1,584,735	1,659,903	1,719,566	1,730,080	1,691,206	1,660,981	1,628,515	1,609,008	1,601,188	1,605,571	1,587,878
Oklahoma	560,993	548,065	543,170	586,266	587,188	591,486	596,172	596,450	603,375	610,019	616,775	624,410	630,766
Oregon	436,736	418,593	419,771	479,321	506,638	513,650	516,258	515,834	518,119	515,644	517,373	518,896	520,326
Pennsylvania	2,169,225	1,808,630	1,524,839	1,684,913	1,698,795	1,702,566	1,701,044	1,693,569	1,680,772	1,661,990	1,668,916	1,659,616	1,649,205
Rhode Island	163,205	139,195	125,934	144,422	143,939	139,001	138,993	134,737	131,963	131,538	131,494	131,379	139,494
South Carolina	600,292	569,612	569,029	624,456	639,950	647,703	652,803	656,996	662,231	664,136	664,133	673,850	681,402
South Dakota	158,543	124,934	119,823	122,252	115,148	114,673	114,863	114,723	114,209	115,242	119,449	120,950	123,220
Tennessee	836,010	806,696	761,766	844,878	868,129	881,414	889,312	891,430	895,335	896,130	899,382	903,695	910,540
Texas	2,432,420	2,608,817	3,075,333	3,706,550	4,084,792	4,186,812	4,255,963	4,322,975	4,393,893	4,473,236	4,551,084	4,634,133	4,699,372
Utah	287,405	312,813	408,917	448,096	464,645	478,233	488,514	503,562	513,884	528,608	540,683	556,885	567,605
Vermont	97,772	95,045	87,832	98,894	93,608	92,508	91,437	89,880	87,931	86,378	85,501	85,184	84,326
Virginia	995,580	955,105	989,197	1,195,123	1,133,882	1,141,790	1,142,342	1,150,316	1,154,689	1,159,105	1,165,907	1,177,274	1,180,497
Washington	764,735	710,929	755,141	925,696	941,238	946,824	947,857	947,791	953,719	960,084	965,191	964,255	968,149
West Virginia	372,278	353,264	301,947	273,277	271,197	271,780	272,045	267,989	269,623	268,872	270,961	273,355	273,305
Wisconsin	880,609	770,554	711,466	825,699	831,809	834,177	835,072	823,754	823,595	817,284	825,622	825,949	829,261
Wyoming	81,293	89,471	91,277	86,092	77,878	77,757	79,090	79,788	81,006	80,717	81,654	83,131	83,983
Other jurisdictions													
American Samoa	—	—	11,448	15,102	15,302	15,237	14,606	14,646	14,646	14,403	15,451	15,541	13,355
Guam	20,315	—	23,883	—	—	29,617	29,515	28,358	28,521	28,075	28,765	28,735	29,591
Northern Marianas	—	—	6,809	8,712	10,301	10,871	10,277	9,927	9,815	9,900	9,965	9,731	9,564
Puerto Rico	—	656,709	597,436	540,676	540,365	522,655	531,273	494,880	477,918	466,483	411,164	429,799	422,560
U.S. Virgin Islands	—	—	18,924	18,676	15,841	15,241	14,927	15,903	15,768	15,493	15,747	15,711	15,192

—Not available.

[1]Data for California for 1989–90 and earlier years are not strictly comparable with those for other states because California's attendance figures included excused absences.

[2]Excludes average daily attendance for regional occupational programs and summer school programs that were reported in prior years.

NOTE: Some data have been revised from previously published figures.

SOURCE: U.S. Department of Education, National Center for Education Statistics, *Statistics of State School Systems, 1969–70; Revenues and Expenditures for Public Elementary and Secondary Education, 1979–80*; and Common Core of Data (CCD), "National Public Education Financial Survey," 1989–90 through 2012–13. (This table was prepared September 2015.)

Table 203.90. Average daily attendance (ADA) as a percentage of total enrollment, school day length, and school year length in public schools, by school level and state: 2007–08 and 2011–12

[Standard errors appear in parentheses]

State	2007–08		2011–12: Total elementary, secondary, and combined elementary/secondary schools				Elementary schools		Secondary schools	
	ADA as percent of enrollment	Average hours in school day	ADA as percent of enrollment	Average hours in school day	Average days in school year	Average hours in school year	ADA as percent of enrollment	Average hours in school day	ADA as percent of enrollment	Average hours in school day
1	2	3	4	5	6	7	8	9	10	11
United States	**93.1 (0.22)**	**6.6 (0.02)**	**93.9 (0.12)**	**6.7 (0.01)**	**179 (0.1)**	**1,203 (2.0)**	**94.9 (0.12)**	**6.7 (0.01)**	**91.7 (0.34)**	**6.7 (0.02)**
Alabama	93.8 (1.24)	7.0 (0.07)	94.4 (0.94)	7.0 (0.04)	181 (0.8)	1,271 (8.5)	95.3 (0.92)	7.1 (0.04)	94.6 (0.65)	6.9 (0.13)
Alaska	89.9 (1.22)	6.5 (0.05)	91.4 (1.19)	6.7 (0.17)	177 (1.3)	1,183 (37.3)	‡ (†)	‡ (†)	‡ (†)	‡ (†)
Arizona	89.0 (2.95)	6.4 (0.09)	91.7 (0.99)	6.7 (0.08)	179 (1.3)	1,201 (12.5)	93.5 (0.53)	6.9 (0.06)	87.9 (2.40)	6.5 (0.26)
Arkansas	91.8 (1.35)	6.9 (0.06)	94.2 (0.58)	7.0 (0.07)	180 (0.5)	1,261 (14.1)	94.7 (0.36)	7.0 (0.08)	92.9 (1.93)	6.9 (0.14)
California	93.2 (0.71)	6.2 (0.07)	93.1 (0.46)	6.2 (0.05)	180 (0.3)	1,121 (9.0)	94.7 (0.51)	6.3 (0.06)	89.7 (1.08)	6.3 (0.08)
Colorado	93.9 (0.44)	7.0 (0.05)	93.1 (0.71)	7.1 (0.06)	172 (1.4)	1,215 (7.7)	94.6 (0.59)	7.0 (0.07)	88.0 (2.57)	7.1 (0.10)
Connecticut	87.9 (2.98)	6.5 (0.09)	94.9 (0.47)	6.6 (0.04)	181 (0.1)	1,201 (7.5)	95.4 (0.61)	6.6 (0.05)	94.3 (0.33)	6.7 (0.09)
Delaware	89.8 (1.75)	6.7 (0.09)	93.5 (0.50)	7.0 (0.10)	182 (1.2)	1,269 (23.7)	94.1 (0.50)	7.0 (0.12)	93.8 (0.71)	7.0 (0.09)
District of Columbia	91.2 (1.27)	6.9 (0.21)	‡ (†)	‡ (†)	‡ (†)	‡ (†)	‡ (†)	‡ (†)	‡ (†)	‡ (†)
Florida	92.7 (0.74)	6.4 (0.08)	93.2 (0.52)	6.6 (0.06)	181 (1.2)	1,193 (14.2)	94.3 (0.49)	6.6 (0.08)	90.7 (0.84)	6.7 (0.09)
Georgia	93.3 (1.28)	6.8 (0.06)	94.3 (0.53)	7.0 (0.04)	178 (0.4)	1,242 (8.5)	95.0 (0.59)	6.9 (0.05)	‡ (†)	‡ (†)
Hawaii	90.7 (4.58)	6.3 (0.10)	‡ (†)	‡ (†)	‡ (†)	‡ (†)	‡ (†)	‡ (†)	‡ (†)	‡ (†)
Idaho	92.4 (2.27)	6.6 (0.09)	94.1 (1.01)	6.7 (0.13)	166 (5.1)	1,110 (21.7)	94.4 (0.75)	6.7 (0.08)	93.1 (0.83)	6.7 (0.20)
Illinois	94.0 (0.71)	6.5 (0.05)	94.1 (0.40)	6.5 (0.04)	176 (0.4)	1,151 (7.7)	95.1 (0.29)	6.5 (0.05)	92.4 (1.29)	6.8 (0.08)
Indiana	95.7 (0.51)	6.8 (0.06)	95.9 (0.20)	6.8 (0.05)	180 (0.1)	1,226 (9.1)	96.1 (0.25)	6.7 (0.05)	95.5 (0.31)	7.0 (0.07)
Iowa	94.8 (0.65)	6.9 (0.09)	95.7 (0.36)	6.7 (0.12)	180 (0.2)	1,213 (21.8)	96.4 (0.21)	6.9 (0.05)	93.6 (1.39)	6.3 (0.47)
Kansas	95.4 (0.52)	7.0 (0.07)	94.9 (0.42)	7.0 (0.03)	177 (2.6)	1,245 (17.9)	95.5 (0.53)	7.0 (0.04)	94.0 (0.42)	7.1 (0.04)
Kentucky	93.1 (1.89)	6.7 (0.06)	93.2 (1.33)	6.8 (0.06)	179 (1.0)	1,211 (11.6)	95.9 (0.22)	6.8 (0.07)	87.0 (4.87)	6.8 (0.14)
Louisiana	90.3 (2.31)	7.1 (0.08)	92.8 (0.70)	7.2 (0.07)	178 (1.1)	1,283 (10.7)	93.0 (0.88)	7.3 (0.07)	93.5 (0.42)	7.1 (0.14)
Maine	90.3 (2.41)	6.5 (0.06)	94.2 (0.73)	6.6 (0.06)	176 (0.2)	1,156 (10.7)	94.4 (1.00)	6.6 (0.07)	93.8 (0.45)	6.3 (0.08)
Maryland	94.1 (0.44)	6.6 (0.07)	‡ (†)	‡ (†)	‡ (†)	‡ (†)	‡ (†)	‡ (†)	‡ (†)	‡ (†)
Massachusetts	94.6 (0.58)	6.5 (0.05)	93.5 (0.62)	6.4 (0.07)	180 (0.2)	1,157 (13.3)	94.4 (0.63)	6.4 (0.07)	90.3 (2.55)	6.6 (0.05)
Michigan	93.0 (1.01)	6.6 (0.08)	91.6 (0.71)	6.8 (0.03)	177 (0.5)	1,196 (5.9)	92.3 (0.99)	6.8 (0.03)	89.4 (1.28)	6.7 (0.07)
Minnesota	93.1 (0.91)	6.3 (0.12)	93.1 (0.49)	6.4 (0.08)	173 (1.3)	1,111 (14.0)	96.1 (0.19)	6.6 (0.07)	89.5 (1.21)	6.0 (0.20)
Mississippi	92.1 (2.00)	7.0 (0.12)	94.4 (0.47)	7.2 (0.09)	181 (0.4)	1,312 (16.4)	94.9 (0.57)	7.3 (0.06)	93.7 (0.86)	7.2 (0.24)
Missouri	94.8 (0.26)	6.7 (0.05)	95.1 (0.20)	6.9 (0.03)	175 (0.3)	1,197 (5.3)	95.6 (0.24)	6.9 (0.04)	94.3 (0.24)	6.8 (0.11)
Montana	91.3 (1.39)	6.8 (0.05)	93.9 (0.81)	6.6 (0.06)	179 (0.4)	1,189 (11.2)	94.3 (0.79)	6.6 (0.09)	93.0 (0.48)	6.7 (0.08)
Nebraska	94.9 (1.21)	6.9 (0.08)	94.8 (0.60)	7.1 (0.05)	177 (1.0)	1,257 (9.6)	96.0 (0.53)	7.1 (0.04)	94.5 (0.66)	6.8 (0.19)
Nevada	93.5 (1.27)	6.3 (0.06)	93.9 (0.39)	6.5 (0.07)	180 (1.1)	1,164 (10.9)	94.5 (0.30)	6.4 (0.10)	93.9 (0.70)	6.5 (0.07)
New Hampshire	92.2 (1.75)	6.5 (0.06)	91.1 (2.86)	6.6 (0.05)	180 (0.3)	1,181 (10.3)	95.9 (0.45)	6.5 (0.07)	75.1 (12.63)	6.7 (0.05)
New Jersey	94.6 (0.59)	6.4 (0.05)	93.5 (1.13)	6.6 (0.06)	181 (0.2)	1,201 (11.8)	93.7 (1.40)	6.6 (0.07)	92.6 (1.29)	6.7 (0.07)
New Mexico	91.9 (1.76)	6.8 (0.08)	92.8 (0.80)	6.9 (0.09)	177 (0.6)	1,216 (15.7)	93.8 (0.80)	6.7 (0.08)	88.5 (2.41)	7.1 (0.14)
New York	92.7 (1.30)	6.6 (0.09)	92.7 (0.94)	6.6 (0.06)	182 (0.2)	1,206 (10.6)	93.6 (1.28)	6.6 (0.07)	90.0 (1.32)	6.8 (0.07)
North Carolina	92.6 (1.73)	6.7 (0.06)	94.7 (0.37)	6.9 (0.04)	181 (0.2)	1,240 (7.4)	95.2 (0.23)	6.8 (0.04)	‡ (†)	‡ (†)
North Dakota	95.9 (0.59)	6.6 (0.04)	95.2 (0.46)	6.5 (0.06)	177 (0.3)	1,159 (10.0)	96.4 (0.35)	6.4 (0.08)	95.5 (0.45)	6.6 (0.14)
Ohio	91.8 (2.01)	6.6 (0.10)	93.8 (0.48)	6.6 (0.03)	180 (0.5)	1,191 (6.2)	95.0 (0.30)	6.6 (0.04)	91.0 (1.45)	6.7 (0.07)
Oklahoma	92.1 (2.24)	6.6 (0.06)	94.4 (0.32)	6.7 (0.04)	174 (0.7)	1,176 (8.6)	94.9 (0.38)	6.7 (0.04)	93.3 (0.74)	6.8 (0.10)
Oregon	94.4 (0.59)	6.6 (0.06)	94.2 (0.40)	6.6 (0.05)	170 (0.9)	1,118 (7.9)	95.1 (0.29)	6.5 (0.06)	91.1 (1.41)	6.7 (0.06)
Pennsylvania	94.9 (0.39)	6.4 (0.12)	94.4 (0.29)	6.7 (0.05)	181 (0.3)	1,212 (9.5)	94.9 (0.38)	6.7 (0.06)	92.9 (0.56)	6.9 (0.14)
Rhode Island	93.7 (1.27)	6.3 (0.03)	94.6 (0.36)	6.4 (0.05)	180 (0.1)	1,150 (8.2)	95.1 (0.38)	6.3 (0.05)	‡ (†)	‡ (†)
South Carolina	94.9 (0.71)	6.9 (0.07)	95.6 (0.26)	7.0 (0.04)	181 (0.4)	1,263 (7.3)	96.2 (0.27)	6.9 (0.05)	93.9 (0.84)	7.1 (0.05)
South Dakota	93.6 (2.53)	6.8 (0.08)	96.1 (0.24)	7.0 (0.07)	170 (1.1)	1,180 (6.7)	96.7 (0.30)	6.9 (0.08)	93.6 (0.53)	6.9 (0.17)
Tennessee	94.9 (0.23)	7.0 (0.05)	94.6 (0.30)	7.1 (0.03)	179 (0.4)	1,272 (7.8)	95.0 (0.28)	7.1 (0.04)	94.2 (0.45)	7.0 (0.02)
Texas	94.1 (1.34)	7.2 (0.11)	95.2 (0.43)	7.3 (0.04)	179 (0.7)	1,297 (8.8)	95.9 (0.41)	7.3 (0.03)	94.8 (0.29)	7.3 (0.06)
Utah	91.4 (1.56)	6.3 (0.29)	93.3 (0.80)	6.5 (0.08)	179 (0.3)	1,165 (13.5)	94.4 (0.80)	6.5 (0.08)	93.6 (0.74)	6.6 (0.09)
Vermont	92.7 (3.39)	6.7 (0.07)	94.0 (0.95)	6.7 (0.04)	178 (0.3)	1,183 (7.2)	93.7 (1.30)	6.8 (0.04)	94.7 (0.35)	6.2 (0.12)
Virginia	94.7 (0.46)	6.6 (0.05)	95.0 (0.32)	6.6 (0.03)	185 (3.4)	1,222 (18.8)	95.8 (0.32)	6.7 (0.03)	93.3 (0.65)	6.6 (0.10)
Washington	82.9 (3.06)	6.2 (0.08)	92.2 (0.67)	6.3 (0.06)	179 (0.3)	1,129 (11.3)	94.3 (0.55)	6.4 (0.04)	88.0 (2.00)	6.1 (0.19)
West Virginia	94.0 (0.99)	6.9 (0.07)	94.9 (0.46)	7.0 (0.05)	181 (0.4)	1,272 (9.8)	96.2 (0.27)	7.0 (0.07)	89.8 (1.98)	7.3 (0.09)
Wisconsin	95.0 (0.57)	6.9 (0.04)	94.9 (0.31)	6.9 (0.11)	179 (0.2)	1,234 (19.2)	95.7 (0.21)	7.0 (0.03)	91.9 (1.08)	7.0 (0.12)
Wyoming	92.4 (1.15)	6.9 (0.05)	93.6 (0.81)	7.0 (0.04)	174 (0.5)	1,209 (6.5)	94.8 (0.78)	6.9 (0.05)	89.9 (2.19)	7.0 (0.08)

†Not applicable.
‡Reporting standards not met. Either the response rate is under 50 percent or there are too few cases for a reliable estimate.
NOTE: Averages reflect data reported by schools rather than state requirements. School-reported length of day may exceed state requirements, and there is a range of statistical error in reported estimates.

SOURCE: U.S. Department of Education, National Center for Education Statistics, Schools and Staffing Survey (SASS), "Public School Data File," 2007–08 and 2011–12. (This table was prepared May 2013.)

Table 219.10. High school graduates, by sex and control of school: Selected years, 1869–70 through 2025–26

School year	High school graduates							Averaged freshman graduation rate for public schools[3]	Population 17 years old[4]	Graduates as a ratio of 17-year-old population
		Sex		Control						
				Public[2]						
	Total[1]	Males	Females	Total	Males	Females	Private, total			
1	2	3	4	5	6	7	8	9	10	11
1869–70	16,000	7,064	8,936	—	—	—	—	—	815,000	2.0
1879–80	23,634	10,605	13,029	—	—	—	—	—	946,026	2.5
1889–90	43,731	18,549	25,182	21,882	—	—	21,849 [5]	—	1,259,177	3.5
1899–1900	94,883	38,075	56,808	61,737	—	—	33,146 [5]	—	1,489,146	6.4
1909–10	156,429	63,676	92,753	111,363	—	—	45,066 [5]	—	1,786,240	8.8
1919–20	311,266	123,684	187,582	230,902	—	—	80,364 [5]	—	1,855,173	16.8
1929–30	666,904	300,376	366,528	591,719	—	—	75,185 [5]	—	2,295,822	29.0
1939–40	1,221,475	578,718	642,757	1,143,246	538,273	604,973	78,229 [5]	—	2,403,074	50.8
1949–50	1,199,700	570,700	629,000	1,063,444	505,394	558,050	136,256 [5]	—	2,034,450	59.0
1959–60	1,858,023	895,000	963,000	1,627,050	791,426	835,624	230,973	—	2,672,000	69.5
1969–70	2,888,639	1,430,000	1,459,000	2,588,639	1,285,895	1,302,744	300,000 [5]	78.7	3,757,000	76.9
1975–76	3,142,120	1,552,000	1,590,000	2,837,129	1,401,064	1,436,065	304,991	74.9	4,272,000	73.6
1979–80	3,042,214	1,503,000	1,539,000	2,747,678	—	—	294,536	71.5	4,262,000	71.4
1980–81	3,020,285	1,492,000	1,528,000	2,725,285	—	—	295,000 [5]	72.2	4,212,000	71.7
1981–82	2,994,758	1,479,000	1,515,000	2,704,758	—	—	290,000 [5]	72.9	4,134,000	72.4
1982–83	2,887,604	1,426,000	1,461,000	2,597,604	—	—	290,000 [5]	73.8	3,962,000	72.9
1983–84	2,766,797	—	—	2,494,797	—	—	272,000 [5]	74.5	3,784,000	73.1
1984–85	2,676,917	—	—	2,413,917	—	—	263,000 [5]	74.2	3,699,000	72.4
1985–86	2,642,616	—	—	2,382,616	—	—	260,000 [5]	74.3	3,670,000	72.0
1986–87	2,693,803	—	—	2,428,803	—	—	265,000 [5]	74.3	3,754,000	71.8
1987–88	2,773,020	—	—	2,500,020	—	—	273,000 [5]	74.2	3,849,000	72.0
1988–89	2,743,743	—	—	2,458,800	—	—	284,943	73.4	3,842,000	71.4
1989–90[6]	2,574,162	—	—	2,320,337	—	—	253,825 [7]	73.6	3,505,000	73.4
1990–91	2,492,988	—	—	2,234,893	—	—	258,095	73.7	3,417,913	72.9
1991–92	2,480,399	—	—	2,226,016	—	—	254,383 [7]	74.2	3,398,884	73.0
1992–93	2,480,519	—	—	2,233,241	—	—	247,278	73.8	3,449,143	71.9
1993–94	2,463,849	—	—	2,220,849	—	—	243,000 [5]	73.1	3,442,521	71.6
1994–95	2,519,084	—	—	2,273,541	—	—	245,543	71.8	3,635,803	69.3
1995–96	2,518,109	—	—	2,273,109	—	—	245,000 [5]	71.0	3,640,132	69.2
1996–97	2,611,988	—	—	2,358,403	—	—	253,585	71.3	3,792,207	68.9
1997–98	2,704,050	—	—	2,439,050	1,187,647	1,251,403	265,000 [5]	71.3	4,008,416	67.5
1998–99	2,758,655	—	—	2,485,630	1,212,924	1,272,706	273,025	71.1	3,917,885	70.4
1999–2000	2,832,844	—	—	2,553,844	1,241,631	1,312,213	279,000 [5]	71.7	4,056,639	69.8
2000–01	2,847,973	—	—	2,569,200	1,251,931	1,317,269	278,773	71.7	4,023,686	70.8
2001–02	2,906,534	—	—	2,621,534	1,275,813	1,345,721	285,000 [5]	72.6	4,023,968	72.2
2002–03	3,015,735	—	—	2,719,947	1,330,973	1,388,974	295,788	73.9	4,125,087	73.1
2003–04[6,8]	3,054,438	—	—	2,753,438	1,347,800	1,405,638	301,000 [5]	74.3	4,113,074	74.3
2004–05	3,106,499	—	—	2,799,250	1,369,749	1,429,501	307,249	74.7	4,120,073	75.4
2005–06[6]	3,122,544	—	—	2,815,544	1,376,458	1,439,086	307,000 [5]	73.4	4,200,554	74.3
2006–07	3,199,650	—	—	2,893,045	1,414,069	1,478,976	306,605	73.9	4,297,239	74.5
2007–08	3,312,337	—	—	3,001,337	1,467,180	1,534,157	311,000 [5]	74.7	4,436,955	74.7
2008–09[6]	3,347,828	—	—	3,039,015	1,490,317	1,548,698	308,813	75.5	4,336,950	77.2
2009–10	3,439,102	—	—	3,128,022	1,542,684 [9]	1,585,338 [9]	311,080	78.2	4,311,831	79.8
2010–11	3,449,940	—	—	3,144,100	1,552,981	1,591,113	305,840 [5]	79.6	4,368,154	79.0
2011–12	3,455,405	—	—	3,149,185	1,558,489	1,590,694	306,220	80.8	4,294,956	80.5
2012–13	3,478,027	—	—	3,169,257	1,569,675	1,599,579	308,770 [5]	81.9	4,257,599	81.7
2013–14[10]	3,480,130	—	—	3,168,650	—	—	311,480	—	4,187,691	83.1
2014–15[10]	3,477,620	—	—	3,166,260	—	—	311,360	—	4,172,212	83.4
2015–16[10]	3,505,920	—	—	3,192,220	—	—	313,700	—	—	—
2016–17[10]	3,510,330	—	—	3,195,630	—	—	314,700	—	—	—
2017–18[10]	3,558,100	—	—	3,242,620	—	—	315,480	—	—	—
2018–19[10]	3,549,010	—	—	3,242,630	—	—	306,380	—	—	—
2019–20[10]	3,509,360	—	—	3,208,110	—	—	301,250	—	—	—
2020–21[10]	3,535,980	—	—	3,233,840	—	—	302,140	—	—	—
2021–22[10]	3,543,910	—	—	3,248,980	—	—	294,930	—	—	—
2022–23[10]	3,558,600	—	—	3,272,620	—	—	285,980	—	—	—
2023–24[10]	3,604,410	—	—	3,326,230	—	—	278,180	—	—	—
2024–25[10]	3,658,340	—	—	3,378,810	—	—	279,530	—	—	—
2025–26[10]	3,650,620	—	—	3,371,680	—	—	278,940	—	—	—

—Not available.

[1]Includes graduates of public and private schools.

[2]Data for 1929–30 and preceding years are from *Statistics of Public High Schools* and exclude graduates from high schools that failed to report to the Office of Education. Includes estimates for jurisdictions not reporting counts of graduates by sex.

[3]The averaged freshman graduation rate provides an estimate of the percentage of students who receive a regular diploma within 4 years of entering ninth grade. The rate uses aggregate student enrollment data to estimate the size of an incoming freshman class and aggregate counts of the number of diplomas awarded 4 years later. Averaged freshman graduation rates in this table are based on reported totals of enrollment by grade and high school graduates, rather than on details reported by race/ethnicity.

[4]Derived from Current Population Reports, Series P-25. For years 1869–70 through 1989–90, 17-year-old population is an estimate of the October 17-year-old population based on July data. Data for 1990–91 and later years are October resident population estimates prepared by the Census Bureau.

[5]Estimated.

[6]Includes imputations for nonreporting states.

[7]Projected by private schools responding to the Private School Universe Survey.

[8]Includes estimates for public schools in New York and Wisconsin. Without estimates for these two states, the averaged freshman graduation rate for the remaining 48 states and the District of Columbia is 75.0 percent.

[9]Includes estimate for Connecticut, which did not report graduates by sex.

[10]Projected by NCES.

NOTE: Includes graduates of regular day school programs. Excludes graduates of other programs, when separately reported, and recipients of high school equivalency certificates. Some data have been revised from previously published figures. Detail may not sum to totals because of rounding and adjustments to protect student privacy.

SOURCE: U.S. Department of Education, National Center for Education Statistics, *Annual Report of the Commissioner of Education*, 1870 through 1910; *Biennial Survey of Education in the United States*, 1919–20 through 1949–50; *Statistics of State School Systems*, 1951–52 through 1957–58; *Statistics of Public Elementary and Secondary School Systems*, 1958–59 through 1980–81; *Statistics of Nonpublic Elementary and Secondary Schools*, 1959 through 1980; Common Core of Data (CCD), "State Nonfiscal Survey of Public Elementary/Secondary Education," 1981–82 through 2009–10; "State Dropout and Completion Data File," 2005–06 through 2012–13; *Public School Graduates and Dropouts From the Common Core of Data*, 2007–08 and 2008–09; Private School Universe Survey (PSS), 1989 through 2013; and National High School Graduates Projection Model, 1972–73 through 2025–26. U.S. Department of Commerce, Census Bureau, Population Estimates, retrieved August 11, 2011, from http://www.census.gov/popest/data/national/asrh/2009/2009-nat-res.html and Population Estimates, retrieved December 18, 2015, from http://www.census.gov/popest/data/national/asrh/2014/2014-nat-res.html. (This table was prepared January 2016.)

Table 219.20. Public high school graduates, by region, state, and jurisdiction: Selected years, 1980–81 through 2025–26

Region, state, and jurisdiction	Actual data											Projected data												Percent change, 2012–13 to 2025–26
	1980–81	1989–90	1999–2000	2006–07	2007–08	2008–09	2009–10	2010–11	2011–12	2012–13	2013–14	2014–15	2015–16	2016–17	2017–18	2018–19	2019–20	2020–21	2021–22	2022–23	2023–24	2024–25	2025–26	
1	2	3	4	5	6	7	8	9	10	11	12	13	14	15	16	17	18	19	20	21	22	23	24	25
United States	2,725,285	2,320,337[1]	2,553,844	2,893,045	3,001,337	3,039,015[1]	3,128,022	3,144,100	3,149,185	3,169,257	3,168,650	3,166,260	3,192,220	3,195,630	3,242,620	3,242,630	3,208,110	3,233,840	3,248,980	3,272,620	3,326,230	3,378,810	3,371,680	6.4
Region																								
Northeast	593,727	446,045	453,814	536,697	552,289	552,973	556,400	556,611	554,705	555,202	546,940	541,890	539,000	534,910	536,910	532,910	525,990	530,150	529,890	526,380	532,020	541,880	535,840	-3.5
Midwest	784,071	616,700	648,020	702,987	721,220	717,536	726,844	718,779	716,072	713,662	705,590	702,490	704,950	703,690	715,240	713,800	701,690	705,420	714,230	709,600	717,080	724,370	718,480	0.7
South	868,068	796,385	861,498	986,801	1,031,773	1,068,270	1,104,770	1,119,414	1,121,400	1,138,965	1,145,650	1,154,890	1,176,960	1,188,240	1,213,240	1,220,330	1,206,310	1,210,460	1,213,120	1,234,320	1,257,450	1,299,490	1,303,110	14.4
West	479,419	461,207	590,512	666,560	696,055	700,236	740,008	749,296	757,008	761,428	770,470	766,990	771,310	768,800	777,230	775,590	774,120	787,810	791,740	802,310	819,690	813,070	814,240	6.9
State																								
Alabama	44,894	40,485	37,819	38,912	41,346	42,082	43,166	46,035	45,394	44,233	44,540	45,210	44,450	44,660	45,200	44,250	43,020	42,590	42,440	42,620	43,000	44,510	44,140	-0.2
Alaska	5,343	5,386	6,615	7,666	7,855	8,008	8,245	8,064	7,989	7,860	7,720	7,450	7,360	7,520	7,430	7,370	7,130	7,130	7,350	7,540	7,810	8,000	7,980	1.6
Arizona	28,416	32,103	38,304	55,954	61,667	62,374	61,145	64,472	63,208	62,208	66,710	65,520	65,740	63,730	64,390	64,220	64,670	66,470	67,500	69,390	70,890	72,600	72,970	17.3
Arkansas	29,577	26,475	27,335	27,166	28,725	28,057	28,276	28,205	28,419	28,928	29,610	30,360	30,520	30,330	30,330	30,480	30,320	29,910	30,040	29,850	29,690	31,820	31,490	8.8
California	242,172	236,291	309,866	356,641	374,561	372,310[2]	404,987	410,467	418,664	422,125	424,110	420,920	420,140	415,710	420,520	416,700	414,980	422,540	422,530	427,010	436,140	417,570	417,430	-1.1
Colorado	35,897	32,967	38,924	45,628	46,082	47,459	49,321	50,122	50,087	50,968	51,310	51,890	53,470	54,340	55,580	56,580	57,260	58,550	58,600	59,360	60,440	61,580	61,550	20.8
Connecticut	38,369	27,878	31,562	37,541	38,419	34,968	34,495	38,854	38,681	38,722	37,860	36,660	36,650	36,520	35,910	35,580	34,750	35,330	34,360	34,200	33,490	33,910	33,130	-14.4
Delaware	7,349	5,550	6,108	7,205	7,388	7,839	8,133	8,043	8,247	8,070	8,240	8,150	8,090	8,330	8,360	8,350	8,480	8,860	8,830	9,050	9,290	9,190	9,160	13.5
District of Columbia[3]	4,848	3,626	2,695	2,944	3,352	3,517	3,602	3,477	3,860	3,961	3,880	3,920	3,910	3,830	3,920	3,940	3,750	3,750	3,830	4,160	4,300	4,710	4,880	23.1
Florida	88,755	88,934	106,708	142,284	149,046	153,461	156,130	155,493	151,964	158,029	158,450	162,200	162,630	165,540	167,270	168,390	164,800	164,770	166,960	170,250	174,690	181,370	183,470	16.1
Georgia	62,963	56,605	62,563	77,829	83,505	88,003	91,561	92,338	90,582	92,416	94,390	96,530	99,150	100,540	102,560	103,750	102,380	101,700	102,220	103,710	105,840	108,930	109,110	18.1
Hawaii	11,472	10,325	10,437	11,063	11,613	11,508	10,998	10,716	11,360	10,790	11,050	10,900	10,760	10,660	11,080	10,640	11,140	11,350	11,400	11,670	11,640	12,170	12,100	12.1
Idaho	12,679	11,971	16,170	16,242	16,567	16,807	17,793	17,525	17,568	17,198	19,120	18,800	19,820	20,790	20,930	21,340	21,160	21,430	22,250	23,110	23,770	25,190	25,150	46.2
Illinois	136,795	108,119	111,835	130,220	135,143	131,670	139,035	134,956	139,575	139,228	137,650	139,000	136,900	137,350	141,510	141,890	139,730	142,530	145,760	143,530	143,900	143,390	139,980	0.5
Indiana	73,381	60,012	57,012	59,887	61,901	63,663	64,551	66,133	65,667	66,595	67,560	66,840	66,890	67,120	67,700	69,160	66,250	64,380	65,710	64,220	65,020	66,210	65,920	-1.0
Iowa	42,635	31,796	33,926	34,127	34,573	33,926	34,462	33,853	33,230	32,548	32,600	32,640	32,820	33,000	33,490	33,120	33,180	33,550	33,630	34,210	34,960	35,660	35,730	9.8
Kansas	29,397	25,367	29,102	30,139	30,737	30,368	31,642	31,370	31,898	31,922	32,150	31,750	32,750	32,650	33,530	33,630	33,430	34,080	34,120	34,600	35,210	36,250	36,040	12.9
Kentucky	41,714	38,005	36,830	39,099	39,339	41,851	42,664	43,031	42,642	42,888	42,400	41,640	41,900	41,440	41,890	41,980	40,710	41,480	41,450	40,530	40,640	41,370	41,110	-4.2
Louisiana	46,199	36,053	38,430	34,274	34,401	35,622	36,573	35,844	36,675	37,508	38,190	37,240	38,440	38,170	39,780	38,900	38,840	38,250	37,840	38,260	38,880	40,300	40,090	6.9
Maine	15,554	13,839	12,211	13,151	14,350[4]	14,093[4]	14,069	13,653	13,473	13,170	12,730	12,650	12,730	12,410	12,240	12,110	11,830	11,780	11,930	11,890	11,720	11,820	11,630	-11.7
Maryland	54,050	41,566	47,849	57,564	59,171	58,304	59,078	58,745	58,811	58,896	58,130	57,350	57,290	56,300	57,550	57,020	58,930	59,420	60,260	61,010	62,600	64,900	65,310	10.9
Massachusetts	74,831	55,941[5]	52,950	63,903	65,197	65,258	64,462	64,724	65,157	66,360	65,200	65,570	66,560	65,730	65,850	65,830	65,210	65,450	65,100	64,300	64,880	66,130	64,750	-2.4
Michigan	124,372	93,807	97,679	111,838	115,183	112,742	110,682	106,017	105,446	104,210	102,520	101,310	101,840	100,160	101,570	99,430	96,400	96,040	96,850	94,090	94,610	94,670	93,490	-10.3
Minnesota	64,166	49,087	57,372	59,497	60,409	59,729	59,667	59,357	57,501	58,255	56,380	57,150	56,590	57,300	58,200	59,130	58,620	60,270	61,880	62,390	63,860	65,150	64,690	11.0
Mississippi	28,083	25,182	24,232	24,186	24,795	24,505	25,478	27,321	26,158	26,502	26,650	25,910	25,890	26,070	26,830	25,820	25,370	24,480	24,730	24,620	25,370	26,770	26,230	-1.0
Missouri	60,359	48,957	52,848	60,275	61,717	62,969	63,994	62,994	61,313	61,407	60,900	60,780	61,640	60,860	61,060	60,530	59,650	59,580	59,880	60,290	60,820	62,260	62,050	1.0
Montana	11,634	9,370	10,903	10,122	10,396	10,077	10,075	9,732	9,750	9,369	9,470	9,420	9,480	9,480	9,250	9,480	9,530	9,530	9,690	9,720	10,190	10,160	10,330	10.2
Nebraska	21,411	17,664	20,149	19,873	20,035	19,501	19,370	20,331	20,464	20,442	20,580	20,860	21,120	21,420	22,030	22,350	22,760	22,970	23,490	23,420	23,790	22,450	23,190	13.4
Nevada	9,069	9,477	14,551	17,149	18,815	19,904[2]	20,956	21,182	21,891	23,038	22,720	22,100	22,490	22,860	23,040	23,420	23,390	23,520	23,640	24,270	24,940	26,210	26,520	15.1
New Hampshire	11,552	10,766	11,829	14,452	14,982	14,757	15,034	14,495	14,426	14,262	13,790	13,560	13,510	13,050	12,970	12,690	12,660	12,400	12,410	12,130	12,080	11,960	11,740	-17.7
New Jersey	93,168	69,824	74,420	93,013	94,994	95,085	96,225	95,186	93,819	96,490	95,230	95,640	95,400	94,520	94,950	94,780	93,810	94,440	94,980	93,870	94,710	96,890	95,970	-0.5
New Mexico	17,915	14,884	18,031	16,131	18,264	17,931	18,595	19,352	20,315	19,232	18,590	19,180	18,690	19,100	19,090	19,440	19,290	19,020	19,290	19,450	19,550	20,100	19,850	3.2
New York	198,465	143,318	141,731	168,333	176,310	180,917	183,826	182,759	180,806	180,351	178,820	179,220	178,550	177,440	179,510	176,920	175,600	177,800	176,870	177,240	181,430	185,130	183,720	1.9
North Carolina	69,395	64,782	62,140	76,031	83,307	86,712	88,704	89,892	93,977	94,339	96,220	96,520	98,260	98,540	100,790	101,870	100,130	100,090	93,300	100,230	103,100	105,800	105,360	11.7
North Dakota	9,924	7,690	8,606	7,159	6,999	7,232	7,155	7,156	6,942	6,900	6,960	7,020	7,200	7,250	7,080	7,420	7,540	7,810	8,290	8,460	9,230	9,540	9,940	44.0
Ohio	143,503	114,513	111,668	117,658	120,758	122,203	123,437	124,229	123,135	122,491	119,520	116,970	118,530	117,520	119,010	117,970	115,700	115,150	114,750	114,380	115,230	116,470	115,580	-5.6
Oklahoma	38,875	35,606	37,646	37,100	37,630	37,219	38,503	37,744	37,305	37,033	37,260	37,640	38,930	39,530	40,060	40,160	40,210	40,910	41,150	41,350	42,140	43,800	43,870	18.5
Oregon	28,729	25,473	30,151	33,446	34,949	35,138	34,671	34,723	34,261	33,899	34,450	34,010	34,620	34,400	34,410	34,300	34,050	34,440	34,650	34,800	35,730	36,880	37,070	9.4
Pennsylvania	144,645	110,527	113,959	128,603	130,298	130,658	131,182	130,284	131,733	129,777	127,210	122,630	119,790	120,200	120,440	119,470	116,730	117,680	118,720	117,430	118,670	120,470	119,630	-7.8
Rhode Island	10,719	7,825	8,477	10,384	10,347	10,028	9,908	9,724	9,751	9,579	9,730	9,630	9,630	8,750	9,020	9,530	9,500	9,420	9,610	9,280	9,240	9,600	9,420	-1.6

See notes at end of table.

Table 219.20. Public high school graduates, by region, state, and jurisdiction: Selected years, 1980–81 through 2025–26—Continued

Region, state, and jurisdiction	Actual data							Projected data																
	1980–81	1989–90	1999–2000	2006–07	2007–08	2008–09	2009–10	2010–11	2011–12	2012–13	2013–14	2014–15	2015–16	2016–17	2017–18	2018–19	2019–20	2020–21	2021–22	2022–23	2023–24	2024–25	2025–26	Percent change, 2012–13 to 2025–26
1	2	3	4	5	6	7	8	9	10	11	12	13	14	15	16	17	18	19	20	21	22	23	24	25
South Carolina	38,347	32,483	31,617	35,108	35,303	39,114	40,438	40,708	41,442	42,246	41,720	42,300	43,500	44,600	45,630	45,830	44,800	44,760	45,220	46,000	47,810	49,850	50,160	18.7
South Dakota	10,385	7,650	9,278	8,346	8,582	8,123	8,162	8,248	8,196	8,239	7,960	7,910	7,800	7,880	8,040	7,830	7,970	8,100	8,280	8,750	8,820	9,120	9,180	11.4
Tennessee	50,648	46,094	41,568	54,502	57,486	60,368	62,408	61,862	62,454	61,323	60,980	60,770	61,180	62,040	62,310	62,080	61,210	61,220	61,460	62,400	63,910	64,850	64,930	5.9
Texas	171,665	172,480	212,925	241,193	252,121	264,275	280,894	290,470	292,531	301,390	304,380	308,820	320,520	325,890	336,640	344,000	340,310	345,840	349,080	355,970	360,340	372,450	375,720	24.7
Utah	19,886	21,196	32,501	28,276	28,167	30,463	31,481	30,888	31,157	33,186	33,400	34,260	35,550	36,970	37,770	38,360	39,050	40,210	40,750	41,040	42,180	43,400	43,420	30.8
Vermont	6,424	6,127	6,675	7,317	7,392	7,209	7,199	6,932	6,859	6,491	6,360	6,330	6,170	6,300	6,020	5,990	5,900	5,850	5,910	6,040	5,810	5,970	5,850	-9.8
Virginia	67,126	60,605	65,596	73,997	77,369	79,651	81,511	82,895	83,336	83,279	83,100	82,900	84,560	85,030	86,650	86,570	86,180	86,010	87,720	87,890	89,570	92,150	91,550	9.9
Washington	50,046	45,941	57,597	62,801	61,625	62,764	66,046	66,453	65,205	66,066	66,240	66,990	67,500	67,540	68,000	67,980	66,730	67,550	68,060	68,670	69,930	72,530	73,190	10.8
West Virginia	23,580	21,854	19,437	17,407	17,489	17,690	17,651	17,311	17,603	17,924	17,520	17,420	17,740	17,400	17,470	16,940	16,870	16,420	16,590	16,410	16,270	16,720	16,540	-7.7
Wisconsin	67,743	52,038	58,545	63,968	65,183	65,410	64,687	64,135	62,705	61,425	60,820	60,240	60,850	61,180	62,020	61,350	60,470	60,950	61,610	61,240	61,630	63,200	62,710	2.1
Wyoming	6,161	5,823	6,462	5,441	5,494	5,493	5,695	5,600	5,553	5,489	5,590	5,560	5,700	5,700	5,730	5,750	5,750	6,070	6,030	6,300	6,480	6,670	6,690	21.9
Jurisdiction																								
Bureau of Indian Education	—	—	—	—	—	—	—	—	—	—	—	—	—	—	—	—	—	—	—	—	—	—	—	—
DoD, overseas	—	—	2,642	—	—	—	—	—	—	—	—	—	—	—	—	—	—	—	—	—	—	—	—	—
DoD, domestic	—	—	560	—	—	—	—	—	—	—	—	—	—	—	—	—	—	—	—	—	—	—	—	—
Other jurisdictions																								
American Samoa	—	703	698	954	—	—	—	—	—	—	—	—	—	—	—	—	—	—	—	—	—	—	—	—
Guam	—	1,033	1,406	—	—	—	—	—	—	—	—	—	—	—	—	—	—	—	—	—	—	—	—	—
Northern Marianas	—	227	360	643	—	—	—	—	—	—	—	—	—	—	—	—	—	—	—	—	—	—	—	—
Puerto Rico	—	29,049	30,856	31,718	30,016	29,286	25,514	26,231	25,720	—	—	—	—	—	—	—	—	—	—	—	—	—	—	—
U.S. Virgin Islands	—	1,260	1,060	820	820	940	958	1,014	1,046	897	—	—	—	—	—	—	—	—	—	—	—	—	—	—

—Not available.
[1]U.S. total includes estimates for nonreporting states.
[2]Estimated high school graduates from NCES 2011-312, *Public School Graduates and Dropouts from the Common Core of Data: School Year 2008–09.*
[3]Beginning in 1989–90, graduates from adult programs are excluded.
[4]Includes 1,161 graduates in 2007–08 and 1,169 graduates in 2008–09 from private high schools that received a majority of their funding from public sources.
[5]Projected data from NCES 91-490, *Projections of Education Statistics to 2002.*

NOTE: Data include regular diploma recipients, but exclude students receiving a certificate of attendance and persons receiving high school equivalency certificates. DoD = Department of Defense. Some data have been revised from previously published figures. Detail may not sum to totals because of rounding.
SOURCE: U.S. Department of Education, National Center for Education Statistics, Common Core of Data (CCD), "State Nonfiscal Survey of Public Elementary/Secondary Education," 1981–82 through 2005–06; "State Dropout and Completion Data File," 2005–06 through 2012–13; *Public School Graduates and Dropouts From the Common Core of Data,* 2007–08 and 2008–09; and State High School Graduates Projection Model, 1980–81 through 2025–26. (This table was prepared January 2016.)

Table 219.30. Public high school graduates, by race/ethnicity: 1998–99 through 2025–26

Year	Number of high school graduates							Percentage distribution of graduates						
	Total	White	Black	Hispanic	Asian/ Pacific Islander	American Indian/ Alaska Native	Two or more races	Total	White	Black	Hispanic	Asian/ Pacific Islander	American Indian/ Alaska Native	Two or more races
1	2	3	4	5	6	7	8	9	10	11	12	13	14	15
1998–99	2,485,630	1,749,561	325,708	270,836	115,216	24,309	—	100.0	70.4	13.1	10.9	4.6	1.0	†
1999–2000	2,553,844	1,778,370	338,116	289,139	122,344	25,875	—	100.0	69.6	13.2	11.3	4.8	1.0	†
2000–01	2,569,200	1,775,036	339,578	301,740	126,465	26,381	—	100.0	69.1	13.2	11.7	4.9	1.0	†
2001–02	2,621,534	1,796,110	348,969	317,197	132,182	27,076	—	100.0	68.5	13.3	12.1	5.0	1.0	†
2002–03	2,719,947	1,856,454	359,920	340,182	135,588	27,803	—	100.0	68.3	13.2	12.5	5.0	1.0	†
2003–04	2,753,438	1,829,177	383,443	374,492	137,496	28,830	—	100.0	66.4	13.9	13.6	5.0	1.0	†
2004–05	2,799,250	1,855,198	385,987	383,714	143,729	30,622	—	100.0	66.3	13.8	13.7	5.1	1.1	†
2005–06	2,815,544	1,838,765	399,406	396,820	150,925	29,628	—	100.0	65.3	14.2	14.1	5.4	1.1	†
2006–07	2,893,045	1,868,056	418,113	421,036	154,837	31,003	—	100.0	64.6	14.5	14.6	5.4	1.1	†
2007–08	3,001,337	1,898,367	429,840	448,887	159,410	32,036	32,797 [1]	100.0	63.3	14.3	15.0	5.3	1.1	1.1 [1]
2008–09	3,039,015	1,883,382	451,384	481,698	163,575	32,213	26,763 [1]	100.0	62.0	14.9	15.9	5.4	1.1	0.9 [1]
2009–10	3,128,022	1,871,980	472,261	545,518	167,840	34,131	36,292 [1]	100.0	59.8	15.1	17.4	5.4	1.1	1.2 [1]
2010–11	3,144,100	1,835,332	471,461	583,907	168,875	32,768	51,748	100.0	58.4	15.0	18.6	5.4	1.0	1.6
2011–12	3,149,185	1,807,528	467,932	608,726	173,835	32,450	58,703	100.0	57.4	14.9	19.3	5.5	1.0	1.9
2012–13	3,169,257	1,791,147	461,919	640,413	179,101	31,100	65,569	100.0	56.5	14.6	20.2	5.7	1.0	2.1
2013–14[2]	3,168,650	1,771,690	453,800	657,520	183,210	30,230	72,190	100.0	55.9	14.3	20.8	5.8	1.0	2.3
2014–15[2]	3,166,260	1,754,090	457,250	673,030	186,540	29,800	65,560	100.0	55.4	14.4	21.3	5.9	0.9	2.1
2015–16[2]	3,192,220	1,754,840	462,620	690,090	186,490	30,370	67,810	100.0	55.0	14.5	21.6	5.8	1.0	2.1
2016–17[2]	3,195,630	1,749,280	461,500	696,570	188,240	30,040	70,000	100.0	54.7	14.4	21.8	5.9	0.9	2.2
2017–18[2]	3,242,620	1,743,650	467,080	729,510	201,350	29,370	71,650	100.0	53.8	14.4	22.5	6.2	0.9	2.2
2018–19[2]	3,242,630	1,724,920	461,930	752,130	201,860	28,560	73,230	100.0	53.2	14.2	23.2	6.2	0.9	2.3
2019–20[2]	3,208,110	1,684,190	450,920	765,430	204,560	27,810	75,200	100.0	52.5	14.1	23.9	6.4	0.9	2.3
2020–21[2]	3,233,840	1,681,980	443,170	791,050	213,430	26,900	77,310	100.0	52.0	13.7	24.5	6.6	0.8	2.4
2021–22[2]	3,248,980	1,668,640	440,250	817,460	217,020	26,410	79,190	100.0	51.4	13.6	25.2	6.7	0.8	2.4
2022–23[2]	3,272,620	1,648,490	446,110	853,780	216,980	25,980	81,290	100.0	50.4	13.6	26.1	6.6	0.8	2.5
2023–24[2]	3,326,230	1,645,150	457,510	896,570	217,630	25,860	83,510	100.0	49.5	13.8	27.0	6.5	0.8	2.5
2024–25[2]	3,378,810	1,651,690	471,750	922,660	221,420	25,500	85,790	100.0	48.9	14.0	27.3	6.6	0.8	2.5
2025–26[2]	3,371,680	1,635,040	473,570	920,630	228,750	25,420	88,260	100.0	48.5	14.0	27.3	6.8	0.8	2.6

—Not available.
†Not applicable.
[1]Data on students of Two or more races were not reported by all states; therefore, the data are not comparable to figures for 2010–11 and later years.
[2]Projected.
NOTE: Race categories exclude persons of Hispanic ethnicity. Prior to 2007–08, data on students of Two or more races were not collected separately. Some data have been revised from previously published figures. Detail may not sum to totals because of rounding and statistical methods used to prevent the identification of individual students.
SOURCE: U.S. Department of Education, National Center for Education Statistics, Common Core of Data (CCD), "State Nonfiscal Survey of Public Elementary/Secondary Education," 1999–2000 through 2005–06; "State Dropout and Completion Data File," 2005–06 through 2012–13; and National Public High School Graduates by Race/Ethnicity Projection Model, 1995–96 through 2025–26. (This table was prepared January 2016.)

Table 219.32. Public high school graduates, by sex, race/ethnicity, and state or jurisdiction: 2012–13

State or jurisdiction	Total, male and female									Male							Female						
					Asian/Pacific Islander																		
	Total	White	Black	Hispanic	Total	Asian	Pacific Islander	American Indian/ Alaska Native	Two or more races	Total	White	Black	Hispanic	Asian/ Pacific Islander	American Indian/ Alaska Native	Two or more races	Total	White	Black	Hispanic	Asian/ Pacific Islander	American Indian/ Alaska Native	Two or more races
1	2	3	4	5	6	7	8	9	10	11	12	13	14	15	16	17	18	19	20	21	22	23	24
United States	**3,169,257**	**1,791,147**	**461,919**	**640,413**	**179,101**	**168,782**	**10,319**	**31,100**	**65,569**	**1,569,675**	**899,883**	**219,989**	**312,878**	**90,150**	**15,407**	**31,370**	**1,599,579**	**891,264**	**241,930**	**327,535**	**88,959**	**15,692**	**34,200**
Alabama	44,233	26,963	14,709	1,338	595	574	21	486	142	21,701	13,618	6,815	675	284	246	63	22,532	13,345	7,894	663	311	240	79
Alaska	7,860	4,428	271	482	725	567	158	1,495	459	3,945	2,224	133	238	379	738	233	3,915	2,204	138	244	346	757	226
Arizona	62,208	29,357	3,332	23,542	2,313	2,166	147	2,837	827	30,337	14,505	1,635	11,281	1,185	1,348	383	31,871	14,852	1,697	12,261	1,128	1,489	444
Arkansas	28,928	19,426	6,007	2,413	513	428	85	180	389	14,369	9,787	2,815	1,235	262	90	180	14,559	9,639	3,192	1,178	251	90	209
California	422,125	125,492	27,069	198,993	57,667	55,083	2,584	2,998	9,906	208,126	62,954	13,102	96,324	29,437	1,441	4,868	213,999	62,538	13,967	102,669	28,230	1,557	5,038
Colorado	50,968	31,552	2,441	13,219	1,916	1,797	119	432	1,408	25,170	15,703	1,234	6,434	911	213	675	25,798	15,849	1,207	6,785	1,005	219	733
Connecticut	38,722	25,828	4,758	5,838	1,707	1,642	65	142	449	19,435	13,084	2,368	2,859	831	75	218	19,287	12,744	2,390	2,979	876	67	231
Delaware	8,070	4,334	2,561	805	295	292	≤3	26	46	3,948	2,144	1,229	381	159	13	22	4,122	2,190	1,332	424	139	13	24
District of Columbia	3,961	142	3,028	422	59	54	5	7	303	1,732	64	1,285	192	26	≤3	164	2,228	78	1,743	230	34	4	139
Florida	158,029	73,953	32,454	42,010	4,804	4,652	152	629	4,179	77,301	36,500	15,484	20,638	2,372	326	1,981	80,728	37,453	16,970	21,372	2,432	303	2,198
Georgia	92,416	44,875	32,811	8,275	3,776	3,699	77	207	2,472	44,872	22,315	15,271	4,062	1,954	101	1,169	47,544	22,560	17,540	4,213	1,822	106	1,303
Hawaii	10,790	1,379	224	504	8,017	4,753	3,264	42	624	5,350	659	103	240	3,997	21	330	5,440	720	121	264	4,020	21	294
Idaho	17,198	13,883	199	2,375	329	258	71	198	214	8,524	6,914	102	1,137	168	99	104	8,674	6,969	97	1,238	161	99	110
Illinois	139,228	80,496	22,016	26,687	6,390	6,278	112	363	3,276	68,855	40,673	10,235	12,992	3,199	201	1,555	70,373	39,823	11,781	13,695	3,191	162	1,721
Indiana	66,595	51,519	6,877	4,643	1,209	1,176	33	223	2,124	32,674	25,530	3,150	2,263	593	106	1,032	33,921	25,989	3,727	2,380	616	117	1,092
Iowa	32,548	27,495	1,314	2,228	724	687	37	154	633	16,388	13,871	674	1,095	358	76	314	16,160	13,624	640	1,133	366	78	319
Kansas	31,922	22,933	2,235	4,352	801	756	45	369	1,232	16,057	11,654	1,125	2,131	396	196	555	15,865	11,279	1,110	2,221	405	173	677
Kentucky	42,888	35,865	4,581	1,236	577	550	27	119	510	21,653	18,215	2,237	609	297	56	239	21,235	17,650	2,344	627	280	63	271
Louisiana	37,508	19,635	15,307	1,259	747	722	25	272	288	17,728	9,529	6,974	600	379	130	116	19,780	10,106	8,333	659	368	142	172
Maine	13,170	12,175	319	191	294	284	10	92	99	6,660	6,162	157	104	145	47	45	6,510	6,013	162	87	149	45	54
Maryland	58,896	27,409	20,361	5,463	3,752	3,700	52	246	1,665	29,049	13,791	9,715	2,756	1,863	133	791	29,847	13,618	10,646	2,707	1,889	113	874
Massachusetts	66,360	47,254	5,870	7,941	3,874	3,800	74	153	1,268	33,048	23,642	2,859	3,937	1,934	82	594	33,312	23,612	3,011	4,004	1,940	71	674
Michigan	104,210	77,503	16,949	3,324	3,087	2,973	114	833	2,514	51,453	38,637	7,974	1,658	1,582	418	1,184	52,757	38,866	8,975	1,666	1,505	415	1,330
Minnesota	58,255	46,012	4,231	2,827	3,670	3,644	26	664	851	29,164	23,177	2,113	1,398	1,773	322	381	29,091	22,835	2,118	1,429	1,897	342	470
Mississippi	26,502	12,883	12,740	448	304	297	7	44	83	12,382	6,256	5,687	230	154	21	34	14,120	6,627	7,053	218	150	23	49
Missouri	61,407	47,112	9,671	2,317	1,273	1,202	71	283	751	31,258	24,158	4,764	1,172	666	142	356	30,149	22,954	4,907	1,145	607	141	395
Montana	9,369	8,041	65	281	128	109	19	738	116	4,794	4,122	34	154	60	366	58	4,575	3,919	31	127	68	372	58
Nebraska	20,442	15,329	1,264	2,666	413	393	20	230	540	10,340	7,815	615	1,318	207	124	261	10,102	7,514	649	1,348	206	106	279
Nevada	23,038	10,028	1,873	7,548	2,064	1,735	329	230	1,295	10,953	4,820	904	3,480	1,030	111	608	12,085	5,208	969	4,068	1,034	119	687
New Hampshire	14,262	13,022	261	457	353	344	9	37	132	7,176	6,569	143	214	175	15	60	7,086	6,453	118	243	178	22	72
New Jersey	96,490	54,591	14,930	17,711	8,788	8,555	233	111	359	48,698	27,864	7,409	8,736	4,453	48	188	47,792	26,727	7,521	8,975	4,335	63	171
New Mexico	19,232	5,509	426	10,628	303	288	15	2,146	220	9,390	2,745	218	5,114	155	1,054	104	9,842	2,764	208	5,514	148	1,092	116
New York[1]	180,351	98,641	30,059	33,532	16,496	16,295	201	785	838	88,740	49,507	14,149	16,174	8,169	376	365	91,611	49,134	15,910	17,358	8,327	409	473
North Carolina	94,339	52,914	25,497	9,078	2,568	2,482	86	1,301	2,981	46,526	26,687	12,125	4,412	1,239	660	1,403	47,813	26,227	13,372	4,666	1,329	641	1,578
North Dakota	6,900	6,051	164	134	103	92	11	417	31	3,486	3,073	81	70	56	194	12	3,414	2,978	83	64	47	223	19
Ohio	122,491	96,889	16,229	3,286	2,100	2,054	46	154	3,833	61,315	48,901	7,768	1,659	1,030	86	1,871	61,176	47,988	8,461	1,627	1,070	68	1,962
Oklahoma	37,033	21,386	3,434	3,601	928	857	71	6,441	1,243	18,444	10,761	1,670	1,756	450	3,205	602	18,589	10,625	1,764	1,845	478	3,236	641
Oregon	33,899	23,534	848	5,807	1,723	1,535	188	514	1,473	16,610	11,688	379	2,737	846	232	728	17,289	11,846	469	3,070	877	282	745
Pennsylvania	129,777	97,199	17,765	8,706	4,429	4,344	85	163	1,515	65,092	49,267	8,544	4,285	2,207	78	711	64,685	47,932	9,221	4,421	2,222	85	804
Rhode Island	9,579	6,582	770	1,740	298	282	16	36	153	4,749	3,305	371	842	141	19	71	4,830	3,277	399	898	157	17	82
South Carolina	42,246	23,802	14,769	2,070	707	647	60	123	775	20,566	11,845	6,945	1,022	351	65	338	21,680	11,957	7,824	1,048	356	58	437
South Dakota	8,239	7,025	209	229	149	144	5	543	83	4,147	3,553	104	101	75	274	40	4,092	3,472	105	128	75	269	43
Tennessee	61,323	42,682	14,509	2,800	1,185	1,113	72	147	—	30,378	21,452	6,836	1,408	601	82	—	30,943	21,230	7,673	1,392	584	65	—
Texas	301,390	104,466	38,772	139,783	12,044	11,650	394	1,311	5,014	151,002	53,036	19,177	69,495	6,174	701	2,419	150,388	51,430	19,595	70,288	5,870	610	2,595
Utah	33,186	26,757	402	4,100	1,135	669	466	373	419	16,436	13,259	212	1,994	613	165	193	16,750	13,498	190	2,106	522	208	226
Vermont	6,491	5,949	135	83	152	143	9	12	160	3,317	3,051	57	43	71	4	91	3,174	2,898	78	40	81	8	69
Virginia	83,279	47,825	18,565	8,055	5,293	5,183	110	265	3,276	41,383	24,168	8,820	4,000	2,710	130	1,555	41,896	23,657	9,745	4,055	2,583	135	1,721
Washington	66,066	43,132	2,905	10,092	5,826	5,380	446	740	3,371	32,368	21,235	1,416	4,860	2,865	381	1,611	33,698	21,897	1,489	5,232	2,961	359	1,760
West Virginia	17,924	16,572	917	174	134	131	≤3	19	105	9,033	8,344	475	84	69	13	48	8,891	8,228	442	90	68	6	57
Wisconsin	61,425	48,675	4,754	4,155	2,297	2,268	29	682	862	30,832	24,717	2,263	2,024	1,070	341	417	30,593	23,958	2,491	2,131	1,227	341	445
Wyoming	5,489	4,643	62	565	67	55	12	88	64	2,721	2,333	34	255	29	40	30	2,768	2,310	28	310	38	48	34

See notes at end of table.

Table 219.32. Public high school graduates, by sex, race/ethnicity, and state or jurisdiction: 2012–13—Continued

State or jurisdiction	Total, male and female									Male							Female						
	Total	White	Black	Hispanic	Asian/Pacific Islander			American Indian/ Alaska Native	Two or more races	Total	White	Black	Hispanic	Asian/ Pacific Islander	American Indian/ Alaska Native	Two or more races	Total	White	Black	Hispanic	Asian/ Pacific Islander	American Indian/ Alaska Native	Two or more races
					Total	Asian	Pacific Islander																
1	2	3	4	5	6	7	8	9	10	11	12	13	14	15	16	17	18	19	20	21	22	23	24
Bureau of Indian Education	—	—	—	—	—	—	—	—	—	—	—	—	—	—	—	—	—	—	—	—	—	—	—
DoD, overseas	—	—	—	—	—	—	—	—	—	—	—	—	—	—	—	—	—	—	—	—	—	—	—
DoD, domestic	—	—	—	—	—	—	—	—	—	—	—	—	—	—	—	—	—	—	—	—	—	—	—
Other jurisdictions																							
American Samoa	—	—	—	—	—	—	—	—	—	—	—	—	—	—	—	—	—	—	—	—	—	—	—
Guam	—	—	—	—	—	—	—	—	—	—	—	—	—	—	—	—	—	—	—	—	—	—	—
Northern Marianas	—	—	—	—	—	—	—	—	—	—	—	—	—	—	—	—	—	—	—	—	—	—	—
Puerto Rico	—	—	—	—	—	—	—	—	—	—	—	—	—	—	—	—	—	—	—	—	—	—	—
U.S. Virgin Islands	897	7	727	139	≤3	≤3	≤3	≤3	20	383	≤3	321	55	≤3	≤3	≤3	514	4	406	84	≤3	≤3	17

—Not available.
[1]Distribution of Asian and Pacific Islander students is estimated by the National Center for Education Statistics.
NOTE: Race categories exclude persons of Hispanic ethnicity. DoD = Department of Defense. To protect the confidentiality of individual students, small cell sizes have been bottom coded to less than or equal to three. Detail may not sum to totals because of statistical methods used to prevent the identification of individual students.
SOURCE: U.S. Department of Education, National Center for Education Statistics, Common Core of Data (CCD), State Dropout and Completion Data File, 2012–13. (This table was prepared January 2016.)

Table 219.35. Public high school averaged freshman graduation rate (AFGR), by state or jurisdiction: Selected years, 1990–91 through 2012–13

State or jurisdiction	1990–91	1995–96	1999–2000	2000–01	2002–03	2003–04	2004–05	2005–06	2006–07	2007–08	2008–09	2009–10	2010–11	2011–12	2012–13
1	2	3	4	5	6	7	8	9	10	11	12	13	14	15	16
United States	**73.7**	**71.0**	**71.7**	**71.7**	**73.9**	**74.3** [1]	**74.7**	**73.4** [2]	**73.9**	**74.7**	**75.5** [2]	**78.2**	**79.6**	**80.8**	**81.9**
Alabama	69.8	62.7	64.1	63.7	64.7	65.0	65.9	66.2	67.1	69.0	69.9	71.8	76.1	75.1	74.2
Alaska	74.6	68.3	66.7	68.0	68.0	67.2	64.1	66.5	69.0	69.1	72.6	75.5	77.9	78.6	79.9
Arizona	76.7	60.8	63.6	74.2	75.9	66.8	84.7	70.5	69.6	70.7	72.5	74.7	78.9	77.3	76.5
Arkansas	76.6	74.2	74.6	73.9	76.6	76.8	75.7	80.4	74.4	76.4	74.0	75.0	77.0	78.1	80.1
California	69.6	67.6	71.7	71.6	74.1	73.9	74.6	69.2	70.7	71.2	71.0 [3]	78.2	79.7	81.7	83.6
Colorado	76.3	74.8	74.1	73.2	76.4	78.7	76.7	75.5	76.6	75.4	77.6	79.8	82.0	82.3	83.3
Connecticut	80.2	76.1	81.9	77.5	80.9	80.7	80.9	80.9	81.8	82.2	75.4	75.1	84.7	86.1	87.4
Delaware	72.5	70.4	66.8	71.0	73.0	72.9	73.0	76.3	71.9	72.1	73.7	75.5	76.1	77.1	77.0
District of Columbia	54.5	49.7	54.5	60.2	59.6	68.2	66.3	65.4 [4]	54.8	56.0	62.4	59.9	64.9	70.8	77.7
Florida	65.6	62.3	61.0	61.2	66.7	66.4	64.6	63.6	65.0	66.9	68.9	70.8	72.0	74.7	75.8
Georgia	70.3	61.9	59.7	58.7	60.8	61.2	61.7	62.4	64.1	65.4	67.8	69.9	69.6	69.6	70.5
Hawaii	75.9	74.5	70.9	68.3	71.3	72.6	75.1	75.5	75.4	76.0	75.3	75.4	73.7	77.9	78.0
Idaho	79.6	80.5	79.4	79.6	81.4	81.5	81.0	80.5	80.4	80.1	80.6	84.0	83.2	83.9	82.1
Illinois	76.6	75.2	76.3	75.6	75.9	80.3	79.4	79.7	79.5	80.4	77.7	81.9	80.0	82.1	82.7
Indiana	76.9	73.6	71.8	72.1	75.5	73.5	73.2	73.3	73.9	74.1	75.2	77.2	79.9	80.0	81.0
Iowa	84.4	84.3	83.1	82.8	85.3	85.8	86.6	86.9	86.5	86.4	85.7	87.9	89.0	89.3	89.4
Kansas	80.8	77.1	77.1	76.5	76.9	77.9	79.2	77.5	78.8	79.0	80.2	84.5	86.5	88.3	88.4
Kentucky	72.9	71.3	69.7	69.8	71.7	73.0	75.9	77.2	76.4	74.4	77.6	79.9	80.9	81.9	83.1
Louisiana	57.5	61.7	62.2	63.7	64.1	69.4	63.9	59.5	61.3	63.5	67.3	68.8	71.2	71.9	72.7
Maine	80.7	73.7	75.9	76.4	76.3	77.6	78.6	76.3	78.5	79.1 [5]	79.9 [5]	82.8 [6]	85.7	86.7	87.5
Maryland	77.5	78.3	77.6	78.7	79.2	79.5	79.3	79.9	80.0	80.4	80.1	82.2	83.8	84.5	85.6
Massachusetts	79.1	78.0	78.0	78.9	75.7	79.3	78.7	79.5	80.8	81.5	83.3	82.6	85.4	86.5	88.4
Michigan	72.1	71.4	75.3	75.4	74.0	72.5	73.0	72.2	77.0	76.3	75.3	75.9	74.7	77.5	78.3
Minnesota	90.8	86.1	84.9	83.6	84.8	84.7	85.9	86.2	86.5	86.4	87.4	88.2	89.2	88.4	91.0
Mississippi	63.3	59.7	59.4	59.7	62.7	62.7	63.3	63.5	63.5	63.9	62.0	63.8	68.5	67.3	68.4
Missouri	76.0	75.0	76.3	75.5	78.3	80.4	80.6	81.0	81.9	82.4	83.1	83.7	84.7	85.9	86.6
Montana	84.4	83.9	80.8	80.0	81.0	80.4	81.5	81.9	81.5	82.0	82.0	81.9	83.7	85.7	84.7
Nebraska	86.7	85.6	85.7	83.8	85.2	87.6	87.8	87.0	86.3	83.8	82.9	83.8	89.8	92.7	93.3
Nevada	77.0	65.8	69.7	70.0	72.3	57.4	55.8	55.8	54.2	56.3	56.3 [3]	57.8	58.7	59.5	67.5
New Hampshire	78.6	77.5	76.1	77.8	78.2	78.7	80.1	81.1	81.7	83.3	84.3	86.3	86.6	87.0	87.3
New Jersey	81.4	82.8	83.6	85.4	87.0	86.3	85.1	84.8	84.4	84.6	85.3	87.2	86.6	86.4	89.1
New Mexico	70.1	63.7	64.7	65.9	63.1	67.0	65.4	67.3	59.1	66.8	64.8	67.3	70.7	74.3	71.6
New York	66.1	63.6	61.8	61.5	60.9	60.9 [7]	65.3	67.4	68.9	70.9	73.5	76.0	77.6	77.1	78.5
North Carolina	71.3	66.5	65.8	66.5	70.1	71.4	72.6	71.8	68.6	72.8	75.1	76.9	76.8	78.7	80.5
North Dakota	87.6	89.5	86.0	85.4	86.4	86.1	86.3	82.2	83.1	83.8	87.4	88.4	90.2	91.1	91.4
Ohio	77.5	74.5	75.2	76.5	79.0	81.3	80.2	79.2	78.7	79.0	79.6	81.4	82.3	83.9	84.9
Oklahoma	76.5	75.6	75.8	75.8	76.0	77.0	76.9	77.8	77.8	78.0	77.3	78.5	79.9	79.3	79.4
Oregon	72.7	68.3	69.6	68.3	73.7	74.2	74.2	73.0	73.8	76.7	76.5	76.3	78.1	78.0	76.8
Pennsylvania	79.7	80.0	78.7	79.0	81.7	82.2	82.5	83.5 [4]	83.0	82.7	80.5	84.1	85.8	88.3	88.4
Rhode Island	75.0	72.7	72.8	73.5	77.7	75.9	78.4	77.8	78.4	76.4	75.3	76.4	76.6	77.1	79.0
South Carolina	66.6	60.9	58.6	56.5	59.7	60.6	60.1	61.0 [4]	58.9	62.2	66.0	68.2	69.0	71.6	74.2
South Dakota	83.8	84.5	77.6	77.4	83.0	83.7	82.3	84.5	82.5	84.4	81.7	81.8	81.6	83.1	83.8
Tennessee	69.8	66.6	59.5	59.0	63.4	66.1	68.5	70.7	72.6	74.9	77.4	80.4	81.1	83.6	82.4
Texas	72.2	66.1	71.0	70.8	75.5	76.7	74.0	72.5	71.9	73.1	75.4	78.9	81.4	83.0	83.6
Utah	77.5	76.9	82.5	81.6	80.2	83.0	84.4	78.6	76.6	74.3	79.4	78.6	78.5	77.6	81.6
Vermont	79.5	85.3	81.0	80.2	83.6	85.4	86.5	82.3	88.5	89.3	89.6	91.4	92.7	91.9	89.3
Virginia	76.2	76.2	76.9	77.5	80.6	79.3	79.6	74.5	75.5	77.0	78.4	81.2	82.7	83.9	84.8
Washington	75.7	75.5	73.7	69.2	74.2	74.6	75.0	72.9	74.8	71.9	73.7	77.2	79.0	79.2	80.4
West Virginia	76.6	77.0	76.7	75.9	75.7	76.9	77.3	76.9	78.2	77.3	77.0	78.3	78.1	80.3	81.5
Wisconsin	85.2	83.6	82.7	83.3	85.8	85.8 [7]	86.7	87.5	88.5	89.6	90.7	91.1	92.2	92.2	93.0
Wyoming	81.1	77.7	76.3	73.4	73.9	76.0	76.7	76.1	75.8	76.0	75.2	80.3	80.4	80.2	82.5
Other jurisdictions															
American Samoa	85.3	79.7	71.9	77.0	81.0	80.2	81.1	81.0	84.6	—	—	—	—	—	—
Guam	48.2	44.6	52.9	51.7	56.3	48.4	—	—	—	—	—	—	—	—	—
Northern Marianas	—	63.3	61.1	62.7	65.2	75.3	75.4	80.3	73.6	—	—	—	—	—	—
Puerto Rico	60.9	60.8	64.7	65.7	67.8	64.8	61.7	68.6	66.7	64.5	67.2	60.2	61.6	61.7	—
U.S. Virgin Islands	53.2	54.2	53.8	57.3	53.5	—	—	—	57.8	58.3	63.1	65.5	96.8	72.5	67.8

—Not available.

[1]Includes estimates for New York and Wisconsin. Without estimates for these two states, the averaged freshman graduation rate for the remaining 48 states and the District of Columbia is 75.0 percent.

[2]U.S. total includes estimates for nonreporting states.

[3]Estimated high school graduates from NCES 2011-312, *Public School Graduates and Dropouts From the Common Core of Data: School Year 2008–09.*

[4]Projected high school graduates from NCES 2009-062, *Projections of Education Statistics to 2018.*

[5]Includes 1,161 graduates in 2007–08 and 1,169 graduates in 2008–09 from private high schools that received a majority of their funding from public sources.

[6]Includes 1,419 fall 2006 9th-graders who attended publicly funded private schools that were not reported in the 2006–07 Common Core of Data, but were reported in data for later years.

[7]Estimated high school graduates from NCES 2006-606rev, *The Averaged Freshman Graduation Rate for Public High Schools From the Common Core of Data: School Years 2002–03 and 2003–04.*

NOTE: The averaged freshman graduation rate provides an estimate of the percentage of students who receive a regular diploma within 4 years of entering ninth grade. The rate uses aggregate student enrollment data to estimate the size of an incoming freshman class and aggregate counts of the number of diplomas awarded 4 years later. Averaged freshman graduation rates in this table are based on reported totals of enrollment by grade and high school graduates, rather than on details reported by race/ethnicity.

SOURCE: U.S. Department of Education, National Center for Education Statistics, Common Core of Data (CCD), "State Nonfiscal Survey of Public Elementary/Secondary Education," 1986–87 through 2010–11; "State Dropout and Completion Data File," 2005–06 through 2012–13; *The Averaged Freshman Graduation Rate for Public High Schools From the Common Core of Data: School Years 2002–03 and 2003–04; Public School Graduates and Dropouts From the Common Core of Data*, 2007–08 and 2008–09; and *Projections of Education Statistics to 2018.* (This table was prepared January 2016.)

Table 219.40. Public high school averaged freshman graduation rate (AFGR), by sex, race/ethnicity, and state or jurisdiction: 2012–13

State or jurisdiction	Total, male and female						Male						Female					
	Total[1]	White	Black	Hispanic	Asian/ Pacific Islander	American Indian/ Alaska Native	Total[1]	White	Black	Hispanic	Asian/ Pacific Islander	American Indian/ Alaska Native	Total[1]	White	Black	Hispanic	Asian/ Pacific Islander	American Indian/ Alaska Native
1	2	3	4	5	6	7	8	9	10	11	12	13	14	15	16	17	18	19
United States	**81.9**	**85.6**	**69.4**	**78.2**	**94.6**	**67.7**	**78.8**	**83.5**	**64.3**	**74.1**	**92.6**	**65.3**	**85.2**	**87.8**	**74.8**	**82.6**	**96.7**	**70.2**
Alabama	74.2	78.1	67.6	67.5	87.2	84.7	70.5	75.8	61.3	64.9	86.7	83.4	78.2	80.6	74.3	70.5	87.8	86.0
Alaska	79.9	82.3	74.7	87.6	94.1	68.6	77.7	80.7	67.3	87.7	92.1	64.7	82.2	83.9	83.6	87.6	96.5	72.8
Arizona	76.5	80.1	70.0	72.1	90.1	64.2	72.7	77.1	67.3	66.9	89.0	61.3	80.6	83.1	72.8	77.6	91.4	67.0
Arkansas	80.1	81.0	74.5	81.1	87.8	67.0	77.1	78.8	69.0	78.5	86.7	65.5	83.3	83.5	80.2	83.9	89.0	68.5
California	83.6	88.7	72.7	79.7	97.3	73.5	80.1	86.3	68.9	75.2	95.5	68.9	87.3	91.3	76.8	84.4	99.2	78.4
Colorado	83.3	84.5	68.7	77.7	90.4	62.7	79.8	81.7	66.5	73.0	87.2	60.3	87.0	87.6	71.1	82.7	93.5	65.2
Connecticut	87.4	90.4	76.6	77.7	100.0	79.5	84.9	89.1	72.0	73.0	99.6	80.1[2]	90.0	91.7	81.8	82.8	100.0	78.8[2]
Delaware	77.0	79.8	70.6	75.8	94.2	83.0[2]	72.7	76.1	65.2	71.8	92.8	‡	81.6	83.8	76.5	79.7	98.1	‡
District of Columbia	77.7	94.8	69.8	80.7	87.1[2]	‡	68.9	84.6[2]	59.8	76.8	82.9[2]	‡	86.2	100.0[2]	79.7	84.3	93.5[2]	‡
Florida	75.8	77.8	67.2	79.1	93.3	85.2	72.1	74.4	62.3	75.7	91.7	82.3	79.7	81.4	72.5	82.6	95.0	88.7
Georgia	70.5	76.5	63.7	64.4	90.8	66.9	66.5	73.3	58.0	60.9	89.3	63.3	74.9	79.8	69.6	68.1	92.5	70.8
Hawaii	78.0	57.5	70.6	84.8	79.8	57.0[2]	74.8	53.9	60.2	76.2	77.0	49.1[2]	81.4	61.3	82.8	94.4	82.9	67.7[2]
Idaho	82.1	82.4	77.3	78.7	88.8	55.2	79.8	80.0	84.5	75.1	87.8	55.1	84.5	84.8	71.0	82.2	89.8	55.2
Illinois	82.7	90.6	63.6	78.3	97.8	78.5	80.7	90.5	58.1	75.1	96.7	81.8	84.7	90.7	69.4	81.6	98.9	74.7
Indiana	81.0	83.1	66.4	85.7	99.2	92.7	77.0	79.8	59.3	80.2	96.8	89.6	85.2	86.6	73.9	91.6	100.0	95.6
Iowa	89.4	90.2	69.0	85.5	98.0	67.2	87.3	88.3	65.9	82.1	96.1	69.1	91.6	92.2	72.6	89.0	100.0	65.5
Kansas	88.4	89.6	75.5	85.9	95.9	68.8	86.3	88.6	73.6	79.8	94.2	68.1	90.6	90.6	77.5	92.7	97.5	69.6
Kentucky	83.1	83.4	79.5	86.8	99.7	100.0[2]	81.7	81.6	75.0	79.8	100.0	100.0[2]	86.6	85.4	84.4	94.9	99.0	100.0[2]
Louisiana	72.7	78.0	64.3	94.4	97.1	69.5	67.3	73.7	57.7	87.4	94.5	64.6	78.4	82.6	71.1	100.0	99.9	74.7
Maine	87.5	86.5	92.7	92.9	100.0	76.9	86.0	85.0	95.7	87.6	100.0	79.2[2]	89.1	88.2	90.0	100.0[2]	100.0	74.6[2]
Maryland	85.6	88.6	76.2	84.5	99.3	85.0	81.8	86.5	70.7	79.8	97.8	83.6	89.7	90.9	82.1	89.9	100.0	86.7
Massachusetts	88.4	90.9	87.0	72.7	100.0	67.6	86.1	89.3	81.2	69.6	100.0	71.5	90.8	92.6	93.4	76.0	100.0	63.6
Michigan	78.3	83.4	60.6	52.6	95.3	68.2	74.5	80.3	54.8	49.8	93.3	66.6	82.3	86.7	67.0	55.7	97.5	69.8
Minnesota	91.0	93.2	74.2	77.1	97.8	50.7	88.5	91.3	70.4	73.1	94.3	48.5	93.6	95.3	78.4	81.6	100.0	53.0
Mississippi	68.4	74.2	63.1	64.7	88.7	60.8[2]	63.1	70.5	56.4	62.5	85.1	52.6[2]	73.7	78.1	69.8	67.1	92.7	71.1[2]
Missouri	86.6	88.2	73.6	91.2	95.7	86.8	84.8	87.0	69.9	89.9	96.6	84.2	88.4	89.6	77.6	92.6	94.7	89.6
Montana	84.7	86.9	66.6[2]	94.6	92.3	60.1	83.7	85.8	66.7[2]	94.1	90.9[2]	59.1	85.8	88.0	66.4[2]	95.3	93.6[2]	61.2
Nebraska	93.3	94.6	71.3	90.7	93.4	65.5	91.3	93.4	67.4	85.7	90.5	66.0	95.5	95.9	75.5	96.1	96.6	64.9
Nevada	67.5	69.5	48.6	62.0	73.4	45.1	63.2	65.6	45.6	56.9	70.9	42.0	71.9	73.7	51.7	67.2	76.1	48.5
New Hampshire	87.3	86.7	85.9	87.0	97.3	68.5[2]	84.9	84.5	85.3	77.6	99.6	‡	89.8	89.1	86.8	97.3	95.2	71.0[2]
New Jersey	89.1	92.7	79.4	83.3	98.6	70.3	86.9	91.3	75.7	79.9	98.5	60.5[2]	91.4	94.3	83.4	86.8	98.8	80.2[2]
New Mexico	71.6	76.9	64.9	68.3	94.8	71.8	67.6	73.7	58.4	63.9	92.6	67.8	76.0	80.2	73.6	73.0	97.2	76.2
New York	78.5	87.1	65.2	66.4	90.9	71.9	76.1	87.1	60.5	62.1	86.1	65.2	81.0	87.1	70.1	70.9	96.1	79.4
North Carolina	80.5	83.4	69.7	79.9	91.9	76.3	76.6	80.8	64.3	74.7	89.5	72.5	84.7	86.2	75.4	85.7	94.3	80.6
North Dakota	91.4	93.8	100.0	85.4	100.0[2]	59.1	89.1	91.8	100.0[2]	89.7[2]	100.0[2]	54.5	93.8	95.8	100.0[2]	81.0[2]	100.0[2]	63.7
Ohio	84.9	89.4	65.2	85.7	98.8	73.9	82.7	87.7	60.5	84.0	96.5	81.6	87.3	91.1	70.3	87.6	100.0	66.0
Oklahoma	79.4	81.0	66.2	76.6	92.8	71.5	76.9	78.7	63.1	73.0	92.4	70.0	82.0	83.5	69.5	80.3	93.2	73.1
Oregon	76.8	76.7	66.4	76.0	87.3	56.5	73.2	73.7	59.9	70.3	86.2	49.2	80.6	80.0	72.7	82.0	88.4	64.3
Pennsylvania	88.4	90.8	76.4	77.4	100.0	68.4	86.0	89.2	71.7	73.2	100.0	63.0	91.0	92.6	81.2	81.9	100.0	74.3
Rhode Island	79.0	80.5	69.7	74.6	81.1	46.2[2]	75.3	77.2	64.0	70.4	77.8	53.3[2]	83.0	84.1	76.0	79.1	84.3	40.2[2]
South Carolina	74.2	78.2	66.3	74.7	86.3	57.4	69.4	74.4	60.0	70.7	85.6	56.2	79.5	82.3	73.1	79.0	87.0	58.8[2]
South Dakota	83.8	87.9	76.7	80.5	100.0	47.7	81.3	85.3	72.6	71.0	100.0[2]	47.9	86.3	90.7	81.4	90.1	100.0[2]	47.6
Tennessee	82.4	83.8	77.6	82.7	100.0	96.1	79.2	81.6	71.6	78.4	100.0	100.0[2]	85.8	86.2	83.8	87.5	100.0	85.2[2]
Texas	83.6	85.8	77.0	82.1	97.4	71.5	80.9	84.3	73.1	78.6	96.9	71.5	86.6	87.4	81.2	85.7	98.0	71.4
Utah	81.6	83.2	67.4	71.4	82.5	62.5	78.9	80.9	66.3	67.2	85.2	55.3	84.4	85.7	68.7	75.9	79.6	69.6
Vermont	89.3	89.2	88.0	97.3[2]	100.0	‡	88.9	88.9	79.2[2]	100.0[2]	100.0[2]	‡	89.7	89.6	95.9[2]	83.9[2]	100.0[2]	‡
Virginia	84.8	86.4	72.7	89.7	98.5	76.2	81.5	84.2	67.2	84.5	97.1	74.4	88.4	88.7	78.6	95.5	100.0	78.0
Washington	80.4	80.1	62.7	80.7	84.5	40.3	76.8	76.8	58.5	74.8	82.1	40.5	84.6	83.7	67.2	86.9	87.0	40.1
West Virginia	81.5	81.5	73.5	83.4	93.7	‡	79.7	79.7	73.5	80.0	92.8[2]	‡	83.3	83.5	73.5	86.8	99.0[2]	‡
Wisconsin	93.0	96.3	68.1	83.7	97.7	72.9	90.7	95.1	61.5	78.5	93.5	68.6	95.5	97.5	75.5	89.3	100.0	77.9
Wyoming	82.5	84.0	75.3[2]	77.9	100.0[2]	42.6	80.0	82.1	73.9[2]	69.4	‡	41.0[2]	85.0	85.9	77.1[2]	86.8	100.0[2]	44.2
Bureau of Indian Education	—	—	—	—	—	—	—	—	—	—	—	—	—	—	—	—	—	—
DoD, overseas	—	—	—	—	—	—	—	—	—	—	—	—	—	—	—	—	—	—
DoD, domestic	—	—	—	—	—	—	—	—	—	—	—	—	—	—	—	—	—	—
Other jurisdictions																		
American Samoa	—	—	—	—	—	—	—	—	—	—	—	—	—	—	—	—	—	—
Guam	—	—	—	—	—	—	—	—	—	—	—	—	—	—	—	—	—	—
Northern Marianas	—	—	—	—	—	—	—	—	—	—	—	—	—	—	—	—	—	—
Puerto Rico	—	—	—	—	—	—	—	—	—	—	—	—	—	—	—	—	—	—
U.S. Virgin Islands	67.8	‡	67.2	63.8	‡	‡	59.1	‡	59.6	54.5	‡	‡	76.1	‡	74.7	71.8	‡	‡

—Not available.
‡Reporting standards not met (too few cases).
[1]Total averaged freshman graduation rate (AFGR) is based on reported totals of enrollment by grade and high school graduates, rather than on details reported by race/ethnicity.
[2]AFGR is based on an estimate of 30 to 99 students entering ninth grade and may show large variation from year to year.
NOTE: The AFGR provides an estimate of the percentage of students who receive a regular diploma within 4 years of entering ninth grade. The rate uses aggregate student enrollment data to estimate the size of an incoming freshman class and aggregate counts of the number of diplomas awarded 4 years later. The enrollment data used in computing the AFGR for race/ethnicity categories include only students for whom race/ethnicity was reported. Race categories exclude persons of Hispanic ethnicity. DoD = Department of Defense.
SOURCE: U.S. Department of Education, National Center for Education Statistics, Common Core of Data (CCD), "State Dropout and Completion Data File," 2012–13. (This table was prepared January 2016.)

Table 219.50. Number and percentage of 9th- to 12th-graders who dropped out of public schools (event dropout rate), by race/ethnicity, grade, and state or jurisdiction: 2009–10

State or jurisdiction	Percent of 9th- to 12th-graders who dropped out (event dropout rate), by race/ethnicity							Number and percent of 9th- to 12th-graders who dropped out (event dropout rate), by grade							
								Grade 9		Grade 10		Grade 11		Grade 12	
	Total	White	Black	Hispanic	Asian/ Pacific Islander	American Indian/ Alaska Native	Two or more races	Number of dropouts	Event dropout rate	Number of dropouts	Event dropout rate	Number of dropouts	Event dropout rate	Number of dropouts	Event dropout rate
1	2	3	4	5	6	7	8	9	10	11	12	13	14	15	16
United States	**3.4**	**2.3**	**5.5**	**5.0**	**1.9**	**6.7**	**‡**	**104,756**	**2.6**	**113,370**	**3.0**	**117,536**	**3.3**	**175,806**	**5.1**
Alabama	1.8	1.6	2.0	0.9	1.4	1.3	—	864	1.4	1,128	2.0	1,048	2.1	862	1.8
Alaska	6.9	5.1	6.4	6.1	4.8	11.6	9.6	404	4.0	551	5.5	1,014	9.3	851	8.7
Arizona	7.8	6.8	8.8	8.1	4.9	14.6	—	4,207	5.1	4,594	5.7	5,269	7.0	10,795	13.6
Arkansas	3.6	3.1	5.0	4.1	2.0	4.9	3.1	720	1.9	1,130	3.2	1,427	4.4	1,613	5.3
California	4.6	2.8	8.4	5.8	2.0	6.5	5.0	13,849	2.6	15,518	3.1	20,625	4.2	42,587	8.9
Colorado	5.3	3.2	8.6	9.9	2.4	10.1	—	1,957	3.1	2,216	3.7	3,045	5.3	5,673	9.7
Connecticut	3.0	1.4	6.8	6.9	1.1	3.0	—	1,316	2.8	1,127	2.6	1,452	3.4	1,299	3.2
Delaware	3.9	3.1	4.9	4.7	3.2	10.3	—	546	4.7	386	3.7	299	3.4	288	3.5
District of Columbia[1]	7.0	4.9	6.9	8.3	5.4	#	—	501	8.1	262	5.9	153	4.2	133	4.0
Florida	2.3	1.6	3.5	2.8	0.8	2.7	—	4,189	1.9	4,348	2.2	4,678	2.4	4,816	2.8
Georgia	3.8	3.1	4.6	4.3	1.5	4.2	3.4	5,800	4.0	5,095	4.2	4,074	3.8	2,800	2.9
Hawaii	5.2	6.4	7.9	5.9	4.7	9.0	—	562	3.7	816	5.7	726	5.8	632	6.0
Idaho	1.4	1.2	1.9	2.2	1.2	2.5	—	211	1.0	235	1.1	301	1.5	386	2.0
Illinois	2.9	1.8	5.7	3.8	0.9	3.0	—	3,482	2.0	5,287	3.1	3,970	2.7	5,801	4.0
Indiana	1.6	1.3	3.1	2.4	1.1	2.2	—	373	0.4	945	1.2	1,349	1.7	2,346	3.2
Iowa	3.4	2.8	9.1	6.9	2.1	8.9	4.9	363	1.0	713	1.9	1,276	3.5	2,747	7.1
Kansas	2.1	1.8	3.7	2.9	0.7	4.1	2.0	442	1.2	661	1.9	765	2.3	1,105	3.3
Kentucky	3.2	2.9	5.5	5.6	2.0	1.9	—	1,076	2.0	1,769	3.5	1,762	3.8	1,615	3.7
Louisiana	4.8	3.2	6.8	3.9	2.0	4.8	—	3,229	5.7	1,920	4.2	1,663	4.1	1,892	4.9
Maine	4.2	4.2	4.9	5.0	3.8	8.6	—	252	1.7	349	2.3	703	4.8	1,260	8.3
Maryland	2.7	2.0	3.4	4.2	0.9	3.2	—	1,998	2.7	2,029	3.0	1,686	2.7	1,369	2.2
Massachusetts	2.8	1.7	5.0	7.3	1.7	3.3	3.1	2,356	3.0	2,045	2.8	1,837	2.6	1,847	2.7
Michigan	4.3	2.7	9.2	6.2	3.1	5.4	—	4,305	3.1	6,661	4.9	5,318	4.2	6,699	5.3
Minnesota	1.6	1.0	3.9	4.2	1.6	5.7	—	337	0.5	453	0.7	796	1.2	2,752	3.7
Mississippi	7.4	5.6	9.3	5.9	2.8	4.6	#	2,399	6.0	2,651	7.3	2,339	7.3	2,023	7.0
Missouri	3.5	2.4	8.4	4.1	1.5	3.0	—	2,139	2.9	2,009	2.9	2,449	3.6	3,245	4.8
Montana	4.3	3.5	7.0	6.2	2.0	10.3	—	340	2.9	435	3.9	527	4.9	599	5.7
Nebraska	2.2	1.6	4.1	4.0	1.8	7.0	—	186	0.8	372	1.7	538	2.5	825	3.7
Nevada	4.5	3.4	6.5	5.4	3.1	4.7	—	790	2.3	1,389	4.0	1,294	4.4	2,071	8.0
New Hampshire	1.2	1.1	1.6	2.9	1.1	1.5	1.0	3	#	6	#	90	0.6	667	4.3
New Jersey	1.6	0.9	3.5	2.8	0.4	1.5	3.4	1,696	1.6	1,667	1.6	1,522	1.5	1,594	1.6
New Mexico	6.9	5.3	9.0	7.2	4.6	8.8	4.7	2,229	7.5	2,075	7.8	1,484	6.6	1,021	5.1
New York	3.6	1.7	6.5	5.9	2.4	5.6	—	7,354	3.1	8,222	3.5	6,674	3.4	8,931	4.7
North Carolina	4.7	4.0	5.4	6.1	2.0	6.1	—	6,553	5.1	5,535	4.9	4,769	4.8	3,338	3.8
North Dakota	2.2	1.7	2.6	3.5	0.9	7.5	—	40	0.5	174	2.3	207	2.7	259	3.4
Ohio	4.2	2.8	9.4	7.4	1.4	7.8	—	6,968	4.4	3,853	2.8	4,574	3.7	7,011	5.9
Oklahoma	2.4	2.1	3.3	3.5	1.1	2.5	—	949	1.9	1,062	2.3	1,188	2.8	1,086	2.7
Oregon	3.4	2.9	6.2	4.7	1.4	6.7	—	465	1.0	771	1.7	1,451	3.3	3,299	7.2
Pennsylvania	2.1	1.5	3.7	5.1	1.3	2.2	—	1,643	1.1	3,029	2.0	3,268	2.3	4,302	3.1
Rhode Island	4.6	3.8	6.6	6.8	4.5	8.5	—	573	4.4	613	5.0	509	4.7	471	4.4
South Carolina	3.0	2.7	3.3	3.6	1.3	5.6	—	1,691	2.7	1,811	3.3	1,547	3.2	1,220	2.7
South Dakota	2.6	1.6	3.4	5.2	2.7	10.5	—	184	1.8	267	2.7	258	2.8	291	3.3
Tennessee	2.7	1.8	4.9	3.3	1.2	2.7	—	1,370	1.8	1,579	2.1	1,790	2.6	2,843	4.3
Texas	2.7	1.2	4.2	3.6	0.5	3.6	—	6,945	1.8	8,253	2.5	6,824	2.2	14,048	4.8
Utah	2.6	2.1	3.8	5.5	2.8	5.7	—	207	0.5	555	1.4	927	2.3	2,444	6.1
Vermont	2.4	2.4	1.5	2.6	2.0	#	4.1	76	1.0	180	2.4	215	3.0	250	3.4
Virginia	2.1	1.4	3.0	4.6	1.2	1.6	—	1,741	1.7	1,857	1.9	1,934	2.1	2,467	2.8
Washington	4.2	3.6	6.1	5.8	3.0	8.2	—	2,881	3.4	2,792	3.4	3,472	4.4	4,815	5.8
West Virginia	4.0	4.0	4.6	4.6	0.5	3.6	1.9	809	3.4	848	4.1	839	4.4	798	4.3
Wisconsin	2.2	1.2	7.5	4.7	1.6	5.2	—	971	1.4	611	0.9	1,222	1.7	3,260	4.6
Wyoming	6.0	5.0	13.1	#	1.7	20.8	94.9	215	3.2	516	7.3	389	6.1	460	7.5
Bureau of Indian Education	—	—	—	—	—	—	—	—	—	—	—	—	—	—	—
DoD, overseas	—	—	—	—	—	—	—	—	—	—	—	—	—	—	—
DoD, domestic	—	—	—	—	—	—	—	—	—	—	—	—	—	—	—
Other jurisdictions															
American Samoa	—	—	—	—	—	—	—	—	—	—	—	—	—	—	—
Guam	—	—	—	—	—	—	—	—	—	—	—	—	—	—	—
Northern Marianas	—	—	—	—	—	—	—	—	—	—	—	—	—	—	—
Puerto Rico	—	—	—	—	—	—	—	—	—	—	—	—	—	—	—
U.S. Virgin Islands	5.5	#	5.3	7.4	#	#	—	122	7.2	68	5.5	53	4.7	38	3.7

—Not available.
#Rounds to zero.
‡Reporting standards not met (too few cases for a reliable estimate).
[1]Data were imputed based on prior year rates.
NOTE: Race categories exclude persons of Hispanic ethnicity. Event dropout rates measure the percentage of public school students in grades 9 through 12 who dropped out of school between one October and the next. Enrollment and dropout data for ungraded students were prorated into grades 9 through 12 based on the counts for graded students. DoD stands for Department of Defense.
SOURCE: U.S. Department of Education, National Center for Education Statistics, Common Core of Data (CCD), "State Dropout and Completion Data File," 2009–10. (This table was prepared November 2012.)

Table 219.55. Among 15- to 24-year-olds enrolled in grades 10 through 12, percentage who dropped out (event dropout rate), by sex and race/ethnicity: 1972 through 2014

[Standard errors appear in parentheses]

Year	Event dropout rate[1]											
			Sex				Race/ethnicity					
	Total[2]		Male		Female		White		Black		Hispanic	
1	2		3		4		5		6		7	
1972	6.1	(0.34)	5.9	(0.47)	6.3	(0.49)	5.3	(0.35)	9.6	(1.36)	11.2 !	(3.70)
1973	6.3	(0.34)	6.8	(0.50)	5.7	(0.46)	5.5	(0.35)	10.0	(1.39)	10.0 !	(3.50)
1974	6.7	(0.35)	7.4	(0.52)	6.0	(0.47)	5.8	(0.36)	11.6	(1.44)	9.9 !	(3.34)
1975	5.8	(0.32)	5.4	(0.45)	6.1	(0.47)	5.1	(0.34)	8.7	(1.28)	10.9 !	(3.30)
1976	5.9	(0.33)	6.6	(0.49)	5.2	(0.44)	5.6	(0.36)	7.4	(1.18)	7.3 !	(2.71)
1977	6.5	(0.34)	6.9	(0.49)	6.1	(0.47)	6.1	(0.37)	8.6	(1.21)	7.8 !	(2.79)
1978	6.7	(0.35)	7.5	(0.52)	5.9	(0.46)	5.8	(0.36)	10.2	(1.32)	12.3	(3.60)
1979	6.7	(0.35)	6.8	(0.50)	6.7	(0.49)	6.1	(0.37)	10.0	(1.34)	9.8 !	(3.20)
1980	6.1	(0.33)	6.7	(0.49)	5.5	(0.45)	5.3	(0.35)	8.3	(1.22)	11.7	(3.36)
1981	5.9	(0.33)	6.0	(0.47)	5.8	(0.46)	4.9	(0.34)	9.7	(1.30)	10.7	(3.00)
1982	5.5	(0.34)	5.8	(0.50)	5.2	(0.47)	4.8	(0.37)	7.8	(1.23)	9.2 !	(3.04)
1983	5.2	(0.34)	5.8	(0.50)	4.7	(0.46)	4.4	(0.36)	7.0	(1.20)	10.1 !	(3.18)
1984	5.1	(0.34)	5.5	(0.50)	4.8	(0.47)	4.5	(0.37)	5.8	(1.08)	11.1	(3.28)
1985	5.3	(0.35)	5.4	(0.51)	5.1	(0.49)	4.4	(0.37)	7.8	(1.29)	9.8	(2.58)
1986	4.7	(0.33)	4.7	(0.46)	4.7	(0.46)	3.8	(0.34)	5.5	(1.08)	11.9	(2.70)
1987	4.1	(0.31)	4.4	(0.45)	3.8	(0.42)	3.6	(0.33)	6.4	(1.16)	5.6 !	(1.94)
1988	4.8	(0.37)	5.4	(0.55)	4.6	(0.53)	4.4	(0.42)	6.3	(1.28)	11.0	(3.08)
1989	4.5	(0.35)	4.6	(0.50)	4.6	(0.50)	3.6	(0.37)	8.2	(1.40)	8.1	(2.43)
1990	4.0	(0.33)	4.2	(0.49)	4.1	(0.49)	3.5	(0.37)	5.2	(1.17)	8.4	(2.41)
1991	4.0	(0.33)	3.9	(0.47)	4.4	(0.51)	3.3	(0.37)	6.4	(1.27)	7.8	(2.33)
1992	4.4	(0.35)	3.9	(0.46)	4.9	(0.53)	3.7	(0.38)	5.0	(1.09)	8.2	(2.23)
1993	4.5	(0.36)	4.6	(0.51)	4.3	(0.50)	3.9	(0.40)	5.8	(1.20)	6.7 !	(2.02)
1994	5.3	(0.37)	5.2	(0.51)	5.4	(0.53)	4.2	(0.40)	6.6	(1.21)	10.0	(2.18)
1995	5.7	(0.35)	6.2	(0.51)	5.3	(0.48)	4.5	(0.38)	6.4	(1.01)	12.4	(1.62)
1996	5.0	(0.34)	5.0	(0.48)	5.1	(0.49)	4.1	(0.38)	6.7	(1.05)	9.0	(1.49)
1997	4.6	(0.32)	5.0	(0.47)	4.1	(0.43)	3.6	(0.35)	5.0	(0.91)	9.5	(1.45)
1998	4.8	(0.33)	4.6	(0.45)	4.9	(0.47)	3.9	(0.36)	5.2	(0.91)	9.4	(1.46)
1999	5.0	(0.33)	4.6	(0.44)	5.4	(0.49)	4.0	(0.36)	6.5	(0.99)	7.8	(1.27)
2000	4.8	(0.33)	5.5	(0.49)	4.1	(0.43)	4.1	(0.37)	6.1	(1.00)	7.4	(1.24)
2001	5.0	(0.32)	5.6	(0.46)	4.3	(0.42)	4.1	(0.35)	6.3	(0.96)	8.8	(1.31)
2002	3.5	(0.27)	3.7	(0.39)	3.4	(0.37)	2.6	(0.28)	4.9	(0.87)	5.8	(1.01)
2003	4.0	(0.28)	4.2	(0.40)	3.8	(0.38)	3.2	(0.31)	4.8	(0.85)	7.1	(1.06)
2004	4.7	(0.30)	5.1	(0.44)	4.3	(0.41)	3.7	(0.34)	5.7	(0.94)	8.9	(1.20)
2005	3.8	(0.27)	4.2	(0.40)	3.4	(0.36)	2.8	(0.29)	7.3	(1.03)	5.0	(0.87)
2006	3.8	(0.27)	4.1	(0.39)	3.4	(0.36)	2.9	(0.30)	3.8	(0.77)	7.0	(1.01)
2007	3.5	(0.26)	3.7	(0.37)	3.3	(0.35)	2.2	(0.26)	4.5	(0.80)	6.0	(0.98)
2008	3.5	(0.26)	3.1	(0.34)	4.0	(0.39)	2.3	(0.27)	6.4	(0.94)	5.3	(0.85)
2009	3.4	(0.25)	3.5	(0.36)	3.4	(0.35)	2.4	(0.28)	4.8	(0.83)	5.8	(0.87)
2010	3.0	(0.24)	3.0	(0.33)	2.9	(0.34)	2.3	(0.27)	3.6	(0.70)	4.1	(0.75)
2011	3.4	(0.25)	3.6	(0.36)	3.1	(0.35)	2.7	(0.30)	4.4	(0.77)	4.6	(0.75)
2012	3.4	(0.32)	3.6	(0.48)	3.3	(0.49)	1.6	(0.24)	6.8	(1.35)	5.4	(0.93)
2013	4.7	(0.40)	4.8	(0.53)	4.5	(0.55)	4.3	(0.51)	5.8	(1.17)	5.7	(0.95)
2014	5.2	(0.38)	5.4	(0.58)	5.0	(0.53)	4.7	(0.43)	5.7	(1.21)	7.9	(1.05)

!Interpret data with caution. The coefficient of variation (CV) for this estimate is between 30 and 50 percent.

[1]The event dropout rate is the percentage of 15- to 24-year-olds in grades 10 through 12 who dropped out between one October and the next (e.g., the 2014 data refer to 10th- through 12th-graders who were enrolled in October 2013 but had dropped out by October 2014). Dropping out is defined as leaving school without a high school diploma or alternative credential such as a GED certificate.

[2]Includes other racial/ethnic groups not separately shown.

NOTE: Data are based on sample surveys of the civilian noninstitutionalized population, which excludes persons in prisons, persons in the military, and other persons not living in households. Because of changes in data collection procedures, data for 1992 and later years may not be comparable with figures for prior years. Beginning in 2010, standard errors were computed using replicate weights, which produced more precise values than the generalized variance function methodology used in prior years. Race categories exclude persons of Hispanic ethnicity. Detail may not sum to totals because of rounding.

SOURCE: U.S. Department of Commerce, Census Bureau, Current Population Survey (CPS), October, 1972 through 2014. (This table was prepared March 2016.)

Table 219.57. Population of 15- to 24-year-olds enrolled in grades 10 through 12, number who dropped out (event dropouts), percentage who dropped out (event dropout rate), and percentage distribution, by selected characteristics: 2014

[Standard errors appear in parentheses]

Selected characteristic	15- to 24-year-olds enrolled in grades 10 through 12									
	Number (in thousands)						Percentage distribution			
	Total population[1]		Event dropouts[2]		Event dropout rate (percent)[3]		Total population[1]		Event dropouts[2]	
1	2		3		4		5		6	
Total	**10,889**	**(138.4)**	**567**	**(42.4)**	**5.2**	**(0.38)**	**100.0**	**(†)**	**100.0**	**(†)**
Sex										
Male	5,558	(88.5)	300	(32.7)	5.4	(0.58)	51.0	(0.54)	53.0	(3.99)
Female	5,330	(92.9)	267	(29.3)	5.0	(0.53)	49.0	(0.54)	47.0	(3.99)
Race/ethnicity										
White	6,104	(94.2)	285	(27.4)	4.7	(0.43)	56.1	(0.64)	50.2	(3.90)
Black	1,463	(46.3)	83	(17.9)	5.7	(1.21)	13.4	(0.38)	14.6	(2.84)
Hispanic	2,274	(67.4)	179	(25.6)	7.9	(1.05)	20.9	(0.52)	31.5	(3.52)
Asian	507	(34.5)	‡	(†)	‡	(†)	4.7	(0.30)	‡	(†)
Pacific Islander	‡	(†)	‡	(†)	‡	(†)	‡	(†)	‡	(†)
American Indian/Alaska Native	118	(21.0)	12 !	(4.9)	10.1 !	(3.91)	1.1	(0.19)	2.1 !	(0.86)
Two or more races	378	(32.5)	‡	(†)	‡	(†)	3.5	(0.30)	‡	(†)
Family income[4]										
Low income	1,603	(76.5)	150	(23.9)	9.4	(1.41)	14.7	(0.65)	26.5	(3.43)
Middle income	6,273	(123.3)	339	(30.6)	5.4	(0.48)	57.6	(0.90)	59.8	(3.76)
High income	3,012	(90.8)	78	(15.8)	2.6	(0.50)	27.7	(0.77)	13.7	(2.55)
Age[5]										
15–16	3,058	(84.0)	190	(25.8)	6.2	(0.82)	28.1	(0.62)	33.5	(3.85)
17	3,684	(56.1)	120	(22.3)	3.3	(0.60)	33.8	(0.49)	21.2	(3.51)
18	2,871	(63.2)	121	(21.4)	4.2	(0.73)	26.4	(0.54)	21.3	(3.39)
19	930	(56.1)	68	(14.1)	7.4	(1.38)	8.5	(0.48)	12.1	(2.35)
20–24	346	(39.8)	68	(16.1)	19.5	(4.25)	3.2	(0.35)	11.9	(2.73)
Recency of immigration[6]										
Born outside the United States										
Hispanic	387	(35.5)	72	(16.8)	18.7	(3.82)	3.6	(0.32)	12.8	(2.74)
Non-Hispanic	480	(42.5)	24 !	(10.5)	4.9 !	(2.11)	4.4	(0.38)	4.2 !	(1.75)
First generation										
Hispanic	1,183	(60.6)	63	(15.7)	5.3	(1.29)	10.9	(0.54)	11.0	(2.65)
Non-Hispanic	952	(60.8)	27 !	(9.3)	2.8 !	(0.96)	8.7	(0.56)	4.7 !	(1.58)
Second or later generation										
Hispanic	703	(47.6)	44 !	(14.6)	6.2 !	(1.95)	6.5	(0.41)	7.7 !	(2.43)
Non-Hispanic	7,183	(117.9)	338	(27.8)	4.7	(0.37)	66.0	(0.72)	59.6	(3.66)
Disability status[7]										
With a disability	450	(40.8)	18 !	(6.2)	4.0 !	(1.39)	4.1	(0.37)	3.2 !	(1.10)
Without a disability	10,439	(136.3)	549	(42.3)	5.3	(0.39)	95.9	(0.37)	96.8	(1.10)
Region										
Northeast	1,983	(80.2)	96	(20.3)	4.8	(0.98)	18.2	(0.69)	16.9	(3.29)
Midwest	2,533	(75.8)	118	(17.2)	4.6	(0.68)	23.3	(0.65)	20.7	(2.90)
South	3,715	(100.2)	190	(25.9)	5.1	(0.67)	34.1	(0.82)	33.5	(3.93)
West	2,659	(84.5)	164	(26.0)	6.2	(0.93)	24.4	(0.69)	28.9	(3.80)

†Not applicable.
!Interpret data with caution. The coefficient of variation (CV) for this estimate is between 30 and 50 percent.
‡Reporting standards not met. Either there are too few cases for a reliable estimate or the coefficient of variation (CV) is 50 percent or greater.
[1]Includes all 15- to 24-year-olds who were enrolled in grades 10 through 12 in October 2013.
[2]Includes only those 15- to 24-year-olds who dropped out of grades 10 through 12 between October 2013 and October 2014. Dropping out is defined as leaving school without a high school diploma or alternative credential such as a GED certificate.
[3]Among 15- to 24-year-olds who were enrolled in grades 10 through 12 in October 2013, the percentage who had dropped out by October 2014.
[4]Low income refers to the bottom 20 percent of all family incomes; high income refers to the top 20 percent of all family incomes; and middle income refers to the 60 percent in between. In 2014, low income was defined as $19,716 or less, and high income was defined as $95,433 or more.
[5]Age at the time of data collection. A person's age at the time of dropping out may be 1 year younger, because the dropout event could occur at any time over the previous 12-month period.
[6]The United States includes the 50 states and the District of Columbia. Individuals defined as "first generation" were born in the United States, but one or both of their parents were born outside the United States. Individuals defined as "second or later generation" were born in the United States, as were both of their parents.
[7]Individuals identified as having a disability reported difficulty with at least one of the following: hearing, seeing even when wearing glasses, walking or climbing stairs, dressing or bathing, doing errands alone, concentrating, remembering, or making decisions.
NOTE: Data are based on sample surveys of the civilian noninstitutionalized population, which excludes persons in prisons, persons in the military, and other persons not living in households. Race categories exclude persons of Hispanic ethnicity. Detail may not sum to totals because of rounding. Standard errors were computed using replicate weights.
SOURCE: U.S. Department of Commerce, Census Bureau, Current Population Survey (CPS), October 2014. (This table was prepared March 2016.)

Table 219.60. Number of people taking the GED test and percentage distribution of those who passed, by age group: 1971 through 2013

Year	Number of test takers (in thousands)			Percentage distribution of test passers, by age group[1]				
	Total[2]	Completing test battery[3]	Passing tests[4]	16 to 18 years old	19 to 24 years old	25 to 29 years old	30 to 34 years old	35 years old or over
1	2	3	4	5	6	7	8	9
1971[5]	377	—	227	—	—	—	—	—
1972[5]	419	—	245	—	—	—	—	—
1973[5]	423	—	249	—	—	—	—	—
1974	—	—	294	35 [6]	27 [6]	13	9	17
1975	—	—	340	33 [6]	26 [6]	14	9	18
1976	—	—	333	31 [6]	28 [6]	14	10	17
1977	—	—	330	40 [6]	24 [6]	13	8	14
1978	—	—	381	31 [6]	27 [6]	13	10	18
1979	—	—	426	37 [6]	28 [6]	12	13	11
1980	—	—	479	37 [6]	27 [6]	13	8	15
1981	—	—	489	37 [6]	27 [6]	13	8	14
1982	—	—	486	37 [6]	28 [6]	13	8	15
1983	—	—	465	34 [6]	29 [6]	14	8	15
1984	—	—	427	32 [6]	28 [6]	15	9	16
1985	—	—	413	32 [6]	26 [6]	15	10	16
1986	—	—	428	32 [6]	26 [6]	15	10	17
1987	—	—	444	33 [6]	24 [6]	15	10	18
1988	—	—	410	35 [6]	22 [6]	14	10	18
1989	632	541	357	22	37	13	—	—
1990	714	615	410	22	39	13	10	15
1991	755	657	462	20	40	13	10	16
1992	739	639	457	22	39	13	9	17
1993	746	651	469	22	38	13	10	16
1994	774	668	491	25	37	13	10	15
1995	787	682	504	27	36	13	9	15
1996	824	716	488	27	37	13	9	14
1997	785	681	460	31	36	12	8	13
1998	776	673	481	32	36	11	7	13
1999	808	702	498	32	37	11	7	13
2000	811	699	487	33	37	11	7	13
2001[7]	1,016	928	648	29	38	11	8	14
2002[7]	557	467	330	38	36	10	6	11
2003	657	552	387	35	37	10	7	11
2004	666	570	406	35	38	11	6	10
2005	681	588	424	34	37	12	7	11
2006	676	580	398	35	36	12	6	11
2007	692	600	429	35	35	12	7	11
2008	737	642	469	34	35	13	7	11
2009	748	645	448	31	36	13	8	12
2010	720	623	452	27	37	14	9	14
2011	691	602	434	27	37	13	9	14
2012	674	581	401	26	37	14	9	13
2013	816	714	541	22	35	15	11	17

—Not available.

[1]Age data for 1988 and prior years are for all test takers and may not be comparable to data for later years. For 1989 and later years, age data are only for test passers. The less than 1 percent of people who failed to report their date of birth—2,948 of the 540,535 test passers in 2013—were excluded from the calculation.

[2]All people taking the GED tests (one or more subtests).

[3]People completing the entire GED battery of five tests.

[4]Data for 2002 and later years are for people passing the GED tests (i.e., earning both a passing total score on the test battery and a passing score on each individual test). Data for 2001 and prior years are for high school equivalency credentials issued by the states to GED test passers. In order to receive high school equivalency credentials in some states, GED test passers must meet additional state requirements (e.g., complete an approved course in civics or government).

[5]Includes other jurisdictions, such as Puerto Rico, Guam, and American Samoa.

[6]For 1988 and prior years, 19-year-olds are included with the 16- to 18-year-olds instead of the 19- to 24-year-olds.

[7]A revised GED test was introduced in 2002. In 2001, test takers were required to successfully complete all five components of the GED or else begin the five-part series again with the new test that was introduced in 2002.

NOTE: Data are for the United States only and exclude other jurisdictions, except where noted. Detail may not sum to totals because of rounding.

SOURCE: American Council on Education, General Educational Development Testing Service, the GED annual *Statistical Report*, 1971 through 1992; *Who Took the GED?* 1993 through 2001; *Who Passed the GED Tests?* 2002 through 2005; and *GED Testing Program Statistical Report*, 2006 through 2013, retrieved November 5, 2014, from http://www.gedtestingservice.com/educators/historical-testing-data. (This table was prepared November 2014.)

Table 219.67. High school completion rate of 18- to 24-year-olds not enrolled in high school (status completion rate) and number and percentage distribution of 18- to 24-year-olds not enrolled in high school, by selected characteristics: Selected years, 2004 through 2014

[Standard errors appear in parentheses]

Selected characteristic	Status completion rate[1]								2014: Number of 18- to 24-year-olds not enrolled in high school (in thousands)				2014: Percentage distribution of 18- to 24-year-olds not enrolled in high school			
	2004		2009		2013		2014		Total population[2]		Status completers only[3]		Total population[2]		Status completers only[3]	
1	2		3		4		5		6		7		8		9	
Total	**86.9**	**(0.30)**	**89.8**	**(0.27)**	**92.0**	**(0.35)**	**92.4**	**(0.32)**	**28,402**	**(99.9)**	**26,255**	**(137.6)**	**100.0**	**(†)**	**100.0**	**(†)**
Sex																
Male	84.9	(0.46)	88.3	(0.40)	91.4	(0.47)	91.8	(0.46)	14,151	(70.1)	12,986	(94.1)	49.8	(0.20)	49.5	(0.26)
Female	88.8	(0.40)	91.2	(0.35)	92.6	(0.45)	93.1	(0.38)	14,251	(81.9)	13,269	(99.3)	50.2	(0.20)	50.5	(0.26)
Race/ethnicity																
White	91.7	(0.31)	93.8	(0.27)	94.3	(0.38)	94.2	(0.40)	15,767	(123.5)	14,847	(136.0)	55.5	(0.40)	56.6	(0.45)
Black	83.5	(0.98)	87.1	(0.84)	91.5	(1.13)	91.7	(0.91)	4,092	(102.0)	3,750	(102.8)	14.4	(0.35)	14.3	(0.38)
Hispanic	69.9	(1.12)	76.8	(1.00)	85.0	(0.98)	87.1	(0.88)	6,101	(76.5)	5,313	(88.9)	21.5	(0.26)	20.2	(0.32)
Asian	95.2	(1.00)	97.6	(0.72)	96.3	(1.27)	98.8	(0.47)	1,467	(44.6)	1,450	(45.5)	5.2	(0.16)	5.5	(0.17)
Pacific Islander	94.7	(4.07)	77.2	(6.63)	99.3	(0.79)	94.3	(5.59)	97	(22.4)	91	(21.7)	0.3	(0.08)	0.3	(0.08)
American Indian/Alaska Native	76.7	(4.70)	82.4	(4.47)	91.7	(2.97)	78.7	(4.18)	244	(25.2)	192	(24.0)	0.9	(0.09)	0.7	(0.09)
Two or more races	93.1	(1.86)	89.2	(2.18)	93.6	(1.83)	96.6	(1.16)	633	(42.5)	612	(41.9)	2.2	(0.15)	2.3	(0.16)
Race/ethnicity by sex																
Male																
White	91.2	(0.46)	92.4	(0.42)	93.8	(0.48)	93.7	(0.53)	7,911	(75.4)	7,411	(85.6)	55.9	(0.43)	57.1	(0.50)
Black	79.9	(1.56)	85.0	(1.31)	90.3	(1.41)	91.2	(1.30)	1,944	(39.4)	1,773	(46.3)	13.7	(0.27)	13.7	(0.34)
Hispanic	64.2	(1.59)	74.9	(1.43)	83.8	(1.35)	86.0	(1.22)	3,095	(51.4)	2,663	(53.4)	21.9	(0.37)	20.5	(0.40)
Asian	96.7	(1.18)	98.7	(0.74)	97.6	(1.17)	98.0	(0.86)	755	(32.7)	739	(33.3)	5.3	(0.23)	5.7	(0.25)
Pacific Islander	‡	(†)	‡	(†)	‡	(†)	‡	(†)	41 !	(12.3)	36 !	(11.1)	0.3 !	(0.09)	0.3 !	(0.09)
American Indian/Alaska Native	81.0	(6.37)	85.0	(6.06)	90.5	(6.44)	78.0	(5.79)	115	(16.2)	89	(14.3)	0.8	(0.11)	0.7	(0.11)
Two or more races	92.1	(2.79)	90.0	(3.00)	94.7	(2.65)	94.7	(2.14)	290	(26.2)	275	(25.6)	2.1	(0.18)	2.1	(0.20)
Female																
White	92.2	(0.43)	95.1	(0.34)	94.7	(0.45)	94.7	(0.52)	7,856	(75.2)	7,436	(83.7)	55.1	(0.55)	56.0	(0.61)
Black	86.5	(1.22)	88.9	(1.09)	92.6	(1.39)	92.0	(1.16)	2,148	(84.5)	1,977	(81.9)	15.1	(0.55)	14.9	(0.57)
Hispanic	76.5	(1.52)	78.8	(1.40)	86.2	(1.30)	88.1	(1.16)	3,006	(47.6)	2,649	(61.2)	21.1	(0.31)	20.0	(0.42)
Asian	93.6	(1.62)	96.5	(1.23)	94.9	(1.94)	99.6	(0.31)	713	(27.1)	710	(26.9)	5.0	(0.19)	5.4	(0.20)
Pacific Islander	‡	(†)	‡	(†)	‡	(†)	100.0	(#)	56	(16.4)	56	(16.4)	0.4	(0.11)	0.4	(0.12)
American Indian/Alaska Native	73.0	(6.79)	80.1	(6.50)	92.5	(4.02)	79.4	(4.56)	129	(17.5)	103	(16.5)	0.9	(0.12)	0.8	(0.12)
Two or more races	94.2	(2.45)	88.5	(3.16)	92.5	(2.88)	98.2	(1.05)	343	(29.4)	337	(29.3)	2.4	(0.21)	2.5	(0.22)
Age																
18–19	85.9	(0.63)	89.0	(0.55)	91.4	(0.69)	90.7	(0.70)	6,643	(71.6)	6,028	(81.5)	23.4	(0.20)	23.0	(0.25)
20–21	87.2	(0.55)	89.8	(0.50)	92.4	(0.63)	92.8	(0.53)	8,369	(171.4)	7,765	(166.7)	29.5	(0.60)	29.6	(0.61)
22–24	87.1	(0.44)	90.2	(0.39)	92.1	(0.51)	93.1	(0.44)	13,389	(167.8)	12,463	(162.9)	47.1	(0.59)	47.5	(0.61)
Recency of immigration[4]																
Born outside the United States																
Hispanic	54.7	(1.84)	63.0	(1.88)	73.0	(2.36)	74.7	(2.29)	1,462	(76.0)	1,093	(63.3)	5.1	(0.27)	4.2	(0.24)
Non-Hispanic	91.0	(1.06)	92.5	(0.99)	93.3	(1.34)	95.7	(1.08)	1,669	(91.1)	1,597	(88.4)	5.9	(0.32)	6.1	(0.34)
First generation																
Hispanic	81.0	(1.70)	83.7	(1.49)	89.1	(1.36)	91.3	(1.05)	2,718	(97.9)	2,481	(90.1)	9.6	(0.34)	9.4	(0.34)
Non-Hispanic	95.9	(0.77)	95.2	(0.74)	95.3	(1.22)	97.9	(0.69)	1,883	(82.1)	1,843	(82.0)	6.6	(0.29)	7.0	(0.31)
Second generation or higher																
Hispanic	82.0	(1.86)	86.7	(1.53)	89.8	(1.46)	90.5	(1.46)	1,921	(91.0)	1,739	(92.0)	6.8	(0.32)	6.6	(0.35)
Non-Hispanic	90.0	(0.32)	92.3	(0.28)	93.8	(0.38)	93.4	(0.36)	18,748	(137.9)	17,502	(149.0)	66.0	(0.42)	66.7	(0.47)
Disability[5]																
With a disability	—	(†)	80.0	(1.90)	81.3	(2.27)	83.7	(2.10)	1,050	(64.1)	878	(57.3)	3.7	(0.23)	3.3	(0.22)
Without a disability	—	(†)	90.1	(0.27)	92.4	(0.33)	92.8	(0.31)	27,352	(115.1)	25,377	(144.9)	96.3	(0.23)	96.7	(0.22)
Region																
Northeast	88.7	(0.62)	90.9	(0.62)	93.4	(0.79)	94.3	(0.71)	5,017	(125.5)	4,731	(120.4)	17.7	(0.43)	18.0	(0.45)
Midwest	89.7	(0.55)	90.3	(0.58)	93.2	(0.71)	93.6	(0.70)	5,897	(145.8)	5,520	(146.8)	20.8	(0.50)	21.0	(0.54)
South	85.5	(0.57)	89.3	(0.47)	91.2	(0.60)	91.2	(0.62)	10,459	(166.6)	9,538	(174.3)	36.8	(0.58)	36.3	(0.63)
West	84.5	(0.73)	89.1	(0.56)	91.2	(0.70)	92.0	(0.68)	7,029	(135.9)	6,466	(139.7)	24.7	(0.48)	24.6	(0.53)

—Not available.
†Not applicable.
#Rounds to zero.
!Interpret data with caution. The coefficient of variation for this estimate is between 30 and 50 percent.
‡Reporting standards not met (too few cases for a reliable estimate).
[1]The status completion rate is the number of 18- to 24-year-olds who are high school completers as a percentage of the total number of 18- to 24-year-olds who are not enrolled in high school or a lower level of education. High school completers include those with a high school diploma, as well as those with an alternative credential, such as a GED.
[2]Includes all 18- to 24-year-olds who are not enrolled in high school or a lower level of education.
[3]Status completers are 18- to 24-year-olds who are not enrolled in high school or a lower level of education and who also are high school completers—that is, have either a high school diploma or an alternative credential, such as a GED.
[4]The United States includes the 50 states and the District of Columbia. Individuals defined as "first generation" were born in the United States, but one or both of their parents were born outside the United States. Individuals defined as "second generation or higher" were born in the United States, as were both of their parents.
[5]Individuals identified as having a disability reported difficulty in at least one of the following: hearing, seeing even when wearing glasses, walking or climbing stairs, dressing or bathing, doing errands alone, concentrating, remembering, or making decisions.
NOTE: Data are based on sample surveys of the civilian noninstitutionalized population, which excludes persons in prisons, persons in the military, and other persons not living in households. Race categories exclude persons of Hispanic ethnicity. Detail may not sum to totals because of rounding.
SOURCE: U.S. Department of Commerce, Census Bureau, Current Population Survey (CPS), October, 2004 through 2014. (This table was prepared March 2016.)

Table 219.70. Percentage of high school dropouts among persons 16 to 24 years old (status dropout rate), by sex and race/ethnicity: Selected years, 1960 through 2014

[Standard errors appear in parentheses]

Year	Total status dropout rate				Male status dropout rate				Female status dropout rate			
	All races[1]	White	Black	Hispanic	All races[1]	White	Black	Hispanic	All races[1]	White	Black	Hispanic
1	2	3	4	5	6	7	8	9	10	11	12	13
1960[2]	27.2 (—)	— (†)	— (†)	— (†)	27.8 (—)	— (†)	— (†)	— (†)	26.7 (—)	— (†)	— (†)	— (†)
1967[3]	17.0 (—)	15.4 (—)	28.6 (—)	— (†)	16.5 (—)	14.7 (—)	30.6 (—)	— (†)	17.3 (—)	16.1 (—)	26.9 (—)	— (†)
1968[3]	16.2 (—)	14.7 (—)	27.4 (—)	— (†)	15.8 (—)	14.4 (—)	27.1 (—)	— (†)	16.5 (—)	15.0 (—)	27.6 (—)	— (†)
1969[3]	15.2 (—)	13.6 (—)	26.7 (—)	— (†)	14.3 (—)	12.6 (—)	26.9 (—)	— (†)	16.0 (—)	14.6 (—)	26.7 (—)	— (†)
1970[3]	15.0 (0.29)	13.2 (0.30)	27.9 (1.22)	— (†)	14.2 (0.42)	12.2 (0.42)	29.4 (1.82)	— (†)	15.7 (0.41)	14.1 (0.42)	26.6 (1.65)	— (†)
1971[3]	14.7 (0.28)	13.4 (0.29)	24.0 (1.14)	— (†)	14.2 (0.41)	12.6 (0.41)	25.5 (1.70)	— (†)	15.2 (0.40)	14.2 (0.42)	22.6 (1.54)	— (†)
1972	14.6 (0.28)	12.3 (0.29)	21.3 (1.07)	34.3 (2.22)	14.1 (0.40)	11.6 (0.40)	22.3 (1.59)	33.7 (3.23)	15.1 (0.39)	12.8 (0.41)	20.5 (1.44)	34.8 (3.05)
1973	14.1 (0.27)	11.6 (0.28)	22.2 (1.06)	33.5 (2.24)	13.7 (0.38)	11.5 (0.39)	21.5 (1.53)	30.4 (3.16)	14.5 (0.38)	11.8 (0.39)	22.8 (1.47)	36.4 (3.16)
1974	14.3 (0.27)	11.9 (0.28)	21.2 (1.05)	33.0 (2.08)	14.2 (0.39)	12.0 (0.40)	20.1 (1.51)	33.8 (2.99)	14.3 (0.38)	11.8 (0.39)	22.1 (1.45)	32.2 (2.90)
1975	13.9 (0.27)	11.4 (0.27)	22.9 (1.06)	29.2 (2.02)	13.3 (0.37)	11.0 (0.38)	23.0 (1.56)	26.7 (2.84)	14.5 (0.38)	11.8 (0.39)	22.9 (1.44)	31.6 (2.86)
1976	14.1 (0.27)	12.0 (0.28)	20.5 (1.00)	31.4 (2.01)	14.1 (0.38)	12.1 (0.39)	21.2 (1.49)	30.3 (2.94)	14.2 (0.37)	11.8 (0.39)	19.9 (1.35)	32.3 (2.76)
1977	14.1 (0.27)	11.9 (0.28)	19.8 (0.99)	33.0 (2.02)	14.5 (0.38)	12.6 (0.40)	19.5 (1.45)	31.6 (2.89)	13.8 (0.37)	11.2 (0.38)	20.0 (1.36)	34.3 (2.83)
1978	14.2 (0.27)	11.9 (0.28)	20.2 (1.00)	33.3 (2.00)	14.6 (0.38)	12.2 (0.40)	22.5 (1.52)	33.6 (2.88)	13.9 (0.37)	11.6 (0.39)	18.3 (1.31)	33.1 (2.78)
1979	14.6 (0.27)	12.0 (0.28)	21.1 (1.01)	33.8 (1.98)	15.0 (0.39)	12.6 (0.40)	22.4 (1.52)	33.0 (2.83)	14.2 (0.37)	11.5 (0.38)	20.0 (1.35)	34.5 (2.77)
1980	14.1 (0.26)	11.4 (0.27)	19.1 (0.97)	35.2 (1.89)	15.1 (0.39)	12.3 (0.40)	20.8 (1.47)	37.2 (2.72)	13.1 (0.36)	10.5 (0.37)	17.7 (1.28)	33.2 (2.61)
1981	13.9 (0.26)	11.3 (0.27)	18.4 (0.93)	33.2 (1.80)	15.1 (0.38)	12.5 (0.40)	19.9 (1.40)	36.0 (2.61)	12.8 (0.35)	10.2 (0.36)	17.1 (1.24)	30.4 (2.48)
1982	13.9 (0.27)	11.4 (0.29)	18.4 (0.97)	31.7 (1.93)	14.5 (0.40)	12.0 (0.42)	21.2 (1.50)	30.5 (2.73)	13.3 (0.38)	10.8 (0.40)	15.9 (1.26)	32.8 (2.71)
1983	13.7 (0.27)	11.1 (0.29)	18.0 (0.97)	31.6 (1.93)	14.9 (0.41)	12.2 (0.43)	19.9 (1.46)	34.3 (2.84)	12.5 (0.37)	10.1 (0.39)	16.2 (1.28)	29.1 (2.61)
1984	13.1 (0.27)	11.0 (0.29)	15.5 (0.91)	29.8 (1.91)	14.0 (0.40)	11.9 (0.43)	16.8 (1.37)	30.6 (2.78)	12.3 (0.37)	10.1 (0.39)	14.3 (1.22)	29.0 (2.63)
1985	12.6 (0.27)	10.4 (0.29)	15.2 (0.92)	27.6 (1.93)	13.4 (0.40)	11.1 (0.42)	16.1 (1.37)	29.9 (2.76)	11.8 (0.37)	9.8 (0.39)	14.3 (1.23)	25.2 (2.68)
1986	12.2 (0.27)	9.7 (0.28)	14.2 (0.90)	30.1 (1.88)	13.1 (0.40)	10.3 (0.42)	15.0 (1.33)	32.8 (2.66)	11.4 (0.37)	9.1 (0.39)	13.5 (1.21)	27.2 (2.63)
1987	12.6 (0.28)	10.4 (0.30)	14.1 (0.90)	28.6 (1.84)	13.2 (0.40)	10.8 (0.43)	15.0 (1.35)	29.1 (2.57)	12.1 (0.38)	10.0 (0.41)	13.3 (1.21)	28.1 (2.64)
1988	12.9 (0.30)	9.6 (0.31)	14.5 (1.00)	35.8 (2.30)	13.5 (0.44)	10.3 (0.46)	15.0 (1.48)	36.0 (3.19)	12.2 (0.42)	8.9 (0.43)	14.0 (1.36)	35.4 (3.31)
1989	12.6 (0.31)	9.4 (0.32)	13.9 (0.98)	33.0 (2.19)	13.6 (0.45)	10.3 (0.47)	14.9 (1.46)	34.4 (3.08)	11.7 (0.42)	8.5 (0.43)	13.0 (1.32)	31.6 (3.11)
1990	12.1 (0.29)	9.0 (0.30)	13.2 (0.94)	32.4 (1.91)	12.3 (0.42)	9.3 (0.44)	11.9 (1.30)	34.3 (2.71)	11.8 (0.41)	8.7 (0.42)	14.4 (1.34)	30.3 (2.70)
1991	12.5 (0.30)	8.9 (0.31)	13.6 (0.95)	35.3 (1.93)	13.0 (0.43)	8.9 (0.44)	13.5 (1.37)	39.2 (2.74)	11.9 (0.41)	8.9 (0.43)	13.7 (1.31)	31.1 (2.70)
1992[4]	11.0 (0.28)	7.7 (0.29)	13.7 (0.95)	29.4 (1.86)	11.3 (0.41)	8.0 (0.42)	12.5 (1.32)	32.1 (2.67)	10.7 (0.39)	7.4 (0.40)	14.8 (1.36)	26.6 (2.56)
1993[4]	11.0 (0.28)	7.9 (0.29)	13.6 (0.94)	27.5 (1.79)	11.2 (0.40)	8.2 (0.42)	12.6 (1.32)	28.1 (2.54)	10.9 (0.40)	7.6 (0.41)	14.4 (1.34)	26.9 (2.52)
1994[4]	11.4 (0.26)	7.7 (0.27)	12.6 (0.75)	30.0 (1.16)	12.3 (0.38)	8.0 (0.38)	14.1 (1.14)	31.6 (1.60)	10.6 (0.36)	7.5 (0.37)	11.3 (0.99)	28.1 (1.66)
1995[4]	12.0 (0.27)	8.6 (0.28)	12.1 (0.74)	30.0 (1.15)	12.2 (0.38)	9.0 (0.40)	11.1 (1.05)	30.0 (1.59)	11.7 (0.37)	8.2 (0.39)	12.9 (1.05)	30.0 (1.66)
1996[4]	11.1 (0.27)	7.3 (0.27)	13.0 (0.80)	29.4 (1.19)	11.4 (0.38)	7.3 (0.38)	13.5 (1.18)	30.3 (1.67)	10.9 (0.38)	7.3 (0.39)	12.5 (1.08)	28.3 (1.69)
1997[4]	11.0 (0.27)	7.6 (0.28)	13.4 (0.80)	25.3 (1.11)	11.9 (0.39)	8.5 (0.41)	13.3 (1.16)	27.0 (1.55)	10.1 (0.36)	6.7 (0.37)	13.5 (1.11)	23.4 (1.59)
1998[4]	11.8 (0.27)	7.7 (0.28)	13.8 (0.81)	29.5 (1.12)	13.3 (0.40)	8.6 (0.41)	15.5 (1.24)	33.5 (1.59)	10.3 (0.36)	6.9 (0.37)	12.2 (1.05)	25.0 (1.56)
1999[4]	11.2 (0.26)	7.3 (0.27)	12.6 (0.77)	28.6 (1.11)	11.9 (0.38)	7.7 (0.39)	12.1 (1.10)	31.0 (1.58)	10.5 (0.36)	6.9 (0.37)	13.0 (1.08)	26.0 (1.54)
2000[4]	10.9 (0.26)	6.9 (0.26)	13.1 (0.78)	27.8 (1.08)	12.0 (0.38)	7.0 (0.37)	15.3 (1.20)	31.8 (1.56)	9.9 (0.35)	6.9 (0.37)	11.1 (1.00)	23.5 (1.48)
2001[4]	10.7 (0.25)	7.3 (0.26)	10.9 (0.71)	27.0 (1.06)	12.2 (0.38)	7.9 (0.39)	13.0 (1.12)	31.6 (1.55)	9.3 (0.34)	6.7 (0.36)	9.0 (0.90)	22.1 (1.42)
2002[4]	10.5 (0.24)	6.5 (0.24)	11.3 (0.70)	25.7 (0.93)	11.8 (0.35)	6.7 (0.35)	12.8 (1.07)	29.6 (1.32)	9.2 (0.32)	6.3 (0.34)	9.9 (0.91)	21.2 (1.27)
2003[4,5]	9.9 (0.23)	6.3 (0.24)	10.9 (0.69)	23.5 (0.90)	11.3 (0.34)	7.1 (0.35)	12.5 (1.05)	26.7 (1.29)	8.4 (0.30)	5.6 (0.32)	9.5 (0.89)	20.1 (1.23)
2004[4,5]	10.3 (0.23)	6.8 (0.24)	11.8 (0.70)	23.8 (0.89)	11.6 (0.34)	7.1 (0.35)	13.5 (1.08)	28.5 (1.30)	9.0 (0.31)	6.4 (0.34)	10.2 (0.92)	18.5 (1.18)
2005[4,5]	9.4 (0.22)	6.0 (0.23)	10.4 (0.66)	22.4 (0.87)	10.8 (0.33)	6.6 (0.34)	12.0 (1.02)	26.4 (1.26)	8.0 (0.29)	5.3 (0.31)	9.0 (0.86)	18.1 (1.16)
2006[4,5]	9.3 (0.22)	5.8 (0.23)	10.7 (0.66)	22.1 (0.86)	10.3 (0.33)	6.4 (0.33)	9.7 (0.91)	25.7 (1.25)	8.3 (0.30)	5.3 (0.31)	11.7 (0.96)	18.1 (1.15)
2007[4,5]	8.7 (0.21)	5.3 (0.22)	8.4 (0.59)	21.4 (0.83)	9.8 (0.32)	6.0 (0.32)	8.0 (0.82)	24.7 (1.22)	7.7 (0.29)	4.5 (0.28)	8.8 (0.84)	18.0 (1.13)
2008[4,5]	8.0 (0.20)	4.8 (0.21)	9.9 (0.63)	18.3 (0.78)	8.5 (0.30)	5.4 (0.30)	8.7 (0.85)	19.9 (1.12)	7.5 (0.28)	4.2 (0.28)	11.1 (0.93)	16.7 (1.08)
2009[4,5]	8.1 (0.20)	5.2 (0.21)	9.3 (0.61)	17.6 (0.76)	9.1 (0.31)	6.3 (0.33)	10.6 (0.93)	19.0 (1.10)	7.0 (0.27)	4.1 (0.27)	8.1 (0.80)	16.1 (1.06)
2010[4,5,6]	7.4 (0.27)	5.1 (0.30)	8.0 (0.76)	15.1 (0.87)	8.5 (0.40)	5.9 (0.42)	9.5 (1.11)	17.3 (1.24)	6.3 (0.28)	4.2 (0.35)	6.7 (0.85)	12.8 (0.97)
2011[4,5,6]	7.1 (0.26)	5.0 (0.31)	7.3 (0.67)	13.6 (0.78)	7.7 (0.36)	5.4 (0.41)	8.3 (0.98)	14.6 (1.09)	6.5 (0.34)	4.6 (0.38)	6.4 (0.94)	12.4 (0.97)
2012[4,5,6]	6.6 (0.25)	4.3 (0.31)	7.5 (0.76)	12.7 (0.72)	7.3 (0.36)	4.8 (0.40)	8.1 (1.15)	13.9 (1.04)	5.9 (0.33)	3.8 (0.37)	7.0 (1.01)	11.3 (1.00)
2013[4,5,6]	6.8 (0.28)	5.1 (0.31)	7.3 (0.87)	11.7 (0.74)	7.2 (0.37)	5.5 (0.39)	8.2 (1.11)	12.6 (1.01)	6.3 (0.34)	4.7 (0.36)	6.6 (1.07)	10.8 (0.98)
2014[4,5,6]	6.5 (0.25)	5.2 (0.32)	7.4 (0.74)	10.6 (0.68)	7.1 (0.37)	5.7 (0.42)	7.1 (1.02)	11.8 (1.04)	5.9 (0.29)	4.8 (0.41)	7.7 (1.02)	9.3 (0.84)

—Not available.
†Not applicable.
[1]Includes other racial/ethnic categories not separately shown.
[2]Based on the April 1960 decennial census.
[3]For 1967 through 1971, White and Black include persons of Hispanic ethnicity.
[4]Because of changes in data collection procedures, data may not be comparable with figures for years prior to 1992.
[5]White and Black exclude persons identifying themselves as Two or more races.
[6]Beginning in 2010, standard errors were computed using replicate weights, which produced more precise values than the generalized variance function methodology used in prior years.

NOTE: "Status" dropouts are 16- to 24-year-olds who are not enrolled in school and who have not completed a high school program, regardless of when they left school. People who have received GED credentials are counted as high school completers. All data except for 1960 are based on October counts. Data are based on sample surveys of the civilian noninstitutionalized population, which excludes persons in prisons, persons in the military, and other persons not living in households. Race categories exclude persons of Hispanic ethnicity except where otherwise noted.
SOURCE: U.S. Department of Commerce, Census Bureau, Current Population Survey (CPS), October, 1967 through 2014. (This table was prepared August 2015.)

Table 219.71. Population 16 to 24 years old and number of 16- to 24-year-old high school dropouts (status dropouts), by sex and race/ethnicity: 1970 through 2014

[Standard errors appear in parentheses]

Year	Total								Males								Females							
	All races[1]		White		Black		Hispanic		All races[1]		White		Black		Hispanic		All races[1]		White		Black		Hispanic	
1	2		3		4		5		6		7		8		9		10		11		12		13	
	Population 16 to 24 years old (in thousands)																							
1970[2]	30,251	(260.7)	26,241	(245.8)	3,669	(93.6)	—	(†)	14,260	(175.6)	12,403	(165.7)	1,703	(62.5)	—	(†)	15,991	(177.3)	13,838	(167.3)	1,966	(63.7)	—	(†)
1971[2]	31,538	(265.1)	27,299	(249.9)	3,871	(95.5)	—	(†)	15,060	(179.5)	13,076	(169.4)	1,809	(64.0)	—	(†)	16,478	(179.4)	14,223	(169.2)	2,062	(64.8)	—	(†)
1972	32,643	(268.8)	26,502	(246.8)	4,024	(96.9)	1,774	(81.5)	15,787	(183.0)	12,913	(168.5)	1,878	(64.8)	830	(55.2)	16,856	(181.0)	13,589	(166.1)	2,145	(65.7)	944	(55.3)
1973	33,430	(271.4)	27,100	(249.1)	4,190	(98.3)	1,718	(80.4)	16,248	(185.1)	13,259	(170.4)	1,976	(66.0)	821	(54.9)	17,182	(182.3)	13,841	(167.4)	2,214	(66.4)	896	(54.1)
1974	33,968	(273.1)	27,301	(249.9)	4,153	(98.0)	1,981	(85.6)	16,508	(186.2)	13,361	(171.0)	1,921	(65.3)	972	(59.2)	17,460	(183.4)	13,941	(167.8)	2,232	(66.6)	1,009	(57.0)
1975	34,700	(275.4)	27,867	(252.0)	4,310	(99.3)	1,962	(85.3)	16,925	(188.0)	13,711	(172.8)	1,992	(66.2)	940	(58.3)	17,775	(184.7)	14,157	(168.9)	2,319	(67.4)	1,022	(57.3)
1976	35,222	(277.0)	28,146	(253.1)	4,429	(100.2)	2,060	(87.1)	17,210	(189.3)	13,925	(173.9)	2,054	(66.9)	944	(58.4)	18,012	(185.6)	14,221	(169.2)	2,375	(67.9)	1,115	(59.4)
1977	35,658	(278.3)	28,393	(254.0)	4,516	(100.9)	2,123	(88.3)	17,431	(190.2)	14,027	(174.4)	2,086	(67.2)	1,018	(60.4)	18,227	(186.4)	14,366	(169.9)	2,430	(68.4)	1,106	(59.2)
1978	35,931	(279.1)	28,490	(254.3)	4,584	(101.4)	2,183	(89.3)	17,582	(190.8)	14,084	(174.7)	2,113	(67.5)	1,059	(61.5)	18,349	(186.9)	14,406	(170.1)	2,471	(68.8)	1,123	(59.6)
1979	36,131	(279.7)	28,602	(254.8)	4,618	(101.7)	2,242	(90.4)	17,708	(191.4)	14,172	(175.2)	2,128	(67.7)	1,085	(62.1)	18,423	(187.2)	14,430	(170.2)	2,490	(69.0)	1,157	(60.3)
1980	36,143	(279.7)	28,253	(253.5)	4,651	(101.9)	2,518	(95.0)	17,715	(191.4)	13,979	(174.2)	2,148	(67.9)	1,240	(65.8)	18,428	(187.2)	14,274	(169.5)	2,503	(69.1)	1,277	(62.8)
1981	36,945	(282.1)	28,483	(254.3)	4,895	(103.7)	2,684	(97.5)	18,167	(193.2)	14,111	(174.9)	2,286	(69.2)	1,333	(67.8)	18,778	(188.5)	14,372	(169.9)	2,608	(69.9)	1,352	(64.3)
1982	36,452	(296.5)	27,979	(266.7)	4,912	(109.6)	2,598	(103.0)	17,938	(203.2)	13,841	(183.3)	2,303	(73.3)	1,263	(70.9)	18,514	(198.1)	14,139	(178.4)	2,609	(73.9)	1,335	(64.0)
1983	35,884	(294.7)	27,385	(264.3)	4,907	(109.6)	2,587	(101.9)	17,712	(202.2)	13,616	(182.0)	2,329	(73.6)	1,242	(69.8)	18,172	(196.7)	13,769	(176.4)	2,578	(73.6)	1,345	(68.1)
1984	35,204	(292.6)	26,758	(261.8)	4,890	(109.5)	2,558	(101.4)	17,387	(200.8)	13,325	(180.4)	2,329	(73.6)	1,226	(69.4)	17,817	(195.3)	13,433	(174.7)	2,561	(73.5)	1,332	(67.8)
1985	34,382	(289.9)	25,772	(257.7)	4,749	(108.4)	2,887	(86.4)	16,892	(198.5)	12,715	(176.9)	2,239	(72.7)	1,472	(60.7)	17,490	(193.9)	13,057	(172.6)	2,510	(73.0)	1,415	(69.4)
1986	33,945	(288.4)	24,959	(254.2)	4,698	(108.0)	3,206	(93.7)	16,709	(197.7)	12,276	(174.3)	2,222	(72.5)	1,667	(66.4)	17,236	(192.9)	12,684	(170.5)	2,476	(72.7)	1,538	(60.5)
1987	33,452	(286.8)	24,479	(252.1)	4,631	(107.5)	3,234	(94.1)	16,458	(196.5)	12,058	(173.0)	2,176	(72.0)	1,680	(66.6)	16,994	(191.8)	12,420	(169.1)	2,455	(72.5)	1,554	(60.7)
1988	32,893	(310.4)	23,908	(272.0)	4,584	(116.7)	3,267	(107.8)	16,134	(212.5)	11,725	(186.3)	2,156	(78.2)	1,696	(76.3)	16,759	(207.9)	12,184	(182.7)	2,429	(78.7)	1,571	(61.0)
1989	32,007	(291.9)	22,947	(254.0)	4,593	(111.1)	3,459	(98.1)	15,783	(200.2)	11,314	(174.4)	2,193	(74.8)	1,783	(69.1)	16,224	(195.2)	11,634	(170.3)	2,399	(74.6)	1,676	(69.8)
1990	31,443	(289.8)	22,360	(251.1)	4,487	(110.2)	3,443	(99.8)	15,502	(198.8)	11,059	(172.7)	2,117	(73.9)	1,773	(70.4)	15,941	(193.8)	11,302	(168.2)	2,370	(74.3)	1,669	(64.6)
1991	31,171	(288.8)	21,883	(248.8)	4,475	(110.1)	3,519	(100.7)	15,408	(198.3)	10,819	(171.0)	2,126	(74.0)	1,829	(71.2)	15,763	(193.0)	11,064	(166.7)	2,350	(74.1)	1,690	(64.9)
1992[3]	30,944	(287.9)	21,697	(247.9)	4,527	(110.6)	3,476	(100.2)	15,375	(198.1)	10,826	(171.1)	2,169	(74.5)	1,760	(70.2)	15,569	(192.0)	10,871	(165.5)	2,358	(74.2)	1,716	(65.3)
1993[3]	30,845	(287.5)	21,499	(246.9)	4,536	(110.7)	3,595	(101.5)	15,355	(198.0)	10,742	(170.5)	2,179	(74.6)	1,802	(70.8)	15,490	(191.6)	10,757	(164.7)	2,357	(74.2)	1,793	(66.3)
1994[3]	32,560	(293.9)	22,080	(249.8)	4,805	(112.8)	4,411	(109.3)	16,304	(202.8)	11,016	(172.4)	2,298	(75.9)	2,355	(77.9)	16,257	(195.3)	11,064	(166.7)	2,507	(75.7)	2,056	(69.5)
1995[3]	32,379	(293.2)	21,991	(249.3)	4,732	(112.2)	4,485	(109.9)	16,208	(202.3)	11,062	(172.7)	2,236	(75.3)	2,338	(77.7)	16,170	(194.9)	10,929	(165.8)	2,496	(75.6)	2,147	(70.5)
1996[3]	32,452	(304.7)	21,527	(256.4)	4,745	(116.6)	4,481	(115.4)	16,296	(210.5)	10,836	(177.7)	2,251	(78.2)	2,313	(81.4)	16,156	(202.3)	10,690	(170.5)	2,494	(78.4)	2,168	(70.7)
1997[3]	32,960	(306.6)	21,800	(257.8)	4,847	(117.4)	4,660	(115.6)	16,619	(212.1)	11,001	(178.8)	2,308	(78.9)	2,487	(82.3)	16,341	(203.2)	10,799	(171.3)	2,540	(78.8)	2,173	(73.4)
1998[3]	33,445	(308.3)	21,920	(258.4)	4,893	(117.7)	5,034	(118.5)	16,854	(213.3)	11,067	(179.3)	2,305	(78.8)	2,683	(84.2)	16,592	(204.4)	10,854	(171.6)	2,588	(79.3)	2,351	(75.2)
1999[3]	34,169	(310.9)	22,408	(260.9)	4,939	(118.1)	5,060	(118.7)	17,106	(214.5)	11,325	(181.1)	2,336	(79.2)	2,603	(83.5)	17,063	(206.6)	11,084	(173.2)	2,603	(79.4)	2,457	(76.2)
2000[3]	34,568	(312.4)	22,574	(261.8)	5,058	(119.0)	5,237	(120.0)	17,402	(215.9)	11,390	(181.5)	2,417	(80.0)	2,725	(84.6)	17,166	(207.0)	11,184	(173.9)	2,641	(79.7)	2,513	(76.7)
2001[3]	35,167	(298.5)	22,874	(249.9)	5,119	(113.3)	5,344	(112.0)	17,663	(206.1)	11,598	(173.6)	2,418	(75.9)	2,744	(78.6)	17,504	(198.0)	11,276	(165.6)	2,701	(76.2)	2,601	(77.4)
2002[3]	35,495	(299.6)	22,358	(247.4)	4,991	(112.4)	6,120	(118.9)	17,893	(207.2)	11,183	(170.9)	2,375	(75.5)	3,281	(84.3)	17,602	(198.4)	11,175	(165.0)	2,617	(75.5)	2,838	(75.0)
2003[3,4]	36,017	(301.3)	22,565	(248.4)	4,973	(115.6)	6,103	(118.8)	18,099	(208.1)	11,329	(171.9)	2,385	(78.1)	3,214	(83.9)	17,918	(199.7)	11,236	(165.4)	2,588	(77.7)	2,888	(75.3)
2004[3,4]	36,504	(302.8)	22,654	(248.8)	5,048	(116.3)	6,301	(119.8)	18,406	(209.4)	11,395	(172.3)	2,425	(78.5)	3,326	(84.6)	18,097	(200.5)	11,259	(165.5)	2,623	(78.0)	2,975	(75.8)
2005[3,4]	36,761	(303.6)	22,806	(249.6)	5,111	(116.8)	6,364	(120.1)	18,547	(210.0)	11,492	(173.0)	2,457	(78.9)	3,341	(84.6)	18,214	(201.0)	11,314	(165.9)	2,654	(78.4)	3,023	(76.0)
2006[3,4]	37,047	(304.5)	22,863	(249.8)	5,260	(118.0)	6,439	(120.4)	18,707	(210.7)	11,537	(173.3)	2,573	(80.1)	3,357	(84.7)	18,340	(201.5)	11,327	(165.9)	2,688	(78.7)	3,083	(76.3)
2007[3,4]	37,480	(305.9)	22,962	(250.3)	5,363	(118.7)	6,632	(121.2)	18,940	(211.6)	11,641	(173.9)	2,639	(80.7)	3,447	(85.2)	18,541	(202.3)	11,320	(165.9)	2,724	(79.1)	3,186	(76.8)
2008[3,4]	37,569	(306.2)	22,956	(250.3)	5,387	(118.9)	6,721	(121.5)	18,948	(211.7)	11,628	(173.8)	2,616	(80.5)	3,472	(85.3)	18,621	(202.6)	11,328	(165.9)	2,771	(79.5)	3,249	(77.1)
2009[3,4]	37,616	(306.3)	22,809	(249.6)	5,445	(119.4)	6,809	(121.9)	18,949	(211.7)	11,542	(173.3)	2,633	(80.7)	3,497	(85.4)	18,667	(202.8)	11,267	(165.6)	2,812	(79.9)	3,313	(77.3)
2010[3,4,5]	37,949	(#)	22,607	(38.0)	5,450	(33.5)	7,193	(10.0)	19,126	(#)	11,437	(27.6)	2,609	(24.1)	3,714	(5.8)	18,823	(#)	11,170	(24.6)	2,841	(20.2)	3,479	(8.6)
2011[3,4,5]	38,205	(133.8)	22,359	(138.0)	5,444	(86.7)	7,656	(59.0)	19,430	(40.3)	11,290	(36.9)	2,627	(58.2)	4,123	(41.9)	18,775	(135.4)	11,068	(133.6)	2,817	(36.2)	3,533	(23.1)
2012[3,4,5]	38,800	(306.3)	21,708	(137.5)	5,540	(64.1)	8,201	(73.5)	19,557	(266.3)	10,963	(120.5)	2,699	(47.9)	4,241	(85.8)	19,243	(54.1)	10,745	(44.8)	2,841	(35.0)	3,959	(22.9)
2013[3,4,5]	38,804	(210.7)	21,542	(196.8)	5,570	(48.4)	8,263	(43.2)	19,561	(150.8)	10,911	(119.0)	2,708	(40.5)	4,248	(30.3)	19,243	(71.7)	10,631	(89.5)	2,863	(33.1)	4,015	(22.0)
2014[3,4,5]	38,650	(67.1)	21,290	(111.6)	5,590	(99.2)	8,345	(61.6)	19,484	(46.7)	10,775	(67.6)	2,739	(31.6)	4,278	(41.7)	19,166	(57.8)	10,515	(57.9)	2,851	(81.4)	4,066	(26.8)

See notes at end of table.

Table 219.71. Population 16 to 24 years old and number of 16- to 24-year-old high school dropouts (status dropouts), by sex and race/ethnicity: 1970 through 2014—Continued

[Standard errors appear in parentheses]

Year	Total				Males				Females			
	All races[1]	White	Black	Hispanic	All races[1]	White	Black	Hispanic	All races[1]	White	Black	Hispanic
1	2	3	4	5	6	7	8	9	10	11	12	13
	Number of 16- to 24-year-old (status) dropouts (in thousands)											
1970[2]	4,525 (108.5)	3,459 (95.1)	1,022 (53.6)	— (†)	2,022 (71.1)	1,508 (61.6)	500 (36.8)	— (†)	2,503 (76.3)	1,951 (67.6)	522 (36.0)	— (†)
1971[2]	4,641 (109.8)	3,663 (97.8)	919 (50.9)	— (†)	2,137 (73.0)	1,649 (64.3)	462 (35.5)	— (†)	2,504 (76.3)	2,013 (68.6)	456 (33.8)	— (†)
1972	4,770 (111.3)	3,250 (92.2)	858 (49.3)	609 (49.4)	2,226 (74.5)	1,504 (61.5)	419 (33.9)	280 (33.1)	2,545 (76.9)	1,745 (64.0)	439 (33.2)	329 (34.0)
1973	4,716 (110.7)	3,150 (90.8)	930 (51.2)	576 (48.1)	2,220 (74.4)	1,519 (61.8)	425 (34.1)	250 (31.3)	2,496 (76.2)	1,631 (61.9)	504 (35.4)	326 (33.9)
1974	4,849 (112.2)	3,240 (92.1)	878 (49.9)	653 (51.1)	2,343 (76.4)	1,601 (63.4)	386 (32.6)	328 (35.7)	2,505 (76.3)	1,638 (62.0)	493 (35.0)	325 (33.9)
1975	4,824 (111.9)	3,185 (91.3)	987 (52.7)	573 (48.0)	2,248 (74.9)	1,509 (61.6)	457 (35.3)	251 (31.3)	2,577 (77.4)	1,676 (62.7)	530 (36.3)	323 (33.7)
1976	4,981 (113.7)	3,366 (93.8)	908 (50.7)	646 (50.8)	2,432 (77.8)	1,688 (65.1)	435 (34.5)	286 (33.4)	2,549 (77.0)	1,678 (62.8)	473 (34.4)	360 (35.5)
1977	5,031 (114.2)	3,374 (94.0)	893 (50.3)	701 (52.9)	2,519 (79.1)	1,767 (66.5)	407 (33.4)	322 (35.4)	2,512 (76.4)	1,607 (61.5)	487 (34.8)	379 (36.4)
1978	5,114 (115.1)	3,384 (94.1)	928 (51.2)	728 (53.8)	2,572 (79.9)	1,715 (65.6)	475 (36.0)	356 (37.1)	2,541 (76.9)	1,670 (62.6)	453 (33.7)	371 (36.1)
1979	5,265 (116.8)	3,433 (94.8)	975 (52.4)	758 (54.9)	2,650 (81.1)	1,779 (66.8)	477 (36.0)	358 (37.2)	2,614 (77.9)	1,653 (62.3)	499 (35.2)	400 (37.4)
1980	5,085 (114.8)	3,211 (91.7)	889 (50.2)	885 (59.1)	2,672 (81.4)	1,715 (65.6)	446 (34.9)	462 (42.0)	2,413 (75.0)	1,496 (59.3)	444 (33.3)	424 (38.4)
1981	5,143 (115.4)	3,232 (92.0)	901 (50.5)	891 (59.3)	2,746 (82.5)	1,762 (66.5)	454 (35.2)	480 (42.8)	2,397 (74.7)	1,470 (58.8)	447 (33.4)	411 (37.9)
1982	5,055 (121.0)	3,202 (96.7)	902 (53.4)	823 (60.7)	2,601 (84.9)	1,668 (68.3)	488 (38.5)	386 (41.0)	2,454 (79.8)	1,534 (63.5)	414 (34.1)	437 (39.0)
1983	4,905 (119.2)	3,053 (94.5)	882 (52.8)	816 (60.3)	2,631 (85.4)	1,661 (68.2)	463 (37.6)	426 (42.9)	2,274 (76.9)	1,392 (60.5)	418 (34.2)	391 (39.2)
1984	4,626 (115.8)	2,952 (92.9)	758 (49.1)	762 (58.4)	2,438 (82.3)	1,592 (66.8)	391 (34.7)	375 (40.4)	2,188 (75.5)	1,360 (59.8)	367 (32.2)	387 (39.0)
1985	4,324 (112.1)	2,688 (88.8)	719 (47.9)	797 (49.8)	2,264 (79.4)	1,406 (62.8)	360 (33.3)	440 (36.4)	2,060 (73.3)	1,282 (58.1)	360 (31.9)	357 (37.6)
1986	4,142 (109.8)	2,418 (84.2)	667 (46.2)	966 (55.1)	2,183 (78.0)	1,260 (59.5)	333 (32.1)	547 (40.7)	1,959 (71.5)	1,158 (55.2)	334 (30.7)	419 (34.2)
1987	4,230 (110.9)	2,538 (86.3)	653 (45.7)	926 (54.0)	2,169 (77.7)	1,299 (60.4)	326 (31.8)	490 (38.7)	2,061 (73.3)	1,239 (57.1)	327 (30.4)	437 (34.8)
1988	4,232 (120.9)	2,301 (89.6)	664 (50.2)	1,168 (67.8)	2,184 (85.0)	1,214 (63.7)	323 (34.5)	611 (48.3)	2,049 (79.7)	1,087 (58.4)	341 (33.9)	557 (39.0)
1989	4,038 (112.3)	2,152 (82.4)	639 (46.9)	1,142 (61.4)	2,145 (80.1)	1,160 (59.2)	327 (32.9)	613 (44.2)	1,893 (72.9)	991 (53.0)	312 (30.8)	529 (42.6)
1990	3,797 (108.9)	2,007 (79.6)	594 (45.2)	1,114 (61.0)	1,909 (75.6)	1,027 (55.8)	252 (29.1)	608 (44.3)	1,887 (72.8)	980 (52.7)	342 (32.2)	506 (38.7)
1991	3,881 (110.1)	1,953 (78.5)	609 (45.8)	1,241 (64.2)	2,001 (77.4)	967 (54.1)	288 (31.0)	717 (47.8)	1,880 (72.6)	985 (52.8)	321 (31.3)	525 (39.3)
1992[3]	3,410 (103.4)	1,676 (72.8)	621 (46.2)	1,022 (58.6)	1,742 (72.3)	866 (51.3)	271 (30.1)	565 (42.8)	1,668 (68.5)	810 (48.0)	350 (32.6)	457 (36.9)
1993[3]	3,396 (103.1)	1,707 (73.4)	615 (46.0)	989 (57.7)	1,715 (71.8)	884 (51.8)	275 (30.3)	507 (40.7)	1,681 (68.7)	823 (48.3)	340 (32.1)	483 (37.8)
1994[3]	3,727 (108.0)	1,709 (73.5)	607 (45.7)	1,322 (66.1)	2,000 (77.4)	880 (51.6)	324 (32.8)	744 (48.6)	1,727 (69.7)	829 (48.5)	284 (29.4)	578 (41.1)
1995[3]	3,876 (110.1)	1,887 (77.2)	571 (44.4)	1,345 (66.6)	1,978 (77.0)	996 (54.9)	249 (28.9)	701 (47.3)	1,898 (73.0)	891 (50.3)	322 (31.3)	644 (43.2)
1996[3]	3,611 (110.3)	1,569 (73.1)	615 (47.8)	1,315 (68.6)	1,854 (77.4)	792 (50.9)	304 (33.0)	701 (49.3)	1,757 (72.9)	777 (48.8)	312 (32.0)	614 (42.3)
1997[3]	3,624 (110.6)	1,656 (75.1)	649 (49.0)	1,180 (65.1)	1,970 (79.7)	934 (55.2)	306 (33.2)	671 (48.2)	1,654 (70.8)	722 (47.0)	343 (33.5)	509 (40.3)
1998[3]	3,942 (115.2)	1,697 (76.0)	675 (50.0)	1,487 (72.4)	2,241 (84.9)	950 (55.7)	358 (35.7)	899 (55.0)	1,701 (71.8)	747 (47.8)	317 (32.2)	587 (43.0)
1999[3]	3,829 (113.6)	1,636 (74.7)	621 (48.0)	1,445 (71.5)	2,032 (81.0)	873 (53.4)	282 (31.9)	807 (52.4)	1,797 (73.7)	763 (48.3)	338 (33.3)	638 (44.7)
2000[3]	3,776 (112.8)	1,564 (73.0)	663 (49.5)	1,456 (71.7)	2,082 (81.9)	795 (51.0)	369 (36.3)	866 (54.1)	1,694 (71.6)	769 (48.5)	294 (31.1)	590 (43.1)
2001[3]	3,766 (106.9)	1,668 (71.6)	557 (43.2)	1,442 (67.5)	2,151 (79.0)	916 (51.9)	314 (31.8)	865 (51.0)	1,615 (66.4)	752 (45.6)	243 (26.9)	577 (42.7)
2002[3]	3,721 (106.3)	1,457 (66.9)	564 (43.5)	1,572 (70.5)	2,108 (78.2)	752 (47.1)	305 (31.4)	971 (54.0)	1,612 (66.4)	705 (44.1)	259 (27.7)	601 (41.3)
2003[3,4]	3,552 (103.9)	1,431 (66.3)	544 (42.8)	1,437 (67.7)	2,045 (77.1)	802 (48.6)	298 (31.2)	858 (51.1)	1,506 (64.2)	630 (41.7)	246 (27.1)	579 (40.6)
2004[3,4]	3,766 (106.9)	1,530 (68.5)	594 (44.7)	1,499 (69.0)	2,140 (78.8)	808 (48.8)	326 (32.6)	949 (53.5)	1,626 (66.6)	722 (44.6)	268 (28.3)	549 (39.6)
2005[3,4]	3,458 (102.5)	1,358 (64.6)	534 (42.4)	1,429 (67.5)	2,009 (76.4)	760 (47.3)	295 (31.0)	883 (51.8)	1,449 (63.0)	599 (40.7)	239 (26.7)	546 (39.5)
2006[3,4]	3,462 (102.6)	1,337 (64.1)	565 (43.6)	1,421 (67.3)	1,935 (75.0)	739 (46.7)	250 (28.6)	864 (51.3)	1,527 (64.6)	598 (40.7)	315 (30.6)	557 (39.8)
2007[3,4]	3,278 (99.9)	1,210 (61.0)	451 (39.1)	1,422 (67.3)	1,859 (73.6)	704 (45.6)	212 (26.4)	850 (50.9)	1,419 (62.3)	507 (37.4)	239 (26.8)	572 (40.3)
2008[3,4]	3,010 (95.8)	1,103 (58.3)	535 (42.5)	1,232 (63.0)	1,606 (68.5)	623 (42.9)	227 (27.3)	690 (46.3)	1,403 (62.0)	480 (36.5)	308 (30.3)	541 (39.3)
2009[3,4]	3,030 (96.1)	1,188 (60.5)	508 (41.4)	1,199 (62.2)	1,731 (71.0)	725 (46.2)	280 (30.2)	665 (45.5)	1,299 (59.7)	464 (35.8)	228 (26.2)	534 (39.1)
2010[3,4,5]	2,816 (100.8)	1,147 (67.9)	437 (41.5)	1,090 (62.3)	1,625 (77.3)	675 (48.4)	247 (29.2)	644 (46.2)	1,192 (53.0)	472 (38.7)	190 (24.1)	446 (33.9)
2011[3,4,5]	2,714 (99.1)	1,118 (68.1)	400 (37.5)	1,040 (60.1)	1,501 (69.9)	614 (46.0)	218 (26.4)	602 (44.9)	1,213 (64.6)	505 (42.9)	182 (27.2)	439 (34.0)
2012[3,4,5]	2,562 (101.1)	930 (67.7)	418 (42.3)	1,040 (59.0)	1,427 (74.2)	526 (43.8)	219 (31.2)	591 (46.1)	1,135 (63.8)	404 (39.4)	199 (28.9)	449 (39.6)
2013[3,4,5]	2,622 (109.3)	1,100 (66.7)	409 (48.4)	969 (61.2)	1,406 (73.6)	596 (42.8)	221 (29.9)	536 (43.1)	1,216 (66.0)	504 (38.5)	188 (31.1)	432 (39.5)
2014[3,4,5]	2,527 (94.9)	1,114 (68.1)	415 (42.8)	882 (57.4)	1,389 (71.1)	612 (44.6)	195 (27.9)	506 (45.4)	1,138 (55.7)	502 (43.2)	219 (30.5)	377 (33.9)

—Not available.
†Not applicable.
#Rounds to zero.
[1]Includes other racial/ethnic categories not separately shown.
[2]For 1970 and 1971, White and Black include persons of Hispanic ethnicity.
[3]Because of changes in data collection procedures, data may not be comparable with figures for years prior to 1992.
[4]White and Black exclude persons of Two or more races.
[5]Beginning in 2010, standard errors were computed using replicate weights, which produced more precise values than the generalized variance function methodology used in prior years.

NOTE: "Status" dropouts are 16- to 24-year-olds who are not enrolled in school and who have not completed a high school program, regardless of when they left school. People who have received GED credentials are counted as high school completers. All data are based on October counts. Data are based on sample surveys of the civilian noninstitutionalized population, which excludes persons in prisons, persons in the military, and other persons not living in households. Race categories exclude persons of Hispanic ethnicity except where otherwise noted. Detail may not sum to totals because of rounding.
SOURCE: U.S. Department of Commerce, Census Bureau, Current Population Survey (CPS), October, 1970 through 2014. (This table was prepared August 2015.)

Table 219.73. Percentage of high school dropouts among persons 16 to 24 years old (status dropout rate) and number and percentage distribution of 16- to 24-year-olds, by selected characteristics: Selected years, 2004 to 2014

Selected characteristic	Status dropout rate[1]								2014							
									Number of 16- to 24-year-olds (in thousands)				Percentage distribution of 16- to 24-year-olds			
	2004		2009		2013		2014		Total population[2]		Status dropouts only[3]		Total population[2]		Status dropouts only[3]	
1	2		3		4		5		6		7		8		9	
Total	**10.3**	**(0.23)**	**8.1**	**(0.20)**	**6.8**	**(0.28)**	**6.5**	**(0.25)**	**38,650**	**(67.1)**	**2,527**	**(94.9)**	**100.0**	**(†)**	**100.0**	**(†)**
Sex																
Male	11.6	(0.34)	9.1	(0.31)	7.2	(0.37)	7.1	(0.37)	19,484	(46.7)	1,389	(71.1)	50.4	(0.10)	55.0	(1.66)
Female	9.0	(0.31)	7.0	(0.27)	6.3	(0.34)	5.9	(0.29)	19,166	(57.8)	1,138	(55.7)	49.6	(0.10)	45.0	(1.66)
Race/ethnicity																
White	6.8	(0.24)	5.2	(0.21)	5.1	(0.31)	5.2	(0.32)	21,290	(111.6)	1,114	(68.1)	55.1	(0.28)	44.1	(2.03)
Black	11.8	(0.70)	9.3	(0.61)	7.3	(0.87)	7.4	(0.74)	5,590	(99.2)	415	(42.8)	14.5	(0.26)	16.4	(1.60)
Hispanic	23.8	(0.89)	17.6	(0.76)	11.7	(0.74)	10.6	(0.68)	8,345	(61.6)	882	(57.4)	21.6	(0.16)	34.9	(1.85)
Asian	3.5	(0.74)	2.1	(0.58)	3.2	(0.95)	1.0 !	(0.35)	1,966	(43.1)	21 !	(6.8)	5.1	(0.11)	0.8 !	(0.27)
Pacific Islander	‡	(†)	18.4	(5.42)	‡	(†)	12.1 !	(6.05)	125	(26.3)	‡	(†)	0.3	(0.07)	‡	(†)
American Indian/Alaska Native	17.0	(3.46)	13.2	(3.28)	7.0 !	(2.27)	15.7	(3.02)	339	(32.9)	53	(10.6)	0.9	(0.08)	2.1	(0.42)
Two or more races	6.1	(1.47)	6.5	(1.41)	5.7	(1.37)	2.7	(0.80)	996	(51.7)	27	(7.8)	2.6	(0.13)	1.1	(0.30)
Race/ethnicity by sex																
Male																
White	7.1	(0.35)	6.3	(0.33)	5.5	(0.39)	5.7	(0.42)	10,775	(67.6)	612	(44.6)	55.3	(0.28)	44.1	(2.48)
Black	13.5	(1.08)	10.6	(0.93)	8.2	(1.11)	7.1	(1.02)	2,739	(31.6)	195	(27.9)	14.1	(0.17)	14.1	(1.89)
Hispanic	28.5	(1.30)	19.0	(1.10)	12.6	(1.01)	11.8	(1.04)	4,278	(41.7)	506	(45.4)	22.0	(0.24)	36.4	(2.41)
Asian	2.1 !	(0.82)	‡	(†)	2.3 !	(0.96)	1.9 !	(0.66)	978	(29.8)	18 !	(6.4)	5.0	(0.15)	1.3 !	(0.47)
Pacific Islander	‡	(†)	26.9 !	(8.45)	‡	(†)	‡	(†)	58	(13.6)	‡	(†)	0.3	(0.07)	‡	(†)
American Indian/Alaska Native	12.6 !	(4.26)	12.3 !	(4.59)	‡	(†)	13.7	(3.48)	186	(24.3)	25	(7.3)	1.0	(0.12)	1.8	(0.53)
Two or more races	6.3 !	(2.09)	5.5 !	(1.86)	4.2 !	(2.01)	4.1 !	(1.45)	469	(29.5)	19 !	(6.7)	2.4	(0.15)	1.4 !	(0.47)
Female																
White	6.4	(0.34)	4.1	(0.27)	4.7	(0.36)	4.8	(0.41)	10,515	(57.9)	502	(43.2)	54.9	(0.34)	44.1	(2.98)
Black	10.2	(0.92)	8.1	(0.80)	6.6	(1.07)	7.7	(1.02)	2,851	(81.4)	219	(30.5)	14.9	(0.40)	19.3	(2.48)
Hispanic	18.5	(1.18)	16.1	(1.06)	10.8	(0.98)	9.3	(0.84)	4,066	(26.8)	377	(33.9)	21.2	(0.12)	33.1	(2.62)
Asian	4.9	(1.24)	3.0 !	(0.99)	4.1 !	(1.35)	‡	(†)	988	(22.2)	‡	(†)	5.2	(0.11)	‡	(†)
Pacific Islander	‡	(†)	‡	(†)	‡	(†)	‡	(†)	67	(18.6)	‡	(†)	0.3	(0.10)	‡	(†)
American Indian/Alaska Native	21.7	(5.44)	14.1 !	(4.69)	8.0 !	(3.56)	18.1	(4.01)	153	(19.3)	28	(6.2)	0.8	(0.10)	2.4	(0.56)
Two or more races	5.8 !	(2.06)	7.5	(2.10)	7.2	(2.07)	1.5 !	(0.72)	527	(32.3)	8 !	(3.8)	2.8	(0.17)	0.7 !	(0.33)
Age																
16	3.8	(0.42)	2.7	(0.37)	5.2	(0.64)	5.2	(0.62)	4,101	(50.9)	213	(25.1)	10.6	(0.13)	8.4	(0.96)
17	5.2	(0.51)	4.4	(0.46)	4.7	(0.62)	5.2	(0.67)	4,245	(50.0)	223	(28.6)	11.0	(0.13)	8.8	(1.10)
18	10.6	(0.73)	7.8	(0.59)	5.4	(0.64)	7.0	(0.72)	4,145	(45.9)	291	(30.4)	10.7	(0.12)	11.5	(1.15)
19	11.2	(0.74)	9.3	(0.65)	7.1	(0.78)	7.2	(0.76)	4,116	(46.5)	297	(31.5)	10.7	(0.13)	11.7	(1.12)
20 to 24	12.6	(0.34)	9.7	(0.30)	7.6	(0.38)	6.8	(0.33)	22,043	(65.5)	1,503	(72.9)	57.0	(0.08)	59.5	(1.72)
Recency of immigration[4]																
Born outside the United States																
Hispanic	38.4	(1.61)	31.3	(1.64)	22.8	(1.97)	21.0	(1.84)	1,889	(88.1)	397	(41.3)	4.9	(0.23)	15.7	(1.51)
Non-Hispanic	6.5	(0.81)	6.2	(0.81)	5.5	(1.06)	3.9	(0.91)	2,134	(102.5)	84	(20.2)	5.5	(0.27)	3.3	(0.79)
First generation																
Hispanic	14.7	(1.27)	11.8	(1.04)	8.2	(0.98)	7.1	(0.82)	3,808	(112.6)	270	(33.3)	9.9	(0.29)	10.7	(1.25)
Non-Hispanic	2.6	(0.51)	3.9	(0.57)	3.9	(0.90)	2.2	(0.59)	2,689	(106.8)	60	(15.8)	7.0	(0.27)	2.4	(0.61)
Second generation or higher																
Hispanic	13.7	(1.39)	10.2	(1.13)	8.3	(1.10)	8.1	(1.17)	2,648	(109.4)	215	(31.7)	6.9	(0.28)	8.5	(1.22)
Non-Hispanic	8.0	(0.24)	6.1	(0.21)	5.6	(0.31)	5.9	(0.29)	25,483	(135.2)	1,500	(74.1)	65.9	(0.34)	59.4	(1.94)
Disability[5]																
With a disability	—	(†)	15.5	(1.44)	14.9	(1.87)	13.9	(1.59)	1,530	(75.0)	212	(26.4)	4.0	(0.19)	8.4	(0.98)
Without a disability	—	(†)	7.8	(0.21)	6.4	(0.27)	6.2	(0.24)	37,121	(103.8)	2,314	(89.0)	96.0	(0.19)	91.6	(0.98)
Region																
Northeast	8.8	(0.47)	7.1	(0.47)	5.5	(0.61)	5.3	(0.54)	6,750	(134.1)	359	(37.4)	17.5	(0.34)	14.2	(1.42)
Midwest	8.0	(0.42)	7.6	(0.44)	6.0	(0.60)	5.4	(0.52)	8,186	(149.1)	443	(43.4)	21.2	(0.38)	17.5	(1.62)
South	11.4	(0.44)	8.4	(0.36)	7.6	(0.48)	7.6	(0.49)	14,294	(171.5)	1,083	(70.8)	37.0	(0.45)	42.9	(2.05)
West	12.2	(0.56)	8.6	(0.44)	7.1	(0.53)	6.8	(0.55)	9,420	(153.4)	642	(52.5)	24.4	(0.39)	25.4	(1.92)

—Not available.
†Not applicable.
!Interpret data with caution. The coefficient of variation (CV) for this estimate is 30 percent or greater.
‡Reporting standards not met. Either there are too few cases for a reliable estimate or the coefficient of variation (CV) is 50 percent or greater.
[1]The status dropout rate is the percentage of 16- to 24-year-olds who are not enrolled in high school and who lack a high school credential. High school credentials include high school diplomas and alternative credentials, such as a GED certificate.
[2]Includes all 16- to 24-year-olds.
[3]Status dropouts are 16- to 24-year-olds who are not enrolled in high school and who lack a high school credential. High school credentials include high school diplomas and alternative credentials, such as a GED certificate.
[4]The United States includes the 50 states and the District of Columbia. Individuals defined as "first generation" were born in the United States, but one or both of their parents were born outside the United States. Individuals defined as "second generation or higher" were born in the United States, as were both of their parents.
[5]Individuals identified as having a disability reported difficulty in at least one of the following: hearing, seeing even when wearing glasses, walking or climbing stairs, dressing or bathing, doing errands alone, concentrating, remembering, or making decisions.
NOTE: Data are based on sample surveys of the civilian noninstitutionalized population, which excludes persons in prisons, persons in the military, and other persons not living in households. Race categories exclude persons of Hispanic ethnicity. Detail may not sum to totals because of rounding.
SOURCE: U.S. Department of Commerce, Census Bureau, Current Population Survey (CPS), October, 2004 through 2014. (This table was prepared March 2016.)

Table 219.75. Percentage of high school dropouts among persons 16 to 24 years old (status dropout rate), by income level, and percentage distribution of status dropouts, by labor force status and years of school completed: 1970 through 2014

[Standard errors appear in parentheses]

Year	Status dropout rate	Status dropout rate, by family income quartile: Lowest quartile	Middle low quartile	Middle high quartile	Highest quartile	Percentage distribution of status dropouts, by labor force status: Total	Employed[1]	Unemployed	Not in labor force	Percentage distribution of status dropouts, by years of school completed: Total	Less than 9 years	9 years	10 years	11 or 12 years
1	2	3	4	5	6	7	8	9	10	11	12	13	14	15
1970	15.0 (0.29)	28.0 (0.92)	21.2 (0.65)	11.7 (0.50)	5.2 (0.34)	100.0 (†)	49.8 (1.06)	10.3 (0.65)	39.9 (1.04)	100.0 (†)	28.5 (0.96)	20.6 (0.86)	26.8 (0.94)	24.0 (0.91)
1971	14.7 (0.28)	28.8 (0.90)	20.7 (0.63)	10.9 (0.49)	5.1 (0.32)	100.0 (†)	49.5 (1.05)	10.9 (0.65)	39.6 (1.02)	100.0 (†)	27.9 (0.94)	21.7 (0.86)	27.8 (0.94)	22.7 (0.88)
1972	14.6 (0.28)	27.6 (0.85)	20.8 (0.62)	10.2 (0.46)	5.4 (0.33)	100.0 (†)	51.2 (1.03)	10.2 (0.63)	38.6 (1.01)	100.0 (†)	27.5 (0.92)	20.8 (0.84)	29.0 (0.94)	22.7 (0.87)
1973	14.1 (0.27)	28.0 (0.85)	19.6 (0.60)	9.9 (0.45)	4.9 (0.31)	100.0 (†)	53.2 (1.04)	9.2 (0.60)	37.5 (1.01)	100.0 (†)	26.5 (0.92)	20.9 (0.84)	27.4 (0.93)	25.3 (0.90)
1974	14.3 (0.27)	— (†)	— (†)	— (†)	— (†)	100.0 (†)	51.8 (1.02)	12.3 (0.67)	35.9 (0.98)	100.0 (†)	25.4 (0.89)	20.1 (0.82)	28.7 (0.93)	25.8 (0.90)
1975	13.9 (0.27)	28.8 (0.82)	18.0 (0.58)	10.2 (0.45)	5.0 (0.30)	100.0 (†)	46.0 (1.02)	15.6 (0.74)	38.4 (1.00)	100.0 (†)	23.5 (0.87)	21.1 (0.84)	27.5 (0.92)	27.9 (0.92)
1976	14.1 (0.27)	28.1 (0.79)	19.2 (0.60)	10.1 (0.45)	4.9 (0.29)	100.0 (†)	48.8 (1.01)	16.0 (0.74)	35.2 (0.97)	100.0 (†)	24.3 (0.87)	20.1 (0.81)	27.8 (0.91)	27.8 (0.91)
1977	14.1 (0.27)	28.5 (0.80)	19.0 (0.60)	10.4 (0.46)	4.5 (0.29)	100.0 (†)	52.9 (1.02)	13.6 (0.70)	33.6 (0.96)	100.0 (†)	24.3 (0.87)	21.7 (0.84)	27.3 (0.91)	26.6 (0.90)
1978	14.2 (0.27)	28.2 (0.80)	18.9 (0.60)	10.5 (0.46)	5.5 (0.31)	100.0 (†)	54.3 (1.01)	12.4 (0.67)	33.3 (0.95)	100.0 (†)	22.9 (0.85)	20.2 (0.81)	28.2 (0.91)	28.8 (0.91)
1979	14.6 (0.27)	28.1 (0.79)	18.5 (0.60)	11.5 (0.47)	5.6 (0.32)	100.0 (†)	54.0 (0.99)	12.7 (0.66)	33.3 (0.94)	100.0 (†)	22.6 (0.83)	21.0 (0.81)	28.6 (0.90)	27.8 (0.89)
1980	14.1 (0.26)	27.0 (0.77)	18.1 (0.60)	10.7 (0.46)	5.7 (0.32)	100.0 (†)	50.4 (1.01)	17.0 (0.76)	32.6 (0.95)	100.0 (†)	23.6 (0.86)	19.7 (0.80)	29.8 (0.93)	27.0 (0.90)
1981	13.9 (0.26)	26.4 (0.75)	17.8 (0.57)	11.1 (0.47)	5.2 (0.30)	100.0 (†)	49.8 (1.01)	18.3 (0.78)	31.9 (0.94)	100.0 (†)	24.3 (0.86)	18.6 (0.78)	30.2 (0.92)	26.9 (0.89)
1982	13.9 (0.27)	27.2 (0.78)	18.3 (0.63)	10.2 (0.48)	4.4 (0.29)	100.0 (†)	45.2 (1.06)	21.1 (0.87)	33.7 (1.01)	100.0 (†)	22.9 (0.90)	20.8 (0.87)	28.8 (0.96)	27.6 (0.95)
1983	13.7 (0.27)	26.5 (0.77)	17.8 (0.62)	10.5 (0.50)	4.1 (0.29)	100.0 (†)	48.4 (1.08)	18.2 (0.83)	33.4 (1.02)	100.0 (†)	23.0 (0.91)	19.3 (0.85)	28.8 (0.98)	28.8 (0.98)
1984	13.1 (0.27)	25.9 (0.76)	16.5 (0.61)	9.9 (0.48)	3.8 (0.29)	100.0 (†)	49.7 (1.11)	17.3 (0.84)	32.9 (1.05)	100.0 (†)	23.6 (0.95)	21.4 (0.91)	27.5 (1.00)	27.5 (0.99)
1985	12.6 (0.27)	27.1 (0.78)	14.7 (0.60)	8.3 (0.46)	4.0 (0.29)	100.0 (†)	50.1 (1.15)	17.5 (0.88)	32.4 (1.08)	100.0 (†)	23.9 (0.98)	21.0 (0.94)	27.9 (1.03)	27.2 (1.03)
1986	12.2 (0.27)	25.4 (0.75)	14.8 (0.60)	8.0 (0.45)	3.4 (0.28)	100.0 (†)	51.1 (1.18)	16.4 (0.87)	32.5 (1.10)	100.0 (†)	25.4 (1.03)	21.5 (0.97)	25.7 (1.03)	27.4 (1.05)
1987	12.6 (0.28)	25.5 (0.76)	16.6 (0.63)	8.0 (0.46)	3.6 (0.28)	100.0 (†)	52.4 (1.16)	13.6 (0.80)	34.0 (1.10)	100.0 (†)	25.9 (1.02)	20.7 (0.94)	26.0 (1.02)	27.5 (1.04)
1988	12.9 (0.30)	27.2 (0.85)	15.4 (0.68)	8.2 (0.51)	3.4 (0.30)	100.0 (†)	52.9 (1.27)	— (†)	— (†)	100.0 (†)	28.9 (1.15)	19.3 (1.00)	25.1 (1.10)	26.8 (1.12)
1989	12.6 (0.31)	25.0 (0.84)	16.2 (0.71)	8.7 (0.52)	3.3 (0.31)	100.0 (†)	53.2 (1.30)	13.8 (0.90)	33.0 (1.22)	100.0 (†)	29.4 (1.18)	20.8 (1.05)	24.9 (1.12)	25.0 (1.13)
1990	12.1 (0.29)	24.3 (0.82)	15.1 (0.65)	8.7 (0.51)	2.9 (0.28)	100.0 (†)	52.5 (1.29)	13.3 (0.88)	34.2 (1.23)	100.0 (†)	28.6 (1.17)	20.9 (1.05)	24.4 (1.11)	26.1 (1.14)
1991	12.5 (0.30)	25.9 (0.83)	15.5 (0.66)	7.7 (0.49)	3.0 (0.29)	100.0 (†)	47.5 (1.28)	15.8 (0.93)	36.7 (1.23)	100.0 (†)	28.6 (1.15)	20.5 (1.03)	26.1 (1.12)	24.9 (1.10)
1992[2]	11.0 (0.28)	23.4 (0.79)	12.9 (0.62)	7.3 (0.48)	2.4 (0.26)	100.0 (†)	47.6 (1.36)	15.0 (0.97)	37.4 (1.32)	100.0 (†)	21.6 (1.12)	17.5 (1.04)	24.4 (1.17)	36.5 (1.31)
1993[2]	11.0 (0.28)	22.9 (0.77)	12.7 (0.62)	6.6 (0.46)	2.9 (0.29)	100.0 (†)	48.7 (1.37)	12.8 (0.91)	38.5 (1.33)	100.0 (†)	20.5 (1.10)	16.6 (1.02)	24.1 (1.17)	38.8 (1.33)
1994[2]	11.4 (0.26)	20.7 (0.71)	13.7 (0.58)	8.7 (0.45)	4.9 (0.33)	100.0 (†)	49.5 (1.21)	13.0 (0.81)	37.5 (1.17)	100.0 (†)	23.9 (1.03)	16.2 (0.89)	20.3 (0.97)	39.6 (1.18)
1995[2]	12.0 (0.27)	23.2 (0.69)	13.8 (0.59)	8.3 (0.46)	3.6 (0.29)	100.0 (†)	48.9 (1.19)	14.2 (0.83)	37.0 (1.14)	100.0 (†)	22.2 (0.99)	17.0 (0.89)	22.5 (0.99)	38.3 (1.15)
1996[2]	11.1 (0.27)	22.0 (0.72)	13.6 (0.60)	7.0 (0.45)	3.2 (0.28)	100.0 (†)	47.3 (1.28)	15.0 (0.91)	37.7 (1.24)	100.0 (†)	20.3 (1.03)	17.7 (0.98)	22.6 (1.07)	39.4 (1.25)
1997[2]	11.0 (0.27)	21.8 (0.71)	13.5 (0.59)	6.2 (0.42)	3.4 (0.29)	100.0 (†)	53.3 (1.28)	13.2 (0.86)	33.5 (1.21)	100.0 (†)	19.9 (1.02)	15.7 (0.93)	22.3 (1.06)	42.1 (1.26)
1998[2]	11.8 (0.27)	22.3 (0.71)	14.9 (0.62)	7.7 (0.45)	3.5 (0.29)	100.0 (†)	55.1 (1.22)	10.3 (0.74)	34.6 (1.17)	100.0 (†)	21.0 (1.00)	14.9 (0.87)	21.4 (1.01)	42.6 (1.21)
1999[2]	11.2 (0.26)	21.0 (0.70)	14.3 (0.60)	7.4 (0.44)	3.9 (0.30)	100.0 (†)	55.6 (1.24)	10.0 (0.75)	34.4 (1.18)	100.0 (†)	22.2 (1.03)	16.3 (0.92)	22.5 (1.04)	39.0 (1.21)
2000[2]	10.9 (0.26)	20.7 (0.70)	12.8 (0.56)	8.3 (0.46)	3.5 (0.29)	100.0 (†)	56.9 (1.24)	12.3 (0.82)	30.8 (1.16)	100.0 (†)	21.5 (1.03)	15.3 (0.90)	23.1 (1.06)	40.0 (1.23)
2001[2]	10.7 (0.25)	19.3 (0.68)	13.4 (0.57)	9.0 (0.47)	3.2 (0.27)	100.0 (†)	58.3 (1.24)	14.8 (0.89)	26.9 (1.11)	100.0 (†)	18.4 (0.97)	16.8 (0.94)	23.8 (1.07)	40.9 (1.23)
2002[2]	10.5 (0.24)	18.8 (0.62)	12.3 (0.53)	8.4 (0.43)	3.8 (0.28)	100.0 (†)	57.4 (1.18)	13.3 (0.81)	29.2 (1.09)	100.0 (†)	22.8 (1.00)	17.1 (0.90)	21.3 (0.98)	38.9 (1.17)
2003[2]	9.9 (0.23)	19.5 (0.64)	10.8 (0.49)	7.3 (0.40)	3.4 (0.26)	100.0 (†)	53.5 (1.22)	13.7 (0.84)	32.9 (1.15)	100.0 (†)	21.2 (1.00)	18.2 (0.94)	20.7 (0.99)	40.0 (1.20)
2004[2]	10.3 (0.23)	18.0 (0.60)	12.7 (0.52)	8.2 (0.42)	3.7 (0.27)	100.0 (†)	53.0 (1.19)	14.3 (0.83)	32.7 (1.12)	100.0 (†)	21.4 (0.97)	15.9 (0.87)	22.5 (0.99)	40.3 (1.17)
2005[2]	9.4 (0.22)	17.9 (0.60)	11.5 (0.51)	7.1 (0.39)	2.7 (0.23)	100.0 (†)	56.9 (1.23)	11.9 (0.80)	31.2 (1.15)	100.0 (†)	18.9 (0.97)	16.8 (0.93)	21.4 (1.02)	42.9 (1.23)
2006[2]	9.3 (0.22)	16.5 (0.58)	12.1 (0.51)	6.3 (0.37)	3.8 (0.27)	100.0 (†)	56.4 (1.23)	11.7 (0.80)	32.0 (1.16)	100.0 (†)	22.1 (1.03)	13.4 (0.85)	20.7 (1.01)	43.9 (1.23)
2007[2]	8.7 (0.21)	16.7 (0.59)	10.5 (0.48)	6.4 (0.36)	3.2 (0.25)	100.0 (†)	55.5 (1.27)	11.2 (0.80)	33.3 (1.20)	100.0 (†)	21.2 (1.04)	16.9 (0.96)	22.9 (1.07)	39.0 (1.24)
2008[2]	8.0 (0.20)	16.4 (0.58)	9.4 (0.45)	5.4 (0.34)	2.2 (0.21)	100.0 (†)	46.8 (1.33)	16.3 (0.98)	36.9 (1.28)	100.0 (†)	18.4 (1.03)	15.2 (0.96)	23.8 (1.13)	42.6 (1.32)
2009[2]	8.1 (0.20)	15.8 (0.57)	9.7 (0.45)	5.4 (0.34)	2.5 (0.22)	100.0 (†)	43.2 (1.31)	19.9 (1.06)	36.9 (1.28)	100.0 (†)	17.7 (1.01)	13.6 (0.91)	24.4 (1.14)	44.3 (1.32)
2010[2,3]	7.4 (0.27)	13.8 (0.83)	8.9 (0.54)	5.1 (0.48)	2.5 (0.31)	100.0 (†)	45.8 (1.64)	18.7 (1.38)	35.5 (1.70)	100.0 (†)	19.2 (1.48)	13.1 (1.07)	22.5 (1.59)	45.2 (1.89)
2011[2,3]	7.1 (0.26)	13.0 (0.73)	9.0 (0.53)	4.8 (0.45)	2.3 (0.32)	100.0 (†)	49.8 (1.77)	16.0 (1.33)	34.2 (1.69)	100.0 (†)	18.1 (1.72)	12.9 (1.15)	21.2 (1.39)	47.7 (1.87)
2012[2,3]	6.6 (0.25)	11.8 (0.70)	8.7 (0.65)	4.1 (0.44)	1.9 (0.31)	100.0 (†)	44.8 (2.07)	18.1 (1.49)	37.1 (1.83)	100.0 (†)	18.3 (1.76)	10.2 (1.21)	21.9 (1.57)	49.6 (2.20)
2013[2,3]	6.8 (0.28)	10.7 (0.73)	8.8 (0.67)	5.0 (0.44)	3.2 (0.36)	100.0 (†)	41.1 (2.01)	16.8 (1.58)	42.1 (1.84)	100.0 (†)	18.3 (1.70)	13.3 (1.34)	21.1 (1.63)	47.4 (2.31)
2014[2,3]	6.5 (0.25)	11.6 (0.68)	7.6 (0.57)	4.7 (0.43)	2.8 (0.31)	100.0 (†)	44.7 (1.84)	17.0 (1.41)	38.3 (1.61)	100.0 (†)	15.0 (1.58)	13.7 (1.28)	21.3 (1.56)	50.0 (1.94)

—Not available.
†Not applicable.
[1]Includes persons who were employed but not at work during the survey week.
[2]Because of changes in data collection procedures, data may not be comparable with figures for years prior to 1992.
[3]Beginning in 2010, standard errors were computed using replicate weights, which produced more precise values than the generalized variance function methodology used in prior years.

NOTE: "Status" dropouts are 16- to 24-year-olds who are not enrolled in school and who have not completed a high school program, regardless of when they left school. People who have received GED credentials are counted as high school completers. Data are based on sample surveys of the civilian noninstitutionalized population, which excludes persons in prisons, persons in the military, and other persons not living in households. Detail may not sum to totals because of rounding.
SOURCE: U.S. Department of Commerce, Census Bureau, Current Population Survey (CPS), October, 1970 through 2014. (This table was prepared August 2015.)

Table 219.80. Percentage of high school dropouts among persons 16 to 24 years old (status dropout rate) and number of status dropouts, by noninstitutionalized or institutionalized status, birth in or outside of the United States, and selected characteristics: Selected years, 2006 through 2014

[Standard errors appear in parentheses]

Selected characteristic	Total status dropout rate: 2006	Total status dropout rate: 2009	Total status dropout rate: 2013	Total status dropout rate: 2014	2014, Noninstitutionalized population[1]: Number of status dropouts (in thousands)	2014, Noninstitutionalized population[1]: Percentage distribution of status dropouts	2014, Noninstitutionalized population[1], Status dropout rate: Total for noninstitutionalized population	2014, Noninstitutionalized population[1], Status dropout rate: For those born in the United States[3]	2014, Noninstitutionalized population[1], Status dropout rate: For those born outside of the United States[3]	2014, Institutionalized population[2]: Number of status dropouts (in thousands)	2014, Institutionalized population[2]: Status dropout rate
1	2	3	4	5	6	7	8	9	10	11	12
Total	**9.7 (0.07)**	**8.6 (0.08)**	**6.8 (0.06)**	**6.3 (0.05)**	**2,346 (21.5)**	**100.0 (†)**	**6.0 (0.05)**	**5.3 (0.05)**	**12.4 (0.27)**	**151 (3.4)**	**33.1 (0.64)**
Sex											
Male	11.3 (0.11)	10.1 (0.10)	8.0 (0.08)	7.2 (0.09)	1,343 (17.2)	57.2 (0.46)	6.7 (0.09)	5.9 (0.08)	14.2 (0.35)	138 (3.6)	34.1 (0.72)
Female	7.9 (0.08)	7.1 (0.09)	5.6 (0.08)	5.2 (0.07)	1,003 (13.3)	42.8 (0.46)	5.2 (0.07)	4.7 (0.07)	10.4 (0.33)	13 (1.1)	24.7 (1.76)
Race/ethnicity											
White	6.4 (0.07)	5.6 (0.07)	4.7 (0.06)	4.4 (0.06)	936 (12.5)	39.9 (0.41)	4.3 (0.06)	4.3 (0.06)	4.0 (0.36)	33 (1.7)	23.9 (1.18)
Black	11.5 (0.21)	10.7 (0.18)	9.0 (0.19)	7.9 (0.17)	385 (9.5)	16.4 (0.38)	6.8 (0.17)	6.9 (0.17)	5.7 (0.59)	74 (2.6)	39.2 (1.12)
Hispanic	21.0 (0.26)	17.9 (0.22)	11.8 (0.20)	10.7 (0.15)	872 (12.5)	37.2 (0.39)	10.4 (0.15)	7.6 (0.15)	20.8 (0.47)	38 (1.6)	37.2 (1.30)
Cuban	7.2 (0.83)	7.0 (0.87)	6.2 (0.63)	6.3 (0.85)	14 (2.0)	0.6 (0.08)	6.1 (0.85)	4.3 (0.68)	10.4 (1.89)	‡ (†)	‡ (†)
Dominican	10.0 (0.92)	10.8 (0.94)	8.3 (0.70)	8.0 (0.67)	22 (2.2)	1.0 (0.09)	7.7 (0.70)	6.2 (0.78)	10.7 (1.35)	‡ (†)	30.8 (8.29)
Mexican	23.6 (0.31)	19.3 (0.26)	12.8 (0.26)	11.0 (0.16)	592 (9.2)	25.2 (0.34)	10.6 (0.16)	7.8 (0.17)	22.0 (0.61)	26 (1.5)	39.2 (1.55)
Puerto Rican	15.2 (0.64)	14.1 (0.58)	9.5 (0.49)	9.6 (0.51)	76 (3.9)	3.2 (0.16)	9.4 (0.51)	9.3 (0.51)	13.3 ! (5.35)	3 (0.7)	25.9 (3.82)
Spaniard	6.9 (1.50)	7.4 (1.46)	4.9 (1.04)	4.5 (0.90)	4 (0.9)	0.2 (0.04)	4.1 (0.86)	4.0 (0.88)	‡ (†)	‡ (†)	‡ (†)
Central American[4]	29.8 (0.93)	27.0 (0.83)	17.1 (0.69)	17.8 (0.73)	123 (5.6)	5.2 (0.23)	17.4 (0.75)	6.5 (0.51)	32.7 (1.53)	4 (0.7)	46.0 (5.36)
Costa Rican	13.6 (3.84)	12.5 (3.59)	4.7 ! (2.06)	6.1 ! (2.38)	‡ (†)	# (†)	6.1 ! (2.38)	5.6 ! (2.56)	‡ (†)	‡ (†)	‡ (†)
Guatemalan	43.4 (2.17)	41.0 (1.57)	27.0 (1.75)	28.7 (1.66)	52 (3.8)	2.2 (0.16)	28.4 (1.68)	7.8 (1.21)	46.3 (2.51)	‡ (†)	50.5 (9.24)
Honduran	34.2 (2.75)	32.0 (2.45)	19.9 (1.66)	19.5 (1.76)	20 (2.2)	0.9 (0.09)	18.7 (1.78)	6.3 (1.55)	28.7 (3.07)	‡ (†)	67.4 (9.27)
Nicaraguan	13.6 (2.41)	7.5 (1.51)	7.6 (1.55)	7.3 (1.24)	4 (0.7)	0.2 (0.03)	7.4 (1.25)	6.4 (1.34)	11.3 ! (3.99)	‡ (†)	‡ (†)
Panamanian	7.4 ! (2.95)	5.6 ! (2.07)	3.0 ! (1.13)	1.8 ! (0.81)	‡ (†)	# (†)	1.8 ! (0.82)	‡ (†)	‡ (†)	‡ (†)	‡ (†)
Salvadoran	23.9 (1.46)	23.1 (1.36)	13.4 (0.95)	14.9 (0.92)	45 (3.1)	1.9 (0.13)	14.6 (0.93)	6.8 (0.80)	27.8 (1.94)	‡ (†)	41.9 (9.74)
South American	8.1 (0.71)	6.8 (0.63)	4.3 (0.43)	4.1 (0.45)	17 (1.9)	0.7 (0.08)	3.9 (0.43)	2.7 (0.40)	5.4 (0.79)	‡ (†)	38.3 ! (11.97)
Chilean	4.9 ! (2.19)	‡ (†)	4.3 ! (1.81)	‡ (†)	‡ (†)	‡ (†)	‡ (†)	‡ (†)	‡ (†)	‡ (†)	‡ (†)
Colombian	5.6 (0.89)	6.1 (0.80)	3.4 (0.56)	3.4 (0.79)	5 (1.1)	0.2 (0.05)	3.1 (0.73)	2.2 (0.53)	4.3 ! (1.37)	‡ (†)	‡ (†)
Ecuadorian	14.1 (2.31)	13.8 (2.08)	10.8 (1.67)	7.3 (1.38)	6 (1.2)	0.3 (0.05)	7.1 (1.37)	3.3 ! (1.07)	12.8 (2.76)	‡ (†)	‡ (†)
Peruvian	6.2 ! (1.88)	3.5 (0.96)	1.7 (0.42)	3.1 (0.88)	‡ (†)	0.1 (0.03)	3.0 (0.87)	‡ (†)	4.4 (1.28)	‡ (†)	‡ (†)
Venezuelan	5.1 ! (1.69)	2.6 ! (1.00)	‡ (†)	4.1 ! (1.26)	‡ (†)	# (†)	4.1 ! (1.26)	3.8 ! (1.85)	4.3 ! (1.66)	‡ (†)	‡ (†)
Other South American	9.5 (2.38)	6.5 (1.50)	1.5 (0.41)	2.7 (0.79)	‡ (†)	0.1 ! (0.02)	2.5 ! (0.75)	2.7 ! (1.05)	2.3 ! (1.03)	‡ (†)	‡ (†)
Other Hispanic	13.4 (0.70)	11.9 (0.87)	9.0 (0.75)	10.0 (0.77)	24 (2.2)	1.0 (0.09)	9.6 (0.80)	9.0 (0.86)	15.1 (3.14)	‡ (†)	27.8 (6.34)
Asian	3.1 (0.20)	3.3 (0.17)	2.5 (0.16)	2.5 (0.14)	51 (2.9)	2.2 (0.12)	2.5 (0.14)	1.8 (0.14)	3.4 (0.28)	‡ (†)	21.5 ! (10.04)
Chinese[5]	3.1 (0.45)	2.1 (0.34)	1.6 (0.25)	1.2 (0.18)	6 (1.0)	0.3 (0.04)	1.2 (0.18)	1.0 (0.23)	1.3 (0.25)	‡ (†)	‡ (†)
Filipino	2.6 (0.37)	3.2 (0.43)	1.9 (0.35)	1.9 (0.35)	6 (1.1)	0.2 (0.05)	1.9 (0.35)	1.4 (0.37)	2.5 (0.62)	‡ (†)	‡ (†)
Japanese	1.0 ! (0.39)	2.5 ! (0.82)	1.6 ! (0.60)	1.3 ! (0.51)	‡ (†)	# (†)	1.3 ! (0.51)	1.5 ! (0.72)	‡ (†)	‡ (†)	‡ (†)
Korean	0.9 (0.21)	2.4 (0.56)	1.0 ! (0.36)	0.9 ! (0.28)	‡ (†)	0.1 ! (0.02)	0.9 ! (0.28)	1.3 ! (0.47)	‡ (†)	‡ (†)	‡ (†)
South Asian[6]	2.7 (0.41)	2.4 (0.35)	2.8 (0.40)	3.2 (0.38)	14 (1.8)	0.6 (0.08)	3.1 (0.39)	1.4 (0.34)	4.6 (0.65)	‡ (†)	‡ (†)
Asian Indian	2.6 (0.47)	2.1 (0.34)	1.8 (0.31)	2.0 (0.31)	7 (1.1)	0.3 (0.05)	1.9 (0.31)	1.3 (0.38)	2.6 (0.51)	‡ (†)	‡ (†)
Bangladeshi	‡ (†)	‡ (†)	‡ (†)	6.1 ! (2.34)	‡ (†)	# (†)	5.2 ! (2.35)	‡ (†)	8.0 ! (3.45)	‡ (†)	‡ (†)
Bhutanese	— (†)	— (†)	36.8 (8.18)	‡ (†)	‡ (†)	‡ (†)	‡ (†)	‡ (†)	‡ (†)	‡ (†)	‡ (†)
Nepalese	— (†)	— (†)	11.1 ! (3.36)	19.6 (5.67)	‡ (†)	0.2 ! (0.06)	19.9 (5.80)	‡ (†)	21.6 (6.24)	‡ (†)	‡ (†)
Pakistani	3.5 ! (1.22)	4.1 (1.18)	1.8 ! (0.60)	2.6 (0.76)	‡ (†)	0.1 (0.02)	2.6 (0.76)	2.4 ! (1.14)	2.8 ! (1.01)	‡ (†)	‡ (†)
Southeast Asian	5.7 (0.55)	6.0 (0.55)	4.7 (0.48)	5.3 (0.50)	21 (2.1)	0.9 (0.09)	5.2 (0.50)	3.4 (0.45)	8.5 (1.24)	‡ (†)	‡ (†)
Burmese	— (†)	— (†)	20.7 (4.13)	27.5 (5.70)	‡ (†)	0.2 (0.06)	27.5 (5.70)	‡ (†)	28.4 (5.91)	‡ (†)	‡ (†)
Cambodian	6.5 (1.59)	9.7 (2.10)	6.2 (1.49)	8.4 (1.71)	‡ (†)	0.1 (0.03)	8.3 (1.71)	8.2 (2.00)	8.9 ! (4.45)	‡ (†)	‡ (†)
Hmong	6.7 (1.56)	7.3 (1.33)	4.3 (1.12)	5.8 (1.20)	‡ (†)	0.1 (0.03)	5.8 (1.20)	3.3 (0.91)	17.6 ! (5.64)	‡ (†)	‡ (†)
Laotian	8.0 (1.93)	9.7 (2.15)	5.7 ! (1.91)	8.9 (2.51)	‡ (†)	0.1 (0.03)	8.8 (2.53)	8.9 ! (2.80)	‡ (†)	‡ (†)	‡ (†)
Thai	2.5 ! (1.24)	‡ (†)	‡ (†)	6.3 ! (2.02)	‡ (†)	# (†)	5.5 ! (1.98)	‡ (†)	10.6 ! (4.41)	‡ (†)	‡ (†)
Vietnamese	5.4 (0.76)	4.6 (0.74)	3.5 (0.55)	2.4 (0.45)	6 (1.0)	0.2 (0.04)	2.5 (0.45)	1.6 (0.37)	4.0 (1.08)	‡ (†)	‡ (†)
Other Southeast Asian[7]	‡ (†)	‡ (†)	‡ (†)	‡ (†)	‡ (†)	‡ (†)	‡ (†)	‡ (†)	‡ (†)	‡ (†)	‡ (†)
Other Asian	3.0 (0.69)	6.0 (1.01)	1.7 (0.49)	2.2 (0.64)	‡ (†)	0.1 (0.02)	2.2 (0.64)	1.0 ! (0.51)	6.3 ! (2.41)	‡ (†)	‡ (†)
Pacific Islander	7.4 (1.13)	9.5 (1.45)	5.0 (1.03)	10.6 (1.66)	8 (1.4)	0.3 (0.06)	10.2 (1.67)	7.1 (1.37)	23.4 (5.65)	‡ (†)	‡ (†)
American Indian/Alaska Native[8]	15.1 (0.63)	15.9 (0.83)	12.8 (0.76)	11.5 (0.77)	32 (2.3)	1.4 (0.09)	11.3 (0.77)	11.1 (0.77)	21.8 ! (7.44)	2 (0.5)	22.2 (5.70)
American Indian	15.0 (0.79)	16.3 (0.95)	13.2 (0.83)	11.5 (0.83)	27 (2.0)	1.2 (0.08)	11.2 (0.82)	11.0 (0.84)	‡ (†)	‡ (†)	23.8 ! (7.36)
Alaska Native	17.2 (3.93)	19.5 (3.42)	9.1 (1.73)	10.6 (1.73)	2 (0.3)	0.1 (0.01)	10.7 (1.78)	10.7 (1.78)	‡ (†)	‡ (†)	‡ (†)

See notes at end of table.

Table 219.80. Percentage of high school dropouts among persons 16 to 24 years old (status dropout rate) and number of status dropouts, by noninstitutionalized or institutionalized status, birth in or outside of the United States, and selected characteristics: Selected years, 2006 through 2014—Continued

[Standard errors appear in parentheses]

Selected characteristic	Total status dropout rate: 2006		2009		2013		2014		2014, Noninstitutionalized population[1]: Number of status dropouts (in thousands)		Percentage distribution of status dropouts		Status dropout rate: Total for noninstitutionalized population		For those born in the United States[3]		For those born outside of the United States[3]		Institutionalized population[2]: Number of status dropouts (in thousands)		Status dropout rate	
1	2		3		4		5		6		7		8		9		10		11		12	
Some other race[9]	10.2	(1.23)	9.1	(1.48)	5.1	(1.13)	5.6	(1.03)	5	(1.0)	0.2	(0.04)	5.4	(1.03)	3.8	(1.05)	10.9	(2.94)	‡	(†)	‡	(†)
Two or more races	7.8	(0.39)	6.5	(0.36)	5.2	(0.28)	5.0	(0.26)	56	(3.2)	2.4	(0.14)	4.8	(0.26)	4.7	(0.27)	5.4	(1.04)	3	(0.4)	20.8	(2.67)
Race/ethnicity by sex																						
Male																						
White	7.2	(0.10)	6.3	(0.10)	5.4	(0.08)	5.0	(0.08)	528	(9.2)	39.3	(0.52)	4.8	(0.08)	4.8	(0.09)	4.6	(0.59)	29	(1.6)	25.3	(1.38)
Black	14.0	(0.31)	13.1	(0.27)	10.9	(0.27)	9.5	(0.22)	211	(6.7)	15.7	(0.42)	7.6	(0.23)	7.7	(0.23)	5.6	(0.84)	69	(2.6)	39.5	(1.22)
Hispanic	24.8	(0.36)	21.2	(0.31)	13.9	(0.26)	12.7	(0.23)	526	(9.9)	39.1	(0.56)	12.2	(0.23)	8.8	(0.23)	23.6	(0.60)	35	(1.6)	37.6	(1.41)
Asian	3.5	(0.28)	3.7	(0.26)	2.8	(0.19)	2.5	(0.19)	25	(2.0)	1.9	(0.14)	2.5	(0.19)	2.0	(0.20)	3.1	(0.36)	‡	(†)	21.5 !	(10.04)
Pacific Islander	7.7	(1.54)	9.4	(2.06)	4.2	(1.00)	12.6	(2.45)	‡	(†)	0.4	(0.08)	11.9	(2.48)	7.8	(1.82)	24.9 !	(8.06)	‡	(†)	‡	(†)
American Indian/Alaska Native	17.3	(1.08)	17.6	(1.20)	14.3	(1.11)	13.1	(1.13)	18	(1.5)	1.3	(0.11)	12.6	(1.08)	12.5	(1.12)	‡	(†)	‡	(†)	24.4	(6.33)
Some other race[9]	11.4	(1.78)	12.0	(2.43)	6.2	(1.75)	5.5	(1.36)	‡	(†)	0.2	(0.05)	5.3	(1.37)	3.6 !	(1.25)	10.3 !	(3.79)	‡	(†)	‡	(†)
Two or more races	8.8	(0.59)	7.4	(0.56)	5.5	(0.43)	5.0	(0.34)	27	(2.1)	2.0	(0.16)	4.7	(0.35)	4.7	(0.37)	4.5 !	(1.48)	3	(0.4)	19.6	(2.97)
Female																						
White	5.5	(0.08)	4.9	(0.08)	4.0	(0.08)	3.9	(0.09)	408	(9.3)	40.7	(0.68)	3.8	(0.09)	3.9	(0.09)	3.3	(0.41)	5	(0.7)	17.5	(2.49)
Black	9.0	(0.23)	8.2	(0.21)	7.1	(0.23)	6.3	(0.21)	174	(5.8)	17.3	(0.60)	6.1	(0.21)	6.1	(0.22)	5.9	(0.82)	5	(0.7)	35.0	(4.13)
Hispanic	16.7	(0.29)	14.3	(0.26)	9.6	(0.23)	8.5	(0.20)	347	(7.9)	34.5	(0.60)	8.5	(0.20)	6.3	(0.19)	17.3	(0.59)	3	(0.5)	31.9	(4.88)
Asian	2.7	(0.22)	2.1	(0.22)	2.1	(0.22)	2.6	(0.21)	26	(2.1)	2.6	(0.20)	2.6	(0.21)	1.5	(0.21)	3.8	(0.39)	‡	(†)	‡	(†)
Pacific Islander	7.2	(1.49)	9.7	(2.00)	5.8 !	(1.76)	8.3	(1.64)	3	(0.6)	0.3	(0.06)	8.4	(1.63)	6.4	(1.73)	20.6	(6.14)	‡	(†)	‡	(†)
American Indian/Alaska Native	12.9	(0.98)	14.2	(1.18)	11.3	(0.96)	9.9	(0.93)	15	(1.4)	1.4	(0.14)	9.9	(0.93)	9.7	(0.92)	‡	(†)	‡	(†)	‡	(†)
Some other race[9]	8.9	(1.72)	6.4	(1.60)	3.9	(1.16)	5.6	(1.48)	‡	(†)	0.3	(0.07)	5.6	(1.48)	4.1 !	(1.70)	11.8 !	(4.54)	‡	(†)	‡	(†)
Two or more races	6.8	(0.51)	5.6	(0.43)	4.8	(0.36)	5.0	(0.39)	29	(2.4)	2.8	(0.24)	4.9	(0.39)	4.8	(0.39)	6.5	(1.62)	‡	(†)	27.8	(7.47)
Age																						
16	3.3	(0.10)	2.8	(0.10)	2.2	(0.08)	2.2	(0.10)	88	(4.2)	3.8	(0.17)	2.1	(0.10)	2.0	(0.10)	4.3	(0.58)	3	(0.5)	7.2	(1.32)
17	5.5	(0.14)	4.4	(0.12)	3.1	(0.09)	3.0	(0.12)	121	(4.8)	5.2	(0.20)	2.9	(0.12)	2.8	(0.12)	4.6	(0.57)	5	(0.8)	14.0	(1.88)
18	8.0	(0.18)	7.5	(0.17)	5.0	(0.17)	4.8	(0.15)	207	(6.4)	8.8	(0.24)	4.6	(0.14)	4.3	(0.14)	7.6	(0.63)	11	(1.1)	35.7	(3.00)
19	10.0	(0.18)	9.1	(0.20)	6.4	(0.16)	6.0	(0.18)	237	(7.6)	10.1	(0.30)	5.6	(0.18)	5.3	(0.19)	9.7	(0.72)	16	(1.1)	41.3	(2.35)
20–24	12.2	(0.11)	10.8	(0.11)	8.7	(0.09)	7.9	(0.07)	1,693	(15.6)	72.2	(0.42)	7.5	(0.07)	6.6	(0.07)	15.4	(0.34)	117	(3.2)	37.0	(0.87)
English speaking ability																						
Spoke English at home or spoke English very well	7.9	(0.06)	7.2	(0.07)	6.0	(0.06)	5.5	(0.05)	1,946	(20.4)	82.9	(0.39)	5.2	(0.05)	5.2	(0.05)	5.5	(0.18)	140	(3.3)	32.2	(0.64)
Spoke a language other than English at home and spoke English less than very well	34.7	(0.47)	32.8	(0.42)	23.5	(0.53)	21.8	(0.47)	400	(9.8)	17.1	(0.39)	21.5	(0.47)	12.7	(0.53)	25.8	(0.65)	11	(1.0)	49.4	(3.17)
Region																						
Northeast	7.4	(0.14)	6.8	(0.12)	5.4	(0.12)	5.2	(0.11)	337	(7.4)	14.4	(0.30)	4.9	(0.11)	4.3	(0.11)	10.2	(0.50)	22	(1.4)	30.3	(1.65)
Midwest	8.1	(0.13)	7.4	(0.13)	5.9	(0.12)	5.7	(0.10)	454	(8.5)	19.4	(0.29)	5.4	(0.10)	5.1	(0.09)	10.7	(0.76)	26	(1.5)	30.0	(1.44)
South	11.0	(0.13)	9.7	(0.13)	7.8	(0.11)	6.9	(0.10)	956	(14.5)	40.8	(0.45)	6.5	(0.10)	5.8	(0.09)	13.7	(0.46)	74	(2.7)	36.8	(1.02)
West	10.7	(0.13)	9.5	(0.14)	7.1	(0.10)	6.6	(0.10)	599	(9.4)	25.5	(0.37)	6.3	(0.10)	5.4	(0.10)	13.2	(0.43)	29	(1.7)	30.0	(1.61)

—Not available.
†Not applicable.
#Rounds to zero.
!Interpret data with caution. The coefficient of variation (CV) for this estimate is between 30 and 50 percent.
‡Reporting standards not met. Either there are too few cases for a reliable estimate or the coefficient of variation (CV) is 50 percent or greater.
[1]Persons living in households as well as persons living in noninstitutionalized group quarters. Noninstitutionalized group quarters include college and university housing, military quarters, facilities for workers and religious groups, and temporary shelters for the homeless.
[2]Persons living in institutionalized group quarters, including adult and juvenile correctional facilities, nursing facilities, and other health care facilities.
[3]United States refers to the 50 states and the District of Columbia, Puerto Rico, American Samoa, Guam, the U.S. Virgin Islands, and the Northern Marianas.
[4]Includes other Central American subgroups not shown separately.
[5]Includes Taiwanese.
[6]In addition to the subgroups shown, also includes Sri Lankan.
[7]Consists of Indonesian and Malaysian.
[8]Includes persons reporting American Indian alone, persons reporting Alaska Native alone, and persons from American Indian and/or Alaska Native tribes specified or not specified.
[9]Respondents who wrote in some other race that was not included as an option on the questionnaire.
NOTE: "Status" dropouts are 16- to 24-year-olds who are not enrolled in school and who have not completed a high school program, regardless of when they left school and whether they ever attended school in the United States. People who have received GED credentials are counted as high school completers. Detail may not sum to totals because of rounding. Race categories exclude persons of Hispanic ethnicity. Status dropout rates in this table may differ from those in tables based on the Current Population Survey (CPS) because of differences in survey design and target populations.
SOURCE: U.S. Department of Commerce, Census Bureau, American Community Survey (ACS), 2006, 2009, 2013, and 2014. (This table was prepared November 2015.)

Table 219.90. Number and percentage distribution of 14- through 21-year-old students served under Individuals with Disabilities Education Act (IDEA), Part B, who exited school, by exit reason, sex, race/ethnicity, age, and type of disability: 2011–12 and 2012–13

Year, sex, race/ethnicity, age, and type of disability	Exited school						Transferred to regular education[4]	Moved, known to be continuing[5]
	Total	Graduated with regular diploma	Received alternative certificate[1]	Reached maximum age[2]	Dropped out[3]	Died		
1	2	3	4	5	6	7	8	9
2011–12								
Total number	**392,200**	**250,672**	**53,914**	**5,567**	**80,469**	**1,578**	**64,709**	**175,719**
Percentage distribution of total	100.0	63.9	13.7	1.4	20.5	0.4	†	†
Number by sex								
Male	256,276	161,429	34,184	3,709	55,866	1,088	43,014	118,347
Female	135,924	89,243	19,730	1,858	24,603	490	21,695	57,372
Number by race/ethnicity								
White	207,262	147,512	22,073	2,945	33,945	787	36,934	85,875
Black	87,018	46,782	15,744	1,281	22,839	372	11,060	46,587
Hispanic	77,201	42,954	13,578	989	19,351	329	12,714	32,690
Asian	6,131	4,297	1,002	213	591	28	1,388	1,701
Pacific Islander	1,542	1,026	180	32	297	7	404	452
American Indian/Alaska Native	6,105	3,634	536	46	1,863	26	895	3,723
Two or more races	6,941	4,467	801	61	1,583	29	1,314	4,691
Number by type of disability								
Autism	16,732	10,806	3,791	847	1,224	64	1,815	4,958
Deaf-blindness	83	39	15	12	12	5	6	28
Emotional disturbance	40,966	21,190	3,671	362	15,589	154	6,072	32,505
Hearing impairment	4,704	3,452	696	60	482	14	726	1,505
Intellectual disability	38,622	15,546	13,388	2,197	7,243	248	2,210	14,196
Multiple disabilities	8,712	4,235	2,121	717	1,375	264	338	3,048
Orthopedic impairment	3,737	2,308	731	183	425	90	505	1,183
Other health impairment[6]	54,515	38,080	5,439	270	10,443	283	9,712	25,030
Specific learning disability	209,813	144,445	22,520	768	41,667	413	34,197	87,482
Speech or language impairment	9,997	7,462	910	51	1,563	11	8,736	4,651
Traumatic brain injury	2,583	1,771	412	60	319	21	204	671
Visual impairment	1,735	1,337	220	40	127	11	188	460
2012–13								
Total number	**396,292**	**258,028**	**56,404**	**5,846**	**74,575**	**1,439**	**57,677**	**162,901**
Percentage distribution of total	100.0	65.1	14.2	1.5	18.8	0.4	†	†
Number by sex								
Male	258,321	166,023	35,705	3,786	51,810	997	38,328	109,036
Female	137,971	92,005	20,699	2,060	22,765	442	19,349	53,865
Number by race/ethnicity								
White	208,030	149,809	22,314	3,035	32,105	767	33,817	79,442
Black	84,905	46,520	16,360	1,296	20,391	338	9,795	42,779
Hispanic	82,015	47,671	15,032	1,062	18,007	243	10,548	30,722
Asian	6,450	4,547	1,054	264	555	30	1,263	1,638
Pacific Islander	1,617	1,061	159	50	338	9	300	474
American Indian/Alaska Native	5,645	3,559	518	51	1,498	19	754	3,092
Two or more races	7,630	4,861	967	88	1,681	33	1,200	4,754
Number by age[7]								
14	2,687	13	21	†	2,461	192	15,210	33,807
15	5,280	46	32	†	4,974	228	13,229	34,883
16	15,964	3,537	560	†	11,574	293	12,766	35,506
17	147,525	111,224	15,493	5	20,525	278	10,158	31,521
18	149,844	107,060	22,095	1	20,467	221	4,464	18,570
19	43,275	25,284	8,319	73	9,483	116	1,126	5,915
20	18,536	7,624	5,512	1,588	3,741	71	506	1,981
21	13,181	3,240	4,372	4,179	1,350	40	218	718
Number by type of disability								
Autism	19,429	12,467	4,506	1,027	1,375	54	1,802	5,276
Deaf-blindness	82	46	13	9	12	2	2	18
Emotional disturbance	39,493	21,249	3,787	344	13,984	129	5,557	29,392
Hearing impairment	4,623	3,335	768	70	441	9	637	1,470
Intellectual disability	40,690	17,384	13,438	2,315	7,302	251	1,781	15,880
Multiple disabilities	9,205	4,184	2,602	718	1,397	304	320	2,901
Orthopedic impairment	3,586	2,268	708	165	382	63	414	1,093
Other health impairment[6]	58,413	41,526	5,814	267	10,550	256	9,245	24,801
Specific learning disability	206,054	144,530	23,260	754	37,191	319	28,869	76,001
Speech or language impairment	10,488	7,990	907	45	1,525	21	8,622	4,845
Traumatic brain injury	2,525	1,741	405	81	280	18	219	758
Visual impairment	1,704	1,308	196	51	136	13	209	466

†Not applicable.

[1]Received a certificate of completion, modified diploma, or some similar document, but did not meet the same standards for graduation as those for students without disabilities.

[2]Students may exit special education services due to maximum age beginning at age 18, depending on state law or practice or order of any court.

[3]"Dropped out" is defined as the total who were enrolled at some point in the reporting year, were not enrolled at the end of the reporting year, and did not exit for any of the other reasons described. Includes students previously categorized as "moved, not known to continue."

[4]"Transferred to regular education" was previously labeled "no longer receives special education."

[5]"Moved, known to be continuing" is the total number of students who moved out of the administrative area or transferred to another district and are known to be continuing in an educational program.

[6]Other health impairments include having limited strength, vitality, or alertness due to chronic or acute health problems such as a heart condition, tuberculosis, rheumatic fever, nephritis, asthma, sickle cell anemia, hemophilia, epilepsy, lead poisoning, leukemia, or diabetes.

[7]Age data are as of fall of the school year, so some students may have been 1 year older at the time they exited school.

NOTE: Data are for the 50 states, the District of Columbia, the Bureau of Indian Education, American Samoa, the Federated States of Micronesia, Guam, the Northern Marianas, Puerto Rico, the Republic of Palau, the Republic of the Marshall Islands, and the U.S. Virgin Islands. Data on number by age are not available for 2011–12, so these rows have been omitted. Detail may not sum to totals because of rounding.

SOURCE: U.S. Department of Education, Office of Special Education Programs, Individuals with Disabilities Education Act (IDEA) Section 618 Data Products: State Level Data Files. Retrieved November 30, 2015, from http://www2.ed.gov/programs/osepidea/618-data/state-level-data-files/index.html. (This table was prepared December 2015.)

Table 206.10. Number and percentage of homeschooled students ages 5 through 17 with a grade equivalent of kindergarten through 12th grade, by selected child, parent, and household characteristics: 2003, 2007, and 2012

[Standard errors appear in parentheses]

Selected child, parent, or household characteristic	2003			2007			2012		
	Number of students[1] (in thousands)	Number homeschooled[2] (in thousands)	Percent homeschooled[2]	Number of students[1] (in thousands)	Number homeschooled[2] (in thousands)	Percent homeschooled[2]	Number of students[1] (in thousands)	Number homeschooled[2] (in thousands)	Percent homeschooled[2]
1	2	3	4	5	6	7	8	9	10
Total	**50,707 (89.3)**	**1,096 (92.3)**	**2.2 (0.18)**	**51,135 (155.3)**	**1,520 (118.0)**	**3.0 (0.23)**	**51,657 (98.7)**	**1,773 [3] (115.7)**	**3.4 [3] (0.23)**
Sex of child									
Male	25,819 (286.8)	569 (61.9)	2.2 (0.24)	26,286 (355.6)	639 (75.1)	2.4 (0.28)	26,620 (318.2)	499 (48.0)	1.9 (0.18)
Female	24,888 (277.7)	527 (58.2)	2.1 (0.23)	24,849 (386.9)	881 (97.4)	3.5 (0.39)	25,037 (314.0)	583 (63.4)	2.3 (0.25)
Race/ethnicity of child									
White	31,584 (187.2)	843 (77.5)	2.7 (0.25)	29,815 (197.9)	1,171 (102.2)	3.9 (0.34)	26,978 (161.7)	893 (81.2)	3.3 (0.30)
Black	7,985 (45.7)	‡ (†)	‡ (†)	7,523 (114.0)	‡ (†)	‡ (†)	7,191 (45.8)	‡ (†)	‡ (†)
Hispanic	8,075 (35.1)	‡ (†)	‡ (†)	9,589 (84.8)	147 (27.5)	1.5 (0.29)	11,814 (55.1)	72 (17.3)	0.6 (0.15)
Asian/Pacific Islander	1,432 (114.5)	‡ (†)	‡ (†)	1,580 (122.9)	‡ (†)	‡ (†)	2,849 (118.4)	‡ (†)	‡ (†)
Other	1,631 (127.7)	‡ (†)	‡ (†)	2,629 (141.0)	‡ (†)	‡ (†)	2,825 (120.0)	‡ (†)	‡ (†)
Grade equivalent[4]									
Kindergarten through grade 5	24,269 (24.7)	472 (55.3)	1.9 (0.23)	23,529 (68.1)	717 (83.8)	3.0 (0.36)	25,842 (141.1)	423 (61.1)	1.6 (0.24)
Kindergarten	3,643 (24.7)	‡ (†)	‡ (†)	3,669 (67.9)	‡ (†)	‡ (†)	5,295 (136.2)	‡ (†)	‡ (†)
Grades 1 through 3	12,098 (#)	214 (33.3)	1.8 (0.28)	11,965 (2.4)	406 (64.5)	3.4 (0.54)	12,101 (135.0)	203 (45.6)	1.7 (0.38)
Grades 4 through 5	8,528 (#)	160 (30.1)	1.9 (0.35)	7,895 (2.1)	197 (41.4)	2.5 (0.52)	8,446 (128.1)	142 (26.1)	1.7 (0.31)
Grades 6 through 8	12,472 (6.5)	302 (44.9)	2.4 (0.36)	12,435 (0.7)	371 (65.3)	3.0 (0.53)	12,006 (139.1)	317 (44.3)	2.6 (0.37)
Grades 9 through 12	13,958 (81.8)	315 (47.0)	2.3 (0.33)	15,161 (129.3)	422 (58.2)	2.8 (0.38)	13,808 (112.0)	341 (42.8)	2.5 (0.31)
Number of children in the household									
One child	8,033 (218.1)	110 (22.3)	1.4 (0.27)	8,463 (227.1)	197 (32.5)	2.3 (0.38)	10,899 (182.6)	179 (21.4)	1.6 (0.19)
Two children	20,530 (319.4)	306 (45.1)	1.5 (0.22)	20,694 (295.3)	414 (67.2)	2.0 (0.32)	20,337 (251.8)	314 (44.5)	1.5 (0.22)
Three or more children	22,144 (362.8)	679 (80.2)	3.1 (0.36)	21,979 (331.0)	909 (102.4)	4.1 (0.46)	20,421 (209.6)	589 (63.5)	2.9 (0.30)
Number of parents in the household									
Two parents	35,936 (315.1)	886 (82.7)	2.5 (0.23)	37,219 (300.7)	1,357 (111.5)	3.6 (0.30)	34,252 (254.7)	908 (79.2)	2.7 (0.23)
One parent	13,260 (319.2)	196 (42.6)	1.5 (0.32)	11,777 (296.8)	118 (28.4)	1.0 (0.24)	15,436 (250.8)	137 (34.5)	0.9 (0.22)
Nonparental guardians	1,511 (100.1)	‡ (†)	‡ (†)	2,139 (203.2)	‡ (†)	‡ (†)	1,968 (112.5)	‡ (†)	‡ (†)
Parent participation in the labor force									
Two parents—both in labor force	25,108 (373.1)	274 (44.1)	1.1 (0.18)	26,055 (318.3)	518 (76.2)	2.0 (0.29)	22,884 (293.3)	295 (41.3)	1.3 (0.18)
Two parents—one in labor force	10,545 (297.2)	594 (73.7)	5.6 (0.67)	10,754 (286.1)	808 (94.3)	7.5 (0.82)	11,581 (275.2)	618 (70.1)	5.3 (0.60)
One parent—in labor force	12,045 (267.9)	174 (39.8)	1.4 (0.33)	10,020 (277.1)	127 (29.5)	1.3 (0.30)	13,083 (238.6)	96 (19.2)	0.7 (0.15)
No parent participation in labor force	3,008 (171.4)	‡ (†)	‡ (†)	4,308 (228.9)	‡ (†)	‡ (†)	4,108 (187.3)	74 ! (26.9)	1.8 ! (0.65)
Highest education level of parents									
High school diploma or less	16,106 (272.3)	269 (51.6)	1.7 (0.32)	14,306 (292.9)	208 (35.5)	1.5 (0.24)	16,762 (83.8)	270 (53.3)	1.6 (0.32)
Vocational/technical or some college	16,068 (323.4)	338 (57.7)	2.1 (0.36)	14,581 (326.5)	559 (77.5)	3.8 (0.52)	15,621 (173.9)	344 (38.4)	2.2 (0.24)
Bachelor's degree/some graduate school	10,849 (275.0)	309 (48.5)	2.8 (0.45)	11,448 (276.5)	444 (64.7)	3.9 (0.57)	11,675 (168.4)	275 (41.9)	2.4 (0.36)
Graduate/professional degree	7,683 (239.5)	180 (41.6)	2.3 (0.55)	10,800 (236.0)	309 (50.0)	2.9 (0.46)	7,599 (34.1)	192 (26.5)	2.5 (0.35)
Household income									
$20,000 or less	9,079 (146.2)	164 (38.9)	1.8 (0.43)	8,488 (201.2)	186 (42.1)	2.2 (0.50)	7,593 (39.6)	59 (12.1)	0.8 (0.16)
$20,001 to $50,000	16,515 (336.1)	430 (60.3)	2.6 (0.36)	13,648 (306.1)	420 (59.8)	3.1 (0.42)	13,973 (84.7)	321 (44.2)	2.3 (0.32)
$50,001 to $75,000	10,961 (282.2)	264 (51.1)	2.4 (0.46)	10,289 (232.9)	414 (58.8)	4.0 (0.57)	9,406 (23.9)	278 (40.8)	3.0 (0.44)
$75,001 to $100,000	6,432 (238.0)	169 (42.9)	2.6 (0.66)	6,899 (210.8)	264 (57.2)	3.8 (0.83)	6,916 (29.5)	211 (42.4)	3.0 (0.61)
Over $100,000	7,718 (212.6)	‡ (†)	‡ (†)	11,811 (228.2)	236 (57.5)	2.0 (0.49)	13,769 (56.5)	214 (34.4)	1.6 (0.25)
Locale									
City	— (†)	— (†)	— (†)	15,998 (292.3)	327 (40.4)	2.0 (0.26)	15,191 (236.0)	226 (28.0)	1.5 (0.18)
Suburb	— (†)	— (†)	— (†)	18,988 (291.3)	503 (78.8)	2.6 (0.41)	19,356 (330.6)	303 (44.6)	1.6 (0.22)
Town	— (†)	— (†)	— (†)	5,574 (209.4)	168 (37.1)	3.0 (0.65)	4,839 (197.9)	112 (30.8)	2.3 (0.63)
Rural	— (†)	— (†)	— (†)	10,576 (110.9)	523 (75.9)	4.9 (0.71)	12,271 (249.1)	441 (65.0)	3.6 (0.52)

—Not available.
†Not applicable.
#Rounds to zero.
‡Reporting standards not met (too few cases for a reliable estimate).
[1]Refers to all students in public and private schools and homeschooled students.
[2]Numbers and percentages of homeschoolers exclude students who were enrolled in school for more than 25 hours a week or who were homeschooled only due to a temporary illness.
[3]The National Center for Education Statistics uses a statistical adjustment for estimates of total homeschoolers in 2012. For more information about this adjustment, please see *Homeschooling in the United States: 2012* (NCES 2015-019, forthcoming). All other estimates about homeschoolers do not use a statistical adjustment.
[4]Students whose grade equivalent was "ungraded" were excluded from the grade analysis. The percentage of students with an "ungraded" grade equivalent was 0.02 percent in 2003 and 2007. There were no students with an "ungraded" grade equivalent in 2012.
NOTE: While National Household Education Surveys Program (NHES) administrations prior to 2012 were administered via telephone with an interviewer, NHES:2012 used self-administered paper-and-pencil questionnaires that were mailed to respondents. Measurable differences in estimates between 2012 and prior years could reflect actual changes in the population, or the changes could be due to the mode change from telephone to mail. Race categories exclude persons of Hispanic ethnicity. Detail may not sum to totals because of rounding. Some data have been revised from previously published figures.
SOURCE: U.S. Department of Education, National Center for Education Statistics, Parent and Family Involvement in Education Survey of the National Household Education Surveys Program (PFI-NHES:2003, 2007, and 2012). (This table was prepared November 2014.)

Table 206.30. Percentage distribution of students enrolled in grades 1 through 12, by public school type and charter status, private school type, and selected child and household characteristics: 2012

[Standard errors appear in parentheses]

Selected child or household characteristic and public school type	Total	Public school: Total	Public school: Assigned or chosen type[1]: Assigned	Public school: Assigned or chosen type[1]: Chosen	Public school: Traditional or charter status: Traditional[2]	Public school: Traditional or charter status: Charter	Private school: Total	Private school: Religious	Private school: Nonsectarian
1	2	3	4	5	6	7	8	9	10
Total	100.0 (†)	100.0 (†)	100.0 (†)	100.0 (†)	100.0 (†)	100.0 (†)	100.0 (†)	100.0 (†)	100.0 (†)
Sex of child									
Male	51.6 (0.60)	51.5 (0.63)	51.9 (0.68)	50.2 (1.48)	51.7 (0.63)	45.4 (3.46)	52.7 (1.89)	52.8 (2.24)	51.8 (3.71)
Female	48.4 (0.60)	48.5 (0.63)	48.1 (0.68)	49.8 (1.48)	48.3 (0.63)	54.6 (3.46)	47.3 (1.89)	47.2 (2.24)	48.2 (3.71)
Race/ethnicity of child									
White	52.3 (0.39)	51.3 (0.43)	53.1 (0.49)	40.2 (1.36)	51.9 (0.43)	31.5 (2.85)	65.0 (1.77)	63.3 (1.94)	72.8 (3.35)
Black	14.4 (0.19)	14.7 (0.24)	13.5 (0.31)	21.6 (1.19)	14.3 (0.26)	29.9 (3.24)	10.2 (1.05)	11.0 (1.18)	6.6 (1.82)
Hispanic	22.7 (0.26)	23.3 (0.28)	22.7 (0.37)	27.4 (1.21)	23.1 (0.31)	30.8 (3.13)	15.2 (1.38)	16.8 (1.57)	7.6 (1.93)
Asian/Pacific Islander	5.2 (0.22)	5.2 (0.23)	5.1 (0.25)	5.5 (0.68)	5.2 (0.23)	5.4 ! (1.83)	5.2 (0.62)	5.1 (0.73)	6.0 (1.40)
Other	5.4 (0.26)	5.5 (0.27)	5.5 (0.30)	5.3 (0.55)	5.6 (0.28)	2.4 ! (0.84)	4.4 (0.70)	3.8 (0.79)	7.0 (1.95)
Disability status of child as reported by parent									
Has a disability	17.3 (0.46)	17.7 (0.47)	17.7 (0.55)	17.7 (0.98)	17.8 (0.49)	15.5 (2.04)	12.2 (1.16)	11.1 (1.14)	17.7 (2.78)
Does not have a disability	82.7 (0.46)	82.3 (0.47)	82.3 (0.55)	82.3 (0.98)	82.2 (0.49)	84.5 (2.04)	87.8 (1.16)	88.9 (1.14)	82.3 (2.78)
Grade level									
Grades 1 through 5	43.4 (0.26)	43.2 (0.32)	43.5 (0.40)	40.6 (1.19)	43.0 (0.33)	47.0 (3.65)	46.7 (1.73)	47.2 (1.84)	44.0 (3.84)
Grades 6 through 8	25.2 (0.33)	25.4 (0.34)	25.2 (0.42)	27.2 (1.05)	25.2 (0.36)	32.5 (3.12)	22.7 (1.42)	22.7 (1.60)	23.0 (3.26)
Grades 9 through 12	31.3 (0.23)	31.4 (0.30)	31.3 (0.34)	32.2 (1.13)	31.7 (0.30)	20.5 (2.41)	30.6 (1.74)	30.1 (1.84)	33.0 (3.77)
Number of parents in the household									
Two parents	65.7 (0.50)	64.6 (0.54)	65.0 (0.62)	61.5 (1.29)	64.8 (0.55)	57.8 (3.61)	78.9 (1.18)	79.0 (1.33)	78.7 (2.54)
One parent	30.6 (0.49)	31.6 (0.53)	31.2 (0.63)	34.3 (1.37)	31.4 (0.55)	38.0 (3.61)	18.4 (1.19)	18.3 (1.35)	19.0 (2.40)
Nonparental guardians	3.8 (0.18)	3.8 (0.20)	3.8 (0.22)	4.2 (0.53)	3.8 (0.20)	4.2 ! (1.31)	2.7 (0.47)	2.8 (0.57)	2.3 ! (0.89)
Highest education level of parents									
Less than a high school diploma	11.7 (0.21)	12.3 (0.23)	12.1 (0.28)	12.4 (1.06)	12.3 (0.24)	12.3 (3.08)	4.8 (1.09)	4.9 (1.11)	‡ (†)
High school diploma or GED	20.3 (0.22)	21.2 (0.26)	21.9 (0.33)	18.1 (1.26)	21.0 (0.27)	25.8 (3.53)	9.8 (1.30)	10.5 (1.44)	6.6 ! (2.24)
Vocational/technical or some college	30.4 (0.39)	31.3 (0.42)	31.6 (0.46)	30.4 (1.25)	31.4 (0.43)	26.4 (2.75)	20.0 (1.44)	20.7 (1.69)	16.8 (2.68)
Bachelor's degree/some graduate school	22.7 (0.34)	21.6 (0.35)	21.1 (0.41)	23.9 (1.27)	21.6 (0.36)	22.9 (2.72)	36.1 (1.68)	37.6 (1.92)	29.4 (3.97)
Graduate/professional degree	14.8 (0.13)	13.6 (0.17)	13.3 (0.21)	15.3 (0.65)	13.7 (0.18)	12.6 (1.82)	29.3 (1.38)	26.3 (1.48)	43.2 (3.30)
Poverty status of household[3]									
Poor	18.6 (0.29)	19.5 (0.32)	19.6 (0.42)	19.3 (1.08)	19.4 (0.34)	25.2 (3.62)	7.1 (1.07)	6.9 (1.24)	8.1 ! (2.82)
Near-poor	22.1 (0.39)	23.0 (0.43)	23.1 (0.49)	22.9 (1.00)	22.9 (0.44)	27.7 (3.14)	10.7 (1.23)	11.2 (1.39)	8.0 (1.93)
Nonpoor	59.3 (0.30)	57.4 (0.37)	57.3 (0.42)	57.9 (1.21)	57.8 (0.39)	47.2 (3.19)	82.2 (1.54)	81.8 (1.71)	83.9 (3.18)
Locale									
City	29.0 (0.49)	28.5 (0.48)	25.3 (0.49)	45.9 (1.41)	27.7 (0.46)	51.6 (3.10)	34.8 (1.81)	33.8 (2.03)	39.2 (3.41)
Suburban	38.0 (0.63)	37.7 (0.65)	38.5 (0.71)	33.8 (1.41)	37.9 (0.64)	30.8 (3.45)	41.6 (1.44)	42.8 (1.75)	35.7 (3.36)
Town	9.4 (0.34)	9.8 (0.36)	10.6 (0.43)	5.9 (0.82)	9.9 (0.37)	5.2 ! (2.08)	5.0 (0.65)	4.8 (0.72)	5.9 (1.63)
Rural	23.6 (0.49)	24.0 (0.50)	25.6 (0.57)	14.4 (1.03)	24.4 (0.50)	12.3 (2.18)	18.7 (1.50)	18.5 (1.68)	19.2 (2.99)
Region									
Northeast	17.5 (0.39)	17.0 (0.39)	18.2 (0.44)	10.0 (0.79)	17.1 (0.41)	13.1 (2.05)	24.7 (1.53)	23.9 (1.88)	28.4 (4.04)
South	35.9 (0.57)	36.3 (0.60)	36.2 (0.69)	37.1 (1.36)	36.5 (0.61)	30.3 (3.20)	30.6 (1.52)	28.6 (1.69)	39.6 (3.32)
Midwest	22.2 (0.53)	22.1 (0.54)	22.4 (0.58)	20.0 (1.16)	22.0 (0.53)	23.8 (3.26)	23.2 (1.61)	26.6 (1.93)	7.2 (1.73)
West	24.4 (0.51)	24.7 (0.55)	23.2 (0.57)	33.0 (1.32)	24.4 (0.55)	32.8 (3.01)	21.5 (1.48)	20.8 (1.67)	24.8 (3.71)
Public school type[1]									
Assigned	84.6 [4] (0.46)	84.6 (0.46)	100.0 (†)	† (†)	87.3 (0.40)	† (†)	† (†)	† (†)	† (†)
Chosen	15.4 [4] (0.46)	15.4 (0.46)	† (†)	100.0 (†)	12.7 (0.40)	100.0 (†)	† (†)	† (†)	† (†)

†Not applicable.
!Interpret data with caution. The coefficient of variation (CV) for this estimate is between 30 and 50 percent.
‡Reporting standards not met. The coefficient of variation (CV) for this estimate is 50 percent or greater.
[1]In 160 cases, questions about whether the school was assigned were not asked because parents reported the school as a private school, and it was only later found to be a public school. These cases were excluded from the analysis of assigned versus chosen public schools, but were included in the charter school analysis as well as in the public school and overall totals.
[2]Includes all types of public noncharter schools.
[3]Poor children are those whose family incomes were below the Census Bureau's poverty threshold in the year prior to data collection; near-poor children are those whose family incomes ranged from the poverty threshold to 199 percent of the poverty threshold; and nonpoor children are those whose family incomes were at or above 200 percent of the poverty threshold. The poverty threshold is a dollar amount that varies depending on a family's size and composition and is updated annually to account for inflation. In 2011, for example, the poverty threshold for a family of four with two children was $22,811. Survey respondents are asked to select the range within which their income falls, rather than giving the exact amount of their income; therefore, the measure of poverty status is an approximation.
[4]Includes only students enrolled in public schools.
NOTE: Data exclude homeschooled children. Race categories exclude persons of Hispanic ethnicity. Detail may not sum to totals because of rounding.
SOURCE: U.S. Department of Education, National Center for Education Statistics, Parent and Family Involvement in Education Survey of the National Household Education Surveys Program (PFI-NHES:2012). (This table was prepared September 2014.)

Table 206.40. Percentage of students enrolled in grades 1 through 12 whose parents reported having public school choice, considered other schools, reported current school was their first choice, or moved to their current neighborhood for the public school, by school type and selected child and household characteristics: 2012

[Standard errors appear in parentheses]

School type and selected child or household characteristic	Public choice available		Considered other schools		School was parent's first choice		Moved to neighborhood for public school[1]	
1		2		3		4		5
Total	**37.3**	**(0.54)**	**30.5**	**(0.51)**	**78.6**	**(0.43)**	**18.6**	**(0.54)**
School type[2]								
Public, assigned	27.8	(0.58)	24.2	(0.59)	77.5	(0.50)	20.3	(0.64)
Public, chosen[3]	100.0	(†)	53.1	(1.49)	79.3	(1.05)	9.8	(0.97)
Private, religious	20.7	(1.57)	46.5	(1.92)	87.2	(1.51)	†	(†)
Private, nonsectarian	21.2	(3.58)	61.5	(3.63)	88.9	(2.37)	†	(†)
Sex of child								
Male	36.3	(0.78)	29.9	(0.78)	79.0	(0.56)	17.6	(0.67)
Female	38.5	(0.71)	31.2	(0.81)	78.1	(0.71)	19.7	(0.79)
Race/ethnicity of child								
White	34.2	(0.64)	26.5	(0.67)	83.4	(0.60)	20.5	(0.60)
Black	43.2	(1.56)	40.1	(1.56)	69.4	(1.69)	15.0	(1.70)
Hispanic	38.9	(1.25)	31.5	(1.20)	74.3	(1.04)	16.5	(1.33)
Asian/Pacific Islander	42.8	(2.51)	33.2	(2.50)	77.2	(2.12)	24.4	(1.75)
Other	40.5	(2.33)	36.4	(2.55)	75.6	(1.99)	14.9	(1.55)
Disability status of child as reported by parent								
Has a disability	37.8	(1.25)	32.5	(1.32)	75.4	(1.15)	18.3	(1.22)
Does not have a disability	37.2	(0.56)	30.1	(0.55)	79.2	(0.50)	18.7	(0.62)
Grade level								
Grades 1 through 5	35.0	(0.87)	30.9	(0.94)	78.4	(0.81)	18.7	(0.86)
Grades 6 through 8	39.0	(1.11)	30.3	(0.92)	78.1	(0.83)	19.4	(1.05)
Grades 9 through 12	39.2	(0.86)	30.1	(0.80)	79.1	(0.73)	17.9	(1.06)
Number of parents in the household								
Two parents	37.2	(0.62)	30.7	(0.61)	81.3	(0.45)	19.2	(0.57)
One parent	37.4	(1.01)	30.4	(0.97)	73.1	(1.04)	18.5	(1.08)
Nonparental guardians	38.5	(2.63)	27.9	(2.67)	75.3	(2.87)	10.6	(1.74)
Highest education level of parents								
Less than a high school diploma	37.3	(1.71)	25.8	(1.63)	75.7	(1.65)	16.3	(1.89)
High school diploma or GED	34.7	(1.45)	23.9	(1.46)	77.9	(1.10)	13.5	(1.03)
Vocational/technical or some college	37.5	(0.90)	28.5	(0.74)	75.3	(0.87)	17.0	(0.85)
Bachelor's degree/some graduate school	38.4	(1.17)	35.1	(1.22)	81.9	(0.85)	21.6	(0.97)
Graduate/professional degree	39.0	(0.93)	40.2	(0.99)	83.3	(0.67)	27.8	(0.84)
Poverty status of household[4]								
Poor	37.7	(1.35)	26.8	(1.32)	72.5	(1.18)	14.8	(1.06)
Near-poor	39.2	(1.14)	28.4	(1.13)	76.6	(1.01)	14.6	(0.92)
Nonpoor	36.5	(0.67)	32.4	(0.75)	81.2	(0.56)	21.5	(0.69)
Locale								
City	48.8	(1.07)	39.7	(1.05)	73.6	(0.77)	17.0	(0.80)
Suburban	32.0	(0.88)	30.0	(0.72)	78.1	(0.80)	22.5	(0.90)
Town	33.1	(1.91)	19.6	(1.46)	82.2	(1.33)	14.0	(1.77)
Rural	33.6	(1.15)	24.3	(1.02)	84.0	(0.88)	16.4	(0.96)
Region								
Northeast	22.4	(1.01)	29.5	(1.08)	76.5	(1.13)	18.4	(1.10)
South	34.2	(0.93)	28.9	(0.90)	78.3	(0.79)	18.3	(0.96)
Midwest	41.8	(1.01)	28.5	(1.24)	80.1	(1.08)	21.1	(1.13)
West	48.6	(1.21)	35.3	(0.98)	79.2	(0.80)	17.1	(0.89)

†Not applicable.
[1]This column shows percentages of public school students only. Private school students are excluded from the analysis.
[2]There were 160 cases excluded from the school type analysis because parents reported the school as a private school when it was later found to be a public school, and therefore questions about whether the school was assigned were not asked.
[3]Students who attended chosen public schools were automatically coded as yes for whether or not their district allowed public school choice.
[4]Poor children are those whose family incomes were below the Census Bureau's poverty threshold in the year prior to data collection; near-poor children are those whose family incomes ranged from the poverty threshold to 199 percent of the poverty threshold; and nonpoor children are those whose family incomes were at or above 200 percent of the poverty threshold. The poverty threshold is a dollar amount that varies depending on a family's size and composition and is updated annually to account for inflation. In 2011, for example, the poverty threshold for a family of four with two children was $22,811. Survey respondents are asked to select the range within which their income falls, rather than giving the exact amount of their income; therefore, the measure of poverty status is an approximation.
NOTE: Data exclude homeschooled children. Race categories exclude persons of Hispanic ethnicity.
SOURCE: U.S. Department of Education, National Center for Education Statistics, Parent and Family Involvement in Education Survey of the National Household Education Surveys Program (PFI-NHES:2012). (This table was prepared September 2014.)

Table 206.50. Percentage of students enrolled in grades 3 through 12 whose parents were satisfied or dissatisfied with various aspects of their children's schools, by public and private school type: 2003, 2007, and 2012

[Standard errors appear in parentheses]

Parent satisfaction	2003				2007				2012			
	Public school		Private school		Public school		Private school		Public school		Private school	
	Assigned	Chosen	Religious	Nonsectarian	Assigned	Chosen	Religious	Nonsectarian	Assigned	Chosen	Religious	Nonsectarian
1	2	3	4	5	6	7	8	9	10	11	12	13
Very satisfied												
School	53.7 (0.79)	64.2 (1.72)	77.0 (2.01)	71.7 (3.65)	52.1 (0.96)	62.1 (2.34)	78.7 (1.97)	78.6 (3.57)	52.5 (0.58)	56.2 (1.30)	80.0 (1.44)	77.8 (3.36)
Teachers	56.4 (0.74)	64.5 (1.62)	72.5 (1.88)	70.3 (3.68)	56.6 (0.88)	63.5 (2.32)	76.3 (1.96)	74.0 (3.67)	52.3 (0.65)	51.7 (1.48)	72.1 (1.80)	76.3 (3.23)
Academic standards	54.5 (0.78)	63.8 (1.75)	79.5 (1.77)	77.3 (3.32)	56.3 (0.84)	65.9 (2.09)	81.9 (1.70)	78.8 (3.81)	52.7 (0.58)	58.8 (1.48)	79.2 (1.76)	83.5 (2.89)
Order and discipline	55.9 (0.78)	64.8 (1.81)	81.2 (1.81)	80.5 (3.23)	55.0 (0.97)	60.9 (2.21)	82.7 (1.95)	80.5 (3.15)	52.4 (0.64)	57.9 (1.64)	82.2 (1.49)	79.8 (3.68)
Staff interaction with parents	— (†)	— (†)	— (†)	— (†)	47.7 (1.00)	56.7 (2.24)	75.4 (1.85)	73.0 (4.03)	44.7 (0.72)	48.8 (1.67)	72.2 (1.66)	72.8 (3.53)
Somewhat satisfied												
School	35.3 (0.74)	27.6 (1.40)	18.7 (1.84)	22.6 (3.33)	34.9 (0.82)	30.5 (2.01)	18.4 (1.82)	17.8 (3.40)	37.6 (0.68)	34.0 (1.57)	16.4 (1.42)	19.4 (3.16)
Teachers	35.4 (0.71)	29.3 (1.57)	23.4 (1.69)	23.6 (3.25)	34.1 (0.84)	29.8 (1.87)	21.1 (1.90)	23.1 (3.78)	38.4 (0.64)	38.7 (1.47)	23.6 (1.70)	20.4 (3.16)
Academic standards	35.4 (0.79)	29.1 (1.59)	16.4 (1.52)	17.7 (2.97)	32.7 (0.84)	28.2 (1.99)	15.8 (1.58)	18.6 (3.67)	38.0 (0.67)	33.0 (1.49)	17.2 (1.56)	14.0 (2.70)
Order and discipline	30.5 (0.72)	26.0 (1.67)	14.7 (1.70)	15.6 (3.13)	30.1 (0.85)	27.6 (2.57)	14.6 (1.83)	16.8 (2.89)	35.3 (0.67)	30.8 (1.50)	15.2 (1.53)	16.9 (3.37)
Staff interaction with parents	— (†)	— (†)	— (†)	— (†)	36.4 (0.92)	33.5 (2.03)	21.1 (1.83)	22.9 (3.92)	40.1 (0.79)	35.4 (1.69)	23.6 (1.54)	23.4 (3.40)
Somewhat dissatisfied												
School	7.4 (0.37)	5.6 (0.75)	3.2 (0.69)	4.5 ! (1.98)	8.4 (0.45)	5.5 (0.98)	2.6 (0.58)	3.3 ! (1.50)	7.4 (0.37)	7.6 (0.95)	2.9 (0.68)	‡ (†)
Teachers	6.2 (0.38)	4.1 (0.52)	3.4 (0.69)	3.8 ! (1.67)	6.6 (0.48)	5.6 (1.11)	1.7 (0.50)	2.9 ! (1.35)	7.2 (0.33)	7.7 (0.84)	4.0 (0.84)	2.0 ! (0.88)
Academic standards	6.6 (0.37)	4.3 (0.56)	3.3 (0.77)	4.5 ! (1.94)	6.8 (0.47)	4.9 (0.83)	2.0 ! (0.74)	‡ (†)	7.0 (0.40)	6.3 (0.77)	3.5 (0.92)	‡ (†)
Order and discipline	7.8 (0.42)	5.0 (0.69)	2.1 (0.52)	3.7 ! (1.45)	8.6 (0.50)	7.0 (1.00)	2.1 (0.52)	‡ (†)	8.6 (0.36)	7.3 (0.75)	1.8 (0.48)	‡ (†)
Staff interaction with parents	— (†)	— (†)	— (†)	— (†)	10.7 (0.59)	6.7 (0.93)	2.3 (0.57)	‡ (†)	11.0 (0.41)	11.9 (1.03)	3.0 (0.58)	1.9 ! (0.77)
Very dissatisfied												
School	3.6 (0.26)	2.6 (0.54)	1.1 ! (0.50)	‡ (†)	4.6 (0.44)	1.8 (0.51)	0.4 ! (0.20)	‡ (†)	2.5 (0.21)	2.3 (0.39)	0.7 ! (0.33)	‡ (†)
Teachers	2.0 (0.16)	2.1 (0.45)	‡ (†)	‡ (†)	2.7 (0.39)	1.1 ! (0.34)	0.9 ! (0.32)	# (†)	2.0 (0.18)	2.0 (0.47)	‡ (†)	‡ (†)
Academic standards	3.4 (0.28)	2.7 (0.59)	‡ (†)	‡ (†)	4.3 (0.43)	1.0 ! (0.30)	‡ (†)	‡ (†)	2.3 (0.21)	1.8 (0.33)	‡ (†)	‡ (†)
Order and discipline	5.8 (0.38)	4.2 (0.72)	2.0 ! (0.80)	‡ (†)	8.6 (0.50)	4.5 (0.82)	‡ (†)	‡ (†)	3.6 (0.22)	4.1 (0.59)	0.7 ! (0.35)	‡ (†)
Staff interaction with parents	— (†)	— (†)	— (†)	— (†)	5.3 (0.48)	3.2 (0.62)	1.2 ! (0.38)	‡ (†)	4.3 (0.28)	3.9 (0.55)	1.2 ! (0.42)	‡ (†)

—Not available.
†Not applicable.
#Rounds to zero.
!Interpret data with caution. The coefficient of variation (CV) for this estimate is between 30 and 50 percent.
‡Reporting standards not met. Either there are too few cases for a reliable estimate or the coefficient of variation (CV) is 50 percent or greater.
NOTE: Data exclude homeschooled children. While National Household Education Surveys Program (NHES) administrations prior to 2012 were administered via telephone with an interviewer, NHES:2012 used self-administered paper-and-pencil questionnaires that were mailed to respondents. Measurable differences in estimates between 2012 and prior years could reflect actual changes in the population, or the changes could be due to the mode change from telephone to mail. Detail may not sum to totals because of rounding.
SOURCE: U.S. Department of Education, National Center for Education Statistics, Parent and Family Involvement in Education Survey of the National Household Education Surveys Program (PFI-NHES:2003, 2007, and 2012). (This table was prepared September 2014.)

Table 205.10. Private elementary and secondary school enrollment and private enrollment as a percentage of total enrollment in public and private schools, by region and grade level: Selected years, fall 1995 through fall 2013

[Standard errors appear in parentheses]

Grade level and year	Total private enrollment: In thousands	Total private enrollment: Percent of total enrollment	Northeast: In thousands	Northeast: Percent of total enrollment in Northeast	Midwest: In thousands	Midwest: Percent of total enrollment in Midwest	South: In thousands	South: Percent of total enrollment in South	West: In thousands	West: Percent of total enrollment in West
1	2	3	4	5	6	7	8	9	10	11
Total, all grades										
1995	5,918 (31.8)	11.7 (0.06)	1,509 (18.8)	16.0 (0.20)	1,525 (14.2)	12.7 (0.12)	1,744 (12.8)	9.8 (0.07)	1,141 (11.5)	10.0 (0.10)
1997	5,944 (18.5)	11.4 (0.04)	1,496 (8.3)	15.6 (0.09)	1,528 (11.6)	12.5 (0.10)	1,804 (11.3)	9.8 (0.06)	1,116 (5.2)	9.4 (0.04)
1999	6,018 (30.2)	11.4 (0.06)	1,507 (7.9)	15.5 (0.08)	1,520 (10.3)	12.4 (0.09)	1,863 (26.7)	10.0 (0.14)	1,127 (5.4)	9.2 (0.04)
2001	6,320 (40.3)	11.7 (0.08)	1,581 (9.5)	16.1 (0.10)	1,556 (22.9)	12.6 (0.19)	1,975 (21.4)	10.3 (0.11)	1,208 (23.4)	9.6 (0.19)
2003	6,099 (41.2)	11.2 (0.08)	1,513 (25.8)	15.4 (0.27)	1,460 (15.1)	11.9 (0.12)	1,944 (21.0)	9.9 (0.11)	1,182 (19.1)	9.1 (0.15)
2005	6,073 (42.4)	11.0 (0.08)	1,430 (7.7)	14.8 (0.08)	1,434 (21.0)	11.7 (0.17)	1,976 (24.7)	9.8 (0.12)	1,234 (26.3)	9.4 (0.20)
2007	5,910 (28.4)	10.7 (0.05)	1,426 (11.0)	14.9 (0.12)	1,352 (8.3)	11.2 (0.07)	1,965 (21.5)	9.6 (0.11)	1,167 (12.3)	8.9 (0.09)
2009	5,488 (35.9)	10.0 (0.07)	1,310 (15.7)	14.0 (0.17)	1,296 (25.9)	10.8 (0.22)	1,842 (17.6)	9.1 (0.09)	1,041 (8.0)	8.0 (0.06)
2011	5,268 (24.9)	9.7 (0.04)	1,252 (18.0)	13.7 (0.17)	1,263 (17.1)	10.7 (0.13)	1,747 (2.6)	8.5 (0.01)	1,006 (0.4)	7.8 (#)
2013	5,396 (50.3)	9.8 (0.08)	1,201 (9.5)	13.2 (0.09)	1,326 (45.2)	11.2 (0.34)	1,840 (8.3)	8.7 (0.04)	1,028 (18.3)	7.9 (0.13)
Prekindergarten through grade 8										
1995	4,756 (28.4)	12.8 (0.08)	1,174 (16.8)	17.2 (0.25)	1,238 (13.5)	14.3 (0.16)	1,413 (11.9)	10.7 (0.09)	931 (9.2)	11.1 (0.11)
1997	4,759 (17.3)	12.6 (0.05)	1,165 (8.3)	16.8 (0.12)	1,235 (11.0)	14.1 (0.13)	1,449 (10.0)	10.8 (0.07)	909 (4.4)	10.5 (0.05)
1999	4,789 (23.1)	12.5 (0.06)	1,168 (7.5)	16.7 (0.11)	1,222 (8.4)	13.9 (0.10)	1,487 (19.6)	10.9 (0.14)	913 (4.4)	10.4 (0.05)
2001	5,023 (36.1)	12.9 (0.09)	1,216 (9.4)	17.3 (0.14)	1,253 (21.2)	14.3 (0.24)	1,584 (17.8)	11.3 (0.13)	969 (21.2)	10.6 (0.23)
2003	4,788 (30.3)	12.3 (0.08)	1,131 (7.8)	16.4 (0.11)	1,167 (13.6)	13.5 (0.16)	1,547 (18.6)	10.9 (0.13)	944 (18.1)	10.2 (0.20)
2005	4,724 (33.0)	12.1 (0.09)	1,063 (6.6)	15.9 (0.10)	1,142 (19.3)	13.3 (0.23)	1,551 (21.2)	10.7 (0.15)	969 (15.0)	10.5 (0.16)
2007	4,546 (21.9)	11.7 (0.06)	1,047 (6.3)	16.0 (0.10)	1,065 (7.7)	12.6 (0.09)	1,525 (17.7)	10.4 (0.12)	909 (8.1)	9.9 (0.09)
2009	4,179 (33.2)	10.8 (0.09)	938 (12.6)	14.6 (0.20)	1,016 (25.1)	12.1 (0.30)	1,424 (16.2)	9.8 (0.11)	802 (7.2)	8.8 (0.08)
2011	3,977 (18.2)	10.3 (0.04)	898 (12.8)	14.1 (0.17)	967 (12.8)	11.7 (0.14)	1,337 (1.8)	9.0 (0.01)	774 (0.3)	8.6 (#)
2013	4,084 (42.4)	10.5 (0.10)	859 (8.8)	13.5 (0.12)	1,036 (37.9)	12.4 (0.40)	1,403 (7.9)	9.2 (0.05)	786 (15.0)	8.6 (0.15)
Grades 9 through 12										
1995	1,163 (4.6)	8.5 (0.03)	335 (2.9)	13.0 (0.11)	287 (0.9)	8.6 (0.03)	331 (2.1)	7.1 (0.04)	209 (2.3)	6.8 (0.08)
1997	1,185 (2.4)	8.3 (0.02)	331 (0.5)	12.5 (0.02)	293 (0.7)	8.5 (0.02)	354 (1.7)	7.2 (0.03)	207 (1.2)	6.4 (0.04)
1999	1,229 (8.3)	8.4 (0.06)	340 (1.1)	12.6 (0.04)	299 (2.5)	8.6 (0.07)	376 (7.6)	7.5 (0.15)	215 (1.8)	6.3 (0.05)
2001	1,296 (6.7)	8.6 (0.04)	365 (0.8)	13.1 (0.03)	302 (2.0)	8.6 (0.06)	390 (4.4)	7.5 (0.08)	239 (4.5)	6.8 (0.13)
2003	1,311 (24.7)	8.4 (0.16)	382 (24.0)	13.1 (0.83)	294 (4.1)	8.2 (0.11)	397 (3.0)	7.4 (0.06)	238 (3.5)	6.4 (0.09)
2005	1,349 (18.1)	8.3 (0.11)	367 (1.7)	12.3 (0.06)	292 (5.0)	7.9 (0.14)	425 (7.2)	7.5 (0.13)	265 (15.7)	6.7 (0.40)
2007	1,364 (12.0)	8.3 (0.07)	379 (8.8)	12.7 (0.30)	287 (1.3)	7.8 (0.04)	440 (5.5)	7.6 (0.10)	257 (5.7)	6.5 (0.14)
2009	1,309 (6.5)	8.0 (0.04)	372 (5.7)	12.6 (0.20)	280 (2.2)	7.7 (0.06)	418 (1.7)	7.3 (0.03)	239 (1.1)	6.1 (0.03)
2011	1,291 (15.4)	8.1 (0.09)	353 (5.2)	12.6 (0.16)	295 (14.4)	8.4 (0.38)	411 (1.8)	7.1 (0.03)	232 (0.1)	5.9 (#)
2013	1,312 (14.9)	8.2 (0.09)	342 (0.8)	12.4 (0.03)	291 (13.1)	8.4 (0.35)	437 (1.3)	7.4 (0.02)	242 (7.0)	6.2 (0.17)

#Rounds to zero.

NOTE: Includes enrollment in prekindergarten through grade 12 in schools that offer kindergarten or higher grade. Ungraded students are prorated into prekindergarten through grade 8 and grades 9 through 12. Detail may not sum to totals because of rounding.

SOURCE: U.S. Department of Education, National Center for Education Statistics, Private School Universe Survey (PSS), 1995–96 through 2013–14; and Common Core of Data (CCD), "State Nonfiscal Survey of Public Elementary/Secondary Education," 1995–96 through 2013–14. (This table was prepared February 2016.)

Table 205.20. Enrollment and percentage distribution of students enrolled in private elementary and secondary schools, by school orientation and grade level: Selected years, fall 1995 through fall 2013

[Standard errors appear in parentheses]

Grade level and year	Total private enrollment	Catholic				Other religious				Nonsectarian
		Total	Parochial	Diocesan	Private	Total	Conservative Christian	Affiliated[1]	Unaffiliated[1]	
1	2	3	4	5	6	7	8	9	10	11
	Enrollment									
Total, all grades										
1995	5,918,040 (31,815)	2,660,450 (6,878)	1,458,990 (2,079)	850,560 (5,674)	350,900 (1,176)	2,094,690 (16,956)	786,660 (8,815)	697,280 (4,886)	610,750 (11,831)	1,162,900 (18,443)
1997	5,944,320 (18,543)	2,665,630 (5,472)	1,438,860 (5,331)	873,780 (761)	352,990 (1,405)	2,097,190 (13,733)	823,610 (7,342)	646,500 (3,104)	627,080 (11,133)	1,181,510 (12,013)
1999	6,018,280 (30,179)	2,660,420 (4,831)	1,397,570 (4,421)	880,650 (†)	382,190 (1,945)	2,193,370 (27,176)	871,060 (4,827)	646,280 (4,894)	676,030 (24,593)	1,164,500 (8,156)
2001	6,319,650 (40,272)	2,672,650 (12,460)	1,309,890 (5,626)	979,050 (6,976)	383,710 (3,152)	2,328,160 (17,281)	937,420 (6,070)	663,190 (8,636)	727,550 (13,303)	1,318,840 (27,300)
2003	6,099,220 (41,219)	2,520,120 (10,580)	1,183,250 (9,937)	963,140 (4,754)	373,740 (3,996)	2,228,230 (19,674)	889,710 (8,852)	650,530 (5,860)	688,000 (14,805)	1,350,870 (29,197)
2005	6,073,240 (42,446)	2,402,800 (9,293)	1,062,950 (6,355)	956,610 (6,325)	383,230 (3,996)	2,303,330 (22,368)	957,360 (9,561)	696,910 (6,677)	649,050 (14,200)	1,367,120 (27,558)
2007	5,910,210 (28,363)	2,308,150 (6,083)	945,860 (5,361)	969,940 (1,788)	392,340 (3,432)	2,283,210 (20,628)	883,180 (6,616)	527,040 (3,512)	872,990 (18,217)	1,318,850 (18,235)
2009	5,488,490 (35,857)	2,160,220 (3,494)	856,440 (3,088)	909,010 (4,393)	394,770 (1,087)	2,076,220 (32,751)	737,020 (1,891)	516,310 (4,366)	822,890 (31,180)	1,252,050 (8,849)
2011	5,268,090 (24,908)	2,087,870 (14,426)	804,410 (3,686)	899,810 (14,320)	383,650 (459)	1,991,950 (21,814)	730,570 (4,721)	565,340 (2,990)	696,040 (20,419)	1,188,270 (5,376)
2013	5,395,740 (50,342)	2,055,140 (37,142)	739,850 (18,829)	936,320 (32,000)	378,970 (980)	2,030,930 (30,090)	707,100 (7,544)	565,490 (5,884)	758,350 (28,152)	1,309,670 (14,800)
Prekindergarten through grade 8										
1995	4,755,540 (28,435)	2,041,990 (5,249)	1,368,340 (2,079)	575,190 (3,528)	98,460 (1,176)	1,752,510 (14,834)	651,050 (7,219)	574,820 (4,581)	526,630 (11,121)	961,040 (17,471)
1997	4,759,060 (17,323)	2,046,620 (5,469)	1,352,620 (5,331)	598,380 (761)	95,620 (1,393)	1,744,500 (12,194)	678,660 (5,957)	529,050 (2,504)	536,790 (10,120)	967,940 (11,050)
1999	4,788,990 (23,055)	2,033,900 (4,830)	1,317,300 (4,421)	607,860 (†)	108,740 (1,943)	1,818,260 (19,897)	713,020 (3,748)	529,280 (3,866)	575,970 (17,632)	936,820 (7,302)
2001	5,023,160 (36,096)	2,032,080 (10,751)	1,226,960 (4,494)	687,540 (6,976)	117,580 (2,978)	1,926,870 (15,459)	765,080 (5,110)	535,850 (7,370)	625,940 (12,240)	1,064,210 (24,703)
2003	4,788,070 (30,338)	1,886,530 (11,055)	1,108,320 (9,937)	670,910 (4,754)	107,300 (337)	1,835,930 (16,931)	722,460 (6,517)	519,310 (4,134)	594,160 (13,504)	1,065,620 (15,379)
2005	4,724,310 (33,034)	1,779,830 (9,318)	993,390 (6,355)	673,110 (6,286)	113,330 (2,896)	1,865,430 (19,380)	764,920 (8,028)	561,320 (5,730)	539,190 (12,633)	1,079,050 (15,497)
2007	4,545,910 (21,853)	1,685,220 (5,288)	878,830 (4,562)	688,260 (1,640)	118,130 (3,104)	1,833,540 (18,364)	698,930 (5,885)	417,610 (3,218)	717,000 (16,573)	1,027,150 (11,379)
2009	4,179,060 (33,168)	1,541,830 (3,250)	782,050 (3,085)	642,720 (846)	117,050 (578)	1,665,680 (30,216)	579,190 (1,685)	401,430 (3,952)	685,050 (28,928)	971,550 (8,113)
2011	3,976,960 (18,241)	1,481,620 (3,867)	737,090 (3,675)	630,970 (321)	113,560 (459)	1,583,610 (16,558)	568,150 (3,607)	443,780 (2,604)	571,690 (15,197)	911,730 (3,469)
2013	4,083,860 (42,441)	1,466,550 (27,646)	680,370 (18,826)	666,260 (20,228)	119,930 (843)	1,615,120 (29,311)	544,610 (5,638)	446,050 (5,316)	624,470 (27,948)	1,002,180 (11,849)
Grades 9 through 12										
1995	1,162,500 (4,625)	618,460 (2,786)	90,650 (†)	275,370 (2,786)	252,440 (†)	342,180 (3,174)	135,610 (2,338)	122,460 (645)	84,120 (1,720)	201,860 (1,495)
1997	1,185,260 (2,374)	619,010 (96)	86,240 (†)	275,400 (†)	257,370 (96)	352,690 (2,261)	144,950 (1,660)	117,450 (848)	90,290 (1,221)	213,560 (1,860)
1999	1,229,290 (8,260)	626,520 (70)	80,270 (†)	272,790 (†)	273,460 (70)	375,100 (7,920)	158,040 (1,640)	117,000 (1,237)	100,060 (7,461)	227,670 (2,208)
2001	1,296,480 (6,669)	640,570 (2,317)	82,930 (2,293)	291,520 (†)	266,130 (338)	401,290 (3,527)	172,340 (2,633)	127,340 (1,625)	101,600 (1,852)	254,620 (4,465)
2003	1,311,150 (24,733)	633,590 (3,888)	74,930 (†)	292,230 (†)	266,430 (3,888)	392,310 (4,195)	167,250 (3,144)	131,220 (1,924)	93,840 (2,031)	285,250 (23,952)
2005	1,348,930 (18,073)	622,970 (1,538)	69,560 (†)	283,510 (700)	269,900 (1,341)	437,900 (6,541)	192,440 (3,404)	135,590 (1,493)	109,860 (5,190)	288,070 (16,551)
2007	1,364,300 (11,958)	622,930 (1,377)	67,030 (1,201)	281,680 (566)	274,210 (364)	449,680 (3,796)	184,260 (1,768)	109,430 (374)	156,000 (3,052)	291,700 (11,156)
2009	1,309,430 (6,480)	618,390 (4,409)	74,380 (42)	266,290 (4,311)	277,720 (920)	410,540 (4,285)	157,830 (362)	114,880 (1,074)	137,840 (4,111)	280,500 (1,880)
2011	1,291,130 (15,396)	606,250 (14,313)	67,320 (10)	268,840 (14,313)	270,090 (†)	408,330 (5,747)	162,420 (1,349)	121,560 (513)	124,350 (5,792)	276,550 (3,485)
2013	1,311,880 (14,936)	588,580 (13,452)	59,480 (358)	270,060 (13,416)	259,040 (905)	415,810 (2,774)	162,490 (1,942)	119,440 (1,862)	133,880 (1,762)	307,490 (6,938)
	Percentage distribution									
Total, all grades										
1995	100.0 (†)	45.0 (0.19)	24.7 (0.13)	14.4 (0.08)	5.9 (0.03)	35.4 (0.19)	13.3 (0.12)	11.8 (0.08)	10.3 (0.18)	19.7 (0.23)
1997	100.0 (†)	44.8 (0.13)	24.2 (0.09)	14.7 (0.05)	5.9 (0.03)	35.3 (0.18)	13.9 (0.12)	10.9 (0.06)	10.5 (0.17)	19.9 (0.17)
1999	100.0 (†)	44.2 (0.24)	23.2 (0.14)	14.6 (0.07)	6.4 (0.04)	36.4 (0.28)	14.5 (0.09)	10.7 (0.08)	11.2 (0.36)	19.3 (0.11)
2001	100.0 (†)	42.3 (0.25)	20.7 (0.14)	15.5 (0.12)	6.1 (0.04)	36.8 (0.22)	14.8 (0.13)	10.5 (0.13)	11.5 (0.18)	20.9 (0.33)
2003	100.0 (†)	41.3 (0.27)	19.4 (0.17)	15.8 (0.14)	6.1 (0.07)	36.5 (0.25)	14.6 (0.13)	10.7 (0.10)	11.3 (0.22)	22.1 (0.36)
2005	100.0 (†)	39.6 (0.26)	17.5 (0.13)	15.8 (0.14)	6.3 (0.07)	37.9 (0.25)	15.8 (0.14)	11.5 (0.09)	10.7 (0.20)	22.5 (0.34)
2007	100.0 (†)	39.1 (0.20)	16.0 (0.11)	16.4 (0.09)	6.6 (0.06)	38.6 (0.25)	14.9 (0.12)	8.9 (0.06)	14.8 (0.26)	22.3 (0.25)
2009	100.0 (†)	39.4 (0.25)	15.6 (0.11)	16.6 (0.13)	7.2 (0.05)	37.8 (0.37)	13.4 (0.09)	9.4 (0.07)	15.0 (0.48)	22.8 (0.16)
2011	100.0 (†)	39.6 (0.25)	15.3 (0.09)	17.1 (0.25)	7.3 (0.04)	37.8 (0.28)	13.9 (0.09)	10.7 (0.08)	13.2 (0.34)	22.6 (0.15)
2013	100.0 (†)	38.1 (0.50)	13.7 (0.33)	17.4 (0.51)	7.0 (0.07)	37.6 (0.44)	13.1 (0.16)	10.5 (0.13)	14.1 (0.47)	24.3 (0.28)

See notes at end of table.

Table 205.20. Enrollment and percentage distribution of students enrolled in private elementary and secondary schools, by school orientation and grade level: Selected years, fall 1995 through fall 2013—Continued

[Standard errors appear in parentheses]

Grade level and year	Total private enrollment	Catholic				Other religious				Nonsectarian
		Total	Parochial	Diocesan	Private	Total	Conservative Christian	Affiliated[1]	Unaffiliated[1]	
1	2	3	4	5	6	7	8	9	10	11
Prekindergarten through grade 8										
1995	100.0 (†)	42.9 (0.20)	28.8 (0.17)	12.1 (0.06)	2.1 (0.02)	36.9 (0.22)	13.7 (0.13)	12.1 (0.09)	11.1 (0.21)	20.2 (0.28)
1997	100.0 (†)	43.0 (0.15)	28.4 (0.12)	12.6 (0.05)	2.0 (0.03)	36.7 (0.20)	14.3 (0.13)	11.1 (0.06)	11.3 (0.19)	20.3 (0.19)
1999	100.0 (†)	42.5 (0.23)	27.5 (0.16)	12.7 (0.06)	2.3 (0.04)	38.0 (0.26)	14.9 (0.09)	11.1 (0.07)	12.0 (0.32)	19.6 (0.12)
2001	100.0 (†)	40.5 (0.27)	24.4 (0.17)	13.7 (0.14)	2.3 (0.05)	38.4 (0.25)	15.2 (0.15)	10.7 (0.14)	12.5 (0.20)	21.2 (0.37)
2003	100.0 (†)	39.4 (0.25)	23.1 (0.18)	14.0 (0.13)	2.2 (0.01)	38.3 (0.23)	15.1 (0.12)	10.8 (0.09)	12.4 (0.24)	22.3 (0.22)
2005	100.0 (†)	37.7 (0.25)	21.0 (0.14)	14.2 (0.15)	2.4 (0.06)	39.5 (0.21)	16.2 (0.16)	11.9 (0.09)	11.4 (0.22)	22.8 (0.23)
2007	100.0 (†)	37.1 (0.20)	19.3 (0.13)	15.1 (0.09)	2.6 (0.07)	40.3 (0.27)	15.4 (0.14)	9.2 (0.07)	15.8 (0.30)	22.6 (0.21)
2009	100.0 (†)	36.9 (0.29)	18.7 (0.15)	15.4 (0.12)	2.8 (0.03)	39.9 (0.43)	13.9 (0.11)	9.6 (0.10)	16.4 (0.57)	23.2 (0.20)
2011	100.0 (†)	37.3 (0.18)	18.5 (0.11)	15.9 (0.08)	2.9 (0.02)	39.8 (0.24)	14.3 (0.08)	11.2 (0.08)	14.4 (0.32)	22.9 (0.11)
2013	100.0 (†)	35.9 (0.53)	16.7 (0.42)	16.3 (0.44)	2.9 (0.04)	39.5 (0.52)	13.3 (0.17)	10.9 (0.15)	15.3 (0.59)	24.5 (0.31)
Grades 9 through 12										
1995	100.0 (†)	53.2 (0.20)	7.8 (0.03)	23.7 (0.20)	21.7 (0.09)	29.4 (0.20)	11.7 (0.18)	10.5 (0.06)	7.2 (0.14)	17.4 (0.12)
1997	100.0 (†)	52.2 (0.10)	7.3 (0.01)	23.2 (0.05)	21.7 (0.04)	29.8 (0.16)	12.2 (0.13)	9.9 (0.08)	7.6 (0.10)	18.0 (0.14)
1999	100.0 (†)	51.0 (0.34)	6.5 (0.04)	22.2 (0.15)	22.2 (0.15)	30.5 (0.45)	12.9 (0.14)	9.5 (0.11)	8.1 (0.56)	18.5 (0.19)
2001	100.0 (†)	49.4 (0.26)	6.4 (0.17)	22.5 (0.12)	20.5 (0.10)	31.0 (0.19)	13.3 (0.17)	9.8 (0.12)	7.8 (0.13)	19.6 (0.28)
2003	100.0 (†)	48.3 (0.91)	5.7 (0.11)	22.3 (0.42)	20.3 (0.44)	29.9 (0.59)	12.8 (0.32)	10.0 (0.23)	7.2 (0.20)	21.8 (1.43)
2005	100.0 (†)	46.2 (0.60)	5.2 (0.07)	21.0 (0.28)	20.0 (0.27)	32.5 (0.52)	14.3 (0.28)	10.1 (0.16)	8.1 (0.37)	21.4 (0.97)
2007	100.0 (†)	45.7 (0.40)	4.9 (0.09)	20.6 (0.18)	20.1 (0.17)	33.0 (0.33)	13.5 (0.16)	8.0 (0.07)	11.4 (0.22)	21.4 (0.65)
2009	100.0 (†)	47.2 (0.25)	5.7 (0.03)	20.3 (0.27)	21.2 (0.12)	31.4 (0.25)	12.1 (0.06)	8.8 (0.08)	10.5 (0.28)	21.4 (0.15)
2011	100.0 (†)	47.0 (0.63)	5.2 (0.06)	20.8 (0.88)	20.9 (0.25)	31.6 (0.49)	12.6 (0.18)	9.4 (0.13)	9.6 (0.43)	21.4 (0.35)
2013	100.0 (†)	44.9 (0.64)	4.5 (0.06)	20.6 (0.83)	19.7 (0.24)	31.7 (0.42)	12.4 (0.19)	9.1 (0.17)	10.2 (0.19)	23.4 (0.47)

†Not applicable.
[1]Affiliated schools belong to associations of schools with a specific religious orientation other than Catholic or conservative Christian. Unaffiliated schools have a religious orientation or purpose but are not classified as Catholic, conservative Christian, or affiliated.

NOTE: Includes enrollment in prekindergarten through grade 12 in schools that offer kindergarten or higher grade. Ungraded students are prorated into prekindergarten through grade 8 and grades 9 through 12. Detail may not sum to totals because of rounding.

SOURCE: U.S. Department of Education, National Center for Education Statistics, Private School Universe Survey (PSS), 1995–96 through 2013–14. (This table was prepared December 2015.)

Table 205.30. Percentage distribution of students enrolled in private elementary and secondary schools, by school orientation and selected characteristics: Fall 2011 and fall 2013

[Standard errors appear in parentheses]

Selected characteristic	Total		Catholic								Other religious								Nonsectarian	
			Total		Parochial		Diocesan		Private		Total		Conservative Christian		Affiliated[1]		Unaffiliated[1]			
1	2		3		4		5		6		7		8		9		10		11	
	Fall 2011																			
Total	**100.0**	**(†)**	**39.6**	**(0.25)**	**15.3**	**(0.09)**	**17.1**	**(0.25)**	**7.3**	**(0.04)**	**37.8**	**(0.28)**	**13.9**	**(0.09)**	**10.7**	**(0.08)**	**13.2**	**(0.34)**	**22.6**	**(0.15)**
School level[2]																				
Elementary	100.0	(†)	49.8	(0.16)	25.7	(0.12)	21.5	(0.07)	2.7	(0.02)	29.5	(0.19)	7.1	(0.05)	9.5	(0.05)	12.9	(0.23)	20.6	(0.12)
Secondary	100.0	(†)	74.0	(0.52)	8.1	(0.15)	34.3	(1.24)	31.6	(0.60)	14.1	(0.28)	2.6	(0.05)	5.9	(0.11)	5.7	(0.12)	11.9	(0.31)
Combined	100.0	(†)	8.3	(0.11)	1.7	(0.02)	2.6	(0.05)	4.1	(0.04)	61.4	(0.48)	29.6	(0.34)	14.8	(0.24)	17.1	(0.89)	30.3	(0.39)
Student race/ethnicity[3]																				
White	100.0	(†)	41.9	(0.35)	15.9	(0.14)	18.3	(0.33)	7.7	(0.06)	39.5	(0.45)	14.3	(0.13)	11.5	(0.12)	13.7	(0.55)	18.7	(0.19)
Black	100.0	(†)	35.4	(0.15)	11.9	(0.05)	14.9	(0.08)	8.6	(0.03)	41.8	(0.18)	17.7	(0.08)	10.5	(0.10)	13.6	(0.06)	22.8	(0.30)
Hispanic	100.0	(†)	60.2	(0.22)	24.3	(0.12)	24.5	(0.32)	11.4	(0.05)	24.4	(0.19)	11.1	(0.19)	6.9	(0.04)	6.4	(0.06)	15.4	(0.10)
Asian	100.0	(†)	36.6	(0.10)	13.8	(0.02)	15.2	(0.11)	7.5	(0.01)	31.2	(0.05)	12.3	(0.04)	10.1	(0.01)	8.9	(0.01)	32.2	(0.07)
Pacific Islander	100.0	(†)	46.3	(0.33)	16.2	(0.08)	20.9	(0.36)	9.2	(0.04)	38.1	(0.28)	12.2	(0.18)	13.0	(0.06)	12.9	(0.06)	15.6	(0.30)
American Indian/Alaska Native	100.0	(†)	43.9	(0.18)	11.0	(0.05)	18.0	(0.08)	15.0	(0.06)	30.4	(0.29)	16.1	(0.35)	7.2	(0.03)	7.2	(0.06)	25.7	(0.11)
Two or more races	100.0	(†)	44.1	(0.14)	15.5	(0.04)	19.9	(0.14)	8.7	(0.06)	27.6	(0.10)	11.0	(0.04)	9.4	(0.02)	7.3	(0.09)	28.3	(0.12)
School enrollment																				
Less than 50	100.0	(†)	2.9	(0.21)	0.8	(0.03)	0.8	(0.02)	1.4	(0.19)	54.4	(1.45)	14.5	(0.57)	8.2	(0.30)	31.7	(1.65)	42.7	(1.38)
50 to 149	100.0	(†)	15.4	(0.15)	6.7	(0.06)	6.5	(0.08)	2.2	(0.02)	46.9	(0.78)	16.1	(0.37)	11.1	(0.11)	19.7	(0.52)	37.7	(0.69)
150 to 299	100.0	(†)	44.0	(0.10)	21.2	(0.08)	19.5	(0.05)	3.3	(0.01)	37.3	(0.10)	14.4	(0.03)	10.8	(0.11)	12.2	(0.03)	18.7	(0.12)
300 to 499	100.0	(†)	51.2	(0.10)	23.1	(0.15)	21.6	(0.08)	6.5	(0.02)	31.9	(0.12)	12.9	(0.05)	9.6	(0.17)	9.4	(0.03)	16.8	(0.06)
500 to 749	100.0	(†)	55.6	(0.80)	18.6	(0.34)	24.9	(1.36)	12.2	(0.22)	29.7	(0.54)	12.5	(0.23)	9.5	(0.17)	7.7	(0.14)	14.7	(0.27)
750 or more	100.0	(†)	38.4	(0.80)	5.7	(0.12)	15.7	(0.33)	16.9	(0.35)	39.6	(1.25)	13.0	(0.27)	13.5	(0.28)	13.0	(1.80)	22.1	(0.46)
Region																				
Northeast	100.0	(†)	43.3	(0.66)	17.0	(0.25)	16.5	(0.27)	9.8	(0.14)	30.9	(0.89)	4.7	(0.07)	11.9	(0.30)	14.2	(1.24)	25.8	(0.28)
Midwest	100.0	(†)	56.8	(0.79)	24.3	(0.38)	24.5	(0.94)	8.0	(0.13)	31.5	(0.90)	10.2	(0.32)	8.9	(0.18)	12.4	(0.66)	11.6	(0.43)
South	100.0	(†)	27.8	(0.04)	9.8	(0.01)	12.9	(0.02)	5.1	(0.01)	47.9	(0.07)	20.2	(0.06)	12.2	(0.02)	15.5	(0.02)	24.3	(0.09)
West	100.0	(†)	34.0	(0.01)	11.2	(0.01)	15.8	(0.01)	7.0	(0.00)	36.8	(0.02)	18.8	(0.01)	9.0	(0.01)	9.0	(0.02)	29.2	(0.01)
School locale																				
City	100.0	(†)	44.2	(0.37)	15.4	(0.10)	19.3	(0.53)	9.5	(0.06)	33.9	(0.23)	10.4	(0.07)	11.1	(0.10)	12.4	(0.08)	21.9	(0.17)
Suburban	100.0	(†)	40.9	(0.14)	16.8	(0.15)	17.0	(0.06)	7.2	(0.02)	35.0	(0.08)	13.8	(0.05)	11.1	(0.10)	10.2	(0.04)	24.0	(0.15)
Town	100.0	(†)	49.4	(0.43)	23.9	(0.21)	23.4	(0.20)	2.1	(0.02)	39.3	(0.53)	16.8	(0.36)	8.6	(0.08)	14.0	(0.67)	11.3	(0.10)
Rural	100.0	(†)	16.7	(0.47)	6.3	(0.18)	7.2	(0.20)	3.2	(0.09)	57.2	(1.41)	23.4	(0.76)	9.7	(0.28)	24.1	(2.10)	26.2	(0.98)
	Fall 2013																			
Total	**100.0**	**(†)**	**38.1**	**(0.50)**	**13.7**	**(0.33)**	**17.4**	**(0.51)**	**7.0**	**(0.07)**	**37.6**	**(0.44)**	**13.1**	**(0.16)**	**10.5**	**(0.13)**	**14.1**	**(0.47)**	**24.3**	**(0.28)**
School level[2]																				
Elementary	100.0	(†)	47.4	(0.64)	23.1	(0.57)	21.6	(0.37)	2.8	(0.04)	30.3	(0.73)	6.3	(0.08)	9.5	(0.20)	14.5	(0.85)	22.2	(0.38)
Secondary	100.0	(†)	71.4	(0.72)	6.9	(0.10)	34.1	(0.64)	30.3	(0.41)	15.3	(0.31)	2.5	(0.03)	6.5	(0.23)	6.3	(0.17)	13.3	(0.79)
Combined	100.0	(†)	9.8	(1.61)	1.7	(0.03)	3.9	(1.71)	4.2	(0.08)	58.3	(1.08)	28.2	(0.59)	13.6	(0.27)	16.6	(0.37)	31.9	(0.65)
Student race/ethnicity[3]																				
White	100.0	(†)	40.2	(0.62)	14.0	(0.21)	18.9	(0.67)	7.3	(0.10)	39.7	(0.63)	13.5	(0.20)	11.6	(0.18)	14.6	(0.75)	20.1	(0.27)
Black	100.0	(†)	35.5	(1.81)	12.7	(2.34)	14.4	(0.45)	8.4	(0.26)	40.3	(1.27)	16.0	(0.50)	10.0	(0.40)	14.4	(0.55)	24.2	(1.35)
Hispanic	100.0	(†)	57.5	(0.50)	21.8	(0.25)	24.2	(0.39)	11.4	(0.10)	25.9	(0.49)	11.9	(0.41)	6.7	(0.06)	7.3	(0.16)	16.6	(0.17)
Asian	100.0	(†)	35.0	(0.48)	11.0	(0.14)	16.5	(0.56)	7.5	(0.07)	31.6	(0.33)	12.2	(0.18)	10.2	(0.17)	9.2	(0.09)	33.4	(0.31)
Pacific Islander	100.0	(†)	39.4	(0.43)	14.1	(0.19)	18.0	(0.53)	7.3	(0.08)	43.7	(0.33)	12.4	(0.14)	6.8	(0.05)	24.5	(0.25)	16.9	(0.20)
American Indian/Alaska Native	100.0	(†)	39.1	(0.37)	12.1	(0.11)	15.6	(0.28)	11.3	(0.10)	34.6	(0.49)	16.2	(0.14)	6.8	(0.65)	11.5	(0.11)	26.3	(0.36)
Two or more races	100.0	(†)	43.1	(0.43)	14.4	(0.30)	19.1	(0.32)	9.6	(0.08)	27.8	(0.41)	11.7	(0.25)	8.2	(0.22)	7.9	(0.12)	29.1	(0.34)
School enrollment																				
Less than 50	100.0	(†)	2.9	(0.40)	0.8	(0.14)	0.9	(0.08)	1.2	(0.30)	58.4	(4.14)	10.5	(1.04)	6.4	(0.68)	41.6	(5.71)	38.7	(3.88)
50 to 149	100.0	(†)	14.8	(0.58)	6.0	(0.59)	6.8	(0.22)	2.0	(0.05)	46.9	(0.56)	14.5	(0.28)	10.9	(0.17)	21.6	(0.56)	38.3	(0.46)
150 to 299	100.0	(†)	42.9	(0.60)	20.3	(0.73)	18.9	(0.22)	3.7	(0.07)	36.5	(0.46)	13.2	(0.16)	10.5	(0.26)	12.8	(0.21)	20.6	(0.52)
300 to 499	100.0	(†)	50.7	(0.28)	21.0	(0.12)	23.0	(0.23)	6.6	(0.04)	32.3	(0.35)	14.1	(0.30)	9.6	(0.33)	8.6	(0.05)	17.0	(0.10)
500 to 749	100.0	(†)	51.8	(0.80)	16.4	(0.60)	23.6	(0.84)	11.8	(0.19)	30.7	(0.46)	12.2	(0.48)	9.9	(0.16)	8.6	(0.14)	17.5	(0.36)
750 or more	100.0	(†)	38.8	(2.22)	4.7	(0.17)	18.8	(2.92)	15.4	(0.57)	35.7	(1.31)	12.1	(0.45)	12.8	(0.47)	10.8	(0.40)	25.5	(1.10)

See notes at end of table.

Table 205.30. Percentage distribution of students enrolled in private elementary and secondary schools, by school orientation and selected characteristics: Fall 2011 and fall 2013—Continued

[Standard errors appear in parentheses]

Selected characteristic	Total		Catholic								Other religious								Nonsectarian	
			Total		Parochial		Diocesan		Private		Total		Conservative Christian		Affiliated[1]		Unaffiliated[1]			
1	2		3		4		5		6		7		8		9		10		11	
Region																				
Northeast	100.0	(†)	42.0	(0.34)	15.1	(0.12)	16.5	(0.13)	10.3	(0.09)	29.9	(0.21)	4.8	(0.21)	11.4	(0.12)	13.7	(0.10)	28.1	(0.47)
Midwest	100.0	(†)	56.1	(1.68)	22.4	(1.27)	26.0	(1.90)	7.6	(0.27)	31.5	(1.69)	8.8	(1.69)	8.6	(0.36)	14.1	(1.83)	12.5	(0.47)
South	100.0	(†)	25.9	(0.29)	8.4	(0.28)	13.0	(0.06)	4.5	(0.04)	48.4	(0.30)	19.0	(0.30)	12.4	(0.18)	17.0	(0.32)	25.7	(0.21)
West	100.0	(†)	32.2	(0.60)	10.2	(0.18)	15.0	(0.36)	7.0	(0.12)	35.4	(0.52)	17.8	(0.52)	8.4	(0.26)	9.2	(0.17)	32.5	(0.65)
School locale																				
City	100.0	(†)	42.1	(0.85)	13.9	(0.28)	19.3	(1.16)	8.9	(0.14)	33.6	(0.54)	10.0	(0.16)	11.5	(0.23)	12.2	(0.29)	24.2	(0.46)
Suburban	100.0	(†)	38.2	(0.38)	13.9	(0.12)	17.5	(0.34)	6.8	(0.07)	35.9	(0.37)	14.1	(0.27)	10.1	(0.19)	11.6	(0.14)	25.9	(0.30)
Town	100.0	(†)	48.2	(2.81)	25.2	(3.99)	20.9	(1.13)	2.1	(0.12)	38.6	(2.12)	15.6	(0.85)	8.2	(0.45)	14.8	(0.96)	13.2	(1.04)
Rural	100.0	(†)	14.4	(0.73)	4.8	(0.24)	6.3	(0.32)	3.3	(0.17)	61.1	(1.96)	20.4	(1.04)	9.1	(0.50)	31.5	(3.48)	24.5	(1.24)

†Not applicable.
[1]Affiliated schools belong to associations of schools with a specific religious orientation other than Catholic or conservative Christian. Unaffiliated schools have a religious orientation or purpose but are not classified as Catholic, conservative Christian, or affiliated.
[2]Elementary schools have grade 6 or lower and no grade higher than 8. Secondary schools have no grade lower than 7. Combined schools include those that have grades lower than 7 and higher than 8, as well as those that do not classify students by grade level.
[3]Race/ethnicity was not collected for prekindergarten students (773,240 out of 5,268,090 students in 2011 and 819,320 out of 5,395,740 students in 2013). Percentage distribution is based on the students for whom race/ethnicity was reported.
NOTE: Includes enrollment in prekindergarten through grade 12 in schools that offer kindergarten or higher grade. Race categories exclude persons of Hispanic ethnicity. Detail may not sum to totals because of rounding.
SOURCE: U.S. Department of Education, National Center for Education Statistics, Private School Universe Survey (PSS), 2011–12 and 2013–14. (This table was prepared December 2015.)

Table 205.40. Number and percentage distribution of private elementary and secondary students, teachers, and schools, by orientation of school and selected characteristics: Fall 1999, fall 2009, and fall 2013

[Standard errors appear in parentheses]

Selected characteristic	Fall 1999, total number		Fall 2009, total number		Fall 2013															
					Total				Catholic				Other religious				Nonsectarian			
					Number		Percent		Number		Percent		Number		Percent		Number		Percent	
1	2		3		4		5		6		7		8		9		10		11	
Students[1]																				
Total	**6,018,280**	**(30,179)**	**5,488,490**	**(35,857)**	**5,395,740**	**(50,342)**	**100.0**	**(†)**	**2,055,140**	**(37,142)**	**100.0**	**(†)**	**2,030,930**	**(30,090)**	**100.0**	**(†)**	**1,309,670**	**(14,800)**	**100.0**	**(†)**
School level[2]																				
Elementary	3,595,020	(11,516)	2,937,090	(26,807)	2,848,140	(36,022)	52.8	(0.47)	1,351,380	(20,818)	65.8	(1.14)	863,250	(28,166)	42.5	(0.80)	633,510	(9,546)	48.4	(0.51)
Secondary	806,640	(2,395)	785,810	(4,810)	737,950	(9,211)	13.7	(0.19)	526,640	(6,315)	25.6	(0.51)	112,990	(2,036)	5.6	(0.13)	98,330	(6,627)	7.5	(0.46)
Combined	1,616,620	(23,949)	1,765,590	(15,909)	1,809,650	(34,220)	33.5	(0.48)	177,120	(32,247)	8.6	(1.45)	1,054,690	(7,776)	51.9	(0.72)	577,840	(7,819)	44.1	(0.54)
School enrollment																				
Less than 50	238,980	(5,691)	296,000	(22,889)	292,310	(26,965)	5.4	(0.47)	8,360	(878)	0.4	(0.04)	170,830	(27,269)	8.4	(1.23)	113,130	(3,839)	8.6	(0.25)
50 to 149	939,110	(10,717)	950,050	(12,053)	925,150	(10,930)	17.1	(0.23)	136,820	(6,136)	6.7	(0.30)	434,100	(7,789)	21.4	(0.44)	354,230	(3,796)	27.0	(0.35)
150 to 299	1,615,970	(7,315)	1,423,220	(9,951)	1,378,460	(16,204)	25.5	(0.29)	591,210	(12,394)	28.8	(0.57)	502,810	(5,399)	24.8	(0.40)	284,430	(8,403)	21.7	(0.50)
300 to 499	1,419,360	(13,203)	1,154,950	(10,730)	1,102,200	(6,197)	20.4	(0.21)	558,370	(2,871)	27.2	(0.50)	356,170	(5,492)	17.5	(0.33)	187,660	(†)	14.3	(0.16)
500 to 749	917,670	(2,330)	768,540	(†)	782,570	(12,660)	14.5	(0.24)	405,250	(9,585)	19.7	(0.51)	240,020	(4,550)	11.8	(0.24)	137,300	(3,720)	10.5	(0.26)
750 or more	887,190	(18,232)	895,720	(6,538)	915,060	(33,650)	17.0	(0.54)	355,130	(32,844)	17.3	(1.35)	327,000	(†)	16.1	(0.24)	232,930	(7,318)	17.8	(0.49)
Student race/ethnicity[3]																				
White	4,061,870	(24,242)	3,410,360	(31,067)	3,185,550	(38,542)	69.6	(0.31)	1,280,320	(25,768)	67.7	(0.51)	1,264,370	(28,385)	73.9	(0.45)	640,860	(6,026)	65.8	(0.47)
Black	494,530	(5,079)	430,970	(2,579)	424,480	(13,148)	9.3	(0.27)	150,840	(11,300)	8.0	(0.55)	170,950	(1,699)	10.0	(0.19)	102,690	(6,582)	10.5	(0.60)
Hispanic	435,890	(1,592)	443,290	(4,113)	468,790	(4,024)	10.2	(0.11)	269,520	(2,234)	14.2	(0.19)	121,310	(3,071)	7.1	(0.20)	77,960	(908)	8.0	(0.09)
Asian	239,510	(877)	239,320	(1,894)	268,690	(2,346)	5.9	(0.05)	94,100	(1,786)	5.0	(0.04)	84,790	(1,046)	5.0	(0.09)	89,790	(879)	9.2	(0.08)
Pacific Islander	[4]	(†)	28,020	(884)	29,790	(221)	0.7	(0.01)	11,730	(200)	0.6	(0.01)	13,010	(80)	0.8	(0.01)	5,050	(57)	0.5	(0.01)
American Indian/ Alaska Native	22,690	(164)	21,080	(162)	22,030	(193)	0.5	(0.01)	8,610	(66)	0.5	(0.01)	7,620	(155)	0.4	(0.01)	5,800	(90)	0.6	(0.01)
Two or more races	—	(†)	127,090	(781)	177,090	(1,538)	3.9	(0.03)	76,250	(837)	4.0	(0.04)	49,310	(953)	2.9	(0.06)	51,530	(763)	5.3	(0.05)
School locale																				
City	—	(†)	2,252,780	(12,708)	2,294,730	(35,960)	42.5	(0.50)	967,070	(33,365)	47.1	(1.01)	771,220	(5,625)	38.0	(0.59)	556,440	(9,732)	42.5	(0.47)
Suburban	—	(†)	2,137,800	(20,891)	2,212,320	(18,866)	41.0	(0.44)	844,740	(8,428)	41.1	(0.85)	793,610	(12,105)	39.1	(0.66)	573,970	(8,821)	43.8	(0.52)
Town	—	(†)	387,920	(9,565)	341,840	(18,483)	6.3	(0.33)	164,660	(18,120)	8.0	(0.82)	132,000	(2,105)	6.5	(0.14)	45,180	(2,976)	3.4	(0.21)
Rural	—	(†)	709,990	(26,462)	546,850	(27,453)	10.1	(0.47)	78,660	(†)	3.8	(0.07)	334,100	(27,449)	16.5	(1.14)	134,090	(459)	10.2	(0.11)
Teachers[5]																				
Total	**408,400**	**(2,977)**	**437,410**	**(3,222)**	**441,500**	**(3,456)**	**100.0**	**(†)**	**138,990**	**(2,177)**	**100.0**	**(.00)**	**171,460**	**(2,192)**	**100.0**	**(†)**	**131,050**	**(1,516)**	**100.0**	**(†)**
School level[2]																				
Elementary	200,910	(735)	194,480	(1,878)	193,580	(2,206)	43.8	(0.40)	84,580	(1,000)	60.8	(1.08)	62,520	(1,957)	36.5	(0.73)	46,480	(394)	35.5	(0.43)
Secondary	62,740	(229)	67,530	(553)	64,770	(459)	14.7	(0.13)	39,460	(325)	28.4	(0.47)	12,030	(140)	7.0	(0.12)	13,280	(321)	10.1	(0.17)
Combined	144,750	(2,682)	175,410	(1,853)	183,150	(2,656)	41.5	(0.42)	14,960	(2,191)	10.8	(1.43)	96,910	(815)	56.5	(0.66)	71,280	(1,229)	54.4	(0.41)
School enrollment																				
Less than 50	25,970	(488)	34,120	(1,642)	34,030	(1,966)	7.7	(0.41)	1,290	(192)	0.9	(0.14)	18,580	(1,933)	10.8	(1.01)	14,160	(420)	10.8	(0.25)
50 to 149	70,800	(983)	82,460	(1,102)	79,420	(703)	18.0	(0.21)	11,600	(283)	8.3	(0.31)	37,180	(606)	21.7	(0.39)	30,650	(282)	23.4	(0.31)
150 to 299	102,240	(486)	107,490	(1,873)	104,450	(883)	23.7	(0.23)	39,860	(708)	28.7	(0.54)	39,730	(439)	23.2	(0.33)	24,850	(244)	19.0	(0.26)
300 to 499	90,010	(1,316)	86,850	(751)	85,620	(395)	19.4	(0.17)	36,150	(164)	26.0	(0.42)	28,990	(360)	16.9	(0.27)	20,490	(†)	15.6	(0.18)
500 to 749	57,930	(79)	56,920	(†)	60,950	(711)	13.8	(0.17)	26,150	(499)	18.8	(0.41)	19,640	(444)	11.5	(0.25)	15,150	(†)	11.6	(0.14)
750 or more	61,440	(2,143)	69,570	(566)	77,030	(2,510)	17.4	(0.48)	23,950	(†)	17.2	(1.36)	27,340	(†)	15.9	(0.20)	25,740	(†)	19.6	(0.70)
School locale																				
City	—	(†)	176,740	(799)	187,910	(2,369)	42.6	(0.42)	64,630	(2,242)	46.5	(1.00)	66,360	(307)	38.7	(0.52)	56,920	(463)	43.4	(0.36)
Suburban	—	(†)	166,170	(2,463)	175,370	(1,730)	39.7	(0.39)	56,380	(520)	40.6	(0.82)	64,900	(1,033)	37.8	(0.59)	54,090	(1,231)	41.3	(0.51)
Town	—	(†)	30,390	(663)	26,640	(803)	6.0	(0.18)	11,600	(789)	8.3	(0.53)	10,940	(98)	6.4	(0.09)	4,100	(112)	3.1	(0.09)
Rural	—	(†)	64,120	(1,960)	51,580	(1,942)	11.7	(0.40)	6,380	(†)	4.6	(0.07)	29,270	(1,939)	17.1	(0.94)	15,940	(105)	12.2	(0.15)
Schools																				
Total	**33,000**	**(301)**	**33,370**	**(834)**	**33,620**	**(1,665)**	**100.0**	**(†)**	**6,700**	**(93)**	**100.0**	**(.00)**	**16,390**	**(1,665)**	**100.0**	**(†)**	**10,540**	**(171)**	**100.0**	**(†)**
School level[2]																				
Elementary	22,300	(242)	21,420	(745)	22,510	(1,657)	67.0	(1.66)	5,290	(95)	79.0	(0.45)	10,240	(1,660)	62.5	(3.91)	6,980	(131)	66.3	(0.51)
Secondary	2,540	(62)	2,780	(39)	2,700	(59)	8.0	(0.43)	990	(11)	14.8	(0.25)	790	(39)	4.8	(0.56)	920	(41)	8.7	(0.31)
Combined	8,150	(160)	9,160	(153)	8,410	(142)	25.0	(1.28)	410	(21)	6.2	(0.32)	5,360	(130)	32.7	(3.42)	2,640	(59)	25.0	(0.56)
School enrollment																				
Less than 50	9,160	(210)	11,070	(801)	11,990	(1,657)	35.7	(3.19)	250	(21)	3.8	(0.31)	7,620	(1,663)	46.5	(5.56)	4,130	(131)	39.2	(0.68)
50 to 149	10,260	(134)	10,470	(154)	10,120	(118)	30.1	(1.51)	1,300	(50)	19.5	(0.54)	4,730	(86)	28.9	(3.02)	4,090	(51)	38.8	(0.63)
150 to 299	7,440	(34)	6,690	(46)	6,480	(69)	19.3	(0.97)	2,680	(44)	40.1	(0.21)	2,400	(29)	14.7	(1.54)	1,390	(42)	13.2	(0.31)
300 to 499	3,730	(41)	3,010	(30)	2,880	(16)	8.6	(0.43)	1,450	(8)	21.6	(0.32)	940	(13)	5.7	(0.60)	490	(†)	4.7	(0.08)
500 to 749	1,530	(3)	1,280	(†)	1,300	(20)	3.9	(0.20)	680	(16)	10.1	(0.26)	400	(6)	2.4	(0.25)	230	(6)	2.1	(0.06)
750 or more	870	(20)	850	(7)	850	(22)	2.5	(0.14)	330	(†)	5.0	(0.32)	300	(†)	1.8	(0.19)	210	(8)	2.0	(0.08)
School locale																				
City	—	(†)	10,810	(171)	10,630	(138)	31.6	(1.60)	2,720	(26)	40.6	(0.66)	4,100	(75)	25.0	(2.63)	3,810	(84)	36.1	(0.60)
Suburban	—	(†)	11,610	(176)	12,110	(141)	36.0	(1.82)	2,570	(33)	38.3	(0.65)	4,490	(66)	27.4	(2.87)	5,050	(87)	47.9	(0.76)
Town	—	(†)	3,340	(154)	2,890	(136)	8.6	(0.59)	920	(89)	13.8	(1.14)	1,410	(51)	8.6	(0.93)	560	(90)	5.3	(0.79)
Rural	—	(†)	7,610	(799)	7,990	(1,662)	23.8	(3.80)	490	(†)	7.2	(0.10)	6,390	(1,662)	39.0	(6.33)	1,120	(21)	10.6	(0.21)

—Not available.
†Not applicable.
[1]Includes students in prekindergarten through grade 12 in schools that offer kindergarten or higher grade.
[2]Elementary schools have grade 6 or lower and no grade higher than 8. Secondary schools have no grade lower than 7. Combined schools include those that have grades lower than 7 and higher than 8, as well as those that do not classify students by grade level.
[3]Race/ethnicity was not collected for prekindergarten students (819,320 in fall 2013). Percentage distribution is based on the students for whom race/ethnicity was reported.
[4]For 1999, Pacific Islander students are included under Asian. Prior to 2009, data were not collected on Pacific Islander students as a separate category.
[5]Reported in full-time equivalents (FTE). Excludes teachers who teach only prekindergarten students.
NOTE: Tabulation includes schools that offer kindergarten or higher grade. Detail may not sum to totals because of rounding.
SOURCE: U.S. Department of Education, National Center for Education Statistics, Private School Universe Survey (PSS), 1999–2000, 2009–10, and 2013–14. (This table was prepared December 2015.)

Table 205.50. Private elementary and secondary enrollment, number of schools, and average tuition, by school level, orientation, and tuition: Selected years, 1999–2000 through 2011–12

[Standard errors appear in parentheses]

School orientation and tuition	Kindergarten through 12th-grade enrollment[1] Total	Elementary	Secondary	Combined	Total schools	Average tuition charged[2] (in current dollars) Total	Elementary	Secondary	Combined	Average tuition charged[2] (in constant 2014–15 dollars), total
1	2	3	4	5	6	7	8	9	10	11
1999–2000										
Total	**5,262,850 (131,001)**	**2,920,680 (55,057)**	**818,920 (34,102)**	**1,523,240 (88,816)**	**27,220 (239)**	**$4,980 (157)**	**$3,740 (249)**	**$6,080 (175)**	**$6,760 (261)**	**$6,960 (220)**
Catholic	2,548,710 (23,352)	1,810,330 (18,134)	616,200 (25,935)	122,190 (15,613)	8,100 (24)	3,340 (57)	2,600 (47)	4,830 (92)	6,890 (690)	4,670 (80)
Other religious	1,871,850 (86,782)	831,060 (41,035)	115,010 (10,981)	925,780 (66,926)	13,270 (237)	4,440 (153)	4,070 (130)	6,400 (456)	4,520 (280)	6,210 (215)
Nonsectarian	842,290 (61,373)	279,290 (28,987)	87,720 (11,774)	475,270 (43,377)	5,850 (76)	11,120 (775)	10,130 (1,921)	14,450 (1,461)	11,090 (801)	15,550 (1,083)
2003–04										
Total	**5,059,450 (104,287)**	**2,675,960 (55,714)**	**832,320 (54,051)**	**1,551,170 (82,059)**	**28,380 (262)**	**$6,600 (145)**	**$5,050 (120)**	**$8,410 (433)**	**$8,300 (290)**	**$8,390 (184)**
Catholic	2,320,040 (49,156)	1,645,680 (41,231)	584,250 (32,236)	90,110 (14,746)	7,920 (35)	4,250 (96)	3,530 (106)	6,050 (131)	5,800 (883)	5,410 (122)
Other religious	1,746,460 (63,090)	714,860 (28,935)	107,980 ! (33,776)	923,630 (48,379)	13,660 (203)	5,840 (144)	5,400 (161)	9,540 (963)	5,750 (230)	7,430 (183)
Nonsectarian	992,940 (71,519)	315,430 (30,820)	140,080 (27,556)	537,440 (59,332)	6,810 (136)	13,420 (379)	12,170 (468)	17,410 (1,988)	13,110 (480)	17,070 (482)
2007–08										
Total	**5,165,280 (104,435)**	**2,462,980 (58,830)**	**850,750 (38,553)**	**1,851,550 (91,348)**	**28,220 (328)**	**$8,550 (176)**	**$6,730 (181)**	**$10,550 (356)**	**$10,050 (372)**	**$9,560 (197)**
Less than $3,500	1,122,300 (50,988)	750,020 (35,402)	‡ (†)	342,100 (35,615)	10,030 (344)	2,710 (61)	2,900 (54)	‡ (†)	2,350 (134)	3,030 (68)
$3,500 to $5,999	1,790,410 (77,850)	1,066,750 (45,444)	143,510 (19,815)	580,150 (53,528)	9,110 (341)	5,210 (42)	5,220 (49)	5,080 (80)	5,210 (89)	5,820 (46)
$6,000 to $9,999	1,155,290 (60,342)	366,470 (37,396)	455,840 (33,376)	332,980 (36,574)	4,460 (232)	8,260 (101)	9,230 (287)	7,660 (105)	8,030 (192)	9,230 (113)
$10,000 to $14,999	503,380 (45,776)	169,970 (26,731)	‡ (†)	237,850 (37,089)	1,980 (154)	13,640 (319)	15,730 (696)	‡ (†)	12,910 (318)	15,250 (357)
$15,000 or more	593,900 (50,049)	109,770 (19,266)	125,660 (15,623)	358,470 (43,060)	2,650 (187)	25,890 (768)	25,360 (1,940)	28,400 (1,327)	25,180 (1,061)	28,940 (858)
Catholic	2,224,470 (49,385)	1,457,960 (32,114)	620,840 (32,581)	145,680 (25,445)	7,400 (34)	6,020 (180)	4,940 (212)	7,830 (232)	9,070 (964)	6,730 (202)
Less than $3,500	619,410 (37,867)	571,560 (34,303)	‡ (†)	‡ (†)	2,810 (132)	2,980 (55)	3,010 (57)	‡ (†)	‡ (†)	3,330 (61)
$3,500 to $5,999	826,120 (37,974)	683,980 (32,576)	111,770 (16,043)	‡ (†)	3,040 (131)	4,900 (49)	4,860 (57)	5,150 (80)	‡ (†)	5,480 (55)
$6,000 to $9,999	607,980 (49,329)	165,120 (28,123)	395,900 (30,158)	‡ (†)	1,170 (102)	7,680 (116)	7,790 (240)	7,650 (117)	‡ (†)	8,590 (130)
$10,000 to $14,999	‡ (†)	‡ (†)	‡ (†)	‡ (†)	‡ (†)	‡ (†)	‡ (†)	‡ (†)	‡ (†)	‡ (†)
$15,000 or more	‡ (†)	‡ (†)	‡ (†)	‡ (†)	‡ (†)	‡ (†)	‡ (†)	‡ (†)	‡ (†)	‡ (†)
Other religious	1,975,980 (81,216)	709,730 (36,666)	128,550 (15,136)	1,137,700 (75,038)	13,950 (282)	7,120 (237)	6,580 (241)	10,490 (1,336)	7,070 (359)	7,960 (265)
Less than $3,500	430,010 (31,875)	172,660 (14,154)	‡ (†)	252,490 (29,920)	6,180 (291)	2,520 (106)	2,550 (167)	‡ (†)	2,510 (133)	2,820 (118)
$3,500 to $5,999	860,370 (59,588)	340,150 (27,800)	‡ (†)	489,390 (49,116)	5,030 (257)	5,370 (75)	5,570 (111)	‡ (†)	5,270 (101)	6,000 (84)
$6,000 to $9,999	384,850 (39,687)	103,280 (15,561)	57,150 (10,809)	224,420 (33,273)	1,640 (137)	8,050 (155)	8,810 (430)	7,680 (188)	7,790 (164)	9,000 (173)
$10,000 to $14,999	167,770 (25,960)	‡ (†)	‡ (†)	‡ (†)	620 (83)	13,230 (401)	‡ (†)	‡ (†)	‡ (†)	14,790 (448)
$15,000 or more	132,980 (24,657)	‡ (†)	‡ (†)	‡ (†)	480 (91)	22,880 (1,053)	‡ (†)	‡ (†)	‡ (†)	25,580 (1,178)
Nonsectarian	964,830 (55,074)	295,280 (25,191)	101,370 (12,739)	568,180 (48,321)	6,860 (119)	17,320 (555)	15,940 (702)	27,300 (1,506)	16,250 (795)	19,360 (621)
Less than $3,500	72,890 (10,998)	‡ (†)	‡ (†)	59,910 (10,584)	1,030 (125)	1,610 (387)	‡ (†)	‡ (†)	1,640 (467)	1,800 (432)
$3,500 to $5,999	103,930 (18,494)	42,610 (7,809)	‡ (†)	‡ (†)	1,040 (143)	6,290 (352)	8,090 (687)	‡ (†)	‡ (†)	7,030 (394)
$6,000 to $9,999	162,450 (24,872)	98,070 (16,434)	‡ (†)	‡ (†)	1,650 (168)	10,960 (530)	12,110 (792)	‡ (†)	‡ (†)	12,250 (593)
$10,000 to $14,999	208,670 (29,194)	77,450 (15,769)	‡ (†)	126,610 (25,784)	1,150 (124)	14,890 (567)	17,750 (1,501)	‡ (†)	13,230 (336)	16,650 (634)
$15,000 or more	416,900 (39,779)	71,360 (14,776)	85,870 (13,205)	259,670 (38,826)	2,000 (157)	26,500 (943)	25,010 (1,422)	31,220 (1,647)	25,350 (1,334)	29,630 (1,055)
2011–12										
Total	**4,479,530 (105,651)**	**2,133,810 (59,964)**	**731,620 (53,646)**	**1,614,100 (98,602)**	**26,230 (541)**	**$10,740 (316)**	**$7,770 (211)**	**$13,030 (727)**	**$13,640 (753)**	**$11,170 (328)**
Less than $3,500	618,710 (45,753)	404,700 (36,956)	42,580 ! (13,642)	171,430 (23,140)	7,950 (581)	2,190 (112)	2,410 (139)	1,370 (392)	1,870 (182)	2,280 (117)
$3,500 to $5,999	1,351,550 (64,739)	946,810 (56,403)	‡ (†)	364,520 (30,056)	7,800 (326)	5,300 (58)	5,350 (67)	‡ (†)	5,250 (118)	5,510 (60)
$6,000 to $9,999	1,167,820 (80,517)	467,040 (41,842)	275,980 (29,528)	424,800 (62,852)	5,070 (279)	8,560 (124)	9,090 (230)	7,980 (172)	8,360 (251)	8,900 (129)
$10,000 to $14,999	534,560 (45,926)	143,500 (18,976)	208,750 (38,977)	182,310 (36,985)	1,840 (150)	13,400 (207)	15,050 (454)	11,960 (225)	13,750 (348)	13,940 (216)
$15,000 or more	806,880 (69,846)	171,760 (25,237)	164,090 (32,298)	471,040 (65,345)	3,570 (194)	27,820 (951)	24,020 (960)	28,000 (2,487)	29,140 (1,274)	28,930 (989)
Catholic	1,892,480 (59,899)	1,244,480 (36,762)	511,870 (43,761)	136,130 (19,283)	6,760 (39)	6,890 (185)	5,330 (128)	9,790 (405)	10,230 (1,230)	7,170 (192)
Less than $3,500	307,610 (35,036)	259,330 (33,704)	‡ (†)	‡ (†)	1,730 (170)	2,580 (123)	2,690 (122)	‡ (†)	‡ (†)	2,680 (128)
$3,500 to $5,999	781,420 (53,974)	716,630 (50,260)	‡ (†)	‡ (†)	3,070 (187)	5,110 (68)	5,120 (72)	‡ (†)	‡ (†)	5,310 (71)
$6,000 to $9,999	516,660 (48,765)	243,570 (35,924)	234,460 (29,418)	‡ (†)	1,320 (126)	7,850 (139)	7,820 (210)	7,970 (199)	‡ (†)	8,160 (144)
$10,000 to $14,999	221,150 (36,032)	‡ (†)	177,560 (34,919)	‡ (†)	440 (68)	12,290 (240)	‡ (†)	12,020 (252)	‡ (†)	12,780 (250)
$15,000 or more	‡ (†)	‡ (†)	‡ (†)	‡ (†)	‡ (†)	‡ (†)	‡ (†)	‡ (†)	‡ (†)	‡ (†)

See notes at end of table.

Table 205.50. Private elementary and secondary enrollment, number of schools, and average tuition, by school level, orientation, and tuition: Selected years, 1999–2000 through 2011–12—Continued

[Standard errors appear in parentheses]

School orientation and tuition	Kindergarten through 12th-grade enrollment[1]				Total schools	Average tuition charged[2] (in current dollars)				Average tuition charged[2] (in constant 2014–15 dollars), total
	Total	Elementary	Secondary	Combined		Total	Elementary	Secondary	Combined	
1	2	3	4	5	6	7	8	9	10	11
Other religious	1,604,900 (84,424)	609,930 (38,479)	116,660 (31,187)	878,320 (77,923)	13,040 (550)	8,690 (397)	7,960 (447)	16,520 (2,288)	8,160 (518)	9,040 (413)
Less than $3,500	243,840 (25,511)	136,240 (19,015)	‡ (†)	103,980 (13,231)	5,190 (518)	2,090 (156)	1,860 (245)	‡ (†)	2,440 (169)	2,170 (163)
$3,500 to $5,999	507,660 (38,017)	214,270 (23,446)	‡ (†)	286,370 (28,337)	4,280 (259)	5,540 (101)	5,980 (183)	‡ (†)	5,220 (123)	5,760 (105)
$6,000 to $9,999	532,720 (61,948)	144,110 (26,978)	40,740 (7,928)	347,870 (59,370)	2,220 (228)	8,460 (186)	9,010 (269)	8,030 (196)	8,280 (260)	8,800 (194)
$10,000 to $14,999	165,130 (32,486)	‡ (†)	‡ (†)	‡ (†)	630 (89)	13,490 (359)	‡ (†)	‡ (†)	‡ (†)	14,030 (373)
$15,000 or more	155,550 (33,317)	‡ (†)	‡ (†)	‡ (†)	720 (126)	25,000 (2,243)	‡ (†)	‡ (†)	‡ (†)	26,000 (2,333)
Nonsectarian	982,140 (67,032)	279,400 (21,508)	103,090 (19,049)	599,650 (61,512)	6,430 (68)	21,510 (1,018)	18,170 (906)	25,180 (2,907)	22,440 (1,503)	22,370 (1,059)
Less than $3,500	67,260 (15,092)	‡ (†)	‡ (†)	47,370 ! (14,470)	1,040 (140)	740 ! (285)	‡ (†)	‡ (†)	490 ! (244)	770 ! (297)
$3,500 to $5,999	‡ (†)	‡ (†)	‡ (†)	‡ (†)	‡ (†)	‡ (†)	‡ (†)	‡ (†)	‡ (†)	‡ (†)
$6,000 to $9,999	118,440 (21,597)	79,370 (7,976)	‡ (†)	‡ (†)	1,530 (119)	12,130 (628)	13,140 (683)	‡ (†)	‡ (†)	12,620 (653)
$10,000 to $14,999	148,280 (33,642)	59,130 (11,788)	‡ (†)	‡ (†)	770 (106)	14,950 (418)	15,960 (908)	‡ (†)	‡ (†)	15,550 (435)
$15,000 or more	585,680 (66,696)	115,850 (20,781)	74,630 (16,406)	395,200 (61,972)	2,640 (165)	29,160 (1,092)	25,490 (1,219)	32,120 (3,206)	29,670 (1,368)	30,330 (1,136)

†Not applicable.
!Interpret data with caution. The coefficient of variation (CV) for this estimate is between 30 and 50 percent.
‡Reporting standards not met. Either there are too few cases for a reliable estimate or the coefficient of variation (CV) is 50 percent or greater.
[1]Only includes kindergarten students who attend schools that offer first or higher grade.
[2]Each school reports the highest annual tuition charged for a full-time student; this amount does not take into account discounts that individual students may receive. This amount is weighted by the number of students enrolled in each school and averaged.

NOTE: Excludes schools not offering first or higher grade. Elementary schools have grade 6 or lower and no grade higher than 8. Secondary schools have no grade lower than 7. Combined schools include those that have grades lower than 7 and higher than 8, as well as those that do not classify students by grade level. Excludes prekindergarten students. Includes a small percentage of schools reporting tuition of 0; these private schools are often under contract to public school districts to provide special education services. Detail may not sum to totals because of rounding and cell suppression. Some data have been revised from previously published figures.
SOURCE: U.S. Department of Education, National Center for Education Statistics, Schools and Staffing Survey (SASS), "Private School Data File," 1999–2000, 2003–04, 2007–08, and 2011–12. (This table was prepared in December 2015.)

Table 205.60. Private elementary and secondary school full-time-equivalent (FTE) staff and student to FTE staff ratios, by orientation of school, school level, and type of staff: 2007–08 and 2011–12

[Standard errors appear in parentheses]

Type of staff	Total, 2007–08	2011–12							
		Total				Catholic			
		Total	Elementary[1]	Secondary[2]	Combined[3]	Total	Elementary[1]	Secondary[2]	Combined[3]
1	2	3	4	5	6	7	8	9	10
Number of schools	28,220 (328)	26,230 (541)	15,000 (434)	2,820 (153)	8,400 (220)	6,760 (39)	5,300 (24)	1,040 (37)	410 (26)
Enrollment (in thousands)	5,165 (104)	4,480 (106)	2,134 (60)	732 (54)	1,614 (99)	1,892 (60)	1,244 (37)	512 (44M)	136 (19)
	Number of FTE staff								
Total FTE staff	**786,250 (16,261)**	**733,560 (17,373)**	**296,720 (8,627)**	**118,740 (8,321)**	**318,100 (17,125)**	**224,790 (7,201)**	**138,980 (3,830)**	**62,650 (5,069)**	**23,160 (2,739)**
Principals	30,550 (463)	26,290 (497)	12,670 (319)	3,040 (159)	10,580 (410)	7,070 (115)	5,240 (83)	1,250 (50)	580 (66)
Assistant principals	13,120 (487)	11,280 (418)	4,160 (274)	2,510 (253)	4,610 (326)	3,270 (208)	1,470 (147)	1,460 (138)	350 (68)
Other managers	26,110 (952)	25,950 (872)	9,710 (511)	5,160 (479)	11,070 (707)	6,690 (410)	3,010 (252)	2,710 (312)	970 (142)
Instruction coordinators	7,850 (538)	7,630 (733)	2,310 (296)	1,440 ! (443)	3,880 (572)	1,280 (176)	550 (124)	500 (107)	230 (54)
Teachers	436,910 (8,665)	413,140 (9,516)	174,930 (4,690)	64,390 (4,936)	173,810 (10,001)	130,210 (3,981)	82,300 (2,281)	36,000 (2,853)	11,900 (1,567)
Teacher aides	53,740 (2,591)	52,440 (3,563)	25,210 (1,664)	2,370 (384)	24,860 (2,940)	14,260 (1,102)	11,350 (720)	450 ! (136)	2,460 ! (763)
Other aides	11,350 (1,251)	11,060 (2,290)	3,480 (374)	1,250 ! (400)	6,330 ! (2,122)	2,040 (281)	1,800 (260)	70 ! (28)	‡ (†)
Guidance counselors	11,780 (506)	11,040 (501)	2,140 (188)	3,590 (288)	5,310 (390)	4,220 (259)	1,390 (146)	2,320 (209)	500 (86)
Librarians/media specialists	12,190 (351)	11,190 (393)	5,230 (228)	1,610 (134)	4,350 (319)	4,300 (164)	3,080 (147)	900 (78)	320 (51)
Library/media center aides	4,150 (261)	2,650 (443)	1,320 (246)	‡ (†)	900 (152)	1,210 (215)	910 (220)	200 (46)	100 ! (30)
Nurses	8,340 (399)	7,600 (372)	3,010 (203)	1,680 (246)	2,900 (279)	2,890 (180)	2,070 (158)	600 (122)	230 (51)
Student support staff[4]	24,920 (1,236)	23,010 (1,629)	5,510 (482)	4,190 (617)	13,300 (1,516)	4,420 (468)	2,210 (230)	1,350 (254)	860 ! (298)
Secretaries/clerical staff	50,360 (1,441)	42,730 (1,382)	15,420 (586)	8,210 (753)	19,090 (1,203)	13,460 (584)	7,080 (208)	5,160 (471)	1,220 (186)
Food service personnel	28,080 (1,019)	25,040 (1,196)	9,620 (549)	5,220 (583)	10,210 (998)	10,470 (625)	6,530 (435)	3,000 (383)	940 (142)
Custodial and maintenance	45,660 (1,469)	38,300 (1,482)	14,450 (614)	7,230 (527)	16,630 (1,369)	12,820 (576)	7,410 (325)	4,210 (393)	1,210 (185)
Other employees[5]	21,140 (2,717)	24,230 (3,023)	7,550 (1,820)	6,420 (1,602)	10,260 (1,975)	6,180 (1,381)	2,570 ! (921)	2,480 (735)	1,120 ! (508)
	Students per FTE staff member								
Total FTE staff	**7 (0.1)**	**6 (0.1)**	**7 (0.1)**	**6 (0.3)**	**5 (0.2)**	**8 (0.1)**	**9 (0.1)**	**8 (0.2)**	**6 (0.6)**
Principals	169 (2.9)	170 (3.4)	168 (4.1)	241 (16.1)	153 (6.4)	268 (7.7)	237 (7.2)	409 (28.9)	235 (23.1)
Assistant principals	394 (12.3)	397 (14.5)	512 (30.9)	292 (20.2)	350 (23.5)	579 (28.4)	847 (77.4)	352 (19.1)	394 (69.0)
Other managers	198 (6.0)	173 (6.0)	220 (11.2)	142 (11.0)	146 (9.3)	283 (14.1)	413 (33.4)	189 (15.0)	140 (21.5)
Instruction coordinators	658 (43.1)	587 (54.5)	925 (125.5)	507 (128.0)	416 (64.9)	1,480 (198.3)	2,253 (653.7)	1,022 (226.7)	605 ! (223.6)
Teachers	12 (0.1)	11 (0.2)	12 (0.2)	11 (0.5)	9 (0.2)	15 (0.2)	15 (0.3)	14 (0.3)	11 (0.5)
Teacher aides	96 (4.8)	85 (5.9)	85 (5.0)	308 (57.9)	65 (8.9)	133 (10.6)	110 (6.3)	‡ (†)	‡ (†)
Other aides	455 (52.2)	405 (78.2)	614 (64.7)	‡ (†)	255 ! (80.4)	929 (144.9)	692 (107.9)	‡ (†)	‡ (†)
Guidance counselors	439 (16.1)	406 (15.0)	998 (84.7)	204 (9.3)	304 (16.0)	448 (21.0)	894 (96.6)	220 (7.9)	270 (34.6)
Librarians/media specialists	424 (9.5)	400 (13.0)	408 (15.7)	455 (35.2)	371 (20.6)	440 (17.9)	404 (22.0)	571 (30.4)	421 (46.3)
Library/media center aides	1,243 (75.1)	1,692 (229.0)	1,615 (281.5)	1,696 ! (636.7)	1,803 (329.9)	1,570 (259.6)	1,374 (328.5)	2,512 (665.0)	1,416 ! (510.9)
Nurses	619 (26.1)	590 (31.8)	709 (41.8)	434 (83.1)	556 (55.8)	654 (45.4)	602 (39.8)	860 ! (269.8)	594 (152.5)
Student support staff[4]	207 (9.9)	195 (14.1)	387 (32.3)	174 (26.7)	121 (12.7)	428 (49.0)	562 (61.8)	380 (98.6)	‡ (†)
Secretaries/clerical staff	103 (2.1)	105 (2.6)	138 (4.2)	89 (4.9)	85 (3.5)	141 (4.6)	176 (5.9)	99 (5.2)	112 (13.1)
Food service personnel	184 (6.2)	179 (7.8)	222 (12.1)	140 (15.9)	158 (13.9)	181 (9.1)	191 (12.0)	171 (17.8)	144 (26.5)
Custodial and maintenance	113 (2.8)	117 (3.8)	148 (5.0)	101 (5.4)	97 (6.2)	148 (4.5)	168 (5.8)	122 (6.2)	113 (15.5)
Other employees[5]	244 (29.0)	185 (24.0)	283 (62.5)	114 (32.0)	157 (37.1)	306 (71.6)	‡ (†)	206 ! (66.7)	‡ (†)

See notes at end of table.

Table 205.60. Private elementary and secondary school full-time-equivalent (FTE) staff and student to FTE staff ratios, by orientation of school, school level, and type of staff: 2007–08 and 2011–12—Continued

[Standard errors appear in parentheses]

Type of staff	2011–12: Other religious orientation: Total	Other religious orientation: Elementary[1]	Other religious orientation: Secondary[2]	Other religious orientation: Combined[3]	Nonsectarian: Total	Nonsectarian: Elementary[1]	Nonsectarian: Secondary[2]	Nonsectarian: Combined[3]
1	11	12	13	14	15	16	17	18
Number of schools	13,040 (550)	6,860 (433)	890 (146)	5,290 (226)	6,430 (68)	2,840 (48)	890 (19)	2,700 (65)
Enrollment (in thousands)	1,605 (84)	610 (38)	117 (31)	878 (78)	982 (67)	279 (22)	103 (19)	600 (62)
	Number of FTE staff							
Total FTE staff	**254,000 (11,431)**	**92,610 (6,078)**	**25,040 (6,246)**	**136,350 (10,252)**	**254,770 (14,961)**	**65,140 (3,983)**	**31,050 (4,110)**	**158,590 (13,610)**
Principals	11,990 (419)	4,760 (291)	840 (141)	6,390 (350)	7,230 (249)	2,670 (106)	950 (63)	3,610 (215)
Assistant principals	4,000 (300)	1,320 (177)	540 ! (228)	2,140 (221)	4,020 (338)	1,380 (165)	510 (108)	2,130 (278)
Other managers	8,790 (592)	3,230 (280)	1,120 ! (377)	4,440 (375)	10,470 (734)	3,470 (322)	1,330 (238)	5,670 (620)
Instruction coordinators	2,790 (470)	790 (135)	‡ (†)	1,470 (236)	3,560 (529)	960 (200)	410 ! (125)	2,190 (487)
Teachers	154,650 (6,944)	56,490 (3,508)	13,990 (3,896)	84,170 (6,547)	128,280 (8,136)	36,140 (2,384)	14,400 (2,231)	77,740 (7,508)
Teacher aides	12,200 (1,070)	7,250 (987)	310 ! (132)	4,630 (522)	25,980 (3,077)	6,610 (809)	1,610 (354)	17,760 (2,705)
Other aides	2,990 (585)	780 (158)	320 ! (140)	1,900 (512)	6,020 ! (2,194)	900 (203)	870 ! (384)	4,260 ! (2,068)
Guidance counselors	3,080 (276)	370 (67)	600 ! (183)	2,120 (208)	3,740 (370)	380 (104)	670 (112)	2,690 (328)
Librarians/media specialists	3,630 (240)	1,290 (134)	390 (112)	1,960 (199)	3,260 (283)	870 (98)	320 (63)	2,070 (252)
Library/media center aides	730 ! (330)	240 (63)	‡ (†)	320 (88)	710 (146)	170 ! (60)	‡ (†)	470 (132)
Nurses	1,740 (182)	530 (71)	400 ! (121)	810 (115)	2,960 (310)	410 (74)	690 (190)	1,860 (258)
Student support staff[4]	4,050 (436)	1,550 (245)	810 ! (405)	1,680 (335)	14,540 (1,529)	1,750 (342)	2,030 (448)	10,760 (1,372)
Secretaries/clerical staff	16,000 (966)	5,510 (457)	1,610 ! (593)	8,890 (730)	13,270 (1,017)	2,830 (293)	1,450 (333)	8,980 (900)
Food service personnel	8,290 (813)	2,300 (238)	1,050 (264)	4,940 (718)	6,280 (886)	790 (155)	1,170 ! (392)	4,320 (756)
Custodial and maintenance	13,150 (904)	4,250 (358)	1,410 (323)	7,480 (804)	12,330 (1,101)	2,790 (347)	1,600 (348)	7,930 (998)
Other employees[5]	5,910 (1,690)	‡ (†)	970 ! (450)	2,990 (762)	12,130 (2,194)	3,020 (831)	2,970 ! (1,293)	6,150 (1,810)
	Students per FTE staff member							
Total FTE staff	**6 (0.2)**	**7 (0.2)**	**5 (0.5)**	**6 (0.2)**	**4 (0.1)**	**4 (0.2)**	**3 (0.4)**	**4 (0.2)**
Principals	134 (5.5)	128 (6.4)	140 (26.9)	137 (8.9)	136 (7.6)	105 (7.9)	108 (21.6)	166 (13.0)
Assistant principals	402 (30.3)	464 (58.8)	217 (49.8)	410 (44.2)	245 (18.1)	203 (23.1)	202 (42.8)	282 (30.8)
Other managers	183 (11.8)	189 (16.7)	104 (17.1)	198 (16.3)	94 (6.1)	80 (5.5)	78 (16.8)	106 (11.1)
Instruction coordinators	575 (88.4)	769 (136.5)	‡ (†)	598 (107.7)	276 (40.2)	291 (64.2)	250 ! (116.8)	274 (66.3)
Teachers	10 (0.3)	11 (0.3)	8 (1.1)	10 (0.4)	8 (0.2)	8 (0.3)	7 (0.7)	8 (0.3)
Teacher aides	132 (12.6)	84 (9.7)	‡ (†)	190 (23.3)	38 (4.8)	42 (5.9)	64 (16.6)	34 (6.1)
Other aides	536 (110.3)	785 (171.8)	‡ (†)	462 ! (141.0)	163 ! (64.9)	310 (82.7)	‡ (†)	‡ (†)
Guidance counselors	520 (36.9)	1,653 (313.9)	195 (46.5)	415 (24.6)	263 (20.3)	743 (219.1)	154 (22.6)	223 (20.8)
Librarians/media specialists	442 (26.3)	475 (37.3)	301 ! (99.7)	448 (39.1)	301 (15.9)	322 (29.6)	319 (44.4)	290 (20.1)
Library/media center aides	2,196 (593.2)	2,512 (626.7)	‡ (†)	2,711 ! (866.0)	1,381 (257.5)	‡ (†)	‡ (†)	1,262 (352.2)
Nurses	922 (107.2)	1,154 (131.9)	‡ (†)	1,080 (160.3)	331 (34.0)	679 (160.0)	149 ! (54.5)	322 (46.9)
Student support staff[4]	396 (43.6)	394 (51.9)	143 ! (65.7)	521 (105.2)	68 (7.4)	160 (33.7)	51 (14.7)	56 (7.4)
Secretaries/clerical staff	100 (4.6)	111 (6.7)	73 (11.9)	99 (6.0)	74 (3.5)	99 (7.3)	71 (11.0)	67 (4.6)
Food service personnel	194 (17.2)	265 (27.7)	‡ (†)	178 (21.3)	156 (19.4)	354 (82.1)	88 ! (32.9)	139 (24.1)
Custodial and maintenance	122 (6.7)	143 (10.7)	82 (16.4)	117 (9.1)	80 (4.6)	100 (9.0)	64 (11.3)	76 (6.7)
Other employees[5]	271 (64.9)	311 ! (131.9)	‡ (†)	294 ! (90.0)	81 (18.5)	93 ! (36.7)	‡ (†)	98 ! (45.5)

†Not applicable.
!Interpret data with caution. The coefficient of variation (CV) for this estimate is between 30 and 50 percent.
‡Reporting standards not met. The coefficient of variation (CV) for this estimate is 50 percent or greater.
[1]Includes schools beginning with grade 6 or below and with no grade higher than 8.
[2]Schools with no grade lower than 7.
[3]Schools with grades lower than 7 and higher than 8, as well as schools that do not classify students by grade level.
[4]Includes student support services professional staff, such as school psychologists, social workers, and speech therapists or pathologists.
[5]Includes other employees not identified by function.

NOTE: FTE staff consists of the total number of full-time staff, plus 48 percent of the part-time staff; this percentage was estimated based on the number of hours that part-time staff reported working. Data are based on a sample survey and may not be strictly comparable with data reported elsewhere. Excludes all prekindergarten students from calculations, but includes kindergarten students attending schools that offer first or higher grade. Includes only schools that offer first or higher grade. Detail may not sum to totals because of rounding. Some data have been revised from previously published figures.
SOURCE: U.S. Department of Education, National Center for Education Statistics, Schools and Staffing Survey (SASS), "Private School Data File," 2007–08 and 2011–12. (This table was prepared June 2013.)

Table 205.70. Enrollment and instructional staff in Catholic elementary and secondary schools, by level: Selected years, 1919–20 through 2014–15

School year	Number of schools			Enrollment[1]				Instructional staff[2]		
	Total	Elementary[3]	Secondary	Total	Prekindergarten	Elementary	Secondary	Total	Elementary[3]	Secondary
1	2	3	4	5	6	7	8	9	10	11
1919–20	8,103	6,551	1,552	1,925,521	([4])	1,795,673	129,848	49,516	41,592	7,924
1929–30	10,046	7,923	2,123	2,464,467	([4])	2,222,598	241,869	72,552	58,245	14,307
1939–40	10,049	7,944	2,105	2,396,305	([4])	2,035,182	361,123	81,057	60,081	20,976
1949–50	10,778	8,589	2,189	3,066,387	([4])	2,560,815	505,572	94,295	66,525	27,770
Fall 1960	12,893	10,501	2,392	5,253,791	([4])	4,373,422	880,369	151,902	108,169	43,733
1969–70	11,352	9,366	1,986	4,367,000	([4])	3,359,000	1,008,000	195,400 [5]	133,200 [5]	62,200 [5]
1970–71	11,350	9,370	1,980	4,363,566	([4])	3,355,478	1,008,088	166,208	112,750	53,458
1974–75	10,127	8,437	1,690	3,504,000	([4])	2,602,000	902,000	150,179	100,011	50,168
1975–76	9,993	8,340	1,653	3,415,000	([4])	2,525,000	890,000	149,276	99,319	49,957
1979–80	9,640	8,100	1,540	3,139,000	([4])	2,293,000	846,000	147,294	97,724	49,570
1980–81	9,559	8,043	1,516	3,106,000	([4])	2,269,000	837,000	145,777	96,739	49,038
1981–82	9,494	7,996	1,498	3,094,000	([4])	2,266,000	828,000	146,172	96,847	49,325
1982–83	9,432	7,950	1,482	3,007,189	([4])	2,211,412	795,777	146,460	97,337	49,123
1983–84	9,401	7,937	1,464	2,969,000	([4])	2,179,000	790,000	146,913	98,591	48,322
1984–85	9,325	7,876	1,449	2,903,000	([4])	2,119,000	784,000	149,888	99,820	50,068
1985–86	9,220	7,790	1,430	2,821,000	([4])	2,061,000	760,000	146,594	96,741	49,853
1986–87	9,102	7,693	1,409	2,726,000	([4])	1,998,000	728,000	141,930	93,554	48,376
1987–88	8,992	7,601	1,391	2,690,668	67,637	1,942,148	680,883	139,887	93,199	46,688
1988–89	8,867	7,505	1,362	2,627,745	76,626	1,911,911	639,208	137,700	93,154	44,546
1989–90	8,719	7,395	1,324	2,588,893	90,023	1,892,913	605,957	136,900	94,197	42,703
1990–91	8,587	7,291	1,296	2,575,815	100,376	1,883,906	591,533	131,198	91,039	40,159
1991–92	8,508	7,239	1,269	2,550,863	107,939	1,856,302	586,622	153,334	109,084	44,250
1992–93	8,423	7,174	1,249	2,567,630	122,788	1,860,937	583,905	154,816	109,825	44,991
1993–94	8,345	7,114	1,231	2,576,845	132,236	1,859,947	584,662	157,201	112,199	45,002
1994–95	8,293	7,055	1,238	2,618,567	143,360	1,877,782	597,425	164,219	117,620	46,599
1995–96	8,250	7,022	1,228	2,635,210	144,099	1,884,461	606,650	166,759	118,753	48,006
1996–97	8,231	7,005	1,226	2,645,462	148,264	1,885,037	612,161	153,276	107,548	45,728
1997–98	8,223	7,004	1,219	2,648,859	150,965	1,879,737	618,157	152,259	105,717	46,542
1998–99	8,217	6,990	1,227	2,648,844	152,356	1,876,211	620,277	153,081	105,943	47,138
1999–2000	8,144	6,923	1,221	2,653,038	152,622	1,877,236	623,180	157,134	109,404	47,730
2000–01	8,146	6,920	1,226	2,647,301	155,742	1,863,682	627,877	160,731	111,937	48,794
2001–02	8,114	6,886	1,228	2,616,330	159,869	1,827,319	629,142	155,658	108,485	47,173
2002–03	8,000	6,785	1,215	2,553,277	157,250	1,765,893	630,134	163,004	112,884	50,120
2003–04	7,955	6,727	1,228	2,484,252	150,422	1,708,501	625,329	162,337	112,303	50,034
2004–05	7,799	6,574	1,225	2,420,590	150,905	1,642,868	626,817	160,153	107,764	52,389
2005–06	7,589	6,386	1,203	2,325,220	146,327	1,568,687	610,206	152,502 [6]	103,481 [6]	49,021 [6]
2006–07	7,498	6,288	1,210	2,320,651	152,429	1,544,695	623,527	159,135	107,682	51,453
2007–08	7,378	6,165	1,213	2,270,913	152,980	1,494,979	622,954	160,075	107,217	52,858
2008–09	7,248	6,028	1,220	2,192,531	153,325	1,434,949	604,257	157,615	105,518	52,097
2009–10	7,094	5,889	1,205	2,119,341	150,262	1,375,982	593,097	154,316	103,460	50,856
2010–11	6,980	5,774	1,206	2,065,872	152,846	1,336,560	576,466	151,473	102,365	49,108
2011–12	6,841	5,636	1,205	2,031,455	154,282	1,303,028	574,145	151,395	100,365	51,030
2012–13	6,685	5,472	1,213	2,001,740	156,233	1,278,010	567,497	151,405	100,633	50,772
2013–14	6,594	5,399	1,195	1,974,578	158,537	1,252,397	563,644	151,351	100,244	51,107
2014–15	6,568	5,368	1,200	1,939,574	156,380	1,359,969	579,605	150,709	99,388	51,321

[1]Elementary enrollment is for kindergarten through grade 8, and secondary enrollment is for grades 9 through 12.
[2]From 1919–20 through fall 1960, includes part-time teachers. From 1969–70 through 1993–94, excludes part-time teachers. Beginning in 1994–95, reported in full-time equivalents (FTE). Prekindergarten teachers not counted separately but may be included with elementary teachers.
[3]Includes middle schools.
[4]Prekindergarten enrollment was not reported separately, but may be included in elementary enrollment.
[5]Includes estimates for the nonreporting schools.
[6]Excludes the Archdiocese of New Orleans.

NOTE: Data collected by the National Catholic Educational Association and data collected by the National Center for Education Statistics are not directly comparable because survey procedures and definitions differ.

SOURCE: National Catholic Educational Association, *A Statistical Report on Catholic Elementary and Secondary Schools for the Years 1967–68 to 1969–70; A Report on Catholic Schools*, 1970–71 through 1973–74; *A Statistical Report on U.S. Catholic Schools*, 1974–75 through 1980–81; and *United States Catholic Elementary and Secondary Schools*, 1981–82 through 2014–15, retrieved August 11, 2015, from http://www.ncea.org/data-information/catholic-school-data. (This table was prepared August 2015.)

Table 205.80. Private elementary and secondary schools, enrollment, teachers, and high school graduates, by state: Selected years, 2003 through 2013

[Standard errors appear in parentheses]

State	Schools, fall 2013		Enrollment in prekindergarten through grade 12												Teachers,[1] fall 2013		High school graduates, 2012–13	
			Fall 2003		Fall 2005		Fall 2007		Fall 2009		Fall 2011		Fall 2013					
1	2		3		4		5		6		7		8		9		10	
United States	**33,620**	**(1,665)**	**6,099,220**	**(41,219)**	**6,073,240**	**(42,446)**	**5,910,210**	**(28,363)**	**5,488,490**	**(35,857)**	**5,268,090**	**(24,908)**	**5,395,740**	**(50,342)**	**441,500**	**(3,456)**	**308,770**	**(3,801)**
Alabama	400	(37)	99,580	(12,130)	92,280	(5,892)	83,840	(103)	95,570	(11,745)	81,070	(49)	76,400	(295)	6,180	(15)	4,770	(37)
Alaska	50	(†)	7,370	(424)	7,500	(1,028)	4,990	(†)	7,510 !	(2,740)	5,170	(†)	5,080	(†)	410	(†)	200	(†)
Arizona	340	(†)	75,360	(16,426)	66,840	(†)	64,910	(†)	55,390	(†)	53,120	(229)	55,070	(†)	4,060	(†)	3,010	(†)
Arkansas	190	(47)	31,300	(†)	35,390	(5,858)	40,120	(11,961)	28,900	(1,371)	29,930	(1,245)	30,340	(1,496)	2,530	(196)	1,600	(62)
California	3,390	(39)	740,460	(8,703)	737,490	(15,529)	703,810	(6,129)	623,150	(4,185)	608,070	(69)	596,160	(3,500)	45,710	(239)	32,700	(†)
Colorado	430	(33)	62,080	(476)	70,770	(1,160)	64,740	(†)	63,720	(3,486)	61,140	(148)	60,690	(4,498)	4,640	(137)	2,520	(50)
Connecticut	400	(34)	102,960	(25,024)	76,220	(1,619)	85,150	(9,241)	72,540	(464)	66,320	(142)	72,770	(8,293)	8,560	(1,410)	6,070	(17)
Delaware	120	(†)	33,020	(2,649)	29,830	(†)	32,520	(2,701)	26,640	(†)	25,090	(†)	23,640	(†)	2,070	(†)	1,790	(†)
District of Columbia	90	(9)	23,510	(6,121)	19,880	(†)	19,640	(†)	17,810	(†)	16,950	(†)	19,790	(277)	2,460	(57)	1,820	(†)
Florida	2,140	(41)	398,720	(14,590)	396,790	(7,429)	391,660	(6,123)	343,990	(1,023)	340,960	(230)	372,790	(2,812)	29,420	(104)	19,440	(73)
Georgia	740	(26)	144,850	(6,527)	152,600	(10,394)	157,430	(9,185)	150,300	(6,251)	138,080	(†)	150,360	(2,250)	13,760	(26)	9,370	(†)
Hawaii	130	(3)	39,940	(†)	32,810	(†)	37,300	(290)	37,130	(†)	37,530	(†)	33,820	(32)	2,850	(9)	2,610	(†)
Idaho	200 !	(66)	12,570	(†)	15,320	(2,518)	24,700 !	(11,608)	18,680	(4,814)	13,670	(193)	18,580	(3,090)	1,360	(190)	670	(†)
Illinois	1,550	(8)	316,430	(1,698)	317,940	(4,263)	312,270	(6,638)	289,720	(9,237)	271,030	(1,289)	281,360	(6,026)	19,050	(323)	14,030	(†)
Indiana	870	(89)	124,500	(455)	139,370	(17,870)	119,910	(2,284)	120,770	(5,919)	129,120	(12,177)	121,230	(3,928)	8,390	(314)	5,100	(259)
Iowa	‡	(†)	53,850	(4,634)	60,960	(8,311)	47,820	(†)	45,160	(†)	63,840	(14,665)	56,150	(9,338)	4,580	(1,097)	2,400	(†)
Kansas	360 !	(160)	47,710	(2,151)	47,130	(1,654)	47,780	(2,414)	44,680	(1,668)	43,100	(1,640)	41,520	(3,286)	3,060	(240)	2,180	(†)
Kentucky	470	(83)	82,100	(1,525)	78,880	(1,228)	76,140	(2,074)	70,590	(2,132)	69,410	(12)	74,750	(4,226)	5,490	(166)	4,800	(783)
Louisiana	420	(52)	155,780	(3,515)	138,270	(525)	137,460	(†)	147,040	(9,890)	125,720	(108)	129,720	(2,606)	9,230	(52)	7,900	(†)
Maine	190	(27)	24,740	(3,629)	20,680	(337)	21,260	(143)	18,310	(†)	18,350	(†)	18,380	(272)	2,040	(120)	2,630	(†)
Maryland	770	(36)	172,360	(†)	170,350	(4,201)	165,760	(1,160)	145,690	(160)	137,450	(564)	143,530	(2,030)	13,490	(208)	8,970	(†)
Massachusetts	800	(27)	164,390	(6,636)	157,770	(3,273)	151,640	(2,516)	137,110	(1,169)	130,940	(1,596)	134,560	(943)	15,050	(197)	11,020	(†)
Michigan	780	(6)	180,080	(†)	166,950	(407)	159,100	(2,047)	153,230	(5,828)	135,580	(544)	141,590	(6,240)	10,150	(296)	9,810	(1,735)
Minnesota	500	(†)	106,010	(3,011)	104,730	(3,467)	101,740	(3,903)	89,530	(†)	87,620	(†)	85,260	(†)	6,420	(†)	4,390	(†)
Mississippi	310 !	(97)	57,110	(2,981)	57,930	(4,104)	55,270	(†)	54,650	(2,458)	52,060	(†)	50,330	(3,333)	4,170	(386)	3,590	(193)
Missouri	‡	(†)	141,530	(9,966)	137,810	(10,580)	125,610	(3,685)	117,970	(2,065)	130,130	(8,715)	139,570	(25,980)	10,860	(1,695)	7,740	(326)
Montana	140	(21)	12,510	(2,091)	‡	(†)	15,030 !	(5,465)	10,390	(1,221)	10,550	(†)	10,560	(521)	880	(41)	390	(†)
Nebraska	220	(†)	41,650	(†)	42,420	(†)	40,320	(†)	39,040	(†)	40,750	(†)	42,300	(†)	3,000	(†)	2,380	(†)
Nevada	140	(†)	23,930	(†)	29,120	(†)	29,820	(2,009)	25,060	(†)	26,130	(†)	21,980	(†)	1,370	(†)	840	(†)
New Hampshire	280	(†)	33,780	(†)	33,220	(†)	30,920	(†)	26,470	(†)	27,350	(†)	26,700	(†)	2,690	(†)	2,460	(†)
New Jersey	1,270	(87)	269,530	(7,577)	256,160	(8,439)	253,250	(5,016)	232,020	(16,536)	210,220	(1,211)	211,150	(4,607)	17,440	(371)	13,100	(†)
New Mexico	170	(†)	29,310	(3,928)	25,030	(141)	27,290	(1,388)	23,730	(507)	22,680	(10)	21,750	(†)	2,020	(†)	1,060	(†)
New York	1,870	(25)	515,620	(4,071)	510,750	(3,596)	518,850	(7,196)	486,310	(5,211)	487,810	(19,574)	452,380	(901)	41,580	(415)	28,410	(†)
North Carolina	690	(31)	126,230	(11,439)	117,280	(11,681)	121,660	(2,226)	110,740	(1,851)	119,070	(†)	118,090	(492)	11,050	(31)	7,120	(†)
North Dakota	50	(†)	6,840	(†)	7,290	(†)	7,430	(†)	7,750	(†)	7,770	(†)	8,290	(†)	680	(†)	380	(†)
Ohio	1,160	(97)	270,660	(7,094)	254,530	(9,821)	239,520	(2,741)	246,250	(24,214)	213,990	(3,419)	238,620	(19,487)	16,890	(914)	12,750	(457)
Oklahoma	170	(†)	34,300	(2,013)	35,350	(1,194)	40,320	(5,032)	34,000	(716)	35,750	(847)	32,740	(†)	2,950	(†)	1,990	(†)
Oregon	480	(42)	54,320	(†)	69,620	(14,139)	66,260	(5,188)	56,820	(3,502)	53,200	(†)	58,830	(3,109)	4,310	(213)	3,040	(313)
Pennsylvania	2,320	(43)	357,580	(3,364)	332,740	(3,918)	324,020	(6,253)	301,640	(5,036)	276,300	(3,668)	253,800	(756)	20,510	(43)	14,760	(†)
Rhode Island	130	(†)	31,960	(†)	30,600	(†)	28,260	(1,096)	24,940	(†)	25,420	(†)	22,180	(†)	1,970	(†)	1,750	(†)
South Carolina	430	(37)	73,800	(†)	70,240	(1,797)	71,430	(1,043)	62,320	(311)	60,890	(†)	65,350	(4,447)	5,310	(100)	3,010	(†)
South Dakota	70	(†)	11,980	(†)	12,700	(†)	12,280	(†)	11,470	(†)	12,490	(†)	9,950	(†)	780	(†)	260	(†)
Tennessee	560	(30)	93,390	(†)	105,240	(2,531)	117,540	(12,851)	98,310	(4,176)	92,430	(34)	93,990	(3,210)	8,720	(316)	5,510	(†)
Texas	1,740	(97)	271,380	(2,758)	304,170	(20,453)	296,540	(4,132)	313,360	(11,968)	285,320	(2,046)	312,640	(5,896)	26,600	(385)	14,060	(76)
Utah	160	(†)	19,990	(†)	21,220	(†)	20,860	(†)	21,990	(1,558)	18,660	(55)	23,310	(†)	1,720	(†)	1,600	(†)
Vermont	110	(†)	12,730	(†)	11,530	(†)	12,600	(232)	10,350	(†)	9,030	(†)	8,890	(†)	1,230	(†)	930	(†)
Virginia	910	(11)	131,160	(6,936)	155,220	(14,290)	143,140	(7,988)	128,140	(2,581)	123,780	(82)	131,330	(1,828)	12,080	(143)	6,530	(†)
Washington	800	(124)	101,130	(7,935)	119,640	(13,187)	104,070	(3,054)	94,340	(625)	93,630	(234)	119,730	(17,349)	8,720	(990)	5,960	(967)
West Virginia	130	(†)	15,300	(†)	16,120	(†)	14,980	(†)	13,860	(†)	13,430	(1)	14,350	(†)	1,230	(†)	780	(†)
Wisconsin	900	(44)	159,240	(11,743)	142,280	(137)	138,290	(1,597)	130,510	(†)	127,250	(†)	160,650	(32,980)	11,500	(2,244)	8,520 !	(3,248)
Wyoming	40	(†)	2,600	(†)	2,310	(†)	2,930	(†)	2,910	(†)	2,740	(†)	2,780	(†)	270	(†)	50	(†)

†Not applicable.
!Interpret data with caution. The coefficient of variation (CVV) for this estimate is between 30 and 50 percent.
‡Reporting standards not met. The coefficient of variation (CV) for this estimate is 50 percent or greater.
[1]Reported in full-time equivalents (FTE). Excludes teachers who teach only prekindergarten students.

NOTE: Includes special education, vocational/technical education, and alternative schools. Tabulation includes schools that offer kindergarten or higher grade. Includes enrollment of students in prekindergarten through grade 12 in schools that offer kindergarten or higher grade. Detail may not sum to totals because of rounding.
SOURCE: U.S. Department of Education, National Center for Education Statistics, Private School Universe Survey (PSS), 2003–04 through 2013–14. (This table was prepared December 2015.)

Table 235.10. Revenues for public elementary and secondary schools, by source of funds: Selected years, 1919–20 through 2012–13

School year	Revenues (in thousands)							Revenues per pupil						
				Local (including intermediate sources below the state level)							Local (including intermediate sources below the state level)			
	Total	Federal	State	Total	Property taxes	Other public revenue	Private[1]	Total	Federal	State	Total	Property taxes	Other public revenue	Private[1]
1	2	3	4	5	6	7	8	9	10	11	12	13	14	15
							Current dollars							
1919–20	$970,121	$2,475	$160,085	$807,561	—	—	—	$45	#	$7	$37	—	—	—
1929–30	2,088,557	7,334	353,670	1,727,553	—	—	—	81	#	14	67	—	—	—
1939–40	2,260,527	39,810	684,354	1,536,363	—	—	—	89	$2	27	60	—	—	—
1949–50	5,437,044	155,848	2,165,689	3,115,507	—	—	—	217	6	86	124	—	—	—
1959–60	14,746,618	651,639	5,768,047	8,326,932	—	—	—	419	19	164	237	—	—	—
1969–70	40,266,922	3,219,557	16,062,776	20,984,589	—	—	—	884	71	353	461	—	—	—
1979–80	96,881,164	9,503,537	45,348,814	42,028,813	—	—	—	2,326	228	1,089	1,009	—	—	—
1989–90	208,547,573	12,700,784	98,238,633	97,608,157	$74,867,627	$17,084,494	$5,656,036	5,144	313	2,423	2,408	$1,847	$421	$140
1991–92	234,581,384	15,493,330	108,783,449	110,304,605	85,874,700	18,213,748	6,216,157	5,579	368	2,587	2,623	2,042	433	148
1992–93	247,626,168	17,261,252	113,403,436	116,961,481	87,143,955	23,116,567	6,700,958	5,783	403	2,648	2,731	2,035	540	156
1993–94	260,159,468	18,341,483	117,474,209	124,343,776	97,762,990	19,661,128	6,919,657	5,986	422	2,703	2,861	2,249	452	159
1994–95	273,149,449	18,582,157	127,729,576	126,837,717	97,978,129	21,560,162	7,299,425	6,192	421	2,896	2,875	2,221	489	165
1995–96	287,702,844	19,104,019	136,670,754	131,928,071	101,785,858	22,522,345	7,619,869	6,416	426	3,048	2,942	2,270	502	170
1996–97	305,065,192	20,081,287	146,435,584	138,548,321	106,545,881	24,288,693	7,713,747	6,688	440	3,211	3,038	2,336	533	169
1997–98	325,925,708	22,201,965	157,645,372	146,078,370	111,184,150	26,676,244	8,217,977	7,066	481	3,418	3,167	2,410	578	178
1998–99	347,377,993	24,521,817	169,298,232	153,557,944	119,483,487	25,348,879	8,725,578	7,464	527	3,638	3,300	2,567	545	187
1999–2000	372,943,802	27,097,866	184,613,352	161,232,584	124,735,516	27,628,923	8,868,145	7,959	578	3,940	3,441	2,662	590	189
2000–01	401,356,120	29,100,183	199,583,097	172,672,840	132,575,925	30,889,273	9,207,643	8,503	616	4,228	3,658	2,809	654	195
2001–02	419,501,976	33,144,633	206,541,793	179,815,551	141,095,685	28,924,825	9,795,041	8,800	695	4,333	3,772	2,960	607	205
2002–03	440,111,653	37,515,909	214,277,407	188,318,337	148,511,786	29,579,240	10,227,310	9,134	779	4,447	3,908	3,082	614	212
2003–04	462,026,099	41,923,435	217,384,191	202,718,474	160,602,055	31,651,489	10,464,930	9,518	864	4,478	4,176	3,309	652	216
2004–05	487,753,525	44,809,532	228,553,579	214,390,414	167,909,883	35,433,486	11,047,044	9,996	918	4,684	4,394	3,441	726	226
2005–06	520,621,788	47,553,778	242,151,076	230,916,934	178,279,408	41,111,066	11,526,460	10,600	968	4,930	4,702	3,630	837	235
2006–07	555,710,762	47,150,608	263,608,741	244,951,413	188,287,298	44,806,422	11,857,694	11,281	957	5,351	4,972	3,822	910	241
2007–08	584,683,686	47,788,467	282,622,523	254,272,697	196,521,569	45,314,965	12,436,163	11,879	971	5,742	5,166	3,993	921	253
2008–09	592,422,033	56,670,261	276,525,603	259,226,169	205,821,844	41,195,313	12,209,012	12,032	1,151	5,616	5,265	4,180	837	248
2009–10	596,390,664	75,997,858	258,863,973	261,528,833	210,837,095	38,771,186	11,920,551	12,089	1,540	5,247	5,301	4,274	786	242
2010–11	604,228,585	75,549,471	266,786,402	261,892,711	211,649,523	38,558,755	11,684,433	12,218	1,528	5,395	5,296	4,280	780	236
2011–12[2]	597,885,111	60,921,462	269,043,077	267,920,572	215,830,316	40,290,007	11,800,249	12,075	1,230	5,434	5,411	4,359	814	238
2012–13	603,686,987	55,862,552	273,101,724	274,722,710	221,961,238	41,141,278	11,620,194	12,130	1,122	5,487	5,520	4,460	827	233
							Constant 2014–15 dollars[3]							
1919–20	$12,047,714	$30,736	$1,988,059	$10,028,918	—	—	—	$558	$1	$92	$465	—	—	—
1929–30	28,878,507	101,407	4,890,200	23,886,900	—	—	—	1,125	4	190	930	—	—	—
1939–40	38,283,703	674,212	11,590,043	26,019,448	—	—	—	1,505	27	456	1,023	—	—	—
1949–50	54,335,315	1,557,473	21,642,899	31,134,943	—	—	—	2,164	62	862	1,240	—	—	—
1959–60	118,782,470	5,248,884	46,461,017	67,072,569	—	—	—	3,376	149	1,321	1,906	—	—	—
1969–70	252,289,988	20,171,942	100,640,361	131,477,686	—	—	—	5,539	443	2,209	2,886	—	—	—
1979–80	295,358,201	28,973,099	138,253,336	128,131,766	—	—	—	7,091	696	3,319	3,076	—	—	—
1989–90	388,725,450	23,673,821	183,113,407	181,938,222	$139,550,663	$31,844,906	$10,542,654	9,588	584	4,517	4,488	$3,442	$785	$260
1991–92	401,713,492	26,531,857	186,288,351	188,893,284	147,057,815	31,190,490	10,644,980	9,554	631	4,430	4,492	3,497	742	253
1992–93	411,207,989	28,664,033	188,317,734	194,226,222	144,711,243	38,387,369	11,127,610	9,602	669	4,398	4,536	3,379	896	260
1993–94	421,112,199	29,688,800	190,151,920	201,271,479	158,245,971	31,824,869	11,200,638	9,689	683	4,375	4,631	3,641	732	258
1994–95	429,818,841	29,240,261	200,990,990	199,587,590	154,175,108	33,926,351	11,486,131	9,744	663	4,556	4,525	3,495	769	260
1995–96	440,729,100	29,265,255	209,364,556	202,099,289	155,924,735	34,501,754	11,672,800	9,829	653	4,669	4,507	3,477	769	260
1996–97	454,362,992	29,908,996	218,100,628	206,353,368	158,689,049	36,175,491	11,488,827	9,962	656	4,782	4,524	3,479	793	252
1997–98	476,926,950	32,488,126	230,682,406	213,756,417	162,695,719	39,035,336	12,025,362	10,339	704	5,001	4,634	3,527	846	261
1998–99	499,668,056	35,272,150	243,518,357	220,877,548	171,864,893	36,461,795	12,550,860	10,737	758	5,233	4,746	3,693	783	270
1999–2000	521,390,379	37,883,903	258,096,864	225,409,613	174,385,250	38,626,341	12,398,022	11,127	808	5,508	4,811	3,722	824	265
2000–01	542,524,858	39,335,572	269,782,336	233,406,950	179,206,772	41,753,937	12,446,241	11,493	833	5,715	4,945	3,796	885	264

See notes at end of table.

Table 235.10. Revenues for public elementary and secondary schools, by source of funds: Selected years, 1919–20 through 2012–13—Continued

School year	Revenues (in thousands)							Revenues per pupil						
				Local (including intermediate sources below the state level)							Local (including intermediate sources below the state level)			
	Total	Federal	State	Total	Property taxes	Other public revenue	Private[1]	Total	Federal	State	Total	Property taxes	Other public revenue	Private[1]
1	2	3	4	5	6	7	8	9	10	11	12	13	14	15
2001–02	557,188,141	44,023,145	274,331,574	238,833,422	187,405,178	38,418,340	13,009,904	11,688	923	5,755	5,010	3,931	806	273
2002–03	571,991,926	48,757,621	278,486,029	244,748,276	193,013,619	38,442,715	13,291,942	11,871	1,012	5,780	5,080	4,006	798	276
2003–04	587,617,690	53,319,395	276,475,281	257,823,014	204,258,176	40,255,248	13,309,590	12,106	1,098	5,696	5,312	4,208	829	274
2004–05	602,216,268	55,325,134	282,189,008	264,702,126	207,313,855	43,748,780	13,639,491	12,342	1,134	5,783	5,425	4,249	897	280
2005–06	619,216,867	56,559,487	288,009,519	274,647,861	212,041,868	48,896,658	13,709,335	12,608	1,152	5,864	5,592	4,317	996	279
2006–07	644,289,432	54,666,277	305,627,203	283,995,952	218,299,742	51,948,434	13,747,776	13,079	1,110	6,204	5,765	4,431	1,055	279
2007–08	653,660,243	53,426,188	315,964,189	284,269,865	219,705,696	50,660,882	13,903,288	13,280	1,085	6,419	5,775	4,464	1,029	282
2008–09	653,190,980	62,483,333	304,890,804	285,816,843	226,934,457	45,421,009	13,461,377	13,267	1,269	6,193	5,805	4,609	923	273
2009–10	651,265,154	82,990,496	282,682,301	285,592,357	230,236,423	42,338,561	13,017,373	13,201	1,682	5,730	5,789	4,667	858	264
2010–11	646,835,901	80,876,859	285,598,906	280,360,136	226,574,037	41,277,735	12,508,364	13,080	1,635	5,775	5,669	4,582	835	253
2011–12[2]	621,825,212	63,360,837	279,815,914	278,648,462	224,472,444	41,903,271	12,272,746	12,559	1,280	5,651	5,628	4,534	846	248
2012–13	617,581,975	57,148,334	279,387,672	281,045,969	227,070,092	42,088,222	11,887,655	12,409	1,148	5,614	5,647	4,562	846	239
	Percentage distribution													
1919–20	100.0	0.3	16.5	83.2	—	—	—	100.0	0.3	16.5	83.2	—	—	—
1929–30	100.0	0.4	16.9	82.7	—	—	—	100.0	0.4	16.9	82.7	—	—	—
1939–40	100.0	1.8	30.3	68.0	—	—	—	100.0	1.8	30.3	68.0	—	—	—
1949–50	100.0	2.9	39.8	57.3	—	—	—	100.0	2.9	39.8	57.3	—	—	—
1959–60	100.0	4.4	39.1	56.5	—	—	—	100.0	4.4	39.1	56.5	—	—	—
1969–70	100.0	8.0	39.9	52.1	—	—	—	100.0	8.0	39.9	52.1	—	—	—
1979–80	100.0	9.8	46.8	43.4	—	—	—	100.0	9.8	46.8	43.4	—	—	—
1989–90	100.0	6.1	47.1	46.8	35.9	8.2	2.7	100.0	6.1	47.1	46.8	35.9	8.2	2.7
1991–92	100.0	6.6	46.4	47.0	36.6	7.8	2.6	100.0	6.6	46.4	47.0	36.6	7.8	2.6
1992–93	100.0	7.0	45.8	47.2	35.2	9.3	2.7	100.0	7.0	45.8	47.2	35.2	9.3	2.7
1993–94	100.0	7.1	45.2	47.8	37.6	7.6	2.7	100.0	7.1	45.2	47.8	37.6	7.6	2.7
1994–95	100.0	6.8	46.8	46.4	35.9	7.9	2.7	100.0	6.8	46.8	46.4	35.9	7.9	2.7
1995–96	100.0	6.6	47.5	45.9	35.4	7.8	2.6	100.0	6.6	47.5	45.9	35.4	7.8	2.6
1996–97	100.0	6.6	48.0	45.4	34.9	8.0	2.5	100.0	6.6	48.0	45.4	34.9	8.0	2.5
1997–98	100.0	6.8	48.4	44.8	34.1	8.2	2.5	100.0	6.8	48.4	44.8	34.1	8.2	2.5
1998–99	100.0	7.1	48.7	44.2	34.4	7.3	2.5	100.0	7.1	48.7	44.2	34.4	7.3	2.5
1999–2000	100.0	7.3	49.5	43.2	33.4	7.4	2.4	100.0	7.3	49.5	43.2	33.4	7.4	2.4
2000–01	100.0	7.3	49.7	43.0	33.0	7.7	2.3	100.0	7.3	49.7	43.0	33.0	7.7	2.3
2001–02	100.0	7.9	49.2	42.9	33.6	6.9	2.3	100.0	7.9	49.2	42.9	33.6	6.9	2.3
2002–03	100.0	8.5	48.7	42.8	33.7	6.7	2.3	100.0	8.5	48.7	42.8	33.7	6.7	2.3
2003–04	100.0	9.1	47.1	43.9	34.8	6.9	2.3	100.0	9.1	47.1	43.9	34.8	6.9	2.3
2004–05	100.0	9.2	46.9	44.0	34.4	7.3	2.3	100.0	9.2	46.9	44.0	34.4	7.3	2.3
2005–06	100.0	9.1	46.5	44.4	34.2	7.9	2.2	100.0	9.1	46.5	44.4	34.2	7.9	2.2
2006–07	100.0	8.5	47.4	44.1	33.9	8.1	2.1	100.0	8.5	47.4	44.1	33.9	8.1	2.1
2007–08	100.0	8.2	48.3	43.5	33.6	7.8	2.1	100.0	8.2	48.3	43.5	33.6	7.8	2.1
2008–09	100.0	9.6	46.7	43.8	34.7	7.0	2.1	100.0	9.6	46.7	43.8	34.7	7.0	2.1
2009–10	100.0	12.7	43.4	43.9	35.4	6.5	2.0	100.0	12.7	43.4	43.9	35.4	6.5	2.0
2010–11	100.0	12.5	44.2	43.3	35.0	6.4	1.9	100.0	12.5	44.2	43.3	35.0	6.4	1.9
2011–12[2]	100.0	10.2	45.0	44.8	36.1	6.7	2.0	100.0	10.2	45.0	44.8	36.1	6.7	2.0
2012–13	100.0	9.3	45.2	45.5	36.8	6.8	1.9	100.0	9.3	45.2	45.5	36.8	6.8	1.9

—Not available.
#Rounds to zero.
[1]Includes revenues from gifts, and tuition and fees from patrons.
[2]Data have been revised from previously published figures.
[3]Constant dollars based on the Consumer Price Index, prepared by the Bureau of Labor Statistics, U.S. Department of Labor, adjusted to a school-year basis.

NOTE: Beginning in 1989–90, revenues for state education agencies were excluded and new survey collection procedures were initiated; data may not be entirely comparable with figures for earlier years. Detail may not sum to totals because of rounding.
SOURCE: U.S. Department of Education, National Center for Education Statistics, *Biennial Survey of Education in the United States*, 1919–20 through 1949–50; *Statistics of State School Systems*, 1959–60 and 1969–70; *Revenues and Expenditures for Public Elementary and Secondary Education, 1979–80*; and Common Core of Data (CCD), "National Public Education Financial Survey," 1989–90 through 2012–13. (This table was prepared September 2015.)

Table 235.20. Revenues for public elementary and secondary schools, by source of funds and state or jurisdiction: 2012–13
[In current dollars]

State or jurisdiction	Total (in thousands)	Federal: Amount (in thousands)	Federal: Per pupil	Federal: Percent of total	State: Amount (in thousands)	State: Percent of total	Local (including intermediate sources below the state level): Amount (in thousands)[1]	Local: Percent of total	Property taxes: Amount (in thousands)	Property taxes: Percent of total	Private[2]: Amount (in thousands)	Private[2]: Percent of total
1	2	3	4	5	6	7	8	9	10	11	12	13
United States	**$603,686,987**	**$55,862,552**	**$1,128**	**9.3**	**$273,101,724**	**45.2**	**$274,722,710**	**45.5**	**$221,961,238**	**36.8**	**$11,620,194**	**1.9**
Alabama	7,188,210	850,523	1,142	11.8	3,936,486	54.8	2,401,201	33.4	1,099,433	15.3	321,517	4.5
Alaska	2,670,758	324,045	2,464	12.1	1,830,051	68.5	516,661	19.3	299,136	11.2	19,536	0.7
Arizona	9,385,733	1,278,835	1,174	13.6	3,965,426	42.2	4,141,471	44.1	3,013,964	32.1	228,247	2.4
Arkansas	5,051,804	612,256	1,259	12.1	2,624,126	51.9	1,815,421	35.9	1,568,431	31.0	148,938	2.9
California	66,026,445	7,388,302	1,173	11.2	35,878,654	54.3	22,759,489	34.5	18,324,216	27.8	402,845	0.6
Colorado	8,905,156	702,772	814	7.9	3,765,335	42.3	4,437,048	49.8	3,599,102	40.4	340,019	3.8
Connecticut	10,549,973	461,506	838	4.4	4,163,960	39.5	5,924,506	56.2	5,757,213	54.6	109,174	1.0
Delaware	1,909,503	192,422	1,491	10.1	1,123,567	58.8	593,514	31.1	506,397	26.5	15,084	0.8
District of Columbia	2,094,445	200,097	2,628	9.6	†	†	1,894,347	90.4	611,079	29.2	10,909	0.5
Florida	24,506,837	3,087,261	1,147	12.6	9,455,551	38.6	11,964,026	48.8	9,907,489	40.4	1,020,457	4.2
Georgia	17,492,816	1,864,121	1,094	10.7	7,620,092	43.6	8,008,603	45.8	5,396,960	30.9	468,040	2.7
Hawaii	2,331,839	310,777	1,682	13.3	1,962,993	84.2	58,069	2.5	0	0.0	31,653	1.4
Idaho	2,103,804	251,215	882	11.9	1,347,311	64.0	505,278	24.0	426,539	20.3	35,519	1.7
Illinois	26,879,107	2,313,498	1,116	8.6	7,003,524	26.1	17,562,085	65.3	15,453,409	57.5	499,742	1.9
Indiana	11,887,836	1,036,984	996	8.7	6,654,115	56.0	4,196,737	35.3	2,825,697	23.8	320,866	2.7
Iowa	6,033,012	472,925	946	7.8	3,118,397	51.7	2,441,689	40.5	1,988,380	33.0	138,259	2.3
Kansas	5,866,415	502,059	1,027	8.6	3,229,626	55.1	2,134,730	36.4	1,604,032	27.3	136,348	2.3
Kentucky	7,120,960	875,760	1,278	12.3	3,878,756	54.5	2,366,445	33.2	1,711,443	24.0	99,046	1.4
Louisiana	8,439,545	1,280,583	1,801	15.2	3,651,777	43.3	3,507,185	41.6	1,510,093	17.9	65,839	0.8
Maine	2,584,962	196,780	1,059	7.6	1,032,121	39.9	1,356,060	52.5	1,288,470	49.8	38,403	1.5
Maryland	13,800,320	831,092	967	6.0	6,093,647	44.2	6,875,581	49.8	3,349,654	24.3	118,938	0.9
Massachusetts	16,436,188	936,545	981	5.7	6,479,966	39.4	9,019,677	54.9	8,433,566	51.3	215,274	1.3
Michigan	18,632,336	1,819,682	1,170	9.8	10,938,995	58.7	5,873,659	31.5	4,950,705	26.6	275,054	1.5
Minnesota	11,215,788	709,817	840	6.3	7,233,164	64.5	3,272,807	29.2	2,104,741	18.8	331,571	3.0
Mississippi	4,394,942	707,620	1,433	16.1	2,213,480	50.4	1,473,842	33.5	1,216,479	27.7	108,453	2.5
Missouri	10,311,473	927,013	1,010	9.0	3,382,862	32.8	6,001,597	58.2	4,730,986	45.9	345,634	3.4
Montana	1,657,908	213,213	1,492	12.9	797,417	48.1	647,279	39.0	409,351	24.7	58,990	3.6
Nebraska	3,800,737	358,790	1,182	9.4	1,217,700	32.0	2,224,247	58.5	1,969,368	51.8	143,380	3.8
Nevada	4,140,625	401,968	902	9.7	1,397,295	33.7	2,341,362	56.5	1,080,253	26.1	40,006	1.0
New Hampshire	2,875,406	164,398	870	5.7	1,020,239	35.5	1,690,769	58.8	1,616,304	56.2	45,830	1.6
New Jersey	27,087,144	1,184,706	863	4.4	11,052,695	40.8	14,849,743	54.8	14,002,457	51.7	540,858	2.0
New Mexico	3,695,203	561,650	1,661	15.2	2,535,796	68.6	597,756	16.2	483,289	13.1	54,107	1.5
New York	59,007,178	3,234,775	1,193	5.5	23,665,880	40.1	32,106,522	54.4	28,771,765	48.8	325,359	0.6
North Carolina	13,107,879	1,652,625	1,088	12.6	8,150,584	62.2	3,304,670	25.2	2,754,510	21.0	220,079	1.7
North Dakota	1,354,505	159,520	1,578	11.8	690,150	51.0	504,835	37.3	377,577	27.9	59,087	4.4
Ohio	22,609,388	1,944,765	1,124	8.6	9,830,868	43.5	10,833,755	47.9	8,917,668	39.4	653,040	2.9
Oklahoma	5,912,975	732,453	1,088	12.4	2,906,491	49.2	2,274,031	38.5	1,650,554	27.9	266,078	4.5
Oregon	6,160,158	569,756	970	9.2	3,041,818	49.4	2,548,584	41.4	2,056,350	33.4	152,807	2.5
Pennsylvania	27,446,614	2,186,130	1,240	8.0	9,841,441	35.9	15,419,043	56.2	12,199,033	44.4	424,679	1.5
Rhode Island	2,336,776	202,770	1,423	8.7	909,689	38.9	1,224,317	52.4	1,194,407	51.1	19,658	0.8
South Carolina	8,414,913	845,279	1,148	10.0	3,904,090	46.4	3,665,545	43.6	2,693,565	32.0	244,930	2.9
South Dakota	1,323,242	198,333	1,520	15.0	413,443	31.2	711,466	53.8	585,913	44.3	38,339	2.9
Tennessee	9,084,504	1,182,985	1,191	13.0	4,151,138	45.7	3,750,381	41.3	1,828,701	20.1	435,060	4.8
Texas	50,053,709	5,872,123	1,156	11.7	20,134,113	40.2	24,047,473	48.0	21,886,177	43.7	985,247	2.0
Utah	4,860,217	449,443	733	9.2	2,527,828	52.0	1,882,946	38.7	1,466,486	30.2	204,466	4.2
Vermont	1,641,315	116,847	1,304	7.1	1,459,459	88.9	65,009	4.0	956	0.1	23,197	1.4
Virginia	15,106,627	1,108,890	876	7.3	5,880,122	38.9	8,117,614	53.7	4,899,822	32.4	256,811	1.7
Washington	12,142,892	1,042,169	991	8.6	7,160,382	59.0	3,940,341	32.4	3,326,713	27.4	322,510	2.7
West Virginia	3,543,326	380,192	1,343	10.7	2,089,304	59.0	1,073,830	30.3	957,233	27.0	25,682	0.7
Wisconsin	10,809,097	850,329	975	7.9	4,858,710	45.0	5,100,059	47.2	4,673,928	43.2	216,894	2.0
Wyoming	1,694,441	113,949	1,252	6.7	881,087	52.0	699,405	41.3	481,248	28.4	17,734	1.0
Other jurisdictions												
American Samoa	64,420	54,272	—	84.2	9,890	15.4	258	0.4	0	0.0	36	0.1
Guam	290,408	69,078	2,215	23.8	0	0.0	221,330	76.2	0	0.0	554	0.2
Northern Marianas	61,275	28,024	2,632	45.7	33,251	54.3	0	0.0	0	0.0	0	0.0
Puerto Rico	3,577,365	1,234,613	2,841	34.5	2,342,270	65.5	481	#	0	0.0	481	#
U.S. Virgin Islands	206,300	35,112	2,311	17.0	0	0.0	171,188	83.0	0	0.0	24	#

—Not available.
†Not applicable.
#Rounds to zero.
[1]Includes other categories of revenue not separately shown.
[2]Includes revenues from gifts, and tuition and fees from patrons.

NOTE: Excludes revenues for state education agencies. Detail may not sum to totals because of rounding.
SOURCE: U.S. Department of Education, National Center for Education Statistics, Common Core of Data (CCD), "National Public Education Financial Survey," 2012–13. (This table was prepared August 2015.)

Table 235.40. Public elementary and secondary revenues and expenditures, by locale, source of revenue, and purpose of expenditure: 2012–13

Source of revenue and purpose of expenditure	Total	City, large[1]	City, midsize[2]	City, small[3]	Suburban, large[4]	Suburban, midsize[5]	Suburban, small[6]	Town, fringe[7]	Town, distant[8]	Town, remote[9]	Rural, fringe[10]	Rural, distant[11]	Rural, remote[12]
1	2	3	4	5	6	7	8	9	10	11	12	13	14
Revenue amounts (in millions of current dollars)													
Total revenue[13]	$606,778	$83,757	$28,720	$35,386	$189,618	$17,923	$8,362	$12,447	$24,745	$17,814	$37,849	$29,026	$11,289
Federal	55,104	9,596	3,383	3,465	12,127	1,376	667	978	2,471	2,082	3,136	2,530	1,266
Title I	14,213	3,228	959	903	2,600	323	146	212	627	545	685	628	328
Child Nutrition Act	14,020	2,269	837	863	3,238	392	169	262	677	492	853	715	277
Children with disabilities (IDEA)	11,249	1,341	559	686	3,242	310	165	215	470	356	686	440	162
Impact aid	1,522	108	83	65	195	26	3	63	35	120	118	72	170
Bilingual education	361	37	15	17	63	3	1	2	4	5	9	3	1
Indian education	107	5	2	3	6	1	0	2	8	12	5	7	10
Math, science, and professional development	1,577	230	95	95	253	38	18	26	75	78	87	78	45
Safe and drug-free schools	141	7	11	12	23	1	2	2	9	7	12	5	5
Vocational and technical education	555	89	32	35	137	15	9	9	29	26	40	19	8
Other and unclassified	11,361	2,283	789	786	2,371	267	152	184	537	440	640	563	258
State	274,732	34,269	13,383	17,304	74,286	8,711	3,920	6,307	12,905	9,084	18,487	15,529	5,386
Special education programs	18,323	2,460	808	1,043	6,001	485	251	392	698	433	963	710	249
Compensatory and basic skills	5,610	659	177	415	1,635	195	43	83	182	102	278	184	81
Bilingual education	893	49	33	54	592	52	6	5	23	7	30	7	3
Gifted and talented	935	24	55	62	585	33	7	12	32	9	73	26	7
Vocational education	988	25	52	65	342	35	23	22	77	59	115	78	29
Other	247,982	31,052	12,257	15,666	65,132	7,911	3,591	5,794	11,892	8,474	17,028	14,525	5,017
Local[13]	276,942	39,892	11,955	14,617	103,205	7,836	3,775	5,162	9,369	6,648	16,226	10,967	4,638
Property tax[14]	176,222	16,779	7,352	9,731	72,452	4,623	2,861	3,834	6,708	4,938	10,642	7,833	3,527
Parent government contribution[14]	48,335	14,845	2,199	2,189	16,167	1,808	148	249	661	151	2,342	874	166
Private (fees from individuals)	14,052	979	629	718	5,279	562	203	354	633	414	1,061	737	306
Other[13]	38,333	7,289	1,776	1,979	9,306	843	563	725	1,367	1,145	2,182	1,523	638
Percentage distribution of revenue													
Total revenue	100.0	100.0	100.0	100.0	100.0	100.0	100.0	100.0	100.0	100.0	100.0	100.0	100.0
Federal	9.1	11.5	11.8	9.8	6.4	7.7	8.0	7.9	10.0	11.7	8.3	8.7	11.2
State	45.3	40.9	46.6	48.9	39.2	48.6	46.9	50.7	52.2	51.0	48.8	53.5	47.7
Local	45.6	47.6	41.6	41.3	54.4	43.7	45.1	41.5	37.9	37.3	42.9	37.8	41.1
Expenditure amounts (in millions of current dollars)													
Total expenditures	$618,331	$88,215	$28,979	$36,218	$190,912	$17,940	$8,617	$12,802	$25,154	$18,108	$38,076	$29,063	$11,467
Current expenditures for schools	526,937	72,281	24,946	30,913	164,730	15,638	7,410	10,881	21,720	15,583	33,164	25,359	9,734
Instruction	319,544	45,795	14,673	18,712	100,943	9,468	4,461	6,584	13,045	9,348	19,843	15,057	5,719
Support services, students	29,395	2,999	1,598	1,922	10,180	900	471	590	1,123	853	1,828	1,143	409
Support services, instructional staff	24,563	3,026	1,479	1,571	7,367	733	307	449	1,024	673	1,436	1,000	337
Administration	39,620	4,804	1,827	2,194	11,951	1,098	554	870	1,778	1,325	2,606	2,297	971
Operation and maintenance	49,918	7,023	2,249	2,871	15,331	1,484	672	996	2,010	1,503	3,111	2,398	962
Transportation	23,692	3,187	1,033	1,205	7,958	737	387	549	1,001	650	1,870	1,509	561
Food service	21,400	2,783	1,105	1,264	5,792	676	306	467	1,052	782	1,455	1,228	487
Other	18,804	2,664	981	1,175	5,208	542	252	377	686	449	1,014	728	287
Other current expenditures	22,478	2,828	1,135	1,324	6,172	708	321	483	1,076	811	1,540	1,263	525
Interest on school debt	17,067	2,680	714	923	5,458	471	205	403	585	336	1,014	613	168
Capital outlay	47,281	7,551	2,323	3,028	12,885	1,235	611	1,034	1,986	1,663	2,527	1,997	964
Percentage distribution of current expenditures for schools													
All current expenditures for schools	100.0	100.0	100.0	100.0	100.0	100.0	100.0	100.0	100.0	100.0	100.0	100.0	100.0
Instruction	60.6	63.4	58.8	60.5	61.3	60.5	60.2	60.5	60.1	60.0	59.8	59.4	58.8
Support services	10.2	8.3	12.3	11.3	10.7	10.4	10.5	9.5	9.9	9.8	9.8	8.5	7.7
Administration	7.5	6.6	7.3	7.1	7.3	7.0	7.5	8.0	8.2	8.5	7.9	9.1	10.0
Operation and maintenance	9.5	9.7	9.0	9.3	9.3	9.5	9.1	9.1	9.3	9.6	9.4	9.5	9.9
Transportation	4.5	4.4	4.1	3.9	4.8	4.7	5.2	5.0	4.6	4.2	5.6	5.9	5.8
Food service and other	7.6	7.5	8.4	7.9	6.7	7.8	7.5	7.8	8.0	7.9	7.4	7.7	8.0
Per student amounts (in current dollars)													
Current expenditure per student	$10,628	$12,169	$10,052	$10,803	$11,233	$10,115	$10,837	$10,178	$9,988	$9,836	$10,355	$10,334	$11,402
Instruction expenditure per student	6,445	7,710	5,913	6,539	6,884	6,124	6,523	6,158	5,999	5,901	6,196	6,136	6,699

[1]Located inside an urbanized area and inside a principal city with a population of at least 250,000.
[2]Located inside an urbanized area and inside a principal city with a population of at least 100,000, but less than 250,000.
[3]Located inside an urbanized area and inside a principal city with a population less than 100,000.
[4]Located inside an urbanized area and outside a principal city with a population of 250,000 or more.
[5]Located inside an urbanized area and outside a principal city with a population of at least 100,000, but less than 250,000.
[6]Located inside an urbanized area and outside a principal city with a population less than 100,000.
[7]Located inside an urban cluster that is 10 miles or less from an urbanized area.
[8]Located inside an urban cluster that is more than 10 but less than or equal to 35 miles from an urbanized area.
[9]Located inside an urban cluster that is more than 35 miles from an urbanized area.
[10]Located outside any urbanized area or urban cluster, but 5 miles or less from an urbanized area or 2.5 miles or less from an urban cluster.
[11]Located outside any urbanized area or urban cluster and more than 5 miles but less than or equal to 25 miles from an urbanized area, or more than 2.5 miles but less than or equal to 10 miles from an urban cluster.
[12]Located outside any urbanized area or urban cluster, more than 25 miles from an urbanized area, and more than 10 miles from an urban cluster.
[13]Excludes revenues from other in-state school systems.
[14]Property tax and parent government contributions are determined on the basis of independence or dependence of the local school system and are mutually exclusive.

NOTE: Total includes data for some school districts not identified by locale. Detail may not sum to totals because of rounding.

SOURCE: U.S. Department of Education, National Center for Education Statistics, Common Core of Data (CCD), "Local Education Agency (School District) Finance Survey (F33)," 2012–13. (This table was prepared January 2016.)

Table 236.15. Current expenditures and current expenditures per pupil in public elementary and secondary schools: 1989–90 through 2025–26

School year	Current expenditures in unadjusted dollars[1]			Current expenditures in constant 2014–15 dollars[2]					
				Total current expenditures		Per pupil in fall enrollment		Per pupil in average daily attendance (ADA)	
	Total, in billions	Per pupil in fall enrollment	Per pupil in average daily attendance (ADA)	In billions	Annual percentage change	Per pupil enrolled	Annual percentage change	Per pupil in ADA	Annual percentage change
1	2	3	4	5	6	7	8	9	10
1989–90	$188.2	$4,643	$4,980	$350.9	3.8	$8,654	2.9	$9,282	2.3
1990–91	202.0	4,902	5,258	357.1	1.8	8,663	0.1	9,292	0.1
1991–92	211.2	5,023	5,421	361.7	1.3	8,602	-0.7	9,283	-0.1
1992–93	220.9	5,160	5,584	366.9	1.4	8,568	-0.4	9,272	-0.1
1993–94	231.5	5,327	5,767	374.8	2.1	8,623	0.6	9,336	0.7
1994–95	243.9	5,529	5,989	383.8	2.4	8,700	0.9	9,424	0.9
1995–96	255.1	5,689	6,147	390.8	1.8	8,715	0.2	9,416	-0.1
1996–97	270.2	5,923	6,393	402.4	3.0	8,822	1.2	9,521	1.1
1997–98	285.5	6,189	6,676	417.8	3.8	9,057	2.7	9,768	2.6
1998–99	302.9	6,508	7,013	435.7	4.3	9,361	3.4	10,088	3.3
1999–2000	323.9	6,912	7,394	452.8	3.9	9,664	3.2	10,337	2.5
2000–01	348.4	7,380	7,904	470.9	4.0	9,976	3.2	10,684	3.4
2001–02	368.4	7,727	8,259	489.3	3.9	10,264	2.9	10,969	2.7
2002–03	387.6	8,044	8,610	503.7	3.0	10,455	1.9	11,190	2.0
2003–04	403.4	8,310	8,900	513.0	1.8	10,569	1.1	11,319	1.2
2004–05	425.0	8,711	9,316	524.8	2.3	10,755	1.8	11,502	1.6
2005–06	449.1	9,145	9,778	534.2	1.8	10,877	1.1	11,630	1.1
2006–07	476.8	9,679	10,336	552.8	3.5	11,222	3.2	11,983	3.0
2007–08	506.9	10,298	10,982	566.7	2.5	11,513	2.6	12,278	2.5
2008–09	518.9	10,540	11,239	572.2	1.0	11,621	0.9	12,391	0.9
2009–10	524.7	10,636	11,427	573.0	0.1	11,615	-0.1	12,478	0.7
2010–11	527.3	10,663	11,433	564.5	-1.5	11,414	-1.7	12,240	-1.9
2011–12	527.2	10,648	11,362	548.3	-2.9	11,074	-3.0	11,817	-3.5
2012–13	535.7	10,763	11,503	548.0	-0.1	11,011	-0.6	11,768	-0.4
2013–14[3]	530.0	10,590	11,330	533.9	-2.6	10,667	-3.1	11,410	-3.0
2014–15[3]	544.9	10,870	11,630	544.9	2.1	10,870	1.9	11,630	1.9
2015–16[3]	560.5	11,150	11,930	557.4	2.3	11,090	2.0	11,860	2.0
2016–17[3]	584.4	11,600	12,410	567.1	1.7	11,260	1.5	12,040	1.5
2017–18[3]	611.9	12,120	12,970	578.8	2.1	11,470	1.9	12,270	1.9
2018–19[3]	637.8	12,620	13,500	589.6	1.9	11,670	1.8	12,480	1.8
2019–20[3]	663.6	13,110	14,020	599.0	1.6	11,830	1.4	12,660	1.4
2020–21[3]	690.7	13,600	14,550	608.3	1.5	11,980	1.2	12,820	1.2
2021–22[3]	718.5	14,110	15,090	616.3	1.3	12,100	1.0	12,950	1.0
2022–23[3]	747.0	14,620	15,640	623.8	1.2	12,210	0.9	13,060	0.9
2023–24[3]	775.5	15,140	16,190	630.9	1.1	12,320	0.9	13,180	0.9
2024–25[3]	803.2	15,640	16,740	637.8	1.1	12,420	0.9	13,290	0.9
2025–26[3]	822.8	16,000	17,120	642.2	0.7	12,490	0.5	13,360	0.5

[1]Unadjusted (or "current") dollars have not been adjusted to compensate for inflation.
[2]Constant dollars based on the Consumer Price Index, prepared by the Bureau of Labor Statistics, U.S. Department of Labor, adjusted to a school-year basis.
[3]Projected.
NOTE: Current expenditures include instruction, support services, food services, and enterprise operations. Some data have been revised from previously published figures.

SOURCE: U.S. Department of Education, National Center for Education Statistics, Common Core of Data (CCD), "National Public Education Financial Survey," 1989–90 through 2012–13; National Elementary and Secondary Enrollment Projection Model, 1972 through 2025; and Public Elementary and Secondary Education Current Expenditure Projection Model, 1973–74 through 2025–26. (This table was prepared April 2016.)

Table 236.65. Current expenditure per pupil in fall enrollment in public elementary and secondary schools, by state or jurisdiction: Selected years, 1969–70 through 2012–13

State or jurisdiction	Unadjusted dollars[1]														
	1969–70	1979–80	1989–90	1999–2000	2002–03	2003–04	2004–05	2005–06	2006–07	2007–08	2008–09	2009–10	2010–11	2011–12	2012–13
1	2	3	4	5	6	7	8	9	10	11	12	13	14	15	16
United States	**$751**	**$2,088**	**$4,643**	**$6,912**	**$8,044**	**$8,310**	**$8,711**	**$9,145**	**$9,679**	**$10,298**	**$10,540**	**$10,636**	**$10,663**	**$10,648**	**$10,763**
Alabama	512	1,520	3,144	5,638	6,300	6,581	7,073	7,683	8,398	9,197	8,964	8,907	8,726	8,577	8,773
Alaska	1,059	4,267	7,577	8,806	9,870	10,116	10,847	11,476	12,324	14,641	15,363	15,829	16,663	17,475	18,217
Arizona	674	1,865	3,717	5,030	6,283	5,999	6,307	6,515	7,316	7,727	8,022	7,870	7,782	7,383	7,495
Arkansas	511	1,472	3,229	5,277	6,482	6,842	7,659	8,030	8,391	8,677	8,854	9,281	9,496	9,536	9,538
California	833	2,227	4,502	6,314	7,552	7,673	7,905	8,301	8,952	9,706	9,503	9,300	9,146	9,220	9,258
Colorado	686	2,258	4,357	6,215	7,384	7,478	7,826	8,166	8,286	9,152	8,782	8,926	8,786	8,594	8,693
Connecticut	911	2,167	7,463	9,753	11,057	11,436	12,263	13,072	13,659	14,610	15,353	15,698	16,224	16,855	17,321
Delaware	833	2,587	5,326	8,310	9,693	10,212	10,911	11,621	11,760	12,153	12,109	12,222	12,467	13,580	13,653
District of Columbia	947	2,811	7,872	10,107	11,847	12,959	13,915	13,752	15,511	16,353	19,698	20,910	20,793	19,847	20,530
Florida	683	1,834	4,597	5,831	6,439	6,793	7,215	7,812	8,567	9,084	8,867	8,863	9,030	8,520	8,623
Georgia	539	1,491	4,000	6,437	7,774	7,742	8,065	8,595	9,102	9,718	9,649	9,432	9,259	9,272	9,121
Hawaii	792	2,086	4,130	6,530	8,100	8,533	8,997	9,876	11,316	11,800	12,400	11,855	11,924	11,973	11,743
Idaho	573	1,548	2,921	5,315	6,081	6,168	6,319	6,469	6,648	6,951	7,118	7,100	6,821	6,626	6,761
Illinois	816	2,241	4,521	7,133	8,287	8,606	8,896	9,113	9,596	10,353	11,097	11,739	11,742	12,011	12,443
Indiana	661	1,708	4,270	7,192	8,057	8,431	8,919	8,929	9,080	8,867	9,254	9,479	9,251	9,588	9,421
Iowa	798	2,164	4,190	6,564	7,574	7,626	7,962	8,355	8,791	9,520	9,704	9,748	9,795	10,027	10,291
Kansas	699	1,963	4,290	6,294	7,454	7,776	7,926	8,640	9,243	9,894	10,204	9,972	9,802	10,021	10,011
Kentucky	502	1,557	3,384	5,921	6,661	6,864	7,132	7,668	7,941	8,740	8,786	8,957	9,228	9,327	9,274
Louisiana	589	1,629	3,625	5,804	6,922	7,271	7,669	8,486	8,937	10,006	10,625	10,701	10,799	10,726	10,539
Maine	649	1,692	4,903	7,667	9,344	9,746	10,342	10,841	11,644	11,761	12,183	12,525	12,576	12,335	12,655
Maryland	809	2,293	5,573	7,731	9,153	9,433	10,031	10,909	11,989	13,257	13,737	14,007	13,946	13,875	14,086
Massachusetts	791	2,548	5,766	8,816	10,460	11,015	11,642	12,087	12,784	13,690	14,534	13,956	14,612	14,844	15,321
Michigan	841	2,495	5,090	8,110	8,781	9,094	9,338	9,575	9,876	10,075	10,373	10,447	10,577	10,477	10,515
Minnesota	855	2,296	4,698	7,190	8,109	8,405	8,718	9,159	9,589	10,060	10,983	10,665	10,674	10,781	11,065
Mississippi	457	1,568	2,934	5,014	5,792	6,199	6,548	7,173	7,459	7,890	8,064	8,104	7,926	8,097	8,117
Missouri	596	1,724	4,071	6,187	7,495	7,542	7,858	8,273	8,848	9,532	9,617	9,721	9,461	9,514	9,702
Montana	728	2,264	4,240	6,314	7,496	7,825	8,133	8,626	9,191	9,786	10,120	10,565	10,719	10,569	10,662
Nebraska	700	2,025	4,553	6,683	8,074	8,452	8,794	9,324	10,068	10,565	10,846	11,339	11,704	11,492	11,743
Nevada	706	1,908	3,816	5,760	6,092	6,410	6,804	7,177	7,796	8,187	8,321	8,376	8,411	8,130	8,026
New Hampshire	666	1,732	4,786	6,860	8,579	9,161	9,771	10,396	11,036	11,951	12,583	13,072	13,548	13,774	14,050
New Jersey	924	2,825	7,546	10,337	12,568	13,338	14,117	14,954	16,163	17,620	16,973	17,379	16,855	17,982	18,523
New Mexico	665	1,870	3,446	5,825	7,125	7,572	7,834	8,354	8,849	9,291	9,648	9,621	9,250	9,013	9,164
New York	1,194	2,950	7,051	9,846	11,961	12,638	13,703	14,615	15,546	16,794	17,746	18,167	18,857	19,396	19,529
North Carolina	570	1,635	4,018	6,045	6,562	6,613	7,098	7,396	7,878	7,798	8,463	8,225	8,267	8,160	8,342
North Dakota	662	1,941	3,899	5,667	6,870	7,333	8,279	8,728	8,671	9,324	9,802	10,519	10,898	11,246	11,615
Ohio	677	1,894	4,531	7,065	8,632	9,029	9,330	9,692	9,937	10,340	10,669	11,224	11,395	11,323	11,276
Oklahoma	554	1,810	3,293	5,395	6,092	6,154	6,610	6,941	7,430	7,683	7,878	7,929	7,631	7,763	7,914
Oregon	843	2,412	4,864	7,149	7,491	7,618	8,069	8,645	8,958	9,565	9,611	9,268	9,516	9,485	9,183
Pennsylvania	815	2,328	5,737	7,772	8,997	9,708	10,235	10,723	10,905	11,741	12,299	12,729	13,096	13,091	13,445
Rhode Island	807	2,340	5,908	8,904	10,349	11,078	11,667	12,609	13,453	14,459	14,719	14,723	14,948	15,172	14,889
South Carolina	567	1,597	3,769	6,130	7,040	7,177	7,549	8,120	8,507	9,060	9,228	9,080	8,908	9,102	9,444
South Dakota	656	1,781	3,511	5,632	6,547	7,068	7,464	7,775	8,064	8,535	8,543	9,020	8,931	8,593	8,630
Tennessee	531	1,523	3,405	5,383	6,118	6,466	6,850	7,004	7,129	7,820	7,992	8,117	8,330	8,348	8,588
Texas	551	1,740	3,835	6,288	7,136	7,151	7,246	7,480	7,850	8,350	8,562	8,788	8,685	8,213	8,261
Utah	595	1,556	2,577	4,378	4,838	4,991	5,216	5,464	5,709	5,978	6,612	6,452	6,440	6,312	6,432
Vermont	790	1,930	5,770	8,323	10,454	11,211	11,972	12,805	13,629	14,421	15,096	15,666	14,707	16,651	17,286
Virginia	654	1,824	4,690	6,841	7,822	8,219	8,886	9,452	10,214	10,664	10,928	10,594	10,363	10,656	10,960
Washington	853	2,387	4,382	6,376	7,252	7,391	7,717	7,984	8,524	9,058	9,585	9,497	9,619	9,604	9,714
West Virginia	621	1,749	4,020	7,152	8,319	8,588	9,024	9,440	9,727	10,059	10,606	11,774	11,978	11,579	11,257
Wisconsin	793	2,225	5,020	7,806	9,004	9,240	9,755	9,993	10,372	10,791	11,183	11,507	11,947	11,233	11,186
Wyoming	805	2,369	5,239	7,425	8,985	9,308	10,190	11,437	13,266	13,856	14,628	15,232	15,815	15,988	15,815
Other jurisdictions															
American Samoa	—	—	1,781	2,739	2,976	3,493	3,607	3,561	3,481	—	—	—	—	—	—
Guam	766	—	3,817	—	—	5,781	—	6,781	—	—	—	—	8,443	9,300	8,949
Northern Marianas	—	—	3,356	5,120	4,519	4,241	5,034	4,924	4,707	4,535	5,753	5,676	7,623	6,246	5,733
Puerto Rico	—	—	1,605	3,404	4,260	4,147	4,979	5,470	6,006	6,520	6,955	7,021	7,429	7,403	7,981
U.S. Virgin Islands	—	—	6,043	6,478	6,840	7,239	8,387	8,768	9,669	12,358	12,768	14,215	13,226	11,669	10,661

See notes at end of table.

Table 236.65. Current expenditure per pupil in fall enrollment in public elementary and secondary schools, by state or jurisdiction: Selected years, 1969–70 through 2012–13—Continued

State or jurisdiction	Constant 2014–15 dollars[2]														
	1969–70	1979–80	1989–90	1999–2000	2002–03	2003–04	2004–05	2005–06	2006–07	2007–08	2008–09	2009–10	2010–11	2011–12	2012–13
1	17	18	19	20	21	22	23	24	25	26	27	28	29	30	31
United States	**$4,707**	**$6,367**	**$8,654**	**$9,664**	**$10,455**	**$10,569**	**$10,755**	**$10,877**	**$11,222**	**$11,513**	**$11,621**	**$11,615**	**$11,414**	**$11,074**	**$11,011**
Alabama	3,206	4,635	5,860	7,882	8,187	8,370	8,733	9,138	9,737	10,282	9,883	9,727	9,341	8,920	8,974
Alaska	6,636	13,009	14,124	12,312	12,828	12,866	13,392	13,650	14,289	16,368	16,939	17,285	17,838	18,175	18,636
Arizona	4,225	5,686	6,929	7,032	8,166	7,630	7,787	7,749	8,483	8,639	8,845	8,594	8,331	7,679	7,667
Arkansas	3,201	4,487	6,019	7,378	8,425	8,701	9,456	9,551	9,729	9,701	9,762	10,135	10,166	9,918	9,758
California	5,221	6,788	8,392	8,828	9,815	9,759	9,760	9,873	10,379	10,851	10,477	10,155	9,791	9,589	9,472
Colorado	4,298	6,884	8,121	8,689	9,596	9,511	9,662	9,713	9,606	10,232	9,682	9,747	9,406	8,938	8,893
Connecticut	5,706	6,606	13,910	13,634	14,371	14,544	15,141	15,547	15,837	16,333	16,928	17,143	17,368	17,530	17,720
Delaware	5,222	7,886	9,928	11,617	12,598	12,988	13,471	13,822	13,635	13,586	13,351	13,347	13,346	14,124	13,967
District of Columbia	5,933	8,571	14,673	14,130	15,397	16,482	17,181	16,356	17,984	18,282	21,719	22,834	22,259	20,641	21,002
Florida	4,277	5,592	8,569	8,152	8,369	8,640	8,908	9,291	9,933	10,155	9,776	9,678	9,667	8,861	8,822
Georgia	3,376	4,546	7,456	8,999	10,104	9,847	9,958	10,223	10,553	10,864	10,639	10,300	9,912	9,643	9,331
Hawaii	4,962	6,361	7,698	9,129	10,528	10,853	11,108	11,746	13,120	13,192	13,671	12,945	12,765	12,452	12,013
Idaho	3,591	4,720	5,444	7,430	7,904	7,844	7,802	7,694	7,707	7,771	7,848	7,754	7,302	6,892	6,916
Illinois	5,111	6,833	8,427	9,972	10,770	10,946	10,983	10,839	11,125	11,575	12,235	12,819	12,570	12,492	12,730
Indiana	4,143	5,207	7,960	10,055	10,472	10,723	11,011	10,620	10,527	9,913	10,203	10,351	9,903	9,972	9,638
Iowa	5,001	6,598	7,810	9,177	9,843	9,699	9,830	9,937	10,193	10,643	10,700	10,645	10,485	10,428	10,528
Kansas	4,378	5,984	7,996	8,799	9,688	9,889	9,785	10,276	10,716	11,062	11,250	10,890	10,493	10,422	10,242
Kentucky	3,145	4,748	6,307	8,278	8,657	8,730	8,806	9,121	9,206	9,771	9,687	9,782	9,878	9,700	9,488
Louisiana	3,693	4,966	6,756	8,114	8,997	9,247	9,469	10,093	10,362	11,186	11,715	11,686	11,560	11,156	10,781
Maine	4,067	5,159	9,140	10,719	12,144	12,395	12,769	12,894	13,500	13,149	13,432	13,678	13,463	12,828	12,946
Maryland	5,070	6,990	10,388	10,809	11,895	11,997	12,385	12,974	13,900	14,821	15,146	15,296	14,930	14,431	14,410
Massachusetts	4,954	7,767	10,748	12,325	13,594	14,009	14,374	14,375	14,822	15,305	16,025	15,240	15,642	15,438	15,673
Michigan	5,272	7,608	9,487	11,338	11,412	11,566	11,530	11,388	11,450	11,263	11,437	11,408	11,323	10,896	10,757
Minnesota	5,356	7,001	8,757	10,052	10,539	10,689	10,764	10,894	11,118	11,247	12,110	11,646	11,426	11,212	11,320
Mississippi	2,862	4,781	5,468	7,009	7,528	7,884	8,085	8,531	8,648	8,820	8,891	8,849	8,485	8,422	8,303
Missouri	3,734	5,256	7,587	8,650	9,741	9,592	9,702	9,840	10,258	10,657	10,604	10,615	10,128	9,894	9,926
Montana	4,559	6,901	7,903	8,827	9,742	9,952	10,042	10,260	10,657	10,941	11,158	11,538	11,475	10,993	10,907
Nebraska	4,384	6,172	8,486	9,343	10,493	10,750	10,857	11,090	11,673	11,811	11,958	12,382	12,529	11,952	12,013
Nevada	4,422	5,817	7,112	8,053	7,918	8,153	8,401	8,536	9,039	9,152	9,174	9,147	9,004	8,456	8,211
New Hampshire	4,173	5,281	8,920	9,590	11,150	11,652	12,064	12,365	12,796	13,360	13,874	14,274	14,503	14,326	14,373
New Jersey	5,788	8,614	14,065	14,452	16,334	16,964	17,430	17,786	18,740	19,699	18,714	18,978	18,043	18,702	18,949
New Mexico	4,167	5,702	6,423	8,144	9,260	9,630	9,672	9,936	10,260	10,387	10,638	10,506	9,902	9,374	9,375
New York	7,483	8,995	13,142	13,765	15,546	16,073	16,919	17,383	18,024	18,776	19,567	19,839	20,187	20,173	19,979
North Carolina	3,573	4,986	7,490	8,452	8,529	8,410	8,763	8,797	9,133	8,718	9,331	8,981	8,850	8,486	8,534
North Dakota	4,150	5,919	7,268	7,923	8,928	9,327	10,222	10,380	10,053	10,424	10,808	11,487	11,667	11,696	11,882
Ohio	4,239	5,775	8,445	9,877	11,219	11,484	11,520	11,527	11,521	11,559	11,763	12,256	12,198	11,776	11,535
Oklahoma	3,470	5,517	6,138	7,542	7,917	7,827	8,162	8,256	8,614	8,589	8,686	8,659	8,170	8,074	8,096
Oregon	5,283	7,354	9,067	9,994	9,736	9,689	9,962	10,282	10,386	10,693	10,596	10,121	10,187	9,864	9,395
Pennsylvania	5,108	7,099	10,694	10,866	11,692	12,347	12,637	12,754	12,643	13,126	13,561	13,900	14,020	13,616	13,755
Rhode Island	5,055	7,135	11,013	12,449	13,450	14,090	14,405	14,996	15,597	16,165	16,229	16,078	16,002	15,780	15,232
South Carolina	3,554	4,870	7,026	8,570	9,149	9,127	9,321	9,658	9,863	10,129	10,175	9,916	9,536	9,467	9,661
South Dakota	4,111	5,429	6,545	7,874	8,509	8,990	9,216	9,248	9,349	9,542	9,419	9,850	9,561	8,938	8,828
Tennessee	3,326	4,644	6,346	7,525	7,951	8,224	8,458	8,331	8,266	8,742	8,812	8,864	8,918	8,682	8,785
Texas	3,453	5,304	7,148	8,790	9,275	9,094	8,946	8,897	9,101	9,335	9,440	9,596	9,297	8,542	8,451
Utah	3,729	4,744	4,803	6,121	6,287	6,348	6,441	6,499	6,619	6,684	7,291	7,046	6,894	6,565	6,580
Vermont	4,947	5,885	10,756	11,635	13,587	14,258	14,782	15,230	15,801	16,123	16,644	17,108	15,744	17,318	17,684
Virginia	4,100	5,561	8,742	9,564	10,166	10,454	10,971	11,242	11,842	11,922	12,049	11,569	11,094	11,082	11,212
Washington	5,345	7,277	8,169	8,914	9,425	9,401	9,527	9,496	9,882	10,126	10,569	10,371	10,297	9,989	9,938
West Virginia	3,893	5,331	7,493	9,998	10,812	10,922	11,141	11,228	11,277	11,245	11,694	12,858	12,823	12,042	11,516
Wisconsin	4,969	6,783	9,356	10,914	11,702	11,751	12,044	11,885	12,025	12,064	12,330	12,566	12,790	11,683	11,443
Wyoming	5,044	7,223	9,765	10,381	11,678	11,838	12,581	13,602	15,381	15,491	16,129	16,634	16,930	16,628	16,179
Other jurisdictions															
American Samoa	—	—	3,321	3,830	3,868	4,443	4,453	4,236	4,036	—	—	—	—	—	—
Guam	4,802	—	7,115	—	—	7,352	—	8,065	—	—	—	—	9,038	9,673	9,155
Northern Marianas	—	—	6,256	7,159	5,873	5,393	6,215	5,856	5,457	5,070	6,344	6,198	8,161	6,496	5,864
Puerto Rico	—	—	2,992	4,758	5,537	5,274	6,147	6,506	6,964	7,289	7,668	7,667	7,953	7,699	8,165
U.S. Virgin Islands	—	—	11,264	9,057	8,890	9,207	10,355	10,429	11,210	13,816	14,078	15,523	14,158	12,136	10,906

—Not available.
[1]Unadjusted (or "current") dollars have not been adjusted to compensate for inflation.
[2]Constant dollars based on the Consumer Price Index (CPI), prepared by the Bureau of Labor Statistics, U.S. Department of Labor, adjusted to a school-year basis. The CPI does not account for differences in inflation rates from state to state.
NOTE: Current expenditures include instruction, support services, food services, and enterprise operations. Expenditures for state administration are excluded in all years except 1969–70 and 1979–80. Beginning in 1989–90, extensive changes were made in the data collection procedures. Some data have been revised from previously published figures.
SOURCE: U.S. Department of Education, National Center for Education Statistics, *Statistics of State School Systems*, 1969–70; *Revenues and Expenditures for Public Elementary and Secondary Schools*, 1979–80; and Common Core of Data (CCD), "National Public Education Financial Survey," 1989–90 through 2012–13. (This table was prepared September 2015.)

Table 236.70. Current expenditure per pupil in average daily attendance in public elementary and secondary schools, by state or jurisdiction: Selected years, 1969–70 through 2012–13

	Unadjusted dollars[1]														
State or jurisdiction	1969–70	1979–80	1989–90	1999–2000	2002–03	2003–04	2004–05	2005–06	2006–07	2007–08	2008–09	2009–10	2010–11	2011–12	2012–13
1	2	3	4	5	6	7	8	9	10	11	12	13	14	15	16
United States	**$816**	**$2,272**	**$4,980**	**$7,394**	**$8,610**	**$8,900**	**$9,316**	**$9,778**	**$10,336**	**$10,982**	**$11,239**	**$11,427**	**$11,433**	**$11,362**	**$11,503**
Alabama	544	1,612	3,327	5,758	6,642	6,812	7,309	7,980	8,743	9,345	9,385	9,554	9,296	8,927	9,486
Alaska	1,123	4,728	8,431	9,668	10,770	11,074	11,851	12,537	13,508	16,002	16,822	17,350	18,352	19,134	19,982
Arizona	720	1,971	4,053	5,478	6,784	6,908	7,218	7,637	8,038	8,630	8,732	8,756	8,646	8,224	8,388
Arkansas	568	1,574	3,485	5,628	6,981	7,307	8,243	8,748	9,152	9,460	9,651	10,237	10,332	10,397	9,853
California	867	2,268	4,391	6,401	7,601	7,708	7,989	8,416	9,029	9,673	9,439	9,680	9,540	9,608	9,686
Colorado	738	2,421	4,720	6,702	7,826	8,416	8,558	8,938	9,110	9,977	9,611	9,747	9,709	9,415	9,572
Connecticut	951	2,420	7,837	10,122	11,302	11,755	12,655	13,461	14,143	15,063	15,840	16,133	16,932	17,472	17,859
Delaware	900	2,861	5,799	8,809	10,257	11,049	11,770	12,330	12,612	12,789	12,753	12,928	13,228	14,253	14,129
District of Columbia	1,018	3,259	8,955	11,935	14,735	15,414	15,074	17,877	18,285	20,807	19,766	21,283	21,304	20,399	20,437
Florida	732	1,889	4,997	6,383	6,922	7,269	7,731	8,376	9,055	9,711	9,452	9,363	9,394	8,825	8,925
Georgia	588	1,625	4,275	6,903	8,308	8,278	8,577	9,164	9,615	10,263	10,178	9,855	9,577	9,492	9,437
Hawaii	841	2,322	4,448	7,090	8,770	9,341	9,705	10,747	12,364	12,774	13,397	12,887	12,603	12,735	12,535
Idaho	603	1,659	3,078	5,644	6,454	6,559	6,698	6,861	7,074	7,402	7,567	7,481	7,155	7,041	7,273
Illinois	909	2,587	5,118	8,084	9,309	9,710	10,020	10,282	10,816	11,624	12,489	13,083	13,180	13,459	13,808
Indiana	728	1,882	4,606	7,652	8,582	9,033	9,640	9,558	9,727	9,569	9,946	10,160	9,924	10,220	10,037
Iowa	844	2,326	4,453	6,925	7,943	8,017	8,341	8,460	8,789	9,128	10,482	10,524	10,565	10,748	10,915
Kansas	771	2,173	4,752	6,962	8,373	8,804	9,037	9,905	10,280	11,065	11,485	10,859	10,700	10,712	10,789
Kentucky	545	1,701	3,745	6,784	7,728	7,976	8,379	8,975	9,303	9,940	10,054	10,376	10,469	10,700	10,269
Louisiana	648	1,792	3,903	6,256	7,492	7,846	8,288	8,568	9,650	10,797	11,410	11,492	11,500	11,352	11,121
Maine	692	1,824	5,373	8,247	10,114	10,504	11,153	11,760	12,628	13,177	13,558	14,090	14,406	14,000	14,303
Maryland	918	2,598	6,275	8,273	9,801	10,140	10,790	11,719	12,836	14,122	14,612	14,937	14,876	14,746	15,010
Massachusetts	859	2,819	6,237	9,375	11,161	11,583	12,208	12,629	13,263	14,373	15,249	14,632	15,334	15,607	16,111
Michigan	904	2,640	5,546	8,886	9,847	10,049	10,328	10,598	10,932	11,155	11,493	11,661	11,560	11,462	11,495
Minnesota	904	2,387	4,971	7,499	8,440	8,934	9,273	9,761	10,185	10,663	11,602	11,366	11,368	11,424	11,754
Mississippi	501	1,664	3,094	5,356	6,186	6,601	6,994	7,699	7,988	8,448	8,610	8,670	8,436	8,623	8,685
Missouri	709	1,936	4,507	6,764	8,002	8,022	8,360	8,834	9,266	10,007	10,341	10,468	10,348	10,370	10,555
Montana	782	2,476	4,736	6,990	8,391	8,771	9,108	9,653	10,244	10,541	10,881	11,463	11,599	11,290	11,493
Nebraska	736	2,150	4,842	7,360	8,550	9,270	9,638	10,170	10,711	11,217	11,457	11,920	12,324	12,114	12,374
Nevada	769	2,088	4,117	6,148	6,496	6,780	7,198	7,720	8,372	8,891	8,865	8,869	9,035	8,677	8,525
New Hampshire	723	1,916	5,304	7,082	8,900	9,391	10,043	10,698	11,347	12,280	12,912	13,424	13,964	14,215	14,463
New Jersey	1,016	3,191	8,139	10,903	13,093	13,776	14,666	15,362	16,650	18,174	17,466	18,060	17,654	18,197	19,020
New Mexico	707	2,034	3,515	5,835	7,126	7,653	7,933	8,426	8,876	9,377	9,727	9,716	9,356	9,069	9,230
New York	1,327	3,462	8,062	10,957	13,211	13,926	15,054	16,095	17,182	18,423	19,373	19,965	20,517	20,881	21,172
North Carolina	612	1,754	4,290	6,505	7,057	7,114	7,628	7,940	8,373	8,415	9,167	8,930	8,943	8,828	9,041
North Dakota	690	1,920	4,189	6,078	7,315	7,791	8,776	9,239	9,203	9,637	10,113	10,976	11,356	11,643	12,090
Ohio	730	2,075	5,045	7,816	9,427	9,799	9,984	10,306	10,792	11,374	11,905	12,307	12,484	12,271	12,284
Oklahoma	604	1,926	3,508	5,770	6,540	6,599	7,086	7,449	7,968	8,270	8,423	8,511	8,165	8,281	8,450
Oregon	925	2,692	5,474	8,129	8,514	8,640	8,799	9,294	9,762	10,487	10,673	10,476	10,497	10,386	10,370
Pennsylvania	882	2,535	6,228	8,380	9,648	10,393	11,014	11,530	11,995	12,493	12,989	13,678	14,072	13,973	14,378
Rhode Island	891	2,601	6,368	9,646	11,377	12,279	12,685	13,917	14,674	15,843	16,211	16,243	16,346	16,498	15,208
South Carolina	613	1,752	4,082	6,545	7,759	7,893	8,302	8,795	9,226	9,823	10,007	9,887	9,735	9,823	10,200
South Dakota	690	1,908	3,731	6,037	7,192	7,607	7,960	8,273	8,506	9,047	9,457	9,683	9,431	9,095	9,138
Tennessee	566	1,635	3,664	5,837	6,674	7,047	7,426	7,580	7,843	8,459	8,676	8,810	9,146	9,235	9,370
Texas	624	1,916	4,150	6,771	7,714	7,711	7,814	8,085	8,484	9,029	9,260	9,528	9,418	8,862	8,926
Utah	626	1,657	2,764	4,692	5,247	5,427	5,654	5,809	6,116	6,841	7,081	6,877	6,851	6,787	6,950
Vermont	807	1,997	6,227	8,799	10,903	11,675	12,579	13,377	14,219	15,089	16,073	16,586	16,661	17,575	18,372
Virginia	708	1,970	4,672	6,491	8,300	8,761	9,441	10,046	10,913	11,410	11,696	11,383	11,123	11,385	11,748
Washington	915	2,568	4,702	6,914	7,882	8,051	8,362	8,702	9,233	9,846	10,423	10,242	10,402	10,413	10,553
West Virginia	670	1,920	4,360	7,637	9,025	9,076	9,321	9,756	10,080	10,605	11,122	12,378	12,505	11,982	11,658
Wisconsin	883	2,477	5,524	8,299	9,538	9,834	10,141	10,484	10,813	11,370	11,773	12,194	12,515	11,750	11,768
Wyoming	856	2,527	5,577	7,944	9,906	10,351	11,087	12,415	14,219	14,936	15,658	16,535	17,126	17,228	17,135
Other jurisdictions															
American Samoa	—	—	1,908	2,807	3,121	3,671	3,801	3,842	3,909	4,309	4,468	4,881	4,877	5,154	4,870
Guam	820	—	4,234	—	—	6,449	—	7,095	7,450	8,084	8,264	8,393	9,280	10,112	9,431
Northern Marianas	—	—	3,007	5,720	5,221	4,746	5,669	5,307	5,356	5,162	6,397	6,284	8,495	7,068	6,381
Puerto Rico	—	—	1,750	3,859	4,743	4,534	5,304	5,897	6,152	6,937	7,329	7,426	8,560	7,798	8,209
U.S. Virgin Islands	—	—	6,767	7,238	7,747	8,077	8,698	9,637	10,548	12,358	12,768	14,215	13,014	11,669	10,661

See notes at end of table.

Table 236.70. Current expenditure per pupil in average daily attendance in public elementary and secondary schools, by state or jurisdiction: Selected years, 1969–70 through 2012–13—Continued

State or jurisdiction	Constant 2014–15 dollars[2]														
	1969–70	1979–80	1989–90	1999–2000	2002–03	2003–04	2004–05	2005–06	2006–07	2007–08	2008–09	2009–10	2010–11	2011–12	2012–13
1	17	18	19	20	21	22	23	24	25	26	27	28	29	30	31
United States	**$5,112**	**$6,926**	**$9,282**	**$10,337**	**$11,190**	**$11,319**	**$11,502**	**$11,630**	**$11,983**	**$12,278**	**$12,391**	**$12,478**	**$12,240**	**$11,817**	**$11,768**
Alabama	3,408	4,914	6,202	8,051	8,632	8,664	9,024	9,491	10,136	10,447	10,348	10,433	9,951	9,285	9,705
Alaska	7,033	14,413	15,715	13,516	13,997	14,085	14,632	14,911	15,661	17,890	18,547	18,946	19,646	19,900	20,442
Arizona	4,512	6,008	7,555	7,659	8,817	8,786	8,912	9,083	9,319	9,648	9,628	9,562	9,255	8,554	8,581
Arkansas	3,556	4,800	6,496	7,868	9,073	9,293	10,178	10,405	10,611	10,576	10,641	11,179	11,060	10,813	10,080
California	5,433	6,913	8,184	8,948	9,879	9,803	9,863	10,010	10,469	10,814	10,407	10,571	10,213	9,992	9,909
Colorado	4,623	7,380	8,799	9,369	10,171	10,703	10,566	10,631	10,562	11,154	10,596	10,644	10,394	9,792	9,793
Connecticut	5,960	7,378	14,608	14,151	14,688	14,950	15,625	16,010	16,397	16,841	17,465	17,617	18,126	18,172	18,270
Delaware	5,639	8,722	10,809	12,315	13,331	14,053	14,532	14,665	14,623	14,298	14,061	14,118	14,161	14,823	14,454
District of Columbia	6,380	9,936	16,691	16,685	19,150	19,604	18,612	21,262	21,200	23,261	21,793	23,241	22,806	21,216	20,907
Florida	4,588	5,759	9,315	8,924	8,996	9,245	9,545	9,963	10,499	10,857	10,422	10,225	10,056	9,179	9,131
Georgia	3,684	4,955	7,968	9,651	10,797	10,529	10,590	10,899	11,147	11,474	11,222	10,762	10,252	9,872	9,654
Hawaii	5,266	7,078	8,292	9,912	11,398	11,880	11,982	12,782	14,335	14,281	14,771	14,072	13,492	13,245	12,823
Idaho	3,780	5,058	5,737	7,891	8,388	8,341	8,270	8,161	8,201	8,276	8,343	8,170	7,659	7,323	7,440
Illinois	5,698	7,886	9,539	11,302	12,098	12,349	12,372	12,230	12,540	12,996	13,770	14,287	14,109	13,998	14,126
Indiana	4,561	5,739	8,586	10,698	11,154	11,489	11,902	11,368	11,277	10,698	10,966	11,095	10,624	10,630	10,268
Iowa	5,289	7,092	8,300	9,681	10,324	10,196	10,299	10,062	10,189	10,204	11,557	11,492	11,310	11,179	11,166
Kansas	4,831	6,625	8,857	9,733	10,882	11,197	11,157	11,781	11,918	12,370	12,664	11,858	11,454	11,141	11,037
Kentucky	3,416	5,186	6,981	9,485	10,044	10,144	10,345	10,674	10,786	11,113	11,085	11,331	11,207	11,129	10,506
Louisiana	4,060	5,463	7,276	8,746	9,737	9,979	10,233	10,191	11,189	12,070	12,580	12,549	12,311	11,806	11,376
Maine	4,339	5,559	10,015	11,529	13,145	13,360	13,770	13,987	14,641	14,731	14,949	15,386	15,421	14,561	14,632
Maryland	5,754	7,920	11,697	11,566	12,738	12,896	13,322	13,938	14,881	15,788	16,111	16,312	15,925	15,336	15,356
Massachusetts	5,382	8,595	11,626	13,107	14,506	14,731	15,073	15,021	15,377	16,069	16,813	15,979	16,415	16,232	16,482
Michigan	5,664	8,050	10,338	12,423	12,797	12,780	12,751	12,605	12,674	12,471	12,672	12,734	12,375	11,921	11,759
Minnesota	5,661	7,277	9,265	10,484	10,969	11,363	11,449	11,609	11,808	11,921	12,792	12,412	12,170	11,882	12,025
Mississippi	3,138	5,072	5,766	7,487	8,040	8,396	8,635	9,157	9,261	9,445	9,493	9,467	9,031	8,969	8,885
Missouri	4,439	5,903	8,401	9,457	10,400	10,202	10,322	10,507	10,743	11,187	11,402	11,431	11,077	10,785	10,798
Montana	4,899	7,550	8,829	9,772	10,905	11,155	11,246	11,481	11,876	11,784	11,997	12,518	12,416	11,742	11,757
Nebraska	4,614	6,554	9,025	10,289	11,112	11,790	11,900	12,096	12,419	12,540	12,632	13,017	13,193	12,599	12,659
Nevada	4,821	6,366	7,674	8,595	8,443	8,623	8,887	9,182	9,707	9,940	9,774	9,686	9,672	9,024	8,721
New Hampshire	4,530	5,841	9,886	9,902	11,567	11,943	12,400	12,724	13,155	13,729	14,237	14,659	14,948	14,784	14,796
New Jersey	6,367	9,729	15,171	15,242	17,016	17,521	18,108	18,271	19,303	20,318	19,258	19,721	18,899	18,926	19,458
New Mexico	4,430	6,200	6,551	8,157	9,261	9,733	9,794	10,022	10,290	10,483	10,725	10,610	10,016	9,432	9,443
New York	8,313	10,555	15,026	15,318	17,170	17,711	18,587	19,143	19,920	20,597	21,360	21,802	21,963	21,717	21,660
North Carolina	3,837	5,348	7,997	9,094	9,172	9,048	9,418	9,444	9,708	9,408	10,108	9,752	9,574	9,182	9,249
North Dakota	4,321	5,854	7,809	8,497	9,507	9,908	10,835	10,989	10,670	10,774	11,150	11,986	12,157	12,110	12,368
Ohio	4,574	6,325	9,403	10,928	12,252	12,462	12,327	12,257	12,512	12,716	13,126	13,439	13,364	12,762	12,567
Oklahoma	3,787	5,873	6,538	8,066	8,499	8,393	8,749	8,860	9,239	9,246	9,287	9,295	8,741	8,613	8,644
Oregon	5,794	8,207	10,204	11,364	11,065	10,988	10,864	11,054	11,318	11,724	11,768	11,439	11,237	10,802	10,609
Pennsylvania	5,524	7,727	11,609	11,716	12,539	13,219	13,599	13,714	13,907	13,967	14,322	14,937	15,064	14,533	14,709
Rhode Island	5,584	7,930	11,869	13,486	14,787	15,616	15,662	16,552	17,013	17,712	17,874	17,738	17,498	17,158	15,558
South Carolina	3,838	5,341	7,608	9,151	10,084	10,038	10,250	10,461	10,697	10,982	11,033	10,796	10,422	10,216	10,435
South Dakota	4,322	5,816	6,955	8,440	9,347	9,674	9,828	9,840	9,862	10,114	10,427	10,574	10,096	9,460	9,348
Tennessee	3,547	4,986	6,829	8,161	8,673	8,962	9,169	9,016	9,093	9,457	9,566	9,620	9,790	9,605	9,586
Texas	3,911	5,840	7,736	9,467	10,026	9,808	9,648	9,617	9,836	10,094	10,210	10,405	10,083	9,217	9,132
Utah	3,924	5,051	5,151	6,560	6,820	6,902	6,981	6,910	7,091	7,648	7,807	7,509	7,334	7,059	7,110
Vermont	5,057	6,088	11,606	12,302	14,170	14,849	15,531	15,910	16,486	16,869	17,722	18,112	17,836	18,279	18,795
Virginia	4,435	6,006	8,708	9,075	10,787	11,142	11,657	11,949	12,652	12,757	12,896	12,430	11,907	11,841	12,018
Washington	5,735	7,829	8,765	9,665	10,244	10,240	10,325	10,351	10,705	11,007	11,492	11,184	11,136	10,830	10,796
West Virginia	4,197	5,854	8,128	10,676	11,730	11,544	11,508	11,604	11,687	11,856	12,262	13,517	13,387	12,461	11,926
Wisconsin	5,530	7,551	10,296	11,602	12,396	12,507	12,521	12,469	12,537	12,711	12,981	13,316	13,398	12,221	12,039
Wyoming	5,363	7,703	10,396	11,106	12,875	13,164	13,689	14,766	16,485	16,698	17,264	18,056	18,334	17,918	17,529
Other jurisdictions															
American Samoa	—	—	3,556	3,925	4,056	4,669	4,693	4,569	4,532	4,817	4,926	5,330	5,221	5,361	4,982
Guam	5,136	—	7,893	—	—	8,202	—	8,438	8,637	9,038	9,112	9,165	9,935	10,517	9,648
Northern Marianas	—	—	5,605	7,997	6,785	6,036	7,000	6,312	6,210	5,771	7,053	6,862	9,094	7,351	6,528
Puerto Rico	—	—	3,262	5,395	6,164	5,766	6,548	7,014	7,132	7,756	8,081	8,109	9,164	8,110	8,398
U.S. Virgin Islands	—	—	12,614	10,119	10,069	10,273	10,740	11,462	12,229	13,816	14,078	15,523	13,932	12,136	10,906

—Not available.

[1]Unadjusted (or "current") dollars have not been adjusted to compensate for inflation.

[2]Constant dollars based on the Consumer Price Index (CPI), prepared by the Bureau of Labor Statistics, U.S. Department of Labor, adjusted to a school-year basis. The CPI does not account for differences in inflation rates from state to state.

NOTE: Current expenditures include instruction, support services, food services, and enterprise operations. Expenditures for state administration are excluded in all years except 1969–70 and 1979–80. Beginning in 1989–90, extensive changes were made in the data collection procedures. There are discrepancies in average daily attendance reporting practices from state to state. Some data have been revised from previously published figures.

SOURCE: U.S. Department of Education, National Center for Education Statistics, *Statistics of State School Systems*, 1969–70; *Revenues and Expenditures for Public Elementary and Secondary Education*, 1979–80; and Common Core of Data (CCD), "National Public Education Financial Survey," 1989–90 through 2012–13. (This table was prepared September 2015.)

Table 236.75. Total and current expenditures per pupil in fall enrollment in public elementary and secondary education, by function and state or jurisdiction: 2012–13

State or jurisdiction	Current expenditures, capital expenditures, and interest on school debt per pupil														
		Current expenditures													
				Support services											
	Total[1]	Total	Instruction	Total	Student support[4]	Instructional staff[5]	General administration	School administration	Operation and maintenance	Student transportation	Other support services	Food services	Enterprise operations[3]	Capital outlay[2]	Interest on school debt
1	2	3	4	5	6	7	8	9	10	11	12	13	14	15	16
United States	**$12,020**	**$10,763**	**$6,543**	**$3,759**	**$600**	**$501**	**$217**	**$593**	**$1,018**	**$467**	**$363**	**$439**	**$22**	**$910**	**$347**
Alabama	9,824	8,773	5,039	3,121	504	400	199	539	832	457	191	612	0	867	184
Alaska	20,397	18,217	10,115	7,525	1,521	1,260	259	1,113	2,149	556	667	509	68	1,891	288
Arizona	8,546	7,495	4,081	3,026	541	387	128	399	929	332	311	386	2	837	215
Arkansas	10,908	9,538	5,361	3,602	490	805	232	487	930	377	282	564	11	1,109	260
California	10,617	9,258	5,527	3,313	499	541	97	613	939	218	406	395	24	970	389
Colorado	10,092	8,693	5,038	3,292	425	470	141	606	803	263	583	319	44	883	516
Connecticut	18,797	17,321	10,965	5,798	1,092	516	362	1,008	1,533	886	401	412	146	1,242	235
Delaware	15,090	13,653	8,477	4,713	593	257	186	733	1,460	726	759	462	0	1,256	182
District of Columbia	26,670	20,530	11,229	8,103	790	1,046	1,152	1,598	1,754	1,318	444	1,148	50	5,645	495
Florida	9,403	8,623	5,286	2,912	372	535	77	479	882	351	217	425	0	524	256
Georgia	10,218	9,121	5,656	2,933	424	469	116	556	675	421	271	506	27	959	138
Hawaii	12,536	11,743	6,918	4,124	1,086	452	63	732	1,125	373	294	700	0	793	0
Idaho	7,455	6,761	4,071	2,322	379	286	156	381	615	331	174	366	1	504	190
Illinois	13,880	12,443	7,511	4,548	836	498	502	632	1,068	581	430	385	0	1,007	429
Indiana	10,605	9,421	5,478	3,498	461	364	239	574	1,043	583	236	445	0	864	320
Iowa	12,110	10,291	6,317	3,491	584	494	259	590	877	383	304	473	9	1,580	238
Kansas	11,703	10,011	6,043	3,479	594	410	283	573	941	401	277	489	0	1,300	392
Kentucky	10,614	9,274	5,323	3,355	429	507	213	536	839	586	244	574	23	1,041	299
Louisiana	11,648	10,539	5,960	4,002	648	533	265	638	981	627	311	576	1	949	161
Maine	13,471	12,655	7,524	4,689	795	646	424	703	1,312	653	156	439	3	537	279
Maryland	15,423	14,086	8,756	4,939	633	755	115	977	1,276	773	412	390	0	1,145	192
Massachusetts	16,483	15,321	9,871	5,032	1,092	682	241	643	1,349	652	373	418	0	910	253
Michigan	11,810	10,515	6,079	4,043	804	515	221	580	951	441	531	393	0	736	559
Minnesota	12,746	11,065	7,228	3,318	296	482	349	442	797	628	324	486	32	1,234	446
Mississippi	8,637	8,117	4,620	2,986	400	407	259	482	834	410	193	510	1	403	117
Missouri	10,975	9,702	5,753	3,488	455	424	325	566	971	508	238	462	0	924	349
Montana	11,577	10,662	6,353	3,838	680	408	330	586	1,056	525	251	455	16	801	113
Nebraska	13,068	11,743	7,470	3,487	511	383	372	548	981	367	325	487	298	984	341
Nevada	8,997	8,026	4,613	3,092	430	482	103	590	846	342	300	320	1	498	472
New Hampshire	14,663	14,050	9,023	4,653	1,050	434	471	769	1,158	614	158	373	0	383	230
New Jersey	19,639	18,523	11,106	6,828	1,851	594	369	874	1,802	918	419	403	186	667	449
New Mexico	10,410	9,164	5,262	3,459	928	248	199	549	950	305	280	437	6	1,246	0
New York	20,636	19,529	13,540	5,589	667	496	374	764	1,709	1,019	560	401	0	696	410
North Carolina	8,745	8,342	5,174	2,694	395	293	130	528	717	369	263	473	0	398	6
North Dakota	14,022	11,615	6,718	3,932	497	419	520	592	1,082	509	313	616	348	2,218	190
Ohio	12,807	11,276	6,438	4,449	729	696	340	616	991	548	529	389	1	1,151	380
Oklahoma	8,813	7,914	4,378	2,945	529	344	261	431	856	272	253	510	81	828	71
Oregon	10,375	9,183	5,321	3,516	655	336	121	591	763	445	605	342	4	584	607
Pennsylvania	14,934	13,445	8,276	4,652	716	462	403	610	1,301	674	486	455	62	919	569
Rhode Island	15,476	14,889	9,204	5,290	1,553	488	210	703	1,163	611	561	390	5	262	325
South Carolina	11,091	9,444	5,333	3,580	707	564	97	591	909	387	324	505	26	1,149	499
South Dakota	10,225	8,630	5,057	3,054	472	344	288	421	888	321	320	479	39	1,380	215
Tennessee	9,336	8,588	5,291	2,827	362	547	203	505	724	324	162	470	0	548	201
Texas	9,923	8,261	4,873	2,899	405	416	126	475	906	243	329	488	0	1,077	585
Utah	7,905	6,432	4,068	1,981	242	256	62	408	617	207	187	357	26	1,248	224
Vermont	18,038	17,286	10,894	5,888	1,312	734	386	1,077	1,422	559	399	490	15	622	130
Virginia	11,959	10,960	6,674	3,852	543	703	170	643	1,031	588	173	432	2	865	134
Washington	11,456	9,714	5,630	3,633	650	588	175	572	870	400	377	334	118	1,367	374
West Virginia	11,536	11,257	6,539	4,047	554	459	218	606	1,160	853	197	671	0	205	74
Wisconsin	11,972	11,186	6,714	4,048	538	540	303	547	1,018	489	613	424	0	596	190
Wyoming	18,187	15,815	9,329	6,005	929	937	314	866	1,560	783	617	474	6	2,350	23
Other jurisdictions															
American Samoa	—	—	—	—	—	—	—	—	—	—	—	—	—	—	—
Guam	10,928	8,949	4,624	3,810	840	164	71	541	1,436	236	522	515	0	1,906	73
Northern Marianas	5,755	5,733	2,652	2,246	429	514	229	384	462	150	78	834	0	23	0
Puerto Rico	8,125	7,981	3,522	3,328	538	403	134	372	740	319	822	1,132	0	143	0
U.S. Virgin Islands	10,667	10,661	5,395	4,693	893	338	485	565	752	464	1,196	556	16	6	0

—Not available.

[1]Excludes "Other current expenditures," such as community services, private school programs, adult education, and other programs not allocable to expenditures per pupil in public schools.

[2]Includes expenditures for property and for buildings and alterations completed by school district staff or contractors.

[3]Includes expenditures for operations funded by sales of products or services (e.g., school bookstore or computer time).

[4]Includes expenditures for guidance, health, attendance, and speech pathology services.

[5]Includes expenditures for curriculum development, staff training, libraries, and media and computer centers.

NOTE: Excludes expenditures for state education agencies. "0" indicates none or less than $0.50. Detail may not sum to totals because of rounding.

SOURCE: U.S. Department of Education, National Center for Education Statistics, Common Core of Data (CCD), "National Public Education Financial Survey," 2012–13. (This table was prepared September 2015.)

Table 236.90. Students transported at public expense and current expenditures for transportation: Selected years, 1929–30 through 2012–13

School year	Average daily attendance, all students	Students transported at public expense: Number	Students transported at public expense: Percent of total	Expenditures for transportation (in unadjusted dollars)[1]: Total[3] (in thousands)	Expenditures for transportation (in unadjusted dollars)[1]: Average per student transported	Expenditures for transportation (in constant 2014–15 dollars)[2]: Total[3] (in thousands)	Expenditures for transportation (in constant 2014–15 dollars)[2]: Average per student transported
1	2	3	4	5	6	7	8
1929–30	21,265,000	1,902,826	8.9	$54,823	$29	$758,038	$398
1931–32	22,245,000	2,419,173	10.9	58,078	24	953,439	394
1933–34	22,458,000	2,794,724	12.4	53,908	19	963,509	345
1935–36	22,299,000	3,250,658	14.6	62,653	19	1,079,066	332
1937–38	22,298,000	3,769,242	16.9	75,637	20	1,249,671	332
1939–40	22,042,000	4,144,161	18.8	83,283	20	1,410,459	340
1941–42	21,031,000	4,503,081	21.4	92,922	21	1,410,499	313
1943–44	19,603,000	4,512,412	23.0	107,754	24	1,463,581	324
1945–46	19,849,000	5,056,966	25.5	129,756	26	1,683,492	333
1947–48	20,910,000	5,854,041	28.0	176,265	30	1,790,467	306
1949–50	22,284,000	6,947,384	31.2	214,504	31	2,143,654	309
1951–52	23,257,000	7,697,130	33.1	268,827	35	2,420,773	315
1953–54	25,643,871	8,411,719	32.8	307,437	37	2,705,759	322
1955–56	27,740,149	9,695,819	35.0	353,972	37	3,116,357	321
1957–58	29,722,275	10,861,689	36.5	416,491	38	3,451,707	318
1959–60	32,477,440	12,225,142	37.6	486,338	40	3,917,402	320
1961–62	34,682,340	13,222,667	38.1	576,361	44	4,538,272	343
1963–64	37,405,058	14,475,778	38.7	673,845	47	5,170,988	357
1965–66	39,154,497	15,536,567	39.7	787,358	51	5,840,213	376
1967–68	40,827,965	17,130,873	42.0	981,006	57	6,827,263	399
1969–70	41,934,376	18,198,577	43.4	1,218,557	67	7,634,796	420
1971–72	42,254,272	19,474,355	46.1	1,507,830	77	8,672,386	445
1973–74	41,438,054	21,347,039	51.5	1,858,141	87	9,432,262	442
1975–76	41,269,720	21,772,483	52.8	2,377,313	109	10,145,611	466
1977–78	40,079,590	21,800,000 [4]	54.4	2,731,041	125 [4]	10,320,032	473 [4]
1979–80	38,288,911	21,713,515	56.7	3,833,145	177	11,685,975	538
1980–81	37,703,744	22,272,000 [4]	59.1	4,408,000 [4]	198 [4]	12,043,547 [4]	541 [4]
1981–82	37,094,652	22,246,000 [4]	60.0	4,793,000 [4]	215 [4]	12,054,160 [4]	542 [4]
1982–83	36,635,868	22,199,000 [4]	60.6	5,000,000 [4]	225 [4]	12,056,903 [4]	543 [4]
1983–84	36,362,978	22,031,000 [4]	60.6	5,284,000 [4]	240 [4]	12,286,937 [4]	558 [4]
1984–85	36,404,261	22,320,000 [4]	61.3	5,722,000 [4]	256 [4]	12,804,238 [4]	574 [4]
1985–86	36,523,103	22,041,000 [4]	60.3	6,123,000 [4]	278 [4]	13,317,526 [4]	604 [4]
1986–87	36,863,867	22,397,000 [4]	60.8	6,551,000 [4]	292 [4]	13,938,948 [4]	622 [4]
1987–88	37,050,707	22,158,000 [4]	59.8	6,888,000 [4]	311 [4]	14,072,885 [4]	635 [4]
1988–89	37,268,072	22,635,000 [4]	60.7	7,550,000 [4]	334 [4]	14,744,466 [4]	651 [4]
1989–90	37,799,296	22,459,000 [4]	59.4	8,030,990	358 [4]	14,969,488	667 [4]
1990–91	38,426,543	22,000,000 [4]	57.3	8,678,954	394 [4]	15,338,672	697 [4]
1991–92	38,960,783	23,165,000 [4]	59.5	8,769,754	379 [4]	15,017,937	648 [4]
1992–93	39,570,462	23,439,000 [4]	59.2	9,252,300	395 [4]	15,364,369	656 [4]
1993–94	40,146,393	23,858,000 [4]	59.4	9,627,155	404 [4]	15,583,182	653 [4]
1994–95	40,720,763	23,693,000 [4]	58.2	9,889,034	417 [4]	15,561,053	657 [4]
1995–96	41,501,596	24,155,000 [4]	58.2	10,396,426	430 [4]	15,926,180	659 [4]
1996–97	42,262,004	24,090,000 [4]	57.0	10,989,809	456 [4]	16,368,182	679 [4]
1997–98	42,765,774	24,342,000 [4]	56.9	11,465,658	471 [4]	16,777,693	689 [4]
1998–99	43,186,715	24,898,000 [4]		12,224,454	491 [4]	17,583,639	706 [4]
1999–2000	43,806,726	24,951,000 [4]	57.0	13,007,625	521 [4]	18,185,182	729 [4]
2000–01	44,075,930	24,471,000 [4]	55.5	14,052,654	574 [4]	18,995,386	776 [4]
2001–02	44,604,592	24,529,000 [5]	55.0	14,799,365	603 [5]	19,656,715	801 [5]
2002–03	45,017,360	24,621,000 [5]	54.7	15,648,821	636 [5]	20,338,019	826 [5]
2003–04	45,325,731	25,159,000 [5]	55.5	16,348,784	650 [5]	20,792,839	826 [5]
2004–05	45,625,458	25,318,000 [5]	55.5	17,459,659	690 [5]	21,556,975	851 [5]
2005–06	45,931,617	25,252,000 [5]	55.0	18,850,234	746 [5]	22,420,081	888 [5]
2006–07	46,132,663	25,285,000 [5]	54.8	19,979,068	790 [5]	23,163,673	916 [5]
2007–08	46,155,880	25,221,000 [5]	54.6	21,536,978	854 [4]	24,077,748	955 [4]
2008–09	46,173,477	—	—	21,679,876	860 [4]	23,903,735	948 [4]
2009–10	45,919,206	—	—	21,819,304	870 [4]	23,826,919	950 [4]
2010–11	46,118,737	—	—	22,370,807	888 [4]	24,429,167	970 [4]
2011–12	46,400,465	—	—	22,926,700	905 [4]	24,543,381	969 [4]
2012–13	46,567,834	—	—	23,233,698	914 [4]	24,164,005	950 [4]

—Not available.
[1]Unadjusted (or "current") dollars have not been adjusted to compensate for inflation.
[2]Constant dollars based on the Consumer Price Index, prepared by the Bureau of Labor Statistics, U.S. Department of Labor, adjusted to a school-year basis.
[3]Excludes capital outlay for years through 1979–80, and 1989–90 to the latest year. From 1980–81 to 1988–89, total transportation figures include capital outlay.
[4]Estimate based on data appearing in January issues of *School Bus Fleet*.
[5]Estimate based on data reported by *School Transportation News*.
NOTE: Some data have been revised from previously published figures.

SOURCE: U.S. Department of Education, National Center for Education Statistics, *Statistics of State School Systems*, 1929–30 through 1975–76; *Revenues and Expenditures for Public Elementary and Secondary Education*, 1977–78 and 1979–80; Common Core of Data (CCD), "National Public Education Financial Survey," 1987–88 through 2012–13; Bobit Publishing Co., *School Bus Fleet*, "School Transportation: 2000–2001 School Year" and "2010 Fact Book"; *School Transportation News*, "K–12 Enrollment/Transportation Data," 2001–02 through 2007–08; and unpublished data. (This table was prepared September 2015.)

Table 228.10. School-associated violent deaths of all persons, homicides and suicides of youth ages 5–18 at school, and total homicides and suicides of youth ages 5–18, by type of violent death: 1992–93 to 2012–13

Year	School-associated violent deaths[1] of all persons (includes students, staff, and other nonstudents)					Homicides of youth ages 5–18		Suicides of youth ages 5–18	
	Total	Homicides	Suicides	Legal interventions	Unintentional firearm-related deaths	Homicides at school[2]	Total homicides	Suicides at school[2]	Total suicides[3]
1	2	3	4	5	6	7	8	9	10
1992–93	57	47	10	0	0	34	2,721	6	1,680
1993–94	48	38	10	0	0	29	2,932	7	1,723
1994–95	48	39	8	0	1	28	2,696	7	1,767
1995–96	53	46	6	1	0	32	2,545	6	1,725
1996–97	48	45	2	1	0	28	2,221	1	1,633
1997–98	57	47	9	1	0	34	2,100	6	1,626
1998–99	47	38	6	2	1	33	1,777	4	1,597
1999–2000	37[4]	26[4]	11[4]	0[4]	0[4]	14[4]	1,567	8[4]	1,415
2000–01	34[4]	26[4]	7[4]	1[4]	0[4]	14[4]	1,509	6[4]	1,493
2001–02	36[4]	27[4]	8[4]	1[4]	0[4]	16[4]	1,498	5[4]	1,400
2002–03	36[4]	25[4]	11[4]	0[4]	0[4]	18[4]	1,553	10[4]	1,331
2003–04	45[4]	37[4]	7[4]	1[4]	0[4]	23[4]	1,474	5[4]	1,285
2004–05	52[4]	40[4]	10[4]	2[4]	0[4]	22[4]	1,554	8[4]	1,471
2005–06	44[4]	37[4]	6[4]	1[4]	0[4]	21[4]	1,697	3[4]	1,408
2006–07	63[4]	48[4]	13[4]	2[4]	0[4]	32[4]	1,801	9[4]	1,296
2007–08	48[4]	39[4]	7[4]	2[4]	0[4]	21[4]	1,744	5[4]	1,231
2008–09	44[4]	29[4]	15[4]	0[4]	0[4]	18[4]	1,605	7[4]	1,344
2009–10	35[4]	27[4]	5[4]	3[4]	0[4]	19[4]	1,410	2[4]	1,467
2010–11	32[4]	26[4]	6[4]	0[4]	0[4]	11[4]	1,339	3[4]	1,456
2011–12	45[4]	26[4]	14[4]	5[4]	0[4]	15[4]	1,201	5[4]	1,568
2012–13	53[4]	41[4]	11[4]	1[4]	0[4]	31[4]	1,186	6[4]	1,590

[1]A school-associated violent death is defined as "a homicide, suicide, or legal intervention (involving a law enforcement officer), in which the fatal injury occurred on the campus of a functioning elementary or secondary school in the United States," while the victim was on the way to or from regular sessions at school, or while the victim was attending or traveling to or from an official school-sponsored event.

[2]"At school" includes on school property, on the way to or from regular sessions at school, and while attending or traveling to or from a school-sponsored event.

[3]Total youth suicides are reported for calendar years 1992 through 2012 (instead of school years 1992–93 through 2012–13).

[4]Data from 1999–2000 onward are subject to change until interviews with school and law enforcement officials have been completed. The details learned during the interviews can occasionally change the classification of a case.

NOTE: Unless otherwise noted, data are reported for the school year, defined as July 1 through June 30. Some data have been revised from previously published figures.

SOURCE: Centers for Disease Control and Prevention (CDC), 1992–2013 School-Associated Violent Deaths Surveillance Study (SAVD) (partially funded by the U.S. Department of Education, Office of Safe and Healthy Students), previously unpublished tabulation (September 2015); CDC, National Center for Injury Prevention and Control, Web-based Injury Statistics Query and Reporting System Fatal (WISQARS™ Fatal), 1999–2012, retrieved September 2015 from http://www.cdc.gov/injury/wisqars/index.html; and Federal Bureau of Investigation and Bureau of Justice Statistics, Supplementary Homicide Reports (SHR), preliminary data (November 2015). (This table was prepared December 2015.)

Table 228.20. Number of nonfatal victimizations against students ages 12–18 and rate of victimization per 1,000 students, by type of victimization, location, and year: 1992 through 2014

[Standard errors appear in parentheses]

Location and year	Number of nonfatal victimizations				Rate of victimization per 1,000 students			
			Violent				Violent	
	Total	Theft	All violent	Serious violent[1]	Total	Theft	All violent	Serious violent[1]
1	2	3	4	5	6	7	8	9
At school[2]								
1992	4,281,200 (225,600)	2,679,400 (147,660)	1,601,800 (121,630)	197,600 (35,430)	181.5 (7.99)	113.6 (5.64)	67.9 (4.77)	8.4 (1.48)
1993	4,692,800 (321,220)	2,477,100 (121,200)	2,215,700 (194,520)	535,500 (76,050)	193.5 (11.02)	102.1 (4.61)	91.4 (7.23)	22.1 (3.02)
1994	4,721,000 (271,730)	2,474,100 (121,260)	2,246,900 (165,530)	459,100 (58,110)	187.7 (9.04)	98.4 (4.46)	89.3 (5.95)	18.3 (2.24)
1995	4,400,700 (267,610)	2,468,400 (120,690)	1,932,200 (152,670)	294,500 (42,890)	172.2 (8.82)	96.6 (4.37)	75.6 (5.44)	11.5 (1.64)
1996	4,130,400 (281,640)	2,205,200 (107,650)	1,925,300 (166,690)	371,900 (54,150)	158.4 (9.17)	84.5 (3.88)	73.8 (5.81)	14.3 (2.01)
1997	3,610,900 (282,430)	1,975,000 (111,830)	1,635,900 (164,530)	376,200 (60,990)	136.6 (9.25)	74.7 (3.95)	61.9 (5.74)	14.2 (2.24)
1998	3,247,300 (254,250)	1,635,100 (104,210)	1,612,200 (155,840)	314,500 (49,770)	121.3 (8.27)	61.1 (3.69)	60.2 (5.34)	11.7 (1.80)
1999	3,152,400 (258,560)	1,752,200 (104,970)	1,400,200 (148,230)	281,100 (50,060)	117.0 (8.43)	65.1 (3.69)	52.0 (5.11)	10.4 (1.81)
2000	2,301,000 (211,140)	1,331,500 (95,940)	969,500 (115,680)	214,200 (40,980)	84.9 (7.00)	49.1 (3.34)	35.8 (4.02)	7.9 (1.48)
2001	2,521,300 (202,890)	1,348,500 (93,240)	1,172,700 (120,560)	259,400 (44,110)	92.3 (6.67)	49.4 (3.23)	42.9 (4.14)	9.5 (1.58)
2002	2,082,600 (212,520)	1,088,800 (77,110)	993,800 (126,210)	173,500 (37,300)	75.4 (6.96)	39.4 (2.69)	36.0 (4.29)	6.3 (1.32)
2003	2,308,800 (210,930)	1,270,500 (88,550)	1,038,300 (121,490)	188,400 (38,240)	87.4 (7.16)	48.1 (3.18)	39.3 (4.32)	7.1 (1.42)
2004	1,762,200 (154,390)	1,065,400 (75,160)	696,800 (83,090)	107,300 (25,110)	67.2 (5.40)	40.6 (2.76)	26.6 (3.03)	4.1 (0.95)
2005	1,678,600 (169,040)	875,900 (70,140)	802,600 (102,360)	140,300 (32,400)	63.2 (5.85)	33.0 (2.56)	30.2 (3.66)	5.3 (1.20)
2006[3]	1,799,900 (170,490)	859,000 (68,730)	940,900 (109,880)	249,900 (45,670)	67.5 (5.86)	32.2 (2.52)	35.3 (3.90)	9.4 (1.68)
2007	1,801,200 (188,450)	896,700 (66,230)	904,400 (114,320)	116,100 (25,430)	67.8 (6.40)	33.7 (2.41)	34.0 (4.02)	4.4 (0.94)
2008	1,435,500 (161,330)	648,000 (61,170)	787,500 (108,480)	128,700 (34,370)	54.3 (5.67)	24.5 (2.26)	29.8 (3.91)	4.9 (1.28)
2009	1,322,800 (168,370)	594,500 (54,480)	728,300 (111,550)	233,700 (51,610)	51.0 (6.00)	22.9 (2.05)	28.1 (4.08)	9.0 (1.94)
2010	892,000 (124,260)	469,800 (45,300)	422,300 (73,310)	155,000 (36,500)	34.9 (4.55)	18.4 (1.75)	16.5 (2.75)	6.1 (1.40)
2011	1,246,200 (139,940)	647,700 (61,500)	598,600 (84,090)	89,500 (23,360)	49.3 (5.11)	25.6 (2.36)	23.7 (3.16)	3.5 (0.91)
2012	1,364,900 (133,810)	615,600 (51,440)	749,200 (90,250)	89,000 (23,850)	52.4 (4.78)	23.6 (1.93)	28.8 (3.31)	3.4 (0.91)
2013	1,420,900 (176,390)	454,900 (43,390)	966,000 (134,140)	125,500 (32,110)	55.0 (6.24)	17.6 (1.65)	37.4 (4.84)	4.9 (1.22)
2014	850,100 (109,100)	363,700 (39,120)	486,400 (74,790)	93,800 (25,550)	33.0 (4.00)	14.1 (1.50)	18.9 (2.79)	3.6 (0.98)
Away from school								
1992	4,084,100 (218,910)	1,857,600 (118,610)	2,226,500 (149,210)	1,025,100 (92,600)	173.1 (7.81)	78.7 (4.66)	94.4 (5.70)	43.5 (3.72)
1993	3,835,900 (280,790)	1,731,100 (96,700)	2,104,800 (187,960)	1,004,300 (114,870)	158.2 (9.90)	71.4 (3.75)	86.8 (7.01)	41.4 (4.47)
1994	4,147,100 (249,260)	1,713,900 (96,250)	2,433,200 (174,580)	1,074,900 (101,370)	164.9 (8.44)	68.1 (3.61)	96.7 (6.24)	42.7 (3.80)
1995	3,626,600 (234,640)	1,604,800 (92,000)	2,021,800 (157,470)	829,700 (85,830)	141.9 (7.91)	62.8 (3.41)	79.1 (5.59)	32.5 (3.19)
1996	3,483,200 (250,620)	1,572,700 (87,830)	1,910,600 (165,810)	870,000 (96,510)	133.5 (8.32)	60.3 (3.22)	73.3 (5.79)	33.4 (3.50)
1997	3,717,600 (288,080)	1,710,700 (101,810)	2,006,900 (189,180)	853,300 (105,660)	140.7 (9.41)	64.7 (3.62)	75.9 (6.51)	32.3 (3.79)
1998	3,047,800 (243,270)	1,408,000 (94,900)	1,639,800 (157,700)	684,900 (85,520)	113.8 (7.96)	52.6 (3.38)	61.3 (5.40)	25.6 (3.04)
1999	2,713,800 (233,350)	1,129,200 (79,770)	1,584,500 (161,350)	675,400 (90,150)	100.8 (7.71)	41.9 (2.85)	58.8 (5.53)	25.1 (3.20)
2000	2,303,600 (211,310)	1,228,900 (90,770)	1,074,800 (124,280)	402,100 (62,950)	85.0 (7.01)	45.3 (3.17)	39.6 (4.30)	14.8 (2.24)
2001	1,780,300 (160,090)	961,400 (74,230)	819,000 (94,590)	314,800 (50,070)	65.2 (5.39)	35.2 (2.60)	30.0 (3.30)	11.5 (1.79)
2002	1,619,500 (178,050)	820,100 (64,530)	799,400 (108,260)	341,200 (59,590)	58.6 (5.92)	29.7 (2.27)	28.9 (3.71)	12.4 (2.09)
2003	1,824,100 (179,240)	780,900 (64,210)	1,043,200 (121,880)	412,800 (64,660)	69.1 (6.19)	29.6 (2.34)	39.5 (4.33)	15.6 (2.37)
2004	1,371,800 (130,480)	718,000 (59,070)	653,700 (79,660)	272,500 (45,080)	52.3 (4.63)	27.4 (2.19)	24.9 (2.91)	10.4 (1.68)
2005	1,429,000 (151,460)	637,700 (57,740)	791,300 (101,380)	257,100 (47,950)	53.8 (5.29)	24.0 (2.12)	29.8 (3.63)	9.7 (1.77)
2006[3]	1,413,100 (144,660)	714,200 (61,900)	698,900 (89,980)	263,600 (47,280)	53.0 (5.04)	26.8 (2.27)	26.2 (3.22)	9.9 (1.73)
2007	1,371,700 (154,740)	614,300 (52,740)	757,400 (100,440)	337,700 (55,630)	51.6 (5.34)	23.1 (1.94)	28.5 (3.55)	12.7 (2.01)
2008	1,132,600 (137,840)	498,500 (52,350)	634,100 (94,160)	258,600 (52,980)	42.8 (4.90)	18.9 (1.94)	24.0 (3.42)	9.8 (1.96)
2009	857,200 (124,770)	484,200 (48,320)	372,900 (70,660)	176,800 (42,890)	33.1 (4.54)	18.7 (1.83)	14.4 (2.63)	6.8 (1.62)
2010	689,900 (103,620)	378,800 (40,200)	311,200 (59,190)	167,300 (38,460)	27.0 (3.83)	14.8 (1.55)	12.2 (2.24)	6.5 (1.47)
2011	966,100 (117,200)	541,900 (55,160)	424,300 (66,350)	137,600 (31,000)	38.2 (4.33)	21.4 (2.13)	16.8 (2.52)	5.4 (1.20)
2012	991,200 (108,370)	470,800 (44,070)	520,400 (71,280)	169,900 (35,260)	38.0 (3.93)	18.1 (1.66)	20.0 (2.64)	6.5 (1.33)
2013	778,500 (115,110)	403,000 (40,470)	375,500 (68,800)	151,200 (36,490)	30.1 (4.19)	15.6 (1.54)	14.5 (2.56)	5.8 (1.38)
2014	621,300 (88,190)	288,900 (34,370)	332,400 (58,000)	165,000 (36,650)	24.1 (3.27)	11.2 (1.32)	12.9 (2.18)	6.4 (1.40)

[1]Serious violent victimization is also included in all violent victimization.

[2]"At school" includes inside the school building, on school property, and on the way to and from school.

[3]Due to methodological differences, use caution when comparing 2006 estimates to other years.

NOTE: "Serious violent victimization" includes the crimes of rape, sexual assault, robbery, and aggravated assault. "All violent victimization" includes serious violent crimes as well as simple assault. "Theft" includes attempted and completed purse-snatching, completed pickpocketing, and all attempted and completed thefts, with the exception of motor vehicle thefts. Theft does not include robbery, which involves the threat or use of force and is classified as a violent crime. "Total victimization" includes theft and violent crimes. Data in this table are from the National Crime Victimization Survey (NCVS); due to differences in time coverage and administration between the NCVS and the School Crime Supplement (SCS) to the NCVS, data in this table cannot be compared with data in tables that are based on the SCS. Detail may not sum to totals because of rounding.

SOURCE: U.S. Department of Justice, Bureau of Justice Statistics, National Crime Victimization Survey (NCVS), 1992 through 2014. (This table was prepared August 2015).

Table 228.25. Number of nonfatal victimizations against students ages 12–18 and rate of victimization per 1,000 students, by type of victimization, location, and selected student characteristics: 2014

[Standard errors appear in parentheses]

Location and student characteristic	Number of nonfatal victimizations: Total	Number: Theft	Number: Violent: All violent	Number: Violent: Serious violent[1]	Rate of victimization per 1,000 students: Total	Rate: Theft	Rate: Violent: All violent	Rate: Violent: Serious violent[1]
1	2	3	4	5	6	7	8	9
At school[2]								
Total	**850,100 (109,100)**	**363,700 (39,120)**	**486,400 (74,790)**	**93,800 (25,550)**	**33.0 (4.00)**	**14.1 (1.50)**	**18.9 (2.79)**	**3.6 (0.98)**
Sex								
Male	461,800 (72,230)	202,000 (28,180)	259,900 (49,290)	69,500 ! (21,170)	34.8 (5.12)	15.2 (2.09)	19.6 (3.57)	5.2 ! (1.57)
Female	388,300 (64,320)	161,800 (24,940)	226,600 (45,040)	24,300 ! (11,190)	31.0 (4.85)	12.9 (1.97)	18.1 (3.46)	1.9 ! (0.89)
Age								
12–14	421,200 (67,910)	182,600 (26,650)	238,700 (46,610)	18,700 ! (9,580)	33.9 (5.13)	14.7 (2.11)	19.2 (3.60)	1.5 ! (0.77)
15–18	428,900 (68,740)	181,200 (26,540)	247,700 (47,770)	75,100 (22,220)	32.2 (4.86)	13.6 (1.96)	18.6 (3.44)	5.6 (1.64)
Race/ethnicity[3]								
White	473,400 (73,440)	211,500 (28,900)	262,000 (49,550)	59,800 ! (19,280)	34.6 (5.04)	15.4 (2.08)	19.1 (3.47)	4.4 ! (1.39)
Black	111,300 (28,460)	51,600 (13,470)	59,700 (19,260)	10,800 ! (6,980)	27.6 (6.73)	12.8 (3.31)	14.8 (4.64)	2.7 ! (1.72)
Hispanic	102,600 (27,040)	48,200 (12,980)	54,500 (18,200)	13,700 ! (7,990)	17.3 (4.40)	8.1 (2.17)	9.2 (3.00)	2.3 ! (1.34)
Other	162,800 (36,330)	52,500 (13,600)	110,300 ! (28,300)	9,600 ! (6,520)	76.5 (15.41)	24.7 (6.27)	51.8 ! (12.34)	4.5 ! (3.03)
Urbanicity[4]								
Urban	245,800 (47,520)	121,100 (21,290)	124,800 (30,620)	31,300 ! (12,990)	32.5 (5.91)	16.0 (2.77)	16.5 (3.90)	4.1 ! (1.69)
Suburban	391,100 (64,630)	189,700 (27,220)	201,500 (41,720)	16,900 ! (9,050)	27.6 (4.33)	13.4 (1.90)	14.2 (2.85)	1.2 ! (0.64)
Rural	213,200 (43,290)	53,000 (13,660)	160,200 (35,950)	45,600 ! (16,330)	52.8 (9.88)	13.1 (3.34)	39.7 (8.34)	11.3 ! (3.95)
Household income								
Less than $15,000	125,800 (30,770)	41,400 (11,980)	84,400 ! (23,890)	8,400 ! (6,070)	66.9 (14.94)	22.0 (6.26)	44.9 ! (11.89)	4.5 ! (3.20)
$15,000–29,999	75,900 (22,360)	44,200 (12,410)	31,700 (13,100)	14,100 ! (8,120)	26.1 (7.36)	15.2 (4.22)	10.9 (4.41)	4.8 ! (2.77)
$30,000–49,999	156,500 (35,420)	61,200 (14,750)	95,300 (25,810)	10,700 ! (6,960)	35.6 (7.58)	13.9 (3.31)	21.7 (5.63)	2.4 ! (1.57)
$50,000–74,999	119,200 (29,740)	35,600 (11,070)	83,600 (23,760)	6,000 ! (5,020)	36.1 (8.48)	10.8 (3.32)	25.3 (6.88)	1.8 ! (1.51)
$75,000 or more	202,300 (41,830)	128,400 (21,990)	73,800 (21,980)	9,700 ! (6,570)	27.1 (5.33)	17.2 (2.90)	9.9 (2.88)	1.3 ! (0.88)
Not reported	170,500 (37,430)	52,900 (13,650)	117,600 (29,480)	44,800 ! (16,160)	29.2 (6.08)	9.1 (2.32)	20.1 (4.85)	7.7 ! (2.71)
Away from school								
Total	**621,300 (88,190)**	**288,900 (34,370)**	**332,400 (58,000)**	**165,000 (36,650)**	**24.1 (3.27)**	**11.2 (1.32)**	**12.9 (2.18)**	**6.4 (1.40)**
Sex								
Male	332,100 (57,970)	150,100 (23,930)	182,000 (39,060)	107,100 (27,780)	25.0 (4.16)	11.3 (1.78)	13.7 (2.85)	8.1 (2.05)
Female	289,200 (52,890)	138,800 (22,940)	150,300 (34,510)	57,900 (18,900)	23.1 (4.03)	11.1 (1.81)	12.0 (2.68)	4.6 (1.49)
Age								
12–14	269,400 (50,470)	116,800 (20,880)	152,600 (34,840)	69,600 (21,180)	21.7 (3.88)	9.4 (1.66)	12.3 (2.72)	5.6 (1.67)
15–18	351,900 (60,240)	172,100 (25,800)	179,800 (38,740)	95,400 (25,820)	26.4 (4.29)	12.9 (1.91)	13.5 (2.81)	7.2 (1.90)
Race/ethnicity[3]								
White	373,200 (62,640)	191,900 (27,400)	181,300 (38,950)	79,300 (22,990)	27.2 (4.34)	14.0 (1.97)	13.2 (2.76)	5.8 (1.65)
Black	103,300 (27,140)	36,600 (11,240)	66,600 (20,620)	32,500 ! (13,310)	25.7 (6.43)	9.1 (2.77)	16.6 (4.95)	8.1 ! (3.24)
Hispanic	100,600 (26,700)	37,000 (11,300)	63,600 (20,030)	42,900 (15,730)	17.0 (4.35)	6.2 (1.89)	10.7 (3.30)	7.2 (2.61)
Other	44,200 (16,020)	23,300 (8,870)	20,900 ! (10,230)	10,200 ! (6,780)	20.8 (7.26)	11.0 (4.13)	9.8 ! (4.71)	4.8 ! (3.15)
Urbanicity[4]								
Urban	193,300 (40,610)	95,400 (18,710)	97,900 (26,240)	37,600 ! (14,530)	25.5 (5.10)	12.6 (2.44)	12.9 (3.36)	5.0 ! (1.89)
Suburban	308,400 (55,180)	139,400 (22,990)	169,000 (37,210)	100,900 (26,750)	21.8 (3.73)	9.8 (1.61)	11.9 (2.55)	7.1 (1.85)
Rural	119,600 (29,810)	54,100 (13,810)	65,500 (20,410)	26,400 ! (11,760)	29.6 (7.00)	13.4 (3.38)	16.2 (4.89)	6.5 ! (2.87)
Household income								
Less than $15,000	85,800 (24,140)	20,800 ! (8,360)	64,900 (20,290)	22,900 ! (10,810)	45.6 (12.00)	11.1 ! (4.41)	34.5 (10.23)	12.2 ! (5.62)
$15,000–29,999	105,600 (27,520)	49,500 (13,180)	56,000 (18,520)	34,000 ! (13,670)	36.4 (8.94)	17.1 (4.48)	19.3 (6.15)	11.7 ! (4.60)
$30,000–49,999	93,000 (25,400)	40,200 (11,800)	52,800 (17,850)	23,400 ! (10,920)	21.1 (5.54)	9.1 (2.66)	12.0 (3.95)	5.3 ! (2.45)
$50,000–74,999	103,600 (27,200)	51,000 (13,390)	52,600 (17,810)	19,100 ! (9,720)	31.4 (7.81)	15.5 (4.00)	15.9 (5.23)	5.8 ! (2.90)
$75,000 or more	109,700 (28,210)	57,300 (14,240)	52,400 (17,770)	35,500 ! (14,020)	14.7 (3.66)	7.7 (1.90)	7.0 (2.34)	4.8 ! (1.86)
Not reported	123,700 (30,450)	70,000 (15,840)	53,700 (18,050)	30,100 ! (12,690)	21.2 (5.00)	12.0 (2.68)	9.2 (3.02)	5.1 ! (2.14)

! Interpret data with caution. Estimate based on 10 or fewer sample cases, or the coefficient of variation is greater than 50 percent.

[1] Serious violent victimization is also included in all violent victimization.

[2] "At school" includes inside the school building, on school property, and on the way to and from school.

[3] Race categories exclude persons of Hispanic ethnicity. "Other" includes Asians, Pacific Islanders, American Indians/Alaska Natives, and persons of Two or more races.

[4] Refers to the Standard Metropolitan Statistical Area (MSA) status of the respondent's household as defined in 2000 by the U.S. Census Bureau. Categories include "central city of an MSA (Urban)," "in MSA but not in central city (Suburban)," and "not MSA (Rural)."

NOTE: "Serious violent victimization" includes the crimes of rape, sexual assault, robbery, and aggravated assault. "All violent victimization" includes serious violent crimes as well as simple assault. "Theft" includes attempted and completed purse-snatching, completed pickpocketing, and all attempted and completed thefts, with the exception of motor vehicle thefts. Theft does not include robbery, which involves the threat or use of force and is classified as a violent crime. "Total victimization" includes theft and violent crimes. Data in this table are from the National Crime Victimization Survey (NCVS) and are reported in accordance with Bureau of Justice Statistics standards. Detail may not sum to totals because of rounding and missing data on student characteristics. The population size for students ages 12–18 was 25,773,800 in 2014.

SOURCE: U.S. Department of Justice, Bureau of Justice Statistics, National Crime Victimization Survey (NCVS), 2014. (This table was prepared August 2015.)

Table 228.30. Percentage of students ages 12–18 who reported criminal victimization at school during the previous 6 months, by type of victimization and selected student and school characteristics: Selected years, 1995 through 2013

[Standard errors appear in parentheses]

Type of victimization and student or school characteristic	1995	1999	2001	2003	2005	2007	2009	2011	2013
1	2	3	4	5	6	7	8	9	10
Total	**9.5 (0.35)**	**7.6 (0.35)**	**5.5 (0.31)**	**5.1 (0.24)**	**4.3 (0.31)**	**4.3 (0.30)**	**3.9 (0.28)**	**3.5 (0.28)**	**3.0 (0.25)**
Sex									
Male	10.0 (0.46)	7.8 (0.46)	6.1 (0.41)	5.4 (0.33)	4.6 (0.42)	4.5 (0.43)	4.6 (0.40)	3.7 (0.35)	3.2 (0.40)
Female	9.0 (0.47)	7.3 (0.46)	4.9 (0.39)	4.8 (0.36)	3.9 (0.38)	4.0 (0.39)	3.2 (0.35)	3.4 (0.38)	2.8 (0.34)
Race/ethnicity[1]									
White	9.8 (0.37)	7.5 (0.44)	5.8 (0.39)	5.4 (0.31)	4.7 (0.35)	4.3 (0.38)	3.9 (0.37)	3.6 (0.35)	3.0 (0.32)
Black	10.2 (1.04)	9.9 (0.85)	6.1 (0.78)	5.3 (0.80)	3.8 (0.80)	4.3 (0.83)	4.4 (0.74)	4.6 (0.89)	3.2 (0.71)
Hispanic	7.6 (0.90)	5.7 (0.77)	4.6 (0.64)	3.9 (0.50)	3.9 (0.70)	3.6 (0.54)	3.9 (0.75)	2.9 (0.47)	3.2 (0.46)
Asian	— (†)	— (†)	— (†)	— (†)	1.5 ! (0.68)	3.6 ! (1.38)	‡ (†)	2.5 ! (1.23)	2.6 ! (1.08)
Other	8.8 (1.54)	6.4 (1.28)	3.1 (0.91)	5.0 (1.08)	4.3 ! (2.00)	8.1 (2.01)	‡ (†)	3.7 ! (1.37)	2.2 ! (1.08)
Grade									
6th	9.6 (0.97)	8.0 (1.24)	5.9 (0.90)	3.8 (0.77)	4.6 (0.83)	4.1 (0.87)	3.7 (0.91)	3.8 (0.85)	4.1 (0.92)
7th	11.2 (0.81)	8.2 (0.81)	5.8 (0.66)	6.3 (0.74)	5.4 (0.71)	4.7 (0.69)	3.4 (0.70)	3.1 (0.61)	2.5 (0.51)
8th	10.5 (0.78)	7.6 (0.84)	4.3 (0.61)	5.2 (0.65)	3.6 (0.63)	4.4 (0.63)	3.8 (0.78)	3.8 (0.67)	2.3 (0.52)
9th	11.9 (0.88)	8.9 (0.79)	7.9 (0.81)	6.3 (0.70)	4.7 (0.69)	5.3 (0.75)	5.3 (0.85)	5.1 (0.83)	4.1 (0.76)
10th	9.1 (0.76)	8.0 (0.82)	6.5 (0.77)	4.8 (0.63)	4.3 (0.71)	4.4 (0.67)	4.2 (0.79)	3.0 (0.58)	3.3 (0.57)
11th	7.3 (0.74)	7.2 (0.88)	4.8 (0.62)	5.1 (0.68)	3.6 (0.51)	4.0 (0.75)	4.7 (0.88)	3.1 (0.65)	3.3 (0.65)
12th	6.1 (0.74)	4.8 (0.81)	2.9 (0.52)	3.6 (0.71)	3.8 (0.85)	2.7 (0.70)	2.0 (0.52)	2.9 (0.68)	2.0 ! (0.67)
Urbanicity[2]									
Urban	9.3 (0.64)	8.4 (0.69)	5.9 (0.58)	6.1 (0.58)	5.3 (0.65)	4.5 (0.58)	4.2 (0.56)	4.3 (0.56)	3.3 (0.47)
Suburban	10.3 (0.49)	7.6 (0.43)	5.7 (0.40)	4.8 (0.33)	4.2 (0.34)	4.1 (0.38)	4.0 (0.36)	3.3 (0.34)	3.2 (0.35)
Rural	8.3 (0.79)	6.4 (0.96)	4.7 (0.93)	4.7 (0.75)	2.8 (0.69)	4.4 (0.55)	3.1 (0.66)	2.8 (0.57)	2.0 (0.58)
Sector									
Public	9.8 (0.38)	7.9 (0.37)	5.7 (0.34)	5.2 (0.26)	4.4 (0.32)	4.6 (0.32)	4.1 (0.30)	3.7 (0.29)	3.1 (0.27)
Private	6.6 (0.90)	4.5 (0.80)	3.4 (0.72)	4.9 (0.79)	2.7 (0.77)	1.1 ! (0.50)	1.8 ! (0.76)	1.9 ! (0.68)	2.8 ! (0.89)
Theft	**7.1 (0.29)**	**5.7 (0.32)**	**4.2 (0.24)**	**4.0 (0.21)**	**3.1 (0.27)**	**3.0 (0.23)**	**2.8 (0.23)**	**2.6 (0.23)**	**1.9 (0.20)**
Sex									
Male	7.1 (0.38)	5.7 (0.41)	4.5 (0.34)	4.0 (0.27)	3.1 (0.34)	3.0 (0.34)	3.4 (0.36)	2.6 (0.29)	2.0 (0.30)
Female	7.1 (0.41)	5.7 (0.43)	3.8 (0.33)	4.1 (0.32)	3.2 (0.36)	3.0 (0.33)	2.1 (0.28)	2.6 (0.33)	1.8 (0.28)
Race/ethnicity[1]									
White	7.4 (0.32)	5.8 (0.43)	4.2 (0.30)	4.3 (0.28)	3.4 (0.32)	3.1 (0.29)	2.9 (0.31)	2.5 (0.28)	1.6 (0.22)
Black	7.1 (0.85)	7.4 (0.77)	5.0 (0.68)	4.0 (0.66)	2.7 (0.65)	3.0 (0.70)	2.5 (0.61)	3.7 (0.78)	2.7 (0.67)
Hispanic	5.8 (0.78)	3.9 (0.61)	3.7 (0.69)	3.0 (0.41)	3.1 (0.64)	2.2 (0.47)	3.0 (0.63)	2.0 (0.41)	1.8 (0.39)
Asian	— (†)	— (†)	— (†)	— (†)	‡ (†)	3.2 ! (1.32)	‡ (†)	2.5 ! (1.23)	2.6 ! (1.08)
Other	6.5 (1.40)	4.4 (0.98)	2.9 (0.87)	4.4 (1.04)	‡ (†)	4.5 ! (1.57)	‡ (†)	2.8 ! (1.21)	‡ (†)
Grade									
6th	5.4 (0.66)	5.2 (0.97)	4.0 (0.70)	2.2 (0.63)	2.8 (0.75)	2.7 (0.77)	1.3 ! (0.52)	2.7 (0.70)	1.4 ! (0.57)
7th	8.1 (0.71)	6.0 (0.73)	3.4 (0.51)	4.8 (0.67)	2.9 (0.50)	2.7 (0.54)	2.1 (0.57)	1.9 (0.44)	1.4 (0.38)
8th	7.9 (0.72)	5.9 (0.81)	3.3 (0.50)	4.1 (0.56)	2.4 (0.53)	2.5 (0.54)	2.0 (0.55)	2.0 (0.48)	1.0 ! (0.33)
9th	9.1 (0.77)	6.5 (0.71)	6.2 (0.76)	5.3 (0.62)	3.7 (0.61)	4.6 (0.70)	4.9 (0.80)	4.4 (0.78)	2.7 (0.58)
10th	7.7 (0.72)	6.5 (0.73)	5.7 (0.72)	3.7 (0.59)	3.8 (0.66)	3.6 (0.63)	3.5 (0.72)	2.1 (0.50)	2.6 (0.48)
11th	5.5 (0.66)	5.5 (0.67)	3.8 (0.57)	4.1 (0.64)	2.8 (0.45)	2.6 (0.61)	3.3 (0.74)	2.7 (0.58)	2.3 (0.50)
12th	4.6 (0.67)	4.0 (0.71)	2.3 (0.45)	3.1 (0.68)	3.5 (0.85)	1.9 (0.55)	1.5 (0.44)	2.4 (0.62)	1.6 ! (0.62)
Urbanicity[2]									
Urban	6.6 (0.51)	6.9 (0.59)	4.5 (0.52)	4.5 (0.47)	3.6 (0.51)	2.8 (0.48)	2.9 (0.45)	3.0 (0.45)	2.4 (0.44)
Suburban	7.6 (0.40)	5.4 (0.36)	4.3 (0.32)	3.8 (0.27)	3.2 (0.31)	3.0 (0.31)	2.8 (0.32)	2.5 (0.30)	1.9 (0.27)
Rural	6.8 (0.66)	5.0 (0.95)	3.4 (0.65)	3.9 (0.66)	2.2 ! (0.68)	3.2 (0.46)	2.3 (0.59)	2.0 (0.47)	0.8 (0.24)
Sector									
Public	7.3 (0.32)	5.9 (0.34)	4.4 (0.26)	4.0 (0.22)	3.3 (0.28)	3.2 (0.25)	2.9 (0.25)	2.7 (0.24)	1.9 (0.21)
Private	5.2 (0.74)	4.3 (0.78)	2.5 (0.67)	4.0 (0.77)	1.3 ! (0.48)	1.1 ! (0.50)	‡ (†)	1.2 ! (0.52)	2.0 ! (0.76)
Violent	**3.0 (0.21)**	**2.3 (0.18)**	**1.8 (0.19)**	**1.3 (0.15)**	**1.2 (0.15)**	**1.6 (0.18)**	**1.4 (0.17)**	**1.1 (0.15)**	**1.2 (0.15)**
Sex									
Male	3.5 (0.27)	2.5 (0.26)	2.1 (0.26)	1.8 (0.24)	1.6 (0.25)	1.7 (0.26)	1.6 (0.25)	1.2 (0.21)	1.3 (0.23)
Female	2.4 (0.25)	2.0 (0.22)	1.5 (0.24)	0.9 (0.16)	0.8 (0.15)	1.4 (0.23)	1.1 (0.21)	0.9 (0.17)	1.1 (0.23)
Race/ethnicity[1]									
White	3.0 (0.23)	2.1 (0.22)	2.0 (0.24)	1.4 (0.18)	1.3 (0.20)	1.5 (0.22)	1.2 (0.21)	1.2 (0.17)	1.5 (0.24)
Black	3.4 (0.61)	3.5 (0.55)	1.3 ! (0.40)	1.6 (0.41)	1.3 ! (0.46)	1.6 ! (0.50)	2.3 (0.62)	1.1 ! (0.42)	‡ (†)
Hispanic	2.7 (0.43)	1.9 (0.38)	1.5 (0.41)	1.1 (0.28)	0.9 (0.24)	1.4 (0.42)	1.3 ! (0.40)	1.0 (0.28)	1.5 (0.26)
Asian	— (†)	— (†)	— (†)	— (†)	‡ (†)	‡ (†)	# (†)	# (†)	‡ (†)
Other	2.5 ! (0.87)	2.2 ! (0.81)	‡ (†)	‡ (†)	‡ (†)	4.5 ! (1.50)	‡ (†)	‡ (†)	‡ (†)
Grade									
6th	5.1 (0.73)	3.8 (0.76)	2.6 (0.66)	1.9 (0.53)	1.9 (0.55)	1.5 ! (0.54)	2.6 ! (0.83)	1.3 ! (0.49)	2.7 (0.73)
7th	3.8 (0.54)	2.6 (0.43)	2.6 (0.47)	1.7 (0.43)	2.6 (0.53)	2.4 (0.50)	1.2 ! (0.42)	1.2 ! (0.41)	1.2 ! (0.38)
8th	3.1 (0.44)	2.4 (0.44)	1.3 (0.34)	1.5 (0.35)	1.4 (0.39)	2.1 (0.47)	2.0 (0.60)	2.1 (0.50)	1.4 (0.42)
9th	3.4 (0.50)	3.2 (0.47)	2.4 (0.46)	1.5 (0.31)	1.0 (0.29)	1.2 ! (0.37)	0.9 ! (0.37)	1.1 ! (0.35)	1.4 ! (0.44)
10th	2.1 (0.36)	1.7 (0.39)	1.2 (0.31)	1.4 (0.36)	0.5 ! (0.24)	1.2 ! (0.39)	1.0 ! (0.37)	0.9 ! (0.34)	1.0 ! (0.35)
11th	1.9 (0.40)	1.8 ! (0.58)	1.6 (0.39)	1.0 ! (0.33)	0.7 ! (0.31)	1.5 ! (0.46)	1.5 ! (0.51)	‡ (†)	1.0 ! (0.43)
12th	1.9 (0.41)	0.8 ! (0.31)	0.9 ! (0.31)	0.5 ! (0.26)	‡ (†)	0.8 ! (0.35)	‡ (†)	‡ (†)	‡ (†)
Urbanicity[2]									
Urban	3.3 (0.40)	2.3 (0.38)	1.7 (0.29)	1.8 (0.32)	1.8 (0.34)	2.0 (0.35)	1.8 (0.41)	1.4 (0.31)	0.9 (0.21)
Suburban	3.5 (0.30)	2.4 (0.26)	1.7 (0.20)	1.2 (0.19)	1.1 (0.18)	1.3 (0.23)	1.3 (0.23)	0.9 (0.16)	1.4 (0.21)
Rural	1.8 (0.31)	1.9 (0.50)	2.0 ! (0.64)	0.9 ! (0.31)	0.6 ! (0.26)	1.7 (0.36)	0.8 ! (0.32)	1.0 ! (0.31)	1.1 ! (0.46)
Sector									
Public	3.1 (0.22)	2.5 (0.20)	1.9 (0.20)	1.4 (0.15)	1.2 (0.15)	1.7 (0.20)	1.4 (0.19)	1.1 (0.15)	1.2 (0.16)
Private	1.7 (0.45)	‡ (†)	1.0 ! (0.32)	0.9 ! (0.39)	1.4 ! (0.60)	‡ (†)	‡ (†)	‡ (†)	‡ (†)

See notes at end of table.

Table 228.30. Percentage of students ages 12–18 who reported criminal victimization at school during the previous 6 months, by type of victimization and selected student and school characteristics: Selected years, 1995 through 2013—Continued

[Standard errors appear in parentheses]

Type of victimization and student or school characteristic	1995	1999	2001	2003	2005	2007	2009	2011	2013
1	2	3	4	5	6	7	8	9	10
Serious violent[3]	**0.7 (0.09)**	**0.5 (0.09)**	**0.4 (0.08)**	**0.2 (0.06)**	**0.3 (0.07)**	**0.4 (0.08)**	**0.3 (0.09)**	**0.1 ! (0.05)**	**0.2 ! (0.07)**
Sex									
Male	0.9 (0.14)	0.6 (0.12)	0.5 (0.11)	0.3 ! (0.10)	0.3 ! (0.10)	0.5 ! (0.14)	0.6 (0.16)	0.2 ! (0.08)	0.2 ! (0.10)
Female	0.4 (0.10)	0.5 (0.12)	0.4 ! (0.12)	‡ (†)	0.3 (0.07)	0.2 ! (0.08)	‡ (†)	‡ (†)	0.2 ! (0.10)
Race/ethnicity[1]									
White	0.6 (0.09)	0.4 (0.09)	0.4 (0.08)	0.2 ! (0.06)	0.3 ! (0.09)	0.2 ! (0.08)	0.3 ! (0.10)	0.2 ! (0.07)	0.2 ! (0.09)
Black	1.0 ! (0.31)	1.2 (0.33)	0.5 ! (0.25)	‡ (†)	‡ (†)	‡ (†)	‡ (†)	‡ (†)	‡ (†)
Hispanic	0.9 ! (0.30)	0.6 ! (0.22)	0.8 ! (0.33)	0.4 ! (0.18)	0.4 ! (0.16)	0.8 ! (0.32)	‡ (†)	‡ (†)	0.4 ! (0.17)
Asian	— (†)	— (†)	— (†)	— (†)	‡ (†)	‡ (†)	# (†)	# (†)	‡ (†)
Other	‡ (†)	# (†)	# (†)	‡ (†)	‡ (†)	‡ (†)	# (†)	# (†)	‡ (†)
Grade									
6th	1.5 (0.42)	1.3 ! (0.40)	‡ (†)	# (†)	‡ (†)	‡ (†)	‡ (†)	‡ (†)	0.8 ! (0.42)
7th	0.9 (0.24)	0.9 ! (0.27)	0.6 ! (0.24)	‡ (†)	‡ (†)	0.4 ! (0.20)	‡ (†)	0.5 ! (0.23)	‡ (†)
8th	0.8 ! (0.23)	0.5 ! (0.22)	0.3 ! (0.14)	0.3 ! (0.15)	‡ (†)	‡ (†)	‡ (†)	# (†)	‡ (†)
9th	0.7 (0.21)	0.6 ! (0.18)	0.8 ! (0.31)	0.6 ! (0.21)	‡ (†)	‡ (†)	‡ (†)	‡ (†)	‡ (†)
10th	0.4 ! (0.17)	‡ (†)	0.4 ! (0.18)	# (†)	‡ (†)	‡ (†)	‡ (†)	# (†)	‡ (†)
11th	0.4 ! (0.16)	‡ (†)	‡ (†)	‡ (†)	‡ (†)	0.6 ! (0.27)	‡ (†)	# (†)	‡ (†)
12th	‡ (†)	‡ (†)	‡ (†)	# (†)	‡ (†)	‡ (†)	‡ (†)	# (†)	‡ (†)
Urbanicity[2]									
Urban	1.3 (0.24)	0.7 (0.19)	0.5 (0.15)	0.4 ! (0.14)	0.4 ! (0.17)	0.7 ! (0.23)	0.6 ! (0.22)	‡ (†)	0.3 ! (0.16)
Suburban	0.6 (0.12)	0.5 (0.11)	0.4 (0.09)	0.1 ! (0.05)	0.3 ! (0.08)	0.2 ! (0.09)	0.3 ! (0.11)	‡ (†)	0.2 ! (0.08)
Rural	0.3 ! (0.10)	0.4 ! (0.18)	0.5 ! (0.24)	‡ (†)	‡ (†)	‡ (†)	‡ (†)	‡ (†)	‡ (†)
Sector									
Public	0.7 (0.10)	0.6 (0.10)	0.5 (0.09)	0.2 (0.06)	0.3 (0.06)	0.4 (0.09)	0.4 (0.10)	0.1 ! (0.06)	0.2 ! (0.08)
Private	‡ (†)	# (†)	# (†)	# (†)	‡ (†)	‡ (†)	‡ (†)	# (†)	‡ (†)

—Not available.
†Not applicable.
#Rounds to zero.
!Interpret data with caution. The coefficient of variation (CV) for this estimate is between 30 and 50 percent.
‡Reporting standards not met. Either there are too few cases for a reliable estimate or the coefficient of variation (CV) is 50 percent or greater.
[1]Race categories exclude persons of Hispanic ethnicity. "Other" includes American Indians/Alaska Natives, Asians (prior to 2005), Pacific Islanders, and, from 2003 onward, persons of Two or more races. Due to changes in racial/ethnic categories, comparisons of race/ethnicity across years should be made with caution.
[2]Refers to the Standard Metropolitan Statistical Area (MSA) status of the respondent's household as defined in 2000 by the U.S. Census Bureau. Categories include "central city of an MSA (Urban)," "in MSA but not in central city (Suburban)," and "not MSA (Rural)."
[3]Serious violent victimization is also included in violent victimization.
NOTE: "Total victimization" includes theft and violent victimization. A single student could report more than one type of victimization. In the total victimization section, students who reported both theft and violent victimization are counted only once. "Theft" includes attempted and completed purse-snatching, completed pickpocketing, and all attempted and completed thefts, with the exception of motor vehicle thefts. Theft does not include robbery, which involves the threat or use of force and is classified as a violent crime. "Serious violent victimization" includes the crimes of rape, sexual assault, robbery, and aggravated assault. "Violent victimization" includes the serious violent crimes as well as simple assault. "At school" includes the school building, on school property, on a school bus, and, from 2001 onward, going to and from school.
SOURCE: U.S. Department of Justice, Bureau of Justice Statistics, School Crime Supplement (SCS) to the National Crime Victimization Survey, selected years, 1995 through 2013. (This table was prepared August 2014.)

Table 228.40. Percentage of students in grades 9–12 who reported being threatened or injured with a weapon on school property during the previous 12 months, by selected student characteristics and number of times threatened or injured: Selected years, 1993 through 2013

[Standard errors appear in parentheses]

Number of times and year	Total	Sex		Race/ethnicity[1]							Grade			
		Male	Female	White	Black	Hispanic	Asian[2]	Pacific Islander[2]	American Indian/ Alaska Native[2]	Two or more races[2]	9th grade	10th grade	11th grade	12th grade
1	2	3	4	5	6	7	8	9	10	11	12	13	14	15
At least once														
1993	7.3 (0.44)	9.2 (0.64)	5.4 (0.40)	6.3 (0.58)	11.2 (0.95)	8.6 (0.83)	— (†)	— (†)	11.7 (2.50)	— (†)	9.4 (0.92)	7.3 (0.59)	7.3 (0.64)	5.5 (0.62)
1995	8.4 (0.52)	10.9 (0.57)	5.8 (0.68)	7.0 (0.53)	11.0 (1.61)	12.4 (1.44)	— (†)	— (†)	11.4 ! (4.22)	— (†)	9.6 (0.96)	9.6 (1.03)	7.7 (0.64)	6.7 (0.57)
1997	7.4 (0.45)	10.2 (0.71)	4.0 (0.32)	6.2 (0.56)	9.9 (0.91)	9.0 (0.63)	— (†)	— (†)	12.5 ! (5.15)	— (†)	10.1 (1.02)	7.9 (1.14)	5.9 (0.70)	5.8 (0.80)
1999	7.7 (0.42)	9.5 (0.80)	5.8 (0.64)	6.6 (0.35)	7.6 (0.85)	9.8 (1.09)	7.7 (1.05)	15.6 (4.46)	13.2 ! (5.45)	9.3 (1.22)	10.5 (0.95)	8.2 (0.92)	6.1 (0.46)	5.1 (0.79)
2001	8.9 (0.55)	11.5 (0.66)	6.5 (0.52)	8.5 (0.66)	9.3 (0.71)	8.9 (1.05)	11.3 (2.73)	24.8 (7.16)	15.2 ! (4.57)	10.3 (2.33)	12.7 (0.89)	9.1 (0.75)	6.9 (0.65)	5.3 (0.52)
2003	9.2 (0.75)	11.6 (0.96)	6.5 (0.61)	7.8 (0.77)	10.9 (0.80)	9.4 (1.23)	11.5 (2.66)	16.3 (4.31)	22.1 (4.79)	18.7 (3.11)	12.1 (1.25)	9.2 (1.02)	7.3 (0.69)	6.3 (0.92)
2005	7.9 (0.35)	9.7 (0.42)	6.1 (0.41)	7.2 (0.46)	8.1 (0.69)	9.8 (0.86)	4.6 (1.10)	14.5 ! (4.93)	9.8 (2.67)	10.7 (2.33)	10.5 (0.63)	8.8 (0.72)	5.5 (0.43)	5.8 (0.52)
2007	7.8 (0.44)	10.2 (0.59)	5.4 (0.41)	6.9 (0.52)	9.7 (0.86)	8.7 (0.60)	7.6 ! (2.29)	8.1 ! (2.45)	5.9 (1.24)	13.3 (2.25)	9.2 (0.69)	8.4 (0.51)	6.8 (0.57)	6.3 (0.64)
2009	7.7 (0.37)	9.6 (0.59)	5.5 (0.37)	6.4 (0.43)	9.4 (0.80)	9.1 (0.61)	5.5 (0.91)	12.5 (3.11)	16.5 (2.68)	9.2 (1.50)	8.7 (0.53)	8.4 (0.72)	7.9 (0.60)	5.2 (0.53)
2011	7.4 (0.31)	9.5 (0.39)	5.2 (0.37)	6.1 (0.35)	8.9 (0.64)	9.2 (0.81)	7.0 (0.99)	11.3 (3.23)	8.2 (1.52)	9.9 (1.35)	8.3 (0.63)	7.7 (0.58)	7.3 (0.61)	5.9 (0.45)
2013	6.9 (0.38)	7.7 (0.54)	6.1 (0.40)	5.8 (0.32)	8.4 (0.82)	8.5 (0.73)	5.3 (1.41)	8.7 ! (2.71)	18.5 (5.24)	7.7 (2.11)	8.5 (0.75)	7.0 (0.67)	6.8 (0.60)	4.9 (0.61)
Number of times, 2013														
0 times	93.1 (0.38)	92.3 (0.54)	93.9 (0.40)	94.2 (0.32)	91.6 (0.82)	91.5 (0.73)	94.7 (1.41)	91.3 (2.71)	81.5 (5.24)	92.3 (2.11)	91.5 (0.75)	93.0 (0.67)	93.2 (0.60)	95.1 (0.61)
1 time	3.0 (0.22)	3.0 (0.25)	3.0 (0.33)	2.7 (0.27)	3.8 (0.51)	3.3 (0.51)	1.7 ! (0.51)	2.0 (0.59)	9.6 ! (3.14)	3.1 ! (0.96)	3.5 (0.50)	3.0 (0.52)	3.4 (0.39)	2.0 (0.27)
2 or 3 times	1.7 (0.14)	1.7 (0.21)	1.6 (0.20)	1.6 (0.17)	1.8 (0.35)	1.6 (0.29)	‡ (†)	‡ (†)	‡ (†)	2.2 ! (0.67)	2.5 (0.37)	1.7 (0.26)	1.3 (0.24)	1.1 (0.21)
4 to 11 times	1.3 (0.14)	1.7 (0.21)	0.9 (0.18)	0.8 (0.12)	1.7 (0.36)	2.3 (0.34)	‡ (†)	‡ (†)	4.9 ! (2.34)	1.5 ! (0.63)	1.5 (0.22)	1.4 (0.30)	1.3 (0.28)	1.0 (0.21)
12 or more times	0.9 (0.11)	1.3 (0.19)	0.6 (0.08)	0.7 (0.17)	1.2 (0.23)	1.2 (0.25)	‡ (†)	‡ (†)	‡ (†)	‡ (†)	1.0 (0.20)	0.9 (0.20)	0.9 (0.22)	0.9 (0.25)

—Not available.
†Not applicable.
!Interpret data with caution. The coefficient of variation (CV) for this estimate is between 30 and 50 percent.
‡Reporting standards not met. Either there are too few cases for a reliable estimate or the coefficient of variation (CV) is 50 percent or greater.
[1]Race categories exclude persons of Hispanic ethnicity.
[2]Before 1999, Asian students and Pacific Islander students were not categorized separately, and students could not be classified as Two or more races. Because the response categories changed in 1999, caution should be used in comparing data on race from 1993, 1995, and 1997 with data from later years.
NOTE: Survey respondents were asked about being threatened or injured "with a weapon such as a gun, knife, or club on school property." "On school property" was not defined for respondents. Detail may not sum to totals because of rounding.
SOURCE: Centers for Disease Control and Prevention, Division of Adolescent and School Health, Youth Risk Behavior Surveillance System (YRBSS), 1993 through 2013. (This table was prepared June 2014.)

Table 228.50. Percentage of public school students in grades 9–12 who reported being threatened or injured with a weapon on school property at least one time during the previous 12 months, by state: Selected years, 2003 through 2013

[Standard errors appear in parentheses]

State	2003		2005		2007		2009		2011		2013	
1	2		3		4		5		6		7	
United States[1]	**9.2**	**(0.75)**	**7.9**	**(0.35)**	**7.8**	**(0.44)**	**7.7**	**(0.37)**	**7.4**	**(0.31)**	**6.9**	**(0.38)**
Alabama	7.2	(0.91)	10.6	(0.86)	—	(†)	10.4	(1.56)	7.6	(1.20)	9.9	(1.17)
Alaska	8.1	(1.01)	—	(†)	7.7	(0.88)	7.3	(0.90)	5.6	(0.70)	—	(†)
Arizona	9.7	(1.10)	10.7	(0.55)	11.2	(0.79)	9.3	(0.92)	10.4	(0.74)	9.1	(1.32)
Arkansas	—	(†)	9.6	(1.06)	9.1	(1.03)	11.9	(1.38)	6.3	(0.85)	10.9	(1.14)
California	—	(†)	—	(†)	—	(†)	—	(†)	—	(†)	—	(†)
Colorado	—	(†)	7.6	(0.75)	—	(†)	8.0	(0.74)	6.7	(0.80)	—	(†)
Connecticut	—	(†)	9.1	(0.91)	7.7	(0.59)	7.0	(0.62)	6.8	(0.71)	7.1	(0.74)
Delaware	7.7	(0.60)	6.2	(0.63)	5.6	(0.50)	7.8	(0.63)	6.4	(0.62)	5.6	(0.46)
District of Columbia	12.7	(1.42)	12.1	(0.78)	11.3	(0.98)	—	(†)	8.7	(0.92)	—	(†)
Florida	8.4	(0.44)	7.9	(0.45)	8.6	(0.57)	8.2	(0.39)	7.2	(0.31)	7.1	(0.37)
Georgia	8.2	(0.75)	8.3	(2.08)	8.1	(0.81)	8.2	(0.83)	11.7	(2.08)	7.2	(0.81)
Hawaii	—	(†)	6.8	(0.87)	6.4	(1.10)	7.7	(1.03)	6.3	(0.62)	—	(†)
Idaho	9.4	(0.82)	8.3	(0.59)	10.2	(1.07)	7.9	(0.62)	7.3	(0.99)	5.8	(0.59)
Illinois	—	(†)	—	(†)	7.8	(0.69)	8.8	(0.86)	7.6	(0.48)	8.5	(0.82)
Indiana	6.7	(0.91)	8.8	(0.96)	9.6	(0.68)	6.5	(0.66)	6.8	(1.14)	—	(†)
Iowa	—	(†)	7.8	(1.02)	7.1	(0.86)	—	(†)	6.3	(0.85)	—	(†)
Kansas	—	(†)	7.4	(0.82)	8.6	(1.12)	6.2	(0.62)	5.6	(0.68)	5.3	(0.65)
Kentucky	5.2	(0.72)	8.0	(0.75)	8.3	(0.53)	7.9	(1.00)	7.4	(0.98)	5.4	(0.57)
Louisiana	—	(†)	—	(†)	—	(†)	9.5	(1.29)	8.7	(1.18)	10.5	(0.99)
Maine	8.5	(0.78)	7.1	(0.68)	6.8	(0.84)	7.7	(0.32)	6.8	(0.26)	5.3	(0.29)
Maryland	—	(†)	11.7	(1.30)	9.6	(0.86)	9.1	(0.75)	8.4	(0.67)	9.4	(0.22)
Massachusetts	6.3	(0.54)	5.4	(0.44)	5.3	(0.47)	7.0	(0.58)	6.8	(0.67)	4.4	(0.38)
Michigan	9.7	(0.57)	8.6	(0.81)	8.1	(0.77)	9.4	(0.63)	6.8	(0.50)	6.7	(0.52)
Minnesota	—	(†)	—	(†)	—	(†)	—	(†)	—	(†)	—	(†)
Mississippi	6.6	(0.82)	—	(†)	8.3	(0.59)	8.0	(0.69)	7.5	(0.63)	8.8	(0.78)
Missouri	7.5	(0.93)	9.1	(1.19)	9.3	(1.03)	7.8	(0.76)	—	(†)	—	(†)
Montana	7.1	(0.46)	8.0	(0.64)	7.0	(0.51)	7.4	(0.99)	7.5	(0.53)	6.3	(0.40)
Nebraska	8.8	(0.80)	9.7	(0.68)	—	(†)	—	(†)	6.4	(0.54)	6.4	(0.57)
Nevada	6.0	(0.65)	8.1	(0.96)	7.8	(0.70)	10.7	(0.84)	—	(†)	6.4	(0.80)
New Hampshire	7.5	(0.98)	8.6	(0.91)	7.3	(0.69)	—	(†)	—	(†)	—	(†)
New Jersey	—	(†)	8.0	(1.07)	—	(†)	6.6	(0.75)	5.7	(0.51)	6.2	(0.81)
New Mexico	—	(†)	10.4	(0.96)	10.1	(0.68)	—	(†)	—	(†)	—	(†)
New York	7.2	(0.44)	7.2	(0.47)	7.3	(0.57)	7.5	(0.55)	7.3	(0.60)	7.3	(0.61)
North Carolina	7.2	(0.74)	7.9	(0.92)	6.6	(0.62)	6.8	(0.61)	9.1	(0.95)	6.9	(0.45)
North Dakota	5.9	(0.89)	6.6	(0.58)	5.2	(0.59)	—	(†)	—	(†)	—	(†)
Ohio[2]	7.7	(1.30)	8.2	(0.67)	8.3	(0.77)	—	(†)	—	(†)	—	(†)
Oklahoma	7.4	(1.10)	6.0	(0.65)	7.0	(0.72)	5.8	(0.66)	5.7	(0.88)	4.6	(0.53)
Oregon	—	(†)	—	(†)	—	(†)	—	(†)	—	(†)	—	(†)
Pennsylvania	—	(†)	—	(†)	—	(†)	5.6	(0.73)	—	(†)	—	(†)
Rhode Island	8.2	(0.84)	8.7	(0.87)	8.3	(0.42)	6.5	(0.65)	—	(†)	6.4	(0.51)
South Carolina	—	(†)	10.1	(0.93)	9.8	(0.85)	8.8	(1.48)	9.2	(0.92)	6.5	(0.83)
South Dakota[2]	6.5	(0.71)	8.1	(1.04)	5.9	(0.87)	6.8	(0.87)	6.1	(0.77)	5.0	(0.69)
Tennessee	8.4	(1.17)	7.4	(0.79)	7.3	(0.76)	7.0	(0.71)	5.8	(0.52)	9.3	(0.73)
Texas	—	(†)	9.3	(0.84)	8.7	(0.52)	7.2	(0.52)	6.8	(0.40)	7.1	(0.62)
Utah	7.3	(1.44)	9.8	(1.32)	11.4	(1.92)	7.7	(0.88)	7.0	(0.98)	5.5	(0.59)
Vermont	7.3	(0.20)	6.3	(0.46)	6.2	(0.56)	6.0	(0.30)	5.5	(0.37)	6.4	(0.43)
Virginia	—	(†)	—	(†)	—	(†)	—	(†)	7.0	(0.86)	6.1	(0.43)
Washington	—	(†)	—	(†)	—	(†)	—	(†)	—	(†)	—	(†)
West Virginia	8.5	(1.26)	8.0	(0.78)	9.7	(0.77)	9.2	(0.77)	6.6	(0.93)	5.6	(0.51)
Wisconsin	5.5	(0.70)	7.6	(0.73)	5.6	(0.66)	6.7	(0.75)	5.1	(0.48)	4.3	(0.64)
Wyoming	9.7	(1.00)	7.8	(0.67)	8.3	(0.67)	9.4	(0.58)	7.3	(0.58)	6.8	(0.47)

—Not available.
†Not applicable.
[1]Data for the U.S. total include both public and private schools and were collected through a national survey representing the entire country.
[2]Data include both public and private schools.
NOTE: Survey respondents were asked about being threatened or injured "with a weapon such as a gun, knife, or club on school property." "On school property" was not defined for respondents. State-level data include public schools only, with the exception of data for Ohio and South Dakota. Data for the U.S. total, Ohio, and South Dakota include both public and private schools. For specific states, a given year's data may be unavailable (1) because the state did not participate in the survey that year; (2) because the state omitted this particular survey item from the state-level questionnaire; or (3) because the state had an overall response rate of less than 60 percent (the overall response rate is the school response rate multiplied by the student response rate).
SOURCE: Centers for Disease Control and Prevention, Division of Adolescent and School Health, Youth Risk Behavior Surveillance System (YRBSS), 2003 through 2013. (This table was prepared June 2014.)

Table 228.70. Number and percentage of public and private school teachers who reported that they were threatened with injury or physically attacked by a student from school during the previous 12 months, by selected teacher and school characteristics: Selected years, 1993–94 through 2011–12

[Standard errors appear in parentheses]

Year	Total	Sex: Male	Sex: Female	Race/ethnicity: White	Race/ethnicity: Black	Race/ethnicity: Hispanic	Race/ethnicity: Other[2]	Instructional level[1]: Elementary	Instructional level[1]: Secondary	Control of school: Public[3]	Control of school: Private
1	2	3	4	5	6	7	8	9	10	11	12
						Number of teachers					
Threatened with injury											
1993–94	342,700 (7,140)	115,900 (3,870)	226,800 (5,570)	295,700 (6,320)	23,900 (1,380)	15,900 (1,850)	7,300 (680)	135,200 (4,520)	207,500 (5,380)	326,800 (7,040)	15,900 (1,130)
1999–2000	304,900 (7,090)	95,100 (3,610)	209,800 (5,490)	252,500 (5,670)	28,300 (2,150)	17,200 (1,980)	7,000 (850)	148,100 (5,560)	156,900 (4,360)	287,400 (7,060)	17,500 (1,700)
2003–04	252,800 (8,750)	78,400 (3,930)	174,400 (7,260)	198,900 (6,980)	32,500 (3,050)	12,400 (1,810)	9,000 (1,250)	113,600 (7,240)	139,200 (5,280)	242,100 (7,840)	10,700 (1,780)
2007–08	289,900 (10,660)	88,300 (5,970)	201,600 (8,140)	234,700 (8,850)	28,700 (3,080)	17,900 (3,230)	8,600 (1,630)	130,000 (7,720)	160,000 (7,220)	276,600 (10,570)	13,300 (1,460)
2011–12	352,900 (17,080)	84,500 (5,220)	268,400 (15,450)	279,900 (13,300)	34,200 (4,380)	27,100 (4,660)	11,800 (2,200)	189,800 (13,430)	163,200 (7,520)	338,400 (17,290)	14,500 (1,450)
Physically attacked											
1993–94	121,100 (3,950)	30,800 (1,770)	90,300 (3,900)	104,300 (4,020)	7,700 (860)	6,200 (1,290)	2,800 (450)	77,300 (3,240)	43,800 (1,980)	112,400 (3,730)	8,700 (860)
1999–2000	134,800 (4,820)	30,600 (1,990)	104,200 (4,390)	111,700 (3,810)	11,600 (1,540)	8,800 (1,660)	2,600 (460)	102,200 (4,360)	32,600 (2,270)	125,000 (4,630)	9,800 (1,070)
2003–04	129,200 (7,810)	23,600 (2,610)	105,700 (6,460)	102,200 (5,920)	15,100 (2,300)	7,000 (1,860)	5,000 (1,110)	89,800 (6,680)	39,400 (3,410)	121,400 (7,180)	7,800 (1,450)
2007–08	156,000 (8,090)	34,900 (4,760)	121,100 (6,120)	132,300 (6,860)	12,300 (2,350)	8,200 (2,040)	3,200 ! (1,250)	114,700 (7,220)	41,300 (3,220)	146,400 (8,200)	9,600 (1,170)
2011–12	209,800 (11,880)	32,500 (3,330)	177,300 (11,310)	171,300 (10,950)	18,800 (3,580)	11,800 (2,890)	7,900 (1,990)	160,700 (10,210)	49,100 (4,310)	197,400 (11,730)	12,400 (1,490)
						Percent of teachers					
Threatened with injury											
1993–94	11.7 (0.23)	14.7 (0.40)	10.5 (0.25)	11.5 (0.24)	11.9 (0.61)	13.1 (1.32)	13.4 (1.08)	8.7 (0.30)	15.0 (0.28)	12.8 (0.26)	4.2 (0.29)
1999–2000	8.8 (0.20)	11.0 (0.38)	8.1 (0.20)	8.6 (0.19)	11.6 (0.84)	9.1 (1.01)	8.3 (0.98)	8.0 (0.29)	9.9 (0.26)	9.6 (0.22)	3.9 (0.35)
2003–04	6.8 (0.24)	8.5 (0.39)	6.2 (0.27)	6.4 (0.24)	11.8 (0.96)	5.5 (0.82)	8.7 (1.25)	5.7 (0.37)	8.0 (0.27)	7.4 (0.24)	2.3 (0.40)
2007–08	7.4 (0.26)	9.3 (0.59)	6.8 (0.27)	7.2 (0.26)	11.1 (0.93)	6.7 (1.19)	7.6 (1.36)	6.6 (0.38)	8.4 (0.36)	8.1 (0.30)	2.7 (0.30)
2011–12	9.2 (0.42)	9.2 (0.49)	9.2 (0.50)	8.8 (0.40)	13.8 (1.72)	9.4 (1.54)	9.1 (1.54)	9.6 (0.67)	8.7 (0.34)	10.0 (0.48)	3.1 (0.32)
Physically attacked											
1993–94	4.1 (0.13)	3.9 (0.21)	4.2 (0.18)	4.1 (0.16)	3.9 (0.40)	5.2 (0.99)	5.2 (0.76)	5.0 (0.20)	3.2 (0.14)	4.4 (0.14)	2.3 (0.23)
1999–2000	3.9 (0.14)	3.5 (0.22)	4.0 (0.17)	3.8 (0.13)	4.8 (0.59)	4.6 (0.83)	3.1 (0.54)	5.5 (0.23)	2.1 (0.14)	4.2 (0.15)	2.2 (0.22)
2003–04	3.\5 (0.21)	2.6 (0.27)	3.8 (0.24)	3.3 (0.20)	5.5 (0.78)	3.1 (0.85)	4.8 (1.10)	4.5 (0.35)	2.3 (0.19)	3.7 (0.22)	1.7 (0.32)
2007–08	4.0 (0.21)	3.7 (0.49)	4.1 (0.21)	4.1 (0.22)	4.7 (0.89)	3.1 (0.73)	2.8 ! (0.97)	5.8 (0.38)	2.2 (0.16)	4.3 (0.24)	2.0 (0.24)
2011–12	5.4 (0.30)	3.5 (0.35)	6.0 (0.37)	5.4 (0.33)	7.6 (1.41)	4.1 (0.96)	6.1 (1.43)	8.2 (0.50)	2.6 (0.21)	5.8 (0.33)	2.7 (0.33)

!Interpret data with caution. The coefficient of variation (CV) for this estimate is between 30 and 50 percent.
[1]Teachers were classified as elementary or secondary on the basis of the grades they taught, rather than on the level of the school in which they taught. In general, elementary teachers include those teaching prekindergarten through grade 5 and those teaching multiple grades, with a preponderance of grades taught being kindergarten through grade 6. In general, secondary teachers include those teaching any of grades 7 through 12 and those teaching multiple grades, with a preponderance of grades taught being grades 7 through 12 and usually with no grade taught being lower than grade 5.
[2]Includes American Indians/Alaska Natives, Asians, and Pacific Islanders; for 2003–04 and later years, also includes persons of Two or more races.
[3]Includes traditional public and public charter schools.
NOTE: Teachers who taught only prekindergarten students are excluded. Instructional level divides teachers into elementary or secondary based on a combination of the grades taught, main teaching assignment, and the structure of the teachers' class(es). Race categories exclude persons of Hispanic ethnicity. Detail may not sum to totals because of rounding. Some data have been revised from previously published figures.
SOURCE: U.S. Department of Education, National Center for Education Statistics, Schools and Staffing Survey (SASS), "Public School Teacher Data File" and "Private School Teacher Data File," 1993–94, 1999–2000, 2003–04, 2007–08, and 2011–12; and "Charter School Teacher Data File," 1999–2000. (This table was prepared October 2013.)

Table 228.80. Percentage of public school teachers who reported that they were threatened with injury or physically attacked by a student from school during the previous 12 months, by state: Selected years, 1993–94 through 2011–12

[Standard errors appear in parentheses]

State	Threatened with injury					Physically attacked				
	1993–94	1999–2000	2003–04	2007–08	2011–12	1993–94	1999–2000	2003–04	2007–08	2011–12
1	2	3	4	5	6	7	8	9	10	11
United States	**12.8 (0.26)**	**9.6 (0.22)**	**7.4 (0.24)**	**8.1 (0.30)**	**10.0 (0.48)**	**4.4 (0.14)**	**4.2 (0.15)**	**3.7 (0.22)**	**4.3 (0.24)**	**5.8 (0.33)**
Alabama	13.3 (1.29)	8.8 (0.99)	6.1 (0.88)	6.8 (1.41)	7.6 (1.92)	3.2 (0.84)	3.8 (0.57)	2.7 (0.75)	3.2 ! (1.12)	3.1 ! (0.94)
Alaska	13.7 (0.92)	10.9 (0.80)	8.9 (1.25)	7.8 (1.24)	12.3 (2.82)	6.5 (0.48)	5.2 (0.51)	6.0 (0.94)	6.7 (1.50)	5.1 ! (1.78)
Arizona	13.0 (1.07)	9.5 (1.16)	6.8 (0.98)	6.4 (1.04)	9.1 (2.08)	3.6 (0.67)	4.5 (0.95)	2.6 (0.58)	4.9 (1.29)	4.7 ! (1.43)
Arkansas	13.8 (1.38)	10.1 (1.18)	4.8 (0.81)	5.9 (1.18)	7.8 (1.48)	3.0 (0.67)	2.5 (0.59)	2.7 (0.72)	4.1 (1.07)	5.2 ! (1.80)
California	7.4 (0.91)	5.8 (0.70)	6.0 (1.00)	8.5 (1.31)	7.7 (1.17)	2.9 (0.61)	2.5 (0.46)	2.0 (0.53)	3.6 (0.78)	4.4 (0.95)
Colorado	13.1 (1.29)	6.6 (0.97)	3.8 (0.82)	6.8 (1.64)	7.3 (1.69)	4.9 (0.82)	3.1 (0.60)	1.5 ! (0.45)	4.7 (1.33)	3.6 ! (1.26)
Connecticut	11.8 (0.86)	9.1 (0.88)	6.9 (1.28)	7.2 (1.39)	7.5 ! (3.03)	3.5 (0.46)	4.1 (0.55)	2.8 (0.70)	3.3 ! (1.04)	6.2 ! (2.91)
Delaware	18.7 (1.56)	11.4 (1.37)	7.7 (1.35)	11.7 (1.93)	15.8 (3.49)	7.2 (1.10)	5.3 (0.92)	3.2 ! (1.00)	5.4 (1.46)	9.8 (2.80)
District of Columbia	24.0 (1.80)	22.3 (1.30)	17.3 (2.63)	16.9 (3.06)	‡ (†)	8.3 (1.34)	9.1 (0.83)	5.2 (1.24)	7.3 (2.00)	‡ (†)
Florida	20.1 (1.65)	12.2 (1.07)	11.2 (1.26)	11.4 (2.11)	‡ (†)	4.9 (0.78)	6.7 (0.91)	6.5 (1.58)	4.0 (1.04)	‡ (†)
Georgia	14.0 (1.29)	9.5 (1.42)	6.4 (1.21)	5.8 (1.18)	9.5 ! (2.98)	3.4 (0.66)	3.6 (0.84)	4.6 (1.30)	4.0 (1.04)	6.3 ! (2.60)
Hawaii	9.9 (1.48)	9.4 (0.99)	9.0 (1.33)	8.0 (1.84)	‡ (†)	2.9 (0.57)	3.2 (0.57)	5.7 (1.18)	4.5 (1.30)	‡ (†)
Idaho	9.7 (1.02)	7.8 (0.44)	5.4 (0.98)	5.9 (1.24)	6.7 (1.42)	4.2 (0.76)	4.3 (0.39)	2.5 ! (0.75)	2.9 ! (0.87)	3.6 ! (1.34)
Illinois	10.9 (0.76)	8.2 (0.89)	7.9 (1.60)	8.1 (1.42)	7.3 (1.41)	4.5 (0.50)	2.7 (0.39)	2.3 ! (0.77)	3.9 (0.90)	4.1 (1.11)
Indiana	13.8 (1.28)	7.6 (1.12)	7.2 (1.18)	10.2 (1.78)	11.2 (2.87)	3.0 (0.66)	3.0 (0.75)	4.1 ! (1.28)	4.7 (0.93)	6.4 (1.88)
Iowa	9.4 (1.19)	10.7 (0.93)	4.9 (1.13)	7.2 (1.32)	11.7 (2.43)	4.3 (0.88)	3.9 (0.73)	2.4 (0.64)	3.4 (0.93)	7.6 (2.11)
Kansas	10.9 (0.91)	6.0 (0.78)	3.9 (0.81)	5.7 (1.07)	7.2 (1.66)	3.8 (0.61)	2.9 (0.55)	3.3 (0.79)	5.0 (1.36)	5.5 ! (1.77)
Kentucky	14.0 (1.33)	12.6 (1.22)	7.8 (1.46)	9.8 (1.86)	10.6 (1.48)	3.8 (0.72)	4.5 (0.62)	2.7 (0.79)	5.8 (1.60)	7.0 (1.25)
Louisiana	17.0 (1.17)	13.4 (2.31)	9.8 (1.42)	10.3 (2.35)	18.3 (2.95)	6.6 (0.82)	5.0 (1.31)	2.7 (0.69)	4.0 ! (1.40)	7.2 ! (2.27)
Maine	9.0 (1.11)	11.7 (1.13)	5.2 (1.09)	9.5 (1.49)	9.1 (1.98)	2.4 (0.62)	6.3 (0.96)	3.3 ! (1.00)	5.2 (1.37)	5.2 (1.55)
Maryland	19.8 (2.15)	10.7 (1.31)	13.5 (2.24)	12.6 (2.47)	‡ (†)	8.6 (1.34)	4.6 (0.93)	6.5 (1.40)	8.4 (1.57)	‡ (†)
Massachusetts	10.8 (0.83)	11.3 (1.48)	6.4 (1.23)	9.7 (1.98)	6.2 (1.69)	4.7 (0.64)	4.3 (0.67)	3.8 (0.75)	4.1 (0.93)	5.3 (1.51)
Michigan	10.7 (1.54)	8.0 (0.93)	9.2 (1.55)	6.0 (1.15)	11.8 (1.62)	6.4 (1.13)	3.8 (0.91)	5.4 (1.04)	3.5 ! (1.32)	9.0 (2.00)
Minnesota	9.6 (1.13)	9.5 (1.11)	8.1 (1.17)	7.3 (1.16)	11.4 (1.49)	4.5 (0.85)	4.4 (1.04)	3.6 (0.68)	6.5 (1.38)	6.5 (1.27)
Mississippi	13.4 (1.48)	11.1 (0.99)	5.5 (0.92)	10.7 (1.59)	7.7 (1.42)	4.1 (0.78)	3.7 (0.58)	0.9 ! (0.34)	2.9 (0.83)	3.1 ! (1.14)
Missouri	12.6 (1.11)	11.3 (1.73)	8.3 (1.27)	8.7 (1.17)	12.3 (2.25)	3.2 (0.73)	5.6 (1.41)	5.5 (1.43)	5.3 (1.15)	7.5 (1.73)
Montana	7.7 (0.58)	8.3 (0.97)	6.0 (0.78)	6.3 (1.25)	7.6 (2.24)	2.7 (0.48)	2.7 (0.38)	1.9 (0.47)	4.0 (0.81)	4.2 ! (1.37)
Nebraska	10.4 (0.61)	9.9 (0.70)	7.5 (1.12)	7.2 (1.27)	8.0 (1.46)	3.6 (0.64)	3.8 (0.57)	4.1 (0.89)	4.2 (1.11)	5.8 (1.36)
Nevada	13.2 (1.22)	11.6 (1.34)	7.3 (1.89)	9.2 (2.21)	9.1 (2.65)	4.5 (0.86)	8.1 (1.07)	4.1 ! (1.28)	3.7 ! (1.41)	4.7 ! (2.25)
New Hampshire	11.1 (1.30)	8.8 (1.43)	5.8 (1.37)	6.5 (1.47)	5.6 ! (2.11)	3.0 (0.70)	4.2 (1.09)	2.8 ! (0.91)	2.2 ! (0.91)	‡ (†)
New Jersey	7.9 (0.87)	7.5 (0.80)	4.3 (1.20)	4.6 (1.26)	6.9 (1.08)	2.4 (0.45)	3.4 (0.78)	2.0 ! (0.67)	2.2 ! (0.82)	3.6 (0.97)
New Mexico	12.8 (1.27)	10.2 (1.75)	7.8 (1.25)	12.8 (1.85)	10.0 (2.76)	4.4 (0.72)	6.8 (1.77)	5.9 (0.97)	4.5 (1.33)	9.9 ! (3.17)
New York	16.2 (1.32)	11.5 (1.06)	10.4 (1.62)	10.5 (1.85)	11.9 (1.86)	6.7 (0.97)	5.2 (0.79)	6.5 (1.12)	6.4 (1.56)	7.0 (1.48)
North Carolina	17.1 (1.32)	12.8 (1.63)	8.7 (1.44)	9.6 (1.71)	13.4 (2.79)	6.0 (0.95)	5.5 (1.23)	4.4 (0.95)	5.9 ! (1.84)	6.3 (1.58)
North Dakota	5.5 (0.62)	5.7 (0.57)	5.0 (0.95)	2.5 (0.70)	6.1 (1.48)	2.9 (0.66)	2.1 (0.37)	2.1 (0.49)	1.6 ! (0.50)	3.3 ! (1.06)
Ohio	15.2 (1.48)	9.6 (1.35)	6.2 (1.14)	8.7 (1.59)	9.9 (1.20)	3.6 (0.69)	2.9 (0.83)	2.5 ! (0.83)	2.2 ! (0.70)	3.9 (0.88)
Oklahoma	11.0 (1.21)	8.5 (1.17)	6.0 (0.79)	7.4 (0.87)	9.6 (2.12)	4.1 (0.81)	4.5 (1.12)	3.0 (0.53)	3.2 (0.63)	6.2 (1.66)
Oregon	11.5 (1.00)	6.9 (1.33)	5.5 (1.11)	6.3 (1.30)	5.3 (1.56)	3.4 (0.64)	3.0 (0.60)	1.4 ! (0.55)	3.9 ! (1.18)	3.4 ! (1.27)
Pennsylvania	11.0 (1.75)	9.5 (1.28)	9.5 (1.29)	4.6 (1.04)	10.1 (1.54)	3.6 (1.02)	4.5 (0.97)	5.0 (0.82)	3.8 (0.90)	4.4 (0.99)
Rhode Island	13.4 (1.78)	10.2 (0.64)	4.6 ! (1.39)	8.6 (2.13)	‡ (†)	4.2 (0.91)	4.8 (0.59)	2.4 ! (0.92)	‡ (†)	‡ (†)
South Carolina	15.2 (1.62)	11.5 (1.10)	8.5 (1.30)	8.5 (1.46)	13.1 (2.70)	3.8 (0.92)	5.3 (0.94)	3.1 (0.82)	2.9 ! (1.18)	‡ (†)
South Dakota	6.5 (0.83)	7.7 (0.91)	4.7 (1.23)	6.9 (1.88)	10.0 (2.28)	2.6 (0.46)	3.9 (0.50)	2.9 (0.79)	4.3 (0.88)	5.2 ! (1.66)
Tennessee	12.4 (1.45)	13.3 (1.65)	6.5 (1.24)	7.7 (1.26)	9.4 (2.11)	3.5 (0.91)	2.6 (0.67)	3.7 (1.02)	4.1 (1.11)	3.2 ! (1.04)
Texas	12.6 (1.15)	8.9 (0.89)	7.6 (1.13)	7.6 (1.31)	10.0 (1.81)	4.2 (0.65)	4.8 (0.75)	3.9 (0.92)	4.2 (1.18)	5.7 (1.30)
Utah	11.1 (0.87)	8.0 (1.15)	5.2 (0.82)	5.7 (1.18)	7.2 (1.96)	7.2 (0.72)	2.6 (0.58)	4.1 (0.90)	3.8 ! (1.26)	5.4 (1.53)
Vermont	12.4 (1.28)	9.9 (1.46)	4.9 (1.18)	7.6 (1.82)	8.7 (1.86)	8.6 (1.38)	5.3 (0.94)	1.8 ! (0.90)	4.2 (1.22)	5.3 (1.29)
Virginia	14.9 (1.37)	12.1 (1.19)	6.5 (1.11)	8.1 (1.38)	9.9 (1.58)	6.9 (1.23)	4.9 (0.76)	2.9 ! (0.88)	6.0 (1.32)	6.5 (1.68)
Washington	13.0 (1.33)	10.0 (0.98)	6.7 (1.29)	7.0 (1.34)	7.4 (1.36)	4.9 (0.74)	5.0 (0.61)	4.1 (0.85)	4.4 (1.28)	6.8 (1.80)
West Virginia	11.7 (0.86)	10.0 (1.19)	7.4 (1.13)	8.1 (1.67)	9.4 (2.08)	3.4 (0.67)	3.4 (0.67)	3.4 (0.82)	4.0 (1.07)	4.3 ! (1.72)
Wisconsin	13.7 (1.82)	10.1 (0.99)	4.7 (0.99)	8.8 (1.51)	13.7 (2.37)	3.9 (0.77)	4.4 (0.79)	2.5 (0.71)	6.5 (1.29)	11.3 (2.56)
Wyoming	9.0 (0.79)	6.7 (0.96)	3.8 ! (1.31)	5.1 (1.00)	10.9 (3.10)	2.7 (0.49)	2.6 (0.47)	2.5 ! (1.04)	3.0 (0.86)	‡ (†)

†Not applicable.
!Interpret data with caution. The coefficient of variation (CV) for this estimate is between 30 and 50 percent.
‡Reporting standards not met. Data may be suppressed because the response rate is under 50 percent, there are too few cases for a reliable estimate, or the coefficient of variation (CV) is 50 percent or greater.

NOTE: Teachers who taught only prekindergarten students are excluded. Includes traditional public and public charter schools. Detail may not sum to totals because of rounding. Some data have been revised from previously published figures.
SOURCE: U.S. Department of Education, National Center for Education Statistics, Schools and Staffing Survey (SASS), "Public School Teacher Data File," 1993–94, 1999–2000, 2003–04, 2007–08, and 2011–12; and "Charter School Teacher Data File," 1999–2000. (This table was prepared October 2013.)

Table 229.10. Percentage of public schools recording incidents of crime at school and reporting incidents to police, number of incidents, and rate per 1,000 students, by type of crime: Selected years, 1999–2000 through 2013–14

[Standard errors appear in parentheses]

Type of crime recorded or reported to police	Percent of schools										2013–14[1]					
	1999–2000		2003–04		2005–06		2007–08		2009–10		Percent of schools		Number of incidents		Rate per 1,000 students[2]	
1	2		3		4		5		6		7		8		9	
Recorded incidents																
Total[3]	**86.4**	**(1.23)**	**88.5**	**(0.85)**	**85.7**	**(1.07)**	**85.5**	**(0.87)**	**85.0**	**(0.87)**	—	(†)	—	(†)	—	(†)
Violent incidents	**71.4**	**(1.37)**	**81.4**	**(1.05)**	**77.7**	**(1.11)**	**75.5**	**(1.09)**	**73.8**	**(1.09)**	**65.0**	**(1.46)**	**757,000**	**(48,540)**	**15.4**	**(1.04)**
Serious violent incidents	19.7	(0.98)	18.3	(0.99)	17.1	(0.91)	17.2	(1.06)	16.4	(1.06)	13.1	(1.00)	25,700	(2,730)	0.5	(0.06)
Rape or attempted rape	0.7	(0.10)	0.8	(0.17)	0.3	(0.07)	0.8	(0.17)	0.5	(0.17)	0.2 !	(0.10)	‡	(†)	#	(†)
Sexual battery other than rape	2.5	(0.33)	3.0	(0.32)	2.8	(0.24)	2.5	(0.33)	2.3	(0.33)	1.7	(0.37)	1,800	(480)	#	(†)
Physical attack or fight with a weapon	5.2	(0.60)	4.0	(0.46)	3.0	(0.38)	3.0	(0.33)	3.9	(0.33)	1.8	(0.34)	2,900	(700)	0.1	(0.01)
Threat of physical attack with a weapon	11.1	(0.70)	8.6	(0.71)	8.8	(0.66)	9.3	(0.77)	7.7	(0.77)	8.7	(0.78)	15,100	(1,820)	0.3	(0.04)
Robbery with a weapon	0.5 !	(0.15)	0.6	(0.15)	0.4	(0.12)	0.4 !	(0.14)	0.2	(0.14)	‡	(†)	‡	(†)	‡	(†)
Robbery without a weapon	5.3	(0.56)	6.3	(0.60)	6.4	(0.59)	5.2	(0.56)	4.4	(0.56)	2.5	(0.42)	5,200	(920)	0.1	(0.02)
Physical attack or fight without a weapon	63.7	(1.52)	76.7	(1.21)	74.3	(1.20)	72.7	(1.07)	70.5	(1.07)	57.5	(1.43)	453,100	(41,330)	9.1	(0.87)
Threat of physical attack without a weapon	52.2	(1.47)	53.0	(1.34)	52.2	(1.27)	47.8	(1.19)	46.4	(1.19)	47.1	(1.50)	278,100	(13,820)	5.7	(0.30)
Theft[4]	**45.6**	**(1.37)**	**46.0**	**(1.29)**	**46.0**	**(1.07)**	**47.3**	**(1.29)**	**44.1**	**(1.29)**	—	(†)	—	(†)	—	(†)
Other incidents[5]	**72.7**	**(1.30)**	**64.0**	**(1.27)**	**68.2**	**(1.07)**	**67.4**	**(1.13)**	**68.1**	**(1.13)**	—	(†)	—	(†)	—	(†)
Possession of a firearm/explosive device	5.5	(0.44)	6.1	(0.49)	7.2	(0.60)	4.7	(0.38)	4.7	(0.38)	—	(†)	—	(†)	—	(†)
Possession of a knife or sharp object	42.6	(1.28)	—	(†)	42.8	(1.23)	40.6	(1.10)	39.7	(1.10)	—	(†)	—	(†)	—	(†)
Distribution of illegal drugs[6]	12.3	(0.50)	12.9	(0.55)	—	(†)	—	(†)	—	(†)	—	(†)	—	(†)	—	(†)
Possession or use of alcohol or illegal drugs[6]	26.6	(0.72)	29.3	(0.87)	—	(†)	—	(†)	—	(†)	—	(†)	—	(†)	—	(†)
Distribution, possession, or use of illegal drugs[7]	—	(†)	—	(†)	25.9	(0.68)	23.2	(0.68)	24.6	(0.68)	—	(†)	—	(†)	—	(†)
Inappropriate distribution, possession, or use of prescription drugs[8]	—	(†)	—	(†)	—	(†)	—	(†)	12.1	(†)	—	(†)	—	(†)	—	(†)
Distribution, possession, or use of alcohol[7]	—	(†)	—	(†)	16.2	(0.68)	14.9	(0.57)	14.1	(0.57)	—	(†)	—	(†)	—	(†)
Sexual harassment	36.3	(1.26)	—	(†)	—	(†)	—	(†)	—	(†)	—	(†)	—	(†)	—	(†)
Vandalism	51.4	(1.61)	51.4	(1.17)	50.5	(1.17)	49.3	(1.16)	45.8	(1.16)	—	(†)	—	(†)	—	(†)
Reported incidents to police																
Total	**62.5**	**(1.37)**	**65.2**	**(1.35)**	**60.9**	**(1.15)**	**62.0**	**(1.24)**	**60.0**	**(1.24)**	—	(†)	—	(†)	—	(†)
Violent incidents	**36.0**	**(1.26)**	**43.6**	**(1.15)**	**37.7**	**(1.09)**	**37.8**	**(1.16)**	**39.9**	**(1.16)**	—	(†)	—	(†)	—	(†)
Serious violent incidents	14.8	(0.82)	13.3	(0.88)	12.6	(0.70)	12.6	(0.86)	10.4	(0.86)	—	(†)	—	(†)	—	(†)
Rape or attempted rape	0.6	(0.10)	0.8	(0.17)	0.3	(0.07)	0.8	(0.17)	0.5	(0.17)	—	(†)	—	(†)	—	(†)
Sexual battery other than rape	2.3	(0.34)	2.6	(0.28)	2.6	(0.26)	2.1	(0.29)	1.4	(0.29)	—	(†)	—	(†)	—	(†)
Physical attack or fight with a weapon	3.9	(0.50)	2.8	(0.38)	2.2	(0.27)	2.1	(0.27)	2.2	(0.27)	—	(†)	—	(†)	—	(†)
Threat of physical attack with a weapon	8.5	(0.59)	6.0	(0.55)	5.9	(0.49)	5.7	(0.59)	4.5	(0.59)	—	(†)	—	(†)	—	(†)
Robbery with a weapon	0.3 !	(0.09)	0.6	(0.15)	0.4	(0.12)	0.4 !	(0.14)	0.2	(0.14)	—	(†)	—	(†)	—	(†)
Robbery without a weapon	3.4	(0.41)	4.2	(0.51)	4.9	(0.48)	4.1	(0.42)	3.5	(0.42)	—	(†)	—	(†)	—	(†)
Physical attack or fight without a weapon	25.8	(0.91)	35.6	(0.98)	29.2	(1.00)	28.2	(0.90)	34.3	(0.90)	—	(†)	—	(†)	—	(†)
Threat of physical attack without a weapon	18.9	(0.94)	21.0	(0.82)	19.7	(0.69)	19.5	(0.76)	15.2	(0.76)	—	(†)	—	(†)	—	(†)
Theft[4]	**28.5**	**(1.04)**	**30.5**	**(1.17)**	**27.9**	**(0.97)**	**31.0**	**(1.12)**	**25.4**	**(1.12)**	—	(†)	—	(†)	—	(†)
Other incidents[5]	**52.0**	**(1.14)**	**50.0**	**(1.18)**	**50.6**	**(1.00)**	**48.7**	**(1.17)**	**46.3**	**(1.17)**	—	(†)	—	(†)	—	(†)
Possession of a firearm/explosive device	4.5	(0.41)	4.9	(0.44)	5.5	(0.51)	3.6	(0.32)	3.1	(0.32)	—	(†)	—	(†)	—	(†)
Possession of a knife or sharp object	23.0	(0.84)	—	(†)	25.0	(1.00)	23.3	(0.69)	20.0	(0.69)	—	(†)	—	(†)	—	(†)
Distribution of illegal drugs[6]	11.4	(0.48)	12.4	(0.57)	—	(†)	—	(†)	—	(†)	—	(†)	—	(†)	—	(†)
Possession or use of alcohol or illegal drugs[6]	22.2	(0.67)	26.0	(0.76)	—	(†)	—	(†)	—	(†)	—	(†)	—	(†)	—	(†)
Distribution, possession, or use of illegal drugs[7]	—	(†)	—	(†)	22.8	(0.62)	20.7	(0.60)	21.4	(0.60)	—	(†)	—	(†)	—	(†)
Inappropriate distribution, possession, or use of prescription drugs[8]	—	(†)	—	(†)	—	(†)	—	(†)	9.6	(†)	—	(†)	—	(†)	—	(†)
Distribution, possession, or use of alcohol[7]	—	(†)	—	(†)	11.6	(0.61)	10.6	(0.55)	10.0	(0.55)	—	(†)	—	(†)	—	(†)
Sexual harassment	14.7	(0.78)	—	(†)	—	(†)	—	(†)	—	(†)	—	(†)	—	(†)	—	(†)
Vandalism	32.7	(1.10)	34.3	(1.06)	31.9	(1.02)	30.8	(1.18)	26.8	(1.18)	—	(†)	—	(†)	—	(†)

—Not available.

†Not applicable.

#Rounds to zero.

!Interpret data with caution. The coefficient of variation (CV) for this estimate is between 30 and 50 percent.

‡Reporting standards not met. Either there are too few cases for a reliable estimate or the coefficient of variation (CV) is 50 percent or greater.

[1]Data for 2013–14 were collected using the Fast Response Survey System, while data for earlier years were collected using the School Survey on Crime and Safety (SSOCS). The 2013–14 survey was designed to allow comparisons with SSOCS data. However, respondents to the 2013–14 survey could choose either to complete the survey on paper (and mail it back) or to complete the survey online, whereas respondents to SSOCS did not have the option of completing the survey online. The 2013–14 survey also relied on a smaller sample. The smaller sample size and change in survey administration may have impacted 2013–14 results.

[2]Because the 2013–14 survey did not collect school enrollment counts, the rate per 1,000 students was calculated by dividing the number of incidents by the total number of students obtained from the Common Core of Data.

[3]Total not presented for 2013–14 because the survey did not collect information regarding theft and other incidents. Therefore, the total incident rate is not comparable with earlier years.

[4]Theft/larceny (taking things worth over $10 without personal confrontation) was defined for respondents as "the unlawful taking of another person's property without personal confrontation, threat, violence, or bodily harm." This includes pocket picking, stealing a purse or backpack (if left unattended or no force was used to take it from owner), theft from a building, theft from a motor vehicle or motor vehicle parts or accessories, theft of a bicycle, theft from a vending machine, and all other types of thefts.

[5]Caution should be used when making direct comparisons of "Other incidents" between years because the survey questions about alcohol and drugs changed, as outlined in footnotes 6, 7, and 8.

[6]The survey items "Distribution of illegal drugs" and "Possession or use of alcohol or illegal drugs" appear only on the 1999–2000 and 2003–04 questionnaires. Different alcohol- and drug-related survey items were used on the questionnaires for later years.

[7]The survey items "Distribution, possession, or use of illegal drugs" and "Distribution, possession, or use of alcohol" appear only on the questionnaires for 2005–06 and later years.

[8]The 2009–10 questionnaire was the first to include the survey item "Inappropriate distribution, possession, or use of prescription drugs."

NOTE: Responses were provided by the principal or the person most knowledgeable about crime and safety issues at the school. "At school" was defined to include activities that happen in school buildings, on school grounds, on school buses, and at places that hold school-sponsored events or activities. Respondents were instructed to include incidents that occurred before, during, and after normal school hours or when school activities or events were in session. Detail may not sum to totals because of rounding and because schools that recorded or reported more than one type of crime incident were counted only once in the total percentage of schools recording or reporting incidents.

SOURCE: U.S. Department of Education, National Center for Education Statistics, 1999–2000, 2003–04, 2005–06, 2007–08, and 2009–10 School Survey on Crime and Safety (SSOCS), 2000, 2004, 2006, 2008, and 2010; Fast Response Survey System (FRSS), "School Safety and Discipline: 2013–14," FRSS 106, 2014; and Common Core of Data (CCD), "Public Elementary/Secondary School Universe Survey," 2013–14. (This table was prepared September 2015.)

Table 229.30. Percentage of public schools recording violent incidents of crime at school, number of incidents, and rate per 1,000 students, by category of violent incident and selected school characteristics: 2009–10 and 2013–14

[Standard errors appear in parentheses]

School characteristic	2009–10							2013–14[1]						
	Total number of public schools	All violent incidents[2]			Serious violent incidents[3]			Total number of public schools	All violent incidents[2]			Serious violent incidents[3]		
		Percent of schools recording	Number of incidents	Rate per 1,000 students	Percent of schools recording	Number of incidents	Rate per 1,000 students		Percent of schools recording	Number of incidents	Rate per 1,000 students[4]	Percent of schools recording	Number of incidents	Rate per 1,000 students[4]
1	2	3	4	5	6	7	8	9	10	11	12	13	14	15
Total	**82,800 (460)**	**73.8 (1.07)**	**1,183,700 (44,390)**	**25.0 (0.91)**	**16.4 (0.94)**	**52,500 (5,510)**	**1.1 (0.12)**	**84,100 (840)**	**65.0 (1.46)**	**757,000 (48,540)**	**15.4 (1.04)**	**13.1 (1.00)**	**25,700 (2,730)**	**0.5 (0.06)**
School level[5]														
Primary	48,900 (340)	64.4 (1.63)	482,100 (37,320)	21.3 (1.64)	13.0 (1.42)	21,900 (3,780)	1.0 (0.17)	49,700 (800)	52.8 (2.18)	318,300 (43,530)	13.0 (1.85)	9.2 (1.25)	7,700 (1,250)	0.3 (0.05)
Middle	15,300 (100)	90.5 (1.10)	375,200 (19,310)	40.0 (2.04)	18.9 (1.46)	13,600 (2,360)	1.5 (0.25)	16,100 (250)	87.6 (1.93)	228,700 (15,050)	23.3 (1.58)	18.3 (1.92)	7,600 (1,150)	0.8 (0.12)
High school/combined	— (†)	— (†)	— (†)	— (†)	— (†)	— (†)	— (†)	18,400 (330)	78.0 (2.53)	209,900 (15,680)	13.9 (0.98)	19.3 (1.85)	10,400 (1,960)	0.7 (0.13)
High school	12,200 (70)	90.9 (1.21)	264,400 (12,910)	21.4 (1.05)	27.6 (1.35)	13,500 (1,690)	1.1 (0.14)	— (†)	— (†)	— (†)	— (†)	— (†)	— (†)	— (†)
Combined	6,400 (200)	73.7 (5.33)	62,000 (7,570)	20.8 (2.21)	15.5 (3.72)	‡ (†)	‡ (†)	— (†)	— (†)	— (†)	— (†)	— (†)	— (†)	— (†)
Enrollment size														
Less than 300	18,900 (400)	62.8 (3.25)	111,300 (17,230)	27.2 (4.08)	10.4 (2.11)	6,100 ! (2,100)	1.5 ! (0.51)	19,500 (1,540)	54.6 (4.18)	72,200 (15,010)	16.0 (2.74)	11.3 (2.58)	‡ (†)	0.8 (0.19)
300–499	25,200 (180)	71.3 (2.34)	274,400 (25,110)	26.5 (2.44)	15.7 (2.14)	14,200 (3,560)	1.4 (0.35)	25,400 (1,250)	60.7 (2.80)	202,700 (38,450)	19.5 (3.80)	10.7 (1.77)	5,000 (1,090)	0.5 (0.10)
500–999	29,800 (100)	76.4 (1.75)	487,900 (35,630)	25.0 (1.78)	15.9 (1.42)	16,400 (2,420)	0.8 (0.12)	30,700 (950)	69.1 (1.98)	316,200 (24,810)	14.9 (1.14)	12.9 (1.57)	11,500 (2,290)	0.5 (0.11)
1,000 or more	8,900 (60)	95.4 (1.22)	310,100 (16,110)	23.2 (1.19)	32.8 (1.61)	15,700 (2,080)	1.2 (0.15)	8,500 (300)	86.4 (2.18)	165,900 (12,860)	12.7 (0.92)	25.3 (2.57)	6,300 (900)	0.5 (0.07)
Locale														
City	21,500 (190)	74.9 (2.12)	396,300 (27,430)	28.8 (2.11)	21.7 (2.12)	17,400 (2,830)	1.3 (0.21)	21,100 (570)	68.0 (2.96)	300,200 (39,830)	20.7 (2.87)	17.5 (2.30)	10,100 (2,010)	0.7 (0.15)
Suburban	23,800 (240)	73.5 (2.21)	371,000 (33,010)	22.4 (1.92)	15.5 (1.80)	16,200 (3,070)	1.0 (0.18)	23,500 (630)	60.4 (3.13)	192,100 (20,140)	11.9 (1.23)	11.2 (1.62)	6,000 (1,010)	0.4 (0.06)
Town	12,100 (110)	80.3 (3.14)	166,300 (21,190)	28.2 (3.36)	15.6 (2.33)	6,300 (1,390)	1.1 (0.23)	10,800 (750)	76.4 (3.51)	103,100 (12,540)	18.3 (2.01)	17.4 (3.46)	4,400 (1,040)	0.8 (0.18)
Rural	25,300 (300)	70.2 (1.91)	250,100 (15,910)	22.5 (1.49)	13.2 (1.51)	12,600 (2,920)	1.1 (0.26)	28,600 (1,030)	62.2 (3.21)	161,700 (16,780)	12.4 (1.23)	9.9 (1.51)	5,200 (840)	0.4 (0.07)
Percent combined enrollment of Black, Hispanic, Asian/Pacific Islander, and American Indian/ Alaska Native students														
Less than 5 percent	11,700 (980)	69.6 (3.33)	108,500 (20,340)	23.3 (3.62)	12.6 (2.52)	5,400 ! (2,090)	1.2 ! (0.44)	7,300 (920)	59.7 (5.75)	30,500 (4,910)	11.6 (1.37)	5.7 ! (2.37)	‡ (†)	0.2 ! (0.09)
5 percent to less than 20 percent	20,900 (1,080)	67.9 (2.82)	192,800 (15,450)	17.2 (1.19)	9.9 (1.29)	6,500 (1,490)	0.6 (0.13)	22,800 (1,130)	62.1 (3.55)	111,600 (10,320)	10.3 (0.93)	10.2 (1.80)	5,400 (1,080)	0.5 (0.10)
20 percent to less than 50 percent	20,000 (650)	75.9 (2.14)	293,600 (20,960)	23.1 (1.76)	18.6 (1.58)	15,100 (3,000)	1.2 (0.23)	22,700 (1,290)	62.1 (2.81)	173,500 (15,540)	11.9 (1.01)	14.9 (2.06)	6,800 (1,020)	0.5 (0.07)
50 percent or more	30,100 (1,270)	78.2 (1.75)	588,800 (43,670)	31.4 (1.96)	21.1 (1.82)	25,400 (4,360)	1.4 (0.23)	31,300 (1,120)	70.4 (2.29)	441,400 (44,490)	20.9 (2.13)	15.7 (1.62)	13,000 (2,170)	0.6 (0.11)
Percent of students eligible for free or reduced-price lunch[4]														
0–25	17,100 (690)	62.6 (3.07)	141,700 (11,440)	11.9 (0.82)	10.5 (1.22)	6,700 (1,400)	0.6 (0.11)	15,100 (1,090)	50.8 (3.79)	62,400 (9,970)	6.1 (0.93)	10.3 (2.01)	3,200 (680)	0.3 (0.06)
26–50	22,700 (1,050)	76.0 (2.13)	290,500 (20,440)	22.1 (1.48)	16.2 (1.89)	12,500 (1,970)	1.0 (0.16)	22,900 (1,290)	66.9 (2.82)	141,200 (12,280)	10.7 (0.89)	10.9 (1.69)	4,600 (770)	0.4 (0.06)
51–75	23,800 (1,020)	73.8 (2.49)	334,400 (24,050)	27.3 (1.82)	15.8 (1.67)	13,100 (2,840)	1.1 (0.24)	23,200 (1,200)	67.4 (3.00)	219,300 (19,270)	17.2 (1.29)	14.6 (1.88)	8,500 (1,460)	0.7 (0.11)
76–100	19,100 (940)	81.4 (2.49)	417,200 (42,360)	41.3 (3.73)	22.9 (2.60)	20,100 (4,550)	2.0 (0.45)	19,800 (1,100)	71.2 (2.91)	301,800 (43,350)	27.6 (3.94)	16.2 (2.16)	8,700 (1,920)	0.8 (0.18)

—Not available.
†Not applicable.
!Interpret data with caution. The coefficient of variation (CV) for this estimate is between 30 and 50 percent.
‡Reporting standards not met. Either there are too few cases for a reliable estimate or the coefficient of variation (CV) is 50 percent or greater.
[1]Data for 2013–14 were collected using the Fast Response Survey System, while data for 2009–10 were collected using the School Survey on Crime and Safety (SSOCS). The 2013–14 survey was designed to allow comparisons with SSOCS data. However, respondents to the 2013–14 survey could choose either to complete the survey on paper (and mail it back) or to complete the survey online, whereas respondents to SSOCS did not have the option of completing the survey online. The 2013–14 survey also relied on a smaller sample. The smaller sample size and change in survey administration may have impacted 2013–14 results.
[2]All violent incidents include serious violent incidents (see footnote 3) as well as physical attack or fight without a weapon and threat of physical attack without a weapon.
[3]Serious violent incidents include rape, sexual battery other than rape, physical attack or fight with a weapon, threat of physical attack with a weapon, and robbery with or without a weapon.
[4]The 2013–14 survey collected neither school enrollment counts nor data on the percentage of students eligible for free or reduced-price lunch. For 2013–14, the rate per 1,000 students was calculated by dividing the number of incidents by the total number of students obtained from the Common Core of Data (CCD). For 2013–14, the classification of schools by the percentage of students eligible for free or reduced-price lunch was also computed from CCD data.
[5]Primary schools are defined as schools in which the lowest grade is not higher than grade 3 and the highest grade is not higher than grade 8. Middle schools are defined as schools in which the lowest grade is not lower than grade 4 and the highest grade is not higher than grade 9. High schools are defined as schools in which the lowest grade is not lower than grade 9 and the highest grade is not higher than grade 12. Combined schools include all other combinations of grades, including K–12 schools. Separate data on high schools and combined schools are not available for 2013–14.
NOTE: Responses were provided by the principal or the person most knowledgeable about crime and safety issues at the school. "At school" was defined to include activities that happen in school buildings, on school grounds, on school buses, and at places that hold school-sponsored events or activities. Respondents were instructed to include incidents that occurred before, during, or after normal school hours or when school activities or events were in session. Detail may not sum to totals because of rounding.
SOURCE: U.S. Department of Education, National Center for Education Statistics, 2009–10 School Survey on Crime and Safety (SSOCS), 2010; Fast Response Survey System (FRSS), "School Safety and Discipline: 2013–14," FRSS 106, 2014; and Common Core of Data (CCD), "Public Elementary/Secondary School Universe Survey," 2013–14. (This table was prepared September 2015.)

Table 230.10. Percentage of public schools reporting selected discipline problems that occurred at school, by frequency and selected school characteristics: Selected years, 1999–2000 through 2013–14

[Standard errors appear in parentheses]

Year and school characteristic	Happens at least once a week[1]: Student racial/ethnic tensions[3]	Student bullying	Student sexual harassment of other students	Student harassment of other students based on sexual orientation or gender identity	Student verbal abuse of teachers	Widespread disorder in classrooms	Student acts of disrespect for teachers other than verbal abuse	Happens at all[2]: Gang activities	Cult or extremist group activities
1	2	3	4	5	6	7	8	9	10
All schools									
1999–2000	3.4 (0.41)	29.3 (1.21)	— (†)	— (†)	12.5 (0.69)	3.1 (0.44)	— (†)	18.7 (0.85)	6.7 (0.46)
2003–04	2.1 (0.28)	26.8 (1.09)	4.0 (0.40)	— (†)	10.7 (0.80)	2.8 (0.39)	— (†)	16.7 (0.78)	3.4 (0.35)
2005–06	2.8 (0.31)	24.5 (1.14)	3.5 (0.40)	— (†)	9.5 (0.61)	2.3 (0.24)	— (†)	16.9 (0.76)	3.7 (0.41)
2007–08	3.7 (0.49)	25.3 (1.11)	3.0 (0.39)	— (†)	6.0 (0.48)	4.0 (0.45)	10.5 (0.71)	19.8 (0.88)	2.6 (0.36)
2009–10									
All schools	**2.8 (0.39)**	**23.1 (1.12)**	**3.2 (0.55)**	**2.5 (0.41)**	**4.8 (0.49)**	**2.5 (0.37)**	**8.6 (0.67)**	**16.4 (0.84)**	**1.7 (0.31)**
School level[4]									
Primary	2.1 (0.62)	19.6 (1.75)	1.8 ! (0.70)	0.8 ! (0.35)	3.4 (0.67)	1.9 ! (0.60)	6.1 (0.92)	7.5 (1.11)	1.4 ! (0.48)
Middle	5.4 (0.81)	38.6 (1.60)	6.1 (0.89)	6.2 (0.92)	6.8 (0.83)	4.1 (0.67)	13.7 (1.15)	29.2 (1.48)	1.4 (0.36)
High school	3.3 (0.56)	19.8 (1.41)	3.2 (0.58)	3.1 (0.55)	8.6 (1.00)	4.4 (0.80)	14.3 (1.27)	38.4 (1.50)	3.9 (0.48)
Combined	‡ (†)	18.6 (4.38)	7.5 ! (2.92)	6.0 ! (2.74)	‡ (†)	# (†)	4.4 ! (2.05)	11.1 (2.89)	‡ (†)
Enrollment size									
Less than 300	‡ (†)	16.5 (2.48)	4.5 ! (1.38)	4.3 ! (1.33)	‡ (†)	‡ (†)	3.3 ! (1.09)	6.5 (1.34)	‡ (†)
300–499	2.5 (0.72)	24.0 (2.19)	2.4 ! (0.75)	1.0 (0.28)	5.2 (1.03)	2.4 (0.70)	9.5 (1.57)	11.9 (1.49)	‡ (†)
500–999	3.0 (0.54)	25.3 (1.55)	2.6 (0.55)	2.4 (0.48)	4.3 (0.64)	2.6 (0.60)	8.3 (1.00)	16.4 (1.24)	1.3 ! (0.44)
1,000 or more	5.5 (1.10)	27.0 (2.12)	4.7 (1.01)	3.8 (0.82)	11.2 (1.37)	4.3 (0.96)	18.2 (1.64)	49.8 (1.72)	5.6 (0.95)
Locale									
City	5.3 (1.14)	27.0 (2.08)	3.6 ! (1.16)	2.9 ! (1.06)	9.1 (1.38)	4.5 (0.85)	11.7 (1.46)	28.3 (2.10)	2.5 (0.72)
Suburban	2.7 (0.61)	19.9 (1.96)	2.6 (0.69)	2.0 (0.42)	4.7 (0.92)	3.0 (0.77)	8.1 (1.10)	14.6 (1.16)	1.2 ! (0.41)
Town	1.0 ! (0.36)	26.2 (2.71)	2.9 ! (0.99)	2.0 (0.56)	3.3 ! (1.24)	0.6 ! (0.26)	11.6 (2.16)	13.9 (1.56)	1.7 ! (0.75)
Rural	1.6 ! (0.63)	21.2 (2.11)	3.6 (1.01)	2.9 (0.69)	1.9 ! (0.58)	1.3 ! (0.62)	5.0 (0.93)	9.1 (1.13)	1.6 ! (0.70)
Percent combined enrollment of Black, Hispanic, Asian/Pacific Islander, and American Indian/Alaska Native students									
Less than 5 percent	‡ (†)	22.0 (3.36)	4.5 ! (1.91)	2.7 ! (1.19)	‡ (†)	‡ (†)	3.6 ! (1.18)	1.5 (0.39)	0.4 ! (0.19)
5 percent to less than 20 percent	1.5 (0.33)	21.3 (1.66)	1.8 ! (0.58)	1.9 (0.46)	1.8 (0.48)	0.5 ! (0.16)	6.1 (1.22)	5.8 (0.80)	1.8 ! (0.75)
20 percent to less than 50 percent	3.2 (0.96)	22.3 (1.70)	2.6 (0.45)	2.6 (0.47)	4.5 (1.08)	1.1 ! (0.48)	9.6 (1.12)	16.9 (1.40)	1.4 (0.23)
50 percent or more	4.3 (0.95)	25.2 (2.35)	4.1 ! (1.25)	2.9 ! (0.87)	8.5 (1.17)	5.7 (0.94)	11.7 (1.22)	29.1 (1.88)	2.4 (0.64)
Percent of students eligible for free or reduced-price lunch									
0–25	1.9 (0.40)	19.7 (1.99)	2.6 (0.74)	2.1 (0.55)	1.5 (0.28)	0.7 ! (0.21)	3.6 (0.60)	7.9 (0.91)	1.4 (0.39)
26–50	2.6 ! (0.85)	21.9 (1.58)	3.2 (0.80)	3.0 (0.67)	2.3 (0.52)	1.3 ! (0.43)	6.9 (0.91)	13.2 (1.33)	1.9 ! (0.68)
51–75	2.4 ! (0.83)	24.1 (2.24)	3.2 ! (0.98)	2.7 ! (0.86)	5.6 (0.95)	1.0 ! (0.37)	10.7 (1.42)	17.4 (1.46)	1.3 ! (0.57)
76–100	4.3 (1.16)	26.1 (3.07)	3.9 ! (1.47)	2.1 ! (0.87)	9.6 (1.64)	7.5 (1.38)	12.5 (1.49)	26.5 (2.19)	2.3 ! (0.87)
2013–14[5]									
All schools	**1.4 (0.31)**	**15.7 (1.12)**	**1.4 (0.26)**	**0.8 (0.19)**	**5.1 (0.54)**	**2.3 (0.45)**	**8.6 (0.74)**	**— (†)**	**— (†)**
School level[4]									
Primary	1.2 ! (0.47)	12.2 (1.64)	‡ (†)	‡ (†)	4.4 (0.83)	2.1 ! (0.64)	6.2 (1.11)	— (†)	— (†)
Middle	2.5 ! (0.84)	24.5 (2.11)	3.4 (0.84)	2.4 ! (0.81)	6.1 (1.08)	2.5 ! (0.87)	11.1 (1.58)	— (†)	— (†)
High school/combined	1.1 ! (0.37)	17.2 (1.84)	1.8 ! (0.54)	1.4 ! (0.54)	6.2 (1.10)	2.8 (0.76)	12.8 (1.68)	— (†)	— (†)
Enrollment size									
Less than 300	‡ (†)	13.5 (2.93)	‡ (†)	‡ (†)	‡ (†)	‡ (†)	5.1 ! (1.72)	— (†)	— (†)
300–499	‡ (†)	14.6 (2.10)	1.8 ! (0.69)	0.7 ! (0.34)	6.1 (1.41)	3.7 ! (1.20)	7.8 (1.53)	— (†)	— (†)
500–999	2.1 ! (0.73)	16.1 (1.54)	1.3 (0.36)	0.4 ! (0.22)	5.4 (0.94)	2.4 (0.71)	9.5 (1.23)	— (†)	— (†)
1,000 or more	3.7 (1.01)	22.1 (2.40)	3.8 ! (1.19)	2.0 ! (0.74)	8.4 (1.47)	2.6 ! (0.85)	15.6 (2.53)	— (†)	— (†)
Locale									
City	3.1 ! (1.08)	14.8 (2.11)	2.5 ! (0.84)	‡ (†)	8.1 (1.52)	4.9 (1.38)	12.5 (1.72)	— (†)	— (†)
Suburban	2.0 ! (0.59)	12.9 (1.66)	1.5 ! (0.47)	1.0 ! (0.35)	6.2 (1.35)	2.4 ! (0.99)	9.0 (1.81)	— (†)	— (†)
Town	‡ (†)	24.0 (3.39)	‡ (†)	‡ (†)	3.9 ! (1.67)	‡ (†)	8.6 (2.08)	— (†)	— (†)
Rural	‡ (†)	15.4 (2.35)	‡ (†)	‡ (†)	2.5 (0.70)	1.2 ! (0.52)	5.4 (1.15)	— (†)	— (†)

See notes at end of table.

Table 230.10. Percentage of public schools reporting selected discipline problems that occurred at school, by frequency and selected school characteristics: Selected years, 1999–2000 through 2013–14—Continued

[Standard errors appear in parentheses]

Year and school characteristic	Happens at least once a week[1]							Happens at all[2]	
	Student racial/ ethnic tensions[3]	Student bullying	Student sexual harassment of other students	Student harassment of other students based on sexual orientation or gender identity	Student verbal abuse of teachers	Widespread disorder in classrooms	Student acts of disrespect for teachers other than verbal abuse	Gang activities	Cult or extremist group activities
1	2	3	4	5	6	7	8	9	10
Percent combined enrollment of Black, Hispanic, Asian/Pacific Islander, and American Indian/Alaska Native students									
Less than 5 percent	‡ (†)	14.6 ! (4.52)	‡ (†)	‡ (†)	‡ (†)	‡ (†)	‡ (†)	— (†)	— (†)
5 percent to less than 20 percent	‡ (†)	11.9 (2.03)	‡ (†)	‡ (†)	1.6 ! (0.71)	‡ (†)	4.1 (1.00)	— (†)	— (†)
20 percent to less than 50 percent	1.5 ! (0.57)	18.1 (2.52)	2.2 ! (0.79)	‡ (†)	6.0 (1.36)	3.6 ! (1.13)	10.1 (1.72)	— (†)	— (†)
50 percent or more	2.5 (0.72)	16.8 (1.67)	1.5 (0.38)	1.1 ! (0.39)	7.8 (1.15)	3.4 (0.86)	11.6 (1.51)	— (†)	— (†)
Percent of students eligible for free or reduced-price lunch[6]									
0–25	‡ (†)	8.2 (2.15)	‡ (†)	‡ (†)	‡ (†)	‡ (†)	2.0 (0.59)	— (†)	— (†)
26–50	1.4 ! (0.56)	14.2 (2.02)	1.2 ! (0.42)	1.0 ! (0.45)	3.0 ! (0.94)	1.6 ! (0.76)	6.7 (1.28)	— (†)	— (†)
51–75	‡ (†)	18.3 (2.26)	2.2 ! (0.69)	‡ (†)	6.2 (1.19)	1.9 ! (0.70)	11.1 (1.75)	— (†)	— (†)
76–100	3.4 ! (1.18)	20.2 (2.36)	1.4 ! (0.67)	‡ (†)	8.2 (1.80)	5.1 (1.39)	12.4 (1.72)	— (†)	— (†)

—Not available.
†Not applicable.
#Rounds to zero.
!Interpret data with caution. The coefficient of variation (CV) for this estimate is between 30 and 50 percent.
‡Reporting standards not met. Either there are too few cases for a reliable estimate or the coefficient of variation (CV) is 50 percent or greater.
[1]Includes schools that reported the activity happens either at least once a week or daily.
[2]Includes schools that reported the activity happens at all at their school during the school year. In the 1999–2000 survey administration, the questionnaire specified "undesirable" gang activities and "undesirable" cult or extremist group activities.
[3]Prior to the 2007–08 survey administration, the questionnaire wording was "student racial tensions."
[4]Primary schools are defined as schools in which the lowest grade is not higher than grade 3 and the highest grade is not higher than grade 8. Middle schools are defined as schools in which the lowest grade is not lower than grade 4 and the highest grade is not higher than grade 9. High schools are defined as schools in which the lowest grade is not lower than grade 9 and the highest grade is not higher than grade 12. Combined schools include all other combinations of grades, including K–12 schools. Separate data on high schools and combined schools are not available for 2013–14.
[5]Data for 2013–14 were collected using the Fast Response Survey System, while data for earlier years were collected using the School Survey on Crime and Safety (SSOCS). The 2013–14 survey was designed to allow comparisons with SSOCS data. However, respondents to the 2013–14 survey could choose either to complete the survey on paper (and mail it back) or to complete the survey online, whereas respondents to SSOCS did not have the option of completing the survey online. The 2013–14 survey also relied on a smaller sample. The smaller sample size and change in survey administration may have impacted 2013–14 results.
[6]Because the 2013–14 survey did not collect data on the percentage of students eligible for free or reduced-price lunch, the classification of schools by the percentage of students eligible for free or reduced-price lunch was computed based on data obtained from the Common Core of Data.
NOTE: Responses were provided by the principal or the person most knowledgeable about crime and safety issues at the school. "At school" was defined to include activities that happen in school buildings, on school grounds, on school buses, and at places that hold school-sponsored events or activities. Respondents were instructed to respond only for those times that were during normal school hours or when school activities or events were in session, unless the survey specified otherwise.
SOURCE: U.S. Department of Education, National Center for Education Statistics, 1999–2000, 2003–04, 2005–06, 2007–08, and 2009–10 School Survey on Crime and Safety (SSOCS), 2000, 2004, 2006, 2008, and 2010; Fast Response Survey System (FRSS), "School Safety and Discipline: 2013–14," FRSS 106, 2014; and Common Core of Data (CCD), "Public Elementary/Secondary School Universe Survey," 2013–14. (This table was prepared September 2015.)

Table 230.20. Percentage of students ages 12–18 who reported that gangs were present at school during the school year, by selected student and school characteristics and urbanicity: Selected years, 2001 through 2013

Year and urbanicity	Total	Sex: Male	Sex: Female	Race/ethnicity[1]: White	Black	Hispanic	Asian	Other	Grade: 6th grade	7th grade	8th grade	9th grade	10th grade	11th grade	12th grade	Control of school: Public	Private
1	2	3	4	5	6	7	8	9	10	11	12	13	14	15	16	17	18
2001																	
Total	**20.1 (0.71)**	**21.4 (0.86)**	**18.8 (0.90)**	**15.5 (0.72)**	**28.6 (1.90)**	**32.0 (1.82)**	**— (†)**	**21.4 (2.18)**	**11.2 (1.28)**	**15.7 (1.09)**	**17.3 (1.22)**	**24.3 (1.27)**	**23.6 (1.48)**	**24.2 (1.56)**	**21.1 (1.54)**	**21.6 (0.77)**	**4.9 (1.05)**
Urban	28.9 (1.23)	31.9 (1.62)	25.9 (1.52)	20.5 (1.28)	32.4 (2.79)	40.3 (2.45)	— (†)	27.0 (4.41)	14.9 (2.45)	23.7 (2.54)	24.0 (2.66)	35.3 (2.77)	33.1 (3.08)	34.2 (3.18)	34.1 (3.21)	31.9 (1.35)	5.0 (1.38)
Suburban	18.3 (0.72)	18.9 (0.92)	17.5 (1.08)	15.4 (0.75)	25.4 (2.79)	27.1 (2.25)	— (†)	20.0 (2.95)	9.0 (1.52)	13.7 (1.16)	16.6 (1.50)	20.8 (1.48)	22.3 (1.58)	22.7 (1.71)	18.6 (1.81)	19.5 (0.80)	4.3 ! (1.45)
Rural	13.3 (1.71)	14.0 (2.08)	12.5 (1.84)	12.1 (1.70)	22.5 (5.78)	16.8 ! (7.49)	— (†)	‡ (†)	11.0 (2.78)	8.9 (1.87)	10.1 (2.24)	18.9 (3.03)	14.4 (3.05)	15.8 (3.85)	11.5 ! (4.51)	13.7 (1.80)	‡ (†)
2003																	
Total	**20.9 (0.70)**	**22.3 (0.95)**	**19.5 (0.79)**	**14.2 (0.59)**	**29.5 (2.14)**	**37.2 (1.76)**	**— (†)**	**22.0 (2.54)**	**10.9 (1.28)**	**16.3 (1.14)**	**17.9 (1.29)**	**26.1 (1.44)**	**26.3 (1.37)**	**23.4 (1.64)**	**22.2 (1.50)**	**22.5 (0.78)**	**3.9 (0.82)**
Urban	30.9 (1.33)	32.1 (1.71)	29.7 (1.84)	19.8 (1.71)	32.8 (2.43)	42.6 (2.17)	— (†)	30.6 (4.09)	21.6 (3.42)	25.5 (2.32)	25.2 (2.63)	38.2 (3.25)	35.3 (2.82)	34.6 (2.81)	34.8 (2.75)	33.7 (1.50)	6.0 (1.62)
Suburban	18.4 (0.84)	20.5 (1.07)	16.3 (0.92)	13.8 (0.67)	28.3 (3.93)	34.6 (2.14)	— (†)	18.2 (2.96)	7.5 (1.25)	13.2 (1.28)	16.2 (1.65)	24.3 (1.58)	24.1 (1.72)	20.4 (2.34)	19.3 (1.91)	19.9 (0.91)	2.4 ! (0.78)
Rural	12.3 (1.81)	12.2 (2.00)	12.4 (2.34)	10.7 (1.42)	21.8 ! (7.17)	12.7 ! (4.11)	— (†)	‡ (†)	‡ (†)	9.4 (2.56)	10.9 ! (3.26)	13.8 (3.00)	18.0 (3.50)	15.0 (3.30)	13.3 (3.60)	12.8 (2.02)	‡ (†)
2005																	
Total	**24.2 (0.93)**	**25.3 (1.07)**	**22.9 (1.09)**	**16.8 (0.83)**	**37.6 (2.41)**	**38.9 (2.69)**	**20.2 (2.59)**	**27.7 (4.62)**	**12.1 (1.41)**	**17.3 (1.21)**	**19.1 (1.79)**	**28.3 (1.59)**	**32.6 (1.89)**	**28.0 (1.89)**	**27.9 (2.16)**	**25.8 (1.01)**	**4.2 (0.94)**
Urban	36.2 (2.00)	37.4 (2.31)	35.0 (2.42)	23.7 (1.87)	41.8 (2.93)	48.9 (4.44)	25.0 (5.16)	33.9 (8.68)	19.9 (3.11)	24.2 (2.64)	30.5 (3.81)	40.3 (3.70)	50.6 (3.79)	44.3 (3.89)	39.5 (3.73)	39.1 (2.12)	7.7 (2.26)
Suburban	20.8 (0.93)	22.4 (1.14)	19.1 (1.15)	16.0 (0.87)	36.2 (4.41)	32.1 (2.52)	18.1 (2.87)	29.0 (6.12)	8.9 (1.52)	14.9 (1.46)	14.6 (2.01)	24.8 (1.92)	27.9 (2.37)	25.5 (2.21)	25.1 (2.60)	22.3 (1.01)	3.0 ! (1.02)
Rural	16.4 (2.53)	16.1 (3.20)	16.7 (2.79)	14.1 (2.46)	24.4 (6.75)	26.2 (6.51)	19.0 ! (9.22)	‡ (†)	8.3 (3.29)	15.2 (3.46)	14.7 (4.22)	21.0 (4.00)	22.0 (3.61)	13.3 ! (4.36)	15.8 ! (5.82)	17.2 (2.67)	‡ (†)
2007[2]																	
Total	**23.2 (0.80)**	**25.1 (1.07)**	**21.3 (0.87)**	**16.0 (0.70)**	**37.6 (2.26)**	**36.1 (2.04)**	**17.4 (2.72)**	**26.4 (3.63)**	**15.3 (1.99)**	**17.4 (1.28)**	**20.6 (1.68)**	**28.0 (1.51)**	**28.1 (1.73)**	**25.9 (1.61)**	**24.4 (1.69)**	**24.9 (0.87)**	**5.2 (1.14)**
Urban	32.3 (1.49)	35.3 (2.01)	29.2 (1.62)	23.4 (1.98)	39.7 (3.07)	40.4 (2.90)	18.4 (4.30)	31.9 (6.10)	17.8 (3.45)	24.1 (2.96)	25.9 (2.90)	41.1 (3.40)	38.6 (3.36)	34.7 (3.05)	38.4 (4.01)	35.6 (1.61)	7.3 (2.07)
Suburban	21.0 (0.97)	23.1 (1.36)	18.9 (1.19)	15.9 (0.92)	35.5 (3.16)	33.3 (2.66)	16.3 (3.63)	29.0 (5.14)	14.0 (2.40)	15.4 (1.67)	19.6 (2.23)	23.1 (1.78)	26.6 (2.01)	23.6 (2.22)	22.4 (2.26)	22.7 (1.05)	2.8 ! (1.09)
Rural	15.5 (2.78)	14.9 (2.69)	16.1 (3.18)	10.9 (1.59)	36.8 (10.42)	27.5 ! (10.34)	‡ (†)	14.3 ! (6.01)	15.6 ! (6.21)	13.1 (2.79)	14.7 (4.26)	21.7 (4.43)	15.2 (3.39)	18.7 (3.98)	7.6 ! (2.90)	15.6 (2.91)	11.8 ! (5.84)
2009[2]																	
Total	**20.4 (0.85)**	**20.9 (1.12)**	**19.9 (1.03)**	**14.1 (0.79)**	**31.4 (2.62)**	**33.0 (2.20)**	**17.2 (3.21)**	**15.3 (4.07)**	**11.0 (1.76)**	**14.8 (1.70)**	**15.9 (1.60)**	**24.9 (2.01)**	**27.7 (1.75)**	**22.6 (1.53)**	**21.9 (2.02)**	**22.0 (0.89)**	**2.3 ! (0.82)**
Urban	30.7 (1.86)	32.8 (2.35)	28.6 (2.29)	19.4 (1.99)	40.0 (3.76)	38.9 (3.31)	18.9 (4.63)	23.2 ! (9.05)	14.5 (4.13)	21.0 (3.37)	24.4 (3.24)	34.2 (4.01)	44.8 (3.41)	34.9 (4.08)	36.0 (4.32)	33.7 (1.94)	4.1 ! (1.83)
Suburban	16.6 (0.80)	17.2 (1.10)	16.0 (1.17)	13.5 (0.91)	20.2 (2.75)	28.3 (2.64)	14.5 (3.95)	14.8 ! (6.41)	9.7 (1.90)	11.2 (1.89)	11.8 (1.73)	22.4 (2.10)	21.0 (2.07)	19.4 (1.88)	17.6 (2.29)	18.1 (0.85)	‡ (†)
Rural	16.0 (3.08)	13.7 (3.37)	18.1 (3.18)	11.8 (2.09)	35.4 (9.77)	27.3 ! (10.84)	‡ (†)	‡ (†)	8.3 ! (3.11)	16.5 (4.19)	14.2 ! (4.41)	18.8 (5.04)	19.6 (5.02)	13.4 (3.50)	17.3 ! (5.37)	16.2 (3.18)	‡ (†)
2011[2]																	
Total	**17.5 (0.71)**	**17.5 (0.95)**	**17.5 (0.88)**	**11.1 (0.67)**	**32.7 (2.23)**	**26.4 (1.55)**	**9.9 (2.24)**	**9.9 (2.12)**	**8.2 (1.20)**	**10.2 (1.08)**	**11.3 (1.02)**	**21.7 (1.47)**	**23.0 (1.63)**	**23.2 (1.74)**	**21.3 (1.82)**	**18.9 (0.77)**	**1.9 ! (0.69)**
Urban	22.8 (1.34)	23.0 (1.90)	22.6 (1.53)	13.9 (1.60)	31.6 (2.75)	31.0 (2.34)	7.6 ! (2.29)	12.3 (3.41)	5.4 ! (1.98)	11.7 (2.02)	16.2 (2.29)	27.5 (3.12)	31.1 (3.13)	28.1 (3.17)	32.9 (3.88)	25.7 (1.47)	‡ (†)
Suburban	16.1 (0.97)	16.5 (1.24)	15.6 (1.18)	11.3 (0.89)	33.5 (4.08)	23.2 (1.95)	12.0 ! (3.69)	10.4 ! (3.54)	8.6 (1.79)	9.3 (1.37)	9.0 (1.22)	18.9 (1.79)	21.5 (2.10)	23.7 (2.46)	18.5 (2.27)	17.1 (1.01)	2.9 ! (1.20)
Rural	12.1 (2.42)	10.2 (2.23)	14.1 (3.18)	7.7 (1.31)	34.5 (6.62)	22.1 ! (10.47)	‡ (†)	‡ (†)	11.1 (2.97)	10.1 (2.64)	9.6 ! (2.89)	19.3 (4.99)	13.9 (4.02)	10.6 (3.69)	9.2 ! (3.04)	12.5 (2.49)	‡ (†)
2013[2]																	
Total	**12.4 (0.62)**	**12.9 (0.85)**	**12.0 (0.73)**	**7.5 (0.63)**	**18.6 (1.72)**	**20.1 (1.34)**	**9.4 (1.85)**	**14.3 (2.68)**	**5.0 (1.15)**	**7.7 (0.96)**	**7.8 (0.96)**	**13.9 (1.43)**	**17.7 (1.46)**	**17.1 (1.65)**	**14.6 (1.58)**	**13.3 (0.67)**	**2.3 ! (0.94)**
Urban	18.3 (1.23)	18.6 (1.61)	18.0 (1.38)	14.3 (1.73)	20.6 (2.36)	22.6 (2.15)	10.4 (2.61)	17.9 ! (5.59)	9.6 (2.75)	12.0 (2.44)	13.2 (2.30)	19.6 (2.53)	24.8 (2.86)	26.7 (3.21)	18.2 (3.07)	19.9 (1.35)	4.6 ! (2.08)
Suburban	10.8 (0.76)	11.7 (1.09)	9.8 (0.92)	6.5 (0.76)	17.3 (3.02)	19.3 (1.69)	8.2 ! (2.59)	13.0 (3.29)	3.0 ! (1.25)	6.6 (1.14)	6.3 (1.19)	12.2 (1.95)	15.4 (1.91)	15.1 (2.00)	14.1 (2.06)	11.7 (0.82)	‡ (†)
Rural	6.8 (1.44)	5.7 (1.38)	7.9 (1.92)	4.1 (1.20)	16.1 (4.49)	9.4 ! (4.52)	‡ (†)	11.9 ! (5.43)	‡ (†)	4.2 ! (1.88)	‡ (†)	8.0 ! (3.19)	11.3 (3.37)	8.1 ! (3.32)	9.0 ! (3.56)	6.8 (1.47)	‡ (†)

—Not available.
†Not applicable.
!Interpret data with caution. The coefficient of variation (CV) for this estimate is between 30 and 50 percent.
‡Reporting standards not met. Either there are too few cases for a reliable estimate or the coefficient of variation (CV) is 50 percent or greater.
[1]Race categories exclude persons of Hispanic ethnicity. "Other" includes American Indians/Alaska Natives, Asians (prior to 2005), Pacific Islanders, and, from 2003 onward, persons of Two or more races. Due to changes in racial/ethnic categories, comparisons of race/ethnicity across years should be made with caution.
[2]Starting in 2007, the reference period was the school year, whereas in prior survey years the reference period was the previous 6 months. Cognitive testing showed that estimates from 2007 onward are comparable to previous years.
NOTE: Urbanicity refers to the Standard Metropolitan Statistical Area (MSA) status of the respondent's household as defined in 2000 by the U.S. Census Bureau. Categories include "central city of an MSA (Urban)," "in MSA but not in central city (Suburban)," and "not MSA (Rural)." All gangs, whether or not they are involved in violent or illegal activity, are included. "At school" includes in the school building, on school property, on a school bus, and going to and from school.
SOURCE: U.S. Department of Justice, Bureau of Justice Statistics, School Crime Supplement (SCS) to the National Crime Victimization Survey, selected years, 2001 through 2013. (This table was prepared August 2014.)

Table 230.30. Percentage of students ages 12–18 who reported being the target of hate-related words and seeing hate-related graffiti at school during the school year, by selected student and school characteristics: Selected years, 1999 through 2013

[Standard errors appear in parentheses]

Student or school characteristic	1999		2001		2003		2005		2007[1]		2009[1]		2011[1]		2013[1]	
1	2		3		4		5		6		7		8		9	
Hate-related words																
Total	**—**	**(†)**	**12.3**	**(0.46)**	**11.7**	**(0.47)**	**11.2**	**(0.50)**	**9.7**	**(0.43)**	**8.7**	**(0.52)**	**9.1**	**(0.48)**	**6.6**	**(0.40)**
Sex																
Male	—	(†)	12.8	(0.65)	12.0	(0.61)	11.7	(0.68)	9.9	(0.61)	8.5	(0.62)	9.0	(0.60)	6.6	(0.51)
Female	—	(†)	11.7	(0.52)	11.3	(0.64)	10.7	(0.64)	9.6	(0.57)	8.9	(0.72)	9.1	(0.68)	6.7	(0.53)
Race/ethnicity[2]																
White	—	(†)	12.1	(0.58)	10.9	(0.56)	10.3	(0.60)	8.9	(0.50)	7.2	(0.59)	8.3	(0.59)	5.3	(0.43)
Black	—	(†)	13.9	(1.08)	14.2	(1.35)	15.1	(1.48)	11.4	(1.35)	11.1	(1.35)	10.7	(1.30)	7.8	(1.20)
Hispanic	—	(†)	11.0	(1.15)	11.4	(0.96)	10.5	(1.15)	10.6	(1.18)	11.2	(1.13)	9.8	(0.98)	7.4	(0.84)
Asian	—	(†)	—	(†)	—	(†)	10.9	(2.56)	11.1	(1.97)	10.7	(2.81)	9.0	(2.00)	10.3	(2.19)
Other	—	(†)	13.6	(2.05)	14.1	(2.03)	14.2	(3.27)	10.6	(2.71)	10.0	(2.37)	10.4	(2.61)	11.2	(2.47)
Grade																
6th	—	(†)	12.1	(1.26)	11.9	(1.31)	11.1	(1.58)	12.1	(1.54)	8.3	(1.39)	9.0	(1.43)	6.7	(1.33)
7th	—	(†)	14.1	(1.13)	12.5	(1.04)	13.1	(1.16)	10.7	(1.02)	9.6	(1.22)	9.9	(1.02)	7.5	(0.89)
8th	—	(†)	13.0	(1.07)	12.8	(0.92)	11.2	(1.04)	11.0	(1.19)	10.9	(1.22)	8.4	(0.94)	7.4	(1.01)
9th	—	(†)	12.1	(1.00)	13.5	(1.23)	12.8	(1.12)	10.9	(1.08)	8.0	(1.09)	10.2	(1.10)	6.6	(0.94)
10th	—	(†)	13.1	(0.95)	11.6	(1.12)	10.9	(1.04)	9.0	(0.99)	9.7	(1.18)	9.6	(1.14)	6.4	(0.97)
11th	—	(†)	12.7	(1.13)	8.3	(0.97)	9.0	(1.17)	8.6	(1.01)	8.4	(1.14)	8.7	(1.01)	7.5	(1.01)
12th	—	(†)	7.9	(0.87)	10.8	(1.25)	9.7	(1.35)	6.0	(0.98)	5.8	(0.96)	7.5	(1.01)	4.1	(0.78)
Urbanicity[3]																
Urban	—	(†)	11.9	(0.73)	13.2	(0.83)	12.2	(0.86)	9.7	(0.83)	9.9	(0.93)	8.0	(0.77)	7.2	(0.76)
Suburban	—	(†)	12.4	(0.63)	10.7	(0.58)	9.4	(0.52)	9.3	(0.62)	8.3	(0.64)	9.8	(0.71)	6.6	(0.50)
Rural	—	(†)	12.4	(1.11)	12.2	(1.35)	15.5	(1.74)	11.0	(1.07)	8.1	(1.37)	8.5	(1.00)	5.7	(0.80)
Control of school																
Public	—	(†)	12.7	(0.51)	11.9	(0.49)	11.6	(0.53)	10.1	(0.46)	8.9	(0.54)	9.3	(0.50)	6.6	(0.41)
Private	—	(†)	8.2	(1.13)	9.7	(1.11)	6.8	(1.18)	6.1	(1.25)	6.6	(1.62)	6.9	(1.29)	6.7	(1.41)
Hate-related graffiti																
Total	**36.3**	**(0.94)**	**35.5**	**(0.75)**	**36.3**	**(0.84)**	**38.4**	**(0.83)**	**34.9**	**(0.89)**	**29.2**	**(0.96)**	**28.4**	**(0.88)**	**24.6**	**(0.88)**
Sex																
Male	33.8	(1.06)	34.9	(0.89)	35.0	(0.97)	37.7	(1.10)	34.4	(1.12)	29.0	(1.26)	28.6	(1.11)	24.1	(1.11)
Female	38.9	(1.14)	36.1	(0.92)	37.6	(1.06)	39.1	(0.93)	35.4	(1.12)	29.3	(1.09)	28.1	(1.07)	25.1	(1.05)
Race/ethnicity[2]																
White	36.4	(1.20)	36.2	(0.95)	35.2	(0.86)	38.5	(0.96)	35.5	(1.05)	28.3	(1.10)	28.2	(1.19)	23.7	(1.20)
Black	37.6	(1.71)	33.6	(1.52)	38.1	(1.95)	38.0	(2.29)	33.7	(2.37)	29.0	(2.44)	28.1	(1.90)	26.3	(2.10)
Hispanic	35.6	(1.46)	35.1	(1.87)	40.3	(2.24)	38.0	(1.78)	34.8	(1.76)	32.2	(1.61)	29.1	(1.33)	25.6	(1.52)
Asian	—	(†)	—	(†)	—	(†)	34.5	(3.76)	28.2	(3.01)	31.2	(3.59)	29.9	(4.56)	20.8	(3.22)
Other	32.2	(2.53)	32.1	(2.82)	31.4	(2.83)	46.9	(4.68)	38.7	(3.44)	25.8	(4.20)	25.9	(3.79)	28.4	(3.52)
Grade																
6th	30.3	(1.82)	34.9	(1.88)	35.7	(1.83)	34.0	(2.24)	35.5	(2.30)	28.1	(2.26)	25.9	(2.13)	21.9	(1.77)
7th	34.9	(1.43)	34.9	(1.36)	37.2	(1.41)	37.0	(1.63)	32.3	(1.52)	27.9	(1.88)	26.0	(1.70)	21.7	(1.49)
8th	35.6	(1.51)	36.7	(1.40)	34.2	(1.53)	35.7	(1.61)	33.5	(1.81)	30.8	(1.80)	25.9	(1.55)	24.0	(1.80)
9th	39.2	(1.55)	35.7	(1.55)	37.0	(1.48)	41.6	(1.64)	34.5	(1.77)	28.1	(1.83)	28.7	(1.69)	27.2	(1.74)
10th	38.9	(1.77)	36.2	(1.49)	40.7	(1.67)	40.7	(1.83)	36.4	(1.69)	31.0	(2.03)	33.3	(1.78)	26.0	(1.58)
11th	37.0	(1.74)	36.1	(1.76)	36.6	(1.74)	40.2	(1.70)	35.3	(1.81)	27.4	(2.01)	32.1	(1.70)	25.8	(2.03)
12th	35.6	(2.04)	33.0	(1.79)	32.2	(1.78)	37.8	(2.34)	37.7	(2.03)	30.4	(2.00)	25.7	(1.51)	24.2	(1.91)
Urbanicity[3]																
Urban	37.0	(1.18)	35.7	(1.21)	38.6	(1.27)	40.9	(1.43)	34.4	(1.36)	31.1	(1.56)	27.5	(1.49)	27.8	(1.48)
Suburban	37.3	(1.12)	36.0	(0.87)	35.9	(1.16)	38.0	(1.02)	34.2	(1.03)	28.6	(1.15)	29.9	(1.08)	23.7	(1.11)
Rural	32.7	(2.60)	33.8	(2.56)	33.9	(1.97)	35.8	(2.40)	37.8	(3.06)	27.7	(2.43)	24.9	(2.25)	21.6	(2.71)
Control of school																
Public	38.0	(0.97)	37.3	(0.80)	37.9	(0.90)	40.0	(0.87)	36.4	(0.93)	30.7	(1.01)	29.7	(0.95)	25.6	(0.94)
Private	20.7	(1.85)	16.8	(1.34)	19.5	(1.75)	18.6	(1.97)	18.5	(2.07)	11.8	(1.93)	13.4	(1.56)	12.6	(1.74)

—Not available.
†Not applicable.
[1]Starting in 2007, the reference period was the school year, whereas in prior survey years the reference period was the previous 6 months. Cognitive testing showed that estimates from 2007 onward are comparable to previous years.
[2]Race categories exclude persons of Hispanic ethnicity. "Other" includes American Indians/Alaska Natives, Asians (prior to 2005), Pacific Islanders, and, from 2003 onward, persons of Two or more races. Due to changes in racial/ethnic categories, comparisons of race/ethnicity across years should be made with caution.
[3]Refers to the Standard Metropolitan Statistical Area (MSA) status of the respondent's household as defined in 2000 by the U.S. Census Bureau. Categories include "central city of an MSA (Urban)," "in MSA but not in central city (Suburban)," and "not MSA (Rural)."
NOTE: "At school" includes in the school building, on school property, on a school bus, and, from 2001 onward, going to and from school. "Hate-related" refers to derogatory terms used by others in reference to students' personal characteristics.
SOURCE: U.S. Department of Justice, Bureau of Justice Statistics, School Crime Supplement (SCS) to the National Crime Victimization Survey, selected years, 1999 through 2013. (This table was prepared August 2014.)

Table 230.35. Percentage of students ages 12–18 who reported being the target of hate-related words at school, by type of hate-related word and selected student and school characteristics: 2013

[Standard errors appear in parentheses]

Student or school characteristic	Total[1]		Hate-related words related to student's characteristic: Race		Ethnicity		Religion		Disability		Gender		Sexual orientation	
1	2		3		4		5		6		7		8	
Total	**6.6**	**(0.40)**	**3.3**	**(0.31)**	**1.9**	**(0.21)**	**1.2**	**(0.15)**	**0.8**	**(0.14)**	**1.0**	**(0.14)**	**1.1**	**(0.13)**
Sex														
Male	6.6	(0.51)	3.5	(0.41)	1.9	(0.27)	1.0	(0.19)	0.7	(0.16)	0.3	(0.09)	0.9	(0.16)
Female	6.7	(0.53)	3.1	(0.40)	1.9	(0.30)	1.4	(0.22)	0.9	(0.21)	1.7	(0.29)	1.3	(0.22)
Race/ethnicity[2]														
White	5.3	(0.43)	1.6	(0.25)	0.8	(0.18)	1.2	(0.22)	1.2	(0.22)	1.1	(0.20)	1.3	(0.22)
Black	7.8	(1.20)	5.8	(1.03)	1.9	(0.48)	1.0 !	(0.39)	‡	(†)	1.0 !	(0.41)	1.1 !	(0.43)
Hispanic	7.4	(0.84)	3.9	(0.64)	3.7	(0.62)	1.0	(0.27)	‡	(†)	0.9	(0.25)	0.8 !	(0.27)
Asian	10.3	(2.19)	8.5	(2.05)	7.1	(2.00)	2.1 !	(0.87)	‡	(†)	‡	(†)	‡	(†)
Other	11.2	(2.47)	8.3	(2.10)	‡	(†)	‡	(†)	‡	(†)	‡	(†)	‡	(†)
Grade														
6th	6.7	(1.33)	3.5	(0.98)	1.9 !	(0.67)	1.1 !	(0.52)	‡	(†)	‡	(†)	‡	(†)
7th	7.5	(0.89)	3.6	(0.64)	2.0	(0.46)	0.8 !	(0.32)	1.1 !	(0.35)	1.1 !	(0.36)	0.9 !	(0.35)
8th	7.4	(1.01)	3.3	(0.72)	1.8 !	(0.54)	1.7	(0.48)	1.0 !	(0.33)	1.4	(0.40)	1.4 !	(0.43)
9th	6.6	(0.94)	3.0	(0.68)	2.0	(0.58)	2.1	(0.56)	0.9 !	(0.36)	0.9 !	(0.33)	0.8 !	(0.31)
10th	6.4	(0.97)	3.9	(0.76)	2.0	(0.50)	1.2 !	(0.39)	0.9 !	(0.32)	0.7 !	(0.28)	0.8 !	(0.32)
11th	7.5	(1.01)	3.9	(0.74)	1.9	(0.53)	1.1 !	(0.40)	‡	(†)	1.4 !	(0.45)	2.3	(0.48)
12th	4.1	(0.78)	1.8	(0.55)	1.9	(0.53)	‡	(†)	‡	(†)	0.6 !	(0.32)	0.8 !	(0.36)
Urbanicity[3]														
Urban	7.2	(0.76)	4.2	(0.65)	2.2	(0.37)	0.9	(0.21)	0.6 !	(0.23)	0.8	(0.23)	1.2	(0.25)
Suburban	6.6	(0.50)	3.1	(0.39)	1.9	(0.29)	1.3	(0.21)	0.8	(0.19)	1.0	(0.18)	0.9	(0.18)
Rural	5.7	(0.80)	2.3	(0.56)	1.5 !	(0.49)	1.5 !	(0.45)	1.2 !	(0.44)	1.4 !	(0.46)	1.4	(0.39)
Control of school														
Public	6.6	(0.41)	3.3	(0.30)	1.9	(0.21)	1.2	(0.15)	0.8	(0.14)	1.0	(0.15)	1.1	(0.13)
Private	6.7	(1.41)	3.7	(1.08)	1.9 !	(0.79)	‡	(†)	‡	(†)	1.2 !	(0.55)	‡	(†)

†Not applicable.
!Interpret data with caution. The coefficient of variation (CV) for this estimate is between 30 and 50 percent.
‡Reporting standards not met. Either there are too few cases for a reliable estimate or the coefficient of variation (CV) is 50 percent or greater.
[1]Students who indicated that they had been called a hate-related word were asked to choose the specific characteristics that the hate-related word or words targeted. Students were allowed to choose more than one characteristic. If a student chose more than one characteristic, he or she is counted only once in the total percentage of students who reported being called a hate-related word; therefore, the total is less than the sum of the students' individual characteristics.
[2]Race categories exclude persons of Hispanic ethnicity. "Other" includes American Indians/Alaska Natives, Pacific Islanders, and persons of Two or more races.
[3]Refers to the Standard Metropolitan Statistical Area (MSA) status of the respondent's household as defined in 2000 by the U.S. Census Bureau. Categories include "central city of an MSA (Urban)," "in MSA but not in central city (Suburban)," "and not MSA (Rural)."
NOTE: "At school" includes in the school building, on school property, on a school bus, or going to and from school. "Hate-related" refers to derogatory terms used by others in reference to students' personal characteristics. Detail may not sum to totals because of rounding and because students may have reported being targets of hate-related words related to more than one student characteristic.
SOURCE: U.S. Department of Justice, Bureau of Justice Statistics, School Crime Supplement (SCS) to the National Crime Victimization Survey, 2013. (This table was prepared August 2014.)

Table 230.40. Percentage of students ages 12–18 who reported being bullied at school or cyber-bullied anywhere during the school year, by type of bullying at school, reports of injury, and selected student and school characteristics: 2013

[Standard errors appear in parentheses]

Student or school characteristic	Bullied at school or cyber-bullied anywhere: Total bullied at school or cyber-bullied anywhere[2]	Bullied at school or cyber-bullied anywhere: Total cyber-bullied anywhere[3]	Bullied at school or cyber-bullied anywhere: Total bullied at school[4]	Type of bullying at school: Made fun of, called names, or insulted	Type of bullying at school: Subject of rumors	Type of bullying at school: Threatened with harm	Type of bullying at school: Tried to make do things did not want to do	Type of bullying at school: Excluded from activities on purpose	Type of bullying at school: Property destroyed on purpose	Type of bullying at school: Pushed, shoved, tripped, or spit on	Of students who were pushed, shoved, tripped, or spit on, percent reporting injury[1]
1	2	3	4	5	6	7	8	9	10	11	12
Total	**23.1 (0.67)**	**6.9 (0.42)**	**21.5 (0.66)**	**13.6 (0.51)**	**13.2 (0.50)**	**3.9 (0.27)**	**2.2 (0.21)**	**4.5 (0.30)**	**1.6 (0.20)**	**6.0 (0.39)**	**20.8 (2.48)**
Sex											
Male	21.1 (0.84)	5.2 (0.43)	19.5 (0.81)	12.6 (0.70)	9.6 (0.60)	4.1 (0.38)	2.4 (0.30)	3.5 (0.34)	1.8 (0.28)	7.4 (0.59)	20.6 (3.21)
Female	25.2 (0.99)	8.6 (0.63)	23.7 (0.98)	14.7 (0.75)	17.0 (0.80)	3.7 (0.37)	1.9 (0.27)	5.5 (0.47)	1.3 (0.25)	4.6 (0.42)	21.1 (3.63)
Race/ethnicity[5]											
White	25.3 (0.94)	7.6 (0.57)	23.7 (0.93)	15.6 (0.74)	14.6 (0.76)	4.4 (0.40)	2.0 (0.28)	5.4 (0.46)	1.5 (0.24)	6.1 (0.49)	22.3 (3.39)
Black	21.2 (1.85)	4.5 (0.94)	20.3 (1.81)	10.5 (1.22)	12.7 (1.40)	3.2 (0.68)	2.7 (0.59)	2.7 (0.71)	2.0 (0.54)	6.0 (0.97)	15.6 ! (6.04)
Hispanic	20.5 (1.32)	5.8 (0.78)	19.2 (1.30)	12.1 (1.13)	11.5 (1.02)	4.0 (0.58)	1.6 (0.32)	3.5 (0.53)	1.4 (0.38)	6.3 (0.79)	18.3 (4.15)
Asian	11.8 (2.02)	5.8 (1.67)	9.2 (1.67)	7.5 (1.63)	3.7 (0.95)	‡ (†)	3.8 ! (1.32)	2.2 ! (0.71)	1.6 ! (0.78)	2.0 ! (0.85)	‡ (†)
Other	29.7 (3.83)	13.4 (2.43)	25.2 (3.60)	16.5 (2.99)	17.3 (3.05)	4.3 ! (1.56)	4.0 ! (1.38)	6.5 (1.85)	2.1 ! (1.00)	8.5 (1.90)	‡ (†)
Grade											
6th	29.9 (2.31)	5.9 (1.20)	27.8 (2.31)	21.3 (2.15)	16.1 (1.61)	5.9 (1.13)	3.4 (0.88)	6.5 (1.20)	3.1 (0.77)	11.0 (1.46)	26.8 (6.90)
7th	27.3 (1.65)	7.0 (0.91)	26.4 (1.65)	17.9 (1.35)	15.5 (1.35)	6.1 (0.88)	3.0 (0.52)	6.3 (0.86)	2.2 (0.52)	11.6 (1.12)	24.0 (4.11)
8th	22.7 (1.43)	6.4 (0.86)	21.7 (1.42)	14.5 (1.23)	12.7 (1.11)	3.9 (0.68)	2.3 (0.54)	5.2 (0.80)	1.5 ! (0.45)	6.5 (0.85)	20.8 (5.92)
9th	24.4 (1.46)	6.7 (0.97)	23.0 (1.42)	13.7 (1.16)	13.8 (1.22)	3.6 (0.61)	2.6 (0.58)	4.3 (0.70)	1.2 ! (0.40)	4.9 (0.83)	18.2 ! (7.32)
10th	21.4 (1.52)	8.6 (1.16)	19.5 (1.48)	12.9 (1.21)	12.9 (1.28)	4.3 (0.73)	1.7 (0.47)	4.6 (0.72)	1.3 (0.37)	3.7 (0.68)	21.2 ! (7.78)
11th	22.4 (1.50)	6.8 (0.87)	20.0 (1.50)	11.2 (1.20)	12.5 (1.31)	3.0 (0.60)	1.5 (0.45)	2.4 (0.61)	1.6 ! (0.50)	3.4 (0.72)	‡ (†)
12th	15.4 (1.45)	5.9 (0.93)	14.1 (1.51)	6.4 (1.04)	9.7 (1.15)	1.0 ! (0.43)	1.3 ! (0.48)	2.5 (0.67)	0.7 ! (0.31)	3.0 (0.71)	‡ (†)
Urbanicity[6]											
Urban	22.6 (1.10)	7.1 (0.73)	20.7 (1.10)	12.8 (0.80)	12.7 (0.87)	3.9 (0.47)	2.7 (0.45)	4.1 (0.51)	1.4 (0.27)	5.6 (0.60)	20.9 (4.99)
Suburban	23.5 (0.93)	7.0 (0.61)	22.0 (0.90)	14.2 (0.69)	13.4 (0.71)	3.9 (0.39)	2.0 (0.28)	4.7 (0.43)	1.3 (0.24)	6.4 (0.52)	21.8 (3.31)
Rural	22.7 (1.87)	5.9 (1.02)	21.4 (1.86)	13.2 (1.49)	13.3 (1.45)	4.1 (0.67)	1.7 (0.42)	4.2 (0.73)	2.8 (0.66)	5.8 (0.88)	16.7 ! (5.31)
Control of school											
Public	23.0 (0.69)	6.9 (0.45)	21.5 (0.67)	13.5 (0.53)	13.2 (0.52)	3.9 (0.28)	2.2 (0.22)	4.3 (0.31)	1.6 (0.19)	6.1 (0.41)	20.3 (2.57)
Private	23.8 (2.79)	6.4 (1.44)	22.4 (2.71)	15.3 (2.01)	13.4 (2.20)	3.9 (1.14)	2.7 ! (0.82)	6.7 (1.31)	1.3 ! (0.60)	5.2 (1.24)	‡ (†)

†Not applicable.

!Interpret data with caution. The coefficient of variation (CV) for this estimate is between 30 and 50 percent.

‡Reporting standards not met. Either there are too few cases for a reliable estimate or the coefficient of variation (CV) is 50 percent or greater.

[1]Only students who reported that they were pushed, shoved, tripped, or spit on were asked if they suffered injuries as a result of the incident.

[2]Students who reported that they were both bullied at school and cyber-bullied anywhere were counted only once in the total for students bullied at school or cyber-bullied anywhere.

[3]Students who reported being cyber-bullied are those who responded that another student had done one or more of the following: posted hurtful information about them on the Internet; purposely shared private information about them on the Internet; threatened or insulted them through instant messaging; threatened or insulted them through text messaging; threatened or insulted them through e-mail; threatened or insulted them while gaming; or excluded them online. Students who reported more than one of these types of cyber-bullying were counted only once in the total for students cyber-bullied anywhere.

[4]Students who reported experiencing more than one type of bullying at school were counted only once in the total for students bullied at school.

[5]Race categories exclude persons of Hispanic ethnicity. "Other" includes American Indians/Alaska Natives, Pacific Islanders, and persons of Two or more races.

[6]Refers to the Standard Metropolitan Statistical Area (MSA) status of the respondent's household as defined in 2000 by the U.S. Census Bureau. Categories include "central city of an MSA (Urban)," "in MSA but not in central city (Suburban)," and "not MSA (Rural)."

NOTE: "At school" includes the school building, on school property, on a school bus, or going to and from school. Bullying types do not sum to totals because students could have experienced more than one type of bullying.

SOURCE: U.S. Department of Justice, Bureau of Justice Statistics, School Crime Supplement (SCS) to the National Crime Victimization Survey, 2013. (This table was prepared August 2014.)

Table 230.45. Percentage of students ages 12–18 who reported being bullied at school during the school year, by type of bullying and selected student and school characteristics: Selected years, 2005 through 2013

[Standard errors appear in parentheses]

Year and student or school characteristic	Total bullied at school		Type of bullying at school: Made fun of, called names, or insulted		Subject of rumors		Threatened with harm		Tried to make do things did not want to do		Excluded from activities on purpose		Property destroyed on purpose		Pushed, shoved, tripped, or spit on	
1	2		3		4		5		6		7		8		9	
2005																
Total	**28.1**	**(0.70)**	**18.7**	**(0.58)**	**14.7**	**(0.53)**	**4.8**	**(0.31)**	**3.5**	**(0.27)**	**4.6**	**(0.30)**	**3.4**	**(0.29)**	**9.0**	**(0.45)**
Sex																
Male	27.1	(0.90)	18.5	(0.73)	11.0	(0.64)	5.2	(0.51)	3.9	(0.39)	4.1	(0.40)	3.5	(0.41)	10.9	(0.70)
Female	29.2	(0.84)	19.0	(0.79)	18.5	(0.74)	4.4	(0.37)	3.1	(0.32)	5.2	(0.40)	3.3	(0.35)	7.1	(0.50)
Race/ethnicity[1]																
White	30.0	(0.84)	20.1	(0.72)	15.8	(0.66)	5.1	(0.47)	3.6	(0.35)	5.3	(0.36)	3.4	(0.35)	9.7	(0.62)
Black	28.5	(2.21)	18.5	(1.72)	14.2	(1.36)	4.9	(0.76)	4.7	(1.00)	4.5	(0.91)	4.6	(0.89)	8.9	(1.14)
Hispanic	22.3	(1.28)	14.7	(1.11)	12.4	(1.00)	4.6	(0.64)	2.6	(0.55)	3.0	(0.53)	2.7	(0.49)	7.6	(0.94)
Asian	—	(†)	—	(†)	—	(†)	—	(†)	—	(†)	—	(†)	—	(†)	—	(†)
Other	24.6	(2.06)	16.3	(1.82)	11.6	(1.71)	2.1	(0.59)	2.1 !	(0.74)	2.5 !	(0.79)	2.5 !	(0.77)	6.8	(1.19)
Grade																
6th	36.6	(1.99)	26.3	(2.05)	16.4	(1.60)	6.4	(1.18)	4.4	(0.92)	7.4	(1.19)	3.9	(0.91)	15.1	(1.75)
7th	35.0	(1.72)	25.2	(1.57)	18.9	(1.27)	6.3	(0.80)	4.7	(0.83)	7.1	(0.85)	4.6	(0.79)	15.4	(1.25)
8th	30.4	(1.50)	20.4	(1.30)	14.3	(1.10)	4.3	(0.64)	3.8	(0.71)	5.4	(0.68)	4.5	(0.75)	11.3	(1.23)
9th	28.1	(1.57)	18.9	(1.33)	13.8	(1.23)	5.3	(0.67)	3.2	(0.58)	3.8	(0.63)	2.7	(0.53)	8.2	(0.91)
10th	24.9	(1.43)	15.5	(1.14)	13.6	(1.19)	4.9	(0.82)	3.6	(0.64)	3.6	(0.63)	2.9	(0.64)	6.8	(0.78)
11th	23.0	(1.58)	14.7	(1.32)	13.4	(1.29)	3.2	(0.61)	2.8	(0.59)	3.3	(0.61)	2.6	(0.56)	4.2	(0.69)
12th	19.9	(1.75)	11.3	(1.52)	12.5	(1.54)	3.5	(0.71)	1.8	(0.51)	2.2 !	(0.72)	2.4	(0.63)	2.9	(0.66)
Urbanicity[2]																
Urban	26.0	(1.29)	17.7	(0.95)	13.3	(1.07)	5.5	(0.49)	4.1	(0.53)	4.9	(0.63)	3.9	(0.58)	8.5	(0.73)
Suburban	28.9	(0.81)	18.9	(0.75)	14.6	(0.64)	4.4	(0.42)	3.1	(0.33)	4.5	(0.37)	3.0	(0.32)	9.0	(0.56)
Rural	29.0	(1.96)	19.8	(1.76)	17.2	(1.32)	5.0	(1.10)	3.7	(0.74)	4.5	(0.88)	3.8	(0.87)	9.9	(1.23)
Control of school[3]																
Public	28.6	(0.74)	19.0	(0.61)	14.9	(0.55)	5.1	(0.33)	3.5	(0.27)	4.5	(0.30)	3.5	(0.31)	9.3	(0.48)
Private	22.7	(2.09)	15.3	(1.67)	12.4	(1.66)	0.9 !	(0.40)	3.0 !	(0.90)	6.2	(1.06)	2.0 !	(0.70)	5.5	(1.03)
2007																
Total	**31.7**	**(0.74)**	**21.0**	**(0.62)**	**18.1**	**(0.61)**	**5.8**	**(0.35)**	**4.1**	**(0.27)**	**5.2**	**(0.30)**	**4.2**	**(0.28)**	**11.0**	**(0.42)**
Sex																
Male	30.3	(0.96)	20.3	(0.83)	13.5	(0.73)	6.0	(0.50)	4.8	(0.43)	4.6	(0.40)	4.0	(0.35)	12.2	(0.58)
Female	33.2	(0.99)	21.7	(0.89)	22.8	(0.91)	5.6	(0.45)	3.4	(0.32)	5.8	(0.43)	4.4	(0.41)	9.7	(0.59)
Race/ethnicity[1]																
White	34.1	(0.97)	23.5	(0.84)	20.3	(0.84)	6.3	(0.47)	4.8	(0.36)	6.1	(0.44)	4.2	(0.35)	11.5	(0.56)
Black	30.4	(2.18)	19.5	(1.71)	15.7	(1.51)	5.8	(0.89)	3.2	(0.69)	3.7	(0.72)	5.6	(0.96)	11.3	(1.42)
Hispanic	27.3	(1.53)	16.1	(1.25)	14.4	(1.27)	4.9	(0.75)	3.0	(0.71)	4.0	(0.60)	3.6	(0.67)	9.9	(1.05)
Asian	18.1	(2.60)	10.6	(2.19)	8.2	(1.93)	‡	(†)	‡	(†)	‡	(†)	1.8 !	(0.89)	3.8 !	(1.25)
Other	34.1	(3.03)	20.1	(3.12)	20.8	(2.98)	7.7	(2.01)	3.1 !	(1.23)	7.7	(2.08)	3.4 !	(1.30)	14.4	(2.73)
Grade																
6th	42.7	(2.23)	31.2	(2.00)	21.3	(1.84)	7.0	(1.13)	5.4	(0.98)	7.4	(1.20)	5.2	(0.98)	17.6	(1.56)
7th	35.6	(1.78)	27.6	(1.58)	20.2	(1.33)	7.4	(0.92)	4.1	(0.64)	7.7	(0.92)	6.0	(0.81)	15.8	(1.28)
8th	36.9	(1.84)	25.1	(1.65)	19.7	(1.41)	6.9	(0.84)	3.6	(0.64)	5.4	(0.77)	4.6	(0.79)	14.2	(1.23)
9th	30.6	(1.72)	20.3	(1.39)	18.1	(1.45)	4.6	(0.77)	5.1	(0.67)	4.5	(0.69)	3.5	(0.63)	11.4	(1.13)
10th	27.7	(1.44)	17.7	(1.22)	15.0	(1.13)	5.8	(0.81)	4.6	(0.68)	4.6	(0.74)	3.4	(0.59)	8.6	(0.89)
11th	28.5	(1.48)	15.3	(1.25)	18.7	(1.40)	4.9	(0.80)	4.2	(0.73)	3.9	(0.68)	4.4	(0.78)	6.5	(0.92)
12th	23.0	(1.60)	12.1	(1.36)	14.1	(1.38)	4.3	(0.83)	2.1	(0.53)	3.5	(0.75)	2.4	(0.61)	4.1	(0.81)
Urbanicity[2]																
Urban	30.7	(1.36)	20.0	(1.09)	15.5	(1.02)	5.2	(0.54)	3.6	(0.46)	4.9	(0.57)	4.2	(0.59)	9.2	(0.76)
Suburban	31.2	(1.07)	21.1	(0.84)	17.4	(0.87)	5.7	(0.48)	4.1	(0.37)	5.0	(0.42)	4.0	(0.38)	11.2	(0.60)
Rural	35.2	(1.73)	22.1	(1.43)	24.1	(1.42)	7.0	(0.78)	5.1	(0.69)	6.3	(0.79)	4.9	(0.63)	13.1	(0.98)
Control of school[3]																
Public	32.0	(0.76)	21.1	(0.65)	18.3	(0.64)	6.2	(0.38)	4.2	(0.28)	5.2	(0.32)	4.1	(0.28)	11.4	(0.45)
Private	29.1	(2.10)	20.1	(1.79)	16.0	(1.76)	1.3 !	(0.50)	3.6	(0.92)	5.9	(1.11)	5.0	(1.11)	6.5	(1.14)
2009																
Total	**28.0**	**(0.83)**	**18.8**	**(0.65)**	**16.5**	**(0.66)**	**5.7**	**(0.34)**	**3.6**	**(0.28)**	**4.7**	**(0.34)**	**3.3**	**(0.28)**	**9.0**	**(0.48)**
Sex																
Male	26.6	(1.04)	18.4	(0.89)	12.8	(0.79)	5.6	(0.50)	4.0	(0.43)	3.8	(0.39)	3.4	(0.40)	10.1	(0.65)
Female	29.5	(1.08)	19.2	(0.95)	20.3	(0.92)	5.8	(0.50)	3.2	(0.37)	5.7	(0.52)	3.2	(0.39)	7.9	(0.64)
Race/ethnicity[1]																
White	29.3	(1.03)	20.5	(0.89)	17.4	(0.86)	5.4	(0.40)	3.7	(0.38)	5.2	(0.44)	3.3	(0.32)	9.1	(0.61)
Black	29.1	(2.29)	18.4	(1.78)	17.7	(1.60)	7.8	(1.20)	4.8	(0.92)	4.6	(0.97)	4.6	(0.99)	9.9	(1.55)
Hispanic	25.5	(1.71)	15.8	(1.34)	14.8	(1.44)	5.8	(0.87)	2.7	(0.59)	3.6	(0.68)	2.6	(0.55)	9.1	(0.97)
Asian	17.3	(3.01)	9.6	(2.38)	8.1	(2.11)	‡	(†)	‡	(†)	3.4 !	(1.41)	‡	(†)	5.5 !	(1.75)
Other	26.7	(4.61)	17.4	(3.83)	12.9	(3.21)	9.7 !	(3.01)	4.5 !	(1.97)	4.5 !	(1.85)	3.8 !	(1.67)	7.1 !	(2.39)
Grade																
6th	39.4	(2.60)	30.6	(2.32)	21.4	(2.20)	9.3	(1.34)	4.2 !	(1.27)	6.6	(1.31)	4.0	(1.00)	14.5	(1.89)
7th	33.1	(1.87)	23.6	(1.76)	17.3	(1.58)	5.7	(1.00)	4.6	(0.82)	5.6	(0.95)	4.6	(0.85)	13.1	(1.34)
8th	31.7	(1.85)	22.8	(1.64)	18.1	(1.50)	6.8	(0.94)	5.4	(0.91)	6.9	(1.04)	6.1	(0.92)	12.8	(1.29)
9th	28.0	(1.90)	19.2	(1.66)	16.6	(1.53)	7.1	(1.00)	4.0	(0.74)	4.5	(0.78)	2.9	(0.71)	9.7	(1.24)
10th	26.6	(1.71)	15.0	(1.41)	17.0	(1.32)	5.8	(0.91)	3.1	(0.63)	4.0	(0.76)	2.9	(0.63)	7.3	(1.03)
11th	21.1	(1.69)	13.9	(1.42)	13.9	(1.42)	4.8	(0.84)	2.5	(0.63)	3.6	(0.76)	1.5 !	(0.49)	4.4	(0.84)
12th	20.4	(1.63)	11.1	(1.20)	13.1	(1.32)	2.0	(0.57)	1.7 !	(0.52)	2.6	(0.64)	1.3 !	(0.46)	3.0	(0.65)
Urbanicity[2]																
Urban	27.4	(1.25)	17.0	(1.00)	16.5	(1.01)	6.6	(0.67)	4.2	(0.59)	4.0	(0.57)	4.2	(0.63)	9.0	(0.98)
Suburban	27.5	(1.06)	19.3	(0.87)	15.5	(0.97)	5.2	(0.44)	3.2	(0.33)	5.0	(0.46)	2.9	(0.34)	8.9	(0.56)
Rural	30.7	(1.99)	20.2	(1.60)	19.9	(1.56)	6.1	(0.79)	4.1	(0.80)	5.2	(0.85)	3.3	(0.64)	9.5	(1.27)
Control of school[3]																
Public	28.8	(0.88)	19.3	(0.68)	16.9	(0.69)	5.9	(0.37)	3.8	(0.30)	4.7	(0.36)	3.4	(0.29)	9.4	(0.52)
Private	18.9	(2.16)	13.3	(1.87)	11.6	(1.75)	4.4	(1.12)	1.9 !	(0.76)	4.9	(1.16)	1.8 !	(0.68)	4.5	(1.14)

See notes at end of table.

Table 230.45. Percentage of students ages 12–18 who reported being bullied at school during the school year, by type of bullying and selected student and school characteristics: Selected years, 2005 through 2013—Continued

[Standard errors appear in parentheses]

Year and student or school characteristic	Total bullied at school	Type of bullying at school: Made fun of, called names, or insulted	Subject of rumors	Threatened with harm	Tried to make do things did not want to do	Excluded from activities on purpose	Property destroyed on purpose	Pushed, shoved, tripped, or spit on
1	2	3	4	5	6	7	8	9
2011								
Total	**27.8 (0.76)**	**17.6 (0.62)**	**18.3 (0.61)**	**5.0 (0.30)**	**3.3 (0.26)**	**5.6 (0.34)**	**2.8 (0.23)**	**7.9 (0.38)**
Sex								
Male	24.5 (0.91)	16.2 (0.73)	13.2 (0.66)	5.0 (0.44)	3.6 (0.34)	4.8 (0.41)	3.3 (0.34)	8.9 (0.57)
Female	31.4 (0.99)	19.1 (0.84)	23.8 (0.93)	5.1 (0.41)	3.0 (0.36)	6.4 (0.49)	2.3 (0.30)	6.8 (0.49)
Race/ethnicity[1]								
White	31.5 (1.07)	20.6 (0.89)	20.3 (0.81)	5.8 (0.44)	3.3 (0.35)	7.1 (0.51)	3.1 (0.33)	8.6 (0.55)
Black	27.2 (1.97)	16.4 (1.45)	18.6 (1.79)	5.5 (0.83)	4.3 (0.79)	4.7 (0.90)	3.3 (0.72)	9.3 (1.00)
Hispanic	21.9 (1.07)	12.7 (0.93)	15.1 (0.87)	3.3 (0.53)	2.9 (0.46)	2.8 (0.52)	2.4 (0.52)	6.2 (0.75)
Asian	14.9 (2.70)	9.0 (2.04)	7.7 (2.03)	‡ (†)	2.7 ! (1.10)	2.9 ! (1.13)	‡ (†)	2.1 ! (0.95)
Other	23.7 (3.38)	15.0 (2.47)	17.0 (2.94)	6.5 (1.73)	‡ (†)	5.0 ! (1.62)	‡ (†)	7.2 (1.81)
Grade								
6th	37.0 (2.17)	27.0 (2.03)	23.1 (1.90)	4.9 (0.94)	3.9 (0.85)	6.6 (1.19)	3.7 (0.87)	12.7 (1.56)
7th	30.3 (1.64)	22.4 (1.35)	18.3 (1.31)	6.9 (0.89)	4.5 (0.72)	7.8 (0.95)	4.0 (0.68)	12.6 (1.16)
8th	30.7 (1.68)	20.7 (1.51)	19.0 (1.40)	5.3 (0.75)	2.9 (0.56)	6.4 (0.80)	4.0 (0.73)	10.8 (1.07)
9th	26.5 (1.66)	16.4 (1.28)	16.3 (1.38)	5.4 (0.73)	3.3 (0.64)	4.1 (0.87)	2.5 (0.60)	7.3 (0.85)
10th	28.0 (1.56)	16.9 (1.26)	19.6 (1.24)	5.1 (0.75)	3.9 (0.65)	5.3 (0.71)	2.2 (0.48)	6.7 (0.82)
11th	23.8 (1.72)	12.7 (1.17)	17.1 (1.48)	4.0 (0.68)	2.4 (0.60)	4.7 (0.71)	1.8 (0.50)	3.9 (0.73)
12th	22.0 (1.34)	10.6 (1.12)	16.7 (1.23)	3.5 (0.65)	2.3 (0.55)	4.3 (0.75)	1.9 (0.51)	2.7 (0.59)
Urbanicity[2]								
Urban	24.8 (1.28)	15.9 (1.07)	16.1 (1.05)	4.4 (0.49)	3.1 (0.38)	4.6 (0.50)	2.5 (0.38)	7.6 (0.66)
Suburban	29.0 (1.07)	18.4 (0.85)	18.7 (0.86)	5.0 (0.47)	3.2 (0.33)	6.0 (0.46)	3.0 (0.35)	8.2 (0.56)
Rural	29.7 (1.82)	18.4 (1.33)	21.4 (1.47)	6.3 (0.69)	3.9 (0.80)	5.8 (0.89)	3.0 (0.54)	7.3 (0.78)
Control of school[3]								
Public	28.4 (0.82)	17.9 (0.66)	18.8 (0.65)	5.3 (0.33)	3.3 (0.28)	5.5 (0.37)	2.9 (0.24)	8.1 (0.42)
Private	21.5 (1.91)	13.9 (1.68)	12.6 (1.59)	1.6 ! (0.62)	2.9 (0.76)	5.6 (1.07)	2.1 ! (0.71)	4.7 (1.03)
2013								
Total	**21.5 (0.66)**	**13.6 (0.51)**	**13.2 (0.50)**	**3.9 (0.27)**	**2.2 (0.21)**	**4.5 (0.30)**	**1.6 (0.20)**	**6.0 (0.39)**
Sex								
Male	19.5 (0.81)	12.6 (0.70)	9.6 (0.60)	4.1 (0.38)	2.4 (0.30)	3.5 (0.34)	1.8 (0.28)	7.4 (0.59)
Female	23.7 (0.98)	14.7 (0.75)	17.0 (0.80)	3.7 (0.37)	1.9 (0.27)	5.5 (0.47)	1.3 (0.25)	4.6 (0.42)
Race/ethnicity[1]								
White	23.7 (0.93)	15.6 (0.74)	14.6 (0.76)	4.4 (0.40)	2.0 (0.28)	5.4 (0.46)	1.5 (0.24)	6.1 (0.49)
Black	20.3 (1.81)	10.5 (1.22)	12.7 (1.40)	3.2 (0.68)	2.7 (0.59)	2.7 (0.71)	2.0 (0.54)	6.0 (0.97)
Hispanic	19.2 (1.30)	12.1 (1.13)	11.5 (1.02)	4.0 (0.58)	1.6 (0.32)	3.5 (0.53)	1.4 (0.38)	6.3 (0.79)
Asian	9.2 (1.67)	7.5 (1.63)	3.7 (0.95)	‡ (†)	3.8 ! (1.32)	2.2 ! (0.71)	1.6 ! (0.78)	2.0 ! (0.85)
Other	25.2 (3.60)	16.5 (2.99)	17.3 (3.05)	4.3 ! (1.56)	4.0 ! (1.38)	6.5 (1.85)	2.1 ! (1.00)	8.5 (1.90)
Grade								
6th	27.8 (2.31)	21.3 (2.15)	16.1 (1.61)	5.9 (1.13)	3.4 (0.88)	6.5 (1.20)	3.1 (0.77)	11.0 (1.46)
7th	26.4 (1.65)	17.9 (1.35)	15.5 (1.35)	6.1 (0.88)	3.0 (0.52)	6.3 (0.86)	2.2 (0.52)	11.6 (1.12)
8th	21.7 (1.42)	14.5 (1.23)	12.7 (1.11)	3.9 (0.68)	2.3 (0.54)	5.2 (0.80)	1.5 ! (0.45)	6.5 (0.85)
9th	23.0 (1.42)	13.7 (1.16)	13.8 (1.22)	3.6 (0.61)	2.6 (0.58)	4.3 (0.70)	1.2 ! (0.40)	4.9 (0.83)
10th	19.5 (1.48)	12.9 (1.21)	12.9 (1.28)	4.3 (0.73)	1.7 (0.47)	4.6 (0.72)	1.3 (0.37)	3.7 (0.68)
11th	20.0 (1.50)	11.2 (1.20)	12.5 (1.31)	3.0 (0.60)	1.5 (0.45)	2.4 (0.61)	1.6 ! (0.50)	3.4 (0.72)
12th	14.1 (1.51)	6.4 (1.04)	9.7 (1.15)	1.0 ! (0.43)	1.3 ! (0.48)	2.5 (0.67)	0.7 ! (0.31)	3.0 (0.71)
Urbanicity[2]								
Urban	20.7 (1.10)	12.8 (0.80)	12.7 (0.87)	3.9 (0.47)	2.7 (0.45)	4.1 (0.51)	1.4 (0.27)	5.6 (0.60)
Suburban	22.0 (0.90)	14.2 (0.69)	13.4 (0.71)	3.9 (0.39)	2.0 (0.28)	4.7 (0.43)	1.3 (0.24)	6.4 (0.52)
Rural	21.4 (1.86)	13.2 (1.49)	13.3 (1.45)	4.1 (0.67)	1.7 (0.42)	4.2 (0.73)	2.8 (0.66)	5.8 (0.88)
Control of school[3]								
Public	21.5 (0.67)	13.5 (0.53)	13.2 (0.52)	3.9 (0.28)	2.2 (0.22)	4.3 (0.31)	1.6 (0.19)	6.1 (0.41)
Private	22.4 (2.71)	15.3 (2.01)	13.4 (2.20)	3.9 (1.14)	2.7 ! (0.82)	6.7 (1.31)	1.3 ! (0.60)	5.2 (1.24)

—Not available.
†Not applicable.
!Interpret data with caution. The coefficient of variation (CV) for this estimate is between 30 and 50 percent.
‡Reporting standards not met. Either there are too few cases for a reliable estimate or the coefficient of variation (CV) is 50 percent or greater.
[1]Race categories exclude persons of Hispanic ethnicity. "Other" includes American Indians/Alaska Natives, Pacific Islanders, and persons of Two or more races.
[2]Refers to the Standard Metropolitan Statistical Area (MSA) status of the respondent's household as defined in 2000 by the U.S. Census Bureau. Categories include "central city of an MSA (Urban)," "in MSA but not in central city (Suburban)," and "not MSA (Rural)." These data by metropolitan status were based on the location of households and differ from those published in *Student Reports of Bullying and Cyber-Bullying: Results from the 2011 School Crime Supplement to the National Crime Victimization Survey*, which were based on the urban-centric measure of the location of the school that the child attended.
[3]Control of school as reported by the respondent. These data differ from those based on a matching of the respondent-reported school name to the Common Core of Data's Public Elementary/Secondary School Universe Survey or the Private School Survey, as reported in *Student Reports of Bullying and Cyber-Bullying: Results from the 2011 School Crime Supplement to the National Crime Victimization Survey*.
NOTE: "At school" includes the school building, on school property, on a school bus, or going to and from school. Bullying types do not sum to totals because students could have experienced more than one type of bullying.
SOURCE: U.S. Department of Justice, Bureau of Justice Statistics, School Crime Supplement (SCS) to the National Crime Victimization Survey, selected years, 2005 through 2013. (This table was prepared August 2014.)

Table 230.50. Percentage of students ages 12–18 who reported being bullied at school during the school year and, among bullied students, percentage who reported being bullied in various locations, by selected student and school characteristics: 2013

[Standard errors appear in parentheses]

Student or school characteristic	Total		Among students who were bullied, percent by location[1]													
			Inside classroom		In hallway or stairwell		In bathroom or locker room		Cafeteria		Somewhere else in school building		Outside on school grounds		On school bus	
1	2		3		4		5		6		7		8		9	
Total	**21.5**	**(0.66)**	**33.6**	**(1.54)**	**45.6**	**(1.73)**	**9.1**	**(0.84)**	**18.9**	**(1.17)**	**0.8 !**	**(0.30)**	**22.9**	**(1.44)**	**7.8**	**(0.86)**
Sex																
Male	19.5	(0.81)	31.1	(2.13)	45.8	(2.37)	11.6	(1.46)	17.9	(1.76)	‡	(†)	22.3	(1.85)	8.9	(1.41)
Female	23.7	(0.98)	35.8	(2.03)	45.3	(2.37)	7.0	(1.01)	19.7	(1.69)	1.2 !	(0.54)	23.4	(1.92)	6.9	(1.12)
Race/ethnicity[2]																
White	23.7	(0.93)	33.9	(2.08)	46.9	(2.09)	11.0	(1.24)	19.8	(1.53)	0.8 !	(0.34)	22.9	(1.89)	9.6	(1.18)
Black	20.3	(1.81)	28.7	(4.03)	39.5	(4.27)	5.1 !	(2.00)	19.2	(3.36)	‡	(†)	18.7	(3.10)	6.4 !	(2.15)
Hispanic	19.2	(1.30)	35.6	(3.02)	44.8	(3.47)	7.1	(1.66)	15.5	(2.45)	‡	(†)	26.4	(3.08)	2.3 !	(1.00)
Asian	9.2	(1.67)	‡	(†)	‡	(†)	‡	(†)	‡	(†)	‡	(†)	‡	(†)	‡	(†)
Other	25.2	(3.60)	31.9	(5.92)	48.3	(7.19)	‡	(†)	14.3 !	(5.14)	‡	(†)	25.1	(5.03)	17.0 !	(5.47)
Grade																
6th	27.8	(2.31)	34.9	(4.23)	40.9	(4.91)	7.3 !	(2.57)	11.6	(2.98)	‡	(†)	36.4	(4.37)	17.1	(3.61)
7th	26.4	(1.65)	32.4	(2.88)	43.6	(3.35)	12.9	(2.25)	20.8	(2.63)	‡	(†)	26.8	(3.03)	10.2	(1.92)
8th	21.7	(1.42)	38.0	(4.12)	41.2	(4.00)	7.7	(2.06)	18.0	(2.97)	‡	(†)	26.1	(3.53)	8.7	(2.40)
9th	23.0	(1.42)	29.9	(3.44)	42.0	(3.61)	9.5	(2.01)	23.9	(3.22)	‡	(†)	19.0	(2.76)	5.7 !	(1.80)
10th	19.5	(1.48)	40.1	(4.32)	52.6	(4.63)	9.0	(2.24)	19.2	(3.15)	‡	(†)	20.0	(3.79)	7.9	(2.17)
11th	20.0	(1.50)	29.5	(3.66)	52.2	(4.05)	8.2	(2.43)	18.8	(3.35)	‡	(†)	16.6	(3.52)	‡	(†)
12th	14.1	(1.51)	30.1	(5.29)	47.4	(5.92)	6.2 !	(2.47)	14.9	(4.18)	‡	(†)	14.1	(3.80)	‡	(†)
Urbanicity[3]																
Urban	20.7	(1.10)	34.3	(3.05)	42.2	(3.07)	7.9	(1.59)	21.5	(2.35)	‡	(†)	26.2	(2.86)	4.8	(1.29)
Suburban	22.0	(0.90)	32.9	(2.01)	48.3	(2.18)	9.5	(1.12)	18.0	(1.61)	‡	(†)	22.3	(1.89)	9.0	(1.25)
Rural	21.4	(1.86)	35.1	(4.17)	41.9	(3.93)	10.2	(2.07)	17.0	(2.79)	‡	(†)	18.7	(3.57)	9.2	(1.84)
Control of school																
Public	21.5	(0.67)	33.3	(1.61)	46.1	(1.80)	9.3	(0.90)	18.7	(1.22)	0.8 !	(0.33)	22.3	(1.47)	8.2	(0.91)
Private	22.4	(2.71)	36.7	(5.32)	39.2	(5.26)	6.7 !	(2.64)	20.5	(4.47)	‡	(†)	30.1	(5.17)	‡	(†)

†Not applicable.

!Interpret data with caution. The coefficient of variation (CV) for this estimate is between 30 and 50 percent.

‡Reporting standards not met. Either there are too few cases for a reliable estimate or the coefficient of variation (CV) is 50 percent or greater.

[1]Includes only students who indicated the location of bullying. Excludes students who indicated that they were bullied but did not answer the question about where the bullying occurred.

[2]Race categories exclude persons of Hispanic ethnicity. "Other" includes American Indians/Alaska Natives, Pacific Islanders, and persons of Two or more races.

[3]Refers to the Standard Metropolitan Statistical Area (MSA) status of the respondent's household as defined in 2000 by the U.S. Census Bureau. Categories include "central city of an MSA (Urban)," "in MSA but not in central city (Suburban)," and "not MSA (Rural)."

NOTE: "At school" includes the school building, on school property, on a school bus, or going to and from school. Location totals may sum to more than 100 percent because students could have been bullied in more than one location.

SOURCE: U.S. Department of Justice, Bureau of Justice Statistics, School Crime Supplement (SCS) to the National Crime Victimization Survey, 2013. (This table was prepared August 2014.)

Table 230.55. Percentage of students ages 12–18 who reported being cyber-bullied anywhere during the school year, by type of cyber-bullying and selected student and school characteristics: 2013

[Standard errors appear in parentheses]

Student or school characteristic	Total cyber-bullying[1]		Type of cyber-bullying: Hurtful information on Internet		Private information purposely shared on Internet		Subject of harassing instant messages		Subject of harassing text messages		Subject of harassing e-mails		Subject of harassment while gaming		Excluded online	
1	2		3		4		5		6		7		8		9	
Total	**6.9**	**(0.42)**	**2.8**	**(0.24)**	**0.9**	**(0.15)**	**2.1**	**(0.22)**	**3.2**	**(0.28)**	**0.9**	**(0.15)**	**1.5**	**(0.18)**	**0.9**	**(0.13)**
Sex																
Male	5.2	(0.43)	1.2	(0.22)	0.4	(0.12)	1.0	(0.19)	1.6	(0.25)	0.2 !	(0.09)	2.5	(0.31)	0.9	(0.18)
Female	8.6	(0.63)	4.5	(0.42)	1.5	(0.27)	3.4	(0.39)	4.9	(0.51)	1.7	(0.30)	0.4 !	(0.14)	0.9	(0.18)
Race/ethnicity[2]																
White	7.6	(0.57)	2.9	(0.35)	1.0	(0.22)	2.2	(0.27)	3.8	(0.42)	0.8	(0.19)	1.8	(0.26)	1.0	(0.18)
Black	4.5	(0.94)	2.2	(0.63)	‡	(†)	1.8 !	(0.57)	1.9	(0.49)	0.8 !	(0.35)	‡	(†)	‡	(†)
Hispanic	5.8	(0.78)	2.6	(0.52)	1.0 !	(0.34)	1.9	(0.41)	2.6	(0.52)	0.8 !	(0.28)	0.9 !	(0.30)	1.0	(0.29)
Asian	5.8	(1.67)	1.8 !	(0.85)	‡	(†)	‡	(†)	‡	(†)	‡	(†)	3.1 !	(1.20)	‡	(†)
Other	13.4	(2.43)	6.9	(1.86)	1.9 !	(0.96)	4.9 !	(1.63)	6.2	(1.69)	4.7 !	(1.62)	3.2 !	(1.30)	‡	(†)
Grade																
6th	5.9	(1.20)	1.4 !	(0.58)	‡	(†)	1.2 !	(0.54)	2.3 !	(0.78)	‡	(†)	1.5 !	(0.61)	‡	(†)
7th	7.0	(0.91)	2.1	(0.53)	1.1 !	(0.36)	2.3	(0.51)	3.8	(0.74)	1.0 !	(0.35)	1.8	(0.44)	0.8 !	(0.30)
8th	6.4	(0.86)	3.1	(0.59)	0.9 !	(0.26)	2.3	(0.55)	3.2	(0.64)	1.5 !	(0.48)	1.7	(0.50)	1.5 !	(0.46)
9th	6.7	(0.97)	2.0	(0.49)	‡	(†)	2.9	(0.58)	2.8	(0.62)	‡	(†)	1.6	(0.48)	1.4 !	(0.43)
10th	8.6	(1.16)	4.1	(0.84)	1.2 !	(0.41)	2.8	(0.61)	4.5	(0.81)	1.4 !	(0.41)	1.0 !	(0.35)	1.0 !	(0.34)
11th	6.8	(0.87)	3.9	(0.71)	1.3 !	(0.41)	1.1 !	(0.43)	2.7	(0.55)	‡	(†)	1.3	(0.39)	‡	(†)
12th	5.9	(0.93)	2.6	(0.67)	‡	(†)	1.9	(0.55)	2.3	(0.59)	1.1 !	(0.40)	1.4 !	(0.51)	‡	(†)
Urbanicity[3]																
Urban	7.1	(0.73)	3.4	(0.50)	1.1	(0.32)	2.4	(0.45)	3.1	(0.50)	1.4	(0.34)	1.5	(0.25)	1.2	(0.33)
Suburban	7.0	(0.61)	2.7	(0.35)	0.9	(0.20)	2.0	(0.27)	3.3	(0.40)	0.8	(0.18)	1.6	(0.27)	0.9	(0.17)
Rural	5.9	(1.02)	2.2	(0.43)	0.8 !	(0.29)	2.0 !	(0.62)	2.9	(0.72)	0.7 !	(0.31)	1.0 !	(0.48)	‡	(†)
Control of school																
Public	6.9	(0.45)	2.9	(0.26)	0.9	(0.16)	2.2	(0.23)	3.2	(0.30)	0.9	(0.16)	1.5	(0.19)	0.9	(0.14)
Private	6.4	(1.44)	2.0 !	(0.76)	1.2 !	(0.54)	‡	(†)	2.9 !	(0.98)	‡	(†)	‡	(†)	‡	(†)

†Not applicable.

!Interpret data with caution. The coefficient of variation (CV) for this estimate is between 30 and 50 percent.

‡Reporting standards not met. Either there are too few cases for a reliable estimate or the coefficient of variation (CV) is 50 percent or greater.

[1]Students who reported experiencing more than one type of cyber-bullying were counted only once in the total for students cyber-bullied.

[2]Race categories exclude persons of Hispanic ethnicity. "Other" includes American Indians/Alaska Natives, Pacific Islanders, and persons of Two or more races.

[3]Refers to the Standard Metropolitan Statistical Area (MSA) status of the respondent's household as defined in 2000 by the U.S. Census Bureau. Categories include "central city of an MSA (Urban)," "in MSA but not in central city (Suburban)," and "not MSA (Rural)."

NOTE: Detail may not sum to totals because of rounding and because students could have experienced more than one type of cyber-bullying.

SOURCE: U.S. Department of Justice, Bureau of Justice Statistics, School Crime Supplement (SCS) to the National Crime Victimization Survey, 2013. (This table was prepared August 2014.)

Table 230.60. Among students ages 12–18 who reported being bullied at school or cyber-bullied anywhere during the school year, percentage reporting various frequencies of bullying and the notification of an adult at school, by selected student and school characteristics: 2013

[Standard errors appear in parentheses]

	Among students who reported being bullied at school					Among students who reported being cyber-bullied anywhere[1]				
	Frequency of bullying					Frequency of cyber-bullying				
Student or school characteristic	Once or twice in the school year	Once or twice a month	Once or twice a week	Almost every day	Adult at school was notified[2]	Once or twice in the school year	Once or twice a month	Once or twice a week	Almost every day	Adult at school was notified[2]
1	2	3	4	5	6	7	8	9	10	11
Total	**67.3 (1.53)**	**19.4 (1.32)**	**7.6 (0.78)**	**5.7 (0.71)**	**38.9 (1.45)**	**73.2 (2.72)**	**15.0 (2.08)**	**7.9 (1.46)**	**3.8 (1.05)**	**23.3 (2.55)**
Sex										
Male	68.0 (2.19)	19.2 (1.98)	7.4 (1.09)	5.5 (1.01)	38.5 (2.01)	75.2 (3.80)	9.3 (2.62)	8.1 (2.24)	7.4 ! (2.23)	10.5 (2.53)
Female	66.6 (2.13)	19.6 (1.89)	7.8 (1.11)	6.0 (0.94)	39.3 (2.20)	71.9 (3.40)	18.8 (2.90)	7.9 (1.82)	‡ (†)	31.6 (3.54)
Race/ethnicity[3]										
White	64.6 (2.04)	20.6 (1.70)	9.1 (1.20)	5.7 (0.87)	40.5 (2.04)	76.9 (3.27)	15.2 (2.80)	4.6 ! (1.53)	3.3 ! (1.23)	24.4 (3.08)
Black	70.2 (3.93)	18.0 (3.40)	5.6 ! (2.07)	6.2 ! (2.13)	40.0 (3.44)	68.2 (7.99)	18.9 ! (6.71)	‡ (†)	‡ (†)	24.5 ! (10.44)
Hispanic	73.8 (3.24)	17.9 (2.88)	4.4 (1.30)	4.0 ! (1.26)	37.5 (3.15)	73.5 (6.28)	8.9 ! (3.78)	12.5 ! (4.48)	‡ (†)	23.7 (4.92)
Asian	‡ (†)	‡ (†)	‡ (†)	‡ (†)	‡ (†)	‡ (†)	‡ (†)	‡ (†)	‡ (†)	‡ (†)
Other	66.9 (7.42)	15.2 ! (5.49)	‡ (†)	12.8 ! (5.30)	36.8 (6.34)	‡ (†)	‡ (†)	‡ (†)	‡ (†)	‡ (†)
Grade										
6th	62.4 (4.19)	22.7 (3.64)	6.5 ! (2.00)	8.4 ! (3.10)	58.3 (4.71)	‡ (†)	‡ (†)	‡ (†)	‡ (†)	‡ (†)
7th	63.8 (2.92)	17.3 (2.60)	11.4 (2.18)	7.5 (1.69)	52.3 (3.53)	65.5 (6.74)	24.9 (6.48)	‡ (†)	‡ (†)	28.0 (5.87)
8th	64.0 (3.74)	19.1 (3.05)	7.9 (2.12)	9.1 (2.30)	38.1 (3.82)	70.5 (6.04)	17.1 ! (5.69)	8.6 ! (3.16)	‡ (†)	30.4 (6.05)
9th	67.4 (3.49)	24.7 (3.48)	3.7 ! (1.41)	4.2 ! (1.59)	35.2 (3.89)	79.6 (5.43)	7.7 ! (3.68)	9.2 ! (3.89)	‡ (†)	12.4 ! (4.90)
10th	65.6 (4.11)	21.5 (3.56)	7.8 (2.29)	5.0 ! (1.79)	34.6 (3.84)	73.8 (5.76)	16.7 ! (5.09)	6.7 ! (3.30)	‡ (†)	23.9 (5.47)
11th	75.8 (3.60)	12.9 (2.83)	8.2 (2.09)	3.2 ! (1.41)	25.8 (3.37)	71.4 (7.36)	14.2 ! (5.62)	12.3 ! (5.36)	‡ (†)	26.7 (6.87)
12th	75.2 (5.35)	17.4 (4.42)	6.1 ! (2.63)	‡ (†)	22.4 (4.32)	74.6 (7.15)	13.3 ! (5.46)	‡ (†)	‡ (†)	21.0 ! (6.70)
Urbanicity[4]										
Urban	71.8 (2.86)	14.9 (2.21)	7.0 (1.36)	6.3 (1.46)	36.6 (2.64)	68.4 (4.76)	15.1 (3.76)	11.9 (3.17)	4.6 ! (1.99)	21.7 (4.81)
Suburban	67.0 (1.94)	20.6 (1.64)	7.1 (1.09)	5.2 (0.85)	40.7 (2.01)	77.9 (3.29)	13.2 (2.67)	5.0 ! (1.59)	3.9 ! (1.48)	24.1 (3.25)
Rural	59.7 (4.96)	23.4 (3.83)	10.2 (2.51)	6.6 (1.66)	36.9 (4.03)	65.2 (8.87)	22.2 (5.79)	10.8 ! (4.91)	‡ (†)	24.1 (5.37)
Control of school										
Public	67.2 (1.63)	19.7 (1.40)	7.4 (0.81)	5.7 (0.74)	38.9 (1.48)	72.0 (2.78)	16.1 (2.20)	7.8 (1.48)	4.1 (1.13)	22.5 (2.61)
Private	67.9 (5.01)	16.7 (3.74)	9.6 ! (2.96)	5.8 ! (2.09)	39.5 (5.50)	‡ (†)	‡ (†)	‡ (†)	‡ (†)	‡ (†)
Total indicating adult at school notified,[2] by frequency of bullying	**36.9 (1.86)**	**38.3 (3.29)**	**55.0 (5.81)**	**50.0 (6.95)**	**† (†)**	**20.2 (2.57)**	**21.6 (6.11)**	**‡ (†)**	**‡ (†)**	**† (†)**
Males indicating adult notified	39.4 (2.55)	31.8 (4.54)	45.9 (9.12)	‡ (†)	† (†)	8.6 ! (2.75)	‡ (†)	‡ (†)	‡ (†)	† (†)
Females indicating adult notified	34.7 (2.64)	43.8 (4.83)	62.5 (7.39)	43.7 (8.65)	† (†)	28.2 (4.02)	28.6 (7.67)	‡ (†)	‡ (†)	† (†)

†Not applicable.
!Interpret data with caution. The coefficient of variation (CV) for this estimate is between 30 and 50 percent.
‡Reporting standards not met. Either there are too few cases for a reliable estimate or the coefficient of variation (CV) is 50 percent or greater.
[1]Students who reported being cyber-bullied are those who responded that another student had done one or more of the following: posted hurtful information about them on the Internet; purposely shared private information about them on the Internet; threatened or insulted them through instant messaging; threatened or insulted them through text messaging; threatened or insulted them through e-mail; threatened or insulted them while gaming; or excluded them online.
[2]Teacher or other adult at school notified.
[3]Race categories exclude persons of Hispanic ethnicity. "Other" includes American Indians/Alaska Natives, Pacific Islanders, and persons of Two or more races.
[4]Refers to the Standard Metropolitan Statistical Area (MSA) status of the respondent's household as defined in 2000 by the U.S. Census Bureau. Categories include "central city of an MSA (Urban)," "in MSA but not in central city (Suburban)," and "not MSA (Rural)."
NOTE: "At school" includes the school building, on school property, on a school bus, or going to and from school. Detail may not sum to totals because of rounding.
SOURCE: U.S. Department of Justice, Bureau of Justice Statistics, School Crime Supplement (SCS) to the National Crime Victimization Survey, 2013. (This table was prepared September 2014.)

Table 230.62. Percentage of public school students in grades 9–12 who reported having been bullied on school property or electronically bullied during the previous 12 months, by state: Selected years, 2009 through 2013

[Standard errors appear in parentheses]

State	Bullied on school property[1]						Electronically bullied[2]					
	2009		2011		2013		2009		2011		2013	
1	2		3		4		5		6		7	
United States[3]	**19.9**	**(0.58)**	**20.1**	**(0.68)**	**19.6**	**(0.55)**	**—**	**(†)**	**16.2**	**(0.45)**	**14.8**	**(0.54)**
Alabama	19.3	(1.45)	14.1	(1.22)	20.8	(1.28)	—	(†)	12.3	(1.64)	13.5	(0.95)
Alaska	20.7	(1.29)	23.0	(1.32)	20.7	(1.35)	—	(†)	15.3	(1.04)	14.7	(1.10)
Arizona	—	(†)	—	(†)	—	(†)	—	(†)	—	(†)	—	(†)
Arkansas	—	(†)	21.9	(1.74)	25.0	(1.51)	—	(†)	16.7	(1.48)	17.6	(1.05)
California	—	(†)	—	(†)	—	(†)	—	(†)	—	(†)	—	(†)
Colorado	18.8	(1.60)	19.3	(1.33)	—	(†)	—	(†)	14.4	(1.09)	—	(†)
Connecticut	—	(†)	21.6	(1.09)	21.9	(0.96)	—	(†)	16.3	(0.81)	17.5	(1.23)
Delaware	15.9	(1.11)	16.5	(1.03)	18.5	(0.96)	—	(†)	—	(†)	13.4	(0.78)
District of Columbia	—	(†)	—	(†)	—	(†)	—	(†)	—	(†)	—	(†)
Florida	13.4	(0.51)	14.0	(0.54)	15.7	(0.50)	—	(†)	12.4	(0.53)	12.3	(0.54)
Georgia	—	(†)	19.1	(1.66)	19.5	(1.36)	—	(†)	13.6	(1.09)	13.9	(0.93)
Hawaii	—	(†)	20.3	(1.29)	18.7	(1.00)	—	(†)	14.9	(0.80)	15.6	(0.98)
Idaho	22.3	(1.03)	22.8	(1.76)	25.4	(1.12)	—	(†)	17.0	(1.18)	18.8	(1.18)
Illinois	19.6	(1.46)	19.3	(1.31)	22.2	(1.00)	—	(†)	16.0	(1.38)	16.9	(0.77)
Indiana	22.8	(1.69)	25.0	(1.38)	—	(†)	—	(†)	18.7	(1.15)	—	(†)
Iowa	—	(†)	22.5	(1.47)	—	(†)	—	(†)	16.8	(0.97)	—	(†)
Kansas	18.5	(1.21)	20.5	(1.31)	22.1	(1.57)	—	(†)	15.5	(0.88)	16.9	(0.97)
Kentucky	20.8	(1.30)	18.9	(1.24)	21.4	(1.41)	—	(†)	17.4	(1.14)	13.2	(1.06)
Louisiana	15.9	(1.88)	19.2	(1.40)	24.2	(1.64)	—	(†)	18.0	(1.53)	16.9	(1.91)
Maine	22.4	(0.49)	22.4	(0.43)	24.2	(0.66)	—	(†)	19.7	(0.55)	20.6	(0.61)
Maryland	20.9	(0.96)	21.2	(1.28)	19.6	(0.25)	—	(†)	14.2	(0.78)	14.0	(0.22)
Massachusetts	19.4	(0.89)	18.1	(1.04)	16.6	(0.98)	—	(†)	—	(†)	13.8	(0.79)
Michigan	24.0	(1.77)	22.7	(1.40)	25.3	(1.47)	—	(†)	18.0	(0.91)	18.8	(1.20)
Minnesota	—	(†)	—	(†)	—	(†)	—	(†)	—	(†)	—	(†)
Mississippi	16.0	(1.04)	15.6	(1.32)	19.2	(0.93)	—	(†)	12.5	(0.93)	11.9	(0.74)
Missouri	22.8	(1.74)	—	(†)	25.2	(1.72)	—	(†)	—	(†)	—	(†)
Montana	23.1	(1.32)	26.0	(1.06)	26.3	(0.68)	—	(†)	19.2	(0.92)	18.1	(0.62)
Nebraska	—	(†)	22.9	(0.85)	20.8	(1.10)	—	(†)	15.8	(0.81)	15.7	(0.91)
Nevada	—	(†)	—	(†)	19.7	(1.09)	—	(†)	—	(†)	15.0	(1.28)
New Hampshire	22.1	(1.53)	25.3	(1.21)	22.8	(1.05)	—	(†)	21.6	(1.27)	18.1	(1.02)
New Jersey	20.7	(1.44)	20.0	(1.57)	21.3	(1.12)	—	(†)	15.6	(1.65)	14.8	(1.25)
New Mexico	19.5	(0.80)	18.7	(0.72)	18.2	(0.95)	—	(†)	13.2	(0.66)	13.1	(0.67)
New York	18.2	(1.01)	17.7	(0.66)	19.7	(1.43)	—	(†)	16.2	(0.68)	15.3	(0.89)
North Carolina	16.6	(1.00)	20.5	(1.34)	19.2	(0.94)	—	(†)	15.7	(0.83)	12.5	(1.11)
North Dakota	21.1	(1.29)	24.9	(1.24)	25.4	(1.28)	—	(†)	17.4	(1.15)	17.1	(0.82)
Ohio[4]	—	(†)	22.7	(1.83)	20.8	(1.40)	—	(†)	14.7	(1.08)	15.1	(1.31)
Oklahoma	17.5	(1.25)	16.7	(1.27)	18.6	(1.08)	—	(†)	15.6	(1.21)	14.3	(1.33)
Oregon	—	(†)	—	(†)	—	(†)	—	(†)	—	(†)	—	(†)
Pennsylvania	19.2	(1.18)	—	(†)	—	(†)	—	(†)	—	(†)	—	(†)
Rhode Island	16.3	(0.85)	19.1	(1.74)	18.1	(1.00)	—	(†)	15.3	(1.14)	14.3	(1.11)
South Carolina	15.1	(1.53)	18.3	(1.36)	20.2	(1.33)	—	(†)	15.6	(1.44)	13.8	(1.00)
South Dakota[4]	—	(†)	26.7	(1.25)	24.3	(2.05)	—	(†)	19.6	(0.94)	17.8	(1.05)
Tennessee	17.3	(1.24)	17.5	(0.88)	21.1	(1.22)	—	(†)	13.9	(0.69)	15.5	(0.94)
Texas	18.7	(1.06)	16.5	(0.73)	19.1	(1.06)	—	(†)	13.0	(0.66)	13.8	(1.04)
Utah	18.8	(1.05)	21.7	(0.97)	21.8	(0.99)	—	(†)	16.6	(1.12)	16.9	(0.87)
Vermont	—	(†)	—	(†)	—	(†)	—	(†)	15.2	(0.54)	18.0	(0.32)
Virginia	—	(†)	20.3	(1.37)	21.9	(0.87)	—	(†)	14.8	(1.49)	14.5	(0.61)
Washington	—	(†)	—	(†)	—	(†)	—	(†)	—	(†)	—	(†)
West Virginia	23.5	(1.33)	18.6	(1.71)	22.1	(1.72)	—	(†)	15.5	(1.18)	17.2	(0.89)
Wisconsin	22.5	(1.28)	24.0	(1.35)	22.7	(1.23)	—	(†)	16.6	(0.74)	17.6	(0.86)
Wyoming	24.4	(0.93)	25.0	(0.98)	23.3	(0.82)	—	(†)	18.7	(0.80)	16.1	(0.71)

—Not available.
†Not applicable.
[1]Bullying was defined for respondents as "when one or more students tease, threaten, spread rumors about, hit, shove, or hurt another student over and over again." "On school property" was not defined for survey respondents.
[2]Survey respondents were asked about being electronically bullied ("being bullied through e-mail, chat rooms, instant messaging, websites, or texting"). Data on electronic bullying were not collected in 2009.
[3]Data for the U.S. total include both public and private schools and were collected through a national survey representing the entire country.
[4]Data include both public and private schools.

NOTE: State-level data include public schools only, with the exception of data for Ohio and South Dakota. Data for the U.S. total, Ohio, and South Dakota include both public and private schools. For specific states, a given year's data may be unavailable (1) because the state did not participate in the survey that year; (2) because the state omitted this particular survey item from the state-level questionnaire; or (3) because the state had an overall response rate of less than 60 percent (the overall response rate is the school response rate multiplied by the student response rate).
SOURCE: Centers for Disease Control and Prevention, Division of Adolescent and School Health, Youth Risk Behavior Surveillance System (YRBSS), 2009 through 2013. (This table was prepared September 2014.)

Table 230.65. Percentage of public schools reporting selected types of cyber-bullying problems occurring at school or away from school at least once a week, by selected school characteristics: 2009–10

[Standard errors appear in parentheses]

School characteristic	Cyber-bullying among students		School environment is affected by cyber-bullying		Staff resources are used to deal with cyber-bullying	
1	2		3		4	
All public schools	**7.9**	**(0.49)**	**4.4**	**(0.34)**	**3.8**	**(0.39)**
School level[1]						
Primary	1.5	(0.43)	0.9 !	(0.38)	0.9 !	(0.34)
Middle	18.6	(1.48)	9.8	(1.07)	8.5	(1.01)
High school	17.6	(1.11)	9.9	(0.85)	8.6	(0.81)
Combined	12.6	(3.34)	7.4 !	(2.64)	‡	(†)
Enrollment size						
Less than 300	4.8	(1.21)	3.2 !	(1.05)	2.9 !	(0.89)
300–499	4.6	(0.74)	2.8	(0.57)	2.7	(0.64)
500–999	9.3	(0.63)	4.6	(0.57)	3.7	(0.58)
1,000 or more	19.2	(1.42)	10.7	(1.26)	9.4	(0.96)
Locale						
City	5.7	(0.62)	3.8	(0.57)	3.6	(0.70)
Suburban	8.5	(0.85)	4.0	(0.48)	3.7	(0.46)
Town	9.6	(1.45)	5.8	(1.15)	4.1	(1.06)
Rural	8.4	(1.07)	4.5	(0.89)	4.0	(0.82)
Percent combined enrollment of Black, Hispanic, Asian/Pacific Islander, and American Indian/Alaska Native students						
Less than 5 percent	12.8	(2.05)	7.7	(1.66)	4.7	(1.32)
5 percent to less than 20 percent	10.1	(0.90)	5.1	(0.59)	4.7	(0.72)
20 percent to less than 50 percent	6.7	(0.77)	3.6	(0.67)	3.9	(0.74)
50 percent or more	5.3	(0.60)	3.1	(0.41)	2.8	(0.54)
Percent of students eligible for free or reduced-price lunch						
0–25	10.8	(1.08)	5.0	(0.62)	4.9	(0.72)
26–50	9.7	(1.14)	4.3	(0.55)	3.4	(0.48)
51–75	6.8	(0.83)	4.9	(0.78)	4.1	(0.78)
76–100	4.5	(0.96)	3.3	(0.91)	3.0	(0.73)
Student/teacher ratio[2]						
Less than 12	6.8	(1.36)	4.1	(1.20)	3.5	(1.02)
12–16	7.4	(0.71)	4.0	(0.48)	3.8	(0.66)
More than 16	8.7	(0.75)	4.8	(0.60)	3.9	(0.56)
Prevalence of violent incidents[3]						
No violent incidents	2.4 !	(0.90)	‡	(†)	‡	(†)
Any violent incidents	9.9	(0.53)	5.6	(0.40)	5.1	(0.53)

†Not applicable.
!Interpret data with caution. The coefficient of variation (CV) for this estimate is between 30 and 50 percent.
‡Reporting standards not met. Either there are too few cases for a reliable estimate or the coefficient of variation (CV) is 50 percent or greater.
[1]Primary schools are defined as schools in which the lowest grade is not higher than grade 3 and the highest grade is not higher than grade 8. Middle schools are defined as schools in which the lowest grade is not lower than grade 4 and the highest grade is not higher than grade 9. High schools are defined as schools in which the lowest grade is not lower than grade 9 and the highest grade is not higher than grade 12. Combined schools include all other combinations of grades, including K–12 schools.
[2]Student/teacher ratio was calculated by dividing the total number of students enrolled in the school by the total number of full-time-equivalent (FTE) teachers. Information regarding the total number of FTE teachers was obtained from the Common Core of Data (CCD), the sampling frame for SSOCS.
[3]"Violent incidents" include rape or attempted rape, sexual battery other than rape, physical attack or fight with or without a weapon, threat of physical attack or fight with or without a weapon, and robbery with or without a weapon. "At school" was defined for respondents to include activities that happen in school buildings, on school grounds, on school buses, and at places that hold school-sponsored events or activities. Respondents were instructed to respond only for those times that were during normal school hours or when school activities and events were in session.
NOTE: Includes schools reporting that cyber-bullying happens either "daily" or "at least once a week." "Cyber-bullying" was defined for respondents as occurring "when willful and repeated harm is inflicted through the use of computers, cell phones, or other electronic devices." Responses were provided by the principal or the person most knowledgeable about crime and safety issues at the school. Respondents were instructed to include cyber-bullying "problems that can occur anywhere (both at your school and away from school)."
SOURCE: U.S. Department of Education, National Center for Education Statistics, 2009–10 School Survey on Crime and Safety (SSOCS), 2010. (This table was prepared September 2013.)

Table 230.70. Percentage of students ages 12–18 who reported being afraid of attack or harm, by location and selected student and school characteristics: Selected years, 1995 through 2013

[Standard errors appear in parentheses]

Student or school characteristic	1995	1999	2001	2003	2005	2007[1]	2009[1]	2011[1]	2013[1]
1	2	3	4	5	6	7	8	9	10
At school									
Total	**11.8 (0.39)**	**7.3 (0.37)**	**6.4 (0.31)**	**6.1 (0.31)**	**6.4 (0.39)**	**5.3 (0.33)**	**4.2 (0.33)**	**3.7 (0.28)**	**3.5 (0.33)**
Sex									
Male	10.8 (0.51)	6.5 (0.44)	6.4 (0.38)	5.3 (0.34)	6.1 (0.56)	4.6 (0.42)	3.7 (0.38)	3.7 (0.41)	3.1 (0.38)
Female	12.8 (0.58)	8.2 (0.53)	6.4 (0.43)	6.9 (0.48)	6.7 (0.47)	6.0 (0.45)	4.8 (0.51)	3.8 (0.36)	4.0 (0.48)
Race/ethnicity[2]									
White	8.1 (0.36)	5.0 (0.32)	4.9 (0.35)	4.1 (0.35)	4.6 (0.39)	4.2 (0.37)	3.3 (0.35)	3.0 (0.31)	2.6 (0.33)
Black	20.3 (1.31)	13.5 (1.27)	8.9 (0.87)	10.7 (1.22)	9.2 (1.19)	8.6 (1.18)	7.0 (1.12)	4.9 (1.03)	4.6 (0.85)
Hispanic	20.9 (1.27)	11.7 (1.20)	10.6 (1.07)	9.5 (0.65)	10.3 (1.16)	7.1 (0.88)	4.9 (0.89)	4.8 (0.59)	4.9 (0.78)
Asian	— (†)	— (†)	— (†)	— (†)	6.2 ! (2.09)	2.3 ! (1.05)	5.9 ! (2.25)	4.2 ! (1.52)	3.1 ! (1.09)
Other	13.5 (1.58)	6.7 (1.09)	6.4 (1.11)	5.0 (1.31)	5.7 (1.63)	3.3 ! (1.09)	‡ (†)	4.1 ! (1.31)	3.8 ! (1.44)
Grade									
6th	14.3 (1.13)	10.9 (1.37)	10.6 (1.26)	10.0 (1.35)	9.5 (1.14)	9.9 (1.33)	6.4 (1.20)	5.6 (1.08)	4.7 (1.01)
7th	15.3 (1.02)	9.5 (0.79)	9.2 (0.95)	8.2 (0.86)	9.1 (1.04)	6.7 (0.86)	6.2 (1.06)	4.5 (0.69)	4.3 (0.69)
8th	13.0 (0.84)	8.1 (0.74)	7.6 (0.69)	6.3 (0.68)	7.1 (0.95)	4.6 (0.71)	3.5 (0.75)	4.6 (0.71)	3.3 (0.78)
9th	11.6 (0.82)	7.1 (0.74)	5.5 (0.63)	6.3 (0.61)	5.9 (0.71)	5.5 (0.87)	4.6 (0.75)	4.2 (0.66)	3.4 (0.71)
10th	11.0 (0.82)	7.1 (0.77)	5.0 (0.71)	4.4 (0.67)	5.5 (0.89)	5.2 (0.87)	4.6 (0.79)	3.9 (0.63)	4.4 (0.75)
11th	8.9 (0.80)	4.8 (0.68)	4.8 (0.65)	4.7 (0.66)	4.6 (0.73)	3.1 (0.63)	3.3 (0.74)	1.8 (0.48)	2.6 (0.55)
12th	7.8 (0.94)	4.8 (0.88)	2.9 (0.55)	3.7 (0.53)	3.3 (0.69)	3.1 (0.65)	1.9 ! (0.57)	2.2 (0.57)	2.0 (0.56)
Urbanicity[3]									
Urban	18.4 (0.84)	11.6 (0.81)	9.7 (0.59)	9.5 (0.68)	10.5 (0.92)	7.1 (0.81)	6.9 (0.84)	5.2 (0.60)	4.5 (0.60)
Suburban	9.8 (0.49)	6.2 (0.42)	4.8 (0.33)	4.8 (0.30)	4.7 (0.41)	4.4 (0.41)	3.0 (0.33)	3.1 (0.39)	3.0 (0.38)
Rural	8.6 (0.80)	4.8 (0.70)	6.0 (0.97)	4.7 (0.93)	5.1 (0.97)	4.9 (0.59)	3.9 (0.63)	3.0 (0.63)	3.3 (0.62)
Control of school									
Public	12.2 (0.43)	7.7 (0.38)	6.6 (0.33)	6.4 (0.34)	6.6 (0.42)	5.5 (0.34)	4.4 (0.35)	3.9 (0.30)	3.5 (0.35)
Private	7.3 (1.01)	3.6 (0.81)	4.6 (0.92)	3.0 (0.73)	3.8 (0.82)	2.5 ! (0.89)	1.9 ! (0.74)	1.5 ! (0.64)	2.6 ! (0.83)
Away from school									
Total	**— (†)**	**5.7 (0.32)**	**4.6 (0.28)**	**5.4 (0.29)**	**5.2 (0.33)**	**3.5 (0.29)**	**3.3 (0.32)**	**2.4 (0.23)**	**2.7 (0.35)**
Sex									
Male	— (†)	4.1 (0.34)	3.7 (0.31)	4.0 (0.30)	4.6 (0.42)	2.4 (0.31)	2.5 (0.34)	2.0 (0.27)	2.4 (0.40)
Female	— (†)	7.4 (0.49)	5.6 (0.42)	6.8 (0.48)	5.8 (0.48)	4.5 (0.40)	4.1 (0.51)	2.7 (0.30)	3.0 (0.44)
Race/ethnicity[2]									
White	— (†)	4.3 (0.32)	3.7 (0.29)	3.8 (0.31)	4.2 (0.40)	2.5 (0.28)	2.2 (0.28)	1.6 (0.24)	1.6 (0.30)
Black	— (†)	8.7 (1.00)	6.3 (0.87)	10.0 (1.13)	7.3 (0.96)	4.9 (0.73)	5.7 (1.10)	3.5 (0.86)	3.6 (0.78)
Hispanic	— (†)	8.9 (1.03)	6.5 (0.75)	7.4 (0.80)	6.2 (0.84)	5.9 (0.80)	3.9 (0.70)	3.3 (0.50)	4.5 (0.86)
Asian	— (†)	— (†)	— (†)	— (†)	7.4 ! (2.89)	‡ (†)	7.1 ! (2.50)	3.2 ! (1.15)	2.9 ! (1.03)
Other	— (†)	5.4 (1.04)	6.6 (1.32)	3.9 (1.02)	3.1 ! (1.28)	‡ (†)	4.0 ! (1.79)	2.5 ! (1.05)	3.2 ! (1.42)
Grade									
6th	— (†)	7.8 (1.11)	6.3 (1.15)	6.8 (1.01)	5.6 (0.99)	5.9 (1.20)	3.3 (0.89)	3.0 (0.86)	3.9 (0.88)
7th	— (†)	6.1 (0.72)	5.5 (0.80)	6.7 (0.80)	7.5 (0.89)	3.0 (0.55)	4.0 (0.78)	2.7 (0.58)	2.2 (0.54)
8th	— (†)	5.5 (0.66)	4.4 (0.61)	5.3 (0.71)	5.0 (0.72)	3.6 (0.65)	3.3 (0.72)	2.1 (0.43)	2.4 ! (0.80)
9th	— (†)	4.6 (0.63)	4.5 (0.62)	4.3 (0.55)	3.8 (0.61)	4.0 (0.75)	2.6 (0.62)	3.5 (0.65)	2.8 (0.59)
10th	— (†)	4.8 (0.63)	4.2 (0.63)	5.3 (0.67)	4.7 (0.66)	3.0 (0.60)	5.5 (0.96)	1.7 (0.46)	4.4 (0.83)
11th	— (†)	5.9 (0.72)	4.7 (0.62)	4.7 (0.69)	4.2 (0.74)	2.3 (0.56)	2.2 (0.56)	2.9 (0.70)	2.2 (0.47)
12th	— (†)	6.1 (0.86)	3.3 (0.62)	4.9 (0.72)	5.4 (0.98)	3.2 (0.61)	2.1 (0.63)	1.0 ! (0.37)	1.3 ! (0.46)
Urbanicity[3]									
Urban	— (†)	9.1 (0.82)	7.4 (0.68)	8.1 (0.60)	6.7 (0.61)	5.3 (0.67)	5.8 (0.87)	3.4 (0.42)	4.0 (0.54)
Suburban	— (†)	5.0 (0.31)	3.8 (0.33)	4.4 (0.34)	4.6 (0.43)	2.7 (0.36)	2.5 (0.33)	2.2 (0.30)	2.2 (0.42)
Rural	— (†)	3.0 (0.71)	3.0 (0.59)	4.0 (0.69)	4.7 (0.98)	2.8 (0.54)	1.9 (0.48)	1.0 ! (0.35)	1.7 (0.49)
Control of school									
Public	— (†)	5.8 (0.32)	4.6 (0.30)	5.4 (0.31)	5.2 (0.34)	3.6 (0.30)	3.5 (0.33)	2.4 (0.23)	2.7 (0.36)
Private	— (†)	5.0 (0.92)	5.1 (1.08)	4.7 (0.89)	4.9 (1.41)	2.1 ! (0.72)	1.8 ! (0.71)	1.6 ! (0.68)	2.0 ! (0.70)

—Not available.
†Not applicable.
!Interpret data with caution. The coefficient of variation (CV) for this estimate is between 30 and 50 percent.
‡Reporting standards not met. Either there are too few cases for a reliable estimate or the coefficient of variation (CV) is 50 percent or greater.
[1]Starting in 2007, the reference period was the school year, whereas in prior survey years the reference period was the previous 6 months. Cognitive testing showed that estimates from 2007 onward are comparable to previous years.
[2]Race categories exclude persons of Hispanic ethnicity. "Other" includes American Indians/Alaska Natives, Asians (prior to 2005), Pacific Islanders, and, from 2003 onward, persons of Two or more races. Due to changes in racial/ethnic categories, comparisons of race/ethnicity across years should be made with caution.
[3]Refers to the Standard Metropolitan Statistical Area (MSA) status of the respondent's household as defined in 2000 by the U.S. Census Bureau. Categories include "central city of an MSA (Urban)," "in MSA but not in central city (Suburban)," and "not MSA (Rural)."
NOTE: "At school" includes the school building, on school property, on a school bus, and, from 2001 onward, going to and from school. Students were asked if they "never," "almost never," "sometimes," or "most of the time" feared that someone would attack or harm them at school or away from school. Students responding "sometimes" or "most of the time" were considered fearful. For the 2001 survey only, the wording was changed from "attack or harm" to "attack or threaten to attack."
SOURCE: U.S. Department of Justice, Bureau of Justice Statistics, School Crime Supplement (SCS) to the National Crime Victimization Survey, selected years, 1995 through 2013. (This table was prepared September 2014.)

Table 230.80. Percentage of students ages 12–18 who reported avoiding one or more places in school or avoiding school activities or classes because of fear of attack or harm, by selected student and school characteristics: Selected years, 1995 through 2013

[Standard errors appear in parentheses]

Type of avoidance and student or school characteristic	1995		1999		2001		2003		2005		2007[1]		2009[1]		2011[1]		2013[1]	
1	2		3		4		5		6		7		8		9		10	
Total, any avoidance	**—**	**(†)**	**6.9**	**(0.34)**	**6.1**	**(0.32)**	**5.0**	**(0.30)**	**5.5**	**(0.32)**	**7.2**	**(0.36)**	**5.0**	**(0.35)**	**5.5**	**(0.34)**	**4.7**	**(0.31)**
Avoided one or more places in school																		
Total	8.7	(0.29)	4.6	(0.29)	4.7	(0.27)	4.0	(0.27)	4.5	(0.28)	5.8	(0.31)	4.0	(0.32)	4.7	(0.30)	3.7	(0.27)
Entrance to the school	2.1	(0.15)	1.1	(0.14)	1.2	(0.11)	1.2	(0.11)	1.0	(0.14)	1.5	(0.15)	0.9	(0.15)	0.9	(0.13)	0.8	(0.14)
Hallways or stairs in school	4.2	(0.21)	2.1	(0.17)	2.1	(0.18)	1.7	(0.17)	2.1	(0.21)	2.6	(0.21)	2.2	(0.23)	2.5	(0.21)	1.7	(0.18)
Parts of the school cafeteria	2.5	(0.18)	1.3	(0.15)	1.4	(0.16)	1.2	(0.13)	1.8	(0.16)	1.9	(0.19)	1.1	(0.17)	1.8	(0.18)	1.4	(0.19)
Any school restrooms	4.4	(0.22)	2.1	(0.19)	2.2	(0.19)	2.0	(0.16)	2.1	(0.20)	2.6	(0.24)	1.4	(0.19)	1.7	(0.19)	1.3	(0.16)
Other places inside the school building	2.5	(0.18)	1.4	(0.17)	1.4	(0.14)	1.2	(0.14)	1.4	(0.18)	1.5	(0.17)	1.0	(0.16)	1.1	(0.15)	0.8	(0.13)
Sex																		
Male	8.8	(0.43)	4.6	(0.35)	4.7	(0.40)	3.9	(0.34)	4.9	(0.46)	6.1	(0.47)	3.9	(0.45)	3.9	(0.42)	3.4	(0.34)
Female	8.5	(0.46)	4.6	(0.39)	4.6	(0.35)	4.1	(0.37)	4.1	(0.40)	5.5	(0.41)	4.0	(0.42)	5.5	(0.40)	3.9	(0.43)
Race/ethnicity[2]																		
White	7.1	(0.32)	3.8	(0.27)	3.9	(0.30)	3.0	(0.27)	3.6	(0.30)	5.3	(0.36)	3.3	(0.38)	4.4	(0.38)	3.0	(0.34)
Black	12.1	(1.01)	6.7	(0.90)	6.6	(0.75)	5.1	(0.79)	7.2	(0.98)	8.3	(1.02)	6.1	(1.04)	4.5	(0.80)	3.3	(0.79)
Hispanic	12.9	(0.97)	6.2	(0.73)	5.5	(0.71)	6.3	(0.70)	6.0	(0.80)	6.8	(0.82)	4.8	(0.86)	6.0	(0.68)	4.9	(0.63)
Asian	—	(†)	—	(†)	—	(†)	—	(†)	2.5 !	(0.87)	‡	(†)	3.7 !	(1.53)	2.7 !	(1.06)	3.8 !	(1.26)
Other	11.1	(1.61)	5.4	(0.99)	6.2	(1.16)	4.4	(1.02)	4.3 !	(1.86)	3.5 !	(1.22)	‡	(†)	3.3 !	(1.04)	5.9	(1.72)
Grade																		
6th	11.6	(0.99)	5.9	(0.92)	6.8	(0.93)	5.6	(0.94)	7.9	(1.27)	7.8	(1.20)	7.1	(1.13)	6.9	(0.99)	4.4	(0.92)
7th	11.8	(0.89)	6.1	(0.72)	6.2	(0.79)	5.7	(0.73)	5.8	(0.93)	7.5	(0.86)	5.5	(0.86)	5.1	(0.76)	4.6	(0.72)
8th	8.8	(0.77)	5.5	(0.70)	5.2	(0.62)	4.7	(0.63)	4.5	(0.67)	5.9	(0.84)	4.8	(0.93)	5.2	(0.75)	2.7	(0.62)
9th	9.5	(0.71)	5.3	(0.63)	5.0	(0.61)	5.1	(0.62)	5.2	(0.78)	6.7	(0.81)	4.5	(0.89)	3.7	(0.67)	5.1	(0.78)
10th	7.8	(0.75)	4.7	(0.61)	4.2	(0.64)	3.1	(0.54)	4.2	(0.65)	5.5	(0.80)	4.2	(0.88)	5.4	(0.72)	4.0	(0.72)
11th	6.9	(0.64)	2.5	(0.46)	2.8	(0.43)	2.5	(0.53)	3.3	(0.58)	4.2	(0.70)	1.2 !	(0.44)	3.6	(0.65)	2.5	(0.61)
12th	4.1	(0.74)	2.4	(0.51)	3.0	(0.64)	1.2 !	(0.41)	1.3 !	(0.41)	3.2	(0.71)	1.6 !	(0.50)	3.7	(0.71)	2.3	(0.62)
Urbanicity[3]																		
Urban	11.7	(0.73)	5.8	(0.48)	6.0	(0.52)	5.7	(0.59)	6.3	(0.67)	6.1	(0.65)	5.5	(0.69)	5.3	(0.61)	4.3	(0.54)
Suburban	7.9	(0.40)	4.7	(0.38)	4.3	(0.38)	3.5	(0.30)	3.8	(0.36)	5.2	(0.38)	3.1	(0.38)	4.6	(0.36)	3.3	(0.33)
Rural	7.0	(0.65)	3.0	(0.56)	3.9	(0.70)	2.8	(0.53)	4.2	(0.74)	6.9	(0.69)	4.3	(0.80)	3.5	(0.54)	3.5	(0.68)
School control																		
Public	9.3	(0.33)	5.0	(0.31)	4.9	(0.29)	4.2	(0.29)	4.8	(0.30)	6.2	(0.35)	4.2	(0.34)	4.9	(0.32)	3.9	(0.29)
Private	2.2	(0.47)	1.6	(0.45)	2.0 !	(0.69)	1.5 !	(0.49)	1.4 !	(0.55)	1.4 !	(0.54)	1.8 !	(0.73)	2.1 !	(0.70)	1.0 !	(0.49)
Avoided school activities or classes																		
Total	—	(†)	3.2	(0.22)	2.3	(0.18)	1.9	(0.18)	2.1	(0.23)	2.6	(0.23)	2.1	(0.25)	2.0	(0.20)	2.0	(0.21)
Any activities[4]	1.7	(0.15)	0.8	(0.10)	1.1	(0.12)	1.0	(0.11)	1.0	(0.16)	1.8	(0.20)	1.3	(0.20)	1.2	(0.16)	1.0	(0.13)
Any classes	—	(†)	0.6	(0.09)	0.6	(0.09)	0.6	(0.10)	0.7	(0.13)	0.7	(0.12)	0.6	(0.13)	0.7	(0.10)	0.5	(0.10)
Stayed home from school	—	(†)	2.3	(0.19)	1.1	(0.13)	0.8	(0.11)	0.7	(0.11)	0.8	(0.13)	0.6	(0.14)	0.8	(0.12)	0.9	(0.13)

—Not available.

†Not applicable.

!Interpret data with caution. The coefficient of variation (CV) for this estimate is between 30 and 50 percent.

‡Reporting standards not met. Either there are too few cases for a reliable estimate or the coefficient of variation (CV) is 50 percent or greater.

[1]Starting in 2007, the reference period was the school year, whereas in prior survey years the reference period was the previous 6 months. Cognitive testing showed that estimates from 2007 onward are comparable to previous years.

[2]Race categories exclude persons of Hispanic ethnicity. "Other" includes American Indians/Alaska Natives, Asians (prior to 2005), Pacific Islanders, and, from 2003 onward, persons of Two or more races. Due to changes in racial/ethnic categories, comparisons of race/ethnicity across years should be made with caution.

[3]Refers to the Standard Metropolitan Statistical Area (MSA) status of the respondent's household as defined in 2000 by the U.S. Census Bureau. Categories include "central city of an MSA (Urban)," "in MSA but not in central city (Suburban)," and "not MSA (Rural)."

[4]Before 2007, students were asked whether they avoided "any extracurricular activities." Starting in 2007, the survey wording was changed to "any activities."

NOTE: Students were asked whether they avoided places or activities because they thought that someone might attack or harm them. For the 2001 survey only, the wording was changed from "attack or harm" to "attack or threaten to attack." Detail may not sum to totals because of rounding and because students reporting more than one type of avoidance were counted only once in the totals.

SOURCE: U.S. Department of Justice, Bureau of Justice Statistics, School Crime Supplement (SCS) to the National Crime Victimization Survey, selected years, 1995 through 2013. (This table was prepared September 2014.)

Table 230.90. Percentage of public and private school teachers who agreed that student misbehavior and student tardiness and class cutting interfered with their teaching, by selected teacher and school characteristics: Selected years, 1987–88 through 2011–12

[Standard errors appear in parentheses]

Teacher or school characteristic	Student misbehavior interfered with teaching							Student tardiness and class cutting interfered with teaching						
	1987–88	1990–91	1993–94	1999–2000	2003–04	2007–08	2011–12	1987–88	1990–91	1993–94	1999–2000	2003–04	2007–08	2011–12
1	2	3	4	5	6	7	8	9	10	11	12	13	14	15
Total	**40.2 (0.33)**	**33.8 (0.31)**	**41.3 (0.34)**	**38.6 (0.39)**	**35.1 (0.58)**	**34.1 (0.50)**	**38.5 (0.61)**	**32.6 (0.28)**	**— (†)**	**25.4 (0.28)**	**29.3 (0.30)**	**31.3 (0.44)**	**31.5 (0.60)**	**35.3 (0.46)**
Years of teaching experience														
3 or fewer	42.1 (0.95)	35.5 (0.75)	44.8 (0.98)	41.5 (0.79)	39.2 (2.15)	37.3 (1.00)	43.2 (1.21)	34.6 (0.89)	— (†)	27.8 (0.71)	32.3 (0.73)	34.0 (1.20)	34.3 (1.01)	38.5 (1.28)
4 to 9	40.1 (0.65)	33.6 (0.69)	41.9 (0.61)	40.5 (0.66)	36.2 (0.75)	35.1 (1.02)	39.8 (1.05)	31.4 (0.50)	— (†)	25.5 (0.59)	30.1 (0.55)	32.0 (0.70)	32.6 (1.01)	36.0 (0.96)
10 to 19	39.5 (0.41)	33.0 (0.52)	40.7 (0.57)	36.4 (0.65)	34.0 (0.83)	33.6 (0.83)	38.0 (0.92)	31.7 (0.35)	— (†)	24.3 (0.48)	26.7 (0.55)	30.7 (0.75)	30.9 (1.04)	35.3 (0.93)
20 or more	40.7 (0.73)	34.1 (0.70)	40.1 (0.53)	37.6 (0.57)	32.8 (0.68)	31.5 (0.82)	35.4 (0.97)	34.3 (0.61)	— (†)	25.5 (0.35)	29.3 (0.51)	29.7 (0.67)	29.1 (0.90)	33.0 (0.95)
School level[1]														
Elementary	39.2 (0.53)	34.1 (0.45)	40.9 (0.54)	39.1 (0.57)	33.8 (0.74)	32.6 (0.73)	38.6 (0.92)	22.6 (0.35)	— (†)	17.2 (0.41)	24.2 (0.42)	26.5 (0.57)	25.6 (0.76)	31.0 (0.71)
Secondary	43.2 (0.43)	34.9 (0.43)	43.7 (0.35)	39.5 (0.42)	40.0 (0.60)	38.8 (0.74)	40.5 (0.80)	49.9 (0.45)	— (†)	43.0 (0.37)	41.5 (0.46)	43.8 (0.65)	45.4 (0.81)	45.3 (0.69)
School control														
Public[2]	42.3 (0.36)	35.7 (0.34)	44.1 (0.40)	40.8 (0.42)	37.2 (0.52)	36.0 (0.57)	40.7 (0.65)	34.7 (0.29)	— (†)	27.9 (0.32)	31.5 (0.35)	33.4 (0.45)	33.4 (0.64)	37.6 (0.51)
Private	24.2 (0.95)	20.0 (0.63)	22.4 (0.43)	24.1 (0.61)	20.7 (2.47)	20.6 (0.72)	22.0 (1.05)	17.2 (0.73)	— (†)	8.6 (0.42)	15.0 (0.43)	16.9 (1.11)	17.9 (0.72)	18.8 (1.06)
School enrollment														
Under 200	31.9 (0.89)	25.0 (0.82)	31.1 (0.72)	32.5 (0.93)	29.4 (2.44)	29.9 (1.10)	33.9 (1.27)	24.5 (0.94)	— (†)	14.7 (0.51)	21.7 (0.71)	24.9 (1.52)	26.1 (0.91)	29.4 (1.03)
200 to 499	36.6 (0.52)	30.6 (0.60)	36.9 (0.72)	36.4 (0.57)	30.7 (0.91)	32.9 (0.87)	37.3 (0.87)	23.9 (0.37)	— (†)	16.9 (0.52)	25.0 (0.60)	26.2 (0.73)	27.4 (0.94)	32.1 (0.92)
500 to 749	41.2 (0.63)	34.9 (0.64)	41.9 (0.74)	40.0 (0.82)	34.0 (0.94)	34.4 (1.28)	37.4 (1.38)	29.0 (0.66)	— (†)	21.2 (0.67)	27.1 (0.63)	28.2 (0.83)	28.4 (1.25)	32.5 (1.02)
750 to 999	44.6 (1.10)	39.3 (1.03)	47.6 (0.85)	39.8 (1.32)	37.2 (1.45)	32.4 (1.34)	41.9 (1.82)	35.6 (1.05)	— (†)	30.2 (1.19)	27.7 (1.00)	31.0 (1.15)	29.6 (1.24)	36.7 (1.87)
1,000 or more	47.0 (0.75)	38.8 (0.76)	48.0 (0.69)	41.9 (0.65)	43.7 (0.85)	37.9 (1.01)	40.9 (0.97)	54.2 (0.72)	— (†)	46.8 (0.70)	41.7 (0.77)	44.9 (0.97)	43.1 (1.13)	44.2 (0.92)
Locale[3]														
City	— (†)	— (†)	— (†)	— (†)	41.8 (1.14)	39.9 (1.08)	‡ (†)	— (†)	— (†)	— (†)	— (†)	37.3 (0.89)	38.5 (0.95)	‡ (†)
Suburban	— (†)	— (†)	— (†)	— (†)	32.3 (0.77)	31.7 (0.78)	‡ (†)	— (†)	— (†)	— (†)	— (†)	28.5 (0.74)	28.8 (0.86)	‡ (†)
Town	— (†)	— (†)	— (†)	— (†)	34.7 (1.32)	34.7 (1.32)	‡ (†)	— (†)	— (†)	— (†)	— (†)	31.7 (1.12)	34.0 (1.68)	‡ (†)
Rural	— (†)	— (†)	— (†)	— (†)	31.1 (1.31)	30.8 (0.97)	‡ (†)	— (†)	— (†)	— (†)	— (†)	27.9 (0.88)	26.4 (0.92)	‡ (†)

—Not available.
†Not applicable.
‡Reporting standards not met. Data may be suppressed because the response rate is under 50 percent, there are too few cases for a reliable estimate, or the coefficient of variation (CV) is 50 percent or greater.
[1]Elementary schools are those with any of grades kindergarten through grade 6 and none of grades 9 through 12. Secondary schools have any of grades 7 through 12 and none of grades kindergarten through grade 6. Combined elementary/secondary schools are included in totals but are not shown separately.
[2]Includes traditional public and public charter schools.
[3]Substantial improvements in geocoding technology and changes in the Office of Management and Budget's definition of metropolitan and nonmetropolitan areas allow for more precision in describing an area as of 2003–04. Comparisons with earlier years are not possible.
NOTE: Teachers who taught only prekindergarten students are excluded. Includes both teachers who "strongly" agreed and those who "somewhat" agreed that student misbehavior or student tardiness and class cutting interfered with their teaching. Some data have been revised from previously published figures.
SOURCE: U.S. Department of Education, National Center for Education Statistics, Schools and Staffing Survey (SASS), "Public School Teacher Data File" and "Private School Teacher Data File," 1987–88, 1990–91, 1993–94, 1999–2000, 2003–04, 2007–08, and 2011–12; and "Charter School Teacher Data File," 1999–2000. (This table was prepared October 2013.)

Table 230.92. Percentage of public and private school teachers who agreed that other teachers and the principal enforced school rules, by selected teacher and school characteristics: Selected years, 1987–88 through 2011–12

[Standard errors appear in parentheses]

Teacher or school characteristic	Other teachers enforced school rules[1]							Principal enforced school rules[2]						
	1987–88	1990–91	1993–94	1999–2000	2003–04	2007–08	2011–12	1987–88	1990–91	1993–94	1999–2000	2003–04	2007–08	2011–12
1	2	3	4	5	6	7	8	9	10	11	12	13	14	15
Total	**65.1 (0.30)**	**73.4 (0.34)**	**63.8 (0.36)**	**64.4 (0.35)**	**72.4 (0.41)**	**71.8 (0.47)**	**68.8 (0.48)**	**83.7 (0.22)**	**87.4 (0.26)**	**81.8 (0.31)**	**83.0 (0.28)**	**87.8 (0.30)**	**88.5 (0.34)**	**84.4 (0.41)**
Years of teaching experience														
3 or fewer	68.6 (0.93)	76.1 (0.88)	68.8 (0.92)	69.4 (0.71)	76.6 (0.91)	73.6 (1.07)	70.2 (1.27)	85.0 (0.52)	88.1 (0.49)	85.1 (0.59)	84.5 (0.52)	88.6 (0.66)	89.9 (0.68)	86.6 (1.15)
4 to 9	65.3 (0.71)	72.7 (0.69)	63.0 (0.78)	61.6 (0.62)	70.6 (0.70)	69.5 (0.88)	66.6 (0.88)	84.1 (0.45)	87.4 (0.55)	80.7 (0.63)	82.7 (0.49)	86.9 (0.57)	88.2 (0.61)	84.6 (0.72)
10 to 19	64.3 (0.49)	72.9 (0.48)	63.1 (0.55)	64.6 (0.65)	71.4 (0.76)	71.0 (0.73)	68.3 (0.86)	83.9 (0.35)	87.5 (0.43)	82.4 (0.41)	83.1 (0.49)	87.8 (0.53)	87.2 (0.62)	82.3 (0.74)
20 or more	64.9 (0.58)	73.5 (0.57)	63.1 (0.58)	63.6 (0.59)	72.5 (0.64)	73.8 (0.80)	71.1 (0.84)	82.8 (0.56)	86.9 (0.41)	80.6 (0.38)	82.4 (0.41)	88.3 (0.43)	89.4 (0.55)	85.9 (0.79)
School level[3]														
Elementary	74.2 (0.41)	80.5 (0.52)	72.2 (0.48)	72.2 (0.49)	79.5 (0.54)	79.4 (0.61)	75.6 (0.71)	85.1 (0.36)	88.0 (0.41)	82.8 (0.45)	84.2 (0.41)	88.3 (0.45)	89.5 (0.44)	85.0 (0.60)
Secondary	49.9 (0.60)	60.2 (0.43)	47.0 (0.34)	47.2 (0.46)	55.7 (0.55)	56.1 (0.64)	54.4 (0.69)	81.5 (0.37)	85.8 (0.37)	79.0 (0.31)	80.0 (0.39)	86.2 (0.41)	86.3 (0.48)	82.5 (0.56)
School control														
Public[4]	63.8 (0.31)	71.9 (0.36)	61.8 (0.42)	62.6 (0.39)	71.1 (0.46)	70.6 (0.55)	67.6 (0.51)	83.1 (0.22)	86.7 (0.29)	80.8 (0.35)	82.2 (0.33)	87.2 (0.34)	88.0 (0.37)	83.7 (0.43)
Private	75.4 (0.98)	84.3 (0.61)	77.6 (0.50)	75.9 (0.51)	81.0 (1.52)	80.1 (0.81)	77.4 (1.49)	88.6 (0.57)	92.0 (0.42)	88.4 (0.41)	88.3 (0.39)	92.2 (0.75)	92.2 (0.57)	89.4 (0.98)
School enrollment														
Under 200	76.1 (0.90)	83.7 (0.60)	76.5 (0.84)	75.4 (0.81)	84.0 (1.54)	81.0 (0.85)	78.7 (0.91)	86.6 (0.54)	89.3 (0.54)	85.2 (0.61)	87.1 (0.48)	90.9 (0.86)	90.8 (0.60)	88.7 (0.84)
200 to 499	72.6 (0.42)	79.4 (0.55)	71.2 (0.65)	71.6 (0.58)	78.9 (0.62)	78.6 (0.71)	74.2 (1.00)	84.6 (0.38)	88.1 (0.42)	83.5 (0.47)	84.2 (0.46)	89.3 (0.48)	89.4 (0.60)	84.7 (0.87)
500 to 749	66.6 (0.74)	75.8 (0.74)	66.8 (0.81)	67.7 (0.66)	75.8 (0.68)	74.1 (1.04)	72.2 (1.06)	84.4 (0.55)	88.5 (0.53)	82.3 (0.76)	83.5 (0.55)	87.7 (0.66)	88.6 (0.68)	85.2 (0.75)
750 to 999	59.8 (1.00)	68.5 (1.01)	58.6 (1.10)	63.0 (0.97)	69.4 (1.32)	71.7 (1.50)	66.0 (1.33)	83.0 (0.80)	85.7 (0.81)	79.6 (0.87)	82.5 (0.83)	86.0 (1.14)	88.4 (0.89)	82.7 (1.30)
1,000 or more	48.1 (0.89)	57.5 (0.67)	45.8 (0.77)	47.3 (0.75)	56.3 (0.88)	57.1 (1.17)	55.4 (1.04)	80.7 (0.62)	84.9 (0.66)	78.0 (0.58)	79.4 (0.57)	85.8 (0.63)	86.5 (0.73)	82.3 (0.81)
Locale[5]														
City	— (†)	— (†)	— (†)	— (†)	69.6 (0.86)	69.4 (0.98)	‡ (†)	— (†)	— (†)	— (†)	— (†)	85.5 (0.60)	86.5 (0.72)	‡ (†)
Suburban	— (†)	— (†)	— (†)	— (†)	73.5 (0.70)	72.6 (0.76)	‡ (†)	— (†)	— (†)	— (†)	— (†)	89.1 (0.47)	89.7 (0.53)	‡ (†)
Town	— (†)	— (†)	— (†)	— (†)	72.4 (1.03)	71.7 (1.32)	‡ (†)	— (†)	— (†)	— (†)	— (†)	88.9 (0.71)	87.5 (1.26)	‡ (†)
Rural	— (†)	— (†)	— (†)	— (†)	74.3 (0.74)	73.6 (0.81)	‡ (†)	— (†)	— (†)	— (†)	— (†)	88.5 (0.61)	89.5 (0.58)	‡ (†)

—Not available.

†Not applicable.

‡Reporting standards not met. Data may be suppressed because the response rate is under 50 percent, there are too few cases for a reliable estimate, or the coefficient of variation (CV) is 50 percent or greater.

[1]Respondents were asked whether "rules for student behavior are consistently enforced by teachers in this school, even for students not in their classes."

[2]Respondents were asked whether their "principal enforces school rules for student conduct and backs me up when I need it."

[3]Elementary schools are those with any of grades kindergarten through grade 6 and none of grades 9 through 12. Secondary schools have any of grades 7 through 12 and none of grades kindergarten through grade 6. Combined elementary/secondary schools are included in totals but are not shown separately.

[4]Includes traditional public and public charter schools.

[5]Substantial improvements in geocoding technology and changes in the Office of Management and Budget's definition of metropolitan and nonmetropolitan areas allow for more precision in describing an area as of 2003–04. Comparisons with earlier years are not possible.

NOTE: Teachers who taught only prekindergarten students are excluded. Includes both teachers who "strongly" agreed and those who "somewhat" agreed that rules were enforced by other teachers and the principal. Some data have been revised from previously published figures.

SOURCE: U.S. Department of Education, National Center for Education Statistics, Schools and Staffing Survey (SASS), "Public School Teacher Data File" and "Private School Teacher Data File," 1987–88, 1990–91, 1993–94, 1999–2000, 2003–04, 2007–08, and 2011–12; and "Charter School Teacher Data File," 1999–2000. (This table was prepared October 2013.)

Table 230.95. Percentage of public school teachers who agreed that student misbehavior and student tardiness and class cutting interfered with their teaching and that other teachers and the principal enforced school rules, by state: 2011–12

[Standard errors appear in parentheses]

State	Interfered with teaching				Enforced school rules			
	Student misbehavior		Student tardiness and class cutting		Other teachers[1]		Principal[2]	
1	2		3		4		5	
United States	**40.7**	**(0.65)**	**37.6**	**(0.51)**	**67.6**	**(0.51)**	**83.7**	**(0.43)**
Alabama	40.9	(3.36)	38.6	(2.82)	71.8	(2.84)	86.8	(2.26)
Alaska	35.8	(5.73)	56.8	(6.73)	72.2	(4.41)	83.2	(5.16)
Arizona	41.3	(2.56)	44.5	(2.67)	67.9	(2.72)	83.4	(2.06)
Arkansas	39.5	(3.56)	38.5	(3.80)	74.0	(2.60)	90.0	(2.16)
California	38.9	(2.47)	39.7	(2.36)	69.7	(1.83)	83.0	(1.63)
Colorado	45.5	(3.54)	47.6	(4.02)	61.7	(3.39)	80.6	(3.28)
Connecticut	37.2	(2.35)	28.6	(3.81)	61.7	(3.91)	80.7	(2.98)
Delaware	46.7	(4.47)	35.2	(4.58)	68.7	(3.58)	82.9	(3.32)
District of Columbia	‡	(†)	‡	(†)	‡	(†)	‡	(†)
Florida	‡	(†)	‡	(†)	‡	(†)	‡	(†)
Georgia	38.2	(3.56)	32.1	(3.36)	71.9	(2.64)	85.5	(2.29)
Hawaii	‡	(†)	‡	(†)	‡	(†)	‡	(†)
Idaho	34.6	(3.54)	36.1	(3.08)	74.7	(2.48)	87.9	(2.18)
Illinois	40.0	(2.96)	33.9	(3.07)	66.0	(3.18)	83.6	(2.31)
Indiana	38.8	(3.33)	41.0	(2.95)	68.4	(2.47)	81.8	(2.99)
Iowa	37.9	(3.12)	34.6	(3.18)	68.5	(2.77)	81.8	(2.40)
Kansas	32.0	(3.57)	24.9	(2.34)	70.9	(3.29)	91.8	(1.61)
Kentucky	42.8	(3.06)	32.8	(2.92)	67.4	(2.80)	86.9	(2.47)
Louisiana	55.1	(3.92)	36.1	(3.60)	62.5	(3.19)	82.1	(3.89)
Maine	39.1	(3.00)	39.2	(3.02)	62.9	(2.90)	83.2	(3.06)
Maryland	‡	(†)	‡	(†)	‡	(†)	‡	(†)
Massachusetts	37.2	(3.07)	32.0	(2.74)	66.6	(3.04)	83.1	(2.80)
Michigan	46.6	(2.87)	40.9	(2.63)	67.6	(2.12)	84.4	(2.08)
Minnesota	43.7	(2.49)	37.3	(2.50)	68.7	(1.88)	84.5	(1.84)
Mississippi	37.4	(3.30)	35.6	(3.40)	72.4	(2.96)	84.5	(2.51)
Missouri	33.2	(2.10)	33.6	(2.87)	68.9	(2.17)	86.6	(1.76)
Montana	41.3	(3.43)	45.3	(4.08)	66.5	(3.65)	83.1	(2.97)
Nebraska	38.2	(3.01)	33.6	(2.81)	70.9	(2.73)	86.7	(1.66)
Nevada	45.5	(3.77)	42.3	(4.86)	65.5	(3.42)	79.3	(3.22)
New Hampshire	38.3	(4.36)	30.9	(3.11)	62.0	(3.93)	83.2	(2.66)
New Jersey	35.9	(2.36)	29.9	(2.29)	66.8	(2.06)	84.4	(1.70)
New Mexico	39.0	(4.55)	54.5	(5.87)	64.2	(3.80)	78.7	(4.23)
New York	40.3	(2.91)	45.3	(3.06)	65.9	(2.47)	80.7	(2.46)
North Carolina	41.9	(3.13)	37.0	(2.94)	69.0	(2.58)	84.0	(2.34)
North Dakota	34.6	(3.26)	33.5	(3.52)	70.4	(2.77)	86.7	(2.45)
Ohio	41.8	(1.95)	38.8	(1.96)	66.4	(1.73)	84.7	(1.55)
Oklahoma	40.1	(2.74)	40.8	(2.87)	72.5	(2.47)	86.5	(2.12)
Oregon	33.1	(3.24)	35.6	(3.73)	77.3	(2.90)	88.1	(1.77)
Pennsylvania	40.0	(2.64)	33.4	(2.55)	65.2	(2.18)	82.5	(1.88)
Rhode Island	‡	(†)	‡	(†)	‡	(†)	‡	(†)
South Carolina	40.9	(3.22)	33.7	(3.40)	71.8	(3.23)	86.8	(2.15)
South Dakota	40.1	(3.10)	37.2	(3.92)	73.2	(2.91)	84.8	(2.53)
Tennessee	41.5	(3.56)	40.0	(3.56)	71.4	(3.14)	88.7	(2.14)
Texas	45.6	(2.29)	35.1	(2.13)	65.8	(2.56)	81.8	(1.99)
Utah	39.7	(3.67)	45.1	(4.30)	75.8	(3.56)	89.9	(2.27)
Vermont	39.9	(2.61)	36.2	(2.62)	59.2	(2.59)	80.5	(2.28)
Virginia	40.8	(3.46)	35.6	(3.06)	64.9	(2.87)	82.5	(2.52)
Washington	39.2	(2.89)	39.5	(3.16)	73.1	(2.60)	85.6	(2.18)
West Virginia	43.9	(3.87)	42.4	(4.09)	73.4	(2.90)	90.4	(2.58)
Wisconsin	42.7	(2.70)	34.2	(3.07)	69.5	(2.87)	85.8	(1.70)
Wyoming	30.7	(4.76)	40.0	(4.78)	73.9	(3.55)	89.1	(3.41)

†Not applicable.
‡Reporting standards not met. Data may be suppressed because the response rate is under 50 percent, there are too few cases for a reliable estimate, or the coefficient of variation (CV) is 50 percent or greater.
[1]Respondents were asked whether "rules for student behavior are consistently enforced by teachers in this school, even for students not in their classes."
[2]Respondents were asked whether their "principal enforces school rules for student conduct and backs me up when I need it."
NOTE: Teachers who taught only prekindergarten students are excluded. Includes traditional public and public charter school teachers. Includes both teachers who "strongly" agreed and those who "somewhat" agreed.
SOURCE: U.S. Department of Education, National Center for Education Statistics, Schools and Staffing Survey (SASS), "Public School Teacher Data File," 2011–12. (This table was prepared July 2013.)

Table 232.50. Percentage distribution of students in grades 9–12, by number of times they reported using marijuana anywhere or on school property during the previous 30 days and selected student characteristics: Selected years, 2009 through 2013

[Standard errors appear in parentheses]

Year and student characteristic	Anywhere (including on school property)[1]								On school property[2]							
	0 times		1 or 2 times		3 to 39 times		40 or more times		0 times		1 or 2 times		3 to 39 times		40 or more times	
1	2		3		4		5		6		7		8		9	
2009																
Total	**79.2**	**(0.70)**	**7.2**	**(0.30)**	**9.7**	**(0.37)**	**3.8**	**(0.27)**	**95.4**	**(0.35)**	**2.1**	**(0.16)**	**1.8**	**(0.18)**	**0.7**	**(0.10)**
Sex																
Male	76.6	(0.80)	6.8	(0.38)	10.8	(0.48)	5.8	(0.46)	93.7	(0.54)	2.6	(0.24)	2.6	(0.27)	1.1	(0.18)
Female	82.1	(0.87)	7.7	(0.39)	8.5	(0.56)	1.7	(0.20)	97.2	(0.32)	1.7	(0.19)	1.0	(0.21)	0.2	(0.06)
Race/ethnicity[3]																
White	79.3	(0.93)	7.4	(0.43)	9.6	(0.49)	3.7	(0.38)	96.2	(0.38)	1.9	(0.21)	1.4	(0.18)	0.5	(0.10)
Black	77.8	(1.44)	6.7	(0.62)	10.9	(0.90)	4.6	(0.68)	94.4	(0.64)	2.2	(0.31)	2.8	(0.44)	0.6 !	(0.24)
Hispanic	78.4	(1.04)	8.2	(0.57)	9.8	(0.71)	3.6	(0.37)	93.5	(0.76)	3.2	(0.43)	2.3	(0.39)	1.0	(0.22)
Asian	92.5	(1.40)	3.0	(0.69)	3.3	(0.85)	1.2 !	(0.55)	98.0	(0.54)	‡	(†)	1.1 !	(0.50)	‡	(†)
Pacific Islander	75.2	(5.50)	5.0 !	(1.61)	13.0	(2.95)	6.8 !	(2.56)	91.0	(2.40)	4.4 !	(1.59)	3.7 !	(1.58)	‡	(†)
American Indian/Alaska Native	68.4	(5.26)	6.7 !	(2.47)	19.6	(3.43)	5.3 !	(2.11)	97.1	(1.25)	‡	(†)	‡	(†)	#	(†)
Two or more races	78.3	(2.33)	7.8	(1.40)	9.8	(1.51)	4.1 !	(1.27)	94.6	(1.34)	1.4 !	(0.51)	2.2 !	(0.90)	1.8 !	(0.66)
Grade																
9th	84.5	(0.97)	5.8	(0.55)	7.6	(0.55)	2.1	(0.29)	95.7	(0.38)	2.3	(0.22)	1.4	(0.21)	0.6	(0.15)
10th	78.9	(1.11)	7.9	(0.59)	9.6	(0.64)	3.6	(0.44)	95.4	(0.50)	1.9	(0.28)	2.1	(0.35)	0.6	(0.12)
11th	76.8	(1.52)	7.9	(0.66)	11.2	(0.89)	4.1	(0.42)	95.0	(0.55)	2.5	(0.37)	2.0	(0.31)	0.5	(0.12)
12th	75.4	(1.49)	7.7	(0.60)	10.9	(0.86)	6.0	(0.64)	95.4	(0.49)	1.9	(0.30)	1.9	(0.27)	0.8	(0.23)
2011																
Total	**76.9**	**(0.80)**	**7.4**	**(0.30)**	**10.9**	**(0.42)**	**4.8**	**(0.30)**	**94.1**	**(0.39)**	**2.8**	**(0.22)**	**2.3**	**(0.21)**	**0.7**	**(0.09)**
Sex																
Male	74.1	(1.01)	7.1	(0.40)	11.8	(0.57)	7.0	(0.47)	92.5	(0.56)	3.1	(0.28)	3.2	(0.31)	1.2	(0.17)
Female	79.9	(0.95)	7.7	(0.48)	9.9	(0.56)	2.4	(0.26)	95.9	(0.32)	2.5	(0.21)	1.4	(0.19)	0.2	(0.04)
Race/ethnicity[3]																
White	78.3	(1.09)	6.9	(0.42)	10.2	(0.59)	4.6	(0.44)	95.5	(0.42)	2.2	(0.26)	1.9	(0.23)	0.4	(0.09)
Black	74.9	(1.35)	7.9	(0.69)	12.5	(0.81)	4.7	(0.63)	93.3	(0.77)	3.2	(0.43)	2.8	(0.52)	0.7	(0.18)
Hispanic	75.6	(1.27)	8.3	(0.59)	11.5	(0.67)	4.7	(0.46)	92.3	(0.54)	3.6	(0.26)	3.1	(0.40)	1.0	(0.21)
Asian	86.4	(3.75)	‡	(†)	5.5	(0.96)	3.2 !	(1.34)	95.5	(1.34)	2.4 !	(1.15)	‡	(†)	1.5 !	(0.70)
Pacific Islander	68.9	(7.08)	11.3	(3.34)	13.2 !	(5.20)	6.6 !	(2.27)	87.5	(4.94)	5.6 !	(2.24)	‡	(†)	‡	(†)
American Indian/Alaska Native	52.6	(3.20)	10.5	(2.82)	23.6	(2.57)	13.2	(1.81)	79.1	(4.05)	8.6	(2.18)	9.8	(1.79)	2.5	(0.67)
Two or more races	73.2	(2.10)	7.2	(1.20)	12.9	(1.44)	6.7	(1.33)	91.9	(1.79)	3.7	(0.98)	2.4 !	(0.86)	2.0 !	(0.69)
Grade																
9th	82.0	(1.11)	6.2	(0.47)	8.2	(0.63)	3.6	(0.42)	94.6	(0.65)	2.7	(0.41)	2.2	(0.33)	0.5	(0.11)
10th	78.4	(1.15)	7.4	(0.60)	10.0	(0.65)	4.3	(0.50)	93.8	(0.63)	3.2	(0.38)	2.3	(0.40)	0.7	(0.16)
11th	74.5	(1.44)	8.0	(0.59)	12.9	(0.82)	4.5	(0.50)	93.8	(0.70)	3.2	(0.47)	2.3	(0.35)	0.7	(0.16)
12th	72.0	(1.08)	8.3	(0.59)	13.0	(0.69)	6.7	(0.53)	94.6	(0.39)	2.2	(0.30)	2.4	(0.30)	0.8	(0.18)
2013[4]																
Total	**76.6**	**(1.08)**	**7.1**	**(0.42)**	**11.3**	**(0.68)**	**5.0**	**(0.39)**	**—**	**(†)**	**—**	**(†)**	**—**	**(†)**	**—**	**(†)**
Sex																
Male	75.0	(1.14)	6.5	(0.42)	12.0	(0.72)	6.5	(0.53)	—	(†)	—	(†)	—	(†)	—	(†)
Female	78.1	(1.28)	7.8	(0.59)	10.7	(0.77)	3.4	(0.36)	—	(†)	—	(†)	—	(†)	—	(†)
Race/ethnicity[3]																
White	79.6	(1.36)	6.3	(0.63)	9.7	(0.75)	4.4	(0.42)	—	(†)	—	(†)	—	(†)	—	(†)
Black	71.1	(1.30)	8.2	(0.52)	14.3	(0.90)	6.3	(0.71)	—	(†)	—	(†)	—	(†)	—	(†)
Hispanic	72.4	(1.50)	8.6	(0.52)	13.4	(1.22)	5.6	(0.70)	—	(†)	—	(†)	—	(†)	—	(†)
Asian	83.6	(2.99)	4.1	(1.02)	7.6	(1.32)	4.7 !	(2.03)	—	(†)	—	(†)	—	(†)	—	(†)
Pacific Islander	76.6	(7.35)	4.9 !	(2.31)	17.1 !	(5.82)	‡	(†)	—	(†)	—	(†)	—	(†)	—	(†)
American Indian/Alaska Native	64.5	(6.37)	8.8 !	(2.70)	18.9	(4.54)	7.9 !	(2.77)	—	(†)	—	(†)	—	(†)	—	(†)
Two or more races	71.2	(2.55)	9.7	(1.36)	12.4	(1.45)	6.7	(1.29)	—	(†)	—	(†)	—	(†)	—	(†)
Grade																
9th	82.3	(1.13)	6.3	(0.59)	8.6	(0.70)	2.8	(0.38)	—	(†)	—	(†)	—	(†)	—	(†)
10th	76.5	(1.89)	7.2	(0.65)	11.3	(1.35)	5.0	(0.81)	—	(†)	—	(†)	—	(†)	—	(†)
11th	74.5	(1.37)	7.6	(0.68)	12.0	(0.85)	6.0	(0.56)	—	(†)	—	(†)	—	(†)	—	(†)
12th	72.3	(1.58)	7.6	(0.68)	13.8	(1.00)	6.4	(0.63)	—	(†)	—	(†)	—	(†)	—	(†)

—Not available.
†Not applicable.
#Rounds to zero.
!Interpret data with caution. The coefficient of variation (CV) for this estimate is between 30 and 50 percent.
‡Reporting standards not met. Either there are too few cases for a reliable estimate or the coefficient of variation (CV) is 50 percent or greater.
[1]The term "anywhere" is not used in the Youth Risk Behavior Survey (YRBS) questionnaire; students were simply asked how many times during the previous 30 days they had used marijuana.
[2]In the question about using marijuana at school, "on school property" was not defined for survey respondents.
[3]Race categories exclude persons of Hispanic ethnicity.
[4]Data on marijuana use at school were not collected in 2013.
NOTE: Detail may not sum to totals because of rounding.
SOURCE: Centers for Disease Control and Prevention, Division of Adolescent and School Health, Youth Risk Behavior Surveillance System (YRBSS), 2009 through 2013. (This table was prepared September 2014.)

Table 232.60. Percentage of public school students in grades 9–12 who reported using marijuana at least one time during the previous 30 days, by location and state: Selected years, 2003 through 2013

[Standard errors appear in parentheses]

State	Anywhere (including on school property)[1]						On school property[2]					
	2003	2005	2007	2009	2011	2013	2003	2005	2007	2009	2011	2013
1	2	3	4	5	6	7	8	9	10	11	12	13
United States[3]	**22.4 (1.09)**	**20.2 (0.84)**	**19.7 (0.97)**	**20.8 (0.70)**	**23.1 (0.80)**	**23.4 (1.08)**	**5.8 (0.68)**	**4.5 (0.32)**	**4.5 (0.46)**	**4.6 (0.35)**	**5.9 (0.39)**	**— (†)**
Alabama	17.7 (1.38)	18.5 (1.49)	— (†)	16.2 (1.28)	20.8 (1.62)	19.2 (1.46)	2.6 (0.54)	3.5 (0.80)	— (†)	4.6 (0.81)	4.0 (0.68)	— (†)
Alaska	23.9 (1.29)	— (†)	20.5 (1.47)	22.7 (1.65)	21.2 (1.68)	19.7 (1.35)	6.5 (0.80)	— (†)	5.9 (0.70)	5.9 (0.69)	4.3 (0.59)	— (†)
Arizona	25.6 (1.08)	20.0 (1.08)	22.0 (1.38)	23.7 (1.90)	22.9 (1.59)	23.5 (1.75)	6.5 (0.52)	5.1 (0.63)	6.1 (0.68)	6.4 (0.74)	5.6 (0.75)	— (†)
Arkansas	— (†)	18.9 (1.70)	16.4 (1.08)	17.8 (1.24)	16.8 (1.72)	19.0 (0.98)	— (†)	4.1 (0.61)	2.8 (0.50)	4.5 (1.02)	3.9 (0.78)	— (†)
California	— (†)	— (†)	— (†)	— (†)	— (†)	— (†)	— (†)	— (†)	— (†)	— (†)	— (†)	— (†)
Colorado	— (†)	22.7 (2.99)	— (†)	24.8 (2.22)	22.0 (1.16)	— (†)	— (†)	6.0 (0.88)	— (†)	6.1 (0.89)	6.0 (0.77)	— (†)
Connecticut	— (†)	23.1 (1.37)	23.2 (1.35)	21.8 (1.52)	24.2 (1.44)	26.1 (1.44)	— (†)	5.1 (0.49)	5.9 (0.77)	6.2 (0.76)	5.2 (0.68)	— (†)
Delaware	27.3 (1.13)	22.8 (1.12)	25.1 (1.03)	25.8 (1.30)	27.6 (1.37)	25.6 (1.17)	6.0 (0.54)	5.6 (0.57)	5.4 (0.53)	5.6 (0.71)	6.1 (0.65)	— (†)
District of Columbia	23.5 (1.23)	14.5 (1.08)	20.8 (1.33)	— (†)	26.1 (1.29)	— (†)	7.5 (0.88)	4.8 (0.62)	5.8 (0.66)	— (†)	7.9 (0.91)	— (†)
Florida	21.4 (0.89)	16.8 (0.86)	18.9 (0.88)	21.4 (0.72)	22.5 (0.86)	22.0 (0.81)	4.9 (0.41)	4.0 (0.31)	4.7 (0.40)	5.2 (0.39)	6.3 (0.39)	— (†)
Georgia	19.5 (0.94)	18.9 (1.59)	19.6 (0.96)	18.3 (1.02)	21.2 (1.23)	20.3 (1.64)	3.2 (0.45)	3.3 (0.58)	3.6 (0.58)	3.4 (0.62)	5.6 (0.70)	— (†)
Hawaii	— (†)	17.2 (1.73)	15.7 (1.78)	22.1 (2.03)	22.0 (1.32)	18.9 (1.54)	— (†)	7.2 (1.14)	5.7 (0.85)	8.3 (1.86)	7.6 (0.67)	— (†)
Idaho	14.7 (1.56)	17.1 (1.32)	17.9 (1.73)	13.7 (1.07)	18.8 (1.76)	15.3 (1.10)	2.7 (0.55)	3.9 (0.61)	4.7 (0.80)	3.0 (0.44)	4.9 (0.73)	— (†)
Illinois	— (†)	— (†)	20.3 (1.38)	21.0 (1.53)	23.1 (1.59)	24.0 (1.70)	— (†)	— (†)	4.2 (0.76)	5.0 (0.77)	4.7 (0.50)	— (†)
Indiana	22.1 (1.19)	18.9 (1.38)	18.9 (1.19)	20.9 (1.83)	20.0 (1.13)	— (†)	3.8 (0.67)	3.4 (0.57)	4.1 (0.45)	4.4 (0.62)	3.3 (0.66)	— (†)
Iowa	— (†)	15.6 (1.74)	11.5 (1.53)	— (†)	14.6 (1.99)	— (†)	— (†)	2.7 (0.64)	2.5 (0.66)	— (†)	3.4 (0.88)	— (†)
Kansas	— (†)	15.6 (1.46)	15.3 (0.93)	14.7 (1.19)	16.8 (0.87)	14.3 (1.19)	— (†)	3.2 (0.51)	3.8 (0.53)	2.7 (0.35)	2.9 (0.53)	— (†)
Kentucky	21.1 (1.09)	15.8 (1.19)	16.4 (1.07)	16.1 (1.15)	19.2 (1.47)	17.7 (1.50)	4.3 (0.55)	3.2 (0.45)	3.9 (0.44)	3.1 (0.54)	4.2 (0.65)	— (†)
Louisiana	— (†)	— (†)	— (†)	16.3 (1.29)	16.8 (1.02)	17.5 (1.38)	— (†)	— (†)	— (†)	3.6 (0.89)	4.1 (0.59)	— (†)
Maine	26.4 (1.69)	22.2 (2.13)	22.0 (1.55)	20.5 (0.57)	21.2 (0.72)	21.3 (0.89)	6.3 (0.76)	4.6 (0.72)	5.2 (0.65)	— (†)	— (†)	— (†)
Maryland	— (†)	18.5 (2.25)	19.4 (1.91)	21.9 (1.57)	23.2 (1.51)	19.8 (0.36)	— (†)	3.7 (0.82)	4.7 (1.13)	5.0 (0.65)	5.7 (0.70)	— (†)
Massachusetts	27.7 (1.39)	26.2 (1.22)	24.6 (1.43)	27.1 (1.24)	27.9 (1.31)	24.8 (0.92)	6.3 (0.44)	5.3 (0.54)	4.8 (0.44)	5.9 (0.79)	6.3 (0.51)	— (†)
Michigan	24.0 (1.96)	18.8 (1.29)	18.0 (1.10)	20.7 (0.91)	18.6 (1.15)	18.2 (0.73)	7.0 (1.20)	3.7 (0.50)	4.0 (0.57)	4.8 (0.59)	3.3 (0.44)	— (†)
Minnesota	— (†)	— (†)	— (†)	— (†)	— (†)	— (†)	— (†)	— (†)	— (†)	— (†)	— (†)	— (†)
Mississippi	20.6 (1.57)	— (†)	16.7 (1.02)	17.7 (1.21)	17.5 (1.18)	17.7 (1.28)	4.4 (0.90)	— (†)	2.7 (0.35)	2.5 (0.46)	3.2 (0.58)	— (†)
Missouri	21.8 (1.37)	18.1 (2.23)	19.0 (1.23)	20.6 (2.02)	— (†)	20.5 (1.69)	3.0 (0.58)	4.0 (0.82)	3.6 (0.63)	3.4 (0.48)	— (†)	— (†)
Montana	23.1 (1.45)	22.3 (1.43)	21.0 (1.44)	23.1 (1.58)	21.2 (1.50)	21.0 (1.18)	6.4 (0.70)	6.1 (0.70)	5.0 (0.49)	5.8 (0.67)	5.5 (0.59)	— (†)
Nebraska	18.3 (1.23)	17.5 (1.05)	— (†)	— (†)	12.7 (1.06)	11.7 (1.10)	3.9 (0.51)	3.1 (0.41)	— (†)	— (†)	2.7 (0.43)	— (†)
Nevada	22.3 (1.31)	17.3 (1.34)	15.5 (1.07)	20.0 (1.36)	— (†)	18.7 (1.57)	5.3 (0.69)	5.7 (0.81)	3.6 (0.55)	4.9 (0.53)	— (†)	— (†)
New Hampshire	30.6 (2.51)	25.9 (1.69)	22.9 (1.39)	25.6 (1.86)	28.4 (1.82)	24.4 (1.36)	6.6 (0.86)	— (†)	4.7 (0.64)	6.8 (0.78)	7.3 (0.87)	— (†)
New Jersey	— (†)	19.9 (2.18)	— (†)	20.3 (1.53)	21.1 (1.33)	21.0 (1.20)	— (†)	3.4 (0.67)	— (†)	— (†)	— (†)	— (†)
New Mexico	— (†)	26.2 (2.00)	25.0 (2.07)	28.0 (1.52)	27.6 (1.58)	27.8 (1.70)	— (†)	8.4 (0.98)	7.9 (0.86)	9.7 (1.06)	9.7 (0.84)	— (†)
New York	20.7 (1.05)	18.3 (1.13)	18.6 (0.78)	20.9 (1.32)	20.6 (1.07)	21.4 (1.04)	4.5 (0.41)	3.6 (0.41)	4.1 (0.44)	— (†)	— (†)	— (†)
North Carolina	24.3 (1.99)	21.4 (1.61)	19.1 (1.27)	19.8 (1.67)	24.2 (1.25)	23.2 (1.83)	3.5 (0.71)	4.1 (0.65)	4.3 (0.54)	4.0 (0.63)	5.2 (0.91)	— (†)
North Dakota	20.6 (1.58)	15.5 (1.62)	14.8 (1.18)	16.9 (1.55)	15.3 (1.52)	15.9 (1.26)	6.3 (0.98)	4.0 (0.71)	2.7 (0.43)	3.8 (0.59)	3.4 (0.45)	— (†)
Ohio[4]	21.4 (2.33)	20.9 (1.79)	17.7 (1.50)	— (†)	23.6 (1.95)	20.7 (2.30)	4.2 (0.96)	4.3 (0.62)	3.7 (0.67)	— (†)	— (†)	— (†)
Oklahoma	22.0 (2.20)	18.7 (1.12)	15.9 (1.37)	17.2 (2.04)	19.1 (1.90)	16.3 (1.57)	4.3 (0.70)	3.0 (0.38)	2.6 (0.40)	2.9 (0.70)	2.4 (0.58)	— (†)
Oregon	— (†)	— (†)	— (†)	— (†)	— (†)	— (†)	— (†)	— (†)	— (†)	— (†)	— (†)	— (†)
Pennsylvania	— (†)	— (†)	— (†)	19.3 (1.43)	— (†)	— (†)	— (†)	— (†)	— (†)	3.5 (0.58)	— (†)	— (†)
Rhode Island	27.6 (1.11)	25.0 (1.16)	23.2 (1.85)	26.3 (1.33)	26.3 (1.35)	23.9 (1.92)	7.4 (0.70)	7.2 (0.65)	6.5 (0.93)	5.1 (0.60)	— (†)	— (†)
South Carolina	— (†)	19.0 (1.24)	18.6 (1.44)	20.4 (1.56)	24.1 (1.99)	19.7 (1.22)	— (†)	4.6 (0.64)	3.3 (0.52)	3.7 (0.63)	5.2 (0.75)	— (†)
South Dakota[4]	21.5 (3.35)	16.8 (1.87)	17.7 (3.72)	15.2 (1.36)	17.8 (3.57)	16.1 (3.01)	4.5 ! (1.50)	2.9 (0.73)	5.0 ! (2.41)	2.9 (0.49)	— (†)	— (†)
Tennessee	23.6 (2.10)	19.5 (1.38)	19.4 (1.29)	20.1 (1.31)	20.6 (0.96)	21.4 (1.70)	4.1 (0.86)	3.5 (0.67)	4.1 (0.60)	3.8 (0.65)	3.6 (0.40)	— (†)
Texas	— (†)	21.7 (0.99)	19.3 (1.01)	19.5 (0.71)	20.8 (1.30)	20.5 (1.26)	— (†)	3.8 (0.52)	3.6 (0.30)	4.6 (0.51)	4.8 (0.47)	— (†)
Utah	11.4 (1.28)	7.6 (1.18)	8.7 (2.00)	10.0 (1.53)	9.6 (1.26)	7.6 (0.79)	3.7 (0.59)	1.7 (0.42)	3.8 ! (1.24)	2.5 (0.48)	4.0 (0.72)	— (†)
Vermont	28.2 (1.58)	25.3 (1.59)	24.1 (0.88)	24.6 (1.14)	24.4 (1.43)	25.7 (0.83)	8.0 (0.44)	7.0 (0.80)	6.3 (0.63)	6.3 (0.57)	6.0 (0.84)	— (†)
Virginia	— (†)	— (†)	— (†)	— (†)	18.0 (1.79)	17.9 (0.85)	— (†)	— (†)	— (†)	— (†)	3.5 (0.70)	— (†)
Washington	— (†)	— (†)	— (†)	— (†)	— (†)	— (†)	— (†)	— (†)	— (†)	— (†)	— (†)	— (†)
West Virginia	23.1 (2.13)	19.6 (1.70)	23.5 (1.05)	20.3 (1.73)	19.7 (1.61)	18.9 (1.39)	4.5 (0.72)	4.9 (0.85)	5.8 (0.97)	3.9 (0.37)	3.0 (0.45)	— (†)
Wisconsin	21.8 (1.18)	15.9 (1.07)	20.3 (1.30)	18.9 (1.64)	21.6 (1.78)	17.3 (1.12)	— (†)	— (†)	— (†)	— (†)	— (†)	— (†)
Wyoming	20.4 (1.56)	17.8 (1.05)	14.4 (0.79)	16.9 (0.91)	18.5 (1.23)	17.8 (0.81)	5.1 (0.66)	4.0 (0.43)	4.7 (0.52)	5.3 (0.45)	4.7 (0.44)	— (†)

—Not available.

†Not applicable.

!Interpret data with caution. The coefficient of variation (CV) for this estimate is between 30 and 50 percent.

[1]The term "anywhere" is not used in the Youth Risk Behavior Survey (YRBS) questionnaire; students were simply asked how many times during the previous 30 days they had used marijuana.

[2]In the question about using marijuana at school, "on school property" was not defined for survey respondents. Data on marijuana use at school were not collected in 2013.

[3]Data for the U.S. total include both public and private schools and were collected through a national survey representing the entire country.

[4]Data include both public and private schools.

NOTE: State-level data include public schools only, with the exception of data for Ohio and South Dakota. Data for the U.S. total, Ohio, and South Dakota include both public and private schools. For specific states, a given year's data may be unavailable (1) because the state did not participate in the survey that year; (2) because the state omitted this particular survey item from the state-level questionnaire; or (3) because the state had an overall response rate of less than 60 percent (the overall response rate is the school response rate multiplied by the student response rate).

SOURCE: Centers for Disease Control and Prevention, Division of Adolescent and School Health, Youth Risk Behavior Surveillance System (YRBSS), 2003 through 2013. (This table was prepared June 2014.)

Table 232.70. Percentage of students in grades 9–12 who reported that illegal drugs were made available to them on school property during the previous 12 months, by selected student characteristics: Selected years, 1993 through 2013

[Standard errors appear in parentheses]

Student characteristic	1993		1995		1997		1999		2001		2003		2005		2007		2009		2011		2013	
1	2		3		4		5		6		7		8		9		10		11		12	
Total	**24.0**	**(1.33)**	**32.1**	**(1.55)**	**31.7**	**(0.90)**	**30.2**	**(1.23)**	**28.5**	**(1.01)**	**28.7**	**(1.95)**	**25.4**	**(1.05)**	**22.3**	**(1.04)**	**22.7**	**(1.04)**	**25.6**	**(0.99)**	**22.1**	**(0.96)**
Sex																						
Male	28.5	(1.50)	38.8	(1.73)	37.4	(1.19)	34.7	(1.69)	34.6	(1.20)	31.9	(2.07)	28.8	(1.23)	25.7	(1.15)	25.9	(1.36)	29.2	(1.10)	24.5	(1.21)
Female	19.1	(1.31)	24.8	(1.43)	24.7	(1.22)	25.7	(1.26)	22.7	(1.03)	25.0	(1.92)	21.8	(1.03)	18.7	(1.16)	19.3	(1.01)	21.7	(1.17)	19.7	(0.89)
Race/ethnicity[1]																						
White	24.1	(1.69)	31.7	(2.24)	31.0	(1.36)	28.8	(1.50)	28.3	(1.31)	27.5	(2.68)	23.6	(1.32)	20.8	(1.23)	19.8	(1.13)	22.7	(0.96)	20.4	(1.11)
Black	17.5	(1.49)	28.5	(1.98)	25.4	(1.69)	25.3	(2.03)	21.9	(1.72)	23.1	(1.42)	23.9	(2.22)	19.2	(1.36)	22.2	(1.42)	22.8	(1.82)	18.6	(1.11)
Hispanic	34.1	(1.58)	40.7	(2.45)	41.1	(2.04)	36.9	(2.10)	34.2	(1.17)	36.5	(1.91)	33.5	(1.18)	29.1	(1.94)	31.2	(1.53)	33.2	(1.70)	27.4	(1.42)
Asian[2]	—	(†)	—	(†)	—	(†)	25.7	(2.65)	25.7	(2.92)	22.5	(3.71)	15.9	(2.68)	21.0	(2.78)	18.3	(2.03)	23.3	(2.46)	22.6	(2.57)
Pacific Islander[2]	—	(†)	—	(†)	—	(†)	46.9	(4.33)	50.2	(5.73)	34.7	(6.19)	41.3	(5.75)	38.5	(5.45)	27.6	(5.10)	38.9	(5.01)	27.7	(3.68)
American Indian/Alaska Native	20.9	(4.55)	22.8	(4.78)	30.1	(4.54)	30.6	(5.90)	34.5	(5.15)	31.3	(5.64)	24.4	(3.57)	25.1	(2.04)	34.0	(4.81)	40.5	(2.80)	25.5	(4.10)
Two or more races[2]	—	(†)	—	(†)	—	(†)	36.0	(2.72)	34.5	(3.22)	36.6	(3.99)	31.6	(3.13)	24.6	(3.55)	26.9	(2.62)	33.3	(2.79)	26.4	(2.67)
Grade																						
9th	21.8	(1.24)	31.1	(1.69)	31.4	(2.33)	27.6	(2.51)	29.0	(1.59)	29.5	(2.39)	24.0	(1.21)	21.2	(1.23)	22.0	(1.32)	23.7	(1.22)	22.4	(1.15)
10th	23.7	(1.86)	35.0	(1.54)	33.4	(1.71)	32.1	(1.94)	29.0	(1.39)	29.2	(2.02)	27.5	(1.68)	25.3	(1.29)	23.7	(1.11)	27.8	(1.21)	23.2	(1.54)
11th	27.5	(1.61)	32.8	(1.88)	33.2	(1.42)	31.1	(2.16)	28.7	(1.39)	29.9	(2.33)	24.9	(1.03)	22.8	(1.42)	24.3	(1.44)	27.0	(1.51)	23.2	(1.32)
12th	23.0	(1.82)	29.1	(2.63)	29.0	(1.80)	30.5	(1.11)	26.9	(1.30)	24.9	(2.24)	24.9	(1.40)	19.6	(1.26)	20.6	(1.21)	23.8	(1.13)	18.8	(1.11)
Urbanicity[3]																						
Urban	—	(†)	—	(†)	31.2	(1.11)	30.3	(1.50)	32.0	(1.36)	31.1	(2.12)	—	(†)	—	(†)	—	(†)	—	(†)	—	(†)
Suburban	—	(†)	—	(†)	34.2	(0.94)	29.7	(1.87)	26.6	(1.34)	28.4	(2.16)	—	(†)	—	(†)	—	(†)	—	(†)	—	(†)
Rural	—	(†)	—	(†)	22.7	(1.91)	32.1	(5.76)	28.2	(3.10)	26.2	(5.08)	—	(†)	—	(†)	—	(†)	—	(†)	—	(†)

—Not available.
†Not applicable.
[1]Race categories exclude persons of Hispanic ethnicity.
[2]Before 1999, Asian students and Pacific Islander students were not categorized separately, and students were not given the option of choosing Two or more races. Because the response categories changed in 1999, caution should be used in comparing data on race from 1993, 1995, and 1997 with data from later years.
[3]Refers to the Standard Metropolitan Statistical Area (MSA) status of the respondent's household as defined in 2000 by the U.S. Census Bureau. Categories include "central city of an MSA (Urban)," "in MSA but not in central city (Suburban)," and "not MSA (Rural)."
NOTE: "On school property" was not defined for survey respondents.
SOURCE: Centers for Disease Control and Prevention, Division of Adolescent and School Health, Youth Risk Behavior Surveillance System (YRBSS), 1993 through 2013. (This table was prepared June 2014.)

Table 232.80. Percentage of public school students in grades 9–12 who reported that illegal drugs were made available to them on school property during the previous 12 months, by state: Selected years, 2003 through 2013

[Standard errors appear in parentheses]

State	2003		2005		2007		2009		2011		2013	
1		2		3		4		5		6		7
United States[1]	**28.7**	**(1.95)**	**25.4**	**(1.05)**	**22.3**	**(1.04)**	**22.7**	**(1.04)**	**25.6**	**(0.99)**	**22.1**	**(0.96)**
Alabama	26.0	(1.78)	26.2	(1.90)	—	(†)	27.6	(1.30)	20.3	(1.32)	25.3	(1.11)
Alaska	28.4	(1.24)	—	(†)	25.1	(1.36)	24.8	(1.25)	23.2	(0.98)	—	(†)
Arizona	28.6	(1.23)	38.7	(1.18)	37.1	(1.45)	34.6	(1.43)	34.6	(1.55)	31.3	(1.46)
Arkansas	—	(†)	29.2	(1.35)	28.1	(1.28)	31.4	(1.56)	26.1	(1.30)	27.4	(1.28)
California	—	(†)	—	(†)	—	(†)	—	(†)	—	(†)	—	(†)
Colorado	—	(†)	21.2	(1.81)	—	(†)	22.7	(1.52)	17.2	(1.28)	—	(†)
Connecticut	—	(†)	31.5	(0.90)	30.5	(1.52)	28.9	(1.25)	27.8	(1.43)	27.1	(0.85)
Delaware	27.9	(0.90)	26.1	(1.05)	22.9	(0.99)	20.9	(0.87)	23.1	(1.20)	19.1	(0.83)
District of Columbia	30.2	(1.46)	20.3	(1.18)	25.7	(1.20)	—	(†)	22.6	(1.53)	—	(†)
Florida	25.7	(0.81)	23.2	(0.85)	19.0	(0.80)	21.8	(0.72)	22.9	(0.84)	20.0	(0.64)
Georgia	33.3	(1.00)	30.7	(1.25)	32.0	(1.23)	32.9	(1.22)	32.1	(1.34)	26.5	(1.32)
Hawaii	—	(†)	32.7	(1.74)	36.2	(2.46)	36.1	(1.51)	31.7	(1.48)	31.2	(0.99)
Idaho	19.6	(1.26)	24.8	(1.52)	25.1	(1.63)	22.7	(1.39)	24.4	(1.56)	22.1	(1.31)
Illinois	—	(†)	—	(†)	21.2	(1.18)	27.5	(1.97)	27.3	(1.46)	27.2	(1.06)
Indiana	28.3	(1.55)	28.9	(1.33)	20.5	(1.02)	25.5	(1.24)	28.3	(1.33)	—	(†)
Iowa	—	(†)	15.5	(1.37)	10.1	(1.08)	—	(†)	11.9	(1.16)	—	(†)
Kansas	—	(†)	16.7	(1.27)	15.0	(1.24)	15.1	(0.78)	24.9	(1.19)	19.4	(1.06)
Kentucky	30.4	(1.51)	19.8	(1.23)	27.0	(1.11)	25.6	(1.49)	24.4	(1.40)	20.6	(1.15)
Louisiana	—	(†)	—	(†)	—	(†)	22.8	(1.66)	25.1	(1.82)	—	(†)
Maine	32.6	(1.73)	33.5	(1.89)	29.1	(1.67)	21.2	(0.51)	21.7	(0.80)	18.4	(0.87)
Maryland	—	(†)	28.9	(2.04)	27.4	(1.46)	29.3	(1.35)	30.4	(1.99)	29.1	(0.37)
Massachusetts	31.9	(1.08)	29.9	(1.09)	27.3	(1.06)	26.1	(1.34)	27.1	(1.04)	23.0	(0.90)
Michigan	31.3	(1.50)	28.8	(1.37)	29.1	(1.07)	29.5	(0.90)	25.4	(0.90)	23.8	(0.94)
Minnesota	—	(†)	—	(†)	—	(†)	—	(†)	—	(†)	—	(†)
Mississippi	22.3	(1.31)	—	(†)	15.6	(1.53)	18.0	(1.07)	15.9	(0.89)	12.1	(1.00)
Missouri	21.6	(2.09)	18.2	(1.92)	17.8	(1.49)	17.3	(1.32)	—	(†)	—	(†)
Montana	26.9	(1.23)	25.3	(1.09)	24.9	(0.83)	20.7	(1.10)	25.2	(0.93)	22.8	(0.71)
Nebraska	23.3	(1.04)	22.0	(0.82)	—	(†)	—	(†)	20.3	(1.01)	19.2	(1.15)
Nevada	34.5	(1.30)	32.6	(1.53)	28.8	(1.39)	35.6	(1.30)	—	(†)	31.2	(1.90)
New Hampshire	28.2	(1.87)	26.9	(1.40)	22.5	(1.25)	22.1	(1.44)	23.2	(1.44)	20.1	(1.03)
New Jersey	—	(†)	32.6	(1.32)	—	(†)	32.2	(1.38)	27.3	(1.41)	30.7	(1.70)
New Mexico	—	(†)	33.5	(1.37)	31.3	(1.39)	30.9	(1.54)	34.5	(1.24)	32.8	(1.04)
New York	23.0	(0.97)	23.7	(0.76)	26.6	(1.09)	24.0	(1.05)	—	(†)	—	(†)
North Carolina	31.9	(1.74)	27.4	(1.66)	28.5	(1.37)	30.2	(1.51)	29.8	(1.87)	23.6	(1.61)
North Dakota	21.3	(1.07)	19.6	(1.10)	18.7	(1.05)	19.5	(1.16)	20.8	(1.03)	14.1	(0.79)
Ohio[2]	31.1	(1.68)	30.9	(1.88)	26.7	(1.26)	—	(†)	24.3	(1.70)	19.9	(1.41)
Oklahoma	22.2	(1.23)	18.4	(1.49)	19.1	(1.12)	16.8	(1.50)	17.2	(1.36)	14.0	(1.07)
Oregon	—	(†)	—	(†)	—	(†)	—	(†)	—	(†)	—	(†)
Pennsylvania	—	(†)	—	(†)	—	(†)	16.1	(1.07)	—	(†)	—	(†)
Rhode Island	26.0	(1.26)	24.1	(1.11)	25.3	(1.33)	25.2	(1.52)	22.4	(0.95)	22.6	(1.16)
South Carolina	—	(†)	29.1	(1.45)	26.6	(1.58)	27.6	(1.74)	29.3	(1.83)	24.5	(1.43)
South Dakota[2]	22.1	(1.25)	20.9	(2.30)	21.1	(1.98)	17.7	(0.64)	16.0	(1.81)	15.4	(1.70)
Tennessee	24.3	(2.25)	26.6	(1.21)	21.6	(1.35)	18.8	(1.06)	16.6	(0.88)	24.8	(1.57)
Texas	—	(†)	30.7	(1.73)	26.5	(0.83)	25.9	(1.25)	29.4	(1.34)	26.4	(1.24)
Utah	24.7	(2.04)	20.6	(1.36)	23.2	(1.83)	19.7	(1.52)	21.4	(1.55)	20.0	(1.57)
Vermont	29.4	(1.67)	23.1	(1.59)	22.0	(0.99)	21.1	(1.21)	17.6	(1.51)	—	(†)
Virginia	—	(†)	—	(†)	—	(†)	—	(†)	24.0	(1.67)	—	(†)
Washington	—	(†)	—	(†)	—	(†)	—	(†)	—	(†)	—	(†)
West Virginia	26.5	(2.06)	24.8	(1.36)	28.6	(2.76)	28.0	(1.27)	17.3	(1.04)	17.1	(1.16)
Wisconsin	26.3	(1.18)	21.7	(1.18)	22.7	(1.34)	20.5	(1.03)	20.9	(1.29)	18.3	(1.01)
Wyoming	18.1	(0.99)	22.7	(0.97)	24.7	(1.08)	23.7	(0.93)	25.2	(0.97)	20.2	(0.74)

— Not available.
†Not applicable.
[1]Data for the U.S. total include both public and private schools and were collected through a national survey representing the entire country.
[2]Data include both public and private schools.
NOTE: "On school property" was not defined for survey respondents. State-level data include public schools only, with the exception of data for Ohio and South Dakota. Data for the U.S. total, Ohio, and South Dakota include both public and private schools. For specific states, a given year's data may be unavailable (1) because the state did not participate in the survey that year; (2) because the state omitted this particular survey item from the state-level questionnaire; or (3) because the state had an overall response rate of less than 60 percent (the overall response rate is the school response rate multiplied by the student response rate).
SOURCE: Centers for Disease Control and Prevention, Division of Adolescent and School Health, Youth Risk Behavior Surveillance System (YRBSS), 2003 through 2013. (This table was prepared June 2014.)

Table 232.90. Percentage of high school seniors reporting use of alcohol and illicit drugs, by frequency of use and substance used: Selected years, 1975 through 2015

[Standard errors appear in parentheses]

Frequency of use and substance used	1975	1980	1985	1990	1995	2000	2005	2009	2010	2011	2012	2013	2014	2015
1	2	3	4	5	6	7	8	9	10	11	12	13	14	15
Ever used														
Alcohol[1]	90.4 (0.69)	93.2 (0.46)	92.2 (0.48)	89.5 (0.57)	80.7 (0.73)	80.3 (0.80)	75.1 (0.81)	72.3 (0.85)	71.0 (0.84)	70.0 (0.88)	69.4 (0.90)	68.2 (0.95)	66.0 (0.95)	64.0 (0.94)
Any illicit drug	55.2 (1.68)	65.4 (1.23)	60.6 (1.26)	47.9 (1.33)	48.4 (1.32)	54.0 (1.44)	50.4 (1.35)	46.7 (1.36)	48.2 (1.33)	49.9 (1.38)	49.1 (1.40)	49.8 (1.46)	49.1 (1.43)	48.9 (1.40)
Marijuana only	19.0 (1.32)	26.7 (1.15)	20.9 (1.05)	18.5 (1.03)	20.3 (1.06)	25.0 (1.25)	23.0 (1.14)	22.7 (1.15)	23.5 (1.13)	25.0 (1.19)	25.0 (1.21)	25.0 (1.26)	26.5 (1.27)	27.8 (1.25)
Any illicit drug other than marijuana[2]	36.2 (1.33)	38.7 (1.04)	39.7 (1.04)	29.4 (0.99)	28.1 (0.97)	29.0 (1.08)	27.4 (0.99)	24.0 (0.96)	24.7 (0.94)	24.9 (0.98)	24.1 (0.98)	24.8 (1.03)	22.6 (0.98)	21.1 (0.94)
Selected drugs														
Cocaine	9.0 (0.73)	15.7 (0.72)	17.3 (0.74)	9.4 (0.59)	6.0 (0.48)	8.6 (0.62)	8.0 (0.56)	6.0 (0.49)	5.5 (0.46)	5.2 (0.47)	4.9 (0.46)	4.5 (0.46)	4.6 (0.46)	4.0 (0.42)
Heroin	2.2 (0.21)	1.1 (0.12)	1.2 (0.12)	1.3 (0.13)	1.6 (0.14)	2.4 (0.19)	1.5 (0.14)	1.2 (0.13)	1.6 (0.14)	1.4 (0.14)	1.1 (0.13)	1.0 (0.13)	1.0 (0.12)	0.8 (0.11)
LSD	11.3 (0.81)	9.3 (0.57)	7.5 (0.52)	8.7 (0.57)	11.7 (0.64)	11.1 (0.69)	3.5 (0.38)	3.1 (0.36)	4.0 (0.40)	4.0 (0.41)	3.8 (0.41)	3.9 (0.43)	3.7 (0.41)	4.3 (0.43)
Marijuana/hashish	47.3 (1.68)	60.3 (1.27)	54.2 (1.83)	40.7 (1.30)	41.7 (1.30)	48.8 (1.45)	44.8 (1.34)	42.0 (1.35)	43.8 (1.32)	45.5 (1.37)	45.2 (1.39)	45.5 (1.45)	44.4 (1.43)	44.7 (1.39)
PCP	— (†)	9.6 (0.33)	4.9 (0.24)	2.8 (0.19)	2.7 (0.18)	3.4 (0.23)	2.4 (0.18)	1.7 (0.15)	1.8 (0.15)	2.3 (0.18)	1.6 (0.15)	1.3 (0.14)	— (†)	— (†)
Used during past 12 months														
Alcohol[1]	84.8 (0.84)	87.9 (0.59)	85.6 (0.63)	80.6 (0.73)	73.7 (0.81)	73.2 (0.89)	68.6 (0.87)	66.2 (0.90)	65.2 (0.88)	63.5 (0.92)	63.5 (0.94)	62.0 (0.99)	60.2 (0.98)	58.2 (0.96)
Any illicit drug	45.0 (1.64)	53.1 (1.26)	46.3 (1.26)	32.5 (1.21)	39.0 (1.26)	40.9 (1.39)	38.4 (1.28)	36.5 (1.29)	38.3 (1.26)	40.0 (1.32)	39.7 (1.34)	40.1 (1.39)	38.7 (1.36)	38.6 (1.33)
Marijuana only	18.8 (1.29)	22.7 (1.06)	18.9 (0.99)	14.6 (0.91)	19.6 (1.02)	20.5 (1.14)	18.8 (1.03)	19.5 (1.06)	21.0 (1.06)	22.4 (1.12)	22.7 (1.14)	22.3 (1.18)	22.8 (1.18)	23.4 (1.16)
Any illicit drug other than marijuana[2]	26.2 (1.15)	30.4 (0.92)	27.4 (0.89)	17.9 (0.79)	19.4 (0.81)	20.4 (0.90)	19.7 (0.83)	17.0 (0.79)	17.3 (0.78)	17.6 (0.81)	17.0 (0.81)	17.8 (0.86)	15.9 (0.81)	15.2 (0.78)
Selected drugs														
Cocaine	5.6 (0.52)	12.3 (0.58)	13.1 (0.59)	5.3 (0.40)	4.0 (0.35)	5.0 (0.43)	5.1 (0.40)	3.4 (0.34)	2.9 (0.30)	2.9 (0.31)	2.7 (0.31)	2.6 (0.31)	2.6 (0.31)	2.5 (0.30)
Heroin	1.0 (0.13)	0.5 (0.07)	0.6 (0.07)	0.5 (0.07)	1.1 (0.10)	1.5 (0.13)	0.8 (0.09)	0.7 (0.09)	0.9 (0.09)	0.8 (0.09)	0.6 (0.08)	0.6 (0.08)	0.6 (0.08)	0.5 (0.07)
LSD	7.2 (0.59)	6.5 (0.43)	4.4 (0.36)	5.4 (0.41)	8.4 (0.49)	6.6 (0.49)	1.8 (0.24)	1.9 (0.25)	2.6 (0.29)	2.7 (0.30)	2.4 (0.29)	2.2 (0.29)	2.5 (0.30)	2.9 (0.32)
Marijuana/hashish	40.0 (1.61)	48.8 (1.27)	40.6 (1.24)	27.0 (1.15)	34.7 (1.23)	36.5 (1.36)	33.6 (1.24)	32.8 (1.25)	34.8 (1.24)	36.4 (1.29)	36.4 (1.31)	36.4 (1.37)	35.1 (1.34)	34.9 (1.30)
PCP	— (†)	4.4 (0.20)	2.9 (0.16)	1.2 (0.11)	1.8 (0.13)	2.3 (0.16)	1.3 (0.11)	1.0 (0.10)	1.0 (0.10)	1.3 (0.12)	0.9 (0.10)	0.7 (0.09)	0.8 (0.10)	1.4 (0.12)
Used during past 30 days														
Alcohol[1]	68.2 (1.10)	72.0 (0.81)	65.9 (0.85)	57.1 (0.92)	51.3 (0.92)	50.0 (1.01)	47.0 (0.94)	43.5 (0.95)	41.2 (0.91)	40.0 (0.94)	41.5 (0.96)	39.2 (0.99)	37.4 (0.97)	35.3 (0.93)
Any illicit drug	30.7 (1.35)	37.2 (1.09)	29.7 (1.03)	17.2 (0.87)	23.8 (0.98)	24.9 (1.09)	23.1 (0.99)	23.3 (1.01)	23.8 (0.99)	25.2 (1.04)	25.2 (1.06)	25.2 (1.10)	23.7 (1.06)	23.6 (1.03)
Marijuana only	15.3 (1.06)	18.8 (0.88)	14.8 (0.80)	9.2 (0.67)	13.8 (0.79)	14.5 (0.89)	12.8 (0.78)	14.7 (0.84)	15.2 (0.83)	16.3 (0.89)	16.8 (0.91)	17.0 (0.95)	16.0 (0.92)	16.0 (0.89)
Any illicit drug other than marijuana[2]	15.4 (0.80)	18.4 (0.66)	14.9 (0.60)	8.0 (0.47)	10.0 (0.52)	10.4 (0.58)	10.3 (0.54)	8.6 (0.50)	8.6 (0.49)	8.9 (0.51)	8.4 (0.51)	8.2 (0.52)	7.7 (0.50)	7.6 (0.49)
Selected drugs														
Cocaine	1.9 (0.25)	5.2 (0.31)	6.7 (0.35)	1.9 (0.20)	1.8 (0.19)	2.1 (0.23)	2.3 (0.22)	1.3 (0.17)	1.3 (0.16)	1.1 (0.16)	1.1 (0.16)	1.1 (0.17)	1.0 (0.16)	1.1 (0.16)
Heroin	0.4 (0.08)	0.2 (0.04)	0.3 (0.05)	0.2 (0.04)	0.6 (0.08)	0.7 (0.09)	0.5 (0.07)	0.4 (0.06)	0.4 (0.06)	0.4 (0.07)	0.3 (0.06)	0.3 (0.06)	0.4 (0.07)	0.3 (0.06)
LSD	2.3 (0.28)	2.3 (0.21)	1.6 (0.18)	1.9 (0.20)	4.0 (0.28)	1.6 (0.20)	0.7 (0.12)	0.5 (0.11)	0.8 (0.13)	0.8 (0.13)	0.8 (0.14)	0.8 (0.14)	1.0 (0.16)	1.1 (0.16)
Marijuana/hashish	27.1 (1.30)	33.7 (1.07)	25.7 (0.98)	14.0 (0.80)	21.2 (0.94)	21.6 (1.04)	19.8 (0.94)	20.6 (0.96)	21.4 (0.95)	22.6 (1.00)	22.9 (1.02)	22.7 (1.06)	21.2 (1.02)	21.3 (1.00)
PCP	— (†)	1.4 (0.11)	1.6 (0.12)	0.4 (0.06)	0.6 (0.08)	0.9 (0.10)	0.7 (0.08)	0.5 (0.07)	0.8 (0.09)	0.8 (0.09)	0.5 (0.07)	0.4 (0.07)	— (†)	— (†)

—Not available.
†Not applicable.
[1]Survey question changed in 1993; later data are not comparable to figures for earlier years.
[2]Other illicit drugs include any use of LSD or other hallucinogens, crack or other cocaine, or heroin, or any use of other narcotics, amphetamines, barbiturates, or tranquilizers not under a doctor's orders.

NOTE: Detail may not sum to totals because of rounding. Standard errors were calculated from formulas to perform trend analysis over an interval greater than 1 year (for example, a comparison between 1975 and 1990). A revised questionnaire was used in 1982 and later years to reduce the inappropriate reporting of nonprescription stimulants. This slightly reduced the positive responses for some types of drug abuse.
SOURCE: University of Michigan, Institute for Social Research, Monitoring the Future, selected years, 1975 through 2015, retrieved January 29, 2016, from http://monitoringthefuture.org/data/data.html. (This table was prepared February 2016.)

Table 232.95. Percentage of 12- to 17-year-olds reporting use of illicit drugs, alcohol, and cigarettes during the past 30 days and the past year, by substance used, sex, and race/ethnicity: Selected years, 1985 through 2014

[Standard errors appear in parentheses]

Year, sex, and race/ethnicity	Percent reporting use during past 30 days					Percent reporting use during past year				
	Illicit drugs					Illicit drugs				
	Any[1]	Marijuana	Cocaine	Alcohol	Cigarettes	Any[1]	Marijuana	Cocaine	Alcohol	Cigarettes
1	2	3	4	5	6	7	8	9	10	11
1985	13.2 (—)	10.2 (—)	1.5 (—)	41.2 (—)	29.4 (—)	20.7 (—)	16.7 (—)	3.4 (—)	52.7 (—)	29.9 (—)
1990	7.1 (—)	4.4 (—)	0.6 (—)	32.5 (—)	22.4 (—)	14.1 (—)	9.6 (—)	1.9 (—)	41.8 (—)	26.2 (—)
1995	10.9 (—)	8.2 (—)	0.8 (—)	21.1 (—)	20.2 (—)	18.0 (—)	14.2 (—)	1.7 (—)	35.1 (—)	26.6 (—)
1999	9.8 (0.23)	7.2 (0.20)	0.5 (0.06)	16.5 (0.30)	14.9 (0.31)	19.8 (0.32)	14.2 (0.29)	1.6 (0.10)	34.1 (0.41)	23.4 (0.37)
2000	9.7 (0.24)	7.2 (0.21)	0.6 (0.07)	16.4 (0.29)	13.4 (0.28)	18.6 (0.31)	13.4 (0.27)	1.7 (0.12)	33.0 (0.39)	20.8 (0.34)
2001	10.8 (0.26)	8.0 (0.24)	0.4 (0.06)	17.3 (0.33)	13.0 (0.28)	20.8 (0.36)	15.2 (0.32)	1.5 (0.10)	33.9 (0.39)	20.0 (0.35)
2002	11.6 (0.29)	8.2 (0.24)	0.6 (0.07)	17.6 (0.32)	13.0 (0.30)	22.2 (0.38)	15.8 (0.32)	2.1 (0.13)	34.6 (0.42)	20.3 (0.35)
2003	11.2 (0.27)	7.9 (0.24)	0.6 (0.06)	17.7 (0.33)	12.2 (0.29)	21.8 (0.36)	15.0 (0.31)	1.8 (0.11)	34.3 (0.42)	19.0 (0.36)
2004	10.6 (0.27)	7.6 (0.23)	0.5 (0.06)	17.6 (0.32)	11.9 (0.30)	21.0 (0.34)	14.5 (0.31)	1.6 (0.11)	33.9 (0.41)	18.4 (0.35)
2005	9.9 (0.25)	6.8 (0.22)	0.6 (0.06)	16.5 (0.32)	10.8 (0.28)	19.9 (0.35)	13.3 (0.30)	1.7 (0.11)	33.3 (0.41)	17.3 (0.36)
2006	9.8 (0.27)	6.7 (0.21)	0.4 (0.05)	16.6 (0.32)	10.4 (0.26)	19.6 (0.37)	13.2 (0.31)	1.6 (0.11)	32.9 (0.42)	17.0 (0.35)
2007	9.5 (0.27)	6.7 (0.22)	0.4 (0.05)	15.9 (0.34)	9.8 (0.26)	18.7 (0.35)	12.5 (0.30)	1.5 (0.11)	31.8 (0.42)	15.7 (0.34)
2008	9.3 (0.24)	6.7 (0.22)	0.4 (0.05)	14.6 (0.31)	9.1 (0.24)	19.0 (0.35)	13.0 (0.29)	1.2 (0.10)	30.8 (0.40)	15.0 (0.31)
2009	10.0 (0.27)	7.3 (0.24)	0.3 (0.05)	14.7 (0.32)	8.9 (0.26)	19.5 (0.36)	13.6 (0.31)	1.0 (0.09)	30.3 (0.42)	15.0 (0.33)
2010	10.1 (0.29)	7.4 (0.25)	0.2 (0.05)	13.6 (0.33)	8.4 (0.26)	19.5 (0.38)	14.0 (0.34)	1.0 (0.09)	28.7 (0.43)	14.2 (0.34)
2011	10.1 (0.27)	7.9 (0.24)	0.3 (0.05)	13.3 (0.31)	7.8 (0.24)	19.0 (0.37)	14.2 (0.33)	0.9 (0.08)	27.8 (0.43)	13.2 (0.31)
2012	9.5 (0.25)	7.2 (0.22)	0.1 ! (0.03)	12.9 (0.31)	6.6 (0.22)	17.9 (0.33)	13.5 (0.30)	0.7 (0.08)	26.3 (0.42)	11.8 (0.29)
2013	8.8 (0.25)	7.1 (0.23)	0.2 (0.04)	11.6 (0.29)	5.6 (0.20)	17.2 (0.35)	13.4 (0.31)	0.5 (0.06)	24.6 (0.40)	10.3 (0.27)
Sex										
Male	9.6 (0.36)	7.9 (0.33)	0.2 (0.05)	11.2 (0.41)	5.7 (0.28)	17.8 (0.51)	14.1 (0.45)	0.6 (0.09)	23.5 (0.56)	10.3 (0.37)
Female	8.0 (0.34)	6.2 (0.30)	0.2 ! (0.06)	11.9 (0.43)	5.5 (0.30)	16.6 (0.50)	12.8 (0.44)	0.5 (0.09)	25.8 (0.58)	10.3 (0.40)
Race/ethnicity										
White	8.8 (0.32)	7.1 (0.29)	0.2 (0.05)	12.9 (0.40)	7.2 (0.31)	17.0 (0.43)	13.5 (0.40)	0.6 (0.09)	27.1 (0.52)	12.2 (0.38)
Black	10.5 (0.73)	7.4 (0.59)	‡ (†)	9.7 (0.71)	3.2 (0.39)	20.1 (0.90)	14.7 (0.83)	‡ (†)	21.6 (0.97)	6.4 (0.57)
Hispanic	8.7 (0.58)	7.2 (0.52)	0.3 (0.08)	10.7 (0.66)	3.7 (0.37)	17.2 (0.83)	13.5 (0.76)	0.6 (0.13)	23.2 (0.91)	9.0 (0.60)
Asian	3.8 (0.91)	3.6 (0.90)	‡ (†)	8.0 (1.48)	2.5 (0.71)	9.1 (1.37)	7.1 (1.26)	‡ (†)	15.8 (2.25)	5.1 (1.12)
Pacific Islander	‡ (†)	‡ (†)	‡ (†)	8.2 ! (2.90)	3.6 ! (1.48)	‡ (†)	‡ (†)	‡ (†)	‡ (†)	6.0 ! (2.52)
American Indian/Alaska Native	‡ (†)	9.1 (2.58)	‡ (†)	9.3 (2.39)	7.5 (1.95)	27.8 (4.94)	20.1 (3.52)	‡ (†)	20.3 (3.90)	16.1 (3.13)
Two or more races	10.3 (1.25)	8.6 (1.15)	‡ (†)	9.0 (1.10)	7.0 (1.18)	19.0 (1.73)	15.5 (1.59)	‡ (†)	21.8 (1.79)	10.3 (1.36)
2014	9.4 (0.30)	7.4 (0.27)	0.2 (0.04)	11.5 (0.33)	4.9 (0.21)	17.4 (0.38)	13.1 (0.33)	0.7 (0.09)	24.0 (0.42)	8.9 (0.29)
Sex										
Male	9.6 (0.41)	7.9 (0.38)	‡ (†)	10.8 (0.42)	5.1 (0.28)	16.7 (0.52)	13.2 (0.46)	0.7 (0.13)	22.0 (0.56)	9.1 (0.41)
Female	9.1 (0.41)	6.8 (0.35)	0.2 ! (0.06)	12.3 (0.47)	4.6 (0.28)	18.2 (0.53)	13.0 (0.46)	0.7 (0.13)	26.1 (0.61)	8.7 (0.38)
Race/ethnicity										
White	9.3 (0.41)	7.7 (0.37)	‡ (†)	13.2 (0.47)	6.3 (0.31)	17.0 (0.51)	13.2 (0.45)	0.7 (0.12)	26.7 (0.57)	10.6 (0.39)
Black	9.8 (0.76)	6.9 (0.65)	‡ (†)	8.6 (0.71)	2.2 (0.31)	19.2 (0.94)	13.6 (0.83)	‡ (†)	18.7 (0.97)	4.4 (0.44)
Hispanic	10.5 (0.69)	7.9 (0.62)	0.4 ! (0.14)	11.2 (0.71)	3.8 (0.42)	18.9 (0.85)	14.1 (0.74)	1.2 (0.27)	23.9 (0.97)	8.4 (0.63)
Asian	3.5 (0.84)	2.5 (0.69)	‡ (†)	4.5 (0.97)	1.3 ! (0.55)	9.1 (1.40)	6.2 (1.15)	‡ (†)	12.3 (1.57)	3.4 (0.88)
Pacific Islander	‡ (†)	‡ (†)	‡ (†)	‡ (†)	‡ (†)	‡ (†)	‡ (†)	‡ (†)	‡ (†)	‡ (†)
American Indian/Alaska Native	10.6 (2.78)	9.4 (2.78)	‡ (†)	‡ (†)	8.6 ! (2.83)	23.2 (4.29)	20.2 (4.28)	‡ (†)	22.3 (5.06)	17.5 (4.55)
Two or more races	10.0 (1.29)	6.9 (1.05)	‡ (†)	9.7 (1.35)	4.4 (0.87)	19.3 (1.79)	13.0 (1.43)	‡ (†)	22.1 (1.92)	9.3 (1.31)

—Not available.
†Not applicable.
!Interpret data with caution. The coefficient of variation (CV) for this estimate is between 30 and 50 percent.
‡Reporting standards not met. Either there are too few cases for a reliable estimate or the coefficient of variation (CV) is 50 percent or greater.
[1]Includes other illegal drug use not shown separately—specifically, the use of heroin, hallucinogens, and inhalants, as well as the nonmedical use of prescription-type pain relievers, tranquilizers, stimulants, and sedatives.

NOTE: Marijuana includes hashish usage. Data for 1999 and later years were gathered using Computer Assisted Interviewing (CAI) and may not be directly comparable to previous years. Because of survey improvements in 2002, the 2002 data constitute a new baseline for tracking trends. Valid trend comparisons can be made for 1985 through 1995, 1999 through 2001, and 2002 through 2014. Race categories exclude persons of Hispanic ethnicity.

SOURCE: U.S. Department of Health and Human Services, Substance Abuse and Mental Health Services Administration, *National Household Survey on Drug Abuse: Main Findings*, selected years, 1985 through 2001, and National Survey on Drug Use and Health, 2002 through 2014. Retrieved March 4, 2016, from http://www.samhsa.gov/data/population-data-nsduh/reports?tab=38. (This table was prepared March 2016.)

Table 231.10. Percentage of students in grades 9–12 who reported having been in a physical fight at least one time during the previous 12 months, by location and selected student characteristics: Selected years, 1993 through 2013

[Standard errors appear in parentheses]

Location and student characteristic	1993		1995		1997		1999		2001		2003		2005		2007		2009		2011		2013	
1	2		3		4		5		6		7		8		9		10		11		12	
Anywhere (including on school property)[1]																						
Total	**41.8**	**(0.99)**	**38.7**	**(1.14)**	**36.6**	**(1.01)**	**35.7**	**(1.17)**	**33.2**	**(0.71)**	**33.0**	**(0.99)**	**35.9**	**(0.77)**	**35.5**	**(0.77)**	**31.5**	**(0.70)**	**32.8**	**(0.65)**	**24.7**	**(0.74)**
Sex																						
Male	51.2	(1.05)	46.1	(1.09)	45.5	(1.07)	44.0	(1.27)	43.1	(0.84)	40.5	(1.32)	43.4	(1.01)	44.4	(0.89)	39.3	(1.20)	40.7	(0.74)	30.2	(1.10)
Female	31.7	(1.19)	30.6	(1.49)	26.0	(1.26)	27.3	(1.70)	23.9	(0.95)	25.1	(0.85)	28.1	(0.94)	26.5	(0.99)	22.9	(0.74)	24.4	(0.92)	19.2	(0.72)
Race/ethnicity[2]																						
White	40.3	(1.13)	36.0	(1.06)	33.7	(1.29)	33.1	(1.45)	32.2	(0.95)	30.5	(1.11)	33.1	(0.88)	31.7	(0.96)	27.8	(0.88)	29.4	(0.74)	20.9	(0.70)
Black	49.5	(1.82)	41.6	(1.99)	43.0	(1.92)	41.4	(3.12)	36.5	(1.60)	39.7	(1.23)	43.1	(1.74)	44.7	(1.33)	41.1	(1.71)	39.1	(1.52)	34.7	(1.67)
Hispanic	43.2	(1.58)	47.9	(2.69)	40.7	(1.68)	39.9	(1.65)	35.8	(0.91)	36.1	(0.98)	41.0	(1.64)	40.4	(1.25)	36.2	(0.95)	36.8	(1.44)	28.4	(1.15)
Asian[3]	—	(†)	—	(†)	—	(†)	22.7	(2.71)	22.3	(2.73)	25.9	(2.99)	21.6	(2.43)	24.3	(3.50)	18.9	(1.72)	18.4	(1.87)	16.1	(1.87)
Pacific Islander[3]	—	(†)	—	(†)	—	(†)	50.7	(3.42)	51.7	(6.25)	30.0	(5.21)	34.4	(5.58)	42.6	(7.74)	32.6	(3.50)	43.0	(5.14)	22.0	(4.95)
American Indian/Alaska Native	49.8	(4.79)	47.2	(6.44)	54.7	(5.75)	48.7	(6.78)	49.2	(6.58)	46.6	(6.53)	44.2	(3.40)	36.0	(1.49)	42.4	(5.23)	42.4	(2.12)	32.1	(7.39)
Two or more races[3]	—	(†)	—	(†)	—	(†)	40.2	(2.76)	39.6	(2.85)	38.2	(3.64)	46.9	(4.16)	47.8	(3.30)	34.2	(3.51)	45.0	(2.60)	28.5	(2.31)
Grade																						
9th	50.4	(1.54)	47.3	(2.22)	44.8	(1.98)	41.1	(1.96)	39.5	(1.27)	38.6	(1.38)	43.5	(1.15)	40.9	(1.16)	37.0	(1.21)	37.7	(1.11)	28.3	(1.17)
10th	42.2	(1.45)	40.4	(1.49)	40.2	(1.91)	37.7	(2.11)	34.7	(1.37)	33.5	(1.20)	36.6	(1.09)	36.2	(1.34)	33.5	(1.19)	35.3	(1.35)	26.4	(1.42)
11th	40.5	(1.52)	36.9	(1.48)	34.2	(1.72)	31.3	(1.55)	29.1	(1.10)	30.9	(1.38)	31.6	(1.44)	34.8	(1.36)	28.6	(0.93)	29.7	(1.14)	24.0	(1.04)
12th	34.8	(1.56)	31.0	(1.71)	28.8	(1.36)	30.4	(1.91)	26.5	(1.01)	26.5	(1.08)	29.1	(1.26)	28.0	(1.42)	24.9	(0.99)	26.9	(0.95)	18.8	(1.19)
Urbanicity[4]																						
Urban	—	(†)	—	(†)	38.2	(2.00)	37.0	(2.66)	36.8	(1.53)	35.5	(2.17)	—	(†)	—	(†)	—	(†)	—	(†)	—	(†)
Suburban	—	(†)	—	(†)	36.7	(1.59)	35.0	(1.56)	31.3	(0.80)	33.1	(1.23)	—	(†)	—	(†)	—	(†)	—	(†)	—	(†)
Rural	—	(†)	—	(†)	32.9	(2.91)	36.6	(2.14)	33.8	(2.58)	29.7	(1.61)	—	(†)	—	(†)	—	(†)	—	(†)	—	(†)
On school property[5]																						
Total	**16.2**	**(0.59)**	**15.5**	**(0.79)**	**14.8**	**(0.64)**	**14.2**	**(0.62)**	**12.5**	**(0.49)**	**12.8**	**(0.76)**	**13.6**	**(0.56)**	**12.4**	**(0.48)**	**11.1**	**(0.54)**	**12.0**	**(0.39)**	**8.1**	**(0.35)**
Sex																						
Male	23.5	(0.71)	21.0	(0.90)	20.0	(1.04)	18.5	(0.66)	18.0	(0.74)	17.1	(0.92)	18.2	(0.93)	16.3	(0.60)	15.1	(1.05)	16.0	(0.58)	10.7	(0.55)
Female	8.6	(0.73)	9.5	(1.03)	8.6	(0.78)	9.8	(0.95)	7.2	(0.47)	8.0	(0.70)	8.8	(0.52)	8.5	(0.62)	6.7	(0.42)	7.8	(0.43)	5.6	(0.38)
Race/ethnicity[2]																						
White	15.0	(0.68)	12.9	(0.62)	13.3	(0.84)	12.3	(0.86)	11.2	(0.60)	10.0	(0.73)	11.6	(0.66)	10.2	(0.56)	8.6	(0.58)	9.9	(0.51)	6.4	(0.45)
Black	22.0	(1.39)	20.3	(1.25)	20.7	(1.20)	18.7	(1.51)	16.8	(1.26)	17.1	(1.30)	16.9	(1.39)	17.6	(1.10)	17.4	(0.99)	16.4	(0.89)	12.8	(0.84)
Hispanic	17.9	(1.75)	21.1	(1.68)	19.0	(1.50)	15.7	(0.91)	14.1	(0.89)	16.7	(1.14)	18.3	(1.62)	15.5	(0.81)	13.5	(0.82)	14.4	(0.79)	9.4	(0.44)
Asian[3]	—	(†)	—	(†)	—	(†)	10.4	(0.95)	10.8	(1.92)	13.1	(2.26)	5.9	(1.53)	8.5	(1.99)	7.7	(1.09)	6.2	(1.06)	5.5	(1.39)
Pacific Islander[3]	—	(†)	—	(†)	—	(†)	25.3	(4.60)	29.1	(7.63)	22.2	(4.82)	24.5	(5.60)	9.6 !	(3.47)	14.8	(2.37)	20.9	(4.41)	7.1 !	(2.58)
American Indian/Alaska Native	18.6	(2.74)	31.4	(5.58)	18.9	(5.55)	16.2 !	(5.23)	18.2	(4.41)	24.2	(5.03)	22.0	(3.16)	15.0	(1.12)	20.7	(3.73)	12.0	(1.77)	10.7	(3.13)
Two or more races[3]	—	(†)	—	(†)	—	(†)	16.9	(2.40)	14.7	(1.97)	20.2	(3.83)	15.8	(2.61)	19.6	(2.39)	12.4	(2.19)	16.6	(1.41)	10.0	(1.04)
Grade																						
9th	23.1	(1.55)	21.6	(1.79)	21.3	(1.29)	18.6	(1.02)	17.3	(0.77)	18.0	(1.24)	18.9	(0.93)	17.0	(0.67)	14.9	(0.98)	16.2	(0.77)	10.9	(0.78)
10th	17.2	(1.07)	16.5	(1.57)	17.0	(1.67)	17.2	(1.23)	13.5	(0.88)	12.8	(0.89)	14.4	(1.08)	11.7	(0.86)	12.1	(0.83)	12.8	(0.86)	8.3	(0.61)
11th	13.8	(1.27)	13.6	(1.00)	12.5	(0.87)	10.8	(1.01)	9.4	(0.71)	10.4	(0.89)	10.4	(0.75)	11.0	(0.73)	9.5	(0.63)	9.2	(0.55)	7.5	(0.53)
12th	11.4	(0.66)	10.6	(0.73)	9.5	(0.73)	8.1	(1.00)	7.5	(0.56)	7.3	(0.70)	8.5	(0.70)	8.6	(0.62)	6.6	(0.59)	8.8	(0.69)	4.9	(0.63)
Urbanicity[4]																						
Urban	—	(†)	—	(†)	15.8	(1.50)	14.4	(1.08)	14.8	(0.90)	14.8	(1.31)	—	(†)	—	(†)	—	(†)	—	(†)	—	(†)
Suburban	—	(†)	—	(†)	14.2	(0.95)	13.7	(0.86)	11.0	(0.75)	12.8	(1.23)	—	(†)	—	(†)	—	(†)	—	(†)	—	(†)
Rural	—	(†)	—	(†)	14.7	(2.09)	16.3	(2.33)	13.8	(1.10)	10.0	(1.36)	—	(†)	—	(†)	—	(†)	—	(†)	—	(†)

—Not available.
†Not applicable.
!Interpret data with caution. The coefficient of variation (CV) for this estimate is between 30 and 50 percent.
[1]The term "anywhere" is not used in the Youth Risk Behavior Survey (YRBS) questionnaire; students were simply asked how many times in the past 12 months they had been in a physical fight.
[2]Race categories exclude persons of Hispanic ethnicity.
[3]Before 1999, Asian students and Pacific Islander students were not categorized separately, and students could not be classified as Two or more races. Because the response categories changed in 1999, caution should be used in comparing data on race from 1993, 1995, and 1997 with data from later years.
[4]Refers to the Standard Metropolitan Statistical Area (MSA) status of the respondent's household as defined in 2000 by the U.S. Census Bureau. Categories include "central city of an MSA (Urban)," "in MSA but not in central city (Suburban)," and "not MSA (Rural)."
[5]In the question asking students about physical fights at school, "on school property" was not defined for survey respondents.
SOURCE: Centers for Disease Control and Prevention, Division of Adolescent and School Health, Youth Risk Behavior Surveillance System (YRBSS), 1993 through 2013. (This table was prepared June 2014.)

Table 231.20. Percentage distribution of students in grades 9–12, by number of times they reported having been in a physical fight anywhere or on school property during the previous 12 months and selected student characteristics: 2013

[Standard errors appear in parentheses]

Student characteristic	Anywhere (including on school property)[1]								On school property[2]							
	0 times		1 to 3 times		4 to 11 times		12 or more times		0 times		1 to 3 times		4 to 11 times		12 or more times	
1	2		3		4		5		6		7		8		9	
Total	**75.3**	**(0.74)**	**18.8**	**(0.59)**	**4.0**	**(0.26)**	**1.9**	**(0.18)**	**91.9**	**(0.35)**	**7.1**	**(0.34)**	**0.6**	**(0.08)**	**0.5**	**(0.07)**
Sex																
Male	69.8	(1.10)	22.1	(0.82)	5.4	(0.43)	2.7	(0.30)	89.3	(0.55)	9.1	(0.48)	0.8	(0.15)	0.7	(0.12)
Female	80.8	(0.72)	15.6	(0.64)	2.6	(0.21)	1.0	(0.17)	94.4	(0.38)	5.1	(0.38)	0.3 !	(0.09)	0.3	(0.07)
Race/ethnicity[3]																
White	79.1	(0.70)	16.5	(0.61)	3.2	(0.30)	1.2	(0.18)	93.6	(0.45)	5.7	(0.44)	0.4	(0.11)	0.3	(0.08)
Black	65.3	(1.67)	26.3	(1.49)	5.9	(0.66)	2.5	(0.31)	87.2	(0.84)	11.1	(0.90)	1.2	(0.30)	0.5	(0.13)
Hispanic	71.6	(1.15)	20.4	(1.30)	5.2	(0.55)	2.8	(0.44)	90.6	(0.44)	7.9	(0.41)	0.7	(0.17)	0.7	(0.14)
Asian	83.9	(1.87)	10.4	(1.55)	2.1 !	(0.80)	3.7 !	(1.28)	94.5	(1.39)	3.1 !	(0.94)	‡	(†)	‡	(†)
Pacific Islander	78.0	(4.95)	19.9	(3.98)	‡	(†)	‡	(†)	92.9	(2.58)	7.1 !	(2.58)	‡	(†)	‡	(†)
American Indian/Alaska Native	67.9	(7.39)	23.0	(5.74)	‡	(†)	‡	(†)	89.3	(3.13)	9.1 !	(3.14)	‡	(†)	‡	(†)
Two or more races	71.5	(2.31)	22.3	(2.03)	3.7	(0.83)	2.6 !	(0.81)	90.0	(1.04)	9.1	(1.03)	‡	(†)	‡	(†)
Grade																
9th	71.7	(1.17)	20.8	(1.02)	5.1	(0.38)	2.4	(0.35)	89.1	(0.78)	9.5	(0.77)	0.9	(0.24)	0.5	(0.12)
10th	73.6	(1.42)	20.8	(1.21)	3.8	(0.46)	1.8	(0.31)	91.7	(0.61)	7.4	(0.59)	0.4	(0.10)	0.5	(0.14)
11th	76.0	(1.04)	18.7	(0.82)	3.4	(0.46)	1.9	(0.31)	92.5	(0.53)	6.4	(0.52)	0.4 !	(0.15)	0.6	(0.17)
12th	81.2	(1.19)	14.5	(0.91)	3.1	(0.45)	1.1	(0.19)	95.1	(0.63)	4.1	(0.54)	0.5 !	(0.14)	0.4	(0.10)

†Not applicable.
!Interpret data with caution. The coefficient of variation (CV) for this estimate is between 30 and 50 percent.
‡Reporting standards not met. Either there are too few cases for a reliable estimate or the coefficient of variation (CV) is 50 percent or greater.
[1]The term "anywhere" is not used in the Youth Risk Behavior Survey (YRBS) questionnaire; students were simply asked how many times in the past 12 months they had been in a physical fight.
[2]In the question asking students about physical fights at school, "on school property" was not defined for respondents.
[3]Race categories exclude persons of Hispanic ethnicity.
NOTE: Detail may not sum to totals because of rounding.
SOURCE: Centers for Disease Control and Prevention, Division of Adolescent and School Health, Youth Risk Behavior Surveillance System (YRBSS), 2013. (This table was prepared June 2014.)

Table 231.30. Percentage of public school students in grades 9–12 who reported having been in a physical fight at least one time during the previous 12 months, by location and state: Selected years, 2003 through 2013

[Standard errors appear in parentheses]

State	Anywhere (including on school property)[1]						On school property[2]					
	2003	2005	2007	2009	2011	2013	2003	2005	2007	2009	2011	2013
1	2	3	4	5	6	7	8	9	10	11	12	13
United States[3]	**33.0 (0.99)**	**35.9 (0.77)**	**35.5 (0.77)**	**31.5 (0.70)**	**32.8 (0.65)**	**24.7 (0.74)**	**12.8 (0.76)**	**13.6 (0.56)**	**12.4 (0.48)**	**11.1 (0.54)**	**12.0 (0.39)**	**8.1 (0.35)**
Alabama	30.0 (1.78)	31.7 (1.84)	— (†)	31.7 (2.44)	28.4 (1.79)	29.2 (2.32)	12.9 (1.21)	14.6 (1.29)	— (†)	13.1 (1.41)	11.8 (1.30)	10.9 (0.93)
Alaska	27.1 (1.55)	— (†)	29.2 (1.77)	27.8 (1.52)	23.7 (1.17)	22.7 (1.64)	8.6 (0.92)	— (†)	10.4 (1.17)	9.8 (1.04)	7.7 (0.90)	— (†)
Arizona	32.4 (1.79)	32.4 (1.43)	31.3 (1.54)	35.9 (1.83)	27.7 (1.41)	23.9 (1.48)	11.4 (0.86)	11.7 (0.87)	11.3 (0.72)	12.0 (0.82)	10.8 (0.78)	8.8 (0.94)
Arkansas	— (†)	32.1 (1.67)	32.8 (1.79)	34.7 (2.08)	29.1 (1.76)	27.0 (1.30)	— (†)	13.9 (1.33)	13.0 (1.03)	14.8 (1.30)	11.0 (1.36)	11.4 (0.89)
California	— (†)	— (†)	— (†)	— (†)	— (†)	— (†)	— (†)	— (†)	— (†)	— (†)	— (†)	— (†)
Colorado	— (†)	32.2 (1.54)	— (†)	32.0 (1.51)	24.9 (1.69)	— (†)	— (†)	12.1 (0.89)	— (†)	10.7 (0.83)	— (†)	— (†)
Connecticut	— (†)	32.7 (1.45)	31.4 (1.39)	28.3 (1.26)	25.1 (1.53)	22.4 (1.23)	— (†)	10.5 (0.72)	10.5 (0.83)	9.6 (0.79)	8.7 (0.84)	— (†)
Delaware	34.9 (1.15)	30.3 (1.38)	33.0 (1.31)	30.4 (1.22)	28.0 (1.59)	25.1 (1.24)	11.4 (0.70)	9.8 (0.82)	10.5 (0.72)	8.6 (0.72)	8.8 (1.02)	9.3 (0.82)
District of Columbia	38.0 (1.61)	36.3 (1.26)	43.0 (1.45)	— (†)	37.9 (1.71)	— (†)	15.2 (1.07)	16.4 (0.88)	19.8 (1.21)	— (†)	15.8 (1.55)	— (†)
Florida	32.1 (0.74)	30.0 (0.94)	32.3 (1.24)	29.8 (0.83)	28.0 (0.72)	22.0 (0.77)	13.3 (0.65)	11.5 (0.77)	12.5 (0.84)	10.5 (0.47)	10.2 (0.44)	8.1 (0.52)
Georgia	31.4 (1.20)	33.8 (1.40)	34.0 (1.26)	32.3 (1.76)	33.1 (1.65)	21.4 (1.24)	11.1 (0.74)	12.1 (1.01)	13.1 (1.07)	11.7 (1.21)	11.9 (1.07)	10.3 (1.37)
Hawaii	— (†)	27.0 (1.37)	28.6 (2.20)	29.5 (1.92)	22.3 (1.11)	16.7 (0.87)	— (†)	10.0 (1.01)	7.0 (0.78)	10.2 (0.99)	8.2 (0.75)	— (†)
Idaho	28.3 (2.00)	32.3 (1.38)	30.0 (1.39)	29.0 (1.08)	26.4 (1.45)	21.6 (1.18)	11.7 (1.20)	12.1 (1.14)	12.3 (0.98)	10.2 (0.79)	9.4 (0.81)	7.3 (0.75)
Illinois	— (†)	— (†)	33.9 (1.91)	33.0 (1.38)	29.5 (1.41)	24.6 (1.67)	— (†)	— (†)	11.3 (1.11)	11.5 (0.82)	9.8 (0.69)	8.2 (0.66)
Indiana	30.6 (2.01)	29.3 (1.51)	29.5 (1.35)	29.1 (1.51)	29.0 (1.34)	— (†)	10.9 (1.14)	11.2 (0.98)	11.5 (0.92)	9.5 (1.18)	8.9 (0.80)	— (†)
Iowa	— (†)	28.3 (1.61)	24.0 (1.39)	— (†)	24.4 (1.87)	— (†)	— (†)	11.3 (1.12)	9.1 (0.96)	— (†)	9.6 (0.89)	— (†)
Kansas	— (†)	27.9 (1.51)	30.3 (1.62)	27.8 (1.37)	22.4 (1.40)	20.4 (1.21)	— (†)	10.1 (0.92)	10.6 (1.04)	9.0 (0.81)	7.8 (0.84)	7.2 (0.72)
Kentucky	26.4 (1.66)	29.6 (1.17)	27.0 (0.98)	28.7 (1.66)	28.7 (1.65)	21.2 (1.20)	10.1 (1.05)	12.7 (0.81)	10.6 (0.65)	9.5 (0.93)	11.4 (0.93)	6.0 (0.94)
Louisiana	— (†)	— (†)	— (†)	36.1 (1.60)	36.0 (2.72)	30.8 (2.59)	— (†)	— (†)	— (†)	13.7 (1.28)	15.8 (2.17)	12.0 (1.68)
Maine	26.5 (1.39)	28.2 (1.11)	26.5 (1.93)	22.8 (0.55)	19.5 (0.46)	17.0 (0.40)	9.1 (1.01)	10.0 (1.03)	10.1 (1.09)	9.1 (0.33)	7.9 (0.27)	5.7 (0.29)
Maryland	— (†)	36.6 (1.83)	35.7 (2.62)	32.5 (2.23)	29.1 (1.80)	— (†)	— (†)	14.9 (1.33)	12.4 (1.69)	11.2 (1.30)	11.1 (1.24)	14.3 (0.32)
Massachusetts	30.7 (1.05)	28.6 (1.33)	27.5 (1.34)	29.2 (1.24)	25.4 (0.92)	20.3 (0.91)	10.2 (0.67)	10.2 (0.67)	9.1 (0.81)	8.7 (0.68)	7.1 (0.65)	4.6 (0.49)
Michigan	30.8 (1.51)	30.1 (2.02)	30.7 (1.89)	31.6 (1.72)	27.4 (1.32)	21.6 (0.88)	12.2 (1.02)	11.4 (1.11)	11.4 (0.89)	11.3 (1.02)	9.1 (0.68)	6.9 (0.55)
Minnesota	— (†)	— (†)	— (†)	— (†)	— (†)	— (†)	— (†)	— (†)	— (†)	— (†)	— (†)	— (†)
Mississippi	30.6 (1.66)	— (†)	30.6 (1.43)	34.1 (1.73)	29.3 (1.72)	31.0 (1.84)	10.2 (1.26)	— (†)	11.9 (0.96)	12.6 (1.02)	12.3 (1.06)	13.6 (1.40)
Missouri	28.2 (2.07)	29.8 (2.12)	30.9 (2.18)	28.7 (1.34)	— (†)	— (†)	9.8 (0.95)	10.2 (1.31)	10.7 (1.21)	9.0 (0.97)	— (†)	— (†)
Montana	28.6 (1.16)	30.5 (1.19)	32.8 (1.08)	31.7 (2.25)	25.4 (0.73)	22.8 (0.90)	10.3 (0.68)	10.9 (0.67)	12.0 (0.75)	10.8 (1.33)	9.1 (0.51)	7.3 (0.37)
Nebraska	29.6 (1.14)	28.5 (1.02)	— (†)	— (†)	26.7 (1.09)	20.1 (1.22)	10.6 (0.81)	9.3 (0.60)	— (†)	— (†)	7.4 (0.68)	5.7 (0.70)
Nevada	35.0 (1.56)	34.5 (1.78)	31.6 (1.53)	35.0 (1.45)	— (†)	23.6 (1.93)	12.6 (1.01)	14.2 (1.32)	11.3 (1.10)	10.0 (0.82)	— (†)	6.8 (1.12)
New Hampshire	30.5 (1.84)	26.4 (1.84)	27.0 (1.40)	25.9 (1.59)	23.8 (1.27)	— (†)	11.6 (1.20)	10.7 (1.06)	11.3 (0.70)	9.1 (0.87)	9.9 (0.89)	6.9 (0.81)
New Jersey	— (†)	30.7 (2.18)	— (†)	27.5 (1.46)	23.9 (1.56)	21.8 (1.34)	— (†)	10.1 (1.31)	— (†)	— (†)	— (†)	— (†)
New Mexico	— (†)	36.7 (1.47)	37.1 (1.06)	37.3 (1.07)	31.5 (1.02)	27.2 (1.27)	— (†)	15.6 (1.19)	16.9 (0.70)	15.0 (0.85)	11.3 (0.78)	9.7 (0.61)
New York	32.1 (0.82)	32.1 (1.07)	31.7 (1.08)	29.6 (1.23)	27.0 (1.25)	22.8 (1.10)	14.6 (0.73)	12.5 (0.74)	12.2 (0.91)	11.4 (0.91)	— (†)	— (†)
North Carolina	30.9 (1.41)	29.9 (1.41)	30.1 (1.54)	28.6 (0.96)	27.6 (1.37)	24.1 (1.49)	10.7 (1.00)	11.6 (0.85)	10.4 (0.84)	9.4 (0.43)	10.6 (1.01)	7.6 (0.94)
North Dakota	27.2 (1.60)	— (†)	— (†)	— (†)	— (†)	— (†)	8.6 (0.96)	10.7 (1.13)	9.6 (0.79)	7.4 (0.78)	8.2 (0.73)	8.8 (0.75)
Ohio[4]	31.5 (2.83)	30.2 (1.95)	30.4 (1.57)	— (†)	31.2 (1.58)	19.8 (1.49)	11.3 (1.67)	10.2 (1.17)	9.4 (0.82)	— (†)	8.8 (0.68)	6.2 (0.88)
Oklahoma	28.4 (2.61)	31.1 (1.63)	29.2 (1.37)	30.8 (2.10)	28.5 (1.96)	25.1 (1.79)	11.4 (1.15)	12.1 (1.13)	10.6 (0.81)	12.8 (1.43)	9.4 (1.25)	7.2 (1.05)
Oregon	— (†)	— (†)	— (†)	— (†)	— (†)	— (†)	— (†)	— (†)	— (†)	— (†)	— (†)	— (†)
Pennsylvania	— (†)	— (†)	— (†)	29.6 (1.76)	— (†)	— (†)	— (†)	— (†)	— (†)	9.9 (1.01)	— (†)	— (†)
Rhode Island	27.6 (1.59)	28.4 (1.34)	26.3 (1.61)	25.1 (0.83)	23.5 (0.81)	18.8 (1.12)	11.4 (1.18)	11.2 (0.80)	9.6 (0.93)	9.1 (0.73)	7.8 (0.52)	6.4 (0.52)
South Carolina	— (†)	31.3 (1.68)	29.1 (1.37)	36.4 (2.06)	32.6 (2.04)	26.7 (1.42)	— (†)	12.7 (1.18)	10.8 (0.86)	12.1 (1.43)	12.2 (1.48)	9.6 (1.17)
South Dakota[4]	27.0 (2.72)	26.5 (2.86)	29.8 (2.00)	27.1 (1.36)	24.5 (2.22)	24.2 (2.04)	9.0 (1.12)	8.4 (1.56)	9.3 (1.32)	8.3 (0.52)	8.2 (0.92)	6.6 (0.52)
Tennessee	28.3 (1.94)	30.9 (1.66)	31.8 (1.55)	32.3 (1.31)	30.8 (1.24)	25.7 (1.69)	12.2 (1.33)	10.9 (1.00)	12.4 (1.13)	11.3 (0.96)	10.5 (0.83)	10.4 (1.02)
Texas	— (†)	34.2 (1.57)	34.9 (1.17)	33.3 (1.05)	34.1 (0.92)	25.4 (1.33)	— (†)	14.5 (0.94)	13.9 (0.90)	13.2 (0.67)	12.5 (0.65)	9.1 (0.79)
Utah	28.7 (2.74)	25.9 (1.84)	30.1 (2.01)	28.2 (1.61)	23.9 (1.88)	21.3 (1.16)	11.9 (1.80)	10.4 (1.57)	11.6 (1.36)	10.6 (0.84)	8.1 (1.18)	6.9 (0.65)
Vermont	26.9 (0.92)	24.3 (1.36)	26.0 (1.44)	25.6 (0.71)	23.1 (1.42)	— (†)	12.2 (0.71)	12.2 (0.98)	11.5 (0.88)	11.0 (0.36)	8.8 (0.72)	9.4 (0.50)
Virginia	— (†)	— (†)	— (†)	— (†)	24.9 (1.71)	23.5 (0.90)	— (†)	— (†)	— (†)	— (†)	7.9 (0.93)	— (†)
Washington	— (†)	— (†)	— (†)	— (†)	— (†)	— (†)	— (†)	— (†)	— (†)	— (†)	— (†)	— (†)
West Virginia	26.5 (1.62)	29.1 (1.88)	29.9 (2.39)	31.7 (1.96)	25.7 (1.66)	25.2 (1.84)	10.3 (1.39)	12.1 (1.41)	12.9 (1.70)	11.3 (1.07)	10.3 (1.02)	9.1 (1.08)
Wisconsin	31.4 (1.68)	32.6 (1.51)	31.2 (1.46)	25.8 (1.52)	25.3 (1.72)	22.4 (1.46)	11.6 (0.92)	12.2 (1.03)	11.4 (0.97)	9.6 (0.87)	9.1 (0.95)	6.8 (0.69)
Wyoming	31.2 (1.23)	30.4 (1.08)	27.9 (1.12)	30.9 (1.17)	26.5 (1.08)	24.3 (1.11)	12.7 (0.93)	12.2 (0.72)	11.6 (0.83)	12.6 (0.73)	11.3 (0.65)	8.9 (0.60)

—Not available.
†Not applicable.
[1]The term "anywhere" is not used in the Youth Risk Behavior Survey (YRBS) questionnaire; students were simply asked how many times in the past 12 months they had been in a physical fight.
[2]In the question asking students about physical fights at school, "on school property" was not defined for survey respondents.
[3]Data for the U.S. total include both public and private schools and were collected through a national survey representing the entire country.
[4]Data include both public and private schools.

NOTE: State-level data include public schools only, with the exception of data for Ohio and South Dakota. Data for the U.S. total, Ohio, and South Dakota include both public and private schools. For specific states, a given year's data may be unavailable (1) because the state did not participate in the survey that year; (2) because the state omitted this particular survey item from the state-level questionnaire; or (3) because the state had an overall response rate of less than 60 percent (the overall response rate is the school response rate multiplied by the student response rate).
SOURCE: Centers for Disease Control and Prevention, Division of Adolescent and School Health, Youth Risk Behavior Surveillance System (YRBSS), 2003 through 2013. (This table was prepared June 2014.)

Table 231.40. Percentage of students in grades 9–12 who reported carrying a weapon at least 1 day during the previous 30 days, by location and selected student characteristics: Selected years, 1993 through 2013

[Standard errors appear in parentheses]

Location and student characteristic	1993		1995		1997		1999		2001		2003		2005		2007		2009		2011		2013	
1	2		3		4		5		6		7		8		9		10		11		12	
Anywhere (including on school property)[1]																						
Total	**22.1**	**(1.18)**	**20.0**	**(0.66)**	**18.3**	**(0.91)**	**17.3**	**(0.97)**	**17.4**	**(0.99)**	**17.1**	**(0.90)**	**18.5**	**(0.80)**	**18.0**	**(0.87)**	**17.5**	**(0.73)**	**16.6**	**(0.65)**	**17.9**	**(0.73)**
Sex																						
Male	34.3	(1.68)	31.1	(1.03)	27.7	(1.57)	28.6	(1.71)	29.3	(1.67)	26.9	(1.31)	29.8	(1.35)	28.5	(1.41)	27.1	(1.45)	25.9	(1.07)	28.1	(1.31)
Female	9.2	(0.85)	8.3	(0.72)	7.0	(0.54)	6.0	(0.56)	6.2	(0.41)	6.7	(0.60)	7.1	(0.43)	7.5	(0.66)	7.1	(0.38)	6.8	(0.41)	7.9	(0.56)
Race/ethnicity[2]																						
White	20.6	(1.43)	18.9	(0.93)	17.0	(1.29)	16.4	(1.36)	17.9	(1.30)	16.7	(0.95)	18.7	(1.13)	18.2	(1.28)	18.6	(1.16)	17.0	(1.05)	20.8	(0.90)
Black	28.5	(1.24)	21.8	(2.03)	21.7	(1.99)	17.2	(2.68)	15.2	(1.23)	17.3	(1.77)	16.4	(0.81)	17.2	(1.05)	14.4	(1.33)	14.2	(0.85)	12.5	(0.96)
Hispanic	24.4	(1.35)	24.7	(1.87)	23.3	(1.44)	18.7	(1.35)	16.5	(0.78)	16.5	(1.31)	19.0	(1.10)	18.5	(1.21)	17.2	(0.94)	16.2	(0.82)	15.5	(0.95)
Asian[3]	—	(†)	—	(†)	—	(†)	13.0	(2.01)	10.6	(2.10)	11.6	(2.67)	7.0	(1.70)	7.8	(1.41)	8.4	(1.28)	9.1	(1.57)	8.7	(1.79)
Pacific Islander[3]	—	(†)	—	(†)	—	(†)	25.3	(5.02)	17.4	(4.35)	16.3 !	(6.37)	20.0 !	(6.52)	25.5	(4.35)	20.3	(3.40)	20.7	(5.00)	12.6 !	(3.98)
American Indian/Alaska Native	34.2	(8.08)	32.0	(5.69)	26.2	(3.65)	21.8	(5.68)	31.2	(5.52)	29.3	(4.58)	25.6	(3.79)	20.6	(3.02)	20.7	(3.40)	27.6	(2.41)	17.8	(4.01)
Two or more races[3]	—	(†)	—	(†)	—	(†)	22.2	(3.34)	25.2	(3.41)	29.8	(5.03)	26.7	(3.11)	19.0	(2.46)	17.9	(1.61)	23.7	(2.58)	18.8	(2.09)
Grade																						
9th	25.5	(1.42)	22.6	(1.24)	22.6	(1.34)	17.6	(1.58)	19.8	(1.44)	18.0	(1.81)	19.9	(1.21)	20.1	(1.41)	18.0	(0.87)	17.3	(1.07)	17.5	(0.99)
10th	21.4	(1.11)	21.1	(0.94)	17.4	(1.33)	18.7	(1.31)	16.7	(1.11)	15.9	(1.14)	19.4	(1.19)	18.8	(1.21)	18.4	(1.51)	16.6	(0.89)	17.8	(1.09)
11th	21.5	(1.66)	20.3	(1.40)	18.2	(1.69)	16.1	(1.31)	16.8	(1.26)	18.2	(1.21)	17.1	(1.13)	16.7	(1.08)	16.2	(0.93)	16.2	(0.84)	17.9	(1.43)
12th	19.9	(1.46)	16.1	(0.93)	15.4	(1.65)	15.9	(1.44)	15.1	(1.28)	15.5	(1.06)	16.9	(0.95)	15.5	(1.28)	16.6	(0.85)	15.8	(0.90)	18.3	(1.17)
Urbanicity[4]																						
Urban	—	(†)	—	(†)	18.7	(1.34)	15.8	(0.85)	15.3	(0.99)	17.0	(1.32)	—	(†)	—	(†)	—	(†)	—	(†)	—	(†)
Suburban	—	(†)	—	(†)	16.8	(1.02)	17.0	(1.34)	17.4	(1.39)	16.5	(1.36)	—	(†)	—	(†)	—	(†)	—	(†)	—	(†)
Rural	—	(†)	—	(†)	22.3	(2.12)	22.3	(2.19)	23.0	(1.86)	18.9	(1.91)	—	(†)	—	(†)	—	(†)	—	(†)	—	(†)
On school property[5]																						
Total	**11.8**	**(0.73)**	**9.8**	**(0.45)**	**8.5**	**(0.79)**	**6.9**	**(0.60)**	**6.4**	**(0.52)**	**6.1**	**(0.57)**	**6.5**	**(0.46)**	**5.9**	**(0.37)**	**5.6**	**(0.32)**	**5.4**	**(0.35)**	**5.2**	**(0.44)**
Sex																						
Male	17.9	(0.96)	14.3	(0.76)	12.5	(1.50)	11.0	(1.07)	10.2	(0.88)	8.9	(0.74)	10.2	(0.83)	9.0	(0.65)	8.0	(0.52)	8.2	(0.59)	7.6	(0.70)
Female	5.1	(0.65)	4.9	(0.53)	3.7	(0.37)	2.8	(0.38)	2.9	(0.27)	3.1	(0.50)	2.6	(0.30)	2.7	(0.33)	2.9	(0.24)	2.3	(0.19)	3.0	(0.40)
Race/ethnicity[2]																						
White	10.9	(0.86)	9.0	(0.65)	7.8	(1.16)	6.4	(0.87)	6.1	(0.62)	5.5	(0.57)	6.1	(0.66)	5.3	(0.55)	5.6	(0.44)	5.1	(0.40)	5.7	(0.65)
Black	15.0	(0.85)	10.3	(1.13)	9.2	(0.98)	5.0	(0.50)	6.3	(0.92)	6.9	(0.96)	5.1	(0.66)	6.0	(0.46)	5.3	(0.74)	4.6	(0.67)	3.9	(0.42)
Hispanic	13.3	(1.09)	14.1	(1.63)	10.4	(0.99)	7.9	(0.73)	6.4	(0.53)	6.0	(0.56)	8.2	(0.91)	7.3	(0.82)	5.8	(0.58)	5.8	(0.70)	4.7	(0.61)
Asian[3]	—	(†)	—	(†)	—	(†)	6.5	(1.44)	7.2	(2.05)	6.6 !	(2.44)	2.8 !	(1.24)	4.1	(1.01)	3.6	(0.84)	4.3 !	(1.66)	3.8	(1.13)
Pacific Islander[3]	—	(†)	—	(†)	—	(†)	9.3	(2.66)	10.0 !	(3.05)	4.9 !	(2.05)	15.4 !	(6.10)	9.5 !	(3.40)	9.8	(2.33)	10.9 !	(3.73)	4.0 !	(1.95)
American Indian/Alaska Native	17.6 !	(5.70)	13.0 !	(4.35)	15.9	(3.68)	11.6 !	(5.13)	16.4	(4.02)	12.9	(3.40)	7.2	(1.60)	7.7	(2.08)	4.2 !	(1.50)	7.5	(1.62)	7.0 !	(3.22)
Two or more races[3]	—	(†)	—	(†)	—	(†)	11.4	(2.76)	13.2	(3.61)	13.3 !	(4.10)	11.9	(2.99)	5.0	(1.11)	5.8	(1.35)	7.5	(1.87)	6.3	(1.58)
Grade																						
9th	12.6	(0.73)	10.7	(0.76)	10.2	(0.90)	7.2	(1.07)	6.7	(0.66)	5.3	(1.13)	6.4	(0.75)	6.0	(0.59)	4.9	(0.46)	4.8	(0.50)	4.8	(0.69)
10th	11.5	(0.97)	10.4	(0.78)	7.7	(0.99)	6.6	(0.83)	6.7	(0.60)	6.0	(0.53)	6.9	(0.70)	5.8	(0.61)	6.1	(0.57)	6.1	(0.72)	4.8	(0.58)
11th	11.9	(1.41)	10.2	(0.94)	9.4	(1.33)	7.0	(0.60)	6.1	(0.74)	6.6	(0.80)	5.9	(0.71)	5.5	(0.68)	5.2	(0.44)	4.7	(0.44)	5.9	(1.19)
12th	10.8	(0.83)	7.6	(0.68)	7.0	(0.91)	6.2	(0.78)	6.1	(0.71)	6.4	(0.64)	6.7	(0.64)	6.0	(0.58)	6.0	(0.57)	5.6	(0.51)	5.3	(0.88)
Urbanicity[4]																						
Urban	—	(†)	—	(†)	7.0	(0.67)	7.2	(1.09)	6.0	(0.67)	5.6	(0.81)	—	(†)	—	(†)	—	(†)	—	(†)	—	(†)
Suburban	—	(†)	—	(†)	8.7	(0.68)	6.2	(0.74)	6.3	(0.68)	6.4	(1.01)	—	(†)	—	(†)	—	(†)	—	(†)	—	(†)
Rural	—	(†)	—	(†)	11.2	(2.19)	9.6	(1.61)	8.3	(1.48)	6.3	(0.67)	—	(†)	—	(†)	—	(†)	—	(†)	—	(†)

—Not available.
†Not applicable.
!Interpret data with caution. The coefficient of variation (CV) for this estimate is between 30 and 50 percent.
[1]The term "anywhere" is not used in the Youth Risk Behavior Survey (YRBS) questionnaire; students were simply asked how many days they carried a weapon during the past 30 days.
[2]Race categories exclude persons of Hispanic ethnicity.
[3]Before 1999, Asian students and Pacific Islander students were not categorized separately, and students could not be classified as Two or more races. Because the response categories changed in 1999, caution should be used in comparing data on race from 1993, 1995, and 1997 with data from later years.
[4]Refers to the Standard Metropolitan Statistical Area (MSA) status of the respondent's household as defined in 2000 by the U.S. Census Bureau. Categories include "central city of an MSA (Urban)," "in MSA but not in central city (Suburban)," and "not MSA (Rural)."
[5]In the question asking students about carrying a weapon at school, "on school property" was not defined for survey respondents.
NOTE: Respondents were asked about carrying "a weapon such as a gun, knife, or club."
SOURCE: Centers for Disease Control and Prevention, Division of Adolescent and School Health, Youth Risk Behavior Surveillance System (YRBSS), 1993 through 2013. (This table was prepared June 2014.)

Table 231.50. Percentage distribution of students in grades 9–12, by number of days they reported carrying a weapon anywhere or on school property during the previous 30 days and selected student characteristics: 2013

[Standard errors appear in parentheses]

Student characteristic	Anywhere (including on school property)[1]				On school property[2]			
	0 days	1 day	2 to 5 days	6 or more days	0 days	1 day	2 to 5 days	6 or more days
1	2	3	4	5	6	7	8	9
Total	**82.1 (0.73)**	**3.4 (0.19)**	**5.5 (0.22)**	**9.0 (0.67)**	**94.8 (0.44)**	**1.4 (0.14)**	**1.2 (0.13)**	**2.6 (0.42)**
Sex								
Male	71.9 (1.31)	5.0 (0.31)	8.9 (0.45)	14.2 (1.23)	92.4 (0.70)	2.0 (0.23)	1.9 (0.23)	3.7 (0.64)
Female	92.1 (0.56)	1.8 (0.20)	2.2 (0.19)	3.8 (0.39)	97.0 (0.40)	0.8 (0.15)	0.5 (0.14)	1.6 (0.33)
Race/ethnicity[3]								
White	79.2 (0.90)	3.4 (0.31)	6.1 (0.30)	11.3 (0.97)	94.3 (0.65)	1.3 (0.19)	1.1 (0.15)	3.3 (0.67)
Black	87.5 (0.96)	2.8 (0.42)	4.2 (0.63)	5.5 (0.57)	96.1 (0.42)	1.6 (0.29)	1.4 (0.31)	0.9 (0.18)
Hispanic	84.5 (0.95)	4.0 (0.37)	5.1 (0.46)	6.4 (0.59)	95.3 (0.61)	1.5 (0.33)	1.3 (0.28)	1.9 (0.29)
Asian	91.3 (1.79)	1.5 ! (0.55)	2.5 ! (0.76)	4.7 ! (1.49)	96.2 (1.13)	0.8 ! (0.41)	‡ (†)	2.4 ! (1.01)
Pacific Islander	87.4 (3.98)	‡ (†)	6.8 (1.95)	4.5 ! (1.99)	96.0 (1.95)	‡ (†)	‡ (†)	‡ (†)
American Indian/Alaska Native	82.2 (4.01)	‡ (†)	‡ (†)	9.9 (2.12)	93.0 (3.22)	‡ (†)	‡ (†)	2.7 ! (1.31)
Two or more races	81.2 (2.09)	5.3 (1.26)	6.8 (1.14)	6.6 (1.08)	93.7 (1.58)	2.4 ! (0.93)	‡ (†)	2.6 (0.69)
Grade								
9th	82.5 (0.99)	4.0 (0.37)	5.7 (0.69)	7.8 (0.69)	95.2 (0.69)	1.6 (0.28)	1.1 (0.28)	2.1 (0.38)
10th	82.2 (1.09)	3.8 (0.42)	5.9 (0.72)	8.0 (0.64)	95.2 (0.58)	1.7 (0.26)	1.0 (0.21)	2.1 (0.44)
11th	82.1 (1.43)	2.8 (0.34)	5.5 (0.49)	9.6 (1.29)	94.1 (1.19)	1.3 (0.34)	1.4 (0.25)	3.3 ! (1.10)
12th	81.7 (1.17)	2.9 (0.37)	4.9 (0.60)	10.5 (0.86)	94.7 (0.88)	0.9 (0.18)	1.4 (0.37)	3.1 (0.60)

†Not applicable.

!Interpret data with caution. The coefficient of variation (CV) for this estimate is between 30 and 50 percent.

‡Reporting standards not met. Either there are too few cases for a reliable estimate or the coefficient of variation (CV) is 50 percent or greater.

[1]The term "anywhere" is not used in the Youth Risk Behavior Survey (YRBS) questionnaire; students were simply asked how many days they carried a weapon during the past 30 days.

[2]In the question asking students about carrying a weapon at school, "on school property" was not defined for survey respondents.

[3]Race categories exclude persons of Hispanic ethnicity.

NOTE: Respondents were asked about carrying "a weapon such as a gun, knife, or club." Detail may not sum to totals because of rounding.

SOURCE: Centers for Disease Control and Prevention, Division of Adolescent and School Health, Youth Risk Behavior Surveillance System (YRBSS), 2013. (This table was prepared June 2014.)

Table 231.60. Percentage of public school students in grades 9–12 who reported carrying a weapon at least 1 day during the previous 30 days, by location and state: Selected years, 2003 through 2013

[Standard errors appear in parentheses]

State	Anywhere (including on school property)[1]						On school property[2]					
	2003	2005	2007	2009	2011	2013	2003	2005	2007	2009	2011	2013
1	2	3	4	5	6	7	8	9	10	11	12	13
United States[3]	**17.1 (0.90)**	**18.5 (0.80)**	**18.0 (0.87)**	**17.5 (0.73)**	**16.6 (0.65)**	**17.9 (0.73)**	**6.1 (0.57)**	**6.5 (0.46)**	**5.9 (0.37)**	**5.6 (0.32)**	**5.4 (0.35)**	**5.2 (0.44)**
Alabama	19.9 (1.44)	21.0 (1.72)	— (†)	22.9 (2.27)	21.5 (1.54)	23.1 (1.55)	7.3 (1.35)	8.4 (1.44)	— (†)	8.7 (1.42)	8.2 (1.02)	5.5 (0.56)
Alaska	18.4 (1.14)	— (†)	24.4 (1.61)	20.0 (1.30)	19.0 (1.19)	19.2 (1.31)	7.1 (0.81)	— (†)	8.4 (1.07)	7.8 (0.83)	5.7 (0.72)	6.1 (0.80)
Arizona	18.4 (0.82)	20.6 (0.84)	20.5 (0.91)	19.9 (1.25)	17.5 (1.17)	17.5 (1.17)	5.8 (0.68)	7.4 (0.53)	7.0 (0.75)	6.5 (0.64)	5.7 (0.59)	4.8 (0.86)
Arkansas	— (†)	25.9 (1.15)	20.7 (1.36)	22.9 (1.82)	21.1 (1.76)	27.1 (1.76)	— (†)	10.5 (1.10)	6.8 (0.85)	8.4 (1.02)	6.5 (0.95)	9.1 (1.10)
California	— (†)	— (†)	— (†)	— (†)	— (†)	— (†)	— (†)	— (†)	— (†)	— (†)	— (†)	— (†)
Colorado	— (†)	17.0 (1.57)	— (†)	16.7 (1.27)	15.5 (1.31)	— (†)	— (†)	5.4 (0.81)	— (†)	5.5 (0.90)	5.5 (0.69)	— (†)
Connecticut	— (†)	16.3 (1.30)	17.2 (1.72)	12.4 (0.89)	— (†)	— (†)	— (†)	6.4 (0.83)	5.5 (1.03)	3.9 (0.45)	6.6 (0.67)	6.6 (0.82)
Delaware	16.0 (0.88)	16.6 (1.04)	17.1 (1.00)	18.5 (0.92)	13.5 (0.88)	14.4 (0.80)	5.0 (0.47)	5.7 (0.54)	5.4 (0.55)	5.1 (0.59)	5.2 (0.57)	3.1 (0.34)
District of Columbia	25.0 (1.40)	17.2 (1.11)	21.3 (1.45)	— (†)	18.9 (1.34)	— (†)	10.6 (0.96)	6.7 (0.60)	7.4 (0.76)	— (†)	5.5 (0.88)	— (†)
Florida	17.2 (0.76)	15.2 (0.68)	18.0 (0.93)	17.3 (0.60)	15.6 (0.76)	15.7 (0.67)	5.3 (0.38)	4.7 (0.41)	5.6 (0.41)	4.7 (0.35)	— (†)	— (†)
Georgia	18.7 (1.17)	22.1 (1.99)	19.5 (0.96)	18.8 (1.11)	22.8 (2.25)	18.5 (1.51)	5.0 (0.52)	7.5 (1.50)	5.3 (0.48)	6.0 (0.90)	8.6 (1.80)	4.2 (0.66)
Hawaii	— (†)	13.3 (1.03)	14.8 (1.56)	15.9 (2.06)	13.9 (0.81)	10.5 (0.87)	— (†)	4.9 (0.72)	3.7 (0.92)	4.7 (0.63)	4.2 (0.45)	— (†)
Idaho	— (†)	23.9 (1.45)	23.6 (1.35)	21.8 (1.15)	22.8 (1.30)	27.1 (1.31)	7.7 (0.90)	— (†)	8.9 (0.96)	6.7 (0.59)	6.3 (0.78)	6.5 (0.92)
Illinois	— (†)	— (†)	14.3 (1.01)	16.0 (1.04)	12.6 (0.91)	15.8 (1.22)	— (†)	— (†)	3.7 (0.67)	4.8 (0.59)	3.9 (0.53)	4.7 (0.57)
Indiana	17.8 (1.93)	19.2 (1.25)	20.9 (0.80)	18.1 (1.58)	17.0 (1.46)	— (†)	6.2 (0.91)	5.8 (0.71)	6.9 (0.64)	5.7 (0.80)	3.7 (0.46)	— (†)
Iowa	— (†)	15.7 (1.49)	12.8 (1.13)	— (†)	15.8 (1.26)	— (†)	— (†)	4.3 (0.70)	4.4 (0.61)	— (†)	4.5 (0.76)	— (†)
Kansas	— (†)	16.2 (1.37)	18.4 (1.19)	16.0 (1.26)	— (†)	16.1 (0.87)	— (†)	4.9 (0.85)	5.7 (0.75)	5.1 (0.65)	5.2 (0.72)	— (†)
Kentucky	18.5 (1.20)	23.1 (1.49)	24.4 (1.08)	21.7 (1.72)	22.8 (1.72)	20.7 (1.35)	7.4 (0.86)	6.8 (0.72)	8.0 (0.59)	6.5 (0.77)	7.4 (1.25)	6.4 (0.73)
Louisiana	— (†)	— (†)	— (†)	19.6 (1.73)	22.2 (0.98)	22.8 (2.78)	— (†)	— (†)	— (†)	5.8 (1.12)	4.2 (1.01)	7.0 (1.37)
Maine	16.5 (1.20)	18.3 (2.00)	15.0 (1.47)	— (†)	— (†)	— (†)	6.6 (0.91)	5.9 (1.03)	4.9 (0.70)	— (†)	8.0 (0.45)	7.1 (0.46)
Maryland	— (†)	19.1 (1.59)	19.3 (1.51)	16.6 (1.19)	15.9 (1.10)	15.8 (0.27)	— (†)	6.9 (0.88)	5.9 (0.81)	4.6 (0.58)	5.3 (0.55)	4.8 (0.13)
Massachusetts	13.5 (0.89)	15.2 (0.88)	14.9 (0.88)	12.8 (1.00)	12.3 (0.95)	11.6 (0.83)	5.0 (0.50)	5.8 (0.59)	5.0 (0.48)	4.4 (0.58)	3.7 (0.46)	3.1 (0.50)
Michigan	15.2 (0.89)	15.8 (1.49)	17.9 (1.30)	16.6 (0.69)	15.7 (0.94)	15.5 (1.06)	5.1 (0.66)	4.7 (0.54)	5.0 (0.66)	5.4 (0.33)	3.5 (0.37)	3.8 (0.35)
Minnesota	— (†)	— (†)	— (†)	— (†)	— (†)	— (†)	— (†)	— (†)	— (†)	— (†)	— (†)	— (†)
Mississippi	20.0 (1.78)	— (†)	17.3 (1.33)	17.2 (1.02)	18.0 (1.39)	19.1 (1.56)	5.2 (0.78)	— (†)	4.8 (0.60)	4.5 (0.48)	4.2 (0.76)	4.1 (0.66)
Missouri	16.8 (1.87)	19.4 (1.79)	18.6 (1.48)	16.0 (1.44)	— (†)	22.2 (1.93)	5.5 (1.04)	7.3 (0.99)	4.6 (0.83)	5.3 (1.02)	— (†)	— (†)
Montana	19.4 (0.88)	21.4 (1.20)	22.1 (0.76)	23.0 (1.07)	23.5 (0.96)	25.7 (0.84)	7.2 (0.56)	10.2 (0.89)	9.7 (0.57)	7.9 (0.67)	9.3 (0.69)	9.9 (0.58)
Nebraska	16.0 (1.06)	17.9 (0.89)	— (†)	— (†)	18.6 (0.90)	— (†)	5.0 (0.53)	4.8 (0.48)	— (†)	— (†)	3.8 (0.45)	— (†)
Nevada	14.9 (1.09)	18.4 (1.32)	14.5 (1.08)	19.1 (1.08)	— (†)	16.0 (1.50)	6.3 (0.67)	6.8 (0.91)	4.7 (0.61)	6.2 (0.62)	— (†)	3.3 (0.64)
New Hampshire	15.1 (1.59)	16.2 (1.26)	18.1 (1.46)	— (†)	14.5 (1.04)	— (†)	5.8 (1.00)	6.5 (0.93)	5.8 (0.61)	8.8 (1.00)	— (†)	— (†)
New Jersey	— (†)	10.5 (0.95)	— (†)	9.6 (0.81)	9.6 (1.17)	10.2 (1.08)	— (†)	3.1 (0.53)	— (†)	3.1 (0.45)	— (†)	2.7 (0.34)
New Mexico	— (†)	24.5 (1.44)	27.5 (1.20)	27.4 (0.90)	22.8 (0.93)	22.2 (0.88)	— (†)	8.0 (0.29)	9.3 (0.66)	8.1 (0.59)	6.5 (0.51)	5.4 (0.42)
New York	13.5 (1.01)	14.3 (0.74)	14.2 (0.76)	13.9 (0.98)	12.6 (0.76)	12.8 (0.82)	5.2 (0.51)	5.2 (0.42)	4.7 (0.41)	4.8 (0.64)	4.2 (0.32)	4.0 (0.38)
North Carolina	19.2 (1.49)	21.5 (1.35)	21.2 (1.19)	19.6 (0.95)	20.8 (1.24)	20.6 (1.34)	6.3 (0.79)	6.4 (0.77)	6.8 (0.94)	4.7 (0.57)	6.1 (0.64)	4.5 (0.67)
North Dakota	— (†)	— (†)	— (†)	— (†)	— (†)	— (†)	5.7 (0.98)	6.0 (0.74)	5.0 (0.57)	5.4 (0.64)	5.7 (0.73)	6.4 (0.75)
Ohio[4]	12.5 (1.40)	15.2 (1.27)	16.6 (1.42)	— (†)	16.4 (1.37)	14.2 (1.61)	3.6 (0.75)	4.4 (0.63)	4.1 (0.51)	— (†)	— (†)	— (†)
Oklahoma	21.8 (1.72)	18.9 (1.38)	22.3 (1.65)	19.0 (1.44)	19.4 (1.86)	19.9 (1.41)	8.0 (1.01)	7.0 (0.77)	9.0 (1.43)	5.6 (0.79)	6.1 (1.14)	6.0 (0.77)
Oregon	— (†)	— (†)	— (†)	— (†)	— (†)	— (†)	— (†)	— (†)	— (†)	— (†)	— (†)	— (†)
Pennsylvania	— (†)	— (†)	— (†)	14.8 (1.28)	— (†)	— (†)	— (†)	— (†)	— (†)	3.3 (0.47)	— (†)	— (†)
Rhode Island	12.3 (1.01)	12.4 (0.90)	12.0 (0.74)	10.4 (0.50)	11.2 (0.82)	— (†)	5.9 (0.85)	4.9 (0.41)	4.9 (0.63)	4.0 (0.33)	4.0 (0.39)	5.0 (0.78)
South Carolina	— (†)	20.5 (1.42)	19.8 (1.69)	20.4 (2.22)	23.4 (1.86)	21.2 (1.25)	— (†)	6.7 (0.82)	4.8 (0.79)	4.6 (0.67)	6.3 (0.89)	3.7 (0.48)
South Dakota[4]	— (†)	— (†)	— (†)	— (†)	— (†)	— (†)	7.1 (0.73)	8.3 (0.72)	6.3 (0.80)	9.2 (0.76)	5.7 (0.52)	6.8 (0.87)
Tennessee	21.3 (2.06)	24.1 (1.58)	22.6 (1.41)	20.5 (1.64)	21.1 (1.34)	19.2 (1.70)	5.4 (0.80)	8.1 (0.92)	5.6 (0.70)	5.1 (0.70)	5.2 (0.80)	5.4 (0.79)
Texas	— (†)	19.3 (0.93)	18.8 (0.71)	18.2 (0.89)	17.6 (0.73)	18.4 (1.33)	— (†)	7.9 (0.63)	6.8 (0.55)	6.4 (0.76)	4.9 (0.45)	5.6 (0.68)
Utah	15.3 (1.80)	17.7 (1.70)	17.1 (1.38)	16.0 (1.40)	16.8 (1.48)	17.2 (1.19)	5.6 (1.24)	7.0 (1.03)	7.5 (1.00)	4.6 (0.63)	5.9 (1.01)	5.0 (0.57)
Vermont	— (†)	— (†)	— (†)	— (†)	— (†)	— (†)	8.3 (0.31)	9.1 (0.90)	9.6 (1.05)	9.0 (0.61)	9.1 (0.73)	10.4 (1.28)
Virginia	— (†)	— (†)	— (†)	— (†)	20.4 (1.26)	15.8 (0.69)	— (†)	— (†)	— (†)	— (†)	5.7 (0.64)	— (†)
Washington	— (†)	— (†)	— (†)	— (†)	— (†)	— (†)	— (†)	— (†)	— (†)	— (†)	— (†)	— (†)
West Virginia	20.7 (1.37)	22.3 (1.32)	21.3 (1.52)	24.4 (1.05)	20.7 (1.64)	24.3 (2.16)	6.6 (1.25)	8.5 (1.00)	6.9 (0.89)	6.5 (0.72)	5.5 (0.75)	5.5 (0.99)
Wisconsin	13.2 (0.81)	15.8 (1.19)	12.7 (0.76)	10.9 (0.81)	10.4 (0.66)	14.4 (1.32)	3.2 (0.43)	3.9 (0.54)	3.6 (0.49)	3.4 (0.50)	3.1 (0.41)	3.2 (0.52)
Wyoming	24.6 (1.49)	28.0 (1.17)	26.8 (1.28)	26.0 (1.04)	27.1 (1.19)	28.8 (0.95)	10.1 (0.91)	10.0 (0.71)	11.4 (0.76)	11.5 (0.81)	10.5 (0.71)	9.9 (0.62)

—Not available.
†Not applicable.
[1]The term "anywhere" is not used in the Youth Risk Behavior Survey (YRBS) questionnaire; students were simply asked how many days they carried a weapon during the past 30 days.
[2]In the question asking students about carrying a weapon at school, "on school property" was not defined for survey respondents.
[3]Data for the U.S. total include both public and private schools and were collected through a national survey representing the entire country.
[4]Data include both public and private schools.
NOTE: Respondents were asked about carrying "a weapon such as a gun, knife, or club." State-level data include public schools only, with the exception of data for Ohio and South Dakota. Data for the U.S. total, Ohio, and South Dakota include both public and private schools. For specific states, a given year's data may be unavailable (1) because the state did not participate in the survey that year; (2) because the state omitted this particular survey item from the state-level questionnaire; or (3) because the state had an overall response rate of less than 60 percent (the overall response rate is the school response rate multiplied by the student response rate).
SOURCE: Centers for Disease Control and Prevention, Division of Adolescent and School Health, Youth Risk Behavior Surveillance System (YRBSS), 2003 through 2013. (This table was prepared June 2014.)

Table 231.65. Number of incidents of students bringing firearms to or possessing firearms at a public school and rate of incidents per 100,000 students, by state: 2009–10 through 2013–14

State	Number of firearm incidents					Rate of firearm incidents per 100,000 students				
	2009–10	2010–11	2011–12	2012–13	2013–14	2009–10	2010–11	2011–12	2012–13	2013–14
1	2	3	4	5	6	7	8	9	10	11
United States	**1,749**	**1,685**	**1,333**	**1,556**	**1,501**	**3.5**	**3.4**	**2.7**	**3.1**	**3.0**
Alabama	23	15	5	46	29	3.1	2.0	0.7	6.2	3.9
Alaska	7	3	5	5	4	5.3	2.3	3.8	3.8	3.1
Arizona	18	7	22	18	17	1.7	0.7	2.0	1.7	1.5
Arkansas	32	45	50	65	51	6.7	9.3	10.3	13.4	10.4
California	267	220	79	129	92	4.3	3.5	1.3	2.0	1.5
Colorado	23	19	17	23	21	2.8	2.3	2.0	2.7	2.4
Connecticut	29	12	21	19	7	5.1	2.1	3.8	3.4	1.3
Delaware	7	2	1	2	5	5.5	1.5	0.8	1.6	3.8
District of Columbia	2	2	2	0	2	2.9	2.8	2.7	0.0	2.6
Florida	66	63	51	62	71	2.5	2.4	1.9	2.3	2.6
Georgia	132	154	104	118	83	7.9	9.2	6.2	6.9	4.8
Hawaii	1	2	1	0	0	0.6	1.1	0.5	0.0	0.0
Idaho	12	—	10	5	4	4.3	—	3.6	1.8	1.3
Illinois	21	5	5	9	4	1.0	0.2	0.2	0.4	0.2
Indiana	42	28	26	27	25	4.0	2.7	2.5	2.6	2.4
Iowa	5	2	2	3	3	1.0	0.4	0.4	0.6	0.6
Kansas	32	20	9	28	19	6.7	4.1	1.9	5.7	3.8
Kentucky	12	15	23	20	43	1.8	2.2	3.4	2.9	6.3
Louisiana	50	49	43	66	80	7.2	7.0	6.1	9.3	11.2
Maine	2	2	4	2	0	1.1	1.1	2.1	1.1	0.0
Maryland	8	8	10	11	7	0.9	0.9	1.2	1.3	0.8
Massachusetts	11	12	7	10	19	1.1	1.3	0.7	1.0	2.0
Michigan	37	80	60	70	41	2.2	5.0	3.8	4.5	2.6
Minnesota	21	23	10	19	22	2.5	2.7	1.2	2.2	2.6
Mississippi	42	32	32	38	49	8.5	6.5	6.5	7.7	9.9
Missouri	104	120	81	110	88	11.3	13.1	8.8	12.0	9.6
Montana	14	11	9	8	8	9.9	7.8	6.3	5.6	5.6
Nebraska	8	13	10	16	14	2.7	4.4	3.3	5.3	4.6
Nevada	18	14	14	8	29	4.2	3.2	3.2	1.8	6.4
New Hampshire	2	5	6	4	9	1.0	2.6	3.1	2.1	4.8
New Jersey	5	5	6	5	5	0.4	0.4	0.4	0.4	0.4
New Mexico	18	25	18	13	15	5.4	7.4	5.3	3.8	4.4
New York	17[1]	18[1]	46	28	45	0.6[1]	0.7[1]	1.7	1.0	1.6
North Carolina	23	9	9	11	19	1.6	0.6	0.6	0.7	1.2
North Dakota	2	11	2	5	6	2.1	11.4	2.0	4.9	5.8
Ohio	103	91	76	71	102	5.8	5.2	4.4	4.1	5.9
Oklahoma	37	22	27	39	21	5.7	3.3	4.1	5.8	3.1
Oregon	14	17	19	16	15	2.4	3.0	3.3	2.7	2.5
Pennsylvania	27	24	23	34	23	1.5	1.3	1.3	1.9	1.3
Rhode Island	3	7	1	0	2	2.1	4.9	0.7	0.0	1.4
South Carolina	32	8	26	49	51	4.4	1.1	3.6	6.7	6.8
South Dakota	8	2	10	9	4	6.5	1.6	7.8	6.9	3.1
Tennessee	79	43	82	64	57	8.1	4.4	8.2	6.4	5.7
Texas	103	93	85	100	103	2.1	1.9	1.7	2.0	2.0
Utah	5	76	99[2]	49	45	0.9	13.0	16.5[2]	8.0	7.2
Vermont	1	3	1	2	9	1.1	3.1	1.1	2.2	10.1
Virginia	34	30	32	31	22	2.7	2.4	2.5	2.4	1.7
Washington	162	173	26	33	46	15.6	16.6	2.5	3.1	4.3
West Virginia	4	3	14	1	16	1.4	1.1	4.9	0.4	5.7
Wisconsin	19	33	8	37	40	2.2	3.8	0.9	4.2	4.6
Wyoming	5	9	4	18	9	5.7	10.1	4.4	19.7	9.7

—Not available.
[1]Data for New York City Public Schools were not reported.
[2]The state reported a total state-level firearm incident count that was less than the sum of its reported district-level counts. The sum of the district-level firearm incident counts is displayed instead of the reported state-level count.
NOTE: Separate counts were collected for incidents involving handguns, rifles/shotguns, other firearms, and multiple types of firearms. The counts reported here exclude the "other firearms" category.

SOURCE: U.S. Department of Education, National Center for Education Statistics, ED*Facts* file 094, Data Group 601, extracted September 23, 2015, from the ED*Facts* Data Warehouse (internal U.S. Department of Education source); Common Core of Data (CCD), "State Nonfiscal Survey of Public Elementary and Secondary Education," 2009–10 through 2013–14. (This table was prepared September 2015.)

Table 231.70. Percentage of students ages 12–18 who reported having access to a loaded gun, without adult permission, at school or away from school during the school year, by selected student and school characteristics: Selected years, 2007 through 2013

[Standard errors appear in parentheses]

Student or school characteristic	2007		2009		2011		2013	
1	2		3		4		5	
Total	**6.7**	**(0.40)**	**5.5**	**(0.47)**	**4.7**	**(0.43)**	**3.7**	**(0.38)**
Sex								
Male	8.4	(0.56)	7.6	(0.72)	5.6	(0.59)	3.9	(0.56)
Female	5.0	(0.47)	3.4	(0.44)	3.6	(0.44)	3.4	(0.35)
Race/ethnicity[1]								
White	7.7	(0.55)	6.4	(0.60)	5.3	(0.50)	4.2	(0.45)
Black	6.2	(0.98)	3.9	(0.92)	4.1	(0.86)	3.4	(0.78)
Hispanic	4.8	(0.79)	4.9	(0.90)	4.1	(0.89)	3.0	(0.71)
Asian	‡	(†)	‡	(†)	‡	(†)	‡	(†)
Other	9.3	(2.30)	5.4 !	(2.40)	‡	(†)	4.7 !	(1.79)
Grade								
6th	2.4	(0.64)	0.8 !	(0.40)	2.0 !	(0.89)	‡	(†)
7th	2.6	(0.56)	3.6	(0.84)	3.0	(0.63)	2.0	(0.50)
8th	3.2	(0.63)	3.2	(0.63)	2.9	(0.60)	2.4	(0.62)
9th	6.8	(0.98)	4.4	(0.80)	4.0	(0.75)	3.3	(0.80)
10th	9.2	(1.13)	7.3	(1.02)	5.3	(0.70)	4.7	(0.80)
11th	9.9	(1.00)	7.6	(1.16)	6.4	(1.06)	5.9	(0.99)
12th	12.3	(1.33)	9.8	(1.44)	8.2	(1.06)	5.8	(0.99)
Urbanicity[2]								
Urban	5.8	(0.67)	4.7	(0.72)	4.1	(0.61)	3.2	(0.54)
Suburban	6.4	(0.59)	5.5	(0.57)	4.9	(0.55)	3.7	(0.46)
Rural	9.1	(1.04)	7.1	(1.39)	4.9	(0.92)	4.6	(0.91)
Control of school								
Public	6.9	(0.44)	5.8	(0.49)	4.8	(0.42)	3.7	(0.40)
Private	4.5	(0.88)	2.3 !	(0.83)	3.2 !	(0.98)	3.6	(1.01)

†Not applicable.
!Interpret data with caution. The coefficient of variation (CV) for this estimate is between 30 and 50 percent.
‡Reporting standards not met. Either there are too few cases for a reliable estimate or the coefficient of variation (CV) is 50 percent or greater.
[1]Race categories exclude persons of Hispanic ethnicity. "Other" includes American Indians/Alaska Natives, Pacific Islanders, and persons reporting that they are of Two or more races.
[2]Refers to the Standard Metropolitan Statistical Area (MSA) status of the respondent's household as defined in 2000 by the U.S. Census Bureau. Categories include "central city of an MSA (Urban)," "in MSA but not in central city (Suburban)," and "not MSA (Rural)."
SOURCE: U.S. Department of Justice, Bureau of Justice Statistics, School Crime Supplement (SCS) to the National Crime Victimization Survey, 2007 through 2013. (This table was prepared October 2014.)

Table 214.10. Number of public school districts and public and private elementary and secondary schools: Selected years, 1869–70 through 2013–14

School year	Regular public school districts[1]	Total, all public and private schools	Public schools[2]: Total, all public schools[4]	Public schools[2]: Total, schools with reported grade spans[5]	Public schools[2]: Schools with elementary grades: Total	Public schools[2]: Schools with elementary grades: One-teacher	Public schools[2]: Schools with secondary grades	Private schools[2,3]: Total, all private schools	Private schools[2,3]: Schools with elementary grades	Private schools[2,3]: Schools with secondary grades
1	2	3	4	5	6	7	8	9	10	11
1869–70	—	—	116,312	—	—	—	—	—	—	—
1879–80	—	—	178,122	—	—	—	—	—	—	—
1889–90	—	—	224,526	—	—	—	—	—	—	—
1899–1900	—	—	248,279	—	—	—	—	—	—	—
1909–10	—	—	265,474	—	—	212,448	—	—	—	—
1919–20	—	—	271,319	—	—	187,948	—	—	—	—
1929–30	—	—	248,117	—	238,306	148,712	23,930	—	9,275 [6]	3,258 [6]
1939–40	117,108 [7]	—	226,762	—	—	113,600	—	—	11,306 [6]	3,568 [6]
1949–50	83,718 [7]	—	—	—	128,225	59,652	24,542	—	10,375 [6]	3,331 [6]
1951–52	71,094 [7]	—	—	—	123,763	50,742	23,746	—	10,666 [6]	3,322 [6]
1959–60	40,520 [7]	—	—	—	91,853	20,213	25,784	—	13,574 [6]	4,061 [6]
1961–62	35,676 [7]	125,634	107,260	—	81,910	13,333	25,350	18,374	14,762 [6]	4,129 [6]
1963–64	31,705 [7]	—	104,015	—	77,584	9,895	26,431	—	—	4,451 [6]
1965–66	26,983 [7]	117,662	99,813	—	73,216	6,491	26,597	17,849 [6]	15,340 [6]	4,606 [6]
1967–68	22,010 [7]	—	—	94,197	70,879	4,146	27,011	—	—	—
1970–71	17,995 [7]	—	—	89,372	65,800	1,815	25,352	—	14,372 [6]	3,770 [6]
1973–74	16,730 [7]	—	—	88,655	65,070	1,365	25,906	—	—	—
1975–76	16,376 [7]	—	88,597	87,034	63,242	1,166	25,330	—	—	—
1976–77	16,271 [7]	—	—	86,501	62,644	1,111	25,378	19,910 [6]	16,385 [6]	5,904 [6]
1978–79	16,014 [7]	—	—	84,816	61,982	1,056	24,504	19,489 [6]	16,097 [6]	5,766 [6]
1979–80	15,944 [7]	—	87,004	—	—	—	—	—	—	—
1980–81	15,912 [7]	106,746	85,982	83,688	61,069	921	24,362	20,764 [6]	16,792 [6]	5,678 [6]
1982–83	15,824 [7]	—	84,740	82,039	59,656	798	23,988	—	—	—
1983–84	15,747 [7]	111,872	84,178	81,418	59,082	838	23,947	27,694	20,872	7,862
1984–85	—	—	84,007	81,147	58,827	825	23,916	—	—	—
1985–86	—	—	—	—	—	—	—	25,616	20,252	7,387
1986–87	15,713	—	83,421	82,316	60,811	763	23,481	—	—	—
1987–88	15,577	110,055	83,248	81,416	59,754	729	23,841	26,807	22,959	8,418
1988–89	15,376	—	83,165	81,579	60,176	583	23,638	—	—	—
1989–90	15,367	110,137	83,425	81,880	60,699	630	23,461	26,712	24,221	10,197
1990–91	15,358	109,228	84,538	82,475	61,340	617	23,460	24,690	22,223	8,989
1991–92	15,173	110,576	84,578	82,506	61,739	569	23,248	25,998	23,523	9,282
1992–93	15,025	—	84,497	82,896	62,225	430	23,220	—	—	—
1993–94	14,881	111,486	85,393	83,431	62,726	442	23,379	26,093	23,543	10,555
1994–95	14,772	—	86,221	84,476	63,572	458	23,668	—	—	—
1995–96	14,766	121,519	87,125	84,958	63,961	474	23,793	34,394	32,401	10,942
1996–97	14,841	—	88,223	86,092	64,785	487	24,287	—	—	—
1997–98	14,805	123,403	89,508	87,541	65,859	476	24,802	33,895	31,408	10,779
1998–99	14,891	—	90,874	89,259	67,183	463	25,797	—	—	—
1999–2000	14,928	125,007	92,012	90,538	68,173	423	26,407	32,995	30,457	10,693
2000–01	14,859	—	93,273	91,691	69,697	411	27,090	—	—	—
2001–02	14,559	130,007	94,112	92,696	70,516	408	27,468	35,895	33,191	11,846
2002–03	14,465	—	95,615	93,869	71,270	366	28,151	—	—	—
2003–04	14,383	130,407	95,726	93,977	71,195	376	28,219	34,681	31,988	11,188
2004–05	14,205	—	96,513	95,001	71,556	338	29,017	—	—	—
2005–06	14,166	132,436	97,382	95,731	71,733	326	29,705	35,054	32,127	12,184
2006–07	13,856	—	98,793	96,362	72,442	313	29,904	—	—	—
2007–08	13,838	132,656	98,916	97,654	73,011	288	30,542	33,740	30,808	11,870
2008–09	13,809	—	98,706	97,119	72,771	237	29,971	—	—	—
2009–10	13,625	132,183	98,817	97,521	72,870	217	30,381	33,366	30,590	11,491
2010–11	13,588	—	98,817	97,767	73,323	224	30,681	—	—	—
2011–12	13,567	129,189	98,328	97,357	73,000	205	30,668	30,861	28,184	11,165
2012–13	13,515	—	98,454	97,369	73,089	196	30,651	—	—	—
2013–14	13,491	131,890	98,271	97,292	73,239	193	30,258	33,619	30,919	11,110

—Not available.

[1]Regular districts exclude regional education service agencies and supervisory union administrative centers, state-operated agencies, federally operated agencies, and other types of local education agencies, such as independent charter schools.

[2]Schools with both elementary and secondary grades are included under elementary schools and also under secondary schools.

[3]Data for most years prior to 1976–77 are partly estimated. Prior to 1995–96, excludes schools with highest grade of kindergarten.

[4]Includes schools not classified by grade span, which are not shown separately.

[5]Includes elementary, secondary, and combined elementary/secondary schools.

[6]These data cannot be compared directly with the data for years after 1980–81.

[7]Because of expanded survey coverage, data are not directly comparable with figures after 1983–84.

SOURCE: U.S. Department of Education, National Center for Education Statistics, *Annual Report of the Commissioner of Education*, 1870 through 1910; *Biennial Survey of Education in the United States*, 1919–20 through 1949–50; *Statistics of State School Systems*, 1951–52 through 1967–68; *Statistics of Public Elementary and Secondary School Systems*, 1970–71 through 1980–81; *Statistics of Public and Nonpublic Elementary and Secondary Day Schools, 1968–69; Statistics of Nonpublic Elementary and Secondary Schools*, 1970–71; *Private Schools in American Education*; Schools and Staffing Survey (SASS), "Private School Questionnaire," 1987–88 and 1990–91; Private School Universe Survey (PSS), 1989–90 through 2013–14; and Common Core of Data (CCD), "Local Education Agency Universe Survey" and "Public Elementary/Secondary School Universe Survey," 1982–83 through 2013–14. (This table was prepared January 2016.)

Table 214.20. Number and percentage distribution of regular public school districts and students, by enrollment size of district: Selected years, 1979–80 through 2013–14

Year	Enrollment size of district									
	Total	25,000 or more	10,000 to 24,999	5,000 to 9,999	2,500 to 4,999	1,000 to 2,499	600 to 999	300 to 599	1 to 299	Size not reported
1	2	3	4	5	6	7	8	9	10	11
	Number of districts									
1979–80	15,944	181	478	1,106	2,039	3,475	1,841	2,298	4,223	303
1989–90	15,367	179	479	913	1,937	3,547	1,801	2,283	3,910	318
1999–2000	14,928	238	579	1,036	2,068	3,457	1,814	2,081	3,298	357
2001–02	14,559	243	573	1,067	2,031	3,429	1,744	2,015	3,127	330
2002–03	14,465	248	587	1,062	2,033	3,411	1,745	1,987	3,117	275
2003–04	14,383	256	594	1,058	2,031	3,421	1,728	1,981	2,994	320
2004–05	14,205	264	589	1,056	2,018	3,391	1,739	1,931	2,881	336
2005–06	14,166	269	594	1,066	2,015	3,335	1,768	1,895	2,857	367
2006–07	13,856	275	598	1,066	2,006	3,334	1,730	1,898	2,685	264
2007–08	13,838	281	589	1,062	2,006	3,292	1,753	1,890	2,692	273
2008–09	13,809	280	594	1,049	1,995	3,272	1,766	1,886	2,721	246
2009–10	13,625	284	598	1,044	1,985	3,242	1,750	1,891	2,707	124
2010–11	13,588	282	600	1,052	1,975	3,224	1,738	1,887	2,687	143
2011–12	13,567	286	592	1,044	1,952	3,222	1,755	1,911	2,676	129
2012–13	13,515	290	588	1,048	1,924	3,227	1,751	1,908	2,678	101
2013–14	13,491	286	596	1,046	1,920	3,186	1,791	1,894	2,668	104
	Percentage distribution of districts									
1979–80	100.0	1.1	3.0	6.9	12.8	21.8	11.5	14.4	26.5	1.9
1989–90	100.0	1.2	3.1	5.9	12.6	23.1	11.7	14.9	25.4	2.1
1999–2000	100.0	1.6	3.9	6.9	13.9	23.2	12.2	13.9	22.1	2.4
2001–02	100.0	1.7	3.9	7.3	14.0	23.6	12.0	13.8	21.5	2.3
2002–03	100.0	1.7	4.1	7.3	14.1	23.6	12.1	13.7	21.5	1.9
2003–04	100.0	1.8	4.1	7.4	14.1	23.8	12.0	13.8	20.8	2.2
2004–05	100.0	1.9	4.1	7.4	14.2	23.9	12.2	13.6	20.3	2.4
2005–06	100.0	1.9	4.2	7.5	14.2	23.5	12.5	13.4	20.2	2.6
2006–07	100.0	2.0	4.3	7.7	14.5	24.1	12.5	13.7	19.4	1.9
2007–08	100.0	2.0	4.3	7.7	14.5	23.8	12.7	13.7	19.5	2.0
2008–09	100.0	2.0	4.3	7.6	14.4	23.7	12.8	13.7	19.7	1.8
2009–10	100.0	2.1	4.4	7.7	14.6	23.8	12.8	13.9	19.9	0.9
2010–11	100.0	2.1	4.4	7.7	14.5	23.7	12.8	13.9	19.8	1.1
2011–12	100.0	2.1	4.4	7.7	14.4	23.7	12.9	14.1	19.7	1.0
2012–13	100.0	2.1	4.4	7.8	14.2	23.9	13.0	14.1	19.8	0.7
2013–14	100.0	2.1	4.4	7.8	14.2	23.6	13.3	14.0	19.8	0.8
	Number of students									
1979–80	41,882,000	11,415,000	7,004,000	7,713,000	7,076,000	5,698,000	1,450,000	1,005,000	521,000	†
1989–90	40,069,756	11,209,889	7,107,362	6,347,103	6,731,334	5,763,282	1,402,623	997,434	510,729	†
1999–2000	46,318,635	14,886,636	8,656,672	7,120,704	7,244,407	5,620,962	1,426,280	911,127	451,847	†
2001–02	46,906,607	15,356,867	8,756,777	7,393,237	7,129,358	5,576,508	1,375,571	885,061	433,228	†
2002–03	47,379,395	15,690,805	8,957,891	7,348,643	7,150,205	5,547,189	1,375,070	874,163	435,429	†
2003–04	47,685,982	15,939,776	9,039,697	7,342,745	7,160,367	5,558,125	1,355,563	867,599	422,110	†
2004–05	47,800,967	16,182,672	8,980,096	7,346,960	7,134,861	5,533,156	1,368,546	851,455	403,221	†
2005–06	48,013,931	16,376,213	9,055,547	7,394,010	7,114,942	5,442,588	1,391,314	835,430	403,887	†
2006–07	48,105,666	16,496,573	9,083,944	7,395,889	7,092,532	5,433,770	1,363,287	840,032	399,639	†
2007–08	48,096,140	16,669,611	8,946,432	7,408,553	7,103,274	5,358,492	1,381,342	834,295	394,141	†
2008–09	48,033,126	16,634,807	9,043,665	7,324,565	7,079,061	5,329,406	1,392,110	832,262	397,250	†
2009–10	48,021,335	16,788,789	9,053,144	7,265,111	7,034,640	5,266,945	1,381,415	835,035	396,256	†
2010–11	48,059,830	16,803,247	9,150,912	7,318,413	6,973,720	5,215,389	1,372,759	833,764	391,626	†
2011–12	47,973,834	16,934,369	9,031,528	7,266,770	6,907,658	5,218,533	1,381,289	842,134	391,553	†
2012–13	48,033,002	17,101,040	8,967,874	7,300,285	6,817,724	5,232,487	1,377,490	841,150	394,952	†
2013–14	48,124,386	17,125,416	9,128,194	7,270,070	6,792,172	5,169,748	1,412,987	832,091	393,708	†
	Percentage distribution of students									
1979–80	100.0	27.3	16.7	18.4	16.9	13.6	3.5	2.4	1.2	†
1989–90	100.0	28.0	17.7	15.8	16.8	14.4	3.5	2.5	1.3	†
1999–2000	100.0	32.1	18.7	15.4	15.6	12.1	3.1	2.0	1.0	†
2001–02	100.0	32.7	18.7	15.8	15.2	11.9	2.9	1.9	0.9	†
2002–03	100.0	33.1	18.9	15.5	15.1	11.7	2.9	1.8	0.9	†
2003–04	100.0	33.4	19.0	15.4	15.0	11.7	2.8	1.8	0.9	†
2004–05	100.0	33.9	18.8	15.4	14.9	11.6	2.9	1.8	0.8	†
2005–06	100.0	34.1	18.9	15.4	14.8	11.3	2.9	1.7	0.8	†
2006–07	100.0	34.3	18.9	15.4	14.7	11.3	2.8	1.7	0.8	†
2007–08	100.0	34.7	18.6	15.4	14.8	11.1	2.9	1.7	0.8	†
2008–09	100.0	34.6	18.8	15.2	14.7	11.1	2.9	1.7	0.8	†
2009–10	100.0	35.0	18.9	15.1	14.6	11.0	2.9	1.7	0.8	†
2010–11	100.0	35.0	19.0	15.2	14.5	10.9	2.9	1.7	0.8	†
2011–12	100.0	35.3	18.8	15.1	14.4	10.9	2.9	1.8	0.8	†
2012–13	100.0	35.6	18.7	15.2	14.2	10.9	2.9	1.8	0.8	†
2013–14	100.0	35.6	19.0	15.1	14.1	10.7	2.9	1.7	0.8	†

†Not applicable.

NOTE: Size not reported (column 11) includes school districts reporting enrollment of zero and school districts whose enrollment counts were suppressed because they failed data quality edits. Regular districts exclude regional education service agencies and supervisory union administrative centers, state-operated agencies, federally operated agencies, and other types of local education agencies, such as independent charter schools. Enrollment totals differ from other tables because this table represents data reported by regular school districts rather than states or schools. Detail may not sum to totals because of rounding.

SOURCE: U.S. Department of Education, National Center for Education Statistics, Common Core of Data (CCD), "Local Education Agency Universe Survey," 1979–80 through 2013–14. (This table was prepared September 2015.)

Table 214.30. Number of public elementary and secondary education agencies, by type of agency and state or jurisdiction: 2012–13 and 2013–14

State or jurisdiction	Total agencies		Type of agency									
			Regular school districts[1]		Regional education service agencies and supervisory union administrative centers		State-operated agencies		Federally operated agencies		Independent charter schools and other agencies	
	2012–13	2013–14	2012–13	2013–14	2012–13	2013–14	2012–13	2013–14	2012–13	2013–14	2012–13	2013–14
1	2	3	4	5	6	7	8	9	10	11	12	13
United States	**18,087**	**18,194**	**13,515**	**13,491**	**1,540**	**1,522**	**265**	**255**	**3**	**3**	**2,764**	**2,923**
Alabama	173	177	135	137	0	0	38	40	0	0	0	0
Alaska	54	54	53	53	0	0	1	1	0	0	0	0
Arizona	665	684	223	223	19	19	10	10	0	0	413	432
Arkansas	288	288	238	237	15	15	5	5	0	0	30	31
California	1,181	1,172	948	944	198	197	4	4	0	0	31	27
Colorado	259	261	178	178	79	81	1	1	0	0	1	1
Connecticut	200	201	169	169	6	6	7	7	0	0	18	19
Delaware	44	43	19	19	1	1	2	2	0	0	22	21
District of Columbia	60	62	1	1	0	0	2	1	0	0	57	60
Florida	76	76	67	67	0	0	3	3	0	0	6	6
Georgia	218	218	180	180	16	16	7	7	0	0	15	15
Hawaii	1	1	1	1	0	0	0	0	0	0	0	0
Idaho	149	152	116	115	0	2	3	3	0	0	30	32
Illinois	1,070	1,068	863	861	197	195	5	5	0	0	5	7
Indiana	407	408	297	295	32	31	4	4	0	0	74	78
Iowa	357	355	348	346	9	9	0	0	0	0	0	0
Kansas	321	321	309	309	0	0	12	12	0	0	0	0
Kentucky	194	194	174	174	18	18	2	2	0	0	0	0
Louisiana	131	133	70	70	0	0	6	6	0	0	55	57
Maine	255	254	231	237	18	8	4	4	0	0	2	5
Maryland	25	25	24	24	0	0	1	1	0	0	0	0
Massachusetts	404	409	237	238	89	89	1	1	0	0	77	81
Michigan	890	907	550	548	56	56	6	6	0	0	278	297
Minnesota	553	548	336	332	66	63	3	3	0	0	148	150
Mississippi	162	162	151	151	0	0	11	11	0	0	0	0
Missouri	567	568	521	521	0	0	5	5	0	0	41	42
Montana	496	493	410	407	77	77	4	4	0	0	5	5
Nebraska	286	287	249	249	32	33	5	5	0	0	0	0
Nevada	18	19	17	18	0	0	0	0	0	0	1	1
New Hampshire	288	292	178	179	93	95	0	0	0	0	17	18
New Jersey	691	680	601	590	1	0	3	3	0	0	86	87
New Mexico	146	150	89	89	0	0	6	6	0	0	51	55
New York[2]	950	970	696	694	37	37	6	6	0	0	211	233
North Carolina	244	265	115	115	0	0	4	4	2	2	123	144
North Dakota	223	222	177	176	43	43	3	3	0	0	0	0
Ohio	1,093	1,116	616	618	105	104	4	4	0	0	368	390
Oklahoma	584	598	521	517	0	0	3	3	0	0	60	78
Oregon	220	220	180	180	19	19	4	4	0	0	17	17
Pennsylvania	799	789	500	500	103	99	19	8	0	0	177	182
Rhode Island	54	61	32	35	4	4	5	6	0	0	13	16
South Carolina	103	102	84	84	12	11	4	4	0	0	3	3
South Dakota	170	170	151	151	15	15	4	4	0	0	0	0
Tennessee	141	140	141	140	0	0	0	0	0	0	0	0
Texas	1,254	1,252	1,029	1,027	20	20	3	3	0	0	202	202
Utah	132	138	41	41	4	4	3	3	0	0	84	90
Vermont	361	360	294	294	60	59	2	2	0	0	5	5
Virginia	227	227	134	134	71	71	21	21	1	1	0	0
Washington	322	318	295	298	9	9	2	0	0	0	16	11
West Virginia	57	57	55	55	0	0	2	2	0	0	0	0
Wisconsin	464	466	423	422	16	16	3	3	0	0	22	25
Wyoming	60	61	48	48	0	0	12	13	0	0	0	0
Bureau of Indian Education	196	196	174	174	22	22	0	0	0	0	0	0
DoD, domestic and overseas	16	16	0	0	0	0	0	0	16	16	0	0
Other jurisdictions												
American Samoa	1	1	1	1	0	0	0	0	0	0	0	0
Guam	1	1	1	1	0	0	0	0	0	0	0	0
Northern Marianas	1	1	1	1	0	0	0	0	0	0	0	0
Puerto Rico	1	1	1	1	0	0	0	0	0	0	0	0
U.S. Virgin Islands	2	2	2	2	0	0	0	0	0	0	0	0

[1]Regular school districts include both independent districts and those that are a dependent segment of a local government. Also includes components of supervisory unions that operate schools, but share superintendent services with other districts.
[2]New York City counted as one school district.

NOTE: DoD = Department of Defense.
SOURCE: U.S. Department of Education, National Center for Education Statistics, Common Core of Data (CCD), "Local Education Agency Universe Survey," 2012–13 and 2013–14. (This table was prepared September 2015.)

Table 215.30. Enrollment, poverty, and federal funds for the 120 largest school districts, by enrollment size in 2013: Selected years, 2012–13 through 2015

							Revenues by source of funds, 2012–13				Revenue from selected federal programs (in thousands), 2012–13						Federal Title I allocations (in thousands), federal fiscal year 2015[2]				
Name of district	State	Rank order	Enrollment, fall 2013	5- to 17-year-old population, 2014	5- to 17-year-olds in poverty, 2014[1]	Poverty rate of 5- to 17-year-olds, 2014[1]	Total (in thousands)	Federal (in thousands)	Federal as a percent of total	Federal revenue per student[3]	Title I basic and concentration grants	School lunch	Individuals with Disabilities Education Act (IDEA)	Eisenhower math and science	Vocational education	Drug-free schools	Total	Basic grants	Concentration grants	Targeted grants	Education finance incentive grants
1	2	3	4	5	6	7	8	9	10	11	12	13	14	15	16	17	18	19	20	21	22
New York City	NY	1	989,012	1,229,623	371,720	30.2	$23,438,719	$1,780,098	7.6	$1,799	$661,541	$401,378	$282,453	—	$11,907	$117	$701,094	$262,524	$63,969	$197,973	$176,629
Los Angeles Unified	CA	2	653,826	740,867	232,853	31.4	8,318,105	1,091,741	13.1	1,666	362,695	299,444	128,108	$52,933	8,893	617	344,219	119,183	28,242	95,019	101,776
City of Chicago (SD 299)	IL	3	396,641	420,432	138,024	32.8	5,388,477	806,318	15.0	2,036	304,801	190,093	106,902	33,204	8,268	—	279,268	96,913	22,964	75,399	83,992
Dade	FL	4	356,233	390,870	101,841	26.1	3,266,516	488,124	14.9	1,378	163,180	122,149	80,223	—	4,935	—	126,439	47,391	11,230	36,089	31,730
Clark County	NV	5	320,532	356,617	77,378	21.7	2,964,019	281,548	9.5	889	99,076	86,172	50,043	9,017	3,720	—	93,091	36,308	8,604	26,964	21,215
Broward	FL	6	262,666	293,180	51,909	17.7	2,302,764	263,763	11.5	1,014	69,820	72,166	55,480	10,563	2,813	84	62,226	24,328	5,765	17,100	15,034
Houston ISD	TX	7	211,552	237,925	79,916	33.6	1,987,654	301,816	15.2	1,484	110,863	98,315	36,563	12,776	2,452	—	105,461	37,265	8,919	27,752	31,526
Hillsborough	FL	8	203,439	219,108	49,055	22.4	1,845,716	279,601	15.1	1,395	62,793	68,507	41,644	10,700	3,316	—	58,474	22,980	5,445	15,990	14,058
Orange	FL	9	187,092	203,372	49,895	24.5	1,879,014	206,990	11.0	1,131	56,709	64,616	42,287	5,245	2,162	—	58,949	23,151	5,486	16,131	14,182
Hawaii Department of Education	HI	10	186,825	216,496	29,375	13.6	2,331,770	310,778	13.3	1,682	46,636	43,837	38,832	962	2,225	—	47,116	19,490	4,588	11,414	11,624
Fairfax County	VA	11	183,417	195,333	13,643	7.0	2,543,509	110,231	4.3	610	19,176	31,405	33,797	4,251	1,663	—	20,550	8,205	1,944	4,746	5,655
Palm Beach	FL	12	182,895	199,881	42,336	21.2	1,778,291	178,941	10.1	997	54,120	52,677	39,119	—	1,669	—	49,530	19,768	4,684	13,345	11,733
Gwinnett County	GA	13	169,150	178,365	32,573	18.3	1,582,099	132,604	8.4	804	32,880	59,527	26,917	3,007	1,136	200	38,079	15,319	3,630	9,818	9,312
Dallas ISD	TX	14	159,713	190,136	70,878	37.3	1,632,183	255,315	15.6	1,606	85,861	79,876	30,211	9,194	2,655	—	92,559	33,055	7,833	24,285	27,386
Wake County	NC	15	153,534	181,251	24,013	13.2	1,216,116	97,321	8.0	645	24,655	27,656	30,521	2,710	—	—	28,156	11,216	2,658	7,012	7,271
Montgomery County	MD	16	151,295	173,396	15,202	8.8	2,764,729	105,027	3.8	706	20,951	29,211	30,081	3,929	1,230	—	25,876	10,672	2,529	6,297	6,379
Shelby County	TN	17	149,832	172,997	54,891	31.7	1,179,930	253,751	21.5	2,358	92,876	53,789	26,564	—	3,200	793	69,472	25,911	6,140	18,403	19,019
Charlotte-Mecklenburg	NC	18	142,991	174,930	34,323	19.6	1,235,570	129,228	10.5	894	37,718	44,442	26,927	3,387	—	—	40,660	15,962	3,782	10,269	10,647
Philadelphia City	PA	19	137,674	236,225	79,210	33.5	2,743,433	429,562	15.7	2,985	222,083	71,108	—	29,863	5,798	—	170,023	58,117	13,761	43,633	54,512
San Diego Unified	CA	20	130,303	139,328	31,967	22.9	1,427,717	164,044	11.5	1,259	46,889	48,420	26,953	9,128	995	267	39,812	16,032	3,799	10,274	9,707
Duval	FL	21	127,653	143,628	31,807	22.1	1,106,654	152,989	13.8	1,217	48,470	38,221	33,981	5,686	1,265	1	36,213	14,843	3,517	9,501	8,353
Prince George's County	MD	22	125,136	142,561	18,373	12.9	2,138,117	141,722	6.6	1,145	34,793	42,789	25,907	4,208	1,129	—	31,665	12,883	3,053	7,814	7,915
Cypress-Fairbanks ISD	TX	23	111,440	113,304	17,037	15.0	982,181	77,092	7.8	701	14,588	31,397	13,911	1,173	977	—	19,358	7,944	1,882	4,767	4,764
Cobb County	GA	24	110,001	121,444	19,620	16.2	1,091,899	86,718	7.9	800	20,382	27,476	20,398	2,517	790	1,830	22,795	9,311	2,206	5,696	5,582
Baltimore County	MD	25	108,191	128,226	14,754	11.5	1,579,381	96,279	6.1	900	22,849	25,954	24,085	3,778	960	174	25,860	10,666	2,527	6,293	6,374
Pinellas	FL	26	103,411	118,224	26,051	22.0	921,475	106,001	11.5	1,023	28,112	28,698	30,506	3,841	1,859	—	29,490	12,182	2,887	7,675	6,747
Northside ISD	TX	27	102,129	103,742	16,738	16.1	917,293	85,183	9.3	850	17,647	29,838	14,519	2,140	970	—	19,503	7,965	1,886	4,848	4,803
Jefferson County	KY	28	100,529	123,168	25,043	20.3	1,241,582	162,705	13.1	1,622	46,151	38,217	—	—	—	—	37,683	14,048	3,323	8,903	11,408
DeKalb County	GA	29	99,388	109,957	31,444	28.6	1,120,290	120,025	10.7	1,213	45,081	39,054	17,802	3,142	785	518	38,216	14,995	3,551	9,643	10,027
Polk	FL	30	97,953	105,795	29,108	27.5	913,627	110,493	12.1	1,140	28,396	32,206	21,066	3,219	1,268	—	33,100	13,610	3,225	8,655	7,609
Fulton County	GA	31	95,232	111,576	19,273	17.3	1,090,818	74,519	6.8	794	24,424	22,916	17,889	2,353	578	—	22,025	9,081	2,152	5,539	5,253
Albuquerque	NM	32	93,202	114,253	28,822	25.2	964,205	106,368	11.0	1,131	35,713	11	25,909	4,658	1,089	—	35,282	13,737	3,255	8,742	9,549
Lee	FL	33	87,425	92,340	24,017	26.0	795,969	92,386	11.6	1,077	19,261	29,041	21,314	—	983	—	27,011	11,200	2,654	7,001	6,155
Denver	CO	34	86,046	91,237	26,159	28.7	1,057,142	125,850	11.9	1,509	40,506	31,377	16,663	4,637	1,299	—	32,896	12,527	2,968	7,901	9,500
Jefferson County, No. R1	CO	35	86,011	88,260	10,463	11.9	842,074	53,795	6.4	629	11,596	13,195	14,082	1,083	432	—	12,297	5,132	1,216	2,826	3,123
Prince William County	VA	36	85,451	88,432	7,606	8.6	1,004,075	47,983	4.8	572	6,299	16,309	14,273	1,166	730	—	10,311	4,559	1,080	2,261	2,410
Austin ISD	TX	37	85,372	98,159	24,367	24.8	1,054,072	146,954	13.9	1,699	39,323	28,258	17,354	3,165	1,166	—	29,892	11,899	2,817	7,536	7,639
Baltimore City	MD	38	84,730	89,707	26,703	29.8	1,432,281	178,834	12.5	2,110	62,103	37,902	26,897	8,151	1,692	—	49,459	19,660	4,655	12,500	12,644
Fort Worth ISD	TX	39	84,588	91,520	29,068	31.8	841,701	129,752	15.4	1,554	46,882	34,116	14,942	3,156	1,128	—	34,506	13,611	3,320	8,674	8,901
Davidson County	TN	40	82,806	96,427	27,359	28.4	904,316	113,884	12.6	1,404	28,917	32,509	18,155	—	3,016	—	32,165	12,748	3,021	8,063	8,333
Long Beach Unified	CA	41	81,155	87,044	22,571	25.9	810,505	116,859	14.4	1,421	33,912	27,744	15,651	4,672	736	—	27,575	11,316	2,681	7,038	6,540
Milwaukee	WI	42	78,516	111,407	44,749	40.2	1,184,781	204,823	17.3	2,614	100,835	35,590	21,129	—	1,886	—	74,998	26,825	6,356	18,337	23,480
Anne Arundel County	MD	43	78,489	91,526	7,502	8.2	1,125,008	60,765	5.4	781	10,642	12,350	17,500	2,116	580	—	11,731	5,250	1,244	2,602	2,635
Greenville, 01	SC	44	74,475	84,024	19,048	22.7	739,657	63,797	8.6	866	21,428	20,145	14,975	1,983	1,116	—	25,126	9,735	2,307	5,937	7,148
Alpine	UT	45	73,975	82,407	7,913	9.6	473,461	40,700	8.6	562	4,374	10,668	12,232	1,157	633	—	8,734	3,775	895	1,906	2,158

See notes at end of table.

Table 215.30. Enrollment, poverty, and federal funds for the 120 largest school districts, by enrollment size in 2013: Selected years, 2012–13 through 2015—Continued

Name of district	State	Rank order	Enrollment, fall 2013	5- to 17-year-old population, 2014	5- to 17-year-olds in poverty, 2014[1]	Poverty rate of 5- to 17-year-olds, 2014[1]	Revenues by source of funds, 2012–13: Total (in thousands)	Federal (in thousands)	Federal as a percent of total	Federal revenue per student[3]	Revenue from selected federal programs (in thousands), 2012–13: Title I basic and concentration grants	School lunch	Individuals with Disabilities Education Act (IDEA)	Eisenhower math and science	Vocational education	Drug-free schools	Federal Title I allocations (in thousands), federal fiscal year 2015[2]: Total	Basic grants	Concentration grants	Targeted grants	Education finance incentive grants
1	2	3	4	5	6	7	8	9	10	11	12	13	14	15	16	17	18	19	20	21	22
Fresno Unified	CA	46	73,353	79,385	39,743	50.1	775,739	128,551	16.6	1,745	55,287	35,393	15,624	6,701	1,144	—	50,504	19,796	4,691	13,245	12,772
Guilford County	NC	47	72,081	84,854	23,052	27.2	686,284	99,692	14.5	1,344	25,763	25,671	18,110	1,896	—	—	26,822	10,709	2,538	6,664	6,910
Brevard	FL	48	71,232	78,341	15,442	19.7	599,412	62,930	10.5	884	14,626	17,346	15,685	2,618	619	—	16,940	7,214	1,709	4,266	3,751
Fort Bend ISD	TX	49	70,931	82,427	10,001	12.1	613,872	39,064	6.4	561	7,876	11,646	10,015	896	598	—	10,903	4,767	1,129	2,587	2,420
Loudoun County	VA	50	70,759	76,328	2,780	3.6	1,027,126	21,204	2.1	311	1,183	6,127	9,774	579	241	—	1,687	1,687	—	—	—
Virginia Beach City	VA	51	70,556	73,625	8,265	11.2	765,695	70,068	9.2	997	12,139	12,735	18,683	2,499	837	—	11,525	5,008	1,187	2,552	2,778
Davis	UT	52	70,411	78,643	6,769	8.6	502,664	38,175	7.6	544	2,702	11,420	10,685	1,376	553	—	7,232	3,182	754	1,560	1,737
Granite	UT	53	70,407	81,256	15,402	19.0	491,011	62,052	12.6	895	15,923	19,048	14,446	2,700	932	—	18,594	7,216	1,710	4,267	5,402
North East ISD	TX	54	68,205	76,118	12,276	16.1	650,475	55,278	8.5	814	11,850	16,783	12,847	1,478	688	—	13,641	5,796	1,373	3,293	3,179
Pasco	FL	55	68,109	73,537	13,030	17.7	596,027	62,571	10.5	932	15,284	20,731	12,233	1,864	593	81	14,168	6,117	1,449	3,513	3,089
Aldine ISD	TX	56	67,381	63,532	23,699	37.3	626,345	86,783	13.9	1,321	19,622	37,024	11,253	2,454	944	—	27,624	11,051	2,619	6,899	7,055
Katy ISD	TX	57	67,213	63,833	6,287	9.8	630,967	39,276	6.2	608	4,694	10,345	7,029	736	456	—	6,214	2,939	610	1,426	1,239
Douglas County, No. RE1	CO	58	66,230	69,001	2,343	3.4	603,241	18,184	3.0	281	1,065	3,599	10,681	458	182	—	1,115	1,115	—	—	—
Washoe County	NV	59	65,550	72,033	12,408	17.2	594,199	60,924	10.3	937	14,019	14,445	10,200	1,811	786	96	14,801	6,591	1,561	3,907	2,742
Seminole	FL	60	64,851	71,952	11,369	15.8	522,697	50,596	9.7	785	10,290	15,911	15,317	1,960	444	—	12,131	5,310	1,258	2,960	2,602
Arlington ISD	TX	61	64,688	68,697	15,593	22.7	574,291	66,478	11.6	1,023	14,107	23,234	12,012	1,727	766	—	17,542	7,262	1,721	4,299	4,260
Mesa Unified	AZ	62	64,161	81,861	20,782	25.4	549,773	74,829	13.6	1,166	24,497	22,105	12,299	3,293	1,354	510	24,242	10,057	2,383	6,217	5,586
Elk Grove Unified	CA	63	62,499	68,820	13,407	19.5	549,526	54,840	10.0	883	12,988	17,783	9,552	3,249	524	—	15,708	6,742	1,598	3,900	3,468
El Paso ISD	TX	64	61,620	63,519	20,205	31.8	590,906	94,183	15.9	1,490	30,492	23,110	11,408	4,201	988	—	26,610	10,475	2,670	6,966	6,498
Volusia	FL	65	61,238	67,567	15,988	23.7	548,917	61,284	11.2	1,004	18,064	17,811	14,535	—	659	—	19,165	8,056	1,908	4,910	4,291
Knox County	TN	66	59,236	69,627	13,253	19.0	524,707	60,904	11.6	1,034	12,471	16,909	12,690	—	1,041	364	15,139	6,280	1,488	3,625	3,746
Chesterfield County	VA	67	59,186	61,727	5,808	9.4	581,811	32,908	5.7	559	6,832	7,773	12,144	1,490	583	—	6,917	3,483	—	1,670	1,765
Mobile County	AL	68	58,808	67,973	19,338	28.4	552,138	78,340	14.2	1,336	29,650	24,557	18,069	3,111	907	461	23,185	9,036	2,141	5,516	6,492
Osceola	FL	69	58,204	56,477	17,946	31.8	492,781	61,964	12.6	1,098	18,559	21,804	9,222	—	585	2	19,815	8,352	1,979	5,047	4,437
San Francisco Unified	CA	70	57,620	73,913	10,527	14.2	752,645	80,673	10.7	1,416	31,718	14,168	—	3,514	347	211	12,017	5,255	1,245	2,924	2,592
Garland ISD	TX	71	57,616	61,166	13,227	21.6	516,152	49,404	9.6	851	12,180	17,632	10,671	1,110	706	—	14,623	6,165	1,461	3,546	3,451
Santa Ana Unified	CA	72	57,499	54,420	17,084	31.4	554,940	85,915	15.5	1,497	29,500	26,037	11,810	3,728	443	—	20,195	8,472	2,007	5,086	4,630
Conroe ISD	TX	73	55,009	56,948	7,463	13.1	460,425	27,482	6.0	510	6,765	8,719	6,998	1,135	408	—	7,570	3,496	828	1,732	1,513
Plano ISD	TX	74	54,822	65,316	6,230	9.5	588,710	31,117	5.3	564	5,360	8,003	8,713	1,172	381	—	5,579	2,926	—	1,419	1,233
Pasadena ISD	TX	75	54,535	55,870	15,902	28.5	523,346	74,357	14.2	1,386	20,564	24,955	10,758	1,638	729	—	17,950	7,415	1,757	4,404	4,374
Boston	MA	76	54,300	72,057	20,458	28.4	1,262,641	98,227	7.8	1,782	24,779	17,134	20,657	—	1,452	—	39,078	14,511	3,438	8,931	12,198
Cherry Creek, No. 5	CO	77	54,228	55,930	5,520	9.9	548,930	26,039	4.7	487	4,820	7,565	9,503	804	220	—	5,152	2,631	—	1,254	1,268
San Antonio ISD	TX	78	53,857	58,889	22,093	37.5	582,725	135,767	23.3	2,502	36,312	35,652	13,475	4,311	832	—	27,710	11,187	2,786	7,012	6,725
Capistrano Unified	CA	79	53,833	63,230	5,751	9.1	413,762	22,301	5.4	415	3,916	4,672	10,194	783	240	—	5,296	2,852	—	1,367	1,078
San Bernardino City Unified	CA	80	53,785	56,077	21,197	37.8	558,440	90,300	16.2	1,669	43,826	23,733	10,908	4,283	557	—	26,908	11,009	2,607	6,855	6,438
Corona-Norco Unified	CA	81	53,782	55,882	7,540	13.5	457,589	31,925	7.0	597	5,969	10,648	9,259	1,446	259	—	8,129	3,805	902	1,890	1,532
Winston-Salem/Forsyth County	NC	82	53,413	62,708	16,346	26.1	477,178	55,778	11.7	1,035	17,434	16,466	9,217	1,596	—	—	19,010	7,675	1,817	4,649	4,868
Jordan	UT	83	53,355	60,105	4,934	8.2	362,061	23,316	6.4	444	3,057	7,787	7,585	579	426	—	4,641	2,338	—	1,096	1,206
Howard County	MD	84	52,806	57,534	3,268	5.7	934,547	23,580	2.5	453	2,885	4,842	9,900	1,346	322	—	4,247	2,286	—	974	987
Lewisville ISD	TX	85	52,801	60,889	5,274	8.7	525,467	34,064	6.5	648	3,538	9,251	8,750	611	384	—	4,659	2,475	—	1,172	1,011
Clayton County	GA	86	52,296	53,836	18,335	34.1	471,535	59,213	12.6	1,144	14,319	26,058	8,788	895	488	—	23,200	9,378	2,221	5,760	5,842
Cumberland County	NC	87	51,471	54,436	13,857	25.5	425,630	65,617	15.4	1,240	17,728	17,926	11,953	2,792	—	—	15,900	6,564	1,555	3,820	3,961
Omaha	NE	88	51,069	63,358	13,793	21.8	613,144	97,243	15.9	1,923	35,653	20,674	11,354	2,932	503	—	23,901	9,054	2,145	5,306	7,395
Wichita	KS	89	50,629	57,069	14,452	25.3	597,576	73,149	12.2	1,453	28,987	18,597	—	—	—	202	21,881	8,295	1,966	4,891	6,729
Henrico County	VA	90	50,629	54,985	6,700	12.2	545,496	34,931	6.4	697	4,370	10,460	9,548	1,813	1,234	—	9,049	4,030	955	1,971	2,093

See notes at end of table.

Table 215.30. Enrollment, poverty, and federal funds for the 120 largest school districts, by enrollment size in 2013: Selected years, 2012–13 through 2015—Continued

							Revenues by source of funds, 2012–13				Revenue from selected federal programs (in thousands), 2012–13						Federal Title I allocations (in thousands), federal fiscal year 2015[2]				
Name of district	State	Rank order	Enrollment, fall 2013	5- to 17-year-old population, 2014	5- to 17-year-olds in poverty, 2014[1]	Poverty rate of 5- to 17-year-olds, 2014[1]	Total (in thousands)	Federal (in thousands)	Federal as a percent of total	Federal revenue per student[3]	Title I basic and concentration grants	School lunch	Individuals with Disabilities Education Act (IDEA)	Eisenhower math and science	Vocational education	Drug-free schools	Total	Basic grants	Concentration grants	Targeted grants	Education finance incentive grants
1	2	3	4	5	6	7	8	9	10	11	12	13	14	15	16	17	18	19	20	21	22
Seattle	WA	91	50,509	64,156	9,766	15.2	703,137	52,494	7.5	1,036	11,899	9,626	11,831	153	376	—	12,740	5,254	1,245	2,825	3,415
Columbus City	OH	92	50,478	70,736	27,741	39.2	855,757	63,211	7.4	1,255	0	24,785	11,983	—	2,054	—	46,439	17,424	4,129	11,061	13,826
Atlanta	GA	93	50,131	57,606	20,970	36.4	771,985	84,743	11.0	1,710	30,480	21,009	10,400	4,783	499	1,270	31,528	12,228	2,983	7,662	8,655
Brownsville ISD	TX	94	49,370	47,291	20,521	43.4	501,016	110,950	22.1	2,256	37,154	33,573	10,941	3,198	968	—	24,905	9,835	2,402	6,358	6,310
Tucson Unified	AZ	95	49,308	73,274	19,315	26.4	470,812	58,134	12.3	1,145	22,803	17,108	13	3,907	1,416	813	23,894	9,559	2,263	5,939	6,133
Detroit City	MI	96	49,043	128,676	65,949	51.3	851,989	228,390	26.8	4,638	126,653	37,999	14,987	—	2,197	—	139,667	45,887	11,696	36,374	45,710
San Juan Unified	CA	97	49,035	49,829	10,698	21.5	436,242	45,645	10.5	956	13,324	9,876	9,380	1,800	339	406	12,326	5,439	1,289	3,006	2,593
Klein ISD	TX	98	48,253	49,135	7,135	14.5	432,348	31,330	7.2	666	6,088	10,024	8,092	556	215	—	7,186	3,328	789	1,640	1,431
Anchorage	AK	99	48,159	53,216	4,994	9.4	770,180	76,535	9.9	1,569	13,938	15,529	12,306	3,206	967	—	12,763	5,118	651	3,464	3,529
Portland, SD1J	OR	100	47,323	55,527	9,319	16.8	534,955	55,347	10.3	1,184	15,777	10,498	13,107	2,697	435	—	12,056	4,936	1,170	2,622	3,329
Oakland Unified	CA	101	47,194	57,818	14,988	25.9	604,008	74,530	12.3	1,604	26,581	15,427	11,515	3,098	489	323	17,582	7,464	1,769	4,395	3,953
Sacramento City Unified	CA	102	47,031	52,506	16,515	31.5	488,458	82,038	16.8	1,723	22,342	19,862	10,365	3,863	544	535	19,817	8,297	1,966	4,974	4,580
Garden Grove Unified	CA	103	46,936	50,483	13,318	26.4	506,887	52,738	10.4	1,108	14,586	19,494	9,126	1,561	357	—	15,348	6,604	1,565	3,805	3,375
Manatee	FL	104	46,705	50,242	13,063	26.0	415,726	48,375	11.6	1,048	11,210	15,279	9,750	1,486	660	—	14,098	6,089	1,443	3,494	3,072
Round Rock ISD	TX	105	46,666	51,345	4,095	8.0	442,949	29,811	6.7	652	3,043	7,504	6,489	466	318	—	3,568	1,941	—	878	749
Jefferson Parish	LA	106	46,312	68,154	18,877	27.7	557,140	85,506	15.3	1,855	29,878	17,183	9,675	2,343	721	—	26,469	10,548	2,499	6,414	7,008
Alief ISD	TX	107	46,258	52,409	18,767	35.8	452,367	63,375	14.0	1,384	16,130	20,850	8,830	1,085	673	—	21,504	8,751	2,074	5,321	5,359
Frisco ISD	TX	108	46,053	40,585	2,184	5.4	431,286	9,830	2.3	230	1,013	2,845	4,820	117	219	—	1,696	1,020	—	376	300
Charleston, 01	SC	109	45,650	52,565	13,179	25.1	707,221	72,128	10.2	1,617	27,445	16,264	10,421	2,448	646	—	16,571	6,683	1,584	3,843	4,461
District of Columbia	DC	110	44,942	70,507	20,544	29.1	1,300,036	129,874	10.0	2,940	32,760	22,088	13,622	7,795	2,527	320	42,820	17,744	3,994	10,557	10,525
Socorro ISD	TX	111	44,517	44,018	10,791	24.5	383,072	40,997	10.7	926	9,285	17,728	6,670	999	578	—	11,520	4,999	1,184	2,746	2,591
Collier	FL	112	44,418	46,316	10,384	22.4	491,985	55,854	11.4	1,276	17,776	16,115	8,987	1,309	515	—	10,933	4,836	1,146	2,635	2,316
United ISD	TX	113	43,575	42,174	13,223	31.4	395,105	50,435	12.8	1,176	14,065	19,433	7,413	1,050	409	—	14,583	6,150	1,457	3,536	3,440
Hamilton County	TN	114	43,540	53,541	12,166	22.7	398,221	50,421	12.7	1,154	16,521	14,689	9,826	—	729	529	13,776	5,762	1,365	3,270	3,379
Ysleta ISD	TX	115	43,063	38,453	13,819	35.9	423,790	61,548	14.5	1,409	19,099	19,418	8,184	2,571	674	—	15,793	6,416	1,635	4,006	3,736
Riverside Unified	CA	116	42,587	46,032	9,624	20.9	382,543	42,841	11.2	1,007	10,804	15,392	8,189	2,835	347	—	10,817	4,857	1,151	2,606	2,202
Adams 12 Five Star Schools	CO	117	42,230	44,089	4,834	11.0	405,051	22,447	5.5	519	4,651	6,112	6,995	1,162	199	—	4,656	2,337	—	1,122	1,197
Marion	FL	118	42,107	46,865	12,945	27.6	361,558	51,208	14.2	1,220	13,801	17,540	9,932	1,642	585	—	13,932	6,023	1,427	3,449	3,033
East Baton Rouge Parish	LA	119	41,937	60,888	17,228	28.3	565,614	71,584	12.7	1,665	24,044	20,549	8,668	4,879	679	25	24,139	9,650	2,287	5,798	6,404
Lake	FL	120	41,794	46,136	10,094	21.9	340,131	38,288	11.3	923	10,350	13,244	9,025	1,385	483	—	10,580	4,697	1,113	2,539	2,232

—Not available.

[1]Poverty is defined based on the number of persons and related children in the family and their income. For information on poverty thresholds, see http://www.census.gov/hhes/www/poverty/data/threshld/.

[2]Fiscal year 2015 Department of Education funds available for spending by school districts in the 2015–16 school year.

[3]Federal revenue per student is based on fall enrollment collected through the "Local Education Agency (School District) Finance Survey (F33)."

NOTE: Detail may not sum to totals because of rounding. ISD = independent school district.

SOURCE: U.S. Department of Education, National Center for Education Statistics, Common Core of Data (CCD), "Local Education Agency Universe Survey," 2013–14; "Local Education Agency (School District) Finance Survey (F33)," 2012–13; and unpublished Department of Education budget data. U.S. Department of Commerce, Census Bureau, Small Area Income and Poverty Estimates (SAIPE) Program, 2014 Poverty Estimates for School Districts. (This table was prepared January 2016.)

Table 216.10. Public elementary and secondary schools, by level of school: Selected years, 1967–68 through 2013–14

Year	Total, all public schools	Schools with reported grade spans												Other schools[1]
		Total	Elementary schools				Secondary schools					Combined elementary/ secondary schools[2]	
			Total[3]	Middle schools[4]	One-teacher schools	Other elementary schools	Total[5]	Junior high[6]	3-year or 4-year high schools	5-year or 6-year high schools	Other secondary schools		
1	2	3	4	5	6	7	8	9	10	11	12	13	14
1967–68	—	94,197	67,186	—	4,146	63,040	23,318	7,437	10,751	4,650	480	3,693	—
1970–71	—	89,372	64,020	2,080	1,815	60,125	23,572	7,750	11,265	3,887	670	1,780	—
1972–73	—	88,864	62,942	2,308	1,475	59,159	23,919	7,878	11,550	3,962	529	2,003	—
1974–75	—	87,456	61,759	3,224	1,247	57,288	23,837	7,690	11,480	4,122	545	1,860	—
1975–76	88,597	87,034	61,704	3,916	1,166	56,622	23,792	7,521	11,572	4,113	586	1,538	1,563
1976–77	—	86,501	61,123	4,180	1,111	55,832	23,857	7,434	11,658	4,130	635	1,521	—
1978–79	—	84,816	60,312	5,879	1,056	53,377	22,834	6,282	11,410	4,429	713	1,670	—
1980–81	85,982	83,688	59,326	6,003	921	52,402	22,619	5,890	10,758	4,193	1,778	1,743	2,294
1982–83	84,740	82,039	58,051	6,875	798	50,378	22,383	5,948	11,678	4,067	690	1,605	2,701
1983–84	84,178	81,418	57,471	6,885	838	49,748	22,336	5,936	11,670	4,046	684	1,611	2,760
1984–85	84,007	81,147	57,231	6,893	825	49,513	22,320	5,916	11,671	4,021	712	1,596	2,860
1986–87	83,421	82,316	58,835	7,483	763	50,589	21,505	5,109	11,430	4,196	770	1,976	1,105 [7]
1987–88	83,248	81,416	57,575	7,641	729	49,205	21,662	4,900	11,279	4,048	1,435	2,179	1,832 [7]
1988–89	83,165	81,579	57,941	7,957	583	49,401	21,403	4,687	11,350	3,994	1,372	2,235	1,586 [7]
1989–90	83,425	81,880	58,419	8,272	630	49,517	21,181	4,512	11,492	3,812	1,365	2,280	1,545 [7]
1990–91	84,538	82,475	59,015	8,545	617	49,853	21,135	4,561	11,537	3,723	1,314	2,325	2,063
1991–92	84,578	82,506	59,258	8,829	569	49,860	20,767	4,298	11,528	3,699	1,242	2,481	2,072
1992–93	84,497	82,896	59,676	9,152	430	50,094	20,671	4,115	11,651	3,613	1,292	2,549	1,601
1993–94	85,393	83,431	60,052	9,573	442	50,037	20,705	3,970	11,858	3,595	1,282	2,674	1,962
1994–95	86,221	84,476	60,808	9,954	458	50,396	20,904	3,859	12,058	3,628	1,359	2,764	1,745
1995–96	87,125	84,958	61,165	10,205	474	50,486	20,997	3,743	12,168	3,621	1,465	2,796	2,167
1996–97	88,223	86,092	61,805	10,499	487	50,819	21,307	3,707	12,424	3,614	1,562	2,980	2,131
1997–98	89,508	87,541	62,739	10,944	476	51,319	21,682	3,599	12,734	3,611	1,738	3,120	1,967
1998–99	90,874	89,259	63,462	11,202	463	51,797	22,076	3,607	13,457	3,707	1,305	3,721	1,615
1999–2000	92,012	90,538	64,131	11,521	423	52,187	22,365	3,566	13,914	3,686	1,199	4,042	1,474
2000–01	93,273	91,691	64,601	11,696	411	52,494	21,994	3,318	13,793	3,974	909	5,096	1,582
2001–02	94,112	92,696	65,228	11,983	408	52,837	22,180	3,285	14,070	3,917	908	5,288	1,416
2002–03	95,615	93,869	65,718	12,174	366	53,178	22,599	3,263	14,330	4,017	989	5,552	1,746
2003–04	95,726	93,977	65,758	12,341	376	53,041	22,782	3,251	14,595	3,840	1,096	5,437	1,749
2004–05	96,513	95,001	65,984	12,530	338	53,116	23,445	3,250	14,854	3,945	1,396	5,572	1,512
2005–06	97,382	95,731	66,026	12,545	326	53,155	23,998	3,249	15,103	3,910	1,736	5,707	1,651
2006–07	98,793	96,362	66,458	12,773	313	53,372	23,920	3,112	15,043	4,048	1,717	5,984	2,431
2007–08	98,916	97,654	67,112	13,014	288	53,810	24,643	3,117	16,146	3,981	1,399	5,899	1,262
2008–09	98,706	97,119	67,148	13,060	237	53,851	24,348	3,037	16,246	3,761	1,304	5,623	1,587
2009–10	98,817	97,521	67,140	13,163	217	53,760	24,651	2,953	16,706	3,778	1,214	5,730	1,296
2010–11	98,817	97,767	67,086	13,045	224	53,817	24,544	2,855	16,321	4,047	1,321	6,137	1,050
2011–12	98,328	97,357	66,689	12,963	205	53,521	24,357	2,865	16,586	3,899	1,007	6,311	971
2012–13	98,454	97,369	66,718	13,061	196	53,461	24,280	2,810	16,657	3,871	942	6,371	1,085
2013–14	98,271	97,292	67,034	13,322	193	53,519	24,053	2,719	16,937	3,498	899	6,205	979

—Not available.
[1]Includes special education, alternative, and other schools not reported by grade span.
[2]Includes schools beginning with grade 6 or below and ending with grade 9 or above.
[3]Includes schools beginning with grade 6 or below and with no grade higher than 8.
[4]Includes schools with grade spans beginning with 4, 5, or 6 and ending with 6, 7, or 8.
[5]Includes schools with no grade below 7, and at least one higher grade.
[6]Includes schools with grades 7 and 8 or grades 7 through 9.
[7]Because of revision in data collection procedures, figures not comparable to data for other years.
SOURCE: U.S. Department of Education, National Center for Education Statistics, *Statistics of State School Systems*, 1967–68 and 1975–76; *Statistics of Public Elementary and Secondary Day Schools*, 1970–71, 1972–73, 1974–75, and 1976–77 through 1980–81; and Common Core of Data (CCD), "Public Elementary/Secondary School Universe Survey," 1982–83 through 2013–14. (This table was prepared September 2015.)

Table 216.20. Number and enrollment of public elementary and secondary schools, by school level, type, and charter and magnet status: Selected years, 1990–91 through 2013–14

School level, type, and charter and magnet status	Number of schools										Enrollment									
	1990–91	2000–01	2003–04	2007–08	2008–09	2009–10	2010–11	2011–12	2012–13	2013–14	1990–91	2000–01	2003–04	2007–08	2008–09	2009–10	2010–11	2011–12	2012–13	2013–14
1	2	3	4	5	6	7	8	9	10	11	12	13	14	15	16	17	18	19	20	21
Total, all schools	**84,538**	**93,273**	**95,726**	**98,916**	**98,706**	**98,817**	**98,817**	**98,328**	**98,454**	**98,271**	**41,141,366**	**47,060,714**	**48,353,523**	**48,910,025**	**49,053,786**	**49,081,519**	**49,177,617**	**49,256,120**	**49,474,030**	**49,709,977**
School type																				
Regular	80,395	85,422	86,340	88,274	88,801	89,018	88,929	88,663	89,031	89,183	40,599,943	46,194,730	47,415,655	47,962,492	48,168,727	48,186,142	48,259,245	48,273,539	48,539,891	48,800,105
Special education	1,932	2,008	2,328	2,267	2,289	2,089	2,206	2,087	2,034	2,010	209,145	174,577	211,623	207,030	164,874	192,989	190,910	195,161	198,417	213,077
Vocational	1,060	1,025	1,100	1,409	1,409	1,417	1,485	1,434	1,403	1,380	198,117	199,669	182,343	163,003	156,390	129,840	164,013	159,905	159,917	148,451
Alternative[1]	1,151	4,818	5,958	6,966	6,207	6,293	6,197	6,144	5,986	5,698	134,161	491,738	543,902	577,500	563,795	572,548	563,449	627,515	575,805	548,344
School level and type																				
Elementary[2]	59,015	64,601	65,758	67,112	67,148	67,140	67,086	66,689	66,718	67,034	26,503,677	30,673,453	31,204,774	31,225,474	31,446,040	31,547,988	31,581,751	31,724,573	31,893,347	32,183,080
Regular	58,440	63,674	64,721	65,721	65,999	65,947	65,874	65,461	65,581	65,948	26,400,740	30,582,610	31,088,893	31,093,502	31,325,566	31,413,221	31,441,027	31,545,886	31,747,440	32,040,651
Special education	419	496	487	583	538	520	587	544	540	543	58,204	42,127	44,908	63,371	49,661	56,959	58,987	58,844	59,537	62,580
Vocational	31	8	5	7	1	24	16	17	15	7	17,686	2,409	1,917	1,634	16	1,892	3,495	4,558	3,734	1,791
Alternative[1]	125	423	545	801	610	649	609	667	582	536	27,047	46,307	69,056	66,967	70,797	75,916	78,242	115,285	82,636	78,058
Secondary[3]	21,135	21,994	22,782	24,643	24,348	24,651	24,544	24,357	24,280	24,053	13,569,787	15,038,171	15,751,624	16,184,724	16,055,123	15,930,401	15,692,610	15,708,815	15,644,214	15,618,300
Regular	19,459	18,456	18,810	19,371	19,349	19,604	19,449	19,441	19,470	19,409	13,313,097	14,567,969	15,279,073	15,680,507	15,568,281	15,454,043	15,197,786	15,194,153	15,137,814	15,148,323
Special education	165	219	274	375	325	354	359	339	330	329	11,913	12,607	17,743	30,680	24,266	30,443	27,990	27,905	27,731	28,014
Vocational	1,010	997	1,069	1,356	1,326	1,343	1,387	1,349	1,324	1,311	174,105	193,981	176,022	159,270	154,522	126,827	154,088	154,187	154,275	144,070
Alternative[1]	501	2,322	2,629	3,541	3,348	3,350	3,349	3,228	3,156	3,004	70,672	263,614	278,786	314,267	308,054	319,088	312,746	332,570	324,394	297,893
Combined elementary/secondary[4]	2,325	5,096	5,437	5,899	5,623	5,730	6,137	6,311	6,371	6,205	925,887	1,266,778	1,310,435	1,472,248	1,520,246	1,542,734	1,897,712	1,818,020	1,934,697	1,896,908
Regular	1,784	2,780	2,657	2,786	2,793	3,028	3,363	3,435	3,572	3,448	855,814	1,007,368	1,030,665	1,187,281	1,253,785	1,288,109	1,620,031	1,533,002	1,654,256	1,610,750
Special education	376	715	801	904	938	847	964	970	960	951	43,992	86,253	98,668	88,000	80,245	76,691	99,120	104,344	109,992	111,175
Vocational	19	20	26	46	82	50	82	68	64	62	6,326	3,279	4,404	2,099	1,852	1,121	6,430	1,160	1,908	2,590
Alternative[1]	146	1,581	1,953	2,163	1,810	1,805	1,728	1,838	1,775	1,744	19,755	169,878	176,698	194,868	184,364	176,813	172,131	179,514	168,541	172,393
Other (not classified by grade span)	2,063	1,582	1,749	1,262	1,587	1,296	1,050	971	1,085	979	142,015	82,312	86,690	27,579	32,377	60,396	5,544	4,712	1,772	11,689
Regular	712	512	152	396	660	439	243	326	408	378	30,292	36,783	17,024	1,202	21,095	30,769	401	498	381	381
Special education	972	578	766	405	488	368	296	234	204	187	95,036	33,590	50,304	24,979	10,702	28,896	4,813	4,068	1,157	11,308
Vocational	0	0	0	0	0	0	0	0	0	0	0	0	0	0	0	0	0	0	0	0
Alternative[1]	379	492	831	461	439	489	511	411	473	414	16,687	11,939	19,362	1,398	580	731	330	146	234	0
Charter status and level																				
All charter schools[5]	—	1,993	2,977	4,388	4,694	4,952	5,274	5,696	6,079	6,465	—	448,343	789,479	1,276,731	1,433,116	1,610,285	1,787,091	2,057,599	2,267,814	2,519,065
Elementary[2]	—	1,011	1,549	2,340	2,513	2,679	2,866	3,127	3,391	3,636	—	249,101	414,225	674,990	746,950	824,297	905,575	1,045,492	1,156,384	1,287,378
Secondary[3]	—	467	779	1,218	1,255	1,329	1,368	1,418	1,463	1,521	—	79,588	158,999	264,402	291,016	327,289	341,534	386,482	398,430	441,762
Combined elementary/secondary[4]	—	448	626	803	865	929	1,027	1,112	1,204	1,269	—	117,377	215,462	337,195	395,122	458,075	539,653	625,429	712,634	789,777
Other (not classified by grade span)	—	67	23	27	61	15	13	39	21	39	—	2,277	793	144	28	624	329	196	366	148
Magnet status and level																				
All magnet schools[5]	—	1,469	2,108	2,793	3,021	2,213	2,722	2,949	3,151	3,254	—	1,213,976	1,619,779	2,132,395	2,307,712	1,515,562	2,055,133	2,248,177	2,479,188	2,554,828
Elementary[2]	—	1,111	1,566	2,015	2,193	1,530	1,849	2,012	2,150	2,164	—	704,763	946,815	1,157,470	1,267,944	799,546	1,035,288	1,158,405	1,287,589	1,298,904
Secondary[3]	—	328	478	688	728	582	746	802	862	939	—	484,684	633,080	926,314	976,483	668,832	944,434	1,015,267	1,119,369	1,177,869
Combined elementary/secondary[4]	—	29	59	83	92	79	103	116	121	133	—	24,529	39,011	48,593	63,285	46,467	75,411	74,505	72,192	78,055
Other (not classified by grade span)	—	1	5	7	8	22	24	19	18	18	—	0	873	18	0	717	0	0	38	0

—Not available.
[1]Includes schools that provide nontraditional education, address needs of students that typically cannot be met in regular schools, serve as adjuncts to regular schools, or fall outside the categories of regular, special education, or vocational education.
[2]Includes schools beginning with grade 6 or below and with no grade higher than 8.
[3]Includes schools with no grade lower than 7.
[4]Includes schools beginning with grade 6 or below and ending with grade 9 or above.
[5]Magnet and charter schools are also included under regular, special education, vocational, or alternative schools as appropriate.
SOURCE: U.S. Department of Education, National Center for Education Statistics, Common Core of Data (CCD), "Public Elementary/Secondary School Universe Survey," 1990–91 through 2013–14. (This table was prepared September 2015.)

Table 216.30. Number and percentage distribution of public elementary and secondary students and schools, by traditional or charter school status and selected characteristics: Selected years, 1999–2000 through 2013–14

Selected characteristic	1999–2000			2003–04			Charter schools				2013–14		
	Total, all public schools	Traditional (noncharter) schools	Charter schools	Total, all public schools	Traditional (noncharter) schools	Charter schools	2007–08	2009–10	2011–12	2012–13	Total, all public schools	Traditional (noncharter) schools	Charter schools
1	2	3	4	5	6	7	8	9	10	11	12	13	14
Enrollment (in thousands)	46,689	46,350	340	48,354	47,564	789	1,277	1,610	2,058	2,268	49,710	47,191	2,519
Percentage distribution of students													
Sex	100.0	100.0	100.0	100.0	100.0	100.0	100.0	100.0	100.0	100.0	100.0	100.0	100.0
Male	51.4	51.4	51.0	51.4	51.5	50.3	49.5	49.5	49.6	49.6	51.4	51.4	49.6
Female	48.6	48.6	49.0	48.6	48.5	49.7	50.5	50.5	50.4	50.4	48.6	48.6	50.4
Race/ethnicity	100.0	100.0	100.0	100.0	100.0	100.0	100.0	100.0	100.0	100.0	100.0	100.0	100.0
White	61.8	61.9	42.5	58.4	58.7	41.8	38.8	37.3	35.6	35.4	50.3	51.1	34.9
Black	17.1	16.9	33.5	17.1	16.9	31.9	31.8	30.3	28.7	27.6	15.6	15.0	27.1
Hispanic	15.9	15.9	19.6	18.8	18.7	21.5	24.5	26.0	28.0	29.1	24.9	24.6	30.0
Asian/Pacific Islander	4.1	4.1	2.8	4.5	4.5	3.2	3.8	3.9	4.0	4.2	5.2	5.2	4.1
American Indian/Alaska Native	1.2	1.2	1.5	1.2	1.2	1.5	1.2	1.0	0.9	0.8	1.0	1.1	0.8
Two or more races	—	—	—	—	—	—	—	1.4	2.8	2.9	3.0	3.0	3.0
Percent of students eligible for free or reduced-price lunch program[1]	100.0	100.0	100.0	100.0	100.0	100.0	100.0	100.0	100.0	100.0	100.0	100.0	100.0
0 to 25.0	44.9	45.0	36.9	31.7	31.6	33.2	19.8	20.6	21.9	19.5	20.2	20.2	19.7
25.1 to 50.0	25.4	25.5	12.7	26.0	26.1	17.1	16.5	18.8	18.4	19.8	27.1	27.6	18.9
50.1 to 75.0	16.0	16.1	13.0	18.1	18.2	16.1	18.9	20.2	21.0	22.0	26.9	27.1	21.8
More than 75.0	12.2	12.2	14.3	13.4	13.3	18.4	21.2	30.7	30.8	35.5	24.8	24.2	36.7
Missing/school does not participate	1.4	1.2	23.2	10.8	10.7	15.2	23.6	9.7	7.9	3.1	1.0	0.8	3.0
Number of teachers[2]	2,636,277	2,622,678	13,599	2,714,733	2,678,327	36,406	69,725	84,983	107,929	117,037	2,973,522	2,844,844	128,678
Pupil/teacher ratio[2]	16.6	16.6	18.8	16.4	16.4	17.6	15.9	17.3	17.6	17.7	16.3	16.2	17.9
Total number of schools	92,012	90,488	1,524	95,726	92,749	2,977	4,388	4,952	5,696	6,079	98,271	91,806	6,465
Percentage distribution of schools													
School level	100.0	100.0	100.0	100.0	100.0	100.0	100.0	100.0	100.0	100.0	100.0	100.0	100.0
Elementary[3]	69.7	70.0	54.6	68.7	69.2	52.0	53.3	54.1	54.9	55.8	68.2	69.1	56.2
Secondary[4]	24.3	24.3	25.9	23.8	23.7	26.2	27.8	26.8	24.9	24.1	24.5	24.5	23.5
Combined[5]	4.4	4.2	18.6	5.7	5.2	21.0	18.3	18.8	19.5	19.8	6.3	5.4	19.6
Other	1.6	1.6	0.9	1.8	1.9	0.8	0.6	0.3	0.7	0.3	1.0	1.0	0.6
Size of enrollment	100.0	100.0	100.0	100.0	100.0	100.0	100.0	100.0	100.0	100.0	100.0	100.0	100.0
Less than 300	31.4	30.7	77.1	32.4	31.2	71.1	65.6	61.5	55.8	54.1	30.2	28.6	51.7
300 to 499	26.4	26.7	12.0	26.6	27.0	15.6	19.3	20.8	23.1	23.5	27.3	27.5	24.3
500 to 999	32.6	33.0	8.6	31.0	31.7	10.1	12.0	14.0	17.0	18.0	33.4	34.4	19.0
1,000 or more	9.5	9.7	2.4	9.9	10.2	3.2	3.1	3.7	4.2	4.4	9.1	9.4	4.9
Racial/ethnic concentration													
More than 50 percent White	70.9	71.2	51.1	67.2	67.8	48.7	43.2	40.3	37.5	36.6	58.2	59.8	35.8
More than 50 percent Black	11.1	10.8	26.5	11.4	10.9	24.5	26.5	25.8	25.3	24.9	10.1	9.1	24.4
More than 50 percent Hispanic	8.8	8.7	11.4	10.8	10.7	13.6	17.8	19.8	21.8	22.6	15.8	15.3	23.4
Percent of students eligible for free or reduced-price lunch program[1]	100.0	100.0	100.0	100.0	100.0	100.0	100.0	100.0	100.0	100.0	100.0	100.0	100.0
0 to 25.0	42.3	42.3	44.5	26.9	26.8	28.7	20.2	19.3	18.7	18.3	17.5	17.5	17.7
25.1 to 50.0	25.6	25.9	11.1	25.8	26.1	16.0	15.5	17.2	17.9	18.7	25.6	26.1	18.0
50.1 to 75.0	16.8	16.9	10.2	18.9	19.0	16.0	18.8	20.9	19.9	20.9	27.0	27.4	20.6
More than 75.0	11.9	11.9	12.4	14.1	13.9	19.9	22.4	32.8	33.8	36.9	25.0	24.1	38.9
Missing/school does not participate	3.3	3.0	21.9	14.3	14.1	19.5	23.0	9.8	9.7	5.2	4.9	4.9	4.8
Locale	—	—	—	100.0	100.0	100.0	100.0	100.0	100.0	100.0	100.0	100.0	100.0
City	—	—	—	25.7	24.8	52.7	54.3	54.8	55.4	56.7	27.0	25.0	56.5
Suburban	—	—	—	27.8	28.0	22.0	22.0	21.1	21.2	25.5	31.5	31.9	26.1
Town	—	—	—	15.2	15.4	9.6	8.5	8.0	7.4	7.0	13.7	14.2	7.0
Rural	—	—	—	31.3	31.8	15.8	15.2	16.1	16.0	10.8	27.7	29.0	10.4
Region	100.0	100.0	100.0	100.0	100.0	100.0	100.0	100.0	100.0	100.0	100.0	100.0	100.0
Northeast	16.1	16.3	7.2	16.0	16.2	9.2	8.6	9.1	9.7	10.0	15.4	15.8	10.1
Midwest	28.9	29.0	24.9	28.1	28.3	23.7	26.5	24.0	22.3	21.9	25.9	26.2	21.7
South	33.1	33.2	28.9	33.6	33.8	26.7	28.2	29.5	30.8	30.7	35.1	35.4	31.2
West	21.8	21.6	38.9	22.3	21.8	40.3	36.6	37.4	37.2	37.3	23.6	22.7	37.0

—Not available.

[1]The National School Lunch Program is a federally assisted meal program. To be eligible for free lunch under the program, a student must be from a household with an income at or below 130 percent of the poverty threshold; to be eligible for reduced-price lunch, a student must be from a household with an income between 130 percent and 185 percent of the poverty threshold.

[2]Pupil/teacher ratio based on schools that reported both enrollment and teacher data.

[3]Includes schools beginning with grade 6 or below and with no grade higher than 8.

[4]Includes schools with no grade lower than 7.

[5]Includes schools beginning with grade 6 or below and ending with grade 9 or above.

NOTE: Detail may not sum to totals because of rounding. Race categories exclude persons of Hispanic ethnicity.

SOURCE: U.S. Department of Education, National Center for Education Statistics, Common Core of Data (CCD), "Public Elementary/Secondary School Universe Survey," 1999–2000 through 2013–14. (This table was prepared September 2015.)

Table 216.40. Number and percentage distribution of public elementary and secondary schools and enrollment, by level, type, and enrollment size of school: 2011–12, 2012–13, and 2013–14

Enrollment size of school	Number and percentage distribution of schools, by level and type						Enrollment totals and percentage distribution, by level and type of school[1]					
			Secondary[4]		Combined elementary/ secondary[5]				Secondary[4]		Combined elementary/ secondary[5]	
	Total[2]	Elementary[3]	All schools	Regular schools[7]		Other[6]	Total[2]	Elementary[3]	All schools	Regular schools[7]		Other[6]
1	2	3	4	5	6	7	8	9	10	11	12	13
2011–12												
Total	98,328	66,689	24,357	19,441	6,311	971	49,256,120	31,724,573	15,708,815	15,194,153	1,818,020	4,712
Percent[8]	**100.00**	**100.00**	**100.00**	**100.00**	**100.00**	**100.00**	**100.00**	**100.00**	**100.00**	**100.00**	**100.00**	**100.00**
Under 100	10.32	5.46	17.47	9.31	37.92	67.86	0.89	0.57	1.08	0.65	4.80	35.93
100 to 199	9.09	7.65	11.57	10.59	15.72	28.57	2.62	2.43	2.47	2.00	7.05	49.79
200 to 299	10.96	11.68	9.12	9.36	10.02	1.79	5.31	6.18	3.29	2.96	7.68	4.69
300 to 399	13.79	16.20	8.12	8.88	8.45	0.00	9.29	11.88	4.10	3.93	9.10	0.00
400 to 499	13.92	17.08	6.56	7.40	6.55	1.79	12.00	16.00	4.26	4.21	9.16	9.59
500 to 599	11.65	14.14	5.87	6.68	5.90	0.00	12.27	16.17	4.66	4.64	10.01	0.00
600 to 699	8.58	10.23	4.92	5.56	4.04	0.00	10.67	13.82	4.61	4.56	8.12	0.00
700 to 799	6.13	6.98	4.48	5.12	2.96	0.00	8.80	10.88	4.85	4.85	6.80	0.00
800 to 999	6.56	6.77	6.79	7.87	3.13	0.00	11.17	12.49	8.80	8.94	8.65	0.00
1,000 to 1,499	5.40	3.48	11.51	13.30	3.28	0.00	12.42	8.42	20.53	20.76	12.20	0.00
1,500 to 1,999	2.02	0.29	7.26	8.53	1.24	0.00	6.71	1.02	18.24	18.77	6.49	0.00
2,000 to 2,999	1.33	0.03	5.36	6.29	0.44	0.00	6.03	0.13	18.26	18.78	3.27	0.00
3,000 or more	0.25	#	0.97	1.13	0.35	0.00	1.80	0.01	4.85	4.93	6.67	0.00
Average enrollment[8]	520	479	690	788	322	84	520	479	690	788	322	84
2012–13												
Total	98,454	66,718	24,280	19,470	6,371	1,085	49,474,030	31,893,347	15,644,214	15,137,814	1,934,697	1,772
Percent[8]	**100.00**	**100.00**	**100.00**	**100.00**	**100.00**	**100.00**	**100.00**	**100.00**	**100.00**	**100.00**	**100.00**	**100.00**
Under 100	10.14	5.34	17.35	9.30	36.73	86.21	0.88	0.56	1.08	0.65	4.42	57.73
100 to 199	9.20	7.74	11.66	10.60	16.30	6.90	2.63	2.44	2.48	1.99	6.94	12.64
200 to 299	10.90	11.50	9.30	9.66	10.23	6.90	5.28	6.08	3.36	3.07	7.52	29.63
300 to 399	13.62	16.05	7.95	8.65	8.11	0.00	9.15	11.71	4.02	3.84	8.37	0.00
400 to 499	13.86	16.93	6.87	7.72	6.07	0.00	11.91	15.80	4.46	4.40	8.06	0.00
500 to 599	11.72	14.24	5.85	6.63	5.93	0.00	12.28	16.19	4.64	4.62	9.63	0.00
600 to 699	8.64	10.35	4.91	5.54	3.71	0.00	10.70	13.90	4.62	4.57	7.13	0.00
700 to 799	6.14	7.06	4.23	4.87	3.21	0.00	8.78	10.94	4.59	4.64	7.10	0.00
800 to 999	6.70	6.94	6.70	7.76	3.87	0.00	11.36	12.74	8.69	8.84	10.13	0.00
1,000 to 1,499	5.47	3.52	11.60	13.37	3.68	0.00	12.53	8.47	20.74	20.97	13.08	0.00
1,500 to 1,999	2.04	0.29	7.38	8.64	1.17	0.00	6.77	1.00	18.63	19.13	5.88	0.00
2,000 to 2,999	1.30	0.03	5.23	6.12	0.49	0.00	5.86	0.14	17.85	18.34	3.29	0.00
3,000 or more	0.27	#	0.97	1.14	0.51	0.00	1.87	0.02	4.84	4.95	8.44	0.00
Average enrollment[8]	522	481	689	785	337	61	522	481	689	785	337	61
2013–14												
Total	98,271	67,034	24,053	19,409	6,205	979	49,709,977	32,183,080	15,618,300	15,148,323	1,896,908	11,689
Percent[8]	**100.00**	**100.00**	**100.00**	**100.00**	**100.00**	**100.00**	**100.00**	**100.00**	**100.00**	**100.00**	**100.00**	**100.00**
Under 100	10.12	5.35	17.33	9.46	37.63	45.45	0.88	0.56	1.10	0.67	4.49	6.07
100 to 199	9.04	7.68	11.29	10.28	16.23	11.36	2.58	2.41	2.39	1.93	6.86	5.40
200 to 299	10.91	11.49	9.35	9.61	10.28	18.18	5.25	6.04	3.34	3.03	7.44	16.39
300 to 399	13.40	15.70	8.00	8.76	7.83	9.09	8.96	11.41	4.03	3.88	8.06	11.94
400 to 499	13.90	16.95	6.88	7.72	5.88	2.27	11.89	15.75	4.45	4.40	7.77	4.12
500 to 599	11.81	14.41	5.80	6.52	5.06	4.55	12.32	16.33	4.57	4.52	8.13	8.74
600 to 699	8.71	10.35	4.98	5.61	4.32	2.27	10.74	13.85	4.64	4.61	8.24	5.62
700 to 799	6.13	7.07	4.10	4.71	3.20	0.00	8.72	10.91	4.42	4.48	7.03	0.00
800 to 999	6.85	7.13	6.89	7.95	3.41	2.27	11.57	13.04	8.86	9.01	9.01	7.98
1,000 to 1,499	5.49	3.57	11.58	13.33	3.84	2.27	12.52	8.56	20.54	20.83	13.66	10.77
1,500 to 1,999	2.04	0.29	7.44	8.64	1.25	0.00	6.73	0.99	18.61	19.03	6.35	0.00
2,000 to 2,999	1.33	0.03	5.37	6.27	0.55	2.27	5.95	0.13	18.19	18.70	3.92	22.96
3,000 or more	0.27	#	0.98	1.13	0.52	0.00	1.88	0.02	4.86	4.91	9.05	0.00
Average enrollment[8]	525	483	694	788	339	266	525	483	694	788	339	266

#Rounds to zero.
[1]Totals differ from those reported in other tables because this table represents data reported by schools rather than by states or school districts. Percentage distribution and average enrollment calculations exclude data for schools not reporting enrollment.
[2]Includes elementary, secondary, combined elementary/secondary, and other schools.
[3]Includes schools beginning with grade 6 or below and with no grade higher than 8.
[4]Includes schools with no grade lower than 7.
[5]Includes schools beginning with grade 6 or below and ending with grade 9 or above.
[6]Includes special education, alternative, and other schools not reported by grade span.
[7]Excludes special education schools, vocational schools, and alternative schools.
[8]Data are for schools reporting enrollments greater than zero. Enrollments greater than zero were reported for 94,743 out of 98,328 schools in 2011–12, 94,771 out of 98,454 in 2012–13, and 94,758 out of 98,271 in 2013–14.
NOTE: Detail may not sum to totals because of rounding.
SOURCE: U.S. Department of Education, National Center for Education Statistics, Common Core of Data (CCD), "Public Elementary/Secondary School Universe Survey," 2011–12, 2012–13, 2013–14. (This table was prepared September 2015.)

Table 216.45. Average enrollment and percentage distribution of public elementary and secondary schools, by level, type, and enrollment size: Selected years, 1982–83 through 2013–14

Year	Average enrollment in schools, by level and type						Percentage distribution of schools, by enrollment size							
			Secondary[3]											
	Total[1]	Elementary[2]	All schools	Regular schools[6]	Combined elementary/ secondary[4]	Other[5]	Under 200	200 to 299	300 to 399	400 to 499	500 to 599	600 to 699	700 to 999	1,000 or more
1	2	3	4	5	6	7	8	9	10	11	12	13	14	15
1982–83	478	399	719	—	478	142	21.9	13.8	15.5	13.1	10.2	7.1	10.2	8.3
1983–84	480	401	720	—	475	145	21.7	13.7	15.5	13.2	10.2	7.1	10.3	8.3
1984–85	482	403	721	—	476	146	21.5	13.6	15.5	13.2	10.3	7.1	10.4	8.4
1986–87	489	416	707	714	426	118	21.1	13.1	15.0	13.5	10.8	7.5	10.7	8.1
1987–88	490	424	695	711	420	122	20.3	12.9	14.9	13.8	11.1	7.8	11.2	8.0
1988–89	494	433	689	697	412	142	20.0	12.5	14.7	13.8	11.4	8.0	11.6	8.0
1989–90	493	441	669	689	402	142	19.8	12.2	14.5	13.7	11.5	8.3	12.0	7.9
1990–91	497	449	663	684	398	150	19.7	11.9	14.2	13.6	11.7	8.5	12.3	8.1
1991–92	507	458	677	717	407	152	19.1	11.7	14.1	13.5	11.8	8.6	12.8	8.5
1992–93	513	464	688	733	423	135	18.6	11.6	13.9	13.5	11.9	8.7	13.1	8.7
1993–94	518	468	693	748	418	136	18.6	11.5	13.6	13.5	11.7	8.8	13.3	9.0
1994–95	520	471	696	759	412	131	18.6	11.4	13.6	13.4	11.8	8.7	13.3	9.2
1995–96	525	476	703	771	401	136	18.5	11.2	13.5	13.4	11.8	8.8	13.4	9.4
1996–97	527	478	703	777	387	135	18.7	11.3	13.2	13.2	11.8	8.8	13.6	9.5
1997–98	525	478	699	779	374	121	19.3	11.2	13.1	13.3	11.6	8.6	13.4	9.6
1998–99	524	478	707	786	290	135	19.6	11.2	13.1	13.2	11.5	8.5	13.3	9.6
1999–2000	521	477	706	785	282	123	20.0	11.3	13.3	13.2	11.2	8.4	13.1	9.5
2000–01	519	477	714	795	274	136	20.4	11.4	13.2	13.3	11.0	8.2	12.9	9.6
2001–02	520	477	718	807	270	138	20.5	11.5	13.3	13.1	10.9	8.1	12.7	9.7
2002–03	519	476	720	813	265	136	20.7	11.6	13.4	13.0	10.9	8.1	12.4	9.8
2003–04	521	476	722	816	269	142	20.7	11.6	13.5	13.2	10.8	8.0	12.3	9.9
2004–05	521	474	713	815	298	143	20.7	11.6	13.5	13.2	10.8	8.1	12.2	9.9
2005–06	521	473	709	819	318	128	20.7	11.5	13.6	13.2	11.0	8.1	12.2	9.8
2006–07	521	473	711	818	325	138	20.3	11.5	13.8	13.4	11.0	8.2	12.2	9.6
2007–08	516	469	704	816	292	136	20.4	11.5	13.9	13.6	11.1	8.1	12.0	9.3
2008–09	517	470	704	807	308	177	20.0	11.4	13.8	13.9	11.3	8.3	12.2	9.1
2009–10	516	473	692	796	300	191	20.0	11.3	13.7	13.9	11.4	8.5	12.3	9.0
2010–11	517	475	684	790	343	57	19.8	11.0	13.9	13.9	11.5	8.5	12.5	9.0
2011–12	520	479	690	788	322	84	19.4	11.0	13.8	13.9	11.7	8.6	12.7	9.0
2012–13	522	481	689	785	337	61	19.3	10.9	13.6	13.9	11.7	8.6	12.8	9.1
2013–14	525	483	694	788	339	266	19.2	10.9	13.4	13.9	11.8	8.7	13.0	9.1

—Not available.
[1]Includes elementary, secondary, combined elementary/secondary, and other schools.
[2]Includes schools beginning with grade 6 or below and with no grade higher than 8.
[3]Includes schools with no grade lower than 7.
[4]Includes schools beginning with grade 6 or below and ending with grade 9 or above.
[5]Includes special education, alternative, and other schools not reported by grade span.
[6]Excludes special education schools, vocational schools, and alternative schools.

NOTE: Data reflect reports by schools rather than by states or school districts. Percentage distribution and average enrollment calculations include data only for schools reporting enrollments greater than zero. Enrollments greater than zero were reported for 94,758 out of 98,271 schools in 2013–14. Detail may not sum to totals because of rounding.
SOURCE: U.S. Department of Education, National Center for Education Statistics, Common Core of Data (CCD), "Public Elementary/Secondary School Universe Survey," 1982–83 through 2013–14. (This table was prepared September 2015.)

Table 216.50. Number and percentage distribution of public elementary and secondary school students, by percentage of minority enrollment in the school and student's racial/ethnic group: Selected years, fall 1995 through fall 2013

Year and racial/ethnic group	Number of students in racial/ethnic group, by percent minority enrollment in the school							Percentage distribution of students in racial/ethnic group, by percent minority enrollment in the school						
	Total	Less than 10 percent	10 to 24 percent	25 to 49 percent	50 to 74 percent	75 to 89 percent	90 percent or more	Total	Less than 10 percent	10 to 24 percent	25 to 49 percent	50 to 74 percent	75 to 89 percent	90 percent or more
1	2	3	4	5	6	7	8	9	10	11	12	13	14	15
Total, 1995	**44,424,467**	**14,508,573**	**8,182,484**	**8,261,110**	**5,467,784**	**2,876,302**	**5,128,214**	**100.0**	**32.7**	**18.4**	**18.6**	**12.3**	**6.5**	**11.5**
White	28,736,961	13,939,633	6,812,196	5,246,785	2,094,440	499,884	144,023	100.0	48.5	23.7	18.3	7.3	1.7	0.5
Minority	15,687,506	568,940	1,370,288	3,014,325	3,373,344	2,376,418	4,984,191	100.0	3.6	8.7	19.2	21.5	15.1	31.8
Black	7,510,678	198,386	598,716	1,588,850	1,622,448	941,335	2,560,943	100.0	2.6	8.0	21.2	21.6	12.5	34.1
Hispanic	6,016,293	174,140	415,761	932,949	1,289,184	1,099,109	2,105,150	100.0	2.9	6.9	15.5	21.4	18.3	35.0
Asian/Pacific Islander	1,656,787	142,886	259,335	367,888	379,110	297,680	209,888	100.0	8.6	15.7	22.2	22.9	18.0	12.7
American Indian/Alaska Native	503,748	53,528	96,476	124,638	82,602	38,294	108,210	100.0	10.6	19.2	24.7	16.4	7.6	21.5
Total, 2000	**46,120,425**	**12,761,478**	**8,736,252**	**8,760,300**	**6,013,131**	**3,472,083**	**6,377,181**	**100.0**	**27.7**	**18.9**	**19.0**	**13.0**	**7.5**	**13.8**
White	28,146,613	12,218,862	7,271,285	5,566,681	2,303,106	596,478	190,201	100.0	43.4	25.8	19.8	8.2	2.1	0.7
Minority	17,973,812	542,616	1,464,967	3,193,619	3,710,025	2,875,605	6,186,980	100.0	3.0	8.2	17.8	20.6	16.0	34.4
Black	7,854,032	178,185	561,488	1,485,130	1,652,393	1,043,907	2,932,929	100.0	2.3	7.1	18.9	21.0	13.3	37.3
Hispanic	7,649,728	181,685	505,612	1,121,809	1,542,982	1,432,639	2,865,001	100.0	2.4	6.6	14.7	20.2	18.7	37.5
Asian/Pacific Islander	1,924,875	132,813	295,437	441,769	423,175	353,395	278,286	100.0	6.9	15.3	23.0	22.0	18.4	14.5
American Indian/Alaska Native	545,177	49,933	102,430	144,911	91,475	45,664	110,764	100.0	9.2	18.8	26.6	16.8	8.4	20.3
Total, 2005	**48,584,980**	**10,711,307**	**9,283,783**	**9,865,121**	**6,839,850**	**4,149,802**	**7,735,117**	**100.0**	**22.0**	**19.1**	**20.3**	**14.1**	**8.5**	**15.9**
White	27,742,612	10,208,608	7,720,632	6,259,485	2,604,846	707,603	241,438	100.0	36.8	27.8	22.6	9.4	2.6	0.9
Minority	20,842,368	502,699	1,563,151	3,605,636	4,235,004	3,442,199	7,493,679	100.0	2.4	7.5	17.3	20.3	16.5	36.0
Black	8,366,722	162,455	560,928	1,513,020	1,752,207	1,176,649	3,201,463	100.0	1.9	6.7	18.1	20.9	14.1	38.3
Hispanic	9,638,712	182,039	581,533	1,388,496	1,873,877	1,803,567	3,809,200	100.0	1.9	6.0	14.4	19.4	18.7	39.5
Asian/Pacific Islander	2,242,628	115,084	319,524	543,952	496,515	406,788	360,765	100.0	5.1	14.2	24.3	22.1	18.1	16.1
American Indian/Alaska Native	594,306	43,121	101,166	160,168	112,405	55,195	122,251	100.0	7.3	17.0	27.0	18.9	9.3	20.6
Total, 2010	**49,212,031**	**7,395,549**	**9,177,649**	**11,236,328**	**7,904,340**	**4,718,126**	**8,780,039**	**100.0**	**15.0**	**18.6**	**22.8**	**16.1**	**9.6**	**17.8**
White	25,801,021	6,987,898	7,614,557	7,097,284	3,003,599	808,637	289,046	100.0	27.1	29.5	27.5	11.6	3.1	1.1
Minority	23,411,010	407,651	1,563,092	4,139,044	4,900,741	3,909,489	8,490,993	100.0	1.7	6.7	17.7	20.9	16.7	36.3
Black	7,873,809	95,108	415,807	1,335,674	1,697,727	1,236,333	3,093,160	100.0	1.2	5.3	17.0	21.6	15.7	39.3
Hispanic	11,367,157	142,927	583,019	1,654,084	2,238,071	2,063,492	4,685,564	100.0	1.3	5.1	14.6	19.7	18.2	41.2
Asian	2,281,908	63,974	259,910	585,447	552,633	390,731	429,213	100.0	2.8	11.4	25.7	24.2	17.1	18.8
Pacific Islander	169,678	4,958	13,772	27,478	32,241	41,652	49,577	100.0	2.9	8.1	16.2	19.0	24.5	29.2
American Indian/Alaska Native	561,126	26,066	77,990	157,300	116,787	58,476	124,507	100.0	4.6	13.9	28.0	20.8	10.4	22.2
Two or more races	1,157,332	74,618	212,594	379,061	263,282	118,805	108,972	100.0	6.4	18.4	32.8	22.7	10.3	9.4
Total, 2011	**49,246,537**	**6,943,209**	**9,090,845**	**11,325,084**	**8,087,862**	**4,909,344**	**8,890,193**	**100.0**	**14.1**	**18.5**	**23.0**	**16.4**	**10.0**	**18.1**
White	25,464,162	6,549,257	7,535,852	7,154,879	3,086,247	842,317	295,610	100.0	25.7	29.6	28.1	12.1	3.3	1.2
Minority	23,782,375	393,952	1,554,993	4,170,205	5,001,615	4,067,027	8,594,583	100.0	1.7	6.5	17.5	21.0	17.1	36.1
Black	7,782,146	85,682	393,118	1,302,027	1,686,653	1,255,240	3,059,426	100.0	1.1	5.1	16.7	21.7	16.1	39.3
Hispanic	11,693,788	141,593	594,874	1,678,320	2,302,100	2,161,819	4,815,082	100.0	1.2	5.1	14.4	19.7	18.5	41.2
Asian	2,321,362	58,414	249,943	587,291	570,921	415,832	438,961	100.0	2.5	10.8	25.3	24.6	17.9	18.9
Pacific Islander	177,871	5,170	13,635	27,828	34,546	42,851	53,841	100.0	2.9	7.7	15.6	19.4	24.1	30.3
American Indian/Alaska Native	541,986	23,215	69,953	152,088	112,568	58,106	126,056	100.0	4.3	12.9	28.1	20.8	10.7	23.3
Two or more races	1,265,222	79,878	233,470	422,651	294,827	133,179	101,217	100.0	6.3	18.5	33.4	23.3	10.5	8.0
Total, 2012	**49,460,399**	**6,512,145**	**9,106,399**	**11,465,619**	**8,280,130**	**4,994,550**	**9,101,556**	**100.0**	**13.2**	**18.4**	**23.2**	**16.7**	**10.1**	**18.4**
White	25,238,825	6,136,381	7,549,183	7,233,482	3,153,892	859,415	306,472	100.0	24.3	29.9	28.7	12.5	3.4	1.2
Minority	24,221,574	375,764	1,557,216	4,232,137	5,126,238	4,135,135	8,795,084	100.0	1.6	6.4	17.5	21.2	17.1	36.3
Black	7,745,244	76,614	377,613	1,275,975	1,690,994	1,260,621	3,063,427	100.0	1.0	4.9	16.5	21.8	16.3	39.6
Hispanic	12,028,116	137,254	601,847	1,721,620	2,374,944	2,210,057	4,982,394	100.0	1.1	5.0	14.3	19.7	18.4	41.4
Asian	2,358,015	52,671	244,691	595,541	589,235	417,742	458,135	100.0	2.2	10.4	25.3	25.0	17.7	19.4
Pacific Islander	179,353	4,899	13,819	28,583	34,480	40,876	56,696	100.0	2.7	7.7	15.9	19.2	22.8	31.6
American Indian/Alaska Native	528,024	20,847	65,566	147,080	110,908	59,210	124,413	100.0	3.9	12.4	27.9	21.0	11.2	23.6
Two or more races	1,382,822	83,479	253,680	463,338	325,677	146,629	110,019	100.0	6.0	18.3	33.5	23.6	10.6	8.0
Total, 2013	**49,700,391**	**6,121,290**	**9,029,047**	**11,604,239**	**8,505,389**	**5,179,379**	**9,261,047**	**100.0**	**12.3**	**18.2**	**23.3**	**17.1**	**10.4**	**18.6**
White	25,002,213	5,761,258	7,482,233	7,319,117	3,241,142	886,628	311,835	100.0	23.0	29.9	29.3	13.0	3.5	1.2
Minority	24,698,178	360,032	1,546,814	4,285,122	5,264,247	4,292,751	8,949,212	100.0	1.5	6.3	17.3	21.3	17.4	36.2
Black	7,743,485	69,458	360,023	1,251,977	1,696,184	1,298,309	3,067,534	100.0	0.9	4.6	16.2	21.9	16.8	39.6
Hispanic	12,363,677	132,910	603,028	1,755,809	2,448,589	2,304,721	5,118,620	100.0	1.1	4.9	14.2	19.8	18.6	41.4
Asian	2,401,305	48,171	238,017	603,725	613,063	430,727	467,602	100.0	2.0	9.9	25.1	25.5	17.9	19.5
Pacific Islander	175,236	4,200	13,249	28,616	35,507	39,899	53,765	100.0	2.4	7.6	16.3	20.3	22.8	30.7
American Indian/Alaska Native	516,705	18,685	61,576	142,536	110,727	59,304	123,877	100.0	3.6	11.9	27.6	21.4	11.5	24.0
Two or more races	1,497,770	86,608	270,921	502,459	360,177	159,791	117,814	100.0	5.8	18.1	33.5	24.0	10.7	7.9

NOTE: Data reflect racial/ethnic data reported by schools. Because some schools do not report complete racial/ethnic data, totals may differ from figures in other tables. Excludes 1995 data for Idaho and 2000 data for Tennessee because racial/ethnic data were not reported. Race categories exclude persons of Hispanic ethnicity. Detail may not sum to totals because of rounding.

SOURCE: U.S. Department of Education, National Center for Education Statistics, Common Core of Data (CCD), "Public Elementary/Secondary School Universe Survey," 1995–96 through 2013–14. (This table was prepared January 2016.)

Table 216.55. Number and percentage distribution of public elementary and secondary school students, by percentage of student's racial/ethnic group enrolled in the school and student's racial/ethnic group: Selected years, fall 1995 through fall 2013

Year and racial/ethnic group	Number of students in each racial/ethnic group, by percent of that racial/ethnic group in the school							Percentage distribution of students in each racial/ethnic group, by percent of that racial/ethnic group in the school						
	Total	Less than 10 percent of group	10 to 24 percent of group	25 to 49 percent of group	50 to 74 percent of group	75 to 89 percent of group	90 percent or more of group	Total	Less than 10 percent of group	10 to 24 percent of group	25 to 49 percent of group	50 to 74 percent of group	75 to 89 percent of group	90 percent or more of group
1	2	3	4	5	6	7	8	9	10	11	12	13	14	15
1995														
White	28,736,961	143,787	498,649	2,084,689	5,244,015	6,813,804	13,952,017	100.0	0.5	1.7	7.3	18.2	23.7	48.6
Black	7,510,678	657,403	1,119,556	1,873,303	1,386,802	811,898	1,661,716	100.0	8.8	14.9	24.9	18.5	10.8	22.1
Hispanic	6,016,293	646,364	847,792	1,359,649	1,360,020	874,878	927,590	100.0	10.7	14.1	22.6	22.6	14.5	15.4
Asian/Pacific Islander	1,656,787	703,101	435,495	301,984	135,001	67,558	13,648	100.0	42.4	26.3	18.2	8.1	4.1	0.8
American Indian/Alaska Native	503,748	223,244	75,019	63,070	39,200	15,084	88,131	100.0	44.3	14.9	12.5	7.8	3.0	17.5
2000														
White	28,146,613	189,779	595,137	2,294,232	5,556,108	7,279,301	12,232,056	100.0	0.7	2.1	8.2	19.7	25.9	43.5
Black	7,854,032	735,459	1,199,865	1,899,982	1,366,363	871,399	1,780,964	100.0	9.4	15.3	24.2	17.4	11.1	22.7
Hispanic	7,649,728	738,509	1,054,396	1,696,944	1,739,038	1,134,466	1,286,375	100.0	9.7	13.8	22.2	22.7	14.8	16.8
Asian/Pacific Islander	1,924,875	799,220	524,279	331,576	171,739	81,461	16,600	100.0	41.5	27.2	17.2	8.9	4.2	0.9
American Indian/Alaska Native	545,177	251,983	81,119	75,831	39,944	15,363	80,937	100.0	46.2	14.9	13.9	7.3	2.8	14.8
2005														
White	27,742,612	240,614	705,300	2,596,310	6,256,109	7,718,175	10,226,104	100.0	0.9	2.5	9.4	22.6	27.8	36.9
Black	8,366,722	849,399	1,396,670	2,004,856	1,453,759	884,663	1,777,375	100.0	10.2	16.7	24.0	17.4	10.6	21.2
Hispanic	9,638,712	848,160	1,316,558	2,071,303	2,218,616	1,545,322	1,638,753	100.0	8.8	13.7	21.5	23.0	16.0	17.0
Asian/Pacific Islander	2,242,628	925,411	616,762	363,562	214,304	100,845	21,744	100.0	41.3	27.5	16.2	9.6	4.5	1.0
American Indian/Alaska Native	594,306	276,846	86,978	84,665	43,272	21,275	81,270	100.0	46.6	14.6	14.2	7.3	3.6	13.7
2010														
White	25,801,021	288,136	807,107	2,991,928	7,090,581	7,620,071	7,003,198	100.0	1.1	3.1	11.6	27.5	29.5	27.1
Black	7,873,809	904,777	1,453,068	1,907,158	1,328,164	859,843	1,420,799	100.0	11.5	18.5	24.2	16.9	10.9	18.0
Hispanic	11,367,157	896,796	1,603,546	2,473,080	2,657,108	1,791,161	1,945,466	100.0	7.9	14.1	21.8	23.4	15.8	17.1
Asian	2,281,908	944,657	633,149	431,446	219,381	43,509	9,766	100.0	41.4	27.7	18.9	9.6	1.9	0.4
Pacific Islander	169,678	104,646	15,170	27,558	14,860	5,146	2,298	100.0	61.7	8.9	16.2	8.8	3.0	1.4
American Indian/Alaska Native	561,126	276,859	76,874	78,978	38,349	21,156	68,910	100.0	49.3	13.7	14.1	6.8	3.8	12.3
Two or more races	1,157,332	996,181	128,813	15,347	6,709	3,286	6,996	100.0	86.1	11.1	1.3	0.6	0.3	0.6
2011														
White	25,464,162	294,998	840,764	3,072,182	7,153,778	7,543,427	6,559,013	100.0	1.2	3.3	12.1	28.1	29.6	25.8
Black	7,782,146	909,399	1,448,983	1,912,335	1,301,165	864,856	1,345,408	100.0	11.7	18.6	24.6	16.7	11.1	17.3
Hispanic	11,693,788	909,247	1,658,024	2,543,266	2,720,777	1,877,108	1,985,366	100.0	7.8	14.2	21.7	23.3	16.1	17.0
Asian	2,321,362	946,520	644,479	441,656	232,408	43,530	12,769	100.0	40.8	27.8	19.0	10.0	1.9	0.6
Pacific Islander	177,871	112,805	14,759	28,211	15,688	4,471	1,937	100.0	63.4	8.3	15.9	8.8	2.5	1.1
American Indian/Alaska Native	541,986	267,993	72,148	77,142	36,010	22,095	66,598	100.0	49.4	13.3	14.2	6.6	4.1	12.3
Two or more races	1,265,222	1,107,727	139,250	8,444	3,484	5,324	993	100.0	87.6	11.0	0.7	0.3	0.4	0.1
2012														
White	25,238,825	306,146	857,049	3,139,878	7,229,221	7,552,960	6,153,571	100.0	1.2	3.4	12.4	28.6	29.9	24.4
Black	7,745,244	912,607	1,458,854	1,902,995	1,326,005	854,903	1,289,880	100.0	11.8	18.8	24.6	17.1	11.0	16.7
Hispanic	12,028,116	918,483	1,709,042	2,610,291	2,818,279	1,916,973	2,055,048	100.0	7.6	14.2	21.7	23.4	15.9	17.1
Asian	2,358,015	954,868	649,405	460,219	235,915	44,832	12,776	100.0	40.5	27.5	19.5	10.0	1.9	0.5
Pacific Islander	179,353	115,282	14,614	28,687	14,860	4,542	1,368	100.0	64.3	8.1	16.0	8.3	2.5	0.8
American Indian/Alaska Native	528,024	260,268	70,477	77,044	33,558	20,767	65,910	100.0	49.3	13.3	14.6	6.4	3.9	12.5
Two or more races	1,382,822	1,205,382	164,423	7,702	1,229	3,114	972	100.0	87.2	11.9	0.6	0.1	0.2	0.1
2013														
White	25,002,213	311,182	883,277	3,231,085	7,315,466	7,487,804	5,773,399	100.0	1.2	3.5	12.9	29.3	29.9	23.1
Black	7,743,485	911,504	1,477,015	1,921,631	1,336,048	860,336	1,236,951	100.0	11.8	19.1	24.8	17.3	11.1	16.0
Hispanic	12,363,677	919,255	1,750,152	2,690,698	2,918,707	1,969,011	2,115,854	100.0	7.4	14.2	21.8	23.6	15.9	17.1
Asian	2,401,305	956,000	661,825	479,668	243,021	48,169	12,622	100.0	39.8	27.6	20.0	10.1	2.0	0.5
Pacific Islander	175,236	112,227	14,772	30,051	12,430	5,136	620	100.0	64.0	8.4	17.1	7.1	2.9	0.4
American Indian/Alaska Native	516,705	254,656	69,669	74,838	33,702	18,951	64,889	100.0	49.3	13.5	14.5	6.5	3.7	12.6
Two or more races	1,497,770	1,290,200	195,092	8,046	2,822	1,397	213	100.0	86.1	13.0	0.5	0.2	0.1	#

#Rounds to zero.

NOTE: Data reflect racial/ethnic data reported by schools. Because some schools do not report complete racial/ethnic data, totals may differ from figures in other tables. Excludes 1995 data for Idaho and 2000 data for Tennessee because racial/ethnic data were not reported. Race categories exclude persons of Hispanic ethnicity. Detail may not sum to totals because of rounding.

SOURCE: U.S. Department of Education, National Center for Education Statistics, Common Core of Data (CCD), "Public Elementary/Secondary School Universe Survey," 1995–96 through 2013–14. (This table was prepared January 2016.)

Table 216.60. Number and percentage distribution of public school students, by percentage of students in school who are eligible for free or reduced-price lunch, school level, locale, and student race/ethnicity: 2013–14

School level, locale, and student race/ethnicity	Number of students, by percent of students in school eligible for free or reduced-price lunch						Percentage distribution of students, by percent of students in school eligible for free or reduced-price lunch					
	Total[1]	0 to 25.0 percent	25.1 to 50.0 percent	50.1 to 75.0 percent	More than 75.0 percent	Missing/ school does not participate	Total[1]	0 to 25.0 percent	25.1 to 50.0 percent	50.1 to 75.0 percent	More than 75.0 percent	Missing/ school does not participate
1	2	3	4	5	6	7	8	9	10	11	12	13
Total[2]	**49,700,391**	**10,034,137**	**13,490,958**	**13,356,867**	**12,343,741**	**474,688**	**100.0**	**20.2**	**27.1**	**26.9**	**24.8**	**1.0**
White	25,002,213	7,301,646	8,960,889	6,541,027	1,885,498	313,153	100.0	29.2	35.8	26.2	7.5	1.3
Black	7,743,485	512,623	1,259,165	2,261,276	3,652,903	57,518	100.0	6.6	16.3	29.2	47.2	0.7
Hispanic	12,363,677	942,396	2,053,535	3,386,043	5,913,177	68,526	100.0	7.6	16.6	27.4	47.8	0.6
Asian	2,401,305	880,078	598,242	499,840	408,341	14,804	100.0	36.6	24.9	20.8	17.0	0.6
Pacific Islander	175,236	20,511	47,529	63,727	42,877	592	100.0	11.7	27.1	36.4	24.5	0.3
American Indian/ Alaska Native	516,705	42,312	112,860	171,850	182,777	6,906	100.0	8.2	21.8	33.3	35.4	1.3
Two or more races	1,497,770	334,571	458,738	433,104	258,168	13,189	100.0	22.3	30.6	28.9	17.2	0.9
School level[3]												
Elementary[4]	32,175,213	6,018,352	7,704,642	8,635,843	9,508,930	307,446	100.0	18.7	23.9	26.8	29.6	1.0
White	15,751,282	4,346,966	5,151,807	4,511,613	1,533,505	207,391	100.0	27.6	32.7	28.6	9.7	1.3
Black	5,043,598	273,226	675,159	1,304,427	2,753,907	36,879	100.0	5.4	13.4	25.9	54.6	0.7
Hispanic	8,344,356	564,016	1,151,154	2,056,521	4,530,456	42,209	100.0	6.8	13.8	24.6	54.3	0.5
Asian	1,542,059	578,232	350,545	302,863	302,864	7,555	100.0	37.5	22.7	19.6	19.6	0.5
Pacific Islander	110,748	11,644	24,699	40,143	33,945	317	100.0	10.5	22.3	36.2	30.7	0.3
American Indian/ Alaska Native	322,836	20,935	58,245	105,048	134,925	3,683	100.0	6.5	18.0	32.5	41.8	1.1
Two or more races	1,060,334	223,333	293,033	315,228	219,328	9,412	100.0	21.1	27.6	29.7	20.7	0.9
Secondary[5]	15,617,444	3,659,280	5,332,383	4,163,053	2,352,910	109,818	100.0	23.4	34.1	26.7	15.1	0.7
White	8,269,298	2,695,839	3,499,775	1,730,805	274,026	68,853	100.0	32.6	42.3	20.9	3.3	0.8
Black	2,341,741	211,470	544,303	853,299	718,123	14,546	100.0	9.0	23.2	36.4	30.7	0.6
Hispanic	3,604,199	343,316	832,614	1,212,456	1,196,949	18,864	100.0	9.5	23.1	33.6	33.2	0.5
Asian	797,676	284,628	232,735	183,865	92,575	3,873	100.0	35.7	29.2	23.1	11.6	0.5
Pacific Islander	56,269	7,656	21,128	20,677	6,657	151	100.0	13.6	37.5	36.7	11.8	0.3
American Indian/ Alaska Native	161,158	18,197	50,293	56,978	33,990	1,700	100.0	11.3	31.2	35.4	21.1	1.1
Two or more races	387,103	98,174	151,535	104,973	30,590	1,831	100.0	25.4	39.1	27.1	7.9	0.5
School locale												
City	15,114,922	1,791,693	2,913,971	3,785,675	6,504,136	119,447	100.0	11.9	19.3	25.0	43.0	0.8
White	4,527,499	1,071,551	1,534,934	1,214,590	654,696	51,728	100.0	23.7	33.9	26.8	14.5	1.1
Black	3,615,068	123,521	395,180	889,890	2,176,775	29,702	100.0	3.4	10.9	24.6	60.2	0.8
Hispanic	5,305,056	240,032	605,356	1,238,056	3,195,421	26,191	100.0	4.5	11.4	23.3	60.2	0.5
Asian	1,015,350	256,116	217,399	253,019	283,364	5,452	100.0	25.2	21.4	24.9	27.9	0.5
Pacific Islander	58,778	5,432	12,953	20,425	19,690	278	100.0	9.2	22.0	34.7	33.5	0.5
American Indian/ Alaska Native	109,831	10,176	24,126	30,327	43,628	1,574	100.0	9.3	22.0	27.6	39.7	1.4
Two or more races	483,340	84,865	124,023	139,368	130,562	4,522	100.0	17.6	25.7	28.8	27.0	0.9
Suburban	19,773,710	6,348,192	5,559,004	4,193,326	3,516,067	157,121	100.0	32.1	28.1	21.2	17.8	0.8
White	10,187,181	4,643,800	3,354,988	1,626,949	459,771	101,673	100.0	45.6	32.9	16.0	4.5	1.0
Black	2,699,895	322,694	628,336	851,530	879,443	17,892	100.0	12.0	23.3	31.5	32.6	0.7
Hispanic	4,902,880	579,961	999,072	1,330,180	1,969,636	24,031	100.0	11.8	20.4	27.1	40.2	0.5
Asian	1,185,234	565,708	313,550	191,845	106,161	7,970	100.0	47.7	26.5	16.2	9.0	0.7
Pacific Islander	74,107	12,703	24,457	22,824	13,990	133	100.0	17.1	33.0	30.8	18.9	0.2
American Indian/ Alaska Native	91,282	19,167	30,600	25,322	15,413	780	100.0	21.0	33.5	27.7	16.9	0.9
Two or more races	633,131	204,159	208,001	144,676	71,653	4,642	100.0	32.2	32.9	22.9	11.3	0.7
Town	5,680,267	421,943	1,829,156	2,276,395	1,071,025	81,748	100.0	7.4	32.2	40.1	18.9	1.4
White	3,679,384	357,329	1,477,785	1,472,132	310,858	61,280	100.0	9.7	40.2	40.0	8.4	1.7
Black	574,829	12,060	63,536	218,362	276,423	4,448	100.0	2.1	11.1	38.0	48.1	0.8
Hispanic	1,043,352	28,783	179,093	422,734	401,853	10,889	100.0	2.8	17.2	40.5	38.5	1.0
Asian	73,932	7,992	26,247	28,864	10,215	614	100.0	10.8	35.5	39.0	13.8	0.8
Pacific Islander	24,429	608	5,558	13,628	4,549	86	100.0	2.5	22.8	55.8	18.6	0.4
American Indian/ Alaska Native	124,378	5,073	27,656	49,931	39,308	2,410	100.0	4.1	22.2	40.1	31.6	1.9
Two or more races	159,963	10,098	49,281	70,744	27,819	2,021	100.0	6.3	30.8	44.2	17.4	1.3
Rural	9,131,492	1,472,309	3,188,827	3,101,471	1,252,513	116,372	100.0	16.1	34.9	34.0	13.7	1.3
White	6,608,149	1,228,966	2,593,182	2,227,356	460,173	98,472	100.0	18.6	39.2	33.7	7.0	1.5
Black	853,693	54,348	172,113	301,494	320,262	5,476	100.0	6.4	20.2	35.3	37.5	0.6
Hispanic	1,112,389	93,620	270,014	395,073	346,267	7,415	100.0	8.4	24.3	35.5	31.1	0.7
Asian	126,789	50,262	41,046	26,112	8,601	768	100.0	39.6	32.4	20.6	6.8	0.6
Pacific Islander	17,922	1,768	4,561	6,850	4,648	95	100.0	9.9	25.4	38.2	25.9	0.5
American Indian/ Alaska Native	191,214	7,896	30,478	66,270	84,428	2,142	100.0	4.1	15.9	34.7	44.2	1.1
Two or more races	221,336	35,449	77,433	78,316	28,134	2,004	100.0	16.0	35.0	35.4	12.7	0.9

[1]Includes students enrolled in schools that did not report free or reduced-price lunch eligibility.
[2]Excludes 9,586 students whose race/ethnicity was not available. Includes students who attended combined elementary/secondary schools and schools not reported by grade span, which are not shown separately.
[3]Combined elementary/secondary schools and schools not reported by grade span are not shown separately.
[4]Includes schools beginning with grade 6 or below and with no grade higher than 8.
[5]Includes schools with no grade lower than 7.
NOTE: Students with household incomes under 185 percent of the poverty threshold are eligible for free or reduced price lunch under the National School Lunch Program (NSLP). In addition, some groups of children—such as foster children, children participating in the Head Start and Migrant Education programs, and children receiving services under the Runaway and Homeless Youth Act—are assumed to be categorically eligible to participate in the NSLP. Also, under the Community Eligibility option, some nonpoor children who attend school in a low-income area may participate if the district decides that it would be more efficient to provide free lunch to all children in the school. For more information, see http://www.fns.usda.gov/nslp/national-school-lunch-program-nslp. Race categories exclude persons of Hispanic ethnicity. Detail may not sum to totals because of rounding.
SOURCE: U.S. Department of Education, National Center for Education Statistics, Common Core of Data (CCD), "Public Elementary/Secondary School Universe Survey," 2013–14. (This table was prepared September 2015.)

Table 216.70. Public elementary and secondary schools, by level, type, and state or jurisdiction: 1990–91, 2000–01, 2010–11, and 2013–14

State or jurisdiction	Total, all schools, 1990–91	Total, all schools, 2000–01	Total, all schools, 2010–11	Schools by level, 2013–14: Total, all schools	Elementary[1]	Secondary[2]	Combined elementary/secondary[3]: Total	Prekindergarten, kindergarten, or 1st grade to grade 12	Other schools ending with grade 12	Other combined schools	Other[4]	Selected types of schools, 2013–14: Alternative[5]	Special education[5]	One-teacher schools[5]
1	2	3	4	5	6	7	8	9	10	11	12	13	14	15
United States	**84,538**	**93,273**	**98,817**	**98,271**	**67,034**	**24,053**	**6,205**	**3,123**	**2,484**	**598**	**979**	**5,698**	**2,010**	**193**
Alabama	1,297	1,517	1,600	1,637	990	434	182	118	60	4	31	119	44	1
Alaska	498	515	509	507	199	83	225	210	12	3	0	61	3	7
Arizona	1,049	1,724	2,265	2,252	1,335	734	157	83	50	24	26	61	21	3
Arkansas	1,098	1,138	1,110	1,112	718	368	24	6	11	7	2	9	4	0
California	7,913	8,773	10,124	10,276	6,954	2,606	601	452	135	14	115	1,238	151	36
Colorado	1,344	1,632	1,796	1,832	1,300	389	143	61	67	15	0	92	6	2
Connecticut	985	1,248	1,157	1,152	815	286	41	9	19	13	10	50	44	0
Delaware	173	191	214	219	159	36	19	11	6	2	5	7	19	0
District of Columbia	181	198	228	225	166	39	11	4	4	3	9	11	5	0
Florida	2,516	3,316	4,131	4,295	2,829	695	631	245	367	19	140	398	186	1
Georgia	1,734	1,946	2,449	2,379	1,776	457	61	16	29	16	85	72	60	1
Hawaii	235	261	289	288	208	52	28	24	3	1	0	1	1	1
Idaho	582	673	748	706	449	197	57	38	15	4	3	51	13	8
Illinois	4,239	4,342	4,361	4,204	3,107	937	159	46	100	13	1	144	137	0
Indiana	1,915	1,976	1,936	1,928	1,370	460	98	56	32	10	0	9	27	0
Iowa	1,588	1,534	1,436	1,382	969	371	42	6	36	0	0	26	7	3
Kansas	1,477	1,430	1,378	1,346	943	352	49	13	35	1	2	2	10	0
Kentucky	1,400	1,526	1,554	1,565	983	422	142	40	98	4	18	152	5	0
Louisiana	1,533	1,530	1,471	1,412	930	281	117	67	39	11	84	97	30	0
Maine	747	714	631	619	453	149	13	10	2	1	4	0	3	3
Maryland	1,220	1,383	1,449	1,442	1,130	246	51	20	24	7	15	54	38	1
Massachusetts	1,842	1,905	1,829	1,865	1,430	382	47	12	30	5	6	22	22	1
Michigan	3,313	3,998	3,877	3,538	2,213	939	378	203	157	18	8	310	183	4
Minnesota	1,590	2,362	2,392	2,414	1,280	836	297	144	140	13	1	479	279	0
Mississippi	972	1,030	1,083	1,066	626	325	106	65	40	1	9	62	4	0
Missouri	2,199	2,368	2,410	2,410	1,591	642	157	73	82	2	20	104	63	0
Montana	900	879	827	824	485	339	0	0	0	0	0	4	2	62
Nebraska	1,506	1,326	1,096	1,102	730	307	13	11	1	1	52	52	26	4
Nevada	354	511	645	653	480	132	41	13	28	0	0	35	13	12
New Hampshire	439	526	480	482	376	106	0	0	0	0	0	0	0	0
New Jersey	2,272	2,410	2,607	2,508	1,956	494	56	34	18	4	2	23	58	0
New Mexico	681	765	862	880	611	238	30	9	18	3	1	40	8	0
New York	4,010	4,336	4,757	4,801	3,307	1,130	330	128	140	62	34	30	128	0
North Carolina	1,955	2,207	2,567	2,588	1,899	536	146	60	69	17	7	82	26	0
North Dakota	663	579	516	512	297	183	0	0	0	0	32	0	33	5
Ohio	3,731	3,916	3,758	3,656	2,488	1,013	150	49	63	38	5	4	50	1
Oklahoma	1,880	1,821	1,785	1,789	1,222	561	6	2	4	0	0	4	4	0
Oregon	1,199	1,273	1,296	1,246	882	277	87	57	29	1	0	39	1	9
Pennsylvania	3,260	3,252	3,233	3,068	2,165	805	96	47	43	6	2	10	5	0
Rhode Island	309	328	317	304	224	73	6	3	2	1	1	5	1	0
South Carolina	1,097	1,127	1,214	1,243	914	288	34	11	17	6	7	20	9	0
South Dakota	802	769	710	699	437	239	23	9	13	1	0	31	9	12
Tennessee	1,543	1,624	1,784	1,855	1,387	384	82	37	42	3	2	23	16	0
Texas	5,991	7,519	8,732	8,748	5,983	2,097	663	294	215	154	5	977	21	0
Utah	714	793	1,016	1,006	649	261	96	43	8	45	0	26	69	6
Vermont	397	393	320	316	232	68	16	11	5	0	0	1	0	1
Virginia	1,811	1,969	2,175	2,166	1,495	406	34	24	9	1	231	187	53	0
Washington	1,936	2,305	2,338	2,381	1,504	617	260	158	72	30	0	325	96	0
West Virginia	1,015	840	757	758	568	124	66	43	18	5	0	30	3	0
Wisconsin	2,018	2,182	2,238	2,249	1,576	560	109	36	71	2	4	95	11	3
Wyoming	415	393	360	366	244	97	25	12	6	7	0	24	3	6
Bureau of Indian Education	—	189	173	174	110	19	45	39	3	3	0	0	0	—
DoD, domestic and overseas	—	227	191	191	141	35	14	10	4	0	1	0	0	—
Other jurisdictions														
American Samoa	30	31	28	28	22	6	0	0	0	0	0	0	0	—
Guam	35	38	40	38	32	4	2	1	0	1	0	0	0	0
Northern Marianas	26	29	30	29	22	6	0	0	0	0	1	0	0	0
Puerto Rico	1,619	1,543	1,473	1,452	852	398	171	4	1	166	31	10	23	0
U.S. Virgin Islands	33	36	32	31	22	9	0	0	0	0	0	0	0	0

—Not available.
[1]Includes schools beginning with grade 6 or below and with no grade higher than 8.
[2]Includes schools with no grade lower than 7.
[3]Includes schools beginning with grade 6 or below and ending with grade 9 or above.
[4]Includes schools not reported by grade span.
[5]Schools are also included under elementary, secondary, combined, or other as appropriate.
NOTE: DoD = Department of Defense.
SOURCE: U.S. Department of Education, National Center for Education Statistics, Common Core of Data (CCD), "Public Elementary/Secondary School Universe Survey," 1990–91, 2000–01, 2010–11, and 2013–14. (This table was prepared September 2015.)

Table 216.75. Public elementary schools, by grade span, average school enrollment, and state or jurisdiction: 2013–14

State or jurisdiction	Total, all elementary schools	Total, all regular elementary schools[1]	Schools, by grade span: Prekindergarten, kindergarten, or 1st grade to grades 3 or 4	Prekindergarten, kindergarten, or 1st grade to grade 5	Prekindergarten, kindergarten, or 1st grade to grade 6	Prekindergarten, kindergarten, or 1st grade to grade 8	Grade 4, 5, or 6 to grade 6, 7, or 8	Other grade spans	Average school enrollment[2]: All elementary schools	Regular elementary schools[1]
1	2	3	4	5	6	7	8	9	10	11
United States	**67,034**	**65,948**	**5,090**	**25,309**	**10,213**	**6,553**	**13,322**	**6,547**	**483**	**488**
Alabama	990	977	91	331	141	74	229	124	496	499
Alaska	199	190	2	45	89	26	25	12	333	329
Arizona	1,335	1,316	44	243	355	453	167	73	516	518
Arkansas	718	715	116	164	156	9	161	112	431	432
California	6,954	6,765	134	2,443	2,124	1,006	1,045	202	559	569
Colorado	1,300	1,295	28	617	212	121	248	74	441	441
Connecticut	815	805	93	251	72	99	153	147	428	432
Delaware	159	154	15	78	6	9	37	14	560	570
District of Columbia	166	164	11	68	6	32	26	23	347	345
Florida	2,829	2,765	33	1,675	138	255	593	135	656	668
Georgia	1,776	1,774	38	1,057	30	36	463	152	676	677
Hawaii	208	208	0	84	86	9	28	1	573	573
Idaho	449	439	35	152	129	26	76	31	410	415
Illinois	3,107	3,067	288	782	312	664	583	478	437	441
Indiana	1,370	1,369	174	467	310	42	264	113	476	476
Iowa	969	966	125	334	136	12	234	128	338	338
Kansas	943	939	89	354	175	65	197	63	340	342
Kentucky	983	971	26	488	104	82	202	81	477	482
Louisiana	930	890	68	321	119	104	193	125	488	487
Maine	453	453	61	98	51	87	85	71	264	264
Maryland	1,130	1,113	13	667	82	92	221	55	532	538
Massachusetts	1,430	1,418	193	482	115	98	297	245	437	438
Michigan	2,213	2,166	243	782	201	237	473	277	419	422
Minnesota	1,280	1,127	108	376	285	75	245	191	431	471
Mississippi	626	623	71	134	96	37	160	128	511	511
Missouri	1,591	1,580	149	502	295	115	319	211	381	382
Montana	485	482	19	59	206	111	60	30	189	190
Nebraska	730	723	57	171	273	26	105	98	277	278
Nevada	480	470	9	263	81	23	89	15	627	638
New Hampshire	376	376	54	115	36	54	81	36	329	329
New Jersey	1,956	1,940	271	566	141	293	371	314	463	466
New Mexico	611	600	19	256	115	33	129	59	369	373
New York	3,307	3,273	300	1,260	351	268	724	404	518	519
North Carolina	1,899	1,886	79	1,088	66	120	461	85	537	539
North Dakota	297	296	14	72	111	61	29	10	227	228
Ohio	2,488	2,467	372	619	346	262	545	344	431	433
Oklahoma	1,222	1,218	84	297	166	283	237	155	385	385
Oregon	882	876	30	410	120	118	177	27	410	410
Pennsylvania	2,165	2,165	301	660	389	188	421	206	488	488
Rhode Island	224	223	32	83	37	3	41	28	411	412
South Carolina	914	911	40	459	53	39	224	99	559	561
South Dakota	437	433	17	134	68	91	101	26	209	210
Tennessee	1,387	1,376	168	548	54	177	326	114	508	511
Texas	5,983	5,841	610	2,763	463	140	1,356	651	571	581
Utah	649	612	13	114	399	33	42	48	552	575
Vermont	232	232	13	25	103	62	18	11	235	235
Virginia	1,495	1,495	47	839	150	12	312	135	575	575
Washington	1,504	1,428	42	579	414	88	257	124	440	456
West Virginia	568	568	73	265	35	39	115	41	350	350
Wisconsin	1,576	1,566	155	606	134	150	333	198	365	367
Wyoming	244	242	23	63	77	14	44	23	231	232
Bureau of Indian Education	110	110	6	5	25	68	4	2	—	—
DoD, domestic and overseas	141	141	20	43	26	9	28	15	—	—
Other jurisdictions										
American Samoa	22	22	0	0	0	22	0	0	—	—
Guam	32	32	0	4	20	0	7	1	615	615
Northern Marianas	22	22	0	1	11	0	1	9	266	266
Puerto Rico	852	852	38	4	782	2	18	8	226	226
U.S. Virgin Islands	22	22	1	1	17	1	2	0	390	390

—Not available.
[1]Excludes special education and alternative schools.
[2]Average for schools reporting enrollment data. Enrollment data were available for 66,605 out of 67,034 public elementary schools in 2013–14.

NOTE: Includes schools beginning with grade 6 or below and with no grade higher than 8. Excludes schools not reported by grade level, such as some special education schools for the disabled. DoD = Department of Defense.
SOURCE: U.S. Department of Education, National Center for Education Statistics, Common Core of Data (CCD), "Public Elementary/Secondary School Universe Survey," 2013–14. (This table was prepared September 2015.)

Table 216.80. Public secondary schools, by grade span, average school enrollment, and state or jurisdiction: 2013–14

State or jurisdiction	Total, all secondary schools	Total, all regular secondary schools[1]	Schools, by grade span: Grades 7 to 8 and 7 to 9	Grades 7 to 12	Grades 8 to 12	Grades 9 to 12	Grades 10 to 12	Other spans ending with grade 12	Other grade spans	Vocational schools[2]	Average school enrollment[3]: All secondary schools	Regular secondary schools[1]
1	2	3	4	5	6	7	8	9	10	11	12	13
United States	**24,053**	**19,409**	**2,719**	**3,002**	**496**	**16,361**	**576**	**321**	**578**	**1,380**	**694**	**788**
Alabama	434	326	40	78	8	262	32	3	11	72	706	721
Alaska	83	60	12	21	1	47	1	1	0	3	436	549
Arizona	734	491	70	43	7	584	12	5	13	227	617	713
Arkansas	368	335	47	119	12	136	35	0	19	26	499	507
California	2,606	1,642	372	300	10	1,819	63	27	15	76	860	1,234
Colorado	389	330	39	43	2	292	5	1	7	6	642	722
Connecticut	286	207	30	13	7	195	10	21	10	16	638	815
Delaware	36	28	1	1	12	22	0	0	0	6	1,033	1,067
District of Columbia	39	31	1	1	0	31	0	0	6	2	405	460
Florida	695	513	16	44	39	571	6	15	4	51	1,210	1,489
Georgia	457	424	17	5	7	391	4	1	32	1	1,074	1,147
Hawaii	52	51	12	7	0	33	0	0	0	0	1,134	1,155
Idaho	197	141	33	39	2	119	3	1	0	9	501	622
Illinois	937	819	138	72	15	675	9	13	15	0	716	802
Indiana	460	439	73	95	4	272	3	5	8	27	813	820
Iowa	371	346	37	73	0	243	10	2	6	0	430	456
Kansas	352	346	38	88	4	218	1	2	1	1	443	449
Kentucky	422	245	25	35	7	350	2	1	2	122	676	819
Louisiana	281	243	28	42	53	135	4	12	7	8	707	776
Maine	149	120	10	11	4	121	1	0	2	27	461	463
Maryland	246	190	5	3	2	221	3	6	6	26	1,077	1,244
Massachusetts	382	327	34	36	15	288	1	5	3	39	799	819
Michigan	939	695	73	96	34	681	32	15	8	6	542	680
Minnesota	836	448	46	276	26	394	48	42	4	11	393	606
Mississippi	325	227	24	58	2	212	23	2	4	90	645	645
Missouri	642	560	59	184	1	362	15	9	12	64	536	540
Montana	339	336	168	0	0	171	0	0	0	0	155	156
Nebraska	307	301	29	160	1	112	1	4	0	0	364	364
Nevada	132	117	21	7	2	96	2	4	0	1	1,023	1,129
New Hampshire	106	106	14	0	0	88	2	0	2	0	585	585
New Jersey	494	410	50	37	4	390	2	3	8	57	918	1,032
New Mexico	238	207	35	35	1	153	8	0	6	1	478	519
New York	1,130	1,057	70	133	21	825	20	2	59	25	736	749
North Carolina	536	509	25	7	5	480	2	6	11	7	826	858
North Dakota	183	171	7	93	0	78	1	1	3	12	202	202
Ohio	1,013	934	136	142	37	655	17	11	15	69	593	603
Oklahoma	561	557	91	1	0	429	29	1	10	0	364	366
Oregon	277	255	27	49	3	195	1	2	0	0	654	693
Pennsylvania	805	711	112	143	12	511	17	3	7	85	805	816
Rhode Island	73	59	10	0	1	59	1	0	2	12	704	737
South Carolina	288	234	20	9	1	237	10	4	7	42	880	922
South Dakota	239	222	61	2	0	173	1	2	0	3	167	173
Tennessee	384	361	14	18	1	328	11	3	9	19	813	834
Texas	2,097	1,535	283	166	50	1,322	40	44	192	0	751	986
Utah	261	234	84	45	8	67	42	1	14	4	856	922
Vermont	68	52	7	19	0	27	0	0	15	15	493	502
Virginia	406	343	33	4	28	337	2	0	2	58	1,160	1,176
Washington	617	432	71	55	38	398	26	18	11	20	633	833
West Virginia	124	105	2	18	4	92	2	0	6	30	634	727
Wisconsin	560	497	51	63	4	401	14	23	4	4	497	541
Wyoming	97	80	18	13	1	63	2	0	0	0	332	383
Bureau of Indian Education	19	19	1	5	0	13	0	0	0	0	—	—
DoD, domestic and overseas	35	35	3	11	0	21	0	0	0	0	—	—
Other jurisdictions												
American Samoa	6	5	0	0	0	6	0	0	0	1	—	—
Guam	4	4	0	0	0	4	0	0	0	0	1,853	1,853
Northern Marianas	6	6	1	2	0	3	0	0	0	0	787	787
Puerto Rico	398	367	196	26	1	5	159	0	11	30	431	416
U.S. Virgin Islands	9	8	4	0	0	5	0	0	0	1	798	798

—Not available.
[1]Excludes vocational, special education, and alternative schools.
[2]Vocational schools are also included under appropriate grade span. Includes vocational schools not classified as secondary schools.
[3]Average for schools reporting enrollment data. Enrollment data were available for 22,513 out of 24,053 public secondary schools in 2013–14.

NOTE: Includes schools with no grade lower than 7. Excludes schools not reported by grade level, such as some special education schools for the disabled. DoD = Department of Defense.
SOURCE: U.S. Department of Education, National Center for Education Statistics, Common Core of Data (CCD), "Public Elementary/Secondary School Universe Survey," 2013–14. (This table was prepared September 2015.)

Table 216.90. Public elementary and secondary charter schools and enrollment, by state: Selected years, 1999–2000 through 2013–14

State	Number of charter schools					Charter school enrollment					Charter schools as a percent of total public schools				Charter school enrollment as a percent of total public school enrollment			
	1999–2000	2003–04	2009–10	2012–13	2013–14	1999–2000	2003–04	2009–10	2012–13	2013–14	1999–2000	2003–04	2009–10	2013–14	1999–2000	2003–04	2009–10	2013–14
1	2	3	4	5	6	7	8	9	10	11	12	13	14	15	16	17	18	19
United States	**1,524**	**2,977**	**4,952**	**6,079**	**6,465**	**339,678**	**789,479**	**1,610,285**	**2,267,814**	**2,519,065**	**1.7**	**3.1**	**5.0**	**6.6**	**0.7**	**1.6**	**3.3**	**5.1**
Alabama	0	0	0	0	0	0	0	0	0	0	0.0	0.0	0.0	0.0	0.0	0.0	0.0	0.0
Alaska	18	19	25	27	27	2,300	3,476	5,196	5,869	6,118	3.6	3.7	4.9	5.3	1.7	2.6	3.9	4.7
Arizona	245	505	504	542	600	31,176	81,725	113,974	151,086	195,027	14.9	25.0	22.4	26.6	3.7	8.1	10.6	17.8
Arkansas	0	13	38	45	52	0	2,719	8,662	13,261	17,176	0.0	1.1	3.4	4.7	0.0	0.6	1.8	3.5
California	238	444	813	1,085	1,125	104,730	166,208	316,658	470,880	513,350	2.8	4.8	8.1	10.9	1.8	2.6	5.1	8.3
Colorado	69	96	158	187	200	17,822	31,529	66,826	89,451	95,860	4.3	5.7	8.8	10.9	2.5	4.2	8.0	10.9
Connecticut	16	12	18	17	18	2,148	2,222	5,215	6,518	7,094	1.5	1.0	1.5	1.6	0.4	0.4	0.9	1.3
Delaware	1	13	18	22	21	115	6,241	9,173	9,942	11,064	0.5	6.4	8.3	9.6	0.1	5.3	7.3	8.4
District of Columbia	27	37	99	102	109	6,432	12,958	25,813	31,580	33,158	14.3	18.0	42.5	48.4	8.3	16.6	37.3	42.4
Florida	113	257	412	581	623	17,251	67,472	137,887	204,132	230,173	3.5	7.5	10.2	14.5	0.7	2.6	5.2	8.5
Georgia	18	51	63	93	94	11,005	26,756	37,545	64,233	70,544	1.0	2.1	2.6	4.0	0.8	1.8	2.3	4.1
Hawaii	2	26	31	32	33	790	4,502	7,869	9,635	9,816	0.8	9.2	10.7	11.5	0.4	2.5	4.4	5.3
Idaho	8	17	36	47	49	915	4,811	14,529	18,188	19,375	1.2	2.5	4.9	6.9	0.4	1.9	5.3	6.6
Illinois	17	28	39	58	65	6,152	11,750	35,836	53,829	59,817	0.4	0.6	0.9	1.5	0.3	0.6	1.7	2.9
Indiana	0	17	53	72	76	0	2,908	18,488	33,297	35,676	0.0	0.9	2.7	3.9	0.0	0.3	1.8	3.4
Iowa	0	0	9	3	3	0	0	593	352	315	0.0	0.0	0.6	0.2	0.0	0.0	0.1	0.1
Kansas	0	17	35	16	11	0	1,395	4,684	2,888	2,518	0.0	1.2	2.5	0.8	0.0	0.3	1.0	0.5
Kentucky	0	0	0	0	0	0	0	0	0	0	0.0	0.0	0.0	0.0	0.0	0.0	0.0	0.0
Louisiana	16	16	77	104	118	2,449	4,585	31,467	45,293	50,049	1.0	1.0	5.2	8.4	0.3	0.6	4.6	7.2
Maine	0	0	0	2	5	0	0	0	106	384	0.0	0.0	0.0	0.8	0.0	0.0	0.0	0.2
Maryland	0	1	42	52	53	0	196	11,995	18,943	20,269	0.0	0.1	2.9	3.7	0.0	#	1.4	2.3
Massachusetts	40	51	62	77	81	12,518	17,971	27,393	31,830	34,631	2.1	2.7	3.4	4.3	1.3	1.8	2.9	3.6
Michigan	193	212	294	346	370	46,078	72,096	110,504	126,602	139,110	4.9	5.3	7.6	10.5	2.8	4.1	6.8	9.2
Minnesota	62	105	181	176	186	7,794	14,256	35,375	41,615	43,937	2.6	4.1	7.4	7.7	0.9	1.7	4.2	5.2
Mississippi	1	1	1	0	0	347	338	375	0	0	0.1	0.1	0.1	0.0	0.1	0.1	0.1	0.0
Missouri	15	26	48	57	59	4,303	10,304	18,415	17,925	19,462	0.6	1.1	2.0	2.4	0.5	1.1	2.0	2.1
Montana	0	0	0	0	0	0	0	0	0	0	0.0	0.0	0.0	0.0	0.0	0.0	0.0	0.0
Nebraska	0	0	0	0	0	0	0	0	0	0	0.0	0.0	0.0	0.0	0.0	0.0	0.0	0.0
Nevada	5	15	35	40	41	898	3,917	11,613	22,199	24,621	1.0	2.7	5.5	6.3	0.3	1.0	2.7	5.4
New Hampshire	0	0	15	22	23	0	0	816	1,739	2,097	0.0	0.0	3.1	4.8	0.0	0.0	0.4	1.1
New Jersey	0	51	70	86	87	0	12,806	22,981	29,540	33,430	0.0	2.1	2.7	3.5	0.0	0.9	1.7	2.4
New Mexico	1	34	72	94	95	22	6,225	13,090	19,916	21,485	0.1	4.2	8.4	10.8	#	1.9	3.9	6.3
New York	5	50	140	211	233	—	14,572	43,963	78,139	92,143	0.1	1.1	3.0	4.9	—	0.5	1.6	3.4
North Carolina	82	93	96	108	128	12,691	21,955	38,973	50,060	58,307	3.8	4.1	3.8	4.9	1.0	1.6	2.6	3.9
North Dakota	0	0	0	0	0	0	0	0	0	0	0.0	0.0	0.0	0.0	0.0	0.0	0.0	0.0
Ohio	48	165	323	368	390	9,809	46,130	90,989	114,459	120,224	1.2	4.2	8.5	10.7	0.5	2.5	5.2	7.0
Oklahoma	0	12	18	23	25	0	3,491	6,315	12,037	13,473	0.0	0.7	1.0	1.4	0.0	0.6	1.0	2.0
Oregon	1	24	102	123	124	109	2,487	18,334	27,077	28,241	0.1	1.9	7.8	10.0	#	0.5	3.3	5.1
Pennsylvania	47	102	134	175	181	11,413	41,114	79,167	118,430	128,701	1.5	3.1	4.1	5.9	0.6	2.3	4.5	7.4
Rhode Island	2	8	12	18	23	446	1,024	3,233	5,131	5,950	0.6	2.3	3.7	7.6	0.3	0.7	2.3	4.2
South Carolina	7	18	39	55	60	327	3,155	13,035	20,067	23,432	0.6	1.6	3.2	4.8	#	0.5	1.8	3.2
South Dakota	0	0	0	0	0	0	0	0	0	0	0.0	0.0	0.0	0.0	0.0	0.0	0.0	0.0
Tennessee	0	4	20	51	72	0	324	4,343	11,698	15,690	0.0	0.2	1.1	3.9	0.0	#	0.4	1.6
Texas	176	274	536	628	658	25,687	60,833	148,392	215,082	235,634	2.4	3.4	6.2	7.5	0.6	1.4	3.1	4.6
Utah	6	19	72	88	95	390	3,253	33,968	50,694	54,795	0.8	2.1	6.9	9.4	0.1	0.7	5.8	8.8
Vermont	0	0	0	0	0	0	0	0	0	0	0.0	0.0	0.0	0.0	0.0	0.0	0.0	0.0
Virginia	0	6	3	4	6	0	478	179	399	603	0.0	0.3	0.1	0.3	0.0	#	#	#
Washington	0	0	0	0	0	0	0	0	0	0	0.0	0.0	0.0	0.0	0.0	0.0	0.0	0.0
West Virginia	0	0	0	0	0	0	0	0	0	0	0.0	0.0	0.0	0.0	0.0	0.0	0.0	0.0
Wisconsin	45	137	206	238	242	3,561	21,165	36,153	43,323	44,853	2.1	6.2	9.2	10.8	0.4	2.4	4.1	5.1
Wyoming	0	1	3	4	4	0	132	269	369	463	0.0	0.3	0.8	1.1	0.0	0.2	0.3	0.5

—Not available.
#Rounds to zero.
NOTE: Some data have been revised from previously published figures.

SOURCE: U.S. Department of Education, National Center for Education Statistics, Common Core of Data (CCD), "Public Elementary/Secondary School Universe Survey," 1999–2000 through 2013–14. (This table was prepared September 2015.)

Table 216.95. Number and enrollment of public elementary and secondary schools that have closed, by school level, type, and charter status: Selected years, 1995–96 through 2013–14

School level, type, and charter status	1995–96	2000–01	2001–02	2002–03	2003–04	2004–05	2005–06	2006–07	2007–08	2008–09	2009–10	2010–11	2011–12	2012–13	2013–14
1	2	3	4	5	6	7	8	9	10	11	12	13	14	15	16
	Number of schools that closed														
Total, all schools	**954**	**1,193**	**1,412**	**1,368**	**2,168**	**1,913**	**1,553**	**1,877**	**2,120**	**1,515**	**1,822**	**1,929**	**1,840**	**1,493**	**1,737**
School type															
Regular	686	908	1,018	985	1,248	1,190	1,171	1,348	1,450	1,059	1,321	1,486	1,340	1,075	1,179
Special education	110	84	118	91	114	271	88	160	195	99	235	72	87	83	90
Vocational	17	17	90	27	33	18	28	14	30	15	11	7	11	66	20
Alternative[1]	141	184	186	265	773	434	266	355	445	342	255	364	402	269	448
School level and type															
Elementary[2]	497	601	697	721	947	901	770	846	844	769	936	1,073	1,020	776	864
Regular	449	563	648	660	870	847	725	771	804	713	893	1,010	959	726	778
Special education	28	20	21	26	23	25	13	53	20	22	13	18	18	18	33
Vocational	0	2	0	0	0	0	1	1	0	1	0	0	0	0	1
Alternative[1]	20	16	28	35	54	29	31	21	20	33	30	45	43	32	52
Secondary[3]	199	302	313	245	347	302	342	308	394	368	346	436	451	421	502
Regular	114	173	141	127	144	177	192	171	233	186	212	237	238	204	231
Special education	12	19	12	9	10	4	11	24	19	21	12	15	15	24	15
Vocational	17	14	89	27	33	18	27	13	29	13	11	7	10	64	19
Alternative[1]	56	96	71	82	160	103	112	100	113	148	111	177	188	129	237
Combined elementary/secondary[4]	42	146	168	124	158	321	184	193	172	164	91	157	207	170	183
Regular	10	83	76	57	54	68	82	65	65	50	42	74	82	64	67
Special education	13	22	29	22	30	28	38	45	48	34	16	24	34	34	33
Vocational	0	1	1	0	0	0	0	0	1	1	0	0	1	2	0
Alternative[1]	19	40	62	45	74	225	64	83	58	79	33	59	90	70	83
Other (not classified by grade span)	216	144	234	278	716	389	257	530	710	214	449	263	162	126	188
Regular	113	89	153	141	180	98	172	341	348	110	174	165	61	81	103
Special education	57	23	56	34	51	214	26	38	108	22	194	15	20	7	9
Vocational	0	0	0	0	0	0	0	0	0	0	0	0	0	0	0
Alternative[1]	46	32	25	103	485	77	59	151	254	82	81	83	81	38	76
All charter schools[5]	—	72	111	85	74	171	206	267	133	161	189	216	202	183	284
	Prior year enrollment of schools that have closed														
Total, enrollment	**173,766**	**209,228**	**171,669**	**195,033**	**262,183**	**297,487**	**229,259**	**242,388**	**268,212**	**243,166**	**306,806**	**321,246**	**300,764**	**240,704**	**274,397**
School type															
Regular	151,574	198,699	161,663	185,536	242,383	282,432	216,360	227,260	253,409	227,714	292,915	304,001	281,961	227,444	252,172
Special education	4,475	1,665	2,840	1,789	4,144	2,799	3,068	4,745	4,060	1,916	2,173	1,709	3,765	1,168	4,331
Vocational	1,613	632	75	223	719	2,975	73	429	183	1,665	767	22	26	289	1,578
Alternative[1]	16,104	8,232	7,091	7,485	14,937	9,281	9,758	9,954	10,560	11,871	10,951	15,514	15,012	11,803	16,316
School level and type															
Elementary[2]	112,328	134,934	125,753	146,709	194,752	213,607	161,649	172,403	179,554	171,722	221,681	242,193	225,205	174,885	195,776
Regular	108,440	134,060	124,170	144,013	192,117	211,822	158,744	169,895	176,862	169,815	219,469	239,913	222,186	173,272	190,138
Special education	2,991	338	591	1,020	1,040	1,153	1,158	1,892	2,131	651	727	404	1,539	272	2,042
Vocational	0	2	0	0	0	0	0	9	0	569	0	0	0	0	308
Alternative[1]	897	534	992	1,676	1,595	632	1,747	607	561	687	1,485	1,876	1,480	1,341	3,288
Secondary[3]	48,074	47,950	30,817	33,243	52,437	60,029	54,489	55,834	66,163	55,261	68,548	56,935	54,558	51,820	59,920
Regular	39,307	42,666	27,752	30,271	42,750	51,547	49,335	48,797	60,085	45,800	60,734	48,430	46,345	43,775	49,374
Special education	398	121	175	357	172	108	83	1,126	440	501	508	520	404	500	633
Vocational	1,613	592	72	223	719	2,975	73	420	183	1,096	767	22	19	202	1,270
Alternative[1]	6,756	4,571	2,818	2,392	8,796	5,399	4,998	5,491	5,455	7,864	6,539	7,963	7,790	7,343	8,643
Combined elementary/secondary[4]	12,418	25,031	12,622	12,957	13,150	22,022	12,993	12,157	19,349	16,093	12,151	21,360	20,931	13,963	18,614
Regular	3,743	21,973	8,999	9,451	7,484	18,415	8,281	7,682	16,295	12,081	8,342	14,941	13,430	10,361	12,660
Special education	326	701	410	365	1,328	840	1,791	1,293	1,008	692	882	744	1,752	396	1,569
Vocational	0	38	3	0	0	0	0	0	0	0	0	0	7	87	0
Alternative[1]	8,349	2,319	3,210	3,141	4,338	2,767	2,921	3,182	2,046	3,320	2,927	5,675	5,742	3,119	4,385
Other (not classified by grade span)	946	1,313	2,477	2,124	1,844	1,829	128	1,994	3,146	90	4,426	758	70	36	87
Regular	84	0	742	1,801	32	648	0	886	167	18	4,370	717	0	36	0
Special education	760	505	1,664	47	1,604	698	36	434	481	72	56	41	70	0	87
Vocational	0	0	0	0	0	0	0	0	0	0	0	0	0	0	0
Alternative[1]	102	808	71	276	208	483	92	674	2,498	0	0	0	0	0	0
All charter schools[5]	—	5,925	11,134	11,894	6,797	21,505	14,118	15,340	12,226	20,537	17,954	24,165	29,095	24,437	38,327

—Not available.

[1]Includes schools that provide nontraditional education, address needs of students that typically cannot be met in regular schools, serve as adjuncts to regular schools, or fall outside the categories of regular, special education, or vocational education.

[2]Includes schools beginning with grade 6 or below and with no grade higher than 8.

[3]Includes schools with no grade lower than 7.

[4]Includes schools beginning with grade 6 or below and ending with grade 9 or above.

[5]Charter schools are also included under the school level and type categories, as appropriate.

NOTE: This table indicates the school year by which the school no longer operated (generally it closed between that school year and the prior school year). The closure of a school does not necessarily mean that a building is no longer used for educational purposes. A single school may share a building with another school, or one school may be housed in several buildings.

SOURCE: U.S. Department of Education, National Center for Education Statistics, Common Core of Data (CCD), "Public Elementary/Secondary School Universe Survey," 1995–96 through 2013–14. (This table was prepared February 2016.)

Table 234.10. Age range for compulsory school attendance and special education services, and policies on year-round schools and kindergarten programs, by state: Selected years, 2000 through 2014

	Compulsory attendance								Year-round schools, 2008		Kindergarten programs, 2014		
											School districts required to offer		
State	2000	2002	2004	2006	2008	2010	2014	Compulsory special education services, 2004[1]	Has policy on year-round schools	Has districts with year-round schools	Program	Full-day program	Attendance required
1	2	3	4	5	6	7	8	9	10	11	12	13	14
Alabama	7 to 16	7 to 16	7 to 16 [2]	7 to 16	7 to 16	7 to 17	6 to 17 [3]	6 to 21		Yes	X	X	
Alaska	7 to 16	7 to 16	7 to 16 [2]	7 to 16	7 to 16	7 to 16	7 to 16 [2]	3 to 22		Yes			
Arizona	6 to 16 [2]	6 to 16 [2]	6 to 16 [2]	6 to 16 [2]	6 to 16 [2]	6 to 16 [2]	6 to 16 [2]	3 to 21	—	—	X		
Arkansas	5 to 17 [2,3]	5 to 17 [2,3]	5 to 17 [2,3]	5 to 17 [2,3]	5 to 17 [2,3]	5 to 17 [2,3]	5 to 18	5 to 21	X	Yes	X	X	X
California	6 to 18 [2]	6 to 18	6 to 18	6 to 18	6 to 18	6 to 18	6 to 18	Birth to 21 [4]	X	Yes	X		
Colorado	—	—	7 to 16	7 to 16	6 to 17	6 to 17	6 to 17	3 to 21		Yes	X		
Connecticut	7 to 16	7 to 18 [2]	7 to 18 [2]	5 to 18 [3]	5 to 18 [3]	5 to 18 [3]	5 to 18 [3]	3 to 21		—	X		X
Delaware	5 to 16	5 to 16	5 to 16 [2]	5 to 16	5 to 16	5 to 16	5 to 16	Birth to 20		Yes	X	X	X
District of Columbia	—	5 to 18 [5]	5 to 18	5 to 18	5 to 18	5 to 18	5 to 18	—	—	—	X	X	X
Florida	6 to 16 [5]	6 to 16 [5]	6 to 16 [5]	6 to 16 [5]	6 to 16 [5]	6 to 16 [5]	6 to 16	3 to 21	X	Yes	X		
Georgia	6 to 16	6 to 16	6 to 16	6 to 16	6 to 16	6 to 16	6 to 16	Birth to 21 [6]		Yes	X		
Hawaii	6 to 18	6 to 18	6 to 18	6 to 18	6 to 18	6 to 18	5 to 18	Birth to 19		[7]	X		
Idaho	7 to 16	7 to 16	7 to 16	7 to 16	7 to 16	7 to 16	7 to 16	3 to 21		Yes			
Illinois	7 to 16	7 to 16	7 to 17	7 to 17	7 to 17	7 to 17	6 to 17	3 to 21	X	Yes	X		
Indiana	7 to 16	7 to 16	7 to 16	7 to 18 [2]	7 to 18 [2]	7 to 18 [2]	7 to 18	3 to 22		Yes	X		
Iowa	6 to 16 [2]	6 to 16 [2]	6 to 16	6 to 16	6 to 16	6 to 16	6 to 16 [8]	Birth to 21	X	Yes	X		
Kansas	7 to 18 [2]	7 to 18 [2]	7 to 18 [2]	7 to 18 [2]	7 to 18 [2]	7 to 18 [2]	7 to 18	3 to 21 [9]		—	X		
Kentucky	6 to 16	6 to 16	6 to 16 [2]	6 to 16	6 to 16	6 to 16	6 to 18 [10]	Birth to 21		Yes	X		
Louisiana	7 to 17	7 to 17	7 to 17 [2]	7 to 18 [2]	7 to 18 [2]	7 to 18 [2]	7 to 18	3 to 21 [11]		Yes	X	X	X
Maine	7 to 17	7 to 17	7 to 17 [2]	7 to 17 [2]	7 to 17 [2]	7 to 17 [2]	7 to 17	5 to 19 [11,12]		—	X		
Maryland	5 to 16	5 to 16	5 to 16	5 to 16	5 to 16	5 to 16 [3]	5 to 17	Birth to 21	X	—	X	X	X
Massachusetts	6 to 16	6 to 16	6 to 16	6 to 16 [2]	6 to 16 [2]	6 to 16 [2]	6 to 16	3 to 21 [6]	[13]	—	X		
Michigan	6 to 16	6 to 16	6 to 16	6 to 16	6 to 16	6 to 18	6 to 18	Birth to 25	X	Yes	X		
Minnesota	7 to 18 [2]	7 to 16	7 to 16	7 to 16 [2]	7 to 16 [2]	7 to 16 [2]	7 to 17	Birth to 21	X	Yes	X		
Mississippi	6 to 17	6 to 17	6 to 16	6 to 16	6 to 17	6 to 17	6 to 17	Birth to 20		—	X	X	
Missouri	7 to 16	7 to 16	7 to 16	7 to 16	7 to 16	7 to 17	7 to 17 [2,3]	Birth to 20		Yes [14]	X		
Montana	7 to 16 [2]	7 to 16 [2]	7 to 16 [2]	7 to 16 [2]	7 to 16 [2]	7 to 16 [2]	7 to 16 [2]	3 to 18 [11]		—	X		
Nebraska	7 to 16	7 to 16	7 to 16	6 to 18	6 to 18	6 to 18	6 to 18	Birth to 20		Yes	X		
Nevada	7 to 17	7 to 17	7 to 17	7 to 17	7 to 18 [2]	7 to 18 [2]	7 to 18	Birth to 21 [4]		Yes	X	[15]	X
New Hampshire	6 to 16	6 to 16	6 to 16	6 to 16	6 to 16	6 to 18	6 to 18	3 to 21		—	X		
New Jersey	6 to 16	6 to 16	6 to 16	6 to 16	6 to 16	6 to 16	6 to 16	5 to 21		—		[16]	
New Mexico	5 to 18	5 to 18	5 to 18 [2]	5 to 18 [2]	5 to 18 [2]	5 to 18 [2]	5 to 18	3 to 21	X	Yes	X		X
New York	6 to 16 [2]	6 to 16	6 to 16	6 to 16 [17]	6 to 16 [17]	6 to 16 [17]	6 to 16 [17]	Birth to 20		—			
North Carolina	7 to 16	7 to 16	7 to 16	7 to 16	7 to 16	7 to 16	7 to 16	5 to 20	X	Yes	X	X	
North Dakota	7 to 16	7 to 16	7 to 16	7 to 16	7 to 16	7 to 16	7 to 16	3 to 21		No	X		
Ohio	6 to 18	6 to 18	6 to 18	6 to 18	6 to 18	6 to 18	6 to 18	3 to 21	X	—	X		X
Oklahoma	5 to 18	5 to 18	5 to 18	5 to 18	5 to 18	5 to 18	5 to 18	Birth to 21 [11]		Yes	X	X	X
Oregon	7 to 18	7 to 18	7 to 18 [2]	7 to 18	7 to 18	7 to 18 [2]	7 to 18	3 to 20		Yes	X		
Pennsylvania	8 to 17	8 to 17	8 to 17 [2]	8 to 17 [2]	8 to 17 [2]	8 to 17 [2]	8 to 17	6 to 21	X [14]	— [14]			
Rhode Island	6 to 16	6 to 16	6 to 16	6 to 16	6 to 16	6 to 16	6 to 18 [2]	3 to 21		—	X		X
South Carolina	5 to 16	5 to 16	5 to 16	5 to 17 [3]	5 to 17 [3]	5 to 17 [3]	5 to 17	3 to 21 [18]		—	X	X	X
South Dakota	6 to 16	6 to 16	6 to 16	6 to 16	6 to 16	6 to 18 [2]	6 to 18 [2]	Birth to 21	X	—	X		X [19]
Tennessee	6 to 17	6 to 17	6 to 17	6 to 17 [3]	6 to 17 [3]	6 to 17 [3]	6 to 18	3 to 21 [4]	X	Yes	X	X	X
Texas	6 to 18	6 to 18	6 to 18	6 to 18	6 to 18	6 to 18	6 to 18	3 to 21	X	Yes	X		
Utah	6 to 18	6 to 18	6 to 18	6 to 18	6 to 18	6 to 18	6 to 18	3 to 22		Yes	X		
Vermont	7 to 16	6 to 16	6 to 16	6 to 16 [2]	6 to 16 [2]	6 to 16 [2]	6 to 16 [2]	3 to 21		— [14]	X		
Virginia	5 to 18	5 to 18	5 to 18	5 to 18 [2]	5 to 18 [2]	5 to 18 [2,3]	5 to 18	2 to 21	X	Yes	X		X
Washington	8 to 17 [2]	8 to 17 [2]	8 to 16 [2]	8 to 18	8 to 18	8 to 18	8 to 18	3 to 21 [18]		Yes	X	[20]	
West Virginia	6 to 16	6 to 16	6 to 16	6 to 16	6 to 16	6 to 17	6 to 17	5 to 21 [21]	X	Yes	X	X	X
Wisconsin	6 to 18	6 to 18	6 to 18	6 to 18	6 to 18	6 to 18	6 to 18	3 to 21		Yes	X		
Wyoming	6 to 16 [2]	6 to 16 [2]	7 to 16 [2]	7 to 16 [2]	7 to 16 [2]	7 to 16 [2]	7 to 16 [2]	3 to 21		—	X	[22]	

—Not available.

X Denotes that the state has a policy. A blank denotes that the state does not have a policy.

[1]Most states have a provision whereby education is provided up to a certain age or completion of secondary school, whichever comes first.

[2]Child may be exempted from compulsory attendance if he/she meets state requirements for early withdrawal with or without meeting conditions for a diploma or equivalency.

[3]Parent/guardian may delay child's entry until a later age per state law/regulation.

[4]Student may continue in the program if 22nd birthday falls before the end of the school year.

[5]Attendance is compulsory until age 18 for Manatee County students, unless they earn a high school diploma prior to reaching their 18th birthday.

[6]Through age 21 or until child graduates with a high school or special education diploma or equivalent.

[7]Some schools operate on a multitrack system; the schools are open year-round, but different cohorts start and end at different times.

[8]Children enrolled in preschool programs (4 years old on or before September 15) are considered to be of compulsory school attendance age.

[9]To be determined by rules and regulations adopted by the state board.

[10]All districts have adopted a policy to raise the upper compulsory school age from 16 to 18. The policy will take effect for most districts in the 2015–16 school year.

[11]Children from birth through age 2 are eligible for additional services.

[12]Must be age 5 before October 15, and not age 20 before start of school year.

[13]Policies about year-round schools are decided locally.

[14]State did not participate in 2008 online survey. Data are from 2006.

[15]In certain school districts in Nevada, the lowest performing schools with the highest numbers of limited English proficient students will start offering full-day kindergarten programs.

[16]The Abbott District is required to offer full-day kindergarten.

[17]Local boards of education can require school attendance until age 17 unless employed. The boards of education of Syracuse, New York City, Rochester, Utica, and Buffalo are authorized to require kindergarten attendance at age 5 unless the parents elect not to enroll their child until the following September or the child is enrolled in nonpublic school or in home instruction.

[18]Student may complete school year if 21st birthday occurs while attending school.

[19]All children must attend kindergarten before age 7.

[20]Full-day kindergarten is being phased in beginning in the 2012–13 school year, starting with the highest poverty schools. Statewide implementation will be achieved by 2017–18.

[21]Children with severe disabilities may begin receiving services at age 3.

[22]Statute requires one full-day program per district.

NOTE: The Education of the Handicapped Act (EHA) Amendments of 1986 make it mandatory for all states receiving EHA funds to serve all 3- to 18-year-old disabled children.

SOURCE: Council of Chief State School Officers, *Key State Education Policies on PK–12 Education*, 2000, 2002, 2004, and 2008; Education Commission of the States (ECS), ECS StateNotes, *Compulsory School Age Requirements*, retrieved August 9, 2010, from http://www.ecs.org/clearinghouse/86/62/8662.pdf; ECS StateNotes, *Special Education: State Special Education Definitions, Ages Served*, retrieved August 9, 2010, from http://www.ecs.org/clearinghouse/52/29/5229.pdf; ECS StateNotes, *Compulsory School Age Requirements*, retrieved May 19, 2015, from http://www.ecs.org/clearinghouse/01/18/68/11868.pdf; ESC StateNotes, *District Must Offer Kindergarten*, retrieved April 18, 2014, from http://ecs.force.com/mbdata/mbquestRT?rep=Kq1416; ESC StateNotes, *Child Must Attend Kindergarten*, retrieved April 18, 2014, from http://ecs.force.com/mbdata/mbquestRT?rep=Kq1403; and supplemental information retrieved from various state websites. (This table was prepared May 2015.)

Table 234.20. Minimum amount of instructional time per year and policies on textbooks, by state: Selected years, 2000 through 2014

State	Minimum amount of instructional time per year: In days, 2000	In days, 2006	In days, 2011	In days, 2014	In hours, 2014	Policies on textbooks, 2014: Textbook selection level, State	Textbook selection level, Local education agency	Free textbooks provided to students
1	2	3	4	5	6	7	8	9
Alabama	175	175	180	180 [1]	†	X		X
Alaska	180	180	170 [2]	180 [3]	740 (K–3); 900 (4–12)		X	X
Arizona	—	180	180 [1]	180 [1]	356 (K); 712 (1–3); 890 (4–6); 1,000 (7–8); 720[4] (9–12)		X	X [5]
Arkansas	178	178	178 [2]	178 [3]	†		X [6]	X
California	175	180	180/175 [7]	180/175 [7]	600 (K); 840 (1–3); 900 (4–8); 1,080 (9–12)	X [8]		X
Colorado	[9]	160	160	160	435/870[2] (K); 968[2] (1–5); 1,056[2] (6–12)		X	
Connecticut	180	180	180	180	450/900 (K); 900 (1–12)		X	X
Delaware	[9]	†	†	†	1,060 (K–11); 1,032 (12)		X	X
District of Columbia	180 [10]	180	178	180	†			X
Florida	180	180	180	180	720[11] (K–3); 900[11] (4–12)	X		X
Georgia	180 [10]	180	180	180	810 (K–3); 900 (4–5); 990 (6–12)	X		X
Hawaii	184	179	180 [12]	180 [12]	915 (K–6)[12,13]; 990 (7–12)[12,13]	X		X [14]
Idaho	180	†	†	†	450[3] (K); 810[3] (1–3); 900[3] (4–8); 990[3,15] (9–12)	X		X
Illinois	180 [16]	176	176	180 [3]	†		X	[17]
Indiana	180	180	180	180	†		X	
Iowa	180	180	180	180	1,080		X	
Kansas	186	186 (K–11);181 (12)	186 (K–11);181 (12)	186 (K–11);181 (12)	465 (K); 1,116 (1–11); 1,086 (12)		X	
Kentucky	175	175	175 [2]	170 [2]	1,062	X		X [18]
Louisiana	175	177	177 [2]	177 [2,15]	1,062	X		X
Maine	175	175	175 [2]	175 [2]	†		X	X
Maryland	180	180	180	180	1,080; 1,170 (8–12)		X	X
Massachusetts	180	180	180	180	425 (K); 900 (1–5); 990 (6–12)		X	X
Michigan	180	†	165	175	1,098		X	X [19]
Minnesota	[9]	[9]	†	†	425/850 (K); 935 (1–6); 1,020 (7–12)		X	X
Mississippi	180	180	180	180	†	X		X
Missouri	174	174	174/142 [20]	174/142 [20]	1,044		X	X
Montana	180	90 (K);180 (K–12)	†	†	360/720[3] (K); 720[3] (1–3); 1,080[3,15] (4–12)		X	X
Nebraska	[9]	†	†	†	400 (K); 1,032 (1–8); 1,080 (9–12)		X	X
Nevada	180	180	180	180	†	X		[14]
New Hampshire	180	180	180	180	450 (K); 945 (1–5); 990[15] (6–12)		X	X
New Jersey	180	180	180	180	†		X	X
New Mexico	180	180	180	†	450/990 (K); 990 (1–6); 1,080 (7–12)	X		X
New York	180 [10]	180	180	180	†		X	X
North Carolina	180	180	180	185	1,025	X		X
North Dakota	173	173	175 [2]	175 [2]	951.5 (K–8); 1,038 (9–12)		X	X [19]
Ohio	182	182	182 [3]	†	455/910[3] (K); 910[3] (1–6); 1,001[3] (7–12)		X	X
Oklahoma	180	180	180 [3]	180	1,083[3]	X		X
Oregon	[9]	†	†	†	405 (K); 810 (1–3); 900 (4–8); 990[15] (9–12)	X		X
Pennsylvania	180	180	180	180	450 (K); 900 (1–8); 990 (9–12)		X	X
Rhode Island	180	180	180	180	1,080		X	X [19]
South Carolina	180	180	180 [2]	180 [2]	†	X		
South Dakota	—	†	†	†	437.5 (K); 875 (1–5); 962.5[15] (6–12)		X	X
Tennessee	180	180	180 [2]	180 [2]	†	X		X
Texas	187	180	180	180	†	X		X
Utah	180	180	180	180	450 (K); 810 (1); 990 (2–12)	X	([21])	

See notes at end of table.

Table 234.20. Minimum amount of instructional time per year and policies on textbooks, by state: Selected years, 2000 through 2014—Continued

State	Minimum amount of instructional time per year					Policies on textbooks, 2014		
	In days				In hours	Textbook selection level		Free textbooks provided to students
	2000	2006	2011	2014	2014	State	Local education agency	
1	2	3	4	5	6	7	8	9
Vermont	175	175	175	175	†		X	X
Virginia	180	180	180	180	540 (K); 990 (1–12)	X		X
Washington	180 [16]	180	180	180	450[22] (K); 1,000[22] (1–12)		X	([23])
West Virginia	180	180	180	180	†	X		X
Wisconsin	180	180	180	†	437/1,050[2] (K); 1,050[2] (1–6); 1,137[2] (7–12)		X	
Wyoming	175	175	180	175	450 (K); 900 (Elementary); 1,050 (Middle/Jr. High); 1,100 (Secondary)		X	X

—Not available.
†Not applicable.
X Denotes that the state has a policy. A blank denotes that the state does not have a policy.
[1]Or an equivalent number of hours or minutes of instruction per year.
[2]Does not include time for in-service or staff development or parent-teacher conferences.
[3]Includes time for in-service or staff development or parent-teacher conferences.
[4]Students must enroll in at least 4 subjects that meet at least 720 hours.
[5]Fees permitted at the high school level for nonrequired or supplementary textbooks.
[6]State Department of Education prepares a list of suggestions, but the districts choose.
[7]Through 2014–15, districts are allowed to shorten the 180-day instructional year to 175 days without fiscal penalty.
[8]Statewide textbook adoption is only at the elementary level. Adoption practices have been suspended until the 2015–16 school year.
[9]No statewide policy; varies by district.
[10]1996 data.
[11]For schools on double-session or approved experimental calendar: 630 (K–3); 810 (4–12).
[12]Does not apply to charter and multitrack schools.
[13]For the 2014–15 and 2015–16 school years.
[14]Fees for lost or damaged books permitted.
[15]Instructional time for graduating seniors may be reduced.
[16]1998 data.
[17]Fees permitted, but if 5 percent or more of the voters in a district petition the school board, a majority of the district's voters may decide to furnish free textbooks to students.
[18]Fees permitted for students in grades 9–12, but students who qualify for free or reduced-price lunch are exempted.
[19]Refundable or security deposits permitted.
[20]174 days required for a 5-day week; 142 days required for a 4-day week.
[21]Local districts may select textbooks not on the state recommended list provided the textbooks meet specific criteria and the selection is based on recommendations by the district's curriculum materials review committee.
[22]Starting in the 2015–16 school year, grades 9 through 12 will transition to 1,080 hours and kindergarten will transition to 1,000 hours statewide by the 2017–18 school year.
[23]A district may provide free textbooks to students when, in its judgment, the best interests of the district will be served.
NOTE: Minimum number of instructional days refers to the actual number of days that pupils have contact with a teacher. Some states allow for different types of school calendars by setting instructional time in both days and hours, while others use only days or only hours. For states in which the number of days or hours varies by grade, the relevant grade(s) appear in parentheses.
SOURCE: Council of Chief State School Officers, *Key State Education Policies on PK–12 Education*, 2000 and 2006; Education Commission of the States, StateNotes, *Number of Instructional Days/Hours in the School Year* (October 2014 revision), retrieved May 19, 2015, from http://www.ecs.org/clearinghouse/01/15/05/11505.pdf; *State Textbook Adoption* (September 2013 edition), retrieved May 19, 2015, from http://www.ecs.org/clearinghouse/01/09/23/10923.pdf; and supplemental information retrieved from various state websites. (This table was prepared May 2015.)

Table 234.30. Course credit requirements and exit exam requirements for a standard high school diploma and the use of other high school completion credentials, by state: 2013

State	Course credits (in Carnegie units)						High school exit exams				Other completion credentials	
	Total required credits for standard diploma, all courses	Required credits in selected subject areas: English/ language arts	Social studies	Science	Mathematics	Other credits	Exit exam required for standard diploma	Characteristics of required exams: Subjects tested[1]	Exam based on standards for 10th grade or higher	Appeals or alternative route to standard diploma if exam failed	Advanced recognition for exceeding standard requirements	Alternative credential for not meeting all standard requirements[2]
1	2	3	4	5	6	7	8	9	10	11	12	13
Alabama	24.0	4.0	4.0	4.0	4.0	8.0	Yes	EMSH	Yes	Yes	Yes	Yes
Alaska	21.0	4.0	3.0	2.0	2.0	10.0	Yes	EM	Yes	Yes	No	Yes
Arizona	22.0	4.0	3.0	3.0	4.0	8.0	Yes	EM	Yes	Yes	Yes	No
Arkansas	22.0	4.0	3.0	3.0	4.0	8.0	Yes	M	No	Yes	Yes	No
California	13.0	3.0	3.0	2.0	2.0	3.0	Yes	EM	Yes	Yes	Yes	Yes
Colorado	—	—	0.5	—	—	—	No	†	†	†	No	No
Connecticut	20.0	4.0	3.0	2.0	3.0	8.0	No[3]	†	†	†	No	No
Delaware	22.0	4.0	3.0	3.0	4.0	8.0	No	†	†	†	No	Yes
District of Columbia	24.0	4.0	4.0	4.0	4.0	8.0	No	†	†	†	No	Yes
Florida	24.0	4.0	3.0	3.0	4.0	10.0	Yes	EM	Yes	Yes	No	Yes
Georgia	23.0	4.0	3.0	4.0	4.0	8.0	Yes	EMSH	Yes	Yes	No	Yes
Hawaii	24.0	4.0	4.0	3.0	3.0	10.0	No	†	†	†	Yes	Yes
Idaho	23.0	4.5	2.5	3.0	3.0	10.0	Yes	EM	Yes	Yes	No	No
Illinois	16.0	4.0	2.0	2.0	3.0	5.0	No	†	†	†	No	No
Indiana	20.0	4.0	3.0	3.0	3.0	7.0	Yes	EM	Yes	Yes	Yes	Yes
Iowa	14.0	4.0	3.0	3.0	3.0	1.0	No	†	†	†	Yes	No
Kansas	21.0	4.0	3.0	3.0	3.0	8.0	No	†	†	†	No	No
Kentucky	22.0	4.0	3.0	3.0	3.0	9.0	No	†	†	†	Yes	Yes
Louisiana	24.0	4.0	4.0	4.0	4.0	8.0	Yes	EMSH[4]	Yes	Yes	Yes	Yes
Maine	16.0	4.0	2.0	2.0	2.0	6.0	No	†	†	†	No	Yes
Maryland	21.0	4.0	3.0	3.0	3.0	8.0	Yes	EMS	Yes	Yes	Yes	Yes
Massachusetts	—	—	—	—	—	—	Yes	EMS	Yes	Yes	No	No
Michigan	16.0	4.0	3.0	3.0	4.0	2.0	No	†	†	†	No	No
Minnesota	21.5	4.0	3.5	3.0	3.0	8.0	Yes	EM[5]	Yes	Yes	No	No
Mississippi	24.0	4.0	4.0	4.0	4.0	8.0	Yes	EMSH	Yes	Yes	No	Yes
Missouri	24.0	4.0	3.0	3.0	3.0	11.0	No	†	†	†	No	No
Montana	20.0	4.0	2.0	2.0	2.0	10.0	No	†	†	†	No	No
Nebraska	200.0[6]	—	—	—	—	—	No	†	†	†	No	No
Nevada	22.5	4.0	2.0	2.0	3.0	11.5	Yes	EMS	Yes	Yes	Yes	Yes
New Hampshire	20.0	4.0	2.5	2.0	3.0	8.5	No	†	†	†	Yes	Yes
New Jersey	24.0	4.0	3.0	3.0	3.0	11.0	Yes	EM	Yes	Yes	No	No
New Mexico	24.0	4.0	3.5	3.0	4.0	9.5	Yes	EMSH	Yes	Yes	No	Yes
New York	22.0	4.0	4.0	3.0	3.0	8.0	Yes	EMSH	Yes	Yes	Yes	Yes
North Carolina	21.0	4.0	3.0	3.0	4.0	7.0	No	†	†	†	Yes	Yes
North Dakota	22.0	4.0	3.0	3.0	3.0	9.0	No	†	†	†	No	No
Ohio	20.0	4.0	3.0	3.0	3.0	7.0	Yes	EMSH	Yes	Yes	Yes	No
Oklahoma	23.0	4.0	3.0	3.0	3.0	10.0	Yes	EMSH[7]	Yes	Yes	Yes	No
Oregon	24.0	4.0	3.0	3.0	3.0	11.0	No	†	†	†	No	Yes
Pennsylvania	—	—	—	—	—	—	No	†	†	†	No	No
Rhode Island	20.0	4.0	3.0	3.0	4.0	6.0	No[8]	†	†	†	No	No
South Carolina	24.0	4.0	3.0	3.0	4.0	10.0	Yes	EM	Yes	No	Yes	Yes
South Dakota	22.0	4.0	3.0	3.0	3.0	9.0	No	†	†	†	Yes	No
Tennessee	22.0	4.0	3.0	3.0	4.0	8.0	No	†	†	No	Yes	Yes
Texas	26.0	4.0	4.0	4.0	4.0	10.0	Yes	EMSH	Yes	Yes	Yes	Yes
Utah	24.0	4.0	3.0	3.0	3.0	11.0	No	†	†	†	No	Yes
Vermont	20.0	4.0	3.0	3.0	3.0	7.0	No	†	†	†	No	No
Virginia	22.0	4.0	3.0	3.0	3.0	9.0	Yes	EMSH[9]	Yes	Yes	Yes	Yes
Washington	20.0	3.0	2.5	2.0	3.0	9.5	Yes	EM	Yes	Yes	No	No
West Virginia	24.0	4.0	4.0	3.0	4.0	9.0	No	†	†	†	Yes	Yes
Wisconsin	13.0	4.0	3.0	2.0	2.0	2.0	No	†	†	†	No	Yes
Wyoming	13.0	4.0	3.0	3.0	3.0	0.0	No	†	†	†	Yes	No

—Not available.
†Not applicable.
[1]Exit exam subjects tested: E = English (including writing), M = Mathematics, S = Science, and H = History/social studies.
[2]A certificate of attendance is an example of an alternative credential for students who do not meet all requirements for a standard diploma. Depending on an individual state's policies, alternative credentials may be offered to students with disabilities, students who fail exit exams, or other students who do not meet all requirements.
[3]Requirement takes effect for class of 2020.
[4]Students must pass either the science or social studies components of the Graduation Exit Examination (GEE) to receive a standard diploma.
[5]Students can graduate by passing statewide reading and writing assessments and either passing mathematics assessments or meeting other requirements.
[6]Expressed in semester credits instead of Carnegie units.
[7]To receive the standard diploma, students must pass tests in algebra 1, English 2, and two of the following five subjects: algebra 2, biology 1, English 3, geometry, and U.S. history.
[8]Requirement takes effect for class of 2014.
[9]To receive the standard diploma, students must earn at least six verified credits by passing end-of-course assessments. One of those credits may be earned by passing a student-selected test in computer science, technology, career and technical education, or other areas.
NOTE: Local school districts frequently have other graduation requirements in addition to state requirements. The Carnegie unit is a standard of measurement that represents one credit for the completion of a 1-year course.
SOURCE: Editorial Projects in Education Research Center, custom table, retrieved August 27, 2013, from Education Counts database (http://www.edcounts.org/createtable/step1.php). (This table was prepared August 2013.)

Table 234.40. States that use criterion-referenced tests (CRTs) aligned to state standards, by subject area and level: 2006–07

State	Aligned to state standards		Off-the-shelf/ norm-referenced test (NRT)[1]	CRTs,[2] by subject area and level			
	CRT[2]	Augmented or hybrid test[3]		English/ language arts	Mathematics	Science	Social studies/ history
1	2	3	4	5	6	7	8
Alabama	X		X	ES, MS, HS	ES, MS, HS	HS	HS
Alaska	X		X	ES, MS, HS	ES, MS, HS		
Arizona	X	X	X	ES, MS, HS	ES, MS, HS		
Arkansas	X		X	ES, MS, HS	ES, MS, HS	ES, MS	
California	X		X	ES, MS, HS	ES, MS, HS	ES, MS, HS	MS, HS
Colorado	X		X	ES, MS, HS	ES, MS, HS	ES, MS, HS	
Connecticut	X			ES, MS, HS	ES, MS, HS	HS	
Delaware		X		ES, MS, HS	ES, MS, HS	ES, MS, HS	ES, MS, HS
District of Columbia	X			ES, MS, HS	ES, MS, HS		
Florida	X		X	ES, MS, HS	ES, MS, HS	ES, MS, HS	
Georgia	X		X	ES, MS, HS	ES, MS, HS	ES, MS, HS	ES, MS, HS
Hawaii		X		ES, MS, HS	ES, MS, HS		
Idaho	X			ES, MS, HS	ES, MS, HS		
Illinois	X	X		ES, MS, HS	ES, MS, HS	HS	
Indiana	X			ES, MS, HS	ES, MS, HS	ES, MS	
Iowa			X	ES, MS, HS	ES, MS, HS	ES, MS, HS	
Kansas	X			ES, MS, HS	ES, MS, HS		
Kentucky	X		X	ES, MS, HS	ES, MS, HS	ES, MS, HS	ES, MS, HS
Louisiana	X	X		ES, MS, HS	ES, MS, HS	ES, MS, HS	ES, MS, HS
Maine	X		X	ES, MS, HS	ES, MS, HS	ES, MS	
Maryland	X	X		ES, MS, HS	ES, MS, HS	HS	HS
Massachusetts	X			ES, MS, HS	ES, MS, HS	ES, MS, HS	
Michigan	X		X	ES, MS, HS	ES, MS, HS	ES, MS, HS	MS, HS
Minnesota	X			ES, MS, HS	ES, MS, HS		
Mississippi	X		X	ES, MS, HS	ES, MS, HS	ES, MS, HS	HS
Missouri		X		ES, MS, HS	ES, MS, HS		
Montana	X		X	ES, MS, HS	ES, MS, HS		
Nebraska	X			ES, MS, HS			
Nevada	X		X	ES, MS, HS	ES, MS, HS		
New Hampshire	X			ES, MS	ES, MS		
New Jersey	X			ES, MS, HS	ES, MS, HS	ES, MS	
New Mexico	X		X	ES, MS, HS	ES, MS, HS	ES, MS, HS	
New York	X			ES, MS, HS	ES, MS, HS	ES, MS, HS	ES, MS, HS
North Carolina	X			ES, MS, HS	ES, MS, HS	HS	HS
North Dakota	X			ES, MS, HS	ES, MS, HS	ES, MS, HS	
Ohio	X			ES, MS, HS	ES, MS, HS	ES, MS, HS	ES, MS, HS
Oklahoma	X			ES, MS, HS	ES, MS, HS	ES, MS, HS	ES, MS, HS
Oregon	X			ES, MS, HS	ES, MS, HS	MS, HS	
Pennsylvania	X			ES, MS, HS	ES, MS, HS		
Rhode Island	X	X		ES, MS, HS	ES, MS, HS		
South Carolina	X			ES, MS, HS	ES, MS, HS	ES, MS, HS	ES, MS, HS
South Dakota		X	X	ES, MS, HS	ES, MS, HS	ES, MS, HS	
Tennessee	X			ES, MS, HS	ES, MS, HS	ES, MS, HS	ES, MS, HS
Texas	X			ES, MS, HS	ES, MS, HS	ES, MS, HS	MS, HS
Utah	X		X	ES, MS, HS	ES, MS, HS	ES, MS, HS	
Vermont	X			ES, MS	ES, MS		
Virginia	X			ES, MS, HS	ES, MS, HS	ES, MS, HS	ES, MS, HS
Washington	X			ES, MS, HS	ES, MS, HS	ES, MS, HS	
West Virginia	X		X	ES, MS, HS	ES, MS, HS	ES, MS, HS	ES, MS
Wisconsin		X		ES, MS, HS	ES, MS, HS	ES, MS, HS	ES, MS, HS
Wyoming	X			ES, MS, HS	ES, MS, HS		

X State has a test. A blank denotes that the state does not have this type of test.
[1]Off-the-shelf/norm-referenced tests (NRTs) are commercially developed tests that have not been modified to reflect state content standards.
[2]Criterion-referenced tests (CRTs) are custom-developed and explicitly designed to measure state content standards.
[3]Augmented or hybrid tests incorporate elements of both NRTs and CRTs. These tests include NRTs that have been augmented or modified to reflect state standards.
NOTE: ES = elementary school, MS = middle school, and HS = high school.
SOURCE: Quality Counts 2007, Cradle to Career, *Education Week,* 2007. (This table was prepared September 2008.)

Table 234.50. Required testing for initial certification of elementary and secondary school teachers, by type of assessment and state: 2014 and 2015

State	Assessment for certification, 2014				Assessment for certification, 2015			
	Basic skills exam	Subject-matter exam	Knowledge of teaching exam	Assessment of teaching performance	Basic skills exam	Subject-matter exam	Knowledge of teaching exam	Assessment of teaching performance
1	2	3	4	5	6	7	8	9
Alabama	X	X	X	X	X	X	X	X
Alaska	X				X			
Arizona		X	X			X	X	
Arkansas	X	X	X	X	X	X	X	
California	X	—		X	X	—		X
Colorado		X				X		
Connecticut	X	X	—	—	X	X	—	—
Delaware	X	X			X	X		
District of Columbia	X	X	X		X	X	X	
Florida	X			X	X			X
Georgia	X	X			X	X		
Hawaii	X	X		—	X	X		
Idaho		X		X		X		X
Illinois	X	X	X		X	X	X	X[1]
Indiana	X	X		X	X	X		X
Iowa						X	X	
Kansas		X	X			X	X	
Kentucky	X	X	X	X	X	X	X	X
Louisiana	X	X	X	X	X	X	X	X
Maine	—	—	—	—	X	X	X	
Maryland	X	X	X	X	X	X	X	
Massachusetts	X	X		X	X	X		X
Michigan	X	X		X	X	X		X
Minnesota	X	X	X		X	X	X	
Mississippi	—	—	—	—	X	X	X	X
Missouri	X	X		X	X	X	X	X
Montana								
Nebraska	X				X			
Nevada	—	X	—	—	X	X		
New Hampshire	X	X			X	X		
New Jersey	—	—	—	—	X	X		
New Mexico	X	X	X	X	X	X	X	X
New York		X	X		X	X	X	X
North Carolina	—	—	—	—	X	X	X	X
North Dakota	—	X	—	—	X	X	X	X
Ohio		X	X	X		X	X	X
Oklahoma	—	—	—	—	—	—	—	—
Oregon	X	X		X	X	X		X
Pennsylvania	X	X	X	X	X	X		X
Rhode Island			X	X	X	X	X	X
South Carolina		X	X			X	X	
South Dakota	X	X	X	X	X	X	X	X
Tennessee	X	X	X		X	X	X	
Texas	X	X	X	X	X	X	X	X
Utah		X		X		X		X
Vermont	X	X			X			
Virginia	X	X	X		X	X	X	
Washington	X	X		X	X	X		X
West Virginia	X	X	X	X	X	X	X	X
Wisconsin	X	X			X	X		X
Wyoming	—		—	—				

—Not available.
X Denotes that the state requires testing. A blank denotes that the state does not require testing.
[1]Beginning September 1, 2015.

SOURCE: National Association of State Directors of Teacher Education and Certification (NASDTEC), NASDTEC Knowledgebase, retrieved July 9, 2015, from https://www.nasdtec.net/. (This table was prepared July 2015.)

Table 227.40. Percentage of elementary and secondary school students who do homework, average time spent, percentage whose parents check that homework is done, and percentage whose parents help with homework, by frequency and selected characteristics: 2007 and 2012

[Standard errors appear in parentheses]

Year and selected characteristic	Percent of students who do homework outside of school	Students who do homework outside of school										
		Average hours spent per week doing homework	Percentage distribution by how frequently they do homework				Percent whose parents[1] check that homework is done[2]	Percentage distribution by how frequently their parents[1] help with homework				
			Less than once per week	1 to 2 days per week	3 to 4 days per week	5 or more days per week		No help given	Less than once per week	1 to 2 days per week	3 to 4 days per week	5 or more days per week
1	2	3	4	5	6	7	8	9	10	11	12	13
2007												
All students	**94.4 (0.30)**	**5.4 (0.06)**	**3.1 (0.34)**	**13.1 (0.47)**	**43.6 (0.62)**	**40.2 (0.60)**	**85.4 (0.46)**	**10.2 (0.41)**	**20.3 (0.51)**	**31.7 (0.64)**	**25.3 (0.59)**	**12.4 (0.41)**
All elementary school students (kindergarten through grade 8)	**95.0 (0.37)**	**4.7 (0.07)**	**2.1 (0.23)**	**12.3 (0.56)**	**46.2 (0.73)**	**39.4 (0.68)**	**95.0 (0.34)**	**4.3 (0.34)**	**13.1 (0.52)**	**32.6 (0.77)**	**32.9 (0.76)**	**17.0 (0.56)**
Sex												
Male	94.6 (0.51)	4.6 (0.09)	2.1 (0.31)	12.4 (0.71)	47.9 (1.19)	37.6 (1.09)	95.3 (0.47)	4.3 (0.39)	12.9 (0.63)	32.3 (1.02)	32.7 (1.28)	17.8 (0.85)
Female	95.4 (0.53)	4.9 (0.10)	2.1 (0.31)	12.2 (0.96)	44.4 (1.13)	41.3 (1.08)	94.6 (0.48)	4.3 (0.56)	13.4 (0.76)	32.9 (1.17)	33.2 (1.17)	16.1 (0.79)
Race/ethnicity												
White	94.7 (0.48)	4.4 (0.07)	2.7 (0.36)	13.7 (0.74)	48.3 (1.05)	35.3 (0.99)	94.0 (0.42)	3.8 (0.37)	15.7 (0.74)	34.9 (0.94)	31.3 (0.92)	14.3 (0.63)
Black	95.5 (1.07)	5.6 (0.27)	1.3 ! (0.53)	7.0 (1.19)	44.4 (3.40)	47.2 (3.11)	98.1 (0.63)	3.5 (1.03)	7.4 (1.14)	25.2 (2.22)	38.3 (3.36)	25.5 (2.38)
Hispanic	94.8 (0.85)	4.7 (0.11)	1.3 (0.33)	13.5 (1.39)	40.7 (1.94)	44.4 (1.74)	96.1 (0.70)	7.1 (0.95)	10.3 (0.91)	30.1 (1.79)	34.0 (1.78)	18.6 (1.52)
Asian/Pacific Islander	95.9 (2.14)	5.7 (0.36)	‡ (†)	4.7 (1.35)	40.1 (4.35)	54.3 (4.73)	89.4 (3.22)	3.7 ! (1.35)	15.4 (4.07)	34.7 (4.39)	29.3 (4.03)	17.0 (2.54)
Asian	97.7 (0.97)	5.7 (0.39)	‡ (†)	5.1 ! (1.53)	39.1 (4.31)	54.8 (4.48)	88.5 (3.44)	3.1 ! (1.36)	12.8 (2.84)	37.5 (4.52)	30.7 (4.22)	15.9 (2.56)
Pacific Islander	‡ (†)	‡ (†)	‡ (†)	‡ (†)	‡ (†)	‡ (†)	‡ (†)	‡ (†)	‡ (†)	‡ (†)	‡ (†)	‡ (†)
American Indian/Alaska Native	‡ (†)	‡ (†)	‡ (†)	‡ (†)	‡ (†)	‡ (†)	‡ (†)	‡ (†)	‡ (†)	‡ (†)	‡ (†)	‡ (†)
Other	96.7 (1.24)	4.8 (0.25)	1.2 ! (0.56)	8.5 (1.73)	57.1 (3.81)	33.1 (3.69)	95.1 (1.81)	‡ (†)	12.3 (2.30)	35.5 (3.99)	33.8 (3.81)	16.1 (2.71)
School control												
Public	95.1 (0.38)	4.7 (0.08)	2.0 (0.25)	12.4 (0.62)	46.1 (0.76)	39.4 (0.73)	95.4 (0.36)	4.4 (0.38)	13.1 (0.55)	32.4 (0.86)	32.9 (0.81)	17.2 (0.64)
Private	94.0 (1.01)	4.8 (0.19)	2.7 (0.63)	11.4 (1.96)	46.7 (2.64)	39.2 (2.46)	91.5 (1.19)	3.6 (0.85)	13.6 (1.48)	34.3 (2.10)	33.5 (2.36)	15.2 (1.68)
Poverty status[3]												
Poor	94.2 (0.99)	4.7 (0.20)	2.9 (0.72)	16.3 (2.18)	39.0 (2.53)	41.7 (2.21)	97.9 (0.55)	6.1 (1.01)	8.8 (1.29)	28.5 (2.44)	35.2 (2.41)	21.3 (1.90)
Near-poor	93.1 (1.03)	4.7 (0.16)	2.2 (0.49)	13.4 (1.37)	47.0 (1.89)	37.5 (1.91)	95.8 (1.05)	5.2 (0.92)	11.5 (1.13)	31.8 (1.79)	33.3 (1.63)	18.2 (1.60)
Nonpoor	95.9 (0.38)	4.8 (0.08)	1.8 (0.24)	10.7 (0.59)	48.3 (0.94)	39.2 (0.89)	93.7 (0.48)	3.5 (0.32)	15.1 (0.68)	34.2 (0.85)	32.1 (0.79)	15.2 (0.59)
Locale												
City	95.2 (0.65)	5.1 (0.13)	1.5 (0.31)	9.1 (0.91)	43.4 (1.58)	46.0 (1.43)	95.4 (0.54)	4.8 (0.67)	11.3 (1.02)	29.1 (1.39)	36.0 (1.41)	18.7 (1.15)
Suburb	95.4 (0.51)	4.9 (0.11)	1.9 (0.37)	9.3 (0.71)	46.1 (1.24)	42.7 (1.19)	93.5 (0.67)	4.4 (0.55)	14.5 (0.85)	33.1 (1.05)	30.8 (1.14)	17.1 (0.91)
Town	93.0 (1.50)	4.1 (0.14)	2.7 (0.79)	18.8 (1.98)	46.4 (2.29)	32.2 (2.08)	96.0 (1.04)	3.2 (0.80)	14.2 (1.62)	35.7 (2.68)	31.1 (2.31)	15.7 (1.62)
Rural	95.0 (0.85)	4.2 (0.15)	3.2 (0.69)	19.5 (1.79)	50.6 (1.90)	26.8 (1.63)	96.3 (0.72)	4.1 (0.94)	13.1 (1.30)	35.5 (2.29)	32.8 (2.23)	14.6 (1.37)
All secondary school students (grades 9 through 12)	**93.0 (0.55)**	**6.8 (0.11)**	**5.4 (0.85)**	**14.8 (0.96)**	**38.0 (1.15)**	**41.9 (1.18)**	**64.6 (1.21)**	**23.1 (1.08)**	**35.9 (1.26)**	**29.7 (1.19)**	**8.8 (0.81)**	**2.5 (0.34)**
Sex												
Male	91.2 (0.80)	6.0 (0.19)	7.4 (1.53)	18.3 (1.59)	38.2 (1.78)	36.0 (1.64)	67.8 (1.88)	24.1 (1.56)	36.9 (1.97)	29.1 (1.84)	8.2 (1.11)	1.8 (0.41)
Female	94.9 (0.79)	7.5 (0.16)	3.3 (0.72)	11.2 (1.10)	37.7 (1.79)	47.9 (1.85)	61.4 (1.78)	22.0 (1.32)	35.0 (1.44)	30.4 (1.35)	9.3 (1.11)	3.3 (0.60)
Race/ethnicity												
White	94.5 (0.52)	6.8 (0.13)	4.2 (0.58)	12.9 (0.91)	38.6 (1.51)	44.3 (1.42)	57.2 (1.54)	22.5 (1.28)	41.1 (1.36)	27.7 (1.43)	6.3 (0.66)	2.3 (0.42)
Black	91.8 (1.98)	6.3 (0.38)	‡ (†)	20.1 (3.86)	41.0 (4.72)	29.7 (3.43)	83.1 (2.84)	19.5 (2.97)	26.5 (4.77)	34.4 (4.03)	16.7 (4.45)	2.9 ! (1.13)
Hispanic	90.7 (2.11)	6.4 (0.34)	5.9 (1.29)	17.7 (3.55)	36.6 (2.93)	39.9 (3.03)	75.6 (2.71)	26.2 (2.94)	25.8 (2.38)	33.8 (3.49)	11.0 (1.76)	3.3 ! (1.00)
Asian/Pacific Islander	94.2 (4.66)	10.9 (1.22)	‡ (†)	12.2 ! (4.84)	22.3 (6.26)	63.6 (7.16)	65.0 (7.41)	27.1 (7.15)	34.0 (6.73)	27.0 (6.87)	9.2 ! (3.24)	‡ (†)
Asian	93.6 (5.45)	10.3 (1.37)	# (†)	13.8 ! (5.51)	18.5 ! (6.12)	67.7 (7.18)	59.0 (7.69)	26.4 (7.58)	36.1 (7.55)	26.8 (7.61)	7.6 ! (3.11)	‡ (†)
Pacific Islander	‡ (†)	‡ (†)	‡ (†)	‡ (†)	‡ (†)	‡ (†)	‡ (†)	‡ (†)	‡ (†)	‡ (†)	‡ (†)	‡ (†)
American Indian/Alaska Native	‡ (†)	‡ (†)	‡ (†)	‡ (†)	‡ (†)	‡ (†)	‡ (†)	‡ (†)	‡ (†)	‡ (†)	‡ (†)	‡ (†)
Other	86.7 (4.90)	7.2 (0.72)	‡ (†)	9.9 (2.55)	34.1 (4.90)	50.2 (5.29)	64.4 (6.36)	27.2 (6.80)	35.6 (5.57)	27.8 (5.30)	7.9 ! (2.41)	‡ (†)
School control												
Public	92.3 (0.60)	6.5 (0.11)	5.9 (0.96)	15.9 (1.06)	39.7 (1.26)	38.5 (1.17)	66.1 (1.24)	22.8 (1.16)	35.4 (1.29)	30.0 (1.26)	9.1 (0.87)	2.7 (0.37)
Private	98.5 (0.54)	9.3 (0.39)	0.8 ! (0.35)	5.9 (1.34)	24.0 (2.72)	69.4 (2.89)	53.1 (3.98)	25.0 (2.64)	40.1 (3.68)	27.5 (4.07)	6.1 (1.36)	1.4 ! (0.61)
Poverty status[3]												
Poor	89.5 (2.21)	5.5 (0.32)	‡ (†)	19.2 (3.62)	38.7 (4.32)	33.7 (3.69)	81.0 (3.03)	24.2 (3.80)	24.0 (4.21)	36.1 (3.76)	14.0 (3.21)	1.7 ! (0.63)
Near-poor	89.5 (1.86)	6.4 (0.35)	6.6 (1.58)	20.5 (3.32)	44.2 (3.43)	28.7 (3.10)	70.8 (3.38)	22.9 (2.90)	32.4 (2.97)	28.7 (3.42)	13.0 (2.22)	3.0 ! (1.02)
Nonpoor	94.9 (0.57)	7.2 (0.13)	4.3 (0.54)	12.1 (0.74)	36.1 (1.41)	47.5 (1.34)	58.9 (1.28)	22.8 (1.11)	39.9 (1.29)	28.4 (1.17)	6.3 (0.68)	2.6 (0.45)

See notes at end of table.

Table 227.40. Percentage of elementary and secondary school students who do homework, average time spent, percentage whose parents check that homework is done, and percentage whose parents help with homework, by frequency and selected characteristics: 2007 and 2012—Continued

[Standard errors appear in parentheses]

Year and selected characteristic	Percent of students who do homework outside of school	Students who do homework outside of school: Average hours spent per week doing homework	Percentage distribution by how frequently they do homework: Less than once per week	1 to 2 days per week	3 to 4 days per week	5 or more days per week	Percent whose parents[1] check that homework is done[2]	Percentage distribution by how frequently their parents[1] help with homework: No help given	Less than once per week	1 to 2 days per week	3 to 4 days per week	5 or more days per week
1	2	3	4	5	6	7	8	9	10	11	12	13
Coursework												
Enrolled in AP classes	96.9 (0.59)	8.5 (0.22)	2.4 (0.70)	7.5 (0.93)	31.9 (1.81)	58.2 (1.97)	56.3 (2.06)	27.4 (1.90)	36.3 (1.69)	28.3 (1.74)	6.0 (0.99)	1.9 (0.43)
Not enrolled in AP classes	90.6 (0.81)	5.7 (0.13)	7.3 (1.31)	19.5 (1.40)	41.9 (1.56)	31.2 (1.42)	70.1 (1.46)	20.2 (1.14)	35.7 (1.70)	30.7 (1.59)	10.5 (1.23)	2.9 (0.51)
Locale												
City	92.8 (1.01)	6.8 (0.22)	6.3 ! (2.46)	14.1 (1.90)	35.9 (2.32)	43.7 (2.53)	71.5 (1.89)	22.6 (1.88)	33.4 (2.64)	29.3 (2.00)	12.0 (1.80)	2.7 (0.55)
Suburb	93.6 (0.95)	7.5 (0.17)	4.8 (0.86)	11.4 (1.27)	36.5 (1.71)	47.4 (2.07)	58.9 (2.00)	23.6 (1.74)	39.1 (1.79)	27.8 (1.68)	7.5 (1.01)	2.0 (0.47)
Town	89.7 (2.16)	6.4 (0.27)	5.4 (1.48)	13.2 (1.74)	45.9 (3.46)	35.5 (3.17)	64.8 (3.12)	24.3 (2.81)	34.4 (2.96)	27.9 (3.41)	9.3 (1.80)	4.2 ! (1.54)
Rural	93.9 (1.23)	5.6 (0.29)	5.1 (1.20)	22.7 (2.76)	39.6 (3.04)	32.6 (2.79)	65.5 (2.94)	22.1 (2.69)	34.4 (2.71)	34.8 (3.43)	6.2 (1.53)	2.5 ! (0.88)
2012												
All students	**96.0 (0.27)**	**5.2 (0.05)**	**5.3 (0.22)**	**15.3 (0.46)**	**43.5 (0.58)**	**35.9 (0.59)**	**96.6 (0.18)**	**8.5 (0.24)**	**22.0 (0.43)**	**26.5 (0.43)**	**26.5 (0.52)**	**16.6 (0.41)**
All elementary school students (kindergarten through grade 8)	**96.3 (0.29)**	**4.7 (0.06)**	**4.1 (0.27)**	**12.8 (0.50)**	**46.7 (0.74)**	**36.3 (0.68)**	**99.0 (0.12)**	**3.0 (0.24)**	**14.5 (0.40)**	**27.0 (0.54)**	**33.7 (0.64)**	**21.9 (0.57)**
Sex												
Male	96.2 (0.37)	4.5 (0.09)	4.7 (0.41)	13.5 (0.64)	46.7 (0.91)	35.1 (0.90)	99.1 (0.18)	3.3 (0.35)	14.7 (0.60)	26.0 (0.73)	34.5 (0.88)	21.5 (0.83)
Female	96.5 (0.46)	4.8 (0.09)	3.4 (0.37)	12.1 (0.69)	46.8 (1.21)	37.7 (1.04)	98.9 (0.15)	2.7 (0.31)	14.3 (0.59)	28.0 (0.90)	32.7 (1.03)	22.3 (0.88)
Race/ethnicity												
White	95.4 (0.54)	4.4 (0.07)	5.3 (0.40)	14.3 (0.69)	47.4 (0.95)	33.0 (0.91)	98.8 (0.16)	2.5 (0.27)	17.7 (0.61)	27.5 (0.68)	33.4 (0.92)	18.9 (0.82)
Black	96.2 (0.83)	5.5 (0.19)	3.5 (0.86)	14.0 (1.63)	47.9 (2.16)	34.7 (1.75)	99.1 (0.37)	3.7 (0.92)	9.8 (1.62)	24.3 (1.80)	37.0 (2.40)	25.1 (1.80)
Hispanic	98.1 (0.40)	4.7 (0.12)	3.0 (0.57)	10.0 (0.82)	44.7 (1.65)	42.3 (1.53)	99.6 (0.13)	3.8 (0.46)	11.0 (0.96)	28.1 (1.25)	32.7 (1.58)	24.4 (1.34)
Asian	97.3 (0.85)	5.6 (0.27)	1.0 ! (0.39)	11.1 (2.03)	39.1 (3.03)	48.7 (3.11)	98.4 (0.64)	4.1 (0.91)	14.0 (1.64)	25.7 (2.60)	26.9 (2.49)	29.3 (3.15)
Asian	97.0 (0.93)	5.7 (0.29)	1.1 ! (0.42)	11.6 (1.98)	37.2 (2.71)	50.1 (2.96)	98.2 (0.70)	3.9 (0.99)	14.9 (1.73)	27.4 (2.55)	26.5 (2.54)	27.3 (3.10)
Pacific Islander	‡ (†)	‡ (†)	‡ (†)	‡ (†)	‡ (†)	‡ (†)	‡ (†)	‡ (†)	‡ (†)	‡ (†)	‡ (†)	‡ (†)
American Indian/Alaska Native	97.9 (2.15)	4.5 (0.41)	‡ (†)	8.1 ! (3.18)	71.2 (7.78)	14.5 ! (4.82)	100.0 (†)	‡ (†)	9.3 ! (3.95)	18.8 ! (6.52)	48.0 (11.41)	23.2 ! (10.28)
Other	96.9 (0.79)	4.6 (0.25)	2.3 ! (0.73)	11.2 (1.97)	51.7 (2.94)	34.7 (2.48)	99.1 (0.42)	1.8 ! (0.58)	14.3 (2.12)	26.8 (2.95)	35.9 (2.76)	21.2 (2.40)
School control												
Public	96.7 (0.30)	4.7 (0.06)	4.1 (0.26)	13.3 (0.54)	47.0 (0.78)	35.7 (0.72)	99.1 (0.12)	3.0 (0.25)	14.5 (0.45)	27.4 (0.57)	33.5 (0.69)	21.6 (0.60)
Private	92.5 (1.23)	4.8 (0.15)	4.0 (1.15)	8.5 (1.19)	43.9 (1.77)	43.5 (1.95)	98.7 (0.49)	3.0 (0.78)	14.2 (1.41)	23.0 (1.83)	35.5 (1.88)	24.3 (1.70)
Poverty status[3]												
Poor	94.9 (1.00)	4.7 (0.16)	4.2 (0.64)	13.7 (1.15)	42.2 (1.87)	39.9 (1.68)	99.2 (0.33)	4.7 (0.74)	10.0 (0.87)	24.9 (1.50)	31.9 (1.83)	28.5 (1.49)
Near-poor	95.4 (0.71)	4.6 (0.14)	4.4 (0.56)	14.6 (1.10)	46.9 (1.51)	34.1 (1.44)	99.1 (0.26)	3.6 (0.57)	12.5 (1.12)	27.2 (1.58)	35.3 (1.61)	21.4 (1.38)
Nonpoor	97.2 (0.30)	4.7 (0.07)	3.9 (0.36)	11.9 (0.60)	48.3 (1.00)	35.9 (0.88)	99.0 (0.14)	2.2 (0.25)	16.8 (0.56)	27.7 (0.68)	33.7 (0.79)	19.7 (0.72)
Locale												
City	96.0 (0.49)	5.0 (0.12)	3.3 (0.51)	11.4 (0.90)	43.7 (1.47)	41.5 (1.39)	98.9 (0.21)	4.0 (0.60)	12.3 (0.77)	26.8 (1.21)	32.0 (1.17)	24.9 (1.21)
Suburb	96.8 (0.64)	4.8 (0.08)	2.9 (0.34)	11.0 (0.84)	46.2 (1.25)	39.9 (1.19)	99.1 (0.18)	2.7 (0.26)	15.6 (0.84)	27.2 (0.93)	32.6 (1.22)	21.9 (0.92)
Town	97.1 (0.65)	4.2 (0.21)	6.2 (1.25)	15.5 (1.52)	49.9 (2.66)	28.3 (2.44)	99.2 (0.36)	2.0 (0.53)	13.7 (1.95)	25.4 (2.12)	35.8 (2.64)	23.1 (2.25)
Rural	95.6 (0.62)	4.3 (0.14)	6.1 (0.73)	16.5 (1.15)	50.2 (1.31)	27.2 (1.35)	99.0 (0.22)	2.7 (0.48)	15.9 (1.03)	27.5 (1.34)	36.6 (1.35)	17.2 (1.08)
All secondary school students (grades 9 through 12)	**95.1 (0.58)**	**6.6 (0.10)**	**8.4 (0.48)**	**21.8 (0.92)**	**35.0 (0.91)**	**34.9 (0.97)**	**90.4 (0.55)**	**22.7 (0.70)**	**41.5 (1.00)**	**25.3 (0.84)**	**7.8 (0.63)**	**2.8 (0.28)**
Sex												
Male	93.4 (1.02)	5.7 (0.15)	10.8 (0.73)	24.7 (1.28)	35.2 (1.24)	29.3 (1.19)	92.5 (0.59)	22.4 (0.92)	41.7 (1.25)	23.9 (1.01)	8.7 (1.07)	3.3 (0.41)
Female	97.0 (0.42)	7.5 (0.15)	5.8 (0.64)	18.7 (1.15)	34.7 (1.19)	40.7 (1.42)	88.2 (0.92)	23.0 (1.13)	41.3 (1.59)	26.6 (1.43)	6.8 (0.62)	2.2 (0.42)
Race/ethnicity												
White	94.9 (1.01)	6.5 (0.10)	8.6 (0.59)	21.2 (0.88)	34.6 (1.04)	35.6 (1.22)	89.0 (0.85)	20.1 (0.85)	48.1 (1.21)	24.2 (1.07)	5.8 (0.49)	1.8 (0.32)
Black	94.5 (0.94)	6.3 (0.24)	7.7 (1.28)	27.2 (2.52)	34.4 (2.51)	30.7 (2.31)	95.2 (0.93)	20.5 (2.12)	32.0 (3.05)	28.7 (2.51)	12.1 (2.23)	6.7 (1.23)
Hispanic	95.3 (0.86)	6.1 (0.22)	8.9 (1.32)	22.3 (2.29)	36.4 (2.72)	32.4 (2.10)	91.7 (1.27)	27.9 (2.10)	33.7 (1.80)	27.6 (1.80)	7.6 (1.54)	3.2 (0.59)
Asian/Pacific Islander	98.4 (0.59)	10.5 (0.76)	5.5 ! (1.78)	10.0 ! (3.24)	30.6 (3.66)	53.9 (3.64)	87.3 (3.15)	38.4 (3.90)	33.4 (3.72)	14.8 (2.49)	11.5 (2.25)	‡ (†)
Asian	98.6 (0.61)	10.9 (0.82)	5.0 ! (1.85)	10.4 ! (3.58)	31.0 (3.96)	53.7 (3.83)	87.0 (3.44)	40.8 (4.08)	34.7 (3.97)	14.4 (2.52)	9.2 (1.78)	‡ (†)
Pacific Islander	‡ (†)	‡ (†)	‡ (†)	‡ (†)	‡ (†)	‡ (†)	‡ (†)	‡ (†)	‡ (†)	‡ (†)	‡ (†)	‡ (†)
American Indian/Alaska Native	99.7 (0.33)	‡ (†)	‡ (†)	‡ (†)	‡ (†)	‡ (†)	‡ (†)	‡ (†)	‡ (†)	‡ (†)	‡ (†)	‡ (†)
Other	93.9 (2.11)	6.6 (0.63)	6.8 (1.84)	24.6 (6.65)	37.7 (5.27)	31.0 (4.48)	90.2 (3.09)	17.5 (3.71)	38.7 (4.64)	27.0 (4.28)	15.9 ! (6.95)	‡ (†)

See notes at end of table.

Table 227.40. Percentage of elementary and secondary school students who do homework, average time spent, percentage whose parents check that homework is done, and percentage whose parents help with homework, by frequency and selected characteristics: 2007 and 2012—Continued

[Standard errors appear in parentheses]

Year and selected characteristic	Percent of students who do homework outside of school	Students who do homework outside of school: Average hours spent per week doing homework	Percentage distribution by how frequently they do homework: Less than once per week	1 to 2 days per week	3 to 4 days per week	5 or more days per week	Percent whose parents[1] check that homework is done[2]	Percentage distribution by how frequently their parents[1] help with homework: No help given	Less than once per week	1 to 2 days per week	3 to 4 days per week	5 or more days per week
1	2	3	4	5	6	7	8	9	10	11	12	13
School control												
Public	94.9 (0.63)	6.3 (0.11)	8.9 (0.52)	22.9 (1.00)	35.8 (0.95)	32.4 (1.04)	90.8 (0.56)	22.7 (0.77)	41.0 (1.07)	25.6 (0.91)	7.9 (0.67)	2.8 (0.31)
Private	97.5 (0.88)	9.4 (0.28)	1.9 ! (0.69)	8.7 (1.32)	25.4 (2.07)	64.0 (2.52)	85.8 (1.87)	22.4 (2.41)	47.4 (2.70)	21.5 (1.94)	6.5 (1.37)	2.2 ! (0.76)
Poverty status[3]												
Poor	90.8 (1.20)	5.5 (0.26)	14.3 (1.36)	24.1 (2.02)	33.8 (1.96)	27.8 (2.37)	90.1 (1.87)	28.2 (2.12)	28.8 (2.12)	27.7 (2.18)	11.3 (1.36)	4.1 (0.91)
Near-poor	94.9 (0.73)	5.8 (0.23)	9.6 (1.05)	26.9 (2.04)	36.6 (2.14)	26.8 (1.58)	90.7 (1.32)	25.8 (2.19)	35.4 (2.36)	27.5 (2.24)	7.1 (1.33)	4.2 (0.84)
Nonpoor	96.3 (0.83)	7.1 (0.12)	6.4 (0.55)	19.2 (0.88)	34.6 (1.12)	39.8 (1.15)	90.4 (0.56)	20.1 (0.82)	47.1 (1.27)	23.8 (0.97)	7.1 (0.86)	1.9 (0.26)
Coursework												
Enrolled in AP classes	98.7 (0.32)	8.3 (0.16)	4.6 (0.50)	13.6 (0.93)	34.3 (1.35)	47.5 (1.30)	88.1 (0.81)	26.5 (1.23)	45.2 (1.44)	21.6 (1.08)	4.6 (0.60)	2.2 (0.39)
Not enrolled in AP classes	92.9 (0.95)	5.4 (0.14)	11.0 (0.79)	27.6 (1.27)	35.5 (1.12)	25.9 (1.18)	92.2 (0.73)	19.9 (1.05)	39.0 (1.34)	28.0 (1.21)	9.9 (0.98)	3.2 (0.39)
Locale												
City	95.1 (0.66)	7.1 (0.21)	7.3 (0.78)	20.0 (1.54)	33.7 (1.85)	39.0 (1.61)	92.8 (0.78)	24.4 (1.49)	37.8 (1.96)	25.4 (1.51)	9.1 (1.23)	3.2 (0.57)
Suburb	96.4 (0.43)	7.0 (0.16)	5.8 (0.66)	19.9 (1.62)	34.9 (1.31)	39.4 (1.42)	89.7 (1.05)	23.4 (1.25)	41.4 (1.48)	24.0 (1.33)	8.1 (1.24)	3.0 (0.51)
Town	94.9 (1.13)	5.1 (0.21)	14.1 (2.02)	26.9 (2.75)	36.5 (2.99)	22.5 (2.89)	89.0 (2.16)	19.7 (2.21)	41.3 (3.45)	28.8 (2.72)	7.3 (1.56)	2.9 ! (0.98)
Rural	93.1 (2.06)	5.8 (0.20)	11.7 (1.13)	25.1 (1.89)	35.9 (1.92)	27.3 (1.55)	89.3 (1.09)	20.5 (1.41)	46.2 (2.07)	25.9 (1.77)	5.7 (0.70)	1.8 (0.49)

†Not applicable.
#Rounds to zero.
!Interpret data with caution. The coefficient of variation (CV) for this estimate is between 30 and 50 percent.
‡Reporting standards not met. Either there are too few cases for a reliable estimate or the coefficient of variation (CV) is 50 percent or greater.
[1]Refers to one or more parent or other household adult.
[2]The wording of the questionnaire item changed from 2007 to 2012. In 2007, parents responded "yes" or "no" to an item asking whether they check that homework is done. In 2012, parents responded to a multiple-choice question asking how often they check that homework is done, and the 2012 estimates include all parents who "rarely," "sometimes," or "always" check. Therefore, the 2007 and 2012 estimates are not comparable.
[3]Poor children are those whose family incomes were below the Census Bureau's poverty threshold in the year prior to data collection; near-poor children are those whose family incomes ranged from the poverty threshold to 199 percent of the poverty threshold; and nonpoor children are those whose family incomes were at or above 200 percent of the poverty threshold. The poverty threshold is a dollar amount that varies depending on a family's size and composition and is updated annually to account for inflation. In 2011, for example, the poverty threshold for a family of four with two children was $22,811. Survey respondents are asked to select the range within which their income falls, rather than giving the exact amount of their income; therefore, the measure of poverty status is an approximation.
NOTE: While National Household Education Surveys Program (NHES) administrations prior to 2012 were administered via telephone with an interviewer, NHES:2012 used self-administered paper-and-pencil questionnaires that were mailed to respondents. Measurable differences in estimates between 2012 and prior years could reflect actual changes in the population, or the changes could be due to the mode change from telephone to mail. Includes children enrolled in kindergarten through grade 12 and ungraded students. Excludes homeschooled students. Data based on responses of the parent most knowledgeable about the student's education. Race categories exclude persons of Hispanic ethnicity. Detail may not sum to totals because of rounding.
SOURCE: U.S. Department of Education, National Center for Education Statistics, Parent and Family Involvement in Education Survey of the National Household Education Surveys Program (PFI-NHES:2007 and 2012). (This table was prepared May 2015.)

Table 227.50. Average National Assessment of Educational Progress (NAEP) reading and mathematics scale scores of 4th-, 8th-, and 12th-graders and percentage absent from school, by selected characteristics and number of days absent in the last month: 2013 and 2015

[Standard errors appear in parentheses]

Grade level and days absent from school in the last month	All students	Sex		Race/ethnicity							Eligibility for free or reduced-price lunch (public schools only)			Control of school		
		Male	Female	White	Black	Hispanic	Asian	Pacific Islander	American Indian/ Alaska Native	Two or more races	Eligible	Not eligible	Unknown	Public	Catholic	Other private
1	2	3	4	5	6	7	8	9	10	11	12	13	14	15	16	17
	Average mathematics scale score[1]															
4th-graders (2015)																
0 days	245 (0.3)	246 (0.4)	244 (0.3)	252 (0.3)	229 (0.6)	235 (0.5)	264 (1.2)	240 (3.1)	232 (1.5)	249 (1.1)	233 (0.3)	257 (0.4)	250 (3.0)	245 (0.3)	250 (1.3)	‡ (†)
1–2 days	240 (0.4)	240 (0.5)	239 (0.4)	248 (0.4)	223 (0.7)	230 (0.7)	255 (1.4)	231 (3.5)	228 (1.7)	244 (1.3)	230 (0.4)	252 (0.4)	245 (2.6)	239 (0.4)	246 (1.6)	‡ (†)
3–4 days	233 (0.4)	234 (0.6)	232 (0.6)	241 (0.6)	220 (0.8)	225 (1.0)	250 (2.8)	223 (4.3)	226 (1.9)	240 (2.0)	225 (0.5)	247 (0.7)	238 (2.7)	233 (0.5)	240 (2.6)	‡ (†)
5–10 days	231 (0.6)	231 (0.8)	231 (0.8)	242 (0.7)	215 (1.1)	221 (1.6)	240 (5.4)	218 (5.3)	220 (4.6)	232 (4.4)	220 (0.9)	247 (1.1)	239 (4.4)	230 (0.6)	‡ (†)	‡ (†)
More than 10 days	216 (1.0)	215 (1.5)	216 (1.1)	227 (1.3)	204 (1.7)	208 (2.0)	232 (4.8)	‡ (†)	203 (4.1)	219 (3.4)	209 (1.0)	231 (1.8)	‡ (†)	215 (1.0)	‡ (†)	‡ (†)
8th-graders (2015)																
0 days	288 (0.4)	288 (0.4)	288 (0.5)	297 (0.4)	266 (0.7)	275 (0.7)	311 (1.8)	282 (4.7)	272 (2.4)	292 (1.4)	274 (0.5)	300 (0.5)	299 (3.4)	288 (0.4)	296 (2.1)	‡ (†)
1–2 days	283 (0.4)	282 (0.5)	283 (0.5)	292 (0.4)	261 (0.8)	271 (0.8)	306 (1.9)	278 (6.0)	270 (2.8)	282 (1.6)	268 (0.4)	296 (0.4)	297 (3.5)	282 (0.4)	295 (1.9)	‡ (†)
3–4 days	272 (0.5)	271 (0.7)	272 (0.6)	282 (0.6)	252 (1.1)	261 (0.8)	295 (3.8)	270 (8.2)	262 (2.6)	281 (2.4)	260 (0.6)	287 (0.7)	281 (4.6)	271 (0.4)	281 (3.2)	‡ (†)
5–10 days	266 (0.8)	266 (1.0)	265 (1.1)	277 (1.0)	249 (1.5)	255 (1.7)	281 (5.9)	270 (7.4)	264 (5.6)	269 (6.0)	256 (0.9)	282 (1.1)	273 (6.0)	265 (0.8)	‡ (†)	‡ (†)
More than 10 days	251 (1.5)	250 (2.2)	252 (2.2)	264 (2.0)	235 (2.6)	240 (2.4)	‡ (†)	‡ (†)	236 (7.0)	261 (8.4)	241 (1.5)	269 (2.5)	‡ (†)	250 (1.5)	‡ (†)	‡ (†)
12th-graders (2013)																
0 days	157 (0.6)	159 (0.7)	156 (0.8)	165 (0.7)	135 (1.2)	146 (0.9)	176 (1.8)	‡ (†)	156 (5.5)	159 (3.3)	143 (0.9)	165 (0.7)	142 (6.1)	— (†)	— (†)	— (†)
1–2 days	155 (0.7)	157 (0.8)	154 (0.8)	163 (0.7)	134 (1.3)	141 (1.1)	174 (2.0)	‡ (†)	146 (6.6)	157 (2.5)	140 (0.9)	163 (0.7)	140 (6.2)	— (†)	— (†)	— (†)
3–4 days	147 (0.9)	149 (1.1)	146 (1.1)	157 (1.0)	126 (1.5)	133 (1.3)	167 (3.3)	‡ (†)	131 (6.7)	150 (4.1)	134 (1.1)	156 (1.1)	‡ (†)	— (†)	— (†)	— (†)
5–10 days	144 (1.4)	145 (2.0)	143 (2.0)	150 (1.7)	125 (2.4)	133 (2.5)	172 (6.3)	‡ (†)	‡ (†)	‡ (†)	131 (1.8)	152 (1.9)	‡ (†)	— (†)	— (†)	— (†)
More than 10 days	135 (2.2)	133 (2.9)	137 (2.9)	139 (3.2)	113 (3.5)	126 (3.8)	‡ (†)	‡ (†)	‡ (†)	‡ (†)	124 (3.3)	142 (2.5)	‡ (†)	— (†)	— (†)	— (†)
	Average reading scale score[2]															
4th-graders (2015)																
0 days	227 (0.4)	224 (0.5)	231 (0.4)	236 (0.4)	212 (0.5)	213 (0.8)	244 (1.5)	216 (4.1)	212 (2.1)	233 (1.6)	213 (0.4)	240 (0.4)	232 (3.3)	226 (0.4)	240 (1.3)	‡ (†)
1–2 days	222 (0.5)	219 (0.7)	225 (0.6)	232 (0.5)	206 (0.8)	208 (1.1)	238 (2.7)	217 (8.5)	209 (2.7)	225 (2.0)	210 (0.6)	236 (0.6)	228 (4.3)	221 (0.5)	237 (1.8)	‡ (†)
3–4 days	215 (0.6)	211 (0.8)	219 (0.9)	226 (0.7)	200 (1.2)	202 (1.5)	230 (3.7)	218 (5.6)	200 (2.7)	222 (1.9)	204 (0.8)	232 (0.8)	225 (5.0)	214 (0.6)	232 (3.0)	‡ (†)
5–10 days	214 (0.7)	209 (1.4)	218 (1.0)	225 (0.9)	195 (2.1)	203 (1.8)	237 (4.4)	203 (6.2)	200 (5.5)	221 (3.8)	202 (1.1)	231 (1.2)	‡ (†)	213 (0.8)	‡ (†)	‡ (†)
More than 10 days	192 (1.4)	189 (2.2)	197 (1.7)	206 (1.6)	184 (2.7)	181 (2.6)	204 (7.7)	‡ (†)	182 (6.0)	199 (4.3)	186 (1.4)	208 (2.1)	‡ (†)	192 (1.3)	‡ (†)	‡ (†)
8th-graders (2015)																
0 days	270 (0.3)	266 (0.4)	275 (0.4)	278 (0.4)	253 (0.6)	258 (0.6)	284 (1.4)	265 (3.1)	260 (2.2)	273 (1.4)	257 (0.5)	279 (0.4)	277 (3.0)	269 (0.3)	287 (1.2)	‡ (†)
1–2 days	266 (0.3)	261 (0.4)	271 (0.4)	275 (0.3)	248 (0.6)	254 (0.6)	280 (1.8)	249 (4.7)	256 (2.5)	271 (1.7)	254 (0.4)	277 (0.4)	276 (3.3)	265 (0.3)	283 (1.7)	‡ (†)
3–4 days	257 (0.5)	252 (0.8)	262 (0.7)	267 (0.6)	241 (1.0)	247 (1.1)	269 (3.0)	251 (4.6)	249 (2.8)	261 (3.1)	247 (0.6)	269 (0.8)	268 (4.6)	256 (0.5)	275 (3.1)	‡ (†)
5–10 days	251 (1.0)	244 (1.2)	257 (1.3)	262 (1.1)	236 (1.8)	240 (1.8)	271 (5.8)	236 (7.3)	239 (8.0)	257 (4.1)	241 (1.1)	266 (1.6)	250 (8.3)	250 (1.0)	‡ (†)	‡ (†)
More than 10 days	236 (1.5)	232 (2.0)	240 (2.1)	246 (2.2)	224 (2.7)	227 (2.6)	256 (7.8)	‡ (†)	223 (10.6)	‡ (†)	229 (1.7)	248 (2.7)	‡ (†)	235 (1.5)	‡ (†)	‡ (†)
12th-graders (2013)																
0 days	292 (0.7)	287 (0.8)	297 (0.8)	301 (0.8)	271 (1.4)	280 (1.1)	298 (2.4)	‡ (†)	266 (6.5)	300 (4.8)	276 (1.1)	299 (0.8)	281 (3.1)	— (†)	— (†)	— (†)
1–2 days	290 (0.6)	286 (0.8)	295 (0.7)	299 (0.8)	269 (1.2)	276 (1.1)	300 (2.3)	‡ (†)	288 (4.4)	289 (4.4)	275 (0.7)	298 (0.7)	284 (6.0)	— (†)	— (†)	— (†)
3–4 days	286 (0.8)	281 (1.1)	290 (1.1)	295 (1.0)	264 (1.7)	273 (1.7)	291 (4.8)	‡ (†)	270 (9.3)	285 (4.3)	272 (1.2)	294 (1.0)	‡ (†)	— (†)	— (†)	— (†)
5–10 days	278 (1.4)	271 (1.6)	283 (2.1)	285 (1.8)	265 (4.2)	266 (2.7)	‡ (†)	‡ (†)	‡ (†)	‡ (†)	270 (2.3)	283 (1.9)	‡ (†)	— (†)	— (†)	— (†)
More than 10 days	259 (3.0)	251 (3.6)	269 (3.9)	266 (4.6)	239 (4.4)	247 (4.3)	‡ (†)	‡ (†)	‡ (†)	‡ (†)	252 (3.3)	260 (4.0)	‡ (†)	— (†)	— (†)	— (†)

See notes at end of table.

Table 227.50. Average National Assessment of Educational Progress (NAEP) reading and mathematics scale scores of 4th-, 8th-, and 12th-graders and percentage absent from school, by selected characteristics and number of days absent in the last month: 2013 and 2015—Continued

[Standard errors appear in parentheses]

Grade level and days absent from school in the last month	All students	Sex		Race/ethnicity							Eligibility for free or reduced-price lunch (public schools only)			Control of school		
		Male	Female	White	Black	Hispanic	Asian	Pacific Islander	American Indian/ Alaska Native	Two or more races	Eligible	Not eligible	Unknown	Public	Catholic	Other private
1	2	3	4	5	6	7	8	9	10	11	12	13	14	15	16	17
	Percent of students absent[3]															
4th-graders (2015)																
0 days	52 (0.2)	54 (0.3)	50 (0.4)	52 (0.3)	49 (0.6)	51 (0.6)	67 (1.3)	45 (4.4)	44 (1.9)	49 (1.4)	48 (0.3)	56 (0.4)	59 (3.2)	52 (0.3)	55 (1.6)	‡ (†)
1–2 days	29 (0.2)	28 (0.2)	31 (0.3)	30 (0.3)	28 (0.5)	29 (0.5)	22 (1.0)	28 (3.0)	31 (1.8)	31 (1.4)	30 (0.3)	29 (0.3)	24 (2.2)	29 (0.2)	28 (1.3)	‡ (†)
3–4 days	11 (0.1)	11 (0.2)	12 (0.2)	11 (0.2)	13 (0.3)	12 (0.3)	7 (0.5)	17 (3.0)	15 (0.9)	12 (0.9)	13 (0.2)	9 (0.2)	12 (1.5)	11 (0.1)	11 (0.9)	‡ (†)
5–10 days	5 (0.1)	5 (0.1)	5 (0.2)	5 (0.1)	6 (0.3)	5 (0.2)	3 (0.3)	6 (1.8)	7 (0.8)	5 (0.5)	5 (0.1)	4 (0.2)	4 (1.1)	5 (0.1)	4 (0.6)	‡ (†)
More than 10 days	3 (0.1)	3 (0.1)	2 (0.1)	2 (0.1)	4 (0.3)	3 (0.2)	2 (0.2)	3 (0.7)	4 (0.6)	3 (0.4)	4 (0.1)	2 (0.1)	1 (0.4)	3 (0.1)	1 (0.4)	‡ (†)
8th-graders (2015)																
0 days	45 (0.3)	47 (0.4)	43 (0.4)	44 (0.3)	45 (0.6)	44 (0.7)	65 (1.3)	47 (4.0)	32 (1.7)	45 (1.5)	41 (0.4)	49 (0.4)	45 (1.5)	45 (0.3)	51 (1.6)	‡ (†)
1–2 days	36 (0.2)	35 (0.3)	38 (0.3)	38 (0.3)	33 (0.4)	37 (0.5)	26 (1.1)	28 (2.7)	40 (1.7)	35 (1.2)	36 (0.3)	37 (0.3)	35 (1.4)	36 (0.2)	36 (1.4)	‡ (†)
3–4 days	12 (0.2)	12 (0.2)	13 (0.3)	12 (0.2)	14 (0.4)	13 (0.4)	6 (0.6)	14 (2.4)	20 (1.2)	14 (0.9)	15 (0.2)	10 (0.2)	14 (1.1)	13 (0.1)	10 (0.9)	‡ (†)
5–10 days	4 (0.1)	4 (0.1)	5 (0.1)	4 (0.1)	6 (0.3)	5 (0.2)	2 (0.3)	7 (1.5)	6 (0.9)	5 (0.5)	6 (0.1)	3 (0.1)	5 (0.9)	5 (0.1)	2 (0.5)	‡ (†)
More than 10 days	1 (0.1)	2 (0.1)	1 (0.1)	1 (0.1)	2 (0.2)	2 (0.1)	1 (0.1)	5 (1.8)	3 (0.6)	1 (0.3)	2 (0.1)	1 (0.1)	1 (0.3)	2 (0.1)	1 (0.2)	‡ (†)
12th-graders (2013)																
0 days	36 (0.4)	40 (0.6)	32 (0.6)	35 (0.6)	41 (1.1)	35 (0.8)	50 (1.7)	44 (6.8)	24 (4.5)	34 (3.3)	34 (0.7)	37 (0.6)	41 (4.3)	— (†)	— (†)	— (†)
1–2 days	40 (0.4)	38 (0.6)	42 (0.5)	42 (0.5)	36 (0.9)	40 (0.7)	34 (1.5)	36 (6.7)	42 (4.2)	40 (3.0)	39 (0.6)	40 (0.5)	31 (4.1)	— (†)	— (†)	— (†)
3–4 days	16 (0.3)	14 (0.3)	17 (0.4)	16 (0.4)	16 (0.7)	16 (0.6)	11 (1.3)	15 (4.8)	21 (4.0)	17 (2.6)	17 (0.4)	16 (0.4)	20 (3.5)	— (†)	— (†)	— (†)
5–10 days	6 (0.2)	5 (0.2)	6 (0.3)	6 (0.2)	6 (0.6)	6 (0.5)	4 (0.7)	5 (2.8)	11 (3.5)	6 (1.4)	7 (0.4)	5 (0.3)	6 (2.3)	— (†)	— (†)	— (†)
More than 10 days	2 (0.1)	2 (0.2)	2 (0.2)	2 (0.2)	2 (0.2)	2 (0.3)	1 (0.3)	# (†)	2 (0.9)	3 (1.6)	2 (0.2)	2 (0.1)	1 (0.4)	— (†)	— (†)	— (†)

—Not available.
†Not applicable.
#Rounds to zero.
‡Reporting standards not met (too few cases for a reliable estimate).
[1]For grades 4 and 8, mathematics scale ranges from 0 to 500. For grade 12, mathematics scale ranges from 0 to 300.
[2]Reading scale ranges from 0 to 500.
[3]Absenteeism percentages based on the 2015 Reading Assessment for 4th- and 8th-graders and the 2013 Reading Assessment for 12th-graders, who were not assessed in 2015.

NOTE: Includes public and private schools except where otherwise noted. Includes students tested with accommodations (9 to 13 percent of all students, depending on assessment, grade level, and year); excludes only those students with disabilities and English language learners who were unable to be tested even with accommodations (2 percent of all students). Race categories exclude persons of Hispanic ethnicity. Some data have been revised from previously published figures. Detail may not sum to totals because of rounding.
SOURCE: U.S. Department of Education, National Center for Education Statistics, National Assessment of Educational Progress (NAEP), 2013 and 2015 Mathematics and Reading Assessments, retrieved November 4, 2015, from the Main NAEP Data Explorer (http://nces.ed.gov/nationsreportcard/naepdata/). (This table was prepared November 2015.)

Table 208.10. Public elementary and secondary pupil/teacher ratios, by selected school characteristics: Selected years, fall 1990 through fall 2013

Selected school characteristic	1990	1994	1995	1996	1997	1998	1999	2000	2001	2002	2003	2004	2005	2006	2007	2008	2009	2010[1]	2011	2012	2013
1	2	3	4	5	6	7	8	9	10	11	12	13	14	15	16	17	18	19	20	21	22
All schools	**17.4**	**17.7**	**17.8**	**17.6**	**17.2**	**16.9**	**16.6**	**16.4**	**16.3**	**16.2**	**16.4**	**16.2**	**16.0**	**15.8**	**15.7**	**15.7**	**16.0**	**16.4**	**16.3**	**16.2**	**16.3**
Enrollment size of school																					
Under 300	14.0	14.1	14.1	14.0	13.7	13.6	13.3	13.1	12.9	12.8	13.0	12.8	12.7	12.7	12.7	12.5	12.6	12.9	12.8	12.7	12.7
300 to 499	17.0	17.2	17.1	16.9	16.5	16.2	15.8	15.5	15.4	15.3	15.5	15.2	15.0	14.9	15.0	14.8	15.2	15.4	15.4	15.3	15.4
500 to 999	18.0	18.1	18.2	17.9	17.5	17.1	16.8	16.7	16.5	16.5	16.6	16.4	16.2	15.9	15.9	15.9	16.3	16.7	16.7	16.6	16.7
1,000 to 1,499	17.9	18.6	18.7	18.5	18.1	17.7	17.6	17.4	17.4	17.4	17.6	17.3	16.9	16.7	16.5	16.5	16.8	17.3	17.1	17.0	17.1
1,500 or more	19.2	19.9	20.0	20.0	19.7	19.3	19.3	19.1	19.0	18.9	19.2	19.1	18.8	18.6	18.1	18.3	18.7	19.5	19.0	18.8	19.1
Type																					
Regular schools	17.6	17.8	17.9	17.7	17.3	17.0	16.7	16.5	16.4	16.3	16.5	16.3	16.1	15.9	15.8	15.8	16.1	16.5	16.4	16.4	16.5
Alternative	14.2	18.0	16.6	16.6	16.5	16.4	15.8	15.2	14.9	14.9	15.0	14.4	14.0	14.7	13.5	14.2	14.3	14.8	14.7	14.7	14.3
Special education	6.5	6.9	7.2	7.4	7.6	7.3	7.2	7.0	6.4	7.0	7.3	7.4	6.2	6.6	7.1	6.8	7.1	6.9	7.1	6.9	6.6
Vocational	13.0	12.9	12.7	12.9	12.9	13.1	13.0	12.7	12.7	9.9	10.3	11.5	12.0	13.3	11.3	10.7	10.2	11.7	11.8	11.6	11.7
Percent of students eligible for free or reduced-price lunch																					
25 percent or less	—	—	—	—	—	—	—	—	—	—	—	16.8	16.4	16.4	16.3	16.1	16.5	16.9	17.5	16.4	16.4
26 percent to 50 percent	—	—	—	—	—	—	—	—	—	—	—	16.2	16.1	15.8	15.7	15.7	16.1	16.5	16.2	16.3	16.3
51 percent to 75 percent	—	—	—	—	—	—	—	—	—	—	—	15.9	15.6	15.3	15.2	15.4	15.8	16.2	15.8	16.1	16.2
More than 75 percent	—	—	—	—	—	—	—	—	—	—	—	15.9	15.5	15.4	15.0	15.1	15.6	16.0	15.5	16.2	16.4
Level and size																					
Elementary schools	18.1	18.0	18.1	17.8	17.4	17.0	16.7	16.5	16.3	16.2	16.3	16.0	15.8	15.6	15.6	15.5	15.9	16.3	16.3	16.3	16.3
Regular	18.2	18.0	18.1	17.9	17.4	17.0	16.7	16.5	16.3	16.2	16.3	16.0	15.8	15.6	15.6	15.5	15.9	16.3	16.3	16.3	16.4
Under 300	16.0	15.7	15.7	15.6	15.3	15.1	14.6	14.4	14.1	13.9	14.0	13.7	13.6	13.5	13.7	13.5	13.7	14.0	14.0	13.9	14.0
300 to 499	17.6	17.5	17.5	17.2	16.8	16.4	16.1	15.8	15.6	15.5	15.6	15.3	15.2	15.1	15.2	15.0	15.4	15.6	15.7	15.6	15.6
500 to 999	18.8	18.5	18.6	18.3	17.8	17.4	17.1	16.9	16.8	16.7	16.8	16.5	16.3	16.0	16.0	16.0	16.5	16.9	16.9	16.9	17.0
1,000 to 1,499	19.5	19.6	19.7	19.4	18.8	18.4	18.3	18.1	18.0	18.0	18.1	17.7	17.2	17.0	16.7	16.8	17.2	17.8	17.7	17.7	17.7
1,500 or more	19.9	20.4	20.9	21.2	20.7	19.9	20.0	20.5	20.2	20.3	20.8	20.5	19.6	19.4	18.0	18.1	18.5	19.3	19.0	18.7	19.0
Secondary schools	16.6	17.5	17.6	17.5	17.3	17.0	16.8	16.6	16.6	16.7	16.9	16.8	16.6	16.4	16.3	16.2	16.4	16.8	16.5	16.5	16.6
Regular	16.7	17.6	17.7	17.6	17.4	17.1	16.9	16.7	16.7	16.8	17.0	16.9	16.8	16.6	16.4	16.3	16.6	16.9	16.7	16.6	16.7
Under 300	12.3	12.7	12.8	12.7	12.5	12.5	12.0	12.0	11.9	12.0	12.3	12.0	12.2	12.0	12.1	11.9	11.9	12.2	12.0	12.0	12.0
300 to 499	14.9	15.7	15.7	15.5	15.3	15.1	14.6	14.5	14.4	14.4	14.7	14.7	14.6	14.4	14.4	14.3	14.3	14.6	14.6	14.5	14.4
500 to 999	16.1	16.8	16.9	16.7	16.4	16.2	16.0	15.8	15.7	15.8	16.0	15.9	15.8	15.6	15.4	15.4	15.6	15.8	15.7	15.6	15.7
1,000 to 1,499	17.2	17.9	18.0	17.9	17.5	17.2	17.1	16.8	16.8	16.9	17.2	17.0	16.8	16.5	16.5	16.3	16.6	16.9	16.6	16.5	16.6
1,500 or more	19.3	19.9	20.0	20.0	19.7	19.3	19.2	18.9	18.8	18.8	19.0	19.0	18.8	18.5	18.2	18.2	18.6	19.3	18.8	18.7	18.9
Combined schools	14.5	15.1	15.0	14.7	14.4	13.4	13.4	13.7	13.4	13.5	13.8	13.9	14.1	14.7	13.4	13.9	14.0	15.4	14.4	14.3	14.6
Under 300	8.9	9.3	9.0	8.7	8.6	8.9	9.1	9.2	9.1	9.1	9.5	9.2	9.5	10.1	9.2	8.9	9.1	9.2	9.4	9.1	9.1
300 to 499	14.2	14.4	14.7	14.3	14.0	13.6	13.8	13.5	13.1	13.1	14.4	13.4	13.9	14.3	13.7	13.9	13.8	13.6	13.3	13.2	13.5
500 to 999	16.3	16.6	16.6	16.6	16.2	15.5	14.9	15.8	15.6	16.0	15.4	15.8	15.9	16.0	15.2	15.6	15.8	16.9	15.6	15.5	15.5
1,000 to 1,499	17.8	18.3	18.2	18.4	18.0	16.9	16.9	17.5	18.1	17.7	17.5	17.4	16.4	17.3	15.9	16.7	17.9	19.2	18.1	17.8	17.9
1,500 or more	17.7	19.5	19.6	19.3	19.3	18.7	19.2	18.6	18.9	19.1	19.2	18.7	20.0	20.3	18.0	21.7	21.7	25.7	23.4	23.0	24.6
Ungraded	6.4	6.7	6.9	5.9	6.2	5.9	5.3	7.0	6.3	6.8	9.6	8.0	7.7	7.2	7.3	5.5	8.5	5.3	6.0	5.6	2.9
Level, type, and percent of students eligible for free or reduced-price lunch																					
Elementary, regular																					
25 percent or less	—	—	—	—	—	—	—	—	—	—	—	16.6	16.4	16.2	16.2	16.0	16.4	16.8	17.4	16.4	16.4
26 to 50 percent	—	—	—	—	—	—	—	—	—	—	—	16.0	15.8	15.5	15.6	15.6	16.0	16.4	16.3	16.3	16.3
51 to 75 percent	—	—	—	—	—	—	—	—	—	—	—	15.7	15.5	15.1	15.2	15.2	15.7	16.0	15.9	16.1	16.1
More than 75 percent	—	—	—	—	—	—	—	—	—	—	—	16.0	15.6	15.4	15.1	15.2	15.8	16.1	15.7	16.4	16.6
Secondary, regular																					
25 percent or less	—	—	—	—	—	—	—	—	—	—	—	17.5	17.0	16.9	16.8	16.6	16.8	17.2	17.8	16.6	16.7
26 to 50 percent	—	—	—	—	—	—	—	—	—	—	—	16.9	16.8	16.4	16.4	16.2	16.5	16.8	16.4	16.6	16.5
51 to 75 percent	—	—	—	—	—	—	—	—	—	—	—	16.9	16.7	16.3	16.1	16.4	16.5	17.1	16.1	16.7	16.8
More than 75 percent	—	—	—	—	—	—	—	—	—	—	—	16.2	16.7	16.2	15.7	15.9	16.0	16.5	15.5	16.5	16.9

—Not available.
[1]Includes imputations for California and Wyoming.
NOTE: Pupil/teacher ratios are based on data reported by types of schools rather than by instructional programs within schools. Only includes schools that reported both enrollment and teacher data. Ratios are based on data reported by schools and may differ from data reported in other tables that reflect aggregate totals reported by states.

SOURCE: U.S. Department of Education, National Center for Education Statistics, Common Core of Data (CCD), "Public Elementary/Secondary School Universe Survey," 1990–91 through 2013–14. (This table was prepared October 2015.)

Table 208.20. Public and private elementary and secondary teachers, enrollment, pupil/teacher ratios, and new teacher hires: Selected years, fall 1955 through fall 2025

Year	Teachers (in thousands)			Enrollment (in thousands)			Pupil/teacher ratio			Number of new teacher hires (in thousands)[1]		
	Total	Public	Private	Total	Public	Private	Total	Public	Private	Total	Public	Private
1	2	3	4	5	6	7	8	9	10	11	12	13
1955	1,286	1,141	145 [2]	35,280	30,680	4,600 [2]	27.4	26.9	31.7 [2]	—	—	—
1960	1,600	1,408	192 [2]	42,181	36,281	5,900 [2]	26.4	25.8	30.7 [2]	—	—	—
1965	1,933	1,710	223	48,473	42,173	6,300	25.1	24.7	28.3	—	—	—
1970	2,292	2,059	233	51,257	45,894	5,363	22.4	22.3	23.0	—	—	—
1975	2,453	2,198	255 [2]	49,819	44,819	5,000 [2]	20.3	20.4	19.6 [2]	—	—	—
1976	2,457	2,189	268	49,478	44,311	5,167	20.1	20.2	19.3	—	—	—
1977	2,488	2,209	279	48,717	43,577	5,140	19.6	19.7	18.4	—	—	—
1978	2,479	2,207	272	47,637	42,551	5,086	19.2	19.3	18.7	—	—	—
1979	2,461	2,185	276 [2]	46,651	41,651	5,000 [2]	19.0	19.1	18.1 [2]	—	—	—
1980	2,485	2,184	301	46,208	40,877	5,331	18.6	18.7	17.7			
1981	2,440	2,127	313 [2]	45,544	40,044	5,500 [2]	18.7	18.8	17.6 [2]	—	—	—
1982	2,458	2,133	325 [2]	45,166	39,566	5,600 [2]	18.4	18.6	17.2 [2]	—	—	—
1983	2,476	2,139	337	44,967	39,252	5,715	18.2	18.4	17.0	—	—	—
1984	2,508	2,168	340 [2]	44,908	39,208	5,700 [2]	17.9	18.1	16.8 [2]	—	—	—
1985	2,549	2,206	343	44,979	39,422	5,557	17.6	17.9	16.2	—	—	—
1986	2,592	2,244	348 [2]	45,205	39,753	5,452 [2]	17.4	17.7	15.7 [2]	—	—	—
1987	2,631	2,279	352	45,488	40,008	5,479	17.3	17.6	15.6	—	—	—
1988	2,668	2,323	345 [2]	45,430	40,189	5,242 [2]	17.0	17.3	15.2 [2]	—	—	—
1989	2,713	2,357	356	46,141	40,543	5,599	17.0	17.2	15.7	—	—	—
1990	2,759	2,398	361 [2]	46,864	41,217	5,648 [2]	17.0	17.2	15.6 [2]	—	—	—
1991	2,797	2,432	365	47,728	42,047	5,681	17.1	17.3	15.6	—	—	—
1992	2,823	2,459	364 [2]	48,694	42,823	5,870 [2]	17.2	17.4	16.1 [2]	—	—	—
1993	2,868	2,504	364	49,532	43,465	6,067	17.3	17.4	16.7	—	—	—
1994	2,922	2,552	370 [2]	50,106	44,111	5,994 [2]	17.1	17.3	16.2 [2]	—	—	—
1995	2,974	2,598	376	50,759	44,840	5,918	17.1	17.3	15.7	—	—	—
1996	3,051	2,667	384 [2]	51,544	45,611	5,933 [2]	16.9	17.1	15.5 [2]	—	—	—
1997	3,138	2,746	391	52,071	46,127	5,944	16.6	16.8	15.2	—	—	—
1998	3,230	2,830	400 [2]	52,526	46,539	5,988 [2]	16.3	16.4	15.0 [2]	—	—	—
1999	3,319	2,911	408	52,875	46,857	6,018	15.9	16.1	14.7	305	222	83
2000	3,366	2,941	424 [2]	53,373	47,204	6,169 [2]	15.9	16.0	14.5 [2]	—	—	—
2001	3,440	3,000	441	53,992	47,672	6,320	15.7	15.9	14.3	—	—	—
2002	3,476	3,034	442 [2]	54,403	48,183	6,220 [2]	15.7	15.9	14.1 [2]	—	—	—
2003	3,490	3,049	441	54,639	48,540	6,099	15.7	15.9	13.8	311	236	74
2004	3,536	3,091	445 [2]	54,882	48,795	6,087 [2]	15.5	15.8	13.7 [2]	—	—	—
2005	3,593	3,143	450	55,187	49,113	6,073	15.4	15.6	13.5	—	—	—
2006	3,622	3,166	456 [2]	55,307	49,316	5,991 [2]	15.3	15.6	13.2 [2]	—	—	—
2007	3,656	3,200	456	55,201	49,291	5,910	15.1	15.4	13.0	241	173	68
2008	3,670	3,222	448 [2]	54,973	49,266	5,707 [2]	15.0	15.3	12.8 [2]	—	—	—
2009	3,647	3,210	437	54,849	49,361	5,488	15.0	15.4	12.5	—	—	—
2010	3,529	3,099	429 [2]	54,867	49,484	5,382 [2]	15.5	16.0	12.5 [2]	—	—	—
2011	3,524	3,103	421	54,790	49,522	5,268	15.5	16.0	12.5	241	173	68
2012	3,540	3,109	431 [2]	55,104	49,771	5,333 [2]	15.6	16.0	12.4 [2]	338	247	91
2013	3,555	3,114	441	55,440	50,045	5,396	15.6	16.1	12.2	334	244	90
2014[3]	3,555	3,119	435	55,454	50,132	5,322	15.6	16.1	12.2	322	246	76
2015[3]	3,560	3,128	432	55,546	50,268	5,278	15.6	16.1	12.2	328	251	77
2016[3]	3,563	3,135	428	55,620	50,385	5,235	15.6	16.1	12.2	325	249	76
2017[3]	3,565	3,141	424	55,661	50,477	5,183	15.6	16.1	12.2	322	247	76
2018[3]	3,592	3,168	424	55,665	50,528	5,136	15.5	15.9	12.1	347	268	78
2019[3]	3,615	3,192	424	55,726	50,618	5,108	15.4	15.9	12.1	343	265	79
2020[3]	3,636	3,213	423	55,862	50,774	5,088	15.4	15.8	12.0	342	263	79
2021[3]	3,661	3,237	424	55,998	50,928	5,070	15.3	15.7	12.0	346	267	79
2022[3]	3,686	3,261	425	56,146	51,084	5,062	15.2	15.7	11.9	348	268	80
2023[3]	3,712	3,285	427	56,291	51,225	5,065	15.2	15.6	11.9	350	269	82
2024[3]	3,739	3,309	430	56,416	51,338	5,078	15.1	15.5	11.8	353	270	83
2025[3]	3,761	3,327	433	56,510	51,420	5,090	15.0	15.5	11.8	350	267	83

—Not available.

[1]A teacher is considered to be a new hire for a public or private school if the teacher had not taught in that control of school in the previous year. A teacher who moves from a public to private or a private to public school is considered a new teacher hire, but a teacher who moves from one public school to another public school or one private school to another private school is not considered a new teacher hire.

[2]Estimated.

[3]Projected.

NOTE: Data for teachers are expressed in full-time equivalents (FTE). Counts of private school teachers and enrollment include prekindergarten through grade 12 in schools offering kindergarten or higher grades. Counts of public school teachers and enrollment include prekindergarten through grade 12. The pupil/teacher ratio includes teachers for students with disabilities and other special teachers, while these teachers are generally excluded from class size calculations. Ratios for public schools reflect totals reported by states and differ from totals reported for schools or school districts. Some data have been revised from previously published figures. Detail may not sum to totals because of rounding.

SOURCE: U.S. Department of Education, National Center for Education Statistics, *Statistics of Public Elementary and Secondary Day Schools*, 1955–56 through 1980–81; Common Core of Data (CCD), "State Nonfiscal Survey of Public Elementary/Secondary Education," 1981–82 through 2013–14; Private School Universe Survey (PSS), 1989–90 through 2013–14; Schools and Staffing Survey (SASS), "Public School Teacher Data File" and "Private School Teacher Data File," 1999–2000 through 2011–12; Elementary and Secondary Teacher Projection Model, 1973 through 2025; and New Teacher Hires Projection Model, 1988 through 2025. (This table was prepared February 2016.)

Table 208.30. Public elementary and secondary teachers, by level and state or jurisdiction: Selected years, fall 2000 through fall 2013

State or jurisdiction	Fall 2000	Fall 2005	Fall 2009	Fall 2010	Fall 2011	Fall 2012				Fall 2013			
						Total	Elementary	Secondary	Ungraded	Total	Elementary	Secondary	Ungraded
1	2	3	4	5	6	7	8	9	10	11	12	13	14
United States	**2,941,461[1]**	**3,143,003[1]**	**3,209,672[1]**	**3,099,095[1]**	**3,103,263[1]**	**3,109,101[1]**	**1,719,764[1]**	**1,215,042[1]**	**174,295**	**3,113,764[1]**	**1,736,644[1]**	**1,207,774[1]**	**169,347**
Alabama	48,194[2]	57,757	47,492	49,363	47,723	51,877	30,428	21,450	0	47,162	33,029	14,133	0
Alaska	7,880	7,912	8,083	8,171	8,088	7,682	4,191	3,491	0	7,898	4,255	3,643	0
Arizona	44,438	51,376	51,947	50,031	50,800	48,866	34,248	14,619	0	48,359	33,890	14,468	0
Arkansas	31,947	32,997	37,240	34,273	33,983	34,131	17,619	13,929	2,583	34,933	18,198	14,216	2,518
California	298,021[2]	309,222[2]	316,299[2]	260,806[2]	268,689[2]	266,255[2]	172,533[2]	87,675	6,048	259,506[2]	175,937[2]	80,911	2,657
Colorado	41,983	45,841	49,060	48,543	48,078	48,922	28,033	20,889	0	50,157	28,807	21,350	0
Connecticut	41,044	39,687	43,593	42,951	43,805	43,931	29,256	13,365	1,311	43,443	28,951	13,268	1,225
Delaware	7,469	7,998	8,640	8,933	8,587	9,257	4,661	4,596	0	9,388	4,782	4,606	0
District of Columbia	4,949	5,481[3]	5,854	5,925	6,278	5,925	2,975	2,295	655	5,991	3,068	1,726	1,198
Florida	132,030	158,962	183,827	175,609	175,006	176,537	76,564	66,930	33,043	177,853	77,076	66,896	33,881
Georgia	91,043	108,535	115,918	112,460	111,133	109,365	50,808	42,795	15,763	109,441	50,826	42,831	15,785
Hawaii	10,927	11,226	11,472	11,396	11,458	11,608	6,378	5,149	81	11,781	6,467	5,240	74
Idaho	13,714	14,521	15,201	15,673	15,990	14,563	6,997	7,566	0	15,002	7,163	7,839	0
Illinois	127,620	133,857	138,483	132,983	131,777	135,701[4]	92,561[5]	42,044[3]	1,095	136,355[6]	91,826[5]	43,459	1,070[3]
Indiana	59,226	60,592	62,258	58,121[2]	62,339	59,863	31,187	28,676	0	59,823	31,188	28,635	0
Iowa	34,636	35,181	35,842	34,642	34,658	35,080	24,443	10,637	0	35,397	24,719	10,677	0
Kansas	32,742	33,608	34,700	34,644	37,407	41,243	20,833	19,608	802	38,153	19,360	18,298	496
Kentucky	39,589	42,413	41,981	42,042	41,860	42,769	21,874	10,120	10,776	41,820	24,751	9,959	7,110
Louisiana	49,915	44,660	49,646	48,655	48,657	46,493	31,715	14,778	0	46,437	31,650	14,787	0
Maine	16,559	16,684	16,331	15,384	14,888	15,222	10,561	4,661	0	15,452	10,699	4,744	9
Maryland	52,433	56,685	58,463	58,428	57,589	57,718	34,453	23,266	0	58,611	35,332	23,279	0
Massachusetts	67,432	73,596	69,909	68,754	69,342	70,636	46,678	23,958	0	70,490	46,284	24,206	0
Michigan	97,031	98,069	92,691	88,615	86,997	86,154	35,430	33,967	16,757	85,786	35,535	33,666	16,585
Minnesota	53,457	51,107	52,839	52,672	52,832	53,585	28,561	23,413	1,611	54,413	29,197	23,650	1,565
Mississippi	31,006	31,433	33,103	32,255	32,007	32,613	15,401	13,187	4,026	32,292	15,291	13,068	3,934
Missouri	64,735	67,076	67,796	66,735	66,252	66,248	34,219	32,029	0	66,651	34,510	32,141	0
Montana	10,411	10,369	10,521	10,361	10,153	10,200	7,079	3,121	0	10,310	7,143	3,150	18
Nebraska	20,983	21,359	22,256	22,345	22,182	22,103	13,805	8,298	0	22,401	14,095	8,306	0
Nevada	18,293	21,744	22,104	21,839	21,132	20,695	10,088	7,683	2,924	21,921	10,760	8,071	3,090
New Hampshire	14,341	15,536	15,491	15,365	15,049	14,925	9,983	4,941	0	14,826	10,052	4,774	0
New Jersey	99,061	112,673	115,248	110,202	109,719	110,929	58,569	37,481	14,879	114,581	60,466	38,638	15,477
New Mexico	21,042	22,021	22,724	22,437	21,957	22,201	9,806	8,339	4,056	22,239	9,825	8,332	4,082
New York	206,961	218,989	214,804	211,606	209,527	207,060	109,082	97,751	227	206,693	109,430	97,055	208
North Carolina	83,680	95,664	105,036[7]	98,357	97,308	98,590	68,745	28,772	1,073	99,327	68,076	30,249	1,002
North Dakota	8,141	8,003	8,366	8,417	8,525	8,677	5,595	3,082	0	8,805	5,754	3,051	0
Ohio	118,361	117,982	111,378	109,282	107,972	106,000	50,217	47,953	7,830	106,010	49,680	47,207	9,123
Oklahoma	41,318	41,833	42,615	41,278	41,349	41,775	22,948	18,827	0	41,983	23,239	18,743	0
Oregon	28,094	28,346	28,768	28,109	26,791	26,410	18,541	7,869	0	26,733	18,776	7,957	0
Pennsylvania	116,963	122,397	130,984	129,911	124,646	123,147	58,769	54,682	9,696	121,330	58,121	53,270	9,938
Rhode Island	10,645	14,180[2]	11,366	11,212	11,414	9,871	5,359	4,512	0	9,824	5,280	4,544	0
South Carolina	45,380	48,212	46,980	45,210	46,782	48,072	33,640	14,432	0	48,151	33,849	14,303	0
South Dakota	9,397	9,129	9,326	9,512	9,247	9,334	5,967	2,505	862	9,510	6,157	2,518	834
Tennessee	57,164	59,596	65,361	66,558	66,382	66,406	45,229	19,103	2,075	65,847	45,018	18,937	1,892
Texas	274,826	302,425	333,164	334,997	324,282	327,357	165,006	133,053	29,298	334,580	167,594	137,971	29,015
Utah	22,008	22,993	25,615	25,677	25,970	26,610	13,318	10,642	2,649	27,247	13,464	11,219	2,564
Vermont	8,414	8,851	8,734	8,382	8,364	8,403	3,377	3,186	1,840	8,375	3,369	3,152	1,854
Virginia	86,977[2]	103,944	70,827	70,947	90,832	89,389	41,852	47,536	0	90,098	42,088	48,009	0
Washington	51,098	53,508	53,448	53,934	53,119	53,699	28,139	23,575	1,985	54,867	29,057	24,060	1,750
West Virginia	20,930	19,940	20,299	20,338	20,247	20,101	9,433	10,668	0	19,978	9,392	10,586	0
Wisconsin	60,165	60,127	58,426	57,625	56,245	57,551	28,658	28,543	350	57,980	29,092	28,496	392
Wyoming	6,783	6,706	7,166	7,127	7,847	7,350	3,952	3,397	0	7,555	4,078	3,477	0
Bureau of Indian Education	—	—	—	—	—	5,308	4,282	1,027	0	—	—	—	—
DoD, overseas	5,105	5,726	—	—	—	—	—	—	—	—	—	—	—
DoD, domestic	2,399	2,033	—	—	—	—	—	—	—	—	—	—	—
Other jurisdictions													
American Samoa	820	989	—	—	—	—	—	—	—	—	—	—	—
Guam	1,975	1,804	—	1,843	2,291	2,291	925	991	375	2,291	925	991	375
Northern Marianas	526	614	552	607	496	409	249	156	4	417	243	170	4
Puerto Rico	37,620	42,036	39,102	36,506	33,079	30,986	14,293	11,765	4,928	33,412	15,209	12,642	5,560
U.S. Virgin Islands	1,511	1,434	1,425	1,457	1,217	1,129	489	351	289	1,082	470	276	336

—Not available.
[1]Includes imputed values for states.
[2]Includes imputations to correct for underreporting of prekindergarten teachers.
[3]Imputed.
[4]Includes imputations to correct for underreporting of prekindergarten, kindergarten, and secondary teachers.
[5]Includes imputations to correct for underreporting of prekindergarten and kindergarten teachers.
[6]Includes imputations to correct for underreporting of prekindergarten, kindergarten, and ungraded teachers.
[7]Includes imputations to correct for underreporting of kindergarten teachers.
NOTE: Distribution of elementary and secondary teachers determined by reporting units. DoD = Department of Defense.
SOURCE: U.S. Department of Education, National Center for Education Statistics, Common Core of Data (CCD), "State Nonfiscal Survey of Public Elementary/Secondary Education," 2000–01 through 2013–14. (This table was prepared August 2015.)

Table 208.40. Public elementary and secondary teachers, enrollment, and pupil/teacher ratios, by state or jurisdiction: Selected years, fall 2000 through fall 2013

State or jurisdiction	Pupil/teacher ratio				Fall 2011			Fall 2012			Fall 2013		
	Fall 2000	Fall 2008	Fall 2009	Fall 2010	Teachers	Enrollment	Pupil/ teacher ratio	Teachers	Enrollment	Pupil/ teacher ratio	Teachers	Enrollment	Pupil/ teacher ratio
1	2	3	4	5	6	7	8	9	10	11	12	13	14
United States	**16.0** [1]	**15.3** [1]	**15.4** [1]	**16.0** [1]	**3,103,263** [1]	**49,521,669**	**16.0** [1]	**3,109,101** [1]	**49,771,118**	**16.0** [1]	**3,113,764** [1]	**50,044,522**	**16.1** [1]
Alabama	15.4 [2]	15.6	15.8	15.3	47,723	744,621	15.6	51,877	744,637	14.4	47,162	746,204	15.8
Alaska	16.9	16.5	16.3	16.2	8,088	131,167	16.2	7,682	131,489	17.1	7,898	130,944	16.6
Arizona	19.8	19.9	20.7	21.4	50,800	1,080,319	21.3	48,866	1,089,384	22.3	48,359	1,102,445	22.8
Arkansas	14.1	12.9	12.9	14.1	33,983	483,114	14.2	34,131	486,157	14.2	34,933	489,979	14.0
California	20.6 [2]	20.8 [2]	19.8 [2]	24.1 [2]	268,689 [2]	6,287,834	23.4 [2]	266,255 [2]	6,299,451	23.7 [2]	259,506 [2]	6,312,623	24.3 [2]
Colorado	17.3	16.8	17.0	17.4	48,078	854,265	17.8	48,922	863,561	17.7	50,157	876,999	17.5
Connecticut	13.7	11.7	12.9	13.1	43,805	554,437	12.7	43,931	550,954	12.5	43,443	546,200	12.6
Delaware	15.4	15.1	14.7	14.5	8,587	128,946	15.0	9,257	129,026	13.9	9,388	131,687	14.0
District of Columbia	13.9	12.9	11.9	12.0	6,278	73,911	11.8	5,925	76,140	12.9	5,991	78,153	13.0
Florida	18.4	14.1	14.3	15.1	175,006	2,668,156	15.2	176,537	2,692,162	15.2	177,853	2,720,744	15.3
Georgia	15.9	13.9	14.4	14.9	111,133	1,685,016	15.2	109,365	1,703,332	15.6	109,441	1,723,909	15.8
Hawaii	16.9	15.9	15.7	15.8	11,458	182,706	15.9	11,608	184,760	15.9	11,781	186,825	15.9
Idaho	17.9	18.2	18.2	17.6	15,990	279,873	17.5	14,563	284,834	19.6	15,002	296,476	19.8
Illinois	16.1	15.6	15.2	15.7	131,777	2,083,097	15.8	135,701 [3]	2,072,880	15.3 [3]	136,355 [4]	2,066,990	15.2 [4]
Indiana	16.7	16.7	16.8	18.0 [2]	62,339	1,040,765	16.7 [2]	59,863	1,041,369	17.4	59,823	1,047,385	17.5
Iowa	14.3	13.6	13.7	14.3	34,658	495,870	14.3	35,080	499,825	14.2	35,397	502,964	14.2
Kansas	14.4	13.1	13.7	14.0	37,407	486,108	13.0	41,243	489,043	11.9	38,153	496,440	13.0
Kentucky	16.8	15.4	16.2	16.0	41,860	681,987	16.3	42,769	685,167	16.0	41,820	677,389	16.2
Louisiana	14.9	13.9	13.9	14.3	48,657	703,390	14.5	46,493	710,903	15.3	46,437	711,491	15.3
Maine	12.5	12.1	11.6	12.3	14,888	188,969	12.7	15,222	185,739	12.2	15,452	183,995	11.9
Maryland	16.3	14.3	14.5	14.6	57,589	854,086	14.8	57,718	859,638	14.9	58,611	866,169	14.8
Massachusetts	14.5	13.6	13.7	13.9	69,342	953,369	13.7	70,636	954,773	13.5	70,490	955,739	13.6
Michigan	17.7 [2]	17.5	17.8	17.9	86,997	1,573,537	18.1	86,154	1,555,370	18.1	85,786	1,548,841	18.1
Minnesota	16.0	15.7	15.8	15.9	52,832	839,738	15.9	53,585	845,404	15.8	54,413	850,973	15.6
Mississippi	16.1	14.7	14.9	15.2	32,007	490,619	15.3	32,613	493,650	15.1	32,292	492,586	15.3
Missouri	14.1	13.5	13.5	13.8	66,252	916,584	13.8	66,248	917,900	13.9	66,651	918,288	13.8
Montana	14.9	13.6	13.5	13.7	10,153	142,349	14.0	10,200	142,908	14.0	10,310	144,129	14.0
Nebraska	13.6	13.3	13.3	13.4	22,182	301,296	13.6	22,103	303,505	13.7	22,401	307,677	13.7
Nevada	18.6	19.7	19.4	20.0	21,132	439,634	20.8	20,695	445,707	21.5	21,921	451,831	20.6
New Hampshire	14.5	12.6	12.7	12.7	15,049	191,900	12.8	14,925	188,974	12.7	14,826	186,310	12.6
New Jersey	13.3	12.0	12.1	12.7	109,719	1,356,431	12.4	110,929	1,372,203	12.4	114,581	1,370,295	12.0
New Mexico	15.2	14.5	14.7	15.1	21,957	337,225	15.4	22,201	338,220	15.2	22,239	339,244	15.3
New York	13.9	12.6	12.9	12.9	209,527	2,704,718	12.9	207,060	2,710,703	13.1	206,693	2,732,770	13.2
North Carolina	15.5	13.6	14.1 [5]	15.2	97,308	1,507,864	15.5	98,590	1,518,465	15.4	99,327	1,530,857	15.4
North Dakota	13.4	11.6	11.4	11.4	8,525	97,646	11.5	8,677	101,111	11.7	8,805	103,947	11.8
Ohio	15.5	16.1	15.8	16.1	107,972	1,740,030	16.1	106,000	1,729,916	16.3	106,010	1,724,111	16.3
Oklahoma	15.1	13.9	15.4	16.0	41,349	666,120	16.1	41,775	673,483	16.1	41,983	681,848	16.2
Oregon	19.4	19.1	20.3	20.3	26,791	568,208	21.2	26,410	587,564	22.2	26,733	593,000	22.2
Pennsylvania	15.5	13.7	13.6	13.8	124,646	1,771,395	14.2	123,147	1,763,677	14.3	121,330	1,755,236	14.5
Rhode Island	14.8	12.8	12.8	12.8	11,414	142,854	12.5	9,871	142,481	14.4	9,824	142,008	14.5
South Carolina	14.9	14.4	15.4	16.1	46,782	727,186	15.5	48,072	735,998	15.3	48,151	745,657	15.5
South Dakota	13.7	13.7	13.3	13.3	9,247	128,016	13.8	9,334	130,471	14.0	9,510	130,890	13.8
Tennessee	15.9 [2]	15.0	14.9	14.8	66,382	999,693	15.1	66,406	993,496	15.0	65,847	993,556	15.1
Texas	14.8	14.5	14.6	14.7	324,282	5,000,470	15.4	327,357	5,077,659	15.5	334,580	5,153,702	15.4
Utah	21.9	23.7	22.3	22.8	25,970	598,832	23.1	26,610	613,279	23.0	27,247	625,461	23.0
Vermont	12.1	10.7	10.5	11.6	8,364	89,908	10.7	8,403	89,624	10.7	8,375	88,690	10.6
Virginia	13.2 [2]	17.3	17.6	17.6	90,832	1,257,883	13.8	89,389	1,265,419	14.2	90,098	1,273,825	14.1
Washington	19.7	19.1	19.4	19.4	53,119	1,045,453	19.7	53,699	1,051,694	19.6	54,867	1,058,936	19.3
West Virginia	13.7	14.0	13.9	13.9	20,247	282,870	14.0	20,101	283,044	14.1	19,978	280,958	14.1
Wisconsin	14.6	14.7	14.9	15.1	56,245	871,105	15.5	57,551	872,436	15.2	57,980	874,414	15.1
Wyoming	13.3	12.5	12.3	12.5	7,847	90,099	11.5	7,350	91,533	12.5	7,555	92,732	12.3
Bureau of Indian Education	—	—	—	—	—	—	—	5,308	—	—	—	—	—
DoD, overseas	14.4	12.5	—	—	—	—	—	—	—	—	—	—	—
DoD, domestic	14.2	13.1	—	—	—	—	—	—	—	—	—	—	—
Other jurisdictions													
American Samoa	19.1	—	—	—	—	—	—	—	—	—	—	—	—
Guam	16.4	—	—	17.2	2,291	31,243	13.6	2,291	31,186	13.6	2,291	33,414	14.6
Northern Marianas	19.0	21.2	19.9	18.3	496	11,011	22.2	409	10,646	26.0	417	10,638	25.5
Puerto Rico	16.3	12.8	12.6	13.0	33,079	452,740	13.7	30,986	434,609	14.0	33,412	423,934	12.7
U.S. Virgin Islands	12.9	11.8	10.9	10.6	1,217	15,711	12.9	1,129	15,192	13.5	1,082	14,953	13.8

—Not available.
[1]Includes imputed values for states.
[2]Includes imputations to correct for underreporting of prekindergarten teachers/enrollment.
[3]Includes imputations to correct for underreporting of prekindergarten, kindergarten, and secondary teachers.
[4]Includes imputations to correct for underreporting of prekindergarten, kindergarten, and unclassified teachers.
[5]Includes imputations to correct for underreporting of kindergarten teachers.

NOTE: Teachers reported in full-time equivalents (FTE). DoD = Department of Defense. The pupil/teacher ratio includes teachers for students with disabilities and other special teachers, while these teachers are generally excluded from class size calculations. Ratios reflect totals reported by states and differ from totals reported for schools or school districts.
SOURCE: U.S. Department of Education, National Center for Education Statistics, Common Core of Data (CCD), "State Nonfiscal Survey of Public Elementary/Secondary Education," 2000–01 through 2013–14. (This table was prepared August 2015.)

Table 211.50. Estimated average annual salary of teachers in public elementary and secondary schools: Selected years, 1959–60 through 2014–15

School year	Current dollars					Average public school teachers' salary in constant 2014–15 dollars[1]		
	Average public school teachers' salary			Wage and salary accruals per full-time-equivalent (FTE) employee[2]	Ratio of average teachers' salary to accruals per FTE employee			
	All teachers	Elementary teachers[3]	Secondary teachers[4]			All teachers	Elementary teachers[3]	Secondary teachers[4]
1	2	3	4	5	6	7	8	9
1959–60	$4,995	$4,815	$5,276	$4,749	1.05	$40,234	$38,784	$42,498
1961–62	5,515	5,340	5,775	5,063	1.09	43,425	42,047	45,472
1963–64	5,995	5,805	6,266	5,478	1.09	46,005	44,547	48,084
1965–66	6,485	6,279	6,761	5,934	1.09	48,102	46,574	50,150
1967–68	7,423	7,208	7,692	6,533	1.14	51,660	50,164	53,532
1969–70	8,626	8,412	8,891	7,486	1.15	54,046	52,705	55,706
1970–71	9,268	9,021	9,568	7,998	1.16	55,218	53,746	57,005
1971–72	9,705	9,424	10,031	8,521	1.14	55,819	54,203	57,694
1972–73	10,174	9,893	10,507	9,056	1.12	56,250	54,696	58,091
1973–74	10,770	10,507	11,077	9,667	1.11	54,670	53,335	56,229
1974–75	11,641	11,334	12,000	10,411	1.12	53,196	51,794	54,837
1975–76	12,600	12,280	12,937	11,194	1.13	53,773	52,407	55,211
1976–77	13,354	12,989	13,776	11,971	1.12	53,850	52,378	55,552
1977–78	14,198	13,845	14,602	12,811	1.11	53,651	52,317	55,178
1978–79	15,032	14,681	15,450	13,807	1.09	51,938	50,725	53,382
1979–80	15,970	15,569	16,459	15,050	1.06	48,687	47,465	50,178
1980–81	17,644	17,230	18,142	16,461	1.07	48,207	47,076	49,568
1981–82	19,274	18,853	19,805	17,795	1.08	48,473	47,414	49,809
1982–83	20,695	20,227	21,291	18,873	1.10	49,903	48,775	51,341
1983–84	21,935	21,487	22,554	19,781	1.11	51,006	49,964	52,445
1984–85	23,600	23,200	24,187	20,694	1.14	52,810	51,915	54,124
1985–86	25,199	24,718	25,846	21,685	1.16	54,808	53,762	56,215
1986–87	26,569	26,057	27,244	22,700	1.17	56,532	55,443	57,969
1987–88	28,034	27,519	28,798	23,777	1.18	57,276	56,224	58,837
1988–89	29,564	29,022	30,218	24,752	1.19	57,736	56,677	59,013
1989–90	31,367	30,832	32,049	25,762	1.22	58,467	57,470	59,738
1990–91	33,084	32,490	33,896	26,935	1.23	58,471	57,421	59,906
1991–92	34,063	33,479	34,827	28,169	1.21	58,332	57,332	59,640
1992–93	35,029	34,350	35,880	29,245	1.20	58,169	57,042	59,582
1993–94	35,737	35,233	36,566	30,030	1.19	57,846	57,030	59,188
1994–95	36,675	36,088	37,523	30,857	1.19	57,710	56,787	59,045
1995–96	37,642	37,138	38,397	31,822	1.18	57,663	56,891	58,820
1996–97	38,443	38,039	39,184	33,058	1.16	57,257	56,655	58,360
1997–98	39,350	39,002	39,944	34,635	1.14	57,581	57,072	58,450
1998–99	40,544	40,165	41,203	36,277	1.12	58,318	57,773	59,266
1999–2000	41,807	41,306	42,546	38,144	1.10	58,448	57,747	59,481
2000–01	43,378	42,910	44,053	39,727	1.09	58,635	58,003	59,548
2001–02	44,655	44,177	45,310	40,589	1.10	59,311	58,676	60,181
2002–03	45,686	45,408	46,106	41,629	1.10	59,376	59,014	59,922
2003–04	46,542	46,187	46,976	43,259	1.08	59,193	58,742	59,745
2004–05	47,516	47,122	47,688	44,908	1.06	58,667	58,180	58,879
2005–06	49,086	48,573	49,496	46,626	1.05	58,382	57,772	58,869
2006–07	51,052	50,740	51,529	48,713	1.05	59,189	58,828	59,743
2007–08	52,800	52,385	53,262	50,504	1.05	59,029	58,565	59,545
2008–09	54,319	53,998	54,552	51,409	1.06	59,891	59,537	60,148
2009–10	55,202	54,918	55,595	52,413	1.05	60,281	59,971	60,710
2010–11	55,623	55,217	56,225	53,975	1.03	59,545	59,110	60,190
2011–12	55,418	54,704	56,226	55,435	1.00	57,637	56,894	58,477
2012–13	56,103	55,344	57,077	56,361	1.00	57,394	56,618	58,391
2013–14	56,610	56,395	56,886	57,081	0.99	57,022	56,806	57,300
2014–15	57,379	57,225	57,609	—	—	57,379	57,225	57,609

—Not available.

[1]Constant dollars based on the Consumer Price Index, prepared by the Bureau of Labor Statistics, U.S. Department of Labor, adjusted to a school-year basis.

[2]The average monetary remuneration earned by FTE employees across all industries in a given year, including wages, salaries, commissions, tips, bonuses, voluntary employee contributions to certain deferred compensation plans, and receipts in kind that represent income. Calendar-year data from the U.S. Department of Commerce, Bureau of Economic Analysis, have been converted to a school-year basis by averaging the two appropriate calendar years in each case.

[3]Teachers at schools that are classified as elementary by state and local practice and composed of any span of grades not above grade 8. Preschool or kindergarten schools are included only if they are an integral part of an elementary school or a regularly established school system.

[4]Teachers at schools comprising any span of grades beginning with the next grade following an elementary or middle school (usually 7, 8, or 9) and ending with or below grade 12. Includes both junior high schools and senior high schools.

NOTE: Some data have been revised from previously published figures. Standard errors are not available for these estimates, which are based on state reports.

SOURCE: National Education Association, *Estimates of School Statistics*, 1959–60 through 2014–15; and unpublished tabulations. U.S. Department of Commerce, Bureau of Economic Analysis, National Income and Product Accounts, tables 6.6D, retrieved September 2, 2015, from http://www.bea.gov/iTable/iTable.cfm?ReqID=9&step=1#reqid=9&step=1&isuri=1. (This table was prepared September 2015.)

Table 211.60. Estimated average annual salary of teachers in public elementary and secondary schools, by state: Selected years, 1969–70 through 2014–15

	Current dollars							Constant 2014–15 dollars[1]							
State	1969–70	1979–80	1989–90	1999–2000	2009–10	2013–14	2014–15	1969–70	1979–80	1989–90	1999–2000	2009–10	2013–14	2014–15	Percent change, 1999–2000 to 2014–15
1	2	3	4	5	6	7	8	9	10	11	12	13	14	15	16
United States	**$8,626**	**$15,970**	**$31,367**	**$41,807**	**$55,202**	**$56,610**	**$57,379**	**$54,046**	**$48,687**	**$58,467**	**$58,448**	**$60,281**	**$57,022**	**$57,379**	**-1.8**
Alabama	6,818	13,060	24,828	36,689	47,571	48,720	49,497	42,718	39,815	46,278	51,293	51,948	49,075	49,497	-3.5
Alaska	10,560	27,210	43,153	46,462	59,672	65,891	66,755	66,163	82,954	80,436	64,956	65,162	66,371	66,755	2.8
Arizona	8,711	15,054	29,402	36,902	46,952	45,335	45,406	54,578	45,894	54,804	51,590	51,272	45,665	45,406	-12.0
Arkansas	6,307	12,299	22,352	33,386	46,700	47,319	48,017	39,516	37,495	41,663	46,675	50,997	47,664	48,017	2.9
California	10,315	18,020	37,998	47,680	68,203	71,396	72,535	64,628	54,937	70,827	66,659	74,478	71,916	72,535	8.8
Colorado	7,761	16,205	30,758	38,163	49,202	49,615	49,828	48,626	49,403	57,332	53,353	53,729	49,976	49,828	-6.6
Connecticut	9,262	16,229	40,461	51,780	64,350	70,583	71,709	58,030	49,476	75,418	72,391	70,271	71,097	71,709	-0.9
Delaware	9,015	16,148	33,377	44,435	57,080	59,305	59,195	56,483	49,230	62,213	62,122	62,332	59,737	59,195	-4.7
District of Columbia	10,285	22,190	38,402	47,076	64,548	73,162	75,490	64,440	67,649	71,580	65,814	70,487	73,695	75,490	14.7
Florida	8,412	14,149	28,803	36,722	46,708	47,780	48,992	52,705	43,135	53,688	51,339	51,006	48,128	48,992	-4.6
Georgia	7,276	13,853	28,006	41,023	53,112	52,924	53,382	45,587	42,233	52,202	57,352	57,999	53,309	53,382	-6.9
Hawaii	9,453	19,920	32,047	40,578	55,063	56,291	57,189	59,227	60,729	59,734	56,730	60,129	56,701	57,189	0.8
Idaho	6,890	13,611	23,861	35,547	46,283	44,465	45,218	43,169	41,495	44,476	49,696	50,541	44,789	45,218	-9.0
Illinois	9,569	17,601	32,794	46,486	62,077	60,124	61,083	59,954	53,659	61,127	64,989	67,789	60,562	61,083	-6.0
Indiana	8,833	15,599	30,902	41,850	49,986	50,289	50,502	55,343	47,556	57,600	58,508	54,585	50,655	50,502	-13.7
Iowa	8,355	15,203	26,747	35,678	49,626	52,032	52,862	52,348	46,349	49,855	49,879	54,192	52,411	52,862	6.0
Kansas	7,612	13,690	28,744	34,981	46,657	48,221	48,990	47,692	41,736	53,578	48,905	50,950	48,572	48,990	0.2
Kentucky	6,953	14,520	26,292	36,380	49,543	50,560	51,093	43,564	44,266	49,007	50,861	54,101	50,928	51,093	0.5
Louisiana	7,028	13,760	24,300	33,109	48,903	49,067	47,886	44,033	41,949	45,294	46,288	53,402	49,424	47,886	3.5
Maine	7,572	13,071	26,881	35,561	46,106	49,232	50,017	47,442	39,849	50,105	49,716	50,348	49,590	50,017	0.6
Maryland	9,383	17,558	36,319	44,048	63,971	64,546	64,845	58,789	53,528	67,697	61,581	69,857	65,016	64,845	5.3
Massachusetts	8,764	17,253	34,712	46,580	69,273	73,195	74,805	54,910	52,598	64,702	65,121	75,647	73,728	74,805	14.9
Michigan	9,826	19,663	37,072	49,044	57,958	62,166	62,778	61,564	59,946	69,101	68,565	63,291	62,619	62,778	-8.4
Minnesota	8,658	15,912	32,190	39,802	52,431	54,752	56,670	54,246	48,510	60,001	55,645	57,255	55,151	56,670	1.8
Mississippi	5,798	11,850	24,292	31,857	45,644	42,187	42,564	36,327	36,126	45,279	44,537	49,844	42,494	42,564	-4.4
Missouri	7,799	13,682	27,094	35,656	45,317	46,750	47,394	48,864	41,712	50,502	49,849	49,487	47,090	47,394	-4.9
Montana	7,606	14,537	25,081	32,121	45,759	49,893	50,999	47,655	44,318	46,750	44,906	49,969	50,256	50,999	13.6
Nebraska	7,375	13,516	25,522	33,237	46,227	49,539	50,318	46,208	41,206	47,572	46,467	50,480	49,900	50,318	8.3
Nevada	9,215	16,295	30,590	39,390	51,524	55,813	56,703	57,736	49,678	57,019	55,069	56,265	56,219	56,703	3.0
New Hampshire	7,771	13,017	28,986	37,734	51,443	57,057	58,554	48,689	39,684	54,029	52,754	56,176	57,472	58,554	11.0
New Jersey	9,130	17,161	35,676	52,015	65,130	68,238	69,038	57,203	52,318	66,499	72,719	71,123	68,735	69,038	-5.1
New Mexico	7,796	14,887	24,756	32,554	46,258	45,727	46,003	48,845	45,385	46,144	45,512	50,514	46,060	46,003	1.1
New York	10,336	19,812	38,925	51,020	71,633	76,409	77,628	64,759	60,400	72,555	71,328	78,224	76,965	77,628	8.8
North Carolina	7,494	14,117	27,883	39,404	46,850	44,990	47,783	46,953	43,038	51,973	55,088	51,161	45,318	47,783	-13.3
North Dakota	6,696	13,263	23,016	29,863	42,964	48,666	50,025	41,953	40,434	42,901	41,750	46,917	49,020	50,025	19.8
Ohio	8,300	15,269	31,218	41,436	55,958	55,913	56,172	52,003	46,550	58,189	57,929	61,107	56,320	56,172	-3.0
Oklahoma	6,882	13,107	23,070	31,298	47,691	44,549	44,628	43,119	39,959	43,002	43,756	52,079	44,873	44,628	2.0
Oregon	8,818	16,266	30,840	42,336	55,224	58,638	59,811	55,249	49,589	57,485	59,187	60,305	59,065	59,811	1.1
Pennsylvania	8,858	16,515	33,338	48,321	59,156	63,701	64,717	55,499	50,348	62,141	67,555	64,599	64,165	64,717	-4.2
Rhode Island	8,776	18,002	36,057	47,041	59,686	64,696	65,918	54,985	54,882	67,209	65,765	65,178	65,167	65,918	0.2
South Carolina	6,927	13,063	27,217	36,081	47,508	48,430	48,709	43,401	39,824	50,731	50,443	51,879	48,783	48,709	-3.4
South Dakota	6,403	12,348	21,300	29,071	38,837	40,023	40,661	40,118	37,645	39,702	40,642	42,410	40,314	40,661	#
Tennessee	7,050	13,972	27,052	36,328	46,290	47,742	48,503	44,171	42,596	50,424	50,788	50,549	48,090	48,503	-4.5
Texas	7,255	14,132	27,496	37,567	48,261	49,690	50,576	45,456	43,083	51,252	52,520	52,701	50,052	50,576	-3.7
Utah	7,644	14,909	23,686	34,946	45,885	45,695	45,848	47,893	45,452	44,150	48,856	50,107	46,028	45,848	-6.2
Vermont	7,968	12,484	29,012	37,758	49,084	55,958	57,642	49,923	38,059	54,077	52,787	53,600	56,365	57,642	9.2
Virginia	8,070	14,060	30,938	38,744	50,015	49,826	50,620	50,562	42,864	57,667	54,166	54,617	50,189	50,620	-6.5
Washington	9,225	18,820	30,457	41,043	53,003	52,969	53,714	57,799	57,376	56,771	57,380	57,880	53,355	53,714	-6.4
West Virginia	7,650	13,710	22,842	35,009	45,959	45,086	45,647	47,931	41,797	42,577	48,944	50,188	45,414	45,647	-6.7
Wisconsin	8,963	16,006	31,921	41,153	51,264	53,679	54,535	56,157	48,797	59,500	57,534	55,981	54,070	54,535	-5.2
Wyoming	8,232	16,012	28,141	34,127	55,861	56,583	57,715	51,577	48,815	52,454	47,711	61,001	56,995	57,715	21.0

#Rounds to zero.
[1]Constant dollars based on the Consumer Price Index (CPI), prepared by the Bureau of Labor Statistics, U.S. Department of Labor, adjusted to a school-year basis. The CPI does not account for differences in inflation rates from state to state.

NOTE: Some data have been revised from previously published figures. Standard errors are not available for these estimates, which are based on state reports.
SOURCE: National Education Association, *Estimates of School Statistics*, 1969–70 through 2014–15. (This table was prepared September 2015.)

Table 401.10. Federal support and estimated federal tax expenditures for education, by category: Selected fiscal years, 1965 through 2015

[In thousands of dollars]

Fiscal year	Total on-budget support, off-budget support, and nonfederal funds generated by federal legislation	On-budget support[1]					Off-budget support and nonfederal funds generated by federal legislation								Estimated federal tax expenditures for education[2]
		Total	Elementary and secondary	Post-secondary	Other education[3]	Research at educational institutions	Total	Off-budget support: Direct Loan Program[4]	Nonfederal funds: Federal Family Education Loan Program[5]	Perkins Loans[6]	Income Contingent Loans[7]	Leveraging Educational Assistance Partnerships[8]	Supplemental Educational Opportunity Grants[9]	Work-Study Aid[10]	
1	2	3	4	5	6	7	8	9	10	11	12	13	14	15	16
							Current dollars								
1965	$5,324,767	$5,331,016	$1,942,577	$1,197,511	$374,652	$1,816,276	-$6,249	†	†	$16,111	†	†	†	-$22,360	—
1970	13,365,315	12,526,499	5,830,442	3,447,697	964,719	2,283,641	838,816	†	$770,000	20,976	†	†	†	47,840	—
1975	24,451,787	23,288,120	10,617,195	7,644,037	1,608,478	3,418,410	1,163,667	†	1,233,000	35,667	†	$20,000	†	-125,000	$8,605,000
1980	39,310,241	34,493,502	16,027,686	11,115,882	1,548,730	5,801,204	4,816,739	†	4,598,000	31,778	†	76,800	†	110,161	13,320,000
1985	47,655,763	39,027,876	16,901,334	11,174,379	2,107,588	8,844,575	8,627,887	†	8,467,000	21,387	†	76,000	†	63,500	19,105,000
1986	48,260,015	39,962,901	17,049,940	11,283,589	2,620,021	9,009,351	8,297,114	†	8,142,000	20,203	†	72,700	†	62,211	20,425,000
1987	50,606,736	41,194,718	17,535,707	10,299,998	2,820,407	10,538,606	9,412,018	†	9,272,000	20,889	$556	76,000	†	42,573	20,830,000
1988	53,965,521	43,454,424	18,564,859	10,657,530	2,981,571	11,250,464	10,511,097	†	10,380,000	20,637	479	72,800	†	37,181	17,025,000
1989	59,418,905	48,269,575	19,809,528	13,269,888	3,180,334	12,009,825	11,149,330	†	10,938,000	20,390	549	71,900	$65,140	53,351	17,755,000
1990	62,778,792	51,624,342	21,984,361	13,650,915	3,383,031	12,606,035	11,154,450	†	10,826,000	15,014	500	59,181	127,719	126,036	19,040,000
1991	70,349,116	57,599,477	25,418,031	14,707,407	3,698,617	13,775,422	12,749,639	†	12,372,000	17,349	500	63,530	131,115	165,145	18,995,000
1992	74,481,656	60,483,092	27,926,887	14,387,387	3,991,955	14,176,863	13,998,564	†	13,568,000	17,333	542	72,000	175,656	165,033	19,950,000
1993	84,692,869	67,740,617	30,834,326	17,844,015	4,107,193	14,955,083	16,952,252	†	16,524,000	29,255	†	72,429	172,023	154,545	21,010,000
1994	92,718,577	68,254,205	32,304,356	16,177,051	4,483,704	15,289,094	24,464,372	$813,000	23,214,000	52,667	†	72,429	172,000	140,276	22,630,000
1995	95,763,287	71,639,520	33,623,809	17,618,137	4,719,655	15,677,919	24,123,767	5,161,000	18,519,000	52,667	†	63,400	181,000	146,700	24,600,000
1996	96,795,962	71,327,362	34,391,501	15,775,508	4,828,038	16,332,315	25,468,600	8,357,000	16,711,000	31,100	†	31,400	179,000	159,100	26,340,000
1997	103,140,145	73,731,845	35,478,905	15,959,425	5,021,163	17,272,352	29,408,300	9,838,000	19,163,000	52,700	†	50,000	228,200	76,400	28,125,000
1998	107,706,075	76,909,233	37,486,166	15,799,570	5,148,492	18,475,005	30,796,842	10,400,100	20,002,500	45,000	†	25,000	240,950	83,292	29,540,000
1999	113,285,097	82,863,597	39,937,911	17,651,199	5,318,020	19,956,467	30,421,500	9,953,000	20,107,000	33,300	†	25,000	255,900	47,300	37,360,000
2000	119,367,271	85,944,203	43,790,783	15,008,715	5,484,571	21,660,134	33,423,068	10,347,000	22,711,000	33,300	†	50,000	276,743	5,025	39,475,000
2001	130,618,224	94,846,476	48,530,061	14,938,278	5,880,007	25,498,130	35,771,748	10,635,000	24,694,000	25,000	†	80,000	316,655	21,093	41,460,000
2002	150,030,786	109,211,479	52,754,118	22,964,176	6,297,697	27,195,488	40,819,307	11,689,000	28,606,000	25,000	†	104,000	308,811	86,496	—
2003	170,677,327	124,374,489	59,274,219	29,499,694	6,532,502	29,068,074	46,302,838	11,969,000	33,791,000	33,000	†	103,000	304,671	102,167	—
2004	185,040,371	132,420,703	62,653,231	32,432,974	6,576,821	30,757,677	52,619,668	12,840,000	39,266,000	33,000	†	102,000	295,143	83,525	—
2005	204,558,951	147,878,146	68,957,711	38,587,287	6,913,451	33,419,698	56,680,805	12,930,000	43,284,000	0	†	101,000	305,644	60,161	—
2006[11]	226,951,151	166,495,661	70,948,229	57,757,738	7,074,484	30,715,210	60,455,490	12,677,000	47,307,000	0	†	100,000	309,608	61,882	—
2007	210,509,705	145,697,988	70,735,875	37,465,287	7,214,906	30,281,920	64,811,717	13,022,000	51,320,000	0	†	100,000	287,126	82,591	—
2008	220,360,440	144,338,889	71,272,580	36,386,271	7,882,220	28,797,817	76,021,551	18,213,000	57,296,000	0	†	98,000	281,812	132,739	—
2009[12]	368,486,844	271,297,568	172,660,784	53,085,401	8,853,694	36,697,689	97,189,276	29,738,000	66,778,000	0	†	98,000	309,058	266,218	—
2010	288,081,805	183,189,989	86,681,783	50,188,459	9,326,441	36,993,306	104,891,816	84,703,000	19,618,000	0	†	98,000	255,108	217,708	—
2011	293,297,670	183,942,414	76,406,315	64,422,753	11,096,234	32,017,112	109,355,256	108,926,300	0	0	†	0	231,480	197,476	—
2012	295,441,149	190,400,108	78,529,067	70,304,347	9,390,511	32,176,184	105,041,041	104,613,008	0	0	†	0	243,871	184,162	—
2013	284,367,652	182,297,588	78,965,899	63,353,225	9,638,631	30,339,833	102,070,064	101,731,079	0	0	†	0	192,116	146,869	—
2014	291,094,418	190,498,209	79,411,320	69,439,861	9,443,392	32,203,636	100,596,209	100,156,082	0	0	†	0	244,918 [13]	195,209 [13]	—
2015	297,974,582	196,456,123	77,565,989	76,955,169	9,467,086	32,467,878 [13]	101,518,459	101,088,453	0	0	†	0	243,383 [13]	186,622 [13]	—
							Constant fiscal year 2015 dollars[14]								
1965	$37,612,810	$37,656,951	$13,721,874	$8,458,915	$2,646,447	$12,829,715	-$44,141	†	†	$113,804	†	†	†	-$157,945	—
1970	77,207,744	72,362,135	33,680,858	19,916,396	5,572,916	13,191,965	4,845,609	†	$4,448,078	121,173	†	†	†	276,359	—
1975	99,494,104	94,759,153	43,201,272	31,103,519	6,544,883	13,909,480	4,734,951	†	5,017,066	145,129	†	$81,380	†	-508,624	$35,013,668
1980	109,090,145	95,723,177	44,478,552	30,847,768	4,297,892	16,098,965	13,366,969	†	12,759,944	88,187	†	213,128	†	305,709	36,964,432
1985	97,298,291	79,682,821	34,507,283	22,814,617	4,303,041	18,057,880	17,615,470	†	17,286,989	43,666	†	155,168	†	129,647	39,006,486
1986	96,484,849	79,896,669	34,087,451	22,558,952	5,238,132	18,012,134	16,588,179	†	16,278,065	40,391	†	145,347	†	124,377	40,835,110
1987	98,362,136	80,068,401	34,083,399	20,019,663	5,481,904	20,483,435	18,293,734	†	18,021,588	40,601	$1,081	147,718	†	82,747	40,486,375
1988	101,457,029	81,695,807	34,902,571	20,036,522	5,605,456	21,151,258	19,761,222	†	19,514,756	38,798	900	136,866	†	69,902	32,007,584
1989	107,579,697	87,393,504	35,865,741	24,025,528	5,758,089	21,744,146	20,186,194	†	19,803,575	36,917	994	130,177	$117,938	96,594	32,145,956

See notes at end of table.

Table 401.10. Federal support and estimated federal tax expenditures for education, by category: Selected fiscal years, 1965 through 2015—Continued

[In thousands of dollars]

Fiscal year	Total on-budget support, off-budget support, and nonfederal funds generated by federal legislation	On-budget support[1]					Off-budget support and nonfederal funds generated by federal legislation								Estimated federal tax expenditures for education[2]
		Total	Elementary and secondary	Post-secondary	Other education[3]	Research at educational institutions	Total	Off-budget support: Direct Loan Program[4]	Nonfederal funds: Federal Family Education Loan Program[5]	Perkins Loans[6]	Income Contingent Loans[7]	Leveraging Educational Assistance Partnerships[8]	Supplemental Educational Opportunity Grants[9]	Work-Study Aid[10]	
1	2	3	4	5	6	7	8	9	10	11	12	13	14	15	16
1990	110,401,306	90,785,353	38,661,180	24,006,178	5,949,319	22,168,676	19,615,953	†	19,038,349	26,403	879	104,074	224,604	221,644	33,483,296
1991	118,236,526	96,808,068	42,720,362	24,718,899	6,216,306	23,152,502	21,428,457	†	20,793,755	29,159	840	106,776	220,366	277,561	31,925,103
1992	120,653,244	97,976,893	45,238,918	23,306,207	6,466,590	22,965,178	22,676,351	†	21,978,878	28,078	878	116,633	284,546	267,338	32,317,115
1993	133,239,749	106,570,281	48,508,900	28,072,400	6,461,481	23,527,500	26,669,469	†	25,995,738	46,024	†	113,946	270,628	243,132	33,053,162
1994	143,256,731	105,457,553	49,912,505	24,994,683	6,927,638	23,622,727	37,799,178	$1,256,142	35,867,265	81,374	†	111,908	265,752	216,736	34,964,944
1995	143,769,435	107,552,420	50,479,429	26,450,111	7,085,619	23,537,262	36,217,014	7,748,210	27,802,577	79,069	†	95,182	271,735	220,241	36,931,983
1996	142,339,370	104,887,555	50,573,025	23,198,033	7,099,675	24,016,822	37,451,815	12,289,047	24,573,682	45,733	†	46,174	263,221	233,958	38,733,217
1997	148,639,962	106,258,321	51,130,266	22,999,854	7,236,227	24,891,973	42,381,641	14,177,990	27,616,672	75,948	†	72,057	328,869	110,104	40,532,219
1998	153,825,757	109,841,725	53,537,722	22,564,937	7,353,073	26,385,992	43,984,033	14,853,417	28,567,560	64,269	†	35,705	344,125	118,958	42,189,012
1999	159,775,972	116,869,846	56,327,961	24,895,044	7,500,473	28,146,367	42,906,127	14,037,594	28,358,677	46,966	†	35,260	360,918	66,711	52,692,106
2000	164,277,878	118,279,752	60,266,578	20,655,577	7,548,080	29,809,518	45,998,125	14,239,944	31,255,761	45,829	†	68,812	380,864	6,916	54,327,029
2001	175,083,323	127,134,145	65,050,680	20,023,572	7,881,681	34,178,212	47,949,178	14,255,370	33,100,340	33,511	†	107,234	424,451	28,273	55,573,827
2002	197,817,034	143,996,385	69,556,812	30,278,487	8,303,574	35,857,512	53,820,649	15,412,059	37,717,286	32,963	†	137,125	407,170	114,046	—
2003	218,858,010	159,484,295	76,006,801	37,827,194	8,376,569	37,273,731	59,373,715	15,347,742	43,329,897	42,316	†	132,076	390,677	131,008	—
2004	231,221,423	165,469,314	78,289,776	40,527,364	8,218,217	38,433,958	65,752,108	16,044,515	49,065,727	41,236	†	127,456	368,803	104,371	—
2005	247,056,225	178,599,941	83,283,726	46,603,824	8,349,725	40,362,665	68,456,284	15,616,217	52,276,283	0	†	121,983	369,142	72,659	—
2006[11]	264,969,575	194,386,697	82,833,341	67,433,204	8,259,588	35,860,563	70,582,878	14,800,627	55,231,778	0	†	116,752	361,473	72,248	—
2007	239,453,698	165,730,706	80,461,691	42,616,570	8,206,918	34,445,527	73,722,992	14,812,457	58,376,234	0	†	113,749	326,604	93,947	—
2008	242,195,574	158,641,179	78,334,857	39,991,724	8,663,256	31,651,343	83,554,395	20,017,695	62,973,361	0	†	107,711	309,736	145,892	—
2009[12]	404,230,067	297,613,432	189,408,880	58,234,685	9,712,502	40,257,365	106,616,636	32,622,586	73,255,466	0	†	107,506	339,037	292,041	—
2010	312,309,260	198,596,124	93,971,653	54,409,269	10,110,788	40,104,414	113,713,136	91,826,456	21,267,858	0	†	106,242	276,562	236,017	—
2011	311,831,308	195,565,835	81,234,471	68,493,662	11,797,411	34,040,291	116,265,474	115,809,412	0	0	†	0	246,107	209,955	—
2012	308,313,300	198,695,699	81,950,520	73,367,455	9,799,648	33,578,077	109,617,601	109,170,919	0	0	†	0	254,496	192,186	—
2013	292,664,710	187,616,525	81,269,904	65,201,696	9,919,859	31,225,065	105,048,185	104,699,309	0	0	†	0	197,721	151,154	—
2014	294,993,604	193,049,917	80,475,028	70,370,002	9,569,885	32,635,001	101,943,687	101,497,665	0	0	†	0	248,199 [13]	197,823 [13]	—
2015	297,974,582	196,456,123	77,565,989	76,955,169	9,467,086	32,467,878 [13]	101,518,459	101,088,453	0	0	†	0	243,383 [13]	186,622 [13]	—

—Not available.
†Not applicable.
[1]On-budget support includes federal funds for education programs tied to appropriations. Excludes federal support for medical education benefits under Medicare in the U.S. Department of Health and Human Services. Benefits excluded because data before fiscal year (FY) 1990 are not available. This program existed since Medicare began, but was not available as a separate budget item until FY 1990. Excluded amounts range from an estimated $4,440,000,000 in FY 1990 to an estimated $11,800,000,000 in FY 2015.
[2]Losses of tax revenue attributable to provisions of the federal income tax laws that allow a special exclusion, exemption, or deduction from gross income or provide a special credit, preferential rate of tax, or a deferral of tax liability affecting individual or corporate income tax liabilities.
[3]Other education includes libraries, museums, cultural activities, and miscellaneous research.
[4]The William D. Ford Federal Direct Loan Program (commonly referred to as the Direct Loan Program) provides students with the same benefits they were eligible to receive under the Federal Family Education Loan (FFEL) Program, but provides loans to students through federal capital rather than through private lenders.
[5]The Federal Family Education Loan (FFEL) Program, formerly known as the Guaranteed Student Loan Program, provided student loans guaranteed by the federal government and disbursed to borrowers. After June 30, 2010, no new FFEL loans have been originated; all new loans are originated through the Direct Loan Program.
[6]Student loans created from institutional matching funds (since 1993 one-third of federal capital contributions). Excludes repayments of outstanding loans.
[7]Student loans created from institutional matching funds (one-ninth of federal contributions). This was a demonstration project that involved only 10 institutions and had unsubsidized interest rates. Program repealed in fiscal year 1992.
[8]Formerly the State Student Incentive Grant Program. Starting in fiscal year 2000, amounts under $30.0 million have required dollar-for-dollar state matching contributions, while amounts over $30.0 million have required two-to-one state matching contributions.
[9]Institutions award grants to undergraduate students, and the federal share of such grants may not exceed 75 percent of the total grant.
[10]Employer contributions to student earnings are generally one-third of federal allocation.
[11]The increase in postsecondary expenditures in 2006 resulted primarily from an accounting adjustment.
[12]All education funds from the American Recovery and Reinvestment Act of 2009 (ARRA) are included in the FY 2009 row of this table. Most of these funds had a 2-year availability, meaning that they were available for the Department of Education to obligate during FY 2009 and FY 2010.
[13]Estimated.
[14]Data adjusted by the federal budget composite deflator, as reported in the U.S. Office of Management and Budget's *Budget of the U.S. Government, Historical Tables, Fiscal Year 2016.*
NOTE: To the extent possible, federal education funds data do not represent obligations, but instead represent appropriations or (especially for earlier years) outlays. Negative amounts occur when program receipts exceed outlays. Some data have been revised from previously published figures. Detail may not sum to totals because of rounding.
SOURCE: U.S. Department of Education, Budget Service, unpublished tabulations. U.S. Department of Education, National Center for Education Statistics, unpublished tabulations. U.S. Office of Management and Budget, *Budget of the U.S. Government, Appendix,* fiscal years 1967 through 2016. National Science Foundation, *Federal Funds for Research and Development,* fiscal years 1967 through 2015. (This table was prepared May 2016.)

Table 401.20. Federal on-budget funds for education, by agency: Selected fiscal years, 1970 through 2014

[In thousands of dollars]

Agency	1970	1980	1990[1]	2000[1]	2005[1]	2010[1]	2011[1]	2012[1]	2013[1]	2014[1]
1	2	3	4	5	6	7	8	9	10	11
	Current dollars									
Total	**$12,526,499**	**$34,493,502**	**$51,624,342**	**$85,944,203**	**$147,878,146**	**$183,189,989**	**$183,942,414**	**$190,400,108**	**$182,297,588**	**$190,498,209**
Department of Education[2]	4,625,224	13,137,785	23,198,575	34,106,697	72,893,301	91,893,199	93,777,295	99,129,939	91,129,538	95,665,940
Department of Agriculture	960,910	4,562,467	6,260,843	11,080,031	13,817,553	19,260,881	20,241,295	22,120,982	23,135,596	23,145,081
Department of Commerce	13,990	135,561	53,835	114,575	243,948	303,000	242,778	205,085	235,936	275,521
Department of Defense	821,388	1,560,301	3,605,509	4,525,080	7,986,654	7,686,288	7,617,359	7,400,880	7,036,469	7,297,021
Department of Energy	551,527	1,605,558	2,561,950	3,577,004	4,339,879	3,402,600	2,994,903	2,983,055	2,941,159	3,288,681
Department of Health and Human Services	1,796,854	5,613,930	7,956,011	17,670,867	26,112,807	31,961,852	28,359,740	28,578,464	27,074,506	28,904,559
Department of Homeland Security	†	†	†	†	624,860	540,229	2,006,390	333,630	358,580	372,386
Department of Housing and Urban Development	114,709	5,314	118	1,400	1,100	400	1,600	300	4,500	100
Department of the Interior	190,975	440,547	630,537	959,802	1,254,533	1,042,901	1,041,115	971,805	904,600	975,564
Department of Justice	15,728	60,721	99,775	278,927	608,148	205,692	203,988	217,850	229,791	237,025
Department of Labor	424,494	1,862,738	2,511,380	4,696,100	5,764,500	6,826,000	6,121,000	5,802,000	5,188,004	5,463,123
Department of State	59,742	25,188	51,225	388,349	533,309	778,180	741,670	725,222	797,102	819,041
Department of Transportation	27,534	54,712	76,186	117,054	126,900	160,243	160,741	173,888	178,502	168,000
Department of the Treasury	18	1,247,463	41,715	83,000	†	†	†	†	†	†
Department of Veterans Affairs	1,032,918	2,351,233	757,476	1,577,374	4,293,624	8,795,010	10,581,209	10,905,478	12,616,642	13,104,028
Other agencies and programs										
ACTION	†	2,833	8,472	†	†	†	†	†	†	†
Agency for International Development	88,034	176,770	249,786	332,500	602,100	557,900	621,900	629,900	603,900	594,039
Appalachian Regional Commission	37,838	19,032	93	7,243	8,542	5,070	11,902	11,124	13,070	13,073
Barry Goldwater Scholarship and Excellence in Education Foundation	†	†	1,033	3,000	3,000	4,000	3,000	4,000	4,000	3,000
Corporation for National and Community Service	†	†	†	386,000	472,000	965,000	983,000	750,252	711,009	756,849
Environmental Protection Agency	19,446	41,083	87,481	98,900	83,400	54,700	79,200	87,200	73,700	86,100
Estimated education share of federal aid to the District of Columbia	33,019	81,847	104,940	127,127	154,962	159,670	155,643	151,381	217,160	210,732
Federal Emergency Management Agency[3]	290	1,946	215	14,894	†	†	†	†	†	†
General Services Administration	14,775	34,800	†	†	†	†	†	†	†	†
Harry S Truman Scholarship fund	†	-1,895	2,883	3,000	3,000	2,000	1,000	1,200	1,500	1,000
Institute of American Indian and Alaska Native Culture and Arts Development	†	†	4,305	2,000	6,000	8,000	8,284	8,500	9,550	11,369
Institute of Museum and Library Services	†	†	†	166,000	250,000	265,000	274,000	242,605	231,954	225,813
James Madison Memorial Fellowship Foundation	†	†	191	7,000	2,000	2,000	2,000	2,000	2,000	2,000
Japanese-United States Friendship Commission	†	2,294	2,299	3,000	3,000	2,000	3,700	3,700	3,700	3,000
Library of Congress	29,478	151,871	189,827	299,000	430,000	516,000	521,000	521,000	470,202	485,757
National Aeronautics and Space Administration	258,366	255,511	1,093,303	2,077,830	2,763,120	1,585,500	1,430,761	2,289,837	2,200,143	2,287,755
National Archives and Records Administration	†	†	77,397	121,879	276,000	339,000	349,000	339,000	373,000	370,706
National Commission on Libraries and Information Science	†	2,090	3,281	2,000	1,000	†	†	†	†	†
National Endowment for the Arts	340	5,220	5,577	10,048	10,976	14,413	13,495	16,595	13,910	15,426
National Endowment for the Humanities	8,459	142,586	141,048	100,014	117,825	142,654	131,135	136,100	114,171	117,533
National Science Foundation	295,628	808,392	1,588,891	2,955,244	3,993,216	5,560,700	5,127,990	5,534,426	5,302,011	5,478,258
Nuclear Regulatory Commission	†	32,590	42,328	12,200	15,100	14,500	14,000	8,600	5,400	9,400
Office of Economic Opportunity	1,092,410	†	†	†	†	†	†	†	†	†
Smithsonian Institution	2,461	5,153	5,779	25,764	45,890	63,107	67,322	65,109	65,483	68,529
U.S. Arms Control and Disarmament Agency	100	661	25	†	†	†	†	†	†	†
United States Information Agency	8,423	66,210	201,547	†	†	†	†	†	†	†
United States Institute of Peace	†	†	7,621	13,000	28,000	58,000	47,000	44,000	47,000	37,000
Other agencies	1,421	990	885	300	7,900	14,300	6,000	5,000	3,800	4,800

See notes at end of table.

Table 401.20. Federal on-budget funds for education, by agency: Selected fiscal years, 1970 through 2014—Continued

[In thousands of dollars]

Agency	1970	1980	1990[1]	2000[1]	2005[1]	2010[1]	2011[1]	2012[1]	2013[1]	2014[1]
1	2	3	4	5	6	7	8	9	10	11
	Constant fiscal year 2015 dollars[4]									
Total	**$72,362,135**	**$95,723,177**	**$90,785,353**	**$118,279,752**	**$178,599,941**	**$198,596,124**	**$195,565,835**	**$198,695,699**	**$187,616,525**	**$193,049,917**
Department of Education[2]	26,718,645	36,458,766	40,796,468	46,938,962	88,036,938	99,621,345	99,703,133	103,448,957	93,788,445	96,947,378
Department of Agriculture	5,550,912	12,661,336	11,010,171	15,248,769	16,688,159	20,880,706	21,520,353	23,084,777	23,810,628	23,455,107
Department of Commerce	80,816	376,196	94,673	157,683	294,628	328,482	258,119	214,020	242,820	279,212
Department of Defense	4,744,932	4,330,003	6,340,563	6,227,591	9,645,887	8,332,699	8,098,704	7,723,331	7,241,774	7,394,764
Department of Energy	3,186,020	4,455,596	4,505,385	4,922,812	5,241,492	3,688,756	3,184,152	3,113,024	3,026,974	3,332,732
Department of Health and Human Services	10,379,931	15,579,259	13,991,253	24,319,334	31,537,762	34,649,819	30,151,807	29,823,606	27,864,465	29,291,733
Department of Homeland Security	†	†	†	†	754,675	585,662	2,133,175	348,166	369,043	377,374
Department of Housing and Urban Development	662,642	14,747	208	1,927	1,329	434	1,701	313	4,631	101
Department of the Interior	1,103,210	1,222,565	1,108,848	1,320,917	1,515,163	1,130,608	1,106,904	1,014,146	930,993	988,631
Department of Justice	90,856	168,507	175,462	383,870	734,491	222,991	216,878	227,342	236,495	240,200
Department of Labor	2,452,185	5,169,298	4,416,454	6,462,955	6,962,079	7,400,061	6,507,789	6,054,789	5,339,376	5,536,301
Department of State	345,113	69,899	90,083	534,461	644,104	843,624	788,537	756,819	820,359	830,012
Department of Transportation	159,056	151,832	133,979	161,094	153,264	173,719	170,898	181,464	183,710	170,250
Department of the Treasury	104	3,461,844	73,359	114,228	†	†	†	†	†	†
Department of Veterans Affairs	5,966,883	6,524,924	1,332,079	2,170,843	5,185,628	9,534,663	11,249,841	11,380,622	12,984,761	13,279,555
Other agencies and programs										
ACTION	†	7,862	14,899	†	†	†	†	†	†	†
Agency for International Development	508,548	490,556	439,268	457,599	727,187	604,819	661,198	657,344	621,520	601,996
Appalachian Regional Commission	218,580	52,816	164	9,968	10,317	5,496	12,654	11,609	13,451	13,248
Barry Goldwater Scholarship and Excellence in Education Foundation	†	†	1,817	4,129	3,623	4,336	3,190	4,174	4,117	3,040
Corporation for National and Community Service	†	†	†	531,228	570,058	1,046,156	1,045,116	782,940	731,754	766,987
Environmental Protection Agency	112,334	114,010	153,842	136,110	100,726	59,300	84,205	90,999	75,850	87,253
Estimated education share of federal aid to the District of Columbia	190,742	227,134	184,545	174,957	187,155	173,098	165,478	157,977	223,496	213,555
Federal Emergency Management Agency[3]	1,675	5,400	378	20,498	†	†	†	†	†	†
General Services Administration	85,351	96,574	†	†	†	†	†	†	†	†
Harry S Truman Scholarship fund	†	-5,259	5,070	4,129	3,623	2,168	1,063	1,252	1,544	1,013
Institute of American Indian and Alaska Native Culture and Arts Development	†	†	7,571	2,752	7,247	8,673	8,807	8,870	9,829	11,521
Institute of Museum and Library Services	†	†	†	228,456	301,938	287,286	291,314	253,175	238,722	228,837
James Madison Memorial Fellowship Foundation	†	†	336	9,634	2,416	2,168	2,126	2,087	2,058	2,027
Japanese-United States Friendship Commission	†	6,366	4,043	4,129	3,623	2,168	3,934	3,861	3,808	3,040
Library of Congress	170,286	421,458	333,825	411,495	519,333	559,395	553,922	543,700	483,921	492,264
National Aeronautics and Space Administration	1,492,509	709,070	1,922,657	2,859,590	3,337,160	1,718,839	1,521,171	2,389,604	2,264,337	2,318,399
National Archives and Records Administration	†	†	136,109	167,735	333,339	367,510	371,053	353,770	383,883	375,672
National Commission on Libraries and Information Science	†	5,800	5,770	2,752	1,208	†	†	†	†	†
National Endowment for the Arts	1,964	14,486	9,808	13,828	13,256	15,625	14,348	17,318	14,316	15,633
National Endowment for the Humanities	48,865	395,691	248,044	137,644	142,303	154,651	139,421	142,030	117,502	119,107
National Science Foundation	1,707,762	2,243,375	2,794,186	4,067,122	4,822,810	6,028,351	5,452,030	5,775,557	5,456,709	5,551,639
Nuclear Regulatory Commission	†	90,441	74,437	16,790	18,237	15,719	14,885	8,975	5,558	9,526
Office of Economic Opportunity	6,310,552	†	†	†	†	†	†	†	†	†
Smithsonian Institution	14,217	14,300	10,163	35,457	55,424	68,414	71,576	67,946	67,394	69,447
U.S. Arms Control and Disarmament Agency	578	1,834	44	†	†	†	†	†	†	†
United States Information Agency	48,657	183,740	354,436	†	†	†	†	†	†	†
United States Institute of Peace	†	†	13,402	17,891	33,817	62,878	49,970	45,917	48,371	37,496
Other agencies	8,209	2,747	1,556	413	9,541	15,503	6,379	5,218	3,911	4,864

†Not applicable.

[1]Excludes federal support for medical education benefits under Medicare in the U.S. Department of Health and Human Services. Benefits excluded from total because data before fiscal year (FY) 1990 are not available. This program existed since Medicare began, but was not available as a separate budget item until FY 1990. Excluded amounts are estimated as follows: $4,440,000,000 in FY 1990, $8,020,000,000 in FY 2000, $8,290,000,000 in FY 2005, $9,080,000,000 in FY 2010, $9,200,000,000 in FY 2011, $9,800,000,000 in FY 2012, $10,000,000,000 in FY 2013, and $11,330,000,000 in FY 2014.

[2]The U.S. Department of Education was created in May 1980. It formerly was the Office of Education in the U.S. Department of Health, Education, and Welfare. All education funds from the American Recovery and Reinvestment Act of 2009 (ARRA) are included in the Department of Education amount for FY 2009. Most of these funds had a 2-year availability, meaning that they were available for the Department of Education to obligate during FY 2009 and FY 2010.

[3]The Federal Emergency Management Agency (FEMA) was created in 1979, representing a combination of five existing agencies. The FY 1970 funds shown for FEMA were in other agencies. FEMA was transferred to the U.S. Department of Homeland Security in March of 2003.

[4]Data adjusted by the federal budget composite deflator, as reported in the U.S. Office of Management and Budget's *Budget of the U.S. Government, Historical Tables, Fiscal Year 2016.*

NOTE: To the extent possible, amounts reported do not represent obligations, but instead represent appropriations or (especially for earlier years) outlays. Negative amounts occur when program receipts exceed outlays. Some data have been revised from previously published figures. Detail may not sum to totals because of rounding.

SOURCE: U.S. Department of Education, National Center for Education Statistics, unpublished tabulations. U.S. Office of Management and Budget, *Budget of the U.S. Government, Appendix,* fiscal years 1972 through 2015. National Science Foundation, Federal Funds for Research and Development, fiscal years 1970 to 2014. (This table was prepared May 2016.)

Table 401.30. Federal on-budget funds for education, by level/educational purpose, agency, and program: Selected fiscal years, 1970 through 2015

[In thousands of current dollars]

Level/educational purpose, agency, and program	1970	1980	1990[1]	1995[1]	2000[1]	2005[1]	2010[1]	2011[1]	2012[1]	2013[1]	2014[1]	2015[1,2]
1	2	3	4	5	6	7	8	9	10	11	12	13
Total	**$12,526,499**	**$34,493,502**	**$51,624,342**	**$71,639,520**	**$85,944,203**	**$147,878,146**	**$183,189,989**	**$183,942,414**	**$190,400,108**	**$182,297,588**	**$190,498,209**	**$196,456,123**
Elementary/secondary education	**5,830,442**	**16,027,686**	**21,984,361**	**33,623,809**	**43,790,783**	**68,957,711**	**86,681,783**	**76,406,315**	**78,529,067**	**78,965,899**	**79,411,320**	**77,565,989**
Department of Education[3]	2,719,204	6,629,095	9,681,313	14,029,000	20,039,563	37,477,594	49,621,475	38,652,240	38,600,066	38,705,852	37,771,972	37,394,190
Education for the disadvantaged	1,339,014	3,204,664	4,494,111	6,808,000	8,529,111	14,635,566	15,864,666	15,515,444	15,741,703	15,590,733	15,552,693	15,536,107
Impact aid program[4]	656,372	690,170	816,366	808,000	877,101	1,262,174	1,276,183	1,273,631	1,291,186	1,299,088	1,288,603	1,288,603
School improvement programs[5]	288,304	788,918	1,189,158	1,397,000	2,549,971	7,918,091	16,999,862	6,738,485	6,327,886	6,543,628	5,883,351	5,478,097
Indian education	†	93,365	69,451	71,000	65,285	121,911	127,282	127,027	130,779	131,579	123,939	123,939
English Language Acquisition	21,250	169,540	188,919	225,000	362,662	667,485	750,000	733,530	732,144	736,624	723,400	737,400
Special education	79,090	821,777	1,616,623	3,177,000	4,948,977	10,940,312	12,587,035	12,526,672	12,640,709	12,661,256	12,497,300	12,522,358
Vocational and adult education	335,174	860,661	1,306,685	1,482,000	1,462,977	1,967,086	2,016,447	1,737,451	1,735,659	1,742,944	1,702,686	1,707,686
Education Reform—Goals 2000[6]	†	†	†	61,000	1,243,479	-35,031	†	†	†	†	†	†
Hurricane Education Recovery	†	†	†	†	†	†	†	†	†	†	†	†
Department of Agriculture	760,477	4,064,497	5,528,950	8,201,294	10,051,278	12,577,265	17,875,561	18,843,607	20,849,143	21,931,420	21,818,519	20,617,097
Child nutrition programs[7]	299,131	3,377,056	4,977,075	7,644,789	9,554,028	11,901,943	16,383,421	17,290,601	19,504,343	20,487,229	20,487,299	19,287,957
McGovern-Dole International Food for Education and Child Nutrition Program[8]	†	†	†	†	†	86,000	210,000	343,500	196,400	197,126	260,000	192,000
Agricultural Marketing Service—commodities[9]	341,597	388,000	350,441	400,000	400,000	399,322	1,100,000	1,006,000	952,000	1,053,000	888,000	1,029,000
Special Milk Program	83,800	159,293	18,707	(7)	(7)	(7)	(7)	(7)	(7)	(7)	(7)	(7)
Estimated education share of Forest Service permanent appropriations	35,949	140,148	182,727	156,505	97,250	190,000	182,140	203,506	196,400	194,065	183,220	108,140
Department of Commerce	†	54,816	†	†	†	†	†	†	†	†	†	†
Local public works program—school facilities[10]	†	54,816	†	†	†	†	†	†	†	†	†	†
Department of Defense	143,100	370,846	1,097,876	1,295,547	1,485,611	1,786,253	1,981,321	2,047,825	2,132,046	2,220,611	2,193,877	2,134,713
Junior Reserve Officers Training Corps (JROTC)	12,100	32,000	39,300	155,600	210,432	315,122	359,689	377,526	391,682	407,335	450,229	381,306
Overseas dependents schools	131,000	338,846	864,958	855,772	904,829	1,060,920	1,186,560	1,193,636	1,235,707	1,262,545	1,187,691	1,170,596
Domestic schools[4]	†	†	193,618	284,175	370,350	410,211	435,072	476,663	504,657	550,731	555,957	582,811
Department of Energy	200	77,633	15,563	12,646	†	†	†	†	†	†	†	†
Energy conservation for school buildings[11]	†	77,240	15,213	10,746	†	†	†	†	†	†	†	†
Pre-engineering program	200	393	350	1,900	†	†	†	†	†	†	†	†
Department of Health and Human Services	167,333	1,077,000	2,396,793	5,116,559	6,011,036	8,003,348	8,547,000	8,871,364	9,298,710	8,894,300	9,963,200	9,981,200
Head Start[12]	†	735,000	1,447,758	3,534,000	5,267,000	6,842,348	7,234,000	7,559,164	7,969,210	7,573,000	8,598,000	8,598,000
Payments to states for Aid to Families with Dependent Children (AFDC) work programs[13]	†	†	459,221	953,000	15,000	—	—	—	—	—	—	—
Social Security student benefits[14]	167,333	342,000	489,814	629,559	729,036	1,161,000	1,313,000	1,312,200	1,329,500	1,321,300	1,365,200	1,383,200
Department of Homeland Security	†	†	†	†	†	500	505	504	454	364	341	346
Tuition assistance for educational accreditation—Coast Guard personnel[15]	†	†	†	†	†	500	505	504	454	364	341	346
Department of the Interior	140,705	318,170	445,267	493,124	725,423	938,506	781,075	815,877	782,335	742,546	782,405	807,193
Mineral Leasing Act and other funds												
Payments to states—estimated education share	12,294	62,636	123,811	18,750	24,610	60,290	23,000	24,380	26,450	24,770	28,100	24,100
Payments to counties—estimated education share	16,359	48,953	102,522	37,490	53,500	79,686	50,000	53,000	58,000	53,970	61,300	52,500
Indian Education												
Bureau of Indian Education schools	95,850	178,112	192,841	411,524	466,905	517,647	580,492	583,572	631,477	597,412	622,382	641,353
Johnson-O'Malley assistance[16]	16,080	28,081	25,556	24,359	17,387	16,510	13,589	13,415	13,304	12,615	14,338	14,739
Education construction	†	†	†	†	161,021	263,373	112,994	140,509	52,104	52,779	55,285	74,501
Education expenses for children of employees, Yellowstone National Park	122	388	538	1,000	2,000	1,000	1,000	1,000	1,000	1,000	1,000	†
Department of Justice	8,237	23,890	65,997	128,850	224,800	554,500	137,529	140,525	149,587	160,684	151,630	—
Advanced occupational education	†	†	†	†	†	†	137,529	140,525	149,587	160,684	151,630	—
Vocational training expenses for prisoners in federal prisons	2,720	4,966	2,066	3,000	1,000	0	†	†	†	†	†	†
Inmate programs[17]	5,517	18,924	63,931	125,850	223,800	554,500	†	†	†	†	†	†

See notes at end of table.

Table 401.30. Federal on-budget funds for education, by level/educational purpose, agency, and program: Selected fiscal years, 1970 through 2015—Continued

[In thousands of current dollars]

Level/educational purpose, agency, and program	1970	1980	1990[1]	1995[1]	2000[1]	2005[1]	2010[1]	2011[1]	2012[1]	2013[1]	2014[1]	2015[1,2]
1	2	3	4	5	6	7	8	9	10	11	12	13
Department of Labor	420,927	1,849,800	2,505,487	3,957,800	4,683,200	5,654,000	6,826,000	6,121,000	5,802,000	5,188,004	5,463,123	5,314,155
Job Corps	†	469,800	739,376	1,029,000	1,256,000	1,521,000	1,850,000	1,660,000	1,789,000	1,650,004	1,691,123	1,688,155
Training programs—estimated funds for education programs[18]	420,927	1,380,000	1,766,111	2,928,800	3,427,200	4,133,000	4,976,000	4,461,000	4,013,000	3,538,000	3,772,000	3,626,000
Department of Transportation	45	60	46	62	188	†	†	†	†	†	†	†
Tuition assistance for educational accreditation—Coast Guard personnel[15]	45	60	46	62	188	†	†	†	†	†	†	†
Department of the Treasury	†	935,903	†	†	†	†	†	†	†	†	†	†
Estimated education share of general revenue sharing[19]												
State[20]	†	525,019	†	†	†	†	†	†	†	†	†	†
Local	†	410,884	†	†	†	†	†	†	†	†	†	†
Department of Veterans Affairs	338,910	545,786	155,351	311,768	445,052	1,815,000	760,476	759,457	790,688	930,750	1,079,667	1,201,493
Noncollegiate and job training programs[21]	281,640	439,993	12,848	†	†	†	†	†	†	†	†	†
Vocational rehabilitation for disabled veterans[22]	41,700	87,980	136,780	298,132	438,635	1,815,000	760,476	759,457	790,688	930,750	1,079,667	1,201,493
Veteran Dependents' education[23]	15,570	17,813	5,723	5,961	6,417	—	—	—	—	—	—	—
Service members occupational conversion training act of 1992	†	†	†	7,675	†	†	†	†	†	†	†	†
Other agencies												
Appalachian Regional Commission	33,161	9,157	93	2,173	2,588	2,962	986	2,290	962	1,689	3,163	1,574
National Endowment for the Arts[24]	†	4,989	4,641	7,117	6,002	8,470	11,530	12,125	10,450	10,427	10,924	9,777
Arts in education	†	4,989	4,641	7,117	6,002	8,470	11,530	12,125	10,450	10,427	10,924	9,777
National Endowment for the Humanities	20	330	404	997	812	603	125	75	100	333	181	243
Office of Economic Opportunity	1,072,375	†	†	†	†	†	†	†	†	†	†	†
Head Start[25]	325,700	†	†	†	†	†	†	†	†	†	†	†
Other elementary and secondary programs[26]	42,809	†	†	†	†	†	†	†	†	†	†	†
Job Corps[27]	144,000	†	†	†	†	†	†	†	†	†	†	†
Youth Corps and other training programs[27]	553,368	†	†	†	†	†	†	†	†	†	†	†
Volunteers in Service to America (VISTA)[28]	6,498	†	†	†	†	†	†	†	†	†	†	†
Other programs												
Estimated education share of federal aid to the District of Columbia	25,748	65,714	86,579	66,871	115,230	138,710	138,200	139,426	112,526	178,919	172,318	104,008
Postsecondary education	**$3,447,697**	**$11,115,882**	**$13,650,915**	**$17,618,137**	**$15,008,715**	**$38,587,287**	**$50,188,459**	**$64,422,753**	**$70,304,347**	**$63,353,225**	**$69,439,861**	**$76,955,169**
Department of Education[3]	1,187,962	5,682,242	11,175,978	14,234,000	10,727,315	31,420,023	36,539,655	49,260,330	54,470,178	46,130,198	51,896,533	57,908,189
Student financial assistance	†	3,682,789	5,920,328	7,047,000	9,060,317	15,209,515	25,959,478	43,753,247	43,324,872	37,319,312	30,589,493	30,278,081
Direct Loan Program[29]	†	†	†	840,000	-2,862,240	3,020,992	3,481,859	2,781,709	6,917,373	3,273,880	16,254,117	23,660,742
Federal Family Education Loan Program[30]	2,323	1,407,977	4,372,446	5,190,000	2,707,473	10,777,470	3,932,994	-91,796	1,498,353	2,787,755	2,269,320	1,362,692
Higher education	1,029,131	399,787	659,492	871,000	1,530,779	2,053,288	2,740,665	2,388,946	2,297,656	2,302,753	2,322,592	2,161,224
Facilities—loans and insurance	114,199	-19,031	19,219	-6,000	-2,174	-1,464	-8,360	-4,607	-8,513	-156	-109	-156
College housing loans[31]	†	14,082	-57,167	-46,000	-41,886	-33,521	-16,725	-13,265	-16,725	-1,176	-1,176	-1,176
Educational activities overseas	774	3,561	82	†	†	†	†	†	†	†	†	†
Historically Black Colleges and Universities Capital Financing, Program Account	†	†	†	†	150	169	23,330	23,289	32,160	20,227	55,184	37,670
Gallaudet College and Howard University	38,559	176,829	230,327	292,000	291,060	339,823	357,977	357,261	359,580	361,781	340,821	342,096
National Technical Institute for the Deaf	2,976	16,248	31,251	46,000	43,836	53,751	68,437	65,546	65,422	65,822	66,291	67,016
Department of Agriculture	†	10,453	31,273	33,373	30,676	61,957	80,697	81,658	81,658	75,387	82,986	82,986
Agriculture Extension Service, Second Morrill Act payments to agricultural and mechanical colleges and Tuskegee Institute	†	10,453	31,273	33,373	30,676	61,957	80,697	81,658	81,658	75,387	82,986	82,986
Department of Commerce	8,277	29,971	3,312	3,487	3,800	—	—	—	—	—	—	—
Sea Grant Program[32]	†	3,123	3,312	3,487	3,800	—	—	—	—	—	—	—
Merchant Marine Academy[33]	6,160	14,809	†	†	†	†	†	†	†	†	†	†
State marine schools[33]	2,117	12,039	†	†	†	†	†	†	†	†	†	†

See notes at end of table.

Table 401.30. Federal on-budget funds for education, by level/educational purpose, agency, and program: Selected fiscal years, 1970 through 2015—Continued

[In thousands of current dollars]

Level/educational purpose, agency, and program	1970	1980	1990[1]	1995[1]	2000[1]	2005[1]	2010[1]	2011[1]	2012[1]	2013[1]	2014[1]	2015[1,2]
1	2	3	4	5	6	7	8	9	10	11	12	13
Department of Defense	322,100	545,000	635,769	729,500	1,147,759	1,858,301	2,550,667	2,297,234	2,407,629	2,420,958	2,314,444	2,204,083
Tuition assistance for military personnel	57,500	—	95,300	127,000	263,303	608,109	669,892	567,412	590,626	564,604	580,848	520,817
Service academies	78,700	106,100	120,613	163,300	212,678	300,760	402,640	348,836	375,250	372,726	225,163	227,413
Senior Reserve Officers Training Corps (SROTC)	108,100	—	193,056	219,400	363,461	537,525	885,500	851,910	844,498	843,018	856,900	840,384
Professional development education[34]	77,800	—	226,800	219,800	308,317	411,907	592,635	529,076	597,255	640,610	651,533	615,469
Department of Energy	3,000	57,701	25,502	28,027	†	†	†	†	†	†	†	†
University laboratory cooperative program	3,000	2,800	9,402	8,552	†	†	†	†	†	†	†	†
Teacher development projects	†	1,400	†	†	†	†	†	†	†	†	†	†
Energy conservation for buildings—higher education[11]	†	53,501	7,459	7,381	†	†	†	†	†	†	†	†
Minority honors vocational training	†	†	†	†	†	†	†	†	†	†	†	†
Honors research program	†	†	6,472	2,221	†	†	†	†	†	†	†	†
Students and teachers	†	†	2,169	9,873	†	†	†	†	†	†	†	†
Department of Health and Human Services	981,483	2,412,058	578,542	796,035	954,190	1,433,516	1,278,936	1,368,129	1,311,009	1,254,548	1,308,245	1,302,908
Health professions training programs[35]	353,029	460,736	230,600	298,302	340,361	581,661	406,000	498,000	459,000	438,039	469,236	438,721
Indian health manpower	†	7,187	9,508	27,000	16,000	27,000	46,000	41,000	41,000	32,000	32,000	48,000
National Health Service Corps scholarships	†	70,667	4,759	78,206	33,300	45,000	41,000	46,400	38,300	39,800	43,300	38,500
National Institutes of Health training grants[36]	†	176,388	241,356	380,502	550,220	756,014	775,186	772,000	762,000	734,000	753,000	767,000
National Institute of Occupational Safety and Health training grants[37]	8,088	12,899	10,461	11,660	14,198	23,841	10,750	10,729	10,709	10,709	10,709	10,687
Alcohol, drug abuse, and mental health training programs[38]	118,366	122,103	81,353	†	†	†	†	†	†	†	†	†
Health teaching facilities[39]	†	3,078	505	365	110	†	†	†	†	†	†	†
Social Security postsecondary students' benefits[40]	502,000	1,559,000	†	†	†	†	†	†	†	†	†	†
Department of Homeland Security	†	†	†	†	†	36,400	45,824	49,604	48,592	43,468	36,142	35,905
Coast Guard Academy[15]	†	†	†	†	†	16,400	26,326	27,581	26,803	24,359	25,407	23,905
Postgraduate training for Coast Guard officers[41]	†	†	†	†	†	8,700	4,645	4,883	5,891	6,198	5,417	5,345
Tuition assistance to Coast Guard military personnel[15]	†	†	†	†	†	11,300	14,853	17,140	15,898	12,911	5,318	6,655
Department of Housing and Urban Development[31]	114,199	†	†	†	†	†	†	†	†	†	†	†
College housing loans[31]	114,199	†	†	†	†	†	†	†	†	†	†	†
Department of the Interior	31,749	80,202	135,480	159,054	187,179	249,227	177,626	116,465	124,065	110,702	116,337	115,172
Shared revenues, Mineral Leasing Act and other receipts—estimated education share	6,949	35,403	69,980	82,810	98,740	146,235	16,250	20,430	29,900	20,310	23,100	19,800
Indian programs												
Continuing education	9,380	16,909	34,911	43,907	57,576	76,271	126,791	61,603	61,435	58,832	61,887	64,182
Higher education scholarships	15,420	27,890	30,589	32,337	30,863	26,721	34,585	34,432	32,730	31,560	31,350	31,190
Department of State	30,850	†	2,167	3,000	319,000	424,000	657,660	620,050	601,770	577,864	567,811	589,900
Educational exchange[42]	30,850	†	†	†	319,000	424,000	657,660	620,050	601,770	577,864	567,811	589,900
Mutual educational and cultural exchange activities	30,454	†	†	†	303,000	402,000	635,000	599,550	583,200	559,180	567,811	589,900
International educational exchange activities[43]	396	†	†	†	16,000	22,000	22,660	20,500	18,570	18,684	†	†
Russian, Eurasian, and East European Research and Training	†	†	2,167	3,000	†	†	†	†	†	†	†	†
Department of Transportation	11,197	12,530	46,025	59,257	60,300	73,000	89,997	95,806	102,268	97,993	96,800	97,650
Merchant Marine Academy[33]	†	†	20,926	30,850	34,000	61,000	74,057	79,897	85,168	81,787	79,500	79,150
State marine schools[33]	†	†	8,269	8,980	7,000	12,000	15,940	15,909	17,100	16,206	17,300	18,500
Coast Guard Academy[15]	9,342	10,000	12,074	13,500	15,500	†	†	†	†	†	†	†
Postgraduate training for Coast Guard officers[41]	1,655	2,230	4,173	5,513	2,500	†	†	†	†	†	†	†
Tuition assistance to Coast Guard military personnel[15]	200	300	582	414	1,300	†	†	†	†	†	†	†
Department of the Treasury	†	296,750	†	†	†	†	†	†	†	†	†	†
General revenue sharing—estimated state share to higher education[19,20]	†	296,750	†	†	†	†	†	†	†	†	†	†
Department of Veterans Affairs	693,490	1,803,847	599,825	1,010,114	1,132,322	2,478,624	8,034,534	9,821,752	10,114,790	11,685,892	12,024,361	13,605,271
Vietnam-era veterans	638,260	1,579,974	46,998	†	†	†	†	†	†	†	†	†
College student support	†	1,560,081	39,458	†	†	†	†	†	†	†	†	†
Work-study	†	19,893	7,540	†	†	†	†	†	†	†	†	†

See notes at end of table.

Table 401.30. Federal on-budget funds for education, by level/educational purpose, agency, and program: Selected fiscal years, 1970 through 2015—Continued

[In thousands of current dollars]

Level/educational purpose, agency, and program	1970	1980	1990[1]	1995[1]	2000[1]	2005[1]	2010[1]	2011[1]	2012[1]	2013[1]	2014[1]	2015[1,2]
1	2	3	4	5	6	7	8	9	10	11	12	13
Service persons college support	18,900	46,617	8,911	†	†	†	†	†	†	†	†	†
Post-Vietnam veterans	†	922	161,475	33,596	3,958	1,136	1,496	1,343	932	615	425	398
All-volunteer-force educational assistance	†	†	269,947	868,394	984,068	2,070,996	1,854,917	1,587,376	1,086,585	928,847	680,312	605,763
Veterans	†	†	183,765	760,390	876,434	1,887,239	1,659,694	1,385,943	931,756	775,382	530,508	478,735
Reservists	†	†	86,182	108,004	107,634	183,757	195,223	201,433	154,829	153,465	149,804	127,028
Post 9-11 GI Bill[44]	†	†	†	†	†	†	5,542,843	7,656,490	8,476,227	10,184,499	10,754,649	12,407,886
Veteran dependents' education	36,330	176,334	100,494	95,124	131,296	388,719	507,294	462,877	455,318	483,281	513,633	540,801
Payments to state education agencies	†	†	12,000	13,000	13,000	17,773	18,958	18,342	18,738	18,980	18,985	19,000
Reserve Education Assistance Program (REAP)[45]	†	†	†	†	†	†	109,026	95,324	76,990	69,670	56,357	31,423
Other agencies												
Appalachian Regional Commission	4,105	1,751	—	2,741	2,286	4,407	2,464	6,098	6,653	4,443	7,471	17,062
National Endowment for the Humanities	3,349	56,451	50,938	56,481	28,395	29,253	47,949	40,168	45,000	39,399	39,824	42,900
National Science Foundation	42,000	64,583	161,884	211,800	389,000	490,000	646,000	636,060	937,160	858,130	894,000	893,350
Science and engineering education programs	37,000	64,583	161,884	211,800	389,000	490,000	646,000	636,060	937,160	858,130	894,000	893,350
Sea Grant Program[32]	5,000	†	†	†	†	†	†	†	†	†	†	†
United States Information Agency[46]	8,423	51,095	181,172	260,800	†	†	†	†	†	†	†	†
Educational and cultural affairs[42]	†	49,546	35,862	13,600	†	†	†	†	†	†	†	†
Educational and cultural exchange programs[47]	†	†	145,307	247,200	†	†	†	†	†	†	†	†
Educational exchange activities, international	†	1,549	3	†	†	†	†	†	†	†	†	†
Information center and library activities	8,423	†	†	†	†	†	†	†	†	†	†	†
Other programs												
Barry Goldwater Scholarship and Excellence in Education Foundation	†	†	1,033	3,000	3,000	3,000	4,000	3,000	4,000	4,000	3,000	3,000
Estimated education share of federal aid to the District of Columbia[48]	5,513	13,143	14,637	9,468	11,493	14,578	20,450	15,115	37,875	37,193	37,538	42,324
Harry S Truman Scholarship fund	†	-1,895	2,883	3,000	3,000	3,000	2,000	1,000	1,200	1,500	1,000	1,000
Institute of American Indian and Alaska Native Culture and Arts Development	†	†	4,305	13,000	2,000	6,000	8,000	8,284	8,500	9,550	11,369	11,469
James Madison Memorial Fellowship Foundation	†	†	191	2,000	7,000	2,000	2,000	2,000	2,000	2,000	2,000	2,000
Other education	**$964,719**	**$1,548,730**	**$3,383,031**	**$4,719,655**	**$5,484,571**	**$6,913,451**	**$9,326,441**	**$11,096,234**	**$9,390,511**	**$9,638,631**	**$9,443,392**	**$9,467,086**
Department of Education[3]	630,235	747,706	2,251,801	2,861,000	3,223,355	3,538,862	5,073,063	5,255,939	5,466,031	5,696,191	5,420,500	5,457,928
Administration	47,456	187,317	328,293	404,000	458,054	548,842	1,531,232	1,755,384	1,928,821	2,048,098	1,971,955	1,965,715
Libraries[49]	108,284	129,127	137,264	117,000	†	†	†	†	†	†	†	†
Rehabilitative services and disability research	473,091	426,886	1,780,360	2,333,000	2,755,468	2,973,346	3,506,861	3,474,718	3,511,281	3,622,925	3,422,749	3,466,393
American Printing House for the Blind	1,404	4,349	5,736	7,000	9,368	16,538	24,600	24,551	24,505	24,655	24,456	24,931
Trust funds and contributions	0	27	148	0	465	136	10,370	1,286	1,424	513	1,340	889
Department of Agriculture	135,637	271,112	352,511	422,878	444,477	468,631	567,423	552,030	547,081	549,989	545,676	548,176
Extension Service	131,734	263,584	337,907	405,371	424,174	445,631	543,423	530,030	526,081	528,989	521,676	524,176
National Agricultural Library	3,903	7,528	14,604	17,507	20,303	23,000	24,000	22,000	21,000	21,000	24,000	24,000
Department of Commerce	1,226	2,479	†	†	†	†	†	†	†	†	†	†
Maritime Administration												
Training for private sector employees[33]	1,226	2,479	†	†	†	†	†	†	†	†	†	†
Department of Health and Human Services	24,273	37,819	77,962	138,000	214,000	317,947	339,716	339,716	338,278	337,639	327,723	336,939
National Library of Medicine	24,273	37,819	77,962	138,000	214,000	317,947	339,716	339,716	338,278	337,639	327,723	336,939
Department of Homeland Security	†	†	†	†	†	278,243	341,100	1,851,832	215,884	243,111	258,730	259,595
Federal Law Enforcement Training Center[50]	†	†	†	†	†	159,000	323,000	270,832	271,413	243,111	258,730	259,595
Estimated disaster relief[51]	†	†	†	†	†	119,243	18,100	1,581,000	-55,529	—	—	—
Department of Justice	5,546	27,642	26,920	36,296	34,727	26,148	33,563	33,563	33,563	30,207	30,095	30,814
Federal Bureau of Investigation National Academy	2,066	7,234	6,028	12,831	22,479	15,619	19,443	19,443	19,443	21,268	21,291	21,409
Federal Bureau of Investigation Field Police Academy	2,500	7,715	10,548	11,140	11,962	10,456	14,120	14,120	14,120	8,939	8,804	9,405
Narcotics and dangerous drug training	980	2,416	850	325	286	73	†	†	†	†	†	†
National Institute of Corrections	†	10,277	9,494	12,000	†	†	†	†	†	†	†	†

See notes at end of table.

Table 401.30. Federal on-budget funds for education, by level/educational purpose, agency, and program: Selected fiscal years, 1970 through 2015—Continued

[In thousands of current dollars]

Level/educational purpose, agency, and program	1970	1980	1990[1]	1995[1]	2000[1]	2005[1]	2010[1]	2011[1]	2012[1]	2013[1]	2014[1]	2015[1,2]
1	2	3	4	5	6	7	8	9	10	11	12	13
Department of State	20,672	25,000	47,539	51,648	69,349	109,309	120,520	121,620	123,452	219,238	251,230	234,337
Foreign Service Institute	15,857	25,000	47,539	51,648	69,349	109,309	120,520	121,620	123,452	219,238	251,230	234,337
Center for Cultural and Technical Interchange[42]	4,815	†	†	†	†	†	†	†	†	†	†	†
Department of Transportation	3,964	10,212	1,507	650	700	1,100	146	135	120	—	—	—
Highways training and education grants	2,418	3,412	—	—	—	—	—	—	—	—	—	—
Maritime Administration												
Training for private sector employees[31]	†	†	1,507	650	700	1,100	146	135	120	—	—	—
Urban mass transportation—managerial training grants	1,546	500	†	†	†	†	†	†	†	†	†	†
Federal Aviation Administration												
Air traffic controllers second career program	—	6,300	—	—	—	—	—	—	—	—	—	—
Department of the Treasury	18	14,584	41,488	48,000	83,000	†	†	†	†	†	†	†
Federal Law Enforcement Training Center[50]	18	14,584	41,488	48,000	83,000	†	†	†	†	†	†	†
Other agencies												
ACTION[52]	†	2,833	8,472	†	†	†	†	†	†	†	†	†
Estimated education funds	†	2,833	8,472	†	†	†	†	†	†	†	†	†
Agency for International Development	88,034	99,707	170,371	260,408	299,000	574,000	542,700	599,500	598,800	574,000	576,439	589,900
Education and human resources	61,570	80,518	142,801	248,408	299,000	574,000	542,700	599,500	598,800	574,000	576,439	589,900
American schools and hospitals abroad	26,464	19,189	27,570	12,000	†	†	†	†	†	†	†	†
Appalachian Regional Commission	572	8,124	†	5,709	2,369	1,173	1,620	3,514	3,510	6,938	2,439	5,045
Corporation for National and Community Service[52]	†	†	†	214,600	386,000	472,000	965,000	983,000	750,252	711,009	756,849	758,349
Federal Emergency Management Agency[53]	290	281	215	170,400	14,894	†	†	†	†	†	†	†
Estimated architect/engineer student development program	40	31	200	—	—	†	†	†	†	†	†	†
Estimated other training programs[54]	250	250	15	—	—	†	†	†	†	†	†	†
Estimated disaster relief[51]	—	—	—	170,400	14,894	†	†	†	†	†	†	†
General Services Administration	14,775	34,800	†	†	†	†	†	†	†	†	†	†
Libraries and other archival activities[55]	14,775	34,800	†	†	†	†	†	†	†	†	†	†
Institute of Museum and Library Services[49]	†	†	†	†	166,000	250,000	265,000	274,000	242,605	231,954	225,813	226,448
Japanese-United States Friendship Commission	†	2,294	2,299	2,000	3,000	3,000	2,000	3,700	3,700	3,700	3,000	3,000
Library of Congress	29,478	151,871	189,827	241,000	299,000	430,000	516,000	521,000	521,000	470,202	485,757	469,605
Salaries and expenses	20,700	102,364	148,985	198,000	247,000	383,000	439,000	446,000	442,000	422,625	433,830	419,357
Books for the blind and the physically handicapped	6,195	31,436	37,473	39,000	46,000	47,000	77,000	75,000	79,000	47,577	51,927	50,248
Special foreign currency program	2,273	3,492	10	†	†	†	†	†	†	†	†	†
Furniture and furnishings	310	14,579	3,359	4,000	6,000	—	—	—	—	—	—	—
National Aeronautics and Space Administration	350	882	3,300	5,923	6,800	—	—	—	—	—	—	—
Aerospace education services project	350	882	3,300	5,923	6,800	—	—	—	—	—	—	—
National Archives and Records Administration	†	†	77,397	105,172	121,879	276,000	339,000	349,000	339,000	373,000	370,706	360,000
Libraries and other archival activities[55]	†	†	77,397	105,172	121,879	276,000	339,000	349,000	339,000	373,000	370,706	360,000
National Commission on Libraries and Information Science[56]	†	2,090	3,281	1,000	2,000	1,000	†	†	†	†	†	†
National Endowment for the Arts[24]	340	231	936	2,304	4,046	2,506	2,883	1,370	6,145	3,483	4,502	3,732
National Endowment for the Humanities	5,090	85,805	89,706	94,249	70,807	87,969	94,580	90,891	91,000	74,439	77,528	77,073
Smithsonian Institution	2,461	5,153	5,779	9,961	25,764	45,890	63,107	67,322	65,109	65,483	68,529	70,053
Museum programs and related research	2,261	3,254	690	3,190	18,000	32,000	52,000	56,000	54,000	54,313	57,915	59,553
National Gallery of Art extension service	200	426	474	771	764	890	107	119	122	115	114	—
Woodrow Wilson International Center for Scholars	†	1,473	4,615	6,000	7,000	13,000	11,000	11,203	10,987	11,055	10,500	10,500

See notes at end of table.

Table 401.30. Federal on-budget funds for education, by level/educational purpose, agency, and program: Selected fiscal years, 1970 through 2015—Continued

[In thousands of current dollars]

Level/educational purpose, agency, and program	1970	1980	1990[1]	1995[1]	2000[1]	2005[1]	2010[1]	2011[1]	2012[1]	2013[1]	2014[1]	2015[1,2]
1	2	3	4	5	6	7	8	9	10	11	12	13
United States Information Agency—Center for Cultural and Technical Interchange[42]	†	15,115	20,375	34,000	†	†	†	†	†	†	†	†
United States Institute of Peace	†	†	7,621	12,000	13,000	28,000	58,000	47,000	44,000	47,000	37,000	35,000
Other programs												
Estimated education share of federal aid for the District of Columbia	1,758	2,990	3,724	2,457	404	1,674	1,020	1,102	980	1,048	876	1,092
Research programs at universities and related institutions[57]	**$2,283,641**	**$5,801,204**	**$12,606,035**	**$15,677,919**	**$21,660,134**	**$33,419,698**	**$36,993,306**	**$32,017,112**	**$32,176,184**	**$30,339,833**	**$32,203,636**	**$32,467,878**
Department of Education[58]	87,823	78,742	89,483	279,000	116,464	456,822	659,006	608,786	593,664	$597,297	$576,935	$573,935
Department of Agriculture	64,796	216,405	348,109	434,544	553,600	709,700	737,200	764,000	643,100	578,800	697,900	794,100
Department of Commerce	4,487	48,295	50,523	85,442	110,775	243,948	303,000	242,778	205,085	235,936	275,521	294,768
Department of Defense	356,188	644,455	1,871,864	1,853,955	1,891,710	4,342,100	3,154,300	3,272,300	2,861,205	2,394,900	2,788,700	2,940,200
Department of Energy	548,327	1,470,224	2,520,885	2,651,641	3,577,004	4,339,879	3,402,600	2,994,903	2,983,055	2,941,159	3,288,681	3,099,413
Department of Health and Human Services	623,765	2,087,053	4,902,714	6,418,969	10,491,641	16,357,996	21,796,200	17,780,531	17,630,467	16,588,019	17,305,391	17,416,327
Department of Homeland Security	†	†	†	†	†	309,717	152,800	104,450	68,700	71,637	77,173	78,176
Department of Housing and Urban Development	510	5,314	118	1,613	1,400	1,100	400	1,600	300	4,500	100	1,500
Department of the Interior	18,521	42,175	49,790	50,618	47,200	66,800	84,200	108,774	65,405	51,352	76,822	52,400
Department of Justice	1,945	9,189	6,858	7,204	19,400	27,500	34,600	29,900	34,700	38,900	55,300	54,800
Department of Labor	3,567	12,938	5,893	10,114	12,900	110,500	†	†	†	†	†	†
Department of State	8,220	188	1,519	23	†	†	†	†	†	†	†	†
Department of Transportation	12,328	31,910	28,608	75,847	55,866	52,800	70,100	64,800	71,500	80,509	71,200	6,800
Department of the Treasury	†	226	227	1,496	†	†	†	†	†	†	†	†
Department of Veterans Affairs	518	1,600	2,300	2,500	†	†	†	†	†	†	†	†
Agency for International Development	†	77,063	79,415	30,172	33,500	28,100	15,200	22,400	31,100	29,900	17,600	17,900
Environmental Protection Agency	19,446	41,083	87,481	125,721	98,900	83,400	54,700	79,200	87,200	73,700	86,100	68,000
Federal Emergency Management Agency	†	1,665	†	†	†	†	†	†	†	†	†	†
National Aeronautics and Space Administration	258,016	254,629	1,090,003	1,751,977	2,071,030	2,763,120	1,585,500	1,430,761	2,289,837	2,200,143	2,287,755	2,333,069
National Science Foundation	253,628	743,809	1,427,007	1,874,395	2,566,244	3,503,216	4,914,700	4,491,930	4,597,266	4,443,881	4,584,258	4,723,391
Nuclear Regulatory Commission	†	32,590	42,328	22,188	12,200	15,100	14,500	14,000	8,600	5,400	9,400	6,200
Office of Economic Opportunity	20,035	†	†	†	†	†	†	†	†	†	†	†
U.S. Arms Control and Disarmament Agency	100	661	25	†	†	†	†	†	†	†	†	†
Other agencies	1,421	990	885	500	300	7,900	14,300	6,000	5,000	3,800	4,800	6,900

See notes at end of table.

Table 401.30. Federal on-budget funds for education, by level/educational purpose, agency, and program: Selected fiscal years, 1970 through 2014—Continued

—Not available.
†Not applicable.
[1]Excludes federal support for medical education benefits under Medicare in the U.S. Department of Health and Human Services. Benefits excluded from total because data before fiscal year (FY) 1990 are not available. This program existed since Medicare began, but was not available as a separate budget item until FY 1990. Excluded amounts are estimated as follows: $4,440,000,000 in FY 1990, $7,510,000,000 in FY 1995, $8,020,000,000 in FY 2000, $8,290,000,000 in FY 2005, $9,080,000,000 in FY 2010, $9,200,000,000 in FY 2011, $9,800,000,000 in FY 2012, $10,000,000,000 in FY 2013, $11,330,000,000 in FY 2014, and $11,800,000,000 in FY 2015.
[2]Data for research programs at universities and related institutions are estimated.
[3]The U.S. Department of Education was created in May 1980. It formerly was the Office of Education in the U.S. Department of Health, Education, and Welfare.
[4]Arranges for the education of children who reside on federal property when no suitable local school district can or will provide for the education of these children.
[5]Includes many programs, such as No Child Left Behind, 21st Century Community Learning Centers, Class Size Reduction, Charter Schools, Safe and Drug-Free Schools, and Innovative programs.
[6]Included the School-To-Work Opportunities program, which initiated a national system to be administered jointly by the U.S. Departments of Education and Labor. Programs in the Education Reform program were transferred to the school improvement programs or discontinued in FY 2002. Amounts after FY 2002 reflect balances that are spending out from prior-year appropriations.
[7]Starting in FY 1994, the Special Milk Program has been included in the child nutrition programs.
[8]The Farm Security and Rural Investment Act of 2002 (Public Law 107-171) carries out preschool and school feeding programs in foreign countries to help reduce the incidence of hunger and malnutrition, and improve literacy and primary education.
[9]These commodities are purchased under Section 32 of the Agricultural Adjustment Act of 1935 (Public Law 74-320), for use in the child nutrition programs.
[10]Assisted in the construction of public facilities, such as vocational schools, through grants or loans. No funds have been appropriated for this program since FY 1977, and it was completely phased out in FY 1984.
[11]Established in 1979, with funds first appropriated in FY 1980.
[12]Formerly in the Office of Economic Opportunity. In FY 1972, funds were transferred to the U.S. Department of Health, Education, and Welfare, Office of Child Development.
[13]Created by the Family Support Act of 1988 (Public Law 100-485) to provide funds for the Job Opportunities and Basic Skills Training program. Later incorporated into Temporary Assistance for Needy Families program.
[14]After age 18, benefits terminate at the end of the school term or in 3 months, whichever comes first.
[15]Transferred from the U.S. Department of Transportation to the U.S. Department of Homeland Security in March 2003.
[16]Provides funding for supplemental programs for eligible American Indian students in public schools.
[17]Finances the cost of academic, social, and occupational education courses for inmates in federal prisons.
[18]Some of the work and training programs were in the Office of Economic Opportunity and were transferred to the U.S. Department of Labor in FYs 1971 and 1972. From FY 1994 through FY 2001, included the School-to-Work Opportunities program, which was administered jointly by the U.S. Departments of Education and Labor.
[19]Established in FY 1972 and closed in FY 1986.
[20]The states' share of revenue-sharing funds could not be spent on education in FYs 1981 through 1986.
[21]Provided educational assistance allowances in order to restore lost educational opportunities to those individuals whose careers were interrupted or impeded by reason of active military service between January 31, 1955, and January 1, 1977.
[22]This program is in Readjustment Benefits program, Chapter 31, and covers the costs of subsistence, tuition, books, supplies, and equipment for disabled veterans requiring vocational rehabilitation.
[23]This program is in Readjustment Benefits program, Chapter 35, and provides benefits to children and spouses of veterans.
[24]"Elementary/secondary" obligations for FYs 2014 and 2015 include those items that impact elementary and secondary (K–12) students, and that are standards based. "Other education" obligations include all other arts education items not meeting the terms of "elementary/secondary."
[25]Head Start program funds were transferred to the U.S. Department of Health, Education, and Welfare, Office of Child Development, in FY 1972.
[26]Most of these programs were transferred to the U.S. Department of Health, Education, and Welfare, Office of Education, in FY 1972.
[27]Transferred to the U.S. Department of Labor in FYs 1971 and 1972.
[28]Transferred to the ACTION Agency in FY 1972.
[29]Under the William D. Ford Federal Direct Loan Program (commonly referred to as the Direct Loan Program), the federal government uses Treasury funds to provide loan capital directly to schools, which then disburse loan funds to students.
[30]The Federal Family Education Loan (FFEL) Program eliminated the authorization to originate new FFEL loans after June 30, 2010; all new loans are originated through the Direct Loan Program. The FFEL Program made loan capital available to students and their families through private lenders. State and private nonprofit guaranty agencies administer the federal guarantee protecting FFEL lenders against losses related to borrower default. These agencies also collect on defaulted loans and provide other services to lenders.
[31]Transferred from the U.S. Department of Housing and Urban Development to the U.S. Department of Health, Education, and Welfare, Office of Education, in FY 1979.
[32]Transferred from the National Science Foundation to the U.S. Department of Commerce in October 1970.
[33]Transferred from the U.S. Department of Commerce to the U.S. Department of Transportation in FY 1981.
[34]Includes special education programs (military and civilian); legal education program; flight training; advanced degree program; college degree program (officers); and Armed Forces Health Professions Scholarship program.
[35]Does not include Health Education Assistance Loans (HEAL).
[36]Alcohol, drug abuse, and mental health training programs are included starting in FY 1992.
[37]From 2008 onward, funding came from Harwood Training Grants.
[38]Beginning in FY 1992, data were included in the National Institutes of Health training grants program.
[39]This program closed in FY 2004.
[40]Postsecondary student benefits were ended by the Omnibus Budget Reconciliation Act of 1981 (Public Law 97-35) and were completely phased out by August 1985.
[41]Includes flight training. Transferred to the U.S. Department of Homeland Security in March 2003.
[42]Transferred from the U.S. Department of State to the United States Information Agency in 1977, then transferred back to the U.S. Department of State in FY 1998.
[43]In FY 2014, the Regional Graduate Fellowship program was consolidated with the Fulbright Program.
[44]Chapter 33 was enacted in the Post 9-11 Veterans Educational Assistance Act of 2008 (Public Law 110-252).
[45]Part of the Ronald W. Reagan National Defense Authorization Act for FY 2005 (Public Law 108-375), enacted October 28, 2004. The Reserve Education Assistance Program (REAP) provides educational assistance to members of the National Guard and Reserves who serve on active duty in support of a contingency operation under federal authority on or after September 11, 2001.
[46]Abolished in FY 1998, with functions transferred to the U.S. Department of State and the newly created Broadcasting Board of Governors.
[47]Included in the Educational and Cultural Affairs program in FYs 1980 through 1983, and became an independent program in FY 1984.
[48]Includes funding for D.C. College Tuition Assistance Grant (DC TAG), D.C. Adoption Scholarship Program, Robert C. Byrd Honors Scholarship Program, United States Senate Youth Program (USSYP), Advanced Placement Test Fee Program, the Early College Grant, and the College Access Challenge Grant.
[49]Transferred from U.S. Department of Education to the Institute of Museum and Library Services in FY 1997.
[50]Transferred to the U.S. Department of Homeland Security in FY 2003.
[51]The disaster relief program repairs and replaces damaged and destroyed school buildings. This program was transferred from the Federal Emergency Management Agency to the U.S. Department of Homeland Security in FY 2003.
[52]The National Service Trust Act of 1993 (Public Law 103-82) established the Corporation for National and Community Service. In 1993, ACTION became part of this agency.
[53]The Federal Emergency Management Agency was created in 1979, representing a combination of five existing agencies. The funds for the Federal Emergency Management Agency in FY 1970 were in other agencies. This agency was transferred to the U.S. Department of Homeland Security in March 2003.
[54]These programs include the Fall-Out Shelter Analysis, Blast Protection Design through FY 1992. Starting in FY 1993, earthquake training and safety for teachers and administrators for grades 1 through 12 are included.
[55]Transferred from the General Services Administration to the National Archives and Records Administration in April 1985.
[56]The Consolidated Appropriations Act of 2008 (Public Law 110-161) transferred the National Commission on Libraries and Information Science to the Institute of Museum and Library Services starting in FY 2008.
[57]Includes federal obligations for research and development centers and R & D plant administered by colleges and universities. FY 2015 data are estimated, except the U.S Department of Education data, which are actual numbers.
[58]FY 1970 includes outlays for the Research and Training program. FY 1980 includes outlays for the National Institute of Education program. FY 1990 through FY 2000 amounts are outlays for the Office of Educational Research and Improvement. Amounts for FY 2005 and later years are for the Institute of Education Sciences; these amounts are outlays for years prior to FY 2010 and appropriations for later years.
NOTE: To the extent possible, amounts reported do not represent obligations, but instead represent appropriations or (especially for earlier years) outlays. Negative amounts occur when program receipts exceed outlays. Some data have been revised from previously published figures. Detail may not sum to totals because of rounding.
SOURCE: U.S. Department of Education, Budget Service, unpublished tabulations. U.S. Office of Management and Budget, *Budget of the U.S. Government, Appendix*, fiscal years 1972 through 2016. National Science Foundation, Federal Funds for Research and Development, fiscal years 1970 through 2015. (This table was prepared May 2016.)

Table 401.60. U.S. Department of Education appropriations for major programs, by state or jurisdiction: Fiscal year 2014
[In thousands of current dollars]

State or jurisdiction	Total	Grants for the disadvantaged[1]	Block grants to states for school improvement[2]	School assistance in federally affected areas[3]	Career/technical and adult education[4]	Special education[5]	Language assistance[6]	American Indian education	Student financial assistance[7]	Rehabilitation services[8]
1	2	3	4	5	6	7	8	9	10	11
Total, 50 states and D.C.[9]	**$69,873,570**	**$14,676,651**	**$4,024,201**	**$1,040,434**	**$1,622,315**	**$11,984,134**	**$664,423**	**$100,381**	**$32,759,496**	**$3,001,536**
Total, 50 states, D.C., other activities, and other jurisdictions	**72,342,512**	**15,312,923**	**4,260,867**	**1,216,955**	**1,681,553**	**12,264,584**	**723,400**	**100,381**	**33,627,028**	**3,154,820**
Alabama	1,161,215	231,586	67,627	2,452	28,375	190,766	3,971	1,530	574,052	60,855
Alaska	313,248	47,029	21,209	127,825	5,244	39,443	1,189	12,383	47,768	11,159
Arizona	2,437,713	343,891	76,305	147,376	36,272	201,977	15,178	10,437	1,540,434	65,843
Arkansas	711,121	169,775	45,574	385	16,807	119,386	3,218	260	306,858	48,859
California	8,559,688	1,879,925	443,404	55,870	209,783	1,294,029	150,817	5,691	4,212,432	307,737
Colorado	1,016,228	165,139	48,310	26,283	22,508	166,020	8,610	651	536,532	42,177
Connecticut	669,449	120,173	38,574	4,684	14,674	139,786	6,309	30	318,441	26,777
Delaware	197,628	46,342	21,024	42	6,341	37,787	1,465	0	70,218	14,409
District of Columbia	277,732	44,795	20,702	295	5,475	19,698	881	0	167,499	18,387
Florida	4,176,246	828,823	191,393	6,632	98,948	673,866	43,667	107	2,156,419	176,390
Georgia	2,273,371	534,528	122,548	18,064	56,142	351,312	15,158	0	1,112,356	63,264
Hawaii	274,353	56,161	21,318	41,186	7,616	42,300	3,813	0	87,910	14,050
Idaho	362,890	64,187	24,004	4,893	8,587	59,750	1,911	424	181,063	18,071
Illinois	3,004,056	671,808	172,075	13,320	60,609	532,649	27,322	192	1,413,737	112,345
Indiana	1,584,207	274,577	72,532	95	34,343	272,346	8,481	0	860,467	61,366
Iowa	767,564	89,710	35,338	102	15,439	128,308	3,785	286	465,285	29,312
Kansas	628,563	121,743	36,755	34,010	13,834	113,564	4,269	1,022	282,234	21,131
Kentucky	1,006,424	237,294	67,783	664	26,299	171,261	3,613	0	450,755	48,754
Louisiana	1,093,089	305,731	87,403	8,903	30,016	198,564	3,035	918	421,834	36,684
Maine	297,411	55,033	24,081	1,445	7,163	58,537	726	158	131,860	18,410
Maryland	1,021,494	205,957	58,240	5,618	24,347	211,224	9,835	80	457,474	48,718
Massachusetts	1,267,565	224,262	69,702	494	27,597	297,178	13,702	86	580,576	53,967
Michigan	2,326,922	547,272	152,205	3,418	50,529	417,505	11,225	2,418	1,049,031	93,318
Minnesota	1,152,830	152,368	55,384	18,393	22,305	201,289	8,532	3,589	637,694	53,274
Mississippi	800,922	194,644	60,428	1,184	19,356	126,255	1,589	459	351,547	45,459
Missouri	1,348,099	248,958	75,727	23,352	30,120	237,637	5,288	76	663,001	63,941
Montana	260,828	47,344	26,340	39,978	6,380	40,115	556	3,532	82,288	14,296
Nebraska	392,765	78,682	25,920	10,215	9,114	78,595	2,965	875	165,714	20,686
Nevada	429,325	119,908	27,232	2,735	15,142	76,587	7,155	731	161,638	18,196
New Hampshire	278,924	45,065	23,433	5	7,128	50,466	1,054	0	139,612	12,161
New Jersey	1,586,588	320,298	89,114	10,487	37,291	378,446	20,953	33	669,182	60,784
New Mexico	602,877	115,332	34,657	77,601	12,091	95,903	4,306	7,855	232,662	22,471
New York	4,721,724	1,136,338	304,225	37,531	92,151	805,320	59,771	1,797	2,137,598	146,994
North Carolina	1,993,777	433,807	104,617	14,181	52,451	350,292	14,187	3,560	913,061	107,621
North Dakota	184,294	34,715	21,758	22,527	5,177	30,865	646	1,878	55,819	10,909
Ohio	2,440,942	589,882	155,217	1,194	57,985	456,491	10,101	0	1,057,605	112,466
Oklahoma	851,266	162,123	56,234	31,961	21,063	155,168	5,020	23,995	350,469	45,233
Oregon	855,630	163,730	45,017	2,060	18,775	135,369	7,008	1,867	430,905	50,898
Pennsylvania	2,450,301	578,464	156,003	840	58,209	448,310	15,157	0	1,068,228	125,090
Rhode Island	274,035	50,589	21,180	1,288	7,683	46,898	2,460	0	129,562	14,375
South Carolina	1,005,723	224,026	57,202	1,033	26,658	187,372	3,550	18	448,248	57,615
South Dakota	285,822	44,520	22,017	46,119	5,397	36,863	995	3,729	115,273	10,909
Tennessee	1,335,678	286,904	76,995	2,731	34,279	249,249	5,273	0	607,178	73,068
Texas	5,775,497	1,424,950	352,539	88,180	146,182	1,043,902	103,674	510	2,371,373	244,188
Utah	736,374	94,422	29,848	8,414	15,390	118,330	4,113	1,357	424,518	39,983
Vermont	167,601	35,519	20,762	7	5,100	29,914	500	217	58,474	17,109
Virginia	1,539,662	243,292	72,344	31,030	36,311	299,534	12,284	11	771,305	73,550
Washington	1,190,650	239,359	68,203	38,295	29,985	234,506	16,666	4,104	504,135	55,395
West Virginia	515,150	92,212	34,799	11	11,980	80,406	680	0	257,127	37,935
Wisconsin	1,108,889	217,398	68,041	12,074	26,647	221,362	7,260	2,612	488,596	64,898
Wyoming	159,220	36,059	20,861	12,952	5,018	31,432	500	904	41,445	10,050
Other activities/jurisdictions										
Indian Tribe Set-Aside	273,856	95,732	22,661	0	13,970	99,219	5,000	0	0	37,275
Other nonstate allocations	416,742	45,462	80,957	176,521	11,875	15,000	47,021	0	0	39,905
American Samoa	31,875	11,226	4,785	0	579	6,956	1,104	0	6,089	1,136
Freely Associated States[10]	24,586	0	0	0	171	6,579	0	0	17,835	0
Guam	62,578	16,777	7,435	0	1,059	15,560	1,350	0	17,556	2,841
Northern Marianas	23,639	7,174	3,361	0	689	5,290	1,068	0	4,940	1,117
Puerto Rico	1,599,444	447,492	112,610	0	29,818	122,107	3,339	0	815,270	68,808
U.S. Virgin Islands	36,221	12,409	4,858	0	1,076	9,740	95	0	5,842	2,201

[1]Title I grants. Includes Grants to Local Education Agencies (Basic, Concentration, Targeted, and Education Finance Incentive Grants); School Turnaround Grants; Migrant Education Grants; and Neglected and Delinquent Children Grants.
[2]Title VI grants. Includes Improving Teacher Quality State Grants; Mathematics and Science Partnerships; 21st Century Community Learning Centers; Assessing Achievement, including No Child Left Behind; Rural and Low-Income Schools Program; Small, Rural School Achievement Program; and Homeless Children and Youth Education.
[3]Includes Impact Aid—Basic Support Payments; Impact Aid—Payments for Children with Disabilities; and Impact Aid—Construction.
[4]Includes Career and Technical Education State Grants; Adult Basic and Literacy Education State Grants; and English Literacy and Civics Education State Grants.
[5]Includes Special Education—Grants to States; Special Education—Preschool Grants; and Grants for Infants and Families.
[6]Includes English Language Acquisition.
[7]Includes Pell Grants; Federal Supplemental Educational Opportunity Grants; Federal Work-Study; College Access Challenge Grant; and Student Loan Program interest subsidies.
[8]Includes Vocational Rehabilitation State Grants; Client Assistance State Grants; Protection and Advocacy of Individual Rights; Supported Employment State Grants; and Services for Older Blind Individuals.
[9]Total excludes other activities and other jurisdictions.
[10]Includes the Marshall Islands, the Federated States of Micronesia, and Palau.
NOTE: Data reflect revisions to figures in the *Budget of the United States Government, Fiscal Year 2016*. Detail may not sum to totals because of rounding.
SOURCE: U.S. Department of Education, Budget Service, retrieved November 25, 2015, from http://www2.ed.gov/about/overview/budget/statetables/index.html; and unpublished tabulations. (This table was prepared November 2015.)

Table 401.70. Appropriations for Title I and selected other programs under the No Child Left Behind Act of 2001, by program and state or jurisdiction: Fiscal years 2014 and 2015

[In thousands of current dollars]

State or jurisdiction	Title I total, 2014	Title I, 2015: Total	Title I, 2015: Grants to local education agencies[1]	Title I, 2015: State agency programs: Neglected and Delinquent	Title I, 2015: State agency programs: Migrant	Title I, 2015: Turn-around Grants	Assessing Achievement, 2015	Improving Teacher Quality State Grants, 2015
1	2	3	4	5	6	7	8	9
Total, 50 states and D.C.[2]	**$14,676,651**	**$14,717,694**	**$13,843,293**	**$45,928**	**$364,751**	**$463,722**	**$360,104**	**$2,190,206**
Total, 50 states, D.C., other activities, and other jurisdictions	**15,312,923**	**15,337,923**	**14,409,802**	**47,614**	**374,751**	**505,756**	**378,000**	**2,349,830**
Alabama	231,586	231,649	221,675	669	2,038	7,267	6,135	36,285
Alaska	47,029	45,994	37,335	325	6,895	1,440	3,508	10,833
Arizona	343,891	341,799	322,822	1,835	6,506	10,636	7,592	35,496
Arkansas	169,775	165,232	154,451	481	5,218	5,082	4,987	22,040
California	1,879,925	1,874,266	1,684,977	1,215	128,658	59,416	28,595	254,340
Colorado	165,139	162,514	150,086	405	6,965	5,057	6,515	25,437
Connecticut	120,173	120,861	115,996	1,064	0	3,801	5,260	21,574
Delaware	46,342	46,376	44,349	288	289	1,450	3,570	10,833
District of Columbia	44,795	44,391	42,820	177	0	1,394	3,279	10,833
Florida	828,823	825,820	775,326	1,567	22,495	26,432	14,450	102,926
Georgia	534,528	525,067	499,248	1,580	7,809	16,430	10,059	59,838
Hawaii	56,161	49,798	47,045	409	794	1,550	3,837	10,833
Idaho	64,187	63,373	57,304	537	3,532	2,000	4,223	10,853
Illinois	671,808	688,240	663,791	640	1,887	21,922	11,475	93,723
Indiana	274,577	272,993	258,436	558	5,437	8,562	7,483	38,852
Iowa	89,710	96,206	91,259	314	1,591	3,043	5,046	17,873
Kansas	121,743	119,543	104,127	237	11,413	3,766	5,013	18,241
Kentucky	237,294	227,306	211,876	1,091	7,310	7,029	5,840	35,840
Louisiana	305,731	298,550	284,811	2,010	2,443	9,287	6,104	52,095
Maine	55,033	53,123	50,087	230	1,156	1,649	3,749	10,833
Maryland	205,957	204,400	195,845	1,524	500	6,531	6,782	33,206
Massachusetts	224,262	243,232	231,735	2,160	1,591	7,745	6,950	41,946
Michigan	547,272	523,850	498,742	1,029	8,459	15,620	9,376	91,173
Minnesota	152,368	156,404	148,649	753	2,046	4,956	6,599	31,236
Mississippi	194,644	198,203	190,654	397	1,024	6,128	5,071	34,059
Missouri	248,958	251,840	240,817	1,621	1,499	7,902	6,927	39,456
Montana	47,344	48,148	45,473	187	995	1,494	3,632	10,833
Nebraska	78,682	76,709	68,871	376	5,032	2,431	4,297	11,110
Nevada	119,908	121,131	116,689	358	234	3,851	4,877	11,417
New Hampshire	45,065	41,851	39,727	682	144	1,297	3,781	10,833
New Jersey	320,298	344,633	330,260	1,438	1,938	10,996	8,705	52,363
New Mexico	115,332	121,289	116,205	350	910	3,823	4,407	18,096
New York	1,136,338	1,153,476	1,104,146	2,776	9,764	36,789	14,739	188,307
North Carolina	433,807	437,051	416,987	609	5,567	13,888	9,479	49,793
North Dakota	34,715	34,938	33,486	123	231	1,098	3,453	10,833
Ohio	589,882	580,183	558,414	1,054	2,621	18,094	10,511	85,802
Oklahoma	162,123	163,261	156,253	356	1,515	5,137	5,650	26,237
Oregon	163,730	157,216	140,708	1,515	10,121	4,872	5,424	22,084
Pennsylvania	578,464	571,697	544,019	836	8,946	17,895	10,658	93,503
Rhode Island	50,589	51,444	49,334	476	0	1,634	3,609	10,833
South Carolina	224,026	235,440	225,816	1,554	554	7,515	6,063	28,553
South Dakota	44,520	45,878	43,470	140	827	1,441	3,578	10,833
Tennessee	286,904	293,915	283,633	359	568	9,355	7,219	38,844
Texas	1,424,950	1,425,719	1,320,435	2,199	58,218	44,867	22,896	186,990
Utah	94,422	93,035	87,185	1,046	1,823	2,982	5,514	14,923
Vermont	35,519	35,073	33,196	148	626	1,102	3,352	10,833
Virginia	243,292	254,065	243,634	1,563	784	8,084	8,222	40,760
Washington	239,359	254,977	230,297	1,706	14,921	8,054	7,458	37,521
West Virginia	92,212	92,927	89,209	793	0	2,925	4,071	19,680
Wisconsin	217,398	217,429	208,522	1,380	627	6,900	6,697	37,733
Wyoming	36,059	35,178	33,060	788	230	1,100	3,386	10,833
Other activities/jurisdictions								
Indian Tribe Set-Aside	95,732	98,993	95,806	0	0	3,187	1,845	11,690
Other nonstate allocations	45,462	45,462	8,984	1,190	10,000	25,288	8,949	65,795
American Samoa	11,226	10,662	10,321	0	0	342	359	2,673
Guam	16,777	15,925	15,424	0	0	502	809	4,496
Northern Marianas	7,174	6,808	6,595	0	0	213	262	1,644
Puerto Rico	447,492	431,198	418,467	496	0	12,235	5,257	70,448
U.S. Virgin Islands	12,409	11,180	10,913	0	0	267	415	2,878

[1]Includes Basic, Concentration, Targeted, and Education Finance Incentive Grants.
[2]Total excludes other activities and other jurisdictions.
NOTE: Detail may not sum to totals because of rounding. Data for fiscal year 2014 are revised from previously published figures. Estimates for fiscal year 2015 are preliminary.

SOURCE: U.S. Department of Education, Budget Service, Elementary, Secondary, and Vocational Education Analysis Division, retrieved September 15, 2015, from http://www2.ed.gov/about/overview/budget/statetables/16stbyprogram.pdf. (This table was prepared September 2015.)

Table 501.10. Labor force participation, employment, and unemployment of persons 25 to 64 years old, by sex, race/ethnicity, age group, and educational attainment: 2012, 2013, and 2014

[Standard errors appear in parentheses]

Sex, race/ethnicity, age group, and educational attainment	Labor force participation: Labor force participation rate[1] 2012	Labor force participation rate[1] 2013	Labor force participation rate[1] 2014	Number of participants (in thousands) 2014	Employment: Employment to population ratio[2] 2012	Employment to population ratio[2] 2013	Employment to population ratio[2] 2014	Number employed (in thousands) 2014	Unemployment: Unemployment rate[3] 2012	Unemployment rate[3] 2013	Unemployment rate[3] 2014	Number unemployed (in thousands) 2014
1	2	3	4	5	6	7	8	9	10	11	12	13
All persons 25 to 64 years old, all education levels	**77.5 (0.04)**	**77.2 (0.04)**	**77.1 (0.04)**	**128,728 (86.0)**	**71.5 (0.04)**	**71.9 (0.04)**	**72.5 (0.05)**	**121,021 (91.3)**	**7.8 (0.03)**	**7.0 (0.03)**	**6.0 (0.03)**	**7,706 (39.6)**
Less than high school completion	60.7 (0.14)	60.7 (0.14)	60.2 (0.15)	11,804 (52.3)	52.1 (0.14)	53.0 (0.16)	53.6 (0.15)	10,511 (50.1)	14.1 (0.14)	12.7 (0.14)	11.0 (0.13)	1,293 (15.6)
High school completion[4]	73.2 (0.09)	72.8 (0.09)	72.3 (0.09)	31,787 (77.6)	65.9 (0.09)	66.2 (0.09)	66.7 (0.09)	29,320 (72.0)	10.0 (0.07)	9.1 (0.06)	7.8 (0.07)	2,467 (24.4)
Some college, no degree	78.0 (0.09)	77.5 (0.09)	77.5 (0.09)	27,877 (64.6)	71.2 (0.10)	71.5 (0.09)	72.4 (0.10)	26,054 (59.8)	8.7 (0.07)	7.7 (0.07)	6.5 (0.06)	1,824 (18.0)
Associate's degree	82.2 (0.13)	82.0 (0.13)	81.6 (0.13)	12,122 (46.3)	76.7 (0.15)	77.2 (0.15)	77.5 (0.15)	11,508 (46.0)	6.6 (0.09)	5.8 (0.09)	5.1 (0.08)	614 (9.2)
Bachelor's or higher degree	86.1 (0.06)	86.0 (0.05)	85.8 (0.06)	45,138 (110.6)	82.5 (0.07)	82.7 (0.06)	83.0 (0.07)	43,629 (106.6)	4.2 (0.04)	3.8 (0.03)	3.3 (0.04)	1,509 (17.4)
Sex												
Male, all education levels	**82.9 (0.05)**	**82.7 (0.05)**	**82.6 (0.05)**	**67,901 (51.1)**	**76.4 (0.05)**	**76.8 (0.06)**	**77.6 (0.06)**	**63,846 (60.3)**	**7.9 (0.04)**	**7.0 (0.04)**	**6.0 (0.04)**	**4,055 (27.1)**
Less than high school completion	69.7 (0.19)	69.8 (0.18)	69.9 (0.18)	7,466 (38.9)	60.7 (0.20)	61.7 (0.21)	63.0 (0.19)	6,730 (37.5)	13.0 (0.14)	11.5 (0.16)	9.9 (0.16)	736 (12.4)
High school completion[4]	79.2 (0.11)	78.7 (0.10)	78.3 (0.12)	18,407 (53.7)	71.0 (0.12)	71.4 (0.12)	72.2 (0.13)	16,980 (53.3)	10.4 (0.10)	9.2 (0.09)	7.8 (0.09)	1,428 (16.8)
Some college, no degree	83.0 (0.10)	82.6 (0.13)	82.7 (0.12)	14,335 (47.8)	76.1 (0.13)	76.5 (0.14)	77.5 (0.12)	13,442 (46.0)	8.3 (0.09)	7.4 (0.11)	6.2 (0.08)	893 (12.1)
Associate's degree	86.6 (0.16)	86.4 (0.16)	86.4 (0.19)	5,444 (29.2)	81.0 (0.18)	81.5 (0.20)	82.0 (0.21)	5,170 (29.2)	6.5 (0.11)	5.8 (0.13)	5.0 (0.11)	274 (6.1)
Bachelor's or higher degree	91.5 (0.06)	91.4 (0.06)	91.1 (0.07)	22,248 (60.5)	87.8 (0.08)	87.9 (0.07)	88.2 (0.08)	21,524 (58.4)	4.0 (0.05)	3.8 (0.05)	3.3 (0.05)	725 (11.5)
Female, all education levels	**72.2 (0.06)**	**72.0 (0.06)**	**71.8 (0.05)**	**60,827 (54.9)**	**66.7 (0.07)**	**67.0 (0.06)**	**67.5 (0.06)**	**57,175 (59.9)**	**7.7 (0.04)**	**6.9 (0.04)**	**6.0 (0.04)**	**3,651 (27.2)**
Less than high school completion	49.8 (0.23)	49.8 (0.21)	48.7 (0.19)	4,338 (25.1)	41.8 (0.23)	42.5 (0.22)	42.4 (0.19)	3,781 (24.5)	15.9 (0.26)	14.7 (0.25)	12.9 (0.20)	558 (8.9)
High school completion[4]	66.5 (0.14)	66.1 (0.13)	65.3 (0.12)	13,379 (45.8)	60.1 (0.15)	60.2 (0.14)	60.2 (0.12)	12,340 (43.5)	9.6 (0.10)	8.9 (0.11)	7.8 (0.10)	1,040 (13.9)
Some college, no degree	73.4 (0.14)	72.7 (0.13)	72.7 (0.12)	13,542 (43.8)	66.7 (0.15)	66.9 (0.13)	67.7 (0.13)	12,612 (40.6)	9.1 (0.10)	7.9 (0.09)	6.9 (0.10)	931 (14.4)
Associate's degree	78.9 (0.16)	78.7 (0.17)	78.1 (0.17)	6,677 (31.4)	73.6 (0.20)	74.0 (0.18)	74.2 (0.17)	6,338 (30.7)	6.7 (0.13)	5.9 (0.11)	5.1 (0.10)	339 (6.9)
Bachelor's or higher degree	81.3 (0.09)	81.2 (0.08)	81.3 (0.09)	22,889 (67.0)	77.8 (0.11)	78.1 (0.10)	78.5 (0.09)	22,105 (64.7)	4.3 (0.05)	3.8 (0.05)	3.4 (0.05)	784 (12.8)
Race/ethnicity												
White, all education levels	**78.5 (0.05)**	**78.2 (0.05)**	**78.1 (0.05)**	**82,330 (52.9)**	**73.4 (0.06)**	**73.7 (0.05)**	**74.2 (0.05)**	**78,284 (58.0)**	**6.5 (0.04)**	**5.8 (0.03)**	**4.9 (0.03)**	**4,046 (25.6)**
Less than high school completion	54.3 (0.23)	54.3 (0.23)	53.3 (0.26)	3,546 (27.9)	45.7 (0.21)	46.6 (0.23)	46.5 (0.26)	3,092 (25.4)	15.8 (0.20)	14.2 (0.24)	12.8 (0.23)	455 (8.9)
High school completion[4]	73.5 (0.11)	72.9 (0.11)	72.2 (0.11)	19,845 (54.5)	67.1 (0.12)	67.2 (0.11)	67.5 (0.11)	18,551 (51.1)	8.7 (0.08)	7.9 (0.07)	6.5 (0.07)	1,293 (15.6)
Some college, no degree	78.0 (0.10)	77.4 (0.10)	77.4 (0.10)	17,951 (48.2)	72.3 (0.13)	72.4 (0.10)	73.1 (0.10)	16,958 (45.1)	7.3 (0.09)	6.5 (0.07)	5.5 (0.06)	993 (12.0)
Associate's degree	82.5 (0.16)	82.0 (0.15)	81.8 (0.17)	8,446 (36.1)	77.8 (0.19)	77.8 (0.17)	78.3 (0.19)	8,082 (36.6)	5.8 (0.12)	5.1 (0.10)	4.3 (0.10)	364 (8.1)
Bachelor's or higher degree	86.1 (0.07)	86.1 (0.06)	86.0 (0.07)	32,542 (75.0)	83.0 (0.08)	83.2 (0.06)	83.5 (0.07)	31,601 (72.5)	3.7 (0.04)	3.3 (0.04)	2.9 (0.03)	941 (11.6)
Black, all education levels	**72.9 (0.13)**	**72.9 (0.12)**	**72.9 (0.14)**	**14,977 (33.4)**	**62.9 (0.15)**	**63.9 (0.12)**	**65.0 (0.14)**	**13,357 (33.4)**	**13.6 (0.11)**	**12.3 (0.11)**	**10.8 (0.10)**	**1,620 (15.0)**
Less than high school completion	47.3 (0.43)	47.8 (0.40)	47.1 (0.40)	1,236 (15.2)	34.9 (0.39)	35.8 (0.39)	36.8 (0.40)	964 (13.5)	26.2 (0.48)	25.1 (0.52)	22.0 (0.51)	272 (7.1)
High school completion[4]	68.3 (0.26)	68.1 (0.20)	68.1 (0.25)	4,428 (32.1)	57.1 (0.24)	58.0 (0.23)	58.9 (0.27)	3,831 (29.3)	16.4 (0.22)	14.9 (0.24)	13.5 (0.23)	597 (11.0)
Some college, no degree	76.8 (0.24)	76.4 (0.22)	76.5 (0.26)	4,141 (25.2)	66.2 (0.30)	67.4 (0.26)	68.5 (0.26)	3,705 (22.7)	13.7 (0.26)	11.8 (0.21)	10.5 (0.21)	435 (9.5)
Associate's degree	81.9 (0.40)	82.6 (0.41)	81.0 (0.33)	1,429 (17.5)	73.3 (0.46)	75.0 (0.48)	74.6 (0.41)	1,314 (16.8)	10.5 (0.32)	9.2 (0.32)	8.0 (0.30)	114 (4.5)
Bachelor's or higher degree	88.5 (0.20)	88.1 (0.18)	88.2 (0.19)	3,744 (26.2)	82.7 (0.27)	82.4 (0.22)	83.4 (0.20)	3,542 (26.6)	6.5 (0.19)	6.4 (0.16)	5.4 (0.17)	202 (6.3)
Hispanic, all education levels	**77.3 (0.09)**	**76.9 (0.11)**	**76.9 (0.11)**	**20,834 (33.3)**	**70.3 (0.11)**	**70.7 (0.13)**	**71.7 (0.11)**	**19,424 (33.1)**	**9.1 (0.09)**	**8.0 (0.09)**	**6.8 (0.08)**	**1,410 (17.2)**
Less than high school completion	70.1 (0.19)	69.8 (0.21)	69.6 (0.21)	6,130 (38.6)	62.6 (0.22)	63.3 (0.25)	64.1 (0.23)	5,650 (38.8)	10.7 (0.19)	9.3 (0.17)	7.8 (0.16)	480 (9.8)
High school completion[4]	77.3 (0.20)	76.8 (0.23)	76.5 (0.22)	5,740 (32.3)	69.6 (0.21)	70.1 (0.25)	70.9 (0.23)	5,320 (31.1)	10.0 (0.16)	8.8 (0.15)	7.3 (0.16)	420 (9.7)
Some college, no degree	80.8 (0.23)	80.1 (0.25)	80.4 (0.25)	4,040 (24.8)	73.4 (0.28)	73.5 (0.28)	75.2 (0.24)	3,778 (22.5)	9.1 (0.19)	8.2 (0.20)	6.5 (0.15)	261 (6.6)
Associate's degree	83.7 (0.38)	83.4 (0.41)	83.2 (0.41)	1,418 (16.7)	77.5 (0.38)	78.2 (0.44)	78.1 (0.48)	1,331 (16.7)	7.4 (0.27)	6.3 (0.28)	6.1 (0.30)	87 (4.3)
Bachelor's or higher degree	87.1 (0.23)	86.8 (0.22)	86.4 (0.18)	3,507 (27.8)	82.4 (0.26)	82.5 (0.26)	82.4 (0.23)	3,345 (26.6)	5.4 (0.16)	5.0 (0.17)	4.6 (0.17)	162 (6.2)
Asian, all education levels	**78.4 (0.16)**	**78.6 (0.15)**	**78.1 (0.13)**	**7,528 (19.8)**	**73.5 (0.18)**	**74.3 (0.17)**	**74.4 (0.15)**	**7,176 (20.8)**	**6.2 (0.12)**	**5.5 (0.10)**	**4.7 (0.10)**	**352 (7.4)**
Less than high school completion	64.5 (0.52)	63.8 (0.50)	63.1 (0.55)	663 (9.8)	58.5 (0.54)	57.8 (0.49)	58.5 (0.55)	615 (8.8)	9.3 (0.43)	9.3 (0.45)	7.3 (0.38)	48 (2.8)
High school completion[4]	74.3 (0.49)	73.8 (0.43)	73.6 (0.48)	1,019 (12.5)	67.9 (0.50)	68.8 (0.48)	68.6 (0.53)	951 (11.9)	8.6 (0.37)	6.8 (0.31)	6.7 (0.38)	69 (4.1)
Some college, no degree	78.0 (0.48)	78.2 (0.49)	76.5 (0.51)	952 (13.4)	71.3 (0.49)	72.6 (0.51)	72.1 (0.53)	898 (13.2)	8.6 (0.39)	7.2 (0.32)	5.7 (0.30)	54 (2.9)
Associate's degree	76.4 (0.68)	79.1 (0.56)	78.7 (0.69)	529 (8.7)	71.3 (0.70)	74.3 (0.61)	75.0 (0.67)	504 (8.4)	6.6 (0.41)	6.1 (0.43)	4.8 (0.33)	25 (1.8)
Bachelor's or higher degree	82.7 (0.21)	82.8 (0.22)	82.5 (0.20)	4,365 (22.7)	79.0 (0.21)	79.4 (0.24)	79.6 (0.22)	4,209 (22.2)	4.5 (0.13)	4.2 (0.11)	3.6 (0.11)	156 (4.8)
American Indian/Alaska Native, all education levels	**66.2 (0.56)**	**65.1 (0.58)**	**64.4 (0.51)**	**696 (8.8)**	**57.2 (0.60)**	**56.7 (0.60)**	**57.2 (0.54)**	**618 (8.6)**	**13.7 (0.44)**	**12.9 (0.45)**	**11.2 (0.42)**	**78 (3.0)**
Less than high school completion	44.0 (1.21)	45.8 (1.50)	43.0 (1.43)	72 (3.2)	33.0 (1.13)	35.3 (1.47)	33.3 (1.31)	56 (2.7)	24.9 (1.88)	22.9 (1.59)	22.5 (1.26)	16 (1.1)
High school completion[4]	64.7 (0.96)	62.5 (0.84)	60.9 (0.83)	224 (5.2)	54.4 (1.03)	52.4 (0.97)	53.0 (0.94)	196 (5.4)	16.0 (0.94)	16.1 (0.96)	12.9 (0.90)	29 (2.0)
Some college, no degree	68.5 (1.14)	67.2 (0.98)	67.5 (0.99)	196 (4.9)	59.0 (1.13)	59.1 (1.05)	60.6 (1.10)	176 (4.8)	13.8 (0.85)	12.0 (0.77)	10.2 (0.73)	20 (1.5)
Associate's degree	75.0 (1.75)	74.8 (1.55)	75.5 (1.68)	73 (3.0)	67.4 (1.69)	68.3 (1.64)	67.9 (1.72)	66 (2.8)	10.0 (1.04)	8.6 (1.18)	10.0 (1.10)	7 (0.9)
Bachelor's or higher degree	84.4 (1.13)	82.1 (1.25)	82.3 (1.16)	131 (4.9)	79.9 (1.16)	78.0 (1.35)	78.9 (1.24)	125 (4.9)	5.2 (0.65)	5.0 (0.71)	4.2 (0.67)	6 (0.9)

See notes at end of table.

Table 501.10. Labor force participation, employment, and unemployment of persons 25 to 64 years old, by sex, race/ethnicity, age group, and educational attainment: 2012, 2013, and 2014—Continued

[Standard errors appear in parentheses]

Sex, race/ethnicity, age group, and educational attainment	Labor force participation				Employment				Unemployment			
	Labor force participation rate[1]			Number of participants (in thousands)	Employment to population ratio[2]			Number employed (in thousands)	Unemployment rate[3]			Number unemployed (in thousands)
	2012	2013	2014	2014	2012	2013	2014	2014	2012	2013	2014	2014
1	2	3	4	5	6	7	8	9	10	11	12	13
Age group												
25 to 34, all education levels	**82.0 (0.06)**	**81.8 (0.08)**	**81.8 (0.07)**	**35,094 (39.1)**	**74.1 (0.07)**	**74.6 (0.09)**	**75.6 (0.09)**	**32,436 (46.4)**	**9.7 (0.06)**	**8.7 (0.06)**	**7.6 (0.07)**	**2,658 (22.4)**
Less than high school completion	65.5 (0.29)	65.3 (0.30)	64.6 (0.32)	3,011 (23.6)	53.7 (0.32)	54.4 (0.30)	55.0 (0.33)	2,566 (22.5)	18.0 (0.31)	16.7 (0.26)	14.8 (0.30)	445 (9.4)
High school completion[4]	78.0 (0.17)	77.1 (0.18)	76.9 (0.16)	7,919 (38.6)	67.2 (0.17)	67.5 (0.21)	68.5 (0.19)	7,045 (36.8)	13.9 (0.15)	12.5 (0.15)	11.0 (0.16)	874 (12.9)
Some college, no degree	82.0 (0.17)	81.8 (0.19)	82.0 (0.15)	8,050 (36.1)	72.9 (0.20)	73.8 (0.20)	75.0 (0.19)	7,358 (33.3)	11.2 (0.15)	9.8 (0.14)	8.6 (0.15)	692 (13.0)
Associate's degree	86.7 (0.22)	86.6 (0.21)	86.5 (0.22)	3,279 (21.8)	80.1 (0.26)	80.8 (0.23)	81.2 (0.30)	3,078 (21.4)	7.7 (0.22)	6.7 (0.15)	6.1 (0.20)	200 (6.7)
Bachelor's or higher degree	89.7 (0.10)	89.6 (0.11)	89.4 (0.11)	12,835 (51.8)	85.8 (0.11)	85.9 (0.11)	86.3 (0.11)	12,388 (50.0)	4.3 (0.08)	4.1 (0.06)	3.5 (0.07)	447 (9.6)
35 to 44, all education levels	**82.5 (0.08)**	**82.1 (0.08)**	**82.1 (0.10)**	**33,412 (45.3)**	**76.3 (0.09)**	**76.6 (0.09)**	**77.3 (0.09)**	**31,460 (41.9)**	**7.5 (0.06)**	**6.7 (0.06)**	**5.8 (0.06)**	**1,952 (19.5)**
Less than high school completion	68.4 (0.24)	68.0 (0.28)	67.3 (0.28)	3,349 (23.2)	59.3 (0.26)	59.8 (0.31)	60.1 (0.30)	2,989 (23.3)	13.4 (0.22)	12.0 (0.27)	10.8 (0.25)	361 (8.4)
High school completion[4]	79.0 (0.18)	78.4 (0.18)	78.0 (0.18)	7,701 (33.8)	70.9 (0.18)	71.1 (0.20)	71.6 (0.20)	7,075 (33.3)	10.3 (0.16)	9.3 (0.15)	8.1 (0.13)	626 (10.6)
Some college, no degree	83.1 (0.18)	82.3 (0.17)	82.4 (0.18)	6,990 (36.1)	76.1 (0.23)	76.0 (0.20)	77.1 (0.20)	6,538 (34.5)	8.5 (0.15)	7.7 (0.14)	6.5 (0.12)	452 (8.5)
Associate's degree	86.5 (0.24)	86.1 (0.23)	86.2 (0.24)	3,168 (22.5)	80.8 (0.27)	81.2 (0.30)	82.0 (0.28)	3,012 (23.0)	6.6 (0.22)	5.7 (0.21)	4.9 (0.18)	155 (5.7)
Bachelor's or higher degree	89.1 (0.11)	89.1 (0.10)	89.1 (0.11)	12,204 (43.3)	85.8 (0.12)	86.2 (0.11)	86.5 (0.11)	11,847 (41.8)	3.7 (0.08)	3.2 (0.06)	2.9 (0.06)	357 (8.0)
45 to 54, all education levels	**80.3 (0.07)**	**80.0 (0.07)**	**79.8 (0.08)**	**34,557 (44.9)**	**74.6 (0.08)**	**75.0 (0.08)**	**75.6 (0.08)**	**32,731 (47.7)**	**7.0 (0.05)**	**6.3 (0.05)**	**5.3 (0.05)**	**1,826 (17.4)**
Less than high school completion	61.9 (0.26)	62.1 (0.29)	62.2 (0.27)	3,299 (23.6)	53.8 (0.27)	55.0 (0.30)	56.2 (0.27)	2,980 (22.8)	13.0 (0.22)	11.5 (0.23)	9.7 (0.21)	319 (7.2)
High school completion[4]	76.9 (0.16)	76.4 (0.14)	75.8 (0.15)	9,266 (35.8)	70.3 (0.17)	70.5 (0.15)	70.9 (0.16)	8,665 (34.0)	8.6 (0.10)	7.7 (0.09)	6.5 (0.10)	601 (10.0)
Some college, no degree	81.3 (0.13)	80.9 (0.18)	80.6 (0.17)	7,273 (30.4)	75.3 (0.16)	75.7 (0.19)	76.3 (0.18)	6,885 (30.3)	7.3 (0.11)	6.5 (0.11)	5.3 (0.11)	388 (7.9)
Associate's degree	84.6 (0.21)	84.7 (0.22)	84.4 (0.24)	3,298 (23.2)	79.5 (0.27)	80.3 (0.22)	80.6 (0.24)	3,150 (21.7)	6.0 (0.17)	5.2 (0.13)	4.5 (0.12)	148 (4.3)
Bachelor's or higher degree	89.4 (0.12)	89.0 (0.11)	89.0 (0.11)	11,422 (37.7)	85.9 (0.14)	85.7 (0.13)	86.1 (0.12)	11,051 (35.9)	4.0 (0.07)	3.8 (0.08)	3.2 (0.05)	371 (6.1)
55 to 64, all education levels	**64.1 (0.08)**	**64.3 (0.08)**	**64.1 (0.08)**	**25,665 (32.3)**	**59.9 (0.08)**	**60.5 (0.09)**	**60.9 (0.08)**	**24,394 (34.5)**	**6.6 (0.06)**	**5.9 (0.06)**	**4.9 (0.06)**	**1,270 (14.3)**
Less than high school completion	45.5 (0.26)	46.0 (0.26)	46.1 (0.26)	2,145 (18.7)	40.5 (0.26)	41.5 (0.27)	42.5 (0.26)	1,975 (18.1)	10.8 (0.24)	9.9 (0.25)	7.9 (0.22)	169 (4.8)
High school completion[4]	59.3 (0.15)	59.8 (0.17)	59.5 (0.16)	6,900 (28.6)	54.9 (0.15)	55.8 (0.17)	56.3 (0.16)	6,534 (27.3)	7.4 (0.11)	6.6 (0.12)	5.3 (0.11)	366 (8.2)
Some college, no degree	64.4 (0.19)	64.1 (0.19)	64.4 (0.18)	5,565 (26.1)	59.8 (0.20)	60.1 (0.19)	61.0 (0.19)	5,273 (25.1)	7.2 (0.12)	6.2 (0.13)	5.2 (0.10)	291 (6.0)
Associate's degree	69.2 (0.31)	69.1 (0.28)	68.4 (0.32)	2,378 (17.7)	65.0 (0.34)	65.2 (0.30)	65.2 (0.32)	2,268 (17.0)	6.2 (0.19)	5.7 (0.18)	4.6 (0.17)	110 (4.1)
Bachelor's or higher degree	74.5 (0.15)	74.6 (0.14)	74.2 (0.13)	8,677 (30.1)	71.0 (0.16)	71.5 (0.14)	71.4 (0.15)	8,344 (30.8)	4.8 (0.08)	4.2 (0.07)	3.8 (0.08)	334 (6.7)

[1]Percentage of the civilian population who are employed or seeking employment.
[2]Number of persons employed as a percentage of the civilian population.
[3]The percentage of persons in the civilian labor force who are not working and who made specific efforts to find employment sometime during the prior 4 weeks.
[4]Includes equivalency credentials, such as the GED credential.

NOTE: Race categories exclude persons of Hispanic ethnicity. Totals include racial/ethnic groups not separately shown. Standard errors were computed using replicate weights.

SOURCE: U.S. Department of Commerce, Census Bureau, American Community Survey (ACS), 2012, 2013, and 2014, unpublished tabulations. (This table was prepared February 2016.)

Table 501.20. Labor force participation, employment, and unemployment of persons 16 to 24 years old who are not enrolled in school, by age group, sex, race/ethnicity, and educational attainment: 2012, 2013, and 2014

[Standard errors appear in parentheses]

Age group, sex, race/ethnicity, and educational attainment	Labor force participation: Labor force participation rate[1] 2012	Labor force participation rate[1] 2013	Labor force participation rate[1] 2014	Number of participants (in thousands) 2014	Employment: Employment to population ratio[2] 2012	Employment to population ratio[2] 2013	Employment to population ratio[2] 2014	Number employed (in thousands) 2014	Unemployment: Unemployment rate[3] 2012	Unemployment rate[3] 2013	Unemployment rate[3] 2014	Number unemployed (in thousands) 2014
1	2	3	4	5	6	7	8	9	10	11	12	13
16 to 19 years old												
All persons, all education levels	64.1 (0.39)	64.3 (0.40)	65.0 (0.39)	1,573 (15.1)	43.5 (0.41)	45.5 (0.39)	48.2 (0.43)	1,166 (13.6)	32.1 (0.50)	29.2 (0.48)	25.8 (0.46)	406 (8.1)
Less than high school completion	47.9 (0.72)	47.1 (0.81)	49.3 (0.86)	338 (9.1)	27.6 (0.63)	28.4 (0.76)	32.0 (0.73)	220 (6.8)	42.5 (1.06)	39.7 (1.19)	35.0 (1.06)	119 (4.9)
High school completion[4]	70.3 (0.53)	70.2 (0.52)	70.6 (0.53)	1,020 (12.8)	48.6 (0.54)	50.3 (0.53)	53.4 (0.58)	770 (11.4)	30.8 (0.61)	28.4 (0.57)	24.5 (0.54)	249 (6.1)
At least some college	77.1 (1.03)	76.4 (1.09)	74.3 (1.00)	215 (5.8)	61.1 (1.22)	62.7 (1.09)	61.0 (1.11)	176 (5.3)	20.8 (1.12)	18.0 (0.92)	17.8 (1.15)	38 (2.7)
Male, all education levels	66.0 (0.52)	66.9 (0.61)	66.9 (0.48)	903 (11.7)	44.9 (0.49)	46.6 (0.55)	49.4 (0.52)	667 (10.3)	32.0 (0.59)	30.4 (0.56)	26.1 (0.56)	236 (5.8)
Less than high school completion	51.2 (1.09)	50.1 (1.13)	51.5 (1.11)	209 (7.1)	30.1 (0.90)	30.1 (0.96)	34.0 (0.90)	138 (5.5)	41.2 (1.30)	40.0 (1.37)	33.9 (1.24)	71 (3.4)
High school completion[4]	72.5 (0.63)	73.9 (0.71)	73.1 (0.64)	588 (9.8)	50.7 (0.65)	52.1 (0.66)	55.1 (0.71)	443 (8.9)	30.1 (0.75)	29.5 (0.72)	24.6 (0.68)	145 (4.3)
At least some college	77.2 (1.43)	76.6 (1.68)	75.4 (1.51)	106 (4.1)	60.2 (1.58)	62.6 (1.74)	61.2 (1.70)	86 (3.7)	22.1 (1.75)	18.2 (1.42)	18.8 (1.61)	20 (1.9)
Female, all education levels	61.5 (0.66)	60.9 (0.56)	62.7 (0.62)	670 (9.7)	41.6 (0.65)	44.1 (0.65)	46.7 (0.69)	499 (9.0)	32.3 (0.82)	27.5 (0.75)	25.5 (0.78)	171 (5.8)
Less than high school completion	43.0 (1.05)	42.7 (1.16)	46.0 (1.31)	129 (5.1)	23.8 (0.89)	26.0 (1.04)	29.0 (1.11)	82 (3.5)	44.7 (1.70)	39.1 (1.76)	36.8 (1.86)	48 (3.4)
High school completion[4]	67.2 (0.78)	65.5 (0.87)	67.6 (0.85)	432 (7.8)	45.8 (0.92)	48.0 (0.87)	51.2 (0.95)	327 (7.5)	31.8 (1.03)	26.8 (0.88)	24.3 (0.93)	105 (4.2)
At least some college	77.0 (1.34)	76.3 (1.33)	73.2 (1.36)	109 (4.1)	62.0 (1.56)	62.7 (1.68)	60.8 (1.39)	91 (3.8)	19.5 (1.57)	17.8 (1.48)	16.9 (1.56)	18 (1.8)
White, all education levels	68.8 (0.51)	68.5 (0.57)	69.2 (0.56)	818 (11.3)	50.4 (0.58)	51.4 (0.53)	53.8 (0.56)	636 (9.4)	26.7 (0.57)	24.9 (0.58)	22.2 (0.48)	182 (4.7)
Less than high school completion	49.6 (1.07)	49.5 (1.19)	50.9 (1.14)	155 (5.9)	29.1 (1.01)	31.2 (1.00)	34.6 (1.00)	105 (4.4)	41.3 (1.47)	36.9 (1.64)	32.1 (1.47)	50 (3.1)
High school completion[4]	74.8 (0.64)	74.1 (0.66)	75.3 (0.68)	545 (9.4)	56.3 (0.71)	56.1 (0.66)	59.3 (0.80)	429 (8.6)	24.8 (0.70)	24.3 (0.62)	21.2 (0.68)	115 (4.0)
At least some college	81.8 (1.20)	79.5 (1.30)	76.6 (1.46)	119 (4.4)	68.5 (1.36)	69.2 (1.22)	65.7 (1.50)	102 (4.0)	16.2 (1.27)	13.0 (1.18)	14.3 (1.16)	17 (1.5)
Black, all education levels	55.6 (1.12)	55.7 (0.82)	57.5 (1.15)	233 (7.1)	27.6 (1.02)	30.4 (0.97)	34.9 (0.96)	141 (5.0)	50.3 (1.39)	45.5 (1.55)	39.4 (1.43)	92 (4.6)
Less than high school completion	35.4 (1.75)	36.0 (1.65)	35.9 (2.13)	40 (3.0)	12.6 (1.25)	14.1 (1.41)	17.6 (1.81)	20 (2.2)	64.4 (2.97)	61.0 (3.33)	50.9 (3.68)	21 (2.0)
High school completion[4]	63.2 (1.36)	64.0 (1.34)	65.1 (1.36)	161 (5.6)	31.8 (1.47)	35.9 (1.38)	40.4 (1.35)	100 (4.3)	49.6 (1.85)	43.9 (1.90)	37.9 (1.77)	61 (3.7)
At least some college	75.8 (2.88)	68.6 (2.20)	69.8 (2.87)	31 (2.5)	50.1 (2.69)	46.7 (2.78)	47.6 (3.87)	21 (2.2)	33.9 (2.90)	31.9 (3.60)	31.8 (4.54)	10 (1.6)
Hispanic, all education levels	61.9 (0.72)	63.3 (0.88)	62.8 (0.82)	418 (9.8)	42.1 (0.67)	46.0 (0.83)	47.6 (0.87)	316 (8.4)	32.0 (0.96)	27.4 (0.96)	24.3 (0.86)	101 (4.2)
Less than high school completion	52.8 (1.48)	51.9 (1.66)	53.4 (1.57)	119 (5.2)	34.7 (1.27)	34.1 (1.60)	36.4 (1.52)	81 (4.2)	34.2 (1.79)	34.3 (1.97)	31.8 (1.90)	38 (2.8)
High school completion[4]	66.6 (1.05)	67.6 (1.19)	66.9 (1.10)	253 (7.2)	44.8 (1.11)	50.0 (1.13)	51.9 (1.14)	196 (6.2)	32.7 (1.33)	26.0 (1.18)	22.4 (0.99)	57 (2.9)
At least some college	71.2 (2.70)	75.9 (2.13)	71.8 (2.49)	46 (3.0)	56.1 (2.83)	61.4 (2.61)	60.9 (2.58)	39 (2.8)	21.2 (2.42)	19.1 (2.27)	15.2 (1.89)	7 (0.9)
Asian, all education levels	57.5 (3.08)	49.6 (3.11)	54.3 (3.21)	25 (2.3)	48.3 (3.36)	34.5 (2.34)	40.7 (3.11)	19 (1.9)	16.0 (2.76)	30.5 (3.48)	25.1 (3.45)	6 (1.0)
Less than high school completion	34.6 (5.69)	29.3 (3.44)	34.4 (4.91)	4 (0.8)	27.5 (5.25)	20.3 (3.55)	24.1 (4.95)	‡ (†)	20.5 (5.60)	30.8 (7.86)	29.7 (8.25)	‡ (†)
High school completion[4]	65.3 (4.12)	57.4 (4.60)	60.2 (4.60)	15 (1.7)	56.0 (4.27)	35.2 (3.77)	45.3 (4.41)	11 (1.4)	14.3 (3.29)	38.7 (5.59)	24.8 (4.55)	4 (0.8)
At least some college	61.8 (7.32)	67.4 (5.89)	64.2 (6.71)	6 (1.1)	49.6 (8.50)	56.7 (5.60)	49.6 (7.32)	5 (1.0)	19.8 ! (8.49)	15.9 ! (5.22)	22.7 ! (7.26)	‡ (†)
American Indian/Alaska Native, all education levels	56.1 (3.26)	53.2 (3.11)	54.3 (3.43)	14 (1.4)	28.3 (3.43)	34.1 (3.22)	37.4 (3.56)	10 (1.3)	49.6 (5.04)	35.8 (4.24)	31.2 (4.61)	4 (0.7)
Less than high school completion	45.7 (5.02)	42.0 (4.72)	41.9 (4.97)	4 (0.6)	17.3 (3.98)	26.3 (4.69)	25.3 (5.26)	‡ (†)	62.1 (8.22)	37.5 (7.65)	39.5 (9.25)	‡ (†)
High school completion[4]	63.6 (4.40)	61.8 (4.20)	55.1 (4.80)	7 (1.0)	36.4 (4.67)	40.1 (5.21)	37.5 (4.77)	5 (0.9)	42.7 (5.70)	35.1 (6.01)	31.9 (6.20)	2 (0.5)
At least some college	66.7 (7.65)	58.2 (8.60)	79.1 (6.33)	3 (0.7)	38.3 (8.74)	38.0 (8.31)	63.3 (8.90)	‡ (†)	42.6 (11.01)	‡ (†)	20.0 ! (9.31)	‡ (†)
20 to 24 years old												
All persons, all education levels	80.5 (0.13)	80.7 (0.15)	80.7 (0.15)	10,595 (38.5)	66.6 (0.18)	67.9 (0.19)	69.5 (0.19)	9,122 (39.1)	17.3 (0.18)	15.9 (0.18)	13.9 (0.17)	1,473 (18.1)
Less than high school completion	64.2 (0.47)	63.3 (0.51)	63.5 (0.48)	1,148 (12.0)	45.3 (0.44)	46.7 (0.53)	48.4 (0.51)	874 (11.1)	29.5 (0.58)	26.2 (0.50)	23.9 (0.55)	274 (6.9)
High school completion[4]	78.4 (0.24)	78.5 (0.27)	77.9 (0.19)	4,209 (24.9)	62.4 (0.30)	63.6 (0.34)	64.7 (0.25)	3,494 (23.4)	20.4 (0.30)	18.9 (0.28)	17.0 (0.27)	716 (12.3)
Some college, no degree	85.3 (0.27)	85.8 (0.31)	85.4 (0.26)	2,842 (21.8)	72.7 (0.36)	74.0 (0.34)	75.6 (0.35)	2,515 (21.1)	14.7 (0.33)	13.7 (0.27)	11.5 (0.29)	327 (8.4)
Associate's degree	89.4 (0.60)	90.8 (0.43)	90.8 (0.46)	611 (11.4)	81.2 (0.72)	82.9 (0.54)	84.5 (0.60)	569 (10.8)	9.2 (0.53)	8.7 (0.53)	6.9 (0.39)	42 (2.5)
Bachelor's or higher degree	93.8 (0.25)	93.4 (0.21)	93.3 (0.27)	1,785 (18.6)	87.0 (0.35)	87.1 (0.27)	87.3 (0.34)	1,670 (18.1)	7.2 (0.27)	6.7 (0.25)	6.4 (0.25)	115 (4.5)

See notes at end of table.

Table 501.20. Labor force participation, employment, and unemployment of persons 16 to 24 years old who are not enrolled in school, by age group, sex, race/ethnicity, and educational attainment: 2012, 2013, and 2014—Continued

[Standard errors appear in parentheses]

Age group, sex, race/ethnicity, and educational attainment	Labor force participation: Labor force participation rate[1], 2012	Labor force participation rate[1], 2013	Labor force participation rate[1], 2014	Number of participants (in thousands), 2014	Employment: Employment to population ratio[2], 2012	Employment to population ratio[2], 2013	Employment to population ratio[2], 2014	Number employed (in thousands), 2014	Unemployment: Unemployment rate[3], 2012	Unemployment rate[3], 2013	Unemployment rate[3], 2014	Number unemployed (in thousands), 2014
1	2	3	4	5	6	7	8	9	10	11	12	13
Male, all education levels	**83.0 (0.17)**	**82.9 (0.18)**	**83.0 (0.22)**	**5,839 (27.8)**	**67.8 (0.24)**	**69.1 (0.24)**	**71.0 (0.26)**	**4,997 (26.7)**	**18.2 (0.23)**	**16.6 (0.23)**	**14.4 (0.21)**	**842 (12.8)**
Less than high school completion	69.7 (0.57)	68.4 (0.62)	68.4 (0.59)	734 (10.8)	50.7 (0.65)	52.0 (0.68)	53.7 (0.65)	576 (9.6)	27.1 (0.74)	24.0 (0.61)	21.5 (0.68)	158 (5.6)
High school completion[4]	81.9 (0.27)	81.8 (0.30)	81.3 (0.29)	2,567 (19.7)	65.1 (0.39)	66.3 (0.40)	67.5 (0.33)	2,129 (17.4)	20.5 (0.38)	19.0 (0.36)	17.1 (0.32)	438 (9.1)
Some college, no degree	88.2 (0.31)	88.4 (0.37)	88.1 (0.36)	1,495 (17.8)	74.7 (0.45)	75.6 (0.49)	78.0 (0.48)	1,323 (16.5)	15.2 (0.41)	14.5 (0.40)	11.5 (0.37)	172 (5.9)
Associate's degree	92.2 (0.70)	93.2 (0.59)	92.1 (0.74)	280 (7.4)	82.8 (1.02)	85.3 (0.88)	85.9 (0.95)	261 (7.1)	10.2 (0.85)	8.5 (0.77)	6.8 (0.56)	19 (1.6)
Bachelor's or higher degree	94.9 (0.30)	94.1 (0.34)	94.9 (0.31)	763 (11.2)	87.0 (0.50)	87.3 (0.49)	88.0 (0.42)	707 (10.7)	8.4 (0.39)	7.2 (0.42)	7.2 (0.38)	55 (3.1)
Female, all education levels	**77.7 (0.21)**	**78.2 (0.22)**	**78.1 (0.20)**	**4,756 (23.8)**	**65.1 (0.27)**	**66.5 (0.26)**	**67.8 (0.27)**	**4,125 (24.8)**	**16.2 (0.24)**	**15.0 (0.22)**	**13.3 (0.26)**	**632 (12.3)**
Less than high school completion	56.0 (0.81)	55.5 (0.76)	56.4 (0.72)	415 (7.7)	37.0 (0.74)	38.6 (0.73)	40.6 (0.70)	298 (6.4)	33.9 (1.07)	30.4 (0.90)	28.1 (0.95)	117 (4.7)
High school completion[4]	73.6 (0.39)	73.9 (0.45)	73.1 (0.37)	1,642 (16.3)	58.6 (0.48)	59.9 (0.51)	60.7 (0.48)	1,365 (16.5)	20.4 (0.46)	18.8 (0.42)	16.9 (0.48)	277 (7.9)
Some college, no degree	82.3 (0.42)	83.1 (0.46)	82.7 (0.39)	1,347 (14.0)	70.7 (0.54)	72.3 (0.51)	73.2 (0.51)	1,192 (13.8)	14.0 (0.47)	13.0 (0.40)	11.5 (0.43)	155 (6.0)
Associate's degree	87.0 (0.89)	88.6 (0.72)	89.7 (0.66)	331 (8.0)	79.7 (1.01)	80.7 (0.84)	83.4 (0.80)	308 (7.7)	8.3 (0.65)	8.9 (0.74)	7.0 (0.54)	23 (1.9)
Bachelor's or higher degree	93.0 (0.32)	93.0 (0.31)	92.2 (0.41)	1,022 (13.7)	87.0 (0.41)	87.1 (0.42)	86.8 (0.49)	962 (13.3)	6.4 (0.33)	6.3 (0.32)	5.9 (0.32)	60 (3.4)
White, all education levels	**84.1 (0.17)**	**84.0 (0.19)**	**83.8 (0.18)**	**5,903 (28.5)**	**72.4 (0.20)**	**73.0 (0.25)**	**74.4 (0.22)**	**5,238 (28.3)**	**14.0 (0.20)**	**13.2 (0.21)**	**11.3 (0.20)**	**665 (12.0)**
Less than high school completion	64.6 (0.80)	64.1 (0.70)	63.9 (0.78)	424 (7.9)	45.0 (0.70)	46.6 (0.78)	49.3 (0.85)	328 (7.1)	30.2 (1.00)	27.4 (0.81)	22.8 (0.86)	97 (4.0)
High school completion[4]	81.1 (0.34)	81.0 (0.34)	80.1 (0.27)	2,215 (20.8)	66.6 (0.39)	67.4 (0.44)	68.3 (0.34)	1,889 (19.7)	17.8 (0.35)	16.7 (0.37)	14.7 (0.33)	325 (7.7)
Some college, no degree	86.7 (0.35)	87.1 (0.38)	86.5 (0.35)	1,578 (15.9)	76.7 (0.45)	77.1 (0.50)	78.2 (0.39)	1,427 (15.6)	11.6 (0.38)	11.4 (0.38)	9.6 (0.32)	151 (5.2)
Associate's degree	91.5 (0.61)	92.2 (0.55)	91.8 (0.59)	408 (8.5)	84.5 (0.78)	85.8 (0.69)	86.6 (0.71)	385 (8.3)	7.7 (0.59)	6.9 (0.55)	5.7 (0.46)	23 (1.9)
Bachelor's or higher degree	95.6 (0.24)	94.9 (0.25)	95.1 (0.24)	1,278 (14.3)	89.9 (0.31)	89.6 (0.32)	90.0 (0.35)	1,209 (13.4)	6.0 (0.27)	5.6 (0.28)	5.4 (0.28)	68 (3.8)
Black, all education levels	**73.0 (0.45)**	**74.0 (0.48)**	**74.5 (0.44)**	**1,583 (17.2)**	**50.4 (0.61)**	**53.8 (0.52)**	**56.0 (0.50)**	**1,190 (15.7)**	**30.9 (0.61)**	**27.4 (0.55)**	**24.8 (0.51)**	**393 (9.0)**
Less than high school completion	53.3 (1.09)	51.3 (1.09)	52.9 (1.05)	183 (5.7)	25.6 (0.95)	27.4 (1.04)	29.1 (0.91)	101 (4.0)	52.1 (1.60)	46.6 (1.43)	45.0 (1.47)	82 (3.8)
High school completion[4]	71.1 (0.61)	73.2 (0.69)	72.6 (0.69)	704 (13.4)	47.7 (0.76)	51.3 (0.71)	52.0 (0.80)	505 (11.3)	32.9 (0.81)	29.9 (0.72)	28.3 (0.78)	199 (6.5)
Some college, no degree	84.0 (0.72)	84.7 (0.69)	84.2 (0.78)	493 (11.0)	63.0 (1.08)	66.1 (0.90)	69.4 (0.93)	406 (10.4)	25.0 (1.01)	22.0 (0.91)	17.7 (0.77)	87 (4.0)
Associate's degree	86.3 (1.98)	89.7 (1.66)	88.4 (1.83)	63 (4.0)	73.0 (2.75)	77.1 (2.23)	76.8 (2.44)	55 (3.6)	15.4 (2.47)	14.1 (2.21)	13.2 (2.27)	8 (1.6)
Bachelor's or higher degree	92.9 (1.03)	92.9 (1.08)	92.1 (1.08)	141 (5.3)	81.1 (1.46)	83.0 (1.51)	81.3 (1.40)	124 (5.1)	12.7 (1.37)	10.7 (1.24)	11.7 (1.10)	16 (1.6)
Hispanic, all education levels	**77.8 (0.32)**	**78.3 (0.34)**	**79.1 (0.33)**	**2,390 (17.8)**	**64.5 (0.38)**	**66.6 (0.44)**	**68.8 (0.42)**	**2,080 (18.7)**	**17.1 (0.38)**	**15.0 (0.38)**	**13.0 (0.36)**	**310 (8.6)**
Less than high school completion	69.4 (0.72)	69.2 (0.79)	69.5 (0.77)	477 (9.2)	55.0 (0.83)	57.1 (0.88)	58.2 (0.85)	400 (8.6)	20.7 (0.81)	17.5 (0.74)	16.2 (0.83)	77 (4.3)
High school completion[4]	78.3 (0.51)	78.0 (0.48)	78.4 (0.41)	1,057 (13.8)	64.3 (0.60)	65.3 (0.64)	67.3 (0.52)	908 (12.9)	17.9 (0.57)	16.2 (0.51)	14.1 (0.50)	149 (5.6)
Some college, no degree	83.4 (0.54)	84.7 (0.69)	84.9 (0.72)	585 (11.1)	71.2 (0.73)	74.1 (0.81)	75.8 (0.91)	522 (10.9)	14.6 (0.67)	12.5 (0.69)	10.7 (0.64)	63 (3.8)
Associate's degree	84.0 (1.80)	87.6 (1.34)	88.9 (1.22)	102 (4.4)	74.5 (1.90)	76.7 (1.81)	82.1 (1.34)	94 (3.9)	11.4 (1.46)	12.5 (1.66)	7.6 (1.25)	8 (1.4)
Bachelor's or higher degree	91.2 (0.85)	91.7 (0.89)	92.3 (0.85)	170 (6.1)	81.7 (1.31)	83.3 (1.13)	84.9 (1.16)	156 (5.9)	10.4 (1.30)	9.1 (0.94)	8.0 (0.80)	14 (1.4)
Asian, all education levels	**78.9 (0.73)**	**77.3 (0.77)**	**78.6 (0.86)**	**324 (7.0)**	**68.3 (0.97)**	**68.4 (0.94)**	**70.6 (1.00)**	**291 (6.8)**	**13.4 (0.83)**	**11.5 (0.79)**	**10.2 (0.74)**	**33 (2.5)**
Less than high school completion	61.2 (3.18)	60.2 (3.95)	61.9 (3.49)	24 (2.0)	49.3 (3.69)	50.7 (3.99)	49.6 (3.14)	19 (1.6)	19.5 (3.45)	15.8 (3.50)	19.9 (3.10)	5 (0.9)
High school completion[4]	78.9 (1.75)	71.8 (1.68)	71.7 (1.96)	69 (3.9)	65.6 (2.13)	61.4 (2.19)	64.0 (2.22)	62 (3.8)	16.9 (1.93)	14.4 (1.85)	10.7 (1.48)	7 (1.0)
Some college, no degree	80.0 (2.00)	75.3 (2.27)	82.9 (1.77)	68 (3.2)	68.2 (2.29)	67.3 (2.31)	72.7 (2.23)	60 (3.0)	14.8 (1.70)	10.6 (1.40)	12.3 (1.68)	8 (1.2)
Associate's degree	81.2 (3.87)	80.7 (4.04)	87.3 (2.87)	18 (1.5)	71.8 (4.44)	70.7 (5.08)	82.2 (3.39)	17 (1.4)	11.5 (3.42)	12.3 (3.61)	5.9 ! (2.06)	‡ (†)
Bachelor's or higher degree	82.7 (1.23)	83.8 (1.03)	83.2 (1.06)	145 (4.0)	74.5 (1.42)	75.5 (1.20)	76.7 (1.14)	133 (3.8)	10.0 (1.07)	9.9 (1.01)	7.8 (0.80)	11 (1.2)
American Indian/Alaska Native, all education levels	**71.8 (1.39)**	**67.9 (1.75)**	**67.1 (1.53)**	**85 (3.4)**	**50.6 (1.72)**	**48.0 (1.72)**	**51.2 (1.75)**	**65 (3.3)**	**29.5 (1.82)**	**29.3 (1.94)**	**23.6 (1.76)**	**20 (1.5)**
Less than high school completion	55.9 (3.41)	52.5 (3.50)	56.2 (2.98)	14 (1.5)	32.1 (3.53)	30.6 (3.32)	34.3 (2.93)	9 (1.1)	42.5 (4.49)	41.8 (5.16)	38.9 (4.09)	6 (0.8)
High school completion[4]	73.0 (1.68)	65.4 (2.44)	65.0 (2.15)	41 (2.2)	50.3 (2.25)	45.2 (2.58)	50.2 (2.22)	31 (2.1)	31.0 (2.44)	30.8 (3.13)	22.8 (2.31)	9 (1.0)
Some college, no degree	79.0 (2.84)	79.8 (2.32)	75.4 (3.02)	23 (2.2)	61.2 (3.13)	60.7 (3.32)	60.2 (3.41)	18 (2.0)	22.5 (2.76)	23.9 (3.62)	20.2 (3.27)	5 (0.9)
Associate's degree	86.3 (5.12)	89.8 (5.17)	85.7 (6.60)	‡ (†)	76.3 (7.99)	83.0 (6.10)	75.2 (8.81)	‡ (†)	‡ (†)	‡ (†)	‡ (†)	‡ (†)
Bachelor's or higher degree	89.7 (4.84)	87.7 (4.03)	87.6 (6.14)	4 (0.9)	72.4 (10.74)	66.7 (7.86)	83.8 (6.73)	‡ (†)	‡ (†)	23.9 ! (9.08)	‡ (†)	‡ (†)

†Not applicable.
!Interpret data with caution. The coefficient of variation (CV) for this estimate is between 30 and 50 percent.
‡Reporting standards not met. Either there are too few cases for a reliable estimate or the coefficient of variation (CV) is 50 percent or greater.
[1]Percentage of the civilian population who are employed or seeking employment.
[2]Number of persons employed as a percentage of the civilian population.
[3]The percentage of persons in the civilian labor force who are not working and who made specific efforts to find employment sometime during the prior 4 weeks.
[4]Includes equivalency credentials, such as the GED credential.
NOTE: Table excludes persons enrolled in school. Race categories exclude persons of Hispanic ethnicity. Totals include racial/ethnic groups not separately shown. Standard errors were computed using replicate weights.
SOURCE: U.S. Department of Commerce, Census Bureau, American Community Survey (ACS), 2012, 2013, and 2014, unpublished tabulations. (This table was prepared February 2016.)

Table 501.30. Number and percentage of persons 18 to 24 years old who were neither enrolled in school nor working, by educational attainment, age group, sex, family poverty status, and race/ethnicity: 2015

[Standard errors appear in parentheses]

Age group, sex, family poverty status, and race/ethnicity	Total (in thousands)		Neither enrolled in school nor working: Number (in thousands)		Percentage distribution		Percent, by educational attainment: Total		Less than high school completion		High school completion[1]		Some college, no bachelor's degree[2]		Bachelor's or higher degree	
1	2		3		4		5		6		7		8		9	
Total, 18 and 19 years old	**7,900**	**(82.2)**	**1,018**	**(44.4)**	**100.0**	**(†)**	**12.9**	**(0.54)**	**10.4**	**(0.81)**	**24.6**	**(1.28)**	**4.8**	**(0.56)**	**‡**	**(†)**
Male	3,962	(59.1)	534	(31.9)	52.5	(2.16)	13.5	(0.77)	10.5	(0.92)	24.2	(1.72)	5.9	(1.00)	‡	(†)
Female	3,938	(61.3)	484	(30.5)	47.5	(2.16)	12.3	(0.74)	10.3	(1.24)	25.1	(1.90)	4.0	(0.71)	‡	(†)
White	4,293	(61.3)	476	(31.4)	46.7	(2.21)	11.1	(0.69)	7.9	(0.89)	23.8	(1.85)	3.6	(0.68)	‡	(†)
Black	1,094	(35.6)	196	(19.2)	19.2	(1.68)	17.9	(1.63)	15.2	(2.40)	30.3	(3.89)	7.7 !	(2.57)	‡	(†)
Hispanic	1,771	(39.3)	285	(21.8)	28.0	(1.78)	16.1	(1.19)	14.4	(1.63)	25.0	(2.59)	7.6	(1.65)	‡	(†)
Asian	379	(21.2)	‡	(†)	1.8 !	(0.55)	4.8	(1.42)	‡	(†)	8.3 !	(3.56)	3.9 !	(1.82)	‡	(†)
Pacific Islander	36	(8.6)	‡	(†)	‡	(†)	‡	(†)	‡	(†)	‡	(†)	‡	(†)	‡	(†)
American Indian/Alaska Native	76	(11.0)	‡	(†)	1.3 !	(0.44)	18.0	(5.00)	8.5 !	(3.94)	‡	(†)	‡	(†)	‡	(†)
Two or more races	251	(17.9)	‡	(†)	2.6	(0.71)	10.6	(2.80)	‡	(†)	22.0	(6.20)	‡	(†)	‡	(†)
Poor[3]	1,503	(57.8)	386	(28.1)	37.9	(2.11)	25.7	(1.61)	21.6	(2.57)	43.8	(3.44)	9.3	(2.28)	‡	(†)
Nonpoor[3]	6,398	(91.0)	632	(33.9)	62.1	(2.11)	9.9	(0.50)	7.3	(0.71)	19.8	(1.38)	4.1	(0.56)	‡	(†)
Total, 20 to 24 years old	**22,215**	**(21.7)**	**3,852**	**(96.9)**	**100.0**	**(†)**	**17.3**	**(0.44)**	**41.2**	**(1.91)**	**28.4**	**(0.89)**	**8.7**	**(0.42)**	**7.8**	**(0.76)**
Male	11,201	(21.1)	1,741	(72.7)	45.2	(1.27)	15.5	(0.65)	32.9	(2.46)	24.8	(1.24)	7.5	(0.66)	6.5	(1.21)
Female	11,014	(3.9)	2,112	(63.6)	54.8	(1.27)	19.2	(0.58)	50.4	(2.99)	32.9	(1.24)	9.8	(0.63)	8.8	(1.06)
White	12,219	(33.8)	1,793	(74.1)	46.5	(1.26)	14.7	(0.60)	43.3	(3.66)	25.8	(1.34)	8.0	(0.66)	6.3	(0.93)
Black	3,249	(23.7)	755	(38.9)	19.6	(0.94)	23.2	(1.20)	48.0	(4.29)	35.8	(2.39)	10.9	(1.34)	10.8	(3.15)
Hispanic	4,717	(7.4)	1,014	(42.9)	26.3	(1.02)	21.5	(0.91)	36.9	(2.54)	28.9	(1.63)	10.0	(0.95)	11.6	(2.29)
Asian	1,268	(29.6)	115	(15.6)	3.0	(0.39)	9.1	(1.21)	‡	(†)	12.4 !	(3.75)	5.8	(1.30)	11.1	(2.43)
Pacific Islander	81	(14.2)	‡	(†)	0.5 !	(0.14)	22.1	(6.00)	‡	(†)	24.0 !	(8.88)	‡	(†)	‡	(†)
American Indian/Alaska Native	204	(23.9)	78	(13.2)	2.0	(0.34)	38.4	(5.05)	61.6	(11.93)	57.8	(7.42)	15.7 !	(6.97)	‡	(†)
Two or more races	476	(26.6)	79	(13.5)	2.1	(0.35)	16.6	(2.57)	‡	(†)	29.0	(5.37)	7.2 !	(2.78)	14.9 !	(5.24)
Family poverty status																
Poor[3]	4,451	(111.1)	1,368	(57.5)	100.0	(†)	30.7	(1.17)	53.7	(2.52)	44.8	(2.05)	13.4	(1.40)	12.2	(2.60)
White	2,098	(83.7)	592	(42.7)	43.2	(2.28)	28.2	(1.88)	57.5	(5.71)	46.9	(3.38)	13.0	(2.07)	10.2 !	(3.06)
Black	915	(42.4)	332	(28.6)	24.3	(1.75)	36.3	(2.63)	53.4	(6.21)	48.8	(4.34)	17.1	(3.51)	‡	(†)
Hispanic	1,017	(47.5)	352	(26.1)	25.7	(1.84)	34.6	(2.12)	49.3	(3.60)	38.2	(3.79)	14.0	(2.72)	35.3 !	(12.11)
Asian	265	(31.0)	‡	(†)	1.8	(0.53)	9.4	(2.62)	‡	(†)	‡	(†)	6.8 !	(2.79)	‡	(†)
Pacific Islander	‡	(†)	‡	(†)	0.7 !	(0.31)	49.2	(13.84)	‡	(†)	‡	(†)	‡	(†)	‡	(†)
American Indian/Alaska Native	45	(9.5)	‡	(†)	1.9 !	(0.59)	59.6	(10.63)	‡	(†)	‡	(†)	‡	(†)	‡	(†)
Two or more races	91	(16.1)	‡	(†)	2.2	(0.64)	33.9	(7.98)	‡	(†)	‡	(†)	‡	(†)	‡	(†)
Nonpoor[3]	17,764	(114.3)	2,484	(80.7)	100.0	(†)	14.0	(0.44)	32.7	(2.28)	23.8	(0.95)	7.7	(0.44)	7.2	(0.79)
White	10,122	(85.3)	1,201	(60.7)	48.4	(1.62)	11.9	(0.59)	33.6	(4.12)	21.3	(1.31)	7.0	(0.69)	5.7	(0.97)
Black	2,334	(46.6)	423	(33.2)	17.0	(1.29)	18.1	(1.35)	43.4	(6.07)	29.3	(2.68)	9.0	(1.31)	9.3 !	(3.26)
Hispanic	3,700	(48.3)	662	(37.1)	26.7	(1.30)	17.9	(0.94)	28.9	(3.21)	26.3	(1.81)	9.3	(1.00)	8.5	(2.11)
Asian	1,003	(38.0)	90	(14.3)	3.6	(0.55)	9.0	(1.35)	‡	(†)	13.3	(3.99)	5.5	(1.39)	12.6	(2.92)
Pacific Islander	60	(13.1)	‡	(†)	0.3 !	(0.15)	12.8 !	(5.74)	‡	(†)	‡	(†)	‡	(†)	‡	(†)
American Indian/Alaska Native	160	(21.4)	52	(10.9)	2.1	(0.44)	32.5	(5.72)	‡	(†)	55.4	(8.33)	14.8 !	(7.40)	‡	(†)
Two or more races	386	(25.2)	49	(10.1)	2.0	(0.41)	12.6	(2.40)	‡	(†)	21.1	(5.38)	7.1 !	(2.99)	14.7 !	(5.32)

†Not applicable.
!Interpret data with caution. The coefficient of variation (CV) for this estimate is between 30 and 50 percent.
‡Reporting standards not met. Either there are too few cases for a reliable estimate or the coefficient of variation (CV) is 50 percent or greater.
[1]Includes equivalency credentials, such as the GED credential.
[2]Includes persons with no college degree as well as those with an associate's degree.
[3]Poor is defined to include families with incomes below the poverty threshold. Nonpoor is defined to include families with incomes at or above the poverty threshold. For information about how the Census Bureau determines who is in poverty, see http://www.census.gov/hhes/www/poverty/about/overview/measure.html.
NOTE: Race categories exclude persons of Hispanic ethnicity. Standard errors were computed using replicate weights. Detail may not sum to totals because of rounding.
SOURCE: U.S. Department of Commerce, Census Bureau, Current Population Survey (CPS), Annual Social and Economic Supplement, 2015. (This table was prepared October 2015.)

Table 501.40. Percentage distribution of 25- to 34-year-olds with various levels of educational attainment, by labor force status, sex, race/ethnicity, and U.S. nativity and citizenship status: 2014

[Standard errors appear in parentheses]

Sex, race/ethnicity, and U.S. nativity and citizenship status	All 25- to 34-year-olds			Less than high school completion			High school completion[1]			Some college, no bachelor's degree[2]			Bachelor's or higher degree		
	In labor force			In labor force			In labor force			In labor force			In labor force		
	Employed	Unemployed (seeking employment)	Not in labor force	Employed	Unemployed (seeking employment)	Not in labor force	Employed	Unemployed (seeking employment)	Not in labor force	Employed	Unemployed (seeking employment)	Not in labor force	Employed	Unemployed (seeking employment)	Not in labor force
1	2	3	4	5	6	7	8	9	10	11	12	13	14	15	16
Total	**75.6 (0.09)**	**6.2 (0.05)**	**18.2 (0.07)**	**55.0 (0.33)**	**9.5 (0.20)**	**35.4 (0.32)**	**68.5 (0.19)**	**8.5 (0.12)**	**23.1 (0.16)**	**76.7 (0.15)**	**6.6 (0.10)**	**16.7 (0.13)**	**86.3 (0.11)**	**3.1 (0.07)**	**10.6 (0.11)**
Sex															
Male	80.2 (0.11)	6.6 (0.07)	13.3 (0.09)	65.2 (0.40)	9.5 (0.24)	25.4 (0.39)	74.4 (0.21)	8.6 (0.16)	16.9 (0.16)	81.7 (0.22)	6.6 (0.14)	11.7 (0.16)	90.3 (0.16)	3.4 (0.10)	6.3 (0.14)
Female	71.0 (0.13)	5.8 (0.07)	23.2 (0.11)	41.2 (0.48)	9.6 (0.30)	49.2 (0.48)	60.3 (0.34)	8.3 (0.18)	31.4 (0.30)	72.1 (0.21)	6.5 (0.13)	21.4 (0.21)	83.1 (0.19)	2.9 (0.08)	14.0 (0.17)
Race/ethnicity															
White	78.7 (0.12)	5.2 (0.07)	16.1 (0.10)	49.1 (0.59)	11.5 (0.35)	39.4 (0.53)	70.1 (0.26)	7.6 (0.16)	22.3 (0.24)	78.1 (0.19)	5.6 (0.10)	16.3 (0.18)	88.2 (0.13)	2.6 (0.07)	9.2 (0.12)
Black	67.5 (0.28)	11.3 (0.18)	21.2 (0.21)	35.6 (0.81)	16.9 (0.66)	47.6 (0.85)	59.2 (0.48)	14.0 (0.39)	26.8 (0.42)	73.8 (0.46)	10.6 (0.32)	15.6 (0.33)	86.8 (0.53)	5.3 (0.32)	7.9 (0.41)
Hispanic	73.2 (0.21)	6.2 (0.11)	20.6 (0.20)	64.3 (0.44)	6.5 (0.27)	29.2 (0.42)	71.8 (0.41)	6.8 (0.26)	21.4 (0.37)	77.0 (0.37)	6.2 (0.20)	16.7 (0.35)	84.4 (0.42)	4.3 (0.24)	11.3 (0.35)
Asian	74.5 (0.32)	4.0 (0.16)	21.5 (0.29)	61.2 (1.72)	6.3 (0.76)	32.6 (1.79)	69.6 (1.10)	5.8 (0.67)	24.6 (1.07)	71.2 (0.82)	5.0 (0.31)	23.8 (0.76)	77.5 (0.41)	3.1 (0.16)	19.4 (0.40)
Pacific Islander	72.3 (1.96)	6.8 (1.18)	20.9 (1.96)	56.9 (5.39)	3.7 ! (1.81)	39.3 (5.45)	72.0 (3.40)	7.9 (2.12)	20.0 (2.95)	73.4 (3.51)	7.0 (1.85)	19.7 (3.00)	85.0 (3.75)	5.9 ! (2.37)	9.1 ! (2.92)
American Indian/Alaska Native[3]	56.6 (0.91)	10.7 (0.63)	32.7 (0.92)	32.2 (2.26)	14.6 (1.67)	53.3 (2.46)	49.6 (1.68)	13.6 (1.15)	36.8 (1.50)	64.6 (1.79)	8.3 (1.03)	27.2 (1.76)	82.1 (2.42)	5.0 ! (1.61)	12.9 (1.92)
American Indian	56.7 (1.02)	10.2 (0.71)	33.1 (1.04)	30.0 (2.49)	15.2 (1.87)	54.7 (2.62)	48.8 (1.81)	12.4 (1.22)	38.8 (1.79)	64.9 (1.91)	8.0 (1.12)	27.2 (1.88)	84.5 (2.23)	5.3 ! (1.77)	10.2 (1.61)
Alaska Native	54.6 (3.84)	15.6 (2.38)	29.8 (3.56)	24.0 ! (8.39)	27.3 ! (8.61)	48.7 (10.99)	57.3 (5.61)	16.2 (3.32)	26.6 (5.07)	61.7 (7.33)	13.1 ! (4.03)	25.2 (5.83)	‡ (†)	‡ (†)	‡ (†)
Two or more races	73.2 (0.62)	7.5 (0.38)	19.3 (0.49)	46.3 (2.51)	9.1 (1.55)	44.6 (2.41)	65.3 (1.45)	9.8 (0.91)	24.9 (1.18)	72.6 (0.99)	8.3 (0.71)	19.1 (0.77)	83.8 (0.80)	4.9 (0.52)	11.3 (0.66)
Race/ethnicity by sex															
Male															
White	83.1 (0.15)	5.8 (0.10)	11.1 (0.11)	57.9 (0.79)	12.4 (0.45)	29.7 (0.70)	76.3 (0.30)	8.1 (0.22)	15.6 (0.24)	84.2 (0.24)	5.6 (0.15)	10.2 (0.19)	91.7 (0.16)	3.0 (0.10)	5.2 (0.14)
Black	64.4 (0.41)	12.0 (0.29)	23.7 (0.34)	30.4 (1.04)	17.3 (0.88)	52.3 (1.14)	58.3 (0.69)	13.8 (0.54)	27.9 (0.57)	73.6 (0.76)	11.0 (0.51)	15.4 (0.55)	86.9 (0.80)	5.4 (0.49)	7.7 (0.58)
Hispanic	82.1 (0.24)	5.9 (0.17)	12.0 (0.20)	79.5 (0.45)	5.5 (0.29)	15.0 (0.41)	81.4 (0.43)	6.4 (0.34)	12.2 (0.34)	82.9 (0.47)	6.2 (0.30)	10.9 (0.40)	88.7 (0.53)	4.5 (0.39)	6.8 (0.46)
Asian	82.1 (0.44)	4.4 (0.23)	13.5 (0.40)	71.0 (2.24)	8.5 (1.29)	20.5 (2.05)	78.9 (1.31)	6.3 (1.01)	14.8 (0.92)	74.5 (1.11)	6.4 (0.53)	19.1 (1.00)	86.4 (0.52)	3.0 (0.25)	10.6 (0.48)
Pacific Islander	80.5 (2.83)	6.6 (1.79)	12.9 (2.53)	82.1 (6.48)	‡ (†)	14.6 ! (5.11)	78.1 (4.29)	8.9 ! (3.12)	13.0 (3.53)	80.1 (5.51)	‡ (†)	15.5 ! (4.90)	90.0 (4.86)	‡ (†)	‡ (†)
American Indian/Alaska Native[3]	57.5 (1.48)	12.6 (1.11)	29.9 (1.21)	36.4 (3.04)	14.7 (2.08)	48.9 (3.16)	52.2 (2.49)	16.1 (1.89)	31.6 (2.00)	66.2 (2.88)	9.2 (1.86)	24.6 (2.43)	80.7 (4.09)	7.5 ! (3.46)	11.7 (2.72)
American Indian	58.0 (1.54)	12.0 (1.16)	30.0 (1.39)	32.7 (3.45)	15.4 (2.37)	51.9 (3.58)	53.7 (2.67)	14.3 (1.86)	32.0 (2.47)	66.3 (3.13)	9.3 (2.04)	24.4 (2.59)	83.0 (4.07)	8.0 ! (3.90)	9.0 (2.30)
Alaska Native	51.5 (5.48)	17.3 (3.24)	31.2 (4.59)	‡ (†)	‡ (†)	‡ (†)	54.5 (8.17)	17.2 (3.93)	28.3 (7.00)	‡ (†)	‡ (†)	‡ (†)	‡ (†)	‡ (†)	‡ (†)
Two or more races	76.2 (0.95)	8.0 (0.63)	15.9 (0.66)	53.6 (3.25)	8.8 (1.99)	37.5 (3.04)	70.3 (1.85)	10.1 (1.33)	19.6 (1.41)	75.9 (1.60)	8.4 (1.10)	15.8 (1.24)	86.4 (1.19)	5.7 (0.85)	7.9 (0.96)
Female															
White	74.3 (0.16)	4.6 (0.09)	21.1 (0.15)	36.8 (0.85)	10.2 (0.55)	53.0 (0.84)	61.1 (0.47)	6.8 (0.25)	32.1 (0.42)	72.2 (0.27)	5.5 (0.15)	22.2 (0.28)	85.3 (0.22)	2.3 (0.08)	12.4 (0.20)
Black	70.4 (0.38)	10.7 (0.25)	18.9 (0.30)	42.4 (1.31)	16.3 (0.83)	41.3 (1.33)	60.2 (0.86)	14.2 (0.58)	25.5 (0.80)	73.9 (0.49)	10.3 (0.36)	15.7 (0.42)	86.7 (0.63)	5.3 (0.38)	8.1 (0.53)
Hispanic	63.5 (0.36)	6.5 (0.16)	30.0 (0.33)	43.0 (0.66)	7.8 (0.42)	49.2 (0.73)	59.6 (0.68)	7.2 (0.37)	33.2 (0.62)	71.8 (0.57)	6.3 (0.26)	21.9 (0.55)	81.2 (0.63)	4.2 (0.28)	14.5 (0.54)
Asian	67.6 (0.51)	3.6 (0.19)	28.8 (0.49)	51.5 (2.55)	4.1 (0.86)	44.4 (2.58)	60.6 (1.67)	5.2 (0.71)	34.2 (1.83)	68.1 (1.20)	3.7 (0.43)	28.2 (1.20)	69.9 (0.60)	3.2 (0.19)	26.8 (0.58)
Pacific Islander	64.7 (3.17)	7.0 (1.54)	28.4 (3.09)	35.5 (8.53)	‡ (†)	60.5 (8.72)	64.8 (5.56)	6.8 ! (2.05)	28.5 (5.14)	68.0 (4.40)	9.0 ! (2.87)	23.0 (3.79)	81.6 (5.39)	‡ (†)	13.2 ! (4.73)
American Indian/Alaska Native[3]	55.8 (1.32)	8.8 (0.73)	35.4 (1.29)	27.4 (3.13)	14.5 (2.84)	58.1 (3.38)	46.5 (2.45)	10.5 (1.41)	42.9 (2.51)	63.2 (2.46)	7.4 (1.12)	29.4 (2.43)	83.0 (2.87)	3.2 (0.96)	13.7 (2.80)
American Indian	55.4 (1.44)	8.5 (0.76)	36.0 (1.43)	27.2 (3.35)	15.1 (3.08)	57.8 (3.63)	43.1 (2.62)	10.3 (1.54)	46.5 (2.79)	63.6 (2.54)	6.8 (1.12)	29.6 (2.54)	85.6 (2.46)	3.4 ! (1.09)	11.0 (2.27)
Alaska Native	57.7 (5.36)	14.0 (3.60)	28.4 (5.39)	‡ (†)	‡ (†)	‡ (†)	60.6 (7.51)	15.0 ! (5.20)	24.5 (6.94)	59.9 (9.42)	14.9 ! (6.12)	25.2 (7.49)	‡ (†)	‡ (†)	‡ (†)
Two or more races	70.5 (0.86)	7.0 (0.50)	22.5 (0.80)	37.3 (3.57)	9.4 (2.53)	53.3 (3.97)	58.2 (2.00)	9.4 (1.36)	32.4 (1.99)	69.9 (1.27)	8.3 (0.92)	21.9 (1.12)	81.7 (1.15)	4.3 (0.62)	14.0 (1.01)
Nativity															
Hispanic															
Born within United States[4]	73.5 (0.25)	7.1 (0.17)	19.4 (0.21)	53.3 (0.82)	10.6 (0.59)	36.1 (0.81)	70.1 (0.54)	8.3 (0.39)	21.6 (0.44)	77.2 (0.45)	6.3 (0.24)	16.5 (0.40)	86.4 (0.48)	4.3 (0.29)	9.3 (0.40)
Born outside United States[4]	72.8 (0.33)	5.1 (0.15)	22.2 (0.33)	68.9 (0.49)	4.7 (0.24)	26.4 (0.46)	73.8 (0.53)	5.1 (0.28)	21.1 (0.53)	76.6 (0.71)	6.0 (0.44)	17.4 (0.68)	79.3 (0.98)	4.5 (0.44)	16.2 (0.84)
Asian															
Born within United States[4]	81.3 (0.55)	4.6 (0.27)	14.1 (0.48)	49.2 (3.70)	10.2 (2.58)	40.6 (3.51)	70.5 (1.88)	8.1 (1.28)	21.4 (1.63)	75.7 (1.29)	5.8 (0.58)	18.6 (1.18)	86.9 (0.61)	3.3 (0.30)	9.7 (0.52)
Born outside United States[4]	71.4 (0.37)	3.7 (0.18)	24.9 (0.36)	63.5 (1.88)	5.5 (0.77)	31.0 (1.98)	69.2 (1.39)	4.8 (0.77)	26.0 (1.32)	68.5 (1.01)	4.6 (0.36)	27.0 (1.00)	73.5 (0.48)	3.0 (0.21)	23.5 (0.48)
Citizenship status															
U.S.-born citizen	76.3 (0.10)	6.5 (0.06)	17.3 (0.08)	46.2 (0.40)	12.7 (0.28)	41.2 (0.43)	67.7 (0.21)	9.1 (0.14)	23.2 (0.19)	77.1 (0.16)	6.7 (0.10)	16.2 (0.14)	88.5 (0.11)	3.0 (0.07)	8.5 (0.10)
Naturalized citizen	78.9 (0.35)	4.8 (0.19)	16.3 (0.35)	66.2 (1.47)	5.2 (0.67)	28.6 (1.46)	74.6 (0.77)	5.3 (0.45)	20.0 (0.75)	77.8 (0.62)	5.5 (0.40)	16.7 (0.61)	84.7 (0.51)	3.9 (0.26)	11.4 (0.52)
Noncitizen	69.7 (0.26)	4.9 (0.12)	25.4 (0.26)	68.0 (0.47)	5.0 (0.22)	27.0 (0.43)	71.5 (0.54)	5.5 (0.29)	23.1 (0.49)	70.2 (0.62)	5.9 (0.40)	23.9 (0.59)	69.9 (0.42)	3.6 (0.20)	26.5 (0.45)

†Not applicable.

!Interpret data with caution. The coefficient of variation (CV) for this estimate is between 30 and 50 percent.

‡Reporting standards not met. Either there are too few cases for a reliable estimate or the coefficient of variation (CV) is 50 percent or greater.

[1]Data are for all persons with high school completion as their highest level of education, including those with equivalency credentials, such as the GED credential.

[2]Includes persons with no college degree as well as those with an associate's degree.

[3]Includes persons reporting American Indian alone, persons reporting Alaska Native alone, and persons from American Indian and/or Alaska Native tribes specified or not specified.

[4]United States refers to the 50 states, the District of Columbia, Puerto Rico, American Samoa, Guam, the U.S. Virgin Islands, and the Northern Marianas. Children born abroad to U.S. citizen parents are also counted as born within the United States.

NOTE: Estimates are for the entire population in the indicated age range, including persons living in households and persons living in group quarters (such as college residence halls, residential treatment centers, military barracks, and correctional facilities). The labor force consists of all employed persons plus those seeking employment. Standard errors were computed using replicate weights. Detail may not sum to totals because of rounding. Race categories exclude persons of Hispanic ethnicity.

SOURCE: U.S. Department of Commerce, Census Bureau, American Community Survey (ACS), 2014. (This table was prepared May 2016.)

Table 501.50. Employment to population ratios of persons 16 to 64 years old, by age group and highest level of educational attainment: Selected years, 1975 through 2015

[Standard errors appear in parentheses]

Age group and highest level of educational attainment	1975	1980	1985	1990	1995	2000	2005	2008	2009	2010	2011	2012	2013	2014	2015
1	2	3	4	5	6	7	8	9	10	11	12	13	14	15	16
16 to 19 years old, all education levels[1]	**— (†)**	**— (†)**	**— (†)**	**60.8 (2.03)**	**58.0 (2.13)**	**62.6 (2.09)**	**53.7 (1.40)**	**53.5 (1.41)**	**46.6 (1.36)**	**43.2 (1.30)**	**44.8 (1.40)**	**45.8 (1.43)**	**46.3 (1.40)**	**51.0 (1.67)**	**49.2 (1.36)**
Less than high school completion	— (†)	— (†)	— (†)	44.2 (3.08)	44.0 (3.13)	52.2 (3.19)	39.4 (2.01)	37.5 (1.90)	31.1 (1.89)	29.4 (1.83)	31.1 (2.21)	28.5 (2.05)	32.6 (2.03)	39.7 (2.63)	35.3 (2.03)
High school completion[2]	— (†)	— (†)	— (†)	74.2 (2.54)	70.1 (2.99)	70.1 (2.92)	65.0 (2.04)	64.3 (1.96)	53.6 (1.72)	51.1 (1.84)	50.3 (2.01)	53.6 (1.90)	52.7 (2.15)	58.5 (2.22)	56.1 (1.83)
At least some college	— (†)	— (†)	— (†)	76.8 (9.32)	71.6 (6.38)	78.2 (6.22)	66.6 (4.54)	65.3 (3.89)	65.4 (3.70)	57.5 (3.99)	61.5 (3.63)	64.3 (4.07)	63.5 (3.96)	60.5 (5.27)	65.7 (3.40)
20 to 24 years old, all education levels[1]	**— (†)**	**— (†)**	**— (†)**	**75.6 (0.90)**	**73.7 (0.93)**	**77.4 (0.93)**	**73.2 (0.66)**	**73.4 (0.60)**	**68.3 (0.66)**	**65.5 (0.72)**	**67.0 (0.59)**	**68.7 (0.67)**	**68.5 (0.72)**	**69.4 (0.74)**	**71.4 (0.66)**
Less than high school completion	— (†)	— (†)	— (†)	54.4 (2.29)	52.7 (2.41)	60.8 (2.43)	55.7 (1.27)	55.1 (1.73)	50.6 (1.60)	44.4 (1.58)	46.8 (1.71)	47.7 (1.95)	46.8 (1.88)	46.6 (2.62)	51.4 (2.17)
High school completion[2]	— (†)	— (†)	— (†)	76.6 (1.26)	72.2 (1.46)	76.5 (1.46)	72.3 (0.91)	69.8 (0.97)	63.9 (1.03)	61.5 (1.01)	62.9 (1.07)	64.2 (0.99)	63.5 (1.16)	63.7 (1.31)	66.9 (1.01)
Some college, no bachelor's degree[3]	— (†)	— (†)	— (†)	85.6 (1.69)	83.6 (1.52)	86.6 (1.49)	80.3 (1.19)	81.8 (1.09)	74.9 (1.32)	72.9 (1.27)	73.2 (1.01)	75.3 (1.19)	75.3 (1.15)	75.0 (1.29)	76.4 (1.03)
Bachelor's or higher degree	— (†)	— (†)	— (†)	93.3 (1.57)	90.9 (1.76)	87.8 (2.07)	89.3 (1.16)	89.6 (1.21)	87.2 (1.26)	86.5 (1.37)	85.2 (1.41)	87.3 (1.16)	86.6 (1.46)	88.1 (1.47)	88.9 (1.05)
25 to 64 years old, all education levels	**65.8 (0.33)**	**70.2 (0.30)**	**71.6 (0.30)**	**75.0 (0.29)**	**75.5 (0.28)**	**77.7 (0.27)**	**75.0 (0.19)**	**75.5 (0.16)**	**72.2 (0.19)**	**71.5 (0.19)**	**71.2 (0.19)**	**71.7 (0.18)**	**72.1 (0.19)**	**72.3 (0.26)**	**73.1 (0.19)**
Less than high school completion	55.3 (0.62)	55.5 (0.66)	53.1 (0.74)	54.9 (0.80)	53.8 (0.85)	57.8 (0.91)	57.2 (0.51)	56.2 (0.51)	52.5 (0.57)	52.1 (0.60)	51.1 (0.56)	52.9 (0.60)	53.2 (0.60)	54.9 (0.78)	54.7 (0.58)
High school completion[2]	65.7 (0.53)	70.4 (0.48)	70.7 (0.48)	74.4 (0.46)	73.3 (0.49)	75.5 (0.49)	71.5 (0.34)	71.6 (0.28)	67.8 (0.33)	67.0 (0.36)	66.2 (0.39)	66.5 (0.35)	66.7 (0.38)	67.0 (0.44)	67.3 (0.37)
Some college, no bachelor's degree[3]	71.7 (0.86)	76.1 (0.70)	77.8 (0.66)	80.2 (0.60)	79.5 (0.51)	80.7 (0.50)	77.7 (0.33)	77.5 (0.31)	73.9 (0.33)	72.7 (0.30)	72.2 (0.30)	72.2 (0.30)	73.1 (0.31)	72.6 (0.44)	74.1 (0.32)
Bachelor's or higher degree	82.5 (0.68)	84.5 (0.55)	85.6 (0.51)	86.7 (0.47)	86.5 (0.44)	86.4 (0.42)	83.7 (0.26)	84.4 (0.27)	82.2 (0.25)	81.6 (0.24)	81.5 (0.26)	82.1 (0.24)	81.9 (0.26)	82.0 (0.34)	82.8 (0.26)
25 to 34 years old, all education levels	**67.7 (0.59)**	**74.5 (0.49)**	**76.2 (0.48)**	**78.6 (0.47)**	**78.5 (0.48)**	**81.6 (0.49)**	**76.8 (0.31)**	**78.1 (0.31)**	**74.2 (0.36)**	**73.2 (0.34)**	**73.0 (0.35)**	**73.8 (0.31)**	**74.6 (0.33)**	**74.5 (0.43)**	**76.0 (0.35)**
Less than high school completion	52.9 (1.43)	58.3 (1.46)	57.0 (1.54)	60.3 (1.50)	59.8 (1.59)	64.1 (1.76)	62.0 (0.95)	60.4 (0.93)	54.6 (1.07)	55.1 (0.95)	54.2 (1.17)	56.2 (1.14)	57.4 (1.03)	57.8 (1.37)	56.5 (1.11)
High school completion[2]	65.5 (0.92)	72.0 (0.81)	74.3 (0.78)	77.7 (0.74)	77.0 (0.84)	80.2 (0.91)	73.1 (0.60)	74.0 (0.60)	69.0 (0.66)	68.1 (0.72)	67.9 (0.67)	68.7 (0.75)	68.2 (0.68)	68.2 (0.73)	70.4 (0.72)
Some college, no bachelor's degree[3]	71.7 (1.33)	77.8 (1.01)	80.1 (0.97)	81.6 (0.96)	80.5 (0.87)	82.8 (0.90)	79.4 (0.54)	79.9 (0.52)	75.9 (0.60)	72.9 (0.57)	73.0 (0.62)	72.7 (0.68)	74.9 (0.65)	74.5 (0.74)	76.4 (0.60)
Bachelor's or higher degree	82.0 (1.04)	85.4 (0.82)	86.6 (0.79)	88.1 (0.76)	88.1 (0.75)	89.0 (0.73)	84.4 (0.52)	86.8 (0.46)	84.5 (0.49)	84.0 (0.49)	83.4 (0.45)	84.3 (0.45)	84.4 (0.45)	84.0 (0.59)	84.8 (0.48)
35 to 44 years old, all education levels	**70.3 (0.66)**	**76.5 (0.58)**	**78.1 (0.54)**	**81.6 (0.48)**	**80.2 (0.46)**	**81.8 (0.45)**	**79.9 (0.26)**	**80.1 (0.30)**	**76.7 (0.29)**	**76.0 (0.30)**	**76.0 (0.35)**	**76.9 (0.35)**	**77.0 (0.35)**	**77.1 (0.40)**	**78.3 (0.31)**
Less than high school completion	61.4 (1.31)	63.4 (1.39)	60.0 (1.58)	62.5 (1.69)	58.6 (1.66)	64.8 (1.64)	64.9 (0.93)	64.3 (1.05)	60.2 (1.01)	58.2 (1.13)	57.5 (1.04)	59.6 (1.13)	61.6 (1.03)	61.3 (1.25)	62.3 (0.84)
High school completion[2]	69.6 (1.02)	76.6 (0.90)	76.6 (0.88)	80.0 (0.80)	78.6 (0.82)	81.0 (0.79)	78.0 (0.52)	76.9 (0.57)	72.6 (0.63)	72.4 (0.64)	71.8 (0.64)	72.1 (0.68)	72.6 (0.66)	72.6 (0.80)	72.5 (0.63)
Some college, no bachelor's degree[3]	74.5 (1.74)	80.9 (1.33)	81.6 (1.15)	85.0 (0.93)	83.3 (0.81)	84.4 (0.80)	82.0 (0.48)	82.4 (0.58)	78.5 (0.53)	76.9 (0.53)	76.9 (0.62)	78.2 (0.61)	77.0 (0.64)	77.3 (0.68)	79.6 (0.53)
Bachelor's or higher degree	84.5 (1.31)	87.1 (1.00)	88.8 (0.80)	89.5 (0.72)	88.5 (0.71)	87.6 (0.74)	85.9 (0.41)	86.4 (0.40)	84.8 (0.42)	84.7 (0.39)	84.8 (0.43)	85.0 (0.41)	84.8 (0.43)	85.0 (0.57)	86.7 (0.39)
45 to 54 years old, all education levels	**68.4 (0.65)**	**71.7 (0.65)**	**73.5 (0.67)**	**77.6 (0.62)**	**78.8 (0.55)**	**81.2 (0.50)**	**78.4 (0.32)**	**78.4 (0.33)**	**75.2 (0.34)**	**74.7 (0.35)**	**74.3 (0.32)**	**74.6 (0.30)**	**74.9 (0.30)**	**76.2 (0.43)**	**75.9 (0.33)**
Less than high school completion	59.8 (1.14)	61.8 (1.24)	58.7 (1.52)	60.7 (1.63)	58.4 (1.79)	60.3 (1.89)	59.0 (1.04)	56.0 (1.02)	54.0 (1.13)	52.5 (1.05)	51.7 (0.84)	54.7 (1.06)	53.3 (1.04)	59.4 (1.50)	56.8 (1.16)
High school completion[2]	68.8 (1.03)	72.0 (1.02)	74.0 (1.03)	77.5 (0.97)	75.9 (1.01)	78.2 (0.95)	75.1 (0.64)	75.4 (0.57)	71.6 (0.53)	71.0 (0.65)	70.1 (0.58)	70.4 (0.62)	70.1 (0.60)	70.7 (0.84)	70.9 (0.63)
Some college, no bachelor's degree[3]	74.7 (1.81)	76.5 (1.72)	79.2 (1.63)	81.9 (1.38)	81.7 (1.03)	83.4 (0.91)	80.4 (0.57)	80.2 (0.51)	77.3 (0.58)	77.3 (0.54)	76.6 (0.53)	76.2 (0.53)	77.4 (0.53)	77.4 (0.76)	77.1 (0.60)
Bachelor's or higher degree	87.1 (1.36)	87.3 (1.21)	87.9 (1.16)	89.4 (0.97)	89.5 (0.78)	89.7 (0.71)	87.5 (0.45)	88.1 (0.45)	85.2 (0.45)	84.4 (0.45)	84.9 (0.45)	84.7 (0.48)	84.7 (0.47)	85.9 (0.54)	85.7 (0.43)
55 to 64 years old, all education levels	**54.6 (0.77)**	**54.1 (0.73)**	**52.1 (0.77)**	**53.4 (0.81)**	**55.0 (0.82)**	**58.1 (0.79)**	**60.8 (0.48)**	**62.8 (0.41)**	**60.8 (0.42)**	**60.6 (0.41)**	**60.2 (0.43)**	**60.6 (0.41)**	**61.3 (0.43)**	**60.9 (0.52)**	**61.9 (0.37)**
Less than high school completion	48.5 (1.11)	43.2 (1.16)	41.8 (1.29)	39.5 (1.46)	38.1 (1.67)	40.4 (1.84)	39.4 (1.13)	41.0 (1.24)	38.2 (1.19)	40.0 (1.19)	39.4 (1.15)	39.1 (1.08)	38.5 (1.32)	39.6 (1.34)	42.4 (1.12)
High school completion[2]	56.5 (1.32)	57.5 (1.19)	52.1 (1.22)	54.0 (1.29)	53.7 (1.34)	55.4 (1.34)	55.3 (0.79)	57.8 (0.69)	55.8 (0.73)	55.1 (0.71)	54.4 (0.81)	54.6 (0.75)	56.3 (0.74)	57.6 (0.90)	56.9 (0.74)
Some college, no bachelor's degree[3]	62.6 (2.48)	62.5 (2.08)	58.9 (2.21)	60.4 (2.12)	62.0 (1.74)	62.4 (1.64)	64.8 (0.90)	64.8 (0.80)	61.6 (0.74)	61.8 (0.76)	61.2 (0.78)	61.2 (0.70)	62.3 (0.72)	60.5 (0.99)	63.2 (0.68)
Bachelor's or higher degree	72.6 (2.34)	71.9 (1.96)	71.3 (1.83)	70.5 (1.79)	70.0 (1.72)	71.9 (1.49)	73.5 (0.74)	74.0 (0.68)	72.7 (0.63)	72.0 (0.65)	71.8 (0.71)	73.1 (0.66)	72.4 (0.67)	71.7 (0.90)	72.3 (0.62)

—Not available.
†Not applicable.
[1]Data for 16- to 19-year-olds and 20- to 24-year-olds exclude persons enrolled in school.
[2]Includes equivalency credentials, such as the GED credential.
[3]Includes persons with no college degree as well as those with an associate's degree.

NOTE: For each age group, the employment to population ratio is the number of persons in that age group who are employed as a percentage of the civilian population in that age group.
SOURCE: U.S. Department of Commerce, Census Bureau, Current Population Survey (CPS), Annual Social and Economic Supplement, selected years, 1975 through 2015. (This table was prepared October 2015.)

Table 501.60. Employment to population ratios of males 16 to 64 years old, by age group and highest level of educational attainment: Selected years, 1975 through 2015

[Standard errors appear in parentheses]

Age group and highest level of educational attainment	1975	1980	1985	1990	1995	2000	2005	2008	2009	2010	2011	2012	2013	2014	2015
1	2	3	4	5	6	7	8	9	10	11	12	13	14	15	16
16 to 19 years old, all education levels[1]	— (†)	— (†)	— (†)	65.3 (2.82)	63.6 (2.87)	69.2 (2.70)	56.2 (2.10)	58.7 (1.72)	45.8 (1.77)	44.0 (1.72)	47.0 (1.94)	48.1 (2.00)	48.1 (1.92)	51.9 (2.37)	51.2 (1.92)
Less than high school completion	— (†)	— (†)	— (†)	51.5 (4.20)	50.6 (4.26)	63.1 (4.09)	47.0 (3.07)	45.8 (2.44)	34.0 (2.70)	31.5 (2.64)	37.4 (3.03)	34.7 (3.25)	33.9 (2.63)	43.6 (3.64)	37.2 (2.72)
High school completion[2]	— (†)	— (†)	— (†)	78.7 (3.51)	76.1 (3.87)	74.4 (3.77)	63.1 (2.88)	67.1 (2.47)	51.1 (2.35)	51.0 (2.37)	51.2 (2.84)	52.5 (2.51)	55.8 (2.86)	58.1 (3.28)	58.7 (2.49)
At least some college	— (†)	— (†)	— (†)	83.1 (13.41)	75.9 (8.99)	77.0 (9.81)	70.4 (5.98)	74.3 (4.67)	62.9 (5.37)	61.4 (6.00)	60.2 (5.67)	64.2 (5.72)	65.9 (5.64)	57.6 (8.04)	63.9 (4.71)
20 to 24 years old, all education levels[1]	— (†)	— (†)	— (†)	83.5 (1.10)	81.2 (1.16)	83.3 (1.16)	78.9 (0.86)	79.1 (0.68)	70.6 (0.86)	68.4 (0.97)	69.5 (0.84)	72.1 (0.96)	71.4 (0.95)	72.4 (1.04)	74.9 (0.98)
Less than high school completion	— (†)	— (†)	— (†)	70.0 (2.84)	69.3 (2.99)	72.1 (2.93)	69.5 (1.80)	68.2 (2.11)	59.2 (2.28)	52.9 (2.06)	57.3 (2.43)	56.6 (2.42)	57.0 (2.54)	58.3 (3.16)	60.3 (2.76)
High school completion[2]	— (†)	— (†)	— (†)	84.6 (1.50)	81.1 (1.73)	82.7 (1.78)	78.0 (1.21)	76.9 (1.05)	66.9 (1.38)	66.0 (1.31)	66.2 (1.31)	68.0 (1.43)	67.3 (1.47)	66.6 (1.77)	71.1 (1.39)
Some college, no bachelor's degree[3]	— (†)	— (†)	— (†)	91.8 (1.98)	87.5 (1.97)	92.6 (1.65)	84.6 (1.43)	85.2 (1.38)	77.7 (1.69)	74.8 (1.71)	75.2 (1.66)	80.5 (1.59)	77.9 (1.51)	78.6 (1.82)	79.9 (1.57)
Bachelor's or higher degree	— (†)	— (†)	— (†)	94.9 (2.07)	91.1 (2.70)	89.1 (3.07)	90.6 (1.82)	92.4 (1.51)	86.4 (1.94)	86.3 (2.04)	84.7 (2.16)	88.7 (1.77)	86.1 (2.11)	90.6 (1.93)	90.6 (1.71)
25 to 64 years old, all education levels	84.6 (0.36)	85.0 (0.34)	83.1 (0.36)	84.5 (0.34)	83.0 (0.34)	84.6 (0.33)	81.9 (0.25)	81.6 (0.22)	77.0 (0.25)	76.3 (0.27)	76.3 (0.27)	77.4 (0.25)	78.2 (0.27)	78.2 (0.35)	79.4 (0.26)
Less than high school completion	74.3 (0.77)	72.4 (0.84)	67.6 (0.98)	67.9 (1.04)	64.2 (1.13)	69.6 (1.17)	69.7 (0.70)	66.6 (0.78)	61.6 (0.80)	61.2 (0.93)	61.0 (0.81)	63.0 (0.77)	64.0 (0.75)	66.3 (1.04)	67.2 (0.75)
High school completion[2]	87.2 (0.56)	87.0 (0.54)	83.5 (0.58)	85.1 (0.55)	81.9 (0.61)	82.9 (0.61)	78.6 (0.44)	78.3 (0.42)	72.1 (0.49)	71.7 (0.50)	71.8 (0.50)	72.6 (0.45)	73.1 (0.51)	73.6 (0.59)	74.7 (0.48)
Some college, no bachelor's degree[3]	88.8 (0.83)	88.3 (0.73)	87.1 (0.75)	87.9 (0.70)	86.1 (0.63)	86.1 (0.63)	83.7 (0.44)	82.9 (0.42)	78.1 (0.41)	76.6 (0.42)	75.9 (0.45)	77.3 (0.43)	78.3 (0.46)	77.5 (0.59)	79.6 (0.48)
Bachelor's or higher degree	93.8 (0.55)	93.6 (0.48)	92.4 (0.50)	92.5 (0.48)	91.4 (0.48)	91.8 (0.47)	89.4 (0.35)	90.0 (0.31)	87.6 (0.34)	86.9 (0.33)	86.9 (0.35)	87.5 (0.33)	88.0 (0.33)	87.7 (0.42)	88.0 (0.32)
25 to 34 years old, all education levels	87.4 (0.59)	88.1 (0.52)	86.9 (0.54)	87.9 (0.52)	87.1 (0.55)	89.4 (0.55)	84.6 (0.40)	84.6 (0.41)	79.1 (0.46)	78.4 (0.48)	78.5 (0.51)	80.1 (0.48)	81.3 (0.46)	80.9 (0.56)	83.2 (0.44)
Less than high school completion	76.2 (1.78)	76.3 (1.80)	75.1 (1.87)	75.6 (1.77)	73.7 (1.91)	78.4 (2.04)	78.1 (1.23)	73.5 (1.40)	66.2 (1.45)	66.6 (1.42)	66.3 (1.47)	70.1 (1.51)	70.2 (1.32)	73.1 (1.88)	73.1 (1.59)
High school completion[2]	88.4 (0.93)	88.4 (0.86)	86.1 (0.88)	88.6 (0.80)	86.6 (0.94)	89.1 (0.98)	81.7 (0.77)	81.7 (0.83)	73.4 (0.87)	73.0 (0.85)	74.3 (0.91)	76.5 (0.90)	77.3 (0.82)	77.2 (0.93)	79.6 (0.87)
Some college, no bachelor's degree[3]	87.7 (1.31)	88.5 (1.06)	89.7 (1.04)	89.7 (1.08)	89.6 (0.98)	90.7 (1.02)	86.4 (0.82)	86.3 (0.73)	81.4 (0.82)	78.7 (0.83)	77.5 (0.90)	78.2 (0.97)	80.7 (0.95)	79.1 (1.25)	83.0 (0.86)
Bachelor's or higher degree	93.5 (0.87)	93.4 (0.76)	92.2 (0.85)	93.1 (0.83)	93.0 (0.83)	93.6 (0.82)	89.6 (0.69)	91.7 (0.62)	89.5 (0.68)	89.2 (0.74)	89.0 (0.70)	89.3 (0.67)	89.8 (0.57)	88.8 (0.78)	89.6 (0.59)
35 to 44 years old, all education levels	90.1 (0.61)	91.1 (0.55)	89.1 (0.57)	90.2 (0.52)	86.8 (0.55)	88.8 (0.52)	87.2 (0.37)	87.1 (0.41)	82.7 (0.41)	82.3 (0.42)	82.4 (0.43)	83.3 (0.43)	84.7 (0.47)	83.8 (0.56)	85.6 (0.42)
Less than high school completion	81.6 (1.48)	80.1 (1.65)	74.6 (1.99)	73.9 (2.13)	66.7 (2.15)	76.5 (2.00)	75.9 (1.26)	73.3 (1.51)	69.4 (1.47)	69.5 (1.61)	70.9 (1.59)	70.6 (1.47)	74.8 (1.38)	73.9 (1.75)	76.9 (1.24)
High school completion[2]	91.3 (0.95)	92.3 (0.85)	88.6 (1.00)	89.1 (0.91)	85.9 (0.98)	87.1 (0.93)	83.7 (0.71)	83.3 (0.76)	77.6 (0.80)	77.6 (0.92)	76.8 (0.83)	78.2 (0.97)	79.4 (0.88)	78.2 (1.17)	80.4 (0.82)
Some college, no bachelor's degree[3]	93.8 (1.34)	93.8 (1.13)	90.2 (1.25)	92.6 (0.97)	88.8 (0.99)	90.2 (0.95)	89.4 (0.60)	89.0 (0.71)	83.9 (0.74)	82.7 (0.73)	83.1 (0.86)	83.9 (0.76)	84.6 (0.78)	83.9 (1.04)	85.4 (0.85)
Bachelor's or higher degree	97.0 (0.77)	97.1 (0.65)	96.3 (0.62)	96.3 (0.59)	95.1 (0.66)	95.1 (0.67)	94.6 (0.45)	94.9 (0.41)	92.3 (0.56)	91.9 (0.55)	91.4 (0.51)	92.2 (0.51)	92.9 (0.48)	92.4 (0.75)	93.6 (0.53)
45 to 54 years old, all education levels	86.6 (0.68)	87.4 (0.67)	85.8 (0.76)	87.1 (0.70)	84.9 (0.68)	86.5 (0.62)	83.9 (0.45)	83.7 (0.43)	78.8 (0.44)	78.3 (0.50)	78.9 (0.45)	79.9 (0.44)	79.7 (0.38)	81.8 (0.61)	81.3 (0.46)
Less than high school completion	78.2 (1.34)	79.6 (1.42)	73.2 (1.90)	74.3 (2.05)	66.4 (2.41)	68.5 (2.52)	69.9 (1.55)	65.5 (1.49)	61.4 (1.50)	58.8 (1.48)	58.6 (1.25)	62.5 (1.45)	61.1 (1.33)	67.3 (1.96)	65.0 (1.56)
High school completion[2]	90.3 (1.01)	89.3 (1.08)	87.3 (1.18)	87.5 (1.15)	82.1 (1.35)	84.6 (1.21)	80.7 (0.86)	80.4 (0.81)	74.2 (0.80)	74.6 (0.91)	75.4 (0.78)	75.2 (0.88)	74.2 (0.78)	76.4 (1.12)	76.7 (0.86)
Some college, no bachelor's degree[3]	91.0 (1.66)	89.4 (1.78)	89.3 (1.76)	88.9 (1.58)	87.2 (1.29)	86.4 (1.18)	84.5 (0.84)	85.6 (0.64)	80.1 (0.84)	79.4 (0.80)	79.2 (0.81)	81.9 (0.74)	82.1 (0.69)	83.5 (0.95)	82.4 (0.87)
Bachelor's or higher degree	95.6 (1.02)	96.0 (0.88)	94.8 (1.00)	95.2 (0.88)	93.8 (0.80)	94.6 (0.72)	92.2 (0.53)	93.5 (0.46)	90.2 (0.58)	89.4 (0.58)	90.5 (0.53)	90.2 (0.60)	90.7 (0.51)	91.4 (0.65)	91.2 (0.50)
55 to 64 years old, all education levels	71.3 (1.00)	69.7 (0.98)	64.6 (1.05)	64.0 (1.12)	63.2 (1.13)	64.9 (1.09)	67.3 (0.66)	68.0 (0.54)	65.2 (0.59)	64.4 (0.61)	64.1 (0.61)	65.1 (0.58)	66.0 (0.54)	65.7 (0.76)	67.1 (0.53)
Less than high school completion	64.5 (1.51)	58.3 (1.65)	53.4 (1.85)	49.6 (2.13)	46.9 (2.46)	51.2 (2.71)	48.8 (1.70)	48.3 (1.60)	44.3 (1.75)	45.0 (1.81)	45.2 (1.68)	44.6 (1.48)	45.5 (1.73)	48.4 (1.96)	52.6 (1.61)
High school completion[2]	74.9 (1.73)	74.6 (1.61)	66.1 (1.80)	66.0 (1.89)	62.7 (1.99)	61.0 (1.97)	61.8 (1.15)	62.9 (1.10)	59.3 (1.19)	58.5 (1.12)	58.2 (1.12)	59.1 (1.05)	61.1 (1.04)	62.6 (1.34)	62.2 (1.03)
Some college, no bachelor's degree[3]	80.8 (2.87)	77.2 (2.53)	67.5 (3.01)	67.7 (2.93)	67.8 (2.41)	66.6 (2.31)	69.6 (1.31)	67.9 (1.10)	64.5 (1.06)	63.9 (1.10)	63.0 (1.08)	64.3 (1.11)	64.9 (1.02)	63.3 (1.29)	67.6 (1.00)
Bachelor's or higher degree	84.1 (2.52)	83.8 (2.04)	80.7 (1.98)	77.9 (2.03)	74.9 (2.04)	77.0 (1.82)	78.6 (0.89)	78.6 (0.81)	77.4 (0.83)	76.2 (0.82)	76.3 (0.84)	77.7 (0.85)	77.8 (0.91)	77.2 (1.18)	76.8 (0.87)

—Not available.
†Not applicable.
[1]Data for 16- to 19-year-olds and 20- to 24-year-olds exclude persons enrolled in school.
[2]Includes equivalency credentials, such as the GED credential.
[3]Includes persons with no college degree as well as those with an associate's degree.

NOTE: For each age group, the employment to population ratio of males is the number of males in that age group who are employed as a percentage of the male civilian population in that age group.
SOURCE: U.S. Department of Commerce, Census Bureau, Current Population Survey (CPS), Annual Social and Economic Supplement, selected years, 1975 through 2015. (This table was prepared October 2015.)

Table 501.70. Employment to population ratios of females 16 to 64 years old, by age group and highest level of educational attainment: Selected years, 1975 through 2015

[Standard errors appear in parentheses]

Age group and highest level of educational attainment	1975	1980	1985	1990	1995	2000	2005	2008	2009	2010	2011	2012	2013	2014	2015
1	2	3	4	5	6	7	8	9	10	11	12	13	14	15	16
16 to 19 years old, all education levels[1]	**— (†)**	**— (†)**	**— (†)**	**56.6 (2.72)**	**52.2 (2.93)**	**55.1 (2.98)**	**51.0 (1.88)**	**47.3 (2.14)**	**47.7 (1.81)**	**42.3 (1.88)**	**42.3 (2.14)**	**43.1 (2.03)**	**44.3 (1.90)**	**50.0 (2.39)**	**46.9 (1.88)**
Less than high school completion	— (†)	— (†)	— (†)	36.0 (4.13)	36.5 (4.23)	38.9 (4.42)	30.3 (2.72)	25.9 (2.84)	27.3 (2.57)	26.8 (2.75)	23.5 (2.92)	22.6 (2.88)	31.0 (3.10)	34.5 (3.67)	33.3 (2.82)
High school completion[2]	— (†)	— (†)	— (†)	70.5 (3.38)	64.1 (4.22)	65.2 (4.22)	67.0 (2.60)	61.2 (2.94)	56.7 (2.54)	51.2 (2.99)	49.1 (2.91)	55.2 (2.97)	48.9 (2.96)	59.0 (3.35)	52.8 (2.83)
At least some college	— (†)	— (†)	— (†)	73.1 (11.73)	68.3 (8.37)	79.1 (7.56)	63.6 (6.23)	55.9 (5.75)	67.6 (4.82)	54.4 (5.29)	62.5 (5.31)	64.3 (5.68)	61.7 (4.61)	63.0 (7.14)	67.7 (5.08)
20 to 24 years old, all education levels[1]	**— (†)**	**— (†)**	**— (†)**	**68.2 (1.29)**	**66.3 (1.34)**	**71.5 (1.35)**	**67.0 (1.01)**	**67.2 (0.97)**	**65.8 (0.94)**	**62.4 (1.01)**	**64.1 (0.92)**	**65.0 (0.94)**	**65.2 (1.01)**	**66.3 (1.06)**	**67.7 (0.88)**
Less than high school completion	— (†)	— (†)	— (†)	36.7 (3.08)	33.6 (3.18)	46.2 (3.57)	38.5 (2.20)	37.5 (2.47)	38.6 (2.32)	33.3 (2.50)	33.2 (2.31)	36.2 (2.84)	33.4 (2.55)	30.5 (3.57)	42.0 (3.18)
High school completion[2]	— (†)	— (†)	— (†)	68.8 (1.84)	62.2 (2.19)	70.0 (2.15)	65.0 (1.47)	60.8 (1.55)	59.9 (1.53)	55.6 (1.43)	58.5 (1.77)	59.2 (1.55)	58.4 (1.78)	60.2 (1.86)	61.6 (1.41)
Some college, no bachelor's degree[3]	— (†)	— (†)	— (†)	80.9 (2.39)	80.3 (2.12)	81.4 (2.23)	76.6 (1.72)	78.7 (1.56)	72.4 (1.67)	71.2 (1.65)	71.2 (1.47)	70.6 (1.64)	72.9 (1.64)	71.6 (1.89)	72.9 (1.54)
Bachelor's or higher degree	— (†)	— (†)	— (†)	92.0 (2.12)	90.8 (2.19)	86.9 (2.61)	88.4 (1.53)	87.8 (1.55)	87.7 (1.60)	86.7 (1.67)	85.5 (1.81)	86.4 (1.53)	87.0 (1.64)	86.3 (1.96)	87.6 (1.42)
25 to 64 years old, all education levels	**48.5 (0.46)**	**56.5 (0.44)**	**60.8 (0.43)**	**66.0 (0.42)**	**68.3 (0.40)**	**71.2 (0.39)**	**68.4 (0.23)**	**69.6 (0.23)**	**67.6 (0.24)**	**66.9 (0.23)**	**66.2 (0.24)**	**66.3 (0.25)**	**66.4 (0.23)**	**66.6 (0.32)**	**67.1 (0.24)**
Less than high school completion	37.7 (0.80)	39.8 (0.86)	39.1 (0.97)	41.8 (1.06)	43.2 (1.15)	45.8 (1.24)	43.4 (0.72)	43.8 (0.74)	41.9 (0.67)	41.6 (0.81)	39.7 (0.71)	41.6 (0.89)	40.6 (0.82)	41.5 (0.89)	40.5 (0.81)
High school completion[2]	50.1 (0.70)	58.2 (0.65)	60.8 (0.65)	65.6 (0.64)	65.7 (0.69)	68.6 (0.70)	64.2 (0.44)	64.7 (0.43)	63.2 (0.42)	61.9 (0.44)	60.1 (0.51)	60.0 (0.49)	59.8 (0.47)	59.7 (0.58)	59.1 (0.48)
Some college, no bachelor's degree[3]	53.8 (1.30)	63.7 (1.07)	69.0 (0.98)	73.2 (0.88)	73.8 (0.71)	76.0 (0.70)	72.8 (0.42)	73.0 (0.43)	70.4 (0.44)	69.4 (0.45)	69.1 (0.37)	67.9 (0.43)	68.6 (0.46)	68.3 (0.58)	69.3 (0.45)
Bachelor's or higher degree	65.6 (1.29)	71.8 (1.01)	76.7 (0.88)	79.8 (0.78)	80.8 (0.71)	80.8 (0.66)	78.1 (0.40)	79.1 (0.40)	77.3 (0.38)	76.9 (0.36)	76.6 (0.39)	77.2 (0.38)	76.6 (0.40)	77.1 (0.47)	78.2 (0.35)
25 to 34 years old, all education levels	**49.3 (0.83)**	**61.6 (0.73)**	**65.9 (0.72)**	**69.6 (0.70)**	**70.2 (0.71)**	**74.1 (0.74)**	**69.0 (0.48)**	**71.7 (0.47)**	**69.3 (0.51)**	**68.0 (0.44)**	**67.5 (0.42)**	**67.7 (0.44)**	**68.0 (0.45)**	**68.2 (0.55)**	**69.0 (0.51)**
Less than high school completion	33.7 (1.74)	42.3 (1.91)	38.7 (2.05)	42.5 (2.12)	43.5 (2.25)	47.6 (2.56)	42.7 (1.44)	42.4 (1.37)	39.5 (1.50)	40.2 (1.35)	37.5 (1.55)	38.9 (1.69)	40.7 (1.49)	40.2 (1.86)	36.5 (1.73)
High school completion[2]	48.1 (1.22)	59.4 (1.12)	63.9 (1.11)	67.5 (1.11)	67.2 (1.27)	70.7 (1.43)	62.5 (0.99)	64.3 (0.92)	63.2 (0.98)	61.4 (1.14)	59.5 (0.94)	59.1 (1.05)	57.1 (1.07)	56.3 (1.19)	58.6 (1.08)
Some college, no bachelor's degree[3]	53.6 (2.06)	66.3 (1.58)	71.0 (1.46)	74.5 (1.40)	73.0 (1.26)	76.3 (1.31)	73.0 (0.81)	74.4 (0.81)	70.8 (0.86)	67.7 (0.80)	69.1 (0.79)	67.7 (0.90)	69.7 (0.84)	70.3 (0.91)	70.6 (0.83)
Bachelor's or higher degree	66.3 (1.88)	75.5 (1.42)	80.6 (1.26)	83.2 (1.18)	83.4 (1.16)	84.7 (1.11)	80.1 (0.72)	82.8 (0.66)	80.7 (0.73)	79.9 (0.63)	78.8 (0.60)	80.3 (0.63)	80.1 (0.67)	80.2 (0.77)	80.9 (0.67)
35 to 44 years old, all education levels	**51.9 (0.95)**	**62.8 (0.87)**	**67.7 (0.80)**	**73.3 (0.72)**	**73.8 (0.68)**	**75.1 (0.67)**	**72.8 (0.38)**	**73.3 (0.40)**	**70.9 (0.42)**	**69.9 (0.42)**	**69.8 (0.48)**	**70.7 (0.48)**	**69.6 (0.47)**	**70.7 (0.57)**	**71.3 (0.42)**
Less than high school completion	42.8 (1.76)	48.2 (1.90)	46.4 (2.13)	51.0 (2.35)	49.7 (2.33)	52.5 (2.35)	51.5 (1.33)	53.1 (1.57)	48.9 (1.47)	44.8 (1.54)	42.5 (1.41)	47.0 (1.49)	45.8 (1.52)	45.6 (1.61)	45.5 (1.44)
High school completion[2]	53.9 (1.38)	64.7 (1.28)	67.8 (1.22)	72.7 (1.13)	71.7 (1.19)	74.7 (1.18)	71.6 (0.74)	69.6 (0.78)	66.9 (0.94)	66.3 (0.87)	65.8 (0.87)	64.9 (1.02)	64.8 (0.92)	65.8 (1.07)	62.8 (0.99)
Some college, no bachelor's degree[3]	55.1 (2.67)	67.8 (2.14)	73.6 (1.73)	77.9 (1.44)	78.5 (1.16)	79.4 (1.16)	76.1 (0.67)	76.9 (0.81)	74.0 (0.79)	72.2 (0.74)	71.8 (0.87)	73.4 (0.85)	70.3 (0.90)	71.7 (1.06)	74.5 (0.70)
Bachelor's or higher degree	63.2 (2.73)	73.0 (1.97)	78.5 (1.53)	81.2 (1.30)	81.5 (1.19)	80.2 (1.20)	78.1 (0.66)	78.9 (0.63)	78.1 (0.61)	78.3 (0.59)	78.9 (0.68)	78.8 (0.64)	78.0 (0.71)	79.0 (0.80)	81.0 (0.57)
45 to 54 years old, all education levels	**51.5 (0.93)**	**57.1 (0.94)**	**62.1 (0.98)**	**68.6 (0.92)**	**72.9 (0.80)**	**76.0 (0.73)**	**73.2 (0.40)**	**73.2 (0.46)**	**71.8 (0.46)**	**71.3 (0.44)**	**70.0 (0.44)**	**69.6 (0.42)**	**70.3 (0.41)**	**70.8 (0.58)**	**70.8 (0.46)**
Less than high school completion	41.5 (1.55)	43.9 (1.71)	44.3 (2.06)	47.6 (2.22)	50.6 (2.43)	52.3 (2.57)	47.8 (1.40)	44.6 (1.30)	45.5 (1.47)	45.2 (1.61)	44.1 (1.25)	45.8 (1.53)	43.8 (1.52)	49.6 (2.11)	47.3 (1.50)
High school completion[2]	53.8 (1.37)	60.2 (1.37)	64.2 (1.41)	69.9 (1.35)	71.1 (1.36)	72.9 (1.33)	69.5 (0.83)	70.1 (0.80)	68.8 (0.85)	67.1 (0.72)	64.4 (0.89)	65.5 (0.82)	65.7 (0.84)	64.8 (1.17)	64.5 (0.93)
Some college, no bachelor's degree[3]	58.1 (2.78)	64.7 (2.56)	69.7 (2.45)	75.2 (2.08)	76.9 (1.46)	80.6 (1.28)	76.9 (0.72)	75.9 (0.74)	75.0 (0.73)	75.5 (0.74)	74.4 (0.71)	71.4 (0.77)	73.6 (0.78)	72.6 (1.03)	72.8 (0.80)
Bachelor's or higher degree	72.2 (2.87)	72.3 (2.55)	77.3 (2.24)	81.8 (1.76)	83.8 (1.36)	84.5 (1.17)	82.8 (0.72)	83.0 (0.73)	80.5 (0.69)	79.7 (0.69)	79.6 (0.68)	79.6 (0.72)	79.2 (0.71)	80.6 (0.83)	80.8 (0.63)
55 to 64 years old, all education levels	**39.7 (0.99)**	**40.5 (0.94)**	**41.1 (0.99)**	**44.0 (1.05)**	**47.5 (1.08)**	**51.9 (1.06)**	**54.8 (0.61)**	**58.1 (0.55)**	**56.7 (0.55)**	**57.1 (0.53)**	**56.4 (0.51)**	**56.5 (0.57)**	**57.1 (0.57)**	**56.4 (0.63)**	**57.0 (0.49)**
Less than high school completion	33.5 (1.39)	29.4 (1.41)	31.2 (1.60)	30.5 (1.80)	30.3 (2.07)	30.9 (2.26)	30.5 (1.33)	34.1 (1.70)	32.1 (1.47)	35.1 (1.54)	33.6 (1.46)	34.0 (1.57)	32.1 (1.57)	30.4 (1.69)	32.1 (1.42)
High school completion[2]	42.6 (1.65)	45.8 (1.48)	42.8 (1.48)	45.7 (1.60)	47.5 (1.66)	51.3 (1.69)	50.5 (0.95)	53.8 (0.90)	52.9 (0.97)	52.2 (0.92)	51.1 (0.95)	50.6 (0.97)	52.0 (0.93)	52.9 (1.09)	51.8 (0.99)
Some college, no bachelor's degree[3]	45.9 (3.37)	48.2 (2.87)	51.1 (2.95)	54.1 (2.81)	57.0 (2.32)	58.8 (2.17)	60.9 (1.06)	62.0 (1.04)	59.1 (1.02)	59.9 (1.08)	59.6 (1.08)	58.7 (1.01)	60.2 (1.03)	58.2 (1.19)	59.4 (0.92)
Bachelor's or higher degree	57.8 (3.72)	54.0 (3.27)	55.1 (3.18)	58.6 (2.98)	61.9 (2.81)	65.1 (2.28)	67.5 (1.22)	68.7 (1.04)	67.5 (0.96)	67.5 (0.98)	67.0 (1.04)	68.3 (1.03)	67.2 (0.93)	66.6 (1.25)	68.1 (0.86)

—Not available.
†Not applicable.
[1]Data for 16- to 19-year-olds and 20- to 24-year-olds exclude persons enrolled in school.
[2]Includes equivalency credentials, such as the GED credential.
[3]Includes persons with no college degree as well as those with an associate's degree.

NOTE: For each age group, the employment to population ratio of females in that age group is the number of females who are employed as a percentage of the female civilian population in that age group.
SOURCE: U.S. Department of Commerce, Census Bureau, Current Population Survey (CPS), Annual Social and Economic Supplement, selected years, 1975 through 2015. (This table was prepared October 2015.)

Table 501.80. Unemployment rates of persons 16 to 64 years old, by age group and highest level of educational attainment: Selected years, 1975 through 2015

[Standard errors appear in parentheses]

Age group and highest level of educational attainment	1975	1980	1985	1990	1995	2000	2005	2008	2009	2010	2011	2012	2013	2014	2015
1	2	3	4	5	6	7	8	9	10	11	12	13	14	15	16
16 to 19 years old, all education levels[1]	**— (†)**	**— (†)**	**— (†)**	**17.0 (1.83)**	**21.0 (2.06)**	**17.2 (1.89)**	**22.8 (1.39)**	**20.9 (1.36)**	**30.3 (1.58)**	**31.9 (1.59)**	**28.8 (1.62)**	**30.6 (1.57)**	**29.4 (1.57)**	**22.9 (1.83)**	**22.5 (1.35)**
Less than high school completion	— (†)	— (†)	— (†)	26.2 (3.54)	30.3 (3.67)	21.4 (3.23)	30.3 (2.34)	30.8 (2.40)	38.9 (3.05)	41.7 (3.14)	35.1 (3.42)	41.1 (3.01)	36.3 (2.70)	22.9 (3.38)	25.6 (2.67)
High school completion[2]	— (†)	— (†)	— (†)	11.7 (2.05)	15.1 (2.59)	15.3 (2.54)	19.1 (2.02)	17.2 (1.62)	29.1 (1.80)	29.6 (2.08)	28.9 (2.18)	28.7 (2.00)	29.2 (2.12)	25.0 (2.32)	23.3 (1.90)
At least some college	— (†)	— (†)	— (†)	‡ ! (†)	12.4 ! (5.19)	‡ ! (†)	15.8 (3.54)	11.3 (2.99)	18.1 (3.68)	18.1 (3.65)	16.2 (3.55)	19.6 (3.83)	16.2 (3.32)	15.1 (4.16)	13.2 (2.96)
20 to 24 years old, all education levels[1]	**— (†)**	**— (†)**	**— (†)**	**8.2 (0.63)**	**10.7 (0.72)**	**9.2 (0.70)**	**10.9 (0.48)**	**10.7 (0.43)**	**17.0 (0.62)**	**18.8 (0.66)**	**18.1 (0.60)**	**15.5 (0.55)**	**15.2 (0.62)**	**14.9 (0.70)**	**12.3 (0.53)**
Less than high school completion	— (†)	— (†)	— (†)	17.4 (2.15)	19.5 (2.37)	16.6 (2.18)	18.9 (1.24)	19.2 (1.66)	29.0 (1.69)	32.3 (1.80)	30.1 (1.95)	27.6 (2.12)	29.2 (2.27)	25.3 (2.75)	19.9 (1.99)
High school completion[2]	— (†)	— (†)	— (†)	7.8 (0.88)	12.0 (1.18)	10.0 (1.12)	12.0 (0.73)	13.0 (0.70)	20.3 (1.05)	22.3 (0.95)	21.6 (1.02)	18.3 (0.96)	17.5 (0.91)	18.9 (1.18)	15.8 (0.92)
Some college, no bachelor's degree[3]	— (†)	— (†)	— (†)	4.8 (1.09)	7.3 (1.13)	5.2 (1.02)	7.3 (0.76)	6.8 (0.67)	12.1 (0.94)	14.2 (1.07)	14.0 (0.98)	12.7 (0.89)	12.2 (1.02)	12.2 (1.16)	9.6 (0.89)
Bachelor's or higher degree	— (†)	— (†)	— (†)	3.1 ! (1.12)	4.1 ! (1.26)	5.0 (1.43)	5.4 (0.91)	4.5 (0.78)	7.9 (1.02)	7.9 (1.15)	8.7 (1.05)	6.0 (0.95)	7.0 (1.09)	6.7 (1.09)	5.1 (0.72)
25 to 64 years old, all education levels	**6.8 (0.21)**	**5.0 (0.17)**	**6.1 (0.18)**	**3.6 (0.14)**	**4.8 (0.15)**	**3.3 (0.13)**	**4.4 (0.09)**	**4.4 (0.09)**	**8.1 (0.12)**	**9.1 (0.13)**	**8.3 (0.13)**	**7.4 (0.11)**	**6.6 (0.12)**	**5.8 (0.14)**	**4.7 (0.10)**
Less than high school completion	10.5 (0.49)	8.4 (0.48)	11.4 (0.61)	7.7 (0.55)	10.0 (0.66)	7.9 (0.63)	9.0 (0.36)	10.1 (0.44)	15.8 (0.54)	16.8 (0.54)	16.2 (0.55)	14.3 (0.49)	12.7 (0.46)	10.6 (0.63)	9.2 (0.44)
High school completion[2]	6.8 (0.34)	5.1 (0.27)	6.9 (0.31)	3.8 (0.23)	5.2 (0.28)	3.8 (0.25)	5.5 (0.17)	5.8 (0.18)	10.4 (0.21)	12.1 (0.26)	10.9 (0.27)	9.2 (0.25)	8.7 (0.27)	7.4 (0.29)	6.2 (0.21)
Some college, no bachelor's degree[3]	5.5 (0.50)	4.3 (0.38)	4.7 (0.37)	3.1 (0.29)	4.5 (0.29)	3.0 (0.24)	4.2 (0.17)	4.2 (0.17)	8.0 (0.22)	8.8 (0.23)	8.1 (0.20)	7.9 (0.24)	6.5 (0.21)	6.1 (0.27)	4.9 (0.16)
Bachelor's or higher degree	2.4 (0.30)	1.9 (0.23)	2.4 (0.24)	1.7 (0.19)	2.5 (0.21)	1.5 (0.16)	2.3 (0.13)	2.1 (0.11)	4.3 (0.15)	4.7 (0.15)	4.4 (0.15)	4.1 (0.14)	3.8 (0.13)	3.4 (0.16)	2.4 (0.11)
25 to 34 years old, all education levels	**8.6 (0.41)**	**6.8 (0.32)**	**7.3 (0.33)**	**4.8 (0.27)**	**5.8 (0.30)**	**4.0 (0.27)**	**5.8 (0.18)**	**5.9 (0.21)**	**10.1 (0.27)**	**10.8 (0.28)**	**10.0 (0.28)**	**9.2 (0.26)**	**8.0 (0.23)**	**7.4 (0.30)**	**5.9 (0.20)**
Less than high school completion	17.2 (1.36)	13.7 (1.24)	15.5 (1.38)	12.0 (1.21)	12.9 (1.32)	10.3 (1.33)	11.6 (0.69)	14.2 (0.93)	19.9 (1.05)	20.3 (1.02)	19.7 (1.18)	16.8 (1.09)	15.1 (0.97)	13.7 (1.24)	12.5 (1.01)
High school completion[2]	9.4 (0.67)	7.9 (0.55)	9.1 (0.57)	5.1 (0.44)	6.8 (0.56)	4.8 (0.54)	7.7 (0.41)	8.5 (0.49)	14.1 (0.57)	15.9 (0.62)	14.3 (0.55)	12.8 (0.57)	12.1 (0.57)	10.5 (0.68)	8.9 (0.50)
Some college, no bachelor's degree[3]	6.7 (0.85)	6.0 (0.64)	5.4 (0.60)	3.8 (0.51)	5.0 (0.52)	3.6 (0.49)	5.4 (0.36)	5.0 (0.33)	9.8 (0.46)	10.6 (0.44)	10.1 (0.46)	10.1 (0.51)	8.0 (0.42)	7.8 (0.52)	6.5 (0.39)
Bachelor's or higher degree	2.9 (0.50)	2.5 (0.39)	2.8 (0.41)	1.9 (0.34)	2.7 (0.40)	1.6 (0.31)	2.6 (0.26)	2.2 (0.21)	4.5 (0.29)	4.5 (0.28)	4.3 (0.31)	4.1 (0.28)	3.6 (0.25)	3.7 (0.30)	2.4 (0.20)
35 to 44 years old, all education levels	**6.4 (0.41)**	**4.3 (0.31)**	**5.6 (0.33)**	**3.3 (0.24)**	**4.6 (0.27)**	**3.5 (0.23)**	**4.2 (0.14)**	**4.3 (0.17)**	**7.9 (0.18)**	**9.2 (0.24)**	**8.2 (0.23)**	**7.1 (0.22)**	**6.4 (0.19)**	**5.7 (0.24)**	**4.4 (0.17)**
Less than high school completion	11.2 (1.02)	9.0 (1.00)	12.4 (1.29)	8.3 (1.17)	10.5 (1.28)	8.4 (1.14)	8.7 (0.63)	9.1 (0.79)	15.3 (0.87)	17.8 (1.07)	15.9 (1.04)	14.1 (0.88)	11.5 (0.80)	11.5 (1.08)	8.4 (0.74)
High school completion[2]	5.7 (0.60)	4.2 (0.48)	6.1 (0.55)	3.7 (0.41)	5.1 (0.48)	3.9 (0.43)	5.2 (0.31)	6.0 (0.35)	10.6 (0.44)	11.9 (0.51)	11.3 (0.44)	9.1 (0.48)	8.5 (0.50)	7.4 (0.48)	6.3 (0.41)
Some college, no bachelor's degree[3]	4.6 (0.95)	3.1 (0.64)	4.8 (0.69)	2.8 (0.47)	4.7 (0.49)	3.1 (0.41)	3.9 (0.25)	3.8 (0.27)	7.2 (0.36)	9.2 (0.42)	7.5 (0.39)	7.4 (0.44)	6.7 (0.40)	6.1 (0.49)	4.5 (0.31)
Bachelor's or higher degree	2.3 (0.59)	1.6 (0.41)	2.2 (0.39)	1.6 (0.31)	2.2 (0.34)	1.8 (0.31)	2.0 (0.19)	1.9 (0.17)	4.2 (0.26)	4.6 (0.26)	4.6 (0.29)	3.6 (0.26)	3.6 (0.23)	2.8 (0.30)	2.1 (0.20)
45 to 54 years old, all education levels	**5.9 (0.39)**	**3.9 (0.32)**	**5.4 (0.39)**	**2.5 (0.26)**	**3.9 (0.29)**	**2.4 (0.22)**	**3.9 (0.16)**	**3.9 (0.16)**	**7.4 (0.21)**	**8.4 (0.22)**	**7.5 (0.20)**	**6.8 (0.18)**	**6.0 (0.18)**	**4.9 (0.24)**	**4.1 (0.15)**
Less than high school completion	8.5 (0.81)	6.6 (0.78)	10.2 (1.16)	4.7 (0.89)	7.9 (1.24)	6.1 (1.16)	7.0 (0.66)	8.9 (0.74)	13.6 (0.95)	15.6 (0.98)	16.3 (0.92)	13.5 (0.92)	12.3 (0.94)	8.0 (0.95)	8.6 (0.80)
High school completion[2]	5.6 (0.60)	3.4 (0.48)	5.4 (0.60)	2.3 (0.39)	4.0 (0.53)	2.7 (0.42)	4.6 (0.33)	4.7 (0.34)	8.8 (0.42)	11.0 (0.43)	9.3 (0.42)	7.8 (0.36)	7.8 (0.40)	6.1 (0.50)	5.2 (0.34)
Some college, no bachelor's degree[3]	4.7 (1.00)	3.0 (0.78)	3.2 (0.79)	2.6 (0.62)	3.9 (0.56)	2.4 (0.40)	3.7 (0.30)	4.0 (0.32)	7.5 (0.39)	7.6 (0.40)	7.1 (0.35)	6.9 (0.36)	5.2 (0.35)	4.8 (0.44)	4.1 (0.30)
Bachelor's or higher degree	2.0 ! (0.61)	1.3 ! (0.44)	2.1 (0.54)	1.4 (0.38)	2.4 (0.41)	1.3 (0.28)	2.5 (0.26)	1.9 (0.18)	4.3 (0.29)	4.8 (0.30)	4.0 (0.27)	3.9 (0.27)	3.8 (0.26)	3.2 (0.29)	2.2 (0.18)
55 to 64 years old, all education levels	**5.5 (0.46)**	**3.2 (0.35)**	**4.6 (0.44)**	**2.8 (0.36)**	**3.9 (0.42)**	**2.8 (0.35)**	**3.7 (0.20)**	**3.3 (0.18)**	**6.7 (0.25)**	**7.3 (0.25)**	**6.9 (0.25)**	**6.6 (0.23)**	**5.7 (0.23)**	**5.2 (0.28)**	**4.2 (0.20)**
Less than high school completion	7.1 (0.79)	5.2 (0.77)	7.1 (1.01)	3.9 (0.90)	6.7 (1.35)	5.2 (1.28)	7.5 (0.90)	5.6 (0.77)	12.7 (1.25)	10.1 (0.99)	10.0 (1.02)	11.5 (1.05)	11.2 (1.19)	8.2 (1.21)	6.9 (0.84)
High school completion[2]	5.1 (0.76)	2.7 (0.51)	4.5 (0.69)	3.0 (0.59)	3.4 (0.65)	3.1 (0.62)	4.3 (0.39)	3.4 (0.35)	7.8 (0.50)	9.3 (0.56)	8.4 (0.58)	7.1 (0.50)	6.4 (0.47)	5.6 (0.53)	4.4 (0.38)
Some college, no bachelor's degree[3]	4.1 ! (1.26)	2.0 ! (0.77)	3.0 ! (1.00)	2.2 ! (0.82)	3.2 (0.80)	2.8 (0.70)	3.5 (0.37)	3.7 (0.37)	7.0 (0.50)	7.7 (0.52)	7.3 (0.45)	7.1 (0.44)	5.8 (0.40)	5.5 (0.54)	4.3 (0.40)
Bachelor's or higher degree	1.5 ! (0.75)	‡ ! (†)	2.2 ! (0.70)	1.8 ! (0.62)	3.3 (0.79)	1.4 ! (0.46)	2.3 (0.30)	2.4 (0.26)	4.3 (0.33)	5.0 (0.34)	4.9 (0.35)	4.8 (0.38)	4.2 (0.29)	4.0 (0.39)	3.3 (0.30)

—Not available.
†Not applicable.
!Interpret data with caution. The coefficient of variation (CV) for this estimate is between 30 and 50 percent.
‡Reporting standards not met. The coefficient of variation (CV) for this estimate is 50 percent or greater.
[1]Data for 16- to 19-year-olds and 20- to 24-year-olds exclude persons enrolled in school.
[2]Includes equivalency credentials, such as the GED credential.
[3]Includes persons with no college degree as well as those with an associate's degree.
NOTE: The unemployment rate is the percentage of persons in the civilian labor force who are not working and who made specific efforts to find employment sometime during the prior 4 weeks. The civilian labor force consists of all civilians who are employed or seeking employment.
SOURCE: U.S. Department of Commerce, Census Bureau, Current Population Survey (CPS), Annual Social and Economic Supplement, selected years, 1975 through 2015. (This table was prepared October 2015.)

Table 501.85. Unemployment rates of males 16 to 64 years old, by age group and highest level of educational attainment: Selected years, 1975 through 2015

[Standard errors appear in parentheses]

Age group and highest level of educational attainment	1975	1980	1985	1990	1995	2000	2005	2008	2009	2010	2011	2012	2013	2014	2015
1	2	3	4	5	6	7	8	9	10	11	12	13	14	15	16
16 to 19 years old, all education levels[1]	**— (†)**	**— (†)**	**— (†)**	**18.9 (2.58)**	**21.3 (2.71)**	**16.0 (2.36)**	**25.2 (1.83)**	**22.3 (1.79)**	**35.1 (2.08)**	**35.6 (2.07)**	**31.2 (2.10)**	**31.4 (2.05)**	**29.7 (2.00)**	**24.4 (2.40)**	**22.5 (1.79)**
Less than high school completion	— (†)	— (†)	— (†)	27.9 (4.45)	30.6 (4.60)	17.6 (3.69)	29.9 (2.88)	30.7 (2.87)	41.2 (3.89)	44.7 (4.07)	32.0 (4.05)	37.1 (3.82)	36.1 (3.57)	23.1 (4.25)	26.6 (3.61)
High school completion[2]	— (†)	— (†)	— (†)	12.1 (2.96)	14.4 (3.38)	15.0 (3.30)	23.4 (2.77)	18.9 (2.43)	34.4 (2.46)	33.0 (2.59)	32.7 (2.96)	31.8 (2.68)	28.8 (2.70)	26.7 (3.29)	23.0 (2.47)
At least some college	— (†)	— (†)	— (†)	‡ (†)	‡ (†)	‡ (†)	12.7 (4.34)	9.1 ! (3.09)	22.4 (5.43)	19.0 (5.64)	21.4 ! (5.91)	20.2 ! (5.03)	17.5 (4.79)	17.7 ! (7.00)	11.5 (3.68)
20 to 24 years old, all education levels[1]	**— (†)**	**— (†)**	**— (†)**	**8.4 (0.86)**	**11.1 (0.97)**	**9.4 (0.94)**	**11.4 (0.61)**	**11.5 (0.58)**	**19.8 (0.85)**	**21.4 (0.88)**	**19.7 (0.81)**	**16.6 (0.83)**	**16.5 (0.80)**	**17.0 (0.92)**	**13.6 (0.75)**
Less than high school completion	— (†)	— (†)	— (†)	16.9 (2.53)	17.4 (2.68)	16.5 (2.61)	16.1 (1.37)	18.2 (1.89)	29.2 (2.06)	32.4 (2.20)	27.0 (2.23)	27.8 (2.48)	26.4 (2.72)	23.6 (3.04)	19.0 (2.52)
High school completion[2]	— (†)	— (†)	— (†)	7.4 (1.15)	11.6 (1.48)	9.6 (1.45)	12.4 (0.97)	13.3 (0.85)	22.7 (1.31)	23.7 (1.25)	22.9 (1.31)	19.0 (1.28)	19.0 (1.24)	21.1 (1.60)	16.6 (1.16)
Some college, no bachelor's degree[3]	— (†)	— (†)	— (†)	4.6 ! (1.54)	8.0 (1.65)	4.8 (1.36)	7.8 (1.04)	7.1 (0.97)	13.7 (1.39)	16.4 (1.58)	15.2 (1.46)	12.0 (1.23)	12.8 (1.36)	13.8 (1.56)	11.5 (1.46)
Bachelor's or higher degree	— (†)	— (†)	— (†)	‡ (†)	5.6 ! (2.22)	5.5 ! (2.32)	6.8 (1.54)	4.7 (1.19)	10.1 (1.71)	9.8 (1.82)	10.8 (1.82)	6.6 (1.54)	8.5 (1.89)	7.3 (1.71)	5.1 (1.18)
25 to 64 years old, all education levels	**6.5 (0.26)**	**4.9 (0.22)**	**6.1 (0.24)**	**3.6 (0.19)**	**5.1 (0.21)**	**3.3 (0.18)**	**4.7 (0.14)**	**4.9 (0.13)**	**9.5 (0.18)**	**10.5 (0.19)**	**9.2 (0.18)**	**8.0 (0.16)**	**6.9 (0.16)**	**5.9 (0.19)**	**5.0 (0.14)**
Less than high school completion	10.3 (0.59)	8.2 (0.58)	11.2 (0.76)	7.3 (0.68)	10.9 (0.86)	7.1 (0.75)	7.9 (0.44)	10.9 (0.60)	16.5 (0.72)	17.8 (0.79)	16.7 (0.70)	13.6 (0.59)	11.9 (0.58)	9.4 (0.70)	8.4 (0.54)
High school completion[2]	6.6 (0.43)	5.3 (0.37)	7.2 (0.43)	3.8 (0.32)	5.7 (0.40)	3.9 (0.34)	6.0 (0.25)	6.3 (0.24)	12.4 (0.32)	13.8 (0.39)	12.2 (0.38)	10.1 (0.33)	9.2 (0.37)	7.8 (0.37)	6.7 (0.27)
Some college, no bachelor's degree[3]	5.0 (0.59)	4.4 (0.49)	4.5 (0.49)	3.0 (0.38)	4.4 (0.39)	3.1 (0.34)	4.3 (0.27)	4.2 (0.25)	9.3 (0.31)	10.2 (0.35)	8.7 (0.33)	8.2 (0.34)	6.5 (0.30)	5.9 (0.37)	4.9 (0.23)
Bachelor's or higher degree	2.1 (0.34)	1.7 (0.26)	2.4 (0.30)	1.8 (0.25)	2.6 (0.28)	1.6 (0.22)	2.5 (0.19)	2.0 (0.15)	4.7 (0.23)	5.1 (0.22)	4.6 (0.20)	4.3 (0.20)	3.7 (0.18)	3.4 (0.25)	2.8 (0.16)
25 to 34 years old, all education levels	**8.3 (0.50)**	**6.8 (0.41)**	**7.3 (0.43)**	**4.5 (0.35)**	**5.9 (0.40)**	**4.2 (0.37)**	**6.0 (0.27)**	**6.5 (0.28)**	**11.9 (0.40)**	**12.6 (0.40)**	**11.3 (0.38)**	**10.0 (0.38)**	**8.4 (0.31)**	**7.5 (0.41)**	**6.2 (0.27)**
Less than high school completion	17.3 (1.65)	13.4 (1.53)	13.9 (1.60)	10.3 (1.36)	12.5 (1.57)	8.8 (1.51)	9.7 (0.84)	14.8 (1.18)	19.2 (1.27)	20.7 (1.36)	19.2 (1.30)	14.3 (1.17)	13.2 (1.19)	10.8 (1.37)	10.2 (1.15)
High school completion[2]	9.0 (0.85)	8.2 (0.75)	9.5 (0.77)	4.6 (0.55)	6.6 (0.72)	4.9 (0.70)	7.8 (0.52)	8.5 (0.64)	16.1 (0.77)	17.8 (0.77)	15.2 (0.74)	13.5 (0.70)	11.8 (0.69)	10.1 (0.81)	9.1 (0.63)
Some college, no bachelor's degree[3]	6.6 (1.03)	6.0 (0.81)	4.9 (0.76)	3.6 (0.68)	4.6 (0.70)	3.8 (0.69)	5.6 (0.57)	5.0 (0.48)	11.3 (0.68)	11.8 (0.69)	11.2 (0.71)	11.1 (0.75)	8.5 (0.63)	7.8 (0.76)	6.1 (0.51)
Bachelor's or higher degree	2.6 (0.57)	2.4 (0.48)	2.8 (0.54)	1.9 (0.46)	2.8 (0.55)	1.8 (0.46)	2.7 (0.36)	2.1 (0.30)	5.1 (0.52)	4.8 (0.45)	4.5 (0.47)	4.2 (0.45)	3.9 (0.40)	3.8 (0.51)	2.8 (0.34)
35 to 44 years old, all education levels	**6.0 (0.50)**	**4.1 (0.39)**	**5.7 (0.44)**	**3.2 (0.32)**	**4.9 (0.37)**	**3.4 (0.31)**	**4.4 (0.20)**	**4.7 (0.24)**	**9.2 (0.30)**	**10.1 (0.33)**	**8.9 (0.32)**	**7.6 (0.31)**	**6.3 (0.29)**	**5.7 (0.33)**	**4.6 (0.26)**
Less than high school completion	10.8 (1.24)	8.4 (1.22)	12.3 (1.63)	7.9 (1.46)	11.8 (1.69)	6.3 (1.27)	7.8 (0.76)	9.9 (1.05)	16.5 (1.23)	18.4 (1.42)	15.8 (1.34)	13.5 (1.13)	10.3 (0.97)	9.8 (1.22)	7.5 (0.90)
High school completion[2]	5.8 (0.80)	4.2 (0.65)	6.5 (0.79)	3.4 (0.56)	5.6 (0.68)	4.2 (0.58)	5.7 (0.46)	6.4 (0.45)	12.2 (0.62)	12.9 (0.71)	12.4 (0.66)	9.7 (0.66)	8.8 (0.63)	8.2 (0.68)	6.3 (0.54)
Some college, no bachelor's degree[3]	3.3 ! (1.01)	2.9 (0.81)	5.3 (0.96)	2.8 (0.63)	4.8 (0.69)	2.9 (0.56)	4.1 (0.38)	4.1 (0.43)	8.3 (0.61)	9.9 (0.63)	7.4 (0.60)	7.4 (0.64)	6.1 (0.58)	5.5 (0.69)	4.9 (0.46)
Bachelor's or higher degree	1.9 ! (0.61)	1.3 ! (0.44)	2.2 (0.49)	1.7 (0.41)	2.0 (0.43)	1.7 (0.42)	2.1 (0.27)	1.7 (0.24)	4.6 (0.40)	4.6 (0.38)	4.7 (0.39)	4.1 (0.40)	3.1 (0.33)	2.6 (0.43)	2.2 (0.28)
45 to 54 years old, all education levels	**5.5 (0.48)**	**3.7 (0.40)**	**5.4 (0.51)**	**2.7 (0.36)**	**4.6 (0.42)**	**2.5 (0.30)**	**4.1 (0.25)**	**4.3 (0.23)**	**8.6 (0.31)**	**9.9 (0.32)**	**8.2 (0.30)**	**7.0 (0.22)**	**6.5 (0.26)**	**4.9 (0.33)**	**4.5 (0.23)**
Less than high school completion	8.3 (0.97)	6.1 (0.92)	10.9 (1.48)	4.7 (1.12)	9.4 (1.74)	6.9 (1.60)	6.3 (0.81)	9.7 (0.97)	14.1 (1.24)	16.8 (1.29)	16.6 (1.15)	13.7 (1.12)	12.3 (1.23)	8.7 (1.17)	8.8 (1.05)
High school completion[2]	4.9 (0.76)	3.3 (0.64)	5.5 (0.84)	2.8 (0.61)	5.5 (0.87)	2.4 (0.55)	5.1 (0.51)	5.4 (0.47)	10.7 (0.59)	12.6 (0.67)	10.3 (0.56)	8.7 (0.51)	8.9 (0.58)	6.2 (0.65)	5.7 (0.49)
Some college, no bachelor's degree[3]	4.4 (1.21)	3.5 ! (1.11)	2.6 ! (0.94)	2.5 ! (0.82)	4.0 (0.79)	2.6 (0.58)	3.8 (0.47)	3.9 (0.45)	8.6 (0.64)	9.5 (0.63)	8.1 (0.56)	6.3 (0.49)	5.0 (0.47)	4.3 (0.48)	4.1 (0.48)
Bachelor's or higher degree	1.8 ! (0.67)	1.1 ! (0.47)	2.0 ! (0.63)	1.4 ! (0.49)	2.7 (0.55)	1.3 (0.38)	2.7 (0.38)	1.9 (0.28)	4.8 (0.43)	5.3 (0.42)	3.9 (0.37)	3.8 (0.34)	3.7 (0.33)	3.1 (0.39)	2.4 (0.25)
55 to 64 years old, all education levels	**5.5 (0.58)**	**3.6 (0.46)**	**4.7 (0.57)**	**3.3 (0.51)**	**4.3 (0.59)**	**3.2 (0.49)**	**3.9 (0.30)**	**3.4 (0.25)**	**7.6 (0.36)**	**8.6 (0.37)**	**7.9 (0.34)**	**7.1 (0.33)**	**6.1 (0.32)**	**5.6 (0.37)**	**4.6 (0.28)**
Less than high school completion	6.9 (0.96)	5.9 (1.01)	7.4 (1.28)	4.6 (1.24)	7.7 (1.84)	5.5 ! (1.67)	6.7 (1.01)	5.7 (1.06)	14.8 (1.75)	11.6 (1.48)	13.4 (1.53)	12.1 (1.27)	11.7 (1.56)	7.2 (1.50)	6.9 (1.05)
High school completion[2]	5.5 (1.02)	2.8 (0.70)	4.6 (0.96)	3.7 (0.91)	3.6 (0.95)	3.5 (0.93)	5.2 (0.63)	4.0 (0.48)	9.4 (0.78)	11.1 (0.88)	10.2 (0.88)	7.7 (0.68)	6.7 (0.64)	6.5 (0.76)	5.1 (0.56)
Some college, no bachelor's degree[3]	3.1 ! (1.39)	2.5 ! (1.06)	3.6 ! (1.43)	‡ (†)	3.7 ! (1.16)	3.4 ! (1.06)	3.3 (0.52)	3.5 (0.51)	8.5 (0.80)	9.2 (0.77)	7.5 (0.65)	8.0 (0.70)	6.2 (0.62)	5.9 (0.80)	4.1 (0.48)
Bachelor's or higher degree	‡ (†)	‡ (†)	2.2 ! (0.80)	2.1 ! (0.78)	3.6 (1.00)	1.7 ! (0.63)	2.6 (0.41)	2.4 (0.34)	4.3 (0.47)	5.8 (0.48)	5.3 (0.47)	5.2 (0.55)	4.4 (0.42)	4.3 (0.53)	3.9 (0.50)

—Not available.
†Not applicable.
!Interpret data with caution. The coefficient of variation (CV) for this estimate is between 30 and 50 percent.
‡Reporting standards not met. The coefficient of variation (CV) for this estimate is 50 percent or greater.
[1]Data for 16- to 19-year-olds and 20- to 24-year-olds exclude persons enrolled in school.
[2]Includes equivalency credentials, such as the GED credential.
[3]Includes persons with no college degree as well as those with an associate's degree.

NOTE: The unemployment rate is the percentage of persons in the civilian labor force who are not working and who made specific efforts to find employment sometime during the prior 4 weeks. The civilian labor force consists of all civilians who are employed or seeking employment.

SOURCE: U.S. Department of Commerce, Census Bureau, Current Population Survey (CPS), Annual Social and Economic Supplement, selected years, 1975 through 2015. (This table was prepared October 2015.)

Table 501.90. Unemployment rates of females 16 to 64 years old, by age group and highest level of educational attainment: Selected years, 1975 through 2015

[Standard errors appear in parentheses]

Age group and highest level of educational attainment	1975	1980	1985	1990	1995	2000	2005	2008	2009	2010	2011	2012	2013	2014	2015
1	2	3	4	5	6	7	8	9	10	11	12	13	14	15	16
16 to 19 years old, all education levels[1]	**— (†)**	**— (†)**	**— (†)**	**14.7 (2.39)**	**20.6 (2.93)**	**18.9 (2.85)**	**19.7 (1.86)**	**18.8 (2.01)**	**23.8 (2.10)**	**26.9 (2.14)**	**25.5 (2.45)**	**29.6 (2.48)**	**28.9 (2.31)**	**20.9 (2.54)**	**22.4 (2.07)**
Less than high school completion	— (†)	— (†)	— (†)	23.4 (5.31)	29.7 (5.57)	27.9 (5.53)	31.0 (3.88)	30.9 (4.44)	34.9 (4.60)	36.4 (4.75)	40.4 (5.78)	46.2 (5.08)	36.5 (4.27)	22.5 (4.49)	24.4 (4.00)
High school completion[2]	— (†)	— (†)	— (†)	11.3 (2.64)	16.0 (3.69)	15.7 (3.66)	14.2 (2.34)	15.0 (2.09)	22.2 (2.59)	24.9 (3.03)	23.8 (2.91)	24.5 (3.01)	29.6 (3.16)	22.9 (3.54)	23.7 (2.88)
At least some college	— (†)	— (†)	— (†)	‡ (†)	‡ (†)	‡ (†)	18.3 (5.47)	14.2 ! (5.49)	14.0 (4.16)	17.3 (4.41)	11.8 ! (4.28)	18.7 ! (5.62)	15.2 (3.92)	12.9 ! (4.87)	14.8 (4.26)
20 to 24 years old, all education levels[1]	**— (†)**	**— (†)**	**— (†)**	**7.8 (0.86)**	**10.2 (1.00)**	**8.9 (0.96)**	**10.3 (0.73)**	**9.7 (0.63)**	**13.5 (0.78)**	**15.6 (0.86)**	**16.0 (0.75)**	**14.1 (0.78)**	**13.4 (0.85)**	**12.4 (0.89)**	**10.7 (0.69)**
Less than high school completion	— (†)	— (†)	— (†)	18.6 (3.70)	24.3 (4.34)	17.0 (3.60)	24.5 (2.79)	21.6 (3.02)	28.4 (2.94)	32.2 (3.38)	36.3 (3.46)	27.3 (3.57)	34.9 (3.85)	29.3 (5.22)	21.2 (3.60)
High school completion[2]	— (†)	— (†)	— (†)	8.1 (1.26)	12.7 (1.78)	10.6 (1.63)	11.5 (1.14)	12.5 (1.17)	16.6 (1.37)	19.9 (1.46)	19.5 (1.43)	17.1 (1.31)	15.1 (1.44)	15.8 (1.72)	14.6 (1.38)
Some college, no bachelor's degree[3]	— (†)	— (†)	— (†)	4.9 (1.43)	6.7 (1.43)	5.7 (1.42)	6.8 (1.01)	6.5 (0.94)	10.5 (1.18)	12.1 (1.33)	12.8 (1.27)	13.4 (1.28)	11.5 (1.36)	10.6 (1.41)	7.5 (0.97)
Bachelor's or higher degree	— (†)	— (†)	— (†)	3.5 ! (1.47)	3.1 ! (1.35)	4.6 ! (1.70)	4.4 (1.05)	4.4 (1.01)	6.1 (1.13)	6.3 (1.29)	7.2 (1.27)	5.6 (1.14)	5.6 (1.01)	6.3 (1.38)	5.2 (1.01)
25 to 64 years old, all education levels	**7.3 (0.33)**	**5.0 (0.25)**	**6.0 (0.26)**	**3.7 (0.20)**	**4.4 (0.21)**	**3.2 (0.18)**	**4.2 (0.12)**	**4.0 (0.12)**	**6.6 (0.12)**	**7.5 (0.15)**	**7.2 (0.17)**	**6.8 (0.15)**	**6.3 (0.15)**	**5.7 (0.19)**	**4.3 (0.13)**
Less than high school completion	10.8 (0.79)	8.9 (0.76)	11.7 (0.96)	8.3 (0.88)	8.6 (0.95)	9.1 (1.00)	10.9 (0.65)	8.5 (0.62)	14.5 (0.72)	15.0 (0.71)	15.2 (0.74)	15.4 (0.83)	14.1 (0.84)	12.7 (0.98)	10.6 (0.68)
High school completion[2]	7.1 (0.49)	5.0 (0.37)	6.5 (0.41)	3.9 (0.32)	4.6 (0.36)	3.6 (0.33)	4.8 (0.23)	5.1 (0.27)	7.9 (0.26)	9.8 (0.30)	9.1 (0.36)	8.1 (0.31)	8.1 (0.35)	6.8 (0.42)	5.6 (0.31)
Some college, no bachelor's degree[3]	6.3 (0.84)	4.1 (0.54)	4.8 (0.53)	3.2 (0.40)	4.5 (0.38)	2.9 (0.31)	4.0 (0.22)	4.2 (0.21)	6.7 (0.27)	7.5 (0.27)	7.5 (0.27)	7.7 (0.30)	6.4 (0.26)	6.3 (0.36)	5.0 (0.23)
Bachelor's or higher degree	3.1 (0.57)	2.2 (0.39)	2.5 (0.36)	1.6 (0.27)	2.4 (0.30)	1.4 (0.22)	2.2 (0.17)	2.1 (0.15)	4.0 (0.19)	4.3 (0.19)	4.3 (0.21)	3.8 (0.19)	3.8 (0.19)	3.4 (0.22)	2.1 (0.13)
25 to 34 years old, all education levels	**9.1 (0.65)**	**6.8 (0.47)**	**7.3 (0.47)**	**5.1 (0.39)**	**5.7 (0.42)**	**3.9 (0.37)**	**5.6 (0.27)**	**5.3 (0.29)**	**8.0 (0.28)**	**8.7 (0.33)**	**8.6 (0.33)**	**8.2 (0.32)**	**7.5 (0.32)**	**7.3 (0.36)**	**5.6 (0.29)**
Less than high school completion	17.0 (2.18)	14.2 (1.93)	18.5 (2.37)	15.1 (2.17)	13.7 (2.20)	12.9 (2.33)	15.7 (1.36)	12.8 (1.53)	21.5 (1.79)	19.5 (1.52)	20.8 (1.84)	22.0 (1.99)	19.3 (1.65)	19.1 (2.42)	17.5 (1.85)
High school completion[2]	10.0 (1.01)	7.6 (0.76)	8.6 (0.78)	5.7 (0.65)	6.9 (0.81)	4.8 (0.78)	7.6 (0.62)	8.7 (0.67)	10.8 (0.67)	12.6 (0.86)	12.9 (0.78)	11.6 (0.82)	12.5 (0.88)	11.1 (1.04)	8.7 (0.74)
Some college, no bachelor's degree[3]	6.9 (1.38)	5.9 (0.94)	6.0 (0.88)	4.0 (0.72)	5.4 (0.73)	3.5 (0.63)	5.1 (0.46)	5.1 (0.45)	8.2 (0.56)	9.3 (0.57)	9.0 (0.61)	9.1 (0.59)	7.4 (0.57)	7.7 (0.68)	6.9 (0.58)
Bachelor's or higher degree	3.5 (0.88)	2.6 (0.60)	2.7 (0.57)	2.0 (0.47)	2.6 (0.53)	1.4 (0.39)	2.5 (0.31)	2.3 (0.29)	4.1 (0.37)	4.3 (0.35)	4.1 (0.35)	3.9 (0.38)	3.3 (0.33)	3.6 (0.38)	1.9 (0.26)
35 to 44 years old, all education levels	**7.1 (0.66)**	**4.7 (0.47)**	**5.4 (0.46)**	**3.5 (0.34)**	**4.3 (0.36)**	**3.7 (0.33)**	**3.9 (0.20)**	**3.8 (0.22)**	**6.4 (0.25)**	**8.2 (0.29)**	**7.4 (0.30)**	**6.5 (0.29)**	**6.6 (0.27)**	**5.6 (0.34)**	**4.1 (0.20)**
Less than high school completion	11.9 (1.65)	10.0 (1.56)	12.7 (1.95)	8.9 (1.79)	8.4 (1.75)	11.3 (1.94)	10.1 (1.02)	7.7 (1.03)	13.0 (1.33)	16.7 (1.32)	16.1 (1.51)	15.2 (1.29)	13.6 (1.57)	14.9 (1.99)	10.2 (1.26)
High school completion[2]	5.7 (0.85)	4.1 (0.65)	5.7 (0.72)	4.0 (0.57)	4.5 (0.63)	3.6 (0.58)	4.5 (0.40)	5.3 (0.50)	8.4 (0.63)	10.5 (0.67)	9.6 (0.66)	8.3 (0.71)	8.1 (0.70)	6.2 (0.68)	6.3 (0.61)
Some college, no bachelor's degree[3]	6.8 (1.76)	3.3 (0.97)	4.3 (0.91)	2.8 (0.64)	4.7 (0.66)	3.3 (0.57)	3.7 (0.36)	3.6 (0.35)	6.2 (0.46)	8.5 (0.51)	7.6 (0.56)	7.4 (0.54)	7.3 (0.53)	6.7 (0.70)	4.2 (0.39)
Bachelor's or higher degree	3.5 ! (1.29)	2.3 ! (0.76)	2.2 (0.61)	1.4 ! (0.42)	2.4 (0.52)	1.8 (0.44)	1.9 (0.26)	2.1 (0.24)	3.7 (0.35)	4.5 (0.35)	4.5 (0.41)	3.1 (0.31)	4.0 (0.35)	3.0 (0.40)	2.1 (0.25)
45 to 54 years old, all education levels	**6.5 (0.62)**	**4.1 (0.49)**	**5.3 (0.56)**	**2.3 (0.35)**	**3.1 (0.36)**	**2.4 (0.30)**	**3.6 (0.19)**	**3.5 (0.20)**	**6.1 (0.23)**	**6.8 (0.27)**	**6.7 (0.29)**	**6.5 (0.28)**	**5.6 (0.25)**	**4.9 (0.32)**	**3.7 (0.19)**
Less than high school completion	9.0 (1.33)	7.6 (1.32)	9.2 (1.71)	4.7 (1.33)	5.8 (1.55)	5.1 ! (1.52)	8.2 (1.08)	7.3 (1.08)	12.7 (1.38)	13.6 (1.41)	15.8 (1.50)	13.1 (1.49)	12.1 (1.43)	6.7 (1.32)	8.3 (1.09)
High school completion[2]	6.3 (0.88)	3.6 (0.66)	5.4 (0.80)	1.8 (0.46)	2.7 (0.57)	3.0 (0.59)	4.0 (0.39)	3.7 (0.41)	6.6 (0.50)	9.0 (0.56)	8.0 (0.62)	6.7 (0.48)	6.4 (0.45)	6.1 (0.69)	4.4 (0.51)
Some college, no bachelor's degree[3]	5.3 ! (1.61)	2.3 ! (0.99)	4.0 ! (1.23)	2.7 ! (0.89)	3.7 (0.73)	2.2 (0.52)	3.6 (0.41)	4.2 (0.40)	6.5 (0.47)	5.9 (0.43)	6.2 (0.43)	7.5 (0.57)	5.4 (0.44)	5.3 (0.64)	4.1 (0.39)
Bachelor's or higher degree	2.6 ! (1.18)	1.9 ! (0.90)	2.4 ! (0.92)	1.3 ! (0.56)	2.1 (0.57)	1.3 ! (0.39)	2.2 (0.33)	1.9 (0.24)	3.8 (0.34)	4.3 (0.36)	4.1 (0.40)	4.1 (0.38)	3.9 (0.38)	3.3 (0.40)	2.0 (0.25)
55 to 64 years old, all education levels	**5.4 (0.71)**	**2.5 (0.47)**	**4.5 (0.63)**	**2.2 (0.47)**	**3.3 (0.55)**	**2.4 (0.45)**	**3.4 (0.29)**	**3.2 (0.24)**	**5.6 (0.33)**	**6.0 (0.32)**	**5.9 (0.34)**	**6.0 (0.31)**	**5.4 (0.33)**	**4.7 (0.38)**	**3.7 (0.26)**
Less than high school completion	7.3 (1.28)	3.7 (1.06)	6.7 (1.49)	2.9 ! (1.17)	5.3 ! (1.78)	4.8 ! (1.84)	8.6 (1.51)	5.6 (1.10)	9.7 (1.45)	8.0 (1.36)	4.8 (1.05)	10.8 (1.78)	10.5 (1.69)	9.8 (2.00)	7.0 (1.51)
High school completion[2]	4.6 (1.05)	2.6 (0.69)	4.5 (0.93)	2.2 ! (0.68)	3.2 (0.84)	2.8 (0.77)	3.3 (0.46)	2.9 (0.45)	6.3 (0.64)	7.5 (0.68)	6.7 (0.65)	6.5 (0.69)	6.0 (0.64)	4.6 (0.65)	3.5 (0.54)
Some college, no bachelor's degree[3]	5.6 ! (2.23)	‡ (†)	‡ (†)	2.4 ! (1.15)	2.8 ! (1.00)	2.2 ! (0.84)	3.7 (0.54)	3.9 (0.51)	5.5 (0.63)	6.3 (0.65)	7.1 (0.66)	6.3 (0.58)	5.5 (0.50)	5.1 (0.68)	4.5 (0.55)
Bachelor's or higher degree	‡ (†)	‡ (†)	‡ (†)	‡ (†)	2.6 ! (1.16)	‡ (†)	1.9 (0.39)	2.3 (0.36)	4.3 (0.50)	4.1 (0.49)	4.4 (0.52)	4.4 (0.51)	4.0 (0.44)	3.6 (0.58)	2.7 (0.36)

—Not available.
†Not applicable.
!Interpret data with caution. The coefficient of variation (CV) for this estimate is between 30 and 50 percent.
‡Reporting standards not met. The coefficient of variation (CV) for this estimate is 50 percent or greater.
[1]Data for 16- to 19-year-olds and 20- to 24-year-olds exclude persons enrolled in school.
[2]Includes equivalency credentials, such as the GED credential.
[3]Includes persons with no college degree as well as those with an associate's degree.

NOTE: The unemployment rate is the percentage of persons in the civilian labor force who are not working and who made specific efforts to find employment sometime during the prior 4 weeks. The civilian labor force consists of all civilians who are employed or seeking employment.

SOURCE: U.S. Department of Commerce, Census Bureau, Current Population Survey (CPS), Annual Social and Economic Supplement, selected years, 1975 through 2015. (This table was prepared October 2015.)

Table 502.10. Occupation of employed persons 25 years old and over, by highest level of educational attainment and sex: 2014 and 2015

[Standard errors appear in parentheses]

Sex and occupation	Total employed (in thousands)		Percentage distribution, by highest level of educational attainment: Total	Less than high school completion		High school completion (includes equivalency)		College: Some college, no degree		College: Associate's degree		College: Bachelor's degree		College: Master's or higher degree	
1	2		3	4		5		6		7		8		9	
2014															
All persons	**127,863**	**(227.9)**	**100.0**	**7.7**	**(0.09)**	**26.5**	**(0.14)**	**16.5**	**(0.12)**	**11.1**	**(0.10)**	**24.1**	**(0.14)**	**14.1**	**(0.11)**
Management, professional, and related	52,674	(224.1)	100.0	1.2	(0.05)	10.5	(0.15)	11.1	(0.16)	10.4	(0.15)	36.9	(0.24)	29.9	(0.23)
Management, business, and financial operations	22,144	(161.3)	100.0	2.0	(0.11)	15.6	(0.28)	14.2	(0.27)	8.9	(0.22)	39.0	(0.38)	20.3	(0.31)
Professional and related	30,531	(184.4)	100.0	0.6	(0.05)	6.8	(0.17)	8.8	(0.19)	11.5	(0.21)	35.4	(0.32)	36.9	(0.32)
Education, training, and library	7,972	(100.9)	100.0	0.5	(0.09)	6.0	(0.31)	6.4	(0.32)	5.6	(0.30)	34.7	(0.62)	46.9	(0.65)
Preschool and kindergarten teachers	591	(28.1)	100.0	‡	(†)	12.7	(1.58)	13.2	(1.61)	14.4	(1.67)	40.3	(2.33)	18.8	(1.86)
Elementary and middle school teachers	2,955	(62.3)	100.0	0.2 !	(0.10)	2.1	(0.30)	2.6	(0.34)	2.5	(0.33)	42.8	(1.05)	49.7	(1.06)
Secondary school teachers	1,044	(37.2)	100.0	‡	(†)	1.1 !	(0.37)	1.5	(0.44)	1.1 !	(0.38)	41.3	(1.76)	54.7	(1.78)
Special education teachers	320	(20.7)	100.0	‡	(†)	3.4 !	(1.18)	2.5 !	(1.01)	5.3	(1.45)	34.4	(3.07)	54.7	(3.22)
Postsecondary teachers	1,170	(39.4)	100.0	‡	(†)	0.9 !	(0.33)	2.0	(0.47)	3.2	(0.60)	13.4	(1.15)	80.3	(1.35)
Other education, training, and library workers	1,892	(50.0)	100.0	1.2	(0.29)	16.2	(0.98)	16.3	(0.98)	11.4	(0.85)	30.0	(1.22)	24.9	(1.15)
Service occupations	20,013	(154.4)	100.0	15.9	(0.30)	36.7	(0.39)	20.2	(0.33)	11.8	(0.26)	12.7	(0.27)	2.7	(0.13)
Sales and office occupations	27,778	(177.5)	100.0	4.1	(0.14)	31.3	(0.32)	23.2	(0.29)	12.4	(0.23)	24.0	(0.30)	5.0	(0.15)
Natural resources, construction, and maintenance	12,097	(122.9)	100.0	20.1	(0.42)	42.3	(0.52)	17.2	(0.40)	12.2	(0.34)	7.0	(0.27)	1.2	(0.12)
Production, transportation, and material moving	15,301	(136.9)	100.0	16.3	(0.35)	46.7	(0.47)	18.0	(0.36)	9.0	(0.27)	8.5	(0.26)	1.5	(0.12)
Males	**68,284**	**(152.2)**	**100.0**	**9.4**	**(0.13)**	**28.4**	**(0.20)**	**16.3**	**(0.16)**	**9.6**	**(0.13)**	**23.0**	**(0.18)**	**13.3**	**(0.15)**
Management, professional, and related	25,606	(154.8)	100.0	1.5	(0.09)	11.2	(0.22)	11.4	(0.23)	8.1	(0.19)	37.1	(0.34)	30.7	(0.33)
Management, business, and financial operations	12,569	(118.6)	100.0	2.4	(0.16)	16.5	(0.38)	14.0	(0.35)	7.9	(0.27)	38.3	(0.49)	20.9	(0.41)
Professional and related	13,037	(120.4)	100.0	0.7	(0.08)	6.0	(0.24)	8.9	(0.28)	8.3	(0.27)	36.0	(0.48)	40.1	(0.49)
Education, training, and library	2,052	(51.0)	100.0	0.3 !	(0.15)	3.0	(0.43)	4.7	(0.53)	2.9	(0.42)	32.9	(1.18)	56.2	(1.25)
Service occupations	8,642	(100.7)	100.0	16.2	(0.45)	34.8	(0.58)	20.4	(0.49)	10.4	(0.37)	15.2	(0.44)	3.0	(0.21)
Sales and office occupations	10,535	(109.9)	100.0	4.5	(0.23)	28.1	(0.50)	21.7	(0.46)	10.0	(0.33)	29.3	(0.50)	6.4	(0.27)
Natural resources, construction, and maintenance	11,562	(114.4)	100.0	19.9	(0.42)	42.7	(0.52)	17.2	(0.40)	12.3	(0.35)	6.8	(0.27)	1.1	(0.11)
Production, transportation, and material moving	11,939	(116.0)	100.0	15.3	(0.38)	47.3	(0.52)	18.4	(0.40)	9.1	(0.30)	8.5	(0.29)	1.5	(0.12)
Females	**59,579**	**(158.8)**	**100.0**	**5.8**	**(0.11)**	**24.3**	**(0.19)**	**16.8**	**(0.17)**	**12.8**	**(0.15)**	**25.3**	**(0.20)**	**15.1**	**(0.16)**
Management, professional, and related	27,069	(152.0)	100.0	0.8	(0.06)	10.0	(0.20)	10.8	(0.21)	12.6	(0.22)	36.7	(0.32)	29.1	(0.30)
Management, business, and financial operations	9,575	(101.9)	100.0	1.5	(0.14)	14.5	(0.40)	14.5	(0.40)	10.1	(0.34)	39.9	(0.55)	19.4	(0.45)
Professional and related	17,494	(131.0)	100.0	0.5	(0.06)	7.4	(0.22)	8.8	(0.24)	13.9	(0.29)	34.9	(0.40)	34.4	(0.40)
Education, training, and library	5,919	(81.9)	100.0	0.5	(0.10)	7.0	(0.37)	7.0	(0.37)	6.5	(0.35)	35.3	(0.68)	43.6	(0.71)
Service occupations	11,371	(109.9)	100.0	15.6	(0.37)	38.2	(0.50)	20.0	(0.41)	13.0	(0.35)	10.8	(0.32)	2.5	(0.16)
Sales and office occupations	17,243	(130.2)	100.0	3.8	(0.16)	33.3	(0.40)	24.1	(0.36)	13.9	(0.29)	20.7	(0.34)	4.2	(0.17)
Natural resources, construction, and maintenance	534	(25.4)	100.0	24.5	(2.05)	33.5	(2.25)	16.5	(1.77)	9.9	(1.42)	12.4	(1.57)	3.4	(0.86)
Production, transportation, and material moving	3,362	(62.7)	100.0	19.7	(0.75)	44.8	(0.94)	16.5	(0.70)	8.5	(0.53)	8.7	(0.53)	1.8	(0.25)
2015															
All persons	**130,077**	**(225.3)**	**100.0**	**7.8**	**(0.09)**	**25.7**	**(0.14)**	**16.6**	**(0.12)**	**10.9**	**(0.10)**	**24.4**	**(0.14)**	**14.6**	**(0.11)**
Management, professional, and related	54,504	(226.3)	100.0	1.3	(0.06)	10.2	(0.15)	11.1	(0.16)	10.2	(0.15)	37.0	(0.24)	30.3	(0.23)
Management, business, and financial operations	23,093	(164.3)	100.0	2.2	(0.11)	15.1	(0.27)	14.3	(0.27)	8.8	(0.22)	39.1	(0.37)	20.5	(0.31)
Professional and related	31,410	(186.5)	100.0	0.6	(0.05)	6.6	(0.16)	8.8	(0.18)	11.1	(0.21)	35.5	(0.31)	37.4	(0.32)
Education, training, and library	8,124	(101.9)	100.0	0.5	(0.09)	6.1	(0.31)	6.5	(0.32)	4.9	(0.28)	34.8	(0.61)	47.2	(0.64)
Preschool and kindergarten teachers	605	(28.4)	100.0	1.0 !	(0.47)	12.9	(1.57)	13.1	(1.58)	13.4	(1.60)	38.2	(2.28)	21.5	(1.93)
Elementary and middle school teachers	2,994	(62.7)	100.0	0.3 !	(0.11)	1.9	(0.29)	2.2	(0.31)	2.1	(0.31)	43.7	(1.05)	49.9	(1.06)
Secondary school teachers	1,079	(37.9)	100.0	‡	(†)	0.9 !	(0.34)	2.2	(0.52)	1.2 !	(0.38)	37.5	(1.70)	57.9	(1.74)
Special education teachers	321	(20.7)	100.0	‡	(†)	4.0 !	(1.27)	3.4 !	(1.17)	3.4 !	(1.17)	34.9	(3.08)	53.9	(3.22)
Postsecondary teachers	1,233	(40.5)	100.0	‡	(†)	0.9 !	(0.31)	1.7	(0.43)	2.6	(0.52)	15.4	(1.19)	79.2	(1.34)
Other education, training, and library workers	1,892	(50.0)	100.0	1.3	(0.30)	17.1	(1.00)	17.1	(1.00)	10.6	(0.82)	30.9	(1.23)	22.9	(1.12)
Service occupations	20,042	(154.5)	100.0	16.2	(0.30)	36.2	(0.39)	19.9	(0.33)	12.0	(0.27)	12.8	(0.27)	2.9	(0.14)
Sales and office occupations	27,800	(177.6)	100.0	4.0	(0.14)	30.3	(0.32)	23.6	(0.29)	12.5	(0.23)	24.3	(0.30)	5.3	(0.16)
Natural resources, construction, and maintenance	12,271	(123.7)	100.0	20.5	(0.42)	41.2	(0.51)	17.1	(0.39)	11.9	(0.34)	7.7	(0.28)	1.5	(0.13)
Production, transportation, and material moving	15,461	(137.6)	100.0	16.4	(0.34)	45.9	(0.46)	18.6	(0.36)	8.7	(0.26)	8.6	(0.26)	1.8	(0.13)
Males	**69,604**	**(149.4)**	**100.0**	**9.4**	**(0.13)**	**27.7**	**(0.19)**	**16.2**	**(0.16)**	**9.6**	**(0.13)**	**23.5**	**(0.18)**	**13.6**	**(0.15)**
Management, professional, and related	26,577	(156.6)	100.0	1.6	(0.09)	10.8	(0.22)	11.4	(0.22)	8.1	(0.19)	37.6	(0.34)	30.4	(0.32)
Management, business, and financial operations	13,085	(120.6)	100.0	2.7	(0.16)	16.0	(0.36)	14.0	(0.34)	8.0	(0.27)	39.0	(0.49)	20.3	(0.40)
Professional and related	13,492	(122.1)	100.0	0.6	(0.07)	5.8	(0.23)	8.9	(0.28)	8.1	(0.27)	36.3	(0.47)	40.3	(0.48)
Education, training, and library	2,141	(52.0)	100.0	‡	(†)	3.2	(0.43)	4.8	(0.52)	2.8	(0.41)	32.6	(1.15)	56.4	(1.22)
Service occupations	8,623	(100.6)	100.0	16.7	(0.46)	34.6	(0.58)	19.5	(0.49)	10.9	(0.38)	15.2	(0.44)	3.1	(0.21)
Sales and office occupations	10,612	(110.3)	100.0	4.2	(0.22)	27.6	(0.49)	21.7	(0.45)	10.5	(0.34)	29.4	(0.50)	6.6	(0.27)
Natural resources, construction, and maintenance	11,717	(115.1)	100.0	20.3	(0.42)	41.7	(0.52)	17.1	(0.40)	11.9	(0.34)	7.5	(0.28)	1.5	(0.13)
Production, transportation, and material moving	12,074	(116.6)	100.0	15.5	(0.37)	46.6	(0.52)	18.9	(0.41)	8.8	(0.29)	8.4	(0.29)	1.9	(0.14)
Females	**60,474**	**(157.7)**	**100.0**	**5.8**	**(0.10)**	**23.3**	**(0.19)**	**17.0**	**(0.17)**	**12.5**	**(0.15)**	**25.5**	**(0.20)**	**15.8**	**(0.16)**
Management, professional, and related	27,926	(153.4)	100.0	0.9	(0.06)	9.6	(0.19)	10.9	(0.20)	12.1	(0.22)	36.4	(0.32)	30.1	(0.30)
Management, business, and financial operations	10,008	(103.9)	100.0	1.5	(0.14)	13.9	(0.38)	14.8	(0.39)	9.9	(0.33)	39.1	(0.54)	20.8	(0.45)
Professional and related	17,918	(132.2)	100.0	0.6	(0.06)	7.2	(0.21)	8.7	(0.23)	13.4	(0.28)	34.8	(0.39)	35.3	(0.39)
Education, training, and library	5,983	(82.3)	100.0	0.7	(0.11)	7.1	(0.36)	7.1	(0.37)	5.7	(0.33)	35.6	(0.68)	43.9	(0.71)
Service occupations	11,419	(110.1)	100.0	15.8	(0.38)	37.4	(0.50)	20.3	(0.41)	12.9	(0.34)	11.0	(0.32)	2.7	(0.17)
Sales and office occupations	17,188	(130.1)	100.0	3.9	(0.16)	32.0	(0.39)	24.7	(0.36)	13.7	(0.29)	21.2	(0.34)	4.5	(0.17)
Natural resources, construction, and maintenance	554	(25.8)	100.0	24.9	(2.02)	31.0	(2.16)	15.9	(1.71)	11.2	(1.47)	14.1	(1.63)	2.5	(0.73)
Production, transportation, and material moving	3,387	(62.9)	100.0	19.5	(0.75)	43.6	(0.94)	17.5	(0.72)	8.3	(0.52)	9.4	(0.55)	1.7	(0.25)

†Not applicable.
!Interpret data with caution. The coefficient of variation (CV) for this estimate is between 30 and 50 percent.
‡Reporting standards not met. Either there are too few cases for a reliable estimate or the coefficient of variation (CV) is 50 percent or greater.

NOTE: Detail may not sum to totals because of rounding.
SOURCE: U.S. Department of Labor, Bureau of Labor Statistics, Office of Employment and Unemployment Statistics, unpublished 2014 and 2015 annual average data from the Current Population Survey (CPS). (This table was prepared May 2016.)

Table 502.20. Median annual earnings, number, and percentage of full-time year-round workers 25 years old and over, by highest level of educational attainment and sex: 1990 through 2014

[Standard errors appear in parentheses]

Sex and year	Total	Elementary/secondary			College						
		Less than 9th grade	Some high school, no completion[1]	High school completion (includes equivalency)[2]	Some college, no degree[3]	Associate's degree	Bachelor's or higher degree[4]				
							Total	Bachelor's degree[5]	Master's degree	Professional degree	Doctor's degree
1	2	3	4	5	6	7	8	9	10	11	12
	Current dollars										
Males											
1990	$30,730 (—)	$17,390 (—)	$20,900 (—)	$26,650 (—)	$31,730 (—)	[6] (†)	$42,670 (—)	$39,240 (—)	[6] (†)	[6] (†)	[6] (†)
1991	31,610 (—)	17,620 (—)	21,400 (—)	26,780 (—)	31,660 (—)	$33,820 (—)	45,140 (—)	40,910 (—)	$49,730 (—)	$74,000 (—)	$57,190 (—)
1992	32,060 (120)	17,290 (—)	21,270 (—)	27,280 (175)	32,100 (—)	33,430 (—)	45,800 (—)	41,360 (304)	49,970 (—)	76,220 (—)	57,420 (—)
1993	32,360 (124)	16,860 (—)	21,750 (—)	27,370 (204)	32,080 (—)	33,690 (—)	47,740 (—)	42,760 (536)	51,870 (—)	80,550 (—)	63,150 (—)
1994	33,440 (246)	17,530 (453)	22,050 (319)	28,040 (322)	32,280 (300)	35,790 (430)	49,230 (707)	43,660 (633)	53,500 (854)	75,010 (3,040)	61,920 (1,619)
1995	34,550 (275)	18,350 (545)	22,190 (342)	29,510 (358)	33,880 (517)	35,200 (535)	50,480 (312)	45,270 (510)	55,220 (973)	79,670 (2,582)	65,340 (2,188)
1996	35,620 (150)	17,960 (594)	22,720 (414)	30,710 (184)	34,850 (456)	37,130 (435)	51,440 (303)	45,850 (458)	60,510 (945)	85,960 (3,317)	71,230 (3,362)
1997	36,680 (149)	19,290 (629)	24,730 (466)	31,220 (171)	35,950 (293)	38,020 (774)	53,450 (755)	48,620 (851)	61,690 (771)	85,010 (4,253)	76,230 (3,611)
1998	37,910 (291)	19,380 (600)	23,960 (547)	31,480 (169)	36,930 (291)	40,270 (539)	56,520 (421)	51,410 (349)	62,240 (847)	94,740 (12,105)	75,080 (2,507)
1999	40,330 (144)	20,430 (444)	25,040 (535)	33,180 (388)	39,220 (581)	41,640 (459)	60,200 (439)	52,990 (722)	66,240 (690)	100,000 ! (37,836)	81,690 (3,953)
2000	41,060 (156)	20,790 (376)	25,100 (436)	34,300 (457)	40,340 (312)	41,950 (460)	61,870 (303)	56,330 (573)	68,320 (1,506)	99,410 (20,832)	80,250 (2,446)
2001	41,620 (104)	21,360 (235)	26,210 (251)	34,720 (299)	41,050 (214)	42,780 (561)	62,220 (279)	55,930 (335)	70,900 (687)	100,000 (—)	86,970 (3,013)
2002	41,150 (100)	20,920 (213)	25,900 (207)	33,210 (311)	40,850 (195)	42,860 (673)	61,700 (201)	56,080 (385)	67,280 (1,294)	100,000 (—)	83,310 (2,076)
2003	41,940 (90)	21,220 (227)	26,470 (280)	35,410 (168)	41,350 (182)	42,870 (719)	62,080 (187)	56,500 (365)	70,640 (562)	100,000 (—)	87,130 (2,528)
2004	42,090 (89)	21,660 (191)	26,280 (234)	35,730 (148)	41,900 (175)	44,400 (931)	62,800 (798)	57,220 (393)	71,530 (490)	100,000 (—)	82,400 (2,423)
2005	43,320 (367)	22,330 (220)	27,190 (237)	36,300 (141)	42,420 (323)	47,180 (367)	66,170 (356)	60,020 (653)	75,030 (1,229)	100,000 (—)	85,860 (3,061)
2006	45,760 (134)	22,710 (398)	27,650 (573)	37,030 (164)	43,830 (812)	47,070 (390)	66,930 (346)	60,910 (235)	75,430 (859)	100,000 (—)	100,000 (—)
2007	47,000 (130)	23,380 (544)	29,320 (590)	37,860 (406)	44,900 (585)	49,040 (801)	70,400 (241)	62,090 (236)	76,280 (416)	100,000 (—)	92,090 (1,894)
2008	49,000 (339)	24,260 (631)	29,680 (458)	39,010 (399)	45,820 (276)	50,150 (344)	72,220 (236)	65,800 (388)	80,960 (468)	100,000 (—)	100,000 (—)
2009	49,990 (201)	23,950 (394)	28,020 (542)	39,480 (379)	47,100 (347)	50,300 (238)	71,470 (239)	62,440 (707)	79,340 (1,568)	123,240 (2,539)	100,740 (519)
2010	50,360 (93)	24,450 (597)	29,440 (684)	40,060 (237)	46,430 (348)	50,280 (245)	71,780 (267)	63,740 (1,115)	80,960 (453)	115,300 (4,891)	101,220 (653)
2011	50,660 (25)	25,220 (23)	30,420 (300)	40,450 (87)	47,070 (78)	50,930 (212)	73,850 (490)	66,200 (25)	83,030 (755)	119,470 (1,917)	100,770 (192)
2012	50,950 (144)	25,130 (440)	30,330 (430)	40,350 (194)	47,190 (407)	50,960 (329)	75,320 (565)	66,150 (570)	85,120 (1,412)	116,350 (5,632)	106,470 (4,656)
2013	51,120 (149)	26,160 (531)	30,570 (551)	40,290 (227)	47,650 (739)	51,000 (493)	76,110 (485)	67,240 (992)	86,310 (1,429)	126,730 (8,647)	105,280 (4,631)
2014	51,400 (133)	26,580 (382)	30,840 (382)	40,930 (197)	46,900 (429)	51,110 (345)	75,910 (391)	68,160 (1,282)	84,760 (1,988)	121,750 (5,986)	100,710 (852)
Females											
1990	21,370 (—)	12,250 (—)	14,430 (—)	18,320 (—)	22,230 (—)	[6] (†)	30,380 (—)	28,020 (—)	[6] (†)	[6] (†)	[6] (†)
1991	22,040 (—)	12,070 (—)	14,460 (—)	18,840 (—)	22,140 (—)	25,000 (—)	31,310 (—)	29,080 (—)	34,950 (—)	46,740 (—)	43,300 (—)
1992	23,140 (159)	12,960 (—)	14,560 (—)	19,430 (176)	23,160 (—)	25,620 (—)	32,300 (—)	30,330 (294)	36,040 (—)	46,260 (—)	45,790 (—)
1993	23,630 (166)	12,420 (—)	15,390 (—)	19,960 (173)	23,060 (—)	25,880 (—)	34,310 (—)	31,200 (310)	38,610 (—)	50,210 (—)	47,250 (—)
1994	24,400 (165)	12,430 (427)	15,130 (328)	20,370 (158)	23,510 (327)	25,940 (295)	35,380 (280)	31,740 (314)	39,460 (606)	50,620 (2,154)	51,120 (2,888)
1995	24,880 (160)	13,580 (490)	15,830 (293)	20,460 (162)	24,000 (274)	27,310 (428)	35,260 (313)	32,050 (273)	40,260 (556)	50,000 (2,532)	48,140 (2,373)
1996	25,810 (131)	14,410 (559)	16,950 (333)	21,180 (143)	25,170 (267)	28,080 (526)	36,460 (296)	33,530 (437)	41,900 (564)	57,620 (3,635)	56,270 (3,300)
1997	26,970 (134)	14,160 (492)	16,700 (335)	22,070 (148)	26,340 (291)	28,810 (660)	38,040 (481)	35,380 (295)	44,950 (837)	61,050 (4,737)	53,040 (3,626)
1998	27,960 (199)	14,470 (429)	16,480 (322)	22,780 (254)	27,420 (271)	29,920 (513)	39,790 (408)	36,560 (305)	45,280 (760)	57,570 (1,705)	57,800 (1,881)
1999	28,840 (216)	15,100 (492)	17,020 (298)	23,060 (279)	27,760 (369)	30,920 (318)	41,750 (275)	37,990 (614)	48,100 (862)	59,900 (4,479)	60,080 (3,130)
2000	30,330 (138)	15,800 (327)	17,920 (434)	24,970 (236)	28,700 (364)	31,070 (307)	42,710 (439)	40,420 (284)	50,140 (735)	58,960 (3,552)	57,080 (2,999)
2001	31,360 (91)	16,690 (255)	19,160 (359)	25,300 (132)	30,420 (186)	32,150 (231)	44,780 (367)	40,990 (231)	50,670 (328)	61,750 (3,976)	62,120 (2,228)
2002	31,010 (83)	16,510 (297)	19,310 (360)	25,180 (121)	29,400 (299)	31,630 (211)	43,250 (568)	40,850 (173)	48,890 (595)	57,020 (2,421)	65,720 (2,268)
2003	31,570 (85)	16,910 (256)	18,940 (327)	26,070 (118)	30,140 (176)	32,250 (241)	45,120 (291)	41,330 (204)	50,160 (454)	66,490 (3,469)	67,210 (2,462)
2004	31,990 (80)	17,020 (241)	19,160 (319)	26,030 (116)	30,820 (135)	33,480 (489)	45,910 (229)	41,680 (172)	51,320 (263)	75,040 (2,436)	68,880 (2,450)
2005	33,080 (242)	16,140 (250)	20,130 (274)	26,290 (134)	31,400 (165)	33,940 (497)	46,950 (232)	42,170 (179)	51,410 (283)	80,460 (2,774)	66,850 (2,490)
2006	35,100 (113)	18,130 (408)	20,130 (270)	26,740 (136)	31,950 (165)	35,160 (376)	49,570 (441)	45,410 (259)	52,440 (561)	76,240 (2,488)	70,520 (1,779)
2007	36,090 (105)	18,260 (461)	20,400 (292)	27,240 (133)	32,840 (415)	36,330 (283)	50,400 (158)	45,770 (262)	55,430 (412)	71,100 (910)	68,990 (2,155)
2008	36,700 (109)	18,630 (494)	20,410 (295)	28,380 (283)	32,630 (355)	36,760 (243)	51,410 (145)	47,030 (237)	57,510 (745)	71,300 (2,859)	74,030 (2,144)
2009	37,260 (107)	18,480 (451)	21,230 (301)	29,150 (273)	34,090 (483)	37,270 (310)	51,880 (169)	46,830 (260)	61,070 (304)	83,910 (3,210)	76,580 (912)
2010	38,290 (272)	18,240 (592)	20,880 (334)	29,860 (260)	33,400 (410)	37,770 (588)	51,940 (159)	47,440 (336)	59,100 (1,021)	76,740 (2,723)	77,390 (2,174)
2011	38,910 (216)	20,100 (250)	21,110 (131)	30,010 (145)	34,590 (512)	39,290 (40)	52,140 (88)	49,110 (103)	60,300 (533)	80,720 (135)	77,460 (21)
2012	39,980 (294)	20,060 (514)	21,390 (285)	30,410 (165)	35,060 (452)	37,320 (455)	53,690 (888)	50,170 (290)	60,930 (464)	94,470 (6,655)	77,900 (3,616)
2013	40,610 (134)	19,840 (502)	22,250 (544)	30,800 (173)	35,240 (312)	37,700 (751)	55,720 (416)	50,750 (341)	61,280 (561)	85,400 (6,196)	75,090 (3,515)
2014	40,830 (151)	20,990 (279)	21,990 (322)	30,650 (151)	34,380 (891)	37,480 (591)	55,940 (333)	51,350 (230)	60,830 (442)	91,810 (8,587)	80,540 (2,875)

See notes at end of table.

Table 502.20. Median annual earnings, number, and percentage of full-time year-round workers 25 years old and over, by highest level of educational attainment and sex: 1990 through 2014—Continued

[Standard errors appear in parentheses]

Sex and year	Elementary/secondary: Total	Elementary/secondary: Less than 9th grade	Elementary/secondary: Some high school, no completion[1]	Elementary/secondary: High school completion (includes equivalency)[2]	College: Some college, no degree[3]	College: Associate's degree	College: Bachelor's or higher degree[4]: Total	Bachelor's or higher degree[4]: Bachelor's degree[5]	Bachelor's or higher degree[4]: Master's degree	Bachelor's or higher degree[4]: Professional degree	Bachelor's or higher degree[4]: Doctor's degree
1	2	3	4	5	6	7	8	9	10	11	12
					Constant 2014 dollars[7]						
Males											
1990	$55,000 (—)	$31,130 (—)	$37,410 (—)	$47,700 (—)	$56,790 (—)	[6] (†)	$76,370 (—)	$70,220 (—)	[6] (†)	[6] (†)	[6] (†)
1991	54,290 (—)	30,270 (—)	36,760 (—)	45,990 (—)	54,380 (—)	$58,080 (—)	77,520 (—)	70,250 (—)	$85,420 (—)	$127,080 (—)	$98,220 (—)
1992	53,450 (200)	28,830 (—)	35,470 (—)	45,480 (292)	53,520 (—)	55,740 (—)	76,360 (—)	68,950 (507)	83,320 (—)	127,080 (—)	95,730 (—)
1993	52,380 (201)	27,300 (—)	35,210 (—)	44,310 (330)	51,930 (—)	54,540 (—)	77,280 (—)	69,210 (868)	83,960 (—)	130,390 (—)	102,230 (—)
1994	52,780 (388)	27,670 (715)	34,800 (504)	44,250 (508)	50,950 (474)	56,500 (679)	77,700 (1,116)	68,920 (999)	84,440 (1,348)	118,390 (4,798)	97,730 (2,555)
1995	53,030 (422)	28,170 (837)	34,050 (525)	45,290 (549)	52,010 (794)	54,030 (821)	77,480 (479)	69,480 (783)	84,750 (1,493)	122,280 (3,963)	100,280 (3,358)
1996	53,110 (224)	26,780 (886)	33,870 (617)	45,780 (274)	51,950 (680)	55,360 (649)	76,680 (452)	68,350 (683)	90,210 (1,409)	128,160 (4,945)	106,190 (5,012)
1997	53,460 (217)	28,120 (917)	36,040 (679)	45,490 (249)	52,390 (427)	55,410 (1,128)	77,900 (1,100)	70,850 (1,240)	89,910 (1,124)	123,900 (6,198)	111,100 (5,263)
1998	54,400 (418)	27,810 (861)	34,380 (785)	45,170 (243)	53,000 (418)	57,800 (774)	81,120 (604)	73,770 (501)	89,320 (1,216)	135,950 (17,371)	107,740 (3,598)
1999	56,630 (202)	28,680 (623)	35,150 (751)	46,590 (545)	55,070 (816)	58,460 (644)	84,530 (616)	74,390 (1,014)	93,010 (969)	140,410 ! (53,124)	114,690 (5,550)
2000	55,770 (212)	28,240 (511)	34,090 (592)	46,600 (621)	54,790 (424)	56,990 (625)	84,040 (412)	76,520 (778)	92,810 (2,046)	135,040 (28,298)	109,010 (3,323)
2001	54,970 (137)	28,210 (310)	34,620 (332)	45,860 (395)	54,210 (283)	56,500 (741)	82,180 (369)	73,870 (442)	93,640 (907)	132,080 (—)	114,860 (3,980)
2002	53,510 (130)	27,200 (277)	33,680 (269)	43,180 (404)	53,120 (254)	55,720 (875)	80,230 (261)	72,910 (501)	87,480 (1,683)	130,030 (—)	108,320 (2,699)
2003	53,320 (114)	26,970 (289)	33,650 (356)	45,020 (214)	52,560 (231)	54,500 (914)	78,910 (238)	71,830 (464)	89,800 (714)	127,130 (—)	110,770 (3,214)
2004	52,110 (110)	26,820 (237)	32,540 (290)	44,240 (183)	51,880 (217)	54,990 (1,153)	77,760 (988)	70,860 (487)	88,580 (607)	123,830 (—)	102,040 (3,000)
2005	51,880 (440)	26,750 (263)	32,560 (284)	43,480 (169)	50,810 (387)	56,510 (440)	79,250 (426)	71,890 (782)	89,860 (1,472)	119,770 (—)	102,840 (3,666)
2006	53,090 (155)	26,350 (462)	32,090 (665)	42,970 (190)	50,860 (942)	54,620 (453)	77,660 (401)	70,670 (273)	87,520 (997)	116,030 (—)	116,030 (—)
2007	53,030 (147)	26,370 (614)	33,070 (666)	42,710 (458)	50,650 (660)	55,330 (904)	79,420 (272)	70,040 (266)	86,060 (469)	112,820 (—)	103,890 (2,137)
2008	53,240 (368)	26,350 (686)	32,240 (498)	42,380 (433)	49,780 (300)	54,480 (374)	78,460 (256)	71,490 (422)	87,960 (508)	108,650 (—)	108,650 (—)
2009	54,510 (219)	26,110 (430)	30,550 (591)	43,040 (413)	51,350 (378)	54,850 (259)	77,920 (261)	68,080 (771)	86,510 (1,710)	134,380 (2,768)	109,840 (566)
2010	54,020 (100)	26,230 (640)	31,580 (734)	42,970 (254)	49,810 (373)	53,940 (263)	77,000 (286)	68,370 (1,196)	86,850 (486)	123,680 (5,247)	108,580 (700)
2011	52,680 (26)	26,230 (24)	31,640 (312)	42,060 (90)	48,950 (81)	52,960 (220)	76,800 (510)	68,840 (26)	86,340 (785)	124,240 (1,994)	104,790 (200)
2012	51,910 (147)	25,600 (448)	30,900 (438)	41,110 (198)	48,070 (415)	51,920 (335)	76,740 (576)	67,400 (581)	86,720 (1,439)	118,540 (5,738)	108,470 (4,744)
2013	51,920 (151)	26,570 (539)	31,050 (560)	40,930 (231)	48,400 (751)	51,800 (501)	77,310 (493)	68,300 (1,008)	87,670 (1,452)	128,730 (8,784)	106,940 (4,704)
2014	51,400 (133)	26,580 (382)	30,840 (382)	40,930 (197)	46,900 (429)	51,110 (345)	75,910 (391)	68,160 (1,282)	84,760 (1,988)	121,750 (5,986)	100,710 (852)
Females											
1990	38,250 (—)	21,930 (—)	25,820 (—)	32,790 (—)	39,780 (—)	[6] (†)	54,370 (—)	50,140 (—)	[6] (†)	[6] (†)	[6] (†)
1991	37,860 (—)	20,720 (—)	24,830 (—)	32,350 (—)	38,030 (—)	42,940 (—)	53,770 (—)	49,940 (—)	60,020 (—)	80,280 (—)	74,370 (—)
1992	38,580 (265)	21,600 (—)	24,270 (—)	32,390 (293)	38,610 (—)	42,720 (—)	53,860 (—)	50,560 (490)	60,080 (—)	77,120 (—)	76,340 (—)
1993	38,250 (269)	20,100 (—)	24,910 (—)	32,320 (280)	37,320 (—)	41,900 (—)	55,540 (—)	50,500 (502)	62,500 (—)	81,280 (—)	76,480 (—)
1994	38,510 (260)	19,620 (674)	23,890 (518)	32,160 (249)	37,110 (516)	40,940 (466)	55,840 (442)	50,100 (496)	62,280 (956)	79,890 (3,400)	80,690 (4,558)
1995	38,180 (246)	20,840 (752)	24,290 (450)	31,410 (249)	36,830 (421)	41,920 (657)	54,120 (480)	49,190 (419)	61,800 (853)	76,740 (3,886)	73,890 (3,642)
1996	38,480 (195)	21,490 (833)	25,270 (496)	31,570 (213)	37,520 (398)	41,870 (784)	54,360 (441)	49,980 (652)	62,470 (841)	85,910 (5,419)	83,890 (4,920)
1997	39,310 (195)	20,640 (717)	24,330 (488)	32,160 (216)	38,380 (424)	41,990 (962)	55,440 (701)	51,560 (430)	65,510 (1,220)	88,980 (6,904)	77,300 (5,285)
1998	40,120 (286)	20,760 (616)	23,650 (462)	32,690 (365)	39,350 (389)	42,940 (736)	57,100 (586)	52,460 (438)	64,980 (1,091)	82,610 (2,447)	82,940 (2,699)
1999	40,500 (303)	21,200 (691)	23,890 (418)	32,380 (392)	38,970 (518)	43,410 (446)	58,620 (386)	53,340 (862)	67,530 (1,210)	84,110 (6,289)	84,350 (4,395)
2000	41,200 (187)	21,460 (444)	24,340 (590)	33,920 (321)	38,980 (494)	42,210 (417)	58,010 (596)	54,900 (386)	68,110 (998)	80,090 (4,825)	77,540 (4,074)
2001	41,420 (120)	22,050 (337)	25,300 (474)	33,420 (174)	40,180 (246)	42,470 (305)	59,140 (485)	54,150 (305)	66,920 (433)	81,560 (5,252)	82,050 (2,943)
2002	40,320 (108)	21,470 (386)	25,100 (468)	32,740 (157)	38,230 (389)	41,120 (274)	56,230 (739)	53,120 (225)	63,570 (774)	74,140 (3,148)	85,450 (2,949)
2003	40,130 (108)	21,490 (325)	24,080 (416)	33,150 (150)	38,320 (224)	41,000 (306)	57,360 (370)	52,540 (259)	63,770 (577)	84,530 (4,410)	85,450 (3,130)
2004	39,610 (99)	21,080 (298)	23,730 (395)	32,230 (144)	38,160 (167)	41,460 (606)	56,850 (284)	51,610 (213)	63,540 (326)	92,920 (3,017)	85,290 (3,034)
2005	39,610 (290)	19,330 (299)	24,100 (328)	31,490 (160)	37,610 (198)	40,650 (595)	56,230 (278)	50,510 (214)	61,580 (339)	96,370 (3,322)	80,070 (2,982)
2006	40,720 (131)	21,040 (473)	23,360 (313)	31,020 (158)	37,080 (191)	40,790 (436)	57,520 (512)	52,690 (301)	60,840 (651)	88,460 (2,887)	81,820 (2,064)
2007	40,710 (118)	20,600 (520)	23,010 (329)	30,730 (150)	37,050 (468)	40,990 (319)	56,860 (178)	51,640 (296)	62,530 (465)	80,210 (1,027)	77,830 (2,431)
2008	39,870 (118)	20,240 (537)	22,170 (321)	30,840 (307)	35,450 (386)	39,940 (264)	55,850 (158)	51,090 (257)	62,480 (809)	77,460 (3,106)	80,420 (2,329)
2009	40,630 (117)	20,150 (492)	23,140 (328)	31,780 (298)	37,170 (527)	40,630 (338)	56,560 (184)	51,060 (283)	66,580 (331)	91,480 (3,500)	83,500 (994)
2010	41,080 (292)	19,570 (635)	22,400 (358)	32,030 (279)	35,830 (440)	40,520 (631)	55,720 (171)	50,890 (360)	63,400 (1,095)	82,320 (2,921)	83,020 (2,332)
2011	40,460 (225)	20,900 (260)	21,960 (136)	31,210 (151)	35,970 (532)	40,850 (42)	54,220 (92)	51,070 (107)	62,710 (554)	83,940 (140)	80,550 (22)
2012	40,730 (300)	20,440 (524)	21,790 (290)	30,980 (168)	35,720 (460)	38,020 (464)	54,700 (905)	51,120 (295)	62,070 (473)	96,250 (6,780)	79,370 (3,684)
2013	41,250 (136)	20,150 (510)	22,600 (553)	31,290 (176)	35,800 (317)	38,300 (763)	56,600 (423)	51,550 (346)	62,250 (570)	86,740 (6,294)	76,280 (3,571)
2014	40,830 (151)	20,990 (279)	21,990 (322)	30,650 (151)	34,380 (891)	37,480 (591)	55,940 (333)	51,350 (230)	60,830 (442)	91,810 (8,587)	80,540 (2,875)

See notes at end of table.

Table 502.20. Median annual earnings, number, and percentage of full-time year-round workers 25 years old and over, by highest level of educational attainment and sex: 1990 through 2014—Continued

[Standard errors appear in parentheses]

Sex and year	Total	Elementary/secondary: Less than 9th grade	Elementary/secondary: Some high school, no completion[1]	Elementary/secondary: High school completion (includes equivalency)[2]	College: Some college, no degree[3]	College: Associate's degree	College: Bachelor's or higher degree[4]: Total	Bachelor's degree[5]	Master's degree	Professional degree	Doctor's degree
1	2	3	4	5	6	7	8	9	10	11	12
	Number of persons with earnings who worked full time, year round (in thousands)										
Males											
1990	44,406 (268.6)	2,250 (73.9)	3,315 (89.3)	16,394 (188.0)	9,113 (144.6)	[6] (†)	13,334 (171.8)	7,569 (132.6)	[6] (†)	[6] (†)	[6] (†)
1991	44,199 (268.3)	1,807 (66.3)	3,083 (86.2)	15,025 (181.1)	8,034 (136.4)	2,899 (83.6)	13,350 (171.9)	8,456 (139.7)	3,073 (86.1)	1,147 (53.0)	674 (40.7)
1992	44,752 (269.1)	1,815 (66.5)	3,009 (85.2)	14,722 (179.5)	8,067 (136.6)	3,203 (87.8)	13,937 (175.2)	8,719 (141.7)	3,178 (87.5)	1,295 (56.3)	745 (42.8)
1993	45,873 (270.6)	1,790 (66.0)	3,083 (86.2)	14,604 (178.9)	8,493 (140.0)	3,557 (92.4)	14,346 (177.5)	9,178 (145.1)	3,131 (86.8)	1,231 (54.9)	808 (44.5)
1994	47,566 (303.0)	1,895 (69.2)	3,057 (87.6)	15,109 (188.5)	8,783 (146.2)	3,735 (96.6)	14,987 (187.8)	9,636 (152.8)	3,225 (89.9)	1,258 (56.4)	868 (46.9)
1995	48,500 (306.1)	1,946 (72.8)	3,335 (94.9)	15,331 (195.6)	8,908 (152.3)	3,926 (102.8)	15,054 (194.0)	9,597 (157.8)	3,395 (95.7)	1,208 (57.5)	853 (48.4)
1996	49,764 (301.1)	2,041 (69.2)	3,441 (89.6)	15,840 (186.5)	9,173 (144.2)	3,931 (95.6)	15,339 (183.7)	9,898 (149.6)	3,272 (87.4)	1,277 (54.8)	893 (45.9)
1997	50,807 (299.0)	1,914 (67.0)	3,548 (90.9)	16,225 (187.8)	9,170 (143.9)	4,086 (97.4)	15,864 (185.9)	10,349 (152.4)	3,228 (86.7)	1,321 (55.8)	966 (47.7)
1998	52,381 (306.4)	1,870 (66.3)	3,613 (91.7)	16,442 (189.7)	9,375 (145.7)	4,347 (100.4)	16,733 (191.2)	11,058 (157.6)	3,414 (89.2)	1,264 (54.6)	998 (48.5)
1999	53,062 (307.8)	1,993 (68.4)	3,295 (87.7)	16,589 (190.5)	9,684 (148.0)	4,359 (100.6)	17,142 (193.3)	11,142 (158.2)	3,725 (93.1)	1,267 (54.6)	1,008 (48.8)
2000	54,065 (309.7)	1,968 (68.0)	3,354 (88.4)	16,834 (191.7)	9,792 (148.8)	4,729 (104.7)	17,387 (194.6)	11,395 (159.9)	3,680 (92.6)	1,274 (54.8)	1,038 (49.5)
2001	54,013 (224.8)	2,207 (51.4)	3,503 (64.5)	16,314 (135.4)	9,494 (104.9)	4,714 (74.7)	17,780 (140.9)	11,479 (114.8)	3,961 (68.5)	1,298 (39.5)	1,041 (35.4)
2002	54,108 (225.0)	2,154 (50.7)	3,680 (66.1)	16,005 (134.2)	9,603 (105.5)	4,399 (72.2)	18,267 (142.7)	11,829 (116.5)	4,065 (69.4)	1,308 (39.6)	1,065 (35.8)
2003	54,253 (225.2)	2,209 (51.4)	3,369 (63.3)	16,285 (135.3)	9,340 (104.1)	4,696 (74.5)	18,354 (143.0)	11,846 (116.6)	4,124 (69.9)	1,348 (40.2)	1,037 (35.3)
2004	55,469 (227.0)	2,427 (53.8)	3,468 (64.2)	17,067 (138.3)	9,257 (103.6)	4,913 (76.2)	18,338 (142.9)	11,701 (115.9)	4,243 (70.9)	1,305 (39.6)	1,088 (36.1)
2005	56,717 (228.7)	2,425 (53.8)	3,652 (65.9)	17,266 (139.0)	9,532 (105.1)	5,022 (77.0)	18,820 (144.7)	12,032 (117.4)	4,275 (71.2)	1,369 (40.5)	1,144 (37.1)
2006	58,109 (230.6)	2,361 (53.1)	3,872 (67.8)	17,369 (139.4)	9,493 (104.9)	5,110 (77.7)	19,903 (148.4)	12,764 (120.7)	4,542 (73.3)	1,425 (41.3)	1,172 (37.5)
2007	58,147 (230.7)	2,142 (50.6)	3,451 (64.0)	17,224 (138.9)	9,867 (106.8)	5,244 (78.7)	20,218 (149.5)	12,962 (121.6)	4,800 (75.3)	1,332 (40.0)	1,125 (36.7)
2008	55,655 (227.2)	1,982 (48.7)	3,118 (60.9)	16,195 (135.0)	9,515 (105.0)	5,020 (77.0)	19,825 (148.1)	12,609 (120.0)	4,709 (74.6)	1,388 (40.8)	1,119 (36.7)
2009	52,445 (222.5)	1,561 (43.2)	2,795 (57.7)	15,258 (131.3)	8,609 (100.1)	4,828 (75.5)	19,395 (146.7)	12,290 (118.6)	4,575 (73.6)	1,319 (39.8)	1,212 (38.1)
2010	52,890 (223.2)	1,600 (43.8)	2,615 (55.9)	15,104 (130.7)	8,541 (99.7)	5,042 (77.2)	19,990 (148.7)	12,836 (121.1)	4,670 (74.3)	1,237 (38.5)	1,246 (38.7)
2011	54,279 (225.2)	1,848 (47.0)	2,715 (56.9)	15,335 (131.6)	8,752 (100.9)	5,206 (78.4)	20,423 (150.1)	13,013 (121.8)	4,839 (75.6)	1,300 (39.5)	1,271 (39.0)
2012	55,208 (226.6)	1,793 (46.3)	2,671 (56.4)	15,295 (131.4)	8,974 (102.1)	5,423 (80.0)	21,052 (152.2)	13,315 (123.2)	5,003 (76.9)	1,301 (39.5)	1,433 (41.4)
2013	56,703 (289.3)	1,944 (61.0)	2,910 (74.5)	16,034 (170.0)	8,960 (129.0)	5,605 (102.8)	21,249 (193.4)	13,378 (156.2)	5,146 (98.6)	1,249 (49.0)	1,476 (53.2)
2014	58,435 (256.1)	1,994 (54.0)	3,012 (66.2)	16,429 (150.3)	9,281 (114.7)	5,622 (90.0)	22,098 (172.1)	13,969 (139.3)	5,401 (88.2)	1,359 (44.6)	1,369 (44.8)
Females											
1990	28,636 (234.7)	847 (45.6)	1,861 (67.3)	11,810 (162.8)	6,462 (123.1)	[6] (†)	7,655 (133.3)	4,704 (105.8)	[6] (†)	[6] (†)	[6] (†)
1991	29,474 (237.1)	733 (42.4)	1,819 (66.5)	10,959 (157.4)	5,633 (115.3)	2,523 (78.1)	7,807 (134.6)	5,263 (111.6)	2,025 (70.1)	312 (27.7)	206 (22.5)
1992	30,346 (239.6)	734 (42.4)	1,659 (63.6)	11,039 (157.9)	5,904 (117.9)	2,655 (80.1)	8,355 (138.9)	5,604 (115.0)	2,192 (72.9)	334 (28.7)	225 (23.5)
1993	30,683 (240.5)	765 (43.3)	1,576 (62.0)	10,513 (154.4)	6,279 (121.4)	3,067 (86.0)	8,483 (139.9)	5,735 (116.3)	2,166 (72.5)	323 (28.2)	260 (25.3)
1994	31,379 (259.2)	696 (42.0)	1,675 (65.1)	10,785 (161.2)	6,256 (124.2)	3,210 (89.7)	8,756 (146.0)	5,901 (120.8)	2,174 (74.0)	398 (31.8)	283 (26.8)
1995	32,673 (268.2)	774 (46.1)	1,763 (69.3)	11,064 (168.6)	6,329 (129.5)	3,336 (94.9)	9,406 (156.3)	6,434 (130.5)	2,268 (78.5)	421 (34.0)	283 (27.9)
1996	33,549 (259.0)	750 (42.1)	1,751 (64.1)	11,363 (159.7)	6,582 (122.9)	3,468 (89.9)	9,636 (147.7)	6,689 (123.9)	2,213 (72.0)	413 (31.2)	322 (27.6)
1997	34,624 (260.1)	791 (43.2)	1,765 (64.4)	11,475 (160.0)	6,628 (123.2)	3,538 (90.7)	10,427 (153.0)	7,173 (128.0)	2,448 (75.7)	488 (34.0)	318 (27.4)
1998	35,628 (265.4)	814 (43.8)	1,878 (66.4)	11,613 (161.3)	7,070 (127.3)	3,527 (90.7)	10,725 (155.4)	7,288 (129.2)	2,639 (78.6)	468 (33.3)	329 (27.9)
1999	37,091 (269.7)	886 (45.7)	1,883 (66.5)	11,824 (162.7)	7,453 (130.6)	3,804 (94.1)	11,242 (158.9)	7,607 (131.9)	2,818 (81.2)	470 (33.3)	346 (28.6)
2000	37,762 (271.6)	930 (46.8)	1,950 (67.7)	11,789 (162.5)	7,391 (130.0)	4,118 (97.8)	11,584 (161.1)	7,899 (134.3)	2,823 (81.2)	509 (34.7)	353 (28.9)
2001	38,228 (197.0)	927 (33.4)	1,869 (47.3)	11,690 (115.8)	7,283 (92.3)	4,190 (70.5)	12,269 (118.5)	8,257 (98.1)	3,089 (60.6)	531 (25.3)	392 (21.7)
2002	38,510 (197.6)	858 (32.1)	1,841 (46.9)	11,687 (115.8)	7,354 (92.7)	4,285 (71.2)	12,484 (119.5)	8,229 (97.9)	3,281 (62.5)	572 (26.2)	402 (22.0)
2003	38,681 (197.9)	882 (32.6)	1,739 (45.6)	11,587 (115.3)	7,341 (92.6)	4,397 (72.2)	12,735 (120.6)	8,330 (98.5)	3,376 (63.4)	567 (26.1)	462 (23.6)
2004	39,072 (198.7)	917 (33.2)	1,797 (46.4)	11,392 (114.4)	7,330 (92.6)	4,505 (73.0)	13,131 (122.4)	8,664 (100.4)	3,451 (64.0)	564 (26.0)	452 (23.3)
2005	40,021 (200.6)	902 (32.9)	1,740 (45.6)	11,419 (114.5)	7,452 (93.3)	4,751 (74.9)	13,758 (125.1)	9,074 (102.6)	3,591 (65.3)	657 (28.1)	437 (22.9)
2006	41,311 (203.2)	934 (33.5)	1,802 (46.4)	11,652 (115.6)	7,613 (94.3)	4,760 (75.0)	14,549 (128.4)	9,645 (105.7)	3,746 (66.7)	662 (28.2)	497 (24.5)
2007	42,196 (204.9)	823 (31.5)	1,649 (44.4)	11,447 (114.7)	7,916 (96.1)	4,891 (76.0)	15,469 (132.1)	9,931 (107.2)	4,389 (72.1)	666 (28.3)	484 (24.1)
2008	40,979 (202.5)	814 (31.3)	1,568 (43.3)	10,851 (111.8)	7,456 (93.3)	4,955 (76.5)	15,335 (131.6)	9,856 (106.8)	4,176 (70.3)	753 (30.1)	550 (25.7)
2009	40,376 (201.4)	776 (30.5)	1,519 (42.7)	10,467 (109.9)	7,164 (91.6)	4,924 (76.3)	15,526 (132.4)	10,066 (107.9)	4,261 (71.0)	606 (27.0)	592 (26.7)
2010	40,196 (201.0)	732 (29.7)	1,371 (40.5)	10,117 (108.1)	7,150 (91.5)	4,999 (76.8)	15,826 (133.5)	9,903 (107.0)	4,576 (73.6)	622 (27.4)	725 (29.5)
2011	40,885 (202.4)	779 (30.6)	1,380 (40.7)	10,040 (107.7)	6,989 (90.5)	5,131 (77.8)	16,566 (136.4)	10,537 (110.2)	4,700 (74.6)	635 (27.6)	694 (28.9)
2012	41,319 (203.2)	690 (28.8)	1,351 (40.3)	9,870 (106.8)	6,899 (89.9)	5,246 (78.7)	17,263 (139.0)	10,961 (112.3)	4,887 (76.0)	670 (28.4)	745 (29.9)
2013	42,021 (258.8)	788 (38.9)	1,309 (50.1)	9,990 (135.9)	7,070 (115.1)	5,253 (99.6)	17,611 (177.5)	11,124 (143.1)	4,963 (96.9)	793 (39.1)	732 (37.5)
2014	42,957 (228.5)	796 (34.2)	1,356 (44.6)	9,802 (117.7)	7,241 (101.7)	5,426 (88.4)	18,336 (158.1)	11,420 (126.6)	5,310 (87.5)	776 (33.8)	830 (34.9)

See notes at end of table.

Table 502.20. Median annual earnings, number, and percentage of full-time year-round workers 25 years old and over, by highest level of educational attainment and sex: 1990 through 2014—Continued

[Standard errors appear in parentheses]

Sex and year	Total	Elementary/secondary: Less than 9th grade	Elementary/secondary: Some high school, no completion[1]	Elementary/secondary: High school completion (includes equivalency)[2]	College: Some college, no degree[3]	College: Associate's degree	College: Bachelor's or higher degree[4]: Total	Bachelor's or higher degree[4]: Bachelor's degree[5]	Bachelor's or higher degree[4]: Master's degree	Bachelor's or higher degree[4]: Professional degree	Bachelor's or higher degree[4]: Doctor's degree
1	2	3	4	5	6	7	8	9	10	11	12
	Percent of persons with earnings who worked full time, year round[8]										
Males											
1996	78.2 (0.25)	64.5 (1.31)	66.9 (1.01)	77.2 (0.45)	78.8 (0.58)	83.8 (0.83)	82.9 (0.43)	83.2 (0.53)	80.6 (0.95)	85.4 (1.40)	85.1 (1.69)
1997	81.6 (0.24)	63.9 (1.35)	69.5 (0.99)	78.7 (0.44)	79.5 (0.58)	81.7 (0.84)	83.3 (0.42)	83.9 (0.51)	80.8 (0.96)	85.4 (1.38)	83.4 (1.68)
1998	81.0 (0.24)	66.8 (1.37)	73.5 (0.97)	80.3 (0.43)	81.0 (0.56)	85.3 (0.76)	84.6 (0.39)	85.9 (0.47)	81.6 (0.92)	86.0 (1.39)	80.0 (1.74)
1999	81.1 (0.24)	70.3 (1.32)	71.5 (1.02)	80.3 (0.43)	81.3 (0.55)	84.2 (0.78)	84.7 (0.39)	85.3 (0.48)	83.5 (0.86)	85.6 (1.40)	81.8 (1.69)
2000	81.7 (0.23)	69.2 (1.33)	71.8 (1.01)	80.9 (0.42)	82.2 (0.54)	86.6 (0.71)	84.8 (0.39)	85.6 (0.47)	82.8 (0.87)	85.8 (1.39)	82.5 (1.65)
2001	80.1 (0.17)	69.7 (0.90)	70.9 (0.71)	79.4 (0.31)	80.2 (0.40)	84.1 (0.54)	83.3 (0.28)	83.6 (0.35)	82.4 (0.60)	84.6 (1.01)	82.2 (1.18)
2002	79.4 (0.17)	70.1 (0.91)	71.3 (0.69)	77.8 (0.32)	78.8 (0.41)	81.4 (0.58)	83.9 (0.27)	84.4 (0.34)	82.2 (0.60)	85.7 (0.99)	82.8 (1.16)
2003	79.5 (0.17)	71.5 (0.89)	70.1 (0.73)	78.7 (0.31)	78.8 (0.41)	82.1 (0.56)	83.1 (0.28)	84.0 (0.34)	81.1 (0.60)	84.4 (1.00)	80.3 (1.22)
2004	80.0 (0.17)	74.7 (0.84)	71.2 (0.71)	79.1 (0.30)	79.3 (0.41)	83.6 (0.53)	83.0 (0.28)	83.1 (0.35)	83.1 (0.58)	83.3 (1.03)	81.7 (1.16)
2005	80.3 (0.16)	74.0 (0.84)	73.8 (0.69)	79.5 (0.30)	80.0 (0.40)	82.5 (0.54)	82.9 (0.27)	83.0 (0.34)	82.7 (0.58)	83.7 (1.00)	82.4 (1.12)
2006	81.1 (0.16)	73.6 (0.85)	72.9 (0.67)	79.6 (0.30)	80.1 (0.40)	85.3 (0.50)	84.7 (0.26)	85.2 (0.32)	83.5 (0.55)	85.9 (0.94)	83.4 (1.09)
2007	80.5 (0.16)	71.1 (0.91)	70.8 (0.72)	79.4 (0.30)	79.5 (0.40)	83.3 (0.52)	84.5 (0.26)	85.1 (0.32)	83.5 (0.54)	83.1 (1.03)	83.5 (1.11)
2008	77.0 (0.17)	66.3 (0.95)	64.6 (0.76)	74.6 (0.32)	76.5 (0.42)	79.4 (0.56)	82.6 (0.27)	83.2 (0.33)	80.9 (0.57)	82.4 (1.02)	83.1 (1.12)
2009	73.9 (0.18)	56.2 (1.03)	61.8 (0.79)	70.1 (0.34)	73.4 (0.45)	77.9 (0.58)	80.8 (0.28)	79.9 (0.35)	82.0 (0.56)	85.1 (0.99)	81.2 (1.11)
2010	74.8 (0.18)	58.8 (1.04)	61.6 (0.82)	71.9 (0.34)	72.9 (0.45)	78.2 (0.56)	81.4 (0.27)	81.8 (0.34)	80.0 (0.58)	81.4 (1.10)	82.2 (1.08)
2011	76.6 (0.17)	67.2 (0.98)	64.2 (0.81)	74.2 (0.33)	75.2 (0.44)	78.0 (0.56)	82.0 (0.27)	82.1 (0.33)	82.3 (0.55)	81.6 (1.07)	81.0 (1.09)
2012	76.5 (0.17)	65.4 (1.00)	64.4 (0.82)	74.5 (0.33)	73.7 (0.44)	78.8 (0.54)	82.1 (0.26)	82.5 (0.33)	80.8 (0.55)	84.4 (1.01)	81.4 (1.02)
2013	78.1 (0.21)	69.3 (1.21)	68.9 (0.99)	76.5 (0.41)	76.2 (0.55)	79.6 (0.67)	82.4 (0.33)	82.6 (0.41)	82.5 (0.67)	83.2 (1.34)	79.7 (1.30)
2014	79.2 (0.18)	72.2 (1.03)	69.4 (0.85)	78.3 (0.35)	76.7 (0.47)	79.9 (0.58)	83.3 (0.28)	83.7 (0.35)	82.7 (0.57)	83.5 (1.12)	81.2 (1.15)
Females											
1996	60.7 (0.32)	47.9 (1.94)	49.4 (1.29)	60.0 (0.55)	62.0 (0.73)	63.7 (1.00)	63.5 (0.60)	63.4 (0.72)	62.4 (1.25)	68.4 (2.91)	70.0 (3.29)
1997	61.7 (0.32)	48.7 (1.91)	49.3 (1.29)	61.0 (0.55)	61.9 (0.72)	64.3 (0.99)	65.4 (0.58)	64.6 (0.70)	65.7 (1.20)	73.6 (2.63)	72.1 (3.29)
1998	62.5 (0.31)	51.8 (1.94)	53.1 (1.29)	61.9 (0.55)	63.3 (0.70)	64.9 (1.00)	65.0 (0.57)	64.0 (0.69)	66.2 (1.15)	71.9 (2.71)	68.5 (3.26)
1999	63.7 (0.31)	53.0 (1.88)	54.0 (1.30)	63.0 (0.54)	64.8 (0.69)	65.1 (0.96)	66.2 (0.56)	65.9 (0.68)	66.5 (1.12)	68.4 (2.73)	68.2 (3.18)
2000	64.6 (0.30)	53.5 (1.84)	56.5 (1.30)	64.1 (0.54)	65.3 (0.69)	66.6 (0.92)	66.5 (0.55)	66.7 (0.67)	64.9 (1.11)	70.6 (2.61)	71.5 (3.13)
2001	64.3 (0.22)	54.0 (1.32)	55.3 (0.94)	63.5 (0.39)	65.1 (0.49)	65.8 (0.65)	66.6 (0.38)	66.6 (0.47)	65.6 (0.76)	70.3 (1.83)	70.9 (2.12)
2002	64.1 (0.22)	52.6 (1.36)	55.5 (0.95)	63.2 (0.39)	65.0 (0.49)	65.6 (0.65)	66.5 (0.38)	65.9 (0.47)	66.1 (0.74)	74.3 (1.73)	73.8 (2.07)
2003	64.4 (0.21)	56.5 (1.38)	53.8 (0.96)	64.4 (0.39)	64.2 (0.49)	65.6 (0.64)	66.4 (0.37)	65.8 (0.46)	66.3 (0.73)	72.3 (1.75)	71.9 (1.95)
2004	64.5 (0.21)	56.3 (1.35)	56.1 (0.96)	64.5 (0.40)	64.2 (0.49)	64.6 (0.63)	66.7 (0.37)	66.3 (0.45)	66.3 (0.72)	71.5 (1.77)	71.2 (1.97)
2005	65.3 (0.21)	56.5 (1.36)	54.5 (0.97)	65.1 (0.40)	63.5 (0.49)	67.2 (0.61)	68.2 (0.36)	68.0 (0.44)	68.3 (0.70)	71.2 (1.64)	67.3 (2.02)
2006	66.2 (0.21)	58.5 (1.35)	56.0 (0.96)	65.6 (0.39)	65.9 (0.48)	67.3 (0.61)	68.6 (0.35)	68.4 (0.43)	67.5 (0.69)	73.6 (1.61)	74.0 (1.86)
2007	66.7 (0.21)	56.8 (1.43)	55.3 (1.00)	65.7 (0.39)	66.7 (0.48)	67.3 (0.60)	69.3 (0.34)	68.4 (0.42)	70.6 (0.63)	74.1 (1.60)	71.2 (1.91)
2008	64.4 (0.21)	51.6 (1.38)	52.8 (1.01)	62.4 (0.40)	64.7 (0.49)	65.5 (0.60)	67.9 (0.34)	67.8 (0.43)	66.9 (0.65)	74.0 (1.51)	70.0 (1.80)
2009	64.3 (0.21)	52.0 (1.42)	54.5 (1.04)	62.4 (0.41)	63.9 (0.50)	64.5 (0.60)	68.0 (0.34)	68.3 (0.42)	67.5 (0.65)	66.4 (1.72)	68.3 (1.74)
2010	64.4 (0.21)	51.7 (1.46)	52.4 (1.07)	62.6 (0.42)	63.3 (0.50)	64.3 (0.60)	68.5 (0.34)	67.7 (0.42)	68.5 (0.62)	73.9 (1.66)	76.3 (1.51)
2011	65.0 (0.21)	52.2 (1.42)	49.1 (1.04)	63.0 (0.42)	62.9 (0.50)	66.3 (0.59)	69.6 (0.33)	69.4 (0.41)	69.0 (0.62)	72.8 (1.65)	73.6 (1.58)
2012	64.8 (0.21)	50.0 (1.48)	51.1 (1.07)	62.3 (0.42)	61.7 (0.50)	64.7 (0.58)	70.0 (0.32)	70.6 (0.40)	68.0 (0.60)	73.2 (1.61)	73.9 (1.52)
2013	65.6 (0.26)	56.0 (1.84)	52.3 (1.07)	63.8 (0.46)	63.4 (0.62)	65.1 (0.79)	69.6 (0.40)	70.4 (0.50)	67.4 (0.82)	73.9 (1.86)	69.4 (1.97)
2014	66.1 (0.23)	53.5 (1.57)	54.1 (1.21)	63.6 (0.47)	64.3 (0.55)	66.5 (0.63)	70.0 (0.34)	70.3 (0.44)	69.2 (0.64)	73.8 (1.65)	68.1 (1.62)

—Not available.
†Not applicable.
!Interpret data with caution. The coefficient of variation (CV) for this estimate is between 30 and 50 percent.
[1]Includes 1 to 3 years of high school for 1990.
[2]Includes 4 years of high school for 1990.
[3]Includes 1 to 3 years of college and associate's degrees for 1990.
[4]Includes 4 or more years of college for 1990.
[5]Includes 4 years of college for 1990.
[6]Not reported separately for 1990.
[7]Constant dollars based on the Consumer Price Index, prepared by the Bureau of Labor Statistics, U.S. Department of Labor.
[8]Data not available for 1990 through 1995.
NOTE: Detail may not sum to totals because of rounding.
SOURCE: U.S. Department of Commerce, Census Bureau, Current Population Reports, Series P-60, *Money Income of Households, Families, and Persons in the United States* and *Income, Poverty, and Valuation of Noncash Benefits*, 1990 through 1994; Series P-60, *Money Income in the United States*, 1995 through 2002; and Current Population Survey (CPS), Annual Social and Economic Supplement, 2004 through 2015. Retrieved January 28, 2016, from http://www.census.gov/hhes/www/cpstables/032015/perinc/pinc03_000.htm. (This table was prepared January 2015.)

Table 502.30. Median annual earnings of full-time year-round workers 25 to 34 years old and full-time year-round workers as a percentage of the labor force, by sex, race/ethnicity, and educational attainment: Selected years, 1995 through 2014

[Amounts in constant 2014 dollars. Standard errors appear in parentheses]

Sex, race/ethnicity, and educational attainment	1995	2000	2004	2005	2007	2009	2010	2011	2012	2013	2014
1	2	3	4	5	6	7	8	9	10	11	12
Total, all full-time year-round workers 25 to 34 years old											
Median annual earnings, all education levels	**$38,840 (215)**	**$41,240 (131)**	**$40,700 (939)**	**$39,980 (1,092)**	**$39,960 (#)**	**$41,890 (1,090)**	**$40,580 (840)**	**$39,940 (99)**	**$39,180 (901)**	**$40,650 (#)**	**$40,000 (80)**
Less than high school completion	24,620 (391)	24,880 (540)	25,030 (23)	24,900 (776)	25,030 (707)	22,990 (797)	22,790 (853)	24,060 (869)	23,630 (840)	24,330 (726)	24,960 (1,440)
High school completion[1]	32,290 (308)	34,360 (241)	33,740 (457)	33,810 (1,136)	33,070 (716)	33,020 (17)	32,470 (33)	31,520 (25)	30,890 (16)	30,480 (2)	30,000 (2)
Some college, no degree	36,110 (673)	39,660 (516)	39,060 (1,017)	38,030 (777)	37,530 (880)	36,600 (1,264)	35,720 (937)	33,670 (526)	33,870 (740)	34,630 (1,185)	31,810 (827)
Associate's degree	38,550 (632)	41,240 (390)	41,180 (1,313)	41,170 (1,044)	39,730 (157)	39,610 (1,062)	40,150 (1,118)	38,980 (1,525)	36,830 (1,495)	38,150 (2,157)	34,970 (455)
Bachelor's or higher degree	51,230 (874)	54,980 (284)	53,860 (1,381)	53,180 (1,077)	54,640 (1,467)	54,990 (35)	52,910 (1,090)	52,620 (359)	51,510 (17)	50,810 (1,298)	51,980 (783)
Bachelor's degree	48,100 (391)	54,870 (406)	51,210 (1,111)	49,460 (1,336)	51,180 (905)	49,640 (299)	48,850 (675)	47,330 (661)	48,360 (920)	49,320 (1,737)	49,880 (150)
Master's or higher degree	61,590 (1,132)	65,870 (2,034)	62,190 (288)	60,540 (54)	63,560 (2,243)	65,340 (2,231)	59,340 (1,076)	62,340 (1,581)	61,480 (1,168)	60,540 (454)	59,080 (1,258)
Percent,[2] all education levels	**63.6 (0.44)**	**68.4 (0.32)**	**66.2 (0.38)**	**66.6 (0.37)**	**67.8 (0.36)**	**61.0 (0.41)**	**61.9 (0.42)**	**63.3 (0.41)**	**64.2 (0.44)**	**65.1 (0.49)**	**67.1 (0.40)**
Less than high school completion	49.6 (1.37)	59.4 (1.02)	60.1 (1.26)	60.0 (1.32)	56.5 (1.26)	47.0 (1.25)	44.9 (1.52)	48.1 (1.43)	48.6 (1.38)	53.3 (1.72)	55.1 (1.51)
High school completion[1]	62.8 (0.79)	67.2 (0.59)	65.6 (0.71)	66.9 (0.75)	67.0 (0.71)	55.3 (0.74)	57.0 (0.80)	59.1 (0.78)	60.3 (0.80)	61.7 (1.07)	65.3 (0.87)
Some college, no degree	61.5 (0.99)	67.8 (0.71)	63.1 (0.93)	63.5 (0.83)	64.8 (0.92)	58.7 (0.91)	58.1 (0.92)	59.0 (0.99)	59.2 (1.00)	59.0 (1.10)	61.6 (0.84)
Associate's degree	67.4 (1.41)	70.9 (1.01)	65.8 (1.16)	67.8 (1.16)	67.8 (1.23)	65.1 (1.18)	63.6 (1.29)	65.4 (1.17)	64.8 (1.18)	67.5 (1.51)	65.8 (1.17)
Bachelor's or higher degree	70.4 (0.79)	72.3 (0.55)	70.7 (0.70)	70.2 (0.67)	73.5 (0.59)	69.4 (0.63)	71.4 (0.59)	71.4 (0.62)	72.8 (0.62)	72.1 (0.71)	73.5 (0.63)
Bachelor's degree	70.5 (0.90)	73.1 (0.62)	70.9 (0.74)	70.9 (0.76)	73.2 (0.70)	69.1 (0.77)	71.2 (0.71)	71.1 (0.72)	72.9 (0.75)	71.9 (0.84)	73.4 (0.72)
Master's or higher degree	69.8 (1.65)	69.6 (1.18)	70.1 (1.42)	68.2 (1.27)	74.4 (1.21)	70.0 (1.10)	71.7 (1.23)	72.2 (1.25)	72.5 (1.20)	72.6 (1.32)	73.5 (1.14)
Male											
Median annual earnings, all education levels	**41,840 (286)**	**43,980 (210)**	**43,870 (#)**	**42,430 (#)**	**43,320 (100)**	**44,140 (#)**	**43,290 (31)**	**42,010 (34)**	**41,240 (1)**	**40,650 (355)**	**40,950 (1,006)**
Less than high school completion	27,590 (728)	27,390 (342)	26,040 (129)	26,560 (1,055)	26,250 (572)	25,000 (1,075)	26,050 (842)	26,270 (1,115)	25,360 (1,008)	24,780 (393)	25,000 (829)
High school completion[1]	37,190 (611)	39,610 (650)	37,560 (150)	36,220 (49)	35,200 (1,067)	36,290 (1,245)	35,610 (909)	34,150 (870)	33,850 (742)	32,220 (485)	32,970 (1,154)
Some college, no degree	40,310 (555)	43,720 (369)	43,660 (501)	42,320 (319)	41,880 (1,567)	42,670 (982)	41,120 (999)	38,610 (1,257)	38,840 (868)	38,960 (1,438)	35,790 (822)
Associate's degree	40,070 (1,029)	48,080 (751)	46,310 (1,115)	47,130 (1,880)	45,360 (379)	46,000 (1,697)	43,330 (466)	44,040 (1,822)	45,000 (2,828)	42,420 (2,467)	40,060 (1,548)
Bachelor's or higher degree	57,750 (895)	63,120 (570)	62,580 (720)	60,580 (1,934)	58,880 (1,119)	60,060 (606)	57,280 (1,931)	57,220 (1,089)	56,540 (529)	57,870 (2,179)	57,890 (1,704)
Bachelor's degree	54,330 (719)	61,550 (824)	57,600 (1,616)	54,510 (1,303)	56,950 (52)	55,700 (1,416)	54,050 (165)	52,370 (128)	51,530 (602)	52,790 (1,277)	54,710 (559)
Master's or higher degree	68,760 (2,204)	75,460 (2,043)	65,070 (3,830)	66,660 (4,044)	70,440 (3,434)	76,410 (3,202)	69,660 (1,521)	71,560 (2,473)	67,020 (2,435)	67,850 (2,567)	64,630 (1,440)
Percent,[2] all education levels	**69.7 (0.57)**	**75.1 (0.40)**	**72.3 (0.52)**	**72.5 (0.48)**	**72.2 (0.51)**	**62.8 (0.58)**	**64.5 (0.56)**	**67.4 (0.57)**	**68.4 (0.53)**	**69.5 (0.62)**	**72.4 (0.55)**
Less than high school completion	54.3 (1.71)	67.8 (1.22)	67.0 (1.43)	66.7 (1.54)	61.1 (1.51)	49.2 (1.71)	47.4 (1.81)	55.5 (1.74)	54.1 (1.88)	59.9 (2.06)	63.0 (1.85)
High school completion[1]	69.3 (1.00)	73.6 (0.73)	71.0 (0.95)	73.5 (0.91)	71.9 (0.94)	57.4 (1.01)	60.6 (1.01)	63.8 (1.00)	65.5 (1.00)	67.0 (1.27)	71.4 (1.00)
Some college, no degree	68.5 (1.31)	76.1 (0.91)	69.7 (1.22)	70.7 (1.13)	71.1 (1.31)	62.7 (1.31)	62.0 (1.17)	64.2 (1.33)	64.3 (1.41)	63.9 (1.56)	67.8 (1.19)
Associate's degree	78.6 (1.81)	80.9 (1.31)	74.9 (1.63)	75.1 (1.67)	73.4 (1.70)	70.1 (1.65)	68.6 (1.77)	71.6 (1.61)	71.8 (1.70)	76.3 (2.03)	71.0 (1.79)
Bachelor's or higher degree	75.9 (1.04)	78.0 (0.72)	77.1 (0.82)	74.6 (0.93)	77.7 (0.94)	71.8 (0.94)	75.0 (0.80)	75.3 (0.84)	77.1 (0.87)	75.7 (1.01)	78.7 (0.87)
Bachelor's degree	76.4 (1.19)	78.8 (0.81)	77.2 (0.93)	74.5 (1.01)	78.0 (1.07)	70.6 (1.15)	75.4 (0.91)	74.7 (0.98)	77.3 (0.94)	74.8 (1.34)	78.5 (1.02)
Master's or higher degree	74.6 (2.11)	75.3 (1.58)	76.7 (1.72)	75.1 (2.00)	76.8 (1.93)	75.6 (1.61)	74.0 (1.88)	77.3 (1.63)	76.4 (1.82)	78.0 (1.83)	79.2 (1.61)
Female											
Median annual earnings, all education levels	**33,880 (279)**	**38,100 (327)**	**37,550 (17)**	**36,320 (35)**	**37,610 (442)**	**38,530 (230)**	**37,880 (37)**	**36,790 (21)**	**36,090 (810)**	**37,530 (800)**	**35,960 (695)**
Less than high school completion	20,100 (784)	20,590 (576)	22,060 (951)	20,360 (774)	20,340 (922)	20,930 (639)	19,300 (716)	19,930 (494)	18,460 (797)	20,230 (587)	19,950 (324)
High school completion[1]	27,360 (461)	30,120 (329)	29,900 (815)	28,970 (197)	27,440 (1,103)	27,530 (28)	27,110 (68)	27,270 (772)	25,760 (9)	25,390 (14)	25,000 (353)
Some college, no degree	31,050 (449)	34,330 (336)	34,950 (1,561)	33,840 (481)	34,150 (820)	32,220 (1,080)	32,040 (1,102)	30,460 (1,152)	30,260 (647)	30,230 (139)	28,040 (1,016)
Associate's degree	37,200 (1,386)	36,620 (492)	37,310 (314)	35,550 (433)	35,390 (1,186)	34,090 (1,331)	37,630 (927)	33,760 (1,405)	32,590 (999)	32,950 (1,040)	29,740 (271)
Bachelor's or higher degree	46,250 (654)	49,490 (343)	50,050 (135)	48,200 (127)	48,990 (1,093)	49,600 (26)	47,760 (1,276)	47,250 (60)	48,300 (715)	47,560 (1,554)	49,810 (957)
Bachelor's degree	43,340 (939)	47,970 (383)	47,210 (802)	45,460 (1,109)	45,490 (106)	44,240 (1,283)	43,410 (1,226)	43,100 (1,403)	44,280 (1,274)	45,340 (490)	44,990 (144)
Master's or higher degree	53,660 (1,482)	57,160 (1,151)	56,150 (1,419)	56,910 (2,229)	57,300 (1,725)	59,580 (2,331)	54,100 (96)	54,160 (1,635)	55,190 (1,504)	54,790 (1,480)	54,590 (644)
Percent,[2] all education levels	**56.6 (0.67)**	**60.7 (0.49)**	**58.9 (0.56)**	**59.6 (0.57)**	**62.7 (0.57)**	**58.9 (0.53)**	**58.7 (0.53)**	**58.6 (0.52)**	**59.3 (0.63)**	**59.9 (0.76)**	**60.8 (0.56)**
Less than high school completion	41.3 (2.24)	45.3 (1.68)	47.0 (1.95)	45.9 (1.83)	45.9 (2.22)	42.7 (2.03)	39.4 (2.22)	34.1 (2.03)	37.8 (1.96)	41.1 (2.70)	38.5 (1.98)
High school completion[1]	54.4 (1.23)	58.5 (0.96)	57.4 (1.23)	57.0 (1.11)	59.4 (1.13)	51.8 (1.12)	51.1 (1.19)	51.6 (1.19)	51.9 (1.24)	52.4 (1.64)	54.9 (1.29)
Some college, no degree	53.9 (1.46)	59.2 (1.08)	55.8 (1.35)	55.7 (1.19)	57.9 (1.22)	54.1 (1.28)	53.6 (1.29)	53.3 (1.33)	53.3 (1.22)	53.4 (1.69)	54.6 (1.28)
Associate's degree	57.6 (2.05)	62.7 (1.45)	56.9 (1.54)	60.8 (1.57)	62.7 (1.75)	60.8 (1.65)	59.1 (1.67)	59.5 (1.75)	58.8 (1.69)	59.6 (2.13)	61.1 (1.51)
Bachelor's or higher degree	64.7 (1.17)	66.8 (0.82)	64.9 (1.03)	66.0 (0.99)	69.9 (0.76)	67.2 (0.82)	68.0 (0.77)	68.0 (0.84)	68.9 (0.90)	68.9 (0.98)	68.7 (0.83)
Bachelor's degree	64.9 (1.32)	67.6 (0.93)	65.0 (1.10)	67.4 (1.18)	68.7 (0.92)	67.9 (1.04)	67.2 (0.94)	67.8 (1.06)	68.5 (1.13)	69.1 (1.16)	68.6 (0.94)
Master's or higher degree	63.9 (2.57)	64.2 (1.71)	64.4 (2.05)	62.6 (1.76)	72.6 (1.52)	65.7 (1.58)	70.0 (1.63)	68.6 (1.76)	69.7 (1.71)	68.5 (1.79)	68.9 (1.58)

See notes at end of table.

Table 502.30. Median annual earnings of full-time year-round workers 25 to 34 years old and full-time year-round workers as a percentage of the labor force, by sex, race/ethnicity, and educational attainment: Selected years, 1995 through 2014—Continued

[Amounts in constant 2014 dollars. Standard errors appear in parentheses]

Sex, race/ethnicity, and educational attainment	1995	2000	2004	2005	2007	2009	2010	2011	2012	2013	2014
1	2	3	4	5	6	7	8	9	10	11	12
White											
Median annual earnings, all education levels	**40,380** (244)	**44,990** (386)	**44,950** (290)	**42,430** (94)	**45,640** (1,357)	**44,140** (#)	**43,380** (24)	**42,090** (152)	**42,230** (1,268)	**42,640** (333)	**42,940** (745)
Less than high school completion	27,300 (1,089)	28,580 (567)	30,640 (498)	27,820 (1,587)	27,350 (1,642)	27,210 (1,082)	27,130 (430)	29,170 (1,244)	25,400 (1,112)	30,490 (2,007)	28,540 (1,945)
High school completion[1]	34,140 (384)	37,960 (508)	37,570 (14)	36,270 (44)	34,230 (20)	35,240 (785)	34,690 (928)	33,620 (651)	33,340 (712)	32,190 (635)	32,940 (1,216)
Some college, no degree	37,280 (703)	41,110 (353)	40,590 (903)	38,650 (411)	39,860 (858)	38,610 (213)	37,810 (823)	36,530 (1,159)	36,010 (1,148)	35,540 (806)	34,940 (162)
Associate's degree	40,270 (784)	43,570 (425)	43,350 (427)	42,000 (453)	41,980 (1,509)	43,970 (1,620)	43,070 (815)	41,610 (1,403)	39,840 (1,926)	40,630 (15)	36,490 (1,346)
Bachelor's or higher degree	52,750 (927)	54,990 (314)	55,150 (1,304)	54,100 (914)	54,740 (1,084)	55,000 (39)	53,780 (862)	52,250 (94)	51,500 (19)	50,810 (1,503)	52,840 (1,111)
Bachelor's degree	49,700 (482)	54,890 (362)	52,520 (273)	49,670 (1,086)	51,270 (68)	49,650 (873)	49,850 (1,228)	49,400 (1,223)	48,910 (1,093)	50,520 (2,046)	49,920 (50)
Master's or higher degree	61,750 (1,076)	65,770 (2,260)	62,130 (905)	60,540 (61)	62,400 (952)	63,540 (1,873)	58,980 (931)	61,820 (1,692)	58,720 (2,551)	59,740 (835)	57,850 (1,475)
Percent,[2] all education levels	**64.5** (0.52)	**68.2** (0.39)	**66.1** (0.52)	**66.9** (0.49)	**68.3** (0.47)	**62.5** (0.52)	**63.3** (0.52)	**65.6** (0.54)	**66.0** (0.54)	**66.3** (0.68)	**68.7** (0.49)
Less than high school completion	48.6 (2.03)	55.2 (1.76)	55.6 (2.31)	58.7 (2.29)	51.8 (2.28)	41.0 (2.43)	39.5 (2.78)	41.2 (2.70)	45.0 (2.44)	47.3 (3.27)	47.1 (2.69)
High school completion[1]	62.7 (0.94)	66.2 (0.75)	64.2 (0.94)	66.6 (0.92)	66.9 (0.89)	55.9 (1.04)	57.1 (1.08)	60.8 (1.15)	61.7 (1.10)	62.4 (1.41)	66.6 (1.17)
Some college, no degree	62.3 (1.18)	67.6 (0.88)	62.7 (1.19)	64.2 (1.02)	63.7 (1.18)	59.0 (1.14)	57.0 (1.20)	60.7 (1.25)	59.2 (1.39)	60.5 (1.53)	62.1 (1.23)
Associate's degree	66.7 (1.63)	68.2 (1.23)	63.4 (1.36)	66.9 (1.41)	69.6 (1.51)	65.4 (1.54)	63.9 (1.60)	65.7 (1.29)	66.2 (1.45)	66.9 (1.85)	67.1 (1.44)
Bachelor's or higher degree	70.5 (0.87)	72.2 (0.63)	71.4 (0.77)	69.8 (0.79)	72.8 (0.65)	69.5 (0.77)	71.7 (0.69)	72.4 (0.76)	72.8 (0.74)	71.9 (0.91)	74.2 (0.74)
Bachelor's degree	70.6 (0.99)	72.9 (0.72)	71.6 (0.81)	70.1 (0.92)	72.7 (0.77)	69.4 (0.90)	71.5 (0.79)	72.2 (0.84)	73.2 (0.88)	72.0 (1.03)	73.9 (0.87)
Master's or higher degree	70.3 (1.84)	69.9 (1.36)	71.0 (1.66)	68.8 (1.56)	73.3 (1.48)	69.5 (1.43)	72.3 (1.47)	72.8 (1.44)	71.9 (1.38)	71.7 (1.76)	74.9 (1.35)
Black											
Median annual earnings, all education levels	**32,550** (559)	**34,360** (362)	**34,420** (1,135)	**34,630** (1,227)	**34,170** (44)	**33,090** (134)	**34,300** (778)	**33,560** (765)	**32,780** (482)	**33,830** (1,713)	**30,810** (1,015)
Less than high school completion	21,460 (1,689)	22,780 (1,066)	24,340 (934)	24,710 (1,436)	21,440 (2,087)	24,500 (3,868)	22,010 (2,005)	20,470 (772)	21,740 (1,748)	20,810 (1,299)	20,480 (2,189)
High school completion[1]	27,890 (896)	30,050 (497)	29,800 (724)	27,820 (1,223)	29,490 (1,496)	27,540 (957)	27,140 (794)	26,620 (1,103)	27,260 (1,371)	25,420 (1,370)	24,970 (681)
Some college, no degree	34,130 (1,321)	35,660 (714)	37,370 (1,848)	35,190 (1,697)	34,100 (172)	32,020 (1,703)	31,780 (421)	30,860 (609)	30,930 (1,331)	32,190 (1,535)	27,270 (1,258)
Associate's degree	34,050 (1,406)	34,220 (980)	35,950 (1,731)	33,740 (1,528)	33,630 (830)	30,600 (2,106)	34,110 (2,347)	35,420 (2,478)	32,580 (2,611)	34,730 (4,480)	30,980 (1,631)
Bachelor's or higher degree	42,540 (1,453)	47,520 (1,285)	48,690 (1,781)	46,960 (1,758)	45,430 (1,252)	49,180 (944)	44,540 (1,553)	43,700 (1,889)	45,450 (2,008)	45,320 (766)	46,800 (2,441)
Bachelor's degree	40,340 (1,322)	45,020 (1,968)	44,730 (1,682)	42,760 (2,606)	44,530 (1,304)	44,140 (1,715)	42,870 (534)	41,200 (1,036)	40,690 (846)	40,580 (3,074)	44,840 (1,712)
Master's or higher degree	51,440 (1,938)	55,510 (2,553)	59,030 (4,952)	52,200 (3,680)	51,320 (2,668)	58,590 (2,959)	53,310 (6,466)	52,620 (1,090)	56,360 (2,279)	55,400 (5,867)	49,170 (1,237)
Percent,[2] all education levels	**62.4** (1.30)	**69.7** (1.28)	**64.3** (1.12)	**64.5** (1.19)	**65.0** (1.21)	**57.4** (1.13)	**57.7** (1.26)	**55.7** (1.33)	**58.5** (1.23)	**59.6** (1.51)	**61.7** (1.12)
Less than high school completion	42.4 (4.02)	48.8 (4.46)	48.6 (4.06)	40.3 (3.98)	43.9 (4.11)	38.1 (4.26)	30.5 (3.73)	30.3 (3.80)	27.5 (4.20)	40.9 (5.90)	39.0 (5.19)
High school completion[1]	60.7 (2.11)	68.3 (2.16)	64.5 (1.92)	64.0 (2.01)	60.4 (2.11)	48.9 (1.93)	53.6 (2.03)	50.8 (2.16)	51.4 (2.22)	51.2 (2.64)	58.5 (1.78)
Some college, no degree	62.2 (2.51)	69.8 (2.57)	61.5 (2.28)	59.3 (2.65)	65.5 (2.78)	57.7 (2.21)	56.2 (2.42)	50.8 (2.40)	58.0 (2.18)	54.6 (2.94)	58.9 (2.36)
Associate's degree	69.2 (4.29)	78.0 (3.79)	68.6 (4.20)	72.2 (3.57)	57.9 (3.78)	63.2 (3.58)	61.5 (3.25)	69.0 (3.32)	58.9 (3.34)	64.2 (4.19)	59.3 (3.23)
Bachelor's or higher degree	77.3 (2.85)	78.6 (2.58)	72.0 (2.16)	79.0 (1.94)	82.0 (1.95)	73.5 (2.05)	72.4 (2.11)	69.1 (2.13)	76.2 (2.12)	78.2 (2.27)	74.2 (2.07)
Bachelor's degree	76.1 (3.15)	79.4 (2.80)	71.7 (2.66)	79.9 (2.14)	82.5 (2.44)	73.1 (2.46)	71.1 (2.70)	68.5 (2.41)	75.1 (2.47)	74.3 (2.99)	73.4 (2.52)
Master's or higher degree	84.0 (6.41)	74.9 (6.52)	72.8 (4.96)	76.5 (3.95)	80.5 (3.78)	74.7 (3.60)	76.5 (3.65)	70.6 (4.32)	79.3 (3.96)	88.6 (3.30)	76.4 (3.53)
Hispanic											
Median annual earnings, all education levels	**29,110** (679)	**30,790** (460)	**30,080** (1,090)	**30,290** (10)	**30,810** (769)	**31,810** (1,399)	**32,530** (642)	**31,520** (22)	**30,830** (45)	**30,120** (123)	**30,000** (103)
Less than high school completion	23,100 (626)	23,370 (482)	24,520 (1,675)	24,100 (75)	23,500 (819)	21,950 (83)	21,630 (282)	22,800 (989)	23,130 (1,205)	23,180 (1,800)	23,820 (909)
High school completion[1]	29,250 (1,214)	31,570 (820)	29,900 (650)	29,020 (1,055)	29,460 (947)	28,390 (877)	30,220 (980)	29,410 (1,353)	28,430 (788)	28,730 (1,138)	29,990 (822)
Some college, no degree	30,320 (1,384)	36,360 (968)	37,580 (1,445)	37,990 (1,727)	35,290 (1,096)	35,610 (1,013)	34,440 (1,493)	31,550 (821)	32,760 (1,398)	30,370 (1,077)	31,060 (1,338)
Associate's degree	36,910 (2,218)	40,710 (1,746)	37,250 (1,757)	41,110 (1,969)	34,230 (1,484)	33,910 (1,609)	36,790 (1,422)	36,510 (1,523)	34,370 (1,791)	33,130 (2,304)	29,920 (1,540)
Bachelor's or higher degree	46,280 (1,802)	49,960 (1,770)	49,510 (1,896)	49,370 (2,270)	49,440 (1,804)	50,290 (1,657)	47,880 (2,144)	43,350 (1,846)	46,040 (592)	46,560 (1,500)	47,390 (2,413)
Bachelor's degree	43,590 (2,076)	48,130 (1,319)	46,430 (2,750)	47,830 (841)	45,670 (2,380)	48,930 (1,074)	45,290 (3,273)	41,690 (313)	44,000 (2,105)	45,690 (1,485)	44,220 (1,400)
Master's or higher degree	64,830 (8,743)	52,470 (3,216)	61,580 (2,300)	60,970 (4,268)	66,100 (3,068)	58,400 (4,377)	53,010 (3,882)	53,550 (2,628)	51,560 (4,168)	50,350 (5,655)	57,130 (2,404)
Percent,[2] all education levels	**60.5** (1.32)	**68.7** (1.14)	**68.0** (0.84)	**68.1** (0.82)	**67.9** (0.86)	**58.2** (0.96)	**59.4** (0.85)	**61.4** (0.89)	**61.8** (0.87)	**64.7** (1.04)	**65.9** (0.94)
Less than high school completion	53.5 (2.27)	64.4 (2.00)	64.8 (1.52)	64.9 (1.67)	61.1 (1.72)	51.8 (1.67)	50.4 (1.77)	54.9 (1.69)	54.4 (1.81)	58.9 (2.15)	62.0 (1.96)
High school completion[1]	66.0 (2.31)	70.5 (2.00)	70.8 (1.57)	71.3 (1.40)	72.1 (1.31)	58.2 (1.57)	59.0 (1.64)	61.5 (1.49)	63.3 (1.53)	66.9 (1.78)	67.8 (1.70)
Some college, no degree	58.4 (3.18)	69.5 (2.89)	67.3 (2.16)	66.6 (1.93)	67.9 (2.06)	61.1 (2.28)	64.5 (1.85)	63.0 (2.09)	61.7 (2.13)	58.2 (2.44)	63.3 (1.79)
Associate's degree	67.0 (5.34)	79.0 (3.95)	73.1 (2.69)	70.0 (2.63)	65.6 (3.15)	66.2 (3.03)	65.1 (2.70)	65.3 (3.06)	65.2 (2.90)	73.5 (2.81)	64.4 (2.84)
Bachelor's or higher degree	66.9 (3.73)	70.1 (3.27)	68.9 (2.11)	69.5 (2.11)	73.5 (1.92)	64.4 (2.12)	68.1 (2.10)	68.3 (1.84)	68.4 (1.96)	71.1 (2.00)	70.8 (1.84)
Bachelor's degree	66.3 (4.12)	71.1 (3.57)	68.8 (2.52)	69.3 (2.40)	71.6 (2.15)	64.2 (2.23)	68.1 (2.29)	68.6 (2.13)	67.6 (2.21)	72.2 (2.27)	70.6 (2.10)
Master's or higher degree	69.8 (8.84)	65.5 (8.05)	69.3 (4.88)	70.4 (4.19)	80.2 (3.55)	65.3 (4.32)	68.2 (3.89)	67.1 (3.97)	71.3 (4.09)	67.5 (4.31)	71.5 (4.16)

See notes at end of table.

Table 502.30. Median annual earnings of full-time year-round workers 25 to 34 years old and full-time year-round workers as a percentage of the labor force, by sex, race/ethnicity, and educational attainment: Selected years, 1995 through 2014—Continued

[Amounts in constant 2014 dollars. Standard errors appear in parentheses]

Sex, race/ethnicity, and educational attainment	1995	2000	2004	2005	2007	2009	2010	2011	2012	2013	2014
1	2	3	4	5	6	7	8	9	10	11	12
Asian[3]											
Median annual earnings, all education levels	**39,290 (1,094)**	**49,290 (836)**	**49,350 (1,238)**	**48,310 (1,966)**	**51,080 (2,088)**	**54,290 (814)**	**49,640 (2,781)**	**51,800 (2,763)**	**55,510 (2,577)**	**51,260 (2,011)**	**49,520 (681)**
Less than high school completion	‡ (†)	25,290 (2,268)	24,120 (3,963)	‡ (†)	‡ (†)	‡ (†)	‡ (†)	‡ (†)	‡ (†)	‡ (†)	‡ (†)
High school completion[1]	30,840 (2,256)	34,360 (1,244)	31,440 (1,391)	32,610 (1,712)	31,830 (2,915)	28,550 (2,232)	31,700 (1,870)	26,250 (1,354)	30,440 (841)	28,390 (2,562)	29,810 (1,870)
Some college, no degree	28,770 (2,706)	39,550 (2,047)	37,110 (3,288)	35,960 (2,524)	39,750 (2,748)	41,910 (3,622)	37,720 (1,549)	32,510 (1,892)	34,240 (2,716)	35,240 (4,790)	29,410 (2,938)
Associate's degree	31,070 (1,905)	40,560 (2,026)	36,100 (5,890)	41,250 (5,116)	40,100 (5,198)	40,040 (4,221)	38,960 (2,914)	36,400 (6,856)	44,440 (3,260)	32,110 (3,058)	33,840 (3,942)
Bachelor's or higher degree	51,110 (2,202)	67,800 (1,402)	61,960 (1,169)	60,600 (1,103)	62,740 (5,200)	65,410 (1,548)	64,980 (1,173)	64,310 (2,488)	66,220 (1,726)	60,880 (2,420)	61,190 (3,195)
Bachelor's degree	46,840 (988)	61,650 (2,483)	59,530 (2,581)	60,590 (3,939)	56,280 (1,955)	54,960 (1,240)	58,640 (4,306)	53,980 (3,488)	61,130 (1,985)	59,080 (2,765)	55,960 (2,275)
Master's or higher degree	58,950 (5,643)	78,640 (6,034)	64,130 (2,676)	65,970 (4,839)	73,940 (2,483)	77,240 (3,319)	74,140 (5,325)	77,060 (4,698)	71,890 (2,024)	75,860 (5,396)	73,080 (4,500)
Percent,[2] all education levels	**63.4 (2.98)**	**68.5 (1.78)**	**67.1 (1.79)**	**64.8 (1.57)**	**71.2 (1.63)**	**66.7 (1.51)**	**65.1 (1.46)**	**65.1 (1.73)**	**67.9 (1.57)**	**66.0 (1.79)**	**68.2 (1.46)**
Less than high school completion	46.6 (9.98)	61.6 (8.31)	61.8 (6.81)	49.4 (7.62)	58.3 (8.93)	52.4 (11.87)	46.6 (11.24)	56.2 (6.80)	50.9 (7.17)	53.3 (9.35)	50.8 (7.91)
High school completion[1]	66.9 (7.05)	68.9 (4.59)	73.6 (4.04)	62.5 (4.82)	68.5 (4.09)	59.3 (4.15)	55.9 (3.97)	53.7 (4.47)	64.6 (3.36)	62.4 (5.45)	66.8 (4.47)
Some college, no degree	51.8 (8.46)	63.4 (4.59)	62.4 (5.22)	66.5 (4.65)	73.4 (4.48)	57.4 (5.03)	58.2 (4.93)	58.3 (4.37)	51.7 (4.31)	57.2 (5.79)	58.6 (5.25)
Associate's degree	77.1 (8.01)	72.2 (5.92)	65.1 (6.35)	66.3 (5.93)	70.6 (5.49)	70.3 (4.25)	56.5 (5.57)	55.1 (5.88)	60.6 (5.79)	69.3 (5.81)	72.8 (5.10)
Bachelor's or higher degree	65.6 (4.18)	69.9 (2.35)	67.1 (2.55)	66.0 (2.07)	72.4 (2.04)	70.5 (1.84)	71.1 (1.89)	70.4 (2.08)	72.9 (1.80)	68.5 (2.24)	70.5 (1.65)
Bachelor's degree	68.0 (5.27)	70.8 (2.87)	67.6 (2.65)	68.7 (2.69)	71.6 (2.40)	69.7 (2.46)	72.2 (2.22)	69.6 (2.59)	73.7 (2.31)	67.6 (3.04)	72.9 (2.14)
Master's or higher degree	62.0 (6.80)	67.9 (4.11)	66.1 (3.98)	61.3 (3.08)	73.6 (3.25)	71.6 (3.17)	69.4 (3.15)	71.8 (3.20)	71.7 (2.85)	70.0 (3.51)	66.9 (2.83)
Median annual earnings for other race groups, all education levels											
Pacific Islander[4]	[3] (†)	[3] (†)	38,260 (8,298)	36,630 (3,907)	39,250 (3,695)	32,050 (5,746)	37,180 (1,428)	36,040 (2,705)	33,090 (5,056)	39,630 (4,420)	34,110 (3,654)
American Indian/Alaska Native[4]	30,800 (3,084)	34,350 (1,506)	32,280 (2,607)	35,760 (2,065)	35,040 (1,992)	33,110 (4,351)	34,190 (3,434)	30,830 (1,763)	33,910 (2,799)	32,750 (6,664)	29,830 (1,358)
Two or more races[4]	— (†)	— (†)	38,920 (2,300)	41,210 (1,729)	37,020 (3,516)	37,080 (2,970)	37,780 (1,511)	38,620 (1,733)	36,680 (1,563)	37,170 (3,416)	34,360 (1,974)
Percent[2] for other race groups, all education levels											
Pacific Islander[4]	[3] (†)	[3] (†)	64.3 (6.81)	53.7 (6.81)	70.2 (5.06)	46.9 (7.15)	62.2 (6.71)	56.9 (5.50)	69.4 (6.03)	77.2 (6.48)	63.9 (5.09)
American Indian/Alaska Native[4]	46.9 (8.10)	57.6 (4.94)	54.3 (4.25)	60.2 (4.01)	64.3 (4.58)	59.8 (4.30)	52.9 (4.14)	52.2 (4.58)	55.8 (5.05)	59.4 (5.26)	61.0 (3.84)
Two or more races[4]	— (†)	— (†)	60.7 (2.46)	61.9 (3.46)	59.5 (3.21)	50.2 (2.95)	60.2 (2.87)	58.1 (2.93)	59.0 (2.94)	61.0 (3.73)	61.6 (3.23)

—Not available.
†Not applicable.
#Rounds to zero.
‡Reporting standards not met (too few cases for a reliable estimate).
[1]Includes equivalency credentials, such as the GED credential.
[2]Full-time year-round workers as a percentage of the population ages 25 through 34 who reported working or looking for work in the given year.
[3]For 1995 and 2000, data for Asians and Pacific Islanders were not reported separately; therefore, Pacific Islanders are included with Asians for 1995 and 2000.
[4]For Pacific Islanders, American Indians/Alaska Natives, and persons of Two or more races, data by educational attainment are omitted because these data did not meet reporting standards. All data shown for these three race categories are for persons of all education levels.
NOTE: Beginning in 2004, standard errors were computed using replicate weights, which produced more precise values than the generalized variance function methodology used in prior years. Race categories exclude persons of Hispanic ethnicity. Constant dollars based on the Consumer Price Index, prepared by the Bureau of Labor Statistics, U.S. Department of Labor.
SOURCE: U.S. Department of Commerce, Census Bureau, Current Population Survey (CPS), Annual Social and Economic Supplement, 1996 through 2015. (This table was prepared November 2015.)

Table 502.40. Annual earnings of persons 25 years old and over, by highest level of educational attainment and sex: 2014

[Standard errors appear in parentheses]

Sex and earnings		Elementary/secondary			College						
							Bachelor's or higher degree				
	Total	Less than 9th grade	Some high school, no completion	High school completion (includes equivalency)	Some college, no degree	Associate's degree	Total	Bachelor's degree	Master's degree	Professional degree	Doctor's degree
1	2	3	4	5	6	7	8	9	10	11	12
Number of persons (in thousands)	**212,132 (231.8)**	**9,896 (120.5)**	**14,686 (145.3)**	**62,575 (268.3)**	**35,164 (215.0)**	**20,867 (171.0)**	**68,945 (276.9)**	**43,500 (234.6)**	**18,471 (161.7)**	**3,365 (71.2)**	**3,609 (73.7)**
With earnings	138,766 (310.2)	4,249 (79.8)	6,846 (100.8)	36,388 (218.1)	23,370 (180.0)	15,202 (147.7)	52,712 (252.5)	32,928 (209.1)	14,201 (143.0)	2,680 (63.6)	2,903 (66.2)
For persons with earnings											
Percentage distribution, by total annual earnings[1]	100.0 (†)	100.0 (†)	100.0 (†)	100.0 (†)	100.0 (†)	100.0 (†)	100.0 (†)	100.0 (†)	100.0 (†)	100.0 (†)	100.0 (†)
$1 to $4,999 or loss[2]	4.7 (0.07)	6.7 (0.47)	8.2 (0.41)	5.1 (0.14)	5.6 (0.19)	5.1 (0.22)	3.3 (0.10)	3.5 (0.13)	3.0 (0.18)	2.5 (0.38)	2.5 (0.36)
$5,000 to $9,999	4.5 (0.07)	7.9 (0.51)	9.0 (0.43)	5.5 (0.15)	5.5 (0.18)	4.1 (0.20)	2.8 (0.09)	2.9 (0.11)	2.6 (0.17)	2.2 (0.35)	2.5 (0.36)
$10,000 to $14,999	6.2 (0.08)	14.4 (0.66)	12.9 (0.50)	7.9 (0.17)	7.0 (0.21)	5.8 (0.23)	3.3 (0.10)	3.7 (0.13)	3.0 (0.18)	1.6 (0.30)	2.0 (0.32)
$15,000 to $19,999	6.5 (0.08)	16.5 (0.70)	12.9 (0.50)	8.5 (0.18)	7.3 (0.21)	6.0 (0.24)	3.1 (0.09)	3.6 (0.13)	2.4 (0.16)	2.2 (0.35)	2.3 (0.34)
$20,000 to $24,999	8.1 (0.09)	16.3 (0.70)	14.0 (0.52)	10.8 (0.20)	9.7 (0.24)	8.4 (0.28)	4.1 (0.11)	4.7 (0.14)	3.7 (0.20)	2.0 (0.34)	2.3 (0.34)
$25,000 to $29,999	7.0 (0.08)	9.4 (0.55)	9.5 (0.44)	9.8 (0.19)	8.5 (0.23)	7.5 (0.26)	3.8 (0.10)	4.6 (0.14)	2.9 (0.17)	1.9 (0.32)	1.6 (0.29)
$30,000 to $34,999	7.7 (0.09)	9.8 (0.56)	8.1 (0.41)	10.4 (0.20)	8.9 (0.23)	8.4 (0.28)	4.8 (0.11)	5.6 (0.16)	3.8 (0.20)	1.6 (0.30)	2.9 (0.38)
$35,000 to $39,999	6.3 (0.08)	4.4 (0.39)	4.6 (0.31)	7.7 (0.17)	7.2 (0.21)	7.4 (0.26)	5.1 (0.12)	6.1 (0.16)	3.9 (0.20)	2.0 (0.33)	2.3 (0.34)
$40,000 to $49,999	11.4 (0.11)	5.3 (0.43)	8.4 (0.42)	11.2 (0.20)	12.0 (0.26)	14.0 (0.35)	11.5 (0.17)	12.3 (0.22)	11.1 (0.33)	6.9 (0.61)	8.3 (0.63)
$50,000 to $74,999	18.4 (0.13)	6.0 (0.45)	8.1 (0.41)	14.8 (0.23)	16.5 (0.30)	19.9 (0.40)	23.7 (0.23)	23.7 (0.29)	25.7 (0.45)	16.1 (0.88)	20.3 (0.92)
$75,000 to $99,999	8.3 (0.09)	1.4 (0.23)	2.3 (0.22)	5.0 (0.14)	6.2 (0.20)	7.5 (0.26)	13.2 (0.18)	12.3 (0.22)	15.4 (0.37)	10.9 (0.74)	14.5 (0.81)
$100,000 or more	10.7 (0.10)	1.9 (0.26)	2.0 (0.21)	3.3 (0.12)	5.7 (0.19)	5.8 (0.23)	21.3 (0.22)	17.0 (0.26)	22.5 (0.43)	50.2 (1.19)	38.4 (1.12)
Median annual earnings[1]	$38,430 (343)	$20,940 (207)	$21,860 (223)	$30,730 (138)	$32,330 (162)	$37,320 (322)	$56,470 (283)	$51,310 (185)	$61,390 (352)	$100,070 (5,533)	$77,750 (2,772)
Number of males (in thousands)	**101,887 (143.3)**	**4,911 (84.7)**	**7,278 (102.1)**	**30,997 (186.6)**	**16,772 (148.1)**	**9,006 (112.6)**	**32,923 (190.1)**	**20,696 (161.3)**	**8,157 (107.6)**	**1,965 (54.3)**	**2,105 (56.2)**
With earnings	73,743 (204.5)	2,761 (64.1)	4,338 (79.8)	20,972 (162.1)	12,106 (128.7)	7,040 (100.5)	26,526 (177.0)	16,681 (147.8)	6,533 (97.0)	1,628 (49.5)	1,685 (50.3)
For males with earnings											
Percentage distribution, by total annual earnings[1]	100.0 (†)	100.0 (†)	100.0 (†)	100.0 (†)	100.0 (†)	100.0 (†)	100.0 (†)	100.0 (†)	100.0 (†)	100.0 (†)	100.0 (†)
$1 to $4,999 or loss[2]	3.3 (0.08)	4.0 (0.46)	6.0 (0.45)	3.7 (0.16)	3.6 (0.21)	3.4 (0.27)	2.3 (0.11)	2.4 (0.15)	1.9 (0.21)	2.1 (0.44)	2.6 (0.47)
$5,000 to $9,999	3.2 (0.08)	5.4 (0.53)	6.3 (0.46)	3.6 (0.16)	4.0 (0.22)	2.8 (0.24)	1.8 (0.10)	1.9 (0.13)	1.5 (0.19)	1.8 (0.41)	2.0 (0.42)
$10,000 to $14,999	4.7 (0.10)	10.5 (0.72)	9.8 (0.56)	5.6 (0.20)	5.3 (0.25)	4.2 (0.30)	2.4 (0.12)	2.5 (0.15)	2.5 (0.24)	0.9 ! (0.29)	1.5 (0.37)
$15,000 to $19,999	5.4 (0.10)	15.9 (0.86)	11.0 (0.59)	6.6 (0.21)	6.0 (0.27)	3.8 (0.28)	2.6 (0.12)	2.9 (0.16)	1.8 (0.20)	2.2 (0.45)	2.7 (0.49)
$20,000 to $24,999	6.7 (0.11)	16.2 (0.87)	13.8 (0.65)	8.4 (0.24)	7.3 (0.29)	6.0 (0.35)	3.1 (0.13)	3.5 (0.17)	3.0 (0.26)	1.9 (0.42)	1.8 (0.40)
$25,000 to $29,999	6.3 (0.11)	10.6 (0.73)	10.3 (0.57)	9.0 (0.24)	6.7 (0.28)	5.4 (0.33)	3.1 (0.13)	3.8 (0.18)	2.0 (0.21)	1.3 (0.35)	1.5 (0.36)
$30,000 to $34,999	7.1 (0.12)	12.5 (0.78)	9.5 (0.55)	10.0 (0.26)	7.9 (0.30)	6.8 (0.37)	3.7 (0.14)	4.4 (0.20)	2.8 (0.25)	1.5 (0.38)	1.7 (0.38)
$35,000 to $39,999	6.3 (0.11)	5.2 (0.52)	5.8 (0.44)	8.2 (0.23)	7.5 (0.30)	7.5 (0.39)	4.1 (0.15)	5.0 (0.21)	3.0 (0.26)	1.0 (0.31)	1.7 (0.38)
$40,000 to $49,999	11.3 (0.14)	7.0 (0.60)	10.9 (0.58)	13.2 (0.29)	12.8 (0.37)	14.3 (0.52)	8.8 (0.22)	10.1 (0.29)	7.1 (0.39)	4.7 (0.65)	7.1 (0.77)
$50,000 to $74,999	20.5 (0.18)	8.6 (0.66)	10.7 (0.58)	19.8 (0.34)	21.0 (0.46)	25.2 (0.64)	22.5 (0.32)	23.9 (0.41)	22.1 (0.63)	14.9 (1.09)	17.8 (1.15)
$75,000 to $99,999	10.2 (0.14)	1.9 (0.32)	3.3 (0.33)	7.2 (0.22)	9.1 (0.32)	10.8 (0.46)	15.0 (0.27)	14.5 (0.34)	17.3 (0.58)	11.1 (0.96)	13.6 (1.03)
$100,000 or more	15.0 (0.16)	2.4 (0.36)	2.5 (0.29)	4.7 (0.18)	8.8 (0.32)	9.7 (0.44)	30.7 (0.35)	25.0 (0.41)	35.0 (0.73)	56.5 (1.52)	46.1 (1.50)
Median annual earnings[1]	$45,390 (205)	$23,880 (786)	$25,970 (385)	$36,290 (228)	$40,730 (274)	$46,410 (449)	$69,400 (1,051)	$61,730 (269)	$76,690 (702)	$106,450 (5,279)	$90,910 (2,388)

See notes at end of table.

Table 502.40. Annual earnings of persons 25 years old and over, by highest level of educational attainment and sex: 2014—Continued

[Standard errors appear in parentheses]

Sex and earnings	Total		Elementary/secondary						College													
			Less than 9th grade		Some high school, no completion		High school completion (includes equivalency)		Some college, no degree		Associate's degree		Bachelor's or higher degree									
													Total		Bachelor's degree		Master's degree		Professional degree		Doctor's degree	
1	2		3		4		5		6		7		8		9		10		11		12	
Number of females (in thousands)	**110,245**	**(149.6)**	**4,985**	**(85.5)**	**7,408**	**(103.2)**	**31,578**	**(190.3)**	**18,391**	**(154.9)**	**11,861**	**(128.1)**	**36,021**	**(198.5)**	**22,804**	**(169.0)**	**10,314**	**(120.3)**	**1,400**	**(46.0)**	**1,504**	**(47.6)**
With earnings	65,023	(220.2)	1,488	(47.4)	2,508	(61.3)	15,415	(143.8)	11,263	(125.2)	8,163	(108.0)	26,186	(178.1)	16,248	(147.1)	7,668	(104.9)	1,052	(39.9)	1,218	(42.9)
For females with earnings																						
Percentage distribution, by total annual earnings[1]	100.0	(†)	100.0	(†)	100.0	(†)	100.0	(†)	100.0	(†)	100.0	(†)	100.0	(†)	100.0	(†)	100.0	(†)	100.0	(†)	100.0	(†)
$1 to $4,999 or loss[2]	6.3	(0.12)	11.8	(1.03)	11.8	(0.80)	7.0	(0.25)	7.7	(0.31)	6.6	(0.34)	4.3	(0.16)	4.7	(0.20)	4.0	(0.28)	3.2	(0.67)	2.5	(0.55)
$5,000 to $9,999	6.1	(0.12)	12.5	(1.06)	13.6	(0.84)	8.0	(0.27)	7.0	(0.30)	5.2	(0.30)	3.7	(0.14)	3.9	(0.19)	3.6	(0.26)	2.9	(0.63)	3.2	(0.62)
$10,000 to $14,999	8.0	(0.13)	21.6	(1.32)	18.4	(0.96)	11.0	(0.31)	8.9	(0.33)	7.2	(0.35)	4.3	(0.16)	5.0	(0.21)	3.5	(0.26)	2.8	(0.62)	2.6	(0.57)
$15,000 to $19,999	7.7	(0.13)	17.5	(1.22)	16.1	(0.91)	11.2	(0.31)	8.7	(0.33)	7.9	(0.37)	3.7	(0.14)	4.3	(0.20)	2.8	(0.23)	2.1	(0.54)	1.8	(0.47)
$20,000 to $24,999	9.8	(0.14)	16.6	(1.19)	14.3	(0.86)	14.0	(0.35)	12.3	(0.38)	10.4	(0.42)	5.1	(0.17)	5.9	(0.23)	4.3	(0.29)	2.2	(0.56)	3.0	(0.61)
$25,000 to $29,999	7.8	(0.13)	7.0	(0.82)	8.1	(0.67)	10.8	(0.31)	10.4	(0.35)	9.3	(0.40)	4.6	(0.16)	5.3	(0.22)	3.7	(0.26)	2.8	(0.62)	1.8	(0.47)
$30,000 to $34,999	8.2	(0.13)	4.8	(0.69)	5.7	(0.57)	10.9	(0.31)	10.0	(0.35)	9.8	(0.41)	5.9	(0.18)	6.9	(0.25)	4.6	(0.30)	1.7	(0.49)	4.5	(0.73)
$35,000 to $39,999	6.4	(0.12)	3.0	(0.54)	2.7	(0.40)	7.1	(0.26)	7.0	(0.30)	7.3	(0.36)	6.0	(0.18)	7.1	(0.25)	4.6	(0.30)	3.4	(0.69)	3.2	(0.62)
$40,000 to $49,999	11.6	(0.16)	2.4	(0.49)	4.2	(0.50)	8.5	(0.28)	11.1	(0.37)	13.7	(0.47)	14.2	(0.27)	14.6	(0.34)	14.5	(0.50)	10.3	(1.16)	9.9	(1.06)
$50,000 to $74,999	16.0	(0.18)	1.2	(0.35)	3.5	(0.45)	8.1	(0.27)	11.6	(0.37)	15.3	(0.49)	24.8	(0.33)	23.5	(0.41)	28.7	(0.64)	17.9	(1.46)	23.8	(1.51)
$75,000 to $99,999	6.2	(0.12)	0.5 !	(0.23)	0.6 !	(0.18)	1.9	(0.14)	3.1	(0.20)	4.7	(0.29)	11.4	(0.24)	10.0	(0.29)	13.8	(0.49)	10.6	(1.17)	15.7	(1.29)
$100,000 or more	5.9	(0.11)	0.9 !	(0.31)	1.0	(0.25)	1.4	(0.12)	2.4	(0.18)	2.5	(0.21)	11.8	(0.25)	8.7	(0.27)	11.8	(0.46)	40.3	(1.87)	27.9	(1.59)
Median annual earnings[1]	$31,680	(124)	$15,960	(377)	$16,630	(341)	$24,300	(350)	$27,090	(273)	$31,020	(231)	$47,690	(527)	$42,440	(458)	$51,920	(372)	$75,960	(5,396)	$66,650	(2,560)

†Not applicable.
!Interpret data with caution. The coefficient of variation (CV) for this estimate is between 30 and 50 percent.
[1]Excludes persons without earnings.
[2]A negative amount (a net loss) may be reported by self-employed persons.

NOTE: Detail may not sum to totals because of rounding.
SOURCE: U.S. Department of Commerce, Census Bureau, Current Population Survey (CPS), Annual Social and Economic Supplement, 2015; retrieved April 15, 2016, from http://www.census.gov/hhes/www/cpstables/032015/perinc/pinc03_000.htm. (This table was prepared April 2016.)

Table 503.10. Percentage of high school students age 16 and over who were employed, by age group, sex, race/ethnicity, family income, nativity, and hours worked per week: Selected years, 1970 through 2014

[Standard errors appear in parentheses]

Year	Total	Age group: 16 and 17 years old	Age group: 18 years old and over	Sex: Male	Sex: Female	Race/ethnicity: White	Race/ethnicity: Black	Race/ethnicity: Hispanic	Family income[1]: Low income	Family income[1]: Middle income	Family income[1]: High income	Nativity: U.S.-born	Nativity: Foreign-born
1	2	3	4	5	6	7	8	9	10	11	12	13	14
						Percent employed[2]							
1970	31.9 (0.88)	30.8 (0.93)	39.7 (2.55)	35.2 (1.24)	28.3 (1.22)	— (†)	— (†)	— (†)	22.0 (2.51)	31.5 (1.12)	35.9 (1.64)	— (†)	— (†)
1975	33.2 (0.85)	32.9 (0.91)	34.9 (2.40)	35.0 (1.19)	31.2 (1.22)	38.0 (1.00)	13.9 (1.63)	21.8 (3.59)	18.4 (2.22)	31.8 (1.10)	40.4 (1.59)	— (†)	— (†)
1980	35.6 (0.87)	34.9 (0.94)	39.6 (2.28)	36.9 (1.22)	34.2 (1.24)	41.2 (1.03)	15.0 (1.64)	24.1 (3.65)	19.4 (2.10)	35.2 (1.15)	42.3 (1.59)	— (†)	— (†)
1985	31.6 (0.93)	30.8 (1.00)	36.1 (2.47)	32.1 (1.29)	31.0 (1.33)	37.9 (1.15)	15.0 (1.85)	17.6 (2.63)	14.7 (1.85)	31.0 (1.23)	41.1 (1.81)	— (†)	— (†)
1990	32.3 (0.98)	31.2 (1.08)	37.1 (2.33)	33.1 (1.37)	31.3 (1.39)	37.8 (1.24)	17.3 (2.05)	26.4 (2.86)	21.4 (2.16)	33.1 (1.29)	36.8 (1.97)	— (†)	— (†)
1995	33.6 (0.92)	32.7 (1.02)	37.5 (2.19)	33.1 (1.26)	34.2 (1.35)	40.8 (1.18)	18.0 (1.91)	22.2 (2.41)	17.4 (1.82)	34.4 (1.23)	42.1 (1.88)	34.9 (0.97)	20.1 (2.65)
2000	34.1 (0.93)	33.3 (1.03)	37.7 (2.15)	33.2 (1.28)	35.1 (1.36)	41.3 (1.20)	21.3 (2.14)	20.9 (2.18)	22.0 (2.11)	34.1 (1.22)	40.7 (1.85)	35.1 (0.99)	24.4 (2.74)
2001	32.4 (0.86)	31.1 (0.95)	37.8 (1.99)	30.6 (1.17)	34.5 (1.27)	38.9 (1.11)	18.7 (1.85)	23.6 (2.23)	21.4 (2.04)	33.3 (1.12)	36.1 (1.70)	33.3 (0.90)	23.0 (2.64)
2002	30.6 (0.84)	29.2 (0.93)	35.9 (1.92)	28.0 (1.13)	33.4 (1.24)	37.5 (1.11)	16.9 (1.81)	21.1 (1.94)	18.4 (1.83)	31.4 (1.11)	35.3 (1.64)	31.6 (0.89)	21.3 (2.34)
2003	27.0 (0.79)	25.3 (0.86)	34.6 (1.97)	26.7 (1.09)	27.3 (1.15)	33.3 (1.07)	15.2 (1.68)	18.8 (1.82)	14.3 (1.64)	27.8 (1.05)	31.8 (1.57)	28.0 (0.84)	17.7 (2.17)
2004	27.2 (0.80)	25.6 (0.87)	34.7 (2.03)	26.2 (1.09)	28.3 (1.17)	32.9 (1.08)	15.1 (1.71)	21.2 (1.92)	12.0 (1.55)	27.5 (1.05)	34.4 (1.64)	27.8 (0.85)	20.8 (2.43)
2005	26.4 (0.77)	25.2 (0.84)	32.2 (1.95)	25.3 (1.05)	27.6 (1.14)	31.8 (1.05)	13.7 (1.63)	19.4 (1.78)	14.8 (1.61)	26.9 (1.03)	31.7 (1.55)	26.8 (0.81)	21.7 (2.49)
2006	27.6 (0.79)	26.0 (0.86)	34.1 (1.87)	26.5 (1.08)	28.8 (1.16)	33.6 (1.08)	20.1 (1.85)	17.5 (1.72)	17.8 (1.72)	27.5 (1.04)	33.5 (1.59)	27.9 (0.82)	23.9 (2.64)
2007	26.2 (0.78)	24.8 (0.85)	32.2 (1.87)	25.0 (1.06)	27.6 (1.14)	31.3 (1.06)	15.1 (1.68)	21.1 (1.83)	17.3 (1.74)	25.9 (1.01)	32.1 (1.62)	26.0 (0.81)	28.5 (2.64)
2008	22.6 (0.74)	21.0 (0.80)	29.5 (1.83)	20.0 (0.99)	25.4 (1.10)	27.7 (1.04)	15.5 (1.69)	15.1 (1.54)	13.5 (1.54)	22.6 (0.96)	28.4 (1.59)	23.1 (0.78)	18.0 (2.35)
2009	17.0 (0.67)	15.2 (0.72)	23.8 (1.65)	16.0 (0.91)	18.1 (0.98)	21.5 (0.96)	10.5 (1.43)	11.9 (1.39)	9.7 (1.33)	16.3 (0.85)	23.5 (1.51)	17.0 (0.70)	16.9 (2.32)
2010[3]	16.2 (0.55)	15.0 (0.59)	20.8 (1.52)	14.0 (0.78)	18.5 (0.86)	20.9 (0.86)	9.6 (1.28)	10.4 (1.18)	8.5 (1.01)	16.5 (0.80)	20.9 (1.31)	16.4 (0.60)	13.4 (2.20)
2011[3]	16.9 (0.67)	16.4 (0.77)	18.7 (1.28)	14.7 (0.76)	19.4 (1.09)	22.2 (1.07)	10.2 (1.43)	11.3 (1.11)	10.2 (1.29)	17.5 (0.83)	19.6 (1.39)	17.3 (0.74)	12.4 (1.91)
2012[3]	18.0 (0.71)	16.0 (0.75)	24.5 (1.88)	16.6 (0.83)	19.4 (1.13)	23.2 (0.97)	12.7 (2.17)	11.4 (1.23)	13.0 (1.42)	16.4 (0.88)	24.9 (1.55)	18.6 (0.76)	12.0 (2.01)
2013[3]	17.9 (0.65)	15.8 (0.69)	24.7 (1.73)	17.6 (0.89)	18.3 (0.94)	23.3 (0.99)	11.8 (1.42)	14.0 (1.19)	9.7 (1.26)	16.9 (0.90)	25.4 (1.69)	17.8 (0.66)	19.0 (2.67)
2014[3]	19.2 (0.70)	17.3 (0.71)	25.5 (1.63)	18.1 (0.90)	20.3 (1.03)	23.2 (1.00)	14.0 (1.65)	14.7 (1.47)	12.6 (1.52)	19.3 (0.88)	23.2 (1.54)	19.2 (0.75)	18.8 (2.20)
						Percent working less than 15 hours per week[4]							
1970	13.6 (0.64)	14.5 (0.71)	7.5 (1.37)	12.3 (0.85)	14.9 (0.97)	— (†)	— (†)	— (†)	9.9 (1.81)	12.6 (0.80)	16.8 (1.28)	— (†)	— (†)
1975	13.4 (0.62)	14.0 (0.67)	8.8 (1.43)	12.5 (0.82)	14.3 (0.92)	15.5 (0.75)	5.3 (1.05)	6.6 ! (2.15)	6.8 (1.44)	12.3 (0.78)	17.4 (1.23)	— (†)	— (†)
1980	14.0 (0.63)	14.9 (0.70)	8.9 (1.33)	13.7 (0.87)	14.2 (0.91)	16.4 (0.77)	4.6 (0.96)	9.4 (2.49)	7.7 (1.41)	13.2 (0.82)	17.7 (1.23)	— (†)	— (†)
1985	12.3 (0.65)	12.8 (0.72)	9.5 (1.51)	11.7 (0.89)	12.9 (0.96)	15.2 (0.85)	6.2 (1.25)	3.0 ! (1.18)	3.6 (0.97)	11.8 (0.86)	17.5 (1.40)	— (†)	— (†)
1990	11.7 (0.67)	12.9 (0.78)	6.8 (1.21)	11.3 (0.92)	12.2 (0.98)	14.7 (0.90)	6.0 (1.28)	4.8 (1.39)	5.9 (1.24)	11.5 (0.88)	15.6 (1.48)	— (†)	— (†)
1995	11.9 (0.63)	13.1 (0.73)	6.8 (1.14)	11.1 (0.84)	12.9 (0.96)	14.8 (0.85)	6.5 (1.22)	6.5 (1.42)	4.4 (0.98)	11.3 (0.82)	18.1 (1.47)	12.6 (0.68)	5.1 (1.46)
2000	11.9 (0.64)	12.9 (0.73)	7.8 (1.19)	11.2 (0.86)	12.6 (0.94)	15.4 (0.88)	6.3 (1.27)	3.7 (1.01)	5.4 (1.15)	11.3 (0.82)	16.5 (1.40)	12.6 (0.68)	5.2 (1.42)
2001	11.6 (0.59)	12.6 (0.68)	7.7 (1.10)	9.8 (0.75)	13.7 (0.91)	15.0 (0.82)	4.3 (0.96)	6.1 (1.26)	5.7 (1.15)	10.8 (0.74)	16.4 (1.31)	12.2 (0.63)	5.5 (1.43)
2002	11.1 (0.57)	12.1 (0.66)	7.2 (1.04)	9.7 (0.74)	12.7 (0.87)	15.0 (0.82)	4.5 (1.00)	3.6 (0.89)	6.0 (1.12)	10.0 (0.72)	16.1 (1.26)	11.9 (0.62)	4.1 (1.13)
2003	9.6 (0.52)	10.0 (0.59)	7.8 (1.11)	9.0 (0.70)	10.2 (0.78)	12.4 (0.75)	4.5 (0.96)	5.5 (1.06)	4.8 (1.00)	9.1 (0.67)	13.1 (1.14)	10.2 (0.57)	3.7 (1.07)
2004	10.4 (0.55)	10.9 (0.62)	8.4 (1.18)	9.9 (0.74)	11.0 (0.82)	14.0 (0.80)	4.9 (1.03)	4.4 (0.96)	3.5 (0.87)	8.5 (0.66)	18.1 (1.33)	11.0 (0.59)	5.2 (1.33)
2005	10.1 (0.53)	10.7 (0.60)	7.2 (1.08)	8.9 (0.69)	11.4 (0.81)	13.4 (0.77)	3.7 (0.89)	5.0 (0.99)	3.7 (0.85)	9.9 (0.69)	13.9 (1.16)	10.6 (0.56)	4.6 (1.26)
2006	9.9 (0.53)	10.7 (0.61)	6.4 (0.97)	8.8 (0.69)	11.0 (0.80)	12.8 (0.76)	5.2 (1.03)	4.2 (0.91)	3.7 (0.85)	9.2 (0.67)	14.7 (1.20)	10.5 (0.56)	3.0 ! (1.06)
2007	10.6 (0.54)	11.4 (0.63)	7.0 (1.02)	9.5 (0.72)	11.7 (0.82)	14.2 (0.80)	3.0 (0.80)	6.0 (1.06)	6.1 (1.10)	9.6 (0.68)	15.3 (1.25)	11.1 (0.58)	5.7 (1.36)
2008	9.2 (0.51)	9.9 (0.59)	6.1 (0.96)	8.1 (0.68)	10.3 (0.77)	12.4 (0.77)	3.2 (0.82)	4.1 (0.85)	3.1 (0.78)	9.1 (0.66)	13.0 (1.18)	9.6 (0.54)	4.6 (1.28)
2009	7.6 (0.47)	8.0 (0.54)	6.2 (0.94)	6.8 (0.62)	8.4 (0.71)	10.1 (0.71)	3.6 (0.86)	4.7 (0.91)	3.6 (0.83)	6.9 (0.58)	11.8 (1.15)	7.8 (0.50)	5.2 (1.38)
2010[3]	7.3 (0.42)	7.5 (0.49)	6.8 (0.94)	6.3 (0.50)	8.4 (0.69)	9.5 (0.65)	4.1 (0.82)	4.5 (0.79)	3.0 (0.63)	7.1 (0.54)	10.9 (1.01)	7.7 (0.45)	3.4 ! (1.21)
2011[3]	7.3 (0.40)	8.1 (0.50)	4.4 (0.71)	5.8 (0.51)	9.0 (0.66)	11.0 (0.66)	2.2 (0.60)	2.7 (0.54)	3.7 (0.81)	7.0 (0.55)	10.2 (0.94)	7.7 (0.44)	2.8 ! (0.98)
2012[3]	8.2 (0.46)	8.5 (0.53)	7.3 (0.95)	7.1 (0.57)	9.4 (0.73)	12.2 (0.73)	3.7 (0.92)	2.4 (0.58)	4.2 (0.89)	7.2 (0.53)	13.3 (1.27)	8.8 (0.50)	2.4 ! (0.75)
2013[3]	7.9 (0.50)	8.2 (0.54)	6.8 (0.99)	6.9 (0.61)	8.9 (0.77)	12.2 (0.81)	2.6 (0.71)	3.4 (0.62)	2.9 (0.78)	7.0 (0.54)	13.1 (1.38)	8.1 (0.50)	5.5 ! (1.75)
2014[3]	7.8 (0.43)	8.4 (0.49)	5.7 (0.85)	6.5 (0.54)	9.1 (0.67)	10.7 (0.67)	3.5 (0.91)	3.5 (0.65)	3.8 (0.90)	7.6 (0.57)	10.9 (1.04)	8.2 (0.46)	3.7 ! (1.14)
						Percent working 15 or more hours per week[4]							
1970	17.5 (0.71)	15.6 (0.73)	30.8 (2.41)	22.1 (1.08)	12.6 (0.90)	— (†)	— (†)	— (†)	10.6 (1.87)	18.4 (0.93)	18.1 (1.32)	— (†)	— (†)
1975	19.2 (0.71)	18.2 (0.75)	25.7 (2.20)	21.7 (1.03)	16.4 (0.97)	21.8 (0.85)	8.3 (1.30)	14.7 (3.08)	11.3 (1.81)	19.0 (0.93)	22.1 (1.34)	— (†)	— (†)
1980	20.5 (0.73)	19.0 (0.77)	29.4 (2.12)	22.1 (1.05)	18.9 (1.02)	23.5 (0.89)	10.1 (1.39)	14.3 (2.99)	11.4 (1.69)	21.0 (0.98)	23.1 (1.36)	— (†)	— (†)
1985	18.4 (0.77)	17.2 (0.81)	25.5 (2.24)	19.5 (1.09)	17.3 (1.09)	21.7 (0.97)	8.4 (1.44)	13.7 (2.37)	10.0 (1.57)	18.4 (1.03)	22.6 (1.54)	— (†)	— (†)
1990	19.7 (0.83)	17.5 (0.88)	29.1 (2.19)	21.0 (1.19)	18.3 (1.16)	22.1 (1.06)	10.6 (1.67)	21.5 (2.66)	15.0 (1.88)	20.8 (1.11)	20.2 (1.64)	— (†)	— (†)
1995	20.5 (0.79)	18.4 (0.84)	29.7 (2.07)	20.8 (1.09)	20.2 (1.14)	24.5 (1.03)	10.9 (1.55)	15.1 (2.07)	12.7 (1.60)	21.9 (1.07)	22.5 (1.59)	21.1 (0.83)	14.9 (2.35)

See notes at end of table.

Table 503.10. Percentage of high school students age 16 and over who were employed, by age group, sex, race/ethnicity, family income, nativity, and hours worked per week: Selected years, 1970 through 2014—Continued

[Standard errors appear in parentheses]

Year	Total		Age group: 16 and 17 years old		Age group: 18 years old and over		Sex: Male		Sex: Female		Race/ethnicity: White		Race/ethnicity: Black		Race/ethnicity: Hispanic		Family income[1]: Low income		Family income[1]: Middle income		Family income[1]: High income		Nativity: U.S.-born		Nativity: Foreign-born	
1	2		3		4		5		6		7		8		9		10		11		12		13		14	
2000	21.1	(0.80)	19.2	(0.86)	28.8	(2.01)	21.1	(1.11)	21.0	(1.16)	24.6	(1.05)	13.8	(1.80)	16.3	(1.98)	15.6	(1.85)	21.5	(1.06)	23.1	(1.59)	21.3	(0.84)	19.0	(2.50)
2001	19.4	(0.73)	17.1	(0.77)	28.3	(1.85)	19.6	(1.01)	19.1	(1.05)	22.2	(0.95)	13.4	(1.62)	17.0	(1.97)	14.6	(1.76)	20.9	(0.97)	18.4	(1.37)	19.6	(0.76)	16.9	(2.35)
2002	18.5	(0.71)	16.1	(0.75)	27.9	(1.80)	17.5	(0.95)	19.7	(1.04)	21.4	(0.94)	11.9	(1.57)	16.8	(1.78)	12.3	(1.55)	20.7	(0.97)	17.4	(1.30)	18.7	(0.75)	16.5	(2.12)
2003	16.4	(0.66)	14.3	(0.69)	25.9	(1.82)	16.8	(0.92)	16.0	(0.94)	19.5	(0.90)	10.4	(1.42)	13.1	(1.57)	9.1	(1.35)	17.6	(0.89)	17.7	(1.29)	16.7	(0.70)	13.6	(1.95)
2004	16.0	(0.66)	13.8	(0.68)	26.2	(1.88)	15.5	(0.90)	16.6	(0.97)	17.8	(0.88)	10.2	(1.45)	16.6	(1.75)	8.1	(1.30)	18.3	(0.91)	15.2	(1.24)	16.1	(0.69)	15.2	(2.15)
2005	15.2	(0.63)	13.4	(0.66)	23.5	(1.77)	15.5	(0.88)	14.8	(0.90)	17.0	(0.84)	9.6	(1.40)	13.6	(1.55)	10.8	(1.40)	15.9	(0.85)	16.1	(1.23)	15.1	(0.66)	16.5	(2.24)
2006	17.0	(0.66)	14.4	(0.69)	27.0	(1.75)	16.8	(0.91)	17.1	(0.96)	19.5	(0.90)	14.5	(1.63)	13.3	(1.54)	13.8	(1.55)	17.7	(0.89)	17.3	(1.27)	16.6	(0.68)	20.8	(2.51)
2007	15.0	(0.63)	12.8	(0.66)	24.2	(1.72)	14.8	(0.87)	15.2	(0.92)	16.2	(0.85)	11.4	(1.49)	14.9	(1.59)	10.9	(1.44)	15.6	(0.83)	15.8	(1.27)	14.3	(0.65)	22.2	(2.43)
2008	12.8	(0.59)	10.3	(0.60)	22.7	(1.68)	11.4	(0.79)	14.1	(0.88)	14.3	(0.82)	11.9	(1.51)	10.6	(1.32)	9.9	(1.34)	12.8	(0.77)	14.4	(1.23)	12.7	(0.62)	13.0	(2.06)
2009	8.7	(0.50)	6.4	(0.49)	17.3	(1.47)	8.4	(0.69)	9.1	(0.73)	10.4	(0.71)	6.5	(1.15)	7.2	(1.11)	5.9	(1.06)	8.9	(0.66)	9.9	(1.07)	8.4	(0.52)	11.7	(1.99)
2010[3]	8.3	(0.45)	6.9	(0.47)	13.4	(1.24)	7.2	(0.62)	9.4	(0.70)	10.5	(0.67)	5.3	(1.01)	5.6	(0.84)	5.3	(0.88)	9.0	(0.58)	8.7	(1.16)	8.1	(0.46)	9.6	(1.83)
2011[3]	9.0	(0.52)	7.7	(0.56)	13.6	(1.10)	8.4	(0.63)	9.8	(0.78)	10.5	(0.77)	7.4	(1.30)	8.4	(1.06)	6.3	(1.10)	10.0	(0.69)	8.5	(0.94)	9.0	(0.55)	9.6	(1.84)
2012[3]	8.9	(0.55)	6.7	(0.51)	16.5	(1.62)	8.4	(0.62)	9.5	(0.84)	10.0	(0.69)	8.2	(1.97)	8.4	(1.04)	8.3	(1.22)	8.7	(0.68)	9.9	(1.30)	8.9	(0.59)	9.6	(1.76)
2013[3]	9.7	(0.56)	7.3	(0.53)	17.4	(1.57)	10.3	(0.85)	9.1	(0.67)	10.6	(0.81)	9.1	(1.37)	10.6	(1.10)	6.7	(1.19)	9.7	(0.82)	11.7	(1.12)	9.4	(0.60)	13.4	(2.15)
2014[3]	10.7	(0.55)	8.2	(0.48)	19.3	(1.49)	10.8	(0.72)	10.6	(0.81)	11.6	(0.75)	9.4	(1.52)	11.0	(1.30)	8.6	(1.34)	11.1	(0.73)	11.1	(1.25)	10.2	(0.56)	15.1	(2.12)

—Not available.
†Not applicable.
!Interpret data with caution. The coefficient of variation (CV) for this estimate is between 30 and 50 percent.
[1]Low income refers to the bottom 20 percent of all family incomes; high income refers to the top 20 percent of all family incomes; and middle income refers to the 60 percent in between.
[2]Percent employed includes those who were employed but not at work during the survey week.
[3]Beginning in 2010, standard errors were computed using replicate weights, which produced more precise values than the generalized variance function methodology used in prior years.
[4]Hours worked per week refers to the number of hours the respondent worked at all jobs during the survey week. The estimates of the percentage of high school students age 16 and over who worked less than 15 hours per week or 15 or more hours per week exclude those who were employed but not at work during the survey week. Therefore, detail may not sum to total percentage employed.
NOTE: Race categories exclude persons of Hispanic ethnicity. Totals include racial/ethnic groups not shown separately.
SOURCE: U.S. Department of Commerce, Census Bureau, Current Population Survey (CPS), October, 1970 through 2014. (This table was prepared November 2015.)

Table 503.20. Percentage of college students 16 to 24 years old who were employed, by attendance status, hours worked per week, and control and level of institution: Selected years, October 1970 through 2014

[Standard errors appear in parentheses]

Control and level of institution and year	Full-time students: Percent employed[1]	Full-time: Hours worked per week[2]: Less than 20 hours	Full-time: 20 to 34 hours	Full-time: 35 or more hours	Part-time students: Percent employed[1]	Part-time: Hours worked per week[2]: Less than 20 hours	Part-time: 20 to 34 hours	Part-time: 35 or more hours
1	2	3	4	5	6	7	8	9
Total, all institutions								
1970	33.8 (0.88)	19.0 (0.73)	10.4 (0.57)	3.7 (0.35)	82.1 (1.81)	5.0 (1.03)	15.9 (1.72)	60.1 (2.31)
1975	35.3 (0.83)	18.0 (0.67)	12.0 (0.56)	4.6 (0.36)	80.8 (1.55)	6.0 (0.94)	19.4 (1.56)	52.6 (1.97)
1980	40.0 (0.84)	21.3 (0.70)	14.0 (0.59)	3.9 (0.33)	84.7 (1.38)	7.9 (1.04)	22.5 (1.60)	52.7 (1.91)
1985	44.2 (0.88)	21.7 (0.73)	17.3 (0.67)	4.3 (0.36)	85.9 (1.41)	5.7 (0.94)	26.9 (1.80)	52.2 (2.03)
1990	45.7 (0.89)	20.6 (0.73)	19.3 (0.71)	4.8 (0.38)	83.7 (1.50)	4.0 (0.80)	26.0 (1.78)	52.7 (2.03)
1991	47.2 (0.88)	20.9 (0.72)	19.8 (0.70)	5.6 (0.41)	85.9 (1.45)	8.2 (1.15)	25.4 (1.82)	51.0 (2.09)
1992	47.2 (0.87)	20.3 (0.70)	20.3 (0.70)	5.5 (0.40)	83.4 (1.50)	7.5 (1.06)	27.2 (1.79)	47.8 (2.01)
1993	46.3 (0.89)	20.8 (0.72)	19.5 (0.71)	5.1 (0.39)	84.6 (1.43)	8.5 (1.10)	31.4 (1.84)	43.7 (1.96)
1994	48.6 (0.87)	20.1 (0.70)	21.7 (0.72)	5.8 (0.41)	86.3 (1.28)	9.8 (1.10)	31.1 (1.72)	43.8 (1.84)
1995	47.2 (0.87)	19.1 (0.69)	20.3 (0.70)	6.5 (0.43)	82.9 (1.45)	8.6 (1.08)	30.4 (1.77)	42.3 (1.90)
1996	49.2 (0.88)	18.2 (0.68)	22.3 (0.74)	7.0 (0.45)	84.8 (1.47)	8.3 (1.13)	27.5 (1.83)	48.0 (2.05)
1997	47.8 (0.86)	18.3 (0.67)	21.4 (0.71)	7.4 (0.45)	84.4 (1.46)	9.4 (1.17)	26.2 (1.77)	47.7 (2.01)
1998	50.2 (0.86)	20.2 (0.69)	20.6 (0.70)	8.0 (0.47)	84.1 (1.45)	7.0 (1.01)	26.8 (1.76)	49.3 (1.98)
1999	50.4 (0.86)	19.0 (0.68)	22.3 (0.72)	7.8 (0.46)	82.3 (1.55)	6.2 (0.98)	28.8 (1.85)	45.9 (2.03)
2000	52.0 (0.86)	20.1 (0.69)	21.7 (0.71)	8.9 (0.49)	84.9 (1.38)	8.6 (1.08)	27.8 (1.73)	47.5 (1.93)
2001	47.1 (0.80)	17.4 (0.61)	20.6 (0.65)	7.9 (0.43)	84.4 (1.29)	8.0 (0.97)	25.8 (1.56)	48.9 (1.78)
2002	47.8 (0.78)	17.3 (0.59)	20.9 (0.64)	8.5 (0.44)	78.9 (1.51)	8.7 (1.04)	25.3 (1.61)	43.4 (1.84)
2003	47.7 (0.78)	17.1 (0.59)	20.7 (0.63)	8.8 (0.44)	79.0 (1.44)	7.8 (0.95)	27.2 (1.58)	42.8 (1.75)
2004	49.0 (0.76)	17.7 (0.58)	21.6 (0.62)	8.6 (0.43)	81.5 (1.44)	8.5 (1.04)	27.4 (1.66)	44.1 (1.84)
2005	49.1 (0.75)	17.8 (0.58)	21.1 (0.61)	9.0 (0.43)	85.0 (1.30)	10.2 (1.10)	27.1 (1.62)	47.1 (1.82)
2006	46.5 (0.76)	15.1 (0.55)	22.0 (0.63)	8.1 (0.42)	81.0 (1.41)	7.3 (0.94)	27.6 (1.61)	45.5 (1.80)
2007	45.5 (0.74)	15.4 (0.54)	20.7 (0.60)	8.7 (0.42)	81.2 (1.39)	6.8 (0.90)	27.2 (1.59)	45.9 (1.78)
2008	45.3 (0.72)	15.6 (0.53)	20.1 (0.58)	8.7 (0.41)	79.4 (1.51)	9.3 (1.09)	24.7 (1.61)	44.4 (1.86)
2009	40.6 (0.69)	15.6 (0.51)	17.6 (0.54)	6.2 (0.34)	76.2 (1.57)	10.1 (1.11)	27.5 (1.65)	36.9 (1.78)
2010[3]	39.8 (1.01)	14.9 (0.57)	17.2 (0.77)	6.6 (0.46)	73.4 (2.03)	10.7 (1.24)	28.3 (1.92)	32.8 (2.19)
2011[3]	41.3 (0.94)	15.8 (0.67)	17.4 (0.66)	7.0 (0.44)	75.5 (1.93)	9.7 (1.21)	28.4 (1.99)	35.5 (2.16)
2012[3]	41.0 (0.83)	15.1 (0.72)	17.8 (0.71)	7.2 (0.44)	71.7 (2.07)	9.0 (1.27)	29.5 (2.09)	32.1 (2.07)
2012[3]	39.5 (1.00)	14.0 (0.67)	18.5 (0.77)	6.6 (0.50)	75.7 (2.06)	10.5 (1.44)	28.7 (1.76)	35.4 (2.11)
2014[3]	41.3 (0.97)	15.6 (0.69)	17.9 (0.80)	6.6 (0.48)	80.3 (1.81)	13.8 (1.58)	26.9 (2.33)	38.5 (2.36)
Public 4-year institutions								
1990	43.0 (1.18)	19.8 (0.95)	18.6 (0.93)	3.7 (0.45)	87.4 (2.25)	4.2 ! (1.37)	27.9 (3.05)	54.7 (3.39)
1995	48.8 (1.16)	19.4 (0.92)	22.6 (0.97)	5.6 (0.53)	86.7 (2.08)	9.6 (1.80)	30.8 (2.83)	45.0 (3.05)
2000	50.5 (1.15)	19.1 (0.90)	21.5 (0.94)	9.0 (0.66)	87.3 (1.91)	8.5 (1.60)	26.4 (2.53)	50.9 (2.87)
2005	49.6 (0.99)	17.8 (0.76)	22.7 (0.83)	8.0 (0.54)	86.3 (1.90)	9.0 (1.58)	26.8 (2.45)	49.7 (2.76)
2008	44.1 (0.96)	15.1 (0.70)	19.2 (0.76)	8.8 (0.55)	83.9 (2.25)	9.3 (1.78)	24.7 (2.64)	49.5 (3.06)
2009	40.6 (0.91)	14.7 (0.66)	18.7 (0.73)	5.8 (0.44)	78.7 (2.45)	11.1 (1.88)	25.7 (2.61)	39.8 (2.92)
2010[3]	40.8 (1.27)	15.2 (0.88)	18.0 (0.93)	6.6 (0.64)	70.4 (3.58)	10.5 (2.04)	26.9 (2.82)	32.1 (3.59)
2011[3]	41.0 (1.20)	15.0 (0.91)	17.6 (0.85)	7.4 (0.63)	77.5 (3.27)	7.8 (1.65)	28.4 (3.18)	39.7 (3.29)
2012[3]	41.0 (1.13)	14.9 (0.95)	18.6 (0.99)	6.7 (0.57)	77.6 (3.20)	9.9 (2.41)	28.0 (3.44)	38.8 (3.36)
2013[3]	40.1 (1.31)	13.9 (0.88)	19.2 (0.98)	6.6 (0.63)	78.8 (2.88)	9.8 (1.94)	26.6 (2.80)	41.1 (3.84)
2014[3]	41.1 (1.31)	14.6 (0.91)	18.4 (0.99)	6.9 (0.69)	83.4 (2.86)	12.2 (2.61)	28.4 (3.69)	42.3 (3.81)
Private 4-year institutions								
1990	38.1 (1.89)	24.0 (1.66)	9.9 (1.17)	3.5 (0.72)	89.9 (4.27)	‡ (†)	31.9 (6.62)	53.1 (7.09)
1995	38.6 (1.78)	21.6 (1.51)	10.7 (1.13)	4.6 (0.77)	80.1 (4.85)	14.9 (4.32)	26.8 (5.38)	36.5 (5.84)
2000	45.8 (1.88)	23.6 (1.60)	14.9 (1.34)	5.4 (0.85)	78.0 (5.36)	‡ (†)	18.5 (5.02)	52.6 (6.46)
2005	42.3 (1.64)	20.1 (1.33)	13.8 (1.15)	7.0 (0.85)	88.5 (3.32)	10.6 ! (3.20)	34.5 (4.94)	43.2 (5.15)
2008	38.0 (1.68)	18.5 (1.35)	12.4 (1.14)	5.6 (0.80)	84.4 (4.44)	‡ (†)	21.4 (5.01)	55.3 (6.08)
2009	35.2 (1.64)	18.6 (1.33)	10.7 (1.06)	5.1 (0.76)	93.9 (2.89)	7.5 ! (3.17)	22.1 (5.00)	62.4 (5.84)
2010[3]	35.6 (2.37)	15.7 (1.63)	12.2 (1.52)	6.0 (1.08)	78.6 (7.00)	‡ (†)	23.4 ! (7.49)	45.6 (9.01)
2011[3]	36.3 (2.07)	20.0 (1.61)	10.1 (1.34)	4.5 (0.82)	79.4 (6.01)	‡ (†)	34.2 (7.03)	38.2 (7.67)
2012[3]	40.4 (2.39)	19.9 (1.80)	12.2 (1.40)	6.7 (1.13)	84.4 (5.35)	9.5 ! (4.53)	33.9 (6.58)	36.9 (7.38)
2013[3]	34.0 (2.27)	14.9 (1.55)	12.8 (1.33)	5.6 (1.13)	86.9 (4.71)	21.9 (6.40)	29.8 (7.01)	35.2 (6.56)
2014[3]	37.8 (2.29)	18.7 (1.72)	12.0 (1.62)	5.3 (1.00)	77.1 (6.82)	12.9 ! (4.92)	13.5 ! (5.59)	50.8 (8.76)
Public 2-year institutions								
1990	61.2 (1.94)	19.1 (1.57)	31.2 (1.85)	9.2 (1.15)	81.5 (2.17)	4.1 (1.12)	24.9 (2.42)	51.1 (2.80)
1995	52.9 (1.97)	15.6 (1.43)	25.3 (1.72)	10.9 (1.23)	81.1 (2.21)	6.1 (1.35)	32.5 (2.64)	40.5 (2.77)
2000	63.9 (1.79)	20.6 (1.51)	29.9 (1.71)	11.9 (1.21)	85.5 (2.09)	9.9 (1.77)	30.0 (2.72)	44.9 (2.95)
2005	54.2 (1.69)	15.6 (1.23)	24.2 (1.46)	13.4 (1.16)	82.0 (2.20)	10.8 (1.77)	25.8 (2.50)	44.8 (2.84)
2008	52.9 (1.43)	14.6 (1.01)	26.9 (1.27)	10.7 (0.89)	74.8 (2.29)	9.7 (1.56)	25.9 (2.31)	37.8 (2.56)
2009	45.4 (1.45)	16.0 (1.07)	20.5 (1.18)	7.8 (0.78)	71.8 (2.36)	10.3 (1.60)	30.6 (2.42)	29.4 (2.39)
2010[3]	40.6 (1.90)	14.0 (1.20)	19.1 (1.50)	6.8 (0.78)	74.7 (2.51)	11.6 (1.93)	30.1 (2.86)	31.0 (3.08)
2011[3]	45.6 (2.00)	14.7 (1.45)	22.1 (1.47)	8.1 (1.01)	73.6 (2.58)	11.3 (1.73)	27.5 (3.12)	32.4 (3.21)
2012[3]	41.2 (1.76)	12.0 (1.17)	19.8 (1.44)	8.4 (0.95)	66.1 (2.98)	8.3 (1.60)	30.0 (2.70)	26.9 (2.79)
2013[3]	41.8 (1.89)	13.8 (1.37)	20.5 (1.55)	7.1 (1.05)	71.1 (3.02)	8.8 (1.92)	29.8 (2.85)	31.2 (3.09)
2014[3]	45.0 (2.28)	15.9 (1.57)	21.3 (1.82)	6.9 (0.91)	77.5 (2.64)	15.2 (2.35)	28.3 (3.35)	32.4 (3.58)

†Not applicable.
!Interpret data with caution. The coefficient of variation (CV) for this estimate is between 30 and 50 percent.
‡Reporting standards not met. Either there are too few cases for a reliable estimate or the coefficient of variation (CV) is 50 percent or greater.
[1]Includes those who were employed but not at work during the survey week.
[2]Excludes those who were employed but not at work during the survey week; therefore, detail may not sum to total percentage employed. "Hours worked per week" refers to the number of hours worked at all jobs during the survey week.
[3]Beginning in 2010, standard errors were computed using replicate weights, which produced more precise values than the generalized variance function methodology used in prior years.
NOTE: Students were classified as full time if they were taking at least 12 hours of classes (or at least 9 hours of graduate classes) during an average school week and as part time if they were taking fewer hours.
SOURCE: U.S. Department of Commerce, Census Bureau, Current Population Survey (CPS), October, selected years, 1970 through 2014. (This table was prepared September 2015.)

Table 503.30. Percentage of college students 16 to 24 years old who were employed, by attendance status, hours worked per week, and selected characteristics: October 2012 through 2014

[Standard errors appear in parentheses]

Year and selected characteristic	Full-time students: Percent employed[1]		Full-time: Hours worked per week[2]: Less than 20 hours		20 to 34 hours		35 or more hours		Part-time students: Percent employed[1]		Part-time: Hours worked per week[2]: Less than 20 hours		20 to 34 hours		35 or more hours	
1	2		3		4		5		6		7		8		9	
2012																
Total	**41.0**	**(0.83)**	**15.1**	**(0.72)**	**17.8**	**(0.71)**	**7.2**	**(0.44)**	**71.7**	**(2.07)**	**9.0**	**(1.27)**	**29.5**	**(2.09)**	**32.1**	**(2.07)**
Sex																
Male	39.1	(1.27)	13.0	(0.93)	17.0	(1.08)	7.9	(0.69)	74.0	(2.68)	7.9	(2.04)	30.9	(3.08)	35.1	(3.26)
Female	42.7	(1.19)	17.0	(0.98)	18.4	(0.98)	6.5	(0.57)	69.9	(2.61)	9.9	(1.72)	28.3	(2.60)	29.5	(2.46)
2013																
Total	**39.5**	**(1.00)**	**14.0**	**(0.67)**	**18.5**	**(0.77)**	**6.6**	**(0.50)**	**75.7**	**(2.06)**	**10.5**	**(1.44)**	**28.7**	**(1.76)**	**35.4**	**(2.11)**
Sex																
Male	35.9	(1.36)	12.2	(0.94)	16.6	(1.05)	6.6	(0.78)	70.9	(3.16)	7.4	(1.95)	28.8	(2.84)	33.9	(2.98)
Female	42.7	(1.31)	15.6	(0.99)	20.2	(0.97)	6.6	(0.67)	79.4	(2.50)	12.9	(1.93)	28.6	(2.49)	36.5	(2.93)
Level and control of institution																
2-year	42.0	(1.84)	13.6	(1.32)	20.7	(1.52)	7.3	(1.01)	71.3	(2.90)	9.0	(1.92)	30.0	(2.75)	31.0	(2.99)
Public	41.8	(1.89)	13.8	(1.37)	20.5	(1.55)	7.1	(1.05)	71.1	(3.02)	8.8	(1.92)	29.8	(2.85)	31.2	(3.09)
Private	45.1	(8.22)	10.1 !	(4.13)	24.5	(6.99)	10.5 !	(5.01)	‡	(†)	‡	(†)	‡	(†)	‡	(†)
4-year	38.7	(1.15)	14.1	(0.76)	17.8	(0.87)	6.3	(0.53)	80.4	(2.59)	12.2	(2.03)	27.2	(2.45)	39.9	(3.29)
Public	40.1	(1.31)	13.9	(0.88)	19.2	(0.98)	6.6	(0.63)	78.8	(2.88)	9.8	(1.94)	26.6	(2.80)	41.1	(3.84)
Private	34.0	(2.27)	14.9	(1.55)	12.8	(1.33)	5.6	(1.13)	86.9	(4.71)	21.9	(6.40)	29.8	(7.01)	35.2	(6.56)
2014																
Total	**41.3**	**(0.97)**	**15.6**	**(0.69)**	**17.9**	**(0.80)**	**6.6**	**(0.48)**	**80.3**	**(1.81)**	**13.8**	**(1.58)**	**26.9**	**(2.33)**	**38.5**	**(2.36)**
Sex																
Male	37.3	(1.40)	12.9	(0.98)	17.2	(1.13)	6.1	(0.63)	82.8	(2.83)	13.6	(2.35)	25.0	(3.20)	42.5	(3.15)
Female	44.9	(1.36)	18.0	(0.99)	18.6	(1.02)	7.1	(0.63)	78.4	(2.48)	14.0	(2.10)	28.4	(3.23)	35.5	(3.12)
Race/ethnicity																
White	46.1	(1.26)	18.2	(0.93)	19.4	(1.02)	7.2	(0.62)	85.9	(2.40)	15.3	(2.24)	28.9	(3.07)	40.6	(3.18)
Black	32.2	(2.64)	8.4	(1.60)	14.9	(2.00)	6.7	(1.45)	69.2	(6.11)	11.5 !	(5.03)	26.1	(6.89)	31.6	(7.22)
Hispanic	41.5	(2.36)	14.5	(1.71)	19.4	(1.87)	6.9	(1.17)	76.6	(3.67)	9.1	(2.55)	27.0	(4.05)	38.9	(4.48)
Asian	23.6	(2.71)	11.4	(2.00)	9.2	(2.06)	3.0 !	(1.09)	80.6	(6.88)	25.5 !	(7.87)	20.7 !	(7.52)	34.4	(8.68)
Pacific Islander	‡	(†)	‡	(†)	‡	(†)	‡	(†)	‡	(†)	‡	(†)	‡	(†)	‡	(†)
American Indian/Alaska Native	15.0 !	(6.42)	‡	(†)	‡	(†)	‡	(†)	‡	(†)	‡	(†)	‡	(†)	‡	(†)
Two or more races	40.1	(5.79)	14.1 !	(4.45)	21.5	(5.10)	‡	(†)	‡	(†)	‡	(†)	‡	(†)	‡	(†)
Level and control of institution																
2-year	44.5	(2.15)	15.7	(1.42)	21.0	(1.72)	7.0	(0.89)	78.5	(2.57)	15.2	(2.33)	27.8	(3.24)	33.9	(3.49)
Public	45.0	(2.28)	15.9	(1.57)	21.3	(1.82)	6.9	(0.91)	77.5	(2.64)	15.2	(2.35)	28.3	(3.35)	32.4	(3.58)
Private	39.4	(6.92)	13.6 !	(5.65)	17.5 !	(5.75)	8.3 !	(3.25)	‡	(†)	‡	(†)	‡	(†)	‡	(†)
4-year	40.3	(1.15)	15.5	(0.81)	17.0	(0.86)	6.5	(0.59)	82.4	(2.57)	12.3	(2.23)	25.9	(3.25)	43.7	(3.32)
Public	41.1	(1.31)	14.6	(0.91)	18.4	(0.99)	6.9	(0.69)	83.4	(2.86)	12.2	(2.61)	28.4	(3.69)	42.3	(3.81)
Private	37.8	(2.29)	18.7	(1.72)	12.0	(1.62)	5.3	(1.00)	77.1	(6.82)	12.9 !	(4.92)	13.5 !	(5.59)	50.8	(8.76)
Student enrollment level																
Undergraduate	40.9	(1.00)	15.8	(0.74)	17.9	(0.85)	6.0	(0.47)	80.1	(2.00)	14.4	(1.72)	29.0	(2.47)	35.6	(2.45)
Sex																
Male	36.8	(1.42)	13.2	(1.04)	17.2	(1.20)	5.4	(0.62)	83.3	(2.96)	14.8	(2.58)	26.1	(3.37)	40.4	(3.32)
Female	44.6	(1.41)	18.1	(1.05)	18.5	(1.10)	6.5	(0.64)	77.6	(2.78)	14.0	(2.22)	31.3	(3.60)	31.8	(3.14)
Race/ethnicity																
White	45.4	(1.30)	18.2	(0.97)	19.4	(1.08)	6.4	(0.61)	84.7	(2.71)	15.7	(2.55)	31.7	(3.38)	35.9	(3.31)
Black	31.7	(2.78)	9.1	(1.76)	14.3	(2.05)	6.0	(1.46)	71.6	(6.58)	12.4 !	(5.45)	28.2	(7.41)	31.0	(7.71)
Hispanic	40.8	(2.40)	14.8	(1.74)	19.0	(1.87)	6.3	(1.15)	76.2	(3.80)	9.0	(2.66)	28.2	(4.26)	37.3	(4.64)
Asian	23.6	(2.83)	12.0	(2.23)	9.0	(2.28)	2.6 !	(1.08)	87.3	(5.94)	31.6	(9.04)	22.2 !	(7.86)	33.5	(9.36)
Pacific Islander	‡	(†)	‡	(†)	‡	(†)	‡	(†)	‡	(†)	‡	(†)	‡	(†)	‡	(†)
American Indian/Alaska Native	18.0 !	(7.69)	‡	(†)	‡	(†)	‡	(†)	‡	(†)	‡	(†)	‡	(†)	‡	(†)
Two or more races	41.3	(6.03)	14.3 !	(4.70)	22.4	(5.23)	‡	(†)	‡	(†)	‡	(†)	‡	(†)	‡	(†)
Level and control of institution																
2-year	43.6	(2.20)	15.4	(1.45)	20.8	(1.76)	6.7	(0.87)	79.8	(2.57)	16.2	(2.50)	29.8	(3.38)	32.1	(3.62)
Public	44.0	(2.33)	15.5	(1.59)	21.0	(1.85)	6.7	(0.89)	78.9	(2.65)	16.3	(2.51)	30.3	(3.50)	30.7	(3.68)
Private	38.7	(7.16)	14.1 !	(5.95)	17.9 !	(5.90)	6.7 !	(2.83)	‡	(†)	‡	(†)	‡	(†)	‡	(†)
4-year	40.0	(1.20)	15.9	(0.88)	17.0	(0.94)	5.8	(0.56)	80.6	(3.01)	12.0	(2.58)	27.9	(3.66)	40.2	(3.75)
Public	40.5	(1.39)	14.9	(0.98)	18.2	(1.07)	6.2	(0.67)	81.2	(3.29)	13.0	(2.97)	29.4	(4.09)	38.2	(4.12)
Private	38.0	(2.32)	19.7	(1.96)	12.3	(1.78)	4.1	(0.87)	76.3	(8.81)	‡	(†)	18.3 !	(7.54)	52.2	(10.87)
Graduate	46.1	(3.29)	13.2	(2.09)	18.3	(2.37)	14.2	(2.56)	81.6	(5.25)	9.9 !	(4.15)	12.2 !	(4.54)	59.6	(5.76)

†Not applicable.

!Interpret data with caution. The coefficient of variation (CV) for this estimate is between 30 and 50 percent.

‡Reporting standards not met. Either there are too few cases for a reliable estimate or the coefficient of variation (CV) is 50 percent or greater.

[1]Includes those who were employed but not at work during the survey week.

[2]Excludes those who were employed but not at work during the survey week; therefore, detail may not sum to total percentage employed. "Hours worked per week" refers to the number of hours worked at all jobs during the survey week.

NOTE: Students were classified as full time if they were taking at least 12 hours of classes (or at least 9 hours of graduate classes) during an average school week and as part time if they were taking fewer hours. Race categories exclude persons of Hispanic ethnicity.

SOURCE: U.S. Department of Commerce, Census Bureau, Current Population Survey (CPS), October, 2011 through 2012 through 2014. (This table was prepared September 2015.)

Table 326.10. Graduation rate from first institution attended for first-time, full-time bachelor's degree-seeking students at 4-year postsecondary institutions, by race/ethnicity, time to completion, sex, control of institution, and acceptance rate: Selected cohort entry years, 1996 through 2008

Time to completion, sex, control of institution, cohort entry year, and acceptance rate	Total	White	Black	Hispanic	Asian/Pacific Islander			American Indian/ Alaska Native	Two or more races	Nonresident alien
					Total	Asian	Pacific Islander			
1	2	3	4	5	6	7	8	9	10	11
Graduating within 4 years after start, males and females										
All 4-year institutions										
1996 starting cohort	33.7	36.3	19.5	22.8	37.5	—	—	18.8	—	41.7
2000 starting cohort	36.1	38.9	21.3	25.9	41.0	—	—	21.0	—	41.9
2002 starting cohort	36.4	39.3	20.4	26.4	42.8	—	—	20.5	—	38.7
2003 starting cohort	37.0	40.2	20.2	26.7	43.9	—	—	20.6	—	39.4
2004 starting cohort	38.0	41.3	20.5	27.9	45.0	—	—	21.8	—	43.7
2005 starting cohort	38.3	41.8	20.2	28.2	45.1	45.5	22.2	21.8	44.1	44.0
2006 starting cohort	39.1	42.7	20.6	29.3	46.0	46.4	24.2	21.9	46.6	44.1
2007 starting cohort	39.4	43.3	20.8	29.8	46.2	46.7	25.8	23.0	49.1	44.6
2008 starting cohort	39.8	43.7	21.4	30.4	47.1	47.7	26.7	23.0	46.5	46.4
Public institutions										
1996 starting cohort	26.0	28.3	15.0	15.8	28.5	—	—	14.5	—	30.9
2000 starting cohort	29.0	31.4	17.9	18.9	33.7	—	—	16.4	—	32.7
2002 starting cohort	29.9	32.3	16.9	20.1	35.8	—	—	16.0	—	33.4
2003 starting cohort	30.7	33.5	16.5	20.7	37.5	—	—	17.0	—	33.8
2004 starting cohort	31.4	34.2	16.4	21.5	38.0	—	—	17.2	—	34.4
2005 starting cohort	32.0	35.1	16.8	22.4	38.7	39.1	16.9	17.9	28.7	33.5
2006 starting cohort	32.9	36.1	17.2	23.1	40.0	40.4	18.6	17.9	30.5	33.9
2007 starting cohort	33.5	36.9	17.4	24.0	39.8	40.2	20.9	19.5	35.9	34.4
2008 starting cohort	34.4	37.9	18.6	24.8	41.1	41.6	22.1	19.1	35.2	38.0
Nonprofit institutions										
1996 starting cohort	48.6	51.3	29.3	39.9	57.9	—	—	33.7	—	50.4
2000 starting cohort	50.3	53.5	28.2	42.9	58.8	—	—	36.0	—	50.3
2002 starting cohort	51.0	54.0	29.4	44.1	61.0	—	—	36.6	—	54.8
2003 starting cohort	51.6	54.7	29.8	44.0	61.5	—	—	34.4	—	55.3
2004 starting cohort	52.6	55.5	30.6	46.2	62.8	—	—	39.0	—	57.4
2005 starting cohort	52.2	55.4	29.2	45.1	62.3	62.8	34.9	35.2	59.9	57.4
2006 starting cohort	52.9	56.2	29.7	47.4	62.8	63.5	37.2	38.3	62.1	56.8
2007 starting cohort	52.8	56.4	29.7	46.7	63.6	64.2	40.1	37.0	62.6	56.9
2008 starting cohort	52.7	56.3	29.7	47.2	63.4	63.9	44.8	37.0	59.3	57.1
For-profit institutions										
1996 starting cohort	21.8	26.3	14.8	20.1	24.6	—	—	16.5	—	33.8
2000 starting cohort	25.7	30.3	22.5	27.4	42.7	—	—	28.0	—	36.5
2002 starting cohort	14.2	17.5	10.0	19.1	29.4	—	—	11.2	—	3.4
2003 starting cohort	14.8	18.2	10.4	19.5	25.5	—	—	8.4	—	4.7
2004 starting cohort	20.6	27.3	13.3	20.7	31.4	—	—	9.4	—	10.6
2005 starting cohort	20.0	27.9	11.0	19.6	31.7	33.8	15.4	15.2	24.7	15.4
2006 starting cohort	22.8	32.5	12.7	23.0	30.1	32.4	9.4	13.0	27.6	22.4
2007 starting cohort	22.5	32.7	11.6	22.7	32.2	36.4	8.2	12.6	27.2	24.4
2008 starting cohort	17.5	26.4	9.6	20.9	30.7	34.8	8.7	12.8	30.1	19.7
Graduating within 4 years after start, males										
All 4-year institutions										
1996 starting cohort	28.5	30.6	13.9	19.0	32.2	—	—	15.1	—	38.6
2000 starting cohort	31.1	33.4	15.5	21.8	35.7	—	—	17.1	—	39.3
2002 starting cohort	31.3	33.8	14.7	21.8	37.4	—	—	17.2	—	36.6
2003 starting cohort	32.2	34.8	14.7	22.5	39.0	—	—	17.7	—	37.7
2004 starting cohort	33.0	35.7	15.1	23.3	39.9	—	—	18.9	—	39.7
2005 starting cohort	33.5	36.4	15.0	24.2	39.9	40.2	19.6	18.8	40.2	40.1
2006 starting cohort	34.3	37.2	15.7	24.9	41.2	41.6	21.6	17.6	43.2	39.6
2007 starting cohort	34.5	37.7	15.7	25.4	41.1	41.5	24.0	18.6	44.7	39.3
2008 starting cohort	34.8	38.1	16.2	25.7	42.1	42.5	25.0	18.9	40.7	41.0
Public institutions										
1996 starting cohort	20.8	22.6	9.9	12.5	23.4	—	—	10.9	—	28.6
2000 starting cohort	23.6	25.5	11.7	14.5	27.8	—	—	11.9	—	30.2
2002 starting cohort	24.5	26.6	11.0	15.8	30.4	—	—	12.7	—	30.3
2003 starting cohort	25.7	27.9	10.9	16.4	32.5	—	—	14.1	—	30.8
2004 starting cohort	26.2	28.5	11.2	16.9	32.9	—	—	14.5	—	30.1
2005 starting cohort	27.1	29.6	11.7	18.3	33.5	33.8	14.1	15.0	26.4	29.8
2006 starting cohort	27.9	30.4	12.1	18.8	34.9	35.2	15.4	13.8	29.2	29.7
2007 starting cohort	28.3	31.1	12.1	19.5	34.8	35.0	18.8	14.7	33.8	29.4
2008 starting cohort	29.3	32.1	13.3	20.0	36.1	36.5	18.7	15.3	30.7	33.1
Nonprofit institutions										
1996 starting cohort	43.6	46.2	22.1	35.0	53.5	—	—	28.9	—	47.0
2000 starting cohort	46.0	48.9	22.3	38.2	56.1	—	—	33.2	—	48.0
2002 starting cohort	46.3	49.1	22.9	38.8	57.6	—	—	32.1	—	50.6
2003 starting cohort	47.0	49.8	23.1	39.9	58.6	—	—	30.7	—	51.3
2004 starting cohort	47.8	50.6	23.2	41.2	59.0	—	—	35.4	—	53.2
2005 starting cohort	47.5	50.5	22.6	40.7	58.8	59.3	29.4	30.8	55.7	52.7
2006 starting cohort	48.2	51.2	23.4	42.4	60.2	60.8	34.5	34.2	58.4	52.2
2007 starting cohort	47.8	51.4	23.0	42.3	60.0	60.5	37.3	32.2	57.8	51.4
2008 starting cohort	47.7	51.3	23.0	42.4	59.5	59.9	43.5	31.5	53.9	51.6

See notes at end of table.

Table 326.10. Graduation rate from first institution attended for first-time, full-time bachelor's degree-seeking students at 4-year postsecondary institutions, by race/ethnicity, time to completion, sex, control of institution, and acceptance rate: Selected cohort entry years, 1996 through 2008—Continued

Time to completion, sex, control of institution, cohort entry year, and acceptance rate	Total	White	Black	Hispanic	Asian/Pacific Islander			American Indian/ Alaska Native	Two or more races	Nonresident alien
					Total	Asian	Pacific Islander			
1	2	3	4	5	6	7	8	9	10	11
For-profit institutions										
1996 starting cohort	22.3	25.5	16.1	23.0	27.7	—	—	25.6	—	33.1
2000 starting cohort	30.1	34.3	23.7	30.9	44.5	—	—	28.7	—	36.7
2002 starting cohort	17.0	20.9	11.8	20.1	33.3	—	—	17.6	—	4.0
2003 starting cohort	17.4	20.9	11.8	20.8	28.1	—	—	11.1	—	6.4
2004 starting cohort	23.5	30.5	15.0	21.6	36.6	—	—	12.1	—	10.7
2005 starting cohort	23.6	31.4	12.0	22.2	32.2	33.2	24.0	20.8	25.2	16.7
2006 starting cohort	27.8	37.2	16.6	26.0	33.7	35.2	17.2	14.7	30.1	23.7
2007 starting cohort	28.4	39.3	15.3	25.7	35.8	38.3	14.1	19.0	25.8	26.9
2008 starting cohort	20.7	30.5	11.1	22.0	34.0	35.9	16.2	12.4	27.8	14.9
Graduating within 4 years after start, females										
All 4-year institutions										
1996 starting cohort	38.0	41.1	23.2	25.8	42.2	—	—	21.7	—	45.8
2000 starting cohort	40.2	43.5	25.2	29.0	45.7	—	—	24.0	—	45.3
2002 starting cohort	40.5	43.9	24.3	29.9	47.4	—	—	23.0	—	41.0
2003 starting cohort	41.0	44.8	23.9	29.8	48.1	—	—	22.8	—	41.1
2004 starting cohort	42.2	45.9	24.2	31.4	49.4	—	—	24.0	—	48.1
2005 starting cohort	42.2	46.4	23.7	31.3	49.6	50.1	24.2	24.1	47.3	48.4
2006 starting cohort	43.1	47.4	23.9	32.5	50.2	50.8	26.2	25.2	49.1	49.3
2007 starting cohort	43.5	48.0	24.3	33.1	50.7	51.3	27.0	26.3	52.3	50.8
2008 starting cohort	43.9	48.6	24.9	33.9	51.6	52.4	27.8	26.0	50.6	52.5
Public institutions										
1996 starting cohort	30.3	33.3	18.3	18.4	33.2	—	—	17.3	—	34.1
2000 starting cohort	33.5	36.3	22.0	22.2	39.1	—	—	19.9	—	36.2
2002 starting cohort	34.3	37.2	20.9	23.4	40.8	—	—	18.5	—	37.0
2003 starting cohort	35.0	38.3	20.2	23.9	42.0	—	—	19.2	—	37.2
2004 starting cohort	35.7	39.2	19.9	24.9	42.6	—	—	19.3	—	39.6
2005 starting cohort	36.2	39.9	20.2	25.5	43.5	43.9	19.0	20.1	30.7	37.7
2006 starting cohort	37.2	41.1	20.6	26.4	44.7	45.1	21.3	21.1	31.5	39.1
2007 starting cohort	37.8	42.0	21.0	27.5	44.6	45.1	22.5	23.1	37.5	40.8
2008 starting cohort	38.8	43.1	22.2	28.5	45.8	46.4	24.5	21.9	38.7	44.0
Nonprofit institutions										
1996 starting cohort	52.6	55.5	34.2	43.5	61.6	—	—	37.5	—	54.4
2000 starting cohort	53.7	57.3	32.3	46.2	60.9	—	—	38.1	—	53.2
2002 starting cohort	54.7	57.8	34.0	47.8	63.6	—	—	39.9	—	59.2
2003 starting cohort	55.3	58.6	34.4	46.7	63.7	—	—	37.0	—	59.7
2004 starting cohort	56.4	59.4	35.9	49.6	65.6	—	—	41.5	—	61.9
2005 starting cohort	55.9	59.2	34.1	48.1	64.9	65.5	38.6	38.5	63.1	62.7
2006 starting cohort	56.7	60.1	34.4	50.8	64.9	65.7	39.2	40.9	64.4	61.8
2007 starting cohort	56.7	60.4	34.7	49.8	66.4	67.2	41.8	40.6	65.6	62.8
2008 starting cohort	56.7	60.4	34.8	50.5	66.5	67.1	45.8	41.0	62.5	62.8
For-profit institutions										
1996 starting cohort	21.1	27.5	13.7	16.1	20.3	—	—	9.6	—	34.6
2000 starting cohort	20.7	24.5	21.4	23.1	39.3	—	—	27.2	—	36.3
2002 starting cohort	11.6	14.0	8.7	18.1	23.9	—	—	6.0	—	3.1
2003 starting cohort	12.8	15.9	9.5	18.3	22.8	—	—	6.7	—	3.7
2004 starting cohort	17.8	23.8	12.2	19.9	25.0	—	—	7.4	—	10.5
2005 starting cohort	16.9	24.1	10.4	17.3	30.9	34.6	5.9	11.4	24.0	14.4
2006 starting cohort	18.1	26.7	10.1	20.3	26.2	29.3	3.7	11.8	24.1	21.3
2007 starting cohort	17.0	24.5	9.2	19.9	28.8	34.4	5.1	8.1	29.4	22.3
2008 starting cohort	14.7	22.2	8.6	19.9	27.5	33.7	5.6	13.1	33.3	23.7
Graduating within 5 years after start, males and females										
All 4-year institutions										
1996 starting cohort	50.2	53.3	33.3	38.9	56.4	—	—	33.3	—	54.3
2000 starting cohort	52.6	55.7	36.0	42.4	60.1	—	—	35.1	—	55.2
2002 starting cohort	52.3	55.7	34.3	42.5	61.0	—	—	33.8	—	50.6
2003 starting cohort	53.2	56.9	34.2	43.0	62.1	—	—	33.7	—	52.1
2004 starting cohort	54.1	57.7	34.5	44.0	62.9	—	—	34.7	—	57.2
2005 starting cohort	54.2	58.0	34.2	44.6	63.2	63.6	40.6	34.7	58.6	58.1
2006 starting cohort	54.9	58.7	34.9	45.8	64.4	64.9	41.7	35.6	61.8	59.0
2007 starting cohort	55.1	59.1	35.5	46.4	64.2	64.7	42.6	36.3	63.9	58.9
2008 starting cohort	55.3	59.5	35.7	47.1	65.1	65.7	43.8	36.3	60.5	60.8
Public institutions										
1996 starting cohort	45.9	49.0	30.5	34.1	51.3	—	—	30.0	—	46.5
2000 starting cohort	49.1	51.9	34.6	38.0	56.8	—	—	31.9	—	49.8
2002 starting cohort	49.2	52.2	32.9	38.8	57.7	—	—	30.8	—	50.4
2003 starting cohort	50.3	53.6	32.4	39.5	59.0	—	—	31.6	—	51.4
2004 starting cohort	50.7	54.1	32.2	40.2	59.3	—	—	31.6	—	51.9
2005 starting cohort	51.1	54.7	32.6	41.4	59.9	60.2	39.1	32.5	47.6	51.3
2006 starting cohort	51.9	55.5	33.5	42.2	61.6	62.0	41.3	32.9	50.1	51.9
2007 starting cohort	52.3	56.0	34.1	43.3	61.0	61.4	41.1	34.4	54.9	51.9
2008 starting cohort	53.1	56.7	35.0	44.4	62.1	62.6	41.8	34.1	52.1	55.1

See notes at end of table.

Table 326.10. Graduation rate from first institution attended for first-time, full-time bachelor's degree-seeking students at 4-year postsecondary institutions, by race/ethnicity, time to completion, sex, control of institution, and acceptance rate: Selected cohort entry years, 1996 through 2008—Continued

Time to completion, sex, control of institution, cohort entry year, and acceptance rate	Total	White	Black	Hispanic	Asian/Pacific Islander			American Indian/ Alaska Native	Two or more races	Nonresident alien
					Total	Asian	Pacific Islander			
1	2	3	4	5	6	7	8	9	10	11
Nonprofit institutions										
1996 starting cohort	59.2	61.8	40.2	51.4	68.7	—	—	45.2	—	60.4
2000 starting cohort	60.8	63.8	39.9	55.1	70.0	—	—	46.9	—	60.4
2002 starting cohort	61.3	64.2	40.2	55.7	71.1	—	—	46.7	—	64.7
2003 starting cohort	62.3	65.2	41.2	56.1	72.0	—	—	44.4	—	65.6
2004 starting cohort	63.0	65.8	41.8	57.8	73.1	—	—	47.9	—	67.9
2005 starting cohort	62.6	65.6	40.5	56.6	73.1	73.6	49.4	44.0	71.5	67.9
2006 starting cohort	63.2	66.1	41.2	59.0	73.5	74.2	47.4	48.8	74.5	68.6
2007 starting cohort	63.1	66.3	41.5	58.5	74.2	74.8	53.9	45.9	74.1	68.2
2008 starting cohort	63.2	66.4	41.4	58.6	74.3	74.7	57.7	46.6	70.7	68.6
For-profit institutions										
1996 starting cohort	25.4	30.1	17.8	23.1	27.3	—	—	19.8	—	51.6
2000 starting cohort	30.0	34.8	28.0	31.3	45.1	—	—	29.4	—	44.0
2002 starting cohort	17.2	20.7	12.5	22.7	32.0	—	—	12.6	—	6.0
2003 starting cohort	20.2	23.6	15.6	24.4	30.4	—	—	11.4	—	10.0
2004 starting cohort	25.9	32.9	19.1	25.8	36.5	—	—	15.5	—	17.7
2005 starting cohort	25.5	33.3	15.8	26.0	38.2	40.2	23.1	18.9	27.3	24.1
2006 starting cohort	28.0	37.2	17.8	29.8	38.0	40.2	18.7	16.8	30.5	30.3
2007 starting cohort	27.8	37.6	16.7	29.1	38.9	43.1	14.4	16.2	31.0	34.6
2008 starting cohort	22.9	31.7	14.8	27.7	37.4	40.7	19.6	16.7	34.7	33.3
Graduating within 5 years after start, males										
All 4-year institutions										
1996 starting cohort	46.2	49.2	27.0	34.4	51.8	—	—	31.2	—	51.5
2000 starting cohort	49.0	52.0	29.9	37.8	56.5	—	—	31.6	—	53.0
2002 starting cohort	48.7	52.1	28.2	37.5	57.4	—	—	30.9	—	49.3
2003 starting cohort	49.9	53.5	28.5	38.6	58.6	—	—	31.1	—	50.9
2004 starting cohort	50.6	54.2	28.8	39.3	59.3	—	—	31.9	—	53.5
2005 starting cohort	50.9	54.7	28.8	40.7	59.4	59.7	39.0	33.1	55.6	54.2
2006 starting cohort	51.6	55.2	29.8	41.4	61.1	61.5	39.7	31.8	59.3	54.5
2007 starting cohort	51.6	55.5	29.9	42.2	60.3	60.7	42.1	32.6	60.4	53.9
2008 starting cohort	51.6	55.6	30.1	42.3	61.4	61.8	42.8	32.9	56.1	55.5
Public institutions										
1996 starting cohort	41.6	44.6	24.0	29.4	46.4	—	—	27.7	—	44.1
2000 starting cohort	44.8	47.6	27.4	32.6	52.1	—	—	27.7	—	47.2
2002 starting cohort	45.3	48.3	26.0	33.7	53.7	—	—	27.5	—	47.0
2003 starting cohort	46.7	50.0	26.3	34.7	55.1	—	—	28.7	—	48.2
2004 starting cohort	47.0	50.4	26.3	35.2	55.4	—	—	28.6	—	47.2
2005 starting cohort	47.8	51.3	26.9	37.2	56.0	56.3	37.1	31.2	44.9	46.9
2006 starting cohort	48.4	51.8	27.8	37.4	57.7	58.0	38.8	29.0	48.5	47.0
2007 starting cohort	48.6	52.2	28.1	38.6	56.9	57.2	40.7	30.2	53.5	46.8
2008 starting cohort	49.1	52.7	29.1	39.0	58.1	58.5	39.1	31.2	47.4	50.3
Nonprofit institutions										
1996 starting cohort	55.8	58.5	34.0	47.4	65.9	—	—	42.9	—	57.7
2000 starting cohort	58.5	61.3	35.1	51.7	69.9	—	—	45.9	—	58.9
2002 starting cohort	58.5	61.5	34.7	51.4	70.0	—	—	44.0	—	61.9
2003 starting cohort	59.3	62.3	35.0	53.2	70.7	—	—	41.5	—	62.2
2004 starting cohort	60.1	62.9	35.6	54.0	71.2	—	—	46.0	—	64.4
2005 starting cohort	59.5	62.5	34.7	53.3	70.6	71.0	45.2	40.4	69.3	63.9
2006 starting cohort	60.2	63.2	35.6	55.4	72.1	72.9	44.6	45.7	72.8	64.4
2007 starting cohort	59.7	63.2	35.0	55.1	71.5	72.0	50.8	42.5	70.9	63.1
2008 starting cohort	59.6	63.1	35.0	54.8	72.1	72.5	56.9	41.7	68.6	63.0
For-profit institutions										
1996 starting cohort	25.6	29.2	18.1	25.4	29.9	—	—	30.8	—	51.0
2000 starting cohort	33.6	38.1	27.6	34.4	46.4	—	—	28.7	—	43.1
2002 starting cohort	19.9	24.1	14.3	23.6	35.4	—	—	18.5	—	6.3
2003 starting cohort	22.6	26.3	16.0	24.9	32.0	—	—	16.0	—	10.2
2004 starting cohort	27.8	35.1	19.1	25.9	41.6	—	—	15.0	—	16.8
2005 starting cohort	28.7	36.4	16.4	27.4	38.1	38.7	33.3	23.8	28.5	24.9
2006 starting cohort	32.5	41.5	20.9	32.0	40.8	42.1	25.9	18.2	34.0	32.4
2007 starting cohort	32.7	43.3	19.5	30.7	41.8	44.2	21.1	23.1	27.7	34.8
2008 starting cohort	25.0	34.9	14.7	27.4	40.3	42.0	25.0	14.2	31.1	26.7
Graduating within 5 years after start, females										
All 4-year institutions										
1996 starting cohort	53.6	56.8	37.5	42.4	60.5	—	—	34.9	—	57.9
2000 starting cohort	55.6	58.8	40.2	45.9	63.4	—	—	37.8	—	58.0
2002 starting cohort	55.2	58.6	38.4	46.2	64.1	—	—	36.0	—	52.0
2003 starting cohort	55.9	59.7	38.0	46.2	65.1	—	—	35.8	—	53.5
2004 starting cohort	56.9	60.7	38.3	47.6	66.0	—	—	36.8	—	61.4
2005 starting cohort	56.8	60.8	37.8	47.5	66.5	66.9	41.9	35.9	61.2	62.4
2006 starting cohort	57.6	61.7	38.4	49.0	67.4	68.0	43.2	38.5	63.7	64.2
2007 starting cohort	58.1	62.2	39.3	49.7	67.7	68.4	42.9	39.0	66.3	64.9
2008 starting cohort	58.5	62.8	39.6	50.8	68.4	69.1	44.5	38.8	63.6	66.8

See notes at end of table.

Table 326.10. Graduation rate from first institution attended for first-time, full-time bachelor's degree-seeking students at 4-year postsecondary institutions, by race/ethnicity, time to completion, sex, control of institution, and acceptance rate: Selected cohort entry years, 1996 through 2008—Continued

Time to completion, sex, control of institution, cohort entry year, and acceptance rate	Total	White	Black	Hispanic	Asian/Pacific Islander: Total	Asian/Pacific Islander: Asian	Asian/Pacific Islander: Pacific Islander	American Indian/ Alaska Native	Two or more races	Nonresident alien
1	2	3	4	5	6	7	8	9	10	11
Public institutions										
1996 starting cohort	49.5	52.7	34.8	37.8	56.0	—	—	31.8	—	50.0
2000 starting cohort	52.7	55.5	39.3	42.1	61.0	—	—	35.1	—	53.5
2002 starting cohort	52.5	55.4	37.6	42.6	61.5	—	—	33.2	—	54.4
2003 starting cohort	53.3	56.8	36.5	43.1	62.6	—	—	33.9	—	55.0
2004 starting cohort	53.8	57.4	36.2	44.0	62.9	—	—	34.0	—	57.6
2005 starting cohort	53.9	57.7	36.3	44.5	63.4	63.7	40.5	33.5	50.0	56.5
2006 starting cohort	54.9	58.7	37.2	45.7	65.2	65.6	43.3	36.0	51.3	58.0
2007 starting cohort	55.5	59.4	38.1	46.8	64.8	65.3	41.4	37.6	56.0	58.4
2008 starting cohort	56.5	60.3	39.1	48.4	65.9	66.6	43.7	36.2	55.7	61.0
Nonprofit institutions										
1996 starting cohort	61.8	64.5	44.5	54.3	71.0	—	—	47.0	—	63.7
2000 starting cohort	62.7	65.8	43.2	57.4	70.0	—	—	47.7	—	62.3
2002 starting cohort	63.5	66.4	44.0	58.7	71.9	—	—	48.6	—	67.7
2003 starting cohort	64.6	67.5	45.5	58.0	73.0	—	—	46.5	—	69.3
2004 starting cohort	65.4	68.0	46.3	60.4	74.6	—	—	49.3	—	71.6
2005 starting cohort	65.1	68.0	44.8	58.8	75.0	75.5	52.3	46.7	73.1	72.4
2006 starting cohort	65.7	68.5	45.4	61.5	74.5	75.2	49.5	50.8	75.5	73.3
2007 starting cohort	65.9	68.9	46.4	60.7	76.3	76.9	55.8	48.5	76.2	73.7
2008 starting cohort	66.0	69.0	46.1	61.3	76.0	76.5	58.2	50.1	71.9	74.5
For-profit institutions										
1996 starting cohort	25.1	31.4	17.6	20.0	23.7	—	—	11.5	—	52.2
2000 starting cohort	25.9	30.0	28.4	27.5	42.6	—	—	30.4	—	45.1
2002 starting cohort	14.7	17.3	11.2	21.7	27.1	—	—	8.0	—	5.8
2003 starting cohort	18.3	21.4	15.3	23.9	28.8	—	—	8.5	—	9.9
2004 starting cohort	24.2	30.5	19.1	25.6	30.3	—	—	15.8	—	18.3
2005 starting cohort	22.6	29.9	15.5	24.7	38.3	42.3	11.8	15.5	26.0	23.5
2006 starting cohort	23.8	31.8	15.8	27.8	35.1	38.1	13.6	15.8	25.9	28.5
2007 starting cohort	23.2	30.5	14.8	27.6	36.1	42.0	10.9	11.4	35.8	34.4
2008 starting cohort	21.2	28.5	14.8	27.9	34.5	39.4	17.3	18.7	39.8	38.9
Graduating within 6 years after start, males and females										
All 4-year institutions										
1996 starting cohort	55.4	58.1	38.9	45.7	63.4	—	—	38.0	—	58.0
2000 starting cohort	57.5	60.2	42.1	49.1	66.7	—	—	40.2	—	59.6
2002 starting cohort	57.2	60.2	40.1	48.9	67.1	—	—	38.3	—	55.3
2003 starting cohort	57.8	61.1	39.5	49.1	68.1	—	—	38.7	—	56.1
2004 starting cohort	58.4	61.6	39.6	50.2	68.7	—	—	39.4	—	61.6
2005 starting cohort	58.6	62.0	39.5	51.0	69.2	69.6	48.3	39.3	64.2	62.6
2006 starting cohort	59.2	62.5	40.2	51.9	70.1	70.6	48.5	40.2	66.6	63.6
2007 starting cohort	59.4	62.9	40.8	52.5	70.0	70.5	49.6	40.6	67.8	63.9
2008 starting cohort[1]	59.6	63.2	40.9	53.5	70.6	71.2	50.0	41.0	65.2	65.6
Open admissions	36.3	43.3	23.9	32.0	45.0	46.4	32.6	18.1	37.0	44.8
90 percent or more accepted	43.8	47.7	27.9	36.2	43.3	42.9	51.5	27.5	41.0	52.5
75.0 to 89.9 percent accepted	56.0	58.4	38.0	51.8	62.1	62.5	47.8	41.2	54.7	56.3
50.0 to 74.9 percent accepted	61.7	65.2	44.4	53.6	68.0	68.6	50.4	42.7	64.0	64.4
25.0 to 49.9 percent accepted	68.9	74.6	47.1	62.7	77.7	77.8	65.9	58.8	79.5	72.8
Less than 25.0 percent accepted	88.6	88.7	79.2	86.3	94.9	94.9	89.2	73.7	92.7	89.9
Public institutions										
1996 starting cohort	51.7	54.3	36.8	42.1	59.5	—	—	35.3	—	51.3
2000 starting cohort	54.8	57.1	40.8	46.0	64.1	—	—	37.5	—	54.6
2002 starting cohort	54.9	57.4	39.4	46.3	64.7	—	—	35.7	—	55.5
2003 starting cohort	55.8	58.7	38.6	47.0	65.9	—	—	37.2	—	56.4
2004 starting cohort	56.1	59.0	38.5	47.9	66.3	—	—	37.0	—	57.2
2005 starting cohort	56.6	59.6	38.8	48.9	67.0	67.2	49.7	37.8	55.7	57.3
2006 starting cohort	57.2	60.3	39.7	49.5	68.2	68.5	49.1	38.2	57.0	57.7
2007 starting cohort	57.7	60.7	40.3	50.7	68.0	68.3	49.6	39.5	60.4	58.2
2008 starting cohort[1]	58.5	61.4	41.2	52.3	68.9	69.4	49.2	39.7	58.9	61.0
Open admissions	34.5	39.9	23.6	26.7	39.4	41.2	18.2	13.3	32.3	42.5
90 percent or more accepted	42.7	46.4	26.5	35.2	40.8	40.7	46.7	25.8	36.7	51.4
75.0 to 89.9 percent accepted	55.0	56.9	38.5	51.8	62.7	63.1	47.0	40.5	51.4	55.5
50.0 to 74.9 percent accepted	61.4	64.8	45.1	52.6	67.9	68.5	47.2	42.0	60.2	63.0
25.0 to 49.9 percent accepted	66.1	71.9	45.2	61.2	74.6	74.6	69.0	60.6	79.8	64.0
Less than 25.0 percent accepted	85.0	83.1	71.8	81.9	93.9	93.9	87.8	59.5	87.2	87.0
Nonprofit institutions										
1996 starting cohort	63.1	65.7	44.6	55.7	73.5	—	—	48.1	—	63.4
2000 starting cohort	64.5	67.0	45.9	59.0	75.2	—	—	50.9	—	64.5
2002 starting cohort	64.6	67.2	44.9	59.5	75.3	—	—	49.8	—	68.3
2003 starting cohort	65.1	67.8	45.0	59.4	76.0	—	—	47.6	—	69.3
2004 starting cohort	65.5	67.9	45.0	60.6	76.2	—	—	50.8	—	71.3
2005 starting cohort	65.2	67.8	43.9	60.4	76.5	77.0	52.6	46.5	75.2	71.0
2006 starting cohort	65.5	68.1	44.5	62.0	76.8	77.5	52.6	51.3	77.5	71.9
2007 starting cohort	65.3	68.3	44.7	60.9	77.0	77.5	58.2	47.9	76.8	71.5

See notes at end of table.

Table 326.10. Graduation rate from first institution attended for first-time, full-time bachelor's degree-seeking students at 4-year postsecondary institutions, by race/ethnicity, time to completion, sex, control of institution, and acceptance rate: Selected cohort entry years, 1996 through 2008—Continued

Time to completion, sex, control of institution, cohort entry year, and acceptance rate	Total	White	Black	Hispanic	Asian/Pacific Islander: Total	Asian/Pacific Islander: Asian	Asian/Pacific Islander: Pacific Islander	American Indian/ Alaska Native	Two or more races	Nonresident alien
1	2	3	4	5	6	7	8	9	10	11
2008 starting cohort[1]	65.4	68.3	44.6	61.5	76.9	77.3	60.6	48.7	73.2	72.1
Open admissions	41.4	49.7	25.1	42.4	56.2	56.1	57.5	26.0	51.4	49.6
90 percent or more accepted	50.0	53.0	33.7	45.7	53.4	53.4	53.6	42.5	48.6	54.8
75.0 to 89.9 percent accepted	59.7	63.0	38.5	52.9	60.4	60.9	48.8	45.3	59.8	57.6
50.0 to 74.9 percent accepted	62.8	66.4	43.2	57.2	68.8	68.9	63.4	46.1	69.2	66.7
25.0 to 49.9 percent accepted	74.7	78.9	51.7	70.8	84.5	84.8	62.8	57.3	80.9	78.0
Less than 25.0 percent accepted	90.2	91.0	81.5	89.0	95.6	95.7	90.9	79.6	93.8	90.5
For-profit institutions										
1996 starting cohort	28.0	33.2	19.2	24.6	28.9	—	—	23.1	—	54.0
2000 starting cohort	32.6	38.1	29.7	33.8	47.3	—	—	30.4	—	47.5
2002 starting cohort	22.0	25.5	16.3	27.5	35.5	—	—	17.1	—	12.5
2003 starting cohort	23.5	27.3	18.3	26.8	33.3	—	—	13.9	—	11.8
2004 starting cohort	28.6	35.5	21.4	29.0	38.8	—	—	19.0	—	21.8
2005 starting cohort	29.1	36.2	19.8	30.2	42.3	44.3	27.3	22.3	27.8	28.4
2006 starting cohort	31.5	40.3	21.1	33.7	42.5	44.4	25.2	18.8	32.4	35.5
2007 starting cohort	31.9	39.9	22.4	35.0	43.1	46.9	21.2	19.6	32.5	41.1
2008 starting cohort	26.5	34.5	18.8	31.7	41.2	44.1	26.1	19.8	35.5	41.3
Graduating within 6 years after start, males										
All 4-year institutions										
1996 starting cohort	52.0	54.8	32.8	41.3	59.5	—	—	36.2	—	55.4
2000 starting cohort	54.3	57.1	35.6	44.6	62.9	—	—	37.1	—	56.8
2002 starting cohort	54.1	57.3	34.0	44.1	64.0	—	—	35.1	—	53.9
2003 starting cohort	55.1	58.4	34.1	44.9	65.1	—	—	36.7	—	55.0
2004 starting cohort	55.6	58.9	34.3	45.7	65.7	—	—	37.5	—	58.5
2005 starting cohort	56.0	59.4	34.2	47.2	66.3	66.6	48.6	37.9	61.3	59.2
2006 starting cohort	56.5	59.8	35.2	47.8	67.4	67.8	46.4	37.2	64.5	60.1
2007 starting cohort	56.5	60.0	35.3	48.6	66.7	67.1	50.0	37.3	64.8	59.8
2008 starting cohort[1]	56.5	60.1	35.3	48.9	67.6	68.0	49.9	38.6	61.7	61.6
Open admissions	34.7	41.7	20.5	29.1	43.3	43.9	33.9	18.5	33.0	40.1
90 percent or more accepted	39.8	43.9	23.9	32.1	39.3	38.4	60.0	21.9	35.2	49.2
75.0 to 89.9 percent accepted	52.8	55.1	33.4	47.3	59.7	60.2	42.4	39.9	52.4	51.9
50.0 to 74.9 percent accepted	58.3	61.9	39.2	48.6	64.9	65.2	50.2	40.5	59.9	60.2
25.0 to 49.9 percent accepted	65.6	71.7	39.0	57.7	74.4	74.5	62.0	51.9	75.8	69.6
Less than 25.0 percent accepted	87.2	88.0	72.7	84.6	93.8	93.9	86.4	72.4	90.1	87.7
Public institutions										
1996 starting cohort	48.1	50.8	30.3	37.5	55.2	—	—	33.1	—	48.8
2000 starting cohort	51.3	53.8	34.1	41.1	60.0	—	—	33.6	—	52.1
2002 starting cohort	51.7	54.4	32.9	41.4	61.3	—	—	32.2	—	52.5
2003 starting cohort	52.9	55.9	32.9	42.4	62.7	—	—	35.0	—	53.5
2004 starting cohort	53.2	56.2	32.9	43.1	63.0	—	—	34.9	—	53.1
2005 starting cohort	53.9	57.0	33.3	44.9	64.0	64.2	50.9	36.8	52.7	53.3
2006 starting cohort	54.4	57.4	34.2	45.0	65.1	65.4	47.2	35.3	56.1	53.7
2007 starting cohort	54.6	57.7	34.7	46.3	64.4	64.7	49.5	35.8	59.1	54.1
2008 starting cohort[1]	55.2	58.2	35.4	47.3	65.6	65.9	47.7	37.9	54.9	57.4
Open admissions	31.9	37.1	19.8	22.5	38.0	39.2	20.8	14.0	27.2	39.4
90 percent or more accepted	39.1	42.9	23.3	30.9	36.8	36.6	50.0	18.9	30.7	47.7
75.0 to 89.9 percent accepted	52.1	54.0	33.6	47.3	60.3	60.8	40.0	40.2	50.0	51.5
50.0 to 74.9 percent accepted	58.2	61.6	40.0	47.6	64.7	65.1	46.8	40.4	54.5	59.4
25.0 to 49.9 percent accepted	61.9	67.8	36.9	55.6	70.8	70.8	68.0	53.5	74.3	61.6
Less than 25.0 percent accepted	83.1	82.5	64.4	80.0	92.3	92.4	84.6	69.0	85.4	83.9
Nonprofit institutions										
1996 starting cohort	60.4	63.0	38.9	52.1	71.5	—	—	46.7	—	60.9
2000 starting cohort	61.7	64.4	39.3	55.3	73.1	—	—	50.1	—	61.7
2002 starting cohort	61.9	64.8	38.6	55.4	73.8	—	—	46.6	—	65.4
2003 starting cohort	62.5	65.3	38.9	56.7	74.2	—	—	45.4	—	65.8
2004 starting cohort	63.0	65.7	39.3	57.1	74.5	—	—	49.5	—	68.3
2005 starting cohort	62.5	65.3	38.2	57.2	74.6	75.1	49.2	42.8	73.5	67.4
2006 starting cohort	62.9	65.6	39.2	58.7	75.6	76.3	49.1	48.6	76.2	68.8
2007 starting cohort	62.3	65.5	38.3	58.1	74.9	75.3	58.1	44.5	74.3	67.3
2008 starting cohort[1]	62.3	65.6	38.3	57.8	75.0	75.3	60.7	44.3	72.2	67.9
Open admissions	38.8	48.4	20.4	35.3	51.4	51.1	57.1	25.4	59.1	45.7
90 percent or more accepted	44.7	48.1	26.2	40.8	48.1	44.9	64.5	45.9	44.8	52.7
75.0 to 89.9 percent accepted	55.2	58.8	34.2	48.1	57.3	57.8	48.1	39.1	56.9	52.3
50.0 to 74.9 percent accepted	59.0	62.9	38.1	52.5	65.7	65.8	62.9	42.1	68.2	62.0
25.0 to 49.9 percent accepted	73.1	77.6	44.3	68.1	82.7	83.0	55.3	50.6	79.8	74.2
Less than 25.0 percent accepted	89.2	90.7	75.4	87.2	94.9	94.9	88.9	74.1	91.8	88.5
For-profit institutions										
1996 starting cohort	28.0	32.3	19.4	26.7	31.7	—	—	30.8	—	53.0
2000 starting cohort	35.5	40.2	29.8	36.2	48.4	—	—	30.3	—	46.3
2002 starting cohort	23.6	27.8	16.6	26.7	38.4	—	—	23.5	—	11.7
2003 starting cohort	25.7	29.3	18.5	26.9	35.0	—	—	18.8	—	12.1
2004 starting cohort	30.3	37.2	21.5	29.0	43.6	—	—	18.6	—	23.7
2005 starting cohort	31.6	38.8	19.5	30.4	42.5	43.3	36.0	27.7	28.5	29.4
2006 starting cohort	35.4	43.9	23.5	35.4	44.0	45.5	27.6	19.6	34.6	37.4
2007 starting cohort	35.7	45.0	23.4	36.0	43.7	45.9	23.9	27.2	28.9	41.4
2008 starting cohort	27.8	37.1	17.9	30.7	43.0	44.5	29.4	18.9	31.8	33.4

See notes at end of table.

Table 326.10. Graduation rate from first institution attended for first-time, full-time bachelor's degree-seeking students at 4-year postsecondary institutions, by race/ethnicity, time to completion, sex, control of institution, and acceptance rate: Selected cohort entry years, 1996 through 2008—Continued

Time to completion, sex, control of institution, cohort entry year, and acceptance rate	Total	White	Black	Hispanic	Asian/Pacific Islander			American Indian/ Alaska Native	Two or more races	Nonresident alien
					Total	Asian	Pacific Islander			
1	2	3	4	5	6	7	8	9	10	11
Graduating within 6 years after start, females										
All 4-year institutions										
1996 starting cohort	58.2	60.9	43.0	49.1	66.8	—	—	39.5	—	61.5
2000 starting cohort	60.2	62.8	46.4	52.4	70.1	—	—	42.7	—	63.1
2002 starting cohort	59.7	62.5	44.2	52.5	69.8	—	—	40.7	—	56.7
2003 starting cohort	60.0	63.3	43.2	52.2	70.7	—	—	40.2	—	57.3
2004 starting cohort	60.7	63.9	43.3	53.5	71.3	—	—	40.9	—	65.0
2005 starting cohort	60.8	64.2	43.0	53.8	71.8	72.2	48.1	40.3	66.7	66.6
2006 starting cohort	61.4	64.9	43.6	54.9	72.6	73.1	50.2	42.5	68.1	67.6
2007 starting cohort	61.9	65.4	44.6	55.5	73.0	73.6	49.3	43.1	69.9	68.7
2008 starting cohort[1]	62.3	65.9	44.8	57.0	73.4	74.1	50.1	42.8	67.6	70.2
Open admissions	37.9	45.0	26.9	34.6	46.7	49.1	32.0	17.9	40.4	50.6
90 percent or more accepted	47.4	51.2	31.2	39.9	47.5	47.7	44.4	32.5	44.8	57.3
75.0 to 89.9 percent accepted	58.8	61.2	41.2	55.3	64.3	64.7	52.2	42.3	56.6	61.8
50.0 to 74.9 percent accepted	64.4	68.0	47.9	57.3	70.9	71.5	50.5	44.4	66.6	69.2
25.0 to 49.9 percent accepted	71.5	77.1	52.2	66.4	80.5	80.7	67.9	63.7	81.8	76.1
Less than 25.0 percent accepted	90.0	89.4	84.5	87.8	95.8	95.8	93.3	74.8	95.0	92.3
Public institutions										
1996 starting cohort	54.7	57.4	41.0	45.7	63.5	—	—	37.0	—	54.9
2000 starting cohort	57.7	59.9	45.2	49.7	67.8	—	—	40.5	—	58.1
2002 starting cohort	57.5	59.9	43.7	50.0	67.7	—	—	38.3	—	59.0
2003 starting cohort	58.2	61.0	42.4	50.4	68.8	—	—	38.9	—	59.7
2004 starting cohort	58.6	61.5	42.3	51.5	69.2	—	—	38.5	—	62.3
2005 starting cohort	58.8	61.8	42.4	51.9	69.7	70.0	48.7	38.5	58.4	62.0
2006 starting cohort	59.6	62.7	43.3	52.9	71.1	71.5	50.7	40.5	57.8	62.6
2007 starting cohort	60.3	63.3	44.1	54.1	71.3	71.8	49.7	42.3	61.4	63.4
2008 starting cohort[1]	61.2	64.3	45.1	56.1	72.0	72.6	50.3	41.1	62.0	65.3
Open admissions	36.8	42.6	26.6	30.1	40.9	43.3	16.1	12.8	36.0	46.5
90 percent or more accepted	45.9	49.6	29.1	39.0	45.0	45.0	43.8	31.8	41.0	57.0
75.0 to 89.9 percent accepted	57.5	59.5	41.8	55.4	65.0	65.4	52.9	40.8	52.5	60.5
50.0 to 74.9 percent accepted	64.0	67.6	48.3	56.2	70.9	71.7	47.5	43.2	64.2	67.5
25.0 to 49.9 percent accepted	69.5	75.5	50.7	65.2	78.0	78.2	69.4	65.7	84.0	66.3
Less than 25.0 percent accepted	87.1	84.0	79.0	83.6	95.2	95.2	93.3	48.6	91.2	91.1
Nonprofit institutions										
1996 starting cohort	65.4	67.9	48.4	58.3	75.0	—	—	49.2	—	66.4
2000 starting cohort	66.7	69.1	50.4	61.7	76.7	—	—	51.5	—	67.9
2002 starting cohort	66.7	69.1	49.4	62.2	76.3	—	—	52.1	—	71.5
2003 starting cohort	67.2	69.8	49.2	61.3	77.3	—	—	49.3	—	73.2
2004 starting cohort	67.4	69.7	49.2	63.0	77.6	—	—	51.7	—	74.5
2005 starting cohort	67.3	69.8	48.1	62.6	77.9	78.4	54.9	49.2	76.5	75.1
2006 starting cohort	67.6	70.1	48.5	64.2	77.7	78.4	55.1	53.0	78.3	75.4
2007 starting cohort	67.7	70.4	49.4	62.9	78.7	79.3	58.2	50.5	78.4	76.0
2008 starting cohort[1]	67.8	70.5	49.4	64.1	78.4	78.9	60.6	51.8	73.8	76.5
Open admissions	43.9	51.0	29.5	48.6	61.2	61.5	57.7	26.4	48.0	54.5
90 percent or more accepted	54.7	57.4	40.4	49.8	58.1	60.9	44.7	38.9	50.6	57.5
75.0 to 89.9 percent accepted	63.0	66.0	42.3	56.2	62.5	63.1	49.3	50.2	61.7	64.2
50.0 to 74.9 percent accepted	65.7	69.1	47.2	60.3	71.0	71.3	63.8	48.9	69.8	71.4
25.0 to 49.9 percent accepted	76.1	80.0	56.2	72.8	85.8	86.2	66.7	61.9	81.5	81.7
Less than 25.0 percent accepted	91.2	91.3	86.4	90.6	96.3	96.3	93.3	83.8	95.4	92.5
For-profit institutions										
1996 starting cohort	27.9	34.5	19.0	21.9	24.9	—	—	17.3	—	55.1
2000 starting cohort	29.1	35.1	29.7	30.9	45.2	—	—	30.4	—	48.9
2002 starting cohort	20.5	23.1	16.1	28.3	31.3	—	—	12.0	—	13.0
2003 starting cohort	21.8	25.6	18.2	26.7	31.6	—	—	10.8	—	11.6
2004 starting cohort	26.9	33.6	21.3	28.9	33.1	—	—	19.3	—	20.4
2005 starting cohort	26.9	33.3	20.0	30.0	42.1	45.8	17.6	18.7	26.9	27.7
2006 starting cohort	28.0	35.8	19.5	32.1	40.8	43.3	23.5	18.2	29.3	33.9
2007 starting cohort	28.3	33.7	21.7	34.1	42.6	48.0	19.7	14.3	37.6	40.8
2008 starting cohort	25.4	31.9	19.4	32.7	39.5	43.7	24.7	20.6	40.7	48.0

—Not available.

[1]Includes data for institutions not reporting admissions data, which are not separately shown.

NOTE: Data are for 4-year degree-granting postsecondary institutions participating in Title IV federal financial aid programs. Graduation rates refer to students receiving bachelor's degrees from their initial institutions of attendance only. Totals include data for persons whose race/ethnicity was not reported. Race categories exclude persons of Hispanic ethnicity. Some data have been revised from previously published figures.

SOURCE: U.S. Department of Education, National Center for Education Statistics, Integrated Postsecondary Education Data System (IPEDS), Spring 2002 through Spring 2013, Winter 2013–14, and Winter 2014–15, Graduation Rates component; and IPEDS Fall 2008, Institutional Characteristics component. (This table was prepared December 2015.)

Table 326.20. Graduation rate from first institution attended within 150 percent of normal time for first-time, full-time degree/certificate-seeking students at 2-year postsecondary institutions, by race/ethnicity, sex, and control of institution: Selected cohort entry years, 2000 through 2011

Sex, control of institution, and cohort entry year	Percent graduating with a certificate or associate's degree within 150 percent of normal time: Total	White	Black	Hispanic	Asian/Pacific Islander: Total	Asian/Pacific Islander: Asian	Asian/Pacific Islander: Pacific Islander	American Indian/ Alaska Native	Two or more races	Nonresident alien
1	2	3	4	5	6	7	8	9	10	11
Males and females										
All 2-year institutions										
2000 starting cohort	30.5	31.5	26.1	30.1	33.3	—	—	29.3	—	25.5
2002 starting cohort	29.3	30.4	24.2	30.7	31.4	—	—	26.3	—	26.7
2003 starting cohort	29.1	29.9	24.2	30.2	31.7	—	—	25.9	—	27.2
2004 starting cohort	27.8	29.0	22.9	26.3	30.2	—	—	26.7	—	32.9
2005 starting cohort	27.5	28.5	22.6	25.7	31.5	—	—	24.9	—	32.2
2006 starting cohort	29.2	29.3	24.4	30.7	33.9	—	—	24.4	—	30.1
2007 starting cohort	29.8	29.4	25.4	33.3	33.1	—	—	25.5	—	30.9
2008 starting cohort	31.2	30.1	27.6	35.1	34.3	35.2	24.1	25.7	33.3	33.7
2009 starting cohort	30.9	30.1	26.4	36.3	35.1	36.0	25.0	25.7	30.5	34.6
2010 starting cohort	29.4	29.4	23.7	33.8	35.4	35.2	37.9	24.0	26.0	36.2
2011 starting cohort	27.9	29.1	20.2	29.9	33.6	33.7	32.1	22.5	24.5	34.3
Public institutions										
2000 starting cohort	23.6	25.7	17.8	16.8	25.5	—	—	19.6	—	23.2
2002 starting cohort	21.9	24.5	13.2	16.7	23.8	—	—	18.8	—	25.5
2003 starting cohort	21.5	24.1	12.7	16.3	24.8	—	—	17.9	—	25.8
2004 starting cohort	20.3	22.9	11.5	15.0	24.2	—	—	17.8	—	30.5
2005 starting cohort	20.6	22.9	12.1	15.6	25.8	—	—	18.2	—	29.9
2006 starting cohort	20.4	23.1	12.0	15.5	25.4	—	—	16.9	—	25.0
2007 starting cohort	20.3	22.9	11.8	15.9	25.3	—	—	17.4	—	25.5
2008 starting cohort	20.2	22.8	11.8	15.8	26.2	27.2	15.2	15.4	17.0	30.5
2009 starting cohort	19.8	22.5	11.3	15.9	26.1	27.3	11.9	15.9	18.5	32.6
2010 starting cohort	19.5	22.4	10.8	16.2	26.7	27.5	15.6	15.0	17.4	32.6
2011 starting cohort	20.0	23.4	9.8	17.5	27.2	28.1	14.0	14.4	17.6	31.0
Nonprofit institutions										
2000 starting cohort	50.1	49.6	37.5	56.3	61.4	—	—	62.1	—	43.1
2002 starting cohort	49.1	55.1	36.5	46.1	49.5	—	—	20.3	—	45.3
2003 starting cohort	49.0	56.0	35.8	39.4	50.1	—	—	17.9	—	64.2
2004 starting cohort	44.4	48.9	37.3	35.6	36.6	—	—	19.5	—	54.7
2005 starting cohort	48.2	52.3	41.6	47.3	41.6	—	—	14.8	—	51.7
2006 starting cohort	52.8	55.0	46.5	47.5	51.2	—	—	22.6	—	69.3
2007 starting cohort	51.0	56.1	43.6	46.1	51.0	—	—	15.3	—	63.9
2008 starting cohort	56.6	59.7	53.4	62.4	52.9	53.9	‡	25.0	55.8	59.5
2009 starting cohort	62.3	66.0	59.7	68.3	57.9	57.7	‡	30.4	66.5	50.0
2010 starting cohort	53.6	55.9	51.0	62.1	51.7	52.2	‡	18.2	39.5	52.5
2011 starting cohort	51.2	56.3	46.5	57.5	47.0	48.0	35.7	21.6	45.6	51.5
For-profit institutions										
2000 starting cohort	59.1	63.1	47.6	60.3	64.4	—	—	60.3	—	55.4
2002 starting cohort	57.1	61.0	49.3	59.7	61.7	—	—	58.1	—	58.9
2003 starting cohort	57.2	61.8	48.4	60.0	55.8	—	—	59.1	—	36.5
2004 starting cohort	58.2	64.3	48.4	59.6	65.4	—	—	59.0	—	71.1
2005 starting cohort	57.7	62.9	47.8	61.4	65.8	—	—	55.8	—	57.7
2006 starting cohort	58.3	62.8	46.9	62.7	72.1	—	—	57.5	—	65.6
2007 starting cohort	60.6	65.0	49.7	65.1	68.8	—	—	59.0	—	67.6
2008 starting cohort	61.7	64.1	52.6	67.9	69.9	70.2	66.2	60.3	57.4	62.0
2009 starting cohort	62.7	65.1	52.9	68.4	70.8	71.6	64.0	60.7	59.9	61.7
2010 starting cohort	62.8	65.8	53.3	68.3	72.4	73.4	68.9	61.4	59.0	69.7
2011 starting cohort	58.4	62.6	48.5	62.3	65.8	66.3	63.6	55.5	56.7	63.6
Males										
All 2-year institutions										
2000 starting cohort	28.7	30.0	23.1	27.9	30.1	—	—	28.3	—	22.9
2002 starting cohort	27.2	28.6	21.3	27.0	28.7	—	—	23.7	—	22.5
2003 starting cohort	27.2	28.5	20.6	26.8	29.4	—	—	22.4	—	22.6
2004 starting cohort	25.7	27.3	19.1	22.6	27.9	—	—	23.6	—	30.1
2005 starting cohort	25.3	27.0	18.6	21.8	28.4	—	—	23.4	—	29.4
2006 starting cohort	26.3	27.2	20.3	25.4	30.5	—	—	22.6	—	27.4
2007 starting cohort	26.2	27.0	20.3	26.6	29.3	—	—	23.7	—	27.1
2008 starting cohort	27.4	27.7	22.7	29.1	30.3	30.9	23.8	23.0	28.8	30.5
2009 starting cohort	27.2	27.8	22.1	30.0	30.9	31.7	21.6	23.6	24.6	31.5
2010 starting cohort	26.2	27.6	19.4	27.7	31.5	31.5	31.8	21.4	22.3	33.2
2011 starting cohort	25.3	27.5	16.9	25.7	29.8	29.9	28.7	20.6	21.7	31.5
Public institutions										
2000 starting cohort	22.2	24.2	16.5	15.4	22.6	—	—	19.3	—	20.4
2002 starting cohort	20.9	23.2	13.1	15.2	21.8	—	—	16.9	—	21.4
2003 starting cohort	20.8	23.0	12.5	15.2	22.7	—	—	16.4	—	21.3
2004 starting cohort	19.6	21.8	11.5	13.8	22.6	—	—	17.5	—	27.8
2005 starting cohort	19.9	22.1	12.0	14.6	23.5	—	—	18.7	—	27.4
2006 starting cohort	19.8	22.2	12.2	14.7	23.7	—	—	16.3	—	22.5
2007 starting cohort	19.8	22.2	11.9	15.1	23.6	—	—	18.6	—	22.1
2008 starting cohort	19.6	22.1	12.0	14.9	24.3	25.1	15.2	15.2	16.7	28.1
2009 starting cohort	19.3	22.0	11.4	14.8	24.4	25.4	12.4	16.0	16.8	29.9
2010 starting cohort	19.0	21.9	10.7	15.1	24.6	25.4	14.6	14.1	16.2	30.2
2011 starting cohort	19.5	23.0	9.8	16.4	24.6	25.4	13.0	14.2	16.3	28.2

See notes at end of table.

Table 326.20. Graduation rate from first institution attended within 150 percent of normal time for first-time, full-time degree/certificate-seeking students at 2-year postsecondary institutions, by race/ethnicity, sex, and control of institution: Selected cohort entry years, 2000 through 2011—Continued

Sex, control of institution, and cohort entry year	Percent graduating with a certificate or associate's degree within 150 percent of normal time									
					Asian/Pacific Islander					
	Total	White	Black	Hispanic	Total	Asian	Pacific Islander	American Indian/ Alaska Native	Two or more races	Nonresident alien
1	2	3	4	5	6	7	8	9	10	11
Nonprofit institutions										
2000 starting cohort	49.5	49.3	31.7	54.3	62.5	—	—	64.5	—	42.6
2002 starting cohort	51.1	58.8	33.0	42.9	56.0	—	—	21.7	—	35.3
2003 starting cohort	49.6	57.0	31.4	42.4	48.1	—	—	16.8	—	51.6
2004 starting cohort	43.2	46.4	38.3	36.4	40.3	—	—	17.5	—	52.0
2005 starting cohort	44.5	49.1	38.7	42.9	43.7	—	—	10.4	—	47.7
2006 starting cohort	51.3	52.6	45.1	45.6	54.0	—	—	21.8	—	68.2
2007 starting cohort	50.1	56.4	45.5	41.1	49.3	—	—	10.3	—	58.1
2008 starting cohort	49.8	53.8	47.3	49.4	45.4	46.3	‡	14.6	46.7	52.1
2009 starting cohort	53.6	57.5	51.0	58.2	47.4	47.7	‡	22.4	56.1	45.1
2010 starting cohort	46.2	49.4	42.5	52.1	47.6	48.8	‡	19.8	27.0	44.0
2011 starting cohort	45.7	52.0	38.0	48.9	41.1	42.8	‡	19.2	42.0	50.3
For-profit institutions										
2000 starting cohort	59.3	63.7	45.6	58.2	63.1	—	—	55.9	—	55.0
2002 starting cohort	56.6	62.0	45.9	56.1	59.7	—	—	58.4	—	61.9
2003 starting cohort	58.0	63.7	45.7	56.9	62.0	—	—	59.5	—	36.7
2004 starting cohort	58.1	65.4	44.6	55.4	64.3	—	—	59.6	—	69.4
2005 starting cohort	57.7	64.8	43.1	57.5	65.7	—	—	56.3	—	56.3
2006 starting cohort	56.5	62.2	42.3	57.6	69.7	—	—	57.5	—	63.8
2007 starting cohort	58.4	65.1	45.0	59.5	66.8	—	—	56.7	—	67.9
2008 starting cohort	58.9	63.9	48.2	63.1	67.7	68.1	65.1	54.6	58.2	54.6
2009 starting cohort	59.6	63.7	49.3	63.8	67.7	68.7	59.2	59.4	55.2	59.9
2010 starting cohort	60.8	65.9	49.4	63.4	71.2	72.8	65.5	59.4	57.4	66.4
2011 starting cohort	57.7	63.3	45.7	60.0	65.8	65.5	67.1	53.6	56.2	62.6
Females										
All 2-year institutions										
2000 starting cohort	32.1	33.0	28.1	31.8	36.3	—	—	30.0	—	28.3
2002 starting cohort	30.9	32.0	26.1	33.4	33.9	—	—	28.2	—	30.4
2003 starting cohort	30.7	31.2	26.3	32.7	33.9	—	—	28.4	—	31.5
2004 starting cohort	29.6	30.5	25.2	29.0	32.6	—	—	28.8	—	35.3
2005 starting cohort	29.3	29.9	25.2	28.6	34.6	—	—	25.9	—	34.8
2006 starting cohort	31.5	31.2	26.9	34.5	37.4	—	—	25.7	—	32.5
2007 starting cohort	32.7	31.5	28.5	37.9	37.0	—	—	26.8	—	34.4
2008 starting cohort	34.4	32.3	30.9	39.4	38.3	39.6	24.3	27.9	36.2	36.7
2009 starting cohort	34.1	32.3	29.4	40.9	39.3	40.3	28.0	27.3	35.0	37.6
2010 starting cohort	32.2	31.1	26.7	38.2	39.4	38.9	43.2	26.0	28.8	39.0
2011 starting cohort	30.1	30.5	22.6	33.2	37.6	37.9	35.2	24.0	26.8	37.1
Public institutions										
2000 starting cohort	24.8	27.1	18.8	17.9	28.4	—	—	19.9	—	26.2
2002 starting cohort	22.8	25.8	13.2	17.8	25.9	—	—	20.2	—	29.2
2003 starting cohort	22.2	25.1	12.8	17.3	27.1	—	—	19.0	—	30.0
2004 starting cohort	21.0	24.0	11.5	16.0	26.1	—	—	17.9	—	32.8
2005 starting cohort	21.2	23.8	12.1	16.4	28.2	—	—	17.8	—	32.2
2006 starting cohort	20.9	23.9	11.8	16.2	27.3	—	—	17.5	—	27.3
2007 starting cohort	20.7	23.6	11.7	16.7	27.1	—	—	16.4	—	28.7
2008 starting cohort	20.7	23.5	11.7	16.5	28.3	29.6	15.2	15.6	17.3	32.9
2009 starting cohort	20.2	23.0	11.2	16.8	28.0	29.5	11.4	15.8	20.0	35.4
2010 starting cohort	20.0	23.0	10.8	17.2	29.0	30.0	16.7	15.7	18.6	35.0
2011 starting cohort	20.4	23.8	9.7	18.5	30.3	31.3	15.2	14.6	18.8	33.9
Nonprofit institutions										
2000 starting cohort	50.7	50.0	43.1	58.3	60.1	—	—	60.2	—	43.8
2002 starting cohort	47.3	51.4	39.2	48.9	44.3	—	—	19.3	—	55.0
2003 starting cohort	48.5	55.0	38.8	37.5	51.4	—	—	18.7	—	75.4
2004 starting cohort	45.4	51.1	36.3	35.1	34.3	—	—	21.0	—	57.4
2005 starting cohort	51.3	54.9	44.9	49.6	40.1	—	—	18.0	—	55.2
2006 starting cohort	54.0	56.7	47.7	48.5	48.8	—	—	23.2	—	70.4
2007 starting cohort	51.8	55.8	41.6	49.5	52.2	—	—	18.9	—	69.9
2008 starting cohort	59.9	63.2	55.8	67.7	56.8	57.7	‡	31.5	58.3	66.8
2009 starting cohort	66.6	70.8	63.4	72.5	63.2	62.7	‡	34.5	70.3	54.5
2010 starting cohort	57.7	60.0	55.0	66.8	54.5	54.5	‡	17.3	45.5	58.7
2011 starting cohort	54.1	59.2	50.2	60.8	50.0	50.6	‡	23.6	47.7	52.7
For-profit institutions										
2000 starting cohort	58.9	62.6	48.6	61.8	65.3	—	—	63.8	—	55.7
2002 starting cohort	57.4	60.3	50.8	61.7	63.3	—	—	58.0	—	56.7
2003 starting cohort	56.8	60.4	49.4	61.9	52.1	—	—	59.0	—	36.4
2004 starting cohort	58.3	63.4	49.9	61.9	66.2	—	—	58.7	—	72.3
2005 starting cohort	57.7	61.6	49.4	63.3	65.8	—	—	55.7	—	58.6
2006 starting cohort	59.3	63.2	48.8	65.1	73.7	—	—	57.4	—	67.0
2007 starting cohort	61.6	64.9	51.4	67.4	70.0	—	—	60.0	—	67.5
2008 starting cohort	63.2	64.2	54.7	70.3	71.2	71.4	67.3	64.0	57.1	67.6
2009 starting cohort	64.4	66.0	54.7	70.7	72.7	73.4	66.9	61.5	61.9	62.8
2010 starting cohort	63.8	65.8	55.0	70.7	73.1	73.8	71.0	62.6	59.8	72.7
2011 starting cohort	58.9	62.2	49.8	63.4	65.8	66.9	61.4	56.6	57.0	64.5

—Not available.
‡Reporting standards not met (too few cases).
NOTE: Data are for 2-year degree-granting postsecondary institutions participating in Title IV federal financial aid programs. Graduation rates refer to students receiving associate's degrees or certificates from their initial institutions of attendance only. Totals include data for persons whose race/ethnicity was not reported. Race categories exclude persons of Hispanic ethnicity. Some data have been revised from previously published figures.
SOURCE: U.S. Department of Education, National Center for Education Statistics, Integrated Postsecondary Education Data System (IPEDS), Spring 2002 through Spring 2013, Winter 2013–14, and Winter 2014–15, Graduation Rates component. (This table was prepared December 2015.)

Table 326.30. Retention of first-time degree-seeking undergraduates at degree-granting postsecondary institutions, by attendance status, level and control of institution, and percentage of applications accepted: Selected years, 2006 to 2014

Attendance status, level, control, and percent of applications accepted	First-time degree-seekers (adjusted entry cohort),[1] by entry year							Students from adjusted cohort returning in the following year							Percent of first-time undergraduates retained						
	2006	2008	2009	2010	2011	2012	2013	2007	2009	2010	2011	2012	2013	2014	2006 to 2007	2008 to 2009	2009 to 2010	2010 to 2011	2011 to 2012	2012 to 2013	2013 to 2014
1	2	3	4	5	6	7	8	9	10	11	12	13	14	15	16	17	18	19	20	21	22
Full-time students																					
All institutions	**2,171,714**	**2,294,973**	**2,371,220**	**2,340,415**	**2,271,908**	**2,223,481**	**2,221,384**	**1,542,175**	**1,646,507**	**1,705,242**	**1,678,241**	**1,631,396**	**1,621,301**	**1,642,199**	**71.0**	**71.7**	**71.9**	**71.7**	**71.8**	**72.9**	**73.9**
Public institutions	1,524,044	1,654,851	1,732,822	1,698,150	1,666,828	1,637,612	1,646,239	1,072,644	1,167,982	1,222,688	1,192,140	1,170,856	1,168,799	1,192,882	70.4	70.6	70.6	70.2	70.2	71.4	72.5
Nonprofit institutions	466,139	476,059	478,755	487,746	484,388	483,953	483,621	369,084	378,339	381,364	389,124	386,563	388,539	392,197	79.2	79.5	79.7	79.8	79.8	80.3	81.1
For-profit institutions	181,531	164,063	159,643	154,519	120,692	101,916	91,524	100,447	100,186	101,190	96,977	73,977	63,963	57,120	55.3	61.1	63.4	62.8	61.3	62.8	62.4
4-year institutions	1,458,731	1,511,258	1,452,575	1,460,795	1,472,189	1,466,842	1,482,853	1,115,529	1,176,183	1,146,534	1,151,786	1,159,681	1,167,016	1,193,644	76.5	77.8	78.9	78.8	78.8	79.6	80.5
Public institutions	912,401	973,212	936,840	940,660	957,744	957,853	977,381	711,490	765,335	745,703	746,121	758,616	765,747	789,743	78.0	78.6	79.6	79.3	79.2	79.9	80.8
Open admissions	62,724	76,596	45,458	43,031	41,111	35,041	34,566	38,839	49,281	28,675	26,485	24,978	21,189	21,413	61.9	64.3	63.1	61.5	60.8	60.5	61.9
90 percent or more accepted	68,835	63,404	63,453	74,553	50,200	47,775	55,149	49,274	45,743	46,280	53,975	35,197	33,969	40,118	71.6	72.1	72.9	72.4	70.1	71.1	72.7
75.0 to 89.9 percent accepted	244,177	213,394	212,573	205,403	230,328	226,673	261,407	185,457	162,454	163,639	158,677	176,676	174,316	203,267	76.0	76.1	77.0	77.3	76.7	76.9	77.8
50.0 to 74.9 percent accepted	417,093	464,239	462,554	469,026	451,184	469,245	461,424	336,199	375,310	376,021	379,353	363,305	381,576	381,505	80.6	80.8	81.3	80.9	80.5	81.3	82.7
25.0 to 49.9 percent accepted	103,118	133,409	131,241	131,782	169,908	164,067	147,849	88,908	113,365	112,209	112,006	145,215	141,671	127,595	86.2	85.0	85.5	85.0	85.5	86.3	86.3
Less than 25.0 percent accepted	7,716	14,540	14,326	13,996	9,468	8,843	15,315	7,048	13,780	13,649	13,302	9,013	8,357	14,651	91.3	94.8	95.3	95.0	95.2	94.5	95.7
Information not available	8,738	7,630	7,235	2,869	5,545	6,209	1,671	5,765	5,402	5,230	2,323	4,232	4,669	1,194	66.0	70.8	72.3	81.0	76.3	75.2	71.5
Nonprofit institutions	457,566	468,126	470,795	476,794	473,690	476,215	476,441	363,760	373,610	376,668	382,427	380,126	383,984	387,721	79.5	79.8	80.0	80.2	80.2	80.6	81.4
Open admissions	26,679	23,712	22,613	22,853	21,972	22,493	12,549	16,116	16,124	14,349	14,304	13,835	14,351	7,653	60.4	68.0	63.5	62.6	63.0	63.8	61.0
90 percent or more accepted	13,684	15,241	15,135	14,102	13,537	12,348	22,841	9,549	10,835	10,953	9,859	9,292	8,516	16,881	69.8	71.1	72.4	69.9	68.6	69.0	73.9
75.0 to 89.9 percent accepted	102,218	82,985	80,301	83,326	80,566	79,817	86,040	78,495	63,646	62,196	64,730	62,725	62,184	68,481	76.8	76.7	77.5	77.7	77.9	77.9	79.6
50.0 to 74.9 percent accepted	190,079	214,266	218,072	222,880	218,224	220,080	207,435	148,781	166,608	170,232	175,151	170,519	173,261	162,951	78.3	77.8	78.1	78.6	78.1	78.7	78.6
25.0 to 49.9 percent accepted	93,560	95,727	98,312	92,723	93,743	95,784	98,202	81,880	82,558	84,941	79,654	80,260	81,876	85,506	87.5	86.2	86.4	85.9	85.6	85.5	87.1
Less than 25.0 percent accepted	26,696	32,644	32,980	38,511	44,290	44,735	45,222	25,639	31,409	31,790	37,056	42,698	43,215	43,522	96.0	96.2	96.4	96.2	96.4	96.6	96.2
Information not available	4,650	3,551	3,382	2,399	1,358	958	4,152	3,300	2,430	2,207	1,673	797	581	2,727	71.0	68.4	65.3	69.7	58.7	60.6	65.7
For-profit institutions	88,764	69,920	44,940	43,341	40,755	32,774	29,031	40,279	37,238	24,163	23,238	20,939	17,285	16,180	45.4	53.3	53.8	53.6	51.4	52.7	55.7
Open admissions	45,273	21,906	16,826	16,783	20,710	16,811	19,206	18,735	12,545	9,260	9,034	10,769	8,331	10,053	41.4	57.3	55.0	53.8	52.0	49.6	52.3
90 percent or more accepted	6,285	15,104	3,722	2,475	5,380	3,337	700	3,454	6,916	1,311	1,460	2,511	1,650	504	55.0	45.8	35.2	59.0	46.7	49.4	72.0
75.0 to 89.9 percent accepted	3,703	2,544	3,224	2,536	2,857	1,880	2,920	2,081	1,408	1,549	1,369	1,352	1,224	1,865	56.2	55.3	48.0	54.0	47.3	65.1	63.9
50.0 to 74.9 percent accepted	12,845	18,996	12,061	10,122	4,849	6,245	3,690	6,536	9,685	6,839	5,443	2,691	3,608	2,472	50.9	51.0	56.7	53.8	55.5	57.8	67.0
25.0 to 49.9 percent accepted	18,142	8,662	6,098	7,214	6,687	2,908	419	8,036	5,229	3,423	3,942	3,451	1,554	293	44.3	60.4	56.1	54.6	51.6	53.4	69.9
Less than 25.0 percent accepted	0	15	3	0	0	0	0	0	7	2	0	0	0	0	†	46.7	66.7	†	†	†	†
Information not available	2,516	2,693	3,006	4,211	272	1,593	2,096	1,437	1,448	1,779	1,990	165	918	993	57.1	53.8	59.2	47.3	60.7	57.6	47.4
2-year institutions	712,983	783,715	918,645	879,620	799,719	756,639	738,531	426,646	470,324	558,708	526,455	471,715	454,285	448,555	59.8	60.0	60.8	59.9	59.0	60.0	60.7
Public institutions	611,643	681,639	795,982	757,490	709,084	679,759	668,858	361,154	402,647	476,985	446,019	412,240	403,052	403,139	59.0	59.1	59.9	58.9	58.1	59.3	60.3
Public institutions	8,573	7,933	7,960	10,952	10,698	7,738	7,180	5,324	4,729	4,696	6,697	6,437	4,555	4,476	62.1	59.6	59.0	61.1	60.2	58.9	62.3
Nonprofit institutions	92,767	94,143	114,703	111,178	79,937	69,142	62,493	60,168	62,948	77,027	73,739	53,038	46,678	40,940	64.9	66.9	67.2	66.3	66.3	67.5	65.5
Part-time students																					
All institutions	**463,234**	**518,634**	**545,635**	**548,178**	**532,017**	**516,025**	**490,022**	**191,586**	**210,937**	**229,566**	**228,329**	**224,401**	**222,420**	**213,497**	**41.4**	**40.7**	**42.1**	**41.7**	**42.2**	**43.1**	**43.6**
Public institutions	419,006	476,800	497,453	500,615	494,294	483,211	461,845	171,746	192,636	209,164	210,466	209,013	209,110	202,505	41.0	40.4	42.0	42.0	42.3	43.3	43.8
Nonprofit institutions	14,585	11,199	10,359	9,805	9,788	9,935	9,341	7,018	5,472	4,892	4,325	4,395	3,996	3,884	48.1	48.9	47.2	44.1	44.9	40.2	41.6
For-profit institutions	29,643	30,635	37,823	37,758	27,935	22,879	18,836	12,822	12,829	15,510	13,538	10,993	9,314	7,108	43.3	41.9	41.0	35.9	39.4	40.7	37.7
4-year institutions	82,367	96,353	72,046	69,397	57,810	53,825	49,367	38,257	45,400	32,344	29,023	25,142	23,701	22,328	46.4	47.1	44.9	41.8	43.5	44.0	45.2
Public institutions	48,353	63,869	33,327	29,934	28,281	27,517	26,540	23,631	31,962	16,944	15,354	14,044	13,803	13,921	48.9	50.0	50.8	51.3	49.7	50.2	52.5
Open admissions	20,223	38,361	8,356	6,303	5,971	5,553	5,243	8,298	18,048	3,586	2,616	2,249	1,991	2,093	41.0	47.0	42.9	41.5	37.7	35.9	39.9
90 percent or more accepted	3,745	4,199	4,004	4,974	2,294	2,223	2,098	1,909	2,023	1,959	2,796	1,008	1,005	1,061	51.0	48.2	48.9	56.2	43.9	45.2	50.6
75.0 to 89.9 percent accepted	8,969	7,192	6,493	5,650	6,003	5,226	7,386	4,196	3,572	3,268	2,856	3,109	2,595	3,946	46.8	49.7	50.3	50.5	51.8	49.7	53.4
50.0 to 74.9 percent accepted	11,599	10,805	11,254	10,650	10,785	10,671	9,154	6,766	6,189	6,053	5,690	5,798	5,840	5,149	58.3	57.3	53.8	53.4	53.8	54.7	56.2
25.0 to 49.9 percent accepted	3,373	3,062	3,046	2,262	2,947	2,854	2,553	2,223	1,989	1,982	1,330	1,739	1,774	1,617	65.9	65.0	65.1	58.8	59.0	62.2	63.3
Less than 25.0 percent accepted	65	57	44	43	41	49	51	50	43	35	35	27	38	33	76.9	75.4	79.5	81.4	65.9	77.6	64.7
Information not available	379	193	130	52	240	941	55	189	98	61	31	114	560	22	49.9	50.8	46.9	59.6	47.5	59.5	40.0

See notes at end of table.

Table 326.30. Retention of first-time degree-seeking undergraduates at degree-granting postsecondary institutions, by attendance status, level and control of institution, and percentage of applications accepted: Selected years, 2006 to 2014—Continued

Attendance status, level, control, and percent of applications accepted	First-time degree-seekers (adjusted entry cohort),[1] by entry year							Students from adjusted cohort returning in the following year							Percent of first-time undergraduates retained						
	2006	2008	2009	2010	2011	2012	2013	2007	2009	2010	2011	2012	2013	2014	2006 to 2007	2008 to 2009	2009 to 2010	2010 to 2011	2011 to 2012	2012 to 2013	2013 to 2014
1	2	3	4	5	6	7	8	9	10	11	12	13	14	15	16	17	18	19	20	21	22
Nonprofit institutions	12,828	9,869	9,599	9,046	8,833	9,195	8,502	6,045	4,767	4,491	3,951	3,881	3,628	3,449	47.1	48.3	46.8	43.7	43.9	39.5	40.6
Open admissions	5,446	3,566	3,821	3,896	4,226	4,433	2,434	2,579	1,639	1,693	1,575	1,634	1,400	848	47.4	46.0	44.3	40.4	38.7	31.6	34.8
90 percent or more accepted	523	321	393	474	843	915	1,159	237	122	199	175	358	377	468	45.3	38.0	50.6	36.9	42.5	41.2	40.4
75.0 to 89.9 percent accepted	2,459	1,873	1,164	975	1,278	1,177	1,332	1,047	1,033	550	462	683	521	622	42.6	55.2	47.3	47.4	53.4	44.3	46.7
50.0 to 74.9 percent accepted	3,131	3,123	3,256	2,924	1,869	1,829	1,516	1,406	1,423	1,531	1,330	844	865	702	44.9	45.6	47.0	45.5	45.2	47.3	46.3
25.0 to 49.9 percent accepted	853	766	715	647	466	584	606	452	398	366	319	240	278	305	53.0	52.0	51.2	49.3	51.5	47.6	50.3
Less than 25.0 percent accepted	112	77	93	84	116	126	115	86	70	78	67	104	106	101	76.8	90.9	83.9	79.8	89.7	84.1	87.8
Information not available	304	143	157	46	35	131	1,340	238	82	74	23	18	81	403	78.3	57.3	47.1	50.0	51.4	61.8	30.1
For-profit institutions	21,186	22,615	29,120	30,417	20,696	17,113	14,325	8,581	8,671	10,909	9,718	7,217	6,270	4,958	40.5	38.3	37.5	31.9	34.9	36.6	34.6
Open admissions	10,515	11,179	10,926	13,567	10,634	9,561	10,395	4,105	4,164	4,299	4,875	4,253	3,909	3,751	39.0	37.2	39.3	35.9	40.0	40.9	36.1
90 percent or more accepted	2,212	1,623	1,372	2,159	2,234	360	121	639	548	375	504	637	137	59	28.9	33.8	27.3	23.3	28.5	38.1	48.8
75.0 to 89.9 percent accepted	2,838	3,026	3,151	2,407	4,145	854	1,232	1,342	1,218	1,093	527	1,106	250	353	47.3	40.3	34.7	21.9	26.7	29.3	28.7
50.0 to 74.9 percent accepted	2,774	4,886	4,591	6,237	524	1,819	2,471	1,134	2,049	2,249	1,996	220	594	755	40.9	41.9	49.0	32.0	42.0	32.7	30.6
25.0 to 49.9 percent accepted	2,033	1,675	1,099	1,826	2,932	2,537	73	627	629	342	583	936	727	25	30.8	37.6	31.1	31.9	31.9	28.7	34.2
Less than 25.0 percent accepted	0	0	0	0	0	0	0	0	0	0	0	0	0	0	†	†	†	†	†	†	†
Information not available	814	226	7,981	4,221	227	1,982	33	734	63	2,551	1,233	65	653	15	90.2	27.9	32.0	29.2	28.6	32.9	45.5
2-year institutions	380,867	422,281	473,589	478,781	474,207	462,200	440,655	153,329	165,537	197,222	199,306	199,259	198,719	191,169	40.3	39.2	41.6	41.6	42.0	43.0	43.4
Public institutions	370,653	412,931	464,126	470,681	466,013	455,694	435,305	148,115	160,674	192,220	195,112	194,969	195,307	188,584	40.0	38.9	41.4	41.5	41.8	42.9	43.3
Public institutions	1,757	1,330	760	759	955	740	839	973	705	401	374	514	368	435	55.4	53.0	52.8	49.3	53.8	49.7	51.8
Nonprofit institutions	8,457	8,020	8,703	7,341	7,239	5,766	4,511	4,241	4,158	4,601	3,820	3,776	3,044	2,150	50.1	51.8	52.9	52.0	52.2	52.8	47.7

†Not applicable.

[1]Adjusted student counts exclude students who died or were totally and permanently disabled, served in the armed forces (including those called to active duty), served with a foreign aid service of the federal government (e.g., Peace Corps), or served on official church missions.

NOTE: Returning students data for 2-year institutions include returning students, plus students who completed their program

SOURCE: U.S. Department of Education, National Center for Education Statistics, Integrated Postsecondary Education Data System (IPEDS), Spring 2008 through Spring 2015, Fall Enrollment component; and IPEDS Fall 2006 through Fall 2013, Institutional Characteristics component. (This table was prepared December 2015.)

Table 326.40. Percentage distribution of first-time postsecondary students starting at 2- and 4-year institutions during the 2003–04 academic year, by highest degree attained, enrollment status, and selected characteristics: Spring 2009

[Standard errors appear in parentheses]

Selected characteristic	Students starting at 2-year institutions: Highest degree attained: Total, any degree[1]	Certificate	Associate's	Bachelor's[2]	No degree, still enrolled	No degree, not enrolled	Students starting at 4-year institutions: Highest degree attained: Total, any degree[1]	Certificate	Associate's	Bachelor's[2]	No degree, still enrolled	No degree, not enrolled
1	2	3	4	5	6	7	8	9	10	11	12	13
Total	**35.1 (0.86)**	**9.5 (0.68)**	**15.0 (0.63)**	**10.6 (0.63)**	**18.5 (0.98)**	**46.4 (1.01)**	**64.2 (1.18)**	**1.7 (0.24)**	**4.6 (0.49)**	**58.0 (1.34)**	**12.2 (0.60)**	**23.6 (0.97)**
Sex												
Male	33.3 (1.54)	9.4 (1.19)	13.7 (1.00)	10.3 (0.79)	19.1 (1.64)	47.6 (1.54)	61.4 (1.40)	1.2 (0.29)	5.1 (0.72)	55.1 (1.54)	13.9 (0.86)	24.8 (1.18)
Female	36.5 (1.18)	9.6 (0.90)	16.0 (0.92)	10.9 (0.83)	18.1 (0.93)	45.4 (1.37)	66.5 (1.45)	2.1 (0.34)	4.2 (0.51)	60.2 (1.58)	10.9 (0.71)	22.6 (1.24)
Age when first enrolled												
18 years old or younger	39.4 (1.63)	6.1 (0.78)	15.5 (1.24)	17.9 (1.36)	20.6 (1.70)	40.0 (1.58)	69.1 (1.27)	1.6 (0.29)	3.7 (0.45)	63.8 (1.41)	11.2 (0.76)	19.8 (1.07)
19 years old	37.7 (2.04)	8.9 (2.01)	16.2 (1.46)	12.6 (1.21)	17.7 (1.57)	44.6 (1.75)	65.1 (1.43)	1.0 (0.24)	4.2 (0.63)	59.9 (1.51)	12.3 (0.92)	22.6 (1.16)
20 to 23 years old	29.1 (1.94)	10.3 (1.38)	14.6 (1.68)	4.1 (0.69)	21.9 (1.92)	49.0 (2.10)	41.9 (3.78)	4.1 ! (1.62)	8.4 (1.74)	29.4 (3.71)	17.8 (2.91)	40.3 (3.49)
24 to 29 years old	28.8 (4.04)	15.6 (3.98)	10.8 (1.98)	2.5 (0.74)	17.2 (2.62)	53.9 (4.05)	32.7 (5.77)	‡ (†)	9.4 ! (4.28)	20.4 (5.06)	18.8 (4.87)	48.6 (5.81)
30 years old or over	31.7 (2.43)	14.4 (2.08)	15.0 (1.89)	‡ (†)	10.4 (1.97)	57.9 (2.65)	33.7 (7.09)	3.9 ! (1.84)	13.4 ! (5.05)	16.4 ! (6.14)	14.8 (3.97)	51.4 (7.32)
Race/ethnicity												
White	38.9 (1.16)	9.8 (1.00)	16.6 (0.82)	12.5 (0.85)	16.2 (1.21)	44.9 (1.31)	68.9 (1.04)	1.5 (0.31)	4.8 (0.54)	62.6 (1.31)	9.8 (0.58)	21.4 (0.94)
Black	28.1 (2.60)	11.3 (1.66)	11.4 (2.12)	5.3 (1.10)	22.0 (2.04)	50.0 (2.79)	46.9 (3.16)	2.2 ! (0.91)	4.2 ! (1.48)	40.5 (3.03)	19.6 (2.21)	33.6 (3.08)
Hispanic	28.3 (2.18)	8.2 (1.67)	12.7 (1.51)	7.4 (1.10)	18.8 (2.03)	52.9 (2.58)	48.8 (3.24)	2.2 ! (0.83)	5.1 (1.39)	41.5 (2.96)	18.6 (2.36)	32.5 (3.34)
Asian/Pacific Islander	38.3 (4.50)	6.5 ! (2.29)	14.6 (2.91)	17.2 (3.50)	29.0 (4.58)	32.7 (3.51)	72.8 (3.21)	1.4 ! (0.67)	2.1 ! (0.94)	69.3 (3.22)	11.9 (2.23)	15.2 (2.59)
American Indian/Alaska Native	32.1 (9.62)	‡ (†)	‡ (†)	‡ (†)	28.4 ! (10.89)	39.6 (10.68)	51.5 (9.53)	‡ (†)	‡ (†)	39.3 (9.11)	19.3 ! (8.63)	29.3 ! (10.85)
Two or more races	33.9 (5.51)	9.0 ! (3.65)	14.6 ! (4.39)	10.3 (2.87)	21.4 (4.98)	44.7 (5.50)	57.1 (5.42)	‡ (†)	4.0 ! (1.83)	50.4 (5.57)	19.2 (4.71)	23.6 (4.32)
Highest education level of parents												
High school diploma or less	32.0 (1.42)	11.0 (1.30)	14.3 (1.05)	6.7 (0.72)	17.1 (1.18)	50.9 (1.51)	49.9 (2.12)	2.9 (0.83)	6.6 (0.97)	40.4 (2.01)	15.4 (1.33)	34.7 (1.98)
Some college/vocational	38.3 (2.24)	9.6 (1.48)	17.6 (1.17)	11.1 (1.07)	18.0 (1.70)	43.8 (2.06)	59.1 (1.90)	2.3 ! (0.76)	7.0 (1.08)	49.8 (2.11)	13.4 (1.24)	27.5 (1.84)
Bachelor's degree	39.4 (1.91)	8.2 (1.60)	14.1 (1.87)	17.2 (1.74)	20.6 (2.09)	40.0 (2.53)	70.1 (1.60)	1.2 (0.28)	3.4 (0.58)	65.6 (1.62)	11.0 (0.87)	18.9 (1.41)
Advanced (higher than bachelor's) degree	37.2 (3.03)	6.2 (1.70)	13.7 (1.81)	17.2 (2.09)	22.4 (2.56)	40.4 (3.74)	75.8 (1.44)	0.6 ! (0.24)	2.1 (0.39)	73.1 (1.51)	9.2 (0.78)	15.0 (1.35)
Dependency status when first enrolled												
Dependent	39.4 (1.26)	7.5 (0.76)	16.7 (0.85)	15.2 (0.88)	19.6 (1.19)	41.0 (1.15)	68.3 (1.06)	1.4 (0.22)	4.2 (0.45)	62.7 (1.22)	11.6 (0.63)	20.1 (0.90)
Independent	28.3 (1.44)	12.8 (1.26)	12.3 (1.13)	3.3 (0.60)	16.8 (1.42)	54.9 (1.75)	31.4 (3.08)	3.7 (1.10)	7.5 (1.92)	20.2 (2.84)	17.3 (2.61)	51.3 (3.25)
Dependent student family income in 2002												
Less than $25,000	34.6 (2.35)	8.4 (1.48)	14.5 (1.54)	11.7 (1.73)	18.0 (1.91)	47.4 (2.43)	52.7 (2.28)	2.8 ! (1.09)	5.0 (1.00)	44.9 (2.40)	15.9 (1.63)	31.4 (2.38)
$25,000 to $44,999	36.0 (2.12)	7.3 (1.36)	16.4 (1.75)	12.3 (1.60)	19.0 (2.24)	45.0 (2.67)	62.7 (2.31)	1.9 (0.53)	5.4 (1.03)	55.3 (2.50)	13.1 (1.69)	24.2 (1.97)
$45,000 to $69,999	41.3 (2.13)	7.1 (1.29)	17.6 (1.59)	16.6 (1.58)	22.0 (1.92)	36.7 (1.86)	67.1 (1.94)	1.5 (0.34)	5.1 (0.77)	60.6 (2.00)	12.8 (1.27)	20.1 (1.86)
$70,000 to $99,999	43.1 (3.50)	7.6 ! (3.67)	16.3 (2.58)	19.1 (2.14)	18.4 (2.75)	38.5 (2.76)	71.9 (1.64)	0.9 ! (0.30)	4.4 (0.88)	66.7 (1.85)	9.4 (0.83)	18.7 (1.37)
$100,000 or more	45.0 (3.56)	6.6 (1.77)	19.6 (3.74)	18.8 (2.40)	20.5 (3.25)	34.4 (3.61)	80.0 (1.30)	0.7 ! (0.29)	1.9 (0.37)	77.5 (1.38)	8.5 (0.94)	11.4 (0.99)
Timing of postsecondary enrollment												
Delayed entry	29.1 (1.25)	11.0 (1.11)	13.2 (1.02)	4.9 (0.63)	17.2 (1.26)	53.7 (1.44)	36.6 (2.80)	3.8 (1.01)	7.9 (1.54)	24.9 (2.53)	17.8 (2.06)	45.6 (2.75)
Did not delay entry[3]	41.0 (1.36)	7.8 (0.86)	17.0 (0.99)	16.2 (1.00)	20.1 (1.44)	38.8 (1.16)	69.2 (1.05)	1.3 (0.21)	4.0 (0.40)	64.0 (1.17)	11.1 (0.61)	19.6 (0.91)
Intensity of enrollment through 2009												
Always full-time	44.9 (1.66)	11.4 (1.50)	18.0 (1.42)	15.5 (1.11)	10.1 (0.87)	44.9 (1.65)	73.7 (1.15)	1.2 (0.26)	3.8 (0.55)	68.7 (1.41)	6.7 (0.46)	19.6 (1.03)
Always part-time	13.9 (2.80)	8.4 ! (2.79)	5.5 (1.12)	‡ (†)	13.3 (1.79)	72.8 (2.68)	12.5 ! (4.93)	‡ (†)	‡ (†)	‡ (†)	13.8 ! (4.23)	73.6 (6.59)
Mixed	36.6 (1.32)	8.7 (0.83)	16.6 (1.10)	11.4 (0.99)	26.1 (1.34)	37.2 (1.69)	48.3 (1.59)	2.7 (0.47)	6.1 (0.72)	39.5 (1.60)	23.3 (1.39)	28.4 (1.42)
Remedial course taken in 2003–04												
No	35.4 (0.95)	10.0 (0.84)	14.5 (0.81)	10.9 (0.78)	17.6 (0.99)	47.0 (1.21)	65.2 (1.23)	1.8 (0.28)	4.4 (0.53)	59.0 (1.43)	11.5 (0.62)	23.4 (1.05)
Yes	34.3 (2.10)	8.3 (1.62)	16.2 (1.37)	9.8 (0.98)	21.0 (1.70)	44.7 (1.92)	59.6 (1.98)	1.2 (0.32)	5.4 (0.92)	53.0 (2.13)	15.7 (1.44)	24.6 (1.81)

See notes at end of table.

Table 326.40. Percentage distribution of first-time postsecondary students starting at 2- and 4-year institutions during the 2003–04 academic year, by highest degree attained, enrollment status, and selected characteristics: Spring 2009—Continued

[Standard errors appear in parentheses]

Selected characteristic	Students starting at 2-year institutions						Students starting at 4-year institutions					
	Highest degree attained						Highest degree attained					
	Total, any degree[1]	Certificate	Associate's	Bachelor's[2]	No degree, still enrolled	No degree, not enrolled	Total, any degree[1]	Certificate	Associate's	Bachelor's[2]	No degree, still enrolled	No degree, not enrolled
1	2	3	4	5	6	7	8	9	10	11	12	13
Highest degree expected in 2003–04												
No degree or certificate	‡ (†)	‡ (†)	‡ (†)	# (†)	‡ (†)	87.3 (4.75)	‡ (†)	‡ (†)	‡ (†)	‡ (†)	‡ (†)	‡ (†)
Certificate	44.8 (5.47)	42.8 (5.28)	‡ (†)	‡ (†)	6.9 (2.02)	48.3 (5.60)	41.2 ! (18.43)	‡ (†)	‡ (†)	‡ (†)	‡ (†)	‡ (†)
Associate's degree	34.6 (2.38)	13.9 (2.05)	19.3 (1.86)	1.4 ! (0.49)	12.3 (1.69)	53.1 (2.80)	43.7 (8.43)	16.2 ! (5.50)	21.3 ! (7.06)	6.1 ! (2.93)	12.8 ! (5.09)	43.5 (7.70)
Bachelor's degree[4]	32.7 (1.81)	8.0 (1.49)	15.4 (1.02)	9.3 (1.03)	18.1 (1.50)	49.3 (1.60)	55.2 (2.02)	2.2 (0.52)	6.8 (1.02)	46.2 (2.07)	15.1 (1.37)	29.7 (1.59)
Master's degree[4]	38.2 (1.72)	7.0 (1.32)	14.8 (1.21)	16.4 (1.19)	22.7 (1.63)	39.1 (1.66)	66.7 (1.42)	1.0 (0.25)	4.1 (0.62)	61.7 (1.42)	11.2 (0.77)	22.1 (1.32)
Doctoral/first-professional degree[4]	34.7 (2.30)	4.8 (0.93)	13.8 (2.02)	16.0 (1.65)	22.4 (2.54)	42.9 (3.25)	70.6 (1.57)	1.3 (0.36)	1.9 (0.36)	67.4 (1.69)	11.0 (0.95)	18.3 (1.35)
Work intensity (including work-study) in 2003–04												
Did not work	34.7 (1.79)	11.2 (1.57)	15.8 (1.20)	7.7 (0.85)	19.9 (1.80)	45.3 (2.16)	69.9 (1.35)	0.8 (0.18)	3.4 (0.55)	65.8 (1.47)	10.9 (0.92)	19.1 (1.08)
Worked part time	39.9 (2.08)	7.9 (1.20)	17.4 (1.00)	14.6 (1.04)	17.2 (1.28)	42.8 (1.70)	66.2 (1.42)	1.7 (0.31)	5.2 (0.69)	59.3 (1.44)	12.1 (0.85)	21.7 (1.21)
Worked full time	28.6 (1.96)	10.6 (1.63)	10.9 (1.08)	7.2 (0.94)	19.3 (1.53)	52.1 (2.10)	40.1 (2.93)	4.1 (1.22)	5.9 (1.20)	30.1 (2.60)	16.5 (1.77)	43.4 (2.86)
Control of first institution												
Public	34.4 (0.95)	8.5 (0.68)	14.4 (0.61)	11.6 (0.68)	19.6 (1.03)	46.0 (1.00)	64.8 (1.22)	1.6 (0.23)	3.8 (0.45)	59.5 (1.32)	12.9 (0.73)	22.2 (0.98)
Private, nonprofit	46.2 (8.52)	13.3 ! (6.56)	21.5 ! (6.76)	11.3 ! (4.99)	10.4 ! (3.32)	43.4 (8.28)	69.9 (1.45)	1.5 (0.37)	3.8 (0.95)	64.6 (1.89)	11.1 (1.02)	19.0 (1.18)
Private, for profit	39.5 (3.70)	19.6 (4.78)	19.5 (3.51)	‡ (†)	9.6 (2.61)	50.9 (4.64)	33.9 (4.37)	‡ (†)	14.6 (3.45)	15.7 (3.78)	11.3 (2.44)	54.8 (3.82)
Income quartile in 2003–04[5]												
Lowest quartile	30.6 (1.45)	9.4 (1.27)	13.0 (1.14)	8.3 (0.84)	18.4 (1.46)	51.0 (1.78)	49.5 (1.91)	2.7 (0.73)	4.6 (0.74)	42.2 (2.15)	16.2 (1.37)	34.3 (1.75)
Second quartile	37.1 (1.58)	10.5 (1.56)	15.8 (1.26)	10.8 (0.97)	19.7 (1.58)	43.2 (1.86)	60.5 (2.04)	2.4 (0.51)	6.5 (1.10)	51.6 (2.20)	13.5 (1.16)	26.0 (1.82)
Third quartile	36.3 (2.51)	9.6 (1.71)	15.0 (1.35)	11.6 (1.53)	18.7 (1.64)	45.0 (2.18)	67.2 (1.58)	1.3 (0.31)	4.9 (0.80)	61.0 (1.85)	11.2 (0.88)	21.6 (1.55)
Highest quartile	38.6 (2.51)	8.1 (1.49)	17.3 (1.96)	13.2 (1.65)	16.5 (2.30)	45.0 (3.20)	76.8 (1.37)	0.6 ! (0.25)	2.4 (0.46)	73.8 (1.42)	8.7 (0.80)	14.4 (1.18)

†Not applicable.
#Rounds to zero.
!Interpret data with caution. The coefficient of variation (CV) for this estimate is between 30 and 50 percent.
‡Reporting standards not met. Either there are too few cases for a reliable estimate or the coefficient of variation (CV) is 50 percent or greater.
[1]Includes a small percentage of students who had attained a degree and were still enrolled. Includes recipients of degrees not shown separately.
[2]Includes a small percentage of students who had attained an advanced degree.
[3]Includes students with a standard high school diploma who enrolled in postsecondary education in the same year as their graduation.
[4]Students starting at 2-year institutions include students whose goal was to transfer to a 4-year institution.
[5]Indicates the income quartile of the student, based on the student's total income in 2002 for independent students or the parents' total income in 2002 for dependent students. Income quartiles were determined separately for dependent and independent students based on percentile rankings and then combined into one variable.
NOTE: Race categories exclude persons of Hispanic ethnicity. Detail may not sum to totals because of rounding.
SOURCE: U.S. Department of Education, National Center for Education Statistics, 2004/09 Beginning Postsecondary Students Longitudinal Study (BPS:04/09). (This table was prepared November 2011.)

Table 318.10. Degrees conferred by postsecondary institutions, by level of degree and sex of student: Selected years, 1869–70 through 2025–26

Year	Associate's degrees				Bachelor's degrees				Master's degrees				Doctor's degrees[1]			
	Total	Males	Females	Percent female	Total	Males	Females	Percent female	Total	Males	Females	Percent female	Total	Males	Females	Percent female
1	2	3	4	5	6	7	8	9	10	11	12	13	14	15	16	17
1869–70	—	—	—	—	9,371[2]	7,993[2]	1,378[2]	14.7	0	0	0	—	1	1	0	0.0
1879–80	—	—	—	—	12,896[2]	10,411[2]	2,485[2]	19.3	879	868	11	1.3	54	51	3	5.6
1889–90	—	—	—	—	15,539[2]	12,857[2]	2,682[2]	17.3	1,015	821	194	19.1	149	147	2	1.3
1899–1900	—	—	—	—	27,410[2]	22,173[2]	5,237[2]	19.1	1,583	1,280	303	19.1	382	359	23	6.0
1909–10	—	—	—	—	37,199[2]	28,762[2]	8,437[2]	22.7	2,113	1,555	558	26.4	443	399	44	9.9
1919–20	—	—	—	—	48,622[2]	31,980[2]	16,642[2]	34.2	4,279	2,985	1,294	30.2	615	522	93	15.1
1929–30	—	—	—	—	122,484[2]	73,615[2]	48,869[2]	39.9	14,969	8,925	6,044	40.4	2,299	1,946	353	15.4
1939–40	—	—	—	—	186,500[2]	109,546[2]	76,954[2]	41.3	26,731	16,508	10,223	38.2	3,290	2,861	429	13.0
1949–50	—	—	—	—	432,058[2]	328,841[2]	103,217[2]	23.9	58,183	41,220	16,963	29.2	6,420	5,804	616	9.6
1959–60	—	—	—	—	392,440[2]	254,063[2]	138,377[2]	35.3	74,435	50,898	23,537	31.6	9,829	8,801	1,028	10.5
1969–70	206,023	117,432	88,591	43.0	792,316	451,097	341,219	43.1	213,589	130,799	82,790	38.8	59,486	53,792	5,694	9.6
1970–71	252,311	144,144	108,167	42.9	839,730	475,594	364,136	43.4	235,564	143,083	92,481	39.3	64,998	58,137	6,861	10.6
1971–72	292,014	166,227	125,787	43.1	887,273	500,590	386,683	43.6	257,201	155,010	102,191	39.7	71,206	63,353	7,853	11.0
1972–73	316,174	175,413	140,761	44.5	922,362	518,191	404,171	43.8	268,654	159,569	109,085	40.6	79,512	69,959	9,553	12.0
1973–74	343,924	188,591	155,333	45.2	945,776	527,313	418,463	44.2	282,074	162,606	119,468	42.4	82,591	71,131	11,460	13.9
1974–75	360,171	191,017	169,154	47.0	922,933	504,841	418,092	45.3	297,545	166,318	131,227	44.1	84,904	71,025	13,879	16.3
1975–76	391,454	209,996	181,458	46.4	925,746	504,925	420,821	45.5	317,477	172,519	144,958	45.7	91,007	73,888	17,119	18.8
1976–77	406,377	210,842	195,535	48.1	919,549	495,545	424,004	46.1	323,025	173,090	149,935	46.4	91,730	72,209	19,521	21.3
1977–78	412,246	204,718	207,528	50.3	921,204	487,347	433,857	47.1	317,987	166,857	151,130	47.5	92,345	70,283	22,062	23.9
1978–79	402,702	192,091	210,611	52.3	921,390	477,344	444,046	48.2	307,686	159,111	148,575	48.3	94,971	70,452	24,519	25.8
1979–80	400,910	183,737	217,173	54.2	929,417	473,611	455,806	49.0	305,196	156,882	148,314	48.6	95,631	69,526	26,105	27.3
1980–81	416,377	188,638	227,739	54.7	935,140	469,883	465,257	49.8	302,637	152,979	149,658	49.5	98,016	69,567	28,449	29.0
1981–82	434,526	196,944	237,582	54.7	952,998	473,364	479,634	50.3	302,447	151,349	151,098	50.0	97,838	68,630	29,208	29.9
1982–83	449,620	203,991	245,629	54.6	969,510	479,140	490,370	50.6	296,415	150,092	146,323	49.4	99,335	67,757	31,578	31.8
1983–84	452,240	202,704	249,536	55.2	974,309	482,319	491,990	50.5	291,141	149,268	141,873	48.7	100,799	67,769	33,030	32.8
1984–85	454,712	202,932	251,780	55.4	979,477	482,528	496,949	50.7	293,472	149,276	144,196	49.1	100,785	66,269	34,516	34.2
1985–86	446,047	196,166	249,881	56.0	987,823	485,923	501,900	50.8	295,850	149,373	146,477	49.5	100,280	65,215	35,065	35.0
1986–87	436,304	190,839	245,465	56.3	991,264	480,782	510,482	51.5	296,530	147,063	149,467	50.4	98,477	62,790	35,687	36.2
1987–88	435,085	190,047	245,038	56.3	994,829	477,203	517,626	52.0	305,783	150,243	155,540	50.9	99,139	63,019	36,120	36.4
1988–89	436,764	186,316	250,448	57.3	1,018,755	483,346	535,409	52.6	316,626	153,993	162,633	51.4	100,571	63,055	37,516	37.3
1989–90	455,102	191,195	263,907	58.0	1,051,344	491,696	559,648	53.2	330,152	158,052	172,100	52.1	103,508	63,963	39,545	38.2
1990–91	481,720	198,634	283,086	58.8	1,094,538	504,045	590,493	53.9	342,863	160,842	182,021	53.1	105,547	64,242	41,305	39.1
1991–92	504,231	207,481	296,750	58.9	1,136,553	520,811	615,742	54.2	358,089	165,867	192,222	53.7	109,554	66,603	42,951	39.2
1992–93	514,756	211,964	302,792	58.8	1,165,178	532,881	632,297	54.3	375,032	173,354	201,678	53.8	112,072	67,130	44,942	40.1
1993–94	530,632	215,261	315,371	59.4	1,169,275	532,422	636,853	54.5	393,037	180,571	212,466	54.1	112,636	66,773	45,863	40.7
1994–95	539,691	218,352	321,339	59.5	1,160,134	526,131	634,003	54.6	403,609	183,043	220,566	54.6	114,266	67,324	46,942	41.1
1995–96	555,216	219,514	335,702	60.5	1,164,792	522,454	642,338	55.1	412,180	183,481	228,699	55.5	115,507	67,189	48,318	41.8
1996–97	571,226	223,948	347,278	60.8	1,172,879	520,515	652,364	55.6	425,260	185,270	239,990	56.4	118,747	68,387	50,360	42.4
1997–98	558,555	217,613	340,942	61.0	1,184,406	519,956	664,450	56.1	436,037	188,718	247,319	56.7	118,735	67,232	51,503	43.4
1998–99	564,984	220,508	344,476	61.0	1,202,239	519,961	682,278	56.8	446,038	190,230	255,808	57.4	116,700	65,340	51,360	44.0
1999–2000	564,933	224,721	340,212	60.2	1,237,875	530,367	707,508	57.2	463,185	196,129	267,056	57.7	118,736	64,930	53,806	45.3
2000–01	578,865	231,645	347,220	60.0	1,244,171	531,840	712,331	57.3	473,502	197,770	275,732	58.2	119,585	64,171	55,414	46.3
2001–02	595,133	238,109	357,024	60.0	1,291,900	549,816	742,084	57.4	487,313	202,604	284,709	58.4	119,663	62,731	56,932	47.6
2002–03	634,016	253,451	380,565	60.0	1,348,811	573,258	775,553	57.5	518,699	215,172	303,527	58.5	121,579	62,730	58,849	48.4
2003–04	665,301	260,033	405,268	60.9	1,399,542	595,425	804,117	57.5	564,272	233,056	331,216	58.7	126,087	63,981	62,106	49.3
2004–05	696,660	267,536	429,124	61.6	1,439,264	613,000	826,264	57.4	580,151	237,155	342,996	59.1	134,387	67,257	67,130	50.0
2005–06	713,066	270,095	442,971	62.1	1,485,242	630,600	854,642	57.5	599,731	241,656	358,075	59.7	138,056	68,912	69,144	50.1
2006–07	728,114	275,187	452,927	62.2	1,524,092	649,570	874,522	57.4	610,597	242,189	368,408	60.3	144,690	71,308	73,382	50.7
2007–08	750,164	282,521	467,643	62.3	1,563,069	667,928	895,141	57.3	630,666	250,169	380,497	60.3	149,378	73,453	75,925	50.8
2008–09	787,243	298,066	489,177	62.1	1,601,399	685,422	915,977	57.2	662,082	263,515	398,567	60.2	154,564	75,674	78,890	51.0
2009–10	848,856	322,747	526,109	62.0	1,649,919	706,660	943,259	57.2	693,313	275,317	417,996	60.3	158,590	76,610	81,980	51.7
2010–11	943,506	361,408	582,098	61.7	1,716,053	734,159	981,894	57.2	730,922	291,680	439,242	60.1	163,827	79,672	84,155	51.4
2011–12	1,021,718	393,479	628,239	61.5	1,792,163	765,772	1,026,391	57.3	755,967	302,484	453,483	60.0	170,217	82,670	87,547	51.4
2012–13	1,007,427	389,195	618,232	61.4	1,840,381	787,408	1,052,973	57.2	751,718	301,552	450,166	59.9	175,026	85,080	89,946	51.4
2013–14	1,003,364	390,805	612,559	61.1	1,869,814	801,692	1,068,122	57.1	754,475	302,807	451,668	59.9	177,580	85,587	91,993	51.8
2014–15[3]	979,000	379,000	600,000	61.3	1,868,000	802,000	1,066,000	57.1	763,000	308,000	454,000	59.6	178,000	85,000	92,000	51.9
2015–16[3]	999,000	389,000	610,000	61.0	1,853,000	794,000	1,058,000	57.1	773,000	319,000	454,000	58.7	179,000	86,000	93,000	52.1
2016–17[3]	1,018,000	385,000	633,000	62.1	1,863,000	796,000	1,067,000	57.3	798,000	333,000	465,000	58.3	181,000	86,000	94,000	52.2
2017–18[3]	1,074,000	401,000	673,000	62.7	1,830,000	780,000	1,050,000	57.4	823,000	342,000	481,000	58.5	183,000	89,000	95,000	51.7
2018–19[3]	1,104,000	407,000	697,000	63.1	1,854,000	785,000	1,069,000	57.6	846,000	352,000	494,000	58.4	188,000	91,000	97,000	51.7
2019–20[3]	1,135,000	414,000	721,000	63.5	1,888,000	795,000	1,093,000	57.9	867,000	362,000	505,000	58.3	192,000	92,000	100,000	52.0
2020–21[3]	1,162,000	420,000	742,000	63.8	1,920,000	807,000	1,113,000	58.0	887,000	370,000	517,000	58.3	195,000	94,000	102,000	52.0
2021–22[3]	1,188,000	427,000	761,000	64.1	1,947,000	817,000	1,130,000	58.0	908,000	378,000	529,000	58.3	199,000	95,000	103,000	52.1
2022–23[3]	1,213,000	432,000	780,000	64.3	1,968,000	825,000	1,144,000	58.1	929,000	387,000	542,000	58.3	201,000	96,000	105,000	52.2
2023–24[3]	1,240,000	439,000	801,000	64.6	1,993,000	834,000	1,159,000	58.2	950,000	396,000	554,000	58.3	204,000	97,000	107,000	52.3
2024–25[3]	1,266,000	445,000	821,000	64.9	2,015,000	843,000	1,173,000	58.2	968,000	403,000	565,000	58.4	207,000	99,000	108,000	52.4
2025–26[3]	1,290,000	451,000	840,000	65.1	2,037,000	851,000	1,187,000	58.2	982,000	408,000	573,000	58.4	209,000	100,000	110,000	52.4

—Not available.

[1] Includes Ph.D., Ed.D., and comparable degrees at the doctoral level. Includes most degrees formerly classified as first-professional, such as M.D., D.D.S., and law degrees.

[2] Includes some degrees classified as master's or doctor's degrees in later years.

[3] Projected.

NOTE: Data through 1994–95 are for institutions of higher education, while later data are for degree-granting institutions. Degree-granting institutions grant associate's or higher degrees and participate in Title IV federal financial aid programs. Some data have been revised from previously published figures. Detail may not sum to totals because of rounding.

SOURCE: U.S. Department of Education, National Center for Education Statistics, *Earned Degrees Conferred*, 1869–70 through 1964–65; Higher Education General Information Survey (HEGIS), "Degrees and Other Formal Awards Conferred" surveys, 1965–66 through 1985–86; Integrated Postsecondary Education Data System (IPEDS), "Completions Survey" (IPEDS-C:87–99); IPEDS Fall 2000 through Fall 2014, Completions component; and Degrees Conferred Projection Model, 1980–81 through 2025–26. (This table was prepared March 2016.)

Table 318.30. Bachelor's, master's, and doctor's degrees conferred by postsecondary institutions, by sex of student and discipline division: 2013–14

Discipline division	Bachelor's degrees			Master's degrees			Doctor's degrees[1]		
	Total	Males	Females	Total	Males	Females	Total	Males	Females
1	2	3	4	5	6	7	8	9	10
All fields, total	**1,869,814**	**801,692**	**1,068,122**	**754,475**	**302,807**	**451,668**	**177,580**	**85,587**	**91,993**
Agriculture and natural resources	35,116	17,249	17,867	6,544	2,966	3,578	1,407	739	668
Agriculture, agriculture operations, and related sciences	18,036	8,437	9,599	2,704	1,201	1,503	823	426	397
Agriculture, general	1,854	975	879	282	105	177	16	8	8
Agricultural business and management, general	1,171	762	409	73	47	26	0	0	0
Agribusiness/agricultural business operations	1,533	999	534	18	7	11	0	0	0
Agricultural economics	1,555	1,113	442	420	234	186	153	89	64
Farm/farm and ranch management	130	89	41	12	8	4	0	0	0
Agricultural/farm supplies retailing and wholesaling	71	31	40	0	0	0	0	0	0
Agricultural business technology	17	10	7	0	0	0	0	0	0
Agricultural business and management, other	31	12	19	3	1	2	0	0	0
Agricultural mechanization, general	339	313	26	1	1	0	0	0	0
Agricultural mechanics and equipment/machine technology	5	5	0	0	0	0	0	0	0
Agricultural production operations, general	108	62	46	11	5	6	0	0	0
Animal/livestock husbandry and production	205	70	135	0	0	0	0	0	0
Aquaculture	53	38	15	32	17	15	12	8	4
Crop production	45	37	8	2	2	0	3	3	0
Dairy husbandry and production	6	1	5	0	0	0	0	0	0
Horse husbandry/equine science and management	123	5	118	5	0	5	0	0	0
Agroecology and sustainable agriculture	97	58	39	55	24	31	13	7	6
Viticulture and enology	98	52	46	10	4	6	0	0	0
Agricultural and food products processing	92	48	44	0	0	0	0	0	0
Equestrian/equine studies	334	11	323	0	0	0	0	0	0
Agricultural and domestic animal services, other	0	0	0	0	0	0	0	0	0
Applied horticulture/horticultural operations, general	174	104	70	33	13	20	4	0	4
Ornamental horticulture	49	35	14	8	5	3	2	2	0
Landscaping and groundskeeping	142	101	41	8	3	5	0	0	0
Plant nursery operations and management	1	1	0	0	0	0	0	0	0
Turf and turfgrass management	108	105	3	10	9	1	0	0	0
Floriculture/floristry operations and management	3	2	1	0	0	0	0	0	0
Applied horticulture/horticultural business services, other	19	16	3	0	0	0	0	0	0
International agriculture	35	15	20	50	18	32	0	0	0
Agricultural and extension education services	58	21	37	75	22	53	5	1	4
Agricultural communication/journalism	332	81	251	23	5	18	0	0	0
Agricultural public services, other	89	44	45	3	0	3	0	0	0
Animal sciences, general	5,108	1,034	4,074	382	139	243	152	68	84
Agricultural animal breeding	0	0	0	5	0	5	5	1	4
Animal health	2	2	0	2	1	1	0	0	0
Animal nutrition	0	0	0	0	0	0	2	1	1
Dairy science	142	63	79	10	3	7	2	1	1
Livestock management	15	7	8	1	0	1	2	1	1
Poultry science	79	39	40	15	8	7	9	4	5
Animal sciences, other	72	10	62	4	2	2	0	0	0
Food science	1,414	471	943	447	144	303	125	48	77
Food technology and processing	6	4	2	16	5	11	3	2	1
Food science and technology, other	2	0	2	12	4	8	2	0	2
Plant sciences, general	432	290	142	105	56	49	45	23	22
Agronomy and crop science	570	449	121	212	144	68	93	64	29
Horticultural science	600	363	237	90	36	54	39	21	18
Agricultural and horticultural plant breeding	2	1	1	11	5	6	12	10	2
Plant protection and integrated pest management	42	28	14	18	10	8	2	2	0
Range science and management	149	93	56	33	14	19	9	3	6
Plant sciences, other	37	25	12	54	27	27	31	14	17
Soil science and agronomy, general	211	144	67	107	56	51	65	37	28
Soil chemistry and physics	22	19	3	0	0	0	0	0	0
Soil sciences, other	28	16	12	13	7	6	6	4	2
Agriculture, agriculture operations, and related sciences, other	226	163	63	33	10	23	11	4	7
Natural resources and conservation	17,080	8,812	8,268	3,840	1,765	2,075	584	313	271
Natural resources/conservation, general	1,385	739	646	602	253	349	73	46	27
Environmental studies	5,925	2,679	3,246	893	410	483	79	37	42
Environmental science	5,542	2,697	2,845	1,017	438	579	169	88	81
Natural resources conservation and research, other	25	12	13	77	39	38	21	10	11
Natural resources management and policy	616	390	226	428	191	237	36	20	16
Natural resource economics	60	35	25	9	5	4	14	7	7
Water, wetlands, and marine resources management	90	60	30	146	50	96	2	1	1
Land use planning and management/development	56	41	15	51	21	30	10	2	8
Natural resource recreation and tourism	67	46	21	27	14	13	3	1	2
Natural resources law enforcement and protective services	33	29	4	0	0	0	0	0	0
Natural resources management and policy, other	189	96	93	11	4	7	1	0	1
Fishing and fisheries sciences and management	347	206	141	36	19	17	17	10	7
Forestry, general	600	466	134	140	83	57	28	18	10
Forest sciences and biology	218	175	43	126	81	45	58	31	27
Forest management/forest resources management	177	147	30	50	26	24	13	7	6
Urban forestry	9	3	6	8	4	4	0	0	0
Wood science and wood products/pulp and paper technology	46	40	6	13	11	2	6	6	0
Forest resources production and management	5	5	0	17	9	8	7	6	1
Forest technology/technician	5	5	0	0	0	0	0	0	0
Forestry, other	43	34	9	13	5	8	8	3	5
Wildlife, fish, and wildlands science and management	1,374	757	617	150	90	60	34	17	17
Natural resources and conservation, other	268	150	118	26	12	14	5	3	2
Architecture and related services	9,144	5,173	3,971	8,048	4,122	3,926	247	134	113
Architecture	5,952	3,444	2,508	4,285	2,436	1,849	119	63	56
City/urban, community and regional planning	827	502	325	2,222	1,030	1,192	90	44	46
Environmental design/architecture	595	339	256	125	54	71	21	12	9
Interior architecture	416	50	366	205	33	172	0	0	0
Landscape architecture	871	540	331	738	290	448	5	5	0
Architectural history and criticism, general	71	30	41	43	12	31	3	3	0
Architectural technology/technician	214	145	69	0	0	0	0	0	0
Architectural and building sciences/technology	62	50	12	85	53	32	5	4	1
Real estate development	0	0	0	232	174	58	0	0	0
Architecture and related services, other	136	73	63	113	40	73	4	3	1

See notes at end of table.

Table 318.30. Bachelor's, master's, and doctor's degrees conferred by postsecondary institutions, by sex of student and discipline division: 2013–14—Continued

Discipline division	Bachelor's degrees			Master's degrees			Doctor's degrees[1]		
	Total	Males	Females	Total	Males	Females	Total	Males	Females
1	2	3	4	5	6	7	8	9	10
Area, ethnic, cultural, gender, and group studies	8,275	2,466	5,809	1,824	623	1,201	336	130	206
African studies	87	26	61	36	12	24	8	2	6
American/United States studies/civilization	1,303	501	802	247	89	158	103	39	64
Asian studies/civilization	755	317	438	111	37	74	3	1	2
East Asian studies	428	180	248	172	58	114	18	10	8
Russian, Central European, East European and Eurasian studies	20	9	11	33	11	22	0	0	0
European studies/civilization	100	26	74	30	13	17	0	0	0
Latin American studies	384	140	244	218	78	140	5	1	4
Near and Middle Eastern studies	196	65	131	168	87	81	40	20	20
Pacific Area/Pacific Rim studies	18	10	8	7	3	4	0	0	0
Russian studies	81	39	42	48	23	25	0	0	0
Scandinavian studies	13	4	9	3	2	1	4	3	1
South Asian studies	26	8	18	17	10	7	5	2	3
Southeast Asian studies	2	1	1	20	7	13	0	0	0
Western European studies	5	1	4	35	11	24	0	0	0
Canadian studies	2	1	1	0	0	0	0	0	0
Slavic studies	4	0	4	1	1	0	1	0	1
Ural-Altaic and Central Asian studies	0	0	0	9	6	3	3	2	1
Regional studies (U.S., Canadian, foreign)	32	5	27	24	8	16	4	3	1
Chinese studies	47	19	28	14	7	7	0	0	0
French studies	54	10	44	18	8	10	15	8	7
German studies	81	30	51	12	3	9	6	3	3
Italian studies	34	12	22	12	6	6	1	0	1
Japanese studies	51	22	29	5	5	0	0	0	0
Korean studies	0	0	0	4	2	2	0	0	0
Spanish and Iberian studies	28	8	20	0	0	0	0	0	0
Irish studies	0	0	0	2	0	2	0	0	0
Latin American and Caribbean studies	46	14	32	21	6	15	0	0	0
Area studies, other	784	244	540	59	26	33	4	1	3
Ethnic studies	140	39	101	16	5	11	6	3	3
African-American/Black studies	639	205	434	75	23	52	25	10	15
American Indian/Native American studies	228	79	149	32	6	26	8	1	7
Hispanic-American, Puerto Rican, and Mexican-American/Chicano studies	456	125	331	30	17	13	15	8	7
Asian-American studies	120	49	71	11	2	9	0	0	0
Women's studies	1,357	94	1,263	184	13	171	22	1	21
Gay/lesbian studies	19	0	19	0	0	0	0	0	0
Folklore studies	17	6	11	26	9	17	13	6	7
Disability studies	5	1	4	41	12	29	2	1	1
Ethnic, cultural minority, gender, and group studies, other	713	176	537	83	17	66	25	5	20
Biological and biomedical sciences	104,633	43,427	61,206	13,960	6,072	7,888	8,302	3,884	4,418
Biology/biological sciences, general	69,402	27,668	41,734	3,465	1,453	2,012	1,053	488	565
Biomedical sciences, general	2,922	1,145	1,777	1,503	760	743	504	226	278
Biochemistry	7,312	3,785	3,527	280	136	144	530	257	273
Biophysics	142	101	41	28	18	10	139	88	51
Molecular biology	717	343	374	212	96	116	268	128	140
Molecular biochemistry	439	239	200	82	19	63	62	33	29
Molecular biophysics	0	0	0	3	2	1	17	11	6
Structural biology	0	0	0	2	2	0	6	4	2
Radiation biology/radiobiology	11	1	10	8	7	1	11	5	6
Biochemistry and molecular biology	800	449	351	97	54	43	182	103	79
Biochemistry, biophysics and molecular biology, other	198	99	99	5	5	0	23	17	6
Botany/plant biology	212	113	99	87	35	52	120	50	70
Plant pathology/phytopathology	13	4	9	74	31	43	85	39	46
Plant physiology	0	0	0	3	3	0	7	6	1
Plant molecular biology	0	0	0	0	0	0	13	10	3
Botany/plant biology, other	17	7	10	9	2	7	0	0	0
Cell/cellular biology and histology	415	205	210	46	20	26	149	56	93
Anatomy	365	145	220	142	73	69	43	28	15
Developmental biology and embryology	42	19	23	29	8	21	48	20	28
Cell/cellular and molecular biology	2,330	1,088	1,242	193	91	102	474	221	253
Cell biology and anatomy	5	1	4	10	5	5	46	22	24
Cell/cellular biology and anatomical sciences, other	127	56	71	105	43	62	137	50	87
Microbiology, general	1,752	850	902	183	77	106	207	90	117
Medical microbiology and bacteriology	603	284	319	155	60	95	127	50	77
Virology	0	0	0	0	0	0	20	13	7
Parasitology	0	0	0	1	0	1	0	0	0
Immunology	0	0	0	38	16	22	183	80	103
Microbiology and immunology	92	34	58	33	9	24	74	24	50
Microbiological sciences and immunology, other	125	46	79	55	16	39	63	28	35
Zoology/animal biology	1,633	527	1,106	179	56	123	79	34	45
Entomology	118	54	64	170	79	91	99	55	44
Animal physiology	72	33	39	59	21	38	25	11	14
Animal behavior and ethology	49	10	39	6	2	4	1	1	0
Wildlife biology	361	178	183	16	7	9	9	8	1
Zoology/animal biology, other	36	12	24	34	13	21	4	2	2
Genetics, general	247	89	158	57	18	39	153	67	86
Molecular genetics	162	62	100	20	10	10	72	31	41
Animal genetics	22	5	17	25	11	14	51	16	35
Plant genetics	5	4	1	7	3	4	23	10	13
Human/medical genetics	0	0	0	115	14	101	84	32	52
Genome sciences/genomics	0	0	0	1	1	0	7	3	4
Genetics, other	0	0	0	3	0	3	12	7	5
Physiology, general	1,505	645	860	554	313	241	159	83	76
Molecular physiology	0	0	0	5	3	2	21	14	7
Cell physiology	0	0	0	23	12	11	25	9	16
Endocrinology	0	0	0	2	2	0	9	3	6
Reproductive biology	0	0	0	9	5	4	2	1	1
Cardiovascular science	0	0	0	7	2	5	11	9	2
Exercise physiology	2,252	1,113	1,139	241	98	143	56	32	24
Vision science/physiological optics	21	13	8	26	10	16	10	5	5
Pathology/experimental pathology	27	9	18	91	33	58	207	94	113
Oncology and cancer biology	0	0	0	35	20	15	111	48	63
Physiology, pathology, and related sciences, other	0	0	0	1	1	0	6	5	1

See notes at end of table.

Table 318.30. Bachelor's, master's, and doctor's degrees conferred by postsecondary institutions, by sex of student and discipline division: 2013–14—Continued

Discipline division	Bachelor's degrees			Master's degrees			Doctor's degrees[1]		
	Total	Males	Females	Total	Males	Females	Total	Males	Females
1	2	3	4	5	6	7	8	9	10
Pharmacology	55	34	21	166	80	86	243	106	137
Molecular pharmacology	0	0	0	5	0	5	39	18	21
Neuropharmacology	0	0	0	14	9	5	0	0	0
Toxicology	122	30	92	44	17	27	95	47	48
Molecular toxicology	0	0	0	0	0	0	4	2	2
Environmental toxicology	30	13	17	33	7	26	42	17	25
Pharmacology and toxicology	62	28	34	72	26	46	54	29	25
Biometry/biometrics	20	7	13	29	20	9	20	14	6
Biostatistics	25	10	15	458	187	271	181	82	99
Bioinformatics	141	88	53	262	148	114	129	85	44
Computational biology	41	23	18	8	6	2	31	20	11
Biomathematics, bioinformatics, and computational biology, other	31	16	15	37	27	10	19	11	8
Biotechnology	656	319	337	1,213	546	667	8	2	6
Ecology	759	331	428	125	43	82	172	74	98
Marine biology and biological oceanography	1,200	421	779	254	86	168	55	29	26
Evolutionary biology	125	51	74	15	7	8	32	18	14
Aquatic biology/limnology	79	41	38	13	6	7	0	0	0
Environmental biology	285	119	166	48	18	30	11	9	2
Population biology	0	0	0	3	1	2	1	1	0
Conservation biology	141	45	96	118	36	82	17	7	10
Systematic biology/biological systematics	0	0	0	1	0	1	9	4	5
Epidemiology	24	6	18	1,073	315	758	273	100	173
Ecology and evolutionary biology	360	157	203	40	14	26	89	37	52
Ecology, evolution, systematics and population biology, other	136	50	86	22	7	15	38	6	32
Molecular medicine	0	0	0	16	8	8	58	23	35
Neuroscience	4,006	1,529	2,477	150	69	81	548	278	270
Neuroanatomy	0	0	0	0	0	0	0	0	0
Neurobiology and anatomy	606	272	334	11	5	6	106	59	47
Neurobiology and behavior	82	29	53	26	12	14	11	1	10
Neurobiology and neurosciences, other	4	1	3	0	0	0	5	1	4
Biological and biomedical sciences, other	1,092	371	721	1,170	597	573	185	77	108
Business, management, marketing, and personal and culinary services	358,079	188,418	169,661	189,328	101,043	88,285	3,039	1,722	1,317
Business, management, marketing, and related support services	356,747	187,818	168,929	189,284	101,036	88,248	3,039	1,722	1,317
Business/commerce, general	23,248	12,502	10,746	10,562	6,336	4,226	349	181	168
Business administration and management, general	134,243	70,929	63,314	109,368	60,891	48,477	1,589	962	627
Purchasing, procurement/acquisitions and contracts management	627	360	267	568	307	261	4	2	2
Logistics, materials, and supply chain management	3,314	2,313	1,001	782	518	264	3	1	2
Office management and supervision	261	102	159	0	0	0	0	0	0
Operations management and supervision	3,030	1,948	1,082	759	472	287	11	8	3
Nonprofit/public/organizational management	486	173	313	1,809	574	1,235	11	4	7
Customer service management	93	28	65	1	0	1	0	0	0
E-commerce/electronic commerce	181	105	76	189	96	93	1	1	0
Transportation/mobility management	295	236	59	121	85	36	1	0	1
Research and development management	8	7	1	47	7	40	0	0	0
Project management	1,064	819	245	1,242	754	488	16	11	5
Retail management	231	31	200	10	1	9	0	0	0
Organizational leadership	2,305	1,060	1,245	2,878	1,321	1,557	222	103	119
Business administration, management and operations, other	10,329	4,962	5,367	5,949	3,016	2,933	41	25	16
Accounting	49,421	24,046	25,375	18,354	8,537	9,817	47	30	17
Accounting technology/technician and bookkeeping	99	54	45	0	0	0	0	0	0
Auditing	34	10	24	66	30	36	0	0	0
Accounting and finance	527	306	221	1,299	475	824	0	0	0
Accounting and business/management	2,188	627	1,561	289	154	135	0	0	0
Accounting and related services, other	203	116	87	266	149	117	2	2	0
Administrative assistant and secretarial science, general	56	23	33	0	0	0	0	0	0
Business/office automation/technology/data entry	55	24	31	0	0	0	0	0	0
General office occupations and clerical services	13	3	10	0	0	0	0	0	0
Parts, warehousing, and inventory management operations	0	0	0	0	0	0	0	0	0
Business operations support and secretarial services, other	0	0	0	49	21	28	0	0	0
Business/corporate communications	655	250	405	158	38	120	0	0	0
Business/managerial economics	4,858	3,330	1,528	294	140	154	70	43	27
Entrepreneurship/entrepreneurial studies	2,234	1,516	718	715	472	243	14	10	4
Small business administration/management	61	38	23	20	14	6	0	0	0
Entrepreneurial and small business operations, other	41	23	18	13	7	6	2	1	1
Finance, general	31,365	21,875	9,490	6,705	4,118	2,587	48	31	17
Banking and financial support services	499	302	197	49	35	14	0	0	0
Financial planning and services	251	176	75	339	192	147	7	6	1
International finance	6	3	3	35	21	14	0	0	0
Investments and securities	81	64	17	224	136	88	0	0	0
Public finance	24	19	5	0	0	0	0	0	0
Finance and financial management services, other	154	111	43	283	193	90	1	0	1
Hospitality administration/management, general	7,930	2,437	5,493	475	141	334	22	12	10
Tourism and travel services management	564	144	420	130	34	96	0	0	0
Hotel/motel administration/management	1,867	656	1,211	180	59	121	4	3	1
Restaurant/food services management	799	361	438	0	0	0	0	0	0
Resort management	214	92	122	0	0	0	0	0	0
Meeting and event planning	429	38	391	0	0	0	0	0	0
Casino management	6	3	3	0	0	0	0	0	0
Hotel, motel, and restaurant management	154	54	100	0	0	0	0	0	0
Hospitality administration/management, other	476	186	290	69	25	44	2	0	2
Human resources management/personnel administration, general	7,120	1,993	5,127	4,457	1,129	3,328	38	12	26
Labor and industrial relations	766	380	386	794	249	545	20	7	13
Organizational behavior studies	2,878	1,255	1,623	2,010	749	1,261	267	123	144
Labor studies	43	15	28	25	11	14	1	1	0
Human resources development	539	149	390	1,191	336	855	19	9	10
Human resources management and services, other	222	53	169	1,179	436	743	0	0	0
International business/trade/commerce	5,334	2,651	2,683	2,424	1,444	980	33	23	10
Management information systems, general	7,477	5,581	1,896	2,950	2,051	899	41	27	14
Information resources management	224	172	52	630	441	189	27	20	7
Knowledge management	12	8	4	53	42	11	0	0	0
Management information systems and services, other	188	128	60	19	13	6	0	0	0
Management science, general	2,762	1,683	1,079	1,346	781	565	28	20	8
Business statistics	84	55	29	106	54	52	0	0	0

See notes at end of table.

Table 318.30. Bachelor's, master's, and doctor's degrees conferred by postsecondary institutions, by sex of student and discipline division: 2013–14—Continued

Discipline division	Bachelor's degrees			Master's degrees			Doctor's degrees[1]		
	Total	Males	Females	Total	Males	Females	Total	Males	Females
1	2	3	4	5	6	7	8	9	10
Actuarial science	1,099	650	449	378	216	162	0	0	0
Management sciences and quantitative methods, other	289	183	106	559	354	205	10	7	3
Marketing/marketing management, general	29,769	14,238	15,531	1,997	771	1,226	23	11	12
Marketing research	60	26	34	117	51	66	0	0	0
International marketing	156	33	123	103	27	76	5	2	3
Marketing, other	932	451	481	221	98	123	3	1	2
Real estate	536	391	145	755	554	201	1	1	0
Taxation	0	0	0	1,787	893	894	0	0	0
Insurance	773	514	259	94	49	45	2	1	1
Sales, distribution, and marketing operations, general	1,231	682	549	314	106	208	2	0	2
Merchandising and buying operations	13	0	13	23	0	23	0	0	0
Retailing and retail operations	247	55	192	3	0	3	0	0	0
Selling skills and sales operations	339	225	114	0	0	0	0	0	0
General merchandising/sales/related marketing operations, other	107	52	55	7	6	1	0	0	0
Fashion merchandising	2,511	128	2,383	17	2	15	0	0	0
Apparel and accessories marketing operations	755	72	683	7	3	4	0	0	0
Tourism and travel services marketing operations	35	19	16	0	0	0	0	0	0
Tourism promotion operations	67	7	60	0	0	0	0	0	0
Vehicle and vehicle parts and accessories marketing operations	66	61	5	0	0	0	0	0	0
Special products marketing operations	204	81	123	15	5	10	0	0	0
Hospitality and recreation marketing operations	81	67	14	0	0	0	0	0	0
Specialized merchandising/sales/related marketing operations, other	83	32	51	57	17	40	0	0	0
Construction management	1,862	1,695	167	277	212	65	0	0	0
Telecommunications management	1	1	0	3	2	1	0	0	0
Business/management/marketing/related support services, other	2,903	1,570	1,333	1,069	565	504	52	21	31
Personal and culinary services	1,332	600	732	44	7	37	0	0	0
Funeral service and mortuary science, general	113	35	78	0	0	0	0	0	0
Funeral direction/service	24	7	17	0	0	0	0	0	0
Cosmetology/cosmetologist, general	0	0	0	0	0	0	0	0	0
Cooking and related culinary arts, general	0	0	0	0	0	0	0	0	0
Baking and pastry arts/baker/pastry chef	76	10	66	0	0	0	0	0	0
Culinary arts/chef training	332	154	178	0	0	0	0	0	0
Restaurant, culinary, and catering management/manager	716	364	352	0	0	0	0	0	0
Food service, waiter/waitress, and dining room management	0	0	0	0	0	0	0	0	0
Culinary science/culinology	26	15	11	0	0	0	0	0	0
Culinary arts and related services, other	43	15	28	44	7	37	0	0	0
Personal and culinary services, other	2	0	2	0	0	0	0	0	0
Communication and communications technologies	92,591	34,370	58,221	9,928	3,129	6,799	614	267	347
Communication, journalism, and related programs	87,604	30,955	56,649	9,347	2,807	6,540	611	266	345
Communication, general	8,037	2,582	5,455	504	141	363	60	20	40
Speech communication and rhetoric	31,812	11,163	20,649	2,076	646	1,430	244	100	144
Mass communication/media studies	9,522	3,438	6,084	944	277	667	141	64	77
Communication and media studies, other	1,806	600	1,206	777	224	553	59	24	35
Journalism	12,009	3,947	8,062	1,751	536	1,215	34	20	14
Broadcast journalism	1,014	443	571	58	22	36	0	0	0
Photojournalism	147	48	99	23	11	12	0	0	0
Journalism, other	796	257	539	193	57	136	0	0	0
Radio and television	5,161	2,779	2,382	184	79	105	8	2	6
Digital communication and media/multimedia	2,154	1,133	1,021	380	185	195	27	23	4
Radio, television, and digital communication, other	846	475	371	17	11	6	0	0	0
Public relations, advertising, and applied communication	1,213	328	885	42	13	29	0	0	0
Organizational communication, general	1,167	380	787	121	28	93	2	1	1
Public relations/image management	4,634	974	3,660	600	161	439	0	0	0
Advertising	4,625	1,486	3,139	327	112	215	4	0	4
Political communication	74	21	53	22	7	15	0	0	0
Health communication	53	6	47	146	12	134	6	1	5
Sports communication	100	71	29	14	8	6	0	0	0
International and intercultural communication	31	12	19	84	14	70	0	0	0
Technical and scientific communication	42	10	32	12	4	8	7	3	4
Public relations, advertising and applied communication, other	1,029	266	763	180	52	128	0	0	0
Publishing	4	1	3	173	24	149	0	0	0
Communication, journalism, and related programs, other	1,328	535	793	719	183	536	19	8	11
Communications technologies/technicians and support services	4,987	3,415	1,572	581	322	259	3	1	2
Communications technology/technician	91	62	29	42	17	25	3	1	2
Photographic and film/video technology/technician and assistant	77	56	21	0	0	0	0	0	0
Radio and television broadcasting technology/technician	472	298	174	122	43	79	0	0	0
Recording arts technology/technician	1,248	1,101	147	33	22	11	0	0	0
Audiovisual communications technologies/technicians, other	153	123	30	0	0	0	0	0	0
Graphic communications, general	293	101	192	0	0	0	0	0	0
Printing management	88	41	47	2	2	0	0	0	0
Prepress/desktop publishing and digital imaging design	65	24	41	0	0	0	0	0	0
Animation/interactive technology/video graphics/special effects	2,228	1,483	745	355	225	130	0	0	0
Graphic and printing equipment operator, general production	35	17	18	0	0	0	0	0	0
Printing press operator	12	6	6	0	0	0	0	0	0
Graphic communications, other	42	13	29	13	5	8	0	0	0
Communications technologies/technicians and support services, other	183	90	93	14	8	6	0	0	0
Computer and information sciences and support services	55,367	45,393	9,974	24,532	17,484	7,048	1,982	1,566	416
Computer and information sciences, general	12,523	10,546	1,977	5,188	3,917	1,271	667	537	130
Artificial intelligence	0	0	0	112	85	27	39	32	7
Information technology	6,833	5,484	1,349	3,203	2,172	1,031	63	44	19
Informatics	649	505	144	319	114	205	13	9	4
Computer and information sciences, other	329	265	64	99	74	25	27	14	13
Computer programming/programmer, general	1,229	1,047	182	78	56	22	2	1	1
Computer programming, specific applications	242	228	14	37	32	5	0	0	0
Computer programming, other	0	0	0	0	0	0	0	0	0
Data processing and data processing technology/technician	75	69	6	0	0	0	0	0	0
Information science/studies	6,097	4,730	1,367	4,487	2,774	1,713	163	107	56
Computer systems analysis/analyst	1,542	1,204	338	358	248	110	0	0	0
Computer science	13,220	11,306	1,914	6,689	5,114	1,575	954	783	171
Web page, digital/multimedia and information resources design	1,667	1,025	642	252	120	132	0	0	0
Data modeling/warehousing and database administration	186	123	63	93	60	33	0	0	0
Computer graphics	1,626	1,056	570	177	111	66	0	0	0
Modeling, virtual environments and simulation	217	192	25	50	47	3	1	1	0

See notes at end of table.

Table 318.30. Bachelor's, master's, and doctor's degrees conferred by postsecondary institutions, by sex of student and discipline division: 2013–14—Continued

Discipline division	Bachelor's degrees			Master's degrees			Doctor's degrees[1]		
	Total	Males	Females	Total	Males	Females	Total	Males	Females
1	2	3	4	5	6	7	8	9	10
Computer software and media applications, other	250	228	22	38	23	15	0	0	0
Computer systems networking and telecommunications	1,779	1,602	177	666	530	136	3	3	0
Network and system administration/administrator	668	595	73	45	30	15	0	0	0
System, networking, and LAN/WAN management/manager	244	205	39	22	14	8	0	0	0
Computer and information systems security/information assurance	4,432	3,832	600	1,804	1,424	380	16	13	3
Web/multimedia management and webmaster	417	257	160	13	8	5	0	0	0
Information technology project management	371	306	65	190	119	71	6	5	1
Computer support specialist	34	28	6	0	0	0	0	0	0
Computer/information tech. services admin. and management, other	420	313	107	212	141	71	0	0	0
Computer and information sciences and support services, other	317	247	70	400	271	129	28	17	11
Education	98,854	20,353	78,501	154,636	35,984	118,652	10,920	3,464	7,456
Education, general	3,761	645	3,116	22,071	5,190	16,881	2,048	585	1,463
Bilingual and multilingual education	227	19	208	328	52	276	12	2	10
Multicultural education	0	0	0	172	38	134	37	16	21
Indian/Native American education	4	1	3	0	0	0	0	0	0
Bilingual, multilingual, and multicultural education, other	0	0	0	3	0	3	0	0	0
Curriculum and instruction	215	45	170	15,442	2,751	12,691	1,325	305	1,020
Educational leadership and administration, general	2	2	0	18,226	6,427	11,799	3,972	1,460	2,512
Administration of special education	0	0	0	69	8	61	17	2	15
Adult and continuing education administration	7	4	3	876	242	634	55	19	36
Educational, instructional, and curriculum supervision	43	9	34	976	265	711	65	12	53
Higher education/higher education administration	7	4	3	2,712	793	1,919	523	206	317
Community college education	0	0	0	46	15	31	40	14	26
Elementary and middle school administration/principalship	69	5	64	649	294	355	27	8	19
Secondary school administration/principalship	0	0	0	448	182	266	0	0	0
Urban education and leadership	113	44	69	485	127	358	53	17	36
Superintendency and educational system administration	0	0	0	520	183	337	58	30	28
Educational administration and supervision, other	1	0	1	1,270	435	835	317	124	193
Educational/instructional technology	53	32	21	4,388	1,299	3,089	147	46	101
Educational evaluation and research	0	0	0	49	10	39	69	25	44
Educational statistics and research methods	0	0	0	48	18	30	39	15	24
Educational assessment, testing, and measurement	0	0	0	70	6	64	9	4	5
Learning sciences	50	6	44	23	6	17	2	0	2
Educational assessment, evaluation, and research, other	14	3	11	103	28	75	32	10	22
International and comparative education	35	6	29	267	47	220	16	3	13
Social and philosophical foundations of education	30	6	24	512	139	373	113	39	74
Special education and teaching, general	7,697	884	6,813	11,869	1,955	9,914	226	30	196
Education/teaching of individuals with hearing impairments/deafness	102	7	95	140	12	128	8	3	5
Education/teaching of the gifted and talented	0	0	0	318	29	289	2	1	1
Education/teaching of individuals with emotional disturbances	81	17	64	83	21	62	11	1	10
Education/teaching of individuals with mental retardation	141	15	126	97	15	82	3	0	3
Education/teaching of individuals with multiple disabilities	131	10	121	294	45	249	0	0	0
Educ./teach. of individuals with orthopedic/physical health impair.	0	0	0	17	2	15	0	0	0
Education/teaching of individuals with vision impairments/blindness	27	5	22	127	24	103	0	0	0
Educ./teach. of individuals with specific learning disabilities	193	21	172	356	45	311	1	0	1
Education/teaching of individuals with speech/language impairments	192	9	183	221	12	209	0	0	0
Education/teaching of individuals with autism	0	0	0	351	31	320	0	0	0
Education/teaching of individuals who are developmentally delayed	15	0	15	156	25	131	0	0	0
Educ./teach. of individuals in early childhood spec. educ. programs	444	16	428	1,143	110	1,033	0	0	0
Education/teaching of individuals in elementary special educ. programs	219	15	204	1,426	132	1,294	0	0	0
Educ./teach. of individuals in jr. high/middle school special educ. prog.	16	5	11	241	76	165	0	0	0
Education/teaching of individuals in secondary special educ. prog.	45	14	31	376	111	265	0	0	0
Special education and teaching, other	335	44	291	576	80	496	6	2	4
Counselor education/school counseling and guidance services	6	0	6	11,614	2,027	9,587	295	74	221
College student counseling and personnel services	0	0	0	1,059	289	770	25	7	18
Student counseling and personnel services, other	2	0	2	300	48	252	6	0	6
Adult and continuing education and teaching	32	7	25	1,117	312	805	152	40	112
Elementary education and teaching	31,772	2,915	28,857	9,810	1,166	8,644	74	12	62
Junior high/intermediate/middle school education and teaching	3,165	852	2,313	876	219	657	2	1	1
Secondary education and teaching	3,849	1,594	2,255	6,498	2,525	3,973	26	8	18
Teacher education, multiple levels	1,626	297	1,329	3,474	871	2,603	19	4	15
Montessori teacher education	6	0	6	213	13	200	0	0	0
Waldorf/Steiner teacher education	0	0	0	0	0	0	0	0	0
Kindergarten/preschool education and teaching	1,384	67	1,317	267	11	256	12	5	7
Early childhood education and teaching	13,855	542	13,313	3,047	96	2,951	21	0	21
Teacher educ. and prof. dev., specific levels and methods, other	166	26	140	3,532	832	2,700	69	21	48
Agricultural teacher education	577	229	348	251	86	165	29	9	20
Art teacher education	1,178	181	997	893	151	742	25	5	20
Business teacher education	230	89	141	113	51	62	0	0	0
Driver and safety teacher education	0	0	0	5	3	2	0	0	0
English/language arts teacher education	2,445	503	1,942	790	204	586	10	3	7
Foreign language teacher education	108	15	93	183	29	154	12	3	9
Health teacher education	1,609	460	1,149	644	149	495	35	13	22
Family and consumer sciences/home economics teacher education	257	10	247	62	4	58	3	1	2
Technology teacher education/industrial arts teacher education	330	281	49	331	137	194	1	1	0
Sales and marketing operations/marketing and dist. teacher educ.	11	4	7	9	4	5	0	0	0
Mathematics teacher education	2,056	703	1,353	1,609	527	1,082	60	22	38
Music teacher education	3,835	1,577	2,258	1,145	460	685	92	43	49
Physical education teaching and coaching	8,175	4,806	3,369	1,957	1,172	785	36	19	17
Reading teacher education	85	12	73	6,018	352	5,666	78	8	70
Science teacher education/general science teacher education	617	264	353	891	303	588	55	14	41
Social science teacher education	500	289	211	111	56	55	0	0	0
Social studies teacher education	1,618	940	678	479	254	225	3	1	2
Technical teacher education	219	121	98	231	92	139	58	28	30
Trade and industrial teacher education	686	407	279	222	96	126	4	2	2
Computer teacher education	59	10	49	233	66	167	10	4	6
Biology teacher education	430	139	291	292	93	199	1	0	1
Chemistry teacher education	85	30	55	67	27	40	2	1	1
Drama and dance teacher education	131	12	119	72	16	56	0	0	0
French language teacher education	43	6	37	30	7	23	0	0	0
German language teacher education	12	5	7	0	0	0	0	0	0
Health occupations teacher education	10	0	10	74	9	65	67	1	66
History teacher education	598	347	251	93	43	50	0	0	0

See notes at end of table.

Table 318.30. Bachelor's, master's, and doctor's degrees conferred by postsecondary institutions, by sex of student and discipline division: 2013–14—Continued

Discipline division	Bachelor's degrees			Master's degrees			Doctor's degrees[1]		
	Total	Males	Females	Total	Males	Females	Total	Males	Females
1	2	3	4	5	6	7	8	9	10
Physics teacher education	60	38	22	62	42	20	0	0	0
Spanish language teacher education	398	75	323	149	44	105	0	0	0
Speech teacher education	20	5	15	46	8	38	11	3	8
Geography teacher education	2	0	2	2	0	2	0	0	0
Latin teacher education	4	0	4	14	7	7	0	0	0
School librarian/library media specialist	1	1	0	145	14	131	0	0	0
Psychology teacher education	12	3	9	0	0	0	0	0	0
Earth science teacher education	55	18	37	66	30	36	0	0	0
Environmental education	3	2	1	4	1	3	0	0	0
Teacher educ. and prof. dev., specific subject areas, other	300	111	189	1,852	381	1,471	35	14	21
Teaching English as a second/foreign language/ESL language instructor	325	59	266	3,301	653	2,648	27	11	16
Teaching French as a second or foreign language	0	0	0	0	0	0	0	0	0
Teaching English or French as a second or foreign lang., other	35	13	22	0	0	0	0	0	0
Teacher assistant/aide	1	1	0	17	5	12	0	0	0
Adult literacy tutor/instructor	0	0	0	10	1	9	1	0	1
Education, other	1,602	394	1,208	2,812	718	2,094	331	107	224
Engineering and engineering technologies	108,969	88,938	20,031	47,326	35,777	11,549	10,117	7,820	2,297
Engineering	92,162	73,903	18,259	42,372	32,158	10,214	10,010	7,739	2,271
Engineering, general	2,171	1,671	500	2,083	1,596	487	417	330	87
Pre-engineering	17	10	7	0	0	0	0	0	0
Aerospace, aeronautical and astronautical engineering	3,565	3,077	488	1,311	1,104	207	336	283	53
Agricultural engineering	971	639	332	305	162	143	145	99	46
Architectural engineering	675	493	182	129	95	34	14	10	4
Bioengineering and biomedical engineering	5,430	3,255	2,175	1,925	1,165	760	955	590	365
Ceramic sciences and engineering	81	64	17	9	6	3	7	4	3
Chemical engineering	7,969	5,320	2,649	1,473	989	484	980	694	286
Chemical and biomolecular engineering	134	73	61	37	27	10	12	10	2
Chemical engineering, other	0	0	0	8	5	3	0	0	0
Civil engineering, general	12,794	9,976	2,818	5,107	3,738	1,369	936	704	232
Geotechnical and geoenvironmental engineering	0	0	0	1	1	0	0	0	0
Structural engineering	173	142	31	217	163	54	9	9	0
Transportation and highway engineering	0	0	0	95	59	36	9	6	3
Water resources engineering	9	2	7	65	32	33	12	6	6
Civil engineering, other	17	7	10	16	13	3	6	6	0
Computer engineering, general	5,061	4,540	521	1,964	1,508	456	332	289	43
Computer hardware engineering	0	0	0	71	65	6	0	0	0
Computer software engineering	660	612	48	1,197	827	370	6	4	2
Computer engineering, other	1	1	0	9	8	1	4	4	0
Electrical and electronics engineering	13,757	12,052	1,705	9,537	7,595	1,942	2,267	1,906	361
Laser and optical engineering	15	12	3	36	30	6	16	11	5
Telecommunications engineering	3	3	0	205	161	44	0	0	0
Electrical, electronics and communications engineering, other	77	68	9	51	39	12	18	16	2
Engineering mechanics	94	75	19	89	66	23	67	54	13
Engineering physics/applied physics	499	427	72	103	83	20	64	48	16
Engineering science	474	362	112	298	219	79	131	95	36
Environmental/environmental health engineering	1,261	720	541	905	484	421	166	98	68
Materials engineering	1,185	868	317	925	657	268	589	437	152
Mechanical engineering	24,301	21,265	3,036	6,182	5,248	934	1,387	1,183	204
Metallurgical engineering	104	72	32	43	35	8	16	11	5
Mining and mineral engineering	277	241	36	52	47	5	15	14	1
Naval architecture and marine engineering	440	393	47	48	40	8	12	11	1
Nuclear engineering	572	482	90	299	243	56	162	138	24
Ocean engineering	175	146	29	121	94	27	15	13	2
Petroleum engineering	1,406	1,206	200	458	367	91	110	92	18
Systems engineering	808	619	189	2,088	1,632	456	118	92	26
Textile sciences and engineering	252	71	181	43	19	24	32	13	19
Polymer/plastics engineering	98	81	17	113	86	27	61	42	19
Construction engineering	387	349	38	97	72	25	0	0	0
Forest engineering	24	22	2	2	2	0	1	0	1
Industrial engineering	4,101	2,892	1,209	2,286	1,615	671	342	236	106
Manufacturing engineering	339	303	36	257	220	37	4	1	3
Operations research	436	281	155	667	437	230	65	47	18
Surveying engineering	28	27	1	15	12	3	0	0	0
Geological/geophysical engineering	197	138	59	159	127	32	18	14	4
Paper science and engineering	9	5	4	6	2	4	2	1	1
Electromechanical engineering	59	53	6	0	0	0	0	0	0
Mechatronics, robotics, and automation engineering	32	29	3	86	72	14	17	16	1
Biochemical engineering	60	33	27	2	1	1	0	0	0
Engineering chemistry	3	2	1	0	0	0	0	0	0
Biological/biosystems engineering	210	134	76	21	9	12	15	11	4
Engineering, other	751	590	161	1,156	881	275	120	91	29
Engineering technologies/construction trades/mechanics and repairers	16,807	15,035	1,772	4,954	3,619	1,335	107	81	26
Engineering technologies and engineering-related fields	16,221	14,495	1,726	4,954	3,619	1,335	107	81	26
Engineering technology, general	1,309	1,156	153	270	219	51	7	5	2
Architectural engineering technology/technician	386	332	54	15	12	3	0	0	0
Civil engineering technology/technician	532	460	72	0	0	0	0	0	0
Electrical/electronic/communications eng. technology/technician	1,736	1,615	121	39	32	7	0	0	0
Laser and optical technology/technician	0	0	0	0	0	0	0	0	0
Telecommunications technology/technician	73	58	15	94	76	18	0	0	0
Electrical/electronic eng. technologies/technicians, other	793	731	62	2	2	0	0	0	0
Biomedical technology/technician	117	90	27	5	4	1	3	0	3
Electromechanical technology/electromechanical eng. technology	84	80	4	5	3	2	0	0	0
Instrumentation technology/technician	47	41	6	0	0	0	0	0	0
Robotics technology/technician	4	4	0	0	0	0	0	0	0
Automation engineer technology/technician	49	47	2	0	0	0	0	0	0
Electromechanical/instrumentation and maintenance technol./tech.	12	9	3	0	0	0	0	0	0
Heating, ventilation, air conditioning and refrig. eng. technol./tech.	2	2	0	0	0	0	0	0	0
Energy management and systems technology/technician	102	95	7	77	55	22	0	0	0
Solar energy technology/technician	63	61	2	12	11	1	0	0	0
Water quality/wastewater treatment manage./recycling technol./tech.	15	6	9	0	0	0	0	0	0
Environmental engineering technology/environmental technology	112	86	26	77	39	38	3	3	0
Hazardous materials management and waste technology/technician	0	0	0	0	0	0	0	0	0
Environmental control technologies/technicians, other	8	6	2	57	35	22	0	0	0

See notes at end of table.

Table 318.30. Bachelor's, master's, and doctor's degrees conferred by postsecondary institutions, by sex of student and discipline division: 2013–14—Continued

Discipline division	Bachelor's degrees			Master's degrees			Doctor's degrees[1]		
	Total	Males	Females	Total	Males	Females	Total	Males	Females
1	2	3	4	5	6	7	8	9	10
Plastics and polymer engineering technology/technician	83	75	8	7	4	3	0	0	0
Industrial technology/technician	1,649	1,491	158	240	170	70	14	13	1
Manufacturing engineering technology/technician	535	510	25	47	41	6	0	0	0
Welding engineering technology/technician	8	7	1	0	0	0	0	0	0
Industrial production technologies/technicians, other	257	222	35	2	2	0	0	0	0
Occupational safety and health technology/technician	1,268	1,048	220	487	352	135	0	0	0
Quality control technology/technician	21	13	8	113	57	56	0	0	0
Industrial safety technology/technician	113	95	18	25	23	2	0	0	0
Quality control and safety technologies/technicians, other	43	40	3	0	0	0	0	0	0
Aeronautical/aerospace engineering technology/technician	98	88	10	46	37	9	0	0	0
Automotive engineering technology/technician	249	241	8	28	21	7	1	1	0
Mechanical engineering/mechanical technology/technician	1,574	1,486	88	29	20	9	0	0	0
Mechanical engineering related technologies/technicians, other	183	165	18	0	0	0	0	0	0
Mining technology/technician	4	3	1	0	0	0	0	0	0
Petroleum technology/technician	18	17	1	0	0	0	0	0	0
Mining and petroleum technologies/technicians, other	0	0	0	0	0	0	0	0	0
Construction engineering technology/technician	1,680	1,538	142	148	115	33	3	2	1
Surveying technology/surveying	159	145	14	2	1	1	8	6	2
Hydraulics and fluid power technology/technician	6	6	0	0	0	0	0	0	0
Engineering-related technologies, other	0	0	0	0	0	0	0	0	0
Computer engineering technology/technician	488	439	49	0	0	0	0	0	0
Computer technology/computer systems technology	287	249	38	6	4	2	1	1	0
Computer hardware technology/technician	0	0	0	0	0	0	0	0	0
Computer software technology/technician	39	36	3	0	0	0	1	1	0
Computer engineering technologies/technicians, other	13	13	0	0	0	0	0	0	0
Drafting and design technologies/technicians, general	69	54	15	0	0	0	0	0	0
CAD/CADD drafting and/or design technology/technician	86	72	14	1	1	0	0	0	0
Architectural drafting and architectural CAD/CADD	2	2	0	0	0	0	0	0	0
Civil drafting and civil engineering CAD/CADD	3	3	0	0	0	0	0	0	0
Mechanical drafting and mechanical drafting CAD/CADD	33	24	9	0	0	0	0	0	0
Drafting/design engineering technologies/technicians, other	7	1	6	0	0	0	0	0	0
Nuclear engineering technology/technician	169	153	16	0	0	0	0	0	0
Engineering/industrial management	705	580	125	2,886	2,152	734	52	40	12
Engineering design	0	0	0	40	23	17	3	2	1
Packaging science	285	214	71	38	23	15	4	4	0
Engineering-related fields, other	12	10	2	4	1	3	7	3	4
Nanotechnology	4	4	0	26	18	8	0	0	0
Engineering tech. and engineering-related fields, other	627	572	55	126	66	60	0	0	0
Construction trades	268	243	25	0	0	0	0	0	0
Construction trades, general	0	0	0	0	0	0	0	0	0
Mason/masonry	0	0	0	0	0	0	0	0	0
Electrician	0	0	0	0	0	0	0	0	0
Building/property maintenance	0	0	0	0	0	0	0	0	0
Building/construction site management/manager	156	139	17	0	0	0	0	0	0
Building construction technology	63	59	4	0	0	0	0	0	0
Building/construction finishing, mgmt., and inspection, other	49	45	4	0	0	0	0	0	0
Construction trades, other	0	0	0	0	0	0	0	0	0
Mechanic and repair technologies/technicians	318	297	21	0	0	0	0	0	0
Communications systems installation and repair technology	0	0	0	0	0	0	0	0	0
Industrial electronics technology/technician	1	1	0	0	0	0	0	0	0
Heating, air conditioning, ventilation and refrig. main. tech.	1	1	0	0	0	0	0	0	0
Heavy equipment maintenance technology/technician	10	10	0	0	0	0	0	0	0
Autobody/collision and repair technology/technician	0	0	0	0	0	0	0	0	0
Automobile/automotive mechanics technology/technician	49	48	1	0	0	0	0	0	0
Diesel mechanics technology/technician	29	28	1	0	0	0	0	0	0
Airframe mechanics and aircraft maintenance technology/technician	55	51	4	0	0	0	0	0	0
Aircraft powerplant technology/technician	66	61	5	0	0	0	0	0	0
Avionics maintenance technology/technician	104	94	10	0	0	0	0	0	0
Vehicle maintenance and repair technologies, other	3	3	0	0	0	0	0	0	0
English language and literature/letters	50,404	15,809	34,595	9,292	3,113	6,179	1,393	557	836
English language and literature, general	39,996	12,168	27,828	5,044	1,604	3,440	1,196	481	715
Writing, general	602	230	372	125	41	84	0	0	0
Creative writing	2,937	1,010	1,927	3,215	1,212	2,003	9	6	3
Professional, technical, business, and scientific writing	682	218	464	314	94	220	24	10	14
Rhetoric and composition	4,946	1,832	3,114	264	82	182	116	46	70
Rhetoric and composition/writing studies, other	31	6	25	7	2	5	0	0	0
General literature	225	60	165	34	9	25	8	3	5
American literature (United States)	32	3	29	7	0	7	0	0	0
English literature (British and Commonwealth)	244	67	177	117	25	92	10	2	8
Children's and adolescent literature	9	0	9	0	0	0	0	0	0
Literature, other	10	2	8	0	0	0	0	0	0
English language and literature/letters, other	690	213	477	165	44	121	30	9	21
Family and consumer sciences/human sciences	24,722	3,014	21,708	3,121	422	2,699	335	62	273
Work and family studies	1	0	1	0	0	0	0	0	0
Family and consumer sciences/human sciences, general	3,650	343	3,307	528	94	434	69	14	55
Business family and consumer sciences/human sciences	169	55	114	4	2	2	0	0	0
Family and consumer sciences/human sciences communication	17	0	17	0	0	0	0	0	0
Consumer merchandising/retailing management	170	24	146	6	3	3	2	0	2
Family and consumer sciences/human sciences business services, other	7	0	7	0	0	0	0	0	0
Family resource management studies, general	748	217	531	58	14	44	6	1	5
Consumer economics	194	73	121	0	0	0	0	0	0
Consumer services and advocacy	19	2	17	0	0	0	0	0	0
Family and consumer economics and related services, other	359	45	314	4	0	4	8	1	7
Foods, nutrition, and wellness studies, general	2,645	535	2,110	581	85	496	34	8	26
Human nutrition	790	152	638	357	63	294	23	6	17
Food service systems administration/management	1,010	398	612	8	0	8	0	0	0
Foods, nutrition, and related services, other	14	1	13	34	3	31	0	0	0
Housing and human environments, general	226	39	187	24	5	19	5	0	5
Facilities planning and management	59	56	3	11	8	3	0	0	0
Housing and human environments, other	13	3	10	0	0	0	0	0	0
Human development and family studies, general	8,191	650	7,541	602	61	541	112	23	89
Adult development and aging	18	1	17	171	18	153	1	0	1
Family systems	506	47	459	24	1	23	7	0	7

See notes at end of table.

Table 318.30. Bachelor's, master's, and doctor's degrees conferred by postsecondary institutions, by sex of student and discipline division: 2013–14—Continued

Discipline division	Bachelor's degrees			Master's degrees			Doctor's degrees[1]		
	Total	Males	Females	Total	Males	Females	Total	Males	Females
1	2	3	4	5	6	7	8	9	10
Child development	1,808	63	1,745	235	14	221	16	1	15
Family and community services	1,121	151	970	212	21	191	31	4	27
Child care and support services management	223	8	215	39	1	38	0	0	0
Child care provider/assistant	13	0	13	5	0	5	0	0	0
Human development, family studies, and related services, other	470	40	430	58	8	50	8	1	7
Apparel and textiles, general	1,868	88	1,780	72	11	61	9	3	6
Apparel and textile manufacture	49	4	45	0	0	0	0	0	0
Textile science	1	0	1	0	0	0	0	0	0
Apparel and textile marketing management	321	16	305	46	4	42	4	0	4
Fashion and fabric consultant	2	0	2	0	0	0	0	0	0
Apparel and textiles, other	15	0	15	1	0	1	0	0	0
Family and consumer sciences/human sciences, other	25	3	22	41	6	35	0	0	0
Foreign languages, literatures, and linguistics	20,335	6,266	14,069	3,482	1,222	2,260	1,231	498	733
Foreign languages and literatures, general	1,586	469	1,117	256	61	195	22	6	16
Linguistics	2,068	670	1,398	665	268	397	231	94	137
Language interpretation and translation	39	16	23	152	41	111	7	3	4
Comparative literature	788	235	553	136	49	87	156	71	85
Applied linguistics	18	5	13	16	6	10	4	0	4
Linguistic/comparative/related language studies and serv., other	139	33	106	33	8	25	5	0	5
African languages, literatures, and linguistics	6	1	5	3	2	1	4	2	2
East Asian languages, literatures, and linguistics, general	157	60	97	77	36	41	32	15	17
Chinese language and literature	497	255	242	46	5	41	3	0	3
Japanese language and literature	625	290	335	25	11	14	4	2	2
Korean language and literature	32	12	20	10	3	7	8	0	8
East Asian languages, literatures, and linguistics, other	102	35	67	19	11	8	22	8	14
Slavic languages, literatures, and linguistics, general	66	28	38	46	13	33	34	14	20
Russian language and literature	371	191	180	14	8	6	1	0	1
Polish language and literature	4	3	1	0	0	0	0	0	0
Slavic/Baltic/Albanian languages, lit., and linguistics, other	0	0	0	1	0	1	0	0	0
Germanic languages, literatures, and linguistics, general	68	26	42	23	9	14	32	17	15
German language and literature	878	408	470	123	44	79	44	21	23
Scandinavian languages, literatures, and linguistics	7	3	4	3	0	3	4	0	4
Danish language and literature	2	0	2	0	0	0	0	0	0
Dutch/Flemish language and literature	1	0	1	0	0	0	0	0	0
Norwegian language and literature	9	5	4	0	0	0	0	0	0
Swedish language and literature	1	0	1	0	0	0	0	0	0
Germanic languages, literatures, and linguistics, other	1	1	0	0	0	0	0	0	0
Modern Greek language and literature	2	2	0	0	0	0	1	1	0
South Asian languages, literatures, and linguistics, general	2	2	0	2	2	0	4	1	3
Iranian languages, literatures, and linguistics	13	9	4	2	1	1	0	0	0
Romance languages, literatures, and linguistics, general	152	34	118	74	23	51	53	22	31
French language and literature	2,044	492	1,552	308	91	217	107	31	76
Italian language and literature	271	85	186	58	14	44	29	10	19
Portuguese language and literature	50	23	27	19	7	12	6	3	3
Spanish language and literature	8,034	2,029	6,005	832	250	582	193	66	127
Hispanic and Latin American languages, lit., and linguistics, general	85	23	62	21	8	13	14	6	8
Romance languages, literatures, and linguistics, other	68	17	51	40	11	29	47	16	31
American Indian/Native American languages, literatures, and linguistics	0	0	0	9	2	7	0	0	0
Middle/Near Eastern and Semitic languages, lit., and linguistics, general	20	11	9	27	15	12	16	8	8
Arabic language and literature	165	87	78	6	4	2	0	0	0
Hebrew language and literature	60	26	34	30	20	10	9	3	6
Ancient Near Eastern and biblical languages, lit., and linguistics	39	26	13	26	21	5	4	3	1
Middle/Near Eastern and Semitic languages, lit., and ling., other	80	29	51	38	18	20	29	17	12
Classics and classical languages, lit., and linguistics, general	994	456	538	194	106	88	87	50	37
Ancient/classical Greek language and literature	17	7	10	1	0	1	0	0	0
Latin language and literature	55	22	33	20	11	9	0	0	0
Classics and classical languages, lit., and linguistics, other	19	9	10	23	16	7	1	1	0
Celtic languages, literatures, and linguistics	2	1	1	0	0	0	2	0	2
Filipino/Tagalog language and literature	6	2	4	0	0	0	0	0	0
Turkish language and literature	0	0	0	0	0	0	0	0	0
Uralic languages, literatures, and linguistics	0	0	0	0	0	0	0	0	0
American sign language (ASL)	124	9	115	31	12	19	0	0	0
Sign language interpretation and translation	313	36	277	29	5	24	0	0	0
American sign language, other	2	1	1	0	0	0	0	0	0
Foreign languages, literatures, and linguistics, other	253	82	171	44	10	34	16	7	9
Health professions and related programs	198,770	30,931	167,839	97,403	17,749	79,654	67,448	28,084	39,364
Health and wellness, general	9,944	2,394	7,550	672	258	414	177	51	126
Chiropractic	0	0	0	0	0	0	2,420	1,464	956
Communication sciences and disorders, general	4,852	258	4,594	1,898	87	1,811	32	6	26
Audiology/audiologist	253	19	234	119	9	110	605	100	505
Speech-language pathology/pathologist	1,383	49	1,334	2,881	118	2,763	25	2	23
Audiology/audiologist and speech-language pathology/pathologist	4,539	228	4,311	2,649	120	2,529	212	30	182
Communication disorders sciences and services, other	80	2	78	110	3	107	14	4	10
Dentistry	0	0	0	0	0	0	5,407	2,839	2,568
Dental clinical sciences, general	0	0	0	347	199	148	7	3	4
Advanced general dentistry	0	0	0	8	6	2	0	0	0
Oral biology and oral maxillofacial pathology	0	0	0	92	50	42	16	8	8
Dental public health and education	0	0	0	8	1	7	1	0	1
Dental materials	0	0	0	0	0	0	0	0	0
Endodontics/endodontology	0	0	0	30	20	10	2	1	1
Oral/maxillofacial surgery	0	0	0	0	0	0	0	0	0
Orthodontics/orthodontology	0	0	0	84	40	44	5	3	2
Pediatric dentistry/pedodontics	0	0	0	26	9	17	0	0	0
Periodontics/periodontology	0	0	0	36	20	16	1	1	0
Prosthodontics/prosthodontology	0	0	0	25	17	8	5	3	2
Advanced/graduate dentistry and oral sciences, other	0	0	0	57	27	30	4	3	1
Dental assisting/assistant	1	0	1	0	0	0	0	0	0
Dental hygiene/hygienist	2,059	72	1,987	82	4	78	0	0	0
Dental laboratory technology/technician	0	0	0	13	8	5	0	0	0
Dental services and allied professions, other	13	0	13	4	2	2	0	0	0
Health/health care administration/management	9,249	1,826	7,423	7,836	2,359	5,477	189	58	131
Hospital and health care facilities administration/management	4,400	572	3,828	938	308	630	1	1	0
Health unit manager/ward supervisor	0	0	0	4	1	3	0	0	0

See notes at end of table.

Table 318.30. Bachelor's, master's, and doctor's degrees conferred by postsecondary institutions, by sex of student and discipline division: 2013–14—Continued

Discipline division	Bachelor's degrees			Master's degrees			Doctor's degrees[1]		
	Total	Males	Females	Total	Males	Females	Total	Males	Females
1	2	3	4	5	6	7	8	9	10
Medical office management/administration	10	1	9	0	0	0	0	0	0
Health information/medical records administration/administrator	1,577	258	1,319	295	108	187	0	0	0
Health information/medical records technology/technician	42	15	27	29	4	25	0	0	0
Medical office assistant/specialist	5	2	3	0	0	0	0	0	0
Medical/health management and clinical assistant/specialist	111	24	87	6	1	5	0	0	0
Medical staff services technology/technician	0	0	0	0	0	0	0	0	0
Long term care administration/management	472	43	429	11	2	9	0	0	0
Clinical research coordinator	9	0	9	62	12	50	0	0	0
Health and medical administrative services, other	571	128	443	294	70	224	14	5	9
Medical/clinical assistant	4	1	3	13	5	8	0	0	0
Occupational therapist assistant	0	0	0	0	0	0	0	0	0
Pharmacy technician/assistant	0	0	0	0	0	0	0	0	0
Physical therapy technician/assistant	8	6	2	0	0	0	0	0	0
Veterinary/animal health technology/technician and vet. assistant	384	33	351	0	0	0	0	0	0
Anesthesiologist assistant	0	0	0	124	59	65	0	0	0
Pathology/pathologist assistant	11	3	8	67	13	54	0	0	0
Respiratory therapy technician/assistant	15	8	7	0	0	0	0	0	0
Radiologist assistant	0	0	0	10	3	7	0	0	0
Allied health and medical assisting services, other	356	99	257	156	50	106	0	0	0
Cardiovascular technology/technologist	83	22	61	0	0	0	0	0	0
Emergency medical technology/technician (EMT paramedic)	242	172	70	17	13	4	0	0	0
Nuclear medical technology/technologist	300	99	201	0	0	0	0	0	0
Perfusion technology/perfusionist	6	5	1	62	36	26	0	0	0
Medical radiologic technology/science radiation therapist	1,186	307	879	63	32	31	0	0	0
Respiratory care therapy/therapist	1,100	346	754	25	6	19	0	0	0
Surgical technology/technologist	3	0	3	15	3	12	0	0	0
Diagnostic medical sonography/sonographer and ultrasound technician	647	115	532	9	2	7	0	0	0
Radiologic technology/science radiographer	1,246	326	920	49	23	26	3	2	1
Physician assistant	485	126	359	6,542	1,638	4,904	10	9	1
Athletic training/trainer	3,630	1,495	2,135	548	219	329	1	1	0
Gene/genetic therapy	11	4	7	0	0	0	1	0	1
Cardiopulmonary technology/technologist	6	1	5	0	0	0	0	0	0
Radiation protection/health physics technician	13	2	11	8	7	1	0	0	0
Magnetic resonance imaging (MRI) technology/technician	31	13	18	0	0	0	0	0	0
Allied health diagnostic/intervention/treatment professions, other	325	85	240	13	7	6	143	33	110
Blood bank technology specialist	0	0	0	0	0	0	0	0	0
Cytotechnology/cytotechnologist	45	17	28	8	2	6	0	0	0
Hematology technology/technician	0	0	0	9	5	4	0	0	0
Clinical/medical laboratory technician	125	35	90	0	0	0	0	0	0
Clinical laboratory science/medical technology/technologist	2,700	783	1,917	170	60	110	0	0	0
Histologic technology/histotechnologist	13	1	12	4	0	4	0	0	0
Cytogenetics/genetics/clinical genetics technology/technologist	51	14	37	0	0	0	0	0	0
Clinical/medical laboratory science and allied professions, other	269	80	189	91	31	60	6	4	2
Pre-dentistry studies	13	8	5	0	0	0	0	0	0
Pre-medicine/pre-medical studies	859	367	492	30	13	17	0	0	0
Pre-pharmacy studies	21	8	13	0	0	0	0	0	0
Pre-veterinary studies	302	45	257	0	0	0	0	0	0
Pre-nursing studies	16	2	14	0	0	0	0	0	0
Pre-occupational therapy studies	138	9	129	0	0	0	0	0	0
Pre-optometry studies	1	0	1	0	0	0	0	0	0
Pre-physical therapy studies	215	86	129	0	0	0	0	0	0
Health/medical preparatory programs, other	1,382	394	988	95	38	57	0	0	0
Medicine	0	0	0	0	0	0	17,606	9,234	8,372
Medical scientist	0	0	0	483	245	238	15	8	7
Substance abuse/addiction counseling	457	114	343	421	115	306	0	0	0
Psychiatric/mental health services technician	245	48	197	31	1	30	0	0	0
Clinical/medical social work	212	31	181	586	73	513	5	0	5
Community health services/liaison/counseling	1,104	225	879	245	48	197	9	1	8
Marriage and family therapy/counseling	0	0	0	3,006	463	2,543	113	24	89
Clinical pastoral counseling/patient counseling	38	5	33	95	32	63	34	9	25
Psychoanalysis and psychotherapy	0	0	0	6	3	3	8	2	6
Mental health counseling/counselor	9	1	8	4,891	743	4,148	15	3	12
Genetic counseling/counselor	0	0	0	138	6	132	0	0	0
Mental and social health services and allied professions, other	585	77	508	129	29	100	16	1	15
Optometry	0	0	0	0	0	0	1,523	535	988
Ophthalmic technician/technologist	5	1	4	0	0	0	0	0	0
Orthoptics/orthoptist	2	0	2	0	0	0	0	0	0
Ophthalmic/optometric support services/allied professions, other	10	7	3	20	9	11	3	2	1
Osteopathic medicine/osteopathy	0	0	0	0	0	0	4,990	2,662	2,328
Pharmacy	954	368	586	2	2	0	13,919	5,427	8,492
Pharmacy admin. and pharmacy policy and regulatory affairs	0	0	0	361	139	222	23	9	14
Pharmaceutics and drug design	151	72	79	122	59	63	150	74	76
Medicinal and pharmaceutical chemistry	25	14	11	63	32	31	104	60	44
Natural products chemistry and pharmacognosy	0	0	0	2	1	1	4	3	1
Clinical and industrial drug development	24	6	18	136	36	100	0	0	0
Pharmacoeconomics/pharmaceutical economics	0	0	0	5	2	3	94	41	53
Clinical, hospital, and managed care pharmacy	0	0	0	3	2	1	0	0	0
Industrial and physical pharmacy and cosmetic sciences	2	0	2	14	1	13	0	0	0
Pharmaceutical sciences	613	248	365	210	97	113	157	81	76
Pharmaceutical marketing and management	53	21	32	22	10	12	0	0	0
Pharmacy, pharmaceutical sciences, and administration, other	456	181	275	327	111	216	38	24	14
Podiatric medicine/podiatry	0	0	0	0	0	0	567	338	229
Public health, general	3,050	669	2,381	8,115	2,110	6,005	363	105	258
Environmental health	348	161	187	532	187	345	92	34	58
Health/medical physics	42	23	19	122	87	35	45	29	16
Occupational health and industrial hygiene	152	113	39	114	72	42	15	8	7
Public health education and promotion	2,493	459	2,034	815	104	711	79	14	65
Community health and preventive medicine	1,145	225	920	189	37	152	29	7	22
Maternal and child health	17	0	17	153	4	149	23	2	21
International public health/international health	62	15	47	493	114	379	15	8	7
Health services administration	817	143	674	628	217	411	12	4	8
Behavioral aspects of health	137	43	94	119	13	106	24	4	20
Public health, other	1,045	288	757	553	136	417	78	22	56

See notes at end of table.

Table 318.30. Bachelor's, master's, and doctor's degrees conferred by postsecondary institutions, by sex of student and discipline division: 2013–14—Continued

Discipline division	Bachelor's degrees			Master's degrees			Doctor's degrees[1]		
	Total	Males	Females	Total	Males	Females	Total	Males	Females
1	2	3	4	5	6	7	8	9	10
Art therapy/therapist	194	7	187	452	18	434	4	0	4
Dance therapy/therapist	0	0	0	68	0	68	0	0	0
Music therapy/therapist	293	44	249	115	20	95	1	0	1
Occupational therapy/therapist	890	96	794	5,498	618	4,880	302	25	277
Orthotist/prosthetist	16	10	6	115	44	71	0	0	0
Physical therapy/therapist	304	114	190	179	57	122	10,207	3,416	6,791
Therapeutic recreation/recreational therapy	597	84	513	48	6	42	0	0	0
Vocational rehabilitation counseling/counselor	323	58	265	1,023	220	803	21	3	18
Kinesiotherapy/kinesiotherapist	51	17	34	20	2	18	0	0	0
Assistive/augmentative technology and rehabilitation engineering	0	0	0	10	6	4	0	0	0
Animal-assisted therapy	8	0	8	6	0	6	0	0	0
Rehabilitation science	575	143	432	114	47	67	49	17	32
Rehabilitation and therapeutic professions, other	720	139	581	351	72	279	23	7	16
Veterinary medicine	0	0	0	0	0	0	2,686	565	2,121
Veterinary sciences/veterinary clinical sciences, general	42	4	38	179	55	124	176	63	113
Veterinary physiology	0	0	0	0	0	0	7	4	3
Veterinary microbiology and immunobiology	29	10	19	4	1	3	5	2	3
Veterinary pathology and pathobiology	0	0	0	7	2	5	16	3	13
Large animal/food animal/equine surgery and medicine	0	0	0	1	0	1	1	0	1
Small/companion animal surgery and medicine	0	0	0	4	1	3	0	0	0
Comparative and laboratory animal medicine	0	0	0	36	8	28	0	0	0
Veterinary preventive medicine epidemiology/public health	0	0	0	10	6	4	0	0	0
Veterinary infectious diseases	0	0	0	0	0	0	6	4	2
Medical illustration/medical illustrator	50	4	46	33	5	28	0	0	0
Medical informatics	119	40	79	457	215	242	62	40	22
Dietetics/dietitian	3,096	335	2,761	491	35	456	1	0	1
Clinical nutrition/nutritionist	159	19	140	286	52	234	8	1	7
Dietetic technician	0	0	0	0	0	0	0	0	0
Dietetics and clinical nutrition services, other	313	54	259	89	10	79	0	0	0
Bioethics/medical ethics	13	4	9	246	75	171	21	4	17
Alternative and complementary medicine and medical systems, general	0	0	0	22	7	15	8	2	6
Acupuncture and oriental medicine	91	29	62	1,425	418	1,007	83	37	46
Traditional Chinese medicine and Chinese herbology	0	0	0	251	63	188	16	5	11
Naturopathic medicine/naturopathy	0	0	0	0	0	0	294	73	221
Holistic health	157	33	124	30	7	23	0	0	0
Alternative and complementary medicine and medical systems, other	176	30	146	18	1	17	0	0	0
Direct entry midwifery	20	0	20	14	0	14	0	0	0
Massage therapy/therapeutic massage	0	0	0	0	0	0	0	0	0
Asian bodywork therapy	0	0	0	0	0	0	0	0	0
Movement therapy and movement education	54	30	24	22	0	22	6	2	4
Herbalism/herbalist	12	4	8	16	0	16	0	0	0
Energy and biologically based therapies, other	0	0	0	0	0	0	0	0	0
Registered nursing/registered nurse	110,817	13,454	97,363	14,201	1,442	12,759	643	59	584
Nursing administration	979	80	899	4,552	480	4,072	294	34	260
Adult health nurse/nursing	73	6	67	1,089	97	992	15	0	15
Nurse anesthetist	0	0	0	1,650	648	1,002	80	32	48
Family practice nurse/nursing	298	44	254	5,480	605	4,875	211	17	194
Maternal/child health and neonatal nurse/nursing	0	0	0	235	12	223	1	0	1
Nurse midwife/nursing midwifery	0	0	0	328	0	328	11	0	11
Nursing science	1,145	127	1,018	2,181	233	1,948	643	40	603
Pediatric nurse/nursing	0	0	0	295	12	283	12	0	12
Psychiatric/mental health nurse/nursing	0	0	0	314	52	262	14	1	13
Public health/community nurse/nursing	17	1	16	159	8	151	0	0	0
Perioperative/operating room and surgical nurse/nursing	0	0	0	74	5	69	0	0	0
Clinical nurse specialist	62	6	56	330	43	287	45	4	41
Critical care nursing	0	0	0	233	30	203	13	1	12
Occupational and environmental health nursing	0	0	0	18	3	15	2	0	2
Emergency room/trauma nursing	0	0	0	26	9	17	0	0	0
Nursing education	28	0	28	1,800	112	1,688	21	2	19
Nursing practice	804	98	706	236	17	219	1,768	185	1,583
Palliative care nursing	4	0	4	9	2	7	0	0	0
Clinical nurse leader	11	0	11	336	43	293	0	0	0
Geriatric nurse/nursing	0	0	0	242	37	205	2	0	2
Women's health nurse/nursing	0	0	0	146	0	146	0	0	0
Reg. nursing, nursing admin., nursing research and clinical nursing, other	1,617	187	1,430	1,175	99	1,076	161	15	146
Licensed practical/vocational nurse training	30	5	25	0	0	0	0	0	0
Practical nursing, vocational nursing and nursing assistants, other	73	6	67	23	0	23	0	0	0
Health professions and related clinical sciences, other	4,445	1,043	3,402	736	221	515	40	15	25
Homeland security, law enforcement, firefighting and related prot. services	62,409	33,383	29,026	9,310	4,665	4,645	152	66	86
Corrections	481	209	272	18	5	13	0	0	0
Criminal justice/law enforcement administration	19,363	10,035	9,328	3,039	1,370	1,669	28	11	17
Criminal justice/safety studies	31,415	16,452	14,963	2,869	1,247	1,622	101	41	60
Forensic science and technology	1,184	317	867	612	163	449	0	0	0
Criminal justice/police science	2,854	1,682	1,172	60	17	43	3	2	1
Security and loss prevention services	23	16	7	17	13	4	0	0	0
Juvenile corrections	30	6	24	6	2	4	5	3	2
Criminalistics and criminal science	200	63	137	51	14	37	0	0	0
Securities services administration/management	967	555	412	286	224	62	0	0	0
Corrections administration	90	48	42	11	3	8	0	0	0
Law enforcement investigation and interviewing	10	4	6	0	0	0	0	0	0
Cyber/computer forensics and counterterrorism	201	163	38	110	77	33	0	0	0
Financial forensics and fraud investigation	39	12	27	111	43	68	0	0	0
Law enforcement intelligence analysis	22	17	5	11	5	6	0	0	0
Critical incident response/special police operations	0	0	0	0	0	0	0	0	0
Protective services operations	0	0	0	0	0	0	0	0	0
Corrections and criminal justice, other	1,662	737	925	173	68	105	0	0	0
Fire prevention and safety technology/technician	147	135	12	12	8	4	0	0	0
Fire services administration	533	495	38	122	91	31	2	0	2
Fire science/firefighting	661	619	42	0	0	0	0	0	0
Fire/arson investigation and prevention	15	12	3	0	0	0	0	0	0
Fire protection, other	34	30	4	1	1	0	0	0	0
Homeland security	691	549	142	483	377	106	0	0	0
Crisis/emergency/disaster management	676	470	206	448	308	140	11	7	4

See notes at end of table.

Table 318.30. Bachelor's, master's, and doctor's degrees conferred by postsecondary institutions, by sex of student and discipline division: 2013–14—Continued

Discipline division	Bachelor's degrees			Master's degrees			Doctor's degrees[1]		
	Total	Males	Females	Total	Males	Females	Total	Males	Females
1	2	3	4	5	6	7	8	9	10
Art therapy/therapist	194	7	187	452	18	434	4	0	4
Dance therapy/therapist	0	0	0	68	0	68	0	0	0
Music therapy/therapist	293	44	249	115	20	95	1	0	1
Occupational therapy/therapist	890	96	794	5,498	618	4,880	302	25	277
Orthotist/prosthetist	16	10	6	115	44	71	0	0	0
Physical therapy/therapist	304	114	190	179	57	122	10,207	3,416	6,791
Therapeutic recreation/recreational therapy	597	84	513	48	6	42	0	0	0
Vocational rehabilitation counseling/counselor	323	58	265	1,023	220	803	21	3	18
Kinesiotherapy/kinesiotherapist	51	17	34	20	2	18	0	0	0
Assistive/augmentative technology and rehabilitation engineering	0	0	0	10	6	4	0	0	0
Animal-assisted therapy	8	0	8	6	0	6	0	0	0
Rehabilitation science	575	143	432	114	47	67	49	17	32
Rehabilitation and therapeutic professions, other	720	139	581	351	72	279	23	7	16
Veterinary medicine	0	0	0	0	0	0	2,686	565	2,121
Veterinary sciences/veterinary clinical sciences, general	42	4	38	179	55	124	176	63	113
Veterinary physiology	0	0	0	0	0	0	7	4	3
Veterinary microbiology and immunobiology	29	10	19	4	1	3	5	2	3
Veterinary pathology and pathobiology	0	0	0	7	2	5	16	3	13
Large animal/food animal/equine surgery and medicine	0	0	0	1	0	1	1	0	1
Small/companion animal surgery and medicine	0	0	0	4	1	3	0	0	0
Comparative and laboratory animal medicine	0	0	0	36	8	28	0	0	0
Veterinary preventive medicine epidemiology/public health	0	0	0	10	6	4	0	0	0
Veterinary infectious diseases	0	0	0	0	0	0	6	4	2
Medical illustration/medical illustrator	50	4	46	33	5	28	0	0	0
Medical informatics	119	40	79	457	215	242	62	40	22
Dietetics/dietitian	3,096	335	2,761	491	35	456	1	0	1
Clinical nutrition/nutritionist	159	19	140	286	52	234	8	1	7
Dietetic technician	0	0	0	0	0	0	0	0	0
Dietetics and clinical nutrition services, other	313	54	259	89	10	79	0	0	0
Bioethics/medical ethics	13	4	9	246	75	171	21	4	17
Alternative and complementary medicine and medical systems, general	0	0	0	22	7	15	8	2	6
Acupuncture and oriental medicine	91	29	62	1,425	418	1,007	83	37	46
Traditional Chinese medicine and Chinese herbology	0	0	0	251	63	188	16	5	11
Naturopathic medicine/naturopathy	0	0	0	0	0	0	294	73	221
Holistic health	157	33	124	30	7	23	0	0	0
Alternative and complementary medicine and medical systems, other	176	30	146	18	1	17	0	0	0
Direct entry midwifery	20	0	20	14	0	14	0	0	0
Massage therapy/therapeutic massage	0	0	0	0	0	0	0	0	0
Asian bodywork therapy	0	0	0	0	0	0	0	0	0
Movement therapy and movement education	54	30	24	22	0	22	6	2	4
Herbalism/herbalist	12	4	8	16	0	16	0	0	0
Energy and biologically based therapies, other	0	0	0	0	0	0	0	0	0
Registered nursing/registered nurse	110,817	13,454	97,363	14,201	1,442	12,759	643	59	584
Nursing administration	979	80	899	4,552	480	4,072	294	34	260
Adult health nurse/nursing	73	6	67	1,089	97	992	15	0	15
Nurse anesthetist	0	0	0	1,650	648	1,002	80	32	48
Family practice nurse/nursing	298	44	254	5,480	605	4,875	211	17	194
Maternal/child health and neonatal nurse/nursing	0	0	0	235	12	223	1	0	1
Nurse midwife/nursing midwifery	0	0	0	328	0	328	11	0	11
Nursing science	1,145	127	1,018	2,181	233	1,948	643	40	603
Pediatric nurse/nursing	0	0	0	295	12	283	12	0	12
Psychiatric/mental health nurse/nursing	0	0	0	314	52	262	14	1	13
Public health/community nurse/nursing	17	1	16	159	8	151	0	0	0
Perioperative/operating room and surgical nurse/nursing	0	0	0	74	5	69	0	0	0
Clinical nurse specialist	62	6	56	330	43	287	45	4	41
Critical care nursing	0	0	0	233	30	203	13	1	12
Occupational and environmental health nursing	0	0	0	18	3	15	2	0	2
Emergency room/trauma nursing	0	0	0	26	9	17	0	0	0
Nursing education	28	0	28	1,800	112	1,688	21	2	19
Nursing practice	804	98	706	236	17	219	1,768	185	1,583
Palliative care nursing	4	0	4	9	2	7	0	0	0
Clinical nurse leader	11	0	11	336	43	293	0	0	0
Geriatric nurse/nursing	0	0	0	242	37	205	2	0	2
Women's health nurse/nursing	0	0	0	146	0	146	0	0	0
Reg. nursing, nursing admin., nursing research and clinical nursing, other	1,617	187	1,430	1,175	99	1,076	161	15	146
Licensed practical/vocational nurse training	30	5	25	0	0	0	0	0	0
Practical nursing, vocational nursing and nursing assistants, other	73	6	67	23	0	23	0	0	0
Health professions and related clinical sciences, other	4,445	1,043	3,402	736	221	515	40	15	25
Homeland security, law enforcement, firefighting and related prot. services	62,409	33,383	29,026	9,310	4,665	4,645	152	66	86
Corrections	481	209	272	18	5	13	0	0	0
Criminal justice/law enforcement administration	19,363	10,035	9,328	3,039	1,370	1,669	28	11	17
Criminal justice/safety studies	31,415	16,452	14,963	2,869	1,247	1,622	101	41	60
Forensic science and technology	1,184	317	867	612	163	449	0	0	0
Criminal justice/police science	2,854	1,682	1,172	60	17	43	3	2	1
Security and loss prevention services	23	16	7	17	13	4	0	0	0
Juvenile corrections	30	6	24	6	2	4	5	3	2
Criminalistics and criminal science	200	63	137	51	14	37	0	0	0
Securities services administration/management	967	555	412	286	224	62	0	0	0
Corrections administration	90	48	42	11	3	8	0	0	0
Law enforcement investigation and interviewing	10	4	6	0	0	0	0	0	0
Cyber/computer forensics and counterterrorism	201	163	38	110	77	33	0	0	0
Financial forensics and fraud investigation	39	12	27	111	43	68	0	0	0
Law enforcement intelligence analysis	22	17	5	11	5	6	0	0	0
Critical incident response/special police operations	0	0	0	0	0	0	0	0	0
Protective services operations	0	0	0	0	0	0	0	0	0
Corrections and criminal justice, other	1,662	737	925	173	68	105	0	0	0
Fire prevention and safety technology/technician	147	135	12	12	8	4	0	0	0
Fire services administration	533	495	38	122	91	31	0	0	0
Fire science/firefighting	661	619	42	0	0	0	2	0	2
Fire/arson investigation and prevention	15	12	3	0	0	0	0	0	0
Fire protection, other	34	30	4	1	1	0	0	0	0
Homeland security	691	549	142	483	377	106	0	0	0
Crisis/emergency/disaster management	676	470	206	448	308	140	11	7	4

See notes at end of table.

Table 318.30. Bachelor's, master's, and doctor's degrees conferred by postsecondary institutions, by sex of student and discipline division: 2013–14—Continued

Discipline division	Bachelor's degrees			Master's degrees			Doctor's degrees[1]		
	Total	Males	Females	Total	Males	Females	Total	Males	Females
1	2	3	4	5	6	7	8	9	10
Critical infrastructure protection	55	34	21	86	62	24	0	0	0
Terrorism and counterterrorism operations	0	0	0	12	9	3	0	0	0
Homeland security, other	79	56	23	138	102	36	0	0	0
Homeland sec., law enforcement, firefighting and related prot. serv., other	977	667	310	634	456	178	2	2	0
Legal professions and studies	4,513	1,456	3,057	7,655	3,567	4,088	44,169	23,495	20,674
Pre-law studies	300	156	144	0	0	0	0	0	0
Legal studies, general	1,846	667	1,179	407	127	280	11	2	9
Law	0	0	0	0	0	0	43,772	23,278	20,494
Advanced legal research/studies, general	118	64	54	1,713	766	947	81	51	30
Programs for foreign lawyers	0	0	0	1,064	552	512	0	0	0
American/U.S. law/legal studies/jurisprudence	30	12	18	306	120	186	35	14	21
Banking, corporate, finance, and securities law	0	0	0	280	140	140	1	1	0
Comparative law	0	0	0	51	33	18	0	0	0
Energy, environment, and natural resources law	2	1	1	91	52	39	4	4	0
Health law	0	0	0	215	46	169	4	3	1
International law and legal studies	2	1	1	583	247	336	20	9	11
International business, trade, and tax law	0	0	0	237	129	108	0	0	0
Tax law/taxation	0	0	0	741	477	264	25	12	13
Intellectual property law	0	0	0	137	58	79	24	12	12
Legal research and advanced professional studies, other	0	0	0	801	381	420	104	64	40
Legal administrative assistant/secretary	21	6	15	0	0	0	0	0	0
Legal assistant/paralegal	1,826	421	1,405	103	15	88	0	0	0
Court reporting/court reporter	10	0	10	0	0	0	0	0	0
Legal support services, other	0	0	0	11	4	7	0	0	0
Legal professions and studies, other	358	128	230	915	420	495	88	45	43
Liberal arts and sciences, general studies and humanities	45,260	16,485	28,775	3,002	1,209	1,793	90	29	61
Liberal arts and sciences/liberal studies	24,689	8,175	16,514	1,950	802	1,148	24	8	16
General studies	15,105	6,224	8,881	143	55	88	1	0	1
Humanities/humanistic studies	2,499	806	1,693	574	214	360	60	19	41
Liberal arts and sciences, general studies and humanities, other	2,967	1,280	1,687	335	138	197	5	2	3
Library science	127	14	113	5,839	1,060	4,779	52	14	38
Library and information science	127	14	113	5,703	1,043	4,660	52	14	38
Library science, other	0	0	0	136	17	119	0	0	0
Mathematics and statistics	20,980	11,967	9,013	7,273	4,256	3,017	1,863	1,325	538
Mathematics, general	16,914	9,494	7,420	2,900	1,746	1,154	1,131	846	285
Analysis and functional analysis	1	1	0	0	0	0	0	0	0
Topology and foundations	0	0	0	0	0	0	3	1	2
Mathematics, other	322	192	130	37	14	23	9	4	5
Applied mathematics, general	1,607	1,009	598	802	532	270	250	178	72
Computational mathematics	113	90	23	26	18	8	22	17	5
Computational and applied mathematics	82	50	32	63	42	21	30	25	5
Financial mathematics	107	61	46	773	473	300	1	0	1
Mathematical biology	19	9	10	0	0	0	0	0	0
Applied mathematics, other	111	81	30	119	78	41	9	6	3
Statistics, general	1,205	695	510	2,317	1,207	1,110	374	228	146
Mathematical statistics and probability	178	95	83	112	71	41	14	10	4
Mathematics and statistics	58	24	34	50	30	20	0	0	0
Statistics, other	56	35	21	36	25	11	4	2	2
Mathematics and statistics, other	207	131	76	38	20	18	16	8	8
Military technologies and applied sciences	185	161	24	29	21	8	0	0	0
Intelligence, general	75	72	3	0	0	0	0	0	0
Strategic intelligence	0	0	0	25	18	7	0	0	0
Intelligence, command control and information operations, other	0	0	0	4	3	1	0	0	0
Military applied sciences, other	54	49	5	0	0	0	0	0	0
Military technologies and applied sciences, other	56	40	16	0	0	0	0	0	0
Multi/interdisciplinary studies	48,348	16,119	32,229	8,075	3,061	5,014	769	322	447
Multi/interdisciplinary studies, general	3,356	1,251	2,105	80	30	50	21	13	8
Biological and physical sciences	2,291	971	1,320	428	174	254	49	26	23
Peace studies and conflict resolution	464	162	302	554	180	374	16	9	7
Systems science and theory	258	159	99	221	111	110	24	16	8
Mathematics and computer science	260	200	60	26	16	10	20	14	6
Biopsychology	186	49	137	8	4	4	4	0	4
Gerontology	306	28	278	457	58	399	28	6	22
Historic preservation and conservation	100	25	75	225	51	174	3	2	1
Cultural resource management and policy analysis	0	0	0	26	8	18	0	0	0
Historic preservation and conservation, other	0	0	0	6	0	6	0	0	0
Medieval and renaissance studies	37	12	25	25	11	14	8	6	2
Museology/museum studies	19	1	18	542	64	478	0	0	0
Science, technology and society	666	362	304	124	48	76	29	15	14
Accounting and computer science	2	1	1	4	3	1	0	0	0
Behavioral sciences	5,727	1,097	4,630	46	13	33	22	5	17
Natural sciences	625	234	391	96	40	56	13	8	5
Nutrition sciences	1,932	336	1,596	685	110	575	118	25	93
International/global studies	5,513	2,174	3,339	1,208	715	493	1	0	1
Holocaust and related studies	7	2	5	15	6	9	0	0	0
Ancient studies/civilization	99	35	64	6	1	5	4	1	3
Classical, ancient Mediterranean/Near Eastern studies/archaeology	100	34	66	4	0	4	3	1	2
Intercultural/multicultural and diversity studies	186	49	137	137	37	100	2	0	2
Cognitive science	902	347	555	72	35	37	32	21	11
Cultural studies/critical theory and analysis	137	59	78	37	19	18	2	1	1
Human biology	741	215	526	0	0	0	0	0	0
Dispute resolution	0	0	0	288	112	176	40	20	20
Maritime studies	13	6	7	0	0	0	0	0	0
Computational science	15	11	4	56	43	13	12	11	1
Human computer interaction	37	28	9	130	69	61	3	3	0
Marine sciences	62	25	37	51	15	36	17	12	5
Sustainability studies	312	155	157	327	146	181	1	0	1
Multi/interdisciplinary studies, other	23,995	8,091	15,904	2,191	942	1,249	297	107	190
Parks, recreation, leisure, and fitness studies	46,042	24,713	21,329	7,609	4,338	3,271	317	158	159
Parks, recreation and leisure studies	3,186	1,589	1,597	236	116	120	26	15	11
Parks, recreation and leisure facilities management	3,045	1,517	1,528	412	208	204	23	9	14
Golf course operation and grounds management	12	12	0	0	0	0	0	0	0
Parks, recreation and leisure facilities management, other	3	2	1	0	0	0	0	0	0

See notes at end of table.

Table 318.30. Bachelor's, master's, and doctor's degrees conferred by postsecondary institutions, by sex of student and discipline division: 2013–14—Continued

Discipline division	Bachelor's degrees			Master's degrees			Doctor's degrees[1]		
	Total	Males	Females	Total	Males	Females	Total	Males	Females
1	2	3	4	5	6	7	8	9	10
Health and physical education/fitness, general	9,087	4,592	4,495	1,079	596	483	23	13	10
Sport and fitness administration/management	8,435	6,141	2,294	3,482	2,209	1,273	8	7	1
Kinesiology and exercise science	20,670	9,949	10,721	2,182	1,100	1,082	208	106	102
Physical fitness technician	55	30	25	0	0	0	0	0	0
Sports studies	217	162	55	105	51	54	0	0	0
Health and physical education/fitness, other	1,062	549	513	47	22	25	23	7	16
Outdoor education	99	67	32	52	26	26	0	0	0
Parks, recreation, leisure, and fitness studies, other	171	103	68	14	10	4	6	1	5
Philosophy and religious studies	11,997	7,582	4,415	2,095	1,312	783	698	461	237
Philosophy and religious studies, general	91	54	37	7	2	5	16	7	9
Philosophy	6,774	4,762	2,012	865	656	209	411	294	117
Logic	1	1	0	10	7	3	1	1	0
Ethics	77	21	56	59	29	30	0	0	0
Applied and professional ethics	12	4	8	16	7	9	0	0	0
Philosophy, other	208	113	95	5	4	1	13	9	4
Religion/religious studies	3,904	2,102	1,802	516	287	229	209	133	76
Buddhist studies	0	0	0	2	0	2	1	0	1
Christian studies	365	238	127	364	195	169	0	0	0
Islamic studies	12	4	8	13	8	5	3	1	2
Jewish/Judaic studies	211	76	135	85	31	54	14	6	8
Religion/religious studies, other	87	45	42	45	20	25	11	4	7
Philosophy and religious studies, other	255	162	93	108	66	42	19	6	13
Physical sciences and science technologies	29,304	17,802	11,502	6,984	4,312	2,672	5,806	3,873	1,933
Physical sciences	28,808	17,533	11,275	6,950	4,294	2,656	5,805	3,873	1,932
Physical sciences	396	205	191	58	33	25	49	33	16
Astronomy	220	136	84	103	57	46	100	64	36
Astrophysics	167	103	64	33	21	12	36	27	9
Planetary astronomy and science	9	6	3	12	7	5	24	11	13
Astronomy and astrophysics, other	33	14	19	12	9	3	19	15	4
Atmospheric sciences and meteorology, general	518	332	186	233	131	102	99	68	31
Atmospheric physics and dynamics	0	0	0	0	0	0	1	1	0
Meteorology	206	140	66	29	20	9	19	12	7
Atmospheric sciences and meteorology, other	27	21	6	1	1	0	7	4	3
Chemistry, general	13,730	7,174	6,556	2,234	1,204	1,030	2,673	1,614	1,059
Analytical chemistry	10	1	9	23	10	13	6	3	3
Inorganic chemistry	0	0	0	0	0	0	0	0	0
Organic chemistry	0	0	0	2	2	0	8	5	3
Physical chemistry	1	1	0	1	0	1	3	2	1
Polymer chemistry	1	1	0	51	37	14	40	30	10
Chemical physics	30	23	7	1	1	0	17	14	3
Environmental chemistry	5	2	3	1	0	1	4	3	1
Forensic chemistry	59	14	45	0	0	0	0	0	0
Theoretical chemistry	4	3	1	0	0	0	0	0	0
Chemistry, other	602	288	314	44	20	24	45	28	17
Geology/earth science, general	4,984	3,107	1,877	1,429	852	577	434	234	200
Geochemistry	14	7	7	6	1	5	4	1	3
Geophysics and seismology	126	81	45	134	90	44	88	58	30
Paleontology	1	1	0	4	2	2	0	0	0
Hydrology and water resources science	53	30	23	64	45	19	15	9	6
Geochemistry and petrology	0	0	0	0	0	0	0	0	0
Oceanography, chemical and physical	255	133	122	152	66	86	129	57	72
Geological and earth sciences/geosciences, other	526	274	252	144	73	71	65	43	22
Physics, general	6,002	4,878	1,124	1,666	1,281	385	1,622	1,329	293
Atomic/molecular physics	0	0	0	3	3	0	3	3	0
Elementary particle physics	0	0	0	0	0	0	0	0	0
Nuclear physics	1	1	0	1	1	0	3	2	1
Optics/optical sciences	39	32	7	76	59	17	51	37	14
Condensed matter and materials physics	0	0	0	2	1	1	5	3	2
Acoustics	9	9	0	11	9	2	7	7	0
Theoretical and mathematical physics	11	10	1	0	0	0	1	1	0
Physics, other	199	152	47	107	78	29	76	55	21
Materials science	143	97	46	193	124	69	122	85	37
Materials chemistry	6	6	0	12	10	2	5	4	1
Materials sciences, other	0	0	0	0	0	0	1	1	0
Physical sciences, other	421	251	170	108	46	62	24	10	14
Science technologies/technicians	496	269	227	34	18	16	1	0	1
Science technologies/technicians, general	23	19	4	0	0	0	0	0	0
Biology technician/biotechnology laboratory technician	33	11	22	0	0	0	1	0	1
Nuclear/nuclear power technology/technician	9	8	1	0	0	0	0	0	0
Nuclear and industrial radiologic technologies/technicians, other	0	0	0	0	0	0	0	0	0
Chemical technology/technician	0	0	0	5	2	3	0	0	0
Physical science technologies/technicians, other	0	0	0	0	0	0	0	0	0
Science technologies/technicians, other	431	231	200	29	16	13	0	0	0
Precision production	37	21	16	15	10	5	0	0	0
Tool and die technology/technician	0	0	0	0	0	0	0	0	0
Welding technology/welder	7	7	0	0	0	0	0	0	0
Furniture design and manufacturing	30	14	16	15	10	5	0	0	0
Psychology	117,298	27,304	89,994	27,966	5,731	22,235	6,634	1,680	4,954
Psychology, general	109,165	25,492	83,673	6,368	1,593	4,775	1,895	572	1,323
Cognitive psychology and psycholinguistics	81	22	59	5	2	3	7	6	1
Comparative psychology	0	0	0	5	4	1	0	0	0
Developmental and child psychology	706	65	641	356	29	327	58	8	50
Experimental psychology	860	226	634	180	53	127	123	46	77
Personality psychology	15	3	12	7	1	6	10	1	9
Physiological psychology/psychobiology	1,158	367	791	28	3	25	12	5	7
Social psychology	1,033	224	809	49	19	30	49	15	34
Psychometrics and quantitative psychology	0	0	0	13	3	10	7	4	3
Psychopharmacology	0	0	0	36	15	21	0	0	0
Research and experimental psychology, other	971	271	700	18	6	12	63	24	39
Clinical psychology	101	30	71	2,798	590	2,208	2,564	579	1,985
Community psychology	461	70	391	225	43	182	25	7	18
Counseling psychology	676	106	570	9,193	1,696	7,497	500	113	387
Industrial and organizational psychology	272	90	182	1,044	342	702	140	48	92

See notes at end of table.

Table 318.30. Bachelor's, master's, and doctor's degrees conferred by postsecondary institutions, by sex of student and discipline division: 2013–14—Continued

Discipline division	Bachelor's degrees			Master's degrees			Doctor's degrees[1]		
	Total	Males	Females	Total	Males	Females	Total	Males	Females
1	2	3	4	5	6	7	8	9	10
School psychology	0	0	0	1,675	236	1,439	315	49	266
Educational psychology	117	13	104	1,279	234	1,045	421	115	306
Clinical child psychology	0	0	0	17	1	16	34	3	31
Environmental psychology	31	16	15	71	32	39	13	2	11
Geropsychology	0	0	0	1	1	0	0	0	0
Health/medical psychology	39	7	32	32	8	24	18	1	17
Family psychology	17	3	14	44	10	34	2	2	0
Forensic psychology	538	100	438	831	119	712	100	22	78
Applied psychology	577	108	469	548	88	460	5	1	4
Applied behavior analysis	133	32	101	294	32	262	48	4	44
Clinical, counseling and applied psychology, other	25	6	19	457	92	365	90	12	78
Psychology, other	322	53	269	2,392	479	1,913	135	41	94
Public administration and social service professions	33,483	5,917	27,566	44,490	10,833	33,657	1,047	346	701
Human services, general	7,272	971	6,301	2,499	485	2,014	55	9	46
Community organization and advocacy	1,754	423	1,331	568	180	388	7	3	4
Public administration	3,247	1,608	1,639	13,252	5,489	7,763	282	144	138
Public policy analysis, general	1,319	578	741	2,715	1,200	1,515	205	85	120
Education policy analysis	1	0	1	40	6	34	24	7	17
Health policy analysis	78	14	64	105	52	53	9	3	6
International policy analysis	14	1	13	43	32	11	0	0	0
Public policy analysis, other	1	1	0	57	15	42	9	4	5
Social work	19,400	2,228	17,172	24,460	3,192	21,268	363	74	289
Youth services/administration	90	10	80	60	8	52	0	0	0
Social work, other	29	5	24	167	28	139	0	0	0
Public administration and social service professions, other	278	78	200	524	146	378	93	17	76
Social sciences and history	173,096	88,233	84,863	21,475	10,750	10,725	4,724	2,494	2,230
Social sciences	141,990	69,480	72,510	17,520	8,548	8,972	3,684	1,901	1,783
Social sciences, general	8,166	3,047	5,119	572	188	384	21	6	15
Research methodology and quantitative methods	4	1	3	11	4	7	0	0	0
Anthropology	10,909	3,090	7,819	1,193	380	813	567	218	349
Physical and biological anthropology	26	7	19	18	1	17	1	0	1
Medical anthropology	4	1	3	0	0	0	0	0	0
Cultural anthropology	53	9	44	19	3	16	4	3	1
Anthropology, other	60	21	39	26	9	17	16	4	12
Archeology	215	78	137	60	23	37	18	3	15
Criminology	7,113	3,617	3,496	749	290	459	46	17	29
Demography and population studies	0	0	0	34	12	22	18	8	10
Economics, general	28,382	19,737	8,645	2,883	1,812	1,071	993	676	317
Applied economics	244	164	80	392	246	146	26	13	13
Econometrics and quantitative economics	546	363	183	81	44	37	6	2	4
Development economics and international development	232	65	167	389	160	229	7	3	4
International economics	228	120	108	215	114	101	15	8	7
Economics, other	363	240	123	155	75	80	12	6	6
Geography	4,476	2,855	1,621	792	476	316	289	136	153
Geographic information science and cartography	259	202	57	298	194	104	10	5	5
Geography, other	156	86	70	20	13	7	7	4	3
International relations and affairs	9,331	3,731	5,600	4,398	2,131	2,267	80	39	41
National security policy studies	33	24	9	195	131	64	0	0	0
International relations and national security studies, other	130	76	54	118	65	53	0	0	0
Political science and government, general	36,258	20,401	15,857	2,018	1,160	858	785	452	333
American government and politics (United States)	191	112	79	174	117	57	0	0	0
Political economy	179	99	80	0	0	0	1	1	0
Political science and government, other	733	388	345	102	46	56	6	3	3
Sociology	30,059	9,418	20,641	1,611	519	1,092	674	249	425
Urban studies/affairs	1,044	492	552	444	194	250	53	28	25
Sociology and anthropology	507	145	362	9	4	5	0	0	0
Rural sociology	33	11	22	0	0	0	0	0	0
Social sciences, other	2,056	880	1,176	544	137	407	29	17	12
History	31,106	18,753	12,353	3,955	2,202	1,753	1,040	593	447
History, general	30,361	18,316	12,045	3,327	1,818	1,509	966	550	416
American history (United States)	47	38	9	76	24	52	9	7	2
European history	20	12	8	0	0	0	0	0	0
History and philosophy of science and technology	133	52	81	28	9	19	41	23	18
Public/applied history	32	12	20	141	34	107	0	0	0
Asian history	1	1	0	0	0	0	2	1	1
Military history	64	53	11	207	184	23	0	0	0
History, other	448	269	179	176	133	43	22	12	10
Theology and religious vocations	9,642	6,594	3,048	14,128	9,245	4,883	2,103	1,522	581
Bible/biblical studies	2,728	1,773	955	511	381	130	55	50	5
Missions/missionary studies and missiology	444	158	286	250	129	121	111	98	13
Religious education	965	532	433	503	234	269	61	36	25
Religious/sacred music	320	189	131	114	64	50	0	0	0
Theology/theological studies	999	689	310	4,077	2,772	1,305	603	477	126
Divinity/ministry	248	160	88	5,704	3,834	1,870	514	311	203
Pre-theology/pre-ministerial studies	155	118	37	2	2	0	0	0	0
Rabbinical studies	0	0	0	109	72	37	12	12	0
Talmudic studies	1,777	1,777	0	466	466	0	18	18	0
Theological and ministerial studies, other	350	227	123	678	451	227	313	240	73
Pastoral studies/counseling	500	310	190	788	331	457	127	87	40
Youth ministry	584	370	214	45	25	20	0	0	0
Urban ministry	23	11	12	23	7	16	15	11	4
Women's ministry	2	0	2	0	0	0	0	0	0
Lay ministry	101	55	46	79	26	53	0	0	0
Pastoral counseling and specialized ministries, other	112	36	76	185	88	97	39	26	13
Theology and religious vocations, other	334	189	145	594	363	231	235	156	79
Transportation and materials moving	4,588	4,053	535	1,243	1,020	223	7	6	1
Aeronautics/aviation/aerospace science and technology, general	2,268	2,025	243	937	788	149	5	4	1
Airline/commercial/professional pilot and flight crew	897	813	84	0	0	0	0	0	0
Aviation/airway management and operations	806	681	125	242	187	55	2	2	0
Air traffic controller	240	196	44	0	0	0	0	0	0
Flight instructor	7	7	0	0	0	0	0	0	0

See notes at end of table.

Table 318.30. Bachelor's, master's, and doctor's degrees conferred by postsecondary institutions, by sex of student and discipline division: 2013–14—Continued

Discipline division	Bachelor's degrees			Master's degrees			Doctor's degrees[1]		
	Total	Males	Females	Total	Males	Females	Total	Males	Females
1	2	3	4	5	6	7	8	9	10
Air transportation, other	20	18	2	58	40	18	0	0	0
Marine science/merchant marine officer	348	311	37	0	0	0	0	0	0
Transportation and materials moving, other	2	2	0	6	5	1	0	0	0
Visual and performing arts	97,246	38,081	59,165	17,863	7,711	10,152	1,778	869	909
Visual and performing arts, general	1,746	647	1,099	166	64	102	16	10	6
Digital arts	573	347	226	137	92	45	0	0	0
Crafts/craft design, folk art and artisanry	130	35	95	7	2	5	0	0	0
Dance, general	2,168	239	1,929	215	36	179	6	0	6
Ballet	42	4	38	0	0	0	0	0	0
Dance, other	24	1	23	2	0	2	4	0	4
Design and visual communications, general	3,177	1,067	2,110	508	182	326	3	1	2
Commercial and advertising art	1,326	482	844	88	35	53	0	0	0
Industrial and product design	1,608	976	632	189	111	78	0	0	0
Commercial photography	509	164	345	20	9	11	0	0	0
Fashion/apparel design	2,308	216	2,092	246	18	228	0	0	0
Interior design	3,290	357	2,933	409	66	343	0	0	0
Graphic design	6,186	2,335	3,851	301	103	198	0	0	0
Illustration	1,844	640	1,204	159	68	91	0	0	0
Game and interactive media design	1,331	1,080	251	167	119	48	0	0	0
Design and applied arts, other	667	250	417	272	81	191	7	2	5
Drama and dramatics/theatre arts, general	9,229	3,426	5,803	975	387	588	101	42	59
Technical theatre/theatre design and technology	566	290	276	160	65	95	0	0	0
Playwriting and screenwriting	239	120	119	220	126	94	0	0	0
Theatre literature, history and criticism	35	18	17	8	1	7	3	2	1
Acting	779	310	469	251	129	122	0	0	0
Directing and theatrical production	72	25	47	84	32	52	0	0	0
Musical theatre	429	174	255	0	0	0	0	0	0
Costume design	16	3	13	6	2	4	0	0	0
Dramatic/theatre arts and stagecraft, other	308	108	200	56	25	31	4	1	3
Film/cinema/video studies	3,261	1,912	1,349	322	163	159	42	21	21
Cinematography and film/video production	4,742	3,179	1,563	859	493	366	5	2	3
Photography	1,858	566	1,292	282	153	129	0	0	0
Documentary production	32	10	22	24	11	13	0	0	0
Film/video and photographic arts, other	917	539	378	178	106	72	0	0	0
Art/art studies, general	12,320	3,622	8,698	757	297	460	7	1	6
Fine/studio arts, general	10,247	3,226	7,021	1,521	632	889	0	0	0
Art history, criticism and conservation	3,167	448	2,719	941	119	822	255	57	198
Drawing	302	98	204	21	12	9	0	0	0
Intermedia/multimedia	454	203	251	59	32	27	0	0	0
Painting	693	215	478	190	96	94	0	0	0
Sculpture	279	99	180	62	35	27	0	0	0
Printmaking	172	57	115	44	11	33	0	0	0
Ceramic arts and ceramics	227	61	166	41	15	26	0	0	0
Fiber, textile and weaving arts	218	21	197	30	2	28	2	1	1
Metal and jewelry arts	119	13	106	35	5	30	0	0	0
Fine arts and art studies, other	1,018	302	716	338	118	220	1	1	0
Music, general	7,897	4,234	3,663	2,029	1,057	972	526	313	213
Music history, literature, and theory	97	51	46	44	17	27	18	6	12
Music performance, general	4,226	2,262	1,964	2,345	1,184	1,161	464	227	237
Music theory and composition	816	654	162	291	194	97	67	49	18
Musicology and ethnomusicology	25	16	9	85	41	44	48	23	25
Conducting	9	3	6	107	74	33	47	41	6
Keyboard instruments	140	55	85	189	85	104	47	11	36
Voice and opera	352	89	263	231	87	144	28	18	10
Jazz/jazz studies	340	292	48	137	109	28	7	6	1
Stringed instruments	181	97	84	183	83	100	10	4	6
Music pedagogy	73	19	54	40	11	29	9	2	7
Music technology	277	235	42	64	52	12	5	3	2
Brass instruments	44	34	10	32	23	9	0	0	0
Woodwind instruments	40	16	24	52	29	23	3	2	1
Percussion instruments	24	23	1	17	12	5	1	1	0
Music, other	785	511	274	200	124	76	22	15	7
Arts, entertainment, and media management, general	496	271	225	591	254	337	0	0	0
Fine and studio arts management	800	214	586	455	89	366	5	2	3
Music management	1,450	885	565	30	18	12	0	0	0
Theatre/theatre arts management	119	36	83	55	15	40	0	0	0
Arts, entertainment, and media management, other	25	15	10	1	1	0	0	0	0
Visual and performing arts, other	402	184	218	335	99	236	15	5	10
Not classified by field of study	0	0	0	0	0	0	0	0	0

[1]Includes Ph.D., Ed.D., and comparable degrees at the doctoral level. Includes most degrees formerly classified as first-professional, such as M.D., D.D.S., and law degrees.

NOTE: Data are for postsecondary institutions participating in Title IV federal financial aid programs. Aggregations by field of study derived from the Classification of Instructional Programs developed by the National Center for Education Statistics.

SOURCE: U.S. Department of Education, National Center for Education Statistics, Integrated Postsecondary Education Data System (IPEDS), Fall 2014, Completions component. (This table was prepared September 2015.)

Table 319.10. Degrees conferred by postsecondary institutions, by control of institution, level of degree, and state or jurisdiction: 2013–14

State or jurisdiction	Public				Private nonprofit				Private for-profit			
	Associate's degrees	Bachelor's degrees	Master's degrees	Doctor's degrees[1]	Associate's degrees	Bachelor's degrees	Master's degrees	Doctor's degrees[1]	Associate's degrees	Bachelor's degrees	Master's degrees	Doctor's degrees[1]
1	2	3	4	5	6	7	8	9	10	11	12	13
United States	**793,180**	**1,186,397**	**346,101**	**88,904**	**53,127**	**544,213**	**333,580**	**80,894**	**157,057**	**139,204**	**74,794**	**7,782**
Alabama	9,644	22,617	8,797	1,835	129	3,424	679	445	3,530	3,475	1,870	6
Alaska	1,409	1,855	644	52	12	79	63	8	384	99	0	0
Arizona	18,107	25,718	7,631	1,781	226	806	1,182	730	23,513	34,756	20,016	1,393
Arkansas	8,586	12,671	4,305	895	136	2,633	527	90	128	184	64	0
California	105,374	133,269	28,555	7,080	1,578	38,160	35,415	10,289	23,010	27,829	10,551	950
Colorado	8,651	24,400	7,221	1,783	574	3,967	4,122	643	4,952	5,045	3,592	491
Connecticut	5,882	11,282	3,044	787	929	9,589	6,244	1,262	325	839	233	0
Delaware	1,918	4,299	892	245	158	2,017	1,935	309	4	22	15	0
District of Columbia	263	410	90	103	267	8,386	10,866	3,415	236	455	521	0
Florida	72,474	65,981	17,931	4,686	6,907	22,583	13,230	3,730	16,951	8,440	2,916	697
Georgia	14,269	35,579	10,454	2,504	1,033	10,227	4,602	1,695	3,471	3,025	1,919	447
Hawaii	4,440	4,408	1,179	467	476	2,152	719	0	532	355	177	39
Idaho	3,309	6,482	1,622	400	1,774	4,066	251	12	332	155	15	0
Illinois	34,869	33,688	12,467	3,075	1,285	30,604	24,861	5,191	4,362	10,666	4,349	180
Indiana	12,267	31,065	9,545	2,652	1,504	14,900	4,680	885	3,959	1,021	132	0
Iowa	12,391	12,494	2,732	1,514	645	10,313	2,035	1,318	4,036	5,318	2,914	118
Kansas	9,542	15,256	5,170	1,326	793	4,050	1,699	134	1,464	968	518	0
Kentucky	10,417	17,095	5,735	1,656	439	4,556	3,330	280	2,765	617	442	90
Louisiana	5,827	18,800	5,085	1,563	336	3,331	2,134	932	1,077	408	129	0
Maine	2,638	4,156	898	174	139	3,234	1,135	354	416	86	2	0
Maryland	15,126	25,107	10,553	2,178	16	6,459	7,520	730	616	597	317	0
Massachusetts	11,965	19,748	6,138	773	1,454	38,496	29,774	7,548	704	468	123	0
Michigan	27,533	45,278	16,799	4,426	3,935	12,950	4,346	1,669	861	680	147	0
Minnesota	17,454	21,251	5,227	1,825	609	11,212	4,987	1,192	3,150	3,988	11,868	2,274
Mississippi	12,086	12,012	3,381	995	58	2,247	1,429	264	496	7	12	0
Missouri	12,826	21,472	6,880	1,517	2,989	18,397	13,447	3,234	2,752	941	234	0
Montana	2,231	5,239	1,086	420	186	725	75	0	0	0	0	0
Nebraska	4,983	8,917	2,562	793	268	5,417	2,286	710	501	151	26	0
Nevada	4,600	6,963	1,540	513	0	259	361	409	1,132	858	247	0
New Hampshire	2,069	5,173	1,236	231	556	4,707	3,252	311	345	257	89	0
New Jersey	21,377	30,228	8,620	2,214	138	9,965	6,551	946	995	834	116	0
New Mexico	7,983	8,099	2,923	644	0	114	204	0	665	933	209	0
New York	51,179	61,669	18,712	3,155	7,946	69,241	51,754	11,863	9,467	3,916	1,107	1
North Carolina	26,361	36,981	11,675	2,495	1,103	14,740	6,226	2,102	1,770	881	475	408
North Dakota	1,989	5,425	1,382	437	130	684	443	32	286	59	0	0
Ohio	24,192	45,868	14,776	4,527	3,007	21,380	7,677	1,622	6,274	1,040	327	0
Oklahoma	11,225	16,587	5,129	1,330	189	3,780	1,410	327	1,192	287	77	0
Oregon	12,397	17,179	4,051	1,035	58	5,086	4,351	961	916	474	85	0
Pennsylvania	17,076	48,189	11,849	3,449	3,280	42,679	24,707	6,543	8,061	1,840	335	0
Rhode Island	1,708	4,118	855	241	2,072	7,337	1,763	512	0	0	0	0
South Carolina	9,855	17,647	4,414	1,437	407	5,514	1,047	151	1,623	1,190	417	278
South Dakota	2,243	4,324	1,033	393	214	1,082	278	2	239	270	25	0
Tennessee	9,858	20,870	5,933	1,783	774	12,205	5,691	1,689	2,375	1,059	501	21
Texas	64,939	95,688	35,737	8,408	1,260	20,208	9,487	2,382	4,930	2,889	1,064	20
Utah	11,242	15,291	3,339	826	1,163	13,869	5,867	225	1,204	688	359	220
Vermont	962	3,353	425	220	182	2,806	1,870	138	78	62	0	0
Virginia	18,456	35,779	11,778	3,371	1,315	15,553	10,117	1,849	5,420	4,462	1,949	129
Washington	28,292	24,323	5,744	1,803	79	7,387	3,308	735	693	796	240	20
West Virginia	3,229	9,384	2,591	884	82	1,168	333	125	2,603	4,973	3,882	0
Wisconsin	12,596	27,041	5,257	1,781	304	9,464	3,310	901	2,001	841	188	0
Wyoming	2,871	2,007	476	222	13	5	0	0	261	0	0	0
U.S. Service Academies	0	3,662	3	0	†	†	†	†	†	†	†	†
Other jurisdictions	**2,355**	**7,937**	**927**	**550**	**3,650**	**11,762**	**4,114**	**912**	**3,189**	**1,428**	**280**	**0**
American Samoa	228	3	0	0	0	0	0	0	0	0	0	0
Federated States of Micronesia	267	0	0	0	0	0	0	0	0	0	0	0
Guam	155	414	106	0	0	10	0	0	0	0	0	0
Marshall Islands	106	0	0	0	0	0	0	0	0	0	0	0
Northern Marianas	123	35	0	0	0	0	0	0	0	0	0	0
Palau	88	0	0	0	0	0	0	0	0	0	0	0
Puerto Rico	1,330	7,271	771	550	3,650	11,752	4,114	912	3,189	1,428	280	0
U.S. Virgin Islands	58	214	50	0	0	0	0	0	0	0	0	0

†Not applicable.
[1]Includes Ph.D., Ed.D., and comparable degrees at the doctoral level. Includes most degrees formerly classified as first-professional, such as M.D., D.D.S., and law degrees.
NOTE: Data are for postsecondary institutions participating in Title IV federal financial aid programs.

SOURCE: U.S. Department of Education, National Center for Education Statistics, Integrated Postsecondary Education Data System (IPEDS), Fall 2014, Completions component. (This table was prepared April 2016.)

Table 319.20. Degrees conferred by postsecondary institutions, by level of degree and state or jurisdiction: 2011–12 through 2013–14

State or jurisdiction	2011–12				2012–13				2013–14			
	Associate's degrees	Bachelor's degrees	Master's degrees	Doctor's degrees[1]	Associate's degrees	Bachelor's degrees	Master's degrees	Doctor's degrees[1]	Associate's degrees	Bachelor's degrees	Master's degrees	Doctor's degrees[1]
1	2	3	4	5	6	7	8	9	10	11	12	13
United States	**1,021,718**	**1,792,163**	**755,967**	**170,217**	**1,007,427**	**1,840,381**	**751,718**	**175,026**	**1,003,364**	**1,869,814**	**754,475**	**177,580**
Alabama	14,197	28,277	11,539	2,256	13,758	29,876	11,670	2,297	13,303	29,516	11,346	2,286
Alaska	1,706	1,750	703	50	1,758	1,895	724	54	1,805	2,033	707	60
Arizona	62,994	64,707	36,178	3,533	48,911	66,304	30,579	3,771	41,846	61,280	28,829	3,904
Arkansas	8,645	14,190	5,320	913	8,499	14,317	5,225	980	8,850	15,488	4,896	985
California	114,613	172,419	68,502	17,448	120,550	180,529	69,257	18,761	129,962	199,258	74,521	18,319
Colorado	16,939	31,136	15,406	2,352	15,550	32,446	15,009	2,747	14,177	33,412	14,935	2,917
Connecticut	6,511	20,710	9,457	1,954	6,826	21,470	9,570	1,964	7,136	21,710	9,521	2,049
Delaware	1,947	5,885	2,680	585	2,072	6,230	2,753	558	2,080	6,338	2,842	554
District of Columbia	463	9,212	10,211	3,567	686	9,299	10,995	3,621	766	9,251	11,477	3,518
Florida	103,158	91,225	33,859	9,485	100,877	94,505	32,945	9,029	96,332	97,004	34,077	9,113
Georgia	18,728	45,936	17,674	4,267	18,889	47,655	17,888	4,410	18,773	48,831	16,975	4,646
Hawaii	4,199	6,016	2,115	533	4,402	6,363	1,978	556	5,448	6,915	2,075	506
Idaho	4,952	9,781	2,041	331	5,762	10,336	2,049	398	5,415	10,703	1,888	412
Illinois	41,925	72,541	43,664	8,132	40,584	75,992	43,254	8,598	40,516	74,958	41,677	8,446
Indiana	19,430	45,534	14,230	3,465	18,838	46,551	14,663	3,475	17,730	46,986	14,357	3,537
Iowa	20,515	40,676	12,100	2,957	18,751	41,462	12,127	3,031	17,072	28,125	7,681	2,950
Kansas	10,218	18,999	7,021	1,452	10,647	19,622	6,625	1,474	11,799	20,274	7,387	1,460
Kentucky	14,680	21,531	9,411	1,935	13,853	21,872	9,860	1,951	13,621	22,268	9,507	2,026
Louisiana	7,706	22,015	7,275	2,585	7,150	22,334	7,552	2,532	7,240	22,539	7,348	2,495
Maine	3,321	7,596	1,902	383	3,167	7,335	1,935	489	3,193	7,476	2,035	528
Maryland	15,156	30,863	17,845	2,822	15,387	31,729	18,444	3,043	15,758	32,163	18,390	2,908
Massachusetts	13,645	55,593	35,748	8,146	13,742	57,134	35,438	8,289	14,123	58,712	36,035	8,321
Michigan	33,322	57,815	21,392	5,884	34,187	58,540	21,047	6,053	32,329	58,908	21,292	6,095
Minnesota	21,868	35,428	22,424	4,420	21,664	36,326	22,202	4,813	21,213	36,451	22,082	5,291
Mississippi	12,996	13,516	4,809	1,217	12,140	14,076	4,804	1,261	12,640	14,266	4,822	1,259
Missouri	19,895	43,688	20,979	4,669	19,821	40,963	20,577	4,682	18,567	40,810	20,561	4,751
Montana	2,364	5,384	1,286	372	2,296	5,644	1,280	395	2,417	5,964	1,161	420
Nebraska	5,761	14,248	5,178	1,392	5,944	14,119	5,008	1,495	5,752	14,485	4,874	1,503
Nevada	5,350	7,639	2,604	950	5,375	7,949	2,194	936	5,732	8,080	2,148	922
New Hampshire	3,119	9,270	3,825	480	2,824	9,769	3,878	501	2,970	10,137	4,577	542
New Jersey	21,631	39,804	15,490	3,122	21,647	40,295	14,267	2,335	22,510	41,027	15,287	3,160
New Mexico	7,709	8,259	3,259	614	8,941	8,586	3,239	629	8,648	9,146	3,336	644
New York	69,654	129,429	71,406	14,809	68,104	132,614	70,407	15,332	68,592	134,826	71,573	15,019
North Carolina	27,673	50,737	16,948	4,420	28,591	51,782	17,301	4,824	29,234	52,602	18,376	5,005
North Dakota	2,523	5,742	1,725	480	2,386	5,983	1,676	465	2,405	6,168	1,825	469
Ohio	35,871	66,736	24,148	5,992	33,570	66,193	22,994	6,117	33,473	68,288	22,780	6,149
Oklahoma	11,513	19,846	6,481	1,728	12,405	20,047	6,497	1,658	12,606	20,654	6,616	1,657
Oregon	12,637	21,114	7,541	1,910	14,272	22,085	7,504	1,959	13,371	22,739	8,487	1,996
Pennsylvania	29,875	90,688	36,832	9,384	28,794	91,392	37,151	9,788	28,417	92,708	36,891	9,992
Rhode Island	3,537	11,013	2,566	745	3,727	11,079	2,654	742	3,780	11,455	2,618	753
South Carolina	10,790	22,973	5,972	1,604	11,628	24,004	6,120	1,741	11,885	24,351	5,878	1,866
South Dakota	2,699	5,392	1,467	353	2,610	5,641	1,512	335	2,696	5,676	1,336	395
Tennessee	13,548	32,309	11,929	3,152	13,230	33,766	11,946	3,298	13,007	34,134	12,125	3,493
Texas	67,768	111,312	45,325	10,108	68,898	115,114	46,464	10,426	71,129	118,785	46,288	10,810
Utah	13,280	26,554	7,669	1,184	13,021	28,597	8,412	1,247	13,609	29,848	9,565	1,271
Vermont	1,196	6,283	2,474	415	1,280	6,206	3,191	434	1,222	6,221	2,295	358
Virginia	26,199	52,998	21,516	5,328	25,789	54,749	22,782	5,193	25,191	55,794	23,844	5,349
Washington	28,977	32,376	9,595	2,561	29,281	32,689	9,519	2,601	29,064	32,506	9,292	2,558
West Virginia	4,897	13,284	5,892	986	5,411	14,357	6,409	1,032	5,914	15,525	6,806	1,009
Wisconsin	16,494	36,005	9,856	2,590	15,807	36,927	9,653	2,507	14,901	37,346	8,755	2,682
Wyoming	2,924	2,064	489	197	3,125	2,057	486	199	3,145	2,012	476	222
U.S. Service Academies	0	3,665	9	0	0	3,576	4	0	0	3,662	3	0
Other jurisdictions	**9,135**	**20,358**	**5,309**	**1,405**	**8,293**	**20,870**	**5,224**	**1,471**	**9,194**	**21,127**	**5,321**	**1,462**
American Samoa	269	2	0	0	235	5	0	0	228	3	0	0
Federated States of Micronesia	262	0	0	0	293	0	0	0	267	0	0	0
Guam	278	408	132	0	137	395	113	0	155	424	106	0
Marshall Islands	71	0	0	0	79	0	0	0	106	0	0	0
Northern Marianas	103	14	0	0	133	29	0	0	123	35	0	0
Palau	85	0	0	0	99	0	0	0	88	0	0	0
Puerto Rico	7,994	19,697	5,124	1,405	7,252	20,230	5,055	1,471	8,169	20,451	5,165	1,462
U.S. Virgin Islands	73	237	53	0	65	211	56	0	58	214	50	0

[1]Includes Ph.D., Ed.D., and comparable degrees at the doctoral level. Includes most degrees formerly classified as first-professional, such as M.D., D.D.S., and law degrees.

NOTE: Data are for postsecondary institutions participating in Title IV federal financial aid programs. Some data have been revised from previously published figures.

SOURCE: U.S. Department of Education, National Center for Education Statistics, Integrated Postsecondary Education Data System (IPEDS), Fall 2012 through Fall 2014, Completions component. (This table was prepared April 2016.)

Table 319.30. Bachelor's degrees conferred by postsecondary institutions, by field of study and state or jurisdiction: 2013–14

State or jurisdiction	Total	Humanities[1]	Psychology	Social sciences and history	Natural sciences[2]	Computer sciences	Engineering[3]	Education	Business/ management[4]	Health professions and related programs	Other fields[5]
1	2	3	4	5	6	7	8	9	10	11	12
United States	**1,869,814**	**291,507**	**117,298**	**173,096**	**154,917**	**55,367**	**108,969**	**98,854**	**358,079**	**198,770**	**312,957**
Alabama	29,516	2,513	1,466	1,584	2,166	636	2,496	2,380	7,141	3,324	5,810
Alaska	2,033	336	132	153	192	31	192	100	379	217	301
Arizona	61,280	8,558	2,293	2,763	2,864	3,089	1,769	3,332	14,963	11,009	10,640
Arkansas	15,488	2,347	794	1,057	1,253	282	672	1,504	2,825	1,981	2,773
California	199,258	36,267	15,177	25,816	18,315	5,184	11,534	4,668	36,723	14,812	30,762
Colorado	33,412	4,901	2,054	3,387	3,076	1,254	2,251	273	6,905	3,425	5,886
Connecticut	21,710	4,056	1,730	2,885	1,876	271	941	671	3,495	2,355	3,430
Delaware	6,338	742	353	554	329	160	420	516	1,426	758	1,080
District of Columbia	9,251	1,261	565	2,801	554	192	288	64	1,682	671	1,173
Florida	97,004	12,082	6,429	8,310	6,653	2,943	4,687	5,146	22,070	11,085	17,599
Georgia	48,831	6,931	3,132	4,182	4,382	1,864	2,843	3,824	9,800	4,281	7,592
Hawaii	6,915	1,016	432	701	490	221	183	426	1,568	741	1,137
Idaho	10,703	1,714	512	763	871	294	607	965	1,691	1,391	1,895
Illinois	74,958	11,752	4,291	5,805	5,767	2,500	4,001	4,202	13,919	10,480	12,241
Indiana	46,986	6,424	2,140	3,272	3,259	1,454	3,824	2,936	9,461	6,513	7,703
Iowa	28,125	3,164	1,783	1,771	1,919	789	1,653	1,995	5,822	3,157	6,072
Kansas	20,274	2,831	788	1,269	1,184	405	1,383	1,656	4,805	2,413	3,540
Kentucky	22,268	3,040	1,224	1,501	1,649	415	1,162	2,144	3,497	2,439	5,197
Louisiana	22,539	3,660	1,292	1,621	1,975	362	1,576	1,684	4,398	2,727	3,244
Maine	7,476	1,196	474	889	836	97	440	462	844	1,057	1,181
Maryland	32,163	4,046	2,174	3,861	2,962	2,525	1,550	1,589	5,649	2,675	5,132
Massachusetts	58,712	9,726	4,302	7,391	5,684	1,695	3,775	1,584	10,548	5,546	8,461
Michigan	58,908	7,321	3,523	4,346	5,059	1,713	4,670	3,307	11,380	6,786	10,803
Minnesota	36,451	5,215	2,528	2,960	3,865	1,202	1,430	2,440	7,142	3,879	5,790
Mississippi	14,266	1,763	836	878	1,263	153	800	1,804	2,594	1,701	2,474
Missouri	40,810	5,247	2,615	2,368	3,032	985	2,115	3,174	9,159	5,139	6,976
Montana	5,964	813	303	523	631	105	631	517	798	484	1,159
Nebraska	14,485	1,361	723	854	1,010	508	508	1,462	3,746	1,724	2,589
Nevada	8,080	994	495	626	663	209	442	407	2,179	834	1,231
New Hampshire	10,137	1,724	897	1,113	736	320	541	501	1,969	792	1,544
New Jersey	41,027	7,431	3,605	4,418	3,714	990	2,330	1,819	7,155	3,371	6,194
New Mexico	9,146	1,816	567	615	740	181	715	786	1,589	777	1,360
New York	134,826	26,531	10,578	15,215	11,071	3,723	6,601	6,132	23,876	12,034	19,065
North Carolina	52,602	6,267	3,663	5,250	5,115	1,339	2,850	3,592	8,825	4,725	10,976
North Dakota	6,168	585	255	192	406	116	492	609	1,176	850	1,487
Ohio	68,288	8,939	3,507	5,108	5,076	1,310	4,755	5,430	12,510	10,353	11,300
Oklahoma	20,654	3,550	973	957	1,373	426	1,509	1,607	4,256	2,071	3,932
Oregon	22,739	4,385	1,463	3,008	2,000	466	1,249	615	3,485	2,016	4,052
Pennsylvania	92,708	13,807	5,602	8,494	8,677	3,120	6,161	5,042	16,809	10,725	14,271
Rhode Island	11,455	1,511	612	1,039	870	311	432	441	2,828	813	2,598
South Carolina	24,351	3,281	1,594	2,273	2,710	513	1,211	1,762	5,375	2,001	3,631
South Dakota	5,676	487	228	369	412	189	451	563	733	1,139	1,105
Tennessee	34,134	6,363	1,916	2,589	2,360	654	1,694	2,449	5,880	3,630	6,599
Texas	118,785	23,113	6,242	8,632	9,883	2,513	7,753	2,053	23,209	12,946	22,441
Utah	29,848	3,409	1,221	2,277	1,914	1,937	1,268	3,237	5,522	4,906	4,157
Vermont	6,221	1,283	422	831	572	169	245	300	762	418	1,219
Virginia	55,794	10,757	4,604	6,334	4,547	2,571	3,269	1,425	10,086	4,504	7,697
Washington	32,506	6,204	2,008	4,013	3,595	1,219	2,017	1,404	5,087	2,294	4,665
West Virginia	15,525	3,179	753	1,252	851	572	742	843	2,577	1,045	3,711
Wisconsin	37,346	5,095	1,883	3,263	3,824	1,020	2,252	2,787	7,274	3,494	6,454
Wyoming	2,012	153	117	142	253	18	210	225	235	262	397
U.S. Service Academies	3,662	360	28	821	439	152	1,379	0	252	0	231
Other jurisdictions	**21,127**	**1,036**	**1,224**	**761**	**2,051**	**763**	**1,268**	**1,608**	**4,953**	**4,373**	**3,090**
American Samoa	3	0	0	0	0	0	0	3	0	0	0
Guam	424	43	7	25	29	13	0	74	83	24	126
Northern Marianas	35	0	0	0	0	0	0	35	0	0	0
Puerto Rico	20,451	986	1,196	734	1,981	745	1,268	1,475	4,779	4,338	2,949
U.S. Virgin Islands	214	7	21	2	41	5	0	21	91	11	15

[1]Includes degrees in area, ethnic, cultural, gender, and group studies; English language and literature/letters; foreign languages, literatures, and linguistics; liberal arts and sciences, general studies and humanities; multi/interdisciplinary studies; philosophy and religious studies; theology and religious vocations; and visual and performing arts.

[2]Includes biological and biomedical sciences; physical sciences; science technologies/technicians; and mathematics and statistics.

[3]Includes engineering; engineering technologies/technicians; mechanic and repair technologies/technicians; and construction trades.

[4]Includes business management, marketing, and related support services; and personal and culinary services.

[5]Includes agriculture, agricultural operations, and related sciences; natural resources and conservation; architecture and related services; communication, journalism, and related programs; communications technologies/technicians and support services; family and consumer services/human sciences; legal professions and studies; library science; military technologies and applied sciences; parks, recreation, leisure, and fitness studies; homeland security, law enforcement, and firefighting; public administration and social service professions; transportation and materials moving; and precision production.

NOTE: Data are for postsecondary institutions participating in Title IV federal financial aid programs. This table includes only those jurisdictions with 4-year institutions.

SOURCE: U.S. Department of Education, National Center for Education Statistics, Integrated Postsecondary Education Data System (IPEDS), Fall 2014, Completions component. (This table was prepared April 2016.)

Table 319.40. Master's degrees conferred by postsecondary institutions, by field of study and state or jurisdiction: 2013–14

State or jurisdiction	Total	Humanities[1]	Psychology	Social sciences and history	Natural sciences[2]	Computer sciences	Engineering[3]	Education	Business/ management[4]	Health professions and related programs	Other fields[5]
1	2	3	4	5	6	7	8	9	10	11	12
United States	**754,475**	**59,761**	**27,966**	**21,475**	**28,217**	**24,532**	**47,326**	**154,636**	**189,328**	**97,403**	**103,831**
Alabama	11,346	350	337	213	295	147	982	2,342	2,975	2,041	1,664
Alaska	707	32	32	15	62	2	52	258	107	35	112
Arizona	28,829	808	2,292	249	353	672	957	7,292	9,616	4,252	2,338
Arkansas	4,896	202	39	81	168	81	310	2,051	606	688	670
California	74,521	7,572	4,473	1,992	2,665	2,107	6,305	13,517	16,919	8,201	10,770
Colorado	14,935	907	881	524	524	839	1,041	2,173	5,023	1,239	1,784
Connecticut	9,521	886	329	226	588	272	666	2,086	1,985	1,221	1,262
Delaware	2,842	92	17	61	109	101	86	614	954	387	421
District of Columbia	11,477	1,188	182	1,451	771	405	626	748	2,444	1,020	2,642
Florida	34,077	1,925	1,126	624	1,256	560	2,591	4,697	10,887	4,852	5,559
Georgia	16,975	1,625	345	365	713	601	1,168	3,086	4,625	2,490	1,957
Hawaii	2,075	181	132	51	66	39	61	455	502	209	379
Idaho	1,888	126	12	40	93	19	163	531	295	272	337
Illinois	41,677	2,951	1,364	927	1,526	1,928	2,087	7,773	12,489	4,871	5,761
Indiana	14,357	1,353	290	308	512	375	1,077	2,595	4,468	1,688	1,691
Iowa	7,681	475	397	78	230	407	296	1,497	2,157	1,163	981
Kansas	7,387	670	189	147	193	100	427	1,985	1,721	804	1,151
Kentucky	9,507	703	473	182	255	189	351	2,937	1,364	1,539	1,514
Louisiana	7,348	632	159	171	417	118	305	1,338	1,634	1,311	1,263
Maine	2,035	145	38	10	59	11	34	610	289	459	380
Maryland	18,390	1,198	286	1,002	1,034	1,879	1,257	2,661	5,294	2,245	1,534
Massachusetts	36,035	2,827	951	1,337	1,280	1,122	2,463	7,206	9,392	3,983	5,474
Michigan	21,292	1,324	537	513	926	562	2,127	3,875	5,441	2,670	3,317
Minnesota	22,082	967	1,704	375	425	522	456	5,642	3,972	5,608	2,411
Mississippi	4,822	185	95	93	493	80	135	1,465	958	635	683
Missouri	20,561	1,166	687	567	521	421	909	4,003	7,296	2,660	2,331
Montana	1,161	97	38	44	83	14	55	332	114	191	193
Nebraska	4,874	304	98	317	197	188	100	1,298	1,098	754	520
Nevada	2,148	86	39	70	80	39	100	680	508	298	248
New Hampshire	4,577	212	25	71	72	131	221	907	1,913	610	415
New Jersey	15,287	1,499	466	330	853	662	1,653	3,016	3,270	1,536	2,002
New Mexico	3,336	328	59	123	163	52	277	879	668	455	332
New York	71,573	7,459	1,968	2,622	2,805	2,492	3,990	16,193	14,213	8,071	11,760
North Carolina	18,376	1,646	209	546	875	670	1,240	4,017	4,356	2,473	2,344
North Dakota	1,825	47	70	37	62	29	87	392	396	402	303
Ohio	22,780	1,829	731	566	1,219	388	1,781	4,573	5,184	3,595	2,914
Oklahoma	6,616	765	285	118	220	187	448	1,227	1,778	750	838
Oregon	8,487	773	254	134	308	78	360	3,706	1,239	884	751
Pennsylvania	36,891	2,713	1,357	856	1,361	1,773	2,824	7,319	8,171	5,596	4,921
Rhode Island	2,618	219	101	106	111	64	121	435	832	178	451
South Carolina	5,878	433	138	114	235	86	390	1,446	1,411	728	897
South Dakota	1,336	71	80	27	66	65	101	348	215	163	200
Tennessee	12,125	955	383	204	379	154	478	2,949	2,899	2,389	1,335
Texas	46,288	3,571	1,962	1,323	1,952	1,852	3,260	9,111	12,997	4,969	5,291
Utah	9,565	273	161	110	238	532	350	2,163	3,360	1,612	766
Vermont	2,295	580	83	390	41	37	82	328	267	110	377
Virginia	23,844	3,295	1,228	550	507	811	1,108	5,164	5,320	1,911	3,950
Washington	9,292	707	406	142	438	398	509	1,745	1,865	1,227	1,855
West Virginia	6,806	830	117	782	105	92	168	1,180	1,383	628	1,521
Wisconsin	8,755	514	337	270	247	173	637	1,703	2,397	1,299	1,178
Wyoming	476	65	4	21	66	6	51	88	61	31	83
U.S. Service Academies	3	0	0	0	0	0	3	0	0	0	0
Other jurisdictions	**5,321**	**267**	**356**	**44**	**145**	**103**	**294**	**1,202**	**1,458**	**801**	**651**
American Samoa	0	0	0	0	0	0	0	0	0	0	0
Guam	106	2	5	0	3	0	0	58	6	0	32
Northern Marianas	0	0	0	0	0	0	0	0	0	0	0
Puerto Rico	5,165	265	351	44	142	103	294	1,128	1,430	801	607
U.S. Virgin Islands	50	0	0	0	0	0	0	16	22	0	12

[1]Includes degrees in area, ethnic, cultural, gender, and group studies; English language and literature/letters; foreign languages, literatures, and linguistics; liberal arts and sciences, general studies and humanities; multi/interdisciplinary studies; philosophy and religious studies; theology and religious vocations; and visual and performing arts.
[2]Includes biological and biomedical sciences; physical sciences; science technologies/technicians; and mathematics and statistics.
[3]Includes engineering; engineering technologies/technicians; mechanic and repair technologies/technicians; and construction trades.
[4]Includes business management, marketing, and related support services; and personal and culinary services.
[5]Includes agriculture, agricultural operations, and related sciences; natural resources and conservation; architecture and related services; communication, journalism, and related programs; communications technologies/technicians and support services; family and consumer services/human sciences; legal professions and studies; library science; military technologies and applied sciences; parks, recreation, leisure, and fitness studies; homeland security, law enforcement, and firefighting; public administration and social service professions; transportation and materials moving; and precision production.
NOTE: Data are for postsecondary institutions participating in Title IV federal financial aid programs. This table includes only those jurisdictions with 4-year institutions.
SOURCE: U.S. Department of Education, National Center for Education Statistics, Integrated Postsecondary Education Data System (IPEDS), Fall 2014, Completions component. (This table was prepared April 2016.)

Table 320.10. Certificates below the associate's degree level conferred by postsecondary institutions, by length of curriculum, sex of student, institution level and control, and discipline division: 2013–14

Discipline division	Less-than-1-year certificates								1- to less-than-4-year certificates							
	Total	Sex		Institution level		Institution control			Total	Sex		Institution level		Institution control		
		Males	Females	Non-degree-granting (less-than-2-year)	Degree-granting (2-year and 4-year)	Public	Nonprofit	For-profit		Males	Females	Non-degree-granting (less-than-2-year)	Degree-granting (2-year and 4-year)	Public	Nonprofit	For-profit
1	2	3	4	5	6	7	8	9	10	11	12	13	14	15	16	17
Total	**479,574**	**213,414**	**266,160**	**118,214**	**361,360**	**343,129**	**13,390**	**123,055**	**489,779**	**177,380**	**312,399**	**186,021**	**303,758**	**233,129**	**17,340**	**239,310**
Agriculture and natural resources	3,322	2,095	1,227	90	3,232	3,143	17	162	2,330	1,463	867	178	2,152	2,111	121	98
Agriculture, agriculture operations, and related sciences	2,711	1,701	1,010	90	2,621	2,576	0	135	2,207	1,370	837	176	2,031	1,990	119	98
Natural resources and conservation	611	394	217	0	611	567	17	27	123	93	30	2	121	121	2	0
Architecture and related services	243	148	95	0	243	193	49	1	109	71	38	0	109	72	37	0
Area, ethnic, cultural, gender, and group studies	442	116	326	0	442	422	20	0	151	32	119	0	151	147	4	0
Biological and biomedical sciences	732	202	530	25	707	711	5	16	194	67	127	83	111	117	54	23
Business, management, marketing, and support services	50,889	17,407	33,482	3,401	47,488	45,929	983	3,977	24,198	6,680	17,518	3,154	21,044	20,293	1,198	2,707
Accounting and related services	9,905	2,995	6,910	601	9,304	8,844	75	986	5,597	1,315	4,282	616	4,981	4,837	436	324
Business/commerce, general	2,133	906	1,227	0	2,133	2,086	39	8	1,639	838	801	0	1,639	1,477	7	155
Business administration, management, and operations	10,969	4,295	6,674	17	10,952	10,473	116	380	4,127	1,491	2,636	45	4,082	3,690	47	390
Management information systems and services	949	558	391	274	675	490	62	397	250	132	118	79	171	234	0	16
Business operations support and assistant services	11,499	2,948	8,551	1,691	9,808	10,004	103	1,392	7,771	1,208	6,563	1,908	5,863	6,076	364	1,331
Business and management, other	15,434	5,705	9,729	818	14,616	14,032	588	814	4,814	1,696	3,118	506	4,308	3,979	344	491
Communication, journalism, and related programs	1,993	963	1,030	237	1,756	1,731	106	156	1,860	1,109	751	1,292	568	460	139	1,261
Communications technologies	2,353	1,433	920	465	1,888	1,897	28	428	3,201	2,514	687	1,793	1,408	1,381	15	1,805
Computer and information sciences and support services	23,485	16,647	6,838	2,514	20,971	20,337	240	2,908	10,250	7,719	2,531	2,206	8,044	7,426	236	2,588
Construction trades	12,568	11,916	652	3,355	9,213	10,951	629	988	12,968	12,457	511	3,857	9,111	8,323	530	4,115
Education	5,929	803	5,126	71	5,858	4,754	751	424	3,652	423	3,229	377	3,275	2,480	857	315
Engineering	595	497	98	235	360	486	0	109	329	268	61	39	290	269	50	10
Engineering technologies and engineering-related fields[1]	18,129	15,776	2,353	2,460	15,669	15,710	221	2,198	14,207	12,916	1,291	2,469	11,738	9,012	322	4,873
English language and literature/letters	1,006	324	682	187	819	622	370	14	1,115	390	725	775	340	134	92	889
Family and consumer sciences/human sciences	14,143	1,240	12,903	1,073	13,070	13,986	51	106	3,734	271	3,463	310	3,424	3,664	47	23
Foreign languages, literatures, and linguistics	1,197	256	941	0	1,197	1,041	149	7	598	97	501	1	597	543	55	0
Health professions and related programs	177,063	34,359	142,704	55,211	121,852	102,894	5,330	68,839	183,142	25,921	157,221	60,856	122,286	70,464	8,342	104,336
Dental assisting	8,101	772	7,329	3,232	4,869	1,519	251	6,331	14,113	1,307	12,806	4,222	9,891	4,517	59	9,537
Emergency medical technician (EMT paramedic)	16,457	10,914	5,543	1,122	15,335	15,891	92	474	5,198	3,927	1,271	481	4,717	4,640	265	293
Clinical/medical lab science	9,471	1,392	8,079	2,372	7,099	6,549	182	2,740	2,326	611	1,715	596	1,730	692	666	968
Medical assisting	21,387	2,102	19,285	11,072	10,315	2,682	1,523	17,182	51,708	4,714	46,994	19,774	31,934	6,347	1,625	43,736
Pharmacy assisting	6,473	1,567	4,906	2,967	3,506	2,157	654	3,662	7,788	1,740	6,048	1,676	6,112	1,970	89	5,729
Other allied health assisting	7,470	2,349	5,121	1,841	5,629	4,741	55	2,674	3,297	418	2,879	1,442	1,855	947	221	2,129
Nursing and patient care assistant	46,534	5,911	40,623	11,261	35,273	38,335	754	7,445	982	102	880	317	665	418	0	564
Practical nursing	6,257	682	5,575	852	5,405	5,542	79	636	49,825	5,643	44,182	16,353	33,472	33,836	1,355	14,634
Nursing, registered nurse and other	1,599	198	1,401	0	1,599	1,476	123	0	3,402	473	2,929	2,167	1,235	1,038	2,037	327
Health sciences, other	53,314	8,472	44,842	20,492	32,822	24,002	1,617	27,695	44,503	6,986	37,517	13,828	30,675	16,059	2,025	26,419
Homeland security, law enforcement, and firefighting	27,237	20,160	7,077	3,001	24,236	26,360	429	448	7,159	4,661	2,498	162	6,997	6,514	167	478
Criminal justice and corrections	20,464	14,115	6,349	1,441	19,023	19,911	366	187	5,778	3,470	2,308	152	5,626	5,250	54	474
Fire control and safety	6,096	5,612	484	1,438	4,658	6,073	7	16	1,213	1,112	101	10	1,203	1,213	0	0
Homeland security and related protective services, other	677	433	244	122	555	376	56	245	168	79	89	0	168	51	113	4
Legal professions and studies	2,006	350	1,656	165	1,841	1,228	234	544	3,444	598	2,846	561	2,883	2,642	286	516
Liberal arts and sciences, general studies, and humanities	3,224	1,239	1,985	0	3,224	3,214	10	0	36,266	14,316	21,950	0	36,266	36,193	73	0
Library science	224	31	193	0	224	224	0	0	60	10	50	0	60	60	0	0

See notes at end of table.

Table 320.10. Certificates below the associate's degree level conferred by postsecondary institutions, by length of curriculum, sex of student, institution level and control, and discipline division: 2013–14—Continued

Discipline division	Less-than-1-year certificates								1- to less-than-4-year certificates							
	Total	Sex		Institution level		Institution control			Total	Sex		Institution level		Institution control		
		Males	Females	Non-degree-granting (less-than-2-year)	Degree-granting (2-year and 4-year)	Public	Nonprofit	For-profit		Males	Females	Non-degree-granting (less-than-2-year)	Degree-granting (2-year and 4-year)	Public	Nonprofit	For-profit
1	2	3	4	5	6	7	8	9	10	11	12	13	14	15	16	17
Mathematics and statistics	166	124	42	0	166	146	20	0	17	14	3	0	17	12	5	0
Mechanic and repair technologies/technicians	32,423	30,565	1,858	3,788	28,635	30,143	559	1,721	50,338	48,443	1,895	22,413	27,925	22,360	973	27,005
Military technologies and applied sciences	25	20	5	0	25	9	0	16	36	25	11	0	36	36	0	0
Multi/interdisciplinary studies	1,525	647	878	5	1,520	1,152	55	318	1,203	627	576	0	1,203	1,168	34	1
Parks, recreation, leisure, and fitness studies	2,400	1,121	1,279	687	1,713	1,572	34	794	650	357	293	97	553	431	5	214
Personal and culinary services	38,157	5,545	32,612	27,158	10,999	10,065	276	27,816	98,125	14,332	83,793	78,804	19,321	13,967	1,168	82,990
Philosophy and religious studies	59	27	32	0	59	43	16	0	11	2	9	0	11	5	6	0
Physical sciences and science technologies	886	618	268	73	813	881	5	0	998	671	327	0	998	998	0	0
Physical sciences	197	126	71	0	197	192	5	0	17	13	4	0	17	17	0	0
Science technologies/technicians	689	492	197	73	616	689	0	0	981	658	323	0	981	981	0	0
Precision production	21,616	20,501	1,115	3,421	18,195	19,280	700	1,636	15,900	15,096	804	4,703	11,197	11,740	867	3,293
Psychology	209	35	174	0	209	69	140	0	64	9	55	0	64	59	5	0
Public administration and social services	1,176	279	897	14	1,162	1,034	97	45	1,179	206	973	0	1,179	1,111	63	5
Social sciences and history	1,089	612	477	8	1,081	968	121	0	368	201	167	0	368	353	15	0
Social sciences	1,064	604	460	8	1,056	944	120	0	361	196	165	0	361	346	15	0
History	25	8	17	0	25	24	1	0	7	5	2	0	7	7	0	0
Theology and religious vocations	297	129	168	0	297	2	295	0	819	349	470	437	382	1	818	0
Transportation and materials moving	27,803	25,166	2,637	9,644	18,159	18,298	777	8,728	979	914	65	316	663	631	18	330
Visual and performing arts	4,963	2,063	2,900	926	4,037	3,634	673	656	10,125	4,151	5,974	1,138	8,987	7,952	738	1,435
Fine and studio arts	787	293	494	658	129	116	529	142	5,411	1,999	3,412	5	5,406	5,339	71	1
Music and dance	280	170	110	0	280	197	4	79	431	288	143	93	338	126	148	157
Visual and performing arts, other[2]	3,896	1,600	2,296	268	3,628	3,321	140	435	4,283	1,864	2,419	1,040	3,243	2,487	519	1,277

[1]Excludes "Construction trades" and "Mechanic and repair technologies/technicians," which are listed separately.
[2]Includes design and applied arts, drama and theatre arts, film and photographic arts, and all other arts not included under "Fine and studio arts" or "Music and dance."

NOTE: Data are for postsecondary institutions participating in Title IV federal financial aid programs. Degree-granting institutions grant degrees at the associate's or higher level, while non-degree-granting institutions grant only awards below that level.
SOURCE: U.S. Department of Education, National Center for Education Statistics, Integrated Postsecondary Education Data System (IPEDS), Fall 2014, Completions component. (This table was prepared April 2016.)

Table 320.20. Certificates below the associate's degree level conferred by postsecondary institutions, by race/ethnicity and sex of student: 1998–99 through 2013–14

Year and sex	Number of certificates conferred to U.S. citizens and nonresident aliens								Percentage distribution of certificates conferred to U.S. citizens						
	Total	White	Black	Hispanic	Asian/ Pacific Islander	American Indian/ Alaska Native	Two or more races	Non-resident alien	Total	White	Black	Hispanic	Asian/ Pacific Islander	American Indian/ Alaska Native	Two or more races
1	2	3	4	5	6	7	8	9	10	11	12	13	14	15	16
Total															
1998–99	555,883	345,359	92,800	76,833	27,920	7,510	—	5,461	100.0	62.7	16.9	14.0	5.1	1.4	—
1999–2000	558,129	337,546	97,329	81,132	29,361	6,966	—	5,795	100.0	61.1	17.6	14.7	5.3	1.3	—
2000–01	552,503	333,478	99,397	78,528	28,123	6,598	—	6,379	100.0	61.1	18.2	14.4	5.1	1.2	—
2001–02	584,248	352,559	106,647	83,950	27,490	7,430	—	6,172	100.0	61.0	18.4	14.5	4.8	1.3	—
2002–03	646,425	382,289	120,582	95,499	32,981	8,117	—	6,957	100.0	59.8	18.9	14.9	5.2	1.3	—
2003–04	687,787	402,989	129,891	107,216	32,819	8,375	—	6,497	100.0	59.2	19.1	15.7	4.8	1.2	—
2004–05	710,873	415,670	133,601	114,089	32,783	8,150	—	6,580	100.0	59.0	19.0	16.2	4.7	1.2	—
2005–06	715,401	412,077	135,460	118,853	34,110	8,400	—	6,501	100.0	58.1	19.1	16.8	4.8	1.2	—
2006–07	729,037	420,585	139,995	119,501	32,962	8,793	—	7,201	100.0	58.3	19.4	16.6	4.6	1.2	—
2007–08	749,883	430,187	145,181	122,676	35,985	8,596	—	7,258	100.0	57.9	19.5	16.5	4.8	1.2	—
2008–09	804,620	450,562	161,487	138,301	37,941	9,485	—	6,844	100.0	56.5	20.2	17.3	4.8	1.2	—
2009–10	935,719	511,186	191,657	172,015	41,407	12,003	—	7,451	100.0	55.1	20.6	18.5	4.5	1.3	—
2010–11	1,030,477	557,595	207,693	187,433	44,294	11,204	14,999	7,259	100.0	54.5	20.3	18.3	4.3	1.1	1.5
2011–12	989,061	535,621	190,253	187,014	43,048	10,638	14,140	8,347	100.0	54.6	19.4	19.1	4.4	1.1	1.4
2012–13	967,214	524,000	177,006	186,248	44,196	10,824	17,642	7,298	100.0	54.6	18.4	19.4	4.6	1.1	1.8
2013–14	969,353	523,184	177,881	185,588	43,810	10,817	19,931	8,142	100.0	54.4	18.5	19.3	4.6	1.1	2.1
Males															
1998–99	219,872	144,735	29,875	27,719	11,742	3,061	—	2,740	100.0	66.7	13.8	12.8	5.4	1.4	—
1999–2000	226,110	143,634	33,792	30,337	13,082	2,862	—	2,403	100.0	64.2	15.1	13.6	5.8	1.3	—
2000–01	223,951	143,144	34,381	28,685	12,072	2,719	—	2,950	100.0	64.8	15.6	13.0	5.5	1.2	—
2001–02	235,275	152,226	36,482	29,749	10,938	3,226	—	2,654	100.0	65.4	15.7	12.8	4.7	1.4	—
2002–03	254,238	161,001	40,080	33,925	12,930	3,506	—	2,796	100.0	64.0	15.9	13.5	5.1	1.4	—
2003–04	257,138	161,684	40,809	36,157	12,713	3,135	—	2,640	100.0	63.5	16.0	14.2	5.0	1.2	—
2004–05	259,261	161,126	41,644	38,297	12,448	3,068	—	2,678	100.0	62.8	16.2	14.9	4.9	1.2	—
2005–06	259,737	158,747	41,863	40,752	12,790	3,219	—	2,366	100.0	61.7	16.3	15.8	5.0	1.3	—
2006–07	269,589	164,939	44,870	40,958	12,622	3,527	—	2,673	100.0	61.8	16.8	15.3	4.7	1.3	—
2007–08	283,266	172,398	48,024	43,085	13,527	3,452	—	2,780	100.0	61.5	17.1	15.4	4.8	1.2	—
2008–09	302,449	179,813	53,879	47,860	14,427	3,856	—	2,614	100.0	60.0	18.0	16.0	4.8	1.3	—
2009–10	355,381	205,404	65,487	60,771	15,940	5,067	—	2,712	100.0	58.2	18.6	17.2	4.5	1.4	—
2010–11	391,676	223,755	71,867	66,514	16,944	4,760	4,884	2,952	100.0	57.6	18.5	17.1	4.4	1.2	1.3
2011–12	374,086	213,833	65,224	65,838	16,180	4,507	4,952	3,552	100.0	57.7	17.6	17.8	4.4	1.2	1.3
2012–13	375,928	215,432	61,668	67,377	17,352	4,446	6,511	3,142	100.0	57.8	16.5	18.1	4.7	1.2	1.7
2013–14	390,794	223,229	65,632	68,758	17,283	4,732	7,752	3,408	100.0	57.6	16.9	17.7	4.5	1.2	2.0
Females															
1998–99	336,011	200,624	62,925	49,114	16,178	4,449	—	2,721	100.0	60.2	18.9	14.7	4.9	1.3	—
1999–2000	332,019	193,912	63,537	50,795	16,279	4,104	—	3,392	100.0	59.0	19.3	15.5	5.0	1.2	—
2000–01	328,552	190,334	65,016	49,843	16,051	3,879	—	3,429	100.0	58.5	20.0	15.3	4.9	1.2	—
2001–02	348,973	200,333	70,165	54,201	16,552	4,204	—	3,518	100.0	58.0	20.3	15.7	4.8	1.2	—
2002–03	392,187	221,288	80,502	61,574	20,051	4,611	—	4,161	100.0	57.0	20.7	15.9	5.2	1.2	—
2003–04	430,649	241,305	89,082	71,059	20,106	5,240	—	3,857	100.0	56.5	20.9	16.6	4.7	1.2	—
2004–05	451,612	254,544	91,957	75,792	20,335	5,082	—	3,902	100.0	56.9	20.5	16.9	4.5	1.1	—
2005–06	455,664	253,330	93,597	78,101	21,320	5,181	—	4,135	100.0	56.1	20.7	17.3	4.7	1.1	—
2006–07	459,448	255,646	95,125	78,543	20,340	5,266	—	4,528	100.0	56.2	20.9	17.3	4.5	1.2	—
2007–08	466,617	257,789	97,157	79,591	22,458	5,144	—	4,478	100.0	55.8	21.0	17.2	4.9	1.1	—
2008–09	502,171	270,749	107,608	90,441	23,514	5,629	—	4,230	100.0	54.4	21.6	18.2	4.7	1.1	—
2009–10	580,338	305,782	126,170	111,244	25,467	6,936	—	4,739	100.0	53.1	21.9	19.3	4.4	1.2	—
2010–11	638,801	333,840	135,826	120,919	27,350	6,444	10,115	4,307	100.0	52.6	21.4	19.1	4.3	1.0	1.6
2011–12	614,975	321,788	125,029	121,176	26,868	6,131	9,188	4,795	100.0	52.7	20.5	19.9	4.4	1.0	1.5
2012–13	591,286	308,568	115,338	118,871	26,844	6,378	11,131	4,156	100.0	52.6	19.6	20.2	4.6	1.1	1.9
2013–14	578,559	299,955	112,249	116,830	26,527	6,085	12,179	4,734	100.0	52.3	19.6	20.4	4.6	1.1	2.1

—Not available.

NOTE: Includes less-than-1-year awards and 1- to less-than-4-year awards (excluding associate's degrees) conferred by postsecondary institutions participating in Title IV federal financial aid programs. Race categories exclude persons of Hispanic ethnicity. Reported racial/ethnic distributions of students by level of degree, field of degree, and sex were used to estimate race/ethnicity for students whose race/ethnicity was not reported. Some data have been revised from previously published figures. Detail may not sum to totals because of rounding.

SOURCE: U.S. Department of Education, National Center for Education Statistics, Integrated Postsecondary Education Data System (IPEDS), "Completions Survey" (IPEDS-C:99); and IPEDS Fall 2000 through Fall 2014, Completions component. (This table was prepared September 2015.)

Table 302.10. Recent high school completers and their enrollment in 2-year and 4-year colleges, by sex: 1960 through 2014

[Standard errors appear in parentheses]

Year	Number of high school completers[1] (in thousands)			Percent of recent high school completers[1] enrolled in college[2]								
				Total			Males			Females		
	Total	Males	Females	Total	2-year	4-year	Total	2-year	4-year	Total	2-year	4-year
1	2	3	4	5	6	7	8	9	10	11	12	13
1960	1,679 (43.8)	756 (31.8)	923 (29.6)	45.1 (2.13)	— (†)	— (†)	54.0 (3.18)	— (†)	— (†)	37.9 (2.80)	— (†)	— (†)
1961	1,763 (46.0)	790 (33.2)	973 (31.3)	48.0 (2.09)	— (†)	— (†)	56.3 (3.10)	— (†)	— (†)	41.3 (2.77)	— (†)	— (†)
1962	1,838 (43.6)	872 (31.5)	966 (30.0)	49.0 (2.05)	— (†)	— (†)	55.0 (2.96)	— (†)	— (†)	43.5 (2.80)	— (†)	— (†)
1963	1,741 (44.2)	794 (32.1)	947 (30.0)	45.0 (2.09)	— (†)	— (†)	52.3 (3.11)	— (†)	— (†)	39.0 (2.78)	— (†)	— (†)
1964	2,145 (43.0)	997 (31.9)	1,148 (28.5)	48.3 (1.89)	— (†)	— (†)	57.2 (2.75)	— (†)	— (†)	40.7 (2.54)	— (†)	— (†)
1965	2,659 (47.7)	1,254 (35.1)	1,405 (32.0)	50.9 (1.70)	— (†)	— (†)	57.3 (2.45)	— (†)	— (†)	45.3 (2.33)	— (†)	— (†)
1966	2,612 (45.0)	1,207 (33.8)	1,405 (29.0)	50.1 (1.72)	— (†)	— (†)	58.7 (2.49)	— (†)	— (†)	42.7 (2.32)	— (†)	— (†)
1967	2,525 (37.9)	1,142 (28.4)	1,383 (24.3)	51.9 (1.42)	— (†)	— (†)	57.6 (2.09)	— (†)	— (†)	47.2 (1.92)	— (†)	— (†)
1968	2,606 (37.3)	1,184 (28.2)	1,422 (23.8)	55.4 (1.39)	— (†)	— (†)	63.2 (2.00)	— (†)	— (†)	48.9 (1.89)	— (†)	— (†)
1969	2,842 (36.0)	1,352 (26.8)	1,490 (23.7)	53.3 (1.34)	— (†)	— (†)	60.1 (1.90)	— (†)	— (†)	47.2 (1.85)	— (†)	— (†)
1970	2,758 (37.4)	1,343 (26.1)	1,415 (26.8)	51.7 (1.36)	— (†)	— (†)	55.2 (1.94)	— (†)	— (†)	48.5 (1.90)	— (†)	— (†)
1971	2,875 (38.0)	1,371 (26.6)	1,504 (27.1)	53.5 (1.33)	— (†)	— (†)	57.6 (1.90)	— (†)	— (†)	49.8 (1.84)	— (†)	— (†)
1972	2,964 (37.8)	1,423 (27.0)	1,542 (26.4)	49.2 (1.31)	— (†)	— (†)	52.7 (1.89)	— (†)	— (†)	46.0 (1.81)	— (†)	— (†)
1973	3,058 (37.1)	1,460 (27.6)	1,599 (24.6)	46.6 (1.29)	14.9 (0.92)	31.6 (1.20)	50.0 (1.87)	14.6 (1.32)	35.4 (1.79)	43.4 (1.77)	15.2 (1.28)	28.2 (1.61)
1974	3,101 (38.6)	1,491 (27.8)	1,611 (26.8)	47.6 (1.28)	15.2 (0.92)	32.4 (1.20)	49.4 (1.85)	16.6 (1.37)	32.8 (1.74)	45.9 (1.77)	13.9 (1.23)	32.0 (1.66)
1975	3,185 (38.6)	1,513 (27.3)	1,672 (27.2)	50.7 (1.26)	18.2 (0.98)	32.6 (1.19)	52.6 (1.83)	19.0 (1.44)	33.6 (1.73)	49.0 (1.75)	17.4 (1.32)	31.6 (1.62)
1976	2,986 (39.8)	1,451 (28.9)	1,535 (27.3)	48.8 (1.31)	15.6 (0.95)	33.3 (1.23)	47.2 (1.87)	14.5 (1.32)	32.7 (1.76)	50.3 (1.82)	16.6 (1.35)	33.8 (1.72)
1977	3,141 (40.7)	1,483 (29.7)	1,659 (27.7)	50.6 (1.29)	17.5 (0.98)	33.1 (1.21)	52.1 (1.87)	17.2 (1.41)	35.0 (1.79)	49.3 (1.77)	17.8 (1.36)	31.5 (1.65)
1978	3,163 (39.7)	1,485 (29.3)	1,677 (26.7)	50.1 (1.28)	17.0 (0.96)	33.1 (1.21)	51.1 (1.87)	15.6 (1.36)	35.5 (1.79)	49.3 (1.76)	18.3 (1.36)	31.0 (1.63)
1979	3,160 (40.0)	1,475 (29.2)	1,685 (27.2)	49.3 (1.28)	17.5 (0.98)	31.8 (1.20)	50.4 (1.88)	16.9 (1.41)	33.5 (1.78)	48.4 (1.76)	18.1 (1.35)	30.3 (1.62)
1980	3,088 (39.4)	1,498 (28.4)	1,589 (27.3)	49.3 (1.30)	19.4 (1.03)	29.9 (1.19)	46.7 (1.86)	17.1 (1.40)	29.7 (1.70)	51.8 (1.81)	21.6 (1.49)	30.2 (1.66)
1981	3,056 (42.2)	1,491 (30.4)	1,565 (29.1)	53.9 (1.30)	20.5 (1.05)	33.5 (1.23)	54.8 (1.86)	20.9 (1.52)	33.9 (1.77)	53.1 (1.82)	20.1 (1.46)	33.0 (1.72)
1982	3,100 (40.4)	1,509 (29.0)	1,592 (28.2)	50.6 (1.36)	19.1 (1.07)	31.5 (1.26)	49.1 (1.95)	17.5 (1.48)	31.6 (1.81)	52.0 (1.90)	20.6 (1.54)	31.4 (1.76)
1983	2,963 (41.6)	1,389 (30.4)	1,573 (28.2)	52.7 (1.39)	19.2 (1.10)	33.5 (1.31)	51.9 (2.03)	20.2 (1.63)	31.7 (1.89)	53.4 (1.91)	18.4 (1.48)	35.1 (1.82)
1984	3,012 (36.5)	1,429 (28.7)	1,584 (21.9)	55.2 (1.37)	19.4 (1.09)	35.8 (1.32)	56.0 (1.99)	17.7 (1.53)	38.4 (1.95)	54.5 (1.90)	21.0 (1.55)	33.5 (1.80)
1985	2,668 (40.1)	1,287 (28.7)	1,381 (27.9)	57.7 (1.45)	19.6 (1.16)	38.1 (1.43)	58.6 (2.08)	19.9 (1.69)	38.8 (2.06)	56.8 (2.02)	19.3 (1.61)	37.5 (1.97)
1986	2,786 (38.6)	1,332 (28.5)	1,454 (26.0)	53.8 (1.43)	19.2 (1.13)	34.5 (1.37)	55.8 (2.06)	21.3 (1.70)	34.5 (1.97)	51.9 (1.99)	17.3 (1.50)	34.6 (1.89)
1987	2,647 (40.9)	1,278 (29.8)	1,369 (28.0)	56.8 (1.46)	18.9 (1.15)	37.9 (1.43)	58.3 (2.09)	17.3 (1.60)	41.0 (2.09)	55.3 (2.04)	20.3 (1.65)	35.0 (1.95)
1988	2,673 (47.0)	1,334 (34.1)	1,339 (32.3)	58.9 (1.57)	21.9 (1.32)	37.1 (1.54)	57.1 (2.24)	21.3 (1.85)	35.8 (2.17)	60.7 (2.20)	22.4 (1.88)	38.3 (2.19)
1989	2,450 (46.5)	1,204 (32.9)	1,246 (32.8)	59.6 (1.64)	20.7 (1.35)	38.9 (1.63)	57.6 (2.35)	18.3 (1.84)	39.3 (2.32)	61.6 (2.27)	23.1 (1.97)	38.5 (2.28)
1990	2,362 (43.0)	1,173 (30.6)	1,189 (30.2)	60.1 (1.60)	20.1 (1.31)	40.0 (1.60)	58.0 (2.29)	19.6 (1.85)	38.4 (2.26)	62.2 (2.24)	20.6 (1.87)	41.6 (2.28)
1991	2,276 (41.0)	1,140 (29.0)	1,136 (29.0)	62.5 (1.62)	24.9 (1.44)	37.7 (1.62)	57.9 (2.33)	22.9 (1.98)	35.0 (2.25)	67.1 (2.22)	26.8 (2.09)	40.3 (2.32)
1992	2,397 (40.4)	1,216 (29.1)	1,180 (28.1)	61.9 (1.58)	23.0 (1.37)	38.9 (1.59)	60.0 (2.24)	22.1 (1.89)	37.8 (2.21)	63.8 (2.23)	23.9 (1.98)	40.0 (2.27)
1993	2,342 (41.4)	1,120 (30.6)	1,223 (27.7)	62.6 (1.59)	22.8 (1.38)	39.8 (1.61)	59.9 (2.33)	22.9 (2.00)	37.0 (2.30)	65.2 (2.17)	22.8 (1.91)	42.4 (2.25)
1994	2,517 (38.1)	1,244 (27.9)	1,273 (25.9)	61.9 (1.43)	21.0 (1.20)	40.9 (1.45)	60.6 (2.05)	23.0 (1.76)	37.5 (2.03)	63.2 (1.99)	19.1 (1.63)	44.1 (2.05)
1995	2,599 (40.9)	1,238 (29.9)	1,361 (27.7)	61.9 (1.41)	21.5 (1.19)	40.4 (1.42)	62.6 (2.03)	25.3 (1.82)	37.4 (2.03)	61.3 (1.95)	18.1 (1.54)	43.2 (1.98)
1996	2,660 (40.5)	1,297 (29.5)	1,363 (27.7)	65.0 (1.42)	23.1 (1.26)	41.9 (1.47)	60.1 (2.09)	21.5 (1.76)	38.5 (2.08)	69.7 (1.92)	24.6 (1.80)	45.1 (2.07)
1997	2,769 (41.8)	1,354 (31.0)	1,415 (27.9)	67.0 (1.38)	22.8 (1.23)	44.3 (1.45)	63.6 (2.01)	21.4 (1.71)	42.2 (2.07)	70.3 (1.87)	24.1 (1.75)	46.2 (2.04)
1998	2,810 (43.9)	1,452 (31.0)	1,358 (31.0)	65.6 (1.38)	24.4 (1.25)	41.3 (1.43)	62.4 (1.96)	24.4 (1.74)	38.0 (1.96)	69.1 (1.93)	24.3 (1.79)	44.8 (2.08)
1999	2,897 (41.5)	1,474 (29.9)	1,423 (28.8)	62.9 (1.38)	21.0 (1.17)	41.9 (1.41)	61.4 (1.95)	21.0 (1.63)	40.5 (1.97)	64.4 (1.95)	21.1 (1.67)	43.3 (2.02)
2000	2,756 (45.3)	1,251 (33.6)	1,505 (29.7)	63.3 (1.41)	21.4 (1.20)	41.9 (1.45)	59.9 (2.13)	23.1 (1.83)	36.8 (2.10)	66.2 (1.88)	20.0 (1.59)	46.2 (1.98)
2001	2,549 (46.5)	1,277 (33.7)	1,273 (32.0)	61.8 (1.48)	19.6 (1.21)	42.1 (1.51)	60.1 (2.11)	18.6 (1.68)	41.4 (2.12)	63.5 (2.08)	20.6 (1.75)	42.8 (2.13)
2002	2,796 (42.7)	1,412 (31.3)	1,384 (29.0)	65.2 (1.31)	21.6 (1.14)	43.6 (1.37)	62.1 (1.88)	20.4 (1.57)	41.7 (1.92)	68.4 (1.82)	22.8 (1.65)	45.6 (1.95)
2003	2,677 (42.2)	1,306 (29.9)	1,372 (29.7)	63.9 (1.35)	21.5 (1.16)	42.5 (1.39)	61.2 (1.97)	21.9 (1.67)	39.3 (1.97)	66.5 (1.86)	21.0 (1.61)	45.5 (1.96)
2004	2,752 (40.0)	1,327 (29.1)	1,425 (27.3)	66.7 (1.31)	22.4 (1.16)	44.2 (1.38)	61.4 (1.95)	21.8 (1.65)	39.6 (1.96)	71.5 (1.74)	23.1 (1.63)	48.5 (1.93)
2005	2,675 (40.8)	1,262 (31.5)	1,414 (24.9)	68.6 (1.31)	24.0 (1.21)	44.6 (1.40)	66.5 (1.94)	24.7 (1.77)	41.8 (2.03)	70.4 (1.77)	23.4 (1.64)	47.0 (1.94)
2006	2,692 (44.6)	1,328 (32.7)	1,363 (30.1)	66.0 (1.33)	24.7 (1.21)	41.3 (1.39)	65.8 (1.90)	24.9 (1.73)	40.9 (1.97)	66.1 (1.87)	24.5 (1.70)	41.7 (1.95)
2007	2,955 (42.6)	1,511 (30.0)	1,444 (30.3)	67.2 (1.26)	24.1 (1.15)	43.1 (1.33)	66.1 (1.78)	22.7 (1.57)	43.4 (1.86)	68.3 (1.79)	25.5 (1.67)	42.8 (1.90)
2008	3,151 (42.8)	1,640 (29.6)	1,511 (30.9)	68.6 (1.21)	27.7 (1.16)	40.9 (1.28)	65.9 (1.71)	24.9 (1.56)	41.0 (1.77)	71.6 (1.69)	30.6 (1.73)	40.9 (1.85)
2009	2,937 (45.0)	1,407 (32.8)	1,531 (30.6)	70.1 (1.23)	27.7 (1.21)	42.4 (1.33)	66.0 (1.84)	25.1 (1.69)	40.9 (1.91)	73.8 (1.64)	30.1 (1.71)	43.8 (1.85)
2010[3]	3,160 (91.8)	1,679 (64.6)	1,482 (58.4)	68.1 (1.49)	26.7 (1.52)	41.4 (1.61)	62.8 (1.88)	28.5 (2.03)	34.3 (1.97)	74.0 (2.31)	24.6 (2.32)	49.5 (2.59)
2011[3]	3,079 (88.3)	1,611 (60.6)	1,468 (58.4)	68.2 (1.45)	25.9 (1.49)	42.3 (1.44)	64.7 (2.16)	24.7 (1.79)	40.0 (2.10)	72.2 (1.98)	27.3 (2.17)	44.9 (2.37)
2012[3]	3,203 (96.2)	1,622 (70.1)	1,581 (54.0)	66.2 (1.59)	28.8 (1.57)	37.5 (1.60)	61.3 (2.17)	26.9 (2.20)	34.4 (2.15)	71.3 (2.11)	30.7 (2.09)	40.6 (2.21)
2013[3]	2,977 (84.4)	1,524 (62.9)	1,453 (57.0)	65.9 (1.58)	23.8 (1.44)	42.1 (1.76)	63.5 (2.20)	24.5 (2.14)	39.0 (2.48)	68.4 (2.17)	23.0 (2.15)	45.3 (2.21)
2014[3]	2,868 (78.5)	1,423 (58.1)	1,445 (57.5)	68.4 (1.67)	24.6 (1.56)	43.7 (1.81)	64.0 (2.32)	21.2 (2.07)	42.8 (2.69)	72.6 (2.50)	28.0 (2.35)	44.6 (2.57)

—Not available.
†Not applicable.
[1]Individuals ages 16 to 24 who graduated from high school or completed a GED during the calendar year.
[2]Enrollment in college as of October of each year for individuals ages 16 to 24 who completed high school during the calendar year.
[3]Beginning in 2010, standard errors were computed using replicate weights, which produced more precise values than the generalized variance function methodology used in prior years.

NOTE: Data are based on sample surveys of the civilian noninstitutionalized population. High school completion data in this table differ from figures appearing in other tables because of varying survey procedures and coverage. High school completers include GED recipients. Detail may not sum to totals because of rounding.
SOURCE: American College Testing Program, unpublished tabulations, derived from statistics collected by the Census Bureau, 1960 through 1969. U.S. Department of Commerce, Census Bureau, Current Population Survey (CPS), October, 1970 through 2014. (This table was prepared August 2015.)

Table 302.20. Percentage of recent high school completers enrolled in 2- and 4-year colleges, by race/ethnicity: 1960 through 2014

[Standard errors appear in parentheses]

Year	Percent of recent high school completers[1] enrolled in college[2] (annual data)					3-year moving averages[3]							
						Percent of recent high school completers[1] enrolled in college[2]					Difference between percent enrolled		
	Total	White	Black	Hispanic	Asian	Total	White	Black	Hispanic	Asian	White-Black	White-Hispanic	White-Asian
1	2	3	4	5	6	7	8	9	10	11	12	13	14
1960[4]	45.1 (2.13)	45.8 (2.21)	— (†)	— (†)	— (†)	46.6 (1.49)	47.7 (1.56)	— (†)	— (†)	— (†)	— (†)	— (†)	— (†)
1961[4]	48.0 (2.09)	49.5 (2.19)	— (†)	— (†)	— (†)	47.4 (1.21)	48.7 (1.26)	— (†)	— (†)	— (†)	— (†)	— (†)	— (†)
1962[4]	49.0 (2.05)	50.6 (2.15)	— (†)	— (†)	— (†)	47.4 (1.20)	48.6 (1.25)	— (†)	— (†)	— (†)	— (†)	— (†)	— (†)
1963[4]	45.0 (2.09)	45.6 (2.17)	— (†)	— (†)	— (†)	47.5 (1.16)	48.5 (1.21)	— (†)	— (†)	— (†)	— (†)	— (†)	— (†)
1964[4]	48.3 (1.89)	49.2 (1.98)	— (†)	— (†)	— (†)	48.5 (1.08)	49.2 (1.13)	— (†)	— (†)	— (†)	— (†)	— (†)	— (†)
1965[4]	50.9 (1.70)	51.7 (1.78)	— (†)	— (†)	— (†)	49.9 (1.02)	51.0 (1.07)	— (†)	— (†)	— (†)	— (†)	— (†)	— (†)
1966[4]	50.1 (1.72)	51.7 (1.79)	— (†)	— (†)	— (†)	51.0 (0.99)	52.1 (1.04)	— (†)	— (†)	— (†)	— (†)	— (†)	— (†)
1967[4]	51.9 (1.42)	53.0 (1.50)	— (†)	— (†)	— (†)	52.5 (0.81)	53.8 (0.85)	— (†)	— (†)	— (†)	— (†)	— (†)	— (†)
1968[4]	55.4 (1.39)	56.6 (1.47)	— (†)	— (†)	— (†)	53.6 (0.80)	55.0 (0.84)	— (†)	— (†)	— (†)	— (†)	— (†)	— (†)
1969[4]	53.3 (1.34)	55.2 (1.41)	— (†)	— (†)	— (†)	53.5 (0.79)	54.6 (0.83)	— (†)	— (†)	— (†)	— (†)	— (†)	— (†)
1970[4]	51.7 (1.36)	52.0 (1.44)	— (†)	— (†)	— (†)	52.9 (0.77)	53.8 (0.82)	— (†)	— (†)	— (†)	— (†)	— (†)	— (†)
1971[4]	53.5 (1.33)	54.0 (1.40)	— (†)	— (†)	— (†)	51.5 (0.77)	51.9 (0.82)	— (†)	— (†)	— (†)	— (†)	— (†)	— (†)
1972	49.2 (1.31)	49.7 (1.42)	44.6 (4.62)	45.0 (9.74)	— (†)	49.7 (0.76)	50.5 (0.81)	38.4 (3.18)	49.9 (6.64)	— (†)	12.1 (3.28)	‡ (†)	— (†)
1973	46.6 (1.29)	47.8 (1.40)	32.5 (4.30)	54.1 (9.01)	— (†)	47.8 (0.75)	48.2 (0.81)	41.4 (2.62)	48.8 (5.33)	— (†)	6.8 ! (2.74)	‡ (†)	— (†)
1974	47.6 (1.28)	47.2 (1.39)	47.2 (4.58)	46.9 (8.94)	— (†)	48.3 (0.74)	48.7 (0.80)	40.5 (2.63)	53.1 (5.09)	— (†)	8.3 ! (2.75)	‡ (†)	— (†)
1975	50.7 (1.26)	51.1 (1.37)	41.7 (3.97)	58.0 (8.44)	— (†)	49.1 (0.74)	49.1 (0.81)	44.5 (2.29)	52.7 (4.88)	— (†)	‡ (†)	‡ (†)	— (†)
1976	48.8 (1.31)	48.8 (1.43)	44.4 (4.08)	52.7 (7.97)	— (†)	50.1 (0.74)	50.3 (0.81)	45.3 (2.30)	53.6 (4.68)	— (†)	5.0 ! (2.44)	‡ (†)	— (†)
1977	50.6 (1.29)	50.8 (1.41)	49.5 (4.65)	50.8 (7.96)	— (†)	49.9 (0.75)	50.1 (0.82)	46.8 (2.70)	48.8 (4.72)	— (†)	‡ (†)	‡ (†)	— (†)
1978	50.1 (1.28)	50.5 (1.41)	46.4 (4.51)	42.0 (8.44)	— (†)	50.0 (0.74)	50.4 (0.81)	47.5 (2.67)	46.1 (4.69)	— (†)	‡ (†)	‡ (†)	— (†)
1979	49.3 (1.28)	49.9 (1.41)	46.7 (4.69)	45.0 (7.92)	— (†)	49.6 (0.74)	50.1 (0.82)	45.2 (2.62)	46.3 (4.83)	— (†)	‡ (†)	‡ (†)	— (†)
1980	49.3 (1.30)	49.8 (1.43)	42.7 (4.44)	52.3 (8.70)	— (†)	50.8 (0.75)	51.5 (0.82)	44.0 (2.61)	49.6 (4.78)	— (†)	7.5 ! (2.74)	‡ (†)	— (†)
1981	53.9 (1.30)	54.9 (1.44)	42.7 (4.44)	52.1 (8.19)	— (†)	51.3 (0.75)	52.4 (0.83)	40.3 (2.50)	48.7 (4.68)	— (†)	12.2 (2.64)	‡ (†)	— (†)
1982	50.6 (1.36)	52.7 (1.52)	35.8 (4.33)	43.2 (7.96)	— (†)	52.4 (0.79)	54.2 (0.84)	38.8 (2.57)	49.4 (4.94)	— (†)	15.4 (2.70)	‡ (†)	— (†)
1983	52.7 (1.39)	55.0 (1.55)	38.2 (4.34)	54.2 (8.96)	— (†)	52.8 (0.79)	55.5 (0.89)	38.0 (2.47)	46.7 (4.72)	— (†)	17.5 (2.62)	‡ (†)	— (†)
1984	55.2 (1.37)	59.0 (1.54)	39.8 (4.15)	44.3 (7.67)	— (†)	55.1 (0.81)	57.9 (0.91)	39.9 (2.54)	49.3 (4.89)	— (†)	18.0 (2.70)	‡ (†)	— (†)
1985	57.7 (1.45)	60.1 (1.62)	42.2 (4.78)	51.0 (9.76)	— (†)	55.5 (0.82)	58.6 (0.92)	39.5 (2.55)	46.1 (5.18)	— (†)	19.1 (2.71)	12.5 ! (5.27)	— (†)
1986	53.8 (1.43)	56.8 (1.62)	36.9 (4.38)	44.0 (8.85)	— (†)	56.1 (0.84)	58.5 (0.94)	43.5 (2.71)	42.3 (5.20)	— (†)	15.0 (2.87)	16.2 ! (5.28)	— (†)
1987	56.8 (1.46)	58.6 (1.65)	52.2 (4.82)	33.5 (8.25)	— (†)	56.5 (0.83)	58.8 (0.95)	44.2 (2.65)	45.0 (5.04)	— (†)	14.6 (2.82)	13.8 ! (5.13)	— (†)
1988	58.9 (1.57)	61.1 (1.79)	44.4 (4.91)	57.1 (10.14)	— (†)	58.4 (0.92)	60.1 (0.96)	49.7 (2.98)	48.5 (5.99)	— (†)	10.4 ! (3.13)	‡ (†)	— (†)
1989	59.6 (1.64)	60.7 (1.85)	53.4 (5.27)	55.1 (10.51)	— (†)	59.5 (0.94)	61.6 (1.06)	48.0 (2.98)	52.7 (6.33)	— (†)	13.6 (3.16)	‡ (†)	— (†)
1990	60.1 (1.60)	63.0 (1.80)	46.8 (5.08)	42.7 (10.82)	— (†)	60.7 (0.92)	63.0 (1.08)	48.9 (2.97)	52.5 (5.70)	— (†)	14.0 (3.16)	‡ (†)	— (†)
1991	62.5 (1.62)	65.4 (1.82)	46.4 (5.25)	57.2 (9.58)	— (†)	61.5 (0.92)	64.2 (1.05)	47.2 (2.93)	52.6 (5.52)	— (†)	17.0 (3.11)	11.7 ! (5.62)	— (†)
1992	61.9 (1.58)	64.3 (1.84)	48.2 (4.92)	55.0 (8.50)	— (†)	62.3 (0.92)	64.2 (1.06)	50.0 (2.98)	58.2 (5.04)	— (†)	14.2 (3.16)	‡ (†)	— (†)
1993	62.6 (1.59)	62.9 (1.85)	55.6 (5.28)	62.2 (8.22)	— (†)	62.1 (0.91)	63.9 (1.04)	51.3 (2.97)	55.7 (4.97)	— (†)	12.6 (3.14)	‡ (†)	— (†)
1994	61.9 (1.43)	64.5 (1.61)	50.8 (4.42)	49.1 (6.28)	— (†)	62.1 (0.83)	64.0 (1.03)	52.4 (2.52)	55.0 (3.23)	— (†)	11.5 (2.72)	8.9 ! (3.39)	— (†)
1995	61.9 (1.41)	64.3 (1.64)	51.2 (4.20)	53.7 (4.92)	— (†)	63.0 (0.81)	65.4 (0.93)	52.9 (2.40)	51.6 (3.18)	— (†)	12.5 (2.57)	13.8 (3.31)	— (†)
1996	65.0 (1.42)	67.4 (1.67)	56.0 (4.03)	50.8 (5.79)	— (†)	64.7 (0.82)	66.6 (0.93)	55.4 (2.41)	57.6 (2.96)	— (†)	11.3 (2.58)	9.0 ! (3.10)	— (†)
1997	67.0 (1.38)	68.2 (1.64)	58.5 (4.12)	65.6 (4.53)	— (†)	65.9 (0.80)	68.1 (0.95)	58.8 (2.35)	55.3 (2.93)	— (†)	9.3 (2.53)	12.8 (3.08)	— (†)
1998	65.6 (1.38)	68.5 (1.61)	61.9 (4.05)	47.4 (4.92)	— (†)	65.2 (0.80)	67.7 (0.94)	59.8 (2.31)	51.9 (2.79)	— (†)	7.9 ! (2.50)	15.7 (2.94)	— (†)
1999	62.9 (1.38)	66.3 (1.64)	58.9 (3.86)	42.3 (4.76)	— (†)	64.0 (0.80)	66.8 (0.94)	58.6 (2.31)	47.4 (2.84)	— (†)	8.3 ! (2.50)	19.5 (2.99)	— (†)
2000	63.3 (1.41)	65.7 (1.66)	54.9 (4.11)	52.9 (5.03)	— (†)	62.7 (0.82)	65.4 (0.97)	56.4 (2.33)	48.6 (2.96)	— (†)	9.1 (2.53)	16.9 (3.11)	— (†)
2001	61.8 (1.48)	64.3 (1.72)	55.0 (4.17)	51.7 (5.63)	— (†)	63.5 (0.82)	66.3 (0.97)	56.4 (2.39)	52.8 (2.93)	— (†)	10.0 (2.58)	13.5 (3.09)	— (†)
2002	65.2 (1.31)	69.1 (1.55)	59.4 (3.90)	53.6 (4.46)	— (†)	63.7 (0.78)	66.5 (0.97)	57.3 (2.33)	54.8 (2.75)	— (†)	9.3 (2.52)	11.7 (2.92)	— (†)
2003[5]	63.9 (1.35)	66.2 (1.61)	57.5 (4.25)	58.6 (4.61)	84.1 (5.10)	65.3 (0.77)	68.0 (0.91)	59.9 (2.29)	57.7 (2.66)	80.0 (3.99)	8.1 ! (2.46)	10.3 (2.81)	-11.9 ! (4.10)
2004[5]	66.7 (1.31)	68.8 (1.57)	62.5 (3.77)	61.8 (4.76)	75.6 (6.13)	66.4 (0.77)	69.4 (0.91)	58.8 (2.34)	57.7 (2.60)	81.6 (3.37)	10.6 (2.51)	11.7 (2.75)	-12.2 (3.49)
2005[5]	68.6 (1.31)	73.2 (1.52)	55.7 (4.15)	54.0 (4.18)	86.7 (5.99)	67.1 (0.76)	70.2 (0.90)	58.2 (2.35)	57.5 (2.52)	80.9 (3.64)	12.0 (2.52)	12.6 (2.67)	-10.7 ! (3.75)
2006[5]	66.0 (1.33)	68.5 (1.60)	55.5 (4.33)	57.9 (4.18)	82.3 (5.32)	67.2 (0.75)	70.4 (0.89)	55.6 (2.35)	58.5 (2.43)	85.1 (3.64)	14.7 (2.51)	11.9 (2.59)	-14.7 (3.74)
2007[5]	67.2 (1.26)	69.5 (1.49)	55.7 (3.78)	64.0 (4.22)	88.8 (6.26)	67.3 (0.73)	70.0 (0.87)	55.7 (2.27)	62.0 (2.33)	85.8 (3.45)	14.3 (2.43)	8.0 ! (2.48)	-15.8 (3.56)
2008[5]	68.6 (1.21)	71.7 (1.44)	55.7 (3.78)	63.9 (3.72)	88.4 (5.08)	68.6 (0.71)	70.8 (0.86)	60.3 (2.15)	62.3 (2.25)	90.1 (3.01)	10.5 (2.31)	8.6 (2.41)	-19.2 (3.13)
2009[5]	70.1 (1.23)	71.3 (1.53)	69.5 (3.51)	59.3 (3.80)	92.1 (3.90)	68.9 (0.70)	71.2 (0.86)	62.4 (2.09)	60.9 (2.14)	88.1 (2.85)	8.8 (2.26)	10.3 (2.31)	-16.9 (2.98)
2010[5,6]	68.1 (1.49)	70.5 (1.68)	62.0 (4.81)	59.7 (4.18)	84.7 (5.27)	68.8 (0.71)	70.1 (0.90)	66.1 (2.01)	62.3 (2.01)	87.4 (2.78)	‡ (†)	7.8 (2.21)	-17.3 (2.92)
2011[5,6]	68.2 (1.45)	68.3 (1.86)	67.1 (4.01)	66.6 (3.50)	86.1 (4.25)	67.5 (0.89)	68.2 (1.03)	62.1 (2.86)	66.1 (2.17)	83.9 (2.79)	6.1 ! (3.04)	‡ (†)	-15.7 (2.97)
2012[5,6]	66.2 (1.59)	65.7 (1.94)	56.4 (4.84)	70.3 (3.22)	81.5 (5.15)	66.8 (0.94)	67.6 (1.12)	60.5 (2.64)	65.9 (1.99)	82.3 (3.59)	7.1 ! (2.87)	‡ (†)	-14.7 (3.76)
2013[5,6]	65.9 (1.58)	68.8 (1.90)	56.7 (5.59)	59.8 (3.62)	80.1 (6.52)	66.8 (0.98)	67.4 (1.26)	60.7 (3.09)	65.5 (2.06)	83.6 (3.20)	6.7 ! (3.34)	‡ (†)	-16.2 (3.44)
2014[5,6]	68.4 (1.67)	67.7 (2.25)	70.2 (4.56)	65.2 (4.08)	90.9 (3.91)	67.1 (1.30)	68.3 (1.58)	63.1 (4.17)	62.5 (2.91)	84.8 (4.01)	‡ (†)	‡ (†)	-16.5 (4.31)

—Not available.
†Not applicable.
!Interpret data with caution. The coefficient of variation (CV) for this estimate is between 30 and 50 percent.
‡Reporting standards not met. The coefficient of variation (CV) for this estimate is 50 percent or greater.
[1]Individuals ages 16 to 24 who graduated from high school or completed a GED during the calendar year.
[2]Enrollment in college as of October of each year for individuals ages 16 to 24 who completed high school during the calendar year.
[3]A 3-year moving average is a weighted average of the year indicated, the year immediately preceding, and the year immediately following. For the first and final years of available data, a 2-year moving average is used: The moving average for 1960 reflects an average of 1960 and 1961; for Black and Hispanic data, the moving average for 1972 reflects an average of 1972 and 1973; for Asian data, the moving average for 2003 reflects an average of 2003 and 2004; and the moving average for 2014 reflects an average of 2013 and 2014. Moving averages are used to produce more stable estimates.
[4]Prior to 1972, White data include persons of Hispanic ethnicity.
[5]White, Black, and Asian data exclude persons of Two or more races.
[6]Beginning in 2010, standard errors were computed using replicate weights, which produced more precise values than the generalized variance function methodology used in prior years.
NOTE: Data are based on sample surveys of the civilian noninstitutionalized population. Race categories exclude persons of Hispanic ethnicity except where otherwise noted. Total includes persons of other racial/ethnic groups not separately shown.
SOURCE: American College Testing Program, unpublished tabulations, derived from statistics collected by the Census Bureau, 1960 through 1969. U.S. Department of Commerce, Census Bureau, Current Population Survey (CPS), October, 1970 through 2014. (This table was prepared August 2015.)

Table 302.30. Percentage of recent high school completers enrolled in 2-year and 4-year colleges, by income level: 1975 through 2014

[Standard errors appear in parentheses]

Year	Percent of recent high school completers[1] enrolled in college[2] (annual data)				3-year moving averages[3]					
					Percent of recent high school completers[1] enrolled in college[2]				Difference between percent enrolled	
	Total	Low income	Middle income	High income	Total	Low income	Middle income	High income	High-low income	High-middle income
1	2	3	4	5	6	7	8	9	10	11
1975	50.7 (1.26)	31.2 (3.59)	46.2 (1.69)	64.5 (2.09)	49.1 (0.74)	34.7 (2.74)	43.5 (1.22)	63.7 (1.47)	29.0 (3.11)	20.2 (1.91)
1976	48.8 (1.31)	39.1 (4.20)	40.5 (1.76)	63.0 (2.06)	50.1 (0.74)	32.3 (2.17)	43.8 (1.00)	64.6 (1.18)	32.3 (2.47)	20.8 (1.55)
1977	50.6 (1.29)	27.7 (3.54)	44.2 (1.76)	66.3 (2.01)	49.9 (0.75)	32.4 (2.22)	43.1 (1.02)	64.4 (1.18)	32.1 (2.51)	21.4 (1.56)
1978	50.1 (1.28)	31.4 (3.74)	44.3 (1.74)	64.0 (2.05)	50.0 (0.74)	29.8 (2.13)	43.9 (1.01)	64.5 (1.17)	34.6 (2.43)	20.5 (1.55)
1979	49.3 (1.28)	30.5 (3.78)	43.2 (1.74)	63.2 (2.04)	49.6 (0.74)	31.6 (2.11)	43.4 (1.01)	64.1 (1.19)	32.6 (2.42)	20.8 (1.56)
1980	49.3 (1.30)	32.5 (3.47)	42.5 (1.78)	65.2 (2.08)	50.8 (0.75)	32.2 (2.14)	45.0 (1.02)	65.3 (1.20)	33.0 (2.45)	20.2 (1.57)
1981	53.9 (1.30)	33.6 (3.90)	49.2 (1.75)	67.6 (2.09)	51.3 (0.75)	32.9 (2.11)	44.5 (1.01)	67.9 (1.19)	34.9 (2.42)	23.4 (1.57)
1982	50.6 (1.36)	32.8 (3.81)	41.7 (1.81)	70.9 (2.13)	52.4 (0.79)	33.6 (2.29)	45.4 (1.06)	69.6 (1.25)	36.0 (2.61)	24.2 (1.64)
1983	52.7 (1.39)	34.6 (4.02)	45.2 (1.88)	70.3 (2.17)	52.8 (0.79)	34.0 (2.20)	45.1 (1.08)	71.7 (1.23)	37.8 (2.52)	26.7 (1.63)
1984	55.2 (1.37)	34.5 (3.62)	48.4 (1.89)	74.0 (2.09)	55.1 (0.81)	36.3 (2.26)	48.0 (1.11)	72.9 (1.24)	36.6 (2.58)	24.9 (1.66)
1985	57.7 (1.45)	40.2 (4.14)	50.6 (2.02)	74.6 (2.16)	55.5 (0.82)	35.9 (2.18)	49.1 (1.13)	73.2 (1.26)	37.3 (2.51)	24.1 (1.69)
1986	53.8 (1.43)	33.9 (3.59)	48.5 (1.97)	71.0 (2.28)	56.1 (0.84)	36.8 (2.23)	49.6 (1.17)	73.2 (1.27)	36.4 (2.57)	23.5 (1.72)
1987	56.8 (1.46)	36.9 (3.88)	50.0 (2.07)	73.8 (2.16)	56.5 (0.83)	37.6 (2.21)	51.1 (1.16)	72.6 (1.30)	35.0 (2.57)	21.5 (1.74)
1988	58.9 (1.57)	42.5 (4.39)	54.7 (2.14)	72.8 (2.52)	58.4 (0.92)	42.4 (2.54)	53.4 (1.28)	72.5 (1.44)	30.2 (2.92)	19.1 (1.93)
1989	59.6 (1.64)	48.1 (4.56)	55.4 (2.28)	70.7 (2.61)	59.5 (0.94)	45.6 (2.66)	54.9 (1.28)	73.2 (1.50)	27.6 (3.06)	18.4 (1.97)
1990	60.1 (1.60)	46.7 (4.76)	54.4 (2.14)	76.6 (2.54)	60.7 (0.92)	44.8 (2.63)	56.0 (1.27)	75.0 (1.44)	30.2 (3.00)	19.0 (1.92)
1991	62.5 (1.62)	39.5 (4.50)	58.4 (2.25)	78.2 (2.39)	61.5 (0.92)	42.2 (2.62)	56.5 (1.26)	78.0 (1.40)	35.8 (2.97)	21.4 (1.88)
1992	61.9 (1.58)	40.9 (4.37)	57.0 (2.18)	79.0 (2.35)	62.3 (0.92)	43.6 (2.60)	57.4 (1.26)	78.8 (1.38)	35.3 (2.94)	21.4 (1.87)
1993	62.6 (1.59)	50.4 (4.56)	56.9 (2.15)	79.3 (2.46)	62.1 (0.91)	44.7 (2.55)	57.3 (1.23)	78.7 (1.39)	34.0 (2.90)	21.5 (1.86)
1994	61.9 (1.43)	43.3 (3.96)	57.8 (1.94)	77.9 (2.22)	62.1 (0.83)	42.0 (2.27)	57.0 (1.14)	80.4 (1.22)	38.4 (2.57)	23.4 (1.67)
1995	61.9 (1.41)	34.2 (3.56)	56.0 (2.00)	83.5 (1.86)	63.0 (0.81)	42.1 (2.16)	58.9 (1.12)	79.9 (1.20)	37.8 (2.47)	21.0 (1.64)
1996	65.0 (1.42)	48.6 (3.78)	62.7 (1.95)	78.0 (2.27)	64.7 (0.82)	47.1 (2.18)	59.9 (1.16)	81.3 (1.19)	34.3 (2.49)	21.4 (1.66)
1997	67.0 (1.38)	57.0 (3.66)	60.7 (1.97)	82.2 (1.98)	65.9 (0.80)	50.6 (2.14)	62.7 (1.12)	79.3 (1.24)	28.7 (2.47)	16.6 (1.67)
1998	65.6 (1.38)	46.4 (3.62)	64.7 (1.89)	77.5 (2.21)	65.2 (0.80)	50.3 (2.14)	61.9 (1.10)	78.4 (1.24)	28.1 (2.47)	16.6 (1.66)
1999	62.9 (1.38)	47.6 (3.77)	60.2 (1.87)	75.4 (2.26)	64.0 (0.80)	47.9 (2.13)	61.5 (1.10)	76.6 (1.29)	28.7 (2.49)	15.1 (1.70)
2000	63.3 (1.41)	49.7 (3.67)	59.5 (1.97)	76.9 (2.22)	62.7 (0.82)	47.1 (2.17)	58.8 (1.14)	77.4 (1.29)	30.3 (2.52)	18.6 (1.72)
2001	61.8 (1.48)	43.8 (3.81)	56.4 (2.07)	80.0 (2.19)	63.5 (0.82)	49.9 (2.19)	59.1 (1.14)	78.3 (1.28)	28.4 (2.53)	19.3 (1.71)
2002	65.2 (1.31)	56.3 (3.64)	60.9 (1.78)	78.2 (2.12)	63.7 (0.78)	50.9 (2.14)	58.4 (1.08)	79.5 (1.20)	28.6 (2.45)	21.0 (1.61)
2003	63.9 (1.35)	52.8 (3.83)	57.6 (1.87)	80.1 (2.02)	65.3 (0.77)	52.5 (2.20)	60.6 (1.05)	79.5 (1.18)	27.0 (2.49)	18.9 (1.58)
2004	66.7 (1.31)	47.8 (3.95)	63.3 (1.79)	80.1 (1.98)	66.4 (0.77)	51.4 (2.24)	62.0 (1.05)	80.5 (1.15)	29.0 (2.52)	18.5 (1.56)
2005	68.6 (1.31)	53.5 (3.86)	65.1 (1.81)	81.2 (1.98)	67.1 (0.76)	50.8 (2.26)	63.3 (1.04)	80.7 (1.15)	29.9 (2.53)	17.4 (1.55)
2006	66.0 (1.33)	50.9 (3.92)	61.4 (1.82)	80.7 (2.01)	67.2 (0.75)	54.5 (2.18)	63.3 (1.03)	80.0 (1.15)	25.5 (2.47)	16.7 (1.55)
2007	67.2 (1.26)	58.4 (3.57)	63.3 (1.73)	78.2 (2.01)	67.3 (0.73)	55.3 (2.11)	63.5 (0.99)	80.2 (1.14)	24.9 (2.40)	16.8 (1.51)
2008	68.6 (1.21)	55.9 (3.50)	65.2 (1.62)	81.9 (1.90)	68.6 (0.71)	56.1 (2.08)	65.1 (0.96)	81.4 (1.11)	25.3 (2.36)	16.2 (1.47)
2009	70.1 (1.23)	53.9 (3.75)	66.7 (1.66)	84.2 (1.84)	68.9 (0.70)	53.3 (2.02)	66.2 (0.94)	82.8 (1.10)	29.5 (2.30)	16.6 (1.44)
2010[4]	68.1 (1.49)	50.7 (3.88)	66.7 (2.03)	82.2 (2.34)	68.8 (0.71)	52.6 (1.97)	66.5 (0.94)	83.0 (1.12)	30.4 (2.27)	16.4 (1.46)
2011[4]	68.2 (1.45)	53.5 (4.25)	66.2 (1.94)	82.4 (2.46)	67.5 (0.89)	51.6 (2.47)	65.9 (1.11)	81.7 (1.42)	30.1 (2.85)	15.9 (1.81)
2012[4]	66.2 (1.59)	50.9 (4.39)	64.7 (2.10)	80.7 (2.54)	66.8 (0.94)	50.3 (2.63)	64.9 (1.26)	80.4 (1.59)	30.1 (3.07)	15.5 (2.03)
2013[4]	65.9 (1.58)	45.5 (4.31)	63.8 (2.32)	78.5 (2.68)	66.8 (0.98)	51.6 (2.74)	64.0 (1.36)	80.8 (1.46)	29.2 (3.10)	16.8 (2.00)
2014[4]	68.4 (1.67)	57.8 (4.42)	63.6 (2.31)	83.6 (2.17)	67.1 (1.30)	52.1 (3.19)	63.7 (1.80)	80.9 (1.81)	28.8 (3.66)	17.2 (2.55)

[1]Individuals ages 16 to 24 who graduated from high school or completed a GED during the calendar year.

[2]Enrollment in college as of October of each year for individuals ages 16 to 24 who completed high school during the calendar year.

[3]A 3-year moving average is a weighted average of the year indicated, the year immediately preceding, and the year immediately following. For 1975 and 2014, a 2-year moving average is used: The moving average for income groups in 1975 reflects an average of 1975 and 1976, and the moving average for 2014 reflects an average of 2013 and 2014. Moving averages are used to produce more stable estimates.

[4]Beginning in 2010, standard errors were computed using replicate weights, which produced more precise values than the generalized variance function methodology used in prior years.

NOTE: Data are based on sample surveys of the civilian noninstitutionalized population. Low income refers to the bottom 20 percent of all family incomes, high income refers to the top 20 percent of all family incomes, and middle income refers to the 60 percent in between.

SOURCE: U.S. Department of Commerce, Census Bureau, Current Population Survey (CPS), October, 1975 through 2014. (This table was prepared August 2015.)

Table 302.50. Estimated rate of 2011–12 high school graduates attending degree-granting postsecondary institutions, by state: 2012

State	Number of graduates from high schools located in the state			Number of fall 2012 first-time freshmen graduating from high school in the previous 12 months		Estimated rate of high school graduates going to college	
	Total[1]	Public, 2011–12	Private, 2012–13	State residents enrolled in institutions in any state[2]	State residents enrolled in institutions in their home state[3]	In any state	In their home state
1	2	3	4	5	6	7	8
United States	**3,457,955**	**3,149,185**	**308,770**	**2,132,264** [4]	**1,729,792**	**61.7**	**50.0**
Alabama	50,164	45,394	4,770	29,728	26,567	59.3	53.0
Alaska	8,189	7,989	200	3,732	2,413	45.6	29.5
Arizona	66,218	63,208	3,010	35,181	31,132	53.1	47.0
Arkansas	30,019	28,419	1,600	20,185	18,244	67.2	60.8
California	451,364	418,664	32,700	263,843	231,215	58.5	51.2
Colorado	52,607	50,087	2,520	31,139	23,268	59.2	44.2
Connecticut	44,751	38,681	6,070	31,662	17,396	70.8	38.9
Delaware	10,037	8,247	1,790	6,500	4,632	64.8	46.1
District of Columbia[5]	5,680	3,860	1,820	2,463	450	43.4	7.9
Florida	171,404	151,964	19,440	107,716	94,985	62.8	55.4
Georgia	99,952	90,582	9,370	66,494	55,399	66.5	55.4
Hawaii	13,970	11,360	2,610	9,040	6,091	64.7	43.6
Idaho	18,238	17,568	670	8,782	6,179	48.2	33.9
Illinois	153,605	139,575	14,030	92,394	63,610	60.2	41.4
Indiana	70,767	65,667	5,100	44,612	38,812	63.0	54.8
Iowa	41,550	33,230	2,400	23,488	20,340	56.5	49.0
Kansas	34,078	31,898	2,180	22,239	19,058	65.3	55.9
Kentucky	47,442	42,642	4,800	29,830	26,624	62.9	56.1
Louisiana	44,575	36,675	7,900	28,831	26,024	64.7	58.4
Maine	16,103	13,473	2,630	8,681	5,829	53.9	36.2
Maryland	67,781	58,811	8,970	41,033	25,773	60.5	38.0
Massachusetts	76,177	65,157	11,020	53,836	36,132	70.7	47.4
Michigan	115,256	105,446	9,810	70,843	63,296	61.5	54.9
Minnesota	61,891	57,501	4,390	43,264	30,237	69.9	48.9
Mississippi	29,748	26,158	3,590	23,436	21,752	78.8	73.1
Missouri	69,053	61,313	7,740	42,762	35,648	61.9	51.6
Montana	10,140	9,750	390	5,907	4,598	58.3	45.3
Nebraska	22,844	20,464	2,380	14,750	11,969	64.6	52.4
Nevada	22,731	21,891	840	12,288	9,310	54.1	41.0
New Hampshire	16,886	14,426	2,460	10,418	5,618	61.7	33.3
New Jersey	106,919	93,819	13,100	72,631	41,204	67.9	38.5
New Mexico	21,375	20,315	1,060	14,831	12,903	69.4	60.4
New York	209,216	180,806	28,410	146,458	117,960	70.0	56.4
North Carolina	101,097	93,977	7,120	62,531	55,578	61.9	55.0
North Dakota	7,322	6,942	380	4,751	3,527	64.9	48.2
Ohio	135,885	123,135	12,750	81,428	69,039	59.9	50.8
Oklahoma	39,295	37,305	1,990	22,667	20,207	57.7	51.4
Oregon	37,301	34,261	3,040	17,509	13,343	46.9	35.8
Pennsylvania	146,493	131,733	14,760	87,075	70,625	59.4	48.2
Rhode Island	11,501	9,751	1,750	7,715	5,056	67.1	44.0
South Carolina	44,452	41,442	3,010	29,023	26,154	65.3	58.8
South Dakota	8,456	8,196	260	5,825	4,443	68.9	52.5
Tennessee	67,964	62,454	5,510	41,027	34,318	60.4	50.5
Texas	306,591	292,531	14,060	176,871	156,566	57.7	51.1
Utah	32,757	31,157	1,600	16,650	15,101	50.8	46.1
Vermont	7,789	6,859	930	4,142	2,040	53.2	26.2
Virginia	89,866	83,336	6,530	58,035	47,582	64.6	52.9
Washington	71,165	65,205	5,960	34,168	25,854	48.0	36.3
West Virginia	18,383	17,603	780	10,241	9,110	55.7	49.6
Wisconsin	71,225	62,705	8,520	41,715	33,972	58.6	47.7
Wyoming	5,603	5,553	50	3,170	2,426	56.6	43.3

[1]Total includes public high school graduates for 2011–12 and private high school graduates for 2012–13. Data on private high school graduates are not available for 2011–12.
[2]All U.S. resident students living in a particular state when admitted to an institution in any state. Students may be enrolled in any state.
[3]Students who attend institutions in their home state. Total includes 183 students attending U.S. Service Academies in their home state, not shown separately.
[4]U.S. total includes some U.S. residents whose home state is unknown.
[5]A percentage of the private high school graduates are not residents of the District of Columbia.

NOTE: Degree-granting institutions grant associate's or higher degrees and participate in Title IV federal financial aid programs. Detail may not sum to totals because of rounding.
SOURCE: U.S. Department of Education, National Center for Education Statistics, Common Core of Data (CCD), "NCES Common Core of Data State Dropout and Completion Data File," 2011–12; Private School Universe Survey (PSS), 2013–14; and Integrated Postsecondary Education Data System (IPEDS), Spring 2013, Fall Enrollment component. (This table was prepared January 2016.)

Table 302.60. Percentage of 18- to 24-year-olds enrolled in degree-granting postsecondary institutions, by level of institution and sex and race/ethnicity of student: 1970 through 2014

[Standard errors appear in parentheses]

Year	Total, all students	Level of institution: 2-year	Level of institution: 4-year	Sex: Male	Sex: Female	Race/ethnicity: White	Race/ethnicity: Black	Race/ethnicity: Hispanic	Race/ethnicity: Asian	Race/ethnicity: Pacific Islander	Race/ethnicity: American Indian/Alaska Native	Race/ethnicity: Two or more races	Race/ethnicity by sex: White: Male	Race/ethnicity by sex: White: Female	Race/ethnicity by sex: Black: Male	Race/ethnicity by sex: Black: Female	Race/ethnicity by sex: Hispanic: Male	Race/ethnicity by sex: Hispanic: Female
1	2	3	4	5	6	7	8	9	10	11	12	13	14	15	16	17	18	19
1970[1]	25.7 (0.42)	— (†)	— (†)	32.1 (0.65)	20.3 (0.52)	27.1 (0.45)	15.5 (1.15)	— (†)	— (†)	— (†)	— (†)	— (†)	— (†)	— (†)	— (†)	— (†)	— (†)	— (†)
1971[1]	26.2 (0.41)	— (†)	— (†)	32.5 (0.63)	20.8 (0.52)	27.2 (0.44)	18.2 (1.19)	— (†)	— (†)	— (†)	— (†)	— (†)	— (†)	— (†)	— (†)	— (†)	— (†)	— (†)
1972	25.5 (0.37)	— (†)	— (†)	30.2 (0.56)	21.2 (0.47)	27.2 (0.41)	18.3 (1.18)	13.4 (1.83)	— (†)	— (†)	— (†)	— (†)	32.3 (0.63)	22.5 (0.54)	21.1 (1.83)	15.9 (1.51)	15.1 (2.85)	12.0 (2.37)
1973	24.0 (0.35)	6.9 (0.21)	17.1 (0.31)	27.7 (0.54)	20.5 (0.46)	25.5 (0.40)	15.9 (1.09)	16.1 (2.02)	— (†)	— (†)	— (†)	— (†)	29.6 (0.60)	21.8 (0.53)	18.7 (1.71)	13.5 (1.38)	16.7 (2.94)	15.5 (2.77)
1974	24.6 (0.35)	7.6 (0.22)	17.0 (0.31)	27.7 (0.53)	21.7 (0.47)	25.8 (0.40)	17.6 (1.14)	18.0 (1.95)	— (†)	— (†)	— (†)	— (†)	28.9 (0.60)	22.9 (0.53)	19.8 (1.77)	15.9 (1.47)	19.7 (2.92)	16.5 (2.60)
1975	26.3 (0.36)	9.0 (0.23)	17.3 (0.31)	29.0 (0.53)	23.7 (0.48)	27.4 (0.40)	20.4 (1.18)	20.4 (2.09)	— (†)	— (†)	— (†)	— (†)	30.7 (0.59)	24.3 (0.54)	19.9 (1.74)	20.8 (1.61)	21.4 (3.10)	19.5 (2.81)
1976	26.7 (0.35)	6.4 (0.20)	20.2 (0.32)	28.2 (0.52)	25.2 (0.48)	27.6 (0.40)	22.5 (1.20)	20.0 (2.00)	— (†)	— (†)	— (†)	— (†)	29.3 (0.58)	26.1 (0.55)	22.0 (1.77)	22.9 (1.64)	21.3 (3.05)	18.8 (2.64)
1977	26.1 (0.38)	6.8 (0.22)	19.4 (0.35)	28.1 (0.56)	24.3 (0.52)	27.2 (0.43)	21.1 (1.18)	17.2 (1.87)	— (†)	— (†)	— (†)	— (†)	29.4 (0.64)	25.1 (0.59)	20.3 (1.73)	21.9 (1.61)	18.3 (2.80)	16.3 (2.50)
1978	25.3 (0.38)	6.6 (0.22)	18.7 (0.34)	27.1 (0.55)	23.6 (0.51)	26.5 (0.43)	20.1 (1.15)	15.2 (1.74)	— (†)	— (†)	— (†)	— (†)	28.4 (0.63)	24.6 (0.59)	19.7 (1.70)	20.4 (1.56)	16.1 (2.61)	14.3 (2.33)
1979	25.0 (0.37)	6.3 (0.21)	18.7 (0.34)	25.9 (0.54)	24.2 (0.52)	26.3 (0.43)	19.8 (1.13)	16.7 (1.77)	— (†)	— (†)	— (†)	— (†)	27.1 (0.61)	25.5 (0.59)	19.1 (1.67)	20.3 (1.54)	18.3 (2.65)	15.2 (2.35)
1980	25.7 (0.38)	7.1 (0.22)	18.6 (0.33)	26.4 (0.54)	25.0 (0.52)	27.3 (0.43)	19.4 (1.12)	16.1 (1.64)	— (†)	— (†)	— (†)	— (†)	28.4 (0.63)	26.3 (0.60)	17.5 (1.60)	20.9 (1.55)	15.9 (2.33)	16.2 (2.32)
1981	26.1 (0.37)	7.5 (0.22)	18.6 (0.33)	27.1 (0.54)	25.2 (0.51)	27.7 (0.43)	19.9 (1.09)	16.6 (1.63)	— (†)	— (†)	— (†)	— (†)	28.7 (0.62)	26.6 (0.60)	18.9 (1.58)	20.7 (1.51)	16.6 (2.35)	16.7 (2.27)
1982	26.6 (0.39)	7.7 (0.24)	18.9 (0.35)	27.2 (0.57)	26.0 (0.55)	28.1 (0.46)	19.9 (1.14)	16.8 (1.77)	— (†)	— (†)	— (†)	— (†)	28.9 (0.66)	27.4 (0.64)	18.7 (1.64)	21.0 (1.59)	14.9 (2.45)	18.6 (2.52)
1983	26.2 (0.39)	7.4 (0.23)	18.8 (0.35)	27.3 (0.57)	25.1 (0.54)	27.9 (0.46)	19.2 (1.12)	17.3 (1.77)	— (†)	— (†)	— (†)	— (†)	29.4 (0.66)	26.5 (0.64)	18.1 (1.60)	20.1 (1.56)	15.6 (2.46)	18.8 (2.54)
1984	27.1 (0.40)	7.3 (0.24)	19.8 (0.36)	28.6 (0.58)	25.6 (0.55)	28.9 (0.47)	20.3 (1.15)	17.9 (1.80)	— (†)	— (†)	— (†)	— (†)	30.8 (0.68)	27.1 (0.65)	20.3 (1.67)	20.3 (1.57)	16.1 (2.51)	19.6 (2.57)
1985	27.8 (0.41)	7.4 (0.24)	20.4 (0.37)	28.4 (0.60)	27.2 (0.57)	30.0 (0.49)	19.6 (1.16)	16.9 (1.84)	— (†)	— (†)	— (†)	— (†)	30.9 (0.70)	29.2 (0.67)	20.2 (1.72)	19.1 (1.56)	14.9 (2.46)	18.9 (2.75)
1986	27.9 (0.42)	7.6 (0.25)	20.3 (0.37)	28.2 (0.60)	27.6 (0.58)	29.7 (0.50)	21.9 (1.21)	17.6 (1.76)	— (†)	— (†)	— (†)	— (†)	30.6 (0.72)	28.8 (0.68)	20.0 (1.72)	23.4 (1.69)	16.7 (2.36)	18.7 (2.64)
1987	29.6 (0.43)	8.1 (0.26)	21.5 (0.39)	30.6 (0.62)	28.7 (0.59)	31.9 (0.51)	22.8 (1.25)	17.5 (1.73)	— (†)	— (†)	— (†)	— (†)	33.0 (0.74)	30.8 (0.71)	22.6 (1.83)	22.9 (1.70)	18.5 (2.46)	16.5 (2.43)
1988	30.3 (0.47)	8.8 (0.29)	21.5 (0.42)	30.2 (0.68)	30.4 (0.66)	33.2 (0.57)	21.2 (1.33)	17.0 (2.00)	— (†)	— (†)	— (†)	— (†)	33.4 (0.82)	33.0 (0.79)	18.5 (1.87)	23.5 (1.88)	16.5 (2.74)	17.6 (2.93)
1989	30.9 (0.48)	8.0 (0.28)	22.9 (0.44)	30.2 (0.68)	31.6 (0.67)	34.2 (0.58)	23.4 (1.38)	16.1 (1.90)	46.1 (3.92)	— (†)	15.7 ! (5.33)	— (†)	34.1 (0.83)	34.4 (0.81)	19.7 (1.89)	26.7 (1.97)	14.6 (2.55)	17.6 (2.81)
1990	32.0 (0.47)	8.7 (0.28)	23.3 (0.43)	32.3 (0.68)	31.8 (0.66)	35.1 (0.57)	25.4 (1.37)	15.8 (1.67)	56.9 (3.56)	— (†)	15.8 ! (5.08)	— (†)	35.5 (0.82)	34.7 (0.80)	26.0 (2.03)	24.8 (1.86)	15.3 (2.31)	16.4 (2.42)
1991	33.3 (0.48)	9.7 (0.30)	23.6 (0.43)	32.8 (0.68)	33.6 (0.67)	36.8 (0.58)	23.5 (1.34)	17.9 (1.72)	57.1 (3.19)	— (†)	15.9 ! (5.45)	— (†)	36.5 (0.83)	37.0 (0.82)	23.2 (1.95)	23.8 (1.84)	14.0 (2.15)	22.2 (2.70)
1992	34.4 (0.49)	9.9 (0.31)	24.4 (0.44)	32.7 (0.68)	36.0 (0.69)	37.3 (0.59)	25.2 (1.37)	21.3 (1.87)	58.4 (3.28)	— (†)	18.5 ! (6.18)	— (†)	36.2 (0.83)	38.3 (0.83)	21.3 (1.87)	28.8 (1.96)	17.8 (2.47)	24.7 (2.80)
1993	34.0 (0.49)	9.8 (0.30)	24.2 (0.44)	33.6 (0.69)	34.4 (0.68)	36.8 (0.59)	24.5 (1.35)	21.7 (1.88)	61.2 (3.27)	— (†)	18.9 (5.66)	— (†)	36.5 (0.84)	37.1 (0.83)	22.9 (1.92)	26.0 (1.90)	19.7 (2.59)	23.7 (2.71)
1994	34.6 (0.42)	9.1 (0.26)	25.5 (0.39)	33.1 (0.59)	36.0 (0.60)	38.1 (0.53)	27.7 (1.17)	18.8 (1.10)	62.7 (2.81)	— (†)	29.4 (5.64)	— (†)	37.0 (0.74)	39.2 (0.74)	25.6 (1.66)	29.5 (1.64)	16.5 (1.43)	21.5 (1.71)
1995	34.3 (0.44)	8.9 (0.27)	25.4 (0.41)	33.1 (0.63)	35.5 (0.63)	37.9 (0.55)	27.5 (1.18)	20.7 (1.13)	54.6 (3.10)	— (†)	27.6 (6.14)	— (†)	37.0 (0.78)	38.8 (0.78)	26.0 (1.71)	28.7 (1.62)	18.7 (1.49)	23.0 (1.71)
1996	35.5 (0.47)	9.5 (0.29)	26.1 (0.43)	34.1 (0.66)	37.0 (0.67)	39.5 (0.59)	27.4 (1.23)	20.1 (1.18)	53.9 (2.47)	— (†)	30.3 (5.25)	— (†)	38.3 (0.83)	40.6 (0.84)	25.7 (1.77)	28.8 (1.70)	16.5 (1.52)	24.0 (1.81)
1997	36.8 (0.47)	9.9 (0.29)	27.0 (0.43)	35.0 (0.66)	38.7 (0.67)	40.6 (0.59)	29.8 (1.25)	22.4 (1.21)	55.1 (2.60)	— (†)	27.1 (4.63)	— (†)	39.3 (0.82)	41.8 (0.84)	25.4 (1.75)	33.7 (1.77)	19.2 (1.56)	26.1 (1.88)
1998	36.5 (0.46)	10.2 (0.29)	26.3 (0.42)	34.5 (0.65)	38.6 (0.66)	40.6 (0.59)	29.8 (1.24)	20.4 (1.11)	60.4 (2.49)	— (†)	20.3 (4.91)	— (†)	39.4 (0.82)	41.9 (0.84)	26.1 (1.76)	32.9 (1.73)	16.4 (1.41)	24.9 (1.73)
1999	35.6 (0.46)	9.1 (0.27)	26.5 (0.42)	34.1 (0.64)	37.0 (0.65)	39.4 (0.58)	30.4 (1.24)	18.7 (1.08)	55.7 (2.42)	— (†)	19.5 (4.71)	— (†)	38.3 (0.81)	40.6 (0.82)	28.9 (1.81)	31.6 (1.70)	15.8 (1.41)	21.9 (1.65)
2000	35.5 (0.45)	9.4 (0.28)	26.0 (0.41)	32.6 (0.62)	38.4 (0.65)	38.7 (0.57)	30.5 (1.21)	21.7 (1.12)	55.9 (2.42)	— (†)	15.9 (4.30)	— (†)	36.2 (0.79)	41.3 (0.81)	25.1 (1.67)	35.2 (1.72)	18.5 (1.45)	25.4 (1.72)
2001	36.3 (0.45)	9.8 (0.28)	26.6 (0.41)	33.6 (0.63)	39.0 (0.64)	39.5 (0.57)	31.4 (1.22)	21.7 (1.10)	61.3 (2.35)	— (†)	23.3 (4.29)	— (†)	37.2 (0.79)	41.9 (0.82)	26.7 (1.70)	35.5 (1.71)	17.4 (1.42)	26.1 (1.67)
2002	36.7 (0.43)	9.7 (0.26)	27.0 (0.39)	33.7 (0.59)	39.7 (0.61)	40.9 (0.55)	31.9 (1.18)	19.9 (0.94)	60.9 (2.10)	— (†)	23.6 (3.96)	— (†)	38.9 (0.77)	42.8 (0.78)	26.3 (1.63)	36.9 (1.68)	16.2 (1.17)	24.4 (1.51)
2003[2]	37.8 (0.43)	10.2 (0.27)	27.7 (0.39)	34.3 (0.59)	41.3 (0.61)	41.6 (0.55)	32.3 (1.20)	23.5 (1.02)	61.2 (2.27)	43.3 (9.97)	17.7 (4.45)	41.6 (3.58)	38.5 (0.77)	44.5 (0.78)	28.2 (1.68)	36.0 (1.69)	18.3 (1.27)	29.4 (1.60)
2004[2]	38.0 (0.42)	9.4 (0.25)	28.6 (0.39)	34.7 (0.59)	41.2 (0.61)	41.7 (0.55)	31.8 (1.18)	24.7 (1.02)	60.6 (2.24)	55.8 (8.99)	24.4 (4.52)	36.8 (3.44)	38.4 (0.76)	45.0 (0.78)	26.5 (1.63)	36.6 (1.67)	21.7 (1.33)	28.2 (1.56)
2005[2]	38.9 (0.43)	9.6 (0.26)	29.2 (0.40)	35.3 (0.59)	42.5 (0.61)	42.8 (0.55)	33.1 (1.18)	24.8 (1.02)	61.0 (2.26)	50.6 (10.95)	27.8 (4.88)	41.8 (3.48)	39.4 (0.76)	46.1 (0.79)	28.2 (1.64)	37.6 (1.69)	20.7 (1.31)	29.5 (1.58)
2006[2]	37.3 (0.42)	9.6 (0.25)	27.8 (0.39)	34.1 (0.58)	40.6 (0.60)	41.0 (0.54)	32.6 (1.16)	23.6 (0.99)	58.3 (2.28)	39.1 (8.36)	26.2 (5.18)	38.5 (3.51)	37.9 (0.75)	44.1 (0.78)	28.1 (1.60)	36.9 (1.65)	20.0 (1.29)	27.6 (1.52)
2007[2]	38.8 (0.42)	10.9 (0.27)	27.9 (0.39)	35.5 (0.58)	42.1 (0.60)	42.6 (0.54)	33.1 (1.15)	26.6 (1.02)	57.2 (2.28)	37.1 (9.07)	24.7 (4.63)	39.2 (3.48)	39.6 (0.76)	45.7 (0.78)	32.2 (1.63)	34.0 (1.61)	20.7 (1.29)	33.0 (1.57)
2008[2]	39.6 (0.42)	11.8 (0.28)	27.8 (0.38)	37.0 (0.58)	42.3 (0.60)	44.2 (0.54)	32.1 (1.13)	25.8 (1.01)	59.3 (2.32)	27.3 ! (8.92)	21.9 (4.22)	45.7 (3.55)	41.7 (0.76)	46.9 (0.78)	29.7 (1.61)	34.2 (1.59)	23.0 (1.35)	28.9 (1.50)
2009[2]	41.3 (0.42)	11.7 (0.27)	29.6 (0.39)	38.4 (0.59)	44.2 (0.60)	45.0 (0.55)	37.7 (1.17)	27.5 (1.01)	65.2 (2.17)	33.4 (7.45)	29.8 (5.10)	39.3 (3.32)	42.3 (0.76)	47.7 (0.78)	33.2 (1.64)	41.9 (1.64)	24.2 (1.35)	31.0 (1.50)
2010[2,3]	41.2 (0.57)	12.9 (0.36)	28.2 (0.53)	38.3 (0.78)	44.1 (0.84)	43.3 (0.81)	38.4 (1.66)	31.9 (1.15)	63.6 (2.70)	36.0 (8.36)	41.4 (6.60)	38.3 (4.38)	40.6 (1.00)	46.1 (1.17)	35.2 (2.13)	41.4 (2.16)	27.9 (1.57)	36.1 (1.60)
2011[2,3]	42.0 (0.59)	12.0 (0.35)	30.0 (0.58)	39.1 (0.80)	44.9 (0.80)	44.7 (0.77)	37.1 (1.53)	34.8 (1.20)	60.1 (2.45)	37.8 (7.93)	23.5 (5.30)	38.8 (3.60)	42.4 (0.96)	47.1 (1.08)	34.0 (2.29)	39.9 (1.90)	31.0 (1.63)	39.4 (1.58)
2012[2,3]	41.0 (0.62)	12.7 (0.38)	28.3 (0.58)	37.6 (0.79)	44.5 (0.86)	42.1 (0.83)	36.4 (1.62)	37.5 (1.18)	59.8 (2.61)	50.3 (9.60)	27.8 (4.43)	39.4 (3.64)	38.3 (1.06)	46.0 (1.08)	33.9 (2.04)	38.7 (2.33)	33.5 (1.58)	41.7 (1.73)
2013[2,3]	39.9 (0.63)	11.6 (0.36)	28.3 (0.57)	36.6 (0.85)	43.3 (0.80)	41.6 (0.90)	34.2 (1.58)	33.8 (1.24)	62.3 (2.62)	32.9 (8.26)	31.8 (5.58)	44.7 (3.99)	38.1 (1.11)	45.3 (1.11)	30.6 (2.13)	37.6 (2.18)	29.1 (1.72)	38.8 (1.58)
2014[2,3]	40.0 (0.65)	10.6 (0.40)	29.4 (0.61)	37.3 (0.89)	42.8 (0.79)	42.2 (0.87)	32.6 (1.48)	34.7 (1.21)	65.2 (2.27)	41.0 (11.29)	35.4 (4.63)	31.6 (3.20)	40.2 (1.28)	44.2 (0.99)	28.5 (1.95)	36.6 (2.04)	30.3 (1.65)	39.4 (1.70)

—Not available.
†Not applicable.
!Interpret data with caution. The coefficient of variation (CV) for this estimate is between 30 and 50 percent.
[1]Prior to 1972, White and Black data include persons of Hispanic ethnicity.
[2]After 2002, data for individual race categories exclude persons of Two or more races.
[3]Beginning in 2010, standard errors were computed using replicate weights, which produced more precise values than the generalized variance function methodology used in prior years.
NOTE: Data are based on sample surveys of the civilian noninstitutionalized population. Totals include other racial/ethnic groups not separately shown. Race categories exclude persons of Hispanic ethnicity except where otherwise noted.
SOURCE: U.S. Department of Commerce, Census Bureau, Current Population Survey (CPS), October, 1970 through 2014. (This table was prepared August 2015.)

Table 302.62. Percentage of 18- to 24-year-olds enrolled in degree-granting postsecondary institutions and percentage distribution of those enrolled, by sex, race/ethnicity, and selected racial/ethnic subgroups: 2009 and 2014

[Standard errors appear in parentheses]

Race/ethnicity	2009 Total		2009 Male		2009 Female		2014 Total		2014 Male		2014 Female	
1	2		3		4		5		6		7	
	Percent enrolled											
Total[1]	**41.7**	**(0.12)**	**37.3**	**(0.19)**	**46.3**	**(0.17)**	**42.1**	**(0.13)**	**38.2**	**(0.18)**	**46.3**	**(0.17)**
White	45.7	(0.15)	41.6	(0.23)	50.0	(0.22)	44.4	(0.17)	40.7	(0.23)	48.4	(0.24)
Black	35.3	(0.34)	29.6	(0.52)	41.2	(0.57)	35.6	(0.34)	30.4	(0.46)	41.0	(0.46)
Hispanic	29.1	(0.29)	24.5	(0.35)	34.4	(0.41)	35.4	(0.28)	30.8	(0.35)	40.4	(0.37)
Cuban	45.5	(1.67)	43.1	(2.25)	48.1	(2.59)	45.7	(1.53)	41.8	(2.27)	50.2	(2.04)
Dominican	37.0	(1.66)	32.9	(2.02)	41.2	(2.79)	41.0	(1.49)	33.2	(1.62)	49.2	(2.21)
Mexican	26.2	(0.32)	21.7	(0.41)	31.3	(0.49)	33.4	(0.36)	29.0	(0.44)	38.1	(0.47)
Puerto Rican	29.9	(0.75)	24.6	(1.10)	35.2	(1.03)	32.7	(0.84)	28.6	(1.01)	37.0	(1.26)
Spaniard	43.6	(3.18)	38.3	(4.44)	48.5	(4.35)	47.9	(2.45)	41.6	(3.64)	54.8	(3.88)
Central American[2]	26.8	(0.81)	22.3	(1.05)	33.0	(1.39)	32.9	(0.83)	27.7	(1.15)	39.4	(1.12)
Costa Rican	39.6	(5.44)	41.1	(6.90)	37.1	(9.08)	55.1	(5.75)	50.8	(8.69)	58.9	(6.87)
Guatemalan	18.8	(1.40)	14.1	(1.55)	27.7	(2.72)	27.2	(1.44)	20.0	(1.80)	38.9	(2.19)
Honduran	20.0	(1.87)	13.8	(2.27)	28.5	(2.97)	27.0	(2.00)	25.1	(2.88)	29.3	(3.22)
Nicaraguan	43.4	(3.34)	41.7	(4.61)	45.0	(4.46)	51.5	(2.87)	46.4	(4.53)	56.3	(4.45)
Panamanian	53.1	(4.54)	41.5	(6.75)	63.8	(5.46)	50.3	(4.23)	42.9	(6.62)	57.0	(5.67)
Salvadoran	28.4	(1.37)	26.0	(1.63)	31.3	(1.98)	32.5	(1.27)	29.1	(1.64)	36.5	(1.61)
South American	49.4	(1.38)	45.6	(1.75)	53.3	(1.93)	54.7	(1.17)	50.6	(1.69)	58.9	(1.60)
Chilean	56.1	(4.70)	45.5	(6.99)	68.3	(7.22)	47.1	(6.62)	37.9	(7.19)	56.1	(9.33)
Colombian	50.0	(2.11)	45.4	(2.77)	55.2	(3.00)	57.9	(2.44)	53.7	(3.71)	61.9	(2.47)
Ecuadorian	42.4	(2.80)	34.9	(3.51)	50.0	(4.14)	48.2	(2.32)	44.8	(3.64)	51.9	(3.65)
Peruvian	54.3	(2.92)	50.8	(3.89)	57.7	(4.15)	54.9	(3.16)	50.7	(3.98)	59.7	(3.92)
Venezuelan	57.5	(4.66)	62.3	(7.00)	52.2	(6.32)	58.3	(3.45)	56.8	(6.10)	59.9	(5.05)
Other South American	45.8	(3.87)	48.2	(5.57)	43.4	(4.87)	55.8	(3.26)	51.2	(4.11)	60.3	(4.31)
Other Hispanic	37.0	(1.49)	30.6	(1.76)	43.2	(1.92)	40.1	(1.27)	34.9	(1.75)	45.8	(1.91)
Asian	64.6	(0.56)	64.3	(0.78)	64.9	(0.77)	65.3	(0.44)	65.1	(0.60)	65.5	(0.67)
Chinese[3]	75.5	(0.96)	75.8	(1.39)	75.1	(1.38)	75.5	(0.72)	75.1	(1.03)	76.0	(0.99)
Filipino	55.3	(1.26)	52.5	(1.72)	58.1	(2.03)	55.1	(1.34)	54.7	(1.84)	55.5	(2.04)
Japanese	65.8	(2.92)	66.6	(3.80)	65.2	(3.81)	71.4	(3.00)	67.8	(4.74)	74.4	(3.49)
Korean	67.7	(1.47)	64.2	(2.42)	70.9	(2.10)	68.7	(1.60)	67.5	(2.16)	69.8	(2.56)
South Asian[4]	66.3	(1.18)	68.3	(1.63)	63.9	(1.64)	64.3	(0.97)	65.8	(1.30)	62.7	(1.46)
Asian Indian	66.4	(1.22)	68.8	(1.74)	63.5	(1.76)	67.0	(1.05)	68.2	(1.36)	65.7	(1.69)
Bangladeshi	57.2	(6.29)	52.3	(8.74)	63.9	(8.10)	62.4	(5.41)	79.6	(5.46)	47.4	(8.07)
Bhutanese	—	(†)	—	(†)	—	(†)	‡	(†)	‡	(†)	‡	(†)
Nepalese	—	(†)	—	(†)	—	(†)	45.5	(6.44)	45.6	(8.34)	45.4	(8.11)
Pakistani	67.4	(3.72)	69.1	(4.67)	65.5	(4.49)	58.7	(2.62)	60.5	(4.02)	56.9	(3.73)
Southeast Asian	54.9	(1.26)	53.9	(1.57)	55.8	(1.81)	56.5	(1.21)	54.8	(1.59)	58.1	(1.73)
Burmese	—	(†)	—	(†)	—	(†)	27.5	(5.10)	29.5	(6.79)	25.2	(5.60)
Cambodian	36.2	(3.56)	29.8	(4.34)	43.3	(4.91)	39.9	(3.67)	31.0	(5.18)	46.8	(4.83)
Hmong	40.2	(2.64)	38.7	(4.04)	42.0	(4.52)	43.1	(3.33)	37.9	(4.88)	48.2	(4.51)
Laotian	40.3	(4.69)	37.7	(6.40)	42.5	(5.90)	36.1	(4.67)	24.8	(5.89)	45.4	(6.32)
Thai	61.6	(5.06)	68.6	(7.04)	57.6	(7.13)	50.2	(5.59)	52.6	(7.76)	47.8	(7.74)
Vietnamese	65.1	(1.65)	65.6	(2.09)	64.6	(2.17)	66.9	(1.56)	65.9	(1.95)	67.9	(2.19)
Other Southeast Asian[5]	80.9	(6.16)	83.2	(7.52)	78.6	(7.74)	71.5	(6.19)	84.6	(6.73)	58.4	(10.66)
Other Asian	63.1	(2.35)	63.1	(3.15)	63.1	(3.14)	66.1	(2.27)	67.4	(3.08)	64.8	(3.16)
Pacific Islander	33.2	(2.82)	30.3	(3.50)	36.6	(3.81)	30.5	(2.59)	30.7	(3.95)	30.3	(3.65)
American Indian/Alaska Native	24.8	(0.99)	21.0	(1.41)	28.7	(1.68)	24.9	(0.96)	20.1	(1.42)	29.7	(1.68)
Two or more races	42.1	(0.82)	37.0	(1.29)	47.1	(1.00)	44.5	(0.65)	41.3	(0.91)	47.8	(0.86)
White and Black	40.8	(1.58)	35.6	(2.39)	45.7	(2.26)	38.6	(1.17)	34.1	(1.73)	43.2	(1.50)
White and Asian	54.7	(1.57)	49.9	(2.44)	59.5	(2.05)	57.1	(1.65)	56.4	(1.97)	57.8	(2.20)
White and American Indian/ Alaska Native	34.3	(1.56)	28.2	(2.41)	40.7	(2.18)	33.8	(1.52)	29.3	(1.86)	39.0	(2.28)
Other Two or more races	40.4	(1.69)	36.4	(1.89)	44.3	(2.89)	48.4	(1.55)	46.1	(2.06)	50.6	(1.92)
	Percentage distribution of those enrolled											
Total[1]	**100.0**	**(†)**	**46.1**	**(0.18)**	**53.9**	**(0.18)**	**100.0**	**(†)**	**46.5**	**(0.14)**	**53.5**	**(0.14)**
White	100.0	(†)	46.7	(0.20)	53.3	(0.20)	100.0	(†)	47.0	(0.18)	53.0	(0.18)
Black	100.0	(†)	42.8	(0.62)	57.2	(0.62)	100.0	(†)	43.4	(0.45)	56.6	(0.45)
Hispanic	100.0	(†)	44.6	(0.44)	55.4	(0.44)	100.0	(†)	45.2	(0.36)	54.8	(0.36)
Cuban	100.0	(†)	48.7	(2.27)	51.3	(2.27)	100.0	(†)	48.7	(2.02)	51.3	(2.02)
Dominican	100.0	(†)	45.6	(2.88)	54.4	(2.88)	100.0	(†)	41.3	(1.72)	58.7	(1.72)
Mexican	100.0	(†)	44.2	(0.61)	55.8	(0.61)	100.0	(†)	44.9	(0.47)	55.1	(0.47)
Puerto Rican	100.0	(†)	41.8	(1.45)	58.2	(1.45)	100.0	(†)	44.8	(1.49)	55.2	(1.49)
Spaniard	100.0	(†)	42.5	(4.96)	57.5	(4.96)	100.0	(†)	45.7	(4.17)	54.3	(4.17)
Central American[2]	100.0	(†)	48.0	(1.94)	52.0	(1.94)	100.0	(†)	46.7	(1.53)	53.3	(1.53)
Costa Rican	100.0	(†)	65.8	(8.03)	34.2	(8.03)	100.0	(†)	43.6	(8.07)	56.4	(8.07)
Guatemalan	100.0	(†)	49.3	(3.59)	50.7	(3.59)	100.0	(†)	45.6	(3.13)	54.4	(3.13)
Honduran	100.0	(†)	40.0	(5.16)	60.0	(5.16)	100.0	(†)	52.1	(5.21)	47.9	(5.21)
Nicaraguan	100.0	(†)	48.2	(5.09)	51.8	(5.09)	100.0	(†)	43.9	(4.59)	56.1	(4.59)
Panamanian	100.0	(†)	37.5	(6.74)	62.5	(6.74)	100.0	(†)	40.4	(5.44)	59.6	(5.44)
Salvadoran	100.0	(†)	49.7	(2.53)	50.3	(2.53)	100.0	(†)	47.9	(1.75)	52.1	(1.75)

See notes at end of table.

Table 302.62. Percentage of 18- to 24-year-olds enrolled in degree-granting postsecondary institutions and percentage distribution of those enrolled, by sex, race/ethnicity, and selected racial/ethnic subgroups: 2009 and 2014—Continued

[Standard errors appear in parentheses]

Race/ethnicity	2009						2014					
	Total		Male		Female		Total		Male		Female	
1	2		3		4		5		6		7	
South American	100.0	(†)	47.1	(1.73)	52.9	(1.73)	100.0	(†)	46.7	(1.47)	53.3	(1.47)
Chilean	100.0	(†)	43.3	(7.82)	56.7	(7.82)	100.0	(†)	39.7	(7.55)	60.3	(7.55)
Colombian	100.0	(†)	47.7	(2.73)	52.3	(2.73)	100.0	(†)	45.4	(2.40)	54.6	(2.40)
Ecuadorian	100.0	(†)	41.4	(3.84)	58.6	(3.84)	100.0	(†)	48.4	(3.62)	51.6	(3.62)
Peruvian	100.0	(†)	45.8	(3.37)	54.2	(3.37)	100.0	(†)	49.2	(3.38)	50.8	(3.38)
Venezuelan	100.0	(†)	57.4	(5.57)	42.6	(5.57)	100.0	(†)	49.2	(4.82)	50.8	(4.82)
Other South American	100.0	(†)	52.2	(4.60)	47.8	(4.60)	100.0	(†)	44.7	(4.22)	55.3	(4.22)
Other Hispanic	100.0	(†)	40.6	(2.00)	59.4	(2.00)	100.0	(†)	45.0	(2.24)	55.0	(2.24)
Asian	100.0	(†)	50.8	(0.58)	49.2	(0.58)	100.0	(†)	50.4	(0.52)	49.6	(0.52)
Chinese[3]	100.0	(†)	52.3	(1.12)	47.7	(1.12)	100.0	(†)	51.0	(0.94)	49.0	(0.94)
Filipino	100.0	(†)	46.7	(1.66)	53.3	(1.66)	100.0	(†)	50.4	(1.79)	49.6	(1.79)
Japanese	100.0	(†)	49.4	(3.33)	50.6	(3.33)	100.0	(†)	42.9	(3.64)	57.1	(3.64)
Korean	100.0	(†)	45.7	(1.89)	54.3	(1.89)	100.0	(†)	49.4	(1.91)	50.6	(1.91)
South Asian[4]	100.0	(†)	55.7	(1.45)	44.3	(1.45)	100.0	(†)	52.5	(1.22)	47.5	(1.22)
Asian Indian	100.0	(†)	56.0	(1.75)	44.0	(1.75)	100.0	(†)	52.7	(1.40)	47.3	(1.40)
Bangladeshi	100.0	(†)	52.9	(8.16)	47.1	(8.16)	100.0	(†)	59.3	(5.98)	40.7	(5.98)
Bhutanese	—	(†)	—	(†)	—	(†)	100.0	(†)	‡	(†)	‡	(†)
Nepalese	—	(†)	—	(†)	—	(†)	100.0	(†)	56.8	(7.26)	43.2	(7.26)
Pakistani	100.0	(†)	56.0	(3.25)	44.0	(3.25)	100.0	(†)	51.4	(3.70)	48.6	(3.70)
Southeast Asian	100.0	(†)	49.7	(1.54)	50.3	(1.54)	100.0	(†)	47.4	(1.57)	52.6	(1.57)
Burmese	—	(†)	—	(†)	—	(†)	100.0	(†)	58.3	(7.22)	41.7	(7.22)
Cambodian	100.0	(†)	43.0	(4.59)	57.0	(4.59)	100.0	(†)	33.7	(5.85)	66.3	(5.85)
Hmong	100.0	(†)	52.2	(4.45)	47.8	(4.45)	100.0	(†)	43.7	(4.11)	56.3	(4.11)
Laotian	100.0	(†)	42.4	(6.18)	57.6	(6.18)	100.0	(†)	31.0	(6.44)	69.0	(6.44)
Thai	100.0	(†)	41.1	(6.71)	58.9	(6.71)	100.0	(†)	51.8	(6.84)	48.2	(6.84)
Vietnamese	100.0	(†)	52.0	(1.95)	48.0	(1.95)	100.0	(†)	48.7	(1.69)	51.3	(1.69)
Other Southeast Asian[5]	100.0	(†)	50.9	(6.39)	49.1	(6.39)	100.0	(†)	59.2	(9.89)	40.8	(9.89)
Other Asian	100.0	(†)	49.6	(3.34)	50.4	(3.34)	100.0	(†)	53.2	(3.09)	46.8	(3.09)
Pacific Islander	100.0	(†)	48.9	(4.53)	51.1	(4.53)	100.0	(†)	54.4	(5.58)	45.6	(5.58)
American Indian/Alaska Native	100.0	(†)	42.2	(2.75)	57.8	(2.75)	100.0	(†)	39.9	(2.55)	60.1	(2.55)
Two or more races	100.0	(†)	44.0	(1.38)	56.0	(1.38)	100.0	(†)	47.1	(0.87)	52.9	(0.87)
White and Black	100.0	(†)	42.6	(2.70)	57.4	(2.70)	100.0	(†)	44.3	(2.05)	55.7	(2.05)
White and Asian	100.0	(†)	45.8	(2.38)	54.2	(2.38)	100.0	(†)	50.0	(1.73)	50.0	(1.73)
White and American Indian/ Alaska Native	100.0	(†)	42.6	(3.12)	57.4	(3.12)	100.0	(†)	46.7	(2.49)	53.3	(2.49)
Other Two or more races	100.0	(†)	44.8	(2.87)	55.2	(2.87)	100.0	(†)	47.1	(1.88)	52.9	(1.88)

—Not available.
†Not applicable.
‡Reporting standards not met (too few cases for a reliable estimate).
[1]Total includes other racial/ethnic groups not shown separately.
[2]Includes other Central American subgroups not shown separately.
[3]Includes Taiwanese.
[4]In addition to the subgroups shown, also includes Sri Lankan.
[5]Consists of Indonesian and Malaysian.

NOTE: Data are based on sample surveys of the entire population in the indicated age range, including persons living in households, noninstitutionalized group quarters (such as college or military housing), and institutionalized group quarters (such as correctional or nursing facilities). Enrollment data in this table may differ from data in tables based on the Current Population Survey (CPS) because of differences in survey design and target populations. Race categories exclude persons of Hispanic ethnicity. Detail may not sum to totals because of rounding.

SOURCE: U.S. Department of Commerce, Census Bureau, American Community Survey (ACS), 2009 and 2014. (This table was prepared April 2016.)

Table 303.10. Total fall enrollment in degree-granting postsecondary institutions, by attendance status, sex of student, and control of institution: Selected years, 1947 through 2025

Year	Total enrollment	Attendance status			Sex of student			Control of institution			
		Full-time	Part-time	Percent part-time	Male	Female	Percent female	Public	Private		
									Total	Nonprofit	For-profit
1	2	3	4	5	6	7	8	9	10	11	12
1947[1]	2,338,226	—	—	—	1,659,249	678,977	29.0	1,152,377	1,185,849	—	—
1948[1]	2,403,396	—	—	—	1,709,367	694,029	28.9	1,185,588	1,217,808	—	—
1949[1]	2,444,900	—	—	—	1,721,572	723,328	29.6	1,207,151	1,237,749	—	—
1950[1]	2,281,298	—	—	—	1,560,392	720,906	31.6	1,139,699	1,141,599	—	—
1951[1]	2,101,962	—	—	—	1,390,740	711,222	33.8	1,037,938	1,064,024	—	—
1952[1]	2,134,242	—	—	—	1,380,357	753,885	35.3	1,101,240	1,033,002	—	—
1953[1]	2,231,054	—	—	—	1,422,598	808,456	36.2	1,185,876	1,045,178	—	—
1954[1]	2,446,693	—	—	—	1,563,382	883,311	36.1	1,353,531	1,093,162	—	—
1955[1]	2,653,034	—	—	—	1,733,184	919,850	34.7	1,476,282	1,176,752	—	—
1956[1]	2,918,212	—	—	—	1,911,458	1,006,754	34.5	1,656,402	1,261,810	—	—
1957	3,323,783	—	—	—	2,170,765	1,153,018	34.7	1,972,673	1,351,110	—	—
1959	3,639,847	2,421,016	1,218,831 [2]	33.5	2,332,617	1,307,230	35.9	2,180,982	1,458,865	—	—
1961	4,145,065	2,785,133	1,359,932 [2]	32.8	2,585,821	1,559,244	37.6	2,561,447	1,583,618	—	—
1963	4,779,609	3,183,833	1,595,776 [2]	33.4	2,961,540	1,818,069	38.0	3,081,279	1,698,330	—	—
1964	5,280,020	3,573,238	1,706,782 [2]	32.3	3,248,713	2,031,307	38.5	3,467,708	1,812,312	—	—
1965	5,920,864	4,095,728	1,825,136 [2]	30.8	3,630,020	2,290,844	38.7	3,969,596	1,951,268	—	—
1966	6,389,872	4,438,606	1,951,266 [2]	30.5	3,856,216	2,533,656	39.7	4,348,917	2,040,955	—	—
1967	6,911,748	4,793,128	2,118,620 [2]	30.7	4,132,800	2,778,948	40.2	4,816,028	2,095,720	2,074,041	21,679
1968	7,513,091	5,210,155	2,302,936	30.7	4,477,649	3,035,442	40.4	5,430,652	2,082,439	2,061,211	21,228
1969	8,004,660	5,498,883	2,505,777	31.3	4,746,201	3,258,459	40.7	5,896,868	2,107,792	2,087,653	20,139
1970	8,580,887	5,816,290	2,764,597	32.2	5,043,642	3,537,245	41.2	6,428,134	2,152,753	2,134,420	18,333
1971	8,948,644	6,077,232	2,871,412	32.1	5,207,004	3,741,640	41.8	6,804,309	2,144,335	2,121,913	22,422
1972	9,214,860	6,072,389	3,142,471	34.1	5,238,757	3,976,103	43.1	7,070,635	2,144,225	2,123,245	20,980
1973	9,602,123	6,189,493	3,412,630	35.5	5,371,052	4,231,071	44.1	7,419,516	2,182,607	2,148,784	33,823
1974	10,223,729	6,370,273	3,853,456	37.7	5,622,429	4,601,300	45.0	7,988,500	2,235,229	2,200,963	34,266
1975	11,184,859	6,841,334	4,343,525	38.8	6,148,997	5,035,862	45.0	8,834,508	2,350,351	2,311,448	38,903
1976	11,012,137	6,717,058	4,295,079	39.0	5,810,828	5,201,309	47.2	8,653,477	2,358,660	2,314,298	44,362
1977	11,285,787	6,792,925	4,492,862	39.8	5,789,016	5,496,771	48.7	8,846,993	2,438,794	2,386,652	52,142
1978	11,260,092	6,667,657	4,592,435	40.8	5,640,998	5,619,094	49.9	8,785,893	2,474,199	2,408,331	65,868
1979	11,569,899	6,794,039	4,775,860	41.3	5,682,877	5,887,022	50.9	9,036,822	2,533,077	2,461,773	71,304
1980	12,096,895	7,097,958	4,998,937	41.3	5,874,374	6,222,521	51.4	9,457,394	2,639,501	2,527,787	111,714 [3]
1981	12,371,672	7,181,250	5,190,422	42.0	5,975,056	6,396,616	51.7	9,647,032	2,724,640	2,572,405	152,235 [3]
1982	12,425,780	7,220,618	5,205,162	41.9	6,031,384	6,394,396	51.5	9,696,087	2,729,693	2,552,739	176,954 [3]
1983	12,464,661	7,261,050	5,203,611	41.7	6,023,725	6,440,936	51.7	9,682,734	2,781,927	2,589,187	192,740
1984	12,241,940	7,098,388	5,143,552	42.0	5,863,574	6,378,366	52.1	9,477,370	2,764,570	2,574,419	190,151
1985	12,247,055	7,075,221	5,171,834	42.2	5,818,450	6,428,605	52.5	9,479,273	2,767,782	2,571,791	195,991
1986	12,503,511	7,119,550	5,383,961	43.1	5,884,515	6,618,996	52.9	9,713,893	2,789,618	2,572,479	217,139 [4]
1987	12,766,642	7,231,085	5,535,557	43.4	5,932,056	6,834,586	53.5	9,973,254	2,793,388	2,602,350	191,038 [4]
1988	13,055,337	7,436,768	5,618,569	43.0	6,001,896	7,053,441	54.0	10,161,388	2,893,949	2,673,567	220,382
1989	13,538,560	7,660,950	5,877,610	43.4	6,190,015	7,348,545	54.3	10,577,963	2,960,597	2,731,174	229,423
1990	13,818,637	7,820,985	5,997,652	43.4	6,283,909	7,534,728	54.5	10,844,717	2,973,920	2,760,227	213,693
1991	14,358,953	8,115,329	6,243,624	43.5	6,501,844	7,857,109	54.7	11,309,563	3,049,390	2,819,041	230,349
1992	14,487,359	8,162,118	6,325,241	43.7	6,523,989	7,963,370	55.0	11,384,567	3,102,792	2,872,523	230,269
1993	14,304,803	8,127,618	6,177,185	43.2	6,427,450	7,877,353	55.1	11,189,088	3,115,715	2,888,897	226,818
1994	14,278,790	8,137,776	6,141,014	43.0	6,371,898	7,906,892	55.4	11,133,680	3,145,110	2,910,107	235,003
1995	14,261,781	8,128,802	6,132,979	43.0	6,342,539	7,919,242	55.5	11,092,374	3,169,407	2,929,044	240,363
1996	14,367,520	8,302,953	6,064,567	42.2	6,352,825	8,014,695	55.8	11,120,499	3,247,021	2,942,556	304,465
1997	14,502,334	8,438,062	6,064,272	41.8	6,396,028	8,106,306	55.9	11,196,119	3,306,215	2,977,614	328,601
1998	14,506,967	8,563,338	5,943,629	41.0	6,369,265	8,137,702	56.1	11,137,769	3,369,198	3,004,925	364,273
1999	14,849,691	8,803,139	6,046,552	40.7	6,515,164	8,334,527	56.1	11,375,739	3,473,952	3,055,029	418,923
2000	15,312,289	9,009,600	6,302,689	41.2	6,721,769	8,590,520	56.1	11,752,786	3,559,503	3,109,419	450,084
2001	15,927,987	9,447,502	6,480,485	40.7	6,960,815	8,967,172	56.3	12,233,156	3,694,831	3,167,330	527,501
2002	16,611,711	9,946,359	6,665,352	40.1	7,202,116	9,409,595	56.6	12,751,993	3,859,718	3,265,476	594,242
2003	16,911,481	10,326,133	6,585,348	38.9	7,260,264	9,651,217	57.1	12,858,698	4,052,783	3,341,048	711,735
2004	17,272,044	10,610,177	6,661,867	38.6	7,387,262	9,884,782	57.2	12,980,112	4,291,932	3,411,685	880,247
2005	17,487,475	10,797,011	6,690,464	38.3	7,455,925	10,031,550	57.4	13,021,834	4,465,641	3,454,692	1,010,949
2006	17,758,870	10,957,305	6,801,565	38.3	7,574,815	10,184,055	57.3	13,180,133	4,578,737	3,512,866	1,065,871
2007	18,248,128	11,269,892	6,978,236	38.2	7,815,914	10,432,214	57.2	13,490,780	4,757,348	3,571,150	1,186,198
2008	19,102,814	11,747,743	7,355,071	38.5	8,188,895	10,913,919	57.1	13,972,153	5,130,661	3,661,519	1,469,142
2009	20,313,594	12,605,355	7,708,239	37.9	8,732,953	11,580,641	57.0	14,810,768	5,502,826	3,767,672	1,735,154
2010	21,019,438	13,087,182	7,932,256	37.7	9,045,759	11,973,679	57.0	15,142,171	5,877,267	3,854,482	2,022,785
2011	21,010,590	13,002,531	8,008,059	38.1	9,034,256	11,976,334	57.0	15,116,303	5,894,287	3,926,819	1,967,468
2012	20,644,478	12,734,404	7,910,074	38.3	8,919,006	11,725,472	56.8	14,884,667	5,759,811	3,951,388	1,808,423
2013	20,375,789	12,597,112	7,778,677	38.2	8,860,786	11,515,003	56.5	14,745,558	5,630,231	3,974,004	1,656,227
2014	20,207,369	12,453,975	7,753,394	38.2	8,797,061	11,410,308	57.0	14,655,015	5,552,354	3,996,089	1,556,265

See notes at end of table.

Table 303.10. Total fall enrollment in degree-granting postsecondary institutions, by attendance status, sex of student, and control of institution: Selected years, 1947 through 2025—Continued

Year	Total enrollment	Attendance status			Sex of student			Control of institution			
		Full-time	Part-time	Percent part-time	Male	Female	Percent female	Public	Private		
									Total	Nonprofit	For-profit
1	2	3	4	5	6	7	8	9	10	11	12
2015[5]	20,264,000	12,484,000	7,779,000	38.3	8,760,000	11,503,000	57.3	14,789,000	5,475,000	—	—
2016[5]	20,516,000	12,651,000	7,865,000	38.5	8,808,000	11,708,000	57.6	14,964,000	5,552,000	—	—
2017[5]	20,972,000	12,942,000	8,030,000	38.6	8,944,000	12,028,000	57.9	15,287,000	5,686,000	—	—
2018[5]	21,410,000	13,207,000	8,203,000	38.7	9,118,000	12,292,000	58.1	15,604,000	5,807,000	—	—
2019[5]	21,753,000	13,403,000	8,349,000	38.8	9,260,000	12,493,000	58.2	15,852,000	5,900,000	—	—
2020[5]	22,013,000	13,550,000	8,463,000	38.9	9,364,000	12,648,000	58.4	16,038,000	5,975,000	—	—
2021[5]	22,323,000	13,726,000	8,597,000	39.0	9,496,000	12,827,000	58.5	16,261,000	6,062,000	—	—
2022[5]	22,613,000	13,894,000	8,720,000	39.0	9,625,000	12,989,000	58.7	16,471,000	6,143,000	—	—
2023[5]	22,896,000	14,072,000	8,824,000	39.1	9,747,000	13,149,000	58.8	16,673,000	6,223,000	—	—
2024[5]	23,149,000	14,220,000	8,929,000	39.1	9,859,000	13,290,000	58.8	16,858,000	6,291,000	—	—
2025[5]	23,290,000	14,278,000	9,012,000	39.1	9,937,000	13,353,000	58.8	16,967,000	6,323,000	—	—

—Not available.
[1]Degree-credit enrollment only.
[2]Includes part-time resident students and all extension students (students attending courses at sites separate from the primary reporting campus). In later years, part-time student enrollment was collected as a distinct category.
[3]Large increases are due to the addition of schools accredited by the Accrediting Commission of Career Schools and Colleges of Technology.
[4]Because of imputation techniques, data are not consistent with figures for other years.
[5]Projected.
NOTE: Data through 1995 are for institutions of higher education, while later data are for degree-granting institutions. Degree-granting institutions grant associate's or higher degrees and participate in Title IV federal financial aid programs. The degree-granting classification is very similar to the earlier higher education classification, but it includes more 2-year colleges and excludes a few higher education institutions that did not grant degrees. Some data have been revised from previously published figures.
SOURCE: U.S. Department of Education, National Center for Education Statistics, *Biennial Survey of Education in the United States*; *Opening Fall Enrollment in Higher Education*, 1963 through 1965; Higher Education General Information Survey (HEGIS), "Fall Enrollment in Colleges and Universities" surveys, 1966 through 1985; Integrated Postsecondary Education Data System (IPEDS), "Fall Enrollment Survey" (IPEDS-EF:86–99); IPEDS Spring 2001 through Spring 2015, Fall Enrollment component; and Enrollment in Degree-Granting Institutions Projection Model, 1980 through 2025. (This table was prepared February 2016.)

Table 304.10. Total fall enrollment in degree-granting postsecondary institutions, by state or jurisdiction: Selected years, 1970 through 2014

State or jurisdiction	Fall 1970	Fall 1980	Fall 1990	Fall 2000	Fall 2009	Fall 2010	Fall 2011	Fall 2012	Fall 2013	Fall 2014	Percent change, 2009 to 2014
1	2	3	4	5	6	7	8	9	10	11	12
United States	**8,580,887**	**12,096,895**	**13,818,637**	**15,312,289**	**20,313,594**	**21,019,438**	**21,010,590**	**20,644,478**	**20,375,789**	**20,207,369**	**-0.5**
Alabama	103,936	164,306	218,589	233,962	311,641	327,606	320,349	310,311	305,712	305,028	-2.1
Alaska	9,471	21,296	29,833	27,953	32,406	34,799	34,932	32,797	34,890	34,331	5.9
Arizona	109,619	202,716	264,148	342,490	738,753	793,871	796,974	736,465	694,123	674,746	-8.7
Arkansas	52,039	77,607	90,425	115,172	168,081	175,848	179,345	176,458	172,224	169,571	0.9
California	1,257,245	1,790,993	1,808,740	2,256,708	2,732,147	2,714,699	2,691,852	2,621,606	2,636,921	2,696,415	-1.3
Colorado	123,395	162,916	227,131	263,872	345,034	369,450	365,939	363,170	358,723	353,827	2.5
Connecticut	124,700	159,632	168,604	161,243	191,790	199,384	201,638	201,658	200,966	201,928	5.3
Delaware	25,260	32,939	42,004	43,897	54,735	55,258	56,547	58,127	59,615	60,368	10.3
District of Columbia	77,158	86,675	79,551	72,689	136,792	91,992	90,245	90,150	89,257	90,053	-34.2
Florida	235,525	411,891	588,086	707,684	1,051,917	1,124,778	1,149,160	1,154,506	1,125,810	1,111,018	5.6
Georgia	126,511	184,159	251,786	346,204	531,510	568,916	565,414	545,360	533,424	531,004	-0.1
Hawaii	36,562	47,181	56,436	60,182	74,668	78,073	79,006	78,456	76,434	73,505	-1.6
Idaho	34,567	43,018	51,881	65,594	84,349	85,201	90,142	108,008	109,318	118,953	41.0
Illinois	452,146	644,245	729,246	743,918	893,207	906,845	892,452	866,893	842,888	824,980	-7.6
Indiana	192,668	247,253	284,832	314,334	441,031	459,493	457,506	447,263	444,364	436,327	-1.1
Iowa	108,902	140,449	170,515	188,974	351,036	381,867	372,146	361,189	339,738	282,482	-19.5
Kansas	102,485	136,605	163,733	179,968	210,819	214,849	216,662	213,855	215,855	226,401	7.4
Kentucky	98,591	143,066	177,852	188,341	277,876	291,104	293,766	281,133	273,073	264,197	-4.9
Louisiana	120,728	160,058	186,840	223,800	251,468	263,676	265,740	258,846	251,887	245,938	-2.2
Maine	34,134	43,264	57,186	58,473	70,183	72,406	72,297	73,095	70,849	72,246	2.9
Maryland	149,607	225,526	259,700	273,745	358,775	377,967	380,097	374,496	363,771	365,597	1.9
Massachusetts	303,809	418,415	417,833	421,142	497,234	507,753	508,546	514,119	514,008	510,912	2.8
Michigan	392,726	520,131	569,803	567,631	685,628	697,765	685,420	663,703	643,592	619,438	-9.7
Minnesota	160,788	206,691	253,789	293,445	442,109	465,449	457,737	451,661	441,491	433,854	-1.9
Mississippi	73,967	102,364	122,883	137,389	173,136	179,995	180,576	176,618	173,634	170,728	-1.4
Missouri	183,930	234,421	289,899	321,348	424,541	444,750	456,994	441,186	438,222	419,900	-1.1
Montana	30,062	35,177	35,876	42,240	51,588	53,282	54,042	53,254	52,777	51,942	0.7
Nebraska	66,915	89,488	112,831	112,117	139,594	144,692	142,875	139,558	137,943	135,825	-2.7
Nevada	13,669	40,455	61,728	87,893	124,896	129,360	121,013	118,300	116,738	119,205	-4.6
New Hampshire	29,400	46,794	59,510	61,718	74,234	75,539	77,436	82,678	92,440	106,984	44.1
New Jersey	216,121	321,610	324,286	335,945	431,978	444,092	443,750	439,966	436,939	436,208	1.0
New Mexico	44,461	58,283	85,500	110,739	153,055	162,552	159,058	156,424	153,455	146,246	-4.4
New York	806,479	992,237	1,048,286	1,043,395	1,290,046	1,305,151	1,318,076	1,309,684	1,304,230	1,299,055	0.7
North Carolina	171,925	287,537	352,138	404,652	567,841	585,792	585,013	578,265	575,198	570,045	0.4
North Dakota	31,495	34,069	37,878	40,248	54,456	56,903	56,482	55,242	55,063	54,048	-0.7
Ohio	376,267	489,145	557,690	549,553	712,192	745,115	735,034	710,379	697,647	680,238	-4.5
Oklahoma	110,155	160,295	173,221	178,016	220,377	230,560	230,176	228,492	220,897	215,349	-2.3
Oregon	122,177	157,458	165,741	183,065	243,271	251,708	259,064	254,926	251,106	245,547	0.9
Pennsylvania	411,044	507,716	604,060	609,521	778,054	804,640	787,960	777,350	765,582	750,651	-3.5
Rhode Island	45,898	66,869	78,273	75,450	84,673	85,110	84,647	83,952	83,460	83,499	-1.4
South Carolina	69,518	132,476	159,302	185,931	246,525	257,064	260,002	259,617	257,844	254,629	3.3
South Dakota	30,639	32,761	34,208	43,221	53,342	58,360	55,899	56,058	55,129	53,963	1.2
Tennessee	135,103	204,581	226,238	263,910	332,555	351,762	350,186	343,478	338,197	326,575	-1.8
Texas	442,225	701,391	901,437	1,033,973	1,447,028	1,535,864	1,564,208	1,544,524	1,541,378	1,555,462	7.5
Utah	81,687	93,987	121,303	163,776	236,204	255,653	264,394	267,309	264,255	274,926	16.4
Vermont	22,209	30,628	36,398	35,489	44,975	45,572	45,143	44,697	43,534	43,983	-2.2
Virginia	151,915	280,504	353,442	381,893	544,665	577,922	589,145	588,708	583,755	577,908	6.1
Washington	183,544	303,603	263,384	320,840	382,613	388,116	372,839	365,529	363,377	365,193	-4.6
West Virginia	63,153	81,973	84,790	87,888	142,492	152,431	162,347	162,182	157,954	157,052	10.2
Wisconsin	202,058	269,086	299,774	307,179	373,307	384,181	376,535	369,738	364,021	358,894	-3.9
Wyoming	15,220	21,147	31,326	30,004	37,019	38,298	38,092	37,812	37,084	35,461	-4.2
U.S. Service Academies[1]	17,079	49,808	48,692	13,475	15,748	15,925	15,692	15,227	14,997	14,734	-6.4
Other jurisdictions	**67,237**	**137,749**	**164,618**	**194,633**	**243,447**	**264,240**	**267,159**	**259,975**	**254,543**	**255,843**	**5.1**
American Samoa	0	976	1,219	297	2,189	2,193	2,091	1,795	1,488	1,276	-41.7
Federated States of Micronesia	0	224	975	1,576	3,401	2,699	2,915	2,744	2,446	2,344	-31.1
Guam	2,719	3,217	4,741	5,215	5,755	6,188	6,360	5,955	6,518	6,488	12.7
Marshall Islands	0	0	0	328	847	869	989	1,123	1,000	1,087	28.3
Northern Marianas	0	0	661	1,078	989	1,137	1,046	1,178	1,109	1,186	19.9
Palau	0	0	491	581	651	694	742	680	646	604	-7.2
Puerto Rico	63,073	131,184	154,065	183,290	227,013	247,727	250,402	244,077	239,015	240,578	6.0
U.S. Virgin Islands	1,445	2,148	2,466	2,268	2,602	2,733	2,614	2,423	2,321	2,280	-12.4

[1]Data for 2000 and later years reflect a substantial reduction in the number of Department of Defense institutions included in the IPEDS survey.

NOTE: Data through 1990 are for institutions of higher education, while later data are for degree-granting institutions. Degree-granting institutions grant associate's or higher degrees and participate in Title IV federal financial aid programs. The degree-granting classification is very similar to the earlier higher education classification, but it includes more 2-year colleges and excludes a few higher education institutions that did not grant degrees. Some data have been revised from previously published figures.

SOURCE: U.S. Department of Education, National Center for Education Statistics, Higher Education General Information Survey (HEGIS), "Fall Enrollment in Colleges and Universities" surveys, 1970 and 1980; Integrated Postsecondary Education Data System (IPEDS), "Fall Enrollment Survey" (IPEDS-EF:90); and IPEDS Spring 2001 through Spring 2015, Fall Enrollment component. (This table was prepared October 2015.)

Table 304.15. Total fall enrollment in public degree-granting postsecondary institutions, by state or jurisdiction: Selected years, 1970 through 2014

State or jurisdiction	Fall 1970	Fall 1980	Fall 1990	Fall 2000	Fall 2009	Fall 2010	Fall 2011	Fall 2012	Fall 2013	Fall 2014	Percent change, 2009 to 2014
1	2	3	4	5	6	7	8	9	10	11	12
United States	**6,428,134**	**9,457,394**	**10,844,717**	**11,752,786**	**14,810,768**	**15,142,171**	**15,116,303**	**14,884,667**	**14,745,558**	**14,655,015**	**-1.1**
Alabama	87,884	143,674	195,939	207,435	260,277	267,083	260,523	251,045	248,284	246,989	-5.1
Alaska	8,563	20,561	27,792	26,559	30,493	32,303	32,158	30,595	31,600	29,892	-2.0
Arizona	107,315	194,034	248,213	284,522	350,435	366,976	366,116	359,229	354,462	354,997	1.3
Arkansas	43,599	66,068	78,645	101,775	149,474	155,780	158,824	157,224	153,690	151,399	1.3
California	1,123,529	1,599,838	1,594,710	1,927,771	2,289,427	2,223,163	2,181,675	2,129,152	2,148,147	2,167,444	-5.3
Colorado	108,562	145,598	200,653	217,897	255,438	269,433	269,298	272,444	271,223	268,041	4.9
Connecticut	73,391	97,788	109,556	101,027	123,211	127,194	126,487	124,952	123,093	122,303	-0.7
Delaware	21,151	28,325	34,252	34,194	39,989	39,935	40,729	41,113	40,992	41,012	2.6
District of Columbia	12,194	13,900	11,990	5,499	5,253	5,840	5,312	5,476	5,347	5,115	-2.6
Florida	189,450	334,349	489,081	556,912	759,479	790,027	803,200	804,693	795,860	795,628	4.8
Georgia	101,900	140,158	196,413	271,755	418,037	436,047	428,708	422,189	413,706	413,752	-1.0
Hawaii	32,963	43,269	45,728	44,579	57,945	60,090	60,330	60,295	58,941	57,052	-1.5
Idaho	27,072	34,491	41,315	53,751	63,261	64,204	65,753	78,781	75,910	76,806	21.4
Illinois	315,634	491,274	551,333	534,155	588,741	585,515	577,043	556,890	546,483	529,462	-10.1
Indiana	136,739	189,224	223,953	240,023	325,072	337,705	339,946	333,769	335,923	328,442	1.0
Iowa	68,390	97,454	117,834	135,008	171,283	177,781	178,491	173,558	168,644	169,896	-0.8
Kansas	88,215	121,987	149,117	159,976	182,736	185,623	186,475	183,914	184,075	183,222	0.3
Kentucky	77,240	114,884	147,095	151,973	221,508	229,725	233,427	223,100	218,472	213,043	-3.8
Louisiana	101,127	136,703	158,290	189,213	215,511	224,811	225,210	220,971	215,653	210,943	-2.1
Maine	25,405	31,878	41,500	40,662	49,668	50,903	50,253	50,555	49,602	48,852	-1.6
Maryland	118,988	195,051	220,783	223,797	298,185	309,779	314,383	310,503	301,565	305,156	2.3
Massachusetts	116,127	183,765	186,035	183,248	218,999	224,542	227,006	228,178	228,255	226,158	3.3
Michigan	339,625	454,147	487,359	467,861	553,022	562,448	554,704	540,242	527,740	514,712	-6.9
Minnesota	130,567	162,379	199,211	218,617	270,336	276,176	274,192	272,290	266,440	259,695	-3.9
Mississippi	64,968	90,661	109,038	125,355	155,517	161,493	161,842	157,995	154,916	152,096	-2.2
Missouri	132,540	165,179	200,093	201,509	245,568	256,030	260,585	257,430	254,650	252,980	3.0
Montana	27,287	31,178	31,865	37,387	46,653	48,231	48,912	48,333	47,851	47,024	0.8
Nebraska	51,454	73,509	94,614	88,531	104,149	107,979	106,794	104,166	101,893	99,821	-4.2
Nevada	13,576	40,280	61,242	83,120	112,397	113,103	105,048	103,619	102,538	106,028	-5.7
New Hampshire	15,979	24,119	32,163	35,870	43,507	44,077	43,325	43,289	42,711	43,298	-0.5
New Jersey	145,373	247,028	261,601	266,921	348,934	358,256	359,458	356,457	352,822	351,316	0.7
New Mexico	40,795	55,077	83,403	101,450	143,987	150,844	148,018	146,792	144,381	138,311	-3.9
New York	449,437	563,251	616,884	583,417	712,467	723,500	731,914	722,274	720,934	721,847	1.3
North Carolina	123,761	228,154	285,405	329,422	469,590	475,064	470,989	465,950	460,100	455,178	-3.1
North Dakota	30,192	31,709	34,690	36,014	46,727	48,904	49,578	48,929	48,751	48,292	3.3
Ohio	281,099	381,765	427,613	411,161	522,033	547,551	542,733	524,973	520,039	510,244	-2.3
Oklahoma	91,438	137,188	151,073	153,699	189,953	197,641	197,373	195,118	187,078	182,449	-4.0
Oregon	108,483	140,102	144,427	154,756	201,246	208,001	215,469	212,541	208,317	201,645	0.2
Pennsylvania	232,982	292,499	343,478	339,229	425,979	432,923	428,335	425,890	419,849	413,591	-2.9
Rhode Island	25,527	35,052	42,350	38,458	43,409	43,224	43,254	43,204	42,786	42,765	-1.5
South Carolina	47,101	107,683	131,134	155,519	200,204	205,080	208,302	209,023	207,717	205,756	2.8
South Dakota	23,936	24,328	26,596	34,857	41,674	44,569	43,729	44,185	44,272	44,132	5.9
Tennessee	98,897	156,835	175,049	202,530	231,741	242,486	241,917	235,010	229,302	224,033	-3.3
Texas	365,522	613,552	802,314	896,534	1,258,841	1,334,110	1,366,829	1,352,060	1,349,609	1,365,339	8.5
Utah	49,588	59,598	86,108	123,046	170,921	179,061	179,208	171,001	168,311	167,716	-1.9
Vermont	12,536	17,984	20,910	20,021	27,028	27,524	27,132	26,501	25,852	25,643	-5.1
Virginia	123,279	246,500	291,286	313,780	401,093	409,004	413,761	409,753	405,915	399,359	-0.4
Washington	162,718	276,028	227,632	273,928	328,391	330,853	317,066	311,497	310,192	312,523	-4.8
West Virginia	51,363	71,228	74,108	76,136	94,533	96,104	95,634	93,017	90,782	87,842	-7.1
Wisconsin	170,374	235,179	253,529	249,737	295,090	301,259	296,795	293,416	289,339	286,726	-2.8
Wyoming	15,220	21,121	30,623	28,715	35,608	36,292	36,368	35,859	35,547	34,316	-3.6
U.S. Service Academies[1]	17,079	49,808	48,692	13,475	15,748	15,925	15,692	15,227	14,997	14,734	-6.4
Other jurisdictions	**46,680**	**60,692**	**66,244**	**84,464**	**87,030**	**83,719**	**78,928**	**78,400**	**78,136**	**77,716**	**-10.7**
American Samoa	0	976	1,219	297	2,189	2,193	2,091	1,795	1,488	1,276	-41.7
Federated States of Micronesia	0	224	975	1,576	3,401	2,699	2,915	2,744	2,446	2,344	-31.1
Guam	2,719	3,217	4,741	5,215	5,661	6,103	6,274	5,878	6,439	6,416	13.3
Marshall Islands	0	0	0	328	847	869	989	1,123	1,000	1,087	28.3
Northern Marianas	0	0	661	1,078	989	1,137	1,046	1,178	1,109	1,186	19.9
Palau	0	0	491	581	651	694	742	680	646	604	-7.2
Puerto Rico	42,516	54,127	55,691	73,121	70,690	67,291	62,257	62,579	62,687	62,523	-11.6
U.S. Virgin Islands	1,445	2,148	2,466	2,268	2,602	2,733	2,614	2,423	2,321	2,280	-12.4

[1]Data for 2000 and later years reflect a substantial reduction in the number of Department of Defense institutions included in the IPEDS survey.

NOTE: Data through 1990 are for institutions of higher education, while later data are for degree-granting institutions. Degree-granting institutions grant associate's or higher degrees and participate in Title IV federal financial aid programs. The degree-granting classification is very similar to the earlier higher education classification, but it includes more 2-year colleges and excludes a few higher education institutions that did not grant degrees. Some data have been revised from previously published figures.

SOURCE: U.S. Department of Education, National Center for Education Statistics, Higher Education General Information Survey (HEGIS), "Fall Enrollment in Colleges and Universities" surveys, 1970 and 1980; Integrated Postsecondary Education Data System (IPEDS), "Fall Enrollment Survey" (IPEDS-EF:90); and IPEDS Spring 2001 through Spring 2015, Fall Enrollment component. (This table was prepared October 2015.)

Table 304.20. Total fall enrollment in private degree-granting postsecondary institutions, by state or jurisdiction: Selected years, 1970 through 2014

State or jurisdiction	Fall 1970	Fall 1980	Fall 1990	Fall 2000	Fall 2009	Fall 2010	Fall 2011	Fall 2012	Fall 2013	Fall 2014	Percent change, 2009 to 2014
1	2	3	4	5	6	7	8	9	10	11	12
United States	**2,152,753**	**2,639,501**	**2,973,920**	**3,559,503**	**5,502,826**	**5,877,267**	**5,894,287**	**5,759,811**	**5,630,231**	**5,552,354**	**0.9**
Alabama	16,052	20,632	22,650	26,527	51,364	60,523	59,826	59,266	57,428	58,039	13.0
Alaska	908	735	2,041	1,394	1,913	2,496	2,774	2,202	3,290	4,439	132.0
Arizona	2,304	8,682	15,935	57,968	388,318	426,895	430,858	377,236	339,661	319,749	-17.7
Arkansas	8,440	11,539	11,780	13,397	18,607	20,068	20,521	19,234	18,534	18,172	-2.3
California	133,716	191,155	214,030	328,937	442,720	491,536	510,177	492,454	488,774	528,971	19.5
Colorado	14,833	17,318	26,478	45,975	89,596	100,017	96,641	90,726	87,500	85,786	-4.3
Connecticut	51,309	61,844	59,048	60,216	68,579	72,190	75,151	76,706	77,873	79,625	16.1
Delaware	4,109	4,614	7,752	9,703	14,746	15,323	15,818	17,014	18,623	19,356	31.3
District of Columbia	64,964	72,775	67,561	67,190	131,539	86,152	84,933	84,674	83,910	84,938	-35.4
Florida	46,075	77,542	99,005	150,772	292,438	334,751	345,960	349,813	329,950	315,390	7.8
Georgia	24,611	44,001	55,373	74,449	113,473	132,869	136,706	123,171	119,718	117,252	3.3
Hawaii	3,599	3,912	10,708	15,603	16,723	17,983	18,676	18,161	17,493	16,453	-1.6
Idaho	7,495	8,527	10,566	11,843	21,088	20,997	24,389	29,227	33,408	42,147	99.9
Illinois	136,512	152,971	177,913	209,763	304,466	321,330	315,409	310,003	296,405	295,518	-2.9
Indiana	55,929	58,029	60,879	74,311	115,959	121,788	117,560	113,494	108,441	107,885	-7.0
Iowa	40,512	42,995	52,681	53,966	179,753	204,086	193,655	187,631	171,094	112,586	-37.4
Kansas	14,270	14,618	14,616	19,992	28,083	29,226	30,187	29,941	31,780	43,179	53.8
Kentucky	21,351	28,182	30,757	36,368	56,368	61,379	60,339	58,033	54,601	51,154	-9.2
Louisiana	19,601	23,355	28,550	34,587	35,957	38,865	40,530	37,875	36,234	34,995	-2.7
Maine	8,729	11,386	15,686	17,811	20,515	21,503	22,044	22,540	21,247	23,394	14.0
Maryland	30,619	30,475	38,917	49,948	60,590	68,188	65,714	63,993	62,206	60,441	-0.2
Massachusetts	187,682	234,650	231,798	237,894	278,235	283,211	281,540	285,941	285,753	284,754	2.3
Michigan	53,101	65,984	82,444	99,770	132,606	135,317	130,716	123,461	115,852	104,726	-21.0
Minnesota	30,221	44,312	54,578	74,828	171,773	189,273	183,545	179,371	175,051	174,159	1.4
Mississippi	8,999	11,703	13,845	12,034	17,619	18,502	18,734	18,623	18,718	18,632	5.7
Missouri	51,390	69,242	89,806	119,839	178,973	188,720	196,409	183,756	183,572	166,920	-6.7
Montana	2,775	3,999	4,011	4,853	4,935	5,051	5,130	4,921	4,926	4,918	-0.3
Nebraska	15,461	15,979	18,217	23,586	35,445	36,713	36,081	35,392	36,050	36,004	1.6
Nevada	93	175	486	4,773	12,499	16,257	15,965	14,681	14,200	13,177	5.4
New Hampshire	13,421	22,675	27,347	25,848	30,727	31,462	34,111	39,389	49,729	63,686	107.3
New Jersey	70,748	74,582	62,685	69,024	83,044	85,836	84,292	83,509	84,117	84,892	2.2
New Mexico	3,666	3,206	2,097	9,289	9,068	11,708	11,040	9,632	9,074	7,935	-12.5
New York	357,042	428,986	431,402	459,978	577,579	581,651	586,162	587,410	583,296	577,208	-0.1
North Carolina	48,164	59,383	66,733	75,230	98,251	110,728	114,024	112,315	115,098	114,867	16.9
North Dakota	1,303	2,360	3,188	4,234	7,729	7,999	6,904	6,313	6,312	5,756	-25.5
Ohio	95,168	107,380	130,077	138,392	190,159	197,564	192,301	185,406	177,608	169,994	-10.6
Oklahoma	18,717	23,107	22,148	24,317	30,424	32,919	32,803	33,374	33,819	32,900	8.1
Oregon	13,694	17,356	21,314	28,309	42,025	43,707	43,595	42,385	42,789	43,902	4.5
Pennsylvania	178,062	215,217	260,582	270,292	352,075	371,717	359,625	351,460	345,733	337,060	-4.3
Rhode Island	20,371	31,817	35,923	36,992	41,264	41,886	41,393	40,748	40,674	40,734	-1.3
South Carolina	22,417	24,793	28,168	30,412	46,321	51,984	51,700	50,594	50,127	48,873	5.5
South Dakota	6,703	8,433	7,612	8,364	11,668	13,791	12,170	11,873	10,857	9,831	-15.7
Tennessee	36,206	47,746	51,189	61,380	100,814	109,276	108,269	108,468	108,895	102,542	1.7
Texas	76,703	87,839	99,123	137,439	188,187	201,754	197,379	192,464	191,769	190,123	1.0
Utah	32,099	34,389	35,195	40,730	65,283	76,592	85,186	96,308	95,944	107,210	64.2
Vermont	9,673	12,644	15,488	15,468	17,947	18,048	18,011	18,196	17,682	18,340	2.2
Virginia	28,636	34,004	62,156	68,113	143,572	168,918	175,384	178,955	177,840	178,549	24.4
Washington	20,826	27,575	35,752	46,912	54,222	57,263	55,773	54,032	53,185	52,670	-2.9
West Virginia	11,790	10,745	10,682	11,752	47,959	56,327	66,713	69,165	67,172	69,210	44.3
Wisconsin	31,684	33,907	46,245	57,442	78,217	82,922	79,740	76,322	74,682	72,168	-7.7
Wyoming	0	26	703	1,289	1,411	2,006	1,724	1,953	1,537	1,145	-18.9
Other jurisdictions	**20,557**	**77,057**	**98,374**	**110,169**	**156,417**	**180,521**	**188,231**	**181,575**	**176,407**	**178,127**	**13.9**
American Samoa	0	0	0	0	0	0	0	0	0	0	†
Federated States of Micronesia	0	0	0	0	0	0	0	0	0	0	†
Guam	0	0	0	0	94	85	86	77	79	72	-23.4
Marshall Islands	0	0	0	0	0	0	0	0	0	0	†
Northern Marianas	0	0	0	0	0	0	0	0	0	0	†
Palau	0	0	0	0	0	0	0	0	0	0	†
Puerto Rico	20,557	77,057	98,374	110,169	156,323	180,436	188,145	181,498	176,328	178,055	13.9
U.S. Virgin Islands	0	0	0	0	0	0	0	0	0	0	†

†Not applicable.
NOTE: Data through 1990 are for institutions of higher education, while later data are for degree-granting institutions. Degree-granting institutions grant associate's or higher degrees and participate in Title IV federal financial aid programs. The degree-granting classification is very similar to the earlier higher education classification, but it includes more 2-year colleges and excludes a few higher education institutions that did not grant degrees. Some data have been revised from previously published figures.

SOURCE: U.S. Department of Education, National Center for Education Statistics, Higher Education General Information Survey (HEGIS), "Fall Enrollment in Colleges and Universities" surveys, 1970 and 1980; Integrated Postsecondary Education Data System (IPEDS), "Fall Enrollment Survey" (IPEDS-EF:90); and IPEDS Spring 2001 through Spring 2015, Fall Enrollment component. (This table was prepared October 2015.)

Table 315.10. Number of faculty in degree-granting postsecondary institutions, by employment status, sex, control, and level of institution: Selected years, fall 1970 through fall 2013

Year	Total	Employment status			Sex			Control				Level	
									Private				
		Full-time	Part-time	Percent full-time	Males	Females	Percent female	Public	Total	Nonprofit	For-profit	4-year	2-year
1	2	3	4	5	6	7	8	9	10	11	12	13	14
1970	474,000	369,000	104,000	77.8	—	—	—	314,000	160,000	—	—	382,000	92,000
1971[1]	492,000	379,000	113,000	77.0	—	—	—	333,000	159,000	—	—	387,000	105,000
1972	500,000	380,000	120,000	76.0	—	—	—	343,000	157,000	—	—	384,000	116,000
1973[1]	527,000	389,000	138,000	73.8	—	—	—	365,000	162,000	—	—	401,000	126,000
1974[1]	567,000	406,000	161,000	71.6	—	—	—	397,000	170,000	—	—	427,000	140,000
1975[1]	628,000	440,000	188,000	70.1	—	—	—	443,000	185,000	—	—	467,000	161,000
1976	633,000	434,000	199,000	68.6	—	—	—	449,000	184,000	—	—	467,000	166,000
1977	678,000	448,000	230,000	66.1	—	—	—	492,000	186,000	—	—	485,000	193,000
1979[1]	675,000	445,000	230,000	65.9	—	—	—	488,000	187,000	—	—	494,000	182,000
1980[1]	686,000	450,000	236,000	65.6	—	—	—	495,000	191,000	—	—	494,000	192,000
1981	705,000	461,000	244,000	65.4	—	—	—	509,000	196,000	—	—	493,000	212,000
1982[1]	710,000	462,000	248,000	65.1	—	—	—	506,000	204,000	—	—	493,000	217,000
1983	724,000	471,000	254,000	65.1	—	—	—	512,000	212,000	—	—	504,000	220,000
1984[1]	717,000	462,000	255,000	64.4	—	—	—	505,000	212,000	—	—	504,000	213,000
1985[1]	715,000	459,000	256,000	64.2	—	—	—	503,000	212,000	—	—	504,000	211,000
1986[1]	722,000	459,000	263,000	63.6	—	—	—	510,000	212,000	—	—	506,000	216,000
1987[2]	793,070	523,420	269,650	66.0	529,413	263,657	33.2	552,749	240,321	—	—	547,505	245,565
1989[2]	824,220	524,426	299,794	63.6	534,254	289,966	35.2	577,298	246,922	—	—	583,700	240,520
1991[2]	826,252	535,623	290,629	64.8	525,599	300,653	36.4	580,908	245,344	236,066	9,278	591,269	234,983
1993[2]	915,474	545,706	369,768	59.6	561,123	354,351	38.7	650,434	265,040	254,130	10,910	625,969	289,505
1995[2]	931,706	550,822	380,884	59.1	562,893	368,813	39.6	656,833	274,873	260,900	13,973	647,059	284,647
1997[2]	989,813	568,719	421,094	57.5	587,420	402,393	40.7	694,560	295,253	271,257	23,996	682,650	307,163
1999[2]	1,027,830	590,937	436,893	57.5	602,469	425,361	41.4	713,325	314,505	284,652	29,853	713,823	314,007
2001[2]	1,113,183	617,868	495,315	55.5	644,514	468,669	42.1	771,124	342,059	306,487	35,572	764,172	349,011
2003[2]	1,173,593	630,092	543,501	53.7	663,723	509,870	43.4	791,766	381,827	330,097	51,730	814,289	359,304
2005[2]	1,290,426	675,624	614,802	52.4	714,453	575,973	44.6	841,188	449,238	361,523	87,715	916,996	373,430
2007[2]	1,371,390	703,463	667,927	51.3	743,812	627,578	45.8	877,146	494,244	385,875	108,369	990,849	380,541
2009[2]	1,439,074	729,152	709,922	50.7	761,002	678,072	47.1	913,788	525,286	408,382	116,904	1,038,349	400,725
2011[2]	1,524,469	762,114	762,355	50.0	789,567	734,902	48.2	954,159	570,310	432,630	137,680	1,115,642	408,827
2013[2]	1,545,381	791,378	754,003	51.2	791,971	753,410	48.8	968,734	576,647	449,072	127,575	1,151,638	393,743

—Not available.

[1]Estimated on the basis of enrollment. For methodological details on estimates, see National Center for Education Statistics, *Projections of Education Statistics to 2000*.

[2]Because of revised survey methods, data are not directly comparable with figures for years prior to 1987.

NOTE: Includes faculty members with the title of professor, associate professor, assistant professor, instructor, lecturer, assisting professor, adjunct professor, or interim professor (or the equivalent). Excluded are graduate students with titles such as graduate or teaching fellow who assist senior faculty. Data through 1995 are for institutions of higher education, while later data are for degree-granting institutions. Degree-granting institutions grant associate's or higher degrees and participate in Title IV federal financial aid programs. The degree-granting classification is very similar to the earlier higher education classification, but it includes more 2-year colleges and excludes a few higher education institutions that did not grant degrees. Beginning in 2007, includes institutions with fewer than 15 full-time employees; these institutions did not report staff data prior to 2007. Detail may not sum to totals because of rounding. Some data have been revised from previously published figures.

SOURCE: U.S. Department of Education, National Center for Education Statistics, Higher Education General Information Survey (HEGIS), *Employees in Institutions of Higher Education*, 1970 and 1972, and "Staff Survey" 1976; *Projections of Education Statistics to 2000*; Integrated Postsecondary Education Data System (IPEDS), "Fall Staff Survey" (IPEDS-S:87–99); IPEDS Winter 2001–02 through Winter 2011–12, Human Resources component, Fall Staff section; IPEDS Spring 2014, Human Resources component, Fall Staff section; and U.S. Equal Employment Opportunity Commission, Higher Education Staff Information Survey (EEO-6), 1977, 1981, and 1983. (This table was prepared March 2016.)

Table 315.20. Full-time faculty in degree-granting postsecondary institutions, by race/ethnicity, sex, and academic rank: Fall 2009, fall 2011, and fall 2013

Year, sex, and academic rank	Total	White	Black, Hispanic, Asian, Pacific Islander, American Indian/Alaska Native, and Two or more races: Total	Percent[1]	Black	Hispanic	Asian/Pacific Islander: Total	Asian	Pacific Islander	American Indian/Alaska Native	Two or more races	Race/ethnicity unknown	Nonresident alien[2]
1	2	3	4	5	6	7	8	9	10	11	12	13	14
2009													
Total	**729,152**	**551,230**	**130,903**	**19.2**	**39,706**	**28,022**	**59,480**	**—**	**—**	**3,458**	**—**	**16,059**	**31,197**
Professors	177,566	149,553	24,633	14.1	6,086	4,683	13,281	—	—	580	—	1,923	1,460
Associate professors	148,959	117,241	26,779	18.6	8,162	5,382	12,626	—	—	601	—	2,387	2,560
Assistant professors	171,622	117,794	37,199	24.0	10,974	6,783	18,634	—	—	717	—	4,616	12,104
Instructors	104,554	78,346	20,951	21.1	7,807	6,575	5,546	—	—	1,002	—	3,399	1,879
Lecturers	33,372	24,925	5,851	19.0	1,813	1,583	2,319	—	—	139	—	882	1,711
Other faculty	93,079	63,371	15,490	19.7	4,864	3,016	7,074	—	—	419	—	2,852	11,483
2011													
Total	**762,114**	**564,218**	**147,495**	**20.7**	**41,662**	**31,335**	**66,842**	**65,469**	**1,373**	**3,534**	**4,122**	**16,999**	**33,402**
Professors	181,509	150,364	27,559	15.5	6,517	5,180	14,617	14,425	192	589	656	2,202	1,384
Associate professors	155,201	119,415	30,605	20.4	8,695	6,144	14,364	14,129	235	597	805	2,477	2,704
Assistant professors	174,052	118,022	39,986	25.3	10,994	7,428	19,820	19,445	375	701	1,043	4,926	11,118
Instructors	109,042	80,690	23,162	22.3	8,602	6,907	5,807	5,448	359	981	865	3,262	1,928
Lecturers	34,473	25,821	6,261	19.5	1,688	1,773	2,455	2,420	35	135	210	848	1,543
Other faculty	107,837	69,906	19,922	22.2	5,166	3,903	9,779	9,602	177	531	543	3,284	14,725
Males	427,214	316,133	79,707	20.1	18,636	16,341	40,989	40,368	621	1,752	1,989	9,600	21,774
Professors	128,649	106,069	19,812	15.7	3,984	3,499	11,550	11,420	130	362	417	1,643	1,125
Associate professors	89,742	68,493	17,820	20.6	4,373	3,437	9,260	9,142	118	313	437	1,574	1,855
Assistant professors	88,173	58,538	19,877	25.3	4,458	3,692	10,970	10,820	150	303	454	2,694	7,064
Instructors	48,124	35,864	9,750	21.4	3,138	3,133	2,668	2,525	143	463	348	1,486	1,024
Lecturers	15,690	11,721	2,740	18.9	751	753	1,110	1,090	20	47	79	410	819
Other faculty	56,836	35,448	9,708	21.5	1,932	1,827	5,431	5,371	60	264	254	1,793	9,887
Females	334,900	248,085	67,788	21.5	23,026	14,994	25,853	25,101	752	1,782	2,133	7,399	11,628
Professors	52,860	44,295	7,747	14.9	2,533	1,681	3,067	3,005	62	227	239	559	259
Associate professors	65,459	50,922	12,785	20.1	4,322	2,707	5,104	4,987	117	284	368	903	849
Assistant professors	85,879	59,484	20,109	25.3	6,536	3,736	8,850	8,625	225	398	589	2,232	4,054
Instructors	60,918	44,826	13,412	23.0	5,464	3,774	3,139	2,923	216	518	517	1,776	904
Lecturers	18,783	14,100	3,521	20.0	937	1,020	1,345	1,330	15	88	131	438	724
Other faculty	51,001	34,458	10,214	22.9	3,234	2,076	4,348	4,231	117	267	289	1,491	4,838
2013[3]													
Total	**791,391**	**575,491**	**157,480**	**21.5**	**43,188**	**33,217**	**72,246**	**71,038**	**1,208**	**3,538**	**5,291**	**20,013**	**38,407**
Professors	181,530	148,577	29,111	16.4	6,665	5,604	15,417	15,247	170	573	852	2,323	1,519
Associate professors	155,095	116,817	32,580	21.8	8,812	6,381	15,809	15,626	183	591	987	2,859	2,839
Assistant professors	166,045	112,262	38,011	25.3	10,542	7,130	18,402	18,070	332	683	1,254	5,695	10,077
Instructors	99,304	73,859	20,684	21.9	7,448	6,340	5,236	4,950	286	879	781	3,180	1,581
Lecturers	36,728	27,453	6,591	19.4	1,728	2,015	2,436	2,403	33	117	295	1,151	1,533
Other faculty	152,689	96,523	30,503	24.0	7,993	5,747	14,946	14,742	204	695	1,122	4,805	20,858
Males	436,456	316,912	83,905	20.9	18,905	17,198	43,519	42,928	591	1,736	2,547	10,813	24,826
Professors	125,836	102,520	20,450	16.6	4,018	3,669	11,882	11,772	110	350	531	1,664	1,202
Associate professors	87,420	65,320	18,552	22.1	4,321	3,533	9,897	9,810	87	287	514	1,727	1,821
Assistant professors	82,331	54,700	18,387	25.2	4,169	3,506	9,887	9,725	162	304	521	2,957	6,287
Instructors	42,877	32,014	8,665	21.3	2,714	2,888	2,304	2,179	125	430	329	1,349	849
Lecturers	16,588	12,464	2,756	18.1	760	834	992	983	9	39	131	580	788
Other faculty	81,404	49,894	15,095	23.2	2,923	2,768	8,557	8,459	98	326	521	2,536	13,879
Females	354,935	258,579	73,575	22.2	24,283	16,019	28,727	28,110	617	1,802	2,744	9,200	13,581
Professors	55,694	46,057	8,661	15.8	2,647	1,935	3,535	3,475	60	223	321	659	317
Associate professors	67,675	51,497	14,028	21.4	4,491	2,848	5,912	5,816	96	304	473	1,132	1,018
Assistant professors	83,714	57,562	19,624	25.4	6,373	3,624	8,515	8,345	170	379	733	2,738	3,790
Instructors	56,427	41,845	12,019	22.3	4,734	3,452	2,932	2,771	161	449	452	1,831	732
Lecturers	20,140	14,989	3,835	20.4	968	1,181	1,444	1,420	24	78	164	571	745
Other faculty	71,285	46,629	15,408	24.8	5,070	2,979	6,389	6,283	106	369	601	2,269	6,979

—Not available.
[1]Combined total of faculty who were Black, Hispanic, Asian, Pacific Islander, American Indian/Alaska Native, and of Two or more races as a percentage of total faculty, excluding race/ethnicity unknown and nonresident alien.
[2]Race/ethnicity not collected.
[3]Only instructional faculty were classified by academic rank. Primarily research and primarily public service faculty, as well as faculty without ranks, appear under "other faculty."
NOTE: Degree-granting institutions grant associate's or higher degrees and participate in Title IV federal financial aid programs. Includes institutions with fewer than 15 full-time employees; these institutions did not report staff data prior to 2007. Race categories exclude persons of Hispanic ethnicity. Some data have been revised from previously published figures.
SOURCE: U.S. Department of Education, National Center for Education Statistics, Integrated Postsecondary Education Data System (IPEDS), Winter 2009–10 and Winter 2011–12, Human Resources component, Fall Staff section; and IPEDS Spring 2014, Human Resources component, Fall Staff section. (This table was prepared March 2015.)

Table 316.10. Average salary of full-time instructional faculty on 9-month contracts in degree-granting postsecondary institutions, by academic rank, control and level of institution, and sex: Selected years, 1970–71 through 2014–15

Sex and academic year	All faculty	Academic rank						Public institutions			Private institutions		
		Professor	Associate professor	Assistant professor	Instructor	Lecturer	No rank	Total	4-year	2-year	Total	4-year	2-year
1	2	3	4	5	6	7	8	9	10	11	12	13	14
	Current dollars												
Total													
1970–71	$12,710	$17,958	$13,563	$11,176	$9,360	$11,196	$12,333	$12,953	$13,121	$12,644	$11,619	$11,824	$8,664
1975–76	16,659	22,649	17,065	13,986	13,672	12,906	15,196	16,942	17,400	15,820	15,921	16,116	10,901
1980–81	23,302	30,753	23,214	18,901	15,178	17,301	22,334	23,745	24,373	22,177	22,093	22,325	15,065
1982–83	27,196	35,540	26,921	22,056	17,601	20,072	25,557	27,488	28,293	25,567	26,393	26,691	16,595
1984–85	30,447	39,743	29,945	24,668	20,230	22,334	27,683	30,646	31,764	27,864	29,910	30,247	18,510
1985–86	32,392	42,268	31,787	26,277	20,918	23,770	29,088	32,750	34,033	29,590	31,402	31,732	19,436
1987–88	35,897	47,040	35,231	29,110	22,728	25,977	31,532	36,231	37,840	32,209	35,049	35,346	21,867
1989–90	40,133	52,810	39,392	32,689	25,030	28,990	34,559	40,416	42,365	35,516	39,464	39,817	24,601
1990–91	42,165	55,540	41,414	34,434	26,332	30,097	36,395	42,317	44,510	37,055	41,788	42,224	24,088
1991–92	43,851	57,433	42,929	35,745	30,916	30,456	37,783	43,641	45,638	38,959	44,376	44,793	25,673
1992–93	44,714	58,788	43,945	36,625	28,499	30,543	37,771	44,197	46,515	38,935	45,985	46,427	26,105
1993–94	46,364	60,649	45,278	37,630	28,828	32,729	40,584	45,920	48,019	41,040	47,465	47,880	28,435
1994–95	47,811	62,709	46,713	38,756	29,665	33,198	41,227	47,432	49,738	42,101	48,741	49,379	25,613
1995–96	49,309	64,540	47,966	39,696	30,344	34,136	42,996	48,837	51,172	43,295	50,466	50,819	31,915
1996–97	50,829	66,659	49,307	40,687	31,193	34,962	44,200	50,303	52,718	44,584	52,112	52,443	32,628
1997–98	52,335	68,731	50,828	41,830	32,449	35,484	45,268	51,638	54,114	45,919	54,039	54,379	33,592
1998–99	54,097	71,322	52,576	43,348	33,819	36,819	46,250	53,319	55,948	47,285	55,981	56,284	34,821
1999–2000	55,888	74,410	54,524	44,978	34,918	38,194	47,389	55,011	57,950	48,240	58,013	58,323	35,925
2001–02	59,742	80,792	58,724	48,796	46,959	41,798	46,569	58,524	62,013	50,837	62,818	63,088	33,139
2002–03	61,330	83,466	60,471	50,552	48,304	42,622	46,338	60,014	63,486	52,330	64,533	64,814	34,826
2003–04	62,579	85,333	61,746	51,798	49,065	43,648	47,725	60,874	64,340	53,076	66,666	66,932	36,322
2004–05	64,234	88,158	63,558	53,308	49,730	44,514	48,942	62,346	66,053	53,932	68,755	68,995	37,329
2005–06	66,172	91,208	65,714	55,106	50,883	45,896	50,425	64,158	67,951	55,405	71,016	71,263	38,549
2006–07	68,585	94,870	68,153	57,143	53,278	47,478	52,161	66,566	70,460	57,466	73,419	73,636	41,138
2007–08	71,085	98,548	70,826	59,294	55,325	49,392	54,405	68,981	72,857	59,646	76,133	76,341	43,402
2008–09	73,570	102,346	73,439	61,550	56,918	51,188	56,370	71,237	75,245	61,433	79,147	79,410	43,542
2009–10	74,620	103,682	74,125	62,245	57,791	52,185	56,803	72,178	76,147	62,264	80,379	80,597	44,748
2010–11	75,481	104,961	75,107	63,136	58,003	52,584	56,549	72,715	76,857	62,359	81,897	82,098	45,146
2011–12	76,567	107,090	76,177	64,011	58,350	53,359	56,898	73,496	77,843	62,553	83,540	83,701	47,805
2012–13	77,278	108,074	77,029	64,673	57,674	53,072	58,752	73,877	78,012	62,907	84,932	85,096	44,978
2013–14	78,625	109,905	78,593	66,025	58,080	54,238	58,902	75,241	79,711	63,198	86,265	86,467	44,566
2014–15	80,203	112,697	80,438	67,677	59,211	55,610	58,201	76,963	81,527	64,304	87,617	88,228	38,168
Males													
1975–76	17,414	22,902	17,209	14,174	14,430	13,579	15,761	17,661	18,121	16,339	16,784	16,946	11,378
1980–81	24,499	31,082	23,451	19,227	15,545	18,281	23,170	24,873	25,509	22,965	23,493	23,669	16,075
1982–83	28,664	35,956	27,262	22,586	18,160	21,225	26,541	28,851	29,661	26,524	28,159	28,380	17,346
1984–85	32,182	40,269	30,392	25,330	21,159	23,557	28,670	32,240	33,344	28,891	32,028	32,278	19,460
1985–86	34,294	42,833	32,273	27,094	21,693	25,238	30,267	34,528	35,786	30,758	33,656	33,900	20,412
1987–88	38,112	47,735	35,823	30,086	23,645	27,652	32,747	38,314	39,898	33,477	37,603	37,817	22,641
1989–90	42,763	53,650	40,131	33,781	25,933	31,162	35,980	42,959	44,834	37,081	42,312	42,595	25,218
1990–91	45,065	56,549	42,239	35,636	27,388	32,398	38,036	45,084	47,168	38,787	45,019	45,319	25,937
1991–92	46,848	58,494	43,814	36,969	33,359	32,843	39,422	46,483	48,401	40,811	47,733	48,042	26,825
1992–93	47,866	59,972	44,855	37,842	29,583	32,512	39,365	47,175	49,392	40,725	49,518	49,837	27,402
1993–94	49,579	61,857	46,229	38,794	29,815	34,796	42,251	48,956	50,989	42,938	51,076	51,397	30,783
1994–95	51,228	64,046	47,705	39,923	30,528	35,082	43,103	50,629	52,874	44,020	52,653	53,036	29,639
1995–96	52,814	65,949	49,037	40,858	30,940	36,135	44,624	52,163	54,448	45,209	54,364	54,649	33,301
1996–97	54,465	68,214	50,457	41,864	31,738	36,932	45,688	53,737	56,162	46,393	56,185	56,453	34,736
1997–98	56,115	70,468	52,041	43,017	33,070	37,481	46,822	55,191	57,744	47,690	58,293	58,576	36,157
1998–99	58,048	73,260	53,830	44,650	34,741	38,976	47,610	57,038	59,805	48,961	60,392	60,641	38,040
1999–2000	60,084	76,478	55,939	46,414	35,854	40,202	48,788	58,984	62,030	50,033	62,631	62,905	38,636
2001–02	64,320	83,356	60,300	50,518	48,844	44,519	48,049	62,835	66,577	52,360	67,871	68,100	33,395
2002–03	66,126	86,191	62,226	52,441	50,272	45,469	47,412	64,564	68,322	53,962	69,726	69,976	34,291
2003–04	67,485	88,262	63,466	53,649	50,985	46,214	48,973	65,476	69,248	54,623	72,021	72,250	35,604
2004–05	69,337	91,290	65,394	55,215	51,380	46,929	50,102	67,130	71,145	55,398	74,318	74,540	34,970
2005–06	71,569	94,733	67,654	57,099	52,519	48,256	51,811	69,191	73,353	56,858	76,941	77,143	38,215
2006–07	74,167	98,563	70,168	59,150	55,061	49,641	53,665	71,797	76,072	58,971	79,491	79,663	41,196
2007–08	76,935	102,555	72,940	61,368	57,116	51,804	56,196	74,389	78,673	61,166	82,681	82,850	42,995
2008–09	79,706	106,759	75,634	63,726	58,819	53,777	58,341	76,897	81,394	62,870	86,008	86,205	43,871
2009–10	80,881	108,225	76,400	64,451	59,793	54,947	58,647	77,948	82,423	63,697	87,382	87,546	44,500
2010–11	81,873	109,656	77,429	65,391	59,851	55,457	58,392	78,609	83,279	63,745	89,000	89,160	44,542
2011–12	83,150	112,066	78,560	66,303	60,066	56,367	58,807	79,544	84,444	63,918	90,840	90,976	45,250
2012–13	83,979	113,311	79,423	67,085	59,350	55,759	61,086	80,016	84,700	64,282	92,385	92,530	42,906
2013–14	85,528	115,455	81,156	68,534	59,614	56,920	61,279	81,560	86,562	64,564	94,016	94,177	44,234
2014–15	87,178	118,412	83,001	70,227	60,730	58,633	60,211	83,363	88,459	65,693	95,467	96,058	37,389

See notes at end of table.

Table 316.10. Average salary of full-time instructional faculty on 9-month contracts in degree-granting postsecondary institutions, by academic rank, control and level of institution, and sex: Selected years, 1970–71 through 2014–15—Continued

Sex and academic year	All faculty	Academic rank						Public institutions			Private institutions		
		Professor	Associate professor	Assistant professor	Instructor	Lecturer	No rank	Total	4-year	2-year	Total	4-year	2-year
1	2	3	4	5	6	7	8	9	10	11	12	13	14
Females													
1975–76	14,308	20,308	16,364	13,522	12,572	11,901	14,094	14,762	14,758	14,769	13,030	13,231	10,201
1980–81	19,996	27,959	22,295	18,302	14,854	16,168	20,843	20,673	20,608	20,778	18,073	18,326	13,892
1982–83	23,261	32,221	25,738	21,130	17,102	18,830	23,855	23,892	23,876	23,917	21,451	21,785	15,845
1984–85	25,941	35,824	28,517	23,575	19,362	21,004	26,050	26,566	26,813	26,172	24,186	24,560	17,575
1985–86	27,576	38,252	30,300	24,966	20,237	22,273	27,171	28,299	28,680	27,693	25,523	25,889	18,504
1987–88	30,499	42,371	33,528	27,600	21,962	24,370	29,605	31,215	31,820	30,228	28,621	28,946	21,215
1989–90	34,183	47,663	37,469	31,090	24,320	26,995	32,528	34,796	35,704	33,307	32,650	33,010	24,002
1990–91	35,881	49,728	39,329	32,724	25,534	28,111	34,179	36,459	37,573	34,720	34,359	34,898	22,585
1991–92	37,534	51,621	40,766	34,063	28,873	28,550	35,622	37,800	38,634	36,517	36,828	37,309	24,683
1992–93	38,385	52,755	41,861	35,032	27,700	28,922	35,792	38,356	39,470	36,710	38,460	38,987	25,068
1993–94	40,058	54,746	43,178	36,169	28,136	31,048	38,474	40,118	41,031	38,707	39,902	40,378	26,142
1994–95	41,369	56,555	44,626	37,352	29,072	31,677	38,967	41,548	42,663	39,812	40,908	41,815	22,851
1995–96	42,871	58,318	45,803	38,345	29,940	32,584	41,085	42,871	43,986	41,086	42,871	43,236	30,671
1996–97	44,325	60,160	47,101	39,350	30,819	33,415	42,474	44,306	45,402	42,531	44,374	44,726	30,661
1997–98	45,775	61,965	48,597	40,504	32,011	33,918	43,491	45,648	46,709	43,943	46,106	46,466	30,995
1998–99	47,421	64,236	50,347	41,894	33,152	35,115	44,723	47,247	48,355	45,457	47,874	48,204	31,524
1999–2000	48,997	67,079	52,091	43,367	34,228	36,607	45,865	48,714	50,168	46,340	49,737	50,052	32,951
2001–02	52,662	72,542	56,186	46,824	45,262	39,538	45,003	52,123	53,895	49,290	54,149	54,434	32,921
2002–03	54,105	75,028	57,716	48,380	46,573	40,265	45,251	53,435	55,121	50,717	55,881	56,158	35,296
2003–04	55,378	76,652	59,095	49,689	47,404	41,536	46,519	54,408	56,117	51,591	57,921	58,192	36,896
2004–05	56,926	79,160	60,809	51,154	48,351	42,455	47,860	55,780	57,714	52,566	59,919	60,143	39,291
2005–06	58,665	81,514	62,860	52,901	49,533	43,934	49,172	57,462	59,437	54,082	61,830	62,092	38,786
2006–07	61,016	85,090	65,237	54,974	51,832	45,693	50,812	59,781	61,875	56,127	64,246	64,481	41,099
2007–08	63,347	88,301	67,816	57,111	53,889	47,407	52,837	62,129	64,226	58,318	66,528	66,745	43,670
2008–09	65,638	91,522	70,375	59,286	55,424	49,078	54,649	64,231	66,393	60,195	69,300	69,593	43,344
2009–10	66,647	92,830	71,017	59,997	56,239	49,957	55,206	65,139	67,276	61,047	70,507	70,746	44,892
2010–11	67,473	94,041	72,003	60,888	56,566	50,270	54,985	65,632	67,935	61,193	72,091	72,306	45,518
2011–12	68,468	95,845	73,057	61,763	57,013	50,994	55,299	66,368	68,897	61,417	73,629	73,788	49,382
2012–13	69,124	96,563	73,966	62,321	56,361	50,963	56,777	66,703	69,083	61,774	74,987	75,149	46,407
2013–14	70,355	98,064	75,388	63,599	56,884	52,156	56,916	67,944	70,713	62,079	76,173	76,390	44,769
2014–15	71,943	100,790	77,297	65,225	58,013	53,233	56,508	69,645	72,583	63,164	77,544	78,132	38,841
	Constant 2014–15 dollars[1]												
Total													
1970–71	75,722	106,989	80,809	66,585	55,764	66,705	73,480	77,175	78,176	75,332	69,222	70,448	51,619
1975–76	71,093	96,659	72,829	59,688	58,349	55,078	64,852	72,303	74,258	67,513	67,945	68,780	46,521
1980–81	63,666	84,023	63,425	51,641	41,469	47,270	61,021	64,876	66,592	60,592	60,363	60,996	41,161
1982–83	65,580	85,700	64,917	53,185	42,443	48,401	61,628	66,284	68,225	61,652	63,644	64,362	40,017
1984–85	68,132	88,934	67,009	55,200	45,269	49,977	61,947	68,577	71,079	62,352	66,930	67,684	41,420
1985–86	70,453	91,933	69,137	57,152	45,497	51,700	63,266	71,231	74,022	64,358	68,299	69,017	42,273
1987–88	73,341	96,108	71,981	59,475	46,435	53,073	64,424	74,024	77,311	65,806	71,609	72,215	44,677
1989–90	74,807	98,435	73,426	60,931	46,655	54,037	64,416	75,334	78,966	66,201	73,559	74,218	45,855
1990–91	74,521	98,158	73,192	60,857	46,537	53,192	64,323	74,789	78,664	65,489	73,853	74,625	42,572
1991–92	75,094	98,352	73,514	61,213	52,942	52,154	64,703	74,734	78,153	66,717	75,992	76,706	43,964
1992–93	74,252	97,623	72,974	60,819	47,326	50,719	62,722	73,393	77,243	64,655	76,362	77,097	43,350
1993–94	75,049	98,171	73,289	60,911	46,663	52,977	65,692	74,330	77,727	66,430	76,830	77,502	46,027
1994–95	75,234	98,676	73,506	60,985	46,679	52,239	64,873	74,637	78,266	66,249	76,696	77,701	40,303
1995–96	75,537	98,869	73,479	60,811	46,484	52,292	65,865	74,813	78,390	66,323	77,308	77,849	48,890
1996–97	75,705	99,282	73,438	60,599	46,459	52,072	65,832	74,921	78,517	66,403	77,616	78,109	48,597
1997–98	76,582	100,575	74,377	61,210	47,482	51,924	66,240	75,562	79,186	67,194	79,076	79,573	49,155
1998–99	77,813	102,590	75,625	62,352	48,645	52,960	66,527	76,694	80,475	68,014	80,524	80,959	50,086
1999–2000	78,134	104,029	76,226	62,882	48,817	53,397	66,252	76,908	81,016	67,442	81,104	81,538	50,224
2001–02	79,350	107,309	77,998	64,811	62,372	55,517	61,853	77,732	82,366	67,522	83,435	83,795	44,015
2002–03	79,707	108,477	78,591	65,701	62,778	55,394	60,224	77,997	82,510	68,011	83,871	84,236	45,261
2003–04	79,590	108,529	78,530	65,878	62,402	55,513	60,698	77,421	81,830	67,504	84,787	85,126	46,195
2004–05	79,308	108,847	78,473	65,818	61,400	54,960	60,427	76,976	81,554	66,588	84,890	85,187	46,089
2005–06	78,704	108,481	78,159	65,541	60,519	54,588	59,974	76,309	80,819	65,898	84,465	84,759	45,849
2006–07	79,517	109,992	79,016	66,251	61,770	55,046	60,476	77,176	81,691	66,626	85,122	85,373	47,696
2007–08	79,471	110,174	79,181	66,289	61,852	55,219	60,823	77,119	81,452	66,683	85,114	85,347	48,523
2008–09	81,117	112,844	80,972	67,864	62,756	56,439	62,152	78,545	82,963	67,735	87,265	87,555	48,008
2009–10	81,486	113,222	80,945	67,972	63,108	56,987	62,030	78,820	83,153	67,993	87,775	88,012	48,865
2010–11	80,804	112,363	80,403	67,588	62,093	56,292	60,537	77,843	82,276	66,756	87,672	87,887	48,329
2011–12	79,633	111,378	79,227	66,574	60,686	55,496	59,177	76,439	80,960	65,058	86,885	87,052	49,719
2012–13	79,057	110,561	78,802	66,161	59,001	54,294	60,104	75,577	79,807	64,355	86,887	87,055	46,013
2013–14	79,198	110,705	79,166	66,506	58,502	54,633	59,331	75,789	80,292	63,658	86,894	87,096	44,891
2014–15	80,203	112,697	80,438	67,677	59,211	55,610	58,201	76,963	81,527	64,304	87,617	88,228	38,168

See notes at end of table.

Table 316.10. Average salary of full-time instructional faculty on 9-month contracts in degree-granting postsecondary institutions, by academic rank, control and level of institution, and sex: Selected years, 1970–71 through 2014–15—Continued

Sex and academic year	All faculty	Academic rank						Public institutions			Private institutions		
		Professor	Associate professor	Assistant professor	Instructor	Lecturer	No rank	Total	4-year	2-year	Total	4-year	2-year
1	2	3	4	5	6	7	8	9	10	11	12	13	14
Males													
1975–76	74,316	97,738	73,441	60,491	61,582	57,950	67,262	75,372	77,333	69,731	71,630	72,319	48,556
1980–81	66,936	84,922	64,073	52,532	42,472	49,947	63,305	67,958	69,696	62,745	64,188	64,668	43,920
1982–83	69,120	86,704	65,739	54,463	43,791	51,182	64,000	69,571	71,524	63,959	67,902	68,435	41,828
1984–85	72,014	90,111	68,009	56,681	47,348	52,714	64,155	72,144	74,615	64,650	71,670	72,229	43,546
1985–86	74,589	93,162	70,194	58,929	47,182	54,893	65,831	75,098	77,835	66,899	73,202	73,733	44,396
1987–88	77,866	97,527	73,190	61,470	48,309	56,496	66,905	78,279	81,516	68,397	76,827	77,264	46,258
1989–90	79,710	100,001	74,802	62,966	48,338	58,084	67,065	80,073	83,569	69,119	78,869	79,395	47,006
1990–91	79,646	99,942	74,650	62,980	48,405	57,258	67,222	79,679	83,361	68,550	79,564	80,095	45,839
1991–92	80,226	100,169	75,030	63,307	57,126	56,243	67,509	79,601	82,885	69,888	81,741	82,270	45,936
1992–93	79,485	99,589	74,487	62,840	49,126	53,990	65,370	78,338	82,021	67,627	82,230	82,760	45,503
1993–94	80,252	100,126	74,829	62,794	48,261	56,323	68,390	79,243	82,534	69,502	82,676	83,195	49,828
1994–95	80,611	100,781	75,067	62,821	48,038	55,204	67,826	79,668	83,200	69,269	82,853	83,456	46,640
1995–96	80,906	101,027	75,120	62,590	47,397	55,355	68,360	79,908	83,409	69,255	83,279	83,717	51,014
1996–97	81,120	101,598	75,150	62,352	47,271	55,006	68,048	80,036	83,647	69,097	83,682	84,080	51,735
1997–98	82,114	103,116	76,152	62,946	48,392	54,846	68,514	80,761	84,497	69,785	85,301	85,715	52,909
1998–99	83,496	105,378	77,428	64,224	49,972	56,062	68,483	82,044	86,024	70,426	86,868	87,226	54,717
1999–2000	83,999	106,919	78,205	64,888	50,126	56,204	68,207	82,462	86,720	69,949	87,561	87,943	54,015
2001–02	85,431	110,714	80,091	67,098	64,875	59,131	63,820	83,458	88,429	69,546	90,147	90,451	44,355
2002–03	85,941	112,018	80,872	68,155	65,336	59,093	61,619	83,910	88,795	70,132	90,619	90,944	44,566
2003–04	85,829	112,254	80,718	68,232	64,844	58,776	62,285	83,274	88,071	69,471	91,599	91,889	45,283
2004–05	85,609	112,713	80,740	68,173	63,437	57,942	61,859	82,884	87,841	68,399	91,759	92,033	43,176
2005–06	85,123	112,674	80,466	67,912	62,465	57,395	61,623	82,294	87,245	67,626	91,512	91,752	45,453
2006–07	85,989	114,273	81,352	68,579	63,838	57,553	62,219	83,241	88,197	68,371	92,162	92,361	47,763
2007–08	86,012	114,654	81,545	68,608	63,854	57,915	62,825	83,165	87,955	68,382	92,436	92,624	48,068
2008–09	87,882	117,710	83,393	70,263	64,852	59,293	64,325	84,785	89,743	69,319	94,830	95,048	48,371
2009–10	88,323	118,183	83,430	70,381	65,294	60,003	64,043	85,120	90,006	69,558	95,422	95,601	48,595
2010–11	87,646	117,389	82,889	70,002	64,072	59,368	62,509	84,152	89,152	68,240	95,276	95,447	47,683
2011–12	86,480	116,553	81,705	68,958	62,471	58,624	61,161	82,729	87,825	66,478	94,477	94,618	47,062
2012–13	85,912	115,919	81,251	68,629	60,716	57,043	62,492	81,858	86,649	65,762	94,511	94,659	43,894
2013–14	86,151	116,296	81,747	69,033	60,048	57,334	61,726	82,154	87,192	65,035	94,701	94,863	44,556
2014–15	87,178	118,412	83,001	70,227	60,730	58,633	60,211	83,363	88,459	65,693	95,467	96,058	37,389
Females													
1975–76	61,060	86,668	69,836	57,707	53,652	50,788	60,148	63,001	62,984	63,028	55,610	56,464	43,533
1980–81	54,633	76,390	60,914	50,005	40,584	44,174	56,947	56,483	56,305	56,770	49,379	50,070	37,956
1982–83	56,091	77,697	62,064	50,952	41,239	45,406	57,523	57,613	57,574	57,673	51,727	52,532	38,208
1984–85	58,049	80,164	63,813	52,754	43,327	47,001	58,293	59,447	60,000	58,566	54,122	54,958	39,328
1985–86	59,978	83,198	65,903	54,301	44,015	48,444	59,097	61,550	62,379	60,232	55,513	56,309	40,246
1987–88	62,313	86,568	68,501	56,390	44,870	49,790	60,486	63,775	65,011	61,759	58,476	59,140	43,344
1989–90	63,716	88,842	69,840	57,950	45,331	50,318	60,632	64,859	66,552	62,083	60,858	61,530	44,739
1990–91	63,413	87,887	69,509	57,835	45,127	49,682	60,405	64,436	66,405	61,362	60,724	61,676	39,916
1991–92	64,275	88,399	69,810	58,332	49,444	48,890	61,002	64,731	66,160	62,535	63,066	63,890	42,269
1992–93	63,741	87,606	69,514	58,175	45,999	48,028	59,436	63,693	65,544	60,961	63,866	64,741	41,628
1993–94	64,841	88,616	69,890	58,545	45,543	50,257	62,276	64,937	66,415	62,654	64,589	65,358	42,315
1994–95	65,097	88,993	70,222	58,776	45,747	49,845	61,317	65,378	67,133	62,646	64,371	65,798	35,958
1995–96	65,674	89,336	70,165	58,741	45,865	49,915	62,938	65,673	67,381	62,940	65,674	66,233	46,985
1996–97	66,017	89,602	70,152	58,608	45,902	49,769	63,261	65,989	67,622	63,345	66,090	66,615	45,667
1997–98	66,982	90,673	71,113	59,269	46,842	49,632	63,640	66,797	68,349	64,302	67,467	67,994	45,355
1998–99	68,210	92,397	72,420	60,260	47,686	50,510	64,329	67,960	69,553	65,385	68,863	69,337	45,344
1999–2000	68,500	93,779	72,825	60,629	47,852	51,178	64,121	68,104	70,137	64,785	69,534	69,975	46,067
2001–02	69,946	96,351	74,627	62,192	60,117	52,514	59,773	69,230	71,585	65,467	71,922	72,300	43,726
2002–03	70,317	97,510	75,011	62,877	60,529	52,330	58,811	69,447	71,638	65,915	72,626	72,986	45,873
2003–04	70,431	97,488	75,159	63,196	60,290	52,827	59,164	69,198	71,372	65,615	73,666	74,010	46,926
2004–05	70,285	97,737	75,079	63,159	59,697	52,418	59,091	68,870	71,258	64,902	73,980	74,257	48,511
2005–06	69,775	96,951	74,764	62,920	58,914	52,254	58,485	68,344	70,693	64,325	73,540	73,851	46,132
2006–07	70,741	98,653	75,636	63,737	60,094	52,977	58,911	69,310	71,738	65,073	74,487	74,759	47,651
2007–08	70,820	98,719	75,816	63,849	60,246	53,000	59,071	69,458	71,803	65,198	74,376	74,619	48,822
2008–09	72,371	100,910	77,594	65,368	61,109	54,112	60,255	70,819	73,203	66,370	76,409	76,732	47,790
2009–10	72,779	101,372	77,551	65,517	61,414	54,554	60,285	71,133	73,466	66,664	76,994	77,255	49,022
2010–11	72,231	100,673	77,081	65,181	60,554	53,815	58,862	70,260	72,726	65,508	77,174	77,404	48,728
2011–12	71,210	99,683	75,982	64,236	59,296	53,036	57,513	69,025	71,656	63,877	76,577	76,743	51,359
2012–13	70,715	98,785	75,668	63,756	57,658	52,136	58,084	68,239	70,673	63,196	76,713	76,879	47,475
2013–14	70,868	98,778	75,937	64,062	57,298	52,535	57,330	68,439	71,228	62,531	76,727	76,946	45,095
2014–15	71,943	100,790	77,297	65,225	58,013	53,233	56,508	69,645	72,583	63,164	77,544	78,132	38,841

[1]Constant dollars based on the Consumer Price Index, prepared by the Bureau of Labor Statistics, U.S. Department of Labor, adjusted to an academic-year basis.

NOTE: Data through 1995–96 are for institutions of higher education, while later data are for degree-granting institutions. Degree-granting institutions grant associate's or higher degrees and participate in Title IV federal financial aid programs. Data for 1987–88 and later years include imputations for nonrespondent institutions.

SOURCE: U.S. Department of Education, National Center for Education Statistics, Higher Education General Information Survey (HEGIS), "Faculty Salaries, Tenure, and Fringe Benefits" surveys, 1970–71 through 1985–86; Integrated Postsecondary Education Data System (IPEDS), "Salaries, Tenure, and Fringe Benefits of Full-Time Instructional Faculty Survey" (IPEDS-SA:87–99); and IPEDS, Winter 2001–02 through Winter 2011–12 and Spring 2013 through Spring 2015, Human Resources component, Salaries section. (This table was prepared November 2015.)

Table 316.20. Average salary of full-time instructional faculty on 9-month contracts in degree-granting postsecondary institutions, by academic rank, sex, and control and level of institution: Selected years, 1999–2000 through 2014–15

Academic year, control and level of institution	Constant 2014–15 dollars[1]	Current dollars												
		All faculty			Academic rank									
					Professor			Associate professor						
	All faculty, total	Total	Males	Females	Total	Males	Females	Total	Males	Females	Assistant professor	Instructor	Lecturer	No academic rank
1	2	3	4	5	6	7	8	9	10	11	12	13	14	15
1999–2000														
All institutions	$78,134	$55,888	$60,084	$48,997	$74,410	$76,478	$67,079	$54,524	$55,939	$52,091	$44,978	$34,918	$38,194	$47,389
Public	76,908	55,011	58,984	48,714	72,475	74,501	65,568	54,641	55,992	52,305	45,285	35,007	37,403	47,990
4-year	81,016	57,950	62,030	50,168	75,204	76,530	69,619	55,681	56,776	53,599	45,822	33,528	37,261	40,579
Doctoral[2]	87,032	62,253	66,882	52,287	81,182	82,445	74,653	57,744	58,999	55,156	48,190	33,345	38,883	39,350
Master's[3]	73,779	52,773	55,565	48,235	66,588	67,128	64,863	53,048	53,686	51,977	43,396	33,214	34,448	43,052
Other 4-year	66,920	47,867	49,829	44,577	60,360	60,748	59,052	49,567	50,133	48,548	42,306	35,754	36,088	38,330
2-year	67,442	48,240	50,033	46,340	57,806	59,441	55,501	48,056	49,425	46,711	41,984	37,634	40,061	48,233
Nonprofit	81,326	58,172	62,788	49,881	78,512	80,557	70,609	54,300	55,836	51,687	44,423	34,670	40,761	41,415
4-year	81,680	58,425	63,028	50,117	78,604	80,622	70,774	54,388	55,898	51,809	44,502	34,813	40,783	41,761
Doctoral[2]	100,481	71,873	77,214	59,586	95,182	96,768	87,342	62,503	63,951	59,536	52,134	39,721	42,693	45,887
Master's[3]	69,722	49,871	52,642	45,718	62,539	63,603	59,353	50,176	51,470	48,165	41,447	33,991	37,923	44,153
Other 4-year	65,395	46,776	48,847	43,544	60,200	60,757	58,364	46,822	47,135	46,365	38,775	31,574	33,058	35,120
2-year	52,543	37,583	39,933	34,733	39,454	38,431	40,571	36,349	37,342	35,608	31,818	27,696	25,965	40,373
For-profit	41,303	29,543	30,023	28,942	45,505	44,248	49,693	48,469	53,548	43,389	33,043	29,894	—	27,958
2009–10														
All institutions	81,486	74,620	80,881	66,647	103,682	108,225	92,830	74,125	76,400	71,017	62,245	57,791	52,185	56,803
Public	78,820	72,178	77,948	65,139	99,208	103,746	88,815	73,379	75,687	70,256	62,160	59,310	50,228	55,864
4-year	83,153	76,147	82,423	67,276	103,948	107,191	95,048	75,251	77,282	72,298	63,442	46,028	50,104	54,005
Doctoral[2]	89,381	81,850	89,186	70,307	113,063	115,829	103,793	78,539	80,830	74,963	66,902	44,406	50,313	53,135
Master's[3]	74,522	68,243	71,574	64,239	87,917	88,929	85,883	70,332	71,340	69,036	59,396	44,422	49,746	55,765
Other 4-year	66,834	61,202	63,678	58,349	76,448	79,143	72,073	65,003	66,297	63,338	55,055	54,050	49,432	54,487
2-year	67,993	62,264	63,697	61,047	72,377	74,423	70,429	60,632	61,565	59,852	54,161	65,503	53,548	56,239
Nonprofit	88,002	80,587	87,600	70,676	112,146	116,401	101,119	75,565	77,764	72,502	62,395	47,842	57,508	62,242
4-year	88,167	80,738	87,720	70,834	112,252	116,472	101,290	75,664	77,827	72,642	62,465	47,885	57,520	62,542
Doctoral[2]	104,265	95,480	104,514	80,888	134,776	138,354	123,283	85,864	88,699	81,499	71,973	53,825	58,932	66,634
Master's[3]	71,828	65,776	68,776	62,128	82,516	84,062	79,452	66,524	67,508	65,309	55,469	45,305	53,637	60,591
Other 4-year	70,560	64,614	67,178	61,326	84,869	85,528	83,480	64,747	64,949	64,478	53,130	42,145	52,422	52,775
2-year	49,939	45,731	44,417	46,529	53,063	55,046	51,310	45,768	45,863	45,717	42,706	46,010	32,393	43,562
For-profit	59,888	54,842	56,689	52,925	79,574	81,765	75,817	71,376	72,429	70,199	66,027	41,742	‡	53,705
2013–14														
All institutions	79,198	78,625	85,528	70,355	109,905	115,455	98,064	78,593	81,156	75,388	66,025	58,080	54,238	58,902
Public	75,789	75,241	81,560	67,944	103,587	109,118	92,281	77,106	79,760	73,783	65,659	59,742	51,923	57,233
4-year	80,292	79,711	86,562	70,713	109,541	113,579	99,646	79,151	81,495	76,009	67,387	48,816	52,055	56,528
Doctoral[2]	86,476	85,851	93,677	74,675	118,814	122,452	108,523	83,032	85,507	79,550	71,429	47,822	53,262	56,347
Master's[3]	69,238	68,737	72,067	64,971	87,794	88,863	85,847	71,355	72,678	69,750	61,117	46,288	48,785	55,818
Other 4-year	61,590	61,145	63,227	58,992	74,333	76,927	70,634	66,053	67,918	63,892	56,116	56,123	47,437	57,110
2-year	63,658	63,198	64,564	62,079	72,737	74,264	71,377	62,258	63,168	61,557	55,423	65,524	48,222	57,498
Nonprofit	87,409	86,777	94,498	76,659	121,995	127,064	110,208	81,478	83,869	78,493	66,690	48,088	60,506	70,174
4-year	87,490	86,858	94,572	76,733	122,042	127,097	110,278	81,494	83,882	78,510	66,719	48,005	60,506	70,411
Doctoral[2]	102,425	101,684	111,792	86,884	146,366	151,239	132,794	92,201	95,342	88,010	75,760	51,412	61,601	74,456
Master's[3]	70,145	69,638	72,555	66,299	86,082	87,087	84,255	70,658	71,961	69,164	59,093	48,322	56,837	69,934
Other 4-year	69,796	69,292	71,765	66,384	90,780	91,178	90,028	69,880	70,079	69,641	57,103	41,388	58,445	56,004
2-year	51,160	50,790	47,259	53,092	51,307	49,960	52,415	59,231	47,530	63,689	41,799	52,227	—	49,582
For-profit	51,093	50,723	52,553	49,176	65,002	65,902	63,875	66,921	68,784	65,184	63,354	42,292	62,743	37,673
2014–15														
All institutions	80,203	80,203	87,178	71,943	112,697	118,412	100,790	80,438	83,001	77,297	67,677	59,211	55,610	58,201
Public	76,963	76,963	83,363	69,645	106,474	112,178	95,084	79,068	81,723	75,814	67,510	60,958	53,171	56,882
4-year	81,527	81,527	88,459	72,583	112,384	116,600	102,397	81,188	83,555	78,094	69,399	49,781	53,235	55,955
Doctoral[2]	87,174	87,174	95,158	76,073	121,703	125,480	111,345	84,740	87,352	81,175	73,284	48,553	53,948	55,379
Master's[3]	71,467	71,467	74,791	67,721	91,025	92,314	88,774	73,921	74,984	72,638	63,226	47,174	51,130	51,478
Other 4-year	63,020	63,020	65,252	60,733	77,827	80,664	73,730	68,333	70,131	66,386	58,116	56,695	51,964	57,848
2-year	64,304	64,304	65,693	63,164	74,831	76,675	73,204	63,896	64,692	63,282	56,667	66,791	51,696	57,230
Nonprofit	88,246	88,246	96,100	78,110	124,537	129,826	112,576	83,161	85,544	80,233	68,026	48,602	62,544	67,947
4-year	88,661	88,661	96,513	78,505	124,598	129,878	112,647	83,171	85,549	80,247	68,059	50,423	63,928	68,209
Doctoral[2]	103,587	103,587	113,743	88,984	149,557	154,775	135,574	93,935	96,951	89,982	77,580	54,408	65,543	70,911
Master's[3]	70,912	70,912	73,847	67,544	87,310	88,150	85,774	71,700	72,897	70,323	59,946	49,300	57,570	69,797
Other 4-year	70,023	70,023	72,649	67,061	92,167	92,881	90,893	70,581	70,963	70,147	57,437	43,853	59,224	57,552
2-year	24,824	24,824	21,204	28,094	53,597	51,613	56,021	47,930	41,621	50,033	45,975	23,163	10,199	47,971
For-profit	49,948	49,948	50,770	49,195	67,647	65,843	70,788	66,768	66,233	67,262	60,978	43,524	70,788	45,996

—Not available.
‡Reporting standards not met (too few cases).
[1]Constant dollars based on the Consumer Price Index, prepared by the Bureau of Labor Statistics, U.S. Department of Labor, adjusted to an academic-year basis.
[2]Institutions that awarded 20 or more doctor's degrees during the previous academic year.
[3]Institutions that awarded 20 or more master's degrees, but less than 20 doctor's degrees, during the previous academic year.

NOTE: Degree-granting institutions grant associate's or higher degrees and participate in Title IV federal financial aid programs.
SOURCE: U.S. Department of Education, National Center for Education Statistics, Integrated Postsecondary Education Data System (IPEDS), "Salaries, Tenure, and Fringe Benefits of Full-Time Instructional Faculty Survey" (IPEDS-SA:99); and IPEDS, Winter 2009–10 and Spring 2013 through Spring 2015, Human Resources component, Salaries section. (This table was prepared November 2015.)

Table 316.30. Average salary of full-time instructional faculty on 9-month contracts in degree-granting postsecondary institutions, by control and level of institution and state or jurisdiction: 2014–15

[In current dollars]

State or jurisdiction	All institutions	Public institutions: Total	Public: 4-year institutions: Total	Public: 4-year: Doctoral[1]	Public: 4-year: Master's[2]	Public: 4-year: Other	Public: 2-year	Nonprofit institutions: Total	Nonprofit: 4-year institutions: Total	Nonprofit: 4-year: Doctoral[1]	Nonprofit: 4-year: Master's[2]	Nonprofit: 4-year: Other	Nonprofit: 2-year	For-profit institutions
1	2	3	4	5	6	7	8	9	10	11	12	13	14	15
United States	**$80,203**	**$76,963**	**$81,527**	**$87,174**	**$71,467**	**$63,020**	**$64,304**	**$88,246**	**$88,661**	**$103,587**	**$70,912**	**$70,023**	**$24,824**	**$49,948**
Alabama	68,645	69,968	76,223	83,107	62,522	68,764	53,185	61,408	61,408	75,302	49,298	49,145	†	‡
Alaska	77,679	78,727	78,905	82,390	76,662	†	65,616	51,007	50,774	†	52,329	‡	‡	†
Arizona	81,138	82,568	85,269	86,600	74,523	51,909	75,872	64,203	64,203	†	45,348	76,909	†	49,935
Arkansas	58,886	59,092	64,240	68,787	53,784	59,516	45,035	57,945	58,217	65,248	59,985	53,757	28,193	17,894
California	94,099	90,833	97,637	109,686	76,502	74,420	82,453	106,818	106,818	116,505	83,693	92,586	†	54,712
Colorado	76,469	75,171	79,544	84,995	61,192	71,223	51,598	86,354	86,354	89,116	83,643	69,109	†	30,609
Connecticut	99,655	92,615	98,488	109,408	87,202	†	74,805	107,143	107,143	114,011	94,278	84,580	†	49,737
Delaware	94,034	95,171	102,378	109,361	63,896	†	64,342	80,725	82,122	128,368	62,853	†	53,000	†
District of Columbia	92,005	80,551	80,551	123,188	76,597	†	†	92,727	103,862	104,751	51,645	‡	9,000	‡
Florida	75,397	74,363	75,053	85,139	76,996	59,322	51,986	79,499	79,499	92,234	69,812	61,861	†	56,733
Georgia	72,174	71,069	72,501	79,669	60,266	54,631	45,891	75,956	75,998	92,989	65,981	60,617	30,863	39,010
Hawaii	82,085	83,443	90,127	92,369	†	71,801	69,005	77,853	77,853	†	76,529	88,571	†	49,377
Idaho	61,190	61,651	64,716	66,090	†	50,302	49,331	56,110	56,110	†	52,445	59,458	†	†
Illinois	84,644	79,199	83,276	86,735	69,733	†	72,196	92,302	92,364	108,860	67,652	62,160	36,028	46,041
Indiana	77,163	76,090	81,412	87,618	64,221	53,980	44,347	79,330	79,330	95,068	61,653	70,125	†	†
Iowa	73,926	79,571	90,103	90,103	†	†	57,538	64,383	64,383	72,855	57,111	64,819	†	47,087
Kansas	65,541	67,908	74,892	79,536	60,086	56,169	51,418	50,635	50,802	†	54,753	43,759	46,291	†
Kentucky	64,467	65,720	71,297	72,730	60,627	†	50,656	59,322	59,322	64,680	52,918	61,166	†	68,328
Louisiana	65,488	61,820	66,665	75,204	55,128	47,303	43,592	81,613	81,613	88,661	57,219	58,552	†	36,642
Maine	76,590	72,552	78,621	85,336	†	62,107	54,915	82,337	82,862	67,610	55,207	93,557	56,734	†
Maryland	80,705	80,640	86,123	90,336	72,436	†	68,829	81,098	81,098	90,007	69,746	71,413	†	21,113
Massachusetts	101,455	83,509	90,595	99,032	77,208	†	63,881	110,387	110,392	126,523	84,792	87,530	‡	67,961
Michigan	84,815	87,787	89,732	91,803	75,245	62,673	78,100	66,150	66,150	78,789	64,200	64,873	†	23,494
Minnesota	75,158	75,527	81,908	99,372	71,079	60,454	64,939	74,326	74,326	75,957	67,698	76,284	†	‡
Mississippi	60,032	60,531	66,364	68,713	55,524	†	51,515	56,000	56,000	61,883	57,166	43,687	†	†
Missouri	72,164	67,911	72,000	79,725	61,380	49,419	54,513	79,628	79,704	97,441	61,226	54,053	66,019	51,351
Montana	62,092	66,078	68,488	72,750	59,817	54,772	48,706	42,229	53,232	†	52,803	53,505	13,986	†
Nebraska	71,189	73,056	77,212	82,632	63,375	†	58,941	65,214	65,359	81,555	56,845	55,590	47,847	†
Nevada	82,388	83,269	84,227	90,469	†	69,061	71,469	57,688	57,688	†	57,688	†	†	39,949
New Hampshire	90,149	85,546	92,225	102,219	77,492	88,434	62,811	96,854	96,854	130,855	67,569	70,786	†	†
New Jersey	99,818	96,904	105,652	108,600	98,428	†	73,046	107,288	107,288	124,832	81,703	69,498	†	29,459
New Mexico	65,704	65,449	71,606	77,205	60,744	47,903	51,364	83,973	83,973	†	83,973	†	†	64,025
New York	92,094	81,856	86,878	101,185	83,619	72,171	71,256	101,991	102,052	112,123	78,125	84,421	64,992	39,984
North Carolina	73,083	68,012	78,009	81,657	68,236	69,732	49,357	86,299	86,538	109,027	61,176	59,648	39,340	97,857
North Dakota	66,832	69,110	70,881	77,883	59,302	54,309	54,743	43,241	43,241	25,628	†	44,778	†	†
Ohio	75,089	76,531	80,326	82,726	57,948	64,634	61,880	72,067	72,067	79,140	65,822	72,160	†	42,872
Oklahoma	67,003	66,808	70,743	76,111	62,460	50,531	49,835	68,166	68,166	80,129	57,938	38,478	†	16,245
Oregon	74,060	73,916	76,698	80,253	59,525	65,674	68,435	75,072	75,072	77,993	65,679	79,946	†	50,525
Pennsylvania	86,531	83,650	87,326	94,343	83,884	70,986	63,666	89,859	90,319	102,248	73,434	79,000	47,351	45,270
Rhode Island	94,306	74,350	78,725	84,445	67,705	†	60,577	108,217	108,217	131,442	92,433	†	†	†
South Carolina	66,617	69,181	77,968	90,361	68,235	57,172	51,045	58,274	58,402	68,716	60,021	54,022	51,029	47,241
South Dakota	61,922	63,487	66,755	67,382	68,684	47,724	49,144	54,435	54,435	†	53,410	55,311	†	†
Tennessee	70,602	67,134	72,563	74,176	60,819	†	49,359	77,794	77,794	99,662	57,246	55,084	†	23,459
Texas	74,985	72,842	80,009	83,949	65,285	55,368	57,115	85,616	85,753	98,340	67,396	56,791	33,887	32,028
Utah	69,170	69,021	70,969	79,663	64,904	56,216	51,404	78,643	79,107	92,464	74,849	†	54,193	27,761
Vermont	77,274	78,025	78,025	88,044	56,627	56,242	†	76,579	76,579	†	80,045	54,741	†	†
Virginia	73,443	79,044	84,100	87,458	67,473	70,147	60,785	60,414	60,405	59,903	57,700	63,592	62,640	32,714
Washington	73,684	73,456	78,385	90,704	75,618	56,149	57,082	74,654	74,684	81,483	62,626	69,977	‡	65,144
West Virginia	63,622	65,457	68,347	75,849	58,845	55,994	47,660	51,143	51,143	55,234	50,650	48,420	†	13,521
Wisconsin	71,756	72,881	74,883	85,416	61,487	92,876	68,325	67,481	67,481	76,060	62,526	60,178	†	‡
Wyoming	70,883	71,387	82,753	82,753	†	†	58,577	†	†	†	†	†	†	57,967
U.S. Service Academies	107,888	107,888	107,888	†	†	107,888	†	†	†	†	†	†	†	†
Other jurisdictions	**46,595**	**52,762**	**56,908**	**51,332**	**65,017**	**54,439**	**34,538**	**29,473**	**28,986**	**27,182**	**34,711**	**25,905**	**48,587**	**18,102**
American Samoa	32,891	32,891	32,891	†	†	32,891	†	†	†	†	†	†	†	†
Federated States of Micronesia	26,907	26,907	†	†	†	†	26,907	†	†	†	†	†	†	†
Guam	62,781	62,781	66,547	†	66,547	†	54,355	†	†	†	†	†	†	†
Marshall Islands	†	†	†	†	†	†	†	†	†	†	†	†	†	†
Northern Marianas	42,447	42,447	42,447	†	†	42,447	†	†	†	†	†	†	†	†
Palau	†	†	†	†	†	†	†	†	†	†	†	†	†	†
Puerto Rico	44,418	54,267	56,853	51,332	59,826	58,731	24,964	29,473	28,986	27,182	34,711	25,905	48,587	18,102
U.S. Virgin Islands	63,436	63,436	63,436	†	63,436	†	†	†	†	†	†	†	†	†

†Not applicable.
‡Reporting standards not met (too few cases).
[1]Institutions that awarded 20 or more doctor's degrees during the previous academic year.
[2]Institutions that awarded 20 or more master's degrees, but less than 20 doctor's degrees, during the previous academic year.

NOTE: Degree-granting institutions grant associate's or higher degrees and participate in Title IV federal financial aid programs. Data include imputations for nonrespondent institutions.
SOURCE: U.S. Department of Education, National Center for Education Statistics, Integrated Postsecondary Education Data System (IPEDS), Spring 2015, Human Resources component, Salaries section. (This table was prepared November 2015.)

Table 316.50. Average salary of full-time instructional faculty on 9-month contracts in 4-year degree-granting postsecondary institutions, by control and classification of institution, academic rank of faculty, and state or jurisdiction: 2014–15

[In current dollars]

State or jurisdiction	Public doctoral[1]			Public master's[2]			Nonprofit doctoral[1]			Nonprofit master's[2]		
	Professor	Associate professor	Assistant professor	Professor	Associate professor	Assistant professor	Professor	Associate professor	Assistant professor	Professor	Associate professor	Assistant professor
1	2	3	4	5	6	7	8	9	10	11	12	13
United States	**$121,703**	**$84,740**	**$73,284**	**$91,025**	**$73,921**	**$63,226**	**$149,557**	**$93,935**	**$77,580**	**$87,310**	**$71,700**	**$59,946**
Alabama	120,615	83,192	68,986	79,783	66,346	57,854	81,319	71,201	65,152	60,732	51,763	45,368
Alaska	106,721	84,932	68,928	105,035	81,494	67,505	†	†	†	58,050	56,843	44,961
Arizona	126,064	86,334	74,984	115,551	87,543	78,780	†	†	†	51,791	47,664	48,874
Arkansas	97,262	73,399	65,578	71,002	59,232	51,626	79,132	66,915	60,312	66,723	62,828	54,063
California	142,154	92,562	83,933	91,297	75,276	69,731	157,411	100,512	87,633	103,633	80,556	68,652
Colorado	117,632	87,687	76,391	78,027	64,025	56,725	128,979	90,316	79,512	112,079	80,535	64,560
Connecticut	148,152	99,675	80,479	102,625	83,564	67,297	165,781	89,769	80,293	130,117	92,286	76,681
Delaware	143,824	100,736	85,424	80,845	68,477	54,520	155,301	122,560	‡	74,623	66,564	54,545
District of Columbia	139,420	118,450	94,673	102,609	75,252	61,765	150,218	98,130	82,458	36,103	72,747	60,420
Florida	117,432	82,969	73,912	124,213	85,380	64,999	128,360	87,161	73,392	90,741	74,565	61,071
Georgia	112,413	80,098	68,660	77,113	63,917	56,475	132,761	86,126	70,273	74,930	61,264	52,162
Hawaii	119,253	88,987	77,610	†	†	†	†	†	†	87,800	84,756	69,679
Idaho	87,371	69,222	60,053	†	†	†	†	†	†	60,802	53,785	47,362
Illinois	124,118	85,525	78,561	95,041	74,793	64,737	163,584	95,456	84,638	80,989	69,352	58,509
Indiana	122,173	86,048	74,633	87,760	68,879	60,379	140,001	89,521	73,492	75,705	62,929	53,522
Iowa	121,109	86,190	76,458	†	†	†	92,784	71,310	60,714	68,220	58,029	53,156
Kansas	112,453	78,007	67,283	75,776	61,185	59,308	†	†	†	63,695	55,788	50,433
Kentucky	102,581	73,032	64,063	79,776	64,925	55,947	78,398	62,766	57,100	62,049	54,261	47,098
Louisiana	101,360	74,834	68,614	72,796	60,623	50,318	126,654	84,581	72,855	62,121	57,053	54,270
Maine	106,550	82,239	63,696	†	†	†	87,972	75,778	68,184	70,834	56,707	49,421
Maryland	124,781	91,513	91,100	92,029	74,697	67,197	135,363	87,039	77,875	86,981	70,706	60,693
Massachusetts	133,659	98,527	82,800	91,564	73,805	64,881	174,766	109,314	93,231	100,709	86,905	69,213
Michigan	124,805	87,566	73,733	92,142	79,195	64,653	100,525	78,665	64,547	74,399	62,698	57,392
Minnesota	131,933	92,060	80,948	84,943	71,137	61,134	98,170	76,181	61,338	78,412	66,723	58,819
Mississippi	96,772	74,846	67,232	68,398	57,782	53,741	74,703	68,787	55,750	73,171	58,734	55,353
Missouri	105,730	76,051	65,098	77,630	62,921	53,511	140,395	88,772	76,671	76,471	63,630	52,065
Montana	90,218	71,308	66,387	75,976	68,391	56,534	†	†	†	60,999	51,484	48,140
Nebraska	109,128	82,087	73,136	79,565	63,360	52,888	103,301	81,448	67,633	65,378	57,006	51,870
Nevada	121,793	88,460	71,075	†	†	†	†	†	†	73,157	66,686	51,840
New Hampshire	123,880	95,734	78,792	90,844	75,680	62,512	164,481	106,458	74,330	82,556	69,743	59,140
New Jersey	147,764	101,896	80,693	122,407	97,032	79,822	178,675	97,242	87,567	100,705	85,612	67,347
New Mexico	102,364	75,590	68,533	74,373	62,966	54,569	†	†	†	†	†	†
New York	135,330	94,964	79,050	106,808	82,102	70,356	158,765	101,492	83,859	96,081	76,983	66,643
North Carolina	117,789	80,958	71,797	88,449	69,808	63,170	158,316	95,485	78,073	75,100	63,116	57,228
North Dakota	106,104	81,431	67,075	79,176	64,920	54,363	†	‡	21,301	†	†	†
Ohio	113,660	81,341	70,251	73,059	63,424	53,601	110,879	76,411	65,410	78,643	67,367	56,313
Oklahoma	107,969	75,966	67,373	79,561	66,917	56,726	101,123	73,340	71,717	68,340	59,655	52,044
Oregon	113,524	85,167	75,019	75,338	60,433	49,559	100,720	76,942	63,248	76,544	70,346	58,967
Pennsylvania	136,477	93,478	72,799	108,525	87,534	70,462	148,347	94,417	81,269	93,412	74,065	62,525
Rhode Island	108,353	80,039	73,127	77,387	66,023	57,152	166,274	110,863	91,739	119,124	92,546	74,579
South Carolina	126,492	88,590	79,129	86,671	69,649	60,965	72,514	66,605	64,249	74,406	59,739	53,205
South Dakota	90,489	71,132	65,096	85,549	72,718	62,415	†	†	†	59,895	56,298	51,026
Tennessee	100,290	75,048	63,851	74,904	62,550	54,409	138,351	89,852	74,172	71,204	56,747	49,844
Texas	122,683	84,319	72,045	88,089	72,689	62,599	134,060	91,986	80,810	84,754	69,161	58,326
Utah	105,748	77,010	66,084	80,725	66,964	59,726	117,391	85,497	70,580	90,182	75,885	60,473
Vermont	118,736	88,571	72,597	70,723	52,775	44,060	†	†	†	101,829	75,967	67,687
Virginia	123,255	84,990	71,802	86,755	70,775	61,183	113,154	81,654	44,778	71,505	58,095	50,246
Washington	120,986	88,680	82,968	94,250	79,908	73,376	110,196	82,424	66,804	79,341	65,816	58,715
West Virginia	99,242	76,987	65,455	70,123	62,826	53,397	67,180	58,505	52,903	65,009	54,346	45,668
Wisconsin	110,888	79,077	72,873	74,227	62,742	60,252	103,884	77,330	67,402	76,069	64,534	55,592
Wyoming	112,269	79,174	72,412	†	†	†	†	†	†	†	†	†
U.S. Service Academies	†	†	†	†	†	†	†	†	†	†	†	†
Other jurisdictions	**‡**	**‡**	**53,510**	**84,892**	**68,061**	**52,247**	**†**	**†**	**‡**	**†**	**†**	**38,771**
American Samoa	†	†	†	†	†	†	†	†	†	†	†	†
Federated States of Micronesia	†	†	†	†	†	†	†	†	†	†	†	†
Guam	†	†	†	89,059	70,570	54,299	†	†	†	†	†	†
Marshall Islands	†	†	†	†	†	†	†	†	†	†	†	†
Northern Marianas	†	†	†	†	†	†	†	†	†	†	†	†
Palau	†	†	†	†	†	†	†	†	†	†	†	†
Puerto Rico	‡	‡	53,510	71,880	†	47,771	†	†	‡	†	†	38,771
U.S. Virgin Islands	†	†	†	81,906	64,446	50,873	†	†	†	†	†	†

†Not applicable.
‡Reporting standards not met (too few cases).
[1]Institutions that awarded 20 or more doctor's degrees during the previous academic year.
[2]Institutions that awarded 20 or more master's degrees, but less than 20 doctor's degrees, during the previous academic year.

NOTE: Degree-granting institutions grant associate's or higher degrees and participate in Title IV federal financial aid programs. Data include imputations for nonrespondent institutions.
SOURCE: U.S. Department of Education, National Center for Education Statistics, Integrated Postsecondary Education Data System (IPEDS), Spring 2015, Human Resources component, Salaries section. (This table was prepared November 2015.)

Table 316.80. Percentage of degree-granting postsecondary institutions with a tenure system and of full-time faculty with tenure at these institutions, by control and level of institution and selected characteristics of faculty: Selected years, 1993–94 through 2013–14

Selected characteristic and academic year	All institutions	Public institutions						Nonprofit institutions						For-profit institutions
		Total	4-year institutions				2-year	Total	4-year institutions				2-year	
			Total	Doctoral[1]	Master's[2]	Other			Total	Doctoral[1]	Master's[2]	Other		
1	2	3	4	5	6	7	8	9	10	11	12	13	14	15
Percent of institutions with a tenure system														
1993–94	62.6	73.6	92.6	100.0	98.3	76.4	62.1	62.0	66.3	90.5	76.5	58.3	26.1	7.8
1999–2000	55.0	72.8	94.6	100.0	95.5	86.3	60.3	59.0	63.4	81.2	72.6	54.9	14.0	4.0
2003–04	52.7	71.3	90.9	100.0	98.0	70.9	59.4	57.9	61.2	86.6	71.6	49.5	14.4	3.6
2005–06	50.9	71.5	90.9	99.5	98.0	71.6	59.4	56.5	59.8	85.1	67.1	49.2	11.5	2.0
2007–08	49.5	70.7	91.0	100.0	98.6	71.6	57.4	57.5	60.2	87.8	66.0	49.0	13.0	1.4
2009–10	47.8	71.2	90.9	99.6	98.5	71.3	57.7	57.1	59.5	80.6	64.4	44.6	12.9	1.5
2011–12	45.3	71.6	90.8	99.6	98.5	70.5	57.8	55.6	58.6	79.5	64.0	42.7	8.0	1.3
2013–14	49.3	74.6	95.8	99.6	98.1	86.6	58.9	59.7	61.8	79.6	63.2	49.0	12.5	1.2
Percent of faculty with tenure at institutions with a tenure system														
All full-time faculty (instruction, research, and public service)														
1993–94	56.2	58.9	56.3	54.5	60.5	51.1	69.9	49.5	49.5	47.6	51.8	50.4	47.9	33.8
1999–2000	53.7	55.9	53.2	50.4	59.1	54.7	67.7	48.2	48.1	43.4	52.3	53.5	59.7	77.4
2003–04	50.4	53.0	50.2	48.9	52.9	51.2	65.2	44.6	44.6	40.1	48.7	51.9	47.7	69.2
2005–06	49.6	51.5	48.7	47.2	52.3	49.1	64.1	45.1	45.1	40.7	49.1	52.5	45.2	69.3
2007–08	48.8	50.5	47.8	46.1	51.9	49.1	63.6	44.7	44.7	40.1	49.8	52.7	41.3	51.3
2009–10	48.7	50.6	47.8	45.7	53.6	51.3	64.1	44.3	44.3	40.4	50.5	54.1	38.5	51.0
2011–12	48.5	50.7	48.0	45.8	54.3	53.4	64.7	43.7	43.7	39.7	50.7	54.3	31.4	31.0
2013–14	48.3	50.4	47.3	44.9	55.4	52.2	67.2	43.8	43.8	39.5	51.7	55.9	31.5	19.8
Full-time instructional faculty in 2013–14														
Total	50.7	52.8	50.0	48.1	55.6	53.5	67.2	46.3	46.4	42.9	51.7	55.9	30.5	19.8
Male	56.6	58.5	56.8	55.5	61.9	56.2	69.6	52.7	52.8	49.9	57.2	61.9	36.7	21.7
Female	43.2	45.7	40.8	37.4	48.5	50.6	65.1	37.7	37.7	32.7	45.4	48.7	26.4	18.3
Professor	90.7	91.9	91.7	90.2	97.8	91.8	93.5	88.4	88.4	86.1	92.1	95.4	79.2	61.3
Male	91.1	92.3	92.1	90.8	97.9	92.6	94.4	88.8	88.8	87.0	91.8	95.4	91.7	64.4
Female	89.9	91.1	90.8	88.3	97.6	90.6	92.7	87.4	87.4	83.6	92.6	95.3	66.7	55.9
Associate professor	77.1	80.6	80.7	77.5	90.2	85.8	79.3	70.4	70.4	63.8	78.6	86.2	42.2	22.9
Male	77.2	80.9	81.0	78.2	90.1	86.1	80.4	70.1	70.1	64.1	78.8	84.7	44.4	20.0
Female	76.8	80.1	80.3	76.6	90.3	85.4	78.4	70.7	70.8	63.4	78.5	87.9	41.7	25.0
Assistant professor	6.8	8.7	5.2	2.0	11.6	23.9	45.2	3.4	3.4	2.1	6.7	4.5	11.1	‡
Male	6.5	8.2	5.0	2.0	11.6	23.5	48.1	3.4	3.4	2.2	6.9	4.7	11.5	‡
Female	7.1	9.3	5.4	2.1	11.6	24.3	43.0	3.3	3.3	1.9	6.6	4.3	10.8	†
Instructor	28.4	34.4	2.1	0.9	1.8	11.6	61.7	0.5	0.5	0.4	0.4	1.6	9.1	66.7
Lecturer	1.6	2.0	1.3	0.7	2.9	4.6	20.9	0.3	0.3	0.1	1.0	1.4	†	†
No academic rank	32.3	41.1	20.4	1.0	7.5	64.0	69.1	9.6	9.5	1.2	19.7	42.3	37.1	11.7

†Not applicable.
‡Reporting standards not met (too few cases).
[1]Institutions that awarded 20 or more doctor's degrees during the previous academic year.
[2]Institutions that awarded 20 or more master's degrees, but less than 20 doctor's degrees, during the previous academic year.

NOTE: Degree-granting institutions grant associate's or higher degrees and participate in Title IV federal financial aid programs. Data include imputations for nonrespondent institutions. Some data have been revised from previously published figures.
SOURCE: U.S. Department of Education, National Center for Education Statistics, Integrated Postsecondary Education Data System (IPEDS), "Fall Staff Survey" (IPEDS-S:93–99); and IPEDS Winter 2003–04 through Winter 2011–12 and Spring 2014, Human Resources component, Fall Staff section. (This table was prepared April 2016.)

Table 313.10. Fall enrollment, degrees conferred, and expenditures in degree-granting historically Black colleges and universities, by institution: 2013, 2014, and 2013–14

Institution	State	Level and control[1]	Total enrollment, fall 2013	Enrollment, fall 2014: Total	Enrollment, fall 2014: Black enrollment	Full-time-equivalent enrollment, fall 2014	Degrees conferred, 2013–14: Associate's	Degrees conferred, 2013–14: Bachelor's	Degrees conferred, 2013–14: Master's	Degrees conferred, 2013–14: Doctor's[2]	Total expenditures, 2013–14 (in thousands of current dollars)[3]
1	2	3	4	5	6	7	8	9	10	11	12
Total	**†**	**†**	**303,167**	**294,316**	**231,888**	**254,589**	**4,224**	**33,700**	**7,845**	**2,423**	**$7,619,613**
Alabama A&M University[4]	AL	1	5,020	5,333	4,913	4,925	†	472	223	7	135,120
Alabama State University	AL	1	6,075	5,519	5,024	5,003	†	529	141	55	157,118
Bishop State Community College	AL	2	3,896	3,320	2,123	2,362	286	†	†	†	36,282
Concordia College, Alabama	AL	3	600	546	503	525	29	34	†	†	13,032
Gadsden State Community College	AL	2	5,797	5,289	1,070	3,603	571	†	†	†	54,148
H. Councill Trenholm State Technical College	AL	2	1,351	1,338	786	902	200	†	†	†	18,502
J. F. Drake State Community and Technical College	AL	2	1,383	1,062	608	719	98	†	†	†	13,819
Lawson State Community College, Birmingham Campus	AL	2	3,028	3,090	2,489	2,215	226	†	†	†	35,315
Miles College	AL	3	1,666	1,782	1,736	1,740	†	198	†	†	27,892
Oakwood University	AL	3	1,903	1,939	1,690	1,851	1	321	14	†	51,671
Selma University	AL	3	611	558	551	483	0	23	10	†	2,953
Shelton State Community College	AL	2	5,068	4,978	1,807	3,204	365	†	†	†	45,383
Stillman College	AL	3	863	1,056	955	988	†	114	†	†	20,939
Talladega College	AL	3	932	879	758	802	†	81	†	†	16,379
Tuskegee University[4]	AL	3	3,118	3,103	2,953	3,017	†	327	50	49	152,573
Arkansas Baptist College	AR	3	1,027	899	847	836	82	45	†	†	17,017
Philander Smith College	AR	3	556	567	512	539	†	108	†	†	15,637
Shorter College	AR	4	330	403	395	349	11	†	†	†	2,380
University of Arkansas at Pine Bluff[4]	AR	1	2,615	2,513	2,301	2,337	0	429	26	0	73,048
Delaware State University[4]	DE	1	4,336	4,397	2,974	4,022	†	550	130	6	124,981
Howard University	DC	3	10,297	10,265	8,812	9,589	†	1,033	339	501	848,736
University of the District of Columbia[4]	DC	1	5,011	4,803	3,514	3,195	263	410	86	†	134,230
Bethune-Cookman University	FL	3	3,787	4,044	3,662	3,893	†	480	29	†	76,078
Edward Waters College	FL	3	862	929	838	906	†	106	†	†	22,368
Florida A&M University[4]	FL	1	10,743	10,241	8,956	9,332	113	1,560	277	335	294,167
Florida Memorial University	FL	3	1,560	1,528	1,233	1,470	†	207	19	†	36,310
Albany State University	GA	1	4,260	3,910	3,543	3,344	†	492	108	†	68,270
Clark Atlanta University	GA	3	3,458	3,485	3,306	3,239	†	459	183	42	85,291
Fort Valley State University[4]	GA	1	3,180	2,594	2,375	2,290	†	431	86	†	70,767
Interdenominational Theological Center	GA	3	562	306	295	211	†	†	99	5	8,808
Morehouse College	GA	3	2,170	2,109	2,022	2,045	†	339	†	†	87,058
Morehouse School of Medicine	GA	3	372	398	287	395	†	†	26	44	138,225
Paine College	GA	3	924	848	787	809	†	108	†	†	24,429
Savannah State University	GA	1	4,772	4,915	4,336	4,549	5	442	74	†	95,218
Spelman College	GA	3	2,129	2,135	2,026	2,097	†	464	†	†	86,366
Kentucky State University[4]	KY	1	2,533	1,895	1,137	1,626	49	272	49	†	73,682
Dillard University	LA	3	1,183	1,200	1,155	1,162	†	186	†	†	43,865
Grambling State University	LA	1	5,071	4,504	4,120	3,970	13	697	251	4	97,172
Southern University and A&M College[4]	LA	1	6,777	6,330	5,895	5,499	†	757	272	13	142,446
Southern University at New Orleans	LA	1	2,292	2,103	2,021	1,702	14	303	183	†	43,819
Southern University at Shreveport	LA	2	3,018	2,952	2,617	2,350	273	†	†	†	33,699
Xavier University of Louisiana	LA	3	3,121	2,976	2,116	2,869	†	322	58	159	101,151
Bowie State University	MD	1	5,561	5,695	4,844	4,766	†	741	278	7	98,430
Coppin State College	MD	1	3,383	3,133	2,626	2,562	†	477	83	0	76,693
Morgan State University	MD	1	7,546	7,698	6,320	6,769	†	922	227	52	203,169
University of Maryland, Eastern Shore[4]	MD	1	4,220	4,279	2,891	3,884	†	585	68	101	109,359
Alcorn State University[4]	MS	1	3,848	3,639	3,386	3,083	54	404	128	†	85,187
Coahoma Community College	MS	2	2,073	2,045	1,955	1,877	259	†	†	†	34,533
Hinds Community College, Utica Campus	MS	2	717	711	674	673	75	†	†	†	—
Jackson State University	MS	1	9,134	9,508	8,491	7,843	†	1,093	424	71	193,983
Mississippi Valley State University	MS	1	2,203	2,222	2,111	1,957	†	386	70	†	55,674
Rust College	MS	3	922	963	924	930	5	103	†	†	16,662
Tougaloo College	MS	3	878	900	887	883	5	153	†	†	23,576

See notes at end of table.

Table 313.10. Fall enrollment, degrees conferred, and expenditures in degree-granting historically Black colleges and universities, by institution: 2013, 2014, and 2013–14—Continued

Institution	State	Level and control[1]	Total enroll-ment, fall 2013	Enrollment, fall 2014		Full-time-equivalent enrollment, fall 2014	Degrees conferred, 2013–14				Total expenditures, 2013–14 (in thousands of current dollars)[3]
				Total	Black enrollment		Associate's	Bachelor's	Master's	Doctor's[2]	
1	2	3	4	5	6	7	8	9	10	11	12
Harris-Stowe State University	MO	1	1,298	1,280	1,111	1,095	†	132	†	†	26,168
Lincoln University[4]	MO	1	3,043	3,117	1,298	2,500	80	328	52	†	51,129
Bennett College	NC	3	680	633	595	580	†	105	†	†	18,798
Elizabeth City State University	NC	1	2,421	1,867	1,494	1,727	†	488	55	†	74,329
Fayetteville State University	NC	1	6,179	5,899	3,992	4,912	†	965	193	7	109,956
Johnson C. Smith University	NC	3	1,387	1,402	1,212	1,367	†	248	†	†	44,258
Livingstone College	NC	3	1,175	1,301	1,274	1,296	0	154	†	†	28,663
North Carolina A&T State University[4]	NC	1	10,561	10,725	8,893	9,862	†	1,394	470	43	256,028
North Carolina Central University	NC	1	8,093	7,687	6,073	6,790	†	1,054	427	141	190,426
Saint Augustine's College	NC	3	1,299	1,016	973	1,007	†	226	†	†	34,541
Shaw University	NC	3	2,062	1,802	1,716	1,678	1	286	18	†	47,110
Winston-Salem State University	NC	1	5,399	5,220	3,741	4,707	†	1,371	134	25	142,168
Central State University	OH	1	2,068	1,751	1,686	1,646	†	293	6	†	57,632
Wilberforce University	OH	3	479	387	373	376	†	103	5	†	14,813
Langston University[4]	OK	1	2,533	2,482	2,049	2,185	12	294	110	22	63,156
Cheyney University of Pennsylvania	PA	1	1,212	1,022	924	974	†	150	10	†	46,512
Lincoln University	PA	1	1,963	1,819	1,649	1,668	†	279	160	†	52,246
Allen University	SC	3	651	660	652	649	†	81	†	†	13,369
Benedict College	SC	3	2,512	2,444	2,420	2,420	†	309	†	†	56,967
Claflin College	SC	3	1,884	1,866	1,693	1,825	†	371	25	†	43,663
Clinton College	SC	3	185	194	185	189	26	5	†	†	3,190
Denmark Technical College	SC	2	1,838	1,678	1,615	1,508	82	†	†	†	18,963
Morris College	SC	3	824	780	762	774	†	152	†	†	20,107
South Carolina State University[4]	SC	1	3,463	3,331	3,154	3,002	†	567	112	19	105,507
Voorhees College	SC	3	536	468	461	458	†	117	†	†	16,743
Fisk University	TN	3	646	772	722	749	†	80	6	†	25,817
Lane College	TN	3	1,554	1,262	1,262	1,254	†	239	†	†	24,730
Le Moyne-Owen College	TN	3	1,023	1,006	987	937	†	127	†	†	17,349
Meharry Medical College	TN	3	801	802	645	802	†	†	69	150	132,469
Tennessee State University[4]	TN	1	8,883	9,027	5,798	7,490	104	807	476	85	184,472
Huston-Tillotson University	TX	3	973	1,031	731	967	†	125	†	†	18,737
Jarvis Christian College	TX	3	609	763	623	725	†	65	†	†	15,591
Paul Quinn College	TX	3	243	273	227	265	†	21	†	†	8,124
Prairie View A&M University[4]	TX	1	8,283	8,429	7,236	7,475	†	993	447	22	191,075
Saint Philip's College	TX	2	10,238	10,514	1,119	4,607	511	†	†	†	72,559
Southwestern Christian College	TX	3	172	164	128	157	30	0	†	†	6,307
Texas College	TX	3	971	813	696	792	21	80	†	†	11,543
Texas Southern University	TX	1	8,703	9,233	7,258	8,131	†	867	388	329	199,075
Wiley College	TX	3	1,392	1,351	1,146	1,295	5	176	†	†	23,862
Hampton University	VA	3	4,622	4,393	3,921	4,106	0	710	139	99	151,266
Norfolk State University	VA	1	6,728	6,027	5,163	5,327	95	857	184	9	149,913
Virginia State University[4]	VA	1	5,763	5,025	4,699	4,717	3	793	151	8	138,238
Virginia Union University	VA	3	1,749	1,715	1,669	1,680	†	229	119	9	32,780
Virginia University of Lynchburg	VA	3	582	324	319	249	82	24	11	4	5,377
Bluefield State College	WV	1	1,747	1,563	156	1,377	117	240	†	†	23,364
West Virginia State University[4]	WV	1	2,677	2,884	461	2,343	†	418	17	†	48,268
University of the Virgin Islands[4]	VI	1	2,321	2,280	1,770	1,758	58	214	50	†	78,643

—Not available.
†Not applicable.
[1]1 = 4-year public; 2 = 2-year public; 3 = 4-year private nonprofit; and 4 = 2-year private nonprofit.
[2]Includes Ph.D., Ed.D., and comparable degrees at the doctoral level, as well as such degrees as M.D., D.D.S., and law degrees that were formerly classified as first-professional degrees.
[3]Includes private and some public institutions reporting total expenses and deductions under Financial Accounting Standards Board (FASB) reporting standards and public institutions reporting total expenses and deductions under Governmental Accounting Standards Board (GASB) 34/35 reporting standards.
[4]Land-grant institution.

NOTE: Degree-granting institutions grant associate's or higher degrees and participate in Title IV federal financial aid programs. Excludes historically Black colleges and universities that are not participating in Title IV programs. Historically Black colleges and universities are degree-granting institutions established prior to 1964 with the principal mission of educating Black Americans. Federal regulations, 20 U.S. Code, Section 1061 (2), allow for certain exceptions to the founding date. Totals include persons of other racial/ethnic groups not separately identified. Detail may not sum to totals because of rounding.
SOURCE: U.S. Department of Education, National Center for Education Statistics, Integrated Postsecondary Education Data System (IPEDS), Fall 2014, Completions component; Spring 2014 and Spring 2015, Fall Enrollment component; and Spring 2015, Finance component. (This table was prepared March 2016.)

Table 313.20. Fall enrollment in degree-granting historically Black colleges and universities, by sex of student and level and control of institution: Selected years, 1976 through 2014

Year	Total enrollment	Males	Females	4-year	2-year	Public			Private		
						Total	4-year	2-year	Total	4-year	2-year
1	2	3	4	5	6	7	8	9	10	11	12
	All students										
1976	222,613	104,669	117,944	206,676	15,937	156,836	143,528	13,308	65,777	63,148	2,629
1980	233,557	106,387	127,170	218,009	15,548	168,217	155,085	13,132	65,340	62,924	2,416
1982	228,371	104,897	123,474	212,017	16,354	165,871	151,472	14,399	62,500	60,545	1,955
1984	227,519	102,823	124,696	212,844	14,675	164,116	151,289	12,827	63,403	61,555	1,848
1986	223,275	97,523	125,752	207,231	16,044	162,048	147,631	14,417	61,227	59,600	1,627
1988	239,755	100,561	139,194	223,250	16,505	173,672	158,606	15,066	66,083	64,644	1,439
1990	257,152	105,157	151,995	240,497	16,655	187,046	171,969	15,077	70,106	68,528	1,578
1991	269,335	110,442	158,893	252,093	17,242	197,847	182,204	15,643	71,488	69,889	1,599
1992	279,541	114,622	164,919	261,089	18,452	204,966	188,143	16,823	74,575	72,946	1,629
1993	282,856	116,397	166,459	262,430	20,426	208,197	189,032	19,165	74,659	73,398	1,261
1994	280,071	114,006	166,065	259,997	20,074	206,520	187,735	18,785	73,551	72,262	1,289
1995	278,725	112,637	166,088	259,409	19,316	204,726	186,278	18,448	73,999	73,131	868
1996	273,018	109,498	163,520	253,654	19,364	200,569	182,063	18,506	72,449	71,591	858
1997	269,167	106,865	162,302	248,860	20,307	194,674	175,297	19,377	74,493	73,563	930
1998	273,472	108,752	164,720	248,931	24,541	198,603	174,776	23,827	74,869	74,155	714
1999	274,321	108,301	166,020	249,156	25,165	199,826	175,364	24,462	74,495	73,792	703
2000	275,680	108,164	167,516	250,710	24,970	199,725	175,404	24,321	75,955	75,306	649
2001	289,985	112,874	177,111	260,547	29,438	210,083	181,346	28,737	79,902	79,201	701
2002	299,041	115,466	183,575	269,020	30,021	218,433	189,183	29,250	80,608	79,837	771
2003	306,727	117,795	188,932	274,326	32,401	228,096	196,077	32,019	78,631	78,249	382
2004	308,939	118,129	190,810	276,136	32,803	231,179	198,810	32,369	77,760	77,326	434
2005	311,768	120,023	191,745	272,666	39,102	235,875	197,200	38,675	75,893	75,466	427
2006	308,774	118,865	189,909	272,770	36,004	234,505	198,676	35,829	74,269	74,094	175
2007	306,515	118,640	187,875	270,915	35,600	233,807	198,300	35,507	72,708	72,615	93
2008	313,491	121,873	191,618	274,568	38,923	235,824	197,025	38,799	77,667	77,543	124
2009	322,860	125,728	197,132	280,133	42,727	246,595	204,016	42,579	76,265	76,117	148
2010	326,614	127,437	199,177	283,099	43,515	249,146	205,774	43,372	77,468	77,325	143
2011	323,648	126,160	197,488	281,150	42,498	246,685	204,363	42,322	76,963	76,787	176
2012	312,438	121,719	190,719	273,033	39,405	237,782	198,568	39,214	74,656	74,465	191
2013	303,167	119,291	183,876	264,430	38,737	230,325	191,918	38,407	72,842	72,512	330
2014	294,316	115,837	178,479	256,936	37,380	222,876	185,899	36,977	71,440	71,037	403
	Black students										
1976	190,305	84,492	105,813	179,848	10,457	129,770	121,851	7,919	60,535	57,997	2,538
1980	190,989	81,818	109,171	181,237	9,752	131,661	124,236	7,425	59,328	57,001	2,327
1982	182,639	78,874	103,765	171,942	10,697	126,368	117,562	8,806	56,271	54,380	1,891
1984	180,803	76,819	103,984	171,401	9,402	124,445	116,845	7,600	56,358	54,556	1,802
1986	178,628	74,276	104,352	167,971	10,657	123,555	114,502	9,053	55,073	53,469	1,604
1988	194,151	78,268	115,883	183,402	10,749	133,786	124,438	9,348	60,365	58,964	1,401
1990	208,682	82,897	125,785	198,237	10,445	144,204	134,924	9,280	64,478	63,313	1,165
1991	218,366	87,380	130,986	207,449	10,917	152,864	143,411	9,453	65,502	64,038	1,464
1992	228,963	91,949	137,014	217,614	11,349	159,585	149,754	9,831	69,378	67,860	1,518
1993	231,198	93,110	138,088	219,431	11,767	161,444	150,867	10,577	69,754	68,564	1,190
1994	230,162	91,908	138,254	218,565	11,597	161,098	150,682	10,416	69,064	67,883	1,181
1995	229,418	91,132	138,286	218,379	11,039	159,925	149,661	10,264	69,493	68,718	775
1996	224,201	88,306	135,895	213,309	10,892	156,851	146,753	10,098	67,350	66,556	794
1997	222,331	86,641	135,690	210,741	11,590	153,039	142,326	10,713	69,292	68,415	877
1998	223,745	87,163	136,582	211,822	11,923	154,244	142,985	11,259	69,501	68,837	664
1999	226,592	87,987	138,605	213,779	12,813	156,292	144,166	12,126	70,300	69,613	687
2000	227,239	87,319	139,920	215,172	12,067	156,706	145,277	11,429	70,533	69,895	638
2001	238,638	90,718	147,920	224,417	14,221	164,354	150,831	13,523	74,284	73,586	698
2002	247,292	93,538	153,754	231,834	15,458	172,203	157,507	14,696	75,089	74,327	762
2003	253,257	95,703	157,554	236,753	16,504	180,104	163,977	16,127	73,153	72,776	377
2004	257,545	96,750	160,795	241,030	16,515	184,708	168,619	16,089	72,837	72,411	426
2005	256,584	96,891	159,693	238,030	18,554	186,047	167,916	18,131	70,537	70,114	423
2006	255,150	96,508	158,642	238,446	16,704	185,894	169,365	16,529	69,256	69,081	175
2007	253,415	96,313	157,102	236,885	16,530	185,344	168,906	16,438	68,071	67,979	92
2008	258,403	98,634	159,769	240,133	18,270	186,446	168,299	18,147	71,957	71,834	123
2009	264,092	100,590	163,502	243,956	20,136	194,088	174,099	19,989	70,004	69,857	147
2010	265,908	101,605	164,303	245,158	20,750	193,840	173,233	20,607	72,068	71,925	143
2011	263,435	100,526	162,909	242,881	20,554	192,042	171,664	20,378	71,393	71,217	176
2012	251,527	96,079	155,448	232,897	18,630	183,018	164,578	18,440	68,509	68,319	190
2013	241,476	92,454	149,022	223,481	17,995	175,287	157,619	17,668	66,189	65,862	327
2014	231,888	88,469	143,419	214,630	17,258	167,246	150,383	16,863	64,642	64,247	395

NOTE: Historically Black colleges and universities are degree-granting institutions established prior to 1964 with the principal mission of educating Black Americans. Federal regulations, 20 U.S. Code, Section 1061 (2), allow for certain exceptions to the founding date. Data through 1995 are for institutions of higher education, while later data are for degree-granting institutions. Degree-granting institutions grant associate's or higher degrees and participate in Title IV federal financial aid programs. The degree-granting classification is very similar to the earlier higher education classification, but it includes more 2-year colleges and excludes a few higher education institutions that did not grant degrees. Some data have been revised from previously published figures.

SOURCE: U.S. Department of Education, National Center for Education Statistics, Higher Education General Information Survey (HEGIS), "Fall Enrollment in Colleges and Universities," 1976 through 1985 surveys; Integrated Postsecondary Education Data System (IPEDS), "Fall Enrollment Survey" (IPEDS-EF:86–99); and IPEDS Spring 2001 through Spring 2015, Fall Enrollment component. (This table was prepared March 2016.)

Table 313.30. Selected statistics on degree-granting historically Black colleges and universities, by control and level of institution: Selected years, 1990 through 2014

Selected statistics	Total	Public			Private		
		Total	4-year	2-year	Total	4-year	2-year
1	2	3	4	5	6	7	8
Number of institutions, fall 2014	**100**	**51**	**40**	**11**	**49**	**48**	**1**
Fall enrollment							
Total enrollment, fall 1990	257,152	187,046	171,969	15,077	70,106	68,528	1,578
Males	105,157	76,541	70,220	6,321	28,616	28,054	562
Males, Black	82,897	57,255	54,041	3,214	25,642	25,198	444
Females	151,995	110,505	101,749	8,756	41,490	40,474	1,016
Females, Black	125,785	86,949	80,883	6,066	38,836	38,115	721
Total enrollment, fall 2000	275,680	199,725	175,404	24,321	75,955	75,306	649
Males	108,164	78,186	68,322	9,864	29,978	29,771	207
Males, Black	87,319	60,029	56,017	4,012	27,290	27,085	205
Females	167,516	121,539	107,082	14,457	45,977	45,535	442
Females, Black	139,920	96,677	89,260	7,417	43,243	42,810	433
Total enrollment, fall 2010	326,614	249,146	205,774	43,372	77,468	77,325	143
Males	127,437	95,883	78,528	17,355	31,554	31,482	72
Males, Black	101,605	72,629	65,512	7,117	28,976	28,904	72
Females	199,177	153,263	127,246	26,017	45,914	45,843	71
Females, Black	164,303	121,211	107,721	13,490	43,092	43,021	71
Total enrollment, fall 2014	294,316	222,876	185,899	36,977	71,440	71,037	403
Males	115,837	86,571	71,147	15,424	29,266	29,142	124
Males, Black	88,469	62,428	56,178	6,250	26,041	25,919	122
Females	178,479	136,305	114,752	21,553	42,174	41,895	279
Females, Black	143,419	104,818	94,205	10,613	38,601	38,328	273
Full-time enrollment, fall 2014	231,002	164,824	147,352	17,472	66,178	65,865	313
Males	93,326	66,151	58,425	7,726	27,175	27,073	102
Females	137,676	98,673	88,927	9,746	39,003	38,792	211
Part-time enrollment, fall 2014	63,314	58,052	38,547	19,505	5,262	5,172	90
Males	22,511	20,420	12,722	7,698	2,091	2,069	22
Females	40,803	37,632	25,825	11,807	3,171	3,103	68
Earned degrees conferred, 2013–14							
Associate's	4,224	3,926	980	2,946	298	287	11
Males	1,438	1,285	224	1,061	153	149	4
Males, Black	651	511	107	404	140	136	4
Females	2,786	2,641	756	1,885	145	138	7
Females, Black	1,475	1,340	371	969	135	128	7
Bachelor's	33,700	24,456	24,456	†	9,244	9,244	†
Males	12,092	8,810	8,810	†	3,282	3,282	†
Males, Black	9,927	6,929	6,929	†	2,998	2,998	†
Females	21,608	15,646	15,646	†	5,962	5,962	†
Females, Black	17,955	12,484	12,484	†	5,471	5,471	†
Master's	7,845	6,626	6,626	†	1,219	1,219	†
Males	2,331	1,901	1,901	†	430	430	†
Males, Black	1,647	1,291	1,291	†	356	356	†
Females	5,514	4,725	4,725	†	789	789	†
Females, Black	4,019	3,349	3,349	†	670	670	†
Doctor's[1]	2,423	1,361	1,361	†	1,062	1,062	†
Males	999	580	580	†	419	419	†
Males, Black	563	273	273	†	290	290	†
Females	1,424	781	781	†	643	643	†
Females, Black	918	459	459	†	459	459	†
	In thousands of current dollars						
Financial statistics, 2013–14[2]							
Total revenue	$8,079,150	$5,075,176	$4,693,591	$381,585	$3,003,974	$3,001,508	$2,466
Student tuition and fees	1,825,772	959,451	914,934	44,517	866,321	864,494	1,827
Federal government[3]	2,033,532	1,258,853	1,092,307	166,546	774,679	774,586	93
State governments	1,900,539	1,832,727	1,708,812	123,915	67,812	67,812	0
Local governments	104,177	94,235	63,181	31,054	9,942	9,942	0
Private gifts and grants[4]	265,232	26,610	26,038	572	238,622	238,149	472
Investment return (gain or loss)	470,482	80,163	79,771	392	390,319	390,319	0
Auxiliary (essentially self-supporting) enterprises	868,553	529,742	523,507	6,235	338,811	338,738	74
Hospitals and other sources	610,864	293,395	285,040	8,355	317,469	317,469	0
Total expenditures	7,619,613	4,884,042	4,520,840	363,203	2,735,570	2,733,190	2,380
Instruction	1,914,052	1,330,125	1,210,706	119,419	583,927	583,560	367
Research	403,596	260,769	260,374	395	142,827	142,827	0
Academic support	522,481	373,829	350,680	23,149	148,653	148,496	157
Institutional support	1,093,096	618,368	564,598	53,771	474,728	474,091	636
Auxiliary (essentially self-supporting) enterprises	715,292	532,572	523,458	9,114	182,720	182,589	131
Other expenditures	2,971,095	1,768,379	1,611,024	157,356	1,202,716	1,201,627	1,089

†Not applicable.

[1]Includes Ph.D., Ed.D., and comparable degrees at the doctoral level, as well as such degrees as M.D., D.D.S., and law degrees that were formerly classified as first-professional degrees.

[2]Totals (column 2) of public and private institutions together are approximate because public and private nonprofit institutions fill out different survey forms with different accounting concepts.

[3]Includes independent operations.

[4]Includes contributions from affiliated entities.

NOTE: Degree-granting institutions grant associate's or higher degrees and participate in Title IV federal financial aid programs. Historically Black colleges and universities are degree-granting institutions established prior to 1964 with the principal mission of educating Black Americans. Federal regulations, 20 U.S. Code, Section 1061 (2), allow for certain exceptions to the founding date. Federal, state, and local governments revenue includes appropriations, grants, and contracts. Totals include persons of other racial/ethnic groups not separately identified. Detail may not sum to totals because of rounding.

SOURCE: U.S. Department of Education, National Center for Education Statistics, Integrated Postsecondary Education Data System (IPEDS), "Fall Enrollment Survey" (IPEDS-EF:90); IPEDS Spring 2001, Spring 2011, and Spring 2015, Fall Enrollment component; IPEDS Spring 2015, Finance component; and IPEDS Fall 2014, Completions component. (This table was prepared March 2016.)

Table 317.10. Degree-granting postsecondary institutions, by control and level of institution: Selected years, 1949–50 through 2014–15

Year	All institutions			Public			Private								
										Nonprofit			For-profit		
	Total	4-year	2-year	Total	4-year	2-year	Total	4-year, total	2-year, total	Total	4-year	2-year	Total	4-year	2-year
1	2	3	4	5	6	7	8	9	10	11	12	13	14	15	16
Excluding branch campuses															
1949–50	1,851	1,327	524	641	344	297	1,210	983	227	—	—	—	—	—	—
1959–60	2,004	1,422	582	695	367	328	1,309	1,055	254	—	—	—	—	—	—
1969–70	2,525	1,639	886	1,060	426	634	1,465	1,213	252	—	—	—	—	—	—
1970–71	2,556	1,665	891	1,089	435	654	1,467	1,230	237	—	—	—	—	—	—
1971–72	2,606	1,675	931	1,137	440	697	1,469	1,235	234	—	—	—	—	—	—
1972–73	2,665	1,701	964	1,182	449	733	1,483	1,252	231	—	—	—	—	—	—
1973–74	2,720	1,717	1,003	1,200	440	760	1,520	1,277	243	—	—	—	—	—	—
1974–75	2,747	1,744	1,003	1,214	447	767	1,533	1,297	236	—	—	—	—	—	—
1975–76	2,765	1,767	998	1,219	447	772	1,546	1,320	226	—	—	—	—	—	—
1976–77	2,785	1,783	1,002	1,231	452	779	1,554	1,331	223	—	—	—	—	—	—
1977–78	2,826	1,808	1,018	1,241	454	787	1,585	1,354	231	—	—	—	—	—	—
1978–79	2,954	1,843	1,111	1,308	463	845	1,646	1,380	266	—	—	—	—	—	—
1979–80	2,975	1,863	1,112	1,310	464	846	1,665	1,399	266	—	—	—	—	—	—
1980–81	3,056	1,861	1,195	1,334	465	869	1,722	1,396	326 [1]	—	—	—	—	—	—
1981–82	3,083	1,883	1,200	1,340	471	869	1,743	1,412	331 [1]	—	—	—	—	—	—
1982–83	3,111	1,887	1,224	1,336	472	864	1,775	1,415	360 [1]	—	—	—	—	—	—
1983–84	3,117	1,914	1,203	1,325	474	851	1,792	1,440	352	—	—	—	—	—	—
1984–85	3,146	1,911	1,235	1,329	461	868	1,817	1,450	367	—	—	—	—	—	—
1985–86	3,155	1,915	1,240	1,326	461	865	1,829	1,454	375	—	—	—	—	—	—
Including branch campuses															
1974–75	3,004	1,866	1,138	1,433	537	896	1,571	1,329	242	—	—	—	—	—	—
1975–76	3,026	1,898	1,128	1,442	545	897	1,584	1,353	231	—	—	—	—	—	—
1976–77	3,046	1,913	1,133	1,455	550	905	1,591	1,363	228	1,536	1,348	188	55	15	40
1977–78	3,095	1,938	1,157	1,473	552	921	1,622	1,386	236	—	—	—	—	—	—
1978–79	3,134	1,941	1,193	1,474	550	924	1,660	1,391	269	1,564	1,376	188	96	15	81
1979–80	3,152	1,957	1,195	1,475	549	926	1,677	1,408	269	—	—	—	—	—	—
1980–81	3,231	1,957	1,274	1,497	552	945	1,734	1,405	329 [1]	1,569	1,387	182	165	18	147
1981–82	3,253	1,979	1,274	1,498	558	940	1,755	1,421	334 [1]	—	—	—	—	—	—
1982–83	3,280	1,984	1,296	1,493	560	933	1,787	1,424	363 [1]	—	—	—	—	—	—
1983–84	3,284	2,013	1,271	1,481	565	916	1,803	1,448	355	—	—	—	—	—	—
1984–85	3,331	2,025	1,306	1,501	566	935	1,830	1,459	371	1,616	1,430	186	214	29	185
1985–86	3,340	2,029	1,311	1,498	566	932	1,842	1,463	379	—	—	—	—	—	—
1986–87	3,406	2,070	1,336	1,533	573	960	1,873	1,497	376	1,635	1,462	173	238	35	203
1987–88	3,587	2,135	1,452	1,591	599	992	1,996	1,536	460	1,673	1,487	186	323	49	274
1988–89	3,565	2,129	1,436	1,582	598	984	1,983	1,531	452	1,658	1,478	180	325	53	272
1989–90	3,535	2,127	1,408	1,563	595	968	1,972	1,532	440	1,656	1,479	177	316	53	263
1990–91	3,559	2,141	1,418	1,567	595	972	1,992	1,546	446	1,649	1,482	167	343	64	279
1991–92	3,601	2,157	1,444	1,598	599	999	2,003	1,558	445	1,662	1,486	176	341	72	269
1992–93	3,638	2,169	1,469	1,624	600	1,024	2,014	1,569	445	1,672	1,493	179	342	76	266
1993–94	3,632	2,190	1,442	1,625	604	1,021	2,007	1,586	421	1,687	1,506	181	320	80	240
1994–95	3,688	2,215	1,473	1,641	605	1,036	2,047	1,610	437	1,702	1,510	192	345	100	245
1995–96	3,706	2,244	1,462	1,655	608	1,047	2,051	1,636	415	1,706	1,519	187	345	117	228
1996–97	4,009	2,267	1,742	1,702	614	1,088	2,307	1,653	654	1,693	1,509	184	614	144	470
1997–98	4,064	2,309	1,755	1,707	615	1,092	2,357	1,694	663	1,707	1,528	179	650	166	484
1998–99	4,048	2,335	1,713	1,681	612	1,069	2,367	1,723	644	1,695	1,531	164	672	192	480
1999–2000	4,084	2,363	1,721	1,682	614	1,068	2,402	1,749	653	1,681	1,531	150	721	218	503
2000–01	4,182	2,450	1,732	1,698	622	1,076	2,484	1,828	656	1,695	1,551	144	789	277	512
2001–02	4,197	2,487	1,710	1,713	628	1,085	2,484	1,859	625	1,676	1,541	135	808	318	490
2002–03	4,168	2,466	1,702	1,712	631	1,081	2,456	1,835	621	1,665	1,538	127	791	297	494
2003–04	4,236	2,530	1,706	1,720	634	1,086	2,516	1,896	620	1,664	1,546	118	852	350	502
2004–05	4,216	2,533	1,683	1,700	639	1,061	2,516	1,894	622	1,637	1,525	112	879	369	510
2005–06	4,276	2,582	1,694	1,693	640	1,053	2,583	1,942	641	1,647	1,534	113	936	408	528
2006–07	4,314	2,629	1,685	1,688	643	1,045	2,626	1,986	640	1,640	1,533	107	986	453	533
2007–08	4,352	2,675	1,677	1,685	653	1,032	2,667	2,022	645	1,624	1,532	92	1,043	490	553
2008–09	4,409	2,719	1,690	1,676	652	1,024	2,733	2,067	666	1,629	1,537	92	1,104	530	574
2009–10	4,495	2,774	1,721	1,672	672	1,000	2,823	2,102	721	1,624	1,539	85	1,199	563	636
2010–11	4,599	2,870	1,729	1,656	678	978	2,943	2,192	751	1,630	1,543	87	1,313	649	664
2011–12	4,706	2,968	1,738	1,649	682	967	3,057	2,286	771	1,653	1,553	100	1,404	733	671
2012–13	4,706	2,968	1,738	1,649	682	967	3,057	2,286	771	1,653	1,553	100	1,404	733	671
2013–14	4,724	3,039	1,685	1,625	691	934	3,099	2,348	751	1,675	1,587	88	1,424	761	663
2014–15	4,627	3,011	1,616	1,621	701	920	3,006	2,310	696	1,672	1,584	88	1,334	726	608

—Not available.

[1]Large increases are due to the addition of schools accredited by the Accrediting Commission of Career Schools and Colleges of Technology.

NOTE: Data through 1995–96 are for institutions of higher education, while later data are for degree-granting institutions. Degree-granting institutions grant associate's or higher degrees and participate in Title IV federal financial aid programs. Changes in counts of institutions over time are partly affected by increasing or decreasing numbers of institutions submitting separate data for branch campuses.

SOURCE: U.S. Department of Education, National Center for Education Statistics, *Education Directory, Colleges and Universities*, 1949–50 through 1965–66; Higher Education General Information Survey (HEGIS), "Institutional Characteristics of Colleges and Universities" surveys, 1966–67 through 1985–86; Integrated Postsecondary Education Data System (IPEDS), "Institutional Characteristics Survey" (IPEDS-IC:86–99); and IPEDS Fall 2000 through Fall 2014, Institutional Characteristics component. (This table was prepared October 2015.)

Table 317.20. Degree-granting postsecondary institutions, by control and level of institution and state or jurisdiction: 2014–15

State or jurisdiction	Total	All public institutions	Public 4-year institutions: Total	Public 4-year: Research university, very high[1]	Public 4-year: Research university, high[2]	Public 4-year: Doctoral/research university[3]	Public 4-year: Master's[4]	Public 4-year: Baccalaureate[5]	Public 4-year: Special focus[6]	Public 2-year	All nonprofit institutions	Nonprofit 4-year institutions: Total	Nonprofit 4-year: Research university, very high[1]	Nonprofit 4-year: Research university, high[2]	Nonprofit 4-year: Doctoral/research university[3]	Nonprofit 4-year: Master's[4]	Nonprofit 4-year: Baccalaureate[5]	Nonprofit 4-year: Special focus[6]	Nonprofit 2-year	For-profit institutions: Total	For-profit: 4-year	For-profit: 2-year
1	2	3	4	5	6	7	8	9	10	11	12	13	14	15	16	17	18	19	20	21	22	23
United States	**4,627**	**1,621**	**701**	**73**	**73**	**29**	**274**	**206**	**46**	**920**	**1,672**	**1,584**	**34**	**24**	**48**	**363**	**520**	**595**	**88**	**1,334**	**726**	**608**
Alabama	78	39	14	2	3	0	8	1	0	25	21	20	0	0	0	2	12	6	1	18	11	7
Alaska	10	5	3	0	1	0	2	0	0	2	3	2	0	0	0	1	0	1	1	2	1	1
Arizona	86	28	8	2	1	0	4	0	1	20	14	14	0	0	0	2	4	8	0	44	30	14
Arkansas	52	33	11	1	0	1	6	2	1	22	15	12	0	0	0	1	9	2	3	4	3	1
California	458	149	34	8	1	0	21	2	2	115	144	138	3	1	10	25	24	75	6	165	87	78
Colorado	89	28	14	2	2	1	4	5	0	14	14	14	0	1	0	3	5	5	0	47	26	21
Connecticut	44	21	9	1	0	0	4	4	0	12	19	19	1	0	0	9	5	4	0	4	4	0
Delaware	11	5	2	1	0	0	1	0	0	3	5	4	0	0	1	0	1	2	1	1	1	0
District of Columbia	21	2	2	0	0	0	1	0	1	0	14	13	2	2	1	2	0	6	1	5	4	1
Florida	234	42	38	4	2	2	4	25	1	4	66	62	1	1	3	13	22	22	4	126	65	61
Georgia	131	55	29	3	0	2	9	14	1	26	35	33	1	0	1	4	19	8	2	41	22	19
Hawaii	21	10	4	1	0	0	0	3	0	6	6	6	0	0	0	2	2	2	0	5	3	2
Idaho	19	8	4	0	2	0	1	1	0	4	6	6	0	0	0	1	2	3	0	5	4	1
Illinois	181	60	12	2	2	1	7	0	0	48	83	80	2	2	4	17	19	36	3	38	25	13
Indiana	84	16	15	2	2	1	6	3	1	1	40	39	1	0	0	9	19	10	1	28	18	10
Iowa	65	19	3	2	0	0	1	0	0	16	34	34	0	0	0	6	18	10	0	12	10	2
Kansas	75	33	8	1	2	0	4	0	1	25	26	25	0	0	0	6	12	7	1	16	10	6
Kentucky	76	24	8	2	0	0	5	1	0	16	26	26	0	0	1	6	12	7	0	26	18	8
Louisiana	66	33	17	1	3	0	9	1	3	16	13	11	1	0	0	2	4	4	2	20	5	15
Maine	32	15	8	0	1	0	1	6	0	7	14	12	0	0	0	3	6	3	2	3	2	1
Maryland	60	29	13	1	1	2	7	1	1	16	20	20	1	0	0	6	6	7	0	11	6	5
Massachusetts	124	30	14	1	2	0	7	2	2	16	84	82	5	3	1	16	24	33	2	10	6	4
Michigan	111	46	18	3	2	2	7	4	0	28	50	50	0	0	1	11	22	16	0	15	12	3
Minnesota	115	43	12	1	0	0	8	3	0	31	35	34	0	0	3	6	12	13	1	37	34	3
Mississippi	41	23	8	1	3	0	4	0	0	15	9	9	0	0	0	3	4	2	0	9	2	7
Missouri	129	27	13	1	3	0	6	3	0	14	54	51	1	1	1	11	12	25	3	48	26	22
Montana	22	17	6	1	1	0	1	3	0	11	5	4	0	0	0	0	3	1	1	0	0	0
Nebraska	42	15	7	1	0	1	3	1	1	8	18	16	0	0	0	5	7	4	2	9	5	4
Nevada	24	7	6	0	2	0	0	4	0	1	3	3	0	0	0	1	0	2	0	14	6	8
New Hampshire	27	13	6	0	1	0	2	2	1	7	12	11	1	0	0	5	4	1	1	2	2	0
New Jersey	71	32	13	1	2	0	10	0	0	19	28	28	1	1	1	10	2	13	0	11	6	5
New Mexico	43	28	9	1	1	0	4	1	2	19	3	3	0	0	0	0	3	0	0	12	10	2
New York	302	79	43	4	1	1	21	12	4	36	177	165	6	4	7	39	27	82	12	46	22	24
North Carolina	150	75	16	2	1	3	7	2	1	59	50	49	1	1	0	7	27	13	1	25	17	8
North Dakota	21	14	9	1	1	0	1	4	2	5	6	6	0	0	0	1	1	4	0	1	1	0
Ohio	210	60	35	2	8	0	1	23	1	25	73	68	1	1	2	20	19	25	5	77	29	48
Oklahoma	66	30	17	1	1	0	8	5	2	13	14	14	0	0	1	4	6	3	0	22	11	11
Oregon	64	26	9	2	1	0	3	2	1	17	24	24	0	0	0	5	7	12	0	14	8	6
Pennsylvania	257	62	45	2	1	1	18	21	2	17	118	104	2	3	2	30	35	32	14	77	10	67
Rhode Island	13	3	2	0	1	0	1	0	0	1	10	10	1	0	0	5	1	3	0	0	0	0
South Carolina	78	33	13	1	1	1	5	4	1	20	23	22	0	0	0	5	14	3	1	22	14	8
South Dakota	25	12	7	0	2	0	2	1	2	5	8	7	0	0	0	0	5	2	1	5	5	0
Tennessee	107	22	9	1	1	3	4	0	0	13	50	47	1	0	2	11	16	17	3	35	18	17
Texas	267	107	44	3	6	7	17	4	7	63	68	59	1	2	2	17	14	23	9	92	42	50
Utah	40	8	7	1	1	0	2	3	0	1	11	10	0	1	0	2	3	4	1	21	18	3

See notes at end of table.

Table 317.20. Degree-granting postsecondary institutions, by control and level of institution and state or jurisdiction: 2014–15—Continued

State or jurisdiction	Total	All public institutions	Public 4-year institutions							Public 2-year	All nonprofit institutions	Nonprofit 4-year institutions							Nonprofit 2-year	For-profit institutions		
			Total	Research university, very high[1]	Research university, high[2]	Doctoral/research university[3]	Master's[4]	Baccalaureate[5]	Special focus[6]			Total	Research university, very high[1]	Research university, high[2]	Doctoral/research university[3]	Master's[4]	Baccalaureate[5]	Special focus[6]		Total	4-year	2-year
1	2	3	4	5	6	7	8	9	10	11	12	13	14	15	16	17	18	19	20	21	22	23
Vermont	24	6	5	0	1	0	1	3	0	1	17	17	0	0	0	4	11	2	0	1	1	0
Virginia	130	40	16	3	3	0	7	2	1	24	40	38	0	0	1	7	18	12	2	50	29	21
Washington	87	43	23	2	0	0	6	13	2	20	24	23	0	0	0	10	5	8	1	20	11	9
West Virginia	43	22	13	0	1	0	3	8	1	9	9	9	0	0	0	0	7	2	0	12	3	9
Wisconsin	86	31	14	1	1	0	10	2	0	17	30	30	0	0	3	8	10	9	0	25	23	2
Wyoming	10	8	1	0	1	0	0	0	0	7	1	1	0	0	0	0	0	1	0	1	0	1
U.S. Service Academies	5	5	5	0	0	0	0	5	0	0	†	†	†	†	†	†	†	†	†	†	†	†
Other jurisdictions	**98**	**26**	**18**	**0**	**1**	**1**	**1**	**12**	**3**	**8**	**50**	**46**	**0**	**0**	**3**	**12**	**16**	**15**	**4**	**22**	**12**	**10**
American Samoa	1	1	1	0	0	0	0	1	0	0	0	0	0	0	0	0	0	0	0	0	0	0
Federated States of Micronesia	1	1	0	0	0	0	0	0	0	1	0	0	0	0	0	0	0	0	0	0	0	0
Guam	3	2	1	0	0	0	1	0	0	1	1	1	0	0	0	0	0	1	0	0	0	0
Marshall Islands	1	1	0	0	0	0	0	0	0	1	0	0	0	0	0	0	0	0	0	0	0	0
Northern Marianas	1	1	1	0	0	0	0	1	0	0	0	0	0	0	0	0	0	0	0	0	0	0
Palau	1	1	0	0	0	0	0	0	0	1	0	0	0	0	0	0	0	0	0	0	0	0
Puerto Rico	89	18	14	0	1	1	0	9	3	4	49	45	0	0	3	12	16	14	4	22	12	10
U.S. Virgin Islands	1	1	1	0	0	0	0	1	0	0	0	0	0	0	0	0	0	0	0	0	0	0

†Not applicable.
[1]Research universities with a very high level of research activity.
[2]Research universities with a high level of research activity.
[3]Institutions that award at least 20 doctor's degrees per year, but did not have a high level of research activity.
[4]Institutions that award at least 50 master's degrees per year.
[5]Institutions that primarily emphasize undergraduate education. Also includes institutions classified as 4-year under the IPEDS system, which had been classified as 2-year in the Carnegie classification system because they primarily award associate's degrees.
[6]Four-year institutions that award degrees primarily in single fields of study, such as medicine, business, fine arts, theology, and engineering.

NOTE: Branch campuses are counted as separate institutions. Relative levels of research activity for research universities were determined by an analysis of research and development expenditures, science and engineering research staffing, and doctoral degrees conferred, by field. Further information on the research index ranking may be obtained from http://carnegieclassifications.iu.edu/. Degree-granting institutions grant associate's or higher degrees and participate in Title IV federal financial aid programs.

SOURCE: U.S. Department of Education, National Center for Education Statistics, Integrated Postsecondary Education Data System (IPEDS), Fall 2014, Institutional Characteristics component. (This table was prepared October 2015.)

Table 317.30. Number of non-degree-granting Title IV institutions offering postsecondary education, by control of institution and state or jurisdiction: Selected years, 2000–01 through 2014–15

State or jurisdiction	2000–01, total	2005–06, total	2010–11, total	2012–13 Total	2012–13 Public	2012–13 Private Total	2012–13 Private Non-profit	2012–13 Private For-profit	2013–14 Total	2013–14 Public	2013–14 Private Total	2013–14 Private Non-profit	2013–14 Private For-profit	2014–15 Total	2014–15 Public	2014–15 Private Total	2014–15 Private Non-profit	2014–15 Private For-profit
1	2	3	4	5	6	7	8	9	10	11	12	13	14	15	16	17	18	19
United States	**2,297**	**2,187**	**2,422**	**2,528**	**358**	**2,169**	**168**	**2,001**	**2,512**	**355**	**2,157**	**159**	**1,998**	**2,524**	**343**	**2,181**	**155**	**2,026**
Alabama	10	9	9	12	0	13	1	12	14	0	14	1	13	14	0	14	1	13
Alaska	3	2	3	2	1	1	1	0	0	0	0	0	0	0	0	0	0	0
Arizona	33	34	42	48	2	48	1	47	47	2	45	0	45	48	2	46	0	46
Arkansas	36	32	32	36	2	32	2	30	33	2	31	2	29	31	2	29	1	28
California	230	235	248	262	12	253	24	229	258	14	244	22	222	252	12	240	22	218
Colorado	21	26	33	39	3	37	3	34	39	3	36	3	33	39	3	36	3	33
Connecticut	37	36	59	56	11	39	3	36	48	11	37	3	34	48	10	38	3	35
Delaware	4	6	8	8	0	8	1	7	8	0	8	1	7	8	0	8	1	7
District of Columbia	5	6	5	4	0	4	1	3	4	0	4	1	3	4	0	4	1	3
Florida	124	126	150	153	42	110	4	106	155	43	112	3	109	168	45	123	3	120
Georgia	38	44	46	46	1	44	1	43	46	1	45	2	43	47	1	46	3	43
Hawaii	6	5	5	7	0	6	0	6	5	0	5	0	5	5	0	5	0	5
Idaho	11	13	17	19	1	22	0	22	23	1	22	0	22	23	1	22	0	22
Illinois	88	94	108	117	3	113	10	103	119	2	117	8	109	117	2	115	7	108
Indiana	34	28	42	48	4	45	1	44	48	2	46	1	45	48	1	47	1	46
Iowa	27	26	26	28	0	28	2	26	27	0	27	2	25	27	0	27	2	25
Kansas	23	25	22	22	1	24	0	24	22	1	21	0	21	19	1	18	0	18
Kentucky	52	32	30	32	0	32	2	30	33	0	33	2	31	33	0	33	2	31
Louisiana	57	57	47	51	0	52	2	50	51	0	51	3	48	57	0	57	2	55
Maine	11	9	7	8	0	8	0	8	9	0	9	0	9	8	0	8	0	8
Maryland	34	27	32	33	0	31	0	31	35	0	35	0	35	38	0	38	0	38
Massachusetts	60	61	75	73	11	57	3	54	68	12	56	3	53	67	12	55	3	52
Michigan	72	65	89	86	1	82	2	80	82	1	81	3	78	84	1	83	3	80
Minnesota	20	21	26	26	0	27	2	25	27	0	27	2	25	27	0	27	2	25
Mississippi	16	20	20	20	0	20	0	20	20	0	20	0	20	20	0	20	0	20
Missouri	69	61	74	80	30	47	3	44	77	29	48	2	46	72	23	49	3	46
Montana	10	8	8	9	0	9	0	9	8	0	8	0	8	8	0	8	0	8
Nebraska	12	10	7	7	0	7	1	6	7	0	7	1	6	7	0	7	1	6
Nevada	10	9	18	20	0	23	1	22	23	0	23	1	22	21	0	21	1	20
New Hampshire	11	14	14	15	0	15	1	14	15	0	15	1	14	15	0	15	1	14
New Jersey	89	91	87	90	5	89	8	81	95	5	90	7	83	90	5	85	7	78
New Mexico	6	7	7	8	0	8	0	8	8	0	8	0	8	8	0	8	0	8
New York	152	133	151	156	33	122	30	92	152	33	119	26	93	156	33	123	24	99
North Carolina	36	29	42	43	1	43	2	41	45	1	44	3	41	46	1	45	3	42
North Dakota	5	5	8	8	0	8	0	8	9	0	9	0	9	9	0	9	0	9
Ohio	130	119	138	139	53	87	6	81	138	51	87	6	81	144	50	94	7	87
Oklahoma	84	78	83	82	47	31	0	31	79	49	30	0	30	79	48	31	0	31
Oregon	28	27	26	30	0	29	3	26	30	0	30	3	27	31	0	31	3	28
Pennsylvania	167	131	126	127	34	91	21	70	126	34	92	20	72	126	33	93	21	72
Rhode Island	12	10	11	11	0	11	2	9	11	0	11	2	9	11	0	11	2	9
South Carolina	14	21	27	33	1	32	1	31	33	1	32	1	31	30	1	29	1	28
South Dakota	5	6	6	6	0	6	3	3	6	0	6	3	3	6	0	6	3	3
Tennessee	54	58	66	72	26	46	1	45	72	26	46	1	45	76	26	50	1	49
Texas	161	169	170	174	0	175	4	171	174	0	174	4	170	179	0	179	3	176
Utah	26	24	34	38	7	33	0	33	40	7	33	0	33	40	7	33	0	33
Vermont	3	4	4	4	0	3	0	3	3	0	3	0	3	2	0	2	0	2
Virginia	56	42	33	36	8	32	4	28	40	6	34	3	31	41	6	35	3	32
Washington	42	37	37	37	1	37	3	34	35	1	34	4	30	35	1	34	5	29
West Virginia	36	31	33	32	17	16	5	11	34	17	17	5	12	30	16	14	3	11
Wisconsin	24	22	30	34	0	32	3	29	30	0	30	4	26	29	0	29	3	26
Wyoming	3	2	1	1	0	1	0	1	1	0	1	0	1	1	0	1	0	1
Other jurisdictions	**74**	**74**	**68**	**70**	**2**	**70**	**13**	**57**	**71**	**2**	**69**	**12**	**57**	**61**	**1**	**60**	**6**	**54**
American Samoa	0	0	0	0	0	0	0	0	0	0	0	0	0	0	0	0	0	0
Guam	0	0	0	0	0	0	0	0	0	0	0	0	0	0	0	0	0	0
Northern Marianas	0	0	0	0	0	0	0	0	0	0	0	0	0	0	0	0	0	0
Palau	0	0	0	0	0	0	0	0	0	0	0	0	0	0	0	0	0	0
Puerto Rico	74	74	68	70	2	70	13	57	71	2	69	12	57	61	1	60	6	54
U.S. Virgin Islands	0	0	0	0	0	0	0	0	0	0	0	0	0	0	0	0	0	0

NOTE: Includes all institutions that participated in Title IV federal financial aid programs but did not grant degrees at the associate's or higher level.

SOURCE: U.S. Department of Education, National Center for Education Statistics, Integrated Postsecondary Education Data System (IPEDS), Fall 2000 through Fall 2014, Institutional Characteristics component. (This table was prepared December 2015.)

Table 317.40. Number of degree-granting postsecondary institutions and enrollment in these institutions, by enrollment size, control, and level of institution: Fall 2014

Control and level of institution	Number of institutions, by enrollment size of institution[1]									
	Total	Under 200	200 to 499	500 to 999	1,000 to 2,499	2,500 to 4,999	5,000 to 9,999	10,000 to 19,999	20,000 to 29,999	30,000 or more
1	2	3	4	5	6	7	8	9	10	11
Total	**4,614**	**612**	**791**	**609**	**892**	**643**	**495**	**341**	**142**	**89**
Research university, very high[2]	107	0	0	0	1	0	9	22	32	43
Research university, high[3]	97	0	0	0	1	2	14	42	27	11
Doctoral/research university[4]	88	1	1	4	9	15	21	26	9	2
Master's[5]	675	3	10	21	136	207	178	86	20	14
Baccalaureate[6]	853	28	95	175	356	136	33	18	4	8
Special-focus institutions[7]	1,183	367	375	217	146	55	13	6	3	1
2-year	1,611	213	310	192	243	228	227	141	47	10
Public	1,621	10	34	66	287	361	384	281	125	73
Research university, very high[2]	73	0	0	0	0	0	2	6	25	40
Research university, high[3]	73	0	0	0	0	1	7	32	24	10
Doctoral/research university[4]	29	0	0	0	1	1	4	16	7	0
Master's[5]	274	0	1	0	11	54	112	71	19	6
Baccalaureate[6]	207	0	1	19	59	71	31	16	3	7
Special-focus institutions[7]	45	2	7	10	11	13	2	0	0	0
Art, music, or design	2	0	0	1	1	0	0	0	0	0
Business and management	2	0	0	1	0	0	1	0	0	0
Engineering or technology	2	0	0	0	0	2	0	0	0	0
Law	6	1	3	1	1	0	0	0	0	0
Medical or other health	25	0	2	5	6	11	1	0	0	0
Tribal	8	1	2	2	3	0	0	0	0	0
2-year	920	8	25	37	205	222	226	140	47	10
Private nonprofit	1,666	288	256	233	472	247	99	50	12	9
Research university, very high[2]	34	0	0	0	1	0	7	16	7	3
Research university, high[3]	24	0	0	0	1	2	7	10	3	1
Doctoral/research university[4]	48	1	1	0	5	14	16	9	2	0
Master's[5]	363	2	7	13	112	148	65	12	0	4
Baccalaureate[6]	520	15	51	110	279	63	0	1	0	1
Special-focus institutions[7]	591	240	156	98	71	20	4	2	0	0
Art, music, or design	57	12	13	17	11	3	0	1	0	0
Business and management	40	9	11	11	4	3	2	0	0	0
Engineering or technology	13	6	2	2	2	0	0	1	0	0
Law	21	3	5	7	6	0	0	0	0	0
Medical or other health	141	22	43	29	36	10	1	0	0	0
Theological	298	180	78	26	10	3	1	0	0	0
Tribal	5	0	1	4	0	0	0	0	0	0
Other special focus	16	8	3	2	2	1	0	0	0	0
2-year	86	30	41	12	3	0	0	0	0	0
Private for-profit	1,327	314	501	310	133	35	12	10	5	7
Doctoral/research university[4]	11	0	0	4	3	0	1	1	0	2
Master's[5]	38	1	2	8	13	5	1	3	1	4
Baccalaureate[6]	126	13	43	46	18	2	2	1	1	0
Special-focus institutions[7]	547	125	212	109	64	22	7	4	3	1
Art, music, or design	89	16	25	18	24	4	1	1	0	0
Business and management	220	52	75	40	27	15	5	2	3	1
Engineering or technology	153	30	87	33	0	2	1	0	0	0
Law	9	1	2	3	3	0	0	0	0	0
Medical or other health	71	25	21	15	9	0	0	1	0	0
Other special focus	5	1	2	0	1	1	0	0	0	0
2-year	605	175	244	143	35	6	1	1	0	0

See notes at end of table.

Table 317.40. Number of degree-granting postsecondary institutions and enrollment in these institutions, by enrollment size, control, and level of institution: Fall 2014—Continued

Control and level of institution	Enrollment, by enrollment size of institution: Total	Under 200	200 to 499	500 to 999	1,000 to 2,499	2,500 to 4,999	5,000 to 9,999	10,000 to 19,999	20,000 to 29,999	30,000 or more
1	12	13	14	15	16	17	18	19	20	21
Total	**20,207,369**	**69,031**	**266,824**	**434,332**	**1,480,334**	**2,304,192**	**3,542,720**	**4,717,412**	**3,476,118**	**3,916,406**
Research university, very high[2]	2,963,505	0	0	0	2,209	0	63,677	321,086	824,619	1,751,914
Research university, high[3]	1,807,492	0	0	0	2,160	7,296	107,788	623,645	673,394	393,209
Doctoral/research university[4]	854,781	88	291	3,124	15,054	53,583	152,701	332,439	210,252	87,249
Master's[5]	4,607,954	463	3,329	15,045	247,460	756,900	1,272,104	1,168,696	464,352	679,605
Baccalaureate[6]	2,103,907	3,051	34,715	128,412	573,830	463,848	220,912	260,757	98,240	320,142
Special-focus institutions[7]	1,155,245	40,937	122,818	151,297	220,604	186,888	87,181	81,625	68,836	195,059
2-year	6,714,485	24,492	105,671	136,454	419,017	835,677	1,638,357	1,929,164	1,136,425	489,228
Public	14,655,015	1,506	12,716	52,348	507,752	1,328,046	2,774,495	3,906,638	3,075,542	2,995,972
Research university, very high[2]	2,398,724	0	0	0	0	0	14,361	103,073	653,215	1,628,075
Research university, high[3]	1,502,013	0	0	0	0	0	57,500	480,393	601,395	362,725
Doctoral/research university[4]	420,049	0	0	0	2,200	3,331	31,653	216,857	166,008	0
Master's[5]	2,682,609	0	469	0	21,821	208,793	817,351	958,955	442,794	232,426
Baccalaureate[6]	1,166,559	0	488	14,848	98,899	256,158	206,228	230,715	75,705	283,518
Special-focus institutions[7]	87,296	311	2,349	8,022	18,205	44,145	14,264	0	0	0
Art, music, or design	3,053	0	0	958	2,095	0	0	0	0	0
Business and management	8,879	0	0	891	0	0	7,988	0	0	0
Engineering or technology	6,458	0	0	0	0	6,458	0	0	0	0
Law	2,708	153	908	644	1,003	0	0	0	0	0
Medical or other health	58,830	0	666	4,084	10,117	37,687	6,276	0	0	0
Tribal	7,368	158	775	1,445	4,990	0	0	0	0	0
2-year	6,397,765	1,195	9,410	29,478	366,627	815,619	1,633,138	1,916,645	1,136,425	489,228
Private nonprofit	3,996,089	31,336	85,559	170,750	780,783	859,901	688,786	676,299	287,647	415,028
Research university, very high[2]	564,781	0	0	0	2,209	0	49,316	218,013	171,404	123,839
Research university, high[3]	305,479	0	0	0	2,160	7,296	50,288	143,252	71,999	30,484
Doctoral/research university[4]	322,680	88	291	0	8,532	50,252	114,851	104,422	44,244	0
Master's[5]	1,586,703	359	2,337	9,666	205,265	531,265	447,751	165,979	0	224,081
Baccalaureate[6]	812,195	1,693	18,847	83,961	450,186	201,774	0	19,110	0	36,624
Special-focus institutions[7]	373,886	26,036	50,256	68,830	107,347	69,314	26,580	25,523	0	0
Art, music, or design	60,883	1,268	4,560	11,545	18,966	13,197	0	11,347	0	0
Business and management	40,475	1,236	3,668	7,843	5,871	8,933	12,924	0	0	0
Engineering or technology	20,274	618	722	1,300	3,458	0	0	14,176	0	0
Law	15,406	528	1,852	5,447	7,579	0	0	0	0	0
Medical or other health	132,164	2,581	14,635	20,921	51,951	35,141	6,935	0	0	0
Theological	92,618	18,978	23,551	17,489	16,614	9,265	6,721	0	0	0
Tribal	3,014	0	434	2,580	0	0	0	0	0	0
Other special focus	9,052	827	834	1,705	2,908	2,778	0	0	0	0
2-year	30,365	3,160	13,828	8,293	5,084	0	0	0	0	0
Private for-profit	1,556,265	36,189	168,549	211,234	191,799	116,245	79,439	134,475	112,929	505,406
Doctoral/research university[4]	112,052	0	0	3,124	4,322	0	6,197	11,160	0	87,249
Master's[5]	338,642	104	523	5,379	20,374	16,842	7,002	43,762	21,558	223,098
Baccalaureate[6]	125,153	1,358	15,380	29,603	24,745	5,916	14,684	10,932	22,535	0
Special-focus institutions[7]	694,063	14,590	70,213	74,445	95,052	73,429	46,337	56,102	68,836	195,059
Art, music, or design	96,215	1,771	8,821	13,430	34,590	13,008	9,383	15,212	0	0
Business and management	466,297	6,262	23,978	27,740	41,722	49,748	30,727	22,225	68,836	195,059
Engineering or technology	67,799	3,644	29,202	21,161	0	7,565	6,227	0	0	0
Law	6,492	118	802	2,074	3,498	0	0	0	0	0
Medical or other health	51,590	2,618	6,592	10,040	13,675	0	0	18,665	0	0
Other special focus	5,670	177	818	0	1,567	3,108	0	0	0	0
2-year	286,355	20,137	82,433	98,683	47,306	20,058	5,219	12,519	0	0

[1]Excludes 13 institutions that had no enrollment.
[2]Research universities with a very high level of research activity.
[3]Research universities with a high level of research activity.
[4]Institutions that award at least 20 doctor's degrees per year, but did not have a high level of research activity.
[5]Institutions that award at least 50 master's degrees per year.
[6]Institutions that primarily emphasize undergraduate education. Also includes institutions classified as 4-year under the IPEDS system, which had been classified as 2-year in the Carnegie system because they primarily award associate's degrees.
[7]Four-year institutions that award degrees primarily in single fields of study, such as medicine, business, fine arts, theology, and engineering.

NOTE: Degree-granting institutions grant associate's or higher degrees and participate in Title IV federal financial aid programs. Relative levels of research activity for research universities were determined by an analysis of research and development expenditures, science and engineering research staffing, and doctoral degrees conferred, by field. Further information on the research index ranking may be obtained from http://carnegieclassifications.iu.edu/.

SOURCE: U.S. Department of Education, National Center for Education Statistics, Integrated Postsecondary Education Data System (IPEDS), Spring 2015, Fall Enrollment component. (This table was prepared October 2015.)

Table 317.50. Degree-granting postsecondary institutions that have closed their doors, by control and level of institution: 1969–70 through 2014–15

Year	All institutions			Public			Private								
							Total			Nonprofit			For-profit		
	Total	4-year	2-year	Total	4-year	2-year	Total	4-year	2-year	Total	4-year	2-year	Total	4-year	2-year
1	2	3	4	5	6	7	8	9	10	11	12	13	14	15	16
1969–70	24	10	14	5	1	4	19	9	10	—	—	—	—	—	—
1970–71	35	10	25	11	0	11	24	10	14	—	—	—	—	—	—
1971–72	14	5	9	3	0	3	11	5	6	—	—	—	—	—	—
1972–73	21	12	9	4	0	4	17	12	5	—	—	—	—	—	—
1973–74	20	12	8	1	0	1	19	12	7	—	—	—	—	—	—
1974–75	18	13	5	4	0	4	14	13	1	—	—	—	—	—	—
1975–76	9	7	2	2	1	1	7	6	1	—	—	—	—	—	—
1976–77	9	6	3	0	0	0	9	6	3	—	—	—	—	—	—
1977–78	12	9	3	0	0	0	12	9	3	—	—	—	—	—	—
1978–79	9	4	5	0	0	0	9	4	5	—	—	—	—	—	—
1979–80	6	5	1	0	0	0	6	5	1	—	—	—	—	—	—
1980–81	4	3	1	0	0	0	4	3	1	—	—	—	—	—	—
1981–82	7	6	1	0	0	0	7	6	1	—	—	—	—	—	—
1982–83	7	4	3	0	0	0	7	4	3	—	—	—	—	—	—
1983–84	5	5	0	1	1	0	4	4	0	—	—	—	—	—	—
1984–85	4	4	0	0	0	0	4	4	0	—	—	—	—	—	—
1985–86	12	8	4	1	1	0	11	7	4	—	—	—	—	—	—
1986–87 and 1987–88	26	19	7	1	0	1	25	19	6	—	—	—	—	—	—
1988–89	14	6	8	0	0	0	14	6	8	—	—	—	—	—	—
1989–90	19	8	11	0	0	0	19	8	11	—	—	—	—	—	—
1990–91	18	6	12	0	0	0	18	6	12	7	5	2	11	1	10
1991–92	26	8	18	1	0	1	25	8	17	8	7	1	17	1	16
1992–93	23	6	17	0	0	0	23	6	17	6	5	1	17	1	16
1993–94	38	11	27	1	0	1	37	11	26	13	10	3	24	1	23
1994–95	15	8	7	2	0	2	13	8	5	8	7	1	5	1	4
1995–96	21	8	13	1	1	0	20	7	13	9	7	2	11	0	11
1996–97	36	13	23	2	0	2	34	13	21	14	10	4	20	3	17
1997–98	5	0	5	0	0	0	5	0	5	1	0	1	4	0	4
1998–99	7	1	6	1	0	1	6	1	5	2	0	2	4	1	3
1999–2000	16	3	13	3	0	3	13	3	10	8	3	5	5	0	5
2000–01	14	9	5	0	0	0	14	9	5	8	8	0	6	1	5
2001–02	14	2	12	0	0	0	14	2	12	1	1	0	13	1	12
2002–03	13	7	6	0	0	0	13	7	6	6	6	0	7	1	6
2003–04	12	5	7	0	0	0	12	5	7	8	5	3	4	0	4
2004–05	3	1	2	0	0	0	3	1	2	1	1	0	2	0	2
2005–06	11	6	5	1	1	0	10	5	5	5	4	1	5	1	4
2006–07	13	4	9	0	0	0	13	4	9	6	4	2	7	0	7
2007–08	26	10	16	0	0	0	26	10	16	9	6	3	17	4	13
2008–09	16	6	10	0	0	0	16	6	10	6	5	1	10	1	9
2009–10	17	11	6	0	0	0	17	11	6	9	9	0	8	2	6
2010–11	20	9	11	0	0	0	20	9	11	7	6	1	13	3	10
2011–12	10	5	5	4	0	4	6	5	1	2	2	0	4	3	1
2012–13	21	3	18	1	1	0	20	2	18	4	2	2	16	0	16
2013–14	20	8	12	1	1	0	19	7	12	4	3	1	15	4	11
2014–15	54	7	47	0	0	0	54	7	47	5	3	2	49	4	45

—Not available.

NOTE: This table indicates the year by which the institution no longer operated (generally it closed at the end of or during the prior year). Data through 1995–96 are for institutions of higher education, while later data are for degree-granting institutions. Degree-granting institutions grant associate's or higher degrees and participate in Title IV federal financial aid programs. The degree-granting classification is very similar to the earlier higher education classification, but it includes more 2-year colleges and excludes a few higher education institutions that did not grant degrees.

SOURCE: U.S. Department of Education, National Center for Education Statistics, *Education Directory, Higher Education*, 1969–70 through 1974–75; *Education Directory, Colleges and Universities*, 1975–76 through 1985–86; *1982–83 Supplement to the Education Directory, Colleges and Universities*; Integrated Postsecondary Education Data System (IPEDS), "Institutional Characteristics Survey" (IPEDS-IC:86–99); and IPEDS Fall 2000 through Fall 2014, Institutional Characteristics component. (This table was prepared July 2016.)

Table 333.10. Revenues of public degree-granting postsecondary institutions, by source of revenue and level of institution: 2007–08 through 2013–14

Level of institution and year	Total revenues	Operating revenue							
		Tuition and fees[1]	Grants and contracts			Sales and services of auxiliary enterprises[1]	Sales and services of hospitals	Independent operations	Other operating revenues[2]
			Federal	State	Local and private				
1	2	3	4	5	6	7	8	9	10
	In thousands of current dollars								
All levels									
2007–08	$273,109,306	$48,070,012	$25,522,915	$7,831,530	$8,699,329	$20,488,319	$25,183,379	$1,174,836	$14,108,986
2008–09	267,421,029	51,846,428	26,077,431	7,403,668	9,557,483	21,360,263	27,390,973	1,036,660	14,068,011
2009–10	303,341,758	55,955,342	28,380,803	6,901,666	9,620,236	22,173,993	29,236,931	1,343,230	14,817,094
2010–11	324,473,342	60,268,927	29,821,416	7,019,420	10,110,953	23,605,640	30,998,993	1,330,334	15,758,118
2011–12	317,289,436	65,396,118	29,133,188	6,830,670	10,161,247	24,276,751	33,508,840	1,356,861	16,296,364
2012–13	327,932,633	68,095,088	28,430,717	6,687,856	10,779,776	24,666,058	34,940,780	1,359,043	17,336,700
2013–14	353,095,490	70,498,077	27,533,487	7,093,767	11,186,060	25,476,347	37,596,888	1,432,772	18,204,327
4-year									
2007–08	223,566,529	40,083,063	23,518,933	5,715,188	8,106,887	18,507,934	25,183,379	1,174,836	13,135,633
2008–09	216,470,957	43,478,018	24,172,034	5,527,110	8,988,911	19,391,219	27,390,973	1,036,660	13,193,521
2009–10	248,093,564	46,964,829	26,257,423	5,301,243	9,062,160	20,099,430	29,236,931	1,343,230	13,896,518
2010–11	266,688,058	51,046,786	27,656,656	5,480,573	9,543,780	21,506,767	30,998,993	1,330,334	14,830,150
2011–12	261,158,738	55,978,667	27,235,518	5,352,808	9,590,518	22,240,828	33,508,840	1,356,861	15,343,535
2012–13	272,356,474	58,627,864	26,601,896	5,196,508	10,251,194	22,714,712	34,940,780	1,359,043	16,456,904
2013–14	297,230,653	61,155,700	25,756,710	5,521,827	10,656,459	23,643,409	37,596,888	1,432,772	17,327,733
2-year									
2007–08	49,542,777	7,986,949	2,003,982	2,116,343	592,442	1,980,385	0	0	973,353
2008–09	50,950,072	8,368,411	1,905,397	1,876,558	568,572	1,969,043	0	0	874,490
2009–10	55,248,194	8,990,512	2,123,380	1,600,423	558,076	2,074,563	0	0	920,576
2010–11	57,785,284	9,222,142	2,164,760	1,538,848	567,174	2,098,872	0	0	927,968
2011–12	56,130,698	9,417,451	1,897,670	1,477,862	570,729	2,035,923	0	0	952,830
2012–13	55,576,159	9,467,224	1,828,820	1,491,347	528,582	1,951,346	0	0	879,795
2013–14	55,864,837	9,342,377	1,776,776	1,571,939	529,602	1,832,937	0	0	876,594
	Percentage distribution								
All levels									
2007–08	100.00	17.60	9.35	2.87	3.19	7.50	9.22	0.43	5.17
2008–09	100.00	19.39	9.75	2.77	3.57	7.99	10.24	0.39	5.26
2009–10	100.00	18.45	9.36	2.28	3.17	7.31	9.64	0.44	4.88
2010–11	100.00	18.57	9.19	2.16	3.12	7.28	9.55	0.41	4.86
2011–12	100.00	20.61	9.18	2.15	3.20	7.65	10.56	0.43	5.14
2012–13	100.00	20.76	8.67	2.04	3.29	7.52	10.65	0.41	5.29
2013–14	100.00	19.97	7.80	2.01	3.17	7.22	10.65	0.41	5.16
4-year									
2007–08	100.00	17.93	10.52	2.56	3.63	8.28	11.26	0.53	5.88
2008–09	100.00	20.08	11.17	2.55	4.15	8.96	12.65	0.48	6.09
2009–10	100.00	18.93	10.58	2.14	3.65	8.10	11.78	0.54	5.60
2010–11	100.00	19.14	10.37	2.06	3.58	8.06	11.62	0.50	5.56
2011–12	100.00	21.43	10.43	2.05	3.67	8.52	12.83	0.52	5.88
2012–13	100.00	21.53	9.77	1.91	3.76	8.34	12.83	0.50	6.04
2013–14	100.00	20.58	8.67	1.86	3.59	7.95	12.65	0.48	5.83
2-year									
2007–08	100.00	16.12	4.04	4.27	1.20	4.00	0.00	0.00	1.96
2008–09	100.00	16.42	3.74	3.68	1.12	3.86	0.00	0.00	1.72
2009–10	100.00	16.27	3.84	2.90	1.01	3.75	0.00	0.00	1.67
2010–11	100.00	15.96	3.75	2.66	0.98	3.63	0.00	0.00	1.61
2011–12	100.00	16.78	3.38	2.63	1.02	3.63	0.00	0.00	1.70
2012–13	100.00	17.03	3.29	2.68	0.95	3.51	0.00	0.00	1.58
2013–14	100.00	16.72	3.18	2.81	0.95	3.28	0.00	0.00	1.57
	Revenue per full-time-equivalent student in constant 2014–15 dollars[3]								
All levels									
2007–08	$31,349	$5,518	$2,930	$899	$999	$2,352	$2,891	$135	$1,619
2008–09	29,304	5,681	2,858	811	1,047	2,341	3,002	114	1,542
2009–10	30,824	5,686	2,884	701	978	2,253	2,971	136	1,506
2010–11	31,524	5,855	2,897	682	982	2,293	3,012	129	1,531
2011–12	30,123	6,209	2,766	649	965	2,305	3,181	129	1,547
2012–13	31,115	6,461	2,698	635	1,023	2,340	3,315	129	1,645
2013–14	33,253	6,639	2,593	668	1,053	2,399	3,541	135	1,714
4-year									
2007–08	41,697	7,476	4,386	1,066	1,512	3,452	4,697	219	2,450
2008–09	38,875	7,808	4,341	993	1,614	3,482	4,919	186	2,369
2009–10	41,988	7,948	4,444	897	1,534	3,402	4,948	227	2,352
2010–11	43,023	8,235	4,462	884	1,540	3,470	5,001	215	2,392
2011–12	40,334	8,646	4,206	827	1,481	3,435	5,175	210	2,370
2012–13	41,191	8,867	4,023	786	1,550	3,435	5,284	206	2,489
2013–14	44,088	9,071	3,820	819	1,581	3,507	5,577	213	2,570
2-year									
2007–08	14,788	2,384	598	632	177	591	0	0	291
2008–09	14,322	2,352	536	528	160	554	0	0	246
2009–10	14,049	2,286	540	407	142	528	0	0	234
2010–11	14,114	2,252	529	376	139	513	0	0	227
2011–12	13,832	2,321	468	364	141	502	0	0	235
2012–13	14,152	2,411	466	380	135	497	0	0	224
2013–14	14,411	2,410	458	405	137	473	0	0	226

See notes at end of table.

Table 333.10. Revenues of public degree-granting postsecondary institutions, by source of revenue and level of institution: 2007–08 through 2013–14—Continued

Level of institution and year	Nonoperating revenue: Appropriations: Federal	Appropriations: State	Appropriations: Local	Nonoperating grants: Federal	Nonoperating grants: State	Nonoperating grants: Local	Gifts	Investment income	Other nonoperating revenues	Other revenues and additions: Capital appropriations	Capital grants and gifts	Additions to permanent endowments	Other
1	11	12	13	14	15	16	17	18	19	20	21	22	23
	In thousands of current dollars												
All levels													
2007–08	$1,849,775	$68,375,062	$9,319,219	$10,022,315	$1,909,570	$177,555	$6,070,499	$5,278,643	$2,251,324	$7,578,049	$3,090,589	$1,133,783	$4,973,618
2008–09	2,010,843	65,475,631	9,787,019	12,760,291	2,720,848	265,789	5,893,938	-9,401,624	3,010,295	7,049,628	2,938,605	851,289	5,317,562
2009–10	2,152,228	62,438,851	9,954,504	20,728,610	3,123,358	231,104	5,872,441	10,043,969	5,243,618	6,042,653	3,780,010	873,870	4,427,245
2010–11	1,946,965	63,063,322	10,023,157	24,231,846	3,404,970	228,055	6,287,358	14,215,863	6,888,955	5,645,126	3,745,699	965,007	4,913,217
2011–12	1,835,767	58,789,575	10,214,576	23,204,292	3,559,591	232,167	6,522,320	6,170,822	4,193,110	5,544,504	3,724,162	825,587	5,512,923
2012–13	1,747,391	58,634,067	10,725,798	22,393,312	3,830,396	279,760	7,117,638	11,298,624	4,990,501	5,195,685	3,614,091	928,928	4,880,426
2013–14	1,843,674	62,700,662	11,112,188	21,925,929	4,035,063	300,706	8,114,163	20,024,438	6,543,828	5,313,456	3,835,939	1,123,705	7,200,016
4-year													
2007–08	1,776,452	53,268,648	453,280	5,177,569	1,201,394	103,824	5,798,732	4,430,479	1,770,108	5,637,968	2,762,277	1,120,806	4,639,141
2008–09	1,934,958	50,851,970	484,689	6,425,434	1,729,985	131,427	5,635,304	-9,871,846	2,601,303	5,001,830	2,554,107	838,025	4,975,326
2009–10	2,006,623	48,701,730	431,615	10,308,365	2,088,155	134,608	5,642,265	9,663,671	4,606,436	4,005,260	3,312,752	857,605	4,172,713
2010–11	1,853,109	49,025,814	507,010	11,812,776	2,320,005	130,451	6,061,629	13,781,509	6,061,802	3,884,591	3,249,844	943,748	4,661,730
2011–12	1,715,489	45,755,610	517,219	11,263,074	2,398,688	130,598	6,255,956	5,994,582	3,492,667	3,884,832	3,356,930	815,973	4,969,547
2012–13	1,634,057	45,842,103	551,917	11,126,358	2,516,165	153,773	6,864,121	11,126,073	4,356,413	3,619,996	3,260,502	899,534	4,256,561
2013–14	1,732,216	49,198,717	562,506	11,187,296	2,659,043	179,126	7,867,481	19,709,539	5,873,842	3,867,745	3,563,297	1,106,470	6,631,877
2-year													
2007–08	73,324	15,106,414	8,865,938	4,844,746	708,176	73,731	271,766	848,164	481,216	1,940,082	328,312	12,978	334,477
2008–09	75,885	14,623,660	9,302,330	6,334,857	990,863	134,362	258,634	470,222	408,992	2,047,798	384,498	13,263	342,236
2009–10	145,606	13,737,120	9,522,890	10,420,246	1,035,203	96,496	230,175	380,298	637,182	2,037,393	467,258	16,265	254,532
2010–11	93,856	14,037,508	9,516,147	12,419,069	1,084,965	97,604	225,730	434,353	827,153	1,760,535	495,855	21,258	251,487
2011–12	120,279	13,033,965	9,697,357	11,941,218	1,160,903	101,569	266,364	176,240	700,443	1,659,672	367,232	9,614	543,376
2012–13	113,334	12,791,964	10,173,882	11,266,954	1,314,232	125,987	253,517	172,551	634,088	1,575,688	353,588	29,394	623,866
2013–14	111,459	13,501,945	10,549,682	10,738,632	1,376,020	121,580	246,683	314,899	669,985	1,445,711	272,641	17,236	568,140
	Percentage distribution												
All levels													
2007–08	0.68	25.04	3.41	3.67	0.70	0.07	2.22	1.93	0.82	2.77	1.13	0.42	1.82
2008–09	0.75	24.48	3.66	4.77	1.02	0.10	2.20	-3.52	1.13	2.64	1.10	0.32	1.99
2009–10	0.71	20.58	3.28	6.83	1.03	0.08	1.94	3.31	1.73	1.99	1.25	0.29	1.46
2010–11	0.60	19.44	3.09	7.47	1.05	0.07	1.94	4.38	2.12	1.74	1.15	0.30	1.51
2011–12	0.58	18.53	3.22	7.31	1.12	0.07	2.06	1.94	1.32	1.75	1.17	0.26	1.74
2012–13	0.53	17.88	3.27	6.83	1.17	0.09	2.17	3.45	1.52	1.58	1.10	0.28	1.49
2013–14	0.52	17.76	3.15	6.21	1.14	0.09	2.30	5.67	1.85	1.50	1.09	0.32	2.04
4-year													
2007–08	0.79	23.83	0.20	2.32	0.54	0.05	2.59	1.98	0.79	2.52	1.24	0.50	2.08
2008–09	0.89	23.49	0.22	2.97	0.80	0.06	2.60	-4.56	1.20	2.31	1.18	0.39	2.30
2009–10	0.81	19.63	0.17	4.16	0.84	0.05	2.27	3.90	1.86	1.61	1.34	0.35	1.68
2010–11	0.69	18.38	0.19	4.43	0.87	0.05	2.27	5.17	2.27	1.46	1.22	0.35	1.75
2011–12	0.66	17.52	0.20	4.31	0.92	0.05	2.40	2.30	1.34	1.49	1.29	0.31	1.90
2012–13	0.60	16.83	0.20	4.09	0.92	0.06	2.52	4.09	1.60	1.33	1.20	0.33	1.56
2013–14	0.58	16.55	0.19	3.76	0.89	0.06	2.65	6.63	1.98	1.30	1.20	0.37	2.23
2-year													
2007–08	0.15	30.49	17.90	9.78	1.43	0.15	0.55	1.71	0.97	3.92	0.66	0.03	0.68
2008–09	0.15	28.70	18.26	12.43	1.94	0.26	0.51	0.92	0.80	4.02	0.75	0.03	0.67
2009–10	0.26	24.86	17.24	18.86	1.87	0.17	0.42	0.69	1.15	3.69	0.85	0.03	0.46
2010–11	0.16	24.29	16.47	21.49	1.88	0.17	0.39	0.75	1.43	3.05	0.86	0.04	0.44
2011–12	0.21	23.22	17.28	21.27	2.07	0.18	0.47	0.31	1.25	2.96	0.65	0.02	0.97
2012–13	0.20	23.02	18.31	20.27	2.36	0.23	0.46	0.31	1.14	2.84	0.64	0.05	1.12
2013–14	0.20	24.17	18.88	19.22	2.46	0.22	0.44	0.56	1.20	2.59	0.49	0.03	1.02
	Revenue per full-time-equivalent student in constant 2014–15 dollars[3]												
All levels													
2007–08	$212	$7,848	$1,070	$1,150	$219	$20	$697	$606	$258	$870	$355	$130	$571
2008–09	220	7,175	1,072	1,398	298	29	646	-1,030	330	773	322	93	583
2009–10	219	6,345	1,012	2,106	317	23	597	1,021	533	614	384	89	450
2010–11	189	6,127	974	2,354	331	22	611	1,381	669	548	364	94	477
2011–12	174	5,581	970	2,203	338	22	619	586	398	526	354	78	523
2012–13	166	5,563	1,018	2,125	363	27	675	1,072	474	493	343	88	463
2013–14	174	5,905	1,046	2,065	380	28	764	1,886	616	500	361	106	678
4-year													
2007–08	331	9,935	85	966	224	19	1,082	826	330	1,052	515	209	865
2008–09	347	9,132	87	1,154	311	24	1,012	-1,773	467	898	459	150	894
2009–10	340	8,242	73	1,745	353	23	955	1,635	780	678	561	145	706
2010–11	299	7,909	82	1,906	374	21	978	2,223	978	627	524	152	752
2011–12	265	7,067	80	1,740	370	20	966	926	539	600	518	126	768
2012–13	247	6,933	83	1,683	381	23	1,038	1,683	659	547	493	136	644
2013–14	257	7,298	83	1,659	394	27	1,167	2,923	871	574	529	164	984
2-year													
2007–08	22	4,509	2,646	1,446	211	22	81	253	144	579	98	4	100
2008–09	21	4,111	2,615	1,781	279	38	73	132	115	576	108	4	96
2009–10	37	3,493	2,422	2,650	263	25	59	97	162	518	119	4	65
2010–11	23	3,429	2,324	3,033	265	24	55	106	202	430	121	5	61
2011–12	30	3,212	2,390	2,943	286	25	66	43	173	409	90	2	134
2012–13	29	3,257	2,591	2,869	335	32	65	44	161	401	90	7	159
2013–14	29	3,483	2,721	2,770	355	31	64	81	173	373	70	4	147

[1]After deducting discounts and allowances.
[2]Includes sales and services of educational activities.
[3]Constant dollars based on the Consumer Price Index, prepared by the Bureau of Labor Statistics, U.S. Department of Labor, adjusted to a school-year basis.
NOTE: Degree-granting institutions grant associate's or higher degrees and participate in Title IV federal financial aid programs. Includes data for public institutions reporting data according to either the Governmental Accounting Standards Board (GASB) or the Financial Accounting Standards Board (FASB) questionnaire. Some data have been revised from previously published figures. Detail may not sum to totals because of rounding.
SOURCE: U.S. Department of Education, National Center for Education Statistics, Integrated Postsecondary Education Data System (IPEDS), Spring 2008 through Spring 2014, Fall Enrollment component; and Spring 2009 through Spring 2015, Finance component. (This table was prepared October 2015.)

Table 333.20. Revenues of public degree-granting postsecondary institutions, by source of revenue and state or jurisdiction: 2013–14
[In thousands of current dollars]

State or jurisdiction	Total revenues	Operating revenue: Total	Tuition and fees[2]	Federal grants and contracts	State, local, and private grants and contracts	Sales and services of auxiliary enterprises[2]	Sales and services of hospitals	Independent operations and other[3]	Nonoperating revenue[1]: Total	State appro-priations	Local appro-priations	Other revenues and additions
1	2	3	4	5	6	7	8	9	10	11	12	13
United States	**$353,095,490**	**$199,021,724**	**$70,498,077**	**$27,533,487**	**$18,279,827**	**$25,476,347**	**$37,596,888**	**$19,637,099**	**$136,600,650**	**$62,700,662**	**$11,112,188**	**$17,473,116**
Alabama	7,144,384	4,930,337	1,610,285	656,950	252,855	417,042	1,647,047	346,158	2,099,129	1,317,764	1,895	114,917
Alaska	1,049,003	388,273	126,748	123,150	77,688	40,032	0	20,655	481,384	392,451	10,789	179,345
Arizona	5,841,870	3,053,345	1,793,304	545,626	155,844	398,734	0	159,836	2,679,158	789,580	798,085	109,367
Arkansas	3,801,308	2,361,940	509,171	214,968	204,130	255,140	919,366	259,165	1,356,994	783,427	32,279	82,373
California	49,191,306	27,231,786	6,576,492	3,513,089	2,468,950	1,996,833	8,055,683	4,620,740	19,105,353	8,171,790	3,005,606	2,854,166
Colorado	6,055,720	4,993,088	1,904,190	906,457	579,022	530,689	648,766	423,964	922,089	32,718	83,364	140,543
Connecticut	3,545,779	1,803,353	626,586	176,299	92,853	290,926	308,708	307,982	1,313,433	1,080,009	0	428,993
Delaware	1,391,945	825,566	450,974	138,177	50,194	142,732	0	43,489	558,378	234,102	0	8,000
District of Columbia	159,720	55,507	30,457	12,816	7,639	455	0	4,139	81,314	66,691	0	22,898
Florida	11,473,089	5,427,688	2,352,048	1,039,779	1,070,893	789,818	2,012	173,138	5,586,872	3,356,433	0	458,529
Georgia	7,798,148	4,520,863	1,918,056	782,502	542,361	865,082	189,029	223,833	3,077,695	2,003,786	400	199,591
Hawaii	1,633,045	810,176	249,334	353,524	78,577	97,978	0	30,763	640,799	391,266	0	182,070
Idaho	1,267,010	653,189	324,395	105,750	57,435	115,366	0	50,244	575,706	346,115	27,176	38,115
Illinois	12,306,204	5,906,496	2,353,565	794,628	405,595	898,100	672,662	781,947	6,286,481	1,844,938	1,048,852	113,227
Indiana	7,070,983	4,284,578	2,233,388	544,891	309,494	787,029	0	409,776	2,636,593	1,452,440	7,760	149,812
Iowa	5,506,899	3,888,908	918,065	504,378	159,894	501,764	1,461,969	342,838	1,449,205	818,015	125,607	168,786
Kansas	3,509,730	1,985,657	836,557	317,999	225,276	336,683	0	269,141	1,372,354	731,298	265,604	151,719
Kentucky	5,493,107	3,672,664	1,024,907	396,107	202,452	323,459	1,329,520	396,220	1,711,104	923,182	20,377	109,339
Louisiana	3,947,179	2,467,508	959,277	298,919	515,532	375,069	147,649	171,062	1,338,102	807,568	0	141,569
Maine	905,086	481,252	221,258	64,020	50,888	90,283	0	54,803	397,824	258,412	0	26,011
Maryland	6,505,436	3,790,369	1,556,478	705,175	419,780	699,294	0	409,642	2,338,783	1,480,786	329,689	376,284
Massachusetts	5,010,522	3,124,545	1,296,731	372,668	264,443	497,998	0	692,705	1,671,000	1,168,001	0	214,977
Michigan	16,299,324	10,339,057	3,878,068	1,412,797	467,212	1,072,906	3,001,292	506,784	5,451,403	1,600,635	531,528	508,864
Minnesota	5,466,024	2,918,995	1,281,936	485,747	355,521	620,718	0	175,073	2,303,669	1,183,311	0	243,360
Mississippi	4,271,987	2,456,234	606,824	291,042	193,776	294,110	910,959	159,524	1,612,660	946,620	64,212	203,093
Missouri	5,177,981	3,208,473	1,126,698	238,586	178,200	771,827	733,291	159,870	1,894,030	852,967	147,973	75,478
Montana	1,022,967	652,931	292,172	152,535	36,131	92,129	0	79,964	342,763	211,658	9,156	27,274
Nebraska	2,585,957	1,305,307	432,489	208,582	201,133	322,429	26,081	114,593	1,146,049	666,757	138,933	134,601
Nevada	1,608,047	794,384	372,396	147,181	74,708	92,056	0	108,043	788,386	478,282	0	25,277
New Hampshire	1,093,629	752,685	393,596	74,927	49,586	203,117	0	31,459	214,586	109,724	0	126,359
New Jersey	7,409,557	4,377,767	2,155,396	446,579	403,031	606,433	487,578	278,750	2,772,975	1,569,437	199,631	258,815
New Mexico	3,462,441	1,891,089	288,149	392,974	169,181	114,121	671,214	255,450	1,488,384	749,949	134,655	82,967
New York	15,884,730	7,944,546	2,604,024	740,897	1,199,900	672,664	2,499,595	227,466	7,282,983	4,593,055	803,784	657,202
North Carolina	10,846,550	4,713,325	1,707,181	879,754	330,203	1,579,331	0	216,856	5,689,573	3,474,851	217,480	443,652
North Dakota	1,208,427	714,017	294,322	142,747	68,657	105,321	0	102,970	421,827	334,094	3,082	72,583
Ohio	13,521,773	9,102,680	3,579,698	702,520	548,494	1,127,627	2,808,465	335,877	4,119,231	1,917,249	164,764	299,861
Oklahoma	4,286,400	2,609,029	867,911	274,985	328,923	502,153	77,174	557,883	1,532,249	915,806	56,899	145,121
Oregon	6,427,174	4,445,266	1,228,548	658,589	180,234	489,593	1,624,606	263,696	1,755,374	634,748	230,607	226,534
Pennsylvania	14,288,542	10,362,602	4,042,860	1,239,071	430,688	1,017,593	2,968,771	663,620	3,831,440	1,211,416	111,246	94,499
Rhode Island	775,576	511,979	274,261	74,853	24,538	109,714	0	28,613	219,312	148,310	0	44,284
South Carolina	4,335,333	2,950,170	1,406,699	410,690	397,235	435,158	0	300,387	1,250,492	538,507	64,358	134,672
South Dakota	830,944	505,057	235,110	96,262	49,281	72,473	0	51,931	273,946	180,855	0	51,940
Tennessee	4,540,388	2,248,216	1,083,863	288,249	291,405	306,780	0	277,918	2,040,738	1,117,533	5,707	251,434
Texas	40,011,641	14,917,459	4,968,851	2,013,315	2,288,264	1,362,680	2,215,483	2,068,865	19,907,784	5,394,667	1,623,483	5,186,399
Utah	5,379,665	3,925,547	736,349	395,350	151,950	219,354	1,579,004	843,541	1,293,216	737,380	0	160,902
Vermont	871,552	679,764	358,086	127,324	58,943	104,931	0	30,480	186,815	70,618	0	4,973
Virginia	10,458,605	6,491,774	2,529,739	864,907	211,398	1,292,544	1,262,465	330,723	3,454,418	1,674,472	3,886	512,413
Washington	8,897,290	6,090,617	1,847,536	1,233,600	719,278	632,632	1,206,918	450,653	2,537,607	1,195,297	0	269,067
West Virginia	1,845,096	1,181,613	568,567	128,751	197,567	231,604	0	55,124	594,336	401,966	653	69,147
Wisconsin	6,403,153	3,654,136	1,379,834	672,274	412,368	458,248	0	731,412	2,562,796	1,012,034	795,338	186,221
Wyoming	838,597	301,238	83,823	55,288	65,581	59,212	0	37,334	488,382	327,692	47,331	48,977
U.S. Service Academies	2,438,669	318,678	826	115,239	4,649	56,383	141,582	0	1,463,475	0	0	656,516
Other jurisdictions	**1,746,762**	**421,758**	**92,185**	**169,400**	**43,441**	**12,548**	**67,698**	**36,488**	**1,315,294**	**995,154**	**46,378**	**9,710**
American Samoa	19,401	10,656	3,926	6,316	0	202	0	212	8,745	3,000	0	0
Federated States of Micronesia	28,418	17,425	836	4,802	2,772	1,762	0	7,253	10,993	0	0	0
Guam	140,406	62,096	15,493	33,777	2,942	2,383	0	7,501	78,310	32,131	17,423	0
Marshall Islands	15,630	4,751	492	3,084	0	976	0	200	10,879	2,875	0	0
Northern Marianas	18,834	11,683	1,436	8,997	0	1,248	0	2	7,151	4,114	0	0
Palau	10,361	4,927	2,662	1,707	0	125	0	433	5,434	2,461	0	0
Puerto Rico	1,434,948	273,719	53,015	94,382	35,373	2,812	67,698	20,440	1,155,512	950,573	2,431	5,718
U.S. Virgin Islands	78,762	36,500	14,324	16,335	2,354	3,041	0	447	38,270	0	26,525	3,992

[1]Includes other categories not separately shown.
[2]After deducting discounts and allowances.
[3]Includes sales and services of educational activities.
NOTE: Degree-granting institutions grant associate's or higher degrees and participate in Title IV federal financial aid programs. Includes data for public institutions reporting data according to either the Governmental Accounting Standards Board (GASB) or the Financial Accounting Standards Board (FASB) questionnaire. Detail may not sum to totals because of rounding.
SOURCE: U.S. Department of Education, National Center for Education Statistics, Integrated Postsecondary Education Data System (IPEDS), Spring 2015, Finance component. (This table was prepared October 2015.)

Table 333.30. Appropriations from state and local governments for public degree-granting postsecondary institutions, by state or jurisdiction: Selected years, 1990–91 through 2013–14

[In thousands of current dollars]

State or jurisdiction	State appropriations						Local appropriations					
	1990–91	2000–01	2010–11	2011–12	2012–13	2013–14	1990–91	2000–01	2010–11	2011–12	2012–13	2013–14
1	2	3	4	5	6	7	8	9	10	11	12	13
United States	**$35,898,653**	**$56,268,990**	**$63,063,322**	**$58,789,575**	**$58,634,067**	**$62,700,662**	**$3,159,789**	**$5,582,287**	**$10,023,157**	**$10,214,576**	**$10,725,798**	**$11,112,188**
Alabama	708,191	991,302	1,281,923	1,332,025	1,289,898	1,317,764	6,796	4,829	1,204	1,277	1,337	1,895
Alaska	168,395	190,650	346,644	358,441	377,504	392,451	260	10,340	9,681	10,031	10,031	10,789
Arizona	591,656	903,196	1,006,196	783,210	772,257	789,580	149,337	310,762	746,962	749,180	763,521	798,085
Arkansas	315,372	583,794	753,573	755,308	759,693	783,427	216	9,496	30,375	31,131	30,714	32,279
California	5,313,052	7,891,669	9,367,909	7,397,375	7,353,389	8,171,790	771,160	1,764,717	2,490,057	2,561,870	2,870,210	3,005,606
Colorado	423,710	655,037	33,667	30,648	30,479	32,718	22,400	36,840	82,141	78,374	84,923	83,364
Connecticut	363,427	664,356	1,018,015	892,046	926,224	1,080,009	0	0	0	0	0	0
Delaware	115,729	193,695	214,445	222,253	236,730	234,102	0	0	0	0	0	0
District of Columbia	0	3,019	66,420	67,362	75,405	66,691	73,495	46,933	0	0	0	0
Florida	1,638,218	2,656,376	3,243,232	3,037,050	2,765,668	3,356,433	1,850	2	0	0	0	0
Georgia	915,303	1,826,961	1,938,523	1,847,730	1,887,336	2,003,786	25,705	21,615	23	44	69	400
Hawaii	304,131	395,884	359,077	375,754	372,872	391,266	0	0	0	0	0	0
Idaho	177,918	290,746	312,809	308,986	334,283	346,115	6,161	11,148	13,398	20,559	26,483	27,176
Illinois	1,296,895	1,760,300	1,789,707	1,815,619	1,830,155	1,844,938	284,635	520,136	1,001,566	1,015,855	1,028,222	1,048,852
Indiana	886,124	1,257,919	1,431,488	1,415,835	1,393,030	1,452,440	1,507	6,190	7,951	9,012	8,241	7,760
Iowa	544,945	813,805	731,485	709,408	752,635	818,015	21,624	36,129	107,022	114,880	117,353	125,607
Kansas	437,413	664,201	741,285	719,033	743,076	731,298	87,026	160,873	228,630	233,851	255,347	265,604
Kentucky	617,915	939,047	971,263	969,989	920,031	923,182	4,682	14,930	18,261	17,501	19,349	20,377
Louisiana	566,798	834,643	1,018,696	944,649	874,193	807,568	1,462	517	0	0	0	0
Maine	174,737	212,144	252,786	255,518	251,703	258,412	0	0	0	0	0	0
Maryland	724,223	999,723	1,392,864	1,411,746	1,426,571	1,480,786	117,913	185,034	319,337	310,463	318,138	329,689
Massachusetts	471,368	1,038,998	1,034,211	1,046,090	1,042,983	1,168,001	0	0	0	0	0	0
Michigan	1,326,884	1,991,098	1,713,747	1,490,701	1,551,995	1,600,635	159,202	288,112	551,945	523,771	511,749	531,528
Minnesota	744,381	1,174,797	1,206,301	1,095,626	1,099,848	1,183,311	2,040	0	0	0	0	0
Mississippi	365,574	758,242	868,311	939,075	905,656	946,620	25,670	38,167	58,179	59,716	63,053	64,212
Missouri	563,430	945,746	904,594	836,519	841,745	852,967	38,097	101,562	148,970	146,266	148,724	147,973
Montana	110,199	137,341	173,250	192,319	193,116	211,658	3,310	4,069	8,151	8,404	8,622	9,156
Nebraska	318,482	514,235	621,957	616,412	631,041	666,757	36,569	19,892	120,979	127,737	134,270	138,933
Nevada	161,581	333,117	539,712	466,961	464,295	478,282	0	0	0	0	0	0
New Hampshire	71,226	96,157	131,878	80,192	94,372	109,724	6	0	7	0	0	0
New Jersey	854,989	1,246,554	1,495,505	1,495,920	1,127,237	1,569,437	145,010	172,667	211,638	194,452	194,041	199,631
New Mexico	307,083	538,822	724,046	675,069	711,375	749,949	34,364	60,183	120,930	126,890	128,028	134,655
New York	2,313,128	4,461,671	4,247,113	4,248,791	4,311,984	4,593,055	372,650	431,415	762,484	797,232	802,810	803,784
North Carolina	1,351,111	2,221,600	3,434,423	3,387,420	3,549,146	3,474,851	62,785	113,448	196,168	200,980	206,763	217,480
North Dakota	129,986	188,047	268,488	276,228	312,859	334,094	9	21	2,459	2,686	3,025	3,082
Ohio	1,360,141	1,922,571	1,888,347	1,861,830	1,875,678	1,917,249	63,899	101,647	163,891	158,190	151,995	164,764
Oklahoma	473,898	754,540	924,623	898,544	899,841	915,806	12,822	28,367	49,857	50,986	56,133	56,899
Oregon	377,476	640,347	537,918	583,336	471,202	634,748	118,499	106,436	206,762	210,454	219,987	230,607
Pennsylvania	962,121	1,331,544	1,401,316	1,189,943	1,216,803	1,211,416	62,794	94,338	117,967	111,524	113,607	111,246
Rhode Island	113,614	157,137	137,071	141,208	141,512	148,310	0	0	0	0	0	0
South Carolina	578,794	853,139	480,329	465,402	506,615	538,507	18,670	36,060	62,799	62,126	62,217	64,358
South Dakota	81,859	129,680	157,444	159,652	168,873	180,855	0	0	0	0	0	0
Tennessee	663,536	969,316	1,250,509	1,002,136	1,032,518	1,117,533	1,779	3,824	5,327	5,655	5,684	5,707
Texas	2,627,916	4,236,852	5,179,075	5,022,641	4,891,792	5,394,667	210,934	439,342	1,377,390	1,452,266	1,539,448	1,623,483
Utah	304,738	531,975	661,823	677,217	697,252	737,380	0	0	0	0	0	0
Vermont	40,997	53,605	72,466	67,894	67,725	70,618	4	0	0	0	0	0
Virginia	886,208	1,395,308	1,534,717	1,441,710	1,608,217	1,674,472	973	1,570	3,737	5,141	3,698	3,886
Washington	828,700	1,200,392	1,329,108	1,074,462	1,060,355	1,195,297	2,470	0	0	0	0	0
West Virginia	263,269	382,269	395,050	429,716	439,393	401,966	574	503	316	874	719	653
Wisconsin	841,192	1,186,415	1,151,462	943,010	986,520	1,012,034	197,712	379,648	757,773	769,923	789,097	795,338
Wyoming	120,623	149,009	326,523	333,566	358,988	327,692	12,721	20,525	38,818	45,274	48,190	47,331
U.S. Service Academies	0	0	0	0	0	0	0	0	0	0	0	0
Other jurisdictions	**337,393**	**709,473**	**883,692**	**891,770**	**954,953**	**995,154**	**12,724**	**20,612**	**46,944**	**40,258**	**43,362**	**46,378**
American Samoa	0	0	0	1,948	1,830	3,000	0	0	0	0	0	0
Federated States of Micronesia	0	40	0	0	0	0	0	3,327	0	0	0	0
Guam	28,283	29,122	31,936	34,197	32,661	32,131	10,028	12,826	15,700	14,569	16,156	17,423
Marshall Islands	0	1,924	2,000	2,875	2,901	2,875	0	0	0	0	0	0
Northern Marianas	0	9,055	4,385	3,749	4,474	4,114	0	0	0	0	0	0
Palau	644	2,345	2,039	2,654	2,411	2,461	0	0	0	0	0	0
Puerto Rico	277,295	647,623	843,332	846,348	910,675	950,573	2,375	4,459	1,824	2	2,319	2,431
U.S. Virgin Islands	31,170	19,365	0	0	0	0	320	0	29,420	25,687	24,887	26,525

NOTE: Data for 1990–91 are for institutions of higher education, while later data are for degree-granting institutions. Degree-granting institutions grant associate's or higher degrees and participate in Title IV federal financial aid programs. The degree-granting classification is very similar to the earlier higher education classification, but it includes more 2-year colleges and excludes a few higher education institutions that did not grant degrees. Includes data for public institutions reporting data according to either the Governmental Accounting Standards Board (GASB) or the Financial Accounting Standards Board (FASB) questionnaire. Some data have been revised from previously published figures. Detail may not sum to totals because of rounding.

SOURCE: U.S. Department of Education, National Center for Education Statistics, Integrated Postsecondary Education Data System (IPEDS), "Finance Survey" (IPEDS-F:FY91); and selected years, Spring 2002 through Spring 2015, Finance component. (This table was prepared October 2015.)

Table 333.40. Total revenue of private nonprofit degree-granting postsecondary institutions, by source of funds and level of institution: 1999–2000 through 2013–14

Level of institution and year	Total	Student tuition and fees (net of allowances)	Federal appropriations, grants, and contracts[1]	State and local appropriations, grants, and contracts	Private gifts, grants, and contracts: Total	Private gifts, grants, and contracts: Private grants and contracts	Private gifts, grants, and contracts: Private gifts and contributions from affiliated entities	Investment return (gain or loss)	Educational activities	Auxiliary enterprises (net of allowances)	Hospitals	Other
1	2	3	4	5	6	7	8	9	10	11	12	13
					In thousands of current dollars							
All levels												
1999–2000	$120,625,806	$29,651,812	$12,191,827	$1,697,979	$16,488,984	—	—	$37,763,518	$2,865,606	$8,317,607	$7,208,600	$4,439,874
2000–01	82,174,492	31,318,106	13,378,019	1,684,425	15,859,313	—	—	-3,602,326	3,468,680	8,742,610	7,126,343	4,199,323
2001–02	84,346,652	33,499,121	14,790,235	1,796,930	15,394,353	—	—	-6,545,330	3,220,868	9,317,922	8,083,935	4,788,618
2002–03	105,672,753	36,019,267	16,625,072	1,988,977	14,380,351	—	—	9,340,400	3,056,259	9,833,972	8,942,047	5,486,409
2003–04	134,230,762	38,505,631	18,335,784	1,941,273	15,847,571	—	—	30,896,917	3,290,420	10,325,606	9,657,753	5,429,805
2004–05	140,150,716	41,394,424	19,699,204	1,957,921	16,738,916	—	—	30,431,521	3,595,559	10,823,963	10,377,808	5,131,401
2005–06	152,744,665	44,263,227	19,683,291	2,075,850	18,346,525	—	—	35,634,520	3,716,409	11,610,762	11,536,658	5,877,423
2006–07	182,381,275	47,481,431	20,193,637	2,165,371	20,193,231	—	—	55,907,662	4,105,289	12,291,973	12,636,904	7,405,779
2007–08	139,250,857	50,736,003	20,204,523	2,385,888	20,991,936	—	—	6,446,982	4,849,728	12,928,521	13,299,928	7,407,348
2008–09	69,064,340	53,698,893	21,026,721	2,391,238	17,670,642	—	—	-64,204,943	4,787,360	13,579,506	14,790,231	5,324,691
2009–10	168,688,480	56,386,895	22,913,755	2,193,062	18,019,300	$4,189,574	$13,829,726	28,427,192	4,821,683	14,080,329	16,541,461	5,304,802
2010–11	207,132,349	60,069,691	24,319,663	2,165,584	22,096,853	4,379,206	17,717,647	53,574,169	4,979,595	14,797,601	17,521,091	7,608,102
2011–12	161,843,203	63,010,873	24,147,131	1,964,921	21,619,470	4,446,517	17,172,953	4,538,153	5,082,873	15,500,185	18,658,649	7,320,948
2012–13	202,084,062	65,595,255	23,714,629	1,938,964	22,336,587	4,834,524	17,502,063	38,537,742	5,534,688	15,957,898	19,011,711	9,456,589
2013–14	228,806,703	67,682,150	23,655,533	1,976,193	25,821,258	5,134,270	20,686,988	57,147,116	6,280,766	16,405,110	20,667,484	9,171,093
4-year												
1999–2000	119,708,625	29,257,523	12,133,829	1,673,707	16,346,616	—	—	37,698,219	2,837,784	8,261,507	7,208,600	4,290,841
2000–01	81,568,928	30,996,381	13,318,572	1,659,505	15,788,869	—	—	-3,623,323	3,452,731	8,703,316	7,125,648	4,147,227
2001–02	83,764,907	33,165,965	14,708,582	1,771,383	15,328,974	—	—	-6,547,915	3,206,440	9,263,171	8,083,935	4,784,371
2002–03	105,064,157	35,676,736	16,515,854	1,957,729	14,319,622	—	—	9,338,684	3,041,307	9,779,275	8,942,047	5,492,904
2003–04	133,594,668	38,181,648	18,236,313	1,903,374	15,789,672	—	—	30,854,091	3,277,767	10,287,215	9,657,753	5,406,836
2004–05	139,528,763	41,045,608	19,622,002	1,931,021	16,671,017	—	—	30,408,545	3,581,869	10,784,161	10,377,808	5,106,733
2005–06	152,150,193	43,944,766	19,607,858	2,045,814	18,288,085	—	—	35,603,805	3,699,630	11,573,115	11,536,658	5,850,463
2006–07	181,853,949	47,211,041	20,137,112	2,144,350	20,143,850	—	—	55,857,220	4,097,001	12,253,297	12,636,904	7,373,173
2007–08	138,749,560	50,431,352	20,143,833	2,361,511	20,938,774	—	—	6,459,197	4,838,649	12,890,431	13,299,928	7,385,886
2008–09	68,617,705	53,399,912	20,967,794	2,370,169	17,624,319	—	—	-64,172,755	4,781,845	13,542,690	14,790,231	5,313,500
2009–10	168,169,216	56,087,965	22,843,520	2,179,050	17,968,453	4,185,607	13,782,846	28,406,397	4,814,283	14,044,652	16,541,461	5,283,434
2010–11	206,473,105	59,603,541	24,260,568	2,150,124	22,057,300	4,376,381	17,680,919	53,557,782	4,975,158	14,762,888	17,521,091	7,584,652
2011–12	161,246,877	62,571,879	24,098,863	1,953,307	21,580,612	4,444,004	17,136,608	4,532,992	5,079,866	15,471,860	18,658,649	7,298,849
2012–13	201,568,379	65,246,827	23,668,765	1,925,440	22,294,772	4,832,217	17,462,555	38,524,192	5,531,823	15,928,400	19,011,711	9,436,448
2013–14	228,233,132	67,326,758	23,594,264	1,963,783	25,770,492	5,131,305	20,639,187	57,104,740	6,278,456	16,374,118	20,667,484	9,153,035
2-year												
1999–2000	917,181	394,289	57,998	24,272	142,368	—	—	65,299	27,822	56,100	0	149,033
2000–01	605,564	321,724	59,446	24,920	70,444	—	—	20,996	15,949	39,294	694	52,096
2001–02	581,745	333,156	81,653	25,547	65,379	—	—	2,585	14,429	54,750	0	4,246
2002–03	608,596	342,531	109,217	31,247	60,729	—	—	1,716	14,953	54,697	0	-6,495
2003–04	636,094	323,983	99,471	37,900	57,900	—	—	42,826	12,653	38,391	0	22,969
2004–05	621,953	348,815	77,202	26,900	67,899	—	—	22,976	13,690	39,802	0	24,668
2005–06	594,473	318,460	75,433	30,036	58,441	—	—	30,716	16,778	37,648	0	26,960
2006–07	527,327	270,389	56,525	21,021	49,381	—	—	50,442	8,288	38,675	0	32,606
2007–08	501,297	304,651	60,689	24,377	53,162	—	—	-12,214	11,080	38,091	0	21,462
2008–09	446,635	298,981	58,927	21,069	46,323	—	—	-32,187	5,515	36,816	0	11,191
2009–10	519,264	298,930	70,235	14,012	50,847	3,967	46,880	20,795	7,400	35,677	0	21,368
2010–11	659,244	466,149	59,095	15,460	39,553	2,825	36,727	16,388	4,437	34,712	0	23,450
2011–12	596,326	438,994	48,269	11,614	38,858	2,513	36,345	5,161	3,007	28,325	0	22,099
2012–13	515,683	348,427	45,863	13,524	41,815	2,307	39,508	13,550	2,865	29,498	0	20,140
2013–14	573,571	355,392	61,269	12,409	50,766	2,965	47,800	42,376	2,311	30,991	0	18,058
					Percentage distribution							
All levels												
1999–2000	100.00	24.58	10.11	1.41	13.67	—	—	31.31	2.38	6.90	5.98	3.68
2000–01	100.00	38.11	16.28	2.05	19.30	—	—	-4.38	4.22	10.64	8.67	5.11
2001–02	100.00	39.72	17.54	2.13	18.25	—	—	-7.76	3.82	11.05	9.58	5.68
2002–03	100.00	34.09	15.73	1.88	13.61	—	—	8.84	2.89	9.31	8.46	5.19
2003–04	100.00	28.69	13.66	1.45	11.81	—	—	23.02	2.45	7.69	7.19	4.05
2004–05	100.00	29.54	14.06	1.40	11.94	—	—	21.71	2.57	7.72	7.40	3.66
2005–06	100.00	28.98	12.89	1.36	12.01	—	—	23.33	2.43	7.60	7.55	3.85
2006–07	100.00	26.03	11.07	1.19	11.07	—	—	30.65	2.25	6.74	6.93	4.06
2007–08	100.00	36.43	14.51	1.71	15.07	—	—	4.63	3.48	9.28	9.55	5.32
2008–09	100.00	77.75	30.45	3.46	25.59	—	—	-92.96	6.93	19.66	21.42	7.71
2009–10	100.00	33.43	13.58	1.30	10.68	2.48	8.20	16.85	2.86	8.35	9.81	3.14
2010–11	100.00	29.00	11.74	1.05	10.67	2.11	8.55	25.86	2.40	7.14	8.46	3.67
2011–12	100.00	38.93	14.92	1.21	13.36	2.75	10.61	2.80	3.14	9.58	11.53	4.52
2012–13	100.00	32.46	11.74	0.96	11.05	2.39	8.66	19.07	2.74	7.90	9.41	4.68
2013–14	100.00	29.58	10.34	0.86	11.29	2.24	9.04	24.98	2.75	7.17	9.03	4.01
4-year												
1999–2000	100.00	24.44	10.14	1.40	13.66	—	—	31.49	2.37	6.90	6.02	3.58
2000–01	100.00	38.00	16.33	2.03	19.36	—	—	-4.44	4.23	10.67	8.74	5.08
2001–02	100.00	39.59	17.56	2.11	18.30	—	—	-7.82	3.83	11.06	9.65	5.71
2002–03	100.00	33.96	15.72	1.86	13.63	—	—	8.89	2.89	9.31	8.51	5.23
2003–04	100.00	28.58	13.65	1.42	11.82	—	—	23.10	2.45	7.70	7.23	4.05
2004–05	100.00	29.42	14.06	1.38	11.95	—	—	21.79	2.57	7.73	7.44	3.66
2005–06	100.00	28.88	12.89	1.34	12.02	—	—	23.40	2.43	7.61	7.58	3.85
2006–07	100.00	25.96	11.07	1.18	11.08	—	—	30.72	2.25	6.74	6.95	4.05
2007–08	100.00	36.35	14.52	1.70	15.09	—	—	4.66	3.49	9.29	9.59	5.32
2008–09	100.00	77.82	30.56	3.45	25.68	—	—	-93.52	6.97	19.74	21.55	7.74

See notes at end of table.

Table 333.40. Total revenue of private nonprofit degree-granting postsecondary institutions, by source of funds and level of institution: 1999–2000 through 2013–14—Continued

Level of institution and year	Total	Student tuition and fees (net of allowances)	Federal appropriations, grants, and contracts[1]	State and local appropriations, grants, and contracts	Private gifts, grants, and contracts: Total	Private gifts, grants, and contracts: Private grants and contracts	Private gifts, grants, and contracts: Private gifts and contributions from affiliated entities	Investment return (gain or loss)	Educational activities	Auxiliary enterprises (net of allowances)	Hospitals	Other
1	2	3	4	5	6	7	8	9	10	11	12	13
2009–10	100.00	33.35	13.58	1.30	10.68	2.49	8.20	16.89	2.86	8.35	9.84	3.14
2010–11	100.00	28.87	11.75	1.04	10.68	2.12	8.56	25.94	2.41	7.15	8.49	3.67
2011–12	100.00	38.81	14.95	1.21	13.38	2.76	10.63	2.81	3.15	9.60	11.57	4.53
2012–13	100.00	32.37	11.74	0.96	11.06	2.40	8.66	19.11	2.74	7.90	9.43	4.68
2013–14	100.00	29.50	10.34	0.86	11.29	2.25	9.04	25.02	2.75	7.17	9.06	4.01
2-year												
1999–2000	100.00	42.99	6.32	2.65	15.52	—	—	7.12	3.03	6.12	0.00	16.25
2000–01	100.00	53.13	9.82	4.12	11.63	—	—	3.47	2.63	6.49	0.11	8.60
2001–02	100.00	57.27	14.04	4.39	11.24	—	—	0.44	2.48	9.41	0.00	0.73
2002–03	100.00	56.28	17.95	5.13	9.98	—	—	0.28	2.46	8.99	0.00	-1.07
2003–04	100.00	50.93	15.64	5.96	9.10	—	—	6.73	1.99	6.04	0.00	3.61
2004–05	100.00	56.08	12.41	4.33	10.92	—	—	3.69	2.20	6.40	0.00	3.97
2005–06	100.00	53.57	12.69	5.05	9.83	—	—	5.17	2.82	6.33	0.00	4.54
2006–07	100.00	51.28	10.72	3.99	9.36	—	—	9.57	1.57	7.33	0.00	6.18
2007–08	100.00	60.77	12.11	4.86	10.60	—	—	-2.44	2.21	7.60	0.00	4.28
2008–09	100.00	66.94	13.19	4.72	10.37	—	—	-7.21	1.23	8.24	0.00	2.51
2009–10	100.00	57.57	13.53	2.70	9.79	0.76	9.03	4.00	1.43	6.87	0.00	4.12
2010–11	100.00	70.71	8.96	2.35	6.00	0.43	5.57	2.49	0.67	5.27	0.00	3.56
2011–12	100.00	73.62	8.09	1.95	6.52	0.42	6.09	0.87	0.50	4.75	0.00	3.71
2012–13	100.00	67.57	8.89	2.62	8.11	0.45	7.66	2.63	0.56	5.72	0.00	3.91
2013–14	100.00	61.96	10.68	2.16	8.85	0.52	8.33	7.39	0.40	5.40	0.00	3.15
	Revenue per full-time-equivalent student in constant 2014–15 dollars[2]											
All levels												
1999–2000	$66,422	$16,328	$6,713	$935	$9,080	—	—	$20,794	$1,578	$4,580	$3,969	$2,445
2000–01	42,899	16,350	6,984	879	8,279	—	—	-1,881	1,811	4,564	3,720	2,192
2001–02	42,338	16,815	7,424	902	7,727	—	—	-3,285	1,617	4,677	4,058	2,404
2002–03	50,225	17,120	7,902	945	6,835	—	—	4,439	1,453	4,674	4,250	2,608
2003–04	60,942	17,482	8,325	881	7,195	—	—	14,028	1,494	4,688	4,385	2,465
2004–05	60,304	17,811	8,476	842	7,202	—	—	13,094	1,547	4,657	4,465	2,208
2005–06	62,449	18,097	8,047	849	7,501	—	—	14,569	1,519	4,747	4,717	2,403
2006–07	71,402	18,589	7,906	848	7,906	—	—	21,888	1,607	4,812	4,947	2,899
2007–08	51,282	18,685	7,441	879	7,731	—	—	2,374	1,786	4,761	4,898	2,728
2008–09	24,702	19,206	7,521	855	6,320	—	—	-22,964	1,712	4,857	5,290	1,904
2009–10	58,201	19,455	7,906	757	6,217	$1,445	$4,772	9,808	1,664	4,858	5,707	1,830
2010–11	67,503	19,576	7,926	706	7,201	1,427	5,774	17,459	1,623	4,822	5,710	2,479
2011–12	50,799	19,778	7,579	617	6,786	1,396	5,390	1,424	1,595	4,865	5,857	2,298
2012–13	61,648	20,010	7,234	592	6,814	1,475	5,339	11,756	1,688	4,868	5,800	2,885
2013–14	68,604	20,293	7,093	593	7,742	1,539	6,203	17,135	1,883	4,919	6,197	2,750
4-year												
1999–2000	67,329	16,456	6,825	941	9,194	—	—	21,203	1,596	4,647	4,054	2,413
2000–01	43,248	16,434	7,062	880	8,371	—	—	-1,921	1,831	4,615	3,778	2,199
2001–02	42,674	16,897	7,493	902	7,809	—	—	-3,336	1,634	4,719	4,118	2,437
2002–03	50,607	17,185	7,955	943	6,897	—	—	4,498	1,465	4,710	4,307	2,646
2003–04	61,428	17,556	8,385	875	7,260	—	—	14,187	1,507	4,730	4,441	2,486
2004–05	60,765	17,876	8,545	841	7,260	—	—	13,243	1,560	4,697	4,520	2,224
2005–06	62,882	18,162	8,104	846	7,558	—	—	14,715	1,529	4,783	4,768	2,418
2006–07	71,813	18,643	7,952	847	7,955	—	—	22,058	1,618	4,839	4,990	2,912
2007–08	51,556	18,739	7,485	877	7,780	—	—	2,400	1,798	4,790	4,942	2,744
2008–09	24,751	19,262	7,563	855	6,357	—	—	-23,147	1,725	4,885	5,335	1,917
2009–10	58,499	19,511	7,946	758	6,250	1,456	4,794	9,881	1,675	4,886	5,754	1,838
2010–11	68,010	19,633	7,991	708	7,265	1,442	5,824	17,641	1,639	4,863	5,771	2,498
2011–12	51,114	19,835	7,639	619	6,841	1,409	5,432	1,437	1,610	4,904	5,915	2,314
2012–13	62,007	20,072	7,281	592	6,858	1,487	5,372	11,851	1,702	4,900	5,848	2,903
2013–14	68,984	20,350	7,131	594	7,789	1,551	6,238	17,260	1,898	4,949	6,247	2,767
2-year												
1999–2000	24,074	10,349	1,522	637	3,737	—	—	1,714	730	1,473	0	3,912
2000–01	20,565	10,926	2,019	846	2,392	—	—	713	542	1,334	24	1,769
2001–02	19,838	11,361	2,784	871	2,229	—	—	88	492	1,867	0	145
2002–03	21,813	12,277	3,915	1,120	2,177	—	—	62	536	1,960	0	-233
2003–04	22,909	11,668	3,582	1,365	2,085	—	—	1,542	456	1,383	0	827
2004–05	22,301	12,507	2,768	965	2,435	—	—	824	491	1,427	0	885
2005–06	22,603	12,109	2,868	1,142	2,222	—	—	1,168	638	1,431	0	1,025
2006–07	24,022	12,317	2,575	958	2,250	—	—	2,298	378	1,762	0	1,485
2007–08	20,765	12,620	2,514	1,010	2,202	—	—	-506	459	1,578	0	889
2008–09	18,968	12,697	2,503	895	1,967	—	—	-1,367	234	1,564	0	475
2009–10	21,989	12,659	2,974	593	2,153	168	1,985	881	313	1,511	0	905
2010–11	20,233	14,307	1,814	474	1,214	87	1,127	503	136	1,065	0	720
2011–12	19,055	14,028	1,542	371	1,242	80	1,161	165	96	905	0	706
2012–13	18,871	12,751	1,678	495	1,530	84	1,446	496	105	1,079	0	737
2013–14	21,484	13,312	2,295	465	1,902	111	1,790	1,587	87	1,161	0	676

—Not available.
[1]Includes independent operations.
[2]Constant dollars based on the Consumer Price Index, prepared by the Bureau of Labor Statistics, U.S. Department of Labor, adjusted to a school-year basis.
NOTE: Degree-granting institutions grant associate's or higher degrees and participate in Title IV federal financial aid programs. Some data have been revised from previously published figures. Detail may not sum to totals because of rounding.

SOURCE: U.S. Department of Education, National Center for Education Statistics, Integrated Postsecondary Education Data System (IPEDS), "Fall Enrollment Survey" (IPEDS-EF:99); and Spring 2001 through Spring 2007, Enrollment component; Spring 2008 through Spring 2014, Fall Enrollment component; and Spring 2001 through Spring 2015, Finance component. (This table was prepared November 2015.)

Table 333.50. Total revenue of private nonprofit degree-granting postsecondary institutions, by source of funds and classification of institution: 2013–14

Classification of institution	Total	Student tuition and fees (net of allowances)	Federal appropriations, grants, and contracts[1]	State and local appropriations, grants, and contracts	Private grants and contracts	Private gifts and contributions from affiliated entities	Investment return (gain or loss)	Educational activities	Auxiliary enterprises (net of allowances)	Hospitals	Other
1	2	3	4	5	6	7	8	9	10	11	12
	In thousands of current dollars										
Total	**$228,806,703**	**$67,682,150**	**$23,655,533**	**$1,976,193**	**$5,134,270**	**$20,686,988**	**$57,147,116**	**$6,280,766**	**$16,405,110**	**$20,667,484**	**$9,171,093**
4-year	228,233,132	67,326,758	23,594,264	1,963,783	5,131,305	20,639,187	57,104,740	6,278,456	16,374,118	20,667,484	9,153,035
Research university, very high[2]	116,156,076	14,961,425	18,183,002	883,457	3,577,126	10,173,916	37,247,144	4,757,896	4,317,283	16,196,364	5,858,463
Research university, high[3]	14,928,569	6,349,616	1,156,599	142,768	198,034	1,574,928	2,312,746	633,093	1,572,421	434,199	554,165
Doctoral/research[4]	9,785,706	5,995,835	207,198	75,805	110,719	558,175	1,295,240	65,284	996,374	0	481,077
Master's[5]	33,809,636	21,105,526	985,377	336,513	154,165	2,313,975	3,620,728	164,277	4,266,940	67,503	794,631
Baccalaureate[6]	32,120,799	11,924,551	732,338	179,899	206,514	3,827,690	10,085,520	145,056	4,387,750	342	631,137
Special-focus institutions[7]	21,432,346	6,989,805	2,329,750	345,341	884,748	2,190,504	2,543,363	512,850	833,350	3,969,076	833,561
Art, music, or design	2,707,646	1,586,102	54,046	12,699	23,298	282,302	402,954	17,804	247,440	0	81,001
Business and management	844,297	575,397	24,859	8,346	966	41,587	95,429	6,864	80,854	0	9,994
Engineering or technology	364,804	205,910	3,496	892	204	25,471	90,359	2,167	27,645	0	8,660
Law	611,727	458,984	8,624	2,328	4,564	24,796	89,682	915	14,984	0	6,851
Medical or other health	13,984,306	3,323,005	2,102,246	312,107	805,219	1,089,870	1,127,580	456,313	248,702	3,969,076	550,187
Theological	2,488,360	634,396	44,311	2,640	44,198	690,264	708,395	16,415	188,063	0	159,677
Tribal[8]	107,516	10,379	79,461	2,233	1,634	671	860	611	1,398	0	10,269
Other special focus	323,689	195,632	12,706	4,097	4,664	35,543	28,103	11,760	24,263	0	6,921
2-year	573,571	355,392	61,269	12,409	2,965	47,800	42,376	2,311	30,991	0	18,058
Associate's of arts	553,672	354,704	49,179	11,623	2,772	47,104	42,185	2,311	30,856	0	12,937
Tribal[8]	19,899	688	12,089	786	193	696	191	0	135	0	5,121
	Percentage distribution										
Total	**100.00**	**29.58**	**10.34**	**0.86**	**2.24**	**9.04**	**24.98**	**2.75**	**7.17**	**9.03**	**4.01**
4-year	100.00	29.50	10.34	0.86	2.25	9.04	25.02	2.75	7.17	9.06	4.01
Research university, very high[2]	100.00	12.88	15.65	0.76	3.08	8.76	32.07	4.10	3.72	13.94	5.04
Research university, high[3]	100.00	42.53	7.75	0.96	1.33	10.55	15.49	4.24	10.53	2.91	3.71
Doctoral/research[4]	100.00	61.27	2.12	0.77	1.13	5.70	13.24	0.67	10.18	0.00	4.92
Master's[5]	100.00	62.42	2.91	1.00	0.46	6.84	10.71	0.49	12.62	0.20	2.35
Baccalaureate[6]	100.00	37.12	2.28	0.56	0.64	11.92	31.40	0.45	13.66	#	1.96
Special-focus institutions[7]	100.00	32.61	10.87	1.61	4.13	10.22	11.87	2.39	3.89	18.52	3.89
Art, music, or design	100.00	58.58	2.00	0.47	0.86	10.43	14.88	0.66	9.14	0.00	2.99
Business and management	100.00	68.15	2.94	0.99	0.11	4.93	11.30	0.81	9.58	0.00	1.18
Engineering or technology	100.00	56.44	0.96	0.24	0.06	6.98	24.77	0.59	7.58	0.00	2.37
Law	100.00	75.03	1.41	0.38	0.75	4.05	14.66	0.15	2.45	0.00	1.12
Medical or other health	100.00	23.76	15.03	2.23	5.76	7.79	8.06	3.26	1.78	28.38	3.93
Theological	100.00	25.49	1.78	0.11	1.78	27.74	28.47	0.66	7.56	0.00	6.42
Tribal[8]	100.00	9.65	73.91	2.08	1.52	0.62	0.80	0.57	1.30	0.00	9.55
Other special focus	100.00	60.44	3.93	1.27	1.44	10.98	8.68	3.63	7.50	0.00	2.14
2-year	100.00	61.96	10.68	2.16	0.52	8.33	7.39	0.40	5.40	0.00	3.15
Associate's of arts	100.00	64.06	8.88	2.10	0.50	8.51	7.62	0.42	5.57	0.00	2.34
Tribal[8]	100.00	3.46	60.75	3.95	0.97	3.50	0.96	0.00	0.68	0.00	25.73
	Revenue per full-time-equivalent student in current dollars										
Total	**$68,108**	**$20,147**	**$7,041**	**$588**	**$1,528**	**$6,158**	**$17,011**	**$1,870**	**$4,883**	**$6,152**	**$2,730**
4-year	68,486	20,203	7,080	589	1,540	6,193	17,135	1,884	4,913	6,202	2,747
Research university, very high[2]	229,320	29,538	35,898	1,744	7,062	20,086	73,535	9,393	8,523	31,976	11,566
Research university, high[3]	55,561	23,632	4,305	531	737	5,862	8,607	2,356	5,852	1,616	2,062
Doctoral/research[4]	36,712	22,494	777	284	415	2,094	4,859	245	3,738	0	1,805
Master's[5]	26,981	16,843	786	269	123	1,847	2,889	131	3,405	54	634
Baccalaureate[6]	44,050	16,353	1,004	247	283	5,249	13,831	199	6,017	#	866
Special-focus institutions[7]	69,470	22,657	7,552	1,119	2,868	7,100	8,244	1,662	2,701	12,865	2,702
Art, music, or design	47,436	27,787	947	222	408	4,946	7,059	312	4,335	0	1,419
Business and management	27,825	18,963	819	275	32	1,371	3,145	226	2,665	0	329
Engineering or technology	24,516	13,838	235	60	14	1,712	6,073	146	1,858	0	582
Law	44,035	33,039	621	168	329	1,785	6,456	66	1,079	0	493
Medical or other health	128,407	30,513	19,303	2,866	7,394	10,007	10,354	4,190	2,284	36,445	5,052
Theological	33,743	8,603	601	36	599	9,360	9,606	223	2,550	0	2,165
Tribal[8]	41,803	4,035	30,895	868	635	261	334	238	544	0	3,993
Other special focus	45,629	27,577	1,791	577	657	5,010	3,962	1,658	3,420	0	976
2-year	21,329	13,216	2,278	461	110	1,777	1,576	86	1,152	0	672
Associate's of arts	21,023	13,468	1,867	441	105	1,789	1,602	88	1,172	0	491
Tribal[8]	35,790	1,237	21,743	1,414	348	1,252	343	0	243	0	9,210

#Rounds to zero.
[1]Includes independent operations.
[2]Research universities with a very high level of research activity.
[3]Research universities with a high level of research activity.
[4]Institutions that award at least 20 doctor's degrees per year, but did not have high levels of research activity.
[5]Institutions that award at least 50 master's degrees per year.
[6]Institutions that primarily emphasize undergraduate education. Also includes institutions classified as 4-year under the IPEDS system, which had been classified as 2-year in the Carnegie classification system because they primarily award associate's degrees.
[7]Four-year institutions that award degrees primarily in single fields of study, such as medicine, business, fine arts, theology, and engineering.
[8]Tribally controlled colleges, which are located on reservations and are members of the American Indian Higher Education Consortium.

NOTE: Relative levels of research activity for research universities were determined by an analysis of research and development expenditures, science and engineering research staffing, and doctoral degrees conferred, by field. Further information on the Carnegie 2005 classification system used in this table may be obtained from http://carnegieclassifications.iu.edu/. Degree-granting institutions grant associate's or higher degrees and participate in Title IV federal financial aid programs. Detail may not sum to totals because of rounding.

SOURCE: U.S. Department of Education, National Center for Education Statistics, Integrated Postsecondary Education Data System (IPEDS), Spring 2014, Fall Enrollment component; and Spring 2015, Finance component. (This table was prepared November 2015.)

Table 333.55. Total revenue of private for-profit degree-granting postsecondary institutions, by source of funds and level of institution: Selected years, 1999–2000 through 2013–14

Level of institution and year	Total	Student tuition and fees (net of allowances)	Federal appropriations, grants, and contracts	State and local appropriations, grants, and contracts	Private gifts, grants, and contracts	Investment income and gains (losses)	Educational activities	Auxiliary enterprises (net of allowances)	Other
1	2	3	4	5	6	7	8	9	10
				In thousands of current dollars					
All levels									
1999–2000	$4,321,985	$3,721,032	$198,923	$71,904	$2,151	$18,537	$70,672	$156,613	$82,153
2008–09	19,401,359	16,767,748	1,407,615	130,378	80,345	38,680	368,034	395,589	212,970
2009–10	24,689,264	22,402,076	1,706,901	95,277	37,570	40,115	424,471	485,443	-502,589
2010–11	28,285,216	25,157,459	1,583,370	157,290	31,272	32,551	402,206	542,622	378,447
2011–12	26,922,849	24,344,390	1,220,844	101,443	9,386	36,726	351,917	511,364	346,778
2012–13	24,780,997	22,483,997	1,092,117	96,650	14,700	58,267	312,065	484,747	238,453
2013–14	22,659,062	20,476,030	941,370	77,986	12,206	43,032	256,219	482,560	369,658
4-year									
1999–2000	2,381,042	2,050,136	103,865	39,460	1,109	10,340	33,764	102,103	40,266
2008–09	14,793,302	12,982,049	897,503	80,021	71,601	35,434	327,474	297,626	101,595
2009–10	18,985,251	17,342,058	1,356,142	65,148	35,630	35,949	366,044	372,513	-588,234
2010–11	21,690,069	19,483,895	1,113,186	118,054	29,118	28,671	346,786	405,604	164,755
2011–12	21,204,786	19,251,785	836,741	69,747	7,298	30,546	308,359	404,301	296,009
2012–13	19,574,783	17,783,754	809,567	64,261	12,233	49,224	265,836	395,722	194,187
2013–14	17,845,848	16,187,061	709,416	51,830	10,232	36,012	222,739	395,510	233,049
2-year									
1999–2000	1,940,943	1,670,896	95,058	32,444	1,042	8,197	36,908	54,510	41,888
2008–09	4,608,057	3,785,699	510,112	50,358	8,745	3,246	40,560	97,964	111,374
2009–10	5,704,013	5,060,018	350,759	30,129	1,940	4,166	58,427	112,930	85,644
2010–11	6,595,147	5,673,564	470,183	39,236	2,154	3,880	55,420	137,018	213,692
2011–12	5,718,063	5,092,606	384,103	31,696	2,087	6,180	43,558	107,063	50,770
2012–13	5,206,214	4,700,243	282,550	32,390	2,467	9,043	46,230	89,025	44,266
2013–14	4,813,214	4,288,969	231,954	26,157	1,975	7,021	33,480	87,050	136,609
				Percentage distribution					
All levels									
1999–2000	100.00	86.10	4.60	1.66	0.05	0.43	1.64	3.62	1.90
2008–09	100.00	86.43	7.26	0.67	0.41	0.20	1.90	2.04	1.10
2009–10	100.00	90.74	6.91	0.39	0.15	0.16	1.72	1.97	-2.04
2010–11	100.00	88.94	5.60	0.56	0.11	0.12	1.42	1.92	1.34
2011–12	100.00	90.42	4.53	0.38	0.03	0.14	1.31	1.90	1.29
2012–13	100.00	90.73	4.41	0.39	0.06	0.24	1.26	1.96	0.96
2013–14	100.00	90.37	4.15	0.34	0.05	0.19	1.13	2.13	1.63
4-year									
1999–2000	100.00	86.10	4.36	1.66	0.05	0.43	1.42	4.29	1.69
2008–09	100.00	87.76	6.07	0.54	0.48	0.24	2.21	2.01	0.69
2009–10	100.00	91.34	7.14	0.34	0.19	0.19	1.93	1.96	-3.10
2010–11	100.00	89.83	5.13	0.54	0.13	0.13	1.60	1.87	0.76
2011–12	100.00	90.79	3.95	0.33	0.03	0.14	1.45	1.91	1.40
2012–13	100.00	90.85	4.14	0.33	0.06	0.25	1.36	2.02	0.99
2013–14	100.00	90.70	3.98	0.29	0.06	0.20	1.25	2.22	1.31
2-year									
1999–2000	100.00	86.09	4.90	1.67	0.05	0.42	1.90	2.81	2.16
2008–09	100.00	82.15	11.07	1.09	0.19	0.07	0.88	2.13	2.42
2009–10	100.00	88.71	6.15	0.53	0.03	0.07	1.02	1.98	1.50
2010–11	100.00	86.03	7.13	0.59	0.03	0.06	0.84	2.08	3.24
2011–12	100.00	89.06	6.72	0.55	0.04	0.11	0.76	1.87	0.89
2012–13	100.00	90.28	5.43	0.62	0.05	0.17	0.89	1.71	0.85
2013–14	100.00	89.11	4.82	0.54	0.04	0.15	0.70	1.81	2.84
				Revenue per full-time-equivalent student in constant 2014–15 dollars[1]					
All levels									
1999–2000	$15,710	$13,526	$723	$261	$8	$67	$257	$569	$299
2008–09	16,795	14,515	1,219	113	70	33	319	342	184
2009–10	18,096	16,420	1,251	70	28	29	311	356	-368
2010–11	18,312	16,287	1,025	102	20	21	260	351	245
2011–12	17,370	15,706	788	65	6	24	227	330	224
2012–13	17,913	16,252	789	70	11	42	226	350	172
2013–14	21,557	19,480	896	74	12	41	244	459	352
4-year									
1999–2000	15,945	13,729	696	264	7	69	226	684	270
2008–09	16,645	14,607	1,010	90	81	40	368	335	114
2009–10	18,549	16,944	1,325	64	35	35	358	364	-575
2010–11	18,461	16,583	947	100	25	24	295	345	140
2011–12	17,602	15,980	695	58	6	25	256	336	246
2012–13	18,086	16,431	748	59	11	45	246	366	179
2013–14	23,092	20,946	918	67	13	47	288	512	302
2-year									
1999–2000	15,431	13,284	756	258	8	65	293	433	333
2008–09	17,295	14,209	1,915	189	33	12	152	368	418
2009–10	16,737	14,848	1,029	88	6	12	171	331	251
2010–11	17,837	15,344	1,272	106	6	10	150	371	578
2011–12	16,561	14,750	1,112	92	6	18	126	310	147
2012–13	17,289	15,609	938	108	8	30	154	296	147
2013–14	17,294	15,410	833	94	7	25	120	313	491

[1]Constant dollars based on the Consumer Price Index, prepared by the Bureau of Labor Statistics, U.S. Department of Labor, adjusted to a school-year basis.
NOTE: Degree-granting institutions grant associate's or higher degrees and participate in Title IV federal financial aid programs. Some data have been revised from previously published figures. Detail may not sum to totals because of rounding.

SOURCE: U.S. Department of Education, National Center for Education Statistics, Integrated Postsecondary Education Data System (IPEDS), "Fall Enrollment Survey" (IPEDS-EF:99); Spring 2009 through Spring 2014, Fall Enrollment component; and selected years, Spring 2001 through Spring 2015, Finance component. (This table was prepared November 2015.)

Table 333.60. Total revenue of private for-profit degree-granting postsecondary institutions, by source of funds and classification of institution: 2013–14

Classification of institution	Total	Student tuition and fees (net of allowances)	Federal appropriations, grants, and contracts	State and local appropriations, grants, and contracts	Private gifts, grants, and contracts	Investment income and gains (losses)	Educational activities	Auxiliary enterprises (net of allowances)	Other
1	2	3	4	5	6	7	8	9	10
	In thousands of current dollars								
Total	**$22,659,062**	**$20,476,030**	**$941,370**	**$77,986**	**$12,206**	**$43,032**	**$256,219**	**$482,560**	**$369,658**
4-year	17,845,848	16,187,061	709,416	51,830	10,232	36,012	222,739	395,510	233,049
Doctoral/research[1]	1,238,552	1,178,680	6,132	225	0	13,048	566	1,984	37,917
Master's[2]	4,018,182	3,857,058	24,271	1,081	0	3,277	11,002	95,303	26,191
Baccalaureate[3]	2,132,025	1,927,516	110,337	6,164	6,737	2,266	15,653	39,359	23,992
Special-focus institutions[4]	10,457,089	9,223,807	568,676	44,360	3,494	17,421	195,518	258,863	144,949
Art, music, or design	2,346,574	1,781,444	336,452	32,919	1,703	1,366	120	151,889	40,680
Business and management	5,605,852	5,132,441	194,664	7,140	1,373	4,441	179,412	64,611	21,770
Engineering or technology	1,263,322	1,199,092	24,037	3,945	101	5,170	3,980	17,404	9,594
Law	203,856	203,102	0	0	63	26	306	45	315
Medical or other health	882,290	837,707	13,523	356	255	4,735	8,255	8,108	9,350
Theological	110,629	31,751	0	0	0	1,479	0	14,943	62,455
Other special focus	44,567	38,270	0	0	0	204	3,445	1,864	785
2-year	4,813,214	4,288,969	231,954	26,157	1,975	7,021	33,480	87,050	136,609
	Percentage distribution								
Total	**100.00**	**90.37**	**4.15**	**0.34**	**0.05**	**0.19**	**1.13**	**2.13**	**1.63**
4-year	100.00	90.70	3.98	0.29	0.06	0.20	1.25	2.22	1.31
Doctoral/research[1]	100.00	95.17	0.50	0.02	0.00	1.05	0.05	0.16	3.06
Master's[2]	100.00	95.99	0.60	0.03	0.00	0.08	0.27	2.37	0.65
Baccalaureate[3]	100.00	90.41	5.18	0.29	0.32	0.11	0.73	1.85	1.13
Special-focus institutions[4]	100.00	88.21	5.44	0.42	0.03	0.17	1.87	2.48	1.39
Art, music, or design	100.00	75.92	14.34	1.40	0.07	0.06	0.01	6.47	1.73
Business and management	100.00	91.56	3.47	0.13	0.02	0.08	3.20	1.15	0.39
Engineering or technology	100.00	94.92	1.90	0.31	0.01	0.41	0.32	1.38	0.76
Law	100.00	99.63	0.00	0.00	0.03	0.01	0.15	0.02	0.15
Medical or other health	100.00	94.95	1.53	0.04	0.03	0.54	0.94	0.92	1.06
Theological	100.00	28.70	0.00	0.00	0.00	1.34	0.00	13.51	56.45
Other special focus	100.00	85.87	0.00	0.00	0.00	0.46	7.73	4.18	1.76
2-year	100.00	89.11	4.82	0.54	0.04	0.15	0.70	1.81	2.84
	Revenue per full-time-equivalent student in current dollars								
Total	**$21,401**	**$19,339**	**$889**	**$74**	**$12**	**$41**	**$242**	**$456**	**$349**
4-year	22,925	20,794	911	67	13	46	286	508	299
Doctoral/research[1]	17,459	16,615	86	3	0	184	8	28	535
Master's[2]	17,071	16,386	103	5	0	14	47	405	111
Baccalaureate[3]	19,851	17,947	1,027	57	63	21	146	366	223
Special-focus institutions[4]	28,672	25,291	1,559	122	10	48	536	710	397
Art, music, or design	27,134	20,599	3,890	381	20	16	1	1,756	470
Business and management	32,380	29,645	1,124	41	8	26	1,036	373	126
Engineering or technology	21,292	20,210	405	66	2	87	67	293	162
Law	32,317	32,198	0	0	10	4	49	7	50
Medical or other health	26,040	24,724	399	11	8	140	244	239	276
Theological	36,439	10,458	0	0	0	487	0	4,922	20,571
Other special focus	17,505	15,031	0	0	0	80	1,353	732	308
2-year	17,169	15,299	827	93	7	25	119	311	487
	Revenue per full-time-equivalent student in constant 2014–15 dollars[5]								
Total	**$21,557**	**$19,480**	**$896**	**$74**	**$12**	**$41**	**$244**	**$459**	**$352**
4-year	23,092	20,946	918	67	13	47	288	512	302
Doctoral/research[1]	17,587	16,736	87	3	0	185	8	28	538
Master's[2]	17,195	16,506	104	5	0	14	47	408	112
Baccalaureate[3]	19,996	18,078	1,035	58	63	21	147	369	225
Special-focus institutions[4]	28,881	25,475	1,571	123	10	48	540	715	400
Art, music, or design	27,332	20,749	3,919	383	20	16	1	1,769	474
Business and management	32,616	29,861	1,133	42	8	26	1,044	376	127
Engineering or technology	21,447	20,357	408	67	2	88	68	295	163
Law	32,552	32,432	0	0	10	4	49	7	50
Medical or other health	26,230	24,904	402	11	8	141	245	241	278
Theological	36,704	10,534	0	0	0	491	0	4,958	20,721
Other special focus	17,632	15,141	0	0	0	81	1,363	737	311
2-year	17,294	15,410	833	94	7	25	120	313	491

[1]Institutions that award at least 20 doctor's degrees per year, but did not have high levels of research activity.
[2]Institutions that award at least 50 master's degrees per year.
[3]Institutions that primarily emphasize undergraduate education. Also includes institutions classified as 4-year under the IPEDS system, which had been classified as 2-year in the Carnegie classification system because they primarily award associate's degrees.
[4]Four-year institutions that award degrees primarily in single fields of study, such as medicine, business, fine arts, theology, and engineering.
[5]Constant dollars based on the Consumer Price Index, prepared by the Bureau of Labor Statistics, U.S. Department of Labor, adjusted to a school-year basis.

NOTE: Degree-granting institutions grant associate's or higher degrees and participate in Title IV federal financial aid. Further information on the Carnegie 2005 classification system used in this table may be obtained from http://carnegieclassifications.iu.edu/. Detail may not sum to totals because of rounding.

SOURCE: U.S. Department of Education, National Center for Education Statistics, Integrated Postsecondary Education Data System (IPEDS), Spring 2014, Fall Enrollment component; and Spring 2015, Finance component. (This table was prepared November 2015.)

Table 333.70. Revenue received from the federal government by the 120 degree-granting postsecondary institutions receiving the largest amounts, by control and rank order: 2013–14

Institution	Control[1]	Rank order	Revenue from the federal government[2] (in thousands)
1	2	3	4
United States (all institutions)	†	†	$77,332,765
120 institutions receiving the largest amounts	†	†	45,778,300
Johns Hopkins University (MD)	2	1	2,373,018
California Institute of Technology	2	2	1,865,247
University of Chicago (IL)	2	3	1,486,511
Massachusetts Institute of Technology	2	4	1,273,847
New York University	2	5	1,139,890
University of Washington, Seattle Campus	1	6	1,067,422
Stanford University (CA)	2	7	1,031,747
Weill Cornell Medical College (NY)	2	8	962,303
University of Michigan, Ann Arbor	1	9	855,601
University of Utah	1	10	777,384
University of Pennsylvania	2	11	765,192
Columbia University in the City of New York	2	12	756,604
University of North Carolina at Chapel Hill	1	13	715,272
University of California, San Diego	1	14	687,433
University of Southern California	2	15	656,344
University of California, San Francisco	1	16	648,682
United States Air Force Academy (CO)	1	17	634,201
University of Pittsburgh, Pittsburgh Campus (PA)	1	18	610,717
Harvard University (MA)	2	19	610,580
University of California, Los Angeles	1	20	606,857
University of Wisconsin, Madison	1	21	539,992
Duke University (NC)	2	22	532,977
University of Minnesota, Twin Cities	1	23	525,232
Yale University (CT)	2	24	512,637
Georgia Institute of Technology, Main Campus	1	25	505,556
Pennsylvania State University, Main Campus	1	26	498,597
Vanderbilt University (TN)	2	27	478,563
University of Oklahoma Health Sciences Center	1	28	452,230
University of Illinois at Urbana, Champaign	1	29	451,371
Washington University in St. Louis (MO)	2	30	438,726
University of California, Davis	1	31	436,095
United States Naval Academy (MD)	1	32	430,165
University of Texas at Austin	1	33	425,604
University of Florida	1	34	415,467
Emory University (GA)	2	35	414,915
University of California, Berkeley	1	36	412,589
Northwestern University (IL)	2	37	401,885
Ohio State University, Main Campus	1	38	400,176
University of Arizona	1	39	387,578
Texas A & M University, College Station	1	40	379,176
University of Connecticut	1	41	364,865
University of Maryland, College Park	1	42	362,768
Rutgers University, New Brunswick (NJ)	1	43	356,318
Arizona State University, Tempe	1	44	353,375
Michigan State University	1	45	346,128
University of Colorado, Boulder	1	46	343,974
University of Alabama at Birmingham	1	47	342,701
Cornell University (NY)	2	48	339,697
Carnegie Mellon University (PA)	2	49	337,465
United States Military Academy (NY)	1	50	331,820
Case Western Reserve University (OH)	2	51	314,010
Howard University (DC)	2	52	313,601
University of Tennessee, Knoxville	1	53	307,586
University of Colorado, Denver	1	54	303,220
George Washington University (DC)	2	55	301,120
University of California, Irvine	1	56	298,563
Baylor College of Medicine (TX)	2	57	298,468
University of Illinois at Chicago	1	58	296,729
University of Iowa	1	59	296,334
University of Hawaii at Manoa	1	60	294,655
Icahn School of Medicine at Mount Sinai (NY)	2	61	285,380
Oregon Health & Science University	1	62	284,219
Princeton University (NJ)	2	63	271,319
Purdue University, Main Campus (IN)	1	64	266,069
University of Rochester (NY)	2	65	261,997
Virginia Polytechnic Institute and State University	1	66	254,660
University of Kentucky	1	67	245,970
University of Miami (FL)	2	68	242,029
Boston University (MA)	2	69	240,247
University of South Florida, Main Campus	1	70	235,610
University of New Mexico, Main Campus	1	71	228,861
University of Virginia, Main Campus	1	72	224,687
University of Texas Health Science Center at Houston	1	73	221,941
University of Maryland, Baltimore	1	74	215,629
Colorado State University, Fort Collins	1	75	211,536
Iowa State University	1	76	210,849
Indiana University-Purdue University, Indianapolis	1	77	206,777
University of Massachusetts Medical School, Worcester	1	78	204,290
Ivy Tech Community College (IN)	1	79	202,168
Oregon State University	1	80	200,258
Yeshiva University (NY)	2	81	193,269
University of Kansas	1	82	193,057
Miami-Dade College (FL)	1	83	191,729
North Carolina State University at Raleigh	1	84	190,000
Florida State University	1	85	189,140
University of Texas Southwestern Medical Center	1	86	188,868
Utah State University	1	87	179,405
Virginia Commonwealth University	1	88	176,979
Washington State University	1	89	169,985
University of Central Florida	1	90	166,334
Stony Brook University (NY)	1	91	166,049
Wake Forest University (NC)	2	92	164,873
Florida International University	1	93	163,561
University of California, Santa Barbara	1	94	158,649
University of Missouri, Columbia	1	95	154,141
University of Georgia	1	96	154,068
Indiana University, Bloomington	1	97	149,530
Louisiana State University and Ag. & Mech. College	1	98	148,791
University of Cincinnati, Main Campus (OH)	1	99	147,540
University of South Carolina, Columbia	1	100	147,390
University of Nebraska, Lincoln	1	101	146,552
Tulane University of Louisiana	2	102	146,393
University at Buffalo (NY)	1	103	142,510
Wayne State University (MI)	1	104	142,370
Mississippi State University	1	105	141,556
Medical University of South Carolina	1	106	132,107
New Mexico State University, Main Campus	1	107	131,215
University of Massachusetts, Amherst	1	108	130,515
University of California, Santa Cruz	1	109	129,696
Brown University (RI)	2	110	129,439
Dartmouth College (NH)	2	111	129,198
University of Texas Medical Branch	1	112	127,509
Tufts University (MA)	2	113	126,452
Temple University (PA)	1	114	123,713
University of Vermont	1	115	123,604
Georgetown University (DC)	2	116	123,494
State University of New York at Albany	1	117	120,854
University of Oregon	1	118	119,359
Medical College of Wisconsin	2	119	118,474
University of Houston (TX)	1	120	117,655

†Not applicable.

[1]Publicly controlled institutions are identified by a "1"; private nonprofit, by a "2"; and private for-profit, by a "3."

[2]Includes federal appropriations; operating, nonoperating, unrestricted, and restricted federal contracts and grants; and revenue for independent operations. Independent operations generally include only the revenues associated with major federally funded research and development centers. Pell grants are included for public institutions and may also be included for private nonprofit institutions that do not treat Pell grants as pass-through transactions. Data for public, private nonprofit, and private for-profit institutions are only roughly comparable because they were collected using different survey instruments.

NOTE: Degree-granting institutions grant associate's or higher degrees and participate in Title IV federal financial aid programs.

SOURCE: U.S. Department of Education, National Center for Education Statistics, Integrated Postsecondary Education Data System (IPEDS), Spring 2015, Finance component. (This table was prepared February 2016.)

Table 333.80. Voluntary support for degree-granting postsecondary institutions, by source and purpose of support: Selected years, 1949–50 through 2013–14

Year	Total voluntary support, in millions of constant 2014–15 dollars[1]	In millions of current dollars									Voluntary support as a percent of total expenditures[2]
			Sources						Purpose		
		Total voluntary support	Alumni	Nonalumni individuals	Corporations	Foundations	Religious organizations	Other organizations	Current operations	Capital purposes	
1	2	3	4	5	6	7	8	9	10	11	12
1949–50	$2,398	$240	$60	$60	$28	$60	$16	$16	$101	$139	10.7
1959–60	6,565	815	191	194	130	163	80	57	385	430	14.6
1965–66	10,681	1,440	310	350	230	357	108	85	675	765	11.5
1970–71	11,082	1,860	458	495	259	418	104	126	1,050	810	8.0
1975–76	10,285	2,410	588	569	379	549	130	195	1,480	930	6.2
1980–81	11,557	4,230	1,049	1,007	778	922	140	334	2,590	1,640	6.6
1985–86	16,095	7,400	1,825	1,781	1,702	1,363	211	518	4,022	3,378	7.6
1989–90	18,267	9,800	2,540	2,230	2,170	1,920	240	700	5,440	4,360	7.3
1990–91	18,027	10,200	2,680	2,310	2,230	2,030	240	710	5,830	4,370	7.0
1993–94	19,991	12,350	3,410	2,800	2,510	2,540	240	850	6,710	5,640	7.1
1994–95	20,063	12,750	3,600	2,940	2,560	2,460	250	940	7,230	5,520	7.0
1995–96	21,829	14,250	4,040	3,400	2,800	2,815	255	940	7,850	6,400	7.5
1996–97	23,830	16,000	4,650	3,850	3,050	3,200	250	1,000	8,500	7,500	8.0
1997–98	26,925	18,400	5,500	4,500	3,250	3,800	300	1,050	9,000	9,400	8.8
1998–99	29,343	20,400	5,930	4,810	3,610	4,530	330	1,190	9,900	10,500	9.3
1999–2000	32,434	23,200	6,800	5,420	4,150	5,080	370	1,380	11,270	11,930	9.8
2000–01	32,712	24,200	6,830	5,200	4,350	6,000	370	1,450	12,200	12,000	9.3
2001–02	31,744	23,900	5,900	5,400	4,370	6,300	360	1,570	12,400	11,500	8.5
2002–03	30,672	23,600	6,570	4,280	4,250	6,600	360	1,540	12,900	10,700	7.8
2003–04	31,033	24,400	6,700	5,200	4,400	6,200	350	1,550	13,600	10,800	7.7
2004–05	31,608	25,600	7,100	5,000	4,400	7,000	370	1,730	14,200	11,400	7.6
2005–06	33,303	28,000	8,400	5,700	4,600	7,100	375	1,825	15,000	13,000	7.9
2006–07	34,492	29,750	8,270	5,650	4,800	8,500	380	2,150	16,100	13,650	7.9
2007–08	35,328	31,600	8,700	6,120	4,900	9,100	380	2,400	17,070	14,530	7.7
2008–09	30,707	27,850	7,130	4,995	4,620	8,235	325	2,545	16,955	10,895	6.5
2009–10	30,576	28,000	7,100	4,920	4,730	8,400	305	2,545	17,000	11,000	6.3
2010–11	32,437	30,300	7,800	5,650	5,020	8,675	305	2,850	17,800	12,500	6.4
2011–12	32,241	31,000	7,700	5,825	5,250	9,150	275	2,800	18,900	12,100	6.4
2012–13	34,578	33,800	9,000	6,200	5,100	10,000	300	3,200	20,200	13,600	6.8
2013–14	37,723	37,450	9,850	6,500	5,750	11,200	([3])	4,150	21,800	15,650	7.2

[1]Constant dollars based on the Consumer Price Index, prepared by the Bureau of Labor statistics, U.S. Department of Labor, adjusted to a school-year basis.
[2]Total expenditures include current-fund expenditures and additions to plant value through 1995–96.
[3]For 2013–14, voluntary support from religious organizations is included with that from other organizations.
NOTE: Data rounding is consistent with the original source material. Voluntary support data are from the Council for Aid to Education, while the percentage of total expenditures is based on total expenditures reported through the Integrated Postsecondary Education Data System.
SOURCE: Council for Aid to Education, *Voluntary Support of Education*, selected years, 1949–50 through 2013–14. U.S. Department of Education, National Center for Education Statistics, Higher Education General Information Survey (HEGIS), selected years, 1965–66 through 1985–86; *Financial Statistics of Institutions of Higher Education,* 1949–50 and 1959–60; Integrated Postsecondary Education Data System (IPEDS), "Finance Survey" (IPEDS-F:FY87–99); and IPEDS Spring 2001 through Spring 2015, Finance component. (This table was prepared March 2016.)

Table 333.90. Endowment funds of the 120 degree-granting postsecondary institutions with the largest endowments, by rank order: Fiscal year 2014

Institution	Fiscal year (FY) 2014			
	Rank order, end of FY[1]	Market value of endowment: Beginning of FY (in thousands)	Market value of endowment: End of FY (in thousands)	Market value of endowment: Percent change[2]
1	2	3	4	5
United States (all institutions)	†	**$465,793,112**	**$535,186,040**	**14.9**
120 institutions with the largest amounts	†	**344,599,413**	**398,543,954**	**15.7**
Harvard University (MA)	1	32,689,489	36,429,256	11.4
University of Texas System Office	2	19,740,283	25,445,315	28.9
Yale University (CT)	3	20,708,793	23,858,561	15.2
Stanford University (CA)	4	18,688,868	21,466,006	14.9
Princeton University (NJ)	5	18,786,132	20,576,361	9.5
Massachusetts Institute of Technology	6	10,857,976	12,425,131	14.4
Texas A & M University, College Station	7	8,238,774	10,521,034	27.7
University of Michigan, Ann Arbor	8	8,272,366	9,603,919	16.1
University of Pennsylvania	9	8,174,165	9,582,335	17.2
Columbia University in the City of New York (NY)	10	8,197,880	9,223,047	12.5
University of Notre Dame (IN)	11	6,959,051	8,189,096	17.7
Northwestern University (IL)	12	6,283,130	7,501,116	19.4
University of California System Admin. Central Office	13	6,402,600	7,413,709	15.8
Duke University (NC)	14	6,040,973	7,036,776	16.5
Emory University (GA)	15	6,115,582	6,981,308	14.2
Washington University in St. Louis (MO)	16	5,749,297	6,719,449	16.9
University of Chicago (IL)	17	5,886,968	6,539,290	11.1
University of Virginia, Main Campus	18	5,106,876	5,876,310	15.1
Rice University (TX)	19	4,895,299	5,553,717	13.5
Cornell University (NY)	20	4,133,842	4,646,134	12.4
University of Southern California	21	3,868,355	4,593,014	18.7
Dartmouth College (NH)	22	3,733,596	4,468,220	19.7
Vanderbilt University (TN)	23	3,635,343	4,046,250	11.3
Ohio State University, Main Campus	24	3,130,942	3,595,323	14.8
University of Pittsburgh, Pittsburgh Campus (PA)	25	2,956,739	3,470,665	17.4
New York University	26	2,980,027	3,435,034	15.3
Johns Hopkins University (MD)	27	2,918,546	3,392,529	16.2
University of Texas at Austin	28	3,012,895	3,376,824	12.1
University of Wisconsin, Madison	29	2,295,273	3,133,197	36.5
Brown University (RI)	30	2,669,948	2,999,749	12.4
University of Minnesota, Twin Cities	31	2,610,544	2,992,707	14.6
University of Washington, Seattle Campus	32	2,432,421	2,915,058	19.8
University of North Carolina at Chapel Hill	33	2,344,280	2,659,759	13.5
Michigan State University	34	2,007,498	2,549,137	27.0
Purdue University, Main Campus (IN)	35	2,189,202	2,445,542	11.7
University of Richmond (VA)	36	2,025,996	2,313,305	14.2
Pennsylvania State University, Main Campus	37	1,924,143	2,264,414	17.7
Amherst College (MA)	38	1,823,748	2,149,203	17.8
Williams College (MA)	39	1,902,112	2,143,153	12.7
California Institute of Technology	40	1,960,435	2,118,100	8.0
Boston College (MA)	41	1,868,699	2,105,654	12.7
Pomona College (CA)	42	1,823,441	2,101,461	15.2
University of Rochester (NY)	43	1,730,829	2,015,283	16.4
Georgia Institute of Technology, Main Campus	44	1,714,876	1,889,014	10.2
Swarthmore College (PA)	45	1,634,685	1,876,669	14.8
Wellesley College (MA)	46	1,576,337	1,834,137	16.4
Grinnell College (IA)	47	1,553,629	1,829,521	17.8
Case Western Reserve University (OH)	48	1,595,300	1,758,570	10.2
Smith College (MA)	49	1,557,427	1,755,755	12.7
University of California, Berkeley	50	1,411,707	1,671,939	18.4
University of California, Los Angeles	51	1,411,797	1,616,045	14.5
Boston University (MA)	52	1,403,061	1,616,004	15.2
Tufts University (MA)	53	1,440,527	1,590,045	10.4
George Washington University (DC)	54	1,375,202	1,576,508	14.6
University of Florida	55	1,360,073	1,519,964	11.8
University of Kansas	56	1,310,655	1,494,881	14.1
Washington and Lee University (VA)	57	1,345,356	1,477,923	9.9
Brigham Young University, Provo (UT)	58	1,053,241	1,470,770	39.6
Georgetown University (DC)	59	1,286,322	1,461,276	13.6
Southern Methodist University (TX)	60	1,268,079	1,425,146	12.4
Texas Christian University	61	1,256,030	1,393,241	10.9
University of Delaware	62	1,171,166	1,310,133	11.9
University of Illinois at Urbana-Champaign	63	1,050,492	1,289,584	22.8
University of Iowa	64	1,094,803	1,251,356	14.3
Soka University of America (CA)	65	1,117,424	1,249,761	11.8
Weill Cornell Medical College (NY)	66	1,138,386	1,243,815	9.3
Carnegie Mellon University (PA)	67	1,066,149	1,235,968	15.9
Bowdoin College (ME)	68	1,038,640	1,216,030	17.1
Lehigh University (PA)	69	1,103,449	1,215,926	10.2
University of Kentucky	70	1,054,448	1,215,226	15.2
Trinity University (TX)	71	1,013,929	1,187,929	17.2
Syracuse University (NY)	72	1,053,214	1,183,244	12.3
University of Cincinnati, Main Campus (OH)	73	1,044,198	1,182,040	13.2
Tulane University of Louisiana	74	1,031,661	1,169,060	13.3
Baylor University (TX)	75	1,061,157	1,151,200	8.5
Wake Forest University (NC)	76	1,061,638	1,148,026	8.1
Berea College (KY)	77	1,012,401	1,137,222	12.3
Middlebury College (VT)	78	972,992	1,081,894	11.2
Saint Louis University (MO)	79	956,014	1,076,959	12.7
Princeton Theological Seminary (NJ)	80	941,110	1,042,191	10.7
University of Tulsa (OK)	81	893,055	1,023,412	14.6
Juilliard School (NY)	82	882,012	999,769	13.4
University of Texas Southwestern Medical Center	83	878,855	988,251	12.4
Baylor College of Medicine (TX)	84	844,261	988,247	17.1
Vassar College (NY)	85	868,741	974,180	12.1
University of Oklahoma, Norman Campus	86	845,635	965,937	14.2
Indiana University, Bloomington	87	835,123	961,054	15.1
University of Arkansas	88	819,814	929,693	13.4
Hamilton College (NY)	89	773,828	927,520	19.9
Berry College (GA)	90	861,107	925,698	7.5
University of California, San Francisco	91	766,144	912,957	19.2
North Carolina State University at Raleigh	92	769,404	885,055	15.0
University of Louisville (KY)	93	757,336	876,825	15.8
Washington State University	94	777,644	868,091	11.6
Oberlin College (OH)	95	765,804	866,830	13.2
Colgate University (NY)	96	760,825	865,882	13.8
University of Miami (FL)	97	777,947	865,435	11.2
Brandeis University (MA)	98	766,205	861,152	12.4
Bryn Mawr College (PA)	99	710,168	839,226	18.2
Clemson University (SC)	100	518,606	836,152	61.2
Indiana University, Purdue University, Indianapolis	101	709,877	834,834	17.6
Lafayette College (PA)	102	749,031	832,811	11.2
University of Missouri, Columbia	103	692,853	806,717	16.4
Denison University (OH)	104	691,740	799,108	15.5
College of William and Mary (VA)	105	697,724	797,592	14.3
Wesleyan University (CT)	106	688,643	793,334	15.2
Carleton College (MN)	107	700,540	792,737	13.2
Pepperdine University (CA)	108	715,660	790,483	10.5
Virginia Polytechnic Institute and State U.	109	653,700	788,800	20.7
University of Tennessee, Knoxville	110	662,942	782,734	18.1
Rutgers University, New Brunswick (NJ)	111	655,125	763,561	16.6
University of Arizona	112	611,746	760,679	24.3
Rochester Institute of Technology (NY)	113	669,132	753,951	12.7
Bucknell University (PA)	114	666,563	750,913	12.7
Macalester College (MN)	115	694,311	749,550	8.0
Medical College of Wisconsin	116	597,865	748,637	25.2
Colby College (ME)	117	649,992	740,631	13.9
Northeastern University (MA)	118	631,395	729,034	15.5
College of the Holy Cross (MA)	119	634,912	726,232	14.4
University of Utah	120	642,219	723,827	12.7

†Not applicable.
[1]Institutions ranked by size of endowment at end of 2014 fiscal year.
[2]Change in market value of endowment. Includes growth from gifts and returns on investments, as well as reductions from expenditures and withdrawals.

NOTE: Degree-granting institutions grant associate's or higher degrees and participate in Title IV federal financial aid programs.
SOURCE: U.S. Department of Education, National Center for Education Statistics, Integrated Postsecondary Education Data System (IPEDS), Spring 2015, Finance component. (This table was prepared January 2016.)

Table 334.10. Expenditures of public degree-granting postsecondary institutions, by purpose of expenditure and level of institution: 2007–08 through 2013–14

Level of institution and year	Total expenditures[2]	Instruction		Research	Public service	Academic support	Student services	Institutional support	Operation and maintenance of plant	Depreciation	Scholarships and fellowships[2]	Auxiliary enterprises	Hospitals	Independent operations	Interest	Other
		Total[1]	Salaries and wages													
1	2	3	4	5	6	7	8	9	10	11	12	13	14	15	16	17
	In thousands of current dollars															
All levels																
2007–08	$261,045,829	$71,807,253	$48,691,508	$25,331,167	$10,800,588	$17,871,280	$12,205,110	$22,145,030	$17,032,966	$12,814,049	$9,664,173	$19,533,181	$23,974,721	$931,838	$4,301,708	$12,632,765
2008–09	273,018,676	75,087,547	51,151,497	26,643,578	11,243,089	18,803,731	12,939,241	23,072,985	17,839,425	13,719,433	11,107,945	20,587,662	25,944,900	1,177,848	2,972,642	11,878,652
2009–10	281,390,445	76,331,795	51,808,563	28,102,405	11,511,735	18,890,370	13,124,073	22,679,459	18,037,657	14,307,677	15,494,246	20,482,149	26,595,704	1,236,092	5,062,000	9,535,082
2010–11	296,862,854	79,412,245	53,586,472	29,401,389	12,012,207	19,351,676	13,577,155	23,815,431	18,898,138	15,441,148	17,487,275	21,727,625	27,980,574	1,153,975	5,476,865	11,127,150
2011–12	305,537,590	80,881,773	54,341,187	29,665,476	11,930,514	20,380,843	14,184,601	24,099,951	19,286,569	16,467,330	16,611,881	22,172,526	30,833,717	1,204,016	6,138,489	11,679,905
2012–13	311,424,709	82,946,384	55,555,811	29,860,945	11,905,234	21,259,036	14,688,802	25,269,318	19,717,247	17,436,827	16,221,476	22,490,098	31,838,319	1,224,309	6,364,472	10,202,242
2013–14	323,888,217	85,688,549	57,583,231	29,474,988	12,197,163	22,169,321	15,529,411	26,543,793	20,704,034	18,369,899	15,962,246	23,172,857	34,427,527	1,417,050	6,552,127	11,679,253
4-year																
2007–08	215,474,080	54,371,328	36,618,879	25,312,279	10,055,606	14,471,795	8,051,799	15,812,151	13,047,228	10,959,500	6,467,362	17,296,774	23,974,721	931,838	3,523,683	11,198,015
2008–09	225,343,545	57,273,583	38,666,427	26,621,961	10,497,618	15,298,522	8,612,602	16,500,601	13,802,983	11,719,701	7,146,645	18,292,903	25,944,900	1,177,848	2,354,694	10,098,986
2009–10	230,212,346	58,307,342	39,032,863	28,081,694	10,758,002	15,366,887	8,763,305	16,342,588	13,661,203	12,312,930	9,103,655	18,145,849	26,595,704	1,236,092	4,091,226	7,445,869
2010–11	242,591,219	60,644,416	40,420,752	29,380,202	11,225,195	15,732,164	9,122,182	17,255,818	14,305,617	13,213,721	10,088,873	19,334,526	27,980,574	1,153,975	4,379,246	8,774,710
2011–12	251,518,494	62,225,401	41,334,687	29,645,195	11,174,232	16,732,590	9,659,034	17,376,744	14,805,020	14,102,984	9,737,295	19,801,700	30,833,717	1,204,016	4,779,600	9,440,966
2012–13	257,543,514	64,142,742	42,541,275	29,842,594	11,178,539	17,528,570	10,103,438	18,349,595	15,212,898	14,870,558	9,819,766	20,191,850	31,838,319	1,224,309	5,071,595	8,168,742
2013–14	269,892,768	66,829,678	44,567,421	29,453,355	11,492,915	18,322,501	10,865,041	19,522,528	16,088,167	15,667,606	9,899,892	20,985,004	34,427,527	1,417,050	5,200,722	9,720,781
2-year																
2007–08	45,571,749	17,435,926	12,072,630	18,887	744,982	3,399,485	4,153,311	6,332,879	3,985,738	1,854,549	3,196,811	2,236,407	0	0	778,025	1,434,749
2008–09	47,675,131	17,813,964	12,485,070	21,617	745,470	3,505,209	4,326,639	6,572,385	4,036,442	1,999,732	3,961,299	2,294,759	0	0	617,948	1,779,666
2009–10	51,178,098	18,024,453	12,775,700	20,711	753,733	3,523,483	4,360,768	6,336,871	4,376,455	1,994,747	6,390,591	2,336,300	0	0	970,774	2,089,213
2010–11	54,271,635	18,767,830	13,165,721	21,187	787,012	3,619,512	4,454,973	6,559,613	4,592,521	2,227,427	7,398,402	2,393,099	0	0	1,097,619	2,352,441
2011–12	54,019,096	18,656,373	13,006,500	20,281	756,282	3,648,252	4,525,567	6,723,207	4,481,549	2,364,346	6,874,585	2,370,826	0	0	1,358,889	2,238,939
2012–13	53,881,195	18,803,642	13,014,536	18,351	726,695	3,730,467	4,585,363	6,919,723	4,504,349	2,566,269	6,401,710	2,298,249	0	0	1,292,877	2,033,500
2013–14	53,995,449	18,858,870	13,015,810	21,633	704,248	3,846,819	4,664,370	7,021,265	4,615,867	2,702,294	6,062,353	2,187,853	0	0	1,351,405	1,958,472
	Percentage distribution															
All levels																
2007–08	100.00	27.51	18.65	9.70	4.14	6.85	4.68	8.48	6.52	4.91	3.70	7.48	9.18	0.36	1.65	4.84
2008–09	100.00	27.50	18.74	9.76	4.12	6.89	4.74	8.45	6.53	5.03	4.07	7.54	9.50	0.43	1.09	4.35
2009–10	100.00	27.13	18.41	9.99	4.09	6.71	4.66	8.06	6.41	5.08	5.51	7.28	9.45	0.44	1.80	3.39
2010–11	100.00	26.75	18.05	9.90	4.05	6.52	4.57	8.02	6.37	5.20	5.89	7.32	9.43	0.39	1.84	3.75
2011–12	100.00	26.47	17.79	9.71	3.90	6.67	4.64	7.89	6.31	5.39	5.44	7.26	10.09	0.39	2.01	3.82
2012–13	100.00	26.63	17.84	9.59	3.82	6.83	4.72	8.11	6.33	5.60	5.21	7.22	10.22	0.39	2.04	3.28
2013–14	100.00	26.46	17.78	9.10	3.77	6.84	4.79	8.20	6.39	5.67	4.93	7.15	10.63	0.44	2.02	3.61
4-year																
2007–08	100.00	25.23	16.99	11.75	4.67	6.72	3.74	7.34	6.06	5.09	3.00	8.03	11.13	0.43	1.64	5.20
2008–09	100.00	25.42	17.16	11.81	4.66	6.79	3.82	7.32	6.13	5.20	3.17	8.12	11.51	0.52	1.04	4.48
2009–10	100.00	25.33	16.96	12.20	4.67	6.68	3.81	7.10	5.93	5.35	3.95	7.88	11.55	0.54	1.78	3.23
2010–11	100.00	25.00	16.66	12.11	4.63	6.49	3.76	7.11	5.90	5.45	4.16	7.97	11.53	0.48	1.81	3.62
2011–12	100.00	24.74	16.43	11.79	4.44	6.65	3.84	6.91	5.89	5.61	3.87	7.87	12.26	0.48	1.90	3.75
2012–13	100.00	24.91	16.52	11.59	4.34	6.81	3.92	7.12	5.91	5.77	3.81	7.84	12.36	0.48	1.97	3.17
2013–14	100.00	24.76	16.51	10.91	4.26	6.79	4.03	7.23	5.96	5.81	3.67	7.78	12.76	0.53	1.93	3.60
2-year																
2007–08	100.00	38.26	26.49	0.04	1.63	7.46	9.11	13.90	8.75	4.07	7.01	4.91	0.00	0.00	1.71	3.15
2008–09	100.00	37.37	26.19	0.05	1.56	7.35	9.08	13.79	8.47	4.19	8.31	4.81	0.00	0.00	1.30	3.73
2009–10	100.00	35.22	24.96	0.04	1.47	6.88	8.52	12.38	8.55	3.90	12.49	4.57	0.00	0.00	1.90	4.08
2010–11	100.00	34.58	24.26	0.04	1.45	6.67	8.21	12.09	8.46	4.10	13.63	4.41	0.00	0.00	2.02	4.33
2011–12	100.00	34.54	24.08	0.04	1.40	6.75	8.38	12.45	8.30	4.38	12.73	4.39	0.00	0.00	2.52	4.14
2012–13	100.00	34.90	24.15	0.03	1.35	6.92	8.51	12.84	8.36	4.76	11.88	4.27	0.00	0.00	2.40	3.77
2013–14	100.00	34.93	24.11	0.04	1.30	7.12	8.64	13.00	8.55	5.00	11.23	4.05	0.00	0.00	2.50	3.63

See notes at end of table.

Table 334.10. Expenditures of public degree-granting postsecondary institutions, by purpose of expenditure and level of institution: 2007–08 through 2013–14—Continued

Level of institution and year	Total expenditures	Instruction: Total[1]	Instruction: Salaries and wages	Research	Public service	Academic support	Student services	Institutional support	Operation and maintenance of plant	Depreciation	Scholarships and fellowships[2]	Auxiliary enterprises	Hospitals	Independent operations	Interest	Other
1	2	3	4	5	6	7	8	9	10	11	12	13	14	15	16	17
	Expenditures per full-time-equivalent student in current dollars															
All levels																
2007–08	$26,802	$7,373	$4,999	$2,601	$1,109	$1,835	$1,253	$2,274	$1,749	$1,316	$992	$2,006	$2,462	$96	$442	$1,297
2008–09	27,134	7,463	5,084	2,648	1,117	1,869	1,286	2,293	1,773	1,364	1,104	2,046	2,579	117	295	1,181
2009–10	26,184	7,103	4,821	2,615	1,071	1,758	1,221	2,110	1,678	1,331	1,442	1,906	2,475	115	471	887
2010–11	26,942	7,207	4,863	2,668	1,090	1,756	1,232	2,161	1,715	1,401	1,587	1,972	2,539	105	497	1,010
2011–12	27,891	7,383	4,961	2,708	1,089	1,860	1,295	2,200	1,761	1,503	1,516	2,024	2,815	110	560	1,066
2012–13	28,884	7,693	5,153	2,770	1,104	1,972	1,362	2,344	1,829	1,617	1,505	2,086	2,953	114	590	946
2013–14	30,282	8,011	5,384	2,756	1,140	2,073	1,452	2,482	1,936	1,717	1,492	2,167	3,219	132	613	1,092
4-year																
2007–08	35,947	9,071	6,109	4,223	1,678	2,414	1,343	2,638	2,177	1,828	1,079	2,886	4,000	155	588	1,868
2008–09	36,704	9,329	6,298	4,336	1,710	2,492	1,403	2,688	2,248	1,909	1,164	2,980	4,226	192	384	1,645
2009–10	35,678	9,037	6,049	4,352	1,667	2,382	1,358	2,533	2,117	1,908	1,411	2,812	4,122	192	634	1,154
2010–11	36,558	9,139	6,091	4,428	1,692	2,371	1,375	2,600	2,156	1,991	1,520	2,914	4,217	174	660	1,322
2011–12	37,350	9,240	6,138	4,402	1,659	2,485	1,434	2,580	2,199	2,094	1,446	2,941	4,579	179	710	1,402
2012–13	38,075	9,483	6,289	4,412	1,653	2,591	1,494	2,713	2,249	2,198	1,452	2,985	4,707	181	750	1,208
2013–14	39,743	9,841	6,563	4,337	1,692	2,698	1,600	2,875	2,369	2,307	1,458	3,090	5,070	209	766	1,431
2-year																
2007–08	12,167	4,655	3,223	5	199	908	1,109	1,691	1,064	495	854	597	0	0	208	383
2008–09	12,155	4,542	3,183	6	190	894	1,103	1,676	1,029	510	1,010	585	0	0	158	454
2009–10	11,918	4,197	2,975	5	176	821	1,015	1,476	1,019	465	1,488	544	0	0	226	487
2010–11	12,382	4,282	3,004	5	180	826	1,016	1,497	1,048	508	1,688	546	0	0	250	537
2011–12	12,799	4,420	3,082	5	179	864	1,072	1,593	1,062	560	1,629	562	0	0	322	530
2012–13	13,411	4,680	3,239	5	181	929	1,141	1,722	1,121	639	1,593	572	0	0	322	506
2013–14	13,828	4,830	3,333	6	180	985	1,194	1,798	1,182	692	1,553	560	0	0	346	502
	Expenditures per full-time-equivalent student in constant 2014–15 dollars[3]															
All levels																
2007–08	$29,964	$8,242	$5,589	$2,908	$1,240	$2,051	$1,401	$2,542	$1,955	$1,471	$1,109	$2,242	$2,752	$107	$494	$1,450
2008–09	29,917	8,228	5,605	2,920	1,232	2,061	1,418	2,528	1,955	1,503	1,217	2,256	2,843	129	326	1,302
2009–10	28,593	7,756	5,264	2,856	1,170	1,920	1,334	2,305	1,833	1,454	1,574	2,081	2,703	126	514	969
2010–11	28,841	7,715	5,206	2,856	1,167	1,880	1,319	2,314	1,836	1,500	1,699	2,111	2,718	112	532	1,081
2011–12	29,008	7,679	5,159	2,816	1,133	1,935	1,347	2,288	1,831	1,563	1,577	2,105	2,927	114	583	1,109
2012–13	29,549	7,870	5,271	2,833	1,130	2,017	1,394	2,398	1,871	1,654	1,539	2,134	3,021	116	604	968
2013–14	30,502	8,070	5,423	2,776	1,149	2,088	1,462	2,500	1,950	1,730	1,503	2,182	3,242	133	617	1,100
4-year																
2007–08	40,188	10,141	6,830	4,721	1,875	2,699	1,502	2,949	2,433	2,044	1,206	3,226	4,471	174	657	2,089
2008–09	40,469	10,286	6,944	4,781	1,885	2,747	1,547	2,963	2,479	2,105	1,283	3,285	4,659	212	423	1,814
2009–10	38,961	9,868	6,606	4,753	1,821	2,601	1,483	2,766	2,312	2,084	1,541	3,071	4,501	209	692	1,260
2010–11	39,136	9,783	6,521	4,740	1,811	2,538	1,472	2,784	2,308	2,132	1,628	3,119	4,514	186	706	1,416
2011–12	38,845	9,610	6,384	4,579	1,726	2,584	1,492	2,684	2,287	2,178	1,504	3,058	4,762	186	738	1,458
2012–13	38,951	9,701	6,434	4,513	1,691	2,651	1,528	2,775	2,301	2,249	1,485	3,054	4,815	185	767	1,235
2013–14	40,033	9,913	6,611	4,369	1,705	2,718	1,612	2,896	2,386	2,324	1,468	3,113	5,107	210	771	1,442
2-year																
2007–08	13,603	5,204	3,604	6	222	1,015	1,240	1,890	1,190	554	954	668	0	0	232	428
2008–09	13,402	5,008	3,510	6	210	985	1,216	1,848	1,135	562	1,114	645	0	0	174	500
2009–10	13,014	4,584	3,249	5	192	896	1,109	1,611	1,113	507	1,625	594	0	0	247	531
2010–11	13,256	4,584	3,216	5	192	884	1,088	1,602	1,122	544	1,807	585	0	0	268	575
2011–12	13,311	4,597	3,205	5	186	899	1,115	1,657	1,104	583	1,694	584	0	0	335	552
2012–13	13,720	4,788	3,314	5	185	950	1,168	1,762	1,147	653	1,630	585	0	0	329	518
2013–14	13,928	4,865	3,357	6	182	992	1,203	1,811	1,191	697	1,564	564	0	0	349	505

[1]Includes other categories not separately shown.
[2]Excludes discounts and allowances.
[3]Constant dollars based on the Consumer Price Index, prepared by the Bureau of Labor Statistics, U.S. Department of Labor, adjusted to a school-year basis.

NOTE: Degree-granting institutions grant associate's or higher degrees and participate in Title IV federal financial aid programs. Includes data for public institutions reporting data according to either the Governmental Accounting Standards Board (GASB) or the Financial Accounting Standards Board (FASB) questionnaire. All expenditures reported by institutions for operation and maintenance of plant have been aggregated in the operation and maintenance of plant category, even in cases where they originally were reported by purpose. Similarly, all expenditures reported by institutions for depreciation have been aggregated in the depreciation category, even in cases where they originally were reported by purpose. In addition, all expenditures reported by institutions for interest have been aggregated in the interest category, even in cases where they originally were reported by purpose. Some data have been revised from previously published figures. Detail may not sum to totals because of rounding.

SOURCE: U.S. Department of Education, National Center for Education Statistics, Integrated Postsecondary Education Data System (IPEDS), Spring 2008 through Spring 2014, Fall Enrollment component; and Spring 2009 through Spring 2015, Finance component. (This table was prepared November 2015.)

Table 334.20. Expenditures of public degree-granting postsecondary institutions, by level of institution, purpose of expenditure, and state or jurisdiction: 2010–11 through 2013–14

[In thousands of current dollars]

State or jurisdiction	Total expenditures, 2010–11	Total expenditures, 2011–12	Total expenditures, 2012–13			2013–14					
			All institutions	4-year institutions	2-year institutions	All institutions		4-year institutions		2-year institutions	
						Total[1]	Instruction[2]	Total[1]	Instruction[2]	Total[1]	Instruction[2]
1	2	3	4	5	6	7	8	9	10	11	12
United States	**$296,862,854**	**$305,537,590**	**$311,424,709**	**$257,543,514**	**$53,881,195**	**$323,888,217**	**$85,688,549**	**$269,892,768**	**$66,829,678**	**$53,995,449**	**$18,858,870**
Alabama	6,649,467	6,249,206	6,499,646	5,761,237	738,409	6,762,386	1,525,817	6,030,666	1,252,625	731,720	273,192
Alaska	800,218	829,978	845,578	809,679	35,899	852,991	226,417	823,759	217,287	29,231	9,130
Arizona	4,968,606	5,126,746	5,372,323	3,908,951	1,463,372	5,600,337	1,671,395	4,139,515	1,205,371	1,460,823	466,024
Arkansas	3,454,422	3,592,033	3,614,017	3,115,538	498,479	3,704,972	772,425	3,207,504	608,748	497,468	163,677
California	43,624,464	45,485,482	45,915,560	34,830,021	11,085,538	47,558,693	10,974,319	36,032,725	7,591,689	11,525,968	3,382,630
Colorado	4,837,724	5,145,208	5,342,995	4,756,073	586,922	5,698,854	1,649,462	5,109,318	1,417,891	589,536	231,570
Connecticut	2,974,554	2,931,898	3,030,961	2,565,900	465,062	3,295,856	946,450	2,798,124	749,362	497,732	197,088
Delaware	1,032,228	1,128,190	1,121,660	965,973	155,687	1,153,297	435,992	989,869	363,890	163,428	72,102
District of Columbia	152,640	147,034	141,338	141,338	0	134,230	40,618	134,230	40,618	0	0
Florida	10,413,803	10,559,827	10,659,595	10,272,223	387,372	11,087,586	3,273,040	10,762,561	3,183,978	325,025	89,062
Georgia	7,032,754	7,298,882	7,409,996	6,310,205	1,099,791	7,564,411	1,975,429	6,573,904	1,618,310	990,506	357,119
Hawaii	1,523,301	1,609,315	1,647,129	1,395,933	251,196	1,680,041	488,730	1,426,337	371,762	253,705	116,968
Idaho	1,116,296	1,216,909	1,182,070	974,156	207,914	1,188,089	356,948	981,948	287,096	206,141	69,852
Illinois	10,302,240	10,888,678	11,603,379	8,567,709	3,035,670	11,777,464	3,394,502	8,704,462	2,388,822	3,073,002	1,005,680
Indiana	5,959,191	6,105,284	6,227,063	5,587,045	640,018	6,395,776	2,213,282	5,780,882	2,007,494	614,894	205,789
Iowa	4,332,274	4,726,859	4,846,304	3,957,757	888,547	5,047,472	1,010,442	4,155,763	677,225	891,709	333,217
Kansas	3,053,391	3,214,748	3,306,016	2,562,868	743,148	3,364,787	1,054,428	2,622,331	798,777	742,456	255,651
Kentucky	4,889,725	5,136,705	5,180,174	4,454,346	725,828	5,235,067	1,176,627	4,592,917	952,428	642,150	224,199
Louisiana	4,163,519	4,204,018	4,151,993	3,656,295	495,698	4,010,882	1,154,288	3,509,182	963,131	501,700	191,157
Maine	837,119	844,272	847,717	725,066	122,652	859,812	242,296	732,026	189,034	127,787	53,263
Maryland	5,627,221	5,829,195	5,979,533	4,623,170	1,356,363	6,228,564	1,695,862	4,825,353	1,199,583	1,403,211	496,280
Massachusetts	4,224,820	4,297,014	4,442,564	3,610,605	831,958	4,703,032	1,304,970	3,826,904	972,337	876,128	332,633
Michigan	12,796,769	13,384,740	13,788,962	11,940,315	1,848,647	14,155,072	3,524,124	12,421,602	2,893,847	1,733,470	630,277
Minnesota	4,841,837	4,810,022	5,019,669	3,976,182	1,043,487	5,271,821	1,483,381	4,229,591	1,056,753	1,042,230	426,627
Mississippi	3,717,313	3,800,955	3,855,187	2,976,363	878,824	4,017,008	897,484	3,138,675	599,261	878,333	298,224
Missouri	4,370,406	4,563,353	4,619,674	3,823,178	796,496	4,772,178	1,316,991	3,991,095	1,028,336	781,083	288,655
Montana	961,380	981,509	992,536	866,457	126,079	1,012,355	264,210	885,121	230,207	127,234	34,004
Nebraska	2,119,516	2,176,505	2,226,961	1,838,167	388,794	2,312,160	678,915	1,913,185	529,519	398,975	149,396
Nevada	1,452,203	1,374,536	1,442,757	1,375,441	67,316	1,508,447	520,231	1,439,569	492,907	68,878	27,324
New Hampshire	916,009	894,369	901,393	769,683	131,710	937,896	279,538	803,389	233,204	134,507	46,334
New Jersey	6,814,524	7,080,502	5,474,962	4,147,457	1,327,505	7,090,602	2,105,237	5,771,315	1,654,899	1,319,287	450,338
New Mexico	3,195,659	3,150,710	3,252,357	2,643,255	609,102	3,316,771	652,622	2,689,810	441,810	626,962	210,812
New York	15,481,165	16,037,336	15,844,606	12,689,386	3,155,220	16,292,947	4,802,726	13,020,834	3,484,970	3,272,112	1,317,757
North Carolina	9,639,567	9,563,597	9,964,777	7,766,190	2,198,588	10,156,317	3,138,226	7,973,839	2,255,953	2,182,478	882,273
North Dakota	993,822	1,041,219	1,068,159	977,140	91,019	1,108,117	382,282	1,007,083	347,147	101,034	35,135
Ohio	11,618,184	11,808,427	12,192,587	10,636,363	1,556,224	12,303,835	3,236,387	10,809,969	2,698,065	1,493,866	538,322
Oklahoma	3,721,375	3,859,701	3,924,755	3,432,762	491,994	4,083,901	1,136,627	3,577,738	950,594	506,163	186,033
Oregon	5,209,651	5,531,213	5,744,633	4,529,658	1,214,975	6,000,874	1,275,419	4,812,288	886,843	1,188,585	388,576
Pennsylvania	11,287,473	11,823,354	12,176,869	10,975,980	1,200,889	12,566,618	3,001,192	11,358,294	2,565,821	1,208,324	435,370
Rhode Island	683,831	717,329	719,733	603,025	116,707	746,067	206,859	625,392	154,628	120,675	52,232
South Carolina	3,715,311	3,827,663	4,030,358	3,202,729	827,629	4,168,222	1,318,877	3,332,306	1,031,911	835,916	286,967
South Dakota	707,073	739,971	744,419	669,445	74,974	777,182	239,126	695,739	206,139	81,443	32,987
Tennessee	3,980,862	4,156,217	4,193,989	3,522,799	671,191	4,317,495	1,519,514	3,659,273	1,264,015	658,222	255,499
Texas	26,326,215	26,426,890	27,655,846	22,880,541	4,775,306	29,539,462	7,335,228	24,677,131	5,693,243	4,862,331	1,641,985
Utah	4,232,743	4,461,853	4,744,745	4,539,033	205,712	4,995,994	806,841	4,789,432	724,002	206,562	82,840
Vermont	793,941	799,662	843,550	806,021	37,529	853,311	223,049	817,070	213,154	36,241	9,895
Virginia	7,930,362	8,367,116	8,757,065	7,615,345	1,141,720	9,099,520	2,393,790	7,941,651	1,935,864	1,157,869	457,925
Washington	7,312,805	7,403,283	7,740,652	6,429,794	1,310,858	8,207,793	2,241,170	7,157,286	1,846,327	1,050,507	394,843
West Virginia	1,738,447	1,813,682	1,761,432	1,600,198	161,234	1,762,607	527,757	1,606,576	481,677	156,031	46,080
Wisconsin	5,974,368	5,942,717	6,044,715	4,704,511	1,340,203	6,346,355	1,887,933	5,000,620	1,251,567	1,345,735	636,366
Wyoming	706,777	752,127	744,748	469,004	275,744	761,062	231,331	484,984	141,818	276,078	89,513
U.S. Service Academies	1,653,288	1,679,549	1,585,003	1,585,003	0	1,501,631	477,739	1,501,631	477,739	0	0
Other jurisdictions	**1,698,347**	**1,728,527**	**1,684,136**	**1,591,208**	**92,928**	**1,699,654**	**495,286**	**1,599,556**	**462,634**	**100,099**	**32,653**
American Samoa	15,942	15,097	14,449	14,449	0	14,060	4,537	14,060	4,537	0	0
Federated States of Micronesia	21,048	23,134	22,472	0	22,472	27,695	6,635	0	0	27,695	6,635
Guam	125,565	136,515	129,808	96,962	32,846	136,246	30,303	99,906	18,231	36,340	12,072
Marshall Islands	17,259	18,381	13,552	0	13,552	15,117	3,544	0	0	15,117	3,544
Northern Marianas	20,214	18,085	18,031	18,031	0	17,849	7,647	17,849	7,647	0	0
Palau	4,856	10,488	10,384	0	10,384	9,834	4,097	0	0	9,834	4,097
Puerto Rico	1,406,063	1,418,143	1,393,668	1,379,994	13,674	1,400,211	424,617	1,389,098	418,312	11,113	6,304
U.S. Virgin Islands	87,400	88,683	81,772	81,772	0	78,643	13,906	78,643	13,906	0	0

[1]Includes other categories not separately shown.

[2]Excludes expenditures for operations and maintenance, interest, and depreciation, which are included in the total.

NOTE: Degree-granting institutions grant associate's or higher degrees and participate in Title IV federal financial aid programs. Includes data for public institutions reporting data according to either the Governmental Accounting Standards Board (GASB) or the Financial Accounting Standards Board (FASB) questionnaire. Some data have been revised from previously published figures. Detail may not sum to totals because of rounding.

SOURCE: U.S. Department of Education, National Center for Education Statistics, Integrated Postsecondary Education Data System (IPEDS), Spring 2012 through Spring 2015, Finance component. (This table was prepared November 2015.)

Table 329.10. On-campus crimes, arrests, and referrals for disciplinary action at degree-granting postsecondary institutions, by location of incident, control and level of institution, and type of incident: 2001 through 2013

Control and level of institution and type of incident	Number of incidents														
	Total, in residence halls and at other locations												2013		
	2001	2002	2003	2004	2005	2006	2007	2008	2009	2010	2011	2012	Total	In residence halls	At other locations
1	2	3	4	5	6	7	8	9	10	11	12	13	14	15	16
All institutions															
Selected crimes against persons and property	41,596	42,521	43,064	43,555	42,710	44,492	41,829	40,296	34,054	32,097	30,407	29,832	27,567	13,215	14,352
Murder[1]	17	20	9	15	11	8	44	12	16	15	16	12	23	3	20
Negligent manslaughter[2]	2	0	1	0	2	0	3	3	0	1	1	1	0	0	0
Sex offenses—forcible[3]	2,201	2,327	2,595	2,667	2,674	2,670	2,694	2,639	2,544	2,927	3,375	4,017	4,964	3,627	1,337
Sex offenses—nonforcible[4]	461	261	60	27	42	43	40	35	65	33	46	46	45	20	25
Robbery[5]	1,663	1,802	1,625	1,550	1,551	1,547	1,561	1,576	1,409	1,392	1,285	1,374	1,330	196	1,134
Aggravated assault[6]	2,947	2,804	2,832	2,721	2,656	2,817	2,604	2,495	2,327	2,221	2,239	2,424	2,085	719	1,366
Burglary[7]	26,904	28,038	28,639	29,480	29,256	31,260	29,488	28,737	23,083	21,335	19,472	18,228	15,500	8,285	7,215
Motor vehicle theft[8]	6,221	6,181	6,285	6,062	5,531	5,231	4,619	4,104	3,977	3,441	3,334	3,026	2,993	14	2,979
Arson[9]	1,180	1,088	1,018	1,033	987	916	776	695	633	732	639	704	627	351	276
Weapons-, drug-, and liquor-related arrests and referrals															
Arrests[10]	40,348	43,407	44,581	47,939	49,024	50,187	50,558	50,639	50,066	51,519	54,285	52,819	47,764	24,966	22,798
Illegal weapons possession	1,073	1,142	1,094	1,263	1,316	1,316	1,318	1,190	1,077	1,112	1,023	1,027	1,044	279	765
Drug law violations	11,854	12,041	12,467	12,775	13,707	13,952	14,135	15,146	15,871	18,589	20,729	21,389	20,148	10,744	9,404
Liquor law violations	27,421	30,224	31,020	33,901	34,001	34,919	35,105	34,303	33,118	31,818	32,533	30,403	26,572	13,943	12,629
Referrals for disciplinary action[10]	155,201	167,319	184,915	196,775	202,816	218,040	216,600	217,526	220,987	230,269	249,694	251,724	246,438	222,654	23,784
Illegal weapons possession	1,277	1,287	1,566	1,799	1,882	1,871	1,658	1,455	1,275	1,314	1,282	1,411	1,434	975	459
Drug law violations	23,900	26,038	25,753	25,762	25,356	27,251	28,476	32,469	36,344	42,022	51,562	54,131	54,135	46,222	7,913
Liquor law violations	130,024	139,994	157,596	169,214	175,578	188,918	186,466	183,602	183,368	186,933	196,850	196,182	190,869	175,457	15,412
Public 4-year															
Selected crimes against persons and property	18,710	19,563	19,789	19,984	19,582	20,648	19,579	18,695	15,975	15,503	14,675	14,520	13,240	6,300	6,940
Murder[1]	9	9	5	8	4	5	42	9	8	9	10	7	10	2	8
Negligent manslaughter[2]	2	0	1	0	1	0	2	1	0	0	1	1	0	0	0
Sex offenses—forcible[3]	1,245	1,278	1,358	1,482	1,398	1,400	1,425	1,317	1,214	1,461	1,638	1,972	2,257	1,646	611
Sex offenses—nonforcible[4]	207	113	28	16	25	15	23	12	40	15	17	17	17	9	8
Robbery[5]	584	659	669	612	696	680	722	750	647	662	612	660	641	120	521
Aggravated assault[6]	1,434	1,320	1,381	1,269	1,280	1,338	1,258	1,182	1,134	1,076	1,076	1,192	1,019	355	664
Burglary[7]	11,520	12,523	12,634	13,026	12,935	14,027	13,371	12,970	10,708	10,219	9,373	8,839	7,379	3,919	3,460
Motor vehicle theft[8]	3,072	3,092	3,116	2,964	2,667	2,662	2,266	2,027	1,824	1,604	1,592	1,405	1,513	8	1,505
Arson[9]	637	569	597	607	576	521	470	427	400	457	356	427	404	241	163
Weapons-, drug-, and liquor-related arrests and referrals															
Arrests[10]	31,077	33,831	34,657	36,746	38,051	39,900	39,570	40,607	40,780	41,992	44,891	43,587	38,701	20,060	18,641
Illegal weapons possession	692	745	697	811	878	859	825	759	659	669	629	624	657	209	448
Drug law violations	9,125	9,238	9,389	9,620	10,606	10,850	10,693	11,714	12,186	14,362	16,323	16,931	15,810	8,516	7,294
Liquor law violations	21,260	23,848	24,571	26,315	26,567	28,191	28,052	28,134	27,935	26,961	27,939	26,032	22,234	11,335	10,899
Referrals for disciplinary action[10]	79,152	84,636	94,365	100,588	100,211	107,289	106,148	104,585	108,756	116,029	129,667	132,552	127,851	116,424	11,427
Illegal weapons possession	678	675	847	1,001	1,097	972	867	792	669	664	610	649	623	442	181
Drug law violations	13,179	13,943	13,811	13,658	13,020	13,798	14,458	16,656	18,260	21,451	27,339	29,021	28,732	24,486	4,246
Liquor law violations	65,295	70,018	79,707	85,929	86,094	92,519	90,823	87,137	89,827	93,914	101,718	102,882	98,496	91,496	7,000
Nonprofit 4-year															
Selected crimes against persons and property	14,844	14,859	15,179	15,523	15,574	16,864	15,452	14,892	11,964	11,202	10,740	10,803	10,420	6,116	4,304
Murder[1]	5	9	2	4	5	3	2	1	6	5	3	2	5	0	5
Negligent manslaughter[2]	0	0	0	0	1	0	1	0	0	0	0	0	0	0	0
Sex offenses—forcible[3]	820	914	1,048	1,026	1,088	1,080	1,065	1,083	1,102	1,225	1,431	1,741	2,368	1,876	492
Sex offenses—nonforcible[4]	113	81	14	5	6	10	8	16	11	8	13	10	12	4	8
Robbery[5]	649	735	538	577	500	502	460	437	366	319	320	387	377	53	324
Aggravated assault[6]	882	900	773	838	744	834	768	754	661	641	631	668	690	267	423
Burglary[7]	10,471	10,561	11,066	11,426	11,657	13,051	11,941	11,551	8,810	8,138	7,421	7,058	6,098	3,803	2,295
Motor vehicle theft[8]	1,471	1,273	1,385	1,316	1,248	1,077	984	859	834	641	704	710	694	6	688
Arson[9]	433	386	353	331	325	307	223	191	174	225	217	227	176	107	69
Weapons-, drug-, and liquor-related arrests and referrals															
Arrests[10]	6,329	6,548	6,856	7,722	7,406	6,134	6,732	6,112	5,777	5,459	5,444	5,515	5,729	3,438	2,291
Illegal weapons possession	167	162	166	184	150	146	178	158	148	137	129	127	133	45	88
Drug law violations	1,628	1,723	1,869	1,751	1,691	1,650	1,804	1,883	2,080	2,248	2,425	2,436	2,541	1,658	883
Liquor law violations	4,534	4,663	4,821	5,787	5,565	4,338	4,750	4,071	3,549	3,074	2,890	2,952	3,055	1,735	1,320
Referrals for disciplinary action[10]	71,293	77,641	85,184	90,749	96,646	103,484	103,254	105,289	103,457	104,939	110,607	110,396	110,019	99,314	10,705
Illegal weapons possession	443	424	537	608	590	622	545	457	358	393	417	498	540	430	110
Drug law violations	9,688	11,100	10,885	10,903	11,208	12,114	12,685	14,157	15,845	17,841	21,240	22,197	22,337	19,606	2,731
Liquor law violations	61,162	66,117	73,762	79,238	84,848	90,748	90,024	90,675	87,254	86,705	88,950	87,701	87,142	79,278	7,864
For-profit 4-year															
Selected crimes against persons and property	505	592	720	718	829	641	612	574	525	561	446	384	542	180	362
Murder[1]	0	0	0	0	0	0	0	0	0	0	1	0	1	1	0
Negligent manslaughter[2]	0	0	0	0	0	0	0	0	0	0	0	0	0	0	0
Sex offenses—forcible[3]	4	4	8	5	4	12	12	9	9	22	26	19	20	14	6
Sex offenses—nonforcible[4]	13	1	2	0	1	0	2	0	1	1	0	3	2	0	2
Robbery[5]	64	71	43	46	43	25	31	38	86	70	74	53	90	13	77
Aggravated assault[6]	23	45	41	38	59	31	31	63	43	51	36	47	68	38	30
Burglary[7]	347	376	542	524	607	489	446	385	299	350	249	200	282	113	169
Motor vehicle theft[8]	52	94	80	100	110	78	89	79	85	65	58	61	77	0	77
Arson[9]	2	1	4	5	5	6	1	0	2	2	2	1	2	1	1
Weapons-, drug-, and liquor-related arrests and referrals															
Arrests[10]	11	17	11	41	28	52	28	40	54	165	152	128	86	31	55
Illegal weapons possession	2	3	2	5	2	5	3	8	6	13	11	11	12	2	10
Drug law violations	4	9	4	12	16	14	16	14	22	66	41	50	56	25	31
Liquor law violations	5	5	5	24	10	33	9	18	26	86	100	67	18	4	14
Referrals for disciplinary action[10]	316	399	465	298	529	513	519	566	882	760	718	668	1,166	1,051	115
Illegal weapons possession	11	25	24	11	42	13	11	13	23	9	16	23	18	12	6
Drug law violations	92	133	130	99	128	138	132	159	231	221	233	254	540	476	64
Liquor law violations	213	241	311	188	359	362	376	394	628	530	469	391	608	563	45

See notes at end of table.

Table 329.10. On-campus crimes, arrests, and referrals for disciplinary action at degree-granting postsecondary institutions, by location of incident, control and level of institution, and type of incident: 2001 through 2013—Continued

Control and level of institution and type of incident	Number of incidents														
	Total, in residence halls and at other locations												2013		
	2001	2002	2003	2004	2005	2006	2007	2008	2009	2010	2011	2012	Total	In residence halls	At other locations
1	2	3	4	5	6	7	8	9	10	11	12	13	14	15	16
Public 2-year															
Selected crimes against persons and property	6,817	6,860	6,637	6,637	5,981	5,669	5,381	5,464	4,984	4,396	4,141	3,760	3,117	566	2,551
Murder[1]	2	1	2	3	2	0	0	2	2	1	2	3	7	0	7
Negligent manslaughter[2]	0	0	0	0	0	0	0	0	0	1	0	0	0	0	0
Sex offenses—forcible[3]	118	118	160	142	175	167	181	210	205	210	262	265	304	84	220
Sex offenses—nonforcible[4]	119	61	14	6	10	16	7	7	12	8	16	13	12	5	7
Robbery[5]	245	234	230	213	248	284	279	285	251	298	262	244	194	6	188
Aggravated assault[6]	545	503	589	497	501	546	462	401	431	409	406	437	286	52	234
Burglary[7]	4,132	4,158	3,973	4,068	3,541	3,261	3,202	3,430	2,920	2,398	2,235	1,972	1,615	417	1,198
Motor vehicle theft[8]	1,552	1,661	1,607	1,620	1,428	1,319	1,174	1,059	1,109	1,028	899	777	655	0	655
Arson[9]	104	124	62	88	76	76	76	70	54	43	59	49	44	2	42
Weapons-, drug-, and liquor-related arrests and referrals															
Arrests[10]	2,660	2,844	2,950	3,270	3,416	3,993	4,124	3,764	3,335	3,811	3,723	3,486	3,121	1,365	1,756
Illegal weapons possession	198	221	220	255	278	300	304	258	256	282	248	253	234	21	213
Drug law violations	989	996	1,141	1,312	1,326	1,378	1,563	1,490	1,507	1,866	1,892	1,901	1,652	499	1,153
Liquor law violations	1,473	1,627	1,589	1,703	1,812	2,315	2,257	2,016	1,572	1,663	1,583	1,332	1,235	845	390
Referrals for disciplinary action[10]	3,529	3,744	4,036	4,371	4,688	5,897	5,987	6,425	7,241	8,017	8,174	7,589	6,876	5,369	1,507
Illegal weapons possession	127	146	145	167	133	238	218	183	210	242	228	225	242	85	157
Drug law violations	761	692	679	858	819	908	1,006	1,302	1,745	2,336	2,573	2,469	2,304	1,454	850
Liquor law violations	2,641	2,906	3,212	3,346	3,736	4,751	4,763	4,940	5,286	5,439	5,373	4,895	4,330	3,830	500
Nonprofit 2-year															
Selected crimes against persons and property	248	230	189	166	314	250	258	272	147	120	148	107	61	34	27
Murder[1]	1	0	0	0	0	0	0	0	0	0	0	0	0	0	0
Negligent manslaughter[2]	0	0	0	0	0	0	0	1	0	0	0	0	0	0	0
Sex offenses—forcible[3]	2	7	6	3	8	3	9	16	8	7	11	8	4	1	3
Sex offenses—nonforcible[4]	2	2	0	0	0	1	0	0	0	0	0	0	2	2	0
Robbery[5]	54	56	64	22	9	7	2	13	9	5	1	2	5	2	3
Aggravated assault[6]	23	17	12	17	22	35	52	66	5	9	53	46	9	1	8
Burglary[7]	142	123	83	111	266	187	178	160	120	95	74	47	38	28	10
Motor vehicle theft[8]	23	21	23	13	7	14	14	9	4	2	7	4	3	0	3
Arson[9]	1	4	1	0	2	3	3	7	1	2	2	0	0	0	0
Weapons-, drug-, and liquor-related arrests and referrals															
Arrests[10]	108	39	23	48	76	67	59	93	58	49	52	52	66	34	32
Illegal weapons possession	1	2	3	2	5	3	4	3	4	6	5	5	5	1	4
Drug law violations	21	10	16	16	32	34	27	33	35	18	34	31	49	22	27
Liquor law violations	86	27	4	30	39	30	28	57	19	25	13	16	12	11	1
Referrals for disciplinary action[10]	624	569	552	447	514	537	519	413	348	377	360	300	320	306	14
Illegal weapons possession	2	3	6	5	12	19	10	6	7	4	1	6	7	4	3
Drug law violations	91	65	52	58	47	74	73	85	100	105	109	103	129	121	8
Liquor law violations	531	501	494	384	455	444	436	322	241	268	250	191	184	181	3
For-profit 2-year															
Selected crimes against persons and property	472	417	550	527	430	420	547	399	459	315	257	258	187	19	168
Murder[1]	0	1	0	0	0	0	0	0	0	0	0	0	0	0	0
Negligent manslaughter[2]	0	0	0	0	0	0	0	1	0	0	0	0	0	0	0
Sex offenses—forcible[3]	12	6	15	9	1	8	2	4	6	2	7	12	11	6	5
Sex offenses—nonforcible[4]	7	3	2	0	0	1	0	0	1	1	0	3	0	0	0
Robbery[5]	67	47	81	80	55	49	67	53	50	38	16	28	23	2	21
Aggravated assault[6]	40	19	36	62	50	33	33	29	53	35	37	34	13	6	7
Burglary[7]	292	297	341	325	250	245	350	241	226	135	120	112	88	5	83
Motor vehicle theft[8]	51	40	74	49	71	81	92	71	121	101	74	69	51	0	51
Arson[9]	3	4	1	2	3	3	3	0	2	3	3	0	1	0	1
Weapons-, drug-, and liquor-related arrests and referrals															
Arrests[10]	163	128	84	112	47	41	45	23	62	43	23	51	61	38	23
Illegal weapons possession	13	9	6	6	3	3	4	4	4	5	1	7	3	1	2
Drug law violations	87	65	48	64	36	26	32	12	41	29	14	40	40	24	16
Liquor law violations	63	54	30	42	8	12	9	7	17	9	8	4	18	13	5
Referrals for disciplinary action[10]	287	330	313	322	228	320	173	248	303	147	168	219	206	190	16
Illegal weapons possession	16	14	7	7	8	7	7	4	8	2	10	10	4	2	2
Drug law violations	89	105	196	186	134	219	122	110	163	68	68	87	93	79	14
Liquor law violations	182	211	110	129	86	94	44	134	132	77	90	122	109	109	0

[1]Excludes suicides, fetal deaths, traffic fatalities, accidental deaths, and justifiable homicide (such as the killing of a felon by a law enforcement officer in the line of duty).
[2]Killing of another person through gross negligence (excludes traffic fatalities).
[3]Any sexual act directed against another person forcibly and/or against that person's will.
[4]Includes only statutory rape or incest.
[5]Taking or attempting to take anything of value using actual or threatened force or violence.
[6]Attack upon a person for the purpose of inflicting severe or aggravated bodily injury.
[7]Unlawful entry of a structure to commit a felony or theft.
[8]Theft or attempted theft of a motor vehicle.
[9]Willful or malicious burning or attempt to burn a dwelling house, public building, motor vehicle, or personal property of another.
[10]If an individual is both arrested and referred to college officials for disciplinary action for a single offense, only the arrest is counted.

NOTE: Data are for degree-granting institutions, which are institutions that grant associate's or higher degrees and participate in Title IV federal financial aid programs. Some institutions that report Clery data—specifically, non-degree-granting institutions and institutions outside of the 50 states and the District of Columbia—are excluded from this table. Crimes, arrests, and referrals include incidents involving students, staff, and on-campus guests. Excludes off-campus crimes and arrests even if they involve college students or staff. Some data have been revised from previously published figures.
SOURCE: U.S. Department of Education, Office of Postsecondary Education, Campus Safety and Security Reporting System, 2001 through 2013; and National Center for Education Statistics, Integrated Postsecondary Education Data System (IPEDS), Fall 2002 through Fall 2014, Institutional Characteristics component. (This table was prepared August 2015.)

Table 329.20. On-campus crimes, arrests, and referrals for disciplinary action per 10,000 full-time-equivalent (FTE) students at degree-granting postsecondary institutions, by whether institution has residence halls, control and level of institution, and type of incident: 2001 through 2013

Control and level of institution and type of incident	Number of incidents per 10,000 full-time-equivalent (FTE) students[1]														
	Total, institutions with and without residence halls												2013		
	2001	2002	2003	2004	2005	2006	2007	2008	2009	2010	2011	2012	Total	Institutions with residence halls	Institutions without residence halls
1	2	3	4	5	6	7	8	9	10	11	12	13	14	15	16
All institutions															
Selected crimes against persons and property	35.619	34.649	34.040	33.580	32.864	33.347	30.568	28.987	22.955	20.869	20.027	19.793	18.378	24.209	6.181
Murder[2]	0.015	0.016	0.007	0.012	0.008	0.006	0.032	0.009	0.011	0.010	0.011	0.008	0.015	0.014	0.019
Negligent manslaughter[3]	0.002	0.000	0.001	0.000	0.002	0.000	0.002	0.002	0.000	0.001	0.001	0.001	0.000	0.000	0.000
Sex offenses—forcible[4]	1.885	1.896	2.051	2.056	2.058	2.001	1.969	1.898	1.715	1.903	2.223	2.665	3.309	4.646	0.513
Sex offenses—nonforcible[5]	0.395	0.213	0.047	0.021	0.032	0.032	0.029	0.025	0.044	0.021	0.031	0.031	0.030	0.035	0.019
Robbery[6]	1.424	1.468	1.284	1.195	1.193	1.159	1.141	1.134	0.950	0.905	0.846	0.912	0.887	1.048	0.548
Aggravated assault[7]	2.524	2.285	2.239	2.098	2.044	2.111	1.903	1.795	1.569	1.444	1.475	1.608	1.390	1.792	0.548
Burglary[8]	23.038	22.847	22.638	22.728	22.511	23.429	21.549	20.672	15.559	13.872	12.825	12.094	10.333	13.908	2.857
Motor vehicle theft[9]	5.327	5.037	4.968	4.674	4.256	3.921	3.375	2.952	2.681	2.237	2.196	2.008	1.995	2.191	1.587
Arson[10]	1.010	0.887	0.805	0.796	0.759	0.687	0.567	0.500	0.427	0.476	0.421	0.467	0.418	0.574	0.091
Weapons-, drug-, and liquor-related arrests and referrals															
Arrests[11]	34.550	35.371	35.239	36.960	37.722	37.615	36.947	36.428	33.748	33.497	35.755	35.045	31.842	45.542	3.188
Illegal weapons possession	0.919	0.931	0.865	0.974	1.013	0.986	0.963	0.856	0.726	0.723	0.674	0.681	0.696	0.829	0.418
Drug law violations	10.151	9.812	9.854	9.849	10.547	10.457	10.330	10.895	10.698	12.086	13.653	14.191	13.432	18.809	2.185
Liquor law violations	23.481	24.629	24.520	26.137	26.163	26.172	25.654	24.676	22.324	20.687	21.428	20.172	17.714	25.904	0.585
Referrals for disciplinary action[11]	132.899	136.344	146.165	151.708	156.060	163.421	158.288	156.479	148.959	149.716	164.460	167.017	164.290	241.127	3.576
Illegal weapons possession	1.093	1.049	1.238	1.387	1.448	1.402	1.212	1.047	0.859	0.854	0.844	0.936	0.956	1.284	0.270
Drug law violations	20.466	21.218	20.356	19.862	19.511	20.425	20.810	23.357	24.498	27.322	33.961	35.916	36.090	52.605	1.546
Liquor law violations	111.340	114.077	124.571	130.459	135.101	141.594	136.267	132.076	123.602	121.540	129.654	130.165	127.244	187.238	1.760
Public 4-year															
Selected crimes against persons and property	36.191	36.334	35.725	35.522	34.295	35.532	32.837	30.531	24.898	23.448	21.958	21.652	19.633	20.933	6.306
Murder[2]	0.017	0.017	0.009	0.014	0.007	0.009	0.070	0.015	0.012	0.014	0.015	0.010	0.015	0.015	0.017
Negligent manslaughter[3]	0.004	0.000	0.002	0.000	0.002	0.000	0.003	0.002	0.000	0.000	0.001	0.001	0.000	0.000	0.000
Sex offenses—forcible[4]	2.408	2.374	2.452	2.634	2.448	2.409	2.390	2.151	1.892	2.210	2.451	2.941	3.347	3.624	0.500
Sex offenses—nonforcible[5]	0.400	0.210	0.051	0.028	0.044	0.026	0.039	0.020	0.062	0.023	0.025	0.025	0.025	0.026	0.017
Robbery[6]	1.130	1.224	1.208	1.088	1.219	1.170	1.211	1.225	1.008	1.001	0.916	0.984	0.950	0.990	0.551
Aggravated assault[7]	2.774	2.452	2.493	2.256	2.242	2.302	2.110	1.930	1.767	1.627	1.610	1.778	1.511	1.608	0.517
Burglary[8]	22.283	23.259	22.808	23.154	22.654	24.138	22.425	21.181	16.689	15.456	14.025	13.181	10.942	11.707	3.103
Motor vehicle theft[9]	5.942	5.743	5.625	5.269	4.671	4.581	3.800	3.310	2.843	2.426	2.382	2.095	2.244	2.313	1.535
Arson[10]	1.232	1.057	1.078	1.079	1.009	0.897	0.788	0.697	0.623	0.691	0.533	0.637	0.599	0.651	0.067
Weapons-, drug-, and liquor-related arrests and referrals															
Arrests[11]	60.113	62.833	62.566	65.318	66.641	68.662	66.366	66.315	63.558	63.512	67.169	64.997	57.387	62.562	4.337
Illegal weapons possession	1.339	1.384	1.258	1.442	1.538	1.478	1.384	1.240	1.027	1.012	0.941	0.931	0.974	1.027	0.434
Drug law violations	17.651	17.158	16.950	17.100	18.575	18.671	17.934	19.130	18.993	21.722	24.424	25.248	23.444	25.434	3.036
Liquor law violations	41.123	44.292	44.358	46.776	46.529	48.513	47.048	45.945	43.539	40.778	41.804	38.819	32.969	36.101	0.867
Referrals for disciplinary action[11]	153.104	157.192	170.355	178.800	175.506	184.628	178.029	170.797	169.503	175.490	194.017	197.663	189.581	207.918	1.618
Illegal weapons possession	1.311	1.254	1.529	1.779	1.921	1.673	1.454	1.293	1.043	1.004	0.913	0.968	0.924	1.007	0.067
Drug law violations	25.492	25.896	24.933	24.278	22.803	23.744	24.249	27.201	28.459	32.444	40.907	43.276	42.605	46.663	1.001
Liquor law violations	126.301	130.043	143.893	152.743	150.782	159.211	152.326	142.303	140.001	142.042	152.198	153.419	146.053	160.248	0.551
Nonprofit 4-year															
Selected crimes against persons and property	57.358	55.445	54.891	54.728	54.165	57.681	52.039	49.315	38.613	35.193	33.154	32.730	31.341	33.383	9.371
Murder[2]	0.019	0.034	0.007	0.014	0.017	0.010	0.007	0.003	0.019	0.016	0.009	0.006	0.015	0.013	0.035
Negligent manslaughter[3]	0.000	0.000	0.000	0.000	0.003	0.000	0.003	0.000	0.000	0.000	0.000	0.000	0.000	0.000	0.000
Sex offenses—forcible[4]	3.169	3.410	3.790	3.617	3.784	3.694	3.587	3.586	3.557	3.848	4.417	5.275	7.122	7.686	1.061
Sex offenses—nonforcible[5]	0.437	0.302	0.051	0.018	0.021	0.034	0.027	0.053	0.036	0.025	0.040	0.030	0.036	0.036	0.035
Robbery[6]	2.508	2.743	1.946	2.034	1.739	1.717	1.549	1.447	1.181	1.002	0.988	1.173	1.134	1.154	0.919
Aggravated assault[7]	3.408	3.358	2.795	2.954	2.588	2.853	2.586	2.497	2.133	2.014	1.948	2.024	2.075	2.199	0.743
Burglary[8]	40.460	39.407	40.017	40.284	40.542	44.639	40.214	38.251	28.434	25.567	22.908	21.384	18.341	19.547	5.375
Motor vehicle theft[9]	5.684	4.750	5.008	4.640	4.340	3.684	3.314	2.845	2.692	2.014	2.173	2.151	2.087	2.170	1.202
Arson[10]	1.673	1.440	1.277	1.167	1.130	1.050	0.751	0.632	0.562	0.707	0.670	0.688	0.529	0.579	0.000
Weapons-, drug-, and liquor-related arrests and referrals															
Arrests[11]	24.456	24.433	24.793	27.225	25.758	20.981	22.672	20.240	18.645	17.150	16.805	16.709	17.231	18.656	1.909
Illegal weapons possession	0.645	0.604	0.600	0.649	0.522	0.499	0.599	0.523	0.478	0.430	0.398	0.385	0.400	0.434	0.035
Drug law violations	6.291	6.429	6.759	6.173	5.881	5.644	6.075	6.236	6.713	7.062	7.486	7.380	7.643	8.241	1.202
Liquor law violations	17.520	17.399	17.434	20.403	19.355	14.838	15.997	13.481	11.454	9.657	8.921	8.944	9.189	9.980	0.672
Referrals for disciplinary action[11]	275.480	289.709	308.044	319.945	336.127	353.954	347.734	348.663	333.904	329.679	341.437	334.473	330.910	359.218	26.414
Illegal weapons possession	1.712	1.582	1.942	2.144	2.052	2.127	1.835	1.513	1.155	1.235	1.287	1.509	1.624	1.759	0.177
Drug law violations	37.435	41.418	39.363	38.440	38.981	41.434	42.720	46.881	51.139	56.050	65.567	67.251	67.184	73.026	4.349
Liquor law violations	236.333	246.708	266.740	279.362	295.095	310.392	303.179	300.269	281.609	272.395	274.583	265.713	262.101	284.433	21.888
For-profit 4-year															
Selected crimes against persons and property	19.109	17.840	17.605	13.650	17.049	9.552	8.095	10.320	7.513	6.499	6.003	5.234	7.493	20.129	3.717
Murder[2]	0.000	0.000	0.000	0.000	0.000	0.000	0.000	0.000	0.000	0.000	0.013	0.000	0.014	0.060	0.000
Negligent manslaughter[3]	0.000	0.000	0.000	0.000	0.000	0.000	0.000	0.000	0.000	0.000	0.000	0.000	0.000	0.000	0.000
Sex offenses—forcible[4]	0.151	0.121	0.196	0.095	0.082	0.179	0.159	0.162	0.129	0.255	0.350	0.259	0.277	0.961	0.072
Sex offenses—nonforcible[5]	0.492	0.030	0.049	0.000	0.021	0.000	0.026	0.000	0.014	0.012	0.000	0.041	0.028	0.000	0.036
Robbery[6]	2.422	2.140	1.051	0.875	0.884	0.373	0.410	0.683	1.231	0.811	0.996	0.722	1.244	3.545	0.557
Aggravated assault[7]	0.870	1.356	1.003	0.722	1.213	0.462	0.410	1.133	0.615	0.591	0.485	0.641	0.940	3.004	0.323
Burglary[8]	13.130	11.331	13.253	9.962	12.484	7.287	5.899	6.922	4.279	4.055	3.351	2.726	3.899	10.876	1.814
Motor vehicle theft[9]	1.968	2.833	1.956	1.901	2.262	1.162	1.177	1.420	1.216	0.753	0.781	0.831	1.065	1.622	0.898
Arson[10]	0.076	0.030	0.098	0.095	0.103	0.089	0.013	0.000	0.029	0.023	0.027	0.014	0.028	0.060	0.018
Weapons-, drug-, and liquor-related arrests and referrals															
Arrests[11]	0.416	0.512	0.269	0.779	0.576	0.775	0.370	0.719	0.773	1.911	2.046	1.745	1.189	3.365	0.539
Illegal weapons possession	0.076	0.090	0.049	0.095	0.041	0.075	0.040	0.144	0.086	0.151	0.148	0.150	0.166	0.421	0.090
Drug law violations	0.151	0.271	0.098	0.228	0.329	0.209	0.212	0.252	0.315	0.765	0.552	0.681	0.774	2.343	0.305
Liquor law violations	0.189	0.151	0.122	0.456	0.206	0.492	0.119	0.324	0.372	0.996	1.346	0.913	0.249	0.601	0.144
Referrals for disciplinary action[11]	11.957	12.024	11.370	5.665	10.880	7.645	6.865	10.177	12.623	8.804	9.663	9.104	16.120	68.438	0.485
Illegal weapons possession	0.416	0.753	0.587	0.209	0.864	0.194	0.145	0.234	0.329	0.104	0.215	0.313	0.249	0.901	0.054
Drug law violations	3.481	4.008	3.179	1.882	2.632	2.057	1.746	2.859	3.306	2.560	3.136	3.462	7.466	31.545	0.269
Liquor law violations	8.060	7.263	7.605	3.574	7.383	5.395	4.973	7.084	8.988	6.140	6.312	5.329	8.406	35.991	0.162

See notes at end of table.

Table 329.20. On-campus crimes, arrests, and referrals for disciplinary action per 10,000 full-time-equivalent (FTE) students at degree-granting postsecondary institutions, by whether institution has residence halls, control and level of institution, and type of incident: 2001 through 2013—Continued

Control and level of institution and type of incident	Number of incidents per 10,000 full-time-equivalent (FTE) students[1] — Total, institutions with and without residence halls: 2001	2002	2003	2004	2005	2006	2007	2008	2009	2010	2011	2012	2013: Total	2013: Institutions with residence halls	2013: Institutions without residence halls
1	2	3	4	5	6	7	8	9	10	11	12	13	14	15	16
Public 2-year															
Selected crimes against persons and property	19.867	18.834	18.044	17.903	16.389	15.423	14.388	13.991	11.745	10.195	9.998	9.387	7.994	14.793	6.309
Murder[2]	0.006	0.003	0.005	0.008	0.005	0.000	0.000	0.005	0.005	0.002	0.005	0.007	0.018	0.000	0.022
Negligent manslaughter[3]	0.000	0.000	0.000	0.000	0.000	0.000	0.000	0.000	0.000	0.002	0.000	0.000	0.000	0.000	0.000
Sex offenses—forcible[4]	0.344	0.324	0.435	0.383	0.480	0.454	0.484	0.538	0.483	0.487	0.633	0.662	0.780	1.626	0.570
Sex offenses—nonforcible[5]	0.347	0.167	0.038	0.016	0.027	0.044	0.019	0.018	0.028	0.019	0.039	0.032	0.031	0.090	0.016
Robbery[6]	0.714	0.642	0.625	0.575	0.680	0.773	0.746	0.730	0.591	0.691	0.633	0.609	0.498	0.529	0.490
Aggravated assault[7]	1.588	1.381	1.601	1.341	1.373	1.485	1.235	1.027	1.016	0.949	0.980	1.091	0.734	1.304	0.592
Burglary[8]	12.042	11.416	10.801	10.974	9.703	8.872	8.561	8.783	6.881	5.561	5.396	4.923	4.142	9.746	2.753
Motor vehicle theft[9]	4.523	4.560	4.369	4.370	3.913	3.588	3.139	2.712	2.613	2.384	2.171	1.940	1.680	1.420	1.744
Arson[10]	0.303	0.340	0.169	0.237	0.208	0.207	0.203	0.179	0.127	0.100	0.142	0.122	0.113	0.077	0.122
Weapons-, drug-, and liquor-related arrests and referrals															
Arrests[11]	7.752	7.808	8.020	8.821	9.360	10.863	11.027	9.638	7.859	8.838	8.989	8.703	8.005	25.159	3.751
Illegal weapons possession	0.577	0.607	0.598	0.688	0.762	0.816	0.813	0.661	0.603	0.654	0.599	0.632	0.600	0.839	0.541
Drug law violations	2.882	2.735	3.102	3.539	3.633	3.749	4.179	3.815	3.551	4.328	4.568	4.746	4.237	10.959	2.570
Liquor law violations	4.293	4.467	4.320	4.594	4.965	6.298	6.035	5.162	3.704	3.857	3.822	3.325	3.167	13.360	0.640
Referrals for disciplinary action[11]	10.284	10.279	10.973	11.791	12.846	16.043	16.008	16.451	17.063	18.592	19.735	18.946	17.635	77.865	2.701
Illegal weapons possession	0.370	0.401	0.394	0.450	0.364	0.648	0.583	0.469	0.495	0.561	0.550	0.562	0.621	1.639	0.368
Drug law violations	2.218	1.900	1.846	2.314	2.244	2.470	2.690	3.334	4.112	5.417	6.212	6.164	5.909	22.809	1.719
Liquor law violations	7.697	7.978	8.732	9.026	10.237	12.926	12.735	12.649	12.456	12.614	12.972	12.220	11.105	53.416	0.615
Nonprofit 2-year															
Selected crimes against persons and property	63.955	58.903	51.594	48.535	91.263	81.948	103.819	99.299	55.883	48.448	45.531	34.764	23.425	53.231	10.021
Murder[2]	0.258	0.000	0.000	0.000	0.000	0.000	0.000	0.000	0.000	0.000	0.000	0.000	0.000	0.000	0.000
Negligent manslaughter[3]	0.000	0.000	0.000	0.000	0.000	0.000	0.000	0.365	0.000	0.000	0.000	0.000	0.000	0.000	0.000
Sex offenses—forcible[4]	0.516	1.793	1.638	0.877	2.325	0.983	3.622	5.841	3.041	2.826	3.384	2.599	1.536	2.476	1.113
Sex offenses—nonforcible[5]	0.516	0.512	0.000	0.000	0.000	0.328	0.000	0.000	0.000	0.000	0.000	0.000	0.768	2.476	0.000
Robbery[6]	13.926	14.342	17.471	6.432	2.616	2.295	0.805	4.746	3.421	2.019	0.308	0.650	1.920	3.714	1.113
Aggravated assault[7]	5.931	4.354	3.276	4.970	6.394	11.473	20.925	24.095	1.901	3.634	16.305	14.945	3.456	6.190	2.227
Burglary[8]	36.620	31.500	22.658	32.454	77.312	61.297	71.627	58.411	45.619	38.354	22.766	15.270	14.592	37.138	4.454
Motor vehicle theft[9]	5.931	5.378	6.279	3.801	2.035	4.589	5.634	3.286	1.521	0.807	2.154	1.300	1.152	1.238	1.113
Arson[10]	0.258	1.024	0.273	0.000	0.581	0.983	1.207	2.555	0.380	0.807	0.615	0.000	0.000	0.000	0.000
Weapons-, drug-, and liquor-related arrests and referrals															
Arrests[11]	27.852	9.988	6.279	14.034	22.089	21.962	23.741	33.952	22.049	19.783	15.998	16.895	25.345	66.848	6.680
Illegal weapons possession	0.258	0.512	0.819	0.585	1.453	0.983	1.610	1.095	1.521	2.422	1.538	1.624	1.920	6.190	0.000
Drug law violations	5.416	2.561	4.368	4.678	9.301	11.145	10.865	12.047	13.305	7.267	10.460	10.072	18.816	45.803	6.680
Liquor law violations	22.178	6.915	1.092	8.771	11.335	9.834	11.267	20.809	7.223	10.093	3.999	5.198	4.608	14.855	0.000
Referrals for disciplinary action[11]	160.920	145.722	150.688	130.694	149.393	176.025	208.845	150.774	132.294	152.206	110.752	97.469	122.883	389.948	2.783
Illegal weapons possession	0.516	0.768	1.638	1.462	3.488	6.228	4.024	2.190	2.661	1.615	0.308	1.949	2.688	6.190	1.113
Drug law violations	23.468	16.647	14.195	16.958	13.660	24.257	29.375	31.031	38.016	42.392	33.533	33.464	49.537	157.217	1.113
Liquor law violations	136.937	128.307	134.855	112.274	132.244	145.540	175.446	117.553	91.618	108.200	76.911	62.055	70.658	226.541	0.557
For-profit 2-year															
Selected crimes against persons and property	25.385	21.447	24.700	21.845	17.851	18.237	23.658	14.826	13.033	8.167	7.503	8.744	6.602	21.150	5.916
Murder[2]	0.000	0.051	0.000	0.000	0.000	0.000	0.000	0.000	0.000	0.000	0.000	0.000	0.000	0.000	0.000
Negligent manslaughter[3]	0.000	0.000	0.000	0.000	0.000	0.000	0.000	0.037	0.000	0.000	0.000	0.000	0.000	0.000	0.000
Sex offenses—forcible[4]	0.645	0.309	0.674	0.373	0.042	0.347	0.087	0.149	0.170	0.052	0.204	0.407	0.388	4.700	0.185
Sex offenses—nonforcible[5]	0.376	0.154	0.090	0.000	0.000	0.043	0.000	0.000	0.028	0.026	0.000	0.102	0.000	0.000	0.000
Robbery[6]	3.603	2.417	3.638	3.316	2.283	2.128	2.898	1.969	1.420	0.985	0.467	0.949	0.812	1.567	0.776
Aggravated assault[7]	2.151	0.977	1.617	2.570	2.076	1.433	1.427	1.078	1.505	0.907	1.080	1.152	0.459	4.700	0.259
Burglary[8]	15.704	15.275	15.314	13.472	10.378	10.638	15.138	8.955	6.417	3.500	3.503	3.796	3.107	7.050	2.921
Motor vehicle theft[9]	2.743	2.057	3.323	2.031	2.947	3.517	3.979	2.638	3.436	2.619	2.160	2.338	1.801	3.133	1.738
Arson[10]	0.161	0.206	0.045	0.083	0.125	0.130	0.130	0.000	0.057	0.078	0.088	0.000	0.035	0.000	0.037
Weapons-, drug-, and liquor-related arrests and referrals															
Arrests[11]	8.766	6.583	3.772	4.643	1.951	1.780	1.946	0.855	1.760	1.115	0.671	1.728	2.154	32.900	0.702
Illegal weapons possession	0.699	0.463	0.269	0.249	0.125	0.130	0.173	0.149	0.114	0.130	0.029	0.237	0.106	0.783	0.074
Drug law violations	4.679	3.343	2.156	2.653	1.495	1.129	1.384	0.446	1.164	0.752	0.409	1.356	1.412	21.933	0.444
Liquor law violations	3.388	2.777	1.347	1.741	0.332	0.521	0.389	0.260	0.483	0.233	0.234	0.136	0.636	10.183	0.185
Referrals for disciplinary action[11]	15.435	16.972	14.057	13.348	9.465	13.895	7.482	9.215	8.603	3.811	4.905	7.422	7.273	149.616	0.555
Illegal weapons possession	0.861	0.720	0.314	0.290	0.332	0.304	0.303	0.149	0.227	0.052	0.292	0.339	0.141	1.567	0.074
Drug law violations	4.787	5.400	8.802	7.710	5.563	9.509	5.277	4.087	4.628	1.763	1.985	2.949	3.284	62.666	0.481
Liquor law violations	9.788	10.852	4.940	5.347	3.570	4.082	1.903	4.979	3.748	1.996	2.627	4.135	3.848	85.383	0.000

[1]Although crimes, arrests, and referrals include incidents involving students, staff, and campus guests, they are expressed as a ratio to FTE students because comprehensive FTE counts of all these groups are not available.
[2]Excludes suicides, fetal deaths, traffic fatalities, accidental deaths, and justifiable homicide (such as the killing of a felon by a law enforcement officer in the line of duty).
[3]Killing of another person through gross negligence (excludes traffic fatalities).
[4]Any sexual act directed against another person forcibly and/or against that person's will.
[5]Includes only statutory rape or incest.
[6]Taking or attempting to take anything of value using actual or threatened force or violence.
[7]Attack upon a person for the purpose of inflicting severe or aggravated bodily injury.
[8]Unlawful entry of a structure to commit a felony or theft.
[9]Theft or attempted theft of a motor vehicle.
[10]Willful or malicious burning or attempt to burn a dwelling house, public building, motor vehicle, or personal property of another.
[11]If an individual is both arrested and referred to college officials for disciplinary action for a single offense, only the arrest is counted.

NOTE: Data are for degree-granting institutions, which are institutions that grant associate's or higher degrees and participate in Title IV federal financial aid programs. Some institutions that report Clery data—specifically, non-degree-granting institutions and institutions outside of the 50 states and the District of Columbia—are excluded from this table. Crimes, arrests, and referrals include incidents involving students, staff, and on-campus guests. Excludes off-campus crimes and arrests even if they involve college students or staff. Detail may not sum to totals because of rounding. Some data have been revised from previously published figures.
SOURCE: U.S. Department of Education, Office of Postsecondary Education, Campus Safety and Security Reporting System, 2001 through 2013; and National Center for Education Statistics, Integrated Postsecondary Education Data System (IPEDS), Spring 2002 through Spring 2014, Fall Enrollment component. (This table was prepared August 2015.)

Table 329.30. On-campus hate crimes at degree-granting postsecondary institutions, by level and control of institution, type of crime, and category of bias motivating the crime: 2009 through 2013

Type of crime and category of bias motivating the crime[1]	Total, 2009	Total, 2010	Total, 2011	2012							2013						
					4-year			2-year				4-year			2-year		
				Total	Public	Non-profit	For-profit	Public	Non-profit	For-profit	Total	Public	Non-profit	For-profit	Public	Non-profit	For-profit
1	2	3	4	5	6	7	8	9	10	11	12	13	14	15	16	17	18
All on-campus hate crimes	**672**	**928**	**761**	**787**	**328**	**303**	**12**	**138**	**2**	**4**	**781**	**295**	**349**	**25**	**106**	**1**	**5**
Murder[2]	0	0	0	0	0	0	0	0	0	0	0	0	0	0	0	0	0
Negligent manslaughter[3]	0	0	0	0	0	0	0	0	0	0	0	0	0	0	0	0	0
Sex offenses–forcible[4]	11	7	9	4	1	1	0	2	0	0	7	1	6	0	0	0	0
Race	0	0	0	1	0	0	0	1	0	0	2	0	2	0	0	0	0
Ethnicity	0	0	2	0	0	0	0	0	0	0	0	0	0	0	0	0	0
Religion	0	0	1	2	1	0	0	1	0	0	1	0	1	0	0	0	0
Sexual orientation	0	4	6	1	0	1	0	0	0	0	4	1	3	0	0	0	0
Gender	3	3	0	0	0	0	0	0	0	0	0	0	0	0	0	0	0
Disability	8	0	0	0	0	0	0	0	0	0	0	0	0	0	0	0	0
Sex offenses–nonforcible[5]	0	0	0	0	0	0	0	0	0	0	0	0	0	0	0	0	0
Robbery[6]	5	2	2	5	2	0	0	3	0	0	1	0	1	0	0	0	0
Race	3	1	1	4	2	0	0	2	0	0	0	0	0	0	0	0	0
Ethnicity	0	1	0	0	0	0	0	0	0	0	1	0	1	0	0	0	0
Religion	0	0	0	0	0	0	0	0	0	0	0	0	0	0	0	0	0
Sexual orientation	2	0	1	0	0	0	0	0	0	0	0	0	0	0	0	0	0
Gender	0	0	0	0	0	0	0	0	0	0	0	0	0	0	0	0	0
Disability	0	0	0	1	0	0	0	1	0	0	0	0	0	0	0	0	0
Aggravated assault[7]	9	17	13	14	6	4	1	3	0	0	6	3	1	0	2	0	0
Race	3	6	5	6	3	1	0	2	0	0	4	2	0	0	2	0	0
Ethnicity	1	1	0	0	0	0	0	0	0	0	1	1	0	0	0	0	0
Religion	0	1	2	1	1	0	0	0	0	0	0	0	0	0	0	0	0
Sexual orientation	4	9	6	5	2	2	1	0	0	0	1	0	1	0	0	0	0
Gender	1	0	0	1	0	0	0	1	0	0	0	0	0	0	0	0	0
Disability	0	0	0	1	0	1	0	0	0	0	0	0	0	0	0	0	0
Burglary[8]	8	11	8	5	0	0	0	4	0	1	4	1	2	0	1	0	0
Race	4	7	4	0	0	0	0	0	0	0	1	0	1	0	0	0	0
Ethnicity	2	0	0	0	0	0	0	0	0	0	0	0	0	0	0	0	0
Religion	0	0	2	1	0	0	0	0	0	1	1	0	1	0	0	0	0
Sexual orientation	1	2	1	0	0	0	0	0	0	0	0	0	0	0	0	0	0
Gender	1	1	1	4	0	0	0	4	0	0	2	1	0	0	1	0	0
Disability	0	1	0	0	0	0	0	0	0	0	0	0	0	0	0	0	0
Motor vehicle theft[9]	0	0	0	0	0	0	0	0	0	0	0	0	0	0	0	0	0
Arson[10]	0	0	1	0	0	0	0	0	0	0	0	0	0	0	0	0	0
Race	0	0	0	0	0	0	0	0	0	0	0	0	0	0	0	0	0
Ethnicity	0	0	0	0	0	0	0	0	0	0	0	0	0	0	0	0	0
Religion	0	0	1	0	0	0	0	0	0	0	0	0	0	0	0	0	0
Sexual orientation	0	0	0	0	0	0	0	0	0	0	0	0	0	0	0	0	0
Gender	0	0	0	0	0	0	0	0	0	0	0	0	0	0	0	0	0
Disability	0	0	0	0	0	0	0	0	0	0	0	0	0	0	0	0	0
Simple assault[11]	58	67	67	79	43	19	2	12	1	2	89	39	39	5	6	0	0
Race	23	25	22	36	20	11	1	2	0	2	34	15	14	2	3	0	0
Ethnicity	5	5	10	5	2	1	0	2	0	0	7	5	2	0	0	0	0
Religion	1	4	8	9	6	2	0	1	0	0	5	2	3	0	0	0	0
Sexual orientation	18	23	16	21	13	4	1	3	0	0	26	11	11	1	3	0	0
Gender	7	9	8	5	2	1	0	1	1	0	17	6	9	2	0	0	0
Disability	4	1	3	3	0	0	0	3	0	0	0	0	0	0	0	0	0
Larceny[12]	10	9	15	9	1	4	0	2	1	1	15	1	6	1	3	1	3
Race	0	1	2	2	0	1	0	1	0	0	5	0	2	1	2	0	0
Ethnicity	3	3	3	2	0	1	0	0	1	0	2	0	2	0	0	0	0
Religion	1	1	2	2	1	0	0	0	0	1	3	0	0	0	0	0	3
Sexual orientation	2	1	3	3	0	2	0	1	0	0	3	1	2	0	0	0	0
Gender	4	3	3	0	0	0	0	0	0	0	2	0	0	0	1	1	0
Disability	0	0	2	0	0	0	0	0	0	0	0	0	0	0	0	0	0
Intimidation[13]	175	260	282	268	94	120	7	47	0	0	295	100	139	14	42	0	0
Race	58	79	111	120	47	45	2	26	0	0	110	43	48	4	15	0	0
Ethnicity	23	17	22	23	6	14	1	2	0	0	49	14	29	1	5	0	0
Religion	20	38	24	29	12	14	1	2	0	0	24	7	16	1	0	0	0
Sexual orientation	57	87	91	70	25	31	0	14	0	0	69	26	31	3	9	0	0
Gender	13	37	31	22	1	15	3	3	0	0	37	7	14	5	11	0	0
Disability	4	2	3	4	3	1	0	0	0	0	6	3	1	0	2	0	0
Destruction, damage, and vandalism[14]	396	555	364	403	181	155	2	65	0	0	364	150	155	5	52	0	2
Race	174	257	166	186	91	56	0	39	0	0	151	58	61	5	27	0	0
Ethnicity	28	43	30	34	21	8	1	4	0	0	37	11	19	0	5	0	2
Religion	72	103	57	70	18	43	1	8	0	0	48	21	24	0	3	0	0
Sexual orientation	109	135	104	104	47	46	0	11	0	0	112	57	44	0	11	0	0
Gender	13	17	7	9	4	2	0	3	0	0	14	3	6	0	5	0	0
Disability	0	0	0	0	0	0	0	0	0	0	2	0	1	0	1	0	0

[1]Bias categories correspond to characteristics against which the bias is directed (i.e., race, ethnicity, religion, sexual orientation, gender, or disability).
[2]Excludes suicides, fetal deaths, traffic fatalities, accidental deaths, and justifiable homicide (such as the killing of a felon by a law enforcement officer in the line of duty).
[3]Killing of another person through gross negligence (excludes traffic fatalities).
[4]Any sexual act directed against another person forcibly and/or against that person's will.
[5]Includes only statutory rape or incest.
[6]Taking or attempting to take anything of value using actual or threatened force or violence.
[7]Attack upon a person for the purpose of inflicting severe or aggravated bodily injury.
[8]Unlawful entry of a structure to commit a felony or theft.
[9]Theft or attempted theft of a motor vehicle.
[10]Willful or malicious burning or attempt to burn a dwelling house, public building, motor vehicle, or personal property of another.
[11]A physical attack by one person upon another where neither the offender displays a weapon, nor the victim suffers obvious severe or aggravated bodily injury involving apparent broken bones, loss of teeth, possible internal injury, severe laceration, or loss of consciousness.
[12]The unlawful taking, carrying, leading, or riding away of property from the possession of another.
[13]Placing another person in reasonable fear of bodily harm through the use of threatening words and/or other conduct, but without displaying a weapon or subjecting the victim to actual physical attack.
[14]Willfully or maliciously destroying, damaging, defacing, or otherwise injuring real or personal property without the consent of the owner or the person having custody or control of it.

NOTE: Data are for degree-granting institutions, which are institutions that grant associate's or higher degrees and participate in Title IV federal financial aid programs. Some institutions that report Clery data–specifically, non-degree-granting institutions and institutions outside of the 50 states and the District of Columbia–are excluded from this table. A hate crime is a criminal offense that is motivated, in whole or in part, by the perpetrator's bias against a group of people based on their race, ethnicity, religion, sexual orientation, gender, or disability. Includes on-campus incidents involving students, staff, and on-campus guests. Excludes off-campus crimes and arrests even if they involve college students or staff.

SOURCE: U.S. Department of Education, Office of Postsecondary Education, Campus Safety and Security Reporting System, 2009 through 2013. (This table was prepared August 2015.)

Table 330.10. Average undergraduate tuition and fees and room and board rates charged for full-time students in degree-granting postsecondary institutions, by level and control of institution: 1963–64 through 2014–15

Year and control of institution	Constant 2014–15 dollars[1]												Current dollars											
	Total tuition, fees, room, and board			Tuition and required fees[2]			Dormitory rooms			Board[3]			Total tuition, fees, room, and board			Tuition and required fees[2]			Dormitory rooms			Board[3]		
	All institutions	4-year	2-year	All institutions	4-year	2-year	All institutions	4-year	2-year	All institutions	4-year	2-year	All institutions	4-year	2-year	All institutions	4-year	2-year	All institutions	4-year	2-year	All institutions	4-year	2-year
1	2	3	4	5	6	7	8	9	10	11	12	13	14	15	16	17	18	19	20	21	22	23	24	25
All institutions																								
1963–64	$9,576	$9,869	$5,951	$3,900	$4,240	$1,314	$2,167	$2,138	$1,605	$3,510	$3,491	$3,032	$1,248	$1,286	$775	$508	$553	$171	$282	$279	$209	$457	$455	$395
1964–65	9,722	10,044	6,374	4,016	4,396	1,419	2,240	2,207	1,800	3,465	3,441	3,155	1,283	1,325	841	530	580	187	296	291	238	457	454	416
1965–66	9,819	10,200	6,560	4,069	4,499	1,505	2,303	2,281	1,917	3,447	3,420	3,138	1,324	1,375	884	549	607	203	311	308	258	465	461	423
1966–67	9,908	10,348	6,656	4,127	4,604	1,541	2,362	2,352	2,013	3,419	3,393	3,102	1,378	1,439	926	574	640	214	328	327	280	476	472	431
1967–68	9,849	10,351	6,847	4,089	4,612	1,615	2,380	2,374	2,097	3,380	3,365	3,134	1,415	1,487	984	588	663	232	342	341	301	486	483	450
1968–69	9,679	10,254	6,987	3,957	4,534	1,662	2,391	2,390	2,169	3,331	3,330	3,156	1,459	1,545	1,053	596	683	250	360	360	327	502	502	476
1969–70	9,774	10,491	6,825	4,042	4,730	1,550	2,439	2,455	2,174	3,294	3,306	3,102	1,560	1,674	1,089	645	755	247	389	392	347	526	528	495
1970–71	9,846	10,631	6,675	4,099	4,848	1,486	2,495	2,514	2,201	3,252	3,269	2,988	1,653	1,784	1,120	688	814	249	419	422	369	546	549	501
1971–72	9,953	10,799	6,739	4,163	4,977	1,443	2,559	2,579	2,248	3,231	3,243	3,048	1,730	1,878	1,172	724	865	251	445	448	391	562	564	530
1972–73	10,142	11,227	7,054	4,199	5,254	1,586	2,697	2,723	2,293	3,246	3,251	3,175	1,834	2,031	1,276	759	950	287	488	492	415	587	588	574
1973–74	9,660	10,646	6,895	4,039	4,998	1,667	2,515	2,537	2,181	3,107	3,111	3,047	1,903	2,097	1,358	796	985	328	495	500	430	612	613	600
1974–75	9,062	9,992	6,542	3,699	4,607	1,497	2,413	2,434	2,103	2,951	2,951	2,942	1,983	2,187	1,432	809	1,008	328	528	533	460	646	646	644
1975–76	8,976	10,049	6,288	3,538	4,580	1,268	2,428	2,459	2,023	3,010	3,011	2,997	2,103	2,355	1,473	829	1,073	297	569	576	474	705	706	702
1976–77	9,175	10,391	6,443	3,726	4,913	1,393	2,433	2,463	2,027	3,015	3,015	3,023	2,275	2,577	1,598	924	1,218	346	603	611	503	748	748	750
1977–78	9,110	10,297	6,437	3,720	4,880	1,429	2,438	2,471	1,983	2,951	2,946	3,025	2,411	2,725	1,703	984	1,291	378	645	654	525	781	780	801
1978–79	8,937	10,080	6,316	3,706	4,826	1,420	2,377	2,403	1,987	2,854	2,851	2,910	2,587	2,917	1,828	1,073	1,397	411	688	696	575	826	825	842
1979–80	8,563	9,655	6,035	3,545	4,612	1,375	2,289	2,315	1,914	2,729	2,728	2,745	2,809	3,167	1,979	1,163	1,513	451	751	759	628	895	895	900
1980–81	8,473	9,561	6,093	3,521	4,586	1,437	2,285	2,311	1,925	2,668	2,664	2,731	3,101	3,499	2,230	1,289	1,679	526	836	846	705	976	975	1,000
1981–82	8,776	9,936	6,226	3,663	4,797	1,483	2,389	2,418	1,993	2,723	2,722	2,750	3,489	3,951	2,476	1,457	1,907	590	950	961	793	1,083	1,082	1,094
1982–83	9,348	10,624	6,543	3,920	5,159	1,627	2,565	2,599	2,106	2,863	2,866	2,810	3,877	4,406	2,713	1,626	2,139	675	1,064	1,078	873	1,187	1,189	1,165
1983–84	9,690	11,039	6,638	4,145	5,450	1,698	2,663	2,702	2,130	2,882	2,887	2,809	4,167	4,747	2,854	1,783	2,344	730	1,145	1,162	916	1,239	1,242	1,208
1984–85	10,210	11,548	7,115	4,443	5,745	1,838	2,835	2,869	2,367	2,932	2,933	2,910	4,563	5,160	3,179	1,985	2,567	821	1,267	1,282	1,058	1,310	1,311	1,301
1985–86[4]	10,624	11,972	7,323	4,744	6,056	1,932	2,911	2,947	2,408	2,970	2,969	2,983	4,885	5,504	3,367	2,181	2,784	888	1,338	1,355	1,107	1,365	1,365	1,372
1986–87	11,077	12,690	7,012	4,919	6,473	1,909	2,989	3,035	2,200	3,168	3,182	2,902	5,206	5,964	3,295	2,312	3,042	897	1,405	1,427	1,034	1,489	1,495	1,364
1987–88	11,226	12,815	6,667	5,022	6,540	1,653	3,039	3,098	2,078	3,164	3,178	2,935	5,494	6,272	3,263	2,458	3,201	809	1,488	1,516	1,017	1,549	1,555	1,437
1988–89	11,461	13,134	6,978	5,190	6,781	1,913	3,075	3,142	2,118	3,196	3,212	2,947	5,869	6,725	3,573	2,658	3,472	979	1,575	1,609	1,085	1,636	1,644	1,509
1989–90	11,570	13,442	6,906	5,292	7,083	1,823	3,053	3,122	2,059	3,225	3,237	3,024	6,207	7,212	3,705	2,839	3,800	978	1,638	1,675	1,105	1,730	1,737	1,622
1990–91	11,597	13,435	6,946	5,331	7,085	1,922	3,081	3,149	2,090	3,185	3,200	2,935	6,562	7,602	3,930	3,016	4,009	1,087	1,743	1,782	1,182	1,802	1,811	1,660
1991–92	12,119	14,107	7,007	5,626	7,510	2,036	3,209	3,290	2,073	3,284	3,307	2,898	7,077	8,238	4,092	3,286	4,385	1,189	1,874	1,921	1,210	1,918	1,931	1,692
1992–93	12,376	14,543	6,987	5,841	7,891	2,118	3,220	3,306	2,059	3,315	3,346	2,809	7,452	8,758	4,207	3,517	4,752	1,276	1,939	1,991	1,240	1,996	2,015	1,692
1993–94	12,838	15,048	7,201	6,195	8,286	2,264	3,330	3,416	2,156	3,313	3,345	2,781	7,931	9,296	4,449	3,827	5,119	1,399	2,057	2,111	1,332	2,047	2,067	1,718
1994–95	13,069	15,308	7,291	6,364	8,483	2,341	3,376	3,461	2,197	3,329	3,364	2,753	8,306	9,728	4,633	4,044	5,391	1,488	2,145	2,200	1,396	2,116	2,138	1,750
1995–96	13,481	15,824	7,238	6,645	8,863	2,332	3,468	3,551	2,256	3,368	3,410	2,650	8,800	10,330	4,725	4,338	5,786	1,522	2,264	2,318	1,473	2,199	2,226	1,730
1996–97	13,711	16,146	7,291	6,798	9,113	2,298	3,523	3,607	2,268	3,390	3,427	2,725	9,206	10,841	4,895	4,564	6,118	1,543	2,365	2,422	1,522	2,276	2,301	1,830
1997–98	14,029	16,502	7,597	6,958	9,293	2,480	3,576	3,669	2,338	3,495	3,540	2,780	9,588	11,277	5,192	4,755	6,351	1,695	2,444	2,507	1,598	2,389	2,419	1,900
1998–99	14,493	17,100	7,610	7,211	9,670	2,482	3,678	3,777	2,324	3,604	3,654	2,804	10,076	11,888	5,291	5,013	6,723	1,725	2,557	2,626	1,616	2,506	2,540	1,950
1999–2000	14,582	17,265	7,577	7,300	9,843	2,416	3,755	3,845	2,477	3,527	3,576	2,685	10,430	12,349	5,420	5,222	7,040	1,728	2,686	2,751	1,771	2,523	2,558	1,920
2000–01	14,625	17,468	7,389	7,269	9,964	2,295	3,814	3,910	2,407	3,543	3,593	2,686	10,820	12,922	5,466	5,377	7,372	1,698	2,821	2,893	1,781	2,621	2,658	1,987
2001–02	15,115	18,116	7,595	7,500	10,342	2,390	3,960	4,064	2,455	3,656	3,710	2,750	11,380	13,639	5,718	5,646	7,786	1,800	2,981	3,060	1,848	2,753	2,793	2,070
2002–03	15,613	18,766	8,126	7,801	10,798	2,474	4,132	4,241	2,699	3,681	3,727	2,953	12,014	14,439	6,252	6,002	8,309	1,903	3,179	3,263	2,077	2,832	2,867	2,272
2003–04	16,475	19,720	8,528	8,404	11,483	2,766	4,272	4,385	2,808	3,798	3,852	2,954	12,953	15,505	6,705	6,608	9,029	2,174	3,359	3,448	2,208	2,986	3,028	2,322
2004–05	17,030	20,384	8,760	8,793	11,984	2,886	4,410	4,521	2,906	3,827	3,879	2,968	13,793	16,510	7,095	7,122	9,706	2,338	3,572	3,662	2,354	3,100	3,142	2,404
2005–06	17,405	20,756	8,606	9,041	12,225	2,875	4,532	4,644	2,867	3,832	3,887	2,864	14,634	17,451	7,236	7,601	10,279	2,417	3,810	3,905	2,411	3,222	3,268	2,408
2006–07	17,951	21,415	8,656	9,382	12,673	2,894	4,659	4,772	2,930	3,910	3,970	2,832	15,483	18,471	7,466	8,092	10,931	2,496	4,019	4,116	2,527	3,372	3,424	2,443
2007–08	18,146	21,647	8,538	9,484	12,805	2,817	4,711	4,826	2,946	3,950	4,016	2,776	16,231	19,363	7,637	8,483	11,454	2,519	4,214	4,317	2,635	3,534	3,592	2,483
2008–09	18,845	22,502	9,083	9,805	13,281	2,887	4,902	5,024	3,065	4,139	4,197	3,131	17,092	20,409	8,238	8,893	12,045	2,618	4,446	4,557	2,780	3,754	3,807	2,839
2009–10	19,274	23,070	9,327	9,975	13,545	3,192	5,087	5,225	3,269	4,212	4,299	2,865	17,650	21,126	8,541	9,135	12,404	2,923	4,658	4,785	2,994	3,857	3,937	2,624
2010–11	19,778	23,630	9,493	10,250	13,858	3,275	5,222	5,374	3,291	4,306	4,398	2,927	18,475	22,074	8,868	9,575	12,945	3,060	4,878	5,020	3,074	4,023	4,108	2,734
2011–12	20,178	23,932	9,721	10,586	14,115	3,374	5,289	5,433	3,329	4,303	4,383	3,017	19,401	23,011	9,347	10,179	13,572	3,244	5,085	5,224	3,201	4,138	4,215	2,901
2012–13	20,699	24,420	9,794	10,927	14,424	3,398	5,418	5,558	3,417	4,354	4,438	2,978	20,233	23,871	9,573	10,681	14,099	3,322	5,296	5,433	3,340	4,256	4,338	2,911
2013–14	21,148	24,878	9,959	11,154	14,667	3,394	5,560	5,695	3,566	4,434	4,517	3,000	20,995	24,699	9,887	11,074	14,561	3,370	5,520	5,654	3,540	4,402	4,484	2,978
2014–15	21,728	25,409	10,153	11,487	14,957	3,389	5,719	5,851	3,655	4,523	4,602	3,109	21,728	25,409	10,153	11,487	14,957	3,389	5,719	5,851	3,655	4,523	4,602	3,109

See notes at end of table.

Table 330.10. Average undergraduate tuition and fees and room and board rates charged for full-time students in degree-granting postsecondary institutions, by level and control of institution: 1963–64 through 2014–15—Continued

Year and control of institution	Constant 2014–15 dollars[1]												Current dollars											
	Total tuition, fees, room, and board			Tuition and required fees[2]			Dormitory rooms			Board[3]			Total tuition, fees, room, and board			Tuition and required fees[2]			Dormitory rooms			Board[3]		
	All institutions	4-year	2-year	All institutions	4-year	2-year	All institutions	4-year	2-year	All institutions	4-year	2-year	All institutions	4-year	2-year	All institutions	4-year	2-year	All institutions	4-year	2-year	All institutions	4-year	2-year
1	2	3	4	5	6	7	8	9	10	11	12	13	14	15	16	17	18	19	20	21	22	23	24	25
Public institutions																								
1963–64	7,002	7,126	4,835	1,796	1,867	744	1,917	1,945	1,320	3,290	3,314	2,770	912	929	630	234	243	97	250	253	172	429	432	361
1964–65	7,060	7,208	4,835	1,841	1,938	750	1,979	2,007	1,349	3,240	3,263	2,736	932	951	638	243	256	99	261	265	178	428	431	361
1965–66	7,179	7,385	4,970	1,906	2,061	809	2,037	2,064	1,439	3,236	3,259	2,722	968	996	670	257	278	109	275	278	194	436	439	367
1966–67	7,295	7,542	5,105	1,977	2,174	870	2,094	2,120	1,531	3,224	3,248	2,703	1,015	1,049	710	275	302	121	291	295	213	448	452	376
1967–68	7,346	7,576	5,491	1,970	2,158	1,002	2,159	2,181	1,691	3,217	3,237	2,798	1,055	1,089	789	283	310	144	310	313	243	462	465	402
1968–69	7,376	7,584	5,859	1,958	2,130	1,128	2,217	2,236	1,845	3,201	3,218	2,887	1,112	1,143	883	295	321	170	334	337	278	482	485	435
1969–70	7,497	7,756	5,958	2,024	2,245	1,115	2,293	2,314	1,930	3,181	3,197	2,913	1,197	1,238	951	323	358	178	366	369	308	508	510	465
1970–71	7,603	7,900	5,946	2,091	2,346	1,114	2,367	2,390	2,014	3,144	3,164	2,818	1,276	1,326	998	351	394	187	397	401	338	528	531	473
1971–72	7,747	8,080	6,171	2,163	2,460	1,104	2,449	2,472	2,105	3,136	3,148	2,962	1,347	1,405	1,073	376	428	192	426	430	366	545	547	515
1972–73	8,030	8,589	6,618	2,250	2,779	1,288	2,606	2,633	2,200	3,174	3,177	3,129	1,452	1,553	1,197	407	503	233	471	476	398	574	575	566
1973–74	7,690	8,102	6,467	2,223	2,607	1,391	2,429	2,454	2,076	3,038	3,040	3,000	1,515	1,596	1,274	438	514	274	479	483	409	598	599	591
1974–75	7,134	7,525	6,119	1,974	2,342	1,266	2,309	2,336	1,938	2,852	2,847	2,916	1,561	1,647	1,339	432	512	277	505	511	424	624	623	638
1975–76	7,097	7,594	5,915	1,848	2,314	1,046	2,319	2,355	1,886	2,930	2,926	2,983	1,663	1,780	1,386	433	542	245	543	552	442	687	686	699
1976–77	7,214	7,803	6,011	1,930	2,486	1,143	2,349	2,387	1,874	2,935	2,930	2,993	1,789	1,935	1,491	479	617	283	582	592	465	728	727	742
1977–78	7,133	7,700	6,007	1,933	2,474	1,158	2,346	2,385	1,836	2,853	2,841	3,013	1,888	2,038	1,590	512	655	306	621	631	486	755	752	797
1978–79	6,888	7,410	5,842	1,875	2,376	1,131	2,263	2,294	1,820	2,750	2,740	2,891	1,994	2,145	1,691	543	688	327	655	664	527	796	793	837
1979–80	6,600	7,095	5,553	1,779	2,249	1,082	2,180	2,211	1,749	2,642	2,636	2,722	2,165	2,327	1,822	583	738	355	715	725	574	867	865	893
1980–81	6,484	6,968	5,538	1,735	2,196	1,069	2,182	2,216	1,754	2,568	2,556	2,716	2,373	2,550	2,027	635	804	391	799	811	642	940	936	994
1981–82	6,697	7,220	5,593	1,795	2,287	1,093	2,287	2,328	1,769	2,614	2,605	2,732	2,663	2,871	2,224	714	909	434	909	925	703	1,039	1,036	1,086
1982–83	7,101	7,707	5,762	1,925	2,487	1,141	2,436	2,485	1,821	2,740	2,735	2,801	2,945	3,196	2,390	798	1,031	473	1,010	1,030	755	1,136	1,134	1,162
1983–84	7,339	7,983	5,892	2,073	2,669	1,228	2,528	2,581	1,862	2,738	2,733	2,802	3,156	3,433	2,534	891	1,148	528	1,087	1,110	801	1,178	1,175	1,205
1984–85	7,626	8,238	6,281	2,172	2,748	1,307	2,676	2,723	2,060	2,778	2,768	2,914	3,408	3,682	2,807	971	1,228	584	1,196	1,217	921	1,241	1,237	1,302
1985–86[4]	7,768	8,392	6,484	2,272	2,866	1,394	2,701	2,747	2,088	2,795	2,779	3,002	3,571	3,859	2,981	1,045	1,318	641	1,242	1,263	960	1,285	1,278	1,380
1986–87	8,096	8,804	6,359	2,354	3,008	1,405	2,768	2,814	2,083	2,974	2,982	2,871	3,805	4,138	2,989	1,106	1,414	660	1,301	1,323	979	1,398	1,401	1,349
1987–88	8,274	8,996	6,263	2,489	3,141	1,442	2,815	2,880	1,926	2,970	2,975	2,895	4,050	4,403	3,066	1,218	1,537	706	1,378	1,410	943	1,454	1,456	1,417
1988–89	8,347	9,136	6,216	2,509	3,215	1,426	2,845	2,921	1,884	2,993	3,000	2,906	4,274	4,678	3,183	1,285	1,646	730	1,457	1,496	965	1,533	1,536	1,488
1989–90	8,395	9,274	6,150	2,528	3,317	1,409	2,821	2,903	1,793	3,047	3,054	2,947	4,504	4,975	3,299	1,356	1,780	756	1,513	1,557	962	1,635	1,638	1,581
1990–91	8,407	9,265	6,128	2,570	3,337	1,456	2,849	2,928	1,855	2,988	3,001	2,817	4,757	5,243	3,467	1,454	1,888	824	1,612	1,657	1,050	1,691	1,698	1,594
1991–92	8,799	9,750	6,204	2,788	3,625	1,603	2,964	3,056	1,840	3,048	3,068	2,761	5,138	5,693	3,623	1,628	2,117	936	1,731	1,785	1,074	1,780	1,792	1,612
1992–93	8,932	9,997	6,308	2,958	3,901	1,702	2,916	3,016	1,837	3,057	3,079	2,769	5,379	6,020	3,799	1,782	2,349	1,025	1,756	1,816	1,106	1,841	1,854	1,668
1993–94	9,217	10,303	6,468	3,144	4,106	1,820	3,031	3,130	1,926	3,043	3,067	2,722	5,694	6,365	3,996	1,942	2,537	1,125	1,873	1,934	1,190	1,880	1,895	1,681
1994–95	9,386	10,496	6,509	3,237	4,218	1,876	3,083	3,183	1,938	3,067	3,095	2,694	5,965	6,670	4,137	2,057	2,681	1,192	1,959	2,023	1,232	1,949	1,967	1,712
1995–96	9,583	10,744	6,460	3,338	4,362	1,899	3,152	3,249	1,986	3,094	3,133	2,575	6,256	7,014	4,217	2,179	2,848	1,239	2,057	2,121	1,297	2,020	2,045	1,681
1996–97	9,725	10,924	6,559	3,383	4,449	1,900	3,199	3,297	1,994	3,144	3,177	2,664	6,530	7,334	4,404	2,271	2,987	1,276	2,148	2,214	1,339	2,111	2,133	1,789
1997–98	9,970	11,228	6,599	3,454	4,550	1,923	3,256	3,367	2,050	3,260	3,312	2,626	6,813	7,673	4,509	2,360	3,110	1,314	2,225	2,301	1,401	2,228	2,263	1,795
1998–99	10,222	11,546	6,623	3,496	4,644	1,908	3,351	3,465	2,086	3,376	3,436	2,629	7,107	8,027	4,604	2,430	3,229	1,327	2,330	2,409	1,450	2,347	2,389	1,828
1999–2000	10,217	11,568	6,613	3,500	4,682	1,884	3,411	3,522	2,165	3,305	3,364	2,563	7,308	8,274	4,730	2,504	3,349	1,348	2,440	2,519	1,549	2,364	2,406	1,834
2000–01	10,254	11,697	6,541	3,463	4,732	1,801	3,472	3,588	2,163	3,319	3,378	2,576	7,586	8,653	4,839	2,562	3,501	1,333	2,569	2,654	1,600	2,455	2,499	1,906
2001–02	10,654	12,215	6,824	3,586	4,961	1,833	3,617	3,741	2,287	3,451	3,512	2,704	8,022	9,196	5,137	2,700	3,735	1,380	2,723	2,816	1,722	2,598	2,645	2,036
2002–03	11,049	12,720	7,280	3,772	5,259	1,927	3,808	3,936	2,539	3,469	3,525	2,813	8,502	9,787	5,601	2,903	4,046	1,483	2,930	3,029	1,954	2,669	2,712	2,164
2003–04	11,760	13,576	7,646	4,221	5,833	2,165	3,950	4,085	2,657	3,589	3,657	2,825	9,247	10,674	6,012	3,319	4,587	1,702	3,106	3,212	2,089	2,822	2,876	2,221
2004–05	12,179	14,107	7,871	4,481	6,206	2,283	4,080	4,221	2,684	3,619	3,680	2,905	9,864	11,426	6,375	3,629	5,027	1,849	3,304	3,418	2,174	2,931	2,981	2,353
2005–06	12,434	14,401	7,721	4,607	6,364	2,302	4,217	4,358	2,677	3,610	3,679	2,742	10,454	12,108	6,492	3,874	5,351	1,935	3,545	3,664	2,251	3,035	3,093	2,306
2006–07	12,810	14,837	7,901	4,756	6,569	2,339	4,356	4,497	2,791	3,699	3,771	2,771	11,049	12,797	6,815	4,102	5,666	2,018	3,757	3,878	2,407	3,191	3,253	2,390
2007–08	12,938	15,013	7,798	4,797	6,644	2,304	4,418	4,563	2,801	3,724	3,805	2,693	11,573	13,429	6,975	4,291	5,943	2,061	3,952	4,082	2,506	3,331	3,404	2,409
2008–09	13,513	15,725	8,344	4,975	6,959	2,355	4,619	4,775	2,937	3,919	3,990	3,053	12,256	14,262	7,568	4,512	6,312	2,136	4,190	4,331	2,664	3,554	3,619	2,769
2009–10	13,999	16,419	8,417	5,201	7,335	2,493	4,806	4,984	3,116	3,992	4,101	2,808	12,819	15,036	7,708	4,763	6,717	2,283	4,401	4,564	2,854	3,655	3,755	2,571
2010–11	14,522	17,042	8,648	5,433	7,635	2,613	4,974	5,172	3,164	4,116	4,235	2,872	13,566	15,919	8,079	5,075	7,132	2,441	4,646	4,832	2,955	3,845	3,956	2,683
2011–12	14,934	17,459	8,962	5,786	8,022	2,757	5,044	5,232	3,224	4,104	4,204	2,980	14,359	16,787	8,617	5,563	7,713	2,651	4,849	5,031	3,100	3,946	4,042	2,866
2012–13	15,367	17,877	9,133	6,034	8,256	2,856	5,178	5,362	3,322	4,154	4,259	2,955	15,021	17,475	8,927	5,899	8,070	2,792	5,062	5,241	3,247	4,061	4,163	2,888
2013–14	15,743	18,231	9,349	6,166	8,372	2,903	5,342	5,519	3,472	4,235	4,340	2,974	15,630	18,100	9,281	6,122	8,312	2,882	5,304	5,479	3,447	4,205	4,308	2,953
2014–15	16,188	18,632	9,586	6,371	8,543	2,955	5,504	5,677	3,559	4,313	4,412	3,072	16,188	18,632	9,586	6,371	8,543	2,955	5,504	5,677	3,559	4,313	4,412	3,072

See notes at end of table.

Table 330.10. Average undergraduate tuition and fees and room and board rates charged for full-time students in degree-granting postsecondary institutions, by level and control of institution: 1963–64 through 2014–15—Continued

Year and control of institution	Constant 2014–15 dollars[1]												Current dollars											
	Total tuition, fees, room, and board			Tuition and required fees[2]			Dormitory rooms			Board[3]			Total tuition, fees, room, and board			Tuition and required fees[2]			Dormitory rooms			Board[3]		
	All institutions	4-year	2-year	All institutions	4-year	2-year	All institutions	4-year	2-year	All institutions	4-year	2-year	All institutions	4-year	2-year	All institutions	4-year	2-year	All institutions	4-year	2-year	All institutions	4-year	2-year
1	2	3	4	5	6	7	8	9	10	11	12	13	14	15	16	17	18	19	20	21	22	23	24	25
Private nonprofit and for-profit institutions																								
1963–64	13,928	13,887	10,076	7,766	7,757	4,927	2,425	2,400	1,872	3,737	3,731	3,277	1,815	1,810	1,313	1,012	1,011	642	316	313	244	487	486	427
1964–65	14,451	14,520	11,026	8,245	8,312	5,320	2,508	2,504	2,190	3,698	3,704	3,516	1,907	1,916	1,455	1,088	1,097	702	331	330	289	488	489	464
1965–66	14,872	14,924	11,549	8,560	8,622	5,697	2,641	2,626	2,344	3,672	3,676	3,508	2,005	2,012	1,557	1,154	1,162	768	356	354	316	495	496	473
1966–67	15,272	15,306	12,072	8,865	8,925	6,076	2,768	2,743	2,495	3,638	3,637	3,502	2,124	2,129	1,679	1,233	1,241	845	385	382	347	506	506	487
1967–68	15,346	15,474	12,263	9,026	9,166	6,208	2,728	2,717	2,547	3,591	3,591	3,508	2,205	2,223	1,762	1,297	1,317	892	392	390	366	516	516	504
1968–69	15,402	15,635	12,449	9,177	9,404	6,344	2,681	2,684	2,595	3,543	3,547	3,510	2,321	2,356	1,876	1,383	1,417	956	404	405	391	534	534	529
1969–70	15,836	16,032	12,487	9,605	9,786	6,478	2,720	2,729	2,588	3,511	3,517	3,421	2,527	2,559	1,993	1,533	1,562	1,034	434	436	413	560	561	546
1970–71	16,259	16,411	12,529	10,033	10,166	6,607	2,755	2,765	2,586	3,471	3,480	3,336	2,729	2,754	2,103	1,684	1,706	1,109	462	464	434	583	584	560
1971–72	16,693	16,787	12,573	10,468	10,538	6,741	2,792	2,805	2,582	3,432	3,444	3,250	2,902	2,919	2,186	1,820	1,832	1,172	486	488	449	597	599	565
1972–73	16,786	17,091	12,567	10,494	10,772	6,751	2,891	2,912	2,527	3,401	3,408	3,290	3,036	3,091	2,273	1,898	1,948	1,221	523	527	457	615	616	595
1973–74	16,052	16,354	12,234	10,097	10,378	6,614	2,701	2,715	2,452	3,255	3,261	3,168	3,162	3,222	2,410	1,989	2,045	1,303	532	535	483	641	642	624
1974–75	15,483	15,556	11,840	9,674	9,735	6,247	2,641	2,645	2,577	3,167	3,176	3,016	3,388	3,404	2,591	2,117	2,130	1,367	578	579	564	693	695	660
1975–76	15,552	15,657	11,570	9,696	9,778	6,090	2,669	2,683	2,441	3,187	3,196	3,039	3,644	3,669	2,711	2,272	2,291	1,427	625	629	572	747	749	712
1976–77	15,751	16,037	11,980	9,947	10,219	6,420	2,617	2,627	2,449	3,188	3,192	3,111	3,906	3,977	2,971	2,467	2,534	1,592	649	651	607	790	791	772
1977–78	15,713	16,022	11,895	9,914	10,204	6,445	2,638	2,653	2,386	3,161	3,166	3,064	4,158	4,240	3,148	2,624	2,700	1,706	698	702	631	836	838	811
1978–79	15,597	15,926	11,711	9,908	10,220	6,326	2,618	2,630	2,419	3,072	3,077	2,966	4,514	4,609	3,389	2,867	2,958	1,831	758	761	700	889	890	858
1979–80	14,976	15,282	11,436	9,543	9,832	6,285	2,522	2,533	2,336	2,912	2,917	2,815	4,912	5,013	3,751	3,130	3,225	2,062	827	831	766	955	957	923
1980–81	14,945	15,283	11,756	9,557	9,882	6,593	2,507	2,515	2,381	2,881	2,886	2,783	5,470	5,594	4,303	3,498	3,617	2,413	918	921	871	1,054	1,056	1,019
1981–82	15,506	15,919	11,937	9,941	10,345	6,551	2,609	2,612	2,571	2,956	2,963	2,815	6,166	6,330	4,746	3,953	4,113	2,605	1,038	1,039	1,022	1,175	1,178	1,119
1982–83	16,687	17,183	12,935	10,704	11,186	7,253	2,848	2,849	2,839	3,135	3,148	2,843	6,920	7,126	5,364	4,439	4,639	3,008	1,181	1,181	1,177	1,300	1,306	1,179
1983–84	17,459	18,043	12,954	11,279	11,843	7,206	2,971	2,974	2,913	3,209	3,226	2,835	7,508	7,759	5,571	4,851	5,093	3,099	1,278	1,279	1,253	1,380	1,387	1,219
1984–85	18,354	18,910	13,881	11,892	12,432	7,798	3,191	3,191	3,187	3,271	3,287	2,896	8,202	8,451	6,203	5,315	5,556	3,485	1,426	1,426	1,424	1,462	1,469	1,294
1985–86[4]	19,324	20,071	14,164	12,591	13,312	7,987	3,379	3,386	3,263	3,354	3,373	2,915	8,885	9,228	6,512	5,789	6,121	3,672	1,553	1,557	1,500	1,542	1,551	1,340
1986–87	20,589	21,361	13,583	13,438	14,168	7,838	3,529	3,561	2,694	3,621	3,633	3,051	9,676	10,039	6,384	6,316	6,658	3,684	1,658	1,673	1,266	1,702	1,708	1,434
1987–88	21,476	21,778	14,461	14,278	14,539	8,501	3,571	3,596	2,820	3,627	3,643	3,140	10,512	10,659	7,078	6,988	7,116	4,161	1,748	1,760	1,380	1,775	1,783	1,537
1988–89	21,852	22,408	15,559	14,571	15,080	9,408	3,611	3,639	3,008	3,671	3,689	3,143	11,189	11,474	7,967	7,461	7,722	4,817	1,849	1,863	1,540	1,880	1,889	1,609
1989–90	22,402	22,897	16,161	15,186	15,650	9,686	3,585	3,607	3,100	3,631	3,640	3,375	12,018	12,284	8,670	8,147	8,396	5,196	1,923	1,935	1,663	1,948	1,953	1,811
1990–91	22,816	23,395	16,440	15,504	16,052	9,844	3,647	3,672	3,082	3,666	3,671	3,514	12,910	13,237	9,302	8,772	9,083	5,570	2,063	2,077	1,744	2,074	2,077	1,989
1991–92	23,790	24,416	16,495	16,130	16,713	9,854	3,804	3,837	3,063	3,856	3,865	3,579	13,892	14,258	9,632	9,419	9,759	5,754	2,221	2,241	1,788	2,252	2,257	2,090
1992–93	24,301	24,925	16,446	16,509	17,093	10,061	3,899	3,922	3,271	3,892	3,909	3,113	14,634	15,009	9,903	9,942	10,294	6,059	2,348	2,362	1,970	2,344	2,354	1,875
1993–94	25,082	25,743	16,844	17,112	17,728	10,311	4,030	4,057	3,345	3,940	3,958	3,189	15,496	15,904	10,406	10,572	10,952	6,370	2,490	2,506	2,067	2,434	2,445	1,970
1994–95	25,502	26,124	17,577	17,484	18,066	10,880	4,072	4,093	3,515	3,947	3,965	3,183	16,207	16,602	11,170	11,111	11,481	6,914	2,587	2,601	2,233	2,509	2,520	2,023
1995–96	26,361	26,979	17,714	18,175	18,755	10,868	4,194	4,214	3,632	3,992	4,009	3,214	17,208	17,612	11,563	11,864	12,243	7,094	2,738	2,751	2,371	2,606	2,617	2,098
1996–97	26,867	27,468	17,805	18,614	19,185	10,778	4,286	4,303	3,779	3,967	3,980	3,248	18,039	18,442	11,954	12,498	12,881	7,236	2,878	2,889	2,537	2,663	2,672	2,181
1997–98	27,095	27,905	18,908	18,731	19,527	10,923	4,322	4,337	3,910	4,042	4,041	4,075	18,516	19,070	12,921	12,801	13,344	7,464	2,954	2,964	2,672	2,762	2,761	2,785
1998–99	27,859	28,666	19,158	19,315	20,099	11,296	4,422	4,446	3,713	4,122	4,121	4,149	19,368	19,929	13,319	13,428	13,973	7,854	3,075	3,091	2,581	2,865	2,865	2,884
1999–2000	28,259	28,991	19,635	19,713	20,434	11,499	4,524	4,532	4,288	4,022	4,025	3,848	20,213	20,737	14,045	14,100	14,616	8,225	3,236	3,242	3,067	2,877	2,879	2,753
2000–01	28,891	29,543	20,151	20,276	20,912	12,256	4,572	4,585	4,064	4,043	4,046	3,831	21,373	21,856	14,907	15,000	15,470	9,067	3,382	3,392	3,006	2,991	2,993	2,834
2001–02	29,770	30,411	21,019	20,909	21,532	13,383	4,738	4,750	4,139	4,123	4,129	3,497	22,413	22,896	15,825	15,742	16,211	10,076	3,567	3,576	3,116	3,104	3,109	2,633
2002–03	30,334	30,915	23,073	21,292	21,868	13,842	4,876	4,892	4,201	4,166	4,155	5,030	23,340	23,787	17,753	16,383	16,826	10,651	3,752	3,764	3,232	3,206	3,197	3,870
2003–04	31,317	31,884	24,875	22,021	22,592	14,684	5,018	5,027	4,554	4,278	4,266	5,637	24,624	25,070	19,558	17,315	17,763	11,545	3,945	3,952	3,581	3,364	3,354	4,432
2004–05	31,875	32,422	25,061	22,414	22,970	14,967	5,158	5,152	5,526	4,303	4,301	4,568	25,817	26,260	20,297	18,154	18,604	12,122	4,178	4,173	4,475	3,485	3,483	3,700
2005–06	32,004	32,509	25,457	22,435	22,945	14,808	5,233	5,238	4,964	4,336	4,326	5,686	26,908	27,333	21,404	18,862	19,292	12,450	4,400	4,404	4,173	3,645	3,637	4,781
2006–07	32,972	33,528	23,517	23,243	23,788	14,733	5,341	5,348	4,808	4,389	4,392	3,976	28,439	28,919	20,284	20,048	20,517	12,708	4,606	4,613	4,147	3,785	3,788	3,429
2007–08	33,279	33,792	24,243	23,446	23,955	14,675	5,370	5,375	5,013	4,463	4,462	4,555	29,767	30,226	21,685	20,972	21,427	13,126	4,804	4,808	4,484	3,992	3,991	4,074
2008–09	33,964	34,481	25,057	23,783	24,297	14,954	5,541	5,548	5,002	4,640	4,637	5,101	30,804	31,273	22,726	21,570	22,036	13,562	5,025	5,032	4,537	4,209	4,206	4,627
2009–10	34,225	34,777	26,714	23,766	24,318	16,230	5,731	5,731	5,691	4,728	4,727	4,794	31,341	31,847	24,463	21,764	22,269	14,862	5,248	5,248	5,211	4,329	4,329	4,390
2010–11	34,123	34,810	24,730	23,596	24,276	14,653	5,784	5,791	5,287	4,743	4,742	4,791	31,875	32,517	23,101	22,042	22,677	13,687	5,403	5,410	4,939	4,430	4,430	4,475
2011–12	34,382	35,026	24,550	23,765	24,403	14,520	5,847	5,853	5,376	4,769	4,770	4,654	33,058	33,677	23,605	22,850	23,464	13,961	5,622	5,627	5,169	4,586	4,586	4,475
2012–13	35,277	35,879	23,892	24,495	25,087	14,475	5,965	5,971	5,348	4,817	4,820	4,069	34,483	35,071	23,355	23,943	24,523	14,149	5,831	5,837	5,228	4,709	4,712	3,977
2013–14	36,247	36,854	24,033	25,283	25,883	14,271	6,065	6,070	5,533	4,898	4,901	4,229	35,985	36,587	23,859	25,101	25,696	14,168	6,021	6,026	5,493	4,863	4,865	4,198
2014–15	37,424	37,990	24,317	26,184	26,740	14,254	6,221	6,229	5,504	5,019	5,021	4,560	37,424	37,990	24,317	26,184	26,740	14,254	6,221	6,229	5,504	5,019	5,021	4,560

See notes at end of table.

Table 330.10. Average undergraduate tuition and fees and room and board rates charged for full-time students in degree-granting postsecondary institutions, by level and control of institution: 1963–64 through 2014–15—Continued

Year and control of institution	Constant 2014–15 dollars[1]											
	Total tuition, fees, room, and board			Tuition and required fees[2]			Dormitory rooms			Board[3]		
	All institutions	4-year	2-year	All institutions	4-year	2-year	All institutions	4-year	2-year	All institutions	4-year	2-year
1	2	3	4	5	6	7	8	9	10	11	12	13
Nonprofit												
1999–2000	29,344	29,682	16,340	20,846	21,154	9,636	4,479	4,502	2,957	4,019	4,025	3,747
2000–01	29,649	29,968	15,838	21,082	21,373	9,419	4,524	4,549	2,714	4,043	4,046	3,704
2001–02	30,655	30,890	17,227	21,836	22,053	10,794	4,696	4,708	3,060	4,123	4,129	3,373
2002–03	31,551	31,771	18,769	22,561	22,767	11,576	4,838	4,849	3,439	4,152	4,155	3,755
2003–04	32,667	32,881	19,801	23,438	23,636	12,193	4,969	4,979	3,629	4,260	4,266	3,980
2004–05	33,439	33,651	19,639	24,074	24,264	12,235	5,078	5,086	3,617	4,287	4,301	3,787
2005–06	33,921	34,126	19,421	24,463	24,658	12,272	5,132	5,142	3,588	4,326	4,326	3,561
2006–07	34,973	35,153	20,499	25,323	25,500	12,679	5,255	5,261	4,146	4,395	4,392	3,674
2007–08	35,687	35,831	21,082	25,938	26,081	13,180	5,283	5,288	4,244	4,465	4,462	3,658
2008–09	37,134	37,272	22,350	27,015	27,164	13,896	5,465	5,471	4,288	4,654	4,637	4,167
2009–10	38,133	38,267	22,665	27,732	27,885	13,798	5,649	5,655	4,495	4,751	4,727	4,372
2010–11	38,863	38,984	21,508	28,305	28,456	13,562	5,779	5,786	4,260	4,779	4,742	3,686
2011–12	39,215	39,350	23,844	28,542	28,722	14,642	5,853	5,859	4,452	4,820	4,770	4,750
2012–13	40,072	40,204	22,657	29,224	29,405	14,102	5,973	5,978	4,506	4,876	4,820	4,049
2013–14	40,908	41,003	23,169	29,864	30,016	14,104	6,081	6,086	4,843	4,963	4,901	4,222
2014–15	41,970	42,065	23,576	30,643	30,790	14,287	6,249	6,254	5,038	5,078	5,021	4,252
For-profit												
1999–2000	22,542	23,134	21,996	12,173	12,108	12,255	5,937	6,475	5,469	4,433	4,551	4,273
2000–01	23,909	24,629	23,062	13,777	14,073	13,444	6,092	6,705	5,346	4,040	3,851	4,273
2001–02	24,673	26,262	22,522	14,424	14,702	14,118	6,149	7,168	4,754	4,101	4,392	3,650
2002–03	25,595	26,044	25,219	14,699	14,825	14,464	5,950	6,997	4,588	4,946	4,222	6,168
2003–04	27,753	27,831	28,452	15,616	15,768	15,292	6,476	7,318	5,077	5,661	4,744	8,083
2004–05	28,519	28,910	27,598	16,095	16,295	15,566	6,983	7,239	6,358	5,441	5,377	5,675
2005–06	28,019	27,624	30,532	15,744	15,836	15,413	7,238	7,713	5,681	5,037	4,075	9,438
2006–07	27,832	28,648	24,638	16,553	16,919	15,170	7,194	7,696	5,178	4,085	4,034	4,290
2007–08	27,665	28,042	26,296	16,108	16,372	14,939	7,206	7,581	5,479	4,351	4,090	5,878
2008–09	26,817	26,955	27,199	15,777	15,902	15,133	6,849	7,102	5,402	4,192	3,950	6,664
2009–10	26,338	26,083	28,362	15,320	15,036	16,524	6,816	6,915	6,206	4,201	4,131	5,633
2010–11	24,602	24,488	27,605	14,708	14,695	14,765	5,845	5,865	5,702	4,050	3,928	7,138
2011–12	23,892	23,841	24,426	14,301	14,261	14,502	5,780	5,773	5,852	3,810	3,807	4,072
2012–13	23,699	23,620	24,569	14,087	14,006	14,539	5,872	5,879	5,800	3,739	3,735	4,230
2013–14	23,303	23,213	24,521	13,888	13,812	14,296	5,846	5,837	5,934	3,570	3,564	4,291
2014–15	23,372	23,278	25,615	13,971	13,926	14,248	5,795	5,798	5,773	3,605	3,554	5,594

Year and control of institution	Current dollars											
	Total tuition, fees, room, and board			Tuition and required fees[2]			Dormitory rooms			Board[3]		
	All institutions	4-year	2-year	All institutions	4-year	2-year	All institutions	4-year	2-year	All institutions	4-year	2-year
1	14	15	16	17	18	19	20	21	22	23	24	25
Nonprofit												
1999–2000	20,989	21,231	11,688	14,911	15,131	6,893	3,204	3,221	2,115	2,875	2,879	2,680
2000–01	21,934	22,170	11,717	15,596	15,811	6,968	3,347	3,365	2,008	2,991	2,993	2,740
2001–02	23,080	23,257	12,970	16,440	16,604	8,126	3,536	3,544	2,304	3,104	3,109	2,540
2002–03	24,276	24,446	14,442	17,359	17,517	8,907	3,723	3,731	2,646	3,195	3,197	2,889
2003–04	25,685	25,853	15,569	18,429	18,584	9,587	3,907	3,915	2,853	3,349	3,354	3,129
2004–05	27,083	27,255	15,906	19,498	19,652	9,910	4,113	4,119	2,929	3,472	3,483	3,067
2005–06	28,520	28,692	16,329	20,568	20,732	10,318	4,315	4,323	3,017	3,637	3,637	2,994
2006–07	30,165	30,320	17,681	21,841	21,994	10,936	4,532	4,537	3,576	3,791	3,788	3,169
2007–08	31,921	32,050	18,857	23,201	23,328	11,789	4,725	4,730	3,796	3,994	3,991	3,272
2008–09	33,679	33,804	20,271	24,502	24,636	12,603	4,957	4,962	3,889	4,221	4,206	3,779
2009–10	34,920	35,042	20,756	25,396	25,535	12,636	5,173	5,178	4,116	4,351	4,329	4,004
2010–11	36,304	36,416	20,092	26,441	26,581	12,668	5,398	5,404	3,980	4,464	4,430	3,444
2011–12	37,705	37,835	22,926	27,443	27,616	14,078	5,628	5,633	4,281	4,634	4,586	4,567
2012–13	39,171	39,299	22,148	28,566	28,743	13,785	5,838	5,844	4,405	4,766	4,712	3,958
2013–14	40,612	40,706	23,001	29,648	29,799	14,002	6,037	6,042	4,808	4,927	4,865	4,191
2014–15	41,970	42,065	23,576	30,643	30,790	14,287	6,249	6,254	5,038	5,078	5,021	4,252
For-profit												
1999–2000	16,124	16,547	15,734	8,707	8,661	8,766	4,247	4,631	3,912	3,171	3,255	3,056
2000–01	17,688	18,220	17,061	10,192	10,411	9,945	4,507	4,960	3,955	2,988	2,849	3,161
2001–02	18,576	19,772	16,956	10,860	11,069	10,629	4,629	5,396	3,579	3,087	3,307	2,748
2002–03	19,694	20,039	19,404	11,310	11,407	11,129	4,578	5,384	3,530	3,806	3,249	4,746
2003–04	21,822	21,883	22,371	12,278	12,398	12,024	5,092	5,754	3,992	4,451	3,730	6,355
2004–05	23,098	23,415	22,353	13,036	13,197	12,607	5,655	5,863	5,149	4,407	4,355	4,596
2005–06	23,557	23,225	25,670	13,237	13,315	12,959	6,085	6,485	4,776	4,235	3,426	7,935
2006–07	24,005	24,710	21,250	14,277	14,593	13,085	6,205	6,638	4,466	3,523	3,479	3,700
2007–08	24,745	25,083	23,522	14,409	14,644	13,363	6,445	6,781	4,901	3,892	3,658	5,258
2008–09	24,322	24,447	24,669	14,309	14,423	13,725	6,212	6,441	4,899	3,802	3,583	6,044
2009–10	24,118	23,885	25,973	14,029	13,769	15,132	6,242	6,332	5,683	3,847	3,783	5,158
2010–11	22,982	22,875	25,787	13,739	13,727	13,792	5,460	5,479	5,327	3,783	3,669	6,668
2011–12	22,972	22,923	23,486	13,751	13,712	13,944	5,558	5,551	5,627	3,663	3,660	3,915
2012–13	23,165	23,088	24,016	13,770	13,691	14,212	5,740	5,747	5,669	3,655	3,651	4,135
2013–14	23,135	23,045	24,344	13,787	13,712	14,193	5,803	5,795	5,891	3,544	3,538	4,260
2014–15	23,372	23,278	25,615	13,971	13,926	14,248	5,795	5,798	5,773	3,605	3,554	5,594

[1]Constant dollars based on the Consumer Price Index, prepared by the Bureau of Labor Statistics, U.S. Department of Labor, adjusted to a school-year basis.
[2]For public institutions, in-state tuition and required fees are used.
[3]Data for 1986–87 and later years reflect a basis of 20 meals per week, while data for earlier years are for meals served 7 days a week (the number of meals per day was not specified). Because of this revision in data collection and tabulation procedures, data are not entirely comparable with figures for previous years. In particular, data on board rates are somewhat higher than in earlier years because they reflect the basis of 20 meals per week rather than meals served 7 days a week. Since many institutions serve fewer than 3 meals each day, the 1986–87 and later data reflect a more accurate accounting of total board costs.
[4]Room and board data are estimated.
NOTE: Data are for the entire academic year and are average charges for full-time students. Tuition and fees were weighted by the number of full-time-equivalent undergraduates, but were not adjusted to reflect student residency. Room and board are based on full-time students. Data through 1995–96 are for institutions of higher education, while later data are for degree-granting institutions.

Degree-granting institutions grant associate's or higher degrees and participate in Title IV federal financial aid programs. The degree-granting classification is very similar to the earlier higher education classification, but it includes more 2-year colleges and excludes a few higher education institutions that did not grant degrees. Because of their low response rate, data for private 2-year colleges must be interpreted with caution. Some data have been revised from previously published figures. Detail may not sum to totals because of rounding.
SOURCE: U.S. Department of Education, National Center for Education Statistics, *Projections of Education Statistics to 1986–87*; Higher Education General Information Survey (HEGIS), "Institutional Characteristics of Colleges and Universities" surveys, 1969–70 through 1985–86; "Fall Enrollment in Institutions of Higher Education" surveys, 1963 through 1985; Integrated Postsecondary Education Data System (IPEDS), "Fall Enrollment Survey" (IPEDS-EF:86–99) and "Institutional Characteristics Survey" (IPEDS-IC:86–99); IPEDS Spring 2001 through Spring 2015, Fall Enrollment component; and IPEDS Fall 2000 through Fall 2014, Institutional Characteristics component. (This table was prepared December 2015.)

Table 330.20. Average undergraduate tuition and fees and room and board rates charged for full-time students in degree-granting postsecondary institutions, by control and level of institution and state or jurisdiction: 2013–14 and 2014–15

[In current dollars]

	Public 4-year							Private 4-year						Public 2-year, tuition and required fees		
	In-state, 2013–14		In-state, 2014–15				Out-of-state tuition and required fees, 2014–15	2013–14		2014–15						
State or jurisdiction	Total	Tuition and required fees	Total	Tuition and required fees	Room	Board		Total	Tuition and required fees	Total	Tuition and required fees	Room	Board	In-state, 2013–14	In-state, 2014–15	Out-of-state, 2014–15
1	2	3	4	5	6	7	8	9	10	11	12	13	14	15	16	17
United States	**$18,100**	**$8,312**	**$18,632**	**$8,543**	**$5,677**	**$4,412**	**$23,523**	**$36,587**	**$25,696**	**$37,990**	**$26,740**	**$6,229**	**$5,021**	**$2,882**	**$2,955**	**$7,122**
Alabama	17,245	8,503	17,859	8,871	5,012	3,976	22,499	22,973	14,201	23,883	14,759	4,651	4,473	4,108	4,120	8,096
Alaska	15,693	6,141	16,814	6,356	6,298	4,160	19,185	30,261	20,943	25,961	19,136	3,881	2,944	4,652	3,340	3,340
Arizona	19,781	9,906	19,839	9,775	6,422	3,641	23,180	20,195	11,462	20,928	12,201	4,549	4,178	1,949	2,025	8,086
Arkansas	14,651	6,894	15,320	7,261	4,534	3,526	17,219	26,475	19,104	27,486	19,974	3,918	3,594	2,812	2,973	4,781
California	21,280	8,903	21,749	9,008	7,110	5,630	30,175	41,889	29,678	38,468	27,388	6,179	4,902	1,233	1,244	6,731
Colorado	18,977	8,228	19,710	8,722	5,554	5,434	27,059	31,470	20,359	32,916	21,603	6,254	5,060	3,160	3,347	8,769
Connecticut	21,638	10,128	22,435	10,535	6,416	5,483	31,004	48,715	35,407	49,824	36,304	7,548	5,971	3,824	3,869	11,561
Delaware	22,682	11,278	23,161	11,492	7,008	4,661	28,279	24,221	13,444	24,904	13,720	5,563	5,621	3,380	3,530	8,282
District of Columbia	7,255	7,255	†	5,251	†	†	11,233	49,892	36,723	51,857	37,949	8,869	5,038	†	†	†
Florida	14,369	4,423	14,677	4,456	5,905	4,316	17,771	31,286	20,971	32,418	21,578	6,059	4,781	2,513	2,383	8,862
Georgia	16,060	6,614	16,522	6,753	5,910	3,860	21,739	34,658	23,521	36,107	24,493	6,364	5,250	2,926	3,177	7,769
Hawaii	18,023	8,216	19,131	8,831	5,208	5,092	26,150	27,265	15,073	27,483	15,233	5,344	6,906	2,608	2,800	7,646
Idaho	13,817	6,315	13,644	6,834	3,189	3,621	19,633	14,162	6,736	13,009	6,456	2,449	4,104	2,963	3,023	7,336
Illinois	23,093	12,520	23,792	13,084	6,146	4,561	27,672	38,627	27,504	39,778	28,481	6,596	4,702	3,306	3,499	9,871
Indiana	18,249	8,443	18,393	8,633	5,157	4,603	28,035	37,961	28,035	39,129	29,050	5,211	4,868	3,605	4,055	7,932
Iowa	16,533	7,839	16,708	7,858	4,297	4,554	23,778	24,517	17,492	32,610	24,076	4,075	4,459	4,253	4,355	5,548
Kansas	14,633	7,387	15,584	7,726	3,903	3,956	20,155	27,962	20,122	24,655	16,635	3,865	4,155	2,890	3,015	4,197
Kentucky	17,280	8,715	17,530	9,189	4,404	3,936	21,409	29,526	21,271	31,594	23,039	4,359	4,196	3,487	3,650	12,478
Louisiana	15,238	6,585	16,045	7,296	5,227	3,523	21,409	41,042	30,257	42,620	31,175	6,344	5,100	3,178	3,502	6,659
Maine	19,121	9,368	18,914	9,166	4,687	5,062	25,273	44,057	32,534	44,991	33,205	5,945	5,841	3,545	3,663	6,455
Maryland	18,879	8,320	19,375	8,482	6,151	4,741	21,031	47,022	34,316	49,648	36,402	7,515	5,731	3,550	3,668	8,841
Massachusetts	21,814	10,702	22,214	10,900	6,888	4,426	26,213	51,481	38,009	53,172	39,298	7,953	5,920	4,216	4,333	9,742
Michigan	20,412	11,295	20,843	11,507	4,617	4,720	33,666	27,835	19,372	29,423	20,718	4,270	4,435	2,922	3,062	6,323
Minnesota	18,387	10,355	18,726	10,400	4,575	3,752	17,376	36,246	27,104	37,684	28,123	4,956	4,605	5,387	5,327	5,960
Mississippi	14,411	6,612	15,710	6,880	4,975	3,855	17,262	21,699	15,042	22,844	15,643	3,763	3,438	2,409	2,518	4,676
Missouri	16,785	7,998	17,143	8,065	5,324	3,754	19,410	28,414	19,523	30,402	21,465	4,931	4,007	2,850	2,890	5,514
Montana	14,081	6,323	14,448	6,378	3,713	4,357	21,481	28,731	20,868	29,635	21,630	3,826	4,180	3,202	3,215	8,923
Nebraska	15,635	7,081	16,199	7,223	4,784	4,193	18,180	27,882	19,832	28,930	20,501	4,355	4,074	2,670	2,743	3,743
Nevada	16,034	5,029	15,138	5,016	5,301	4,822	20,064	30,745	16,169	30,812	17,325	7,290	6,198	2,700	2,700	9,345
New Hampshire	25,245	14,469	25,821	14,538	6,435	4,848	26,131	43,487	31,029	44,995	31,868	8,115	5,013	7,230	6,979	15,202
New Jersey	24,243	12,266	24,825	12,541	7,542	4,741	26,556	44,235	32,010	45,434	32,986	7,161	5,288	3,929	3,982	6,926
New Mexico	14,103	5,973	14,778	6,003	4,557	4,217	15,285	27,468	17,657	28,464	18,779	5,441	4,244	1,443	1,475	4,636
New York	19,754	6,892	20,549	7,272	8,582	4,695	18,825	47,053	33,825	48,845	35,095	8,146	5,604	4,507	4,711	8,344
North Carolina	15,195	6,578	15,771	6,658	5,136	3,977	22,676	37,541	27,284	38,918	28,177	5,504	5,236	2,304	2,355	8,269
North Dakota	13,711	6,824	14,217	7,050	2,846	4,320	17,316	18,122	12,408	19,502	13,255	2,761	3,486	3,978	4,283	8,441
Ohio	19,997	9,443	20,537	9,631	5,932	4,974	22,756	36,853	26,917	37,976	27,761	5,273	4,942	3,544	3,610	7,512
Oklahoma	13,493	6,043	14,147	6,345	4,352	3,451	17,633	29,988	21,411	31,093	22,309	4,396	4,388	3,062	3,244	7,940
Oregon	19,152	8,616	19,654	8,891	6,296	4,467	27,341	42,383	31,599	44,215	33,108	5,753	5,354	3,935	4,023	7,552
Pennsylvania	22,575	12,607	23,519	13,171	6,120	4,228	24,741	46,237	34,313	47,894	35,622	6,725	5,547	4,352	4,589	11,732
Rhode Island	21,761	10,809	22,030	10,868	6,953	4,209	27,110	46,704	35,036	48,870	36,205	6,993	5,671	3,944	3,950	10,582
South Carolina	19,502	11,066	20,354	11,448	5,448	3,459	27,814	30,169	21,769	30,957	22,241	4,395	4,321	3,928	4,061	8,537
South Dakota	14,429	7,735	14,983	7,744	3,522	3,718	10,923	27,521	20,114	28,531	21,018	3,659	3,855	4,800	5,014	4,886
Tennessee	16,263	7,958	17,147	8,495	4,700	3,951	23,949	31,707	22,561	33,183	23,893	5,226	4,064	3,637	3,820	14,859
Texas	16,209	7,476	16,872	7,870	4,733	4,269	21,135	36,290	26,382	37,743	27,552	5,690	4,502	1,898	1,948	5,398
Utah	12,800	5,656	12,970	5,942	3,032	3,996	17,899	15,362	7,765	15,435	7,747	3,883	3,805	3,342	3,469	11,011
Vermont	24,071	13,952	24,986	14,495	6,623	3,869	35,241	47,908	36,449	49,211	37,391	6,518	5,301	5,668	5,886	11,622
Virginia	19,845	10,531	20,941	11,057	5,530	4,354	30,416	31,825	22,280	32,501	22,835	4,810	4,856	4,095	4,318	9,019
Washington	19,282	8,766	18,863	8,299	5,515	5,049	28,539	41,863	31,599	43,285	32,964	5,588	4,733	4,026	3,992	6,887
West Virginia	14,834	5,998	15,644	6,420	4,938	4,285	17,882	19,696	11,050	19,681	11,055	4,178	4,447	3,403	3,628	8,215
Wisconsin	15,720	8,406	15,938	8,441	4,422	3,075	20,020	35,653	26,637	37,416	28,094	5,204	4,118	4,233	4,323	7,220
Wyoming	12,949	3,756	13,457	3,968	4,160	5,329	12,152	16,620	16,620	†	16,968	†	†	2,579	2,694	6,658

†Not applicable.

NOTE: Data are for the entire academic year and are average charges for full-time students. In-state tuition and fees were weighted by the number of full-time-equivalent undergraduates, but were not adjusted to reflect the number of students who were state residents. Out-of-state tuition and fees were weighted by the number of first-time freshmen attending the institution in fall 2014 from out of state. Institutional room and board rates are weighted by the number of full-time students. Degree-granting institutions grant associate's or higher degrees and participate in Title IV federal financial aid programs. Some data have been revised from previously published figures. Detail may not sum to totals because of rounding.

SOURCE: U.S. Department of Education, National Center for Education Statistics, Integrated Postsecondary Education Data System (IPEDS), Fall 2013 and Fall 2014, Institutional Characteristics component; and Spring 2014 and Spring 2015, Fall Enrollment component. (This table was prepared December 2015.)

Table 330.30. Average undergraduate tuition, fees, room, and board rates for full-time students in degree-granting postsecondary institutions, by percentile of charges and control and level of institution: Selected years, 2000–01 through 2014–15

Control and level of institution, and year	Current dollars										Constant 2014–15 dollars				
	Tuition, fees, room, and board					Tuition and required fees					Tuition and required fees				
	10th percentile	25th percentile	Median (50th percentile)	75th percentile	90th percentile	10th percentile	25th percentile	Median (50th percentile)	75th percentile	90th percentile	10th percentile	25th percentile	Median (50th percentile)	75th percentile	90th percentile
1	2	3	4	5	6	7	8	9	10	11	12	13	14	15	16
Public institutions[1]															
2000–01	$5,741	$6,880	$8,279	$9,617	$11,384	$612	$1,480	$2,403	$3,444	$4,583	$827	$2,001	$3,248	$4,655	$6,195
2005–06	7,700	9,623	11,348	13,543	16,264	990	2,070	3,329	5,322	6,972	1,177	2,462	3,959	6,330	8,292
2010–11	9,889	12,856	15,234	17,860	21,593	1,230	2,626	4,632	7,115	9,420	1,317	2,811	4,959	7,617	10,084
2012–13	11,283	14,426	17,013	19,481	23,298	1,536	3,048	5,576	8,132	10,514	1,571	3,118	5,704	8,319	10,756
2013–14	11,817	14,954	17,665	20,167	23,943	1,560	3,217	5,963	8,506	10,918	1,571	3,240	6,006	8,568	10,998
2014–15	12,596	15,601	18,012	20,667	24,525	1,630	3,348	6,313	8,878	11,471	1,630	3,348	6,313	8,878	11,471
Public 4-year[1]															
2000–01	6,503	7,347	8,468	9,816	11,611	2,118	2,520	3,314	4,094	5,085	2,863	3,406	4,480	5,534	6,874
2005–06	8,863	10,219	11,596	13,830	16,443	3,094	3,822	5,084	6,458	8,097	3,680	4,546	6,047	7,681	9,630
2010–11	12,048	13,604	15,823	18,419	22,191	4,336	5,091	6,779	8,689	11,029	4,642	5,450	7,257	9,302	11,807
2012–13	13,324	15,102	17,561	19,713	23,686	4,982	6,180	7,554	9,769	12,692	5,097	6,322	7,728	9,994	12,984
2013–14	13,782	15,653	18,239	20,411	24,228	5,086	6,343	7,816	10,037	12,864	5,123	6,389	7,873	10,110	12,958
2014–15	14,289	16,181	18,576	21,080	24,922	5,250	6,497	7,994	10,382	13,160	5,250	6,497	7,994	10,382	13,160
Public 2-year[1]															
2000–01	3,321	3,804	4,627	5,750	6,871	310	724	1,387	1,799	2,460	419	979	1,875	2,432	3,325
2005–06	4,380	4,822	6,234	7,567	8,993	691	1,109	1,920	2,589	3,100	822	1,319	2,284	3,079	3,687
2010–11	5,347	6,327	7,339	9,370	11,312	700	1,412	2,537	3,315	3,840	749	1,512	2,716	3,549	4,111
2012–13	5,812	6,536	8,291	10,282	12,464	1,183	1,627	2,804	3,717	4,352	1,210	1,664	2,869	3,803	4,452
2013–14	6,144	6,952	8,763	10,729	13,369	1,178	1,560	2,954	3,826	4,550	1,187	1,571	2,976	3,854	4,583
2014–15	6,287	7,202	8,815	11,438	14,462	1,183	1,551	3,000	3,963	4,754	1,183	1,551	3,000	3,963	4,754
Private nonprofit institutions															
2000–01	13,514	17,552	22,493	27,430	32,659	7,800	11,730	15,540	19,600	24,532	10,543	15,856	21,006	26,494	33,161
2005–06	18,243	23,258	29,497	35,918	41,707	9,981	15,375	21,070	26,265	31,690	11,871	18,287	25,060	31,239	37,691
2010–11	23,143	29,884	38,063	47,061	52,235	11,930	19,625	26,920	34,536	40,082	12,771	21,009	28,818	36,971	42,908
2012–13	24,955	32,582	41,412	51,744	56,419	11,940	21,140	29,312	37,830	43,204	12,215	21,627	29,987	38,701	44,198
2013–14	26,280	34,020	43,047	53,659	58,612	12,550	22,080	30,390	39,120	44,848	12,641	22,241	30,611	39,405	45,175
2014–15	27,640	35,274	44,582	55,440	60,770	12,525	22,760	31,370	40,660	46,467	12,525	22,760	31,370	40,660	46,467
Nonprofit 4-year															
2000–01	13,972	17,714	22,554	27,476	32,659	8,450	11,920	15,746	19,730	24,532	11,422	16,113	21,284	26,670	33,161
2005–06	18,350	23,322	29,598	36,028	41,774	10,300	15,560	21,190	26,500	31,690	12,251	18,507	25,203	31,519	37,691
2010–11	23,548	30,042	38,129	47,061	52,235	12,220	19,854	27,100	34,580	40,082	13,082	21,254	29,011	37,018	42,908
2012–13	25,183	32,668	41,476	51,750	56,419	12,464	21,496	29,460	38,000	43,204	12,751	21,991	30,138	38,875	44,198
2013–14	26,663	34,095	43,233	53,667	58,612	12,700	22,252	30,579	39,330	44,848	12,792	22,414	30,802	39,616	45,175
2014–15	27,778	35,425	44,775	55,440	60,770	12,920	22,950	31,480	40,670	46,467	12,920	22,950	31,480	40,670	46,467
Nonprofit 2-year															
2000–01	6,850	6,850	9,995	14,209	20,240	2,430	4,825	7,250	8,266	11,100	3,285	6,522	9,800	11,173	15,004
2005–06	8,030	15,680	16,830	20,829	28,643	4,218	8,640	9,940	12,270	14,472	5,017	10,276	11,822	14,594	17,213
2010–11	10,393	19,718	21,186	27,386	30,758	3,840	9,730	12,000	14,640	18,965	4,111	10,416	12,846	15,672	20,302
2012–13	20,135	22,399	24,480	28,882	30,114	7,124	11,640	14,944	16,162	20,050	7,288	11,908	15,288	16,534	20,511
2013–14	21,146	23,815	25,400	29,677	31,200	3,060	10,500	15,533	16,345	20,660	3,082	10,576	15,646	16,464	20,810
2014–15	22,044	23,200	25,705	30,400	32,120	4,200	11,330	15,579	16,678	21,260	4,200	11,330	15,579	16,678	21,260
Private for-profit institutions															
2000–01	13,396	15,778	19,403	21,400	21,845	6,900	8,202	9,644	12,090	14,600	9,327	11,087	13,036	16,342	19,735
2005–06	17,278	19,098	25,589	26,499	31,903	7,632	10,011	12,450	14,335	17,740	9,077	11,907	14,808	17,050	21,100
2010–11	16,097	16,097	17,484	26,175	31,639	10,194	10,194	13,520	15,750	18,048	10,913	10,913	14,473	16,861	19,321
2012–13	16,115	16,115	16,115	22,612	32,239	9,936	11,202	12,685	16,156	18,650	10,165	11,460	12,977	16,528	19,079
2013–14	16,466	16,466	16,745	28,348	34,316	10,312	10,878	13,049	16,156	18,313	10,387	10,957	13,144	16,274	18,446
2014–15	16,942	16,942	23,107	25,619	34,114	10,480	10,702	13,500	17,132	18,748	10,480	10,702	13,500	17,132	18,748
For-profit 4-year															
2000–01	13,396	15,818	20,417	21,400	21,400	7,206	8,305	9,675	12,800	15,090	9,741	11,226	13,078	17,302	20,398
2005–06	17,383	19,098	25,589	26,499	31,903	7,632	10,418	12,900	14,450	17,735	9,077	12,391	15,343	17,187	21,094
2010–11	16,097	16,097	17,484	26,175	31,639	10,194	10,194	13,560	16,500	18,048	10,913	10,913	14,516	17,664	19,321
2012–13	16,115	16,115	16,115	22,612	32,239	9,936	11,202	12,110	16,156	18,650	10,165	11,460	12,389	16,528	19,079
2013–14	16,466	16,466	16,745	28,348	34,316	10,312	10,878	12,435	16,360	18,748	10,387	10,957	12,526	16,479	18,885
2014–15	16,942	16,942	23,107	25,619	34,114	10,480	10,702	12,975	17,173	18,885	10,480	10,702	12,975	17,173	18,885
For-profit 2-year															
2000–01	15,778	15,778	19,403	21,845	21,845	6,025	7,365	9,644	12,000	14,255	8,144	9,955	13,036	16,221	19,269
2005–06	13,010	18,281	43,425	43,425	43,425	7,870	9,285	11,550	14,196	19,425	9,360	11,043	13,737	16,884	23,104
2010–11	23,687	23,687	25,161	25,161	25,161	10,075	12,049	13,418	15,263	17,918	10,785	12,899	14,364	16,339	19,181
2012–13	23,600	23,600	23,600	25,866	25,866	10,425	12,400	13,240	15,552	18,048	10,665	12,685	13,545	15,910	18,463
2013–14	24,019	24,019	26,295	26,295	26,295	10,360	12,307	13,620	15,356	18,000	10,435	12,397	13,719	15,468	18,131
2014–15	25,028	25,028	25,028	25,028	25,028	10,437	12,450	13,620	15,119	17,339	10,437	12,450	13,620	15,119	17,339

[1]Average undergraduate tuition and fees are based on in-state students only.

NOTE: Data are for the entire academic year and are average charges for full-time students. Student charges were weighted by the number of full-time-equivalent undergraduates, but were not adjusted to reflect student residency. Degree-granting institutions grant associate's or higher degrees and participate in Title IV federal financial aid programs. Some data have been revised from previously published figures.

SOURCE: U.S. Department of Education, National Center for Education Statistics, Integrated Postsecondary Education Data System (IPEDS), Fall 2000 through Fall 2014, Institutional Characteristics component; and Spring 2001 through Spring 2015, Fall Enrollment component. (This table was prepared December 2015.)

Table 330.40. Average total cost of attendance for first-time, full-time undergraduate students in degree-granting postsecondary institutions, by control and level of institution, living arrangement, and component of student costs: Selected years, 2009–10 through 2014–15

Level of institution, living arrangement, and component of student costs	2009–10				2011–12				2012–13				2013–14				2014–15			
	All institutions	Public, in-state	Private		All institutions	Public, in-state	Private		All institutions	Public, in-state	Private		All institutions	Public, in-state	Private		All institutions	Public, in-state	Private	
			Nonprofit	For-profit			Nonprofit	For-profit			Nonprofit	For-profit			Nonprofit	For-profit			Nonprofit	For-profit
1	2	3	4	5	6	7	8	9	10	11	12	13	14	15	16	17	18	19	20	21
	Current dollars																			
4-year institutions																				
Average total cost, by living arrangement																				
On campus	$26,283	$19,219	$38,254	$28,916	$28,457	$20,997	$41,375	$29,887	$29,531	$21,677	$42,887	$31,099	$30,177	$22,148	$44,353	$29,816	$31,058	$22,752	$45,763	$30,406
Off campus, living with family	19,091	11,950	30,500	19,318	20,705	13,344	32,982	21,526	21,346	13,595	34,107	23,194	21,522	13,562	35,210	21,975	22,145	13,920	36,319	22,407
Off campus, not living with family	28,829	20,724	38,824	28,836	29,322	22,261	41,413	28,840	30,372	22,655	42,546	31,542	30,116	22,827	43,727	28,393	31,007	23,373	45,249	29,118
Component of student costs																				
Tuition and required fees	13,734	6,773	25,676	12,873	15,077	7,703	27,931	14,609	15,763	7,997	29,029	16,299	16,104	8,199	30,108	15,241	16,628	8,445	31,177	15,463
Books and supplies	1,192	1,165	1,182	1,389	1,237	1,230	1,230	1,373	1,246	1,241	1,239	1,361	1,248	1,250	1,251	1,190	1,266	1,275	1,248	1,283
Room, board, and other expenses																				
On campus																				
Room and board	8,583	8,155	9,114	10,082	9,255	8,839	9,824	9,660	9,598	9,187	10,179	9,228	9,910	9,495	10,506	9,499	10,198	9,760	10,827	9,859
Other	2,774	3,126	2,282	4,573	2,889	3,225	2,389	4,245	2,925	3,253	2,441	4,212	2,916	3,203	2,488	3,886	2,965	3,272	2,511	3,802
Off campus, living with family																				
Other	4,165	4,012	3,642	5,057	4,391	4,411	3,821	5,544	4,337	4,358	3,839	5,534	4,171	4,113	3,850	5,545	4,250	4,200	3,893	5,661
Off campus, not living with family																				
Room and board	8,862	8,722	8,164	8,997	8,572	9,206	8,327	7,898	8,971	9,282	8,410	8,697	8,633	9,435	8,481	7,393	8,873	9,663	8,516	7,760
Other	5,041	4,065	3,801	5,578	4,437	4,122	3,925	4,960	4,393	4,136	3,868	5,184	4,132	3,943	3,886	4,569	4,239	3,990	4,308	4,612
2-year institutions																				
Average total cost, by living arrangement																				
On campus	$14,351	$11,886	$23,352	$27,721	$14,049	$12,796	$26,246	$27,873	$14,436	$13,265	$27,692	$28,035	$14,646	$13,503	$29,373	$28,382	$14,984	$13,847	$29,695	$28,710
Off campus, living with family	9,731	7,581	16,639	18,982	9,115	8,129	19,066	19,810	9,171	8,314	19,990	20,037	9,268	8,469	21,291	19,817	9,408	8,603	21,270	20,072
Off campus, not living with family	17,063	14,758	24,969	26,556	16,562	15,567	27,528	27,015	16,807	15,879	29,752	27,857	16,989	16,157	29,448	27,617	17,241	16,371	29,749	28,297
Component of student costs																				
Tuition and required fees	4,705	2,619	12,326	13,511	3,912	2,940	14,007	14,298	3,925	3,081	14,338	14,510	3,949	3,161	15,354	14,304	4,061	3,270	15,634	14,428
Books and supplies	1,259	1,241	1,205	1,371	1,315	1,311	1,332	1,368	1,341	1,347	1,315	1,254	1,371	1,378	1,264	1,257	1,417	1,422	1,237	1,351
Room, board, and other expenses																				
On campus																				
Room and board	5,481	5,171	7,096	8,729	5,913	5,630	8,011	9,417	6,072	5,765	8,529	9,362	6,317	6,005	9,095	9,767	6,461	6,133	9,459	9,898
Other	2,906	2,856	2,726	4,111	2,910	2,915	2,896	2,789	3,099	3,072	3,510	2,909	3,010	2,959	3,661	3,054	3,046	3,022	3,366	3,032
Off campus, living with family																				
Other	3,767	3,721	3,108	4,101	3,888	3,878	3,726	4,143	3,905	3,886	4,338	4,273	3,948	3,931	4,673	4,256	3,930	3,911	4,399	4,293
Off campus, not living with family																				
Room and board	7,334	7,240	8,095	7,588	7,514	7,524	7,680	7,390	7,656	7,630	9,027	7,723	7,802	7,810	8,258	7,657	7,931	7,918	8,369	8,015
Other	3,765	3,659	3,343	4,087	3,822	3,792	4,508	3,959	3,886	3,821	5,073	4,370	3,867	3,809	4,573	4,399	3,832	3,761	4,509	4,504
	Constant 2014–15 dollars[1]																			
4-year institutions																				
Average total cost, by living arrangement																				
On campus	$28,701	$20,988	$41,774	$31,577	$29,597	$21,838	$43,031	$31,084	$30,211	$22,176	$43,874	$31,815	$30,397	$22,309	$44,676	$30,033	$31,058	$22,752	$45,763	$30,406
Off campus, living with family	20,847	13,049	33,306	21,096	21,534	13,878	34,303	22,388	21,837	13,908	34,892	23,728	21,679	13,661	35,466	22,135	22,145	13,920	36,319	22,407
Off campus, not living with family	31,482	22,631	42,396	31,490	30,497	23,152	43,071	29,995	31,071	23,177	43,525	32,268	30,336	22,994	44,046	28,599	31,007	23,373	45,249	29,118
Tuition and required fees	14,998	7,396	28,038	14,057	15,680	8,012	29,050	15,194	16,126	8,181	29,697	16,674	16,221	8,258	30,327	15,352	16,628	8,445	31,177	15,463
2-year institutions																				
Average total cost, by living arrangement																				
On campus	15,671	12,980	25,501	30,272	14,612	13,309	27,297	28,989	14,768	13,570	28,329	28,680	14,752	13,601	29,587	28,589	14,984	13,847	29,695	28,710
Off campus, living with family	10,626	8,278	18,170	20,729	9,480	8,454	19,829	20,603	9,382	8,505	20,450	20,498	9,336	8,531	21,446	19,961	9,408	8,603	21,270	20,072
Off campus, not living with family	18,633	16,116	27,266	28,999	17,225	16,190	28,630	28,097	17,194	16,245	30,437	28,498	17,112	16,275	29,663	27,818	17,241	16,371	29,749	28,297
Tuition and required fees	5,138	2,860	13,460	14,754	4,068	3,058	14,568	14,871	4,015	3,152	14,668	14,844	3,978	3,184	15,466	14,408	4,061	3,270	15,634	14,428

[1]Constant dollars based on the Consumer Price Index, prepared by the Bureau of Labor Statistics, U.S. Department of Labor, adjusted to a school-year basis.

NOTE: Excludes students who previously attended another postsecondary institution or who began their studies on a part-time basis. Tuition and fees at public institutions are the lower of either in-district or in-state tuition and fees. Data illustrating the average total cost of attendance for all students are weighted by the number of students at the institution receiving Title IV aid. Detail may not sum to totals because of rounding. Some data have been revised from previously published figures.

SOURCE: U.S. Department of Education, National Center for Education Statistics, Integrated Postsecondary Education Data System (IPEDS), Spring 2010 through Spring 2011 and Winter 2011–12 through Winter 2014–15, Student Financial Aid component; and Fall 2009 through Fall 2014, Institutional Characteristics component. (This table was prepared December 2015.)

Table 330.50. Average graduate tuition and required fees in degree-granting postsecondary institutions, by control of institution and percentile of charges: 1989–90 through 2014–15

Year	Total	Public institutions[1]	Private institutions: Total	Private institutions: Nonprofit	Private institutions: For-profit	Public institutions,[1] by percentile: 25th percentile	Public institutions,[1] by percentile: Median (50th percentile)	Public institutions,[1] by percentile: 75th percentile	Nonprofit institutions, by percentile: 25th percentile	Nonprofit institutions, by percentile: Median (50th percentile)	Nonprofit institutions, by percentile: 75th percentile
1	2	3	4	5	6	7	8	9	10	11	12
					Current dollars						
1989–90	$4,135	$1,999	$7,881	—	—	—	—	—	—	—	—
1990–91	4,488	2,206	8,507	—	—	—	—	—	—	—	—
1991–92	5,116	2,524	9,592	—	—	—	—	—	—	—	—
1992–93	5,475	2,791	10,008	—	—	—	—	—	—	—	—
1993–94	5,973	3,050	10,790	—	—	—	—	—	—	—	—
1994–95	6,247	3,250	11,338	—	—	—	—	—	—	—	—
1995–96	6,741	3,449	12,083	—	—	—	—	—	—	—	—
1996–97	7,111	3,607	12,537	—	—	—	—	—	—	—	—
1997–98	7,246	3,744	12,774	—	—	—	—	—	—	—	—
1998–99	7,685	3,897	13,299	—	—	—	—	—	—	—	—
1999–2000	8,069	4,042	13,821	$14,123	$9,611	$2,640	$3,637	$5,163	$7,998	$12,870	$20,487
2000–01	8,429	4,243	14,420	14,457	13,229	2,931	3,822	5,347	8,276	13,200	21,369
2001–02	8,857	4,496	15,165	15,232	13,414	3,226	4,119	5,596	8,583	14,157	22,054
2002–03	9,226	4,842	14,983	15,676	9,644	3,395	4,452	5,927	8,690	14,140	22,700
2003–04	10,312	5,544	16,209	16,807	12,542	3,795	5,103	7,063	9,072	15,030	25,600
2004–05	11,004	6,080	16,751	17,551	13,133	4,236	5,663	7,616	9,300	16,060	26,140
2005–06	11,621	6,493	17,244	18,171	13,432	4,608	6,209	7,977	9,745	16,222	26,958
2006–07	12,312	6,894	18,108	19,033	14,421	4,909	6,594	8,341	10,346	17,057	29,118
2007–08	13,002	7,415	18,878	19,896	14,713	5,176	6,990	9,288	10,705	17,647	30,247
2008–09	13,647	7,999	19,230	20,485	14,418	5,612	7,376	9,912	11,290	18,270	30,514
2009–10	14,542	8,763	20,078	21,317	14,512	6,074	7,983	10,658	12,290	19,460	31,730
2010–11	15,017	9,238	20,397	21,993	13,811	6,550	8,788	10,937	12,510	19,586	33,215
2011–12	15,845	9,978	21,230	22,899	14,285	7,506	9,440	11,954	12,936	20,625	34,680
2012–13	16,407	10,408	21,907	23,642	14,418	7,706	9,900	12,590	12,960	21,352	36,820
2013–14	16,946	10,725	22,607	24,467	14,210	7,791	10,242	12,779	13,567	22,018	36,660
2014–15	17,385	10,979	23,266	25,171	14,265	7,914	10,428	12,829	13,872	22,170	38,948
					Constant 2014–15 dollars						
1989–90	$7,707	$3,726	$14,690	—	—	—	—	—	—	—	—
1990–91	7,932	3,899	15,035	—	—	—	—	—	—	—	—
1991–92	8,761	4,322	16,426	—	—	—	—	—	—	—	—
1992–93	9,092	4,635	16,619	—	—	—	—	—	—	—	—
1993–94	9,668	4,937	17,465	—	—	—	—	—	—	—	—
1994–95	9,830	5,115	17,842	—	—	—	—	—	—	—	—
1995–96	10,326	5,283	18,509	—	—	—	—	—	—	—	—
1996–97	10,591	5,372	18,673	—	—	—	—	—	—	—	—
1997–98	10,603	5,479	18,692	—	—	—	—	—	—	—	—
1998–99	11,054	5,605	19,129	—	—	—	—	—	—	—	—
1999–2000	11,281	5,651	19,322	$19,745	$13,437	$3,691	$5,085	$7,218	$11,182	$17,993	$28,642
2000–01	11,394	5,736	19,492	19,541	17,882	3,962	5,166	7,228	11,187	17,843	28,885
2001–02	11,764	5,971	20,143	20,232	17,816	4,285	5,471	7,433	11,400	18,804	29,292
2002–03	11,990	6,292	19,472	20,373	12,534	4,412	5,786	7,703	11,294	18,377	29,502
2003–04	13,115	7,051	20,615	21,376	15,952	4,827	6,490	8,983	11,538	19,116	32,559
2004–05	13,587	7,507	20,683	21,670	16,215	5,230	6,992	9,403	11,482	19,829	32,274
2005–06	13,822	7,723	20,510	21,612	15,976	5,481	7,385	9,488	11,591	19,294	32,063
2006–07	14,274	7,993	20,994	22,067	16,720	5,691	7,645	9,671	11,995	19,776	33,759
2007–08	14,536	8,290	21,105	22,244	16,449	5,787	7,815	10,384	11,968	19,729	33,815
2008–09	15,047	8,819	21,202	22,587	15,897	6,188	8,133	10,929	12,448	20,144	33,644
2009–10	15,880	9,570	21,926	23,279	15,848	6,633	8,718	11,639	13,421	21,251	34,650
2010–11	16,076	9,889	21,835	23,544	14,785	7,012	9,408	11,708	13,392	20,967	35,557
2011–12	16,479	10,378	22,080	23,816	14,857	7,807	9,818	12,433	13,454	21,451	36,069
2012–13	16,785	10,648	22,411	24,186	14,750	7,883	10,128	12,880	13,258	21,843	37,667
2013–14	17,069	10,803	22,771	24,645	14,313	7,848	10,317	12,872	13,666	22,178	36,927
2014–15	17,385	10,979	23,266	25,171	14,265	7,914	10,428	12,829	13,872	22,170	38,948

—Not available.

[1]Data are based on in-state tuition only.

NOTE: Average graduate student tuition weighted by fall full-time-equivalent graduate enrollment. Excludes doctoral students in professional practice programs. Data through 1995–96 are for institutions of higher education, while later data are for degree-granting institutions. Degree-granting institutions grant associate's or higher degrees and participate in Title IV federal financial aid programs. The degree-granting classification is very similar to the earlier higher education classification, but it includes more 2-year colleges and excludes a few higher education institutions that did not grant degrees. Some data have been revised from previously published figures.

SOURCE: U.S. Department of Education, National Center for Education Statistics, Integrated Postsecondary Education Data System (IPEDS), "Fall Enrollment Survey" (IPEDS-EF:89–99); "Completions Survey" (IPEDS-C:90–99); "Institutional Characteristics Survey" (IPEDS-IC:89–99); IPEDS Fall 2000 through Fall 2014, Institutional Characteristics component; and IPEDS Spring 2001 through Spring 2015, Fall Enrollment component. (This table was prepared December 2015.)

Weighted average tuition fees for full-time Canadian undergraduate students, by field of study, annual (dollars) (1,2,3,4,5,6)

Field of study grouping	2012/2013	2013/2014	2014/2015	2015/2016	2016/2017
Education	4,273	4,394	4,482	4,514	4,580
Visual and performing arts, and communications technologies	5,002	5,138	5,211	5,464	5,640
Humanities	4,941	5,023	5,230	5,346	5,482
Social and behavioural sciences	4,966	5,116	5,294	5,424	5,566
Law, legal professions and studies	9,549	10,039	10,563	10,928	11,385
Business, management and public administration	6,097	6,274	6,366	6,542	6,776
Physical and life sciences and technologies	5,335	5,481	5,701	5,884	6,048
Mathematics, computer and information sciences	6,051	6,245	6,565	6,753	6,978
Engineering	6,560	6,871	7,153	7,511	7,825
Architecture and related technologies	5,340	5,495	5,985	6,346	6,581
Agriculture, natural resources and conservation	5,119	5,251	5,371	5,487	5,651
Dentistry	16,678	17,387	18,118	20,156	21,012
Medicine	12,012	12,470	12,987	13,409	13,858
Nursing	4,985	5,140	5,308	5,401	5,527
Pharmacy	10,463	10,691	11,273	11,928	9,738
Veterinary medicine	6,383	6,680	6,917	7,196	7,419
Other health, parks, recreation and fitness	5,232	5,529	5,757	5,964	6,135

Footnotes:

(1) Data for 2016/2017 are preliminary.

(2) The national and provincial tuition fee averages are weighted with the latest enrolment data (2013). If the number of enrolments is unknown for a given program, that program is excluded from the averages. The same enrolment data are used for the weighting of both years, 2015/2016 and 2016/2017, thereby permitting the comparison of changes in the tuition fees only.

(3) As the distribution of enrolment varies from period to period, caution must be exercised when making long-term historical comparisons.

(4) For Quebec (since 1998/1999) and Nova Scotia (since 2007/2008), the weighted averages take into account the different fees paid by "in province" and "out of province" Canadian students.

(5) It is important to note that tuition fee increases are generally regulated by provincial policies. However, some programs may be exempted from these policies resulting in possible increases that exceed provincial limits.

(6) Data in this release do not take into account financial assistance or tax rebates provided to students. Tuition fees and additional compulsory fees represent only a portion of all costs incurred for attending university.

Source:

Statistics Canada. Table 477-0021 - Weighted average tuition fees for full-time Canadian undergraduate students, by field of study, annual (dollars (accessed: Sept. 5, 2017)

Weighted average tuition fees for full-time Canadian graduate students, by field of study, annual (dollars) (1,2,3,4,5,6,7)

Field of study grouping	2012/2013	2013/2014	2014/2015	2015/2016	2016/2017
Education	5,462	5,536	5,674	5,697	5,834
Visual and performing arts, and communications technologies	4,890	4,700	4,818	5,202	5,311
Humanities	4,522	4,525	4,624	4,619	4,687
Social and behavioural sciences	5,020	5,103	5,325	5,460	5,606
Law, legal professions and studies	5,373	5,834	5,758	6,148	6,303
Business, management and public administration	8,547	8,987	10,378	10,703	11,041
Executive MBA	35,448	38,750	39,413	47,394	48,626
Regular MBA	23,049	26,201	26,989	26,532	27,574
Physical and life sciences and technologies	5,913	6,024	6,100	6,350	6,491
Mathematics, computer and information sciences	5,790	6,001	6,039	6,123	6,240
Engineering	6,040	6,168	6,388	6,777	7,004
Architecture and related technologies	5,290	5,483	5,704	5,807	6,071
Agriculture, natural resources and conservation	5,136	5,236	5,431	5,377	5,486
Dentistry	10,753	11,631	12,135	12,276	12,691
Medicine	(U)	(U)	(U)	n/a	n/a
Nursing	5,746	5,844	6,076	7,321	7,431
Pharmacy	5,199	6,456	6,248	6,044	6,113
Veterinary medicine	3,313	3,650	3,686	3,358	3,429
Other health, parks, recreation and fitness	7,858	7,707	7,868	8,158	8,346

Legend:

n/a Not available

(U) Too unreliable to be published

Footnotes:

(1) Data for 2016/2017 are preliminary.

(2) The national and provincial tuition fee averages are weighted with the latest enrolment data (2013). If the number of enrolments is unknown for a given program, that program is excluded from the averages. The same enrolment data are used for the weighting of both years, 2015/2016 and 2016/2017, thereby permitting the comparison of changes in the tuition fees only.

(3) As the distribution of enrolment varies from period to period, caution must be exercised when making long-term historical comparisons.

(4) For Quebec (since 1998/1999) and Nova Scotia (since 2007/2008), the weighted averages take into account the different fees paid by "in province" and "out of province" Canadian students.

(5) Since 2010/2011, Regular and Executive MBA (master of business administration programs) have been excluded from the national and provincial weighted averages due to their high costs and their effect on the overall tuition fee average. Dental, medical and veterinary

(6) It is important to note that tuition fee increases are generally regulated by provincial policies. However, some programs may be exempted from these policies resulting in possible increases that exceed provincial limits.

(7) Data in this release do not take into account financial assistance or tax rebates provided to students. Tuition fees and additional compulsory fees represent only a portion of all costs incurred for attending university.

Source:

Statistics Canada. Table 477-0022 - Weighted average tuition fees for full-time Canadian graduate students, by field of study, annual (dollars) (accessed: Sept. 5, 2017)

Weighted average tuition fees for full-time international undergraduate students, by field of study, annual (dollars) (1,2,3,4,5)

Field of study grouping	2012/2013	2013/2014	2014/2015	2015/2016	2016/2017
Education	14,133	14,998	15,703	16,712	17,337
Visual and performing arts, and communications technologies	16,677	18,237	18,388	19,766	20,571
Humanities	17,282	18,332	19,300	21,021	22,229
Social and behavioural sciences	17,033	17,629	18,436	20,644	21,604
Law, legal professions and studies	21,793	23,254	25,245	25,864	27,056
Business, management and public administration	18,185	19,525	20,787	22,340	23,555
Physical and life sciences and technologies	18,778	19,877	20,933	22,954	24,456
Mathematics, computer and information sciences	19,265	20,284	21,879	23,643	25,273
Engineering	20,534	21,861	23,443	25,112	26,582
Architecture and related technologies	17,893	18,733	19,868	21,033	22,171
Agriculture, natural resources and conservation	16,402	17,396	17,876	19,327	20,268
Dentistry	44,162	47,243	48,990	50,646	53,105
Medicine	28,600	29,407	29,440	31,881	33,084
Nursing	15,584	16,221	16,704	18,152	18,806
Pharmacy	29,527	30,728	33,434	30,997	32,886
Veterinary medicine	50,493	51,332	51,815	54,326	58,629
Other health, parks, recreation and fitness	16,882	16,966	17,767	19,269	20,117

Footnotes:

(1) Data for 2016/2017 are preliminary.

(2) The national and provincial tuition fee averages are weighted with the latest enrolment data (2013). If the number of enrolments is unknown for a given program, that program is excluded from the averages. The same enrolment data are used for the weighting of both years, 2015/2016 and 2016/2017, thereby permitting the comparison of changes in the tuition fees only.

(3) As the distribution of enrolment varies from period to period, caution must be exercised when making long-term historical comparisons.

(4) It is important to note that tuition fee increases are generally regulated by provincial policies. However, some programs may be exempted from these policies resulting in possible increases that exceed provincial limits.

(5) Data in this release do not take into account financial assistance or tax rebates provided to students. Tuition fees and additional compulsory fees represent only a portion of all costs incurred for attending university.

Source:

Statistics Canada. Table 477-0023 - Weighted average tuition fees for full-time international undergraduate students, by field of study, annual (dollars)
(accessed: Sept. 5, 2017)

Weighted average tuition fees for full-time international graduate students, by field of study, annual (dollars) (1,2,3,4,5,6)

Field of study grouping	2012/2013	2013/2014	2014/2015	2015/2016	2016/2017
Education	12,201	12,802	12,908	13,407	13,962
Visual and performing arts, and communications technologies	11,761	11,840	12,305	13,056	13,150
Humanities	12,189	12,424	12,663	13,154	13,460
Social and behavioural sciences	12,024	12,244	12,650	13,053	13,557
Law, legal professions and studies	14,620	15,396	15,071	16,230	16,549
Business, management and public administration	17,537	18,314	18,960	19,619	20,518
Executive MBA	44,159	44,826	41,127	55,014	56,900
Regular MBA	30,537	33,520	34,597	32,486	34,131
Physical and life sciences and technologies	12,237	12,556	12,978	13,393	13,730
Mathematics, computer and information sciences	11,733	12,099	12,479	12,799	13,067
Engineering	13,806	14,041	14,534	15,281	15,870
Architecture and related technologies	14,534	15,796	16,133	17,240	20,123
Agriculture, natural resources and conservation	11,311	11,370	11,772	12,135	12,416
Dentistry	(U)	19,427	19,711	19,858	20,565
Medicine	(U)	(U)	(U)	n/a	n/a
Nursing	11,212	12,524	12,055	11,877	12,183
Pharmacy	11,966	12,674	13,261	14,178	10,548
Veterinary medicine	8,217	9,268	9,472	8,483	8,640
Other health, parks, recreation and fitness	15,941	15,583	14,909	15,573	16,031

Legend:

(U) Too unreliable to be published

n/a Not available

Footnotes:

(1) Data for 2016/2017 are preliminary.

(2) The national and provincial tuition fee averages are weighted with the latest enrolment data (2013). If the number of enrolments is unknown for a given program, that program is excluded from the averages. The same enrolment data are used for the weighting of both years, 2015/2016 and 2016/2017, thereby permitting the comparison of changes in the tuition fees only.

(3) As the distribution of enrolment varies from period to period, caution must be exercised when making long-term historical comparisons.

(4) Since 2010/2011, Regular and Executive MBA (master of business administration programs) have been excluded from the national and provincial weighted averages due to their high costs and their effect on the overall tuition fee average. Dental, medical and veterinary residency programs offered in teaching hospitals and similar locations that may lead to advanced professional certification have also been excluded.

(5) It is important to note that tuition fee increases are generally regulated by provincial policies. However, some programs may be exempted from these policies resulting in possible increases that exceed provincial limits.

(6) Data in this release do not take into account financial assistance or tax rebates provided to students. Tuition fees and additional compulsory fees represent only a portion of all costs incurred for attending university.

Source:

Statistics Canada. Table 477-0024 - Weighted average tuition fees for full-time international graduate students, by field of study, annual (dollars)

(accessed: Sept. 5, 2017)

School board revenues, by direct source of funds, annual (dollars x 1,000) (1,2,3)

School board revenues by direct source of funds	2010	2011	2012	2013	2014
Total revenues	51,644,180	53,617,497	55,279,523	56,093,476	57,230,208
Local taxation sources	13,062,175	13,143,149	13,422,523	13,881,346	14,389,954
Provincial government sources	34,936,172	36,829,019	38,165,260	38,454,590	39,036,261
Federal government sources	314,175	309,646	304,803	321,498	328,541
Student and other school fees	243,953	280,325	366,047	382,884	417,673
Other private sector sources	3,087,705	3,055,358	3,020,890	3,053,158	3,057,779

Footnotes:

(1) Source: Statistics Canada, Culture, Tourism and the Centre for Education Statistics.

(2) Data are or have been converted to a calendar basis, January 1 to December 31.

(3) School boards represent schools which are a part of the elementary and secondary public school system. The revenues and/or expenditures in this table exclude those of other types of publicly run elementary and secondary schools such as federal schools and special needs education schools as well as the elementary and secondary schools which are in the private school system.

Source:

Statistics Canada. Table 478-0010 - School board revenues, by direct source of funds, annual (dollars) (accessed: Sept. 5, 2017)

School board expenditures, by function and economic classification, annual (dollars x 1,000) (1,2)

Economic classification	2010	2011	2012	2013	2014
Total expenditures by economic classification	51,904,934	53,034,158	54,147,034	55,872,155	57,183,090
Salary and wages expenditures	34,226,301	35,338,155	36,251,844	36,893,635	37,504,944
Fringe benefits expenditures	4,420,034	4,332,646	4,354,706	5,159,119	5,454,589
Supply and services expenditures	4,529,877	4,532,222	4,587,366	4,684,503	4,859,666
Fees and contractual services expenditures	3,034,824	2,911,848	3,528,278	3,581,758	3,630,602
Other operating expenditures	1,114,311	1,291,707	654,308	634,455	636,088
Capital expenditures (non-allocable, outlay and debt charges)	4,579,587	4,627,580	4,770,532	4,918,685	5,097,201

Footnotes:

(1) Source: Statistics Canada, Culture, Tourism and the Centre for Education Statistics.

(2) Data are or have been converted to a calendar basis, January 1 to December 31.

Source:

Statistics Canada. Table 478-0011 - School board expenditures, by function and economic classification, annual (dollars) (accessed: Sept. 5, 2017)

School board expenditures, by function and economic classification, annual (dollars x 1,000) (1,2)

Function	2010	2011	2012	2013	2014
Total expenditures by function	51,904,934	53,034,158	54,147,034	55,872,155	57,183,090
Business administration expenditures	1,544,840	1,538,369	1,525,215	1,545,485	1,582,080
Instruction and educational services expenditures (3)	36,435,142	37,424,240	38,378,213	39,606,290	40,463,204
Adult education expenditures	786,036	7,809,55	819,784	861,275	870,306
Food services expenditures	1,861,807	1,862,813	1,779,191	1,880,867	1,920,401
School facilities service expenditures	4,505,790	4,558,032	4,580,949	4,731,482	4,882,318
Transportation expenditures	2,191,732	2,242,169	2,293,150	2,328,071	2,367,580
Capital outlay expenditures (non-allocable)	3,685,778	3,708,752	3,887,037	4,087,541	4,279,739
Debt charges on capital expenditures (non-allocable)	893,809	918,828	883,495	831,144	817,462

Footnotes:

(1) Source: Statistics Canada, Culture, Tourism and the Centre for Education Statistics.

(2) Data are or have been converted to a calendar basis, January 1 to December 31.

(3) Instruction and education services expenditures include instructional administration expenditures.

Source:

Statistics Canada. Table 478-0011 - School board expenditures, by function and economic classification, annual (dollars) (accessed: Sept. 5, 2017)

Public and private elementary and secondary education expenditures, annual (dollars x 1,000) (1)

Type of expenditures	2010/2011	2011/2012	2012/2013	2013/2014	2014/2015
Public and private elementary and secondary education expenditures	63,844,950	65,025,378	66,326,449	68,235,913	69,941,193
Public elementary and secondary education expenditures	59,927,089	61,023,064	62,244,692	63,919,893	65,529,586
Public school board and direct government expenditures	58,403,764	59,374,575	60,480,272	62,357,553	63,727,886
Public school board expenditures	51,904,934	53,034,158	54,147,034	55,872,155	57,183,090
Public school board expenditures, net	51,854,141	52,981,937	54,093,290	55,816,957	57,126,464
Public school board expenditures transferred to private schools	-50,793	-52,221	-53,744	-55,198	-56,626
Direct government expenditures on public education	6,549,623	6,392,638	6,386,982	6,540,596	6,601,422
Direct government expenditures on services to public school boards (3)	2,165,802	1,898,468	1,533,708	1,470,694	1,326,985
Direct government expenditures on contributions to public school board teachers' pension funds (3)	3,672,903	3,880,756	4,035,930	4,334,584	4,289,835
Direct government expenditures on public education by the Department of National Defence (4)	1,959	365	4,695	20	1,803
Other direct government expenditures on public education (4)	708,959	613,049	812,649	735,298	982,799
Federal school expenditures	1,085,164	1,182,338	1,291,924	1,113,672	1,343,941
Federal school operating expenditures	(T)	(T)	(T)	(T)	(T)
Federal school capital expenditures	(T)	(T)	(T)	(T)	(T)
Special education expenditures on public education	236,880	251,857	248,189	243,710	246,015
Special education expenditures, handicapped outside regular public schools	176,678	182,251	189,548	187,127	186,271
Special education expenditures on provincially licensed correspondence courses	35,103	44,558	33,566	32,591	36,143
Special education expenditures, reform and correctional institutions	4,417	4,465	4,492	3,900	3,923
Special education expenditures on federal penitentiaries	20,682	20,583	20,583	20,092	19,678
Direct provincial government expenditures on administration of public education	201,281	214,294	224,307	204,958	211,744
Private elementary and secondary school expenditures	3,917,861	4,002,314	4,081,757	4,316,020	4,411,607

Symbol legend:

(T) Series is terminated

Footnotes:

(1) Source: Statistics Canada, Tourism and the Centre for Education Statistics.

(3) From 1950 to 1959 there was no separate breakdown available between direct government expenditures on services to public school boards and direct government expenditures on contributions to public school board teachers' pension funds. These were both reported under direct government expenditures on contributions to public school board teachers' pension funds.

(4) From 1950 to 1959, any direct government expenditures on public education by Department of National Defence were reported under other direct government expenditures on public education.

Source:

Statistics Canada. Table 478-0014 - Public and private elementary and secondary education expenditures, annual (dollars) (accessed: Sept. 5, 2017)

Public and private elementary and secondary education expenditures, by direct source of funds, annual (dollars x 1,000) (1)

Public and private elementary and secondary education expenditures by direct source of funds	2010/2011	2011/2012	2012/2013	2013/2014	2014/2015
All sources	63,844,950	65,025,378	66,326,449	68,235,913	69,941,193
All governments' sources	57,271,016	59,242,472	60,993,698	61,864,127	63,292,268
Federal government sources	1,507,560	1,651,550	1,801,463	1,748,728	19,72,055
Provincial government sources	42,695,922	44,442,297	45,764,080	46,228,352	46,924,538
Local government sources	13,067,534	13,148,625	13,428,155	13,887,047	14,395,675
Student and other school fees	2,452,031	2,533,498	2,651,743	2,739,644	2,824,650
Other private sector sources	4,121,903	3,249,408	2,681,008	3,632,142	3,824,275

Footnotes:

(1) Source: Statistics Canada, Tourism and the Centre for Education Statistics.

Source:

Statistics Canada. Table 478-0015 - Public and private elementary and secondary education expenditures, by direct source of funds, annual (dollars)
(accessed: Sept 5, 2017)

Labour force survey estimates (LFS), by educational attainment, sex and age group, annual (18)

Labour force characteristics	Educational attainment (11)	2012	2013	2014	2015	2016
Employment rate (rate) (10)	Total, all education levels	61.7	61.8	61.4	61.3	61.1
Employment rate (rate) (10)	0 to 8 years (12)	20	19.8	19.1	18.8	18.5
Employment rate (rate) (10)	Some high school (13)	39.5	39.5	39.1	38.5	38.1
Employment rate (rate) (10)	High school graduate (14)	61	60.7	60	58.3	58.1
Employment rate (rate) (10)	Some postsecondary (15)	60.5	59.9	58.8	58.6	58.2
Employment rate (rate) (10)	Postsecondary certificate or diploma (16)	70.5	70.6	70.2	69.9	69.2
Employment rate (rate) (10)	University degree (17)	74.8	74.6	74	74.3	73.9
Employment rate (rate) (10)	Bachelor's degree	74.6	74.6	73.9	74.4	73.8
Employment rate (rate) (10)	Above bachelor's degree	75.1	74.6	74.1	74.1	74

Footnotes:

(10) The employment rate (formerly the employment and population ratio) is the number of persons employed expressed as a percentage of the population 15 years of age and over. The employment rate for a particular group (age, sex, marital status) is the number employed in that group expressed as a percentage of the population for that group. Estimates are percentages, rounded to the nearest tenth.

(11) The following categories refer to the highest level of schooling completed. Questions relating to educational attainment were changed in 1990, to better capture the relationship between educational attainment and labour market outcomes. Because this introduced a break in the education series, this table only contains data from 1990 onwards. Beginning January 1990, data on primary and secondary education reflects the highest grade completed. This provides a more consistent measure for those who accelerate or fail a grade than did years of school. A question on high school graduation has also been added since it is generally believed that persons who have never completed their secondary education have greater difficulty competing in the labour market. With the new questions, any education that could be counted towards a degree, certificate or diploma from an educational institution is taken as postsecondary education. The change allows more persons into the postsecondary education category. For example, trades programs offered through apprenticeship, vocational schools or private trade schools do not always require high school graduation. Such education is now considered as postsecondary while only primary or secondary would have been recognized prior to 1990. Finally, more information is collected on the type of postsecondary education: 1) some postsecondary; 2) trades certificate or diploma from a vocational or apprenticeship training; 3) Non-university certificate or diploma from a community college, CEGEP or school of nursing; 4) University certificate below bachelors degree; 5) Bachelors degree; and 6) University degree or certificate above bachelors degree.

(12) Primary education, grade 8 or lower. In Quebec, secondary II or lower.

(13) Attended but did not complete secondary school. In Quebec, attended at least Secondary III but did not complete Secondary V. In Newfoundland and Labrador, attended at least the first year of secondary but did not complete the fourth year.

(14) Received a high school diploma. In Quebec, completed Secondary V. In Newfoundland and Labrador, completed fourth year of secondary.

(15) Worked toward, but did not complete, a degree, certificate (including a trade certificate) or diploma from an educational institution, including a university, beyond the secondary level. This includes vocational schools, apprenticeship training, community college, Collège d'Enseignement Général et Professionnel (CEGEP), and school of nursing.

(16) Completed a certificate (including a trade certificate) or diploma from an educational institution beyond the secondary level. This includes certificates from vocational schools, apprenticeship training, community college, Collège d'Enseignement Général et Professionnel (CEGEP), and school of nursing. Also included are certificates below a Bachelor's degree obtained at a university.

(17) Attained at least a university bachelor's degree.

(18) The Labour force survey collection of tables, starting with number 282-, is large with many possible cross-tabulations for the 10 provinces and other geographic regions. To ensure respondent's confidentiality, detailed data are suppressed. Data for Canada, Quebec, Ontario, Alberta and British Columbia are suppressed if the estimate is below 1,500, for Newfoundland and Labrador, Nova Scotia, New Brunswick, Manitoba and Saskatchewan, if the estimate is below 500, and for Prince Edward Island, under 200. For suppression levels within census metropolitan areas (CMAs) and economic regions (ERs), use the respective provincial suppression levels above. While suppressing to protect respondent confidentiality has the added effect of blocking-out the lowest-quality LFS data, some remaining non-suppressed data in these very large LFS CANSIM tables may be of insufficient quality to allow for accurate interpretation. Please be warned that the more detailed your LFS CANSIM download, the smaller the sample size upon which your LFS estimates will be based, and the greater the risk of downloading poorer quality data.

Source:

Statistics Canada. Table 282-0004 - Labour force survey estimates (LFS), by educational attainment, sex and age group, annual (persons unless otherwise noted)

(accessed: Sept. 5, 2017)

Glossary of Education Terms

Accountability
measurable proof, usually in the form of student results on various tests, that teachers, schools, divisions and states are teaching students efficiently and well, usually in the form of student success rates on various tests; Virginia's accountability programs is known as the Standards of Learning which includes curriculum standards approved by the Board of Education and required state tests based on the standards.

Accreditation
a process used by the Virginia Department of Education to evaluate the educational performance of public schools in accordance regulations.

Achievement gap
the difference between the performance of subgroups of students, especially those defined by gender, race/ethnicity, disability and socioeconomic status.

ACT
one of the two commonly used tests designed to assess high school students' general educational development and their ability to complete college-level work in four skill areas: English, mathematics, reading, and science reasoning.

Adequate yearly progress (AYP)
a measurement indicating whether a school, division or the state met federally approved academic goals required by the federal Elementary and Secondary Education Act/No Child Left Behind Act (ESEA/NCLB).

Adult/Continuing education
a program of instruction provided by an adult/continuing education instructional organization for adults and youth beyond the age of compulsory school attendance including basic education and English literacy, English for speakers of other languages, civics education, GED testing services, adult secondary education and Individualized Student Alternative Education Plan (ISAEP) programs.

Advanced Placement (AP)
college-level courses available to high school students which may allow a student to earn college credit provided through the College Board.

Alignment
effort to ensure that what teachers teach is in accord with what the curriculum says will be taught and what is assessed on official tests.

Alternative assessment
a method to measure student educational attainment other than the typical multiple-choice test which may include portfolios, constructed response items and other performance-measurement tools.

Alternative education
a school or center organized for alternative programs of instruction.

Assessment
method of measuring the learning and performance of students; examples include achievement tests, minimum competency tests, developmental screening tests, aptitude tests, observation instruments, performance tasks, etc.

At-risk students
students who have a higher than average probability of dropping out or failing school.

Average daily membership (ADM)
the K-12 enrollment figure used to distribute state per pupil funding that includes students with disabilities ages 5-21, and students for whom English is a second language who entered school for the first time after reaching their 12th birthday, and who have not reached their 22nd birthday; preschool and post-graduate students are not included in ADM.

Benchmark
a standard for judging performance.

Block scheduling
a way of organizing the school day into blocks of time longer than the typical 50 minute class period; with the 4X4 block students take four 90-minute classes each day allowing for completion of an entire course in one semester instead of a full year; with an A/B or rotating block students take six to eight classes for an entire year but classes in each subject meet on alternate days for 90 minutes.

Charter school
a school controlled by a local school board that provides free public elementary and/or secondary education to eligible students under a specific charter granted by the state legislature or other appropriate authority, and designated by such authority to be a charter school.

Class period
a segment of time in the school day that is approximately 1/6 of the instructional day.

Cohort
a particular group of people with something in common.

College Board
the organization that administers SAT, AP and other standardized tests to high school students planning on continuing their educations at a post-secondary level.

Combined school
a public school that contains any combination of or all K-12 grade levels that are not considered an elementary, middle or secondary school .

Composite index of local ability to pay
a formula to determine the state and local government shares of K-12 education program costs, which is expressed as a ratio, indicating the local percentage share of the cost of education programs; for example, a locality with a composite

index of 0.3000 would pay 30 percent and the state would pay 70 percent of the costs.

Confined
due to physical, medical or emotional impairments based on certification of need, a student is restricted or limited from attendance at a regular public school during the regular school hours; this does not apply to situations where a student is restricted for discipline or non-medically based situations.

Core curriculum
the body of knowledge that all students are expected to learn in the subjects of English, mathematics, history/social science and science.

Curriculum
a plan or document that a school or school division uses to define what will be taught and the methods that will be used to educate and assess students.

Curriculum alignment
occurs when what is taught includes or exceeds the content defined by the Standards of Learning (SOL).

Data-based decision making (also referred to as "research-based decision making")
organizing, analyzing and interpreting existing sources of information and other data to make decisions.

Direct aid to public education
funding appropriated for the operation of public schools including funding for school employee benefits, Standards of Quality, incentive-based programs, allotment of sales tax and lottery revenues and specific appropriations for programs such as Governor's Schools and adult literacy initiatives.

Disaggregated data
presentation of data broken into subgroups of students instead of the entire student body which allows parents and teachers to measure how each student group is performing; typical subgroups include students who are economically disadvantaged, from different racial or ethnic groups, those who have disabilities or have limited English fluency.

Distance learning
method of instruction in locations other than the classroom or places where teachers present the lessons, which uses various forms of technology to provide educational materials and experiences to students.

Dropouts
students who leave high school before receiving a diploma.

Early childhood education
the education of young children, especially under the age of 5.

Economically disadvantaged
a student who is a member of a household that meets the income eligibility guidelines for free or reduced-price school meals (less than or equal to 185% of Federal Poverty Guidelines).

Elementary & Secondary Education Act (ESEA)
the primary federal law affecting K-12 education; the most recent reauthorization of the law is also known as the No Child Left Behind Act of 2001 (NCLB).

Elementary school
a public school with grades kindergarten through five.

Eligible students
the total number of students of school age enrolled in the school at a grade or course with a Standards of Learning test; does not include students who are allowed an exclusion such as limited English proficient (LEP) students or some students with disabilities.

English as a second language (ESL)
a program of instruction and services for non-English-speaking or limited-English-proficient students to help them learn and succeed in schools.

English-language learners (ELL)
a student whose first language is other than English and who is in a special program for learning English.

Enrollment
the act of complying with state and local requirements for registration or admission of a child for attendance in a school within a local school division; also refers to registration for courses within the student's home school or within related schools or programs.

Even Start
a federally funded program that provides family-centered education projects to help parents become full partners in the education of their children.

First time
the student has not been enrolled in the school at any time during the current school year.

Four core subject/academic areas
English, mathematics, science and history/social science for purposes of SOL testing.

Free and appropriate public education (FAPE)
requirement through the federal Individuals with Disabilities Education Act (IDEA) that education of students with disabilities (between the ages of 3 and 22) must be provided at public expense, under public supervision, at no charge to the parents and based on the child's unique needs and not on the child's disability.

General education
K-12 instruction that meets the commonwealth's Standards of Learning and prepares children for elementary, secondary and postsecondary success.

Gifted
programs that provide advanced educational opportunities including accelerated promotion through grades and classes and an enriched curriculum for students who are endowed with a high degree of mental ability.

Governor's school
a school serving gifted high school students who meet specific admissions criteria for advanced educational opportunities in areas including the arts, government and international studies, mathematics, science, and technology; both academic-year and summer governor's schools are offered.

Graduate
a student who has earned a Board of Education recognized diploma: advanced studies, advanced technical, standard, standard technical, modified standard, special or general achievement.

Head Start
a federally funded child-development program that provides health, educational, nutritional, social and other services to pre-school children from economically disadvantaged families.

Home-based instruction
non-reimbursable educational services provided in the home setting (or other agreed upon setting) in accordance with the student's individual education program who were removed from school for disciplinary or other reasons, but not the result of a medical referral.

Homebound instruction
academic instruction provided to students who are confined at home or in a health-care facility for periods that would prevent normal school attendance based upon certification of need by a licensed physician or licensed clinical psychologist. For a student with a disability, the Individual Education Program (IEP) team must determine the delivery of services, including the number of hours of services.

Home instruction (also referred to as "home schooling")
instruction of a student or students by a parent or parents, guardian or other person having control or charge of such student or students as an alternative to attendance in a public or private school in accordance with the provisions of the Code of Virginia provisions (§22.1-254.1).

Home tutoring
instruction by a tutor or teacher with qualifications prescribed by the Virginia Board of Education, as an alternative to attendance in a public or private school and approved by the division superintendent in accordance with the provisions of the Code of Virginia §22.1-254; often used as an alternative form of home schooling.

Individuals with Disabilities Education Act (IDEA)
federal law guiding the delivery of special education services for students with disabilities which includes the guarantee of "free and appropriate public education" for every school-age child with a disability and allows parental involvement in the educational planning process, encourages access to the general curriculum and delineates how school disciplinary rules and the obligation to provide a free appropriate public education for disabled children mesh.

Individualized education program (IEP)
a written plan created for a student with disabilities by the student's teachers, parents or guardians, the school administrator, and other interested parties. The plan is tailored to the student's specific needs and abilities, and outlines attainable goals.

Individualized education program team (IEP Team)
team charged with developing, reviewing and revising a student's IEP and consisting of the parent(s), the child (if appropriate), a regular education teacher, a special education teacher, an administrator qualified to supervise the provision of services and an individual who can interpret the instructional implications of evaluation results.

Individualized family service plan (IFSP)
a written plan outlining the procedure necessary to transition a child with disabilities to preschool or other appropriate services.

International Baccalaureate (IB)
a program established to provide an internationally recognized; interdisciplinary; pre-collegiate course of study offered through the International Baccalaureate Organization, headquartered in Switzerland, and examination results are accepted by more than 100 countries for university admission.

Licensed clinical psychologist
a psychologist licensed by the Virginia Board of Psychology who must either be in a treatment relationship or establishing a treatment relationship with the student to meet eligibility requirements for requesting homebound services.

Licensed physician
an individual who has been licensed by the Virginia Board of Medicine to practice medicine who can certify medical conditions for requesting homebound services.

Licensed teacher
an individual who has met all the current requirements for a teacher in the Virginia and holds a license from the Virginia State Board of Education, or, if teaching on-line, a license from Virginia or another state.

Limited-English proficient (LEP) -see English-language learners Linear weighted average
a calculation, approximating what most school divisions spend to operate their schools, used to establish the funded cost of many components of the Standards of Quality (SOQ), such as instructional salaries.

Literary fund
established in the Constitution of Virginia (Article VIII, § 8) as a permanent and perpetual school fund that provides low-interest loans to school divisions for capital expenditures, such as construction of new buildings or remodeling of existing buildings.

Locally awarded verified credit
a verified unit of credit awarded by a local school board in accordance with the SOA.

Magnet school/center (also referred to as "specialty school/center")
a public school that focuses on a particular area of study, such as performing arts or science and technology but also offer regular school subjects.

Middle school
a public school with grades 6 through 8.

Migrant Education
a program of instruction and services for children who move periodically with their families from one school to another in a different geographical area to secure seasonal employment.

National Assessment of Educational Progress (NAEP) (also referred to as "the Nation's Report Card")
the only nationally representative and continuing assessment of what America's students know and can do in various subject areas including mathematics, reading, science, writing, U.S. history, geography, civics and the arts; the federally funded program (currently contracted to Educational Testing Service in Princeton, N.J.) tests a representative sample of students in grades 4, 8 and 12 and provides information about the achievement of students nationally and state-by-state.

National Blue Ribbon Award
honors public and private K-12 schools that are either academically superior in their states or that demonstrate dramatic gains in student achievement; awarded annually by the U.S. Department of Education through the Blue Ribbon Schools Program.

Nation's Report Card
see "National Assessment of Educational Progress (NAEP)".

No Child Left behind Act of 2001 (NCLB)
see "Elementary & Secondary Education Act".

Norm-referenced tests
standardized tests designed to measure how a student's performance compares with that of other students.

Phonological Awareness Literacy Screening (PALS)
state-provided K-3 screening tool to help reduce the number of children with reading problems by detecting those problems early and providing research-based, small-group intervention.

Pedagogy
the art of teaching.

Planning period
one class period per day (or the equivalent) unencumbered of any teaching or supervisory duties.

Portfolio
a collection of student work chosen to exemplify and document a student's learning progress over time.

Pre-school child care
a school-operated program that provides custodial care of pre-school students enrolled in a school or system before school day starts and/or after a school day ends.

Proficient
test results indicating that the student demonstrated the skills and knowledge outlined in the Standards of Learning (SOL).

Professional/staff development
training for teachers, principals, superintendents, administrative staff, local school board members and Board of Education members designed to enhance student achievement and is required by the Standards of Quality (SOQ).

Psychiatrist
an medical doctor who has been licensed by the Virginia Board of Medicine and trained to practice in the science of treating mental diseases.

Reading First
federal program focuses on putting proven methods of early reading instruction into classrooms to ensure all children learn to read well by the end of third grade.

Recess
a segment of free time during the standard school day in which students are given a break from instruction.

Reconstitution
for a school rated accreditation denied, it is a process to initiate a range of accountability actions to improve pupil performance and to address deficiencies in curriculum and instruction; may include, but is not limited to, restructuring a school's governance, instructional program staff or student population.

Regular school year
the period of time between the opening day of school in the fall and the closing day of school for that school term that is at minimum 180 teaching days or 990 teaching hours.

Remedial program
a program designed to remedy, strengthen and improve the academic achievement of students who demonstrate substandard performance.

Research-based decision making
see "data-based decision making".

Response to intervention (RTI)
a method designed to identify and provide early, effective assistance to children who are having difficulty learning: Tier 1 students need extra help understanding the core curriculum, Tier 2 students consistently showing a discrepancy between their current level of performance and the expected level of performance, and Tier 3 students need even more support.

Restructuring
the implementation of a new organizational pattern or style of leadership and management to bring about renewed, more effective schools. It can mean reorganizing the school day or year and changing conventional practices, such as grouping students by age for an entire school year or giving competitive grades. Or it may refer to changing the roles of teachers and administrators, allocating more decision-making power to teachers, and involving parents in decisions.

Sampling
a way of estimating how a whole group would perform on a test by testing representative members of the group or giving different portions of the test to various subgroups.

SAT
one of the two commonly used tests designed to assess high school students' general educational development and required

for college entrance by many institutions of higher education; administered by The College Board.

School
a publicly funded institution where students are enrolled for all or a majority of the instructional day; those students are reported in fall membership at the institution and the institution, at minimum, meets requirements adopted by the Board of Education.

School age
a child who is age 5 on or before September 30 and has not reached age 20; compulsory attendance school age is 5-18.

Secondary school
a public school with any grades 9 through 12.

Special education (SPED)
a service especially designed and at no cost to the parent/guardian that adapts the curriculum, materials or instruction for students identified as having educational or physical disabilities and tailored to each student's needs and learning style and provided in a general education or special education classroom, home, hospital, separate school or other setting.

Specialty school
see "magnet school/center".

Standardized testing
tests administered and scored under uniform (standardized) conditions. Because most machine-scored, multiple-choice tests are standardized, the term is sometimes used to refer to such tests, but other tests may also be standardized.

Standard school day
a calendar day that averages at least five and one-half instructional hours for students in grades 1-12, excluding breaks for meals and recess, and a minimum of three instructional hours for students in kindergarten.

Standard school year
a school year of at least 180 teaching days or a total of at least 990 teaching hours per year.

Standard unit of credit
earned credit based on a minimum of 140-clock hours of instruction and successful completion of the requirements of the course.

Standards of Accreditation (SOA)
the Board of Education's regulations establishing criteria for approving public schools in Virginia as authorized in the Standards of Quality (SOQ).

Standards of Learning (SOL)
the minimum grade level and subject matter educational objectives, described as the knowledge and skills "necessary for success in school and for preparation for life," that students are expected to meet in Virginia public schools and specified by the Standards of Quality (SOQ).

SOL curriculum frameworks
teacher resource guides for mathematics, science, English and history/social sciences delineating essential knowledge, skills and processes required by the Standards of Learning (SOL).

Standards of Quality (SOQ)
the minimum program that every public school division in Virginia must meet; a major portion of state funding for direct air to public education is based on the SOQ; the standards are established in the Constitution of Virginia, defined in the Code of Virginia and prescribed by the Board of Education, subject to revision only by the General Assembly.

Student
a child age 5 on or before September 30 up to age 18; a child with disabilities age 2-21; a child of limited English proficiency who entered a Virginia school after age 12 but not age 22.

Student periods
means the number of students a teacher instructs per class period multiplied by the number of class periods taught.

Substitute tests
tests approved by the Board of Education as substitutes for SOL end-of-course tests for awarding verified credit for high school; examples include Advanced Placement (AP), International Baccalaureate (IB), SAT II, as well as a number of certifications and licensing examinations in career and technical fields.

Title I
federal funding program authorized by Title I of ESEA/NCLB to support instructional needs of students from low-income families to ensure that all children have a fair and equal opportunity to obtain a high-quality education and reach (at a minimum) proficiency on state academic achievement standards and assessments.

Title 1 school
a school with a high rate of disadvantaged students making it eligible for participation in federal Title I programs.

Title 1 school-wide assistance
Title 1 schools with 40 percent or greater high-poverty, student population may use federal funding to meet the needs of all students at the school.

Title 1 targeted assistance
federal funding is used to meet the needs of the educationally disadvantaged students only and the poverty percentages must be at least 35% or above the district wide average.

Transition plan
plan provided by the licensed physician or licensed clinical psychologist to explain the need for extended homebound instruction which includes the name of the student, justification for the extension of homebound instruction, additional time homebound instruction is anticipated and specific steps planned to return the student to classroom instruction.

Verified unit of credit
earned credit based on a standard unit of credit, plus a passing score on the end-of-course SOL test or substitute test approved by the Board of Education.

Vocational
a school or center organized for a program that offers a sequence of courses that are directly related to the preparation of individuals for paid or unpaid employment in current or emerging occupations requiring other than a baccalaureate or advanced diploma

Source: Virginia Department of Education

A

B

C

D

E

F

G

H

I

J

K

L

M

O

P

Q

R

S

T

U

V

W

X

Y

Z

Alabama

Alaska

Arizona

Arkansas

California

Colorado

Connecticut

Delaware

District of Columbia

Florida

Georgia

Hawaii

Idaho

Illinois

Indiana

Iowa

Kansas

Kentucky

Louisiana

Maine

Maryland

Massachusetts

Michigan

Minnesota

Mississippi

Missouri

Montana

Nebraska

Nevada

New Hampshire

New Jersey

New Mexico

New York

North Carolina

North Dakota

Ohio

Oklahoma

Oregon

Pennsylvania

Rhode Island

South Carolina

South Dakota

Tennessee

Texas

Utah

Vermont

Virginia

Washington

West Virginia

Wisconsin

Wyoming

Arts

Civics & Government

Economics

English

Foreign Language

Geography

History

Mathematics

Reading & Language Arts

Science

Special Education

Technology

Grey House Publishing

2017 Title List

Visit www.GreyHouse.com for Product Information, Table of Contents, and Sample Pages.

General Reference

An African Biographical Dictionary
America's College Museums
American Environmental Leaders: From Colonial Times to the Present
Encyclopedia of African-American Writing
Encyclopedia of Constitutional Amendments
An Encyclopedia of Human Rights in the United States
Encyclopedia of Invasions & Conquests
Encyclopedia of Prisoners of War & Internment
Encyclopedia of Religion & Law in America
Encyclopedia of Rural America
Encyclopedia of the Continental Congress
Encyclopedia of the United States Cabinet, 1789-2010
Encyclopedia of War Journalism
Encyclopedia of Warrior Peoples & Fighting Groups
The Environmental Debate: A Documentary History
The Evolution Wars: A Guide to the Debates
From Suffrage to the Senate: America's Political Women
Gun Debate: An Encyclopedia of Gun Control & Gun Rights
Political Corruption in America
Privacy Rights in the Digital Era
The Religious Right: A Reference Handbook
Speakers of the House of Representatives, 1789-2009
This is Who We Were: 1880-1900
This is Who We Were: A Companion to the 1940 Census
This is Who We Were: In the 1900s
This is Who We Were: In the 1910s
This is Who We Were: In the 1920s
This is Who We Were: In the 1940s
This is Who We Were: In the 1950s
This is Who We Were: In the 1960s
This is Who We Were: In the 1970s
This is Who We Were: In the 1980s
This is Who We Were: In the 1990s
U.S. Land & Natural Resource Policy
The Value of a Dollar 1600-1865: Colonial Era to the Civil War
The Value of a Dollar: 1860-2014
Working Americans 1770-1869 Vol. IX: Revolutionary War to the Civil War
Working Americans 1880-1999 Vol. I: The Working Class
Working Americans 1880-1999 Vol. II: The Middle Class
Working Americans 1880-1999 Vol. III: The Upper Class
Working Americans 1880-1999 Vol. IV: Their Children
Working Americans 1880-2015 Vol. V: Americans At War
Working Americans 1880-2005 Vol. VI: Women at Work
Working Americans 1880-2006 Vol. VII: Social Movements
Working Americans 1880-2007 Vol. VIII: Immigrants
Working Americans 1880-2009 Vol. X: Sports & Recreation
Working Americans 1880-2010 Vol. XI: Inventors & Entrepreneurs
Working Americans 1880-2011 Vol. XII: Our History through Music
Working Americans 1880-2012 Vol. XIII: Education & Educators
Working Americans 1880-2016 Vol. XIV: Industry Through the Ages
World Cultural Leaders of the 20th & 21st Centuries

Education Information

Charter School Movement
Comparative Guide to American Elementary & Secondary Schools
Complete Learning Disabilities Directory
Educators Resource Directory
Special Education: Policy and Curriculum Development

Health Information

Comparative Guide to American Hospitals
Complete Directory for Pediatric Disorders
Complete Directory for People with Chronic Illness
Complete Directory for People with Disabilities
Complete Mental Health Directory
Diabetes in America: Analysis of an Epidemic
Directory of Health Care Group Purchasing Organizations
HMO/PPO Directory
Medical Device Market Place
Older Americans Information Directory

Business Information

Complete Television, Radio & Cable Industry Directory
Directory of Business Information Resources
Directory of Mail Order Catalogs
Directory of Venture Capital & Private Equity Firms
Environmental Resource Handbook
Food & Beverage Market Place
Grey House Homeland Security Directory
Grey House Performing Arts Directory
Grey House Safety & Security Directory
Hudson's Washington News Media Contacts Directory
New York State Directory
Sports Market Place Directory

Statistics & Demographics

American Tally
America's Top-Rated Cities
America's Top-Rated Smaller Cities
Ancestry & Ethnicity in America
The Asian Databook
Comparative Guide to American Suburbs
The Hispanic Databook
Profiles of America
"Profiles of" Series - State Handbooks
Weather America

Financial Ratings Series

TheStreet Ratings' Guide to Bond & Money Market Mutual Funds
TheStreet Ratings' Guide to Common Stocks
TheStreet Ratings' Guide to Exchange-Traded Funds
TheStreet Ratings' Guide to Stock Mutual Funds
TheStreet Ratings' Ultimate Guided Tour of Stock Investing
Weiss Ratings' Consumer Guides
Weiss Ratings' Financial Literary Basic Guides
Weiss Ratings' Guide to Banks
Weiss Ratings' Guide to Credit Unions
Weiss Ratings' Guide to Health Insurers
Weiss Ratings' Guide to Life & Annuity Insurers
Weiss Ratings' Guide to Property & Casualty Insurers

Bowker's Books In Print® Titles

American Book Publishing Record® Annual
American Book Publishing Record® Monthly
Books In Print®
Books In Print® Supplement
Books Out Loud™
Bowker's Complete Video Directory™
Children's Books In Print®
El-Hi Textbooks & Serials In Print®
Forthcoming Books®
Law Books & Serials In Print™
Medical & Health Care Books In Print™
Publishers, Distributors & Wholesalers of the US™
Subject Guide to Books In Print®
Subject Guide to Children's Books In Print®

Canadian General Reference

Associations Canada
Canadian Almanac & Directory
Canadian Environmental Resource Guide
Canadian Parliamentary Guide
Canadian Venture Capital & Private Equity Firms
Financial Post Directory of Directors
Financial Services Canada
Governments Canada
Health Guide Canada
The History of Canada
Libraries Canada
Major Canadian Cities

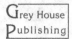

2017 Title List

Visit **www.SalemPress.com** for Product Information, Table of Contents, and Sample Pages.

Science, Careers & Mathematics

Ancient Creatures
Applied Science
Applied Science: Engineering & Mathematics
Applied Science: Science & Medicine
Applied Science: Technology
Biomes and Ecosystems
Careers in The Arts: Fine, Performing & Visual
Careers in Building Construction
Careers in Business
Careers in Chemistry
Careers in Communications & Media
Careers in Environment & Conservation
Careers in Financial Services
Careers in Healthcare
Careers in Hospitality & Tourism
Careers in Human Services
Careers in Law, Criminal Justice & Emergency Services
Careers in Manufacturing
Careers in Overseas Jobs
Careers in Physics
Careers in Sales, Insurance & Real Estate
Careers in Science & Engineering
Careers in Sports & Fitness
Careers in Technology Services & Repair
Computer Technology Innovators
Contemporary Biographies in Business
Contemporary Biographies in Chemistry
Contemporary Biographies in Communications & Media
Contemporary Biographies in Environment & Conservation
Contemporary Biographies in Healthcare
Contemporary Biographies in Hospitality & Tourism
Contemporary Biographies in Law & Criminal Justice
Contemporary Biographies in Physics
Earth Science
Earth Science: Earth Materials & Resources
Earth Science: Earth's Surface and History
Earth Science: Physics & Chemistry of the Earth
Earth Science: Weather, Water & Atmosphere
Encyclopedia of Energy
Encyclopedia of Environmental Issues
Encyclopedia of Environmental Issues: Atmosphere and Air Pollution
Encyclopedia of Environmental Issues: Ecology and Ecosystems
Encyclopedia of Environmental Issues: Energy and Energy Use
Encyclopedia of Environmental Issues: Policy and Activism
Encyclopedia of Environmental Issues: Preservation/Wilderness Issues
Encyclopedia of Environmental Issues: Water and Water Pollution
Encyclopedia of Global Resources
Encyclopedia of Global Warming
Encyclopedia of Mathematics & Society
Encyclopedia of Mathematics & Society: Engineering, Tech, Medicine
Encyclopedia of Mathematics & Society: Great Mathematicians
Encyclopedia of Mathematics & Society: Math & Social Sciences
Encyclopedia of Mathematics & Society: Math Development/Concepts
Encyclopedia of Mathematics & Society: Math in Culture & Society
Encyclopedia of Mathematics & Society: Space, Science, Environment
Encyclopedia of the Ancient World
Forensic Science
Geography Basics
Internet Innovators
Inventions and Inventors
Magill's Encyclopedia of Science: Animal Life
Magill's Encyclopedia of Science: Plant life
Notable Natural Disasters
Principles of Astronomy
Principles of Biology
Principles of Chemistry
Principles of Physical Science
Principles of Physics
Principles of Research Methods
Principles of Sustainability
Science and Scientists
Solar System
Solar System: Great Astronomers
Solar System: Study of the Universe
Solar System: The Inner Planets
Solar System: The Moon and Other Small Bodies
Solar System: The Outer Planets
Solar System: The Sun and Other Stars
World Geography

Literature

American Ethnic Writers
Classics of Science Fiction & Fantasy Literature
Critical Approaches: Feminist
Critical Approaches: Multicultural
Critical Approaches: Moral
Critical Approaches: Psychological
Critical Insights: Authors
Critical Insights: Film
Critical Insights: Literary Collection Bundles
Critical Insights: Themes
Critical Insights: Works
Critical Survey of Drama
Critical Survey of Graphic Novels: Heroes & Super Heroes
Critical Survey of Graphic Novels: History, Theme & Technique
Critical Survey of Graphic Novels: Independents/Underground Classics
Critical Survey of Graphic Novels: Manga
Critical Survey of Long Fiction
Critical Survey of Mystery & Detective Fiction
Critical Survey of Mythology and Folklore: Heroes and Heroines
Critical Survey of Mythology and Folklore: Love, Sexuality & Desire
Critical Survey of Mythology and Folklore: World Mythology
Critical Survey of Poetry
Critical Survey of Poetry: American Poets
Critical Survey of Poetry: British, Irish & Commonwealth Poets
Critical Survey of Poetry: Cumulative Index
Critical Survey of Poetry: European Poets
Critical Survey of Poetry: Topical Essays
Critical Survey of Poetry: World Poets
Critical Survey of Science Fiction & Fantasy
Critical Survey of Shakespeare's Plays
Critical Survey of Shakespeare's Sonnets
Critical Survey of Short Fiction
Critical Survey of Short Fiction: American Writers
Critical Survey of Short Fiction: British, Irish, Commonwealth Writers
Critical Survey of Short Fiction: Cumulative Index
Critical Survey of Short Fiction: European Writers
Critical Survey of Short Fiction: Topical Essays
Critical Survey of Short Fiction: World Writers
Critical Survey of World Literature
Critical Survey of Young Adult Literature
Cyclopedia of Literary Characters
Cyclopedia of Literary Places
Holocaust Literature
Introduction to Literary Context: American Poetry of the 20th Century
Introduction to Literary Context: American Post-Modernist Novels
Introduction to Literary Context: American Short Fiction
Introduction to Literary Context: English Literature
Introduction to Literary Context: Plays
Introduction to Literary Context: World Literature
Magill's Literary Annual 2015
Magill's Survey of American Literature
Magill's Survey of World Literature
Masterplots
Masterplots II: African American Literature
Masterplots II: American Fiction Series
Masterplots II: British & Commonwealth Fiction Series
Masterplots II: Christian Literature
Masterplots II: Drama Series
Masterplots II: Juvenile & Young Adult Literature, Supplement
Masterplots II: Nonfiction Series
Masterplots II: Poetry Series
Masterplots II: Short Story Series
Masterplots II: Women's Literature Series
Notable African American Writers
Notable American Novelists
Notable Playwrights
Notable Poets
Recommended Reading: 600 Classics Reviewed
Short Story Writers

SALEM PRESS

2017 Title List

Visit www.SalemPress.com for Product Information, Table of Contents, and Sample Pages.

History and Social Science

The 2000s in America
50 States
African American History
Agriculture in History
American First Ladies
American Heroes
American Indian Culture
American Indian History
American Indian Tribes
American Presidents
American Villains
America's Historic Sites
Ancient Greece
The Bill of Rights
The Civil Rights Movement
The Cold War
Countries, Peoples & Cultures
Countries, Peoples & Cultures: Central & South America
Countries, Peoples & Cultures: Central, South & Southeast Asia
Countries, Peoples & Cultures: East & South Africa
Countries, Peoples & Cultures: East Asia & the Pacific
Countries, Peoples & Cultures: Eastern Europe
Countries, Peoples & Cultures: Middle East & North Africa
Countries, Peoples & Cultures: North America & the Caribbean
Countries, Peoples & Cultures: West & Central Africa
Countries, Peoples & Cultures: Western Europe
Defining Documents: American Revolution
Defining Documents: American West
Defining Documents: Ancient World
Defining Documents: Civil Rights
Defining Documents: Civil War
Defining Documents: Court Cases
Defining Documents: Dissent & Protest
Defining Documents: Emergence of Modern America
Defining Documents: Exploration & Colonial America
Defining Documents: Immigration & Immigrant Communities
Defining Documents: Manifest Destiny
Defining Documents: Middle Ages
Defining Documents: Nationalism & Populism
Defining Documents: Native Americans
Defining Documents: Postwar 1940s
Defining Documents: Reconstruction
Defining Documents: Renaissance & Early Modern Era
Defining Documents: 1920s
Defining Documents: 1930s
Defining Documents: 1950s
Defining Documents: 1960s
Defining Documents: 1970s
Defining Documents: The 17th Century
Defining Documents: The 18th Century
Defining Documents: Vietnam War
Defining Documents: Women
Defining Documents: World War I
Defining Documents: World War II
The Eighties in America
Encyclopedia of American Immigration
Encyclopedia of Flight
Encyclopedia of the Ancient World
Fashion Innovators
The Fifties in America
The Forties in America
Great Athletes
Great Athletes: Baseball
Great Athletes: Basketball
Great Athletes: Boxing & Soccer
Great Athletes: Cumulative Index
Great Athletes: Football
Great Athletes: Golf & Tennis
Great Athletes: Olympics
Great Athletes: Racing & Individual Sports
Great Events from History: 17th Century
Great Events from History: 18th Century
Great Events from History: 19th Century
Great Events from History: 20th Century (1901-1940)
Great Events from History: 20th Century (1941-1970)
Great Events from History: 20th Century (1971-2000)
Great Events from History: 21st Century (2000-2016)
Great Events from History: African American History
Great Events from History: Cumulative Indexes
Great Events from History: LGBTG
Great Events from History: Middle Ages
Great Events from History: Modern Scandals
Great Events from History: Renaissance & Early Modern Era
Great Lives from History: 17th Century
Great Lives from History: 18th Century
Great Lives from History: 19th Century
Great Lives from History: 20th Century
Great Lives from History: 21st Century (2000-2016)
Great Lives from History: American Women
Great Lives from History: Ancient World
Great Lives from History: Asian & Pacific Islander Americans
Great Lives from History: Cumulative Indexes
Great Lives from History: Incredibly Wealthy
Great Lives from History: Inventors & Inventions
Great Lives from History: Jewish Americans
Great Lives from History: Latinos
Great Lives from History: Notorious Lives
Great Lives from History: Renaissance & Early Modern Era
Great Lives from History: Scientists & Science
Historical Encyclopedia of American Business
Issues in U.S. Immigration
Magill's Guide to Military History
Milestone Documents in African American History
Milestone Documents in American History
Milestone Documents in World History
Milestone Documents of American Leaders
Milestone Documents of World Religions
Music Innovators
Musicians & Composers 20th Century
The Nineties in America
The Seventies in America
The Sixties in America
Survey of American Industry and Careers
The Thirties in America
The Twenties in America
United States at War
U.S. Court Cases
U.S. Government Leaders
U.S. Laws, Acts, and Treaties
U.S. Legal System
U.S. Supreme Court
Weapons and Warfare
World Conflicts: Asia and the Middle East

Health

Addictions & Substance Abuse
Adolescent Health & Wellness
Cancer
Complementary & Alternative Medicine
Community & Family Health
Genetics & Inherited Conditions
Health Issues
Infectious Diseases & Conditions
Magill's Medical Guide
Nutrition
Nursing
Psychology & Behavioral Health
Psychology Basics

WILSON

WILSON

2017 Title List

Visit www.HWWilsonInPrint.com for Product Information, Table of Contents and Sample Pages

Current Biography
Current Biography Cumulative Index 1946-2013
Current Biography Monthly Magazine
Current Biography Yearbook: 2003
Current Biography Yearbook: 2004
Current Biography Yearbook: 2005
Current Biography Yearbook: 2006
Current Biography Yearbook: 2007
Current Biography Yearbook: 2008
Current Biography Yearbook: 2009
Current Biography Yearbook: 2010
Current Biography Yearbook: 2011
Current Biography Yearbook: 2012
Current Biography Yearbook: 2013
Current Biography Yearbook: 2014
Current Biography Yearbook: 2015
Current Biography Yearbook: 2016

Core Collections
Children's Core Collection
Fiction Core Collection
Graphic Novels Core Collection
Middle & Junior High School Core
Public Library Core Collection: Nonfiction
Senior High Core Collection
Young Adult Fiction Core Collection

The Reference Shelf
Aging in America
American Military Presence Overseas
The Arab Spring
The Brain
The Business of Food
Campaign Trends & Election Law
Conspiracy Theories
The Digital Age
Dinosaurs
Embracing New Paradigms in Education
Faith & Science
Families: Traditional and New Structures
The Future of U.S. Economic Relations: Mexico, Cuba, and Venezuela
Global Climate Change
Graphic Novels and Comic Books
Guns in America
Immigration
Immigration in the U.S.
Internet Abuses & Privacy Rights
Internet Safety
LGBTQ in the 21st Century
Marijuana Reform
The News and its Future
The Paranormal
Politics of the Ocean
Prescription Drug Abuse
Racial Tension in a "Postracial" Age
Reality Television
Representative American Speeches: 2008-2009
Representative American Speeches: 2009-2010
Representative American Speeches: 2010-2011
Representative American Speeches: 2011-2012
Representative American Speeches: 2012-2013
Representative American Speeches: 2013-2014
Representative American Speeches: 2014-2015
Representative American Speeches: 2015-2016
Representative American Speeches: 2016-2017
Rethinking Work
Revisiting Gender
Robotics
Russia
Social Networking
Social Services for the Poor
Space Exploration & Development
Sports in America
The Supreme Court
The Transformation of American Cities
U.S. Infrastructure
U.S. National Debate Topic: Educational Reform
U.S. National Debate Topic: Surveillance
U.S. National Debate Topic: The Ocean
U.S. National Debate Topic: Transportation Infrastructure
Whistleblowers

Readers' Guide
Abridged Readers' Guide to Periodical Literature
Readers' Guide to Periodical Literature

Indexes
Index to Legal Periodicals & Books
Short Story Index
Book Review Digest

Sears List
Sears List of Subject Headings
Sears: Lista de Encabezamientos de Materia

Facts About Series
Facts About American Immigration
Facts About China
Facts About the 20th Century
Facts About the Presidents
Facts About the World's Languages

Nobel Prize Winners
Nobel Prize Winners: 1901-1986
Nobel Prize Winners: 1987-1991
Nobel Prize Winners: 1992-1996
Nobel Prize Winners: 1997-2001

World Authors
World Authors: 1995-2000
World Authors: 2000-2005

Famous First Facts
Famous First Facts
Famous First Facts About American Politics
Famous First Facts About Sports
Famous First Facts About the Environment
Famous First Facts: International Edition

American Book of Days
The American Book of Days
The International Book of Days

Monographs
American Reformers
The Barnhart Dictionary of Etymology
Celebrate the World
Guide to the Ancient World
Indexing from A to Z
The Poetry Break
Radical Change: Books for Youth in a Digital Age

Wilson Chronology
Wilson Chronology of Asia and the Pacific
Wilson Chronology of Human Rights
Wilson Chronology of Ideas
Wilson Chronology of the Arts
Wilson Chronology of the World's Religions
Wilson Chronology of Women's Achievements